ROUTLEDGE
MACEDONIAN–ENGLISH
DICTIONARY

'I know of no comparable rival to this dictionary.'

Dr H. Leeming, University of London

'. . . clearly fills the need for a good Macedonian–English dictionary.'

Professor Victor A. Friedman, University of Chicago

The *Macedonian–English Dictionary* is the essential aid to all work involving the two languages.

The *Dictionary* is the most ambitious attempt to date to record English equivalents for the vocabulary of modern Macedonian. It covers the vocabulary met with in a wide variety of settings and literary forms, from modern urban life to traditional folk poetry.

Features include:

- clear, accurate examples of usage
- all necessary grammatical information for Macedonian headwords
- details of stress, where it departs from the regular pattern
- a broad range of idiomatic expressions and proverbs

The work is based on the lexical corpus of the renowned *Rečnik na makendonskiot jazik*. Prepared by scholars at the Australian National University in Canberra, working in collaboration with the compilers of the original *Rečnik*, the content has been brought up to date by the addition of many recent words and new senses which have arisen for older words. The *Dictionary* was initiated by the late **Professor Reginald de Bray**, a leading Slavist at the Australian National University.

Peter Hill is Professor of Slavonic Studies at the University of Hamburg and sometime Visiting Fellow at the Australian National University. **Sunčica Mirčevska** is a research assistant on the Macedonian Dictionary Project. **Kevin Windle** is Senior Lecturer in Russian at the Australian National University.

ROUTLEDGE MACEDONIAN–ENGLISH DICTIONARY

Compiled by Reginald de Bray, Todor Dimitrovski, Blagoja Korubin
and Trajko Stamatoski

Edited and prepared for publication by Peter Hill, Sunčica Mirčevska
and Kevin Windle, at the Australian National University

Routledge
Taylor & Francis Group

LONDON AND NEW YORK

First published 1998
by Routledge
2 Park Square, Milton Park, Abingdon, Oxfordshire OX14 4RN

Simultaneously published in the USA and Canada
by Routledge
711 Third Avenue, New York, NY 10017

First issued in paperback 2016

Typeset in Times by RefineCatch Ltd, Bungay, Suffolk

British Library Cataloguing in Publication Data
A catalogue record for this book is available from the British Library

Library of Congress Cataloguing in Publication Data
Macedonian–English dictionary / edited and prepared for publication
by Peter Hill, Sunčica Mirčevska and Kevin Windle; compiled
by Reginald de Bray . . . [et al.].
p.   cm.
At head of title: Australian National University.
"Simultaneously published in the USA and Canada by Routledge" – CIP
t.p. verso.
Includes bibliographical references.
1. Macedonian language–Dictionaries–English.   I. Hill, Peter M., 1945–
II. Mirčevska, Sunčica, 1956–   .   III. Windle, Kevin, 1947–
IV. De Bray, R. G. A. (Reginald George Arthur)
V. Australian National University.
PG1175.E5M33   1998
491.8′19321—dc21   97–23301

ISBN 13: 978-1-138-98554-4 (pbk)
ISBN 13: 978-0-415-16046-9 (hbk)

Publisher's Note
The publisher has gone to great lengths to ensure the quality
of this reprint but points out that some
imperfections in the original may be apparent

PREFACE

HISTORY OF THE PROJECT

This dictionary has been many years in the making and some account of the origins of the project and its history is called for.

The present Macedonian–English Dictionary was conceived in the early 1980s as an English version of the pioneering Речник на македонскиот јазик (Dictionary of the Macedonian Language), which first appeared in the 1960s. Work on the latter began in 1951, under the general editorship of the well-known linguist Blaže Koneski. Todor Dimitrovski, Blagoja Korubin and Trajko Stamatoski devoted many years to the compilation of this first dictionary of the modern Macedonian language, working in adverse conditions and with no precedent to guide them. The first volume (A–N) appeared in 1961. It was followed by Volume Two (O–P) in 1965, the disastrous Skopje earthquake of 1963 having intervened and caused disruptions to most areas of life, and Volume Three (R–Sh) in 1966.

Despite its title, *Rečnik* is in fact a bilingual dictionary, in which the main purpose was not to provide definitions in Macedonian (though these frequently appeared), but equivalents in Serbo-Croat (Latin script). The reality of this was recognized when Volume Two (O–P) was published in 1965, now bearing the sub-title 'со српскохрватски толкувања' (with glosses in Serbo-Croat). The third and last volume, which was published in 1966, retained the sub-title.

There was, however, another marked difference between the first volume and its successors. In the two later volumes, besides the Serbo-Croat equivalent, definitions in Macedonian were given for far more headwords than was the case in the first. Thus, although the revised title indicated a form of bilingual dictionary, it was possible for the monolingual Macedonian to use it, or large parts of it, to establish the meaning of a word without recourse to a second language.

In addition to this, while the first volume gave few examples of usage, the later two were generous in their provision of examples, some of them drawn from Macedonian literature, as is common practice in authoritative monolingual dictionaries, and from folk poetry.

A later edition of the *Rečnik* (1986) combined the three volumes in one (over 1700 pages long), without, however, making textual changes to regularize the above inconsistencies, which also survived into the 1994 edition.

When in 1983 Professor Reginald de Bray, in collaboration with the original compilers, embarked upon the task of creating an English version of the original *Rečnik na makedonskiot jazik*, he aimed at a complete and literal translation of the latter, reasoning that, since this was the best dictionary available of the Macedonian language and by far the fullest, anything less would fail to do it justice. Accordingly he set out to transcribe faithfully the full contents of the three volumes. Where Macedonian definitions appeared, as they did with reasonable consistency from the beginning of Volume Two, these were retained in the original Macedonian and supplied with an English translation, in addition to an English equivalent (replacing that in Serbo-Croat). Thus a relatively straightforward entry such as 'ставор' (rat) said '(вид голем глушец – a kind of large mouse) rat'. The great majority of the examples, often two or three lines of text each, were rendered in English. This practice was laid down at the beginning of the translation project and continued for several years, during which he was assisted by Sunčica Mirčevska (from 1986) and Peter Hill (from 1991).

It was Professor de Bray's intention, however, to subject the manuscript to rigorous editing, once the initial translation was complete, mainly with a view to improving the English glosses but also in order to ensure a higher degree of consistency and accuracy.

Sadly, Professor de Bray died in May 1993, leaving the project unfinished, and it fell to Sunčica Mirčevska and Peter Hill, now joined by Kevin Windle, to see the work through to the end. After some debate, it was decided that, in the interests of internal consistency and conformity with accepted lexicographical practice, extensive revisions could not be avoided. Since by then the typescript ran to some four thousand A4 pages, the task of revising it (in practice, rewriting the bulk of it) was comparable in scale to that of drafting the first translation. The definitions in Macedonian and English were deleted, except in rare cases where no equivalent could be found, and here only an English explanation was left. In the course of this work, the English equivalents were scrutinized and often modified. The examples were carefully examined to ensure that they clearly illustrated typical usage and the longer examples were radically pruned so as to meet the practical needs of the user. At the same time the structure of the entries was reviewed and the classification of senses by numbers thoroughly revised in order to bring it into line with that in other bilingual dictionaries. Most of the longer entries (those over two lines long) were, in fact, rewritten in the attempt to attain the clarity which Professor de Bray would himself have sought.

The *Rečnik* in its original form is a living reflection of the period in which it was compiled, the early years of Tito's Yugoslavia, the days when fascism had been recently defeated and the future of Yugoslav-style socialism seemed assured. In this period no area of cultural life could escape political intrusions, and linguistics and lexicography were no exception, as can be seen in the profusion of ideological examples about the onward march of socialism and the death throes of capitalist society. Tendentious definitions abound and the quaint and dated flavour of many examples stands out all the more starkly in literal English translation, as found in the typescript, e.g. under претстои: 'a long road awaits you, comrades, in the immediate future'; or учител (teacher): 'Tito is our leader and teacher'. Many other examples, while carrying no ideological burden whatsoever, were uninformative as guides to usage in either language; thus свинче (piglet), illustrated by 'си купивме свинче' (we bought a piglet). The editors of the final English-language text felt it necessary to replace the 'ideologically correct' examples with neutral and more usable phrases, and to delete many others which served little obvious purpose.

These factors apart, the dictionary was clearly in need of updating as the language had undergone much change since the original compilation in the 1950s and '60s. Here a valuable contribution was made by the compilers of the original, who, working with Professor de Bray, deleted many terms deemed too rare to merit inclusion, among them many drawn from the dialects of Macedonian. The editors of the present version have inserted a substantial number of neologisms which have entered the language in more recent times, in addition to new senses for older terms, and some longer-established terms which had escaped inclusion in *Rečnik*. These were culled from a variety of sources, including the press, radio broadcasts and some more recently published mono-lingual and bilingual dictionaries. (See 'Bibliography'.)

Much attention was also devoted to standardizing and amplifying the grammatical information provided in the Dictionary. *Rečnik* gave fairly full coverage of irregular noun plurals, but on other grammatical matters, such as the less predictable aorist forms, it was less informative than some English-speaking users might like. In the latter area, modifications in this version have been extensive. Where *Rečnik* provided scant detail on such matters as the governance of Macedonian verbs, the editors of the Macedonian–English Dictionary have sought to provide as much information as possible regarding transitivity and prepositional usage with particular verbs and to give English translations and examples in which this is clear.

For all of these reasons the resulting work differs in many respects from Professor de Bray's original design. Those who seek to compare it with *Rečnik* will not fail to notice this. They will recognize, however, that the practical considerations which must govern the production of any dictionary militate against a literal and unadorned translation and in favour of a version loosely based upon the lexical corpus laid down in the original work. We in our turn, in revising the manuscript, have endeavoured to be faithful to the spirit of Professor de Bray's intention rather than the letter.

KW
Australian National University
Canberra

1998

ACKNOWLEDGEMENTS

The editors gratefully acknowledge the financial support provided for the project over many years by the Australian Research Council and by the Australian National University in its later stages.

The task of editing was eased and its quality greatly enhanced by the efforts of Margaret Travers, Senior Lecturer in Russian at the Australian National University, who spent many hours checking the near-final text in its entirety. Her painstaking scrutiny led to increased clarity in many entries and spared us many infelicities in the English text as well as typographical errors in both languages. Responsibility for those errors that remain must rest with KW.

Many individuals at the Australian National University and beyond have lent us valuable support, advice and encouragement. We are particularly grateful to the staff of the Australian National Dictionary Centre, headed until 1994 by Dr W. S. (Bill) Ramson, and since then by Dr Bruce Moore.

Our thanks for assistance of various kinds are also due to the following:

Ms Monica Berko, ANDC,
Prof. Richard Campbell, Dean, Faculty of Arts, later Pro-Vice-Chancellor, ANU,
Prof. Victor Friedman, University of Chicago,
Ms Harriet Michell, ANDC,
Dr Lawrence Saha, Dean, Faculty of Arts, ANU,
Mr Peter Scardoni, Business Manager, Faculty of Arts, ANU,
Prof. Roland Sussex, Centre for Language Teaching and Research, University of Queensland

The late Ms Agnese de Bray, who passed away in December 1996, and her children Helen and Serghei followed the progress of work with interest throughout. The editors are grateful for their friendly support.

We also enjoyed welcome support and encouragement from Dr Ilija Čašule, Prof. Olga Mišeska Tomić, Ms Elena Petroska, Prof. Zuzanna Topolińska and Prof. Rina Usikova.

KW is grateful to the ANU for teaching relief and support for travel to Macedonia in 1994, and to Dr Maksim Karanfilovski and the organizers of the Ohrid Seminar on Macedonian Language and Literature. He would also like to express his gratitude to Ludmilla, Rita and Adrian for their patience during the many weekends and long evenings when the revision claimed his full attention.

KW

BIBLIOGRAPHY

In the course of the revision the editors have consulted numerous works of reference. The following were particularly valuable:

Akhmanova, O. S.; Smirnitsky, A. I. *et al.*: *Russian–English Dictionary*. Moscow, 1962
Alford, M. H. T. and V. L.: *Russian–English Scientific and Technical Dictionary*. Oxford, 1970
Atanasova, T. *et al.*: *Bulgarian–English Dictionary*. Sofia, 1983
Benson, Morton: *Serbocroatian–English Dictionary*. Cambridge: (no date)
Bujas, Željko: *Hrvatsko ili srpsko–engleski enciklopedijski rječnik*. Zagreb, 1983
Chambers Twentieth Century Dictionary. London, 1975
The Collins English Dictionary. London, 1991
Delbridge, Arthur (editor-in-chief): *The Macquarie Dictionary*. McMahon's Point, NSW, 1981
Drvodelić, Milan: *Croatian or Serbian–English Dictionary*. Zagreb, 1978
Flavell, Linda and Roger, *Dictionary of Proverbs and their Origins*. London, 1993
Fergusson, Rosalind: *The Penguin Dictionary of Proverbs*. Bungay, 1986
Grad, Anton; Leeming, Henry: *Slovene–English Dictionary*. Ljubljana, 1993
Hessen, Dymitr; Stypuła, Ryszard: *Wielki słownik polsko–rosyjski*. Warsaw–Moscow, 1967
Hughes, J. M.; Michell, P. A.; Ramson, W. S.: *The Australian Concise Oxford Dictionary*. Melbourne, 1992
Langenscheidts Großwörterbuch der englischen und deutschen Sprache. Deutsch–Englisch. Berlin, 1986
Mišeska Tomić, Olga *et al.*: *English–Macedonian Dictionary*. Skopje, 1994
Murgoski, Zoze: *English–Macedonian Macedonian–English Dictionary*. Skopje, 1995
Murgoski, Zoze: *Macedonian–English Dictionary of Idioms*. Skopje, 1993
New Redhouse Turkish–English Dictionary. Istanbul, 1968
Pianka, Włodzimierz; Topolińska, Zuzanna; Vidoeski, Božidar: *Słownik macedońsko–polski i polsko–macedoński*. Warsaw, Skopje, 1990
The Oxford-Duden Pictorial Serbo-Croat & English Dictionary: Oxford, 1988
The Oxford Russian Dictionary, revised and updated by Colin Howlett. Oxford, 1993
The Shorter Oxford English Dictionary. Oxford, 1973
Stanisławski, Jan: *The Great Polish–English Dictionary*. Warsaw, 1988
Uzunov, Nikola; Stevanović-Ančeska, Ljiljana: *English–Macedonian and Macedonian–English Dictionary of Economics and Business*. Skopje, 1994

Гавриш, Ксенија: *Македонско-руски речник*. Скопје, 1969
Китановски, Дано: *Македонско-француски речник*. Скопје, 1974

Ковачевић, Живорад: *Српско-енглески речник идиома, израза и изрека.* Београд, 1992

Конески, Блаже: *Граматика на македонскиот литературен јазик.* Скопје, 1987

Корубин, Благоја: *Интенцијално-синтаксички речник на македонските глаголи, том 1 (А- Ж).* Скопје, 1992

Матица српска; Матица хрватска: *Речник српскохрватскога књижевног језика.* Нови Сад, Загреб, 1967–76

Мићуновић, Љубо: *Современ лексикон на странски зборови и изрази.* Скопје, 1990

Институт за македонски јазик «Крсте Мисирков»: *Правопис на македонскиот литературен јазик.* Скопје, 1986

Симоновић, Драгутин: *Ботанички речник.* Београд, 1959

Српска Академија Наука: *Речник српскохрватског књижевног и народног језика.* Београд, 1959–

Толстой, И. И.: *Сербско-хорватско-русский словарь.* Москва, 1970

Чакалов, Г.; Ляков, Ил.; Станков, Здр.: *Българско-английски речник.* София, 1961

GUIDE TO USE OF THE DICTIONARY

GRAMMATICAL AND PHONOLOGICAL INFORMATION

While it is assumed that the user has a good basic knowledge of Macedonian grammar and phonetics or has access to a textbook of the language, a modicum of grammatical and phonological information about the Macedonian headword is nonetheless provided.

Following the general practice in dictionaries of this type, we do not supply grammatical or phonological information about the English lexemes or phrases used to translate the Macedonian. It is assumed that users who require this information will have access to a textbook of English or to an English–Macedonian dictionary such as that by Olga Mišeska Tomić.

Nouns

Plural forms are indicated after the headword in cases where more than one form is in use and where their formation presents potential difficulties for the English-speaking user, and not otherwise. Thus for риба, решето and парче the plurals are not given, as they follow the regular patterns, giving риби, решета and парчиња. For рид and роб, however, where more than one possible plural exists, these are set out. Thus рид -ови, -је, -ишта.

Forms displaying consonantal change by palatalization are also given, although these changes are of a regular nature. Thus ризик -ци.

Verbal nouns

These are frequently formed from verbs by means of the suffix -ње. Since this process is quite regular not all such nouns are listed in the dictionary. Many will be equivalent to the English verbal noun with the suffix '-ing'. Thus читање – 'reading'.

However, in many other cases where there are additional senses, or where the usual English translation is not formed by the suffix '-ing', the verbal noun will be listed: e.g.

испуштање – 'release; omission'. In such cases it should be realized that the '-ing' senses, i.e. 'releasing, omitting, letting pass, letting slip' etc., still apply.

Verbal nouns in -ост, mostly of an abstract nature and derived from adjectives or passive participles, may often be translated by the English suffix '-ness'. Others may require a more explanatory gloss, including phrases such as 'having the character/quality/ nature of . . . '. The dictionary does not include all possible nouns of this type, as their meaning can usually be established via the adjectives from which they are derived and the forms are largely predictable. In cases where they are given, e.g. смртност (from смртен), the various nominalized senses of the adjective смртен will apply ('deadliness, lethal nature') in addition to the sense given – 'mortality'.

Verbs

As Macedonian lacks an infinitive, verbs are cited in the third person singular of the present tense: тера, чита, etc. The only exception is the Macedonian equivalent of the verb 'to be', which established tradition always refers to as глаголот сум, using the first person singular, rather than глаголот е. The English translation, however, following convention, is in the infinitive ('to drive', 'to read').

In those cases where parts of the Macedonian verb differ greatly from the citation form (as in the verb сум), these parts are listed as separate entries, with a cross reference to the citation form.

For perfective verbs the aorist is indicated in those cases where it differs from the citation form (the present), and the first-person aorist is added in those cases where it might cause difficulty for the English-speaking user.

It will be noted, however, that, as in most dictionaries of Macedonian, there has been no attempt to cover the 'l-participle' of the verb. While predictable for many verbs, in other cases it would have led to unwieldy entries, encumbered by notes on, for example, the correct use of дошол and дојдел – matters which, it was felt, were best left to grammatical manuals.

Governance

The abbreviation *'trans.'* (transitive) is used to signify that the verb so marked may govern a direct object; *'intrans.'* (intransitive) to signify that it cannot. The terms are applied sparingly in the dictionary, only when the English glosses do not themselves make clear whether the Macedonian verb is transitive or intransitive and when an English verb needs to have its sense clarified in this way. When a verb may be used with or without an object, and where Macedonian and English usage coincide, no label is provided. Thus 'чита – to read'.

Prepositional governance is indicated, as far as possible, by placing the Macedonian preposition in brackets following the verb with the corresponding English preposition, where this applies, thus 'поврзе to get in touch (*со – with*)'. Where helpful, such usage will also be illustrated by examples.

Some verbs are marked *'with dat.'*. Since the noun in modern Macedonian does not show case, this is to be read as meaning that the *pronoun* is in the dative case. The noun, if given, will be preceded by the preposition на. Thus: 'допаѓа се *with dat.* to please' indicates that usage will be as follows: 'на учителот му се допаѓа работата the teacher likes his work'.

Certain verbs are marked '*impers. with acc.*'. This should be understood as meaning that the accusative pronoun forms мене/ме, него/го, неа/ја etc. will appear as the object of an impersonal verb, with or without a noun, as in a phrase such as 'ги стемни darkness overtook them.'

Verbal aspect

In general, entries will be found for the perfective and imperfective aspectual forms. This dictionary has in the majority of cases followed the practice laid down in *Rečnik* of treating the perfective as the basic form and stating in the entry for the corresponding imperfective '*impf of* . . . '. Thus тргнува will bear the reference '*impf of* тргне'. The entry трга will be marked '*impf, see* тргне', but since it has additional uses not given under 'тргне', these then follow as separate, numbered senses. This arrangement is not to be taken as implying any comment on the historical evolution of the verbal system, in which the imperfective may precede the perfective. Furthermore, there are numerous aspectual pairs in which the imperfective is more common than the perfective, e.g. лета, which is far less restricted in its application than летне. In such cases the perfective will usually bear a reference to the imperfective, in this case '*see* лета'.

Reflexive verbs

English-speaking users should note that it is usual for the reflexive pronoun 'се' to precede, not follow the verb. For ease of alphabetical reference, however, it has been placed after the headword in the dictionary.

Those verbs which are shown with and without 'се' are subdivided by the Roman numerals **I** and **II** (in bold type), the latter showing uses with 'се'. Within each part of the entry there may be further sub-divisions marked by arabic numerals (in bold type) to separate senses, as in other entries.

As in most other Slavonic languages, the addition of 'се' (self) to a transitive verb may perform a number of functions. It may:

(i)   make the transitive verb intransitive (дига, се дига – to raise/rise), often giving a translation in which the form 'self' will figure;

(ii)   produce a sense best translated by an English passive (се пишува to be written/spelt);

(iii)   denote reciprocal action involving two or more actors (English 'each other' or 'one another');

(iv)   with certain verbs produce impersonal constructions denoting wishes (ми се јаде – I feel peckish; не ми се игра – I don't feel like dancing);

(v)   produce an impersonal statement of a general nature (таму се јаде добро you can get a good meal there);

(vi) produce new senses not immediately apparent from the form without 'се' (јуначи to encourage; се јуначи to strut, to swagger).

The compilers have aimed at the inclusion of the bulk of verbs in which 'се' performs the last of these functions, but it was not felt practical or necessary to indicate all cases in which 'се' gives a passive, intransitive, mutual, impersonal, or truly reflexive sense, as these can readily be identified once the form without 'се' is known.

Participles

In many cases the past participle passive is given as a separate entry, especially when its use is wider than merely participial. When not listed separately its meaning should be clear from the entry for the verb from which it is derived.

Adjectives

Many adjectives of foreign origin are marked *'indecl.'* (indeclinable). As Macedonian nouns and adjectives have no inflection for case, this is to be read as meaning that these adjectives cannot show number or gender agreement. A form such as срмајлија remains unchanged whether its accompanying noun is masculine, feminine or neuter, singular or plural.

Adverbs

Large numbers of Macedonian adverbs are formed simply and regularly from the adjective by the process арен – арно, тажен – тажно, танок – танко. In typical cases their English equivalent is formed by adding the suffix -ly to the adjective: thus 'sad – sadly'. The dictionary does not give systematic coverage of all such adverbs, since the meaning can be derived from the adjective and the English form by a knowledge of this process. However, where there are irregularities in either language, or when useful phrases including such adverbs need to be given, the adverbs will appear as separate entries.

Most adjectives with the ending -ски, -шки, -чки can function as adverbs without any change in form; thus самокритички may serve as both 'self-critical' and 'self-critically'. Since the English adverb can usually be formed by adding -ly to the adjective, the adverbial use will not be mentioned regularly in the entry.

Adverbs which are not derived from adjectives are of course listed.

Prefixes

Verbal prefixes appear as independent headwords (на-, об- etc.), with notes on their possible senses and functions. While most of the more common combinations are accorded separate entries, others are not, and, given that many of these prefixes are highly productive, full coverage is impractical. If the prefixed verb is not listed, the verb should be sought without its prefix, and the sense modified according to the known functions of the prefix. The same applies to nouns derived from prefixed verbs.

Word stress

In standard Macedonian the stress regularly falls on the antepenultimate syllable in words of three or more syllables and on the first in words of two syllables. Stress is therefore marked in the Dictionary only on those words, mostly foreign borrowings, which depart from this rule, e.g. 'скрофулóза scrofula'.

TRANSLATIONS

The stylistic level of a given lexeme or its sphere of use is indicated where necessary in italics, e.g. *colloq.*, *fig.*, *vulg.*, *Tech.* (see Abbreviations).

Where more than one English gloss is provided, close synonyms are separated by a comma, more distant synonyms (words which will not normally be interchangeable) by a semi-colon, and unrelated senses by arabic numerals in bold type.

Where the gloss takes the form of a phrase, a word in parenthesis ( ) within the phrase may freely take the place of the preceding word: 'цел (полн) пансион full board and lodging'. A slash is employed where the second word may be used but with altered sense: 'пали оган/цигара to light a fire/cigarette'.

Pointed brackets <> indicate elements in either language which may be omitted without affecting the meaning: 'подземје <criminal> underworld'.

Supplementary information, such as may be required to disambiguate a gloss, is given in parenthesis and italics: 'пасус passage (*of text*)'. This may appear in English or Macedonian as in each case an attempt has been made to judge which class of user will have the greater need for the information provided.

In the translated examples of usage, 'he' should not normally be taken to exclude 'she' or 'it' unless the sense of a particular example requires this.

Idiomatic expressions, i.e. those which cannot usually be translated literally, are preceded by the symbol ❏.

Preference is given to British English, but variants from the English of North America, Australia and New Zealand also appear, marked as '*Am.*', '*Austral.*', and '*N.Z.*'. The label '*Brit.*' is used to indicate that a translation is used only in Britain. Standard American spelling variants such as 'color' for 'colour' are not shown. Less predictable American forms, such as 'airplane' are given and labelled '*Am.*'.

ABBREVIATIONS

abbr.	abbreviation		*Elec.*	electrical
acc.	accusative		*esp.*	especially
adj	adjective			
adv	adverb		*f*	feminine
Am.	American		*fem.*	feminine
Anat.	anatomy		*fig.*	figurative
aor.	aorist		*folk.*	folklore
arch.	archaic		*freq.*	frequently
Astron.	astronomy		*f.p.*	folk poetry
attrib.	attributively			
augm.	augmentative		*Geog.*	geography
Austral.	Australian		*Geol.*	geology
			Geom.	geometry
Biol.	biology		*Gram.*	grammar
Bot.	botany			
Brit.	British		*Hist.*	historical
			hyp.	hypocoristic
c.	circa			
cf.	compare		i.e.	id est
Chem.	chemistry		*impf*	imperfective
child.	children's language		*imperf.*	imperfect
coll.	collective		*impers.*	impersonal
colloq.	colloquial		*indecl.*	indeclinable
Comm.	commerce		*interj*	interjection
conj	conjunction		*intrans.*	intransitive
Cul.	culinary		*iron.*	ironic
dat.	dative		*joc.*	jocular
dem.	demonstrative			
dial.	dialect		*Leg.*	legal
dim.	diminutive		*Ling.*	linguistics
Econ.	economics		*m*	masculine
e.g.	for example		*Math.*	mathematics

Mech.	mechanical		*prep*	preposition
Med.	medical		*pres.*	present
Mil.	military		*Print.*	printing
Mus.	music		*pron*	pronoun
Myth.	mythology		*prov.*	proverb
			Psychol.	psychology
n	neuter		*pt*	participle
Naut.	nautical			
num	numeral		*Rel.*	religion
N.Z.	New Zealand			
			sg	singular
obs.	obsolete		*sl.*	slang
opp.	opposite		s.o.	someone
o.s.	oneself		*Sport.*	sporting
			s.th.	something
p.	person			
part	particle		*Tech.*	technical
pejor.	pejorative		*trans.*	transitive
perf.	perfect			
pf	perfective		*usu.*	usually
Philos.	philosophy			
Phon.	phonetics		*voc.*	vocative
Phys.	physics		*vulg.*	vulgar
pl	plural			
poet.	poetic		*Zool.*	zoology
Pol.	politics			

THE MACEDONIAN ALPHABET

А а, Б б, В в, Г г, Д д, Ѓ ѓ, Е е, Ж ж, З з, Ѕ ѕ, И и, Ј ј, К к, Л л,
Љ љ, М м, Н н, Њ њ, О о, П п, Р р, С с, Т т, Ќ ќ, У у, Ф ф,
Х х, Ц ц, Ч ч, Џ џ, Ш ш

— A —

a[1] *in expressions:* од А до Ш from A to Z; through and through; all the way; не рече ни а ни бе he didn't say a <single> word

a[2] *conj* **1** (*parallel action*) and; татко му и мајка му разговараа, а тој читаше некаков роман his father and mother were talking, and (while) he was reading a novel **2** (*contrast*) but, and; јас ја чекав, а таа не дојде I was waiting for her, but she did not come **3** (*introducing a new topic*) but; тој се задржа најмногу во Белград, а помина и низ Скопје he stayed mostly in Belgrade, but passed through Skopje too **4** (*contrast reinforced by* пак, камоли) but, still; let alone; а пак тој премногу бара still, he is asking too much; јас не сакам да го видам, а камоли на гости да му одам I don't want to see him, let alone visit him **5** a . . . а *conj* whether . . . or; а тој, а јас – сè едно whether it's him or me, it makes no difference

a[3] *conj* **1** as soon as; а влезе во собата, веднаш седна as soon as he entered the room he sat down **2** a . . . а as soon as; а легнала, а заспала as soon as she lay down, she fell asleep

a[4] *interj* **1** (*indicating surprise, approval, admiration, pain, sorrow, etc.*) ah! oh! а, така значи! oh, so that's it! а што била работата! now I understand! а, одлично! oh, that's wonderful! **2** *f.p., otherwise impolite* (*attracting attention*) а мајко, слушај mother, listen!

аба *f* **1** homespun cloth, *see* шајак **2** aba, man's tasselled waistcoat (*part of traditional costume*)

абажур *f* lampshade

абаџија -ии *m* tailor (*who uses homespun cloth*)

абдал *m arch.* fool, blockhead

абдикација *f* abdication

абдицира *pf & impf* to abdicate

абер *m arch. colloq.* news, message, sign; дојде абер од Скопје news came from Skopje; зеде абер he received news; пушти (прати, стори) абер (на) he informed (*s.o.*), he sent word (*to s.o.*); донесе абер to break the news; немам абер за таа работа I have not the faintest idea (notion) about that; сонцето уште нема абер за заоѓање the sun is nowhere near setting; ѝ даде абер со раката he motioned to her; ❏ абер нема not by a long chalk/shot

аберација *f* aberration; *Optics* сферна аберација spherical aberration; хроматска аберација chromatic aberration

аберција *m arch. see* гласник

абецеда *f* **1** *see* азбука **2** *fig.* rudiments, ABC

аби *impf* **I 1** to wear out *trans.* **2** to blunt; дрварите ги абеа секирите the woodcutters blunted their axes **II**

– **се 1** to wear out *intrans.* **2** to become blunt; ножот се аби the knife is getting blunt

Абисинец -нци *m* Abyssinian

Абисинија *f* Abyssinia, *see* Етиопија

Абисинка *f* (*fem. form*) *see* Абисинец

абисински *adj* Abyssinian

аблатив *m Gram.* ablative

аблаут *m Gram.* ablaut

аблендува *pf & impf* to dip, *Am.* dim (*headlights*)

абнормален -лна *adj* abnormal

абнормалност *f* abnormality

абонент *m* subscriber

абонира *pf & impf* **I** to pay s.o.'s subscription; го абонирав син ми на списанието I took out a subscription to the journal for my son **II** – се to subscribe (*to*) *intrans.*; се абонирав на списанието I subscribed to the journal

абонман *m* subscription, prepayment; износ на абонман subscription rate

абонос *m Bot.* ebony

абортира *pf & impf* to abort, have an abortion; жената абортира the woman had an abortion; *see* пометне

абортус *m* abortion; спонтан абортус miscarriage

абраш *m* **1** fair-haired freckled man **2** piebald horse (*with white hairs under the tail or round its mouth*)

абрашлив *adj* piebald, spotted

ав *interj* (*imitation of a dog barking*) bow wow!

ава *f arch.* air; излезе на ава, зеде ава he went out for some <fresh> air

аван *m* **1** (*vessel for pounding*) mortar **2** tobacco-cutting machine

авангарда *f* avant-garde; *Mil.* advance guard; *fig. Pol.* vanguard

авангарден -дна *adj* avant-garde *attrib.*; *Mil.* in the advance-guard; *fig. Pol.* in the vanguard

аванс *m* advance, down payment; аванс на стока advance on goods; дава аванс to advance money

авансира *pf & impf* to advance

авантура *f* adventure

авантуризам -змот *m* adventurism

авантурист *m* adventurer

авантуристички *adj* adventurous

авантуристка *f* adventuress

Авганистан *m* Afghanistan

Авганистанец -нци *m* Afghan, Afghani

Авганистанка *f* (*fem. form*) *see* Авганистанец

авганистански *adj* Afghan, Afghani

август *m* August; ❏ глуп август clown

августовски *adj* August *attrib.*

аверзија *f* aversion

авијатичар *m* pilot, airman, aviator

авијатичарски *adj* pilot's, airman's

авијација *f* aviation

авион *m* aircraft, plane, *Brit.* aeroplane, *Am.* airplane; ❏ со авион by air; се гледа <и> од авион it sticks out a mile; не се гледа од авион it doesn't show

авионски *adj* air *attrib.*; aircraft *attrib.*; со авионска пошта by air mail; авионски превозник airline, carrier; авионски товар air cargo

авитаминоза *f Med.* avitaminosis, vitamin deficiency

авка *impf* (*see* ав) to bark

авлија[1] -ии *f* **1** yard **2** fence; (*sид околу куќата*) wall

авлија[2] -ии *f* towel

авра *f arch.* synagogue; bedlam; ❑ вреват како во авра they are raising Cain (the roof)

Австралијанец *m see* Австралиец

Австралијанка *f see* Австралијка

австралијански *adj see* австралиски

Австралиец -ијци *m* Australian

Австралија *f* Australia

Австралијка *f (fem. form) see* Австралиец

австралиски *adj* Australian

Австриец -ијци *m* Austrian

Австрија *f* Austria

Австријка *f (fem. form) see* Австриец

австриски *adj* Austrian

Австро-Унгарија *f* Austro-Hungary

автархија *f* autarchy

автархиски *adj* autarchic<al>

автархичен -чна *adj* autarchic<al>, independent

автентичен -чна *adj* authentic, original, true, genuine

автентичност *f* authenticity, genuineness

авто- *prefix* auto-

автобиографија -ии *f* autobiography

автобиографски *adj* autobiographical

автобус *m* (*обично градски*) bus; (*обично меѓуградски*) coach

автобуски *adj* bus/coach *attrib.*; автобуска станица bus-stop; bus (coach) station

автогол *m Sport.* own goal

автограм *m* autograph

автодром *m* racetrack (*for motor racing*)

автокефален -лна *adj* autocephalous, independent (*of a church*)

автокефалност *f* autocephalous status, autocephaly

автократ *m* autocrat

автократија *f* autocracy

автомат *m* **1** automaton, robot **2** slot-machine, *Am.* automat **3** *Mil.* sub-machine gun **4** *fig.* automaton, *colloq.* zombie

автоматизам -змот *m* automatism

автоматизација *f* automation

автоматизира *pf & impf* to automate, automatize

автоматски *adj* automatic

автомобил *m* car, motor car, *Am.* automobile; изнајмување на автомобил car hire; индустрија за автомобили car-manufacturing (motor-vehicle manufacturing) industry, *Am.* automobile (automotive) industry

автомобилизам -змот *m* motoring

автомобилист *m* driver, motorist

автомобилски *adj* car, *Am.* automobile *attrib.*; автомобилска гума car tyre

автономен -мна *adj* autonomous, self-governing

автономија *f* autonomy, self-government

автономист *m* **1** *Hist.* member of the movement for the autonomy of Macedonia **2** advocate of autonomy

автопат *m* motorway, expressway, <major> highway, freeway

автопортрет *m* self-portrait

автор *m* author

авторизира *pf & impf* to authorize; авторизиран превод authorized translation

авторитет *m* **1** (*углед*) authority, prestige, reputation **2** (*угледна личност*) expert, authority

авторитетен -тна *adj* authoritative

авторка *f* author, authoress

авторски *adj* author's; авторско право copyright; film rights; авторска агенција copyright agency; авторски хонорар royalties *pl*; авторски табак *Print.* printer's sheet, 16 pages

авторство *n* authorship

автостоп *n, adv* hitchhiking

автостопер *m* hitchhiker

автостоперство *n* hitchhiking

автостопира *pf & impf* to hitchhike

автострада *f* motorway, expressway, <major> highway, freeway

автосугестија *f* auto-suggestion

автотранспорт *m* road transport

автохтон *adj* indigenous, autochthonous, original, aboriginal

ага *m* aga; master; patron; со лага ага не бидува *prov.* lies have short legs

агент *m* **1** agent, representative **2** detective; agent; таен агент secret agent; агент-провокатор *agent provocateur*

агентура *f* **1** (*од шпиони*) spy ring **2** (*застапништво*) representative's office **3** (*филијала*) branch office **4** (*посредништво*) agency

агенција -ии *f* agency; туристичка агенција travel agency; агенција за вработување employment agency; новинска агенција news (press) agency

агилен -лна *adj* agile, active

агилност *f* agility, energy

агитатор *m* agitator

агитаторка *f (fem. form) see* агитатор

агитација *f Pol.* agitation, propaganda

агитационен -она *adj* propaganda *attrib.*

агитира *impf* to agitate, make propaganda; агитираа против плановите на Комисијата they opposed (agitated against) the Commission's plans

агитка *f* item of propaganda (*play, poster, etc.*)

агица *f* aga's wife

аглест *adj* angular

агломер *m* protractor, goniometer, octant

агломерен -рна *adj* goniometric, for measuring angles

агол -гли *m* corner; angle, aspect; од друг агол from a different angle

агонија *f* agony; death rattle, death throes

аграр *m* agriculture, agronomy

аграрен -рна *adj* agrarian, agricultural; аграрна реформа land (agrarian) reform

агрегат *m* aggregate

агрегатен -тна *adj* aggregate

агресивен -вна *adj* aggressive

агресивност *f* aggressiveness

агресија -ии *f* aggression

агресор *m* aggressor

агрикултурен -рна *adj* agricultural

агроном *m* agronomist

агрономија *f* agronomy

агротехника *f* agricultural practices, agricultural technology; mechanization of agriculture, modern farming methods

агротехнички *adj* mechanized (*of agricultural operations*), agricultural

агува *impf* to act (behave) like an aga, to lord it

ад *m literary* hell, inferno

адаптација *f* adaptation

адаптер & **адаптор** *m Elec.* adaptor

адапти́ра *pf* & *impf* **I** to adapt *trans.* **II – се** to adapt *intrans.*; овие животни се адаптираа на нашата клима these animals have adapted to our climate

адверб *m Gram.* (*прилог*) adverb

адвербија́лен -лна *adj Gram.* adverbial

адвока́т *m* 1 *Leg.* lawyer; (*кој застапува на суд*) *Brit.* barrister, *Am.* attorney; (*кој не застапува на суд*) solicitor; ❑ дрвен адвокат a barrack-room lawyer; a pettifogger; *Austral.* & *N.Z.* bush lawyer 2 *fig.* advocate, protector

адвока́тски *adj* lawyer's; legal

адвокату́ра *f* legal profession; practice of law

адеква́тен -тна *adj* adequate, suitable

адеква́тност *f* adequacy

адет *m colloq.* custom, habit; таков е адетот such is the custom

ади́ра *pf* & *impf* to add up *trans.*

адјектив *m Gram.* adjective, *see* придавка

адјекти́вен -вна *adj Gram.* adjectival

администрати́вен -вна *adj* administrative; office *attrib.*; административен службеник clerical (office) worker

администра́тор *m* administrator

администрација *f* administration

администри́ра *impf* to administrate

адмира́л *m* admiral

адмиралите́т *m* admiralty

адмира́лски *adj* admiral's

адреса *f* address; на адреса care of, c/o; ❑ се јавува на вистинска адреса to come to the right place, be on the right track; се јавува на погрешна адреса to be on the wrong track, be barking up the wrong tree

адреса́нт *m* sender (*of a letter*)

адресар *m* address book; directory; стопански адресар commercial (trade) directory

адреса́т *m* addressee

адреси́ра *pf* & *impf* to address (*a letter, etc.*)

адски *adj literary* hellish, infernal; адска машина infernal machine

адут *m* trump, trump card; ❑ ги држи сите адути to have (hold) all the trump cards; има скриен адут to have a shot in the locker; последен адут an ace up one's sleeve; one's best card

аѓута́нт *m* adjutant

аероби́к *m* aerobics

аеродинамика *f* aerodynamics

аеродинамичен -чна *adj* aerodynamic

аеродро́м *m* airfield, airport, aerodrome

аеросо́л *m* aerosol

аероста́т *m* <hot-air> balloon

аеротра́нспорт *m* air transport

аждер *m* dragon

ажурен -рна *adj* tidy, orderly, exact; regular; prompt; meticulous

ажурност *f* meticulousness, accuracy

азбест *m* asbestos

азбука *f* alphabet

азбучен -чна *adj* alphabetical; азбучен ред alphabetical order

азбучник -ци *m* list, register; alphabetical index; thumb index

азган *adj indecl.* wild, fiery, unbridled; азган жена vamp

аздиса *pf colloq.* to go wild; to get randy (*Am.* horny)

аздисува *impf of* аздиса

Азербејџа́н *m* Azerbaijan

Азербеџа́нец -нци *m* Azerbaijani; Azeri

Азербеџа́нка *f* (*fem. form*) *see* Азербеџанец

азербеџа́нски *adj* Azerbaijani; Azeri

Азиец -ијци *m* Asian

Азија *f* Asia; Мала Азија Asia Minor; Средна Азија Central Asia

Азија́т *m* Asian

Азија́тка *f* (*fem. form*) *see* Азијат

азија́тски *adj* Asian

Азијка *f* (*fem. form*) *see* Азиец

азил *m* asylum, refuge

азила́нт *m* refugee

азиски *adj* Asian

азно *n arch.* treasury; озгора мазно, оздола азно *prov.* a fair face and a foul heart

азот *m Chem.* nitrogen

азотен -тна *adj Chem.* nitrogen *attrib.*; nitrogenous; nitric; азотна киселина nitric acid

азотест *adj Chem.* nitrous; азотеста киселина nitrous acid

азурен -рна *adj* azure, sky-blue

аи *interj* (*expression of surprise*) oh! аи, колкави пораснале децата! oh, how big the children have grown!

аир *m colloq.* 1 <good> luck; аир да не види! *curse* may he come to no good! bad luck to him! (*in a greeting*) аир абер, стари! good luck, old fellow! 2 advantage, profit; каков аир од неа? what help would she be? каков аир од тоа? what advantage does it bring? what's the use of it? 3 *f.p.* good work; <charitable> foundation, endowment

аирлија *colloq.* 1 *adj indecl.* blessed, lucky; аирлија работа! good luck with the job! 2 *adv* happily, with good luck

ај[1] *part see* ајде

ај[2] *part* what if; ај не дошол! what if he hasn't come!

ај[3] *interj* 1 (*as an expression of surprise, regret, alarm, pain*) oh, alas; ај што сторил! oh, what has he done! 2 *f.p.* (*with* бре *and name in voc., or dat. pron., as mode of address*) ај бре гиди, млада невесто! hullo there, young lady!

ајван *m arch.* 1 beast of burden 2 *fig.* blockhead, dunce

ајвар *m* 1 roe 2 paprika relish

ајгар *m arch.* stallion

ајгарува *impf arch.* to grow wanton; to run wild

ајде *part* 1 come on! ајде да одиме come on, let's go! 2 all right; ајде, така нека биде all right, so be it! 3 ајде де you don't say! come off it! ајде да . . . let us . . . ; suppose . . .

ајдук -ци *m* 1 haiduk, rebel against Turkish authority, outlaw 2 highwayman, robber

ајдукува *impf* to lead the life of a haiduk

ајдут<ин> -ти *m see* ајдук

ајдутува *impf see* ајдукува

ајдучки *adj* haiduk's; ајдучка трева *Bot.* yarrow

ајдуштво *n* haiduk way of life; act of brigandry

ајкула *f Zool.* shark

ајљаз *m colloq.* lazybones

ајс *interj* (*exclamation to urge on oxen when ploughing*) come on!

ак *m colloq.* **1** pay, wages; reward; земи го акот твој и оди си take your money and go! **2** right; имаш ак you have every right; имате ак да си ги земете работите you have the right to take your things **3** (*in expressions*) му дојде до ак he ruined him; ак му е he deserves it; *iron.* it serves him right; му го јаде акот he cheats him; he does him an injustice

ака *impf colloq.* **I 1** to wander, roam; по цел ден ака he wanders about all day **2** to push *trans.* **3** to fill; to stuff **II – се 1** to push, shove *intrans.*; децата се акаат the children are pushing and shoving **2** to stuff one's pockets (*со нешто – with s.th.*) **3** *see* I 1

академец -мци *m* cadet

академизам -змот *m* academism

академија -ии *f* **1** academy; академија на науките academy of sciences **2** academy; college; воена академија military academy; трговска академија business college **3** commemoration, formal celebration; свечена академија formal meeting (*with an address*)

академик -ци *m* academician

академиски *adj* academic; academy *attrib.*

академски *adj* academic, learned; академски граѓанин <university/college> graduate

акварел *m* aquarelle, water-colour <painting>

аквариум *m* aquarium

аквизитер *m* collector

акламација *f* acclamation

акламира *impf* to acclaim

аклиматизација *f* acclimatization

аклиматизира *pf & impf* **I** to acclimatize *trans.* **II – се** to acclimatize *intrans.*

акна *f* acne

акне¹ *pf* акна *aor. colloq.* **I 1** to hit; to swipe **2** to push, shove *trans.* **3** to fail; to flop **II – се 1** to hit (*o.s.*) **2** to push, shove (*во – into*) *intrans.*

акне² *pf* акна *aor.* to groan; ❑ да акнеш, да пукнеш! damn and blast you!

акнува¹ (се) *impf of* акне¹ (се)

акнува² *impf of* акне²

ако¹ *conj* **1** if; дојди кај нас ако бидеш слободен come and see us if you are free; ❑ ако даде Господ! God willing! **2** although; ако е болен, тој пак оди на работа although he is ill, he still goes to work

ако² *adv* good, all right; ако, така <тебе> ти треба good, it serves you right

акомодира *pf & impf* **I** to accommodate; to adapt *trans.* **II – се** to accommodate o.s.; to adapt *intrans.*

аконтација -ии *f* advance, down payment

акорд¹ *m Mus.* chord; акорд од четири тонови a chord of four notes

акорд² *m* piece-work, jobbery

акордант *m* piece-rate worker, piece-worker, jobber

акорден -дна *adj* piece-work, piece-rate *attrib.*; акордна работа *see* акорд²; акорден работник *see* акордант; акорден систем piece-rate system; акордна плата piece wage

акредитив *m Comm.* letter of credit

акредитиви *pl Diplomacy* credentials, letter of credence

акредитивен -вна *adj Comm.* accredited

акредитира *pf & impf* to accredit

акреп *m* **1** *Zool.* (Scorpionida) scorpion **2** *fig.* ugly person, fright, monster

акрибија *f* meticulousness, painstaking care; овој научен труд е изработен со акрибија this study has been carried out meticulously (with painstaking care)

акробат *m* acrobat

акробатика *f* acrobatics

акробатски *adj* acrobatic

акробација -ии *f* acrobatics

акроним *m* acronym

акростих *m* acrostic

аксиом *m & аксиома f* axiom

акт *m* **1** act, action, deed **2** document, paper, file, record **3** *Leg.* action, trial, hearing **4** *Painting* nude; женски акт female nude **5** *Drama* act

актив *m* **1** the most active part of an organization; project group **2** success, achievement **3** *Gram.* active <voice>

актива *f Comm.* assets, property; актива и пасива assets and liabilities

активен -вна *adj* **1** industrious, hard-working **2** active, in service or employment; активен офицер serving officer **3** *Gram.* active

активизира & активира *pf & impf* **I 1** to activate; to start, turn on *trans.*; новиот закон ја активизира наставата the new law gave teaching a new impetus; пилотот ги активира моторите the pilot started the engines **2** to stir up (*s.o.*); Претседателството го активира членството the Presidency stirred up the membership **3** *Mil.* to accept (put) back into active service, reactivate **II – се 1** to rouse o.s., take a new lease of life **2** to become active **3** *Mil.* to return to active service

активист *m* activist

активистка *f* (*fem. form*) *see* активист

активност *f* activity; diligence

активно *adv* actively; diligently

актовка *f* **1** one-act play, *see* едночинка **2** briefcase

актуелен -лна *adj* topical, relevant; current, present; up-to-date; актуелно прашање a question of topical interest; a problem of the present day; a relevant question; актуелната власт the present government; the powers that be

актуелност *f* topicality; actuality, reality

актуелно *adv* topically

актчанта *f* briefcase, *see* актовка 2

акузатив *m Gram.* accusative

акумулатор *m* accumulator, battery

акумулација *f* accumulation

акустика *f* acoustics

акустичен -чна *adj* acoustic, resonant; melodious; акустична сала an auditorium with good acoustics

акустички *adj* acoustic

акустичност *f* acoustic properties, sonority

акутен -тна *adj* acute, critical; urgent, pressing; акутно прашање, акутен проблем acute problem; акутни болки acute pains

акушер *m* accoucheur, male midwife; obstetrician

акушерка *f* midwife

акушерски *adj* midwife's; midwifery *attrib.*

акушерство *n* midwifery

акцент *m Phon.* accent; stress; ❑ става акцент на to lay stress on

акценти́ра *pf & impf Phon.* to accent; to stress

акцентски *Phon.* **1** *adj* accentual; stress *attrib.*; акцентска целинка (целост) accentual /stress unit **2** *adv* accentually; in regard to stress/accent

акцентуација *f Phon.* accentuation; stress

акција -ии *f* **1** action, activity; campaign, drive; стапи во акција he went into action; акција за вработување employment campaign; работна акција (што трае подолго) work drive; (што трае покусо) working bee **2** *Comm.* share, *Am.* stock; акциите па́ѓаат shares go down; the market is bearish; акциите растат shares go up; the market is bullish; ❑ му се дигаат/му па́ѓаат акциите his shares are going up/down; *also fig.* his stock is going up/down, his star is rising/sinking

акцио́нен -она *adj* action *attrib.*

акционе́р *m* shareholder, *Am.* stockholder

акционе́рка *f (fem. form) see* акционер

акционе́рски *adj* shareholder's, *Am.* stockholder's; акционерско друштво joint-stock company

акциски *adj Comm.* share, *Am.* stock *attrib.*; акциски капитал share (*Am.* stock) capital, equity, equity capital

ал[1] *m colloq.* bad luck, misfortune; што ал го најде! what bad luck he has had!

ал[2] *adj arch.* bright red, scarlet, vermilion; ал трендафил red rose; ал пипер paprika, *see* црвен 1 (црвен пипер)

ала[1] *f* dragon

ала[2] *impf colloq.* **1** *see* џбара **2** *see* задева

алал *m colloq.* blessing; алал му вера! congratulations to him! нека ти е алал! may you be blessed! good luck to you <with that>! алал ти вера! bravo!

ала́рм *m* alarm

аларма́нтен -тна *adj* alarming

аларми́ра *pf & impf* to alarm

алат *m* tools; ❑ без алат нема занает what is a workman without his tools?

алатен -тна *adj* tool *attrib.*

алатка *f* tool

Албанец -нци *m* Albanian

Албанија *f* Albania

Албанка *f (fem. form) see* Албанец

албански *adj* Albanian

албум *m* album; албум за слики photo album

алва *f* halva; ❑ оди како алва it is selling like hot cakes

алваџија -ии *m* halva maker/seller; алваџија за бозаџија *prov.* it's six of one and half a dozen of the other; scratch my back and I'll scratch yours

алваџиски *adj* halva maker's/seller's; книга алваџиска halva wrapper (*paper in which halva is wrapped when sold*); алваџиски тевтер 1. account book of a halva maker and/or seller 2. *fig.* messy (untidy) account book

алга *f Bot.* alga (*usu. pl* algae)

алгебра *f* algebra

алгебарски *adj* algebraic

Алжир *m* **1** (*земја*) Algeria **2** (*град*) Algiers

Алжирец -рци *m* **1** Algerian **2** person from Algiers

Алжирка *f (fem. form) see* Алжирец

алжирски *adj* **1** Algerian **2** Algiers *attrib.*

алегорија -ии *f* allegory

алегоричен -чна *adj* allegorical

алéја -еи *f* tree-lined path, avenue

ален *adj see* ал[2]

алергија *f* allergy

алергичен -чна *adj* allergic

али *conj colloq.* **1** *see* или **2** *see* дали

алиби *n* alibi

аливце *n dim. of* алиште

алига́тор *m Zool.* alligator

алиментација *f* maintenance, alimony

алинéја -еи *f* <new> paragraph, indented line

алишта *pl* clothing, clothes

алиште *n* garment; dress

алка *f* link; metal ring; (*на врата*) door-knocker; (*накит*) bangle; ❑ алка што недостасува the missing link

алкален -лна *adj* alkaline

алкалии *pl* alkali

алкало́ид *m* alkaloid

алкало́иден -дна *adj* alkaloid *attrib.*, alkaloidal

алкотест *m* breath test

алкохол *m* alcohol; liquor; ❑ држи (носи) алкохол to hold one's drink; под <дејство на> алкохол under the influence of alcohol

алкохолен -лна *adj* alcoholic

алкохоли́зам -змот *m* alcoholism

алкохолизи́ра *pf & impf* **I** to alcoholize; to saturate with alcohol **II** – се to become alcoholized; to become saturated with alcohol; to take to drink

алкохоличар *m* alcoholic

алманах -си *m* almanac

ало *interj* (*on the telephone*) hello!

алов *adj see* ал[2]

аловина *f* bright red colouring, vermilion, scarlet; rosy tint

алоса *pf* **I 1** to hit; to injure **2** to ruin, destroy **II** – се **1** to injure o.s. **2** to ruin o.s.

Алпи *pl* the Alps

алпски *adj* **1** from/of the Alps **2** Alpine

алт *m Mus.* alto, contralto

алтан *m arch.* gold coin

алтернати́ва *f* alternative

алтернати́вен -вна *adj* alternative

алтица *f* patch

алуди́ра *impf* to allude (*на – to*)

алузија -ии *f* allusion

алуминиум *m* aluminium, *Am.* aluminum

алуминиумски *adj* aluminium, *Am.* aluminum *attrib.*

алфа *f* alpha; ❑ алфа и омега alpha and omega; the be-all and end-all

алфабе́т *m* alphabet, *see* азбука

алфабе́тски *adj* alphabetical

алхемичар *m* alchemist

алче[1] *m* sorrel/chestnut <horse>

алче[2] *n dim. of* алка

алчен -чна *adj* greedy; covetous

алчност *f* greed; covetousness

алчо *m* sorrel/chestnut <horse>

ам *m* harness, *see* амут

ама[1] *conj colloq.* but; таа сака да дојде, ама татко ѝ не ја пушта she wants to come, but her father will not let her

ама[2] *interj* **1** oh, what a . . . ! ама жена била! oh, what a woman she is! **2** (*expressing indignation*) ама што знаеш ти! but what do you know about it? a <fat> lot you know! ❏ ама работа! good job! fine! (also iron.); what a to-do!

Амазо́н *m* (*река*) the Amazon

Амазо́нец -нци *m* Amazonian

Амазо́нија *f* (*регион*) the Amazon region, Amazonia

Амазо́нка *f* (*fem. form*) *see* Амазо́нец; амазонка *fig., Myth.* Amazon

амазо́нски *adj* Amazonian

ама́јлија -ии *f* amulet, talisman, charm

ама́л *m* porter

амалга́м *m* amalgam

амалгами́ран *adj* amalgam-coated

ама́лски *adj* porter's

ама́м *m* Turkish bath<house>, steam bath

ама́н *m* 1 mercy, grace, favour; аман не му дава he has no mercy on him 2 (*appeal for mercy, forgiveness, help*) for goodness' (heaven's, God's) sake! аман, помагајте for goodness' sake, help me! 3 (*refrain in folk-songs*) oh! oh! hey-ho!

амандма́н *m* amendment

ама́нет *m* will, testament; charge; trust; ❏ остава аманет (*нешто на некого*) to entrust (*s.th. with s.th.*), leave (*s.th.*) in (*s.o.'s*) safekeeping

ама́нте *interj see* аман 2

амате́р *m* amateur

аматери́зам -змот *m* amateurism

амате́рски *adj* amateur, amateurish

амбала́жа *f* packing/wrapping material; трошоци за амбалажа cost of packing

амбала́жен -жна *adj* packing *attrib.*; wrapping *attrib.*; амбалажна хартија brown paper

амба́р *m* barn, granary

амбаса́да *f* embassy

амбаса́дор *m* ambassador; вонреден и полномоштен амбасадор ambassador extraordinary and plenipotentiary

амбаса́дорски *adj* ambassadorial

амби́ент *m* ambience

амби́с *m* abyss, chasm

амби́ција -ии *f* ambition

амбицио́зен -зна *adj* ambitious

амбицио́зност *f* ambitiousness

амбле́м *m* emblem

амбула́нта *f* clinic; (*во болница*) out-patient department

амбула́нтен -тна *adj* 1 out-patient *attrib.*; амбулантно лекување out-patient treatment 2 itinerant; амбулантен трговец itinerant merchant (trader)

амво́н *m* pulpit, ambo

аме́ба *f Zool.* amoeba

Аме́рика *f* America; Јужна Америка South America; Северна Америка North America; ❏ повторно ја открива Америка to reinvent the wheel

амери́кан *m* unbleached calico, grey cloth

Америка́нец -нци *m* American

Америка́нка *f* (*fem. form*) *see* Американец

америка́нски *adj* American

амети́ст *m* amethyst

ами́[1] *conj* but; ами ако не дојде? but what if he doesn't come? ами сега што ќе правиме? but what are we going to do now?

ами́[2] *part* (*indicates refusal or complete disagreement*) ами! I should say not! *iron.* why, of course!

ами́н *interj* amen

амину́ва *pf & impf* to say amen; *fig.* to say yes, approve

амину́вач *m see* аминџија

амину́ва *m* see амин... [*note: entry reads* аминџија]

амину́вач *m see* аминџија

амка́ *impf* to snap at a suspended piece of food (*usu. a hard-boiled egg*) (*traditional game*)

амне́зија *f* amnesia

амне́стија *f* amnesty

амнести́ра *pf & impf* to amnesty, grant amnesty to; to pardon

амонија́к *m* ammonia

амонија́ков & амонија́чен -чна *adj* of ammonia

амора́лен -лна *adj* amoral; immoral

амора́лност *f* amoral nature; immorality

амортиза́ција *f* 1 writing off 2 *Comm.* amortization, cancelling, extinguishing; depreciation; амортизација на долг debt redemption; амортизација на капиталот depreciation of capital; износ на амортизацијата depreciation charges 3 *Tech.* shock absorption

амортизаци́онен -она *adj* 1 *Comm.* amortizing *attrib.*; depreciation *attrib.*; амортизационен план terms of redemption; амортизационен фонд amortization (sinking) fund 2 *Tech.* shock-absorbing *attrib.*

амортизе́р *m Tech.* shock absorber

амортизи́ра *pf & impf* 1 *Comm.* (*долг*) to amortize, extinguish, pay off; (*инвестиција*) to depreciate 2 to write off 3 *Tech.* to absorb the shocks

аморфен -фна *adj* amorphous

аморфност *f* amorphousness

а́мпа *f arch.* trouble; accident; disaster

ампе́р *m Phys.* ampere

амплиту́да *f* amplitude

амплифика́ција *f* amplification

ампута́ција *f* amputation

ампути́ра *pf & impf* to amputate

аму́т *m* harness

амфи́бија -ии *f* amphibian

амфи́брах *m Prosody* amphibrach

амфитеа́тар -три *m* amphitheatre

ан *m* inn, tavern

Ана́дол & Ана́долија *f* Anatolia

Ана́долец -лци *m* Anatolian

Ана́долка *f* (*fem. form*) *see* Анадолец

анадо́лски *adj* Anatolian

ана́ли *pl* annals

анали́за *f* analysis

анализа́тор *m* (*апарат*) analysing apparatus, analyser; (*лице*) analyst

анализи́ра *pf & impf* to analyse

анали́тика *f* 1 analysis 2 analytical geometry

анали́тичар *m* analyst

анали́тичен -чна *adj* analytical; analytic

ана́логен -гна *adj* analogous

анало́гија -ии *f* analogy; по анологија (со) by analogy (*with*)

ана́логно *adv* analogously, similar

аналфабе́т *m* illiterate <person>

аналфабети́зам -змот *m* illiteracy

аналфабе́тски *adj* illiterate

ана́ма *f* Muslim lady (wife)

анана́с *m Bot.* (Ananas sativus) pineapple

ана́пест *m Prosody* anapaest

анархи́зам -змот *m* anarchism

анархија *f* anarchy

анархист *m* anarchist

анархистичен -чна *adj* anarchistic

анархистички *adj* anarchistic, anarchical

анархичен -чна *adj* anarchic<al>

анасон *m Bot.* (Pimpinella anisum) anise

анасонка *f* aniseed-flavoured spirit (*drink similar to ouzo*)

анатема *f* anathema, curse

анатемиса *pf see* анатемоса

анатемник -ци *m* anathematized person; (*лош човек*) wicked person

анатемоса *pf* to anathematize; to curse

анатемосува *impf of* анатемоса

анатом *m* anatomist

анатомија *f* anatomy

анатомски *adj* anatomical

анахронизам -змот *m* anachronism

ангажира *pf & impf* **I 1** to engage; (*најми*) to hire, take on, retain; ангажираме огромни средства we are employing (applying, bringing to bear) enormous resources; ангажирав адвокат I have retained a lawyer **2** to occupy; (*интересира*) to interest; наставникот ги ангажира учениците во повеќе активности the teacher occupied the pupils in (with) various activities **II – се** (*се впушти во*) to engage o.s. (*with*); (*се нафати на*) to undertake; (*се заинтересира*) to be interested (*за – in*)

ангажман *m* engagement (*at a theatre*); (*ветување, обврска*) voluntary undertaking

ангарија *f* corvée; unpaid work

ангел *m* angel; ❏ ангелот чувар one's guardian angel; вистински ангел е he's an angel, he is kindness itself; не е ангел he's no angel

ангелоса се *pf colloq.* to faint

ангелски *adj* (*на ангел*) angel's; (*како кај ангел*) angelic

ангелче *n* (*dim. of* ангел) cherub

ангина *f Med.* tonsillitis, sore throat; quinsy; angina; ангина пекторис angina pectoris

Англија *f* England

англиски *adj* English

Англичанец -нци *m* Englishman

Англичанка *f* Englishwoman

англикански *adj* Anglican; англиканска црква Anglican church

Ангола *f* Angola

Анголец -лци *m* Angolan

Анголка *f* (*fem. form*) *see* Анголец

анголски *adj* Angolan

ангро *adv* wholesale, gross; трговија на ангро wholesale <trade>

Анди *pl* the Andes

Андора *f* Andorra

Андорец -рци *m* Andorran

Андорка *f* (*fem. form*) *see* Андорец

андорски *adj* Andorran

анегдота *f* anecdote

анегдотичен -чна *adj* anecdotal

анексија *f* annexation

анектира *pf & impf* to annex

анемија *f* anaemia

анемичен -чна *adj* anaemic

анестезија *f* anaesthesia

Анкара *f* Ankara, *arch.* Angora

анкарец -рци *m* person from Ankara

анкарка *f* (*fem. form*) *see* анкарец

анкарски *adj* Ankara *attrib.*

анкета *f* questionnaire; survey, investigation; poll; спроведува анкета to conduct a poll/survey

анкетен -тна *adj* of a questionnaire

анкетира *pf & impf* to conduct a poll/inquiry; to investigate; to ask for an opinion

анласер *m Tech.* starter

анода *f Elec.* anode

аномалија -ии *f* anomaly, irregularity

анонимен -мна *adj* anonymous

анонимност *f* anonymity

ансамбл *m* ensemble; group; фолклорен ансамбл folklore ensemble

ански *adj* inn, tavern *attrib.*

антав *adj* clumsy, awkward

антагонизам -змот *m* antagonism

антагонистички *adj* antagonistic

Антарктик *m* Antarctica, the Antarctic

антарктички *adj* Antarctic

антена *f* antenna, aerial

антерија -ии *f* padded jacket

анти- *prefix* anti-

антибиотик -ци *m Med.* antibiotic

антибиотички *adj Med.* antibiotic

антидржавен -вна *adj* anti-state, subversive, seditious

антика *f* **1** the classical <Greek and Roman> period, antiquity; classical culture/art; the olden days **2** *colloq.* antique **3** *fig. colloq.* антика човек odd person, person with strange habits

антиквар *m* second-hand bookseller; antique dealer

антикварен -рна *adj* antique, ancient; second-hand

антикварница *f* antique shop; second-hand bookshop; curiosity shop

антикварски *adj* antiquarian (*shop, catalogue*)

Антили *pl* the Antilles

антилски *adj* Antilles *attrib.*

антилопа *f Zool.* antelope

антипатија -ии *f* antipathy

антипатичен -чна *adj* repulsive, disgusting

антипод *m* antipode

антисемит *m* anti-Semite

антисемитизам -змот *m* anti-Semitism

антисемитски *adj* anti-Semitic

антисептичен -чна *adj* antiseptic

антитеза *f* antithesis

антифашизам -змот *m* antifascism

антифашист *m* antifascist

антифашистички *adj* antifascist

антихрист *m* Antichrist

антички *adj* classical; antique

антологија -ии *f* anthology

антоним *m Gram.* antonym

антре -éa *n* entrance, hall, vestibule

антропологија *f* anthropology

антрополошки *adj* anthropological

ануитет *m* annuity, yearly instalment

анулира *pf & impf* to annul

анче *n dim. of* ан

анџак *adv colloq.* since, seeing that, as; анџак си тука, да ја свршиме работата since you are here, let's finish the job

анџар *m* long dagger, dirk

анџија -ии *m* innkeeper, tavern owner

аорист *m Gram.* aorist

аóрта *f Anat.* aorta

ап *m colloq.* pill, tablet

апарáт *m* apparatus; фотографски апарат camera; телефонски апарат telephone; апарат за бричење electric shaver; апарати во домаќинството kitchen appliances; државен апарат machinery of State; *Anat.* говорен апарат organs of speech

апаратýра *f* equipment; apparatus

апартмáн *m* suite; luxury flat (*Am.* apartment)

апатија *f* apathy, indifference

апатичен -чна *adj* apathetic

апаш *m* thief; pickpocket; ruffian; good-for-nothing, sponger

апашки *adj* ruffianly; thief's

апе *impf* **1** to bite; to sting; *fig.* to bark; кучето апе the dog bites; директорот апе the boss has a sharp tongue **2** to itch

апеж *m* **1** bite **2** itch, itching

апел *m* appeal, call

апелатѝвен -вна *adj Gram.* appellative; *Leg.* appellate, appeal *attrib.*; апелативен суд court of appeal

апелација *f* <legal> appeal

апелациóнен -она *adj Leg.* appellate; апелационен суд court of appeal

апелѝра *pf & impf* to appeal

Апенѝни *pl* the Apennines

апенински *adj* Apennine *attrib.*; Апенински Полуостров the Apennine Peninsula

аперитѝв *m* aperitif

апетѝт *m* appetite (*also fig.*); ❑ зголемува некому апетит to whet s.o.'s appetite; нема апетит to be off one's food

апетѝтен -тна *adj* appetizing

апла *colloq.* **1** *adv* openly, without beating about the bush **2** *adj indecl.* (*in set expressions*) апла работа obvious thing; it's crystal clear; апла лага bare-faced lie

аплаудѝра *impf* to applaud

аплауз *m* applause; ❑ еден голем аплауз за <to give> (*s.o.*) a big hand; собира аплаузи to bring the house down; to receive a standing ovation

аплив *adj* vicious; апливо куче vicious dog; аплив човек gruff person

апликација *f* **1** application **2** appliqué

апне *pf* апна *aor. see* касне

апнува *impf of* апне

апоéн *m* denomination

апозиција -ии *f Gram.* apposition

апокриф *m* Apocrypha; piece of apocryphal writing

апокрифен -фна *adj* apocryphal

аполитичен -чна *adj* apolitical

аполитичност *f* apolitical nature

апологéт *m* apologist, defender, devotee

апологетика *f* apologetics

апологетичен -чна *adj* apologetic

апологија -ии *f* apologia

апоплексија -ии *f Med.* apoplexy; stroke

апоплектичен -чна *adj Med.* apoplectic

апостол *m* **1** *Rel.* apostle **2** *fig.* champion; апостол на слобода champion of freedom **3** *Rel.* Book/Acts of the Apostles

апостолски *adj* apostolic

апостроф *m* apostrophe

апострофѝра *pf & impf* to apostrophize; (*остро прекине*) to heckle, interrupt; (*искара*) to criticize; (*стави апостроф*) to put in an apostrophe; (*истакне*) to stress, emphasize

апотеóза *f* apotheosis

април *m* April; апри-ли-ли-ли! April fool, April fool!

априлски *adj* April *attrib.*; априлска шега April fool's joke

априóрен -рна *adj* a priori

априóри *adv* a priori

апс *m* **1** *see* апсáна **2** *see* апсеник

апсáна *f* jail, prison

апсеник -ци *m* prisoner

апсење *n* arrest

апси *impf* to arrest

апсолвéнт *m* graduating (final-year) student

апсолвéнтка *f* (*fem. form*) *see* апсолвент

апсолвѝра *pf & impf* **1** to complete course requirements at a university; апсолвирав во јуни месец, дипломирав во септември I completed my studies in June and graduated in September **2** to deal (*with*); тоа прашање сме го апсолвирале we have dealt with that question

апсолýтен -тна *adj* absolute

апсолутѝзам -змот *m* absolutism

апсолутизѝра *pf & impf* to allow (*s.th.*) to predominate; to give precedence (*to*); to override, outweigh

апсолутѝст *m* absolutist

апсолутистички *adj* absolute, absolutistic

апсолýтно *adv* absolutely, completely, unconditionally

апсорбѝра *pf & impf* to absorb

апстинéнт *m* abstainer; teetotaller

апстиненција *f* abstinence

апстрактен -тна *adj* abstract; апстрактна уметност abstract art

апстрактно *adv* abstractly

апстракција -ии *f* abstraction

апстрахѝра *pf & impf* **1** (*издвојува*) to abstract **2** (*занемарува*) to ignore, neglect, overlook

апсурд *m* absurdity, the absurd, nonsense

апсурден -дна *adj* absurd

аптека *f* pharmacy, chemist's shop, *Am.* drugstore

аптекар *m* pharmacist, chemist

аптекарка *f* **1** (*fem. form*) *see* аптекар **2** chemist's wife

аптекарски *adj* pharmaceutical

аптекарство *n* pharmacy

апцигува *pf & impf* **1** to deduct (*money from pay*) **2** *Print.* to take off, pull a proof

апче *n dim. of* ап

ар¹ -ови *m* stable, stall

ар² *m* (*pl* ари) are (*100 square metres*)

арабаџија -ии *m* coachman; carter, waggoner

арабéска *f* arabesque

Арабија *f* Arabia; Саудиска Арабија Saudi Arabia

арабиски *adj* Arabian

Арабјанец -нци *m* Arab, Arabian

Арабјанка *f* (*fem. form*) *see* Арабјанец

арам *colloq.* **1** *m* curse **2** *adj indecl.* cursed; арам ти било млекото со кое сум те доела! cursed be the milk with which I suckled you!

арамбаша *m* 1 *Hist.* komitadji leader 2 *arch. see* арамија 3 *colloq.* scoundrel

арамија -ии *m* robber, bandit; thief, burglar

арамилак -ци *m* robbery

арамиски *adj* robber's, thief's

арамолебец -пци *m colloq.* sponger, idler, loafer, parasite

аранжер *m* arranger; (*на приредба*) organizer, master of ceremonies; (*на излог*) window dresser

аранжира *pf & impf* to arrange (*also Mus.*), organize; to reach an agreement; (*режира*) to rig; аранжира излог to arrange (set up) a display, dress a window; аранжира (*дело*) за оркестар to arrange (*a piece*) for orchestra

аранжман *m* arrangement; agreement; <business> deal; пакет-аранжман package deal; туристички аранжман package tour

аранија -ии *f* large cauldron

арап<ин> -пи *m arch.* Negro; Arab

арапка *f arch.* Negress; Arab woman

арапски *adj arch.* Arabian, Arabic; Negro

арач *m Hist.* tax

арбитер -три *m* arbiter, arbitrator

арбитража *f* arbitration; (*на хартии од вредност*) arbitrage

арбитражен -жна *adj* arbitration *attrib.*; арбитражен суд arbitration court (tribunal); court of conciliation

аргат<ин> -ти *m* day labourer; farm-hand

аргатски *adj* day labourer's; farm-hand's

аргатува *impf* to work as a day labourer/farm-hand

Аргентина *f* Argentina, the Argentine

Аргентинец -нци *m* Argentinian, Argentine

Аргентинка *f* (*fem. form*) *see* Аргентинец

аргентински *adj* Argentinian, Argentine

аргумент *m* argument, debate; proof, reason, justification

аргументација *f* argumentation, debate

аргументира *pf & impf* to argue, discuss; to prove, substantiate

арен -рна *adj* good, worthy; fit, well; strong; diligent; proper; арен сум I am well, I'm fine; не е <нешто> арен he is off colour, he is feeling under par; ❏ од арен поарен excellent, couldn't be better; арен беше, арно го најде one gets what's coming to one; it serves him right; арната стока сама се продава *prov.* good ware makes quick markets

арена *f* arena

аренда *f* renting; rent; lease

ареса *pf dial.* I to like, take a fancy (*to*) II – се to please, catch s.o.'s fancy

аресува (се) *impf of* ареса (се)

арија -ии *f Mus.* aria

аристократ *m* aristocrat

аристократија *f* aristocracy

аристократски *adj* aristocratic

аритметика *m* arithmetic

аритметичар *m* arithmetician

аритметички *adj* arithmetical; arithmetic

арка[1] *f* arch

арка[2] *f* support; protection; ark

Арктик *m* the Arctic <Zone>

арктички *adj* 1 Arctic; Арктичкиот Океан the Arctic Ocean 2 arctic

АРМ *abbr.* (*Армија на Република Македонија*) Army of the Republic of Macedonia

арматура *f* armature; metal framework; accessories

армија -ии *f* army

армиран *adj* reinforced (*concrete, etc.*)

армиски *adj* army *attrib.*

армоника *f see* хармоника

арнина *f see* добрина

арниса *pf colloq.* I to leave, abandon, quit; арнисај ја, бре дете, таа мома give up that girl, my boy! II – се to avoid, keep clear of; to leave alone, give up; најпосле, тој се арниса од таа мисла in the end he gave up that idea

арнисува (се) *impf of* арниса (се)

арно 1 *adv* well, good, fine; од арно поарно couldn't be better, excellent; арно лошо – тоа е, друго нема good or bad, that's it, there's nothing else; арно де! fine! jolly good! со арно nicely; фати го со арно, ќе ти помогне approach him nicely and he will help you 2 *m* good, good luck; арното не иде веднаш, да за лошото дури да трепнеш со окото good luck doesn't come straight away but bad luck comes before you can wink

арнотија -ии *f see* добрина

аро *n arch.* 1 *in the expression:* старо аро *pejor.* old codger; dirty old man 2 evil, bad luck

арогантен -тна *adj* arrogant

ароганција *f* arrogance

арома *f* aroma

аромат *m* aroma

ароматен -тна *adj* aromatic

ароматичен -чна *adj see* ароматен

арпа *f* unhusked rice

арпацик *m* seed onions, *see* кокар

арсен *m Chem.* arsenic

арсенал *m* arsenal

арсеник *m Chem.* arsenic, arsenic trioxide

арслан *m arch.* lion

артерија -ии *f* 1 *Anat.* artery 2 *fig.* main (arterial, *esp. Brit.* trunk) road

артериосклероза *f Med.* arteriosclerosis

артериски *adj Anat.* arterial

артески *adj* artesian; артески бунар artesian well

артикал -кли *m* product, item, <trade> article

артикулација *f* articulation

артикулационен -она *adj* articulatory

артикулира *impf* to articulate

артилерец -рци *m* artilleryman, gunner

артилерија *f* artillery

артилериски *adj* artillery

артист *m* 1 actor 2 artist

артистички *adj* artistic

артистка *f* 1 actress 2 artist

архаизам -змот *m* archaism

архаичен -чна *adj* archaic

архаичност *f* archaic character

археолог -зи *m* archaeologist

археологија *f* archaeology

археолошки *adj* archaeological

архив *m* archives, record office; <public/official> records; annals

архива *f* archive

архивар *m* archivist

архивски *adj* archival

архиѓáкон *m* <Orthodox> archdeacon
архиепископ *m* <Orthodox> archbishop
архиепископија -ии *f* <Orthodox> archbishopric
архиепископски *adj* <Orthodox> archiepiscopal
архиерéj -еи *m* <Orthodox> archpriest
архиерéjски *adj* <Orthodox> archpriest's
архимандрúт *m* <Orthodox> archimandrite
архитéкт *m* architect
архитектоника *f* architectonics
архитектонски *adj* architectonic
архитектýра *f* architecture
архитектýрен -рна *adj* architectural
арч -еви, ови *m colloq.* expense, cost; expenditure
арчлив *adj* wasteful, spendthrift
арчи *impf colloq.* (*троши*) to spend; детето многу арчи the child spends a lot
аршин *m* ell (*measure of length*); ❏ аршините не се за сите еднакви the yardstick is not the same for everyone; двоен аршин double standard
ас *m* 1 *Cards* ace 2 *fig. Sport.* ace
асален -лна *adj see* асолен
асално *adv see* асолно; уште Армијата на Македонија не беше асално заживеала the Macedonian Army was not yet firmly established
асе *n* sheeting (*fine cotton material*)
асимилáтор *m* assimilator
асимилаторски *adj* assimilatory, assimilative
асимилација *f* assimilation
асимилúра *pf & impf* to assimilate
Асирец -рци *m* Assyrian
Асирија *f* Assyria
Асирка *f* (*fem. form*) *see* Асирец
асирски *adj* Assyrian
асистéнт *m* teaching fellow, instructor; research assistant (*at universities, scientific institutions, etc.*); tutor
асистéнтка *f* (*fem. form*) *see* асистент
асистéнтски *adj* teaching fellow's, instructor's, research assistant's; tutor's
асистúра *impf* to assist
аскер *m arch.* 1 soldier 2 army
аскет *m* ascetic
аскетúзам -змот *m* asceticism
аскетски *adj* ascetic
асли 1 *adj indecl. colloq.* real, genuine, *Austral.* dinkum; асли маж a real man 2 *adv* exactly, just, indeed; асли тоа го бараше it was just what he was asking/looking for
АСНОМ *abbr.* (*Антифашистичко собрание на народното ослободување на Македонија*) Antifascist National-Liberation Assembly of Macedonia
асол *m colloq.* good, use; не е за асол it is no good, it is <of> no use
асолен -лна *adj colloq.* useful; worthy, good; асолна жена worthy (good) woman
асолно *adv* well, properly, decently; ни опран, ни закрпен, ни асолно најаден neither washed, nor dressed, nor properly fed
асортимáн *m* assortment, range, selection
асоцијáлен -лна *adj* asocial, antisocial
асоцијација -ии *f* association
асоцúра *pf & impf* to associate
аспект *m* 1 aspect; view, viewpoint, standpoint 2 *Gram.* verbal aspect

аспирáнт *m* candidate, applicant; trainee; clerical assistant
аспирација -ии *f* aspiration, claim
аспра *f* 1 asper (*small Turkish coin*) 2 *colloq.* any small coin, sou, penny; црвена аспра не гине *prov.* he always turns up like a bad penny; the more wicked, the more lucky; the more knave, the better luck
астар *m* 1 *see* постава[1] 2 *arch.* астар на покрив roof construction
астма *f Med.* asthma
астматичар *m Med.* asthmatic
астматичен -чна *adj Med.* asthmatic
астраган *m* astrakhan
астролóг -зи *m* astrologist
астрологија *f* astrology
астронóм *m* astronomer
астрономија *f* astronomy
астронóмски *adj* astronomical (*also fig.*); ❏ бара астрономски цифри he is asking astronomical sums
асфалт *m* asphalt
асфалтен -тна *adj* asphalt *attrib.*, asphalted
асфалтúра *pf & impf* to asphalt
ат *m* 1 Arab <horse> 2 horse
атáка *f* attack
атакува *pf & impf* to attack
аташé -еи *m* attaché
атеúзам -змот *m* atheism
атеúст *m* atheist
атеистичен -чна & атеистички *adj* atheistic
атеúстка *f* (*fem. form*) *see* атеист
ателjé -еа *n* atelier, studio
атентáт *m* assassination; assassination attempt
атентáтор *m* assassin; would-be assassin
атентаторка *f* (*fem. form*) *see* атентатор
атентаторски *adj* assassin's; assassination *attrib.*
атер *m colloq.* love, affection, favour, good will, consideration; за атер на некого for s.o.'s sake; for s.o.'s blue eyes; за атер на татко ти ќе те прими и тебе he will see you because of his affection for your father; од атер as a favour; атер да не ти остане so that you do not feel aggrieved/sorry; му го расипа (скрши) атерот he didn't do his bidding; he didn't humour him; атерот му е голем his good will is very important
атерџија -ии *m colloq.* obliging/tolerant person
атéст & атестáт *m* attestation, certificate
атестúра *pf & impf* to attest, certify
Атина *f* Athens
атински *adj* Athenian
атињанец -нци *m* Athenian
атињанка *f* (*fem. form*) *see* атињанец
Атлантис *m* Atlantis
атлантски *adj* Atlantic; Атлантскиот Океан the Atlantic Ocean
атлас *m* atlas
атлéт *m* athlete
атлетика *f* athletics
атлетичар *m* athlete, *see* атлет
атлéтски *adj* athletic
атмосфéра *f* atmosphere (*also fig.*); mood
атмосфéрски *adj* atmospheric<al>
атом *m* atom
атомизација *f* atomization
атомизúра *pf & impf* to atomize

атоми́ст   *m* **1** atomist **2** atomic scientist
атомски   *adj* atomic
атрибут   *m* attribute
атрофија   *f* atrophy; атрофија на мускулите atrophy of the muscles
атрофи́ра   *pf & impf* to atrophy
ау   *interj* ow!
аугментати́в   *m* augmentative
аудиенција   *f* audience
аудиториум   *m* auditorium
аудиција   *f* audition
аукција   *f* auction; водител на аукција auctioneer; дава на аукција to put up for auction; купува/продава на аукција to buy/sell by auction
аула   *f* auditorium, hall
ауспух   *m* exhaust pipe, exhaust system
аут   *m Sport.* out; ❑ оди в аут to make a faux pas, drop a brick (clanger); to fall into disgrace
ауто   *n colloq. see* автомобил
аутопешки   *adv joc.* on foot; ❑ <оди> аутопешки to go on shanks' pony
афект   *m* strong emotion, excitement; irresistible impulse
афера   *f* illegal/immoral affair; <political> scandal; love affair; ❑ шири афери to chatter; to blab; to gossip
аферим   *interj colloq.* jolly good! bravo!
афери́ст   *m* person prone to get involved in scandals/affairs; sensationalist
афините́т   *m* affinity, attraction
афион   *m* **1** *Bot.* (Papaver somniferum) poppy **2** opium
афионски   *adj* poppy *attrib.*; афионско семе poppy seed; афионски катран opium; афионски нож special knife for collecting dried poppy juice (opium); афионска шапка, афионска чушка poppy seedcase, poppy-head

афирмати́вен   -вна *adj* affirmative
афирмација   *f* affirmation
афирми́ра   *pf & impf* **I** to affirm, assert, establish; го афирмирав институтот I put the institute on the map; писателите го афирмираа македонскиот литературен јазик writers won recognition for the Macedonian standard language **II – се** to establish a reputation; to be recognized; to get accepted; to become known; писателот се афирмира со тој роман the writer established his reputation with that novel
афори́зам   -змот *m* aphorism
афористичен   -чна *adj* aphoristic, concise, pithy
афористички   *adj* aphoristic, concerning *or* containing aphorisms
Африка   *f* Africa
Африканец   -нци *m* African
Африканка   *f* (*fem. form*) *see* Африканец
африкански   *adj* African
ацето́н   *m* acetone; nail-polish remover
ах   *interj* oh!
аџамија   -ии *m colloq.* inexperienced (naive, innocent) person; greenhorn
аџамилак   -ци *m colloq.* lack of experience, immaturity, naivety
аџи   *indecl.* (*title*) Hajji, Hadji; аџи Васил Hadji Vasil
аџија   -ии *m* hajji, hadji; pilgrim
аџилак   *m* hajj, hadj (*Muslim pilgrimage to Mecca*); Christian pilgrimage to Jerusalem
аџиски   *adj* hajji's, hadji's, pilgrim's
аш   *interj child.* all gone! (*when s.th. has disappeared or been hidden*)
ашик[1]   *m arch.* **1** love; ашик се стори he fell in love **2** lover, sweetheart
ашик[2]   -ци *m* knucklebone
ашлак   -ци *m arch.* scoundrel, good-for-nothing

 Б

ба *interj* (*expressing surprise*) oh! ба, ами сега што ќе правиме! oh, but what shall we do now?!

баба *f* **1** grandmother; баба ми my grandmother; ❑ и баба ми го знае тоа anyone can do that, it's a piece of cake **2** old woman; ❑ баба Марта changeable March weather, in March many weathers; баба Зима Jack Frost; баба шарка smallpox; селото гори, бабата се чешла *prov.* Nero fiddles while Rome burns **3** mother-in-law (*wife's mother*), *see* тешта **4** midwife; при многу баби детето килаво излегува *prov.* too many cooks spoil the broth **5** *fig.* weakling, milksop, coward

бабалак -ци *m* **1** father-in-law (*wife's father*) **2** grandfather **3** (*татковнина*) patrimony, inheritance; таа нива ми е бабалак I inherited this field from my father

бабар *m* (*usu. pl*) *see* василичар

бабачко -овци *m colloq.* big (burly) fellow, fat chap, *sl.* fatso

бабешки *adj* old woman's, old wives'

бабилика *f Bot.* (Sorbus torminalis) wild service tree

бабин *adj* old woman's; ❑ бабини прикаски, бабини деветини old wives' tales; бабин ден 8th January (*when midwives pay ritual calls at houses where they have delivered babies*); бабини дни or баби the last three days of March; бабина душица *Bot.* (Thymus serpyllum) wild thyme; бабин заб *Bot.* (Tribulus terrestris) caltrop

бабински *adj* old woman's; бабински работи old women's business (*usu. folk medicine*); fiddle-faddle, rubbish

бабиње *pl* the third evening after the birth of a child; *see* вечер 1: трета вечер

бабица *f* **1** *see* бабичка **2** midwife

бабичка *f hyp.* (*of* баба) granny, grandma

бабнатина *f* bruise, swelling

бабне[1] *impf* to swell up; жилите бабнат the veins are swelling

бабне[2] *pf & impf* бабна *aor.* to bang, strike, thump; ветрот бабнеше по прозорците the wind was drumming on the windows

бабовина *f see* бабалак 3

баботач *m* babbler, chatterbox; noisy person

баботевица *f see* баботење 1 & 2

баботење *n* **1** *from* баботи **2** noise, row **3** *fig.* babble, chatter

баботи *impf* **1** to boom; to rumble **2** to make a noise; не туку баботете кога се починуваат don't keep making a noise when people are resting! **3** (*за оган*) to blaze **4** *fig.* to babble

бабува *impf* to act as a midwife

бабуле[1] *n* bubble; *Anat.* bladder

бабуле[2] *n hyp. of* баба 2

бабулица *f* pimple

бабун *m* **1** s.o. with a wrinkled face **2** *Hist.* Bogomil

бабунов *adj Hist.* Bogomil *attrib.*; бабунов гроб Bogomil grave (tomb)

бабуњоса <ce> *pf* to swell, become swollen

бабуњосан *adj* swollen

бабуњосува <ce> *impf of* бабуњоса <ce>

бабура *f see* бабушка 1

бабушка *f* **1** green pepper **2** large needle (pin) **3** toothless sheep, sheep with missing teeth **4** *Zool.* a fish of the carp family

бавеж *m* delay, dragging out

бавен -вна *adj* slow; sluggish; slow-witted

бави *impf* **I** to delay, protract, drag out; to hold up (back); бави, ама не заборави take your time but don't forget! домашните грижи ме бавеа household worries held me up **II** – ce to be delayed; to be slow; to be late; Мирко се бавеше при приготвувањето Mirko took his time getting ready

бавно *adv* slowly

бавност *f* slowness; sluggishness

бавта *impf* **I** **1** to wade; to plod, trudge **2** *fig.* to chatter, prattle **II** – ce **1** to wade; to trudge; се бавта по кал to trudge through mud **2** to potter; to dabble; по цел ден се бавта со детето she spends all day minding the child; тој сака да се бавта во бавчата he likes pottering about in the garden

бавтанаана *adv in the expression:* на (од) бавтанаана by guesswork, at random

бавча *f* garden; стаклена бавча greenhouse

бавчанџија -ии *m* gardener, market gardener, *Am.* truck farmer; ❑ на бавчанџијата му продава пиперки (краставици) to teach your grandmother to suck eggs

бавчанка *f* (*fem. form*) *see* бавчанџија

бавчанџилак *m* market gardening, *Am.* truck farming

бавчанџиство *n* market gardening, *Am.* truck farming

бавчанџиски *adj* gardener's

багаж *m* luggage, baggage; рачен багаж hand (personal, small) luggage

багажен -жна *adj* luggage, baggage *attrib.*; багажен вагон luggage-van

багажник -ци *m* (*на велосипед, мотор*) carrier, pannier; (*на автомобил*) boot, *Am.* trunk

багатела *f* trifle, bagatelle; bargain; ❑ за багатела dirt cheap, for a song

Багдад *m* Baghdad

багдадски *adj* Baghdad

багдаѓанец -нци *m* person from Baghdad

багдаѓанка *f* (*fem. form*) *see* багдаѓанец

багер *m* dredge, dredger

багерист *m* dredge operator

багра *f* **1** *poet.* colour **2** *poet.* red; purple **3** *colloq.* scum, riff-raff

багрем *m Bot.* (Robinia pseudoacacia) <false> acacia, locust tree, robinia tree; црвен багрем (Robinia hispida) rose acacia

багремарник -ци *m* <false->acacia coppice, acacia grove

багремов *adj* acacia *attrib.*

багри *impf poet.* **1** to colour, paint, dye **2** to make (*s.th.*) red

баде *n* duckling

бадем *m Bot.* (Prunus amygdalus) almond (*tree and fruit*); бадем кајсија large almond-shaped apricot; бадем шеќер sugared almond

бадемов *adj* almond *attrib.*; бадемово масло almond oil

бадијава *adv see* бадијала

бадијала *adj indecl. & adv colloq.* **1** for nothing, free, gratis; за бадијала dirt cheap, for a song **2** in vain; чекам цел ден за бадијала I have waited the whole day in vain (for nothing)

бадијалџија -ии *m colloq.* loafer, *colloq.* lazybones

бадминтон *m* badminton; играат бадминтон they are playing badminton

бадник *m* **1** Christmas Eve **2** yule-log

бадникар *m* person who fetches the yule-log

бадниковица *f see* бадник 2

баднички *adj* Christmas-Eve *attrib.*

бае *impf* to <try to> heal by magic, cast a spell, mumble incantations; to tell tales; to mumble, mutter; ❏ не туку бај! stop grumbling! мижи Асан да ти баам tell that to the marines!

баеги *adv colloq.* rather, quite; баеги скраја quite a distance

баждар *m arch.* **1** collector of fees/tolls **2** inspector of weights and measures **3** public weighing official; gauger

баждари *impf arch.* **1** to check (*weights and measures*); (*инструмент*) to calibrate, gauge **2** to collect a fee/toll **3** (*брод*) to assess the tonnage, gauge

баждарина *f arch.* **1** fee (*for checking weights and measures*), gauging fee **2** toll, charge **3** octroi

баждарница *f arch.* **1** office of weights and measures, gauging office **2** duty office **3** octroi

баждарски *adj* баждарска потврда bill (certificate) of tonnage

баждарџија -ии *m arch. see* баждар

баз -је *m* (*usu. pl*) clod, sod, turf

база *f* **1** base, foundation, basis **2** *Chem.* base

базалт *m* basalt

базалтов *adj* basaltic

базар *m* **1** (*часопис*) fashion magazine **2** (*безистен*) covered market, bazaar

базди *impf* to smell bad, stink; човекот базди од ракија the man reeks of alcohol

базен *m* **1** reservoir; pool; swimming-pool **2** *Geog.* basin

базер *m Bot.* (Asphodelus albus) white asphodel

базика *impf* to tease; не базикај го момето don't tease the girl!

базилика *f* basilica

базира *pf & impf* **I** to base, found, establish (*на – on*) **II – се 1** to base o.s. (*на – on*) **2** *Mil.* to be based

базичен -чна *adj* basic; базична индустрија basic industry

баир *m* hill, hillock

бај *m dial.* (*mode of address for an older person*) бај Петре old Petre; бај Никола Uncle Nikola

бајалец -лци *m see* бајач

бајалка *f see* бајачка

бајалски *adj* fortune-telling *attrib.*; бајалски пари

payment for fortune-telling (*traditionally thrown into a spring or fountain*)

бајарка *f see* бајачка

бајат *adj* stale; бајат леб stale bread

бајати <**се**> *impf* to grow stale, spoil *intrans.*, go bad; се бајати лебот the bread is going stale

бајач *m* sorcerer; faith-healer

бајачка *f* (*fem. form*) *see* бајач; sorceress

бајка¹ *f* **1** pebble **2** bump

бајка² *f* story, tale

бајка³ *f child.* baa-lamb

бајонет *m Mil.* bayonet

бајрак -ци *m* standard, flag, banner

бајрактар *m* standard-bearer

бајрактарка *f* (*fem. form*) *see* бајрактар

Бајрам *m Rel.* Bairam (*Muslim festival*)

бајче *n see* бајка³

бака *f* **1** wooden bucket; wooden basin, small shallow wooden vessel **2** *dial.* trough

бакал *m* grocer

бакалар *m Zool.* (Gadus morhua) cod, codfish

бакалин -ли *m see* бакал

бакалка *f* (*fem. form*) *see* бакал

бакаллак *m* **1** grocer's <trade> **2** grocer's <shop>

бакалница *f* grocer's <shop>, grocery <store>

бакалски *adj* grocer's; бакалска стока groceries

бакам *m Bot.* (Caesalpinia bahamensis) Brazil-wood

бакар *m* copper

бакарен -рна *adj* copper; (*за боја*) coppery; *Chem.* cupric; cuprous

бакари *impf colloq.* to pay attention to, respect; ич не ме бакари he takes no notice of me

бакариса *pf* to copper, coat with copper

бакарлија *adj indecl.* like copper, coppery; blotchy

бакарник -ци *m* copper cauldron/kettle

бакарџија -ии *m* coppersmith

бакелит *m* Bakelite

бакла *f Bot.* (Vicia faba) broad bean

баклава *f* **1** baklava (*sort of sweet pastry*) **2** *colloq.*, *Cards* diamonds

баклица *f* flask

бакне *pf* бакна *aor.* **I** to kiss *trans.*; го бакна татка си в чело (во челото) he kissed his father on the forehead; му бакнал рака he kissed his hand **II – се** to kiss *intrans.*

бакнеж *m* kiss; страстен бакнеж passionate kiss

бакнува (се) *impf of* бакне (се)

бакрдан *m see* бакрданик

бакрданик *m* polenta (*maize-meal porridge*)

бакрен *adj* copper; (*за боја*) coppery

бакрорез *m* copper engraving

бакрорезец -сци *m* engraver (*in copper*); copperplate engraver

баксуз *m colloq.* bad luck; person who has/brings bad luck, *colloq.* jinx; го бие баксуз he's jinxed/out of luck

баксузен -зна *adj colloq.* unlucky, fateful, ill-fated

баксузлак *m colloq.* bad luck, misfortune

бактерија -ии *f* bacterium (*pl* bacteria)

бактериолог -зи *m* bacteriologist

бактериологија *f* bacteriology

бактериолошки *adj* bacteriological; бактериолошка војна bacteriological warfare

бактериски *adj* bacterial

бакшиш *m* tip, gratuity, baksheesh

бал *m* ball, dance; бал под маски fancy-dress ball, masked ball

бала *f see* бале

балабан *m arch.* big fellow

балада *f* ballad

баланс *m* balance, equilibrium; баланс на стопанството economic equilibrium; macro-economic policy; баланс на силите balance of power

балансира *pf & impf* to balance

баласт *m* 1 load 2 ballast

балван *m* 1 log, beam 2 *fig.* blockhead

балган *m* mucus, slime

балдахин *m* canopy, baldachin

балдисан *adj dial.* tired, exhausted

бале *n* bale, pack, bundle; бале тутун a bale of tobacco

балерина *f* ballerina

балет *m* ballet

балетан *m* <male> ballet dancer

балет-мајстор *m* ballet-master, choreographer

балетски *adj* ballet *attrib.*

балист *m Hist.* Albanian fascist

балистика *f* ballistics

Балкан *m* the Balkans

Балканец -нци *m* person from the Balkans

Балканка *f* (*fem. form*) *see* Балканец

балкански *adj* Balkan; Балканскиот Полуостров the Balkan Peninsula

балкон *m* balcony; (*во театар*) прв балкон dress circle, *Am.* balcony, mezzanine; втор балкон balcony, upper circle; трет балкон balcony, gallery

балконски *adj* balcony *attrib.*

балон[1] *m* 1 balloon; ❏ пробен балон trial balloon; се дуе како балон to put on airs 2 *dial.* (*детска играчка*) kite

балон[2] *m* demijohn

балсам *m* balsam

балсамира *pf & impf* to embalm

балски *adj* ball *attrib.*; балски фустан ball gown (dress)

балтија -ии *f* axe, hatchet

Балтик *m* the Baltic

балтички *adj* Baltic; Балтичко Море the Baltic <Sea>

балчак -ци *m* hilt

бам *interj* bang! crash!

бамбадијала *adv colloq.* for next to nothing, for a <mere> trifle; for a song

бамбашка *adj indecl. colloq.* unusual, peculiar; бамбашка човек oddball, crank

бамбус *m Bot.* (Bambusa arundinacea) bamboo

бамбусов *adj* bamboo *attrib.*; бамбусова трска bamboo

бамја *f Bot.* (Hibiscus esculentus) okra

бамка *impf* to hit, beat, knock; *colloq.* to wallop, thrash

бамкалец -лци *m* grumbler

бамња *f see* бамја

бан *m Hist.* ban, viceroy, civil governor

банален -лна *adj* banal, commonplace, stale, trite; crude, in bad taste

банализира *pf & impf* to reduce to banality

баналност *f* banality, triteness

банана *f Bot.* (Musa paradisiaca) banana

бананов *adj* banana *attrib.*

Бангладеш *m* Bangladesh

Бангладешанец -ни *m* Bangladeshi

Бангладешанка *f* (*fem. form*) *see* Бангладешанец

бангладешки *adj* Bangladeshi

банда *f* 1 band <of robbers> 2 *arch. Mus.* band 3 *arch. Mus.* trumpet, bugle

бандера *f* pole; телеграфска бандера telegraph pole

бандит *m* 1 bandit, robber, brigand 2 hired killer 3 *fig.* good-for-nothing

бандитизам -змот *m* banditry, brigandry

бандитски *adj* bandit's; bandit-like, brigandish

бандори *impf* to babble, chatter

баница *f Cul.* cheese past<r>y (*kind of pie made of puff pastry and cheese or other filling*)

баничар *m* 1 *colloq.* person who likes eating banitsa 2 *fig.* idler, parasite, good-for-nothing

баничка *f Cul.* kind of small puff-pastry pie

банка *f* 1 bank; акционерска банка joint-stock bank; става пари во банка to deposit money at a bank; подига пари од банка to withdraw money from a bank; клиент е на некоја банка to be a client of a bank, bank with a particular bank 2 (*во карти, коцка*) bank; ја држи банката to be banker, keep the bank 3 *colloq., obs.* ten-dinar/para coin; ❏ разменува трета/четврта банка to be turning thirty/forty

банкар *m* banker

банкарски *adj* bank *attrib.*; banker's; банкарска сметка bank account; банкарска штедна книшка bank (savings) book, savings-bank deposit book; банкарски влог (депозит) bank deposit; банкарска провизија banker's commission; банкарска тајна banker's duty of secrecy

банкарство *n* banking

банкет *m* banquet

банкин *adj* bank *attrib.*

банкина *f* 1 (*на пат*) shoulder; verge; footpath 2 (*насип*) embankment 3 (*перон*) platform 4 (*греда преку поток*) bridge, catwalk, gangway

банкнота *f* banknote

банковен -вна *adj* bank *attrib.*; извод на состојбата на банковната сметка bank statement

банкрот *m* bankruptcy; bankrupt

банкротира *pf & impf* to become bankrupt

банкротство *n* bankruptcy

бановина *f Hist.* district ruled by a ban

бански *adj Hist.* ban's, viceregal, governor's

банство *n Hist.* viceroy's (governor's) position, vice-royship (governorship)

бантам *m Sport.* (*во боксот*) бантам категорија bantamweight

банува *impf Hist.* to rule as a ban (viceroy)

бања[1] *f* 1 bathroom 2 spa 3 bath; три бањи на ден three baths a day

бања[2] *impf* I to bath *trans.* II – ce to bathe *intrans.*; to take (have) a bath

бањар *m* visitor to a spa

бањарка *f* 1 (*fem. form*) *see* бањар 2 *dial., Austral.* <face> washer, flannel 3 *dial.* bathrobe

бањски *adj* spa *attrib.*, hydrotherapeutic; бањско лекување spa treatment, cure

бапка *f* throat; crop; goitre; бапка да те набабари! *curse* may you choke!

барне *pf* бапна *aor.* **I 1** *trans.* to strike, dash; *intrans.* to fall with a bang, crash; ја бапна чинијата одземи he dashed the plate on the ground; го бапна човекот одземи he knocked him to the ground; ја бапна жената со шишето по глава he struck the woman on the head with the bottle; шишето бапна на подот и се искрши the bottle crashed to the ground and broke **2** *fig.* to put, force, impose, foist (*s.th. on s.o.*); бапни му неколку стотки, ќе те пушти slip him a few hundred and he will let you in/out **II – се 1** to throw o.s., collapse into (*bed, armchair, etc.*) **2** *fig.* to barge in

бапски *adj* old woman's; бапски лек old woman's remedy; бапски прикаски old wives' tales

бар *m* night-club, bar

бара[1] *f* puddle, pool; marsh, bog

бара[2] *impf* **I 1 1** to demand; to look for; to want; to ask; to require; бара работа he is looking for work; колку бараш за коњот? how much do you want for the horse? слободата бара жртви freedom demands sacrifices; тоа бара големи трошоци that requires a big outlay; ❑ тоа се бара that's <just> the job, that's the stuff; си го бара he's asking for it; бара некого и под дрво и под камен to hunt for s.o. high and low; кој бара рогови, ќе ги загуби и ушите *prov.* grasp all, lose all **2** *dial.* to search, ransack **3** *dial.* to mix (*in*) **4** *dial.* to touch, feel **II – се 1** *arch.* to look for a remedy for o.s.; to <try to> cure o.s. **2** *dial.* to feel one's pockets

бараба *m* good-for-nothing, scoundrel

барабан *m Mus.* drum

барабани *impf* to drum; to beat the drum

барабанче *n* small drum

барабанџија -ии *m Mus.* drummer

барабар *adv colloq.* together

барака *f* shack, hut; pre-fab; shanty

барање *n from* бара 1 search, quest **2** demand (*also Comm.*), claim; ❑ на барање on demand (request); по нечие барање at s.o.'s request **3** need, requirement; исполнува (задоволува) барања to meet (satisfy) the requirements

барач *m* seeker; claimant

Барбадос *m* Barbados

Барбадошанец -нци *m* Barbadian

Барбадошанка *f* (*fem. form*) *see* Барбадошанец

барбадошки *adj* Barbadian

бардак -ци *m* earthenware jug, pitcher

бардаклија *f* **1** type of plum **2** brandy made of this

бардакчија -ии *m* maker and/or seller of earthenware jugs (pitchers)

бардаче, барде & бардуле *n dim. of* бардак

баре *adv see* барем

барел *m* (*мерка, околу 160 литри*) barrel

барелјеф *m* bas-relief

барем *adv* at least; if only; барем тоа направи го за мене do at least that for me! зошто барем не се јави why didn't you at least call?

баретка *f* beret

бари *impf* **I** to boil *trans.*, parboil; to simmer *trans.* **II – се** to boil *intrans.*; to simmer *intrans.*

бариера *f* barrier

барикада *f* barricade

барикаден -дна *adj* barricade *attrib.*

барикадира *pf & impf* **I** to barricade **II – се** to barricade o.s.

бариран *adj Comm.* crossed; бариран чек crossed cheque, *Am.* certified check

баритон *m Mus.* baritone

баритонски *adj Mus.* baritone; баритонски глас baritone <voice>

бариум *m Chem.* barium

баричка *f dim. of* бара

бармен *m* barman

барне *pf* барна *aor. dial.* to touch, feel <lightly>

барок *m* baroque

барокен -кна *adj* baroque; барокен стил baroque style

барометар -три *m* barometer

барометарски *adj* barometric<al>

барон *m* baron

баронеса *f* (*ќерка на барон*) baron's daughter

бароница *f* baroness

баронски *adj* baronial

баронство *n* barony

барски *adj* marsh *attrib.*; барски гас marsh gas, methane; барска вода stagnant water; барски растенија marsh plants, reeds

барут *m* gunpowder

барутана *f* powder magazine

барутен -тна *adj* gunpowder *attrib.*

бархет *m* (*вид ткаенина*) fustian

бархетен -тна *adj* fustian

бас[1] *m Mus.* **1** bass <voice> **2** bass <singer> **3** (*гудачки*) double bass; (*дувачки*) bass tuba

бас[2] *m* bet, wager, *see* облог; ај да се фатиме на бас let's bet on it! let's have a bet!

баса *impf* to loiter, roam

басамак -ци *m* step

басара *f Bot.* wheat rust, rust fungus

басен *m Geog.* basin, *see* базен 2

басист *m Mus.* **1** bass <singer> **2** player of a bass instrument

басма *f* chintz

басмар *m* chintz maker/seller

басмен *adj* chintz *attrib.*

басна *f* fable

баснар *m see* бајач

баснарка *f* **1** *see* бајачка **2** witch

баснописец -сци *m* fabulist, writer of fables

баснословен -вна *adj* fabulous; по баснословна цена at a fabulous price; баснословно богатство fabulous wealth

баста *f* fold, crease (*in a dress*)

бастион *m* bastion

бастиса *pf arch.* to search (*s.o.*); to attack; to surround (*with the intention of robbing*)

бастра *f see* басара

бастун *m* walking-stick, cane

батак[1] -ци *m* **1** mud, mire **2** *colloq.* bad debt **3** *fig. see* батакчија

батак[2] -ци *m* (*копан*) leg (*of poultry*), drumstick

батаклив *adj* muddy

батакчија -ии *m colloq.* swindler, con artist, cheat, fraud; fake; good-for-nothing

батал *adj indecl. colloq.* ruined, abandoned, neglected; батал чешма abandoned fountain

батали *pf colloq.* **I** to neglect; to abandon; to

renounce, give up; ги баталил и жената и децата he has abandoned both his wife and his children; го батали пушењето he gave up smoking **II – се** to neglect o.s., let o.s. go

баталјóн *m Mil.* battalion

баталјонски *adj Mil.* battalion *attrib.*; баталјонски командант battalion commander

баталува (се) *impf of* батали (се)

бате *m & n* brother (*mode of address usu. for an elder brother*)

батенце *n see* бате

батерија -ии *f* 1 *Elec.* battery 2 gun-battery 3 torch, *Am.* flashlight

батист *m* batiste

батка *impf* to babble, chatter, prattle

батко -овци *m* elder brother; older boy

бау *interj* bang! crash!

бау-бау 1 *interj* boo! (*exclamation for frightening small children*) 2 *m* bogeyman

бауч *m* bogeyman

Бахамец -мци *m* Bahamian

Бахами *pl* the Bahamas

Бахамка *f* (*fem. form*) *see* Бахамец

бахамски *adj* Bahamian; Бахамски Острови Bahama Islands

баханалија *f* bacchanalia

Бахреин *m* Bahrain

бахреинец -нци *m* Bahraini

Бахреинка *f* (*fem. form*) *see* Бахреинец

бахреински *adj* Bahraini

баца се *impf* to dirty o.s., get dirty

баци *I* to kiss *trans.* **II – се** to kiss *intrans.*

бацил *m* germ, bacillus

бацилен -лна *adj* bacillar<у>

бацилоносител & бацилоносец -сци *m* germ carrier

бацка се *impf see* баца се

бацло -овци *m colloq.* dirty person

бацува (се) *impf of* баци (се)

бацувка *f* kiss

бацунка *f see* бацувка

бач *m* shepherd

бачија -ии *f see* бачило

бачило *n* 1 summer mountain pasture 2 sheepfold 3 mountain dairy

бачува *impf* to work as a shepherd, look after sheep

баца *f* 1 opening in roof/wall (*for smoke or light*) 2 *see* баџанак

баџанак -ци *m* brother-in-law (*husband of wife's sister*)

баш[1] *adj colloq.* chief, senior, first; first-class; баш арамија robber chief; баш ракија first-class brandy

баш[2] *adv* (*токму*) just, exactly; баш сега right now; this minute; не е баш така not exactly, not quite; ама баш си ми некој you are a <right> one; баш ми е гајле *colloq.* I don't give a damn (straw); не баш најдобар механичар not much of a mechanic

башибозук *m* 1 *Hist.* bashi-bazouk (*19th-century Turkish irregular soldier*) 2 *fig.* brutality

башка *colloq.* 1 *adv* separately, apart; таа живее башка од мене she lives apart from me, she lives on her own 2 *adj* separate, other, different; ката ден башка промена different clothes every day

башкари *impf colloq.* 1 to keep to o.s. 2 to be idle, lounge about, take one's ease

башмак -ци *m arch.* kerchief, shawl

бдее *impf* to keep vigil (watch); жената бдееше над детето the woman was keeping watch over the child

бдение -ја *n* vigil, watch

бе[1] *interj* (*expressing anger, impatience, etc. when addressing a man*) you there! кој е нечесен, бе никаквец who says I'm dishonest, you scoundrel!

бе[2] *interj* (*imitating sheep bleating*) baa!

бебе *n* 1 baby, infant; бебе во пелени a babe in arms 2 small bulb (*for pocket torch*)

бебенце *n dim. of* бебе 1

бебешки *adj* baby's

бев *imperf. 1st p. sg of* сум

бег[1] *m* bey (*Turkish title*); governor

бег[2] *m* running away, flight

бега *impf* to flee, run away; to shun; тој бега од лоши другари he shuns bad company; бега од земјата to flee the country; бега од училиште to play truant; ❑ бега како попарен to take to one's heels; to run for one's life; од пишаното не се бега no flying from fate; what must be must be; море бегај таму come off it! get lost!

бегалец -лци *m* fugitive; refugee

бегалка *f* 1 (*fem. form*) *see* бегалец 2 girl who elopes

бегалко -овци *m colloq.* slacker, shirker, *Austral.* bludger; бегалко од училиште truant

беганица *f* flight in panic

беглик -ци *m arch.* 1 bey's estate; поминаа низ бегликот they passed through the bey's property 2 forced labour, corvée 3 tax on livestock (*in Turkish times*)

бегло *adv* hastily, cursorily, superficially

бегов *adj* bey's

беговина *f arch. see* беглик 1

беговица *f* bey's wife

беговски 1 *adj* bey's, of a bey 2 *adv* like a bey

бегол -гла *adj* hasty, cursory, superficial

бегонија *f Bot.* begonia

бегство *n* flight, escape; во бегство е he's on the run; се дава во бегство to take to flight

бегува *impf* to govern as a bey

бегум *adv* 1 running, at a run 2 hastily

беда *f* 1 misfortune, adversity; trouble, bad times 2 poverty, want; plight 3 *dial.* slander, calumny

бедем *m* rampart; bulwark, earthen wall; wall of sandbags; embankment, *Am.* levee; *Mil.* fortified trench

беден -дна *adj* 1 poor, needy 2 pitiable, wretched, miserable; бедната жена the poor woman! 3 meagre, scanty; bad

беди *impf* to slander, calumniate, libel

бедник -ци *m* 1 poor man 2 sufferer, unlucky person, martyr; wretch

бедност *f see* беднотија

беднотија *f* (*сиромаштија*) 1 misery, poverty 2 the poor

бедрен *adj Anat.* thigh *attrib.*, femoral; бедрена коска thigh-bone, femur

бедреница *f Anat.* thigh-bone, femur

бедро *n Anat.* thigh

бедствува *impf* to live in want, in poverty

бедуин *m* Bedouin

беж *n & adj indecl.* beige

бежанец -нци *m see* бегалец

бежица *f see* беговица

без *prep* **1** without; без пари without money; free, gratis; без душа soulless; без многу мислење without much thought; (*with да, as conj*) без да знам without my knowing **2** less, minus; три без дваесет twenty to three; месец без три дена a month less three days; без малку almost, nearly **3** ❑ без време умре, без ден умре he died prematurely, he died young

без- *prefix* un-, in-, non-, dis-, -less

беза *f dial.* sneer, jibe, joke

безалкохолен -лна *adj* non-alcoholic; безалкохолни пијачки (пијалоци) soft drinks

безбеден -дна *adj* safe, secure, protected; безбедно место safe place

безбедно *adv* safely, securely; cautiously

безбедност *f* safety, security, protection; служба за државна безбедност state security police; безбедност на работното место industrial safety

безбели *adv arch.* surely, naturally, indeed

безбоен -јна *adj* colourless

безбожен -жна *adj* godless, irreligious; sinful

безбожие *n* godlessness, atheism

безбожник -ци *m* atheist, non-believer; sinner

безбожница *f* (*fem. form*) *see* безбожник

безбожнички *adj* godless, ungodly

безбожност *f* godlessness, atheism

безбојност *f* **1** colourlessness **2** *fig.* monotony, tedium

безболен -лна *adj* **1** painless; безболно породување painless birth **2** easy, smooth, uncomplicated; безболно решение easy way out

безболност *f* **1** painlessness **2** ease; easiness, smoothness

безбоштво *n* godlessness, atheism

безбрачен -чна *adj* unmarried, single; celibate

безбрачност *f* unmarried (single) state; celibacy

безбрежен -жна *adj* endless, boundless, immense, vast, unlimited

безброен -јна *adj* numberless, countless, numerous

безброј[1] *m* multitude, countless number

безброј[2] **& безбројно** *adv* in large numbers; безброј јунаци countless heroes

безбројност *f see* безброј

безверен -рна *adj* **1** atheistic, godless **2** unfaithful, treacherous

безверец -рци *m see* безверник

безверие *n* **1** unbelief, atheism **2** disbelief, doubt, scepticism, hesitation

безверник -ци *m* **1** non-believer, atheist **2** treacherous/perfidious person

безверница *f* (*fem. form*) *see* безверник

безветрен *adj* calm, still, windless

безветрина *f* calm, stillness

безвкусен -сна *adj* tasteless, insipid

безвластие *n* anarchy

безводен -дна *adj* waterless, arid

безвоздушен -шна *adj* airless; having a vacuum; безвоздушен простор vacuum

безволен -лна *adj* **1** apathetic, indifferent; weak-willed, irresolute; безволен човек apathetic person, person with a weak will **2** involuntary, automatic; безволни движења involuntary movements

безволие *n* indifference, apathy, languor, listlessness

безволник -ци *m* apathetic person

безволно *adv* **1** indifferently, apathetically, listlessly **2** involuntarily

безвредносен -сна *adj* valueless, worthless

безвремен *adj* premature

безвучен -чна *adj* soundless, inaudible; *Phon.* voiceless, unvoiced

безвучност *f* inaudibility

безгаќешко -овци *m colloq.* ragamuffin; poor person

безглав *adj* **1** headless; безглава статуа a headless statue **2** *fig.* (*збунет*) confused, perplexed; (*будалест*) foolish, mad, hysterical

безгласен -сна *adj* soundless, mute; *Phon., fig.* voiceless

безграничен -чна *adj* unlimited, boundless

безгрбичник -ци *m* **1** spineless person, toady **2** *Zool. see* без’рбетник

безгревен -вна *adj* merciless, heartless

безгревник -ци *m* heartless person

безгревница *f* (*fem. form*) *see* безгревник

безгрешен -шна *adj* sinless, innocent, irreproachable

безгрешник -ци *m* innocent person

безгрешница *f* (*fem. form*) *see* безгрешник

безгрижен -жна *adj* carefree, light-hearted; (*за живот*) carefree, untroubled

безгрижник -ци *m* carefree person

безгрижно *adv* in a carefree manner, nonchalantly, light-heartedly

безгрижност *f* carefree state/manner, nonchalance, light-heartedness; (*за живот*) serenity, tranquility

бездарен -рна *adj* untalented, dull

бездарник -ци *m* untalented person

бездарница *f* (*fem. form*) *see* бездарник

бездарност *f* lack of talent

бездеен -јна *adj* inactive

бездејност *f* inactivity; inertness

бездејствие & бездејство *n see* бездејност

бездејствува *impf* to be inactive; to be passive

безделен -лна *adj* idle

безделник -ци *m* idler, *colloq.* lazybones

безделница *f* (*fem. form*) *see* безделник

безделничи *impf* to idle, loaf

безделништво *n* idleness, laziness

бездетен -тна *adj* childless

бездетка *f* childless woman

бездетност *f* childlessness

бездимен -мна *adj* smokeless

бездна *f* abyss

бездожден -дна *adj* rainless, dry

бездомен -мна *adj* homeless, destitute; бездомни деца waifs and strays

бездомник -ци *m* **1** waif, poor/homeless person **2** *fig.* tramp, vagabond, good-for-nothing

бездомница *f* (*fem. form*) *see* бездомник

бездомништво *n* homelessness

бездрвен -вна *adj in the expression:* бездрвна хартија wood-free (rag) paper

бездруго *adv* without fail, certainly, in any case; бездруго дојди come without fail!

бездушен -шна *adj* soulless, heartless, insensitive, merciless, inhuman

бездушник -ци *m* heartless person

бездушница *f* (*fem. form*) *see* бездушник

бездушност *f* heartlessness, mercilessness, inhumanity

безел *m Bot.* (Pisum sativum) pea

безжален -лна *adj* pitiless, unmerciful, heartless, inhuman

безжалосен -сна *adj see* безжален

безживотен -тна *adj* lifeless

безживотност *f* lifelessness

безжитен -тна *adj* barren, sterile, infertile; безжитна година во безжитен крај a barren year in a barren land

безжичен -чна *adj* wireless; безжична телеграфија wireless telegraphy

беззабен -бна *adj* toothless

беззаветен -тна *adj* devoted, self-sacrificing; беззаветна преданост utter/selfless devotion

беззаконен -она *adj* illegal, lawless

беззаконие -ија *n* lawlessness

беззаштитен -тна *adj* defenceless, helpless

безземен -мна *adj* landless

безземјаш *m* landless person

беззлобен -бна *adj* harmless; (*невин*) innocent; (*љубезен*) benevolent, kindly, good-natured

безвезден -дна *adj poet.* starless, dark; безвездно небо starless sky

безидеен -јна *adj* lacking ideas

безидејност *f* lack of ideas

безизлезен -зна *adj* hopeless, desperate; тој се наоѓаше во безизлезна ситуација he was in a desperate situation

безизразен -зна *adj* expressionless, dull; лицето му беше безизразно и тапо his face was expressionless and vacant

безимен *adj* nameless, anonymous, unknown

безимотен -тна *adj* indigent, poor

безистен *m* covered market-place

безлистен -сна *adj* leafless; безлисни растенија aphyllous (leafless) plants

безличен -чна *adj* impersonal, dispassionate; (*среден*) average, undistinguished; *Gram.* impersonal

безличност *f* impersonality

безмерен -рна *adj* infinite, immense, boundless

безмесен -сна *adj* meatless; безмесни дни meatless (fast) days; безмесно јадење meatless (vegetarian) food/dish

безмилосен -сна *adj* merciless, heartless; ruthless

безмилосност *f* mercilessness, heartlessness; ruthlessness

безмирисен -сна *adj* odourless, without smell

безмлечен -чна *adj* milkless; безмлечна крава dry cow; безмлечен сладолед milkless ice-cream, water-ice

безмоќен -ќна *adj* impotent, weak; powerless

безнадежен -жна *adj* hopeless, desperate; forlorn

безнадежност *f* hopelessness, despair

безначаен -јна *adj* insignificant, unimportant

безобѕирен -рна *adj* inconsiderate; arrogant, ruthless

безоблачен -чна *adj* cloudless, clear

безоблачност *f* cloudlessness

безобличен -чна *adj* formless

безобличност *f* formlessness

безобразен -зна *adj* insolent, impudent, shameless

безобразие -ија *n* impudence

безобразник -ци *m* insolent man

безобразница *f* insolent woman, hussy

безобразност *f* insolence, impudence

безогледен -дна *adj see* безобѕирен

безодговорен -рна *adj* irresponsible

безопасен -сна *adj* harmless, safe; безопасна <игла> safety-pin

безопасно *adv* safely

безопасност *f* safety

безосновен -вна *adj* unfounded, groundless, unjustified

безотпорен -рна *adj* frail, weak, non-resistant

безочен -чна *adj* impudent, shameless, insolent

безработен -тна *adj* unemployed

безработица *f* unemployment

безработност *f see* безработица

безрадосен -сна *adj* joyless, sad

безразборен -рна *adj* 1 disorderly, disorganized; slovenly 2 unreasonable, senseless

безразличен -чна *adj* 1 any, no matter which 2 indifferent, apathetic

безразлично *adv* 1 all the same 2 indifferently

безразличност *f* indifference, apathy

безразумен -мна *adj* unreasonable

безрасуден -дна *adj* unwise, imprudent, hasty; reckless, impetuous

без'рбетник -ци *m Zool.* invertebrate

безреден -дна *adj* disorderly, untidy, sloppy

безредие *n* disorder; riot

безредица *f* disorder, *see* безредие

безредно *adv* in a disorderly fashion, untidily

безрезервен -вна *adj* unreserved

безрезултатен -тна *adj* unsuccessful, without result, without effect

безроден -дна *adj* childless, barren

безродница *f* barren woman

безропотен -тна *adj* obedient, submissive, humble, uncomplaining, resigned

безугледен -дна *adj* nondescript, ordinary; unattractive

безумен -мна *adj* mad, insane

безумец -мци *m see* безумник

безуми се *pf* to lose one's senses; to go mad

безумие *n* madness

безумник -ци *m* deranged (mad) person

безумница *f* (*fem. form*) *see* безумник

безумност *f* madness

безуморен -рна *adj* tireless

безуморно *adv* tirelessly

безумство *n* madness

безумствува *impf* to do mad things

безусловен -вна *adj* 1 unconditional; безусловна капитулација unconditional surrender 2 complete, absolute

безуспешен -шна *adj* unsuccessful, vain; безуспешна зделка unsuccessful deal

безуспешност *f* lack of success, vainness

безутешен -шна *adj* inconsolable, disconsolate; desperate

безучество *n* lack of participation; isolation

Бејрут *m* Beirut

бејрутски *adj* Beirut *attrib.*

Бејџинг *m* Beijing, *see* Пекинг

бејџинѓанец -нци *m* person from Beijing

бејџинѓанка *f* (*fem. form*) *see* бејџинѓанец

бејџиншки *adj* Beijing *attrib.*

бек *m Sport.* (*во фудбал и сл.*) <full> back; (*во кошарка*) guard

бекне   *pf* бекна *aor.* **1** to bleat **2** *fig.* to say (utter) a word

бековски   *adj Sport.* <full> back's

бекнува   *impf of* бекне

бекрија   -ии *m* drunkard, drunk; carouser, reveller

бел   *adj* **1** white; бела облека white clothing; бело вино white wine **2** bright, clear; бел ден bright day; broad daylight **3** grey-haired; бела глава head of grey hair **4** (*in botanical names*) бела дреновица the name of a variety of grape; бело грозје white (green) grapes; бел даб (Quercus lanuginosa *or* pubescens) pubescent (downy) oak; бела црница (Morus alba) white mulberry; бел бор (Pinus silvestris) Scots pine; бел слез (Althaea officinalis) marsh mallow; бел трн (Crataegus monogyna *or* oxyacantha) hawthorn **5** ❑ бел вдовец grass widower; бел свет wide world; бели стихови blank (unrhymed) verse; бела недела Shrovetide; Бело Море Aegean Sea; бел дроб (џигер) lung, lights; го остави бел во очите he left him empty-handed; he bled him white; црно на бело in black and white, in writing; бел како тулуп (памук) <as> white as snow; бел ден да не видиш! *curse* may you not see the light of day!

белачка   *f* **1** laundress, washerwoman **2** *joc.* grape-brandy

белвица   *f Zool.* species of trout

Белгиец   -ијци *m* Belgian

Белгија   *f* Belgium

Белгијка   *f* (*fem. form*) *see* Белгиец

белгиски   *adj* Belgian

Белград   *m* Belgrade

белградски   *adj* from/of Belgrade

белграѓанец   -нци *m* person from Belgrade

белграѓанка   *f* (*fem. form*) *see* белграѓанец

белег   -зи *m* (*ознака*) mark, marker; (*особина*) feature, characteristic, trait; (*знак*) sign, signal; (*лузна*) scar; ❑ остава белег to leave one's mark; носи белег (*од нешто*) to bear the mark/scars (*of s.th.*)

белегзија   -ии *f see* белезица

белегија   -ии *f* **1** grindstone, whetstone, hone **2** *arch.* ruler

белее   *impf* I **1** to grow light **2** to turn grey **3** to fade II – се to look (appear) white, shine; сè се белее од чистота everything is sparkling clean

бележан   *pt* **1** marked, indicated **2** *colloq.* vaccinated **3** *fig.* branded, stigmatized, suspected, doubtful

бележи   *pf & impf* **1** to mark, note down, record, register **2** to mark, celebrate, observe **3** *colloq.* to vaccinate

бележит   *adj* significant, important, noted; famous; striking, conspicuous, outstanding

бележник   -ци *m* **1** notebook **2** notary, solicitor

бележува   *impf of* бележи

белезија   -ии *f see* белезица

белезица   *f* **1** bracelet **2** (*лисици*) handcuffs, manacles; (*прангии*) fetters, shackles

белезникав   *adj see* белузлав

беленка   *f* **1** white mark **2** fair-skinned woman **3** white/clear object; чаша беленка clean glass

белетрист   *m* writer of fiction

белетристика   *f* fiction, *belles-lettres*

белец   -лци *m* white man

белешка   *f* **1** line **2** note; memorandum; стенографски белешки shorthand notes; фаќа белешки to take notes **3** (*забелешка*) remark

бели   *impf* I **1** to whiten, make white, bleach (*cloth*) **2** (*варосува*) to whitewash **3** (*лупи*) to peel; (*лупи орев*) to shell II – се **1** to grow light; зора зори, ден се бели it's getting light **2** to powder one's face

белило   *n* **1** (*за лице*) face-powder **2** (*боја од креда*) crushed chalk, whiting; (*за ѕидови*) whitewash; (*за алишта и др.*) bleach

белина   *f* **1** whiteness; ❑ ја види белината на денот to see the light of day **2** (*во книга*) margin

Белисе   *n* **1** (*земја*) Belize **2** (*град*) Belize City

Белисеец   -ејци *m* **1** Belizean **2** person from Belize City

Белисејка   *f* (*fem. form*) *see* Белисеец

белисејски   *adj* Belizean; Belize City *attrib.*

белица   *f* white sheep

белич & беличко   *m* fair-haired/light-skinned person or animal

белка   *f* **1** egg-white, albumen **2** white <of the eye> **3** (*за животно*) white animal

белки   *adv colloq.* perhaps, maybe

белковина   *f* albumen; protein

белне се   *pf* белна се *aor.* to begin to show white

белоборка   *f Bot.* (Pinus silvestris) Scots pine

белобрад   *adj* grey-bearded

белобрадец   -дци *m* greybeard; старец белобрадец grey-bearded old man

беловина   *f* **1** sapwood (*under bark*) **2** white (green) grapes

беловица   *f Bot.* greengage

белоглав   *adj* white-haired, grey-haired

белоглавец   -вци *m* old man

белогрив   *adj* white-maned, with a white mane

белогрлест   *adj* white-necked, white-throated

белодробен   -бна *adj* pulmonary, of the lungs; белодробна туберкулоза pulmonary tuberculosis

белокос   *adj* white-haired; (*as noun*) *f* белокоса spinster, old maid

белокрил   *adj see* белокрилест

белокрилест   *adj* white-winged

белолик   *adj* fair<-skinned>

белоног   *adj* white-legged; white-footed

белообразен   -зна *adj see* белолик

белоперка   *f* **1** (*риба*) roach **2** (*птица*) white bird

белорун   *adj* having a white fleece or coat (*of animals*)

Белорусија   *f* Belorussia, Byelorussia, Belarus

Белорусин   -си   *m*   Belorussian, Byelorussian, Belarusian

Белорусинка   *f* (*fem. form*) *see* Белорусин

белоруски   *adj* Belorussian, Byelorussian, Belarusian

белоса   *pf* to whitewash, *see* вароса

белосветски   *adj* adventurous; (*за жена*) loose, *colloq.* fast; белосветски човек adventurer

белосува   *impf* **1** of белоса, *see* варосува **2** *fig.* to deceive; to lie (*to s.o.*), *sl.* take (*s.o.*) to the cleaners

белотија   *f* whiteness

белоушка   *f Zool.* (Natrix natrix) grass snake

белоцветен   -тна *adj* having white flowers

белтак   -ци *m dial. see* белка 1

белтачина   *f* albumen

белузлав   *adj* whitish

белузнав   *adj see* белузлав

белутрак   -ци *m* quartz

белушина   *f* **1** white clay **2** white (green) grapes

белушка   *f* white goat/sheep/cow

белчо   *m see* белич

беља -ли *f colloq.* misfortune, bad luck, trouble; беља си зедов на глава I have got into trouble, *sl.* I've copped it

бељалија *adj indecl. see* бељачен

бељачен -чна *adj colloq.* **1** fateful, disastrous **2** unfortunate, ill-fated, unlucky

бемка *f see* бенка

бенгалски *adj* Bengal *attrib.*, Bengali; бенгалски пламен Bengal light

бендиса *pf colloq.* **I 1** to like, fancy; девојката го бендиса момчето the girl took a liking to the boy **2** (*with acc. or dat.*) to please; ме (ми) бендиса книгата I liked the book **II – ce** (*with dat. pron. and/or на and noun*) to please; не ми се бендиса тој човек I didn't like the man; филмот не му се бендиса на полицаецот the policeman didn't like the film

бендисува (се) *impf of* бендиса (се)

беневреци *pl* trousers (*in traditional costume*)

Бенелукс *abbr.* (*Белгија, Холандија, Луксембург*) Benelux

бенефиција -ии *f* (*привилегија*) privilege; special rate; (*корист*) benefit; (*намалена возарина*) reduced fare

бенефициран *adj in the expression:* бенефициран стаж occupation with early retirement

бензин *m* petrol, *Am.* gasoline, gas; обичен бензин regular<-grade> petrol; супер бензин super <-grade> petrol; авионски бензин aviation fuel, avgas

бензински *adj* petrol *attrib.*; бензинска пумпа petrol station

бензол *m* benzol

Бенин *m* Benin

Бенинец -нци *m* Beninese

Бенинка *f* (*fem. form*) *see* Бенинец

бенински *adj* Beninese

бенка *f* **1** birthmark; mole **2** spot, freckle **3** sheep with black spots on its head

бенкичав *adj* **1** with birthmarks/moles **2** freckled; бенкичаво лице freckled face

бенкичка *f* & **бенкиче** *n* wrap-over vest (*for a baby*)

бент *m* **1** dam, dyke; weir; fence **2** drainage ditch, channel

берат *m arch.* sultan's decree

берач *m* picker; берач на грозје grape picker

берачка *f* (*fem. form*) *see* берач

берба *f* picking, gathering; (*жетва*) harvest; (*на грозје*) vintage

бербат *colloq.* **1** *adj indecl.* dirty **2** *m* dirt

бербатен -тна *adj colloq.* dirty

бербати се *impf colloq.* to dirty o.s., get dirty

бербер *m* barber

берберка *f* **1** barber's wife **2** (*fem. form*) *see* бербер

берберница *f* barber's shop

берберски *adj* barber's

берберува *impf* to work as a barber

бердана & **берданка** *f* Berdan rifle

бере *impf* **I 1** (*плодови, цвекиња, трева и сл.*) to pick; to harvest; берат јаболка they are picking apples **2** (*збира, содржи*) to hold, contain; ова шише бере еден литар this bottle holds one litre **3** to gather, collect *trans.*; секоја недела ги берев другарите за на лов every Sunday I would collect (round up) my friends to go hunting; бере војска to muster troops; бере данок to collect tax<es>; ❑ бере душа he is not long for this world, he's at death's door; раната бере гној the wound is festering; бере гајле (грижа) (*за*) he is worried (*about*); бери ум! be sensible! да му го бере гревот he is to blame for that (let him suffer for his sins); нигде не го бере he can't settle down anywhere; he is on tenterhooks **II – ce 1** to gather *intrans.*, come together; to huddle together; свет се бере people are gathering **2** (*за платно и сл.*) to shrink *intrans.*

берéтка *n see* баретка

берза *f* stock exchange, bourse; берза на трудот labour-market; црна берза black market

берзански *adj* stock-exchange *attrib.*; stock *attrib.*; берзански работи stock-exchange transactions; берзанска листа exchange (share) list; берзански извештај exchange advice; берзански посредник exchange broker (dealer)

берзијáнец -нци *m* dealer in stocks and shares, stockbroker

беридба *f see* берба

берикéт *m colloq.* bountiful harvest, bumper crop; (*изобилие*) plenty, prosperity; (*благодет, среќа*) boon, blessing

берикéтен -тна *adj colloq.* plentiful, bountiful

Берлин *m* Berlin

берлинец -нци *m* Berliner

берлинка *f* (*fem. form*) *see* берлинец

берлински *adj* Berlin *attrib.*

Бермýди *pl* the Bermudas; бермуди Bermuda shorts, long shorts

Бермудец -дци *m* Bermud<i>an

бермудски *adj* Bermud<i>an

Бермутка *f* (*fem. form*) *see* Бермудец

Берн *m* Bern<e>

бернски *adj* Bernese

бернардúнец -нци *m* St Bernard dog

берокуќник -ци *m* good family man, good provider

берокуќница *f* good home-maker, good housewife

бес *m* **1** evil spirit, devil, fiend; кривиот бес the Devil, *colloq.* Old Nick **2** (*беснило*) rabies **3** (*гнев*) rage, fury, wild anger; истура бес (*врз некого*) to vent one's anger (*on s.o.*), take it out (*on s.o.*) **4** (*бунтовност*) unruliness, recalcitrance; ❑ од бес for kicks (fun), for the hell of it **5** (*страсна желба*) frenzy, craze, craving (*за нешто – for s.th.*)

беса[1] *f arch.* promise, <given> word, oath, troth

беса[2] *f* (*во берза*) decline of the market, slump

бесач *m* hangman, executioner

бесвесен -сна *adj* unconscious; во бесвесна состојба in a state of unconsciousness

бесвесност *f* unconsciousness

беседа *f* (*свечен говор*) oration, speech; (*муабет*) conversation, chat

беседник -ци *m* orator, speaker

беседнички *adj* rhetorical; беседничка дарба gift of eloquence

беседништво *n* oratory, eloquence, rhetoric

бесеже *abbr.* (*вакцина против туберкулоза*) BCG, anti-tuberculosis vaccine

бесен -сна *adj* **1** mad; rabid; бесно куче mad dog **2** angry, furious, enraged; татко ти е бесен your father is furious **3** unruly, unmanageable, restless; бесни деца unruly children

беси *impf* **I** to suspend, hang; на мостот бесат кожи од овци they hang sheepskins from the bridge; секој фатен партизан тие го бесеа they hanged every partisan they caught **II** – **се 1** to hang o.s. **2** *fig.* to hang around, waste time

бесилка *f* gallows

бесилница *f* & **бесило** *n see* бесилка

бескаматен -тна *adj Comm.* interest-free; бескаматен заем interest-free loan

бескарактерен -рна *adj* characterless; тој е бескарактерен човек he has no backbone

бескарактерност *f* weakness of will, spinelessness

бескласен -сна *adj* classless; бескласно општество classless society

бескомпромисен -сна *adj* uncompromising, irreconcilable, implacable

бесконечен -чна *adj* endless, boundless, infinite

бесконечност *f* infinity

бескорисен -сна *adj arch.* **1** (*бесполезен, некорисен*) useless, futile **2** (*несебичен, некористољубив*) unselfish, altruistic, disinterested

бескорисност *f* unselfishness, altruism

бескраен -јна *adj* boundless, infinite

бескрај *m* infinity

бескрајно *adv* infinitely

бескрајност *f* endlessness, infinity

бескрвен -вна *adj* **1** bloodless; бескрвен преврат bloodless coup **2** pallid; *Med.* anaemic; бескрвно лице pallid face **3** *fig.* lifeless

бескрилен -лна *adj* wingless; *Zool.* apterous

бескрупулен -лна *adj see* бескрупулозен

бескрупулозен -зна *adj* unscrupulous; ruthless

бескрупулозност *f* unscrupulousness; ruthlessness

бескуќен -ќна *adj* homeless, destitute, *see* бездомен

бескуќник -ци *m see* бездомник

бескуќница *f see* бездомница

беследен -дна *adj* without <leaving> a trace

бесмислен *adj* (*за зборови*) meaningless; (*за постапка*) senseless, unreasonable, absurd, pointless

бесмислено *adv* senselessly, unreasonably

бесмисленост *f* meaninglessness; senselessness, absurdity

бесмислица *f* nonsense

бесмртен -тна *adj* immortal

бесмртник -ци *m* immortal

бесмртност *f* immortality

беснее *impf* to be rabid; (*се лути*) to rage, fume; (*се улави*) to be crazy; (*за деца, при играње*) to romp about; гостите беснееја до касно во ноќта the guests were making merry until late at night; беснее епидемија на грип an epidemic of influenza is raging

бесни *impf see* беснее

бесник -ци *m* mischievous child; restless person

беснило *n* rabies; кравјо беснило mad cow disease, bovine spongiform encephalopathy (BSE)

беснотија *f* fury, rage; unruliness, disorderly conduct, violence

беспартиен -јна *adj* non-party

беспартиец -јци *m* non-party man, non-party-member

беспатен -тна *adj* **1** trackless; беспатен терен trackless terrain **2** *fig.* desperate, hopeless

беспатица *f* **1** trackless area **2** *fig.* hopeless situation, blind alley

беспаќе *n see* беспатица

бесперспективен -вна *adj* unpromising, hopeless, frustrating

бесплатен -тна *adj* free <of charge>; бесплатно возење free ride; бесплатна услуга free service; favour

бесплатно *adv* free, gratis

бесплатност *f* freedom from charges; lack of charges

бесплоден -дна *adj* **1** barren, sterile; бесплодна почва barren soil **2** *fig.* fruitless, vain, unavailing; бесплодни обиди abortive attempts; бесплодна дискусија sterile (futile) discussion; *Comm.* бесплоден капитал unproductive capital

бесповратен -тна *adj* irreversible, irretrievable; *Comm.* бесповратен заем free grant

бесповратно *adv* irretrievably; отиде бесповратно he has gone never to return

беспогрешен -шна *adj* unerring; faultless

беспокоен -јна *adj* restless; беспокоен поглед troubled look; беспокојно море choppy (rough) sea; беспокојно дете restless (fidgety) child

беспокои *impf* **I** to disturb; to worry *trans.*; to cause (*s.o.*) concern; таа го беспокоеше со својот болен изглед her sickly appearance worried him **II** – **се** to be disturbed (worried); to worry *intrans.*

беспокојност *f* & **беспокојство** *n* restlessness, worry

беспокојува (се) *impf of* беспокои (се)

бесполезен -зна *adj* useless, vain; unproductive, unprofitable; worthless; бесполезни напори unavailing (vain) efforts

бесполов *adj* sexless; *Biol.* agamic, agamous; бесполово размножување asexual reproduction, agamogenesis

беспомошен -шна *adj* helpless, weak, forlorn

беспорен -рна *adj* indisputable, undoubted

беспорно *adv* indisputably, undoubtedly

беспорочен -чна *adj* blameless, irreproachable; unblemished, immaculate, chaste

беспоштеден -дна *adj* unsparing, merciless

бесправен -вна *adj* without rights, deprived of rights; бесправна положба absence of rights

бесправно *adv* without rights; without protection of law

беспрегледен -дна *adj* immense, vast

беспредел *m poet.* immensity, boundlessness, vastness

беспределен -лна *adj* immense, boundless, vast

беспредметен -тна *adj* superfluous, unnecessary; pointless

беспрекорен -рна *adj* irreproachable, impeccable; беспрекорна работа faultless work

беспрестано *adv* ceaselessly, continuously; повторува нешто беспрестано to repeat the same thing over and over again

беспризорен -рна *adj* homeless, neglected

беспримерен -рна *adj* matchless, unparalleled, exceptional

беспринципен -пна *adj* unprincipled; беспринципен човек unscrupulous man

беспристрасен -сна *adj* impartial, objective

беспричинен -ина *adj* unfounded

бесрамен -мна *adj* shameless, indecent

бесрамие *n see* бесрамност

бесрамник -ци *m* shameless man

бесрамница *f* shameless woman, hussy

бесрамност *f* shamelessness

бессилен -лна *adj* helpless, weak, feeble, powerless

бессилие *n* & **бессилност** *f* powerlessness, weakness

бессовесен -сна *adj* unscrupulous

бессовесник -ци *m* unscrupulous person

бессодржаен -јна & **бессодржателен** -лна *adj* insipid, vapid, empty, worthless; бессоддржаен разговор empty talk, *colloq.* hot air

бессонен -она *adj* sleepless

бессоница *f* insomnia, sleeplessness

бестатник -ци *m* fatherless child, orphan

бестелесен -сна *adj* disembodied, incorporeal; immaterial

бестија -ии *f* beast, wild animal; brute (*also as term of abuse*)

бестијален -лна *adj* bestial; brutish

бестијалност *f* bestiality

бестрага *adv* without a trace; very far, out of sight; ❑ фати пустина и бестрага he vanished without a trace

бестрашен -шна *adj* fearless, intrepid

бестрашник -ци *m* fearless person

бестрашност *f* fearlessness, courage, intrepidity

бесформен *adj* formless, shapeless, amorphous

бесформност *f* formlessness, shapelessness

бесцветен -тна *adj* 1 colourless, indefinite, *see* безбоен 2 *see* бесцутен

бесцелен -лна *adj* aimless; useless, vain, senseless; тоа е бесцелно it serves no purpose

бесцелност *f* aimlessness; futility, senselessness

бесцен *adj see* бесценет

бесценет *adj* (*скапоцен*) precious; priceless; invaluable; бесценет камен precious stone

бесцутен -тна *adj* flowerless, without blossom

бесчаден -дна *adj* smokeless

бесчеден -дна *adj see* бездетен

бесчесен -сна *adj* dishonourable; disgraceful, shameful; бесчесна жена promiscuous woman

бесчесник -ци *m* dishonourable (bad) man; rake, libertine

бесчесница *f* dishonourable woman; promiscuous (loose) woman, wanton

бесчести *pf* & *impf* I to deflower, ravish; to disgrace, bring shame (*on s.o.*) II – се to bring shame on o.s.; to fall into disgrace

бесчестие -ја *n* dishonour, shame; dishonesty

бесчествува (се) *impf see* бесчести (се)

бесчовечен -чна *adj see* нечовечен

бесчувствен *adj* insensitive; heartless

бесчувственост *f* insensitivity; heartlessness

бешеќерен -рна *adj* sugarless; бешеќерна храна sugar-free food

бешумен -мна *adj* noiseless, silent

бешумност *f* noiselessness, silence

бета *f* beta; бета-зраци beta rays (particles)

бетер *colloq.* 1 *adj indecl.* worse; ❑ има од бетер побетер to jump out of the frying-pan into the fire 2 *adv* worse

бетон *m* concrete; армиран бетон reinforced concrete

бетонира *pf* & *impf* to concrete; to reinforce with concrete

бетономешалка *f Tech.* concrete mixer

бетонски *adj* concrete *attrib.*; бетонска патека concrete footpath

беќар *m* bachelor; flirt, woman-chaser, playboy; merry-maker, reveller, drunk

беќарлак *m see* беќарство

беќарство *n* bachelorhood, bachelor's life

беќарува *impf* to live as a bachelor

беќарштина *f see* беќарство

бечвар *m* tailor (*who makes trousers for traditional costumes*)

бечви *pl* breeches (*in traditional costumes*)

беше *imperf.* (*2nd & 3rd p. sg*) *of* сум

би *conditional part* would, should

би-би *interj* come on! (*when calling geese*)

бибе *n* duckling; gosling

библија *f* Bible; ❑ стар како библија as old as the hills

библиограф *m* bibliographer

библиографија *f* bibliography

библиографски *adj* bibliographical

библиотека *f* library

библиотекар *m* librarian

библиотекарка *f* (*fem. form*) *see* библиотекар

библиотекарски *adj* library *attrib.*; библиотекарски кадар library staff

библиотекарство *n* 1 librarianship; the work of a librarian 2 library science

библиотечен -чна *adj* library; библиотечен фонд library holdings

библиски *adj* biblical, scriptural

бива *impf dial. see* бидува

бивак -ци *m* bivouac

бивакува *impf* to bivouac, camp

бивол *m Zool.* <water->buffalo

биволар *m* buffalo herdsman

биволарка *f* (*fem. form*) *see* биволар

биволешки *adj dial. see* биволски

биволица *f Zool.* <water->buffalo cow; биволицата е црна, ама бело млеко дава *prov.* a black hen lays a white egg

биволски *adj* buffalo *attrib.*

биволче *n dim. of* бивол; <water->buffalo calf

бивш *adj* former, late, past; бивш претседател ex-president

бигамија *f* bigamy

бигамист *m* bigamist

бигор *m* 1 travertin<e>, calc-sinter; stalactite 2 *fig.* bitterness, torment, pain, trouble

бигорен -рна *adj see* бигорлив 1; бигорен камен limestone

бигорлив *adj* 1 containing lime; бигорлива вода hard water 2 *fig.* bitter, difficult, painful

бигороса *pf* to fur up; садот бигороса lime scale has built up in the the pot

бигоросува *impf of* бигороса

биде *pf of* сум; кој може да биде? who can it be? ❑ така нека биде so be it; that's that; што ќе биде, нека биде come hell or high water; come what may; да се биде или да не се биде to be or not to be; било и поминало it's all over and done with; no use crying over spilled milk; што било било let bygones be bygones; forgive and forget

биде *n* bidet

бидејќи *conj* (*зашто*) seeing that, as, because

биден -дна *adj see* иден

биднина *f see* иднина

бидува *impf* 1 (*usu. 3rd p.*) to happen, take place;

бидувало тоа и другпат that has happened on other occasions **2** *impers.* to be possible, can; should <be>; бидува ли тоа!? is that possible? can it be? тоа не бидува да го правиш you shouldn't do that; виде дека инаку не бидува he saw that it couldn't be otherwise; од него човек не бидува he will never be a real/decent man; крвта вода не бидува *prov.* blood is thicker than water; ❏ бидува! all right! agreed! О.К.! не бидува it's no use; I don't agree **3** *impers.* (*with acc.*) to be fit (за – *for*); to be suitable; за ништо не го бидува he is not fit for anything; го бидува за тоа he's just right for that

бие *impf* **I 1** to beat, hit; (*со камшик*) to whip, flog; го биеше Павлета he was beating Pavle; тапанџијата го бие тапанот the drummer is beating his drum; бијат тапани drums are beating; Неда бие бело платно *f.p.* Neda is beating (washing) a white sheet; ветрот ми (ме) биеше в лице the wind was blowing in my face; на шоферот сонцето му биеше в очи the sun was shining right in the driver's eyes; ова место го бијат силни ветришта strong winds lash this place **2** to destroy, kill; to shoot **3** to strike, attack; to fire (*at, on*); (*со артилерија*) to shell; to pound; непријателот го биеше нашиот одред со минофрлачи the enemy was bombarding our detachment with mortars **4** to beat *intrans.*; to strike *intrans.*; неговото срце бие забрзано his heart is pounding; бие градскиот часовник the town clock is striking **5** to ring, chime, toll; камбаните бијат the bells ring; питропот ја биеше камбаната the church warden was ringing the bell **6** ❏ се бие шега со него he is playing a joke (trick) on him; he is taunting him; тој го бие тапанот 1. he calls the tune 2. he spreads rumours; бие на црвено it's a shade of red **II – се 1** to fight; востаниците се биеја со турската војска the rebels fought the Turkish troops; востаниците се биеја со застарено оружје the rebels fought with outdated weapons **2** to beat against each other

биенáле *n* biennial <event>

биеница *f dial. see* матеница

бижутерија *f coll.* costume jewellery; trinkets

бизмут *m Chem.* bismuth

бизнис *m* business

бизнисмен *m* businessman

бизóн *m Zool.* bison

бик *m* **1** *Zool.* bull; воден бик (Botaurus stellaris) bittern; борба со бикови bullfighting; ❏ здрав како бик fit as a fiddle **2** *Astron.* the Bull, Taurus

бикарбонáт *m* bicarbonate; сода бикарбонат bicarbonate of soda

бикúни *pl* bikini

бил *past pt active of* сум

билáнс *m Comm.* balance <sheet>; financial statement, statement of accounts; биланс на плаќања, платен биланс balance of payments; годишен биланс annual balance sheet, statement of accounts; девизен биланс foreign-exchange statement; енергетски биланс energy supply and demand; книговодствен биланс balance sheet; позитивен (поволен) биланс surplus (favourable) balance; негативен (неповолен) биланс negative (adverse) balance; трговски биланс balance of trade

билáнсен -сна *adj Comm.* balance *attrib.*; билансна ставка balance-sheet item

билансúра *pf & impf Comm.* to balance; to strike a balance

билатерáлен -лна *adj* bilateral; билатерална соработка bilateral cooperation

билбил *m arch. see* славеј

биле & билем *adv colloq.* even, what's more

билен -лна *adj* plant *attrib.*; билен чај herbal tea; билна аптека herbalist, health food shop

билéт *m* ticket; повратен билет return ticket

билетарница *f* ticket office; (*во театар и сл.*) box office

билиóн *m* billion

билјар *m* **1** herbalist; (*берач*) herb-gatherer **2** (*folk name for*) July

билјáрд *m & билјáрдо n* billiards; pool; snooker

билјарка *f* (*fem. form*) *see* билјар **1**

билијáрдски *adj* billiard *attrib.*; билијардски стап billiard cue

билје *n coll.* plants, herbs; железничко билје *Bot.* (Polypodium vulgare) polypody, wall fern; лудо билје *Bot.* (Atropa belladonna) deadly nightshade

билјоса *pf* to drug with herbs, narcotize

билјосува *impf of* билјоса

билјур *m* **1** crystal **2** (*лека*) lens **3** (*двоглед*) binoculars

билка *f* **1** <medicinal> herb **2** *arch.* medicine

билкар *m see* билјар **1**

билмез *m colloq.* fool, ignoramus

билнак -ци *m* demijohn, *see* балон², бинлак

било *n* crest <of a mountain>; ridge; mountain range

билтен *m* bulletin; newsletter; report; метеоролошки билтен weather forecast

биљбиљ *m arch. see* славеј

бим *interj* bang! crash!

бина¹ *f Theatre* stage

бина² *f arch.* building

бинек -ци *m arch.* **1** saddle-horse **2** mounting block (*for a rider*) **3** tipcat

бинлак -ци *m* demijohn

бинóкл *m* (*двоглед*) binoculars

бинóм *m Math.* binomial

бинт *m* **1** bandage **2** belt **3** sanitary towel, pad (*Am.* napkin); tampon

биогрáф *m* biographer

биографија -ии *f* biography

биографски *adj* biographical

биолóг -зи *m* biologist

биологија *f* biology

биолошки *adj* biological; биолошко оружје biological weapons

бир *m dial.* son; boy

бира *impf* **1** to elect; го бираат Стојана за директор they elect Stoyan director **2** to select; бира семе за сеидба to select seed for sowing; ❏ не бира средства to stop at nothing

бирач *m* **1** voter, elector, constituent; бирачи на изборна единица constituency **2** (*на радио и сл.*) selector <knob>

бирачки *adj* voting *attrib.*, electoral; бирачки список electoral register (roll); бирачко право right to vote, voting rights; бирачко тело electorate; бирачко место polling station/booth

биринџија -ии *adj indecl. arch. colloq.* first, first-class, first-rate, excellent; мајстор биринџија master craftsman; first-class mechanic; пијаница биринџија inveterate drunkard

биро[1] *n* **1** bureau, office; branch, section; биро за градежништво construction section (branch); проектантско биро design office; planning office; *Pol.* политичко биро political bureau, politburo; биро за вработување employment bureau; туристичко биро travel agency (bureau); биро за изгубени работи lost-property office **2** desk, writing-desk, secretaire, escritoire

биро[2] *dial. voc. of* бир son! sonny! my boy!

бирокра́т *m* bureaucrat

бирократија *f* bureaucracy; red tape

бирокра́тски *adj* bureaucratic

биртија *f* tavern, inn, pub

бис *interj* encore! again! once more!

бисер *m* pearl; bead

бисерен -рна *adj* pearl *attrib.*; бисерна школка mother-of-pearl

бискви́т *m* biscuit

бискуп *m* (*Catholic*) bishop

бискупија -ии *f* bishopric

бискупски *adj* episcopal

биста *f Art* bust

бистар -тра *adj* **1** clear, limpid, pure; бистра вода clear water; бистар поглед open expression **2** clever, bright, *colloq.* quick on the uptake; бистро дете bright child

бистрее <се> *impf* to look clear; водата на езерото бистрееше the water in the lake was clear; *fig.* очите му бистрееја his eyes were shining

бистри *impf* **I** to make clear, clarify *trans.*; ❑ бистри политика to discuss politics **II** – ce to become clear, clarify *intrans.*; водата се бистри the water is getting clearer; времето се бистри (се пројаснува) the weather is clearing up

бистрина *f* clarity, transparency; cleverness, acumen

бистрота *f* transparency, purity, clarity

бистроумен -мна *adj* quick-witted, clever

бит *m* **1** way of life **2** life (*of a nation, class in society, etc.*); селски бит village (peasant) life

битва *f dial. see* битка

битен -тна *adj* essential, basic, vital, *see* суштествен

битие *n* being; existence; life; општествено битие public life, the life of a community

битиса *pf arch.* **I** to finish, complete *trans.* **II** – ce to end, finish *intrans.*; откако се битиса свадбата, jac се вратив дома when the wedding was over I returned home

битисува (се) *impf of* битиса (се)

битка *f* battle; ❑ битка со време a race against time; води загубена битка to fight a losing battle; жестока битка battle royal, pitched battle

битно *adv* essentially, considerably, substantially

битност *f* essence, substance; importance, *see* суштественост

битов *adj* **1** of life; everyday *attrib.* **2** folklore *attrib.*

битпазар *m arch.* street market, flea market

битумéн *m* bitumen

бифé *n* buffet; snack-bar; canteen

бифеџија -ии *m* manager/owner of a *бифе*; snack-bar operator; canteen lessee

бифтек -ци *m Cul.* beefsteak, steak

бифуркација *f* bifurcation, fork

БиХ *abbr.* (*Босна и Херцеговина*) Bosnia and Hercegovina

бич *m* whip, *see* камшик

бичи *impf* to saw

бичкија -ии *f* **1** saw **2** shoemaker's knife, snob knife (*for cutting leather*)

бичкиџија -ии *m* sawyer

бичува *impf* to whip

бише *n dim. of* бишка; sucking-pig, piglet

бишка[1] *f* **1** *Zool.* sow, *see* свиња **2** children's game

бишка[2] *impf see* кошка

бишкар *m see* свињар

БЈРМ *abbr.* (*Бивша југословенска република Македонија*) *see* ПЈРМ

благ *adj* **1** sweet; чајот е премногу благ the tea is too sweet; благо вино sweet wine; ❑ благ бадем sweet almond (*as opposed to bitter almond*); благ суџук sweet sausage (*made of starch and walnut*); блага пиперка sweet (mild) pepper (capsicum); блага ракија mulled brandy (*drunk by the relatives on the day after a wedding*) **2** mild, gentle; mild-mannered; sweet-tempered

благајна *f* **1** (*на станица*) ticket office, *Brit.* booking-office **2** (*во театар, кино*) box office **3** (*место каде се наплатува*) cash<ier's> desk, till **4** (*организациска единица*) treasury, bursar's office, cashier's office **5** (*средства*) fund

благајник -ци *m* cashier; ticket clerk; (*во банка*) teller, bank clerk; (*на организација*) treasurer

благајница & **благајничка** *f* (*fem. form*) *see* благајник

благајнички *adj* cash *attrib.*, cashier's; благајничка книга cash-book

благар *m* person with a sweet tooth

благден *m* <religious> holiday

благне *pf & impf* благна *aor.* to be/become sweet

благнее *impf* to taste sweet; *fig.* to be/become sweet

благо[1] *n* **1** sweet fruit preserve<s>, *see* слатко[1] **2** sweet, *Am.* candy; cake; dessert

благо[2] *n* property, wealth; рудно благо mineral resources; натрупување на благо hoarding wealth

благо[3] *adv* mildly, gently, sweetly; meekly, quietly; да ти е благо! may things go smoothly for you!

благовиден -дна *adj* charming, sweet, comely

благовремен *adj* timely; punctual; prompt; благовремено известување due notice; *see* навремен

благовремено *adv* on time, in due time, on schedule

благоглаголив *adj* **1** eloquent, mellifluous **2** *iron.* garrulous, voluble; (*проширен*) prolix

благогласен -сна *adj* melodious, harmonious

благодарен -рна *adj* thankful, grateful; многу сум ви благодарен I am very grateful to you

благодарение *adv* thanks to; благодарение на тоа thanks to that

благодари *pf & impf* **I** to thank (*некому за/на нешто – s.o. for s.th.*); благодарам! thank you!; благодарејќи на ... thanks to ..., од срце ви благодарам за помошта I thank you most sincerely for your help **II** – ce to express one's thanks; to be grateful; ти да се благодариш што не те виде никој you can thank your lucky stars that no one saw you

благодарница *f* certificate of gratitude <for services rendered>; letter of thanks; thank-you letter

благодарно *adv* gratefully, thankfully

благодарност *f* gratitude, thanks, thankfulness; должи благодарност to owe a debt of gratitude

благодат *m & f* **1** *Rel.* grace **2** blessing, boon; plenty, wealth

благодатен -тна *adj* beneficial; salutary

благодушен -шна *adj* kind, good-natured, good-hearted, warm-hearted

благозвучен -чна *adj* melodious, pleasant-sounding, euphonious

благозвучност *f* melodiousness, euphony

благонаклонет *adj* favourable, benevolent, gracious; obliging, helpful

благонаклоност *f* favour, benevolence, goodwill

благопријатен -тна *adj* favourable, suitable

благоразумен -мна *adj* reasonable, sensible

благороден -дна *adj* **1** (за човек) noble; (за зборови) exalted, lofty **2** precious; благороден метал precious metal

благородник -ци *m* aristocrat, noble<man>

благороднички *adj* aristocratic; lordly

благороднишство *n* nobility, aristocracy

благородност *f & * **благородство** *n* nobility

благосклон *adj* benevolent, favourable

благослов *m* blessing; дава некому благослов to give s.o. one's blessing

благословен *adj or pt* blessed

благослови *pf* to bless

благословија *f colloq. see* благослов

благословува *impf of* благослови

благосостојба *f* well-being, welfare; prosperity; држава на благосостојба welfare state; општа благосостојба general prosperity

благост *f* **1** sweetness **2** mildness, gentleness

благота *f* **1** sweetness, *see* блажина 1 **2** dairy (milk) products

благотворен -рна *adj* beneficial, salutary; charitable

благува *impf* **1** to enjoy o.s., find pleasure (во – in) **2** *dial. see* блажи 2

благун *m Bot.* (Quercus lanuginosa *or* pubescens) pubescent (downy) oak; бел благун (Quercus sessiliflora *or* petraea) sessile (durmast) oak

блада *impf* to rave, talk nonsense

блаж *m Med.* pleurisy

блажен[1] *adj* blissful, beatific, enraptured

блажен[2] -жна *adj dial. see* мрсен

блаженство *n* bliss

блаженствува *impf* to be in a state of bliss

блажи *impf* **1** to be sweet <to the taste> **2** *dial.* (мрси) to eat foods containing fats

блажина *f* **1** sweetness; море блажина крушиве! oh, how sweet these pears are! **2** *dial.* wealth, property

блазе *interj* lucky! блазе тебе! *and* блазé си ти! lucky you! *Austral.* half your luck!

блазѝран *adj* blasé

блазни *impf* to tempt, provoke, excite

бламáжа *f* **1** shame, disgrace, scandal **2** reproach

бламѝра *pf & impf* **I** to disgrace, compromise; to reproach **II – се** to disgrace o.s., compromise o.s.

бланкéт *m* form (with spaces to be filled), blank

бланко *adj indecl. Comm.* blank; бланко чек blank cheque; бланко кредит blank (open) credit; бланко

меница blank bill

блантав *adj dial. see* блуткав

блатен -тна *adj* marshy, boggy, swampy

блатиште[1] *n augm. of* блато 2

блатиште[2] *n* swamp, marsh, bog

блато *n* **1** marsh, bog, swampy area **2** mud

блатски *adj* marshy, boggy, swampy

блед *adj* pale, pallid, wan; *fig.* colourless; со бледо лице pale-faced; бледо небо a pale sky; бледа слика на стварноста a pale representation of reality; ❏ блед како крпа as white as a sheet, as pale as death

бледен -дна *adj see* блед

бледи *impf see* бледнее

бледило *n* pallor

бледнее *impf* to fade, turn pale; jас бледнеев од бес *colloq.* I was turning livid with rage

бледникав *adj* rather pale

бледност *f* pallor

бледнота & бледнотија *f* pallor

бледожолт *adj* pale yellow, light yellow

бледолик *adj* pale<-faced>, white-faced

блее *impf* to bleat

блека *impf see* блее

блекне *pf* блекна *aor.* to give a bleat

блен *m poet.* dreaming, reverie

бленда *f Photography* stop, f-stop; aperture

блено билје *n Bot.* (Hyoscyamus niger) henbane

бленува *impf poet.* to dream; to day-dream

блеска *impf* to sparkle, glisten; to glare; снегот блескаше the snow was sparkling

блескав *adj* **1** brilliant, radiant, dazzling; блескави очи shining (sparkling) eyes **2** *fig.* splendid, brilliant; блескав успех brilliant success; блескав резултат splendid result

блескот *m* brilliance, sheen; radiance, glow

блескотен *adj see* сјаен, блескав; блескотен успех splendid success

блескоти *impf* to sparkle, glisten; to glow; *fig.* блескоти собата од чистота the room is sparkling clean

блесне *pf* блесна *aor.* to flash

блеснува *impf of* блесне

блесок -ци *m see* блескот

блести *impf see* блескоти

блеф *m* bluff

блефѝра *impf* to bluff

блешти *impf see* блескоти

блештука *impf* to shine faintly, flicker, glimmer; (за звезди) to twinkle; уличните светилки блештукаат the street lights are flickering

ближен -жна *adj* near, neighbouring; (as noun with article) relative, friend

ближи <се> *impf* to come nearer, approach, draw near<er>; авионите <се> ближеа кон (накај) Битола the planes were approaching Bitola; <се> ближи пролетта spring is approaching (coming)

близина *f* closeness, proximity; ❏ од непосредна близина at close quarters; (за пукање) pointblank, at very close range

близнак -ци *m* twin; twin brother; *Astron.* близнаци Gemini

близначе *n dim. of* близнак

близначка *f* twin; twin sister

близни се *impf* to have (bear) twins

близок -ска *adj* **1** near, close; блиските планини the nearby mountains **2** recent; блиското минато the recent past **3** close; intimate; близок роднина a close relative; близок по разбирања near in ideas, kindred in spirit; близок е со некого to be close to s.o.; to be intimate with s.o. **4** (*as noun with article*) relative; friend

близост & **близота** *f see* близина

близу *adv* **1** near<by>, not far; близу до close by; in the neighbourhood; близу до куќата near the house; тој живее близу до мене he lives nearby; ☐ толку близу а сепак далеку so near and yet so far **2** nearly, almost; близу девет километри almost nine kilometres

блик *m poet. see* млаз

блика *impf* **1** to gush, pour; од раната блика крв blood is gushing from the wound **2** to break out, emerge; to sprout **3** (*за река*) to rise, have its source (headwaters) **4** (*за дожд*) to pour, come down **5** *fig.* to boil, seethe *intrans.*; на сите страни блика живот life is in full swing

бликне *pf* бликна *aor.* **1** to spout, gush forth; бликна студена вода cold water gushed out **2** to break out; му бликна пот од снагата he broke into a sweat

бликнува *impf of* бликне

блиндáжа *f* **1** blindage, dug-out, shelter **2** armour-plating

блиндúран *adj* armoured; блиндиран воз armoured train

блинкер *m* spoon-bait; wiggler; fly

блиска *impf see* плиска

блискост *f see* близина

блискот *m see* блескот

блискотен -тна *adj* brilliant, radiant, dazzling, *see* блескав

блиску *adv* near<by>, not far

блисне *pf* блисна *aor. see* плисне

блиснува *impf of* блисне

блиц *m Photography* flash-gun; flash<light>

блок *m* **1** block; (*зграда*) building; (*комплекс згради*) complex of buildings; блокови мраз blocks of ice; изградија нов блок згради they built a new complex **2** *Pol.* bloc; источниот блок the Eastern Bloc **3** (*за цртање*) sketching-pad

блокáда *f* blockade; *Med.* obstruction

блокéј *m* metal plate, cleat (*on a heel or sole of shoe*)

блокúра *pf & impf* to block; to blockade; to obstruct

блоковски *adj Pol.* bloc *attrib.*; блоковска политика bloc politics; блоковска припадност membership of a bloc

блостур *m Bot.* (Verbascum) mullein

блуд *m* fornication, sexual promiscuity; debauchery

блуден -дна *adj* promiscuous; debauched

блудец -дци *m* boiled wheat (*dish prepared for certain religious ceremonies*)

блуди *impf* to wander, roam

блудник -ци *m* libertine, fornicator, lecher

блудница *f* promiscuous (loose) woman

блуднички *impf see* блудствува

блудо *n see* бљудо

блудство *n* debauchery, fornication, lechery

блудствува *impf* to fornicate, be promiscuous

блуе *impf* **I** to vomit, throw up; to belch forth, spew; цела ноќ блуеше he was vomiting all night; блуе крв to vomit blood **II** – **се** *impers.* (*with dat.*) ми се блуе I feel nauseous

блуза *f* blouse

блујавица *f* **1** vomit **2** *fig.* rubbish, *colloq.* bilge **3** *Bot.* (Lolium temulentum) bearded darnel

блуска *f dim. of* блуза

блуткав *adj* lacking flavour, insipid, bland, dull; блуткаво јадење bland food

блуткаво *adv* insipidly, blandly, dully; веќе ми е блуткаво I'm sick of it

бљуд *m see* тарун 1 & 2

бљудо *n* bowl, dish; plate

Б.О. *Med. abbr.* (*без особености*) N.A.D. (no abnormality detected)

боа *f Zool.* boa <constrictor>

боб *m Bot. dial. see* грав

бобúна *f* **1** bobbin **2** *Elec.* coil

бобинка[1] *f* berry, fruit (*with seed*)

бобинка[2] *f Bot. dial. see* боболка, црница

боболка *f* mulberry (*fruit*)

боболкница *f Bot.* (Morus) mulberry tree

боботи *impf see* баботи

боботија *f* roar, boom, din

бовча *f* **1** bundle (*of traveller's personal belongings*), *Austral.* swag **2** *see* бовчалак

бовчалак -ци *m* present (*bundle of clothing traditionally given by the bride to chosen wedding guests*)

бовчиче *n dim. of* бовча

бог, Бог *m* god, God; ☐ Бог да <го> прости! may he rest in peace! помози Бог! God be with us! дал ти Бог добро! God bless you! (*as a reply to* помози Бог *or* Добро утро); Боже поможи! God help us! сполај Богу, фала Богу thank God; до Бога <what> in God's name . . . ? Good God! дај Боже! God grant it! may it please God! само <еден> Бог знае Lord only knows; цар далеку, Бог високо between the devil and the deep blue sea; you're on your own; Богу (на Бога) душа даде to give up the ghost

богами *interj* honest to God, honestly, really; well; surely

богат *adj* **1** rich, wealthy, affluent; зеде жена од богата куќа he married a woman from a wealthy family; ☐ не сум богат евтино да купувам I can't afford false economies **2** abundant, plentiful; богат крај a fertile region; богата берба ample harvest; богат избор a wide choice **3** (*as noun*) rich man; ☐ богати и сиромаси the haves and the have-nots; гнил богат moneybags

богаташ *m* rich man; *sl., pejor.* moneybags

богаташка *f* rich woman

богаташки *adj* rich man's

богатее *impf* **I** to make rich; to enrich **II** – **се** to grow rich, make money

богати (се) *impf see* богатее (се)

богатник -ци *m* rich man

богатница *f see* богаташка

богато *adv* richly, plentifully

богатски *adj see* богаташки

богатство *n* **1** wealth, affluence; riches; <вистинско> мало богатство a small fortune; слава и богатство fame and fortune; стекнува големо богатство to make a pile (packet); цело богатство a fortune; a king's ransom **2** abundance; природни богатства natural resources

богиња *f see* божица

богобојазлив *adj* God-fearing, pious

боговски *adj* magnificent; *fig.* divine

богољубен -бна *adj* pious, devout

богољубец -пци *m arch.* devout person

богољубив *adj see* богољубен

богомил *m* Bogomil

богомилство *n* the Bogomil movement, Bogomilism

богомолец -лци *m* **1** devout person; *pejor.* sanctimonious person **2** *Zool.* (Mantis religiosa) praying mantis

богомрзец -сци *m* atheist

Богородица *f Rel.* the mother of God, the Virgin Mary; Голема богородица the Assumption; Мала богородица the Nativity of the Virgin

богородичен -чна & **богородичин** *adj* of the Virgin, of Our Lady

богослов *m* **1** theologian **2** *see* богословец

богословец -вци *m* theology student, seminary student, seminarian

богословие *n* theology, *see* теологија

богословија *f* seminary

богословски *adj* theological

богослужбен *adj* church *attrib.*; liturgical, for the liturgy

богослужение -ија *n* divine service; religious service

боготвори *impf* to adore, worship

богоугоден -дна *adj* pleasing to God, pious

богохулен -лна *adj* blasphemous

богохулник -ци *m* blasphemer

богохулница *f* (*fem. form*) *see* богохулник

богохулство *n* blasphemy

Богочовек *m* the Son of God, God the Son, Jesus

бод[1] *m* **1** (*шилест врв на остар предмет*) point, tip **2** (*со игла*) stitch

бод[2] *m Sport.* point (*scored*)

бодар -дра *adj* alert; vigorous; lively, cheerful; бодар и здрав hale and hearty; бодар дух high spirits; бодро расположение cheerful mood

боде *impf* **I 1** to prick; (*за брада и сл.*) to be prickly; (*за бик и сл., со рогови*) to butt; (*со остен*) to goad; (*коњ со мамузи*) to spur on **2** (*ранува со нож*) to stab, knife **3** (*за болка*) to stab; нешто ме боде во слабините I feel a stabbing pain in the groin; ❑ ништо не го боде he is well (quite all right) **II – се 1** to prick o.s. **2** (*за рогато животно*) to butt, be inclined to butt; to gore; to lock horns; едниот бик се боде, а другиот не се боде one bull butts, the other does not; со богат не суди се, со рогат не боди се *prov.* be not bold with your biggers and betters **3** to stab each other

бодеж *m* stabbing pain; ❑ од ненадеж бодеж an unexpected blow (misfortune)

бодер -дра *adj see* бодар

бодило *n* awl

бодина *impf* **1** to spur on, ride hard *trans.* **2** to gallop; коњот бодина the horse moves fast (*at a trot or a gallop*)

бодинаница *f* trot; gallop

бодлест *adj* spiky, thorny, prickly

бодлец *m* spike, barb; thorn, spine

бодлив *adj* **1** (*што има боцки*) prickly, thorny, spiky,

spiny; бодлива жица barbed wire **2** (*за рогато животно*) inclined to butt, butting; бодлива крава butting cow

бодлика *f Bot.* thistle

бодликав *adj see* бодлив 1

бодне *pf* бодна *aor.* **I 1** to spur on; го бодна коњот и одјури he put spurs to his horse and galloped away **2** to start to trot/gallop; to gallop off **II – се** to rush off, run off, dash off

боднува (се) *impf of* бодне (се)

бодри *impf* to encourage; to urge on

бодрост *f* cheerfulness, good cheer; courage

боев *adj in the expression:* боева муниција live round<s> (ammunition)

боем *m* bohemian

боемски **1** *adj* bohemian **2** *adv* like a bohemian

боен -јна *adj* battle, combat *attrib.*; бојно поле field of battle, battlefield; бојна кола armoured vehicle

боец -јци *m* fighter; soldier; warrior

божана & божанка *f Bot. see* божурига & божурика

божевен -вна *adj arch.* pious

божем *adv* supposedly; as if, as though

божемен -мна *adj* ostensible, professed; feigned

божествен *adj* divine; *fig.* exquisite, heavenly, marvellous

божество *n* deity, godhead; divine nature

божи *adj see* божји

Божигроб *m* Jerusalem

божигропски *adj* Jerusalem *attrib.*

Божик *m* Christmas

божикен -ќна *adj see* божиќен

божилак -ци *m see* виножито

божило *n* & **божилок** -ци *m see* божилак

Божиќ *m see* Божик

божиќен -ќна *adj* Christmas *attrib.*; божиќни песни Christmas carols; божиќна елка Christmas tree; божиќни честитки Christmas greetings

божица *f* goddess

божјак -ци *m* beggar, *see* питач

божјачи *impf* to beg, ask for charity

божјачка *f* (*fem. form*) *see* божјак

божји *adj* divine, of God; божје право divine right; божја мајка *see* Богородица; служба божја divine service; син божји Jesus Christ; слуга божји clergyman; servant of Christ; царство божје heaven; божја куќа church; десет божји заповеди the Ten Commandments; ❑ божји човек meek (harmless) person; божја бубалка *Zool.* (Coccinella) ladybird, *Am.* ladybug; божја трпеза *Astronomy* the square of Pegasus; во божји раце in the lap of the gods; цел божји ден the livelong day, all day long

божур *m Bot.* (Paeonia officinalis) peony

божурига & божурика *f Bot.* (Papaver rhoeas) poppy

божуриште *n* peony field

божуров *adj* **1** peony *attrib.* **2** (*за боја*) peony-red, crimson

боз *m Bot.* (Sambucus nigra) elder

боза *f boza* (*fermented non-alcoholic drink made from millet*)

бозаџија -ии *m boza maker/seller*; ❑ алваџија за бозаџија it's six of one or half a dozen of the other; it makes no difference

бозаџилница *f* pastry shop (*where boza is also made and sold*)

бозгун *arch.* **1** *m* confusion, disorder **2** *adj indecl.* restless, rebellious

боздиса *pf arch.* **I** to spoil *trans.*; to break *trans.* **II – се** to spoil *intrans.*; to get broken, break *intrans.*; *see* расипе (се)

боздисува (се) *impf of* боздиса (се)

боздоган *m* club, mace

бозе *n Bot. see* боз

бозел *m Bot. see* боз

бозовица *f only in the combination:* пушка бозовица toy gun (*carved from elder-wood*)

бои *impf* to paint; to colour, dye; *see* бојадисува

бои се *impf* to fear, be afraid; од ништо не се боев I was afraid of nothing

боичка *f* **1** *dim. of* боја 1 **2** small coloured pencil, crayon

боиште *n* battlefield

бој¹ -еви *m* battle, fight

бој² *m colloq.* **1** stature, height; бој човечки the height of one man, fathom **2** storey; куќа на два боја two-storey house

боја *f* **1** dye; paint; сина боја blue paint; мрсна боја oil-based paint; oil-paint; водна боја water-based paint; water-colour; боја за чевли shoe polish; пушта боја to run (*of colours*); ❑ *colloq.* премачкан е со сите бои he knows all the tricks of the trade **2** colour; штоф во неколку бои material of several colours; си ја поврати бојата the colour has returned to his face; добива боја to get a tan; ❑ ја мени бојата <на лицето> his face changed colour; he turned pale; he turned all the colours of the rainbow **3** *fig.* colour; (*на глас*) timbre; се покажа во вистинската боја he showed himself in his true colours **4** (*на карти за играње*) suit

бојадиса *pf* to paint; to colour, dye

бојадисува *impf of* бојадиса; бојадисува sидови to paint walls; бојадисува предено to dye yarn

бојазан -зни *f* fear, dread

бојазлив *adj* timid, timorous, fearful

бојазливо *adv* timidly, timorously, fearfully

бојазlivost *f* timidity, fearfulness

бојалија *adj indecl. colloq.* **1** coloured, painted **2** fading; with colours that run

бојар *m see* болјар

бојарски *adj see* болјарски

бојаџија -ии *f* painter; dyer

бојаџилница *f* painter's/dyer's workshop

бојаџиски *adj* painter's; dyer's; painting *attrib.*; dyeing *attrib.*

бојкот *m* boycott

бојкотира *impf* to boycott

бојлија *adj indecl. arch.* **1** tall, well-built, shapely **2** *in the combination:* пушка бојлија long slender rifle

бојник¹ -ци *m Zool.* (Chondrostoma nasus) kind of carp

бојник² -ци *m* fighter, warrior

бојница *f see* бојник¹

бојоса *pf see* бојадиса

бојосува *impf of* бојоса

бок *m* side, flank

бокал *m* pitcher, ewer; carafe

боклук *m* **1** excrement **2** refuse, rubbish, *Am.* trash

бокс¹ *m Sport.* boxing

бокс² *m* calfskin, boxcalf

боксер *m Sport.* boxer

боксира *impf Sport.* **I** to box *trans. & intrans.* **II – се** to box (*со некого – with s.o.*)

боксува (се) *impf. see* боксира (се)

боктиса *pf arch.* to annoy, vex; to bore

бол *m see* болка

болва *f Zool.* (Pulex irritans) flea; ❑ болвата бивол ја прави he makes a mountain out of a molehill

боледува *impf* to be ill (sick); девојката боледува од тифус the girl has typhus

боледување *n* **1** *from* боледува **2** sick-leave

болежливо *adv* painfully, with great anguish; срцето му се свитка болежливо his heart bled

болезлив *adj* **1** sickly, ailing, *see* болникав **2** of pain, pained; болезлива гримаса grimace of pain

болезнен *adj* **1** sickly **2** pertaining to an illness

болен -лна *adj* **1** ill, sick; легнува (паѓа) болен to fall ill, come down with an illness **2** of illness (sickness); болна година a year of illness **3** aching, painful; болни коски aching bones **4** (*as noun*) sick person, patient; ❑ само болен се прашува of course! what a silly question!

болеро *n* **1** (*шпански танц*) bolero **2** (*кусо женско палто*) bolero

болеснички *adj* patient's; sickness *attrib.*; болеснички додаток sickness benefit

болест *f* **1** illness; disease; заразна (префатлива) болест infectious (contagious) disease; душевна болест mental illness; морска болест seasickness; шеќерна болест diabetes; прележа болест he was sick; детски болести children's diseases; *fig.* growing pains, teething troubles; ❑ по смрт болест нема it's no use crying over spilled (spilt) milk **2** *fig.* weakness, passion (*for s.th.*); комарот е болест gambling is a disease

болешка *f dial.* **1** *see* болка **2** wound

болешлив *adj* sickly

болештина *f* **1** severe pain; не се трпат овие болештини I can't stand these pains **2** *fig.* pain, torment, sorrow; worry; изгорев од болештина за детето I am worried to death about the child

боли *impf* (*only 3rd p., with acc. of person*) **1** to hurt, cause to ache; ме боли забот I have toothache; ме боли главата I have a headache; ❑ погоди некого каде најмногу боли to hit s.o. where it hurts most; *colloq.* баш го боли; и тоа го заболе he couldn't care less **2** *fig.* ме боли душата (срцето) my heart aches; овде ме боли за него my heart goes out to him, I am worried about him

боливач *m Bot.* **1** (Glaucium phoeniceum) horned poppy **2** (Anthemis nobilis) camomile

Боливиец -ијци *m* Bolivian

Боливија *f* Bolivia

Боливијка *f* (*fem. form*) *see* Боливиец

боlivиски *adj* Bolivian

болјар *m Hist.* boyar (*member of aristocratic order*), grandee

болјарски *adj* boyar *attrib.*, boyar's

болка *f* **1** pain; ❑ лажни болки false labour **2** illness; ❑ тоа не е болка за умирање you'll live, you won't die of that; it's not so bad

болнав *adj see* болникав

болник -ци *m* patient, sick person

болникав *adj* sickly

болница *f* **1** hospital; стави во болница to send to hospital, hospitalize; лежи во болница to be in hospital; прими во болница to admit to hospital; пушти од болница to discharge from hospital; државна (градска, општа) болница public hospital **2** (*fem. form*) *see* болник

болничав *adj see* болникав

болничар *m* hospital attendant, medical orderly; male nurse

болничен -чна *adj see* болнички

болничарка *f* nurse's aide

болничарски *adj* nurse's; болничарски курс training course for nurses

болнички *adj* hospital *attrib.*; болнички кревет hospital bed; болнички персонал hospital staff

болно *adv* painfully

болска *impf* **1** (за секавица) *see* болсне **1 2** to shine, sparkle, glisten

болскав *adj* shining, sparkling

болскот *m* sparkle, brilliance

болсне *pf* болсна *aor.* **1** (за секавица) to flash **2** (за sвезда) to sparkle, shine for a moment **3** (за сонцето) to rise, start shining

болук *arch.* **1** *m* plenty **2** *adv* many, galore

болшевизам -змот *m* bolshevism

болшевик -ци *m* bolshevik, socialist revolutionary

болшевички 1 *adj* bolshevik *attrib.*, *pejor.* bolshie **2** *adv* like a bolshevik

болши *impf* **I** to hunt for fleas (некого – on s.o.), try to rid (s.o.) of fleas **II** – се to hunt for fleas on o.s., try to rid o.s. of fleas

бомба *f* bomb; атомска бомба atom<ic> bomb; рачна бомба hand-grenade; длабинска бомба depth charge; ❑ бомба! fine! excellent! бомба сум! I'm fine! одекнува како бомба to come as a bombshell

бомбардер *m* bomber

бомбардира *pf & impf* to bombard, bomb

бомбардирање *n* bombing, aerial bombardment

бомбастичен -чна *adj* bombastic

бомбастичност *f* bombast, bombastic quality of expression

бомбаш *m Mil.* grenadier; (терорист) bomber, bomb thrower

бомбашки *adj* grenadier's; бомбашка група grenadier unit

бомбе *n arch.* bowler <hat>, *Am.* derby

бон *m* coupon, ticket; бон за храна meal ticket

бонбон *m & бонбона f* sweet, *Am.* candy, *Austral.* lolly; овошни бонбони fruit drops; чоколадни бонбони chocolates

бонбониера *f* box of chocolates; (порцеланска, кристална) sweet bowl, *bonbonnière*

бонбонџија -ии *m* confectioner

бонсек *m* hacksaw

бонтон *m* good manners, *bon ton*; по бонтон in accordance with etiquette

бонус *m* bonus; девизен бонус bonus for foreign currency

бор[1] *m Bot.* (Pinus) pinetree, pine; црн бор (Pinus nigra) Corsican pine; бел бор (Pinus sylvestris) Scots pine

бор[2] *m Chem.* boron

боравалка *f* ladle; <wooden> mixing spoon

борави *impf* **1** (изведува) to do, perform, carry out **2**

to mix, *see* буричка **I 3** (превртува) to upset, knock over, overturn; to turn over

боралиште *n* wrestling ring

боранија *f* string beans, green beans

борач *m Sport.* wrestler

борачка *f* **1** *Sport.* wrestling, *see* борење **1 2** female wrestler

борачки *adj Sport.* wrestling *attrib.*; борачки вештини martial arts

борба *f* struggle, fray, contest; battle; народно-ослободителна борба national-liberation struggle; борба на живот и смрт fight to the death; борба за опстанок fight for survival; стапи во борба he joined the struggle/campaign; he entered the fray; he took the field

борбен *adj* **1** militant, warlike; combatant; combative; борбени луѓе militant/plucky people; тој играч има добра техника, но не е доволно борбен that player has a good technique, but he is not aggressive enough; борбен дух fighting spirit **2** fighting, combat *attrib.*; борбена сила fighting forces, fighting strength; борбена единица combat unit; борбени средства weapons, weaponry, arms, armaments, munitions

борбеност *f* militancy, aggressiveness; fighting spirit; combativeness

бордеро *n* bordereau

бордо *adj indecl. & n* dark red, burgundy, maroon

борење *n* **1** *Sport.* wrestling **2** struggle, fighting

борец -рци *m* fighter, soldier; combatant; стар борец veteran; борец со бикови bullfighter

боречки *adj* fighting, militant; combatant; боречка пензија veteran's pension

бори се *impf* **1** to fight; to combat, battle (со, против – with, against); се бори со (против) непријателите he fights the enemy **2** *Sport.* to wrestle **3** *fig.* to struggle, fight (with, against, for); to contend (with, against, for); се бори со тешкотии to wrestle with difficulties

борија -ии *f* **1** *arch. Mus.* trumpet, bugle **2** *dial.* pipe (on a stove)

борина *f* **1** *Bot. see* бор[1] **2** pinewood; kindling; *f.p.* torch of pinewood; страк борина a pine switch

боринар *m rare* seller of kindling

бориновина *f* pine fragrance; мириса бориновина it smells of pine

бормашина *f* drill, drilling (boring) machine

боров *adj* pine *attrib.*; борова гора (шума) pine forest; борово дрво pine<wood>, deal

боровина *f* pine<wood>

боровинка *f Bot.* (Vaccinium myrtillus) bilberry, whortleberry, *Am.* blueberry; црвена боровинка cowberry, mountain cranberry, red bilberry

борч -еви, -ови *m colloq.* (долг) debt

борчи *impf colloq.* (должи) to owe

борчлија 1 *adj indecl. colloq.* (должен) in debt, owing **2** *m* debtor

борчува *impf see* борчи

бос *adj* **1** barefoot<ed>; (за нога) bare; босо дете barefooted child; на боса нога on bare feet **2** (за непоткувано животно) unshod **3** *fig.* ignorant, uninformed; ill-trained; и тој е бос во тоа he doesn't know much about this either

босак -ци *m* **1** growth, excrescence; wart **2** nipple

Босанец -нци *m* Bosnian

Босанка _f (fem. form) see_ Босанец

босански _adj_ Bosnian

босилек _m Bot._ (Ocimum basilicum) sweet basil

босилков _adj_ basil _attrib._; _f.p._ китка босилкова a bunch of sweet basil

босилковина _f_ aroma of basil; мириса босилковина it smells of sweet basil

боска _f_ nipple, teat; breast

Босна _f_ Bosnia; _(река)_ the <River> Bosna

босоног _adj_ barefoot<ed>

босота & босотија _f_ **1** state of being barefooted **2** _fig._ ignorance, state of unpreparedness, lack of qualifications (_in a special field_), rawness

бостан _m_ **1** melon field/patch **2** melons; ❏ продава бостан на бостанција to preach to the converted; teach your grandmother to suck eggs; _colloq._ го обра бостанот he is in big trouble, he is on the rocks **3** _Bot._ (Delphinium consolida) larkspur

бостаниште _n_ **1** melon field/patch **2** _augm. of_ бостан

бостанција -ии _m_ melon grower; melon seller

босува _impf_ **1** to go barefoot, lack footwear **2** _fig._ to live in poverty

Босфор _m_ the Bosporus

босфорски _adj_ from/of the Bosporus

ботаника _f_ botany

ботаничар _m_ botanist

ботанички _adj_ botanical

ботее _impf_ to grow luxuriantly, develop, advance, flourish; цвеќето/дрвото ботее the flower/tree is flourishing

Боцвана _f_ Botswana

Боцванец -нци _m_ Botswanan

Боцванка _f (fem. form) see_ Боцванец

боцвански _adj_ Botswanan

боцка[1] _impf_ **I 1** to prick; to sting; (_за болки_) to stab; боцка некого со трн to prick s.o. with a thorn; грубите волнени чорапи многу нѐ боцкаа the coarse woollen socks were very prickly **2** _fig._ to tease, badger, torment, upset **II** - **се** _see_ боцне (се) **II**

боцка[2] _f_ **1** thorn, prickle; sting **2** barb **3** bristle; quill, spine

боцкав _adj_ bristly; barbed; thorny, spiny, prickly

боцкалка _f see_ боцка[2]

боцкало _n see_ боцкач

боцкач _m_ **1** picador **2** _fig._ tease, tormentor; stinging critic

боцлив _adj_ prickly, thorny; боцливо прасе _Zool._ (Hystrix cristata) porcupine

боцне _pf_ боцна _aor._ **I 1** to prick; to jab; to sting; (_за болка_) to stab; го боцна волот со остенот he jabbed the ox with the goad; штркол го боцнал a gadfly stung him **2** _fig._ to tease, needle, torment, upset **II – се 1** to prick o.s.; се боцнав со иглата I pricked myself with (on) the needle **2** _fig._ to tease each other

боцнува (се) _impf of_ боцне (се)

бочва _f_ large barrel; (_за вино_) cask, tun; вино од бочва wine from the wood

бочвар _m_ cooper

бочварница _f_ cooper's shop

бочварство _n_ cooper's trade, cooperage

бочве & бочвичка _f dim. of_ бочва

бочен -чна _adj_ side _attrib._, lateral; бочна страна side

бош _adj indecl. arch._ empty; бош работа worthless job, affair; бош лаф meaningless (empty) word

---

бр. _abbr._ (_број_) number, No.

брав _m_ ram; (_скопен_) wether

брава _f_ lock; брава на врата door lock

бравар _m_ locksmith; (_метални работник_) metalworker

браварница _f_ locksmith's workshop; metalworking shop

браварски _adj_ locksmith's; metalworker's; браварски занает locksmith's trade

браво & бравос _interj_ bravo!

бравски _adj_ ram's; бравско <месо> mutton

брада _f_ **1** chin; дупче на брадата dimple on the chin **2** beard; долга брада long beard; четинеста брада stubble beard; пушта брада to grow a beard; поарно старому под брада, одошто младому под стреа _prov._ better be an old man's darling than a young man's slave **3** (_жилички на корен_) fibres of a root, root-hairs; брада на лук garlic roots

брадавица _f_ **1** wart **2** (_боска_) teat, nipple

брадавичав _adj_ covered in warts, warty

брадат _adj_ bearded

брадва _f_ adze

брадест _adj see_ брадат

брадина 1 _m_ bearded person **2** _f see_ брадиште

брадичка _f dim. of_ брада; tuft; шилеста брадичка goatee

брадиште _n augm. of_ брада

брадоса <се> _pf_ to let one's beard grow, grow a beard

брадосува <се> _impf of_ брадоса <се>

брадуле & брадулче _n dim. of_ брада

брадулка _f dim. of_ брада

бразда _f_ **1** furrow; irrigation ditch; rut; (_жлеб_) groove, flute; трга бразда to make a furrow; моторниот чамец оставаше бразди зад себе the motor boat was leaving a wake; ❏ заора прва бразда to turn the first sod **2** (_поток_) stream, brook **3** wrinkle, fold, furrow; бразди на челото wrinkles on the forehead **4** _Anat._ fissure

браздест _adj_ furrowed; wrinkled; браздеста површина wrinkled surface

бразди _impf_ to furrow, plough; бразди море _poet._ to plough (furrow) the sea; грижите му го браздат лицето his face is lined from worry

Бразил _m_ Brazil

Бразилец -лци _m_ Brazilian

бразилиец -ијци _m_ person from Brasilia

Бразилија _f_ Brasilia

бразилијка _f (fem. form) see_ бразилиец

бразилиски _adj_ from/of Brasilia

Бразилка _f (fem. form) see_ Бразилец

бразилски _adj_ Brazilian

бразлётна _f_ bracelet

брак _m_ **1** marriage; matrimony, wedlock; граѓански брак civil marriage; див брак common-law marriage, de facto relationship; законит брак lawful marriage; неприкладен брак misalliance; брак од користољубие a marriage of convenience; брак на одредено време trial marriage; стапи во брак he/she got married; склучи брак he/she contracted a marriage **2** _dial._ wedding

браколомен -мна _adj_ adulterous

браколомник -ци _m_ adulterer

браколомница _f_ adulteress

браколомство _n_ adultery

бракора́звод *m* divorce

бракоразводен -дна *adj* divorce *attrib.*; бракоразводна парница divorce suit/case

бракува *impf* to scrap; to discard, reject; to condemn <as defective>; (*кораб, авион*) to decommission

бран *m* wave; (*голем*) roller; billow; бран на штрајкови series (wave) of strikes

брана¹ *f* harrow

брана² *f* dam; dyke; (*на река*) weir; (*дрвена*) groyne, *Am.* groin; barrier

браненик -ци *m* reserve, reservation; fenced clearing (*in forest*); *see* забел

браненица *f see* браненик

бранест *adj* wavy; uneven; бранест површина undulating surface; бранест покрив corrugated-iron roof

брани¹ *impf* I 1 to defend, protect; брани свои ставови to defend one's position, uphold one's views; брани некого на суд to defend s.o. in court; карпата нѐ бранеше од ветрот the boulder protected (sheltered) us from the wind 2 to forbid, prevent; мајка му му брани да се дружи со мене his mother forbids him being friends with me 3 *Sport.* to be goalkeeper; тој брани мошне успешно he is very good in goal II – **се** to defend o.s.; to protect o.s.; ❏ се брани со раце и нозе to fight tooth and nail

брани² *impf* to harrow

браник -ци *m* 1 (*на кола*) bumper bar, *Am.* fender 2 rampart (*also fig.*) 3 trigger guard; safety-catch

бранител *m* defender; *fig.* champion; *Leg.* counsel for the defence, *Brit.* defending barrister, *Am.* defense attorney

бранов *adj* wave *attrib.*; бранова должина wavelength; ❏ на иста бранова должина on the same wavelength; speaking the same language

брановит *adj* 1 wavy, turbulent, billowy; брановито море rough sea 2 *see* бранест

браноса *pf* to harrow

браносува *impf see* брани²

бранува¹ *impf see* браносува

бранува² *impf* I to ruffle; (*силно*) to agitate, churn up; ветрот го бранував езерото the wind was ruffling the surface of the lake II – **се** to be choppy (rough); to surge, billow; (*малку*) to ripple; при силен ветер езерото се бранува the lake gets choppy when there is a strong wind; морето се бранува the sea is rough

бранша *f* branch <of business>; speciality, field of specialization; occupation

брат *m* браќа *pl* 1 brother; роден брат blood-brother; ❏ топол брат *pejor.* a queer; мокри браќа drunkards; брат брата не рани, тешко тој што го нема *prov.* blood is thicker than water; брат за брата, сирењето за пари *prov.* business is business 2 friend, comrade, mate; така брате! that's more like it! that's better! now you're talking! 3 monk, friar, *pl* brethren, Brothers 4 *colloq.* man; го гледаш ли братов? do you see this man?

братанец -нци *m dial.* nephew (*brother's son*)

братаница *f dial.* niece (*brother's daughter*)

братенце *n hyp. of* брат

братец *m hyp.* brother; (*in address*) old chap! my boy!

братија *f coll.* brethren, monks of the same order; group, brotherhood, fraternity

братими се *impf* to fraternize (*co – with*); народот се братимеше со војниците the people fraternized with the soldiers; Иван се братимеше со Александар Ivan and Alexander were close

Братислава *f* Bratislava

братиславец -вци *m* person from Bratislava

братиславка *f* (*fem. form*) *see* братиславец

братиславски *adj* Bratislava *attrib.*

братко *m hyp. of* брат

братов *adj* brother's

братовина *f* brother's property, inheritance from a brother

братољубив *adj* brotherly, fraternal

братољубивост *f* brotherly feelings

братоубиец -јци *m* fratricide (*person*)

братоубиствен *adj* fratricidal; братоубиствена војна fratricidal war

братоубиство *n* fratricide (*act*)

братски¹ *adj* fraternal, brotherly; братски народи brother nations; братски народ fraternal (brotherly) people; братска љубов brotherly love; во братска заедница in fraternal union

братски² *adv* fraternally, as/like brothers; братски пружи некому рака to press s.o.'s hand affectionately

братство *n* brotherhood; братство и единство brotherhood and unity; братството за братство, сирењето за пари *prov. see* брат 1

братучед *m* cousin; први братучеди first cousins; втори братучеди second cousins

братучеда & **братучетка** *f* (*fem. form*) *see* братучед

браќа *pl of* брат

брач *m Mus.* alto tambura

брачен -чна *adj* conjugal, marriage *attrib.*; брачна двојка married couple; брачен другар spouse, mate; брачна заедница matrimony; брачно (свадбено) патување honeymoon; брачна состојба married (conjugal) status

брашнар *m* flour merchant

брашнарница *f* flour store

брашнарски *adj* flour-merchant's

брашнен *adj* flour *attrib.*; брашнена алва homemade halva (*made of flour*); брашнена вреќа sack for flour, flour bag; брашнен црв meal-worm

брашненик -ци *m* chest (*for storage of flour*)

брашнест *adj* floury, starchy, mealy; брашнест леб doughy (heavy) bread; брашнести јаболка floury apples

брашник -ци *m see* брашненик

брашно *n* flour; пченично брашно wheat flour; пченкарно (царевно) брашно maize flour, corn meal; крупно брашно meal; ❏ не меле брашно со некого not to see eye to eye with s.o.; легнува на брашно to knuckle under; to eat humble pie; во секое брашно има трици *prov.* there is no wheat without chaff

брашноса *pf* I to sprinkle with flour II – **се** to get flour over o.s.

брашносува (се) *impf of* брашноса (се)

брбашка *f see* брбушка

брбешка *impf* I to dirty, soil; ги брбешка рацете he gets his hands dirty II – **се** to get dirty *intrans.*; to dirty o.s.; детето се брбешка во калта the child gets dirty in the mud

брбешкав *adj* dirty, messy, soiled

брбешко *m* sloven, dirty fellow

брбла & **брблавица** *f* chatterbox, *colloq.* windbag, *sl.* gasbag

брблив *adj* talkative, garrulous

брбливец -вци *m* talker, babbler, *colloq.* windbag, *see* брбло

брбливка *f see* брбла, брблавица

брбливост *f* garrulity, garrulousness

брбло -овци *m* babbler, *colloq.* windbag

брбне *pf* брбна *aor. in the expression:* брбне да се смее to burst out laughing

брбнува *impf of* брбне

брбори *impf* **1** to chatter, babble; брбори глупости to talk bunkum **2** to murmur; to gurgle *intrans.*; потокот брбори the stream murmurs

брборка¹ *f* **1** chatterbox, *sl.* gasbag **2** gurgling spring <of water>

брборка² *impf dim. of* брбори

брборко -овци *m* babbler, *colloq.* windbag

брбулее *impf* to murmur; to gurgle *intrans.*

брбушка *f* animal droppings, dung pellet (*of sheep, goats, hares, etc.*)

брвне *pf* брвна *aor. see* брбне

брго & **бргу** *adv* quickly, soon; брго-брго in haste

бргозборница *f f.p.* babbler, chatterbox

бргошен -шна *adj* recent; imminent, impending

брдар *m* maker of combs (*for looms*)

брдила *pl see* набрдила

брдица *f* **1** mould-board (*of a plough*) **2** spoke (*in a wheel*)

брдо¹ *n* hill; ❑ преку брда и долини over the hills and far away

брдо² *n* reed, comb (*on a loom*)

брдски *adj* hill, mountain *attrib.*; hilly; брдски краишта hilly areas

бре *interj* **1** (*expressing surprise, wonder*) look! well well! gee! бре, што убава куќа! what a lovely house! **2** (*expressing impatience, usu. abrupt*) арно, бре момче all right, young fellow! еј ти бре! hey you! **3** бре . . . бре, . . . now . . . now . . . ; бре овде, бре онде now here, now there

брева & **бревта** *impf* to pant, gasp

брег *m* **1** shore; морски брег coast; речен брег bank; на брегот на реката, езерото on the river bank, lakeside; стигнува до брегот to reach land; ❑ Брег на Слоновата Коска Ivory Coast **2** (*брдо*) hill; ако брегот не сака да дојде кај Мухамед, тогаш Мухамед ќе појде на брегот *prov.* if the mountain will not come to Mahomet, Mahomet must go to the mountain; тивка вода брег рони *prov.* still waters run deep

бреговит *adj* hilly

бре *impf* to roar, bellow (*of a stag*)

брез *adj* (*of animals*) having a white spot on the head

бреза¹ *f*, брезје *coll. Bot.* (Betula) birch, birch-tree

бреза² *f* white spot on the head (*of an animal*)

брезов *adj* birch *attrib.*

брej *interj see* бре

брекина *f Bot.* (Sorbus torminalis) wild service tree

брекне *pf* брекна *aor.* to swell up, become swollen

бреме *n* **1** burden, load **2** *fig.* difficulty, burden

бремен *adj* **1** (*only f*) pregnant, expecting; бремена жена pregnant woman **2** *fig.* (*тежок*) difficult, tiring

бременост *f* pregnancy

бреслика *f* young elm

брест *m Bot.* (Ulmus) elm

брестов *adj* elm *attrib.*

бретéла *f* strap

бреца & **брецка** *impf* **I** to tease; to torment; to offend; (*укорува*) to reproach (*s.o. with s.th.*); to snap at, lash out at; татко ти ме брецаше секогаш your father was forever teasing me **II** – **ce** to tease each other; to torment each other

брецлив *adj* **1** teasing; annoying; (*навредилив*) insulting **2** (*раздразлив*) peevish, touchy, oversensitive

брецне *pf* бреца *aor.* **I** to tease; (*навреди*) to offend, sting, insult; (*укори*) to reproach (*некого за нешто – s.o. with s.th.*); to snap at (*s.o.*) **II** – **ce** to insult each other

бречи *impf* to cry, whine; (*за мали деца*) to scream

бречко -овци *m see* плачко

брешко *m* ox or water-buffalo (*with a white spot on its forehead*)

брз *adj* **1** fast, quick, speedy; swift; rapid; има брзи нозе to be fleet-footed; брз воз fast train; *Comm.* брз обрт quick returns; брза продажба rapid (quick, ready) sale; брза исплата prompt payment; ❑ на брза рака in haste **2** urgent; hasty; брза работа urgent work; брзо решение hasty decision

брза *impf* **I** **1** *intrans.* to hurry, be in a hurry, make haste, rush; тој брзаше he was hurrying (rushing), he was in a hurry; тој не брзаше да одговори he took his time answering; тој брзаше во работата/ јадењето/пишувањето he worked/ate/wrote hastily; побрзај! hurry up! get a move on! **2** *trans.* to hurry (*s.o.*); командирот нè брзаше сите the commander hurried us along **II** – **ce** *see* **I** 1

брзак -ци *m* **1** rapids (*in a river*); (*слап*) cascade; (*водопад*) waterfall **2** *see* брзица **3** early<-ripening> vegetables

брзана *adv only in the expression:* на брзана hastily, in a hurry, in haste

брзаница *f* hurry, rush, haste

брзање *n* **1** *from* брза (се) **2** *see* брзаница; без брзање easy does it! take it easy!

брзга *impf* to spurt, gush; to spray, splash; to sprinkle, water

брзгало *n dial.* watering-can; sprinkler

брзина *f* speed, haste; quickness, rapidity; (*на возило*) gear; *Phys.* velocity; на брзина in a hurry; ограничување на брзина speed limit; смалува брзина to reduce speed, slow down; зголемува брзина to gather speed, speed up; ја става колата во брзина to put the car in gear; сменува во втора/ трета брзина to change into second/third gear; вади од брзина to disengage a gear, put in neutral; со шеметна брзина at a vertiginous (dizzy) speed; *Comm.* брзина на вртењето на парите velocity of circulation of money; со таква брзина at such speed, so rapidly, at so swift a pace; ❑ во петта брзина at full speed; full steam ahead; петта брзина overdrive; фати на брзина to use the opportunity

брзинометар -три *m* speedometer

брзица *f Bot.* (Zea mays) early maize (Indian corn)

брзне *pf* брзна *aor.* (*ѓргне*) to gush (rush) forth, pour out; крв брзна од раната blood came gushing from the wound

брзнува *impf of* брзне

брзо *adv* quickly, fast

брзоговорка & **брзозборка** *f* tongue-twister

брзометен -тна *adj* (*пушка*) rapid-fire *attrib.*, quick-firing

брзометка *f* rapid-fire (semi-automatic) rifle

брзоног *adj* fleet-footed

брзоод *poet.* **1** *adj* fleet-footed **2** *m* fleet-footed person

брзопис *m* **1** cursive handwriting **2** stenography, shorthand

брзострелен -лна *adj* rapid-firing *attrib.*; брзострелно оружје rapid-firing weapon<s>

брзотечен -чна *adj* **1** *poet.* transient, passing, fleeting, momentary **2** (*of tuberculosis*) galloping

брива *impf dial. see* кива

брига *f dial.* care, worry, *see* грижа

брига́да *f* **1** *Mil.* brigade; Првата пролетерска бригада the First Proletarian Brigade **2** *Hist.* работна бригада work brigade, labour collective, work-gang; младинска бригада youth brigade

брига́ден -дна *adj* brigade *attrib.*

бригади́р *m* **1** *Mil.* brigadier **2** work-team leader; ganger, work-team member

бригади́рка *f* (*fem. form*) *see* бригадир 2

брика *impf dial. see* брива

брилија́нт *m* diamond

брилија́нтен -тна & **брилија́нтски** *adj* diamond

брилијанти́н *m* brilliantine, gel

брили́ра *impf literary* to shine *intrans.*, stand out; брилира на испит to shine (do brilliantly) in an exam; тој не брилира со својата скромност modesty is not his strong point

Брисел *m* Brussels

бриселец -лци *m* person from Brussels

бриселка *f* (*fem. form*) *see* бриселец

бриселски *adj* Brussels *attrib.*

Британец -нци *m* Briton

Британија *f* Britain, *see* Велика Британија

Британка *f* (*fem. form*) *see* Британец

британски *adj* British

бритва *f dial.* jug; jar

брич -еви, -ови *m* cutthroat razor

бричач *m see* бербер

бричи *impf* **I** **1** to shave *trans.*; ја бричи брадата he shaves his beard; овој брич бричи добро this razor shaves well, this razor gives a clean (close) shave; ❏ бричи некого на суво to make a fool of s.o., *colloq.* pull a fast one on s.o. **2** *fig.* to flay, fleece, strip **II – се** to shave *intrans.*, shave o.s., have a shave; тој се бричи на бербер (кај берберот) he goes to the barber for a shave

бричко -овци *m colloq.* dandy, smart guy

бричобрад *adj f.p.* **1** who shaves, old enough to shave **2** *iron.* old fogy

бриц *m Cards* **1** bridge **2** rummy

бришалка *f* **1** dishcloth **2** doormat

брише *impf* **I** to wipe; to mop; (*со четка*) to brush *trans.*; (*прав*) to dust; (*со гума*) to erase; брише прав од нешто to wipe the dust off s.th.; брише пот од чело to wipe the sweat from one's brow (forehead); го брише детето she wipes the child <dry>; брише нос to wipe one's nose; бриши го од списокот strike (cross) him off the list! брише садови to dry crockery; брише под to mop the floor **II – се** to wipe o.s.;

to dry o.s.; таа плаче и се брише she weeps and wipes her face/eyes

бришка *f* cloth, dishcloth

брка¹ *impf* **I** to drive, chase, pursue; (*бара*) to look for; (*истерува*) to drive away, throw out; ловците и кучињата го бркаа волкот the hunters and the dogs were chasing the wolf; брка муви to chase away flies; ќе го брка дури е жив he will chase (pursue) him all his life; бркај си ја работата 1. get on with your own work! 2. *fig.* mind your own business! ❏ брка сојки to chase skirts; to sow one's wild oats **II – се** to chase one another; се бркаат еден со друг they chase after one another

брка² *impf* **I** **1** to stir, mix *trans.*; to rummage; јас ќе го бркам бакрданикот I will stir the maize porridge; некој бркал во мојата чанта someone has been rummaging in my handbag **2** to confuse, perplex (*s.o.*) **3** to confuse, mix up; го брка едното прашање со другото he confuses one question with another **II – се 1** to interfere, meddle; не бркај се во моите работи don't interfere in my affairs! **2** to get confused; to get embarrassed **3** (*за животни – се пари*) to mate *intrans.*

бркалка *f* (*wooden*) mixing spoon; ladle, dipper; *see* мешалка 2

брканица *f* **1** chase, rush **2** (*мешаница*) mixing, mixture, stirring up, confusion

бркач *m* pursuer, chaser

бркне *pf* бркна *aor.* **1** to chase off, drive away; дедото ги бркна децата the old man chased the children away **2** to search through; тој бркна во својот џеб he searched through (rummaged in) his pocket

бркнува *impf of* бркне

бркотија -ии *f* confusion; chaos; (*дармар*) uproar, disturbance; (*навалица*) crush

брл *m* gid

брлави <се> *impf see* брливи <се>

брле -евци *m colloq.* madcap, crazy person; брле еден! lunatic!

брлив *adj* **1** (*see* брл) sick (ill) with gid; брлива овца sheep suffering from gid **2** *fig.* mad, crazy

брливи <се> *impf* to behave foolishly; to talk nonsense

брливка *f* (*fem. form*) *see* брливко

брливко -овци *m* crazy person, madman

брливост *f* madness, craziness

брлог -зи *m* **1** pool of mud **2** pigsty; den, lair **3** *fig.* pigsty; moral filth, sleaziness

брмка *impf dim.* (*of* брмчи) to hum/buzz softly

брмне *pf* брмна *aor.* to start humming, buzzing

брмнува *impf of* брмне

брмчи *impf* to hum, buzz; пчелите брмчат the bees are buzzing

брна & **брнка** *f* **1** muzzle (*for an animal*); nose-ring (*for an animal*) **2** ring-shaped protruberance (*on animal's snout or neck*)

брница *f dial.* bunch of various threads

брод¹ *m* ford, shallow place; длабока вода брод нема there are no fords in deep water

брод² *m* **1** ship, boat, *see* кораб; со брод by sea; патнички (лински) брод passenger ship, liner; трговски брод merchant ship (vessel); товарен брод, брод за мешовит товар cargo ship, freighter; брод-ладилник refrigerated cargo vessel; закупен брод chartered vessel; контејнерски брод container ship; вселенски брод spacecraft, spaceship; туристички брод pleasure boat; зема брод под закуп to charter a ship; истоварува брод to unload (clear) a ship; товари брод to load a ship (take goods aboard); на брод on board; ❏ брод што тоне a sinking ship, a lost cause; бродот што тоне глувците први го напуштаат *prov.* the rats are the first to leave a sinking ship **2** nave (*of church*)

бродар *m* ferryman, sailor, seaman; shipowner

бродарски *adj* shipping *attrib.*

бродарство *n* shipping, the shipping industry

броди *impf* **1** to ford (*a river*) **2** to sail (*in/of a ship*) **3** (*скита*) to wander, roam

бродоградилиште *n* shipyard

бродолом *m* shipwreck; доживува бродолом to be shipwrecked; *fig.* to fall through

бродоломен -мна *adj* (*за море, ветер, и сл.*) perilous; shipwreck *attrib.*; wrecking, destructive

бродоломец -мци *&* **бродоломник** -ци *m* shipwreck victim

бродски *adj* ship's; naval; бродска посада ship's crew (company); бродски дневник ship's log; бродска артилерија naval artillery; бродски агент freight agent; бродска агенција shipping agency

броен -јна *adj* numerical, quantitive; бројна состојба quantity, number<s>

броеници *pl see* бројници (*used also in sg:* броеница)

брои *impf* **I 1** to count; to number; брои од еден до десет to count from one to ten; селото брои 200 куќи the village numbers 200 households; ❏ му се бројат ребрата he is skin and bones, he's as thin as a rake **2** to reckon, consider; to include (*in s.th.*) **II – се 1** to number off (*of soldiers on parade*); to count one's money **2** to consider (reckon) o.s.; не се бројам за писател I don't consider (reckon) myself a writer

броител *m Math.* numerator

број -еви *m* number, figure; (*на списание и сл.*) issue, copy; *Gram.* numeral; реден број ordinal <numeral>; *Math.* прости броеви prime numbers; број нема, ни број<от> не им се знае untold numbers; извесен број a number of; во најголем број for the most part; поштенски број post (*Am.* zip) code; ❏ не му се сите на број to lose one's marbles; to be not all there; сите се на број everyone is here, all are present

бројач *m* **1** counter; enumerator; meter reader; (*на пари и сл.*) teller **2** counter, meter; Гајгеров бројач Geiger counter **3** *see* броител

бројачка *f* **1** (*fem. form*) *see* бројач 1 **2** counting

бројка *f* number, figure, digit, cipher; арапски/ римски бројки Arabic/Roman numerals; секој влече по една бројка од кутијата everyone draws a number from the box

бројник -ци *m* (*на саат, телефон и сл.*) face, dial, number pad; (*на километри*) milometer, odometer, counter

бројници *pl* (*used also in sg:* бројница) rosary, counting beads

бројчен *adj see* броен, цифрен

брокат *m* (*вид ткаенина*) brocade

бром *m Chem.* bromine

бронза *f* bronze

бронзен *adj* bronze; бронзена медала bronze medal

бронзов *adj* bronze; бронзова епоха the Bronze Age

бронка *f* pimple

бронкав *&* **бронкичав** *adj* pimply

бронхија -ии *f Anat.* bronchus (*pl* bronchi)

бронхијален -лна *adj* bronchial

бронхитис *m Med.* bronchitis

броска *f dial. see* бронка

брок *&* **брошт** *m Bot.* (Rubia tinctorum) madder

брош *m* brooch, pin

брошира *pf & impf* to bind <in soft covers>, stitch

брошура *f* brochure, pamphlet; пропагандна брошура advertising catalogue

брст *m* (*лисник*) twigs and shoots, forage, fodder, browse

брсти *impf* to browse (*of animals*)

Брунеј *m* Brunei

Брунеец -ејци *m* Bruneian

Брунејка *f* (*fem. form*) *see* Брунеец

брунејски *adj* Bruneian

брунка *f see* бронка

брункав *adj see* бронкав, бронкичав

брунчи се *impf* to come out in pimples; to be covered in pimples; целиот се брунчи по снагата his whole body is breaking out in spots

брус *m* (*точило*) whetstone, grindstone, hone

бруси *impf* (*точи, остри*) to sharpen, grind

брусница *f dial. Bot.* (Vaccinium vitis idaea) red bilberry, cowberry, whimberry

брут *m* бруќе *coll.* nail

бруталeн -лна *adj* brutal

бруталност *f* brutality

бруто *adj indecl.* gross; бруто добивка gross profit; бруто доход gross income; бруто општествен производ gross national product, GNP; бруто за нето <сметано> gross weight for nett

брух *m Med.* hernia

бруцош *m sl.* freshman, *colloq.* fresher

брца (се) *impf see* брцнува (се)

брцка (се) *impf see* брца (се)

брцне *pf* брцна *aor.* **I 1** to dip, moisten; to soak; таа ја брцна кошулата во реката she dipped/soaked the shirt in the river; го брцна прстот во медот и си го оближа he dipped his finger in the honey and licked it **2** to insert, put (*one's hand into s.th.*); тој брцна со раката во џебот he stuck his hand in<to> his pocket **3** *dial.* to spurt; крв брцна од раната blood spurted from the wound **II – се 1** to immerse o.s. **2** *fig.* to intervene, interfere, meddle (*in*)

брцнува (се) *impf of* брцне (се)

брчалка *f* **1** rattle **2** *fig.* (*брблавица*) chatterbox

брчи *impf* **1** (*за инсекти*) *see* брмчи **2** (*за направа, машина*) to throb, roar

брчка¹ *impf* **I** to wrinkle, pucker, crease; го брчка челото he wrinkles his brow; he frowns **II – се** to be wrinkled (creased)

брчка² *f* wrinkle, fold, crease

брчкав *adj* wrinkled

брчне *pf* брчна *aor.* to start buzzing (humming)

бршлан *&* **бршлен** *m Bot.* (Hedera helix) ivy

бршланов *&* **бршленов** *adj* ivy *attrib.*

буба¹ *f* **1** insect, *Am.* bug; свилена (копринена) буба silkworm **2** *child.* bugbear, bugaboo; bogey<man>

буба² *impf* to cram, *colloq.* stew <over>, *Brit. colloq.* swot *intrans.*

бубалка *f* little insect, bug; мирен како бубалка quiet as a mouse; божја бубалка *Zool.* (Coccinella) ladybird, *Am.* ladybug

бубар *m* silkworm breeder

бубарство *n* silkworm breeding, sericulture

бубаќ *m dial.* (*памук*) cotton

бубаќар *m dial.* **1** cotton-grower **2** *fig.* cad, sneak; hypocrite; bloodsucker, extortioner

бубаќарен -рна *adj dial.* (*памучен*) cotton *attrib.*

бубаќарка *f Bot.* (Heliotropium europaneum) heliotrope, turnsole

бубаќлија *adj indecl. see* бубаќарен

бубачка *f see* бубалка

бубин *adj* silkworm *attrib.*; бубина пеперуга silkworm moth; бубини црвци silkworm larvae

бубота *f* fresh maize-flour bread

буботи *impf see* баботи

бубрег -зи *m Anat.* kidney; ❑ живее како бубрег в лој to live in clover

бубрежен -жна *adj* kidney *attrib.*, renal; бубрежен песок kidney stone, gravel, renal calculus; бубрежен лој suet

був *f Zool.* owl; шумски (обичен) був (Strix aluco) tawny owl; голем був (Bubo bubo) eagle owl

бува *impf* **1** to bang, thump, drum, knock **2** *fig.* to try hard, make an effort; to take trouble (*with s. th.*), grind/plod away (*at s. th.*) **3** *fig.* to cough hard, have a bad cough

бувалка *f* **1** mallet **2** pole, bar **3** *see* пиралка

бувка[1] *f* tuft, crest

бувка[2] *impf* **I 1** to push, shove (*s. o.*) **2** *see* бувта 1 **II –** *ce* to push forward (*as in a crowd*)

бувне *pf* бувна *aor.* **I 1** to give (*s. o.*) a shove; го бувна старецот в ребра he shoved (poked) the old man in the ribs **2** *see* бувта I 1 **3** to slam, bang; ја бувна вратата и си отиде he slammed the door and left **II – ce 1** to bump, crash (*into*); се бувна во мене he bumped into me **2** to bang, slam *intrans.* **3** to barge in

бувнува (се) *impf of* бувне (се)

бувта *impf* **I 1** to beat, strike, hit hard, thump *trans.*; pester **2** *fig.* to wander round; бувта наваму-натаму, но не успева he wanders about here and there without getting anywhere **3** *fig. see* бува 2 **4** *fig.* to cough hard **5** to beat *intrans.*; тапани бувтаат drums are beating **II – ce see** бувне (се) II; се бувта в гради to show off, strut; to beat one's breast

бувтаница *f* **1** jostling, crush **2** *see* тепаница **3** *dial.* fist

Бугарија *f* Bulgaria

бугарија *f Mus.* kind of mandolin

Бугарин -ри *m* Bulgarian

Бугарка *f* (*fem. form*) *see* Бугарин

бугарски *adj* Bulgarian

будала *m & f* fool, idiot; ❑ излегува/изигрува будала to make a fool (an ass) of o.s.; кој будала се родил, будала и ќе <си> умре once a fool, always a fool; прави некого будала to play a trick on s.o., make a fool of s.o.; се прави будала to play the innocent, pretend ignorance; *colloq.* што те гледам будала! what a fool you are!

будалак -ци *m* fool, blockhead

будалачка *f* silly woman

будалест *adj* crazy, foolish; rather stupid; будалест човек slightly crazy (*Brit. colloq.* potty, daft) person; будалесто решение stupid decision

будалетинка *m & f* simpleton, naive person, rather stupid person

будали се *impf* to behave foolishly, fool about, play the fool; to talk nonsense

будаличок -чка *adj* crazy, foolish, rather stupid

будалиште *n augm. of* будала

будалски *adj* idiotic, stupid; будалска работа silly business

будалштилак -ци *m see* будалштина

будалштина *f* foolish act; nonsense

буден -дна *adj* **1** awake; уште сум буден I am still awake **2** *fig.* vigilant; будно око watchful eye

буди *impf* **I 1** to wake *trans.*; не буди го don't wake him! **2** *fig.* to evoke; таа песна буди топли чувства that song evokes warm feelings **II – ce** to wake up, awake *intrans.*

будизам -змот *m* Buddhism

будилник -ци *m* alarm clock

будимка *f Bot.* variety of pale red apple

Будимпешта *f* Budapest

будимпештанец -нци *m* person from Budapest

будимпештанка *f* (*fem. form*) *see* будимпештанец

будимпештански *adj* Budapest *attrib.*

будист *m* Buddhist

будистички *adj* Buddhist *attrib.*

будител *m* agitator, inciter, stirrer; evangelist; apostle

будност *f* **1** wakefulness **2** *fig.* attentiveness, vigilance

будоар *m* boudoir

буен -jна *adj* **1** luxuriant, thick, dense; бујна трева rank grass; бујни гради ample bosom; буен развиток rapid development; бујна фантазија vivid imagination **2** hot-tempered, fiery; (*за дете*) unruly; буен човек fiery person; буен темперамент fiery temperament **3** strong, heavy, intense; буен дожд heavy rain; буен ветер high wind; буен оган blazing (bright) fire; бујна река swift-flowing (turbulent) river; бујна смеа loud (uproarious) laughter

буза *f dial.* lip, *see* усна

бузинест *adj dial.* thick-lipped

буи *impf* to grow profusely; на ливаѓе буи трева млада in the meadows young grass is sprouting

буица *f* fever, temperature

бујак -ци *m* thicket

бујат *adj see* буен 1

бујрум *interj arch.* help yourself! come in! here you are!

бук *m poet. see* бука[2]

бука[1] *f* **1** *Bot.* (Fagus silvatica) beech, beech tree **2** gutter **3** *fig.* fool, blockhead; буко една! you idiot!

бука[2] *f* noise, row, uproar, racket

бука се *impf* to mate *intrans.* (*of pigs*)

букагии *pl arch.* fetters, shackles

букал *m see* букар

букар *m* jug

буква *f* letter <of the alphabet>, character; големи букви capital letters, upper case; мали букви small letters, lower case

буквален -лна *adj* literal; буквален превод literal translation; во буквална смисла in the literal sense

буквално *adv* literally; word for word

буквар *m* primer, elementary reader

буквица *f obs.* soldier's identity card

букет *m* bouquet, bunch of flowers, nosegay

букле *n dim. of* букал, букар

буклија -ии *f* flask

буклинка *f* beechmast

букне *pf* буква *aor.* 1 to burst into flames; to flare up; огнот букна the fire flared up 2 (*за растенија*) to shoot up, burst forth; тревата многу букнала the grass has shot up tremendously 3 *fig.* to erupt; букна востание a revolution broke out; тој букна he lost his temper, *colloq.* he flew off the handle; *see* пламне

букнува *impf of* букне

буков *adj* beech *attrib.*; буково дрво beechwood

буковец *m* salt and capsicum condiment, cayenne pepper

буковина *f* beechwood (*timber*)

буковски *adj* Bukovo *attrib.*, *in the expression:* буковски пипер cayenne pepper; *see also* буковец

букоглав *adj* stubborn, obstinate

букурешки *adj* Bucharest *attrib.*

Букурешт *m* Bucharest

букурештанец -нци *m* person from Bucharest

букурештанка *f* (*fem. form*) *see* букурештанец

була[1] *f* 1 (*анама*) Muslim woman 2 *see* божурига

була[2] *f* bull, papal decree

буламач *m* slops

булдог -зи *m* bulldog

булдожер *m* bulldozer

буле *n* kind of flat, round bread (*baked in ashes*)

булевар *m* boulevard

булеварски *adj* boulevard *attrib.*; булеварски печат gutter press; tabloid press

булјон *m Cul.* broth, stock; булјон од зеленчук vegetable stock

булка *f* 1 *dial.* bride 2 *Bot.* (Papaver rhoeas) field poppy 3 lock, kiss-curl (*above the forehead*)

було *n* veil (*also of Muslim women*)

булук -ци *m* 1 herd; flock; pack 2 *Hist.* company (*in the Ottoman army*)

буљбуљ *m see* славеј

буљукбаш & **буљукбаша** *m arch.* company commander, captain (*in the Ottoman army*)

бум[1] *interj* bang! crash!

бум[2] *m Comm.* boom

бумбар *m* 1 bumble-bee 2 *fig.* chubby child 3 *dial. see* дроб<-сарма>

бумбарест *adj* chubby, plump; бумбаресто лице chubby face

бумбаров *adj* bumble-bee *attrib.*

бумеранг *m* boomerang; ❏ му се враќа како бумеранг it comes back to haunt him; it comes home to roost

бумка[1] *f* hillock

бумка[2] *impf* to hit, bang

бумтеж *m* banging, din, boom

буна *f* uproar, disturbance; rebellion, uprising

бунар *m* well; ❏ бунар без дно a bottomless pit; money down the drain; *colloq.* копа бунар крај река to whistle for the wind, beat the air; нов бунар копај, на стариот не плукај *prov.* old fish, old oil and an old friend are the best

бунарски *adj* well *attrib.*; бунарска вода well water

бунарџија -ии *m* well digger, well sinker

бунгалов *m* bungalow, chalet (*in a holiday camp*)

бунгур *m* bulgur; bulgur porridge

бунда *f* fur coat

буни *impf* I 1 to agitate, stir up, incite to rebellion, *see* бунтува I 2 to confuse, perplex; него го буни

таквиот одговор that answer is confusing for him II – се 1 *see* бунтува (се) II 2 to be confused; моето дете многу се буни my child is often confused

бунило *n* delirium

буништарец -рци *m Zool.* dung-beetle

буниште *n* rubbish heap, *Am.* garbage heap, trash heap; dung heap, dunghill; роди ме мајко со среќа, па фрли ме на буниште *prov. said of s.o. starting s.th. with enthusiasm and soon losing interest*

бункер *m* 1 *Mil.* (*за одбрана*) pill-box; bunker 2 (*складиште*) bunker, storage space; бункер за жито grain silo; бункер за сиров јаглен coal bunker

бунт *m* rebellion, uprising, revolt, insurrection; *Mil.*, *Naut.* mutiny; (*метеж*) riot

бунтар *m see* бунтовник

бунтаџија -ии *m colloq.* rebel; *fig.* quarrelsome person, squabbler; bully

бунтовен -вна *adj* rebellious

бунтовник -ци *m* rebel, insurgent; *Mil.*, *Naut.* mutineer

бунтовница *f* (*fem. form*) *see* бунтовник

бунтовнички *adj* rebel, rebellious

бунтовништво *n* rebel activities, rebellion; rebelliousness; *Mil.*, *Naut.* mutiny; mutinous spirit

бунтува *impf* I to stir up, incite to rebellion II – се to rebel, rise up (*against*); *fig.* to be recalcitrant, complain, grumble

бунцав *adj* dishevelled; со бунцава коса with unkempt hair; *see* бушав

бунцоглав *adj see* бунцав

бура *f* storm; (*силна*) tempest; *Naut.* gale; снежна бура snowstorm; ❏ бура се спрема the fat is in the fire; затишје пред бура the calm before the storm

бурбати се *impf impers.* (*with dat.*) to feel sick (nauseous); to feel disgusted

бургија -ии *f* 1 *Mech.* (*сврдел*) borer, gimlet; <small> drill 2 *fig.* nonsense, rubbish; прави бургии 1. to make fun (*со некого* – *of s.o.*) 2. to intrigue

буре *n* barrel, cask; vat; буре за вода water butt; буре за пиво beer barrel; ❏ буре барут powder keg

буревесник -ци *m Zool.*, *fig.* storm petrel

бурек -ци *m* burek (*puff pastry with different fillings*); flaky <minced> meat pie; cheese-filled puff pastry; spinach puff pastry; ❏ *sl.* <не> јади бурек! get stuffed!

бурекчија -ии *m* maker and seller of *burek*, baker

бурекчилница *f* burek shop/stall, bakery

бурен -рна *adj* stormy (*also fig.*); бурно море stormy (rough, heavy) sea; бурно време stormy weather; бурен живот a tempestuous/adventurous life; бурни години stormy/restless years; бурно одобрување vociferous approval; бурен аплауз tumultuous applause, loud cheers

буроносен -сна *adj* storm-bearing, stormy; tempestuous; бороносни облаци storm clouds

буржоазија *f* bourgeoisie; middle class

буржоаски *adj* bourgeois

буржуј -уи *m* bourgeois

буржујка *f* (*fem. form*) *see* буржуј

бурило *n* barrel, cask

буричка *impf* I 1 to mix *trans.*; to stir *trans.*; ja буричкаше кашата he was stirring the porridge 2 to turn over, search thoroughly, rummage; буричкаше по шкафовите he was rummaging through the cupboards **II** – **се** to rummage in one's pockets; to wallow/splash about

буричканица *f* commotion, disturbance

буричне *pf* бурична *aor.* to search (*through s.th.*), pry (*in s.th.*); to rummage; бурична во џебот и извади еден златник he rummaged in his pocket and pulled out a gold coin

бурјан *m Bot.* **1** (Lolium) darnel, rye-grass, *see* плевел **2** (Sambucus ebulus) dwarf elder

бурјаниште *n* place overgrown with weeds, weedy spot

бурјаноса *pf* to become overgrown with weeds

бурјаносува *impf of* бурјаноса

бурлéска *f* burlesque

бурма *f* **1** wedding ring; engagement ring; бурма позлатена gilded (gold-plated) wedding ring **2** screw, bolt

Бурма *f* Burma, *see* Мјанмар

бурмајлија 1 *adj indecl. see* бурмен; бурмајлија прстен wedding ring **2** *f* wedding ring

Бурманец -нци *m* Burmese

Бурманка *f* (*fem. form*) *see* Бурманец

бурмански *adj* Burmese

бурмен *adj* wedding *attrib.*; бурмен прстен wedding ring

бурмут *m* snuff; шмрка бурмут to take snuff

бурмутица *f arch.* snuffbox

бурност *f* storminess

бурум *m Bot. see* боровинка

Бурундец -дци *m* Burundian

Бурýнди *n* Burundi

бурундски *adj* Burundian

Бурунтка *f* (*fem. form*) *see* Бурундец

бусија -ии *f* ambush

бут *m* thigh; leg; haunch; ham (*of an animal*); телешки бут leg of veal

бута (се) *impf see* турка (се)

Бутан *m* Bhutan

Бутанец -нци *m* Bhutanese

Бутанка *f* (*fem. form*) *see* Бутанец

бутански *adj* Bhutanese

бутаница *f* crush, jostling; uproar, *see* турканица

бутин *m* (*канта за млеко*) milk churn; (*за масло*) oil press

бутина *f* **1** *see* бут **2** side; џадето се врежуваше во бутината на ридот the road cut into the side of the hill

бутка *f* kiosk; tobacco shop; бутка за весници newspaper stall

бутка (се) *impf see* бута (се), турка (се)

бутне (се) *pf* бутна *aor. see* турне (се)

бутнува (се) *impf of* бутне (се)

бутур *m butur*, disease in horses (*with coughing*); ❑ *iron.* бутур му е there's nothing wrong with him, he's quite O.K.

бутуриса *pf* to give (*s.o.*) a shove; to shove (push) (*s.o.*) away

бутурлив & **бутурничав** *adj* (*see* бутур) sick with *butur*

буца *impf* **I** to butt (*with horns*) **II** – **се** to butt each other; to lock horns; *see* боде (се)

буцка *f* bump, swelling

буцка *impf dim.* **I 1** *see* буца I, буцне I **2** *fig.* to pick, poke about; to tinker (*with s.th.*); буцкаше со виљушката во салатата he was picking at the salad with his fork **II** – **се** *see* буца (се) II, буцне (се) II

буцкало *n* **1** awl **2** *fig.* instigator; firebrand; goad

буцне *pf* буцна *aor.* **I 1** (*за рогато животно*) to give a butt <with its horns>; (*за човек*) to prod; to poke; to prick; буцне со лакт to nudge; ме буцна со прстот во слабината he poked me in the side with his finger; буцне со игла to prick with a pin **2** *fig.* to incite **3** *fig.* to sting; to tease **II** – **се 1** to butt each other; to nudge each other **2** to prick o.s.; детето се буцна со иглата во прстот the boy pricked his finger with the needle. **3.** *fig.* to incite each other, urge each other on

буцнува (се) *impf of* буцне (се)

бучава & **бучавица** *f* noise, din, roar, boom

бучало *n* **1** drone (*on bagpipes*) **2** waterfall

бучен -чна *adj* noisy; lively; бучна дискусија lively discussion; бучна улица busy street

бучи *impf* to make a noise (din); to roar, boom; надвор силно бучеше ветрот outside the wind was roaring; реката придушено бучи the river is babbling (murmuring) softly; океанот бучеше the ocean was roaring; ми бучи главата there's a ringing in my ears

бучка *f dial.* **1** *see* бутин **2** dasher (*of a churn*)

бучкало *n dial. see* бучка 2

бучук -ци *m see* шиник

бучумиш *m Bot.* (Conium maculatum) hemlock, St. Bennet's herb

буџа *f* **1** club, cudgel **2** *fig.* big shot, *colloq.* bigwig

буџак -ци *m* corner, nook, hole

буџет *m* budget; балансиран буџет balanced budget; нерамнотежен буџет adverse budget

буџетíра *impf* to finance; to budget for

буџетски *adj* budget *attrib.*; budgetary, fiscal; буџетски дефицит budget deficit; буџетски ограничувања budget constraints; буџетски приходи budget receipts; буџетски расходи budget expenses; буџетска година financial (fiscal) year; буџетска политика financial (fiscal) policy; буџетска установа government-financed institution

бушав *adj* dishevelled

бушави *impf* to ruffle *trans.*, tousle

бушавост *f* shagginess; unkempt state

бушарест *adj* hairy, shaggy; куче бушаресто shaggy dog

буштрав *adj see* бушав

В

в¹ *abbr.* **1** (*век*) century, c. **2** (*види*) see

в² *prep see* во

ваби *impf* to call (*animals*); ваби пилиња to call chickens

Вавилóн *m* Babylon

вавилóнец -нци *m* Babylonian

вавилóнка *f* (*fem. form*) *see* вавилонец

вавилóнски *adj* Babylonian

вага¹ *f* **1** scales; децимална вага decimal scales; ❑ стави на вага to judge **2** *Astron.* the Scales, Libra **3** *Gymnastics* forward horizontal stand (arabesque)

вага² *impf* to weigh *trans.* (*also fig.*); си ги вага зборовите he weighs his words

вагабóнт *m* vagabond, tramp

вагабóнтски **1** *adj* vagabond **2** *adv* like/as a vagabond

ваган *m* **1** wooden bowl (*for measuring grain*) **2** *dial.* plate

ваганка *f see* ваган

вагѝна *f Anat.* vagina

вагинáлен -лна *adj* vaginal; вагинална инфекција vaginal infection; вагинален секрет vaginal secretion

вагон *m* **1** railway carriage, *Am.* railroad car; вагон-лѝ, вагон за спиење sleeping-car, sleeper; вагон-ресторáн dining-car; патнички вагон passenger carriage; товарен вагон goods wag<g>on, *Am.* freight car **2** wag<g>on-load; вагон дрва/јаглен a wag<g>on-load of timber/coal

вагонéтка *f* trolley, truck

вагонски *adj* wag<g>on *attrib.*; вагонски прозорец carriage window

вада *f* irrigation channel, ditch

вадалка *f* watering-can

вадачка *f colloq.* wages, pay

вадеж *m dial.* **1** *see* вадачка **2** *fig.* way out

вадење¹ *n* (*from* вади¹); extraction, removal; celebration (*of a requiem*); *Math.* subtraction

вадење² *n* (*from* вади²) irrigation

вади¹ *impf* **I 1** to take out, remove, pull out, draw; to extract; to produce, bring out; вади јаболка од торбата he is taking apples out of his bag; вади нож to draw a knife; вади компири to pull up potatoes; вади маст од млеко to separate cream from milk; нашата куќа секоја година вади некои нови моди our firm brings out new fashions every year; вади палто to take off a coat; вади шапка некому to take off one's hat to s.o.; вади пари од банка to <with>draw money from the bank; вади руда to work a mine, extract ore; вади заклучок to draw a conclusion; вади флеки to remove stains; вади податоци од книга to extract data from a book; вади од

училиште to remove from school; вади заб to pull (extract) a tooth; вади крв to have/administer a blood test; *fig.* to put s.o. through the mill (wringer); ❑ вади некого од такт (умот) to drive (send) s.o. mad; вади леб to earn a living; вади билет to buy (get) a ticket ; вадат некого на суд to sue s.o.; вади очи со некого to be at daggers drawn with s.o.; to fight like cat and dog; вади некому душа to torment the life out of s.o.; to tease s.o.; кај си ги вадиш очите! where are you rushing off to? mind where you are going! вади некому зборови од уста to extract an answer from s.o.; вади од каша to get (*s.o.*) out of a jam; гавран гаврану очи не вади *prov.* there's honour among thieves; на умрено куче нож вади hares may pull dead lions by the beard **2** to celebrate, officiate at; вади парастос to celebrate a requiem **3** to transfer (*pictures, patterns*) **4** *Math.* to subtract (*од – from*); вади корен to extract a root **II – се** to excuse o.s.; to extricate o.s.; to back out of, get out of (*a difficult situation*)

вади² *impf* to water; to irrigate; вади бавча to water the garden; ги вадат ливадите they irrigate the fields

ваѓа *impf dial. see* вади¹

важен -жна *adj* **1** important, significant, prominent; важна личност important person; важно прашање important question; многу важен very important; *iron.* of no account; тоа не е важно it doesn't matter; it makes no difference; **2** *iron.* self-important, conceited; многу е важен he is very conceited; се прави важен to give o.s. airs

важечки *adj literary* valid, current; важечки принципи valid principles; важечки прописи current regulations; *Comm.* важечка каматна стапка current interest rate; важечки пари current money

важи *impf* to be valid, legal; to be in effect, apply; to be considered; договорот важи the contract is valid; the agreement applies; новите одредби важат за сите работници the new regulations apply to all employees; возната карта важи три дена the ticket is valid for three days; тие важат за (како) добри другари they are considered <to be> good friends; важи! OK! agreed! it's a deal! не важи to be out of date, be invalid; не важи! no dice! nothing doing!

важничи *impf* to put on airs, show off

важно *adv* **1** significantly, importantly; важно е it matters; it carries weight; многу важно! so what? big deal! **2** (*надмено*) with an air of importance

важност *f* **1** importance, significance; relevance; си придава важност to put on airs; придава важност на нешто to make much of s.th.; to attach weight to s.th. **2** value; validity; без важност of no value; важноста на пасошот е помината the passport has expired

ваза¹ *f* vase

ваза² *f Bot.* (Ulmus montana) wych-elm

вазал *m Hist.* vassal, liegeman

вазален -лна *adj Hist.* vassal *attrib.*; вазална зависност vassalage

вазалство *n Hist.* vassalage

вазелѝн *m* vaseline

вазна *f* vase

вазне се *pf* вазна се *aor.* (*зјанне*) to start staring; кај си се вазнал? what are you gaping at?

вазнува се *impf of* вазне² се

вај *interj* **1** (*expressing pain or sorrow*) ow! ouch! ooh! вај, боли! ow, that hurts! **2** (*expressing surprise*) good heavens! вај, што е тоа? good heavens, what's that?

ваја¹ -аи *f* (*дадијарка*) nurse

ваја² *impf* to sculpture, sculpt; to carve; (*глина*) to model, mould; (*камен, дрво*) to chisel; ги вајаше од (во) дрво или од (во) камен he carved them in wood or in stone

вајар *m* sculptor

вајарски *adj* sculptural; вајарско длето sculptor's chisel

вајарство *n* sculpture, sculpturing

вака *adv* **1** so, thus, in this way; ❏ вака, така somehow, one way or another; и вака и така 1. whichever is the case; in either event 2. so so **2** *dial.* this way, in this direction, here

ваканција *f* holidays, *Am.* vacation

вакат *m arch.* **1** time **2** Muslim prayer time **3** *Print.* blank (white) page

вакаф *m* Muslim pious foundation; property of a Muslim religious community

ваков *pron* such, of this kind, this kind of

вакол -кла *adj* (*за животно*) spectacled, blotchy-faced; (*за човек*) swarthy

вакуум *m* vacuum

вакцина *f* vaccine

вакцинација *f* vaccination, immunization

вакцинира *pf & impf* to vaccinate, immunize

вала¹ *f dial.* veil, thin transparent material

вала² *impf see* валка I 2 & 3; вала ќотиња во брашно to roll rissoles in flour; студениот ветар ја вала маглата the cold wind rolls away the fog; вала шајак to roll <out> homespun; вала челик to roll steel

валавец *m Bot.* (Eryngium campestre) field eryngo

валавица *f* **1** (*за сукно*) fulling-mill **2** (*за метал*) rolling-shop, rolling-mill **3** roller (*for fulling*)

валавичар *m* **1** (*на сукно*) fuller, felter **2** (*на метал*) roller

вала<ј> *interj* really! I swear!

валанка *f* **1** rolled cloth cap (*traditional costume*) **2** cloth outer garment

валентност & валенција *f Chem.* valence, valency

валеријана *f Bot.* (Valeriana officinalis) valerian

валец -лци *m see* валјак, цилиндар; бојадисува со валец to paint with a roller

вали *impf dial.* to stoke; to heat; вали оган to light the fire; го валеше огнот со слама he stoked the fire with straw

валиден -дна *adj* valid, based on law, legally acceptable

валидитет *m & ***валидност** *f* validity

валија -ии *m* vali (*governor of a vilayet in Turkey*)

валјак -ци *m* roller; валјак за патишта steamroller, roadroller

валка *impf* **I 1** to dirty, soil; мастилото ми ја валка кошулата the ink stains my shirt **2** to roll *trans.*; валка буре to roll a barrel; валка тесто to roll <out> dough **3** (*набива сукно*) to mill, full, felt *trans.* **II – се 1** to get dirty; многу се валка he/it gets dirty easily **2** to roll *intrans.*; to roll about *intrans.*; to wallow; се валка во кал to wallow in mud; ❏ се валка од смеење to roll in the aisles, to split one's sides laughing

валкан *adj* dirty, soiled; ❏ валкана работа dirty business

валканица *f* spot, mark; stain

валмест *adj* **1** spindle-shaped **2** round

валмо *n* **1** spindle **2** axle, spindle (*of water-wheel in a water-mill*) **3** ring, disc

валог -зи *m* arable valley in mountainous country

валоризација *f Comm.* valorization

валоризира *pf & impf Comm.* to valorize

валс *m* waltz; игра валс to dance the waltz, waltz

валта *f* meadow

валуга *f* lump, clod, ball (*of snow, earth, etc.*)

валута *f* currency; здрава валута stable currency; домашна/странска валута local/foreign currency; тврда валута hard (stable) currency

валутен -тна *adj* currency *attrib.*, current; валутна реформа currency reform; валутни побарувања assets in foreign currency; дневна валутна стапка current rate of exchange

валцер *m see* валс

валчевест *adj see* валчест

валчест *adj* round, circular, oval; ball-shaped, globular; rotund; spherical

валчи *impf* to make round, round off

вам *pron* (*long dat. form of* вие. *Used for emphasis with short form* ви) <to> you; прво вам ви кажа, а после нам first he told you and then us

вампир *m* **1** vampire, ghoul; *fig.* bloodsucker **2** *Bot.* (Oenothera biennis) evening primrose **3** vampire bat

вампири се *impf* to behave like a vampire

вампирка *f* (*fem. form*) *see* вампир 1

вампироса се *pf* to start acting like a vampire; to turn into a vampire *intrans.*

вампиросува се *impf of* вампироса се, *see* вампири се

вампирски *adj* vampiric; вампирски поглед vampire's look; вампирска трева *Bot.* (Dipsacus silvestris) wild teasel

вампирција -ии *m arch.* person who drives out vampires, vampire chaser

ваму *adv* here, *arch.* hither

ваму-таму *adv* to and fro, *arch.* hither and thither

вангелоса се *pf* to be frightened, horrified; to give a start; кога го виде, се вангелоса when he saw him he started (was horrified)

вангелосува се *impf of* вангелоса се

вангла *f* basin

вандал *m* vandal

вандализам -змот *m* vandalism, barbaric acts

вандалство *n* act of vandalism

ванила *f Bot.* (Vanilla planifolia) vanilla

ванилија *f see* ванила

ванилин *m* vanilla <sugar>

вапса *pf* **I 1** to colour; to paint; (*предено, платно*) to dye; вапсува велигденски јајца to colour Easter eggs; *f.p.* лице му црно, како со ќумур вапсано his face is black, as if smeared with charcoal **2** *fig.* to deceive, cheat, swindle, defraud **II – се** to paint o.s.

вапсило *n* colouring, paint; (*за платно и сл.*) dye

вапсува (**се**) *impf of* вапса (се)

вапсувач *m* dyer

вапца *pf see* вапса

вар *m & f* lime; негасен<а> вар quicklime, burnt lime; гасен<а> вар slaked lime; пече вар to heat (burn) lime

варај *interj f.p.* hark! beware!

варак *m* gold leaf; tinsel

вараклија *adj indecl.* gold-coloured; gilded

варакоса *pf* to gild

варакосува *impf of* варакоса

варварѝзам -змот *m* **1** barbarous act<s>, barbarity, savagery; barbarism **2** *Ling.* foreign borrowing; barbarism; solecism

варвар<ин> -ри *m* barbarian, savage

варварски[1] *adj* barbarous, savage

варварски[2] *adv* barbarously, like a savage

варварство *n* barbarism; barbarity

варда *interj* beware! look out! stand back! get out of the way! run!

вардар[1] *m see* вардач

Вардар[2] *m* the Vardar

вардарец *m* wind that blows along the Vardar valley

вардарка *f* **1** *Bot.* kind of wheat **2** *Zool.* (Alburnoides bipunctatus) bleak (*fish*)

вардарски *adj* Vardar *attrib.*; Вардарска Македонија Vardar Macedonia

вардач *m* watchman, guard; вардач на деца babysitter, child minder

варди *impf* **I** to defend, protect; to look after; to guard, keep watch (*over*); кучињата ќе ги вардат овците од волци the dogs will protect the sheep from wolves; варди лозје to keep watch over a vineyard **II** – ce **1** to be careful, watch out for o.s.; се вардам да не паднам I am careful not to fall; се варди од настинка to take care not to catch cold **2** to keep away from, abstain from

варел *m &* **варело** *n* big barrel, tun, cask

варен[1] -рна *adj* lime *attrib.*, limy, calcareous; варна вода limewash

варен[2] *pt* cooked, boiled; варена пченка boiled maize, *Am.* corn; варено јајце boiled egg; варено вино mulled wine; ❑ јас сум варен па печен I've been through the mill (through thick and thin)

вареница *f* meal porridge

варзило & **варзилово дрво** *n Bot.* (Caesalpinia brasiliensis) Brazil-wood

вари[1] *impf* **I** **1** to boil *trans.*; to cook *trans.*; (*долго*) to stew *trans.*; (*на тивок оган*) to simmer *trans.*; (*кафе и сл.*) to brew, make *trans.*; (*слатко и др.*) to make *trans.*; вари јајца to boil eggs; вари чај to brew (make) tea; вари манџа to cook a meal; вари вино to mull wine; ❑ вари некому каша to make trouble for s.o. **2** (*ракија и сл.*) to distil **3** (*за желудник*) to digest; мојот стомак тешко го вари гравот my stomach has difficulty digesting beans **4** (*стерилизира*) to sterilize, boil *trans.*; сестрата ги вареше иглите the nurse sterilized the needles **5** to boil *intrans.*; to seethe *intrans.* **6** *fig.* to cook up, devise **II** – ce **1** *see* **I** **5** **2** to feel the heat; се варам! I'm boiling hot! се вари како во котел **1.** to be very hot **2.** *fig.* to be in a tight spot; to be hard-pressed

вари[2] *impf see* to weld

вариво *n* <cooked> vegetables, *see* варило

вариете *n* music hall; variety show; night-club with vaudeville show

вариетет *m* variety; голем вариетет на стоки за широка потрошувачка great variety of consumer goods

варијабила *f* bonus; weighting, *Austral.* loading

варијабилен -лна *adj* variable; варијабилни трошоци variable (direct, running) costs

варијабилност *f* variability

варијанта *f* variant, variety; ❑ резервна варијанта next best thing; fall-back position; има резервна варијанта to have a second string <to one's bow>

варијација -ии *f* **1** *Mus.* variation; варијации на тема variations on a theme (*also fig.*) **2** *Comm.* variation, fluctuation

варикина *f colloq.* bleach

варилец -лци *m* welder

варило *n* <cooked> vegetables

вариометар -три *m* variometer

варира *impf* to vary *intrans.*, fluctuate

варка[1] *f arch.* barque, boat

варка[2] *impf dial.* **I** to guard, watch **II** – ce **1** to guard o.s., watch out

варка[3] *impf dial.* **I** to hurry <up>, hasten *trans.* **II** – ce to hurry <up>, hasten *intrans.*

варница *f* **1** lime quarry, limepit **2** lime-works; limekiln

варов *adj see* варен[1]

варовит *adj* (*за вода*) chalky, limy, calcareous; (*за почва*) limy, chalky; варовит предел area rich in limestone

варовник -ци *m* limestone, lime-rock

вароса *pf* to whitewash

варосува *impf of* вароса

варџија -ии *m* lime-burner

варџилница *f* **1** limekiln; lime-works **2** limepit **3** lime store

Варшава *f* Warsaw

варшавјанец -нци *m* person from Warsaw

варшавјанка *f* (*fem. form*) *see* варшавјанец

варшавски *adj* Warsaw *attrib.*

вас *pron* (*long form for the oblique cases, except dat., of* вие) you; вас ве видов I saw you; со вас with you

васа *impf* **I** to avenge o.s.; со нож ќе им васа he will take his revenge on them in blood **II** – ce to fight, wrestle

васервага *f* spirit-level, *see* либела

Василица *f* St. Basil's Day (*14th January, New Year's Day by the Julian calendar*)

василичар *m* (*usu. pl*) costumed youths who on New Year's Eve (*13th January by the Julian calendar*) go from house to house and play traditional games

васкуларен *adj* vascular; васкуларно ткиво vascular tissue

вастегарка *f* (*ластегарка, остегарка*) stick, cane

ват *m* (*pl* вати) *Phys., Elec.* watt

вата *f* (*медицинска*) cotton wool; (*за поставување*) wadding; хигроскопична вата hygroscopic cotton wool; палто поставено со вата quilted coat

вателин *m* padding (*made from cotton linters*)

ватерполист *m Sport.* water-polo player

ватерполо *n Sport.* water polo

Ватикан *m* Vatican City, the Vatican, the Holy See

ватикански *adj* Vatican

ватира *pf & impf* to pad, wad

вафла *f* wafer

ваш, ваша, ваше, *pl* ваши *possessive pron* your; yours; вашата куќа your house; Ваше Величество Your Majesty; (*as noun*) како се вашите? how are your parents/family?

вашинец -нци *m* fellow villager/townsman/countryman

Вашингтон *m* Washington

вашингтонец -нци *m* Washingtonian

вашингтонка *f* (*fem. form*) *see* вашингтонец

вашингтонски *adj* Washingtonian

вашинка *f* fellow villager/townswoman/countrywoman

вашински *adj* your, your kind of; of your village/town/part of the country

вбеси *pf* I to enrage, madden, exasperate, infuriate II -ce to lose one's temper, fly into a rage

вбесува (**се**) *impf of* вбеси (се)

вбива *impf of* вбие, *see* забива

вбие *pf* to knock (drive)/wedge in, *see* забие; ❑ вбие нешто некому в глава to hammer s.th. into s.o.'s head

вброи *pf* I to include (*во*, *меѓу* – *in*) II – ce to number (*во*, *меѓу* – *among*)

вбројува (**се**) *impf of* вброи (се); романот критиката го вбројува во (меѓу) најуспешните the novel is considered one of the most successful

вгази *pf* to step into; to get stuck, bogged down (*во нешто* – *in s.th.*); to tread in *trans.*; to stamp down

вгазува *impf of* вгази

вглаби *pf* to bite, bite into (*an apple, etc.*)

вглави *pf* I to fit in *trans.*; to stick in *trans.*; ги вглави спиците во главата на тркалото he fitted the spokes into the wheel-hub II – ce 1 to fit in *intrans.*; *Carpentry* to dovetail *intrans.* 2 to stick *intrans.*, get stuck; клучот се вглави во бравата the key <got> stuck in the lock

вглавува (**се**) *impf of* вглави (се)

вгледа се *pf* to stare, gaze, peer, have a good look (*во* – *at*), fix one's eyes (*во* – *on*), look steadily (hard, intently) (*во* – *at*); се вгледа во реката he <stopped and> stared at/into the river

вгледува се *impf of* вгледа се

вгнезди се *pf* 1 to build a nest 2 *fig.* to settle down, strike roots, take root; to bed in; to nestle *intrans.*

вгнездува се *impf of* вгнезди се

вгнете *pf* I to push in, squeeze in, press in *trans.* II – ce to push in, squeeze in *intrans.*; to squeeze (force) one's way in/through

вгнетува (**се**) *impf of* вгнете (се)

вгои *pf* I to fatten <up> *trans.* II – ce to get fat, put on weight; *see* згои (се)

вгојува (**се**) *impf of* вгои (се)

вгорешти се *pf see* згорешти се

вгори се *pf* to get warm, warm up *intrans.*

вгорува се *impf of* вгори се

вграден *adj* built-in; вградени плакари built-in wardrobes

вгради *pf* I to build in; to brick/wall in; to wall up; (*човек*) to immure II – ce to engrave one's name; to set one's seal (stamp) upon; се вградија во темелите на нова Македонија their names are etched in the foundations of the new Macedonia

вградува (**се**) *impf of* вгради (се)

вгребе *pf* to seize, grab

в.д. *abbr.* (*вршител на должноста*) acting

вдава се *impf of* вдаде се

вдаде се *pf* 1 (*with dat.*) to rush off (*no* – *after*); to descend on, turn on, attack; му се вдаде по него he rushed off after him; му се вдаде на брата си he turned (rounded) on his brother 2 *impers.* (*with dat.*) to succeed, manage to; не му се вдаде да избега he didn't manage to escape 3 to get down to work; to become engrossed in a job; се вдаде в работа he got down to work

вдаден *pt* engrossed, preoccupied; тој е вдаден во работата he is engrossed in the work

вдахне *pf* вдахна *aor.* to inspire

вдахновен *pt* inspired

вдахновение *n* inspiration

вдахновител *m* inspirer, source of inspiration (*person*)

вдахновува *impf see* вдахнува

вдахнува *impf of* вдахне

вдене *pf* вдена *aor.* I to insert, pull through; вдене конец во игла to thread a needle; медицинската сестра ја вдена иглата во раката на болниот the nurse inserted the needle into the patient's arm II - ce 1 to stick in *intrans.*; едно трнче му се вдена под ноктот he got a thorn <caught> under his nail 2 to sneak, crawl in; се вдена низ пенџере he sneaked in through the window

вденува (**се**) *impf of* вдене (се)

вдесно *adv* to/on the right

вдише & **вдиши** *pf* вдиша *aor.* to breathe in, inhale

вдишува *impf of* вдише, вдиши

вдлаби *pf* I to deepen *trans.*; to hollow <out> *trans.*; to make concave, depress II – ce 1 to deepen *intrans.*; to recede; to cave in, sink in, subside; патот се вдлаби на неколку места the road subsided in several places 2 to bury o.s.; to penetrate, plunge, sink in *intrans.*; бомбата се вдлаби во меката земја the bomb plunged into the soft ground; се вдлаби во мисли to become engrossed in one's thoughts, bury o.s. in thought

вдлабнат *adj* & *pt* deepened, hollowed; concave; вдлабнато место depression, *see* вдлабнатина

вдлабнатина *f* recess; depression, hollow; groove; (*бразда*) furrow; (*дупче*) dent

вдлабочен *adj* & *pt* engrossed, absorbed

вдлабоченост *f* concentration, absorption, engrossment

вдлабочи се *pf* to become engrossed (absorbed) (*во* – *in*)

вдлабочува се *impf of* вдлабочи се

вдлабува (**се**) *impf of* вдлаби (се)

вдовец -вци *m* widower; ❑ бел вдовец grass widower

вдовечки *adj* widower's

вдовица *f* widow; ❑ бела вдовица grass widow

вдовички *adj* widow's

вдовство *n* widowhood

вдовува *impf* to be a widow/widower, live a widow's/widower's life

вдрвен *adj see* здрвен

вдрви (**се**) *pf see* здрви (се)

вдрвува (**се**) *impf see* здрвува (се)

вдроби *pf* to crumble (*bread into milk, etc.*)

вдробува *impf of* вдроби

вѓаволи се *pf* to become mischievous/skittish

вѓаволува се *impf of* вѓаволи се

ве *pron (short acc. form of* вие*)* you; ве виде he saw you

веалка *f* winnowing machine

веверица *f see* верверица

веверичин *adj see* верверичин

вегетаријанец -нци *m* vegetarian

вегетаријанка *f (fem. form) see* вегетаријанец

вегетаријански *adj* vegetarian; вегетаријанска исхрана vegetarian diet; вегетаријанска кујна vegetarian cuisine

вегетативен -вна *adj* vegetative; вегетативни органи vegetative organs; вегетативно размножување vegetative reproduction; вегетативен нервен систем vegetative nervous system

вегетација *f* vegetating; vegetation

вегетационен -она *adj* vegetating; вегетационен период period of vegetation

вегетира *impf* to vegetate (*also fig.*)

веда *f* 1 lightning, *see* молња, молскавица, секавица[1]; ❑ тој е веда во работата he gets things done in a flash, he is a fast worker 2 witch

ведар -дра *adj* 1 clear, cloudless; ведро небо clear sky; ❑ гром од ведро небо a bolt from the blue; под ведро небо under the open sky 2 *fig.* cheerful, serene; ведра музика cheerful (light) music; ведри мисли cheerful (encouraging) thoughts

веде *impf* I to hatch (*chickens*) *trans.*; to brood II – **се** to hatch *intrans.*; to multiply *intrans.*

ведета *f* 1 star; филмска ведета film star 2 gunboat; patrol boat 3 *Mil.* mounted sentry, sentinel; patrol

ведин *adj* witch's; ведина́ дупка pit, cave

веднаш *adv* at once, straightaway, immediately; веднаш да дојдеш come at once! ❑ веднаш до right next to; веднаш штом as soon as

ведне *impf* I to bend, lean *trans.*; ведне глава (очи) to hang one's head (*in shame, etc.*); to avert one's gaze, to look away; козите ги веднеа гранките the goats pulled (bent) the branches down II – **се** to lean over; to bend down; to bend, lean *intrans.*; to go down

ведно *adv* together; at the same time; *see* наедно

ведреница *f arch.* cup in the shape of a <wooden> pail

ведри *impf* I to clear <up> *trans.*; *fig.* to cheer (*s.o.*) up *trans.* II – **се** to clear up (*of the weather*) *intrans.*

ведрина *f* 1 cloudlessness 2 *fig.* cheerfulness, serenity <of spirit>

ведринка *f dim. of* ведрина

ведро[1] *n* 1 pail, bucket 2 bucketful, pailful

ведро[2] *adv* cheerfully; (*за време*) fine; денес е ведро today it's fine

веѓа *f* eyebrow; ❑ гајтан веѓи arched eyebrows; свие веѓи to knit one's brow, to frown; место веѓи да му тргне, очите ќе му ги извади to play a dirty trick on s.o.

веѓест *adj* bushy-browed

веѓило *n* eyebrow tint (*mixture of coal and fat for accentuating one's eyebrows*)

веѓица *f* edge (*of a piece of cloth*)

веѓосува *impf* I to tint (paint) (*s.o.'s*) eyebrows II – **се** to tint (paint) one's eyebrows

вее *impf* I 1 to blow; ветер вее a wind is blowing, there is a wind; од внатрешноста на пештерата вееше студенило cool air came from inside the cave 2 (*за снег*) to snow heavily; надвор вее снег outside it's snowing heavily (heavy snow is falling) 3 (*за жито*) to winnow; веат пченица they are winnowing wheat 4 to blow about, drive along; ветерот вее лисја the wind is blowing some leaves about; ❑ ветар го вее *see* ветар II – **се** 1 to wave in the wind, flutter *intrans.*; се веат знамиња flags are fluttering <in the wind> 2 *fig.* to wander, roam; каде се вееш? where are you off to?

вежба[1] *f* exercise, practice, drill; (*на факултет*) tutorial; (*во лабораторија*) laboratory session; воена вежба military exercise, manoeuvres; јавна вежба mass callisthenics, gymnastics display

вежба[2] *impf* I to practise *trans.*; to exercise *trans.*; to train *trans.*; вежба пливање to practise swimming; ги вежбаше атлетичарките во фрлање копје he was training the women athletes in javelin throwing II – **се** to exercise, practise *intrans.*

вежбалиште *n* 1 *Sport.* stadium, athletics field 2 *Mil.* exercise ground, drill ground, parade ground

вежбалница *f* gymnasium

вежбанка *f* exercise book

вежбач *m* person who practises; trainee; gymnast

вез *m* embroidery

везач *m* embroiderer

везачка *f* 1 (*fem. form) see* везач 2 needle (*for embroidery*)

везба *f* embroidery

везден *adv* 1 all day <long>; везден те чекам I have been waiting for you all day 2 always; везден тоа ми го зборуваш you are always telling me that

везе *impf* 1 to embroider; to do fancy sewing; везе кошула to embroider a shirt 2 *fig.* to speak fast and eloquently, hold forth; кога ќе го праша учителот, тој везе when the teacher examines him, he speaks brilliantly

везен *adj & pt* 1 embroidered 2 looking like embroidery; везени дињи/пиперки melons/capsicums with a zigzag pattern

везилка *f* embroiderer, *see* везачка 1

везир *m Hist.* vizier; големиот везир the Grand Vizier; ❑ денес везир, утре резил today a prince, tomorrow a pauper; today a man, tomorrow a mouse

везник -ци *m* bundle, load (*carried on the shoulder*); armful; везник дрва faggot; везник сено truss of hay

вејач *m* winnower

вејверица *f see* верверица

вејка *f* twig, small leafless branch; ❑ си станал вејка you've grown as thin as a rake; вејка на ветрот a straw in the wind

вејне *pf* to start blowing (*lightly*)

вејнува *impf of* вејне

век *m* 1 century; дваесеттиот век the twentieth century; на крајот од векот at the turn of the century 2 age, time, epoch, era; стариот век olden days, ancient times; ❑ му помина векот it's gone out of fashion/use; не сме се виделе еден век we haven't seen one another for ages 3 life, lifetime; цел век се мачи he's been struggling all his life; ❑ ни на тој век not on your life; over my dead body; ако има век, има и лек *prov.* while there's life there's hope; векови е скала times change; life has its ups and downs; до век to the end of one's days; *arch.* во веки веков for ever and ever; што нема на векови? it's a rum world;

на тој век in the next life (world); откако се создал веков since the world began, from the beginning of time

векна _f_ loaf

векнина _f_ eternity, _see_ вечност; богатина до пладнина, убавина до векнина _prov._ a thing of beauty is a joy forever

вековен -вна _adj_ centuries-old; age-old, time-honoured; вековна борба eternal struggle

вековечен -чна _adj_ age-old, age-long, eternal

вековит _adj_ centuries-old, eternal

векот _adv_ a great deal, a lot; тој има векот пари he's got a lot of money, _see_ едночудо

векотница _adv see_ векот

вектор _m Math. Phys._ vector; разложување на вектори resolution of vectors; сложување на вектори vector addition

векува _impf_ **1** to live for ages; to last for centuries **2** _fig._ to stay (_somewhere_) for a long time

велеград _m_ big city, metropolis

веледостојник -ци _m_ high<-ranking> dignitary

велелепно _adv_ magnificently

велемајстор _m Chess_ grand master

веленце _n_ little rug

веленье _n from_ вели; ❑ не треба веленье it goes without saying

велепосед _m_ large estate

велепоседник -ци _m_ owner of a large estate, big landowner

велепредавник -ци _m_ person guilty of high treason; traitor

велепредавство _n_ high treason

велесила _f Pol._ great power

велесла́лом _m Sport._ giant slalom

вели[1] _impf_ **I** to say; to tell; јас им велам дека не се прави I tell them that they are wrong; немој тоа никому да го велиш don't tell that to anyone! ајде, не вели! you don't say! што велиш ти за ова? what do you say to that? what do you think of that? вели си ако немаш друга работа you can talk till you're blue in the face **II – се 1** _impers._ се вели дека ќе играат утре I hear they'll play tomorrow; како се вели? how does one say that? што се вели as people say **2** to be called; to call o.s.; ние отсекогаш сме се веле Македонци we have always called ourselves Macedonians

вели[2] -лја _adj_ (_in the names of the days of Holy Week_) Велипеток Good Friday

Велигден _m_ Easter; не е секој ден Велигден _prov._ Christmas comes but once a year

велигденски _adj_ Easter _attrib._, paschal; велигденско јајце Easter egg

велигденче[1] _n Bot._ (Anemone coronaria) poppy anemone

велигденче[2] _n Zool._ (Coccinella) ladybird

велик _adj literary_ great; велики дела great deeds, famous works; велики́ пости Lenten Fast

Велика Британија _f_ Great Britain

великан _m_ giant (_also fig._)

великден _m Bot. see_ велигденче

великобритански _adj_ British

великобугарин _m_ Greater-Bulgarian nationalist, Bulgarian chauvinist

великов _adj_ великови пости _see_ велик: велики пости

великодостојник -ци _m_ dignitary, high-ranking person

великодржавен -вна _adj_ **1** great-power _attrib._; великодржавен шовинизам great-power chauvinism **2** imperialistic

великодушен -шна _adj_ magnanimous, generous; великодушен човек magnanimous person

великодушност _f_ magnanimity, generosity

великолепен -пна _adj_ splendid, magnificent

великолепност _f_ splendour, magnifice

великомаченик -ци _m Rel._ martyr

великомаченички _adj Rel._ martyr's

великосрбин _m_ Greater-Serbian nationalist, Serbian chauvinist

великосрпски _adj_ Greater-Serbian nationalist, Serbian chauvinist _attrib._

великосрпство _n_ Greater-Serbian nationalism, Serbian chauvinism

Велипеток _m_ Good Friday

Велипонеделник _m_ Monday in Holy (Easter) Week

велици́ _adj pl_ велици пости _see_ велик: велики пости

велича _impf_ **I** to extol, exalt, glorify **II – се 1** to extol o.s., glorify o.s., sing one's own praises **2** to be proud (_со – of_), take pride (_in_); мајката се величаше со својот син the mother was proud of her son

величав _adj_ majestic, exalted

величествен _adj_ splendid, magnificent, marvellous, grand; величествен пречек grand reception

величествено _adv_ magnificently, splendidly

величественост _f_ magnificence, splendour, grandeur

величество _n_ majesty; Неговото Величество His Majesty

Величетврток _m_ Maundy (Holy) Thursday

величие _n see_ величина

величина _f_ **1** grandeur, greatness, majesty; lordliness **2** size; amount; _Astronomy_ magnitude; _Math._ quantity; _see_ големина

велможа _m Hist._ noble, magnate, aristocrat

велосипе́д _m_ bicycle, _colloq._ <push->bike; тера велосипед to cycle, ride a bicycle

велосипеди́ст _m_ cyclist

велосипе́дски _adj_ bicycle, cycle _attrib._; велосипедска трка cycle race

Велс _m_ Wales

велтер-категорија _f Sport._ welterweight

велур _m_ velvet; velour<s>

Велшанец -нци _m_ Welshman

Велшанка _f_ (_fem. form_) _see_ Велшанец

велшки _adj_ Welsh

вена _f Anat._ vein; проширени вени varicose veins; _Med._ воспаление на вени phlebitis

венда _impf colloq._ to be idle, loiter

вене _impf_ **1** to fade; цвеќињата венат the flowers are fading **2** _fig._ to pine; вене од тага to fade (pine) away from grief; девојките венеат по (за) него the girls pine for him

венее _impf see_ вене

венеричен -чна _adj Med._ venereal; венерични болести venereal diseases

венероло́г -зи _m Med._ venereologist

венерологија _f Med._ venereology

венец -нци _m_ **1** wreath; garland; (_ореол_) halo; (_знак на слава, за венчавка; врв_) crown; венец од цвеќиња garland of flowers; венец од кромид string of onions; лоboroв венец laurel wreath; ❑ сонатен венец sonnet sequence **2** *Bot.* corolla **3** chain, range; планински венец range of mountains **4** *fig.* marriage **5** (*only pl*) *Anat.* gums, *Med.* gingivae

венециец -нци *m* Venetian, person from Venice

Венеција *f* Venice

Венецијанец -нци *m* Venetian, *Hist.* citizen of <the Republic of> Venice

Венецијанка *f* (*fem. form*) *see* Венецијанец

венецијански *adj* Venetian, *Hist.* from/of the Republic of Venice

венецијка *f* (*fem. form*) *see* венециец

венециски *adj* Venetian

Венецуела *f* Venezuela

Венецуéлец -лци *m* Venezuelan

Венецуéлка *f* (*fem. form*) *see* Венецуелец

венецуéлски *adj* Venezuelan

венóзен -зна *adj* venous

венок -ци *m* bridal garland (*head decoration*)

вентил *m* *Tech.* valve; *fig.* safety-valve; *Tech.* сигурносен вентил safety-valve; издувен вентил exhaust valve

вентилáтор *m* ventilator; fan

вентилација *f* ventilation

вентилира *pf & impf* to ventilate, air

венценосец -сци *m* crowned head, monarch, sovereign

венча *pf & impf* **I 1** to marry, wed (*in church*); попот ги венча the priest married them; ја венчавме Доста за Илко we married <off> Dosta to Ilko **2** to crown; Свети Сава за венча Стефана за крал Saint Sava crowned Stefan king **II – се** to get married (*in church*)

венчава (се) *impf of* венча (се)

венчавка *f* wedding, marriage

венчален -лна *adj* wedding, marriage *attrib.*; венчална облека wedding clothes, wedding dress

венчан *adj* wedding *attrib.*, nuptial; married; венчан прстен wedding ring

венчаник -ци *m* <bride>groom

венчаница *f* **1** bride **2** marriage certificate **3** wedding dress

венчило *n* **1** wedding, marriage **2** topping-out garland (*placed on the roof of a building just completed externally*)

вепар -при *m* boar

вера *f* faith **1** вера во иднината faith in the future **2** confidence, trust; тие имаат вера во нас they have faith in us **3** religion; христијанската вера the Christian faith **4** ❑ му дадов на вера I gave it to him on credit; што вера е овој човек? what kind of a man is he? кучешка вера rogue, scoundrel, *sl.* son of a bitch; алал ти вера well done! congratulations!

верáнда *f Brit.* veranda<h>, *Am.* porch

верба *f see* вера 1 & 2; има верба во to have faith in

вербален -лна *adj* verbal, oral, spoken; вербална нота verbal note; вербален деликт sedition

вербализам -змот *m* verbalism; verbosity

вербалист *m* verbalist, phrasemonger

верверица *f Zool.* (Sciurus) squirrel

верверичин *adj* squirrel's

вергл *m Mus.* barrel-organ

вергла *impf* **1** to play the barrel-organ **2** *fig.* to prattle, babble, chatter

верглар & верглаш *m Mus.* organ-grinder, barrel-organ player

верен -рна *adj* **1** faithful, devoted; loyal, reliable; верен другар faithful friend; верен сојузник staunch ally **2** true, exact, faithful; верна слика a true picture; верни зборови truthful words; верен превод/препис faithful translation/copy

вересија *f* loan, credit; купи на вересија to buy on credit (*colloq.* on tick); ❑ вересија потресија giving loans is certain ruin; од готово прави вересија to throw good money after bad; собери си ја вересијата take your rubbish/clutter away!

верзал *m Print.* **1** capital <letter> **2** text printed in capitals

верзáлен -лна *adj Print.* capital, in capitals

верзија -ии *f* version, variant

верзира *pf & impf* to initiate (*into*); to inform

верзиран *pt* initiated (*во – into*), versed (*in*), skilled, experienced, proficient

верига *f* **1** chain; ги фрли веригите to cast off one's chains **2** <планинска> верига range, ridge, chain <of mountains>

верижен -жна *adj* chain *attrib.*; ❑ верижна реакција chain reaction

верижник -ци *m* (*usu. pl*) pot-hook

верификáтор *m* verifier

верификација *f* verification, check, confirmation

верификува *pf & impf see* верифицира

верифицира *pf & impf* to verify, check, confirm, prove

вермут *m* vermouth

верник -ци *m* believer

верница & верничка *f* (*fem. form*) *see* верник

верно *adv* **1** faithfully, truly, devotedly, loyally; те сака верно he loves you devotedly **2** exactly, accurately, faithfully; го предаде верно ликот (*of portraits*) he produced a true likeness **3** indeed, really, truly; верно, така беше indeed, that's how it was

верност *f* **1** loyalty, devotion, faithfulness, fidelity; верност спрема татковината loyalty to one's country **2** accuracy, correctness; truthfulness; верност на описот accuracy of the description

веровит *adj* trustworthy, reliable

веродостоен -јна *adj* credible, trustworthy, authentic

вероисповед *f* faith, religion; creed; denomination, rite

веројатен -тна *adj* probable

веројатно *adv* probably

веројатност *f* probability, likelihood; ❑ по секоја веројатност in all probability; *Math.* теорија на веројатноста calculus of probability, probability theory, game theory

вероломен -мна *adj* treacherous, perfidious

вероломник -ци *m* treacherous person, traitor

вероломнички *adj* treacherous

вероломно *adv* treacherously, perfidiously

вероломност *f* treachery, perfidy

вероломство *n* treachery, disloyalty, perfidy

веронáл *m* veronal, barbital (*sedative drug*)

веронаука *f* religious instruction

вероотстапник -ци *m* apostate

вероучител -ци *m* teacher of religion, catechist

верс *m* verse

Версај *m* Versailles

версајски *adj* Versailles *attrib.*

версификáтор *m* versifier

версификација *f* versification

версифици́ра & **версификува** *pf* & *impf* to versify, write poetry

верски *adj* religious; верска припадност religious affiliation

вертика́ла *f* vertical, perpendicular

вертика́лен -лна *adj* vertical; upright; perpendicular

вертика́лно *adv* vertically; upright; (*во крстозбор*) down

верува *impf* I to believe (*во – in*); to have faith in, trust; никој не му веруваше no one believed him; верува во духови to believe in ghosts; верува во некого to trust s.o.; to believe in s.o.; не им верува на очите not to believe one's eyes; слепо верува во to have blind faith in; ❏ ќе поверувам кога ќе видам seeing is believing; сит гладен не верува *prov. see* сит II – **се** *impers.* не ми се верува I can't believe it; се верува (*дека*) it is believed (thought) (*that*)

верување *n* (*from* верува) belief; не е за верување it's beyond belief, it's incredible

верују *n* 1 Credo, the Creed 2 *fig.* creed, basic tenets

верушка *f see* врижник

весел *adj* 1 merry, joyful; (*по карактер*) jovial; весело друштво jolly company; весело настроение merry (good) mood; high spirits; весела игра merry dance/ game; весела пошта Chinese whispers 2 *fig.* (*за растенија*) fresh, green

веселба *f* celebration; merry-making; revelry; другарска веселба friendly celebration, party; народна веселба popular festival, public revels; тера веселба to have a good time, enjoy o.s.

весели *impf* I to make (*s.o.*) happy, cheer (*s.o.*) up; to regale, amuse; сончевите утра го веселат the sunny mornings cheer him; со своите шеги ги веселеше своите внучиња with his jokes he kept his grand-children amused II – **се** to rejoice, be glad; to enjoy o.s., have a good time, carouse; се весели на нечиј успех to rejoice at s.o.'s success; свадбарите се веселеа три дни the wedding guests caroused for three days

веселје *n arch. f.p.* 1 *see* веселба 2 *see* веселост

веселко -овци *m* merry/jovial/cheerful fellow

веселник -ци *m see* веселко

веселница *f* merry/jovial/cheerful woman

весело *adv* merrily, gaily

веселост *f* merriment, gaiety; (*на карактер*) joviality

веси *impf* I to hang *trans.*, suspend II – **се** to hang o.s.

весилка *f* gallows, *see* бесилка

весило *n* gallows

весла *impf* to row; to scull; to paddle

веслање *n from* весла; натпревар во веслање rowing competition, rowing race

веслач *m* rower, oarsman

весло *n* oar; (*кусо*) scull; (*кусо и широко*) paddle; чамец со весла rowing-boat

весник -ци *m* 1 newspaper; news bulletin (*on radio, TV*); ѕиден весник wall newspaper; устен (радио) весник radio news bulletin; службен весник <official> gazette 2 herald, messenger, courier

весникар *m* 1 (*новинар*) journalist, newspaperman 2 newspaper-seller, news-vendor, newsagent

весникарница *f* kiosk, newspaper stall, news-stand; newsagency

вест *f* <piece of> news; (*соопштение*) announce-ment, notice; радио-вести radio news bulletin;

спортски вести sports news; ❏ шири вести to spread <the> word (news); лошите вести брзо се шират bad news travels fast

вести *impf see* навестува

вестибил *m* 1 vestibule, entrance-hall, lobby 2 (*предворје на куќа*) porch

ветар -трот, -трови *m* 1 wind; источен ветар east-erly; ❏ зборува на ветар to waste one's breath; ветар работа trivial matter; ветар го вее he is a man of straw, he is a broken reed; ветар фати, ветар пушти useless work; beating the air; кој ветар го довеа?! who the devil brought him here? what on earth brought him here? се врти каде (по) ветрот to swim with the tide (current); во ветар down the drain; пушта ветар to break wind; сфаќа од која страна дува ветрот to see which way the wind is blowing; ветар и магла, глувци во табла a storm in a teacup; кој сее ветар, жнее бура *prov.* to sow the wind and reap the whirlwind 2 *colloq.* air, fresh air; излегов да земам ветар I went out to get some fresh air 3 *Med.* erysipelas

ветарлив *adj* windy, windswept

ветвар *m* second-hand dealer, *see* ветошар

ветварница *f* second-hand shop

ветвее <се> *impf* to wear out, get worn

ветвост *f* worn-out state

ветвотија -ии *f see* ветошина

ветвушинка *f* old things, old clothes, *see* ветошина

ветеник -ци *m* person who has been promised (*to the church, etc.*); betrothed

ветер -трови *m see* ветар

ветера́н *m* veteran

ветерен -рна *adj see* ветрен

ветери́на *f* veterinary science/medicine

ветерина́р *m* veterinarian, veterinary surgeon, *colloq.* vet

ветерина́рен -рна *adj* veterinary; ветеринарен лекар vet

ветерина́рски *adj* veterinary; ветеринарска станица veterinary clinic

ветерлив *adj* windy, windswept

ветерница *f* windmill; ❏ се бори со ветерници to tilt at windmills

ветерничав *adj* scatterbrained, flighty, frivolous

вети *pf* I 1 to promise; вети дека ќе дојде he prom-ised to come; пченицата ни вети добар род the wheat crop looked promising 2 to promise, dedicate; го ветија на манастир they promised him for the monastery II – **се** to promise o.s., dedicate o.s.

ветка *f* branch; twig; од ветка на ветка from branch to branch

веткарка *f* twig collector (*collecting for brooms*)

веткач *m Bot.* scarlet runner <bean>

вето *n* veto; ❏ право на вето right of veto; стави вето to veto (*s.th.*), impose a veto (*on s.th.*)

ветов -тва *adj* old, worn, faded, shabby, threadbare; ветва облека old (worn-out) clothes; ❏ што има ново-ветво? what's new?

ветошар *m* second-hand dealer

ветошина *f* old things, old junk

ветре *n see* ветрец

ветрее *impf* I 1 to air, ventilate 2 to wave *intrans.*, flut-ter, *see* вее II 1; црвено знаме ветрее a red flag is flying (fluttering in the wind) 3 (*за пијалок*) to go off/flat; виното полека ветреело the wine was going off II – **се 1** to be aired; to have an airing; неговата облека се ветрееше his clothing was being aired; дневната соба се ветрееше the living room was being aired **2** *see* I 2 **3** *see* I 3 **4** *fig.* to become senile

ветрен *adj* wind *attrib.*; ветрена воденица windmill

ветреник -ци *m* scatterbrain

ветрец *m dim.* breeze

ветри (се) *impf see* ветрее (се)

ветрило *n* 1 fan 2 *arch.* sail 3 *dial.* триста ветрила! how awful!

ветрина *f* exposed (windy) place

ветришта *pl* strong winds; ❑ ветришта! nonsense! rubbish!

ветровен -вна *adj see* ветровит

ветровит *adj* windy; ветровито време windy weather

ветровка *f* windcheater, *Am.* windbreaker

ветроган *m Bot.* (Eryngium campestre) field eryngo, tumble-weed

ветрогон[1] *m* scatterbrain, frivolous (flighty) person

ветрогон[2] *adj* scatterbrained, *see* ветерничав

ветроказ *m* weather-vane, weathercock; (*на аеродром*) wind-sock (-stocking); (*на едреник*) racing pennant (burgee)

ветромер *m* anemometer, wind-gauge

ветромет *m* **1** strong current of air, draught **2** windy place

ветроса *pf* I to frighten II – **се** to be frightened

ветросува (се) *impf of* ветроса (се)

ветрушка *f* **1** strong wind, gale **2** *Zool.* (Falco tinnunculus) kestrel **3** *dial.* windy place **4** *fig.* scatterbrain

ветува (се) *impf of* вети (се)

ветување *n from* вети (се); promise; празно ветување empty promise

ветувач *m* promiser

ветувачка *f* promise

ветувачки *adj literary* promising

ветушина *f see* ветошина

ветчест *adj* branching

веќава (се) *impf see* ветува (се)

веќавач *m see* ветувач

веќе *adv* already; by now; веќе пет дена не дошол на работа he hasn't come to work for five days now; престани веќе еднаш! why don't you just stop it! веќе не no longer, no more; не можам веќе да го поднесам тоа I can't stand it any longer

вечен -чна *adj* eternal, everlasting; perpetual; вечна мака (мука) eternal torment, hell, *see* вечна *f*; вечен календар church calendar for 100 years; almanac; вечен пат last journey, road to eternity; за вечни времиња *blessing* good luck always! вечна слава eternal glory; вечна му слава (памет) may his memory live forever!

вечер[1] *f* **1** evening; ❑ добро́ вечер good evening! пр́ва вечер the wedding night; трета́ (трека́) вечер the third evening after a birth; Бадна вечер Christmas Eve **2** (*вечерна приредба*) soiree; evening performance; забавна вечер evening of entertainment

вечер[2] *adv* (*вечерва*) this evening, tonight; (*навечер*) in the evening; вечер ќе одиме на кино tonight we are going to the cinema

вечера[1] *f* **1** evening meal; (*лесна*) supper; (*главен*

оброк) dinner, *Brit.* tea; (*свечена*) dinner; *Rel.* тајна вечера the Last Supper **2** (*вечер*) evening; наскоро ќе биде вечера it'll soon be dark

вечера[2] *pf & impf* to have supper; to eat dinner, dine; (*во ресторан и др.*) to dine out

вечерашен -шна *adj* this evening's, tonight's

вечерва *adv* this evening, tonight

вечерен -рна *adj* evening *attrib.*; вечерен весник evening paper; вечерното сонце the evening sun; вечерна молитва evening prayer, vespers; вечерна школа night school

вечерина *f* early evening; eve

вечеринка *f* social evening, party

вечерка *f* evening star, *see* вечерница 1

вечерна *f* evening service, vespers, evensong

вечерник *m* evening breeze

вечерница *f* **1** evening star **2** *Zool.* (Sphingidae) hawk moth

вечерум *adv* in the evenings, every evening

вечит *adj* eternal; constant, permanent; вечит младоженец confirmed bachelor; вечити кавги constant quarrels; вечит студент eternal student

вечито *adv see* вечно

вечна *f arch.* hell, inferno

вечнина *f* eternity

вечно *adv* eternally, forever; constantly

вечнозелен *adj* evergreen; вечнозелено дрво evergreen tree

вечност *f* eternity; ❑ цела вечност forever and a day; a month of Sundays; не сум го видел цела вечност I haven't seen him for ages

вешал *m* (*usu. pl*) bunch of grapes (*picked with the stem so that it can be hung for drying*)

вешалка *f* **1** hanger; rack, stand; *see* закачалка **2** branch (*to which early cherries are fixed, to celebrate a successful harvest*)

вешт *adj* skilled; adroit; вешт <е> во/на to have a good command of; to be versed in; to be good at; вешто лице *see* вештак

вештак -ци *m* expert witness

вештачи *impf* to give an expert opinion; to testify <in court> as an expert

вештачки *adj* artificial; вештачки заби dentures, false teeth; вештачко цвеќе artificial flowers; вештачко дишење resuscitation; artificial respiration

вештачки *adv* artificially; се насмевне вештачки to give a forced (false) smile

вештер *m* sorcerer, *arch.* warlock; поранил како вештер to get up at the crack of dawn

вештери се *impf* to become like a vampire; to turn into a vampire; to rise extremely early

вештерица *f* **1** *see* вештица **2** pustule (*on the tongue*) **3** *Zool.* (Lampiris) *see* светулка[1] **4** *see* вечерница 2

вештерка *f see* вештица

вештина *f* skill, ability; adroitness

вештица *f* **1** witch **2** *fig.* shrew, termagant, hag

вжари *pf* I **1** to make (*s.th.*) red-hot II – **се** to become red-hot

вжарува (се) *impf of* вжари (се)

вжеже (се) *pf see* вжари (се)

вжежува (се) *impf of* вжеже (се)

вжешти *pf* I **1** to heat <up> *trans.*; сонцето го беше вжештило асфалтот the sun had heated the asphalt

2 *fig.* to infuriate, enrage **II – се 1** to heat up *intrans.* **2** *fig.* to lose one's temper

вжештува (се) *impf of* вжешти (се) I 1 & II 1

вживи се *pf* to get accustomed (used) (*во – to*); се вживи во улогата to <begin to> live one's part, feel at home in one's role, enter into one's role

вживува се *impf of* вживи се; тој се вживува во возењето he is getting used to driving

вжили се *pf* to take root

вжилува се *impf of* вжили се

вжолти се *pf* to turn yellow *intrans.*

вжолтува се *impf of* вжолти се

взаемен -мна *adj* mutual, *see* заемен; взаемна зависност interdependence; взаемна корист mutual benefit

взаемност *f* mutuality

взакони *pf* to legalize

взаконува *impf of* взакони

вземи *adv* into the ground; in the ground; ❏ како вземи да пропадна he/it disappeared without a trace

взор *m poet.* look, glance, gaze; expression

взори *adv* at dawn; стигнавме взори we arrived at dawn

ввери се *pf* to become bloodthirsty; to go wild

вверува се *impf of* ввери се

взида *pf* to build in, immure; to build (*into*)

взидува *impf of* взида

ввира се *impf* to examine, observe closely, take a good look (*at*)

ви *pron* **1** (*short dat. form from* вие) <to> you; ви реков I told you **2** (*as dat. of possession*) your; татко ви your father

вибра́тор *m* **1** vibrator **2** pneumatic drill, *Am.* jackhammer

вибра́ција -ии *f* vibration

вибри́ра *impf* to vibrate

вива *impf* to blaze, burn

вивка¹ *f* (*колак, свивка*) head pad (*placed under objects carried on the head*); ball; roll; coil

вивка² *impf* to burn fitfully, smoulder

вивне *pf* вивна *aor.* **I 1** to burst into flame; to flare up; сеното вивна the hay burst into flame; огнот вивна the fire flared up **2** to lay (set, kindle, light) (*fire*) **3** to raise, lift up; to send up; (*летачка*) to fly *trans.*; гулабарот ги вивна своите гулаби the pigeon breeder released (sent off) his pigeons into the sky **II – се 1** *see* I 1 **2** to rise <up>; to take off, fly up; орелот се вивна в облаци the eagle soared into the clouds; балонот се вивна до вишно небо и се изгуби the balloon rose high into the sky and disappeared

вивнува (се) *impf of* вивне (се)

вигна *f* smithy, blacksmith's shop; forge

вид *m* **1** *eyesight*; остар вид good (sharp) vision; ❏ губи од вид to lose sight of **2** aspect, air, appearance; look; form; во вид на in the form of; под вид на on the pretext of; тој има вид на виновник he looks guilty, he has a guilty look **3** *Gram.* aspect; глаголски вид verbal aspect **4** kind, sort, type; *Biol.* species; еден вид риба a kind/species of fish

вида *impf arch.* **I** to heal, cure *trans.* **II – се** to be cured; to heal *intrans.*

видар *m arch.* herbalist

виделен -лна *adj* bright, sparkling

видели се *impf* (*развиделува се*) to dawn

виделија *f in the expression:* вид виделија фатил he has run away, he's gone without a trace

виделина *f* light

видело *n* **1** light, daylight; по видело while it's still light, by daylight; ❏ ќе излезе дело на видело the matter will come to light (will be revealed, will come into the open) **2** sight; му се зеде виделото he lost his sight, he went blind **3** icon lamp **4** petroleum **5** candle; small domestic lamp (*without a glass shield*)

виделце *n dim. of* видело 5

виден -дна *adj* **1** prominent, conspicuous; видна личност prominent personality, outstanding figure **2** notable, significant; видни резултати significant results

видение -ja *n arch.* **1** (*видување*) seeing, meeting **2** (*привидение*) apparition, phantom, ghost

видео *n* video

видеокамера *f* video camera

видеокасе́та *f* video cassette, *colloq.* video

видеокасетофо́н *m* video <cassette> recorder, *colloq.* video

видеоте́ка *f* (*за изнајмување*) video shop

види¹ *interj* look! see!

види² *pf* виде *aor.* **I 1** to see, catch sight of, notice; ❏ книгата виде бел свет the book appeared, saw the light of day; виде не виде willy-nilly; виде не виде се согласи at long last (eventually) he agreed; видов не видов, чув не чув to turn a blind eye (*to*); mum's the word; да видам бел ден give me a break! да видиме! let's see! let's have a look! да ти го видам грбот! get out of my sight! кога ќе си го видам тилот when pigs fly; виде ѕвезди to see stars; не сум му ги видел очите I haven't seen him at all; I've never set eyes on him, I don't know him at all; ќе си ги видиме сметките we'll settle accounts; види со свои очи to see with one's own eyes; живи биле па виделе! we'll see! **2** to understand, realize; видов што мислиш I saw (realized) what you were thinking **3** to perceive, recognize, realize; не може да му го види крајот he can't see it ending, he can't see the end of it **4** to visit; одам да ја видам мајка ми I'm going to see my mother **5** (*за сонување*) to dream; to have a dream; виде чуден сон he had a strange dream **II – се 1** to see o.s. (*in the mirror*) **2** to see, meet; се видов со учителот I saw (met) the teacher; ќе се видиме! I'll be seeing you! see you! **3** to seem, appear, look; му се виде полесно орањето the ploughing seemed easier to him **4** *impf* темница е, не ми се види it's dark, I can't see anything; ❏ да му се не види! damn him/it! blast it!

видик -ци *m* view, perspective; horizon; comprehension, grasp; има широки видици to be broadminded; на видик in sight

видлив *adj* visible, distinct; apparent, obvious

видовит *adj* **1** clairvoyant **2** penetrating, discerning, sagacious

видовитост *f* **1** clairvoyance **2** sagacity

видовиште *n* visit; беф на видовиште кај ќерка ми I went to see my daughter

видоизмени *pf literary* **I** to transform, modify, alter, change *trans.*; современата техника го видоизмени нашиот живот modern technology has transformed our lives; комисијата го видоизмени својот предлог the commission modified their proposal **II** – **ce** to change, alter *intrans.*

видоизменува (се) *impf of* видоизмени (се)

видокруг *m* field of vision; view, perspective; mental outlook, horizon

видра *f* **1** *Zool.* (Lutra lutra) otter; брз <ка>ко видра quick on one's feet **2** *fig.* sensible/capable person

видува *impf* **I** to see, meet (*often*) *trans.* **II** – **ce** to see each other, meet *intrans.*

видувален *m dial.* visitor (*person who calls on a returned migrant worker*)

видување *n* seeing, meeting; до видување goodbye! *au revoir!* see you! до скоро видување! see you soon! познава некого од видување to know s.o. by sight; едно видување – еден век *prov.* a meeting is worth a whole lifetime

видувачка *f* meeting, seeing s.o.

виѓа[1] *f dial.* appearance, look; на виѓа in appearance

виѓа[2] *impf see* гледа

виѓава (се) *impf see* видува (се)

виѓе *n dial.* visit (*to a woman who has just given birth*)

вие[1] *impf* **I 1** to weave *trans.*; вие венец to weave a wreath/garland; вие гнездо to make (build) a nest; вие оро to dance an *oro* **2** to twist, turn, wind *trans.*; to bend *trans.*; вие клопче to wind a ball (skein) (*of wool, etc.*) **3** (*врти*) to hurt, ache; ме вие коленото my knee hurts **4** to wind *intrans.*, meander; патот виеше по ридовите the road wound through the hills **5** (*скопе*) to castrate, geld; вие коњ to geld a stallion **6** (*за знаме*) to wave *trans.* **II** – **ce 1** to wind, weave, twist *intrans.*; to bend *intrans.*; змијата се виеше низ стрништето the snake was slithering through the stubble; змии се вијат во клопче snakes coil up; над локомотивата се виеше чад smoke curled above the locomotive; од (под) тежината на снегот гранките се виеја the branches bent under the weight of the snow; над патот се вие облак од прашина a cloud of dust hangs over the road **2** (*од болки*) to writhe **3** *see* I 3 **4** to turn *intrans.*; орел се виеше над стадото an eagle was wheeling above the flock; светот му се вие пред очи he feels dizzy (giddy), his head is spinning

вие[2] *impf* **1** to howl; волкот вие the wolf is howling **2** to wail, lament; вие над гроб to weep/lament over a grave

вие[3] *pron* (*2nd p. pl*) you; (*dat.* вам, ви; *other cases:* вас, ве)

виеж *m* howl<ing>; wail<ing>; виеж на волци howling of wolves

Виена *f* Vienna

виенчанец -нци *m* Viennese

виенчанка *f* (*fem. form*) *see* виенчанец

виенски *adj* Viennese

Виетнам *m* Vietnam

Виетнамец -мци *m* Vietnamese

Виетнамка *f* (*fem. form*) *see* Виетнамец

виетнамски *adj* Vietnamese

вижди *impf* (*'ржи*) to neigh, whinny

виза *f* visa; влезна виза entry visa; излезна виза exit visa; транзитна виза transit visa

визави **1** *adv* vis-à-vis, face to face **2** *prep* vis-à-vis, across from, facing; opposite; визави нашата куќа има парк opposite our house there is a park

Византиец -ијци *m* Byzantine

Византија *f* Byzantium

Византијка *f* (*fem. form*) *see* Византиец

Византинец -нци *m see* Византиец

Византинка *f see* Византијка

византински *adj see* византиски

византиски *adj* Byzantine

византолог -зи *m* Byzantinist, expert in Byzantium

византологија *f* Byzantine studies

визба *f* cellar, basement

визија -ии *f* vision; phantom, apparition

визионер *m* visionary

визионерство *n* visionary quality; escapism

визир *m* **1** gunsight **2** (*на фотоапарат*) viewfinder

визира *pf & impf* to stamp (*a passport*) with a visa, endorse (*a passport*); to issue a visa

визита *f* visit

визитација *f* **1** doctor's visit **2** medical examination of recruits **3** *Rel.* visitation

визитен -тна *adj* visit, visiting *attrib.*; визитна картичка visiting-card

визит-карта *f* visiting-card

визуелен -лна *adj* visual; apparent

вијадукт *m* viaduct

вијак -ци *m* **1** *Zool.* wether, castrated ram **2** *Mech.* bolt; screw

вик *m* **1** shouting, row, din; даде вик he shouted, he made a row **2** *fig.* call, appeal, *see* повик

вика *impf* **I 1** to shout; to call out; to scream; учителот вика по мене the teacher shouts at me; ❑ вика до што го глас држи to shout at the top of one's voice **2** to call; оваа река ја викаме Сува Река we call this river Suva Reka **3** to call; to summon; нè викаше на помош he was calling on us to help **4** to invite; ќе те викам на вечера I'll invite you to dinner **5** to say; татко вика дека е добро детето father says that the child is good/fine **II** – **ce 1** to be called; ce викам . . . I am called . . . , my name is . . . ; како се викаш? what is your name? **2** што се вика as they say; what is known as . . .

виканица *f* shouting, din, *see* викотница

викар *m* vicar

викач *m* **1** loud person, *colloq.* loud-mouth **2** summoner

викија -ии *f arch.* glass, *see* чаша

викенд *m* weekend

викендица & викендичка *f* weekend cottage, villa

виклер *m* (*за коса*) curler, roller

викло -овци *m see* викач 1

викне *pf* викна *aor.* **1** to give a shout, call out, cry out, yell (*на – то*) **2** to call *trans.*; to summon; to hail; to invite; ме викна да му помогнам he called me to help him; викна лекар he called a doctor **3** to shout (*на некого – at s.o.*), scold, tell (*s.o.*) off **4** to begin, start; to set about; викна да плаче she started to cry

викнува *impf of* викне

викот *m* shouting, screaming, row

викотница *f & викотници pl* shouting, screaming, row; ❑ многу викотници за ништо much ado about nothing

викторија *f* **1** (*победа*) victory **2** *Sport.* (*тренинг*) soccer practice (*playing with one goal only*) **3** (*кочија*) victoria, light four-wheeled carriage

викум *adv* shouting

вила[1] *f* pitchfork

вила[2] *f see* самовила 1

вила³ *f* villa

вилает *m* arch. **1** vilayet (*administrative district in the Ottoman Empire*) **2** province, district

вилаетски *adj* arch. vilayet attrib.

вилар *m* pitchfork-maker

вилен -лна *adj* arch. lively; unrestrained; violent, furious

вилест *adj* forked, pronged

вилица *f* **1** jaw; ❑ јак е во вилиците he is very talkative, he talks too much **2** fork, *see* виљушка

виличар *m* forklift <truck>

виличен -чна *adj* jaw attrib.; вилична коска jawbone

виличест *adj* **1** with big jaws **2** *fig.* (*зборлив*) talkative, garrulous, loquacious

виличи се *impf* to grimace, make faces, grin

виљак -и *m* stack

вилнее *impf* to rage; ветрот вилнее the wind is howling; вилнееше епидемија an epidemic was raging

виловен -вна *adj* arch. lively; unrestrained; violent, furious

виљувче *n dim. of* виљушка; cake fork; cocktail fork

виљушка *f* **1** fork; ❑ виљушка за штимање tuning-fork **2** forkful

виме *n* udder

вимест *adj* having a large udder

вина *f* blame, fault, guilt; префрла вина на друг to put the blame on s.o. else; признава вина to admit one's guilt, *Leg.* plead guilty

винар *m* **1** vintner, wine-merchant; wine-maker, wine-grower, viniculturist **2** wine drinker, winebibber

винарина *f* wine tax

винарница *f* wine shop, wine cellar, winery

винарство *n* wine production, wine-growing

винџакна *f* wind jacket, windcheater, *Am.* windbreaker

винен *adj* vine attrib.; винена лоза grapevine

вененица *f* wineglass

вино *m* wine; бело вино white wine; трпезно вино table wine; црно вино red wine; несортно вино plonk; бокал за вино wine carafe; ❑ ме фати виново this wine has gone to my head; виното раце нема, а за очи фаќа *prov.* there is a devil in every berry of the grape; стар пријател и старо вино не пуштај *prov.* old friends and old wine are best; во виното е вистината *prov.* in vino veritas; what soberness conceals, drunkenness reveals

винов *adj* vine attrib.; винова лоза grapevine

виновен -вна *adj* guilty; тој е виновен за ова he is to blame for this

виновник -ци *m* culprit; lawbreaker

виновност *f* guilt<iness>, culpability

виножито *n* rainbow

винопиец -јци *m* wine drinker, winebibber

винороден -дна *adj* rich in grapes; suitable for wine-growing; винороден крај wine-growing country

вински *adj* wine attrib.; винска чаша wineglass; вински оцет wine vinegar; вински подрум wine cellar; wine bar

винт *m* screw; bolt

винтјага *f see* винџакна

винце *n hyp. of* вино

вињак *m* brandy

вињета *f* vignette

виола *f Mus.* viola

виолетен -тна *adj* violet

виолетка *f Bot.* violet, *see* темјанушка

виолетов *adj* violet<-coloured>, *see* темјанужен

виолина *f Mus.* violin, fiddle; прва виолина **1** *Mus.* first violin **2** *fig.* number one; top dog; *colloq.* big cheese; ❑ свири втора виолина to play second fiddle

виолинист *m Mus.* violinist

виолинистка *f Mus.* (*fem. form*) *see* виолинист

виолински *adj Mus.* violin attrib.; виолински клуч treble clef, G-clef, violin-clef

виолончелист *m Mus.* cellist

виолончело *n Mus.* cello

виор *m* **1** whirlwind, gale; помина како виор he passed (went through) like a whirlwind **2** vortex, eddy **3** *fig.* height; full swing; во виорот на војната at the height of the war

виорен -рна *adj* whirlwind attrib.

виори *impf* **I** to blow about *trans.* **II** - се to fly about; to flutter *intrans.*

виорка *f* girl leader of an *oro*

вир *m* **1** puddle; ❑ вир-вода soaked to the skin **2** millpond; reservoir, cistern, tank **3** *see* вител 1

вирее *impf* to flourish, grow well, do well; кај нас вирее зеленчук vegetables do very well in our region

вирман *m Comm.* transfer, transfer order; банкарски вирман bank transfer

вирмански *adj* transfer attrib.; вирмански промет clearing-house system

виролиште *n* whirlpool, maelstrom

виртуоз *m* virtuoso

виртуозен -зна *adj* virtuoso attrib., masterly

виртуозност *f* virtuosity

вирус *m* virus

вирусен -сна *adj* viral

вирче *n dim. of* вир; капка по капка вирче *prov.* many a mickle makes a muckle

вис *m* **1** height; раце во вис! hands up! **2** summit, mountain peak **3** *Gymnastics* hang

виси *impf* **1** to hang *intrans.*; ламбата виси на таванот the lamp hangs from the ceiling; виси на бесилка he is hanging on the gallows; ❑ виси на конец to hang by a thread (hair); виси некому над глава to hang over s.o.'s head; to breathe down s.o.'s neck; виси во воздух it hangs in the air (balance) **2** to hover **3** *fig.* to hang around; со саати виси на порта he hangs around the door for hours; стално виси со него he always hangs around with him

висина *f see* височина; ❑ на висина е to be up to the mark; to be up to expectations; to be equal to the occasion; to rise to the occasion

висиномéтар -три *m* altimeter

виск *m* **1** neigh **2** shriek, scream

виска *impf* **1** (*'ржи*) to neigh, whinny **2** to shriek, scream, squeal

виски *m* whisky

вискоза *f* viscose

вискозитет & вискозност *f* viscosity

висне¹ *pf* висна aor. **1** to neigh (*once*) **2** (*see* виска 2) to give a shriek

висне² *pf* висна aor. to hang down; to hang loose (limp); над градот виснал облак сив a grey cloud is hanging over the town

висок¹ *adj* **1** high; tall; висок човек tall person;

висока зграда tall building; висок глас high-pitched voice; висока температура high temperature; високи приноси high yields; ❑ висок стил lofty style; висока печка blast furnace; Високата порта the Sublime Porte; високо образование higher (tertiary, university) education; висока школа university; *Elec.* висок напон high tension, high voltage; висок датум end of the month (*when one's salary is almost spent*); на високо ниво high-level *attrib.*, at a high level; живее на висока нога to live in grand style; има високо мислење за некого/нешто to have a high opinion of s.o./s.th., think highly of s.o./s.th. **2** *fig.* high<-ranking>, important, senior; висока личност high official, dignitary; висок гостин important guest, VIP

висок[2] -ци *m* plummet, plumb-line

високо *adv* high; ❑ гледа од високо на некого to look down on s.o.; кој високо лета, ниско паѓа *prov.* the bigger they come, the harder they fall

високоградба *f* **1** high-rise building, skyscraper **2** skyscraper construction

висококвалите́тен -тна *adj* select, top-quality, high-grade

висококвалифику́ван & висококвалифици́ран *adj* highly qualified, skilled; висококвалифику́ван работник skilled worker; висококвалифику́ван труд specialized (skilled) work

високопа́рен -рна *adj* pretentious, pompous, stilted, turgid; високопарен стил grandiloquent (bombastic) style

високопа́рност *f* grandiloquence, pomposity, pretentiousness

високопоставен *adj* high<-ranking>, exalted, senior; eminent

високопреосвештен *adj Rel.* right reverend

високопреосвештенство *n Rel.* Eminence; Grace; Your Grace, My Lord (*title of archbishops and metropolitans of Orthodox Church*)

високопродукти́вен -вна *adj* highly productive

високороден -дна *adj* high-yield; високородна пченица high-yield wheat

високосен -сна *adj* leap<-year> *attrib.*; bissextile; високосна година leap year

високоу́чен *adj* highly educated; very learned, erudite

високоу́ченост *f* erudition

високофреквéнтен -тна *adj* high-frequency *attrib.*

високорамнина *f* plateau, tableland

висост *f* **1** *see* височество **2** *see* висота

висота *f* altitude, height

височество *n* majesty, highness; Ваше Височество Your Majesty (Highness)

височина *f* **1** height; скок во височина *Sport.* high jump **2** altitude; надморска височина height above sea level **3** elevation, hill **4** (*на глас*) pitch **5** sky, heaven; летна во височините it flew very high

височински *adj* altitude *attrib.*; ❑ височинска разлика difference in altitude

височок -чка *adj dim. of* висок[1]

вист *m* whist

вистина[1] *f* truth; апсолутна вистина absolute truth; вистината ќе победи truth will conquer; жива вистина honest (naked) truth; не е вистина it is not true; стара вистина an old truth; сушта вистина the very truth; нема никаква вистина во тоа there is not

a word of truth in it; ❑ за волја на вистината fair is fair; to be honest; frankly speaking

вистина[2] *adv* (*навистина*) really, truly, indeed, it's true; вистина, така беше really, that's how it was; вистина воскресе *see* воскресе

вистинит *adj* true, accurate; authentic; truthful

вистинитост *f* veracity; truthfulness; authenticity

вистинољубив *adj* truthful, veracious

вистинољубивост *f* truthfulness

вистински 1 *adj* real, true; authentic; вистинска мака real torment; вистински другар real friend; вистинска смисла true sense; вистински глупак a complete idiot; тоа е она вистинското just the thing; that's the truth of the matter **2** *adv* really, truly

висулец -лци *m* **1** hanging object; hanging ornament; dangler; (*накит*) pendant **2** (*мразулец*) icicle

висулка *f* **1** (*мразулец*) icicle **2** (*накит, украс*) pendant

вит *adj* slender, slim, thin; flexible, supple; вита снага slim/supple body; вита ела graceful fir-tree; ❑ вити ребра false ribs, floating ribs

витален -лна *adj* vital; тој е многу витален човек he is very vigorous; витално прашање vital question

витали́зам -змот *m Biol.* vitalism

виталитéт & виталност *m* vitality; *fig.* life expectancy

витами́н *m* vitamin

витами́нски *adj* vitamin *attrib.*

витез *m* knight; hero, champion

вител -тли *m* **1** whirlpool, eddy **2** winch, windlass, capstan **3** tool for tying sheaves **4** comber (*for cotton*)

витешки 1 *adj* chivalrous, courtly, knightly; витешка игра knightly sport **2** *adv* chivalrously, gallantly, courteously

вити, вити *interj* (*cry for calling pigeons*) come here!

витка[1] *f* end crust of *pita*

витка[2] *impf* **I 1** to bend, twist *trans.*; to roll <up> *trans.*; витка некому рака to twist s.o.'s arm; витка цигара to roll a cigarette; витка коса to curl (set) hair; витка писмо to fold a letter; ❑ витка грб to bob, duck, bow and scrape; плашливиот витка грб пред посилниот; плашливиот му го витка грбот на посилниот the meek/weak defer to the strong **2** to wrap; витка бонбони во хартија to wrap sweets in paper; витка доенче во (со) пелени to wrap an infant in nappies; витка пари во фишеци to wrap coins in rouleaus **3** to hurt, ache; ме витка коленото my knee hurts **II** – се to curl <up> *intrans.*; to bend *intrans.*; to wriggle *intrans.*; to twist *intrans.*; to roll *intrans.*; (*од болки и сл.*) to squirm, writhe; бршленот се виткаше околу стеблото на крушата the ivy curled round the trunk of the pear tree; змијата се виткаше во клопче the snake would coil up; колоната се виткаше надолу по стрмната падина the column wound <its way> down the steep slope; од силниот ветар трските се виткаа the reeds bent in the strong wind; се витка како змија to wriggle like a snake; се витка од болки to writhe in pain; се витка од смеа to double up with laughter; гранките се виткаа под тежината на плодот the branches hung (bent) down under the weight of the fruit

виткав *adj* winding, twisting, tortuous, sinuous

виткалник -ци *m* cheese pastry (*made of flaky pastry and shaped like a helix*)

витлавица *f* 1 whirlwind, storm 2 (*дожд со снег*) sleet 3 (*растопен снег со кал и вода*) slush

витли *impf* 1 to tie sheaves 2 to swirl, whirl

витло *n see* вител 1

виторог *adj* having twisted horns

витос *interj* be off! get out! get lost!

витоса *pf* I 1 to leave *trans.*; to leave alone; витосај го leave him alone! 2 to lose, leave, put (*s.th. somewhere*); кај го витоса? where did you put it? II – **се** 1 to get out *intrans.*; *sl.* to buzz off; витосај се оттука! get out of here! 2 to collapse *intrans.*, fall in ruins; се витоса целата куќа the whole house went to ruin

витосник -ци *m* (*растурикуќа*) squanderer, spend-thrift, prodigal

витост *f* slenderness

витосува (се) *impf of* витоса (се)

витрина *f* shop window, *Am.* store window; (*шкаф*) showcase, glass case

витриол *m Chem.* vitriol

виулица *f* 1 whirlwind 2 snowstorm, blizzard

виуличав *adj* windswept; (*за време*) stormy

виц *m* joke, witticism; ❑ во тоа е вицот that's the point; кажува вицови to tell (crack) jokes; не е виц it's not a joke

вицеадмирал *m* vice admiral

вицеконзул *m* vice consul

вицекрал *m* viceroy

вицепретседател *m* vice-president

виш -а, -е *adj* higher; виша школа college; higher institute; више образование post-secondary education, diploma studies; виш предавач senior lecturer; виша сила force majeure; Act of God

вишен -шна *adj* high, supreme; вишен Господ Almighty God; го фрли вишно небо he threw it sky high

виши *impf* I 1 to raise, lift; to carry/send up; авионот нè вишеше сè понагоре the plane carried us higher and higher; момчето ја вишеше топката the boy shot the ball into the air; ги вишеше гулабите he was releasing his pigeons <up into the air> 2 *see* II II – **се** to grow *intrans.*; to rise, tower (*над* – *over*); се вишел синот пред очите на мајка си the boy grew before his mother's eyes; се вишеше чад smoke was rising; куполата се вишеше над новата црква the cupola rose above the new church; орлите се вишеа високо into the sky; *see* вивнува (се)

вишина *f* height

вишист *m* <university/college> graduate

вишна *f Bot.* (Prunus cerasus) morello cherry (*tree and fruit*)

вишнов *adj* cherry *attrib.*; cherry-coloured

вишновка *f* cherry brandy

вишок -ци *m* surplus, excess; (*на плата*) pay rise; вишок на вредноста surplus value; вишок на работна сила surplus manpower

вишти *impf see* вижди, виска 1

вјава *impf see* јава

вјавне *pf* вјавна *aor.* to mount (*a horse etc.*)

вјавнува *impf of* вјавне

вјаде се *pf* to eat one's fill

вјадест *adj dial.* cross-eyed, *see* шашлив

вјадува се *impf of* вјаде се

вјаса *impf colloq.* I to hurry, rush; to hurry on *trans.*

& *intrans.* II - **се** 1 to hurry *intrans.*, be in a hurry 2 *impers.* (*with dat.*) му се вјаса he is in a hurry

вјасана *adv colloq.* in a hurry, in a rush, hurriedly; на вјасана in haste, *see* вјасаница

вјасаница *adv colloq.* in a hurry, in a rush, hurriedly, hastily

вјуначи *pf* I to encourage, inspire, spur on; to cheer (*s.o.*) up *trans.* II – **се** to cheer up *intrans.*; to take courage, take heart

вјуначува (се) *impf of* вјуначи (се)

вкалапи *pf* I to mould, shape, form II – **се** to be moulded; to become banal (trite)

вкалапува (се) *impf of* вкалапи (се)

вкамени *pf* I to petrify (*also fig.*); *fig.* to paralyse, confound (*with fear etc.*) II – **се** to turn to stone *intrans.*; to be petrified (*also fig.*); *fig.* to be spellbound

вкаменува (се) *impf of* вкамени (се)

вкачи *pf see* качи² (се)

вкачува (се) *impf of* вкачи (се), *see* качува (се)

вкисели *pf* I to pickle, marinate II – **се** to turn sour, *intrans.*; *see* скисели (се)

вкиселува (се) *impf of* вкисели (се)

вкисне *pf see* скисне <се>

вкиснува *impf see* скиснува <се>

вклешти *pf* I to seize, clutch, grip, squeeze (*as in a vice*) II – **се** to become wedged, stuck; прстот му се вклешти во вратата his finger got stuck in the door

вклештува (се) *impf of* вклешти (се)

вклопи *pf* I to fit (*во* – in) *trans.*; *Carpentry* to join, dovetail *trans.*; to include; ги вклопи цевките една во друга he fitted the tubes into each other; овие двајца ќе ги вклопиме во нашето друштво we'll include these two in our group II – **се** to fit in *intrans.*; *Carpentry* to dovetail *intrans.*; to join in; тој се вклопи во разговорите he joined in the discussions; тие заемки се вклопиле во системот на нашиот јазик these loans have adapted to the system of our language

вклопува (се) *impf of* вклопи (се)

вклучи *pf* I 1 to include; to insert (*во* – in); вклучи во група to include in a group 2 *Tech.* to join, connect; (*радиопренос*) ќе го вклучиме стадионот we will cross to the stadium 3 to turn (switch) on; to plug in; (*мотор*) to start; вклучи радио to turn (switch) on the radio II – **се** to enter, join, join in; to fit in *intrans.*; се вклучи во борба to join in the struggle

вклучителен -лна *adj* inclusive, including

вклучува (се) *impf of* вклучи (се)

вкове *pf* вкова *aor.* I 1 to hammer in 2 to point, aim; to direct; вкова поглед во некого to fix one's gaze (eyes) on s.o. 3 to confound, benumb, transfix; стравот го вкова fear transfixed him II – **се** to become rigid; to be (stand) transfixed (*with fear etc.*)

вкожури се *pf* to form a cocoon; to withdraw into one's shell

вкожурува се *impf of* вкожури се

вкoлчи се *pf* to curl up, coil up *intrans.*; змијата се вколчи the snake coiled up

вколчува се *impf of* вколчи се

вкопа *pf* I to bury, dig (sink) in *trans.*; ги вкопа прстите во нејзиното рамо he dug (sank) his fingers into her shoulder; артилерците беа ги вкопале пушките the gunners had dug their guns in II – **се** 1 to dig in *intrans.*; секирата се вкопа во трупецот the axe bit into the log; нашата чета се вкопа our unit dug in **2** *fig.* to be petrified, rooted to the ground

вкопува (се) *impf of* вкопа (се); работниците ги вкопуваа трупщите за оградата в земја the work-men dug the fence-posts into the ground

вкорави <**се**> *pf see* окорави <се>

вкоравува <**се**> *impf of* вкорави <се>, *see* окоравува <се>

вкорени *pf* **I** to implant **II** – **се** to take root, become established

вкоренува (се) *impf of* вкорени (се)

вкосо *adv* obliquely; crooked; diagonally

вкостени се *pf* to ossify, harden *intrans.*

вкостенува се *impf of* вкостени се

вкотви *pf* **I** to anchor *trans.* **II** – **се** to anchor *intrans.*, cast anchor

вкотвува (се) *impf of* вкотви (се)

вкочани *pf* **I** to make stiff, stiffen *trans.*; to benumb; силниот студ <му> ги вкочани прстите the severe cold had numbed his fingers **II** – **се** to stiffen *intrans.*, become (go, turn) stiff/numb; *see* здрви (се)

вкочанува (се) *impf of* вкочани (се)

вкрсти (се) *pf see* вкрстоса (се); <си> ги вкрсти рацете на гради he crossed (folded) his arms <across his chest>

вкрстоса *pf* **I** to cross *trans.* **II** – **се** to cross *intrans.*; *see* крстоса (се)

вкрстосува (се) *impf of* вкрстоса (се)

вкрстува (се) *impf see* вкрстосува (се); тие две линии се вкрстуваат those two lines cross

вкуп *adv* <all> together, jointly

вкупен -пна *adj* total, whole

вкупно *adv* in total, altogether

вкупност *f* totality

вкус *m* taste, flavour, savour (*also fig.*); без вкус lack-ing flavour, tasteless, insipid; истанчен вкус refined/exquisite taste; остава горчлив вкус во устата to leave a bitter taste in the mouth; по нечиј вкус to s.o.'s taste; to s.o.'s liking; секој има свој вкус every-one to his own taste; за вкусовите да не зборуваме there's no accounting for tastes

вкусен -сна *adj* tasty, nice<-tasting>; вкусно јадење nice food/meal

вкуси *pf* to taste, try

вкусно *adv* tastily; *fig.* tastefully

вкусност *f* palatability, tastiness

вкусува *impf of* вкуси

вкуќи *adv* at home

Влав -си *m* Vlach, Wallach, Wallachian

Влавчиња *pl Astron.* Pleiades, *see* Власи

влага¹ *impf dial. see* влегува

влага² *impf* to put in, insert; to deposit; to invest; влага на штедна книшка to deposit (*money*) in a savings-bank account; влага многу напори во нешто to put much effort into s.th.; *see* вложува

влага³ *f* moisture; humidity; dampness; во воздухот има многу влага the air is very humid; во собата има влага the room is damp; ❑ му држи влага 1. he still has s.th. in reserve 2. it still has a hold on him (*of an experience*)

влагав *adj* moist; humid; damp

влагалиште *n* **1** scabbard, sheath, case, cover **2** *Bot.* calyx **3** *Anat.* vagina

влагомер *m* hygrometer

влада¹ *f* government, cabinet; претседател на владата prime minister; (на одделна држава во Австралија) premier; (на одделна држава во САД) governor

влада² *impf see* владее

влада³ *impf dial.* to stay, reside, *see* престојува

владар *m* ruler

владарка *f* (*fem. form*) *see* владар

владарски *adj* ruler's; владарска палата ruler's palace

владее *impf* **I** **1** to rule, govern; владее земја to rule <over> a country; човекот владее со светот, човекот го владее светот man is master of the world; ❑ раздели и владеј divide and rule! **2** *fig.* to reign; владее ред order reigns; владее тишина silence reigns <supreme>; овде владеат жешки лета hot summers are the rule here **3** to be a master (*of*); владее со својот занает to be a master of one's trade; совршено го владее рускиот јазик he has a perfect command of Russian **II** – **се** **1** to behave; беговите и агите се владееле насилнички кон (спрема) народот the beys and the agas behaved brutally towards the people **2** to control o.s., restrain o.s., abstain, keep cool; тој не се владееше себеси he was not in control of himself (his emotions)

владејач *m* master, ruler

владејачки *adj* ruling

владетел *m see* владејач

владика -ци *m* (*Orthodox*) bishop; ❑ има вујко владика he has influential connections, he has friends in high places

владиков *adj* bishop's

владикува *impf* to rule (act) as <a> bishop

владин *adj* government *attrib.*, governmental

владичи *impf* **I** to appoint as <a> bishop **II** – **се** to be appointed <as a> bishop

влажен -жна *adj* damp; moist; (за време, воздух) humid; (за очи) moist with tears; влажен бран wave of moist air, wave of humidity; влажна соба damp room

влажи *impf* **I** to moisten; to damp<en> *trans.* **II** – **се** to become moist/humid/damp; чорапите му се влажеа од пот his socks became damp with sweat; му се влаже очите <со солзи> his eyes became moist with tears; се влажи воздухот the air is becom-ing humid

влажнее *impf* to become moist; to feel damp

влажни *impf see* влажи

влажникав *adj dim. of* влажен

влажнина & влажност *f* dampness; moisture; (за време, воздух) humidity

Влаинка *f* (*fem. form*) *see* Влав

влак *m* **1** *see* брана¹ **2** seine **3** branches (*which are dif-ficult to load on a cart and are simply dragged on the ground*) **4** *see* влакало

влакало *n* path for dragging branches

влакнав *adj see* влакнест

влакнавост *f* hairiness

влакнен *adj* fibrous

влакнест *adj* **1** fibrous; влакнесто ткиво fibrous tis-sue; влакнест лен fibrous flax; влакнеста боранија stringy (poor quality) beans **2** hairy; shaggy; fila-mentous; влакнест човек hairy person; влакнесто куче shaggy dog

влакно *n* fibre; hair; filament; вештачко влакно artificial fibre; влакно на сијалица electric filament; ❑ прави од влакно – руно to make a mountain out of a molehill; за влакно by a hair's breadth, by a whisker, by the skin of one's teeth; губи/добива за влакно to lose/win by a short head; се фаќа за влакно to split hairs; to pick holes in; нема влакна на јазикот to be very outspoken; повеќе <пати> отколку што имаш влакна на јазикот more than you can shake a stick at; не дава влакно да му падне од главата she looks after him like the apple of her eye

влакноса <ce> *pf* to become covered in hair

влакносува <ce> *impf of* влакноса <ce>

влакоми се *pf* to crave, start hankering after; to become greedy

влакомува се *impf of* влакоми се

влас *m* 1 <strand of> hair 2 carded wool

власеница *f* 1 hair-shirt 2 *Bot.* (Festuca) fescue; (Bromus) brome<-grass> 3 kind of rug

власест *adj* hairy; shaggy; woolly

власи *impf* to card (*wool*)

Власи *pl Astron.* Pleiades

власт *f* 1 power; државна власт state power; дојде на власт to take (come to) power; to take office; држи во власт to hold in one's power; неограничена власт unlimited power; ❑ падна под власта (на) he/it fell under the authority (*of*); he fell into (*s.o.'s*) hands; се наоѓа под власта (на) to be in the power (*of*); to be in (*s.o.'s*) hands; тоа е во мојата власт that is within my power/jurisdiction (competence) 2 authority; regime; administration; законодавна власт legislature; извршна власт executive; народна власт rule by the people; месните власти the local authorities

властелин *m* feudal lord, ruler; landowner

властен -сна *adj* authorized

властодржец -шци *m* autocrat; ruler

властољубец -пци *m* ambitious person; power-hungry person, despot

властољубив *adj* ambitious; power-loving, despotic

властољубје *n* ambition; love of power, craving for power

влачар *m* wool-carder

влачарка *f* (*fem. form*) *see* влачар

влачарница *f* carding machine; carding shed

влачи *impf* 1 to card (*wool*) 2 to harrow (*a field*)

влачило *n* 1 harrow 2 rake

влашки *adj* 1 Vlach, Wallachian 2 Romanian

Влашко *n colloq.* 1 Wallachia 2 Romania

влева[1] (ce) *impf of* влее (ce); Треска се влева во Вардар the Treska flows into the Vardar; полицијата влеваше страв кај луѓето the police inspired fear in the people; со своето однесување тој влева почит he commands respect by his conduct

влева[2] *impf dial. see* влегува

влево *adv* to/on the left

влегува *impf of* влезе; влегува во детали to go into detail; во оваа соба влегуваат пет кревети this room holds five beds; ❑ не ми влегува во главата (умот) it wouldn't enter my head; не ти влегува тоа во работа it doesn't concern you, it's none of your business; it's not part of your duties; од едното уво влегува, од другото излегува it goes in one ear and

out of the other; влегува и излегува <од мода/ употреба> to come and go

вледени *pf* **I** to freeze *trans.* **II** – ce to freeze *intrans.*

вледенува (ce) *impf of* вледени (ce)

влее *pf* влеа *aor.* **I** to pour into; *fig.* to instil, inspire; тоа ми влеа храброст it gave me courage **II** – ce to flow into, empty into

влез *m* 1 entrance, way in; главен влез main entrance 2 entry, entering; влез забранет no entry, no admittance, closed; влез слободен admission free; open; влез 100 денари admission 100 denars

влезе *pf* влегов *1st p. sg aor.* 1 to enter, go/come in; влезе во собата he entered (went/came into) the room; ❑ влезе во беља со некого to get into trouble with s.o.; влезе во врска со некого to get in touch with s.o.; влезе на работа to find a job, start work; влезе во години he's getting old, he's getting on <in years>; влезе во историјата it went down in history; he has gone down in history; влезе во проблемот he investigated the problem; влезе во суштината на работата he dealt with the essence of the problem; влезе во сила it came into force (effect); влезе во долг to get into debt; влезе во навика to become a habit; влези ми во положба understand my position! put yourself in my shoes! влези-излези чинат they mill around, they keep going in and out; му влезе в очи he noticed it, he was struck by it; му влезе во трагата he got on his tracks; му влезе под кожа he won his favour, he ingratiated himself with him 2 to join, become a member (*of*); влезе во комисијата he became a member of the board (commission); влезе во организацијата he joined the organization 3 to move in; влегоа најпосле во куќата they finally moved into the house 4 to fit, go (*in*)

влезен -зна *adj* entrance, entry *attrib.*; влезен билет <entry> ticket; влезна виза entry visa

влезница *f* <entry> ticket

влек *m* 1 *see* влакало 2 *see* влак 2

влекач *m* 1 tractor; prime mover; haulage unit; (*реморкер*) tug, tugboat 2 (*човек*) tower; hauler, haulier 3 *Zool.* reptile

влепи *pf* **I** to glue (paste) in; ❑ му влепи една <шлаканица> he slapped him in the face **II** – ce to stick (adhere) (*во – to*); песок беше ми се влепил во кожата sand had stuck to my skin; таа се влепи во него she clung (stuck) to him like a leech

влепува (ce) *impf of* влепи (ce)

влета *pf* to fly in; to burst in; to dash (*во – into*); авионите влетале во воздушниот простор на непријателот the planes entered enemy airspace; влета во собата he burst into the room; автомобилот влета во излогот the car crashed into the shop-window

влече *impf* **I** 1 to draw; to haul; to pull; to drag *trans.*; (*за реморкер*) to tow; секој влече по една бројка од кутијата everyone draws a number from the box; два коња влечеа една кола two horses were hauling a cart; го влече столот he is dragging the chair; водните струи на морето влечат мраз the ocean currents are carrying ice; оџаците го влечеа чадот од собите the chimneys drew the smoke from the rooms; ❑ влече некого за нос to lead s.o. by the nose; влече некого за јазик to goad s.o. into saying

s.th.; влече по блато to drag into the mire, calumniate; влече конци to pull strings; влече корист од
нешто to derive benefit from s.th. **2** to drag (carry)
about/along *trans.*; во чантата ги влече сите работи
she carries all sorts of things in her handbag; тој
секогаш го влече детето со себе he always drags the
child along with him **3** *fig.* to attract, draw *trans.*; ме
влече љубовта кон него love draws me to him;
срцето го влечеше во татковината he longed to go
home, he was homesick **4** *fig.* to bear, carry *trans.*; to
toil; тој ја влече целата работа the whole thing
depends on him; влече за двајца to work for two;
влече за некого to slave for s.o. **5** to be slow, drag
out; тој сè уште ја влече работата he is still dragging out the whole affair **II – ce 1** to crawl; (*за змија*)
to slither; (*за нешто*) to drag along, draggle *intrans.*;
детето се влече по земја the child is crawling on
(along) the ground; фустанот на невестата се
влечеше по калниот пат the bride's train dragged
along the muddy road **2** to drag o.s., move with difficulty; стариот со мака се влечеше по куќите the
old man struggled from house to house; се влече
како претепан 1. to slouch 2. to drag one's feet, stall
3 *fig.* to have an affair (*со – with*); тој се влече со неа
he's carrying on with her **4** *fig.* to potter; to wander
about; to sneak around; кај се влечеш ти? where are
you wandering off to?

влечение *f* inclination (*за, кон – for, to*), attraction
(*to*)

влечешкум *adv* dragging one's feet; crawling; on all
fours

влечигора *m* untidy/undisciplined person; insolent
person; dissipated (licentious) person, libertine

влечиклашно *m* idler, loafer, *colloq.* lazybones

влечка[1] *f* **1** slipper **2** *fig.* slowcoach **3** *fig.* slattern, slut

влечка[2] **(ce)** *impf see* влече (ce)

влечкар *m* **1** (*папуџија*) slipper-maker **2** *rarely see*
влечко

влечко -овци *m* sloven; slowcoach

влечкома *adv* unwillingly, reluctantly; slothfully

влечуга *f Zool.* reptile

влива (ce) *impf see* влева[1] (ce)

влијае *impf* to influence; влијае врз здравјето it
affects one's health

влијание -ја *n* influence; има влијание врз него he
has an influence on him; се наоѓа под влијание (*на*)
to be under the influence (*of*)

влијателен -лна *adj* influential; влијателна личност
influential person

влице *adv* face to face, openly

влог *m* **1** (*вложени пари*) deposit; investment;
штеден влог savings account; орочен влог term
deposit **2** (*дел*) share; stake (*in a game*); ❑ става влог
to chip in; сигурен влог a safe bet

вложи *pf* **1** to deposit; вложи пари на книшка to
deposit money in a savings bank **2** *fig.* to put in;
вложи време to invest time; вложи напор to make
an effort; вложи многу труд he put in a great deal of
work; вложи протест (жалба) to lodge a protest; ги
вложи сите свои сили he used all his powers

вложува *impf of* вложи

вложувач *m* depositor

влоши *pf* **I 1** to make worse, aggravate **2** to embitter,
make bad-tempered; (*за животно*) to enrage, make

(*an animal*) vicious (fierce, ferocious); тешките
преживеалици го влошија his painful experiences
have soured him **II – ce 1** to get worse, worsen,
deteriorate *intrans.*; му се влоши положбата his position worsened; ќе се влоши времето the weather
will get worse **2** to become embittered; to become
bad-tempered; (*за животно*) to become vicious
(fierce, ferocious)

влошка *f* insert; pad; влошки во чевли insoles;
влошка за хемиско пенкало refill (*for a ball-point
pen*); хигиенска влошка sanitary towel (*Am.* napkin,
Austral. pad), tampon

влошува (ce) *impf of* влоши (ce)

влути се *pf* to get worse (*of illness or wound*); му се
влути раната his wound flared up

влутува се *impf of* влути се

вљубен 1 *pt from* вљуби се; вљубен во in love with;
fond of **2** *m* man in love, lover

вљуби се *pf* to fall in love (*во – with*); вљуби се на
прв поглед to fall in love at first sight

вљубува се *impf of* вљуби се

вметнат *adj & pt* interposed, inserted; *Gram.*
вметната реченица parenthetical clause

вметне *pf* to interpose, insert, add; to interpolate

вметнува *impf of* вметне

вметок -ци *m* insert; преден вметок (на облека)
front panel (of a garment); *Print.* картонски вметок
tympan

вмеша *pf* **I 1** to mix in *trans.*; to introduce, bring in;
овчарот ги вмеша неколкуте мои овци во своето
стадо the shepherd had mixed a few of my sheep into
his flock; **2** *fig.* to involve, implicate; вмешан <е> во
to be involved in; to be mixed up in; не сака да е
вмешан во he doesn't want any part of it **II – ce** to
interfere, meddle; to step in, intervene; to mix in
intrans.; to get mixed up (*во – in, with*); се вмеша
меѓу луѓето и почна да живее нов живот he mixed
<in> with people and began to lead a new life; моите
овци се вмешале во друго стадо my sheep got
mixed up with another flock; се вмеша во разговор
to break into a conversation, butt in

вмешува (ce) *impf of* вмеша (ce)

ВМРО *abbr.* (*Внатрешна македонска револуционерна организација*) Internal Macedonian
Revolutionary Organization

ВМРО–ДПМНЕ *abbr.* (*Внатрешна македонска
револуционерна организација – Демократска
партија за македонско национално единство*)
Internal Macedonian Revolutionary Organization–
Democratic Party for Macedonian National Unity

внатре *adv* **1** inside, indoors; тој е сè внатре he is
always indoors; внатре во организацијата inside
(within) the organization **2** *colloq.* behind bars,
locked up, *sl.* inside; тој е внатре he is doing time

внатрешен -шна *adj* **1** internal; внатрешни борби
internal struggles (strife); (*за лек*) за внатрешна
употреба for internal use; Министерството за
внатрешни работи the Ministry of Internal (Home)
Affairs **2** *fig.* внатрешен човек insider, one of us, one
of our people

внатрешнина *f* interior, inside

внатрешност *f* **1** interior, inside **2** the provinces; град
во внатрешноста a town in the interior, provincial
town

внедоапица *adv arch.* suddenly, unexpectedly

внедри *pf* **I** to introduce; to embed; to inculcate; to implant in s.o.'s mind **II – се** to take root

внедрува (се) *impf of* внедри (се)

внесе *pf* **I 1** to bring in, introduce; to add; го внесовме новиот мебел we brought in the new furniture; новото раководство внесе дисциплина во установата the new management introduced discipline into the institution; внесе измени to make changes; внесе во список to enter in a list; го внесе својот другар во кафеаната he brought his friend into the bar **2** (*увезе*) to import **3** to deposit; целата плата ја внесов во штедната книшка I deposited my whole salary in the savings account **II – се** to become engrossed (*во – in*)

внесува (се) *impf of* внесе (се)

вникне *pf* to penetrate, fathom, grasp, go deeply (*во нешто – into s.th.*)

вникнува *impf of* вникне

внимава *impf* to pay attention (*на – to*), heed, watch; to watch out, be careful; на неговите часови учениците не внимаваат in his lessons the pupils do not pay attention; внимава на своето здравје to look after one's health; четата внимаваше да не падне во некоја заседа the unit was careful not to fall into an ambush; будно внимава на to keep an eye out for; to keep one's ears (eyes) open внимавај! take care! attention, please!

внимание *n* **1** attention; concentration; го слушаа со внимание they listened to him attentively; не му обрнува внимание he pays no attention to him; обрнува (свртува) внимание (*на*) to draw attention (*to*); во центарот на вниманието in the spotlight, in the limelight, in the centre of attention; привлекува нечие внимание to attract (catch, draw) s.o.'s attention; целосно посветува внимание на to be engrossed in **2** respect; consideration; му укажа внимание he gave him special consideration

внимателен -лна *adj* **1** attentive, mindful, heedful **2** kind, polite, obliging, considerate, thoughtful

внимателност *f* attentiveness

внос *m* **1** (*влог*) investment; contribution **2** (*увоз*) import

вноска *f see* внос 1

внук -ци *m* **1** grandson; (*од брат, сестра*) nephew **2** descendant, heir; внуците на Делчев Delchev's heirs

внука *f* granddaughter; (*од брат, сестра*) niece

внуче -иња *n dim. & hyp. of* внук 1

внучка *f see* внука

внуши *pf* **I 1** to suggest; to inspire; кој ви ја внушил таа идеја? who gave you that idea? **2** to persuade, bring (*s.th.*) home (*to s.o.*) **II – се** (*3rd p. only with dat. pron., на and noun*) to disgust, revolt; мене ми се внуши од тоа што го видов I feel sick at what I saw; јадењето им се внуши на затворениците the prisoners were disgusted with the food

внушува *impf of* внуши; командирот им внушуваше доверба на своите борци the commander inspired trust in his soldiers

во *prep* **I 1** (*spatial*) in, at; into, to; живеам во Скопје I live in Skopje; одам во Скопје I'm going to Skopje **2** (*temporal*) in; во јуни оваа година in June this year; во младоста in one's youth **3** (*change of state*)

into; истолче во прав to grind into flour; старото вино се претвора во оцет old wine turns into vinegar **4** (*miscellaneous adverbial phrases*) во четири очи in confidence, in private, between ourselves; во тишина quietly, in silence; го бројам во моите пријатели I count him among my friends; во години getting on in years; долги во нозете long in the leg **II** *Usage of* **во 1** (*when the noun has the article*) во бунарот in the well **2** (*before в, ф*) во вода in water; во фурна in an oven **3** (*with days of the week in certain senses*) во среда on Wednesday<s>, every Wednesday; во средата last Wednesday **4** (*with pronouns*) во мене in me; во нив in them **5** (*with nouns qualified by numerals or adjectival pronouns*) во три села in three villages; во повеќе случаи in several cases; во некои куќи in some houses **III** *Usage of* **в 1** (*when the noun has no article, does not begin with в or ф, and does not emphasize place*) бев в град I was in town; држи в раце to hold in one's hands **2** (*in poetry, even when the noun has the article*) в полето in the field **3** (*with days of the week in certain senses*) в среда on Wednesday, next Wednesday

во- *verbal prefix* (*indicating motion into*)

воајé *n* voyeurism

воајéр *m* voyeur, peeping Tom

воáл *m* veil

вовед *m* introduction; establishment

воведе *pf* **1** (*spatial*) to lead in; to bring in; го воведе во собата he brought/led him into the room **2** to introduce, bring in; to establish; воведе нов начин на работа he introduced a new method of work; се воведе нова тарифа a new tariff has been introduced; воведе ред to establish order; се воведе електрично осветление electric lighting was introduced **3** to introduce, install, induct; го воведе во должноста (работата) he introduced him to his <new> post; го воведе во науката he introduced him to science

воведува *impf of* воведе

вовира (се) *impf of* вовре (се)

вовлекува (се) *impf of* вовлече (се)

вовлече *pf* вовлеков *1st p. sg aor.* **I 1** to drag in, pull in, draw in; to tuck in; вовлече кошула во панталони to tuck a shirt into trousers; го вовлече детето на игралиштето he dragged the child on to the playground; си го вовлече мевот he drew his stomach in **2** *fig.* to involve, draw into; настаните ја вовлекоа земјата во војна the events drew the country into war **II – се** to drag o.s. in; to crawl into; to insinuate o.s. into; to be involved (dragged into); се вовлекоа во вреќи за спиење they crawled into sleeping bags; ❏ му се вовлече на некого под кожа to get into s.o.'s good grace; to worm one's way into s.o.'s confidence; to butter s.o. up, curry favour with s.o.

вовлечува (се) *impf see* вовлекува (се)

вовре *pf* **I** to draw/put through, thread; to slip (*in, under*) *trans.*; ја вовре раката во белезицата she put (threaded) her hand through the bracelet **II – се** to sneak in, squeeze in *intrans.*

воврува (се) *impf see* вовира (се)

вод *m* **1** *Mil.* platoon **2** duct, pipe, tube; електричен вод electrical duct

вода *f* water; вода за пиење drinking-water;

дестилирана вода distilled water; кисела вода mineral water; колонска вода eau-de-Cologne; крстенá вода holy water; минерална вода mineral water; морска вода sea water; слатка вода fresh water; солена вода salt water; ❑ тешка вода *Chem.* heavy water; вир-вода сторен, жива вода сторен soaked to the skin; гола вода watery, like water (*usu. said of tasteless food*); жива вода healing/magical water; жива вода е he is dripping wet, he is drenched with sweat; лесно како вода as easy as ABC; ја знае лекцијата како вода he knows the lesson off pat (by heart); лови во матна вода to fish in troubled waters; мала вода shallow person; мати вода во аван to beat the air, to mill the wind; мати некому вода to muddy the water for s.o., to intrigue against s.o.; оди некому по водата to give in to s.o.; пушта вода некому to waste time to s.o., toady to s.o.; пушта вода некому to have s.o. on; налева вода на туѓа воденица to bring grist to s.o. else's mill; пушта вода to make (pass) water; се чувствува како риба во вода to be in one's element; тивка вода cunning (insincere) person; dissembler, hypocrite, sham; *pl* територијални води territorial waters; брзата вода, брзо истекува more haste, less speed; haste makes waste; вода донела, вода однела easy come easy go; вода не може да му носи he is not a patch on (*s.o.*); меѓу оган и вода between the devil and the deep blue sea; му влегла вода во уши success has gone to his head; му дошла вода до грло he is in dire straits; he is up to his neck in trouble; нема вода во очите <as> poor as a church mouse; носи вода со решето to waste time/effort; паѓа во вода to go up in smoke; to fall flat; to come to nothing; пренесува некого жеден преку вода to lead s.o. by the nose; to pull a fast one on s.o.; фрла пола во вода to find s.th. hard to believe; чува нешто како капка вода на дланка to cherish (treasure) s.th. like the apple of one's eye; водата сè мие, само устата не може *prov.* fair water makes all clean; каде што текла водата, пак ќе тече *prov.* old habits die hard; крвта вода не станува *prov.* blood is thicker than water; мирна вода брег рони *prov.* still waters run deep

водар *m* water-carrier
водарина *f* water-rates
водарка *f* (*fem. form*) *see* водар
водач *m* 1 leader, head; народен водач national leader; leader of the people 2 guide; туристички водач tourist guide, cicerone 3 guidebook
водвиљ -ли *m* vaudeville
воден[1] *pt* (*from* води) led
воден[2] *adj* wet, drenched; ❑ водена фризура set (*hairdressing*)
воден[3] -дна *adj* water *attrib.*, aquatic; водни бои water-colours; воден знак (жиг) watermark (*in paper*); воден пат waterway; водна болест dropsy, oedema; водна енергија water-power; водна заедница water management association; водна стихија flood water; водно пространство expanse of water; *Chem.* воден раствор aqueous solution, воден коњ *Zool.* hippopotamus; водна змија *Zool.* (Natrix natrix) grass snake; водни животни aquatic animals
воден[4] -дна *adj* (*see* вод) platoon *attrib.*; воден офицер platoon commander

Воден *m* Edessa
водени *impf* I to wet; to moisten II – ce to get wet; to get moist<ened>
воденица *f* 1 water-mill; ❑ многу зборови во воденица! you've said enough! донесува вода на своја воденица to bring grist to the mill; празна воденица prattler, chatterbox; туку си тропа како некоја празна воденица he can talk the hind leg off a donkey 2 mill, grinder; воденица за кафе coffee-mill (-grinder) 3 stomach (*of cattle and poultry*)
воденичар *m* miller
воденичарски *adj* mill *attrib.*, *see* воденичен
воденичен -чна *adj* mill *attrib.*; воденичен камен millstone
воденички *adj* mill *attrib.*
воденски *adj* Edessa *attrib.*
воденчанец -ни *m* person from Edessa
воденчанка *f* (*fem. form*) *see* воденчанец
водест *adj* watery, diluted; insipid
водечки *adj* leading; водечки активист leading campaigner; водечка мисла leitmotif
води *impf* I 1 to take; to lead; го води по себе he takes him with him; води некого на училиште to take s.o. to school; момчението водеше за рака еден слепец the little boy was leading a blind man by the hand; води некого под рака to walk arm in arm with s.o.; ова не нè води никаде this is getting us nowhere; сите патишта водат во Рим *prov.* all roads lead to Rome 2 to be the leader (*of*); води оро he leads the *oro* (line-dance); *fig.* to be a ringleader; to rule the roost; to pull the strings; води на табелата it/he heads the league; нашиот тим води our team is in the lead; ја води партијата he leads the party, he is the party leader 3 (*in combination with certain nouns*) to conduct; to run *trans.*; to do, carry out; води војна to wage war; води грижа (*за*) to take care (*of*), attend (*to*); води живот to lead a life, lead one's life; води потекло (*од*) to have one's origin (*in*), hail (*from*); води евиденција to keep a file (*on s.th.*); to keep track (*of s.th.*); води истрага to conduct an investigation; води преговори to conduct negotiations; води разговор to conduct a conversation; води спор to be engaged in a lawsuit; води љубов (*со*) to make love (*to*); to go out (go steady) (*with*); води книги по сметките to keep accounts (books); води финансии to manage finances; води емисија to present a <radio/TV> programme, *Brit.* to compere; води состанок to preside over a meeting; води записник to take minutes; води дневник to keep a diary; *Sport.* води топка to dribble (*a ball*); води куќа to run a household (keep house); води настава to conduct classes (teaching); води сметка за to take into account (consideration), be mindful of; ❑ води сметка! be careful! 4 to have (*s.o.*) as one's spouse; ја водам сестра му I am married to his sister II – ce 1 to follow, be led (guided); to behave; се води од нечиј пример to follow s.o.'s example, be guided by s.o.'s example; се води по (според) обичаите to behave according to local custom; ❑ ни се води, ни се тера you can't please him, there's no pleasing him; се води по инстинкт to follow one's nose 2 to walk; се водевме за рака we walked holding hands; се водевме под рака we walked arm in arm 3 to have a love affair, go out, go steady (*со – with*); се водам со

сестра му I'm going out with his sister **4** to mate (*of animals*) **5** to be listed; to be considered; Пелистер се води како (за) национален парк Pelister is listed as a national park; овој тутун се води во класата (редот) на најдобрите тутуни this tobacco is considered to be among the best

водило *n* headstall; halter

водител *m* leader; водител на емисија presenter, *Brit.* compere; водител на приредба master of ceremonies; водител на записник clerk of the minutes, minute-taker, minuter; водител на курс lecturer; course coordinator

Водици *pl Rel.* Epiphany

водичар *m* (*usu. in pl*) young man who goes from house to house at Epiphany singing traditional songs

водичарка *f* (*fem. form*) *see* водичар

водлест *adj* watery; водлести круши variety of juicy pear

водник[1] -ци *m* **1** place where vessels full of water are kept **2** place where vessels are washed

водник[2] -ци *m Mil.* sergeant

водникав *adj* watery, insipid; *fig.* wishy-washy; водникаво јадење watery food

водовачка *f* small spring (*place where water rises in small amounts*)

водовод *m* water-pipe; water main; water-supply; waterworks; aqueduct; вода од водовод tap water

водоводен -дна *adj* water-supply *attrib.*; водоводна мрежа water-supply network, water-pipes, mains

водоврат *m* watershed, divide

водоврик -ци *m* & **водоврика** *f* marsh, waterlogged land

водовричав *adj see* водовричен

водовричен -чна *adj* swampy, marshy; flood-prone

водовртеж *m* whirlpool

вододел *m see* вододелница

вододелница *f* watershed, divide

водоземен -мна *adj Zool.* amphibious; водоземно животно amphibian

водоземец -мци *m Zool.* amphibian

Водокрст *m Rel.* Epiphany

водолија *f Astron.* Aquarius

водомер *m* (*за количество*) water meter; (*за ниво*) water gauge

водоносец -сци *m* water-carrier

водоóдвод *m* drainpipe; drainage

водоодводен -дна *adj* overflow *attrib.*; водоодводен канал overflow channel

водопад *m* waterfall, cascade

водопиец -јци *m* drinker of water, teetotaller

водопроводен -дна *adj* water-supply *attrib.*; водопроводни цевки water-pipes

водород *m Chem.* hydrogen; водород и кислород hydrogen and oxygen

водороден -дна *adj* hydrogen *attrib.*; водородна бомба hydrogen bomb

водосвет *m Rel.* **1** blessing of <holy> water **2** *see* Водокрст

водоскок -ци *m* fountain, jet of water

водостој *m* water-level

водство *n* **1** leadership **2** *coll.* leaders **3** *Sport.* lead; во водство in the lead

водурина *f* watery stuff, watery dish

водурлив *adj* watery

воедно *adv* together; at the same time, *see* наедно

воен & **военен** воена *adj* **1** military; воено лице serviceman; воени власти military authorities; воена полиција military police; воена обврска compulsory military service; воен обрзник conscript; воен бегалец deserter; воена пошта army post office (АПО); воена школа/академија military school/academy; воени вежби manoeuvres, exercises; воен суд court martial; воени дејствија military operations; hostilities; воен удар military coup **2** war *attrib.*; воен богаташ war profiteer; воен брод warship; воена вештина the art of war; воен заробеник prisoner of war; воен инвалид war invalid; воена штета war damage; воена состојба state of war во воено време in wartime (time of war)

воз *m* train; брз<и> воз fast train; директен воз through train; експресен воз express train; патнички воз passenger train; специјален воз special train; товарен воз goods (*Am.* freight) train

возар *m* carter, carrier; (*скелеџија*) ferryman; (*кочијаш*) coachman

возарина *f* freight <charges>, freightage; возарина за сите видови на стока freight all kinds, FAK; возарина според вредноста на пратката valuation charge

возарински *adj* freight *attrib.*; возаринска стапка freight (transport) rate

возач *m* driver; возач на моторни возила motorist; возач на автобус bus driver; coach driver

возачки *adj* driver's; driving *attrib.*; возачка дозвола driving-licence; возачки испит driving test

возбуда *f* excitement; alarm, disturbance; силна возбуда great excitement/disturbance

возбуден *pt* excited, aroused; disturbed, alarmed

возбудено *adv* excitedly; in a state of agitation

возбуденост *f* excitement; alarm

возбуди *pf* **I** **1** to excite; to alarm, disturb; глетката ќе возбуди и човек со најтврдо срце the sight will disturb even the hardest of hearts **2** to arouse, awake, evoke; тоа возбуди завист кај него it aroused his envy, it excited envy in him **II** – **се** to get excited/disturbed (alarmed)

возбудлив *adj* exciting; возбудлива глетка exciting spectacle; возбудлив натпревар exciting competition (match, game)

возбудливо *adv* excitingly

возбудливост *f* exciting nature (quality)

возбудува (се) *impf of* возбуди (се)

возбунтува *pf* **I** to stir up, incite **II** – **се** to be incited, get stirred up; to rise (*in rebellion*), revolt, rebel

возвишен *adj* lofty, exalted; возвишена цел lofty aim (purpose)

возвишеност *f* elevation; sublimity

возвиши *pf* **I** to raise, elevate, exalt **II** – **се** to tower (*над* – *above, over*), rise <high> (*над* – *above*)

возвишува (се) *impf of* возвиши (се)

возврат *m* return; за возврат in return; in compensation

возврати *pf* to return *trans.*; to reply; возврати поздрав to return a greeting/salute; возврати посета to return a visit; возврати писмо to answer a letter; мајка ми ми пиша и јас ѝ возвратив my mother wrote to me and I replied

возвраќа *impf of* возврати

воздејство *n* effect, influence; морално воздејство moral influence (*на, над, врз – on, over, upon*); физичко воздејство coercion, force

воздејствува *impf* (*на, над, врз*) to affect, influence

воздив *m see* воздишка

воздивне *pf* воздивна *aor.* to sigh, heave a sigh; длабоко воздивна to heave a deep sigh

воздивнува *impf* **1** *of* воздивне **2** to sigh (*по, за – for*), pine (*after, for*), long (*for*); to be fond of, *colloq.* sweet on s.o.

воздига (се) *impf of* воздигне (се)

воздигне *pf* воздигна *aor.* **I 1** to lift, raise; воздигне значење на нешто to enhance the importance of s.th.; воздигне во борба to stir to action; воздигне морал (расположение) to cheer up; воздигне кадри to educate the workforce **2** *fig.* to praise, extol, laud; воздигне некого до небо to praise s.o. to the skies **II – се 1** to rise; се воздигна од урнатини to rise from the ruins **2** to advance, prosper; културно се воздигна he improved his mind

воздишка *f* sigh

воздржан *adj & pt* restrained; reserved; воздржан глас abstention; restrained voice

воздржаност *f* restraint, moderation, temperance; abstention, abstinence; continence

воздржи се *pf* воздржа се *aor.* to abstain, refrain (*од – from*); to restrain o.s.; не можеше да се воздржи he couldn't restrain himself; ќе се воздржи од гласање he will abstain from voting

воздржлив *adj* restrained

воздржливост *f* restraint; temperance

воздржува се *impf of* воздржи се

воздух *m* air; ❑ во воздух in mid air; виси во воздух it is up (hanging) in the air; ѕида кули во воздух to build castles in the air; излезе на воздух to take the air, go out for some <fresh> air; фрла во воздух to throw (*s.th.*) up in the air; дига (крева) во воздух to blow (*s.th.*) up; без воздух out of breath; breathless; живее од воздух to live on <love and> fresh air

воздухопловен -вна *adj* air *attrib.*, aeronautical

воздухопловец -вци *m* pilot, airman, aviator, flier

воздухопловство *n* aeronautics; aviation; air traffic; *Mil.* air force

воздушен -шна *adj* aerial; air *attrib.*; воздушна струја current of air, air current; воздушен притисок air pressure; воздушна дупка air pocket; воздушен напад air raid; воздушен сообраќај air traffic; авионите влетале во воздушниот простор на непријателот the planes entered enemy airspace; воздушна пушка air rifle, airgun

возен -зна *adj* transport *attrib.*, travelling; возен билет <railway/coach> ticket; возен парк rolling stock; car pool; возен ред timetable

вози *impf* **I 1** to drive; (*велосипед и сл.*) to ride; вози камион to drive a lorry; вози бавно! drive slowly! вози десно! drive to/on the right! тој не знае да вози he doesn't <know how to> drive/ride; вози брод to sail a ship **2** to transport, cart, carry; вози песок to transport sand; вози патници to carry passengers **II – се** to drive *intrans.*; to ride *intrans.*; се вози на велосипед to cycle, ride a bicycle; се возевме на брод we went for a trip by boat, we travelled by boat, we took a boat; се вози на ролшуи to roller-skate

возило *n* **1** vehicle; запрежно возило animal-drawn vehicle; моторно возило motor vehicle; возило за итна помош ambulance; оклопно возило armoured car **2** shaft (*of a cart, waggon, etc.*)

возлага *impf of* возложи

возли се *pf* to get angry, furious, upset; жените се возлија the women became furious

возложи *pf* to order, prescribe, impose (*a duty*); возложи некому задача to entrust s.o. with a task

возложува *impf see* возлага

возможен -жна *adj* possible, *see* можен

возможно *adv* possibly, perhaps, *see* можно

возможност *f* **1** possibility **2** opportunity; *see* можност

возмутеност *f* indignation, disgust, revulsion

возмути *pf* **I** to cause indignation, infuriate; тоа силно го возмути that made his blood boil **II – се** to be indignant/amazed; to be disgusted, feel revulsion

возмутува (се) *impf of* возмути (се)

вознемирен *adj & pt* disturbed, troubled, bothered; uneasy, anxious, upset

вознемиреност *f* uneasiness, agitation, anxiety; disturbance, trouble

вознемири *pf* **I** to disturb, trouble, bother; to upset **II – се** to be disturbed; to get upset

вознемирува (се) *impf of* вознемири (се)

вознесе *pf* **I** to raise; to extol, laud **II – се 1** to rise, ascend **2** *fig.* to become conceited

Вознесение *n Rel.* Ascension Day

вознесува (се) *impf of* вознесе (се)

возникне *pf* возникна *aor.* to arise, appear, turn up *intrans.*; возникна спор a dispute arose

возникнува *impf of* возникне

возрази *pf* to object (*на – to*); возрази на предлог to object to a proposal

возразува *impf of* возрази

возрасен -сна *adj* adult, grown-up; elderly; возрасен човек elderly person; мисли како возрасен to have an old head on young shoulders

возраст *f* age; стане на возраст to grow up; на возраст од 8 години at the age of 8, aged 8; зрела возраст maturity

возроди *pf see* прероди

возродува *impf see* преродува

воин *m* warrior

воински *adj* warrior's, warrior *attrib.*, *see* ратнички

воинствен *adj* warlike, militant, belligerent

вој *m poet.* howl, howling

војва се *impf* to loiter, hang about; некој се војва околу куќата s.o. is loitering near the house; се војваше по спортските терени he used to hang about sports grounds

војвода *m* commander; *Hist.* comitadji/haiduk leader; duke, voivode

Војводина *f* Vojvodina, Voivodina

војводински *adj* Vojvodina *attrib.*

војводов *adj* commander's; voivode's

војводски *adj* commander-like; voivode-like

војводство *n* commander's position/dignity; voivodeship

Војвоѓанец -нци *m* person from Vojvodina

Војвоѓанка *f* (*fem. form*) *see* Војвоѓанец

војвотка *f* duchess

војна *f* war; (*војување*) warfare; војна на нерви war

of nerves; граѓанска војна civil war; крстоносна војна crusade; објави војна to declare war; ослободителна војна war of <national> liberation; партизанска војна partisan (guerrilla) war; светска војна world war; студена војна cold war; татковинска војна patriotic war; во војна со at war with; психолошка војна psychological warfare

војник -ци *m* soldier; отиде војник he joined the army; платен војник mercenary

војниклак *m colloq.* military service, soldiering

војников *adj* soldier's

војникува *impf* to be (serve as) a soldier

војнички[1] *adj* soldier's, military; soldierly; војничка дисциплина military discipline; ❏ војнички чекор marching step; јаде војнички леб to be a soldier; соблече војничка униформа to hang up one's uniform, retire from the army

војнички[2] *adv* in a military/soldierly manner; поздрави војнички to salute

војска *f* **1** army, <armed> forces, troops; редовна војска regular army; платена војска mercenary army; род на војска branch of service; ❏ оди како разбиена војска to move as a disorderly mob **2** *arch.* war **3** children's game of war, playing soldiers

војсководач *m see* војсководец

војсководец -дци *m* army commander, military leader

војува *impf* to wage war

војувачки *adj* warring; војувачки страни warring sides (parties), belligerents

вокал *m Gram.* vowel

вокален -лна *adj* **1** *Gram.* vocalic, vowel *attrib.* **2** vocal, sung, choral; вокална музика vocal music; вокален интерпретатор singer

вокализам -змот *m Gram.* vowel system/sound, vocalism

вокализација *f Gram.* vocalization

вокализира *pf & impf Gram.* to vocalize

вокатив *m Gram.* vocative

вол *m* ox **1** *Zool.* ox; ❏ јаде како вол to eat like a horse; како волот за сламата like flies to honey; stubbornly; волот се врзува за рогови, а човекот за јазик *prov.* an ox is taken by the horns and a man by his word **2** *fig.* fool, idiot, dullard, dolt

волан *m* **1** steering-wheel; ❏ зад волан at the wheel **2** (*на фустан и сл.*) flounce, frill

волев *adj literary* voluntary; волеви постапки voluntary actions (acts)

волеј *m Sport.* volley

волен -лна *adj poet.* free

волја *f* will; ❏ железна волја iron will; по своја волја of one's own volition; против својата волја against one's will; слобода на волјата freedom of choice; слободна волја free will; твоја волја as you wish (like); добра волја goodwill; силна волја strong will, will-power; наметнува сопствена волја to get one's own way

волк -ци *m Zool.* wolf; ❏ гладен како волк hungry as a wolf; ние за волкот <а тој на врата> speak of the devil <and he'll appear>; зошто му е на волкот дебел вратот? зашто сам си ја врши работата! self done is well done; и волкот сит, и овците на број pay Peter without robbing Paul; не може <да биде> и волкот сит и овците на број you cannot have your cake and eat it; кога беше волкот куче when pigs fly;

морски волк sea dog, old salt; стар волк old dog (hand); волк во јагнешка кожа a wolf in sheep's clothing; волкот волчиња раѓа eagles do not breed doves; волкот длаката ја менува, табиетот не го менува the wolf may lose his teeth, but never his nature; волкот на ветено не вечера praises fill not the belly; fine words butter no parsnips; волкот на волк ни во планина не удира dog does not eat dog; there is honour among thieves

волна *f* wool; стаклена волна fibreglass

волнар *m* wool processor; wool merchant

волнарница *f* **1** shop for woollens **2** wool mill

волнарство *n* wool production/industry

волнен *adj* woollen; волнен штоф woollen <material>; волнени алишта woollens

волнест *adj* woolly, wool-like

волница *f* wool <for knitting>

волно *adv poet.* freely; волно! *Mil.* (*command*) stand at ease!

воловар *m* **1** herdsman, *Am.* herder (*of oxen*), cowherd, *Austral.* stockman, drover **2** *Astron.* Aldebaran

воловарка *f* **1** (*fem. form*) *see* воловар 1 **2** yellow ribbed pumpkin

воловарник -ци *m* **1** paddock, pasture **2** Christmas-Eve cake

Волови *pl Astron.* Taurus

воловски *adj* ox's, ox-like; bovine; воловско око, *see* волооко

волонтéр *m* volunteer; unsalaried clerk; *see* доброволец

волонтéрски *adj* voluntary, *see* доброволен

волооко *n Bot.* (Malva silvestris) common mallow

волт *m Elec.* volt; струја од 200 волти 200 V (volt) current

волтáжа *f Elec.* voltage

волтмéтар -три *m* voltmeter

волумен *m* volume, capacity, bulk

волуминóзен -зна *adj* voluminous

волунтаризам -змот *m* voluntarism

волунтарист *m* voluntarist

волунтативен -вна *adj* **1** voluntaristic **2** *Gram.* voluntative, desiderative

волфрам *m Chem.* wolfram; tungsten

волчарник -ци *m* wolves' territory/lair

волче *n dim.* wolf-cub

волчешки *adj* wolf's; волчешка дупка wolf's lair

волчи *adj see* волчешки; со волча стрв with the voracity of a wolf

волчи се *impf* to cub, bear (produce) wolf-cubs

волчица *f* she-wolf

волчјак -ци *m* **1** *see* волчарник **2** *Bot.* (Lupinus luteus) yellow lupine **3** *Zool.* Alsatian, German shepherd

волчки *adj see* волчешки

волшебен -бна *adj* magic; enchanting, fascinating, bewitching; Волшебната флејта the Magic Flute; волшебно стапче magic wand; ❏ волшебниот стрелец Cupid

волшебник -ци *m* magician, sorcerer, wizard

волшебница *f* sorceress; enchantress

волшепство *n* magic, sorcery; enchantment

вомјази *pf colloq.* **I** to dumbfound, *colloq.* flabbergast; to shock **II** -се to be dumbfounded (*colloq.* flabbergasted); to get a shock

вомјазува (се) *impf of* вомјази (се)

вон *adv dial. see* надвор[2]; вон од outside; вон од себеси (*од лутина, страв*) beside o.s.; (*од среќа*) over the moon; вон употреба out of use; obsolete

вонблоковски *adj* non-aligned; вонблоковски земји non-aligned countries

вонбрачен -чна *adj* illegitimate; extramarital; вонбрачно дете illegitimate (natural) child; вонбрачна врска extramarital liaison

вонпартиен -јна *adj* non-party

вонпартиец -јци *m* non-party-member

вонпартиски *adj* non-party

вонреден -дна *adj* **1** extraordinary; вонреден професор associate professor; вонредна состојба state of emergency, martial law; вонредни студенти part-time students; external students; вонредно издание special edition; вонредно заседание extraordinary meeting **2** outstanding, excellent, exceptional

воншколски *adj* extra-curricular, out of school

вообичаен *adj* usual, habitual, accepted; вообичаен израз accepted (usual) expression

вообичаено *adv* usually

вообичаеност *f* usual practice/quality

вообичаи *pf* **I** to introduce, establish, make (*s. th.*) customary; to become accustomed (*to s. th.*); носењето на фармерки ние брзо го вообичаивме we quickly established the wearing of jeans; we soon became accustomed to wearing jeans **II** – **ce** to become customary, be accepted; носењето фармерки брзо се вообичаи wearing jeans soon became accepted (established)

вообликува (се) *impf of* вообличи (се)

вообличи *pf* **I** to form, shape, give shape (*to s. th.*); скулпторот го вообличи ликот the sculptor carved the face **II** – **ce** to form, develop *intrans.*

вообразба *f* **1** imagination, fantasy **2** conceit

вообразен *adj* **1** conceited, vain; тој е многу вообразен he is very conceited, he thinks a lot of himself **2** imagined, unreal, imaginary; вообразен лик imaginary character (figure); вообразен болен hypochondriac

вообразеност *f* conceit, vanity, arrogance

вообрази *pf* **I** to imagine **II** – **ce** to become conceited

вообразува (се) *impf of* вообрази (се)

воодушеви *pf* **I** to delight; to inspire **II** – **ce** to be delighted (*од* – *by*), filled with enthusiasm (*од* – *for*); to be inspired (*од* – *by*)

воодушевува (се) *impf of* воодушеви (се); нивната работа воодушевува their work is an inspiration

воопшти *pf* to generalize; to summarize, synthesize

воопшто *adv* in general, generally speaking; воопшто не not at all; jac воопшто не знаев за тоа I knew nothing at all about that

вооружен *adj & pt* armed; вооружени сили armed forces; вооружено востание armed uprising; ❑ вооружен до заби armed to the teeth

вооружение *n* arming; armaments

вооруженост *f* state of being armed

вооружи *pf* **I** to arm *trans.* **II** – **ce** to arm o.s.; to arm *intrans.*; се вооружи со знаење to arm o.s. with knowledge

вооружува (се) *impf of* вооружи (се)

вооружување *n* armaments; атомско вооружување atomic weapons; натпревар во вооружувањето arms race

вопијушт *adj literary* crying for help; ❑ глас на вопијуштиот во пустина voice of one crying in the wilderness

воплоти *pf* to embody, incarnate

воплотува *impf of* воплоти

вопросен -сна *adj* concerned, in question, *see* односен

воскоса *pf* **I 1** to wax, smear with wax **2** *fig.* to become yellow **II** – **ce** *fig.* to become yellow; to grow pale; to become the colour of wax

воскосува (се) *impf of* воскоса (се)

воскресе *pf see* воскресне; ❑ Христос воскресе! Christ is risen! (*Easter greeting*); вистина воскресе! He is risen indeed! (*reply to preceding greeting*)

воскресение *n* resurrection; *Rel.* the Resurrection, Easter

воскресне *pf* воскресна *aor.* to be resurrected, rise from the dead; to come back to life; to resurrect, raise from the dead

воскреснува *impf of* воскресне

воскресува *impf see* воскреснува

восок -ци *m* wax; црвен восок sealing-wax; восок од пчели beeswax

восокар *m* candle-maker, wax-chandler

восоклив *adj* waxy

восочен -чна *adj* wax *attrib.*, waxen; восочно платно oilcloth, waxcloth; восочна свеќа wax candle; восочна хартија wax paper; восочни фигури waxworks

восочи *impf* to wax, smear/polish/treat with wax, *see* вошти

восочина *f* **1** wax candle, *see* воштеница **2** *fig.* weak/pale person

воспален *pt* inflamed (*also fig.*)

воспаление *n Med.* inflammation; воспаление на белите дробови pneumonia; воспаление на слепото црево appendicitis

воспали *pf* **I** to inflame (*also fig.*); to arouse, excite, stir up **II** – **ce 1** *Med.* to become inflamed (*also fig.*); to be aroused (excited, stirred up)

воспалува (се) *impf of* воспали (се)

воспева *impf of* воспее

воспее *pf* воспеа *aor.* to sing s.o.'s praises, acclaim, glorify, extol, laud

воспита *pf* **I** to bring up, raise; to educate; to accustom, habituate (*некого на нешто* – *s.o. to s.th.*); to cultivate **II** – **ce** to be brought up (raised); to receive one's education

воспиталиште *n* educational institution, boarding-school

воспитан *pt* brought up; добро воспитан well-bred, well brought up, polite; лошо воспитан ill-bred, rude, ill-mannered

воспитание *n* upbringing; education; good breeding; домашно воспитание upbringing; човек без воспитание rude person; физичко/музичко воспитание physical/musical education

воспитаник -ци *m* boarding-school pupil

воспитаница & воспитаничка *f* (*fem. form*) *see* воспитаник

воспитаност *f* politeness, breeding, good manners

воспитател *m see* воспитувач

воспитателка *f see* воспитувачка

воспитен -тна *adj* educational; educative; воспитен завод educational institution; воспитен метод method of education, educative method; воспитни средства educational resources

воспитува (се) *impf of* воспита (се); мајсторот ме воспитувал на послушност и трудољубивост the master taught me obedience and industry

воспитувач *m* supervisor, tutor, educator; <school>-master

воспитувачка *f* (*fem. form*) *see* воспитувач; <school>mistress

воспостава *impf see* воспоставува

воспостави *pf* **1** to establish; воспостави врска to make contact (*co – with*); воспостави врски to establish relations; воспостави деловни врски to establish business contacts; воспостави ред to establish order; воспостави тишина to impose silence **2** to re-establish, restore; поштата ги воспостави телефонските врски the Post Office restored the telephone connections; хунтата го воспостави стариот поредок the junta restored the old order

воспоставува *impf of* воспостави

восприема *impf* to perceive, take in, apprehend, to learn, acquire (*knowledge of*); to adopt

восприемлив *adj* receptive, quick on the uptake; (*за нови идеи и сл.*) open-minded

восприемливост *f* receptivity; open-mindedness

воспријатие -ија *n* perception

востане *pf* востана *aor.* to raise a revolt, rise up, rebel; народот востана против османлискиот јарем the people rose <up> against the Ottoman yoke; востане за слобода to rise in defence of freedom

востание -ја *n* rebellion, revolt, uprising, insurrection; антифашистичко востание antifascist uprising; бувна востанието the revolt broke out; дигнаа востание they raised a revolt (rebellion)

востаник -ци *m* rebel, insurgent

востанички *adj* rebel *attrib.*, rebellious

востанови *pf* to restore, reconstitute

востановува *impf of* востанови

востанува *impf of* востане

восторг -зи *m* enthusiasm, fervour, delight, *see* занес

восторжен *adj* enthusiastic, elated, delighted

восхит *m* enthusiasm, fervour, delight, *see* занес

восхити *pf* **I** to delight, thrill, excite, charm **II** – **се** to be delighted/enraptured (*на, од – with*), be in raptures (*на, од – over, about*)

восхитува (се) *impf of* восхити (се)

вотина (се) *impf see* вотнува (се)

вотка *f* vodka

вотне *pf* вотна *aor.* **I** to put in, push in, squeeze in, stick in; to drive in; to plug in; ги вотнаа рацете в појас they stuck their hands in their belts; вотне нешто во торба/ под перница to put s.th. in a bag/ under one's pillow **II** – **се** to push in, squeeze in *intrans.*; to creep in; една оса му се вотна на детето под кошулата и го касна a wasp got under the child's shirt and stung him; вотнал меѓу две карпи he squeezed <in> between two boulders

вотнува (се) *impf of* вотне (се)

вотус *m* silver decoration (*on woman's head-dress*)

вошка *f* **1** louse; бели вошки head lice; зелена вошка aphis, plant-louse; поска вошки to remove lice; to rid (*s.o*) of lice, <de>louse (*s.o.*); ❑ фати вошки he's got infested with lice **2** *fig.* bore, nuisance (*of a person*)

вошкар *m* **1** lice-ridden person **2** *fig. colloq.* louse; wretch

вошла *f* (*fem. form*) *see* вошкар

вошле -евци *m see* вошкар

вошлив *adj* infested with lice

вошло -овци *m see* вошкар

вошлоса *pf* **I** to infest with lice **II** – **се** to become infested with lice

вошлосува (се) *impf of* вошлоса (се)

воштен *adj* wax *attrib.*, waxen; воштена свеќа wax candle

воштеница *f* wax taper (candle)

вошти *impf* to wax, smear/polish/treat with wax

воштинар *m* candle-maker, wax-chandler

воштинка *f* honeycomb, *see* сот

воштиње *n see* воштинка

В.П. *abbr.* (*воена пошта*) Military Post Office Box

впали се *pf* to go bad

впалува се *impf of* впали се

впери *pf* **I** (*насочи, управи*) to point, aim, direct; војниците ги вперија шмајзерите во (*кон*) заробениците the soldiers trained their sub-machine guns on the prisoners **II** - **се** to aim *intrans.*, head (*кон – for*); to become fixed (*во – on*); ракетата се впери кон целта the rocket homed in on its target

вперува (се) *impf of* впери (се); неговите очи се вперуваат во неа his eyes are fixed on her

впечати *pf* **I** to impress, imprint **II** – **се** to impress (imprint) o.s. (*во, на – upon*); му се впечати во сеќавањето it was etched into his memory

впечатлив *adj* striking, impressive

впечатливост *f* impressiveness, striking quality

впечаток -ци *m* impression; прави впечаток he/it makes an impression; првите впечатоци first impressions; остава впечаток to make one's presence felt; to cut a fine figure; има впечаток дека ... to be under the impression that . . .

впечатува (се) *impf of* впечати (се)

впече се *pf* впеков се *1st p. sg aor.* to dry up *intrans.*

впечува се *impf of* впече се

впива (се) *impf of* впие (се); студот му се впива во коските he was chilled to the marrow; нејзините прсти се впиваа во покривката her fingers dug into the blanket; коланот му се впиваше во слабините the belt cut into his sides

впие *pf* впи *aor.* **I 1** to imbibe; to absorb, pick up; впие миризби to absorb odours **2** to press (*нешто во нешто – s.th. into/against s.th.*); to sink (*нешто во нешто – s.th. into s.th.*); впие некого во себе to press s.o. against one's breast; орелот ги впи канџите во вратот на јагнето the eagle sank its talons into the lamb's neck **II** – **се 1** to be absorbed; to penetrate; водата се впи во земјата the water soaked into the ground **2** to press <o.s.> (*во – against*); to cling, stick (*во – to*); to dig (*во – into*); (*за пијавица*) to bite (*во – into*); уста во уста се впила mouth pressed against mouth; старата се беше впила во него the old woman was clinging to him

впика *pf* **I** to squeeze/push in *trans.* **II** – **се** to squeeze/ push in *intrans.*

впикува (се) *impf of* впика (се)

впише *pf* впиша *aor.* **I** to write in, enter *trans.*; *Math.* to inscribe **II – се** to enrol *intrans.*

впишува (се) *impf of* впише (се)

вплете *pf* **I** to weave/knit in, work in, insert (*нешто во нешто – s.th. into s.th.*); си ги вплете прстите he intertwined his fingers **II – се 1** to get entangled (*as of thread*) **2** *fig.* to get involved (*во – in*)

вплетка *pf* **I** to entangle, enmesh; to involve; еден сколовранец беше си ја вплеткал ногата во мрежата a starling had caught its claw in the netting; го вплеткаа и директорот they involved the director as well; ❑ вплетка прсти to get involved **II – се** (*заплетка се*) to become entangled; (*замеша се*) to become involved (*во – in*); to meddle (*во – in*); косата ѝ се вплетка во панделката her hair got caught up in the ribbon

вплеткува (се) *impf of* вплетка (се); милиционерот се вплеткуваше во расправијата the militiaman was becoming involved in the quarrel

вплетува (се) *impf of* вплете (се)

вплови *pf* to sail (*во – into*), enter; бродот вплови во територијалните води на Либија the ship entered (sailed into) Libyan territorial waters

впловува *impf of* вплови

впрега *impf see* впрегнува

впрегне *pf* впрегна *aor.* **I** ⁻**1** to harness, hitch <up>; го впрегна коњчето he harnessed the horse; го впрегна коњот во пајтонот he hitched <up> the horse to the coach **2** *fig.* to saddle (burden) (*s.o.*) with tasks, load (*s.o.*) up **II – се** to get down (*to work*)

впрегнува (се) *impf of* впрегне

впреде *pf* **I** to weave in; to entangle **II – се 1** to get entangled **2** *fig.* to get involved; to become part of s.o.'s life

впредува (се) *impf of* впреде (се)

впрочем *adv* **1** but, however **2** (*патем, меѓу другото*) incidentally, by the way; (*покрај тоа*) besides, moreover **3** (*всушност*) actually, in fact, as a matter of fact

впушта се *impf of* впушти се; не се впушташе во такви деликатни прашања he did not go into such delicate matters

впушти се *pf* **1** to dart, dash, make a dash, rush (*no – after, on*), make a dash/rush (*for*); се впуштија по крадецот they dashed off after the thief; полицајците се впуштија накај шумата the policemen rushed off towards the wood **2** *fig.* to embark (*во – on*); to go (enter)/launch (*во – into*); се впушти во авантура to embark on a venture; се впушти во борба to join battle; се впуштија во акцијата they joined in the campaign

врабец -пци *m Zool.* sparrow; cock-sparrow; ❑ плаши врапци to scare nobody

врабечки & врабешки *adj* sparrow's; like a sparrow

врабица *f* female sparrow, hen sparrow

вработен *adj* employed

вработеност *f* employment

вработи *pf* **I** to employ **II - се** to find employment, get a job

вработува (се) *impf of* вработи (се)

вработување *n* employment; биро за вработување employment bureau

врав *m* grain (*in sheaves*) to be threshed

враг -ови (-зи) *m* **1** (*ѓавол*) devil, fiend **2** (*непријател*) enemy **3** (*итар човек*) crafty fellow, sly rogue

враговштина *f* sly trick, ruse

врагува *impf* to be mischievous, play tricks

вража *impf* **1** to practise sorcery; to foretell the future, tell fortunes; to cure (*by magic*); to put a spell on; *see* бае **2** to wriggle, wiggle; вража со рацете to wave one's hands **3** to teem, swarm, crawl, mill around; луѓето вражаат ваму-таму people are milling around all over the place

вражалец -лци *m* **1** sorcerer, magician; fortune-teller; faith-healer **2** *fig.* prattler, chatterbox

вражалица *f* **1** sorceress; fortune-teller **2** *fig.* chatterbox

вражалка *f* **1** *see* вражалица 1 **2** *Bot.* (Stellaria media) chickweed

вражар *m see* вражалец

вражарка *f see* вражалица 1

вражач *m see* вражалец

вражачка *f* **1** sorcery; spell, charm **2** *see* вражалица 1

вражба *f* sorcery; fortune-telling

вражји *adj* devil's; devilish, fiendish

вразуми *pf* **I** to bring (*s.o.*) to his senses **II – се** to come to one's senses

вразумува (се) *impf of* вразуми (се)

врами *pf* to frame

врамува *impf of* врами

вран[1] *m* raven, *see* гавран

вран[2] *adj* black, raven (*of hair, horse, eyes*)

врана[1] *f Zool.* crow; врана на врана очи не копа *prov.* hawks will not pick hawks' eyes out; there is honour among thieves

врана[2] *f* mark (*on a water melon*)

вранест *adj see* вран[2]

вранец -нци *m* black horse

враноса *pf* **1** to mark (*water melons*), make marks (*on water melons*) **2** to blacken *trans.*

враносува *impf of* враноса

врапит *adj* brisk, agile

врапчар *m* catcher/keeper of small birds

врапчарник -ци *m* place where sparrows gather

врапче *n dim.* baby (young) sparrow; ❑ ми кажа врапчето a little bird told me; и врапчињата тоа го знаат everyone knows that; it's common knowledge; подобро врапче в рака, отколку гулаб на гранка *prov.* a bird in the hand is worth two in the bush

врасне *pf* врасна *aor.* to grow in; ми врасна в месо I have an ingrown toe-nail

враснува *impf of* врасне

врасте *pf see* врасне

врастен *pt* grown in; врастени заби impacted teeth; врастен нокт ingrown nail

врастува *impf see* враснува

врат *m* neck; ❑ зеде некого на врат to drive a nail into s.o.'s coffin, cook s.o.'s goose, cause s.o.'s downfall; кога ќе си го видам вратот when pigs fly; крши вратот! be off! get lost! на волкот вратот му е дебел, зашто сам си ја врши работата *see* волк; нá врат нá нос hastily, headlong, head over heels, helter-skelter; не по врат, а по шија it's six of one and half a dozen of the other; свиткува некому врат to wring s.o.'s neck; зграпчува некого за врат to jump down s.o.'s throat; to bite s.o.'s head off; натовари некому нешто на врат to put/lay the blame for s.th. on s.o.; to lay s.th. at s.o.'s door

врата *f* door; влезна врата entrance door, front door; еднокрилна/двокрилна врата single-/double-leaved door; патна врата front door; gate; царска врата *Rel.* royal gates (*in the middle of the iconostasis*); ❑ заседание зад затворена врата meeting/conference behind closed doors; *Leg.* in-camera session; му ја покажа вратата he showed him the door, he sent him packing; нему сите врати му се отворени for him all doors are open; чука на погрешна врата to beg at the wrong door; to knock at a deaf man's door; треснува врата некому <пред нос> to slam the door in s.o.'s face; to give s.o. the cold shoulder; на голема врата in a grand manner; for all the world to see; на задна (мала) врата by the back door; in a roundabout way; мете прво пред сопствена врата to put (set) one's own house in order; парата железна врата отвора *prov.* money talks

вратар *m* doorman, door-keeper, janitor, *Brit.* commissionaire

вратарка *f* (*fem. form*) *see* вратар

вратарски *adj* doorman's

врате *n dim. see* вратичка

вратен -тна *adj* neck *attrib.*; jugular; cervical; вратни жили jugular veins; вратни пршлени cervical vertebrae

вратец[1] -тци *m see* вратче

вратец[2] *m* return, paying back

врати *pf* **I 1** to return *trans.*, send back; to bring back; to turn back *trans.*; to pay back; го врати писмото he returned the letter; полицијата ја врати колоната the police turned the column back; ми ги врати парите he paid me back the money; на љубовта таа со љубов ми врати she returned my love **2** to reply, rejoin; to retort **II – се** to return *intrans.*, come back; ❑ да ти се врати the same to you (*said in answer to good wishes*)

вратика *f Bot.* (Tanacetum vulgare) tansy

вратило *n* **1** beam (*on a handloom*), *see* кросно **2** *Gymnastics* horizontal bar **3** *Tech., Mech.* shaft

вратичка *f dim. of* врата; hatch; ❑ си остава вратичка to keep an escape route open; to keep one's options open

вратка *f* **1** return, paying back; ❑ ова ти е вратка за твојата навреда this is what you get for being rude **2** return, way back; *in the expression:* нема вратка <отаде> you can't go back, there's no getting out of it

вратница *f* **1** door **2** *dial.* window

вратоврска *f* <neck>tie

вратоломен -мна *adj* headlong, breakneck; вратоломен скок headlong leap; вратоломна брзина breakneck speed

вратче *n dim. of* врат

враќа (се) *impf of* врати (се); ❑ враќа некому мило за драго to give s.o. a taste (dose) of his own medicine; to pay back in kind; се враќа на старо to go back to square one; се враќа со мислите to cast one's mind back

врач *m* magician, sorcerer

врачи *pf* to hand, hand over, deliver; to present (*нешто на некого – s.o. with s.th.*); му го врачи протестот he delivered the protest to him

врачка *f* sorceress; fortune-teller

врачува *impf of* врачи

врацба *f* sorcery; fortune-telling

врашки *adj* devil's; devilish, fiendish

врба *f Bot.* (Salix) willow; црвена врба (Salix purpurea) purple willow/osier; црна врба (Salix fragilis) crack-willow; дива врба (Linaria vulgaris) common toadflax; жалосна врба (Salix babylonica) weeping willow; ❑ кога ќе роди врбата грозје when pigs fly; not in a million years

врбак -ци & **врбалак** -ци *m* willow grove

врбица *f Bot.* (Polygonum) jointweed, knotweed, knot-grass

врбјак -ци *m* willow grove

врбов *adj* willow *attrib.*; willowy; врбова прачка willow switch

врбовина *f* willow timber/osier

врбовка *f Bot.* (Epilobium) willow-herb

врбува *impf* to recruit

врбушка *f* willow rod/switch

врв[1] *m coll.* вршје **1** top, peak, summit (*also fig.*); (*на цигара, чадор, прст, нос*) tip; (*на молив*) point; *fig.* zenith, extreme, height; врвот Љуботен the summit of Ljuboten; на врв планина on the summit of a mountain; врв од нож point of a knife; врв од игла point of a needle, pin; врв на конус apex of a cone; врв на пирамида vertex of a pyramid; врвови на прсти fingertips; се искачува на/до врвот to climb up to (reach) the top (*also fig.*); врв на глупоста the height of folly; состанок на врвот summit meeting; ❑ до врв up to the top; up to the brim, brim-full; земе врв to gain the upper hand, prevail; странските интереси ќе земат врв над домашните foreign interests will dominate (take precedence over) internal (domestic) interests; на врв on <the> top of; на врв јазик ми е it's on the tip of my tongue; на врв глава ми се качи I'm fed up with you **2** cream (*on boiled milk*)

врв[2] *f* string, twine, cord; врв од лен flax cord; *see* врвца

врвчача *f* illness that passes quickly

врвеж *m* **1** walking, motion **2** passing **3** *fig.* circulation **4** *fig.* popularity, good sales

врвен -вна *adj* highest; best; top; врвна точка highest point; врвни играчи best (top) players; врвен квалитет superior quality

врви *impf* **1** to go, walk; to move; (*за моторно возило*) to drive; тој врви бавно he walks slowly **2** to pass, go by; времето ми врви многу брзо time passes very quickly for me; врват покрај црквата they are going past the church; реката врвеше низ неколку градови the river passed (flowed) through several towns **3** to go away; врви си! off with you! **4** to lead (*за, во – то*), take (*to*), go (*to*); овој пат врви за селото this road leads to the village; врне, грми – патот врви *prov.* rain or shine, the roads are busy **5** *fig.* to be in circulation; to be valid; овие пари не врват кај нив this money is not valid currency in their country **6** *fig.* to go well, be successful; to sell well, be popular; работата му врвеше his work was going well; оваа стока врви добро these goods sell well **7** *trans.* to walk/move/drive (*along*); овците ја врвеа истата врвица the sheep walked along the same track

врвица *f* path, way, track

врвка *f* string, cord; shoelace; ❑ врвка му е работата he's in dire trouble

врвлест *adj* pointed, jagged

врвовиње *pl* last crops of fruit and vegetables (*used for preserves and pickling*)

врволица *f* crowd; procession

врволка се *impf* **1** to loiter, hang about; to sneak about; to prowl about; сомнителни луѓе се врволкаа таму по сокаците suspicious people were loitering in the backstreets **2** to potter, tinker; гробарите се врволкаат ваму-таму the grave-diggers are pottering about

врвулица *f see* врволица

врвца *f* string, cord; ❑ папочна врвца umbilical cord

врвчи се *impf* to follow; to pass; to be lined up

врга *f* **1** growth (*on the body*) **2** knot (*on a tree-trunk or in wood*); excrescence, knob **3** (*ѓумка на глава*) bump

вргали се *impf* to gaze, stare (*во – at, into*)

вргалест *adj* **1** knotty, gnarled **2** round

вргалив *adj see* вргалест

врева *f* **1** uproar, shouting, noise, tumult, din; ❑ без многу врева without much ado; многу врева за ништо much ado about nothing; a storm in a teacup **2** *dial.* speech, talking

вревач *m* noisy person, *colloq.* loudmouth

вреви *impf* **1** to make noise; to make a sound **2** *dial.* to talk, tell tales

вред *adv* successively, in turn, one after another; сите вред each in turn, one after another

вреден -дна *adj* **1** industrious, diligent, hard-working; ❑ вреден како пчела (мравка) <as> busy as a bee **2** capable, fit

вреди[1] *impf* to be current, valid; to be worth; to be worthwhile; пет пари не вреди it's not worth a farthing (cent); не ти вреди маката it's not worth the trouble; вреди да се види it's worth seeing; вреди злато it/he is worth its/his weight in gold; ❑ покажува колку вреди to show one's paces; тоа ти вреди you have hit the nail on the head; you have hit the bull's eye; што вреди! what's the use? what's the point?

вреди[2] *pf* **I** to place (*in a class or category*), class, rank (*among*), rate (*as*) *trans.*; го вредија во (меѓу) најперспективните наши поети they rated him among the most promising of our poets **II** - **се** to take one's place (*во – among*), rank (*among*) *intrans.*; со своите трудови тој се вреди во научната елита his works put him among the scholarly elite

вредник -ци *m* hard worker, industrious man

вредница *f* hard worker, industrious woman

вредно *adv* industriously, diligently, hard

вредносен -сна *adj* valuable; вредносни хартии securities, treasury bills; currency, legal tender; coupons

вредносница *f* security, treasury bill; coupon

вредност *f* **1** value (*also Math.*), worth, price; вредност во моментот на продажба realization value; додадена вредност value added; според вредноста ad valorem, according to value; менувачка вредност exchange value; вишок на вредност surplus value; (*на пари*) номинална вредност face value **2** (*важност*) validity

вреднотија *f* diligence, industry

вреднува *impf* to assess, assess the value (*of*), appraise

вреж *m Bot.* (Tamarix gallica) tamarisk

вреже *pf* врежа *aor.* **I** to engrave, inscribe, carve; си го врежал името на каменот he carved his name on the stone **II** – **се** to engrave itself; to cut/sink into *intrans.*; to become impressed (*on the memory etc.*); настаните му се беа врежале во сеќавањето those events became engraved in his memory

врежика *f see* вреж

врежува (се) *impf of* вреже (се); гасениците на тенкот се врежуваа во асфалтот the tank tracks dug into the asphalt

врека *impf* **1** (*за коза*) to bleat **2** *fig.* to whine, whimper; to squall

врекало *n* noisy child/person; bawler; squaller

врекне *pf* врекна *aor.* **1** to give a bleat **2** *fig.* to give a whimper

врекнува *impf of* врекне

врел *adj* **1** boiling, very hot **2** *fig.* passionate, hot-blooded

врелец *m* boiling water/liquid

врелина *f* heat

време *f* **1** time; season; era; умно да си го искористиш времето see that you use your time sensibly (wisely)! вечерно време evening, *poet.* eventide; четири годишни времиња the four seasons; во времето на Наполеона at the time of Napoleon, in Napoleon's day; што време е? what's the time? ❑ во (за) време на војната during (in the course of) the war; во исто време at the same time; во наше време in our time; во последно време recently; во свое време at one time (*in the past*); in one's time (life); губење време waste of time; да добие во време to gain time; до едно време till a certain moment; долго време <for> a long time; духот на времето the spirit of the times; едно време at one time; for some time; забот на времето the ravages of time; за време од две години in the space of two years; извесно време не работеше for a certain <period of> time he didn't work; крајно време <it's> high time; ниедно време, никакво време very late at night, at the dead of night; одвреме-навреме from time to time; по едно време after a certain time, at a certain moment; пред некое време a certain time ago; сè во свое време all in good time; со време in time, gradually; in the long run; со текот на времето with the passage of time; умре без време he died before his time; во вакви времиња at a time like this; во секое (кое било) време any time; трка со времето race against time; времето е на нечија страна; времето работи за некого time is on s.o.'s side; времето е пари time is money; времето е погодно да (за) the time is ripe for; времето лета time flies; времето лечи сè time is a great healer; time cures all things; времето никого не го чека time and tide wait for no man; времето си го прави своето time devours all things; time works wonders; time has taken its toll; времињата се менуваат times change; го издржа тестот на времето to withstand the test of time; дојде некому време да . . . the time has come for s.o. to . . . ; за сè има време there's a time for everything; игра на време to play for time; to play a waiting game; кога <за тоа> ќе дојде време <all> in good time; лошо време hard times; наоѓа време за to get round to doing s.th.; на време on time; in good time; нема време за губење to have no time to spare; оди во чекор со времето to keep pace with the times; to keep abreast of the times; од тоа време since; одзема некому време to waste s.o.'s time; убива време to kill time; стари добри времиња good old days 2 *Gram.* tense; идно време the future tense 3 date, deadline; време за исплата date/term of payment 4 weather; времето е убаво the weather is fine 5 *colloq.* state, position; немаме време we are not in a position to, we haven't the means to, we can't afford to; немаме време да правиме свадба we can't afford a wedding

временен -мена *adj see* привремен

временски *adj* of time, time *attrib.*; of weather, weather *attrib.*; *Gram.* temporal; временска разлика time difference; временски услови weather conditions

временце *n hyp. of* време

времетраење *n* duration

врен *adj see* врел

вреска *impf see* врека

врескало *n see* врекало; детено е големо врескало that child is very noisy, that child makes a lot of noise

вресканица *f* shouting, screaming, shrieking

врескач *m see* врескало

врескот *m see* вресканица

врескоти *impf see* вреска

врескотница *f* shouting, screaming, shrieking; каква е таа врескотница? what is all this screaming about?

вресне *pf* вресна *aor. see* врекне

вреснува *impf of* вресне

вресок -ци *m see* врескот

вретенар *m* 1 spindle maker/seller 2 *fig.* gypsy nomad

вретенарка *f* 1 (*fem. form*) *see* вретенар 2 *Zool.* (Aspro asper) a kind of fresh-water fish

вретенест *adj* spindle-shaped; spindly

вретено *n* 1 spindle; spindleful; *Tech.* axle, pivot, mandrel, shaft 2 yarn, thread

вретеновиден -дна *adj* spindly; spindle-shaped

врека *f* sack, bag; врека брашно a sack of flour; ❏ клава сѐ во една врека he puts all his eggs in one basket; купи мачка во врека to buy a pig in a poke; боксерска врека punchball, punch-bag, *Am.* punching-bag; скината врека a bottomless pit; spendthrift

вреќиче *n dim. of* врека

вреќиште *n augm. of* врека

вреќуле *n dim. see* вреќиче

врз¹ *m see* врзулец

врз² *prep* 1 on, over, upon; целата работа падна врз мене all the work fell on my shoulders; врз кошулата облече џемпер he put on a jumper over his shirt; се нафрли врз него he fell upon him, he attacked him; ❏ врз основа на on the basis of; ми седи врз глава he annoys me, he gets on my nerves 2 one after another; ѝ пишуваше писмо врз писмо he wrote her one letter after another 3 at (*of price*); ќе го сметаме врз десет денари кило let's price it at ten denars a kilo

врзак -ци *m* bundle, *see* врзма, врзоп

врзалка *f* string, lace

врзе *pf* врза *aor.* **I 1** to tie <up>, bind, fix; полицаецот ми ги врза рацете the policeman tied (bound) my hands; му ја врзавме главата we bandaged his head; го врза коњот за дрво he tied the horse to a tree; ја врза китката од цвеќиња he tied the bouquet of flowers; ❏ врзе облог to have a bet; врзе пријателство to make friends; врзе некому раце to tie s.o.'s hands, to render s.o. powerless; врзе некому шлаканица to slap s.o.'s face; си го врза в крпче he took good note of that; he took it for granted; ти што ќе врзеш – врзано your decision will be final; врзе некому и раце и нозе to hamstring s.o.; врзе некого во чвор to tie s.o. up in knots 2 *fig.* to bind, oblige; врзе некого со клетва to bind s.o. by oath 3 to start growing, germinate, take *intrans.*; овошките врзаа плод the fruit has set on the fruit trees; децата врзаа коска the children have grown strong (healthy) **II – се 1** to tie/bind o.s.; се врза со ортомата за едно дрво и се спушти надолу по карпата he hitched his rope to a tree and began climbing down the cliff face; ❏ ми се врза јазикот I am tongue-tied 2 to start, strike up; се врза разговор a conversation started; they struck up a conversation

врзма *f* net for carrying straw

врзоглавка *f* kerchief

врзоп *m* bundle; sheaf

врзува (се) *impf of* врзе (се)

врзувач *m* person who binds (ties)

врзувачка *f* 1 (*fem. form*) *see* врзувач 2 binder <machine>

врзулец -лци *m* bundle; knot

врие *impf* 1 to boil *intrans.*; to seethe; водата врие the water is boiling; ❏ врие од мака he is very upset; му врие крвта he is still young (green) 2 to ferment; виното врие the wine is fermenting 3 to swarm; врие вошки it is swarming with lice 4 to boil *trans.*

вриеж *m* 1 boiling 2 stirring, agitation

вријавец *m* crowd, crush, jostling

вриска *impf see* вреска

врисне *pf* врисна *aor.* to give a shriek

вриснува *impf of* врисне

врисок -ци *m* shriek, scream

врл *adj* 1 (*лош*) evil, bad, malicious 2 (*стрмен*) steep, sheer 3 (*за болка, жалба*) sharp, unbearable 4 (*по вкус*) bitter, sour

врлеж *m* steep slope

врлува *impf* to rage, be rampant; to be rife; (*за човек*) to run wild; врлуваат заразни болести infectious diseases are raging; вооружени банди врлуваат во тој крај that region is infested with armed bands

врне *impf* to fall (*of rain, snow, hail*); *impers.* to rain; it is raining/snowing; врне дожд it is raining; врне снег it is snowing; цело лето не врнело it didn't rain all summer; и да врне и да вее in fair weather or foul; ако не врне, капе *prov.* (*said of wages, earnings, etc.*) half a loaf is better than no bread; врне, грми – патот врви *prov.* rain or shine, the roads are busy; грми, ама не врни *prov.* scold, but don't strike!

врнеж *m* 1 rain 2 precipitation, rainfall; облачно со врнежи cloudy with occasional rain

врнежлив *adj* rainy; врнежливо време rainy weather

вроден *adj* congenital, innate; вродена слабост congenital weakness

врпа *impf* to crunch, munch

врска[1] *f* **1** string, cord, *see* врвца **2** bunch; врска клучеви bunch of keys **3** <neck>tie **4** connection, contact, bond, link; ❑ без врска it doesn't matter, it's not important; брачна врска marriage bond, wedlock; железничка врска rail connection (link); сообраќајна врска communications link; телефонска врска telephone connection (link, line); возот има врска the train connects; во врска со in connection with, as regards ... ; прекине врски to break off relations (*co – with*); роднинска врска family connection; стапи во врска to get in touch, establish contact (*co – with*); трговска врска commercial (business) relations/contacts; нема <блага> врска to have not the faintest idea; to have nothing to do (*co – with*); одржува врска со to maintain contact with, keep in touch with; to have an affair with **5** liaison officer; *Sport.* (*полутка*) inside forward **6** (*pl only*) connections, acquaintances; има големи врски to have many contacts/connections; ❑ бара/фаќа врски to pull the strings

врска[2] *impf* to whip, flog, strike

врсне *pf* врсна *aor.* to whip, strike (*once*)

врсник -ци *m* peer, coeval; ние сме врсници we are of the same age

врсница & **врсничка** *f* (*fem. form*) *see* врсник

врснува *impf of* врсне

врст *f* age; ние сме еднá врст we are of the same age; не ми е од врста he's not my age

врталиште *n* place where one spends one's time, gathering place, meeting-place, haunt; кај ви е врталиштето? where do you usually meet (spend your time)? *colloq.* where do you hang out?

вртачка *f* waste of time

вртеж *m* **1** whirlpool, eddy **2** rheumatic pain

вртелешка *f* **1** top; ❑ се врти како вртелешка he spins around like a top, he is in constant motion **2** merry-go-round **3** *fig.* unstable/ fickle person

вртешка *f* **1** top **2** merry-go-round **3** windlass, winch, capstan

врти *impf* **I 1** to turn *trans. and intrans.*; to spin, rotate, revolve; to twist; to wind; to twirl; (*насочува*) to direct; врти ражен to turn a spit; врти страница to turn a page; врти рака некому to twist s.o.'s arm; врти некого на прав пат to set (put) s.o. on the right road (*also fig.*); патот врти десно the road bends to the right; мушички вртеа околу ламбата gnats were flying round the lamp; врти нечии зборови to twist (distort) s.o.'s words; врти поглед to look round; to turn one's head (*конlод – towardslaway from*); ❑ врти на телефон to dial; песот ја вртеше опашката the dog was wagging its tail; врти очи to roll one's eyes; (*флертува*) to make eyes (*at s.o.*); врти <со> глава to shake one's head; врти глава од нешто to turn one's back on s.th.; врти грб (*на некогоlнешто*) to turn one's back (*on s.o.ls.th.*); врти-сучи to shilly-shally, dither; to beat about the bush; врти некого околу малото прсте to twist s.o. round one's little finger **2** *colloq.* (*мами, лаже*) to deceive, lie to; *Brit.* to lead (s.o.) a dance; врти некого дека нема итн *colloq.* to deceive/manipulate s.o. **3** to manage, maintain, carry on; врти куќа to run a house <well>; врти трговија to ply a trade; to manage a business; ❑ врти пари to save money; надеж врти душа hope springs eternal **4** *fig.* to hurt; ме вртат коските I have shooting pains

in my bones; I ache all over **5** to bore, drill, perforate; црвот го врти дрвото the grub bores into the wood **6** *fig.* to detain, delay, hold up **II – се 1** to turn <round> *intrans.*; сите се вртеа да нè видат everybody turned to look at us; се вртеше де наваму, де натаму he turned this way and that; ❑ се врти каде што дува ветрот to swim with the tide (current) **2** (*се менува*) to change, turn (*на, во – into*) *intrans.*; радоста се врти на жалост joy turns to sorrow **3** (*се движи во круг*) to revolve, rotate, spin *intrans.*; тркалото се врти the wheel turns; *fig.* the wheel of fortune turns; ❑ ми се врти во главата 1. I can't get it out of my mind 2. my head is swimming, I feel dizzy; ми се врти I feel dizzy (giddy), my head is swimming **4** *fig.* to hang around, loiter; to potter; (*се бави, се задржува*) to waste time; постојано се врти околу плоштадот he is continually hanging around the square

вртикапа *m colloq.* fickle person; turncoat

вртикуќа *m see* вртикуќник

вртикуќник -ци *m* good family man

вртикуќница *f* good home-maker (housekeeper)

вртимушка *f* **1** *dial.* top, *see* вртелешка 1 **2** *Zool.* (Sterna hirundo) common tern

вртиопашка *m* **1** *Zool.* wagtail **2** *colloq.* toady, lick-spittle

вртипоп *m Bot.* (Matricaria chamomilla) common camomile

вртка *impf dim.* **I** *of* врти I; вpткам малку пари I am saving some money **2** to splice, intertwine, interweave **II – се** *see* врти се

вртканица *f see* врткање 2

врткање *n* **1** splicing **2** staying, dallying

вртлив *adj* **1** rotating; вртлива столица swivel chair **2** *fig.* unstable, fickle

вртне *pf* вртна *aor.* **1** to swing, shake, twist, twirl **2** to strike s.o. on the neck

вртоверец -рци *m* unreliable/treacherous person

вртоглав *adj* vertiginous, dizzy, dizzying

вртоглавец -вци *m* unstable/unreliable person

вртоглавица *f* giddiness, dizziness, vertigo; ме фаќа вртоглавица I am getting dizzy; I get fits of giddiness; страда од вртоглавица he suffers from giddiness

вртоглавост *f* giddiness, dizziness

вртоперка *m & f* unreliable man/woman

вртушка *f* whirlwind; whirlpool, eddy

вруток *m* spring, rising water

вруќ *adj* hot, *see* жежок

вруќи *impf* **I** to warm, heat *trans.* **II – се** to get warm, warm up *intrans.*

вруќина *f* heat, hot weather, *see* жештина, горештина

вруќица *f* fever

вруши *pf* **I** to demolish, raze, tear down **II – се** to collapse, break up *intrans.*; се вруши танецот the dance broke up

врушува (се) *impf of* вруши (се)

врховен -вна *adj* supreme; врховен командант commander in chief; врховен суд High Court; врховна власт supreme/sovereign power

врцка *impf* **I 1** to twist, wiggle, fidget; врцка со вретеното she twists the spindle **2** *colloq.* to hedge, equivocate, beat about the bush, *colloq.* pussyfoot

<around> **3** *colloq.* (*неодговорно се однесува*) to be unreliable; to be unfaithful, play around **II – ce** to fidget, wriggle; to mince *intrans.*

врчва *f* earthen jug, jar

врша *f* creel

вршалка *f* threshing-machine

вршач *m* thresher

вршачка¹ *f* **1** (*fem. form*) *see* вршач **2** threshing-machine

вршачка² *f see* вршидба²

врши¹ *impf* to thresh

врши² *impf* to carry out, fulfil; врши должност на директор he is acting director; си ja врши работата he is doing his job; врши злосторства to commit atrocities; врши опити to conduct experiments; врши откуп to buy up; врши притисок to put (exert) pressure (*на, врз – on*)

врши³ *impf* to arrange a betrothal (engagement); стројници ja вршеа нашата ќерка за еден трговски син matchmakers were arranging our daughter's engagement to the son of a merchant's family

врши⁴ *impf* to pick the last tobacco leaves, carry out the last picking

вршидба¹ *f* **1** threshing **2** threshing time (season)

вршидба² *f* engagement, betrothal

вршина *f* chaff

вршител *m* performer, doer, executor; вршител на должноста на директор acting manager/director; вршител на работите works contractor; *Diplomacy* chargé d'affaires

вршка *f* summit, peak

вршник -ци *m* cast-iron convex lid (*on which red-hot coals are put for baking bread*); ❑ како под вршник very hot

всади *pf* **I** to plant, put in, insert; to instil, implant **II – ce** to become instilled; *fig.* to strike, take root; лош навик се има всадено во (кај) нив they have picked up a bad habit

всадува (се) *impf of* всади (се)

всали се *pf* to go bad, become rancid; путерот се всали the butter has gone rancid

всалува се *impf of* всали се

всева *impf of* всее

всее *pf* всеа *aor.* to implant, sow (*fear, hatred, etc.*)

вселена *f* universe, space

вселенски *adj* **1** space *attrib.*; вселенски брод spaceship, spacecraft **2** *Rel.* ecumenical, universal; вселенски собор ecumenical council

всели *pf* **I** to move (*s.o.*) in (*into a house, flat*), accommodate, settle *trans.* **II – ce** to move in (*into a house, flat*), settle *intrans.*

вселува (се) *impf of* всели (се)

всипе се *pf* to become covered in pox

всипува се *impf of* всипе се

вслуша се *pf* to pay attention (*во – to*); to be all ears; се вслуша во гласот на разумот to heed the voice of reason

вслушува се *impf of* вслуша се

всоне *adv* in one's sleep

встрана *adv* from one side, on one side, at the side; aside, to one side

всушност *adv* in reality, actually, as a matter of fact

втаса *pf* **I 1** (*пристигне, стигне*) to arrive; to reach *trans.*; втасавме вчера we arrived yesterday; го

втаса и го претваса he caught up with him and overtook him (*also fig.*) **2** (*стигне – only 3rd p.*) to be enough; не ми втаса брашното I ran out of flour **3** to have time (*да – to*); жена ми не втасала да го направи ручекот my wife didn't manage (have time) to make lunch **4** (*of dough*) to prove *intrans.*; to come of age, mature, ripen; лебот втаса the dough <for bread> has proved (risen); втаса за мажење she has come of age for marriage, she is ripe for marriage; втасаа лубениците the water melons are ripe; ❑ ми втасал тоj за таа работа! he's just the man for the job! (*also iron.*) **II – ce** to catch up with each other

втасан *adj* ripe; mature

втасува (се) *impf of* втаса (се)

втврдне *pf* втврдна *aor.* **I** to make hard, harden *trans.* **II – ce** to become hard, harden *intrans.*

втврднува (се) *impf of* втврдне (се)

втера *pf* **I** to drive (*во – in, into*) *trans.*; to force in, squeeze in *trans.*; to herd *trans.*; ги втера магарињата во долот he drove the donkeys into the valley **II – ce** to rush in; to push <o.s.> in, squeeze in *intrans.*; to penetrate, dig in *intrans.*; се втераа внатре they squeezed in; едно трнче ѝ се втера под ноктот a thorn had got under her nail

втерува (се) *impf of* втера (се)

втисне *pf* втисна *aor.* **I** to imprint, impress; to press (*во – in*), sink (*in*) *trans.*; децата ги втиснале своите раце во мекиот малтер the children pressed their hands into the fresh mortar **II – ce** to sink in; to dig o.s. in; to become imprinted (impressed); to squeeze (*o.s.*) in; нозете му се втиснаа во мекиот песок his feet sank into the soft sand

втиснува (се) *impf of* втисне (се); синџирите му се втиснувале во месото the chains cut into his flesh

вткае *pf* втка *aor.* to weave (*s.th. into s.th.*)

втоне *pf* втона *aor.* **1** to sink (*во – into*) *intrans.* **2.** *fig.* to become engrossed (*во – in*); втонал во мисли he became engrossed in thought

вторак -ци *m* two-year-old <child>

втораче *n colloq. hyp.* second-former (*in primary school*)

втор <и> *adj num* second; *Gram.* втор<и> падеж the genitive <case>; ❑ втора природа second nature; втори петли the second cock-crow (*just before first light*); *Rel.* второ пришествие the Second Coming, the Day of Judgement; за вторпат for the second time; *fig.* од втора рака second-hand; свири втора виолина (*also fig.*) to play second violin (fiddle); тоа прашање иде на втор план this matter is of secondary importance

вторичен -чна *adj* secondary; вторично значење secondary meaning/significance; *Gram.* вторичен акцент secondary stress/accent

вторичност *f* secondary quality

вторник -ци *m* Tuesday

вторничен -чна *adj* Tuesday *attrib.*; вторничен ден Tuesday

второкласен -сна *adj* second-class, second-best

второкласник -ци *m* second-form pupil (*Am.* student), second-former (*in high school*)

второстепен *adj* secondary; second-rate; *Med.* second-degree; второстепена пресуда appeal-court verdict; второстепена изгореница second-degree burn

вторпат *adv* <for> the second time

втренчен *pt* fixed (*gaze*)

втренчи се *pf* to fix one's gaze (*во – on*)

втренчува се *impf of* втренчи се

втресе *pf see* стресе

втресува *impf see* стресува

втрештен *pt* stricken; petrified; stunned

втрешти *pf* to strike by lightning; to blast, kill; ровја те втрештила! *curse* may lightning strike you!

втрештува *impf of* втрешти

втрча *pf* I to come running (*во – into*); to run (*во – into*); тој втрча во дворот he came running to the yard II – се to come running (*во – into*); to run (*no – after, кон, накај – towards; на – up to*); детето се втрча кон (накај) мене и ме гушна the child ran up to me and hugged me

втрчува (се) *impf of* втрча (се)

втури се *pf* to bear (*fruit*) abundantly; јаболницата се втури годинава the apple-tree had a big crop this year

втурне се *pf* втурна *aor.* to enter suddenly, rush in, burst (*во – into*); to rush (*no – at*), fall (*no – on*); to turn (*врз – on*); се втурна во собата he burst into the room; старецот се втурна врз полицаецот the old man rounded on the policeman

втурнува се *impf of* втурне се

втурува се *impf of* втури се

вудве *adv* double, twice, twice over; го свитка вудве he folded (bent) it twice (over); ❏ вудве-вутри hastily, hurriedly, in haste

вудвоса *pf* I to double; to cause to stoop; *fig.* to trounce, trample under foot II - се to bend *intrans.*; to stoop (*from old age*)

вудвосува се *impf of* вудвоса се

вујко -овци *m* 1 uncle (*mother's brother or cousin*); ❏ има вујко владика *see* владика; вујко <ми> од Америка the rich uncle 2 mosquito, gnat

вујков *adj* uncle's

вујковец -вци *m* mosquito, gnat, *see* комарец

вујна *f* aunt (*wife of mother's brother or cousin*)

вујнин *adj* aunt's

вујче -евци & вујчо -овци *m hyp. of* вујко

вулва *f Anat.* vulva, *see* срамница²

вулгарен -рна *adj* vulgar

вулгаризам -змот *m* vulgarism

вулгаризатор *m* vulgarizer

вулгаризаторски *adj* vulgarizer's, vulgarizing

вулгаризација *f* vulgarization

вулгаризира *pf & impf* to vulgarize

вулгаритет *m* & **вулгарност** *f* vulgarity

вулкан *m* volcano

вулканизам -змот *m* vulcanology, volcanology

вулканизатор *m* vulcanizer

вулканизација *f* vulcanization

вулканизира *pf & impf* to vulcanize

вулкански *adj* volcanic

вусполница *f* embroidered figures (*on the lower edge of a shirt*)

вутри *adv* treble, threefold; сплетено вутри plaited threefold

вцица *pf* to suck <in>, imbibe

вцицува *impf of* вцица

вцрвени (се) *pf see* вцрви (се)

вцрвенува (се) *impf see* вцрвува (се)

вцрви *pf* I to redden, turn red *trans.*, make (*s.th.*) turn red; to make (*s.o.*) blush; јулското сонце им ги вцрви телата на капачите the July sun reddened the bathers' bodies II – се to go red; to blush; се вцрви од срам he blushed with shame

вцрвоса се *pf* to become wormeaten

вцрвосува се *impf of* вцрвоса се

вцрвува (се) *impf of* вцрви (се)

вцрпе *pf* вцрпи *aor.* 1 (*нешто*) to scoop up, ladle 2 (*некого*) to seize, grab, get hold of

вчади *pf* I to fill with smoke *trans.* II – се to fill with smoke *intrans.*, *see* зачади (се)

вчадува (се) *impf of* вчади (се)

вчас, вчасот & вчасум *adv* suddenly, all of a sudden; at once, immediately; тој вчасот се согласи he agreed immediately

вчекани *pf* I to stop, restrain, obstruct; to petrify II – се to be frozen stiff; to be petrified

вчеканува (се) *impf of* вчекани (се)

вчепи *pf* to grab, seize

вчепка *pf* to grab, seize

вчепкува *impf of* вчепка

вчепува *impf of* вчепи

вчера *adv* yesterday; вчера напладне yesterday afternoon; ❏ не сум од вчера I wasn't born yesterday; you can't fool me

вчеравечер *adv* last night, yesterday evening

вчеранок *adv* last night

вчераутро *adv* yesterday morning

вчерашен -шна *adj* yesterday's; вчерашниот ден да не се повтори! may there never be another day like yesterday! we don't want another yesterday! ❏ не сум вчерашен I wasn't born yesterday; you can't fool me

вчудовиденост *f* 1 astonishment 2 (*непријатна*) shock, unpleasant surprise

вчудовиди *pf* to astonish, astound; (*непријатно*) to shock

вчудовидува *impf of* вчудовиди

вчудоневиди *pf see* вчудовиди

вчудоневидува *impf of* вчудоневиди, *see* вчудовидува

вчуреност *f* <state of> being filled with smoke

вчури *pf* I 1 to fill with smoke *trans.* 2 *fig.* to hit, clout, wallop; му вчури една he hit him II – се to fill with smoke *intrans.*

вчурува (се) *impf of* вчури (се)

вџасеност *f* 1 astonishment, amazement 2 flush; blush

вџаси *pf* I 1 to astonish, amaze, astound; to horrify 2 to embarrass; to fluster *trans.* II - се to blush; to be flushed

вџасува (се) *impf of* вџаси (се)

вџаши (се) *pf see* вџаси (се)

вџашува (се) *impf see* вџасува (се)

вшантрави се *pf* to become bow-legged (bandy-legged)

вшива *impf of* вшие

вшие *pf* вши *aor.* to sew on; to sew in; *fig.* to deal <a blow>; ❏ му вшив една <шлаканица> I slapped his face

вшир *adv see* нашир

— Г —

г *abbr.* (*грам*) gram, g

г. *abbr.* **1** (*година*) year **2** (*господин*) Mr

габа *f dial.* mushroom; fungus

габардѝн *m* gabardine

габардиса *pf colloq.* (*за рана*) to become inflamed; to swell; *see* збувне

габардисува *impf of* габардиса

габер -бри *m Bot.* (Carpinus betulus) hornbeam; ❑ сливи на габер grapes from thorns, figs from thistles

габерлив *adj* hornbeam

габеров *adj see* габров

габичка *n dim. of* габа

Габон *m* Gabon

Габонец -нци *m* Gabonese

Габонка *f* (*fem. form*) Gabonese

габонски *adj* Gabonese

габор *m in the expression:* како габор as ugly as sin

габрак -ци *m* hornbeam grove

габров *adj* hornbeam

гавез *m Bot.* (Symphytum officinale) comfrey

гавра *f dial. see* подбив

гавран *m Zool.* (Corvus corax) raven; ❑ кога ќе обели гавранот when pigs fly, when the sea runs dry; гавран гаврану очи не вади (копа) *prov.* there's honour among thieves;

гавранов *adj* raven's

гаври се *impf dial. see* подбива се

гага[1] *impf dial. see* гака

гага[2] *f dial.* **1** beak, bill **2** *arch.* tailor's pincers

гага[3] *adv sl.* free, gratis; ❑ нема гага! there's no such thing as a free lunch

гад *m* **1** reptile **2** repulsive animal; vermin **3** *fig.* scoundrel, monster; swine

гада *impf see* гата

гаден -дна *adj* disgusting, revolting, repulsive; mean

гади се *impf* **1** to be disgusted; се гадеа од нечистотијата they were revolted by the squalor **2** (*usu. with dat.*) to disgust; нечистотијата им се гади they are revolted by the squalor **3** *impers.* (*with dat.*) ми се гади I feel sick; I am disgusted

гадина *f see* гад

гадинка *f dim. of* гадина; гадинки vermin, pests

гадлив *adj* squeamish; гадлив на јадење choosy (fastidious) about one's food

гадливост *f* squeamishness

гадост *f* filth (*also fig.*), muck; vileness; vile behaviour; foul language; meanness

гадотија *f* **1** *see* гадост **2** *fig.* repulsive woman

гадулар *m* rebec<k> player

гадулица *f see* гадулка

гадулка *f* rebec<k> (*folk string instrument played with a bow*)

гадурија *f dial. see* гадотија

гаѓа *impf* **I** (*trans. or with во or со*) to aim (*at*), fire (*at*), shoot (*at*); артилеријата го гаѓаше градот the artillery was shelling the town; тој гаѓа во мене he is shooting at me; гаѓа со камења (*по, во*) to throw stones (*at*) **II** - се to aim (shoot, fire) at one another

гаѓач *m* marksman; gunner; gun-layer

газ *m colloq./vulg.* backside, behind, bum, *Brit.* arse, *Am.* ass; ❑ валкан му е газот he has dirty hands; газ преку глава head over heels; лиже некому газ to lick s.o.'s arse; мрдни го газот shake a leg! get moving! *Am.* move your ass! не му држи газот to have no guts; to show the white feather; паѓа на газ to be taken aback; седи мадро на газот **1.** sit still and keep quiet! **2.** let sleeping dogs lie; газ и газ е со некого to be like Siamese twins; како да е в газ правен to have the devil's luck; толкав му е газот to have an itching palm; спасува газ to save one's bacon; бесен газ, крвава нос *prov.* (*said to a naughty child*) be careful or you'll hurt yourself/get into trouble!

газа *f* gauze; стерилна газа sterile gauze

газалиште & газало *n* ford, shallow water, shallow place

газда *m* **1** (*чорбаџија*) rich man **2** (*стопан*) master; landlord, owner, proprietor; ❑ покажува кој е газда to show who's the boss; свој газда one's own boss; self-employed

газдарица *f* mistress, proprietress

газѐла *f Zool.* gazelle

газен -зна *adj* of the buttocks; gluteal; газно црево rectum

газер *m* bottom (*of a vessel*)

газета *f* **1** gazette **2** copper coins

газечки *adv colloq.* backwards, back; падне газечки to fall backwards (on one's bottom)

гази *impf* **1** (*trans. or на*) to tread, step <on>; walk, trample <on> (*also fig.*); не гази ја тревата keep off the grass! гази нечии права to trample upon s.o.'s rights; ❑ ќе го гази мечка he'll be in bad trouble; ми гази на лебот he meddles in my affairs **2** (*trans. or по*) to wade through, trudge through; (*река*) to ford; гази снег/вода to be knee-deep in snow/water **3** *trans.* (*of birds*) to tread, copulate with, mate with **4** *colloq.* to walk; гази како мечка he walks like a bear

газија *f colloq. see* гас[2], петролеј

газѝра *pf & impf* **1** to bandage with gauze **2** to carbonate, impregnate with carbon dioxide

газѝран *adj & pt* carbonated, aerated, *colloq.* fizzy

газне *pf* газна *aor. see* гази

газник -ци *m* **1** *see* газ, задник **2** rectum

газо̀за *f arch.* lemonade, fizzy drink

газолѝн *m Chem.* gasoline

газометар *m see* гасометар

гајба *f* **1** crate, wooden box **2** cage, chicken coop

гајгур *m* **1** *arch. Zool.* (Struthio camelus) ostrich, *see* ној; ❑ нѐ од гајгур јајце you won't get anything from me; се запулил како гајгур he started staring like an idiot **2** *fig.* sick/sickly (delicate) person

гајгуров *adj* ostrich, ostrich's; ❑ чува како гајгурово јајце to cherish

гајда *f* bagpipes; ❑ ја надуу гајдата he burst into

tears; се готви да ја дувне гајдата he is about to burst into tears; не му оди на гајдата it doesn't suit him; гајда куќа не храни *prov.* of idleness comes no goodness

гајдар *m* bagpipe player, piper

гајдарски *adj* bagpipe *attrib.*; piper's

гајдаџија -ии *m see* гајдар

гајдуница *f* reed (*in bagpipes*)

гајка *f* loop (*on a belt*)

гајле *n colloq.* care, worry, *see* грижа; немај (не бери) гајле don't worry! *Austral.* no worries! нема гајле it's nothing to worry about; he'll manage; му го бере гајлето he's looking after him; he worries about him; баш ми е гајле I don't care! I don't give a damn! I couldn't care less! не му е гајле за ... he cares nothing for ...

гајлелија *adj indecl. colloq.* worried, depressed; irritable

гајрет *m colloq.* 1 solicitude, care, concern; help, aid; zeal 2 courage, fortitude, stoicism; <чини> гајрет! take courage!

гајтан *m* cord; galloon, braid; *f.p.* гајтан веѓи arched eyebrows

гак *m* cackling, quacking

гака *impf* (*за гуска*) to cackle

гакне[1] *pf* гакна *aor.* to quack

гакне[2] *pf* гакна *aor. trans.* to knock (*s.o.*) to the ground

гакнува[1] *impf of* гакне[1]

гакнува[2] *impf of* гакне[2]

гала *adj indecl.* gala, grand; (*only in combination with certain nouns*) гала-вечера gala evening; gala dinner; гала-претстава gala performance

галаб *m dial. see* гулаб

галабар *m dial. see* гулабар

галаксија & галактика *f* galaxy

галактички *adj* galactic; галактички систем galaxy

галактометар -три *m* lactometer

галант *m* fine gentleman; gallant, ladies' man

гала́нтен -тна *adj* gallant, attentive (*to women*); polite, civil, courtly

галантерија *f* haberdashery; кожна галантерија leather goods

галантериски *adj* haberdashery *attrib.*; галантериска стока haberdashery

гала́нтност *f* gallantry

галатен -тна *adj dial.* 1 dirty 2 indecent; corrupt; ❑ галатен во устата foul-mouthed

галвани́зам -змот *m* galvanism

галванизација *f* galvanization

галванизи́ра *pf & impf* to galvanize

галваноме́тар -три *m Phys.* galvanometer

галванопластика *f Tech.* galvanoplasty

галвански *adj* galvanic, voltaic; сув галвански елемент dry pile (battery); галванска батерија galvanic pile; галванска струја, галвански електрицитет galvanic (direct) <electric> current

галеб *m Zool.* seagull

галебов *adj* seagull's

галежен -жна *adj* tender, gentle; dear, sweet, lovable

галежно *adv* tenderly, gently, sweetly

галежност *f* tenderness, gentleness, sweetness

гален *adj & pt* favourite, pet; галено име pet name; галено дете favourite child; spoilt child

галеник -ци *m* favourite, pet

галеница *f* (*fem. form*) *see* галеник

галениче *n hyp. of* галеник

галено *adv see* галежно

галерија -ии *f* gallery; галерија на слики picture gallery; галерија во рудник gallery in a mine; (*во театар*) прва галерија dress circle, balcony

гали *impf* I to caress, pet; to fondle; (*обично деца*) to spoil *trans.*, pamper, mollycoddle; што го галиш? why do you spoil him? II – се to pet/fondle each other

галиба *adv colloq.* most likely, very probably, *see* веројатно

галија *f Hist.* galley; ропска галија slave galley

галиматијас *m* galimatias, rigmarole

галици́зам -зми *m* Gallicism

галичанец -ни *m* person from Galichnik

галичанка *f* (*fem. form*) *see* галичанец

галички *adj* Galichnik *attrib.*

Галичник *m* Galichnik

галовен -вна *adj rare see* галежен

галовност *f rare see* галежност

галон *m* gallon

галоп *m* gallop; трча во галоп to gallop

галопи́ра *impf* to gallop

галопирачки *adj* galloping; *Med.* галопирачка туберкулоза galloping consumption

гало́ш *m* galosh

гама *f* 1 gamma; гама-зраци *Phys.* gamma-rays 2 *Mus.* scale, gamut; свири гама to play/practise scales; гама Ц-дур scale of C major 3 *Painting* palette, spectrum 4 *fig.* gamut, range; цела гама на чувства whole range of emotions

гамаши *pl* gaiters; leggings; spats; cf. тозлуци

Гамбиец -јци *m* Gambian

Гамбија *f* Gambia

Гамбијка *f* (*fem. form*) *see* Гамбиец

гамбиски *adj* Gambian

гамбит *m Chess* gambit

гамен *m* street urchin, guttersnipe, street arab

гаменски *adj* urchin's, urchin-like

Гана *f* Ghana

ганглија *f Anat.* ganglion (*also fig.*)

ганголи *impf* to talk through the nose; to mumble; to talk with a nasal twang

ганголив *adj* snuffling, mumbling; nasal

гангре́на *f Med.* gangrene

гангрено́зен -зна *adj* gangrenous

гангстер *m* gangster

гангстерски *adj* gangster

Ганец -нци *m* Ghanaian

ганса се *impf* to stagger, waddle; to drag o.s. along, dawdle

гансало *n* 1 person who staggers 2 sluggard

ганслив *adj* 1 staggering 2 sluggish, slow

Ганка *f* (*fem. form*) *see* Ганец

гански *adj* Ghanaian

ганц *adv colloq.* completely; ганц нова облека completely new clothes

гара́жа *f* garage

гара́нт *m* guarantor, guarantee

гара́нтен -тна *adj* <of> guarantee, warranty; гарантен лист written warranty

гаранти́ра *pf & impf* to guarantee, vouch (*за – for*)

гаранција -ии *f* guarantee, warranty; гаранција за лична сигурност safe-conduct; под гаранција under warranty; двогодишна гаранција two-year warranty

гаргара *f* gargle, gargling; прави гаргара to gargle

гарда *f* guard; телесна гарда body guard; *fig.* стара гарда the old guard

гарденија *f Bot.* (Gardenia florida) gardenia, cape jasmine

гардероба *f* **1** (*во театар и др.*) cloakroom, *Am.* checkroom; (*на артист*) dressing-room, make-up room **2** wardrobe, <collection of> clothes **3** (*орман*) wardrobe, cupboard **4** (*на станица*) left-luggage office

гардеробер *m* cloakroom attendant

гардероберка *f* (*fem. form*) *see* гардеробер

гардиски *adj* guard *attrib.*; гардиски полк guards regiment

гардист *m* **1** guardsman, member of an elite guard **2** guard; escort

гарез *m colloq.* quarrel, malice, hatred, grudge; има гарез на него he has a grudge against him, he resents him

гарнизон *m Mil.* garrison

гарнизонски *adj* garrison *attrib.*; гарнизонско место place where soldiers are garrisoned; garrison town

гарнир *m Cul.* garnish; гарнир од зеленчук vegetables

гарнира *pf & impf* **1** *Cul.* to garnish **2** *fig.* to embellish, decorate

гарнитура *f* **1** set; <tool> kit; гарнитура за ручање dinner set; гарнитура шестари pair of compasses **2** suite; гарнитура за седење lounge suite **3** (*луѓе*) set; class; раководна гарнитура leading cadres

гаро[1] -овци *m dial. Zool.* cormorant

гаро[2] *n dial.* custom of lighting fires at carnival time

гарсониера *f* bachelor's flat, *Brit.* bed-sitting-room, *colloq.* bed-sitter, *Am.* one-room apartment

гас[1] *m* gas; отровен гас poison gas; ❑ дава гас to speed off; to take to one's heels; to speed up, step on it; под гас tipsy; под полн гас at full tilt/pelt; flat out; гасови flatulence, wind

гас[2] *m* lamp-oil

гас-генератор *m Tech.* gas generator

гасен[1] *adj & pt* slaked; гасена вар slaked lime

гасен[2] -сна *adj* gas; гасно осветление gaslight; гасна маска gas mask

гасеница *f* **1** *Zool.* caterpillar **2** (*на трактор, тенк*) caterpillar tracks

гасеничав *adj* (*of plant, tree, etc.*) infested with caterpillars

гасеничен -чна *adj* caterpillar's

гаси *impf* **I** to put out, douse, extinguish; ❑ гаси вар to slake lime; гаси жед to quench one's thirst; тој пали, тој гаси he rules the roost, he's the boss **II – ce** *see* гасне I 1 & 3

гасилка *f &* **гасилник** -ци *m see* гасило

гасило *n* extinguisher

гасификација *f* **1** gasification; гасификација на јаглен gasification of coal **2** installation of gas fittings; supply of gas

гас-маска *f* gas mask

гасне *impf* **I** **1** (*за оган, светло*) to go out, die down **2** *trans.* to put out, extinguish **3** *fig.* to fade, weaken,

ebb; гасне неговиот живот his life is ebbing **II - ce** *see* I 1

гасовит *adj* gaseous; гасовита состојба gaseous state

гасовод *m* gas pipe, gas main

гасометар -три *m* gas meter

гастарбајтер *m* migrant worker, Gastarbeiter

гастрит <ис> *m Med.* gastritis

гастроном *m* gourmet, epicure

гастрономија *m* gastronomy

гастроскоп *m* gastroscope

гастроскопија *f Med.* gastroscopy

гата *impf* to tell fortunes; *fig.* to guess

гаталец -лци *m* sorcerer; не прашај гаталец, туку паталец *prov.* experience is the mother of wisdom

гаталка *f* fortune teller

гатанка *f* riddle, puzzle; *fig.* тој е сиот гатанка he's a complete mystery

гатер *m* power saw

гатерист *m* power-saw operator

гатка[1] *impf dim.* to dabble in fortune telling

гатка[2] *f* **1** story, tale, fable, myth **2** riddle

гатка[3] *f see* гадинка

гатне *pf* гатна *aor.* to announce, indicate, predict, *see* загатне

гаќар *m* pigeon or rooster with feathered legs

гаќарест *adj* feather-footed; *fig.* bare, lightly clothed

гаќарка *f* hen with feathered legs

гаќи *pl* **1** <under>pants, *Am.* shorts; (*женски*) panties, knickers; ❑ *colloq., joc.* жити гаќите! well I never! upon my soul! му се запалиле гаќите he's got the wind up, he is in trouble; останува <и> без гаќи to lose everything; полни гаќи to be scared stiff (*vulg.* shitless); to shiver in one's boots/shoes **2** *colloq.* trousers, *Am.* pants **3** pantaloons (*worn by Muslim and Gypsy women*) **4** *Zool.* leg feathers

гаќички *pl* **1** *dim.* of гаќи **2** shorts, swimming trunks

гаќник -ци *m* cord, waistband (*of shorts, swimming trunks*)

Гвајана *f* Guyana

Гвајанец -нци *m* Guyanese

Гвајанка *f* (*fem. form*) *see* Гвајанец

гвајански *adj* Guyanese

Гватемала *f* Guatemala

Гватемалец -лци *m* Guatemalan

Гватемалка *f* (*fem. form*) *see* Гватемалец

гватемалски *adj* Guatemalan

гваца *impf* (*trans. or низ, по*) to wade (*in water, mud*); to trudge (*through snow*)

Гвинеец -јци *m* Guinean

гвинеја[1] *f* **1** *Brit. Hist.* guinea **2** kind of fever

Гвинеја[2] *f* Guinea

Гвинеја Бисау *f* Guinea-Bissau

Гвинејка *f* (*fem. form*) *see* Гвинеец

гвинејски *adj* Guinean

гвинт *m* screw

г-ѓа *abbr.* (*госпоѓа*) Mrs; Ms

гевер *m* machine gun

гега[1] <ce> *impf dial.* to stagger, *see* ганса се

гега[2] *f* shepherd's staff, crook

гегав *adj dial.* bow-legged, bandy-legged

гејзир *m* geyser

гејзирски *adj* geyser *attrib.*

рејша *f* geisha

гелендер *m* railing, handrail, banister, balustrade

гем *m Tennis* game

гемија -ии *f arch.* (*see* лаѓа) boat, vessel, ship; ❑ му пропаднале гемиите he's down in the dumps, he's feeling low

гемиџија -ии *m arch.* (*лаѓар*) boatman, ferryman, mariner

ген *m* gene

генеалогија *f* genealogy

генеалóшки *adj* genealogical

генéза *f* genesis

генерáл *m Mil.* general; генерал-мајор major-general; генерал на армија army commander

генерáлен -лна *adj* general, common, main; генерален директор director general; генерална проба dress rehearsal

генерализација -ии *f* generalization

генерализѝра *pf & impf* to generalize, *see* обопшти, обопштува

генералии *pl* personal details (particulars)

генералисимус *m* generalissimo

генералитéт *m coll.* the generals

генералка *f* **1** dress rehearsal **2** comprehensive map **3** overhaul, major service (*of engine, etc.*)

генерáлски *adj* general's

генералштáб *m* general staff

генералштáбен -бна *adj* staff; генералштабен офицер officer of general staff

генератѝвен -вна *adj* generative

генерáтор *m Tech.* generator

генерација -ии *f* generation, *see* поколение; ❑ јаз меѓу генерации generation gap

генерѝра *pf & impf* to generate

генеричен -чна *adj* generic

генетика *f Biol.* genetics

генетички *adj Biol.* genetic; генетички инженеринг genetic engineering

генѝј -ии *m* genius

генијáлен -лна *adj* of genius, brilliant; генијален поет a poet of genius; генијална творба a work of genius

генитáлен -лна *adj* genital

гениталии *pl* genitals

генитив *m Gram.* genitive

геноцѝд *m* genocide

геноцѝден -дна *adj* genocidal

географ *m* geographer

географија *f* geography; физичка географија physical geography

географски *adj* geographical; географска должина и ширина (широчина) geographical longitude and latitude

геодезија *f* geodesy, surveying

геодéт *m* geodesist, surveyor

геодéтски *adj* geodesic

геолóг -зи *m* geologist

геологија *f* geology

геолóшки *adj* geological; геолошка ера geological era (age); геолошки завод geological institute

геомéтар -три *m* surveyor

геометрија *f* geometry

геометриски *adj* geometric<al>; геометриско тело geometrical body

георгѝна *f Bot. see* ѓурѓина

геофизика *f* geophysics

геофизичар *m* geophysicist

геофизички *adj* geophysical

гепек *m* **1** baggage, luggage **2** (*на автомобил*) boot, *Am.* trunk

геријатрија *f* geriatrics

герила *f* guerilla warfare

герилец -лци *m* guerrilla

герилски *adj* guerrilla *attrib.*; герилска борба guerrilla warfare

Германец -нци *m* German

Германи *pl* Germanic tribes; Germanic peoples

германизација *f* Germanization

германизѝра *pf & impf* to Germanize

Германија *f* Germany

германѝст *m* Germanist

германистика *f* German studies; Germanic studies/ philology

Германка *f* (*fem. form*) *see* Германец

германофѝл *m* Germanophil<e>

германски *adj* German

гесло *n* motto, slogan, watchword; parole, password

гест *m* gesture; убав гест fine gesture; гест на добра волја a sign (gesture) of goodwill

Гестáпо *n* Gestapo

гестаповец -вци *m* member of the Gestapo

гестикулација *f* gesticulation

гестикулѝра *impf* to gesticulate

гети *pl* gaiters

гето *n* ghetto

ги *pron* (*short acc. form of* тие) them; ги видов I saw them

гиба *impf* **I 1** to touch; to feel **2** *fig.* to harass; to tease, bait, bully; to bother; не гибај го! don't tease him! leave him alone! **3** to poke about (*во – in*); гиба некому во џебови to rifle s.o.'s pockets **II - ce 1** to tease one another **2** to touch one another

гибач *m* (*задорица*) tease, teaser

гибел *f* ruin, destruction, disaster, catastrophe

гибелен -лна *adj* ruinous, catastrophic, disastrous

гибне *pf* гибна *aor.* **1** to touch **2** *fig.* to tease; to bait; ❑ без да го гибнеш фитилот, се запали he has a short fuse

гибнува *impf* of гибне

гибóн *m Zool.* (Hylobates) gibbon

Гибралтар *m* Gibraltar

гибралтарски *adj* Gibraltarian

гигáнт *m* giant

гигáнтски *adj* gigantic

гиди *interj colloq.* (*expressing reproach, regret, etc.*) alas! alack! бре гиди! my God!

гидија -ии *m arch.* **1** daring person **2** mischievous person

гиздав *adj* pretty, beautiful, elegant; glorious; gaudy, flamboyant, ornate

гиздавец -вци *m* dandy, fop

гиздавина *f see* гиздавост

гиздавица *f* showy (gaudily dressed) woman

гиздавост *f* elegance, grace, beauty

гизди *impf* **I** to adorn, decorate; to adorn gaudily (showily), overdress **II – ce** to dress up gaudily; to overdress; to adorn each other

Гијáна *f* <French> Guiana

Гијанец -нци *m* Guianese, Guianan

Гијанка   *f* (*fem. form*) *see* Гијанец
гијански   *adj* Guianese, Guianan
гилотина   *f* guillotine
гилотини́ра   *pf & impf* to guillotine
гимназија   -ии *f* secondary school, high school
гимназија́лен   -лна *adj see* гимназиски
гимназија́лец   -лци *m see* гимназист
гимназија́лка   *f see* гимазистка
гимназиски   *adj* secondary-school, high-school
гимнази́ст   *m* secondary-school (high-school) pupil
гимнази́стка   *f* (*fem. form*) *see* гимназист
гимнастика   *f* gymnastics
гимнастици́ра   *impf* to do gymnastics
гимнастичар   *m* gymnast
гимнастичарка   *f* (*fem. form*) *see* гимнастичар
гимнастички   *adj* gymnastic; gymnastics
гина́чка   *f colloq.* 1 death, destruction, ruin 2 loss
гинѓер   *m Bot.* (Notobasis syriaca) variety of thistle
гине   *impf* 1 to perish 2 (*се губи*) to be lost; to disappear; ❑ не ти гине you're in for it; you've had it; црвена аспра не гине *prov.* the more wicked, the more lucky; the more knave, the better luck 3 to lose *trans.*; многу работи гине he's always losing things
гинеа́чка   *f* waste of time
гинее   *impf* to waste time; многу се гинее од ова чекање a lot of time is wasted because of this waiting
гинеж   *m see* гинење; гинеж на месечината the waning of the moon
гинеколо́г   -зи *m* gynaecologist
гинекологија   *f Med.* gynaecology
гинеколо́шки   *adj* gynaecological
гинење   *n* 1 waning 2 loss; death
гипс   *m* gypsum; plaster of Paris
гипсен   *adj* of gypsum; plaster of Paris
гипси́ра   *pf & impf* to plaster, cover with plaster of Paris
гирла́нда   *f* garland, wreath
гита́ра   *f* guitar
гитари́ст   *m* guitarist, guitar-player
глава   *f* 1 head; ме удри по глава he hit me on the head; ме боли главата I have a headache; ❑ мртовечка глава death's head; skull and crossbones; од глава до петици from head to foot; обеси глава to hang one's head; каде му очи таму му и глава he follows his nose, he acts without thinking; со наведната глава on bended knee; наведне глава to hang one's head <in shame>; врти глава to turn one's head; одмавнува со глава to shake one's head; има покрив над глава to have a roof over one's head; горе главата! chin up! courage! крева глава to rebel; не крева глава од работа to have one's hands full, be up to one's ears in work; to keep one's nose to the grindstone; крене глава to become conceited, get above o.s.; зафатен е преку глава со to be up to the ears in (*s. th.*); ја дига главата (*се однесува надмено*) to be overbearing; to hold one's head high; (*се осмелува*) to show one's teeth; to make bold; (*си дава оддишка, здивнува*) to take a break; главата ми е како тапан I have a splitting headache; се фаќа за глава to put one's hand to one's head, clutch one's brow (*in horror, amazement*), *colloq.* be flabbergasted; to be at one's wits' end; никого не го боли главата за (од) тоа no one is any the worse for it; се качува некому на глава to get s.o. thoroughly annoyed, get

on s.o.'s nerves; си зема беља на глава to bring trouble on o.s.; имало глава да пати it was fated to be like this; по врага му глава! to hell with him! крши глава! get lost! *vulg.* bugger off! нека крши глава! good riddance! to hell with him/it! оган му гори на глава he's in great trouble; ми пука главата (*од грижи, работа и сл.*) my head is bursting (*with worry, with jobs to do, etc.*); (*од болка*) I have a splitting headache; му дојде ум в глава he's got some sense into his head; му дојде (се зби) на глава he's had some very bad luck; не се излегува со него на глава no one can cope with him; отсечена глава spitting image, carbon copy; му ја скинал главата на татка си he's the spitting image of his father; како мува без глава hysterical<ly>, like a headless chicken; празна му е главата he has nothing between his ears; преку глава му е од to have a bellyful of; (*in response to good wishes*) и на твоја (ваша) глава! and the same to you! си ја чука (удира) главата в зид to bang (knock) one's head against a brick wall; со глава сид не се турка *prov.* it's no use banging your head against a brick wall; рибата смрди од главата *prov.* fish begins to stink at the head 2 brains, mind, sense (*in certain expressions*); бистра глава lucid mind, bright intellect; clear-headed person; машка глава breadwinner; man of the house; *colloq.* оваа глава не е за две нозе smarty-pants, *Am. colloq.* wise guy; губи глава to lose one's head (*colloq.* cool); to go out of one's mind; to lose one's life; (*се вљуби*) to fall head over heels in love; бута глава во песок to bury one's head in the sand; му сече главата he has a fine brain, he is sharp-witted; мене вака ми сече главата I understand it like this; I think you should . . .; не ми влегува во главата I don't (can't) understand it, it beats me, it's beyond me; дебела глава thickhead; букова (дрвена) глава blockhead; obstinate (pig-headed) person, mule; лукова глава nonentity, nobody; луда глава madcap; умна глава sensible person; бела глава wise (experienced) person; на своја глава 1. on one's own account 2. on one's own head; мисли со своја глава to use one's brains; не знам кај ми е главата I don't know whether I'm coming or going; му се врти главата he is feeling giddy; таа му ја заврти главата she's turned his head; му настинала главата he's become senile; главата му бучи he's hearing noises; си ја чука (удира, тепа, бие) главата to rack one's brains (*about s.th.*); му мина низ главата 1. it occurred to him 2. it went over his head; му ја наполни главата на некого to drive (hammer, knock) (*s.th.*) into s.o.'s head; to put a flea in s.o.'s ear; to brainwash s.o.; избива некому од глава to knock s.th. out of s.o.'s head; мирна да му е главата just to be on the safe side; види му глава, кррој му капа *prov.* the mind is the man; за таква глава – таков брич *prov.* serves him right! колку пријатели толку глави *prov.* the land is never void of counsellors; кој нема во главата, има во нозете *prov.* little wit makes much travel 3 *fig.* life (*in certain expressions*); ќе летаат глави heads will roll; ја спаси главата he saved his skin (neck); извлече жива глава to get out of harm's way; to have a narrow escape, *colloq.* have a close shave; ни за жива глава not on your life; губи глава to lose one's life; клава (става) глава в торба; става глава на коцка to risk one's neck (life), stick one's neck out; to tempt fate; плати со главата to pay with one's life; тоа му ја скина главата it cost him his life; доаѓа некому до глава to seal s.o.'s fate, be the death of s.o., cook s.o.'s goose; главата е во прашање it's a matter of life and death; it's touch and go; глава <од рамена> давам I swear by my very life **4** *fig.* head; leader; глава на семејството head of the family; breadwinner; глава на движењето leader of the movement **5** (*на монета*) head; ❑ глава или писмо heads or tails **6** head; *Mech.* headstock; chuck; глава на шајка head of a nail **7** bulb; глава лук a bulb of garlic; глава кромид an onion **8** (*извор*) source; headwaters; upper reaches; главата на Вардар the source of the Vardar **9** (*во книга*) chapter **10** (*на писмо*) letterhead; (*на весник*) masthead **11** head (*of cattle*); илјада глави добиток a thousand head of cattle **12** head of water (*in a river*), torrent (*after heavy rain*)

главар *m* chief, head, superior

глават *adj* big-headed

главатар *m* chief, head; leader, boss

главатарка *f* (*fem. form*) *see* главатар

главеж *m arch.* (cf. глави I) hiring contract, labouring contract; indenture

главен -вна *adj* chief, main; главен град capital; поминува на главното to get down to business; to get down to brass tacks

главеник -ци *m arch.* servant, hired workman

главеница *f* (*fem. form*) *see* главеник

главечки *adv* headlong, head first; hastily, right away

главешина *m* chief, boss; ringleader

глави *pf* **I** to employ, hire, take on (*for a certain period*); to put to work **II** – се to take work, go into service (*кај – with*), enter service (*with*); се главил <за> овчар he took work as a shepherd

главина *f* **1** hub, nave **2** grapevine **3** decoration on bridal dress

главица *f* **1** *dim. of* глава; бистра водица – мирна главица *prov.* Adam's ale is the best brew; кој прави палица – за своја главица *prov.* he who does evil does it to himself **2** bulb; главица лук bulb (nob, corm) of garlic

главичка *f dim. see* главица; главичка на игла pinhead

главник -ци *m* **1** master of the house, head of the family **2** leader (*e.g. in a children's game*) **3** (*оглав*) headstall **4** (*главина*) hub **5** bottom band (hoop) (*on a vat, cask*); wooden stopper, bung

главнина *f* **1** major part **2** *Mil.* main force

главница *f Comm.* capital, funds; principal; главница и каматата principal and interest

главно *adv* chiefly, mainly, mostly

главоболие -ија *n* **1** headache **2** *fig.* (*usu. pl*) worries, difficulties, headaches; со него имам многу главоболија I have a lot of trouble with him

главоболица *f see* главоболие

главоног *adj Zool.* cephalopod; главоноги животни (Cephalopoda) cephalopods

главорез & **главосек** -ци *m* executioner; *fig.* cut-throat, thug, butcher

главува (се) *impf of* глави (се)

главуш *m* large-headed; *Anthropology* macrocephalic person

глагол *m* **1** *Gram.* verb **2** *dial.* speech; му се зел глаголот he has lost his tongue

глаголаш *m literary* Croatian Catholic priest who uses the Glagolitic missal

глаголи *impf* **1** *dial.* to babble; не туку глаголи! stop babbling! **2** *literary* to administer mass from the Glagolitic missal

глаголив *adj* talkative, garrulous, loquacious

глаголица *f* Glagolitic <script>

глаголски *adj* **1** *Gram.* verbal **2** *literary* Glagolitic

глаголствува *impf see* глаголи

глад *m* hunger; famine; starvation; ❑ умирам од глад I am dying of hunger, I am terribly hungry; глад за земја hunger for land; штрајкува со глад to be on hunger strike

гладен -дна *adj* hungry; (*многу*) famished, starving, ravenous; гладна смрт death from starvation; гладна година a lean year; ❑ *joc.* тој е гладна година he has a huge appetite; на гладно срце on an empty stomach; *fig.* unintentionally; unexpectedly; гладен како пес hungry as a hunter

глади *impf* **1** to smooth <out> *trans.* **2** to stroke, pet; ѝ ја гладеше косата he stroked her hair **3** to whet, grind, sharpen

гладија *f* famine

гладија́тор *m Hist.* gladiator

гладијаторски *adj Hist.* gladiatorial

гладило *n* grindstone, whetstone, hone

гладио́ла *f Bot.* gladiolus

гладник -ци *m* **1** hungry person **2** greedy person, glutton

гладница *f* (*fem. form*) *see* гладник

гладок -тка *adj* smooth, even, *see* мазен

гладост *f* **1** hunger; starvation **2** greed

гладува *impf* **1** to be hungry, hunger, go hungry; to starve **2** to fast

глазира *pf & impf* to glaze; (*торта*) to ice

глазу́ра *f* glaze; (*торта*) icing

гламна[1] *f* burnt (charred) log; firebrand; burnt/smouldering brand; ❑ како гламна се сторил he has become wizened <with age>, he's a shadow of his former self

гламна[2] *f* (Ustilago and Tilletia levis) blight, rust, smut

гламноса *pf* (*за жито*) to be affected by blight (rust)

гламноса се *pf fig.* to turn black; to grow old (*од тага, грижи и сл. – from sorrow, worries, etc.*)

гламносува *impf of* гламноса

гламносува се *impf fig. of* гламноса се

гланц *f colloq.* shine, polish

гланца *impf* to polish, shine *trans.*

глас *m* **1** voice; загуби глас to lose one's voice; глас на совеста voice of conscience; ❑ вика колку глас го држи he's yelling at the top of his voice; крева глас против to raise one's voice against, to speak out against; на глас чита to read aloud; во еден глас with one voice, unanimously; му се слуша гласот he makes his voice heard **2** *Phon.* sound; наука за гласовите phonetics **3** rumour; новост; го бие глас he is rumoured to have ... (to be ...); се пушти глас word spread; се шират (кружат) гласови there are rumours; rumour has it that ...; people say that ...; донесе глас to bring news **4** reputation; ужива добар глас to have (enjoy) a good reputation; стекнува глас to gain fame; стекнува лош глас to fall into disrepute; to acquire a bad name; со светски глас world-famous; of world fame/renown **5** (*бирачки глас*) vote; право на глас <right to> vote, suffrage, franchise; важечки/неважечки глас valid/invalid (spoilt) vote

гласа *impf* **1** *intrans.* to vote; гласа за/против to vote for/against **2** *trans.* (*избира*) to elect

гласање *n from* гласа; тајно гласање secret ballot; гласање со кревање на рака to vote by show of hands; ❏ става на гласање to put to the vote

гласач *m* voter

гласачки *adj* voting, ballot, polling *attrib.*; гласачка кутија ballot box; гласачко место polling station; гласачко ливче ballot paper; гласачки список list of candidates

гласеж *m* **1** sound of voices; voice; cry **2** *Gram.* pronunciation

гласен -сна *adj* **1** audible, clear; гласно читање reading aloud **2** *Phon., Anat.* vocal; гласни жици (струни) vocal cords

гласи[1] *impf* **I 1** *trans.* to call <loudly> **2** to give voice (*to*); гласи песна to sing a song; глас гласи a voice is heard **3** to announce, publicize **II – се 1** to cry out **2** to resound, ring out; се гласи песна a song can be heard

гласи[2] *impf* (*only in 3rd p.*) to say, be worded, run; законов гласи <дека> . . . this law states that . . . ; насловот на романот гласи . . . the title of the novel is . . .

гласи[3] *impf arch.* to tune (*an instrument*), *see* штима

гласилка *f* vocal cord

гласило *n* press organ

гласина *f* rumour; се пушти гласина word spread

гласник -ци *m* messenger, herald

гласно *adv* loudly; aloud; ❏ доволно гласно да ги разбуди и мртвите loud enough to wake the dead

гласноговорник -ци *m* loudspeaker, megaphone, loud hailer; *fig.* mouthpiece

гласност *f* **1** audibility, volume **2** *Phon.* vocality **3** *glasnost*, publicity; openness (*in public affairs*)

гласовен -вна *adj* **1** *Phon.* of sounds, phonetic; гласовен закон sound law **2** *f.p. see* гласовит 2

гласовит *adj* **1** loud-voiced, vociferous, loud-mouthed **2** *f.p.* with a beautiful (good, strong) voice; (*за песна*) melodious

гласом & гласум *adv f.p.* loudly; aloud

гласче *n dim. of* глас

глатко *adv* smoothly, easily, without difficulty; fluently

глаукóма *f Med.* glaucoma

глед *m* **1** look; на глед in appearance; from the look of it **2** *dial.* sight, eyesight **3** *poet.* view; *f.p.* широко море глед нема the eye cannot take in the wide sea

гледа *impf* **I 1** to look; to look (*на, во – at*); to regard; to watch, see; гледа филм to watch a film; гледа поинаку на нешто to take a different view of s.th., to regard s.th. differently; ❏ гледа од високо to look down (*on*); гледа накриво (напреку) to look askance (*at*); гледа низ прсти to be lenient, turn a blind eye; гледа некого бело to look straight through s.o.; гледа од под очи (веѓи) to look furtively (*at*); гледа некого во очите to read s.o. like a book; гледа

некого право в очи to look s.o. in the eye; гледа со добро/друго око на нешто to look with favour on s.th.; to look on s.th. with different eyes; гледа како вол (теле) to gape; ни го гледа ќефот to enjoy life; not to worry; гледај си ја работата! 1. don't worry! 2. mind your own business! кој ти гледа what does that matter? гледа дупло to see double; како што гледаш as you <can> see; гледа од некого to take one's cue from s.o. **2** to see; без очила не гледам I can't see without glasses; ❏ очи до кај ти гледаат as far as the eye can see; не го гледа валмото, го гледа влакното he can't see the wood for the trees; сега гледам дека си бил прав now I see you were right **3** to be careful, watch out, look out, mind; to look after; гледај да не паднеш mind you don't fall! гледа болни to care for the sick; гледа само за себе to look after number one; ❏ ја гледа како црвено јајце he looks after her like the apple of his eye; he mollycoddles her **4** to try, strive; луѓето гледаа да му поможат people tried to help him **5** to face, look out (*на, кон – on*), give (*on*); прозорецот гледа на исток the window faces east; прозорецот гледа на бавчата the window gives on to the garden **6** (*на карти, кафе и др.*) to tell fortunes; to read the cards; to read s.o.'s palm **II – се 1** to look at o.s.; to look at one another **2** to meet, see one another; често се гледаме на улица we often meet in the street **3** *impers.* it is obvious; се гледа дека е болен it's clear that he is ill; ❏ не се гледа прст пред око I can't see a thing **4** *impers.* (*with dat.*) it seems, I think; ми се гледа дека нема да успее I don't think it will work **5** (*with dat.*) to appear, look; како ви се гледам? how do I look to you?

гледалиште *n* auditorium

гледан *adj & pt* cared for, cherished; гледано дете cherished child

гледање *n from* гледа; до гледање! goodbye! *au revoir!* see you! не е баш <многу> за гледање not much to look at

гледач *m* **1** spectator, viewer **2** fortune-teller, soothsayer

гледачка *f* (*fem. form*) *see* гледач

гледен -дна *adj* гледна точка point of view, viewpoint, standpoint

гледичија -ии *f & гледичје n Bot.* (Gleditsia triacanthos) honey locust

гледиште *n* point of view, attitude

гледне *pf dial.* гледна *aor., see* погледне; гледни малце just have a look!

гледник -ци *m* idler, loafer, parasite

гледнува *impf of* гледне

глеѓ *m & f* enamel, glaze; глеѓ на забот <tooth> enamel

глеѓоса *pf* to glaze, enamel

глеѓосува *impf of* глеѓоса

глезен -зна *m* ankle; *see* глужд 1; ❏ ум до глезни feeble-minded (mentally deficient, retarded) person

глези *impf dial.* **I** to spoil, pamper s.o.; to overindulge *trans.*; to oblige, pander to **II – се** to be affected; to indulge o.s.; (*за деме*) to play up, behave badly

глека *impf* to eat slowly

глекав *adj* doughy, half-baked; глекав леб doughy bread

глекавост *f* doughiness

глетка[1] *impf dim. of* гледа **1** to see with difficulty; to see now and then **2** to look now and then; to peep

глетка[2] *f* sight, spectacle; убава глетка beautiful sight; глетка што боде очи eyesore, blot on the landscape

глечер *m* glacier

глечерски *adj* glacier

глиб *m* mud, mire

глибав *adj* muddy, covered with mud

гливар *m Bot.* (Scolymus hispanicus) golden thistle

гликоза *f* glucose

глина *f* clay; бела глина kaolin, china clay; грнчарска глина argil, potter's clay; огноотпорна глина fireclay

глинен *adj* clay, earthenware; глинен сад earthenware (clay) vessel

глинест *adj* clayey; глинеста почва loam

глиновит *adj* clayey

глински *adj* clay *attrib.*; глински шкрилци shale, schist

глисер *m* **1** speedboat **2** glider

глиста *f* worm; фрли глиста да најдеш јагула *prov.* give a little to gain a lot, *see* крапче

глицерин *m Chem.* glycerine

глицерински *adj* glycerine

гличав *adj* **1** tearful, lacrimose **2** capricious

глоб *m* eye socket

глоба *f* **1** fine, penalty **2** *colloq.* damage; море што глоба си! all you do is cause damage! you're a menace!

глобален -лна *adj* global; total, whole

глоби *pf* to fine, penalize, punish

глобува *impf of* глоби

глобус *m* globe

глог *m Bot.* (Crataegus monogyna) hawthorn; од трн та на глог *prov.* out of the frying-pan into the fire

глогина *f* **1** *see* глог **2** *see* глогинка

глогинка *f* haw

глода *impf* **I 1** to gnaw, chew **2** *fig.* to torment, worry; што те глода? what's eating you? **II – се** to quarrel, bicker

глодач *m Zool.* rodent

глоѓе *n* hawthorn thicket

глорија *f* **1** glory **2** halo

глорификација *f* glorification

глорификува *impf see* глорифицира

глорифицира *impf* to glorify, extol, praise

глотеж *m* **1** crumbs, particles **2** (*нечистотија во житото*) smut

глоти *impf* **I 1** to dirty, soil, make a mess **2** *fig.* to be superfluous; to be in the way **II – се** to be smutty; житово се глоти this grain is smutty

глотка *f* **1** particle, bit; глотка во окото mote in the eye **2** uneven (rough) spot

глоцун *m Bot.* (Crataegus oxyacantha) common hawthorn, maytree

глочка *impf in the expression:* окото ме глочка I have s.th. in my eye

глув *adj* **1** deaf; глув на едното уво deaf in one ear; сосема глув, глув како топ stone-deaf, deaf as a post **2** *fig.* insensitive, indifferent, deaf (*за – то*); глув за туѓите страдања indifferent to other people's sufferings **3** (*за звук, глас*) dull, muffled, indistinct **4** remote, secluded, isolated; (*празен, запуштен*) des-

erted, empty; глуво место remote (out-of-the-way) place **5** quiet, silent; глуво оро dance without musical accompaniment; глува доба the dead of night

глуван *m* deaf person

глуварче *n Bot.* (Taraxacum officinale) dandelion

глувее *impf* **1** (*станува глув*) to go deaf, lose one's hearing **2** (*тивок е*) to be silent

глувичок -чка *adj dim. of* глув hard of hearing, a bit deaf

глувне *pf* глувна *aor.* **1** *see* глувее l **2** to fall silent

глуво *adv* quietly, noiselessly; indistinctly; with a dull (muffled) sound

глувонем **1** *adj* deaf and dumb, deaf-mute **2** *m* deaf mute; јазик за глувонеми sign language

глувост & глувота *f* deafness

глувчар *m Zool.* (Buteo) buzzard; обичен глувчар (Buteo buteo) common buzzard

глувчарапче *n Zool.* (Troglodytes troglodytes) wren

глувчарник -ци *m* mouse-hole

глувче[1] *n dim. of* глушец

глувче[2] *n dim. of* глужд; чорапчиња до глувчиња ankle-socks

глужд *m* **1** ankle **2** knot (*in wood*); nodule; *Bot.* node

глуждовит *adj* **1** bony, raw-boned **2** (*за даска и сл.*) knotty, knotted, nodose, nodular; (*за дрво*) snaggy, gnarled, gnarly

глуждовитост *f* **1** boniness **2** knottiness

глужлив *adj see* глуждовит

глумец -мци *m* actor

глумица *f* actress

глуп & глупав *adj* stupid, silly, foolish; dense, doltish; глупа положба silly (awkward) situation

глупаво *adv* stupidly, foolishly

глупавост *f* stupidity, foolishness

глупак -ци *m* idiot, fool, dolt

глупачка *f* (*fem. form*) *see* глупак

глупачки *adj* foolish, idiotic

глупост *f* stupidity; nonsense; foolish act/talk; не правете глупости! don't do anything foolish! не треси глупости don't talk nonsense!

глупчо -овци *m colloq.* fool, idiot

глутница *f* **1** pack (*of wolves*), herd, flock (*of wild beasts*) **2** *fig.* mob, rabble

глуше *n see* глувче[1]

глушец -вци *m Zool.* mouse; ❏ од глушец посилен feeble; timid; *pejor.* канцелариски глушец a pen-pusher; накиснал како глушец like a drowned rat; сиромав како црквен глушец <as> poor as a church mouse

глуши *impf see* заглушува

глушина *f* **1** *Bot.* (Vicia varia) vetch, sweet vetch **2** *Bot.* (Taraxacum officinale) dandelion **3** field overgrown with weeds **4** remote place

гљу-гљу *interj* (*imitating the voice of a turkeycock*) gobble! gobble!

гмечало *n* winepress

гмечи *impf* **1** to press, squeeze **2** *fig.* to oppress

гнас *m only in the expressions:* гнас ми е I loathe (*s.th.*), I am disgusted (*by s.th.*); it makes me sick; I can't stand the sight of (*s.th.*); да ти е гнас you should be disgusted; имам гнас (*за, од*) I have a loathing (*for s.th., s.o.*)

гнаса *f* **1** filth, dirt **2** dirty person, dirty woman **3** *fig.* monster, loathsome person **4** ❏ за гнаса! disgusting!

станал (се сторил, се направил) за гнаса he's got all dirty; *fig.* he's a disgrace!

гнасен -сна *adj* **1** dirty, filthy **2** disgusting, abominable, vile, revolting

гнаси *impf* **I** to make (*s. th.*) dirty, soil; *fig.* to desecrate, besmirch, defile; to stain, sully, tarnish; руба краси, руба гнаси *prov.* the apparel proclaims the man **II –** **се 1** to be disgusted (*од – by s.th., s.o.*), find (*s.th.*) repulsive; to loathe **2** *impers.* (*with dat.*) му се гнаси (*од нешто*) to be revolted, be nauseated (*by s.th.*), feel sick (*about s.th.*)

гнаслив *adj* squeamish; nauseated (*by s.th.*)

гнасник -ци *m* **1** base (vile) person; dirty person **2** foul-mouthed person

гнасница *f* (*fem. form*) *see* гнасник

гнасота *f* **1** filth, dirt **2** *fig.* vileness, baseness, loathesomeness

гнасотија -ии *f see* гнасота

гнасотилак -ци *m colloq.* **1** *see* гнасота **2** (*usu. pl*) private parts

гнев *m* anger, fury, rage

гневен -вна *adj* angry, furious, enraged

гневи *impf* **I** to anger, enrage **II – се** to be angry (furious) (*на – with*)

гневлив *adj* irritable, short-tempered, irascible

гнездест *adj* **1** nest-like **2** *fig.* cosy, pleasant

гнезди се *impf* to nest, make a nest

гнездо *n* **1** (*седело*) nest, perch; ластовичино гнездо swallow's nest **2** *fig.* homeland, birthplace **3** haunt, den, lair; centre; *Mil.* митралеско гнездо machine-gun nest (emplacement)

гнет *m* oppression, tyranny

гнете *impf* **I 1** (*притиска*) to press <down/together>; (*полни*) to cram, stuff; гнете печка со ќумур to fill a stove with coal; гнете облека во врека to cram clothes into a bag **2** *colloq.* to gorge (*on*), eat greedily; ❑ гнете и низ уши he's a terrible glutton **3** *literary* (*потиснува*) to oppress, tyrannize; to squeeze, exploit **II – се** (*се пика*) to push in

гнечи *impf dial. see* гмечи

гнида *f* nit

гнидав *adj* infested with nits

гниди *pl Bot.* (Capsella bursa pastoris) capsell, cassweed, shepherd's purse

гнидоса *pf* to become infested with nits

гнидосува *impf of* гнидоса

гние *impf* to rot (*also fig.*); to decompose; to languish; гние во затвор to languish in prison

гнил *adj* **1** rotten, putrid; *fig.* corrupt; јаболково е гнило this apple is rotten; ❑ се опрел на гнил плот he miscalculated **2** (*за мушмула, оскоруша, вид круши и сл.*) tender, mellow, ripe, soft; гнили круши soft pears

гнилеж *m* rot, decay

гноен -јна *adj* purulent, septic, festering, suppurating; full of manure; well composted; гнојна рана festering wound; гнојно воспаление suppurating inflammation; гноен чир boil; гнојно чирче pustule

гнои *impf* **1** *intrans.* to suppurate, fester, discharge; раната гнои the wound is festering **2** *trans.* to manure

гној *m* **1** pus, matter **2** manure, dung, compost

гнојарник -ци *m* dunghill, dung heap

гнојница *f* pimple, pustule

гнојоса *pf see* загнои

гнојосува *impf see* загнојува

гнома *f* proverb, apophthegm (apothegm), saw

гномски *adj* proverbial

гносеологија *f Philos.* epistemology

гносеолошки *adj Philos.* epistemological

го *pron* (*short acc. form of Toj*) him; го видов I saw him

гоба *f* polyporus <fungus>

гоблéн *m* Gobelin tapestry

говедар *m* herdsman, *Am.* cowboy, *Austral.* stockman

говедарка *f* herdswoman, *Am.* cowgirl

говедарник -ци *m* enclosure, pen

говедарство *n* cattle breeding, cattle raising

говедарче *n dim. of* говедар

говедо *n* **1** a head of cattle; cow; bull; ox; buffalo; calf; *pl* cattle; livestock; ❑ не сум пусто говедо I'm not all alone in the world **2** *fig.* animal, brute; (*простак*) boor, bumpkin; (*глупак*) fool

говедски *adj* cattle, beef *attrib.*; bovine; говедско месо beef

говечки *adj see* говедски; говечка трева *Bot.* (Alchemilla vulgaris) lady's mantle; говечки јазик *Bot.* (Scolopendrium vulgare) hart's tongue fern

говор *m* **1** speech, manner of speaking **2** speech, address; oration; држи говор to hold the floor, hold forth, make a speech **3** dialect; прилепскиот говор the Prilep dialect

говорен -рна *adj* spoken; speech; говорен јазик spoken (colloquial) language; vernacular; говорни органи organs of speech, vocal organs

говори *impf* to talk, speak; *see* зборува¹

говорител *m rare see* зборувач

говорник -ци *m* speaker, orator

говорница *f* speaker's platform, rostrum; pulpit; телефонска говорница telephone booth

говорнички *adj* speaker's; oratorical

говорништво *n* oratory

год. *abbr. see* г. 1

-годе *part* (*in compounds*) -ever, *see* кај-годе wherever; како-годе however; кој-годе whoever; што-годе whatever

годеж *m dial.* engagement, betrothal, *see* свршувачка²

годежник -ци *m dial.* fiancé, *see* свршеник

годежница *f dial.* fiancée, *see* свршеница

годен -дна *adj dial.* **1** (*способен*) capable **2** (*погоден*) suitable, appropriate, convenient, favourable

годеник -ци *m dial.* fiancé, *see* свршеник

годеница *f dial.* fiancée, *see* свршеница

годи¹ *impf* (*with dat.; usu. 3rd p.*) to please, satisfy, accommodate; to suit; тој им годи на муштериите he keeps his customers satisfied; тоа му годи that suits him; he likes it; не му годи it doesn't agree with him; it's not good for him

годи² *impf* to arrange, prepare, fix up; годи куќа за продавање to prepare a house for sale

годи³ *pf* **1** to settle, fix, conclude (*a business*) **2** to guess; to hit upon; ја годив улицата I found the street **3** *dial.* to betrothe

година *f* **1** year; учебна година school year; буџетска година financial (fiscal) year; високосна година leap year; во осумдесеттите години in the eighties; колку години имаш? на колку години си? how old are you?; Нова година New Year; честита Нова година! Happy New Year! за многу години

<денешен>! many happy returns!; Happy New Year!; секоја година every year; за една година in a year; for a year; per annum; in a year's time; тој е на мои години he's my age; на млади години in one's youth (early years); на стари години in one's later years, in one's old age; ја чувствува тежината на годините to feel one's age; ❏ од година на (во) година from year to year; year by year; year in year out; year after year; ден година 1. plenty of time 2. a long <summer> day; со години for years; year by year; <низ, преку> цела година all the year round; годините си го прават своето time takes its toll; влегува во години to be a bit long in the tooth; to be getting on <in years>; зрели години years (age) of discretion; во години човек elderly person; што носи саатот не носи годината *prov.* who can tell what the future will bring; по гладната година иде и берикетлија *prov.* it's a long lane that has no turning **2** requiem, commemorative service (*one year after s.o.'s death*)

годинáва   *adv* this year; ланската година ја бараме годинава, а годинашнава в година *prov.* you can't turn back the clock

годинак   -ци *m* (*дете*) one-year-old; (*прасе, теле и др.*) yearling

годиначе   *n dim. of* годинак

годинашен   -шна *adj* this year's; годинашно вино this year's wine

годинува   *impf* to spend a year

годишен   -шна *adj* yearly, annual; годишно време season; годишно производство yearly output (production); годишно собрание annual <general> meeting

-годишен   -шна *adj* (*with preceding numeral*) -year; -yearly; петгодишен five-yearly; five-year; дванаесетгодишно момченце twelve-year-old boy

годишник   -ци *m* almanac; yearbook, yearly report; статистички годишник statistical yearbook

годишнина   *f* **1** anniversary **2** volume, year's issues (*of a journal*) **3** *dial.* year's supply; тоа му е годишнината that's his year's supplies

-годишнина   *f* (*with preceding numeral*) стогодишнина centenary, hundredth anniversary

годишно   *adv* yearly, a year, per annum

годува   *impf of* годи³

гоен   -јна *adj* fat, fattened

гозба   *f* **1** feast, banquet **2** food

гои   *impf* **I** (*за стока*) to fatten up; to force-feed **II – се** to grow fat, gain weight

гојзерица   *f* (*usu. pl*) <spiked> mountaineering boot, climbing boot

гол¹   *adj* **1** naked, nude, bare; голи дрвја bare trees; ❏ на голо, по голо naked, in the nude; гол како од мајка роден in one's birthday suit; со голо (просто) око to/with the naked eye; со голи раце with one's bare hands; голи зборови mere (empty) words; голи ветувања empty (hollow) promises **2** *fig.* wretched, very poor; ❏ гол и бос destitute, down and out; гол како пиштол, гол како сокол as poor as a church mouse; гол како прст, гол прст <останал> without a bean, penniless; ем гол ем зол *prov.* pride and poverty are ill met, yet often seen together **3** *fig.* plain, pure, unmixed, unadulterated; гола вистина the plain (naked, stark, unvarnished) truth; голо вино pure (unadulterated) wine; гол дуп *Zool.* (Columba palumbus) wood pigeon; гол човек *Bot.* (Arbutus andrachne) bearberry

гол²   *m Sport.* goal

голаб   *m see* гулаб

голак   *m see* голтак

голгетер   *m Sport.* scorer (*of a goal*); striker; *see* стрелец

голее   *impf* to grow bare; гранките голеат the branches are losing their leaves

голеж   *m see* голина

голем   *adj* big, large; great; во голем број in large number<s>; голема буква capital letter; голем настан great event; поголем брат elder brother; ❏ големиот **1**. chief, head, director **2**. God; големите grown-ups; Голема Богородица Assumption of the Blessed Virgin Mary; голем сечко January; големиот прст middle finger; *dial.* голема болест typhus; *Med.* голема кашлица whooping cough; *Med.* голема сипаница smallpox, variola; *Astron.* Големата Мечка, Големиот Одар the Great Bear (Plough); *colloq.* голема сверка (*iron., joc.* клечка) VIP, big shot, bigwig; голем та несолен silly fellow, idiot; голема работа! чудо големо! големо чудо! a lot that matters, that's nothing, *sl.* big deal! голем да пораснеш! God bless you! (*said in answer to a child's greeting*); many happy returns! мало и големо great and small, young and old; не вели голем збор; голем залак лапни, голем збор не вели think before you speak! *colloq.* атерот ти е голем I can't refuse you

големее   *impf* **I 1** *intrans.* to grow, get bigger; денот големее the days are getting longer **2** *trans.* to make bigger/fatter, enlarge **II – се 1** *see* **1 2** *fig.* to put on airs, be haughty

големец   -мци *m colloq.* bigwig; grandee; peer, aristocrat

големина   *f* size, dimensions; extent

големо   *adv in the expressions:* се држи на големо to put on airs; на големо on a large scale

големок   -мка *adj* siz<e>able; largish

големство   *n colloq.* **1** high social position, *colloq.* upper crust, top drawer **2** uppitiness **3** maturity

големџија   -ии *m colloq.* swelled head

големштина   *f* **1** *see* големство **2 2** *colloq., often pejor.* gentlemen, high society

голи   *impf trans.* to strip; to denude; to dress too lightly *trans.*

голијат   *m* giant

голина   *f* **1** bare mountainous terrain **2** exposed place cleared of snow by the wind

голица   *f Bot.* (Cichorium intybus) wild chicory

голич   *m* **1** pauper, destitute person **2** *Zool.* (Limax agrestis) slug

голиштарец   -рци *m* fledg<e>ling, nestling; *fig.* inexperienced person, babe in arms, greenhorn

голман   *m Sport.* goalkeeper

голобрад   *adj* beardless

головрат   *adj* barenecked

гологлав   *adj* bareheaded, hatless

гологлавечки   *adv* **1** with bare head, hatless **2** *fig.* headlong, recklessly

гололедица   *f see* голомразица

голомразен   -зна *adj* frosty, frozen

голомразица *f* frost; black ice; ice-covered ground

голорак *adj* **1** with bare arms **2** (*невооружен*) unarmed, bare-handed

голота *f* nakedness, bareness, nudity

голотија *f* **1** *see* голота **2** *fig.* poverty, destitution; the poor

голта *impf* **1** (*see* голтне) to swallow; (*брзо и алчно*) to bolt, gulp down; (*брзо и шумно*) to gobble; to devour (*also fig.*); голта со очите to devour with one's eyes; ❑ голта букви to omit letters (*when writing*) **2** *fig.* to swallow (*insults*), suffer in silence; ова повеќе не се голта this is too much; enough is enough

голтак -ци *m* pauper, destitute person, down-and-out

голтар *m see* голтак

голтач *m* swallower; голтач на пламен fire-eater

голтачка *f* (*fem. form*) *see* голтак

голтка *f* **1** drink; swallow; nip; (*мала*) sip; (*брза*) gulp; голтка вода drink/sip of water; во една голтка at a draught, at one gulp **2** gullet, throat

голтне *pf* голтна *aor.* **1** to swallow; to bolt; to gobble; to devour (*also fig.*); ❑ голтне јадица to take the bait; си го голтне јазикот to swallow one's tongue, become speechless (*with fear*) **2** *fig.* to take (*s.th.*) by deceit; to defraud (*s.o.*)

голтнува *impf of* голтне

голушка *f* stone, pit (*of plum, apricot, etc.*)

голф *m* golf; топче за голф golf ball; игралиште за голф golf-course

голфски *adj* golf; голфски клуб golf club

Голфска струја *f Geog.* Gulf Stream

голчо -овци *m colloq. see* голтак

гол-човек *m Bot.* (Arbutus andrachine) arbutus, strawberry tree

гомарно *adv colloq.* гомарно му е, му иде гомарно 1. he feels sick (*after eating s.th.*) 2. he shudders (shivers)

гомбел *m Bot.* (Urtica dioica) great nettle

гомжи *pf dial.* to creep, crawl; to teem, swarm, *see* лази, ползи

гомно *n vulg.* shit, crap; ❑ во гомна in the shit; изеде гомна 1. (*оддаде тајна*) to spill the beans, sing 2. (*направи грешка*) to make a mistake

гонг *m* gong; удри гонгот the gong sounded

гондола *f* gondola; гондола со пијалоци drinks trolley; гондоли за лулање swing boats

гондолиéр *m* gondolier

гоненица *f* **1** (*children's game*) tag **2** pursuit; persecution

гони *impf* **I** **1** to chase, harry, pursue; to dog; гони непријател to pursue (harry) the enemy; гони дивеч to hunt game; таа мисла ме гони that thought haunts me **2** (*прогонува*) to persecute; to prosecute **3** (*тера*) to drive; маката го гони да постапува така desperation drives him to act like that **4** *rare* гони цел to pursue an aim **II** – **се** to run around, chase each other

гонител *m* pursuer, hunter

гонорéја *f Med.* gonorrhea

гора *f* **1** wood, forest, *Austral.* bush **2** *rare* mountain; гора со гора се ставува, камо ли човек со човека! *prov.* it's a small world

горд *adj* **1** proud **2** conceited, haughty, arrogant

гордее се *impf* **1** to be proud (*со – of*); to pride o.s.

(*on*), take pride (*in*) **2** to behave haughtily (arrogantly)

горделив *adj* conceited, haughty, arrogant

горделивец -вци *m* conceited (haughty, arrogant) person

горделивост *f* conceit, haughtiness, arrogance

гордост *f* **1** pride **2** conceit, haughtiness, arrogance

горе *adv* above; up; higher up; up there; overhead; (*на погорниот кат*) upstairs; горе на планината up on the mountain, up in the mountains; горе на вториот кат up on the second floor; погоре higher, above; види погоре see above; тој е погоре од сите he is above everybody else; ❑ горе рацете! hands up! горе главата! chin up! courage! горе-долу *see* горедолу; горе високо, долу длабоко *prov.* there's no way out, no solution

горе- (*as prefix*) afore-; гореспоменат aforementioned, above-mentioned; горе-приведен quoted above

горедолу *adv* roughly, about, approximately; more or less; горедолу пет километра about five kilometres

горен -рна *adj* upper, higher, top; (*за облека*) outer; горен дел на куќа upper part of a house; погорен клас higher class; горно алиште outer garment; горните проблеми afore-mentioned problems; *colloq.* (*as noun*) горнион 1. God 2. chief, boss

горешт *adj* **1** hot; torrid; горешта вода boiling water; горешто железо red-hot iron; горешто лето a hot summer **2** *fig.* fiery, passionate, ardent

горешти се *impf* to get excited; to become furious

горештина *f* **1** heat, hot weather, *see* врукина, врелина, жештина; летни горештини summer heat **2** *colloq.* fever, high temperature

гори *impf* **1** to burn *trans. and intrans.* (*also fig.*); to be alight; to shine; куќата гори the house is on fire; гори светло a light is on; гори дрва to burn firewood; небото гори the sky is ablaze; ❑ гори од нетрпение to burn with impatience; гори од желба да to be eager to; гори за вода to be dying of thirst; му гори главата he's in difficulties; оган да го гори! blast him! (*literally* may he be struck by lightning!); село гори (се плени), баба се чешла *prov.* Nero fiddles while Rome burns; стариот пен посилно гори *prov.* there's many a good tune played on an old fiddle **2** to have a temperature; гори од оган to burn with fever

горивен -вна *adj* fuel; горивна ќелија fuel cell

гориво *n* fuel; (*за автомобил*) petrol; течно гориво <fuel> oil

горила *m Zool.* gorilla

горица & горичка *f dim. of* гора

горјанин *m* (*as epithet in f.p.*) highlander; mountaineer; ветар горјанин west wind

горко *adv* bitterly

горни -рна *adj* upper (*in toponyms*); Горни Полог Gorni Polog, Upper Polog

горник -ци *m* upper part (*e.g. of stockings, footwear, garment*)

горница *f* **1** wild pear **2** *dial., f.p.* upper room (chamber) **3** false plaits (*put over a woman's natural hair*)

горниште *n* **1** *see* горник **2** *dial.* hillock, elevation

горнокраец -јци *m* villager (*from the upper part of the village*)

горнокрајка *f* (*fem. form*) *see* горнокраец

горномаалец -лци *m see* горнокраец

горномаалка *f* (*fem. form*) *see* горномаалец

горњак *m* north wind

горок -рка *adj* **1** *rare see* горчлив **2** *fig.* bitter; wretched

гороцвет *m Bot.* (Adonis vernalis) pheasant's eye

горски *adj* forest, woodland; mountain; mountainous; горска самовила oread, mountain nymph; горско дрво forest-tree

горун *m Bot.* (Quercus sessiliflora, Quercus petraea) sessile oak, durmast oak; горун мазник (Quercus robur, Quercus pedunculata) common European oak, English oak

горупла *f Bot.* (Prunus mahaleb) rock cherry

горчи *impf* to be bitter, have a bitter taste; ми горчи it tastes bitter <to me>; ❏ горчи како пелин it's as bitter as wormwood

горчило *n see* горчина

горчина *f* bitterness (*also fig.*), bitter taste; *fig.* grief, sorrow

горчлив *adj* bitter (*also fig.*); горчливо кафе coffee without sugar; горчлива пилула, горчлив ап bitter pill; горчлива трева *Bot.* (Menyanthes trifoliata) bog-bean, buckbean

Господ *voc.* -де, -ди *m* Lord, God; Господ Бог the Lord God; Господи! Господе! Господи Боже! Lord! Good Lord! ❏ го прости Господ he has breathed his last, he has given up the ghost; Господ да го прости God rest his soul! сполај ти Господе thank God! praise be to God! да го прости Господ God grant it! ако даде Господ God willing; дал Господ by the grace of God we have some; имало Господ I also had some luck; thank goodness for that! Господ да чува, да чува Господ God (heaven) forbid! Господ знае God knows; камо тој Господ if only it were so! да види Господ! 1. shame! what a disgrace! 2. what in God's name is this?! што дал Господ <we will eat> whatever we have, we will take pot luck; како што дал Господ as is the custom; со Господ напред God be with us! Господ да те благослови God bless you! Господ да ни е на помош God help us! прости ми Господе! God forgive me! пред Господ сите се еднакви *prov.* we are all equal before the Lord; Господ високо, царот далеку *prov.* between the devil and the deep blue sea

господар *m* master; (*владар*) ruler, sovereign; господар на робови slave master (owner); почитуван господаре! sir! my good sir! сам си е свој господар to be one's own master; летоска измеќар, зимоска господар *prov.* winter eats what summer lays up

господари *impf* to rule, govern; to manage, direct; to be in control; господари со ситуација to be master of the situation

господарка *f* **1** (*fem. form*) *see* господар; mistress **2** master's/ruler's wife

господарски *adj* master's; ruler's

господарство *n* authority, rule, sway, supremacy

господарува *impf see* господари

господен -дна, -дне *adj Rel.* the Lord's; во лето господне in the year of Grace (Our Lord)

господин *pl* господа *m* **1** gentleman; mister, Mr; *pl* gentlemen, sirs; gentry; прав господин a real gentleman; господин Петровски Mr Petrovski; (*во* почеток на деловно писмо) почитуван господине Dear Sir! дами и господа ladies and gentlemen; ❏ господин човек a man of means (substance) **2** *f.p.* master of the house

господиновци *pl only, iron.* the masters, the gentry

господински *adj f.p.* the master's

господов *adj* the Lord's; ❏ господова работа that is in God's hands

господски[1] *adj* gentleman's, gentlemanly; господска вечера sumptuous meal, royal repast; *dial.* господски брат *see* девер

господски[2] *adv* like a gentleman, superbly, magnificently, in <grand> style; generously

господствен *adj* **1** dignified, gentlemanly **2** ruling, dominant; господствена положба dominating (commanding) position

господственост *f* dignity; domination

господство *n* **1** dignity, refinement; Ваше господство Sir; Your Honour **2** rule, domination; господство на капиталот the dominance of capital

господствува *impf* **1** to rule, govern **2** to dominate, prevail (*над – over*)

господствувачки *adj* ruling, governing; господствувачки класи ruling classes

госпоѓа *f* lady; Mrs

госпоѓица *f* young lady; Miss

госпоштина *f* the masters, the gentry, *colloq.* the high-ups

гост -и *m dial. see* гостин; катаден гост како кисел грозд *prov.* fish and guests smell in three days

гости *pf & impf* **I** to entertain, treat, serve (*со јадење/ пиење – with food/drink*); те гостија ли? did they give you anything to eat/drink? гости со разни пијачки to serve various drinks; ❏ *colloq. iron.* го гостив I gave him a good thrashing/dressing down **II** – се to treat o.s. (*со нешто – to s.th.*)

гостилница *f* inn, *literary* tavern; guest-house

гостилничар *n* innkeeper, *literary* tavern-keeper

гостилничарка *f* **1** (*fem. form*) *see* гостилничар **2** innkeeper's wife

гостин -сти *m* guest; visitor; ❏ оди/е на гости to go visiting, visit; to be on a visit; непокането гостин uninvited guest; gatecrasher; почесен гостин guest of honour; *Sport.* во гости away; неканет гостин зад врата седи *prov.* an unbidden guest knows not where to sit; who comes uncalled, sits unserved; и за најмилиот гостин три дена се доста fish and guests smell in three days

гостинка *f* (*fem. form*) *see* гостин

гостински *adj* guest's; гостинска соба guest-room

гостољубив *adj* hospitable

гостољубие & **гостољубје** *n* hospitality; hospitable nature

гостоприемен -мна *adj see* гостољубив

гостоприемство *n see* гостољубие, гостољубје

гостува *impf* to be a guest; to play (perform) on tour, give a guest performance

готварски *adj* cook's, cooking *attrib.*, culinary

готварство *n* cooking, cookery

готвач *m* **1** cook; главен готвач chef **2** cookery book, cookbook

готвачка *f* (*fem. form*) *see* готвач 1

готвачница *f* kitchen, *see* кујна

готвено　*n* cooked food, cooked dish

готви　*impf* **I 1** to prepare *trans.*; готви некого за политичар to groom s.o. for a political career; готви некому стапица to set a trap for s.o. **2** to cook *trans.*; таа знае убаво да готви she is an excellent cook **II – се** to prepare <o.s.>, get ready (*за – for*)

готика　*f* Gothic <style>

готица　*f* Gothic script

готов　*adj* **1** (*довршен, свршен, докрај изработен*) finished; ready-made; готови алишта ready-made (ready-to-wear) clothes **2** (*спремен*) ready, prepared (*за, на, да – for*); ручекот е готов lunch is ready; готов за тргнување ready to go; готов да услужи ready to help; ❏ готов специјалист fully qualified specialist, expert; готови пари cash, ready money; тој е готов! he's finished! there's no hope for him! готов на сè ready for anything; голо здравје – готова болест *prov.* the poor suffer all the wrong

готован　*m* idler, parasite, sponger

готованец　-нци *m see* готован

готованка　*f (fem. form) see* готован

готованство　*n* parasitism

готовина　*f* cash, ready money

готовност　*f* readiness, willingness

готово　*adv* **1** (*свршено*) finished; that's all; ви дадовме толку – и готово we gave you so much and now that's it **2** (*спремно*) ready; готово! почнуваме ready! we're starting; што е попово, да е готово *prov.* pay with the same dish you borrow **3** ❏ за готово for cash; на готово without effort, effortlessly; од готово <прави> вересија to throw good money after bad; зема за готово to take for granted

гоштава　*impf see* гости I

гоштавка　*f* **1** banquet, feast **2** entertainment, treating, regaling

граба　*impf* **I 1** to grab, seize, take; to wrest (*од – from*); to abduct **2** to rob; to plunder, pillage, sack, loot; окупаторската војска грабаше по селата the occupation troops plundered the villages **3** to hurry, rush *intrans.* **II – се 1** to vie (*за – for*), fight (*over*); сите ергени се грабаа за ќерката на попот all the young men were vying for the priest's daughter **2** to seize, grab, hold on (*за – to*); се граба за гранките to hold on to the branches

грабач　*m* **1** predator **2** robber, bandit, plunderer, looter

грабачка　*f* **1** (*fem. form) see* грабач **2** *see* грабеж

грабачки　*adj* predatory

грабеж　*m* **1** robbery, plundering, looting **2** plunder, loot

граби　*pf & impf* **I 1** *see* граба 1 **2** *fig.* (*impf only*) to devour; swallow; граби воздух to gulp in air **II – се** *see* граба (се) II 1

граблив　*adj* grasping, rapacious; (*звер*) predatory

грабливец　-вци *m see* грабач 1

грабливка　*f* rapacious (grasping) woman; (*птица*) bird of prey

грабливост　*f* greediness

грабне　*pf* грабна *aor.* **I 1** to take away, abduct, kidnap; to hijack **2** to snatch, seize, grab; го грабна ножот he grabbed (seized) the knife; ако те грабнам! wait till I get hold of you! **II – се 1** to seize

(grab) one another **2** to grab (*s. th.*), get hold (*of s.th.*); мачето се грабна со ноктите за јорганот the kitten grabbed (took hold of) the quilt with its claws

грабнува (се)　*impf of* грабне (се)

грабнувач　*m* kidnapper; hijacker

грав　*m Bot.* (Phaseolus vulgaris) bean, kidney bean; ❏ го свари гравот to come down with an illness; прост како грав <as> dumb as a fish; <as> light as a cork

гравер　*m* engraver; etcher

гравидна　*adj Med.* pregnant

гравидитет　*m Med.* pregnancy

гравира[1]　*impf* to engrave; (*со киселини*) to etch

гравира[2]　*f see* гравура

гравитација　*f* gravitation

гравитира　*impf* to gravitate (*кон – towards*)

граворика　*f Bot.* (Lathyrus cicera) dwarf chickling-vetch

гравура　*f* (*резба*) engraving; (*отпечаток*) print; (*клише*) etching; (*отпечаток во дрво, дрвено клише*) woodcut

гравушка　*f* **1** bean **2** *fig.* (*јадра капка*) bead, large drop; гравушки пот beads of sweat

гравче　*n dim. of* грав; тавче гравче bean casserole

грагор[1]　*m* gravel

грагор[2]　*m dial.* **1** clamour, racket **2** babbling, chattering

грагорест　*adj* gravelly

грагори　*impf dial.* **1** to make a noise **2** to babble, chatter

грагоровит　*adj* gravelly; gravelled

град[1]　*m* **1** town; city; село фали, в град седи *prov.* hedge your bets! play safe! **2** *f.p. see* тврдина; од град појак stronger than a fortress

град[2]　*m* hail; врне (паѓа) град it is hailing; град глад не носи *prov.* hail doesn't mean starvation; од голема суша и на град благодари се *prov.* any port in a storm; од дожд на град *prov.* from bad to worse; out of the frying-pan into the fire

град[3]　*m* grade, *see* градус

град[4]　*f poet.* (*usu. pl*) breasts

града　*f* breast; (*брадавица*) nipple

градација　*f literary* gradation

градба　*f* **1** (*изградба*) construction, building, erection **2** (*зграда*) building, edifice

градеж　*m see* градба

градежен　-жна *adj* building, construction; градежен материјал building material; градежен инженер civil engineer; градежен претприемач building contractor; градежен работник construction worker; builder

градежник　-ци *m* builder, constructor; contractor; civil engineer

градежништво　*n* construction, civil engineering

граден　-дна *adj* chest *attrib.*; breast *attrib.*; pectoral, thoracic; граден кош thoracic (rib) cage; градна болест tuberculosis; градна коска breastbone, sternum; *Med.* градна жаба angina pectoris; *Sport.* градно пливање breast-stroke

градест　*adj* chesty; (*за жена*) bosomy

гради[1]　*pl* breast<s>, bosom; nipples; chest; ❏ гради со (в) гради hand-to-hand fighting; пречека со гради to welcome with open arms; се удира (чука) в гради to blow one's own trumpet, brag, boast; кокошкини гради pigeon-chest

гради² *impf* **1** to build, construct **2** (*создава*) to create **3** to enclose, fence in **4** *dial.* to make

градиво *n* material; литературно градиво literary material; наставно градиво curriculum

градилиште *n* building site

градина *f* garden; зоолошка градина zoological garden, zoo; детска градина *see* градинка

градинар *m* **1** gardener **2** *colloq.* greengrocer

градинарка *f* (*fem. form*) *see* градинар

градинарски *adj* garden *attrib.*; градинарски производи vegetables

градинарство *n* gardening, horticulture; market gardening

градинка *f* little garden; ❑ детска градинка kindergarten; nursery school; day-care centre

градински *adj* garden *attrib.*; градински цвеќиња garden flowers

гради́ра *pf & impf* **1** to grade, measure, rate **2** to calibrate

градител *m* builder; *fig.* architect, creator

градителски *adj* building, builder's

градиште *n* **1** ruins, site (*of an ancient city, fortress*) **2** *augm. of* град

градник -ци *m* **1** sleeveless jacket, jerkin; vest **2** (*женски*) brassière, bra **3** (*на коњска опрема*) breast collar

градобит *m see* градобитнина

градобитен -тна *adj* hail-bearing; градобитен облак hail-bearing cloud

градобитнина *f* hail damage

градоболен -лна *adj* tubercular

градоначалник -ци *m arch.* mayor

градоносен -сна *adj* hail-bearing; градоносен облак hail-bearing cloud

градски¹ *adj* city, town *attrib.*; urban; municipal; градски сообраќај city transport/traffic; градски совет city council; градско собрание city assembly; градско население urban population; градска управа municipal administration, local government; градски народен одбор *Hist.* People's City Council (*in Skopje only*)

градски² *adv* in urban style, like townspeople; градски се носи he dresses like a townsman

градум *adv f.p.* abundantly, copiously; градум солзи рони to cry one's eyes out, shed bitter tears

градус *m* degree; grade; level

градушка *f dial.* hailstone; hail

граѓа *f* material; building material

граѓанец -ани *m see* граѓанин 1

граѓанин -ани *m* **1** townsman, city dweller **2** citizen; ❑ почесен граѓанин honorary citizen, freeman **3** академски граѓанин graduate, *Am.* university/college graduate;

граѓанка *f* (*fem. form*) *see* граѓанин

граѓански *adj* civil; civic; граѓанска војна civil war; граѓански брак civil marriage; граѓанско право civil law; граѓански права civil rights

граѓанство *n* (*статус*) citizenship; (*граѓаните*) citizenry; ❑ право на граѓанство right of citizenship

граѓанче *n dim. of* граѓанец *and of* граѓанин 1

грак *m* caw, cawing, croak

грака *impf see* грачи

гракне *pf* гракна *aor.* **1** to give a croak (caw) **2** *fig.* to

raise a hue and cry (*на – against*), fly (*на – at*), rail (*на – at, against*)

гракнува *impf of* гракне

грам *m* gram<me>

грамада *f* heap, pile; (*зграда*) mass; ❑ грчка грамада unruly mob; untidy heap

граматика *f* grammar

граматичар *m* grammarian

граматички *adj* grammatical

грамота *f Hist.* Golden Bull; deed, charter

грамотен -тна *adj arch. see* писмен

грамофон *m* gramophone, record-player

грамофонски *adj* gramophone; грамофонска плоча <gramophone> record; грамофонска игла stylus

грана *f dial. see* гранка

грана се *impf* to split, branch, divide *intrans.*

гранат *adj* branching, *see* грановит

грана́та *f Mil.* shell; missile; топовска граната artillery shell; тенковска граната tank shell; рачна граната hand-grenade

грандио́зен -зна *adj* grand, imposing, magnificent

грандио́зност *f* grandeur, magnificence

грандоманија *f* megalomania

гранит *m* granite

гранитен -тна *adj* granite; *fig.* solid, firm; гранитна волја iron will

граница¹ *f* **1** border, frontier; државна граница state frontier, border; ❑ зад граница abroad **2** *fig.* limit; boundary, dividing line, borderline; нема остра граница there is no clear-cut limit; граница на можностите the bounds of possibility; сè има свои граници everything has its limits; во границите на законот within the confines of the law; до крајна граница in/to the extreme; to excess; до одредени граници within limits; to some extent; на граница од on the brink of; on the verge of; не знае за граници to know no bounds; not to know when to stop; преминува <секаква> граница to overstep the bounds; to go too far; to get carried away; сигурносна граница margin of safety; safety factor

граница² *f Bot.* (Quercus robur, Quercus pedunculata) common European oak, English oak, *see* горун мазник

граничар *m* border guard

граничен -чна *adj* frontier, border *attrib.*; boundary *attrib.*; граничен камен border/boundary stone; гранична линија borderline; граничен премин border crossing

граничи <се> *impf* to border (*со – on*) (*also fig.*); to adjoin, abut (*on*); *fig.* to verge (*on*); нашата земја <се> граничи со Грција our country has a common frontier with Greece; тоа граничи со лудост that borders on madness

гранка *f* **1** branch, bough; гранка маслинка olive branch (*also fig.*); ❑ паѓа на ниски гранки to fall on hard times; to come down in the world; не ја сечи гранката на која седиш *prov.* don't cut the bough you are sitting on **2** *fig.* branch, part, division; стопанска гранка sector (branch) of the economy; гранка на наука branch of science

грановит *adj* branching; дрво грановито spreading tree

гранче *n dim. of* гранка 1; twig; branchlet

граор *m Bot.* **1** (Lathyrus) vetchling **2** *dial.* kind of black grape

граорица *m Bot.* (Vicia sativa) common vetch

граорка *f Bot.* (Onobrychis viciifolia) sainfoin

гратче *n dim. of* град

граф *m see* гроф

графа *f* **1** heading, rubric; column (*in a newspaper, etc.*) **2** section, column (*of a form/table*)

графе́ма *f Ling.* grapheme, letter

графика *f* **1** the graphic arts **2** graphics **3** typography

графико́н *m* chart, graph, diagram; timetable, schedule

графиња *f* countess, *see* грофица

графит *m* graphite, plumbago, black lead

графичар *m* **1** graphic artist **2** typographer

графички *adj* graphic; typographic, printing *attrib.*; графички приказ graphic presentation

графоло́г -ози *m* graphologist

грациja -ии *f* **1** *Myth.* Grace **2** *fig.* (*only sg*) grace, gracefulness, elegance

грацио́зен -зна *adj* graceful, elegant

грацио́зност *f* grace, gracefulness

грачи *impf* to caw, croak; to squawk

граше *n* грашец & **грашок**[1] *m hyp. of* грав

грашок[2] *m Bot.* (Pisum sativum) pea

грб[1] *m* back, backbone, spine; back (*of garment*); ❑ да ти го видам грбот! go away! get lost! му го гледа некому грбот to see the back of s.o.; свртува некому грб to turn one's back on s.o.; to leave s.o. in the lurch; не паѓа на грб he doesn't give up, he still insists; го јаде грбот he is looking for a beating; му го направи грбот како мевот he gave him a good hiding; зад нечиj грб behind s.o.'s back; тој ни заби нож в грб he stabbed us in the back; му ја дал кошулата од грбот he gave him the shirt off his back; живее на туѓ грб to live at s.o.'s expense; има грб 1. he has support 2. he's got broad shoulders, he can bear it; се допрел до јак грб he has good connections; на свој грб on his own responsibility; грб со грб back to back; и на грбот има очи to have eyes in the back of one's head; симнува некого/нешто од грб to get s.o./s.th. off one's back; сто стапа по туѓ грб ништо не е *prov.* no skin off my/your, etc. nose

грб[2] *m* coat of arms, crest; државен грб national (state) coat of arms

грба *f dial. see* грпка

грбав *adj* hunchbacked

грбавее <се> *impf* to become hunchbacked

грбави *impf* I *trans. & intrans.* to bend over *intrans.*, stoop; to bend/arch (*one's back*) **II** – ce to become hunchbacked; to stoop

грбач *m* **1** whip; lash, stroke of the whip **2** kind of folk-dance

грбе -евци *m colloq.* hunchback

грбен -бна *adj* back, spinal; *Sport.* грбно пливање backstroke

грбечки *adv* on one's back; плива по грбечки to swim backstroke

грби се *impf* **1** to be hunchbacked **2** to bend over *intrans.*, stoop

грбла *f colloq.* (*fem. form*) *see* грбе

грбло -овци *m colloq. see* грбе

грбник -ци *m* spine, backbone, *see* 'рбет, 'рбетник

грвала[1] *f dial. see* грутка

грвала[2] *impf* I to roll *trans.* **II** – ce to roll *intrans.*; to roll about

грвалавица *f* crush, crowd, *see* мешаница

грвалица *f see* грвалавица

грга *impf* to gush, spurt (*usu. of water*)

гргал *m dial. see* грагор[1], чакал[2]

гргале *n dial.* earthenware water jug with narrow neck

гргалец -лци *m colloq.* person who cannot pronounce the sound *r* clearly, person with a burr

гргалица *f colloq.* (*fem. form*) *see* гргалец

гргне *pf* гргна *aor.* to gush <out>, pour <out> (*usu. of water*)

гргнува *impf of* гргне

гргор *m* **1** *see* кркор **2** gushing, gurgling (*the sound of water*) **3** *fig.* noise, racket

гргори *impf* **1** *see* кркори **2** to gush, gurgle **3** *fig.* to rumble, make a noise/racket

гргот *m see* гргор

гргoтен -тна *adj* noisy, loud

гргoти *impf* to rumble, roar; гргoтеа топовите the cannon thundered

гргуле *n* **1** *Bot.* (Cucurbita ovifera) courgette, *Am., Austral.* zucchini **2** *see* гргале

гргурав *adj dial.* curly (*of hair*)

грд *adj* ugly, hideous; plain <of features>; unsightly

грде -евци *m colloq.* ugly person, fright

грди *impf* I to make ugly, disfigure, deface **II** – ce to grow ugly; to make o.s. ugly

грдо *adv* horribly; ❑ грдо ни е без вас we miss you badly

грдомазен -зна *adj* ugly, *see* грд

грдост *f* ugliness; plainness <of features>; unsightliness; старост – грдост *prov.* an old man is a bed full of bones

грдотиja -ии *f* **1** ugly person, monster, fright **2** *see* грдост

греалка *f* heater

гребалка *f* & **гребало** *n see* струшка

гребаница *f see* гребеница

гребатор *m colloq.* sponger, *Am.* freeloader, *Austral.* bludger

гребачка *f see* струшка

гребе *impf* I **1** to scratch; to scrape; to scrape off; гребе кал од нешто to scrape the mud off s.th. **2** to grind, sharpen, hone **II** – ce **1** to scratch o.s./each other (*од некого* – on s.o.) **2** to sponge

гребен *m* **1** (*за волна*) carding comb, card; *dial.* (*брдо*) comb (*in a loom*); *dial.* comb (*for hair*) **2** (*од бран*) crest; (*од планина*) ridge **3** (*стена*) crag, cliff, sheer rock; (*издаден*) ledge; (*морски*) reef **4** (*од петел*) cock's comb, cockscomb

гребеница *f* scratch

греби се *impf dial. see* грижи се

гребло *n* **1** rake **2** whittling knife; scraper

гребне *pf* гребна *aor. see* гребе

гребнува *impf see* гребе

греботина *f see* гребеница

грев *m* sin, transgression; *fig.* mistake; ❑ смртен грев mortal (deadly) sin; седум смртни гревови the seven deadly sins; влезе во грев he lapsed (fell) into sin; грев ти на душа 1. for God's sake do something! 2. shame on you! ќе те фати гревот you will atone (pay) for this; *joc.* гревот на мевот it came to the same thing, there was no one to blame; гревовите не му се гледаат poor wretch/thing! тој е за грев, тој е за гревови he's a poor wretch; без грев човек pitiless (merciless) person; гревот не ти го дава <as> grasping as a miser; нема ни срам ни грев he's quite shameless; грев ми е I am sorry (*to have to do s.th. to s.o.*); ми падна грев (*за него*) I was sorry (*for him*); I had mercy (*on him*)

гревовен -вна *adj* sinful, *see* грешен 1

гревота *f* shame; немој, гревота е don't! it's wrong; гревота и срамота a shame and a disgrace, a wicked shame

гревотно *adv see* грешно 1; ❏ гревотно и срамотно *see* гревота и срамота

грегор *m Bot.* (Phillyrea media) holly

грегоријански *adj* Gregorian; грегоријански кален-дар Gregorian calendar

греда *f* beam; joist; girder; (*на покрив*) rafter; ❏ нам кожата на греди we've had it, we haven't a hope; на другиот му ја гледа раската, а на себе ни гредата *prov.* he sees the mote (speck) in another's eye and sees not the beam in his own

грее *impf* **I 1** to warm, heat; грее вода to warm water; грее раце to warm one's hands; печката добро грее the stove heats well; ❏ тоа не ме грее (топли) that does not help me **2** to shine; сонцето грее the sun is shining **II – се** to warm o.s.; to warm up *intrans.*; (*на сонце*) to bask; се грееме на струја we use electricity for heating

греење *n from* грее; централно греење central heating

грејач *m* heater

грејне *pf* грејна *aor. of* грее; (*за сонце*) to rise; to start shining (*of the sun*)

грејнува *impf of* грејне

Грена́да *f* Grenada

гренади́р *m* grenadier

гренади́рски *adj* grenadier's

гренадски *adj* Grenadian

Грена́ѓанец -ни *m* Grenadian

Грена́ѓанка *f* (*fem. form*) *see* Грена́ѓанец

Гренланд *m* Greenland

Гренландец -дци *m* Greenlander

гренландски *adj* Greenland *attrib.*

Гренлантка *f* (*fem. form*) *see* Гренландец

грепка¹ *f dial.* **1** *see* гребеница **2** nipple

грепка² *impf* to scratch a little

грешава *impf* to make mistakes, *see* греши 1; и попот в црква грешава *prov.* to err is human

грешен -шна *adj* **1** sinful **2** mistaken, incorrect, wrong; грешна ти е сметката your bill/calculation is wrong (incorrect); *see* погрешен²

греши¹ *impf* **1** (*прави грешка*) to make a mistake, err; тука грешиш that's where you're wrong; човечки е да се греши *prov.* to err is human **2** (*прави грев*) to sin, commit a sin; не греши душа don't commit a sin! don't lie!

греши² *pf* to mistake; си ја грешил вратата you have mistaken the door, you have come to the wrong door; *see* згреши

грешка *f* mistake, error; slip; (*слабост, недостаток*) fault, shortcoming; грешка во чукање typing error; печатна грешка misprint; компјутерска грешка computer (computing) error; фабричка грешка defect in manufacture; по грешка by mistake; ❏ без

грешка first class; above/beyond reproach; грешката е во . . . the fault lies with . . .; грешките се по луѓето *prov.* to err is human

грешник -ци *m* **1** (*оној што прави грев*) sinner **2** *fig.* poor fellow, wretch

грешница *f* (*fem. form*) *see* грешник

грешно *adv* **1** sinfully; грешно е да се убиваат луѓе it is a sin to kill people **2** incorrectly, wrong; грешно го разбра you misunderstood him, you got him wrong

грибла *f see* грибло

грибло *n* **1** curry-comb **2** coarse (wide-toothed) comb

грива *f* **1** mane **2** *dial.* (*снег*) snowdrift

гривест *adj* maned

гривјак -ци *m Zool.* (Columba palumbus) wood-pigeon, ring-dove

гривна *f* **1** bracelet; bangle **2** *Tech.* ring

грижа *f* **1** worry; ❏ бере грижа he is worried; не бери грижа don't worry! не ми е грижа I'm not worried, I don't care; го налегнале грижи he is overcome by worries; мали деца – мала грижа, големи деца – голема грижа *prov.* a little child weighs on your knee, a big one on your heart **2** care; грижа за човекот care for humanity; социјални грижи social services; ❏ без никакви грижи without a care in the world, care-free; има грижа на совест to have a guilty con-science; тоа ми е последна грижа that's the least of my worries

грижд *m Zool.* (Gryllotalpa) mole-cricket

грижен -жна *adj* **1** concerned, worried **2** *see* грижлив

грижи се *impf* **1** to worry; не грижи се don't worry! **2** to take care (*за – of*); се грижи за своите родители he takes care of his parents

грижлив *adj* careful, thoughtful, solicitous

грижливост *f* care, thoughtfulness, solicitude

грижник -ци *m* **1** worried person, worrier, misery **2** attentive (caring) person

гриз¹ *m* bite

гриз² *m dial.* a kind of cloth

гриз³ *m Cul.* semolina; гриз во млеко semolina in milk

гризе *impf* **I 1** to gnaw (*at*); (*по малку*) to nibble; (*за црв*) to bite (*into*); глувци го гризеле mice have been nibbling <at> it; ❏ добро гризе he keeps trying, he doesn't give up **2** (*предизвикува јадеж*) to irritate, cause an irritation, sting; димот ни ги гризеше очите the smoke stung our eyes **3** *fig.* (*за совест*) to prick, torment; to nag; го гризе совеста his con-science is troubling him, he has pangs of conscience **4** to eat away, corrode, rust, rot *trans.*; киселината го гризе и железото the acid will even eat away iron **II – се** to torment o.s.; to be tormented (*by one's con-science*); се гризе сам на себе he is tormented within him-self; ❏ се гризе од бес/лутина to eat one's heart out

гризлив *adj* **1** corrosive, caustic **2** crusty, crunchy

гризне *pf* гризна *aor.* **I 1** to bite, take a bite (*of*); детето го гризна јаболкото the child took a bite of the apple **II – се** to bite o.s. (*on the tongue*), bite one's tongue

гризнува (се) *impf of* гризне (се)

грим *m* <stage> make-up

грима́са *f* grimace; прави гримаси to make (pull) faces, grimace; болезлива гримаса pained grimace

грими́ра *pf & impf* **I** to make (*s.o.*) up **II – се** to make o.s. up, apply make-up

Гринич *m* Greenwich

гринички *adj* Greenwich *attrib.*

грип[1] *m Med.* influenza, *colloq.* flu

грип[2] *m &* **грипа** *f Bot.* (Phillyrea latifolia) phillyrea, mock privet

грипо́зен -зна *adj* influenza *attrib.*, influenzal, *colloq.* flu *attrib.*

грицка *impf* to nibble; грицка нокти to bite one's nails

Грк -рци *m* Greek

Гркинка *f (fem. form) see* Грк

грклан *m Anat.* larynx; throat

гркне *pf* гркна *aor.* to give a muffled squeak; нема ни да гркне! he won't even utter a sound!

гркнува *impf of* гркне

грлат *adj* loud-voiced, *see* грлест

грлашка *f* **1** neck (*of a bottle*) **2** *fig.* empty-headed person **3** *dial.* gourd (*for water*) **4** knitted half-stocking (*without a foot*), leg-warmer

грлашник -ци *m* stocking without a foot; gaiter

грлен *adj* **1** laryngeal **2** (*за глас*) throaty **3** *Phon.* guttural, velar; грлена согласка guttural (velar) consonant

грлест *adj* **1** loud-voiced **2** грлеста круша kind of juicy pear

грлешник *m Bot.* (Sempervivum patens) houseleek

грли *impf* to earth up <the roots of> (*plants*)

грлица[1] *f Zool.* (Streptopelia turtur) turtle-dove

грлица[2] *f see* грлник

грлник *m* anthrax; да го фати грлникот! *curse* a plague on it!

грло *n* **1** throat; го боли грло he has a sore throat; залакот му застана в грло the food stuck in his throat; ❑ лошо грло diphtheria; тесно грло bottle-neck; коска в грло a pain in the neck; накваси грло to wet one's whistle; вика колку го држи грло he shouts at the top of his voice; ни в заб ни в грло *prov.* (*said when there is little to eat*) a bird's portion **2** neck; neck of bottle, etc.; носи ѓердан на грло to wear a necklace **3** (*клисура*) gorge, ravine **4** *Anat.* cervix; рак на грлото на матката cancer of the cervix **5** head (*of cattle*); mouth to feed; храни пет грла to have five mouths to feed;

грмеж *m* **1** thunder, peal of thunder **2** *fig.* crash, bang, explosion

грмежлив *adj* **1** thundery; грмежливо време thundery weather **2** loud, thunderous (*of sounds*)

грми *impf* **1** to thunder; надвор грми it's thundering <outside> **2** *fig.* to roar, boom, resound; грмеа топови и пушки guns and rifles were thundering (roaring); салата грмеше од аплаузи the hall resounded with applause

грмјак *m coll.* bushes, thicket; grove

грмне *pf* грмна *aor.* to thunder <once>; to roar; грмна there was a clap of thunder; there was a loud roar

грмнува *impf of* грмне

грмотевица *f see* грмеж

грмоти *impf see* грми

грмотрн -рње *m Bot.* (Ononis spinosa) rest-harrow

грмушка *f* bush, shrub

грне[1] *n* earthenware pot; ❑ не си грне да се скршиш! don't complain (*Austral.* whinge)! *joc.* ѓупско грне glutton, greedy-guts; се истркалало грнето, си го нашло капачето *prov.* birds of a feather flock together

грне[2] *pf* грна *aor. arch.* to hug, embrace *trans.*, *see* прегрне

грнета *f Mus.* traditional wind instrument (*resembling clarinet*)

грнец -нци *m* large earthenware pot; ❑ *colloq.* прави грнци he's kicked the bucket

грнчар *m* potter; у грнчара ново грне не сакај *prov.* the potter usually uses old pots; the tailor usually wears old clothes

грнчарница *f* potter's shop; pottery

грнчарски *adj* potter's; грнчарски производи pottery <products>

грнчарство *n* pottery, potter's work (trade)

гро *n* (*usu. with the definite article*) the majority; грото на членовите the majority of the members

гроб *m* grave; ❑ му го копа гробот he is out to get him, he has it in for him; молчи како гроб it's silent as the grave; he's as quiet as a mouse; како во гроб е темно it's pitch dark; ќе се преврти в гроб he'll turn in his grave; верен до гроб true unto death; till death do us part; дошол гробу на врата; мириса на гроб; со едната нога е в гроб to be at death's door, be at one's last gasp, have one foot in the grave; *arch.* Божи гроб Jerusalem; отерува некого во гроб to drive s.o. to his grave; to seal s.o.'s fate; сам си го копа гробот to dig one's own grave; тоа е и за оп, и за гроб (*usu. of a garment*) it serves all purposes

гробар *m* gravedigger

гробарски *adj* gravedigger's

гробен -бна *adj* grave, burial *attrib.*; *fig.* funereal; гробна тишина, гробно молчење the silence of the grave

гробишта *pl* cemetery; (*во црковен двор*) graveyard; ❑ помине како покрај турски гробишта to give s.o. the cold shoulder; to cut s.o. dead

гробник -ци *m* vampire, *see* вампир; *fig.* цел гробник е he looks absolutely awful; he's got one foot in the grave

гробнина *f* grave; ❑ ни гробнина ни столнина му се знае no one knows anything about him

гробница *f* **1.** tomb, mausoleum; семејна гробница family vault **2** *fig.* downfall; тука ќе им биде гробницата here they will meet their Waterloo

гровка *impf dim. of* гровта

гровнат *adj* exhausted, worn-out

гровнатост *f* decrepitude; senility

гровне *pf* гровна *aor.* **1** to drop, fall (collapse) with a bang **2** to grow weak, become feeble (decrepit), break down, become worn-out

гровнува *impf of* гровне

гровта *impf* to grunt

гроги *adj* groggy; по нокаутот тој остана гроги he was groggy after the knockout

гроза *f* **1** horror, terror **2** disgust, revulsion; *colloq.* гроза му е he is disgusted (revolted)

грозд *m* bunch (*of grapes*); cluster (*of berries*); катаден гост како кисел грозд *prov.* guests and fish stink after three days

гроздак -ци *&* **гроздален** *m Zool. see* дрозд, дроздален

гроздест *adj* clustered, cluster-like, bunch-like, bunched, *Bot.* racemose, aciniform

гроздобер *m* 1 grape harvest, vintage, grape gathering; grape harvesting season 2 (*popular name for*) September

гроздоберец -рци *m* grape picker, vintager

гроздоберка *f* 1 (*fem. form*) *see* гроздоберец 2 grape-scissors

гроздов *adj* grape; гроздова ракија grape-brandy, *see* гроздовица; гроздов сок grape juice; гроздов шеќер glucose; grape-sugar, dextrose

гроздовица *f* grape-brandy

грозен -зна *adj* 1 (*грд*) ugly 2 horrible, terrible, frightful; грозно убиство a gruesome murder 3 disgusting, revolting 4 (*огромен*) huge, vast, enormous

грози *impf* I 1 (*грди*) to disfigure, make ugly 2 to threaten, menace; им грозеа со палење на селото they threatened to burn down the village 3 *intrans. dial.* to look ugly II – **ce** to be disgusted (*од – by*), feel revulsion (*for*); to detest, loathe

грозјар *m* grape lover

грозјарка *f* (*fem. form*) *see* грозјар

грозје *n coll.* 1 grapes; суво грозје raisins; sultanas; currants; (*affectionately, usu. of children*) грозје мое my little lamb; ❑ кога ќе роди врба грозје when pigs fly; во небрано грозје <to be> at a loss; *colloq.* <to be> caught with one's pants down; каква е лозата такво е грозјето *prov.* like father, like son 2 berry; диво грозје *Bot.* (Vaccinium myrtillus) bilberry, whortleberry; кучешко грозје *Bot.* (Solanum nigrum) black nightshade, morel; мечкино грозје *Bot.* (Vaccinium vitis idaea) red bilberry, cowberry, whimberry; змиино грозје *Bot.* (Muscari botryoides) grape hyacinth

грозјебрање *n see* гроздобер; ❑ лани на грозјебрање ќе ти плати he'll never pay you

грознее *impf* to grow ugly; to become a monster

грозник -ци *m* ugly man, fright, sight, *colloq.* scarecrow

грозница[1] *f* 1 ugly/plain woman, *colloq.* plain Jane 2 *dial.* (*треска*) fever

грозница[2] *f* creeping vine

грозничав *adj dial.* (*трескав*) feverish

грозота *f* 1 (*грдост*) ugliness 2 horror, ghastly scene

грозотија -ии *f see* грозота

гром *m* thunder; thunderbolt; ❑ гром те трештил! go to hell! како гром од ведро небо like a bolt from the blue; out of the blue; како гром да го удрил thunderstruck; не удира гром во коприви the best go first; the good die young

громко *adv* loud<ly>, like thunder

громобран *m* lightning-conductor, lightning-rod

громогласен -сна *adj* loud, noisy

громок -мка *adj* loud; thundering, roaring

громорен -рна *adj* bulky, large; clumsy, awkward; громорна стока bulky goods

гроплан *m* close-up; *colloq.* enlargement, blow-up; ❑ тој секогаш сака да биде во гроплан he always wants to be the centre of attention

гропче *n dim. of* гроб

гросист *m* wholesale dealer, wholesaler

гротвец *m Bot. see* гороцвет

гротéска *f* grotesque

гротéскен -кна *adj* grotesque

гроф *m* count, earl

грофица *f* countess, lady

грофнат *adj see* гровнат

грофне *pf* грофна *aor. see* гровне

грофнува *impf see* гровнува

грофовија *f* county

грош *m* groat (*small Turkish coin of 40 paras*); ❑ без грош е he hasn't got a penny (cent); за свој грош at one's own expense; три за грош му е to chicken out; to show the white feather; to lack the courage (*to do s. th.*); го стори грошот злота *prov.* to throw good money after bad; грош петел шеесет пари крчма *prov.* what you lose on the swings you gain on the roundabouts

грпка *f* hump; bump

грст -и -ови *m* handful (*also fig.*); со грсти by the handful; грст луѓе a handful of people; на еден со грст, на друг со прст *prov.* generous to one, nothing for the other

грсти се *impf* to amass money

грстум *adv* by the handful; зема грстум to take (*s. th.*) by the handful, to help oneself

груб *adj* 1 rough; unvarnished; coarse; boorish; crude; blatant; груб шајак coarse cloth; груб човек rough/ vulgar person, boor; груб одговор rude (curt) reply; груба стварност reality; во груби црти in rough (broad) outline; груб глас rasping/gruff voice; груба грешка flagrant (gross) error, serious mistake 2 *dial.* ugly, *see* грд, грозен 1; ❑ ах, груба јас! oh, woe is me!

груби *impf* I to make ugly, disfigure, *see* грди; го груби изгледот на куќата it spoils the appearance of the house II – **ce** to become ugly/unsightly; to make o.s. ugly, disfigure o.s., spoil one's looks

грубијан *m* boor

грубо *adv* roughly, approximately; грубо пресметано roughly <calculated>, at a guess

грубост *f* roughness; coarseness, coarse quality; vulgarity, boorishness; rudeness, rude conduct; crudity, crudeness; каква грубост! how rude!

грува *impf* 1 to thresh (*grain*) 2 *fig. colloq.* to cram, study hard 3 *fig. see* 'пра[2]

Грузиец -ијци *m* Georgian

Грузија *f* Georgia

Грузијка *f* (*fem. form*) *see* Грузиец

Грузин<ец> *m see* Грузиец

Грузинка *f see* Грузијка

грузи<и>**ски** *adj* Georgian

група *f* group; cluster; clump; department (*at university*); група луѓе a group of people; крвна група blood group (type); група острови cluster of islands; филолошки факултет, група англиски јазик Faculty of Modern Languages and Literatures, English Department

групација -ии *f* 1 grouping; групација на силите distribution (alignment) of forces 2 group, squad, party 3 *Pol.* faction

групаштво *n* factionalism

групен -пна *adj* group; групна терапија group therapy

групúра *pf & impf* I to group, classify II – **ce** to form group<s>, cluster

групно *adv* in groups

грутка *f* soil, sod; lump, clod; родна грутка native

soil, native land; грутка снег lump of snow; snow-ball; грутки-грутки all in lumps, lumpy; *fig.* грутка в грло lump in the throat

грутче   *n dim. of* грутка; small lump; tuber

грутчест   *adj* lumpy

грцизам   -змот *m* 1 philhellenism 2 hellenism

грцизира   *pf & impf* I to hellenize II – се to become hellenized

Грција   *f* Greece

грч   -еви -ови *m* cramp; convulsion, spasm; ме фати грч I've got a cramp; I had a spasm (convulsion); породилни грчеви labour contractions

грчав   *adj* stunted, scrawny, skinny, undeveloped; contorted; sickly, feeble

грчави   *impf* to become stunted; to grow thin, lose weight

грчавина   *f see* грчавост

грчавост   *f* stunted/wasted state

грчи[1]   *impf* I 1 to twist *trans.*, contort; to contract *trans.*; (*прсти*) to clench; (*усни*) to purse; грчи раце to clench one's fists; грчи лице од болки to grimace from pain 2 *dial.* to crease, crumple II – се 1 to contract *intrans.*, become clenched, contorted; to writhe, twist convulsively, wriggle; телото му се грчеше his body was convulsed; лицето му се грчеше од напор his face was contorted with effort 2 *dial.* to be creased, crumpled

грчи[2]   *impf* I to hellenize, make Greek II – се to become hellenized

грчи[3]   *impf* 1 to snore 2 to grunt; to hum, buzz; to rumble; (*за куче*) to growl

грчки   *adj* Greek

губер   *m* coarse woollen blanket, heavy/shaggy homespun rug; ❑ спроти губерот within (according to) one's means

губернатор   *m* 1 *Hist.* prefect 2 (*see* гувернер) governor

губернија   -ии *f Hist.* province; ❑ се однесуваш како да е ова твоја губернија you're treating this like your own property

губи   *impf* I 1 to lose *trans.*; губи сила to lose strength; (*за закон*) to lose its force (validity); губи надеж to lose hope (heart); губи право to forfeit a right; губи партија to lose a game (*e.g. chess*); губи на избори to lose an election; губи на карти to lose at cards; ❑ губи нешто/некого од пред очи to lose sight of s.o./s.th.; губи нешто од предвид to overlook s.th., neglect s.th.; губи глава to lose one's head; губи нерви 1. (*станува нетрпелив*) to become impatient 2. (*избувнува*) to lose one's temper (*colloq.* cool); губи ориентација to lose one's bearings; губи присебност to lose one's temper; губи време to waste time; старо (ветво) крпи, конци губи *prov.* to throw good money after bad 2 *f.p.* (*убива*) to kill; to ruin II – се to get lost, disappear, vanish; (*за звук*) to fade *intrans.*; *fig.* to lose consciousness; се губи во далечината to disappear in the distance; кај се губите? where have you been all this time? губи се! get lost! *vulg.* bugger off! се губи во заборав to fall into oblivion

губилиште   *n* place of execution

гувее   *impf* 1 (*of a bride*) to express respect for one's in-laws and wedding guests by silence 2 *fig.* to stand

dejected (*before s.o.*); to mope (look glum) (*before s.o.*); гувее како млада невеста to be struck dumb

гувернанта   *f* governess

гувернер   *m* governor

гуга   *impf see* гука[2]

гугне   *pf* гугна *aor. see* гукне

гугнува   *impf of* гугне

гугувејче   *n arch.* cruet

гугувка   *f Zool. see* гугутка 1

гугувче   *n* 1 *dim. of* гугувка 2 *fig.* darling, my pet 3 kind of small cake

гугутка   *f* 1 *Zool.* (Streptopelia decaocto) collared dove 2 *dial.* core, nucleus; kernel, *see* јатка 3 wooden spool (*in a loom*)

гугушлија   *adj indecl.* dove-grey, ash-coloured, ashen

гудало   *n Mus.* bow (*for stringed instrument*)

гудач   *m Mus.* player of a bowed string instrument, string player

гудачки   *adj* string; гудачки оркестар string orchestra

гуде   *n hyp.* piglet

гуди[1]   *impf* to play a bowed stringed instrument, fiddle, bow

гуди[2]   *impf dial. see* тркала (се), вала[2] (се), валка (се) 2

гужва   *f* 1 loop (*of plaited twigs or straw*) 2 rowlock 3 *melée*, crush

гуза   *f Zool.* (Fulica atra) coot

гука[1]   *f dial. see* цумка, змучка

гука[2]   *impf* 1 to coo (*also fig.*); тие си гукаат they are billing and cooing 2 (*за дете*) to crow, utter happy cries

гукне   *pf* гукна *aor.* 1 to coo <once> 2 *fig.* to say, utter; тој не гукна he didn't utter a murmur

гукнува   *impf of* гукне

гулаб   *m Zool.* pigeon, dove; див гулаб (Columba livia) rock-dove; гулаб вртало tumbler <pigeon>; *fig.* гулаб! гулабе! my dear! ❑ гулаб на мирот the dove of peace; подобро врапче в рака, отколку гулаб на гранка *prov.* a bird in the hand is worth two in the bush

гулабар   *m* pigeon breeder, pigeon-fancier

гулабарник   -ци *m* pigeon-house, dovecote

гулабица   *f* female pigeon, hen pigeon; *fig.* гулабице! my darling!

гулапче   *n dim. of* гулаб

гулаш   *m Cul.* goulash

гулден   *m* guilder, gulden

гума   *f* rubber; автомобилска гума car tyre; внатрешна <автомобилска> гума inner tube; гума за бришење rubber, eraser; гума за цвакање chewing-gum; гума за пливање float

гумарабика   *f* gum arabic

гумен[1]   *adj* rubber *attrib.*; гумена топка rubber ball; гумени чевли galoshes, rubber overshoes, *Am.* rubbers; гумени чизми gumboots

гумен[2]   *m Zool.* (Athene noctua) little owl

гумира   *pf & impf* to rubberize, cover with rubber; to gum

гумнар   *m* (*popular name for*) August

гумно   *n* 1 threshing-floor 2 *fig.* threshing, threshing season

гуна   *f see* гуња

гунгула   *f* 1 shoving, jostling; disturbance, tumult 2 crowd

гуња *f* shepherd's cloak (*type of long peasant jacket*)

гурабија *f* **1** kind of cake **2** kind of small winter rock melon

гурбет *m* **1** *see* печалба; оди на гурбет to go abroad to make one's living **2** *f.p.* wanderer, nomad, gypsy

гурбетлак *m* life as a migrant worker

гурбетува *impf* to go abroad to earn one's living

гурбетчија -ии *m* migrant worker, *see* печалбар

гурбетчиство *n see* гурбет 1, печалбарство

гурелав *adj* suppurating

гурелави *impf* to suppurate, fester

гурелка *f* (*usu. pl*) matter, suppuration

гурман *m* epicure, gourmand

гурманлак *m* gourmandism, gluttony

гусак -ци *m* gander

гусар *m* pirate, corsair

гусарски *adj* pirate; гусарски брод pirate ship, privateer

гуска *f* **1** *Zool.* goose; дива гуска wild goose **2** *colloq. iron.* (*за жена*) goose, silly woman **3** (*за болни*) bedpan; bottle, urinal

гускар *m* gooseherd

гускарник -ци *m* goose pen

гускин *adj* goose, goose's; гускино јајце goose's egg, goose-egg

гусла *f* *Folk. Mus.* rebec<k>, psaltery

гуслар *m* *Mus.* rebec player, bard

гусли *impf* to play the rebec (psaltery)

гусок -ци *m see* гусак

густ *adj* thick, dense; густа шума dense forest; густо сито fine sieve; густа коса thick hair; густо население dense population; густо млеко rich (creamy) milk; густа каша thick porridge, gruel; густа магла heavy mist, thick fog

густина *f* density; густина на населението density of the population

густира *impf* to enjoy, relish, savour

гутаперка *f* gutta-percha

гутурал *m* *Phon.* guttural <consonant>

гутурален -лна *adj* *Phon.* guttural, velar; гутурални гласови guttural (velar) sounds

гуша *f* **1** (*грло*) throat; (*врат*) neck; (*подбрадок*) double chin, (*на добиток или стар човек*) dewlap, (*на птица*) crop, craw; ❑ на мртвите за душа, на живите в гуша let the dead bury their dead; life goes on; мисли за в гуша he only thinks of his stomach; се фатија гуша за гуша they are at one another's throats, they are at daggers drawn; фаќа некого за гуша to jump down s.o.'s throat; до гуша во долгови up to his neck in debts; доаѓа нешто некому до гуша to be more than one can take (bear) **2** *Med.* goitre

гушав *adj* **1** (*за птица*) with a large crop **2** (*за човек*) goitrous, suffering from goitre

гушавец -вци *m* **1** pouter <pigeon> **2** goitrous person, person suffering from goitre

гушавка *f* *Zool. see* летница 1

гушавост *f* goitre

гушале *n*, **гушалка** *f* & **гушало** *n* kerchief, headscarf

гушар *m* *Zool.* (Ardea cinerea) grey heron

гуши *impf* to clean, gut (*fish*)

гуши се *impf* **1** to snuggle up (*до* – to s.o.) **2** to choke, gasp *intrans.*; се гуши во долгови to be up to one's neck in debts; се гуши во солзи to choke on one's tears

гушка[1] *f* **1** double chin **2** crop (*of birds*) **3** goitre **4** *dial.* kerchief; strap (*on a helmet*)

гушка[2] *impf* **I** to hug, embrace, cuddle *trans.* **II** – се **1** to hug *intrans.*, embrace one another, cuddle *intrans.* **2** *see* гуши се

гушне *pf* гушна *aor.* **I** to give (*s.o.*) a hug **II** – се to give each other a hug, embrace *intrans.*

гушница *f* necklace of old silver coins

гуштер *m* *Zool.* lizard; ❑ блуе <зелени> гуштери (*на некого*) to shower abuse (*on s.o.*), call down fire and brimstone (*on s.o.*)

гуштерица *f* *Zool.* small lizard; кој е каснат од змија, нему му е страв и од гуштерица *prov.* once bitten, twice shy

г-ца *abbr.* (*госпоѓица*) Miss; Ms

Д

да¹ *part* yes

да² *conj* and; and so; so; *see* та, па¹

да³ *part* **1** (*introducing orders, wishes, requests, etc.*) веднаш да си дошол! come at once! да ми донесеше малку вода could you please bring me a little water? голем да пораснеш! many happy returns! да даде Господ! God grant it! да пукнеш! may you croak! **2** (*introducing a question*) да не си нешто болен? are you ill, by any chance? **3** (*adding emphasis*) да врне, да тура it rained cats and dogs

да⁴ *conj* **1** (*often also за да*) <in order> to, so as to; се скри да ја чека he hid in order to wait for her **2** if; да не бев зафатен, ќе дојдев I would have come if I hadn't been busy; арно е да молчиш it will be best if you keep quiet **3** (*linking auxiliary/modal verb with main verb*) сакаше да замине he wanted to set off; почна да плаче he began to weep **4** (*in compound conjunctions*) без да without; дојдов, без да знам што била работата I came without knowing what it was all about; дури да while, until; дури да речеш еден, го снемало before you could say "Jack Robinson," he had disappeared; како да as if; како да спие it looks as though he's asleep; кога да whenever; кога да поминам, сè него го гледам whenever I pass, I see him; колку да however much, no matter how much; колку да мислиш, исто ти се фаќа however much you think about it, the end result will be the same; место да instead of; место да работи, тој цел ден пие instead of working, he drinks the whole day; пред да before; угаси пред да легнеш put out the light/fire before you go to bed!

даб *m Bot.* oak <tree>

дабар *m Zool.* beaver

дабиште *n augm. of* даб

дабјак -ци *m* oak coppice, stand of oaks

Даблин *m* Dublin

даблинец -нци *m* Dubliner

даблинка *f* (*fem. form*) *see* даблинец

даблински *adj* Dublin

дабов *adj* oaken, oak; дабова маса oak table

дабовина *f* oak<-wood>

дабовица *f* oak stick, club, cudgel

дава (се) *impf of* даде (се); ❑ душа дава that is ideal; пет пари не дава he doesn't give a pin (two hoots) <for that>; главата ја давам I'd give my life; животот си го дава to lay down one's life; се дава филм/претстава a film/show is on; не се дава to hold the field; to keep trying/fighting; to take a hard line

давалец *m in the prov.*: давалец – питалец generosity leads to poverty

давање *n from* дава **1** giving **2** debt; имам ли нешто за давање? do I owe <you> anything? **3** marriage; не е момата за давање the girl is not fit/ready for marriage yet **4** *colloq.* давање-земање dealings, business; со него нејќам да имам давање-земање I'll have no truck with him

давач *m* giver; donor

давачка *f* **1** giving **2** duty; taxes; tribute; големи давачки имал народот the people had to pay heavy taxes **3** debt<s> **4** давачка-земачка, *see* давање

давеж *m* drowning; choking, strangling; давеж на кучиња drowning puppies; ❑ *colloq.* вистински (прав) давеж *sl.* a real pain in the neck, a real drag

давеник -ци *m* drowning man; давеник и за сламка се фаќа *prov.* a drowning man will clutch at a straw; any port in a storm

давеница *f* (*fem. form*) *see* давеник

дави *impf* **I 1** (*стега за гуша*) to strangle; (*задушува*) to choke *trans.*, throttle; to smother, suffocate *trans.*; ❑ *colloq.* <ајде>не дави! cut it out! **2** (*во вода*) to drown *trans.* **II** – се **1** to choke, suffocate *intrans.* **2** to drown *intrans.*; кога човек се дави <и> за сламка се фаќа *prov.* a drowning man will clutch at a straw **3** to strangle/choke one another

даволка се *impf* to engage in horseplay, wrestle, fight (*for fun, in play*)

дага *f* **1** (*за бочва*) stave **2** (*во нива и сл.*) layer, stratum, substratum; дага песок substratum of sand

даговит *adj* layered, stratal

дагообразен -зна *adj* stave-shaped, curved

дада *f child.* older sister

даде *pf* **I 1** to give; даде совет/подарок/ветување/одобрение/наредба to give advice/a gift/a promise/approval/an order; ❑ даде дозвола/налог to issue a licence/an order; даде препорака to make a recommendation, recommend; даде под кирија to rent out; даде на чување to hand over for safekeeping; даде збор на говорник to give a speaker the floor; даде кредит/попуст to grant a credit/discount; даде клетва to take (make, swear) an oath; даде слобода to grant freedom; to give a free hand; даде срок to set a deadline; даде суд to give an opinion; шипинки му даде he gave him nothing, he sent him off empty-handed; дај си ја раката! give us your hand!, shake hands!, it's a bargain!; даде збор to give one's word; даде чесен збор to give one's word of honour; даде глас 1. to make o.s. known, give a sign of life 2. to vote; даде вик to call out, give a shout; даде на знаење to make known, announce, inform; даде некому корпа to rebuff s.o.; не му даде мира it gave him no peace; ми даде маки/it gave me a hard time; му даде зорт he had trouble with it; he put pressure on him, he forced him; даде некому изим (дозвола) to give s.o. permission; дај си гајрет calm down! stop worrying! take courage! даде некому благослов to give s.o. one's blessing; што ум ми даваш? what would you advise me to do? даде некому опинците to tell s.o. to be off, to send s.o. packing; даде некому по капа to tell s.o. off, to give s.o. a good dressing down; дај Боже! God grant it! I hope so! не дај Боже! God forbid! дал ти Бог добро! God bless you! (*as a response to a greeting*);

даде сѐ од себе to spare no expense; to do one's best, give one's all **2** to apprentice; to give (*a girl*) in marriage, marry off (*a girl*); го даде сина си на занает за шивач he apprenticed his son to a tailor; го даде сина си на (во) училиште he sent his son to school; даде на суд to take to court; ми ја даде ќерка си за жена he gave me his daughter's hand in marriage **3** to pay; многу си дал за овие чевли you paid a lot for these shoes **4** (*за цена, возраст и сл.*) to set, determine; каква цена даваш? what price do you put‹on this›? колку години ми даваш? how old do you think I am? **5** to sell; ја даде куќата пошто-зашто he sold his house cheaply (for a song) **6** to bear, produce, yield; нивата ни даде колку за јадење this field kept us in food; даде резултати to produce results **7** to arrange, put on, give; (*драма, композиција*) to play *trans.*; даде гозба to arrange a banquet; даде концерт to give a concert **8** to let, allow, permit; не му даде да здивне he gave him no chance to catch his breath; дај ми ти мене да правам што сакам let me do what I like (want)! **9** (*with verbal nouns*) што трчање даде! how he ran! што молење му дадов! how I begged him! **II – се 1** to give in, yield, surrender; не се даде лесно he didn't give in easily **2** to become involved (*на – in*), embark (*on*), devote o.s. (*to*); се даде на учење to devote oneself to one's studies; се даде во потера по to give chase to

даден *adj* given, certain; во дадената ситуација in this case, in such a situation

дадијарка *f* nanny, governess

дажба *f* ration

дајре *n Mus.* tambourine

дајреџија *m Mus.* tambourine player

дактил *m Prosody* dactyl

дактилен -лна *adj Prosody* dactylic; дактилна рима dactylic rhyme

дактилограф *m* ‹male› typist

дактилографија *f* typing

дактилографка *f* ‹woman› typist

дактилологија *f* sign language

дактилоскопија *f* dactyloscopy, identification by study of fingerprints

далавера *f colloq.* fraud, deceit; intrigue

далаве||џија *m colloq.* swindler, cheat

далак *m* **1** spleen **2** oedema (swelling) of the spleen

далга *f see* бран

далековид *adj* **1** *Med.* long-sighted, *Am.* far-sighted **2** *fig.* far-sighted, far-seeing, prescient

далековиден -дна *adj see* далековид 2

далековидност *f see* далековидост 2

далековид||ост *f* **1** *Med.* long sight, long-sightedness, *Am.* far-sightedness **2** *fig.* foresight, prudence, prescience

далекоисточен -чна *adj* Far Eastern

далекосежен -жна *adj* far-reaching; далекосежни последици far-reaching consequences

далекосежност *f* far-reaching consequences; extent

далеку *adv* far; far away; далеку сум од таа работа I am very far from all that; ❏ ни оддалеку nowhere near; далеку отиде to get very far; to go to great lengths; подалеку од мене! keep away from me! don't come near me! далеку дотурка (стигна) to get far; to come a long way; далеку од тоа far from it; not at all; I wouldn't dream of it; далеку од целта

wide of the mark; далеку од очите, далеку од срцето *prov.* out of sight, out of mind

далекум *adv arch. see* далеку

дален -лна *adj see* далечен

далечен -чна *adj* distant, far-away; далечни земји far-off lands, distant countries; далечен пат a long journey; далечното минато the distant past; далечни роднини distant relations

далечина *f* distance; тоне во далечината to disappear in the distance; далечината од сонцето до земјата the distance from the sun to the earth

далечински *adj* remote; далечинско управување remote control

далечко *adv dim. of* далеку; далечко е it's quite a distance (way)

дали 1 *interrogative part.* (*also expressing doubt, uncertainty, hesitation*) дали се дојдени? have they come? дали да одам дали (или) не? should I go or not? **2** *conj* (*in indirect questions*) if, whether; види дали се дома see if they are at home!

далјан *m dial.* fish trap

Далматинец -нци *m* Dalmatian

Далматинка *f* (*fem. form*) *see* Далматинец

далматински *adj* Dalmatian

Далмација *f* Dalmatia

далнина *f poet. see* далечина

далновид *adj see* далековиден

далновод *m* long-distance power (transmission) line; високонапонски далновод high-tension power line

далноглед *adj see* далековиден

далногледност *f see* далековидност

далтонизам -змот *m* colour-blindness, daltonism

далтонист *m* colour-blind person

дама¹ *f* **1** lady; ❏ дами и господа Ladies and Gentlemen; дамите имаат предност! ladies first! **2** (*во карти*) queen; дама пик queen of spades

дама² *f* **1** nine men's morris, merels (*game*) **2** draughts, *Am.* checkers

дамазлак *m* store cattle; (*коњи*) bloodstock; за дамазлак for breeding

дамар *m* **1** blood vesel; (*жила*) vein; (*артерија*) artery; (*пулс*) pulse **2** (*нерв*) nerve **3** (*пукнатина*) crack, fissure

дамаск *m* damask; чаршав од дамаск damask ‹tablecloth›

дамаскин *m* damaskin (*18th-century vernacular homily*)

дамаслија *adj indecl. arch.* сабја дамаслија Damascene sword/blade

дамаџана *f* demijohn

дамаџија -ии *m colloq.* draughts (*Am.* checkers) enthusiast

дамка *f* **1** (*флека*) spot; speckle, speck; stain; blotch; blot (*also fig.*); ❏ дамка на нечиј образ a blot on s.o.'s escutcheon; a skeleton in the cupboard **2** (*на кожата*) spot, speckle; blotch; дамки на лицето freckles; сончеви дамки sunspots; дамки од сипаници pock-marks **3** sign, mark **4** *arch.* tax on the sale of cattle

дамкоса *pf* to mark; to stain; to blot *trans.* (*also fig.*)

дамла *f* **1** stroke; го удри дамлата he had a stroke; *fig.* he was astounded **2** paralysis

дамлоса ‹се› *pf* to become paralysed; *fig.* to be astounded

дамнешен -шна *adj dial. see* одамнешен; ❏ во дамнешни времиња in the olden days; in days of yore

дамски *adj* (*see* дама¹ 1) lady's; дамски кројач dressmaker

дамчест *adj* spotty; dappled, spotted; blotchy

Данец -нци *m* Dane

Данка *f* (*fem. form*) *see* Данец

данок -ци *m* tax; данок на додадена вредност value-added tax, VAT; данок на доход (приход) income tax; данок на приход од капитал capital gains tax; посредни/непосредни даноци direct/indirect taxes; ослободено од плаќање данок tax-free; данок на промет excise tax; sales tax; ❏ плаќа данок на/за to pay the price for; става данок на to impose (put, levy) tax on; данок во крв *Hist.* taking of children as tribute

даночен -чна *adj* tax *attrib.*; даночна стапка tax rate; даночен обврзник taxpayer; даночно олеснување tax deduction

даночник *m* tax collector

Данска *f* Denmark

дански *adj* Danish

дар *m* **1** (*подарок*) gift, present; donation; (*usu. pl*) bride's present (*to best man, future in-laws etc.*) **2** gift, talent, aptitude; дар за музика gift for music; дар за јазици flair for languages

дара *f* tare

дарба *f* **1** gift, talent, aptitude; ❏ има <природна> дарба за to have a natural bent for **2** *arch.* present

дарбука *f Mus.* kind of drum

дарвинизам -змот *m* Darwinism

дарвинист *m* Darwinist, Darwinian

дарвинистички *adj* Darwinian

Дарданели *pl* Dardanelles

дарданелски *adj* Dardanelles *attrib.*

дарежлив *adj* generous

дарежливост *f* generosity

дари *pf see* дарува

дарител *m* donor, contributor; *Leg.* grantor; дарители на крв blood donors

дарителка *f* (*fem. form*) *see* дарител

дармар *m* disorder, bedlam, chaos; вистински дармар absolute chaos; a pretty kettle of fish

даровен -вна *adj* received/intended as a gift

даровит *adj* gifted, talented

даровитост *f* talent

дарпна *f* headscarf, large white kerchief

дарува *pf & impf* to present (*некого со нешто, нешто на некого – s.o. with s.th., s.th. to s.o.*); to shower (*s.o.*) with gifts; to give (*s.th.*) away; сватовите ја даруваа невестата the in-laws gave gifts to the bride; дарува жито to give grain away

дарувач *m* giver, donor

дарчин *m* cinnamon <tree>

даскал *m colloq.* schoolmaster, teacher

даскалица *f* (*fem. form*) schoolmistress, teacher

дата *f see* датум

датив *m Gram.* dative <case>

дативен -вна *adj Gram.* dative

датира *pf & impf* to date; датира писмо to date a letter; спомениците датираат од 14 век the monuments date from the 14th century

датотека *f* data file

датум *m* date; ❏ датум на испорака date of delivery; датум на плаќање date of payment; кој датум е денес? what's the date today?

дафина *f Bot.* (Elaeagnus angustifolia) oleaster, wild olive tree

дафинов *adj* oleaster *attrib.*

дахија -ии *m Hist.* Ottoman governor; *fig.* tyrant

два, две *num* (два *m*, две *f, n*) two; два дена и две ноќи two days and two nights; две деца two children; два и два се четири two and two make four; ❏ како две и две четири as easy (simple) as ABC; не знае колку се два и два not to have enough sense to come out of the rain; ни едно, ни две without mincing words; without beating about the bush; off the cuff; од двете, ниедно neither one thing, nor the other

дваж *adv* twice

дваесет *num* twenty

дваесетгодишен -шна *adj* **1** twenty years old **2** lasting twenty years; twenty-year *attrib.*

дваесетгодишнина *f* twentieth anniversary

дваесетина *num* about twenty

дваесетмина *num* (*of men or mixed groups*) twenty

дваесетти *adj* twentieth

дваесеттина *f* twentieth <part>

двајца *num* **1** couple (*a man and a woman*) **2** (*of m human beings*) two; двајца браќа two brothers; двајца по двајца two by two, in pairs; ❏ каде двајца, тој тројца (*of an uninvited guest*) he turns up like a bad penny; двајца без тројца a thin audience/attendance; потребни се двајца да (за) . . . it takes two to . . .

дванаесет *num* twelve; ❏ пет (минути) до дванаесет eleventh hour

дванаесетгодишен -шна *adj* **1** twelve years old **2** lasting twelve years; twelve-year *attrib.*

дванаесетмина *num* (*of men or mixed groups*) twelve

дванаесетпати *num* twelve times

дванаесетпрсник *m Anat.* duodenum

дванаесетти *adj* twelfth

двапати *adv* twice

два-три *num* two or three

два-триесет *num* twenty or thirty

два-триесетмина *num* twenty or thirty (*people*)

два-тринаесет *num* twelve or thirteen

два-тринаесетмина *num* twelve or thirteen (*people*)

два-тројца *num* two or three (*people*)

две *num see* два

двегодишен -шна *adj* **1** two years old **2** lasting two years; two-year *attrib.*

двенеделен *adj see* двонеделен

двесте *num* two hundred

двестегодишен -шна *adj* **1** two hundred years old **2** lasting two hundred years, bicentennial

двестегодишнина *f* two-hundredth anniversary, bicentenary

двестемина *num* two hundred (*people*)

двестотен -тна & **двести** *adj* two-hundredth

две-три *num* two or three

две-тристотини *num* two or three hundred

двеуми се *impf see* двоуми се

двигател *m* **1** *Tech.* motor, engine; propulsion **2** *fig.* promoter (*of new ideas, etc.*), prime mover; mastermind; moving force

движење *n* 1 movement, motion; движење со глава movement of the head; движење на цените movement of prices; движење на трупите troop movement; пушти (стави) во движење to set in motion; работничко движење workers' movement 2 (*шетање*) walk, stroll; exercise 3 (*сообраќај*) traffic; движење на улиците street traffic

движечки *adj* moving, starting; *Tech.* impellent; движечки сили driving forces, impelling agents

движи *impf* **I 1** to shift, move *trans.*; to drive *trans.*; to draw, pull *trans.*; to set in motion; ветерот ги движеше облаците the wind was driving the clouds; водата го движи колото the water drives the mill-wheel; првите трамваи ги движеле коњи the first trams were horse-drawn 2 *fig.* to move, urge, arouse (*s.o. to do s.th.*); верата во победата нè движи напред belief in victory urges us forward **II** – **се 1** to move *intrans.*; to move about *intrans.*; to exercise *intrans.*; to travel, get about; усните на болниот се движеа the patient's lips were moving; постојано се движи he/it is continually moving; it is in a constant state of flux; се движи меѓу артистите he moves in acting circles 2 to range (*од-до – from-to*), vary *intrans.*; to fluctuate (*between-and*); цената се движи од 1500 до 1700 денари the price varies from 1,500 to 1,700 denars

двобој -ои *m* duel; предизвика на двобој to challenge to a duel

двоглав *adj* two-headed

двоглас<ка> *f Gram.* diphthong

двогласен -сна *adj Mus.* for/in two voices, in two parts, two-part *attrib.*

двогодишен -шна *adj see* двегодишен

двогрб *adj* two-humped; двогрба камила two-humped camel

дводелен -лна *adj* bipartite; two-piece; дводелен костум two-piece suit

дводимензионáлен -лна *adj* two-dimensional

дводомен *adj Pol.* bicameral

дводневен -вна *adj* two days', lasting two days, two-day *attrib.*

двоен *adj* double, twofold; dual; двоен прозорец double window; прозорец со двојно стакло double-glazed window; *Comm.* двојно книговодство double-entry bookkeeping; *Math.* двојна дропка complex fraction

двои *impf* **I 1** to divide <up> *trans.*; to separate *trans.*; двои ливада to divide <up> a field; планината го двои островот the mountain <range> divides the island in two; овчарот ги двоеше нашите овци од овците на соседите the shepherd separated our sheep from the neighbours'; неговата дарба го двои од светот his talent sets him apart from other people 2 (*се разликува*) to be different, differ, stand out; платново двои this linen is different; од сите деца ова двои this child is different from all the others **II** – **се 1** to separate *intrans.*; патот се двои the road forks 2 to move/break away; to branch off; to divide *intrans.*; to split *intrans.*; тој се двои од своите другари he goes his own way; една овца секогаш се двоеше од стадото one sheep kept breaking away from the flock 3 to go away, leave, part with; се двои од куќата to leave home 4 *see* I 2; со својата начитаност тој се двоеше од (меѓу) своите

другари his erudition made him stand out from (among) his comrades

двоина *f Gram.* dual

двојазичен -чна *adj* bilingual; двојазично издание bilingual edition

двојајчан *adj* fraternal, dizygotic, two-egg; двојајчани близнаци fraternal twins

двојак *adj* double, twofold, variant

двојанка *f* 1 (*кола*) two-wheeled cart 2 (*свирка*) double pipe 3 twin sister 4 double fruit

двојка *f* 1 (*цифрата* 2) <figure> two 2 (*школска оцена*) two (*out of five, hence = 'satisfactory'*), pass 3 (*во карти*) two; двојка пик two of spades 4 couple, pair, brace, twosome; брачна двојка married couple 5 (*автобус, трамвај итн.*) <number> two

двојник -ци *m* perfect likeness, double

двојно *adv* doubly

двојство *n* duality; dualism

двојца *num dial. see* двајца

двокатен -тна *adj* 1 two-storeyed; двокатен автобус double-decker bus 2 two-ply; двокатна волница two-ply wool

двокатница *f* two-storeyed house/building

двоколка *f* two-wheeled cart

двокрак *adj* biped<al>; two-legged; two-armed, double; двокрак лост double lever

двократен -тна *adj* occurring twice; double; двократно работно време split shift

двократно *adv* in two periods

двокреветен -тна *adj* with two beds; двокреветна соба double room

двокрилен -лна *adj* two-winged; *Bot., Zool.* dipterous

дволистен -сна *adj* two-leaved

дволичен -чна *adj* two-faced, false, hypocritical

дволичи *impf* to dissemble, act hypocritically

дволичник -ци *m* two-faced person, hypocrite, dissembler, double-dealer

дволичност *f* duplicity, pretence, hypocrisy

двомесечен -чна *adj* two months', lasting two months, two-month *attrib.*; bimonthly

двометраш *m colloq.* tall person, six-footer

двомоторен -рна *adj* with two motors (engines)

двонасочен -чна *adj* two-way; двонасочен сообраќај two-way traffic

двонеделен -лна *adj* two-weeks', fortnight's, lasting two weeks, two-week *attrib.*; fortnightly; двонеделна плата fortnightly payment

двоножен -жна *adj* two-legged; biped<al>

двоножец -шци *m* biped

двоок *adj* two-eyed

двоосен -сна *adj* biaxial

двопартиски *adj* two-party

двопек *m* Melba (thin) toast, rusk

двополов *adj* 1 *Elec., Phys.* bipolar 2 *Biol., Med.* bisexual, hermaphrodite

двополовост *f* 1 *Elec., Phys.* bipolarity 2 *Biol., Med.* bisexuality

двор *m* 1 (*на куќа*) yard; (*во голема зграда*) courtyard 2 (*кралски, царски*) court

двореден -дна *adj* (*за дрва и др.*) in two rows; (*за сако*) double-breasted

дворен -рна *adj* yard *attrib.*; дворно место yard

дворец -рци *m* 1 palace, castle 2 (*sg only*) *dim. of* двор 2

двориште *n augm. of* двор 1

дворјанин -јани *m* noble, lord

дворјанка *f* noblewoman, lady

дворјански *adj* noble

дворјанство *n* nobility

двoрог & двoрожен -жна *adj* two-horned

дворски *adj* (*see* двор 2) court

двосед *m* two-seater; кајак двосед tandem kayak

двосложен -жна *adj* disyllabic

двосмислен *adj* ambiguous

двосмисленост *f* ambiguity

двособен -бна *adj* two-room; двособен стан two-room flat

двостран *adj* bilateral, two-sided

двостраност *f* bilaterality

двострук *adj* double, twofold, *see* двоен

двотомен -мна *adj* two-volume *attrib.*

двотретински *adj* two-thirds

двоумење *n* hesitation, dilemma

двоуми се *impf* to hesitate, waver

двофазен -зна *adj Elec.* two-phase

двоцевен -вна *adj* double-barrelled

двоцевка *f* double-barrelled gun

двоцифрен *adj* double-figure; двоцифрени броеви double figures

двочасовен -вна *adj* of two hours, two hours', two-hour *attrib.*

двочлен *adj* composed of two members; *Math.* binomial

де *part* 1 (*as encouragement, exhortation*) come on! ајде де! get moving! почни де! get on with it! 2 (*expressing displeasure*) доста де! enough of that! cut it out! 3 (*for emphasis*) знам де I know that already

де … де *conj* now … now; едниот де другиот now one, now the other

деба́та *f* debate, discussion

деба́ти́ра *impf* to debate, discuss

дебел *adj* 1 thick; dense; дебел мраз thick ice; дебели веѓи bushy eyebrows; дебела сенка deep shade; ❏ дебела глава pig-headed person; дебела лага outright (shameless, barefaced) lie; дебела кожа thick skin; дебело црево *Anat.* colon, large intestine 2 (*згоен*) fat; obese 3 (*за глас*) deep; (*засипнат*) 4 (*as noun*) fat man

дебелее <се> *impf* to grow fat, put on weight

дебели се *impf see* дебелее <се>

дебелика *f Bot.* (Bryonia alba) white bryony

дебелина *f* thickness; fatness

дебеличок -чка *adj* plump, chubby

дебелка *adj* (*no masculine form*) *dim. of* дебела; plump (chubby) woman/girl

дебелоглавец -вци *m* obtuse person, *colloq.* thick-head

дебелокожен -жна *adj* thick-skinned

дебелокожец -шци *m* thick-skinned person

дебелокорест *adj* with thick rind/peel

дебелокорка *f* thick-rinded melon

дебелуша & дебелушка *f* fat woman/girl

дебелушкам *dim. of* дебел chubby, plump

деби́ *n* debut

деби́л *m* idiot, moron

деби́лен -лна *adj* feeble-minded, moronic

деби́лност *f* feeble-mindedness

дебита́нт *m* debutant; beginner

дебити́ра *pf & impf* to make one's debut

дева *f arch.* maiden, virgin; *Rel.* Света дева Марија Holy (Blessed) Virgin Mary

девалвација *f Econ.* devaluation

девалви́ра *pf & impf Econ.* 1 to devalue 2 to be devalued

деведесет *num* ninety

деведесетгодишен -шна *adj* 1 ninety years old 2 of/for ninety years, ninety-year

деведесетгодишнина *f* ninetieth anniversary

деведесетти *adj* ninetieth

девер *m* 1 dever (*man who chaperones a bride on her wedding day*) 2 brother-in-law (*husband's brother*)

деверица *f* bridesmaid; sister-in-law (*brother-in-law's wife*)

деверичник -ци *m* nephew (*husband's brother's son*)

деверичница *f* niece (*husband's brother's daughter*)

деверов *adj* bridesman's; brother-in-law's; деверова вечера bridesman's supper (*on the day after the wedding, to which the dever and close relatives are invited*)

деверство *n* role (duties) of a *dever*

деверува *impf* to act as *dever*

деверче *n dim. of* девер

девесница *f* spinster, *pejor.* old maid

девет *num* nine

деветгодишен -шна *adj* 1 nine years old 2 of/for nine years, nine-year

деветгодишнина *f* ninth anniversary

деветина *f* 1 nine 2 group of nine 3 ninth <part>

деветини *pl* бабини деветини old wives' tales

деветка *f* 1 <figure> nine 2 (*студентска оцена*) nine (*out of ten*), distinction 3 (*во карти*) nine 4 (*автобус, трамвај итн.*) < number> nine

деветмина *num* (*of men and mixed groups*) nine

деветнаесет *num* nineteen

деветнаесетти *adj* nineteenth

деветстотен -тна & **деветстоти** *adj* nine-hundredth

деветстотини *num* nine hundred

деветти *adj* ninth

деветтина *num see* деветмина

деви́за *f* 1 motto, slogan 2 (*usu. pl*) foreign currency; плаќање во девизи payment in foreign currency

девизен -зна *adj* currency, foreign-currency *attrib.*; девизна берза foreign-currency exchange; девизен курс rate of exchange; девизен прилив export earnings; девизни побарувања currency assets

девијација *f* deviation

девица *f* virgin; *Astron.* Virgo

девојка *f* girl; ❏ девојка за сè maid of all work

девојкин *adj see* девојчин

девоје *n* little girl

девојченце *n see* девоје

девојчин *adj* girl's

девојчински *adj* girls'; girlish

девојчинство *n* girlhood, maidenhood

девојчиште *n augm., pejor. of* девоје

девствен *adj* virginal; virgin

девственик -ци *m* <male> virgin

девственица *f* virgin, *see* девица

девственост *f* virginity

дегажи́ра *pf & impf* 1 *Sport.* to make a throw-in 2 (*од обрски*) to free, discharge 3 (*отпушти од војска*) to discharge

дегажма́н *m* 1 disengagement 2 storeroom, pantry, larder

дегенера́ција *f* degeneration; perversion, depravity

дегене́рик -ци *m* degenerate; freak; monster

дегенери́ра *pf & impf* I 1 to debase, degrade; to deprave, corrupt; to cause to degenerate 2 *see* II II – ce to degenerate, become debased (degraded); to become perverted (depraved)

дегенери́ран *pt* degenerate; perverted, depraved

дегиди *interj see* дејгиди

деградаци́ја *f* degradation, debasement

дегради́ра *pf & impf* to debase, degrade; to demote

дегрес & дегреси́ја *m* degression

дегуста́тор *m* taster; дегустатор на тутун tobacco grader/blender

дегуста́ција *f* tasting, degustation; дегустација на вино wine tasting

дегусти́ра *pf & impf* to taste, degustate

деде & деденце *n hyp.* grandpa, grandad

дедо -овци *m* 1 grandfather; old man (*mode of address to a man two generations older than the speaker*); стар дедо old chap; ❑ дедо Мраз Santa Claus; Jack Frost 2 (*addressing an orthodox priest*) father; дедо попе! Father! дедо владика! Your Grace! My Lord! 3 (*only pl*) ancestors; ❑ останало од дeда прадеда it has remained from time immemorial 4 father-in-law (*of the bridegroom*)

дедов *adj* grandfather's

дедовина *f* patrimony

дедовски *adj* grandfather's; grandfatherly

дедукти́вен -вна *adj* deductive; дедуктивен метод deductive method, deduction

дедукци́ја *f* deduction

деец -јци *m arch.* public figure, advocate; револуционерен деец revolutionary

дежура *pf & impf* to be on duty (call)

дежурен -рна *adj* on duty, on call; дежурна аптека duty pharmacy, all night chemist's; дежурен лекар doctor on duty

дежурство *n* duty, tour of duty

дезаву́ира *pf & impf* to disavow, disown, repudiate

дезен *m* pattern; фустан со цветен дезен dress with a floral pattern

дезерте́р *m* deserter

дезерте́рство *n* desertion

дезерти́ра *pf & impf* to desert; дезертира од својата единица to desert one's unit

дезинсекција *f* fumigation

дезинтереси́ра се *pf & impf* to lose interest (*за – in*)

дезинфекција *f* disinfection

дезинфекцио́нен -она *adj* disinfection; disinfecting

дезинфици́ра *pf & impf* to disinfect

дезинформа́ција *f* misinformation, disinformation

дезинформи́ра *pf & impf* to misinform, mislead

дезодора́нс *m* deodorant

дезоргани́зација *f* disorganization

дезоргани́зира *pf & impf* to disorganize, destabilize

дезориента́ција *f* disorientation

дезориенти́ра *pf & impf* to disorientate, confuse

де́изам -змот *m* deism

де́ист *m* deist

дејгиди & дејди *interj* (*expressing dismay, regret, surprise, esp. f.p.*) oh! alas!

дејност *f* activity; work; непријателска дејност subversive activity; општествени дејности public/ social work

дејство *n* 1 (*pl* -ва) action, effect; дејството на отровот the effect of the poison; под дејство на алкохолот under the influence of alcohol; ❑ во дејство (сила) in force, valid; operative; стапува во дејство to come into effect 2 (*pl* -вија) operation; воени дејствија military operations; hostilities 3 *sg only* (*во литерарно дело*) action; дејството се одвива полека the action unfolds (develops) slowly

дејствува *impf* to act; to function; лекот дејствува брзо the medicine acts (takes effect) quickly; дејствува успокоително to have a soothing effect

дејствувачки *adj* acting, functioning

дека¹ *conj* 1 that; ти ми рече дека дошол you told me that he had come; ❑ *sl.* што дека! so what! big deal! 2 because, as, since; дојдов дека ме повика I came because you called me

дека² *adv dial.* (*see* кај, каде) where; whither; дека си? where are you? дека одиш? where are you going?

декаграм *m* decagramme

дека́да *f* ten days, ten-day period; group of ten; decade

дека́ден -дна *adj* decadal; декаден систем decimal system

декаде́нт *m* decadent

декаде́нтски *adj* decadent

декаденци́ја *f* decadence

декали́тар -три *m* decalitre

декаме́тар -три *m* decametre

декан *m* dean

декана́т *m* dean's office

декар *m* decare, quarter of an acre

деке́мври *m* December

декемвриски *adj* December

деклама́тор *m* orator, reciter

декламаторски *adj* oratorial, declamatory; декламаторско искуство the art of reciting

декламаци́ја -ии *f* declamation, recitation

деклами́ра *impf* to declaim, recite

декларати́вен -вна *adj* declarative, declaratory

деклараци́ја -ии *f* declaration; царинска декларација customs declaration

деклари́ра *pf & impf* to declare

декласи́ра *pf & impf* to declass, degrade

декласи́ран *pt* déclassé

деклинаци́ја -ии *f* 1 *Gram.* declension 2 *Phys., Astron.* declination

деклини́ра *impf* to decline

деколте́ 1 (*pl* -та) décolletage, low-cut (plunging) neckline 2 *adj* décolleté

деколти́ра *pf & impf Dressmaking* to cut a low neckline; to expose the neck and cleavage

деконцентраци́ја *f* 1 decentralization 2 absent-mindedness

декор *m* décor; сценски декор film set

декорате́р *m see* декоратор

декорати́вен -вна *adj* decorative, ornamental

декора́тор *m* (*во театар*) scene painter, scenic artist; (*на куќи*) interior decorator (designer); (*на излог*) <window->dresser

декораци́ја -ии *f* 1 decoration, ornamentation 2

décor **3** (*во театар*) scenery **4** decoration; medal, order **5** *fig.* window-dressing, facade, front

декори́ра *pf & impf* to decorate

декрет *m* decree

декстро́за *f Chem.* dextrose

дел *m* **1** part; помалиот дел the smaller part; ❑ дел по дел bit by bit; inch by inch; најголемиот дел <од> the better part of; the bulk of **2** share, participation; тие имаа дел во таа работа they had a share in that business **3** *Mus.* movement

дела *impf* to trim; to polish, refine

деланка *f* splinter, chip

делач *m* distributor; (*на совети, правда*) dispenser; на делачот оптегачот *prov.* nothing left for the carver (*said when s.o. divides s.th. up among others, leaving nothing for himself*)

делба *f* **1** (*распределување*) distribution, sharing; *Leg.* (*на наследство*) division; (*на недвижен имот*) partition **2** (*дел*) part, share **3** *dial.* (*дарба*) gift, talent; таква делба Бог го делил such is the gift that God gave him **4** (*разделба*) parting, separation

делега́т *m* delegate

делега́ција -ии *f* delegation

делеги́ра *pf & impf* to delegate

дележ *m see* делба

деленик -ци *m* **1** person who has left his family to live alone **2** *Math.* dividend

делени́ца *f* **1** (*fem. form*) *see* деленик 1 **2** divided (shared) house

делење *n from* дели; dividing, division; sharing; separating; *Math.* division; *Comm.* делење на добивка profit sharing

дели[1] *pf & impf* **I 1** to divide, share *trans.*; *Leg.* to partition; дели на два дела to divide into two parts; дели со три to divide by three; дели наследство to share an inheritance; го делам твоето мислење I share your view; ❑ братски го делам алатокот; си го дели залакот to live in each other's pockets; дели тајна со некого to confide in s.o.; дели впечатоци со некого to compare notes with s.o.; делени круши, спокојни заби *prov.* short reckonings make long friends **2** (*раздава*) to distribute, share out, dispense; (*карти*) to deal; дели совети to give advice; дели правда to dispense justice **3** to divide, separate *trans.* (*од – from*); Дрина ја дели Босна од Србија the Drina separates Bosnia from Serbia; многу работи нè делат we are divided by many issues **4** *dial.* to endow; Бог го делил he has God's gift; не му делиле he is not talented **5** (*двои*) to differ (*од – from*); македонскиот јазик дели од српскиот Macedonian differs from Serbian **II – се 1** to divide *intrans.*, be divided (*на – into*); патот се дели the road forks **2** to part (*од – with, from*), take leave (*of*); мома се дели од рода a girl takes leave of her family; превареното месо само се делеше од коските the boiled meat separated (came away) from the bones **3** to set up on one's own; постариот син се дели од таткото the elder son set up on his own

дели[2] *m f.p. see* делија; (*only with names*) Дели Муса Deli Musa, Musa the Bold

делибаша *m Hist.* (*Ottoman*) cavalry commander

делив *adj* divisible

деливост *f* divisibility

делија -ии *m* soldier (*in the Ottoman army*); stout fellow; hero; daredevil

делика́тен -тна *adj* **1** delicate; frail; tender, sensitive **2** attentive, considerate **3** (*за некоја работа*) difficult, delicate, tricky; crucial; деликатно прашање tricky question

деликате́с *m* delicacy

деликате́сен -сна *adj* delicatessen; деликатесна продавница delicatessen (shop)

делика́тност *f* delicacy, tact

деликт *m leg.* offence, misdeed, misdemeanour, felony

делинквент *m* delinquent, offender; малолетни делинквенти juvenile delinquents

делириум *m* delirium; ❑ делириум тременс delirium tremens, chronic alcoholism

делител *m* **1** *Math.* divisor, denominator; најголем заеднички делител highest common denominator **2** distributor; dispenser

делка *impf* **I** to trim; to carve, whittle; делка камења to trim stones; делка нешто од дрво to carve s.th. out of wood; ❑ туку си делка he just potters about **II – се 1** to be suitable for carving; ова дрво не се делка this wood can't be carved **2** *fig.* to learn; се делка кај некого to be apprenticed to s.o.; to learn one's trade from s.o.

делканица *f* **1** trimming; carving **2** s.th. trimmed/carved

делкач *m* trimmer; carver (*of wood, etc.*)

делнат *adj & pt* **1** trimmed; carved; делнато дрво carved wood; trimmed tree **2** *fig.* foolish, crazy, with a screw loose; ❑ делнат во главата a bit touched

делне *pf* делна *aor.* **I 1** to trim; to carve; to make a mark (*on s.th.*) **2** *fig.* to kill **3** ❑ *colloq.* ја делна he did a bunk, he legged it, he did a runner **II – се** to cut o.s.

делник -ци *m* working day

делница *f* **1** allotment, part of a common divided field **2** (*акција*) share **3** section (*of a road, railway*)

делничар *m* part owner; joint heir

делничен -чна *adj* **1** everyday; делничен ден working day; делничен живот daily round **2** *fig.* humdrum, routine

делнички *adj* share; делнички капитал share capital; делничка дивиденда share dividend

делничност *f* (*see* делничен 2) dullness, monotony, everyday routine, daily round; trivia

делнува (се) *impf of* делне (се)

дело *n* **1** deed, act; action, act, work, activity, works; добро дело good deed; уметничко дело work of art; животот и делото на Толстој the life and works of Tolstoy; ❑ во дело in/into action; тоа е негово дело that is his doing; ќе излезе дело на видело the truth will out; it'll come to light; фаќа (затекнува) некого на дело to catch s.o. in the act; to catch s.o. red-handed; крајот делото го краси *prov.* the end crowns the work; all's well that ends well **2** *Leg.* offence; case; кривично дело criminal offence

деловен -вна *adj* business *attrib.*; деловен пријател business friend

деловник -ци *m* correspondence register

деловница *f* office; branch

деловност *f* businesslike manner, efficiency

деловодител *m* clerk, administrative (office) worker

деловодство *n* clerical work; business correspondence

делокруг *m* sphere of activity, field; competence

делотворен -рна *adj* efficient, effective, beneficial

делотворност *f* efficiency, effectiveness

делта *f Geog.* delta; делта крило hang glider

де́лта-зраци *pl Phys.* delta rays

делтойд *m* **1** *Geom.* deltoid, kite **2** *Anat.* deltoid <muscle> **3** *Zool.* deltoid <moth>

делтойден -дна *adj* deltoid

делум *adv* partly, partially

делумен -мна *adj* partial

делфин *m Zool.* dolphin

делче *n dim. of* дел; bit

дема *f* beam, joist, rafter; plank-bridge

демагог -зи *m* demagogue

демагогија *f* demagogy, demagoguery

демаго́шки *adj* demagogic

дема́нти *m* denial

демантира *pf & impf* to deny, refute

демаркацио́нен -она *adj* demarcation; демаркациона линија line of demarcation

дема́рш *m* démarche, step

демаскира *pf & impf* to unmask, expose

дембел *m colloq.* **1** lazybones **2** drone (*also fig.*)

дембелаво *adv colloq.* idly, lazily

дембела́на *f colloq.* laziness, idleness, loafing

дембелски *adj colloq.* idle, lazy

дембелува *impf colloq.* to loaf, idle

демек *conj colloq.* so, therefore, then; (значи) that is

демилитаризација *f* demilitarization

демилитаризира *pf & impf* to demilitarize

деминутив *m Gram.* diminutive

деминутивен -вна *adj Gram.* diminutive

демир *m* iron; демир-капија iron gate

демирли *adj indecl.* with iron bars; демирли пенџере barred window

демисија *f* resignation

демисионира *pf & impf* to resign

демне *impf* to lie in wait (*for s.o.*), watch (*for s.o.*); to watch (над – *over*)

демобилизација *f* demobilization

демобилизира *pf & impf* to demobilize

демоде́ *adj indecl.* outmoded; out of fashion

демодира *pf & impf* to go out of fashion

демокра́т *m* democrat

демократизација *f* democratization

демократизира *pf & impf* to democratize

демократија *f* democracy

демократичност *f* democratic quality; democratic relations

демократски *adj* democratic

демолира *pf & impf* to demolish, destroy

демолиран *pt* demolished, destroyed

демон *m* demon

демонски *adj* demoniac, demonic

демонстра́нт *m* demonstrator, participant in a public demonstration

демонстративен -вна *adj* demonstrative (*also Gram.*)

демонстра́тор *m* demonstrator (*at university*)

демонстрација -ии *f* demonstration; улични демонстрации street demonstrations

демонстрира *pf & impf* to demonstrate

демонтира *pf & impf* to dismantle, take to pieces, take apart, disassemble

деморализација *f* demoralization

деморализира *pf & impf* to demoralize

деморализиран *pt* demoralized

ден -ови, дни *m* day; (*usu. with the definite article*) денот patron saint's day; денот ни е св. Никола our family saint's day is St Nicholas'; што ден е денеска? what day is it today? what's the day today? работен ден working day; ден одење a day's walk away; немал дни да живее he didn't live long; му поминале деновите his time is up; his day is over; работи ден и ноќ to work day and night; ноќта ден ја прави to turn night into day; to work one's fingers to the bone; не гледа бел ден not to see the light of day; to burn the midnight oil; ден година 1. plenty of time 2. a long and boring day (*in summer*); судниот ден Day of Judgement, Judgement Day; до судниот ден till Doomsday; forever and a day; ќе му дојде денот he will have his day; купи ден, помини take life as it comes, live from day to day; цел ден all day; еден ден once, one day; сред ден, по бел ден in broad daylight; од ден на ден from day to day; from one day to the next; ден за ден day by day, day after day; со денови for days on end; преку ден every second day; тој умре без ден he died young (prematurely); *Comm.* на ден per diem, per day; брои денови to count the days; ден за памтење; ден над денови a memorable day; денови на искушение testing times; добри/лоши денови good/bad days; слободен ден day off; претходниот ден the day before; следниот ден the day after; до ден денес, до денешен ден to this day; два пати на ден twice a day; за некој ден; за ден, два in a few days, in a day or two; оној ден the other day; пред некој ден a few days ago; <just> the other day; секој ден every day; day in, day out; точно до ден to the day; има цел ден <на располагање> to have all day; јасно како ден as clear as day; an open-and-shut case; напорен ден a hard day's work; црни (тешки) денови hard times; ми го разубави денот you've made my day; денот се познава уште од утрината *prov.* a good beginning makes a good ending; чувај бели пари за црни дни *prov.* keep something for a rainy day

денар *m* denar

денатурира *pf & impf* to denature, methylate

денгуба *f* waste of time; compensation (*for lost time*); *Naut.* demurrage

денгуби *impf* to waste time; ги денгуби луѓето he is wasting people's time

денгубица *f* waste of time; compensation <for lost time>

денгубник -ци *m* idler, loafer

ден-денес & ден-денеска *adv* nowadays

ден-денешен -шна *adj* today's

денди *m* dandy, fop

дене[1] *impf* **1** to thread (*a needle, etc.*) **2** to string together; дене тутун to string tobacco leaves (*for drying*)

дене[2] *pf* дена *aor.* **I** to put, place, hide; каде да го денам? where can I put it? **II** – се to disappear; кај се дена? where did he go (disappear)?

денес & денеска *adv* today; nowadays; □ денес јас, утре ти scratch my back and I'll scratch yours; денес нѐ има, утре нѐ нема here today, gone tomorrow; денес недела a week from today; денес-утре any day now; pretty soon; one of these days; живее од денес до утре to live from hand to mouth; за денес е доста \<let's\> call it a day; до денес up to now; so far; што можеш денес не оставај за утре *prov.* never put off till tomorrow what you can do today; a stitch in time saves nine

денешен -шна *adj* today's; current; up-to-date; денешен весник today's paper; денешната мода the current fashion

Деница *f* Morning Star, Venus

денк *m* bale, bundle

деновиште *n* place where one spends the day; day site

денонокен -кна *adj* lasting day and night, constant

денонокие -ија *n* a day and a night, 24 hours

денски *adv* by day

дента *adv* that day

денува *impf* to spend (pass) the day

денунцира *pf & impf* to denounce, inform (*on s.o.*)

денчок *m* (*only sg*) *dim. of* ден

дење *adv* by day, during the day; ❏ дење-ноке day and night; night and day

департман *m* department (*administrative district in France and other countries*)

депеша *f* dispatch; telegram

депешира *pf & impf* to send a dispatch/telegram; to telegraph, wire

депилатор *m* depilatory

депилација *f* depilation

депилира *pf & impf* to depilate

депласиран *adj* inappropriate; misplaced

депласман *m Naut.* displacement, tonnage

депо *n* **1** depot; депо за автобуси bus depot **2** store, warehouse

депозит *m* deposit

депозитер *m* depositary, trustee

депонент *m* depositor, investor

депонија *f* **1** dump, rubbish tip **2** depot (*for coal, sand, etc.*)

депонира *pf & impf* to deposit; депонира пари во банка to make a deposit

депортација -ии *f* deportation, expulsion; exile, banishment

депортира *pf & impf* to deport

депортирец -рци *m* deportee

депресивен -вна *adj* depressed; depressive; депресивна состојба depression; депресивен период *Econ.* slump, depression; депресивно подрачје *Meteorology* depression, low; *Econ.* depressed area

депресија -ии *f* **1** (*душевна*) depression, dejection, melancholy, low spirits **2** (*длабнатина*) sunken place, hollow **3** (*економско опаѓање*) depression; slump, decline **4** *Meteorology* depression, low

депримира *pf & impf* to depress; to upset, distress

депримиран *pt* depressed, dejected, upset

депримираност *f* depression, dejection

депутат *m* **1** (*делегат*) delegate, representative; (*пратеник*) envoy; (*член на парламентот*) Member of Parliament, M.P., *Am.* Congressman **2** (*приход во натура*) allowance; emolument; wages in kind

депутација -ии *f* deputation, mission

деранжира *pf & impf* to disturb; to hamper (*usu. Sport.*)

дерач *m* flayer, knacker

дерби *m* **1** *Sport.* final; Derby **2** *Zool.* giant eland

дервен *m arch.* **1** (*клисура*) ravine, gorge **2** (*премин*) mountain pass

дервиш *m* dervish

дервишки *adj* dervish's

дере *impf* **I 1** to skin; to flay; to remove (*hide*); дере овца to skin a sheep; ❏ дере лисици to vomit **2** *fig.* to fleece, swindle; трговците го дерат народот the merchants fleece the public **3** (*пара, кине*) to tear, rip; дере платно to tear linen **4** грлото ме дере I have a tickle in my throat **II – ce** to shout, yell

дереџе *n colloq.* state, plight, pass; на лошо дереџе е he's in a bad way/in a mess

дериват *m* derivative

деривација *f* derivation

дерман *m colloq.* salvation; means of defence; cure; дерман немам од него I get no peace from him; ❏ нема дерман it's hopeless; to be beyond help; to be up against it

дерматолог -зи *m* dermatologist

дерматологија *f* dermatology

дерматолошки *adj* dermatological

дермен *m arch.* water-mill

дерт *m colloq.* care, worry, trouble; sorrow, grief

десант *m Mil.* landing

десантен -тна *adj Mil.* landing *attrib.*; десантен транспорт landing-craft; десантен напад landing

десен -сна *adj* right; ❏ тој ми е десна рака he's my right-hand man; се крсти и со лева и со десна рака to be dumbfounded

десерт *m* dessert

десертен -тна *adj* dessert; sweet; десертно вино sweet wine

десет *num* ten

десетар *m Mil.* corporal; squad leader

десетарски *adj Mil.* corporal's

десетвековен -вна *adj* ten-century

десетгодишен -шна *adj* **1** ten-year-old **2** lasting ten years, ten-year

десетгодишнина *f* tenth anniversary, decennial

десетдневен -вна *adj* ten-day, ten days'

десетина *f* **1** (*of men and mixed groups*) ten **2** group of about ten; *Mil.* squad **3** tenth \<part\>

десетица *f see* десетка 1 & 2

десетка *f* **1** \<number\> ten **2** (*во карти*) ten **3** (*студентска оцена*) ten (*out of ten*), high distinction **4** (*автобус, трамвај итн.*) \<number\> ten **5** ten-denar coin/note

десеткува *pf & impf* to decimate

десетмина *num* (*of men and mixed groups*) ten

десеток *m arch.* tithe

десетпати *adj* ten times

десетти *adj* tenth

десеттина *num see* десетмина

десетчасовен -вна *adj* ten-hour; ten hours'

десиграм *m see* дециграм

десилитар -три *m see* децилитар

десиметар -три *m see* дециметар

дескриптивен -вна *adj* descriptive

дескрипција *f* description

деснак -ци *m* **1** ox (*harnessed on the right side*) **2** mill-stone

десница *f* 1 right hand 2 *Pol.* the right

десничар *m* 1 right-handed person 2 *Pol.* rightist, right-wing politician

десничарка *f* (*fem. form*) *see* десничар

десничарски *adj Pol.* rightist, right-wing *attrib.*

десно *adv* to/on the right; десно од мене to the right of me

деспот *m* despot, tyrant, oppressor

деспотизам -змот *m* despotism

деспотски *adj* despotic

деспотство *n* despotism

деспотува *impf* to rule as a despot; to act despotically

дестилат *m* distillate

дестилација *f* distillation; сува дестилација *Chem.* destructive (dry) distillation

дестилира *pf & impf* to distil

деструктивен -вна *adj* destructive

деструктивност *f* destructiveness

детален -лна *adj* detailed, thorough, exhaustive

детаљ -ли *m* detail, particular; ❑ во детали in detail (depth)

дете *n pl* деца 1 baby, infant, child, *pl* children, offspring; ❑ тројца и дете barely three or four; беспомошен како мало дете <as> helpless as a newborn baby; цело дете a mere child; плаче како дете to weep unashamedly; чека дете to be pregnant; деца како деца boys will be boys; со деца маштеница не се срка *prov.* children are unpredictable 2 *dial.* son; boy, young man; husband

детектив *m* detective

детективски *adj* detective

детектор *m* detector; детектор на лаги lie detector

детел *m Zool.* woodpecker

детелина *f Bot.* (Trifolium) clover; детелина со четири листа four-leaved clover

детенце *n dim. of* дете little child, infant, <tiny> tot, *sl.* kid<dy>

детерминанта *f* determinant

детерминација *f* determination

детерминизам -змот *m* determinism

детерминира *pf & impf* to determine, fix, establish, decide

детерминист *m* determinist

детини се *impf* to act (behave) childishly (like a child)

детински *adj* childish; детински работи childish things; childishness; childish pranks

детинство *n see* детство

детинштина *f* childish behaviour/pranks; childishness; nonsense

детињак -ци *m* youthful-looking person

детиште *n augm. of* дете

детонатор *m* detonator, fuse; blasting cap

детонација -ии *f* detonation, explosion

детошарник -ци *m* childish person

детронизација *f* dethronement

детски *adj* children's; childlike; infantile; детски болести children's (childhood) illnesses; детска парализа infantile paralysis, poliomyelitis; детска градинка day care centre, nursery school; детски јасли crèche; детска соба nursery; детски песнички nursery rhymes; детски додаток child allowance

детство *n* childhood

дефанзива *f* defensive action, defensive

дефанзивен -вна *adj* defensive

дефект *m* 1 defect, fault, shortcoming 2 damage, harm; ❑ остана дефект his vehicle broke down

дефектен -тна *adj* defective, faulty, damaged

дефиле *n* 1 parade 2 gorge, ravine, defile

дефилира *impf* to parade

дефинира *pf & impf* to define

дефинитивен -вна *adj* definitive, final; дефинитивна одлука final decision

дефиниција -ии *f* definition

дефицит *m* deficit, shortfall; shortage; deficiency

дефицитен -тна *adj* deficient, scarce; дефицитна стока commodities in short supply; дефицитни кадри insufficient trained workers

дефлација *f* deflation

дефлационен -она *adj* deflationary

дефлорација *f* defloration

дефлориса *pf* to deflower

деформација -ии *f* deformation, disfigurement

деформира *pf & impf* to deform, disfigure, spoil

дефтер *m dial. see* тефтер

деца *pl of* дете

деценија -ии *f* decade, decennium

децентрализација *f* decentralization

децентрализира *pf & impf* to decentralize

дециграм *m* decigram<me>

децимал *m* decimal

децимален -лна *adj* decimal

децилитар -три *m* decilitre

дециметар -три *m* decimetre

дечар *m* lover of children

дечиња *pl dim. of* деца small children

дечиште *n augm. of* дете

дечка се *impf* to squabble, quarrel, bicker

дечкован *m dial.* boy

дешифрант *m* decoder

дешифрира *pf & impf* to decode, decipher

ди *interj* gee up!

дибек -ци *m* 1 large stone/wooden mortar 2 *fig.* blockhead, fool

дибидус *adv colloq.* altogether, completely

див *m* giant, colossus

див *adj* 1 *Bot., Zool.* wild; feral; дива круша (Pirus piraster *or* silvestris) wild pear-tree; дива свиња wild boar, feral pig 2 (*првобитен*) savage, primitive, uncivilized; диви племиња savage (primitive) tribes 3 (*недруштвен*) unsociable, shy; дива жена unsociable woman 4 rugged, desolate, uncultivated; диво место wild place, wilderness; дива плажа desolate beach; ❑ диви води rough waters; дива работа unreasonable business (act); дива градба unlicensed construction; диво месо proud flesh; див станар squatter

диван *m* 1 sofa, couch; divan 2 *arch.* (oriental) council, meeting; ❑ стои <чапраз> диван to stand demurely; to dance attendance

дивее *impf* to grow (become) wild; to live like a savage; (*за животни*) to run wild; (*за растенија*) to grow rampant, grow rank<ly>, spread <rankly>

дивен -вна *adj poet.* marvellous, beautiful

дивергентен -тна *adj* divergent

дивергенција *f* divergence, divergency

дивергира *pf & impf* to diverge

диверзант *m* saboteur, raider

диверзантски *adj* diversionary, wrecking; диверзантска акција act of sabotage, raid

диверзија -ии *f Mil.* diversion; raid, sabotage

дивеч *m* game (*including deer*); месо од дивеч venison; крадец на дивеч poacher

диви се *impf literary* to admire, wonder (*на – at*)

дивидéнда *f* dividend

дивизија -ии *f Mil.* division

дивизиóн *m Mil.* artillery battalion; cavalry squadron

дивизиски *adj Mil.* division, divisional

дивина *f* **1** wildlife; ❏ во дивина in the wild **2** savagery, brutality **3** (*пустелија*) wilderness

дивинúште *n* game; deer

дивит *m arch.* ink-horn

дивјак -ци *m* **1** (*човек од примитивно племе*) savage **2** *fig.* (*груб човек*) boor **3** (*недруштвен човек*) recluse, hermit; unsociable person

дивјачка *f* wild fruit tree; fruit from wild fruit tree

дивјачки *adj* savage, barbarous

дивјаштво *n* barbarism, savagery

дивјаштина *f* barbarous (savage) act, act of savagery

дивовски *adj* gigantic, colossal

дивотија *f* **1** game; wildfowl **2** barbarous (savage) act **3** (*будалаштилак*) madness, stupidity

дивотина *f* game; wildfowl

дига *impf* **I** to raise, lift; (*буди*) to waken; дига прав to raise dust (*also fig.*); ❏ дига врева to make a din; дига ѓурултија to cause a disturbance; дига тревога to raise the alarm **II – се** to rise; to get up; *fig.* to boast; ❏ се дига на високо to put on airs, look down upon everybody; се дигана борба (*против*) to take up arms (*against*)

дигалка *f Tech.* (*рачна за автомобил*) jack; (*кран*) crane, hoist; подвижна дигалка derrick, mobile crane

дигач *m* **1** lifter; дигач на тегови weightlifter **2** *colloq.* thief, burglar

дигитáлен -лна *adj* digital; дигитален сметач calculator; дигитален телефон digital telephone

дигитрóн *m* calculator

дигне *pf* **I** дигна *aor.* **1** to lift, raise; to pick up; to erect; to elevate; to hoist; ја дигна секирата he raised the axe; дигне раце to raise one's arms; дигне глава to raise one's head, look up; дигне споменик to erect a monument; ❏ дигне раце од to give up on **2** *fig.* to steal, *colloq.* swipe, lift, pinch **3** *fig.* to hide, conceal, put somewhere **II – се** to rise; to get up

дигноглав *adj* proud, insolent, arrogant, conceited

дигнува (се) *impf of* дигне (се)

дигресија *f* digression

дидактика *f* didactics, the art of teaching

дидактичен -чна *adj* didactic

диéта *f* diet; држи строга диета to keep a strict diet; на диета е to be on a diet

диетáлен -лна *adj* dietary, dietetic

дизáјн *m* design

дизáјнер *m* designer

дизг *m see* диск 3

дизгин *m* rein; bridle

дизел *m Tech.* diesel

ди́зел-мóтор *m Tech.* diesel engine

дизентерија *f Med.* dysentery

дизна *f Mech.* injection nozzle, fuel injector

дијабéтес *m Med.* diabetes

дијабетичар *m* diabetic

дијагнóза *f* diagnosis; ❏ дава (поставува) дијагноза to make a diagnosis

дијагностика *f* diagnostics

дијагонáла *f* diagonal; стави по дијагонала to place obliquely

дијагонáлен -лна *adj* diagonal

дијаграм *m* diagram

дијадéма *f* diadem, crown

дијакритички *adj Ling.* diacritic<al>; дијакритички знак diacritical mark

дијалéкт *m* dialect

дијалéктен -тна *adj* dialectal

дијалектика *f Philos.* dialectics

дијалектичар *m Philos.* dialectician

дијалектичен -чна & **дијалектички** *adj Philos.* dialectical; дијалектичен метод dialectical method; дијалектичен материјализам dialectical materalism

дијалектолóг -зи *m Ling.* dialectologist

дијалектологија *f Ling.* dialectology

дијалектолошки *adj Ling.* dialectological

дијалог -зи *m* dialogue; ❏ води дијалог со to negotiate with; to argue with; to exchange words with

дијалошки *adj* dialogic

дијамáнт *m* diamond

дијамáнтски *adj* diamond

дијамéтар -три *m* diameter

дијаметрáлен -лна *adj* diametrical

дијанија -ии *f arch.* creature, being; лоша дијанија cad, scoundrel

дијапазóн *m* range, scope, gamut, compass, diapason; глас со голем дијапазон voice of great range

дијапозитúв *m* slide, transparency

дијатоника *f Mus.* diatonic scale

дијатóнски *adj Mus.* diatonic; дијатонска скала diatonic scale

дијафрáгма *f* diaphragm

дијка *impf* to urge on a horse by calling out *"di!"* (gee up!)

дикел -кли *m* pickaxe; има заби како дикли to have large, protruding teeth

дикотиледóни *pl Bot.* dicotyledons

диктáт *m* **1** dictate, diktat **2** (*наредба*) order **3** (*диктирање*) dictation

диктáтор *m* dictator

диктаторски *adj* dictatorial

диктатýра *f* dictatorship

диктафóн *m* dictaphone

диктúра *impf* to dictate; ❏ диктира мода to set a fashion; диктира темпо to set the pace

дикција *f* diction

дилбер *adj f.p.* fair, bonny, fine

дилéма *f* dilemma; ❏ во дилема е за to be in two minds about; to be in a quandary about; нема дилема to make no bones about

дилетáнт *m* dilettante, amateur

дилетантúзам -змот *m* dilettantism

дилетáнтски *adj* dilettante

дилижáнс *m* & **дилижáнса** *f Hist.* diligence, stagecoach

дилми *conj colloq.* as, since, because; дилми си дошол сега, не враќај се since you're here now, don't go away!

дилувијáлен -лна *adj* diluvial

дилувиум *m* diluvium

дим *m* smoke; испушта дим to blow (exhale) smoke; ❏ дим да го нема he's disappeared, he's run off;

каде има дим, има и оган *prov.* where there is smoke there is fire; there is no smoke without fire

димен -мна *adj* smoke *attrib.*; smoky; димна завеса smokescreen; димни сигнали smoke signals

димензија -ии *f* dimension

дими *impf* **I** 1 to smoke *trans.*, cure 2 to smoke *intrans.*; печката/оцакот дими the stove/chimney smokes; тој само дими he keeps smoking **II – се** to smoke *intrans.*, emit smoke

димии *pl* pantaloons (*worn by Muslim women*)

димлив *adj* smoky, smoking

димљус *m Bot.* (Mentha crispa *or* piperita) peppermint

димник -ци *m see* оцак

диморфен -фна *adj Biol.*, *Chem.*, *Mineralogy* dimorphic, dimorphous

диморфизам -змот *m* & **диморфност** *f Biol.*, *Chem.*, *Mineralogy* dimorphism

динамика *f* 1 dynamics 2 *fig.* dynamism, *see* динамичност

динамит *m* dynamite

динамитен -тна *adj* dynamite

динамитски *adj see* динамитен

динамичен -чна *adj* dynamic, lively; full of action/tension

динамички *adj* dynamic

динамично *adv* dynamically, vividly, forcefully

динамичност *f* dynamism, forcefulness; tension

динамо *n Tech.* dynamo; динамо-машина dynamo-electric generator

динамометар -три *m Tech.* dynamometer

динар *m* dinar; ❏ без скршен динар penniless; *colloq.* flat broke; гледа на секој динар to watch every penny

динарски *adj* in dinars

династија -ии *f* dynasty

династичен -чна *adj* dynastic

диндушман *m arch.* arch-enemy

динствува *impf Cul.* to stew, simmer; динствува месо to stew meat

диња *f Bot.* (Cucumis melo) <musk> melon

диода *f Elec.* diode

диоксид *m Chem.* dioxide

диолен *m* kind of synthetic fabric

диоптер -три *m* diopter

диоптрика *f* dioptrics, study of refraction

дип *colloq.* 1 *adv* much, very, quite; дип лошо very bad 2 *conj* дип ако unless 3 *part* (*for emphasis*) дип не го видов, инаку тешко нему a good thing I didn't see him, otherwise he would have caught it

дипла *f* 1 fold, crease, pleat 2 (*дел од килим и сл.*) strip; веленцето е сошиено од три дипли the quilt is made up of three pieces 3 stack, rick; дипла од сено haystack, hayrick 4 *Mus.* musette 5 *dial.* bouquet 6 mountain slope

дипленица *f f.p.* kind of folding sword

дипли *impf* to fold *trans.*; дипли чаршафи to fold sheets

диплома *f* diploma; (*факултетска*) degree

дипломат *m* diplomat

дипломатија *f* diplomacy

дипломатика *f* study of diplomacy

дипломатски *adj* diplomatic; по дипломатски пат via diplomatic channels; на дипломатски начин diplomatically

дипломира *pf* & *impf* to receive a diploma; (*на факултет*) to graduate

дипломиран *adj* graduate; дипломиран инженер graduate engineer

дипломски *adj* diploma/graduation, final (*examinations, etc.*)

дирек -ци *m* 1 beam, post; prop; support; rafter, joist; ❏ дирек сум I'm fine 2 *fig.* pillar; тој е дирекот на куќата he is the pillar of the household

директен -тна *adj* direct; директен говор *Gram.* direct speech; директен пренос live broadcast; директен одговор direct (straight) answer; директен воз through train

директива *f* directive, instructions, guidelines

директивен -вна *adj* directive; директивна статија guidelines

директно *adv* directly, straight

директор *m* director; manager; managing director; (*на установа*) head; (*на училиште*) headmaster, principal; (*на затвор*) governor

директориум *m* directorate, board of directors

директорка *f* 1 (*fem. form*) *see* директор 2 *iron.* director's wife

директорски *adj* director's; managerial

дирекција -ии *f* main office, head office; department

диригент *m Mus.* conductor

диригентски *adj* conductor's; диригентски пулт conductor's stand

диригира *impf* to conduct

дисаги & **дисаѓи** *pl* saddle-bags

дисертација -ии *f* dissertation, thesis

дисидент *m* dissident

дисидентски *adj* dissident, dissentient

дисидентство *n* dissidence, disagreement

дисимилација -ии *f Gram.* dissimilation

дисјунктивен -вна *adj* disjunctive; дисјунктивен суд *Logic* disjunctive proposition

дисјункција *f* disjunction

диск *m* 1 disc; компјутерски диск floppy disk; *Mech.* диск-кочници disc brakes; *Med.* изместен диск slipped disc; компактен диск compact disc, CD 2 *Sport.* discus 3 (*послужавник*) tray; (*тас*) pan

дискант *m Mus.* treble; descant

дисквалификација *f* disqualification

дисквалификува & **дисквалифицира** *pf* & *impf* to disqualify; to dismiss

дисквалификуван *pt* disqualified

дисконт *m Finance* discount

дисконтен -тна *adj* discount; дисконтен принос discount yield; дисконтна стапка discount rate

дискос *m* 1 *see* диск 2 2 collection (offertory) plate (*in church*)

дискотека *f* discotheque, *colloq.* disco

дискредитира *pf* & *impf* to discredit

дискретен -тна *adj* discreet

дискреција *f* discretion

дискреционен -она *adj* discretionary; дискрециони права discretionary powers

дискриминација *f* discrimination; расна дискриминација racial discrimination

дискриминира *pf* & *impf* to discriminate (*во однос на – against*)

дискусија -ии *f* discussion, debate

дискусио́нен -она *adj* debatable, arguable; controversial, moot; under discussion

дискути́ра *impf* to discuss, debate

дислокација -ии *f* dislocation (*also Med.*); shift, transfer; *Mil.* disposition

дислоци́ра *pf & impf* to dislocate (*also Med.*); *Mil.* to station, post, disposition

дислоци́рање *n see* дислокација

дисона́нс *m* dissonance, discord, disharmony

диспанзе́р *m* health centre, clinic, dispensary

диспечер *m* dispatcher; controller; traffic-manager

диспозити́в *m* court decision, verdict

диспози́ција -ии *f* disposition, arrangement, management; disposition, inclination

диспозицио́нен -она *adj* dispositional; disposable; диспозиционен фонд disposable funding

диспропорција *f* disproportion

диспут *m* (*дебата*) dispute, debate; (*спор*) quarrel, argument

диспути́ра *impf* to dispute, argue, quarrel

диста́нца & дистанција -ии *f* distance; interval, space

дистанци́ра *pf & impf* **I** to move away *trans.*, remove **II – се** to disavow, disown, distance o.s. (*од – from*); се дистанцира од акцијата he dissociated himself from the action

дистинкција -ии *f* distinction, differentiation; difference

дистих -си *m Prosody* distich, couplet

дистракција -ии *f* distraction; recreation, fun, amusement

дистрибуте́р *m* distributor

дистрибуција *f* distribution

дистрикт *m* district, quarter; area, region

дисхармонија *f* disharmony, discord, disagreement

дисхармоничен -чна *adj* disharmonious, discordant

дисхармоничност *f* disharmony, discord

дисципли́на *f* **1** discipline, order; заостри дисциплина to tighten discipline **2** discipline, subject

дисциплини́ра *pf & impf* to discipline

дисциплини́ран *pt* disciplined

дисциплинираност *f* discipline, self-control

дисципли́нски *adj* disciplinary; дисциплински пре-кршок violation of discipline; дисциплинска постапка disciplinary action

дитирамб *m* dithyramb

диференција -ии *f* difference

дифернеција́л *m* differential

диференција́лен -лна *adj* differential; диференцијална тарифа differential tariff; диференцијална сметка *Math.* differential calculus; диференцијална равенка *Math.* differential equation

диференцијација *f* differentiation

диференци́ра *pf & impf* to differentiate, distinguish

дифтерија *f Med.* diphtheria

дифтеричен -чна *adj* diphtherial, diphtheric

дифтик -ци *m* mat with tassels (a fringe)

дифтонг -зи *m Phon.* diphthong

дифузија *f* diffusion, spread

дифузен -зна *adj* diffuse, diffused

дих *m dial. see* здив

дише *impf* to breathe; ❑ го знам како дише I know what makes him tick

дишне *pf* дишна *aor.* to take a breath, draw breath

дишнува *impf of* дишне

длабач *m* **1** gouge **2** carver in wood/bone; sculptor

длабест *adj* hollowed out

длаби *impf* **1** to hollow out, dig out; to carve, gouge; длаб копанка to carve (hollow out) a trough **2** to erode, wear away

длабина *f* depth; bottom

длабински *adj* deep, far-reaching; deep-sea; длабинска бомба depth-charge; *Med.* длабинско снимање gastroscopy

длабнат *adj & pt* hollowed out; grooved; concave

длабнатина *f* hollow, cavity, hole; depression

длабне *pf* длабна *aor. of* длаби

длабнува *impf of* длабне

длабок *adj* deep; profound; длабок бунар deep well; длабока чинија soup-plate; bowl; длабок глас low-pitched (deep) voice; длабока мисла deep thought; длабок сон deep (sound) sleep; длабока ноќ the dead of night; длабока тишина profound silence; ❑ доживува длабока старост to live to a ripe old age; има длабок џеб to have plenty of money; пушти длабоки корења to strike deep roots

длабоко *adv* deeply; profoundly

длабочи *impf see* длаби

длабочина *f* depth

длабочко *adj* deepish, quite deep

длака *f* hair; волкот длаката ја менува, ама ќудта не ја менува *prov.* the leopard cannot change his spots

длакав *adj* hairy, shaggy

дланка *f* palm <of the hand>; ❑ се гледа како на дланка it can be clearly seen; плукнува во дланки to put one's back into s.th.; to get down to work; to take the bit between one's teeth; гледа некому во дланка to read s.o.'s palm; го чеша дланката he's got an itchy palm, he's hoping to get some money (*in a lottery, etc.*)

длапка *f* cavity, hollow; hole, pit

длапчест *adj* uneven; intersected, criss-crossed

длето *n* chisel; gouge

дневен -вна *adj* daily; дневен ред agenda; дневна заповед orders of the day; дневна соба living-room, sitting-room; дневен пазар daily sales; дневна смена day shift; дневна светлина daylight

дневник -ци *m* **1** (*книга*) diary; journal; (*бродски*) log; (*школски*) school register; води дневник to keep a diary **2** (*весник*) daily< newspaper>

дневница *f* daily wage<s>, per diem payment

дневничар *m* day labourer

дневничарка *f* (*fem. form*) *see* дневничар

дневно *adv* daily, per day; два пати дневно twice a day

Днепар *m* the Dnieper

днепарски *adj* Dnieper *attrib.*

дно *n* bottom; од дното на душата from the bottom of one's heart; во дното на душата in the depths of one's soul; во дното на сцената at the back of the stage; испие до дно to drain (drink) to the dregs; без дно bottomless

до[1] *n Mus.* C

до[2] *prep* **1** up to, to, as far as; until, till; дојдоа до реката they got as far as the river, they came to the river; до вчера until yesterday; до ден till dawn, till daylight; for every single day; сите до еден all to a man; до што ги има everyone available; отиде до пазар he went to the market; од понеделник до петок from Monday to Friday; пет до три five <minutes> to three; ❏ до куче, до маче to a man **2** (*покрај*) next to, by, beside; човек до човек side by side; седи до мене sit next to me! до паркот near the park **3** (*of numbers*) under, not over; up to; до десетина души up to about ten people; до дватриесет кила up to twenty or thirty kilos **4** (*in f.p., with numbers, semantically void*) болен лежи до девет години he has lain sick for nine years **5** ❏ не е до мене it's not up to me; it is outside my competence; не ми е до шега I don't feel like joking, I am not in a laughing mood; до Господа! good God! **6** (*before other prepositions*) до над глава out of hand, out of control; over one's head; до пред некој ден until a day or two ago, until recently

до- *verbal prefix* **1** (*completion of an action*) дочита to finish reading **2** (*action or motion to a certain point or destination*) доплови to arrive (*of a ship*) **3** (*action additional to that already performed*) допише to add (*in writing*)

доаѓа *impf of* дојде

доајён *m* doyen

доарчи *pf colloq.* to spend

доарчува *impf of* доарчи

доба *f* **1** time; до никоја (ниедна) доба late at night; until the small hours; глува доба the dead of night; the witching hour; златна доба the golden age; golden days; која доба е сега? what's the time? **2** age; средна доба middle age, mid-life; на моја доба at my age

добаботи *pf* **1** to die down (*of a fire*) **2** *fig.* to stop babbling, fall silent

добаботува *impf of* добаботи

добави *pf* to acquire, obtain

добавува *impf of* добави

добања *pf* **I** to bath, finish bathing *trans.* **II** – **се** to have a bath, finish bathing *intrans.*

добањува (се) *impf of* добања (се)

добар -бра *adj* good; kind; добар човек a kind person; добро јадење good food; добар по математика good at numbers; добар глас good name/reputation; добар изглед good looks; ❏ добар како добар ден good as gold; не е нешто добар he doesn't feel his usual self; he's off colour; добар ден good morning/afternoon! good day! добро утро good morning! добро вечер good evening! добра ноќ good night! бидете со добра мисла don't worry! everything will be all right; кој не е добар за себе не е ни за други<те> *prov.* he helps little that helps not himself; be a friend to thyself and others will befriend thee

добара *pf* to finish searching; to finish demanding

добарка *pf dim. see* добара

добарува *impf of* добара

добега *pf* **1** to run up to **2** to stop running

добеган *adj* добегана мома girl who has eloped

добегува *impf of* добега

добележи *pf* to finish noting (writing down, recording)/marking

добележува *impf of* добележи

добели *pf* to finish bleaching

добелува *impf of* добели

добере *pf* добра *aor.* **I 1** to pick some more **2** to finish

picking (harvesting) **II** – **се** to get hold (*до – оf*); to succeed (in), achieve s.th.; (*се доближи*) to move up close (*до нешто – to s.th.*); (*се пробие*)to get through (*до нешто – to s.th.*)

доберува *impf of* добере

добив *f* prize, winning ticket (*in a lottery, etc.*); gain, profit, earnings, proceeds; (*за инвестиции*) return; (*во карти*) winnings

добива *impf of* добие

добивач *m* recipient

добивка *f see* добив; главна добивка jackpot

добие *pf* доби *aor.* **1** to receive, get, acquire, gain; (*како резултат на труд*) to obtain; (*придобие*) to take on, assume; градот доби современ изглед the town is taking on a modern appearance; ❏ добие врска (*на телефон*) to get through; ќе си го добиеш you'll catch it! добие настинка to catch a cold; добие во време to gain time **2** (*игра, војна и др.*) to win; добие парница to win a suit **3** *dial.* to bear, bring forth; добие дете to have a baby

добира се *impf of* добере се

добиток *m, coll.* добици livestock; крупен добиток cattle; ситен добиток small livestock; товарен добиток beast of burden

добиточен -чна *adj* <live>stock *attrib.*; добиточна храна stock feed, forage; fodder; *see* сточен

добиче *n* beast of burden

добичи *pf* to saw up

добичува *impf of* добичи

доблест *f literary* valour, bravery

доблестен -сна *adj literary* brave, valiant, valorous

доближи *pf* **I 1** to bring near, move closer (*до – to*) *trans.*; ја доближи софрата до гостинот she moved the coffee-table closer to the guest **2** to approach, come near; волците доближија до (кон) трлото the wolves approached (moved closer to) the sheepfold **II** – **се** *see* **I** 2

доближува (се) *impf of* доближи (се)

добојадиса *pf* to finish painting/colouring/dyeing

добојадисува *impf of* добојадиса

доболи *pf* to hurt, cause pain; нејзините зборови го доболеа до дното на срцето her words cut him to the quick

доболува *impf of* доболи

добори се *pf* to stop wrestling

добразди *pf* to finish ploughing

добраздува *impf of* добразди

добрани *pf* **I** to defend successfully, manage to defend, save **II** – **се** to defend o.s. successfully, fend off an attack

добранува (се) *impf of* добрани (се)

добре *adv only in the expressions:* добре дојде! добре најдов! welcome! glad to see you!

добредојде *n* welcome

добредојден *adj* welcome; тој е секогаш добредојден he is always welcome

добрина *f* **1** kindness **2** good deed; favour

добричи *pf* **I** to finish shaving *trans.* **II** – **се** to finish shaving *intrans.*

добричица *m* good-natured (kind) person

добричок -чка *adj dim. of* добар

добричува (се) *impf of* добричи (се)

добрише *pf* **I 1** to wipe, dry (*the rest of s.th.*) **2** to finish wiping **II** – **се** to wipe, dry o.s. completely

добрка *pf* **1** to drive, chase up/in *trans.* **2** to stop driving (chasing) *trans.*

добркува *impf of* добрка

добро[1] *n* **1** goodness, good; good deed, kindness; доброто и злото good and evil; со добро nicely, kindly, in a friendly way; ❏ добро и зло поминале to go through thick and thin; за добро или за лошо for better for worse; во што е доброто од . . . ? what is the good of . . . ? заедничко добро common good; за кое добро? what can I do for you? what brings you here? доброто со добро се враќа one good turn deserves another **2** benefit; welfare; за твое добро for your own good; за нечие добро for s.o.'s sake; to s.o.'s credit; две добра заедно нема *prov.* you can't have your cake and eat it **3** *f.p.* treasure

добро[2] *adv* well; добро доаѓа некому to come in handy/useful; to do good; добро изведува to make a good job; ❏ уште добро се држи he's still going strong; добро се завршува to turn out well; добро стои со некого to be in with s.o.; to be on good terms with s.o.; to get along with s.o.; добро ми е I'm all right; there's nothing wrong with me; не е добро да it's no good to; it doesn't do to; не мириса на добро it bodes no good; тргнува на добро to take a turn for the better; сè е добро штом добро се заврши all's well that ends well; добро! all right! OK!

добровечер (*as greeting*) good evening

доброволен -лна *adj* voluntary

доброволец -лци *m* volunteer

доброволечки *adj* volunteer's; volunteer, voluntary

доброволност *f* volunteer spirit (attitude), voluntariness

добродетел *f literary* virtue

добродиг *pf* to sail (*to a place*); to sail (*до – as far as*), reach (*a place*) by sailing; to float (drift) (*to a place*)

добродува *impf of* добродиг

добродушен -шна *adj* good-natured, kind

добродушност *f* good nature, kindness

доброи *pf* **1** to add in when counting, count in **2** to finish counting; to count up

добројува *impf of* доброи

доброкачествен *adj Med.* benign, non-malignant; доброкачествен тумор benign tumour

добронамерен -рна *adj* well-intentioned

добронамерност *f* good intentions

доброта *f* kindness, goodness

добротвор *m* benefactor, philanthropist

добротворен -рна *adj* charitable, philanthropic

добротворка *f* (*fem. form*) *see* добротвор

добротворство *n* philanthropy; benefaction

добротија *f dial. see* доброта

доброчинец -нци *m see* добротвор

доброчинство *n* good deed, benefaction

добрува *impf* to live well

добрчи *pf* to stop buzzing/humming

добрчува *impf of* добрчи

добута & **добутка** *pf* **1** to push, shove; ја добуткавме колата до гаражата we pushed the car to (as far as) the garage **2** *fig. intrans.* (*with до*) to reach; добутка некако до директор he somehow reached the post of director; добута до осумдесеттата to live to the age of eighty **II - се** to get (*somewhere*); to push through *intrans.*, force one's

way in/through; едвај се добутка до своето седиште во возот he could hardly reach his seat on the train

добучи *pf* to stop making a noise

довади[1] *pf* to take out (remove, extract) completely

довади[2] *pf* to finish watering *trans.*

довадува[1] *impf of* довади[1]

довадува[2] *impf of* довади[2]

довалка[1] *pf* **I** to roll (*up to s.th.*) *trans.* **II – се** to roll (*up to s.th.*) *intrans.*

довалка[2] *pf* **I** to dirty (soil) completely **II – се** to get completely dirty *intrans.*

довалкува (се)[1] *impf of* довалка[1] (се)

довалкува (се)[2] *impf of* довалка[2] (се)

довапса *pf* to finish painting

довапсува *impf of* довапса

доварди *pf* **I 1** to preserve, save **2** to stop guarding (protecting) **II – се** to protect o.s., save o.s.

довардува (се) *impf of* доварди (се)

довари *pf* to complete (finish) boiling/cooking

довароса *pf* to finish whitewashing

доваросува *impf of* довароса

доварува *impf of* довари

довде<ка> *adv* up to here; ❏ довде ми дојде I've had enough <of it /him>

довева *impf of* довее

доведе *pf* to bring, take, lead (*people*); го довеле крадецот во полицијата they took the thief to the police; доведе гости дома to bring guests home; ❏ доведе до голем неред he/it caused great disorder; доведе невеста he got married; доведе до лудило to drive mad (crazy, insane); доведе до питачки стап to reduce to poverty, drive to penury; доведе во опасност to endanger, imperil; доведе во искушение to lead into temptation

доведеник -ци *m* child from a previous marriage (*of remarried mother*), stepchild

доведува *impf of* доведе

довее *pf* **I 1** to winnow (*a quantity of grain*) **2** (*of wind*) to blow, drive up/down/over (*до – as far as*) *trans.* **II – се** to appear/come from somewhere (*unexpectedly*)

довезе[1] *pf* to finish (complete) embroidering; *see* везе

довезе[2] *pf* to drive *trans.*; to transport, deliver; to bring; to take (*by car, lorry, etc.*)

довезува[1] *impf of* довезе[1]

довезува[2] *impf of* довезе[2]

довек<а> *adv* forever

доверба *f* trust, confidence, faith; во доверба in confidence; има доверба во to confide in; to swear by; нема доверба (*во*) to be doubtful (*about*); to distrust; оправдува нечија доверба to justify s.o.'s faith; заслужува доверба to be trustworthy

доверен *pt* entrusted

довери *pf* **I** to entrust; to confide; довери некому тајна to confide a secret to s.o. **II – се** to confide (*in s.o.*); to entrust o.s. (*на – to*), commit o.s.; му се довери дека направил тежок престап he confessed (confided in him) that he had committed a serious offence

доверител *m* creditor, lender

доверлив *adj* confidential; (*полн со доверба*) trusting; (*лековерен*) credulous

доверливо *adv* confidentially; ❏ строго доверливо

top secret; classified; revealed/given in strict confidence

доверливост *f* confidentiality; trustfulness, credulity

доверува (се) *impf of* довери (се); на никого не му се доверуваше he did not confide in anyone; he did not trust anyone

довесла *pf* to row (*to a place*)

довечер *adv* this evening

довечера *pf* to finish one's supper

довечерува *impf of* довечера

довива *impf see* довиткува

довиди *pf* довиде *aor.* 1 to catch sight (*of*), espy 2 to investigate, check; ќе ја довидам таа работа I'll investigate this matter

довие *pf* дови *aor. see* довитка

довика *pf* 1 to call, summon 2 to stop calling/shouting

довикне *pf* довикна *aor.* to call

довикнува *impf of* довикне

довикува *impf* I to call, hail, keep calling II – се to call to each other; to keep calling to each other

довитка *pf* to wind, roll up (*a skein of yarn, etc.*); to finish winding (*a skein of yarn, etc.*); to finish wrapping

довиткува *impf of* довитка

довјава *pf* 1 to come (arrive) on horseback 2 to finish riding

довјаса *pf* to hurry, hasten (*до – to*); to arrive quickly

довлачи *pf* to finish carding (*wool*); to finish harrowing (*a field*)

довлачува *impf of* довлачи

довлегува *impf of* довлезе

довлезе *pf* довлезе *aor.* довлегов *1st sg. aor.* to enter completely, go right in

довлезува *impf of* довлезе, *see* довлегува

довлекува (се) *impf of* довлече (се)

довлет *m arch.* 1 good fortune, prosperity, riches 2 state, kingdom

довлече *pf* довлече *aor.* довлеков *1st p. sg aor.* I to drag/pull up/in; реката довлекла нов песок the river has washed up/down more sand II – се to drag o.s. up/in; to steal (sneak) up (*до некого, до нешто – on s.o., to s.th.*)

довлечка *pf see* довлече

довлечува (се) *impf see* довлекува (се)

довод *m* 1 water mains; main <power> supply, mains 2 argument, reason; (*доказ*) proof, evidence

довоз *m* shipment

довози *pf* 1 to bring, take, drive up/in (*до – to*) 2 to finish driving (bringing)

довозува *impf of* довози

довојува *pf* to finish fighting (waging war)

доволен -лна *adj* 1 sufficient 2 *rare* pleased, satisfied, content

доволно *adv* 1 sufficiently, enough; доволно е да се каже (*дека*) suffice it to say (*that*); доволно глуп да enough of a fool to; доволно и ќе преостане enough and to spare 2 *rare* contentedly

доврага *adv* to the devil, to hell

доврви *pf* to finish swarming; to swarm up/in

довреви *pf* to stop making a noise, quieten down *intrans.*

доврека *pf* to stop bleating/screaming, fall silent

довреска *pf see* доврека

доврзе *pf* доврза *aor.* 1 to tie, bind completely 2 to stop tying, binding

доврзува *impf of* доврзе

доврива *impf of* доврие

доврие *pf* доври *aor.* to boil *intrans.*, come to the boil

доврien *pt* boiled

доврне *pf* доврна *aor.* to stop falling (*of rain, snow, hail*), stop raining/snowing/hailing

доврнува *impf of* доврне

доврти *pf* I 1 to turn/rotate to the end *trans.* 2 to turn over the pages (*to the end*) 3 to save II – се to stop rotating/revolving *intrans.*

довртка *pf* 1 to finish twisting (*yarn, thread*) 2 to protect, preserve; ги довртка овците he saved the sheep

доврткува *impf of* довртка

довртува (се) *impf of* доврти (се)

довршен *pt* finished, completed, concluded

доврши¹ *pf* 1 to finish, complete, conclude 2 (*уништи непријател*) to finish off

доврши² *pf* (*за жито*) to finish threshing (*grain*)

довршок -ци *m* end

довршува¹ *impf of* доврши¹

довршува² *impf of* доврши²

довтаса *pf* 1 to catch up (*with*); таа ја довтаса мајка си she caught up with her mother 2 to come, arrive (*unexpectedly*) 3 (*за река*) *see* дотече 4 to be sufficient; не ми довтасаа пари my money ran out

довтасува *impf of* довтаса

довчерашен -шна *adj* previous, former; yesterday's; recent

догази *pf* 1 to walk/trudge up/in; to wade up/in 2 to finish trampling

доган *m arch.* hawk, falcon

доганса *pf colloq.* to drag o.s. (*somewhere*) with difficulty

доганција -ии *m arch.* falconer

догатка *f* guess, surmise

догледа *pf* 1 to catch sight (*of*), notice, espy 2 to finish looking; to watch to the end, to see all (*of s.th.*); догледа филм to finish watching a film, watch a film to the end 3 (*за очи*) to fail 4 to look (*after s.o.*), take care (*of s.o.*), nurse (*s.o.*) to the end; ги догледа старите родители she looked after her aged parents

догледува *impf* 1 of догледа 2 *only in negative* не догледува not to see clearly

доглода *pf* to gnaw to the end, finish gnawing

доглодува *impf of* доглода

догма *f* dogma

догмати́зам -змот *m* dogmatism

догматика *f Theology* dogmatics

догматичар *m* dogmatist

догматичен -чна *adj* dogmatic

догматски *adj* dogmatic

догмечи *pf* 1 to squeeze/mash/knead completely 2 to finish pressing (*grapes, etc.*)

догмечува *impf of* догмечи

догнаси се *pf* to be disgusted (*од – by*), find (*s.th.*) repulsive, feel disgust (*од – at*)

догнасува се *impf of* догнаси се

догнива *impf of* догние

догние *pf* догни *aor.* to rot completely

договара се *impf* to discuss (*за нешто – s.th.*), seek agreement (*за нешто – on s.th.*); (*преговара*) to negotiate

договарач *m* negotiator; contracting party

договор *m* agreement; understanding; settlement; *Leg.* contract; deed; (*меѓу држави*) treaty, pact; договор за вработување employment contract; договор за заем credit agreement; договор за купување purchase contract; договор за продажба contract of sale; sales contract; договор за дарување deed of gift; хипотекарен договор mortgage deed; царински договор customs treaty; ❏ договор <си> е договор a bargain is a bargain; како по договор as if by agreement; под договор under engagement; работи под договор he works on a contract; постигнува договор to come to an agreement/understanding; прекршува договор to break (breach) an agreement; to break ranks; се држи до договорот to keep one's side of the bargain; договор куќа гради *prov.* united we stand, divided we fall

договорен -рна *adj* agreed; *Leg.* contractual; contracting; *Pol.* treaty, pact *attrib.*; договорен однос/рок contractual relation/term; договорен превозник contracting carrier; договорна страна contracting party; договорна цена agreed price

договорено *adv* agreed, as agreed; договорено! it's a deal!

договори *pf* **I 1** to finish talking **2** to agree (*за нешто – on s.th.*); to arrange (*за нешто – s.th.*); договори средба to arrange a meeting; договори услови to agree on <the> terms **II – се** to agree, come to an understanding

договорник -ци *m* party to an agreement

доголта *pf* to swallow completely

догони *pf* to catch up (*with*)

догонува *impf of* догони

догори *pf* to burn out, burn down *intrans.*

догорува *impf of* догори

догорче *n* butt, end (*of a cigarette, cigar*)

догорчи *pf* (*with dat., often impers.*) ми догорчи I felt a bitter taste in my mouth; јаболкото ми догорчи the apple tasted sour

догорчува *impf of* догорчи

доготви *pf* **1** to prepare, finish off **2** to finish cooking

доготвува *impf of* доготви

дограба *pf* to seize; to seize completely

дограбува *impf of* дограба

дограбба *f* extension; дограбба на куќа extension to a house

догради *pf* to finish <building>; to add, build on; догради куќа to finish building a house; догради кујна до куќата he built on a kitchen

дографува *impf of* догради

дограма *f arch.* woodwork, joinery

дограмаџија -ии *m arch.* carpenter

дограпчи *pf* **I** to seize, grab **II – се 1** (*за*) to seize, grab **2** to get hold (*за – of*)

дограпчува (се) *impf of* дограпчи (се)

догрдее *pf* догрдеа *aor.* to become intolerable (unbearable); (*некому*) to annoy, get on s.o.'s nerves

догребе *pf* догреба *aor.* **1** to reach out to scratch **2** to scratch all over

догребува *impf of* догребе

догрува *pf* **1** (*за жито*) to finish threshing **2** *fig.* to get tired; to become exhausted

додава *impf of* додаде

додаде *pf* **1** to add; to give some more; во таа смеса ќе додадеме малку мед to that mixture we are going to add a little honey; тука ќе додадеме дека . . . here we shall add that . . . ; додаде гас to step on the gas, to accelerate **2** to present; to give, pass, hand; им додадоа на војниците торби со леб they gave the soldiers bags of bread **3** to give in full; ги додаде парите he paid back the money in full; he gave all his money **4** *Sport.* to pass *trans.*

додаток -ци *m* **1** addition, annex, appendix **2** allowance, extra pay, supplement; додаток на плата salary supplement, bonus; додаток за одвоен живот separation allowance; детски додаток children's allowance **3** *Gram.* complement

додева *impf of* додее

додевен -вна *adj* annoying; boring

додевност *f* boring nature (character); (*здодевност*) boredom

додее *pf* додеа *aor.* (*with dat.*) to annoy, bother, make a nuisance of o.s., get on (*s.o.'s*) nerves; to bore

додека *conj* while, until

додели *pf* **1** to award, allot, allocate, grant; to assign; додели награда to award a prize; додели кредит to grant credit/a loan; му доделија на сликарот доживотна плата they granted the painter a life-pension; ми ги додели новите војници he assigned the new soldiers to me **2** to finish awarding (allotting, granting)/assigning

доделува *impf of* додели

додола *f* **1** girl who sings for rain, rain-maker (*in folk ritual*) **2** *fig.* tastelessly dressed woman

додоле *n see* додола

додолу *adv* down

додржи *pf* додржа *aor.* **I 1** to hold on (*to*), keep hold (*of*); to keep, preserve, maintain; додржи поглед на (*некого/нешто*) to keep one's gaze fixed on (*s.o./s.th.*); додржи да не прозбори to manage not to say a word; си го додржа зборот he kept his word; браната не ја додржа водата the dam gave way **2** to stop holding **II – се** to maintain one's position; to stay up; to survive; to keep (*from doing s.th.*); to hold one's ground; to hold out; се додржи на нозе to keep one's feet; се додржи во седлото to stay in the saddle

додржува (се) *impf of* додржи (се)

додрне *pf* додрна *aor.* to touch

додуша *adv* really, truly, indeed, to be sure

доенче *n* suckling; (*бебе*) infant, babe in arms

дожали *pf* **I** to cease mourning **II – се** *impers.* (*with dat.*) (*на некого*) to take pity (*on s.o.*), feel sorry (*for s.o.*)

дожалува (се) *impf of* дожали (се)

дожд *m* rain; дожд се спрема it looks like rain; од дожд на град *prov.* out of the frying-pan, into the fire; по дожд доаѓа сонце *prov.* a foul morning may turn to a fair day; every cloud has a silver lining

дождалец -лци *m Zool.* (Salamandra maculosa) salamander

дожделив *adj* rainy

дождец *m* light rain, shower

дожди *impf impers.* it is raining

дождлив *adj see* дожделив

дождовен -вна *adj* rainy; rain; дождовна глиста rain-worm

дождовит *adj* rainy

дождовник -ци *m Zool. see* дождалец

дождовница *f* rainwater

дожегна *pf* to cause a sudden pain; to sting (*also fig.*)

дожеже *pf impers.* дожежа *aor.* (*with dat.*) ми дожежа I got hot; *fig.* го дожежа he felt a pain

доживее *pf* доживеа *aor.* 1 to live <to see>; доживеа да жени син he lived to see his son married; доживеа длабока старост he lived to a ripe old age 2 to experience; доживее голем срам to experience (feel) great shame; доживее непријатно изненадување to get an unpleasant surprise

доживелица *f* experience; adventure

доживотен -тна *adj* lifelong, for life; осуден на доживотна робија sentenced to life imprisonment; доживотен инвалид permanently disabled person; доживотен член life member

доживува *impf* 1 *see* доживее 2 to live out (one's last years)

доза *f* dose, dosage; *fig.* amount, share; (*јадење*) portion, helping; одредена доза a certain amount of

дозбори *pf* I to finish speaking II – **се** to come to an agreement

дозборува (се) *impf see* дозбори (се)

дозвола *f* (*допуштање*) permission, approval, authorization; (*писмена*) permit, licence (*also fig.*); дозвола за престој residence permit; без дозвола unlicensed, without permission; возачка дозвола driving (driver's) licence; дозвола за слетување/ полетување clearance to land/take off

дозволен *pt* permitted, allowed; licensed, authorized

дозволеност *f* permission

дозволи *pf* (*with dat. of person*) to allow, permit, approve; дозволи да се пуши to permit smoking; ❏ многу си дозволува to take liberties; to get carried away; ако ми дозволите with your permission

дозволува *impf* to дозволи

дозема *impf of* доземе

доземе *pf* дозеде *aor.* 1 to take a little more; доземи си од лебот take some more bread! 2 to take all (the lot, the rest); доземи го лебот take the rest of the bread!

доземи *adv* to the ground, low

дознава *impf of* дознае

дознае *pf* дозна *aor.* to find out, learn

дозрева *impf of* дозрее

дозрее *pf* дозреа *aor.* to ripen, mature

досида *pf* 1 to add to, build on; досидаа уште едно крило на училишната зграда they added another wing to the school building 2 to finish building

досидува *impf of* досида

дои *impf* to breast-feed (*an infant*), suckle

доигра *pf* to finish playing/dancing

доигрува *impf of* доигра

доизрече *pf* доизрече *aor.* доизреков *1st p. aor.* I to say everything II – **се** to come out with everything; to speak one's mind

доилка *f* wet-nurse

доискаже *pf* доискажа *aor.* I to say everything II – **се** to come out with everything; to speak one's mind

доискажува (се) *impf of* доискаже (се)

доислуша *pf* to listen to (*s. o.*) to the end, hear (*s. o.*) out

доиспасе *pf* to graze bare

доиспие *pf* доиспи *aor.* to drink up, finish

доита *pf* to hurry up/down/over/in

дојава *pf* 1 to ride up/down/over (*до – to*); војникот дојава до командантот the soldier rode up to the commander 2 to finish riding

дојаде *pf* I to finish eating, eat up II – **се** *impers.* (*with dat.*) ми се дојаде I feel like eating

дојадува (се) *impf of* дојаде (се)

дојарка *f* wet-nurse

дојде *pf* 1 to come (*до/во/на/кај – to*); to arrive (*at*); to reach; дојде пеш he arrived on foot; дошла на возраст за мажење she reached marriageable age; дојде време за жниење harvest time came; дојде некому на гости, дојде кај некого на гости to visit s.o.; дојде за директор на фабриката he became manager of the factory; дојде наредба an order came; дојде до доказен материјал he got hold of proof; дојде во незгодна ситуација he got into an awkward situation; дојде до кавга there was a row, a row broke out; ❏ си дојде to arrive home; дојде до питачки стап to be reduced to poverty (penury); дојде во судир со to clash with; дојде до израз to find expression; (*за човек*) to make o.s. noticed; си дојдов на себеси I regained consciousness, I came to; добро му дојде it did him good; ми дојде до уши it came to my attention, I heard; ми дојде срцето на место I felt relieved; ми дојде преку глава I've had <more than> enough; ми дојде до гуша I've had <more than> enough; I'm fed up <with it>; ми дојде до рака it fell into my hands; I came across it; појдидојди hastily, in a great rush; иди ми – дојди ми a trifle, something unimportant; wasting time; кој дошол добре дошол it's open house <here>; we welcome all comers; му дојде до ак he ruined him; не можеше да дојде до збор he couldn't get a chance to speak; дојде на власт/до сила to come to power; дојде до заклучок to reach a conclusion; дојде до сознание to realize 2 (*за вода, надојде*) to rise; реката река rose (*припадне*) to come (*to*), be due, make; to weigh; ќе дојде по илјада на човек it will come to a thousand <denars> per person 4 (*стане некаков*) to become, get; дошло поарно it got better 5 *impers.* (*with dat.*) ми дојде жал I felt sorry; ми дојде да плачам I felt like crying

дојдува *impf of* дојде, *see* доаѓа

дојка *f f.p. see* боска

дојница *f* 1 wet-nurse 2 woman who is nursing a baby (*up to the third evening*), nursing mother 3 milk<ing> ewe, milker

Дојранско Езеро *n* Lake Dojran (Doiran)

док *m* dock, wharf

докер *m* docker

докажаност *f* evidence, clearness, obviousness

докаже *pf* докажа *aor.* I 1 to prove; докаже нечија вина to prove s.o.'s guilt; докаже свое право to substantiate one's claim; докаже мислење to prove one's point; to prove the case 2 to say everything 3 to finish speaking II – **се** to prove o.s.; се докаже во to make one's name in

докажок *m* the end of a speech/tale

докажува (се) *impf of* докаже (се)

докажувачка *f colloq.* end of a speech/tale

доказ *m* proof, evidence

доказен -зна *adj* proving, giving evidence; proof *attrib.*; доказен материјал evidence

докај *prep* 1 to, up to, in; докај недела in about a

week; up to about Sunday **2** (*за бројна при-ближност*) up to; roughly, approximately; докај сто <up to> about a hundred **3** to, to s.o.'s place; отидовме докај нив we went to see them

докапе¹ *pf* докапа *aor.* to stop dripping/leaking

докапе² *pf* докапа *aor.* **I 1** to wash /bath everybody **2** to finish bathing *trans.* **II – ce 1** to have a good wash/ bath **2** to finish washing/bathing *intrans.*

докапува (ce) *impf of* докапе² (ce)

докачи *pf* **I 1** to take, grab **2** to lift, raise right up **3** to reach **II – ce 1** to seize **2** to climb to the top **3** to squabble

докачува (ce) *impf of* докачи (ce)

докине *pf* докина *aor.* **I 1** to tear completely **2** to stop tearing **3** to wear out completely *trans.* **II – ce** to wear out completely *intrans.* (*of garments, etc.*)

докинува (ce) *impf of* докине (ce)

доклинка *pf colloq.* **1** to stagger (*до – то*) **2** *fig.* to tire *intrans.*, get tired

доколеници *pl* knee stockings

доколку & до колку *adv* if, in case; доколку . . . дотолку the more . . . the more

докопчи *pf* to grab, seize

докрај & до крај *adv* to the end, completely, utterly; to the utmost

докрајно *adv see* докрај

докрепи *pf* **I 1** to preserve, save **2** to support, hold up **3** to stop supporting **II – ce** to survive, keep going (*in one's old age*)

докрепува (ce) *impf of* докрепи (ce)

доктор *m* doctor, physician; доктор на науките Doctor of Philosophy (*literally* Doctor of Science), Ph. D.; ❏ *colloq.* доктор за an expert in; a dab hand at; <x>рани деца, да не <x>раниш доктор *prov.* sickness soaks the purse

докторáнт *m* candidate for a doctoral degree

докторáт *m* doctorate

докторúра *pf & impf* to receive/be awarded a doctorate; докторира на тема . . . to write a doctoral dissertation on a topic. . .

докторски *adj* doctoral; doctor's, medical

докторува *impf* to practise as a doctor (physician)

доктрúна *f* doctrine

доктринéр *m* doctrinaire

доктринéрство *n* doctrinaire attitude/behaviour

докумéнт *m* document; програмски документ platform; лични документи identity papers

документáрен -рна *adj* documentary; документарен филм documentary

документација *f* documentation

документúра *pf & impf* to document, furnish evidence

докупи *pf* **1** to buy more **2** to buy up

докупува *impf of* докупи

докусури *pf colloq.* to finish off, deal the death blow (*то*)

докусурува *impf of* докусури

докуца & докуцка *pf* to come limping, limp up (*до – то*)

дол *m* valley; ravine; gorge; ditch

долае *pf* долаја *aor.* to stop barking

долази *pf* to crawl (*до – то*)

долазува *impf of* долази

долама *f* dolman

долап *m* **1** closet, cupboard **2** (*кутија за кафе*) coffee box (tin) **3** (*за печење кафе*) coffee-roaster **4** (*за наводнување*) (*for irrigation*) water-wheel **5** revolving barrel (*for washing skins in a river*)

долапа *pf* to eat up everything, *colloq.* wolf down

долар *m* dollar

доларски *adj* dollar

долг *m* debt; државен долг national debt; ❏ ненаплатив долг bad debt; влегува во долгови to get into debt; to incur debts; плива во долгови to be in debt up to one's neck

долг *adj* long; ❏ таа е долга и широка it's a long story; thereby hangs a tale

долгач *m* **1** *Bot.* kind of bean with long seeds **2** tall, thin man, *colloq.* beanpole

долгичок -чка *adj dim. of* долг

долгманест & долгнавест *adj* longish, rather long

долго *adv* long, for a long time

долговечен -чна *adj* lasting, durable, long-lived

долговечност *f* durability; great age

долговремен *adj* of long duration; *Mil.* permanent

долгогодишен -шна *adj* of many years' standing, long-standing, long-range; (*за растение*) perennial

долгоклунест *adj* long-billed

долгокос *adj* long-haired

долголетен -тна *adj* of long duration, lasting many years, long-standing

долгоног *adj* long-legged

долгонос *adj* long-nosed

долгорак *adj* long-armed

долгорочен -чна *adj* long-term

долготраен -јна *adj* long-lasting; lengthy

долготрајност *f* durability

долгоушко *m* long-eared person/animal

долгунест *adj* longish, rather long

долева (ce) *impf of* долее (ce)

долее *pf* долеа *aor.* **I 1** to pour more; to add by pouring; долее вино во чаши to top up wineglasses **2** to pour out; долее вино од шише to empty (drain) a wine bottle **II – ce** *colloq.* to sip

долежи *pf* долежа *aor.* **1** to lie down for a certain time **2** to stop lying down; to serve out a sentence

долежува *impf of* долежи

долен -лна *adj* **1** lower; долна промена underwear; a change of underwear **2** worthless; corrupt **3** poor, weak

долепи *pf* **I 1** to press against; to fit snugly into **2** to stick on to **3** to finish sticking up **II – ce** to stick to; to snuggle up to

долепува (ce) *impf of* долепи (ce)

долет *m* arrival <by air>

долета *pf* **1** to fly up/down/in; to arrive <by air>; долета пеперуга a butterfly flew in **2** to finish flying, land

долетува *impf of* долета

должен -жна *adj* **1** owing <money>, in debt; должен многу пари owing a lot of money, heavily in debt; ❏ не останува должен to give as good as one gets **2** obliged, indebted; должен да стори нешто obliged to do s.th.

должи¹ *impf* **I** to owe; му должам илјада денари I owe him a thousand denars; му должам за животот I owe him my life; ти должам <за ова> I owe you one **II – ce** to be due to (attributable); тоа се должи на повеќе причини this is due to several causes (reasons)

должи[2] *impf* to lengthen, prolong, drag out; to delay; должи со дискусија to prolong a discussion; да не должам повеќе to cut a long story short, to put it briefly

должина *f* length; должина и ширина (широчина) length and breadth

должински *adj* linear; должински мерки linear measures

должник -ци *m* debtor

должност *f* duty; obligation; post, appointment; секојдневни должности the daily round; по службена должност in the line of duty

должностен -тна *adj rare* official

долија -ии *f dial.* big glass, tumbler

доликува *impf (with dat.)* to be appropriate, suitable, fitting, proper; не ти доликува да го кажеш тоа it ill behoves you to say that

долина *f* valley; gully; hollow; ❑ ветува брда и долини to promise pie in the sky (heaven and earth)

долински *adj* valley *attrib.*; valley-like

долма *f* **1** kind of long marrow (*usu. cooked with filling of meat and rice*) **2** kind of large green pepper (capsicum)

долнак *m* **1** south wind **2** *pl* -ци lower of pair of millstones

долница *f* **1** skirt **2** *dial.* pigtail, plait

долниште *n* **1** skirt **2** women's linen, lingerie

долноземец -мци *m* southerner

долноземка *f (fem. form) see* долноземец

долноземски *adj* southern, from the south

долномаалец -лци *m* person from the lower part of a village

долови *pf literary* **1** to perceive; to grasp; to realize **2** to conjure up

доловува *impf literary of* долови

долока *pf* to finish drinking (lapping up)

доломит *m* dolomite

долу *adv* below; ❑ не паѓа подолу од него she's of a piece with him, she's no better than he is; горедолу more or less, roughly, approximately; горе-долу 1. up and down; back and forth; to and fro 2. approximately

долупотпишан *pt* undersigned

долче *n dim. of* дол; gully; depression; glen, coomb

дољум *m arch.* forty by forty arshins, 920 m², about 1/4 acre (*square measure*)

дом *m* **1** house, home; мојот дом my house; ❑ ништо поубаво од дома there's no place like home; home sweet home **2** *fig.* роден дом native country, homeland **3** (*општествена установа*) детски дом children's home; дом на културата cultural centre; Горниот (Долниот) дом Upper (Lower) House <of Parliament>; студентски дом hall of residence, *Am.* <students'> dormitory; дом за старци nursing home; old people's home; здравствен дом health centre; вечен дом the grave

дома *adv* at home; home; се чувствува како дома to feel at home

домаа *pf* домае *aor.* **I** to drive up/down/over *trans.* **II** – се to turn up, appear; се домаа од некаде he appeared out of nowhere

домава *pf* to stop beating

домазет *m* man who lives with his wife's family

домалиот *adj in the expression:* домалиот прст the ring finger

домами *pf* to entice

домамува *impf of* домами

домат *m Bot.* tomato (*plant and fruit*)

доматен -тна *adj* tomato; доматен сос tomato sauce

домаќин *m* **1** (*стопан на куќа*) head of household, householder; (*кој прима гости*) host **2** (*чесен, угледен човек*) good man; good family man; honoured/prominent person, notable **3** (*службеник за набавки и сл.*) supplies manager; steward; manciple **4** *Biol.* host

домаќинка *f* housewife, mistress of the house; hostess; home-maker

домаќински *adj* household; домаќинско дете well-brought-up child

домаќинство *n* **1** household; селско домаќинство farmstead, homestead **2** household duties, housekeeping **3** home, family

домачне *pf (with dat.)* to bore, weary *trans.*

домачнува *impf of* домачне

домашар *m* stay-at-home, homebody, homebird

домашен -шна *adj* **1** domestic, home; household; домашен живот home life; домашни животни domestic animals; домашни работи housework; домашен пријател family friend; домашна посета <physician's> house call **2** home-made; home-grown; домашно платно homespun cloth **3** domestic, national; internal; домашна индустрија national industry **4** *pl* домашните members of a family, household **5** домашно *n colloq.* homework

домет *m* reach, range, scope, *see* досег

домеша *pf* **1** to mix in **2** to finish mixing

домешува *impf of* домеша

доминанта *f* **1** *Mus.* dominant **2** *Arts* dominant theme

доминантен -тна *adj* dominant, predominant, main, prevalent

доминација *f* domination; power, rule; superiority

Доминика *f* Dominica

доминикиски *adj* Dominican, from/of Dominica

доминион *m* dominion

доминира *impf* to dominate, rule, be master; to stand out; exceed, surpass; домашните играчи доминираа the home players were on top

Доминиканец -нци *m* Dominican, person from the Dominican Republic

Доминиканка *f (fem. form) see* Доминиканец

доминикански *adj* Dominican; Доминиканска Република the Dominican Republic

домино *n* **1** (*игра*) dominoes **2** (*карневалска пелерина*) domino <cloak>

домири *pf* to supplement

домирува *impf of* домири

домисли се *pf* to think (*of s.th.*), have an idea, conceive; to guess (*дека – that*)

домислува се *impf* to think (*about s.th.*); wonder; тој се домислуваше кој можел да го напише писмото he was wondering who could have written the letter

домоли *pf* to obtain (*s.th.*) by entreaties, wheedle (*s.th. out of s.o.*)

домолува *impf of* домоли

домороден -дна *adj* home-grown, native

домородец -дци *m* native, aborigine

домрзи *pf impers. (with acc.)* домрзе *aor.* ме домрзе I was overcome by laziness, I felt lazy

домрзува *impf of* домрзи

донде<ка> *adv* so far, that far

донекаде *adv* up to a point, to a degree, to a certain extent; somewhat; up to a certain place/time; up to there

донесе¹ *pf* to bring; to carry; болничарите го донесоа на креветот the orderlies carried him to the bed; донесе вода to fetch water; ❏ донесе вест to bring (bear) news; донесе решение to take (make) a decision; донесе заклучок to draw a conclusion; донесе закон to pass a law; донесе забрана to prohibit; донесе плод to bear fruit; донесе корист to be of benefit

донесе² *pf (за кокошки)* to stop laying eggs

донесеник -ци *m see* доведеник

донесеница *f (fem. form) see* донесеник

донесува *impf of* донесе¹

донесувач *m* bringer

донжуа́н *m* Don Juan, rake

доноси *pf* **1** to wear out *trans.* **2** to carry a child to the full term

доносува *impf of* доноси

донум *m see* дољум

доо́ден *pt* tired, exhausted, worn-out

доо́ди *pf* **1** to walk over to the end **2** to stop walking **3** *fig.* to tire *intrans.*, get tired/ worn-out (exhausted)

доо́дува *impf of* доо́ди

допадне *pf* допадна *aor.* to arrive, enter unexpectedly; to burst in

допадне се *pf* допадна се *aor. (with dat.)* to please, suit, appeal *(to s.o.)*, be to the liking *(of s.o.)*; девојката му се допадна на момчето the boy liked (took a liking to) the girl

допаѓа *pf* to fall completely *(of leaves, etc.)*

допаѓа се *impf of* допадне се

допати *adv* next time; another time

допатува *pf* **1** to arrive **2** to complete a journey

допир *m* contact, touch

допира (се) *impf of* допре (се)

допирен -рна *adj* contact *attrib.*; допирна точка point of contact, common ground

допирна *f* <point of> contact; tangent

допис *m (официјален)* official letter, memorandum, communication; *(новинарски)* report, story

дописен -сна *adj* corresponding *(member)*; postal; дописна карта postcard; дописен курс correspondence course

дописка *f* newspaper report, story

дописник -ци *m* correspondent, reporter

дописница *f* postcard

дописнички *adj* correspondent's, reporter's

дописништво *n* **1** branch office *(of a newspaper)* **2** *coll.* newspapermen, journalists, reporters **3** reporting, journalism *(as a profession)*

допита (се) *pf dial. see* допраша (се)

допитува (се) *impf dial. see* допрашува (се)

допише *pf* допиша *aor.* **1** to add <in writing>; на крајот од писмото допиша уште неколку реченици at the end of the letter he added a few sentences **2** to finish writing

допишува *impf* **I** *of* допише **II** – **се** to correspond *(co – with)*

допишување *n from* допишува; correspondence

доплакува (се) *impf of* доплаче (се)

доплата *f* surcharge, additional payment

доплати *pf* **1** to pay extra; to make an additional payment; доплати разлика во цена to make up a difference in price **2** to pay off, pay in full; ја доплати куќата he paid off the house

доплатува *impf of* доплати

доплаче *pf* доплака *aor.* **I** to stop crying **II** – **се** *impers. (with dat.)* ми се доплака I felt like crying

доплачува (се) *impf see* доплакува (се)

доплива *pf* to swim over/down/up *(до – to)*, swim as far as; to reach <by swimming>

допливува *impf of* доплива

допловии *pf* to arrive, reach *(of/by boat, ship)*; to sail *(to a place)*; со кајчето допловии до брегот he reached the shore by (in his) dinghy

допловува *impf of* допловии

дополнение -нија *n* addition, supplement; amendment

дополни *pf* **I** **1** to fill up/out/in; го дополни со вода he filled it up with water **2** to supplement, add to; to complete; to complement; го дополни кажувањето на мајка си she added to her mother's account **II** – **се** to complement one another, be complementary <to one another>

дополнителен -лна *adj* supplementary, additional, extra; дополнително осигурување additional insurance; дополнителен расход extra disbursement; дополнителен трошок additional charge; extra cost; дополнителна плата extra pay; дополнителен данок surtax; дополнителна работа extra work; дополнително време *Sport.* extra time

дополнително *adv* in addition; later on; extra

дополнува (се) *impf of* дополни (се)

дополу *adv* half; наполни чаша дополу to half-fill a glass

допотопски *adj* antediluvian

допрати *pf* to send; to send word

допратува *impf see* допраќа

допраќа *impf of* допрати

допраша *pf* **I** to ask, enquire further **II** – **се** to consult *(до/со некого за нешто – s.o. on s.th.)*, ask *(s.o.'s)* advice; to talk things over

допраши *pf* to dig round; to dust/pollinate completely

допрашува¹ *impf of* допраши

допрашува² (се) *impf of* допраша (се)

допрва *adv* still (yet) to come; допрва е зимата 1. winter is on its way 2. winter's not over yet

допрвешен -шна *adj* just coming, just starting

допрвин *adv see* допрва

допре *pf* **I** **1** to touch; to make contact *(with)*; слепиот допре со бастунот до ѕидот the blind man touched the wall with his stick **2** to reach *(до некого – s.o.'s ears)* **3** to lean, press *(до, на нешто – against s.th.)* **4** *fig.* to touch on, broach; референтот не го допре тоа прашање the speaker did not touch on that question **II** – **се** **1** to touch; се допре до плотот he touched the fence **2** to lean *(на нешто – against s.th.)*; to snuggle *(до некого – up to s.o.)* **3** *arch.* to rely, depend *(на некого – on s.o.)* **4** *arch.* to resist, offer resistance; му се допреле they resisted him **5** *fig. (with до) see* **I** 4

допринесува *impf see* придонесува

допрува (се) *impf dial. see* допира (се)

допушта *impf of* допушти; ❑ многу си допушта to let o.s. go; to know no limits

допушти *pf* **1** to allow, permit; (*одобри*) to approve, countenance; (*прифати некое тврдење*) to accept; си допуштивме премногу прекршувања на правилата we have allowed ourselves too many breaches of the rules **2** (*допрати*) to send; to send word (*to s.o.*); to inform (*s.o. of s.th.*)

доработи *pf* **1** to finish <working on s.th.>; *fig.* to put the finishing touches (*to s.th.*) **2** to complete one's work, finish one's job **3** (*поради старост и др.*) to stop (give up) working, retire

доработува *impf of* доработи

доразбере *pf* доразбра *aor.* to grasp, understand fully, comprehend

доразвива (се) *impf of* доразвие (се)

доразвие *pf* доразви *aor.* **I 1** to develop further/completely *trans.*; (*мисла*) to elaborate on (*a thought*) **2** (*за цвеќе*) to bloom fully, be in full bloom **II – се** to develop fully *intrans.*; to reach full stature

дорамни *pf* to level, even, smooth <out>

дорамнува *impf of* дорамни

дораснат *adj* equal (*за, на – то*), fit (*for*); ready, mature; дораснат е за то be up to; to be a good match for; дораснат на приликите equal to the occasion

дораснатост *f* maturity

дорасне *pf* дорасна *aor.* **1** to grow up, reach maturity; неговите деца дораснаа his children are (have) grown up **2** to become equal (*to a task*), become a match (*for*); to become ready (mature) (*for*); детето дорасна за (за на) училиште the child is ready for school

дораснува *impf of* дорасне

дорасте *pf see* дорасне

дорастува *impf see* дораснува

дорат *m see* дорија

дореда *adv* next time; another time

дореди *pf* **I** to arrange perfectly; to line up completely *trans.*; to finish arranging **II–се** to line up *intrans.* perfectly, form a perfect line

доредува (се) *impf of* дореди (се)

дорекува *impf of* дорече

дорече *pf* дорече *aor.* дореков *1st sg. aor.* to finish saying

доречува *impf see* дорекува

дорие *pf* дори *aor.* to dig (*to a particular spot*); to finish digging

дорија *m & adj indecl.* bay <horse>

дорине *pf* дорина *aor.* to shovel together (*into a heap*)

доринува *impf of* дорине

дорјанка *f Bot.* chrysanthemum

дорски *adj* Doric, Dorian

доруча *pf* to finish eating (having) lunch, finish one's lunch

доручува *impf of* доруча

дорче & дорчо *m* bay horse

досада *f* boredom, monotony, tedium

досаден -дна *adj* boring, dull; (*непријатен*) irksome, annoying

досади¹ *pf* **I** *see* додее **II – се** (*with dat.*) to bore, weary *trans.*; на сите им се досади од неговите прикаски his stories got on everyone's nerves; ѝ се досади да седи дома she got tired of staying at home

досади² *pf* **1** to finish planting **2** to plant some more; досадивме уште 200 корења пипер we planted 200 more capsicum seedlings

досадно *adv* tediously; (*непријатно*) annoyingly, irritably

досадност *f* dullness, boredom

досадува¹ *impf* **I** *of* досади¹ **II – се** to be bored; се досадуваа чекајќи смена they were bored waiting for the change of shift

досадува² *impf of* досади²

досврши *pf* to finish off/up

досвршува *impf of* досврши

досева *impf of* досее

досег *m* reach, range, scope

досега¹ *impf of* досегне; дворот досегаше до самата плажа the yard reached right down to the beach

досега² *adv* till now, up to now

досегашен -шна *adj* former, one-time, previous; prevailing, to date

досеглив *adj* reachable, attainable

досегне *pf* досегна *aor.* to reach (*до – to, as far as*)

досегнува *impf see* досега¹

доседелка *f dial.* spinster, old maid

доседи *pf* to stay up, sit up (*till*); to sit out

доседува *impf of* доседи

досее *pf* досеа *aor.* to finish sowing

досекува *impf of* досече

доселба *f* settling, immigration

доселеник -ци *m* immigrant

досели *pf* **I** to settle *trans.*; to move *trans.* **II – се** settle *intrans.*; (*во друга држава*) to immigrate; (*во друго живеалиште*) to move <in> *intrans.*; во станот се досели млада брачна двојка a young couple have moved into the flat

доселува (се) *impf of* досели (се)

досети *pf* to realize; (*погоди*) to guess; (*си спомне*) to remember; се досетиле што се случило they realized what had happened

досетка *f* joke, witticism; trick

досетлив *adj* resourceful, clever, quick-witted

досетливост *f* resourcefulness, cleverness, quick wits

досетува се & досеќава се *impf of* досети (се)

досече *pf* to finish cutting (chopping) (*wood*)

досечува *impf of* досече, *see* досекува

досига *impf of* досигне; козата ги досигаше долните гранчиња the goat could reach the lower branches; јажето не досигаше до другиот дирек the rope did not reach the other rafter; *cf.* досега¹

досигне *pf* досигна *aor.* to reach *trans.*, grasp (*with the hand*); ја досигна бравата и ја отвори вратата he reached <up to> the lock and opened the door

досие *n* dossier; чисто досие clean slate, clean record

доскоро *adv* until recently, recently

доскубе *pf* доскуба *aor.* **1** to pluck (*a bird*) completely **2** *fig.* to fleece completely

доскубува *impf of* доскубе

доследен -дна *adj* consistent, logical, persistent; faithful

доследно *adv* consistently; in accordance (*со – with*)

доследност *f* consistency

дословен -вна *adj* literal, word-for-word

дословно *adv* literally

дослужи *pf* to complete one's term of service, complete one's tour of duty

дослужува *impf of* дослужи

дослуша *pf* **1** to listen (*to s.th.*) to the end, hear out **2** to hear, catch; дослуша дека идат другарите he heard his friends coming; одвај ја дослушавме изведбата we could hardly hear the performance

дослушува *impf* **I** *of* дослуша **II – се** *impers.* (*with dat.*) не ми се дослушува I don't hear very well; I won't hear of it

досмрди *pf* досмрде *aor.* (*with dat.*) ми досмрди I noticed a bad smell

досмрдува *impf of* досмрди

досмртен -тна *adj* lifelong, for life; домсртно прогонство lifelong exile

досоли *pf* to add some salt

досолува *impf of* досоли

дососа *pf colloq.* to spend (*money*); to squander

дососува *impf of* дососа

досрка *pf* to lap/sip up completely

досркува *impf of* досрка

доста *adv* enough, sufficiently; a great deal; доста веќе со тоа! enough of that! cut it out! доста е enough; that'll do; <тој> не знае за доста he doesn't know when to stop

достави *pf* **1** to deliver; to supply; to dispatch **2** to notify, inform

доставка *f* delivery; доставка дома home delivery, door-to-door delivery

доставница *f* bill of delivery, delivery note, receipt

доставува *impf of* достави

доставувач *m* supplier; deliverer

достага *f* hardship, difficulty, trouble; torment, pain; sorrow, grief

достап *m* (*право на влегување*) access; approach; слободен достап free access; има достап (*кон*) to have access (*to*)

достапен -пна *adj* accessible; достапни цени reasonable prices; на достапен јазик in intelligible (simple) language

достапност *f* accessibility; approachability; simplicity

достаса *pf* **1** to arrive; to catch up (*with*); to reach; го достаса коњот he caught up with the horse; достаса до дрвјата he got as far as the trees **2** (*за млеко и сл.*) to turn sour; (*за тесто*) to rise, prove *intrans.* **3** to be sufficient; не ми достасаа пари I ran out of money

достасан *adj* due, payable, mature; достасан долг, достасано побарување due (liquid) debt

достасување *n from* достасува; ден на достасување due date, date of expiry; на достасување when due, at maturity

достатен -тна & **достаточен** -чна *adj* sufficient

достига *impf of* достигне

достигање *n from* достига; achievement

достигне *pf* достигна *aor.* **1** *see* достаса 1; арен глас далеку достига – лош уште подалеку *prov.* bad news travels fast **2** *see* досигне; не ја достигна гранката he could not reach the branch; потрошувачката ќе достигне до планираното ниво consumption will reach the projected level **3** *see* достаса 3; овие тули ќе достигнат за една гаража these bricks will be sufficient for one garage

достигнува *impf of* достига

достигнување *n see* достигање; научни достигнувања scientific achievements

достижен -жна *adj* attainable

достиска *pf colloq.* to hold out (*till a certain moment*); стиска, достиска he couldn't stick it any more

достоен -јна *adj* worthy, deserving

достои *pf* достоја *aor.* to stand to the end; to remain standing, stay on one's feet; ❑ не си достоја на зборот he didn't keep <to> his word; си достоја на клетвата she kept her oath

достоинствен *adj* dignified, imposing

достоинственик -ци *m* dignitary, notable

достоинство *n* **1** dignity **2** *pl* merits

достојание *n literary* property

достојно *adv* with dignity; worthily

достојност *f* worth, merit

дострел *m see* досег

достори *pf* to complete, finish

достуди *pf impers.* (*with dat.*) ми достуде I felt cold, I began to feel cold

достудува *impf of* достуди

досуди *pf* **1** to impose a fine/penalty **2** *Leg., Sport.* to award; досуди оштетување to award damages; судот му ја досуди куќата на постариот брат the court awarded the house to the older brother **3** to finish trying (judging)

досудува *impf of* досуди

досуши *pf* **I** to finish drying, dry off **II – се** to dry up/out

досушува (се) *impf of* досуши (се)

дотажи *pf* **I** to cease mourning, keening **II – се** *impers.* (*with dat.*) ми се дотажи I felt sorry

дотажува (се) *impf of* дотажи (се)

дотаму *adv* that far, so far

дотација -ии *f* subsidy, subvention; државна дотација government subsidy

дотегне *pf* дотегна *aor.* **1** to drag (*s.th.*) somewhere **2** (*with dat.*) to annoy, become unbearable; to bore, become boring; децата ѝ дотегнаа на сестра ми my sister could not stand the children any longer; нам ни дотегна од седењето дома we grew tired of staying at home

дотегнува *impf of* дотегне

дотежне *pf* дотежна *aor.* to grow heavy, begin to feel heavy; to be too heavy (*for s.o.*)

дотежнува *impf of* дотежне

дотекува *impf of* дотече

дотепа *pf* to finish off (*also fig.*)

дотепува *impf of* дотепа

дотера *pf* **I 1** to drive up/over/in *trans.*; дотера говеда од пасење to drive cattle from pasture; *fig.* го дотерала маката he was driven to it by circumstances; ❑ дотера до питачки стап to reduce to penury; to be reduced to penury **2** to put right; to refine, touch up, polish, hone; (*јадење*) to do (cook) to a turn; (*разубави*) to decorate, smarten up; дотера текст to polish a text; дотера куќа to decorate (refurbish) a house **3** to set; to adjust, regulate; дотера часовник to set a clock **4** to get somewhere <in life>; тој далеку дотера he has gone a long way; дотера до генерал he reached the rank of general **II – се** to smarten up *intrans.*; to dress up *intrans.*

дотеран *pt* smart, dressed up; (*за стил, изработка*) polished, finished; refined

дотераност *f* smartness; (*за стил, изработка*) polish, finish; refinement

дотерува (се) *impf of* дотера (се)

дотече *pf* **1** to reach (*of water*), flow up (*до – to, as far as*) **2** to rise (*of water*); реката дотекла и однела сè пред себе the river rose and swept everything along **3** to stop flowing

дотечува *impf see* дотекува

дотѝра *pf & impf* to subsidize

дотогај & дотогаш *adv* till then

дотогашен -шна *adj* former, past

дотолку & до толку *adv* that much, to such an extent; <by> so much

дотолче & дотолчи *pf* **1** to grind; to crush completely **2** *fig.* to ruin; to beat up; to finish off

дотолчува *impf of* дотолче & дотолчи

доточка *f* weak raki

дотрае *pf* дотраја *aor.* **1** to last out, endure (hold out) to the end; не дотраја до доаѓањето на другарот he could not wait for his friend to come **2** to remain silent, refrain from speaking, *colloq.* keep mum; дотрајав, не реков ништо I remained silent

дотрајува *impf of* дотрае

дотрапа *pf* to tramp, walk clumsily (*до – towards*)

дотрга *pf* **1** to drag up/down/over/in, bring by dragging **2** to stop dragging

дотркала *pf* **I** to roll up/down/over/in *trans.* **II – се** to roll up/down/over/in *intrans.*

дотркалува (се) *impf of* дотркала (се)

дотрча *pf* **1** to run up/down/over/in, come running; жената дотрча the woman ran up; дотрча до детето he ran over to the child **2** to finish (stop) running

дотрчува *impf of* дотрча

дотука *adv* up to here; *colloq.* up to now; дотука дојдовме we've got up to here, we've got this far

дотура *impf of* дотури

дотури *pf* **1** to pour some more; им дотури супа на децата she poured (served) the children more soup **2** to add **3** to finish pouring **4** (*достави*) to supply, deliver

дотурка *pf* **1** to push up/down/over/in (*до – as far as*); ја дотурка масата до ѕидот he pushed the table over to the wall **2** to demolish completely

дотуркува *impf of* дотурка

доќердоса *pf* to prosper

доуми <се> *pf* to think of, have the idea (*да прави нешто – of doing s.th.*)

дофат *m rare* на дофат на раката within arm's reach; close <at hand>

дофати *pf* to reach; (*се случи некому*) to strike, befall (*s.o.*), happen (*to s.o.*); (*погоди*) to touch, affect

дофрла[1] *impf of* дофрли

дофрла[2] *pf see* дофрли; (*на политички собир*) to heckle, *Brit.* barrack

дофрли *pf* **1.** (*до определено место*) to throw (*to/as far as*); му дофрли на кучето една коска he threw the dog a bone **2** *fig.* to interject, remark, throw in **3** to throw everything out

дофрлува *impf see* дофрла[1]

доход *m* income; revenue; доход на жител per capita income; бруто доход gross income; гарантиран личен доход guaranteed income; годишен доход annual income; данок на доход income tax; трговски доход trade profits (returns)

доходен -дна *adj* **1** income *attrib.*; income-based; доходна политика income policy; доходна стапка rate of income **2** profitable, lucrative; доходна дејност (работа) well-paid job

дохрани *pf* to feed, support, maintain

дохранува *impf of* дохрани

доц. *abbr.* (*доцент*) university lecturer, associate professor, reader

доцврсти *pf* to tighten up; to strengthen, consolidate

доцен -цна *adj* late

доцент *m* university lecturer, associate professor, reader

доцентýра *f* lectureship, associate professorship, readership

доцна *adv* late

доцнежен -жна *adj see* доцен

доцнење *n from* доцни; delay

доцни *impf* **1** to be late, come (arrive) late; доцни на состанок to be late for a meeting **2** (*за часовник*) to be slow

доцнина *f* dead of night, the small hours

доцно *adv dial. see* доцна

доцути *pf* to finish flowering

доцутува *impf of* доцути

дочека *pf* **1** to live to see; to experience; дочека длабока старост to live to a ripe old age; дочека тешки времиња to experience hard times; дочека да жени син he lived <long enough> to see his son married; ❑ што дочекав! Good God! I never expected this! **2** to wait for **3** to take, receive, bear, accept; го дочека ударот во гради he took the blow in the chest **4** to meet, greet, welcome; излезе да го дочека сина си he went out to greet his son **5** to see in; дочека Нова година to see in the New Year **II – се** to fall safely; to land; се дочека на нозе/раце to land on one's feet/hands

дочекува (се) *impf of* дочека (се)

дочисти *pf* to clean out thoroughly

дочистува *impf of* дочисти

дочува[1] *pf* **1** to preserve, save **2** to look (*after s.o.*), take care (*of s.o.*), nurse (*s.o.*) to the end; *see* догледа 4

дочува[2] *impf* **I** *of* дочуе **II – се** *impers.* (*with dat.*) не ми се дочува I can't hear very well; I won't hear of it

дочуди се *pf* **1** to be amazed again/even more **2** to cease being amazed

дочуе *pf* дочу *aor.* **1** to hear, catch; (*без да сака*) to overhear; кучето го дочу мојот глас the dog heard (caught the sound of) my voice **2** to hear (*about s.th.*), find out **3** to hear to the end, hear out; не ја дочу прикаската he did not hear the end of the story

дошантра се *pf* to limp as far as

дошета *pf* **1** to walk as far as **2** to stop walking/strolling

дошива *impf of* дошие

дошие *pf* доши *aor.* **1** to sew on **2** to finish sewing

дошика се *pf arch.* to mind out, look out

дошикува се *impf arch.* of дошика се

дошлак -ци *m* newcomer; immigrant

ДП *abbr.* (*Демократска партија*) Democratic Party

ДПМ *abbr.* (*Демократска партија на Македонија*) Democratic Party of Macedonia

д-р *abbr.* (*доктор*) Dr

драг¹ *m* long stick, pole, bar

драг² *adj* dear, pleasant, sweet; ❑ на драго срце gladly

драго *adv* pleased, delighted; драго ми е I am delighted

драгоман *m arch.* **1** interpreter, dragoman **2** (*на жетвари*) lord of the harvest

драгост *f* preciousness; value

драгоцен *adj* (*скапоцен*) precious, valuable

драгоценост *f* preciousness, high value

драж *f literary rare* charm, allure

дразлив *adj* irritable, excitable

дразливост *f* irritability, excitability

дразни *impf* **I** **1** to tease; to irritate; правот му го дразнеше грлото the dust irritated his throat **2** (*поттикнува*) to stimulate, arouse, excite; миризбата на топло јадење ме дразни the aroma of hot food makes my mouth water **II** – ce **1** to be easily irritable; тој се дразнеше од најобични работи the most ordinary things would irritate him **2** to become aroused

драјка *f Zool.* egret

драка *f Bot.* (Paliurus aculeatus) Christ's thorn

драконски *adj* Draconian; драконски мерки Draconian measures

драм *m arch.* dram; small portion

драма *f* drama

драматизација -ии *f* dramatization

драматизи́ра *pf & impf* to dramatize (*also fig.*)

драматика *f* drama, dramatic art, theatricals, dramatics

драматизам -змот *m* drama, dramatism

драматичен -чна *adj* dramatic

драматичар *m* dramatist, playwright

драматýрг -зи *m* **1** dramatist, playwright **2** dramaturge; repertory director; literary manager

драматургија *f* dramaturgy

драматýршки *adj* dramaturgic

драмски¹ *adj* dramatic, theatrical; драмска уметност dramatic art

драмски² *adv* dramatically, theatrically

дрангулии *pl colloq.* trinkets, knick-knacks

драп *adj indecl. & n* light brown/cream <colour>, beige

драпа *impf* **I** to scratch; си ја драпа главата to scratch one's head; ❑ драпај си мевот go on! that's a tall story; tell that to the marines! **II** – ce **1** to scratch o.s.; to comb o.s. vigorously **2**. *fig.* to make fun (*co некого – of s.o.*), mock, poke fun (*at s.o.*), joke (*at s.o.'s expense*)

драпач *m* **1** person who scratches himself **2** *fig.* mocker

драперија -ии *f* drapery, hangings; curtain; soft furnishings

драпне *pf* драпна *aor.* **1** see драпа **2** *colloq.* to bolt, scram, clear off (out)

драска *impf see* драсне

драсканица *f* **1** scratch **2** scribbling, scribble, scrawl

драскач *m iron.* scribbler

драсне *pf* драсна *aor.* **1** to scratch, graze *trans.*; некој го драснал огледалото someone has scratched the mirror **2** to scribble, scrawl; му драснав неколку збора I scribbled a few words to him

драснува *impf of* драсне

драстичен -чна *adj* drastic

драхма *f* drachma

дрва *pl* firewood; оди на дрва to fetch firewood; ❑ фрла по некого со дрва и камења 1. to jump down s.o.'s throat 2. to speak ill of s.o.

дрвар *m* woodcutter, lumberjack; timber (*Am.* lumber) merchant

дрварина *f* woodcutting fee

дрварник -ци *m* woodpile; timberyard, *Am.* lumberyard

дрварница *f* timberyard, *Am.* lumberyard

дрвен¹ *adj* **1** wooden; дрвена лажица wooden spoon; ❑ дрвена глава blockhead; obstinate person **2** *fig.* stiff; stern, strict; целиот е дрвен he is absolutely inflexible

дрвен² -вна *adj* timber, *Am.* lumber *attrib.*; дрвна индустрија timber industry

дрвенарија *f* woodwork; wooden furniture

дрвенее <ce> *impf* to become wooden

дрвеница¹ *f Zool.* (Cimex lectularis) bedbug

дрвеница² *f* small curved board in a packsaddle

дрвесина *f* timber, wood, wood-pulp

дрво *n* **1** *pl* дрвја tree; ❑ пијан како дрво blind drunk, dead drunk; дрвото се вие дури е младо *prov.* twist the wand while it is green; од секое дрво свирче не бидува *prov.* you can't make a silk purse of a sow's ear **2** *pl* дрва (*за горење, градиво и сл.*) firewood; timber, wood; ❑ камен и дрво пука it's bitterly cold; дрво неделкано blockhead, dolt; да чукнам во дрво touch wood; и под дрво и под камен <search> every nook and cranny; <leave> no stone unturned

дрводелец -лци *m* cabinetmaker, woodworker; carpenter; joiner

дрводелски *adj* cabinetmaker's, carpenter's

дрводелство *n* carpentry, joinery

дрвојад *m* **1** *Zool.* borer **2** *Bot.* dry-rot fungus

дрворед *m* avenue <of trees>

дрворез *m* woodcarving

дрвоса *pf* **1** to become wooden, turn to wood **2** *fig.* to grow stiff/stiff-necked

дрвце *n dim.* **1** *of* дрво; sapling; stick; small piece of wood; дрвца за потпалување kindling **2** *dial.* slate pencil

дрдало *n* **1** drone (*on bagpipes*) **2** *fig.* babbler

дрдори *impf* to babble, chatter a bit

дрдорко -овци *m* babbler, chatterbox

дребен -бна *adj see* дробен

дребина *f* revolving stage

дребнав *adj* petty, hair-splitting

дребнавост *f* pettiness

дреболија -ии *f* knick-knack; *pl* sundries, odds and ends

древен -вна *adj* ancient; antique; old-fashioned

древност *f* ancient times, antiquity

древо *n dial. see* дрво

дреер *m* metalworker

дрезга *f Bot.* (Sium latifolium) water parsnip

дрезгав *adj* hoarse, rasping

дремало *n* sleepyhead

дреме *impf* **I** to doze, slumber; *fig.* to be idle; ❑ дреме како мисир he's standing there like a dummy **II** – ce *impers.* (*with dat.*) ми се дреме I feel drowsy

дремеж *m* drowsiness, sleepiness

дремка *f* sleepiness; doze, snooze
дремла *f* (*fem. form*) *see* дремло
дремлив *adj* drowsy, dreamy, sleepy
дремливко *m* sleepyhead
дремливост *f* drowsiness, sleepiness, dreaminess
дремло -овци *m* sleepyhead
дремне *pf* дремна *aor.* to take a nap
дремнидедо *m* & **дремниче** *n* Bot. (Anemone pulsatilla) pasque-flower, campana
дремнува *impf of* дремне
дрен *m* Bot. (Cornus mas) cornel tree, dogwood; ❏ здрав како дрен fit as a fiddle, fit as a stick
дренажа *f* drainage
дренина *f* dial. see дренка
дренка *f* cornelian cherry
дренковица *f* brandy made from cornelian cherries
дренкукуш *adv* using a queen's seat (*seat made by two pairs of crossing hands in children's games or for carrying injured people*)
дренов *adj* dogwood *attrib.*; cornel<-tree/-wood> *attrib.*
дреновица *f* cornel stick; dogwood cudgel
дренок -ци *m dim. of* дрен
дрес *m Sport.* jersey
дресер *m* trainer; дресер на кучиња dog trainer
дресина *f* rail-inspection car, motor trolley
дресира *impf* to train (*usu. animals*)
дресура *f* training, dressage
дречи *pf* to be loud (gaudy); (*of colours*) to scream, shout
дречлив *adj* loud, gaudy; дречлива боја gaudy (screaming) colour
држава *f* state; (*земја*) country; ❏ држава во држава a state within a state
државен -вна *adj* state *attrib.*; public; national; државен апарат machinery of state; државен долг national debt; државен заем government loan; државен празник public holiday; national holiday; државен сектор public sector; државна сопственост public property; state ownership; државна служба civil service; државен удар coup d'état
државица *f* & **државичка** *f dim. of* држава
државјанин -јани *m* citizen; subject
државјанка *f* (*fem. form*) *see* државјанин
државјански *adj* citizen's
државјанство *n* citizenship
државник -ци *m* statesman
државнички *adj* statesmanlike
државништво *n* state organization; statecraft
државноправен -вна *adj* public-law
државотворен -рна *adj* nation-building; politically constructive
државотворност *f* nation-building qualities
држалје *n see* држалка
држалка *f* 1 (*за перо*) penholder 2 (*дршка*) handle
држало *n see* држалка 1
држана *f* kept woman; mistress
држење *n from* држи 1 holding; support 2 behaviour, conduct; attitude
држи *impf* I 1 to hold, hold on to, take hold of; држете го арамијата stop thief! држи за рака to hold s.o.'s hand; држи глава високо to hold one's head high (*also fig.*) 2 (*крепи*) to hold up, support;

мостот го држеа бетонски столбови the bridge was supported by concrete stanchions; мразот не држи the ice won't hold 3 (*чува*) to keep, hold; држи под стража to keep under guard; држи под клуч to keep under lock and key; држи под своја власт to keep in one's power 4 (*има*) to keep, maintain, own; to run; држи дуќан to run a shop; држи овци to keep sheep; држи слугинка to have a maidservant; ја држи чиста куќата he keeps the house clean 5 to stock, hold, carry; не држиме вино we don't stock wine 6 to observe, uphold, keep to; држи обичај to observe a custom; држи пост to observe a fast; си го држи зборот to keep one's word 7 (*with до*) to set store by, value, prize; држи до нечие пријателство to value s.o.'s friendship; држи многу до себе to have a high opinion of o.s. 8 ❏ убаво време држи the weather is holding; држи предавање to give (deliver) a lecture; држи испит to conduct an examination; држи состанок to hold a meeting; држи сметка (*за*) to keep account (*of s.th.*), take (*s.th.*) into consideration; држи си го јазикот hold your tongue! shut up! држи во тек to keep (*s.o.*) informed; држи <некого> за јунак to consider s.o. a hero; ако му држи! if only he dares! му држи влага he still has a lot to fall back on (*often iron.*); it still has a hold on him; држи во неизвесност to keep in suspense/ignorance; држи <некого> за збор to take s.o. at his word; држи чекор со to keep up with; држи на око to keep an eye on II – се 1 (*за нешто, на нешто*) to hold on (*за – to*); to cling to, maintain, uphold; се држи за гранка to hold on to a branch; држи се! hang on tight! hang in there! се држи за свои обичаи to maintain (cling to) one's customs 2 to hold out, resist; to keep well; уште се држи добро he's still going strong 3 to maintain good relations; to support each other 4 to behave; to hold o.s.; се држи подалеку од некого to keep s.o. at arm's length; to give s.o. a wide berth; се држи понастрана to keep off (away); to steer clear
дрзне <се> *pf* дрзна *aor.* to dare
дрзнува *impf of* дрзне
дрзок -ска *adj* 1 bold, daring, courageous, brave 2 cheeky, impudent, insolent, brazen
дрибла *pf* & *impf Sport.* to dribble
дриблер *m Sport.* dribbler
дриблинг *m Sport.* dribbling
дрипа *f* 1 rags and tatters 2 ragamuffin
дрипав *adj* worn out, ragged, frayed, tattered
дрипло -овци *m see* парталко
дркол *m colloq.* wretched old man
дрла *f dial. see* гурелка
дрлив *adj dial. see* гурелав
дрма *f* small wood, coppice; thicket
дрмка *f* bush
дрмлив *adj* overgrown with bushes
дрмоли *impf* to shake, jolt; to pull; to push
дрмон *m* coarse sieve
дрмоноса *pf* to put through a coarse sieve
дрмоносува *impf of* дрмоноса
дрнат *adj colloq.* crazy, frivolous, *Brit. colloq.* daft
дрнда *impf* 1 to comb, fluff (*wool, cotton, etc.*); (*лен*) to hackle 2 *fig.* to make a noise, chatter, babble
дрндало *n* 1 distaff 2 *fig.* chatterbox, babbler
дрндар *m* babbler, chatterbox

дрне *pf* дрна *aor.* **1** *see* додрне **2** *colloq.* to cheat, swindle, deceive

дрнка *impf colloq.* **1** to strum **2** *fig.* to make a noise, chatter, babble

дрнкач *m colloq.* **1** poor musician, bad player **2** *fig.* babbler, chatterbox

дрнкачка *f colloq.* slut, tart

дрнува *impf of* дрне

дроб *m* offal, fry; intestines, bowels, entrails; internal organs; *Anat.* viscera; црниот дроб liver; белиот дроб lung, lights; *Cul.* (*also* дроб-сарма) lamb's caul stuffed with liver and rice, cf. haggis

дробен -бна *adj* fine, minute, small

дробенка *f* small piece of meat in food; *fig.* (*usu. pl*) nonsense

дроби *impf* **I 1** to break up *trans.*, break into small pieces; (*месо и сл.*) to chop up, dice; (*камен и др.*) to crush; (*леб*) to crumble; што си дробел, ќе сркаш *prov.* as you have sown, so you will reap **2** *fig.* to babble, talk nonsense; ❏ *colloq.* <ајде> не дроби! cut the crap! **II – се** to crumble *intrans.*

дробилка *f* grinder; crusher

дроблив *adj* crushable; crumbly, friable; (*кршлив*) fragile, breakable

дробливост *f* friability; fragility

дробнички *pl dial.* coins threaded and tied into the hair

дроб-сарма *f Cul.* haggis, *see* дроб

дрога *f* drug; опивни дроги narcotics

дрогерија -ии *f* chemist's shop, *Am.* drugstore

дрогерист *m* chemist, pharmacist, *Am.* druggist

дрозд & дроздален *m Zool.* thrush; (Turdus philomelos) song thrush; црн дрозд (Turdus merula) blackbird

дронец -нци *m* (*мразулец*) icicle

дропка[1] *f* **1** wild goose; ❏ ја удри дропката he's been lucky, he hit the jackpot **2** *fig.* fat woman

дропка[2] *f Math.* fraction

дропка[3] *f see* дробенка

дропла *f Zool.* (Otis tarda) great bustard

дрочи *impf* **1** to ripen *intrans.*; грозјето дрочи the grapes are ripening **2** *fig.* to idle; to loaf in bed

дрпа *impf* **I 1** *see* дрпне **1 2** to peck **II – се 1** to scratch o.s. **2** *see* дрпне **II**

дрпав *adj* ragged, tattered; shabby; frayed, torn, worn out

дрпне *pf* дрпна *aor.* **I 1** to jerk, pull; to nip, pinch; to tear; ме дрпна за рака he pulled (tugged) me by the arm, he tugged at my arm **2** *fig.* to take, get, extract; тој дрпна малку he got something out of it **II – се** to tear o.s. away (*од – from*)

дрпнува (се) *impf of* дрпне (се)

дрска *impf* to have diarrhoea, *sl.* to have the runs (trots)

дрскавица *f* diarrhoea, *sl.* the runs (trots)

дрско *adv* **1** boldly, bravely **2** impudently, insolently, shamelessly

дрскост *f* **1** fearlessness, boldness, bravery **2** impudence, insolence, shamelessness

дрсло -овци *m colloq.* coward

дрсне *pf* дрсна *aor.* to get diarrhoea; *colloq.* to be taken short

дрт *adj* old, aged; senile, decrepit, doddering; дрт старец decrepit old man; ❏ дрто магаре old fool

дртало *n colloq.* decrepit old man; *pejor.* old bastard, driveller

дртее *pf colloq.* to grow old; to become senile

дртина *f colloq.* decrepit old woman; *pejor.* old hag

дртла *f colloq.* **1** *see* дртина **2** slattern, slovenly woman

друг *adj* **1** other, another; некој друг someone else; друг ден another day; по друг пат in another way; by another road; на другиот крај at the far end; ❏ од друга страна on the other hand; на друг да му кажеш tell that to someone else! do me a favour! едно-друго various things; едно на друго taking things together; approximately; all things considered; едно по друго one after another; едно за друго continually; еден преку друг in disorder **2** (*инаков*) different; стана друг човек he became a different person; тоа е друга работа that's another matter; со друг збор in other words; настанаа други времиња times have changed **3** (*as noun*) *n & pl* remaining part, the rest; меѓу другото among other things; by the way; нека влезат другите let the others come in! другото е наша работа we'll do the rest; сè друго everything else **4** *dial. f.p.* (*втор*) second; друго венчање second marriage

другаде *adv* elsewhere

другар *m* friend; comrade

другарка *f* (*fem. form*) *see* другар

другарски *adj* friendly; comradely

другарство *n* friendship; comradeship

другарува *impf* to be friends/comrades; to mix (*co – with*)

другачка *f see* другарка

другаш *adv see* другпат

другиден *adv* the day after tomorrow

другипати *adv see* другпат

друговерец -рци *m* person of another faith, heterodox

другореден -дна *adj* second-rate, second-class, inferior; secondary

другоселец -лци *m* person from another village, outsider

другпат *adv* another time, on another occasion

дружба *f* friendship, comradeship; company; лоша дружба bad company

друже *m f.p.* (*only voc.*) comrade! friend!

дружељубив *adj* sociable, friendly

дружељубивост *f* sociability, friendliness

дружен -жна *adj* common, united, joint; со дружни напори by joint efforts

дружи <се> *impf* to be friends (*co – with*); to be friends

дружина *f* (*воена единица, ајдучка чета*) detachment; (*другари, соборци*) band; group; (*трупа глумци*) troupe, company; (*друштво*) club, association

дружно *adv* unanimously; jointly; in harmony; all together

друкер *m* **1** press-stud, snap-fastener **2** *Sport.* fan, supporter **3** metalworker

друм *m* road; main road, highway; ❏ што на ум, тоа на друм to speak one's mind

друмар *m* roadman, roadworker

друмарина *f* <road> toll

друмник -ци *m f.p.* traveller, passenger

друмски *adj* road, highway *attrib.*; друмски превоз road haulage; друмски превозник road carrier (haulier); друмски промет road traffic; друмски транспорт road transport<ation>

друса (се) *impf see* друсне (се)

друсаница *f* shaking

друска (се) *impf see* друса (се)

друсне *pf* друсна *aor.* **I** to shake, jolt *trans.* **II – се** to shake, judder *intrans.*

друснува (се) *impf of* друсне (се)

друшка *f* **1** friend; comrade; *see* другарка **2** couple; тие се двајцата арна друшка they make a good couple

друштво *n* **1** society; (*заедница*) community; company; добро друштво good company (friends); има лошо друштво to keep bad company; прави друштво некому to keep s.o. company; ❑ шарено друштво mixed company **2** *Comm.* company; corporation; акционерско друшто joint-stock company, *Am.* stock company; осигурително друштво insurance company **3** society, association, club; Друштвото на писателите на Македонија Macedonian Writers' Society; добротворно друшто charitable organization; Друшто на народите League of Nations

дрча *f* bad weather, storm; slush

дрчав *adj* дрчаво време *see* дрча

дрчен -чна *adj* **1** greedy, covetous; insatiable **2** дрчно време *see* дрча

дрчност *f* insatiability; greed, cupidity

дршка *f* handle, *see* држалка

дуалѝзам -змот *m* dualism

дуалѝст *m* dualist

дубак -ци *m* baby-walker

дубара *f* **1** twice two (*in backgammon*) **2** *colloq.* fraud, deceit; ми направија дубара they cheated me

дубла *f* Turkish gold coin worth two gold sovereigns (*used as a decoration and worn in a necklace*)

дублѐ *n* gold plate

дублер *m* (*во театар*) understudy; (*во кино*) double, stand-in; (*во опасни сцени*) stunt man

дублѐт *m* doublet

дублѝра *pf & impf* **1** to double; to duplicate **2** (*во театар*) to understudy; (*во кино*) to stand in (*for s.o.*) **3** (*филм*) to dub

Дубровник *m* Dubrovnik

дубровнички *adj* Dubrovnik *attrib.*

дубровчанец -ни *m* person from Dubrovnik

дубровчанка *f* (*fem. form*) *see* дубровчанец

дува *impf* to blow; дува ветер the wind is blowing, it is windy; многу дува низ вратата there is a draught from the door; нè дуваше студен ветар a cold wind was blowing in our faces; ❑ дува низ нос to snort

дувак -ци & **дувек** -ци *m arch.* bride's veil

дувало *n* **1** bellows **2** *Anat.* bladder **3** (*на гајда*) mouthpiece

дувар *m arch. see* ѕид

дувач *m* wind <instrument> player; trumpeter

дувачки *adj* wind; дувачки инструмент wind instrument

дувло *n* den, lair; burrow

дувне *pf* дувна *aor.* **1** to blow, give a puff; дувна ветре a breeze came up; дувна во огништето he blew on the fire **2** to blow *trans.*; to blow away, blow

off/down *trans.*; лисјата од дрвјата ветрот ги дувна the wind blew the leaves from the trees **3** *colloq.* to run away, run off, *sl.* beat it; ја дувна he did a bunk **4** *colloq.* to burst out crying, burst into tears

дувнува *impf of* дувне

дуд *m dial. Bot.* (Morus) mulberry tree

дудинка *f dial. Bot.* mulberry (*tree and fruit*)

дудук -ци *m* **1** wooden pipe (*traditional musical instrument*) **2** *fig.* idiot, fool

дудулка *f* stalk (*of cabbage, tobacco plant, etc.*); (*кочан од пченка*) corncob

дуе *impf* **I** to blow; (*топка*) to blow up, inflate *trans.*; дуе бабулиња to blow bubbles **II – се 1** to inflate *intrans.*; (*се надувува*) to swell <up>, become swollen **2** *fig.* (*се топори*) to put on airs **3** *fig* (*се лути*) to be/get angry; to pout, sulk

дуел *m* duel

дуелѝра се *pf & impf* to duel, fight a duel

дуеница *f dial. Mus.* wooden pipe with two holes

дуѐт *m* duet

дузена & дузина *f* dozen

дукат *m* ducat

дуле *n* **1** earthenware drinking jug **2** (*шопур*) spout

дулец -лци *m* **1** cork **2** (*шопур*) spout

дуљбија -ии *f arch.* field glasses, binoculars; spyglass

дум *interj* bang! thud!

дума[1] *f dial.* **1** thought **2** word

дума[2] *impf dial.* **I 1** to think **2** to remember **3** to speak **II – се** to hesitate

думан *m* **1** (*магла*) mist, fog; haze **2** (*дим*) smoke; (*прав*) dust (*in the air*)

думани[1] *pl arch.* (*in traditional costume*) homespun trousers (*with wide legs coming down to the ankle*)

думани[2] *impf* **I** to raise dust **II – се** to emit smoke

думежлив *adj dial.* talkative, loquacious

думка *impf* **1** to strike with a blunt object; to drum **2** to boom; тапан думка the drum resounds **3** *dial.* to rock, swing (*a small child*)

Дунав *m* the Danube

дунавски *adj* Danubian

дунда *impf dial.* to mutter, mumble crossly (ill-humouredly)

дундест *adj* fat, obese

дундури се *impf dial.* **1** to overdress *intrans.* **2** to get angry (*co – with*); to pout, sulk

дуња[1] *f Bot.* (Cydonia oblonga) quince

дуња[2] *f arch.* world

Дуовден *m Rel.* Pentecost, Whitsun

дупач *m colloq.* agitator, plotter, intriguer; mocker

дупачка *f colloq.* **1** woman agitator, plotter, intriguer **2** mockery, derision

дупачлак -ци *m colloq. see* дупачка 2

дупи *impf* **I 1.** to drill, bore through; to make a hole in; to pierce; дупи ѕид to bore a hole in a wall **2** to push, shove, poke, jab **3** (*also fig.*) to sting, prick; to goad; to spur; дупи коњ to spur on a horse **4** (*шие, везе*) to sew; to embroider **5** *colloq., in the expression:* дупи! go ahead! **II – се 1** to jab/nudge one another **2** *colloq.* to make fun (*co – of*); сите се дупат со него they all make fun of him

дупка *f* **1** hole; (*во закон*) loophole; дупка на чорап hole in a stocking; дупка во земја hole in the ground **2** lair, den; волча (волчка) дупка wolf's lair;

лисичка дупка fox's earth **3** cavity; очна дупка eye socket; усна дупка oral cavity **4** *fig.* grave; од лулка до дупка from the cradle to the grave

дуплекс *m* **1** two-storeyed flat, *Am.* duplex **2** *Radio/ TV* live two-way hook-up **3** *Telephone* party line

дупли *adj indecl.* double; дупли кревет double bed

дупликáт *m* duplicate

дуплѝра *pf & impf* to double; to duplicate

дупне *pf* дупна *aor.* **I** *see* дупи I; ❑ го дупна ѓаволот the devil made him do it **II – се** to develop holes, become perforated; to spring a leak; бурето се дупна the barrel has sprung a leak

дупнува (се) *impf of* дупне (се)

дупчалка *f* drill; drilling <boring> machine/mill; (рачна) hand drill (brace); (за камен) jumper, iron drill; (пневматична) pneumatic drill; jackhammer

дупче *n dim. of* дупка; dent; (на брада, образи) dimple

дупчест *adj* porous; perforated; дупчеста лажица straining spoon

дупчи *impf see* дупи I 1; to perforate; to punch holes in

дупчуле *n dim. see* дупче

дурбин *m* field glasses, binoculars; spyglass; telescopic sight

дур *m Mus.* (тонски род) major

дури **I** *part* **1** even; дури и досега even now; дури и тој even he; дури и да even if; granted that; дури и да е така be that as it may; дури ни not even **2** only (*of time*), just; дури вчера only yesterday; дури сега знам I know only now; дури и сега only now **II** *conj* while; until; дури се разбравме, помина денот the whole day passed before we reached agreement; дури чекавме, заврна while we were waiting it started raining; дури да until; ќе го чекаме, дури да дојде we'll wait until he comes

дурија -ии *f* shovel, spade

дурми се *impf* to frown, scowl; се дурми времето the weather is deteriorating, it is becoming overcast

дурски *adj Mus.* major; дурска скала major

дус *adj indecl. arch.* equal

дустабан *m* flat-footed person

дуќан *m* shop, *Am.* store

дуќански *adj* shop *attrib.*

дуќанче *n dim.* corner shop

дуќанџија -ии *m* shopkeeper, *Am.* storekeeper

дух *m* **1** spirit; дух на пријателство spirit of friendship; без дух without enthusiasm; спортски дух sportsmanship; во духот на времето in the spirit of the times; ❑ духовите се смируваат the dust settles; присуство на дух presence of mind; во здраво тело здрав дух *saying* a healthy mind in a sound body, mens sana in corpore sano **2** (бестелесно суштество) spirit, ghost; духот на покојникот the spirit of the departed; зол дух evil spirit; *Rel.* Свети Дух the Holy Ghost (Spirit)

духовен -вна *adj* spiritual; mental; religious

духовенство *n* clergy

духовит *adj* witty, clever

духовитост *f* wit, humour

духовник -ци *m* clergyman, priest; monk

духовнички *adj* priestly, sacerdotal; monastic

духовништво *n* clergy, the priesthood

душа *f* **1** soul, heart; mind; ❑ добра душа kind soul;

душа човек sweet person, sweetie; an angel; kindness itself; кутра душа! пуста душа! poor fellow! poor chap! мачна душа tormented (suffering) person; ситна душа petty mind; сродна душа a kindred soul (spirit); продадена душа a turncoat; a renegade; a snake in the grass; бере душа; душта во носот си ја носи to be at death's door; to have one foot in the grave; пушта душа to breathe one's last; можеби со душа ќе го затечеме perhaps we'll find him still alive; дури ми колка душа until my last breath; вади душа некому to pick on s.o.; не губи си ја душата don't lose heart! душа дава за нешто to be ideal for; душа дава за некого to go through fire and water for s.o.; ако ти носи душа, сториго т оа if you feel like it, do it! душата ми изгоре I was heartbroken; душата ме боли it breaks my heart; душо моја! my darling! жими душа upon my soul; без душа heartless; од душа ти давам I give <it> you with all my heart; земе (има) некого на душа to have s.o. on one's conscience; to drive a nail into s.o.'s coffin; земе нешто на своја душа to take (accept) the blame; to take it upon o.s.; става нешто некому на душа to lay the blame on s.o.; to hold s.o. responsible for s.th.; ми олесна на душата my heart was eased; I felt relieved; си ја олеснува душата to get s.th. off one's chest; отвора душа to bare one's soul; со душа те чекам I can hardly wait to see you; дотрча со половина душа he ran up breathless (*in panic, in terror*); со мирна душа without remorse/ qualms; во душа at heart; познава некого во душа to know s.o. inside out; за своја душа as a treat; колку што ти сака душа as much as you want; му дојде душата на место to unburden one's mind; на мртвите за душа, на живите в гуша let the dead bury their dead; life goes on; рани душа, да те слуша *prov.* eat well, and then you'll feel well; look after number one! од умрен душа не се бара *prov.* no use flogging a dead horse **2** *fig.* (вдахновител) inspiration, spirit; душа е на to be the moving spirit of; тој е душа на движењето he is the heart and soul of the movement **3** (*with numbers and numeral adverbs*) сто души a hundred people; колку души бевте? how many of you were there? <ни> жива душа нема there's not a soul there **4** (здив) breath; поземa душа he's calming down; he's recovering his composure; душата му мириса на спурено he's got bad breath; his breath smells stale

душалник -ци *m see* душник

душевен -вна *adj* **1** kind, kind-hearted **2** spiritual; mental

душевно *adv* **1** kindly **2** mentally

душевност *f* kindness

душек -ци *m* mattress

душеме *n colloq.* floor

душен -шна *adj* stuffy, suffocating

души[1] *impf* **I** to throttle, choke *trans.*, strangle, smother; срамот ја душеше she was dying of shame **II – се** to choke *intrans.*

души[2] *impf* to sniff, smell; песот ја душеше коската the dog was sniffing <at> the bone

душица & душичка *f dim. of* душа **1** mean-spirited person; ❑ ситна душичка petty little soul **2** poor thing, poor soul

душка   *impf dim. of* души²

душкало   *n* busybody, *colloq.* snooper

душко   *m hyp. (only voc.) of* душа dear! darling!

душман<ин>   -ани *m* enemy, foe; mortal enemy;
(*убиец*) murderer

душмански   *adj* enemy, hostile; (*суров*) cruel, murderous; (*за болка*) intense, strong

душник   -ци *m Anat.* windpipe, trachea

душовадец   -дци *m see* душовадник 1

душовадник   -ци *m* 1 bloodsucker, extortioner; (*убиец*)
murderer 2 *f.p.* Archangel Michael

душогубец   -пци *m see* душогубник

душогубник   -ци *m* usurer, *colloq.* money-grubber

душојадец -   дци *m see* душовадник 1

ѓавол   *m* 1 the Devil, Satan; ❏ црн како ѓавол <as>
black as sin; му влегол ѓаволот the devil has got
into him; he kicked over the traces; ѓавол ќе го знае
the devil only knows; ѓавол да го земе the devil take
him! to hell with it! тука е ѓаволот that's the devil of
it; тоа ти е еден ѓавол 1. he's the very devil <of a
fellow> 2. it comes to the same thing; ѓаволот го
надупил; го дупнал ѓаволот the Devil put him up to
it; кој ѓавол ве тераше да одите таму? what the
devil made you go there? ѓаволот таму го бараше?
who/what the devil (dickens) were you looking for
there? бега како ѓавол од темјан to avoid s.o./s.th.
like the plague; на ѓаволот му ја знае дупката
there's nothing he does not know <how to do>; he's
devilishly clever; оди по ѓаволите! go to hell! пукна
ѓаволот the ice is broken; како на ѓавол му играат
очите he's as crafty as the devil; бега од ѓаволот,
наиде на сатаната out of the frying-pan into the fire;
на ѓаволот му ја продал душата he has sold his
soul to the devil; расте како ѓаволот да го трга за
уши to grow like a weed; го положи ли испитот? –
ѓавола! did you pass the exam? – like hell I did!
ѓаволот си нема работа; ѓаволот ни ора, ни копа
prov. the devil finds work for idle hands 2 *fig.* rogue;
colloq. sly dog; ѓавол жена minx, the devil of a
woman; жив ѓавол a real devil; сиромав човек –
жив ѓавол *prov.* the devil dances in an empty pocket

ѓаволест   *adj* roguish; (*итар*) crafty, cunning, sly; (*за
дете*) mischievous, naughty; impish; ѓаволести очи
eyes full of mischief

ѓаволесто   *adv* seductively, flirtatiously, coquettishly;
го погледна ѓаволесто she gave him a coquettish
look

ѓаволец   *m (only sg) dim.* imp

ѓаволи   *impf* to be mischievous, play pranks

ѓаволија   -ии *f see* ѓаволштина

ѓаволит   *adj see* ѓаволест

ѓаволитост   *f* devilishness; impishness; mischievousness

ѓаволов   *adj* devil's

ѓаволски   *adj* 1 devilish 2 devil's 3 *fig.* (*ужасен*) horrible, terrible, appalling; (*проклет*) accursed;
ѓаволски пари accursed money; ѓаволска работа
appalling business; the hell of a business 4 *see*
ѓаволест

ѓаволува   *impf* to be mischievous, play pranks

ѓаволче   *n dim.* little devil, imp

ѓаволштилак   -ци *m colloq. see* ѓаволштина 1

ѓаволштина   *f* 1 devilry; mischief, prank 2 (*лукавост*)
cunning, guile, craftiness

ѓак -ци *m* **1** novice (*at a monastery*) **2** chorister, choirboy

ѓакон *m* deacon

ѓаконски *adj* deacon's

ѓаконство *n* deaconry; deaconship, deaconate

ѓаконува *impf* to serve as <a> deacon

ѓаур<ин> -ри *m arch. pejor.* infidel, *see* каурин

ѓаурка *f arch. pejor.* (*fem. form*) *see* ѓаур

ѓаче *n* altar boy (*assisting priest at services on special Holy Days*)

ѓевгир *m arch.* **1** stone masonry **2** arch, dome **3** colander, large strainer

ѓеврек -ци *m* sesame ring, *Am.* bagel

ѓеврекчија -ии *m arch.* seller of sesame rings

ѓезве *n* Turkish coffee-pot

ѓем *m* snaffle<-bit>

ѓеран *m* **1** (*на бунар*) sweep; shadoof **2** (*на пат*) toll-gate **3** (*на дигалка*) jib **4** (*на вага*) column

ѓердан *m* necklace

ѓерданест *adj* necklace-like

ѓерѓеф *m* tambour, embroidery frame

ѓериз *m arch.* drain, gutter

ѓоа & ѓоамити *adv colloq.* ostensibly, supposedly, *see* божем; ❑ ѓоа правила тера it only looks as though he is telling the truth

ѓозбоџаџија -ии *m arch.* **1** magician **2** cheat, swindler

ѓозбоџаџилак -ци *m arch.* **1** sorcery, magic; magic spell **2** cheating, faking

ѓок *m see* ѓокат

ѓокат *m* white horse; grey

ѓол *m arch.* bog, marsh; (*езеро*) lake

ѓомлезец *m Cul.* porridge (*oriental dish made of cornmeal and wheatmeal*)

ѓон *m* sole; ❑ лице (образ) како ѓон thick-skinned; insolent, shameless

ѓубралник -ци *m see* ѓубрарник

ѓубрар *m* garbage collector, *Brit.* dustman

ѓубрарник -ци *m* dustpan

ѓубре *n* **1** rubbish, garbage, waste, refuse; trash **2** *fig.* scum, swine; ѓубре едно! filthy pig! you scum! **3** (*гној*) manure, dung; шталско ѓубре stable dung (manure); вештачко ѓубре fertilizer; градско ѓубре urban (town) refuse; природно ѓубре manure; compost

ѓубрелив *adj* fertilized; ѓубрелива нива fertilized field

ѓубри *impf* **1** to make rubbish (garbage) **2** (*гнои*) to manure, fertilize

ѓубриво *n* fertilizer, *see* ѓубре 3

ѓубриште *n* **1** rubbish (garbage) heap; dung heap, dunghill **2** *fig.* pigsty; тоа е цело ѓубриште it's a pigsty! **3** *augm. of* ѓубре

ѓувез *adj indecl. arch.* dark red

ѓувезен -зна *adj arch. see* ѓувез

ѓувеч *m* **1** *Cul.* <lamb-and-vegetable> stew **2** (*мангал*) brazier

ѓузел *adj indecl. f.p.* fair, beautiful

ѓул *m arch. Bot.* rose

ѓуле *n* **1** cannon-ball; any heavy object **2** *Sport.* shot; фрлање ѓуле putting the shot, shot put

ѓулест *adj* ball-shaped, round

ѓулов *adj arch.* rose *attrib.*, *see* ружин; ѓулово масло attar of roses

ѓум *m* copper jug (*for water*)

ѓумрук -ци *m arch.* customs

ѓумче *n dim. of* ѓум

ѓунделак -ци *m arch.* (*daily or hourly*) wages

Ѓупка *f pejor.* (*fem. form*) *see* Ѓуптин

ѓупски *adj* gypsy; *see* цигански¹

Ѓуптин *m pejor.* Gypsy

ѓупчи се *impf colloq. see* циганчи се

ѓупчува *impf colloq. see* циганчи се

ѓупштилак -ци *m colloq. see* циганштилак

ѓурѓина *f Bot.* (Dahlia variabilis) dahlia

Ѓурѓовден *m* St. George's Day (6 May)

ѓурултаџија -ии *m colloq.* rowdy; *colloq.* loud-mouth; hoodlum, troublemaker

ѓурултија -ии *f colloq.* **1** (*бучава*) din, racket, rumpus, uproar **2** (*кавга*) row, set-to, battle royal; чекај си од него кавги и ѓурултии you can expect a lot of trouble with him; со двајца кавга се прави, со тројца – ѓурултија *prov.* two make a quarrel, three – a row, cf. it takes two to make a quarrel

ѓутуре *adv colloq.* roughly; all together; in bulk, *en bloc,* without weighing/counting/ separating, as is; ја купил лубеницата ѓутуре he bought the water melon without its being weighed

ѓутурица *adv colloq. see* ѓутуре

е¹ *part* **1** (*pointing to s.o. or s.th.*) over there; е онаму look over there! **2** (*interrogative*) well <then>? and then? so? е, како ти се чини? well, what do you think? **3** (*in a reply*) well; е добро де! well, all right! **4** (*emphatic*) well <now>; come on; why! really! е арно си сторил! yes, you did quite right! е нема да биде како што сакаш! no, you can't have it your own way!

е² *3rd p. sg pres. of* сум; кај е? where is it/he/she? не е is not, isn't

ебач *m vulg.* fucker

ебачка *f vulg.* fucking

ебе *impf vulg.* **I** to fuck *trans.* **II – се** to fuck *intrans.*; ❑ еби се fuck off!

ебонит *m* vulcanite, ebonite

ебонитен -тна *adj* vulcanite, ebonite *attrib.*

евакуација *f* evacuation

евакуционен -она *adj* evacuation *attrib.*, evacuative; евакуциона станица evacuation centre, casualty-clearing station

евакуира *pf & impf* to evacuate

евангелие -ија *n* gospel

евангелизам -змот *m* evangelism

евангелист *m* evangelist

евангелистички *adj* evangelical, evangelistic

евангелски *adj* evangelical

еве *part* here is/are; look! еве го here he/it is; еве сум јас што барам калфа I am the person who is looking for an assistant; еве, се собравме well, here we are

евентуален -лна *adj* possible, conceivable

евентуалии *pl* (*на дневен ред*) contingencies, unexpected developments; miscellaneous

евентуално *adv* if need be, should the need arise; possibly

евентуалност *f* eventuality; contingency; за секоја евентуалност just in case, to be on the safe side

евидентен -тна *adj* evident, obvious

евидентира *pf & impf* to record; to file; to list, inventory

евидентичар *m* recorder, registrar

евидентност *f* obviousness

евиденција *f* **1** (*податоци, запишување податоци*) files, record<s>, register, list; registration **2** (*востановена состојба, факти*) evidence, facts

евла *f Bot.* (Alnus) alder

евлов *adj* alder

евнух -си *m* (*скопец*) eunuch

евокативен -вна *adj* evocative

евокација *f* evocation; евокација на спомени evocation of memories

еволуира *pf & impf* to evolve

еволуција *f* evolution

еволуционен -она *adj* evolutionary; еволуциона теорија theory of evolution

евоцира *pf & impf* to evoke

Европа *f* Europe

Европеец -ејци *m* European

Европејка *f* (*fem. form*) *see* Европеец

европски *adj* European

евтин *adj* cheap; евтина работна сила cheap labour; евтина шега cheap joke; евтини ефекти cheap effects, gimmicks

евтинија *f* cheapness; low prices; bargain

евтино *adv* cheaply, *colloq.* on the cheap; ❑ евтино помина he got off lightly

евтинџија -ии *m* cheap merchant, cheapjack

егализација *f* equalization

еге *n* file, rasp

Егеец -ејци *m* Aegean <Macedonian>

Егеj *m* the Aegean <Sea>

Егеjка *f* (*fem. form*) *see* Егеец

егеjски *adj* Aegean; Егеjска Македонија Aegean Macedonia; Егеjско Море Aegean <Sea>

егзактен -тна *adj* exact; егзактни науки the exact sciences

егзактност *f* exactness, precision

егзалтација -ии *f* exaltation, raptures

егзалтира *pf & impf* **I** to excite; to thrill; to stir up, arouse **II – се** to be/get excited/ aroused; to work o.s. up, go into raptures

егзалтиран *pt* in a state of exaltation; ecstatic; exalted

егзарх -си *m Rel.* exarch

егзархат *m Rel.* exarchate

егзархија -ии *f Rel.* exarchate

егзархиски *adj Rel.* exarch *attrib.*

егзархист *m Hist.* Exarchist

егзекутива *f* (*извршна власт*) executive <power>

егзекутивен -вна *adj* executive

егзекутира *pf & impf* **1** to execute, put to death **2** (*изврши, извршува*) to carry out, execute

егзекутор *m* **1** executioner, hangman **2** executor

егзекуција -ии *f* execution

егзекуционен -она *adj* executionary

егзема *f Med.* eczema

егземплар *m* copy; (*образец*) example; specimen

егзерцир *m Mil.* drill

егзерцира *pf & impf Mil.* to drill

егзибиција *f* exhibition; ❑ прави егзибиции to make an exhibition of o.s.

егзибиционен -она *adj* exhibition *attrib.*; *Sport.* егзибиционен меч exhibition match

егзибиционизам -змот *m* exhibitionism

егзистенција *f* existence, survival

егзистенцијален -лна *adj* existential

егзистенцијализам -змот *m* existentialism

егзистенцијалист *m* existentialist

егзистенцијалистички *adj* existentialist

егзистенцијалистка *f* (*fem. form*) *see* егзистенцијалист

егзистира *impf* (*постои*) to exist; (*живее*) to live

егзоген *adj* exogenous; exogenetic; *Geol.* егзогени процеси exogenetic processes

егзотика *f* exoticism; exotica, exotic objects

егзотичен -чна *adj* exotic

егиди   *interj see* дегиди, дејгиди

Египет   *m* Egypt

египетски   *adj* Egyptian

Египќанец   -ни *m* Egyptian

Египќанка   *f (fem. form) see* Египќанец

егоизам   -змот *m* egoism, selfishness

егоист   *m* egoist, selfish person

егоистичен   -чна *adj* egoistic, selfish

егоистички   *adv* selfishly, egoistically

егоистка   *f (fem. form) see* егоист

егоцентризам   -змот *m* egocentrism

егоцентрик   -ци *m* egocentric, self-centred person

егоцентричен   -чна *adj* egocentric, self-centred

егоцентричност   *f* egocentricity

егумен   *m* prior, abbot; *see* игумен

егуменија -ии & **егуменка** *f* abbess, prioress

едвај   *adv see* одвај

еделвајс   *m Bot.* (Leontopodium alpinum) edelweiss, lion's foot

еден   -дна *num, pron* **1** one; еден ден one day; some day; once; во еден часот at one o'clock; ❑ еден пат once; еден по еден one by one, one at a time; in single file; еден до друг side by side; huddled up; еден по друг one after another; едно-друго all sorts of things; one thing and another; еден единствен one and only; one of a kind; unique; еден со друг each other; one another; сите до еден to a man; еден за сите, сите за еден one for all and all for one; *(emphatic)* едни зрна како ореви grapes as big as walnuts; на едно рипање in one bound; не е еден единствен not the only pebble on the beach **2** a, an, a certain; some; си беше еден човек there was once a man; сретнав еден пријател I met a friend of mine; те бараше една жена some woman was looking for you **3** the same; од една врст of the same age; од едно село from the same village; ❑ еден и ист one and the same; тоа е сè едно that's all the same; сè едно и исто the same thing over and over again **4** *(as noun)* n one thing; тој едно мисли, а друго зборува he thinks one thing and says another **5** магаре едно! you ass! сверу еден! you beast (brute)!

едикт   *m* edict

Единбург   *m* Edinburgh

единбуржанец   -ни *m* person from Edinburgh

единбуржанка   *f (fem. form) see* единбуржанец

единбуршки   *adj* Edinburgh

единаесет   *num* eleven

единаесетгодишен   -шна *adj* **1** eleven-year-old **2** of/for eleven years, eleven-year

единаесетка   *f* **1** <the figure> eleven **2** number 11 <bus, tram, *etc.*>

единаесетмина   *num (of men or mixed group)* <a group of> eleven

единаесетти   *adj num* eleventh

единак   -ци *m* **1** only son **2** lone wolf *(also fig.)*; solitary/lonely person, loner **3** *(за чешлање лен)* comb, carding-comb, card

единачка   *f* <two-wheeled> country gig

единец   -нци *m* only son

единица   *f* **1** unit; *Math.* unity, one; единица на време unit of time; единица на мерење unit of measurement; единица на трошоци cost unit; изборна единица constituency, electoral district; парична единица monetary unit; воена единица military unit

2 *(школска оценка)* one *(out of five, hence = 'unsatisfactory')*, fail **3** *(единствена ќерка)* only daughter **4** number one <bus, tram, *etc.*>

единичен   -чна *adj* single; individual; isolated; one-man; единично книжење single entry

единичност   *f* singularity

единка   *f* **1** individual **2** only daughter

единствен   *adj* **1** only, one, unique; единствената причина the only reason **2** united; *(изедначен)* uniform; единствени цени uniform prices; единствен пазар unified (integral) market; единствен став common stand/view; единствена стапка flat rate

единствено   *adv* **1** solely, only **2** uniformly

единственост   *f* **1** uniqueness **2** united nature (character)

единство   *n* unity; *(изедначеност)* uniformity; *(едногласност)* unanimity, accord, harmony

единче   *n* only child

едиција   -ии *f* edition

еднаквост   *f* sameness, identity; equality <of rights>

еднаков   -ква *adj* the same, identical; equal

едначење   *n Ling.* assimilation

еднаш<ка>   *adv* once; еднаш има кај мене дојдено he came to my place once; си бил еднаш еден поп once upon a time there was a priest; дај еднаш да ја свршиме оваа работа let's finish this job at last!; еднаш годишно once a year, yearly; ❑ еднаш за секогаш once and for all; еднаш ама вреднаш once and for all; не <е> еднаш many a time

еднина   *f Gram.* singular

еднински   *adj Gram.* singular; еднински форми singular forms

еднипати   *adv* sometimes, occasionally, once in a while

едничок   -чка *adj* <one and> only; едничко чедо only child

едно   **1** *num see* еден **2** *pron* the same; сите луѓе не се едно not all people are alike **3** *adv* roughly, approximately; едно десет кила about ten kilos **4** *conj* as soon as; no sooner than; едно влезе во собата as soon as he entered the room; едно влегување во куќата on entering the house

еднобоен   -јна *adj* monochrome, of one colour; еднобојна светлина monochromatic light; еднобојна слика monochrome picture

еднобожец   -шци *m* monotheist

еднобоштво   *n* monotheism

едновалентен   -тна *adj Chem.* univalent, monovalent

едноверен   -рна *adj* of the same religion

едноверец   -рци *m* co-religionist

едноверка   *f (fem. form) see* едноверец

едноводруго   *adv* one into another, one into the other

едновремен   *adj* simultaneous; contemporaneous

едновременост   *f* simultaneity; contemporaneity

едноврсен   -сна *adj* of the same age; четири едноврсни момчиња four youths of the same age

едногласен   -сна *adj* **1** *Mus.* one-part *attrib.*; едногласно пеење one-part (unison) singing **2** *(еднодушен)* unanimous

едногласно   *adv* **1** *Mus.* in unison; пеат едногласно they sing in unison **2** unanimously; предлогот беше примен едногласно the proposal (motion) was accepted unanimously

едногласност   *f* **1** *Mus.* unison, monophony **2** *(еднодушност)* unanimity

едногодишен -шна *adj* one-year, lasting one year; year-old

едногрб *adj* one-humped; **едногрба камила** one-humped camel, dromedary

едноделен -лна *adj* one-piece; **едноделен костим за капење** one-piece swimming-costume

еднодимензионален -лна *adj* one-dimensional

еднодневен -вна *adj* one-day; ephemeral; **еднодневен излет** day trip

еднододруго *adv* one next to the other; **земено сѐ еднододруго** everything taken together

еднодомен -мна *adj* 1 *Pol.* unicameral; **еднодомен парламент** unicameral (one-chamber) parliament 2 *Bot., Zool.* monoecious

еднодруго *adv* one thing and another

еднодушен -шна *adj* unanimous

еднодушност *f* unanimity

едноженец -нци *m* monogamist

едноженство *n* monogamy

еднозадруго *adv* one after the other, consecutively

еднозначен -чна *adj* synonymous

едноимен *adj* having the same name, eponymous

едноименик -ци & **едноимец** -мци *m* namesake

едноимка *f* (*fem. form*) *see* едноименик

еднојазичен -чна *adj* unilingual, monolingual

еднојајчан *adj* monozygotic; **еднојајчани близнаци** identical twins

еднокатен -тна *adj* single-storey; **еднокатен автобус** single-decker bus

еднокатница *f* single-storey house/building

едноклеточен -чна *adj Biol.* unicellular; *Bot.* single-cell; **едноклеточни животни** unicellular animals

еднокопитар *m Zool.* solidungulate

еднокопитен -тна *adj* solid-hoofed, solidungulate; **еднокопитно животно** solidungulate

еднокрак *adj* one-leg/-arm *attrib.*; **еднокрак лост** simple lever

еднократен -тна *adj* single, one-shot, one-time; **еднократни планови** single-use plans

еднокрвен -вна *adj* consanguineous, agnate; **еднокрвни браќа** half-brothers

еднокреветен -тна *adj* single; **еднокреветна соба** single room

еднокрилен -лна *adj* single-winged; **еднокрилен авион** monoplane

еднолик *adj* 1 with a similar face 2 identical 3 monotonous

едноличен -чна *adj* 1 same, uniform 2 (*здодевен*) monotonous, dull

едноличност *f* 1 uniformity 2 monotony, dullness

едномесечен -чна *adj* one-month, lasting one month; month-old

едноминутен -тна *adj* one-minute, lasting one minute; **едноминутно молчење** one minute's silence

едномисленик -ци *m* like-minded person, sympathizer; **тој е наш едномисленик** he shares our views

едномисленост *f* like-mindedness, sympathy, unanimity; identity/harmony/conformity of views

едномоторен -рна *adj* single-engined

еднонадруго *adv* 1 one on <top of> another; **ги нареди еднонадруго** he stacked them one on top of the other 2 on average; **купив пет овци, еднонадруго по три илјади динари** I bought five sheep at about three thousand dinars each

еднонеделен -лна *adj* one-week, lasting one week; week-old

едноног *adj* one-legged, monopode; one-footed; ❏ **едноногиот** the devil

еднообразен -зна *adj* 1 uniform, similar 2 (*здодевен*) monotonous, dull

еднообразно *adv* 1 uniformly 2 monotonously

еднообразност *f* 1 uniformity 2 monotony

еднаок *adj* one-eyed

еднопартиен -јна & **еднопартиски** *adj* one-party *attrib.*

едноподруго *adv* one after the other, consecutively

еднополов *adj* 1 *Elec.* unipolar; **еднополова индукција** unipolar induction 2 unisexual (*also Bot.*)

еднорак *adj* one-handed, single-handed; one-armed

еднореден -дна *adj* in one row; (*за сако и сл.*) single-breasted

еднорог¹ *adj* one-horned

еднорог² -зи *m Zool.* unicorn

еднороден -дна *adj* homogen<e>ous; (*изедначен*) uniform; (*сличен*) similar; *see* истороден

еднородност *f* homogeneity; uniformity; similarity; *see* историдност

едноселец -лци *m* fellow villager; person from the same village

едноселка *f* (*fem. form*) *see* едноселец

едносложен -жна *adj Gram.* monosyllabic

едносмерен -рна *adj* 1 one-way; **едносмерна улица** one-way street 2 *Elec.* direct; **едносмерна струја** direct current

еднособен -бна *adj* single-room; **еднособен стан** one-room flat

едноставен -вна *adj* 1 simple, easy, uncomplicated 2 (*скромен*) simple; plain, natural

едноставност *f* 1 ease 2 plainness, simplicity

едностоен -јна *adj* (*постојан*) constant, permanent

едностојно *adv* continually, ceaselessly

едностран *adj* 1 unilateral; **едностранa акција** unilateral action 2 *fig.* one-sided, biased, partial; **еднострано мислење** one-sided view

едностраност *f* 1 unilaterality 2 *fig.* one-sidedness

еднотомен -мна *adj* one-volume

едноќелиски *adj see* едноклеточен

едноумие *n pejor.* <communist> party line; rule of the <communist> party, one-party rule

еднофазен -зна *adj Elec.* single-phase, monophase

едноцифрен *adj* one-digit; **едноцифрен број** one-digit number

едночасовен -вна *adj* lasting one hour, one-hour; **едночасовен одмор** one hour's rest; **едночасовен штрајк** one-hour strike

едночинка *f* one-act play

едночлен *adj* having one member, one-man *attrib.*; *Math.* monomial

едночудо & **едно чудо** *adv* many, much, a lot, *colloq.* oodles; **донесе едночудо работи** he brought a lot of things

едреник -ци *m* sailing-boat, yacht

сдри *impf* to sail

едро *n* (*платно*) sail

ЕЕЗ *abbr.* (*Европска економска заедница*) European Economic Community, EEC

еж *m Zool.* hedgehog; **морски еж** (Paracentrotus

lividus) sea-urchin; ❑ го јавнува ежот to be in hot water; to be for the high jump; to be on the rocks

ежави се *impf see* ежи се

еже *n dim. of* еж

ежи се *impf* **1** to bristle; косата ми се ежеше my hair was on end; мачката се ежеше the cat's fur bristled (stood on end) **2** (*наежавува се*) to have goose-flesh (goose-pimples); снагата му се ежеше од такви помисли he got goose-flesh at the thought; ❑ ми се ежи кожата it gives me the creeps; it makes my flesh creep

ежов *adj* hedgehog's

езеро *n* lake

езерски *adj* lake *attrib.*

езерце *n dim. of* езеро; pond

ej *interj* hello, hullo; hey! ej, момче, слушај! hey, young man, listen!

eja *f Zool.* (Circus) harrier; полска eja (Circus cyaneus) hen harrier

ејгиди *interj see* егиди

ек *m* sound; blare, clang; (*на орудија*) throb, roar, thunder; (*на камбани*) peal; (*ехо*) echo; ❑ во ек under way; екна сезона high season

Еквадор *m* Ecuador

Еквадорец -рци *m* Ecuadoran, Ecuadorian

Еквадорка *f (fem. form) see* Еквадорец

еквадорски *adj* Ecuadoran, Ecuadorian

екватор *m Geog.* equator

екваторијален -лна & **екваторски** *adj Geog.* equatorial; екваторијална Африка equatorial Africa; Екваторска Гвинеја Equatorial Guinea

еквивалент *m* equivalent

еквивалентен -тна *adj* equivalent; еквивалентна вредност equivalent value

еквиваленција *f* equivalence

еквилибрист *m* tightrope walker, equilibrist, rope-walker

еквилибристика *f* tightrope walking, rope-walking

еквилибристички *adj* tightrope-walking, rope-walking *attrib.*

еквиноциум *m* (*рамнодневица*) equinox

ЕКГ *abbr.* (*електрокардиограм*) electrocardiogram, ECG

еким *m arch.* doctor

екипа *f* team; екипа за спасување rescue team

екипаж *m* **1** (*раскошна кочија со послуга*) carriage, coach **2** (*на брод, авион, тенк и сл.*) crew **3** *Mil.* (*воена комора*) supply unit; field train

екипен -пна *adj* team; екипно првенство team championship

екипира *pf & impf* **I** to equip, outfit **II** – **се** to equip o.s.

еклатантен -тна *adj* striking, evident, clear

еклектизам -змот & **еклектицизам** -змот *m* eclecticism

еклектичар *m* eclectic

еклектички *adj* eclectic

еклер *m Cul.* éclair

еклипса *f* eclipse

еклиптика *f Astron.* orbit; ecliptic

еклога *f Literature* eclogue

екне *pf* екна *aor.* **1** (*викне*) to scream **2** to ring out, resound, reverberate; (*за камбани*) to peal; (*за топови*) to roar, thunder

екнува *impf of* екне

еколог -зи *m* **1** ecologist **2** environmentalist

екологија *f* ecology

еколошки *adj* ecological; еколошко загадување pollution

економ *m* business manager, steward; housekeeper; (*бродски*) purser; (*болнички*) catering officer, store-keeper

економат *m* **1** (*службата на економот*) stewardship **2** (*канцеларија на економ*) steward's office **3** (*установа во претпријатие*) purchasing (supply) department **4** (*домаќинство*) good housekeeping

економија *f* **1** (*стопанство*) economy; пазарна економија market economy **2** (*наука*) economics; теоретска економија pure economics **3** (*земјоделско стопанство*) agricultural property, farm **4** (*водење имот, домаќинство*) management; housekeeping **5** (*штедење, штедливост*) economy, saving<s>; прави економија to economize, make savings

економика *f* economics, *see* економија 2; економика на туризмот economics of tourism; економика на домаќинството home economics

економист *m* **1** economist **2** economizer; thrifty (frugal) person

економисува *impf* to economize, save; економисува со време to save time

економичен -чна *adj* economical

економичност *f* economy, thriftiness

економски *adj* economic; економски врски economic relations (ties); економски односи economic relations; економски циклус business cycle; економски факултет Economics Faculty, School of Business

екот *m see* ек

екразит *m* (*силен експлозив*) ecrasite

екран *m* screen (*for films, television, computers, etc.*); ❑ на малиот екран on television

екранизира *pf & impf* to film; to adapt for the screen; екранизира роман to make a screen version of a novel

екс *adv sl. in the expression:* пие на екс to down (*a drink*) in one

екс- (*in compounds*) ex-, former; екс-крал former king; екс-министер former minister

екселенција *f* Excellency; Your/His Excellency

ексик *adj indecl. arch., colloq.* lacking, incomplete, deficient; ексик мера short weight; ексик да е, ексик да биде! blast him! blast it!

екскаватор *m Mech.* excavator, power shovel

ексквација *f* excavation

ексклузивен -вна *adj* exclusive, select

ексклузивност *f* exclusiveness

екскомуникација *f Rel.* excommunication

екскурзија -ии *f* **1** excursion; outing **2** *fig.* digression, excursus; ❑ екскурзија на мозокот a flight of fancy

експандер *m* chest-expander

експанзивен -вна *adj* expansive (*able/tending to expand*); expansionist; експанзивна политика expansionist policy

експанзија -ии *f* expansion; expansionism

експедира *pf & impf* to send off, dispatch; (*со пошта*) to post, mail; (*со брод*) to ship <off>

експедитивен -вна *adj* expeditious, efficient

експедити́вно *adv* expeditiously

експедити́вност *f* efficiency

експеди́тор *m* forwarding agent; dispatcher, forwarder; consignor

експедиција -ии *f* **1** forwarding, dispatching; (*по море*) shipping; експедиција на стоки forwarding (dispatching) goods **2** forwarding department; dispatch office, dispatches **3** (*патување*) expedition **4** (*лицата што учествуваат во такво патување*) expedition members, party, team

експедицио́нен -она *adj* expeditionary

експериме́нт *m* experiment, trial, test

експериме́нта́лен -лна *adj* experimental; trial, test *attrib.*; експериментална програма pilot project (programme)

експеримента́тор *m* experimenter

експериментѝра *impf* to experiment, test

експерт *m* expert

експерти́за *f* **1** examination **2** expert opinion, expertise

експирато́рен -рна *adj* expiratory

експирација *f* expiration

експликација *f* explication

експлици́тен -тна *adj* explicit

експлоата́тор *m* exploiter; developer

експлоатација *f* exploitation; development, using

експлоати́ра *impf* to exploit, use

експлоди́ра *pf & impf* to explode

експлози́в *m* explosive

експлози́вен -вна *adj* explosive

експлозија -ии *f* explosion

експозе́ *n* exposé, report, statement

експозиту́ра *f* branch (*of a bank, firm, etc.*)

експозиција *f* **1** exposition **2** *Photography* exposure time; должина на експозиција shutter speed

експона́т *m* exhibit; artefact

експоне́нт *m* exponent (*also Math.*)

експони́ра *pf & impf* to display, exhibit; to expose

експорт *m* export

експортен -тна *adj* export *attrib.*

експорте́р *m* exporter

експорти́ра *pf & impf* to export

експрес 1 *m* express train; special-delivery letter; експрес-ресторан cafeteria; self-service restaurant; fast-food restaurant **2** *adj, adv indecl.* express, fast, rapid; тоа сè оди експрес that all goes very quickly

експресен -сна *adj* express; експресен лонец pressure-cooker

експреси́вен -вна *adj* expressive

експреси́вност *f* expressiveness

експресија *f* expression

експресиони́зам -змот *m* expressionism

експресиони́ст *m* expressionist

експресионистички *adj* expressionist; expressionistic

експроприја́тор *m* expropriator

експропријација *f* expropriation

експропри́ра *pf & impf* to expropriate

екста́з *m & ***екста́за** *f* ecstasy, elation, fervour; inspiration; *Psychol., Med.* trance

екстензи́вен -вна *adj* extensive; екстензивно земјоделство extensive agriculture

екстензија *f* **1** (*протегање*) extension **2** *Med.* traction; му се прави екстензија на ногата his leg is in traction **3** (*продолжување на образование*) extension

екстерен -рна *adj* external, outside

екстерие́р *m* exterior

екстериторија́лен -лна *adj* exterritorial

екстериторија́лност *f* exterritoriality; право на екстериторијалност exterritorial right

екстра[1] *adj indecl.* extra-special, de luxe

екстра[2] *adv* excellently, splendidly

екстравага́нтен -тна *adj* extravagant; extraordinary; odd, queer

екстравага́нтност & екстраваганција *f* extravagance; oddity

екстрадиција *f* extradition

екстра́кт *m* extract

екстракција *f* extraction

екстрем *m* (*крајност*) extreme

екстремен -мна *adj* extreme, exaggerated

екстреми́зам -змот *m* extremism

екстреми́ст *m* extremist

екстремистички *adj* extremist *attrib.*

екстремите́ти *pl* extremities

екстремност *f* extremeness; extremity

ексцентричен -чна *adj* **1** *Geom.* eccentric; *Tech.* cam *attrib.*, off-centre; ексцентрични кругови eccentric circles **2** eccentric, strange, queer, odd

ексцентричност *f* eccentricity

ексцес *m* excess; outrage; (*прекршување*) violation, offence

ектенија -ии *f Rel.* litany; intercession

ела[1] *f Bot.* (Abies alba) silver fir

ела[2] *interj* елате *pl* (*only in the imperative*) come! ела ваму come here! ❑ ела, ако си маж! try it, if you've got the guts!

елабора́т *m* report; proposal

елабори́ра *pf & impf* to elaborate, draft

елан *m* élan, enthusiasm, zest, fervour

еластичен -чна *adj* elastic; stretchy; supple; flexible

еластичност *f* elasticity; flexibility

елева́тор *m* lift; hoist, elevator

елевација *f* elevation

елевацио́нен -она *adj* elevational; елевационен агол <angle of> elevation

елега́нтен -тна *adj* elegant, smart, stylish; fine; distinguished

елега́нтност & елеганција *f* elegance, smartness, stylishness; refinement, distinguished nature

елегија -ии *f* elegy

елегичен -чна *adj* elegiac; *fig.* sad, melancholy

елек -ци *m* waistcoat, *Am.* vest

електризација *f* electrification; electrifying, charging with electricity (*also fig.*)

електризи́ра *impf* to electrify, charge with electricity (*also fig.*)

електрика *f colloq.* **1** <electric> current **2** light-bulb **3** electricity (power) supply

електрификација *f* electrification

електрифици́ра *pf & impf* to supply with electricity, electrify

електрицитет *m* electricity

електричар *m* electrician

електричен -чна *adj* electric<al>; електрично ѕвонче electric bell; електричен удар electric shock; електрична централа power station; електрична енергија electric power; електрично осветление electric lighting; електрични апарати electrical appliances

електро- (*in compounds*) electro-

електрóда *f* electrode

електроенергија *f* electrical energy (power)

електроинженéр *m* electrical engineer

електроинсталáтер *m* electrician

електроинсталација *f* wiring

електрокардиогрáм *m Med.* electrocardiogram, ECG

електролúза *f Chem.* electrolysis

електролúт *m* electrolyte

електромагнет *m* electromagnet

електромагнетúзам -змот *m* electromagnetism

електромагнетски *adj* electromagnetic

електромашински *adj* electrical-engineering

електромéр & **електромéтар** -три *m* electrometer

електромóтор *m* electric motor

електрóн *m* electron

електроника *f* electronics

електронски *adj* electronic; електронска пошта electronic mail, e-mail

електроскóп *m* electroscope

електротерапија *f* electrotherapy

електротехника *f* electrical engineering

електротехничар *m* electrical technician (fitter), electrician

електрофóр *m Phys.* electrophorus

електроцентрáла *f* power station

електрошóк *m Med.* electric shock

елемéнт *m* element (*also fig.*); сомнителни елементи dubious <social> elements; галвански елемент galvanic pile; ❑ во свој елемент е to be in one's element

елементáрен -рна *adj* 1 elementary, initial, basic; елементарни знаења elements, rudiments 2 elemental; елементарна непогода natural disaster; елементарна сила elemental force

елемија -ии *f* windlass

елен *m Zool.* deer, stag; северен елен (Rangifer) reindeer; (Alces alces) elk; канадски елен (Cervus canadensis) wapiti; лов на елени deerstalking

еленски *adj* stag's; еленска кожа deerskin; chamois leather; еленски рогови antlers

еленче *n* 1 *dim. of* елен 2 *Zool.* (Lucanus cervus) stag beetle

елече *n* 1 *dim. of* елек 2 brassière

елизија -ии *f Gram.* elision

еликсúр *m* 1 (*екстракт*) quintessence 2 (*напивка*) elixir

Елим[1] *m f.p.* Hellene, Greek

елим[2] & **елин** *adj indecl. f.p.* sad, mournful

елиминаторен -рна *adj* eliminatory

елиминација *f* elimination

елиминúра *pf & impf* to eliminate, exclude, rule out

елипса *f* 1 *Math.* ellipse 2 *Ling.* ellipsis

елипсовиден -дна *adj* elliptical, oval

елипсóјд *m Math.* ellipsoid

елиптичен -чна *adj* elliptic<al>

елúса *f Tech.* propeller

елúта *f* elite

елитен -тна *adj* elite, select; елитна војска crack troops

елка *f Bot.* fir-tree; (Abies alba) silver fir; Christmas tree

елмаз *m see* дијамант

елов *adj* fir; елова шума fir forest

елоквéнтен -тна *adj* eloquent

елоквенција *f* eloquence

Ел Салвадóр *m* El Salvador

елфа *f Bot.* (Alnus glutinosa) common alder

елха *f dial. see* ела

ем *conj colloq.* and; ем – ем both . . . and; not only . . . but also . . . ; ❑ ем гол ем зол; ем крив ем див the pot calls the kettle black

емáјл *m* enamel

емајлúра *pf & impf* to enamel

емајлúран *pt* enamelled; емајлирани садови enamelware

емалија -ии *f dial. see* амалија

еманација *f* emanation

еманципација *f* emancipation

еманципúра *pf & impf* to emancipate, free

ембáрго *n* embargo

ембриологија *f* embryology

ембриóн *m* embryo; foetus

ембрионáлен -лна *adj* embryonic; foetal; во ембрионална состојба in embryo

емении *pl* brightly-coloured slippers

емигрáнт *m* emigrant; (*обично политички*) émigré

емигрáнтка *f* (*fem. form*) *see* емигрант

емиграција *f* emigration; *coll.* emigrants; émigrés

емигрúра *pf & impf* to emigrate

еминéнтен -тна *adj* eminent, prominent, outstanding

еминенција *f* eminence; Your/His Eminence; ❑ сива еминенција *éminence grise*

емир *m* emir

емирáт *m* emirate

емисáр *m* emissary

емисија -ии *f* 1 broadcast, programme; емисија за деца children's programme 2 *Phys.* (*испракање енергија*) emission 3 *Comm.* issue; емисија на акции issue of shares

емисиóнен -она *adj* issuing; issue *attrib.*; емисиона банка issuing bank; емисионен курс issue price, rate of issue

емитúра *pf & impf* 1 to broadcast 2 *Phys.* (*испрака енергија*) to emit 3 *Comm.* (*издава*) to issue; емитира заем to float a loan

емитува *impf see* емитира

емиш *m see* овошје

емотúвен -вна *adj* emotive, emotional; (*чувствителен*) sensitive, compassionate

емотúвност *f* emotivity; (*чувствителност*) sensitivity

емоција -ии *f* emotion, strong feeling; excitement

емоционáлен -лна *adj* 1 emotional 2 (*возбудлив*) moving, exciting; (*трогателен*) touching

емоционáлност *f* emotion

емпирúзам -змот *m* empiricism

емпириски & **емпирички** *adj* empiric<al>

емпиричар *m* empiricist

ему *n Zool.* (Dromaius novaehollandiae) emu

емулзија *f* emulsion

емфáза *f* emphasis; (*надуен тон*) pretentiousness, pomposity

емфатичен -чна *adj* emphatic; pretentious, pompous

ендек -ци *m* ditch; trench

ене *part* look over there; ене го there he/it is!

енергетика *f* power engineering

енергéтски *adj* power, energy *attrib.*; power engineering *attrib.*; енергетски систем power grid;

енергетски извори power resources; енергетска криза energy crisis

енергија *f* **1** energy, power; потрошувачка на енергија energy consumption; производство на електрична енергија power generation (production); кинетичка енергија kinetic energy **2** energy, vigour

енергичен -чна *adj* energetic, forceful

енигма *f* enigma

енигматичен -чна *adj* enigmatic<al>

енигматичар *m* enigmatist

енклитика *f Gram.* enclitic

енклитичен & енклитички *adj Gram.* enclitic

енорија -ии *f* parish

енормен -мна *adj* enormous

ентериер *m* interior

ентитет *m* entity

ентомолог -зи *m* entomologist

ентомологија *f* entomology

ентомолошки *adj* entomological

ентузијазам -змот *m* enthusiasm; zeal, gusto, zest

ентузијаст *m* enthusiast

енциклопедија -ии *f* encyclopaedia

енциклопедиски *adj* encyclopaedic

енциклопедист *m* encyclopaedist

еп *m* epic, epos

епарх -си *m* eparch, <Orthodox> bishop

епархија -ии *f* eparchy, diocese, bishopric, *see* епископија

епигон *m* epigone, imitator

епигонство *n* epigonism, imitative work; feeble imitation

епиграм *m* epigram

епиграмски *adj* epigrammatic

епиграф *m* epigraph, inscription

епиграфика *f* epigraphy

епидемија -ии *f* epidemic; ❏ се шири како епидемија to spread like wildfire

епидемиолог -зи *m* epidemiologist

епидемиологија *f* epidemiology

епидемиолошки *adj* epidemiological

епидемичен -чна *adj* epidemic

епидерм *m &* **епидерма** *f* epidermis

епизода *f* episode

епизоден -дна *adj* episodic; епизодна личност incidental character; епизодна улога supporting role

епика *f* epic poetry

епикуреец -ејци *m* epicurean

епикурејски *adj* epicurean

епикурејство *m* epicureanism

епилепсија *f Med.* (падавица) epilepsy

епилептичен *m* epileptic

епилептичен -чна *adj* epileptic; епилептични напади epileptic fits

епилог -зи *m* epilogue

Епир *m* Epirus

Епирец -рци *m* person from Epirus

Епирка *f (fem. form) see* Епирец

епирски *adj* of/from Epirus

епископ *m* (*Orthodox*) bishop

епископат *m* episcopate; bishopric

епископија -ии *f* diocese

епископски *adj* bishopric *attrib.*; bishop *attrib.*

епитаф *m* epitaph

епитет *m* epithet

епитрафил *m Rel.* stole, tippet, epitrachelion

епитрахил *m Rel. see* епитрафил

епитроп *m* church warden

епифиза *f Anat.* pineal gland; epiphysis

епицентар -три *m Geol.* epicentre

еполета *f* epaulette

епопеја -еи *f* epos, epic poem; *fig.* epic, saga

епос *m see* еп

епоха *f* epoch, era, period

епохален -лна *adj* epoch-making, epochal

епрувета *f* test-tube

епски *adj* epic

ептен *adv colloq. see* сосем; ептен будала total fool

ера *f* era, period, time; пред нашата ера BC; по нашата ера AD

ербап *adj indecl. colloq.* capable, skilled; resourceful; ербап човек clever person; не прави се толку ербап don't put on airs, don't show off

ергела *f &* **ергеле** *n* stud farm (*for horses*); herd of horses

ерген *m* **1** young man **2** bachelor; стар ерген old bachelor; ерген оди to be a bachelor

ергенлак *m colloq. see* ергенство

ергенски *adj* bachelor's; ергенска забава stag-night (stag-party)

ергенство *n* bachelorhood; bachelor's life

ергенува *impf* to lead a bachelor's life

еребица *f Zool.* (Perdix perdix) partridge

еребичин *adj* partridge's

Ереван *m* Yerevan

ереванец -нци *m* person from Yerevan

ереванка *f (fem. form) see* ереванец

** еревански** *adj* Yerevan *attrib.*

ерекција *f Physiology* erection

ерес *f* heresy; misbelief

еретик -ци *m* heretic

еретички *adj* heretical

Еритреец -ејци *m* Eritrean

Еритреја *f* Eritrea

Еритрејка *f (fem. form) see* Еритреец

еритрејски *adj* Eritrean

еритроцит *m Physiology* erythrocyte

Ерменец -нци *m* Armenian

Ерменија *f* Armenia

Ерменка *f (fem. form) see* Ерменец

ерменски *adj* Armenian

ероген *adj* erogenous; ерогена зона erogenous zone

ерозивен -вна *adj* erosive

ерозија -ии *f* erosion; ерозија на почвата soil erosion

еротизам -змот *m* eroticism

еротик -ци *m* **1** erotic artist/poet **2** rake, libertine

еротика *f* eroticism; erotica

еротичен -чна *adj* erotic

еротичност *f* eroticism

еротичар *m see* еротик

ерудит *m* erudite person, scholar, polymath

ерудиција *f* erudition, learning

еруптивен -вна *adj* eruptive

ерупција -ии *f* eruption

Ерусалим *m* Jerusalem

ерусалимски *adj* Jerusalem *attrib.*

есап *m colloq.* account, bill, *see* сметка[1]; *colloq.* sums; не се есапи it doesn't count; домашниот есап в чаршија не излегува *prov.* don't reckon without your host; don't count your chickens before they are hatched; чист есап, братска љубов *prov.* short reckonings make long friends

есеи́ст *m* essayist

есеи́стика *f (fem. form) see* есеист

есе́ј -еи *m* essay

есен *f* autumn, *Am.* fall

есенен -сена *adj* autumnal, autumn

есенешен -шна *adj* last autumn's; happening every autumn

есеноска *adv* last autumn

есенски *adj see* есенен

есенција *f* **1** essential/volatile oil, essence **2** *fig.* essence, substance

есенција́лен -лна *adj* essential, fundamental

есесовец -вци *m Hist.* SS-man

есетра *f Zool.* (Accipenser sturio) sturgeon

еска́дра *f Mil.* <naval> squadron; *Aviation* wing

ескадри́ла *f Mil.* <air-force> squadron

ескадро́н *m Mil.* <cavalry> troop (squadron)

ескала́тор *m* escalator

ескалација *f* escalation

ескон т *m* discount

есконтен -тна *adj* discount; discounted; есконтна стапка discount rate, rate of discount

есконти́ра *pf & impf* to discount

есна ф *m* guild; еснаф човек *arch.* reliable (trust-worthy) person

еснафлија -ии *m* member of a guild; еснафлија човек *see* еснаф човек

еснафски *adj* **1** guild *attrib.* **2** *fig. pejor.* philistine, narrow-minded

еснафство *n* association of guilds; *coll.* guild members

еснафштина *f* middle-class mentality, philistinism, narrow-mindedness

еспадри́ла *f (usu. pl)* espadrille, light canvas shoe

есперанти́ст *m* Esperantist

еспера́нто *n, adj, adv* Esperanto

есте́т *m* aesthete

естетика *f* aesthetics

естетичар *m* aesthetician

естетички *adj* aesthetic

естетски *adj* **1** aesthetic **2** beautiful

Естонец -нци *m* Estonian

Естонија *f* Estonia

Естонка *f (fem. form) see* Естонец

естонски *adj* Estonian

естра́да *f* stage; variety (*Am.* vaudeville) entertain-ment; entertainment industry

естра́ден -дна *adj* stage/variety *attrib.*; естраден уметник entertainer, stage performer

ета́ж *m (кат)* storey, floor

еталон *m (мерка)* standard

ета́па *f* stage, phase; *Sport.* lap; во етапи by (in) stages

ета́пен -пна *adj* stage, phased

ете *part* **1** there, there it is; you see; ете ти ја книгата there is the book; ете, виде? you see? ете ти реков I told you so; ете зошто that's why; ❑ ете ти бе ља! I can't believe it! it's just my luck! ете ти работа! that's all I need! **2** *(as a filler)* well; ете, што сега? well, what now?

етер *m* ether

етерен -рна *adj* ethereal, ether *attrib.*; volatile, essen-tial; етерно масло essential oil

етерски *adj* ether

ети́да *f Mus.* etude

етика *f* ethics

етике́та *f* label

етикеција *f* etiquette

етил *m Chem.* ethyl; етил алкохол ethyl alcohol

етиле́н *m Chem.* ethylene

етимоло́г -зи *m* etymologist

етимологија *f* etymology

етимолошки *adj* etymological

Етиопија *f* Ethiopia

Етиопјанец -ни *m* Ethiopian

Етиопјанка *f (fem. form) see* Етиопјанец

етиопски *adj* Ethiopian

етичар *m* ethicist; moralist

етички *adj* ethical

еткав *adj* stuttering, *see* тептав

еткави *impf* to stutter, stammer, *see* тептави

етнички *adj* ethnic

етногра́ф *m* ethnographer

етнографија *f* ethnography

етнографски *adj* ethnographical

етноло́г -зи *m* ethnologist

етнологија *f* ethnology

етнолошки *adj* ethnological

ЕУ *abbr.* (*Европска унија*) European Union, EU

еуфеми́зам -змот *m* euphemism

еуфемистичен -чна *adj* euphemistic

еуфонија *f* euphony

еуфониум *m Mus.* euphonium

еуфорија *f* euphoria

ефект *m* efficiency; result, output; effect; impression; работен ефект work output; светлосни/звучни ефекти light/sound effects; ❑ има ефект to work; to take effect; нема ефект to have no effect; to show no result

ефектен -тна *adj* effective; convincing

ефекти́вен -вна *adj* actual, real; ефективна вредност real value

ефекти́вност *f* effectiveness, efficiency; efficacy

ефекти́ви *pl* total strength, manpower

ефеме́рен -рна *adj* ephemeral, transient; (*напразен*) vain, useless

ефеме́рност *f* ephemerality

ефенди<ја> - ии *m arch.* effendi, Sir, master

ефика́сен -сна *adj* efficacious, effective; efficient, successful

ефика́сност *f* efficacy, effectiveness; efficiency

ефла *f Bot. see* елфа

ex *interj (expressing boredom or dismay)* oh dear!

ехла *f Bot. see* елфа

ехо *n* echo, reverberation

ечи *impf see* екнува

ечка *impf (јачи, стенка)* to moan, groan

ечмик *m Bot.* barley, *see* јачмен[1]

ешало́н *m Mil.* transport, train

еша́рпа *f* sash; officer's belt; (*женска*) long scarf

ешек -ци *m colloq. (of a person)* ass

ешко *m f.p.* hedgehog

еште́рица *f* pimple on the end of the tongue

Ж

жаба¹ *f Zool.* frog; зелена жаба (Rana esculenta) edible frog; крастава жаба (Bufo bufo) toad; треварка жаба (Rana temporaria) common frog; ❑ жаба на суво не крека one has to wet one's whistle; човек жаба frogman

жаба² *f Med.* **1** градна жаба angina pectoris; *colloq.* breast pang **2** disease of the throat in cattle

жабар *m* **1** frog eater **2** *pejor.* eyetie, wop, dago **3** *see* жабок, жабор, жаборок

жабарник -ци *m see* жабурнак, жабурник

жабец -пци *m see* жабок, жабор, жаборок

жабешки *adj* frog's, frog *attrib.*

жабин *adj see* жабешки

жабица *f* **1** *dim. of* жаба **2** *Med.* disease in cattle **3** (*за чорапи*) suspender, *Am.* garter

жабјак -ци *m Bot.* duckweed, horned pondweed

жабји *adj* frog's; жабји батак frog's leg; ❑ од жабја перспектива from below

жабо́ *n* jabot

жабок -ци, **жабор & жаборок** -ци *m* male frog

жабокречина *f Bot.* duckweed, horned pondweed

жабра *f* gill

жабуњоса *pf* to become covered with duckweed

жабуњосува *impf of* жабуњоса

жабурка *f* **1** (*меур*) bubble **2** *see* жабра

жабурка *impf* **I 1** to bubble; жабурка сапуница to blow bubbles **2** to rinse one's mouth; to gargle **3** to paddle, dabble (*по вода и сл. – in water, etc.*) **II – се** to froth

жабуркоса <се> *pf* to <begin to> bubble; to go off (*of food*)

жабуркосува <се> *impf of* жабуркоса <се>

жабурлив *adj* covered with duckweed

жабурнак -ци **& жабурник** -ци *m* **1** frog pond **2** frog-spawn **3** *see* жабокречина

жагор *m see* џагор

жагори *impf see* џагори

жад *m* jade

жакет *m* jacket

жал *m* sorrow, sadness, grief; affliction; pity; regret; умирам од жал I am dying of grief; жал ми е за тебе I'm sorry for you; жал ми падна за тебе I felt sorry for you; за жал unfortunately; како не ти е жал? don't you feel sorry?, don't you regret it? тој е за жал he's to be pitied

жала (се) *impf see* жали (се)

жалба *f* **1** sorrow, sadness, grief **2** (*поплака*) complaint; appeal; поднесува жалба to lodge a complaint; to appeal; одбива жалба to reject an appeal; книга за жалби complaints book

жалбен *adj* complaint, complaints *attrib.*; *Leg.* appellate; жалбена книга complaints book; жалбен суд court of appeal

жалевит *adj f.p.* **1** compassionate, kind **2** sad, depressing; pitiable, miserable

жален -лна *adj* **1** (*за расказ, песна*) sad, doleful, mournful; (*за изглед*) sad, woebegone, pitiful; (*за глетка*) piteous, pitiful, woeful; (*за поглед*) sad, doleful, mournful; (*за глас*) sad, plaintive, mournful; ❑ жална врба *Bot.* (Salyx babilonica) weeping willow; жална мајка на мртво дете се радува *prov.* something is better than nothing; any port in a storm **2** (*кутар*) poor, miserable, wretched; pitiful

жалење *n* pity, grief; regret; тој е за жалење he is to be pitied

жали *impf* **I 1** to mourn, grieve; ја жали мајка си she is mourning her mother **2** to regret, be sorry (*за – for*); to pity; жалам што не го видов I regret (I'm sorry) I didn't see him; жалам ама (но) . . . I'm sorry but . . . ; жалеше за младоста he regretted (mourned) his lost youth; жали за Скопје he has fond memories of Skopje **3** (*negated*) not to spare; не жали труд to spare no effort; не жали средства to spare no expense **II – се 1** to complain; to grumble; се жали на некого to complain about s.o.; се жалеше на болки во стомакот he complained of stomachache **2** to appeal; се жали против решение to appeal against a ruling

жалибоже *adv* unfortunately

жалител *m* complainant; plaintiff

жалник -ци *m* wretch, poor devil

жалница *f* (*fem. form*) *see* жалник

жално *adv* sadly; with pity, pityingly; се насмеа жалосно he smiled pitifully; изгледа жално to be a sorry sight

жаловен -вна *adj f.p. see* жален

жаловит *adj* compassionate, kind; sad, depressing; pitiable, miserable

жало́н *m* **1** (*на земјомер*) range (ranging) pole, surveying rod; (*знак*) picket **2** *fig.* landmark, milestone

жалони́ра *pf & impf* to mark out (*with range poles*)

жалосен -сна *adj* pitiful, pitiable

жалослив *adj* **1** pitiful, compassionate **2** (*тажен*) sad

жалосник -ци *m* wretch, poor devil

жалосница *f* (*fem. form*) *see* жалосник

жалост *f* **1** sorrow, grief; regret; pity; на моја жалост to my regret; тој е за жалост he's to be pitied; за жалост unfortunately **2** (*траур*) mourning; народна жалост national mourning

жалости *impf* **I** to sadden, distress; to bereave **II – се** to be sad (distressed)

жалостив *adj see* жалослив

жалузии & жалузини *pl* venetian blinds

жалфија -ии *f Bot.* (Salvia officinalis) sage

жандар *m colloq.* **1** *pejor.* policeman **2** *fig.* bully **3** *Cards* jack; type of card-game

жандарм *m Hist.* gendarme, policeman

жандармерија *f Hist.* gendarmerie

жандарски *adj Hist.* gendarme *attrib.*

жанр *n Literature* genre; епски жанр the epic genre

жапка *f* **1** *dim. of* жаба¹ **2** (*на врата*) spindle (*of a hinge*) **3** *Zool.* (*школка*) mollusc; oyster

жапче *n* **1** *dim. of* жаба¹ **2** tadpole

жар **1** *m & f* live coals, embers; распрета жар to poke a fire; печено на жар grilled, barbecued; ❑ тој е жив жар he is a real live wire; не ќе ти стават жар на мевот! you won't be hung for that! жар се стори во лицето he blushed all over; he blushed to the roots of his hair **2** *fig.* (*m only*) fervour, ardour, passion; зборува со жар to speak heatedly

жаргон *m* jargon; slang; cant

жаргонски *adj* jargon *attrib.*; slang *attrib.*; slangy

жардиниéра *f* jardinière

жари *impf* **I 1** to burn, scorch **2** to heat; жари метал to heat metal **3** to sting; коприватa жари the nettle stings **II – ce** to glow; (*од срам*) to blush

жариште *n* focus; centre; жариште на отпорот centre (hotbed) of resistance; жариште на болеста focus (seat) of infection

жарка *impf see* жари I 2

жаровит *adj* red-hot; glowing

жароса *pf* to make red-hot

жаросува *impf of* жароса

жар-птица *f* phoenix

жарче *n dim. of* жар; ❑ <по>тајно жарче a dark horse; живо (право) жарче a live wire

жбара *impf see* џбара

жбитак -ци *m see* џбитак

жвака *impf see* џвака

жган *m see* џган

жграмоти *impf* to clang, jingle; to clank, clatter, rattle

жгура *f* (*also* џгура¹) *see* згура

ждрака *impf see* штрака

ждракне *pf* ждракна *aor. see* штракне

ждракнува *impf of* ждракне

ждрапа *impf see* штрапа 1

ждреб *m* drawing of lots, draw; die, dice

ждреба *impf* to draw lots; to decide by drawing lots

ждребак -ци *m see* ждребец

ждребе *n* foal

ждребенце *n dim. of* ждребе

ждребец -пци *m* colt

ждреби ce *impf* to foal

ждребица *f* filly

ждребна *adj* (*only f*) in (with) foal

ждрепка *f* drawing of lots; фрли ждрепка to draw (cast) lots

ждрига *impf* to belch, *colloq.* burp

ждригавица *f* belching, belch, eructation

ждригне *pf* ждригна *aor.* to give a belch

ждригнува *impf of* ждригне

ждриговина *f see* ждригавица

ждринга *impf see* ждринготи

ждрингот *m* clang, clank, clink

ждринготи *impf* to clang, clank, clatter, rattle

жебурав *adj* wrinkled, wizened

жебурка *f* (*usu. pl*) bags under the eyes

жебуркоса *pf* to become wrinkled (wizened)

жеволи *impf* to chew the cud, ruminate

жеволка *impf dim. of* жеволи

жег *m* brand, stamp, mark

жега¹ *f* heat, hot weather; голема жега фати a heat wave has begun

жега² *impf* to stab, pierce; ме жега во стомакот I have stabbing pains in my stomach

жегавица *f* **1** stabbing pain; stitch **2** biting insect

жегне *pf* жегна *aor.* **1** to stab, pierce; to poke **2** to bite,

sting; штркелот го жегнал a gad-fly bit him **3** *fig.* to tease, torment; неговите зборови ме жегнаа в срце his words cut me to the quick

жегнува *impf of* жегне

жегол -гли *m* pole (*of a yoke*)

жеголач *m* poker (*for a fire*)

жегоса *pf* to brand, *see* жигоса

жегосува *impf of* жегоса

жегра *f see* жегол

жед *f* thirst (*also fig.*); гаси жед to quench (slake) one's thirst; жед за знаење thirst for knowledge

жеден -дна *adj* thirsty (*also fig.*); ❑ пренесува некого жеден преку вода to lead s.o. by the nose; to pull a fast one on s.o.; жеден коњ матна вода не пребира *prov.* beggars can't be choosers

жеднее *impf* to thirst, yearn, crave (*за – for*)

жедник -ци *m* thirsty person

жедува *impf see* жеднее

жеже *impf* to bake *intrans.*; песоктa жеже the sand is very hot; надвор жеже it is very hot outside

жежне *pf* жежна *aor. of* жеже

жежнува *impf of* жежне

жежок -шка *adj* hot; torrid (*also fig.*); жешки дни hot days; жешка љубов passionate love; *Geog.* жежок појас torrid zone

жезол -зли *m* mace, sceptre; царски жезол royal sceptre

желад *m* acorn

желадар *m* acorn-gatherer

желателен -лна *adj* desirable; desired

желати́н *m* gelatine

желба *f* wish; desire, will; (*барање*) request, demand; ми се исполни желбата my wish came true; по негова желба at his request; губи желба за живот to lose the will to live; има голема желба (*да*) to have a good mind (*to*); гори од желба (*да*) to burn with desire (*to*); пуста желба wishful thinking

желé *n* jelly

желевце *n* **1** *dim. of* железо; piece/scrap of iron **2** (*на чевли и сл.*) heel-plate; toe-plate

железар *m* hardware dealer, *Brit.* ironmonger

железарија *f* hardware, ironware, *Brit.* ironmongery

железарница *f* **1** ironworks, iron-foundry **2** hardware store, *Brit.* ironmongery

железен -зна *adj* iron (*also fig.*); *Chem.* ferrous; железна порта iron ore; ironstone; железна рака hand of iron; железна волја iron will

железница *f* railway, *Am.* railroad; електрична железница electric railway; подземна железница underground <railway>, metro, *Am.* subway; едношинска железница monorail

железничар *m* railway worker

железнички *adj* railway, *Am.* railroad *attrib.*; *colloq.* железничка глава locomotive; железничка станица railway (*Am.* railroad) station

железо *n* iron; ковано железо wrought iron; леано железо cast iron; сирово железо pig-iron; старо железо scrap iron, scrap heap; ❑ рацете му се железо his hands are as cold as ice; фрла во старо железо to scrap, throw on the scrap heap; железото дури е топло се чука, железото се кове додека е жешко *prov.* strike while the iron is hot

желен -лна *adj* **1** desirous; (*нестрплив*) eager, anxious; желен за слава desirous of stardom, ambitious;

желен е да стигне дома што побрзо he is eager to get home as soon as possible **2** (*страден*) lacking, wanting (*за – for*); не сум желен за ништо I'm not wanting for anything

желка *f Zool.* (Testudo) tortoise; морска желка (Chelonia) <marine> turtle; грчка желка (Testudo graeca) Greek tortoise; ❑ jaва на желка to move very slowly, move like a tortoise

желкар *m see* желурок

желкин *adj* tortoise's, tortoise *attrib.*; turtle's

желуд & желудец -дци *m see* желудник & желудок

желудник -ци & **желудок** -ци *m* stomach

желудочен -чна *adj* gastric, stomach *attrib.*; желудочен сок gastric juice

желурок -ци *m* male tortoise/turtle

желче *n dim. of* желка

жена *f* woman; lady; (*сопруга*) wife, spouse; *fig. colloq.* sissy; ❑ машка жена tomboy; лесна жена, шарена жена woman of easy virtue; зема за жена to marry; местото на жената ѝ е дома a woman's place is in the home; жената ја крепи куќата *prov.* men make houses, women make homes; дома од жената, в планина од мечката *prov.* between the devil and the deep blue sea

женачка *f see* женидба

Женева *f* Geneva

женевјанец -ни *m* Genevan, Genevese

женевјанка *f* (*fem. form*) *see* женевјанец

женевски *adj* Genevan, Genevese

женет *adj* married (*of a man*)

жени *impf* **I** to marry off (*a son, etc.*) **II – се** to marry *intrans.*, get married (*of a man*)

женидба *f* marriage

женидбен *adj* marriage, wedding

женин *adj* wife's; woman's; женини роднини wife's relatives

женѝра *impf* **I** to embarrass; to inhibit; to hamper, hinder, restrict; to disrupt **II – се** to be embarrassed/inhibited; to hesitate, restrain o.s., hold back

женица *f dim. hyp. of* жена

женичка *f dim. hyp. of* жена

жениште *f augm. pejor. of* жена

женка *f* **1** female (*of animals*), she-; (*од елен, зајак*) doe; (*птица*) hen **2** *pejor.* female, woman **3** coward, milksop, *colloq.* sissy

женкар *m* rake, libertine, Don Juan, lady's man, womanizer, skirt-chaser

женкарство *n* womanizing

женољубец -пци *m see* женкар

женомразец -сци *m* misogynist

женска *f* female, *colloq.* girl; *pejor.* лесна женска hussy

женски *adj* female; woman's; feminine; womanly; женски пол female sex; *Gram.* женски род feminine gender; женска школа girls' school; ❑ женска́ свадба wedding in the bride's home; женска црница white mulberry; женски водици Feast of St. John the Baptist; женскѝ кромид round<-headed> onion; женскѝ Пејо effeminate man, *colloq., pejor.* pansy

женско *n* female

женсковина *f colloq.* femininity

женскотија *f coll.* females, girls

женствен *adj* feminine, womanly; effeminate; elegant, graceful

женственост *f* femininity; elegance

женче *n dim. hyp. of* жена

жерав *m Zool.* (Grus grus) crane

жерави се *impf* to fidget; to mill around

жерсе́ *n* jersey (*fabric*)

жести се *impf* to flare up, lose one's temper

жестина *f* power; strength; vehemence; со особена жестина with particular vehemence

жесток *adj* **1** severe, bitter; violent, cruel, brutal, savage; жесток човек hard (cruel, merciless) person; жестока постапка cruel (ruthless) act; жестока кавга bitter quarrel; жестоки борби pitched battles, heavy fighting **2** (*за пијалоци*) strong; жестоки пијалоци spirits, hard liquor

жестокост *f* bitterness; violence, cruelty; brutality

жетва *f* harvest; одиме на жетва we are going harvesting; во жетвата at harvest time; богата жетва bumper crop

жетвар *m* **1** harvester, reaper **2** (*popular name for*) July

жетварка *f* **1** (*fem. form*) *see* жетвар 1 **2** harvester, reaping-machine

жетварски *adj* harvest, harvesting

жето́н *m* counter, token; gambling chip; жетони за автобус bus token

жешко *adv* hot; жешко ми е I am hot

жешти се *impf* **1** to get red-hot **2** *fig.* to get excited, flare up

жештина *f* heat, hot weather; голема жештина е надвор it's very hot outside

жи- (*in oaths*) by . . .; жими, жити by my . . ., by your . . .; жити мајка my by your mother's life

жив *adj* **1** alive, living, live; живо суштество living creature; додека сум жив as long as I live; здрав и жив safe and sound, alive and well; сè живо every living thing, everything under the sun; жив јазик living (modern) language; жив збор spoken word; жива историја living history; живо сведоштво living witness; жив жар live coal; *fig.* live wire; жива природа animate nature; ❑ жив умрел; ни жив ни мртов dead scared, more dead than alive; жива душа (жив човек) нема there's not a living soul; да си ми жив good health to you! жив да не сум, ако . . . may God strike me dead if . . . ; жив човек – се лаже to err is human; жив в земи пропаднав I could die of shame; жив в земи не се влегува there is no way out; жив се јаде to eat one's heart out; да сме живи и здрави may we live to see the day; останува жив to survive **2** (*подвижен; прометен*) lively; живо дете lively child; жив ум lively wit/mind; жива фантазија vivid imagination; жива улица busy street; жива трговија brisk trade **3** (*изразит*) vivid, lively; жив опис vivid description; живи бои vivid colours; жива срамота crying shame **4** (*вистински*) true; downright; жив ѓавол real devil, the devil himself; *fig.* жив отров real poison **5** (*суров*) raw, uncooked; живо месо raw meat **6** completely, totally; жив гладен extremely hungry, starving; жив зелен still quite green; жив ненаспан extremely sleepy; жив неразбран extremely self-willed; maverick **7** ❑ жив<а> вар quicklime; жива вода (*in folk-tales*) water of life; живá вода <сторен> soaked (drenched) to the skin; жива мера (*price*) on the hoof; жива ограда hedge, quickset; жива сила *usu. Mil.* men, personnel, troops; живó сребро quicksilver, mercury; жива стока livestock; wealth; жива рана open wound; dangerous disease

жива *f Chem.* mercury, quicksilver

живалец *m colloq.* suckling, infant

живе *adv* на живе, при живе during one's life-<time>, when alive

живеалиште *n* dwelling, residence, domicile, habitation, lodging

живеачка *f colloq.* life, living; life in harmony; нивната живеачка нигде ја нема they get along (on) very well

живее *impf* to live; to reside; to dwell; да живее! long live! живеам во Скопје I live in Skopje; живее човечки to live a decent life; живее од земја to live off the land; живее од плата to live on one's salary; живее за наука to live for learning; живее со некого 1. to get on with s.o. 2. to live with s.o.; ❏ живее на туѓ грб to live at s.o. else's expense; живее како бубрег в лој to live in clover; живее како гроф to live like a lord; живее нашироко (на висока нога) to live in style, *colloq.* to live it up; живее диво со некого to live in sin with s.o.; живеат како куче и маче to lead a cat-and-dog life, fight like cat and dog; живее од денес до утре to live from day to day, live from hand to mouth; живеј и пушти другите да живеат live and let live! само еднаш се живее we only live once; каде живееш ти? do you follow? are you with me?

живец -вци *m* 1 (*кожинка*) cuticle 2 (*usu. pl*) clamp, tie, bracket (*holding together the felloe*)

живин *adj Chem.* mercury *attrib.*; mercuric; живин сулфид mercuric sulphide; живин термометар mercury thermometer

живина *f* 1 *coll.* poultry 2 *colloq.* animal 3 lice; има живина to be infested with lice; се чисти од живина to <de>louse o.s.

живинарник -ци *m* hen-coop, chicken-coop

живинарство *n* poultry raising, poultry breeding

живинче *n* head of cattle; domestic animal

живка *impf* to vegetate, barely exist

живне *pf* живна *aor.* to become lively, perk up, revive *intrans.*

живнува *impf of* живне

живо *adv* in a lively manner; vividly; (*енергично, брзо*) energetically, quickly, briskly; живо работи to work energetically; живо расправа to relate vividly; живо се сеќава to remember clearly; ❏ во/на живо in the flesh; (*за програма*) live; ништо живо не може да го натера wild horses wouldn't drag him there/here

живодер *m* flayer

живожален -лна *adj f.p.* poor, wretched, hapless, *see* кутар

живожарица *f* 1 live coal 2 *fig.* live wire

живоздраво *adv see* здравоживо

живоланче *n see* рулче

живопис *m* painting

живописен -сна *adj* picturesque, vivid

живописец -сци *m* artist, painter

живост *f* liveliness

живот *m* (*colloq. also f*) life; living; начин на живот way of life; животот на Земјата life on earth; го загуби животот to lose one's life; простува некому живот to spare s.o.'s life; живот и здравје *toast* to your health! на живот и смрт to the death; to the bitter end; борба на живот и смрт life-and-death struggle; fight to the finish; долг живот long life; на живот<и> during one's life; така ми мина животот

I lived my life uneventfully; life passed me by; кучешки живот a dog's life; во приватен живот in private life; offstage; нема живот one can't live like this; there's nothing (no life) for us here; удрив на живот I've put my troubles aside; I live for the day; многу животи зеде на душа he's answerable for many lives; црпе мотиви од животот he takes his subjects from real life; полн живот eventful life; полн е со живот to be brimming over with life; ако му е мил животот if he values his life; вдахновува <нов> живот во нешто to breathe new life into s.th.; води двоен живот to lead (live) a double life; животот оди (тече) понатаму life goes on; the show must go on; поврати во живот to bring back to life, revive, resuscitate; спроведува во живот to put into practice/effect; ризикува живот to risk one's life; се пробива во животот to make one's way in life; to go up in the world; услови за живот living conditions; подарува некому живот to grant s.o. his life; си го одзема животот to take one's own life, commit suicide; покажува знаци на живот to show signs of life; таков е животот; тоа ти е животот such is life; that's life; средства за живот means of subsistence, livelihood; способен за живот viable

животворен -рна *adj* life-giving

животен -тна *adj* life *attrib.*; животна способност viability, vitality; животни намирници food, victuals; животно прашање matter of life and death; животно осигурување life insurance; животен стандард standard of living; животен пат life; животно искуство life experience; животна средина the environment; животен век life span; животен минимум subsistence level; животни потреби necessities of life

животец *m iron. dim. of* живот; си го гледа животецот he looks after Number 1

животи *adv* на животи during one's life<time>

животина *f* large animal

животинка *f* small animal

животински *adj* animal; *fig.* brutal; животинско царство animal kingdom; животинска постапка brutal act; животинско однесување beastly behaviour

животинче *n dim. of* животно

животно -тни *n* animal, creature, beast (*also fig.*); товарно животно pack animal, beast of burden; тревопасно животно herbivorous animal, herbivore

животност *f* vitality

животодавен -вна *adj* life-giving, resuscitative

животодавец -вци *m* giver of life, resuscitator

животопис *m* biography

животописец -сци *m* biographer

животоспособен -бна *adj* viable; vital; lively

живува *impf* to get on (*со некого – with s.o.*)

живурка *impf* to vegetate, barely exist

жиг[1] *m* brand; stamp; seal; поштенски жиг postmark; царински жиг customs seal; воден жиг watermark; жиг на благородни метали hallmark

жиг[2] *m in expressions:* жиг ми е I'm sorry

жига *impf see* жега[2]

жиговина *f* heartburn

жиголо *m* gigolo

жигоса *pf* to brand (*also fig.*); to stigmatize, revile, lambast

жигосува *impf of* жигоса; ја жигосува хипокризијата на богатите he attacks the hypocrisy of the wealthy

жижне *pf* жижна *aor.* **1** to burn, scorch **2** *fig.* to cause pain; to sting; to upset; ме жижна твојата мака your trouble upset me

жижнува *impf of* жижне

жизнен *adj literary* vital, life *attrib.*; жизнен сок vital (life-giving) juice; sap

жизнерадосен -сна *adj* joyful, cheerful

жила¹ *f* **1** vein; жили на лист veins in a leaf; рудна жила lode, seam of ore **2** (*на мускул*) tendon, sinew; ми се здрвија жилите my muscles grew stiff; ❏ запнува (се напрегнува) од петни жили to strain every nerve; to pull out all the stops **3** (*на корен*) root hair; го искорна сосе жили he pulled it out by the roots; пушти жили to take root **4** воловска жила oxhide whip

жила² *f* catapult

жилав *adj* sinewy, stringy, tough (*also fig.*); жилаво месо tough meat; жилав човек tough (wiry) person; жилав отпор tough (stubborn) resistance

жилавец *m Bot.* (Plantago major) plantain, waybread

жилавина *f* toughness

жилавка *f* type of grape and wine

жилавост *f* toughness

жилест *adj* veined

жилéт *m* razor blade; safety razor

жилéтка *f arch.* waistcoat

жили *impf* to put down roots

жиличка & жилка *f dim. of* жила¹

жило *n* sting (*of a bee, wasp, etc.*)

жими *see* жи-; жими сè I swear to God! cross my heart!

жипóн *m* petticoat

жир *m see* желад

жирáнт *m* endorser, backer (*of a bill of exchange, draft, etc.*)

жирáфа *f Zool.* giraffe

жири *m* jury, judges

жиро *n Comm.* transfer; жиро-конто giro account, transfer account, drawing account

жироскоп *m* magic lantern

житар *m* grain merchant

житарски *adj* grain *attrib.*

житарство *n* grain-growing; grain trade

жител *m* inhabitant, resident; citizen; постојан/привремен жител permanent/temporary resident

жителка *f* (*fem. form*) *see* жител

жителство *n* **1** population **2** residence, domicile; citizenship

житен -тна *adj* grain *attrib.*; житни растенија cereals; ❏ житна кал droppings, dung; житна трева *see* класатица

жити *see* жи-

житие -ија *n* hagiography

житница *f* granary

жито *n* **1** corn, cereal crops, *Am.* grain; wheat; зрело жито ripe corn **2** ceremonial boiled wheat (*at a slava or requiem*)

житовино *n see* виножито

житороден -дна *adj* rich in grain; житороден крај grain-growing country (region)

жица *f* **1** wire; strand; конец од три жици three-strand thread; боцлива жица barbed wire; телефонска жица telephone line (cable) **2** (*струна*) string; виолинска жица violin string **3** *Geol.* vein, lode; златна жица gold seam; рудна жица ore-bearing seam **4** *fig.* trait; talent; детево има таткова жица this child has inherited some traits from his/her father; поетска жица talent for poetry, poetic strain **5** гласни жици vocal cords **6** (*за стругање*) scouring pad; steel wool

жичара *f* cable railway, cableway, funicular

жичен -чна *adj* wire *attrib.*

жичка *f dim. of* жица

жиш *interj child.* it's hot! (*when warning a child*)

жишка *impf* **I 1** to burn, scorch **2** *fig.* to cause pain; to sting **II** – се to get burnt (scorched); to burn o.s. slightly; *fig.* to get upset

жишне *pf* жишна *aor. see* жижне

жишнува *impf see* жижнува

жлеб¹ *m* groove; gutter; chute; (*на оружје*) rifling; (*на ќерамида*) pantile

жлеб² *m* vat (*for grapes, plums, etc.*)

жлебина *f* (*usu. pl*) *Anat.* gum, *see* венец 5

жлезда *f Anat.* gland; штитовидна жлезда thyroid gland; лимфна жлезда lymph gland; жлезда со внатрешно лачење endocrine gland; надбубрежна жлезда suprarenal gland; има жлезди he has swollen glands

жлезден *adj* glandular

жлездест *adj* glandiform, gland-like; glandular

жмер *m* sediment obtained by rendering down fat

жмерка & жмирка *f Cul.* crackling

жмрка *impf* to gush, squirt

жмурки *pl colloq.* (*мижитамара*) hide-and-seek

жмурне *pf* жмурна *aor.* **I** to immerse, plunge *trans.* **II** – се to dive

жмурнува (се) *impf of* жмурне (се)

жмучка *f* bump, lump, swelling

жнеарка & жнеачка *f see* жетварка

жнее *impf* to reap, harvest (*also fig.*); жнее јачмен to reap barley; жнее успеси to reap success; што ќе сееш, тоа ќе жнееш *prov.* as you sow, so shall you reap

жние *impf see* жнее

жовијáлен -лна *adj* jovial

жовијáлност *f* joviality

жожори *impf* to murmur

жолна *f Zool.* (Picus viridis) green woodpecker

жолт *adj* yellow; ❏ жолт како смил white as a sheet; жолт печат gutter press

жолтее *impf* **I** to appear yellow; to turn yellow/pale *intrans.* **II** – се to make o.s. yellow; to grow yellow<er>; to appear yellow

жолтеникав *adj* yellowish

жолтеница *f* **1** *see* жолтица 1 **2** *Bot.* (Caltha palustris) marsh marigold

жолтеничав *adj see* жолтичав

жолти *impf* **I** to make, paint yellow **II** – се *see* жолтее (се) **II**

жолтикав *adj* yellowish

жолтило *n* & **жолтина** *f* yellowness

жолтица *f* **1** *Med.* jaundice **2** ducat

жолтичав *adj* jaundiced

жолтичок -чка *adj* yellowish

жолтне   *pf* жолтна *aor.* **I 1** to turn yellow/pale *intrans.*; лицето му жолтна his face turned pale **2** to make yellow, turn yellow *trans.* **II – се** *see* жолтее (се) II

жолтникав   *adj see* жолтикав

жолтнува (се)   *impf of* жолтне (се)

жолтозе́лен   *adj* yellowish green

жолток   -ци *m* yolk

жолтокос   *adj* yellow-haired, blond

жолтолик   *adj* yellow-faced; sallow

жолтоок   *adj* yellow-eyed

жолтоса   *pf* **1** to grow yellow, turn yellow/pale *intrans.*; се жолтоса целиот од страв he turned pale with fear **2** to make yellow, turn yellow *trans.*

жолтосува   *impf of* жолтоса

жолточен   -чна *adj* yolk

жолтулав & жолтуњав   *adj see* жолтикав, жолтеникав

жолч   *f see* жолчка 1

жолчен   -чна *adj* **1** gall *attrib.*; жолчен камен gallstone; жолчна кесичка gall-bladder **2** *fig.* bilious, bitter, ill-natured, spiteful, malicious, biting, sarcastic; жолчни зборови scathing words; жолчна расправија bitter quarrel

жолчка   *f* **1** gall, bile (*also fig.*); ❏ му пукна жолчката од мака he was very upset **2** yolk

жолчлив   *adj see* жолчен 2

жолчност   *f* spite, malice, sarcasm, bitterness

жонглер   *m* juggler

жонгли́ра   *impf* to juggle

жорже́т   *m* georgette (*fabric*)

жребе   *n see* ждребе

жрепка   *f see* ждрепка

жрец   *m* pagan priest

жртва   *f* **1** sacrifice; (*за принесување*) offering; принесува жртва to make a sacrifice **2** victim; casualty; жртва на клеветата a victim of slander; ❏ лесна жртва easy target, easy mark

жртвен   *adj* sacrificial

жртвеник   -ци *m* sacrificial altar; (*во антички театар*) thymele

жртвува   *impf* to sacrifice

жуберка   *impf* **1** to ripple, gurgle **2** to chew the cud, *see* жеволи **3** *fig.* to work slowly

жуберлив   *adj* rippling, murmuring; жуберлива вода rippling water

жубори   *impf* to ripple, gurgle

жуборка   *impf* to ripple, gurgle

жуга   *impf see* жугне

жугне   *pf* жугна *aor.* **1** to sprout *intrans.*; жугна пченицата the wheat has sprouted **2** to begin to grow; to get stronger; жугна детето the child has grown stronger **3** to recover (*after an illness*) **4** to become lively **5** *dial.* (*шепне*) to whisper

жугнува   *impf of* жугне

жудлив   *adj* pungent, acerbic, astringent; жудливо грозје acid grapes

жужален   *m dial. see* жужалец

жужалец   -лци *m* Zool. (Gryllus campestris) cricket

жужел   -жли *m* Zool. (Carabus) bombardier beetle

жука   *f* Bot. (Cyperus longus) <English> galingale, sweet cyperus

жулав   *adj* sickly

жулавица   *f* kind of mushroom

жули   *impf* to pinch (*of shoes, etc.*); to rub

жулне   *pf* жулна *aor.* **I** to rub, scrub; to fray, rub holes (*in*); to start pinching/rubbing **II – се** to rub o.s.; to fray, wear through *intrans.*

жулнува (се)   *impf of* жулне (се)

жунжуле   *n see* цунцуле

жупа   *f* **1** district, region **2** *Hist.* tribal state **3** *Rel.* (*Roman Catholic*) parish

жупан   *m Hist.* head of a tribal state

жупник   -ци *m* (*Roman Catholic*) parish priest

жур[1]   *m see* глужд

жур[2]   *m* party, at-home

жури   *impf* (*of nettles*) to sting

журка[1]   *f* Bot. (Gallinula chloropus) moorhen, water-hen

журка[2]   *impf see* жури

журлив   *adj see* глужлив

журна́л   *m* **1** journal, magazine; моден журнал fashion magazine **2** (*филмски*) newsreel

журнали́ст   *m* journalist, reporter

журналистика   *f* journalism

журнали́стка   *f* (*fem. form*) *see* журналист

З

за *prep* **1** (*expressing purpose, reason, target, destination*) for; to; се спрема за Божиќ to get ready for Christmas; патува за Скопје to leave for Skopje; подарок за син ми a present for my son; четка за заби toothbrush; машина за пишување typewriter; за и против pro and contra **2** (*expressing exchange, price*) for; око за око an eye for an eye; купи за готово to buy for cash; за сто денари for a hundred denars **3** (*expressing measurements*) by; за глава повисок taller by a head, a head taller; за километар подалеку a kilometre further **4** (*expressing wish, toast*) to; за ваше здравје! <to> your health! **5** (*with verbs of grasping, holding, etc.*) by; води за рака to lead by the hand; фати за коса to seize by the hair; задене некого за појас to catch s.o. by the belt **6** (*with verbs of appointing, naming, considering, etc.*) избере некого за пратеник to elect s.o. to parliament; смета некого за чесен човек to consider s.o. an honest man **7** (*expressing period of time*) in, within; ја сврши работата за два дена he finished the job in two days; за една година in a year's time **8** about, of, concerning; разговаравме за училиштето we were talking about the school; мисли за мене! think of me! знае за нешто to know about s.th. **9** (*of sequence, succession*) after; ден за ден day after (by) day; нога за нога step by step **10** (*with да*) so that, in order that; за да не lest; тој работи за да се истакне he works in order to be noticed **11** (*with дека*) because, since **12** (*preceding and modifying sense of other prepositions*) лек за од сипаница medicine for measles; за од мисла to keep one's mind off things **13** (*miscellaneous*) за име Божје in God's name, for God's sake; за малку almost; за права Бога for God's sake; blamelessly; for no reason; за чудо големо amazingly, astonishingly; за среќа fortunately; за жал unfortunately

за- *verbal prefix indicating* **1** *beginning of action*; запее to start singing **2** *perfectivization*; заангажира to engage **3** (*with ce*) *intensity, absorption*; се замисли to become lost in thought

заака *pf* **1** to lose one's way; to wander <off>, go astray, stray; заакале во гората they got lost in the forest **2** to begin to wander (roam)

заакува *impf of* заака

заангажи́ра (се) *pf see* ангажира (се)

заапе *pf* заапа *aor.* **I 1** to begin to bite/eat; to bite into **2** (*за куче и др.*) to bite, snap **II – ce** to <start to> bite each other

заапува (се) *impf of* заапе (се)

заарни се *pf colloq.* **1** to restore/improve relations; to make friends **2** (*with dat.*) тоа му се заарни he took a liking to it

заарнува се *impf of* заарни се

заб -и *m* **1** tooth; (*кај слон*) tusk; (*на змија*) fang; катни заби molars; кучешки (песји) заби canine teeth, eye-teeth; млечни заби milk teeth; вештачки заби false teeth; детето вади заб (заби) the child is cutting its teeth; ме болат заб I have toothache; паста за заби toothpaste; ❑ вооружен до заби armed to the teeth; има заб на некого to have it in for s.o.; земе некого на заб to develop a grudge against s.o.; заб не обелува he's as quiet as a mouse; не му дава заб да обели he doesn't give him a chance to open his mouth; скрца (чкрта) со заби to gnash one's teeth; стиска заби to grit one's teeth; му дошла душата во забите he is very tired; he is very ill; he is at his last gasp; мрмори низ заби to mutter (mumble) under one's breath; забот на времето the ravages of time; носи некого в заби to run rings round s.o.; покажува заби to show one's teeth; око за око, заб за заб *prov.* an eye for an eye, a tooth for a tooth; кај те боли забот, таму ти оди јазикот *prov.* the tongue ever turns to the aching tooth; на подарено коњ (подарено магаре) забите не му се гледаат *prov.* never look a gift-horse in the mouth **2** *see* забец

забава *f* **1** fun, pleasure, amusement **2** party

забава (се) *impf of* забави¹ (се)

забаваче *n* pre-school child, preschooler

забавен -вна *adj* amusing, entertaining; забавна музика light music; забавно четиво light reading; забавен парк amusement park, pleasure ground, *Brit.* funfair

забави¹ *pf* **I 1** to slow down *trans.* **2** to detain, hold up, make (*s.o.*) late **II – ce** to be late; се забави, уште го нема he's late, he's not here yet

забави² *pf* **I** to amuse, entertain **II – ce** to amuse o.s., have fun

забавиште *n* pre-school, kindergarten

забавко -овци *m dial.* shilly-shallier

забавник -ци *m* illustrated magazine

забавност *f* interesting item, curio; entertainment value

забавува (се)¹ *impf dial. of* забави¹ (се)

забавува (се)² *impf of* забави² (се) лудо се забавува to paint the town red; се забавува со некого to go steady with s.o.

забадијава & забадијала *adv colloq.* **1** (*бесплатно*) gratis, free, for nothing **2** (*залудно*) in vain; сè забадијала all in vain

забамка *pf* **I 1** to begin to beat (strike) **2** to start walloping (thrashing) **II – ce** to get into a fight

забан *m* short-sleeved/sleeveless jerkin, waistcoat (*part of a national costume*)

забандори *pf* **I 1** to start chattering **2** to tire (*s.o.*) with chatter **II – ce** to become engrossed in conversation

забандорува (се) *impf of* забандори (се)

забар *m* dentist; оди на забар to go to the dentist

забара *pf* **I 1** to start seeking (looking for)/demanding **2** *dial.* to start rummaging/rifling **3** *dial.* to start mixing **4** *dial.* to start touching, feeling **II – ce 1** to rummage in one's pockets **2** to get carried away searching

забарикади́ра *pf* **I** to barricade **II – ce** to barricade o.s. (*in*)

забарка *f* (*fem. form*) *see* забар
забарски *adj* dentist's
забарство *n* dentistry
забарува (се) *impf of* забара (се)
забат *adj* 1 with prominent (projecting) teeth, buck-toothed 2 *fig.* sharp-tongued, sarcastic, cutting, caustic; ❑ забато сонце winter sun
забатали *pf colloq.* I to leave, abandon; to neglect II – ce to neglect o.s., go to seed, go downhill
забаталува (се) *impf of* забатали (се)
забега *pf* 1 to start running 2 to run far away
забегне *pf* забегна *aor.* to escape; to run away, flee; to emigrate
забегнува *impf of* забегне
забел *m* reserve, reservation; fenced clearing (*in forest*)
забелее се *pf* to begin to show white; to glimmer, shine
забележи *pf* забележи, забележа *aor.* 1 (*здогледа, виде*) to notice, catch sight of; to observe, note; забележав дека не е дојден I noticed he hadn't come 2 (*приговори*) to remark, note; to comment 3 (*запише*) to write (note) down; to register, record
забележителен -лна *adj* outstanding, notable, remarkable, significant
забележлив *adj* noticeable; visible; забележлива разлика noticeable difference
забележливост *f* prominence, conspicuousness
забележува *impf of* забележи
забелешка *f* 1 remark, observation; му направи забелешка he reproached him 2 (*во книга*) note 3 (*во весник*) brief note, report
забели *pf* I 1 to paint white, whitewash <a little> 2 to begin to paint (*s.th.*) white II – ce *see* забелее се
забелува (се) *impf of* забели (се)
забен -бна *adj* dental; забен камен tartar (*on teeth*); забен лекар *see* забар, заболекар; забна клиника dental clinic; забен глас dental consonant
забер *m dial.* cliff, bluff, crag, rock
забере *pf* забра *aor.* I 1 to start taking/picking; ❑ му го забрал гајлето he started taking care/heed of him 2 to collect, round up, muster; забрале сè пред себе they drove all before them 3 to bother, pester; беше го забрал да му донесе млеко he had pestered him to bring him some milk 4 (*за рана*) to start festering II – ce to assemble/gather *intrans.* for a journey; ce забере на излет to set out on an excursion
заберува *impf of* забере I
забест *adj* 1 with prominent (projecting) teeth, buck-toothed 2 *fig.* sarcastic, cutting, caustic, biting 3 toothlike, toothed, serrated; jagged
забец -пци *m* 1 *Tech.* tooth; cog; (*на тркало*) cam; (*шилец*) prong 2 (*in pl*) reed (*on a loom*)
заби се *impf* to snarl (*also fig.*), show one's teeth
забива (се) *impf of* забие (се)
забие[1] *pf* заби *aor.* I to knock in, ram in; to thrust, plunge, stick (*во – into*); ❑ му заби нож во грбот he stabbed him in the back; му заби стрела he shot him with an arrow II – ce (*во*) to run into; (*за куршум*) to become embedded
забие[2] *pf* заби *aor.* I to start beating II – ce to start fighting
забиште *n augm. of* заб
забла *f colloq.* (*fem. form*) *see* забло

заблагодари <ce> *pf* to thank
заблагодарува <ce> *impf* заблагодари <ce>
заблажи *pf* I 1 to sweeten; to make milder 2 *dial.* to break one's fast II – ce to eat s.th. sweet, have a treat
заблажува *impf of* заблажи
заблазни *pf* (*with dat.*) to envy; to begin to envy; ❑ да му заблазниш на зборот he has the gift of eloquence
заблазнува *impf of* заблазни
заблеска *pf* to begin to glisten, sparkle, shine
заблескоти *pf see* заблеска
заблесне *pf* заблесна *aor.* to flash
заблеснува *impf of* заблесне
заблест *adj see* забест
забло -овци *m colloq.* 1 person with prominent teeth 2 *fig.* sharp-tongued/sarcastic person 3 *fig.* chatterbox
заблуда *f* mistake, error; држи во заблуда to keep s.o. misinformed; доведе во заблуда to mislead
заблуди *pf* I 1 to mislead, misinform, deceive 2 *rarely* to begin to wander (roam) II – ce to lose one's way, take the wrong road, go off course
заблудува (се) *impf of* заблуди (се)
забобол *m* toothache
забогати *pf* I to enrich II – ce to get rich
забоде *pf* I 1 to stick, thrust, drive in 2 (*прободе*) to stab, jab 3 to start pricking/stinging II – ce to stick (*во – into*) *intrans.*
забодина *pf* 1 to drive (*a horse*) faster, spur on 2 (*за коњ*) to gallop off; to start galloping
забодува *impf of* забоде
заболекар *m* dentist
заболи *pf* 1 to fall ill 2 *impers.* (*with dat.*) to start aching; ме заболи глава I have a headache; ❑ и тоа ме заболи! *sl.* I don't give a damn!
заболсне *pf* заболсна *aor. dial. see* заблесне
заболува *impf of* заболи
заболување *n* illness
заборав *m* oblivion; (*заборавност*) forgetfulness; падне во заборав to fall into oblivion
заборава (се) *impf of* заборави (се)
заборавен[1] *adj & pt* enthralled, carried away; целиот е заборавен he's quite carried away
заборавен[2] -вна *adj* forgetful
заборави *pf* I 1 to forget; го заборавив клучот I forgot my key; заборавив да се поздрава I forgot to say hello 2 (*пренебрегне*) to neglect, forget, abandon; го заборави својот долг he forgot his duty II – ce 1 (*занесе се*) to get carried away 2 (*претера со своето држење*) to forget o.s.
заборавност *f* forgetfulness
забори *pf* I to start knocking down II – ce to start fighting/wrestling
заборува (се) *impf of* забори (се)
заборчи (се) *pf colloq. see* задолжи (се) I 1, II 1
заборчува (се) *impf of* заборчи (се)
забошоти *pf* 1 to cover up, hush up; to suppress, keep secret 2 (*with dat.*) to cheat; to short-change; to give short weight
забошотува *impf of* забошоти
забради *pf* I to cover with a kerchief II – ce to put on a kerchief
забрадник -ци *m see* забратка
забрадува (се) *impf of* забради (се)
забразди *pf* 1 to begin to furrow 2 to cover with furrows; ❑ далеку си забраздил you've gone too far

забраздува *impf see* забразди 2

забрана *f* 1 prohibition, ban; embargo; забрана на увоз/извоз import/export ban; стави забрана to place a ban; стави забрана на имовината на должник to distrain a debtor's property 2 *dial.* fence

забранет *pt* forbidden; забранет влез/пристап no entry/admittance; забранети книги forbidden (banned) books; забрането е пушењето no smoking

забрани *pf* 1 to forbid, prescribe, ban; цензурата го забрани филмот the censor banned the film 2 *dial.* to defend, protect, preserve

забранува[1] *impf of* забрани

забранува[2] *pf* to <begin to> disturb, ruffle, agitate

забратка *f* kerchief, shawl

забрбори *pf* I 1 to babble; to start babbling 2 (*за вода*) to start gurgling/rippling/murmuring II – **се** to get carried away chattering

забрборува (се) *impf of* забрбори (се)

забремени *pf* to become pregnant, conceive *intrans.*

забременува *impf of* забремени

забрза *pf* I 1 to speed up, hurry *intrans.*, accelerate, start hurrying 2 to quicken *trans.*; ги забрза чекорите he quickened his pace; забрза темпо to accelerate; to step up the pace II – **се** *see* I 1

забрзан *pt* accelerated, fast; забрзано движење accelerated movement; забрзан пулс raised pulse rate

забрзува (се) *impf of* забрза (се)

забричи *pf* I 1 to start shaving *trans.* 2 to shave quickly *trans.* II – **се** 1 to start shaving *intrans.* 2 to shave quickly *intrans.*

забричува (се) *impf of* забричи (се)

забрише *pf* забриша *aor.* 1 to start wiping 2 to wipe lightly/superficially

забришува (се) *impf of* забрише (се)

забрка[1] *pf* I 1 to start driving/chasing 2 to drive/chase (*s.o., s.th.*) far away; го забрка в поле he chased him off into a field II – **се** to start rushing/hurrying

забрка[2] *pf* I 1 to confuse, mess up; to entangle 2 to start mixing, stirring 3 to embarrass, confuse II – **се** 1 to interfere 2 to get confused; to be embarrassed

забркува[1] **(се)** *impf of* забрка[1] (се)

забркува[2] **(се)** *impf of* забрка[2] (се)

забрлави & **забрливи** *pf* I 1 to infect with gid 2 *fig.* to confuse, embarrass II – **се** 1 to become infected with gid 2 to get confused/embarrassed

забрмчи *pf dial. see* забрчи

забрмчува *impf see* забрчува

заброди *pf* 1 to start floating/drifting/sailing 2 to start wandering (roaming)

заброи *pf* I to start counting II – **се** 1 to become engrossed in counting 2 (*згреши во броењето*) to miscount, make a mistake in counting

забројува (се) *impf of* заброи (се)

забрчи *pf* 1 to start humming/buzzing/muttering/ grumbling; пчелите забрчија the bees started buzzing 2 to start throbbing/roaring; моторот забрчи the engine started throbbing

забрчува *impf of* забрчи

забули *pf* to veil, mask, conceal (*also fig.*)

забулува *impf of* забули

забуна *f* confusion, embarrassment; error

забуни *pf* I 1 to confuse, perplex, embarrass 2 to begin to agitate (stir up) II – **се** 1 to get confused/rattled; to make a mistake 2 to rebel

забунува (се) *impf of* забунуи (се)

забуричка *pf* I 1 to <start to> stir/mix/muddle 2 to <start to> rummage II – **се** 1 to <start to> get into a muddle; to become confused 2 to get agitated

забуричкува (се) *impf of* забуричка (се)

забута *pf* I 1 to start pushing *trans.* 2 to tuck away, mislay, misplace; не знам кај сум ја забутал книгата I don't know what I did with the book II – **се** 1 to start pushing (shoving) *intrans.* 2 to get lost/ mislaid 3 to isolate o.s.; to bury o.s., hide away; to disappear; кај ли се забутал? where did he get to?

забуца *pf* I to prick, sting, to hammer in; забуца колец во земја to drive a stake into the ground II – **се** to plunge (*во – into*) *intrans.*

заваби *pf* to <start to> entice, lure

завади[1] *pf* 1 to start taking out 2 *colloq.* to start earning; си го завади лебот he's started to earn his living 3 to make (*people*) quarrel; завади комшии to set neighbour against neighbour II – **се** to be on bad-terms (*со – with*); to <start to> quarrel

завади[2] *pf* to start watering

завадува[1] **(се)** *impf of* завади[1] (се)

завадува[2] *impf of* завади[2]

завал *f.p.* 1 *m* pain; evil deed; misfortune; ништо завал да не сторам (чинам) I do no evil; I cause no trouble 2 *adj, indecl* wretched, miserable, pitiful 3 *interj* (*to express pity, sympathy*) alas, woe

завала *pf* I to start rolling *trans.* II – **се** to start rolling *intrans.*

завали *pf* to light (*a fire*); ја завали печката he lit the stove

завалка[1] *pf* I to soil, stain II – **се** to get dirty *intrans.*

завалка[2] **(се)** *pf see* завала (се)

завалува[1] *impf of* завали

завалува[2] **(се)** *impf of* завала (се)

заварди *pf* I 1 to preserve, guard, watch over 2 to start looking after; to start guarding II – **се** to keep away *intrans.* (*од – from*), keep clear (*of*); добро е да се завардиш it'll be best if you keep away

завардува (се) *impf of* заварди (се)

заварен *pt & adj* step-; заварени деца stepchildren

завареник -ци *m* stepson

завареница *f* stepdaughter

завари[1] *pf* 1 to find, come upon; to catch; ноќта ги завари в поле night caught (overtook) them in the fields; *fig.* ги завари на дело he caught them in the act 2 to acquire (*stepchildren*)

завари[2] *pf* I 1 to start cooking *trans.* 2 to boil up *trans.* 3 to weld; to solder II – **се** to start cooking *intrans.*

заварува[1] *impf of* завари[1]

заварува[2] **(се)** *impf of* завари[2] (се)

заварувач *m* 1 welder 2 soldering-iron

заведан *pt & adj* 1 covered, blocked with snow 2 absent-minded, distracted 3 crazy

завеаност *f* 1 absent-mindedness 2 craziness

завева (се) *impf of* завее (се)

заведе *pf* 1 to mislead, lead astray 2 (*девојка*) to seduce 3 (*запише*) to write down, record; ги заведе оценките he recorded the marks 4 (*воспостави*) to establish; заведе ред и мир he established law and order 5 *dial.* to lead, guide; го заведе дома he took him home

заведен *pt* misled, misguided

заведри се *pf impers.* to start clearing up (*of the weather*)

заведрува се *impf of* заведри се

заведува *impf of* заведе

завее *pf* завеа *aor.* I 1 (*за ветар*) to start blowing; завеа малку a light breeze sprang up 2 (*за снег*) to drift, block, make snowbound; снегот ги завеал патиштата the roads are blocked by snow 3 (*за снег*) to start falling; to start drifting 4 to start winnowing (*corn, grain*) II – се 1 *fig.* to wander off 2 *fig.* to get carried away 3 to become forgetful (absent-minded) 4 to go crazy

завејува (се) *impf of* завее (се)

завене *pf* завена *aor.* 1 to start fading 2 *fig.* to lie down, have a nap; само малку да завенам let me lie down for a while

завенее *pf* завенеа *aor. see* завене

завенува *impf of* завене & завенее

завера *f* plot, conspiracy

завери *pf* I to certify, attest, verify; to endorse, countersign; заверен препис certified copy, transcript II – се 1 (*даде завет*) to take (swear) an oath, give one's word 2 (*стани во завера*) to conspire

заверка *f* attestation, authentication

заверува¹ (се) *impf of* завери (се)

заверува² *pf* to believe; to begin to believe, gain belief in

заверувач *m* notary; verifier; заверувачи на записникот authorizers of the minutes/records

завеса *f* curtain, screen; димна завеса smoke-screen; ❑ крене завеса to raise a curtain

завет¹ *m* leeward side; sheltered spot; прави завет to shelter from the wind

завет² *m literary* 1 oath, promise; даде завет to swear an oath 2 testament; Стариот/Новиот завет the Old/New Testament 3 legacy, bequest

заветен¹ -тна *adj* sheltered <from the wind>

заветен² -тна *adj* cherished; hidden, arcane; заветна мисла innermost thought

заветрина *f* lee, sheltered side

заветува *pf & impf* I to promise II – се to take an oath, swear

завешта *pf* to bequeath

завештава *impf of* завешта

завештание -ија *n* will, testament, legacy

завештател *m* testator

завива¹ *impf of* завие¹

завива² *impf of* завие²

завивка *f* 1 wrapping, cover; (*јорган, ќебе*) blanket 2 (*завој, преврска*) bandage

завидели се *pf impers.* to dawn, *see* осамне

завиден -дна *adj* enviable; завиден успех enviable success 2 (*виден, забележителен*) noteworthy, notable, significant; prominent, eminent; завиден напредок significant improvement

завиди *pf* to envy (*некому за нешто – s.o. s.th.*), feel envy (*некому – of s.o.*)

завидлив *adj see* завислив

завидливец -вци *m see* зависливец, зависник

завидливка *f see* зависливка, зависница

завидливост *f see* зависливост

завидност *f* envy

завидува *impf* to envy

завие¹ *pf* зави *aor.* I 1 to wrap; to roll; to twist *trans.*,

see завитка I; *fig.* ги зави во црно he caused them sorrow 2 to turn, begin to turn *intrans.* 3 (*за пат*) to bend, twist *intrans.* II – се 1 to wrap o.s.; (*со покривка*) to cover o.s. 2 to curl up *intrans.* (*of animals*), *see* завитка се 3 to twist *intrans.*

завие² *pf* зави *aor.* (*почне да вие*) to start howling

завика *pf* 1 to start shouting; to shout out 2 *rarely* to start calling (summoning)

завира *impf of* завре

зависен -сна *adj* 1 dependent; зависна положба dependent position; зависна територија dependency; *Gram.* зависни реченици subordinate clauses 2 addicted; зависен од хероин addicted to heroin

зависи *impf* to depend (*од – on*); to be subject to; тоа не зависи од мене that doesn't depend on me

завислив *adj* envious

зависливец -вци *m* envious person

зависливка *f* (*fem. form*) *see* зависливец

зависливост *f* envy, envious nature

зависник -ци *m* 1 *see* зависливец 2 addict

зависница *f see* зависливка

зависништво *n* addiction

зависно *adv* depending; зависно од нешто depending on s.th.

зависност *f* dependence, dependency; (*потчинетост*) subordination

завист *f* envy; тоа го стори од завист he did that out of envy

завитка *pf* I to start rolling/wrapping; to wrap; to roll *trans.*; завитка нешто во хартија to wrap s.th. in paper II – се to roll up *intrans.*; to wrap o.s. <up>

завиткува (се) *impf of* завитка (се)

завитли *pf* I to turn *trans.* II – се to turn *intrans.*

завишти *pf* to neigh

завјаса (се) *pf colloq. see* забрза (се)

завлада *pf see* завладее

завладее *pf* завладеа *aor.* 1 to conquer, occupy; (*град, крепост*) to seize, take, capture 2 to <start to> reign; *fig.* завладеа мир peace reigned again

завладичи *pf* I to appoint as bishop II – се to be installed as bishop

завладува *impf of* завладее

завлегува *impf of* завлезе

завлезе *pf* 1 (*во*) to start entering 2 to go deeper, delve (*во – into*); тој завлезе во работата he went thoroughly into the matter

завлезува *impf see* завлегува

завлекува *impf of* завлече

завлече *pf* I 1 to carry away, sweep away; водата го завлече the water carried it/him away 2 to drag in, involve, embroil; завлече некого во лоша работа to involve s.o. in a conspiracy 3 to drag out, prolong; ја завлече работата he dragged the matter out II – се 1 to <begin to> drag *intrans.*; to drag o.s. along (*with difficulty*) 2 *rare* to withdraw, hide *intrans.* 3 to drag on *intrans.*; се завлече работата the matter dragged on

завлечка *pf* I 1 to begin to drag (*with difficulty*) *trans.* 2 to drag off (*with difficulty*) 3 *see* завлече 3 II – се 1 to begin to drag o.s. along (*with difficulty*) 2 to withdraw, hide, *see* завре се 3 *see* завлече се 3

завлечкува *impf of* завлечка

завлечува (се) *impf see* завлекува (се)

завод *m* 1 organization, establishment, bureau; завод

за вработување employment office; завод за испитување на пазарот market research institute; завод за осигурување insurance company; завод за патенти Patent Office; завод за социјално осигурување Social Security <Bureau> **2** factory, plant, mill, works

заводлив *adj* seductive; заводлива жена seductive woman

заводник -ци *m* seducer

заводница & **заводничка** *f* seductress, temptress, siren, vamp

заводски *adj* organization's, institutional; factory, works *attrib.*

завој -ои *m* **1** (*свиок*) curve, bend; (*за брод, кола*) turn **2** *see* преврска **3** *fig.* turnabout, U-turn, turning point; завој во политиката a complete change of policy

завојува *pf* **1** to begin a war; to go to war **2** *rare* to capture, take, occupy (*in battle*); *fig.* (*see* извојува) to win, gain (*in a struggle, by work, etc.*)

завојувач *m* conqueror

завојувачки *adj* of conquest; aggressive, aggressor's

завор *m* & **заворна** *f* bolt

заврати *pf* **1** to turn up, roll up (*sleeves, apron, etc.*) **2** to turn *trans.*

завратница *f see* затилница

завратува *impf of* заврати, *see* завраќа

завраќа *impf of* заврати

завре *pf* **I** to hide *trans.*, conceal **II** – **се** to hide o.s., go into hiding, withdraw

заврз *m* **1** knot; network **2** *see* зародок, никулец

заврзе *pf* заврза *aor.* **I 1** to bind, tie; заврзе некому раце to tie s.o.'s hands; заврзе некому очи to blindfold s.o. **2** to start tying **3** (*за плод*) to germinate, set **4** to provoke, start; ❏ заврзе бој to start a fight; заврзе пријателство to form a friendship; заврзе разговор to strike up a conversation **II – се 1** to tie o.s. to start *intrans.*; се заврза разговор a conversation started

заврзок -ци *m* **1** *see* врзулец **2** *see* зародок, никулец

заврзува *impf of* заврзе

заврива *impf of* заврие

заврие *pf* завре *aor.* **1** to start boiling **2** to boil up/over **3** *fig.* to seethe, lose one's temper

заврне[1] *pf* заврна *aor.* to start raining/hailing/snowing; заврна силен дожд/снег it started raining/snowing heavily; *impers.* заврна it started raining/snowing

заврне[2] **(се)** *pf* заврна *aor. dial. see* врати (се)

завpница *f* bolt, bar, latch

заврнува *impf of* заврне[2]

заврска *f* **1** *rare, literary* plot, *see* заплет **2** *dial.* bundle, *see* врзулец

заврти *pf* заврти, заврте *aor.* **I 1** to <start to> turn, twist *trans.*; to turn off; to turn over *trans.*; заврти тркало to turn a wheel; заврти славина to turn off a tap; заврти страница to turn a page; ❏ заврти некому ум to turn s.o.'s head; го заврти листот од другата страна 1. to turn over a new leaf 2. to go to the dogs **2** (*вовре со вртење*) to screw up/on/down **3** to turn *intrans.*; заврти влево to turn left **4** to save (*money*) **5** to start; to set up; заврти куќа to set up house; заврти на песна to start singing; заврти оро to start off the *oro* **6** to start hurting (aching); ногата ме заврте I felt a pain in my leg **II – се 1** to

<start to> turn *intrans.*; to turn round, rotate, revolve **2** to stay for a while; не се заврти дома ни ден he didn't spend so much as a day at home **3** (*with dat.*) to become giddy; ми се заврте умот I felt giddy, my head started spinning

завртка[1] *f Tech.* bolt

завртка[2] *pf* **I** *see* заврти 3 **II – се** *see* заврти се 2

завртува (се) *impf of* заврти (се)

завршен[1] *pt* complete<d>, finished

завршен[2] -шна *adj* concluding, final; завршен испит final exam<ination>; завршен збор closing address; завршна сметка annual balance sheet; завршна обработка finish<ing>

завршеност *f* completeness; perfection

заврши[1] *pf* **I** to complete, finish *trans.*; to conclude; to finish school; to finish talking **II – се** to finish, end *intrans.*

заврши[2] *pf* to start threshing

заврши[3] *pf colloq.* to start arranging an engagement (betrothal)

завршница *f Chess* end-game, ending

завршок -ци *m* **1** *Gram.* suffix; ending **2** end, conclusion

завршува[1] **(се)** *impf of* заврши[1] (се)

завршува[2] *impf of* заврши[2]

завтаса *pf* **I 1** to <start to> catch up (*некого – with s.o.*) **2** to find, come upon, *see* завари[1] **II– се** to catch up with each other

завчас *adv* **1** in a minute, right away **2** very quickly, very soon

завчера *adv* the day before yesterday

завчерашен -шна *adj* the day before yesterday's

загаден *adj* polluted; загадена вода polluted water

загаденост *f* pollution

загади *pf* **I** to pollute; to dirty, soil **II – се** to become polluted; to get dirty

загадочен -чна *adj* enigmatic, mysterious, puzzling; загадочна насмевка enigmatic smile

загадува (се) *impf of* загади (се)

загадување *n* pollution; загадување на околината environmental pollution; заштита од загадување pollution control

загадувач *m* pollutant; загадувач на водите water pollutant

загази *pf* **1** to start treading **2** to step (*into s.th.*); загази во калта he stepped into the mud **3** *fig.* to become involved (*во – in*); загази во војна to become embroiled in war; ❏ загазен сум до гуша во долгови I am up to my neck in debt

загазува *impf of* загази

загалати *pf dial.* **1** to dirty, soil **2** *fig.* to start spoiling **3** *fig.* to start swearing (blaspheming, cursing)

загар *m* hound, hunting dog

загаси *pf* **I** to turn off, extinguish **II – се** to go out (*of a light, fire*)

загасне *pf* загасна *aor. see* загаси (се)

загаснува *impf see* загасува (се)

загасува (се) *impf of* загаси (се)

загатка *f* **1** riddle, mystery; загатка на природата a riddle (mystery) of nature **2** (*предвестување*) hint, sign, indication; portent

загатне *pf* загатна *aor.* **1** to hint at, mention in passing **2** to herald, announce; to presage, foreshadow

загатнува *impf of* загатне

загине *pf* загина *aor.* **I 1** to perish, be killed **2** to disappear, get lost **3** to lose; го загинал прстенот he lost the ring **II – се** to get lost

загинува (се) *impf of* загине (се)

заглавен -вна *adj see* насловен

заглави *pf* **I 1** to wedge, jam *trans.*; (*за секира, мотика и др.*) to fix (*an axe-head in position*) **2** *see* сврши² **3** *fig.* to perish; to get lost; заглавил некаде he has disappeared somewhere **II – се 1** to get wedged (jammed); му се заглавил прстот his finger got stuck **2** *see* сврши² се

заглавие -ија *&* **заглавје** *n* chapter heading, title; (*во писмо*) heading; (*во весник*) headline

заглавка *f* wedge

заглавува (се) *impf of* заглави (се)

заглад *pf* **1** to start stroking **2** to smooth out, smooth over, iron out (*also fig.*)

загладни *pf* to get hungry

загладнува *impf of* загладни

загладува[1] *impf of* заглади

загладува[2] *pf see* загладни

загледа *pf* **I 1** to start looking **2** to start looking after **3** to begin telling fortunes (*by cards, etc.*) **4** to catch sight of, note, notice, discover **II – се 1** to start looking at each other **2** to peer, stare, look hard (*во – at*); to fix (rivet) one's eyes (*во – on*); ❏ кај си се загледал? what are you staring at?

заглиби <се> *pf* to get stuck; *fig.* <се> заглиби во долгови to sink into debt

заглибува <се> *impf of* заглиби <се>

заглувее *pf* заглувеа *aor. see* заглувне

заглувне *pf.* заглувна *aor.* to go deaf; му заглувнаа ушите he went deaf

заглувнува *impf of* заглувне

заглупави *pf see* заглупи

заглупи *pf* **1** to stultify **2** to become stupid

заглупува *impf of* заглупи

заглушен -шна *adj* deafening; заглушна врева deafening noise

заглуши *pf* **1** to deafen **2** to deaden, muffle, smother; to drown out **3** *fig.* to stifle; тој го заглуши гласот на совеста he stifled the voice of conscience **4** (*за растенија*) to choke, overgrow, overrun

заглушува *impf of* заглуши

заглушувачки *adj* deafening

загнаси *pf* to soil, dirty

загнасува *impf of* загнаси

загне се *pf* загна *aor.* (*with dat.*) **1** to pursue, rush (*after s.o.*) **2** to rush (*at s.o.*); ми се загна he rushed (flew) at me

загнезди се *pf* **1** to build a nest **2** *fig.* to settle in; (*се закорени*) to take root **3** to outstay one's welcome

загнездува се *impf of* загнезди се

загнива *impf of* загние

загние *pf* загни *aor.* to begin to rot; to rot, decay, perish

загнои *pf* загноја, загнои *aor.* **I 1** (*за рана*) to start festering, suppurating **2** (*за нива*) to manure, fertilize **II – се** to start festering

загнојува (се) *impf of* загнои (се)

загнува се *impf of* загне се

заговара *impf of* заговори

заговор *m* plot, conspiracy; заговор против државата conspiracy against the state

заговори *pf* **I 1** to start talking **2** to address (*s.o.*), accost (*s.o.*), engage (*s.o.*) in conversation, strike up a conversation (*with s.o.*); to detain/distract s.o. (*by talking*) **II – се** to get carried away talking; to forget the time in conversation

заговорник *m* conspirator, plotter

заговорница *&* **заговорничка** *f* (*fem. form*) *see* заговорник

заговорнички *adj* conspiratorial

заголне *pf* заголна *aor.* заголне душа to fortify o.s. (*with food*)

заголнува *impf of* заголне

загон *m arch.* rood, dönüm (*square measure: 920 m²*)

загори *pf* **1** to start burning *trans.*; to burn *trans.*; загори дрва to start burning wood **2** (*за јадење*) to burn *intrans.*; гравот загорел the beans have <got> burnt **3** *fig.* to be parched; to thirst (*за – for*); загори завода to be dying of thirst

загорува *impf of* загори

загорчи *pf* **1** to become bitter; **2** to make bitter; *fig.* животот ми го загорчи he has made my life a misery

загорчува *impf of* загорчи

заграб *m* armful; load (*on the shoulder – of wood, hay*)

заграби *pf* to rake, pile up (*hay, etc.*)

заграда *f* **1** fence, railing; enclosure **2** bracket; parenthesis; ❏ речено во загради incidentally; by the way

загради *pf* **I 1** (*огради*) to fence <in>, enclose; (*со ѕид*) to wall in; (*опколи*) to surround, encircle **2** (*река*) to dam; (*препречи*) to block **3** to put in brackets/parentheses **II – се** to fence o.s. in

заградува (се) *impf of* загради (се)

загреан *pt* **1** warmed up **2** *fig.* interested

загреб *m* **1** dug-up earth; pawed turf (*as by an animal*) **2** rash, hives

Загреб *m* Zagreb, *arch.* Agram

загребе *pf* загреба *aor.* **I 1** to scrape up; (*застружe*) to <begin> grind (sharpen) **2** to scratch **3** to start-grinding (grating) *intrans.* **II – се 1** to get scratched **2** to scratch o.s.

загребува (се) *impf of* загребе (се)

загрева *impf of* загрее

загревен -вна *adj see* огревен

загрее *pf* загреа *aor.* **I 1** (*затопли*) to warm (heat) up *trans.*; загрее вода to heat water **2** *fig.* to fire with enthusiasm; to catch (*s.o.'s*) imagination **3** (*за сонце*) to start warming/shining **II – се 1** (*затопли се*) to warm up *intrans.*; се загреа собата the room warmed up **2** *fig.* to become enthusiastic; се загреав за таа работа I am very excited about that work

загрепски *adj* Zagreb *attrib.*

загрепчанин -ни *m* person from Zagreb

загрепчанка *f* (*fem. form*) *see* загрепчанин

загреши *pf* **I 1** to start making mistakes **2** *see* згреши 1–3 **II – се** to go awry; се загреши работата things have gone wrong

загрижен *pt* **1** anxious, worried, concerned; загрижено лице worried expression **2** caring; тој е многу загрижен за децата he takes great care of the children

загриженост *f* **1** anxiety, concern **2** conscientiousness

загрижи *pf* **I** to worry, upset, disturb **II – се 1** to get worried (upset, disturbed) **2** to take into consideration; to start caring (*за – for*)

загрижува (се) *impf of* загрижи (се)

загрижувачки *adj* worrying, disturbing

загризе *pf* загриза *aor.* **I 1** to bite <into>; to start biting/chewing **2** to start worrying/tormenting *trans.*; го загриза совеста his conscience started worrying him **II – се 1** to start tormenting o.s. **2** to start quarrelling

загризува (се) *impf of* загризе (се)

загрли *pf* to earth up (*roots, plants*)

загрлува *impf of* загрли

загрми *pf* загрми, загрме *aor.* to start thundering; to roar, boom; загрмеа топови the guns <started to> roar; му загрме гласот his voice started thundering; салата загрме од аплауз the hall rang with applause

загрмува *impf of* загрми

загрне *pf* загрна *aor.* **I 1** to cover, drape, wrap **2** *dial.* to encircle, envelop; (*прегрне*) to embrace **II – се 1** to cover o.s., wrap (cover) up *intrans.*; to wrap o.s. up in a rug/blanket *intrans.* **2** *dial.* (*прегрне се*) to embrace one another

загрнува *impf of* загрне

загрози *pf* **I 1** to endanger, imperil, menace, threaten **2** *dial.* to disfigure, deform **II – се 1** to disfigure o.s. **2** *dial.* to become ugly

загрозува (се) *impf of* загрози (се)

загруби *pf* **1** (*стане груб*) to become coarse (crude, vulgar) **2** (*стане грд*) to grow ugly **2** (*направи груб*) to coarsen *trans.*; to roughen *trans.*; to vulgarize **3** (*направи грд*) to make ugly

загуба *f* loss; продаде со загуба to sell at a loss; тој е во загуба he is losing money; загуба од работењето operating loss

загубен *pt* lost; mislaid; *fig.* (*глупав*) slow, wanting, (*безнадежен*) hopeless; загубен човек hopeless case; nincompoop; загубена работа lost cause

загуби *pf* **I 1** to lose; ❑ загуби свест to lose consciousness, to faint; загуби трпение to lose patience; загуби ум to lose one's reason; загуби пат to lose one's way; загуби на карти to lose at cards; загуби натпревар to lose a game (match); загуби од предвид to lose sight of **2** *arch.* to execute, kill **II – се 1** (*исчезне*) to disappear; (*погреши пат*) to lose one's way **2** (*пропадне сосем*) to be completely ruined, be lost **3** (*загуби свест*) to lose consciousness, faint, pass out **4** *f.p.* to kill o.s.

загубува (се) *impf of* загуби (се)

зад *prep* **1** behind, beyond, on the other side of; зад куќата behind the house; сонцето зајде зад планината the sun set behind the mountain; ❑ зад грб behind s.o.'s back **2** after; зад Велигден after Easter

задава *impf of* зададе

задавен *adj* (*задушен*) strangled, smothered

задави *pf* **I 1** to choke, strangle; to smother; to drown *trans.* **2** to crush **3** to start choking/strangling/smothering *trans.* **II – се 1** to choke *intrans.*; to strangle o.s.; to drown *intrans.* **2** to start choking *intrans.*

зададе *pf* **I 1** (*задача*) to set **2** (*удар, болка*) to inflict; to cause **3** to start setting/causing/inflicting **II – се** to appear; to show o.s.; се зададе темен облак a dark cloud appeared

задача *f* assignment, task, duty; си постави задача to set o.s. a task; домашна задача homework;

писмена задача test paper; задачи во економската политика economic policy targets; изврши задача to accomplish a task

задвижи *pf* **I** to set in motion **II – се** to start moving *intrans.*

задвижува (се) *impf of* задвижи (се)

задгробен -бна *adj* beyond the grave; задгробен живот life after death, life beyond the grave

задебели *pf* **I** to thicken, make thicker **II – се** to become thicker; to swell, bulge *intrans.* (*of muscles, joints*)

задебелува (се) *impf of* задебели (се)

задебелување *n* bump, knot, knob

задева *impf* **I** to tease **II – се** to tease (*со*); не задевај се don't tease!

задека *conj colloq.* because; не дојде, задека беше болен he didn't come, because he was ill

заден -дна *adj* **1** rear, back; задна врата back (rear) door **2** last; заден збор last word **3** *fig.* secret; задна намера ulterior motive, secret objective; secret agenda

задене *pf* задена *aor.* **I** to stick (*into*) *trans.*; to tuck; задене игла во перниче to stick a needle into a cushion; ❑ задене некого за појас to be too good for s.o., outdo s.o. **II – се** to catch, get stuck (*on s.th.*)

задени се *pf impers.* to begin to dawn

заденува (се)[1] *impf of* задене (се)

заденува се[2] *impf of* задени се

задими *pf* **I 1** to fill with smoke *trans.*; задими соба to fill a room with smoke **2** to light (*a cigarette*) **3** to smoke *intrans.*, emit smoke; to start smoking *intrans.* **II – се** to fill with smoke *intrans.*, become smoky

задимува (се) *impf of* задими (се)

задира (се) *impf of* задре (се)

задирен -рна *adj see* задорлив

задирлив *adj see* задорлив

задише & задиши *pf* задиши, задиша *aor.* **I 1** to start breathing **2** to get (*s.o.*) breathing, resuscitate **II – се** to become breathless, get out of breath

задишува (се) *impf of* задиши (се)

задлаби *pf* **I 1** to start digging out, hollowing out **2** to drive (ram) (*s.th.*) deep (*into s.th.*) **3** *fig. see* задлабочи **II – се** to become engrossed (*во – in*)

задлабочен *pt* **1** sunk, engrossed (*in thought, etc.*) **2** profound, thorough

задлабоченост *f* **1** preoccupation **2** thoroughness, depth

задлабочи *pf* **I** to deepen, make more profound (*thoughts, etc.*); (*знаења*) to extend **II – се** to become engrossed (*во – in*)

задлабочува (се) *impf of* задлабочи (се)

задлабува (се) *impf of* задлаби (се)

задник -ци *m* **1** buttocks, backside **2** (*за коњ, магаре*) фрла задници to kick with the hind legs **3** back (*of a garment*)

заднина *f* **1** background **2** *see* тил 2

заднински *adj* rear, back

заднина *f* **1** *see* задник 1 **2** *see* задник 3 **3** back part; tail end; end dancer (*of an oro*)

задобри *pf* **I** to cheer (*s.o.*) up *trans.*; to improve *trans.* **II – се** to improve relations (*со – with*); to improve *intrans.*

задобрува (се) *impf of* задобри (се)

задоволен -лна *adj* pleased; contented; satisfied (*од – with*) ❏ задоволен е и од (со) малку to be thankful for small mercies

задоволеност *f* contentment; satisfaction

задоволи *pf* I to satisfy; to please; задоволи потреба/услов to satisfy (meet) a requirement/condition; задоволи очекувања to live up to expectations II – ce to be satisfied; to satisfy o.s.

задоволителен -лна *adj* satisfactory; задоволително решение satisfactory solution

задоволство *n* satisfaction; contentment; pleasure; ❏ со задоволство with pleasure; за свое задоволство for one's own satisfaction/pleasure; наоѓа задоволство во to take delight in; причинува задоволство to give pleasure

задоволува (се) *impf of* задоволи (се)

задои *pf* 1 to start nursing, start breast-feeding 2 *fig.* to fill, imbue; задои со идеали to imbue with ideals

задојница *f* nursing mother; wet nurse

задолжен *pt* 1 responsible, in charge; тој е задолжен за тоа he is responsible for that 2 indebted, in debt; задолжен во банката in debt to the bank; задолжена земја indebted country

задолжение -ија *n* 1 responsibility; *Comm.* liability; земе (прими) задолжение to undertake (accept) responsibility 2 (*обврска*) obligation, duty

задолжи *pf* I 1 to obligate, make (*s.o.*) one's debtor; тој ме има задолжено he has put me in his debt 2 to mortgage; задолжи имот to mortgage an estate 3 (*запише како долг*) to debit; задолжи сметка to charge (debit) an account II – ce 1 to get into debt, incur debts 2 to undertake; се задолжив да го свршам тоа I undertook to finish that

задолжителен -лна *adj* obligatory, compulsory; binding

задолжува (се) *impf of* задолжи (се)

задоми *pf* I 1 to set up house 2 (*омажи*) to marry off (*a daughter*) II – ce to marry *intrans.*; to settle down

задомува (се) *impf of* задоми (се)

задорица *m & f* restless child; tease; bully

задориче *n dim. of* задорица; naughty, mischievous child

задорлив *adj* cheeky, cocky, pert; (*кавгаџија*) quarrelsome

задоцнет *adj* late, tardy; belated

задоцни *pf* I 1 to be late; гостите задоцнија the guests arrived late; задоцнивме со ракописите we are late with the manuscripts 2 to deliver late; to delay, hold up II – ce to arrive (be) late

задоцнува (се) *impf of* задоцни (се)

задоцнување *n* lateness; delay; задоцнување на испорака delay in delivery

задразни *pf* to anger, irritate, upset

задраска *pf* 1 to start scraping/scratching 2 to start scribbling 3 (*пречкрта*) to cross out

задраскува *impf of* задраска

задре *pf* I to tease, needle II – ce to cause trouble, start a quarrel

задреме *pf* задрема *aor.* 1 to doze a little 2 to nod off, doze off

задржан *pt* detained; сите права задржани all rights reserved

задржи *pf* задржа *aor.* I 1 to detain, hold back, retard, delay; задржи некого на ручек to invite s.o.

to stay for lunch; задржи во притвор to remand in custody 2 (*земе*) to withhold, retain; (*одбие*) to deduct; (*зачува*) to reserve; задржи право to retain one's right; задржи некому место to reserve a seat for s.o. 3 to hold/support for a while II – ce to stay, linger; задржи се на некое прашање to dwell on a question

задржува (се) *impf of* задржи (се)

задрипетле *n colloq.* tease

задроби *pf* I 1 to break up, crumble *trans.* 2 to start crumbling *trans.* 3 to start chattering, start talking nonsense II – ce to start crumbling (breaking up) *intrans.*

задробува (се) *impf of* задроби (се)

задруга *f* 1 collective; co-operative; земјоделска задруга agricultural co-operative; потрошувачка задруга consumers' co-operative; станбена задруга housing co-operative 2 *Hist.* clan

задругар *m* 1 member of a collective (co-operative) 2 clan member

задругарка *f* (*fem. form*) *see* задругар

задругарски *adj* collective, co-operative; clan *attrib.*

задругарство *n* co-operative movement (organization); co-operative sector

задругарува *pf* to begin to be friends, begin to be friendly (*co – with*)

задружен -жна *adj* collective; задружно движење collective movement

задршка *f rare* 1 hindrance, difficulty 2 slow-down, stoppage, hold-up 3 delay

задув *m* asthma

задува *pf* to start blowing; *impers.* пак задува the wind's sprung up

задужбина *f* 1 endowment, charitable foundation 2 requiem, mass

задума *pf dial.* I 1 to remember; to make a mental note of, *see* запамети 2 to cause to think 3 to begin to talk II – ce to become pensive; to become concerned

задумани (се) *pf see* запраши (се)

задумка *pf* 1 to start beating (*a drum*) 2 to start beating; тапаните задумкаа the drums started beating 3 *dial.* (*дете*) to rock, swing *trans.*, dandle

задутре *adv* the day after tomorrow

задутрешен -шна *adj* the day after tomorrow's

задуша *f see* задушница; за задуша му даваат they are celebrating a requiem for him

задушен[1] -шна *adj* of All Souls' Day; задушна недела All Souls' Day; задушни дни days consecrated to remembrance of the dead

задушен[2] *pt* choked, strangled; smothered; (*за звук*) muffled; (*со гас*) asphyxiated; *fig.* задушено чувство suppressed feeling

задуши[1] *pf* I 1 to choke, strangle; to smother, stifle, suffocate 2 *fig.* (*чувство*) to suppress, smother; го задуши во себе чувството на страв he suppressed his fear 3 *fig.* (*востание*) to put down, suppress, stamp out II – ce to choke *intrans.*; to suffocate *intrans.*

задуши[2] *pf* 1 to start sniffing 2 to start spying, prying

задушлив *adj* 1 choking; задушлив гас poisonous (asphyxiating) gas 2 asthmatic 3 (*за воздух*) stuffy; (*за времето*) oppressive, sultry

задушливост *f* choking atmosphere; (*жега*) sweltering heat; (*за воздух*) stuffiness

задушница *f* requiem, requiem service; All Souls' Day

задушува (се) *impf of* задуши¹ (се)

заедница *f* community; society, association; partnership, unit; месна заедница local community; интересна заедница community of interest; деловна заедница business association; работна заедница working collective; брачна заедница married couple; првобитна заедница primitive society (community)

заедничен -чна *adj dial. see* заеднички¹

заеднички¹ *adj* common; shared, joint; communal; заеднички јазик common language; заеднички интереси common interests; заедничка кујна shared kitchen; заедничка акција joint action; заедничка обврска joint liability; заеднички потфат joint venture

заеднички² *adv* in common; jointly; *Leg., Comm.* заеднички и солидарно jointly and severally

заедно *adv* together, jointly; сите заедно all together; сè заедно taken as a whole; all in all; заедно со together with

заем *m* loan; државен заем government loan; хипотекарен заем mortgage; даде (одобри) заем to grant a loan; земе заем to obtain/raise a loan; земе на заем to borrow; даде на заем to lend

заема (се) *impf of* заеме (се), *see* зајмува (се)

заеме (се) *pf see* зајми (се)

заемен -мна *adj* mutual, reciprocal; заемна помош mutual aid

заемка *f* 1 *Ling.* loan-word 2 *Comm.* loan; borrowing

заемник -ци *m* member of a voluntary working party

заемница *f* 1 voluntary working party 2 (*fem. form*) *see* заемник

заемнички *adj* of a voluntary work-group/working party; заемнички член working party member

заемност *f* mutuality, reciprocity

заемобарател *m* loan applicant

заемодавец *m* lender, creditor

заемопримач *m* borrower, debtor

заесени *pf* I 1 to begin to spend the autumn (*Am.* fall); заесенивме на туѓина autumn found us abroad 2 *see* II II – се *impers.* to set in, start (*of autumn*); се заесени веќе autumn has started already

заесенува (се) *impf of* заесени (се)

заечи *pf* to <start to> echo, resound

зажали *pf* 1 to start grieving (mourning) 2 to feel regret

зажалува *impf of* зажали

зажари *pf* I 1 to <start to> heat, make red-hot; (*огин*) to stir, stoke 2 (*за коприва*) to start stinging II – се to become red-hot

зажарува (се) *impf of* зажари (се)

зажегли *pf* 1 to yoke 2 *fig.* to subjugate, enslave

зажеглува *impf of* зажегли

зажеднее *pf see* зажедни

зажедни *pf* 1 to get thirsty 2 *fig.* to <start to> crave for, long for, yearn for

зажеже *pf* зажеже, зажежа *aor.* 1 to start producing heat (burning, being hot) 2 *impers. fig.* (*with acc.*) to hurt; ме зажежа it hurt me 3 to start heating (*iron, etc.*) *trans.*

зажежува *impf of* зажеже

зажени *pf* I to set about marrying off (*a son*) II – се to set about getting married (*of a man*)

заживее *pf* заживеа *aor.* to start living; to get on to

good terms (*со – with*), start getting on (*with*); си заживеаја заедно they started living together

заживи се *pf* to take root; to become settled

заживува *impf of* заживее

зажолтее *pf* зажолтеа *aor.* I *see* зажолти 1 II – се *see* зажолти се

зажолти *pf* I 1 to <begin to> turn yellow *intrans.* 2 to turn yellow *trans.*; to colour/paint yellow II – се to turn yellow

зажолтува (се) *impf of* зажолти (се)

зазабица *f* gingivitis; ❑ го фаќа зазабица his mouth waters

зазбива <се> *pf* to be short/out of breath; to puff and pant

зазбиван *pt & adj* out of breath, panting, breathless

зазбиваност *f* shortness of breath

зазбивта <се> *pf see* зазбива <се>

зазбивтан *adj see* зазбиван

зазбивтаност *f see* зазбиваност

зазбира *pf* I to start collecting/gathering *trans.*; зазбира марки to start collecting stamps II – се to start assembling (gathering together) *intrans.*

зазборува *pf* I 1 to start speaking (talking) 2 to distract (*by talking*) II – се to become engrossed in conversation

зазвучи *pf* to begin to sound; to resound, ring out; зазвучи неговиот глас his voice rang out

зазвучува *impf of* зазвучи

заздравее *pf* заздравеа *aor. see* заздрави 3

заздрави *pf* I 1 to strengthen, consolidate *trans.*; ги заздрави своите позиции he consolidated his position 2 (*за рана*) to heal *trans.* 3 (*за рана*) to heal *intrans.*; раната ми заздрави my wound has healed II – се 1 to strengthen *intrans.* 2 to recover, get well again

заздравува *impf of* заздрави

зазеленее <се> *pf* зазеленеа <се> *aor. see* зазелени <се>

зазелени <се> *pf* to start turning green

зазеленува <се> *impf of* зазелени <се> & зазеленее <се>

зазема¹ *impf of* заземе

зазема² *pf* to start taking

заземе *pf* заземе *aor.* 1 (*завладее*) to occupy, take, seize; го заземоа градот they occupied (took) the town 2 (*земе*) to take up, assume; заземе висока положба to take up an important position; заземе став to adopt a stance/position; to assume an attitude II – се to champion, support, intercede (*за – for*)

заземји *pf Elec.* to earth, *Am.* ground

заземјува *impf of* заземји

зазимее *pf dial. see* зазими

зазими & зазимува *pf* I 1 to start over-wintering; зазимивме на туѓина winter found us abroad 2 *see* II II – се *impers.* to set in, begin (*of winter*)

зазира *impf of* зазре

зазјапа <се> *pf* 1 to stare, gape (*во – at*) 2 to start staring, gaping (*at*)

зазјапува <се> *impf of* зазјапа <се>

зазнае *pf* зазна *aor.* 1 to become conscious (aware) of 2 to get to know, become acquainted (*со – with*)

зазор *m* 1 (*срам*) shame; disgrace; нема зазор he has no shame, he's shameless; зазор ми е да те погледнам I am ashamed to look at you **2** (*одвратност*) revulsion, aversion

зазорен -рна *adj* **1** (*срамен*) shameful, disgraceful **2** (*одвратен*) repulsive, disgusting

зазори <**се**> *pf* to dawn; зора се зазори day has dawned; *impers.* <**се**> зазори веќе it has dawned already

зазорлив *adj* **1** (*срамежлив*) bashful, shy **2** (*бојазлив*) timid, fearful, timorous

зазорува <**се**> *impf of* зазори <**се**>

зазре *pf* **1** (*од срам*) to be ashamed; to feel embarrassed; (*од страв*) to be afraid **2** (*одбегне*) to flee (*од – from*), avoid, shun **3** to feel an aversion (*од – for*); to shrink (*from*), shudder (*at*)

зазрева *impf of* зазрее

зазрее *pf* зазре *aor.* to start ripening; to grow ripe, ripen; *fig. poet.* to mature

зазвони *pf* зазвони *aor.* to ring; зазвонив на вратата I rang the doorbell; зазвони телефонот the telephone rang

зазвонува *impf of* зазвони

засида *pf* **1** (*затвори со ѕид*) to wall in/up **2** to build **3** to start building

засидува *impf of* засида

заигра *pf* **I 1** to start dancing *trans. and intrans*; заигра оро to start dancing an *oro* **2** to start playing *trans. and intrans.*; *fig.* to <start to> flutter; срцето му заигра his heart started fluttering **3** to cause to start dancing/playing; заигра коњ to make a horse prance **II – се** to lose o.s. in dancing/playing

заигрува (**се**) *impf of* заигра (**се**)

заизлегува *impf* to start coming out one by one

заинаети се *pf* to become obstinate; to dig one's heels in; to stick to one's guns

заинаетува се *impf of* заинаети се

заинтереси́ра *pf* **I** to interest (*некого за нешто – s.o. in s.th.*), get (*s.o.*) interested (*in s.th.*) **II – се** to get interested (*за – in*), take an interest (*in*)

заинтереси́ран *pt* interested; заинтересирана страна interested party

заинтереси́раност *f* interest

заинтересува (**се**) *pf see* заинтересира (**се**)

заинтересуван *pt see* заинтересиран

Заир *m* Zaïre

Заирец -рци *m* Zaïrean, Zaïrese

Заирка *f* (*fem. form*) *see* Заирец

заирски *adj* Zaïrean, Zaïrese

заискри *pf* to start sparkling; *fig.* ѝ заискрија очите her eyes began to sparkle

заискрува *impf of* заискри

заита *pf* **1** to start hurrying **2** to hurry off

заитува *impf of* заита

зајаде *pf* **I 1** to start eating **2** *fig.* to be sarcastic **3** *fig.* to pester, bother; to start needling **II – се 1** to start fraying, tearing *intrans.* **2** *fig.* to start squabbling (bickering, quarrelling)

зајадлив *adj* sarcastic, biting, caustic; spiteful, malicious

зајадливец -ци *m* sarcastic/spiteful (malicious) person

зајадливост *f* sarcasm; spite, malice

зајадува (**се**) *impf of* зајаде (**се**)

зајази *pf* **1** to dam <up> **2** *fig.* to satisfy, satiate

зајазува *impf of* зајази

зајак -ци *m Zool.* hare; питом зајак rabbit; ❑

страшлив како зајак as timid as a hare; спие како зајак to sleep with one eye open; тука е зајакот! that's the point! that's the catch! со еден куршум два зајака <to kill> two birds with one stone; тој со кола зајаци фаќа he's got what it takes

зајакне *pf* зајакна *aor.* **I 1** to grow stronger **2** to recover *intrans.* **3** to strengthen *trans.* **II – се 1** *see* I 1 & 2 **2** to increase *intrans.*

зајакнува (**се**) *impf of* зајакне (**се**)

зајаче *n dim. of* зајак; leveret! ќе фати и мојот 'рт зајаче *prov.* every dog has his day

зајачи *pf* **1** to <start to> moan, groan <in pain>; to scream out, howl <from pain> **2** *see* заечи

зајачица *f* doe hare

зајачки *adj* hare, hare's; rabbit *attrib.*; зајачко месо hare's meat; hare/rabbit (*as food*) ❑ има зајачко срце to be chicken-hearted (lily-livered)

зајачковина *f Bot.* **1** (Colutea arborescens *or* melanocalyx) bladder senna **2** (Coronilla emerus) scorpion senna

зајачковица *f Bot. see* зајачковина 2

зајачува *impf of* зајачи

зајде *pf* **1** to set, go down (*of the sun*); сонцето зајде the sun set; *impers.* зајде the sun has set **2** to lose control of o.s., become helpless; детето зајде <од плачење> the child was overcome by tears

зајдисонце *n* sunset; на зајдисонце at sunset; откај зајдисонце from the west

зајдува *impf of* зајде, *see* заоѓа²

зајко -овци *m hyp. of* зајак; bunny; ❑ зајко сезнајко smart alec<k>

зајми *pf* **I 1** (*земе на заем од*) to borrow (*од – from*) **2** (*даде на заем*) to lend (*некому – to s.o.*) **II – се** to borrow *intrans.*, take a loan; се зајмив од него I borrowed from him

зајмица *f see* заемница

зајмува (**се**) *impf of* зајми (**се**)

зајчар *m* hunting dog, harrier

зајчарник -ци *m* rabbit warren

зајчина *f Bot. see* зајачковина 1

закади *pf* **1** to start burning incense **2** to start flattering **3** to fill with the scent of incense *trans.*

закаже *pf* закажа *aor.* **1** (*седница, состанок*) to call, fix, arrange; закаже за на доктор to make an appointment to see a doctor **2** to start telling (relating)

закажува *impf of* закаже

закалапи *pf* to start sorting (*tobacco*)

закален *pt* (*за железо*) tempered; *fig.* hardy, inured; steeled; закален борец seasoned fighter

закаленост *f* (*за железо*) hardening, tempering, temper; *fig.* (*телесна*) fitness, endurance, toughness

закали *pf* **I** to toughen, harden, temper (*also fig.*) **II – се** *fig.* to become hardy (tough)

закалува (**се**) *impf of* закали (**се**)

закалуѓери *pf* **I** to receive as a monk/nun **II – се** to become a monk/nun

закалуѓерува (**се**) *impf of* закалуѓери (**се**)

закамуфли́ра (**се**) *pf see* камуфлира (**се**)

закана *f* threat; ❑ празна закана empty threat

закани *pf* to start inviting

закани се¹ *pf* (*with dat.*) to threaten (*дека, да – to*)

закани се² *pf* to make up one's mind, decide, resolve (*да – to*)

заканува *impf of* закани

заканува се[1] *impf of* закани се[1]
заканува се[2] *impf of* закани се[2]
заканувачки *adj* threatening; заканувачко писмо threatening letter
закапе *pf* закапа *aor.* 1 to start dripping (leaking) 2 *fig.* to start falling; лисјето закапаа the leaves have started falling
закастри *pf* 1 to <start to> trim, prune, clip 2 *fig.* to <start to> scold (reprimand)
закатани *pf colloq.* **I** 1 to padlock; to lock, shut; закатани некому уста to stop s.o.'s mouth 2 to lose; to stuff, shove (*s.th. somewhere*) **II – ce** 1 (*заинаети се*) to become obstinate 2 to get lost; to perish; да се закатани! may he rot (burn) in hell! to hell with him/it!
закатанува (се) *impf of* закатани (се)
закатанчи *pf* **I** *see* закатани 1 **II – ce** *fig.* to choke *intrans.*; да ти се закатанчи! may you choke!
закатанчува (се) *impf of* закатанчи (се)
закачалка *f* hanger; hat-and-coat rack; hallstand; (*за шапки*) <hat> rack; (*на алиште*) tab, loop; ❏ како да виси на закачалка available at all times
закачи[1] *pf* **I** 1 to hook on/up; закачи вагони to couple waggons 2 to hang; to attach; to pin up; закачи слика на ѕид to hang a picture on a wall; закачи орден to pin on a medal 3 (*допре при движење*) to catch *trans.*; to brush, graze, brush against 4 *fig.* to needle, sting **II – ce** 1 (*за*) to seize, catch hold of, catch on, hook on; to stick to 2 (*запне*) to catch *intrans.*, snag, get caught; ми се закачи ѓерданот my necklace caught on s.th. 3 *fig.* (*спречка се*) to quarrel; се закачиле одамна they have been quarrelling for ages
закачи[2] *pf* **I** to start lifting (raising) **II – ce** to start climbing/rising
закачка *f* excuse, pretext
закачлив *adj see* задорлив
закачливост *f* quarrelsome nature
закачува[1] **(се)** *impf of* закачи[1] (се)
закачува[2] **(се)** *impf of* закачи[2] (се)
закашка *pf* **I** *colloq.* to dirty, soil **II – ce** 1 to get dirty; to dirty o.s. 2 to start splashing
закашкува (се) *impf of* закашка (се)
закашла се *pf* to start coughing <hard>
закашлува се *impf of* закашла се
закваси *pf dial.* (*потквали*) to ferment; to leaven (*bread*)
заквасува *impf of* закваси
закима *pf* 1 (*со глава*) to <start to> nod 2 (*замига*) to start winking
закимува *impf of* закима
закине *pf* закина *aor.* **I** 1 (*чевли, облека*) to start wearing out *trans.*; (*хартија, ткаеница*) to start tearing *trans.* 2 to start wearing (*new clothes*) 3 (*цвеќиња и сл.*) to start picking **II – ce** 1 to start wearing out *intrans.*; to start tearing *intrans.* 2 *fig.* to start worrying (fretting)
закинува (се) *impf of* закине (се)
закипи *pf* to boil, seethe, start boiling (*also fig.*) *intrans.*; *fig.* to be in full swing
закипува *impf of* закипи
закисели *pf* 1 to sour *trans.* 2 to turn sour *intrans.* 3 *impers.* (*with dat.*) му закисели he felt a sour taste in his mouth
закиселува *impf of* закисели

закисне *pf* закисна *aor.* to soak *trans.*
закиснува *impf of* закисне
закити *pf* **I** 1 to <start to> decorate/adorn 2 to start dressing garishly *trans.* **II – ce** 1 to <start to> adorn o.s. 2 to start dressing garishly *intrans.*
закитува (се) *impf of* закити (се)
заклан *pt* slaughtered, butchered; ❏ скока како заклан петел to jump about like a cat on hot bricks; спие како заклан to sleep like a log
заклати *pf* **I** to <start to> swing/sway/rock *trans.* **II – ce** to <start to> swing/sway/rock *intrans.*; to <start to> wobble *intrans.*
заклатува (се) *impf of* заклати (се)
заклепа *pf* 1 (*почне да остри*) to <start to> sharpen (*by hammering*) 2 (*почне да удира*) to <start to> strike (*a bell with a clapper*) 3 (*за клепало*) to <start to> strike, ring *intrans.*; to <start to> rattle/clank 4 *fig.* to start chattering (prattling) 5 to start blinking
заклет *adj* implacable; confirmed, inveterate; заклет непријател sworn enemy
заклетва *f* oath; ❏ заклетва на верност oath of allegiance; зема/дава заклетва to take an oath
заклешти *pf* to seize, hold firm; to squeeze
заклешти се *pf* to <start to> make faces, grimace; to grin, laugh maliciously, leer
заклештува *impf of* заклешти
заклештува се *impf of* заклешти се
заклина (се) *impf rare of* заколне (се), *see* заколнува (се)
заклопи *pf* **I** 1 to cover 2 (*затвори*) to shut *trans.*; заклопи очи to shut one's eyes; *fig.* to die **II – ce** to shut, close *intrans.*
заклопка *f* lid
заклучен -чна *adj* concluding, final, closing; заклучен биланс closing balance sheet; *Gram.* заклучни реченици consecutive clauses
заклучи *pf* **I** 1 (*со клуч*) to lock 2 to conclude, infer 3 to close; заклучи седница to close a meeting; заклучил сметки to close accounts 4 to conclude, contract, enter into; заклучи договор to conclude a contract; заклучи зделка to make a deal, strike a bargain **II – ce** to lock o.s. in
заклучно *adv* inclusive; уписот се врши до 10-и заклучно enrolment takes place up to the 10th <of the month> inclusive
заклучок -ци *m* 1 conclusion; дојде до заклучок to reach a conclusion; to come to the conclusion (*дека – that*); изведе заклучок to draw a conclusion; ❏ во заклучок in conclusion, to conclude 2 resolution; донесе заклучок to pass a resolution
заклучува (се) *impf of* заклучи (се)
закоби *pf* to <start to> presage evil; to be ominous
закобува *impf of* закоби
закова *pf see* закове
закован *pt* nailed down; *fig.* motionless
закове *pf* закова *aor.* 1 to <start to> hammer (drive) in 2 to nail on; to nail up; to nail down; to rivet 3 *fig.* to pin down, fix; закова некого со поглед to fix s.o. with a stare 4 *fig.* to shackle, chain
закожурчи се *pf* to form a cocoon; *fig.* to withdraw into one's shell
закожурчува се *impf of* закожурчи се
закокори се *pf* 1 to <start to> show off; to strut, swagger 2 to <start to> stare

закокорува се *impf of* закокори се

закол *m* place on the neck of an animal (*used for slaughtering*); *fig.* Achilles heel; ❑ му го најде заколот he found his weak spot

заколе *pf* закла *aor.* to <start to> slaughter

заколне *pf* заколна *aor.* **I 1** to adjure, make (*s.o.*) take an oath; to swear in; заколне некого да не кажува to swear s.o. to silence **2** *rare* to start to curse **II – се 1** to take an oath; *Leg.* криво се заколне to perjure o.s. **2** (*како сведок*) to bear witness under oath

заколнува (се) *impf of* заколне (се)

заколува *impf of* заколе

закон *m* law; act; Закон за работните односи Industrial Relations Act; кривичен закон criminal law; донесе/укине закон to pass/repeal a law;❑ според законот according to the law; од (во) името на законот in the name of the law; надвор од законот outside the law (illegal); заштитен од законот protected by law; закони на природата laws of nature; Архимедовиот закон Archimedes' principle; законот на гравитацијата the law of gravity; непишани закони unwritten laws; неговиот збор е закон his word is law; закон Божји religion, Bible classes

законачи *pf arch. see* заноќева

законачува *impf of* законачи

законик -ци *m* **1** legal code; граѓански законик civil code (codex); кривичен законик penal (criminal) code **2** *f.p.* person versed in divinity **3** *dial. arch.* (*usu. pl*) bridal party (*at a wedding; father, godfather and witnesses*)

законит *adj* **1** lawful, legal, legitimate; законит наследник legal heir; законит сопственик rightful owner; законито дете legitimate child **2** *rare* (*закономерен*) regular; законита појава regular (natural) phenomenon

законитост *f* **1** legality, legitimacy **2** regularity

законодавен -вна *adj* legislative; законодавен орган legislative body

законодавец -вци *m* legislator

законодавство *n* legislature; legislation

закономерен -рна *adj* regular, natural; закономерна појава regular phenomenon

закономерност *f* regularity, conformity to established laws/practices

законски *adj* legal, statutory; законска мерка legal measure; законска моќ force of law; законски пропис statutory provision; законски предлог draft bill, proposed law

закоп *m colloq.* (*погреб*) burial, funeral

закопа *pf* **I 1** to start digging **2** to bury; ❑ жив закопан buried alive; completely isolated **3** to fill in, cover over; закопа дупка to fill in a hole **4** *fig.* to ruin **II – се** to bury o.s. (*во – in*); *fig.* се закопа во долгови to sink deep into debt

закопча (се) *pf see* запетла (се)

закопчува (се) *impf of* закопча (се)

закоравен *pt* inveterate, confirmed; hardened; закоравен злосторник hardened criminal

закорави <се> *pf* **1** to become hardened, inured, insensitive; to become addicted **2** (*покрие се со корка*) to become encrusted

закоравува <се> *impf of* закорави <се>

закоренет *pt & adj* rooted; *fig.* deep-seated, deep-rooted; закоренет навик set habit

закорени *pf* **1** (*за растение*) to take root **2** *fig.* to instil, inculcate **II – се** to take root (*also fig.*); to become established

закоренува (се) *impf of* закорени (се)

закосај -аи *m* amount of hay etc. mown in one scythe-stroke

закотви *impf* **I** to anchor *trans.* **II – се** to anchor, moor *intrans.*

закотвува (се) *impf of* закотви (се)

закоти *pf* **I** to bear, produce, bring forth (*young*) **II – се 1** to cub, bear young **2** to be born (*of an animal*) **3** *colloq.* to reproduce

закотува (се) *impf of* закоти (се)

закочи *pf* **I 1** to brake, apply the brakes **2** (*за пушка*) to lock *trans.*; закочи пушка to close the breech of a gun **3** to hold up, slow down *trans.*; закочи сообраќај to hold up traffic **II – се 1** to lock *intrans.*; to jam *intrans.* **2** to slow down *intrans.*

закочува (се) *impf of* закочи (се)

закрастави *pf* to become covered with scabs

закрвави *pf* **I** to make bloody, cover with blood **II – се 1** to become covered in blood; (*за очи*) to become bloodshot **2** *see* закрви се

закрвавува (се) *impf of* закрвави (се)

закрви се *pf* to become mortal enemies

закрвува се *impf of* закрви се

закрепи *pf* **I 1** (*нотпе*) to prop up **2** to attach, fasten, fix; to make firm (stable) **3** *fig.* to consolidate, fortify, strengthen, stabilize **II – се 1** to prop o.s. up **2** *fig.* to grow stronger; to take hold

закрепне *pf* закрепна *aor.* **1** to grow stronger, gain strength; to become firm; to stabilize *intrans.* **2** to refresh o.s. **3** to recover, get well

закрепник -ци *m* defender, protector; patron

закрепнува *impf of* закрепне

закрепува (се) *impf of* закрепи (се)

закрива (се) *impf of* закрие (се)

закриви *pf* **1** to bend out of shape, make crooked **2** to start limping

закривува *impf of* закриви

закрие *pf* закри *aor.* **I 1** to cover (*partly*) **2** to hide, conceal **II – се 1** to cover o.s. **2** to hide o.s.

закрила *f* protection, patronage; под закрилата under the wing (*на – of*), with the support (*of*)

закрили *pf* to shelter, protect

закрилник -ци *m* protector, defender, patron

закрилница *f* (*fem. form*) *see* закрилник

закрилува *impf of* закрили

закрпи *pf* **I** to <start to> mend; to darn; to patch, patch up; *fig.* ќе ја закрпиме работата we'll patch things up **II – се 1** to <start to> patch one's clothes **2** *fig.* <со пари> to make ends meet, get by

закрпува (се) *impf of* закрпи (се)

закружи *pf* to <start to> circle, hover, soar

закружува *impf of* закружи

закрши *pf* **I 1** to start breaking off *trans.*; to start cracking/fracturing *trans.*; закрши прсти he started cracking his knuckles **3** to start twisting/swaying/wiggling *trans.*; закрши снага she started wiggling her hips (*when walking*) **II – се 1** to start breaking off *intrans.*; to start cracking/fracturing *intrans.* **2** to start twisting/swaying/wiggling one's body (*when walking*)

закршува (се) *impf of* закрши (се)

закуп *m* lease, rent; земе под закуп to rent; даде под закуп to let; договор за закуп rental agreement

закупен -пна *adj* rental; закупна цена rent

закупец -пци *m* tenant, lessee, leaseholder

закупи *pf* to rent; to hire; to lease

закупник *m see* закупец

закупнина *f* rent

закупница & **закупничка** *f* (*fem. form*) *see* закупник

закупнички *adj* rental

закупува[1] *pf* to start buying

закупува[2] *impf of* закупи

закуси[1] *pf* to have a snack

закуси[2] *pf* **I** **1** to start shortening *trans.*; to start reducing **2** to start giving short weight **II** – **се** to start shortening *intrans.*; to start growing smaller

закуска *f* appetizer, hors-d'oeuvre, entrée; starters; snack, refreshments

закусува[1] *impf of* закуси[1]

закусува[2] (**се**) *impf of* закуси[2] (се)

закуќи *pf* **I** to settle (*s.o.*) in a house **II** – **се** to settle in; to settle down

закуќува (**се**) *impf of* закуќи (се)

залага (**се**) *impf of* заложи (се); се залага на работата he is assiduous at work; се залага за to strive after/towards

залагање *n* **1** effort, striving **2** (*трудољубивост*) industry, assiduity

залагува (**се**) *impf of* залаже (се)

залади *pf* **I** **1** to cool *trans.* **2** (*of the weather, air*) to cool down *intrans.*; to turn cold; *impers.* залади it has cooled down **II** – **се** *see* I 2

заладува (**се**) *impf of* залади (се)

залаже *pf* залажа *aor.* **I** **1** to start lying (telling lies) **2** to deceive, mislead, delude **3** *fig.* to distract, draw attention **4** *fig.* to amuse (*a child*) **II** – **се** **1** to start deceiving each other **2** to deceive (delude) o.s. **3** to be mistaken **4** to start amusing o.s.; to start getting interested **5** *dial.* to start having a love affair

залажува (**се**) *impf see* залагува (се)

залак -ци *m* mouthful; morsel; на залак in one gulp; ❏ си куси од залакот to stint on food; не му се тура (клава) залак в уста he won't touch a morsel; му ги брои залаците she begrudges him every bite; преголем залак too hot to handle; голем залак касни, голем збор не вели *prov.* don't be so sure! од првниот залак послаток нема *prov.* the first mouthful is the sweetest

залангур *m colloq.* **1** wanderer, tramp, vagabond **2** (*безделник*) loafer, idler **3** (*калпав човек*) clumsy person

залаче *n dim. of* залак; ❏ колку едно залаче as tiny as a peppercorn; a tiny little bit

залачка (**се**) *pf dial. see* задре (се)

залачкува (**се**) *impf see* задира (се)

залеби *pf* **I** to employ **II** – **се** to find employment; to secure one's livelihood

залебне се *pf* залебна се *aor.* to choke (*од – from*) (*sobbing, laughter, etc.*)

залебнува се *impf of* залебне се

залева *impf of* залее

заледи *pf* **I** to freeze *trans.* **II** – **се** to freeze *intrans.*

заледува (**се**) *impf of* заледи (се)

залее *pf* залеа *aor.* **1** to water (*flowers, etc.*) **2** to water, wash, clean (*streets*) **3** to draw (*water*)

залежи *pf* залежи, залежа *aor.* **I** to lie down, take to one's bed **II** – **се** to lie for a long time; to get stale

залежува (**се**) *impf of* залежи (се)

залез *m poet. see* заод

залекува *pf* **I** to <start to> treat, cure, heal *trans.* **II** – **се** to <start to> heal *intrans.*; to <start to>treat o.s.

залела (**се**) *pf dial. see* залула (се), заниша (се)

залелее (**се**) *pf* залелеа (се) *aor. see* залула (се), заниша (се)

залепи *pf* **I** **1** to stick on *trans.*, paste on, glue on; to glue together; *fig.* to press; залепи марка на писмо to put a stamp on a letter; го залепил челото до џамот he pressed his forehead to the window-pane;❏ залепи некому шлаканица to slap s.o.'s face **2** *rare* to start sticking (pasting) on **II** – **се** to stick (*на – to*) *intrans.*; *fig.* to attach o.s. (*долна – to*), cling (*to*); детето се залепи до мајка his child clung to his mother; се залепи пред телевизорот to become glued to the television

залепува (**се**) *impf of* залепи (се)

залет *m* running start, jump-off; зеде залет he took a running start

залета *pf* **I** to start flying **II** – **се** **1** to make (take) a running start **2** *fig.* to take (make) a quick step; to rush; кај си се залетал? where are you rushing off to? **3** to fly off (*faraway*)

залетне се *pf* залетна се *aor. see* залебне се

залетнува се *impf of* залетне се, *see* залебнува се

залетува (**се**) *impf of* залета (се)

залечи (**се**) *pf see* залекува (се)

залечува (**се**) *impf of* залечи (се)

залив *m* bay, gulf; Солунскиот Залив the Gulf of Salonika

залиже *pf* залижа *aor.* **1** to start licking; *fig.* зградата ја залижаа пламени јазици tongues of flame started licking the building (*за коса*) to sleek down **II** – **се** **1** to start licking one another **2** *fig.* to start wearing down; ѓонов се залижал this sole has started wearing down **3** (*за коса*) to sleek down one's hair **4** *fig., iron.* to dress up *intrans.*

залижува (**се**) *impf of* залиже (се)

залипне <**се**> *pf* залипна <се> *aor.* to choke *intrans.*

залипнува <**се**> *impf of* залипне <се>

залихи *pl* stocks, reserves, supplies; попис на залихи inventory of stocks

заличи *pf* **1** (*на*) to <start to> resemble, look like; заличи на татко my he grew to resemble his father; ми заличи на сестра ми I almost took her for my sister **2** to decorate, adorn, beautify

заличува *impf of* заличи

залог[1] -зи *m* pledge (*also fig.*); mortgage guarantee; collateral

залог[2] -зи *m Gram.* voice (*in verbs*)

заложен -жна *adj* pawn *attrib.*; заложен завод pawnshop

заложи *pf* **I** to stake; to pawn; (*куќа*) to mortgage; заложи свој авторитет to stake one's authority **II** – **се** **1** to pledge; to pledge o.s. **2** to intercede (*за – for*), stand up (*for*) **3** to strive, take care, make an effort

заложник -ци *m* hostage

заложница *f* **1** (*fem. form*) *see* заложник **2** letter of lien **3** pawn ticket; mortgage bond

заложничап *m* pawnbroker

заложува (**се**) *impf see* залага (се)

залости *pf* to lock, bolt; to latch

залп *m* salvo; volley

залуд *adv poet. see* залудо, залудно

залуден -дна *adj* vain, useless, futile; ❑ залудна работа a wild goose chase; a fool's errand

залуди *pf* **I 1** to drive mad, madden **2** to go crazy; ❑ залуди по некого to get a crush on s.o. **II – се** *see* I 2

залудно *adv* in vain

залудност *f* futility, uselessness

залудо *adv* in vain, uselessly, to no purpose

залудува¹ (се) *impf of* залуди (се)

залудува² *pf* to start going crazy (*no – about*); to start playing the fool

залула *pf* **I** to start rocking/swinging *trans.* **II – се** to start rocking/swinging/swaying; *fig.* to lose one's balance; дрвјата се залулаа the trees started swaying

залулее (се) *impf see* залелее (се)

залута *pf* **1** (*загуби се*) to lose one's way **2** to start wandering (roaming)

залути *pf impers.* (*with dat.*) to be hot (spicy); ми залути <од> пиперкава that pepper (capsicum) was too hot for me

залутува *impf of* залути

заљубен *pt* in love

заљуби *pf* **I** *f.p.* to fall in love (*with s.o.*); си заљубив едно моме I fell in love with a girl **II – се** to fall in love (*во – with*); ❑ се заљуби до уши to fall head over heels in love

заљубува се *impf of* заљуби се

замав *m* **1** stroke, blow, swing; со еден замав with/at one stroke; (*наеднаш*) at one fell swoop; во полн замав in full swing **2** *fig.* verve, vigour, dash, élan, zest **3** scale, sweep, range, scope; пожарот зема голем замав the fire assumed great proportions; замав на движење scope of a movement

замава *pf* **I 1** to start striking (beating) **2** *dial. see* замавта **II – се** to start striking (beating) each other

замавне *pf* замавна *aor.* to swipe, lash (*no – at*); to aim a blow (*no – at*)

замавнува *impf of* замавне

замавта *pf* **1** to swing, wave *trans.* and *intrans.*; ги замавта нозете he swung his legs; замавта со рака he waved his hand **2** to rock *trans.*; замавта нишалка to push a swing

замавтува *impf of* замавта

замаглен *pt & adj* **1** clouded, mist-shrouded; befogged; (*за поглед, очи*) dull, dim; (*нејасен воопшто*) dim, obscure **2** (*за стакло*) misted over, steamed over (up)

замагленост *f* befogged state, *Brit.* fug; dimness, obscurity

замагли *pf* **1** to befog; to shroud with mist; to fill with steam/smoke; замагли соба со <дим од> цигари to fill a room with cigarette smoke **2** *fig.* to dim, obscure, cloud, obfuscate; замагли поглед to cloud s.o.'s view; замагли некоја работа to cloud over an issue

замаглува *impf of* замагли

замае *pf* замаја *aor.* **I 1** (*забави, задржи*) to hold up, detain **2** to inspire, carry away (*with enthusiasm*) **3** (*зашемети*) to amaze, astonish, astound; to enthral; to daze, stun **II – се 1** (*задржи се долго*) to stay, tarry **2** to get carried away; to feel dizzy; to feel faint; главата му се замаја he felt dizzy **3** to be astounded

(dumbfounded); се замаја од чудо he was dumbfounded

замаже (се) *pf* замажа (се) *dial. see* замачка (се)

замажува (се) *impf of* замаже (се), *see* замачкува (се)

замазни *pf* **I 1** to level, smooth down **2** *fig.* to smooth over (*a dispute*); to correct (*an impression*) **3** to start smoothing/stroking/fondling **II – се 1** to smooth down one's hair **2** to start dressing up *intrans.*

замазнува (се) *impf of* замазни (се)

замајан *pt* **1** detained **2** carried away, enthralled **3** (*зашеметен*) amazed, astounded

замајува (се) *impf of* замае (се)

заман *m arch.* time, *arch.* tide; ❑ *colloq.* за зор-заман in case of need; for a rainy day

замандали *pf* to bolt, bar (*a door*)

замандалува *impf of* замандали

замаскира *pf* **I** to mask (*also fig.*); (*прикрие*) to hide, conceal; to camouflage **II – се** to conceal o.s.

замасли (се) *pf see* замасти (се)

замаслува (се) *impf see* замастува (се)

замасти *pf* **I 1** to add butter/fat (*to food*) **2** to grease **II – се** to get covered in fat (grease); to become greasy

замастува (се) *impf of* замасти (се)

заматен *pt & adj* misty, dim; clouded; troubled

заматеност *f* mistiness, dimness

замати *pf* **I 1** to stir up; to confuse **2** to start stirring (mixing) **II – се 1** to become muddy/turbid/troubled; се замати времето the weather has turned dull; се заматија работите/приликите the picture became confused **2** *impers.* (*with dat.*) ми се замати <во главата> I feel dizzy

заматка *pf* **I 1** to start stirring (mixing) **2** *fig.* to start lying (telling lies) **3** to detain (*in conversation, etc.*) **II – се 1** to get carried away (*in conversation, etc.*) **2** *fig.* to start to roam; to start to loiter (hang around)

заматкува (се) *impf of* заматка (се)

заматува (се) *impf of* замати (се)

замачка *pf* **I 1** to cover with grease; to smear, soil; ❑ замачка некому очи to pull the wool over s.o.'s eyes **2** *fig.* to hush up, keep secret, suppress **3** to start smearing **II – се** to smear o.s. (*со – with*)

замачкува (се) *impf of* замачка (се)

замба *f* punch, puncher; perforator

замбак -ци *m Bot.* (Lilium candidum) lily

Замбиец -ијци *m* Zambian

Замбија *f* Zambia

Замбијка *f* (*fem. form*) *see* Замбиец

замбиски *adj* Zambian

замеди *pf* to sweeten with honey

замедува *impf of* замеди

замези *pf* to have a snack

замезува *impf of* замези

замелушен *pt* stunned, astounded, *colloq.* flabbergasted

замелуши *pf* to astonish, amaze, astound

замелушува *impf of* замелуши

замена *f* **1** exchange; swap; (*трампа*) barter; замена на пари currency exchange; замена на стоки barter trade; во замена за in exchange for **2** replacement, substitute; substitution; тој му е замена he is his substitute

замени *pf* **I 1** to exchange, swap; јаболката ги замени за крушки he exchanged the apples for pears

2 *fig.* to confuse, muddle up; сум ги заменил документите I have muddled up the documents **3** to replace, stand in for, take the place of; машинава ќе замени стомина работници this machine will take the place of a hundred workmen **II – се** to replace each other; to exchange, swap; се заменија со марки they swapped stamps

заменик *m* deputy, representative; substitute; заменик директор deputy director; заменик министер deputy minister

заменица *f* **1** (*fem. form*) *see* заменик **2** *see* заемница 1

заменка *f* **1** *Gram.* pronoun; лична/повратна/ показна/прашална заменка personal/reflexive/ demonstrative/interrogative pronoun **2** *dial.* substitute **3** *see* заемница 1

заменува (се) *impf of* замени (се)

замери[1] *pf* **I** (*with dat.*) to criticize, find fault; to take offence; ништо не може да му се замери nothing can be held against him; му замерија на/за неговите зборови they were critical of his speech; не замерете! don't be offended! **II – се 1** to offend/anger each other; to <start to> quarrel, bicker **2** (*with dat.*) to offend; to anger

замери[2] *pf* to start measuring/weighing

замери[3] *pf* to take aim; to aim (*во – at*)

замерка *f* reproach, criticism; objection; без замерка beyond reproach

замерок -ци *m* late-summer milk (*from mountain pastures*)

замерува (се) *impf of* замери[1] (се)

замес *m dial.* (*folk custom*) pre-nuptial baking of special loaves

замеси *pf* **1** to mix/knead (*dough*); to bake (make) (*bread*); ❏ тој го замесил тоа he has made a mess of things **2** to start kneading/baking

замесува *impf of* замеси

замет *m colloq.* trouble; toil, fatigue; ❏ ако не ти е замет if it's no trouble to you

замете *pf* to <start to> sweep a little; to sweep up; to sweep over

заметне *pf* заметна *aor.* to shove somewhere; to lose, mislay

заметнува *impf of* заметне

заметува *impf of* замете

замечтае *pf* **1** to start dreaming/day-dreaming **2** to lose o.s. in reverie

замечтан *pt & adj* lost in reverie; dreamy; замечтан поглед dreamy look

замеша *pf* **I 1** to <start to> mix **2** *fig.* to mess up, complicate; ја замеша работата he complicated matters **3** *fig.* to involve, embroil (*во – in*) **II – се 1** to interfere **2** *fig.* to get messed up **3** *fig.* to become involved

замешува (се) *impf of* замеша (се)

замива (се) *impf of* замие (се)

замига *pf* to start winking

замие *pf* зами *aor.* **I 1** to <start to> wash/scour/scrub (*pots, dishes, floor, etc.*) **2** to wash a little *trans.* **II – се 1** to start washing *intrans.* **2** to wash a little *intrans.*

замижан *pt* **1** sleepy **2** apathetic, weak-willed

замиже *pf* замижа *aor.* **1** to close one's eyes; to blink; to squint **2** *fig.* (*пред*) to overlook; замиже пред нешто to close one's eyes to s.th.

замижува *impf of* замиже

замили се *pf* **1** to become liked; тој ми се замили I came to like him, I became fond of him **2** to grow to like each other; to fall in love (*со – with*); се замилија со Стојана she and Stojan fell in love

замилува *pf* **1** to start liking/loving **2** to start caressing (fondling)

замин *m only in the expression:* на замин in passing, on the way; when you have the chance

замине *pf* замина *aor.* **1** to go away; to depart, leave; замине за (во) странство to go abroad **2** to pass <by>; замина одовде he passed this way **3** to pass, overtake *trans.* **4** to pass by, miss, *colloq.* skip **5** замине си to leave for home; to return home

заминува *impf of* замине

замира *impf of* замре

замисла *f* idea, project, plan; убава замисла good idea

замислен *pt & adj* **1** thoughtful, pensive; preoccupied, worried; што си замислен? a penny for your thoughts **2** imagined, imaginary, fictitious

замисленост *f* pensiveness; preoccupation

замисли *pf* **I** to imagine, contemplate **II – се 1** to become thoughtful (lost in thought); to think seriously (*за – about*); to become concerned; to start thinking **2** to get ideas about o.s.; to get above o.s.

замислува (се) *impf of* замисли (се); тој се замислува he has a high opinion of himself

замк *m arch.* glue (*made from resin*)

замка *m* noose, trap, snare

замласка *pf* to champ, chew noisily

замласкува *impf of* замласка

замлачи *pf* **I** to warm <up> *trans.* **II – се** to warm up *intrans.*; *fig.* to become lukewarm (irresolute, weak-willed)

замлачува (се) *impf of* замлачи (се)

замок -ци *m Hist.* castle

замоли *pf* **I 1** to plead, entreat **2** to start pleading/ entreating **II – се 1** (*with dat.*) to ask, put a request (*to s.o.*) **2** to start praying

замолкне *pf* замолкна *aor.* **1** to fall silent; to die away, fade; замолкнаа звуците на гитарата the sounds of the guitar died away **2** to silence, hush

замолкнува *impf of* замолкне

замолува (се) *impf of* замоли (се)

замолчи *pf* **I 1** to fall silent **2** to silence **II – се** *see* **I** 1

замолчува (се) *impf of* замолчи (се)

замоми *pf* **I** to start treating (*a young girl*) as an adult **II – се** to reach adolescence, grow up (*of a girl*)

замомува (се) *impf of* замоми (се)

замомчи *pf* **I** to start treating (*a boy*) as an adult **II – се** to reach adolescence, grow up (*of a boy*)

замомчува (се) *impf of* замомчи (се)

замор *m* fatigue, tiredness; работа без замор unremitting toil

заморен[1] *adj* tired

заморен[2] -рна *adj* tiring; tiresome; заморна работа tiring work (job)

замореност *f* fatigue, tiredness

замори *pf* **I** to tire *trans.*, fatigue **II – се** to get tired, tire *intrans.*

заморува (се) *impf of* замори (се)

замота *pf* **I 1** to start winding (*a skein of wool, etc.*) **2** *dial.* to wrap **II – се** *dial.* to wrap o.s. up

замотува (се) *impf of* замота (се)

замошоли & замошори *pf* (*за дожд*) to start drizzling; (*за снег*) to start falling; to start snowing

замрази[1] *pf impers.* to start freezing

замрази[2] *pf* **I** to start hating; to come to hate; to take a dislike to **II – се** to start hating one another; to become estranged from one another

замразува[1] *impf of* замрази[1]

замразува[2] **(се)** *impf of* замрази[2] (се)

замрачи *pf* **I** to darken; to black out **II – се** to grow (become) dark; *fig.* to frown; *impers.* се замрачи it got dark

замрачува (се) *impf of* замрачи (се)

замре *pf* замре *aor.* 1 to die down, fade away; срцето му замре his heart sank; животот во градот замре life in the city came to a standstill; огнот замре the fire died down 2 to decline, die out, become extinct; замреа некои занаети certain crafts have died out

замрежи *pf* **I** 1 to cover with a net; to net; пајак го замрежи аголот a spider wove its web in the corner 2 (*чорапи*) to darn, mend 3 to dim, cloud; солзи ѝ го замрежија погледот tears dimmed her sight 4 *fig.* to ruffle; ветре ја замрежи водата a breeze ruffled the water **II – се** to cloud over, become befogged; очите му се замрежија his eyes grew dim

замрежува (се) *impf of* замрежи (се)

замреност *f* moribund state

замрзи *pf impers.* (*with acc.*) to pall (*on*); to become irksome (*to*); го замрзи да работи work palled on him

замрзнат *pt & adj* frozen; замрзнато месо frozen meat; замрзнати средства frozen funds

замрзне *pf* замрзна *aor.* **I** 1 to freeze, freeze over *intrans.*; to freeze to death, die of cold; to grow numb/ stiff; езерото замрзна the lake has frozen over; *fig.* крвта му замрзна во жилите his blood ran cold 2 to freeze *trans.* 3 *fig.* to cause to stop dead **II – се** *rare see* I 1

замрзнува (се) *impf of* замрзне (се)

замрзнување *n* freeze; замрзнување на платите wage freeze; замрзнување на цени price freezing; фрижидер за длабоко замрзнување deep-freeze, freezer

замрзува *impf of* замрзи

замркне *pf* замркна *aor.* 1 to be caught by darkness; замркнавме на пат darkness (night) fell while we were still on the road 2 *impers.* замркна darkness fell; ме замркна I was overtaken by darkness (the night)

замркнува *impf of* замркне

замрсен *adj* complicated; замрсено прашање complicated question (matter)

замрсеност *f* complexity

замрси[1] *pf* **I** 1 to muddle, complicate, confuse 2 (*за коса, конци и др.*) to tangle *trans.* **II – се** 1 to become muddled (complicated, confused) 2 to tangle *intrans.*, get tangled

замрси[2] *pf* to break one's fast

замрсува[1] **(се)** *impf of* замрси[1] (се)

замрсува[2] *impf of* замрси[2]

занает *m* craft, trade; даде некого на занает to enrol s.o. as an apprentice; по занает е ковач he is a blacksmith by trade; ❑ од занаетот му е he knows his trade; го испекол занаетот he's learnt his trade well; најстариот занает the oldest profession

занаетчија -ии *m* craftsman, artisan, skilled tradesman

занаетчиски *adj* 1 craftsman's, artisan's 2 craft, trade *attrib.*; занаетчиско училиште vocational (trade) school

занаетчиство *n* 1 craftsmanship 2 handicrafts; craftsmen, artisans

зандан *m arch. see* зандана

зандана *f arch.* dungeon

занемарен *pt* neglected; занемарени обврски neglected duties, obligations

занемареност *f* <state of> neglect

занемари *pf* **I** to neglect **II – се** to neglect o.s., become slovenly, let o.s. go

занемарува (се) *impf of* занемари (се)

занемее *pf* занемеа *aor. see* занеми; занемее од чудо to be dumbfounded

занемен *pt* silenced; *fig.* struck dumb, speechless

занеменост *f* speechlessness

занеми *pf* занеми, занеме *aor.* 1 to become dumb (mute); to become speechless, lose one's tongue 2 *fig.* to die down, grow quiet, fall silent 3 *fig.* to strike dumb; to silence; со поглед го занеми he silenced him with a look

занеможе *pf* to grow weak

занеможува *impf of* занеможе

занемува *impf of* занеми

занес *m* enthusiasm, fervour; rapture; ❑ паѓа во занес to go into ecstasy

занесе[1] *pf* **I** 1 to carry off (away); to push aside; (*одведе*) to take (*somewhere*); го занесла водата the water carried him away 2 *fig.* to fill with enthusiasm; to enthral, captivate; to delight, thrill **II – се** 1 to reel, stagger, be unsteady on one's legs; се занесе и ќе паднеше he staggered and almost fell 2 (*појави се*) to appear; голем облак се занесе a large cloud appeared 3 (*се замисли*) to become engrossed in thought 4 (*стане расеан*) to become absent-minded 5 (*восхити се*) to be carried away; to be filled with enthusiasm; to be delighted, thrilled

занесе[2] *pf* to start laying (*eggs*)

занесен[1] *pt & adj* 1 carried away, delighted, thrilled 2 (*замислен*) preoccupied; engrossed 3 (*расеан*) absent-minded

занесен[2] -сна *adj* enchanting, delightful

занесеник -ци *m* dreamer; enthusiast; *pejor.* fanatic, (*верски*) bigot

занесено *adv rare* absent-mindedly

занесеност *f* enthusiasm (rapture); (*расеаност*) absent-mindedness

занеслив *adj* captivating; intoxicating

занесува[1] **(се)** *impf of* занесе[1] (се)

занесува[2] *impf of* занесе[2]

Занзибар *m* Zanzibar

Занзибарец -рци *m* Zanzibari

Занзибарка *f* (*fem. form*) *see* Занзибарец

Занзибарски *adj* Zanzibari

заниже *pf* занижа *aor.* **I** to start threading **II – се** 1 to start following one another; се занижаа дните the days followed one after the other 2 to become engrossed in threading

занижува (се) *impf of* заниже (се)

занима *impf* **I** 1 (*интересира*) to interest; тоа не ме занима that doesn't interest me 2 *see* занимава 1 **II –**

се 1 (*интересира се*) to be interested, take an interest (*за – in*); to occupy o.s. (*со – with*), go in (*со – for*); to be occupied (*со – with*) **2** *see* занимава се 2 **3** *colloq.* (*води љубов*) to go steady (*со – with*)

занимава *impf* **I 1** to occupy; to distract; јас нема да ве занимавам со тие прашања I won't trouble (bother) you with these questions **2** (*забавува*) to entertain, amuse **II – се 1** to be interested (*со – in*); to occupy o.s. (*со – with*), go in (*со – for*); to be occupied (*со – with*); се занимава со историја to be interested in history **2** (*се забавува*) to amuse o.s.

занимање *n* **1** (*професија*) occupation; (*интересирање*) interest **2** hobby, pastime

занимлив *adj* interesting, intriguing; занимлива книга interesting book

занимливост *f* interest; s.th. of interest; curio

заниша *pf* **I 1** to start rocking/swinging/shaking *trans.* **II – се 1** to start rocking/swaying/ swinging/shaking *intrans.* **2** *fig.* to care (*за – about*)

занишува (се) *impf of* заниша (се); не се занишува за таа работа he doesn't care a hang about that

заноктица *f Med.* **1** paronychia, whitlow **2** cuticle

заноси *pf* **1** to start wearing **2** to conceive (*a child*)

заносува *impf of* заноси

заноќева *pf* to spend (pass) the night

заноќи *pf impers.* **I** to fall (*of night*); ме заноќи night found me (*somewhere*) **II – се** to fall (*of night*); веќе се заноќи night has already fallen

заноќува (се) *impf of* заноќи (се)

занура *pf* **I 1** to start rummaging; to start groping **2** to stumble, trip, skid **II – се** *see* I 2

занурка (се) *pf see* занура (се)

заобиде *pf dial. see* заобиколи 2

заобидува *impf of* заобиде

заобиколен -лна *adj* circuitous, roundabout; ❑ по заобиколен пат in a roundabout way; заобиколен пат bypass; detour

заобиколи *pf* **I 1** to surround, encircle **2** to bypass, detour; го заобиколи законот to circumvent the law **3** *fig.* to avoid, evade; ја заобиколи вистината to evade the truth **4** to make a detour **II – се** to surround o.s.

заобиколка *f* detour, bypass; *fig.* evasion, evading manoeuvre; ❑ без заобиколки without beating about the bush, directly

заобиколно *adv* circuitously, in a roundabout way

заобиколува *impf of* заобиколи; *fig.* to beat about the bush

заобиоѓа *impf dial. see* заобидува

заоблачи се *pf* to cloud over; небото се заоблачи the sky clouded over

заоблен *pt & adj* rounded, round; oval

заобли *pf* **I** to make round **II – се** to become round; to become plump

заоблува (се) *impf of* заобли (се)

заод *m* sunset; на заод сонце at sunset; ❑ на заодот на животот in the twilight of one's life

заодлив *adj dial. in the expression:* заодлива кашлица a bad cough

заодуваче *n* toddler

заоѓа¹ *f f.p. see* заод, зајдисонце

заоѓа² *impf of* зајде

заокругленост *f* roundness

заокружен *pt* **1** surrounded, encircled **2** rounded off, completed; well-rounded

заокружи *pf* **I 1** to surround, encircle; to circle **2** to round <off>; to round up/down *trans.*; заокружи сума to round off a total **3** *fig.* to sum up *trans.*; to complete **II – се** to round <out> *intrans.*, become round; to become plump

заокружува (се) *impf of* заокружи (се)

заора *pf* to start ploughing; ❑ заора бразда to blaze a trail

заорок -ци *m* first furrows (*in ploughing*)

заортачи *pf* **I 1** to take (*s.o.*) as one's associate, make (*s.o.*) one's partner **2** (*здружи средства*) to unite, pool (*one's resources*) **II – се** to unite *intrans.*; to become partners (associates)

заортачува (се) *impf of* заортачи (се)

заорува *impf of* заора

заостава (се) *impf of* заостави (се)

заостави *pf* **I** to neglect; to ignore, disregard; to overlook **II – се** to neglect o.s.

заоставштина *f* inheritance, estate; *fig.* heritage, legacy; литературна заоставштина literary legacy

заостанат *adj & pt* **1** backward; *Biol.* vestigial; заостаната земја backward country; ментално заостанат mentally retarded **2** (*уште неплатен*) outstanding; заостанати долгови outstanding debts; заостаната плата back pay

заостанатост *f* backwardness

заостане *pf* заостана *aor.* to fall behind; to lag behind (*also fig.*); заостане со исплата на долг to be in arrears; часовникот ми заостана my watch is slow

заостанува *impf of* заостане

заостаток -ци *m* **1** (*остаток*) remainder, remnant **2** (*ненаплатен долг*) unpaid portion, arrears

заострен *pt & adj* tense; заострени односи strained relations

заостреност *f* strain

заостри *pf* **I** to <start to> sharpen **II – се** to become strained (tense)

заофка *pf* to <start to> scream/howl/moan/whine

запад *m* west

западен -дна *adj* western

западне *pf* западна *aor.* **1** (*осиромаши*) to be ruined, become destitute; западне во долгови to get into debt **2** (*исчезне*) to die out, disappear; (*опадне*) to decline, decay, fall into decay **3** (*ослабне*) to become weak, weaken *intrans.*

западнува *impf of* западне, *see* запаѓа²

западњак -ци *m* westerner

западњачки *adj* western

запаѓа¹ *pf* to start falling one after another; to start falling (*of rain, snow*)

запаѓа² *impf of* западне

запазен *pt see* зачуван

запази (се) *pf* **1** *see* зачува (се); запази свое здравје to look after one's health **2** to observe, comply with; запази пост to observe a fast

запазува (се) *impf of* запази (се)

запал *m poet.* ecstasy; inspiration

запален¹ *pt* enthusiastic (*за – about*), keen (*за – on*); ❑ запалени глави hotheads

запален² -лна *adj* incendiary; запална бомба incendiary bomb

запали *pf* **I 1** to light; to set fire to, ignite *trans.*; to kindle *trans.*; запали куќа to set a house on fire;

запали оган to light a fire; **запали** цигара to light a cigarette; **запали** струја to turn (switch) on the light; **запали** кибрит to strike a match; **запали** кола to start a car **2** *fig.* to inspire, fill with enthusiasm; to fire s.o.'s imagination; to excite, get (*s.o.*) interested (*за – in*); to ignite *trans.* **II – се 1** to catch fire, ignite *intrans.*; ❑ му се запалиле гаќите he's in big trouble **2** *fig.* to become enthusiastic (*за – about*); ❑ му се запалила главата he's got very enthusiastic; he's overburdened with work **3** *fig.* to lose one's temper, fly off the handle

запалив *adj* **1** incendiary **2** inflammable; запалива течност inflammable liquid

запалка *f* cigarette lighter

запалува (се) *impf of* запали (се)

запамети *pf* to remember; to commit to memory, memorize

запаметува *impf of* запамети

запара *pf* **I 1** to tear/rip (*slightly*) **2** to start ripping/unstitching **II – се** to start to tear *intrans.*

запари *pf* to steam; to wash with hot water

запарува¹ (се) *impf of* запара (се)

запарува² *impf of* запари

запат *m* increase (*in numbers, due to breeding*)

запати¹ *pf* **I** to <start to> breed, rear *trans.*; запати гуски to start breeding geese **II – се** to multiply, grow, increase *intrans.*

запати² се *pf dial.* to turn (*to s.o.*)

запатка *pf colloq.* to begin to walk (*of a child*), start toddling

запаткува *impf of* запатка

запатува¹ (се) *impf of* запати¹ (се)

запатува² се *impf of* запати² се

запаше *pf* запаша *aor.* **I 1** to put (*s.th.*) round the waist **2** to stick (*s.th.*) in one's belt/girdle **3** to girdle **II – се** to put on a belt, gird<le> o.s.

запашува (се) *impf of* запаше (се)

запев *m poet.* refrain

запева *impf of* запее

запее *pf* запеа *aor.* to start singing, burst into song, strike up a tune

запек *m* constipation

запекува (се) *impf see* запечува (се)

запенет *pt* **1** frothy, foaming **2** *fig.* (*за човек*) furious, foaming at the mouth

запенетост *f* rage, fury

запени се *pf* **1** to foam, froth; коњот се запени the horse was covered in foam; виното се запени во чашата the wine foamed in the glass; ❑ ми се запени устата (*од зборување*) I've talked too much **2** *fig.* to get angry (furious), flare up, fly into a rage; се запени од бес to foam at the mouth

запенува се *impf of* запени се

запере *pf* запра *aor.* to <start to> wash/rinse (*clothes*)

заперува *impf of* запере

запеска *f dial.* embroidered figures (*on shirtsleeves*)

запетла *pf* **I** to button up, do up *trans.* **II – се** to button o.s. up

запетлува (се) *impf of* запетла (се)

запечатен *pt* sealed; запечатено писмо sealed letter; неговата судбина е запечатена his fate is sealed

запечати *pf* to seal <up>; запечати писмо to seal a letter

запечатува *impf of* запечати

запече *pf* **I 1** to brown, scorch slightly **2** (*причини запек*) to constipate, cause constipation **3** to <start to> bake **4** сонцето запече the sun grew hotter **II – се 1** to get browned slightly **2** (*добие запек*) to become constipated

запечува (се) *impf of* запече (се)

запива (се) *impf of* запие (се)

запие *pf* запи *aor.* **I** to start drinking **II – се** *colloq.* to hit the bottle, go on a bender

запизми (се) *pf colloq. see* замрази² (се)

запина (се) *impf see* запнува (се)

запир *m* stop; (*прекин*) pause, break, interruption; без запир without a break, ceaselessly; continually; without delay; ❑ тој запир не знае he knows no rest

запира¹ *impf* **I 1** *of* запре **2** запира со јазикот to stutter, stammer **II – се** *of* запре се

запира² *impf see* заперува

запирка *f* comma; точка и запирка semicolon

запис *m* **1** note; record; благајнички запис treasury bill **2** (*амајлија*) amulet, lucky charm **3** *pl* записи memoirs

записка *f* note, observation; (*во весник*) <brief> report

записник -ци *m* minutes, record; води записник to take minutes; записник од седница minutes of a meeting; записник на штета damage survey (report)

записничар *m* minutes secretary; (*на полициско сослушување*) recording clerk; (*на судот*) clerk of the court

записнички *adj* minutes *attrib.*

запише *pf* запиша *aor.* **I 1** to write down, note down, to jot down; to record; запише лекција to take notes of a lecture; ❑ запиши го на мразот you can write it off **2** to enter, register, enrol; запишаа детево книгата на родените to register the birth of a child; запише дете на училиште to enrol a child at school; запише во црниот тефтер to blacklist (*даде прилог*) to contribute; запише сто денари to contribute a hundred denars **4** to start writing **II – се 1** to sign up (*за – for*) *intrans.*; to enrol *intrans.*; се запише на факултет to enrol at university **2** to become engrossed in writing

запишува (се) *impf of* запише (се)

запишувач *m* record clerk; recording secretary; *Sport.* scorekeeper

запладни *pf* **I 1** to start resting in the shade **2** to drive (*sheep*) to rest in the shade **II – се** *impers.* to reach midday; се запладни веќе it's midday already

запладнува (се) *impf of* запладни (се)

заплакне *pf* заплакна *aor.* to rinse

заплакнува *impf of* заплакне

заплакува <се> *impf see* заплачува <се>

запламти *pf* **I 1** to flare up; to burst into flame **2** *fig.* to flash; to start shining/flashing **3** (*почне да гори во лицето*) to <start to> blush, become flushed **II – се** to flare up

запламтува (се) *impf of* запламти (се)

заплаче <се> *pf* заплака *aor.* to burst into tears

заплачува <се> *impf of* заплаче <се>

заплаши *pf* **I 1** to frighten, scare **2** to threaten **II – се** to be frightened, take fright

заплашува (се) *impf of* заплаши (се)

заплашувачки *adj* threatening, menacing

заплена *f Leg.* confiscation, seizure

запленет *pt* confiscated; запленети стоки seized goods

заплени *pf* **1** to seize; to confiscate; заплени шверцувани стоки to confiscate smuggled goods **2** *rare* to capture, take prisoner **3** *fig. rare* (маѓепса) to captivate, charm

запленува *impf of* заплени

заплеска *pf* **1** to <begin to> applaud (clap) **2** to <start to> thin out (*dough, etc.*) **3** to knead hastily; to do s.th. shoddily, hastily **4** to start slapping/spanking

заплескува *impf of* заплеска

заплесне се *pf* **1** *see* занесе се **2** *see* зазјапа се

заплеснува се *impf of* заплесне се

заплет *m* **1** *Literature* plot **2** *fig.* (компликација) complication

заплете *pf* **I 1** to start knitting **2** *see* заплетка **3** *dial.* (за коса) to plait **II – се 1** *see* заплетка се **2** *dial.* (за коса) to plait one's hair

заплетен *pt see* заплеткан

заплетка *pf* **I 1** to tangle, entangle, mix up **2** *fig.* to complicate; ја заплетка работата to confuse the issue **3** *fig. rare* to involve, entangle, enmesh; заплетка некого во скандал to involve s.o. in scandal **II – се 1** to get tangled (muddled, mixed up) **2** *fig.* to get mixed up, become confused; работите се заплеткаа things became confused **3** *fig. rare* (замеша се) to get involved (*во нешто – in s.th.*); to interfere (*во нешто – in s.th.*)

заплеткан *pt & adj* **1** complicated, confused; complex; заплеткан проблем complicated problem **2** (за човек) confused, bewildered

заплеткува (се) *impf of* заплетка (се)

заплетува (се) *impf of* заплете (се)

заплива *pf* **1** to start swimming **2** *fig.* to be filled with joy **3** *dial.* (за брод; со брод) to sail, set sail

заплиска *pf* **I 1** to <start to> splash; го заплиска со вода he splashed him with water **2** (*of rain*) to start pouring **II – се 1** to start splashing o.s. **2** to start splashing (spraying) one another

заплискува (се) *impf of* заплиска (се)

заплови *pf* to set sail, depart

заплоди (се) *pf see* оплоди (се)

заплодува (се) *impf of* заплоди (се), *see* оплодува (се)

запне *pf* запна *aor.* **I 1** to stick, get stuck, bog down *intrans.*; запна за камен to stumble (trip) on a stone **2** (во говор) to stumble; to stutter **3** (напрегне се) to exert o.s., make an effort; запне со сите сили to try one's hardest **4** to rush, hurry; каде си запнал? where are you rushing off to? take it easy! hold your horses! **5** to tighten *trans.*, make taut; запне јаже to tighten a rope **6** to insist (за – on) ; запне нозе to dig one's heels in **7** to catch, snag, hook *trans.*; ❑ запне некому за око to strike s.o.'s fancy **II – се 1** *see* I 3 **2** (закачи се) to get caught, snagged; се запне на (за) капина to catch one's clothes in brambles

запнува (се) *impf of* запне (се)

заповед *f* order, command

заповеда[1] *pf* to command, give an order, order

заповеда[2] *impf* **1** (*with dat.*) to order, command; и заповеда да дојде веднаш he ordered her to come straight away **2** (владее, повела) to rule, dominate; to give orders; to be in command (*со – of*); јас тука заповедам I'm in charge here; заповеда со војска to command an army

заповеден -дна *adj* commanding; imperious; peremptory; заповеден тон imperious tone; *Gram.* заповеден начин imperative <mood>

заповедник -ци *m* **1** (командант) commander **2** (господар) master, ruler; petty tyrant

заповедница *f* (*fem. form*) *see* заповедник

заповеднички *adj* imperious; peremptory; заповеднички тон peremptory tone

заповедништво *n* headquarters, HQ, High Command

заповедува *impf see* заповеда[2]

заповест *f rare see* заповед

запознава *impf of* запознае

запознае *pf* запозна *aor.* **I 1** to get to know; to acquaint o.s. with; запознае некого to get to know s.o. **2** to introduce (*со – to*); ме запозна со татка си he introduced me to his father **3** to acquaint, familiarize; запознае некого со ситуација to acquaint s.o. with a situation **II – се** to get acquainted (*со – with*); to meet

запомни *pf* to remember; to commit to memory, memorize

запомнува *impf of* запомни

запопи *pf* **I** to ordain **II – се** to take holy orders, enter the priesthood

запопува (се) *impf of* запопи (се)

запори *f* **1** to start to undo (unpick) **2** to rip

запорник -ци *m f.p.* former fiancé

запорува *impf of* запори

запоставен *pt* neglected

запоставеност *f* <state of> neglect

запостави *pf* to neglect

запоставува *impf of* запостави

запоти *pf* to decorate with greenery

запотка *f* the custom of decorating with greenery

запотне *pf* запотна *aor. see* запоти

запотнува *impf see* запотува

запотува *impf of* запоти

започне *pf* започна *aor.* **I 1** to start, begin *trans.* (*or with да – to*); започне да зборува to begin speaking; го започна својот говор he began his speech; започне работа to start work **2** to start, begin *intrans.*; играта започна the dancing started; започна нов живот a new life began **II – се** *rare see* I 2

започнува (се) *impf of* започне (се)

заправа *impf of* заправи

заправи *pf* to start making/building

заправо *adv* rather, more exactly; in fact, in truth, really, actually; *see* поправо

запрати *pf* to <start to> send, dispatch

запраќа *impf of* запрати

запраша *pf* **I 1** to ask, question **2** *rare* to start asking **II – се** to ask o.s.

запраши *pf* **I 1** to cover/sprinkle with dust; to scatter dust over; to dust **2** to raise dust **3** *rare* to start covering/sprinkling with dust **II – се** to get covered in dust

запрашува (се) *impf of* запраши (се)

запре *pf* **I 1** to stop *trans.*; to detain, hold up; запре кола to stop a car; запре некому плата to stop s.o.'s pay **2** to close, lock; to turn off; запре вода to turn off water **3** to stop *intrans.*, stand still; to stop working, break down; запри малку! hold on a moment! запрела трговијата trade has come to a standstill; запре стопанството the economy is stagnant **II – се** *see* I 3; му се запре крвта the blood froze in his veins; му се запре (зеде) здивот he stopped breathing; he lost his breath

запрега[1] *f* team; harness; воловска запрега a team of oxen

запрега[2] *impf of* запрегне

запрегне *pf* запрегна *aor.* I **1** to harness; (*волови*) to yoke **2** *fig.* to burden (*with work*) **3** *dial.* to roll up (*one's sleeves*) **II – се 1** to get down (*to work*) **2** *dial.* to roll up one's sleeves

запрегнува (се) *impf of* запрегне (се)

запреде *pf* I **1** to start spinning **2** to begin twisting thread (*for spinning*) **II – се** to become engrossed in spinning

запредува (се) *impf of* запреде (се)

запрежен -жна *adj* **1** draught (*animal*); запрежен коњ draught-horse **2** animal-drawn; запрежна артилерија horse-drawn artillery

запрепастен *pt rare* astonished, amazed; shocked

запрепасти *pf rare* to astonish, amaze; to shock, *see* вчудовиди

запрепастува *impf of* запрепасти, *see* вчудовидува

запрета[1] *pf* I **1** to build, pile up (*a fire*) **2** to cover, bury **II – се** *fig.* to be overburdened

запрета[2] *pf* **1** (*за кокошка и др.*) to start scratching (*the ground*) **2** *fig.* to start shaking (*one's legs*) **3** *fig. iron.* to start complaining, dig one's heels in

запретува[1] **(се)** *impf of* запрета[1] (се)

запретува[2] *impf of* запрета[2]

запречи *pf* **1** to block, bar; запречи некому пат to bar s.o.'s way **2** to block (*s.o.'s*) view **3** to roll up (*one's sleeves etc.*)

запречува *impf of* запречи

запржи *pf* **1** to fry lightly; to thicken *trans.;* to garnish with browned flour **2** to start frying

запржува *impf of* запржи

заприкаже *pf* заприкажа *aor.* I to detain in conversation; to distract **II – се** to become engrossed in conversation

заприкажува[1] *pf* to start telling (relating)

заприкажува[2] **(се)** *impf of* заприкаже (се)

заприлега *pf* (*на*) to start resembling

запристига *pf* to start arriving (*one after another*); запристигаа гости од сите страни guests started arriving from everywhere

запрли *pf* I **1** to <start to> dirty, soil **2** to singe, scorch **II – се 1** to get dirty **2** to get singed

запрли се *pf* to become pregnant (*of a female donkey*)

запролети се *impf impers.* to come, start (*of spring*); рано се запролети spring has come early

запролетува се *impf of* запролети се

запроси *pf* **1** to start begging **2** *f.p.* to ask (*for a girl*) in marriage

запросува *impf of* запроси

запрска *pf* **1** to start splashing (*s.o./s.th.*); to spurt, gush (*over, onto*) **2** to start flying (*of sparks*); запрскаа искри од сите страни sparks started flying from all sides

запруса *pf* to shorten one's step

запршка *f Cul.* thickening; brown sauce

заптиса *pf colloq.* **1** to confiscate; to seize **2** *impers.* (*with acc.*) ме заптиса во градите I felt a pain in my chest

заптисува *impf colloq.* **1** *of* заптиса **2** to keep a tight rein on

запупи *pf* to <start to> bud/blossom; запупија овошките the fruit trees are in bloom

запурнина *f* sultriness; stuffiness

запурничав *adj* **1** sultry; stuffy **2** (*of fruit*) sharp, astringent

запустен *pt* **1** abandoned, deserted; alone; запустена куќа abandoned/derelict house **2** ravaged, destroyed, ruined **3** neglected

запустеник -ци *m* **1** (*бездомник*) homeless person **2** (*неуреден човек*) sloven

запустеност *f* **1** dereliction **2** slovenliness

запусти *pf* I **1** to abandon, leave empty, leave derelict; to neglect **2** to destroy, ravage, lay waste, ruin **3** (*пари*) to squander **II – се 1** to become derelict, fall into disrepair; се запусти селово this village has become derelict **2** to neglect o.s.

запустикуќа *m & f colloq.* spendthrift, squanderer

запустува (се) *impf of* запусти (се)

запустувачка *f* destruction, ruin

запушта (се) *impf of* запусти (се)

запуштен *pt see* запустен 3

запушти *pf* I *see* запусти 3, занемари **II – се** *see* запусти се 2, занемари се

запче *n dim. of* заб

запчен *adj* cogged; запчена железница rack-and-pinion railway

запченик -ци *m Tech.* toothed wheel, cog; cam-wheel

запчест *adj* denticulated; запчест лист denticulated leaf

зар *part* **1** (*interrogatively, expressing surprise, incredulity*) really? зар и тој е дојден? has he really come too? зар ти не знаеш? don't you know? **2** perhaps, maybe; зар не е дојден човекот perhaps he hasn't come

заработи *pf* I **1** to earn; заработи многу пари to earn a lot of money **2** to start working; to find work **II – се 1** to become engrossed in one's work **2** *rare see* I 2

заработка *f* pay, earnings

заработува (се) *impf of* заработи (се)

заработувачка *f see* заработка

заради *prep* for the sake of, for; for the purpose of; because of; заради децата for the sake of the children; заради остварувањето на нашите задачи in order to achieve our aims

зарадува *pf* I to cheer, gladden, make happy **II – се** to be glad, happy; to rejoice

зараѓа се *impf of* зароди се

зараза *f* infection; contagion

заразен -зна *adj* infectious; заразна болест infectious disease; заразни бактерии infectious bacteria; *fig.* заразна смеа infectious laughter

зарази *pf* I to infect (*со – with*) (*also fig.*); to contaminate; to poison, pollute; зарази бунар to poison a well; *fig.* ги зарази со смеа his laughter infected them **II – се** to become infected (*од – with*) (*also fig.*), catch (*an infection*)

заразност *f* infectiousness

заразува (се) *impf of* зарази (се)

зарамни *pf* **1** to level **2** *rare* to start levelling

зарамнува *impf of* зарамни

зарана *adv dial. see* изутрина[2]

зарасне *pf* зарасна *aor.* **1** (*за градина*) to become overgrown (rank) **2** (*за рана*) to close, heal *intrans.*

зараснува *impf of* зарасне

зарасте *pf* **1** to start growing **2** *see* зарасне

зарастува *impf see* зараснува

зарача *pf* **1** (*даде порака*) to give an order; to order; to tell, ask (*некому да направи нешто – s.o. to do s.th.*); to send word (a message); му зарачав да дојде I sent word for him to come; го каниле магарето на свадба, му зарачале да си го земе самарот they sent him on a busman's holiday **2** *f.p.* (*вети*) to promise

зарачува *impf of* зарача

зарделија -ии *f Bot. see* кајсија

зардечал *m* turmeric

зарегистрира *pf see* регистрира

зареди *pf* **I 1** to start visiting; ги зареди сите пријатели по ред he started visiting all his friends in turn **2** to start speaking/telling; to start enumerating **II** – се to come one after another

заредува (се) *impf of* зареди (се)

зареже *pf* зережа *aor.* **1** to notch **2** to start cutting

зережува *impf see* зарезува

зарез *m* notch, cut

зарезува *impf of* зареже

зарек -ци *m* vow, pledge

зарекува се *impf of* зарече се

зарем *part see* зар

зарече *pf* зареков *aor. 1st p. sg* **I 1** to make (*s.o.*) renounce/swear <off>; ме зарекоа да не одам веќе таму they made me swear not to go there any more **2** to start telling (relating, narrating); само што го зарече словото, сите начулија уши as soon as he started speaking everybody pricked up their ears **II** – се **1** to vow, promise, pledge one's word **2** (*цврсто реши*) to swear <off>; to renounce; се зарекол да не пие веќе he swore off drinking

заречува се *impf see* зарекува се

зарешка *f* notch (*on wood*), cut (*on a tree*)

за'ржи *pf* **1** (*за коњ*) to <start to> neigh **2** (*за куче*) to <start to> growl (snarl) (*also fig.*)

за'ржува *impf of* за'ржи

зарзават *m colloq.* vegetables, greens, *see* зеленчук; ❑ разни зарзавати various things, odds and ends

зарзаватчија *m colloq.* greengrocer

зарине *pf* зарина *aor.* **1** to start shovelling **2** *see* заринка 2

заринка *pf* **1** to <go> bang; to thud **2** (*се забие*) to sink; to plunge; to get stuck; автомобилот заринка во калта the car sank (got stuck) in the mud **3** (*се сопне*) to stumble, trip **4** to start shovelling

заринкува *impf of* заринка

заринува *impf of* зарине

зарипнат *pt see* засипнат

зарипнатост *f see* засипнатост

зарипне *pf* зарипна *aor. see* засипне

зарипнува *impf see* засипнува

заробеник -ци *m* prisoner, captive (*also fig.*); (*осуденик*) convict

заробеница & **заробеничка** *f* (*fem. form*) *see* заробеник

заробенички *adj* prisoner's; заробенички логор POW camp

заробеништво *n* captivity

зароби *pf* **I** to enslave (*also fig.*); to reduce to bondage; (*во војна*) to capture, take prisoner **II** – се *fig.* to become a slave, be enslaved; ❑ се оженив, се заробив wedlock is a padlock

заробува (се) *impf of* зароби (се)

зароди се *pf* **1** *literary* to come into being, arise, appear, spring up; се зароди идеја an idea was born **2** (*стане род еден со друг*) to become related (*by marriage*)

зародиш *m see* зародок; ❑ уште во зародиш while still in embryo/bud; уништи во зародиш to nip in the bud

зародок -ци *m* **1** embryo, foetus **2** *fig.* germ, beginning, inception

зародува се *impf see* зараѓа се

зарои се *pf* to <start to> swarm

заројува се *impf of* зарои се

зарумене <се> зарумена <се> *aor. &* **зарумени** <се> *pf* to grow red; to flush (*of the face*), to blush

заруменува <се> *impf of* зарумене <се> *&* зарумени <се>

засади *pf* to <start to> plant

засадува *impf of* засади

засака *pf* **I 1** to take a liking (fancy) to; to fall in love with **2** to start wanting/wishing **II** – се to fall in love <with each other>

засакува (се) *impf of* засака (се)

засвати се *pf* to become related by marriage <of one's children>

засватува се *impf of* засвати се

засведочи *pf* to witness

засведочува *impf of* засведочи

засвети *pf* to <start to> shine

засветка *pf* to start glittering/gleaming, *impers.* (*of lightning*) to flash

засветкува *impf of* засветка

засветува *impf of* засвети

засвири *pf* to play; to start playing (*a musical instrument*)

засвирка *pf* to whistle; to <start to> whistle

засвирува *impf of* засвири

засвисти *pf* (*of a strong wind, a shot, etc.*) to whistle

засводен *pt* vaulted, arched

засводи *pf* to overarch, vault, cover with a vault

засебен -бна *adj* separate, *see* одделен

засева *impf of* засее

засега[1] *adv* for the time being, for the present, for the moment

засега[2] **(се)** *impf of* засегне (се); тоа не го засега that doesn't concern him; that does not apply to him

засегнат *pt* hurt, offended; deeply concerned

засегне *pf* засегна *aor.* **I 1** to touch **2** to catch, hook, brush against, graze; куршумот не го засегна the bullet missed him **3** *fig.* (*трогне*) to touch, move **4** *fig.* (*навреди*) to offend; to touch (*s.o.*) on the raw **5** to touch (*upon a question*), mention **II** – се to be offended (hurt) (*од – at*), take offence (*at*); to be concerned (*за – about*)

засегнува (се) *impf of* засега (се)

заседа *f* ambush; постави заседа to set an ambush; чека во заседа to lie in wait

заседава *impf* to sit, be in session

заседание -ија *n* session, sitting

заседи се *pf* заседе се *aor.* to sit/remain/stay for too long; to grow stiff <from sitting>

заседла *pf* to saddle

заседлува *impf of* заседла

заседне *pf* заседна *aor.* 1 *see* заседи се 2 *dial.* (*за сонце, месец*) to set

заседнува *impf of* заседне

заседува се *impf of* заседи се

засее *pf* засеа *aor.* to <start to> sow, plant

засек -ци *m* 1 cut, notch 2 a disease in goats, horses, etc.

засека *f* 1 forest clearing 2 (*натрупани дрвја на пат*) barrier, road-block

засеклив *adj* засеклива трева *Bot.* (Hypericum perforatum) Saint John's wort

засекник *m* & **засекница** *f see* засеклив<а трева>

засекогаш *adv* forever, for all time; for good

засекува *impf of* засече

засели *pf* **I** 1 to settle *trans.*, find housing (*for s.o.*) 2 to populate 3 to start moving *trans.* **II – се** 1 to settle (down) *intrans.*, take up residence 2 to start moving *intrans.*

заселува (се) *impf of* засели (се) I 1 & II 1

засени *pf* 1 to shade; to shield against the light; си ги засени очите to shade one's eyes; облаците го засенија сонцето the clouds hid the sun 2 *fig.* to eclipse, overshadow, outshine 3 (*with dat.*) to block out s.o.'s light; ми засени you're in my light

засенува *impf of* засени

засенчи *pf* 1 to shade (*painting, drawing*) 2 *rare see* засени 1 & 2

засенчува *impf of* засенчи

засече *pf* засеков *aor. 1st p. sg* 1 to notch 2 to start cutting

засечка *f see* зарешка

засечува *impf see* засекува

засили *pf* **I** 1 to strengthen, increase *trans.*; (*болка, глад, жед*) to intensify, increase; (*страдања, жед*) to aggravate; (*звук, тон*) to amplify; (*истакне*) to emphasize; засили напори to step up one's efforts 2 to strengthen, consolidate; засили своја позиција to consolidate one's position **II – се** 1 to become stronger (more powerful); (*за звук*) to grow louder, swell; to mount 2 (*запне, напрегне се*) to strain, exert o.s. 3 to dash, rush *intrans.*; кај си се засилил? where are you rushing off to? 4 (*стане груб*) to become arrogant

засилува (се) *impf of* засили (се)

засипе *pf* засипа *aor.* 1 to cover, bury; (*исполни*) to fill up, cover in 2 *fig.* to shower *trans.*; засипе со прашања to bombard with questions 3 (*почне да сипе*) to start pouring

засипнат *pt* hoarse; raucous; со засипнат глас in a hoarse voice

засипнатост *f* hoarseness

засипне *pf* засипна *aor.* to become hoarse; to lose one's voice

засипнува *impf of* засипне

засипува *impf of* засипе

засирен *pt* clotted; curdled; засирена крв clotted (coagulated) blood

засири *pf* **I** to curdle *trans.* **II – се** (*за млеко*) to curdle *intrans.*; (*за крв*) to clot, coagulate

засирува (се) *impf of* засири (се)

заситен *pt* 1 saturated; заситен раствор saturated solution; заситен воздух saturated air, saturated atmosphere 2 *fig.* sated, satiated

заситеност *f* saturation; satiation

засити *pf* **I** 1 to satisfy, sate; засити нечија љубопитност to satisfy s.o.'s curiosity 3 to saturate **II – се** to satisfy o.s., satiate o.s.; to have one's fill

заситни *pf* 1 to start chopping up 2 (*за чекор*) to shorten one's step

заситнува *impf of* заситни

заситува (се) *impf of* засити (се)

заскита <се> *pf* 1 to start wandering (roaming) 2 to wander off

заскитува <се> *impf of* заскита <се>

заскокотка *pf* to <start to> tickle; ова ќе ја заскокотка твојата фантазија this will tickle your fancy

заслаби *pf* 1 to grow a little weaker/thinner 2 to start growing weaker/thinner

заслабува *impf of* заслаби

заслади *pf* **I** to sweeten **II – се** to become sweeter; *fig.*, *impers.* (*with dat.*) му се заслади he got to like it, he liked it

засладува (се) *impf of* заслади (се)

заслепен *pt* blinded

заслепеност *f* blindness

заслепи *pf* **I** 1 to blind, dazzle (*also fig.*); to seduce; to lead astray 2 *fig.* to be blinded; кај заслепивме! how could we have overlooked that? how could we have gone wrong? **II – се** *see* I 2

заслепителен -лна *adj see* заслепувачки

заслепува (се) *impf of* заслепи (се)

заслепувачки *adj* blinding, dazzling; заслепувачка светлина dazzling light

заслуг *m* reception on the eve of a *slava*

заслуга *f* merit; по заслуга by/on merit

заслужен[1] -жна *adj* meritorious, of great merit; deserving; тие се заслужни за татковината they deserve well of their country

заслужен[2] *pt* deserved; заслужена награда well-deserved reward

заслужи[1] *pf* 1 to deserve, merit; заслужи награда to deserve a prize; заслужи ќотек to deserve a good hiding; тоа го заслужи serves him right! 2 *rare* (*спечали*) to earn

заслужи[2] *pf* to start serving

заслужува *impf of* заслужи[1]; си го заслужува лебот to earn one's bread

засмади *pf* to go bad, become rancid; to begin to smell of burning; *impers.* (*with dat.*) му засмади he noticed a rancid smell

засмадува *impf of* засмади

засмева (се) *impf of* засмее (се)

засмее *pf* засмеа *aor.* **I** to make (*s.o.*) laugh; to amuse, entertain **II – се** to burst out laughing; (*заедно*) to joke together

засмета *pf* 1 to start reckoning/calculating 2 to charge to s.o.'s account; ми го засмета пивото he charged me for the beer

засметува *impf of* засмета

засмоли *pf* (*измачка со смола*) to smear (coat) with resin (pitch); (*натопи со смола*) to soak in resin (pitch)

засмолува *impf of* засмоли

засмрди *pf* **I 1** to start stinking **2** to make (*s.th.*) malodorous; to cause to stink **II – се** to start stinking; to put on too much perfume

засмрдува (се) *impf of* засмрди (се)

заснежен *pt* snowbound, snowed under/in/up; (*покриен со снег*) covered in snow

заснежи *pf* **I 1** to begin to snow **2** (*покрие со снег*) to cover with snow **II – се** to get snowed in; to become covered in snow

заснежува (се) *impf of* заснежи (се)

заснова (се)[1] *impf of* заснове (се)[1]

заснова (се)[2] *impf of* заснове (се)[2]

заснове[1] *pf* заснова *aor.* **I 1** (*основе*) to found; to establish **2** (*базира*) to base **II – се** to base o.s. (*на – он*), base one's arguments, take one's stand

заснове[2] *pf* заснова *aor.* **I 1** (*при ткаење*) to start warping (forming a warp) **2** *fig.* to start moving/darting around; to start pottering about **3** to start wandering, roaming **II – се** *see* **I 2**

засновува (се)[1] *impf see* заснова (се)[1]

засновува (се)[2] *impf see* заснова (се)[2]

засолн *m rare see* засолниште

засолнат *pt* **1** hidden, concealed; sheltered **2** blocked, obstructed; засолнат поглед obstructed view

засолне *pf* засолна *aor.* **I 1** to remove **2** to shelter, cover, hide, protect; го засолнал со своето тело he shielded him with his own body **3** to obstruct a view; засолне некому поглед to obstruct s.o.'s view **II – се** (*прикрие се*) to hide *intrans.*, take cover, take shelter

засолниште *n* **1** screen **2** <place of> refuge, shelter

засолнува (се) *impf of* засолне (се)

заспан *adj* **1** (*only as predicate*) asleep, sleeping **2** *fig.* listless, lacking energy

заспаност *f* **1** sleepiness **2** *fig.* listlessness, apathy

заспива *impf of* заспие

заспие *pf* заспа *aor.* **1** to go to sleep, fall asleep **2** to put to bed; to lull to sleep

засрамен *pt* shamed, put to shame, disgraced

засрами *pf* **I** to shame, put to shame, disgrace; to embarrass **II – се** to feel ashamed

засрамува (се) *impf of* засрами (се)

засрка *pf* **I** to <start to> sip/lap **II – се** to become engrossed in sipping

засрклив *adj* prone to choking

засркне *pf* засркна *aor.* **I** to choke *trans.* **II – се** to choke *intrans.*

засркнува (се) *impf of* засркне (се)

заставник -ци *m Mil.* sergeant-major; *Hist.* standard-bearer; ensign

застакли *pf* **I** to glaze, fit with glass **II – се** to <start to> shine like glass

застаклува (се) *impf of* застакли (се)

застане *pf* застана *aor.* **1** to stop *intrans.*, stand still; застани малку wait a minute! застане на прсти to rise on tiptoe; саатот ми застанал my watch has stopped; застане на страна на to side with **2** (*зафати место*) to fit in; не можат да застанат сите овде they can't all get in (find room) here **3** to stop *trans.*; застане кола to stop a car **4** to stand *trans.*; застане кукла <на нозе> to stand a doll up

застанува *impf of* застане

застапен *pt* included; represented

застапи *pf* **I 1** (*замени*) to take the place of, stand in for, replace **2** (*претстави*) to represent **3** (*поддржува*) to support, uphold (*мислење, интереси*) **II – се** (*за*) to take s.o.'s side

застапник -ци *m* **1** representative, agent; (*заменик*) proxy **2** (*покровител*) patron; (*заштитник*) defender, champion; advocate

застапница *f* (*fem. form*) *see* застапник

застапништво *n* **1** representative's office; branch office; agency **2** (*покровителство*) patronage, protection

застапува (се) *impf of* застапи (се)

застарен *adj* old-fashioned; outdated, obsolete; застарен збор archaic word

застари *pf* **1** to become obsolete/old-fashioned, go out of date **2** to grow old; to <start to> grow old

застарлив *adj* obsolescent; of limited validity, limited term

застарливост *f* limited validity

застарува *impf of* застари

застова (се) *impf see* застојува (се)

застои *pf* застоја *aor.* **I** to stand up; to stand still **II – се** to stay; to tarry; to outstay one's welcome

застој -ои *m* stoppage, slow-down; stagnation; застој во работата slow-down at work; застој во производството standstill in production; технички застој technical hitch; застој во стопанскиот развиток stagnation in economic development

застојан *adj* stagnant, stale; застојана вода stagnant water

застојува (се) *impf of* застои (се)

застрани *pf rare* (*скршне*) to digress; to turn aside *intrans.*

застранува *impf of* застрани

застрашеност *f* fright, fear

застраши *pf* **I 1** to frighten **2** (*изложи на опасност*) to endanger, imperil **3** (*загрози*) to threaten, menace **II – се** to take fright

застрашува (се) *impf of* застраши (се)

застрашувачки *adj* **1** frightening **2** (*заканувачки*) threatening

застрела *pf* **I 1** to shoot *trans.* **2** to start shooting **II – се** to shoot o.s.

застрои *pf* застрои, застроја *aor. dial.* to season, spice (*food*)

заструг -зи *m* wooden bowl with a cover

заструга *pf see* застружe

застружe *pf* заструга *aor.* to <start to> sharpen, grind; to scrape; to plane

застружува *impf of* застружe

заструи *pf* to start flowing (*also fig.*); заструи нов живот a new life began

застуди *pf* застуде *aor.* to turn cold *intrans.*; времето застуде the weather has turned cold; *impers.* застуде it has turned cold; ми застуде I felt a chill

застудува *impf of* застуди

засука *pf* **I 1** to <start to> turn up, roll up *trans.*; засука ракави to roll up one's sleeves **2** to <start to> twist, twirl; засука мустаќи to twirl one's moustache **3** to <start to> roll *trans.* (*pastry*) **II – се 1** to roll up one's sleeves **2** to become twisted

засукува (се) *impf of* засука (се)

засуче (се) *pf* засука (се) *aor. see* засука (се)

засучува (се) *impf see* засукува (се)

засуши *pf* **I 1** to <start to> dry *trans.* **2** to dry *intrans.*, dry up/out **II – ce** *see* I 2

засушува (се) *impf of* засуши (се)

затаен *pt* concealed, secret; затаен живот secret life; ❑ со затаен здив with bated breath

затаеност *f* secrecy

затажи *pf* **I** to begin to grieve/lament/wail **II – ce** to feel sorry; to start grieving; (*за*) to miss; ce затажил за децата he missed his children

затажува (се) *impf of* затажи (се)

затаи *pf* **1** to conceal **2** to suppress, hold back; затаи здив to hold one's breath **3** (*проневери*) to embezzle

затајува *impf of* затаи

затакне (се) *pf* затакна *aor. see* задене (се)

затакнува *impf of* затакне

затала *pf see* заталка

заталка *pf* **1** to start wandering (roaming)/loitering **2** (*загуби се*) to get lost, go astray

заталкува *impf of* заталка

заталува *impf of* затала, *see* заталкува

затантен *adj* isolated; (*далечен*) out-of-the-way, remote, godforsaken; затантено село remote village

затантеност *f* remoteness

затанти се *pf* to isolate o.s.; кај си се затантил? where have you been hiding?

затанчи *pf* **I 1** to <start to> thin **2** *fig.* to start telling, relating in detail; to embroider **3** *rare* to <start to> grow thinner **II – ce** *see* I 3

затапен *pt & adj* **1** blunt; blunted **2** *fig.* slow-witted, obtuse

затапеност *f* **1** bluntness **2** *fig.* dullness, obtuseness

затапи *pf* **1** to blunt; *fig.* to deaden; to fuddle **2** to become dull/numb/blunt (*also fig.*); to flag *intrans.*

затапка *pf* **1** to stamp down, trample **2** to start stamping/trampling

затапува *impf of* затапи

затвор *m* **1** prison, jail, gaol; detention, imprisonment; истражен затвор pre-trial detention, remand; строг затвор maximum-security prison; лежи в затвор to be in prison, serve time **2** *dial. see* затворач

затвора (се) *impf of* затвори (се)

затворач *m* lock; cover, lid; (*на пушка*) breech-block; bolt; (*на фотоапарат*) shutter

затворен *pt & adj* **1** closed, shut **2** *fig.* (*молчалив*) reserved, taciturn, reticent **3** (*за боја*) dark **4** (*притворен*) arrested, taken into custody

затвореник -ци *m* prisoner; политички затвореник political prisoner

затвореница & затвореничка *f* (*fem. form*) *see* затвореник

затворенички *adj* prisoner's; затвореничка ќелија prisoner's cell

затвореност *f* reserve, reticence, taciturn nature

затвори *pf* **I 1** to close; to shut; затвори врата to close a door; си ги затвори очите to close one's eyes; ❑ затвори некому уста to stop s.o.'s mouth; затвори некому врата to shut the door on s.o.; затвори некому куќа to ruin s.o.; око не затвори he didn't sleep a wink **2** (*препречи*) to bar, block, stop; затвори пат to close a road; затвори граница to close a border **3** (*прекине дејство*) to turn off; затвори чешма to turn off a tap; затвори телефон to put down the receiver (telephone), hang up **4** to

confine, lock up; to imprison **5** (*заклучи*) to close, conclude; затвори седница to close (conclude) a meeting **II – ce** to close *intrans.*; се затворил в соба he locked himself up in his room; ❑ му се затворило срцето he is mean-spirited/tight-fisted; се затвори во себеси he has withdrawn (retreated) into himself

затворник -ци *m see* затвореник

затворница & затворничка *f see* затвореница & затвореничка

затворнички *adj see* затворенички

затворски *adj* prison

затврден *pt* solid, consolidated, firm; settled, regular; затврдена практика regular (established) practice

затврденост *f* consolidation; regularity; stability

затврди *pf* **I 1** (*зацврсти*) to strengthen, consolidate **2** (*утврди*) to fix, regularize **II – ce 1** to harden *intrans.* **2** to become stable, regular; to become accepted

затврдува (се) *impf of* затврди (се)

затега (се) *impf of* затегне (се)

затегнат *pt & adj* tense, strained; затегнати односи strained relations

затегнатост *f* tension, strain

затегне *pf* затегна *aor.* **I 1** (*напне*) to tighten, to strain; затегне жица to tighten a wire **2** *fig.* to prolong, drag out **II – ce 1** to become strained (tense); односите се затегнаа relations became strained **2** *fig.* to drag on; работата се затегна the affair dragged on

затегнува (се) *impf see* затега (се)

затемни *pf* **I 1** to darken; to black out *trans.* **2** to <start to> get dark **II – ce** to get dark; *impers.* ce затемни darkness has fallen

затемнува (се) *impf of* затемни (се)

затемнување *n* **1** darkening; obscuration; blackout **2** *Med.* shadow; consolidation; затемнување на градите area of consolidation (*on chest X-ray*), shadow on the lung<s> **3** eclipse; затемнување на сонцето eclipse of the sun

затера *pf* to start chasing/driving; како го затерало he's had a hard time

затести се *pf* to become like dough/pastry

затече[1] *pf* to start flowing

затече[2] *pf* затече *aor.*, затеков *aor. 1st p. sg* **I 1** to come (chance) upon, find; to catch; него го затековме таму we found him there; ги затече на дело he caught them in the act **2** to acquire (*stepchildren*) **II – ce** to find o.s. by chance (*somewhere*), chance to be

затечен *pt & adj see* заварен

затечува (се) *impf of* затече[2] (се)

затилница *f* clip (blow) on the back of the head

затина *impf of* затне

затир *m see* затор

затира (се) *impf of* затре (се)

затисне *pf* затисна *aor.* **1** to push, thrust **2** (*затне*) to cork, stop up, block

затиснува *impf of* затисне

затишие & затишје *n* lull; (*безветрина*) calm; ❑ затишје пред бура calm before the storm; живее во затишје to live in a quiet spot

затка *f* plug, stopper; cork

заткае *pf* затка *aor.* to start weaving; ❑ како се заткало така се доткало it ended as it began (*usu. badly*)

заткулисен -сна *adj* behind-the-scenes, secret, clandestine, covert; заткулисни преговори secret negotiations

затлакува (се) *impf of* затлачи (се)

затлачи *pf* I to cover with slime/mire/mud; (со тиња) to silt up *trans.* II – **се** to silt up *intrans.*

затлачува (се) *impf see* затлакува (се)

затне *pf* затна *aor.* to cork, stop up, plug, block; ❑ затне некому уста to shut s.o. up

затоа 1 *adv* so, therefore; затоа не дојдов that's why I didn't come; затоа, потоа all in good time 2 *conj* затоа што because

затолче & **затолчи** *pf* затолчи *aor.* 1 to start pounding/crushing 2 to pound/crush quickly 3 *fig.* to start buffeting (lashing); нè затолчи градот the hail started lashing us

затолчува *impf of* затолче & затолчи

затопли *pf* I to heat (*a room*); to warm up (*food, etc.*) II – **се** 1 to warm o.s. 2 (*за време*) to get warmer; to warm up *intrans.*; времево се затопли the weather has got warmer

затоплува (се) *impf of* затопли (се)

затор *m* destruction, annihilation, extermination, ruin

заточение *n* imprisonment, captivity; exile

заточеник -ци *m* prisoner, captive; exile

заточеница *f (fem. form) see* заточеник

заточенички *adj* prisoner's, captive's; exile's

заточи[1] *pf* 1 to start pouring; to start tapping, selling (*beer, etc.*) 2 to start spinning (*silk*)

заточи[2] *pf* 1 to start sharpening 2 to sharpen a little

заточи[3] *pf* 1 to banish, exile 2 to imprison; to enslave

заточи се *pf* to file <along>, follow one after the other; се заточија колони војници по патиштата columns of troops filed along the roads

заточка се *pf* to straggle <along>; to drag o.s. along

заточник -ци *m literary, rare* advocate, champion

заточува *impf of* заточи[3]

затрава (се) *impf of* затрае[2] (се)

затрае[1] *pf* затраа *aor.* to start

затрае[2] *pf* затраа *aor.* I 1 to fall silent 2 to silence II – **се** *see* I 1

затрајува (се) *impf see* затрава (се)

затре *pf* затра *aor.* I to destroy, exterminate; to annihilate; го затреа селото they obliterated (razed) the village II – **се** to die out, become extinct; се затреа некои обичаи certain customs have died out; да му се затре семето! damn him!

затреба *pf* (*with dat.*) to become necessary; ако затреба if need be

затреви *pf* I to sow with grass II – **се** to become overgrown with grass

затресе *pf* I 1 to shake, shake up *trans.* 2 to start shaking *trans.* 3 *impers.* (*with dat.*) ме затресе I have fever II – **се** 1 to start shaking *intrans.*; се затресе земјата the ground began to quake 2 *fig.* (*за*) to start looking after (caring for)

затресен *pt* & *adj* full of cares, worried (*за* – *about*); тој е многу затресен за децата he is very concerned (worried) about the children

затреска *pf* 1 to bang, knock; to start banging, knocking *trans.* & *intrans.* 2 *fig.* to start eating (*of animals*); to start gulping/gorging II – **се** to lose one's head; се затреска во неа he fell head over heels in love with her

затрешти *pf* 1 to blare out 2 (*за гром*) to crash

затрештува *impf of* затрешти

затрива (се) *impf of* затрие (се)

затрие *pf* затри *aor.* I 1 to start rubbing 2 to rub lightly; to massage II – **се** 1 to start rubbing *intrans.* 2 to rub lightly <together> *intrans.*

затрни *pf* I 1 to close off with thorns 2 *fig.* to ruin II – **се** to become overgrown with thorns

затрнува (се) *impf of* затрни (се)

затроши *pf* I 1 to start spending/consuming 2 to start crumbling *trans.* II – **се** 1 to start crumbling *intrans.*; лебот се затроши the bread has started crumbling 2 to be partially used up

затрошува (се) *impf of* затроши (се)

затрпи *pf* to begin to suffer; затрпи за леб to go hungry

затрудни *pf* to conceive, become pregnant

затруднува *impf of* затрудни

затруе *pf* затру *aor.* to <start to> poison (*also fig.*), contaminate; затруе односи to poison relations

затруен *pt* & *adj* poisoned (*also fig.*); bitter, angry; затруен непријател bitter enemy;

затруеност *f* poisoned state; bitterness, anger

затрупа *pf* 1 to <start to> fill up/in 2 to cover up, bury 3 *fig.* to shower, ply; to overwhelm, swamp; (*со работа*) to overload, overburden; го затрупаа со прашања they bombarded him with questions

затрупан *pt* & *adj* overloaded, overburdened, overworked

затрупува *impf of* затрупа

затрча се *pf* 1 to start running 2 *fig.* (*избрза, истрча се*) to hurry, rush, dash

затрчува (се) *impf of* затрча (се)

затскрива (се) *impf of* затскрие (се)

затскрие *pf* затскри *aor.* I 1 to cover; облаците го затскрија сонцето the clouds obscured the sun 2 to conceal, hide; to shelter *trans.* 3 to remove, put away II – **се** 1 to hide *intrans.*; to take cover/shelter 2 to go away, get away, get out

затсношти *adv see* прексиноќа

затутули *pf* to wrap too warmly

закори се *pf colloq. see* заслепи се

закорува се *impf of* закори се

закути (се) *pf see* замолчи (се)

закутува (се) *impf of* закути (се)

заузди *pf* to curb, bridle; *fig.* to pull up, restrain, subdue; него треба да го зауздиме we must restrain him

зауздува *impf of* заузди

заулави *pf* I 1 to drive mad, madden 2 to <start to> go mad (crazy) II – **се** *see* I 2

зауми *pf* 1 *see* запамети 2 (*спомне*) to mention 3 (*потсети*) to remind; му заумив за тоа I reminded him about that 4 (*забележи*) to notice, observe II – **се** to start thinking, become pensive/concerned

заумува (се) *pf of* зауми (се)

заусти *pf* to open one's mouth (*to speak*); to be on the point of speaking/saying; заусти да рече he was about to say

заустува *impf of* заусти

заутка *pf* to start hooting (*of an owl*)

зауткува *impf of* заутка

заутре *adv see* задутре

заутрешен -шна *adj see* задутрешен

заучи *pf* **1** to start learning **2** to start going to school; заучија децата the children have started going to school

заучува *impf of* заучи

заушен -шна *adj* parotid (near the ear); заушни жлезди parotid glands

зауши *pf dial.* **I 1** (*забележи*) to notice, observe **2** to slap s.o.'s face **II – се** to curl round the ears *intrans.* (*of a lock of hair*)

заушки *pl Med.* mumps

заушници *pf see* заушки

заушува (се) *impf of* зауши (се)

зафали *pf* **I** to start praising **II – се 1** to boast, brag **2** to threaten (*дека – to*)

зафат *m* **1** step, initiative, endeavour **2** intervention; treatment; хируршки зафат surgical operation

зафатен *pt & adj* busy; occupied; (*телефонска линија*) engaged; сите места се зафатени all seats are occupied

зафати *pf* **I 1** (*започне*) to begin, start; to strike up; зафати да прикажува to start telling a story **2** to occupy, take; зафати маса to occupy a table; зафати место to take up space **3** to catch, graze, brush *trans.* **4** (*опфати, обземе*) to seize, take hold of; ги зафатила паника they were seized by panic; огнот ја зафати целата куќа the fire engulfed the whole house **5** (*засегне*) to touch on, broach (*a question, etc.*); тој зафати и ред други прашања he touched on a number of other questions **II – се 1** (*со*) to embark on, set about **2** (*со*) to take up with; се зафати со шефот she took up with the boss **3** (*успее*) to rise in society; to improve one's material position **4** (*за растение*) to take root, establish itself

зафатнина *f* volume, capacity

зафаток -ци *m rare see* почеток

зафаќа (се) *impf of* зафати (се)

зафрла¹ *pf* to start throwing

зафрла² *impf of* зафрли

зафрлен *adj* isolated, remote; зафрлен крај remote region

зафрленост *f* isolation, remoteness

зафрли *pf* **1** to throw away/aside **2** (*заметне*) to put away carelessly, mislay, misplace; кај ги зафрли клучевите? where did you put the keys?

зафрлува *impf dial. see* зафрла²

зафучи *pf* **1** (*за ветар*) to start whistling/howling **2** to throw, hurl, fling

захрани *pf* **I 1** to start feeding **2** to feed; захрани некого со леб to feed s.o. on bread **II – се** to feed (*co – on*) *intrans.*, eat

захранува (се) *impf of* захрани (се)

запапа *pf* **I 1** to start treading; to tread, walk, wade **2** *fig.* to get stuck, bogged down **II – се 1** *see* I 2 **2** *fig. colloq.* to fall madly in love

зацари *pf* **1** to proclaim (*s.o.*) emperor **2** to become ruler, ascend the throne, begin one's reign **3** *fig.* to set in, prevail; зацари тишина silence descended (reigned supreme)

зацарува¹ *impf of* зацари

зацарува² *pf see* зацари 2 & 3

зацврсне (се) *pf* зацврсна (се) *aor. rare see* зацврсти (се)

зацврсти *pf* **I 1** to strengthen, reinforce; to fortify; зацврсти ѕид to reinforce a wall **2** *fig.* to consolidate; зацврсти своја позиција to consolidate one's position **II – се** to establish o.s. firmly; to consolidate *intrans.*

зацврстува (се) *impf of* зацврсти (се)

зацеди *pf* **I 1** to start straining (filtering) **2** to squeeze lightly (*also fig.*); to put pressure on **II – се** to start dripping

зацели (се) *pf literary see* залечи (се)

зацеп *m* notch; cleft, split, crack (*in a tree*)

зацепи *pf* **1** to start chopping (*wood*) **2** (*направи зацеп*) to make a notch; to notch **3** *colloq.* зацепи сè во еден правец to hold stubbornly to one's course

зацивка *pf* to give a squeak

зацрвени *pf* **I** (*поцрвени*) to make red, redden **II – се 1** to turn red *intrans.*; to appear (show) red **2** to start blushing

зацрвенува (се) *impf of* зацрвени (се)

зацрви (се) *pf see* зацрвени (се)

зацрвува (се) *impf of* зацрви (се)

зацрни *pf* **I 1** (*поцрни*) to blacken **2** to start blackening **3** *fig.* to make (*s.o.*) suffer; to hurt *trans* **II – се 1** (*стане црн*) to go (turn) black; се зацрни небото the sky turned black **2** to start going black **3** *fig.* to become distressed; to bring misery on o.s.

зацрнува (се) *impf of* зацрни (се)

зачади (се) *pf see* задими (се)

зачадува (се) *impf see* задимува (се)

зачас *adv* in a moment, in a minute; immediately, right away

зачека *pf* **1** to start waiting **2** to surround; го зачекаа од сите страни they surrounded him from all sides **3** *colloq.* to be enough, suffice; нè зачека брашното до пролет we have enough flour to last till spring

зачекори *pf* to step, take a step; to start stepping/walking

зачекорува *impf of* зачекори

зачели *pf f.p.* to fence round, close off

зачепи *pf* to cork; to block up

зачепува *impf of* зачепи

зачестен *adj* frequent

зачестеност *f* frequency

зачести¹ *pf* **1** (*да*) to take to; зачести да оди кај нив he's taken to visiting them **2** to become more frequent; зачестија посети visits have become more frequent; зачести топовската стрелба the cannon fire intensified

зачести² *pf* **I** to start treating, entertaining (*with food and drink*) **II – се** to start treating o.s. (*co – to*)

зачестува *impf of* зачести¹

зачетен -тна *adj* initial, opening; embryonic

зачеток -ци *m* **1** (*почеток*) beginning, inception **2** (*ембрион*) embryo

зачеша *pf* **I** to start scratching *trans.* **II – се 1** to start scratching *intrans.* **2** to touch, brush (*на – against*)

зачешла *pf* **I 1** to start combing **2** to comb, comb back **3** to comb lightly **II – се** to <start to> comb one's hair

зачешлува (се) *impf of* зачешла (се)

зачешува (се) *impf of* зачеша (се)

зачина *impf of* зачне

зачини *pf* to start doing/making

зачисти *pf* **1** to start cleaning **2** to clean slightly/superficially

зачистува *impf of* зачисти

зачита *pf* **I** to start reading **II** – **се** to become engrossed in reading

зачитува (се) *impf of* зачита (се)

зачкива *pf* **1** to start squinting **2** to <start to> flicker; ламбата зачкива the lamp started flickering

зачкивува *impf of* зачкива

зачкрипи *pf* **1** to start creaking/squeaking **2** *fig.* to start going wrong **3** to start gnashing/grinding (*one's teeth*)

зачкрипува *impf of* зачкрипи

зачкрта *pf* **1** to start gnashing/grinding (*one's teeth*) **2** to start creaking **3** to cross out, delete

зачкртува *impf of* зачкрта

зачлени *pf* **I** to enrol, enlist *trans.* **II** – **се** to become a member; се зачлени во партија to join a party

зачленува (се) *impf of* зачлени (се)

зачмае *pf* зачмаја *aor.* **1** to stay for a long time; to start languishing (pining, wasting away) **2** to become apathetic

зачмаен *pt* lifeless, apathetic, listless, indifferent

зачмаеност *f* listlessness, indifference, apathy

зачмајува *impf of* зачмае

зачне *pf* зачна *aor.* **I** **1** (*започне*) to start, begin *trans.* **2** (*затрудни*) to become pregnant **3** *fig.* to cause (*pain, worry etc.*) **II** – **се** **1** to begin *intrans.* **2** to arise, be born (conceived) *also fig.*; се зачна идејата the idea arose

зачнува (се) *impf see* зачина (се)

зачува *pf* **I** **1** (*заварди, запази*) to preserve, save, keep; *rare* to begin preserving; ти го зачував местото I have kept the place for you; тој го зачува присуството на духот he kept his presence of mind **2** (*заштити*) to save, defend; зачува некому живот to save s.o.'s life **3** (*заштеди*) to save <up> (*money*); има зачувано некоја пара he has saved a bit of money **II** – **се** to save o.s.

зачуван *pt & adj* saved, preserved; well preserved

зачуден *pt & adj* astonished, amazed

зачуденост *f* astonishment, amazement

зачуди *pf* to astonish, amaze

зачудо *adv* surprisingly, strange to say, strangely

зачудува *impf of* зачуди

зачуе *pf* зачу *aor.* **I** to hear (*from afar*), catch **II** – **се** *impers.* (*with dat.*) ми се зачу I seemed to hear, I think I heard; I heard something

зачука *pf* **1** to bang, hit (*with a hammer*); to nail **2** (*зацрпона*) to knock (*на врата* – *on a door*) **3** to knock/beat for a long time **4** to start knocking/beating

зачукува *impf of* зачука

зачуми *pf* to afflict with the plague; to contaminate, infect

зачури *pf* **1** to fill with smoke *trans.* **2** to start smoking *intrans.*; зачури оцакот the chimney started smoking **3** *dial. colloq.* to start smoking (*tobacco*) **II** – **се** *see* задими се, зачади се

зачурува (се) *impf of* зачури (се)

зацапа *pf* (*обично за риба*) to start pulling/biting

зашарок -ци *m* decorative design, pattern; motif

зашеметен *pt* stunned, astounded, *colloq.* flabbergasted

зашеметеност *f* amazement, astonishment

зашемети *pf* to stun; *fig.* to astonish, amaze, astound

зашеметува *impf of* зашемети

зашета *pf* **I** to start strolling **II** – **се** to get carried away with the pleasure of walking

зашеќери *pf* **I** **1** to sugar, sweeten (*also fig.*) **2** to turn (*s. th.*) into sugar **II** – **се** to crystallize, turn into sugar *intrans.*; слатково се зашеќерило this fruit preserve has crystallized

зашеќерува (се) *impf of* зашеќери (се)

зашиба *pf* **1** to start whipping, beating; тој ги зашиба коњите he started whipping the horses **2** *colloq. Sport.* to score (*гол* – *a goal*) **3** *sl.* to start deceiving **4** to start pouring *intrans.*; зашиба еден дожд rain came pelting down **5** *sl.* to start telling lies, lying

зашива *impf of* зашие

зашие *pf* заши *aor.* **1** to sew (stitch) on/up; зашие рана to stitch a wound **2** to sew in; ги зашил парите во палтото he sewed the money into his coat **3** to start sewing

зашили *pf* to <start to> sharpen

зашилува *impf of* зашили

зашлака *pf* **I** **1** *see* заплиска **2** to start slapping **II** – **се** **1** *see* заплиска се **2** *rare* to start slapping one another

зашлапа *pf* **1** to start wading/splashing/paddling **2** to get stuck (*in mud*)

зашлапува *impf of* зашлапа

зашмрка *pf* **I** **1** to start sniffing *trans. & intrans.* **2** to start syphoning/drawing/sucking **II** – **се** to start sniffing *intrans.*

зашмркува (се) *impf of* зашмрка (се)

зашмука *pf* **1** to start sucking <in> **2** *fig.* to start exploiting unscrupulously **3** to start kissing noisily; to start clicking one's tongue

зашрафи *pf* to screw down

зашрафува *impf of* зашрафи

заштеда *f* economies, savings

заштеди *pf* to <start to> save (*money*); to save up; заштеди илјада денари to save a thousand denars; заштеди за куќа to save for a house

заштедува *impf of* заштеди

заштита *f* protection; (*покровителство*) patronage; ги зедоа во заштита they took them under their protection (wing); здравствена заштита health care, public health service; хигиенско-техничка заштита industrial safety, safety at work

заштитен -тна *adj* protective; заштитни средства means of protection; заштитни очила protective glasses (goggles); заштитни мерки protective measures; заштитен знак trade mark

заштити *pf* **I** to protect, defend **II** – **се** to protect/defend o.s.

заштитник -ци *m* champion, patron

заштитница *f* **1** (*fem. form*) *see* заштитник; patroness **2** *Mil.* rearguard

заштитува (се) *impf of* заштити (се)

зашто **1** *conj* because, as **2** *conj dial. see* дека; не знаев зашто си болен I didn't know that you were ill **3** *adv dial.* why, *see* зошто

заштури се *pf* **1** to start moving around, pottering about here and there **2** (*стане штур*) to grow stupid **3** (*се изгуби*) to get lost, disappear

зашутка се *pf* to start pottering about

збабарен *pt & adj* wrinkled, wizened

збабари се *pf* to become wrinkled

збабарува се *impf of* збабари се

збаби се *pf see* збабари се

збабува се   *impf see* збабарува се

збае   *pf dial.* **1** to trample, stamp down **2** to scatter around

збере (се)   *pf* збра (се) *aor. see* собере (се); ❑ збери си го умот think what you are doing! come to your senses!

збеснат   *adj* unmanageable; dissolute, debauched

збеснатик   -ци *m* unmanageable/dissolute person

збеснатост   *f* recalcitrance, unruliness; dissoluteness

збеснее   *pf* збеснеа *aor. see* збесни

збесни   *pf* збесна *aor.* **1** to go mad; to lose one's temper; to become rabid **2** *fig.* to become unmanageable/dissolute/debauched

збеснува   *impf of* збесни

збива¹ (се)   *impf of* збие¹ (се)

збива²   *impf* to pant, gasp

збива³ се   *impf of* збие² се

збива⁴ се   *impf of* збие³ се

збивта   *impf see* збива²

збигороса   *pf* **1** to turn into limestone *intrans.* **2** *dial.* to turn sour *intrans.*; *fig.* to become embittered

збидне се   *pf* збидна се *aor.* to be fulfilled (realized); зборовите му се збиднаа his words came true

збиднува се   *impf of* збидне се

збие¹   *pf* зби *aor.* **I** to compress, press together; to compact; ❑ збие редови to close ranks **II** – се to press together *intrans.*; to become denser

збие² се   *pf* зби се *aor. rare* **1** to fight **2** *f.p.* to start feeling labour pains

збие³ се   *pf* зби се *aor.* to happen, occur, take place; ❑ мене ми се збило misfortune has struck me

збиен   *pt & adj* **1** pressed together; compacted; збиени редови serried ranks **2** (*за стил*) concise, compressed, condensed; збиено излагање succinct presentation/report

збиеност   *f* **1** compactness **2** (*концизност*) conciseness, succinctness

збир   *m* total, sum

збира (се)   *impf of* збере (се)

збиралиште   *n see* собиралиште

збирало   *n see* собиралиште

збирен   -рна *adj* collective; *Gram.* збирна именка collective noun

збирка¹   *f* collection; збирка песни collection of songs

збирка² (се)   *impf dim. of* збира (се)

збирштина   *f iron.* **1** mob, rabble **2** heap (*of junk*)

збит   *adj rare see* збиен; *dial.* збита трева thick grass

збитак   -ци *m see* збиток

збиток   -ци *m* plump person; stocky (thickset) person

збитолист   *adj dial.* with dense foliage

зближи   *pf* **I** to bring nearer (closer) (*also fig.*) **II** – се to get closer (*со – то*); to become close friends (*со – with*)

зближува (се)   *impf of* зближи (се)

збогати   *pf* **I** to enrich, make rich **II** – се to get rich

збогатува (се)   *impf of* збогати (се)

збогува се   *impf* to say goodbye (*со – то*), take one's leave (*of*)

збогум   *adv* goodbye, *literary, poet.* farewell; си зеде збогум he said goodbye, he took his leave; ❑ си земе збогум од, рече збогум на to say goodbye to, write off, kiss goodbye

збодне   *pf* збодна *aor.* **I** to drive (*a horse*) faster (*on*), spur on (*also fig.*) **II** – се to rush, dash forward, race

збоднува (се)   *impf of* збодне (се)

зболи   *pf* **1** to hurt suddenly; to stab, pierce (*of pain*) **2** (*заболи*) to start hurting (aching)

зболсне   *pf dial.* зболсна *aor. see* блесне, заблесне

зболснува   *impf of* зболсне

зболува   *impf of* зболи 1

збор¹   *m* **1** word; празни зборови empty (vain) words; тешки зборови harsh words; зборови на песна lyrics of a song; од збор до збор word for word, literally; со други зборови in other words; that is to say; со еден збор in a word; во вистинска смисла на зборот in the true sense of the word; според неговите зборови in his words; ❑ последен збор на модата the last word in fashion; ама збор <кажа>! what a thing to say! дојде на мојот збор I told you so; збор да нема **1**. without further ado **2**. certainly, of course; no question about it; се вели збор; што се вели зборот as they say; зборот не е за тоа that is not the point; станува збор за the issue is, the point is; чесен збор honestly, on my word of honour; човек од збор a man of his word; дава збор to give one's word; си го повлекува зборот to eat one's words; има последен збор to have the last word; скапи му се зборовите he's a man of few words; слушај ми го зборот listen to what I say; му се јаде (слуша) зборот his word is law; скршивме некој збор we had a little chat; фрли некој збор за мене put in a word for me; си стои на зборот he stands on his word, he keeps to his word; во неколку зборови in sum; in short; to cut a long story short; збор по збор one word leads to another; не бира зборови not to mince words; give it to s.o. straight from the shoulder; срамотни зборови four-letter words; obscenities; многу зборови – торба ореви *prov.* fine words butter no parsnips; прецеди го зборот, после речи го *prov.* weigh your words carefully **2** agreement; не ни беше така зборот that's not what was agreed **3** speech; right to speak; има збор to have the floor; даде некому збор to call upon s.o. to speak; одземе некому збор to cut s.o. off; за тебе збор, за магаре оро *prov.* talking to you is like talking to a brick wall

збор²   *m dial. see* собир, собор

зборави се   *pf impers.* (*with dat.*) му се збораи he felt ill

зборавува се   *impf of* зборави се

зборен   -рна *adj* meeting, assembly *attrib.*; зборно место meeting place, assembly point

збори се   *pf* to start wrestling

зборлест   *adj* talkative; loquacious, garrulous

зборлив   *adj see* зборлест

зборливост   *f* talkativeness; garrulity, loquacity

зборне   *pf* зборна *aor.* to say, utter; зборни нешто за мене put in a word for me

зборник   -ци *m* collection, anthology; miscellany; зборник на народни песни a collection of folk songs

зборнува   *impf of* зборне

зборовен   -вна *adj* **1** lexical; зборовен фонд vocabulary, lexical stock **2** *Gram.* зборовни групи parts of speech, word categories

зборообразување   *n* word formation

зборува¹   *impf* **I** **1** to speak, talk; to converse; to say; to tell; зборува руски to speak Russian; зборува за многу работи to talk of many things; ❑ не зборувај! you don't say! really! зборува како празна воденица; зборува како навиен to talk nineteen to the dozen; зборувај си <на сидот> ако немаш работа 1. it's like talking to a wall 2. tell that to the marines! зборуваат на разни јазици they're speaking different languages, they can't agree 2 *fig.* to indicate, suggest; to testify; сето тоа зборува дека не си прав all this suggests that you are wrong; фактите го зборуваат спротивното the facts suggest the contrary; ❏ само по (од) себе зборува <доволно> it speaks for itself, it goes without saying, it is self-evident 3 *colloq.* to slander, defame, run down 4 *f.p.* to promise (*usu. in marriage*) **II – се 1** it is said; people say; кај (како) се зборувало така! how can you say that? how dare you! **2** *impers.* (*without or with dat.*) не ми се зборува I don't feel like talking; не се зборува така that's no way to talk

зборува² **се** *impf of* збори се

зборувач *m* speaker

збратимен *pt & adj* fraternal; twinned; збратимени градови twin cities

збратими *pf* **I** to take as a brother; to twin *trans.* **II – се** to unite as brothers; to fraternize

збратимува (се) *impf of* збратими (се)

збрбешка *pf dial.* 1 to dirty, soil 2 to roll in the mud *trans.*

збрбори *pf* 1 to start babbling, chattering 2 (*за вода*) to start bubbling

збрден -дна *adj* steep

збрева *pf* 1 to start panting/gasping 2 to start pounding (*of the heart*)

збревта *pf see* збрева

збрише *pf* збриша *aor.* 1 to rub out, erase 2 *fig.* (*уништи*) to destroy; to liquidate 3 to run away; to escape (*од – from*); збрише од затвор to escape from prison

збришува *impf of* збрише

збрка¹ *f* confusion; настана збрка confusion arose

збрка² *pf* **I** 1 to muddle, confuse; to mistake; збрка пат to go the wrong way; ❏ сосем ги збркал конците he's made a complete mess of it 2 to make a mistake **II – се 1** to get confused 2 to lose one's way, get lost

збрка³ *pf* **I** 1 to hustle, hurry (*s.o.*) 2 to throw out, send packing 3 to start chasing **II – се** to start chasing one another

збркан *pt & adj* confused, perplexed; embarrassed; put out

збрканост *f* confusion, perplexity; embarrassment

збркува¹ (се) *impf of* збрка² (се)

збркува² (се) *impf of* збрка³ (се)

збрлави (се) *pf see* збрливи (се)

збрливи *pf* **I** 1 to cause to look foolish; to make a fool of 2 to astound **II – се** *see* збудали (се)

збрчи *pf* 1 (*за пчели и сл.*) to start buzzing 2 (*за мотор*) to start throbbing/roaring; ❏ се збрчи работата the business (job) has got going

збрчка *pf* to wrinkle; to crumple, crease

збрчкан *pt* wrinkled, shrivelled, wizened; crumpled, creased

збрчкоса *pf dial. see* збрчка

збрчкува *impf of* збрчка

збрчува *impf of* збрчи

збува *pf see* збувта

збувне *pf* збувна *aor.* to rise, prove (*usu. of dough*)

збувнува *impf of* збувне

збувта *pf* to start battering/beating

збудали *pf* **I** 1 to stultify; to make a fool of 2 *fig.* to astonish, shock **II – се** to become foolish, go crazy

збудалува (се) *impf of* збудали (се)

збуди *pf f.p.* **I** to wake, awaken *trans.* **II – се** to wake up *intrans.*

збунет *pt* confused, perplexed; embarrassed; put out

збунетост *f* confusion, perplexity; embarrassment

збуни *pf* **I** 1 to confuse, embarrass, perplex 2 *rare* to arouse, stir up; to alarm **II – се** 1 to get confused (embarrassed, perplexed) 2 *rare* to become aroused/alarmed

збунлив *adj* easily confused, embarrassed

збунува (се) *impf of* збуни (се)

збурбати се *pf impers. dial. see* слоши се

збуричка *pf* **I** to stir; to mix up, confuse **II – се** 1 to get confused; to become complicated; се збуричка работата the plot has thickened 2 *rare* to clash, come to blows, pitch into one another; се збуричкаа како петли they went for each other like fighting cocks

збуричкува (се) *impf of* збуричка (се)

збута *pf* **I** 1 to push, shove, jolt 2 to put away, shove somewhere; to push (shove, squeeze) in *trans.* **II – се** 1 to start pushing (shoving) *intrans.* 2 to push in *intrans.*

збуца *pf* **I** 1 to stick (*s.th.*) in 2 (*за волови*) to start butting suddenly

збуцува *impf of* збуца

збучи *pf* to start booming/roaring

збучува *impf of* збучи

зван *adj in the expression:* звани и незвани the deserving and the undeserving; all and sundry

звание *n see* звање

званик -ци *m* <invited> guest, guest of honour

званица *f* 1 (*fem. form*) *see* званик 2 bride's attendants 3 wedding invitation 4 flask of wine or brandy (*traditionally offered when inviting guests to a wedding*)

званичен -чна *adj see* официјален

звање *n* 1 title, rank; profession, vocation, calling; звање <на> полковник rank of colonel; звање на професор title of professor; почесно звање honorary title; високо звање exalted calling 2 (*должност*) duty, position

звечка *f Bot. see* зајачковина

звук -ци -ови *m* sound; (*на филм*) soundtrack; *Phys.* брзината на звукот the speed of sound; до каде што допира звукот within earshot

звукомер *m Tech.* phonometer

звукоподражавање *n* onomatopoeia

звучен -чна *adj* 1 sound *attrib.*; sonic; звучна брзина the speed of sound; звучни ефекти sound effects 2 clear, ringing; resonant; sonorous; melodious; звучна фраза a sonorous phrase 3 *Gram.* voiced; звучни согласки voiced consonants 4 *fig.* звучно име eminent name; звучна титула imposing title

звучи *impf* to sound; to be heard; to ring out; пијаното убаво звучи the piano sounds beautiful; во неговиот глас звучеше радост his voice sounded glad

звучник -ци *m Tech.* megaphone; loud-hailer

звучност *f* sonority, melodiousness

згади **се** *pf* 1 (*with dat.*) to disgust, sicken; нечистотијата ми се згади I was revolted by the squalor 2 *impers.* (*with dat.*) му се згадило he felt revolted

згадува се *impf of* згади се

згази *pf* to trample, stamp (*on*), to crush; *fig.* згази нечии права to trample on s.o.'s rights

згазне *pf* згазна *aor.* 1 to step, tread (*on*) 2 to take one's stand; згазни убаво stand up properly

згазнува *impf of* згазне

згазува *impf of* згази

зган *m see* циган

згасне *pf* згасна *aor.* to go out (*of fire, flame, etc.*); *fig.* неговиот живот згасна his life was extinguished, he gave up the ghost

згаснува *impf of* згасне

згашти *pf* 1 to <start to> chase *trans. or with no*; згашти <по> некого 2 to corner, trap, seize, grab

згаштува *impf of* згашти

згине *pf* згина *aor.* to disappear, get lost

згинува *impf of* згине

зглавје *n* pillow, bolster; head of a bed

зглавка *f see* зглоб

зглавник -ци *m* turning-point in ploughing; head of furrow

зглавница *f see* зглавје

згласи *pf* **I** to harmonize, match, coordinate; to reconcile **II – се** 1 to match *intrans.*; *Mus.* to harmonize *intrans.* 2 *fig.* to agree

згласува (се) *impf of* згласи (се)

згледа *pf* 1 to glance at, look at 2 to catch sight of, notice

згледува *impf of* згледа

зглоб *m* 1 *Anat.* joint; зглоб на нога ankle; рачен зглоб wrist; запаление на зглобовите arthritis 2 *see* глоб

зглобалија *adj indecl. f.p.* сабја зглобалија, *see* зглобница 2

зглобен -бна *adj* jointed, articular; зглобно возило articulated vehicle/lorry, *Austral.* semitrailer

зглоби *pf* to put (fit) together, assemble

зглобница *f* 1 hooded cloak (*kind of woman's outer garment*) 2 *f.p.* сабја зглобница folding sword

зглобува *impf of* зглоби

згмечи *pf* 1 to squeeze; to squash, crush 2 *fig.* (*уништи*) to kill, destroy

згнаси се *pf* 1 to feel disgust 2 *impers.* (*with dat.*) му се згнаси he felt disgusted (revolted)

згнасува се *impf of* згнаси се

згнете *pf* 1 to stuff (jam, cram) in 2 *fig.* to devour, swallow greedily, bolt, gulp down

згнетува *impf of* згнете

згнива *impf of* згние

згние *pf* згни *aor.* to rot, decay, putrefy, fester

зговара (се) *impf of* зговори (се)

зговор *m* 1 (*разбирање*) harmony, peace, agreement 2 (*спогодба*) agreement, accord, pact 3 *dial.* betrothal arrangements

зговорен -рна *adj* united; harmonious

зговори *pf* **I** 1 to arrange, agree (*on*); зговори средба to arrange a meeting; зговори датум to fix a date 2 to reconcile; ги зговорил најпосле he finally reconciled them 3 *dial.* to arrange an engagement (betrothal) **II – се** 1 to come to an agreement, agree 2 to be reconciled, make up *intrans.*

зговорлив *adj* easy-going, tolerant, amenable

зговорливост *f see* зговорност

зговорност *f* 1 amenability, tractability 2 (*слога*) harmony, accord, concord

згода *f* 1 convenience; многу згода имаме во станов we find this flat (*Am.* apartment) very convenient 2 *rare* chance, opportunity; opening; ❏ згоди и незгоди conveniences and inconveniences; peripeteia; жива згода an excellent opportunity

згоден -дна *adj* 1 suitable, appropriate; convenient; во згодно време at an appropriate time; чека згоден момент to wait for the right moment 2 comfortable; згоден стан comfortable flat (*Am.* apartment) 3 (*симпатичен*) likeable; attractive, pretty, cute

згоди *pf* **I** 1 (*затече, завари*) to find, come (chance) upon; не згодив никого дома I didn't find anyone in 2 to guess, hit on; to touch, affect **II – се** 1 to happen (come) to be, find o.s. (*somewhere*); во куќата тогаш никој не се згоди there was nobody in at that time 2 *impers.* to happen; така се згоди that's what happened; it happened like that

згодиток -ци *m* prize, winning <lottery> ticket

згодува (се) *impf of* згоди (се)

згои *pf* згои, згоја *aor.* **I** to fatten <up> *trans.* **II – се** to get fat, put on weight

згојува (се) *impf of* згои (се)

зголеми *pf* **I** to increase, enlarge *trans.* **II – се** 1 to increase, enlarge *intrans.*, get larger 2 *fig.* to become insolent/arrogant (haughty, conceited)

зголемува (се) *impf of* зголеми (се)

згон *m* chase, pursuit, hunt

згони *pf* to drive (*game*) (*to one place*); to chase, beat (*game*); to muster (*cattle*)

згонува *impf of* згони

згора *adv* 1 <from> above; on top 2 outside; лебот беше само згора печен the bread was baked only on the outside 3 in addition; ❏ згора на тоа on top of that; to cap it all; згора на сè, на сето згора on top of everything else; згора́-згора superficially, lightly; in a slapdash manner

згорен -рна *adj* 1 (*за облека*) outer, upper, outside 2 superficial (*also fig.*)

згорешти *pf* **I** to warm up, heat up *trans.* **II – се** 1 to warm up *intrans.*; to get hot 2 *fig.* to get excited/heated (worked up)

згорештува (се) *impf of* згорешти (се)

згори *pf* **I** 1 to set fire (*to s.th.*) 2 to stir up; to start, set (*a fire*) **II – се** to start burning *intrans.*; to flare up

згорник -ци *m see* згорница

згорнина *f* 1 surface 2 *see* згорниште

згорница *f* kind of woman's outer garment

згорниште *n* 1 face, right (front) side (*of cloth, of a garment*) 2 *see* згорница 3 extra, bonus

згорчи *pf* **I** 1 to make bitter 2 *see* **II II – се** to become bitter, *fig.* turn sour; му <се> згорчил живот his life turned sour

згорчува <се> *impf of* згорчи <се>

згости *pf dial. see* нагости

згостува *impf of* згости

згответ *pt* cooked, prepared

згтови *pf* **I** 1 to prepare (*food*), cook 2 *rare* to prepare, make ready *trans.* **II – се** *rare* to prepare o.s., get ready *intrans.*

згтовува (се) *impf of* згтови (се)

зграби *pf* to seize, grab

зграбува *impf of* зграби

зграгори *pf* **I** to terrify, petrify *trans.* **II** – **се** to become petrified

зграда *f* building, edifice; станбена зграда block of flats, *Am.* apartment building

згради *pf f.p.* to build, erect, put up

зграпчи *pf* to clutch, grip, grasp, grapple

зграпчува *impf of* зграпчи

зграчи *pf* **1** to caw, croak **2** *fig.* to make a sudden noise

згрбави *pf* **I** to make (*s.o.*) hunchbacked/round-shouldered **II** – **се** to become hunchbacked/round-shouldered

згрбавува (се) *impf of* згрбави (се)

згрби (се) *pf see* згрбави (се)

згрбува (се) *impf see* згрбавува (се)

згрвали *pf* **I** to knock over (*one on top of another, into a heap*) **II** – **се** to fall over (*one on top of another, into a heap*)

згрвалува (се) *impf of* згрвали (се)

згргори *pf* **1** *see* скркори **2** (*за вода*) to gush **3** (*за оружје*) to start rattling/chattering **4** *fig.* to start making a noise

згргорува *impf of* згргори

згрготи *pf see* згргори

згрготува *impf see* згргорува

згргури *pf dial.* **I** to clench, contract, screw up, twist, contort (*usu. of muscles*) **II** – **се** to contract *intrans.*; to grow stiff

згргурува (се) *impf of* згргури (се)

згрева (се) *impf of* згрее (се)

згрее *pf* згреа *aor.* **I** to warm <up>, heat <up> *trans.* **II** – **се** to warm o.s.; to warm up *intrans.*; се згреа собата the room grew warmer

згрешава *impf of* згреши

згреши *pf* **1** *Rel.* to sin, commit a sin **2** (*with dat.*) to offend, give offence to **3** to make a mistake; to be wrong **4** to confuse; го згрешиле патот they took the wrong road

згрешува *impf see* згрешава

згрижи *pf* to provide (*for*), take care (*of*); згрижи деца to provide for children

згрижува *impf of* згрижи

згрли *pf* to earth up <the roots of> (*plants*)

згрлува *impf of* згрли

згрми *pf* to thunder, roar, resound (*suddenly*); згрмеа топовите the guns suddenly roared

згрмоли *pf* **I** to fling, hurl **II** – **се** to fall with a crash; to collapse, tumble, crash down

згрмоти (се) *pf see* згрмоли (се)

згрмува *impf of* згрми

згрне *pf* згрна *aor.* **1** to rake/shovel together; to gather, pile up **2** to encircle, surround **3** *dial.* (*прегрне*) to embrace, hug

згрнува *impf of* згрне

згроби *pf dial.* **I** to destroy, crush **II** – **се** to grow very weak

згробува (се) *impf of* згроби (се)

згровне *pf see* гровне

згровнува *impf of* згровне

згровта *pf* to grunt (*suddenly*)

згровтува *impf of* згровта

згрозди се *pf* to yield a large crop

згрози се *pf* **1** to be disgusted, feel revulsion **2** *impers.* (*with dat.*) ми се згрози I felt revolted

згрозува се *impf of* згрози се

згрсти *pf* to cup; згрсти раце to cup one's hands

згрстува *impf of* згрсти

згрува *pf* to thresh (*grain*)

згруди се *pf see* згрутчи се

згрудува се *impf see* згрутчува се

згрутчи се *pf* to curdle; млеково се згрутчило this milk has curdled

згрутчува се *impf of* згрутчи се

згрчен *pt* convulsed, writhing; clenched; (*свиен*) twisted, contorted; crumpled, shrivelled

згрченост *f* convulsion; contortion

згрчи *pf* **I** (*собере*) to clench; to clutch; (*свие*) to contort, twist **II** – **се** (*се превие*) to double up, writhe, squirm, wriggle

згрчува (се) *impf of* згрчи (се)

згура *f* slag, dross, scoria

згусне *pf* згусна *aor.* **I** to thicken, condense *trans.* **II** – **се** to thicken, condense *intrans.*

згуснува (се) *impf of* згусне (се)

згусти (се) *pf see* згусне (се)

згустува (се) *impf see* згуснува (се)

згута се *pf see* згутави се

згутави се *pf* to crouch, squat; to cower; to lurk

згутавува се *impf of* згутави се

згутува се *impf see* згутавува се

згуши *pf* **I** to press; (*прегрне*) to hug *trans.* **II** – **се 1** to double up; to shrink (*од* – *from*) **2** to press (*до* – *against*) *intrans.*; to snuggle/cuddle up (*to*); to embrace each other

згушне (се) *pf* згушна (се) *aor. see* згуши (се)

згушува (се) *impf of* згуши (се)

здава се *impf of* здаде се

здави *pf* **I** to grip by the throat, fly at (*s.o.'s*) throat **II** – **се** to start choking *intrans.*; to start gasping, suffocating; to fly at <each other's throats>

здаволка *pf* to start wrestling (*playfully*) with; to grapple with

здавува (се) *impf of* здави (се)

здаде се *pf impers.* (*with dat.*) му се здаде he succeeded (*in doing s.th.*)

здалечи *pf dial. see* оддалечи

здание -ија *n* <large, massive> building, edifice

здебели *pf* **I** to fatten **II** – **се** to get fat, put on weight

зделка[1] *f* business, deal, bargain

зделка[2] *pf* **1** to trim, carve, hew **2** *fig. colloq.* to finish (*a difficult job*)

здене *pf* здена *aor.* to stack, pile

зденува *impf of* здене

здечка се *pf dial.* to get into an argument; to argue, squabble

здечкува се *impf of* здечка се

здив *m* breath; без здив breathless; ми се зеде здивот (*s.th.*) took my breath away; земе здив to take breath, catch one's breath; си го поврати здивот to get one's breath back; to get one's second wind

здиви *pf* **I** to make (*s.o.*) become wild, drive wild, make savage **II** – **се** to become wild/uncivilized/savage

здивне *pf* здивна *aor.* to take a breath; to recover one's breath; to rest; не му дава да здивне he doesn't even let him catch his breath

здивнува *impf of* здивне

здивува (се) *impf of* здиви (се)

здипли *pf* I 1 to fold; to bend 2 *colloq., fig.* to steal, *colloq.* pinch II – **се** 1 to stoop, bend over; to double up (*e.g. with pain*) 2 (*клекне*) to crouch, squat

здиплува (се) *impf of* здипли (се)

здобива се *impf of* здобие се

здобие се *pf* здобие се *aor.* 1 (*со*) to obtain, acquire, achieve; се здоби со нечиј благослов to get s.o.'s blessing 2 *f.p.* to bear, bring forth

здоболи *pf* (*only in the 3rd p.*) *see* доболи

здоболува *impf of* здоболи

здобри *pf* I 1 to reconcile 2 to cheer up *trans.* II – **се** 1 to make friends; *colloq.* to make up 2 *rare* to become good

здобрува (се) *impf of* здобри (се)

здогледа *pf dial. see* забележи 1

здодева се *impf of* здодее се

здодевен -вна *adj* boring, dull, tedious

здодевност *f* boredom, tedium

здодее се *pf impers.* (*with dat.*) ми се здодеа I've had enough, I'm sick of it

здола *adv* below, underneath; from below; at the bottom

здолен -лна *adj* lower, inner, under-; здолна кошула vest, singlet, undershirt

здолник -ци *m see* здолница

здолница *f* skirt

здолниште *n* 1 *see* здолница 2 lining (*of clothes*) 3 *dial.* bottom

здрав *adj* 1 healthy, well; (*душевно*) sane; (*зачуван*) well-preserved, hale <and hearty>; (*силен, јак*) robust; strapping; здрава боја на лицето healthy complexion; ❏ здраво тиќе burly fellow; здрав како дрен fit as a fiddle; да си жив и здрав! God bless you! good health! здрав ми си! *toast* your health! здрав и читав (жив) safe and sound, in one piece, unharmed; трн во здрава нога <не клавај си> *prov.* don't shoot yourself in the foot; don't harm your own interests 2 healthy, wholesome; здрава храна wholesome food; здрава клима healthy climate 3 *fig.* (*правилен, разумен, позитивен*) sound; здрави погледи sound views (opinions); здрав разум common sense; здрав дух sanity 4 whole, complete, undamaged; неколку прозорци останаа здрави a few windows remained undamaged

здравен -вна *adj rare see* здравствен

здравец *m Bot.* (Geranium macrorrhizum) Italian cranesbill

здрави *pf* I 1 to toast (*s.o.'s health*), drink (*to s.o.*) 2 (*поздрави*) to greet II – **се** to greet each other

здравина *f* 1 good health, fitness 2 (*цврстина*) strength, firmness, toughness; stability

здравица[1] *f* a toast; држи здравица to propose a toast 2 flask for wine or brandy; здравица вино flask of wine

здравица[2] *f see* ледина

здравје *n* health; слаб (нежен) е со здравјето he is in poor (delicate) health; пие за здравјето на некого to drink to s.o.'s health; ❏ здравје нека има never mind; don't worry; на здравје! 1. <to> your good health! 2. bless you! *gesundheit!* многу здравје на сите! give my regards to everybody! имаш многу здравје *iron.* tell that to the marines! со здравје goodbye

здраво *adv* 1 firmly, strongly 2 permanently, reliably 3 steadily, unshakably 4 (*поздрав*) greetings! hello! hi!

здравоживо *n* (*only sg*) greetings; праќа некому здравоживо to send greetings to s.o.

здравствен *adj* health; здравствена состојба state of health; од здравствени причини for health reasons; здравствена заштита health care, public health; здравствена служба public-health service

здравство *n* public health; health care <services>

здравува *impf of* здрави

здрач *m dial.* 1 daybreak, dawn 2 twilight, dusk

здрвен *pt & adj* 1 stiff, inflexible 2 *fig.* clumsy, awkward

здрвеност *f* 1 stiffness, inflexibility 2 *fig.* clumsiness, awkwardness

здрви *pf* I 1 to stiffen, make stiff; ❏ го здрви од тепање he gave him a good hiding 2 *fig.* to petrify; to astound; to shock II – **се** 1 to go stiff, stiffen *intrans.* 2 to go numb; ми се здрвија нозете my legs went numb 3 *fig.* to be petrified/astounded/shocked

здрвува (се) *impf of* здрви (се)

здржан *pt & adj* restrained, moderate; reserved; здржан тон restrained tone

здржаност *f* restraint, moderation; reserve

здржи *pf* здржа *aor.* I to restrain, curb II – **се** to restrain o.s.; to master one's feelings; одвај се здржав да не му речам I could hardly refrain from telling him

здржува (се) *impf of* здржи (се)

здржување *n* restraint; composure

здроби *pf* I (*искрши*) to smash *trans.*; (*смепе*) to crush; *fig.* ќе го здроби he will make mincemeat of him II – **се** to smash *intrans.*

здробува (се) *impf of* здроби (се)

здрув *m* motion made by a dancer of an *oro* when he kneels

здрувне *pf* здрувна *aor.* to make a *zdruv*

здружен *pt* united; associated; со здружени сили all together, in concert, with one accord

здружение -ија *n* association; здружение на пензионерите pensioners' association

здружи *pf* I 1 to unite, bring together; ги здружи заедничката работа the work that they shared brought them together; здружи средства to pool resources 2 to introduce (*one person to another*) II – **се** 1 to unite, associate *intrans.*; to team up, band together *intrans.*; (*за претпријатија и сл.*) to amalgamate 2 to make (become) friends

здружува (се) *impf of* здружи (се)

здува *pf* 1 to start blowing (*suddenly, unexpectedly*) 2 *fig.* ја здува he slipped away, escaped, beat it

здувне *pf* здувна *aor. see* здува 2

здупи *pf* 1 to spur, spur on, urge on (*also fig.*) 2 to start pushing (shoving, elbowing) 3 (*за постела, перница*) to start causing discomfort

здупува *impf of* здупи 1

здуши се *pf* to become intimate; (*со злосторничка цел*) to band together (*за да – to*), team up

здушува се *impf of* здуши се

зебра *f Zool.* zebra

зев *m* 1 gap, cleft, crevice, opening, chink 2 *Gram.* hiatus

зева *impf* to yawn; to gape

зејгора *m & f* idler, loafer

зејка *f Bot.* (Antirrhinum majus) antirrhinum, snapdragon

зејко *m Bot. see* зејка

зејтин *m* olive oil; vegetable oil

зелен *adj* green; unripe (*also fig.*), immature, inexperienced; зелени сливи unripe plums; ❑ зелен е како јад livid with fury; зелен појас green belt; млад и зелен young and green; still wet behind the ears; не умри, коњу, до зелена трева *prov.* don't entertain false hopes; don't hold your breath

зеленее <се> *impf* to turn green *intrans.*; to show (appear) green

зелени *pf* **I** to turn green *trans.* **II – се** *see* зеленее <се>

зеленика *f Bot.* name given to various shrubs, *esp.* (Buxus sempervirens) box <bush>

зеленикав *adj* greenish

зеленило *n* **1** green vegetation, greenery **2** <the colour> green; *Chem.* париско зеленило Paris green **3** (*usu. pl*) зеленила green (unripe) fruit

зеленина *f see* зеленило 1 & 2

зелениште *n* **1** greens, vegetables **2** green plant **3** green <colour>

зеленкав *adj see* зеленикав

зелено *n* **1** green (unripe) fruit **2** first days of spring

зеленушка *f Zool.* (Carduelis chloris) greenfinch

зеленушкав *adj see* зеленикав

зеленчица *f* patch of green, island of vegetation

зеленчук *m* vegetables, greens

зелјаник -ци *m see* зелник

зелје *n Bot.* **1** spinach **2** orache; sorrel **3** spring onion shoots **4** puff-pastry layer pie with green vegetable filling

зелка *f* **1** *Bot.* cabbage; head of cabbage **2** *joc.* shaven/bald head

зелник -ци *m* pie with green vegetable filling, pasty; кога има масло, и баба знае да меси зелник *prov.* where there's a will there's a way

зема *impf* **I 1** *of* земе **2** (*минува*) to cover; земам пет колометри на час I can do five kilometres an hour **3** *see* зима² 2 **II – се** *of* земе се

земање *n* taking; ❑ земање-давање 1. bargaining; give and take 2. relations, connections; немам со него земање-давање I have no dealings with him

земачка *f colloq. see* земање; ❑ земачка-давачка *see* земање-давање

зембиљ -ли *m* string bag

земе *pf* зеде *aor.* **I 1** to take; (*однесе*) to take away; земе под наем to hire, rent; земе на служба to hire, employ; земе лек to take medicine; земе жена to marry, take a wife; ❑ земе збор to take the floor; земе курс (правец) за to set course for; земе обврска to take on an obligation; земе одговорност за to assume responsibility for; земе предвид to take into account; земе пример од to follow the example of; си земе збогум to take one's leave; земе некого на грб to take charge of s.o.; земе некого на око to have it in for s.o.; земе при срце to take to heart; повелете, земете! please help yourself! земе здраво за готово to take for granted; си ја зеде белјата he got into trouble; што ќе дадеш – што ќе земеш *prov.* as you sow, so shall you reap **2** (*присвои*) to seize; to arrest; to capture; to confiscate; непријателот го зеде градот the enemy occupied the town **3** to get,

obtain; to buy; колку ги зеде чевлите? how much did you pay for the shoes? **4** (*претпостави*) to suppose, assume; да земеме дека е така let us suppose that it is so **5** (*with да*) to start; зеде да вика he started shouting **6** *dial.* to receive; зеде писмо од сина he received a letter from his son **II – се 1** to marry *intrans.*, get married; тие се земаа they<got> married **2** to hold hands, take each other by the hand **3** (*with dat.*) to lose; ми се зеде здивот I am/was out of breath; му се зеде умот he lost his reason **4** to be taken/received; како ќе се земе it depends how you look at it

земен -мна *adj* **1** earthly, terrestrial; земни задоволства/блага earthly pleasures/possessions; земен рај earthly paradise, paradise on earth; земни останки mortal remains; земно масло petroleum; земен гас natural gas **2** *rare see* Земјин

-земи *adv* (*as part of compound adverbs*) вземи into the ground; наземи on the ground; подземи underground; доземи to the ground

земја *f* **1** the earth; Земјата се движи околу Сонцето the earth moves round the sun; ❑ далеку колку од небото до земјата to the ends of the earth; ни на небо, ни на земја neither in heaven, nor on earth; како небото и земјата like chalk and cheese; земјата скришно (тајна) не држи *prov.* the truth will out **2** (*копно*) <dry> land, mainland; земјата и морето land and sea **3** (*почва*) soil, earth, ground; ровита земја loose (friable) earth; под земја underground; седне на гола земја to sit down on the bare ground; срамни со земја to raze to the ground; ❑ мириса на земја he has one foot in the grave; he is at death's door; лесна да му е земјата! may he rest in peace! **4** landed property, land **5** (*држава*) country, state; ❑ обетована земја promised land; never-never land; земја дембелија land of milk and honey; земја на чудата wonderland; зини земјо, голтни ме I could have sunk through the floor; како в земја да пропадна nowhere to be found

земјак -ци *m* compatriot, fellow-countryman

земјан *adj see* земјен

земјанин -ани *m* **1** inhabitant; citizen; local **2** earthling

земјанка *f* dug-out; mud-hut

земјарина *f* land tax; ground rent

земјачка *f* (*fem. form*) *see* земјак; fellow-countrywoman

земјен *adj* earth; earthen; земјен сад earthenware (clay) vessel; земјени работи excavations, diggings

Земјин *adj* the earth's; Земјината оска the earth's axis; Земјината површина the earth's surface; ❑ Земјината топка (сфера) the globe

земјица & **земјичка** *f dim. of* земја

земјиште *n* **1** plot, lot; field; terrain **2** *rare augm. of* земја

земјиштен -шна *adj* land; земјишни права land rights; земјишна книга *see* катастар

земјовина *f* the smell of earth; ❑ мириса на земјовина he has one foot in the grave; he is at death's door

земјоделец -лци *m* farmer

земјоделски *adj* agricultural; farmer's, farming; земјоделско стопанство agricultural economy; agriculture

земјоделство *n* agriculture; farming

земјомер *m Tech.* surveyor

земјопосед *m* landed property, land

земјоседник *m* landowner

земјопоседнички *adj* landowner's

земјоса се *pf fig.* to grow pale (*from illness*); lose one's colour; сиот се земјосал во лицето 1. he's turned quite pale 2. he has one foot in the grave; he's at death's door

земјосува се *impf of* земјоса се

земјотрес *m* earthquake

земјотресен -сна *adj* seismic

земник -ци *m see* визба

земница *f see* земјанка

земски *adj* land, territorial, provincial; земска влада territorial/provincial government

зенит *m* zenith; *fig.* во зенитот на својата слава at the height of one's fame (glory)

зеница *f Anat.* pupil; ❑ чува (пази, варди) како зеницата на окото to cherish as the apple of one's eye; *dial.* ѓаволска зеница a single grape

зеничен -чна *adj Anat.* of the pupil, pupil<l>ary

зет *m* **1** (маж на сестра) brother-in-law (*sister's husband*); (маж на ќерка) son-in-law (*daughter's husband*) **2** bridegroom; зетот и невестата the bridegroom and bride

зеташин *m f.p. see* зет

зетов *adj* **1** brother-in-law's; son-in-law's **2** bridegroom's

зетовски *adj see* зетов; ❑ зетовското a kind of *oro*

зефир *m poet.* zephyr, light breeze

зигзаг *adv see* цикцак

зијан *m colloq.* harm, damage, loss; стори зијан to cause harm; ❑ ни ќар ни зијан there is neither gain nor loss; some you win and some you lose; ќарот и зијанот се браќа *prov.* what you gain on the swings you lose on the roundabouts

зима[1] *f* winter; ❑ нема зима no problem, not to worry; everything is under control; назад му е зимата *prov.* he was born with a silver spoon in his mouth; назад е зимата the best is yet to come

зима[2] *impf* **1** *dial. see* зема 2 **2** to hold, contain, take; кацава зима сто ведра this tub holds a hundred bucketfuls; не нè зима овде сите we can't all fit in here; него нигде не го зима he can't settle down anywhere

зимáва *adv* this winter; зимава ќе останам дома this winter I'll stay at home

Зимбáбве *n* Zimbabwe

Зимбабвеец -ејци *m* Zimbabwean

Зимбабвејка *f* (*fem. form*) *see* Зимбабвеец

зимбабвејски & зимбáбивиски *adj* Zimbabwean

зиме *adv* in winter; зиме-лете <треба да се работи> <one has to work> the whole year round

зимен -мна *adj* winter, winter's; wintry; зимна вечер winter<'s> evening; ❑ зимно време in winter

зимнина *f see* зимница 1

зимница *f* **1** preserved foodstuffs for winter **2** winter crops

зимо *n dial. see* зима[1]

зимовина *f see* зимница 1

зимовиште *n* winter quarters; winter port; winter stores

зимовник -ци *m* winter quarters for livestock

зимоврав *m* autumn digging in a vineyard (*to loosen the soil*)

зимовраши *impf* to dig over a vineyard (*to loosen the soil*)

зиморлив *adj* sensitive to cold

зиморливост *f* sensitivity to cold

зиморничав *adj see* зиморлив

зиморничавост *f see* зиморливост

зимоска *adv* **1** last winter; уште од зимоска те чекам I have been waiting for you since last winter **2** next winter, this coming winter

зимошен -шна *adj* this winter's

зимски *adj* winter; зимски спортови winter sports; зимски сон hibernation

зимува *impf* to winter, spend the winter; to hibernate

зимување *n* **1** hibernation **2** winter holiday

зимурлив *adj see* зиморлив

зимурливост *f see* зиморливост

зимурничав *adj see* зиморлив

зимурничавост *f see* зиморливост

зине *pf* зина *aor.* to open one's mouth, gape; to yawn; зине од чудо his jaw dropped in amazement; зинала пропаст a chasm yawned; зини да ти кажам curiosity killed the cat; wouldn't you like to know?

зинува *impf of* зине

зифт *m* tar, pitch; bitumen, asphalt; ❑ очи како зифт eyes as black as pitch

зјае *impf* to be open; to gape; вратата зјае the door is ajar; млекото зјае the milk is not covered

зјајка *f Bot. see* зејка

зјапа *impf* **1** to gape, gaze, stare; ❑ зјапа по чавките to stare at the ceiling **2** *rare, fig.* to yawn, gape; зјапа пропаст a chasm yawned (opened up)

зјапало *n see* зјапач

зјапач *m* gaper; idler, loafer

зјапло -овци *m see* зјапач

зјапне *pf* зјапна *aor.* to stare (*во – at*); што си зјапнал во него? why are you staring (gaping) at him?

злат *adj f.p., poet.* golden, gold

златар *m* goldsmith

златарка *f* **1** (*fem. form*) *see* златар **2** goldsmith's wife

златарски *adj* goldsmith's; златарски производи goldsmith's wares (products), gold jewellery

златарство *n* goldsmith's trade/art

златен -тна *adj* **1** gold, golden; *fig.* precious; златен прстен gold ring; златен рудник gold-mine (*also fig.*); златна шипка gold ingot; ❑ златни планини (ридје) ветува to promise the earth; златен век golden age; златна средина golden mean; златна свадба golden wedding; златна рипка *Zool.* goldfish; има злати раце he can do anything; губи златно време to waste valuable time **2** bright yellow, golden; златни коси golden hair; златни зраци golden rays **3** *fig.* (прекрасен, мил) wonderful, dear, beloved; златен човек wonderful (lovable) person; златно срце heart of gold; златна сестро! dear sister

златест *adj* golden (*colour*)

злати *impf* **I** to gild; to gold-plate; *fig.* сончеви зраци ги златат вршините од дрвјето the sun's rays gild the tree-tops **II** – **се** *fig.* to shine, glitter

златка *f Zool.* (Martes martes) pine marten

златник -ци *m* **1** gold coin, ducat, gold piece **2** *fig.* (*as a form of address*) my dear fellow

злато *n* **1** gold; ❑ злато човек wonderful person; the soul of kindness; црно злато black gold (oil); злато мое! my darling! my treasure! вреди суво злато worth its weight in gold; молчењето е злато *prov.* silence is golden; не е злато сè што сјае *prov.* all is not gold that glitters **2** *child.* tin foil, silver paper; златото од чоколадо foil wrapping from chocolate

златоврв[1] *adj poet.* gold-tipped

златоврв[2] *m Bot.* (Lilium martagon) martagon lily, Turk's cap lily

златоглав *adj poet.* golden-headed

златогрив *adj poet.* golden-maned

златоклас *adj poet.* golden-eared (*of corn, grain*)

златокос *adj poet.* golden-haired, golden-tressed

златокрил *adj* **1** *poet.* golden-winged **2** *f.p.* golden-finned; златокрила риба golden-finned fish

златоносен *adj* gold-bearing, auriferous; златоносен песок/поток gold-bearing sand/stream

златопер *adj* golden-feathered, golden-plumed; golden-finned

златорог *adj poet.* golden-horned

златорун *adj poet.* golden-fleeced

златоткан *adj* embroidered in gold, interwoven with gold

златоуст *adj poet.* eloquent; smooth-tongued; soft-spoken

злаќен *adj f.p.* (*позлатен*) gilded; злаќени стрели gilded arrows

злини *pl* wicked/malicious acts

зло[1] *n* evil, wrong; (*несреќа*) misfortune, trouble; добро и зло поминале заедно they went through thick and thin together; доброто ќе триумфира над злото good will triumph over evil; ❏ да спие зло; да не чуе зло let sleeping dogs lie; touch wood; коренот на злото the root of <all> evil; нужно зло a necessary evil; помалото од две зла the lesser of two evils; секое зло за добро *prov.* every cloud has a silver lining; стори добро, најди зло *prov.* virtue is its own reward; ingratitude is the worst of vices

зло[2] *adv arch. see* лошо[2]

злоба *f* malice, malevolence, spite; venom, gall

злобен -бна *adj* malicious, malevolent; злобен поглед malevolent look

злоби *n* **1** to spite **2** to be malicious

злоблив *adj* malicious, spiteful, malevolent; vicious; wicked; harmful

злобник -ци *m* spiteful (malicious) person

злобност *f* spite, malice; nefariousness

злогласност *f* infamy, notoriety

злокачествен *adj Med.* malignant; злокачествен тумор malignant tumour

злокобен -бна *adj* ill-fated, ill-omened, ominous; (*катастрофален*) disastrous

злокобник -ци *m* prophet of doom

злокуќник -ци *m* spendthrift, squanderer; bad manager (*of a household*), bad provider

злокуќница *f* (*fem. form*) *see* злокуќник

зломислен *adj* malevolent, malicious

злонамерен -рна *adj* ill-intentioned; злонамерна постапка hostile (malicious) act

злонамерност *f* malice, malevolence

злопамтило *m & f* vengeful (vindictive) person

злорад *adj* gloating, spiteful, malicious; злорад човек malicious person; злорада насмевка malicious smile

злорадост *f* gloating, spite, malice

злостор *m rare, poet. see* злосторник

злосторен -рна *adj rare* villainous

злосторник -ци *m* malefactor, evil-doer, villain; (*престапник*) criminal, felon; (*крвник*) murderer; воен злосторник war criminal

злосторница *f* (*fem. form*) *see* злосторник

злосторнички *adj* criminal, felonious

злосторство *n* evil-doing; misdeed; malefaction; nefarious activity; (*престап*) crime, felony

злота *f* zloty (*monetary unit in Poland*)

злоупотреба *f* misuse, abuse; злоупотреба на доверба breach of trust

злоупотреби *pf* to misuse, abuse; (*доверба, услужливост*) to abuse, take advantage (*of*); (*пари*) to misappropriate; ја злоупотребил нашата доверба he abused (took advantage) of our trust; злоупотреби нечие гостопримство to trespass on s.o.'s hospitality

злоупотребливост *f* <tendency to> misuse, abuse, misappropriation

злоупотребува *impf of* злоупотреби

злочин *m rare* evil deed; (*престап*) crime; *see* злосторство

змев *m see* змеј

змеиница *f* dragon's wife (*in folk stories*)

змеица *f* she-dragon (*in folk stories*)

змеј -ови *m* **1** dragon (*in folk stories*) **2** *fig.* (*за човек*) demon for work, glutton for punishment, Trojan; fiend

змејче *n dim. of* змеј

змеовски *adj* dragon's

змиест *adj* snakelike, serpentine

змиин *adj* snake's, snake *attrib.*, ophidian; ❏ змиини дни "snake days" (*marking the reappearance of snakes after hibernation*); *Bot.* змиино грозје, змиини лубеници *see* грозје; змиина пченка (Arum maculatum) wild arum <lily>, lords and ladies, cuckoo-pint

змија *f* **1** snake, serpent; *fig.* malicious/cunning person; отровна змија venomous snake; водена змија (Natrix) grass snake; ❏ се витка како змија to wriggle like a snake; чува змија в пазува to nurture a serpent (viper) in one's bosom; со гола рака змија не се фаќа *prov.* discretion is the better part of valour; ако би змија да е, ама од срце да е *prov.* it's the thought that counts; кој паднал в море, и за змија се фаќа *prov.* the drowning man clutches even at a straw **2** *Bot.* (Cereus flagelliformis) serpent (whip) cactus

змијар *m* snake-catcher

змијарник -ци *m* snake's nest; nest of vipers

змијулец *m Bot.* (Ornithogalum) star of Bethlehem

змиски *adj* snake, snake's; змиска кожа snakeskin; змиски цар *Zool.* boa constrictor; *dial.* змиски празник St. George's Day (6 May); змиско млеко *Bot.* (Chelidonium majus) greater celandine

змучка *f see* џумка

знае *impf* **I 1** to know; знам што сакаш I know what you want; знае три јазика to know three languages; ❏ тој не знае <за> грижи (тешкотии) he knows no cares; не знае за починка (одмор, сон)/ умор he doesn't think of rest (sleep)/fatigue; не знае делник ни празник he knows no rest, he works tirelessly; нејќе да знае he doesn't want to know; кој знае, којзнае God knows; не е кој знае што he/it isn't anything special; знаеш, знаете you know; што знам? what do I know? for all I know; how should I know? колку што знам јас for all I know; to my knowledge; не оти знам not that I know; тој пак си го знае своето he's at it again; знае срам he knows when to stop; му ја знае на ѓаволот дупката you can't fool him; како <што> знаеш at all costs; знае книга he knows how to read; знае писмо he knows how to write; откако знае за себе all one's <conscious> life; паси трева кога знаеш! go teach your grandmother to suck eggs! знае на што е to know where one stands; знае нешто на прсти to have s.th. at one's fingertips; знам колку што знаеш и ти your guess is as good as mine; не знае што да прави to be at a loose end; да знаеш you never know; така да знаеш you'd better believe it; take my word for it; многу <којшто> знае, многу ќе пати *prov.* ignorance is bliss **2** (*да*) to know how to, be able to; тој знае да прави чевли he knows how to make shoes **3** to be acquainted (*with*); to recognize; го знаеме ние него добро we know him very well; ❑ те знам што си стока си *iron.* I know what you're worth **II – се 1** to know one another; се знаеме ние одамна we've known each other for a long time **2** to know o.s. **3** *impers.* се знае it is <well> known; it goes without saying; of course! тоа се знае that is <well> known, that is common knowledge; не се знае ни кој јаде, ни кој плаќа one doesn't know whether one is coming or going

знаен -јна *adj* known; ❑ знајни и незнајни known and unknown <people>, everyone

знаење *n* knowledge; знаење на јазици knowledge of languages; има солидни знаења од математика he has a good knowledge of mathematics; даде некому на знаење to inform s.o.; земе на знаење to take into account/on board

знак -ци -ови *m* **1** sign; mark; signal; token; патни знаци road (traffic) signs; знаци на распознавање distinguishing marks; знак на согласност sign of agreement; интерпункциски знаци punctuation marks; воден знак watermark; математички знаци mathematical symbols; ❑ во знак на as a mark (token) of; под знак на under the sign of, in a spirit of **2** seal, stamp; фабрички знак trade mark

зналец -лци *m* expert; connoisseur; секој старец <е> и зналец *prov.* there's many a good tune played on an old fiddle

знаме *n* flag, banner, standard (*also fig.*); државно знаме national flag; ❑ го дигна (крена) високо знамето he raised the banner high; преодно знаме *Sport.* challenge banner; свика под знамето (знамињата) to call to the colours, call up, mobilize; знамето се вие на пола копје the flag flies at half-mast

знамение -ија *n* omen, portent, sign

знаменит *adj* famous, renowned, well-known

знаменитост *f* **1** fame **2** hero; eminent person **3** знаменитости на градот sights of the town

знаменосец -сци *m* standard-bearer (*also fig.*)

знамениче *n dim. from* знаме

знатен -тна *adj* **1** eminent, illustrious, distinguished; (*по род*) noble **2** *see* значителен

значаен -јна *adj* significant, important

значајно *adv* significantly, notably

значење *n* **1** meaning; фигуративно значење figurative (metaphorical) meaning **2** significance, importance; тој настан има историско значење that event has historical significance; ❑ од значење е, има значење (*дека . . .*) it is significant (*that . . .*)

значи *impf* **1** to mean, signify; што значи тој збор? what does that word mean? **2** to be of importance; to play a role; тоа многу значи that means a lot, that is very important **3** (*only in 3rd p. sg*) so, therefore, then; that means; тој е, значи, дојден so he has come

значителен -лна *adj* **1** (*голем*) considerable **2** (*што има значење*) significant

значка *f* badge; спортска значка sports badge

зоб *f Bot.* (Avena sativa) oats

зоба *impf of* зобне

зобне *pf* зобна *aor.* to nibble; (*за птици*) to peck (*at*); ❑ си ја зобнал пченицата he is at death's door

зобник -ци *m & * **зобница** *f* fodder bag, nosebag

зобнува *impf see* зоба

зов *m poet.* call

зове *impf* **1** *poet.* to call, invite **2** *dial.* to invite to a wedding

зовира *impf of* зоврие

зоврива *impf see* зовира

зоврие *pf* зовре *aor.* to boil up/over; to <begin to> boil; to ferment *intrans.*; ❑ зовре вошки to be crawling with lice; крвта му зовре his blood began to boil

зограф *m arch.* icon-painter

зографиса *pf arch.* to decorate (*a church with frescos*)

зографисува *impf of* зографиса

зографски *adj arch.* icon-painter's

зографство *n arch.* icon-painting

зодијак *m* zodiac

зокум *m Bot.* (Nerium oleander) oleander, *see* олеандер

зол, зла, зло, *pl* зли *adj* **1** bad, evil, wicked, malicious, vicious; зол дух evil spirit; зли намери evil (malicious) intentions; зли јазици evil (malicious) tongues **2** *rare* poor, bad; difficult; зло време bad (difficult) time<s>; зла среќа bad luck; зла болест serious illness; на зол трн зла копачка *prov.* like cures like; tit for tat

золва *f* sister-in-law (*husband's sister*)

золвеник -ци *& * **золвин** *m* sister-in-law's husband

золвин *adj* sister-in-law's

золвиче *n* sister-in-law's child

золвичка *f hyp. of* золва

золота *f. obs.* small coin (30 paras); грошот золота го прави *prov.* to throw good money after bad

зона *f* zone; погранична зона frontier zone

зонски *adj* zonal; *Sport.* зонски турнир zonal tournament

зоолог -зи *m* zoologist

зоологија *f* zoology

зоолошки *adj* zoological; зоолошка градина zoological garden, zoo

зопца *f hyp. of* зоб

зора *f* dawn; зора <се> зори dawn is breaking, day is dawning; пукнала зора dawn has broken; в зори at dawn; од рани зори from early dawn; at the crack of dawn

зорен -рна *adj* dawn *attrib.*; зорна доба daybreak

зори *impf* to bake *intrans.* (*on a low fire*)

зори се *impf* to break (*of dawn*); зора <се> зори dawn is breaking

зорле *adv colloq.* by force; зорле го однесле в болница he was taken to hospital by force

зорнина *f* early dawn, daybreak

Зорница *f* (*popular name for*) Morning Star, *see* Деница, Вечерница

зорт *m colloq.* **1** fear, fright; имам зорт I'm afraid **2** (*мака*) suffering, strain, trouble; голем зорт виде he was in great need; на зорт е he is suffering; не си дава зорт he doesn't make much effort; му даде зорт he forced him; it gave him trouble; ❑ за зор<т>-заман for a rainy day, for bad times

зошто *adv* why; what for; зошто <да> не why not? ❑ нема зошто **1.** there is no reason **2.** (*as a reply to an expression of thanks*) you're welcome

зрак -ци *m* **1** ray, beam (*also fig.*); сончев зрак sunbeam, ray of sunshine; ултравиолетови зраци ultraviolet rays; Рентгенови зраци X-rays; зрак на надеж ray of hope **2** *dial.* eyesight; зракот од очите му се зел he has lost his sight

зрачен -чна *adj* **1** bright, shining, luminous; зрачно небо bright sky **2** ray *attrib.*; radiated; radiation *attrib.*; зрачна енергија radiation

зрачење *n* **1** radiation; зрачење на топлина thermal radiation **2** *Med.* radiotherapy; X-ray<s>

зрачи *impf* **1** to radiate *trans. & intrans.*; сонцето зрачи енергија the sun radiates energy; некои елементи зрачат certain elements emit radiation; *fig.* од нивните лица зрачи радост joy radiates from their faces **2** *Med.* to X-ray; to treat with radiotherapy; му го зрачеа коленото they X-rayed his knee **II – се 1** to radiate, emanate *intrans.*; to shine **2** to undergo radiotherapy

зрачка *f see* зрак 1

зрее *impf* to ripen, mature (*also fig.*); житото зрее the corn is ripening; во него зрееше нова идеја a new idea was taking shape in his mind

зрел *adj* **1** ripe; зрело грозје ripe grapes **2** *fig.* mature, grown-up; зрел маж mature man; зрела врст mature age; зрело решение a well-considered decision

зрелост *f* maturity; ripeness; полова зрелост puberty; политичка зрелост political maturity

зрнен *adj* grain, cereal; зрнена храна cereal foods

зрнест *adj* granular; зрнеста структура granular structure

зрнешник *m Bot.* (Physalis alkekengi) strawberry tomato, winter cherry

зрно *n* **1** grain; зрно пченица a grain of wheat; зрно грозје a single grape; *fig.* зрно вистина a grain of truth; зрно по зрно – погача *prov.* many a mickle makes a muckle **2** (*сиен, топчест предмет*) bead; bullet, shell; зрно бисер a pearl **3** grain, crop, harvest; собере зрно to harvest grain

зрнце *n* **1** *dim. of* зрно **2** <blood> corpuscle; бели и црвени крвни зрнца white and red blood corpuscles, *Med.* leucocytes and erythrocytes

зуграфдиса *pf dial. see* зографиса

зуграфдисува *impf of* зуграфдиса

зука *f Bot.* (Heleocharis palustris) common spike-rush, marsh club-rush

зулум *m arch.* outrage, violence; (*штета*) harm, damage; прави зулум to maintain a reign of terror

зулумќар *m arch.* tyrant, despot; plunderer

зулумџија -ии *m arch. see* зулумќар

зулуф *m* (*usu. pl*) sideburns

зумбул *m Bot.* (Hyacinthus orientalis) hyacinth

зурла *f* zurla, shawm (*type of double-reed wood-wind instrument*)

зурлаџија -ии *m* zurla-player

S

сангари *impf dial. see* свечи

ѕвезда *f* star; ѕвезда Зорница (Деница) morning star; ѕвезда Вечерница evening star; петокрака ѕвезда five-pointed star; морска ѕвезда *Zool.* (Asterias) starfish; роден под среќна/несреќна ѕвезда born under a lucky/unlucky star; филмска ѕвезда film star; ❑ патоводна ѕвезда guiding star; ѕвезди симина од небо to promise s.o. the moon (world); брои ѕвезди to star-gaze; to daydream; види ѕвезди сред бел ден to see stars; ѕвездите ги брои he holds his head high; дига (крева) некого до ѕвезди to praise s.o. to the skies; не број ги ѕвездите, да не паднеш в кладенец *prov.* the higher you fly, the lower you fall

ѕвезден *adj* starry, star-studded; starlit; stellar; ѕвездено небо starry sky; ѕвездено јато galaxy, star cluster; ѕвезден прав stardust; cosmic dust

ѕвездест *adj* starlike; ѕвездест шрафцигер Phillips-head screwdriver

ѕвездица & ѕвездичка *f* **1** *dim. of* ѕвезда; хотел со пет ѕвездички five-star hotel **2** asterisk **3** pip, star (*insignia of military rank*)

ѕвездовит *adj* **1** *see* ѕвездест **2** *f.p. see* ѕвезден

ѕвездоденица *f f.p.* morning star

ѕвездочатец -тци *m arch.* star-gazer, astrologer

ѕвездочел *adj f.p.* ѕвездочел коњ horse with a star on its forehead

ѕвек *m* clang, clank, clink

ѕвекало *n see* ѕвечало

ѕвекне *pf* ѕвекна *aor.* **1** *intrans.* to clang, jingle, clink **2** *trans. colloq.* to hit; to smack; го ѕвекнал по глава he cracked him on the head

ѕвекнува *impf of* ѕвекне

ѕвекот *m see* ѕвек; ❑ ѕвекот на оружјето the clash of arms; sabre-rattling

ѕвекоти *impf* to clang, clink, jingle

ѕвер *m* animal, beast (*also fig.*)

ѕвери се *impf* to stare, gape

ѕверилник -ци *m* menagerie

ѕверка *f see* ѕвер; ❑ *colloq.* голема ѕверка big shot, VIP

ѕверски *adj* **1** animal, wild, feral; ѕверски инстинкти savage instincts **2** *fig.* inhuman, brutal, bestial, savage; ѕверско убиство brutal murder

ѕверство *n* atrocity; brutality

ѕверче *n dim. of* ѕвер

ѕверштина *f colloq. see* ѕверство

ѕвечало *n see* ѕвечка

ѕвечи *impf* to clank, jingle, clink; to clatter, rattle

ѕвечка[1] *f* **1** (*играчка*) rattle **2** *Bot.* (Colutea arborescens) bladder-senna, bladder-nut

ѕвечка[2] *impf* to jingle, clink; to rattle; *fig.* ѕвечка со оружје (сабја) to rattle the sabre

ѕвечлив *adj* jingling, clinking, clanging; rattling

ѕвизак -ци *m* two-year-old ram

ѕвизди *impf dial.* (*кисне, кмиши*) to wait for a long time; to hang (stay) around

ѕвизне *pf dial.* ѕвизна *aor. see* ѕвекне 2

ѕвизнува *impf of* ѕвизне

ѕвиска *f* two-year-old ewe

ѕвиска *impf* (*за коњ*) to neigh, whinny

ѕвисне *pf* ѕвисна *aor.* (*за коњ*) to give a neigh, a whinny

ѕвиснува *impf of* ѕвисне

ѕвон *m poet.* peal; tolling; chime; (*погребен*) knell

ѕвонар *m* **1** bell-ringer **2** bell-caster, bell-founder

ѕвонарски *adj* bell-ringer's; bell-caster's

ѕвонец -нци *m* bell; school bell; church bell; cowbell; учениците го чекаа ѕвонецот <да удри> the pupils were waiting for the bell <to ring>; ❑ му прилега како на свиња ѕвонец it doesn't suit him at all

ѕвони *impf* to ring; ѕвони на врата to ring a doorbell; телефонот ѕвони the telephone is ringing; ми ѕвони во ушите my ears are ringing

ѕвонлив *adj* ringing, resounding, resonant, clear; ѕвонлив глас ringing voice

ѕвонливост *f* resonance, clarity

ѕвоно *n* bell

ѕвонче *n dim. of* ѕвонец & ѕвоно; doorbell; електрично ѕвонче electric bell

ѕвончест *adj* bell-like

се *interj child.* cooee! look! peekaboo!

севгар *m* yoke <of oxen for ploughing>

семне *impf* to freeze *intrans.*; ми семнат нозете my feet are freezing; цел ден семнеше на студот he was freezing in the cold the whole day

сенѕа *impf* **I** to rock, shake *trans.*; (*дете*) to dandle **II** – се **1** to rock, shake *intrans.*; to judder, jolt *intrans.*; to stagger **2** *fig.* to work slowly, sluggishly; to dawdle

сенѕало *n colloq.* **1** person who staggers **2** *fig.* sluggard

сенѕер *n see* кајсија

сиври *pl colloq.* long johns

ѕид -ови, -ишта *m* wall; ❑ шпански ѕид folding screen; звучен ѕид sound barrier; жив ѕид human barrier; одбранбен ѕид rampart; затворен меѓу четири ѕида cooped up between four walls; се огради со кинески ѕид to isolate o.s. completely; притисне некого до ѕид to drive s.o. to the wall, bring s.o. to bay; и ѕидот има уши *prov.* walls have ears

ѕида *impf* **1** to build, construct **2** (*создава*) to create

ѕидар *m* **1** builder; bricklayer; mason; слободен ѕидар Freemason **2** *fig.* creator

ѕидарски *adj* builder's; building; ѕидарски работи building works

ѕидарство *n* bricklaying, masonry; слободно ѕидарство Freemasonry

ѕиден -дна *adj* wall; ѕиден саат wall clock; ѕиден весник wall newspaper; ѕидно сликарство <the art of> wall-painting, mural painting; ѕидни тапети wallpaper

ѕидина *f dial.* ramparts

ѕидиница *f dial.* dilapidated wall

ѕидиште *n augm. of* ѕид; rampart

сидоса *pf colloq.* to wall, wall around; to wall up; to wall off

синзирида *f dial. Bot.* (Prunus) kind of sour plum

▬ла *impf dial.* **I 1** (*клоца*) to kick (*of a horse*) **2** to wade, trudge (*во кал – in/through mud*) **II – се** (*клоца се*) to kick *intrans.*; to kick each other

сипаница *f dial. see* клоца, клоцаница

сипне (се) *pf see* клоцне (се)

сирка¹ *impf* to peep

сирка² *f* crack, chink (*in a wall, fence, etc.*)

сирне *pf* сирна *aor.* **I 1** *trans.* to visit (*briefly*), call in (*on*), drop in (*on*); сирни го дедо ми call in and see my grandpa! **2** *intrans.* to glance; to peep **II – се 1** to look at/see each other briefly **2** to peep out, emerge

сирнува (се) *impf of* сирне (се)

ситче *n dim. of* сид

срнзурки *pl* cheap jewellery, trinkets, knick-knacks

срцала *pl arch. see* очила

срцало *n dial.* (*огледало*) mirror

срцки *pl joc.* eyes; срцките ќе ти ги извадам! I'll break your neck!

сумба *f f.p.* music

сун *m poet.* ringing

суни *impf* (*only in 3rd p.*) **1** (*свони*) to ring; сунеше камбаната the church bell was ringing; ми сунеше во ушите there was a ringing in my ears **2** to hum, buzz

суница *f* **1** (*виножито, божилак*) rainbow **2** *Bot.* (Fragaria vesca) wild strawberry

сунлив *adj see* звонлив

сунливост *f see* звонливост

сури *impf* to stare, gape

И

и¹ *conj* **1** and; и така натаму and so on; и . . . и both . . . and; не само . . . туку и not only . . . but also **2** also, too **3** (*as emphatic part.*) even; ќе го направиш тоа, и без да сакаш you will do that even if you don't want to

и² *interj* oh! и, што убаво! oh, how beautiful! и, каков си! you amaze me! I'm shocked!

ѝ *pron* **1** (*short dat. form of* таа, она) to/for her/it; ѝ реков I told her **2** (*as dat. of possession*) her; татко ѝ her father

иако *conj* although, though

ибис *m Zool.* (Threskiornis) ibis

ибрик -ци *m* **1** pitcher; (*copper*) kettle; coffee-pot **2** *fig.* fool; idiot

ибриче *n dim. of* ибрик 1

ибришим *m* twist, fine silk thread

ива *f Bot.* (Salix caprea) pussy willow, sallow

Иванден *m* St John's Day (7 July)

иванденски *adj* St John's Day; иванденски петок the Friday before St John's day (*a rest day for women*); иванденско цвеќе *Bot.* (Salvia sclarea) clary-sage

иверка *f* splinter

ивица *f* (*раб*) edge, border; brink; на ивица на пропаст on the brink of disaster

игла *f* needle; игла шијачка sewing needle; игла плетачка knitting-needle; игли од бор pine needles; магнетна игла magnetic needle; грамофонска игла stylus, gramophone needle; игла за вратоврска tie-pin; ❏ седи како на игли to be on tenterhooks (edge); to be like a cat on hot bricks; игла во сено needle in a haystack; игла нема каде да фрлиш to be packed; bursting at the seams

иглен *adj* needle's; needle-like; иглени уши eye of a needle; *fig.* narrow squeak

иглест *adj* needle-like, acicular

игличка *n dim. of* игла

иглолисен -сна *adj* coniferous; иглолисно дрво conifer

игнорáнт *m* ignoramus, ignorant person

игнорáнтка *f* (*fem. form*) *see* игнорант

игнорáнтски *adj* ignorant

игноранција *f* ignorance

игнорѝра *pf* & *impf* (*нешто*) to ignore, disregard, flout, (*некого*) to cold-shoulder, cut (*s.o.*) dead

иго *n literary* yoke, slavery

игра¹ *f* **1** game; детска игра children's game; *fig.* a piece of cake; шаховска игра chess; хазардни игри games of chance; Олимписки игри Olympic Games; игра на зборови word-game; pun; прифаќа нечија игра to play s.o.'s game; игра на случајот coincidence; a stroke of fate; љубовна игра flirting; игра со рака *Sport.* handling; игра на поединци/двојки *Tennis* singles/doubles 2 dance; народни игри folk-dances 3 (*начин на исполнување*) acting, performance; мајсторска игра brilliant acting

игра² *impf* 1 to play; децата <си> играат the children are playing; игра карти to play cards; си игра со to toy with (trifle with); ❑ не играј си со оган don't play with fire! не играј си со главата don't take any risks! не игра никаква улога it's of no importance 2 to act, perform, play; го играат 'Отело' they are staging 'Othello'; го игра Отело he is playing <the part of> Othello 3 to dance; игра валцер to waltz; ❑ оро ќе играш! you'll dance to my tune! you'll do as I tell you! 4 (*with dat.*) to twitch; ми игра окото my eye is twitching; ❑ срцето ми игра <од радост> my heart is jumping <with joy>; му игра некое ребро his back is itching, he needs a beating, he is spoiling for a fight

игралит *adj f.p.* excited, merry

игралиште *n* playing-field; playground; спортско игралиште sports field; тениско игралиште tennis court; фудбалско игралиште soccer field

игран *pt in the expression:* игран филм feature film

игранка *f* dance, ball

играч *m* 1 player 2 dancer

играчица *f (fem. form) see* играч

играчка *f* 1 toy; plaything; *fig.* trifle; ❑ тој го зеде тоа како на играчка he took it as a joke; не е играчка it's no joke 2 *dial.* (*игра*) game, play; ❑ играчка-плачка this will end badly/in tears (*as a warning*)

игрив *adj* playful; (*пргав*) lively, frisky, sportive, sprightly

игривост *f* playfulness; liveliness; agility

игроорец -рци *m* folk-dancer

игумен *m* abbot, Father Superior

игуменија -ии *f* abbot's residence

игуменица & игуменка *f* abbess, Mother Superior

игуменски *adj* abbot's

иде *impf* 1 to come; еве ги, идат there they are, they're coming; *impers.* (*with dat.*) ми иде <да плачам> I feel like <crying>, it makes me <cry>; ❑ не ми иде в ум it's beyond me; it beats me; тој е целиот иди ми дојди ми he can't make up his mind; one can't take him seriously; што не иде, не иде enough is enough 2 – **си** to come home, return home; си идат од град they are returning home from town 3 *dial.* (*оди*) to go

идеал *m* ideal

идеален -лна *adj* ideal, exemplary, perfect

идеализам -змот *m* idealism

идеализатор *m* idealizer

идеализаторски *adj* idealizing

идеализира *pf & impf* to idealize

идеализирање *n* idealization

идеализација *f* idealization

идеалист *m* idealist

идеалистички *adj* idealistic

идеен -јна *adj* 1 ideological; conceptual 2 dedicated to a cause/idea

идеја -еи *f* idea; notion; генијална идеја brilliant idea; фиксна идеја *idée fixe*, obsession

идејност *f* ideological content

иден -дна *adj* future, coming; идните поколенија future generations

идентитет *m* identity

идентификација *f* identification

идентификува & идентифицира *pf & impf* I to identify *trans.*; to equate *trans.* II – **се** to identify o.s.; to equate o.s. (*со – with*) *intrans.*

идентичен -чна *adj* identical

идентичност *f* identity

идеолог -зи *m* ideologist

идеологија -ии *f* ideology

идеолошки *adj* ideological

идила *f* idyll

идиличен -чна *adj* idyllic

идиом *m* idiom

идиот *m* idiot

идиотизам -змот *m* idiocy

идиотка *f (fem. form) see* идиот

идиотски *adj* idiotic

иднина *f* future; иднината ќе покаже the future will show; во иднина in <the> future

идол *m* idol

идолопоклоник -ци *m* idolater; *fig.* admirer

идолопоклонички *adj* idolatrous

идолопоклонство *n* idolatry

и др. *abbr.* (*и друго*) and so on, et cetera, etc.

из- (ис- *before voiceless consonants*) *verbal prefix indicating* 1 *movement out, movement away*; излезе to go/come out 2 *completion; action performed thoroughly; intensity of action*; избања to finish bathing *trans.*; измеле to grind thoroughly 3 *action affecting many objects*; излови to catch (*many or all*) 4 (*with ce*) *satiety*; се изигра to tire of playing

из *prep dial. see* низ

изаби *pf* I 1 to wear out *trans.* 2 (*истапи*) to blunt *trans.* II – **се** 1 to wear out *intrans.* 2 to get (become) blunt

изабува (се) *impf of* изаби (се)

изарчи *pf colloq.* I to spend, expend; (*испотроши*) to consume, use up II – **се** 1 to spend a lot of money 2 to run out (be used up)

изарчува (се) *impf of* изарчи (се)

изба *f see* визба

избави *pf* I to save, deliver; to rescue (*од – from*) II – **се** 1 to save (rescue) o.s. 2 redeem o.s. 3 to get rid (*од – of*)

избавител *m* rescuer; *Rel.* saviour, redeemer; Messiah

избавиште *n* rescue; *Rel.* salvation; ❑ имало избавиште there was a way out

избакне (се) *pf* избакна (се) *aor. see* избаци (се)

избања *pf* I to bathe *trans.*; to finish bathing *trans.* II – **се** to have/take a bath, bathe *intrans.*

избара *pf colloq.* to find, search (seek) out

избаца (се) *pf see* извалка (се)

избаци *pf* I to kiss warmly; to kiss (*many times or several people*) II – **се** to kiss each other warmly

избега *pf* to run away, flee; to escape; избега од дома to run away from home; избега од затвор to escape from prison

избеган *pt & adj* escaped; (*as noun*) escapee

избегне *pf* избегна *aor.* to avoid, evade, elude; to escape; им избегна на властите he eluded the authorities

избегнува *impf of* избегне; to shun; избегнува друштво to shun company

избегува *impf of* избега

избезумен *adj* mad; hysterical

избезуменост *f* madness; hysteria

избезуми *pf* I to drive mad II – се to go mad; to become hysterical

избезумува (се) *impf of* избезуми (се)

избелее *pf* избелеа *aor.* to turn white *intrans.*; to fade, lose colour

избележи *pf* to record/note (*completely*); ги избележив сите дојдени I noted all those that came

избележува *impf of* избележи

избели *pf* to bleach; (*ѕидови*) to whitewash

избелува *impf of* избелее and избели

избербати (се) *pf see* извалка (се)

избербатува (се) *impf of* избербати (се)

избере *pf* избра *aor.* 1 to choose; to select, pick <out> 2 (*со гласање*) to elect; ❑ се избрале кој од кој there's not much to choose between them

избесни *pf* to become violent; (*се налути*) to become furious (infuriated), fly into a rage

избива *impf of* избие

избие *pf* изби *aor.* I 1 (*натепа*) to beat <up> 2 (*убие*) to kill off, slaughter, massacre 3 (*за млеко и сл.*) to beat, churn <up> 4 (*појави се*) to come to the surface, emerge; to appear; to break out; изби пожар fire broke out; изби епидемија an epidemic broke out; му изби пот на челото sweat broke out on his forehead 5 to strike *intrans.*; изби час the hour has struck, the time has come; изби камбаната the church bell struck II – се to have a fight, come to blows

избира *impf of* избере; ❑ не избира средства to stop at nothing

избирач *m* 1 selector; chooser 2 (*гласач*) voter, elector, constituent

избирачки *adj* electoral; избирачки списоци electoral registers (roll); избирачко место polling station; избирачко тело the electorate

избирок *m* choice; кој пребира, паѓа на избирокот *prov.* a maiden with many wooers often chooses the worst; the wider the choice the greater the trouble

избистри *pf* I to clarify *trans.*, make clear II – се to clarify *intrans.*, grow (become) clear; (*за небото*) to clear (brighten) <up> *intrans.*

избиструва (се) *impf of* избистри (се)

избичи *pf* to saw up

избледи *pf* to turn pale; (*избелее*) to fade, lose colour

избледнее *pf* избледнеа *aor. see* избледи

избледни *pf* избледна *aor. see* избледи

избледнува *impf of* избледнее

избледува *impf of* избледи

izблик -ци *m* outburst, burst, effusion; izблик на јад fit of anger; izблик на радост effusion of joy

избликa *pf* to gush, pour out (forth) (*also fig.*); избликa од радост his face lit up with delight

избликне *pf* избликна *aor. see* избликa

избликнува *impf of* избликне

изблуе *pf* избљу *aor.* I to bring up, vomit *trans.* II – се to vomit, throw up *intrans.*

избоде *pf* to prick, pierce, puncture, stab (*repeatedly*); to perforate; (*со рогови*) to butt (*repeatedly*)

избор *m* 1 (*гласање*) election; ballot; избор на претставник election of a representative 2 choice, selection; assortment; option; добар избор a wise choice; во негов избор at his choice (discretion); нема друг избор there is no other alternative; задржува право на избор to keep one's options open

изборен -рна *adj* electoral, election *attrib.*; elective, elected; изборна единица, изборен округ constituency, *Austral.* electorate; изборна комисија electoral commission; првиот изборен круг the first round of elections; изборно место polling station; изборна кампања election campaign

избори *pf* I to win (*s. th.*) (*in a battle*); избори победа to win a victory II – се to win, gain; се изборив за мојот предлог I succeeded in pushing my proposal through

изботеан *pt & adj* decrepit, worn-out

изботее *pf* изботеа *aor.* 1 to fade 2 *fig.* to become senile

избоцка *pf* to prick, sting (*all over*)

избразди *pf* to furrow

избраздува *impf of* избразди

избраник -ци *m* 1 representative 2 (*сакан*) sweetheart; (*свршеник*) fiancé

избраница *f* (*fem. form*) *see* избраник

избрбешка (се) *pf colloq. see* извалка (се)

избрецне се *pf* избрецна се *aor.* to snap (*на некого – at s.o.*)

избрза *pf* to speed up, hasten (hurry) forward; to act rashly; (*со нешто*) to do (*s. th.*) too early

избрзан *adj* premature; (*непромислен*) hasty, rash

избрзаност *f* prematureness; haste, rashness

избрзне *pf* избрзна *aor. see* избрза

избрзува *impf of* избрза

избричи *pf* I to shave *trans.*; to finish shaving *trans.* II – се to shave *intrans.*, have a shave; to finish shaving

избричува (се) *impf of* избричи (се)

избрише *pf* избриша *aor.* I to wipe <clean/dry>; to wipe off; (*прашина*) to dust; (*со гума*) to erase, rub out; (*прецрта*) to cross out II – се to dry one's face, hands, etc.

избришува (се) *impf of* избрише (се)

избрка¹ *pf* to drive away/out; to expel; избрка од училиште to expel from school

избрка² *pf* I to mix up, confuse II – се to get confused

избрлави се *pf* to become infected with *Taenia Coenurus* (tapeworm cysts); (*избезуми се*) to go crazy

изброи *pf* изброи & изброја *aor.* I 1 to count, number 2 to enumerate; (*наведе*) to quote II – се to number off, *Am.* count off (*of soldiers, etc.*)

избројува *impf of* изброи

избува *pf* (*за тапан, топ и сл.*) to boom, roar

избувлив *adj* 1 explosive 2 *fig.* irascible, short-tempered

избувливост *f* irascibility

избувне *pf* избувна *aor.* to break out; to erupt, burst forth; избувна востание a rebellion broke out

избувнува *impf of* избувне

избудали *pf* I to drive crazy II – се to become foolish; to go crazy

избуричка *pf* 1 to mix up, muddle up 2 *fig.* to mess up, complicate; ја избуричка работата he made a mess of things

избута *pf* I to push <out/aside>, shove away *trans.* II – се to shove *intrans.*; to make one's way (*во толпа – through a crowd*)

избутка *pf* **I 1** *see* избута **I 2** to live (get) through; to manage *intrans.*, pull through; некако ја избуткаа зимата they survived (got through) the winter somehow **II – се** *see* избута се

избуца *pf* to prod (*oxen*)

извади *pf* **I 1** to take out, remove, pull out, draw; to extract; to produce, bring out; извади сабја to draw a sword; извади заб to extract a tooth; извади некому очи to gouge out s.o.'s eyes; *colloq.* извади шапка to take off one's hat; извади пари <од банка> to withdraw money <from the bank>; извади флека to remove a stain; *fig.* му извадија прекар they gave him a nickname **2** to get, obtain; to buy; извади уверение to be issued a certificate; извади карта to buy a ticket **3** *colloq.* (*спечали*) to make, earn; си го извади арчот he recovered (reclaimed) his expenses **4** to celebrate, officiate at; *colloq.* му извадија задуша they celebrated a requiem mass for him **5** *Math.* to subtract; извади четири од десет остануваат шест four from ten leaves six; извади корен to extract a root **II – се** to get out (*од – of*) (*a difficult situation*); to back out (*of*)

извадок -ци *m* excerpt, extract, fragment, passage

извадува *impf of* извади

изваја *pf* to sculpture, sculpt; to carve; (*во глина*) to model, mould; (*во камен, дрво*) to chisel

извала *pf* to mill, full, felt *trans.*; to roll over *trans.*

извалка *pf* **I** to dirty, soil **II – се** to get dirty, dirty o.s.

извалкува (се) *impf of* извалка (се)

изварди *pf* **1** to wait (*for s.o.*); to lie in wait (*for s.o.*), ambush; to surprise, catch unawares **2** (*исчува, дочува*) to keep, save, preserve

извардува *impf of* изварди

извари *pf* to boil (*thoroughly*)

изварка *f* curds

изварува *impf of* извари

извеан *adj* senile; (*расеан*) absent-minded

извева (се) *impf of* извее (се)

изведба *f* performance; rendition; во изведба на performed/played by

изведе[1] *pf* **1** to take/bring <out/up>; to lead <away/off/up>; ги изведе на прошетка he took them for a walk; ги изведе од шумата he led them out of the forest; ❏ изведе некого на прав пат to put s.o. on the right track; изведе некого на суд to take s.o. to court **2** *fig.* (*изврши, исполни*) to do, carry out, perform; добро ја изведе работата he made a good job of it; добро ја изведоа претставата they gave a good performance **3** to deduce; to draw; to derive; од ова може да се изведе from this we may deduce; изведе заклучок to come to the conclusion (*дека – that . . .*)

изведе[2] *pf* **I** to hatch *trans.*; квачката изведе десет пилиња the brood-hen hatched ten chicks **II – се** to hatch *intrans.*

изведеница *f* derivative, derived word, derived form

изведит *adj* slim; supple, lithe изведита става lithe figure

изведри *pf* **I** to cheer (*s.o.*) up, put (*s.o.*) in a good mood **II – се 1** to cheer up *intrans.* **2** (*за времето*) to clear up; се изведри небото the sky cleared

изведрува (се) *impf of* изведри (се)

изведува[1] *impf* **1** *of* изведе[1] **2** to misbehave, play up

изведува[2] *impf of* изведе[2]

извее *pf* извеа *aor.* **I** to winnow **II – се** *fig.* to become senile

извежба *pf* **I** to drill, train, exercise; to practise *trans.*; извежба своја точка to rehearse one's act; извежба ученик to train a pupil thoroughly **II – се** to train, acquire (gain) skill/routine; to practise, learn by practice; се извежбав добро I trained (practised) hard

извежбан *pt* trained, skilled; fit, well-trained; practised

извезе *pf* извеза *aor.* to embroider

извезува *impf of* извезе

извејува (се) *impf see* извева (се)

извесен -сна *adj* certain, some; во извесна смисла in a certain sense; извесни луѓе certain people

извесност *f* certainty

известен *pt* informed, notified; добро известени кругови well-informed circles

извести *pf* to inform, let (*s.o.*) know, advise, notify; извести некого за нешто to inform s.o. of s.th.

известие -ија *n* information, news; announcement, report

известител *m see* известувач

известува *impf of* извести

известување *n* notice; announcement; без претходно известување without prior notice, without warning, unannounced

известувач *m* rapporteur; (*новинар*) reporter, correspondent; informer

известувачки *adj* information *attrib.*, informative; известувачка средба briefing

изветвен *adj* **1** worn, worn-out; изветвени панталони threadbare trousers **2** *fig.* trite, hackneyed

изветви *pf* **I** to wear out *trans.*; (*избледни*) to fade *trans.* **II – се** to wear out *intrans.*; (*избелее*) to fade *intrans.*

изветвува (се) *impf of* изветви (се)

изветреан *pt & adj* **1** evaporated **2** *fig.* absent-minded; senile

изветрее *pf* изветреа *aor.* **1** (*испари*) to evaporate; (*за пијалок*) to go flat **2** *fig.* to become absent-minded; (*стане сенилен*) to become senile

изветрува *impf of* изветрее

извештај -аи *m* report, announcement, advice, notice, notification; банкарски извештај bank statement; годишен извештај annual report

извештачен *adj* affected, artificial, mannered

извештаченост *f* affectation, affectedness, affected manner, airs and graces

извешти се *pf* to become skilled/skilful, acquire skill (*in, at s.th.*); се извешти во електроника he has become an expert in electronics

извив *m* **1** *Mus.* glide, turn, trill, modulation **2** (*на пат*) bend; (*на река*) meander, meandering **3** (*на чад*) puff, plume

извива *impf* **I** to bend, twist, turn, wind *trans.*; извива веѓи to raise one's eyebrows; извива глас to sing melodiously, warble, modulate one's voice **II – се 1** to wind, twist, curve *intrans.*; (*за пченица*) to wave *intrans.*; (*за пат, оро и сл.*) to wind; (*за река*) to meander; (*се грчи*) to writhe; (*за змија*) to coil; (*за црв*) to wriggle; (*за да избегне удар*) to swerve; (*за пат*) to curve **2** (*за птица*) to circle, hover; (*се крева*) to rise, soar **3** (*за луна, ветер*) to rise, come on (up)

извивка *f* **1** bend, twist; (*завој*) curve, bend, turn-<ing>; (*на спирала*) whorl; (*во јаже, црево*) kink; (*на стапалото*) arch **2** *Mus.* glide, turn, trill

извиди¹ *pf* to investigate, look into, enquire about; *Mil.* to reconnoitre

извиди² *pf* **I** (*види многу, сè*) to see everybody/ everything; to meet everybody **II** – **ce** (*со*) to meet everybody

извидник -ци *m* scout

извидница *f* patrol

извиднички *adj* scout; извиднички логор boy scout camp

извидува *impf of* извиди¹

извидувач *m* scout (*usu. Mil.*)

извидувачки *adj* reconnaissance (*plane, etc.*)

извие *pf* изви *aor. see* извива

извик -ци *m* **1** shout, exclamation **2** *Gram.* interjection

извика *pf* **I 1** to shout, exclaim, call out **2** (*повика некого*) to call <in/out>, send (*for s.o.*); (*службено*) to summon; го извика надвор he called him outside **II** – **ce 1** to shout one's fill **2** to shout (*на некого – at s.o.*)

извикне *pf* извикна *aor. see* извика

извикнува *impf of* извикне

извикува (се) *impf of* извика (се)

извиличен *pt* twisted, distorted, contorted, crooked (*of a face*)

извиличи се *pf* to screw up one's face; to pull a face, contort one's face

извини *pf* **I** to excuse; (*прости*) to forgive, pardon; извинете на изразот pardon the expression; извинете! excuse me! sorry! **II** – **ce** to excuse o.s.; to apologize; to beg (*s.o.'s*) pardon, ask forgiveness

извинува (се) *impf of* извини (се)

извинувачки *adj* apologetic

извинување *n* excuse; apology

извир *m f.p.* spring; извир-вода spring water

извира *impf* **1** (*за вода*) to spring; (*за извор*) to issue; (*за река*) to rise, take its source (*од – in, from*); (*изобилно*) to gush out/forth **2** *fig.* to come (spring, result) (*од – from*); to originate; од аргументите извира заклучокот the conclusion flows from the arguments

извиси *pf* **1** *see* извиши **2** to be left in the lurch, come off second best; ти добро помина ама јас извисив you did fine but I got the worst of it **3** *colloq.* (*некого*) to stand (*s.o.*) up

извиска *pf* to neigh, whinny

извискува *impf of* извиска

извисува (се) *impf see* извишува (се)

извитка *pf* **I 1** to bend, fold *trans.*; to roll, curl *trans.* **2** to crease, crumple **II** – **ce** to bend, fold *intrans.*; to roll, curl *intrans.*

извиткува (се) *impf of* извитка (се)

извиши *pf* **I 1** to lift/raise <up>; to throw high into the air; (*за глас*) to raise **2** to grow tall **II** – **ce 1** to rise up high; (*за зграда*) to tower (*над нешто – over s.th.*), dominate **2** (*израсте*) to grow <up>

извишува *impf of* извиши

извлекува *impf of* извлече (се)

извлекување *n* extraction; (*во лотарија*) draw

извлече *pf* **I 1** to drag out; (*сабја*) to draw; го извлече од соба надвор he dragged him out of the room **2** (*за лотарија и сл.*) to draw; извлече премија to draw a prize **3** *fig.* (*спаси*) to save, rescue; извлече некого од опасност to rescue s.o. from danger **4** *fig.* (*добие, постигне*) to obtain; to derive, deduce; to draw; извлече поука to learn one's lesson; ❏ го извлече подебелиот крај to get the worst of a bargain; извлече корист (*од*) to do well out (*of*) **5** *Math.* to extract, find **II** – **ce 1** to get out (*од – of*); (*ce спаси*) to save o.s.; (*ce повлече*) to withdraw; to get away with

извлечка *pf* **I** to pull (drag) out (*with difficulty*) **II** – **ce** to drag o.s. out (*with difficulty*), extricate o.s., withdraw

извлечкува (се) *impf of* извлечка (се)

извод *m* **1** excerpt, extract; (*свидетелство*) certificate; abstract, summary; извод од биланс abstract of balance sheet; извод од сметка statement of an account; извод од матичната книга на родените extract <from a> birth certificate **2** (*заклучок*) conclusion, inference, deduction

изводени *pf* **I** to wet, moisten **II** – **ce** to get wet; to become moist

изводенува (се) *impf of* изводени (се)

изводлив *adj* feasible, practicable, possible; attainable

изводливост *f* feasibility, practicability, possibility; attainability

извоз *m* export

извозен -зна *adj* export *attrib.*; извозна такса export tax; извозни производи exports

извози *pf* **I** to drive (*a certain distance*); to take, carry, transport, convey; to finish carrying (transporting, conveying); ја извозов сам целата релација I drove the whole distance myself **II** – **ce** to have one's fill of riding/driving/conveying; се извозив I've had enough of driving

извозник -ци *m* exporter

извознички *adj* export *attrib.*, exporting

извозува *impf* to export

извојува *pf* to win *trans.*; to conquer; to achieve

извонреден -дна *adj* extraordinary, outstanding, exceptional; (*одличен*) excellent; special, extra

извонредно *adv* exceptionally, specially, by way of an exception; excellently

извор *m* spring; source; изворот на Вардар the source of the Vardar; извор на сите зла the source of all evil; историски извори historical sources; од сигурни извори from reliable sources

изворен -рна *adj* **1** *see* изворски **2** original, authentic; изворен материјал authentic/original material

изворност *f* authenticity

изворски *adj* spring; изворска вода spring water

извргали *pf in the expression*: извргали очи to open one's eyes wide; to stare, gape

изврива *impf see* изврие 1

изврие *pf* изври *aor.* **1** to boil thoroughly *trans. & intrans.* **2** to boil away *trans. & intrans.*

изврти *pf* **I 1** to turn *trans.*; to turn over, invert **2** *fig.* to twist, distort; изврти нечии зборови to distort s.o.'s words **3** (*издлаби*) to hollow (bore) out **4** (*заобиколи*) to pass round, skirt **II** – **ce** (*with dat.*) to turn (*to*) (*usu. irritably, gruffly*)

извртува (се) *impf of* изврти (се)

извршен -шна *adj* **1** (*што извршува*) executive; извршен совет executive council **2** (*правосилен*) final; извршна пресуда final sentence

изврши *pf* I to carry out, fulfil, perform, execute; to realize; to commit; изврши исплата to make payment, effect payment; изврши преглед to conduct an inspection; изврши убиство to commit murder II – **ce** to come true; тој сон се изврши that dream too came true

извршител *m* executor, performer; executioner; perpetrator; извршител на тестамент executor of a will

извршува (се) *impf of* изврши (се)

извршувач *m* executor, performer

изгази *pf* to trample (*all over*), crush; (*со кола и сл.*) to run over

изгазува *impf of* изгази

изгаси *pf* I 1 to extinguish, put out; to extinguish (*one after another*) 2 (*умре*) to die, pass away, expire II – **ce** to go out (*of a fire, light*); to go out one after another

изгасне *pf* изгасна *aor.* I 1 to put out, extinguish 2 to go out (*of a fire, light*) II – **ce** *see* I 2

изгаснува *impf of* изгасне

изгасува (се) *impf of* изгаси (се)

изгине *pf* изгина *aor.* to perish, die

изгинува *impf of* изгине

изглаби *pf dial. see* издлаби

изглади *pf* to smooth <out>, straighten out; *fig.* to settle *trans.*; изглади спор to resolve a dispute

изгладнет *pt & adj* hungry; starved, famished

изгладнетост *f* hunger; starvation

изгладни *pf* to become hungry

изгладнува *impf of* изгладни

изгладува *impf of* изглади

изгласа *pf* to elect; (*нацрт закон*) to pass, adopt; изгласа закон за даноците to pass a tax bill

изгласи се *pf* to cry out

изгласува *impf of* изгласа

изгласува се *impf of* изгласи се

изглед *m* 1 look, appearance; тој е добар на изглед he looks well, seems all right 2 (*поглед, пејсаж*) view; landscape; убав изглед beautiful view 3 (*можност*) outlook, possibility; prospect<s>; има изгледи да успее he/it has a good chance of succeeding; изгледи за успех prospects of success; нема никакви изгледи to stand no chance; слаби изгледи slim chances; long odds

изгледа[1] *pf* 1 to look over, measure with the eye; ❑ изгледа од глава до петици to look over from head-to foot 2 to raise, bring up; таа ги изгледа децата she brought up the children

изгледа[2] *impf* to look, seem; изгледа дека ќе врне it looks like rain; ❑ така изгледа so it seems; по сè изгледа in all likelihood; by the look of it; to all appearances; the odds are

изглода *pf* 1 to gnaw 2 to wear away, erode

изгмечи *pf* to knead; to squeeze <out>

изгнаник -ци *m* exile, expatriate; outcast

изгнаница *f* (*fem. form*) *see* изгнаник

изгнанички *adj* of an exile, outcast

изгнанство *n* exile, banishment

изгнаси *pf* to dirty, soil; *fig.* to sully, desecrate, profane II – **ce** 1 to get dirty 2 to feel sick; to feel revulsion (disgust) (*од нешто – at s.th.*)

изгнива *impf of* изгние

изгние *pf* изгни *aor.* to rot, decay, putrefy

изговара (се) *impf of* изговори (се)

изговор *m* 1 pronunciation; литературен изговор literary (standard) pronunciation 2 (*оправдание*) pretext, excuse; неубедлив изговор lame excuse; со (под) изговор дека on the pretext that

изговори *pf* I to pronounce; to state, say II – **ce** to excuse o.s.; to justify o.s.

изговорлив *adj* pronounceable

изгони *pf* to drive out, banish, expel

изгонува *impf of* изгони

изгор *m* 1 torrid heat, heat wave; денеска е изгор today it's as hot as hell; ❑ цените се изгор the prices are shocking 2 *fig., colloq.* love, the pangs of love; lover 3 *fig., f.p.* sorrow, grief, suffering, misfortune

изгора *f colloq. see* изгор 2

изгорен *pt* 1 burnt; (*од сонце*) sunburnt 2 *fig.* worn-out, exhausted; tormented; poor, pitiable; thirsting (*за нешто – for s.th.*); изгорена душа tormented soul; изгорен сум за неа I am dying of love for her

изгореница *f* burn; (*од врела вода*) scald; (*од сонце*) sunburn

изгоретина *f* 1 *see* изгореница 2 *dial.* charred remains

изгори *pf* изгоре *aor.* I 1 to burn, burn up, burn out, burn down *trans. & intrans.*; изгори многу дрва to burn a lot of wood; изгори на сонце to get sunburnt; свеќата изгоре the candle has burnt down; изгоре куќата the house has burnt down 2 to scald; to burn; го изгорев јазикот I burnt my tongue 3 to scorch; сланата ги изгоре посевите the hoar-frost scorched the crops 4 *fig.* to love passionately; to desire, crave (*за – for*); изгорев за неа I am dying of love for her; изгорев за вода I am dying for some water 5 *fig.* to ruin, destroy; (*измачи*) to drive to despair II – **ce** 1 to get burnt/scalded 2 *fig.* to suffer

изгорува (се) *impf of* изгори (се)

изгости *pf* I to entertain, treat (*many or all*) II – **ce** *fig.* to eat one's fill

изготви *pf* to make; to prepare

изготвува *impf of* изготви

изграба *pf* 1 to steal; to seize (*everything or many things*) 2 to rob; to plunder

изградба *f* construction, building; во изградба under construction

изгради *pf* I 1 to build, construct, erect; изгради ново општество to create a new society 2 *fig.* to train *trans.*; изгради нови кадри to train new personnel II – **ce** to develop one's personality; to improve o.s.; to improve one's mind

изградува (се) *impf of* изгради (се)

изгребе *pf* изгреба *aor.* I 1 to scrape up/out 2 (*огребе, издраска*) to scratch II – **ce** to get scratched; to scratch o.s.

изгребува (се) *impf of* изгребе (се)

изгрев *m* 1 sunrise 2 *dial.* east

изгрева *impf* to rise (*of the sun, etc.*)

изгревање *n* sunrise; на изгревање сонце at sunrise

изгрее *pf* изгреа *aor.* I 1 to rise (*of the sun, moon*) 2 *see* стопли II – **ce** to warm o.s.

изгрејсонце *n* sunrise; на изгрејсонце at sunrise

изгризе *pf* изгриза *aor.* 1 to gnaw clean; to gnaw away (off) 2 *see* прегризе 3 (*нагризе, изеде*) to destroy, eat away, nibble; (*кородира*) to corrode

изгризува *impf of* изгризе

изгрми *pf* 1 to thunder 2 to boom

изгрмува *impf of* изгрми

изгруби *pf* to disfigure

изгрубува *impf of* изгруби

изгрува *pf* to thresh (*grain*)

изгуба *f dial. see* загуба

изгуби (се) *pf dial. see* загуби (се)

изгубува (се) *impf dial. see* загубува (се)

изгуши *pf* to scale (*fish*)

изгушка *pf* **I** to hug, embrace **II – се** to hug (embrace) one another

издава (се) *impf of* издаде (се)

издавач *m* publisher

издавачки *adj* publishing; издавачка куќа publishing house

издаде *pf* **I 1** to issue; to hand out/over; издаде налог to give orders; му издаде уверение he issued a certificate to him **2** to let, lease, rent <out>; ja издаде куќата под наем he let the house **3** to publish; издаде книга to publish a book **4** (*предаде, открие*) to betray, reveal, give away; го издаде кашлицата his cough betrayed him **5** (*звуци*) to emit (*sounds*), produce **6** to give out (*everything, completely*); to spend; ги издале парите they have spent the money **7** to stick out *trans.*; го издаде мевот he stuck out his belly **II – се 1** to give o.s. away **2** (*се покаже*) to show o.s., appear, come into view **3** (*се насре*) to stick out *intrans.*, project

издаден *pt* **1** published **2** prominent, protruding **3** rented, leased

издание -ија *n* edition, publication, issue

издател *m see* издавач

издателство *n* publishing house, publisher<s>

издаток -ци *m* expenditure, expense, outlay, disbursement; прави издатоци to incur expenses

издвои *pf* **I 1** to select, single out **2** to allocate **II – се** to stand out, distinguish o.s.

издвојува (се) *impf of* издвои (се)

издебне *pf* издебна *aor. see* издемне

издејствува *pf* to secure, procure; to work out, manage; (*добие*) to obtain, get

издекламíра *pf* to recite, declaim

издела *pf see* изделка

издели *pf* **I 1** to distribute, divide up, share out (*everything*) **2** to divide off, separate **II – се 1** to stand out **2** to cut o.s. off, isolate o.s. **3** (*создава посебно домаќинство*) to set up house on one's own

изделка *pf* **1** to trim; (*со длето*) to chisel (carve) (*од – out of*) **2** *fig.* to polish, refine

изделкан *pt* **1** trimmed, carved **2** *fig.* polished, refined

изделкува *impf of* изделка

изделува (се) *impf of* издели (се)

издемне *pf* издемна *aor.* to take by surprise, catch unawares; (*можност, прилика*) to seize, take advantage (*of*); издемне време to seize the moment

издемнува *impf of* издемне

изденгуби *pf* to waste (*time*); го изденгубив времето во разговори he wasted all his time talking

издив *m* **1** breath; до последен издив to one's last breath **2** (*воздишка*) sigh

издива *impf see* издивне

издивне *pf* издивна *aor.* **1** to breathe out, exhale **2** (*воздивне*) to sigh, give a sigh **3** (*умре*) to expire

издивнува *impf of* издивне

издига *pf & impf* **I 1** *see* издигне **2** to raise (*everything/everyone completely*) **II – се** *see* издигне се

издигнат *adj* prominent, famous; *fig.* <highly> developed

издигне *pf* издигна *aor.* **I 1** to raise, lift <up>; (*знаме*) to hoist **2** (*потпомогне*) to help, promote **3** (*развие*) to develop **II – се** to raise (lift) o.s.; to rise

издигнува (се) *impf of* издигне (се)

издише & издиши *pf* издиша & издиши *aor.* **I** to breathe out *trans. & intrans.* **II – се 1** to breathe out *intrans.* **2** (*воздивне*) to sigh **3** (*за топка, балон и сл.*) to go down, deflate *intrans.*, become deflated **4** (*умре*) to expire

издишен -шна *adj* **1** deflated **2** egressive, exhalation *attrib.*; издишна струја exhalation, outgoing breath

издишка *f* sigh

издишне *pf* издишна *aor.* to breathe out *trans.*

издишува (се) *impf of* издише (се) & издиши (се)

издлабен *pt* hollowed out

издлаби *pf* to excavate, hollow out; (*мал зарез*) to notch; (*со длето*) to chisel (cut) out, carve

издлабува *impf of* издлаби

издои *pf* издои, издоја *aor. see* измолзе

издолжи *pf* **I** to stretch <out> *trans.* **II – се 1** to stretch *intrans.*; (*се истегнува*) to stretch out *intrans.*, sprawl **2** to grow; to lengthen *intrans.*; to drag <on> *intrans.*

издолжува (се) *impf of* издолжи (се)

издраска *pf* **I** to scratch **II – се** to get scratched (*all over*), get badly scratched

издргне *pf* издргна *aor.* to scrub; to grate; to rub **II – се** *fig.* to become thin, lose weight

издрдори *pf* **I** to blurt out **II – се** to blab, reveal a secret

издржан *adj* satisfactory, up to standard, up to the mark; издржана критика well-founded/soundly-based criticism

издржаност *f* soundness

издржи *pf* издржа *aor.* **1** to stand, endure, bear; (*не отстани*) to withstand; (*истрае*) to persevere, last out; издржа проба he passed (stood) the test; ja издржа казната he endured (bore) his punishment **2** to hold (*a small child*) while it relieves itself

издржлив *adj* persistent, persevering; (*здрав*) hardy, robust; (*долготраен*) durable

издржливост *f* endurance; persistence; staying power; stamina; hardiness; durability

издржува *impf* **I 1** of издржи; не се издржува it can't be endured **2** to maintain, keep (*s.o.*); татко му го издржува his father maintains (keeps) him **II – се** to maintain o.s.

издржување *n* maintenance

издрнда *pf* **1** to fluff (*wool, etc.*) **2** *fig.* to blurt out

издроби *pf* **I** to crush, crumble *trans.*; (*исече на парчиња*) to cut up into small pieces **II – се** *fig.* to work o.s. to exhaustion

издробува (се) *impf of* издроби (се)

издрпа *pf* **I** to tear, tatter, rip **II – се** to get torn

издршка *f* <expenses for> maintenance

издубори се *pf colloq.* to straighten up *intrans.*; to stand straight; to throw out one's chest

издува *pf* **I 1** to blow (*s.th.*) clean **2** (*со дување отстрани*) to blow away **3** (*за ветар: дувне*) to blow **II – се** to vent one's anger (*на – on*)

издувен -вна *adj* exhaust *attrib.*; издувен гас exhaust fumes

издудне *pf* издудна *aor.* **I 1** to draw out (*thread, etc.*) **2** *fig.* (*роди*) to bear a child **II – се** to slip out, be drawn out (*of thread, etc.*)

издуднува (се) *impf of* издудне (се)

издума *pf dial.* **1** *see* изговори **2** (*изнакаже*) to make up, think up, invent

издумува *impf of* издума

издупи *pf* to drill (bore) holes in; to perforate; to riddle with holes

издупува *impf of* издупи

издупчи *pf* to make <small> holes in

издупчува *impf of* издупчи

издутне (се) *pf* издутна (се) *aor. see* издудне (се)

издуши *pf* to deflate (*a balloon, etc.*); (*продупи*) to puncture

издушува *impf of* издуши

изед *m see* изедина

изеде *pf* **I 1** to eat <up>; (*за ѕвер*) to devour; ☐ изеде ќотек to get a beating; да го изедеш he/it is so cute; *joc.* нема да те изеде it won't eat you; жив срам ме изеде I nearly died of shame **2** to bite; го изеде змија he was bitten by a snake **3** *fig.* to squander; го изеде сиот имот he squandered the whole estate **4** *fig.* to ruin, destroy (*s.o.*), be (*s.o.'s*) undoing; to be the death of; ме изеде глава I have a splitting headache **II – се 1** *fig.* to fret; жив се изеде од мака he was worried to death **2** (*за месечина*) to wane; (*за сонце*) to be eclipsed

изедина *f* new (crescent) moon

изедначеност *f* uniformity

изедначи *pf* **I** to equalize *trans.*; to equal; to equate; to standardize; го изедначи со предавство he equated it with treason; *Sport.* изедначи резултат to even the score, equalize **II – се** to equalize *intrans.*; to become equal; to be assimilated; to merge *intrans.*; се изедначив со него I drew level (caught up) with him

изедначува (се) *impf of* изедначи (се)

изедник -ци *m see* јадач

изедува *impf see* изеде

изеслив *adj* voracious, greedy, gluttonous

изесник -ци *m see* јадач

изжала (се) *pf see* изжали (се)

изжали *pf* **I** to mourn, grieve (*for*); to cease mourning **II – се** to complain

изжалува (се) *impf of* изжала (се) & изжали (се)

изжебурка се *pf* to become wrinkled

изжедни *pf* to get thirsty

изжени *pf* to marry off (*several sons*)

изженува *impf of* изжени

изживее *pf* изживеа *aor.* **I** to live through; to undergo, experience; to suffer, endure; го изживее управувањето to learn the ropes; ги изживеа мизерно последните години he spent his last years in poverty **II – се** to go out of use, become old-fashioned

изживува се *impf* **1** to give vent to one's feelings, let off steam **2** to let o.s. go, live it up **3** (*над*) to torment; to mock; се иживува над него he torments him

изжнее *pf* изжна *aor. see* изжние

изжнива *impf of* изжние

изжние *pf* изжни *aor.* to reap, harvest

изжули *pf* **I** (*with acc.*) to pinch, cause discomfort (*of shoes, etc.*) **II – се** to get blisters

иззавитка *pf* **1** to wrap well **2** to fold completely; to fold over (*everything, several times*)

иззаврзе *pf* иззаврза *aor.* to tie <up> (*everything, completely*)

иззагине *pf* иззагина *aor.* **1** to die out; to perish, die **2** (*загуби многу*) to lose (*a lot of things*)

иззимува *pf* to spend the winter

иззвони *pf* to ring, strike

иземнат *pt see* измрзнат

иземне *pf* иземна *aor. see* измрзне

иземница *f* & **иземниште** *n* extreme cold, cold snap, freeze

иземнува *impf of* иземне

изиври се *pf dial.* to dress up *intrans.*

изида *pf* to build <up>; to finish building

изидува *impf of* изида

изира се *impf* to be visible; to be transparent

изигра *pf* **I 1** to finish playing/dancing **2** (*измами, излаже*) to deceive, abuse, cheat; го изигра законот to evade the law **3** to play (*a role, a part*); добро ја изигра улогата he played the part well **II – се** to tire of playing/dancing

изигрува *impf* **1** *of* изигра **2** to pretend, act, play, imitate

изиет *m colloq.* trouble, difficulty, worry; discomfort

изиетлија *adj indecl. colloq.* troublesome, difficult

изим & **изин** *m colloq.* licence, permit, approval

изискашла се *pf* to cough a lot

изискува *impf* to demand, claim, require; работата изискува напор the task requires effort

изитрен *adj* resourceful, adroit; shrewd, cunning; skilled

изитри се *pf* to become skilled; to become cunning

изитрува се *impf of* изитри се

изјава *f* declaration, announcement, statement; изјава под заклетва sworn statement; affidavit; даде изјава to make a statement; изјава на сочуство expression of sympathy

изјави *pf* to declare, state; to announce; изјави благодарност to express one's appreciation; изјави љубов to declare one's love; изјави некому сочуство to express sympathy to s.o.

изјавува *impf of* изјави

изјагни *pf* **I** to bring forth, drop (*a lamb*) **II – се** to lamb

изјадоса се *pf colloq.* to get thoroughly upset; to have one's fill of worries

изјази се *pf* to climb out

изјазува се *impf of* изјази се

изјалови *pf* **I** to cause to miscarry (*of animals*) **II – се 1** to miscarry (*of animals*) **2** to remain without offspring; (*за земја*) to become barren **3** *fig.* to come to nothing, fail; се изјалови работата the whole thing came to nothing

изјаловок -ци *m* aborted foetus; misshapen creature; *fig.* freak

изјаловува (се) *impf of* изјалови (се)

изјари *pf* to tread, impregnate (*a hen*)

изјари се *pf* (*of a goat*) to kid, bring forth a kid

изјарми *pf* to unhitch (*oxen, etc.*) from the yoke

изјаснение -ија *n* explanation; clarification

изјасни *pf* **I** to explain, clarify; го изјаснивме прашањето we have clarified the question **II – се 1** to declare (*за или против – for or against*) to come out (*for or against*); изјасни се! out with it! **2** to clear<up>; времето се изјасни the weather has cleared

изјаснува (се) *impf of* изјасни (се)

изјуди се *pf dial.* to become evil

излабави *pf see* олабави

излабавува *impf of* излабави

излага¹ (се) *impf of* изложи (се)

излага² *impf dial. of* излезе, *see* излегува

излагање *n* **1** exhibition, display, show; layout **2** exposure **3** expression, presentation, explanation, exposition, report

излагач *m* **1** lecturer, speaker **2** exhibitor

излади *pf* **I** to cool *trans.* **II** – се to cool *intrans.*; to cool down; *fig.* to cool off

изладува (се) *impf of* излади (се)

излае *pf* излаја *aor.* **I 1** to start barking **2** *fig.* to blurt out, blab out, reveal (*a secret*) **II** – се **1** to tire of barking **2** *fig.* to blab, let out (give away) a secret; човекот се излаја he spilt the beans, he put his foot in it

излаже *pf* излажа *aor.* **I** to cheat, deceive **II** – се to be mistaken; to make a mistake

излажува (се) *impf of* излаже (се)

излази *pf* to crawl over, creep over; to swarm over

излазува *impf of* излази

излапа *pf* to devour, guzzle, bolt, gulp down

излапува *impf of* излапа

изласка *pf* **I** to polish **II** – се **1** to become shiny (*with wear*) **2** *fig.* to dress up *intrans.*

изласне *pf* изласна *aor. see* изласка

излачи *pf* **I 1** to secrete; to discharge; to exude **2** to separate *trans.* **II** – се **1** to radiate *intrans.* **2** to separate *intrans.*

излачува (се) *impf of* излачи (се)

излева¹ *impf dial. see* излегува

излева² (се) *impf see* излее (се)

излегне *pf* излегна *aor.* to lie down; to get flattened; to flatten *trans.*

излегува *impf of* излезе; ❏ тоа не ми излегува од глава I can't get it out of my head; излегува во пресрет to meet halfway; to meet s.o.'s demands; излегува дека . . . it seems that . . .

излее *pf* излеа *aor.* **I 1** to pour <out> *trans.* **2** (*за метал*) to cast; to mould, found; излее од бронза to cast in bronze **3** *fig.* to vent, unleash, give vent to; го излеа своето срце he unburdened his heart **II** – се to pour out *intrans.*, run out, flow, stream; to overflow, flood *intrans.*

излежи се *pf* to tire of inactivity

излежува се *impf of* излежи се

излез *m* exit, way out (*also fig.*); треба да се најде излез a way out (a solution) must be found; ❏ нема излез there's no way out/solution

излезе *pf* **1** to go/come out; to leave; to emerge; to come forward; излезе од дома to go out of the house; to leave home; излезе на прошетка to go for a walk; излезе сонцето the sun came out; излезе од работа to give up one's job; to go out during working hours; излезе со нова теорија to put forward a new theory; ❏ да не си ми излегол пред очи! don't let me set eyes on you again! излезе на видело (мегдан) to become known; to come out in the open; излезе на двобој to accept a challenge; to take the

field; излезе на крај со to cope with; to manage; излезе од кожа to lose one's temper; излезе од такт to lose one's self-control; излезе од употреба/мода to go out of use/fashion; му излезе име to become famous/notorious; душа му излезе he gave up the ghost **2** to appear, come out; to be issued; излезе книга a book has been published; излезе заповед an order was given **3** *fig.* to result, turn out *intrans.*; to prove *intrans.*; од него излезе човек he has turned out well; излезе дека сум бил прав it turned out that I was right; *colloq.* излезе бош работата it turned out badly; ❏ ќе му излезе тоа на нос he'll pay dearly for that; *colloq.* не ми излезе есапот things didn't work out as I planned **4** (*of colour, stains*) to disappear; излезе бојата the colour has faded; флеката излезе the stain has come out **5** *fig.* to amount to, come to; колку излезе тоа сето? how much does all this come to?

излезен -зна *adj* of departure; излезна точка point of departure; starting point; излезна виза exit visa

излекува *pf* **I** to cure, heal *trans.* **II** – се (*за рана*) to heal *intrans.*; (*за човек*) to get well, recover

излепи *pf* **I 1** to paste; to post (put) up **2** to make sticky **II** – се to become sticky

излепува (се) *impf of* излепи (се)

излет *m* **1** outing, excursion; picnic, hike **2** *fig.* (*extramarital*) affair, escapade

излета *pf* to fly out/off/away (*also fig.*); излета на улица to rush out into the street; ❏ излета како куршум to rush out at breakneck speed; излета од кривина to miss a bend

излетник -ци *m* hiker, picnicker; *Brit.* tripper

излетница & излетничка *f* (*fem. form*) *see* излетник

излетнички *adj* picnic *attrib.*; излетничко место picnic area

излетува *impf of* излета

излечи (се) *pf see* излекува (се)

излечив *adj* curable

излечивост *f* curability

излечува (се) *impf see* излекува (се)

излив *m* **1** outflow; discharge, flow (*of bile, etc.*); излив на крв haemorrhage **2** *fig.* effusion, outpouring, gushing

излива (се) *impf see* излева (се)

излие (се) *pf* изли (се) *aor. see* излее (се)

излиже *pf* излижа (се) *aor.* **I 1** to lick; to lick all over; to finish licking **2** to wear out, use up (*by rubbing*) **II** – се **1** to lick o.s./each other **2** to wear out (*by rubbing*) *intrans.*

излижува (се) *impf of* излиже (се)

излитен *pt* worn-out, shabby; излитени алишта worn-out clothes

излитеност *f* shabbiness

излити се *pf* to wear out, become shabby

излицитира *pf* to sell by auction, auction off

излечи *pf f.p.* to announce

излишави се *pf* to become covered in lichen

излишен -шна *adj* superfluous, unnecessary, excessive

излишност *f* superfluity

излишок -ци *m* remnant, surplus

излови *pf* to catch (*many or all*)

излог -зи *m* display, shop-window; разгледува излози to go window-shopping; уредување на излог window-dressing

изложба *f* exhibition

изложбен *adj* exhibition; изложбен павиљон exhibition pavilion

изложи *pf* **I 1** to exhibit, display; изложи стока to display one's wares **2** (*искаже*) to present, express; (*објасни*) to explain, expound; ги изложи своите мисли he expounded his ideas **3** *fig.* to expose; ги изложи на опасност he exposed them to danger **II – се 1** to expose o.s. (*to danger, etc.*) **2** (*компромитира се*) to discredit o.s.; to make an ass/exhibition of o.s.

изложува (се) *impf see* излага (се)

изложувач *m see* излагач

излока *pf* **1** to lap up **2** *fig.* to drink heavily

излоши се *pf* to worsen, deteriorate, go from bad to worse

излуди <се> *pf* to go mad, become insane, lose one's mind

излупи *pf* **I** to peel; to shell; to finish peeling/shelling *trans.* **II – се** to peel *intrans.*

излупува (се) *impf of* излупи (се)

измава *pf* to beat, thrash, whip

измавне *pf* измавна *aor.* to swing, draw back (*one's arm before striking*)

измавнува *impf of* измавне

измажи *pf* to marry off (*several daughters*)

измажува *impf of* измажи

измазни *pf* to smooth/straighten out; to smooth, plane

измазнува *impf of* измазни

измајсториса *pf colloq.* to make, devise, contrive; to cook up

измака *pf* to mop up (*e.g. gravy with bread*)

измакува *impf of* измака

измама *f* **1** deceit, fraud; trick, ruse **2** illusion

измамен[1] *pt* deceived; tricked

измамен[2] -мна *adj* deceitful, tricky; illusory

измами *pf* **I** to deceive, trick, delude, swindle **II – се** to fall (*for a trick*); to be mistaken

измамник -ци *m* deceiver, swindler, trickster, cheat

измамница *f* (*fem. form*) *see* измамник

измамува (се) *impf of* измами (се)

измати *pf* to mix, whisk, shake up, churn (*milk, etc.*)

изматка *pf colloq.* to deceive, trick

изматува *impf of* измати

**изматуви
 се** *pf colloq.* to become senile

измачи *pf* **I** to torment; (*измори*) to wear out, exhaust **II – се** to suffer, go through hell; (*измори се*) to get worn-out, become exhausted

измачка *pf* **I 1** to smear **2** to rub *trans.* **3** *dial.* to crease, crumple, wrinkle (*clothes*) **II – се** to get smeared; to smear o.s.

измачкува (се) *impf of* измачка (се)

измачува (се) *impf of* измачи (се)

измачување *n* torment, torture

измеле *pf* измле *aor.* to grind/mill (*completely*)

измелува *impf of* измеле

измеѓу *prep dial. see* помеѓу

измена *f* change, modification, alteration

измени *pf* **I** to change, alter, modify *trans.*; го измени дневниот ред he changed the agenda **2** *Gram.* (*именка*) to decline; (*глагол*) to conjugate **II – се 1** to change, alter *intrans.* **2** *Gram.* to decline *intrans.*; to conjugate *intrans.*

изменлив *adj* changeable, variable; изменлива положба unstable situation; изменлив став temporary position

изменливост *f* changeability, variability

изменува (се) *impf of* измени (се)

измери *pf* to measure; (*тежина*) to weigh; ❑ измери некого од глава до петици to eye/measure s.o. from head to toe

измерува *impf of* измери

измеси *pf* **1** to knead thoroughly **2** *fig.* to thrash, give (*s.o.*) a beating

измести *pf* **I 1** to move *trans.*; to displace **2** to dislocate **II – се** to move o.s.; to move away *intrans.*

изместува (се) *impf of* измести (се)

измесува *impf of* измеси

измет *m colloq.* **1** service, care, help; прави (чини) измет (*некому*) to take care (*of s.o.*), wait (*on s.o.*); to look after **2** excrement

измете *pf* **1** to sweep out **2** *fig.* (*истера*) to throw (drive) out

изметиште *n* **1** excrement **2** rubbish (*Am.* garbage) heap, dump, tip

изметка *pf see* заплетка; ❑ им ги изметка конците he spoilt their plans

изметне се *pf* изметна се *aor.* to resemble, take after; се изметна на татка си he takes after his father

изметок -ци *m see* изјаловок

изметува *impf of* измете

измеќар *m colloq.* **1** servant **2** *fig.* lackey, bootlicker, toady, flatterer

измеќарски *adj colloq.* servile

измеќарува *impf* to work as a servant; to toady (*некому – to s.o.*)

измеќарче *n dim. of* измеќар

измеша *pf* **I** to mix, blend *trans.*; to stir; (*карти за играње*) to shuffle **II – се** to mix *intrans.*; to get confused; to mix, mingle (*with people*)

измешува (се) *impf of* измеша (се)

измива (се) *impf of* измие (се); нозете ќе им ги измива, водата ќе им ја испива he will wait on them hand and foot

измивачка *f colloq.* wash<ing>

измие *pf* изми *aor.* **I** to wash *trans.*; (*садови*) to wash up; ❑ го измија they took him to the cleaners **II – се** to wash o.s.

измилува *pf* to caress, fondle

измине *pf* измина *aor.* **I 1** (*помине некој простор*) to travel, cover; измине неколку километри to cover several kilometres **2** (*надмине*) to pass *trans.*, overtake **3** (*за време*) to pass *intrans.*; изминале многу години many years passed **II – се** to pass one another

изминува *impf see* измине

измири *pf* **I** to reconcile **II – се** to make peace; to make up *intrans.*

измисли *pf* to think out (up), invent; to fabricate

измислица *f* fabrication; myth

измислува *impf of* измисли

измислувач *m* fabricator, fibber

измислувачка *f colloq.* tall story, cock-and-bull story

измитари се *pf* to moult

измитарува се *impf of* измитари се

измокри *pf* **I** to wet; (*малку*) to moisten; (*наполно*) to drench, soak **II – се** to get wet/drenched (soaked)

измокрува (се) *impf of* измокри (се)

измолзе *pf* измолзи & измолзе *aor.* to milk; ❑

добро го измолзија they fleeced (milked) him properly

измолзува *impf of* измолзе

измоли *pf* I 1 to beg, ask for, seek; to apply for; to obtain by begging/applying/praying; ги измолив да ми одобрат отсуство I got them to approve my leave 2 (*наговори*) to persuade II – **се** 1 to plead (*за – for*); to apply (*for*); се измолив за стипендија I got a scholarship 2 to seek leave; to get leave 3 to complete one's prayers

измолкне *pf* измолкна *aor.* I to pull out; to draw (*a sword, etc.*) II – **се** 1 to get out; to get through 2 *fig.* to grow bigger/taller

измолкнува (се) *impf of* измолкне (се)

измолува[1] *pf* to paint (*a room, flat, etc.*)

измолува[2] **(се)** *impf of* измоли (се)

измореност *f* exhaustion, fatigue

измори *pf* I to exhaust, wear out II – **се** to tire *intrans.*, become exhausted

изморува (се) *impf of* измори (се)

изморувачка *f colloq.* exhaustion, fatigue

измота (се) *pf see* размота (се)

измотува (се) *impf of* измота (се)

измоча *pf vulg.* I to wet with urine II – **се** to piss; (*за дете и сл.*) to wet o.s.

измочува (се) *impf of* измоча (се)

измрда *pf* I 1 to move *trans.* 2 *fig.* to elude, evade II – **се** to move *intrans.*

измрдува (се) *impf of* измрда (се)

измре *pf see* изумре

измрзнат *pt* frozen, freezing, stiff with cold, frozen stiff; frostbitten

измрзне *pf* измрзна *aor.* to get frozen, freeze *intrans.*

измрзнува *impf of* измрзне

измрмори *pf* to mutter, mumble

измрморува *impf of* измрмори

измрси *pf* I 1 (*конци и сл.*) to entangle, tangle *trans.* 2 (*измачка*) to smear, grease II – **се** 1 to tangle *intrans.*, get tangled 2 (*измачка се*) to grease o.s. 3 (*прекине пост*) to break one's fast

измрсува (се) *impf of* измрси (се)

измудри *pf* I to think up, concoct, fabricate; од кај го измудривте тоа решение? where did you get that idea? II – **се** to grow wiser

измудрува (се) *impf of* измудри (се)

измука *pf* to moo; to start mooing

измушне се *pf* измушна се *aor.* to creep through, steal by; to get away unnoticed

измушнува се *impf of* измушне се

изнаака *pf colloq.* I to amass, accumulate (*large quantities*) II – **се** to tire of wandering

изнабара *pf* to invent/discover (*one thing after another*)

изнабере *pf* изнабра *aor.* to pick a lot (*of fruit, flowers, etc.*)

изнаброи се *pf* to tire of counting (enumerating)

изнабута *pf* I to stuff, ram (*s.th. into s.th.*) II – **се** to squeeze in *intrans.* (*of several people*)

изнаваса *pf colloq.* to manage, have time (*to do s.th.*); не можам да изнавасам I can't manage to finish everything

изнавика *pf* I to invite a lot of people II – **се** to shout one's fill

изнаврне *pf* изнаврна *aor.* 1 *impers.* to rain heavily 2

to get drenched; многу изнаврнав I got wet through in the rain

изнагледа се *pf* to see in quantity; to look at sufficiently (enough); to have one's fill of gazing

изнагледува се *impf of* изнагледа се

изнагости *pf* I to entertain well, serve plenty of food (*to s.o.*) II – **се** 1 to help o.s. lavishly (*as a guest*) 2 to outstay one's welcome

изнајде *pf* I 1 to discover, find 2 to invent, think up, devise II – **се** to find each other; одвај се изнајдовме we only just managed to meet

изнајдува (се) *impf of* изнајде (се)

изнајдување *n* discovery; invention

изнакаже *pf* изнакажа *aor.* to tell a lot of stories (gossip); што не ми изнакажа! 1. what a lot of stories (gossip) he told me! 2. he gave me a good ticking-off

изнакажува *impf of* изнакаже

изнакива се *pf* to sneeze a lot

изнамачи *pf* I to torment, worry, exhaust II – **се** to go through hell

изнамести *pf* I to put, place around; to tidy up II – **се** to settle, make o.s. comfortable; се изнаместија на подот they made themselves comfortable on the floor

изнаоди се *pf* to tire of walking

изнаодува се *impf of* изнаоди се

изнастине *pf* изнастина *aor.* to catch a cold, get chilled

изначуди се *pf* to be extremely surprised; to cease wondering; *colloq.* to get over it

изнашета се *pf* to tire of walking

изнашетува се *impf of* изнашета се

изневера *f* disloyalty, betrayal, treachery

изневери *pf* to betray; to be unfaithful to; ја изневери жената he was unfaithful to his wife; ги изневери своите принципи he betrayed his principles

изневерник -ци *m* treacherous/disloyal man; traitor

изневерница *f* treacherous/disloyal woman; traitress

изневерува *impf of* изневери

изнемоштен *pt & adj* exhausted, worn-out; feeble, decrepit

изнемоштеност *f* exhaustion; weakness

изнемошти *pf* I to weaken, wear out *trans.*, exhaust; болеста го изнемошти the illness wore him down II – **се** to become exhausted; to flag, decline *intrans.*; to weaken *intrans.*

изненада *f* surprise; unexpectedness

изненаден -дна *adj* sudden, unexpected, *see* ненадеен

изненади *pf* I to surprise; to take unawares II – **се** to be surprised, be taken by surprise

изненадува (се) *impf of* изненади (се)

изненадување *n* surprise; по нечие големо изненадување much to s.o.'s surprise

изненадувачки *adj* surprising

изнесе *pf* 1 to carry/take/bring out; изнесоа сè надвор they took everything outside 2 (*fig.* (*соопшти, наведе*) to present, produce, quote, mention; изнесе нови докази to produce new evidence; точно е тоа што го изнесовте what you have mentioned is correct; изнесе свое мислење to state one's opinion 3 *fig.* (*за сметка*) to amount to, come to; to total; сметката изнесе илјада денари the bill came to a thousand denars

изнесува *impf of* изнесе

изниже *pf* изнижа *aor.* **1** to thread, string (*much, many, all*) **2** to undo (*s.th. threaded*)

изникне *pf* изникна *aor.* to appear, come up; to sprout; to spring up; му изникнаа заби he has cut his teeth; *fig.* изникнаа нови луѓе new people have appeared on the scene; ❏ изникне како печурки to spring up like mushrooms

изникнува *impf of* изникне

изниша *pf* to rock for a while *trans.*

изнишува *impf of* изниша

изноктен *adj* newly-made; изноктена облека newly-made clothes

износ *m* total, sum, amount; во износ од to the extent of

износен *pt* worn-out, threadbare

износи *pf* to wear out (*clothes*)

износок -ци *m* small, misshapen egg (*traditional ill omen*)

износува *impf of* износи

изнуди *pf* to extort, extract, force; му изнудив признание I wrung recognition from him

изнудува *impf of* изнуди

изнудувач *m* extortioner

изоба́ра *f* isobar

изобилен -лна *adj* plentiful, abundant, copious

изобилие *n* plenty, abundance; во изобилие in abundance

изобилува *impf* to have in abundance; to abound in, be rich in, be full (*со – of*)

изобичаи се *pf* to fall into disuse

изобичајува се *impf of* изобичаи се

изоблекува (се) *impf of* изоблече (се)

изоблече *pf* **I** to dress up (*many people*) **II** – **се** to get dressed up; to overdress

изобличи *pf* **I** to distort; to disfigure **II** – **се** to become disfigured/distorted

изобличува (се) *impf of* изобличи (се)

изоглави *pf* to take a headstall off (*an animal*)

изодбере *pf* изодбра *aor.* to choose (*from a large selection*), select the best

изодбира *impf of* изодбере

изоди *pf* to walk, cover (*a certain distance*); to pass through (*several places*); изоди пет километри to cover five kilometres; изоди полиња to walk all over the fields

изодува *impf of* изоди

изола́тор *m Elec.* insulator

изолација *f* **1** isolation **2** *Elec.* insulation

изоли́ра *pf & impf* **I** **1** to isolate, separate **2** *Elec.* to insulate **II** – **се** to isolate o.s., withdraw *intrans.*

изоли́ран -pt **1** isolated **2** *Elec.* insulated

изолираност *f* **1** isolation, loneliness **2** *Elec.* insulation

изопачен *adj* distorted, twisted; (*расипан*) perverted

изопаченост *f* distortion; (*расипаност*) perversion, depravity, corruption

изопачи *pf* **1** to distort **2** (*расипе*) to pervert, deprave

изопачува *impf of* изопачи

изора *pf* to plough, plough up

изорува *impf of* изора

изостава *impf of* изостави

изостави *pf* **1** to leave out, omit **2** to leave (*several things*)

изоставува *impf see* изостава

изостане *pf* изостана *aor.* **1** to be absent (missing); изостане од часови to miss classes **2** to lag (fall) behind; изостане од колона to fall behind a column

изостанок -ци *m* absence; неоправдани изостаноци unexplained/inexcusable absences

изостанува *impf of* изостане

изострен *adj & pt* **1** sharpened, sharp **2** (*за сетила*) keen, acute **3** (*напрегнат*) strained; изострени односи strained relations

изостреност *f* **1** sharpness **2** *fig.* keenness, acuity **3** *fig.* tension, strain

изостри *pf* **I** **1** to sharpen, whet **2** *fig.* (*за сетила*) to refine **3** *fig.* (*создаде напрегнатост*) to strain **II** – **се** **1** *fig.* to become refined **2** *fig.* (*стане напрегнат*) to become strained

изострува (се) *impf of* изостри (се)

изоте́рма *f* isotherm

изотиде *pf* **I** to go away (*of several people*) **II** – **си** to disperse, go home (*each to his own place*)

изотидува (си) *impf of* изотиде (си)

изото́п *m Chem.* isotope

изотпадне *pf* изотпадна *aor.* to fall away (*of several things or people*)

изохи́пса *f* contour line

изработен *pt* **1** produced, manufactured **2** (*изморен*) exhausted, worn-out with work

изработеност *f* **1** finish<ed state> **2** exhaustion

изработи *pf* **I** **1** to make, manufacture, produce; (*за план, програма*) to develop, draw up; изработи речник to compile a dictionary **2** *see* одработи **II** – **се** to wear o.s. out

изработка *f* manufacture; work; workmanship, finish; стандардна изработка standard make; мајсторска изработка high-quality work

изработува *impf of* изработи

израдува *pf* **I** to make happy, gladden **II** – **се** to be happy, rejoice

Израел *m* Israel

Израелец -лци *m* Israeli

Израелка *f* (*fem. form*) *see* Израелец

израелски *adj* Israeli

израз *m* **1** (*facial*) expression, look; израз на страв fearful expression **2** expression; phrase; израз на почит expression of respect; израз на добродошлица words of welcome; фразеолошки израз set expression; алгебарски израз algebraic expression; стручен израз <technical> term; ❏ доаѓа до израз to come to the fore; to leave one's mark; to make one's presence felt; наоѓа израз во to find expression in

изразгледа *pf* to examine, look through (*everything*)

изразен[1] -зна *adj* expressive; речнички изразни можности lexical resources; изразен поглед expressive look

изразен[2] *pt* **1** expressed; изразен со зборови expressed in words **2** (*изразит*) prominent; marked, pronounced; изразен нос prominent nose; изразена разлик a marked difference

изразеност *f* expressiveness

изрази *pf* **I** to express; to convey; to render; (*за лице*) to show; изрази благодарност to express gratitude; писмото го изрази нашето мислење the letter voiced our opinion **II** – **се** **1** to express o.s.; погрешно се изразив I made a mistake; I said the wrong thing 2 (*пројави се*) to find expression, become manifest; тоа се изрази во решението that was reflected in the decision

изразит *adj* 1 marked, pronounced; conspicuous; clear, distinct 2 (*истакнат*) outstanding, prominent

изразител *m see* изразувач

изразитост *f* 1 clarity, distinctness 2 eminence

изразлив *adj* expressible; тешко изразлив inexpressible

изразност *f* expressiveness, expressive force

изразува *impf of* изрази; ❑ изразува послушност to show obedience; изразува право на to stake one's claim to

изразувач *m* spokesman; (*на мислења, чувства*) interpreter, mouthpiece, exponent

израмни *pf* I 1 to level, flatten <out> *trans.*; (*изглади*) to smooth out, even out *trans.*; *fig.* to settle *trans.* 2 to align; (*резултат*) to equalize II – се 1 to level off *intrans.*; to even out *intrans.* 2 to catch up, draw level (*со – with*)

израмнува (се) *impf of* израмни (се)

израси *pf see* нараси

израсипе *pf* израсипа *aor.* I 1 to spoil (*totally, everything*) 2 *fig.* to corrupt; to spoil (*a child*) II – се 1 to break down one after another 2 *fig.* to be corrupted, become corrupt (*completely or of several people*)

израсне *pf* израсна *aor.* 1 to grow; to grow up; израсна тревата the grass has grown; децата веќе ми израснаа my children have already grown up 2 *fig.* to develop, arise; израсна големо претпријатие a big enterprise (organization) developed (was created) 3 to outgrow; израсне алишта to grow out of one's clothes

израснува *impf of* израсне

израсте *pf see* израсне

израсток -ци *m* excrescence, growth; protuberance; swelling, tumour

израстува *impf see* израснува

израсува *impf of* израси

израчуна *pf see* пресмета

изꞌрга *pf* I to exhaust, wear out II – се to exhaust, wear o.s. out

изреди *pf* I to enumerate, list II – се to line up *intrans.*, form a line

изредува (се) *impf of* изреди (се)

изреже *pf* изрежа *aor.* to cut out; to cut up

изрежува *impf of* изреже

изрез *m* hole, slit; low neckline, décolletage

изрезок -ци *m* hole, slit

изрека *f* saying, maxim

изрекува *impf of* изрече

изрекување *n* statement, pronouncement

изретчи *pf* to thin, thin out, make less dense

изретчува *impf of* изретчи

изрече *pf* to state, utter; изрече пресуда to pronounce sentence, pass judgement

изречува *impf see* изрекува

изрива *impf of* изрие

изрига & изригне *pf* to belch forth, throw up

изригнува *impf of* изригне

изригува *impf of* изрига

изрие *pf* изри *aor.* to dig out

изрине *pf* изрина *aor.* to shovel off, clear (*e.g. snow*)

изринува *impf of* изрине

изрипа *pf* to jump to one's feet

изрипува *impf of* изрипа

изркне *pf* изркна *aor.* I to spit out, hawk up *trans.* II – се to hawk *intrans.*

изркнува (се) *impf of* изркне (се)

изрод *m* degenerate; freak; monster

изроди *pf* I to bring forth, give birth to (*several offspring*) II – се 1 (*of several offspring*) to be born 2 to degenerate; to turn (*во – into*) 3 to arise; to ensue; се изроди кавга a quarrel ensued

изродува (се) *impf of* изроди (се)

изродување *n* degeneration

изрои (се) *pf* (*of bees*) to form a new swarm, swarm out

изрони *pf* I 1 to wear away, erode *trans.* 2 to crumble *trans.*; изрони леб to crumble bread II – се to wear away, erode *intrans.*; to crumble *intrans.*; брегот се изрони the bank crumbled

изронува (се) *impf of* изрони (се)

изроси *pf* to bedew, sprinkle with dew

изрошка *pf* to find by rummaging

изулави *pf* I to drive mad II – се to go mad, lose one's reason

изуми *pf* I to forget; to overlook II – се to go mad, lose one's reason

изумира *impf of* изумре

изумре *pf* to die out, become extinct

изумува *impf of* изуми I

изусти *pf* to utter, pronounce

изустува *impf of* изусти

изутрина[1] *f* morning; секоја изутрина every morning

изутрина[2] *adv* tomorrow morning; ❑ утре изутрина never! pigs may fly

изучи *pf* I 1 to learn, master; изучи занает to learn a trade 2 to teach, train *trans.* II – се to finish school/ one's studies

изучува *impf of* изучи; to study; to do research

изцарка *pf* to burn, scorch

изцвака *pf* to chew well; to chew up

изцвакува *impf of* изцвака

ИК *abbr.* (*Извршен комитет*) Executive Committee

ика *impf* to hiccup

икавица *f* hiccupping, the hiccups

икеба́на *f* ikebana

икне *pf* икна *aor.* to give a hiccup

икона *f* icon (ikon); убава како икона as pretty as a picture; ❑ застане како икона to stand rooted to the spot

иконоборец -рци *m* iconoclast

иконокласт *m* iconoclast

иконом *f colloq.* estate manager

икономиса *pf colloq.* to economize, save (*on s.th.*)

икономисува *impf of* икономиса

иконопис *m* icon-painting

иконописец -сци *m* icon-painter

иконостас *m Rel.* iconostasis

икра *f* roe; фрла икра to spawn

икс *m Math.*, *fig.* the letter 'x'; unknown quantity/ person

илега́ла *f* 1 clandestine political activity 2 de facto marriage

илега́лен -лна *adj* illegal; *Pol.* underground

илега́лец -лци *m* member of an underground movement; person performing an illegal act; illegal immigrant; resident without permit

илегалство *n* clandestine activity

или *conj* or; ❑ или-или make or break (mar); или . . . или either . . . or; или пак or else

илика *f* buttonhole

Илинден *m* St Elias' Day (*anniversary of the uprising of the Macedonians on 2nd August 1903*)

илјада *f* thousand

илјадагодишен -шна *adj* **1** thousand-year-old **2** lasting a thousand years

илјадарка *f* thousand-denar banknote

илјаден -дна *adj* thousandth

илјадници *adv* by the thousand

илје[1] *n colloq.* fraud, trick; не прави илје don't try any tricks! don't try to cheat!

илје[2] *adv colloq.* in the expression: илје и милје much, many

иловица *f* loam

илузија -ии *f* illusion

илузорен -рна *adj* illusory

илуминација -ии *f* illumination

илуминира *pf & impf* to illuminate

илустративен -вна *adj* illustrative

илустратор *m* illustrator

илустрација -ии *f* illustration

илустрира *pf & impf* to illustrate

илустриран *pt* illustrated; илустрирано списание illustrated magazine

им *pron* **1** (*short dat. form of* тие, они) <to> them; им реков I told them **2** (*as dat. of possession*) their; татко им their father

има *impf* **1** to have; to possess; to own; има работа to have a job; to be busy; ❑ има страв to be afraid; има волја to be willing; има врска со to bear on; има десет години to be ten years old; има за носење to have clothes to wear; има намера (*да*) to intend (*to*); има нужда to be in need; има обврски (*кон*) to be obliged (*to*); има обзир to be mindful; има последен збор to have the last word; има право to be right; има право на нешто to be entitled to s.th.; има предност пред to have the edge on; има (*некого/ нешто*) предвид to have in mind; има уште за земање to be owed a debt; ќе имаш за земање! you can write that off! you can forget it! има нешто против некого to have s.th. against s.o. **2** to have to; има да донесеш нешто you must bring s.th. **3** *impers.* there is, there are; има ли уште нешто? is there anything else? има време there's time; овде има многу луѓе there are a lot of people here; ❑ што има што нема? what's new? има и од пиле млеко; има се што сакаш there's everything you care to name **4** to consider; има некого за да take s.o. for **5** (*as auxiliary verb forming perfect tense*) има дојдено he has come; имаше дојдено he had come

имагинарен -рна *adj* imaginary

имагинација *f* imagination; fantasy

имам *m* imam

имам-бајалди *m* dish made from aubergines (eggplants) with oil

иманентен -тна *adj* immanent, inherent; essential, inseparable

иманенција & иманентност *f* immanence

имање *n* **1** presence (*of s.th.*) **2** property; (*добиток*) cattle, livestock

имашлив *adj* well-to-do, rich

имбецил *m* imbecile

име *n* **1** name; по име by name; даде има to name; ❑ од (во) името на in the name of, on behalf of; под името на under the banner of; стекнува име to gain a reputation; имиња да не спомнуваме name no names; извади некому име to give s.o. a nickname; му излегло име his name is well-known; големо име a great name **2** *colloq. see* именден **3** *Gram.* noun

имела *f* **1** *Bot.* (Viscum album) mistletoe **2** unconsciousness, faint; giddiness; ме фати имела I felt giddy; I had a fainting fit

именден *m* name-day

именик -ци *m* directory; телефонски именик telephone directory

именител *m Math.* denominator

именка *f Gram.* noun, substantive; ❑ мислена именка a castle in the air; a pipe dream

имено *adv* **1** namely **2** just, exactly

именски *adj Gram.* substantival, noun (*clause, etc.*)

именува *impf* **1** to name **2** to appoint, nominate

имењак -ци *m* namesake

имза *f arch.* signature

имигрант *m* immigrant

имиграција *f* immigration

имитатор *m* imitator

имитација *f* imitation; имитација на злато imitation gold

имитира *impf* to imitate

имиџ *m* image

имобилизација *f* immobilization

имобилизира *pf & impf* to immobilize

имовит *adj see* имотен

имот *m* estate, property; assets; недвижен имот real estate

имотен -тна *adj* well-to-do, rich

имотност *f* affluence

императив *m* imperative; категорички императив categorical imperative

императивен -вна *adj* imperative; unconditional

император *m* emperor

императорски *adj* imperial

империја -ии *f* empire

империјализам -змот *m* imperialism

империјалист *m* imperialist

империјалистички *adj* imperialistic

имперфект *m Gram.* imperfect, past continuous tense

имперфективен -вна *adj Gram.* imperfective

импликација *f* implication; involvement

имплицира *pf & impf* **1** to implicate **2** to imply

импозантен -тна *adj* imposing, magnificent, impressive

импозантност *f* impressiveness, magnificence

импонира *impf* to impress

импорт *m* import

импортира *pf & impf* to import

импотентен -тна *adj* impotent

импотентност *f* impotence

импотенција *f* impotence

импрегнација *f* impregnation

импрегнира *pf & impf* to impregnate

импресарио *m* impresario

импресија -ии *f* impression

импресионизам -змот *m* impressionism

импресиони́ст *m Art* impressionist (*painter*)
импресиони́стички *adj* impressionistic
импровиза́тор *m* improviser
импровизација -ии *f* improvisation
импровизи́ра *pf & impf* to improvise
импулс *m* impulse
импулси́вен -вна *adj* impulsive
импулси́вност *f* impulsiveness
имун *adj* immune; non-infectious
имунизација *f* immunization
имунизи́ра *pf & impf* to immunize
имуните́т *m* immunity
имуност *f* immunity
инает *m colloq.* spite, malice; grudge; obstinacy; за инает некому to spite s.o.; од инает out of spite; инает човек spiteful person; stubborn person; ☐ тера инает to be spiteful/pigheaded; како за инает just my luck; to make matters worse; as luck would have it
инаети се *impf colloq.* to be stubborn, obstinate
инаетчија -ии *m colloq.* spiteful person; stubborn person
инаков -ква *adj* different, of another kind, *see* поинаков
инаку *adv* differently; otherwise; by the way; тој инаку ја кажа работата he presented the matter differently; инаку не беше лошо otherwise it wasn't bad
инвазија -ии *f* invasion, incursion
инвали́д *m* disabled person; disabled war veteran
инвалиднина *f* disability pension
инвалидитет *m* disability; делумен инвалидитет partial disability
инвали́дски *adj* war veteran's; disabled person's
инвента́р *m* **1** inventory; stocktaking **2** contents, property, assets; ☐ тој е дел од инвентарот he is a permanent fixture
инвентариса *pf* to inventory
инвентарисува *impf of* инвентариса
инвенту́ра *f* stocktaking
инверзија *f* inversion
инвести́ра *pf & impf* to invest
инвеститор *m* investor
инвестиција -ии *f* investment
инвестицио́нен -она *adj* investment
инволвиран *adj* involved
ингере́нт *m Leg.* prosecutor
ингеренција *f* influence, competence, purview; participation
индат *m arch.* help
индекс *m* **1** index; индекс на цени price index **2** студентски индекс university student's record booklet
индетермини́ст *m* indeterminist
индивидуа *f* individual, single person
индивидуа́лен -лна *adj* individual
индивидуали́зам -змот *m* individualism
индивидуализација *f* individualization
индивидуали́ра *pf & impf* to individualize
индивидуали́ст *m* individualist
индивидуалистички *adj* individualistic
индивидуа́лност *f* individuality
индигнација *f* indignation; disgust, revulsion
индиго *n* **1** indigo **2** carbon copy
Индиец -јци *m* Indian
Индија *f* India

Индија́нец -нци *m* American Indian
Индија́нка *f* (*fem. form*) *see* Индијанец
индија́нски *adj* American Indian
Индијка *f* (*fem. form*) *see* Индиец
индикати́в *m Gram.* indicative (*mood*)
индикати́вен *adj* indicative
индирект *m Soccer* indirect free kick
индиректен -тна *adj* indirect, roundabout; индиректен доказ circumstantial evidence; индиректна загуба consequential loss; *Gram.* индиректен говор indirect speech
индиски *adj* Indian; Индиски Океан Indian Ocean
индискре́тен -тна *adj* indiscreet
индискреција *f* indiscretion
индифере́нтен -тна *adj* indifferent
индифере́нтност *f* indifference
индиција *f* <piece of> evidence, pointer; indication, symptom
Индонезиец -ијци *m* Indonesian
Индонезија *f* Indonesia
Индонезијка *f* (*fem. form*) *see* Индонезиец
индонезиски *adj* Indonesian
индукти́вен -вна *adj* inductive
индукција *f* induction
индустрија *f* industry; (*претпријатие*) works, factory
индустрија́лец -лци *m* industrialist
индустријализација *f* industrialization
индустриски *adj* industrial; индустриска гранка branch of industry; индустриски развиена земја industrialized country
ине́ртен -тна *adj* inert, motionless; sluggish, listless
ине́ртност *f* inertness, immobility; sluggishness, listlessness
инерција *f* inertia; законот на инерцијата the law of inertia; по инерција by inertia
инж. *abbr.* (*инженер*) engineer
инжене́р *m* engineer
инженерија *f Mil.* engineering corps
инжене́ринг *m* **1** engineering **2** engineering company
инжене́рски *adj* engineering (*e.g. works*)
инжене́рство *n* engineering
иниција́л *m* initial
иниција́тива *f* initiative; ☐ презема иницијатива to take the initiative; to lead the way
иниција́тивен -вна *adj* enterprising; initiatory
иниција́тор *m* initiator; promoter; instigator; agitator
иници́ра *pf & impf* to initiate
инјекција -ии *f* injection
инка *f* funnel (*for pouring liquids*); ☐ ум со инка не се тура you can't force anybody to study
инкарнација *f* incarnation
инкарни́ра *pf & impf* to embody, incarnate, personify; (*идеја*) to express; (*оствари*) to give material form to
инкаса́нт & инкаса́тор *m* bill collector
инка́со *n* collection
инквизи́тор *m* inquisitor
инквизиторски *adj* inquisitorial
инквизиција *f* inquisition
инкогнито *adv* incognito
инкримини́ра *pf & impf* to incriminate
инкрустација -ии *f* incrustation
инкуба́тор *m* incubator
инкубација *f* incubation

инкубацио́нен -она *adj* incubation *attrib.*
инова́ција *f* innovation
инови́ра *pf & impf* to innovate
инса́н *m arch.* 1 person, soul 2 people, crowd
инсе́кт *m* insect
инсекта́риум *m* insectarium
инсектици́д *m* insecticide
инсе́рт *m* insert (*in press, film, TV*)
инсинуа́ција -ии *f* insinuation
инсинуи́ра *impf* to insinuate
инсисти́ра *pf & impf* to insist (*на – on*)
инспекти́ра *pf & impf* 1 to inspect, investigate, examine 2 to supervise, observe
инспе́ктор *m* inspector; санита́рен инспектор sanitary inspector; фина́нсиски инспектор auditor
инспектора́т *m* inspectorate
инспе́кторски *adj* inspectorial, inspector's
инспе́кција -ии *f* 1 inspection, review 2 supervision; supervisory body
инспекцио́нен -она *adj* inspecting, inspection
инспира́тор *m* inspirer; instigator
инспира́ција *f* inspiration
инспири́ра *pf & impf* 1 to inspire, give inspiration 2 to instigate, incite; to egg on, urge on; to goad
инстала́тор *m* fitter
инстала́ција -ии *f* installation, electrical system; equipment, appliance, plant
инстали́ра *pf & impf* to install, fit, fix
инста́нт *adj indecl.* instant; инстант супа instant soup
инста́нца & **инста́нција** -ии *f* instance, (*level of*) jurisdiction or authority; суд од прва инстанца court of first jurisdiction; суд од највисока инстанца court of summary jurisdiction; највисоки инстанци highest echelons
инсти́нкт *m* instinct, drive
инстикти́вен -вна *adj* instinctive
институ́т *m* institute
институ́тски *adj* institute
институ́ција -ии *f* institution
институционализи́ра <се> *pf & impf* to institutionalize, establish
инстру́ктор *m* instructor
инстру́кција -ии *f* instruction, direction
инструме́нт *m* instrument
инструмента́л *m Gram.* instrumental (*case*)
инструмента́лен -лна *adj* instrumental; инструментална музика instrumental music
инструмента́ција *f Mus.* instrumentation
инструменти́ра *pf & impf Mus.* to instrument
инсцени́ра *pf* 1 to stage, dramatize, adapt for the stage 2 to fabricate, concoct
инт *m arch.* cotton yarn
интабула́ција *f* 1 registration (*of deeds*) 2 distraint, confiscation of property (*in lieu of debt*)
интегра́л *m* integral (*also fig.*)
интегра́лен -лна *adj* integral, complete
интегра́ција *f* integration, amalgamation, merger
интегри́ра *pf & impf* to integrate, amalgamate, merge
интегрите́т *m* integrity
интеле́кт *m* intellect, mind
интелектуа́лен -лна *adj* intellectual, conceptual, mental
интелектуа́лец -лци *m* intellectual
интелектуа́лка *f* (*fem. form*) *see* интелектуалец

интелиге́нт *m* member of the intelligentsia; intellectual
интелиге́нтен -тна *adj* intelligent, sensible; clever
интелиге́нција *f* 1 intelligence 2 intelligentsia, professional classes
интенда́нт *m* quartermaster
интенда́нтски *adj* quartermaster's
интенданту́ра *f* quartermaster's office; quartermaster corps, supply services
интензи́вен -вна *adj* intensive; powerful; tense; интензивна работа intensive work
интензи́вност *f* & **интензите́т** *m* intensity
инте́нција -ии *f* intention, purpose
интерва́л *m* interval (*in space, time*)
интервени́ра *pf & impf* to intervene; to interfere
интерве́нција -ии *f* intervention; interference; хируршка интервенција surgical operation
интервју́ -а *n* interview
интервју́ира *pf & impf* to interview
интере́гнум *m* interregnum
инте́рен -рна *adj* internal, inside; интерни болести internal illnesses; интерен телефон extension <number>
интере́с *m* 1 interest; во интерес на in the interests of; има интерес за to be interested in; губи интерес to lose interest; ❑ од личен интерес for one's own purposes 2 (*добивка*) advantage, gain 3 (*камата*) interest, interest rate
интере́сен -сна *adj* 1 interesting 2 rare, special; unusual; интересна птица rare bird 3 of interest/ advantage; интересна сфера sphere of interest
интересе́нт *m* interested person; prospective buyer/ customer
интереси́ра *pf & impf* I to interest II – се to be interested (*за, во – in*); to take (show) interest (*за – in*); to enquire about
интереси́рање *n* display of interest
интере́сност *f* interest, curiosity
интересу́ва (се) *pf & impf see* интересира (се)
интерие́р *m* interior
интери́м *adj, adv, m* interim
интерје́кција -ии *f* interjection
интерме́цо *m & n* intermezzo
интерна́т *m* boarding-school
интерна́тски *adj* boarding-school
интерна́ција *f* internment
интернациона́ла *f* <the> International; the Internationale (international anthem)
интернациона́лен -лна *adj* international
интернационали́зам -змот *m* internationalism
интернационали́ст *m* internationalist
интернационалисти́чки *adj* internationalistic
интерни́ра *pf & impf* to intern
интерни́рање *n* internment
интерни́ст *m Med.* internist, specialist in internal illnesses
интерпарламента́рен -рна *adj* interparliamentary
интерпела́ција -ии *f* interpellation
интерпели́ра *pf & impf* to interpellate
интерпланета́рен -рна *adj* interplanetary
интерпрета́тор *m* interpreter; expounder; singer, performer
интерпрета́ција -ии *f* interpretation; exposition; интерпретација на песна interpretation of a song

интерпретíра *pf* & *impf* to interpret, expound; интерпретира улога to interpret a role

интерпункција *f* punctuation

интерференција *f* interference

интерфон *m* intercom

интима *f* 1 private life; personal feelings 2 intimate matter 3 close friendship; friendly feeling 4 intimacy 5 underwear

интимен -мна *adj* intimate; familiar, close

интимност *f* intimacy, familiarity

интонација -ии *f* intonation

интонíра *pf* & *impf* to intone; to strike up

интравенозен -зна *adj* intravenous

интрига *f* 1 intrigue, plot, scheme 2 (*во драма, роман*) plot

интригáнт *m* intriguer, plotter, schemer; troublemaker

интригáнтка *f* (*fem. form*) *see* интригант

интригíра *impf* to intrigue; to make trouble

интригува *impf see* интригира

интроспектíвен -вна *adj* introspective

интроспекција *f* introspection

интуитíвен -вна *adj* intuitive

интуиција *f* intuition

инфантíлен -лна *adj* infantile

инфантíлност *f* infantilism; infantility

инфáркт *m Med.* infarct, infarction, heart attack

инфектíвен -вна *adj* infectious, contagious; инфективни болести infectious diseases

инфекција -ии *f* infection; contagion

инфериóрен -рна *adj* inferior

инфериóрност *f* inferiority

инфилтрáт *m* infiltrate

инфилтрација *f* infiltration

инфинитíв *m Gram.* infinitive (*indefinite mood*)

инфицíра *pf* & *impf* I to infect II – ce to become infected (*co – with*)

инфлација *f* inflation

инфлациски *adj* inflationary

инфлуéнца *f* influenza, *colloq.* flu

информатíвен -вна *adj* informative; information *attrib.*

информатика *f* informatics, information science/ technology

информáтор *m* informant; source of information

информација -ии *f* information; announcement; piece of news, news item

информíра *pf* & *impf* I to inform, notify II – ce to find out; to enquire

инфраструктýра *f* infrastructure

инфузија *f* infusion (*also fig.*)

инфузорија -ии *f* infusoria (*pl*)

инхалáтор *m* inhaler

инхалација *f* inhalation

инхалíра *pf* & *impf* to inhale

инцест *m* incest

инцидéнт *m* incident

инцидéнтен -тна *adj* incidental; chance, accidental; unintentional; unforeseen

инч *m* inch

иперíт *m* (*боен отров*) mustard gas

ираде *n arch.* sultan's decree; document

Ирак *m* Iraq

ирам *m* small thin rug (*usu. of two strips, often used as bed-cover*)

Иран *m* Iran, *arch.* Persia

Иранец -нци *m* Iranian, *arch.* Persian

Иранка *f* (*fem. form*) *see* Иранец

ирански *adj* Iranian, *arch.* Persian

ирационáлен -лна *adj* irrational

ирационáлност *f* irrationality

Ирачанец -ни *m* Iraqi

Ирачанка *f* (*fem. form*) *see* Ирачанец

ирачки *adj* Iraqi

ирвас *m Zool.* reindeer

иреален -лна *adj* unreal

иреалност *f* unreality

иредентíзам -змот *m* irredentism

иредентíст *m* irredentist

Ирец -рци *m* Irishman

иригáтор *m* enema, irrigator

иригација *f* 1 irrigation 2 injection

иригациóнен -она *adj* irrigative

ирис *m* 1 *Anat.* iris 2 *Bot.* iris 3 rainbow

иритација *f* irritation

иритíра *pf* & *impf* to irritate

Ирка *f* Irishwoman

иронизíра *impf* to be ironic

иронија *f* irony

ироничен -чна *adj* ironic

Ирска *f* Ireland

ирски *adj* Irish

ис- *verbal prefix see* из-

исвири *pf* to finish playing (*music*)

исвирува *impf of* исвири

изврши *pf* to finish (*many things*)

исе *n colloq.* bit, part

исева *impf* to flash forth

иседи *pf* to sit out

иседува *impf of* иседи

исее *pf* исеа *aor.* to sift; исее брашно to sift flour

исејува *impf of* исее

исекне *pf* исекна *aor.* I to blow (*nose*); си го исекна носот he blew his nose II – ce to blow one's nose

исекнува (се) *impf of* исекне (се)

исекува (се) *impf of* исече (се)

иселеник -ци *m* emigrant, émigré; expatriate; *Austral.* migrant

иселенички *adj* emigrant's, expatriate, *Austral.* migrant; иселеничка виза migrant visa

иселеништво *n* emigrant population; life as an emigrant; *Austral.* migrants

исели *pf* I to move out *trans.*, expel; to remove II – ce to move <out> *intrans.*; to emigrate

иселува (се) *impf of* исели (се)

исенча *pf Art* to shade

исенчува *impf of* исенча

исере *pf* исра *aor. vulg.* to shit

исече *pf* I 1 to cut; to cut off; to hack to pieces 2 to cut down (*everything, completely*) II – ce to get cut, cut o.s.

исечка *pf* to chop up, dice; to hack to pieces

исечкува *impf of* исечка

исечок -ци *m* 1 cutting; cut-out; исечоци од весници newspaper cuttings (clippings) 2 section; sector

исечува (се) *impf see* исекува (се)

исили се *pf* to rush off; to start running fast

исилува се *impf of* исили се

исипе *pf* исипа *aor.* to spill; to pour out

исипува *impf of* исипе

иситни *pf* to chop up, dice, slice

иситнува *impf of* иситни

иска *impf dial. see* сака

искавти *pf* to peel, husk (*maize*)

искаже *pf* искажа *aor.* **I 1** to state, express **II – се** to explain o.s.; to express one's opinion

искажува (се) *impf of* искаже (се)

исказ *m* statement, testimony

исказен -зна *adj Gram.* исказни реченици indirect statements; object clauses

искалапи *pf* to finish sorting, grading (*esp. tobacco*)

искалеми *pf* to finish grafting

искапе[1] *pf* искапа *aor.* **I 1** to bath, bathe *trans.* (*thoroughly or several people*) **II – се** to take a bath, bathe *intrans.*

искапе[2] *pf* искапа *aor.* **I 1** to <start to> water (*of the eyes*); to weep; очите ми искапаа my eyes started watering; ❏ очите му искапаа 1. to strain one's eyes 2. to look with longing (yearning), hanker (*after s.th.*) **2** to drip **3** to spot, stain (*clothes*) **4** (*за лисје*) to fall **II – се** to spatter o.s. (one's clothes) (*with drops of s.th.*)

искапува[1] **(се)** *impf of* искапе[1] (се)

искапува[2] **(се)** *impf of* искапе[2] (се)

искара *pf* **I 1** to reprimand, scold **2** *dial.* to swear at **II – се** to quarrel (*badly or with several people*)

искарува (се) *impf of* искара (се)

искаса *pf* to bite/sting (*all over or many people*); го искасаа комарци he was bitten all over by mosquitoes

искасапи *pf* **1** to cut up **2** to slaughter (*also fig.*); to butcher **3** *fig.* to mangle, destroy

искасапува *impf of* искасапи

искастри *pf* **1** to prune (*all over*); to finish pruning **2** *fig.* to beat up, thrash

искаструва *impf of* искастри

искача *impf dial.* to go out (*co – with*), date

искачи *pf* **I** to raise, lift **II – се** to climb, ascend

искачува (се) *impf of* искачи (се)

искашка *pf* **I 1** to dirty, soil, mess up **2** *fig.* to mess up; ја искашка работата he made a mess of things **II – се** to dirty o.s.; to get dirty

искашкува (се) *impf of* искашка (се)

искашла *pf* **I** to cough up **II – се** to finish coughing; to clear one's throat

искашлува (се) *impf of* искашла (се)

исквака *pf colloq.* to hatch *trans.*

искива *pf* **I** to sneeze (*all over s.o.*) **II – се** to sneeze

искикоти се *pf* to burst into laughter

искикотува се *impf of* искикоти се

искилави *pf* **I** to rupture *trans.* **II – се** to rupture o.s.

искине *pf* искина *aor.* **I** to tear, rip, lacerate **II – се** to get torn, be lacerated

искинува (се) *impf of* искине (се)

искипи *pf* (*of milk, etc.*) to boil over *intrans.*

искипува *impf of* искипи

искисели *pf* **1** to soak *trans.*, steep; to soften by soaking *trans.* **2** to soak *intrans.*; to become soft, soften *intrans.*

искисне *pf* искисна *aor.* to get soaked, soak *intrans.*

искиснува *impf of* искисне

искити *pf* **I** to decorate, adorn **II – се** to adorn o.s.

искитува (се) *impf of* искити (се)

искласи *pf* to ear, form ears (*of cereal crops*)

искласува *impf of* искласи

исклепа *pf* to hammer, forge (*scythe, sickle*)

исклепува *impf of* исклепа

исклешти *pf colloq.* **I** to bare, show (*one's teeth*); to open wide (*one's mouth*) **II – се** to make faces, grimace; to grin; to bare one's teeth

исклоца *pf* **1** to kick (*several times*) **2** to kick (*s.th. or s.o.*) out

исклучено *adv* excluded; excluding

исклучи *pf* **1** to expel, exclude; го исклучија од училиште he was expelled from school **2** to exclude, preclude, rule out; треба да се исклучи таква можност such an eventuality must be precluded **3** to cut off; to disconnect; to turn off, switch off; исклучи телефон to cut off a telephone <service> **II – се 1** to withdraw *intrans.*; се исклучи од светот to go into seclusion **2** to switch off *intrans.*; струјата се исклучи the power was cut off

исклучив *adj* **1** exclusive; selective; исклучиво право exclusive right **2** solitary, single

исклучиво *adv* exclusively, solely

исклучителен -лна *adj* **1** exclusive; selective **2** exceptional

исклучок -ци *m* exception; ❏ без исклучок without exception; bar none; со исклучок на except for; apart from; исклучокот го потврдува правилото *prov.* the exception proves the rule

исклучува *impf of* исклучи

искоби *pf* to have a presentiment; to foretell, foresee (*evil*)

искова *pf see* искове

искове *pf* искова *aor.* to forge, hammer; *fig.* to fashion, shape

искока *impf* to jump out

искокне *pf* искокна *aor.* to jump out

искокнува *impf of* искокне

искокори *pf* **I** to open (*one's eyes*) wide **II – се** to gape, stare

исколве *pf* исколва *aor.* to peck up

исколе *pf* искла *aor.* to slaughter, kill off

исколува *impf of* исколе

исколчи *pf* **I 1** to dislocate, sprain, twist, wrench **2** *fig.* to distort **II – се** to warp *intrans.*

исколчува (се) *impf of* исколчи (се)

искомати *pf* to divide up; to dismember

искона & искони *adv literary* од искона & од искони from time immemorial

исконски *adj* very old, ancient, primeval, primordial

ископ *m* excavation; ditch; excavation site, dig

ископа *pf* to dig out, excavate; (*мртовец*) to exhume, disinter

ископачи *pf* to clear <away>

ископина *f* excavation, excavation site; excavated object

ископува *impf of* ископа

искорени *pf fig.* to eradicate, destroy, root out

искоренува *impf of* искорени

искористи *pf* to use, exploit, take advantage of

искористува *impf of* искористи

искорне *pf* искорна *aor.* to eradicate, root out, uproot

искорнува *impf of* искорне

искоси *pf* **1** to mow; to reap **2** *fig.* to kill, mow down

искосо *adv* obliquely, askance, aslant

искосува *impf of* искоси

искра *f* spark

искраде *pf* **I** to steal (*everything*) **II** – **ce** to slip (steal) away, slip out

искрадува (ce) *impf of* искраде (ce)

искрај *prep arch.* near, by the side of; along

искрвави *pf* **I 1** to bleed; to lose much blood; to bleed to death **2** to cover/stain with blood **II** – **ce** to stain o.s. with blood

искрви ce *pf* to fight until blood is drawn

искрен *adj* sincere

искрено *adv* sincerely; искрено да кажам; искрено да зборуваме to tell the truth; frankly speaking; to be honest

искреност *f* sincerity

искрест *adj* sparkling

искри *impf* to sparkle, scintillate

искрива (ce) *impf of* искрие (ce)

искривеност *f* distortion

искриви *pf* **I 1** to bend *trans.*; to contort; to distort, twist *trans.* (*also fig.*); искриви нечии зборови to distort s.o.'s words **II** – **ce** to bend <over> *intrans.*; to twist *intrans.*; to become crooked

искривоколчи *pf* **1** to dislocate, sprain, wrench **2** *fig.* to distort; to pervert, corrupt, deprave

искривоколчува *impf of* искривоколчи

искривува (ce) *impf of* искриви (ce)

искрие *pf* искри *aor.* **I** to give shelter to (*all*); to hide, conceal (*all*) **II** – **ce** to take shelter; to hide, conceal o.s. (*of many people, animals, etc.*)

искричав *adj* sparkling; effervescent; искричава светлина sparkling light; искричаво вино sparkling (bubbling) wine; искричав разговор lively conversation

искричавост *f* effervescence; искричавост на духот liveliness of spirit

искришум *adv see* кришум, скришум

искркори *pf* to start buzzing/grunting/growling/ rumbling

искрои *pf* to cut out (*a garment from material*); to prune

искрстоса *pf* to cross, intertwine

искрцка *pf* to crunch; to creak

искрши *pf* **I** to crush, break *trans.*, dash to pieces **II** – **ce 1** to break, smash *intrans.* **2** to hurt o.s. badly

искршка *pf* to dodge, weave, zig-zag

искршува (ce) *impf of* искрши (ce)

искубе *pf* искуба *aor.* to pull out, tear out, pluck

искубува *impf of* искубе

искупи *pf* **1** to purchase in quantity, buy up **2** *fig.* to redeem, save; to liberate, ransom

искупител *m* redeemer, saviour

искуса *pf arch.* to eat (*with a spoon*)

искусен -сна *adj see* опитен 1

искуси *pf* **1** to experience, undergo, go through; искуси на своја кожа to learn from personal experience **2** to try, test; to tempt; to expose to temptation

искуство *n* experience; работно искуство working experience, practical experience

искусува *impf of* искуси

искушава *impf see* искуси 2

искушение -ија *n* temptation; seduction

искушеник -ци *m* novice (*in a monastery*)

искушенички *adj* of/like a novice

искушеништво *n* novitiate, novicehood

искушува *impf see* искушава

и сл. *abbr.* (*и слично*) and similar, et cetera, etc.

ислам *m* Islam

исламизѝра *pf & impf* to Muslimize, convert to Islam

Исланд *m* Iceland

исландски *adj* Icelandic

Исланѓанец -ни *m* Icelander

Исланѓанка *f* (*fem. form*) *see* Исланѓанец

иследен -дна *adj* investigative; иследен судија judge in a court of enquiry

иследи *pf* to investigate

иследник -ци *m* investigator

иследува *impf of* иследи

ислужен *pt* worn-out, old

ислужи *pf* to earn (*by service*)

ислужува *impf of* ислужи

ислуша *pf* **1** to hear out; to listen to; го ислушав внимателно I listened to him attentively **2** to interrogate, question

ислушува *impf of* ислуша

исмева (ce) *impf see* исмее (ce)

исмее *pf* исмеа *aor.* **I** to laugh at, mock **II** – **ce 1** to burst out laughing **2** (*with dat.*) to have a good laugh, laugh to one's heart's content (*at*)

исмејува (ce) *see* исмева (ce)

испад *m* **1** assault, attack, sally; offence, provocation **2** blunder, *faux pas*

испади *pf* to drive out, expel

испадне *pf* испадна *aor.* **1** to fall out/off; испадне од воз to fall from a train; *fig.* испадне од комбинација to be eliminated **2** to come out, turn out, become; убаво испадне to turn out well **3** *dial.* to go out (outside); испадне со некого to go on a date with s.o.

испаднува *impf of* испадне, *see* испаѓа

испаѓа *impf of* испадне

испазари *pf* **1** to buy up (*a lot*) **2** to sell **3** to bargain

испара *impf* to unstitch; to tear open

испарение -ја *n* evaporation, fumes

испари *pf* **I 1** to vaporize, evaporate *trans.* **2** to evaporate *intrans.* **3** to steam *trans.* **II** – **ce** to evaporate *intrans.*

испарлив *adj* evaporable

испарливост *f* evaporability

испартален *adj & pt* shabby, ragged, tattered, worn-out

испартали ce *pf* to become shabby, ragged; to wear out *intrans.*

испарува *impf of* испари

испасе *pf* to graze bare

испасува *impf of* испасе

испати *pf* to exhaust, wear out *trans.*

испашка *pf* to drive out, expel

испева *impf of* испее

испегла *pf* **1** to iron, smooth **2** *fig.* to beat up

испеглува *impf of* испегла

испее *pf* испеа *aor.* **1** to sing; to compose, write (*poetry*) **2** to celebrate, sing of; ❑ му се испеа молитвата his prayer is answered **3** *colloq., arch.* to read out, through

испекува (ce) *impf of* испече (ce)

испердаши *pf colloq.* to beat, thrash

испердашува *impf of* испердаши

испере *pf* испра *aor.* to wash (*clothes*), launder

испече *pf* **I 1** to bake; to roast; (*на скара*) to grill; (*парче леб*) to toast; (*цигли и сл.*) to fire, bake **2** *fig.* to

perfect, master; испече занает to master a trade **II –
се 1** to bake *intrans.*; to get sunburnt; to singe, burn
o.s. **2** *fig.* (*настрада*) to become an expert (past master) (*во – in*) **3** *fig.* to suffer loss; to be a victim

испечен *pt* baked; roast<ed>; grilled

испечува (се) *impf see* испекува (се)

испива *impf of* испие

испие *pf* испи *aor.* **1** to drink <up> **2** *colloq., arch.* to
smoke *trans.*

испика *pf* **I** to push in, stuff in *trans.* **II – се** to push in
intrans.

испили *pf* to saw up

испили се *pf* to hatch *intrans.*

испилува се *impf of* испили се

испипа *pf* to feel (touch) all over

испис *m* **1** excerpt; исписи од архивата excerpts from
the archives **2** exclusion; expulsion; elimination;
испис од училиште expulsion from school

исписка *pf* to yelp; to squeal

исписокува *impf of* исписка

испит *m* examination, test; ❏ <го> положи
испит<от> to pass the test; to pass muster

испита *pf* **1** to examine, test; to question; to crossexamine; испита кандидати to examine candidates;
испита сведоци to question witnesses **2** to check, test,
try out; испита апаратура to test an apparatus **3** to
investigate, explore; to study, research

испитан *pt* investigated, studied; *fig.* неиспитана
област unexplored territory

испитен -тна *adj* examination; испитна такса examination fee

испитува *impf of* испита

испитување *n* investigation; poll; испитување на
јавното мислење public-opinion poll

испитувач *m* **1** examiner **2** researcher, research worker

испитувачки *adj* searching, probing; research;
испитувачки поглед searching look; испитувачка
(истражувачка) работа research work

испише *pf* испиша *aor.* **I 1** to write out, copy **2** to
withdraw, remove; испише дете од училиште to
withdraw a child from school **3** to cover with writing
(*paper, notebook, etc.*) **II – се** to resign, withdraw
intrans.

испишмани *pf colloq.* **I** to dissuade, turn away *trans.* **II
– се** to desist, give up

испишува *impf of* испише

исплави *pf* to rinse, wash (*wool, rice, linen, etc.*)

исплавува *impf of* исплави

исплази *pf* **I** исплази јазик на некого to stick one's
tongue out at s.o. **II – се** to stick one's tongue out

исплакне *pf* исплакна *aor.* to rinse

исплакнува *impf of* исплакне

исплакува (се) *impf of* исплаче (се)

исплата *f* payment; disbursement; settlement;
исплата на долг discharge of a debt; ден на исплата
pay-day

исплати *pf* **I** to pay <off>, clear, repay (*a debt*) **II – се**
to pay *intrans.*, be profitable; to be worthwhile; напорот ќе се исплати the effort will pay
dividends

исплатува (се) *impf of* исплати (се)

исплаќа (се) *impf see* исплатува (се); ❏ исплаќа на
рака to pay in cash

исплаче *pf* исплака *aor.* **I 1** to lament, mourn *trans.* **2**

to obtain by pleading <tearfully> **II – се** to have a
good cry, cry one's eyes out

исплаши *pf* **I** to frighten, startle, give (*s.o.*) a fright **II –
се** to get a fright

исплашува (се) *impf of* исплаши (се)

исплеви *pf* to weed; исплеви градина to weed a
garden

исплевува *impf of* исплеви

исплеска *pf* **1** to thin out (*dough, etc.*) **2** to slap, beat

исплете *pf* **1** to knit; to finish knitting; (*за најак и др.*)
to spin *trans.* **2** *fig.* to think up, spin (*a tale*)

исплетка *pf* **I** to entangle; to complicate; to mess up **II
– се** to become entangled, confused; to get into a mess

исплетува *impf of* исплете

исплива *pf* **1** to swim out **2** *fig.* to get out/away; to
cope, manage; to save o.s.

испливува *impf of* исплива

исплиска *pf* **1** to splash, sprinkle (*s.o. or s.th.*) all over
2 to spill; to pour away (*water*)

исплискува *impf of* исплиска

испливи *pf* to sail out, leave port

исплука *pf* to spit out, expectorate

исплукува *impf of* исплука

исповед *f* confession

исповеда *pf* **I** to confess *trans.* **2** to profess, follow
(*religion, belief*) **II – се** to confess (*one's sins*) *intrans.*

исповеден -дна *adj* of confession

исповедник -ци *m* confessor

исповеднички *adj* confessional

исповедува (се) *impf of* исповеда (се)

исповест *f rare see* исповед

исповрти *pf* **I** to turn (*over*), twist *trans.*; *fig.* to distort;
исповрти глава to turn one's head **II – се** to turn
round *intrans.*

исповртува (се) *impf of* исповрти (се)

испогани *pf* **I** to make dirty; to sully, defile **II – се** to
get dirty; to become corrupt; to become evil, wicked

испоганува (се) *impf of* испогани (се)

испознае *pf* испозна *aor.* **I** to recognize (*everything or
everybody*) **II – се** to recognize each other

испокара *pf* **I** to scold, reprimand; to abuse (*everyone*)
II – се (*со*) to quarrel (*a lot or with everybody*)

испокине *pf* испокина *aor.* (*see* кине) **1** to tear to
pieces; испокина алишта to wear out clothes **2** to
pick, pluck (*all the flowers*) **3** *fig.* to wear out, exhaust;
to ruin; му ги испокина нервите she ruined his
nerves

испол *m see* исполица

исползува *pf & impf* to use; to take advantage of, utilize; to exploit, abuse

исполин *m* giant

исполински *adj* gigantic

исполица *f* sharecropping, *métayage*; даде имот во
исполица to lease out land for sharecropping

исполичар *m* tenant farmer, *métayer*, *Am.* sharecropper

исполни *pf* **1** to fill **2** *fig.* to fulfil, carry out; to satisfy;
исполни услови to meet the conditions; исполни
желба to fulfil a wish **3** to perform

исполнител *m* performer, singer

исполнува *impf of* исполни

исполнување *n* performance; fulfilment; implementation

исполција -ии *m see* исполичар

испомачи *pf* I to torment (*everybody*) II – **се** to suffer greatly

испомоча (се) *pf see* измоча (се)

испопука *pf* to break up, burst, shatter *intrans.*; to split *intrans.*

испорака *f* delivery, transmission; consignment

испорача *pf* to deliver, convey; to supply

испорачува *impf of* испорача

испореди *pf* I to arrange in rows, line up *trans.* II – **се** to line up *intrans.*

испоседне *pf* испоседна *aor.* to sit down (*one after another*)

испоседнува *impf of* испоседне

испосее *pf* испосеа *aor.* to sow (*everywhere, completely*)

испосник -ци *m* monk (*of an ascetic order*)

испосница *f* nun (*of an ascetic order*); group of ascetic monks/nuns

испоснички *adj* ascetic, austere

испостен *pt* having fasted; arid, impoverished; испостена земја exhausted land

испости *pf* I to redeem by fasting; to starve *trans.*; ги испостив гостите I gave my guests vegetarian meals; I let my guests starve II – **се** to become impoverished (*of soil*); to finish fasting; to become thin by fasting; се испости земјата the soil was exhausted

испостува (се) *impf of* испости (се)

испотепа *pf* to kill off

испоти *pf* I to cause to perspire, make (*s.o.*) sweat II – **се** to <start to> sweat, perspire; to break into a sweat

испотува (се) *impf of* испоти (се)

исправа[1] *f* document, identity papers

исправа[2] **(се)** *impf see* исправи (се)

исправен *adj & pt* 1 straightened, put straight 2 vertical, upright, straight

исправен -вна *adj* 1 accurate, correct; in order; во исправна состојба in working order 2 exact; right 3 conscientious

исправи *pf* I 1 to straighten *trans.* 2 to correct, rectify II – **се** 1 to straighten up *intrans.*; се исправи пред to face up to 2 *fig.* to correct o.s.

исправка *f* correction

исправност *f* correctness

исправува (се) *impf of* исправи (се)

испразни *pf* I to empty, clear out *trans.* II – **се** to empty *intrans.*

испразнува (се) *impf of* испразни (се)

испраси *pf* I to bring forth, bear (*piglets*) II – **се** to farrow

испрати *pf* 1 to dispatch, forward, send; испрати претставник to send a representative; испрати со брод to ship; испрати пари to remit money 2 to see off; to accompany; испрати некого до врата to see s.o. to the door 3 to get rid of (*s.o.*), send packing

испраток *m dial.* send-off

испраќа *impf see* испрати

испраќач *m* 1 sender, dispatcher 2 escort, companion (*seeing s.o. off*)

испраша *pf* 1 to ask (about everything) 2 to ask (all or many people) 3 to examine (*students*)

испраши[1] *pf* I to cover with dust II – **се** to become dusty

испраши[2] *pf* to loosen the soil around

испрашува *impf of* испраша 3

испрвути се *pf* to flake <off>

испревари *pf* 1 to pass, overtake 2 to anticipate, forestall; to outwit

испреварува *impf of* испревари

испревитка *pf* to fold (*many times*)

испревиткува *impf of* испревитка

испреврти *pf* to overturn; to disarrange, mess up

испревртува *impf of* испреврти

испрега *impf of* испрегне

испрегледа *pf* to look through (everything); (*за доктор*) to look over (everyone), examine (*many people*)

испрегледува *impf of* испрегледа

испрегне *pf* испрегна *aor.* to unharness; to unhitch

испрегнува *impf see* испрега

испреде *pf* to finish spinning; to spin (*yarn*)

испредува *impf of* испреде

испрекинат *pt* interrupted, broken; (*за говор*) disconnected, disjointed, incoherent; spasmodic, intermittent

испрекинатост *f* disjointedness; incoherence

испрекине *pf* испрекина *aor.* I to interrupt, disconnect, break II – **се** *fig.* (*од жал*) to be heartbroken

испрекинува *impf of* испрекине

испремести *pf* I to shift, move *trans.*, transfer, displace II – **се** to move, shift *intrans.*

испреместува (се) *impf of* испремести (се)

испрета *pf* to find (uncover) by scratching

испретува *impf of* испрета

испречи *pf* I to place across, interpose II – **се** to rise up in front of; to confront; ми се испречи на патот he barred my way; се испречив пред тешкотии I was confronted with difficulties

испречува (се) *impf of* испречи (се)

испржи *pf* I to fry, roast *trans.* II – **се** to fry, roast *intrans.*; се испржив на сонце I got sunburnt

испржува (се) *impf of* испржи (се)

исприкаже *pf* исприкажа *aor.* I to tell, relate (*a great deal*) II – **се** to have a good talk

испришти се *pf* to break out in boils, become covered with boils; to get blisters

испрли *pf* to scorch, burn

испроба *pf* to test, try

испробува *impf of* испроба

испродаде *pf* to sell out; to sell off

испроси *pf* to obtain by begging (pleading); to ask for <and be granted> (*a girl*) in marriage

испрости се *pf* 1 to take leave of, say goodbye to (*usu. of several people*) 2 to forgive each other

испротне *pf dial.* испротна *aor.* I to pull through *trans.* II – **се** to squeeze (*o.s.*) through; to get by, manage

испрпела *pf* to roll *trans.* (*in dust, etc.*)

испрска *pf* I to sprinkle; to spray; to splash; to spatter II – **се** 1 to spray o.s.; (*случајно*) to splash/spatter o.s. 2 *fig.*, *colloq.* to boast, brag

испрскува *impf* испрска II – **се** *see* испрска се 1

испрсне *pf* испрсна *aor.* to burst; to gush

испрснува *impf of* испрсне

испружи *pf* I to stretch out *trans.*, extend; испружи рака to hold out one's hand II – **се** 1 to stretch out, extend *intrans.*; to sprawl 2 *fig.*, *colloq.* to loosen one's purse strings, shell out; не можам толку да се испружам I can't afford it

испружува (се)   *impf of* испружи (се)

испрчи   *pf* **I** to stick out (*one's chest, belly*); ❏ го испрчил носот he stuck his nose up in the air **II – се** to throw out one's chest

испрчува (се)   *impf of* испрчи (се)

испука   *pf* **1** to burst; to crack *intrans.*; to explode **2** to use up, exhaust; испука куршуми to run out of ammunition

испукува   *impf of* испука

испули се   *pf dial.* to stare, open one's eyes wide

испупчен   *adj & pt* convex; protuberant; bulging; испупчено огледало convex mirror

испупченост   *f* bulge; bump (*on a road*); protuberance; convexity

испупчи   *pf* **I** to stick out; to swell *trans.*; ги испупчи градите to throw out one's chest **II – се** to bulge, swell *intrans.*

испустен   *adj & pt* **1** devastated **2** deserted, empty

испусти   *pf* **I** to depopulate; to devastate, ravage **II – се** to become deserted; to become empty

испустува (се)   *impf of* испусти (се)

испуши   *pf* to finish smoking; to smoke

испушта   *impf of* испушти

испуштање   *n* **1** release **2** omission

испушти   *pf* **I 1** to release, let go, let out; не испушта некого од вид to keep a close eye on s.o. **2** to drop, let fall; ја испуштив чашата I dropped the glass **3** to miss; испушта можност to miss an opportunity **4** to omit, leave out **5** *intrans.* (*тиши се*) to lose air, go down; гумата испушта the tyre is going down **II – се 1** to become corrupted; to get spoilt **2** *impers.* (*with dat.*) му се испушти дека . . . he let slip that . . .

испушува   *impf of* испуши

исрка   *pf colloq.* to lap up (*completely*)

исркне се   *pf* исркна *aor.* to blow one's nose

ист   *adj* same, identical; the very; ист татко му he's the spitting image of his father

истава (се)   *impf of* истави (се)

истави   *pf* **I** to move *trans.*; to remove **II – се** to move *intrans.*, remove o.s.; истави ми се од предочи get out of my sight!

иставува (се)   *impf see* истава (се)

истагари се   *pf dial.* to become arrogant, give o.s. airs

истакнат   *adj & pt* **1** prominent **2** pronounced, marked

истакне   *pf* истакна *aor.* **I 1** to hang up, hang out **2** *fig.* to emphasize, underline **II – се** to stand out; to distinguish o.s.

истакнува (се)   *impf of* истакне (се)

Истанбул   *m* Istanbul, *arch.* Constantinople; *see* Цариград

истанбулец   -лци *m* person from Istanbul

истанбулка   *f* (*fem. form*) *see* истанбулец

истанбулски   *adj* Istanbul *attrib.*

истанчен   *pt* refined; истанчен вкус refined taste

истанченост   *f* refinement; daintiness

истанчи   *pf* **I 1** to thin, make thin (thinner) **2** *fig.* to refine **II – се** to become thin; се истанчи простирката the rug has worn thin

истанчува (се)   *impf of* истанчи (се)

истап   *m see* испад

истапи[1]   *pf* to come (step) forward; to come out

истапи[2]   *pf* to dull, blunt, make blunt

истапува   *impf of* истапи[1]

истарски   *adj* Istrian

истега   *impf of* истегне (се)

истегари се   *pf* to stretch out *intrans.*, sprawl

истегне   *pf* истегна *aor.* **I 1** to stretch *trans.* **2** (*мускул*) to strain *trans.* **II – се 1** to stretch out *intrans.*, sprawl **2** to strain *intrans.* **3** to stretch *intrans.* (*of clothes*)

истек   *m* expiration, expiry

истекне   *pf* истекна *aor. impers.* (*with dat.*) to occur to s.o.; како ти истекна таква работа? how did such a thing (idea) occur to you?

истекнува   *impf of* истекне

истекува   *impf* **1** *of* истече **2** to rise, have its headwaters (*of a river*)

истели   *pf* **I** to bring forth, bear (*a calf*) **II – се** to calve

истепа   *pf* **I 1** to beat up, thrash **2** to kill off **II – се 1** to kill each other (*of several or all people*) **2** to have a fight **3** *fig.* to get tired, become exhausted (*e.g. from walking*)

истепува (се)   *impf of* истепа (се)

истера   *pf* **I 1** to drive out; to expel, eject; истера од училиште to expel from school; истера од дома to throw (kick) (*s.o.*) out of the house; истера од работа to dismiss (sack) ❏ истера некому мушички од глава to knock the nonsense out of s.o. **2** to knock out; му ги истераа забите they knocked out his teeth **3** to sprout; јачменот истерал the barley has sprouted **4** *fig.* to achieve; to manage to make/earn; истеравме илјада денари we made a thousand denars **II – се** (*на*) to take after; на кого се истера whom does he take after?

истерува   *impf of* истера

истече   *pf* **1** to flow out, run out **2** to expire; истече срокот the deadline has passed

истечува   *impf see* истекува

истимари   *pf* to groom, curry, comb (*usu. horses*)

истина   *f see* вистина[1]

истиндак   *m arch.* investigation, enquiry, hearing

истине   *pf* истина *aor.* to get cold, cool down; истина јадењето the food has got cold; *fig.* срцето му истина за неа he cooled towards her

истинува   *impf of* истине

истиска   *pf see* истисне

истискува   *impf of* истиска

истисне   *pf* истисна *aor.* to press out, squeeze out; to force out, supplant

истиснува   *impf of* истисне

исткава   *impf see* исткае

исткае   *pf* истка *aor.* to weave

истлева   *impf* **1** to cease to smoulder **2** *fig.* to fade, wither

истлее   *pf* истлеа *aor. see* истлева

исто   *adv* likewise, similarly, in the same way; ❏ исто така also; as well; исто толку колку as much as; исто како и as well as; исто ти се фаќа it comes to the same thing; на исто му доаѓа what you lose on the swings you gain on the roundabouts

истовар   *m* unloading, discharge, landing

истовара   *impf of* истовари

истоварен   -рна *adj* landing, discharging; истоварно место discharging berth, landing stage

истовари   *pf* to unload, land, discharge; *pejor.* to dump (*people*)

истоварува   *impf see* истовара

истовремен   *adj* simultaneous; contemporaneous

истовременост   *f* simultaneity; contemporaneity

истозначен -чна *adj* synonymous

истоименен -мена *adj* having the same name, eponymous

исток *m* east

истокми *pf* I to adjust, arrange; ги истокми нозете to put one's feet together II – **се** to dress up *intrans.*, get dressed up

истолкува *pf* to interpret, explain

истолче & истолчи *pf* истолчи *aor.* to crush, pound

истопи *pf* I to melt *trans.*; to melt down, render; (*руда, метал*) to smelt II – **се** to melt *intrans.*

истопи се *pf* to get wet

истопори се *pf* to throw out one's chest; to strut; to show off

истопорува се *impf of* истопори се

истопува (се) *impf of* истопи (се)

историја *f* 1 history; општа историја world history; ❑ влегува во историја to make history 2 story; affair, event

историк -ци *m see* историчар

историски *adj* historical

историцѝзам -змот *m* historicism

историчар *m* historian

истороден -дна *adj* homogeneous, uniform

истородност *f* homogeneity

источен -чна *adj* eastern

источи[1] *pf* to tap, draw; to pour

источи[2] *pf* to sharpen

источник -ци *m Rel.* source, fount

источува[1] *impf of* источи[1]

источува[2] *impf of* источи[2]

истоштен *adj* exhausted, worn-out, feeble, weak

истоштеност *f* fatigue, exhaustion

истошти *pf* I to tire out, wear out, exhaust II – **се** to become exhausted

истоштува (се) *impf of* истошти (се)

Истра *f* Istria

истрага *f* enquiry, investigation (*in court*)

истрада *pf* to endure, go through, suffer

истрадува *impf of* истрада

истрае *pf* истраја *aor.* to persevere, persist; to hold out, last <out>

истраен -јна *adj* persistent, steadfast; stubborn, tenacious

истражен -жна *adj* investigating; investigative; истражен суд court of enquiry; истражен затвор detention on remand; истражен судија investigative judge

истражи *pf* to investigate, explore; to research

истражува *impf of* истражи to conduct research on

истражување *n* research; exploration; научно истражување scientific research

истражувач *m* investigator; explorer; research worker

истражувачки *adj* research; истражувачка работа research work

истрајност *f* persistence, steadfastness; stubbornness, tenacity

истрајува *impf of* истрае

Истранец -нци *m* Istrian

Истранка *f* (*fem. form*) *see* Истранец

истрбуши *pf* I to disembowel II – **се** *fig.* to ungird; to relax, let o.s. go

истрга *pf* 1 to pull out, extract 2 to measure, weigh 3 *colloq.* to drain, drink up (*usu. alcoholic drink*) 4 *fig.* to

endure, go through, suffer; големи маки истрга to suffer great torments

истргне *pf* истргна *aor.* I 1 to pull out, tear out 2 *f.p.* to abduct II – **се** to fall off, break off *intrans.*

истргнува *impf of* истргне

истреби *pf* 1 to clean (*beans, rice, etc.*) 2 to destroy, exterminate

истребува *impf of* истреби

истрезни *pf* to sober (*s.o.*) up *trans.* II – **се** to sober up *intrans.*

истрезнува (се) *impf of* истрезни (се)

истрел *m* shot, report

истресе *pf* I 1 to shake; истресе килим to shake/beat a carpet 2 to empty; истресе торба to empty a bag II – **се** *fig.* 1 to burst (dash) (*во – in*); ни се истресе едно утро he burst into our room one morning 2 (*with dat.*) to vent one's fury on s.o.

истресок -ци *m* 1 waste matter, *vulg.* crap 2 the last animal (*of a litter*); *pejor.* the youngest child (*in a family*)

истресува *impf of* истресе

истрива *impf of* истрие

истрие *pf* истри *aor.* 1 to erase 2 to rub, massage thoroughly 3 to scour, scrub

истриже *pf* истрижа *aor.* to shear, clip; to trim

истркала *pf* I to roll <away> *trans.* II – **се** 1 to roll away *intrans.* 2 to roll about, wallow

истркалува (се) *impf of* истркала (се)

истрошен *pt* worn-out, used up

истроши *pf* I 1 to use up; to spend 2 to crumble *trans.* II – **се** to crumble *intrans.*

истрошува (се) *impf of* истроши (се)

истрпи *pf* to bear, endure; to stand, put up with

истрпне *pf* истрпна *aor.* to become numb; to freeze on the spot (*from fright*); ми истрпнаа рацете my hands have grown numb (stiff)

истрпнува *impf of* истрпне

истрпува *impf of* истрпи

иструже *pf* иструга *aor.* to grind; to sharpen; to plane

истружува *impf of* иструже

иструпи *pf* to chop (*wood*)

иструпува *impf of* иструпи

истрча *pf* I 1 to run out/away/off; истрча на улица to run out into the street 2 to run across; to run a certain distance, cover II – **се** 1 to tire of running 2 *fig.* to act rashly; to butt in

истрчува (се) *impf of* истрча (се)

истура (се) *impf of* истури (се)

истури *pf* I 1 to spill *trans.*; to pour out *trans.* 2 to stick out; го истури мевот he stuck out his belly II – **се** 1 to spill, pour out *intrans.* 2 се истури силен дожд *or impers.* се истури it started pelting with rain

истурка *pf* I 1 to push out/away, drive out *trans.* 2 to knock down, topple (*one after another*) 3 *fig.* (*избутка*) to manage *intrans.*, pull through; to live (get) through II – **се** to shove *intrans.*, make one's way

истуркува (се) *impf of* истурка (се)

истурне *pf* истурна *aor.* to push, shove aside

истурчи *pf* I to make Turkish; to Muslimize II – **се** to become Turkish; to become a Muslim

истурчува (се) *impf of* истурчи (се)

истутка *pf* I to crumple, crease *trans.* II – **се** to crumple, crease *intrans.*

истуши се *pf* 1 to vent one's anger (*на – on*) 2 to

deflate *intrans.*; to go down; гумата се истуши the tyre has gone down

истушува се   *impf of* истуши се

исука & исуче   *pf* исука *aor.* to roll (*dough*); to twist (*thread*)

исукува   *impf of* исука

исушеност   *f* 1 dryness 2 emaciation

исуши   *pf* I to dry; to drain II – се 1 to dry up *intrans.* 2 *fig.* to become thin, emaciated; to waste away

исушува (се)   *impf of* исуши (се)

исфати   *pf* I to catch (*a number of . . .*) II – се to grasp each other's hands

исфаќа   *pf see* исфати

исфрка   *pf* 1 to whip 2 (за коњ) to snort

исфркува   *impf of* исфрка

исфрла   *impf of* исфрли

исфрли   *pf* 1 to throw out, eject; to expel; to dislodge; to delete 2 to fire (*a shot, a bullet, etc.*)

исфрлува   *impf see* исфрла

исфрчи   *pf* to brush

исфучи   *pf* 1 to rumble, boom, roar; (за ветер) to whistle 2 to snarl (на некого – *at s.o.*)

исфучува   *impf of* исфучи

исход   *m literary* consequence, result

исходен   -дна *adj literary* initial, starting; emerging

исхрана   *f* nutrition; nourishment, sustenance; засилена исхрана high-calorie diet, nourishing diet; недостаточна исхрана undernourishment; вештачка исхрана artificial/intravenous feeding; force-feeding; (на бебе) bottle-feeding

исхрани   *pf* to feed, nourish *trans.*

исхранува   *impf of* исхрани

исцапа   *pf* to tread on; to trample

исцапува   *impf of* исцапа

исцеди   *pf* I to squeeze, extract (*juice, etc.*); to strain, filter II – се to leak; to pour <out> *intrans.*

исцедок   *m* juice (*squeezed*); extract, essence

исцедува   *impf of* исцеди; ❑ исцедува некого <како лимон> to milk/suck s.o. dry

исцели   *pf* I to cure, heal II – се to recover

исцелува (се)   *impf of* исцели (се)

исцело   *adv* completely, entirely, wholly

исцепи   *pf* to chop (*wood*)

исцепува   *impf of* исцепи

исцибри се   *pf* to grow pale (*of the face*)

исцигли се   *pf* to become thin, lose weight

исцимоли   *pf* to whine, moan

исцица   *pf* to suck out

исцицува   *impf of* исцица

исцрка   *pf* to shout (на некого – *at s.o.*)

исцрни   *pf* to blacken; to cover with soot

исцрнува   *impf of* исцрни

исцрпе   *pf* 1 to scoop out, bail out; to draw; исцрпе вода од чамец to bail water out of a boat 2 to drain, use up, exhaust; исцрпе резерви to exhaust reserves; ги исцрпија сите средства they have exhausted all the resources (funds)

исцрпен¹   *pt* exhausted, tired out

исцрпен²   -пна *adj* exhaustive, detailed; extensive

исцрпност   *f* exhaustiveness

исцрпува   *impf of* исцрпе

исцути   *pf* to <begin to> flower, blossom

исчади   *pf* to cover with soot; to smoke *trans.*; to fill with smoke

исчадува   *impf of* исчади

исчанчи   *pf* to dislocate, sprain

исчанчува   *impf of* исчанчи

исчезне   *pf* исчезна *aor.* to disappear, vanish

исчезнува   *impf of* исчезне

исчека   *pf* 1 to wait for 2 (дочека) to receive, welcome 3 to live to see

исчекува   *impf of* исчека

исчекување   *n* expectation; ❑ во исчекување на in anticipation of

исчепати   *pf* I to open (*one's mouth wide*) II – се *fig.* (*with dat.*) to call out (*to s.o.*); to shout (*at s.o.*)

исчепатува (се)   *impf of* исчепати (се)

исчепи се   *pf colloq.* to back out; to free o.s.; to save o.s.

исчепка   *pf* 1 to find by scratching 2 to clear, clean (*wool*)

исчепкува   *impf of* исчепка

исчепува се   *impf of* исчепи се

исчетка   *pf* to brush

исчеткува   *impf of* исчетка

исчеша   *pf* I to scratch raw II – се to scratch o.s.

исчешла   *pf* I to comb <out> II – се to comb one's hair

исчешлува (се)   *impf of* исчешла (се)

исчисти   *pf* I to clean out II – се to clean o.s.; to become clean, clear (*of water, etc.*)

исчистува (се)   *impf of* исчисти (се)

исчита   *pf* 1 to read out 2 *colloq.* to reprimand

исчитува   *impf of* исчита

исчува   *pf* 1 to preserve 2 to bring up, rear

исчуди се   *pf* to be astonished, amazed

исчука   *pf* to knock out

исчукан   *adj fig.* crazy; senile

ишета   *pf* to visit, go round (*several places*); ги ишета селата he went round all the villages

ишива   *impf of* ишие

ишие   *pf* иш и *aor.* to sew (*everything*)

ишилчи   *pf* to make pointed; to sharpen

ита   *impf* to hurry, rush, hasten

Италија   *f* Italy

Италијанец   -нци, -ни *m* Italian

Италијанка   *f* (*fem. form*) *see* Италијанец

италијански   *adj* Italian

итаница¹   *f* hurry, rush

итаница²   *adv* quickly; in haste

итар   -тра *adj* 1 bright, intelligent, clever; resourceful, quick-witted, astute 2 sly, cunning; shrewd

итен   -тна *adj* urgent, pressing

итеративен   -вна *adj Gram.* iterative, frequentative

итн.   *abbr.* (и така натаму) et cetera, etc.

итрец   *m see* итроманец

итрина   *f* 1 resourcefulness 2 shrewdness; cunning

итроманец   -нци *m* rogue, sly dog; clever, shrewd, quick-witted person

итрост   *f see* итрина

итроштина   *f see* итрина

ифтирија   -ии *f colloq.* slander; ❑ му вадат ифтирија (ифтирии) they slander him, they run him down

ифтироса се   *pf colloq.* to get upset; to be worried

ихтиологија   *f* ichthyology, study of fish

их   *interj* oh! ah!

ич   *adv colloq.* nothing, absolutely nothing; <in> no way, not at all; ❑ или ич, или брич make or mar; ич да не ти е гајле it's none of your business; don't worry; ич не му е гајле he couldn't care less; ич не ми се допаѓа I don't like it a bit

ичумен *m Bot. dial. see* јачмен[1]

иш *interj* (*cry to drive away hens*) shoo!

ишала *interj colloq.* may God grant it!

ишарет *m colloq.* sign, wink; му прави (даде) ишарет he winked at him

ишари *pf* to colour, decorate

ишарува *impf of* ишари

ишијас *m Med.* sciatica

ишка *impf* to shoo

ишмрка *pf* to sniff, snuffle

ишмркува *impf of* ишмрка

ишмука *pf* to suck <out>

ишмукува *impf of* ишмука

ишне *pf* ишна *aor.* to shoo

ишпарта *pf* to line, makes lines on

ишпартува *impf of* ишпарта

иштав *m colloq.* appetite; desire, urge; ❏ не знае за иштав to get carried away; not to know when to stop

иштипе *pf* иштипа *aor.* to pinch

иштипува *impf of* иштипе

J

ја[1] *pron dial. see* јас

ја[2] *pron* (*short acc. form of* таа, она) her; ја видов I saw her

ја[3] *interj colloq.* 1 come on! get moving! 2 look! see!

ја[4] *part colloq.* of course; certainly; сака да се жени!? – сака, ја! does he want to get married? Of course he does!

ја – ја *conj colloq.* either . . . or . . .; ја едното ја другото either one or the other

јабана *f arch. see* туѓина

јабанец -нци & **јабанџија** -ии *m see* туѓинец

јаболкница *f Bot.* apple tree

јаболко *n* 1 apple; диво јаболко crab-apple; ❏ јаболко на раздорот bone of contention 2 (*на грлото*) Adam's apple 3 cheekbone 4 *arch.* present, gift

јаболков *adj* apple; јаболков сок apple juice

јаболкце & јаболче *n dim. of* јаболко 1 & 2

јаболчест *adj* apple-like

јаболчина *f Bot.* (Aristolochia clematitis) aristolochia, birthwort

јава *impf* 1 to ride; јава <на> коњ to ride a horse; јава велосипед to cycle, ride a bicycle 2 *fig. colloq.* to oppress, exploit; to ride on s.o.'s back; to ride roughshod over

јаваница *f* 1 riding 2 pack- and saddle-horse 3 (*as adv*) дојдоа јаваница they came on horseback

јавање *n from* јава; чизми за јавање riding boots; школо за јавање riding-school; патека за јавање bridle-path

јавач *m* rider, horseman

јавачки *adj* riding; rider's

јаваш *colloq.* 1 *adj indecl.* (*за тутун*) mild 2 *adv* slowly, gently; idly, nonchalantly; јаваш-јаваш gently, without hurrying

јавашлак *m colloq.* laziness; negligence, carelessness; slovenliness, sloppiness

јаве *in the expression:* на јаве in reality; на сон или на јаве in one's dreams or in reality; излезе на јаве to become known, emerge

јавен -вна *adj* public, open; јавно мислење public opinion; јавен обвинител public prosecutor; јавна куќа brothel; ❏ јавна тајна open secret

јави *pf* I 1 to communicate, announce; јави некому нешто to notify s.o. of s.th.; јави некому со писмо/ по телефон to inform s.o. by letter/telephone; радиото јави дека . . . the radio announced that . . . 2 to announce (*некого – s.o.*), introduce, present II – ce 1 (*with dat. or* на & *noun*) to get in touch (*with*); to announce o.s., report; to telephone; to greet; ce јави со писмо he got in touch by letter; се јави на конкурсот за судија he applied to become a judge; ми се јави на улица he greeted me in the street; се јави некому по телефон to give s.o. a call; се јави на телефон to answer the telephone **2** to appear; to present o.s.; се јави на сцена to come onto the stage

јавка *f* **1** password **2** contact man

јавне *pf* (*see* јава) to mount (*a horse, etc.*); *fig.* to oppress, exploit

јавно *adv* openly, publicly

јавност *f* <the> public; ❑ изнесува во јавност to bring into the open; не е за јавност to be off the record; разгласува во јавност to publicize

јавнува *impf of* јавне

јавор *m Bot.* (Acer pseudoplatanus) sycamore *attrib.*

јаворов *adj* sycamore

јаврија -ии *f* hen which has not yet started laying

јавува *impf of* јави (се)

јагарец -рци *m* (*usu. pl*) lymph gland

јаглак -ци *m* embroidered kerchief

јаглен *m* coal; дрвен јаглен charcoal; камен јаглен hard coal; ❑ црн како јаглен black as coal, coal-black; јаглен диоксид carbon dioxide; јаглен хидрат carbohydrate

јагленар *m* **1** coal merchant; charcoal burner; charcoal pedlar **2** coalminer **3** stoker

јагленарник -ци *m & * **јагленарница** *f* **1** charcoal kiln **2** coal yard

јагленов *adj* **1** coal; јагленова прашина coal dust; јагленов басен coalfield **2** *see* јаглероден *Chem.* carbon

јагленокоп *m* coalmine

јагленоса *pf* to char *trans.*, carbonize

јагленосува *impf of* јагленоса

јагленче *n dim.* small <piece of> coal

јаглење & јаглења *pl* embers, live coals

јаглерод *m Chem.* carbon

јаглероден -дна *adj* carbon; јаглероден диоксид carbon dioxide; јаглероден моноксид carbon monoxide

јаглика *f Bot.* **1** (Primula) primula; (Primula vulgaris) primrose **2** *see* јагличе

јагличе *n & * **јагличка** *f Bot.* (Primula veris) cowslip

јагма *f* crush, scramble

јагми се *impf* to vie (*за – for*), contend for, fight over

јагне *n pl* јагнињa *or* јаганца lamb; ❑ кроток (мирен) како јагне <as> meek as a lamb; кроткото јагне од две мајки цица *prov. cf.* kindness is the noblest weapon to conquer with

јагнешки *adj* lamb's; јагнешка кожа lambskin; јагнешко <месо> lamb

јагни *impf* **I** to yean, produce (*a lamb*) **II** – **се** to lamb

јагнило *n* lambing season

јагода *f see* јаготка

јагодарник -ци *m* strawberry bed; strawberry field

јагодов *adj* strawberry

јаготка *f Bot.* strawberry (*plant and fruit*); шумска јаготка wild strawberry

јагуар *m Zool.* jaguar

јагула *f Zool.* eel

јагулест *adj* eel-like

јагулник -ци *m f.p.* eel pond

јагурида *f* late grapes (*which do not ripen*)

јад *m* **1** sorrow, grief; trouble, worry **2** anger, rage;

❑ јад го фати he flew into a rage **3** *arch.* poison; bile, bitterness

јадало *n* food

јадар -дра *adj* large; sturdy; јадра стока horses and cattle

јадач *m* **1** glutton, big eater **2** *fig. colloq.* bloodsucker, vulture

јадачка *f colloq.* **1** food, eats; јадачки и пијачки food and drink **2** feasting **3** *fig.* worry, vexation, anxiety **4** (*fem. form*) *see* јадач

јаде *impf active pt* јал **I 1** to eat; ❑ јал, не јал, три и пол it makes no difference; *colloq.* не јади многу cut it out! knock it off! јаде ќотек to get a beating **2** to corrode, eat away; 'рѓата го јаде железото rust corrodes iron **3** to bite, sting; комарци ме јадат I'm being bitten by mosquitoes **4** to torment; ❑ јанса го јаде he is tormented by anxiety; што те јаде? what's eating you? **5** (*with dat.*) to itch; ме јаде косата my scalp is itching; ❑ не се чешај каде не те јаде you're asking for trouble **II – се 1** to be edible; ❑ ова <повеќе> не се јаде this is intolerable; ова се јаде this is not too bad **2** *fig.* to fret, chafe *intrans.*; се јаде од мака to be tormented by anxiety; се јаде од љубомора/завист to be consumed by jealousy/ envy; to eat one's heart out **3** *impers.* таму се јаде добро the food is good there **4** *impers.* (*with dat.*) ми се јаде I feel peckish

јадеж *m see* јадење 1 & 3

јаден¹ *pt from* јаде; јаден сум I have eaten

јаден² -дна *adj* **1** sad, sorrowful **2** *see* јадосан

јадење *n* **1** food, dish **2** *fig.* worry, trouble, anxiety **3** itching, itch

јадец *m* wishbone; јадец! you've lost your bet! (*said by winner in wishbone-breaking contest*)

јадица *f* fish-hook; ❑ се фати на јадица to swallow the bait

јадовен -вна *adj* sad, sorrowful

јадовит *adj* ill-tempered; bitter, caustic; angry, irate

јадозлив *adj f.p.* poisonous; змија јадозлива poisonous snake

јадоса *pf* **I** to embitter, exasperate; to anger, infuriate **II – се** to become embittered, exasperated; to get angry, furious

јадосан *pt* embittered, exasperated

јадосува *impf of* јадоса

Јадран *m* the Adriatic <Sea>

јадрански *adj* Adriatic; Јадранско Море Adriatic Sea

јадро *n* **1** nucleus; јадро на клетката nucleus of a cell; атомско јадро atomic nucleus **2** *fig.* essence, core **3** *Mil.* main body

јажар *m* rope-maker; rope dealer/merchant

јажарница *f* rope-yard, ropery

јажарство *n* rope-making

јаже *n* rope; (*дебело*) hawser; ❑ како симнат од јаже <looking> like death warmed up

јаженце *n dim. of* јаже

јажица & јажичка *f* rope made of rye straw (*used for tying sheaves*)

јаз *m* **1** dam, weir; јаз воденичен mill-dam **2** ditch; irrigation channel **3** *fig.* gap, gulf, chasm; јаз на генерации generation gap

јазак *adv colloq.* in the expression: јазак да ти е shame on you!

јазди *impf* 1 to ride (*on horseback*); јазди <на> коњ to ride a horse 2 to trot, canter (*of a horse*)

јазе & **јазека** *pron dial. see* јас

јази се *impf* to climb; се јази по дрвја to climb trees

јазик -ци *m* 1 tongue; ❑ исплази јазик to stick one's tongue out; to get very tired; си го голтне (прекаса) јазикот to bite one's tongue; долг е во јазикот to be talkative; брз е на јазик to speak without thinking; нема периз на јазикот to have a loose tongue; влече некого за јазик to goad s.o. into saying s.th.; на јазик ми стои it's on the tip of my tongue; си го држи јазикот <за заби> to hold one's tongue; му се одврза јазикот to find one's voice; му се врза/ плетка јазикот to be tongue-tied; to be at a loss for words; поган јазик sharp tongue; лоши јазици wagging tongues; го чеша јазикот he is dying to say s.th.; си ги чешаат јазиците to gossip; наоѓа заеднички јазик (со) to see eye to eye (*with*); крши јазик to find s.th. a mouthful to say; не пуштај го јазикот пред умот *prov.* look before you leap! јазикот коски нема, ама коски крши *prov.* a word spoken is past recalling 2 language, tongue; мајчин јазик mother tongue; народен јазик vernacular; мртов јазик dead language 3 pointer, arrow; tongue; јазик на терезии pointer <on scales>; јазик на чевел tongue of shoe

јазичар *m* 1 linguist 2 chatterbox

јазиче *n dim. of* јазик; јазиче на ѕвонче clapper of a small bell

јазичен -чна *adj* 1 linguistic; јазично прашање linguistic question (problem) 2 lingual

јазлест & **јазлив** *adj* knotty, knotted; nodose, nodulose; јазливо јаже knotted rope

јазловен -вна *adj* key, main; јазловни точки key points; јазловни прашања key questions

јазовец -вци *m Zool.* badger

јазол -зли *m* knot; морски јазол hitch; јазол на нерв ganglion; јазол на корен node on a root; железнички/патен јазол railway/road junction; ❑ гордиев јазол Gordian knot

јај -ови *m* spring, coil

јајлија *adj indecl.* јајлија кревет spring bed

јајник -ци *m Anat.* ovary

јајце -јца *n* 1 egg; јајце на око fried egg; пржено јајце scrambled egg; црвено (велигденско) јајце Easter egg; ровко/тврдо варено јајце soft-boiled/hard-boiled egg; лушпа од јајце eggshell; ❑ бара влакно во јајце to split hairs; *vulg.* големи јајца big deal! личи како јајце на јајце to be as like as two peas in a pod; to be the spitting image (*со, на – of*); како да гази на јајца as if walking on eggshells; не учи старец да мака јајца *prov.* don't teach your grandmother how to suck eggs; поарно денеска јајце отколку утре кокошка; поарно своe јајце отколку туѓа кокошка *provs.* a bird in the hand is worth two in the bush 2 *Anat.* (*кај жена*) ovum 3 *vulg.* (*usu. pl*) ball, testicle

јајцевиден -дна *adj see* јајчест

јајцевод *m* oviduct, Fallopian tube

јајценце *n dim. of* јајце

јајчаник -ци & **јајчалник** -ци *m* (*млечник*) kind of pastry

јајчарник -ци *m* egg-box; egg-carton, egg-crate

јајчест *adj* egg-shaped, oval, ovoid

јајчник -ци *m see* јајник

јак *adj* 1 strong, tough; durable; powerful, mighty; burly; sturdy; јак како мечка strong as an ox; јако платно strong (durable) cloth; јак тутун strong tobacco; јака зима severe winter; јак мирис strong odour; јака храна wholesome food; ❑ јака му душа God help him! 2 (*тврд*) hard, firm; лебов е јак како камен this bread is as hard as stone 3 (*плоден*) fertile; јака земја fertile land

јака *f* collar; ❑ фати некого за јака to seize s.o. by the collar; to get hold of s.o.

јакне¹ & **јакнее** *impf* to strengthen *intrans.*, grow stronger

јакне² *pf* јакна *aor.* to moan, groan; to start moaning

јакнува *impf of* јакне

јако *adv* 1 firmly; јако стега to hold fast 2 *rarely* much, a great deal; беше се скарал јако со него he had a bad quarrel with him

јакобинец -нци *m* Jacobin

јакост *f* firmness, strength; јакост на материјали strength of materials

јакотија *f* strength, power; firmness

јакулка & **јакуцка** *f* hood

јалдаз *m* 1 gilding 2 gold coin 3 *Bot.* dahlia

јале *interj colloq.* look! јале го! look at him!

јалнаш *adv colloq.* wrong, mistaken<ly>; јалнаш си you're wrong; јалнаш ме разбра you've got me wrong

јалов *adj* barren; *fig.* futile; јалова земја barren land; јалова овца barren sheep; јалов обид fruitless attempt; јалова работа useless work

јаловак -ци *m* barren animal

јалови се *impf* to become sterile (barren)

јаловица *f* 1 barren animal 2 barren land

јама *f* pit, hole; (*во рудник*) shaft; септичка јама cesspool, cesspit; ❑ копа некому јама to lay a trap (dig a pit) for s.o.; кој на друг јама копа, сам во неа упаѓа *prov.* the deed comes back on the doer

Јамáјка *f* Jamaica

јамајски *adj* Jamaican

Јамáјчанец -ни *m* Jamaican

Јамáјчанка *f* (*fem. form*) see Јамáјчанец

јамак -ци *m* copper vessel (*for water*)

јамаче *n* small copper vessel (*for melting fat or butter*)

јамб *m Prosody* iamb

јамболија -ии *f* shaggy woollen home-made blanket, flokati rug

јамка *f* loop; noose

јампски *adj* iambic

јамски *adj* mine; јамски работник mine-worker, miner

јанѕа *f* anxiety; horror; fever, shivering, chill; јанѕа го јаде he is tormented by anxiety

јанија -ии *f* meat stew with vegetables

јаничар *m Hist.* janissary, janizary

јановденче *n Bot.* (Salvia officinalis) sage, shop-sage

јанта *f* shepherd's leather bag

јантар *m* (*ќилибар*) amber

јануáри *m* January

јануáрски *adj* January

јанцик -ци *m* leather shoulder-bag

Јапонец -нци *m* Japanese

Јапонија *f* Japan

Јапонка *f* (*fem. form*) *see* Јапонец

јапонски *adj* Japanese

јара *adj indecl.* (*во земјоделството*) spring, vernal; јара пченица spring wheat

јаран *m arch.* **1** friend **2** lover

јарбол *m* mast

јард *m* (*англиска мерка за должина*) yard

јаре *n* kid, young goat

јаребица *f Zool.* (Perdix perdix) grey partridge

јарем *m* yoke; *fig.* slavery, bondage

јарец -рци *m* **1** (*прч*) billy-goat; ❑ жртвен јарец scapegoat; whipping boy **2** *Astron.* Capricorn **3** *Gymnastics* buck, vaulting-horse

јарешки *adj* kid's; јарешко <месо> kid's meat

јари (се) *impf see* прчи (се), мрка (се)

јари се *impf see* кози се

јарина *f* wool (*from a lamb or a sheep at the second shearing*); ❑ дрн, дрн јарина nonsense! fiddlesticks!

јарица & **јаричка** *f* young hen (*which has not yet started laying*)

јарко *adv* brightly

јаркост *f* brightness

јарма *f* coarse grain-meal (*used as fodder*)

јарок -рка *adj* bright; јарко сонце bright sun

јаросно *adv* furiously, angrily

јарост *f* fury, anger, rage

јаростен -сна *adj* furious, angry, enraged

јас **1** *pron* (*1st p. sg*) I; (*dat. мене, ми*; *other cases мене, ме*); јас тебе, ти мене you scratch my back and I'll scratch yours **2** *n indecl.* the ego, self; друго јас alter ego; своето јас one's self; ❑ има свое јас to stand one's ground; to stand upon one's dignity

јасен[1] -сна *adj* clear; lucid; (*светол*) bright; (*ведар*) serene; (*разбирлив*) distinct; јасна месечина bright moonlight; јасно небо clear sky; јасен глас clear voice; јасна претстава за нешто clear idea of s.th.

јасен[2] *m Bot.* ash tree

јасенов *adj* ash *attrib.*

јасика *f Bot.* (Populus tremula) aspen

јасиков *adj* aspen; јасиково дрво aspen tree; aspen timber

јасје -сја *n arch.* (*јадење*) food, victuals

јаска *pron dial. see* јас

јасли *pl* **1** trough, manger; ❑ на државни јасли maintained by the state **2** детски јасли day nursery; crèche

јасмин *m Bot.* jasmine

јасни се *impf* **1** to clear <up>, brighten up; времето се јасни the weather is clearing **2** to shine

јасник *m* bitter cold; cold but clear weather

јаснина *f* **1** clear sky/weather **2** clarity; brilliance **3** *f.p.* early morning; од јаснина до пладнина from early morning till midday

јасно *adv* clearly, clear; ❑ јасно и гласно loud and clear; кратко и јасно short and sweet; јасно како еден и еден as plain as a pikestaff; јасно како <бел> ден crystal-clear

јасновиден -дна *adj* clear-sighted, penetrating, discerning, perceptive

јасновидец -дци *m* clear-sighted person

јасност, **јаснота** & **јаснотија** *f* clarity, clearness; lucidity

јастак -ци *m* **1** *see* перница **2** straw mattress, palliasse **3** seed-bed

јастог -зи *m* lobster

јастреб *m Zool.* hawk, *esp.* (Accipter gentilis) goshawk

јатаган *m* yataghan

јатак -ци *m* accomplice, accessory

јатакува *impf* to shelter a criminal or accomplice; to conspire (*co – with*)

јатка *f* core; kernel; *fig.* essence; јатка од орев kernel of a walnut

јато *n* (*птици*) flock; (*риби*) school; (*мноштво*) cluster, swarm; herd

јаток -ци *m* woof, weft

јатор *m* notch, cut

јатрва *f* sister-in-law (*wife of husband's brother*)

јатрвин *adj* sister-in-law's

јаудија -ии *m sl. pejor.* Jew

јахта *f* yacht

јачи *impf* **1** to resound, reverberate, echo; јачат гласови voices echo **2** to groan; јачи на сон to groan in one's sleep

јачина *f* **1** strength, power **2** firmness, hardness

јачка *impf dim. of* јачи 2

јачмен[1] *m Bot.* barley

јачмен[2] & **јачменов** *adj* barley; јачмен леб barley bread; јачмена слама barley straw

јачменик -ци *m* **1** barley bread **2** *see* јачменчок

јачмениште *n* barley field

јачменчок -ци *m*, **јачменче** & **јачменце** *n* stye (*on the eyelid*)

јашмак -ци *m* yashmak, veil

је *pron dial. see* й

Јемен *m* Yemen

Јеменец -нци *m* Yemeni

Јеменка *f* (*fem. form*) *see* Јеменец

јеменски *adj* Yemeni

јереј -еи *m* (*Orthodox*) priest

јерејски *adj* of an Orthodox priest

јогурт *m* yog<h>urt

јога *f* yoga

јод *m Chem.* iodine

јоден -дна *adj Chem.* iodine, iodic; јодна киселина iodic acid; јодна тинктура tincture of iodine

јодоформ *m* iodoform

јок *part colloq.* no

јон *m* ion

јонизација *f* ionization

јонизúра *pf & impf* to ionize

јорган *m* **1** quilt, duvet, *Austral.* doona; испружи ги нозете спроти јорганот *prov.* cut your coat according to your cloth **2** wire/rope on a winch

јоргански *adj* quilt *attrib.*; јоргански чаршав quilt (*Austral.* doona) cover

јорганџија -ии *m* quilt maker, quilter

јорганџилница *f* quilt shop

јоргован *m Bot.* (Syringa vulgaris) lilac, *see* лилјак[2]

Јордан *m* Jordan

Јорданец -нци *m* Jordanian

Јорданка *f* (*fem. form*) *see* Јорданец

јордански *adj* Jordanian

јота *f* the letter ј; iota, jot

јубилáр *m* **1** person whose anniversary/jubilee is being celebrated **2** *see* јубилеј

јубилáрен -рна *adj* jubilee; јубиларна свеченост jubilee celebration

јубилéј -еи *m* jubilee

јува _f_ (*расолница*) cabbage brine (*pickle*)

јувелѝр _m_ jeweller

југ _m_ **1** south **2** south wind

југовица _f Zool._ (Picus viridis) green woodpecker

југозáпад _m_ south-west

југозападен -дна _adj_ south-west; south-westerly; south-western; југозападен ветер south-westerly wind, sou'wester

југоѝсток _m_ south-east

југоисточен -чна _adj_ south-east; south-easterly; south-eastern; југоисточен ветер south-easterly

Југославија _f_ Yugoslavia

Југословен _m_ Yugoslav

Југословенка _f_ (*fem. form*) _see_ Југословен

југословенски _adj_ Yugoslav

јуда _f_ **1** renegade, traitor; infidel **2** _pejor._ Jew

јудин _adj_ Judas'; judina целувка kiss of Judas; judino железо <Judas'> money, gold

јужен -жна _adj_ southern; jужна хемисфера Southern Hemisphere

јужи _impf_ (*only in 3rd p.*) to grow warmer (*of the weather*)

јужноамерикански _adj_ South American

Јужноафриканец -нци _m_ South African

Јужноафриканка _f_ (*fem. form*) _see_ Јужноафриканец

Јужноафриканска Република _f_ Republic of South Africa

јужноафрикански _adj_ South African

јули _m_ July

јулијански _adj_ jулиjански календар Julian Calendar

јулски _adj_ July

јунак -ци _m_ hero; brave man; _Literature_ main character, hero, protagonist; главниот јунак на романот the hero of the novel; ❑ јунак на денот man of the

hour; јунак на збор braggart; спроти јунакот и коњот _prov._ everyone gets his just deserts **2** _colloq._ young man, lad; bridegroom; husband

јунакиња _f_ heroine

јуначен -чна _adj_ heroic; brave, bold, courageous

јуначи _impf_ **I** to inspire <with courage>, spur on, encourage **II** – **ce** to boast, brag; to swagger, strut

јуначки _adj_ heroic; brave, intrepid

јунаштво _n_ heroism, bravery; heroic deed

јунаштина _f_ heroism

јунгфер _m_ (*boy*) virgin

јунгферица _f_ (*girl*) virgin

јуне _n_ heifer; bullock

јунец -нци _m_ young bull, bullock

јунешки _adj_ yearling; jунешко <месо> yearling beef

јуни _m_ June

јуниор _m Sport._ junior, colt

јуниорка _f_ (*fem. form*) _see_ јуниор

јуниорски _adj_ junior; jуниорска репрезентација junior team

јуница & јуничка _f_ heifer

јунски _adj_ June

јунче _n see_ јуне

јури _impf of_ јурне

јурѝст _m_ jurist, lawyer

јуриш _m_ attack, assault, charge, storming; ❑ освојува на јуриш to take by storm

јуриша _impf_ to attack, charge, storm, rush

јурне _pf_ to rush off, run off, race; to start chasing

јуруш _m colloq. see_ јуриш

јута _f_ jute

јуфка _f_ noodles, pasta

Ќ

кааза *f see* каза

каба *adj indecl. colloq.* **1** inferior, poor-quality; каба штоф inferior material **2** weak, feeble, frail

кабадаија -ии *m Hist.* Ottoman deputy governor; *fig.* tyrant

кабает *m colloq.* blame, guilt, fault; нема тој кабает he isn't to blame

кабаетлија *adj indecl. colloq.* guilty, at fault

кабаница *f* cloak, cape

кабардиса *pf* to swell, become swollen; to rise (*of dough*)

кабардисува *impf of* кабардиса

кабаре *n* cabaret

кабаст *adj* bulk, bulky; кабаст товар bulk cargo; кабасти стоки bulky goods

кабел -бли *m* cable; подземен кабел underground cable

кабил *adj indecl. colloq.* capable; *in the expressions:* да е кабил if he is able, if he is capable; кабил сум да . . . I'm ready, I'm prepared to . . .

кабина *f* cabin; booth; телефонска кабина telephone booth; шоферска кабина <driver's> cab; пилотска кабина cockpit; кабина нажичара cable-car

кабинет *m* **1** work-room, study; laboratory; office; кабинет по хемија chemistry laboratory **2** *Pol.* cabinet

кабинетски *adj* <of a> study, laboratory; *fig.* abstract, unpractical; кабинетски научник armchair scientist

каблира *pf & impf* **1** to cable **2** to make cables

кабловски *adj* cable; кабловска телевизија cable television

каблограм *m* cablegram

каботажа *f* cabotage, coastal navigation and trade

каботира *pf & impf* to engage in cabotage

кабриолет *m* cabriolet

кавал *m Mus.* shepherd's pipe

кавалер *m* cavalier, escort, gallant, gentleman

кавалерија *f* cavalry

кавалериски *adj* cavalry

кавалерист *m* cavalryman

кавалерски *adj* gentlemanly; gallant

кавалкада *f* cavalcade

кавалџија -ии *m Mus.* player of the *kaval* (shepherd's pipe)

каватина *f Mus.* cavatina

кавга *f colloq.* quarrel, row, wrangle; brawl; ❑ почнува кавга to pick up a quarrel

кавгаџија -ии *m colloq.* quarrelsome person; brawler

кавгаџика *f* (*fem. form*) *see* кавгаџија; termagant, shrew

кавéрна *f Med.* pulmonary cavity

кавијар *m* caviar

Кавказ *m* the Caucasus

кавкаски *adj* Caucasian

кавурма *f Cul.* dish made of diced pork

кад *m see* чад[1]

када[1] *f* **1** tub, bathtub **2** *dial.* vat, large barrel

када[2] *f* married Turkish woman

кадаиф *m* kind of oriental sweetmeat (*made of pastry, nuts and syrup*)

кадана *f see* када[2]

каданка *f* **1** *dim. of* кадана **2** *Zool.* (Carduelis carduelis) goldfinch **3** *Zool.* (Mustela nivalis) weasel, *see* ласица, невестулка

кадар[1] -дри *m* **1** personnel, staff; научни кадри body of scientists, scientific workforce; партиски кадри party cadre; наставен кадар teaching staff **2** *Mil.* cadre, regular forces **3** *Film* frame; sequence; still

кадар[2] -дра *adj* capable, able, fit; не е кадар за ништо he isn't fit for anything

кадарен -рна *adj see* кадар[2]

каде *adv & conj* **1** where; where to, *arch.* whither; каде одиш? where are you going? ❑ до немај каде in vast numbers; to a great extent; каде <и да> било anywhere, wherever; каде не everywhere; каде ќе му излезе крајот? where will it end? нема каде there's no other solution; од каде? whence? from where? how come? од каде накаде? on what basis? од немај каде out of necessity; каде даваат – земај, каде маваат – бегај get what you can while the going's good **2** *adv* anywhere; каде што сакаш anywhere you please **3** *prep* (*кај*) at, by, near; about, towards; каде мене next to me; at my home; каде пладне towards midday

каде-годе *adv* anywhere, wherever

кадеж *m* **1** smoke **2** fumigation **3** smoking, curing (*of meat, etc.*)

каде-каде *adv* much more

кадела *f* **1** tow, harl **2** distaff-full **3** *dial.* spinning-wheel; distaff

каденца *f Mus.* cadence

кадет *m* cadet

кади *impf* **1** to smoke, cure (*meat, etc.*) **2** to burn incense **3** *fig.* to flatter

кадија -ии *m Hist.* qadi, Muslim judge

кадилак -ци *m Hist.* judgeship, judge's office

кадилница *f* censer, thurible

кадило *n see* кадилница

кадиум *m Chem.* cadmium

кадифе *n* velvet

кадифен *adj* velvet (*also fig.*); кадифен фустан velvet dress; кадифен глас velvet voice

кадра *f* lock, curl (*of hair*)

кадрав *adj* curly; кадрава коса curly hair

кадри *impf* **I** to curl *trans.* **II** – се to curl *intrans.*

кадрил *m* (*танц*) quadrille

кадрица *f see* кадра

кадро *n arch.* photograph; ќе те вадам на кадро I'll take a photograph of you

кадровец -вци *m* regular soldier

кадровик -ци *m* personnel officer

кадровски *adj* personnel *attrib.*, staffing; кадровска служба personnel department (office); референт за кадровски прашања personnel officer; кадровски <с>рок traineeship

кадроса *pf arch.* to photograph

кадросува *impf of* кадроса

кае се *impf* to repent

каже *pf* кажа *aor.* **I 1** to say; to utter; to tell; каже еден збор to say a word; кажи ми една приказна tell me a story; немој никому да кажеш don't tell anyone; ❏ кажи ми да ти кажам I have no idea; кажи-речи more or less, roughly; меѓу нас кажано speaking confidentially; privately; право да ти кажам to tell you the truth, really; сакам кажам не знам речам *iron.* he's talking through his hat; ти ќе ми кажеш look who's talking; it's none of your business **2** (*покаже*) to show; каже некому патот to show s.o. the way **II** – **ce** to introduce o.s.

кажува (се) *impf of* каже (се)

каза *f Hist.* kaaza (*administrative region of the Ottoman empire*)

казалец -лци *m see* показалец

казамат *m arch.* **1** casemate **2** prison

казан *m* cauldron, boiler; (*за ракија*) brandy still

казанарница *f see* казарница

казанџија -ии *m* boilermaker; coppersmith

казанџилница *f* boilermaker's/coppersmith's workshop

казарма *f* barracks; артилериска казарма artillery barracks

казармски *adj* barracks; казармски живот barrack (army) life

казарница *f* distillery

Казах -аси *m* Kazakh

Казахстан *m* Kazakhstan

казахстански *adj* Kazakh

казачóк *m* (*танец*) kazachok (*Russian dance*)

Казашка *f* (*fem. form*) *see* Казах

казашки *adj see* казахстански

казеѝн *m Chem.* casein

казѝно *n* casino

казма *f* pickaxe; mattock

казна *f* punishment; penalty; парична казна fine; смртна казна capital punishment; телесна казна corporal punishment; казна за неправилно паркирање parking ticket

казнен *adj* penal; казнен завод prison; reformatory; казнена експедиција punitive expedition; *Sport.* казнен простор penalty area

казненик -ци *m* convict; criminal; prisoner

казнет *pt* punished, penalized, fined

казни *pf* to punish, penalize; (*парично*) to fine

казнив *adj* punishable; казниво дело punishable act

казнува *impf of* казни

каик -ци *m colloq.* boat

каикчија -ии *m arch.* boatman

каил *adj indecl. colloq.* pleased; agreed, in agreement; се чинам каил I agree

каирец -рци *m* person from Cairo, Cairene

каирка *f* (*fem. form*) *see* каирец

Каиро *n* Cairo

каирски *adj from/of* Cairo, Cairene

каиш *m* (*ремен*) belt; strap; band

кај *prep* **1** at, by, with, beside; among; кај мене next to me; at my home; кај некои народи among certain peoples **2** to; отиде кај еден пријател to go to see a friend **3** about, towards; кај полноќ towards midnight; кај Велигден about Easter time **4** *adv* where; кај беше? where were you?

кајак -ци *m* canoe, kayak; кајак на диви води whitewater kayaking

кајакар *m* canoeist, kayaker

кајакарски *adj* canoe (kayak) *attrib.*; canoeist; кајакарски трки kayak races

кајакарство *n* kayaking, canoeing

кајгана *f* scrambled egg<s>

кајмак *m* froth, foam; clotted cream; ❏ го собира кајмакот to skim the cream off

кајмакам *m Hist.* kajmakam (*governor of a kaaza*)

кајмаклија *adj indecl.* кафе кајмаклија strong Turkish coffee with foam on top

кајсија -ии *f Bot.* (Prunus armeniaca) apricot (*tree and fruit*)

кајче *n dim. of* кајак

кака *impf child.* to <do a> poo

какадý *m Zool.* cockatoo

какалашка *f* poppy seedcase

какáо *n* cocoa

каклица *f see* какол

како *adv & conj* **1** how; ❏ како сте? how are you? како така? how is that? how come? како да ви кажам? how can I put it? како ти се гледа? how does it look to you? what do you think? ; како кога sometimes this way, sometimes that; sometimes yes and sometimes no; it all depends when; како му драго as he pleases; како сакало било it doesn't matter how; како <да> не! of course! (*also iron.*) my foot! било како било however it may have been; како каде it all depends where **2** (*comparative*) as, like; уште како дете even as a child; детето е како татко си the boy is like his father; како што знаете as you know **3** (*of time*) while, as; како што си стоев while I was standing there **4** како да as if; како да е тоа моја работа as if it were any business of mine; како да те познавам it seems to me I know you

како-годе *adv* sloppily, carelessly, superficially

каков -ква *pron* **1** what kind of; what a . . . ! каков човек е? what sort of person is he? каква убава мома! what a pretty girl! каков сум, таков сум I am as I am; каков таков of any kind; каков си! I don't believe you can be like that! каков било, каков да е any kind of; каков човек е! what sort of a man is he? **2** of that kind; човек каков што нема повеќе a man whose like we no longer see

каков-годе *pron* any kind of; worthless; inferior; какви-годе алишта shabby clothing

каков што *see* каков 2

какол *m Bot.* (Agrostemma githago) corn-cockle; во секое жито има и какол *prov.* there's a black sheep in every flock

какологија *f* cacology

какофонија *f* cacophony

кактус *m Bot.* cactus

кал *m & f* **1** mud, mire; ❏ тоне сè подлабоко в кал to sink ever deeper into the mire; вади некого од кал to come to s.o.'s rescue; to bail s.o. out **2** dirt; ушна кал earwax

калабалак *m colloq.* crowd, crush

калаен -јна *adj* tin, stannic

калаиса *pf* to tin, cover with tin

калаисува *impf of* калаиса

калај *m* tin; pewter; ❏ ќе го изеде калајот he will get the worst of it; he will do badly

калајџија -ии *m* tinsmith

каламбур *m* **1** confusion, muddle **2** pun

калап *m* **1** mould, cast; калап за чевли shoe last; калап за тутун tobacco standard; ❏ на еден калап cast in the same mould **2** bar, cake; калап сапун bar (cake) of soap **3** *fig.* stereotype

калапар *m* tobacco sorter

калапарка *f* (*fem. form*) *see* калапар

калапи *impf* **1** to sort (*usu. tobacco*) **2** to mould

калауз *m* **1** master-key, skeleton-key **2** *arch.* guide **3** *arch.* intermediary, mediator, go-between **4** *arch.* watch/clock hand **5** *Astron.* Alpha persei (*the brightest star in the constellation Perseus*)

калаф *m* **1** case, sheath **2** cover (*for furniture, etc.*); pillow-case

калач[1] *m arch.* sword

калач[2] *m colloq. in the expression:* на калач crosswise, diagonally, sideways, to the side

калачка *f see* калач[1]

калвинизам -змот *m* Calvinism

калвинист *m* Calvinist

калдрма *f* road paved with cobblestones; cobble-stones

калдрмиса *pf* to pave with cobblestones

калдрмисува *impf of* калдрмиса

калдрмџија -ии *m* person who lays cobblestones, road-paver

кале *n* fortress, citadel; ❏ сега сум кале no one can touch me now

калезба *f* invitation

калезма *f see* калезба

калеидоскоп *m* kaleidoscope

калем *m* **1** spool, reel **2** cutting, graft, scion **3** *arch.* pencil **4** *arch.* tube

калемар *m* grafter

калемарски *adj* grafting

калеми *impf* to graft, transplant, insert

кален[1] *pt* tempered, hardened (*also fig.*)

кален[2] -лна *adj see* каллив

календар *m* calendar

календарски *adj* calendar; календарска година calendar year

каленик -ци *m see* каленица

каленица *f* clay (earthenware) bowl

калеса *pf* to invite

калесар *m see* калесник

калесарка *f see* калесница

калеска *f see* калезба

калесник -ци *m* **1** person who invites **2** invitation

калесница *f* **1** (*fem. form*) *see* калесник 1 **2** flask of wine or brandy (*traditionally offered when inviting guests to a wedding*)

калесува *impf of* калеса

калец -лци *m* (*usu. pl*) thick knee socks; felt boot lining

калеш *adj* swarthy; калеша овца sheep with black rings round its eyes

калешка *f* **1** sheep with black rings round its eyes **2** swarthy woman

кали *impf* to temper, harden

калибар -бри *m* calibre (*also fig.*), gauge

калиграф *m* (*краснописец*) calligrapher

калиграфија *f* (*краснопис*) calligraphy

калина *f* **1** *Bot.* (Punica granatum) pomegranate (*tree and fruit*) **2** *Bot. see* велигденче[1]

калинка *f see* калина 1

калира *pf & impf* **1** to shrink, dry up, lose weight (*of merchandise*) **2** to strike/lower the sails

калиум *m Chem.* potassium

калиумов *adj* potassium; калиумови соли potassium salts

калифа *m* caliph

калифат *m* caliphate

калица *f* pitcher, ewer

калк *m & * **калка** *f* **1** *Ling.* calque **2** tracing-paper **3** tracing; *fig.* exact copy, imitation

калкан *m* **1** *Zool.* (Pleuronectes platessa) plaice **2** shield **3** roof with eaves on one side

калкулатор *m* calculator

калкулација -ии *f* calculation

калкулира *pf & impf* to calculate

каллив *adj* muddy; каллив терен muddy ground/field

калник -ци *m* mudguard, *Am.* fender

кало *n* **1** ullage, loss (*in weight*), short weight **2** (*за течност*) leakage

каловит *adj* muddy

калодонт *m* toothpaste

калорија -ии *f* calorie; голема калорија large calorie; мала калорија small calorie

калориметар -три *m* calorimeter

калорифер *m* fan heater

калоричен -чна *adj* caloric; калорична храна high-calorie food

калота *f* **1** *Anat.* sinciput **2** skull-cap **3** sector (*of domed surface*)

калофер *m Bot.* (Tanacetum vulgare) tansy

калош *m* (*usu. pl*) galosh, overshoe, *Am.* rubber

калпав *adj colloq.* **1** bad, poor-quality **2** forged, false, counterfeit; калпави пари counterfeit money, forged banknotes

калпазан *m colloq.* bungler; good-for-nothing

калпак -ци *m* **1** fur-lined leather cap **2** helmet

калпакчија -ии *m* fur cap maker

калуѓер *m* monk

калуѓери *impf* **I** to receive as a monk/nun **II** – **ce** to become a monk/nun

калуѓерица *f* nun

калуѓерка *f* **1** nun **2** *Zool.* tadpole **3** *Bot.* (Iris pseudacorus) yellow iris, yellow flag **4** *Zool.* (Vanellus vanellus) lapwing

калуѓерски *adj* monastic

калуѓерство *n* monkhood; nunhood

калфа *f & m* journeyman, assistant craftsman

калфински *adj* <of a> journeyman

калфува *impf* to practise a trade

калца *f dim. of* кал

калцедон *m* chalcedony

калциум *m Chem.* calcium

калчун *m & * **калчун** *m see* калец

кама *f* dagger, knife

камара *f* **1** recess, alcove, niche **2** heap, pile

камарила *f* cabal, camarilla

камата *f* interest; interest rate; камата на камата compound interest; затезна камата default interest; камата по видување interest on ordinary deposits

каматен -тна *adj* interest; каматна сметка interest account

камбаана *f* & **камбáна** *f* church bell

камбанар *m* bell-ringer

камбанарија -ии *f* bell-tower; belfry

Камбóџа *f* Cambodia, *see* Кампучија

Камбоџанец -ни *m* Cambodian

Камбоџанка *f* (*fem. form*) *see* Камбоџанец

камбоџански *adj* Cambodian

камбур *colloq.* 1 *m* hunchback 2 *adj indecl.* hunchbacked

камбурест *adj colloq.* hunchbacked

камгарн *m* worsted

камелеóн *m Zool.* chameleon (*also fig.*)

камелија -ии *f Bot.* camellia

камен¹ -ње -ња, (*rare f.p.* камни) *m* stone, rock; воденички камен millstone; *Med.* камен во жолчка gallstone; *Med.* камен во бубрег kidney (renal) stone; бесценет камен precious stone, gem, jewel; модар камен blue vitriol, copper sulphate; камен темелник foundation-stone; keystone; ❑ камен на мудроста philosopher's stone; камен на сопнување stumbling block; пробен камен touchstone; камен пијан dead drunk, stoned; *Med.* забен камен tartar; бара под дрво и под камен to search high and low; не остава камен на камен to leave no stone unturned; пука дрво и камен it is bitterly cold; со свој камен по своја глава to stew in one's own juice; со твој камен по твоја глава you are hoist with your own petard; фрли камен по нас he doesn't visit us anymore; ако те удри некој со камен, ти удри го со леб *prov.* turn the other cheek; тврд како камен<as> hard as stone/flint

камен² *adj* stone; камен јаглен hard coal; камена сол rock-salt; камено време Stone Age

каменар *m* stonemason

каменарка *f* 1 <woman> stonemason 2 stonemason's wife 3 *Zool.* (Vipera ammodytes) sand viper 4 *Zool.* (Alectoris graeca) rock partridge

каменее *impf* to turn to stone, petrify *intrans.*

каменеење *n* petrification

каменен *adj see* камен²; каменен блок stone tablet (block), slab

камени се *impf see* каменее

каменик -ци *m* stone bridge

каменит *adj* stony, rocky

каменица *f* 1 *colloq. see* каменолом 2 *f.p.* bed of stone

каменичар *m see* каменар

каменлив *adj see* каменит

каменоделец -лци *m see* каменорезец

каменолóм *m* quarry

каменорезец -сци *m* stonemason

каменува *pf* & *impf* to stone, kill/injure by stoning

камењар *m* stony (rocky) ground

камењарник -ци *m see* камењар

камера *f* <movie/TV> camera

камерен -рна *adj Mus.* chamber; камерна музика chamber music; камерен оркестар chamber orchestra

камерман *m* cameraman

камертóн *m Mus.* tuning-fork

Камерун *m* Cameroon

Камерунец -нци *m* Cameroonian

Камерунка *f* (*fem. form*) *see* Камерунец

камерунски *adj* Cameroonian

камила *f Zool.* camel; двогрба камила two-humped (Bactrian) camel; едногрба камила one-humped camel, dromedary

камилавка *f* tall cap (*of priest, monk, chef or Chetnik*)

камилар *m* camel-driver, cameleer

камилица *f Bot.* (Matricaria chamomilla) camomile

камин *m* fireplace, hearth

камиóн *m* lorry, truck; камион со приколка articulated lorry, *Austral.* semi-trailer

камионџија *m* lorry driver, truck driver

камичка *f dim. of* кама

камлив *adj f.p. see* каменлив

камо *adv* where; камо го? where is he/it? камо среќа! if only . . . !

камоли *conj* not to mention, not to speak of; а камоли let alone

камп -ови *m* camp; camp site

кампáња *f* campaign; предизборна кампања election campaign

кампáњски *adj* 1 campaign *attrib.* 2 unsystematic, unplanned; occasional, irregular; кампањска работа work in short bursts (fits and starts); кампањско учење *colloq.* last-minute pre-exam study

кампер *m* camper

кампинг -зи *m* camp site, camping ground

кампíра & **кампува** *pf* & *impf* to camp

Кампучиец -ијци *m* Kampuchean

Кампучија *f* Kampuchea

Кампучијка *f* (*fem. form*) *see* Кампучиец

кампучиски *adj* Kampuchean

камуфлáжа *f* camouflage

камуфлíра *pf* & *impf* I to camouflage *trans.*; to mask, disguise II -се to camouflage *intrans.*; to disguise o.s.

камфор *m* camphor

камфорен -рна *adj* camphor<ic>; камфорна инјекција camphor injection

камфоров *adj* camphor; камфорово стебло trunk of a camphor tree

камче *n dim. of* камен; pebble

камџија -ии *m see* камшик

камшик -ци *m* whip, lash

кан *m* khan

кана¹ *f* 1 *see* покана 2 feast (*on the eve of a slava*) 3 *colloq.* intention

кана² *f* jug; pitcher

кана³ *f* (*за коса*) henna; alkanet

канабé *n* couch; sofa

канава *f* canvas; groundwork (*for embroidery*)

канаваза *f* earthen jug/jar

канаваца *f* sacking; coarse material; buckram

Канáда *f* Canada

канадски *adj* Canadian

Канаѓанец -ни *m* Canadian

Канаѓанка *f* (*fem. form*) *see* Канаѓанец

канал *m* canal, channel (*also fig.*); drain; *Anat.* duct; одводен канал sewer; канал за наводнување irrigation channel; телевизиски канал television channel; *Anat.* мочен канал urethra

канален -лна *adj* <of a> canal, channel; ❑ по канален ред in the ordinary way

канализација *f* sewerage system

канализациóнен -она *adj* sewerage, drainage; канализациона мрежа sewerage network

каналзѝра *pf & impf* **1** to provide with sewerage (drainage) **2** *fig.* to channel

канàлски *adj* canal

канàп *m* string, twine

канàпен -пна *adj* of string, twine

канàрка *f Zool.* canary

канàста *f* canasta

канàт *m* wing (*leaf of a door or window*)

канàта *f* jug, pitcher

канàч *m* person who invites guests to a wedding, etc.

Канбера *f* Canberra

канберец -рци *m* Canberran

канберка *f* (*fem. form*) *see* канберец

канберски *adj* Canberran

кандар<д>иса *pf colloq.* to persuade, win over

кандар<д>исување *n colloq.* persuasion

канделàбар -бри *m* candelabra

кандидàт *m* candidate; examinee; пратенички кандидат candidate for parliament; кандидат на конкурс applicant; кандидат на натпреварување competitor

кандидàтски *adj* candidate<'s>; кандидатски стаж training (probationary) period

кандидатỳра *f* candidature, candidacy

кандидациòнен -она *adj* selection; кандидациона комисија selection committee

кандидѝра *pf & impf* **I** to propose as a candidate, nominate **II** – **ce** to stand for election, run for office; to apply (*for a position*)

кандѝлка¹ *f* **1** censer **2** *Bot.* (Aquilegia vulgaris) columbine

кандѝлка² *impf* **I** to rock, swing *trans.* **II** – **ce** to rock, swing *intrans.*

кандѝло *n* icon lamp

кандѝса *pf colloq.* **I 1** to agree **2** to persuade (*да – то*) **II** – **ce** to agree; to decide (*да – то*)

кандисỳва (ce) *impf of* кандиса (ce)

канèник -ци *m* invited guest (at a wedding, etc.)

канѝ *pf & impf* **1** to invite (*esp. to a wedding*); ❑ го каниле магарето на свадба <та му зарачале да си го земе самарот> they sent him on a busman's holiday **2** to urge (*s.o.*) to help himself/eat

канѝбал *m* cannibal

канибалѝзам -змот *m* cannibalism

канѝја -ии *f* sheath, scabbard

канѝла *f Med.* cannula

канкàн *m* cancan

канòн¹ *m* **1** (*пропис*) canon **2** *Mus.* canon, round **3** *Print.* canon **4** canon (*scripture*)

канòн² *m Mus.* zither (*stringed intrument*)

канонàда *f* cannonade

канонизàција *f* **1** canonization **2** legalization, legitimization

канонзѝра *pf & impf* **1** to canonize **2** to legalize, legitimize

канòник -ци *m* canon; prelate

канòнски *adj* canonical; канонско право canon law

канòса *pf* to dye with henna/alkanet

каносỳва *impf of* каноса

канта *f* can, bin; pail, bucket; канта за ѓубре dustbin, *Am.* trash can

кантàвтор *m* chansonnier

кантàр *m* steelyard, balance; ❑ мери вошки на кантар to split hairs, cavil

кантàрион *m Bot.* **1** (Hypericum perforatum) St John's wort **2** (Centaurium umbellatum) common centaury, lesser centaury, pink centaury

кантàрка *f* kind of pear

кантàрница *f* workshop for making scales (steelyards)

кантàрџија -ии *m* weigher; maker or repairer of scales (steelyards)

кантарџилница *f see* кантарница

кантàта *f Mus.* cantata

кантѝна *f* canteen

кантинèр *m* canteen worker

кантòн *m* canton

кантри-музика *f* country-and-western music

канỳ *n* canoe

кануѝст *m* canoeist

канцелàр *m* chancellor

канцелàрија -ии *f* office, bureau

канцелàриски *adj* office; канцелариска хартија stationery; канцелариско време office hours; ❑ канцелариски стил officialese; *pejor.* канцелариски глушец pen-pusher

канцелàрштина *f* red tape

канцер *m Med.* cancer

канцерогèн *adj Med.* carcinogenic

канцерòзен *adj Med.* cancerous

канцòна *f Mus.* canzone

канџа *f* **1** claw; *fig.* grip **2** boat-hook

кањòн *m* canyon

каолѝн *m* kaolin

капа *f* **1** cap; ❑ си ја има мувата на капата to give the game away; to have a guilty conscience; крои некому капа to decide s.o.'s fate; накриви капа! take it easy! don't worry! при двајца татковци, детето останува без капа *prov.* too many cooks spoil the broth; нема ништо под капата to have nothing between one's ears; полна капа more than enough; quite enough; симнува некому капа to take off one's hat to s.o.

капàвец *m sl.* clap, gonorrhoea

капàвица *f* **1** rain-water **2** drip, leak **3** *fig.* wanderer; tramp, vagabond

капàк -ци *m* **1** cover; lid; ❑ тој става капак на сè he has an answer to everything; како капак на сè to crown (cap) it all **2** (*на прозорец, врата*) shutter **3** (*на око*) eyelid **4** (*на меб*) flap

капàклија *adj indecl. colloq.* having a lid, covered

капàкчија -ии *f colloq.* person who has a ready answer to everything

капàма *f Cul.* stew (*of lamb and spring onions*)

капàн *m* **1** trap, snare, mousetrap; ❑ падне в капан to fall into a trap **2** scales with pans

капàр *m* deposit, security; pledge, earnest; advance payment; down payment

капàроса *pf* to reserve by paying a deposit; *Austral.* to lay-by

капаросỳва *impf of* капароса

капацитèт *m* **1** capacity, capability, ability; творечки капацитет creative capacity **2** capacity, size, volume; *Elec.* capacitance; капацитет на бели дробови lung capacity **3** *fig.* expert, authority

капàче *n dim. of* капак

капе¹ *impf* **I** to bathe, bath *trans.* **II** – **ce** to bathe *intrans.*

капе² *impf* **1** to drip, leak; покривот капе the roof leaks; ❏ крв ми капе my heart bleeds **2** *fig.* (*за лисје*) to fall

капела[1] *f* **1** chapel **2** choir, orchestra **3** mortuary

капела[2] *f colloq., arch.* hat

капелан *m* chaplain

капелник -ци *m* band leader; bandmaster

капетан *m* captain, skipper, master; пристанишен капетан harbour-master

капетанија -ии *f* captaincy; captain's office; пристанишна капетанија harbour-master's office

капец -пци *m* top; peak

капидан *m arch.* leader, captain

капија -ии *f* gate; main entrance, portal

капилар *m* capillary

капиларен -рна *adj* capillary; капиларни садови capillary (blood) vessels

капина *f Bot.* (Rubus) blackberry, bramble (*bush and fruit*)

капинлив *adj* капинливо место, *see* капињак

капинов *adj* blackberry; капинов сок blackberry juice

капињак -ци *m* bramble thicket

капира *pf & impf* to understand, grasp, catch on

каписла *f* cartridge case; percussion cap (*of a toy gun*)

капистра *f* iron headstall (*on a halter*)

капитал *m* capital; ❏ мртов капитал idle capital; прави од нешто капитал to make capital out of s.th.; основен капитал fixed capital; обртен капитал working capital

капитален -лна *adj* capital; капитален ремонт major repairs; капитална изградба capital works; капитални вложувања capital investments;

капитализам -змот *m* capitalism

капитализира *pf & impf* to capitalize

капиталист *m* capitalist

капител *m* **1** capital, head (*of a pillar*) **2** *Print.* small capitals **3** chapter

капитен *m Sport.* captain (*of a team*)

капитулант *m* defeatist

капитулација *f* capitulation, surrender; безусловна капитулација unconditional surrender

капитулира *pf & impf* to capitulate

капица *f* **1** *dim. of* капа **2** pod, shell **3** stack, rick

капиџик -ци *m* side gate

капка *f* **1** drop; ❏ млад како капка as fresh as a daisy; капка во преполна чаша last straw; the straw that broke the camel's back; капка по капка вирче *prov.* many a mickle makes a muckle **2** stain, spot

капладиса *pf* to line; to hem, border

капладисува *impf of* капладиса

каплама *f* lining

каплар *m Mil.* corporal

капнат *pt* exhausted, worn out, tired out

капне *pf* капна *aor.* **1** to drip, leak **2** to get tired, exhausted, worn out; капне од работа to become worn out

капнува *impf of* капне

капнувачка *f* exhaustion

каприц & каприш *m* caprice, whim, capriciousness

каприциозен -зна *adj* capricious, wilful, contrary

каприциозност *f* capriciousness

каприцира се *pf & impf* to become (be) capricious

капричио *n Mus.* capriccio

капс *m see* запек

капсла *f see* каписла

капсула *f* capsule

каптажа *f* collection, catchment (*of water*)

каптира *pf & impf* to collect, catch (*water*)

капула *f* horse-cloth

капут *m* overcoat

капче[1] *n dim. of* капа

капче[2] *n dim. of* капка; droplet

капчест *adj* drop-shaped

кара[1] *f* ammunition waggon

кара[2] *adj indecl. arch.* black; кара севда unrequited love; кара смрт *poet.* tragic death

кара[3] *impf* **I 1** to reprimand, scold, berate **2** *dial.* to swear (*use bad language*) **II – се 1** to get angry **2** to quarrel

кара[4] *impf dial. see* тера

карабатак -ци *m* leg (*of a bird*)

карабин *m* carbine

карабинер *m* carabineer, carabinier

карабинка *f see* карабин

караван *m* **1** caravan, camel-train **2** caravan, house-trailer, mobile home **3** (*кола*) *Am., Austral.* station wagon, *Brit.* estate car

каравана *f* shallow copper vessel for food

карагрош *m arch.* old Turkish silver coin

караконџол *m colloq.* **1** vampire **2** evil person

караконџола *f colloq.* **1** witch, female vampire **2** evil woman

карактер *m* character, nature, disposition; type; лош карактер bad character; тврд карактер firm disposition; човек со карактер strong personality, person with character; прашањето доби поинаков карактер the problem took on a different character

карактерен -рна *adj* honest, reliable; карактерен човек honest person; man of good character

карактеризација *f* characterization

карактеризира *pf & impf* **I** to characterize, describe **II – се** to be characterized (*co – by*)

карактеристика *f* **1** characteristic, distinguishing mark **2** description; reference, letter of recommendation **3** *Math.* characteristic

карактеристичен -чна *adj* characteristic, typical

карактерност *f* honesty, reliability

карамбол *m* collision, crush, clash; (*во билијар*) cannon, *Am.* carom

карамела *f* caramel

карамфил *m see* каранфил

караница *f* quarrel; tiff; bickering

карантин *m* quarantine

каранфил *m Bot.* (Dianthus caryophyllus) carnation

карар *m arch.* measure, order; јаде со карар to eat moderately

карат *m* carat

карате *n* karate

каратист *m* karate expert

караула *f* watch-tower; guardhouse

карачка *f see* караница

караш *Zool.* (Carassius carassius) crucian <carp>

карба *f see* караница

карбид *m Chem.* carbide

карбидски *adj* carbide; карбидска ламба acetylene lamp

карбитен -тна *adj* carbide

карбол *m Chem.* phenol, carbolic acid

карболен -лна *adj* carbolic; карболна киселина carbolic acid

карбон *m* carbon

карбона́т *m Chem.* carbonate

карбонизи́ра *pf & impf* to carbonize

карбони́т *m* explosive used in mining

карбонски *adj* carbon

карбура́тор *m Tech.* carburettor

карван *m* convoy; caravan, camel-train; parade, pageant; (*црковен*) procession

карвански *adj* caravan

карванџија -ии *m* caravan leader

карго *n* cargo

кардан *m Tech.* universal joint

кардина́л *m* cardinal

кардина́лен -лна *adj* cardinal; кардинални измени fundamental changes

кардина́лски *adj* of <a> cardinal; кардиналски чин rank of cardinal

кардиогра́м *m Med.* cardiogram

кардиогра́ф *m Med.* cardiograph

кардиоло́г -зи *m Med.* cardiologist

каре́ *n* 1 square; rectangle 2 *Cul.* loin; јагнешко каре loin of lamb

кариér *m* gallop, career

кариéра *f* career (*at work*); ❏ прави кариера to make a career

кариери́зам -змот *m* careerism

кариери́ст *m* careerist

кариеристички *adj* careerist

кариес *m Med.* caries

каријати́да *f* caryatid

карика *f* 1 link (*also fig.*) 2 (*usu. pl*) *Gymnastics* rings

карикату́ра *f* caricature, cartoon

карикатури́ст *m* caricaturist, cartoonist

карики́ра *pf & impf* to caricature, distort

кари́ра *pf & impf* to chequer (checker)

кари́ран *pt* chequered (checkered); кариран фустан chequered dress

карлица *f Anat.* pelvis

кармин *m* 1 lipstick 2 carmine, crimson

карминиса *pf* (*усни*) to apply lipstick

карминисува *impf of* карминиса

карнева́л *m* carnival, masquerade

карнева́лски *adj* carnival; карневалска вечер carnival evening

карнер *m* frill, flounce

каро *n Cards* diamond

каросерија -ии *f* bodywork, body

карпа *f* 1 rock, boulder; cliff; face; escarpment 2 *fig.* strapping fellow

Карпа́ти *pl* Carpathians, Carpathian Mountains

карпатски *adj* Carpathian

карпест *adj* rocky

карпуз *m dial. see* лубеница

карст *m* karst; rocky soil; rocky terrain

карстен -стна *adj* karst; карстен предел karst region

карта¹ *f* 1 map; топографска карта topographical map; авто карта road map 2 ticket; возна карта rail/bus/tram *etc.* ticket; повратна карта return ticket 3 card; лична карта identity card; членска карта membership card; визит-карта visiting card; business card; дописна карта postcard, *see* картичка 4 playing-card; игра карти to play cards; ❏ гледа на

карти to tell s.o.'s fortune; игра на последната карта to play one's last card; to play one's ace (trump card); игра со отворени карти to put one's cards on the table; му оди на карти he is lucky at cards; to be on a winning streak

карта² *f* wine flask

карта се *impf* to play cards; to gamble

картал *m Zool.* (Aegypius monachus) black vulture

карташија -ии *m colloq.* card-player; gambler

картел *m Econ.* cartel

картер *m Tech.* crankcase

картеч *m* case-shot, canister

картечен -чна *adj* картечен оган machine-gun fire

картечница *f* machine-gun

картичка *f* postcard; card

картогра́ф *m* cartographer

картографија *f* cartography

картон *m* 1 cardboard; pasteboard; millboard 2 card (*for card index*); file

картона́жа *f* 1 cardboard products 2 cardboard factory

картони́ра *pf & impf* to paste on to cardboard; to bind (*a book*) in boards

картоп *m Bot.* (Viburnum opulus sterile) snowball-tree, guelder rose

картоте́ка *f* card index, card catalogue, card file

картоте́чен -чна *adj* (of a) card index (catalogue, file)

карфио́л *m Bot.* cauliflower

карцер *m* jail (*Brit.* gaol), prison

карчо -овци *m* name of black horse or ox

карши *adv & prep colloq.* opposite, vis-à-vis ; across; карши-карши right opposite, vis-à-vis; седна карши мене he sat down opposite me

каршија *adv colloq.* од каршија opposite, vis-à-vis; across; седат од каршија they live opposite (us, each other); карши-каршија, *see* карши-карши

каршилак -ци *m colloq.* 1 dissuasion 2 waistcoat of homespun cloth 3 edge of linen, selvedge

каса¹ *f* cashbox; strong-box; cash register; till; ticket-office; (*во кино, театар*) booking-office

каса² *impf* 1 to bite 2 *fig.* to be sarcastic; to insult; to sting (*verbally*)

касаба *f arch.* provincial town

касај -аи *m* mouthful

касап *m* butcher

касапи *impf* to butcher (*also fig.*), slaughter

касапница *f* 1 (*кланица*) slaughterhouse, abattoir 2 *colloq.* (*месарница*) butcher's shop 3 *fig.* carnage

касапски *adj* butcher's; ❏ касапско куче stray dog

касарма *f see* касарна

касарна *f* barracks

касација *f* cassation; court of cassation

касио́нен -она *adj* cassation; касациона постапка cassation action; касационен суд court of cassation

касач *m* sarcastic person

касела *f arch. see* ковчег 1

касе́та *f* 1 box, strongbox; casket 2 tape, cassette

касиéр *m* cashier

касиéрка *f* (*fem. form*) *see* касиер

каси́на *f see* казино

каси́ра *pf & impf* to quash, annul, rescind

касичка *f* money box

каска *f* helmet

каска́да *f* 1 cascade 2 *Film* stunt

каскадер   *m Film* stunt man

каскандиса   *pf colloq. see* завиди

каскандисува   *impf of* каскандиса

касканџија   -ии *m colloq. see* зависник

каскет   *m see* качкет

каско   *adj indecl. in the expression:* каско осигу-руваље comprehensive insurance

касмет   *m colloq.* (*среќа*) luck, fortune; kismet; ❑ касметот му работи fortune favours him

касметлив   *adj colloq.* lucky

касметлија   *adj indecl. see* касметлив; касметлија човек lucky devil

каснатинка   *f* insect bite

касне   *pf* касна *aor.* **I 1** to bite; to sting (*also fig.*) ❑ змија ме касна I lost my temper; ме касна за срце he stung me to the quick; кој е каснат од змија, се плаши и од гуштерица *prov.* once bitten, twice shy **2** to take a bite of; to taste **II** – **се** to bite o.s. (*one's tongue, lip, etc.*)

касни   *impf* to be late, *see* доцни, задоцнува

касно   *adv* late, *see* доцна

касов   *adj* cash; касова книга ledger

Касписко Море (Езеро)   *n* Caspian Sea

каста   *f* caste

кастанети   *pl Mus.* castanets

кастел   *m* castle; fortress

кастелан   *m Hist.* castellan

кастиле   *adv colloq.* especially; on purpose

кастински   *adj* caste

кастрат   *m* eunuch, castrato; (*коњ*) gelding

кастрација   *f* castration

кастреж   *m* **1** pruning; trimming, clipping **2** pruned tree

кастреник   -ци *m* pruned, trimmed tree

кастреница   *f* stand of pruned trees

кастри   *impf* **1** to prune; to trim, clip, lop **2** *fig.* to scold, berate

кастрира   *pf & impf* to castrate, emasculate, geld

кат[1]   *m* **1** corner; nook; hideaway, retreat **2** place by the hearth (*in village houses*)

кат[2]   -ови, ката *m* **1** storey, floor; layer, ply **2** suit, change (*of clothes*); еден кат алишта two-piece suit **3** *dial.* time<s>; сто ката полошо a hundred times worse; два ката doubly

ката   *indecl. colloq.* every; ката вечер every evening; ката година every year; ❑ ката годинка новинка *joc.* a new baby every year

катадешен   -шна *adj colloq. see* катадневен

катадневен   -вна *adj colloq.* every day, daily

катаклизма   *f* cataclysm (*also fig.*)

катакомба   *f* (*usu. pl*) catacomb

катализа   *f Chem.* catalysis

катализатор   *m* catalyst

каталог   -зи *m* catalogue

каталогизира   *pf & impf* to catalogue

катана   *f colloq.* **1** large horse **2** *fig.* large woman

катанец   -нци *m* padlock

катаплазма   *f* cataplasm, poultice

катапулт   *m* catapult (*for launching carrier-borne aircraft*)

катар   *m Med.* catarrh; бронхијален катар bronchial catarrh

Катар   *m* Qatar

катаракт   *m* cataract (*also Med.*)

катарален   -лна *adj* catarrhal; катарална кашлица catarrhal cough

Катарец   -рци *m* Qatari

катарза   *f literary* catharsis

катарка[1]   *f* mast

катарка[2]   *f see* пуканка

Катарка   *f* (*fem. form*) *see* Катарец

катарски   *adj* Qatari

катастар   -три *m* cadastre, land register

катастрофа   *f* catastrophe

катастрофален   -лна *adj* catastrophic, disastrous

катафалка   *f* catafalque

категоризација   -ии *f* categorization

категорија   -ии *f* category, class; граматичка кате-горија grammatical category; мува категорија *Sport.* flyweight; лесна категорија *Sport.* lightweight

категориса   *pf* to categorize

категоричен   -чна *adj see* категорички

категорички   *adj* categorical; категорички импер-атив categorical imperative; категорички одговор explicit answer

катедра   *f* **1** lecturer's desk; (*подиум*) lectern **2** academic discipline **3** <academic> department; катедра за историја department of history **4** cath-edra (bishop's throne); chair (professorial position) ❑ зборува екс катедра to speak ex cathedra

катедрала   *f* cathedral

катедрален   -лна *adj* cathedral

катен   -тни *adj* катен заб *see* катник

катета   *f Geom.* leg (*of a right-angled triangle*)

кати   *impf* to husk (*maize, Am. corn*)

катил   -ли *m colloq. & adj indecl.* evil-doer, criminal; murderer

катинар   *m see* катанец

катихет   *m* catechist

катихизис   *m* catechism

катник   -ци *m* molar

катода   *f* cathode

католизира   *pf & impf* to convert to Catholicism *trans.*

католик   -ци *m* Catholic

католицизам   -змот *m* Roman Catholicism

католичка   *f* (*fem. form*) *see* католик

католички   *adj* Catholic

катран   *m* **1** tar, pitch; црн како катран as black as pitch/soot **2** grease, lubricant

катраник   -ци *m & катраница   *f* tar can

катраноса   *pf* to tar

катраносува   *impf of* катраноса

катранџија   -ии *m* tar maker; tar dealer

катун[1]   *m* nomad, gypsy

катун[2]   *m* kind of thick cotton material

катунка   *f* (*fem. form*) *see* катун[1]

каубој   -ои *m* cowboy

каубојски   *adj* cowboy; каубојски филм cowboy film, western

кауза   *f* cause, concern

каузален   -лна *adj* causal; causative

каузалитет   *m* causality

каузалност   *f* causality; принципот на каузалноста the principle of causality

каури   *impf arch.* to convert *trans.* to Christianity; to baptize

каурин   -ри *m arch.* non-Muslim, infidel; Christian

каурка   *f arch.* (*fem. form*) *see* каурин

каурма *f see* кавурма

каурски *adj* non-Muslim; Christian

каустичен -чна *adj* caustic; каустична сода caustic soda

кауција *f* deposit, security; (*при притвор*) bail

кауч *m* couch

каучук *m* rubber; природен/синтетички каучук natural/synthetic rubber

кафе *n* 1 coffee 2 café, coffee-house, coffee-shop

кафеав *adj* coffee-coloured, brown

кафеана *f arch.* tavern, inn

кафеански *adj arch.* tavern, inn; ❑ кафеански политичар bar-room politician

кафез *m* cage

кафен *adj* coffee; coffee-coloured, brown; кафена лажица coffee-spoon

кафене *n dial. see* кафе 2, кафеана

кафенце *n hyp. of* кафе

кафеџија -ии *m* 1 tavern (inn) proprietor, manager 2 coffee lover

кафеџика *f* (*fem. form*) *see* кафеџија

кафтан *m* caftan (kaftan)

каца *f* (*wooden*) tub, vat

кацар *m see* качар

кација -ии *f* coal shovel; poker

качак -ци *m arch.* 1 renegade, apostate, turncoat; outlaw 2 smuggled tobacco

качамак -ци *m* polenta

качар *m* cooper, barrel-maker

качарница *f* cooper's workshop, cooperage

каче *n dim.* small barrel, keg

качествен *adj* 1 high-quality, high-grade, top-quality 2 qualitative

качество *n* quality

качи¹ *impf* 1 to hang (*on a nail, etc.*) 2 to knock (drive) in (*a nail, post, etc.*)

качи² *pf* I to lift, raise; to put up; качи цена to raise a price II – се to rise, climb; to go up; (*на*) to get on; to mount; се качи на дрво to climb a tree; се качи в автобус to get on a bus; се качи во авион to board a plane; цените се качија the prices rose; ❑ ми се качи на глава he/it got on my nerves

качкет *m* cap

качор *m* 1 tooth that has grown crooked 2 old ram with crooked horns

качорлив *adj* качорливи заби crooked teeth

качува (се) *impf of* качи (се)

качулка *f* 1 hood 2 tuft, crest

качунка *f Bot.* crocus

каша *f* 1 porridge; mash; mush; gruel; pap; каша од пченкарно брашно maize flour porridge, mush; ❑ каша ми стана во главата I feel confused, I feel all in a muddle; каша ќе те направам! I'll make mincemeat of you! во иста каша in the same boat; во каша е to be in dire straits/hot water; убава каша a fine kettle of fish 2 mixture; blend; mass, pulp; бетонска каша concrete mixture 3 *fig.* confusion, muddle, chaos

кашав *adj* 1 mushy; кашаво време wet weather 2 *fig.* soft, delicate, oversensitive

кашави се *impf* to soften, melt *intrans.*

кашест *adj* mushy; pulpy; кашесто јадење mushy food/dish

каширa *pf & impf* to cover with paper; to conceal

кашка *impf* I to dirty II – се 1 to get dirty 2 to wallow, splash *intrans.*

кашкав *adj* dirty, muddy; soiled

кашкавал *m kashkaval*, hard yellow cheese

кашкаваџија -ии *m* maker of *kashkaval* cheese

кашла *impf* to cough

кашле -евци *m see* кашло

кашлица *f* cough; сува кашлица dry cough; црна (голема, магарешка) кашлица whooping cough; ❑ не е <баш> мачкина кашлица not to be sneezed/sniffed at

кашличав *adj* coughing

кашло -овци *m colloq.* cougher, person who coughs

кашљичар *m Bot.* (Ruscus aculeatus) butcher's broom

кашмир *m* cashmere

квадрант *m Math.* quadrant

квадрат *m Math.* square; ❑ дига на квадрат to square

квадратен -тна *adj* square; квадратен корен square root; квадратен метар square metre

квадратура *f* squaring; quadrature; area (*of room, etc.*); квадратура на кругот squaring the circle

квази- *adv* (*in compounds*) quasi-

квазимодо *m* Quasimodo, hunchback

квак-квак *interj* croak! quack!

квака¹ *f* doorknob; latch

квака² *impf* (*за жаба, гавран*) to croak; (*за патка*) to quack

квакне *pf* квакна *aor.* (*за жаба, гавран*) to croak; (*за патка*) to quack

квакнува *impf of* квакне, *see* квака²

квалитативен -вна *adj* qualitative

квалитет *m* quality

квалитетен -тна *adj* high-quality, high-grade

квалификација -ии *f* qualification

квалификационен -она *adj* qualifying; квалификационен натпревар qualifying match; qualifying competition

квалификува *pf & impf* I to qualify, train, prepare *trans.*; школувањето го квалификува за електричар his training equipped him to be an electrician II – се to qualify *intrans.*; се квалификува за светско првенство to qualify for the world championship

квалификуван *pt & adj* qualified; skilled; квалификуван работник skilled worker;

квалифицира (се) *pf & impf see* квалификува (се)

квант *m Phys.* quantum

квантитативен -вна *adj* quantitative

квантитет *m* quantity

квантум *m* quantum

кварт *m* quarter, neighbourhood

кварта *f Mus.* fourth (*interval*)

квартал *m* quarter (*of a year*), three-month period

квартален -лна *adj* quarterly

квартет *m Mus.* quartet; гудачки квартет string quartet

квартира *f* 1 (*стан*) flat, apartment 2 (*војнички логор*) quarters

кварц *m* quartz; flint

кварцен -цна *adj* quartz; кварцен часовник quartz clock; кварцна ламба (кварц-ламба) quartz lamp

кварцит *m* quartzite

квас *m* 1 yeast, leaven 2 *kvas* (Russian rye beer)

квасец *m* yeast; пивски квасец yeast for making beer; ❑ расте како квасец to feel pleased with o.s.; to act the cock of the walk; to act like a dog with two tails

кваси *impf* to ferment; to put in yeast

квасник -ци *m* leavened bread

квачи *impf* **1** to hatch, brood, incubate *trans.* **2** *fig.* to loaf, idle; to waste time; ❑ квачам јајца (*in reply to што правиш?*) I'm minding my own business

квачка *f* **1** brooding hen **2** *colloq.* Квачката the Pleiades, *see* Власи

квекер *m* Quaker

квестионáр *m* questionnaire

квестор *m* quaestor

квечер *adv* in the evening, towards evening

квечерина[1] *f* eve; во квечерината на војната on the eve of the war

квечерина[2], **квечерју**, **квечерум** *adv see* квечер

квиз *m* quiz; (*occasionally as indec. adj*) квиз емисија quiz programme

квикне *pf* квикна *aor. see* квичи

квикнува *impf of* квикне

квинта *f Mus.* fifth (*interval*)

квинтáл *m* quintal

квинтéт *m Mus.* quintet; вокален квинтет vocal quintet

квислинг -зи *m* quisling

квислиншки *adj* quisling; квислиншка влада quisling government

квит *adv* quits, even; сега сме квит now we are quits

квитанција -ии *f* receipt; acknowledgement

квитíра *pf & impf* **I 1** to settle (*an account*), pay (*a debt*) **2** to break (*со некого – with s.o.*); to terminate **II** – *ce* (*раздолжи се*) to settle accounts

квичи *impf* (*за прасе*) to squeal; (*за куче*) to yelp

кворум *m* quorum

квота *f* quota

кг *abbr.* (*килограм*) kg

кегла *f* bowling pin; tenpin

кедар -дри *m Bot.* (Cedrus) cedar

кеј -јови *m* quay; dock; wharf

кекс *m* biscuit

келнер *m* waiter

келнерка *f* waitress

кељ *m Bot.* (Brassica oleracea acephala) kale, borecole

Кембриџ *m* Cambridge

кембрички *adj* Cambridge *attrib.*, Cantabrigian

кенгур *m Zool.* kangaroo

Кениец -ијци *m* Kenyan

Кенија *f* Kenya

кенијка *f* (*fem. form*) *see* Кениец

кениски *adj* Kenyan

кенка *impf colloq.* to whimper, snivel, whine

кенкало *m colloq.* whimperer, sniveller, complainer

кенозоик *m Geol.* Cenozoic era

кепе *n* coarse felt cape

кепец *m* dwarf, midget; gnome

керал *m see* килер

керамида *f see* ќерамида

керамика *f* ceramics, pottery

керамичар *m* potter, ceramist

керван *m see* карван

кермес *m* fair; fête

керозин *m* kerosene

кеса *f & кесе* *n see* ќесе; ❑ го отвора кесето to splurge

кесон *m Tech.* caisson

кец *m colloq.* (*во карти*) асе; (*школска оцена*) one (*out of five, hence = 'unsatisfactory'*), fail; доаѓа некому како кец на десетка to suit s.o. down to the ground

кеч *m* **1** all-in wrestling **2** *Mus.* catch

кече *n* Albanian (*white*) cap

кечига *f Zool.* (Acipenser ruthenus) sturgeon

кибар *adj indecl. colloq.* noble, fine; polished, refined, pure

кибицéр *m* onlooker, observer; kibitzer

кибицíра *impf* **I** to watch, look at; to ogle **II** – *ce* to ogle (make eyes at) each other

кибрит *m* <safety> match

кибритче *n dim. of* кибрит

кива *impf* to sneeze

кивавица *f* cold (*in the head*)

кивавичав *adj* having a cold; sneezing; prone to colds

кивка *impf* to sneeze

кивне *pf* кивна *aor.* to sneeze

кивнува *impf of* кивне

кивор *m arch.* **1** coffin **2** reliquary (*containing icons and an icon lamp*)

киднапер *m* kidnapper

киднапíра *pf & impf* to kidnap

Киев *m* Kiev

киеванец -нци *m* person from Kiev

киеванка *f* (*fem. form*) *see* киеванец

киевски *adj* Kiev *attrib.*

кијавица *f see* кивавица

кијамет *m colloq.* bad weather

ки-ки *interj* tee-hee!

кикирига *impf see* кукурига

кикирика *f dial. see* кикиритка 1; ❑ нема ни за кикирики to work for peanuts; танте за кикирики you scratch my back, I'll scratch yours

кикиритка *f* **1** *Bot.* (Arachis hypogaea) peanut, ground-nut **2** *see* кикиришка

кикиришка *f* comb, crest (*on a fowl*)

киклоп *m* Cyclops, giant

кикот *m* giggling; giggle

кикоти се *impf* to giggle, titter; to chuckle

кикотница *f* giggling

кикс *m* blunder, *faux pas*

киксер *m* blunderer

киксíра *pf & impf* to blunder, commit a *faux pas*

кила *f Med.* rupture, hernia

килав *adj* **1** hernial; ruptured **2** mediocre, inept; при многу баби детето килаво излегува *prov.* too many cooks spoil the broth

килави се *impf* to rupture o.s.; *fig.* to overwork *intrans.*

килáжа *f* weight; проблем со килажа weight problem

килер *m* pantry; cellar

килерче *n dim. of* килер

килибар *m* amber

килим *m* rug, carpet; персиски килим Persian rug; ❑ црвен килим red carpet

килимар *m* carpet maker/seller

килимарка *f* (*fem. form*) *see* килимар

килимарница *f* carpet workshop/factory

килимарство *n* carpet-making industry

кило *n* 1 kilo, kilogram; кило брашно a kilo of flour 2 measure for grain (*approximately 130 kg*)

киловат *m* kilowatt; киловат-час kilowatt-hour

килограм *m* kilogram

километар -три *m* kilometre

километарски *adj* kilometre<-long>

километра́жа *f* distance in kilometres (cf. mileage)

ким *m Bot.* (Carum carvi) caraway

кима *impf* 1 to nod (*one's head*) 2 to wink

кимка *f colloq.* pique, ill-feeling, resentment; има кимка на некого to nurse a grudge against s.o.

кимне *pf* кимна *aor.* 1 to nod 2 to wink

кимнува *impf of* кимне

кимо́но *n* kimono

Кина *f* China

кине *impf* **I** 1 to tear, rip *trans.* 2 to pick, pluck (*flowers*) 3 *fig.* to anger; to get on s.o.'s nerves **II – се** 1 to tear *intrans.* 2 *fig.* to break *intrans.*; to snap *intrans.*; ми се кине срцево my heart is breaking; ❑ кај што е тенко, таму се кине a chain is as strong as its weakest link 3 *fig.* to get angry, lose one's temper

Кинез *m* Chinese <person>

кинематогра́ф *m obs.* cinematograph; cinema

кинематографија *f* cinematography

Кинеска *adj* (*fem. form*) *see* Кинез

кинески *adj* Chinese

кинетика *f Phys.* kinetics

кинетички *adj* kinetic; кинетичка енергија kinetic energy

кинин *m* quinine

кинис *m colloq.* departure; на кинис on leaving

киниса *pf colloq.* to depart, leave

кинисува *impf of* киниса

кинкалерија -ии *f* ironmongery, hardware

кино *n* cinema; оди на кино to go to the cinema (to the pictures)

киноопера́тор *m Film* projectionist

кинопрое́ктор *m Film* projector

кинотека *f* film library

киоск -ци *m* kiosk

кип *m* statue

кипар *adj f.p.* beautiful, fine

Кипар *m* Cyprus

кипарис *m Bot.* (Cupressus sempervirens) Italian cypress <tree>

кипарски *adj* Cypriot

кипеж *m see* вриеж

кипер *m* dump truck

кипи *impf see* врие

кипне *pf* кипна *aor. fig.* to boil up, flare <up>

кипра *f* beautiful girl, beauty

Кипранец -нци *m* Cypriot

Кипранка *f* (*fem. form*) *see* Кипранец

кипри се *impf* to adorn o.s. excessively; to overdress *intrans.*

кир[1] *m colloq.* uncleanliness (*of body and clothes*)

кир[2] *m arch.* sire, squire, master (*usu. with Christian name*)

кирација -ии *m* 1 carter 2 tenant

кирета́жа *f Med.* curettage

Киргиз *m* Kirghiz

Киргиска *f* (*fem. form*) *see* Киргиз

киргиски *adj* Kirghiz

Киргиста́н *m* Kyrgyzstan, Kirghizia

киргиста́нски *adj* Kyrgyzstani

кирија -ии *f* 1 cartage, freight charges 2 rent; земе куќа под кирија to rent a house

кирилица *f* Cyrillic <script>

кирилски *adj* Cyrillic; кирилско писмо the Cyrillic script

кирјоса *pf see* кирлиса

кирка *f* pickaxe

кирлив *adj colloq.* dirty, filthy

кирлиса *pf colloq.* **I** to soil, dirty **II – се** to get dirty

кирлисува (се) *impf of* кирлиса (се)

кисел *adj* sour (*also fig.*); acid; *fig.* wry; кисела вода mineral water; кисела зелка pickled cabbage (sauerkraut); кисело млеко yog<h>urt; кисела насмевка wry smile; ❑ краставици кисели! rubbish! nonsense! му се стори киселиот his whim has been satisfied; *Chem.* кисела реакција acid reaction; *Bot.* кисело дрво (Rhus coriara/typhina) sumac<h>

киселачка *f* crab-apple

киселец -лци *m* 1 leavened bread 2 *Bot.* (Rumex acetosa) sorrel

кисели *impf* **I** to make sour; to pickle; to marinate; to acidify **II – се** to go (become) sour; *fig.* to get upset

киселина *f* 1 *Chem.* acid 2 sourness 3 vinegar 4 (*во стомак*) heartburn

киселица *f* 1 *see* киселачка 2 *see* киселец 2 3 sour wine

киселичок -чка *adj dim. see* киселкав

киселкав *adj dim.* sourish, tart

киселница *f* sour cabbage, sauerkraut

киска *f see* китка

кискарка *f* tasselled shawl

кислина *f* dressing of garlic, vinegar and oil

кисловина *f* sour odour

кислород *m Chem.* oxygen

кислороден -дна *adj Chem.* oxygen; кислородни соединенија oxygen compounds

кислоса *pf* **I** to pickle, marinate **II – се** to turn sour; *fig.* to get upset

кислосува (се) *impf of* кислоса (се)

кисне *impf* **I** 1 to go sour 2 to get wet; кисне на дождот to get wet in the rain 3 (*за место*) to rise, prove *intrans.*; to ferment *intrans.*; кисне лебот the bread is rising 4 *fig.* to loaf about, be idle; to hang about **II – се** to get wet

кит[1] *m see* укит

кит[2] *m Zool.* whale

кит[3] *m* putty

китаб *m arch.* (*Muslim religious*) book; records

китен[1] *adj f.p.* beautiful; adorned

китен[2] -тна *adj* flowery

китест *adj see* китен -тна

кити *impf* **I** 1 to decorate, adorn, bedeck; кити елка to decorate a Christmas tree 2 to make a bunch (*of flowers*) 3 to dress beautifully/gaudily *trans.* **II – се** 1 to adorn o.s. (*with flowers*); ❑ се кити со туѓи перја to be an impostor 2 to dress beautifully/gaudily *intrans.*

китило *n* ornament, decoration

китица *f* nosegay, posy

китка *f* 1 bunch; bouquet; китка цвеќиња bunch of flowers; китка магдонос bunch of parsley; ❑ таа е китка she's very pretty 2 (*на капа*) tassel 3 (*дланка*) hand, palm 4 *fig.* collection; series; китка народни песни series of folk songs 5 *dial.* flower 6 stanza

киткиритка *f see* кикиритка 1

китнест *adj* ornate, florid

кифла *f* (*type of*) roll, croissant; кифла со путер roll and butter

кич *m* kitsch

киче *n* 1 clapper, tongue (*of a bell*) 2 weight (*on scales*)

кичер *m* 1 lock (*of hair*), tuft 2 bunch, cluster (*of berries, grapes on a twig*)

кишка *f* cleaning cloth (*for rifles, shotguns, etc.*)

клава *impf* (*става*) *of* кладе

клавијатура *f* keyboard

клавир *m Mus.* piano

клавирист *m Mus.* pianist

клавиристка *f Mus.* (*fem. form*) *see* клавирист

клавичембало *n Mus.* harpsichord

клавиш *m* key (*of piano, typewriter, etc.*)

клада *f* log, block (*of wood*)

кладе *pf* (*стави*) to put, place; ❑ кладе крст на нешто to write s.th. off

кладенец -нци *m* spring; well

клади се *impf* to bet, wager; се клади на трки to bet at the races; ❑ се клади во cè to bet one's bottom dollar; to stake everything

кладиво *n Sport.* hammer; фрлач на кладиво hammer thrower

кланик -ци *m* place by the fireplace where firewood is stored

кланица *f* 1 slaughterhouse (*also fig.*), abattoir 2 *colloq.* cattle for slaughtering

кланца се *impf see* клацка се 2

клања *impf* I to bow *trans.*, bend; клања глава to bow one's head II – се 1 (*with dat.*) to bow (*to*); to greet (*s.o.*); to respect, revere 2 to pray (*while bowing; of Muslims*) 3 (*with dat.*) to bow and scrape, cringe (*before*); to curry favour (*with*)

клање *n see* колеж[1]

клапа[1] *f* trap, snare; mousetrap

клапа[2] *impf* 1 to flap, flop, flip-flop; чевлите му клапаат his shoes slap against the floor 2 to drag o.s. along; to totter, stagger 3 *fig.* to babble, chatter; доста клапаше! enough of your chatter!

клапка[1] *f see* клопотарец

клапка[2] *impf see* клапа[2] 1

клапнат *pt* exhausted, worn out; enfeebled

клапне *pf* клапна *aor.* 1 to become exhausted; to tire *intrans.* 2 to flop (*на – down/on*)

клапнува *impf of* клапне

клапушест *adj* clumsy, awkward

клапушко -овци *m see* клапчо

клапчо -овци *m colloq.* oaf; dolt

кларинет *m Mus.* clarinet

кларинетист *m Mus.* clarinettist

клас[1] *m* 1 ear, spike (*of corn, Am. grain*); пченицата пушта клас the wheat is forming ears 2 maize cob, corn-cob

клас[2] *m* 1 class (*in secondary school*) 2 classroom

класа *f* class; работничка класа working class; втора класа (*во воз*) second class (*in a train*); тутун од прва класа first-class tobacco; *Zool.* класа цицачи class of mammals; ❑ за класа подобар a cut above

класатица *f see* класатка

класатка *f Bot.* 1 (Carex) sedge 2 (Stachys) woundwort

класен -сна *adj* class; класна борба class struggle; класен раководител class teacher, form master

класест *adj* ear-like, spike-like

класи *impf* to form ears (*of cereals*); житото класи the wheat is forming ears

класик -ци *m* 1 classic 2 classical scholar

класика *f* the classics, classical literature and art

класина *f* rye straw

класира *pf & impf* to sort, class, classify

класификација *f* classification

класификува & класифицира *pf & impf* to classify

класицизам -змот *m* classicism

класичар *m* classical scholar

класичен -чна *adj* classical, classic; класични јазици classics; класична музика classical music

класов *adj* class; класова борба class struggle

клати *impf* I to shake *trans.*; to swing; to nod; ❑ клати глава to shake one's head; си ги клати нозете to do nothing, be idle II – се 1 to shake, wobble *intrans.*; to be shaky, loose, wobbly; забот се клати the tooth is loose 2 to stagger; to drag o.s. along; to be hardly able to walk

клатно *n* clapper, tongue (*of a bell*); pendulum

клаузула *f* clause, stipulation, rider

клаустрофобија *f* claustrophobia

клацка *impf* I 1 to rock, swing *trans.* 2 to splash, lap, slop (*inside a vessel*) *intrans.* II – се 1 to see-saw 2 to stagger; to drag o.s. along; to be hardly able to walk

клацкалица & клацкалка *f* see-saw

клашен *adj see* клашнен

клашенец -нци *m see* клашеник

клашеник -ци *m* woman's short-sleeved jacket (*of heavy cloth*)

клашна *f* heavy cloth, coarse fabric; felt

клашнар *m* maker of heavy cloth (coarse fabric)

клашнен *adj* of heavy cloth (coarse fabric); клашнени панталони thick trousers

клашненик -ци *m see* клашеник

клашник -ци *m see* клашеник

клашно *n see* клашна

клевета *f* slander, calumny; жртва на клевета victim of slander

клевети *impf* to slander

клеветник -ци *m* slanderer

клеветница *f* (*fem. form*) *see* клеветник

клеветнички *adj* slanderous; клеветничка кампања campaign of slander; клеветнички обвинувања slanderous accusations

клевне *pf* клевне *aor. see* клапне

клевнува *impf of* клевне

клед *m* pantry; cellar

клек *m Bot.* (Pinus montana) mountain pine

клека *f Bot.* (Juniperus communis) <common> juniper

клекав *adj* 1 weak, feeble 2 incapable, unfit; incompetent

клекне *pf* клекна *aor.* 1 to kneel down; to squat, crouch 2 *fig.* to fail, weaken; to become exhausted

клекнува *impf of* клекне

клекум *adv f.p.* kneeling

клекуш -овци *m colloq.* 1 *see* клечо 2 untidy, slovenly person

клекуша *f* kind of folk-dance

клема _f_ clamp; securing bolt

клен _m_ **1** _Bot._ maple, _esp._ (Acer campestre) field maple **2** _Zool._ (Leuciscus/Squalius cephalus) chub

кленѕа _impf see_ кленца

кленца _impf colloq._ to stagger, totter, sway when walking

клепа _impf_ **1** to strike (_a bell_) with a clapper **2** to beat out, sharpen (_scythe, sickle_); to hammer **3** to carve, chisel (_on stone_) **4** _fig._ to babble, chatter **5** _fig._ to slander **6** (_со очи_) to blink

клепало _n_ **1** rattle; clapper **2** _fig._ chatterbox, babbler

клепач[1] _m_ **1** one who strikes/sharpens/carves **2** _fig._ slanderer

клепач[2] _m see_ клепка

клепка _f_ **1** eyelash **2** eyelid

клепне _pf_ клепна _aor._ **1** to strike **2** _fig._ to hit, wallop **3** (_with dat._) to wink (_at_); to blink

клепнува _impf of_ клепне

клептома́н _m_ kleptomaniac

клептоманија _f_ kleptomania

клер _m_ clergy

клерик -ци _m_ cleric, clergyman, priest

клерика́лен -лна _adj Pol._ clerical; клерикална партија clerical party

клерика́лец -лци _m Pol._ clericalist

клерикали́зам -змот _m Pol._ clericalism

клет[1] _m see_ клед

клет[2] _adj_ cursed, damned; wretched, unfortunate

клетва _f_ **1** curse, malediction **2** oath; ❑ даде (положи) клетва to swear an oath; прекрши клетва to break one's word; крива клетва perjury

клетвеник -ци _m_ **1** pledger, s.o. bound by oath **2** _Hist._ vassal

клетвопрестапник -ци _m_ perjurer

клетка _f_ **1** cage, coop **2** square (_in a grid_) **3** cell (_also Biol._); основна клетка basic cell

клетник -ци _m_ wretch, poor chap

клетница _f_ wretched woman

клечавица _f colloq._ diarrhoea; dysentery

клечешкум _adv_ kneeling; squatting, crouching

клечи _impf_ to kneel; to squat, crouch

клечка _f_ **1** splinter **2** toothpick **3** _joc._ bigwig

клечо -овци _m colloq._ weakling; irresolute person, ditherer

клешти _pl_ клешта _f_ pincers; pliers; tongs; забарски клешти dentist's forceps; ковачки клешти blacksmith's tongs

клешти се _impf colloq._ (_with dat._) to grin (_at_); to laugh maliciously; to make faces (_at_)

кливка _impf see_ клинка

клие́нт _m_ client, customer

клиенте́ла _f_ clientèle

клизма _f_ enema

клик _m poet._ cry, shriek (_of joy_); call, scream (_of a bird_)

клика[1] _f_ clique

клика[2] _impf of_ кликне

кликне _pf_ кликна _aor._ to cry, shriek, scream (_with joy, of a bird_)

клима[1] _f_ climate; континентална клима continental climate; клима апарат air-conditioner

клима[2] _impf see_ кима

климакс _m_ climax

климактериум _m_ menopause, climacteric

климат _m see_ клима[1]

климатизација _f_ air-conditioning

климатологија _f_ climatology

климатски _adj_ climatic; климатски услови climatic conditions; климатско место climatic spa

клин _m_ **1** wedge; клин со клин се избива _prov._ like cures like; you have to fight fire with fire **2** (_на облека_) gusset, gore

клинест _adj_ wedge-shaped; клинесто писмо cuneiform script

клинец -нци _m_ nail, peg; ❑ тресе клинци to shiver with cold

клиника _f_ clinic; хируршка клиника surgical clinic

клинички _adj_ clinical; клиничко испитување clinical examination

клинка _impf_ **1** to hop <on one foot>; to hobble **2** _fig._ to drag o.s. along; to stagger; (_no_) to follow; клинка по некого

клинкачка _f_ kind of _oro_ (dance)

клинови _pl Med._ torsion of a testis (_usu. in children_)

клиновиден -дна _adj see_ клинест

клинорога _f_ goat with crumpled horns

клинчар _m_ maker of nails

клинчарница _f_ workshop where nails are made; shop where nails are sold

клинчест _adj see_ клинест

клинчи _impf_ to wait for a long time; to hang around, loaf around

клип _m_ **1** _Tech._ piston; plunger; (_на пумпа_) sucker; хидраулички клип ram (hydraulic) piston **2** curb bit, gag bit

клипен -пна _adj Tech._ piston _attrib._; клипна алка piston-ring

клипница _f Tech._ piston-rod

клирик -ци _m see_ клерик

клиринг _m Finance_ clearing

клириншки _adj_ clearing; клириншка спогодба clearing agreement

клирос _m_ choir (_part of a church_)

клиса _f_ (_usu. pl_) crackling

клисар _m_ sexton

клистир _m_ enema

клисти́ра _pf & impf_ to treat with an enema

клисура _f_ ravine, gorge

клише _n_ cliché

клиши́ра _pf & impf_ to stereotype, print by use of stereotypes (plates)

кло, кло _interj_ (_imitating swallowing or water draining_) gurgle, glug

клобаре _n dim. of_ клопче

клободан _m_ sterling silver; silver ribbon

клобурец -рци _m_ bubble

клобурок -рци _m see_ клобурец

клобучи <се> _impf_ to bubble

клови _impf_ to germinate, sprout; пченицата клови the wheat is sprouting

кловн _m_ clown; buffoon

клозет _m_ lavatory, W.C., toilet

клокне _pf_ клокна _aor._ to gurgle

клокнува _impf of_ колкне

клокот _m_ gurgle, murmur (_of water_)

клокоти _impf_ to murmur, gurgle; to boil _intrans._; to bubble

клон _m_ branch (_of a business, bank, etc._)

клонира *pf & impf* to clone

клопа *impf* **1** to clatter, rattle **2** *fig.*, *colloq.* to gulp down, bolt

клопак -ци *m see* клопче

клопатар *m see* клопотарец

клопец -ци *m see* клопче

клопка *f see* примка, стапица

клопне *pf* клопна *aor. see* клопа 1

клопнува *impf of* клопне

клопот *m* clatter, rattle

клопотавица *f* clatter, rattle

клопотарец -рци *m* cowbell

клопотарник -ци *m see* клопотарец

клопоти *impf* to clatter, rattle, rumble

клопотка *impf dim.* to clatter, rattle, rumble (*intermittently*)

клопче *n* ball, skein

клопчест *adj* ball-like

клоска *impf* to run heavily/with difficulty

клоца[1] *f* kick; му удри една клоца he gave him a kick; *fig.* he kicked him out, he sacked him

клоца[2] *impf* **I 1** to kick *intrans.*; коњов клоца this horse kicks **2** *fig.* to toss and turn in one's sleep, sleep restlessly **II** – **ce** to kick each other

клоцаница *f see* клоца[1]

клоцне *pf* клоца *aor.* **I** to kick; коњот ме клоцна the horse kicked me **II** – **ce** to kick each other

клоцнува (ce) *impf of* клоцне (ce)

клошар *m see* бездомник

клошка *impf see* клоца[2]

клошне *pf* клошна *aor. see* клоцне

клошнува *impf of* клошне

клуб *m* club; фудбалски клуб football (soccer) club

клувка *impf see* колвка

клувне *pf* клувна *aor. see* колвне

клувнува *impf of* клувне

клука *impf* **1** (*чука*, *тропа*) to knock, bang **2** to hurt *trans. & intrans.*; to sting; to tingle; раната го клука his wound hurts **3** *dial.* to peck; to bite **4** to pester, nag **5** to offer (*s.o.*) food (*persistently*); to force-feed; to fatten; to stuff, cram **II** – **ce** to overeat; се клука со таблети to cram pills into o.s.

клукајдрвец -вци *m Zool.* (Dendrocopus) woodpecker

клукалец -лци *m see* клукајдрвец

клукало *n* door knocker

клукне *pf* клукна *aor. see* клука

клукнува *impf of* клукне

клукодрвец -вци *m see* клукајдрвец

клукса *f* mousetrap

клукучар *m Bot.* (Centaurea salonitana) knapweed

клум *interj* plop! splash!

клумбарец -рци *m see* клобурец

клумка *impf* to shake, mix

клумне *pf* клумна *aor.* to shake, mix

клумнува *impf of* клумне

клун *m* **1** beak, bill; ❑ става нешто во клун to have a bite to eat **2** *fig.* (*на брод*) bow, prow

клунар *m Zool.* (Ornithorhynchus anatinus) duckbilled platypus; клунари *Zool.* (Monotremata) monotremes

клундрво *n see* клукајдрвец

клунест *adj* beaked, billed

клунка *f see* клун 1

клупа *f* bench; (*во црква*) pew; обвинителна клупа <prisoner's> dock; училишна клупа school desk; ❑ магарешка клупа dunce's seat

клупиче -иња *n* **1** *dim. of* клупа **2** footrest

клупски *adj* club; клупски просториии club premises

клуч -ови -еви *m* **1** key (*also fig.*); клуч од соба room key; клуч на проблем key to a problem; клуч на шифра key to a code; ❑ држи под клуч to keep under lock and key **2** spanner, wrench; француски клуч monkey-wrench **3** *Mus.* clef, key **4** *Anat.* (*клучна коска*) clavicle, collarbone

клучав *adj* клучав коњ a horse with a narrow croup

клучалка *f* keyhole

клучар *m* **1** locksmith **2** turnkey **3** doorkeeper

клучарка *f* **1** (*fem. form*) *see* клучар **2** bolt; latch

клучен -чна *adj* **1** key; клучна индустрија key industry; клучна позиција key position; *Anat.* клучна коска clavicle, collarbone

клучец *m* loop

клучка *f see* клучец

клучорога *f* goat with crumpled horns

кљака *impf* to rattle; штрковите кљакаат the storks are displaying (*clattering their bills*)

кљакуш -овци, -и *m colloq.* chatterbox, babbler

кљанка *impf colloq.* to talk nonsense; to waste time talking, gossiping

кљанкач *m colloq.* babbler, chatterbox

км *abbr.* (*километар*) km

кмет *m* **1** serf; peasant **2** village elder; селски кмет village mayor

кметува *impf* **1** to work as a farm hand **2** to act as village elder;

кмиши *impf colloq. see* кисне 4

кнап *adj indecl.* just right; just enough; чевлите ми се кнап the shoes fit me perfectly

кнедла *f* dumpling

кнежев *adj* prince's

кнежевина *f see* кнежевство

кнежевски *adj* princely; кнежевски род princely stock, family

кнежевство *n* principality

кнез *m* duke, prince

кнезува *impf* to rule as prince

книвче *n dim. of* книга **1** booklet, *see* книшка **2** small piece of paper, note

книга *f* **1** book **2** register; земјишна книга land register; deed book; касова книга ledger, cash book; книга за жалби complaints book; матична книга record book, register (*of births, marriages, deaths, etc.*); ❑ запише во црната книга to blacklist **3** *arch.* letter, written message **4** *colloq.* paper; книга цигарска cigarette paper **5** *arch.* literacy; тој знае книга he is literate (he can read and write) **6** *arch.* (*usu. pl*) playing-cards

книговезец -сци *m* bookbinder

книговезница *f* bindery, bookbinder's workshop

книговодител *m* book-keeper, accountant; главен книговодител chief book-keeper

книговодствен *adj* account; (of) book-keeping; книговодствена книга account book

книговодство *n* book-keeping; accountancy; двојно книговодство double-entry book-keeping; просто книговодство single-entry book-keeping

книгоиздател *m* publisher

книгоиздателство *n* publishing house

книгољубец -пци *m* book-lover, bookworm

книжар *m* seller of books and stationery

книжарница *f* bookshop and stationer's

книже *n dim. see* книвче

книжевен -вна *adj see* литературен

книжевност *f see* литература

книжен -жна *adj* **1** bookish; book; книжни знаења scholarship, erudition; книжни изрази bookish expressions; книжен фонд holdings (*of a library*) **2** paper; книжни пари paper money, banknotes

книжење *n* **1** booking, entering **2** entry, item; книжење во полза credit entry; книжење на товар debit entry

книжи *impf* to enter, record

книжица *f see* книшка

книжнина *f see* литература

книжница *f* library

книжничар *m* librarian

книжовен -вна *adj see* литературен

книшка *f dim. of* книга; booklet; pamphlet; book; работничка книшка employee's service record; ученичка книшка pupil's (student's) record book; штедна книшка passbook; здравствена книшка health-care booklet

книшки *adj* **1** bookish **2** theoretical; abstract; книшки знаења book learning, theoretical knowledge

книегиња *f* princess, duchess

коала *f Zool.* (Phasolarctos cinereus) koala <bear>

коалира се *pf & impf* to unite (*in a coalition*) *intrans.*; to become associated

коалиција -ии *f* coalition; владина коалиција government coalition

коалиционен -она *adj* coalition; коалициона влада coalition government

коалиционер *m* coalitionist

коб *f & rarely m see* коба

коба *f* foreboding, presentiment; fate, destiny; doom

кобалт *m Chem.* cobalt

кобалтен -тна *adj* cobalt; кобалтна бомба cobalt bomb

кобел -бли *m* wooden bucket (pail)

кобен -бна *adj* fateful, ominous

кобец -бци *m Zool.* (Accipiter nisus) sparrow hawk; ◻ кобец (ламја) е за работа he's a demon for work (glutton for punishment)

коби *impf* to have a presentiment, feel foreboding

кобила *f* **1** mare **2** *fig., pejor.* large woman

кобилица *f* **1** wishbone (*in birds*) **2** bridge (*of stringed instrument*) **3** yoke (*for carrying loads*); bundle carried on the shoulder, *Austral.* swag

коблица *f see* кобел

кобник -ци *m* prophet of doom

кобница *f (fem. form) see* кобник; bird of ill omen

кобра *f Zool.* (Naja) cobra

ков *m* **1** forged metal **2** *fig.* character, cast; stamp; човек од стар ков a man of the old school **3** plates and nails (*for shoeing horses*)

кова *impf* **1** to forge, hammer **2** to mint, coin (*money*); *fig.* кова нови зборови to coin new words **3** to shoe (*horses*) **4** to plot; кова завера против to hatch a plot against

ковало *n* **1** tool for shoeing horses **2** manner of shoeing

кован *pt* **1** forged; wrought; worked; chased (*metal*) **2** coined; ковани пари coins **3** shod; кован коњ shod horse

кованица *f Ling.* newly coined word, neologism

коварен -рна *adj* treacherous, sly, cunning

коварство *n* treachery, cunning

ковач *m* blacksmith; ◻ ковач на својата среќа master of one's destiny

ковачки *adj* blacksmith's; ковачки занает blacksmith's trade

ковачница *f* **1** smithy **2** (*за пари*) mint

кове *impf see* кова

ковен *pt see* кован

коверт *m* envelope

ковертира *pf & impf* **1** to place in an envelope **2** *Chess* to record the last move (*before an interruption*)

ковил *m Bot.* (Stipa pennata) feather-grass

ковина *f* metal

ковне *pf* ковна *aor. see* кова, кове

ковнува *impf of* ковне

ковче *n dim. of* коска

ковчег -зи *m* chest, trunk; мртовечки ковчег coffin

ковчест *adj* bony

кога *adv & conj* **1** when; кога ќе дојде? when will he come? ◻ кога тога sooner or later; нема кога to have no time; уште од кога for a long time now; кога би if only; кога било whenever; any time; ретко кога once in a while; hardly ever; кога сме веќе кај тоа come to think of it **2** sometimes; како кога sometimes this way, sometimes that; it all depends when **3** (*кога да*) whenever; кога <и> да го видам whenever I see him

кога-годе *adv* whenever

когаш *adv usu. in the expression:* когаш тогаш sooner or later

когашен -шна *adj* of what time/date; когашен е весников? what is the date of that paper? когашен е лебов? how old is this bread?

кого *pron* (*oblique case form, except dat., of* кој) whom; од кого from whom; за кого about whom; ◻ со кого си, таков си a man is known by the company he keeps; од кого е, многу е what can you expect from a hog but a grunt?

код *m* code number

кодеин *m Med.* codeine

кодекс *m* code; codex; кривичен кодекс criminal code; кодекс на однесување code of conduct; кодекс на честа code of honour

кодик -ци *m* register of visitors and benefactors (*of a monastery or church*)

кодификација *f* codification

кодифицира *pf & impf* to codify; to legalize

кодош *m colloq.* **1** tell-tale; informer **2** pimp, procurer

кодоши *impf colloq.* **1** to inform on, tell on, *Austral.* dob in **2** to procure (*women*)

кодошка *f colloq.* (*fem. form*) *see* кодош

коегзистенција *f* coexistence; мирољубива коегзистенција peaceful coexistence

коегзистира *impf* to coexist

коефициент *m Math.* coefficient, factor; коефициент на корисно дејствување efficiency

кожа *f* **1** skin; ◻ кожа и коска (коски) skin and bone; си ја чува кожата to look after Number One; кожата ми се наежи од страв (*s.o./s.th.*) gave me the creeps; има дебела кожа to have a thick skin; си ја спаси кожата to save one's skin; од оваа кожа во друга не се влегува there's no way out; what must be, must be; му влезе некому под кожа to get into s.o.'s good graces; одере некому кожа to fleece s.o.; да излезе човек од кожа! it's enough to drive one mad! бери ја кожата на шилец! be prepared for the worst! 2 hide, pelt, skin; leather; телешка кожа calf skin; штавена кожа tanned hide; подврзија во кожа leather binding 3 peel, rind, skin

кожар *m* leather merchant, dealer in hides; tanner; leather-worker

кожарница *f* tannery; leather-goods store

кожарски *adj* tanning *attrib.*; кожарска работилница tannery

кожен -жна *adj* skin; leather; кожна болест skin disease

кожест *adj* leathery, thick

кожлест *adj* thick-skinned; кожлести круши pears with thick skins

кожодер *m* flayer; *fig.* usurer

кожув *m* sheepskin coat; fur-coat

кожувар *m* furrier

кожуварница *f* furrier's workshop/store

кожурек *m* skin (*on milk*)

кожурец -рци *m* 1 cocoon of a silkworm; *fig.* shell 2 bubble; blister

кожурка *f see* кожурец

кожурок *m see* кожурек

коза *f Zool.* goat; nanny-goat; дива коза (Rupicapra rubicapra) chamois; *Astron.* Capricorn

козав *adj see* козинав

козак -ци *m* Cossack

козар *m* goatherd

козарник -ци *m* goat pen

козарница *f see* козарник

козачки *adj* Cossack

козер *m* causeur, conversationalist

козерија -ии *f* conversation, chat, banter

кози се *impf* 1 to kid, bring forth (*a kid*) 2 *fig.* to toil, slave, struggle

козина *f* goat's hide; goat's hair; goat's wool

козинав *adj* made of goat's hair; hairy, shaggy

козинави *impf* I to strew/cover with hair II – ce to become hairy

козинак -ци *m* kind of pastry

козирец -рци *m see* козирог

козирог *m Bot.* (Ceratonia siliqua) carob tree; carob, locust bean

козјавка *f Bot.* (Polygonum aviculare) knotgrass

козји *adj* goat's; козја врвица goat track; козјо млеко goat's milk

козле *n dim. of* коза; kid

козметика *f* cosmetics

козметичар *m* cosmetician, beautician

козметичарка *f* (*fem. form*) *see* козметичар

козметички *adj* cosmetic; козметички салон beauty parlour; козметички средства cosmetic preparations

коинциденција *f* coincidence

коинцидира *pf & impf* to coincide

кој, која, кое, кои *pron* (*acc.* кого, *dat.* кому) 1 (*interrogative*) who; which; кој дошол? who has come? кого барате? whom do you want? со кого? with whom? која рака? which hand? 2 (*relative*) who;

which; прашањата на кои треба да одговориме the questions we must answer 3 кој . . . , кој . . . one, . . . another . . . ; кој спие, кој работи one person is sleeping, another is working 4 (*in expressions*) кој <и да> било, кој <и> да е anyone <you like>; either one; whoever; кој-годе any one, any kind of; кој <го> знае goodness knows; ретко кој very few; со кој ум го стори тоа? how could you do that? what on earth made you do that? кој сака бил! I don't care who it is; whoever it may be; како кој it depends on the person; кој од кој much of a muchness, one not much better than the other; кој како ќе си ја нареди every man for himself; кој му е крив it's his own fault; покажува некому кој е кој to take s.o. down a peg or two

кој-годе *see* кој 4

којнак -ци *m* large walnut (*used in children's game resembling English "conkers"*)

којначка *f see* којнак

којот *m Zool.* (Canis latrans) coyote

којшто, којашто, коешто, коишто *pron see* кој 2

кок *m* (knot of hair)

кока *f* 1 coccus 2 *Bot.* (Erythroxylum coca) coca

кокаин *m* cocaine

кокаинизам -змот *m* cocaine addiction

кокаинист *m* cocaine addict

кокал *m dial. see* коска

кокалест *adj dial. see* ковчест

кокар *m Bot.* (Allium cepa) seed onions

кокарда *f* cockade

кокер *m* cocker <spaniel>

кокерија *f* 1 ship's galley 2 coking works

кокетен -тна *adj* coquettish

кокетерија *f* coquetry

кокетира *impf* to flirt

кокетка *f* coquette, flirt

кокиче *n Bot.* (Galanthus nivalis) snowdrop

коклиш *m* whooping cough

коко *n child.* 1 egg 2 any rounded, edible object, e.g. apple, walnut, sweet

коковче *n dim. of* кокошка; pullet

коковчица *f* pullet

коколи се *impf see* кокори се

кокона *f* 1 *iron.* lady; showy, elegant lady 2 cocoon (*of the silkworm*)

кокорави (се) *impf see* кокори (се)

кокорачко -овци *m colloq.* 1 onlooker 2 spry, vigorous person; conceited person

кокори *impf* I to stare, gape II – ce to show off; to swagger, strut, give o.s. airs

кокос *m Bot.* (Cocos nucifera) coconut palm

кокосов *adj* coconut; кокосов орев coconut

кокошаница *f see* кокошарник

кокошарник -ци *m* 1 chicken coop, hen house 2 *fig.* small, unattractive house

кокошинка *f* bird louse, fowl's louse

кокошка *f Zool.* (Gallina) hen; блатна кокошка (Rallus aquaticus) water rail; црвено клунна блатна кокошка (Gallinula chloropus) moorhen, □ оди со кокошките да спие (легнува со кокошките) to go to bed early; во оваа куќа кокошка пее in this house it's the wife who wears the trousers; јал од кокошка нога he can't keep a secret; гладна кокошка просо сонува *prov.* a dream grants what one covets when awake; ќе дојде кокошката на седало you'll get what you deserve; you'll get what's coming to you

кокошкар *m* **1** chicken thief **2** *fig.* coward; weakling **3** јастреб кокошкар (*Accipiter gentilis*) goshawk

кокошкин *adj* chicken's, hen's; кокошкино сонце the time between sunset and nightfall

кокс *m* coke

коксар *m* coking worker; coke specialist

коктел *m* cocktail party; cocktail

кол -ови *m coll.* колје pole, prop, picket, stake; ❑ набие на кол to drive into a corner; од кол на кол from bad to worse; кој од кол, кој од ортома riffraff

кола[1] *f* **1** cart, waggon; коњска кола horse-drawn waggon; (*вагон*) carriage; кола за спиење sleeping-car, sleeper; ❑ со кола зајци фаќа to do things properly; to have a happy knack of doing things well; откако ќе се скрши колата, многу патчиња се отвораат *prov.* every cloud has a silver lining **2** cartload **3** car, automobile; motor vehicle; бојна кола armoured car; лека кола car **4** *Astron.* Колата Little Bear and Great Bear (Plough, Big Dipper) (*considered as one constellation*)

кола[2] *f* (*штирак*) starch

колабира *pf & impf* to collapse

колаборатор *m* collaborator, associate

колаборација *f* collaboration

колаборира *pf & impf* to collaborate

колаен -јна *adj colloq.* easy

колаж *m* collage

колај[1] **1** *m colloq.* knack, know-how; easy way **2** *adj indecl. see* колаен

колај[2] *adv colloq.* easily; колај му е нему it's easy for him

колајлак *m see* колај[1]

колак -ци *m* **1** flat round loaf (*traditionally offered with wedding invitation*); на царот данокот, на попот колакот *prov.* to each his due; render unto Caesar the things that are Caesar's, and unto God the things that are God's **2** head pad (*for carrying things on one's head*) **3** ball, skein; coil **4** *dial.* roll (*ring of pastry*) **5** *dial.* All Souls' Day offerings (*traditionally taken to cemetery*) **6** (*as adj in the fixed epithet*) колак сабја sabre, scimitar

колан *m* **1** belt **2** saddle-girth

колапс *m Med.* collapse

колар *m* **1** waggon-maker, cartwright **2** coachman

коларница *f* cartwright's workshop

колатерален -лна *adj* collateral

колач[1] *m* cake; pastry; ritual cake (*for slava, etc.*)

колач[2] *m* murderer, cutthroat

колаче *n* small cake

колбас *m* sausage

колбасар *m* sausage maker/seller

колбас<ар>ница *f* sausage shop; sausage-making workshop

колва *impf see* колве

колве *impf of* колвне

колвка *impf dim. of* колве

колвне *pf* колвна *aor.* to peck

коле *impf* **I 1** to slaughter, slay; ❑ тој коле, тој беси he rules the roost **2** *fig.* to worry; to torment; испитот ме коле the exam worries me **II** – **се** to fight <each other>; to kill each other

колеба *impf* to rock (*a child*)

колеба се *impf* **1** to hesitate, vacillate, waver, dither; to be doubtful **2** to vary, fluctuate; температурата се колеба од 20 до 30 степени the temperature varies between 20 and 30 degrees

колебање *n* **1** hesitation **2** fluctuation

колебарка *f see* колепка

колеблив *adj* hesitant, wavering; variable; колеблив елемент variable element

колебливец -вци *m* ditherer

колега *m* colleague, fellow worker/student

колегијален -лна *adj* comradely, friendly; loyal; collegial

колегијалност *f* friendly spirit; loyalty; collegiality

колегиум *m* **1** staff; наставнички колегиум teaching staff; *Am.* faculty **2** board, collegium; редакциски колегиум editorial board

коледа *impf see* коледува

коледар *m* carol-singer

коледарка *f* **1** (*fem. form*) *see* коледар **2** *see* коледачка

коледарски *adj* of carol-singing; коледарски месец (*popular name for*) December; коледарска песна Christmas carol

коледачка *f* baton (*with which carol-singers knock on doors*)

коледашка *f* **1** traditional Christmas buns for children **2** *see* коледачка

коледе *n* **1** Christmas Eve **2** carol-singing **3** *dial.* Christmas

коледува *impf* to go carol-singing

колеж[1] *m* slaughter

колеж[2] *m see* колец

колектив *m* personnel, staff; работен колектив staff (employees)

колективен -вна *adj* collective; колективно раководство collective leadership/management; колективна одговорност joint responsibilty

колективизам -змот *m* collectivism

колективизација *f* collectivization

колективизира *pf & impf* to collectivize

колективизиран *pt* collectivized; колективизирана земја collectivized land

колектор *m* main sewer/drain

колекција -ии *f* collection

колекционер *m* collector

коленик *m Bot.* (Bifora radians) bifora

коленица *f* **1** *see* колено 1; на коленици (*пред*) cap in hand (*to*) **2** коленици knee pads

коленичи *pf & impf* **1** to kneel; to fall on one's knees **2** *fig.* to beseech *trans.*

коленички *adv* kneeling

колено *n* **1** knee; ❑ *Med.* вода во колено water on the knee; мисли дека морето е до колена he thinks he can do anything; не кревај се на големо, да не паднеш на колено the higher you fly, the greater the fall; падне на колена to fall to one's knees; до колена knee-deep; knee-high; му се тресат колената to be weak at the knees **2** (*на цевка*) joint, elbow **3** *fig.* generation; од колено на колено from generation to generation; роднина од деветто колено distant relative/cousin

колепка *f* cradle

колера *f Med.* cholera

колерик -ци *m* choleric (irascible) person

колеричен -чна *adj* choleric, irascible

колесник -ци *m* two-wheeled ox-cart

колесница *f arch.* chariot

колец -лци *m see* кол

колец *m* college

колéшка *f (fem. form) see* колега

колиба *f* hut, cabin; shack; овчарска колиба shepherd's hut

колибар *m* hut dweller

колúбри *m Zool.* (Trochilus) hummingbird

коливо *n* boiled wheat (*traditional dish at certain religious festivals*)

колизија -ии *f* collision, crash; clash

количествен *adj* quantitative; количествена промена quantitative change

количество *n* quantity; количество стоки quantity of goods

количина *f see* количество

количински *adj see* количествен

количка *f dim. of* кола; wheelbarrow; (*инвалидска*) wheelchair; (*за бебе*) pram, *Am.* baby carriage; *Brit.* pushchair, *Am.* stroller

количник -ци *m Math.* quotient

колк *m Anat.* hip

колка *impf* to stuff, fatten; колка со јадење to stuff with food; ❑ дури ми колка душа to my last breath

кóлкав *adj* how big; колкав човек what a big man; колкав-толкав as big as he/it is; no matter how big/small

колку *adv* **1** how much, how many; колку пати (колкупати) how many times, how often; колку е часот (саатот)? what's the time? **2** how big; колку убаво! how beautiful! колку длабоко! how deep! **3** as (*in comparisons*); тој е висок колку мене he is the same height as I am **4** as for, concerning; колку за таа работа as for that matter, as far as that goes **5** (*with да*) however; as much as; колку да сакаш however much you want; as much as you please; колку (колку што) се може as much as possible **6** колку . . . толку the more. . . the more; колку повеќе се секираш, толку полошо за тебе the more you worry, the worse it'll be for you; колку толку however little; to a small extent **7** до колку (доколку) if, provided that, so long as; as far as; до колку знам as far as I know **8** so many, so much; enough; имам колку за лек I have just enough for one dose of medicine; колку да не е без ништо (без ич) just a bare minimum; колку да не ми е после мака just so much that I don't feel bad (regret) about it afterwards; колку за пакост (за бела) just enough to cause trouble; колку за влакно by a hair's breadth; колку-толку a modicum; s.th. at least; колку што as much/many as; however much/little; колку што можам да се сетам to the best of my recollection

колку-годе *adv* just a little

колкумина *adv* (*of men and mixed groups*) how many of them; колкумина работници имаше? how many workers were there?

колкýнsа *adv see* колкуцка

колкýнsав *adj see* колкуцкав

колкупати *adv* how many times

колкýцка *adv dim.* how little; колкуцка ми даде how little he gave me

колкýцкав *adv dim.* how small; види колкуцкав е see how small he/it is

колне *impf* **I 1** to curse, damn **2** to adjure; to entreat; to swear in; колне сведоци to swear in witnesses **II** – **се 1** to curse o.s. **2** to swear (*on, by*); се колне во честа to swear on one's honour; криво се колне to perjure o.s.

колнатик -ци *m* cursed person, wretch

колник -ци *m see* коловоз<ник> 1

коло[1] *n* **1** mill-wheel **2** series, round; коло разговори a round of talks

коло[2] *n* (*laundry*) starch

колобајче *n* marble (*toy*)

колобан *m colloq.* **1** tall, thin man; beanpole **2** *fig.* lazybones

коловоз<ник> *m* **1** road, roadway, lane **2** *dial.* entrance; front door (*of village house*)

коложег *m* (*popular name for*) January

колоúд *m Chem.* colloid

колокација *f* collocation

колоквијáлен -лна *adj* colloquial

колоквúра *pf & impf* to pass/take an intermediate examination

колоквиум *m* intermediate examination

колóна *f* **1** pillar, column **2** (*во весник*) column **3** *Mil.* column, file; во колона по два in double file; стројте се во две колони! form two columns! ❑ петта колона the fifth column

колонáда *f* colonnade

колонизáтор *m* colonizer

колонизација *f* colonization

колонизúра *pf & impf* to colonize

колонија -ии *f* **1** colony (colonial territory) **2** colony, community; македонската колонија во Сиднеј the Macedonian community in Sydney

колонијáл *m* **1** (*колонијални стоки*) groceries **2** (*колонијален дуќан*) grocery shop, grocer's

колонијáлен -лна *adj* **1** grocery; колонијални стоки groceries **2** colonial; колонијални војни colonial wars

колонијалúзам -змот *m* colonialism

колонúст *m* colonist

колонски *adj* cologne; колонска вода eau de Cologne

колор *m* colour; колор-филм colour film

колоратýра *f Mus.* coloratura

колоратýрен -рна *adj Mus.* coloratura; колоратурен сопран coloratura soprano

колорúст *m* colourist

колорúт *m* colour, colouring; локален колорит local colour

колос *m* colossus, giant

колоса *pf* to starch

колосáлен -лна *adj* **1** colossal, enormous, gigantic **2** *fig.* magnificent, majestic

колосан *pt* starched; колосана кошула starched shirt

колосек -ци *m* gauge; track; тесен колосек narrow gauge; широк колосек broad gauge; споредеn колосек siding; ❑ влезе в колосек to get (back) on track; излезе од колосек to go off the track

колосува *impf of* колоса

колофониум *m* rosin, colophony

колоцúра *pf & impf* to collocate

колпите *n* kind of *pita*

колпортáжа *f* sale of newspapers (*on the streets*)

колпортéр *m* newsboy

колски *adj* cart; колски пат cart track, dirt road

Колумбиец -ијци *m* Colombian

Колумбија *f* Colombia

Колумбијка *f* (*fem. form*) *see* Колумбиец

колумбиски *adj* Colombian

колце *n* wheel; ❏ ќе дојде колце на тркалце my/your/his *etc.* turn will come

колчина *adv see* колкумина

колче *n* 1 *dim. of* кол 2 children's game

колчишта *pl* tow, oakum

кома¹ *f Med.* coma

кома² *f Math.* decimal point; comma

комај *adv colloq.* almost, nearly; пладне комај ќе фати it's almost midday

комáнда *f* 1 command, order; дава команда to give an order; ❏ како по команда as one man; in unison 2 command, authority; headquarters; врховна команда supreme command; ❏ под командата на under the command of; преземе (прими) команда to take command 3 band, gang; ❏ боса команда band of ragamuffins, urchins; распашана команда rabble, mob

командáнт *m* commander, commanding officer; commandant; врховен командант supreme commander

команден -дна *adj* command<ing>; командни кадри officer corps (officers' cadres)

командúр *m* commander; командир на батерија battery commander

командúтен -тна *adj* joint-stock; командитно друштво joint-stock company

командос *m* commando

командува *pf & impf* 1 to give orders 2 to command, be in command (*co – of*); командува со баталјон to command a battalion

комар¹ *m see* комарец

комар² *m colloq.* dice, game of chance; игра комар to play dice; to gamble

комарец -рци *m Zool.* (Culex) mosquito, gnat; комарец маларичар malarial mosquito

комарка *f Bot.* (Euonymus japonica) spindle-tree

комарник -ци *m* mosquito-net

комарџија -ии *m colloq.* gambler

комасација *f* re-allotment, land consolidation

комат¹ *m pita* with green vegetables

комат² *m* piece of bread

коматар *m colloq.* 1 voracious eater, glutton 2 parasite, idler

комбáјн *m* combine harvester

комбајнéр *m* combine operator

комби *n* van

комбинáт *m* industrial combine (complex); дрвен комбинат timber combine/works/mill; металургиски комбинат metal works

комбинáтор *m* shrewd operator; schemer, conniver; *Math.* combinatorial analyst

комбинаторен -рна *adj* combinatory

комбинаторика *f Math.* theory of combinations

комбинација -ии *f* 1 combination, grouping, union 2 plan, scheme, concept, idea 3 *fig.* contrivance, manoeuvre, ruse

комбинé *n* slip, petticoat

комбинезóн *m* 1 overalls; jumpsuit 2 *see* комбине

комбинúра *pf & impf* 1 to combine; to group 2 to contrive

комедија -ии *f* comedy

комедијáнт *m* comedian; clown

комедиогрáф *m* comedy-writer

комедиографија *f* comedy-writing

комеморатúвен -вна *adj* commemorative

комеморација -ии *f* commemoration

комендија -ии *f colloq.* comedy, farce

комнтáр *m* commentary; коментари не се потребни no commentary is necessary

комнтáтор *m* commentator

комнтúра *pf & impf* to comment, interpret, explain

комерцијáлен -лна *adj* commercial, trade; комерцијален директор commercial director, business manager

комерцијáлец -лци *m* trade commissioner; sales representative

комерцијализација *f* commercialization

комерцијализúра *pf & impf* to commercialize

комерцијалúст *m see* комерцијалец

комесáр *m* deputy, delegate, commissary; commissar

комесаријáт *m* commissariat

комéта *f* comet

комик -ци *m see* комичар

комика *f* humour; comic element

комина -ње *f* (*usu. pl*) grape/plum skin; ❏ коминье го направи he made mincemeat of him

коминарка *f* grape brandy

коминикé *n* communiqué, official report

коминовица *f see* коминарка

Коминтéрна *f* Comintern, the Third International

комисија -ии *f* committee; board; commission; анкетна комисија commission of enquiry; испитна комисија examination panel; дисциплинска комисија disciplinary committee; советодавна комисија advisory committee

комисиóн *m* commission shop, second-hand shop (*usu. for resale of confiscated goods*)

комисионéр *m* commission agent; broker

комисиски *adj* <of a> committee, board, commission

комита *m Hist.* komitadji, guerilla, rebel (*against Ottoman rule*)

комитéт *m* committee; околиски комитет district committee

комитски *adj* komitadji, rebel

комитува *impf* to engage in rebel (komitadji) activity

комичар *m* comedian

комичен -чна *adj* comic<al>, funny, humorous

комка¹ *f dial.* причесна, причест

комка² (**се**) *pf & impf dial. see* причести (се), причестува (се)

комкалница *f dial.* chalice (*for Communion*)

комов *adj of* grape/plum skins; комова ракија grape brandy

комовица *f see* коминарка

комóда *f* chest of drawers, dresser

комодитéт *m* 1 comfort 2 nonchalance

комоника *f Bot.* (Melilotus officinalis) field-melilot

комора *f* 1 chamber; занаетчиска комора artisans' association; трговска комора chamber of commerce; адвокатска комора bar association; law society 2 chamber, room; compartment; мрачна комора darkroom; комора за длабоко замрзнување deep-freeze compartment 3 *Mil.* ordnance corps, logistics unit 4 *Anat.* chamber, ventricle; коморите на срцето the chambers (ventricles) of the heart

Коморец -рци *m* Comoran

Комори *pl* the Comoros

Коморка *f (fem. form) see* Коморец

коморски *adj* Comoran; Коморски Острови the Comoros

коморџија -ии *m* member of the ordnance corps (supply units)

комотен -тна *adj* 1 comfortable; spacious, roomy 2 *fig.* slow; easy-going, relaxed

комоција -ии *f see* комодитет

компактен -тна *adj* 1 compact 2 *fig.* united; joint

компанија -ии *f* 1 company, firm; авионска компанија airline; трговска компанија trading company 2 company, friendly association; го зедов да ми прави компанија I took him with me to keep me company

компањон *m* companion, friend

компањонка *f (fem. form) see* компањон

компаратив *m Gram.* comparative <degree>

компаративен -вна *adj* comparative

компарација *f* comparison; *Literature* simile

компарира *pf & impf* to compare

компас *m* compass; ❑ без компас aimlessly; губи компас to lose one's bearings

компензација *f* compensation; indemnification

компензациоен -она *adj* compensatory; компензационен договор compensation agreement

компензира *pf & impf* to compensate

компетентен -тна *adj* competent; authoritative, authorized; компетентен орган competent authority

компетенција -ии *f* competence; jurisdiction; field; тоа не е во моја компетенција that is not in my field

компилативен -вна *adj* of compilation; компилативно дело a work of compilation

компилатор *m* compiler

компилација -ии *f* compilation

компилира *pf & impf* to compile

компир *m* 1 *Bot.* potato; салата/супа од компир<и> potato salad/soup; лупи компири to peel potatoes; печени компири baked/roast potatoes; пржени компири potato chips, *Am.* French fries 2 *fig.* fool; dullard

компјутер *m* computer

компјутеризира *pf & impf* to computerize

компјутерски *adj* computer; компјутерска грешка computer error

комплекс *m* complex; комплекс од куќи housing complex; комплекс на помала вредност inferiority complex

комплексен -сна *adj* complex, complicated; confused

комплет *m* set; комплет алатки set of tools; дводелен комплет two-piece suit; плетен комплет twin set

комплотен тна *adj* complete; комплетно издание complete edition

комплетира *pf & impf* to complete, fulfil

компликација -ии *f* complication; прави компликации to create difficulties

компликува *pf & impf see* компликира

комплимент *m* compliment; дава некому комплименти to pay compliments to s.o.

компликира *pf & impf* to complicate

компликиран *pt* complicated, difficult; confused; комплицирано прашање complicated matter

комплот *m* plot, conspiracy

композите *pl Bot.* compositae (*daisies, etc.*)

композитор *m* composer

композиторка *f (fem. form) see* композитор

композиција -ии *f* 1 composition 2 (*вагони*) train

компонента *f* component

компонира *pf & impf* to compose, write music

компот *m* stewed fruit, compote; компот од сливи stewed plums

компрес *m* compress; студени/топли компреси cold/warm compresses

компресор *m* compressor

компромис *m* compromise; прави компромис to split the difference; to meet half-way

компромисен -сна *adj* compromise; компромисно решение compromise solution

компромитира *pf & impf* I to compromise *trans.*; to discredit, expose II – се to compromise (discredit) o.s.

компромитиран *pt* compromised, discredited; компромитирана личност compromised person

Комсомол *m* Komsomol

комсомолец -лци *m* Komsomol member

кому *pron (dat. of* кој) to whom; кому зборуваш? to whom are you speaking?

комуна *f* commune; community; society; Париска комуна the Paris Commune

комунален -лна *adj* communal, community; комунално устројство communal structure/arrangement; utility; комунална услуга/претпријатие public utility

комуналец -лци *m* municipal worker

комуналии *pl (land)* rates

комунар *m Hist.* Communard

комунизам -змот *m* communism

комунизира *pf & impf* to communize

комуникативен -вна *adj* communicative, talkative; approachable

комуникација -ии *f* communication, traffic; слаби комуникации poor communications; масовни комуникации mass media

комуникациоен -она *adj* <of> communication<s>

комунист *m* communist

комунистка *f (fem. form) see* комунист

комунистички *adj* communist

комуницира *impf* to communicate

комфор *m* comfort

комфорен -рна *adj* comfortable; well-appointed; комфорен стан flat with all amenities

комшивка *f colloq. see* сосетка

комшија -ии *m colloq. see* сосед

комшика *f see* комшивка

комшилак *m colloq.* neighbourhood

комшиски *adj colloq.* neighbour's, neighbourly

кон *prep* 1 (*of direction, also fig*) to, towards; патот кон селото the road to the village; љубов кон татковината love for one's homeland; прилог кон првиот број supplement to the first issue/edition 2 roughly, about, approximately; кон илјада луѓе about a thousand people; кон полноќ at about midnight; кон крајот на месецот towards/by the end of the month **3** on, on the occasion of; кон годишнината на . . . on the anniversary of . . .

конак -ци *m arch.* **1** night's lodging, overnight stay, shelter **2** palace; seat of local government (*under Ottoman rule*)

конакува *impf arch.* to pass (stay) the night

конвексен -сна *adj* convex

конвексност *f* convexity

конвенира *impf* (*with dat.*) to suit, be suitable; тоа не ми конвенира that doesn't suit me

конвенција -ии *f* convention, agreement

конвенционален -лна *adj* **1** conditional, agreed **2** customary, usual; конвенционална казна usual (customary) punishment **3** formal, excessively polite

конверзација *f* conversation, communication

конверзационен -она *adj* conversational

конверзија *f* **1** opposite attitude; конверзијата the converse **2** conversion (*of currency, etc.*)

конверзира *impf* to converse

конвертибилен -лна *adj* convertible; конвертибилна валута convertible (hard) currency

конвертибилност *f* convertibility

конвертира *pf & impf* to convert

конвој -ои *m* convoy

конвулзивен -вна *adj* convulsive

конвулзија -ии *f* convulsion

конгенијален -лна *adj* congenial

конгенијалност *f* congeniality

конгломерат *m* conglomerate

Конго *n* the Congo

Конгоанец -нци *m* Congolese

Конгоанка *f* (*fem. form*) *see* Конгоанец

конгоански *adj* Congolese

конгрегација *f* congregation

конгрес *m* congress

конгресен -сна *adj* congress; конгресна сала congress hall

конгресист *m* congress participant; member of congress, congressman

конгруентен -тна *adj* congruent, agreeing; identical

конгруенција *f Gram.* agreement; congruence

кондак -ци *m Rel.* hymn of praise

кондензатор *m Elec., Tech.* condenser

кондензација *f* condensation; compression

кондензира *pf & impf* **I** to condense *trans.* **II – се** to condense *intrans.*

кондензиран *pt* condensed; кондензирано млеко condensed milk

кондил *m arch.* pencil; slate pencil

кондир *m arch.* **1** pitcher **2** goblet

кондиса *pf arch.* to stop, stay, put up *intrans.*

кондисува *impf of* кондиса

кондиција -ии *f* **1** *Sport.* fitness, condition **2** condition, state **3** condition, term

кондиционал *m Gram.* conditional <mood>

кондиционален -лна *adj* conditional

кондиционалност *f Gram.* conditionality

кондом *m* condom

кондор *m Zool.* (Sarcorhamphus gryphus) condor

кондуктер *m* (*train, bus, tram, etc.*) conductor

кондуктерка *f* woman conductor, conductress

кондура *f colloq.* shoe, *see* чевел

кондурација -ии *m colloq. see* чевлар

кондурацилак *m colloq. see* чевларство

конец[1] -нци *m* thread; ❏ каде што е тенок конецот, таму се кине a chain is as strong as its weakest link; животот му виси на конец his life hangs by a thread; има сè, од игла до конец to have everything; како по конец smoothly, without complications; in a straight line; му ги смрси (изметка) конците to foil s.o.'s plans (calculations); to upset s.o.'s apple cart; му ги фати конците to catch s.o.'s drift; скине конци to kick the bucket, to peg out; држи конци во свои раце to pull the strings

конец[2] *m arch.* end; куса болест, благи конец *prov.* short illness, merciful end

конечен -чна *adj* final, definitive

конземи *adv arch.* to the ground; погледне конземи to look down, lower one's eyes

конзерва *f* can, tin; фабрика за конзерви canning factory

конзервативен -вна *adj* conservative; конзервативни погледи old-fashioned views

конзервативец -вци *m* conservative

конзервативизам -змот *m* conservatism

конзерватор *m* preserver, restorer

конзерваторист *m* student at a conservatoire

конзерваториум *m* conservatoire, conservatorium

конзервира *pf & impf* to preserve

конзервиран *pt* preserved, canned; конзервирана риба canned (tinned) fish

конзилиум *m* consultation; concilium; лекарски конзилиум consultative group of doctors

конзорциум *m* consortium, syndicate

конзул *m* consul; генерален конзул consul general

конзулат *m* consulate (*diplomatic mission*)

конзулство *n* consulate (*position*)

конзумација *f see* консумација

конзумен -мна *adj* of a dairy co-operative; конзумна млекара dairy co-operative

конзумира *pf & impf see* консумира

коник -ци *m* horseman, rider; cavalryman

коничен -чна *adj* conical

конјугација *f Gram.* conjugation

конјунктив *m Gram.* subjunctive

конјунктивен -вна *adj Gram.* subjunctive

конјунктура *f* market conditions, juncture; opportunity; висока конјунктура boom

конкавен -вна *adj* concave; конкавно огледало concave mirror

конквечеру *adv* towards evening

конкордат *m* concordat

конкретен -тна *adj* specific, concrete; конкретни факти hard facts; конкретен случај specific case

конкретизира *pf & impf* to specify; to be specific

конкубинат *m* concubinage

конкурент *m* competitor; applicant, candidate; bidder

конкурентен -тна *adj* competitive; конкурентна цена competitive price

конкуренција *f* competition; надвор од конкуренцијата beyond competition, in a class of its own

конкурира *pf & impf* to compete; to apply (за – for), be a candidate (*for*)

конкурс *m* contest, competition; advertisement of a vacant post; објави (распише) конкурс to announce/advertise a vacancy/competition

конкурсен -сна *adj* competition, selection; конкурсна комисија panel (*of judges*), selection committee

коноп *m & f Bot.* (Cannabis sativa) hemp

конопарник -ци *m see* конопиште 2

конопен -пна *adj* hempen; конопно платно <hempen> canvas

конопиште *n* 1 *augm. of* коноп 2 hemp field

конопларче *n Zool.* (Acanthis cannabina) linnet

коносман *m* bill of lading; коносман за воздушен превоз air waybill

консеквентен -тна *adj* consistent

консеквентност *f* consistency

консеквенција -ии *f* consequence, result; повлече консеквенции to have consequences (repercussions)

консекутивен -вна *adj Gram.* (*последичен*) consecutive

консигнација *f* consignment

консолидација *f* consolidation

консолидира *pf & impf* I to consolidate II – се to consolidate *intrans.*; to consolidate one's position

консолидиран *pt* consolidated

консонант *m Phon.* (*согласка*) consonant

консонантен -тна *adj Phon.* consonantal

консонантизам -змот *m Phon.* consonantal system

консонантски *adj Phon. see* консонантен

конспект *m* outline, summary, abstract

конспиративен -вна *adj* conspiratorial, secret; конспиративен состанок conspiratorial meeting

конспиратор *m* conspirator

конспирација *f* conspiracy

конспирира *pf & impf* to conspire, plot

константа *f Math.* constant

константен -тна *adj* constant, permanent

константност *f* constancy, permanence

констатација -ии *f* statement

констатира *pf & impf* to establish, ascertain

констелација *f* constellation

конституант *m* constituent

конституанта *f* constituent assembly

конституира *pf & impf* to constitute

конститутор *m* founder

конституција -ии *f* constitution

конституционен -она *adj* constitutional; конституциона монархија constitutional monarchy

конструира *pf & impf* to construct, put together; to build

конструктивен -вна *adj* constructive; конструктивна критика constructive criticism

конструктор *m* constructor

конструкција -ии *f* 1 structure, construction; бетонска конструкција concrete construction (building) 2 build, physique

консултант *m* consultant

консултативен -вна *adj* consultative; консултативен орган consultative body

консултација -ии *f* consultation

консултационен -она *adj* consultative

консултира *pf & impf* I to consult *trans.*; консултира лекар to consult a doctor II – се to consult *intrans.*; консултира со специјалист to consult a specialist

консумативен -вна *adj* consumer<'s>

консуматор *m* consumer

консумација *f* consumption, use

консумира *pf & impf* to use, consume

контакт *m* 1 *Tech.* connection 2 *fig.* contact; стапи во контакт (со) to get in touch, make contact (*with*)

контакт-леќа *f* contact lens

контаминација *f* contamination

контаминира *pf & impf* to contaminate

конте *n colloq.* dandy, fop

контејнер *m* container

контејнерски *adj* container; контејнерски брод container ship

контекст *m* context

контемплација *f* contemplation

контеса *f* countess

конти *impf* I to adorn; to dress up *trans.* II – се to dress up *intrans.*

контингент *m* 1 (*луѓе*) contingent 2 (*стока*) quota; consignment

континент *m* continent

континентален -лна *adj* continental; континетална клима continental climate

континенталец -лци *m* 1 inland-dweller, inlander 2 *fig. Sport.* star/top player

континуиран *adj* continuous, continual; континуиран развој continuous development

континуитет *m* continuity

конто *n Comm.* account; credit

контра *adv* 1 against, contrary; зошто си секогаш контра? why are you always against everything? 2 (*при бричење*) against the beard; земе некому контра to give s.o. a close shave

контраадмирал *m* rear admiral

контрабанда *f* 1 smuggling 2 contraband, smuggled goods

контрабандист *m* smuggler

контрабас *m Mus.* double bass

контрабасист *m Mus.* double bass player

контрадикторен -рна *adj* contradictory; контрадикторни изјави contradictory statements, declarations

контрадикција *f* contradiction; падне во контрадикција to contradict o.s.

контраиндикација *f Med.* contraindication; side effect

контракција *f* contraction

контраофанзива *f* counter-offensive

контрапункт *m Mus.* counterpoint

контрареволуција *f* counter-revolution

контрареволуционер *m* counter-revolutionary

контраст *m* contrast

контрастен -стна *adj* contrasting; контрастни бои contrasting colours

контрастира *impf* to contrast

контрахира *pf & impf* to contract

контрацепција *f* contraception

контрола *f* checking, inspection, verification, supervision; control; општествена контрола government supervision; служба за општествена контрола auditing office; стави под контрола to put under supervision; to bring under control, bring to heel; <лекарска> контрола <medical> check-up; техничка контрола на возила roadworthiness test

контролен -лна *adj* supervisory; checking; monitoring; контролна станица checkpoint; контролна табла dashboard; контролен уред monitor

контролира *pf & impf* to check, inspect, monitor, supervise

контроло́р *m* inspector; supervisor; контролор на билети ticket inspector; контролор на летови air-traffic controller

контузија -ии *f* contusion, bruise

контузува *pf & impf* to contuse, bruise

контумација -ии *f* *Chess* default; загуби со контумација to lose by default

контумаци́ра *pf & impf* to lose by default

конту́ра *f* contour, outline

конту́рен -рна *adj* contour *attrib.*; контурни линии contour lines

конус *m* cone

конфедерати́вен -вна *adj* confederative

конфедерација -ии *f* confederation, confederacy

конфекција *f* 1 serial production (*of clothing*) 2 ready-to-wear (off-the-peg) clothing 3 shop selling clothes off the peg

конфекционе́р *m* manufacturer/seller of ready-made clothes

конфекциски *adj* ready-to-wear, ready-made; конфекциски дукан shop selling ready-to-wear clothes (clothes off the peg)

конфера́нса *f* programme notes

конферансjе́ *m* master of ceremonies, compère

конференција -ии *f* conference; партиска конференција party conference; конференција на врвот summit meeting

конференциjа́ш *m pejor.* conference delegate

конфери́ра *pf & impf* to confer, attend a meeting

конфесија -ии *f* *Rel.* confession, faith, denomination

конфе́ти *pl* confetti; ❏ дожд од конфети a rain of confetti

конфигурација *f* configuration

конфиде́нт *m* stool pigeon; <police> informer, agent

конфиденција *f.* 1 <police> agent's report 2 assurance, self-confidence

конфирмација *f* 1 confirmation, acknowledgement, corroboration 2 *Rel.* confirmation

конфискација *f* confiscation

конфискува *pf & impf* to confiscate

конфликт *m* conflict, clash; <во>оружен конфликт armed conflict

конфронтација *f* confrontation

конфронти́ра *pf & impf* to confront, face

конфузен -зна *adj* confused, muddled; конфузен одговор confused answer

конфузија *f* confusion, muddle, mix-up

концентра́т *m* concentrate

концентрација *f* concentration; концентрација на капиталот concentration of capital; концентрација на производството concentration of production

концентрацио́нен -она *adj* concentration; концентрационен логор concentration camp

концентри́ра *pf & impf* **I 1** to concentrate *trans.*; концентрира внимание to focus attention **2** *Chem.* to condense, thicken, concentrate *trans.* **3** *Metallurgy* to purify, enrich **II – се 1** to concentrate (*на – on, upon*) *intrans.* **2** to mass, collect *intrans.*

концентри́ран *pt* **1** concentrated, focused; концентрирано внимание concentrated attention **2** *Chem.* condensed, concentrated; концентриран раствор concentrated solution **3** *Metallurgy* enriched; концентрирана руда enriched ore

концентричен -чна *adj* concentric; концентрични кругови concentric circles

концепт *m* sketch, draft, outline; rough copy

концепти́ра *pf & impf* to sketch, draft, outline

концепција -ии *f* conception; idea

концерн *m* *Econ.* concern

концерт *m* concert; concerto

концертен -тна *adj* concert; концертна сала concert hall

концерти́ра *pf & impf* to give a concert

концеси́вен -вна *adj* *Gram.* concessive; концесивни реченици concessive clauses

концесија -ии *f* concession, franchise

концесионе́р *m* concessionaire

концизен -зна *adj* concise, succinct

концил *m* church council

конципи́ра *pf & impf see* концептира

концлогор *m* (*концентрационен логор*) concentration camp

кончина *f arch.* demise, death

коњ *m* **1** horse; коњ за јавање saddle horse; товарен коњ draught horse, *Am.* draft horse; чистокрвен (полнокрвен) коњ thoroughbred <horse>; се качи на коњ to mount one's horse; гимнастички коњ vaulting horse; морски коњ *Zool.* walrus; нилски коњ *Zool.* hippopotamus; ❏ падне од коњ на магаре to come down in the world; работи како коњ to work like a Trojan; сега е на коњ he has the wind in his sails; брзиот коњ се стасува, брзиот збор не се стасува *prov.* think before you speak; на подарен коњ забите не му се гледаат *prov.* you don't look a gift horse in the mouth; не умри, коњу, до зелена трева *prov.* don't entertain false hopes; don't hold your breath **2** *Chess* knight; потер со коњот knight's move

коњак *m* cognac

коњаник -ци *m* horseman, rider; *Mil.* cavalryman; knight

коњар<ин> *m see* коњушар

коњарка *f* (*fem. form*) *see* коњар<ин>

коњарница *f see* коњушница

коњик -ци *m see* коњаник

коњица *f* cavalry; служи <во> коњица to serve in the cavalry

коњички *adj* cavalry

коњогојство *n* horse breeding

коњокрадец -дци *m* horse thief, *Am.* rustler

коњопотковница *f fig.* horseshoe

коњоштип *m* *Zool.* (Gryllotalpa vulgaris) mole-cricket

коњски *adj* horse<'s>; коњско месо horsemeat; коњска сила horsepower; коњска мува *Zool.* (Hippobosca equina) horsefly; коњски босилек *Bot.* (Mentha silvestris) horse-mint, wild mint; ❏ колку за еден коњски нокот plenty of room; quite a lot; коњска работа heavy, difficult work; drudgery

коњушар *m* groom; stable-boy, stable hand

коњушница *f* stable

коњче *n dim. of* коњ; rocking-horse; водно коњче *Zool.* (Libellula depressa) dragonfly

кооперати́в *m & ***кооперати́ва** *f* co-operative

кооперати́вен -вна *adj* co-operative; кооперативно движење co-operative movement

коопера́тор *m* member of a co-operative

кооперација -ии *f* **1** (*соработка*) co-operation **2** (*задруга*) co-operative <society>

коопери́ра *pf & impf* to co-operate; to join a co-operative

кооптација *f* co-optation, co-option

коопти́ра *pf & impf* to co-opt

координа́та *f Geom.* co-ordinate

координација *f* co-ordination, harmonization

координи́ра *pf & impf* to co-ordinate, harmonize

коп *m* digging site; дневен коп open-cast (open-cut) mine, *Am.* strip mine

копа *f* stack, rick

Копенха́ген *m* Copenhagen

копенхагенец -нци *m* person from Copenhagen

копенхагенка *f* (*fem. form*) *see* копенхагенец

копенха́шки *adj* Copenhagen *attrib.*

копилот *m* co-pilot

копа *impf* **1** to dig; to dig up; копа бунар to dig a well; копа јаглен to mine coal; ❑ ѓаволот ни ора ни копа the devil never sleeps; копа некому гроб to dig s.o.'s grave; кој копа гроб другему, сам паѓа во него *prov.* mind you don't fall into your own trap; копа и со раце и со нозе to stop at nothing **2** (*за животно*) to paw (*the ground*)

копалиште *n* digging site

копало *n* digging tool, digging-stick

копан *m* **1** brake (*tool for beating flax*) **2** (*пиралка, пералка*) battledore **3** leg (*of poultry*), drumstick **4** *dial. see* копана

копана *f* trough

копаница *f* wood-carving (*artefact*)

копаничар *m* carver, wood-carver

копаничарство *n* wood-carving (*activity*)

копанка *f dim. of* копана

копар *m Bot.* (Anethum graveolens) dill

копарок -ци *m* heath, place overgrown with scrub

копач *m* **1** digger; miner **2** pickaxe, pick

копачи *impf* to clear (*a forest*)

копачина *f* clearing; cleared land

копачка *f* **1** (*fem. form*) *see* копач 1 **2** pickaxe, pick; на зол трн зла копачка *prov.* you have to fight fire with fire **3** kind of *oro* (folk-dance) **4** digging **5** *Sport.* (*only pl*) soccer boots, cleated shoes, studded boots

копејка *f* kopeck

копелка *impf see* копка

копец -пци *m* clasp; buckle; hook and eye; женски копец female part of a clasp; машки копец male part of a clasp

копидан *m see* копиден

копиден *m Bot.* (Asarum europaeum) hazelwort, asarabacca

копие -ија *n see* копија

копија -ии *f* copy, duplicate; *colloq.* spitting image; копија на писмо copy of a letter; тој е копија на татка си he is the spitting image of his father

копиларка *f* cow/goat/sheep that has recently borne young

копилачка *f* unmarried mother

копиле *n* illegitimate child; bastard

копили се *impf* to bear an illegitimate child

копилјак -ци *m* illegitimate son

копилја́на *pl* illegitimate children

копилка *f* illegitimate daughter

копи́ра *pf & impf* to copy; to imitate, ape

копирач *m* copier; copycat

копирница *f* copying/photocopying room

копитар *m* ungulate, hoofed animal; *pl* копитари *Zool.* (Perissodactyla) ungulates

копитен -тна *adj* копитно животно hoofed animal

копито *n* hoof; коњско копито horse's hoof

копјаник -ци *m arch.* javelineer

копје *n* spear, lance, javelin; (*за знаме*) flagstaff; фрла копје to throw the javelin; ❑ знаме на пола копје flag at half-mast; крши копја to break a lance, cross swords (*за/со – for/with*)

копјевиден -дна *adj see* копјест

копјеносец -сци *m arch.* javelin bearer

копјест *adj* spear-like

копјоносец -сци *m arch. see* копјеносец

копка *impf* **1** to grub, dig, scratch (*soil*) **2** *fig.* to intrigue; to tantalize; ме копкаше да разберам I was dying to find out; ме копка љубопитност I am dying of curiosity

копне[1] *pf* копна *aor.* to strike with a hoe

копне[2] *impf* **1** to melt (*of snow, ice, etc.*) **2** *fig.* to yearn for, long for

копнее *impf* **1** to long for, yearn for; копнее да го види she is longing to see him; копнее по него she is yearning for him **2** to melt, thaw (*of snow, ice*)

копнеж *m* longing, yearning; копнежот кон татковината homesickness, longing for one's homeland

копнежлив *adj* yearning, longing

копнен *adj* land; копнени единици land forces

копно *n* **1** dry land; на копно и на море on land and on sea; дојде на копно to come ashore **2** thawed patch of ground

копнува *impf of* копне[1]

копра *f see* копар

копрал & **копралја** *f* iron-tipped goad

коприва *f Bot.* (Urtica) nettle; мртва (дива) коприва (Lamium) dead nettle; копривата жури (пари, жари) nettle stings; не удира гром во коприви *prov.* only the good die young

копривак -ци *m* bed/patch of stinging nettles

копривалник -ци *m pita* prepared with young nettles

копривар *m* nettle picker

копривен -вна *adj* nettle; копривна треска *Med.* nettle rash; nettle fever

копривка *f Bot.* (Celtis australis) hackberry, nettle-tree

коприна *f see* свила

копринен *adj see* свилен

копродукција *f* co-production

копук -ци *m colloq.* destitute person; homeless person; waif; ❑ копук сум I haven't got a bean

копула *f Gram.* copula

копулати́вен -вна *adj Gram.* copulative, coordinating; coordinate; копулативни сврзници coordinating conjunctions; копулативни реченици coordinate clauses

копчар *m* button-maker

копче *n* **1** button **2** switch, electric button **3** press-stud, patent stud

кор *m* corps; дипломатски кор diplomatic corps

кора *f* **1** bark; crust; peel, skin; rind; (*на рана*) scab; кора од дрво bark of a tree; земјината кора earth's crust; *Anat.* мозочна кора meninx, mem-

brane enveloping the brain; фати кора to crust over
2 rolled layer of filo pastry **3** *colloq. pita*, layer pastry

кораб *m* ship, vessel, boat

корабар & **корабџија** -ии *m arch.* seaman, sailor; boatman

корав *adj* **1** hard **2** *fig.* hard-hearted, insensitive, thick-skinned

коравина *f see* коравост

коравица *f* kind of melon with a hard skin

коравост *f* hardness; insensitivity

корал *m* **1** coral; ornament made of coral **2** chorale

корален -лна *adj* coral; корален ѓердан coral necklace

коралски *adj* coral; коралски острови coral islands

коран *m* Koran

корач *m* blacksmith's shoeing hammer

корбач *m* whip, lash

корвета *f* corvette

кордела *f* ribbon, tape

кордон *m* cordon; кордон од полиција police cordon

Кореец -ејци *m* Korean

Кореја *f* Korea; Јужна Кореја South Korea; Северна Кореја North Korea

Корејка *f* (*fem. form*) *see* Кореец

корејски *adj* Korean

коректен -тна *adj* correct, irreproachable; accurate; коректен човек honest/decent person; коректни односи correct relations

коректив *m* correction fluid; corrective

коректор *m* proof-reader

коректорски *adj* proof-reader's, proof-reading; коректорска грешка proof-reader's error

коректура *f* **1** proof-reading **2** proofs

корекција -ии *f* correction, alteration; корекција на видот correction of eyesight

корелат *m* correlate

корелативен -вна *adj* correlative

корелација *f* correlation

корен -ње, -ња *m* **1** root; корен на коса hair root; *fig.* корен на сите зла root of all evil; ❑ пушти (фати) корен to put down roots; to take root; од корен from the ground up; completely; root and branch **2** *Gram.* root; корен на збор root of a word **3** *Math.* root; квадратен корен square root; кубен корен cube root; вади корен to extract a root **4** *fig.* family, stock, extraction; од добар корен of good family **5** plant (*e.g. grapevine, etc.*); десет корење тутун ten tobacco plants

коренен -ена *adj see* коренит

коренит *adj* radical, fundamental, basic; коренити реформи radical reforms

коренски *adj* root, basic

коренува *impf Math.* to extract the (*square, cube, etc.*) root from

кореограф *m* choreographer

кореографија *f* choreography

корепетира *impf* to coach, train (*musicians, opera-singers*)

корепетитор *m* tutor, coach

корепетиција *f* practice; rehearsal (*of parts*)

кореспондент *m* correspondent; член-кореспондент corresponding member

кореспонденција *f* correspondence; води кореспонденција to carry on a correspondence

кореспондира *impf* to correspond, exchange letters

кореферат *m* supplementary report (paper)

кореферент *m* presenter of a supplementary report (paper)

кореферира *pf* & *impf* to present a supplementary report

корзира се *impf* to stroll on the *corso*; to promenade; to walk around

корзо *n corso*, promenade, walk; strolling on the *corso*

кори *impf* to reproach, scold, berate

коригира *pf* & *impf* to correct

коригиран *pt* corrected; коригиран текст corrected text

коридор *m* corridor

корија -ии *f* grove, wood

корил *m colloq.* collar

корисен -сна *adj* useful, beneficial; корисно за здравјето good (beneficial) for one's health; општествено корисен труд socially useful work

корисник -ци *m* beneficiary; user

корисница & **корисничка** *f* (*fem. form*) *see* корисник

корисност *f* usefulness

корист *f* advantage, benefit, profit; avail; во чија корист to whose advantage; во корист на in favour of; извлече корист (*од*) to benefit (*from*); нема корист! it's useless! it's of no use! општа корист general good

користење *n* use, utilization

користи *impf* **I 1** to profit by, benefit from; го користи знаењето he profits by his knowledge; го користи случајот he takes advantage of the opportunity **2** to use, make use of; to avail o.s. of; користи струја to use electricity; користи годишен одмор to take one's annual leave **3** to help, be beneficial to; овој лек ми користи this medicine helps me **II – се** to avail o.s. (*co – of*), take advantage (*of*)

користољубец -пци *m* greedy (avaricious, covetous) person

користољубив *adj* greedy, avaricious, covetous; self-interested

користољубивост *f* cupidity, covetousness

користољубие & **користољубје** *n* greed, avarice, cupidity

коритар *m* trough-maker

коритница *f arch.* shallow wooden box (*filled with sand, on which children formerly learned to write*)

корито *n* **1** trough **2** (*на река, езеро*) речно корито river bed; езерско корито lake basin

корифеј -еи *m* coryphaeus, leading light

корица *f* **1** (*на книга и сл.*) binding; cover; ❑ од корица до корица from cover to cover **2** (*за нож и сл.*) scabbard, sheath;

коричи *impf* to bind (*books*)

корка¹ *f* crust; корка леб crust of bread; *fig.* daily bread, livelihood

корка² *impf impers. colloq.* (*with dat.*) му корка he's scared

коркач *m colloq.* coward, chicken

кормилар *m* helmsman; coxswain; *fig.* leader

кормило *n* **1** helm, rudder **2** (*на велосипед*) handlebars; (*на автомобил*) steering wheel **3** *fig.* management, leadership; кормилото на државата the leaders of the state; тој е на кормилото he is at the helm

корморан *m Zool.* (Phalacrocorax carbo) cormorant

корна *f colloq. see* корнер

корне *impf* **I** to pull out; to pull up (*of the hair, weeds, etc.*); ❑ смрди корне it stinks terribly, it makes an awful stink **II – ce 1** to tear one's hair; to tear out each other's hair **2** to scuffle

корнер *m Sport.* corner kick

корнет[1] *m* ice-cream cone

корнет[2] *m Mus.* cornet

корниз *m* curtain rail; curtain rod; pelmet, cornice

корозија *f* corrosion

короман *m colloq.* hunk of bread

корона *f see* круна

корониса *pf see* круниса

корпа *f* basket; ❑ *colloq.* дава (удира) некому корпа to dump s.o.; to give s.o. the boot

корпоративен -вна *adj* corporative, group, joint

корпорација -ии *f* corporation

корпулéнтен -тна *adj* corpulent, obese, stout

корпулéнтност *f* corpulence

корпус *m* **1** *Mil.* corps; петнаесеттиот корпус fifteenth <army> corps **2** corpus; корпус деликти corpus delicti **3** *fig.* body; корпус на брод hull

корсет *m* corset

кортеж *m* cortège, procession; escort

кортеш *m pejor.* agitator

кортизóн *m Biochemistry* cortisone

коруба *f see* корупка

корубест *adj* having a rind

коруби се *impf* to warp

корумпúра *pf & impf* to corrupt, spoil; to bribe

корупка *f* **1** (на лубеница, диња) rind **2** (на желка) carapace, shell

корупција *f* corruption, perversion, depravity; bribery

корупционéр *m* bribe-taker

корчи *impf see* мрази

кос *m Zool.* (Turdus merula) blackbird; воден кос (Cinclus cinclus) dipper

кос *adj* oblique, slanting; коса црта slanting line, stroke

коса[1] *f* hair; ❑ косата ми се крева my hair stands on end; се фатија за коси they quarrelled fiercely

коса[2] *f* scythe; клепа коса to sharpen a scythe

коса[3] *f* slope

косар *m* scythe maker

косач *m* reaper; mower, haymaker

косачка *f* **1** (*fem. form*) *see* косач **2** mower (*machine*)

косација -ии *m see* косач

косеж *m* anxiety, worry; problem

косеканс *m Math.* cosecant

косел *m dial.* sulphur, *Am.* sulfur

косенина *f see* косеница

косеница *f* **1** hay-meadow **2** mown hay

косест *adj* hairy, shaggy

коси[1] *impf* **I** to mow; *fig.* to mow down; to massacre **II – ce** to clash, conflict; нашите интереси се косат our interests clash (conflict)

коси[2] *impf* **I** to upset, worry *trans.* **II – ce** to worry *intrans.*; to be upset; не коси се don't worry!

косидба *f* mowing; mowing season

косилен *m dial.* waist-high grass

косило *n* scythe handle

косинус *m Math.* cosine

косир *m* pruning-hook, billhook

косица *f* **1** *dim. of* коса[1] **2** braid, tress; pigtail

косичник -ци *m* woman's ornament (*woollen braid onto which silver coins are sewn*)

коска *f* **1** bone; вилична коска jawbone; клучна коска collarbone; ❑ коска и кожа skin and bone; рибина коска herring-bone pattern; слонова коска ivory; стара коска old hand; широка коска broad-shouldered person; тоа му е коска в грло that sticks in his throat; дошол нож до коска things have come to a head; му ги намести (скрши) коските he gave him a good hiding; миросани да му се коските may he rest in peace; фати коска 1. to gain strength 2. to find a good job (position); смрзнат до коски chilled to the marrow; месо без коски не бива *prov.* there's no rose without a thorn **2** (*кај плодови*) stone, *Am.* pit **3** (*за чевли*) shoehorn

коскарница *f colloq. see* костурница

коскен *adj* bone; коскено копче bone button

коскест *adj see* ковчест

косма *f* hair

космат *adj* hairy; shaggy

космест *adj see* космат

косми *impf arch.* to baptize; to christen

космички *adj* cosmic; космички зраци cosmic rays; космички брод spaceship

космогрáф *m* cosmographer

космографија *f* cosmography

космонáут *m* cosmonaut, astronaut

космополúт *m* cosmopolitan

космополитúзам -змот *m* cosmopolitanism

космос *m* cosmos, space

косне[1] *pf* косна *aor. literary* to touch

косне[2] *pf* косна *aor. dim. of* коси[1]

коснува[1] *impf of* косне[1]

коснува[2] *impf of* косне[1]

косо *adv* obliquely; askance

косовар *m* inhabitant of Kosovo; *Hist.* Kosovo partisan in World War II

Косовец[1] -вци *m* Kosovan, inhabitant of Kosovo

косовец[2] -вци *m dial. see* кос

косовица *f see* кос

Косовка *f* (*fem. form*) *see* Косовец

Косово *n* Kosovo

косовски *adj* Kosovan

косопасец *m* hair-loss (*caused by scalp ringworm*)

косор *m see* косир, сор

Костарúка *f* Costa Rica

Костарикáнец -нци *m* Costa Rican

Костарикáнка *f* (*fem. form*) *see* Костариканец

костарикáнски *adj* Costa Rican

костелив *adj* **1** raw-boned, large-boned; firm **2** (за овошје) having a stone, *Am.* pit

костен[1] -ье *m Bot.* (Castanea sativa) sweet chestnut (*tree and fruit*); див костен (Aesculus hippocastanum) horse-chestnut; ❑ вади костени од жар за некого to pull s.o. else's chestnuts out of the fire

костен[2] -сна *adj Med.* косна туберкулоза tubercular osteomyelitis

костенар *m* seller of roasted chestnuts

костенов *adj* chestnut

костенција -ии *m see* костенар

костец *m* fight; wrestling; wrangle, disagreement; се фатија во костец they started wrangling; се фаќа во костец со работа to get down to work

костим *m* costume; suit; костим за капење bathing costume; ❑ во Евин костим in one's birthday suit

костими́ра *pf & impf* to dress in costume *trans* .

костобол *m Med.* arthritis; gout

кострец *m Zool.* (Perca fluvialitis) perch

костреши се *impf* to bristle

кострушина *f see* кострец

костум *m colloq.* suit

костур *m* skeleton; *fig.* framework

костурница *f* ossuary; charnel house

кот *m* 1 offspring, progeny 2 *fig.* freak, degenerate, runt

кота *f* 1 triangulation point 2 elevation

котангенс *m Math.* cotangent

котар *m* 1 <livestock> pen, enclosure 2 (*folk name for the constellation*) Pegasus

котара *f see* котар 1

котва *f* anchor; дигне котва to weigh anchor; пушти (фрли) котва to cast anchor

коте *n* kitten

котел -тли *m* (*при плетење*) loop; ми се пушти котелец на чорапава I got a ladder (*Am.* run) in my stocking

котелец -лци *m* (*при плетење*) loop; ми се пушти котелец на чорапава I got a ladder (*Am.* run) in my stocking

котерија -ии *f* coterie, clique

котец *m* weir, trap for fish

коти *impf* I to bear, produce, bring forth (*young*) II – се 1 to cub, bear young 2 to be born (*of an animal*) 3 *colloq.* to reproduce

котизација *f* conference fee

котилјо́н *m* (*вид танц*) cotillion

котило *n* 1 breeding ground 2 *pejor.* breed, race

коти́ра <се> *pf & impf* to be in demand; to be rated highly

котка¹ *f* 1 *dial. see* мачка¹ 2 cleat (*on boot*) 3 children's game

котка² *impf* 1 to fondle, cuddle 2 to flatter 3 to amuse, entertain (*children*)

котлар *m* coppersmith; boilermaker

котларница *f* boiler room; coppersmith's workshop

котле *n dim. of* котел

котлет *m* chop, cutlet

котлина *f Geol.* basin, hollow, valley

котловина *f see* котлина

котлоса *pf colloq.* to refuse, reject

котри *pron dial. see* кој

котрул *m* thick unkempt (uncombed) hair

кофа *f* pail, bucket; една кофа вода a pail of water

кофеин *m* caffeine

кофиче *n &* **кофичка** *f dim. of* кофа

кохезија *f* cohesion

коцел -цли *m* plait, pigtail, braid

коцка *f* 1 (*тело*) cube; (*слика*) square; штоф на коцки checkered material 2 dice; фрли коцка to cast lots; ❑ го стави животот на коцка to risk one's life; коцката е фрлена the die is cast; на коцка at stake; in jeopardy; on the line стави сè на коцка to risk (stake) everything 3 gambling

коцка се *impf* to gamble

коцкар *m* gambler

коцкарница *f* gambling house, gambling den, casino

коцкест *adj* cubic; checkered; коцкест штоф checkered material

коцори се *imp* to swagger, strut; to be foolhardy

коч *m Zool.* ram

кочан¹ *m* 1 (*од пченка*) corn-cob; (*на зелка*) heart of cabbage; ❑ нозете му се кочан his feet have gone numb with cold 2 (*на опашка и сл.*) root

кочан² *m* block (*of receipts, entry tickets, etc.*)

кочанка *f* corn-cob

кочи *impf* I to brake, stop II – се to become stiff, stiffen *intrans.*

кочи се *impf* to canoodle, pet

кочија -ии *f* coach, carriage

кочијаш *m* coachman; cab-driver

кочина *f* pigsty (*also fig.*)

кочиџија -ии *m arch.* coachman

кочница *f* brake; воздушна кочница pneumatic brake; рачна кочница hand brake

кочничар *m* bus-driver, trolleybus-driver

коца *adv see* коцамити

коцабашија -ии *m arch.* village elder; mayor

коцамити *adv colloq.* quite, fairly, rather

кош *m* basket; *Anat.* граден кош thoracic cavity, thorax; ❑ става во еден кош to lump together

кошар *m* beehive

кошара *f* basket

кошарест *adj* basket-shaped; basket-like

кошарина *f see* кошар

кошарка *f* 1 *dim. of* кошара 2 beehive 3 *Sport.* basketball

кошаркар *m Sport.* basketball player

кошер *m see* кошар

кошерка *f see* кошарка 2

кошија -ии *f* horse-race; prize for winning a horse-race

кошка *impf* I to kick; кошка топка to kick a ball; to play ball II – се 1 to kick each other 2 to lash out, kick *intrans.* 3 *fig.* to squabble, bicker, quarrel; to live in discord

кошкапа *f* children's game (*played by kicking caps*)

кошмар *m* nightmare

кошне *pf* кошна *aor.* I to kick II – се (*with dat.*) to go for, attack

кошница *f* 1 basket 2 beehive

кошничар *m* basket weaver

кошнува (се) *impf of* кошне (се)

кошоглавица *f f.p.* dishevelled woman

кошта *impf* to cost; колку сака нека кошта money is no object

коштан *m dial. see* костен¹

кошула *f* 1 shirt; долна кошула vest, *Am.* undershirt; змиска кошула cast-off snakeskin, slough; ❑ си ја продаде и кошулата од грбот to sell the shirt off one's back; нема кошула на грбот to be destitute 2 *Anat.* placenta

кошута *f Zool.* doe, hind

КПЈ *abbr.* (*Комунистичка партија на Југославија*) Communist Party of Yugoslavia

крабар *m Zool.* (Carcinus maenas) green crab

крава *f Zool.* cow; крава молзница milch cow; млечна крава milch cow; стелна крава cow in (with) calf; морска крава (Manatus) manatee, sea cow

кравај -аи *m* 1 round loaf, *Austral.* damper 2 *fig.* cake (*of wax, cheese*)

кравар *m* cowherd

краварник -ци *m* cowshed

кравата *f* tie, necktie

кравешки *adj see* кравји

кравичка *f* 1 *dim. of* крава 2 *fig.* quiet, calm person

кравји *adj* cow's; кравјо млеко cow's milk; кравјо беснило mad cow disease, bovine spongiform encephalopathy (BSE)

краг *m* round board (*for kneading dough*)

крагуј -уи *m Zool.* (Gyps fulvus) griffon vulture

крадач *m see* крадец

краде *impf* I to steal *trans.*; (*стока, коњи*) to rustle, *Austral.* duff; (*на карти*) to cheat II – **ce** to steal, creep *intrans.* (*од/до/кон – out/up to/towards*)

крадеж *m* theft; stealing

крадец -дци *m* thief; burglar; shop-lifter

крадечки *adv see* крадешкум

крадешката *adv see* крадешкум

крадешкум *adv* stealthily, furtively, secretly, surreptitiously; влезе крадешкум to steal in

крадла *f colloq.* (*fem. form*) *see* крадло

крадлив *adj* thieving, thievish, light-fingered

крадло -овци *m colloq.* thief

крадум *adv see* крадешкум

краен -jна *adj* last; furthermost, outermost; lowest; extreme, utmost; крајната куќа во улицата the last house in the street; краен срок deadline; крајно време е it is high time; со крајни сили with one's last strength; со крајни напори with a supreme effort; со краен случај at the worst, in the last resort; крајна беда extreme poverty; крајни мерки extreme measures; крајно безобразие the height of impudence (impertinence); краен резултат final result

краешник -ци *m* end crust (*of a loaf of bread*)

кражба *f* theft; shop-lifting; провална кражба burglary

краина *f* 1 outskirts, outlying area 2 province, district 3 end, limit; ❏ правина до краина carrying justice through to the end

краиште *n* edge, brink, margin

крај¹ *m pl* краишта 1 end; edge, brink; на крајот на светот at the end of the world; оди по крај to walk along the edge <of the road>; ❏ без крај endless<ly>; до крај to the end; completely; тажен/весел крај sad/happy ending; на крај<от> (на крајот на краиштата) in the end; finally; at long last; when it comes down to it; од крај време from time immemorial; од крај до крај, од крај на крај, од крај в крај from start to finish; from one end to the other; нема крај there is no end to it; не му се гледа крајот one can't see the end <of it>; му турив крај I put an end to it; му го најде крајот he managed to find a way out (solution); кај ќе му излезе крајот? who knows how it will turn out? who knows how he will manage? излегува на крај со to get the better of; to cope with; врзува крај со крај, излегува на крај to make ends meet; ни на крај ум не ми беше I hadn't the slightest intention, I never even thought of it; over my dead body; му се ближи крајот his end is near; му тури крај на животот he committed suicide; извлекува подебел крај to get the worst of the bargain; издржува до крај to stay the course; крајот делото го краси all's well that ends well; се гледа крајот the end is not far off 2 region,

district; роден крај place of birth, native land, homeland

крај² *prep* by, near; крај мене near me, by my side; крај море by the sea

крајбрежен -жна *adj* coast, coastal, littoral; крајбрежна држава maritime state

крајбрежје *n* coast

крајморје *n* coastal region; seaside

крајник -ци *m* tonsil; воспаление на крајниците tonsillitis

крајнина *f* 1 *see* краиште 2 suburb, outskirts

крајност *f* extreme; до крајност extremely, utterly; оди во крајност to go to extremes

крајречен -чна *adj* riverine, riverside *attrib.*

крајче *n dim. see* краешник

крак -ци *m* 1 *dial.* leg; ❏ пушти краци to step up/out 2 (*на пат, пруга*) spur, branch; (*на река*) branch, arm, fork; краци на шестар arms of a pair of compasses; краци на триаголник sides of a triangle

крака *impf* (*за кокошка*) to cackle, cluck; (*за патка*) to quack; (*за гавран*) to crow, caw

кракел -кли *m* hook

кракле *m colloq.* long-legged man

краклест *adj* long-legged, leggy; краклест човек long-legged person

крал -ови -еви *m* king; *fig.* крал на петролејот oil king; крал пик king of spades

кралица *f* queen

кралски *adj* royal, regal

кралство *n* kingdom

кралува *impf* to reign, rule (*as king*)

кралчиче *n Bot.* (Robinia pseudacacia) (false) acacia, black locust tree

кралштина *f arch.* kingdom

крамп *m* pickaxe, pick

кран *m* crane (*lifting machine*)

кранта *f* 1 nag 2 *fig.* sluggish person

крап *m Zool.* (Cyprinus carpio) carp

крапче *n dim. of* крап; пушти рипче да фатиш крапче *prov.* throw a sprat to catch a mackerel

крас *m* karst, *see* карст

краса *f* snake

красат *adj see* киселкав

красатка -ко *adj* (*rare in m*) красатко време cold clear weather

красен -сна *adj* wonderful, splendid

краси *impf* I to adorn, decorate; руба краси, руба гнаси *prov.* the apparel proclaims the man II – **ce** to adorn o.s.

краснопис *m* calligraphy, penmanship

краснописец -сци *m* calligrapher

красноречив *adj* eloquent

красноречивост *f* eloquence

красноречие *n see* красноречивост

красота *f* beauty, splendour

краста¹ *f* 1 scab, crust 2 *fig.* bad habit; vice; си ја исчеша крастата to indulge one's passion

краста² *f* bare stony place

крастав *adj* scabby, mangy; *fig.* nasty; крастава жаба *Zool.* toad

краставица *f Bot.* (Cucumis sativus) cucumber; gherkin; кисели краставици pickled gherkins; ❏ краставици <кисели>! rubbish! nonsense!

краставичар *m* cucumber seller; ❏ на краставичар

краставици не продавај don't teach your grand-mother to suck eggs!

краставичен -чна *adj* cucumber; краставичен крем cucumber cream (cosmetic)

крастоса <ce> *pf* to become scabby

крастосува <ce> *impf of* крастоса <ce>

крастун *m Bot.* (Quercus pubescens) downy oak

кратенка *f* abbreviation

кратер *m* crater

крати *impf* 1 to shorten, reduce, abbreviate 2 to deprive, deny 3 to prohibit, forbid

кратко *adv* shortly; briefly; кратко и јасно (кратко ама слатко) short and sweet; loud and clear; на/за кратко <време> in the short term

кратковечен -чна *adj* short, short-lived, brief, transient, ephemeral

кратковид <ен> -дна *adj see* кусоглед

кратковидност *f see* кусогледост

кратковремен *adj see* кратковечен

краткодневица *f* winter solstice

краткометражен -жна *adj* short (*of films*); кратко-метражен филм short <film>

краткосрочен -чна *adj* short-term; краткосрочен заем short-term loan

краткост *f* brevity, shortness

краткотраен -јна *adj* brief, short-lived; краткотраен дожд brief shower

краткотрајност *f* brevity; transience

краткоум <ен> -<мн>а *adj* stupid

краткоумност *f* stupidity

краток -тка *adj* short, brief; краток опис brief description; краток пат short cut (*also fig.*); краток спој *Elec.* short circuit

краул *m* crawl <stroke>

крах *m* disaster, ruin; collapse, crash, failure; bankruptcy

крахи́ра *pf & impf* to collapse, to fail (*completely*); to go bankrupt

крачест *adj* long-legged

крбла *f* large wooden tub (vat) (*usu. for pressing grapes*)

крбло *n see* крбла

крв *f* 1 blood (*also fig.*); disposition, temperament; family, kin; човек со бујна крв hot-blooded person; му тече крв he's bleeding; *Hist.* данок во крв tribute in blood (*by taking children*); ❑ до последната капка крв to the last drop of blood; to the bitter end; крв си ми пред очи I can't stand the sight of you; крв за крв an eye for an eye; крвта вода не станува *prov.* blood is thicker than water; ми зовре крвта my blood boiled; ми се фати (здрви) крвта <од страв> the blood froze in my veins; му удри крвта в глава he saw red; пролее крв to shed blood; тоа му е во крвта that's in his blood; пие (цица) некому крв to bleed s.o. white; to torment s.o.; моја крв my own flesh and blood 2 *pl* крви, крвје, крвови pools of blood; целиот е крвови he is all covered in blood 3 *fig., f.p.* killing, murder

крвав *adj* bloody, blood-stained, gory; bloodshot; blood-red; *colloq.* terrific, great; крвави раце blood-stained hands; крвава битка bloody battle; крвави солзи bitter tears; крвава пот sweat and blood; крвав бифтек rare steak

крвави *impf* I to bleed; to shed blood; раната крвави the wound is bleeding; крвави за татковината to shed blood for one's country II – ce to become bloodshot

крвавица *f* blood sausage, black pudding

крваво *adv* painfully; with difficulty; with bitterness

крвен -вна *adj* 1 blood; бели и црвени крвни зрнца (телца) white and red blood corpuscles; крвен притисок blood pressure; крвна група blood group; крвно сродство blood relationship; крвен непријател mortal enemy; крвна одмазда blood feud; крвни интереси vital interests; црвени крвен picture of health 2 full-blooded; pure-bred, thoroughbred

крви се *impf* to quarrel, fight bitterly; се крват околу имотот they are fighting over the estate

крвјоса *pf* to become bloodshot

крвјосан *adj* bloodshot; крвјосани очи bloodshot eyes

крвјосува *impf of* крвјоса

крвник -ци *m* mortal enemy; tormentor, oppressor; hangman, executioner

крвнина *f* 1 bloodshed, murder 2 blood feud 3 relatives, kin, family; kinship

крвнички *adj* filled with hatred; ruthless; крвнички поглед withering look; (*as adv*) го удри крвнички he struck him a swingeing blow

крвно *adv* very much, deeply; крвно заинтересиран vitally interested; крвно се караат they're quarrelling bitterly; крвно сврзан (*co*) closely bound up (*with*)

крвожеден -дна *adj* bloodthirsty; ferocious

крвои́злив *m* haemorrhage, bleeding

крволок -ци *m* bloodsucker, extortioner; murderer

крволочен -чна *adj see* крвожеден

крволочник -ци *m see* крволок

крвоносен -сна *adj* крвоносни садови blood-vessels

крвопиец -јци *m* bloodsucker, extortioner; cutthroat

крвопрелевање *n* blood transfusion

крвопроливање *n* bloodshed

крвополитие -ија *n* bloodshed

крвоса *pf see* крвјоса

крвосер & **крвосерник** -ци *m colloq.* scoundrel; bastard

крвотворен -рна *adj Med.* haematopoietic

крвоток -ци *m* circulation of the blood

крвца *f dim. hyp. of* крв; drop of blood

крдар *m* (*стадо*) herd, flock

крди *impf* (*за стадо*) to rest in the shade

крдо *n see* крдар

креати́вен -вна *adj* creative

креа́тор *m* creator; designer; моден креатор fashion designer

креату́ра *f pejor.* creature

креација -ии *f* creation

крева (ce) *impf see* дига (ce); ❑ крева прашина околу (за) to make a fuss about; крева раце од to give up; се крева на високо to look down upon everyone

кревет *m* bed; (*во воз*) berth, bunk; двоен (дупли) кревет double bed; железен кревет iron bedstead; кревет на спрат bunk-bed

креветски *adj* (*of, for a*) bed; креветски чаршав bed sheet

креветче *n dim. of* кревет; cot

кревок -вка *adj* 1 (*за месо*) tender, without sinews;

(*за зеленчук*) fresh, juicy; кревко месо tender meat **2** *fig.* tender, delicate, weak; кревко здравје delicate health

креда *f* **1** calcium carbonate; chalk **2** *Geol.* the Cretaceous era

креден -дна *adj* **1** chalky; кредна хартија coated paper, chalk-overlay paper **2** *Geol.* Cretaceous; кредна формација Cretaceous formation

креденец -нци *m* buffet, sideboard; cupboard; wall unit

кредит *m* credit; loan; на кредит on credit; отворен кредит open credit; потрошувачки кредит hire purchase

кредитен -тна *adj* credit; кредитен систем credit system; кредитно писмо letter of credit; кредитна картичка credit card

кредитира *pf & impf* to credit; to finance

кредитор *m* creditor

кредитоспособен -бна *adj* creditworthy, solvent

кредо *n* creed, credo

крезол *m* creosote

крејра *pf & impf* to create; to design

крек *m* croak, croaking

крека *impf* **1** to croak; ❑ жаба на суво не крека one has to wet one's whistle **2** *fig.* to speak in a high-pitched voice; to scream

крекав *adj see* креклив

крекалица *f Zool.* (Hula arborea) tree frog

крекла *f colloq. fig.* chatterbox, talkative woman

креклив *adj* croaking; креклив глас croaking voice

крекло -овци *m colloq.* babbler, chatterbox

крекне *pf* крекна *aor.* to croak

крекнува *impf of* крекне

крем *m* **1** cream (*filling for tarts and cakes*) **2** *fig.* cream, elite; крем на општество cream of society **3** cream, ointment; крем за лице facial cream; крем за бричење shaving cream

крематориум *m* crematorium

кремен -ње *m* flint; quartz; здрав како кремен as fit as a fiddle

кременарка *f Hist.* flintlock

кременачка, **кременка** & **кременлија** *f see* кременарка

кремењак -ци *m* quartzite

крене (се) *pf* крена (се) *aor. see* дигне (се)

креол *m* Creole

креолка *f* Creole woman

креон *m* crayon; (*cosmetic*) pencil

креп *m* crêpe <de Chine>

крепа *f* rock; boulder

крепи *impf* **I** **1** to support, hold up; не ме крепат нозете my legs are giving way; ❑ не го крепи земјата he is uncontrollable **2** *fig.* to maintain, support; to care for, look after; таа го крепи детето she looks after the child **II** – **се 1** to support o.s., look after o.s./ one another **2** *fig.* to hold out, last out; старецот уште се крепи the old man is still going strong

крепне *impf* to become stronger, healthier

крепок -пка *adj* strong, robust; healthy; firm, hard

крепон *m* crépon

крепост *f* (*тврдина*) fortress, fortification

крепостен -сна *adj* крепостен селанец serf, peasant; крепосно право serfdom

креска *impf* to squeal; to scream, shriek

крескав *adj* shrieking; croaking; harsh; hoarse; shrill; крескав глас shrill (harsh) voice

крескало *n* child who cries a lot

креслив *adj see* крескав

креснак -ци *m* protective wooden collar (*for cattle*)

кресок -ци *m* scream, shriek

кретен *m* cretin

кретенест *adj* cretinous

кретенизам -змот *m* cretinism

кретон *m* cretonne

крецел -цли *m dial.* garlic clove

креч *m* ми ја фати креч ногата my leg's gone to sleep

кречетало *n* **1** (*во воденица*) shoe, trough, spout **2** child's rattle **3** *fig.* chatterbox; clatterer

крешéндо *adv Mus.* crescendo

крештлив *adj see* креслив

крже *n* child not yet baptized

крз *prep dial. see* низ

крзнар *m* furrier

крзнен *adj* fur; крзнено палто fur coat

крзно *n* fur, pelt, skin

крив *adj* **1** crooked, twisted; криво дрво gnarled tree; криви нозе bow-legs; крива река winding river; ❑ тргне по крив пат to make a bad start; крива кула leaning tower **2** guilty, in the wrong; кој му е крив? whose fault is it? сам си е крив! it's his own fault; ни крив ни должен completely innocent **3** erroneous, wrong; крива сметка miscalculation; крива клетва perjury, false oath **4** lame, limping; кривиот старец the lame old man; ❑ криво магаре, крива магарица leap-frog

крива *f Geom.* curve

кривак -ци *m see* крлук

кривачка[1] *f dial. see* грст

кривачка[2] *f* <very> gnarled tree

кривда *f* injustice; wrong

кривец -вци *m* **1** lawbreaker, culprit; ❑ дежурен кривец scapegoat **2** strong wind (*from varying directions*)

криви *impf* **I** **1** to bend, twist *trans.* **2** to blame, accuse **3** to limp, hobble **II** – **се 1** to twist *intrans.* **2** to grimace, make faces

кривина *f* **1** wrong, injustice; правината ја надможува кривината *prov.* justice will prevail **2** blame; fault; guilt **3** curve, bend; ❑ фаќа кривини to swing the lead; to bunk off

кривица *f* blame; fault; guilt; без моја кривица through no fault of mine; фрли кривица на некого to put the blame on s.o.

кривичен -чна *adj* criminal; кривично право criminal law; кривично дело criminal act

кривка *impf dim.* to limp slightly

кривне *pf* кривна *aor.* **1** to turn slightly *intrans.* **2** to lose one's balance, lurch

кривнува *impf of* кривне

криво *adv* crooked; wrong; unjustly; криво ме разбра you've misunderstood me, *colloq.* you've got me wrong; криво суди to judge unfairly; ❑ криво ми е I am sorry, I regret it; криво-лево be that as it may; one way or another

кривоверен -рна *adj* heretical

кривоверец -рци *m* heretic

кривоврат *adj* wry-necked

кривоглед *adj* (*шашлив*) cross-eyed

кривоклетник -ци *m* perjuror

кривоклетство *n* perjury

криволин␖ски *adj* curved, curving

кривоног *adj* bow-legged, bandy-legged

кривонос *adj* crooked-nosed, hook-nosed

кривооприца *f colloq.* supporter of injustice/wrong

криворог *adj* having twisted (curved) horns

кривоуст *adj* having a crooked mouth

кривошија *m* wryneck <person>

кривулест *adj* winding, twisting; кривулест пат winding road

кривули *impf see* кривулка²

кривулица *f* curve, bend

кривуличав *adj* winding, twisting

кривуличи *impf* to wind, twist *intrans.*

кривулка¹ *f* elbow (*angular joint in a pipe*)

кривулка² *impf* to wind, twist, zigzag; to meander

кривулкав *adj see* кривуличав

кривунделест *adj see* кривулест

кригла *f* glass, mug; кригла пиво mug of beer

крие *impf* **I** to hide *trans.*, conceal; to keep secret; крие нешто од некого to keep s.th. from s.o. **II – се** to hide *intrans.*, conceal o.s.; to lie hidden

криеница *f* hide-and-seek; игра криеница to play hide-and-seek

крижи-мижи *f see* криеница, мижитатара

криза *f* crisis; нервна криза nervous breakdown; станбена криза housing shortage; финансиска криза financial crisis; економска криза recession

кризма *f* confirmation (*of faith*)

кријаница *f see* криеница

крик *m* cry, scream, shriek; ❑ последен крик на модата the last word in fashion, *le dernier cri*

крикет *m Sport.* cricket

крикне *pf* крикна *aor.* to shout out, cry out

крикнува *impf of* крикне

крилат *adj* winged; ❑ крилат збор *see* крилатица

крилатен *adj see* крилат

крилатица *f* catchword, pithy saying, popular saying

крилен -лна *adj* **1** winged **2** wing

крилест *adj* winged

крили *impf* **I** to inspire; to lend wings to **II – се** to take wing

крило *n pl* крила, крилја wing (*also fig.*); крило на авион wing of an aeroplane; крило на зграда wing of a building; крило на врата wing of a door; *Sport., Pol.* лево крило left wing; шири крилја to spread one's wings (*also fig.*); ❑ му ги потсекоа крилата they clipped his wings; под крилото на Бога under God's protection; дава некому крилја to lend s.o. wings

Крим *m* the Crimea

криминал *m* crime, criminal activity

криминален -лна *adj* criminal; криминален роман detective story

криминалец -лци *m* criminal

криминалист *m* criminologist

криминалистика *f* criminology

криминалитет *m* criminality; crime

Кримјанец -нци *m* Crimean

Кримјанка *f* (*fem. form*) *see* Кримјанец

кримски *adj* Crimean

крин *m Bot.* (Lilium candidum) lily

крипта *f* crypt

кристал *m* crystal; чист како кристал as pure as crystal; as clear as glass

кристален -лна *adj* crystal

кристализација *f* crystallization

кристализира *pf & impf* **I** to crystallize *trans.* **II – се** to crystallize *intrans.* (*also fig.*), form crystals

Крит *m* Crete

критериум *m* criterion; научен критериум scientific criterion

критизер *m* carping critic

критизерство *n* captious criticism, cavilling

критизира *impf* to carp at, cavil over

критик -ци *m see* критичар

критика *f* criticism; ❑ не може да издржи критика he can't stand criticism; it cannot stand up to criticism; не трпи критика he doesn't tolerate criticism; под секоја критика beneath all criticism

критикува *impf* to criticize

критицизам -змот *m* criticism

критичар *m* critic; литературен критичар literary critic

критичен -чна *adj* critical; критично издание critical edition; критичен момент critical (decisive) moment

критички *adj see* критичен

критски *adj* Cretan

Криќанец -ни *m* Cretan

Криќанка *f* (*fem. form*) *see* Криќанец

кришен -шна *adj* secret, hidden

кришум *adv* secretly, furtively, surreptitiously; кришум го погледа he looked at him/it furtively

крка *impf* **1** to eat greedily; ❑ <си> го крка <стапот> to take the rap; to carry the can **2** (*крека*) to croak **3** *see* клокоти

кркач¹ *m* **1** glutton **2** *Zool.* (Hula arborea) tree-frog

кркач² *adv* носи некого кркач to carry piggyback

крклеш *adv see* дренкукуш

крклица *f dial. see* какол

кркма *f* **1** goat's hide/hair **2** (*usu. pl*) forelock

кркне *pf* кркна *aor.* **1** to utter a sound; да не си кркнал! not a sound from you! keep quiet! **2** to croak

кркнува *impf of* кркне

кркoлица *f dial.* bend, curve, *see* свијок

кркор *m* wheezing, heavy breathing; growl; croak; snore

кркори *impf* **1** to wheeze, breathe heavily; to make rasping sounds **2** to rumble, growl; цревата ми кркорат my stomach is rumbling **3** *see* крека 1 **4** to snore

кркоти *impf* **I** to wheeze, breathe heavily; to rasp **II – се** to giggle, titter, *see* кикоти се

кркуш *adv see* кркач²

кркушка *f* **1** *Bot.* (Helianthus tuberosus) Jerusalem artichoke **2** *Zool.* (Gobius fluviatilis) gudgeon **3** *fig.* great nuisance

крла *impf* **I 1** to rock *trans.* (*usu. children*) **2** to stagger; to be shaky; to drag o.s. **II – се** to sway, rock *intrans.*

крлави *impf colloq.* **I** to restore (*health*); планинскиот воздух му го крлави здравјето the mountain air restored his health **II – се** to recover

крлеж *m* **1** *Zool.* (Ixodes ricinus) tick **2** *fig.* blood-sucker, parasite, sponger

крлик -ци *m see* крлук

крлук -ци *m* shepherd's crook

крма¹ *f* fodder, forage, cattle feed

крма² *f Naut.* stern; tiller, helm

крма³ *f* sporting gun, shotgun

крмак -ци *m see* крмнак

крмар *m* (кормилар) helmsman

крми *impf* to feed (*cattle, livestock*)

крмнак -ци *m* hog; boar

крндак -ци *m dial.* <tree> stump, *see* пенушка

крни *impf* 1 to disparage, belittle, run down 2 to infringe on, encroach on 3 to mutilate, mangle; to ruin

крнорог *adj* with broken horn<s>

крнорога *f* goat with a broken horn

кринтија -ии *f* wreck (*thing or person*), jalopy

кров *m* roof; shelter; без кров над глава homeless; without a roof over one's head

кроеж *m* 1 cut, style; pattern 2 *fig.* intention, plan

крои *impf* I 1 to cut out; крои алишта to cut clothes; ❑ му крои капа (ќурк) he is deciding his fate; he's making decisions for him 2 *fig.* to think up, devise; крои нешто во главата he's planning s.th. 3 to trim, prune (*a vineyard*)

крој *m* cut (*of clothes*)

кројач *m* tailor; dressmaker

кројачки *adj* tailor's; dressmaker's; кројачка кукла <tailor's> dummy

кројачница *f* tailor's shop

кројка *f see* крој

крокет *m Sport.* croquet

кроки *m indecl.* sketch, drawing

крокира *pf & impf* to sketch, sketch out

крокодил *m Zool.* crocodile

крокодилски *adj* crocodile<'s>; ❑ крокодилски солзи crocodile tears

кромид *m* 1 *Bot.* onion 2 *fig.* fool, idiot, blockhead, dolt

кромидарник -ци *m* 1 place where onions are stored/grown 2 *fig.* саат кромидарник watch of poor quality

кромидушка *f* onion bulb

крондир *m arch.* decanter

крос *m* cross-country running (run)

крос-контри *m see* крос

кросно *n* (weaving) beam

кроти *impf* 1 to tame, domesticate 2 to be still; детето кроти the child is quiet

кроткост *f see* кротост

кроткотија *f see* кротост

кроткум *adv* gently, meekly

кроток -тка *adj* tame; meek, gentle, quiet, mild; obedient; кроток како јагне as meek as a lamb; кротко јагне од две мајки цица *prov. cf.* kindness is the noblest weapon to conquer with

кротост *f* gentleness, meekness

крофна *f* doughnut

кроце *adv* slowly, quietly, carefully; оди кроце to proceed slowly; со кроце со благо nicely, quietly

крошна *f* 1 cradle 2 *dial.* fish trap; creel, small basket

крпа *f* 1 rag; ❑ блед како крпа as pale as death 2 towel 3 kerchief; scarf

крпач *m* repairer; крпач на чевли shoe repairer, cobbler

крпачка *f see* крпеж

крпеж *m* repairs, mending, patching; крпеж и трпеж куќа врти; крпеж и трпеж два века *prov.* a stitch in time saves nine

крпеница *f* mended object

крпи *impf* I 1 to mend, repair 2 *fig.* to scrape along, struggle (*materially*) II – ce 1 to mend one's clothes 2 to make ends meet

крполи *impf* to scrape along, struggle

крпче *n* 1 *dim. of* крпа 2 handkerchief; ❑ си го врза в крпче he took good note of it; he took it for granted; го врза в крпче he has got him tied up, he's got control of him

крсноге *adv* седне крсноге to sit down cross-legged (Turkish fashion)

крст *m* 1 cross; на крст crosswise; ❑ бега како ѓавол од крст to avoid (*s.o./s.th.*) like the plague; кладе (тури) крст на нешто to put an end to s.th; to write s.th. off; тој е со крстот на чело he is very honest/sincere; Црвен Крст Red Cross 2 *Anat.* sacrum, small of the back; lower back; ме боли крстот I have pains in the small of my back

крстат *adj* 1 cross-shaped 2 marked with a cross

крстатен -тна *adj see* крстат 2; крстатен бајрак flag, banner with a cross on it

крстач *m Zool.* (Aquila heliaca) imperial eagle

крстачка *f* folk-dance (*in which legs are crossed in dancing*)

крсташ *m see* крстоносец

крстен¹ *pt* baptized, christened; *arch.* крстена вера Christian faith; *fig.* крстено вино wine diluted with water; ❑ крстен недокрстен fool, crazy

крстен² -сна *adj* of the cross; baptismal; крстен знак sign of the cross

крстец -тци *m* stack (pile) of sheaves

крсти¹ *pl* religious procession (*usu. during a drought*)

крсти² *pf & impf* I 1 to christen, baptize; to name; како го крстивте детето? what name did you give the child? 2 to make the sign of the cross over 3 *fig.* to dilute (*wine*) II – ce to cross o.s.; ❑ нашол црква кај да се крсти he has come to the wrong place; се крсти и со лева и со десна to be taken aback

крстина *f* 1 *see* крст 2 2 *see* крстец

крстител *m* <the> baptist; Јован Крстител John the Baptist

крстица *f see* крстец

Крстовден *m* Holy Cross Day

крстовиден -дна *adj* cross-shaped, cross-like

крстозбор *m* crossword <puzzle>

крстома *adv see* крстум

крстоносен -сна *adj* (of a) crusade; крстоносен поход Crusade; крстоносна војна war of the Crusade<s>

крстоносец -сци *m* Crusader

крстообразен -зна *adj* cross-shaped

крстопат *m* crossroads, junction, intersection

крстоса *pf* I 1 to put (place, lay) crosswise, cross *trans.* 2 to cross-breed, cross *trans.* 3 to travel through, cruise through, traverse II – ce to cross *intrans.* (*e.g. of intersecting roads*)

крстосан *adj & pt* cross, crosswise; крстосан оган cross-fire; крстосано испитување cross-examination

крстословка *f* crossword <puzzle>; решава крстословки to do crosswords

крстосува *impf of* крстоса

крстосувач *m Mil., Naut.* cruiser

крстум *adv* crossed; crosswise; across, crossways

крт *m Zool.* mole; ❑ работи како крт to work like a beaver; to be as busy as a bee

кртала (се) *impf see* тркала (се)

кртечина *f* molehill

кртешница *f see* кртечина

крти *impf* to break; to demolish

кртина *f* lean, boneless meat

кртичав *adj* кртичаво поле field damaged by moles

круг *m* **1** circle; *Sport.* (на тркачка патека) lap; ❑ квадратура на кругот quadrature of the circle; концентрични кругови concentric circles; маѓепсан круг vicious circle; he is caught in a vicious circle; *Mil.* на лево круг! about face! **2** sphere, range; purview; круг на интерес sphere of interest **3** *fig.* group, circle; фамилијарен (семеен) круг family circle; политички кругови political circles **4** grounds, surrounds; болнички круг hospital grounds

кружен -жна *adj* round, circular; кружно патување round trip; кружно движење circular movement

кружест *adj* round, circular; кружеста дамка round spot

кружи *impf* to circulate, spread *intrans.*; кружат разни гласови various rumours are spreading

кружок -ци *m* circle, group, society; литературен кружок literary society

круна *f* **1** crown (*also fig.*); summit; круна на дрво crown of a tree; круна на сета работа the climax of the whole affair **2** *Astron.* corona

круниса *pf* to crown (*also fig.*)

крунисува *impf of* круниса

круп *m Med.* croup

крупен -пна *adj* **1** large; important, serious; prominent; крупно прашање important question; крупна личност prominent person **2** coarse; крупно мелено брашно coarse flour **3** (јак) burly, strapping

крупиé *m* croupier

крупник *m Bot.* (Triticium spelta) spelt, German wheat

крут *adj* stiff, rigid, stern, strict; cruel, merciless; крути мерки stern measures; круто држење unbending attitude/behaviour

крутост *f* stiffness; strictness

круцијáлен -лна *adj* **1** *see* крстосан; круцијални прашања cross-examination **2** crucial, decisive

круша *f Bot.* (Pirus communis) pear (*tree and fruit*); делени круши, спокојни заби *prov.* short reckonings make long friends; кој седи под круша, тој јаде круши *prov.* the early bird catches the worm; круша под круша паѓа *prov.* like father, like son; зрелите круши свињите ги јадат the devil's children have the devil's luck; fortune favours fools

крушар *m* pear-seller; lover of pears

крушарник -ци *m* pear orchard

крушец -вци *m* grain; крушец сол a grain of salt

крушка *f colloq.* light bulb, *Austral.* light globe

крушов *adj* pear; крушово дрво pear tree

крушовиден -дна *adj* pear-shaped

крушовица *f* pear brandy; pear liqueur

крц *interj* crack! creak! squeak!

крца *impf see* крцка

крцка *impf* **1** to crack, break open (*walnuts, hazelnuts*) *trans.* **2** to creak, squeak; креветот крцка the bed creaks; зглобовите крцкаат the joints creak; колата крцка the cart creaks; снегот крцка the snow crunches **3** to grind, gnash (со заби – *one's teeth*)

крцкав *adj* creaky, squeaky

крцкот *m* creaking, squeaking; crunching; gnashing

крцне *pf* крцна *aor. see* крцка

крцнува *impf of* крцне

крцул *m* old breed of domestic pig

крчма *f* **1** inn, tavern; селска крчма village inn **2** *fig.* celebration (*on completion of a job, on sealing a bargain*); у мене е крчмата it's on me, *Austral.* it's my shout

крчмар *m* innkeeper

крчмарица & крчмарка *f* (*fem. form*) *see* крчмар; barmaid

крчми *impf* to keep an inn

крш *m* **1** chaos; крш и лом chaos, disorder; debris; *fig.* chaotic situation; a pretty kettle of fish **2** karst, stony ground

кршеглавечки *adv* headlong, head first; abruptly

кршен -шна *adj* tall; well-built, well-shaped; robust, strong

крши *impf* **I 1** to break off; to break, fracture *trans.*; ❑ крши глава! крши вратот! get out of my sight! get lost! кршат копја околу нешто to cross swords over s.th.; крши прсти to crack one's fingers **2** *fig.* to break, violate; го крши уставот to infringe the constitution **3** *colloq.* крши снага to sway, bend the body (*when walking*) **II – се 1** to break *intrans.*; лесно се крши to be fragile **2** *fig.* to hesitate, waver **3** to sway, bend the body (*when walking*); се крши како некоја ченгија she sways like a Gypsy dancer

кршигора *m f.p.* (*epithet for a*) strong, fast horse

кршјак -ци *m* young hare

кршка *impf* **I 1** to wind, twist, zigzag (*when walking*) **2** to turn *intrans.* **3** *fig.* to hedge, equivocate; to evade, elude; to be unreliable; to be unfaithful **II – се** to bet on the breaking of a wishbone

кршкало *n* **1** unreliable person, double-dealer **2** wishbone

кршканица *f rare* turning; zigzagging

кршла *f* **1** *see* мандра **1 2** *arch.* barracks

кршлив *adj* fragile, brittle

кршне[1] *pf* кршна *aor. of* крши

кршне[2] *pf* кршна *aor. of* кршка to turn slightly *intrans.*

кршгава *impf* to christen, baptize

кршгавање *n* baptism, christening (*also fig.*); ❑ борбено (огнено) кршгавање baptism of fire

кршгалник -ци *m* font

кршгева *impf see* кршгава

кршгелен -лна *adj* baptismal; кршгелно свидетелство baptismal certificate

кршгелница *f* baptismal (birth) certificate

кршгеник -ци *m* godchild, godson

кршгеница *f* goddaughter

кршгенка *f* christening

к.с. *abbr.* (коњска сила) horsepower, h.p.

ксилогрáф *m* wood-engraver; xylographer

ксилографија *f* wood-engraving, wood-carving; xylography

ксилофóн *m Mus.* xylophone

ктитор *m Hist.* founder, church-donor

Куала Лумпур *m* Kuala Lumpur

куалалумпурец -рци *m* person from Kuala Lumpur

куалалумпурка *f* (*fem. form*) *see* куалалумпурец

куалалумпурски *adj* Kuala Lumpur *attrib.*

куб *m* cube; *Math.* дига на куб to cube, raise to the power of three

Куба *f* Cuba

Кубанец -нци *m* Cuban

Кубанка *f* (*fem. form*) *see* Кубанец

кубански *adj* Cuban

кубатура *f* cubic capacity, volume

кубе[1] *n* dome, cupola

кубе[2] *impf* **I 1** to pluck, pull out; кубе веѓи to pluck one's eyebrows; ❏ ги кубе косите to tear one's hair out **2** *fig.* to overcharge, rob, fleece **II** – *ce* to pull out one's hair; to fight

кубен -бна *adj* cube, cubic; *Math.* кубен корен cube root; кубен метар cubic metre

кубизам -змот *m* *Art* cubism

кубик -ци *m* cubic metre

кубира *impf* *Math.* to cube

кубист *m* *Art* cubist

кубне *pf* кубна *aor.* to pluck

кубнува *impf* *of* кубне

кубур *m* *arch.* **1** pistol **2** hardship, adversity

Кувајт *m* Kuwait

кувајтски *adj* Kuwaiti

Кувајќанец -ни *m* Kuwaiti

Кувајќанка *f* (*fem. form*) *see* Кувајќанец

кувенција -ии *m* *see* кујунџија

кувет *m* *colloq.* strength; без кувет without <any> strength; земе кувет to gain strength

куветлија *adj indecl. colloq.* strong, tough

кугла *f* ball; bowling ball; globe

куглана *f* bowling alley

кугла се *impf* to bowl, play bowls

куглагер *m* *Tech.* (*кугличен лагер*) ball bearing

куглица & **кугличка** *f dim. of* кугла; shot; pellet

КУД *abbr.* (*Културно-уметничко друштво*) Cultural and Artistic Society

кудач *m* critic, carper; reviler

куди *impf* **1** to blame; to censure; to deride, run down **2** to criticize, find fault with

кујна *f* **1** kitchen; полска кујна field kitchen **2** cuisine; македонска кујна Macedonian cuisine

кујнски *adj* kitchen; кујнска маса kitchen table

кујунџија -ии *m* goldsmith; silversmith

кујунџиство *n* jeweller's/goldsmith's trade; silversmithing; brassworking; copper chasing

кука[1] *f see* кукачка[1]

кука[2] *impf* to cuckoo

кукавица *f* **1** *Zool.* cuckoo **2** *fig.* coward, *colloq.* chicken

кукавички *adj* cowardly, cravenly; кукавички акт cowardly act

кукавичлук *m* cowardice, cowardliness

кукавичност *f see* кукавичлук

кукалка *f see* кукачка[1]; ❏ кукалка се стори to waste away

кукачка[1] *f* hook

кукачка[2] *f* stacked hay/flax

кукла *f* **1** doll; puppet (*also fig.*); убава како кукла as pretty as a doll; кукло моја! my beauty! надвор кукла, а внатре панукла *prov.* a fair face but a foul heart **2** *colloq.* loaf **3** *dial.* package, bundle **4** cotton (*prepared for spinning*)

куклар *m* doll maker; puppeteer

куклен *adj* *from* кукла; куклен театар puppet <theatre> show

куклест *adj* doll-like, pretty

кукне *pf* кукна *aor.* **1** to cuckoo **2** *fig. see* окука

куков *adj in the expression:* на куков ден until the Greek Calends; till the cows come home

куку & **ку-ку** *interj* cuckoo!

кукул *m* **1** hood **2** tuft, crest; bun

кукумјавка *f* *Zool.* (Athene noctua) little owl

кукурек -ци *m* *Bot.* (Helleborus odorus) stinking hellebore

кукурига *impf* (*за петел*) to crow

кукуригне *pf* кукуригна *aor.* to crow

кукуригнува *impf of* кукуригне

кукуригу *interj* cockadoodledoo!

Кукуш *m* Kilkis

кукушанец -ни *m* person from Kilkis

кукушанка *f* (*fem. form*) *see* кукушанец

кукушки *adj* Kilkis *attrib.*

кула *f* tower (*also Hist.*); ❏ ветува златни кули to promise pie in the sky; ѕида кули во воздух to build castles in the air

кулак -ци *m* kulak, rich peasant

кули *m* coolie, Indian porter

кулик -ци *m* *Zool.* (Burhinus oedicnemus) stone curlew

кулинарски *adj* culinary

кулинарство *n* cookery, culinary art, cuisine

кулиса *f* backdrop, set; ❏ зад кулисите behind the scenes, secretly

кулминација *f* culmination

кулминира *pf & impf* to culminate

кулоар *m* (*usu. pl*) corridor, lobby

кулон *m* *Elec.* coulomb

култ *m* cult; култ на личноста personality cult

култиватор *m* *Tech.* cultivator

култивира *impf* to cultivate

култура *f* **1** culture; духовна култура spiritual culture; човек со висока култура cultured person **2** crop; индустриски култури industrial crops; житни култури grain crops

културен -рна *adj* **1** cultural; cultured; cultivated; културен центар cultural centre; културен човек cultured person; културна средина cultured environment, milieu **2** (*за растенија*) културно растение cultivated plant, cultivar

културтрегер *m* (*usu. iron.*) *Kulturträger*, bearer of culture/civilization

кулук -ци *m* corvée, drudgery

кулукува *impf* to drudge, slave, toil

кулучар *m* labourer, day labourer

кум *m* godfather, witness (*at a wedding*)

кума *f* godmother; witness (*at a wedding*); wife of a *kum*; кума лиса (*in folk-tales*) sly fox

кумаш *m* kind of silken material

кумашин *m* godson; father of one's godson; bridegroom (*in relation to кум – witness*)

куми *impf* to beg, entreat; моли и куми некого to beg and plead with s.o.

кумир *m* idol

кумов *adj* of a godfather/witness (*at a wedding*); ❏ Кумова слама Milky Way

кумрија -ии *f see* гугутка

кумство *n* the duties and relationship of a *kum*

кумува *impf* **1** to act as a *kum* at a wedding or a christening **2** *fig.* to see (*s.th.*) through; to nurture

кумулативен -вна *adj* **1** cumulative **2** *Mil.* hollow-charge; кумулативна граната hollow-charge shell

кумулѝра *pf & impf* to accumulate

кумулус *m* cumulus <cloud>

куна *f Zool.* (Martes martes) pine marten

кунада & **кунатка** *f see* куна

кунг-фу *m* kung fu

кундак -ци *m* rifle butt; потков на кундак butt plate

куп[1] -ови, -ишта *m* **1** heap, pile; куп дрва pile of wood; става на куп to pile up *trans.*; со (на)купишта by the heap/ton/bagful **2** crowd

куп[2] *m* cup, trophy

купар -при *m* deep vessel (*for liquids*), goblet, chalice

купе *n* compartment (*of a railway carriage*)

купел -пли *m Rel.* font

купен *pt* bought; купените стоки не се враќаат no refunds given

купец -пци *m see* купувач

купечки *adj* **1** commercial; купечки леб bread bought in a shop, *Am.* store-bought bread **2** *fig. pejor.* foreign, alien; strange; купечки зборови malapropisms

купи *pf* to buy, purchase; ❑ купи на старо to buy secondhand; купи за готови пари to buy for cash; купина вересија to buy on credit; купи мачка во вреќа to buy a pig in a poke; купи под рака to buy illegally (on the black market)

купиште *n augm. of* куп[1]

куплет *m* **1** stanza, verse **2** (*pl only*) ditties, rhymes

куплетен -тна *adj Prosody* stanzaic

куплетѝст *m* rhymester

куплунг -зи *m Tech.* clutch

куповен -вна *adj* **1** *see* купечки 1 **2** buying, purchase; куповна цена purchase price

купола *f* cupola, dome

купо́н *m* coupon; ration card; stub

купопродажба *f* purchase and sale, buying and selling

купува *impf* **1** *of* купи **2** *fig.* to assimilate, learn, take in; тој само слуша и купува he just listens and takes everything in

купувач *m* buyer, purchaser, customer; постојан купувач regular customer

купувачка *f* purchase, buying; купувачка на стоки за широка потрошувачка purchase of consumer goods

купче *n* **1** *dim. of* куп[1] **2** *pl* купчиња 1. children's game (*with walnuts, fruit stones, etc.*) 2. card game

купчи се *impf* to stoop, crouch

кур -ови *m vulg.* prick, cock

кураж *m* bravery, courage, daring; resolution

куражи *impf* **I** to encourage, cheer up **II** – **се** to summon up courage; to become more courageous

куратѝва *f* treatment, healing, curing

куратѝвен -вна *adj* curative, therapeutic, healing

курбан *m arch.* (*Muslim*) animal sacrifice oblation; sacrifice, offering

курбла *f Tech.* crank <-handle>

курва *f vulg.* **1** whore, prostitute, trollop **2** *fig.* coward

курва се *impf vulg.* to whore around

курвалак -ци *m vulg.* whoredom; immorality, baseness; shameless act

курвар *m vulg.* whore-monger; womanizer

курварница *f vulg.* brothel

курвински *adj vulg.* **1** whorish **2** *fig.* shameless; cowardly; treacherous, perfidious

курвува се *impf vulg. see* курва се

курдела *f see* кордела

курдиса *pf colloq.* **I 1** to wind up (*a watch, clock*) **2** to place, put; to arrange **II** – **се** to settle down, sit down comfortably

курдисува (се) *impf of* курдиса (се)

куре́нтен -тна *adj* in demand, popular, selling well; курентни стоки goods in demand

курешница *f* henhouse, chicken coop

курзив *m Print.* italics

курзивен -вна *adj* italic; курзивни букви italic letters

курија -ии *f Hist.* curia

курио́зен -зна *adj* unusual, strange, curious; inquisitive, curious

куриозите́т *m* curiosity; rarety, unusualness

курир *m* courier; дипломатски курир diplomatic courier

курна *f* stone basin (*in Turkish bath-house*)

курназ *adj indecl. colloq.* insolent; arrogant, conceited; курназ-будала conceited fool; курназ <човек> devil's advocate

курс *m* **1** exchange rate **2** course, trend, direction (*also fig.*) **3** training (educational) course

курсен -сна *adj* курсна листа exchange-rate list

курсѝст *m* student; participant in a course

курсѝстка *f* (*fem. form*) *see* курсист

куртиза́нка *f* courtesan

куртоа́зен -зна *adj* courteous; куртоазна посета a courtesy visit

куртоазија *f* courtesy

куртул *m colloq.* escape, salvation

куртули *pf colloq.* **I** to save, deliver from; to get rid of **II** – **се** to save o.s.; to free o.s. (*од – of*), rid o.s.

куртулија *f see* куртул

куртулиса (се) *pf see* куртули (се)

куртулисува (се) *impf see* куртулува (се)

куртулува (се) *impf of* куртули (се)

куртулувачка *f see* куртул

куртулуш *m see* куртул

куршлус *m* **1** short circuit **2** *fig.* spat, tiff

куршум *m* bullet, cartridge; ❑ летне како куршум to fly like a bullet; со еден куршум два зајака <to kill> two birds with one stone

кус *adj* **1** short, brief, concise; small (*in stature*); куси ракави short sleeves; кусо петле, *see* кускуле; ❑ кус во умот not very bright **2** tailless; short-tailed; ❑ кусиот the devil

кусак -ци *m* short dolman (robe, mantle)

кусале *n see* кусак

кусе *n* **1** dock-tailed dog **2** short person **3** *see* жрепка

куси *impf* **I 1** to shorten; to cut off **2** to give short measure **II** – **се** to become short (shorter); ❑ му се кусат дните his days are numbered

кусичок -чка *adj dim. of* кус; quite short, rather short

кускуле *n iron.* short person; midget

кускун *m see* подопашник

кусо *adv* **1** briefly, concisely **2** lacking; што ти е кусо? what's missing? what are you short of? ❑ уште тоа беше кусо! as if that were not enough! that's the last straw!

кусовечен -чна *adj* short, short-lived

кусоглед *adj* short-sighted, near-sighted, myopic

кусогледост *f* short sight

кусок[1] -ци *m* deficit, shortfall; shortage; кусок во касата cash deficit

кусок[2] -ска *adj dim. of* кус

кусоумен -мна *adj* stupid, dull-witted

кусоумност *f* stupidity

кустос *m* custodian

кусур *m* **1** change (*money*) **2** fault, failing; ❏ не фаќај за кусур don't be offended, don't take it amiss

кутар -тра *adj* poor, miserable; кутриот човек wretched man, poor devil

кутел -тли *m* **1** deep wooden vessel **2** measure (*mainly for grain, 29 kg*)

кутер *m* sloop; cutter

кутија -ии *f* box; една кутија цигари a packet of cigarettes; гласачка кутија ballot box; ❏ како од кутија изваден brand new

кутијка *f* & **кутиче** *n dim. of* кутија

кутина *impf of* кутне I *see* кутне II – **се 1** to wrestle; to struggle **2** *see* кутне се

кутка *impf dim.* I *see* кутне II – **се** *see* кутина се

кутканица *f colloq.* wrestling

кутлица *f* small box for flour

кутне *pf* кутна *aor.* I to knock down, throw to the ground; to floor II – **се** to lie down; to sprawl

кутол -тли *m see* кутел

кутре *n dim.* puppy, whelp

кутри *adj see* кутар

кутура *impf dial. see* вала²

кутурица *adv* in bulk, all together, *see* ѓутуре, ѓутурица

куќа *f* **1** house; куќа на два ката two-storeyed house; зад куќи in the backyard; оди по куќи from house to house; to go visiting; издавачка куќа publishing house; стоковна куќа department store; ❏ вечна куќа the grave; јавна куќа brothel; луда куќа madhouse; нема ни куќа ни куќнина he has nothing in this world; утреш куќа не рани *prov.* don't put off till tomorrow what you can do today **2** *fig., colloq.* household; family; од добра куќа of good family; ❏ врти куќа to run (manage) a household

куќарина *f* house tax

куќарка *f pejor.* dilapidated house, shack

куќарче *n see* куќарка

куќен -ќна *adj* home, domestic, household, family

куќи *impf* I куќи куќа to buy/acquire a house II – **се** to buy/acquire a house; to settle down

куќичка & **куќица** *f dim. of* куќа; small house, cottage; hovel; своја куќичка, своја слободичка *prov.* a man's home is his castle

куќник -ци *m* good family man

куќнина *f* household effects (*furniture, electrical equipment, etc.*)

куќница *f* good housewife; good home-maker; плаче куќа за куќница *prov.* the house depends on the housewife

куќовен -вна *adj see* домашен; куќовни луѓе members of the <same> household

куќовртник -ци *m see* куќник

куфер *m* suitcase; ❏ исфрла некого како куфер to kick s.o. out; to send s.o. packing; лета како куфер to get the sack; to get one's marching orders

куц *adj* lame; куциот the devil, Old Nick

куца *impf* to limp, hobble, be lame (*also fig.*); ми куца работата my business is not going well

куцана *adv* limping; lamely

куцка *impf dim.* **1** to limp a little **2** to hop (*on one leg*)

куцне *pf* куцна *aor.* to limp

куцнува *impf* to limp (*slightly, occasionally*)

Куцовлав -ци *m Kucovlah*, a Macedonian Vlach (Wallach)

куче *n* **1** dog, hound; бесно куче mad dog; домашно куче house dog; ловечко куче hunting dog; полициско куче police dog; ❏ живеат како кучето и мачето they get on together like cat and dog; како на куче му помина the illness passed quickly; he recovered quickly; нема ни куче ни маче he is completely alone in the world; (*also impers.*) there's absolutely no one around; село без кучиња a deserted village; се јадат како кучиња they don't get on; си кладе од куче очи he's become quite shameless; тоа ни кучињата не го јадат even a dog wouldn't eat that; рани куче да те лае to nurture a viper in one's bosom; куче што лае не каса *prov.* the dog that barks a lot doesn't bite **2** little dog, puppy **3** *fig., pejor.* cur, brute; големо куче е тој he's an absolute swine

кученце *n dim. from* куче; puppy, pup

кучешјак -ци *m see* песјак

кучешки *adj* dog's, canine; *fig.* кучешки живот dog's life; кучешки заб canine tooth, eye-tooth, *see* песјак; кучешко грозје *Bot.* (Solanum nigrum) black nightshade, morel

кучи се *impf* (*of a bitch*) to whelp, have puppies

кучило *n* scum, riffraff, vermin

кучински *adj see* кучешки

кучка *f* bitch (*also fig., pejor.*); брзата кучка слепи кучиња раѓа *prov.* haste makes waste

кучкарник -ци *m* kennel, doghouse

куша *impf see* бае

кушачка *f see* бајачка

кушет-кола *f* sleeping-car

Л

ла *f Mus.* A

лаана *f dial.* (*кисела зелка*, *расол*) pickled cabbage, sauerkraut

лабав *adj* **1** loose (*also fig.*); slack (*also fig.*); *fig.* lax, lenient; лабава дисциплина slack discipline; лабав морал loose morals **2** (*за човек*) feeble, flabby, flaccid

лабави *impf* to loosen, make loose

лабавина *f* looseness; slackness

лабаво *adv* loosely; slackly; ❏ нема лабаво no slacking!

лабавост *f see* лабавина

лабед *m see* лебед

лабедов *adj see* лебедов

лабија́л *m Phon.* labial

лабија́лен -лна *adj Phon.* labial

лабилен -лна *adj* unstable; fickle; irresolute; changeable; лабилен карактер unreliable character

лабилност *f* instability; variability

лабис *m* **1** *Med.* forceps **2** *Rel.* spoon used to administer Holy Communion

лабора́нт *m* laboratory technician/assistant

лабора́нтка *f* (*fem. form*) *see* лаборант

лабораторија -ии *f* laboratory

лабораториски *adj* laboratory *attrib.*; лабораториски обид laboratory experiment

лабури́ст *m Pol.* member of the Labour Party, Labourite

лабури́стички *adj Pol.* Labour; лабуристичка партија Labour Party

лав *m Zool.* lion (*also fig.*); *Astron.* Leo; морски лав (Otaria) sea lion; ❏ се бори како лав to fight like a lion/tiger

лава *f* lava; (*ствднатa*) clinker

лавабо *n* (*мијалник*) sink; washbasin

лава́нда *f Bot.* lavender

лавина *f* avalanche (*also fig.*)

лави́ра *impf* **1** to tack, change direction **2** *fig.* to manoeuvre, zigzag; to temporize

лавири́нт *m* labyrinth, maze (*also fig.*)

лавица *f Zool., fig.* lioness

лавне *pf* лавна *aor.* to bark

лавнува *impf of* лавне

лавовски *adj & adv* lion's; leonine; like/as a lion; ❏ лавовски дел lion's share; лавовска борба heroic struggle; со лавовско срце lion-hearted

лавор *m Bot.* (Laurus nobilis) laurel, bay

лаворов *adj see* лавров

лавра *f* monastery (*of the first rank*)

лавров *adj* laurel; лавров лист bay-leaf; ❏ лавров венец laurel wreath

лаг *m* grove, coppice; wood

лага *f* lie, falsehood; ситна лага white lie; невина лага fib; ❏ фаќа некого во лага to catch s.o. out (*in a lie*); лаги со опашки, лаги со рогови barefaced lies; ако е вистина, голема лага believe that if you can! нема лага seriously; во лагата се кратки нозете *prov.* lies have short legs

лагам *m* underground passage; shaft (*in a mine*)

лагер *m* **1** storehouse, warehouse; stock room; ❏ има на лагер to have in stock **2** (*логор*) camp **3** *Tech.* bearing; кугличен лагер ball-bearing

лагу́на *f* lagoon

лад *m* shade; по ладот in the shade; when it's cooler

ладало *n* fan

ладен -дна *adj* cold, cool (*also fig.*); ❏ ладен туш shock, unpleasant surprise; ладно оружје cold steel

лади *impf* **I** to cool, chill *trans.*; ❏ си ја лади душата со некого to go out with s.o. just for fun **II** – **се 1** to cool off (down) **2** *fig.* to lose interest (*во, за нешто – in s.th.*) **3** to laugh at, mock, make fun of, ridicule; сите се ладат со него they all make fun of him (laugh at him)

ладилник -ци *m* icebox; cooler; refrigerator; cool room; refrigerator truck; *Mech.* radiator (*of an engine*)

ладнее *impf* to cool, turn/grow cold; времето ладнее the weather is turning cold

ладнина *f* shade; cool<ness>

ладно *adv* cold<ly>, coolly (*also fig.*); ладно ми е I feel cold; ладно пречека некого to give s.o. a cold reception, give s.o. the cold shoulder

ладнокрвен -вна *adj* cold-blooded; cool, calm

ладнокрвно *adv* coolly; in cold blood

ладнокрвност *f* cold-bloodedness; coolness, composure, equanimity, presence of mind, sang-froid

ладовен -вна *adj* shady; cool

ладовина *f* shade; cool<ness>; cool place

ладовинка *f dim. of* ладовина

ладовиште *n* cool place

ла́ѓа *f* ship; boat

лае *impf* **1** to bark, bay; ❏ куче што лае не каса *prov.* barking dogs seldom bite **2** *fig.* to shout; to quarrel **3** *fig.* to slander, defame, run down; to gossip

лаеж *m* barking, bark

лаж *m* liar, fibber

лажга *f dial. see* лашка

лажго -овци *m dial. see* лашко

лаже *impf* **I 1** to lie, tell lies; ако баба лаже, трап не лаже *prov.* actions speak louder than words; кој лаже, тој краде he that will lie, will steal; *colloq.* лаже – суши to lie through one's teeth; лаже како Циган to lie like a trooper **2** to deceive, cheat; ако не ме лажат очиве if my eyes don't deceive me **3** to amuse, entertain *trans.*; лаже дете to amuse a child **II – се 1** to lie to one another; to cheat one another **2** to be mistaken; to deceive o.s.; ако не се лажам if I'm not mistaken **3** *fig. colloq.* to have a love affair

лажен -жна *adj* false; mock *attrib.*; лажна вера false belief; лажни пари forged (counterfeit) money; лажно свидетелство false certificate; лажно сведочење perjury

лажи́ра *pf & impf Sport.* to fix, rig; лажира натпревар to fix a game лажица *f* **1** spoon; spoonful; супена лажица soup-spoon; две лажици шеќер two spoonfuls of sugar **2** (*за чевли*) shoehorn

лажичар *m* maker of wooden spoons

лажичарник -ци *m* **1** spoon rack **2** water-mill with spoon-shaped spokes in its mill-wheel

лажиче *n dim. of* лажица; teaspoon

лажичка *f* **1** *Anat.* pit of the stomach, epigastrium **2** *see* лажиче

лажлив *adj* lying, untruthful, mendacious; deceitful, treacherous

лажливец -вци *m* liar

лажно *adv* falsely

лажност *f* falsity, falseness

лажовен -вна *adj see* лажлив

лажовник -ци *m* liar; cheat

лажовница *f* (*fem. form*) *see* лажовник

лажоман *m colloq.* liar

лазарет *m Mil.* field hospital

лазач *m Zool.* reptile

лазаче *n* toddler; infant, crawler

лази *impf* to crawl, creep; морници ме лазат I get the shivers; детето лази the child is crawling; возот лази the train crawls along

лазибубе *n Bot.* (Tropaeolum majus) nasturtium, Indian cress

лазина *f &* лазиште *n* clearing (*in a forest*)

лазне *pf* лазна *aor.* to crawl, creep <up>

лазнува *impf of* лазне

лазур *m poet.* azure

лазурен -рна *adj poet.* azure, blue

лаик -ци *m* layman, non-professional

лаички *adj* lay, inexpert, non-professional

лај *m* bark<ing>

лајач *m* **1** barking dog **2** *fig.* chatterbox, babbler; gossip; slanderer

лајкучка *f Bot. see* боливач

лајненица *f vulg.* nonsense, bilge, bull<shit>, crap

лајно *n vulg.* shit

лајтмотив *m* leitmotif

лајца *f dial. see* лажица

лајче *n dial. see* лажиче

лак[1] *m* **1** bow; лак и стрела bow and arrow **2** *Math.* arc

лак[2] *m* varnish, lacquer; чевли од лак patent leather shoes; лак за нокти nail polish

лака *f* water meadow

лакати *impf* **I** to twist, wind *trans.* **II** – се to twist, wind *intrans.*; (*за река*) to meander

лакатиса *pf* to bend into an arc

лакеј -ен *m* **1** footman, manservant **2** *fig.* lackey, flunkey, toady

лакејски *adj* servile, obsequious; лакејска понизност servile humility

лакејство *n* servility, slavishness, toadyism

лакерда *f Zool.* (Petromyzon marinus) lamprey

лакира *pf & impf* to varnish, polish, lacquer

лакмус *m Chem.* litmus

лакмусов *adj Chem.* litmus; лакмусова хартија litmus paper

лаком *adj* greedy, avid; covetous, avaricious; лаком за јадење greedy for food, ravenous; лаком за пари greedy for money

лакомец -мци *m* glutton, greedy person

лакоми се *impf* (*за*) to crave

лакомија *f* greed, insatiability

лакомник -ци *m see* лакомец

лакомница *f* (*fem. form*) *see* лакомник

лакомство *n &* лакомштина *f see* лакомија

лаконизам -змот *m* laconism

лаконски *adj & adv* laconic; laconically

лакот -кти *m* **1** elbow **2** *arch.* ell, cubit

лакрдија -ии *f* **1** *colloq.* conversation, chat; joke; две-три лакрдии two or three words; блага лакрдија kind word<s> **2** farce, comedy

лактиште *n see* наплат

лакто *n see* лакот

лактоза *f Chem.* lactose

лактометар -три *m* lactometer

лале *n Bot.* tulip

лама[1] *f Zool.* (Lama glama) llama

лама[2] *m Rel.* lama

ламарина *f* sheet metal

ламаринен *adj* sheet metal; ламаринен покрив sheet metal roof

ламба *f* lamp

ламбада *f* **1** torch **2** large wax candle

ламбен *adj* lamp *attrib.*; шише ламбено lamp glass

ламбиче *n &* ламбичка *f dim. of* ламба

ламентација *f* lamentation

ламентира *pf & impf* to lament; ламентира над судбината на . . . to lament over the fate of . . .

ламја *f* **1** *Myth.* dragon **2** *fig.* glutton

ламперија *f* wainscot, wooden panelling

лампион *m* paper lampshade; bauble for Christmas tree; lampion

ламтеж *m* greed; craving; lust

ламти *impf* to be greedy; to crave for; to lust after

лангида *f* kind of thick pancake

ландон *m* landau

лани *adv* last year; полани the year before last

ланолин *m* lanolin

лансира *pf & impf* to launch (*also fig.*); to introduce; лансира нова мода to launch a new fashion

лансирен -рна *adj* launching; лансирна рампа launching pad

лански *adj* last year's

ланцета *f* **1** *Med.* lancet **2** (*за дрворез*) whittling knife

Лаос *m* Laos

Лаошанец -ни *m* Laotian

Лаошанка *f* (*fem. form*) *see* Лаошанец

лаошки *adj* Laotian

лапа[1] *f* mash of bran, linseed, etc. (*used as warm compress*)

лапа[2] *f* paw

лапа[3] *impf* to swallow greedily, bolt; ❏ лапа муви to be idle, waste time

лапавица *f* **1** wet snow, sleet **2** *fig.* babbler, chatterbox

лапавичав *adj* sleety

лапало *n see* лапачка

лапарда *f* burning torch (*customarily carried in celebrations on the eve of Lent*)

лапач *m* glutton

лапачка *f colloq.* food, grub, *Austral.* tucker

лапе *n* **1** *pejor.* boy; badly behaved child, brat **2** fool, idiot

лаплив *adj* greedy, gluttonous

лапне *pf* лапна *aor.* **1** *see* лапа; to swallow (*also fig.*);

to take a bite; to snatch, grab; to snap up (*also fig.*); му ги лапна парите she swallowed up his money; ❑ ја лапне јадицата to swallow the bait **2** *fig.*, *colloq.* to make a killing, make a profit

лапниголтни *colloq.* **1** *adv* се најаде на брзина, лапниголтни to bolt down a meal **2** *n* kind of jelly-like cake

лапнува *impf of* лапне

Лапонец -нци *m* Lapp; Laplander

Лапонија *f* Lapland

Лапонка *f* (*fem. form*) *see* Лапонец

лапонски *adj* Lapp

лапорец *m* marl

лапсус *m* mistake, slip, lapse

ларва *f Zool.* larva

ларингитис *m Med.* laryngitis

ларингологија *f* laryngology

ласер *m* laser

ласо *n* lasso

ласица *f Zool.* (Mustela nivalis) weasel

ласка[1] *impf* to flatter; to adulate

ласка[2] *impf* **1** to polish **2** *see* блеска

ласка[3] *f* flattery

ласкав[1] *adj* flattering; (*за човек*) smooth-tongued, smooth-spoken

ласкав[2] *adj* shining, brilliant

ласкавец -вци *m* flatterer; adulator

ласкоти *impf* to shine, sparkle

ласне *pf* ласна *aor.* **1** to polish **2** *see* болсне

ласнува *impf of* ласне

ластар *m* shoot, sprout; пушта ластари to sprout (*of a vine*)

ластарест *adj* slim, slender; ластареста мома slender girl

ластегарка *f* wooden fork (*used for loading and unloading a packhorse*)

ластик -ци *m & ***ластика** *f* elastic; rubber band

ластовечки *adj see* ластовички

ластовица *f Zool.* (Hirundo) swallow; прва ластовица first swallow (*also fig.*); со една ластовица пролет не бидува *prov.* one swallow doesn't make a summer

ластовички *adj* swallow's

ластунка *f* shoot; stem; тиквена ластунка pumpkin vine (stalk); каква семката, таква и ластунката *prov.* like father, like son

Латвиец -ијци *m* Latvian

Латвија *f* Latvia

Латвијка *f* (*fem. form*) *see* Латвиец

латвиски *adj* Latvian

латвица *f* earthenware pot/jug

латéнтен -тна *adj* latent, hidden

латерáлен -лна *adj* lateral

Латин *m see* Латинец

Латинец -нци -ни *m* Latin; Roman; Catholic

латиница *f* Latin script

латински *adj* Latin; латински јазик Latin <language>; латинско писмо Latin script; Латинска Америка Latin America

латифундија -ии *f Hist.* latifundia

латица *f* **1** patch; gusset **2** petal

лауреáт *m* laureate

лаута *f Mus.* lute

лауфер *m Chess* bishop

лаф *m colloq.* word

лафéт *m* gun-carriage, gun limber

лафи *impf colloq.* to talk; to chat

лаф-муабет *m colloq.* talk, chat

лач *m* ray, beam

лачен *adj* varnished, lacquered, polished; лачени чевли patent leather shoes

лачи *impf* **I 1** to secrete; to exude; црниот џигер лачи жолчка the liver secretes bile **2** to separate, divide *trans.*; лачи лозје to trim vines of unwanted shoots **3** to wean **II – се** to separate *intrans.*, secede

лашка *f* (*fem. form*) *see* лашко

лашко -овци *m* liar

ле *part* (*with voc.*) oh; *f.p.* горо ле, горо зелена! oh forest, green forest!

леа *f* flower-bed; vegetable patch

леан *pt* cast; леано железо cast iron

леар *m* smelter

леарница *f* foundry

леарство *n* smelting, casting

леб *m* **1** bread; (*векна*) loaf; меси леб to knead dough; два леба two loaves; црн леб brown bread; rye-bread; ❑ свој леб јаде, туѓо гајле бере to poke one's nose into other people's affairs; на бел леб in limbo; in abeyance; преку леб, бара погача *prov.* half a loaf is better than no bread **2** *fig.* daily bread, bread and butter, one's livelihood; ❑ овде нема леб there is no future in this; forget it; си го вади лебот to earn one's living; кладе некого на леб to give s.o. a job; земе некому леб to take away s.o.'s livelihood; за парче (корка) леб for a crust of bread; насушен леб daily bread; нема леб без мотика no sweet without sweat **3** grain; grain-crop **4** fruit, seed, kernel; леб на лешник hazelnut kernel

лебар *m* **1** baker **2** person who likes bread

лебарка *f Zool.* (Stylopiga orientalis) cockroach

лебарник -ци *m* bread bin

лебарница *f* bakery

лебди *impf* to hang in the air; to float

лебед *m Zool.* swan

лебедов *adj* swan's; лебедови перја swansdown; ❑ лебедова песна swansong

лебен -бна *adj* bread

лебец *m hyp. of* леб

леблебија *f* (*usu. pl*) roasted chick-pea

леблебиџија -ии *m* vendor of roasted chick-peas

леблебиџилница *f* chick-pea vendor's shop

лебороден -дна *adj* rich in grain, fertile

лев *adj* **1** left, left-hand; на левата страна on the left <side>; to the left; ❑ има две леви раце to be all thumbs **2** *Pol. see* левичарски

левак -ци *m see* левучар

левент *m arch.* hero

левица *f* left (*also Pol.*); што знае десницата, да не знае левицата let not thy left hand know what thy right hand doeth

левичар *m* **1** *Pol.* left-winger **2** *see* левучар

левичарка *f* (*fem. form*) *see* левичар

левичарски *adj Pol.* left-wing

левичарство *n Pol.* left-wing views, policies

лево *adv* left, on/to the left; ❑ криво-лево somehow; not quite right, anyhow, one way or another; криво-лево го положи испитот he managed to pass the examination somehow

левтерен -рна *adj colloq.* light; easy; slow

левучар *m* left-handed man, left-hander

левучарка *f (fem. form) see* левучар

легален -лна *adj* legal

легализација *f* legalization

легализира *pf & impf* I to legalize, make legal II – се to become legal

легало *n* 1 bed (*in a hotel, hospital, etc.*) 2 lair, den; nest; ❑ фаќа некого на легало to beard s.o.in his den

легат *m* legate

легација -ии *f* legation, mission

легач *m* loafer, idler; layabout

легачка *f (fem. form) see* легач

легачи *impf* to be idle, loaf (about), loiter

легенда *f* legend; жива легенда a living legend

легендарен -рна *adj* legendary

легија -ии *f & легион m* legion; Легија на странците Foreign Legion

легионер *m* legionnaire

легира¹ *pf & impf* 1 to bequeath 2 to send as envoy

легира² *pf & impf Metallurgy* to alloy

легитимација -ии *f* identity card, identification

легитимен -мна *adj* legitimate, legal

легитимира *pf & impf* I 1 to establish the identity of, identify *trans.* 2 to legalize II – се to prove one's identity, identify o.s.

легло *n see* легало

легне *pf* легна *aor.* 1 to lie down; to settle; си легне to go to bed; житјата легнале the crops are lodged; земјата легна the ground has settled ❑ легне болен to fall ill; си легне на брашното 1. to reconcile o.s. to one's fate 2. to knuckle under; сам легни, сам стани to lead a solitary life; *colloq.* легнало – спие to fit like a glove; како ќе спростреш, така ќе си легнеш *prov.* as you make your bed, so you must lie on it 2 *fig.* to give in, yield; to calm down 3 *fig.* (*with да or на*) to begin, set about; легна на јаде, му легна на јадењето he started eating 4 (*of darkness, fog, etc.*) to fall, close in

легнува *impf of* легне

легура *f* alloy

легуш *m* nest; den; litter, brood

лед *m see* мраз

леден -ена -дна *adj* icy, cold; *fig.* indifferent, insensitive, unfeeling; леден поглед icy look (stare)

леденее *impf poet.* to freeze *intrans.*

леди *f* lady

ледина *f* uncultivated land, virgin soil; meadow; glade, clearing; heath; grassland; moor

лединка *f dim. of* ледина

ледник -ци *m* 1 *see* мразарница 2 *see* мразулец 1

леѓен *m* wash-basin, wash-bowl

лее *impf* I 1 to scoop, scoop up 2 to pour, shed; солзи лее to shed tears; лее крв to shed one's blood; лее дожд it's pouring 3 to pour into a mould; to cast II – се to pour *intrans.*; to flow

лежарина *f* storage charges; demurrage

лежерен -рна *adj* 1 light, easy, not forced, effortless 2 careless; superficial

лежи *impf* to lie; лежи на сонце to lie in the sun; Охрид лежи над езерото Ohrid is situated by the lake; ❑ ми лежи на срце it's close to my heart; I'm concerned about it; лежи на ловорики to rest on one's laurels; лежи болен to be ill in bed, to be sick;

лежи во затвор to languish in jail; to do time; лежи на пари to be rolling in money; тоа мене не ми лежи I am not cut out for that; лежи на јајца to sit on eggs

лежиште *n Mech.* bearing

лезбејка *f* lesbian

лезет *m colloq.* enjoyment, pleasure, delight; без лезет without enthusiasm; without enjoyment; нема лезет there is no pleasure in doing that; there is no point in doing that

лејка *f see* црпка

лек¹ *m* medicine, remedy; лек за (против) маларија medicine (remedy) for malaria; ❑ нема ни за лек not one blessed thing; му нема лек beyond help; beyond hope; beyond repair; за сè има лек *prov.* there is a salve for every sore

лек² *adj see* лесен

лека-полека *adv* slowly; gradually; little by little

лекар *m* doctor, physician; домашен лекар family doctor; (*книга*) medical/first-aid handbook; ветеринарен лекар vet, veterinary surgeon

лекарка *f (fem. form) see* лекар

лекарски *adj* doctor's

лековерен -рна *adj* credulous, gullible

лековерност *f* credulity, gullibility; naivety

лековит *adj* medicinal, curative, healing; лековити билки medicinal herbs; лековита вода mineral water; mineral spring

лекокрил *adj poet.* with light wings

лекокрилен -лна *adj see* лекокрил

лекомислен *adj* reckless, impetuous; frivolous, thoughtless, light-minded, flippant; fickle, capricious

лекомисленост *f* recklessness, impetuousity; frivolity, thoughtlessness, light-mindedness, flippancy, levity; fickleness, capriciousness

лекоумен -мна *adj see* лекомислен

лекоумност *f see* лекомисленост

лексика *f* vocabulary

лексикограф *m* lexicographer

лексикографија *f* lexicography

лексикографски *adj* lexicographical

лексикон *m* lexicon, dictionary

лексички *adj* lexical

лектира *f* reading matter, reading list

лектор *m* 1 lector, reader, lecturer 2 proof-reader

лекторат *m* lectureship

лектура *f* editing, proof-reading

лекува *impf* I to treat, heal II – се to undergo treatment

лекување *n* treatment; лекување со зрачење radiotherapy; несовесно лекување medical malpractice

лекција -ии *f* lesson; ❑ одржи некому една добра лекција to teach s.o. a lesson; to give s.o. a piece of one's mind; ја научи лекцијата to learn one's lesson

леле *interj* (*expressing pain, terror, sorrow or amazement*) ow! oh! alas! ❑ тој е – леле мајко (леле боже) he is awful, he is a terror

лелее *impf* I to rock *trans.*; to swing *trans.*; to wave *trans.* II – се to rock, swing *intrans.*; to wave *intrans.*

лелејка *f see* лулка¹

лелек -ци *m* wailing, weeping, lamentation; moaning; howling

лелека *impf* to wail, lament; to moan; to howl

лелекне *pf* лелекна *aor. see* лелека

лелекнува *impf of* лелекне

лели *conj see* нели

лем *m* **1** (*лепило*) solder **2** (*уред за лемење*) soldering iron

леми *impf* to solder

лемеш *m* ploughshare

лен *m Bot.* (Linum usitatissimum) flax

ленен *adj* flaxen; ленено платно linen

ленинйзам -змот *m* Leninism

ленир *m* ruler, *see* линејка

лениште *n* flax fields

лента *f* ribbon; tape; band; (*на пат*) lane; (*во фабрика*) conveyer belt; производна лента assembly line; магнетофонска лента tape

леопа́рд *m Zool.* leopard

леп *adj dial. f.p. see* убав

лепавица *f* **1** (*popular name for*) sticky, wet snow **2** *fig.* sponger, parasite; leech

лепаец *m Bot.* (Galium aparine) goose-grass, cleavers

лепач *m* (*на плакати*) billposter, billsticker

лепеза *f* **1** fan; се лади со лепеза to fan o.s. **2** *fig.* range; широка лепеза wide range

лепенка *f* patch; sticker; лепенки за автомобилска гума patches for car tyres

лепети се *impf* to flutter, flap; to quiver, shake

лепешка *f* **1** dung, droppings (*of animals*) **2** *Bot.* (Rubia tinctorium) madder

лепешкар *m pejor.* blockhead, dunce

лепи *impf* **I** to stick *trans.*, glue, paste **II** – ce to be sticky; to stick (*до, на – то*) *intrans.*; *fig.* to cling to; to impose on

лепило *n* glue, paste; растително лепило gum; скробно лепило gluten

леплив *adj* sticky; glutinous; леплива трака adhesive tape

лепне *pf* лепна *aor.* to slap, strike; й лепна една шлаканица he slapped her face

лепнува *impf of* лепне

лепра *f* leprosy

лепро́зен -зна *adj* leprous

лепче *n dim. of* леб; bread roll

лер *m* neutral <gear>; во лер in neutral

Лерин *m* Florina

лерински *adj* Florina *attrib.*

леринчанец -ни *m* person from Florina

леринчанка *f* (*fem. form*) *see* леринчанец

леса *f* **1** wattle, wattle fence **2** *fig., arch.* plait **3** bow-net; creel **4** (*брана*) harrow

лесен -сна *adj* **1** light; lightweight; лесен оброк light meal; лесен сон light sleep; лесно оружје light arms; ❑ лесна атлетика field and track athletics; нека му е лесна земјата! may he rest in peace! **2** easy; лесна работа easy work; лесна работа за тоа we'll manage that easily **3** light, slight; лесна болест slight illness; лесен издив slight sigh; лесно четиво light reading; ❑ има лесна рака 1. to have a light touch 2. to be generous **4** light-footed, agile, nimble; лесни нозе agile legs **5** *fig.* light-minded, frivolous, thoughtless; fickle; ❑ лесен-плетен unreliable; scatterbrained; heedless

леска *f Bot.* (Corylus avellana) hazel

лесков *adj* hazel

леснак -ци *m* frivolous/reckless person; scatterbrain

леснее *impf* **I 1** to become lighter, lighten *intrans.* (*of*

weight, pressure) **2** to ease *trans.*, alleviate **II** – ce *fig.* **1** to romp; to behave foolishly **2** to become feeble-minded, become senile

лесник -ци *m* hazel grove

леснина *f* **1** lightness **2** ease; бара леснина to seek the easiest way

лесно *adv* **1** light; lightly; спие лесно to sleep lightly; лесно се извлече to get off lightly **2** easily; не е лесно it's not easy; лесно ти е тебе it's easy for you

леснокрилен -лна *adj see* лекокрил

лесномислен *adj see* лекомислен

леснота & **леснотија** *f see* леснина

лесноумен -мна *adj see* лекоумен

лесонит *m* masonite; fibreboard; gyprock

лествица *f* ladder

лет *m* flight

лета *impf* to fly; времето лета time flies; ❑ лета од радост to be transported with joy; високо лета to fly high; to ride high; не се лета дури не пораснат крилја *prov.* don't run before you can walk; сè што лета не се јаде *prov.* all that glitters is not gold

летален -лна *adj* flying; летален апарат flying machine, aircraft

летало *n* **1** aircraft **2** *see* летачка

летаргија *f* lethargy

летаргичен -чна *adj* lethargic

летач *m* pilot, airman, flyer

летачка *f* kite (*children's toy*)

летачки *adj* flying; летачка чинија flying saucer

летва *f* lath, strip; narrow board

летвичка *f dim. of* летва; slat

лете *adv* in summer; ❑ лете-зиме at any season; all the time; throughout the year

летеж *m* flying, flight

летен -тна *adj* summer; летно време summertime, summer; летна пченица spring wheat

летец -тци *m see* летач

летка *impf dim.* to flit about; to flutter

летне *pf* летна *aor.* (*see* лета) to fly off; to fly up; to take off; ❑ летне да бега to take to one's heels

летник *m* **1** *arch.* festival of the spring equinox **2** (*popular name for*) March

летнина *f* spring sowings (*ripening in summer*)

летница *f* **1** *Zool.* trout **2** kind of pear **3** summer fever

летнува *impf of* летне

лето *n* **1** summer; ❑ ѓупско лето; сиромашко лето Indian summer; средлето high summer **2** *arch.* year; во летото Господово in the year of our Lord

летовиште *n* summer pasture

лето́во *adv* this summer

леток -тци *m* leaflet, handbill, *Am.* flyer

Летонец -нци *m see* Латвиец

Летонија *f see* Латвија

Летонка *f see* Латвијка

летонски *adj see* латвиски

летопис *m* chronicle

летописец -сци *m* chronicler

летоска *adv* last summer

летошен -шна *adj* last summer's

летува *impf* to spend one's summer holidays

летувалиште *n* summer house/residence; summer camp; summer resort; детско летувалиште children's holiday camp

летувач *m* holiday-maker, *Am.* vacationer

лека̄ *f Bot.* (Ervum lens) lentil

леќеница *f* pock; pimple

леукемија *f Med.* leukaemia

леукоци̇т *m* (*usu. pl*) leucocyte, white blood corpuscle

леунка *f* woman who has just given birth

леуса *f dial. see* леунка

лечебен -бна *adj* curative; medical; со лечебна цел for medical purposes

лечење *n see* лекување

лечи (се) *impf see* лекува (се); подобро да се спречи отколку да се лечи *prov.* prevention is better than cure

леш *m* (*животински*) carcass; (*човечки*) corpse

лешник -ци *m* hazelnut

лешникаркa *f Zool.* (Nucifraga) nutcracker

лештарка *f Zool.* (Tetrastes bonasia) hazel hen (grouse)

лештарник -ци *m* hazel bush

лешува *impf* to scrape (*leather for tanning*)

ли I *part* 1 (*interrogative*) слушаш ли? do you hear? are you listening? тука ли си? are you here? 2 (*emphatic*) бега ли, бега he runs and runs II *conj* if; почне ли да бега . . . if he starts to run . . .

Либан *m* <the> Lebanon

Либанец -нци *m* Lebanese

Либанка *f* (*fem. form*) *see* Либанец

либански *adj* Lebanese

либе *n esp. f.p.* sweetheart, darling

либе̇ла *f* spirit-level

либера̇л *m Pol.* liberal

либера̇лен -лна *adj* liberal

либерали̇зам -змот *m* liberalism

Либериец -ијци *m* Liberian

Либерија *f* Liberia

Либеријка *f* (*fem. form*) *see* Либериец

либериски *adj* Liberian

Либиец -ијци *m* Libyan

Либија *f* Libya

Либијка *f* (*fem. form*) *see* Либиец

либиски *adj* Libyan

либре̇то *n Mus.* libretto

лив *m colloq.* wild animal, beast; лив горски beast of the forest

ливада *f* meadow

ливадиште *n augm. of* ливада; meadowland

ливадски *adj* meadow; ливадска трева meadow grass

лива̇ге *n coll.* meadows, meadowland

лива̇нто *n arch.* perfume, scent

ливка се *impf* (*with dat. or на & noun*) to flatter, fawn on, play up to; to court

ливне *pf* ливна *aor.* to pour *intrans.*, gush forth

ливре̇ја -е̇и *f* livery

ливче *n dim. of* лист; small piece of paper; (*метално*) lamina

лига¹ *f* 1 saliva, spittle; ❏ лиги му течат his mouth is watering 2 *see* лигуш 2

лига² *f* league, alliance; society; *Sport.* првата сојузна лига the first division; ❏ прва лига top/first class

лигав *adj* slimy, mucous; slippery (*also fig.*)

лигавец -вци *m see* лигуш

лигави *impf* I to salivate; to slobber; to snivel II – се 1 *see* I 2 *fig.* to blubber; to suck up to

лигавина *f colloq.* 1 *see* лига¹ 1 2 *see* слуз

лигавица *f* 1 *see* лига¹ 2 *fig.* (*of a girl*) sniveller; slip of a girl

лигавка *f* foot-and-mouth disease

лигавче, лиганче & лигарче *n see* лигувче

лигаме̇нт *m Anat.* ligament

лигнит *m* lignite, brown coal

лигувче *n* bib

лигуш *m* 1 sniveller; novice, greenhorn 2 *fig.* lick-spittle, bootlicker, toady, flatterer, sycophant

лигушка *f see* лигавица 2

лида *impf* to wander, roam; to walk about aimlessly

лидер *m Pol.* leader

лие *impf see* лее

лижач *m* licker; *fig.* lickspittle

лиже *impf* I to lick; пламенот ја лижеше стреата the flame was licking the roof II – се 1 to lick one another; to lick o.s.; to be intimate 2 (*за ѓон и сл.*) to wear out *intrans.*

лиживаган & лиживаганко -вци *m colloq. see* лигуш 2

лизарче *n* remnant of a cake of soap

лизга¹ *f* slab

лизга² *impf* I *trans.* to slide *trans.* II – се to skate *intrans.*; to slide *intrans.*; to skid *intrans.*; to trickle; се лизгаше по мразот he slid across the ice; автомобилот се лизгаше the car skidded

лизгав *adj* slippery

лизгавица & лизганица *f* slide, slippery path

лизгалиште *n* skating-rink

лизгалка *f* 1 *see* лизгавица 2 (*usu. pl*) ice-skate

лизгар *m* shovel, spade

лизгач *m* skater

лизгома *adv* sliding, slipping; skidding

лизне *pf* лизна *aor.* to lick (*once*), give a lick; *see* лиже

лизне се *pf* лизна се *aor.* 1 to slide, slide down, slide off; to slip; to skid 2 *fig.* to give o.s. away; to be careless; to fail; to be mistaken; *see* слизне се

лизнува *impf of* лизне

лизнува се *impf of* лизне се

лик *m* 1 face, countenance; appearance 2 (*во уметничко дело и сл.*) image; character; главниот лик на романот the hero of the novel

лика *f* 1 face, countenance; appearance 2 pair; match; ❏ лика-прилика perfect likeness; perfect match 3 shape, form; во лика на . . . in the form of . . .

ликвида̇тор *m* liquidator

ликвидација *f* liquidation; winding up; ликвидација на долг settlement of debt

ликвиден -дна *adj Comm.* liquid, solvent; ликвиден капитал liquid assets

ликвидност *f Comm.* liquidity, solvency

ликвиди̇ра *pf & impf* to liquidate; to wind up; to settle

ликер *m* liqueur

лико *n* bast

ликов *adj* bast *attrib.*

ликовен -вна *adj* imitative, figurative; ликовна уметност fine art

ликува *impf* to rejoice, exult, triumph

лила *f* lilac, violet colour; темно лила purple

лилав *adj* lilac, violet-coloured

лилија -ии *f Bot.* (Lilium candidum) lily

лилјак¹ -ци *m Zool.* bat; ❏ лилјак се стори to get soaked through

лилјак² -ци *m Bot.* (Syringa vulgaris) lilac

лим *m* sheet metal; бел лим tin plate; железен лим sheet iron; *see* ламарина

лима *f Bot.* (Taxus baccata) yew, *see* тиса

лимар *m* tinsmith

лимба *f* lock, curl; tuft

лимен *adj* tin, sheet metal; brass; *Mus.* лимени инструменти brass instruments

лименка *f* tin, can

лимон *m Bot.* lemon (*tree and fruit*); ❑ жолт како лимон as pale as death/ghost; чека лимон to wait for a special invitation; цеди некого како лимон 1. to bleed s.o. white 2. to grill s.o.

лимона́да *f* lemonade; lemon squash

лимони́т *m Mineralogy* limonite

лимонов *adj* lemon; лимонов сок lemon juice

лимон-табиетлија *adj indecl. colloq.* irritable, tetchy, crotchety; touchy

лимонтуз *m* (*usu. pl*) *colloq.* citric acid

лимузи́на *f* limousine

лимфа *f* lymph

лимфатичен -чна *adj* lymphatic; лимфатични садови lymph glands

линар *m Zool.* (Tinca vulgaris) tench

лингви́ст *m* linguist

лингвистика *f* linguistics

лингур *m* poor quality arable land

линеа́рен -рна *adj* linear; линеарно покачување на платите salary increment

линее *impf* 1 (*слабее, ома́ѓа*) to weaken *intrans.* 2 (*за боја, материјал*) to fade; to wear out *intrans.* 3 (*за животни*) to moult

линејка *f* ruler (*for measurement*)

линија -ии *f* line; права линија straight line; автобуска линија bus route; воздушна линија airline; одбранбена линија line of defence; по машка линија by the male line; ❑ држи (чува) линија to watch (keep) one's figure, to be on a diet; линија на помал отпор line of least resistance; скршне од линијата to go wrong; to deviate; во иста линија со in line with; in agreement with; во крајна линија after all; линијата е зафатена the line is engaged; ни се изгуби линијата (*на телефон*) we were cut off

лини́ра *pf & impf* to rule a line

линиски *adj* of a line; линиски брод liner; *Sport.* линиски судија linesman, referee's assistant

линоле́ум *m* linoleum

линч *m* lynching

линчува *pf & impf* to lynch

липа¹ *f Bot.* (Tilia) lime tree, linden

липа² *impf* to sob, moan; to choke; ❑ липа дожд rain is pouring down

липак -ци *m* lime (linden) grove

липало *n* (*на гајда*) chanter, melody-pipe

липица́нер *m* Lipizanner (horse)

липка *f Bot.* 1 (Plumbago europaea) plumbago, leadwort 2 (Prenanthes alba) white lettuce, rattlesnake root

липне *pf* липна *aor. see* липа²

липнува *impf of* липне

липов¹ *adj* lime, linden; липов чај linden tea

липов² *m* (*popular name for*) June

липовина *f* linden wood

липот *m* sob; groan

липта *impf see* липа²

лира¹ *f Mus.* lyre

лира² *f* 1 lira 2 gold coin

лири́зам -змот *m* lyricism

лирик -ци *m see* лиричар

лирика *f* lyric poetry; lyricism

лиричар *m* lyric poet

лирски *adj* lyric, lyrical; лирски поет lyric poet; лирски песни lyric poems

лис *adj see* лисест

лиса *f* 1 fox; кума Лиса Brer Fox 2 sorrel bitch

Лисабон *m* Lisbon

лисабонец -нци *m* person from Lisbon

лисабонка *f* (*fem. form*) *see* лисабонец

лисабонски *adj* Lisbon *attrib.*

лисест *adj* reddish, sorrel; red-haired

лисец -сци *m* dog fox; *fig.* sly person

лисица *f* 1 *Zool.* fox; vixen; *fig.* slyboots; ❑ дере лисици to throw up, vomit; врти како лисица околу стапица to beat about the bush 2 (*крзно*) fox-fur

лисици *pl* handcuffs

лисичар *m* 1 (*ловец*) fox-hunter 2 (*пес*) foxhound

лисиче *n* 1 fox cub 2 *see* лисичина

лисичин & лисичји *adj* foxy; лисичје крзно fox-fur

лисичина *f* fox-grape

лиска *f* 1 mica 2 *see* лизарче 3 *Zool.* (Fulica atrix) coot 4 "Rusty" (*name given to a reddish-coloured domestic animal*)

лискавица *f* mica-schist, mica-slate

лискун *m* mica

лискунов *adj* micaceous; лискунов камен mica-schist, mica-slate

лисне *pf* лисна *aor.* to put out leaves, sprout leaves

лисник -ци *m* (*брст*) forage, fodder, browsing

лиснува *impf of* лисне

лист *m* 1 *pl* лисје; (*на дрво*) leaf; (*на цвет*) petal; *coll.* foliage; листот падна the leaves have fallen; пушта лисје to come into leaf; ❑ се тресе како лист <во гора> to shake like a leaf 2 *pl* -ови; (*од хартија*) leaf, sheet; анкетен лист questionnaire; гарантен лист guarantee; товарен лист consignment note, waybill, bill of lading; ❑ свртува друг лист to turn over a new leaf; to mend one's ways 3 *pl* -ови; sheet, plate; лист од метал sheet of metal 4 *pl* -ови; *Anat.* calf (*of a leg*)

листа *f* list, inventory, roll; листа на чекање waiting list; листа на гласачи list of voters, electoral roll; платна листа payroll; курсна листа exchange list; отпусна листа discharge papers

листеж *m poet.* leafing

листен -сна *adj* 1 of a leaf 2 leafy; лисна гора leafy forest; ❑ лиснато тесто flaky (puff) pastry

листец *m dim. of* лист

листи *impf see* лисне

листовиден -дна *adj* leaf-like, leaf-shaped

листокап & листопад *m* autumn, *Am.* fall; (*popular name for*) October

лит *adj* worn out, shabby, tattered, ragged

литак -ци *m* 1 (*as adj*) worn-out, shabby; литак килим worn-out carpet/rug 2 sleeveless woollen dress with narrow skirt

литанија -ии *f* litany

литар -три *m* litre

Литва *f see* Литванија

Литванец -нци *m* Lithuanian

Литванија *f* Lithuania

Литванка *f* (*fem. form*) *see* Литванец

литвански *adj* Lithuanian

литера́рен -рна *adj* literary; литерарно дело literary work

литера́т & **литера́тор** *m* writer, author; littérateur

литерату́ра *f* literature

литерату́рен -рна *adj* literary; литературен јазик literary language

лити се *impf* **1** (за платно) to fade; to wear out *intrans.* **2** *fig.* to become senile

литија -ии *f* **1** religious procession **2** *fig.* long queue

литица *f* cliff, bluff

литмара *f* **1** *Zool.* (Coccinella) ladybird, *Am.* ladybug **2** *fig.* lightly dressed woman

литогра́ф *m* **1** lithographer **2** lithographic printing machine

литографија *f* **1** lithography **2** lithographic printing workshop

литра *f* ladder-like side of a wagon; cart with such sides, wain

литургија -ии *f* liturgy

литургиски *adj* liturgical

лифера́нт *m* supplier, purveyor

лиферува *pf* & *impf* to supply, deliver

лифт *m* lift, *Am.* elevator

лихва *f* usury; interest

лихвар *m* usurer

лихвари *impf* to practise usury

лихварство *n* usury

лихт *adj indecl.* bright (of colour)

лице *n* **1** face; црти на лицето features; ❏ прави лице to pretend, be hypocritical; како имаш лице! how dare you! покаже свое право лице to show one's true colours, show one's real worth; каже некому нешто в лице to tell s.o. s.th. to his face; на лице место at the scene (of), on the spot **2** person, character, personage; главно лице hero, principal character (of play, novel, etc.); службено лице official; овластено лице proxy, authorized person; правно лице juridical person, legal entity **3** *Gram.* person; трето лице еднина third person singular **4** exterior, outside, face (of material); лице и опачина front and back (of cloth); лице на зграда facade

лицéј -éи *m* lyceum

лицемер *m* hypocrite, dissembler

лицемерен -рна *adj* hypocritical

лицемери *impf* to be hypocritical, dissemble

лицемерка *f* (*fem. form*) *see* лицемер

лицемерство *n* hypocrisy, dissimulation

лиценца *f* licence, licence rights; patent rights; franchise; concession; купува лиценца to acquire patent right; корисник на лиценца licensee

лицитација -ии *f* auction, bidding; учесник на лицитација tenderer, bidder

лицити́ра *impf* to auction; to bid at an auction

личен[1] -чна *adj* personal; private, individual; лична слобода personal (individual) freedom; лични заменки *Gram.* personal pronouns; личен доход <personal> income, salary; лична сопственост private property/ownership; лична карта identity card

личен[2] -чна *adj* beautiful, attractive

личи *impf* **1** (на) to resemble, be like (similar to); тој личи на татка си he is like his father; ❏ на ништо не

личи to look like nothing on earth; на што ти личам? what do you take me for? **2** to be appropriate, suitable, proper; не ти личи тоа it ill befits you **3** to suit, fit; не ти личи палтото that coat doesn't suit you **4** to adorn, beautify; езерото го личи градот the lake enhances the beauty of the city

личнее *impf arch.* to become more beautiful, more handsome

лично *adv* personally, in person; лично го виде he saw it with his own eyes

личност *f* person, individual; personality; (во драма, расказ и др.) character; слобода на личноста freedom of the individual; влијателна личност influential person<ality>, figure; позната личност celebrity, well-known personality

личота & **личотија** *f* beauty, attractiveness

лицба & **лицбина** *f f.p. see* личотија

лишав *adj* lichen-covered; lichenous

лишави се *impf* to become covered with lichen

лишај -аи *m Med., Bot.* lichen

лиши *pf* **I** to deprive (од – of); to bereave (of); лиши од наследство to disinherit; лиши од права to deprive of rights; лиши од сопственост to dispossess **II** – се to deprive o.s., deny o.s. (од – of); to go without; се лиши од животот to commit suicide, take one's own life

лишка *f* wild animal, beast; *fig.* scoundrel

лишува (се) *impf of* лиши (се)

лоби *n* lobby (also Pol.)

лобода *f Bot.* (Atriplex) orach<e>; питома лобода (Atriplex hortense) garden orache; дива (кучешка) лобода (Atriplex patula) wild orache

лободарник -ци *m* place sown with orache

лов *m* **1** hunt, hunting; (на птици) wildfowling; (на риби) fishing; оди на лов to go hunting; лов на вештици witch-hunt **2** game; catch, bag; има многу лов the hunting/fishing is good; богат лов a good catch

ловен -вна *adj* hunting; fishing; ловна сезона hunting/fishing season

ловец -вци *m* **1** (човек) hunter (also fig.), huntsman; ловец на елени deerstalker; ловец на таленти talent-scout **2** (авион) fighter <plane> **3** *Chess* bishop

ловечки *adj* hunting; ловечка пушка sporting gun

лови *impf* to hunt; (риби) to fish; to catch; лови секој збор to catch every word; ❏ лови во матна вода to fish in troubled waters; лови комплименти to fish for compliments

ловидба *f* hunting; fishing

ловиште *n* hunting ground; fishing ground

ловокрадец -дци *m* poacher

ловор *m see* лавор

ловорики *pl.* laurel leaves; ❏ лежи на ловорики to rest on one's laurels

ловоров *adj see* лавров

ловција -ии *m see* ловец 1

ловциски *adj see* ловечки; ❏ ловциска приказна a tall tale

логав *adj see* улогав

логари́там -тми *m Math.* logarithm

логаритамски *adj* logarithmic, logarithm *attrib.*; логаритамски таблици logarithm<ic> tables

логаритмичен -чна *adj see* логаритамски

логика *f* logic

логичен -чна *adj* logical

логички *adj & adv* logical<ly>

логор *m* camp; концентрационен логор concentration camp

логораш *m* camp inmate (*in concentration camp*)

логорски *adj* camp; логорски оган bonfire, camp-fire

логорува *impf* to camp <out>, bivouac

лоен[1] -ена *adj* tallow *attrib.*, fat; свеќа лоена tallow candle

лоен[2] -jна *adj* sebaceous, fatty; лојни жлезди sebaceous glands

ложа *f* **1** (*во театар, кино и сл.*) box **2** масонска ложа Masonic lodge

ложе *n arch. see* легало 1

ложи *impf* **1** to put compresses on **2** to smear with fat

ложник -ци *m* rug (*of wool, goat's hair or hemp, used as bed cover*)

лоз *m* lottery ticket, raffle ticket

лоза *f* **1** *Bot.* (Vitis vinifera) grape vine; дива лоза (Vitis silvestris) wild vine **2** shoot, stem (*esp. of vine*) **3** *fig.* origin, descent, family **4** *colloq.* decoration, ornament (*on a shirt, etc.*)

лозар *m* viticulturist; wine-grower

лозарство *n* viticulture, wine-growing

лозен -зна *adj see* лозов

лози *impf colloq.* to decorate, adorn, embroider

лозина *f see* ластунка

лозинка[1] *f* vine shoot

лозинка[2] *f* slogan, motto; saying; *Mil.* password

лозинков *adj see* лозов

лозиште *n* grape-growing country; vineyard site

лозјар *m see* лозар

лозје *n* vineyard

лозница *f* wild vine; climbing vine

лозов *adj* vine; лозов лист vine leaf

лозунг *m see* лозинка[2]

лои *impf* to smear with fat

лој *m & f* mutton fat, suet; tallow; ❑ како по лој like clockwork; without a hitch; живее како бубрег во лој to live in clover

лојален -лна *adj* loyal, devoted; conscientious, honest

лојалност *f* loyalty; honesty

лока *impf* to drink heavily; ❑ лока некому крв to bleed s.o. white; to suck s.o.'s blood

локал *m* **1** restaurant, bar, pub; ноќен локал night-club **2** location, premises **3** telephone extension **4** *colloq.* local train/bus

локален -лна *adj* local; локална управа local government; локална анестезија local anaesthesia

локализира *pf & impf* to localize; to isolate; локализира пожар to contain a fire

локалитет *m* **1** locality, region **2** *Ling.* localism **3** *Archaeology* excavation site

локација *f* location, site

локан *m* brazier

локач *m colloq.* drunkard, boozer

локва *f* puddle; локва крв pool of blood

локна *f* lock, curl

локне *pf* локна *aor.* (*see* лока) to drink up, gulp; to lap <up>

локнува *impf of* локне

локомобил & локомобила *f* locomobile, portable steam engine

локомотива *f* locomotive

локум *m* Turkish delight; type of sweetmeat

локум-шеќер *m* sugar cube

лом *m* uproar, rumpus; ❑ прави лом to raise hell; to make a scene

ломи (се) *impf see* крши (се)

ломиште *n* place in a river where broken branches have piled up

ломот *m* babble, chatter; mumble, mutter

ломоти *impf* to babble, chatter; to mumble, mutter

Лондон *m* London

лондонец -нци *m* Londoner

лондонка *f* (*fem. form*) *see* лондонец

лондонски *adj* London *attrib.*

лопата *f* **1** shovel, spade; фурнациска лопата baker's paddle; лопата за веење winnowing shovel; ❑ ги има со лопата да ги ринеш you can get them by the shovelful **2** *colloq.* oar

лопатка *f & лопатче n* **1** *dim. of* лопата **2** *see* кација **3** *Anat.* scapula, shoulder-blade

лопеч *m see* лупенига

лопка *f* ball; lump, clod; лопка снег snowball

лопув & лопур *m Bot.* (Quercus frainetto) Hungarian oak

лорбер *m* bay-leaf

лорд *m* lord

лорнет *m* (*очила*) lorgnette

лос *m Zool.* (Cervus alces) elk, *Am.* moose

лосион *m* lotion

лосос *m Zool.* salmon

лост *m* lever; bar; (*на терезија*) beam; (*на врата*) <cross->bar, bolt; *Mech.* спојни лостови connecting-rods

лотарија *f* lottery; raffle; добие на лотарија to win a lottery

лотка *f see* кајче, чун

лото *n* lotto

лотос *m Bot.* (Nymphaea) lotus

лоцира *pf & impf* to locate

лочка[1] *f* **1** puddle; pool; лочка крв pool of blood **2** hoof-print in which water has collected **3** spot, stain

лочка[2] *impf* to soften (*by kneading*); to crush in one's hands; to grind

лош *adj* bad; evil; (*слаб*) poor, inferior; лош дух evil spirit; goblin; лоши очи the evil eye; лоша среќа misfortune, bad luck; лош ден unlucky day; лош знак bad sign, ill omen; лош ветар ill wind; лоша стока inferior goods; лош успех poor result

лоши се *impf* **1** to spoil *intrans.*; to worsen; се лоши времето the weather's getting worse **2** *impers.* (*with dat.*) ми се лоши I feel sick, I want to vomit

лошо[1] *n* (*only sg*) evil; прави (стори) лошо to do evil <things>; ❑ да нè чува Господ од лошо may God preserve us, Lord deliver us from evil! лошото само иде evil comes of its own accord; кој лошо прави, лошо дочекува *prov.* one evil rises out of another; evil be to him who evil thinks

лошо[2] *adv* badly; лошо ми е I feel ill, sick; ❑ лошо ќе си помине he will fare badly; има од лошо полошо it could be worse; лошо му се пишува things are looking black; лошо се завршува to come to a bad end; мириса на лошо there's a bad smell in the air; things bode ill; ми мириса на лошо I smell trouble; тргнува на лошо to go wrong (amiss); не би било лошо (*да/ако/кога*) it wouldn't be amiss; it wouldn't be a bad idea

лошокачествен *adj Med.* malignant; лошокачествен тумор malignant tumour

лошотија -ии *f* **1** malice; baseness, meanness **2** malicious woman, fury, harpy

ЛП *abbr.* (*Либерална партија*) Liberal Party

луб *m* frame for a sieve, sifter or drum

лубеница *f Bot.* (Citrullus vulgaris) water melon; две лубеници под една мишка не се носат *prov.* one thing at a time; you can't have it both ways

луга *f* lye

луд *adj* **1** mad, insane, crazy **2** restless, turbulent; furious; ❑ луда глава madcap; nutcase; се прави луд to play dumb, act innocent; луди млади години carefree/wild youth **3** stupid, silly, crazy

лудак -ци *m* madman, lunatic

лудачки *adj* mad; лудачка кошула straitjacket

лудило *n* insanity, madness; mania; ❑ доведува некого до лудило to drive s.o. crazy; to drive s.o. up the wall

лудница *f* mental hospital; madhouse

лудо[1] *n f.p.* young man; bachelor

лудо[2] *adv* madly; лудо сака некого to be madly in love with s.o.; to be crazy about s.o.; лудо си поминува to have the time of one's life

лудост & **лудотија** -ии *f* madness; младост лудост *prov.* youth is madness

лудува *impf* to be crazy; to rave; лудува по (за) некого to be crazy about s.o.

луѓе *pl* (of човек) people

лузна *f* & **лузно** *n* scar

лук *m Bot.* (Allium sativum) garlic; ❑ лук и вода that's all nonsense; there's nothing to it; milk and water; wishy-washy; ни лук јал, ни лук мирисал *prov.* butter wouldn't melt in his mouth

лукав *adj* cunning, crafty, sly; shrewd, astute

лукавство *n* trick, ruse; shrewdness

лукавштина *f see* лукавство

лукарка & **лукарница** *f see* лучница

луков *adj* garlic *attrib.*

Луксембург *m* Luxembourg, Luxembourg

луксембуршки *adj* Luxembourgeois

луксуз *m* luxury

луксузен -зна *adj* luxurious

лула *impf* **I** to rock *trans.*; to swing *trans.* **II** – **се** to rock *intrans.*, sway

лулашка *f* (*children's*) swing

луле *n* pipe (*for smoking*); едно луле тутун a pipeful of tobacco; луле на мирот pipe of peace

лулее *impf* **I** to rock *trans.*; to swing *trans.* **II** – **се** to rock *intrans.*, sway; to wave; to be ruffled

лулка[1] *f* cradle; ❑ од лулка до дупка from the cradle to the grave, from the womb to the tomb

лулка[2] *impf dim.* to rock (*gently*) *trans.*

лулне (се) *pf* лулна *aor. see* лула (се)

лулнува (се) *impf of* лулне (се)

лумба́го *n Med.* lumbago

лумпераj *m* binge, spree, carousal

лумпува *impf* to carouse, make merry

лумпувач *m* reveller, carouser

луна[1] *f* storm

луна[2] *f poet.* moon

лунав *adj* **1** stormy **2** *see* луничав

луна-парк *m* amusement park, fairground

лунен *adj poet. see* месечев

луничав *adj* short-tempered, hot-headed, fiery, violent

луња *f* **1** *see* луна[1] **2** *Zool.* (Milvus milvus) црвена луња red kite

луњав *adj see* лунав 1

луп *interj* whack! wallop! bang!

лупа *f* magnifying glass, lens; ❑ става под лупа to put under a microscope

лупенига *f Bot.* (Verbascum) mullein

лупешка *f* **1** shell, husk, pod, peel, skin **2** piece of shell, husk, etc.

лупи *impf* **I** **1** to peel; to shell **2** (*за пилиња*) to hatch *trans.* **II** – **се** **1** to peel *intrans.* **2** (*за пилиња*) to hatch *intrans.*

лусне *pf* лусна *aor. in the curse:* да луснеш! drop dead!

лустер *m* chandelier

лустроса *pf colloq.* to lacquer, polish

лут *adj* **1** angry, furious; ill-tempered; fierce, ferocious; severe; лут бој fierce battle; лута зима harsh (fierce, severe) winter; лута змија venomous snake; лут е на некого to be angry with s.o. **2** (*за вкус*) strong, hot, peppery; лута пиперка hot pepper; лута манџа spicy dish; лута ракија strong *raki* **3** hard, stiff; лут камен hard stone

лута *impf* to wander, roam

лутера́н *m* Lutheran

лутера́нство *n* Lutheranism

лути[1] *impf* to burn, sting (*the tongue, skin or eyes*); пиперката лути the capsicum is hot

лути[2] *impf* **I** to anger, infuriate **II** – **се** to get angry, become infuriated

лутина *f* **1** spiciness, pepperiness **2** anger, rage, ferocity

лутица *f Zool.* (Vipera berus) viper, adder, *see* шарка[5]

лутиче *n Bot.* (Ranunculus) buttercup

лутичок -чка & **лутникав** *adj dim. of* лут 2

луфт *m* **1** air **2** gap (*allowing air to pass through*); нема луфт it's airtight

луфти́ра *pf* & *impf* **I** to air <out>, ventilate **II** – **се** to get some fresh air

луцерка *f Bot.* (Medicago sativa) alfalfa, purple medick, lucerne

лучница *f* wooden mortar (*for garlic*)

лушпа *f* **1** shell, husk, pod; peel, skin **2** *coll.* scales (*on fish, etc.*)

Љ

љуба *f f.p.* **1** wife, spouse **2** beloved, sweetheart
љубе *n f.p. see* либе
љубезен -зна *adj* kind; amiable, lovable
љубезно *adv* kindly
љуби *impf* **I 1** to love **2** *f.p.* to kiss **II – се** to love each other
љубимец -мци *m* favourite
љубимка *f* (*fem. form*) *see* љубимец
љубител *m* devotee; lover; fan
љубителка *f* (*fem. form*) *see* љубител
љубичица *f* **1** *dim. of* љуба **2** *Bot.* (Viola tricolor & Viola odorata) violet
Љубљана *f* Ljubljana, *arch.* Laibach
љубљански *adj* Ljubljana *attrib.*
љубљанчанец -ни *m* person from Ljubljana
љубљанчанка *f* (*fem. form*) *see* љубљанчанец
љубов *f* **1** love; се зедоа од/без љубов they married for/without love; љубов кон татковината love for one's native country; љубов кон науката love of learning; ❑ води љубов to have a love affair; to make love **2** beloved; љубов моја my love
љубовен -вна *adj* love; љубовна двојка courting couple
љубовник -ци *m* lover
љубовница *f* (*fem. form*) *see* љубовник; mistress
љубовничар *m* seducer, Don Juan, Casanova
љубовција -ии *m see* љубовничар
љубовџика *f* seductress
љубомора *f* jealousy; envy
љубоморен -рна *adj* jealous; envious
љубоморство *n* jealousy; envy
љубопитен -тна *adj* curious, inquisitive
љубопитност *f* curiosity, inquisitiveness
љубопитствува *impf* to be curious, inquisitive
љубува се *impf poet.* to admire, enjoy looking at, feast one's eyes on
људба *f dial. see* лутина

М

м *abbr.* (*метар*) *m*
ма *interj* (*familiar mode of address to females; not usu. translated*) слушај ма! hey you! listen! look here! ❑ ма немој! (*to males and females*) you don't say! tell me another!
МААК *abbr.* (*Македонска акција*) Movement for Pan-Macedonian Action
маало *n* district of a town, part of a village; quarter
маана *f see* мана[1]
мааниија -ии *m see* манџија
мав[1] *m* stroke; swing; со еден мав at a stroke
мав[2] *m only in the expressions:* мав ќе те сторам! I'll make mincemeat of you! мав ми е работата I'm in big trouble; I'm in a real mess!
мава *impf* **I 1** to strike, beat, hit, thrash **2** *see* мавта **I 1 3** (*со глава*) to nod **II – се 1** to fight **2** *in the expression:* мавај се од очиве мои get out of my sight!
мавање *n* blow, hit; beating, thrashing; на (со) едно мавање два зајака *prov.* to kill two birds with one stone
мавзолéj -éи *m* mausoleum
мавка (се) *impf dim. of* мава (се)
мавнат *adj* crazy, foolish, silly, doltish
мавне *pf* мавна *aor.* **I 1** to hit, strike **2** (*со рака*) to wave; to swing; (*со опашка*) to wag; (*со крилја*) to flap **3** (*со глава*) to nod **4** to move, remove, overthrow; мавни ги оттука! get them out of my sight! **5** *fig., colloq.* to steal, lift, pinch; мавне некому пари to steal s.o.'s money **II – се** to remove o.s., get out; мавни ми се од очиве get out of my sight!
мавнува (се) *impf of* мавне (се)
маврама *f dial. see* марама
Мавританец -нци *m* Mauritanian
Мавританија *f* Mauritania
Мавританка *f* (*fem. form*) *see* Мавританец
мавритански *adj* Mauritanian
Маврициец -ијци *m* Mauritian
Маврицијка *f* (*fem. form*) *see* Маврициец
маврициски *adj* Mauritian
Маврициус *m* Mauritius
мавта *impf* **I 1** to wave; кучето мавта со опашката the dog wags its tail; птицата мавта со крилјата the bird flaps its wings **2** to swing; ❑ ги мавта нозете to do nothing, waste time **3** *fig.* to deceive, dupe, tell lies to (*s.o.*); to pull the wool over s.o.'s eyes **II – се 1** to rock *intrans.*; to wave *intrans.* **2** to wander around; to idle, loiter
мавца *f hyp. of* маст
мавче *n dim. of* маска[1]

маг *m* magician, wizard, sorcerer

магазин *m* **1** (*склад*) storehouse, warehouse; storeroom **2** (*дукан*) shop, store **3** (*списание*) magazine, review

магазине́р *m* warehouseman, storeman

магаре *n* **1** *Zool.* donkey, ass (*also fig.*); ❑ тврдоглав како магаре stubborn as a mule; *pejor.* старо (дрто) магаре dirty old man; *sl.* sugar-daddy; за магаре музика та за некого нешто do not cast pearls before swine; <не трчај> како прле пред магаре 1. look before you leap! 2. don't put the cart before the horse! прави некого магаре to make an ass of s.o.; магарето го канеле на свадба за да носи дрва they sent him on a busman's holiday; паѓа од коњ на магаре *prov.* to come down in the world; човек од магаре да падне ќе се одмори *prov.* Rome was not built in a day; easy does it **2** *see* магарица 2

магаренце *n dim. of* магаре

магарешки *adj* ass's, donkey's; ❑ магарешка кашлица whooping cough; магарешка слива *Bot.* (Prunus domestica) plum; магарешка клупа dunce's seat (*in school*)

магарица *f* **1** female donkey, she-ass; ❑ долга магарица leap-frog **2** trestle, easel, stand, tripod

магаричар *m* muleteer

магарштина *f* blunder; stupidity

магаци́н *m* **1** *see* магазин 1 & 2 **2** (*на пушка*) <gun> magazine

магационе́р *m see* магазинер

магдонос *m Bot.* (Petroselinum sativum *or* Carum petroselinum) parsley; киска магдонос bunch of parsley

магија -ии *f* magic, sorcery; spell; ❑ црна/бела магија black/white magic

магионичар *m* magician

магионичарка *f* (*fem. form*) *see* магионичар

маги́стер -стри *m* Master; магистер по фармација (аптекар) registered pharmacist, chemist; магистер по хуманитарни науки Master of Arts; магистер по природни науки Master of Science

магистра́ла *f* arterial road, highway, *Brit.* motorway

магистра́т *m* **1** magistracy **2** municipality; city administration

магистрату́ра *f* **1** magistrature, magistracy **2** Master's examination/degree

магистри́ра *pf & impf* to obtain a Master's degree

маги́чен -чна *adj* magic, magical; ❑ магичен квадрат magic square; *Tech.* магично око magic eye; магичен круг vicious circle

магла *f* mist, (*густа*) fog; haze; ❑ *Mil.* вештачка магла smokescreen; се сеќава како низ магла to have a vague/dim recollection; му падна магла на очи he saw red; фаќа магла to flee, take to one's heels; ветар и магла! nonsense! bilge!

маглен *m* (*popular name for*) November

магли (се) *impf see* маглосува (се), маглоса (се)

маглив *adj* **1** misty, foggy; hazy **2** *fig.* misty, vague, confused

магличав *adj dim. of* маглив

магловит *adj see* маглив

маглоса *pf* **I 1** to envelop in mist, befog **2** *fig.* to swindle, deceive, trick **II** – се to become enveloped in mist; to mist over; ❑ маглосај се! get lost! beat it!

маглосува (се) *impf of* маглоса (се)

магма *f* magma

магна́т *m* magnate, tycoon

магнезија *f Chem.* magnesia

магнези́т *m Chem.* magnesite

магнезиум *m Chem.* magnesium

магнезиумов *adj* magnesium

магнет *m* **1** magnet **2** magneto

магнетен -тна *adj* magnetic; магнетна стрелка (игла) magnetic needle; магнетно поле magnetic field

магнети́зам -змот *m* magnetism

магнетизи́ра *pf & impf* to magnetize

магнетоско́п *m* video recorder, VCR

магнетоско́пски *adj* video; магнетоскопска снимка video recording; магнетоскопска лента video tape

магнетофо́н *m* tape recorder

магнетофо́нски *adj* tape-recording; магнетофонска лента audio tape

магнетски *adj see* магнетен

магнолија *f Bot.* magnolia

Мадагаскар *m* Madagascar

Мадагаскарец -рци *m* Madagascan, Malagasy

Мадагаскарка *f* (*fem. form*) *see* Мадагаскарец

мадагаскарски *adj* Madagascan, Malagasy

маде *n colloq.* **1** *vulg.* (*usu. pl*) ball **2** clapper, tongue (*of a bell*); ❑ камбана без маде fifth wheel **3** weight, bob (*on scales*)

мадем *m arch.* **1** ore **2** mine **3** *dial. see* молив

мадлест *adj vulg.* spunky, husky

мадрац *m* spring mattress, interior-sprung mattress

мадрига́л *m* madrigal

Мадрид *m* Madrid

мадридски *adj* Madrid *attrib.*

мадриѓанец -ни *m* person from Madrid

мадриѓанка *f* (*fem. form*) *see* мадриѓанец

мадро & мадру *adv* quietly, obediently, meekly; ❑ седи мадро, да не носиш модро don't push your luck! (*usu. as warning to a disobedient child*)

маѓепса *pf* to bewitch, cast a spell on

маѓепсува *impf of* маѓепса

маѓесник -ци *m* magician, wizard, sorcerer

маѓесница *f* witch, sorceress

маѓија -ии *f* spell; magic

мае *impf* **I** to delay *trans.*, hold up **II** – се to delay *intrans.*, dally; to roam; to loiter

маешник -ци *m* slowcoach, dawdler

маж -и *m* man; (*сопруг*) husband; маж четворен big man

мажало *n arch.* marriage (*of a woman*)

мажачка *f* marriage (*of a woman*)

маждрак -ци *m arch.* long spear, lance

мажествен *adj* **1** courageous, manly; resolute **2** virile

мажественост *f* **1** courage, manliness **2** virility

мажи *pf & impf* **I** to marry off (*a daughter, niece, etc.*) *trans.* **II** – се to get married (*of a woman*)

мажиште *n augm. of* маж

мажлец *m Anat.* uvula

мажов *adj* husband's

мажовница *f* married woman

маза *f & m colloq.* spoilt child; мамина маза sissy, mollycoddle, milksop

мазга *f* **1** *arch.* sap (*of tree*) **2** *colloq.* mule

мазгалка *f* embrasure, loophole; long and narrow window (*of warehouse*)

мазен -зна *adj* smooth; ❑ мазна баница toady, lick-spittle; озгора мазно, оздола азно *prov.* a fair face and a foul heart

мазиво *n* lubricant, grease

мазни *impf* **I 1** to smooth (*hair, clothes*); to plane **2** *fig.* to caress, stroke **3** *fig.* to dress up, smarten up *trans.* **4** *fig.* to flatter **II – ce 1** *fig.* to dress up, smarten up *intrans.* **2** *fig.* to fawn (*на – on*)

мазник -ци *m* **1** puff pastry pie (*with cheese filling*) **2** *fig.* toady, lickspittle, flatterer **3** *Bot.* (Quercus robur) English oak

мазникар *m* **1** lover of *maznik* 1 **2** *pejor.* malingering soldier

мазнина *f* fat, grease

мазница *f* (*fem. form*) *see* мазник 2

мазничок -чка *adj dim. of* мазен

мазноглав *adj* smoothly combed, well-groomed

мазурка *f* mazurka

мазут *m* mazut, black oil

мај *m* May; Први мај the First of May, May Day

маја *f* **1** yeast, leaven **2** rennet

мајалница *f* leavened bread (*with egg spread*)

мајасил *m* piles, haemorrhoids; мајасил трева *Bot.* (Arum maculatum) wild arum, lords and ladies, cuckoo-pint

мајка *f* **1** mother; самохрана мајка single mother; ❑ како од мајка роден mother-naked; жими мајка cross my heart; сега му е мајката it's now or never; леле мајко! God help us! God forbid! кара некому мајка to swear at s.o.; ја, мајката! you don't say! на две мајки гладен to fall between two stools; за еден мајка, за друг маштеа there's one law for the rich and another for the poor; каква мајка, таква ќерка like mother, like daughter; <од> трета мајка third time lucky; што мајка бараш? what on earth do you want? **2** (*respectful address to an older woman*) madam, ma'am

мајкин *adj* mother's

мајмун *m Zool.* monkey; мајмун-сурат ugly face; ❑ прави мајмун од некого to make a monkey of s.o.

мајмунест *adj* monkey-like, monkeyish

мајмунлак -ци *m* monkey business

мајмунка *f* female monkey

мајонéз *m* mayonnaise

мајор *m Mil.* major

мајски *adj* May; мајски цвеќиња May flowers

мајстор *m* master; (*занаетчија*) skilled craftsman (artisan); (*механичар*) skilled mechanic; (*ѕидар*) mason; *fig.* expert, master of his trade; *colloq.* boss; мајстор саатчија <master> watchmaker; ❑ мајстор расипи bungler, bodger; си го нашол мајсторот he has met his match; го нема мајсторот nothing will come of that; мајстор за сè jack of all trades; на мајсторот куќата му капе *prov.* the shoemaker's son always goes barefoot

мајсторија -ии *f* **1** mastery, skill; craftsmanship **2** masterpiece, chef d'oeuvre; master-stroke **3** cunning; shrewdness; ruse

мајсторинка *m pejor.* so-called expert; bodger

мајсторка *f* **1** craftsman's wife **2** *Sport.* final, play-off

мајсторлак *m see* мајсторство

мајсторски *adj* craftsman's; masterly; мајсторско писмо (свидетелство) craftsman's certificate (diploma); мајсторско уверение craftsman's (trade) certificate; мајсторско дело masterpiece

мајсторство *n* **1** mastery, skill; craftsmanship **2** master-stroke

мајтап *m colloq.* mockery, derision; joke, jest; си играат мајтап со него they are making fun of him

мајтапи се *impf colloq.* to joke; to mock, ridicule, make fun (*со – of*)

мајтапчија -ии *m colloq.* joker, jokester, comic; mocker

мајче *f voc.* mum, ma

мајчин *adj* mother's, maternal; motherly; мајчин јазик mother tongue; ❑ мајчин сине son of a bitch; *Bot.* мајчина душица (Thymus serpyllum) wild thyme; мајчин дом maternity home; orphanage

мајчинија *f* maternal inheritance

мајчински *adj* mother's, motherly; мајчинска љубов mother love

мајчинство *n* motherhood

мак *m Bot.* poppy

мака[1] *f* **1** pain, suffering, discomfort; torment, torture; многу ми е мака за тоа I regret it very much; мака ми е I feel sick; ❑ судни маки great suffering; вечна мака eternal torment, hell **2** effort, difficulty; со голема мака with great difficulty; без многу мака without much difficulty, effortlessly; без мака нема наука no gain without pain; виде (трга) мака to have a hard time; мака мачи to be in hot water; to strain every nerve

мака[2] *impf* to dip, dunk

макадам *m* macadam

макáо *m* **1** kind of game of chance **2** *Zool.* (Ara) macaw

макар **1** *adv* at least; остани макар еден ден stay at least one day **2** *conj* although, though; макар и да even if, even though; макар што though, although; си отишол, макар што му реков да остане he has gone, although I told him to stay

макара *f* **1** *Tech.* winch, windlass **2** reel, spool; една макара конец one reel of thread

макарóни *pl* macaroni

Македонец -нци *m* Macedonian

македонѝзам -змот *m* **1** *Hist.* the Macedonian National Cause **2** *Gram.* Macedonian linguistic feature

Македонија *f* Macedonia

македонѝст *m Hist.* fighter for the Macedonian National Cause in the 19th century

Македонка *f* (*fem. form*) *see* Македонец

македонски *adj* Macedonian

макéта *f* maquette, model, mock-up

макина *f arch.* *see* машина

макне *pf* to dip, dunk, *see* мака[2]

макнува *impf of* макне

макрó -óа *m* pimp, pander, *sl.* ponce

максима *f* maxim

максимáлен -лна *adj* maximal, maximum; максимални цени maximum prices; top prices; максимална програма maximal programme

максимѝра *pf & impf* to maximize; максимира цени to maximize prices

максимум *m* maximum

мал *adj* small; little; young; slight; (*as noun*) малиот little boy, kid; мала соба small room; малиот прст the little finger; мал по раст short, of small stature; мали деца young children; мала работа trifle, small matter; најмалиот брат the youngest brother; мало и големо big and small, old and young; мала брзина low speed; ❏ на мала врата by the back door; in a roundabout way; за мали пари cheaply; мали сипаници measles; chickenpox; малиот човек the little man; мали огласи classifieds, *colloq.* small ads; мало стопанство small business; трговија на мало retail trade; трговец на мало retailer; ни на малиот прст не можеш да му се фатиш you're not worth his little finger; Мала Богородица the Nativity of the Virgin; *Astron.* Малата Мечка Ursa Minor; мал армас, мал нишан, мал раун, мал строј first exchange of presents (*on the occasion of an engagement*)

Мала́ви *m* Malawi

Малавиец -ијци *m* Malawian

Малавијка *f* (*fem. form*) *see* Малавиец

малависки *adj* Malawian

Мала́ец -ајци *m* Malay

Мала́ја *f* Malaya

Мала́јка *f* (*fem. form*) *see* Малаец

мала́јски *adj* Malay

маларија *f* malaria

маларичен -чна *adj* malarial; маларичен комарец *Zool.* (Anopheles) malarial mosquito; маларична треска malarial fever, ague

малверзација -ии *f* malversation; embezzlement

Малдивец -вци *m* Maldivian

Малди́ви *pl* the Maldives

Малдивка *f* (*fem. form*) *see* Малдивец

малдивски *adj* Maldivian; Малдивски Острови Maldive Islands

Малезиец -ијци *m* Malaysian

Малезија *f* Malaysia

Малезијка *f* (*fem. form*) *see* Малезиец

малезиски *adj* Malaysian

маленсав *adj see* малечкав

малер *m* misfortune, calamity; trouble; accident; го бие малер he has a run of bad luck; he is on a losing streak

малеро́зен -зна *adj* unlucky, unfortunate; accident-prone

малецкав, малецок -цка & **малечек** -чка *adj see* малечкав

малечкав & малечок -чка *adj* tiny, undersized, pint-sized

малечко *n* baby; young animal/bird

Мали *n* Mali

малига *f* pock; rash

малигав *adj* pock-marked

малига́н *m* alcohol content (*of wine*); device for determining alcohol content

малиген *adj* malignant; малиген тумор malignant tumour

Малиец -ијци *m* Malian

Малијка *f* (*fem. form*) *see* малиец

малина *f* *Bot.* (Rubus idaeus) raspberry (*plant and fruit*); *colloq.* raspberry juice

малинка *f* raspberry (*fruit*)

малинов *adj* raspberry; малинов сок raspberry juice

малиски *adj* Malian

малку *adv* a little, a bit; little; зеде од сè по малку he took a little of everything; тој малку знае за таа работа he knows little about that matter; поседе малку to sit for a while; пред малку a little while ago, a moment ago, not long ago; ❏ за малку almost, nearly; shortly; by a hair's breadth; малку по малку little by little; ни најмалку not in the least; малку му треба да пламне to have a short fuse; малку требаше па да . . . it was a close shave

малкумина *adv see* малцина

малку́нsа *adv see* малкуцка

малку́цка *adv* just a little, slightly

малоазиски *adj* Anatolian

малоброен -јна *adj* small in numbers, sparse

маловажен -жна *adj* insignificant, unimportant

маловоден -дна *adj* low in water; waterless; маловодна река waterless river, river low in water

малоградски *adj* provincial

малограѓа́нин -ни *m* petty bourgeois

малограѓа́нка *f* (*fem. form*) *see* малограѓа́нин

малограѓа́нски *adj* petty bourgeois

малограѓа́нство *n* petty bourgeoisie

малограѓа́нштина *f* lower middle class mentality; philistinism, narrow-mindedness

малограничен -чна *adj* of the local border; cross-border; малограничен промет local cross-border trade; малограничен премин local border crossing

малодушен -шна *adj* cowardly, faint-hearted, pusillanimous

малодушност *f* faint-heartedness, pusillanimity

малоимотен -тна *adj* poor, of modest means

малокрвен -вна *adj* anaemic

малолетен -тна *adj* minor, under-age, juvenile

малолетник -ци *m* juvenile, minor

малолетница & малолетничка *f* (*of a girl*) *see* малолетник

малолетство *n* minority, juvenility

малопродажба *f* retail trade

малопродажен -жна *adj* retail; малопродажни цени retail prices

малост *f only in the expressions:* од малост from childhood; на малост in childhood

малоумен -мна *adj* feeble-minded, moronic; mentally retarded

малоумност *f* imbecility, weak-mindedness

Малта *f* Malta

Малтежанец -ни *m* Maltese

Малтежанка *f* (*fem. form*) *see* Малтежанец

малтежански *adj* Maltese

малтер *m* mortar; plaster

малтериса *pf* (*sид, камен*) to plaster, render; to mortar; (*плочки*) to grout; (*надворешен sид*) to pebble-dash

малтерисува *impf of* малтериса

малтерција -ии *m* plasterer; bricklayer

малтешки *adj see* малтежански

малтрети́ра *impf* to mistreat, molest

малу *adv see* малку; ❏ малу-многу some, a few; тој собра малу-многу пари he collected a small amount of money; за малу нешто се скараа they quarrelled about some trifle

малще *adv see* малку

малцемина *adv see* малкумина

малцина *adv* (*of men or mixed company*) few, a few; малцина од нив се вратија few of them returned

малцински *adj* minority; малцински права minority rights

малцинство *n* minority; национално малцинство national minority

мама *f* mum, *Am.* mom

мамалига *f* polenta

мамба *f* **1** mambo (*Latin American dance*) **2** *Zool.* (Dendroaspis angusticeps) mamba

мами *impf* **I 1** to deceive, delude; to cheat; to swindle; мами муштерија to swindle a customer; си ја мами жената to cheat on one's wife; ако не ме мамат очиве if my eyes don't deceive me **2** to lure, entice **II – се** to be mistaken

мамин *adj* mummy's

мамица *f hyp. of* мама; mummy

мамка *f* bait, lure, decoy; *fig.* illusion, deception

мамлив *adj* **1** deceitful, treacherous, false **2** alluring, attractive

мамуз *m & * **мамуза** *f* spur

мамурен -рна *adj see* мамурлив

мамурлак *m* hangover

мамурлив *adj* **1** suffering a hangover **2** drowsy, sleepy

мамурливост *f* **1** hangover **2** drowsiness, sleepiness

мамут *m Zool.* (Elephas primigenius) mammoth

мамутски *adj* mammoth; ❏ мамутска скокалница high ski-jump

мана¹ *f* defect, fault, failing, shortcoming; наоѓа мана на to find fault with; to pick holes in; без мана beyond reproach; impeccable

мана² *f Bot.* rust, *see* пламеница

мана³ *f* manna <from heaven>

манастир *m* monastery; ❏ за на манастир е he's become senile, he's gaga

манастирски *adj* monastery *attrib.*; monastic; манастирска ќелија monastery cell; манастирски сестри nuns

манга *m pejor.* gypsy

мангал *m* brazier

мангар *m arch.* Turkish copper coin; ❏ немам ни мангар I haven't a brass farthing (a cent)

манго -овци *m see* манга

мангуп *m* hooligan, hoodlum, rowdy, young thug; good-for-nothing, rascal

мангупарија -ии *f* hooliganism; *coll.* hooligans

мандало *n* bolt; latch

мандарин *m Hist.* mandarin

мандарина *f Bot.* (Citrus reticulata) mandarin <orange>, tangerine (*tree and fruit*)

мандат *m* **1** (*овластување*) mandate; пратенички мандат parliamentary mandate **2** (*период*) tenure, term of office; пратенички мандат representative's term

мандатен -тна *adj* mandatory; мандатна комисија mandatory commission, Credentials Committee; мандатни земји mandated territories

мандатор *m* mandator

мандолина *f Mus.* mandolin<e>

мандосува *impf colloq.* **I** to deceive **II – се** to deceive one another; to play a trick (*co – on*)

мандра *f* **1** summer mountain pasture **2** (*бачило*) sheepfold

мандрагора *f Bot.* (Mandragora acaulis) mandrake, mandragora

маневар -ври *m* (*more usu.*) **маневра** *f* **1** manoeuvre (*also fig.*); воени маневри military manoeuvres; тоа беше само маневра that was only a stratagem **2** shunting (*of railway cars*)

маневарски & маневрен *adj* used in or involving manoeuvres or shunting; маневарски куршум blank (practice) round; маневарски вежби manoeuvres, exercises; маневарска локомотива shunting engine

маневрира *impf* **1** to manoeuvre **2** to shunt (*railway cars*)

манеж *m* manège, riding school

манекен *m* mannequin, model

манжетна *m* cuff (*of clothes*)

манија -ии *f* mania, craze; passion

манијак -ци *m* maniac

маникер *m* manicurist

маникерка *f* (*fem. form*) *see* маникер

маникир *m* manicure

маникира *pf & impf* to manicure

манипулант *m* **1** operator; манипулант на машина machine operator **2** (*низок службеник*) worker on shop-floor

манипулатор *m* manipulator

манипулативен -вна *adj* manipulation, handling; манипулативни трошоци handling charges

манипулација *f* handling; manipulation; operation

манипулира *impf* to manipulate; to operate; to drive

манир *m* manner, mode, way; behaviour; нема манири to have no manners

манифест *m* manifesto, declaration, proclamation

манифестант *m* demonstrator (*usu. in favour of s. th.*)

манифестација -ии *f* demonstration (*usu. in favour of s. th.*); rally

манифестира *pf & impf* **1** to demonstrate, take part in a demonstration (*usu. in favour of s. th.*) **2** to show, manifest

манлив *adj* defective; imperfect

маноса *pf* to be rust-affected (*of plants*)

маносува *impf of* маноса

мансарда *f* garret, attic, loft

мантија -ии *f* cassock; mantle

мантил *m* overcoat, topcoat; (*за дожд*) raincoat, mackintosh; мантил-палто light overcoat; докторски мантил doctor's smock; лабораториски мантил lab coat

МАНУ *abbr.* (*Македонска академија на науките и уметностите*) Macedonian Academy of Sciences and Arts

мануелен -лна *adj* manual; мануелен работник manual worker

манук -ци *m colloq.* **1** so-and-so (*unnamed person*) **2** *rare* lover

манука *f* (*fem. form*) *see* манук

манускрипт *m* (*scholarly*) manuscript

мануфактура *f* **1** manufacture **2** textiles, drapery

мануфактурен -рна *adj* textile; манифактурно производство manufacture

мануфактурист *m* textile merchant, textile salesman

манџа *f* food, dish; ❏ во туѓа манџа не ставај сол mind your own business! во секоја манџа мирудија *prov.* to have a finger in every pie

манџија -ии *m colloq.* finicky/fastidious person; grumbler, carper; caviller

мапа *f* map

марама *f* (*шамија*) kerchief; shawl; scarf

марамче *n* (*шамиче*) handkerchief

ма́ратóн *m* marathon

маратóнец -нци *m* marathon runner

маргари́н *m* margarine

маргарит *m* **1** *see* бисер **2** *Bot.* (Convallaria majalis) lily of the valley

маргаритка *f see* маргарит 2

марги́на *f* & **маргина́л** *m* margin

маргина́лен -лна *adj* marginal; маргинални трошоци marginal costs

маргиналии *pl* marginalia, marginal notes

маре́ла *f* morello cherry

маржа *f* margin; маржа на профит profit margin; кредитна маржа credit margin

марионе́тка *f* puppet (*also fig.*); marionette

марионе́тен -тна & **марионетски** *adj* puppet; марионетска влада puppet government

марифет *m* *colloq.* skill, mastery; trick; ❏ што марифет what's the good (of), what's the use, what's the point; направи марифет to do the trick

марифетчија -ии *m* *colloq.* past master, clever person; trickster

марихуа́на *f* marijuana

марка *f* **1** stamp; поштенска марка postage stamp; таксена марка tax stamp **2** make, marque, model, type, brand; автомобил марка Застава Zastava car; од најдобра марка top-quality **3** mark; германска марка Deutschmark

марка́нтен -тна *adj* marked, striking, noticeable; prominent, conspicuous

маркиз *m* marquis, marquess

марки́за *f* marchioness, marquise

марки́ра *pf* & *impf* to mark, indicate

маркица *f dim. of* марка 1; tax/duty stamp

маркичка *f dim. of* марка 1

маркси́зам -змот *m* Marxism

маркси́ст *m* Marxist

марксистички *adj* Marxist

маркси́стка *f* (*fem. form*) *see* марксист

маркуч *m* hose (*for pouring liquid from one vessel into another*)

марлив *adj* industrious, diligent, hard-working

мармалад & **мармелад** *m* jam; marmalade

мароде́р *m* marauder, robber, plunderer

Мароканец -нци *m* Moroccan

Мароканка *f* (*fem. form*) *see* Мароканец

марокански *adj* Moroccan

Мароко *n* Morocco

Марс *m* Mars; ❏ како да паднал од Марс lost (*in an unfamiliar situation*)

марсовец -вци *m* Martian

март *m* March

марта *f* (*folk name for*) March; ❏ баба марта changeable March weather, March many-weathers; бела марта *Bot.* (Tussilago farfara) coltsfoot

мартенка & **мартинка** *f* red and white thread (*tied to children's wrists, ankles or round the neck, on 1st March, heralding onset of spring*)

Мартиник *m* Martinique

мартинички *adj* Martinican

мартовски *adj* March

марула & **марулка** *f Bot.* lettuce, salad

марш *m* march; параден марш march past, parade; ❏ марш! get lost! get out! *Mil.* <forward> march!

маршал *m* *Mil.* marshal

маршала́т *m* *Mil.* marshal's headquarters

Маршалски Острови *pl* Marshall Islands

марши́ра *impf* to march

маршру́т *m* & **маршру́та** *f* route; itinerary

маса[1] *f* table; маса за пишување writing-desk; седи на маса to sit at a table; ❏ на зелената маса before the court

маса[2] *f* mass; единица на масата unit of mass; маса свет masses of people

маса́жа *f* massage

маса́кр -кри *m* massacre

масакри́ра *pf* & *impf* to massacre

масат *m* whetstone, grindstone; hone

масен -сна *adj see* мрсен; масна хартија oil-paper; greaseproof paper; *Anat.* масно ткиво fat; *Chem.* масни киселини fatty acids; масно сирење full fat cheese

масер *m* masseur

масерка *f* masseuse

масив *m* *Geog.* massif

масивен -вна *adj* massive, solid; heavy

масивност *f* massiveness

маси́ра *impf* **1** to massage, rub **2** *fig.* to pester, annoy

масиче *n* & **масичка** *f dim. of* маса[1]; coffee-table

маска[1] *f* *Zool.* mule

маска[2] *f* mask; gas mask; ❏ под маската на under the mask of, in the guise of

маскара *f* **1** mockery, ridicule **2** buffoon; laughing-stock **3** masquerade participants **4** mascara

маскара́да *f* masquerade

маскенбал *m* masquerade, masked ball

маски́ра *pf* & *impf* **I** to mask, conceal; to disguise; *Mil.* to camouflage **II** – ce to put on a mask; to camouflage o.s.

маско́та *f* mascot

маслар *m* producer or seller of oil

маслен *adj* **1** oily; oil *attrib.*; маслени бои oil-paints **2** <made> of fat; маслено сирење full fat cheese

маслинен *adj* **1** olive **2** olive coloured; маслинена боја olive colour

маслинест *adj* olive, olive-green

маслинка *f Bot.* (Olea europaea) olive (*tree and fruit*)

маслинов *adj* olive

масло *n* **1** oil; рибино масло cod-liver oil; слика во масло oil-painting; розово масло attar of roses **2** (*маст*) fat; ❏ тое е негово масло that's his doing; he has his a finger in that; ќе му го светам маслото I'll kill him; дотура масло на оган to fan the flames

маслодаен -јна *adj* oleiferous; маслодајни култури oleaginous plants

маслоса *pf* **1** to smear with grease; to soil <with grease> **2** *fig.* to deceive

маслосува *impf of* маслоса

маснотија -ии *f* **1** fat (*on meat*); (*usu. pl*) fat (*fatty substance*) **2** *see* мрсотија

масовен -вна *adj* mass; масовно движење mass movement; масовно производство mass production

масовизи́ра *pf* & *impf* **I** to popularize, spread *trans.* **II** – ce to be popularized; to spread *intrans.*

масолник -ци *m* pot/jar for fat

масолце *n* *hyp. of* масло

масон *m* mason, Freemason

маст *f* **1** fat; топена маст rendered/melted fat; животинска маст animal fat; свинска маст lard; ❑ вади некому маст to pick on s.o.; to drive s.o. up the wall **2** butter; пресна маст fresh (freshly-made) butter **3** grease **4** *Chem.* fat, glyceril ester **5** *Med.* ointment; пеницилинска маст penicillin ointment

мастика **1** *f* mastic (*liquor*) **2** chewing gum

мастилав *adj* ink *attrib.*; мастилав молив ink (copying, indelible) pencil

мастилен *adj see* мастилав

мастило *n* ink

мастраф *m colloq.* expense, outlay; cost

мастрафлија *adj indecl. colloq.* **1** prodigal, spendthrift **2** expensive

мат[1] *adj indecl.* matt, lustreless

мат[2] *m Chess* <check>mate; даде некому мат to checkmate s.o.

матало *n* dasher, beating-stick, paddle (*for churning milk, etc.*)

матарка *f* soldier's flask

матач *m* **1** person who churns milk (*for making butter, etc.*) **2** troublemaker, stirrer **3** *fig.* liar

матежина *f* sediment; dregs

математика *f* mathematics, *colloq.* maths

математичар *m* mathematician

матен -тна *adj* **1** muddy, turbid; opaque; матна вода muddy water; матно стакло frosted glass; матно време stormy weather; *fig.* troubled time; ❑ нека го земе матната he/it can go to hell! who cares about that? лови во матно to fish in troubled waters **2** dim, dull; матни очи lacklustre eyes; матна мисла vague idea

матеница *f* buttermilk; кој се попарил од млекото, дува и на матеницата *prov.* once bitten, twice shy

материја -ии *f* **1** substance; размена на материјата metabolism **2** material, cloth, textile **3** subject <matter>, topic

материјáл *m* material; граделен материјал building material; историски материјал historical material; учебен материјал syllabus; канцелариски материјали office supplies; stationery; доказен материјал evidence

материјáлен -лна *adj* material; материјалниот свет the material (real) world; материјални интереси material interests; материјални средства material goods; resources; funds; *Leg.* материјалната вистина material truth

материјалúзам -змот *m* materialism

материјализúра *pf & impf* to materialize *trans.*, make material

материјалúст *m* materialist

материјално *adv* materially; financially

материца *f Anat.* uterus, womb

материчен -чна *adj* uterine

матерка *f Bot.* (Thymus serpyllum) wild thyme

мати *impf* **1** to stir, mix; to beat; ❑ мати некому вода to confuse s.o.; to make trouble for s.o. **2** to churn (*sour milk*) **3** *see* квачи 1 **4** to pump (*water from a well*) **5** *fig.* to deceive, cheat; to mar, cast a shadow upon; to spoil; ја мати некому среќата to cloud s.o.'s joy **II – се** to become muddy/turbid/troubled; се мати времето the weather is deteriorating

матúра *pf & impf Chess* to checkmate; *fig.* to defeat

матица *f* **1** (*пчела*) queen bee **2** (*на река*) mainstream **3** (*матична книга*) register **4** home; head office; *fig.* cradle; матица на нашата цивилизација the cradle of our civilization **5** society, association; Матица на иселениците на Македонија Cultural Society (*responsible for the interests of Macedonians abroad*); Матица српска Serbian Literary Society **6** *Tech.* nut

матичар *m* registrar, keeper of records

матичен -чна *adj* **1** record; матична книга register (*of births, marriages, deaths, etc.*); матична служба registry office **2** home; main; матично претпријатие home office, head office; матичен брод mother ship; матичен тек mainstream

матичина *f Bot.* **1** (Melissa officinalis) <common/lemon> balm **2** (Melittis melissophyllum) bastard balm

матичник -ци *m see* матичина 2

матка[1] *f* **1** *see* матица 1 & 2 **2** *see* материца

матка[2] *impf* **I** **1** to shake, mix **2** *fig.* to deceive, dupe **3** *fig.* to delay, drag out *trans.* **II – се** to delay *intrans.*; to spend time; to mill around, swarm around; to hang around, loiter

маткало *n* **1** *see* матало **2** *see* маткач

матканица *f* **1** delay; confusion **2** sediment; dregs, slops **3** evasion; deceit

маткач *m* liar; swindler

матнав *adj* dim, vague

матне *pf* матна *aor. see* мати 2, 4, 5

матница *f f.p.* troubled, muddy water

матнува *impf of* матне

матов *adj* dim; opaque; матово стакло opaque glass

маток -ци *m* **1** sediment; dregs **2** rotten egg (*also fig.*)

маторица *f* sow

матоса *pf colloq.* to deceive, cheat

матосува *impf of* матоса

матријархáт *m* matriarchy

матрица *f* stencil; matrix

матрка *f Bot.* (Marrubium vulgare) hoarhound, horehound

матув *m colloq.* senile person

матуви се *impf colloq.* to become senile

матýра *f* school-leaving examination

матурáнт *m* final year pupil; candidate for school-leaving examination; *Am.* high-school graduate

матурáнтка *f* (*fem. form*) *see* матурант

матурúра *pf & impf* to pass the school-leaving examination, *Am.* graduate (*from high school*)

матурски *adj* final examination; secondary-school *attrib.*; матурски предмети final examination subjects; матурски испит school-leaving examination

макеа *f see* маштеа

маузер *m* Mauser (*pistol*)

маузерка *f* repeating rifle

мафија -ии *f* mafia; gang

мафијаш *m* mafioso; gangster

махагóн *m &* **махагóни** *n* mahogany

махер *m colloq.* expert

махинáлен -лна *adj* mechanical, automatic

махинација -ии *f* machination

махмудија -ии *f arch.* old Turkish gold coin

мац, мац *interj* puss, puss!

маца[1] *f hyp. of* мачка; pussy

маца[2] *impf* **I 1** *dim. of* мака **2** to make up (*one's face*) **3** to dirty, soil **II – се 1** to apply make-up **2** to get dirty

мацне *pf* мацна *aor.* to dip

маче & маченце *n dim. of* мачка; kitten; □ се сакаат како кучето и мачето they hate each other's guts; првите мачиња се фрлаат if at first you don't succeed, try, try and try again

мачен -чна *adj* **1** difficult, heavy; мачна работа hard work **2** tormented, wretched, miserable; мачна душа tormented soul; мачни луѓе victims, sufferers

маченик -ци *m* martyr

маченица *f* (*fem. form*) *see* маченик

маченишство *n* martyrdom

мачешки *adj* cat's; feline; □ со мачешки чекори stealthily

мачи[1] *impf* **I** to torment; to worry; што те мачи? what's bothering you? **II – се 1** to be tormented, suffer **2** to labour, persevere

мачи[2] *impf* **I** to kitten *trans.*, bring forth, throw (*kittens*) **II – се** to kitten *intrans.*

мачилиште *n* torture-chamber

мачило *n* cat's offspring, kittens

мачител *m* tormentor

мачка[1] *f Zool.* cat; домашна мачка (Felis domesticus) domestic cat; дива мачка (Felis catus) wild cat; □ нејќе мачка риба (сирење) to pretend one doesn't want s.th.; to feign indifference; купува мачка во врека to buy a pig in a poke; во темница сите мачки се еднакви in the dark all cats are grey; *colloq.* добра мачка nice chick; nice bit of fluff

мачка[2] *impf* **I 1** to spread, smear, put on **2** to squeeze, mash; to crush, crumple **3** *fig.* to lie; to swindle **II – се** to apply make-up

мачкалка *f* oil-can, grease-gun, lubricator; smearing brush

мачканица *f* **1** grease, lubricant **2** smear; paint/grease stain

мачкач *m* **1** bad painter, dauber **2** *fig.* liar

мачкин *adj* cat's, pussy's

мачник -ци *m* sufferer; poor devil, wretch; victim; martyr

мачница *f* (*fem. form*) *see* мачник

мачно *adv* hard, with difficulty; мачно се живее life is hard; мачно ми е I feel sick; мачно ми стана I couldn't stand it any longer

мачнотија -ии *f* difficulty, trouble

мачор *m Zool.* tom-cat

мачорок -ци *m see* мачор

мачорски *adj* tom-cat's

мауп *m* **1** medicine **2** jam

маша *f* tongs; □ тој е туѓа маша he's s.o. else's cat's-paw

машала *interj arch.* **1** bravo! very good! **2** God willing! touch wood! арен е, машала he's quite well, touch wood!

машина *f* **1** machine; *fig.* automaton; машина за шиење sewing-machine; машина за пишување typewriter; машина за перење washing machine; машина за миење садови dishwasher; машина за месо meat-grinder (mincer) **2** locomotive

машинерија -ии *f* machinery

машинист *m* **1** machine-operator, technician **2** engine-driver, *Am.* engineer

машинка *f dim.* **1** *of* машина; машинка за бричење electric razor **2** sub-machine gun

машински *adj* machine; mechanical; машински инженер mechanical engineer; машински факултет school of mechanical engineering

машки[1] *adj* male; manly, masculine; virile; машко дете male child; машки пол male sex; машко одело man's suit; машки кројач tailor; *Gram.* машки род masculine gender; по машка линија on the father's side (*of the family*); машка рака firm hand; *f.p.* машка жена married woman; □ машка Јана, машка Петра tomboy

машки[2] *adv* bravely, heroically

машко -шки *m* boy; young man; □ прво па машко a lucky first; off to a good start

машкост *f* manliness, masculinity

машкотија *f* manliness, masculinity

машкуданка *f* tomboy; virago

маштеа *f* stepmother; □ за еден мајка, за друг маштеа there's one law for the rich and another for the poor

маштеница *f see* матеница

маштија *f coll.* menfolk, males

маштраба & маштрапа *f arch.* mug; jar

МВР *abbr.* (Министерство за внатрешни работи) Ministry of the Interior, *Brit.* Home Office

мг *abbr.* (милиграм) mg

м.г. *abbr.* (минатата година) last year

ме[1] *interj* (*imitating the bleating of goats and sheep*) baa!

ме[2] *pron* (*short acc. form of* јас) me; ме викаат they are calling me; I am called

меана *f arch.* inn, tavern

меанџија -ии *m arch.* innkeeper

меанџика *f arch.* innkeeper's wife; woman innkeeper

мебел *m* furniture; мебел-штоф furniture material (*for upholstery*)

мебелира *pf & impf* to furnish

мев *m* **1** stomach, belly; pot-belly; пушти мев to spread at the waist; ме боли мевот I've got a stomach-ache; □ драпај си мевот! go on, I don't believe you! **2** wineskin **3** blacksmith's bellows **4** (*на гајда*) bag

мевлем & мевлен *m arch.* balm, ointment; □ мевлем на рана a great comfort; a sight for sore eyes

мевце *n hyp. of* месо

мегаломан *m* megalomaniac

мегаломанија *f* megalomania

мегдан *m arch.* **1** square, open place; □ лагата ќе излезе на мегдан the truth will out **2** space, expanse, room; □ дај ми малку мегдан give me a little time, give me a little longer! **3** field of battle **4** fight, duel; contest; □ излегува на мегдан to take the field

мед *m* honey; □ му падна секирата во мед<от> he struck lucky; мед и млеко milk and honey; bed of roses; мед му тече од уста he speaks honeyed words

медал *m* medal; златен медал gold medal; другата страна на медалот the other side of the coin

медалјон *m* medallion

меден -ена & -дна *adj* honey, honeyed (*also fig.*); медени колачиња honey-cakes; медена (медна) уста honeyed words; □ медениот месец honeymoon

медец *m dim. & hyp. of* мед

медика *f Bot.* (Astragalus glycyphyllus/thracicus) milk-vetch

медикамéнт *m* medicine, remedy

медиокритéт *m* mediocrity, limited person

медитација -ии *f* meditation

Медитерáн *m* the Mediterranean <Sea>; *see* Средоземно Море

медитерански *adj* Mediterranean

медитѝра *pf & impf* to meditate

медиум *m* **1** medium (*in various senses*); news media; електронски медиуми electronic media; спиритистички медиум psychic medium **2** *Gram.* middle voice

медицѝна *f* medicine; судска медицина forensic medicine

медицинáр *m* student of medicine

медицѝнски *adj* medical; медицинска сестра medical sister, doctor's assistant, registered nurse

медовина *f* mead

медоносен -сна *adj* honey-bearing; медоносен цут honey-bearing bloom

медреса *f arch.* Muslim religious secondary school

медуза *f* jellyfish

меѓа *f* boundary, boundary-strip

меѓник -ци *m* boundary stone; landmark

меѓу *prep* between, among; меѓу две планини between two mountains; оди меѓу луѓето to go among the people; меѓу двете војни between the wars; се разбраа меѓу себе they came to an agreement between themselves; ❑ меѓу другото among other things, by the way, incidentally; меѓу нас кажано between you and me, confidentially; меѓу нас да си остане let that remain between ourselves

меѓувреме *n* pause, intermission; во меѓувреме in the meantime

меѓуградски *adj* interurban, intercity; меѓуградски <телефонски> разговор trunk call; меѓуградска автобуска станица coach station

меѓудржавен -вна *adj* international; *Austral.* interstate; меѓудржавни односи international relations

меѓукат *m* mezzanine

меѓународен -дна *adj* international; меѓународен саем international fair

меѓунационáлен -лна *adj* international; меѓународни односи/врски international relations/connections

меѓурек *m* interfluve

меѓусебен -бна *adj* mutual; меѓусебно разбирање mutual understanding

меѓутоа *adv* however, but

мездра *f & **мездре** *n* mucous membrane

мезе *n* snack, bite, appetizer

мезетиса се *pf see* мезетисува се

мезетисува се *impf* to have a snack

мезозóик *m* mesozoic

мек *adj* **1** soft; мека постела soft bed; меко дрво soft wood; мек глас soft voice **2** mild, meek, gentle, kind; мек човек kind person; меко срце soft heart; меко време mild weather **3** weak, mild; мека ракија weak *raki* **4** *Gram.* palatalized, palatal; меки согласки soft, palatal<ized> consonants

мека *impf* to bleat

мекам *m colloq.* **1** tune, melody **2** *fig.* pleasure; со мекам with pleasure

мекица *f* doughnut

мекиш *m Bot.* (Hordeum secalinum) mouse-barley, wall barley, wild barley

мекичар *m* doughnut seller

мекне *pf* мекна *aor.* to bleat; to start bleating

мекнее *impf* to become soft, soften

мекнува *impf of* мекне

мекоглавец -вци *m Zool.*(*usu. pl*) mollusc

мекодушен -шна *adj* **1** weak-willed, wavering **2** softhearted

мекодушност *f* **1** weakness of will **2** soft-heartedness, generosity, kindness

мекокрилец лци *m Zool.* member of the insect genus Cantharidae

мекоперка *f Zool.* member of the genus Malacopterygii (soft-finned fishes)

мекост *f* softness; tenderness

мекота & мекотија *f see* мекост

мекотел *adj Zool.* molluscous, soft-bodied

мекотелец -лци *m Zool.* (*usu. pl*) mollusc, molluscoid

Мексикáнец -нци *m* Mexican

Мексикáнка *f* (*fem. form*) *see* Мексиканец

мексикáнски *adj* Mexican

Мексико *n* Mexico

мекуш & мекушко -овци *m* weakling, milksop

мекушав & мекушлив *adj* soft, delicate, weak

меланхолија *f* melancholy

мелáса *f* molasses, *Brit.* treacle

Мелбурн *m* Melbourne

мелбурнец -нци *m* Melburnian

мелбурнка *f* (*fem. form*) *see* мелбурнец

мелбурнски *adj* Melbourne *attrib.*

мелбурнчанец -ни *m see* мелбурнец

мелбурнчанка *f see* мелбурнка

меле *impf* **1** to grind, mill; меле жито to mill grain; меле кафе to grind coffee; меле месо to mince (grind) meat; ❑ не мелеме брашно со тебе you and I can't agree (can't get on); we don't see eye to eye **2** *fig.* to eat; to chew **3** *fig.* to babble; меле како празна воденица to talk the hind leg off a donkey; to talk nineteen to the dozen **II – се** (*with dat.*) *fig.* to spin *intrans.*; ми се меле умот my head is reeling (spinning)

мелез *m* person of mixed race; half-breed; mongrel; hybrid

мелези се *impf* to degenerate

мелем *m see* мевлем, мевлен

мелиоратѝвен -вна *adj* land-reclamation, land-improvement *attrib.*

мелиорација -ии *f* land reclamation

мелиорѝра *pf & impf* to improve, reclaim (*land*)

мелица *f* brake (*for flax or hemp*)

меличник -ци *m* iron teeth on brake (*for flax or hemp*)

мелник -ци *m* millstone

мелница *f* mill; парна мелница steam mill

мелничар *m see* воденичар

мелнички *adj see* воденички

мелодија -ии *f* melody, tune

мелодика *f* **1** melodics, study of melody **2** cadence, music (*of speech, verse*)

мелодичен -чна *adj* melodious

мелодрама *f* melodrama

мелодрамски *adj* melodramatic

мелос *m* music; народен мелос folk music

мембра́на *f* membrane

мемоа́р *m* memorandum, *aide-mémoire*; petition, request; *pl* мемоари memoirs, reminiscences

мемоли *impf* to mumble, mutter

мемора́ндум *m* **1** memorandum (*also Pol.*) **2** letterhead

меморија *f* (*faculty of*) memory; меморија на компјутер computer memory

мена *f* **1** phase (*of the moon*) **2** exchange; substitution **3** change, transformation

мена́жа *f* **1** (*домаќинство*) household, family **2** canteen, staff cafeteria; офицерска менажа officers' mess

менажерија -ии *f* menagerie

менаџмент *m* management

менаџер *m* manager, agent

менгеме *n Tech.* vice

мене *pron* (*long form of* јас *for the oblique cases. Used for emphasis with short forms* ми, ме, *and with prepositions*) me; мене ме виде he saw me; мене ми даде he gave <to> me; за мене **1.** for me **2.** about me; до мене by (next to) me; по мене after me

мененик -ци *m in the expression:* прстен мененик engagement ring

менза *f* dining hall, cafeteria; студентска менза students' refectory, canteen

мензис *m colloq. see* менструација

мени *pf* **I** to change *trans.*; си го мени името to change one's name **II – се** to change *intrans.*

мени́ -ја *n* menu

менинги́тис *m Med.* meningitis

менискус *m* meniscus (*also Anat.*)

меница *f Comm.* negotiable instrument, note; bill of exchange; меница за наплата bill for collection; пристигнување на меница за наплата maturity of a bill

меничен -чна *adj* commercial; меничен посредник bill broker; менична гаранција bill of guarantee

менлив *adj* changeable, variable; менливи зборови *Gram.* inflected words

менливост *f* variability, instability

менструација -ии *f* menstruation

мента *f Bot.* (Mentha) mint

ментален -лна *adj* mental; ментална хигиена mental hygiene

менталите́т *m* mentality

ментол *m* menthol

ментор *m* mentor

менува *impf* **I** to change *trans.*; to exchange; менува кошула to change one's shirt; менува пари to exchange money; ја менува бојата <на лицето> to blush; to go pale; *Gram.* менува глагол to conjugate a verb **II – се 1** to change *intrans.*; времињата се менуваат the times change **2** to change places

менувач *m* **1** money-changer **2** *Mech.* gear-shift, transmission (*on a car*); shift key (*on a typewriter*)

менувачница *f* <currency> exchange office, bureau de change

мера¹ *f* measure; мера за должина linear measure; ми зеде мера he took my measurements; □ земе некому мера to size s.o. up; to deal with s.o.; жива мера (*price*) on the hoof; од мерата надвор extremely, beyond belief; без мера without measure; преку мера excessively; immoderately; до таа мера, во толкава мера to such an extent; во голема мера to a great extent; во значителна мера considerably; во одредена мера up to a point; со мера in moderation; по мера made to measure; tailor-made; надминува секаква мера to exceed all bounds; враќа некому со иста мера to give s.o. a taste of his own medicine

мера² *f* pasture

мерак -ци *m colloq.* wish, desire, passion; fancy, whim; □ за мерак wonderful<ly>, marvellous<ly>; фрлив мерак на неа I took a liking to her; мерак ми е (*да*) I want to, I feel like (*doing s.th.*); I'd like to

мераклија -ии *m colloq.* enthusiast, aficionado; меркалија на шах chess enthusiast; меркалија на жени womanizer

мерач *m* **1** surveyor, measurer **2** measuring device **3** timekeeper

мергур *m Zool.* (Rutilus rutilus) roach, carp

мердивен *m* ladder

мери *impf* **I 1** to measure; to weigh; □ двапати мери, еднаш сечи look before you leap! score twice before you cut once! **2** to aim at; мери цел to aim at a target **II – се 1** to measure/weigh o.s. **2** *fig.* to measure up (*co – to*), compare to *intrans.*, match, equal; to rival; никој не може да се мери со него no one can match (rival) him

меридија́н *m* meridian

мерило *n* measure, scale, standard, criterion

мерино-овца *f* merino <sheep>

мерка¹ *f see* мера¹; □ не знае за мерка not to know when to stop; презема мерки to take precautionary measures; полициски мерки police precautions; казнена мерка sanction

мерка² *impf* to watch, observe; to admire; to inspect

мерка се *impf* to show o.s., appear (*from time to time*); to be visible; to stand out

мерлив *adj* measurable

мермер *m* marble

мермерен -рна *adj* marble; мермерна плоча marble plaque (tablet, slab, gravestone)

мерне се *pf* мерна се *aor.* to show o.s., appear (*for a moment*)

мерник -ци *m* **1** measure **2** dry measure, bushel

меродавен -вна *adj* authoritative; competent

меродавност *f* authority; competence

мерџан *m* coral (*ornament*)

месар *m* **1** butcher **2** meat eater

месарница *f* butcher's shop

месарски *adj* butcher's; месарски нож butcher's knife

месач *m* kneader (*of dough*)

месен¹ *pt* kneaded, prepared for baking

месен² -сна *adj* meat *attrib.*; месен појадок tinned meat; месни поклади, *see* месници; □ нема никаде месен обесен you've got to work for everything

месест *adj* meaty; fleshy

месец *m* **1** month; пред еден месец a month ago; во (за) еден месец in one month; со месеци for months at a time; денес месец; по еден месец a month from today; □ меден месец honeymoon **2** *see* месечина **3** *arch.* menstruation

месечар *m* sleepwalker, somnambulist

месечарка *f* (*fem. form*) *see* месечар

месечарство *n* somnambulism

месечев *adj* moon's; lunar

месечен -чна *adj* monthly; месечна плата salary, monthly pay; месечно списание monthly journal (periodical)

месечина *f* 1 moon 2 moonlight; по месечина in the moonlight, by moonlight

месечко *m poet. see* месечина 1

месечник -ци *m* monthly periodical

месечно *adv* monthly, every month

меси *impf* to knead; (*глина*) to puddle

месија -ии *f* Messiah; Saviour (*also fig.*)

месијанизам -змот *m* Messianism

месинг *m* brass

месингов *adj* brass

меслест *adj see* месест

меснат *adj see* месест

меснатост *f* meatiness

месници *pl* Shrove-tide, carnival

месност *f* region, area, place

месо *n* meat; flesh; (*на овошје*) pulp; говедско месо beef; суво месо smoked meat; месо од круша the flesh of a pear; ❑ диво месо proud flesh; дебелото месо backside, behind

месојад & месојадец -дци *m* carnivorous animal, carnivore

местен -сна *adj* local; местен комитет local committee; месна власт local authority; месниот печат local press

мести *impf* I 1 to arrange, put in order 2 (*преместува*) to move *trans.*, transfer; само ги мести книгите he keeps moving the books II – се 1 to put o.s. in order, tidy o.s. up 2 to move *intrans.*, change one's abode

место[1] *n* 1 place; spot; site; locality; seat; мало место small place (town); направи малку место за некого to make some room for s.o.; место во партер a seat in the stalls; секој да си го знае местото let everybody know his place; место на истовар/утовар discharging/loading berth; ❑ место не го фаќа; место не го држи he's straining at the leash; зборот му фати место what he said produced an effect; не е место; не му е местото that's out of place; на самото место on the spot/scene; then and there; човек на свое место an honest person; на твое место if I were you; in your place; болно место sore spot; место на живеење home address; domicile; residence; место на раѓање birthplace; на прво место in the first place; first of all; to begin with; на друго место somewhere else; elsewhere; нема место за there is no room for; почесно место place of honour; паѓа на место <мртов> to drop dead; прави место за to make way for; се става себе на нечие место to put o.s. in s.o.'s shoes; тапка на едно место to mark time; to be at a standstill; сè доаѓа на свое место everything falls into place; работно место 1. place of work, workplace 2. position, job 2 position, post, job

место[2] *prep* instead of

мета *f* target, bull's-eye

метал *m* metal; благородни метали precious metals; обоени метали non-ferrous metals

метален -лна *adj* metal; metallic; метален звук metallic sound; метален сјај metallic glint

металец -лци *m* metalworker

метализира *pf & impf* to metallize

мет도

метал

метал

метал

метал

металски *adj* metallurgical; метал ски завод metallurgical works; метал ски работник metalworker

металург -рзи *m* metallurgist; metalworker

металургија *f* metallurgy; црна и обоена металургија ferrous and non-ferrous metallurgy

метаморфоза *f* metamorphosis, transformation

метан *m Chem.* methane

метанија -ии *f* bow, bowing (*while praying*); чини метании to bow <down>; *fig.* to grovel

метанисува *impf* to bow, make obeisance; *fig.* to grovel

метар -три *m* metre; квадратен метар square metre; кубен метар cubic metre

метарски *adj* metric

метатеза *f* metathesis

метафизика *f* metaphysics

метафизичар *m* metaphysicist

метафонија *f Gram.* metaphony

метафора *f* metaphor

метафоричен -чна *adj* metaphorical

метафорски *adj* metaphorical

метач *m* sweeper

метачка *f* (*fem. form*) *see* метач

мете *impf* to sweep, clean (*with a broom*)

метеж *m* disturbance, disorder, uproar; chaos, confusion

метеор *m* meteor

метеорит *m* meteorite

метеорологија *f* meteorology

метеоролошки *adj* meteorological; метеоролошки извештај meteorological report, bulletin; weather report, forecast; метеоролошка служба meteorological service

метеорски *adj* meteoric; метеорско железо meteoric iron

метил[1] *m Chem.* methanol; метил-алкохол methyl alcohol, wood alcohol

метил[2] *m* 1 liver fluke 2 (Plasmopara viticola) mildew, grape mildew

метилав *adj* affected by liver fluke

метка[1] *f* besom (*used when threshing corn*); broom, brush

метка[2] *impf* I 1 to throw, scatter 2 to confuse, muddle II – се 1 to sneak, slink; to roam 2 to toss, turn over (*in bed*)

метла *f* 1 broom; ❑ ајде, метла! get out of here! 2 *Bot.* (Artemisia vulgaris) wormwood

метлар *m* broom maker and seller

метларница *f* broom-making <work>shop

метне *pf* метна *aor.* I 1 to throw, hurl; to throw away 2 to miscarry, have a miscarriage II – се (*на*) to resemble, take after; се метна на татка си he takes after his father

метод *m & метода* *f* method

методизам -змот *m Rel.* Methodism

методика *f* teaching methods

методист *m Rel.* Methodist

методичар *m* methodologist

методичен -чна *adj* methodical, orderly, systematic

методологија -ии *f* methodology

методолошки *adj* methodological

методски *adj* methodological, methodic

метонимија -ии *f* metonymy

метох -си *m* land belonging to a monastery or church

метра́жа *f* **1** length in metres **2** yardage, textile (*sold by the metre*)

метре́са *f* mistress, lover

метри *impf* to measure in metres

метрика *f* metrics

метрички *adj* metric

метро[1] *n colloq.* metre

метро́[2] *n* underground <railway>, *Am.* subway

метроно́м *m Mus.* metronome

метропола *f* metropolis; capital

меќава *f* snowstorm, blizzard

меур *m* **1** bubble **2** (*на кожа*) blister **3** *Anat.* bladder

меурче *n dim. of* меур 1, 2

механи́зам -змот *m* mechanism

механизација *f* mechanization; механизација на земјоделството mechanization of agriculture

механизи́ра *pf & impf* to mechanize

механика *f* mechanics

механичар *m* mechanic

механички *adj* mechanical; *fig.* automatic

меца & мецана *f hyp. of* мечка

мецена *m* benefactor, sponsor, Maecenas

мецосо́пран *m Mus.* mezzo-soprano

меч[1] *m* sword; ❑ Дамоклов меч the sword of Damocles; меч со две острици two-edged sword

меч[2] *m Sport.* match, game

мечар *m* (*male*) bear

мече & меченце *n dim. of* мечка; bear cub; (*играчка*) teddy bear

мечешки *adj* bear's, bear-like, ursine; ❑ мечешка услуга disservice

мечи *impf* **I** to bring forth, produce (*bear cubs*) **II – се** to cub (*of a bear*)

мечка *f Zool.* bear (*also fig.*); бела мечка polar bear; тој е цела мечка he's as clumsy as a bear; ❑ *Astron.* Големата Мечка Ursa Major; Great Bear (Plough, Big Dipper); *Astron.* Малата Мечка Ursa Minor; Little Bear; мечка страв, мене ни well, here I go; не чепкај мечка let sleeping dogs lie! don't push it! дури не ја отепаш мечката, не продавај ја кожата *prov.* first catch your hare

мечкар m bear tamer; bear keeper

мечкин *adj* bear's, ursine; мечкино грозје *Bot.* (Vaccinium vitis idaea) red bilberry, cowberry, whimberry

мечоносец -сци *m* sword-bearer

мечта *f* dream, day-dream, reverie

мечтае *impf* to dream, day-dream

мечтател *m* dreamer, day-dreamer

мечтателност *f* dreaminess, reverie

мечува се *impf* to fence

меша *impf* **I 1** to mix, blend; to stir; меша вино со вода to mix wine with water; меша карти to shuffle cards **2** to muddle, confuse; ги мешаш ти тие работи you are confusing those matters **3** *fig.* to slander; to run down, sling mud at **II – се 1** to interfere, meddle (*во – in*); не се меша to draw back; to keep out; to stay away **2** to mingle, mix (*co – with*), associate (*with*)

мешалка *f* **1** mixer (*machine*), бетонска мешалка concrete mixer **2** (*wooden*) mixing spoon, ladle, dipper

мешаница *f* **1** confusion; crush **2** mixture, blend

мешач *m* **1** mixer; stirrer **2** *fig.* slanderer, gossiper, intriguer, plotter

меше *n dim. of* мев; tummy

мешечки *adv* on one's stomach (belly); prone

мешин *m* fine leather, morocco

мешина *f see* мев 2, 4

мешлест *adj* pot-bellied

мешло -овци *m* pot-bellied person

мешница *f* **1** *see* гајда **2** large bellows

мешовит *adj* mixed; мешовит број *Math.* mixed number; продавница со мешовита стока general store

мештанин -ани *m* townsman; local resident

мешунка *f* pod, seedcase

ми[1] *n Mus.* E

ми[2] *pron* **1** (*short dat. form of* јас) <to> me; ми рече he told me; (*also with the long form*) мене ми ја даде куќата he gave the house to me **2** (*as dat. of possession*) my; татко ми my father

мивка *f* dirty dishcloth; *fig. pejor.* dishonest person; spineless person; ❑ си се сторил мивка you've got all dirty

мивне *pf colloq.* мивна *aor.* **I** to drive away; to move away *trans.* **II – се** to move off, go away

мивнува (се) *impf colloq. of* мивне (се)

миг *m* **1** wink **2** moment; ❑ во заден миг in the nick of time; за миг in a second; in no time; in a flash; in a jiffy

мига *impf* to wink; ❑ окото не му мига he doesn't care a hoot

мигач *m* **1** person who winks **2** *see* клепка

мигне *pf* мигна *aor.* **1** to wink **2** *fig.* to take a nap

мигновен -вна *adj* momentary, instantaneous

мигнува *impf of* мигне

миграција *f* migration; масовна миграција mass migration

мигре́на *f* migraine, headache

мидер *m* corset

мие *impf* **I** to wash; мие садови to wash up, wash dishes **II – се** to wash o.s.; се мие раце to wash one's hands; се мие лице to wash one's face

мижав *adj see* мижурлав

миже *impf* to close one's eyes; to keep one's eyes shut; ❑ мижи Асан да ти баам tell that to the marines!

мижеечки *adv* blindfold, with one's eyes shut

мижитатара *f* hide-and-seek

мижурка *impf* to blink

мижурлав *adj* blinking

мизантро́п *m* misanthrope, misanthropist

мизантропија *f* misanthropy

мизерен -рна *adj* miserable, wretched; pitiful; scanty, meagre; мизерна плата scanty pay

мизерија *f* misery, wretchedness; poverty

мијалка *f see* мивка

мијалник -ци *m* washbasin; sink

мијалница *f* wash-room

мијач *m* (*на садови*) washer-up; (*на коли*) car-washer

мијачка *f* **1** (*fem. form*) *see* мијач **2** *see* мивка

микро́б *m* microbe, bacterium, bacillus

микробранов *adj in the expression:* микробранова рерна microwave oven

микро́н *m* micron

микроорга́ни́зам -зми *m* micro-organism

микроскоп *m* microscope; електронски микроскоп electron microscope

микроскопски *adj* microscopic

микрофилм *m* microfilm

микрофо́н   *m* microphone

ми́ксер   *m* **1** <electric> mixer **2** barman

мил[1]   *adj* dear, sweet; nice, pleasant, charming;   ❏ мило за драго paying back in kind; tit for tat; (*при запознавање*) мило ми е! pleased to meet you!

мил[2]   *m* alluvium, silt

миле́е   *impf* **1** to treasure, value **2** to pine for, long for

ми́лен   -лна *adj* dear, sweet, charming, cute

ми́леник   *m* favourite

миле́ниум   *m* millennium

миле́ничка   *f* (*fem. form*) *see* миленик

миле́ниче   *n dim. of* миленик; pet

мили се   *impf* (*with dat.*) to ingratiate o.s. with, curry favour with, play up to (*s.o.*); to like doing s.th.

ми́лиграм   *m* milligram

милија́рда   *f* milliard, one thousand millions, *Am.* billion

милијарде́р   *m* multimillionaire

милиме́тар   -три *m* millimetre

мили́на   *f* pleasure, enjoyment; charm, grace; beauty

милио́н   *m* million

милионе́р   *m* millionaire

милионе́рка   *f* (*fem. form*) *see* милионер

милио́нски   *adj* of millions; million-strong; милионски суми sums (amounts) of money running into millions; милионски град large city

милитари́зам   -змот *m* militarism

милитариза́ција   *f* militarization

милитари́зира   *pf & impf* to militarize

милитари́ст   *m* militarist

милитари́стички   *adj* militarist

мили́ција   *f* police; police station; народна милиција national police

милиционе́р   *m* policeman

мили́циски   *adj* police; милициска станица police station

мили́чок   -чка *adj dim. of* мил[1]

ми́лја   -лји *f* mile; англиска милја (1609 м) statute mile; морска милја (1852 м) nautical mile

милка се   *impf* (*with dat.*) to curry favour with, play up to (*s.o.*); to court, woo

ми́лне   *pf* милна *aor.* to stroke (*once*), caress

милну́ва   *impf of* милне

милови́ден   -дна *adj* pretty, beautiful, comely; gentle

милогла́сен   -сна *adj* sweet-voiced

милозву́чен   -чна *adj* sweet-sounding, melodious, harmonious, mellifluous

мило́злив   *adj see* милослив

мило́лик   *adj* pretty, nice-looking, sweet

ми́лосен   -сна *adj* gracious, kind, friendly

ми́лослив   *adj* compassionate, merciful, kind

ми́лосник   -ци *m* lover; favourite

ми́лосница   *f* (*fem. form*) *see* милосник

ми́лосрден   -дна   *adj*   merciful,   compassionate; милосрдна сестра Sister of Mercy

милосрдие   *n* & милосрдност   *f* mercy, compassion; од милосрдие (*за некого*) out of compassion (*for s.o.*)

ми́лост   *f* **1** mercy; pity; grace, favour, benevolence;   ❏ <остава некого> на милост и немилост <to leave s.o.> at the mercy of/in the lurch **2** compassion **3** love, affection

ми́лостив   *adj* gracious, kind

ми́лостина   *f* charity, alms

милу́ва   *impf* I **1** to caress, fondle; to hug **2** to love; to

like; повеќе ја милува ќерката од синот he loves his daughter more than his son; како што милувате as you like II – **се 1** to caress (fondle) each other; to hug each other **2** to love each other

милу́вка   *f* caresses; целувки и милувки kisses and caresses

ми́лум   *adv in the expression:* милум или силум by hook or by crook

ми́мика   *f* **1** facial expression, play of features **2** mime, mumming

мимикри́ја   *f Biol.* mimicry, mimesis

ми́мичар   *m* mime artist, mummer; mimic

мимо́за   *f Bot.* (Mimosa pudica) mimosa

мимоле́тен   -тна   *adj* fleeting, passing, transitory, transient

мин.   *abbr.* (*минута*) min.

ми́на   *f* **1** *Mil.* mine; mortar bomb, mortar shell **2** (*за пенкало*) refill; (*за молив*) lead; graphite **3** (*во рудник*) gallery

мина́ре   *n* minaret

ми́натиот   -тата *adj* past, last; минатата недела last week; last Sunday

ми́нато   *n* the past; ❏ тоа е минато that's history

минатого́дишен   -шна *adj* last year's

ми́натост   *f see* минато

ми́ндал   *m Bot. see* бадем

ми́ндер   *m* Oriental cushioned wall bench

миндерла́к   -ци *m* sofa

ми́не   *pf* мина *aor. & impf* **1** to go by, pass; (*преку*) to cross over; минавме покрај нејзината куќа we went past her house; патот мине низ клисура the road passes through a ravine; мина болеста the illness has passed; ја минавме реката we crossed the river; мине од предмет на предмет to pass from one subject to another **2** to spend one's time; колку да мине времето just to pass (fill in) the time; не минавме лошо we didn't manage badly, we had quite a good time

мине́ј   -еи *m Rel.* Orthodox monthly calendar (*of saints' days and daily services*)

ми́нер   *m* powder-monkey; *Mil.* sapper

минера́л   *m* mineral

минера́лен   -лна *adj* mineral; минерална вода mineral water

минерало́г   -зи *m* mineralogist

минерало́гија   *m* mineralogy

минерало́шки   *adj* mineralogical

ми́нерски   *adj Mil.* sapper's

мини-вал   *m Hairdressing* soft perm

минијату́ра   *f* miniature

минијату́рен   -рна *adj* miniature

минијатури́ст   *m* miniaturist

минима́лен   -лна *adj* minimal, minimum; минимална температура minimum temperature

минимали́ст   *m* minimalist

ми́нимум   *m* minimum

мини́ра   *pf & impf* **1** to mine, lay mines **2** *fig.* to mine; to undermine

мини́стер   -три *m* minister; министер за надворешни работи foreign minister; ополномоштен министер minister plenipotentiary; министер без портфељ minister without portfolio

министе́рка   *f* **1** minister's wife **2** (*fem. form*) *see* министер

министерски *adj* ministerial; министерски совет council of ministers; cabinet; министерска фотелја minister's position, ministerial offce

министерство *n* ministry; министерство за надворешни работи Ministry of Foreign Affairs, *Am.* State Department, *Brit.* Foreign Office

миноловец -вци *m* mine-sweeper

минонóсец -сци *m Mil.* torpedo boat

миноположувач *m* minelayer

минофрлач *m* & **минофрлачка** *f Mil.* mortar

мински *adj* mine *attrib.*; минско поле minefield

минтан *m folk.* jerkin

минува *impf see* мине

минувалиште *n* passage; entrance

минувач *m* passer-by

минус *m* 1 minus; ❑ во минус е to be in the red 2 *fig.* (*недостаток*) disadvantage, failing, deficiency

минута *f* minute; ❑ во минута до дванаесет at the eleventh hour; секој има свои пет минути every dog has his day

минутен -тна *adj see* моменталон

минуциóзен -зна *adj* meticulous; detailed

минца *f vulg.* cunt

мир *m* peace, calm; harmony; душевен мир peace of mind; оставете ме на мира leave me in peace! leave me alone! мир и тишина peace and quiet; живее во мир и љубов to live in harmony; запазување на мирот preservation of peace; се склучи мир peace has been made; a peace treaty has been concluded

мираз *m* dowry

миразлика *f arch.* girl with a large dowry

мирасчија -ии *m arch.* heir

мирба *f* reconciliation

мирен -рна *adj* peaceful, quiet, calm; placid; мирни деца quiet children; ❑ да ми е мирна главата for the sake of my peace of mind

мири *impf* I to reconcile; to conciliate, pacify II – ce to be reconciled; to make peace with each other

миризба *f* smell; (*пријатна*) scent, aroma; (*непријатна*) bad smell, stench, stink, odour

миризлив *adj* fragrant, aromatic, scented

миризма *f see* миризба

мирис *m* 1 *see* миризба 2 (*парфем*) fragrance, perfume 3 sense of smell

мириса *impf* 1 *intrans.* to smell; цвеќињата мирисаат the flowers smell; тоа ми мириса на старо that strikes me as being out of date; ❑ мириса на лошо it bodes ill; there's a bad smell in the air; тоа ми мириса на старото I think we're back to square one; ми мириса на it looks like; I have a hunch; ни лук јал, ни лук мирисал butter wouldn't melt in his mouth 2 *trans.* to smell; мириса цвеќиња to smell flowers II – ce to smell (sniff) each other; ❑ не се мирисаат they can't stand each other; there's no love lost between them

мирисање *n* smelling; ❑ и тој не е цвеќе за мирисање he's nothing to write home about either

мирисен -сна & **мирислив** *adj see* миризлив

мирисне *pf* мирисна *дол.* to smell *trans.*, sniff

мириснува *impf of* мирисне

мирител *m* peacemaker, conciliator

мирјанин -јани *m Rel.* layman

мирно *adv* peacefully, quietly, calmly; quiet; (*word of command*) *Mil.* attention!

мирнотија *f* calm, tranquillity

миро *n Rel.* chrism (*consecrated oil*)

мировен -вна *adj* 1 of peace, reconciliation; мировен судија Justice of the Peace; мировен совет court of reconciliation, *Am.* court of equity 2 (*световен*) world, secular, lay

мирољубец -пци *m* peace-loving person, peaceable person

мирољубив *adj* peace-loving, peaceable

мироносен -сна *adj* bringing peace

миронóсец -сци *m* messenger/harbinger of peace

миропомазаник -ци *m Rel.* anointed; elect

мироса *pf* I to anoint II – ce ❑ да му се миросаат коските may he rest in peace

миросува (се) *impf of* мироса (се)

миротворец -рци *m* peacemaker

мирта *f Bot.* (Myrtus communis) myrtle

мирува *impf* to be still; to rest, relax; to live in peace

мирудија -ии *f Bot.* (Anethum graveolens) dill; дива мирудија (Pimpinella major) burnet; ❑ тој е во секоја чорба мирудија he has a finger in every pie; he butts into everything

мис *f* Miss, beauty queen; мис на светот Miss World

миса *f Rel.* mass

мисија -ии *f* 1 (*пратеништво*) mission, legation 2 (*задача*) mission, task

мисионéр *m* missionary

мисир *m* 1 *Zool.* turkey, turkeycock; ❑ се дуе како мисир to put on airs; to throw out one's chest 2 *fig.* fool, idiot 3 *see* мисирка 3 4 *dial.* earthenware/ wooden bowl

мисирка *f* 1 *Zool.* turkey<hen> 2 *fig.* stupid woman, fool 3 мисирка царевка kind of maize (*Am.* corn)

мисиркин *adj* turkey<'s>

миск *m* musk

миски *adj* fragrant; миски сапун scented soap

мисла *f* 1 thought; idea; црни мисли dark thoughts; ❑ задни мисли ulterior motive; се даде во мисла to become pensive; тек на мисли train of thought; се помири со мислата to accept an idea; размени мисли to exchange ideas 2 concern, worry, anxiety; мисли ме морат I am very worried; ❑ ме клаваш на мисла you cause me concern; става некого на мисла to get s.o. worried; to give s.o. s.th. to think about 3 intention; се носи со мисла да . . . to intend to . . . ; со мисла е да . . . to toy with the idea of . . . 4 wish, desire; мисла ми остана за тоа I still hanker after it; ❑ бидете добра мисла be of good cheer! all the best! 5 view, opinion; мислата ми е дека . . . I am of the view that . . .

мислен *adj* abstract; мислена именка abstract noun

мислење *n* 1 reflection 2 view, viewpoint, position; belief; opinion; според моето мислење in my opinion; има исто мислење to be of one mind; сменува мислење to change one's mind; јавно мислење public opinion; слобода на мислење freedom of expression 3 concern, worry, anxiety

мисли *impf* I 1 to think; to consider; to believe; to mean; што мислиш ти за тоа? what do you think about that? што мислиш <ти> со тоа? what do you mean by that? Англија, мислам Велика Британија England, I mean Great Britain 2 to intend; мислиме да правиме куќа we are thinking of building (we intend to build) a house 3 to want, wish; ти <го>

мисли добро<то>/лошо<то> he wishes you well/ ill **4** to take care to, be sure to; мисли да дојдеш на време see that you get here on time **II** – **се 1** to think, reflect, consider; to hesitate; се мислам што да направам I am wondering what to do; не мисли му се многу don't spend too long thinking about it/him **2** to consider o.s., imagine o.s.; тој се мисли кој знае што he thinks he is the cat's whiskers

мислител *m* thinker; philosopher

мисловен -вна *adj* abstract, imagined; thoughtful, reflective; мисловна претстава abstract notion

мисловно *adv* in thought, in one's mind

мисловност *f* thoughtfulness

мисол -сли *f see* мисла

мистерија -ии *f* mystery, secret

мистериózен -зна *adj* mysterious, secret

мистика *f* **1** mysticism **2** *fig.* mystery

мистификáтор *m* mystifier

мистификација -ии *f* mystification

мистифицѝра *pf & impf* to mystify

мистицѝзам -змот *m* mysticism

мистичар *m* mystic

мистичен -чна *adj* mystical; enigmatic, secret

мистрија -ии *f* (*builder's*) trowel

мит *m* myth

митари се *impf* to moult (*of birds*)

митинг -зи *m* mass meeting, rally

митка се *impf* (*with dat.*) to flatter, fawn on

миткач *m* flatterer, toady, lickspittle

митница *f* customs-house

мито *n* **1** customs, duty **2** *fig.*, *colloq.* bribe, kickback

митологија *f* mythology

митолошки *adj* mythological

митра *f Rel.* mitre

митралéз *m* machine-gun

митралéзец -сци *m* machine-gunner

митралéски *adj* machine-gun; митралески оган machine-gun fire

Митровден *m* St Dimitrija's Day (*8th November, old style 26th October*)

митровденски *adj* of St Dimitrija's Day

митрополија -ии *f* diocese of a metropolitan (*Orthodox archbishop*); residence of a metropolitan

митрополѝт *m* metropolitan (*Orthodox archbishop*)

митски *adj* mythical

мишка *f* **1** upper arm; biceps; го фати под мишка he put it under his arm; he caught him under his arm; под една мишка две лубеници не се носат *prov.* you can't have it both ways; one thing at a time **2** *dial.* sprig, twig; spray

Мјанмар *m* Myanmar

Мјанмарец -рци *m* person from Myanmar

Мјанмарка *f* (*fem. form*) *see* Мјанмарец

мјанмарски *adj* Myanmar *attrib.*

мјаса *impf colloq.* (*на*) to look like, resemble

мјау *interj* miaow!

мјаука *impf* to mew, miaow

мјаукне *pf* мјаукна *aor.* to mew, miaow

мјаукнува *impf of* мјаукне

мл *abbr.* (*милилитар*) ml

млад *adj* young; на млади години, во младо време in youth; ❏ млада индустрија new industry; млади луди години one's callow youth; млад и надежен up and coming; млад и зелен young and green; дури е

младо дрвото се витка *prov.* twist the wand while it is green

младее *impf* **I** to rejuvenate, renew, make <look> younger **II** – **се 1** to grow young again **2** to pretend to be young

младеж¹ *f coll.* young people, youth, youngsters

младеж² *m* young man, youth; bachelor, boyfriend

младенец -нци *m* **1** *arch.* infant, new-born babe **2** bridegroom

младенци *pl* newly married couple, newly-weds

младенче *n* **1** *see* младенец 1 **2** young of an animal

младешки *adj* youthful; младешки изглед youthfulness; младешки полет youthful enthusiasm

младина *f* **1** youth, young people; студентска младина students **2** youth, early years

младинец -нци *m* youth, young man

младинка *f* young woman

младински *adj* youth; младинска бригада youth brigade

младич *m* young man

младички *adj* youthful; young man's

младоженец -нци *m* bridegroom

младоженка *f* bride

младолик *adj* young-looking, youthful

младост *f* youth, young days; на младост in youth; ❏ втора младост second childhood; ќе те праша младоста кај ти била староста an idle youth, a needy age; provision in season makes rich house; младост лудост *prov.* boys will be boys; youth will have its day; збирај на младост, да имаш на старост *prov.* spare when you're young and spend when you're old

млаз *m* jet, stream

млазен -зна *adj* jet; авион на млазен погон jet plane (aircraft)

млак *adj* **1** tepid, lukewarm; млака вода tepid water; млако време mild weather **2** *fig.* irresolute, wavering, weak-willed

млака *f* swamp, bog, marsh; morass

млаcка *impf* to champ, chew noisily

млачи *impf* **I** to warm up slightly; to make lukewarm **II** – **се** to become warmer (*of the weather, etc.*)

млачиште *n see* млака

млекар *m* milkman, dairyman

млекарка *f* milkmaid, dairymaid

млекарник -ци *m* milk/dairy storage room

млекарница *f* dairy, creamery; конзумна млекарница dairy co-operative

млеко *n* milk; благо млеко fresh milk; кисело млеко yog<h>urt; млеко во прав milk-powder; млеко од кокосов орев coconut milk; ❏ уште мирисаш на млеко you're still wet behind the ears; од пиле млеко everything your heart desires; кој се изгорел на млеко, дува и на матеница *prov.* once bitten twice shy

млеч *m Bot.* (Euphorbia) spurge

млечен -чна *adj* milk; *Chem.* lactic; млечна крава milch cow; млечни производи dairy products; млечна киселина lactic acid; млечен шеќер lactose, milk sugar; млечно чоколадо milk chocolate; ❏ млечни заби milk teeth; млечно стакло opal/frosted glass; млечна сијалица pearl bulb; млечен ресторан milk bar; Млечен пат Milky Way

млечка *f Bot.* dandelion, *see* глушина 2

млечник -ци *m* pie (*with a sweet filling of milk and eggs*), cf. custard pie

мливо *n* grist; meal, flour

млитав *adj* loose; languid, flaccid; irresolute, weak; slack, sluggish

мм *abbr.* (*милиметар*) mm

ММФ *abbr.* (*Меѓународен монетарен фонд*) International Monetary Fund, IMF

мнение -ија *n* opinion, judgement; viewpoint

мним *adj* professed, ostensible; pretended; illusory; insincere, false

многу *adv* **1** much, many, a great deal of, a lot of; многу луѓе many people; ❏ многу бара he's asking a lot; многу знае *iron.* he's a know-all; многу нешто many things **2** very; very much; многу добар (*училишна оценка*) very good (*mark at school*); многу голема загуба a very great loss; многу личен very beautiful; многу ми е жал I am very sorry

многуаголен -лна *adj* polygonal

многуаголник -ци *m* polygon

многубожец -шци *m* polytheist

многубожечки *adj* polytheistic

многубожие & многубоштво *n* polytheism

многуброен -јна *adj* numerous

многуводен -дна *adj* abundant in water, deep; многуводна река deep river

многуглав *adj* many-headed

многуглаголив *adj* talkative, loquacious

многугласен -сна *adj poet.* having many voices; *Mus.* polyphonic, for many voices and/or instruments

многугласност *f poet.*, *Mus.* polyphony

многугодишен -шна *adj* long-standing; long-range; lifelong

многудетен -тна *adj* having many children; многудетно семејство a large (numerous) family

многуженец -нци *m* polygamist

многуженство *n* polygamy

многузначен -чна *adj* polysemantic; ambiguous

многузначност *f* polysemy

многукатен -тна *adj* multi-storey

многукатница *f* multi-storey building

многукратен -тна *adj* repeated; multiple

многулик *adj* many-faced, many-faceted

многумина *adv see* мнозина

многупати *adv* many times, often

многупочитуван *adj* much honoured, highly respected; dear

многурак *adj* many-handed

многустран *adj* many-sided; multilateral

множеник -ци *m Math.* multiplicand

множење *n* **1** multiplication **2** (*размножување*) breeding, reproduction

множество *n* multitude, crowd, large number; *Math.* set

множи *impf* **I** to multiply *trans.* **II** – **се 1** to multiply, increase *intrans.* **2** to breed, multiply, reproduce *intrans.*

множина *f Gram.* plural

множински *adj Gram.* plural; множинска форма plural form

множител *m Math.* multiplier

мнозина *adv* (*of men or mixed groups*) many; мнозина го познаваат many <people> know him; беа мнозина there were many of them

мнозинство *n* majority

мноштво *n* multitude, crowd; large number

МНР *abbr.* (*Министерство за надворешни работи*) Ministry of Foreign Affairs, *Brit.* Foreign Office

МНТ *abbr.* (*Македонски народен театар*) Macedonian National Theatre

мобилен -лна *adj* mobile

мобилизација *f* mobilization

мобилизира *pf & impf* **I** to mobilize *trans.* **II** – **се** to mobilize *intrans.*

мов *f and m* **1** moss **2** *fig.* hair; fuzz, fluff; down **3** (*на ткаенина*) nap; pile

мовлив *adj* hairy, shaggy; fuzzy; mossy

мовче *n dim.* **1** *of* мост **2** *of* мов

могила *f* hillock, hummock; burial mound

мода *f* fashion, vogue; му помина модата it's gone out of fashion; по мода fashionably

модален -лна *adj Gram.* modal

модар -дра *adj* <dark> blue; модар камен blue stone, *Chem.* copper sulphate; модри колца под очите dark rings under the eyes; модар патлиџан aubergine, eggplant

модел *m* **1** sample, model **2** artist's model; designer's model **3** mould, cast

моделар *m* modeller

моделира *pf & impf* to model

моден -дна *adj* fashion; моден журнал (магазин) fashion journal (magazine); моден магазин fashion shop; модна ревија fashion show; моден креатор fashion designer

модерен -рна *adj* modern, trendy, fashionable

модернизам -змот *m* modernism

модернист *m* modernist

модистка *f* milliner

модификација -ии *f* modification

модифицира *pf & impf* to modify

модрее *impf* to turn blue *intrans.*, become blue

модри *impf* to paint blue

модрикав *adj* <dark> bluish

модрило *n* **1** blue paint/dye **2** *see* модрина 2

модрина *f* **1** bruise **2** blueness

модрица *f colloq. see* модрина 1

модровранка *f Zool.* (Coracias garrulus) roller

модроок *adj* blue-eyed

модрушав & модрушкав *adj see* модрикав

може¹ *impf* **I 1** to be able; не можам да го направам тоа I can't do that; ❏ <колку> што може и не може as much as possible; може да бира to have the choice; to have an option; ништо не може да се стори it can't be helped; може и подобро there's room for improvement **2** to be permitted; можам ли да влезам? may I come in? **3** to be likely, may, might; може да стигне доцна he may arrive late **4** (*negative only*) to be unwell; сега нешто не можам I'm not feeling very well at the moment **II – се** *impers.* it is possible; ако се може if possible; ❏ му се може he is in a position to . . . ; he has the power to . . . ; ❏ сè се може кога се сака where there's a will there's a way; сè се може кога се мора necessity is the mother of invention

може² & можеби *adv* perhaps, maybe; тој, може, не знае ништо за тоа perhaps he doesn't know anything about it; можеби уште не дошле maybe they haven't come yet

можен -жна *adj* possible; feasible

можно *adv* possible; можно ли е? is it possible? <до> колку е можно as much as possible; as far as possible

можност *f* possibility; opportunity; според можностите according to (*s.o.'s*) ability; можности за вработување employment opportunities; □ дава некому можност to give s.o. a chance; живее над своите можности to live beyond one's means; по можност if possible

мозаик -ци *m* mosaic

Мозамбик *m* Mozambique

Мозамбичанец -ни *m* Mozambican

Мозамбичанка *f* (*fem. form*) *see* Мозамбичанец

мозамбички *adj* Mozambican

мозок -ци *m* **1** brain; *Anat.* големиот мозок cerebrum; малиот мозок cerebellum; □ ми се врти мозокот my head is spinning; I feel dizzy; пере некому мозок to brainwash s.o.; пушта мозок на пасење to go wool-gathering **2** *Anat.* marrow **3** *fig.* mind, intelligence, intellect; човек без мозок brainless person

мозол *m* & **мозолка** *f* **1** corn, callous **2** pimple

мозолест *adj* **1** calloused **2** pimply

мозолче *n dim. of* мозол & мозолка

мозочен -чна *adj Anat.* brain, cerebral; мозочни центри brain centres

мој, моја, мое, *pl* мои *pron* **1** my, mine; мојот син, синот мој my son; □ *sl.* мој мој – преку мој that settles it! enough is enough! **2** (*as noun*) моите my family, members of my household; мојот мъ husband; □ пак дојде на моето I'm right again

мокар -кра *adj see* воден²

мокри *impf* **1** to urinate, *colloq.* piddle, pee **2** to wet *trans.*

мокрица *f Zool.* (Oniscus murarius) wood-louse

мокрота *f* damp<ness>; wetness; moisture

мол *m Mus.* (*тонски род*) minor

молба *f* **1** request; нема крај на неговите молби there's no end to his requests **2** application; поднесе молба to submit (lodge) an application

молбен *adj* **1** <of> application; молбено барање claim form **2** *see* молежлив

Молдавец -вци *m* Moldavian, Moldovan

Молдавија *f* Moldavia, Moldova

Молдавка *f* (*fem. form*) *see* Молдавец

молдавски *adj* Moldavian, Moldovan

молежлив *adj* entreating, pleading; humble

молекул *m* molecule

молер *m* house painter

молериса *pf* to paint (*houses, etc.*)

молерисува *impf of* молериса

молец -лци *m Zool.* (Tinea) clothes-moth

молзач *m* milker; *fig.* exploiter, bloodsucker

молзга се *impf of* молзне се

молзе *impf* **1** to milk **2** *fig.* to exploit, use

молзен -зна *adj* milked, exploited; молзна крава milch cow

молзне се *pf* молзна се *aor.* to glide, skim, slither, slide

молзница *f* (*за овца*) milch ewe; (*за крава*) milch cow

моли¹ *impf* **I** to request, ask; to beg, plead for, petition; ве молам please; (*in reply to: thank you*) молам! you are welcome! don't mention it! молам, не слушнав I beg your pardon <I didn't hear>; □ моли, коли with the greatest difficulty, by the skin of one's teeth **II** – **се** to pray; to beg, entreat; му се моли на Господа to pray to God; ви се молам <if you> please

моли² *impf* to destroy by eating (*of clothes-moth larvae*)

молив *m* pencil

молира *pf & impf see* молериса

молитва *f* prayer; лозјето не сака молитва, туку мотика *prov.* deeds, not words

молитвен *adj* prayer; молитвена книга prayer-book; □ молитвена вода holy water

молитвеник -ци *m* prayer-book

молител *m* applicant; petitioner; claimant

молителка *f* (*fem. form*) *see* молител

молк **1** *m* silence, quiet; hush **2** *interj* hush! silence! be quiet!

молкне¹ *pf* молкна *aor.* to fall silent, become quiet

молкне² *impf* **I** **1** to haul, drag, draw **2** *fig.* to delay, prolong, drag out **II** – **се 1** to drag o.s. along; одвај се молкне he hardly manages to drag himself along **2** *fig.* to roam, wander; to potter, *Am.* putter

молкнува *impf of* молкне¹

молкома & **молкум** *adv* silently, quietly

молна, **молња** & **молнија** -ии *f* lightning; □ <брз> како молња as quick as lightning

мольоса *pf trans.* to strike (*of lightning*)

молска *impf* to flash (*of lightning*)

молскав *adj* lightning; flashing

молскавица *f* lightning

молскавичен -чна *adj* lightning, as quick as lightning

молскавичност *f* lightning speed

молски *adj Mus.* minor; молска скала minor scale

молскот *m* flash of lightning

молскоти *impf* to flash repeatedly (*of lightning*); to glow, shine

молсне *pf* молсна *aor.* to flash (*of lightning*)

молснува *impf of* молсне

молчалив & **молчелив** *adj* taciturn, silent

молчаливец -вци & **молчеливец** -вци *m* taciturn (silent) man

молчаливка & **молчеливка** *f* taciturn (silent) woman

молчаливост & **молчеливост** *f* taciturnity, reserve

молчење *n* silence; молчењето е злато *prov.* silence is golden

молчешкум *adv see* молкома

молчи *impf* to be silent, say nothing; □ молчи толчи *see* молчитолчи

молчитолчи *m* & *adv* sly person, slyboots; slyly; тој е молчитолчи he is a sly (cunning) person; прави сè молчитолчи to do everything slyly

мома *f* **1** girl, young woman, maiden; □ стара мома old maid, spinster **2** slice (*of bread, etc.*)

моме *n see* момиче

момéнт *m* moment; □ како што налага моментот on the spur of the moment; решавачки момент critical (decisive) moment; breaking-point; преживува тешки моменти to go through a bad patch; момент! just a minute!

момéнтален -лна *adj* momentary; immediate, instant, instantaneous

момéнтално *adv* **1** at the moment **2** instantly, straight away

момéнтен -тна *adj see* моментален

момéнтно *adv see* моменталнo 1

момин *adj* girl's; girlish; момина солза *Bot.* (Convallaria majalis) lily of the valley

моминок *m see* момирок

момински *adj* girl's; girlish

моминство *n* maidenhood, girlhood

момирок *m* mica

момиче *n dim. of* мома

момичка *f* 1 little girl 2 slice (*of bread, etc.*)

момиште *n augm. of* мома 1

момок -ци -мци *m* 1 *arch.* (*слуга*) servant 2 *rare* (*usu. pl*) young men, boys

момува *impf* to live as a girl; момуваше во Скопје as a girl she lived in Skopje

момчак -ци *m* 1 young man; bachelor 2 waiter

момче *n* 1 boy; young man 2 waiter 3 fiancé; bridegroom; (*usu. joc.*) husband

момченце *n* little boy

момчешки *adj* young man's; bachelor's

момчешство *n* youth; bachelorhood

Монáко *n* Monaco

монарх -рси *m* monarch

монархизам -змот *m* monarchism

монархија -ии *f* monarchy; апсолутна монархија absolute monarchy; уставна монархија constitutional monarchy

монархист *m* monarchist

монархистички *adj* monarchial

монаршки *adj* monarchial; монаршка власт monarchial power

монах -си *m* monk

монахиња *f* nun

монашки *adj* monk's; monkish

монаштво *n* monasticism

Монголец -лци *m* Mongolian

Монголи *pl* Mongols

Монголија *f* Mongolia

Монголка *f* (*fem. form*) *see* Монголец

монголски *adj* Mongolian

мондéн *m bon vivant*; dandy, man of fashion

мондéнка *f* woman of fashion, fashionable woman

монéта *f* coin

монетáрен -рна *adj* monetary

монизам -змот *m* monism

монисто *n* bead; (*usu. pl*) trinkets; necklace

монитор *m* 1 monitor (*TV/computer screen*); (*radio/TV*) programme monitor 2 monitor (*warship*) 3 *Zool.* monitor lizard 4 monitor (*official*); school prefect 5 high-pressure pump (*for washing ore*) 6 detector, monitoring device

моногáмен -мна *adj* monogamous

моногамија *f* monogamy

моногамист *m* monogamist

монограм *m* monogram, initials

монографија -ии *f* monograph

монókл -кли *m* monocle

монокотиледóн *m* (*usu. pl*) *Bot.* monocotyledon

монолитен -тна *adj* monolithic

монолог -зи *m* monologue

монолошки *adj* monological

моном *m Math.* monomial

монопол *m* 1 monopoly; монопол на купувачите buyer's monopoly, monopsony 2 tobacco factory; tobacco warehouse

монополизам -змот *m* monopolism

монополизира *pf & impf* to monopolize

монополист *m* monopolist

монополистички *adj* monopolistic

монотеизам -змот *m* monotheism

монотеист *m* monotheist

монотип *m Print.* monotype

монотон *adj* monotonous; dull, boring

монотонија *f* monotony; dullness, boredom

монструм *m* monster

монструóзен -зна *adj* monstrous

монсун *m* monsoon

монтáжа *f* 1 (*на машини и сл.*) installation; assembly, mounting 2 *Film, TV* montage, cutting

монтажен -жна *adj* construction, installation *attrib.*; montage; монтажна куќа prefabricated house, *colloq.* prefab

монтер *m* installer, fitter

монтира *pf & impf* to install, fit; to assemble

монумéнт *m* monument

монументáлен -лна *adj* monumental; magnificent, majestic, stately

мопед *m* motor scooter, moped

мопс *m* (*куче*) pug <dog>

мор *m* epidemic; plague, pestilence

мора[1] *f* 1 nightmare 2 *fig.* torment, worry; difficulty

мора[2] *impf* to have to (*do s.th.*); must; ought to; ❑ кога се мора, се мора what must be, must be; what can't be cured must be endured; што се мора, се мора to make a virtue of necessity

морав *adj* dark-blue; dark (deep) violet

моравина *f* dark-blue colour; dark (deep) violet colour

морал *m* 1 morals, morality 2 morale

морален -лна *adj* moral

морализáтор *m* moralizer

морализира *impf* to moralize

моралист *m* moralist

моралност *f* morality

мораториум *m Comm.* moratorium

море[1] *n* sea; по море by sea; на отворено море on the open sea, on the high seas; на море at sea; оди на море to go to the seaside; ❑ преку море overseas; far away; капка во морето a drop in the ocean; морето му е до колена he couldn't care less

море[2] *interj* (*used only with m and n nouns, often untranslated*) hey, you! look here! море синко, немој така! listen, my boy, don't do that!

морен -рна *adj* 1 tired, exhausted, fatigued 2 sombre, dark, gloomy, dismal; difficult; морна вечер gloomy evening 3 <of> plague, pestilential; морна година plague year

морепловец -вци *m* navigator

морепловство *n* navigation

мори[1] *impf* 1 to fatigue, exhaust 2 to rage, rampage; мори чума a plague is raging 3 to distress, afflict, torture; ме мори тага grief torments me

мори[2] *interj* (*used only with f nouns*) *see* море *interj*

морија *f* plague, pestilence

морков *m Bot.* carrot

морнар *m* sailor, seaman

морнарица *f* fleet; воена морнарица navy; трговска морнарица merchant fleet, mercantile marine

морнарски *adj* sailor's, naval

морници *pl* shivers; gooseflesh, *Am.* goose pimples; морници ме лазат I've got gooseflesh; I've got the shivers; од тоа ми идат морници it gives me the creeps; it sends a chill down my spine

морничав *adj* creepy, spooky

морски *adj* sea, marine; maritime, nautical; морски брег coast, seaside, seaboard; морско дно seabed; морска риба salt-water fish; морско летувалиште seaside resort; морско пристаниште port, harbour; ❑ морска болест seasickness; морска милја nautical mile; морска сол sea salt; морска теснина straits, narrows; морска ластовица *Zool.* (Sterna, *esp.* Sterna hirundo) common tern; морска сабја *Zool.* (Xiphias gladius) swordfish; морска ѕвезда *Zool.* (Asteroidea) starfish; морски коњ *Zool.* (Odobenus rosmarus) walrus; морски лав *Zool.* (Otaria jubata) sea lion; морско куче *Zool.* shark, *see* ајкула; морска крава (Manatus) manatee

морталéла *f* mortadella

морталитет *m* death rate, mortality

мортус *adj indecl. only in the expression:* мортус пијан dead drunk

моруна *f Zool.* (Acipenser huso) beluga, great sturgeon

морфиум *m* morphine

морфологија *f* morphology

морфолошки *adj* morphological

Москва *f* Moscow

московјанец -ни & **московјанин** -ани *m* Muscovite

московјанка *f* (*fem. form*) *see* московјанец & московјанин

московски *adj* Moscow *attrib.*; Muscovite

мост *m* bridge; подвижен мост drawbridge, lifting bridge

мостобран *m* bridgehead

мостра *f* sample; pattern, model

мота *impf* **I 1** to roll up, wind (*a skein, hank*) **2** *fig.* to deceive, mislead **II** – **се 1** to mill around; to roam, wander; to sneak; ми се мота по глава . . . I keep thinking about . . . **2** *colloq.* (со) to ridicule, mock, deride, make fun of; се мота тој со тебе he's making fun of you

мотавило & **мотало** *n see* мотовило

мотаница *f* **1** wound yarn **2** *fig.* roaming, wandering **3** *colloq.* joke; derision, mockery

мотач *m* winder-on (*of yarn, thread, etc.*)

мотачка *f* (*fem. form*) *see* мотач

мотел *m* motel

мотив *m* **1** motive; cause, stimulus; reason **2** (*во уметноста*) motif; љубовен мотив love motif **3** (*во вез*) pattern, design

мотивација -ии *f* motivation

мотивира *pf* & *impf* to motivate; to justify, explain

мотика *f* hoe, mattock

мотка (се) *impf see* мота (се)

мото *n* motto

мотовило *n* windlass

мотор *m* **1** motor, engine; бензински мотор petrol engine **2** *fig.* starter, originator **3** motor cycle, *colloq.* motor bike

моторен -рна *adj* motor; моторно возило motor vehicle; моторен чамец motor boat; *Anat.* моторна функција motor function

моторизира *pf* & *impf* to motorize

моторист *m* **1** motorcyclist **2** motor mechanic

мотоцикл -кли *m* motor cycle, *colloq.* motor bike

моќ *f* power, strength, might; potency; куповна моќ buying power; ❑ прави сè што е во нечија моќ to do one's best

моќен -ќна *adj* powerful, strong, mighty; potent; influential

мохер *adj indecl.* mohair

моч *f* urine

моча <се> *impf vulg.* to piss, pee

мочалник -ци & **мочарник** -ци *m colloq.* lavatory, toilet, latrine; urinal, pissoir

мочало *n vulg.* cock; cunt (*as organs of urination*)

мочка¹ *f* **1** *see* моч **2** *colloq.* piddler (*of a girl*)

мочка² *impf child.* to pee, piddle

мочко -овци *m colloq.* piddler (*of a boy*)

мочла *f see* мочка¹ 2

мочлив *adj* piddling; *fig.* trifling, piddling

мочло -овци *m see* мочко

мочне <се> *pf vulg.* мочна <се> *aor.* to piss

мочнува <се> *impf of* мочне <се>

мочур *m* bog, quagmire, morass, swamp, marsh

мочуриште *n see* мочур

мочуриштен -шна *adj* marshy, swampy, boggy; мочуриштен гас marsh gas

мочурлив *adj* boggy, marshy

мошне *adv* very, extremely; мошне многу very many, very much; мошне убаво extremely beautiful

мошоли & **мошори** *impf* **1** to drizzle **2** to murmur (*of a brook, etc.*)

мошти *pl Rel.* relics; ❑ живи мошти bag of bones, walking skeleton

М.П. *abbr.* (*место за печат*) place stamp here

МПЦ *abbr.* (*Македонска православна црква*) Macedonian Orthodox Church

м-р *abbr.* (*магистер*) Master, M

мрава *f Zool.* ant; ❑ ни на мрава не гази he wouldn't hurt a fly; мрави ме лазат it gives me the creeps

мравјалник -ци *m* anthill

мравји *adj see* мравски

мравка *f dim. of* мрава

мравојад *m Zool.* (Myrmecophaga jubata) great anteater, tamanoir

мравски *adj* ant's; ant-like; мравска киселина formic acid

мраз -еви -ови *m* **1** ice; ❑ крши мраз to break the ice; наведува некого на тенок мраз to cut the ground from under s.o.'s feet **2** frost, <extreme> cold

мразарница *f* **1** ice-house, ice cellar **2** ice-machine, *Am.* artificial ice plant

мразен -зна *adj* frosty, cold

мрази *impf* to hate; to dislike, detest, loathe

мразовен -вна *adj see* мразен

мразовит *adj* frosty

мразулец -лци *m* & **мразулка** *f* **1** icicle **2** *fig.* mucus, snivel

мразурец -рци *m* & **мразурка** *f see* мразулец

мрак *m* darkness, gloom (*also fig.*); ноќен мрак darkness of night; паѓа мрак it's getting dark; ❑ паѓа некому мрак на очи to see red; to fly into a rage; to fly off the handle

мракобесие -ија *n* obscurantism

мракобесник -ци *m* obsurant<ist>; reactionary

мрамор *m see* мермер

мрансул *m see* мразулец

мрачева *f dial.* darkness

мрачен -чна *adj* 1 dark, dismal, sombre, gloomy (*also fig.*); мрачна ноќ dark night; мрачни мисли dark thoughts; мрачни времиња depressing times 2 surly, sullen; malevolent; мрачен поглед a surly look 3 opaque, obscure, unclear; мрачен стил opaque style

мрачи се *impf* to get dark

мрачина *f* darkness, dark; dusk

мрачност *f* darkness, gloom

мрачнотија *f see* мрачност

мрва *f* 1 *see* трошка 2 *see* дробенка

мрва се *impf* to spawn (*of fish*)

мрглав *adj* overcast, dull (*of the weather*), cloudy; lowering

мрглави се *impf* to cloud over, become overcast

мрда *impf* I 1 to move *trans.* and *intrans.*; to fidget; to wriggle; мрда со раце to move one's hands; го мрда кралот to move the king (*in chess*); мрда како живо it moves as if alive; ❑ ич око не ми мрда I don't care a hang about it/him; I'm not afraid of it/him; не мрда од местото he won't budge 2 *fig.* to equivocate, hedge; to be unreliable; to be unfaithful (*in marriage*) II – **се** to move *intrans.*; to fidget; to wriggle

мрдалка *f colloq.* 1 evasion; cunning excuse; сè наоѓа рачки и мрдалки he's always making excuses 2 (*fem. form*) *see* мрдало

мрдало *n colloq.* 1 *see* мрцкало 2 bungler

мрднат *adj* foolish; crazy

мрдне *pf* мрдна *aor.* I 1 to move *trans.* and *intrans.*; не смее да мрдне he doesn't dare to move; мрдне стол to move a chair 2 *fig.* to equivocate, hedge 3 *fig.* to cheat, swindle II – **се** 1 to move *intrans.* 2 *fig.* to make a mistake 3 *fig.* to lose one's wits, go crazy; тој се мрдна од умот he went mad (crazy)

мрднува (се) *impf of* мрдне (се)

мрежа *f* 1 net; mesh; web; рибарска мрежа fishing net; мрежа против комарци mosquito net; пајакова мрежа cobweb; ❑ таа го фати во своите мрежи she caught him in her net; се фати во мрежа to swallow the bait 2 network, grid; телефонска мрежа telephone network; електрична мрежа power grid 3 (на око) cataract 4 membrane 5 bridal veil 6 (за пазарување) string bag 7 *fig.* ring round the moon

мрежар *m* net-maker

мрежест *adj* netlike; reticulated; meshed; мрежеста ткаенина webbing, netting

мрежи *impf* I 1 to cover with a net; to net 2 to darn; мрежи чорапи to darn socks/stockings 3 to dim; to cloud; солзите ѝ го мрежеа погледот the tears dimmed her sight 4 *fig.* to ruffle; ветре ја мрежеше водата a breeze was ruffling the water II – **се** to grow dim; to cloud over; ми се мрежи погледот my sight is becoming blurred; се мрежи небото the sky is clouding over

мрежичка *f dim. of* мрежа

мрежница *f Anat.* retina

мрена *f Zool.* (Barbus fluvialis) barbel (*fish*)

мренка *f see* мрена

мрести се *impf* to spawn (*of fish*)

мрестилиште *n* spawning ground

мрза *f* 1 laziness; го фати мрзата he was overcome by laziness 2 idler, lazybones

мрзел *m see* мрза 1

мрзелив *adj see* мрзлив

мрзелува *impf* to be idle; to loaf about

мрзешен -шна *adj* hateful, odious; disagreeable

мрзешник -ци *m* odious person

мрзи *impf impers.* (*with acc.*) to be too lazy to . . . ; го мрзи да стане he doesn't feel like getting up, he's too lazy to get up

мрзла *f* (*fem. form*) *see* мрзло

мрзлив *adj* lazy

мрзливец -вци *& **мрзливко** -овци *m see* мрзло

мрзливка *f see* мрзла

мрзливост *f* laziness

мрзло -овци *m* idler, lazybones

мрзне *impf* I to freeze *trans.* II – **се** to freeze *intrans.*, get frozen

мрк *adj* dark; brown, tawny; strict; sullen, gloomy

мрка се *impf* to mate, copulate

мркне се *pf impers. see* стемни се

мркушкав *& **мркушлав** *adj* darkish; rather gloomy

мрмоли *impf see* мрмори

мрморец -рци *m Zool.* (Gammarus fluviatilis) amphipod, sand-hopper

мрмори *impf* to mumble, mutter; to grumble

мрморко -овци *m* mumbler; grumbler, complainer

мрсен -сна *adj* 1 fatty, greasy, rich; мрсно јадење rich food; мрсна хартија greaseproof paper 2 oil, oily; мрсна боја oil-paint 3 non-lenten; мрсна среда Ash Wednesday 4 greasy, dirty, soiled; мрсни раце greasy hands 5 *fig.* indecent, smutty, salacious; мрсни приказни risqué stories; мрсен виц dirty joke 6 *Print.* bold; мрсни букви bold face

мрси[1] *impf* to eat non-lenten food

мрси[2] *impf* to tangle (*the hair*); to ruffle/play with (*the hair*)

мрсипетко -овци *m* person who does not fast

мрсници *pl* 1 non-fasting days 2 the days from Christmas to Epiphany

мрсно *n see* мрсотија

мрснотија -ии *f* 1 fat 2 *see* мрсотија

мрсотија *f* fat foods and products

мрсул *m* (*usu. pl*) mucus, snivel, snot

мрсулав *adj* snotty, snivelling

мрсулави се *impf* to snivel, have a runny nose

мрсулка *f* snotty, snivelling girl; immature young girl

мрсулко -овци *m* snotty, snivelling boy; immature young boy

мртвачница *f* mortuary, morgue

мртвен <ден> *m* All Souls' Day

мртвенски *adj* All Souls' Day *attrib.*

мртвило *n* apathy, lethargy; quiet, calm; lifelessness

мртвица *f* 1 stagnant water 2 swamp, marsh

мртвороден *adj* stillborn

мртка *impf see* мрцка

мртов *adj* dead (*also fig.*); падне мртов to drop dead; ❑ мртов уморен dead tired; мртов гладен terribly hungry; мртов пијан dead drunk; мртов ладен cool as a cucumber; мртва тишина dead silence; мртва рка neck and neck; мртва природа still life; мртва уста да јаде to lick one's fingers; <само> преку мене мртов over my dead body; мртво пувало conceited ass; мртва коска excrescence on a bone; мртва точка 1. *Tech.* dead centre 2. *Mil.* dead zone 3. *fig.* deadlock, standstill; на мртва точка at a standstill;

тргнува од мртва точка to get the ball rolling; to get things moving/going; стои на мртва стража to fight to the last ditch; мртов капитал dead (dormant) capital; мртва сезона dead season; претепа на мртво име to beat black and blue

мртовец -вци *m* corpse

мртовечки *adj* death, deathlike; cadaverous; мртовечки сандак coffin; мртовечка кола hearse; мртовечко бледило deathly pallor

мрцина *f* **1** carrion **2** emaciated animal **3** good-for-nothing

мрцка *impf* **1** to stagger **2** to equivocate; to be unreliable **3** to fidget; to wriggle

мрцкало *n* **1** unreliable person; double-dealer **2** fidget

мрцлав *adj* loose; irresolute, weak; sluggish, slow

мрцне *pf* мрцна *aor.* to lurch; *fig.* to hedge

мрцнува *impf of* мрцне

мрчка *impf* to stain, soil, dirty, smear

мрша *f* **1** carrion, carcass **2** corpse; wasted person **3** body **4** *fig.* nakedness; poverty

мршав *adj* thin, lean; skinny, wasted

мршавост *f* thinness, leanness; frailty, debility

мршојад *m see* мршојадец

мршојаден -дна *adj* bloodthirsty

мршојадец -дци *m* vulture (*also fig.*); *fig.* exploiter

мршоли *impf see* мошоли

мршти се *impf see* мурти се

МТВ *abbr.* (*Македонска телевизија*) Macedonian Television

му¹ *pron* **1** (*short dat. form of* тој, он) <to> him; му рече she told him; (*also with the long form*) нему му велам I'm telling *him* **2** (*as dat. of possession*) his; татко му his father

му² *interj* moo!

муабет *m colloq.* chat; ти дојдов на муабет I've come for a chat

муабети *impf colloq.* to talk, chat

мува *f Zool.* fly; домашна мува (Musca domestica) house fly; коњска мува (Hippobosca equi) horse-fly; ❑ му брчат муви во главата he's got a bee in his bonnet; си ја има мувата на капата to give the game away; to have a guilty conscience; како мува без глава like a ship without a rudder; like a headless chicken; од мува лој бара you can't get blood out of a stone; аеродром за муви bald head; мува да се чуе you could hear a pin drop; убива две муви со еден удар to kill two birds with one stone; *Sport.* мува категорија flyweight class

мувла *f* mildew, mould

мувлив *adj* mouldy

мувлоса *pf* to go mouldy

мувлосува *impf of* мувлоса

мувосерка *f* fly droppings

мугра *f* daybreak, dawn; во мугрите at the crack of dawn

мудар -дра *adj* wise; intelligent; prudent

мудбак -ци *m arch.* kitchen; pantry

мудрец *m* wise man, sage; thinker, philosopher; clever person

мудро *adv* wisely; sensibly, reasonably; prudently

мудрост *f* wisdom; prudence

мудроштина *f* **1** wisdom **2** shrewdness, cleverness **3** мудроштиње *pl* tricks, ruses; subtlety, sophistry

мудрува *impf* to philosophize; to theorize

муза *f* muse

музеј -еи *m* museum

музејски *adj* museum; ❑ музејска реткост museum piece

музика *f* **1** music; вокална музика vocal music; инструментална музика instrumental music **2** *colloq.* orchestra, band; воена музика military band **3** mouth-organ

музикален -лна *adj* musical; музикално уво an ear for music; музикален јазик melodious language

музикалии *pl* musical instruments and accessories; sheet music

музикалност *f* musicality

музикант *m* musician, player

музицира *impf* to play music, make music

музичар *m* musician, performing artist

музичарка *f* (*fem. form*) *see* музичар

музички *adj* musical; музички инструмент musical instrument; музичка академија academy of music; музичка вечер musical evening; музички педагог music teacher

мук *m* mooing (*of cattle*), lowing

мука *impf* **1** to moo, low **2** *fig.* to weep, cry

мукава *f* cardboard; pasteboard; millboard

мукавен *adj* cardboard

мукает *adj indecl. colloq.* careful, cautious; considerate; interested; стори се мукает за тоа take that into consideration

мукач *m fig.* cry-baby

муклец *interj colloq.* hush! not a word!

мукне *pf* мукна *aor.* to moo, low; to start mooing, lowing

мукнува *impf of* мукне

мула *m* mullah

мулак -ци *m Zool.* male mule

мулат *m* mulatto

мулатка *f* (*fem. form*) *see* мулат

муле *n Zool.* **1** female mule **2** *dim.* baby mule, young mule

муленце *n dim. of* муле

мулешки *adj* mule; мулешка кожа mule-skin

мулиштар *m* donkey (*which impregnates mares*)

мулти- (*in compounds*) multi-

мултилатерален -лна *adj* multilateral; мултилатерална спогодба multilateral agreement

мултимилионер *m* multimillionaire

мултипликатор *m* multiplier

мумија -ии *f* **1** mummy **2** *fig.* dummy

мунгос *m Zool.* mongoose

мундир *m Mil.* full-dress coat

мунѕа *f* reprimand, rebuke; reproach; scolding

мунѕоса *pf* to reprimand, rebuke; to reproach; to scold

мунѕосува *impf of* мунѕоса

муниција *f coll.* ammunition; боева муниција live ammunition; маневарска муниција blank cartridges

мур *m arch.* seal; stamp

мура *f Bot.* (Pinus abies) fir-tree

муравче *n Zool.* (Muscicapa) flycatcher

мурал *m* mural

мургав *adj* swarthy, dark

мургавина *f* swarthiness

мурго *m* (*name given to a dark-coloured ox or dog*) blackie

муренка *f see* боболка, боболкница

мурти се *impf* to frown, scowl

мурџе & мурџо *m* nickname for a swarthy person or dark-coloured animal

мурџест *adj see* мургав

мусака *f Cul.* moussaka; мусака од компири potato moussaka

мусандра *f* linen cupboard

мускат *m* **1** (*грозје*) muscadine **2** (*вино*) muscat, muscadine

мускéта *f Hist.* musket

мускетáр *m Hist.* musketeer

мускул *m* muscle

мускулатýра *f* musculature

мускулест *adj see* мускулозен

мускулóзен -зна *adj* muscular

муслимáн *m* Muslim (Moslem)

муслимáнка *f* (*fem. form*) *see* муслиман

муслимáнски *adj* Muslim (Moslem)

муслимáнство *n* Islam

муслíн *m* muslin

мустак -ци *m see* мустаќ

мустаклија *adj indecl. see* мустаќлија

мустаќ *m* moustache

мустаќлија *adj indecl.* moustached

мутав *m* goat's-hair mat/blanket

мутавџија -ии *m* maker or seller of goat's-hair blankets

мутација -ии *f* mutation

мутер *m Tech.* (*матица*) nut

мутíра *pf & impf* to mutate

муфлуз *m* **1** bankrupt **2** vagabond

муфте *adv colloq.* <for> free, free of charge, gratis, for nothing; on the house

муфтија -ии *m* mufti

мухамедáнски *adj see* муслимански

муцка¹ *f* snout; *pejor.* mug, gob

муцка² *impf* to grumble, mutter, mumble

муцка³ *impf* to sip; to tipple

муцкало¹ *m* grumbler, mutterer, mumbler

муцкало² *m* tippler, drunkard, alcoholic

муцкач *m see* муцкало¹

муцне¹ *pf* муцна *aor.* to mumble, mutter; ни збор повеќе да не си муцнал don't utter another word!

муцне² *pf* муцна *aor.* to have a drink; to get drunk

мученик -ци *m Rel.* martyr

мученица *f Rel.* female martyr

мучник -ци *m* (*in a water-mill*) container for freshly-ground flour

мушама *f* oilcloth

муши *impf* to pierce, prick, poke

мушичка *f* **1** gnat, midge **2** front sight on a rifle **3** *fig.* caprice, whim

мушка (се) *impf see* мушне (се)

мушмула *f Bot.* (Mespilus germanica) medlar (*tree and fruit*)

мушне *pf* мушна *aor.* **I** to push, shove **II** – **се** to sneak through

мушнува (се) *impf of* мушне (се)

мушта *f* **1** pestle (*used by shoemakers for pounding seams*) **2** tailor's ironing-board

муштерија -ии *m* customer; client; consumer

муштулук -ци *m* present, reward (*given to s.o. who brings good news*)

Н

на¹ *prep* **1** on; на масата on the table; на ѕидот on the wall; тулата му падна на глава the brick fell on<to> his head **2** at, near, by; to; in; на вратата at (by) the door; ќе одиме на море we will go to the seaside; бевме на море we were at the seaside; на овој свет in this world; седи на маса to sit at the table; (*in fixed combinations with certain nouns*) на факултет at the university; оди на кино, на театар to go to the cinema, to the theatre; оди на доктор (на лекар) to go to the doctor; на свадба at/to a wedding; на состанок, на конференција at a meeting, at a conference **3** (*with verbal and other nouns implying purpose*) to, for, into; оди на орање to go out to plough; оди в поле на работа to go into the field to work; бевме на причесна we went to Holy Communion; дојди на вечера come to dinner! оди на вода, на дрва, на лешници to go to fetch water, firewood, pick some hazelnuts; оди на риби to go fishing **4** (*of periods of time*) in, during; на младост, на старост in <one's> youth, in old age; на есен, на пролет in autumn, in spring; на животта, на животи *arch.* during <one's> life **5** (*of holidays, dates*) at; on; на Божиќ, на Велигден at Christmas, at Easter; на 19 мај on 19th May **6** at; на полноќ, на пладне at midnight, at midday; на тој час at that hour (time) **7** (*of conditions, circumstances, manner*) at, by, in, during; на месечина by moonlight; на облачина when it is cloudy; на студ in cold weather; на прва среќа on the first occasion; го фатија на спиење they caught him <while he was> asleep; на враќање on returning, on (at) retirement; на сон in <one's> sleep; на ручање, на јадење while lunching, while eating; на пијанство while drunk; на темница in the dark; на брзина in haste; на некој начин in some way; на две на три somehow, in some fashion, hastily **8** in, into; <исечен> на парчиња <cut> to pieces; <распара> на половина <to cut> in two, in half **9** (*of tools, instruments, means*) by, on, in; текст отчукан на машина typed text; брашно на ситно сито сеано flour sifted in a fine sieve; свири на виолина to play the violin; плете на рака to knit by hand **10** (*of measure, quantity, rate*) at, of, per; десетмина на еден ten against one, ten to one; три леба на ден three loaves a day; по педесет километри на час at fifty kilometres an hour; едно девојче на тринаесет години a girl of thirteen **11** (*in greetings, toasts, wishes, exhortations*) на здравје! <to> your <good> health! на добар час! good luck! have a good journey! *bon voyage!* на јуриш! charge! на борба! into battle!

12 (*indirect object*) му плати на селанецот he paid the farmer; му рече на татка си he told his father; им објасни на учениците he explained to the pupils; му благодарам на мојот пријател I thank my friend **13** (*for 'logical subject' of impersonal expressions*) на детето му се спиеше the child was sleepy; му текнало на момчето дека . . . it occurred to the boy that . . . ; блазе на неа how lucky she is! good for her! *Austral.* good on her! тешко на децата it's hard for the children **14** (*for possession, part of whole; genitive relationship*) of; нивата на попот the priest's field; ќошот на куќата the corner of the house; денот на ослободувањето the day of liberation; продавање на вино the sale of wine **15** (*with certain verbs*) се сети на to remember; свикне на to get used to; одговори на to answer; одговара на прашања he is answering questions; се надева на to trust <in>

на² *interj* here! take it! here you are! на ти here, take this!

на- *verbal prefix indicating* **1** *motion onto*; налета to come across; to step on **2** *perfective in sense of completion*; напише to write **3** (*with transitive verbs*) *action affecting a small part of the object*; нагори to burn slightly **4** (*with transitive verbs*) *action involving large quantities of the grammatical object*; наделка дрва to hew a lot of wood **5** (*with 'ce'*) *action performed to the point of weariness or satiety*; наголта се to swallow in quantity; наигра се to tire of playing

наака *pf* **I** to stuff, cram, jam **II** – **се 1** to force o.s. (*во нешто – into s.th.*) **2** *fig.* to have one's fill of wandering (roaming)

набабари *pf* **I** *see* **II 1**; бапка да те набабари! may you choke! **II** – **се 1** to swell, become swollen (*because of illness*) **2** *fig.* to overdress; to put on a lot of clothes

набабне *pf* набабна *aor.* to swell up, puff up, become swollen

набабнува *impf of* набабне

набабри *pf* to swell up, fill out; оризот набабрел the rice has filled out

набабрува *impf of* набабри

набавен -вна *adj* purchasing; набавно одделение purchasing department; набавна цена purchase price; набавни трошоци cost of acquisition

набави *pf* to procure, acquire; to purchase; to supply; набавив сè што ми беше потребно I got everything I needed; тој ќе ни набави дрва he'll supply us with firewood

набавка *f* **1** supplies **2** acquisition, purchase

набавта *pf* **I 1** to stuff, jam, cram **2** to overdress *trans.* **3** *fig.* to talk a lot of nonsense **4** *fig.* to thrash, whip, beat up **II** – **се 1** to overdress *intrans.* **2** *fig.* to gorge, stuff o.s.

набавтана *adv* (*потамина*) at random; by chance

набавува *impf of* набави

набавувач *m* purchasing agent, procurer; supplier

набара *pf* to find (*s.th.*) by feeling, groping

набастиса *pf* to come across (*s.o./s.th.*) <by chance>

набацува се *pf* to tire of kissing

набеди *pf* to slander, calumniate; to accuse falsely

набедува *impf of* набеди

набележува *impf of* набележи

набележи *pf* набележи & набележа *aor.* **1** to indicate, define, mark **2** to sketch; to explain in outline

набели *pf* **I** to whiten **II – се** to make o.s. white; to put on face-powder

набере *pf* набра *aor.* **I 1** to pick; to collect *trans.*; набравме полна кошница јагоди we've picked a basketful of strawberries **2** to fold, gather, crease *trans.*; to wrinkle *trans.*; to pucker; набран фустан pleated dress; го набра челото he knitted his brow **3** *Print.* to compose, set in type **II – се 1** to pick a lot **2** to wrinkle, crease *intrans.*; to gather in folds **3** to gather, collect *intrans.*

наберува (се) *impf of* набере (се)

набеќарува се *pf* to have one's fling (*of a young man*); to sow one's wild oats; to tire of bachelorhood

набива (се) *impf of* набие (се)

набие *pf* наби *aor.* **I 1** to stamp down, pack down, level (*the ground*); to ram in; (*на колец*) to impale; *arch.* to load (*a firearm*); ❑ набие цена to drive a price up; си набие цена to enhance one's reputation; набие некому рогови to cuckold s.o. **2** to bruise (*limbs*), contuse **II – се** to become bruised

набиен *pt & adj* **1** crammed in, jammed in; stamped down, packed down; impaled; *arch.* loaded (*of a firearm*); bruised **2** thickset, stocky

набиеница *f* bruise, contusion (*on a leg, etc.*)

набира *impf* **I 1** to crease, make folds **2** *Print.* to compose, set in type **II – се** to crease, wrinkle *intrans.*

набирка *f see* набор 1

наблажи *pf* to sweeten a little

наблажне *pf* наблажна *aor.* impers. (*with dat.*) наблажне ми to taste a slight sweetness (*from food, etc.*)

наблажнува *impf* **1** (*only 3rd p.*) to be slightly sweet **2** *of* наблажне

наблажува *impf* **1** to sweeten a little **2** *see* наблажнува

наближи *pf* to approach, move closer; наближија до селото they approached the village; наближи денот на одмаздата the day of reckoning approached (drew near)

наближува *impf of* наближи

наблизу *adv* near, nearby, not far; наблизу има извор there is a spring nearby

набљудателен -лна *adj* observant, watchful; circumspect; набљудателен дух observant spirit

набљудателност *f* power of observation; watchfulness

набљудение -ија *n* observation; observing, watching

набљудува *impf* **1** to observe, watch **2** to look over, supervise

набљудувач *m* observer

набљудувачница *f* lookout

набобне *pf* набобна *aor.* to swell up, puff up

набобнува *impf of* набобне

набобри *pf see* набабри

набобрува *impf of* набобри

набоде *pf* набодов *1st p. sg aor.* **I** to prick, pierce; to haft; to pin; to spit **II – се** to prick o.s.

набодна *f* pitchfork

набодува *impf of* набоде

набожен -жна *adj* pious, devout; religious

набожност *f* piety, devoutness

набој -ои *m* callus (*usu. on sole or heel*)

наболедува се *pf* to have one's share of illnesses; to be ill for a long time

наболи *pf* to <begin to> ache a little; to feel a slight pain

наболува *impf* to ache (*slightly or occasionally*); ме наболува главата I have a slight headache

набор *m* **1** fold; crease **2** *Print.* type, type-face

набосо *adv* barefoot; ги обу чевлите набосо he put his shoes on his bare feet

набоцка *pf* **I** to prick (*of thorns, etc.*) **II – се** to prick o.s.

набразди *pf* **I 1** to furrow, make furrows/grooves **2** to pucker, furrow (*one's forehead, face*) **II – се** to knit one's brow; to grimace; to become wrinkled

набраздува (се) *impf of* набразди (се)

набрашни *pf* **I** to sprinkle with flour **II – се** to sprinkle flour over o.s.

набрбори *pf* **I** to babble a lot **II – се** to babble one's fill

набргу *adv* **1** often, quite often, frequently **2** quickly, hastily; soon, soon after

набрдила *pl* sley, weaver's reed

набрекне *pf* набрекна *aor.* to swell up, puff up; жилите му набрекнаа his veins swelled up

набрекнува *impf of* набрекне

набрзана & набрзина *adv* speedily, hastily

набрзо *adv see* набргу

набрка *pf* **I** to chase away; to dismiss, discharge **II – се** to tire of running about

наброи *pf* наброи & наброја *aor.* **I** to enumerate, list; to count <up> **II – се** to count for a long time *intrans.*; to tire of counting

набројува *impf of* наброи

набрсти се *pf* to graze/browse one's fill (*of animals*)

набрчка *pf* **I** to pucker, furrow (*one's forehead*) **II – се** to wrinkle *intrans.*; to become wrinkled

набрчкува (се) *impf of* набрчка (се)

набувка (се) & набувта (се) *pf see* набавта (се)

набуи *pf poet.* to sprout, spring up, grow rapidly

набута *pf* **I** to cram in, stuff in, push in, squeeze in *trans.* **II – се** to push in, squeeze in *intrans.*

набутува (се) *impf of* набута (се)

набучува *impf* to roar, boom, rumble occasionally (*in the distance*)

навави *pf* to call (*birds, animals*); to lure, entice

навабува *impf of* навави

навади *pf* **I 1** to water; ги навади цвеќињата he watered the flowers **2** to take out, remove in quantity **II– се** *see* I 2

навадува (се) *impf of* навади (се)

навака *adv see* наваму

наваكса *pf colloq.* **1** to manage, succeed **2** to make up for; to retrieve; навакса загубено време to make up for lost time

навал[1] *m* **1** attack, assault; rush **2** crowd, crush, jam

навал[2] *adv* од навал intentionally, purposely, deliberately; on purpose; пцовисала лисицата од навал the fox played dead

навала[1] *f* **1** throng, surge, influx, crush; навала на туристи influx of tourists **2** *Sport.* offence, attack

навала[2] *pf* **I** to roll (*to one spot*) *trans.* **II – се** to roll (*to one spot*) *intrans.*

навала[3] **(се)** *impf see* навалува (се)

навален -лна *adj Sport.* offence *attrib.*; навални играчи attack, attacking players

наваленост *f* steepness; steep slope

навали[1] *pf* **I 1** to press, bend *trans.* **2** to place aslant, lean *trans.*; to incline *trans.* **3** to bother, pester; to pounce (*on*); to insist; навали со прашања to shower with questions **4** to overpower, overcome; го навали тежок сон a deep sleep overcame him **II – ce 1** to bend *intrans.*; to twist *intrans.* **2** to lean (*на – on*)

навали² *pf* to lay <and light> (*a fire*)

навалица *f see* навал¹ 2 & навала¹ 1

навалка (ce) *pf see* извалка (ce)

навалува¹ (ce) *impf of* навали¹ (ce)

навалува² *impf of* навали²

наваму *adv* **1** here, in this direction, *arch.* hither; идат наваму they are coming here; ❑ наваму-натаму to and fro; somehow; наваму-натаму, тој го заврши факултетот somehow or other he finished university **2** until now, up to now; оттогаш наваму since then; ever since; from then on

навари *pf* **1** to rise, boil up *intrans.*; to cook for a long time *intrans.* **2** to cook (*in quantity*), prepare a lot

наварува *impf of* навари

наваса *pf colloq.* **1** *see* навакса **2** to overpower, overcome; ме наваса сонот sleep overcame me

навасува *impf of* наваса

навеалиште *n see* навеиште

навев *m* <snow>drift

навева *impf of* навее

наведе¹ *pf* **I 1** to bend down *trans.* **2** to lower (*one's eyes*), bow (*one's head*) **II – ce** to bend down *intrans.*, stoop down

наведе² *pf* **1** to mention, quote, cite, adduce; да наведам само неколку to name only/but a few **2** to enumerate **3** *fig.* to lead, induce; наведе на погрешен пат to lead astray

наведне (ce) *pf see* наведе¹ (ce)

наведнува (ce) *impf see* наведува¹ (ce)

наведува¹ (ce) *impf of* наведе¹ (ce)

наведува² *impf of* наведе²

навее *pf* навеа *aor.* **1** to sweep (*snow*) into drifts **2** *fig.* to bring, bring on; не испуштај си ја среќата што ти ја навеал случајот don't let slip the good fortune that chance has brought you; кај ми го навеа ѓаволот! why has the devil brought him/it on me!

навезе *pf* навеза *aor.* **I** to embroider **II – ce** to tire of embroidering

навезува (ce) *impf of* навезе (ce)

навеиште *n* **1** place exposed to drifting snow **2** *fig.* reef, trap, pitfall **3** evil, unpleasantness, unpleasant experience

навејчиште *n see* навеиште

навек *adv* always, ever; за навек for ever

навекува се *pf* to live long; to live to a ripe old age

наверно *adv* certainly; by all means; for certain; in any case

навесели се *pf* to have a good time

навести *pf* **1** to hint (*на – at*), allude (*to*); to indicate, point to **2** to predict, foretell; to portend, betoken, herald; to forewarn **3** to announce

навестува *impf of* навести

наветар *adv* in vain; uselessly, to no purpose; му отидоа парите наветар he squandered his money to no purpose

наветво *adv* second-hand; купи нешто наветво to buy s.th. second-hand

навечер *adv* in the evening<s>, every evening; во сабота навечер on Saturday evenings; навечер јас

не можам да читам in the evening I am unable to read

навечера *pf* **I** to give (*s.o.*) supper **II – ce** to have supper

нави *pl arch. Folk.* goblins (*who torment expectant and newly-delivered mothers*)

навива *impf* **I 1** *of* навие **2** *Sport.* to support; навива за 'Вардар' to root (*Austral.* to barrack) for 'Vardar'; to support 'Vardar' **II – ce** *of* навие се

навивалка *f* reel, coiler, spool, bobbin

навивач *m Sport.* fan, *Austral.* barracker (*at a match, game, contest*); supporter

навивка *f* **1** rag; foot-cloth **2** coil, loop (*of thread*)

навига́тор *m* navigator; seaman, sailor

навигација *f* **1** navigation **2** navigation, <act of> sailing **3** navigation season

навигацио́нен -она *adj* navigational; навигационен сателит navigation satellite

навиди *pf* to visit (*s.o.*); to drop in (*кај – on*)

навидува *impf of* навиди

навидум *adv* to all appearances, seemingly, outwardly; apparently; животот си течеше навидум мирно to all appearances life went on peacefully

навие *pf* нави *aor.* **I 1** to wind on **2** to wind<up>; го нави саатот he wound the clock **II – ce** to curl up, coil *intrans.*

навик -ци *m* & **навика** *f* habit; од навик out of habit; добие навик to acquire a habit, get into the habit of (*doing s.th.*); тоа му влезе (помина) во навик that became a habit with him (he got into the habit of doing that); има навика to be in the habit of; се ослободува од навика to kick a habit

навика *pf* **I 1** to scold, berate, tick off; што не му навика he gave him a good talking to; he called him all sorts of names **2** to invite (*several people*) **II – ce 1** to shout one's fill **2** (*with dat.*) *see* **I 1**

навикнат *pt* accustomed, used to; навикнат е на тоа he is used to that

навикне *pf* навикна *aor.* **I 1** to accustom; го навикна детето на ред he instilled in the child a sense of order **2** to get used (*на – to*), grow accustomed to **II – ce** *see* I 2

навикнува (ce) *impf of* навикне (ce)

навикува (ce) *impf of* навика (ce)

навилец -лци *m* amount of hay that can be lifted on a pitchfork, 'pitchforkful'

навили *pf* to get (take) on a pitchfork

навилува *impf of* навили

навине (ce) *pf see* шине (ce)

навинува (ce) *impf see* шинува (ce)

навира¹ *impf of* навре¹

навира² *impf* to swarm, throng; to gush; to well <up>; навираат мисли/спомени thoughts/memories come flooding in; му навираа солзи на очите tears welled in his eyes

навири *pf* **I** ги навири очите his eyes filled with tears **II – ce** (*of eyes*) to be filled with tears

навирува (ce) *impf of* навири (ce)

нависне *pf* нависна *aor.* **1** to hang down; to lean out **2** *trans.* to embrace, throw one's arms round (*s.o.'s neck*)

нависнува *impf of* нависне

нависоко *adv* high <up>, at a great height; ❑ се крева нависоко to put on airs, to show off

навистина *adv* really, truly; навистина беше така it really was so

навистински *adv see* вистински 2

навитка *pf* I to wind <on>; to curl, coil *trans.* II – се to wind (*o.s. round s.th.*), curl up *intrans.*

навиткува (се) *impf of* навитка (се)

навлажи *pf see* навлажни

навлажни *pf* to moisten, wet

навлажнува *impf of* навлажни

навлажува *impf see* навлажнува

навлака *f* cover; pillowcase (pillowslip); crown (*of a tooth*)

навлаклив *adj* heavy; sluggish, slow

навласи *pf* to comb (*hemp*)

навлачи *pf* I to comb (*wool*) II – се to tire of combing (*wool*)

навлачува (се) *impf of* навлачи (се)

навлегува *impf of* навлезе

навлезе *pf* навлегов *1st p. sg aor.* **1** to get in; to penetrate; навлезе чад smoke got in **2** to go in deeper; навлезе во шумата he went deeper into the wood **3** to burst in (*of several people*); to break in (*of several people*); to invade; навлегоа во куќата they broke into the house

навлекува (се) *impf of* навлече (се)

навлече *pf* навлеков *1st p. sg aor.* I **1** to put on, pull on, slip on; to catch (*an illness*) **2** to bring, haul, drag (*a quantity of s.th.*) **3** to draw, deflect; to incur; ја навлече нивната омраза на себе he drew their hatred on to himself II – се to tire of pulling, dragging

навнатре *adv* **1** further, deeper inside (*s.th.*); влеговме навнатре во шумата we went deeper into the forest **2** inward<s>; вратата се отвора навнатре the door opens inwards

навод *m* **1** quotation **2** allegation, claim, statement

наводени *pf* I to soak *trans.*, wet II – се to get wet, soaked

наводни *pf* to irrigate, flood; to water

наводници *pl* inverted commas, quotation marks; меѓу наводници in inverted commas, quotation marks

наводно *adv* supposedly, allegedly; apparently; тој е наводно студент he is supposed to be a student

наводнува *impf of* наводни

навози *pf* I to bring (*in a vehicle*) a lot of s.th. II – се to tire of driving, riding

навозува (се) *impf of* навози (се)

навој -ои *m* **1** *see* навивалка **2** winding mechanism **3** thread (*of screw, bolt*) **4** *Elec.* coil

навол *adv* од навол, *see* навал, од навал

навотка *pf see* напика

навоткува *impf see* напикува

наврапито *adv* hastily, in a rush; anyhow

наврапица *adv see* наврапито

наврат *m* time, *colloq.* go; на неколку (на повеќе) наврати several times, on several occasions; at several attempts/tries/goes

наврати *pf* **1** to direct, divert (*water*) **2** to visit; to drop in (*кај – on*)

навратува *impf of* наврати

навраќа *impf see* наврати

навре[1] *pf* **1** to push in, insert (*into s.th. narrow*) **2** to put on, stick on; навре капа на глава to jam one's cap on one's head **3** to slip on (*hurriedly*); ги навре алиштата he slipped on his clothes

навре[2] *pf* to come in large numbers; to swarm; to well <up>

навреда *f* insult, offence; навреда на честа insult to one's honour; без навреда no offence

навреден *pt* insulted, offended

навреди *pf* I to insult, offend II – се to take offence, be insulted, offended

навредлив *adj* **1** insulting, offensive; навредливи зборови insulting words **2** touchy, sensitive; quick to take offence

навредува (се) *impf of* навреди (се)

навредувач *m* person who insults; offender

навредувачки *adj see* навредлив 1

наврека се *pf* to tire of bleating/yelling/crying

наврекнато *adv* irritably; gruffly, rudely; angrily

навреме *adv* on time, punctually; дојде токму навреме to come exactly on time

навремен *adj* prompt, on time, punctual; timely

навреми *pf* to come (*of time*), reach full term; неговата жена навреми за раѓање his wife's time has come (*to give birth*)

наврзалка *f* **1** little cord, band, strap **2** *fig.* story; chatter

наврзе *pf* наврза *aor.* **1** to attach, fasten, tie on **2** to add to **3** *fig.* to babble, talk, tell many stories

наврзница *f* & **наврзок** -ци *m see* наврзалка 1

наврзува *impf of* наврзе

навриат *pt* drenched, soaked; *fig.* dejected, discouraged, crushed; си остана како навриат he was left dejected (as though crushed)

наврне *pf* наврна *aor.* **1** to fall (*of snow, rain, hail*) **2** to get wet (*in the rain*); наврнал целиот he got wet through (drenched)

наврнува *impf of* наврне

наврти *pf* I **1** to point, aim; му ги навртија пушките they aimed their rifles at him **2** to direct, divert; ❑ ја наврти водата на својата воденица he brought grist to the mill **3** to turn *trans.*; му го наврти грбот he turned his back on him **4** to wind (*on*) II – се **1** to turn *intrans.*; to turn one's back (*на – on*) **2** to begin, get down to; кога му се навртија на ручекот, сѐ изедоа when they got down to lunch they ate everything **3** to tire of winding (*s.th.*)

навртка[1] *f Tech.* nut

навртка[2] *pf* **1** to weave into, work into; to insert **2** to wind (*on*)

навртува (се) *impf of* наврти (се)

наврши[1] *pf* to betroth; му ја наврши ја they betrothed her to him

наврши[2] *pf* I to reach (*a certain age*) II – се (*of time*) to pass, elapse *intrans.*

навршува[1] *impf of* наврши[1]

навршува[2] (се) *impf of* наврши[2] (се)

навтаса *pf colloq.* I **1** to ripen; крушите навтасаа the pears have ripened **2** to catch up with, reach *trans.*; брзо ги навтасавме we soon caught up with them II – се to catch up with each other

навтасува (се) *impf of* навтаса (се)

навтера *pf* I **1** to push in, shove in *trans.* **2** to fill up, cram in, stuff in II – се to push in, shove in *intrans.*

навтерува (се) *impf of* навтера (се)

навчас *adv* immediately, at once

нагаѓа *impf* **1** *see* нагодува **2** to guess, suspect, surmise

нагази *pf* **I 1** to tread, step on; му го нагази прстот he trod on his toe **2** to stamp down, level by treading down **3** *fig.* to come upon, come across (*s.o. by chance*) **4** *fig.* (*only 3rd p.*) to happen to, befall; to meet with; каква несреќа го нагази! what a misfortune befell him! **II – се** to tire of wading, trudging (*through mud, snow, etc.*)

нагазне *pf* нагазна *aor. see* нагази

нагазнува *impf see* нагазува

нагазува (се) *impf of* нагази (се)

нагалено *adv* **1** by nickname, affectionately; тој се вика Петар, но нагалено го викаат Пепе he is called Peter, but his pet name is Pepe **2** sweetly, lovably; fondly; таа го гледаше нагалено she was looking at him fondly

нагали се *pf* (*with dat.*) to caress (*s.o./s.th.*) for a long time; to caress each other for a long time

наган & нагант *m* Nagant (*kind of revolver*)

нагизди *pf* **I** to dress up *trans.*, adorn; to trim **II – се** to dress up *intrans.*, adorn o.s.; to smarten up *intrans.*

нагиздува (се) *impf of* нагизди (се)

наглава & на глава *adv in the expression:* не можеш со него да излезеш наглава he's difficult to manage

наглави *pf* **1** to darn (*using a darning mushroom*) **2** to tether (*a horse, donkey*)

наглавува *impf of* наглави

наглавушка *f* foot of a stocking, sock; vamp (*of a shoe*)

нагладува се *pf* to go hungry for a period

нагласи *pf* **I 1** to arrange, settle, fix; ќе ја нагласиме работата we will settle the matter **2** to accent; to insert accent marks **3** to stress, emphasize, underline **II – се** to get dressed up; to spruce up *intrans.*

нагласок -ци *m* stress; emphasis; ❑ става нагласок на to lay/put emphasis on

нагласува (се) *impf of* нагласи (се)

нагледа *pf* **I** to keep an eye on; to watch <out for>; to take care of, guard (*for a while*); to supervise **II – се** to see a lot; to enjoy looking at, admire

нагледен -дна *adj* **1** obvious, evident **2** visual; нагледна настава teaching with visual aids

нагледно *adv* visually (*in teaching, etc.*)

нагледува (се) *impf of* нагледа (се)

нагледувач *m* supervisor

нагло *adv* suddenly; hastily; quickly

наглост *f* haste, speed; abruptness; suddenness

наглоти *pf* to fill (*eyes, with dust, sand, etc.*); ветрот му ги наглоти очите со прав the wind blew dust into his eyes; ми ги наглоти очите со песок he kicked sand into my eyes

наглув *adj* hard of hearing

наглувост *f* hardness of hearing, slight deafness

нагмечи *pf* **1** to squash, squeeze down; to bruise **2** to press, crush (*grapes, etc.*)

нагмечува *impf of* нагмечи

нагнете *pf* **I 1** to stuff in, ram in, shove in *trans.* **2** *fig.* to feed (*s.o.*) to satiety **II – се 1** to squeeze in *intrans.* **2** *fig.* to eat/drink one's fill; to gorge *intrans.*

нагнетува (се) *impf of* нагнете (се)

нагнива *impf of* нагние

нагние *pf* нагни *aor.* to begin to rot, decay

нагнои *pf* нагнои & нагноја *aor. see* наѓубри

нагнојува *impf of* нагнои

наг097овара (се) *impf see* наговори (се) **I 1 & II 2**

наговор *m poet.* persuading, urging

наговори *pf* **I 1** to persuade, induce, urge, talk into, egg on; to incite **2** to tell a lot of stories; му наговори триста глупости she told him a lot of nonsense **II – се 1** to have one's fill of talking **2** to taunt, tease one another

наговорува (се) *impf see* наговара (се)

нагоди *pf* **1** to arrange, settle **2** to oblige, accommodate; to satisfy; to please; не можам да му нагодам I can't accommodate/please him

нагодува *impf of* нагоди

нагодувачка *f* **1** arranging, settling; satisfying, obliging **2** riddle

наголеми *pf* **I** to increase *trans.*, enlarge; to exaggerate **II – се** to increase, grow *intrans.*; денот се наголеми the day<s> became longer

наголемо *adv* on a large scale; се зголемува наголемо to increase on a large scale; ❑ се крева наголемо, се држи наголемо to put on airs, show off

наголемува (се) *impf of* наголеми (се)

наголо *adv* bareback; го јава коњот наголо he is riding the horse bareback

наголта се *pf* **1** to swallow a lot **2** *fig.* to eat one's fill

наголтува се *impf of* наголта се

нагон *m* instinct, drive; impulse

нагонски¹ *adj* instinctive

нагонски² *adv* instinctively

нагоре *adv* **1** up, upwards **2** uphill; се качуваме нагоре we are climbing up **3** по реката нагоре upstream

нагорен -рна *adj* **1** uphill **2** upward, rising; нагорна линија rising line

нагори *pf* **1** *intrans.* to get slightly burnt **2** *trans.* to singe, burn slightly **3** *arch.* to heat; ќе нагорам една силна фурна I'll stoke up a big fire in the stove

нагорнина & нагорница *f see* нагорниште

нагорниште *n* rise, climb, ascent

нагорува *impf of* нагори

нагорчи *pf see* нагорчува

нагорчува *impf* to taste somewhat bitter; to have a slight tang

нагости *pf* **I** to entertain, serve with food **II – се** to have a good feed, eat one's fill; to treat o.s. (*to plenty of s.th.*)

нагостува (се) *impf of* нагости (се)

награбок -ци *m see* заграб

награда *f* **1** prize, reward; premium; award; прва награда first prize; добие награда to get a prize; додели награда to award a prize; утешна награда consolation prize; second best **2** pay, wages, remuneration; награда за прекувремена работа overtime pay

награди *pf* to reward; to give a prize to

наградник -ци *m* vest, waistcoat, jerkin

наградува *impf of* награди

награмади *pf* to pile up, heap up, accumulate; to cram

награмадува *impf of* награмади

награни *pf* to sprout branches; to spread (*of trees*)

агранува *impf of* награни

нагрби *pf* **I 1** to load (*on s.o.'s back or on to an animal*) **2** *fig.* to set (*s.o.*) a task; to burden (*s.o.*) with s.th.; to make (*s. th.*) incumbent upon (*s. o.*) **II – се 1** to bend down *intrans.*; to shoulder (*a load*) **2** *fig.* to undertake a task

нагрбува (се) *impf of* нагрби (се)

нагрвали <**се**> *pf* **1** to gather together *intrans.*, crowd in **2** to rush, swarm, throng

нагрвалува <**се**> *impf of* нагрвали <се>

нагрден *pt* deformed, disfigured

нагрденост *f* deformity, disfigurement

нагрди *pf* **I** to deform, disfigure, make ugly, maim **II – се** to deform, disfigure o.s., make o.s. ugly

нагрдува (се) *impf of* нагрди (се)

нагребе *pf* нагреба *aor.* **I** to scratch <slightly>; to dent **II – се 1** to get <slightly> scratched **2** to tire of scouring

нагребок -ци *m* scratch

нагребува (се) *impf of* нагребе (се)

нагрева (се) *impf of* нагрее (се)

нагрее *pf* нагреа *aor.* **I** to warm up *trans.* **II – се 1** to warm up *intrans.* (*a little*) **2** to warm up thoroughly *intrans.*

нагрејува (се) *impf see* нагрева (се)

нагрепка *pf dim. of* нагребе

нагризе *pf* нагриза *aor.* **I 1** to gnaw; глувците го нагризале лебот the mice have gnawed <at> the bread **2** *fig.* to corrode; to eat away; киселините го нагризаа садот the acids have corroded the pot **II – се** to have one's fill of gnawing

нагризува (се) *impf of* нагризе (се)

нагрли *pf* to earth up, cover (*potatoes, the roots of maize, etc.*)

нагрлува *impf of* нагрли

нагрне *pf* нагрна *aor.* **I 1** (*наметне*) to throw on, throw on top, throw over **2** to crowd, press, swarm, *see* нагрвали <се> **II – се** to wrap o.s. in a rug/blanket, wrap up *intrans.*; се нагрне со џемпер to put on a pullover

нагрнува (се) *impf of* нагрне (се)

нагрсти се *pf* to pile up, amass (*money*); се нагрстија пари they've made/amassed a lot of money

нагрстува се *impf of* нагрсти се

нагруби (се) *pf see* нагрди (се)

нагрубува (се) *impf see* нагрдува (се)

нагрува *pf* **I** to thresh in quantity (*wheat*) **II – се** to tire of threshing

над *prep* **1** above, over, on top of; more than; над градот летаа авиони aircraft were flying over the city; над селото има еден манастир above the village stands a monastery; над главата overhead; има власт над некого to have authority over s.o.; победа над непријателите victory over the enemy; здравјето над сè health is paramount; тој има над триесет години he is over thirty years old; крал над кралеви king of kings; песна над песните song of songs **2** on, at; работата над речникот the work on the dictionary

над- (**нат-** *before voiceless consonants*) *verbal prefix indicating* **1** *action above*; over-, super-; надбие to overpower **2** *action exceeding*; out-; надбега to outrun **3** (*with ce*) *action in competition*; се надбројува to compete in counting

надава *impf of* нададе

нададе *pf* нададов *1st p. sg aor.* **I 1** to add to, give (*more or in addition*); to attach **2** to add a great deal of

s.th., add in large quantities **3** нададе вик to give voice, start shouting; нададе уши <да слуша> to prick up one's ears **II – се 1** *see* **I 2 2** (*with dat.*) to snap at; *colloq.* to tick off; му се нададов I gave him a piece of my mind

надалеку *adv* far and wide; from afar, at a distance

надарен *adj* gifted, talented

надареност *f* talent, gift; ability

надари *pf* to endow, provide with; го надарил Господ со голем ум the Lord endowed him with a great mind

надарува *impf of* надари

надбега *pf* to overtake, outrun, outstrip

надбегува *impf of* надбега

надбива *impf of* надбие

надбие *pf* надби *aor.* to defeat, overpower, overwhelm

надбискуп *m* archbishop

надбискупија -ии *f* archbishopric, archdiocese

надбори *pf* to overcome, win in wrestling

надборува *impf* **I** *of* надбори **II – се** to compete in wrestling

надбрза *pf* to overtake (*in walking*)

надбрзува *impf* **I** *of* надбрза **II – се** to compete in fast walking

надброи *pf* надброи & надброја *aor.* to miscount, count one or more too many

надбројува *impf* **I** *of* надброи **II – се** to compete in counting

надве *adv* in two, into two parts

надведе се *pf* надведов *1st p. sg aor.* to bend over, lean over; се надведе над бунарот he leaned over the well

надведува се *impf of* надведе се

надве-натри *adv* quickly, hastily, helter-skelter; any-how, carelessly, shoddily

надвива *impf of* надвие

надвие *pf* надви *aor.* to conquer, overcome, defeat; правината ќе надвие justice will prevail, truth will win out

надвика *pf* to outdo in shouting

надвикува *impf* **I** *of* надвика **II – се** to compete in shouting

надвисне <**се**> *pf* надвисна <се> *aor.* to rise; to gather *intrans.*; to lean over, bend over; црни облаци <се> надвиснаа над градот black clouds gathered over the city

надвиснува <**се**> *impf of* надвисне <се>

надвиши *pf* to be higher (taller) than; to exceed, surpass

надвишува *impf of* надвиши

надвладее *pf* надвладеа *aor.* to overpower; to conquer

надвладува *impf of* надвладее

надводен -дна *adj* above-water; надводниот дел на коработ the upper part of the ship (*above the waterline*)

надвојвода *m* archduke

надвојводство *n* archduchy

надвор¹ *m* (*only sg*) *colloq.* **1** diarrhoea **2** motion, stool

надвор² *adv* out; outside; надвор е студено it's cold outside; излезе од порта надвор he went out of the house; надвор! out <with you>! get out! надвор од законот outside the law; ❑ надвор од себеси beside oneself; од мерата надвор beyond measure, excessively; надвор од тоа besides, furthermore, moreover; apart from that

надворешен -шна *adj* **1** external, outward; надворешен изглед external (outward) appearance **2** foreign, alien; министерство за надворешни работи Ministry of Foreign Affairs; надворешен човек foreign person, alien

надворешност *f* exterior, outside, surface

надворешнотрговски *adj* foreign trade *attrib.*

надгласа *pf* to outvote; to outshout

надгласува *impf of* надгласа

надгледува *impf* to supervise, watch, superintend

надгледувач *m* supervisor, superintendent

надградба *f* superstructure

надгробен -бна *adj* grave; надгробен камен gravestone, tombstone; надгробно слово funeral oration

наддава *impf* **I** *of* наддаде **II** – **се 1** to compete **2** to bid at an auction; to haggle

наддавач *m* competitor; bidder at an auction

наддаде *pf* наддадов *1st p. sg aor.* **1** to give, add more than necessary **2** to compete; to bid at an auction

надебелее *pf* надебелеа *aor.* to become stout, grow fat; to gain (put on) weight

надебели *pf* to fatten; to make thicker

надебелува *impf* **1** *of* надебелее **2** *of* надебели

надева се *impf* **1** to hope; се надевам дека сè е во ред I hope everything is all right; се надева на најдобро to hope for the best; се надева на/во to put one's faith in, pin one's hopes on **2** (на) to count on, rely on, have faith in; ние на тебе се надеваме we have faith in you **3** to expect (*s.o. to come*); кога не му се надеваме, тој тогаш доаѓа he comes when we don't expect him

надее се *impf see* надева се

надеж *f* hope; нема веќе надеж there's no hope any more; надежта ми е во него my <only> hope is in him, I pin my hopes on him; ❑ празни (голи) надежи vain (empty) hopes; внесува надеж to strike a hopeful note; губи надеж to yield/give way to despair; живее во надеж to live in hope; зрно (искра) на надеж a ray of hope; му се враќаат надежите one's spirits rise; подгрева нечии надежи to raise s.o.'s hopes; уништува нечии надежи to dash/shatter s.o.'s hopes

надежен -жна *adj* promising, hopeful; trustworthy, faithful; надежен пријател faithful (true) friend

наделка *pf* **I** to hew; to trim; to carve a lot of **II** – **се** to have one's fill of hewing/trimming/carving

наделкува (се) *impf of* наделка (се)

надене *pf* надена *aor.* **I** to put on, shove on, stick on **II** – **се** to catch, get caught (*на – on*); to step (*on*)

наденува (се) *impf of* надене (се)

надере *pf* надра *aor.* **I 1** to tear, rip **2** to skin, flay in quantity **II** – **се 1** to get torn **2** to shout, yell a lot

надерува (се) *impf of* надере (се)

надесно *adv* <to the> right; *Mil.* eyes right!

наджеве *pf* наджевеа *aor.* to outlive, survive *trans.*

наджувува *impf of* наджевее

надзбори *pf see* надзборува

надзборува *pf* to out-talk

надзема *impf of* надземе

надземе *pf* надзема *aor.* to take more (*than one should, more than necessary*); ни надзеде пари he overcharged us

надземен -мна *adj* **1** above-ground **2** unearthly; supernatural

надзира *impf* to supervise

надзирател *m* supervisor

надзирателка *f* (*fem. form*) *see* надзирател

надзор *m* supervision, watch<ing>; под надзор under supervision/surveillance

надзорен -рна *adj* supervisory; надзорна власт supervisory authority; надзорен одбор supervisory committee

надзорник -ци *m* supervisor

надига (се) *impf see* надигне (се)

надигне *pf* надигна *aor.* **I 1** to raise, lift <a little>; надигна глава he raised his head; надигна врева he raised a commotion **2** to raise, rear, bring up; него чичко му го надигна he was brought up by his uncle **3** to take/buy up (*in quantity*); ќе отиде на пазар и ќе надигне многу работи he would go to the market and buy a lot of things **II** – **се 1** to recover (*from an illness, crisis, etc.*) **2** *fig.* to become arrogant, conceited **3** to appear, arise, rise up; се надигна магла a mist formed

надигнува (се) *impf of* надигне (се)

надигра *pf* to outplay, defeat; to outdance

надигрува *impf* **I** *of* надигра **II** – **се** to compete in playing/dancing; to outplay each other; to outdance each other

надитри *pf* to outwit

надитрува *impf* **I** *of* надитри **II** – **се** to try to outwit each other

надише се *pf* надиша се & надиши се *aor.* to get a good breath of; to breathe to one's heart's content

надишува се *impf of* надише се

надјаде *pf* надјадов *1st p. sg aor.* to surpass (*s.o.*) in eating

надјадува *impf* **I** *of* надјаде **II** – **се** to compete in eating

надлаже *pf* надлажа & надлага *aor.* to outdo in telling lies

надлажува *impf* **I** *of* надлаже **II** – **се** to vie with each other in lying

надлежен -жна *adj* competent, authorized; proper, appropriate; надлежен суд competent court of law

надлежност *f* competence, jurisdiction, legal authority; судска надлежност jurisdiction, competence of the courts

надлета *pf* **1** to surpass in flying, outfly **2** (*trans. or with над*) to fly over (*s. th.*), overfly

надлетува *impf* **I** *of* надлета **II** – **се** to compete in flying; to fly over each other

надмен *adj* puffed up, haughty, arrogant

надменост *f* haughtiness, arrogance

надмине *pf* надмина *aor.* **1** to overtake, pass, get ahead of **2** to exceed, surpass

надминува *impf of* надмине

надморски *adj* above sea level; надморска висина (височина) height above sea level

надмоќ *f* superiority, domination, supremacy

надмоќен -ќна *adj* superior, dominant

надмоќност *f* superiority, domination; preponderance

надмудри *pf* to outwit; to play a trick (*on*)

надмудрува *impf* **I** *of* надмудри **II** – **се** to vie with each other in wit

наднесе *pf* **I** to hold over, place over **II** – **ce** to rise over, gather over; to bend over, lean over; се наднесе црн облак a black cloud gathered

наднесува (се) *impf of* наднесе (се)

надница *f* (*daily or hourly*) wages; ❏ надница за страв danger money

надничар *m* day labourer

надничарка *f* (*fem. form*) *see* надничар

надничен -чна *adj* daily (*of pay*)

надничи *impf dial.* to work as a day labourer

наднoси *pf* to carry (*a child*) longer than full term

надносува *impf of* надноси

надоаѓа *impf see* надојдува

надоведе *pf* to bring in (*a lot of people*)

надовлекува *impf of* надовлече

надовлече *pf* to haul (drag) (*s.th.*) in large quantities

надовлечува *impf see* надовлекува

надоврзе *pf* надоврза *aor.* **I** to attach; to add **II** – **ce** to refer (*на – то*)

надоврзува (се) *impf of* надоврзе (се); надоврзувајќи се на претходното писмо further to my previous letter

надодава *impf of* надодаде

надодаде *pf* to add on (*s.th. extra*)

надоди *pf* to outwalk, surpass (exceed) in walking

надодува *impf* **I** *of* надоди **II** – **ce** to compete in walking

надосида *pf* **1** to build on to (above) **2** to add on by building

надосидува *impf of* надосида

надои *pf* надои & надоја *aor.* to breast-feed, nurse a baby (*sufficiently*)

надојде *pf* **1** to arrive in large numbers; му надојдоа селани peasants flocked to him **2** to rise (*of water*); реката надојде the river rose

надојдува *impf of* надојде

надојува *impf of* надои

надокрај *adv* at last, finally; in the end

надолго *adv in the expression:* надолго и нашироко thoroughly, exhaustively, fully, in detail

надолен -лна *adj* **1** downward, sloping; downhill **2** falling (*in tone, pitch*); надолен акцент falling accent

надолж *adv* lengthwise; *prep* along

надолжен -жна *adj* lengthwise, longitudinal; надолжен пресек longitudinal section

надоли *pf* to conquer, overcome, defeat, *see* надвие; дремка го надоли drowsiness overcame him

надолнина & надолница *f see* надолниште

надолниште *n* descent; downhill slope; steep slope

надолу *adv* down, downwards; downhill; (*по скали*) downstairs; по реката надолу down river; падне надолу to fall down; отполу надолу from the waist down

надолува *impf of* надоли

надомест *f see* надоместок

надомести *pf* to compensate; to recompense; to replace, <be a> substitute for; надомести пари to refund/reimburse; надомести штета to indemnify, cover a loss

надоместок -ци *m* compensation; refund; allowance, benefit; indemnity; бара надоместок за штета to claim damages

надоместува *impf of* надомести

надонесе *pf* to bring a lot, in large quantities

надонесува *impf of* надонесе

надополни *pf* **1** to fill up, top up; to add, supplement **2** to compensate; to recompense, make up for; to replace, <be a> substitute for

надополнува *impf of* надополни

надотекува *impf* to rise, come up (*of water*)

надотера *pf* **I** **1** to embellish richly; to dress up *trans.*, deck out **2** to bring, drive in large numbers **II** – **ce** to dress up *intrans.*

надотерува (се) *impf of* надотера (се)

надотече *pf* to rise, come up (*of water*)

надотечува *impf of* надотече

надотокми *pf* **1** to compensate for; to replace **2** to balance out *trans.*; to equalize *trans.*

надотокмува *impf of* надотокми

надработи *pf* **1** to surpass (*s.o.*) in work **2** to work more than necessary; to work long hours

надработува *impf* **I** *of* надработи **II** – **ce** to compete in (at) work

надразлив *adj* **1** irritable **2** excitable

надразни *pf* **I** **1** to irritate **2** to stimulate, excite **II** – **ce** **1** to get irritated/upset; to chafe **2** to become aroused

надразнува (се) *impf of* надразни (се)

надраска *pf* **1** to scratch, scrape **2** *fig.* to scribble, scrawl; to daub

надраскува *impf of* надраска

надрасне *pf* надрасна *aor.* **1** to outgrow **2** *fig.* to surpass, exceed

надраснува *impf of* надрасне

надрдори (се) *pf see* набрбори (се)

надреализам -змот *m* surrealism

надреалист *m* surrealist

надреме се *pf* надрема се *aor.* to have a good nap

надремува се *impf of* надреме се

надрети се *pf rare see* надретува се

надретува се *impf* to tease each other; to taunt each other

надрилекар *m* quack (*doctor*); charlatan

надрилекарство *n* quackery

надрипа *pf* to outjump

надрипува *impf* **I** *of* надрипа **II** – **ce** to compete in jumping

надрнда *pf* **1** to comb, fluff (*wool, cotton, etc.*) **2** *fig. see* надрдори

надрндува *impf of* надрнда

надроби *pf* **1** to crumble *trans.*, crush; to chop up; што си надробил, сега ќе сркаш *prov.* you've made your bed and you must lie on it **2** *fig.* to tell a lot of stories; to babble a lot, talk a lot of nonsense

надробува *impf of* надроби

надрочи *pf* to ripen, mature

надрочува *impf of* надрочи

надрпа *pf* **I** **1** to pull up, jerk (*a quantity of*); to tear up (*a quantity of*) **2** *fig.* to seize, grab a lot **II** – **ce** to seize a lot for o.s.

надрпува (се) *impf of* надрпа (се)

надува¹ (се) *impf of* надуе (се)

надува² се *pf* to swell up

надуе *pf* наду *aor.* **I** to inflate, blow up; *fig.* to exaggerate; to magnify; ❏ го наду носот he got angry; ја наду гајдата he burst into tears **II** – **ce** **1** to swell up **2** *fig.* to become arrogant **3** *fig.* to get angry

надуен *pt & adj* **1** puffed up, arrogant, insolent, conceited **2** angry, irate

надуеност *f* **1** arrogance, haughtiness, insolence, conceit **2** irritability, irascibility; gruffness

надупи *pf colloq.* to talk into, persuade, induce; to incite, egg on

надупува *impf colloq. of* надупи

надупчи *pf* to bore, drill; to bore holes in

надупчува *impf of* надупчи

надурли се *pf colloq.* to have a good sleep; *colloq.* to lie in for a long time

надурми се *pf see* намурти се

надуши *pf* **1** to smell, sniff *trans.* **2** *fig.* to get wind of, sense; надушил што се готви he sensed what was coming

надушка *pf see* надуши

наѓез & **наѓезмо** *n Bot. see* нана¹

наѓубри *pf* to manure, fertilize (*the soil*)

наѓубрува *impf of* наѓубри

наеднаш *adv* **1** suddenly, unexpectedly **2** at once, immediately; quickly

наедно *adv* **1** together, jointly; тие работеа наедно they worked together **2** simultaneously, at the same time

наежави се *pf* to bristle; to have goose-flesh; to shiver, shudder

наежавува се *impf of* наежави се

наежи се *pf see* наежави се

наежува се *impf see* наежавува се

наезда *f* invasion, assault; crowd, multitude, throng

наелектризира *pf see* наелектриса

наелектриса *pf* **I** to charge with electricity, electrify **II** – **се** to become charged with electricity; to get a slight electric shock

наелектрисува (се) *impf of* наелектриса (се)

наем *m* hire, rent, lease; ❑ држи под наем to tenant, occupy as tenant; дава под наем to hire; to let, lease, rent out; зема под наем to take on lease, hire, rent

наема (се) *impf of* наеме (се)

наемател *m* lessee; tenant

наемателка *f* (*fem. form*) *see* наемател

наеме *pf* најми *aor.* **I** to rent; to hire **II** – **се** to accept a job; to become employed (*за – as*); се наеме за слуга to find work as a servant

наемен -мна *pt* & *adj* **1** hired; наемен работник hired worker **2** rental; наемен договор rental agreement

наемне се *pf* наемна се *aor. see* наеме се

наемник -ци *m* employee, hired man; mercenary

наемнина *f* rent, rental fee

наемодавец -вци & **наемодател** *m* lessor

наергенува се *pf* to sow one's wild oats; to enjoy one's youth (*of a young man*); to tire of bachelorhood

наесен *adv* in autumn; next autumn

нажален *pt* & *adj* depressed, sad, forlorn

нажаленост *f* sadness; bereavement

нажали *pf* **I** to sadden, distress; to bereave; to grieve, afflict **II** – **се** to become sad; to be bereaved, afflicted; to grieve *intrans.*

нажалува (се) *impf of* нажали (се)

нажеже *pf* нажежа *aor.* to make red-hot

нажежува *impf of* нажеже

наживее се *pf* наживеа се *aor.* to live long <enough>; to live to a ripe old age

нажнева (се) *impf see* нажнива (се)

нажнее (се) *pf* нажнеа (се) *aor. see* нажние (се)

нажнива (се) *impf of* нажние (се)

нажние *pf* нажни *aor.* **I** to reap (*in quantity*) **II** – **се** to reap a great deal; to reap to one's heart's content

нажолти *pf* to colour (make) yellow

нажолтува *impf of* нажолти

нажули *pf* to pinch, cramp, rub (*of shoes, etc.*)

нажулува *impf of* нажули

назаби *pf* to serrate

назабува *impf of* назаби

назад *adv* **1** back, backwards; врати се назад come back! return! ❑ земи си го зборот назад take that back! (*i.e. take back the insulting thing you have just said*); мисли му за назад think a little ahead! think of the consequences! назад е зимата what will be will be, we can't do anything about it; тој е назад од векови he is behind the times; дотаму и назад there and back; to a fault **2** behind; тој седи назад he is sitting behind, at the back **3** (*comparative and superlative*) поназад further back, right to/at the back; одете поназад go further back! застанавме најназад we stood (stopped) right at the back

назадгазум *adv see* назадечки

назаден -дна *adj* backward, retrograde

назадечки *adv* backward<s>

назадне *pf* назадна *aor.* to begin to regress; to fall behind; to fall into decline

назаднува *impf see* назадува

назадност *f* backwardness

назадува *impf* to regress; to fall behind

назаем *adv* on loan; земе назаем (на заем) to borrow; дава назаем to lend

назал *m Phon.* nasal

назален -лна *adj Phon.* nasal

назборува *pf* **I** to tell, relate a lot **II** – **се 1** to have a good talk; се назборува на некого to tell s.o. a lot of things **2** to scold, reprimand; му се назборував I gave him a piece of my mind

назбувне *pf* назбувна *aor.* to prove *intrans.*, rise (*usu. of dough*)

назбувнува *impf of* назбувне

наздрави *pf* to toast, drink a toast to

наздравица *f* toast

наздраво *adv* firmly, definitely

наздравува *impf of* наздрави

наздравувач *m* proposer of a toast

наземе <**се**> *pf* наземе (се) *aor.* to take (*in quantity*); наземе <се> пари to make a lot of money

наземи *adv* on the ground, on to the ground; седеше наземи he was sitting on the ground (on the floor)

назив *m* name; title; (*scientific, etc.*) term; назив на сметка account title

назималче *n see* назимниче

назимниче *n* sucking-pig

назландиса *pf colloq.* to become spoilt; to become rowdy, ungovernable; to become a libertine

назландисува *impf of* назландиса

назначи *pf* **1** to indicate, mark **2** to appoint, nominate; назначија специјална комисија a special commission was appointed

назначува *impf of* назначи

назоба *pf* **I** to feed (*with grain*) **II** – **се** to eat one's fill (*of grains, cereals, fruit with pips*); коњот се назоба the horse ate plenty of oats; се назобавме грозје we ate a lot of grapes

назобува (се) *impf of* назоба (се)

назоди *pf* to glaze; to enamel

назодува *impf of* назоди

назорум *adv* stealthily, furtively, secretly

назрева *impf of* назрее

назрее *pf* назреа *aor.* to ripen, mature

назрест *adj see* шашлив

наcемне *pf* наcемна *aor. see* наcтине

наcемнува *impf of* наcемне

наcида *pf* to build (*a lot*)

наcидува *impf of* наcида

наcира (се) *impf of* наcпре (се)

наcпре *pf* **1** to peep, peer (*inside, through a crack, etc.*) **2** to look, cast an eye on; наcри ги да ги видиш just look at them! **3** to see, visit; дојдов да ве наcпрам I've come to see you **4** to discern, make out, catch sight of; го наcpеb во далечината I caught sight of him in the distance **II – се** to loom, come into view; може се наcпре крајот the end is in sight

наcрне *pf* наcpна *aor. see* наcпре

наcрница *f* peeper; прислушница и наcрница peeping Tom

наcрнува *impf see* наcира

наивен -вна *adj* naive, simple; inexperienced

наивец -вци *m* naive painter

наивник -ци *m* naive man

наивница *f* (*fem. form*) *see* наивник

наивност *f* naivety, simplicity; inexperience

наигра се *pf* to tire of playing/dancing; to dance/play to one's heart's content

наигрува се *impf of* наигра се

наиде *pf* **1** (*на*) to come across, run into, meet, find; наиде на нафта to strike oil; наиде на одобрување/одсив/отпор to meet with approval/a response/resistance **2** to come, appear; наиде темен облак a dark cloud blew up

наидува *impf of* наиде

наизменичен -чна *adj* alternating; наизменична струја alternating current

наизменично *adv* alternately, by turns

наизменичност *f* alternation

наизуст *adv arch.* by heart; from memory

нај- (*prefix for forming superlatives*) the most; најголем the biggest; најубав the most beautiful, the best; (*sometimes with nouns*) the greatest, the best; најмајстор the greatest craftsman; најјунак the greatest hero

најава се *pf* to tire of riding

најаве *adv* in reality; ❏ на сон и најаве in a dream and in reality, waking and dreaming; излезе најаве to emerge, come to light

најави *pf* to announce

најавне *pf* најавна *aor.* **I 1** to mount (*a horse, etc.*) **2** to weigh down, oppress; го најавнаа тешки маки his worries have got him down **II – се** to lean on each other

најавнува (се) *impf of* најавне (се)

најавува *impf of* најави

најавува се *impf of* најава се

најаде *pf* најадов *1st p. sg aor.* **I 1** to feed *trans.* **2** to eat into, corrode **II – се** to feed *intrans.*; to eat one's fill

најади се *pf f.p.* to become upset, angry, lose one's temper

најадри *pf* најадре *aor.* **1** to ripen, mature **2** to grow longer; денот најадре the days grew longer

најадрува *impf of* најадри

најадува (се) *impf of* најаде (се)

најадувачка *f see* најаска

најазмо *n colloq.* **1** holy water **2** sacred spring, source of holy water **3** *dial.* garden mint

најакне *pf* најакна *aor.* to grow strong, strengthen *intrans.*

најакнува *impf of* најакне

најамчи *pf* **1** to put on a noose **2** *fig.* to impose, foist (*s.th.*) upon

најамчува *impf of* најамчи

најаска *f in the expression:* нема најаска you can never have enough; ова грозје е толку вкусно што нема најаска these grapes are so nice you can't stop eating them

најде *pf* најдов *1st p. sg aor.* **I 1** to find; го најдов дома I found him at home; нашол пари he found some money; ❏ ќе си го најдеш <татко ти>! you'll get what you deserve! најде нешто во некого to see s.th. in s.o.; нашол та зашол he's just gone too far; нашло грнче поклопче *prov.* everybody finds a mate; birds of a feather flock together **2** to obtain, get; јас ќе најдам карти за кино I'll get tickets for the cinema **3** to befall, happen to; леле, што ме најде! alas, what has befallen me! **4** to judge, pronounce a judgement, find, decide; судијата најде дека се тие прави the judge found that they were right **5** *in the expression:* добре нашле! (добренашле!) glad to see you! (*answer to the greeting добре дојде*! welcome!) **II – се 1** to see each other, meet; ќе се најдеме утре we'll meet tomorrow **2** to come in handy; to be of service to; машината ќе ти се најде некогаш this machine will be useful to you one day; тој човек многу ми се најде кога бев болен that man was a godsend when I was ill **3** to find o.s.; се најде на улица he found himself in the street; се најде во чудо he was amazed

најдува (се) *impf see* наоѓа (се)

најлон *m* nylon; најлон чорапи nylon stockings

најлонски *adj* nylon *attrib.*

најлошо *adj, adv* worst; ❏ ако се случи најлошото if the worst comes to to the worst; at the worst

најме (се) *pf* најми *aor. see* наеме (се)

најмалку *adj, adv* least; ❏ ни најмалку not in the least; најмалку што може <некој> да направи the least one can do

најмногу *adj, adv* most; mostly; од сè најмногу most of all

најнакрај *adv* at last, finally; in the end

најнапред *adv* **1** first, first of all **2** in front, first; најнапред одеа децата the children went first

најодзади *adv* **1** *see* најпосле **2** far behind; last of all

најповеќе *adv see* најмногу

најпосле *adv* **1** finally; at last **2** in the end, finally

најпрвин & најпрво *adv* first of all; in the first place

најсетне *adv see* најпосле

накади *pf* to fumigate; to cense, burn incense; to fill with smoke

накадри *pf* to curl (*hair, etc.*)

накадрува *impf of* накадри

накадува *impf of* накади

накаже *pf* накажа *aor.* **1** to punish **2** to talk a lot; to tell a lot of stories **3** *colloq.* to complain about s.o.; to denounce; to tell on (*s.o.*), *Austral.* dob (*s.o.*) in

накажува *impf of* накаже

наказ *m* punishment; *in the expression:* наказ божји, наказ од Бога punishment from God

накај *prep* towards, to; авионот леташе накај Скопје the plane was flying towards Skopje; тој се сврти накај мене he turned to me; фасадата е свртена накај Вардар the facade faces the Vardar

накалеми *pf* **1** to graft **2** *fig.* to add, attach

накалемува *impf of* накалеми

накани *pf* **I** to invite (*usu. many guests*) **II – се** to decide, make up one's mind; се наканив да ти дојдам на гости I decided to visit you

накунува (се) *impf of* накани (се)

накапе *pf* накапа *aor.* **I 1** to leak, drip **2** to extract, squeeze out (*drop by drop*); to instil, put in **3** to bespatter; си ја накапа блузата to stain one's blouse **4** *fig.* to fall (*of leaves*) **5** *fig.* to come across, stumble upon **II – се** to spatter o.s. (one's clothes)

накапува (се) *impf of* накапе (се)

накаса *pf* to bite into (*an apple, etc.*)

накастри *pf* to prune, trim, clip in quantity (*of branches, etc.*)

накаструва *impf of* накастри

накасува *impf of* накаса

накатрани *pf* to tar, smear with tar

накатранува *impf of* накатрани

накачи[1] *pf* **I 1** to drive in, hammer in (*in large numbers*); накачи колје околу бавчата he drove in stakes round the garden **2** to hang out (*laundry, clothes, etc.*) **II – се** to be caught in several places; to catch in several places (*of thorns, barbed wire, etc.*); ми се накачија трње по алиштата thorns caught my clothes in several places

накачи[2] *pf* **I 1** (*покачи*) to raise **2** to lift **3** *f.p.* to climb; накачи горе планина he climbed the mountain **II – се** to climb

накачува[1] **(се)** *impf of* накачи[1] (се)

накачува[2] **(се)** *impf of* накачи[2] (се)

накашла се *pf* **1** to give a cough; се накашла тихо he cleared his throat quietly **2** to tire of coughing; се накашлав од оваа пуста кашлица I'm fed up with this wretched cough

накашлува се *impf of* накашла се

накваси (се) *pf dial. see* натопи (се)

наквасува (се) *impf dial. see* натопува (се)

накисели *pf* **I 1** to become sour; to taste somewhat sour/tart **2** to pickle lightly (*cabbage, etc.*), marinate **3** *fig.* to screw up, pucker (*one's face*); го накисели лицето he made a sour face **II – се** *see* **I** 3

накиселува (се) *impf of* накисели (се)

накисне *pf* накисна *aor.* **1** to wet, moisten, soak, drench **2** to get wet (*in the rain*) **3** *fig.* to become dejected, discouraged, dispirited; to start moping

накиснува *impf of* накисне

накит *m* jewellery; ornament

накити *pf* **I** to adorn **II – се** to adorn o.s.; to dress up *intrans.* (*too much*)

накитува (се) *impf of* накити (се)

наклава *impf of* накладе

накладе *pf* **1** to lay in (*in large quantities*); to set aside; to throw on to; to cram into; накладовме пиперки за зимовиште we've laid in plenty of capsicums for winter; накладе дрва на огнот to throw logs on the fire **2** (*usu. of a pig*) to fatten up *intrans.*; арно ви наклало прасево this pig has fattened up nicely

наклапа *pf* **I** to come across, bump into **II – се** to tire of roaming

наклапува (се) *impf of* наклапа (се)

наклапуши *pf* to shove on, jam on; ја наклапуши капата на глава he jammed his cap on his head

наклевети *pf* to slander, accuse falsely

наклеветува *impf of* наклевети

наклепа *pf* **1** to beat out, hammer (*scythe, sickle*) **2** *fig.* to slander, denounce

наклепува *impf of* наклепа

наклон *m* slope; bow (*in salutation, etc.*)

наклонет *pt & adj* **1** inclined, disposed; well-disposed (*to*), friendly **2** leaning

наклонетост *f* inclination, leaning, predisposition

наклони *pf* **I** to lean, bend, bow *trans.*; наклони глава to bow one's head **II – се** to be inclined to, favour; to bend, bow *intrans.*

наклоност *f* inclination; favour, partiality, liking

наклонува се *impf of* наклони се

наклопа се *pf colloq.* to gorge, stuff o.s.

наклопува се *impf colloq. of* наклопа се

наклука (се) *pf see* наколка (се)

накмишен *adj see* намуртен

накова *impf of* накове

наковална *f* anvil

наковало *n see* наковална

накове *pf* накова *aor.* to forge (*in quantity*); to mint (*a lot of money*)

накодоши *pf colloq.* to denounce, inform on, tell on, *Austral.* dob in; to slander

накодошува *impf of* накодоши

накокори се *pf* **1** to puff o.s. up **2** *fig.* to show off; to strut, swagger

накокорува се *impf of* накокори се

наколве *pf* наколва *aor.* **I** to peck (*a lot of*) **II – се** to peck one's fill

наколе *pf* накла *aor.* to slaughter (*a lot of*)

наколен -лна *adj* pile *attrib.*; наколни живеалишта pile-dwellings, houses on stilts

наколка *pf* **I** (*usu. of turkeys for slaughter*) to fatten up, force-feed **II – се** to have a good feed

наколкува (се) *impf of* наколка (се)

наколува *impf of* наколе

наконти *pf* **I** to adorn, decorate, dress up *trans.* **II – се** to adorn o.s., dress up *intrans.*

наконтува (се) *impf of* наконти (се)

накопа *pf* **I** to dig (*a quantity of*) **II – се** to tire of digging

накопува (се) *impf of* накопа (се)

накорне *pf* накорна *aor.* to uproot, pull up (*grass, etc. in quantity*)

накорнува *impf of* накорне

накоси *pf* **I** to mow, scythe; му накоси малку трева на коњот he mowed some grass for the horse **II – се** to tire of mowing

накосо *adv* at an angle; askew; aslant; askance

накострешен *adj* bristling; *fig.* angry

накострещи се *pf* to bristle (*also fig.*); *fig.* to get angry

накострешува се *impf of* накострещи се

накосува (се) *impf of* накоси (се)

накот *m* brood (*also pejor. of people*)

накоти *pf* **I** to produce, bring forth many young (*of animals*) **II – се** to be born (*of animals*); to multiply *intrans.*

накотува (се) *impf of* накоти (се)

накраен -јна *adj* final, last

накрај *prep* at the end of, at the edge of; накрај село at the end of the village

накратко *adv* in short, in brief, briefly; for a short time

накрвави *pf* to stain, cover with blood

накрева (се) *impf of* накрене (се)

накрене *pf* накрена *aor.* **I 1** to lift, raise (*a little*); во последно време тој ја накрена главата recently he has gained more confidence/he's become conceited **2** to raise a lot (*of s. th.*) **II – се 1** to recover (*from illness*) **2** to rise, stand up; косата му се накрена од страв his hair stood on end from fright **3** to rush in, swarm in; се накрена сè живо everybody came rushing in **4** *fig.* to become conceited, arrogant; to show off

накрепи се *pf* to lean on, support o.s.

накрепува се *impf of* накрепи се

накриви *pf* **I** to make crooked; to bend *trans.*; ја накриви шапката he cocked his hat; го накривил вратот he bent his neck **II – се** to bend, incline *intrans.*; to become crooked, lean over

накривне *pf* накривна *aor. see* накривнува

накривнува *impf* **1** to make slightly crooked **2** to limp a little, hobble

накриво *adv* **1** crooked, awry **2** wrong, incorrect<ly>, falsely; земе (сфати) прашање накриво to misunderstand (misinterpret) a question **3** sideways, askance; ме гледа накриво he's looking at me askance

накривува *impf* **I** *see* накривнува **II – се** *of* накриви се

накрка *pf colloq.* **I** to feed (*s.o.*) copiously **II – се** to eat one's fill; to eat ravenously, gorge o.s.

накркува (се) *impf of* накрка (се)

накрми *pf* to feed (*livestock*), fatten

накрмува *impf of* накрми

накрни *pf* to break <off>, chip <off> *trans.*

накрнува *impf of* накрни

накрст *adv* crosswise

накрши *pf* **I 1** to break off, chip off; to crack *trans.*; to fracture *trans.* **2** to break off (*a lot of, e.g. twigs*) **II – се 1** to crack *intrans.* **2** to break, crack a lot of; се накршив ореви I cracked a lot of walnuts **3** to tire of breaking, cracking

накршува (се) *impf of* накрши (се)

накубе *pf* накуба *aor.* to pull up, pluck (*a lot of*)

накубичи *pf* to stack (*firewood in cubic metres*)

накубичува *impf of* накубичи

накубува *impf of* накубе

накуди *pf* **1** to blame; to censure **2** to criticize, find fault with **3** to deride, revile

накудува *impf of* накуди

накуп *adv* together, altogether

накупец -пци *m* dealer, middleman

накупи *pf* to buy (*in quantity*), buy up

накупува *impf of* накупи

накупчи *pf* **I** to heap up, pile up *trans.* **II – се** to heap up, pile up *intrans.*

накупчува (се) *impf of* накупчи (се)

накусо *adv* in short, in brief, briefly; for a short time

накуцува *impf* to hobble *intrans.*, limp slightly

накучи *pf* **I** to produce, bring forth (*a lot of puppies*) **II – се** (*of puppies*) to be born (*in large numbers*)

накучува (се) *impf of* накучи (се)

налага (се) *impf of* наложи (се)

налази *pf* **I** to crawl (*over s. th.*); to spoil (*s. th.*) by crawling over it; гасеница го налази лебот a caterpillar crawled over the bread **II – се** to tire of crawling

налазува (се) *impf of* налази (се)

налакти се *pf* to lean on one's elbow

налактува се *impf of* налакти се

налан *m* (*usu. pl*) wooden slippers (mules), open-toed clogs

наланџија -ии *m* maker of wooden slippers

налапа *pf* **I** to swallow; to devour **II – се** to gorge <o.s.> *intrans.*

налапува (се) *impf of* налапа (се)

налбат & *more rarely* **налбатин** -ти *m* farrier

налбатница *f* farrier's workshop

налева *impf of* налее

налево *adv* <to the> left; on the left

налегне *pf* налегна *aor.* **1** to lie (*на – on*); to squeeze (*with one's body*), crush, smother **2** *fig.* to oppress

налегнува *impf of* налегне

налее *pf* налеа *aor.* **I 1** to pour <out>; налее чаша вино to pour a glass of wine **2** to draw (*water*) **3** to flood, submerge; реката ги налеа врбите the river flooded the willows **4** to plate (*with metal*) **II – се** *fig.* to drink one's fill; to get drunk; ова мора да се налее we must drink to it

належи се *pf* to lie for a long time; to tire of lying down

належито *adv f.p.* sloping

належува се *impf of* належи се

налепи *pf* **1** to stick on (*sufficient, many*); што си налепил толку марки? why have you stuck on so many stamps? **2** *fig. colloq.* to get into trouble; си налепи беља he got into trouble; си налепи со тоа дете he had a lot of trouble with that child

налепница *f* label; sticker

налепува *impf of* налепи

налет *m* **1** assault, attack, charge **2** *colloq., in the expression:* налет да биде! налет да се стори! damn it! blast it!

налета *pf* **I 1** to rush on, attack; to come across, bump into; to step on (*accidentally*); to collide; налета на мина he stepped on a mine **2** to flock in, fly down (*in numbers*); налетаа врапци a lot of sparrows flew down (flocked in) **II – се** to fly to one's heart's content

налетиште *n colloq.* trouble, misfortune

налетува (се) *impf of* налета (се)

нали *part see* нели

налигави *pf* to dribble on, slaver, drool over

налине *pf* налина *aor.* to incite; to set (*a dog on s.o.*)

налинува *impf of* налине

наличен -чна *adj* available; налична сума ready money (cash)

наличи *pf* to point (*at*); to turn, direct; to aim at

наличност *f* availability

наличува *impf of* наличи

налика *f see* налие

налови *pf* **I** to catch (*a lot of*) **II – се** to tire of fishing/hunting

налог -зи *m* order, command; directive; warrant; патен налог travel warrant; налог за испорачување delivery order; судски налог writ

налогодавач *m* issuer of warrant/order, instructing party, principal

наложи *pf* **I 1** to put compresses on **2** to impose, foist (*нешто на некого* – *s.th. on s.o.*) **3** to order, command, prescribe **II** – **ce** to impose one's own attitude, one's will (*на* – *on*)

наложник -ци *m* lover

наложница *f* concubine, mistress

наложништво *n* concubinage

налои *pf* to smear with tallow

налојува *impf of* налои

налока *pf* **I** to lap up (*enough*) **II** – **ce** *pejor.* to get drunk; to drink one's fill

налокува (ce) *impf of* налока (ce)

налудничав *adj* foolish; crazy

налудничавост *f* foolishness; craziness

налудува се *pf* to let one's hair down, go crazy

налуничав *adj see* налудничав

налута се *pf* to tire of wandering

налутен *pt & adj* angry, cross, furious

налути *pf* **I 1** to anger, infuriate **2** *fig.* (*with dat.*) ми/ му/ни налути it tastes rather hot **II** – **ce** to get angry, lose one's temper

налутува (ce) *impf of* налути (ce)

налче *n* (*на чевли и сл.*) heel-plate; toe-plate

наљубува се *pf* (*на*) to look at with pleasure, enjoy looking at, admire; не можеше да му се наљубува на езерото he couldn't stop admiring the lake

нам *pron* (*long dat. form of* ние. *Used for emphasis with short form* ни) <to> us; прво нам ни кажа, а после вам first he told us and then you

намава *impf see* намавнува

намава се *pf* **1** to tire of beating **2** (*with dat.*) to give a good beating (hiding); арно му се намавав I gave him a good hiding (thrashing)

намавне *pf* намавна *aor.* **1** (*co*) to swing, brandish; намавна со стапот he drew back (swung) his stick **2** (*co*) to wave; му намавна со рака she waved to him

намавнува *impf of* намавне

намавува се *impf of* намава се

намагнетизира *pf* to magnetize

намазни се *pf* to smooth one's hair down

намазнува се *impf of* намазни се

намака *pf* to dip (*bread into soup, etc.*)

намакува *impf of* намака

намали *pf* **I 1** to reduce, cut, cut down; го намалија бројот на работниците they reduced the workforce; нема да ги намалат цените they won't reduce the prices **2** to get shorter, shorten; дните намалија the days had shortened **3** to ease; дождот намали the rain eased **4** to run out, become exhausted (*of supplies*); ни намалило брашното we are running out of flour **II** – **ce 1** to go down, diminish *intrans.* **2** to get shorter

намалува (ce) *impf of* намали (ce)

намами *pf* to lure, entice

намамува *impf of* намами

намачи *pf* **I** to torment; to make difficulties (*for*) **II** – **ce** to suffer, go through hell

намачка *pf* **I 1** to smear **2** *fig.* to run away; ја искористи ноќта и си ја намачка дома he took advantage of the night and ran off home **II** – **ce** to smear o.s.; *pejor.* to apply make-up

намачкува (ce) *impf of* намачка (ce)

намачува (ce) *impf of* намачи (ce)

намекне *pf* намекна *aor.* to soften

намекнува *impf of* намекне

намена *f* purpose, aim

намени *pf* to intend; to set aside (*за* – *for*), earmark; to determine, prescribe

наменски *adj* intended, earmarked; restricted

наменува *impf of* намени

намера *f* **1** intention, intent, purpose; има добри (чесни) намери to mean well; со најдобра намера in all good faith; with the best intentions; има зли (нечесни, задни) намери to mean mischief; to be up to no good; открива свои прави намери to throw off the mask; со намера да in order to **2** *arch.* chance

намерда *pf colloq.* to thrash, drub

намердува *impf of* намерда

намерен -рна *adj* intended; intentional, deliberate

намери *pf* **I 1** to aim (*во* – *at*), point at, direct; ја намери пушката во него he pointed his rifle at him **2** to find; to catch **II** – **ce** to find o.s.; to happen to be; ❏ се намерил јунак на јунак diamond cut diamond

намерник -ци *m* **1** *dial. see* стројник **2** *arch.* chance (unexpected) guest; person met by chance

намерно *adv* intentionally, on purpose, deliberately

намерува *impf of* намери

намесник -ци *m* deputy; regent

намесница *f* (*fem. form*) *see* намесник

намесништво *n* the office (position) of deputy; regency

наместа *adv* in <some> places, here and there; sporadically

наместен *adj* forced, affected, artificial, unnatural

намести *pf* **I 1** to place, put **2** to put in order, arrange; to furnish; to lay (*a table*); to set; to tidy; намести кревет to make a bed; намести соба to tidy a room; ❏ намести некого to frame s.o. **3** *fig.* to arrange, plan; убаво си го наместил тоа you have arranged that nicely **4** to appoint; го наместија <за> чиновник they appointed him as a clerk **II** – **ce 1** to tidy o.s. up **2** to settle down; to establish o.s.

наместо *adv* instead; *prep* instead of

наместува *impf of* намести

намет *m* **1** alluvium, deposit, silt; detritus **2** (*пресна, сосна*) snowdrift **3** tax; duty

наметало *n* cloak, cape; mantle

намете *pf* **1** to sweep together, sweep into a heap **2** to sweep up, sweep away **3** to blow (snow) into drifts

наметиште *n* place where snowdrifts form

наметка *f* **1** *see* наметало **2** (*на очи*) cataract

наметлив *adj* intrusive, meddlesome; obtrusive, officious; importunate, annoying

наметне *pf* наметна *aor.* **I 1** to cover, throw on **2** to impose **II** – **ce 1** (*co*) to cover o.s., throw (*s.th.*) on o.s. **2** to force o.s. (*на* – *on*), impose (*o.s.*) on; to intrude on

наметник -ци *m* intruder; meddler

наметница *f* (*fem. form*) *see* наметник

наметнува (ce) *impf of* наметне (ce)

наметри *pf* to stack firewood (*in cubic metres*)

наметрува *impf of* наметри

наметува *impf of* намете

намеша се *pf* to tire of stirring

намешува се *impf of* намеша се

Намибија *f* Namibia

Намибиец -ијци *m* Namibian

Намибијка *f* (*fem. form*) *see* Намибиец

намибиски *adj* Namibian

намига *impf see* намигнува

намигне *pf* намигна *aor.* (*with dat.*) to wink (*at*)

намигнува *impf of* намигне

намилува *pf* **I** to caress, fondle (*s. o. or s. th.*) for a long time **II** – **се** to caress each other for a long time; to fondle (*s. o./s. th.*) to one's heart's content

намине *pf* намина *aor.* to drop in (*кај* – *on*), come round

наминува *impf of* намине

намири *pf* **1** to prepare, arrange **2** to supply; to satisfy; to settle, pay off **3** to feed

намириса *pf* **I 1** to scent, perfume, make fragrant **2** to smell *trans. and intrans.*; ❏ оттогаш не намириса овде since then he hasn't shown his face here **3** *fig. impers.* (*with dat.*) to sniff out, scent; to get wind of; ми намириса на лук I could smell garlic **II** – **се** to scent o.s., put on perfume

намирисува (се) *impf of* намириса (се)

намирници *f pl* victuals, provisions

намирува *impf of* намири

намисла *f* **1** thought, notion, idea **2** *Leg.* intent, intention, premeditation, design

намисли *pf* **1** to make up one's mind; to take it into one's head; to decide; to intend; to devise; можеш да направиш сè што ќе намислиш you can do anything you fancy **2** to think of (*s. o./s. th.*); to remember (*s. o./ s. th.*); многупати те намислив I often thought of you

намислува *impf of* намисли

намниса *pf colloq.* **1** to mention, talk about; многу работи намниса he mentioned many things **2** to remind (*некого за нешто* – *s. o. of s. th.*); добро што ми намниса за тоа it's a good thing that you reminded me of that

намнисува *impf of* намниса

намножи *pf* **I** to multiply, increase *trans.*, enlarge, magnify **II** – **се** to multiply, increase *intrans.*

намножува (се) *impf of* намножи (се)

намовнат *pt* (*of the skin*) bristling, with goose-flesh

намовне <**се**> *pf* намовна <**се**> *aor.* (*of fur/hair*) to bristle; му се намовна кожата од студ his skin turned to goose-flesh from the cold

намовнува <**се**> *impf of* намовне <**се**>

намодри *pf* to colour blue, paint blue

намодрува *impf of* намодри

намокри *pf* to wet, moisten

намокрува *impf of* намокри

намолзе *pf* намолгов *1st p. sg aor.* to milk

намолзува *impf of* намолзе

намоли *pf* **I** to obtain by pleading, begging; to convince, talk into; одвај го намолив I only just persuaded him **II** – **се 1** to pray a lot **2** (*with dat.*) to beseech, entreat

намолува се *impf of* намоли се

намота *pf* **I 1** to wind <on>, wind up, reel in **2** to wind (*in quantity*); намотала десет клопчиња she wound ten skeins **II** – **се** to wind o.s. <on>; to get wound on

намотува *impf of* намота

намоча *pf vulg.* to piss on

намочува *impf of* намоча

намрази *pf trans.* to take a dislike to; to come to hate

намразува *impf of* намрази

намрди (се) *pf see* намурти (се), стуши (се)

намрежи се *pf* to cloud over lightly; се намрежи небото the sky has slightly clouded over

намрежува се *impf of* намрежи се

намрмори се *pf* to chatter, talk one's fill; to mumble, grumble a lot

намрморува се *impf of* намрмори се

намрси *pf* **1** to grease **2** to soil, smear with grease

намрсува *impf of* намрси

намрсулави *pf* to soil with snivel (mucus)

намршти *pf* **I** to wrinkle, pucker, furrow (*one's brow*) **II** – **се** to frown, scowl

намрштува (се) *impf of* намршти (се)

намќор *m colloq.* curmudgeon, surly, ill-tempered person

намуртен *pt & adj* frowning, scowling; (*за време*) overcast

намурти се *pf* **1** to pucker one's brow; to frown **2** *fig.* to cloud over; небото се намурти the sky clouded over

намуртува се *impf of* намурти се

намуси се *pf* to frown, scowl

намусува се *impf of* намуси се

нана[1] *f Bot.* (Mentha piperita) mint, peppermint; дива нана (Lycopus europaeus) gypsywort

нана[2] *impf see* нани

наназад *adv* backwards; оди наназад to walk backwards; вози наназад to reverse, back; гледа наназад to look back

нане *n see* нана[1]

нанесе *pf* нанесов *1st p. sg. aor.* **1** to do, cause (*harm, pain*); нанесе некому штета to cause s.o. harm **2** to deposit, wash up (*of tide, floodwater*); to blow/drive snow into drifts; реката нанесе многу песок на ливадата the river deposited/washed a lot of sand on the meadow

нанесува *impf of* нанесе

нани *impf child.* to sleep; нани-нани *refrain in a lullaby*: hushabye . . .

наниже *pf* нанижа *aor.* **I 1** to thread, put on a string **2** to adorn, decorate **II** – **се** to thread a lot of; to tire of threading (*tobacco leaves, etc.*)

нанижува *impf of* наниже

наниз *m* thread (*for a necklace of beads, coins, etc.*)

нанишани *pf* to aim at

нанишанува *impf of* нанишани

нанка *impf see* нани

наново *adv* <once> again; afresh; anew

нанос *m* **1** alluvium, deposit, silt; detritus **2** snowdrift

наобеси *pf* to hang <out> (*plenty of laundry, clothes, etc.*)

наобесува *impf of* наобеси

наоблекува (се) *impf of* наоблече (се)

наоблече *pf* наоблеков *1st p. sg aor.* **I 1** to dress well *trans.*; го наоблече детето she dressed the child warmly **2** to dress (*several children, etc.*) **II** – **се** to dress up *intrans.* well, warmly

наобразба *f* education, training

наоглави *pf* **1** *see* наглави **2 2** *fig.* to curb, restrain

наоглавува *impf of* наоглави

наод *m* **1** foundling **2** finding; лекарски наод medical findings

наоди се *pf* **1** to tire of walking, roaming **2** to have many love affairs

наодува се   *impf of* наоди се

наоѓа   *impf* **I** to find, *see* најде **II** – **се 1** to meet (*each other*) **2** to lie, be situated, located; селото се наоѓа меѓу две реки the village lies between two rivers **3** (*with dat.*) to have; ти се наоѓаат ли малку пари? have you got any money?

наоѓалиште   *n* <natural> deposit; наоѓалиште на јаглен coal deposit

наоколу   *adv* all round; in a circle; around, all around; околу-наоколу all around; го опколија езерото околу-наоколу they surrounded the lake

наопаку   *adv* **1** on/from all sides; the wrong way round; upside down; inside out; ја облекол наопаку кошулата he put on the shirt inside out **2** behind, at the back; му ги врзаа рацете наопаку they tied his hands behind his back **3** *fig.* wrong; in the opposite way; ти секогаш наопаку ме разбираш you always misunderstand me, get me wrong

наопачки   *adv* the wrong way round; inside out; upside down

наора[1]   *f Rel.* host, wafer

наора[2]   *pf* **I** to plough (*a lot*) **II** – **се** to plough to one's heart's content; to tire of ploughing

наорува (се)   *impf of* наора (се)

наоружа   *pf* **I 1** (*вооружи*) to arm **2** *arch.* to fit out, equip, prepare; наоружа коњ to fit out a horse **II** – **се 1** (*вооружи се*) to arm o.s. **2** *arch.* to fit o.s. out, equip o.s.

наоружува (се)   *impf of* наоружа (се)

наостреност   *f* strain, tension

наостри   *pf* **I 1** to hone, whet, sharpen **2** *fig.* to spur on, incite, urge, goad, egg on **II** – **се** *fig.* to get very angry, furious

наострува (се)   *impf of* наостри (се)

наотче   *n dim. of* наод 1

напад   *m* **1** assault; raid, attack; ❑ нападот е најдобра одбрана the best form of defence is attack **2** fit, attack, bout; добива напад на кашлица to have a fit of coughing

нападен   -дна *adj* offensive, aggressive; (*за боја*) loud, shocking

напади   *pf* to drive out; to chase away; to expel

нападне   *pf* нападна *aor.* **1** to fall (*in large quantities*); многу снег нападна a lot of snow has fallen **2** to attack, assail, fall upon, charge; to denounce **3** to overcome; дремка ме нападна drowsiness overcame me

нападува   *impf of* напади

напаѓа[1]   *pf see* нападне 1

напаѓа[2]   *impf of* нападне 2 & 3

напаѓач   *m* assailant, attacker; aggressor, invader; *Sport.* forward

напакости   *pf* to play a dirty trick (*on*); to harm *trans.*

напакостува   *impf of* напакости

напамет   *adv* by heart; from memory

напара   *f* bitter experience

напари   *pf* **I 1** to steam *trans.*; to boil *trans.* **2** to scald **II** – **се 1** to be covered with steam; to perspire, steam o.s. (*in steam bath*) **2** to scald o.s.; човек откако ќе се напари на млекото и на маштеницата дува *prov.* once bitten, twice shy **3** *fig.* to burn one's fingers

напарува (се)   *impf of* напари (се)

напасе   *pf* напасов *1st p. sg aor.* **I** to put to graze, put to pasture **II** – **се** to graze one's fill

напасник   -ци *m* tempter, seducer; assailant; mischievous boy; trouble-maker

напаст   *f* trouble, evil, misfortune; ❑ вистинска напаст a pain in the neck; a damn nuisance

напасува (се)   *impf of* напасе (се)

напати   *adv* occasionally, sometimes; now and then

напати се   *pf* to suffer a lot, have a bad time, suffer torment

напатува се   *pf* to tire of travelling

напев   *m* tune, melody

напевен   -вна *adj* melodious, musical, tuneful; напевен говор musical declamation

напердаши   *pf colloq.* to flog, thrash, give a good hiding

напери   *pf* to point at; to aim at; to direct at

наперка   *pf colloq.* **I** to squeeze, stuff (*into s.th.*) *trans.* **II** – **се 1** to squeeze in *intrans.*; се наперкаа сите во собата they all squeezed into the room **2** *fig.* to gorge o.s.

наперкува (се)   *impf of* наперка (се)

напернат   *pt & adj see* наперчен

наперне се   *pf* наперна се *aor. see* наперчи се

напернува се   *impf see* наперчува се

наперува   *impf of* напери

наперчен   *pt & adj* arrogant, haughty; conceited, self-important

наперчи се   *pf* to become arrogant, haughty, self-important

наперчува се   *impf of* наперчи се

напеца се   *pf* to become conceited; ❑ се напецал како вошка he puffed himself up like a turkey-cock

напечали <**се**>   *pf* to earn (make) a lot of money

напечалува <**се**>   *impf of* напечали <се>

напечати   *pf* to print

напечатува   *impf of* напечати

напива (се)   *impf of* напие (се)

напивка   *f* potion, drink; љубовна напивка love potion

напие   *pf* напи *aor.* **I 1** to give (*s.o.*) a drink; го напи болниот со вода he gave the patient a drink of water **2** to make (*s.o.*) drunk **II** – **се 1** to have a drink; ајде да се напиеме малку вино let's drink a little wine **2** to get drunk

напика   *pf* **I 1** to put in, push in, shove in *trans.*; напика еден цел леб в чанта he stuffed a whole loaf into his bag **2** *fig.* to shove, put carelessly; кај ги напикав чорапите? where did I put my socks? **3** *fig.* to give a job to; сите свои роднини ги напика во претпријатието he gave jobs in the company to all his relations **II** – **се 1** to shove, push in *intrans.* **2** *fig.* to go, disappear **3** *fig.* to get into, penetrate, insinuate o.s.

напикува (се)   *impf of* напика (се)

напина (се)   *impf of* напне (се)

напипа   *pf* to find by feeling, groping

напипери   *pf* to season, spice, sprinkle with pepper

напиперува   *impf of* напипери

напипува   *impf of* напипа

напир   *m* flood, rush; напир на вода rush of water; напир на крв rush of blood, congestion of blood

напис   *m* report, article; essay

напишано   *adv* (*писмено*) in writing, written down

напише   *pf* напиша *aor.* to write; напише роман to write a novel; напише писмо to write a letter

напишува   *impf of* напише

наплакан   *pt* tearful, tear-stained

напласка *pf* **1** to throw down, drop; ги напласка дрвата he threw down the firewood **2** *fig.* to talk a lot of nonsense

напласкува *impf of* напласка

напласти *pf* **I** to pile up *trans.*, stack (*in haystacks*); to put in layers, stratify **II** – **се** to pile up, build up *intrans.* in layers; to settle, be deposited in layers

напластува (се) *impf of* напласти (се)

наплат *m* & **наплата**[1] *f* (*на тркало*) felly, felloe

наплата[2] *f* payment; collection, clearance; repayment, reimbursement

наплати[1] *pf* **I 1** to collect payment for; to charge; наплати чек to cash a cheque **2** to pay off, settle *trans.* **II** – **се 1** to pay off one's debts **2** to extract payment

наплати[2] *pf* to assemble (*the sections of a wheel-rim*)

наплатка *f see* наплат

наплатува[1] **(се)** *impf of* наплати[1] (се)

наплатува[2] *impf of* наплати[2]

наплаќа[1] **(се)** *impf see* наплатува[1] (се)

наплаќа[2] **се** *pf* to pay out, pay off (*debts, etc.*); to be chargeable; не можам да се наплаќам I can't pay my debts

наплеска *pf* **1** to applaud **2** *fig.* to slap, smack, spank

наплескува *impf of* наплеска

наплете *pf* наплетов *1st p. sg aor.* **I 1** to knit (*in large quantities*) **2** to knit on; to add by knitting **II** – **се** to knit (*a large quantity*); to tire of knitting

наплетува (се) *impf of* наплете (се)

наплеќи *adv* (*also* на плеќи) on one's back, on to one's back; лежи наплеќи to lie on one's back

наплив *m* crush, crowd; influx

наплиска *pf* to sprinkle; to spray, splash, spatter

наплискува *impf of* наплиска

наплоди се *pf* to breed *intrans.*; to multiply

наплодува се *impf of* наплоди се

наплува *impf of* наплуе

наплувка *f* maggot; fly-blow

наплуе *pf* наплу *aor.* (*of flies*) to cover with larvae; to lay eggs in s.th. (*e.g. food*); to leave unclean; to foul

наплука *pf* **I** to spit all over (*s.o./s.th.*) **II** – **се** to clear one's throat by spitting; to spit on o.s.

наплукува (се) *impf of* наплука (се)

наплуска се *pf colloq.* to get drunk, get tight

напљачка *pf* **I** to plunder, pillage **II** – **се** to tire of plundering, pillaging

напљачкува (се) *impf of* напљачка (се)

напнат *pt* & *adj* **1** tense, strained, taut **2** intense; слуша со напнато внимание to pay close attention **3** *fig.* pompous, arrogant

напнатост *f* **1** tension, strain **2** intensity **3** attentiveness

напне *pf* напна *aor.* **I 1** to tighten; to draw (*a bowstring*) **2** to strain *trans.* **II** – **се 1** to make an effort; to strain *intrans.* **2** to tense **3** *fig.* to become arrogant, pompous

напнува (се) *impf of* напне (се)

напогани *pf* to foul, soil, sully

напоганува *impf of* напогани

напои *pf* напојав *1st p. sg aor.* **I 1** to give (s.o.) a drink; го нахрани и го напои he fed him and gave him a drink **2** *fig.* to imbue (*co – with*) **II** – **се** to quench one's thirst; to be saturated (*with moisture, steam, scent, smell, etc.*); to swell from dampness

напојува (се) *impf of* напои (се)

напокон *adv dial. see* најпосле

напокрива (се) *impf of* напокрие (се)

напокрие *pf* напокри *aor.* **I 1** to cover warmly, well; to tuck in **2** to cover (*several people or things*) **II** – **се** to cover o.s. well

наполни *pf* **I 1** to fill <up> *trans.*; *Cul.* to stuff; наполни чаша to fill a glass; ❑ ги наполни гаќите he dropped his bundle **2** to load (*a rifle, etc.*); to charge (*a battery*) **3** to reach (*an age*); наполни пет години to turn five **II** – **се** to fill <up> *intrans.*

наполно *adv* completely, fully; quite

наполнува (се) *impf of* наполни (се)

наполу *adv* **1** into halves, by halves, half and half **2** halfway, partly

напомни *pf* напомна *aor.* to remind; to mention, remark

напомнува *impf of* напомни

напомпа *pf* to pump <up>

напомпува *impf of* напомпа

напон *m* tightening, effort; tension, strain; електричен напон electrical tension, voltage; во напонот на силите in the prime of life

напонски *adj* tensional; напонска сила tensional force

напор *m* effort; без напор easily; effortlessly; вложува напори да to make an effort to; со голем напор with a great effort

напореден -дна *adj* parallel

напоредно *adv* parallel

напоредност *f* parallelism

напорен -рна *adj* strenuous, tiring, heavy; напорна работа hard work

напоречки *adv* across, diagonally; ме гледа напоречки he looks askance at me

напорка *f* scratch

напорки *adv see* напоречки

напосоки *adv* at random; by guesswork; на сите прашања одговори напосоки he gave random answers to all questions

на пр. *abbr.* (*на пример*) for example, e.g.

направа[1] *f* **1** device, gadget, apparatus, piece of equipment **2** production, manufacture; construction **3** work (*product of work*); убава направа fine workmanship (handiwork)

направа[2] **(се)** *impf of* направи (се)

направи *pf* **I 1** to make, produce, manufacture; направи сам do-it-yourself **2** to build, construct; направи куќа to build a house **3** to do, make; ќе видиш што ќе ти направам! you'll see what I'll do to you! **4** to reach (*of age*); уште малку син ми ќе направи пет години my son will soon be five **5** (*постигне*) to achieve **6** *colloq.* to settle, arrange, fix; ја направивме работата we settled the matter **7** *arch.* to smarten up; to equip; го направи момчето и го испрати на пат he equipped the boy and sent him on his journey **II** – **се 1** to pretend, fake, feign, act as if; се направи <на> болен to feign sickness; се направи <на> удрен to play dumb **2** *arch.* to smarten o.s. up; spruce up

направо *adv* **1** straight, direct, without turning; си оди направо дома to go straight home **2** directly, without beating about the bush; to one's face

напразен -зна *adj* vain, useless, purposeless

напразно *adv* vainly, in vain, to no purpose, uselessly

напрати се *pf* **1** to become accustomed to, get used to; to get into the habit (*of*); се напрати да ми бара пари he's got accustomed to asking me for money **2** to throw o.s. (*на, во нешто – into s.th.*), get down to s.th.; to get to like (*a job*); тој се напрати на таа работа he's come to like that work

напратува се *impf of* напрати се

напраши *pf* **I 1** to dust *trans.* **2** to loosen the soil around **II** – **ce** to get dusty

напрашува (ce) *impf of* напраши (ce)

напрега (ce) *impf of* напрегне (ce)

напрегнато *adv* intensely, tensely, closely

напрегнатост *f* strain, tension

напрегне *pf* напрегна *aor.* **I** to strain, tense *trans.*; напрегне внимание to pay close attention; to concentrate; напрегне очи to strain one's eyes **II** – **ce** to strain *intrans.*; to exert o.s.

напрегнува (ce) *impf of* напрегне (ce)

напред *adv* **1** forward, ahead, in front; се наведе напред to bend forward; јас ќе одам напред I'll go in front; напред! forward! отсега напред, <за>напред henceforth, from now on/onward<s>; ❏ напред-назад back and forth; тргна за напред things have taken a turn for the better **2** (*also in the comparative*) before, formerly, earlier; сега не е таков каков што беше <по>напред now he's not what he was

напреден -дна *adj* **1** advanced; progressive **2** thriving; напредно дете thriving, healthy child

напредие *n*, **напредија** & **напредица** *f arch. see* напредок

напредне *pf* напредна *aor.* to move forward, advance; to prosper, succeed; тој напредна доста he made considerable progress; нашите војски напреднаа малку our forces have advanced a little; во ништо не можеше да напредне he wasn't able to succeed in anything

напредност *f* progressiveness

напреднува *impf of* напредне

напредок *m* progress

напредува *impf of* напредне

напрежен -жна *adj* **1** former, earlier **2** lucky, successful; напрежна ти работа! good luck with your work!

напреки & **напреку** *adv* **1** sideways, askance **2** by a short cut, across

напречен -чна *adj* (*попречен*) cross, transverse

напречно *adv* across, diagonally

напролет *adv* **1** in spring **2** next spring

напросто *adv* simply

напротив *adv* on the contrary; by contrast

напрска *pf* **I** to sprinkle; to water; to spray, splash, spatter **II** – **ce** to spatter o.s.

напрскува (ce) *impf of* напрска (ce)

напрсти *adv* (*also* на прсти) on tiptoe; помина покрај вратата напрсти he tiptoed past the door

напрсток -ци *m* **1** thimble **2** *Bot.* (Digitalis purpurea) foxglove

напрчи *pf* **I 1** to pout; напрчи усни to purse one's lips **2** to raise, hold up; to cock; ❏ напрчи опашка to turn one's nose up **3** напрчи задница *see* **II 1 II** – **ce 1** to stick out one's behind **2** *fig.* to pout; to frown; to get angry **3** *fig.* to puff o.s. up; to show off

напрчува (ce) *impf of* напрчи (ce)

напудри *pf* **I** to powder **II** – **ce** to powder one's face/nose

напудрува (ce) *impf of* напудри (ce)

напука *pf* **I** to anger, infuriate; to upset, worry **II** – **ce 1** to get angry, upset **2** to shoot a lot *intrans.*

напукне *pf* напукна *aor.* to crack, split *intrans.*

напукнува *impf of* напукне

напукува (ce) *impf of* напука (ce)

напулува се *impf dial. see* нагледува се

напумпа *pf see* напомпа

напумпува *impf see* напомпува

напупи *pf see* напупчи

напупува *impf of* напупи

напупчи *pf* to bud; to blossom

напупчува *impf of* напупчи

напусто *adv* in vain, to no purpose, uselessly

напушта[1] *pf see* напушти[1]

напушта[2] *impf of* напушти[2]

напушти[1] *pf* **1** to allow, admit (*many or all*); to let in/out **2** to send many; многу луѓе напуштил да ја молат he sent many people to plead with her **3** to release, let flow copiously (*of water*)

напушти[2] *pf* **1** to leave, abandon; to quit, give up; ја напушти таа работа he left that job **2** to neglect

нар *m Bot.* (Punica granatum) pomegranate

нараби *pf* to hem

нарабува *impf of* нараби

нарав *m* temperament, personality; nature, character; disposition, temper

наравоучение -ија *n* moral; message

нарадува се *pf* to be glad; to rejoice

нараѓа (ce) *pf see* народи (ce)

нараза *f* **1** onset of disease (*in plants*) **2** partial decay (*of fruit, etc.*)

нарази *pf* **I 1** to cause disease (*in plants*); росата го нарази тутунот the dew caused disease in the tobacco **2** to rot, cause rot (*in fruit, etc.*) **II** – **ce** to be slightly ill, feel poorly

наразува (ce) *impf of* нарази (ce)

нараквица *f* **1** glove; (*со еден прст*) mitten; gauntlet; ❏ ја фрли нараквицата to throw down the gauntlet, to challenge **2** bracelet; bangle

нараквичар *m* glove maker

нарами *pf* **I** to shoulder, take on one's shoulder<s>; ja нарами торбата he slung the bag on his shoulder **II** – **ce** *fig.* to undertake (*a task*), take upon o.s.

нарамка *f* **1** pitcher, ewer (*carried on the shoulder*) **2** pad (*on the shoulder, for carrying pitcher*)

нарамник -ци *m* armful, bundle, faggot; нарамник дрва load of firewood

нарамува (ce) *impf of* нарами (ce)

нарани[1] **(ce)** *pf see* нахрани (ce)

нарани[2] *pf* to wound, injure

наранува[1] **(ce)** *impf see* нахранува (ce)

наранува[2] *impf of* нарани[2]

нараси *pf* to sprinkle (*dust, sand, ash*) on; нараси со прав to cover with dust; нараси некого со песок to kick sand over s.o.; ми ги нараси очите **1.** he threw dust in my eyes **2.** ❏ *iron.* he did me a real favour

нарасне *pf* нарасна *aor.* **1** to increase, grow; нарасна бројот на несреќните случаи the number of accidents has increased **2** to rise, prove *intrans.*; лебот нарасна the dough has risen **3** to grow, sprout plentifully; нараснала трева околу куќата grass has grown tall and thick round the house **4** to grow up (*of several children*); децата й нараснаа her children have grown up

нараснува *impf of* нарасне

нарасте *pf* нарастов *1st p. sg aor. see* нарасне

нарасток -ци *m* growth, excrescence, protuberance

нарастува *impf see* нараснува

нарасува *impf of* нараси

наративен -вна *adj* narrative

наратор *m* narrator

нарација *f* narration

нарача *pf* **1** to order; нарача вечера to order dinner **2** to send word, let (*s.o.*) know **3** *arch.* to foretell, predict; to decide (*s.o.'s fate*)

нарачан *pt* ordered, sent for; on order; ❏ како нарачан just the thing/person; made to order

нарачен -чна *adj* handy, convenient, comfortable

нарачува *impf of* нарача

нарачувач *m* person who orders, customer, client, purchaser

наргиле & **нарѓуле** *n* narghile, hookah

наред *adv* one by one, one after another; in order

наредба *f* **1** order, command, decree **2** order, arrangement, system; секоја куќа си има своја наредба every household has its own routine

наредбодавец -вци *m* giver of orders, boss; commander

нареден -дна *adj* next, following

нареди *pf* **1** to order, command, decree **2** to line up *trans.* **3** to put in order, arrange; нареди соба to tidy <up> a room **4** to settle; ќе ја наредиме таа работа we'll settle that matter **5** to adorn; to dress up *trans.* **6** *fig.* to place, find employment for; to appoint; ги нареди сите на служба he placed them all in jobs **II** – **се 1** to line up *intrans.* **2** *fig.* to smarten up *intrans.* **3** *fig.* to fix o.s. up with a job, find o.s. a job

наредник -ци *m Mil.* sergeant-major

наредува (се) *impf of* нареди (се)

нареже *pf* нережа *aor.* **1** to cut up, slice up (*a quantity of*) **2** to sharpen (*a pencil*)

нережува *impf of* нареже

нарекува *impf of* наречe

нареси (се) *pf dial. see* накити (се)

наречe *pf* нареков *1st p. sg aor.* **1** to name, call; го нарекоа премудри Соломон they called him Solomon the Wise **2** to intend (*for s.o.*); to destine (*for s.o.*); тоа е наречено за тебе that is intended for you **3** to foretell; to decide (*s.o.'s*) fate

наречје *n* dialect

наречник -ци *m* the betrothed, promised husband (*destined by fate*)

наречница *f* **1** (*usu. pl*) *Myth.* one of the Parcae, Fates **2** the betrothed, promised wife (*destined by fate*)

наречува *impf see* нарекува

нарилник -ци *m* muzzle; nose-ring (*for an animal*)

нарине *pf* нарина *aor.* to shovel (*a quantity of*)

наринува *impf of* нарине

нарипа *pf* **I 1** to jump on, rush at; to attack; сите нарипаа на него they all rushed at him **2** to jump up, get up (*of several people*); сите со радост нарипаа everybody jumped for joy **II** – **се** to tire of jumping

нарипува (се) *impf of* нарипа (се)

наркоза *f* narcosis; anaesthetic; narcotic, drug

наркоман *m* drug addict

наркоманија *f* drug addiction

наркоманка *f* (*fem. form*) *see* наркоман

наркотизира *pf* & *impf* to drug; to anaesthetize

наркотик -ци *m* narcotic, drug

наркотичен -чна *adj* narcotic

народ *m* people (*in various senses*); nation; македонскиот народ the Macedonian people (nation); работниот народ the working people; многу народ many people

народен -дна *adj* national; folk, popular; народното стопанство the national economy; народните говори popular dialects, vernacular; народниот дух the national spirit; народна поезија folk poetry; народна носија national (folk) costume; народна банка national bank; Народна Република Кина People's Republic of China; народен човек man of the people

народец *m* **1** *dim. of* народ small nation **2** *colloq.* the poor; uneducated people

народи *pf* **I** to bring forth, bear (*in large numbers*) **II** – **се** to be born (*in large numbers*); to multiply *intrans.*

народник -ци *m Hist.* populist, follower of the Populist Movement in 19th century Russia

народништво *n Hist.* populism (*trend in 19th century Russia*)

народнодемократски *adj* of people's democracy

народноослободителен -лна *adj* of national liberation; народноослободителното движење the Movement of National Liberation

народносен -сна *adj* ethnic; народносна група ethnic group

народност *f* nationality; national character; popular character; Македонец по народност a Macedonian by nationality

народски *adj* popular, folk

народува (се) *impf of* народи (се)

нарожи *pf* to grow horns

нарои се *pf* нарои се & нароја се *aor.* to gather in a swarm; to crowd together

наројува се *impf of* нарои се

нарони *pf* to husk (*maize, Am. corn*); to crumble (*bread, etc.*)

наронува *impf of* нарони

нароси *pf* to bedew

наросува *impf of* нароси

нарочен -чна *adj* intentional, not accidental

нарочно *adv* on purpose, deliberately, intentionally

наруга *pf* to scold, reprimand; to insult, offend

наружа & **наружи** *pf arch.* **I** to smarten up *trans.*; to adorn **II** – **се** to smarten up *intrans.*; to adorn o.s.

наружува (се) *impf arch. of* наружа (се)

наруча *pf* **I** to give (*s.o.*) lunch; to feed; ги наруча децата she gave the children their lunch **II** – **се** to have a good lunch; to eat one's fill

наручува (се) *impf of* наруча (се)

наруши *pf* to disrupt, disturb; to break, violate; наруши тишина to disturb the silence; наруши закон to break the law

нарушител *m* disturber; violator, transgressor

нарушува *impf of* наруши

нарушувач *m see* нарушител

на'рга се *pf colloq.* to tire of working hard, of toiling

на'ргува се *impf of* на'рга се

нарцис *m* **1** *Bot.* (Narcissus pseudonarcissus) daffodil; (Narcissus poeticus) narcissus **2** *fig.* narcissist

нарцизам -змот *m* narcissism

нарцисойден -дна *adj* narcissistic

нас *pron* (*long form for the oblique cases, except dat., of* ние) us; нè викна сите нас he called (invited) us all; од нас/со нас from us/with us; прво ве повика вас, а после нас first he invited you, and then us

насад *m* plantation, nursery

насади *pf* **I 1** to plant; насади лозје to plant a vineyard **2** to stack; насади снопје to stack sheaves **3** to plant (*in quantity*); насади дрвја секакви he planted all kinds of trees **4** to set (*domestic fowl on eggs*) **II – се** to tire of planting

насамари *pf* **I** to make a fool of; to cheat **II – се** to make a fool of o.s.

насамо *adv* in private; face to face; by oneself, alone

насапуни *pf* **I** to soap, lather **II – се** to soap o.s.

насапунува (се) *impf of* насапуни (се)

насаска *pf* (*usu. of a dog*) to set on, incite

насаскува *impf of* насаска

насвити (се) *pf see* усвити (се)

насвитува (се) *impf see* усвитува (се)

насева *impf see* насејува

наседне *pf* наседна *aor.* **1** to sit down (*on*); ја наседна кошулата и целата ја истутка he sat down on the shirt and crumpled it **2** (*of blood*) to collect *intrans.*; грлото крв му наседна blood collected in his throat **3** to sit down one after another **4** *fig. colloq.* to be taken in; наседне на провокација to fall for a provocation **5** to take in, dupe, trick; го наседна he tricked him

наседнува *impf of* наседне

насее *pf* насеа *aor.* to sow (*a field*)

насејува *impf of* насее

насекаде *adv* everywhere; in every direction

насекира *pf* **I** to upset, worry **II – се** to get upset, worried; to fret

насекирува (се) *impf of* насекира (се)

насекува (се) *impf of* насече (се)

населба *f* settlement; suburb

населен *pt* inhabited, populated; населено место settlement, inhabited place

население *n* population; попис на населението census

населеник -ци *m* settler

населенички *adj* settler's

населеност *f* <density of> population

насели *pf* **I** to settle *trans.*; to populate **II – се** to settle *intrans.*; to take up residence

населува (се) *impf of* насели (се)

насети *pf* **I** to feel; to have a presentiment (premonition) of; to scent, get wind of **II – се** *impers.* there is a feeling of

насетува (се) *impf of* насети (се)

насече *pf* насеков *1st p. sg aor.* **I 1** to cut (*a certain quantity of*) **2** to nick, cut (*slightly, by accident*); си го насече прстот he cut his finger (*slightly*) **3** to notch, incise **II – се 1** to tire of cutting **2** to cut o.s. (*slightly*)

насечува (се) *impf of* насече (се)

насила *adv* by force; against one's will

насилба *f* violence, force; tyranny, despotism

насилен -лна *adj* violent, forcible; насилна смрт violent death

насили *pf* **1** to force, compel **2** to rape, violate

насилие -ија *n see* насилство

насилник -ци *m* tyrant, despot; rowdy, bully

насилнички *adj* tyrannical, despotic; bullying

насилништво *n* violence, force; tyranny, despotism

насилно *adv* by force; against one's will

насилство *n* violence, force; tyranny, despotism

насилува *impf of* насили

насип *m* bank, embankment; dam, dyke, *Am.* levee; breakwater

насипе *pf* насипа *aor.* **1** to bank up; to fill in **2** to pour in; насипе жито во амбарите to pour grain into the granaries

насипува *impf of* насипе

насит *m see* наситка

наситеност *f* satiety; saturation

насити *pf* **I 1** to satisfy, satiate **2** to saturate (*s. th.*) with **II – се** to satiate o.s., have one's fill

наситка *f* satiation, satiety; нема наситка to be insatiable

наситни *pf* to chop up, dice, mince

наситнува *impf of* наситни

наситок *m see* наситка

наситува (се) *impf of* насити (се)

наскапаност *f* partial decay; incipient rot

наскапе <се> *pf* наскапа <се> *aor.* to begin to decay, rot

наскапува <се> *impf of* наскапе <се>

наскока (се) *pf see* нарипа (се)

наскокува (се) *impf see* нарипува (се)

наскоро *adv* soon

наслага[1] *f* stratum, layer; deposit; stratification

наслага[2] *pf see* наслои

наслада *f* enjoyment; pleasure, delight

наслади се *pf* (*на, со*) to enjoy, take delight in

насладува се *impf of* наслади се

насладувачка *f see* наслада

наслани *pf* to cover with hoarfrost (rime)

насланува *impf of* наслани

наследен -дна *adj* hereditary; наследно право laws of inheritance; наследна болест hereditary disease

наследи *pf* **1** to inherit; наследи куќа to inherit a house **2** to succeed (*s.o.*); ќе го наследи најдобриот ученик his best pupil will succeed him

наследие *n see* наследство

наследник -ци *m* heir, beneficiary; successor

наследница *f* (*fem. form*) *see* наследник; heiress

наследнички *adj* hereditary

наследност *f* heredity

наследство *n* inheritance; heritage; heirloom; legacy; остави во наследство to bequeath

наследува *impf of* наследи

наслика *pf* to paint (*a picture*); to portray

насликува *impf of* наслика

наслов *m* title; heading; под наслов under the title

насловен -вна *adj* title; насловна страна title page

наслои *pf* **I** to deposit (*in layers*) **II – се** to settle *intrans.*, be deposited (*in layers*); to form strata/layers

наслојка *f see* наслага[1]

наслојува (се) *impf of* наслои (се)

наслон *m* rest, support; back (*of a chair, etc.*)

наслути *pf* to foresee, have a presentiment (premonition) of; to sense, perceive

наслутува *impf of* наслути

наслуша *pf* I to listen secretly; to try to hear; to eavesdrop II – **се** to hear <enough> of; to hear a lot

наслушне *pf* наслушна *aor. see* наслуша I

наслушнува *impf see* наслушува

наслушува *impf of* наслушне

наслушувач *m* eavesdropper

насмеан *adj* smiling; секогаш е весел и насмеан he is always cheerful and smiling

насмев *m* smile

насмева (се) *impf of* насмее (се)

насмевка *f* smile; блага насмевка kindly smile; кисела насмевка wry smile

насмевне се *pf* насмевна се *aor.* to smile

насмевнува се *impf of* насмевне се

насмее *pf* насмеа *aor.* I to make (*s.o.*) laugh II – **се 1** to laugh, burst out laughing **2** *fig.* to make fun (*co – of*), mock **3** to joke (*со некого – with s.o.*); to play a joke (*со некого – on s.o.*)

насмејува (се) *impf see* насмева (се)

насмене *pf* насмена *aor.* **1** to mention, talk about **2** to remind (*некому за нешто – s.o. of s.th.*); му насменав за тебе I reminded him of you

насменува *impf of* насмене

насмешка *f* sneer; taunt, jibe; mockery, ridicule

насмешлив *adj* mocking, taunting

насмешливец -вци *m* mocker

насмешливо *adv* mockingly

насмоли *pf* to smear with resin

насмолува *impf of* насмоли

наснова *impf of* наснове

наснове *pf* наснова *aor.* to <form a> warp (*with yarn*)

насновува *impf see* наснова

наснопи *pf* to bind in sheaves

наснопува *impf of* наснопи

насобере *pf* насобра *aor.* I to collect, gather together *trans.* II – **се 1** to collect, gather *intrans.*; се насобраа многу луѓе a lot of people gathered **2** to pile up, accumulate *intrans.* (*also fig.*); се насобраа многу работи a lot of things (business) piled up

насоберува (се) & **насобира (се)** *impf of* насобере (се)

насока *f* **1** direction **2** directive

насолзи *pf* I to bring tears to s.o.'s eyes; неговото раскажување ме насолзи his story brought tears to my eyes II – **се** to be filled with tears

насолзува (се) *impf of* насолзи (се)

насоли *pf* **1** to salt; to corn (*meat, etc.*) **2** to sprinkle, dust (*with powder, etc.*) **3** *fig.* to trick, deceive

насолува *impf of* насоли

насоне *adv* in one's sleep; in a dream; како насоне as in a dream

насоченост *f* direction, aiming

насочи *pf* I to direct, point; to turn *trans.* II – **се** to turn towards *intrans.*

насочува (се) *impf of* насочи (се)

наспива се *impf of* наспие се

наспие се *pf* наспа се *aor.* to have a good sleep

наспичи се *pf* to prick o.s. with a splinter

наспичок -ци *m* splinter

наспомене *pf* наспомена *aor.* to mention; to remind

наспоменува *impf of* наспомене

наспомне *pf* наспомна *aor. see* наспомене

наспомнува *impf see* наспоменува

наспоред *prep see* според

наспореден -дна *adj* parallel

наспоредно *adv* parallel

наспоредност *f* parallelism

наспрема *prep* opposite, as opposed to; in comparison with

наспроти & **наспротив** *prep* **1** *see* наспрема **2** despite; against, contrary to **3** on the eve of; on the other side of

наспротива *adv* on the other side; opposite, across

насрба се *pf* to sip, lap one's fill

насрбува се *impf of* насрба се

насрди (се) *pf see* налути (се)

насрдува (се) *impf of* насрди (се), *see* налутува (се)

насред *prep* (*also* на сред) in the middle of

насреде *adv* in the middle

насрка се *pf* to sip, lap one's fill

насркува се *impf of* насрка се

насрочи *pf* to fix a date (*for a court hearing*); насрочи расправа to set a hearing

насрочува *impf of* насрочи

насрчи *pf* to urge, encourage; to cheer up, give heart to

насрчува *impf of* насрчи

настава *f* teaching, instruction; школска (училишна) настава school teaching

наставен -вна *adj* teaching; наставен план curriculum; наставна програма syllabus

настави *pf* **1** to set, place (*trap, snare*) **2** to add on, put on (*to s.th.*), lengthen (*a pipe, a thread, etc.*); to extend *trans.*

наставка *f* **1** extension, addition; continuation **2** *Gram.* suffix, ending

наставник -ци *m* teacher (*senior primary to lower secondary level*)

наставница & **наставничка** *f* (*fem. form*) *see* наставник

наставнички *adj* teaching; наставнички персонал teaching staff; наставнички колегиум teaching staff (*as a body*)

наставува *impf of* настави

настамени *pf* I to put, place (*s.th. in a certain place; s.o. in a job, etc.*) II – **се** to put, place o.s.

настаменува (се) *impf of* настамени (се)

настан *m* event; настан од историско значење event of historical importance

настане *pf* настана *aor.* **1** to begin; to come, arrive; настана лето summer has come **2** to grow up; децата ми настанаа my children have grown up **3** to rise, rebel; настана народот the people rose in rebellion **4** to originate, develop; to arise; to happen, occur **5** to get up, stand up (*of several people*)

настани *pf* I to quarter, settle, find housing for II – **се** to take up residence, settle down

настанок *m* origin, genesis

настанува[1] *impf of* настане 1, 4 & 5

настанува[2] **(се)** *impf of* настани (се)

настап *m* **1** fit, seizure, attack; настап на лудило fit of madness (insanity) **2** performance, appearance (*on stage*); talk **3** starting date (*of job*)

настапен -пна *adj* coming, approaching; настапнава година the coming year, next year

настапи *pf* **1** to tread on, step on; ми го настапи прстот you trod on my toe **2** to come, arrive; настапи летото summer arrived **3** to appear (*on stage*), perform; играчите настапија вчера the dancers performed yesterday **4** to take up (*a post*)

настапува   *impf of* настапи

настаса   *pf* **I 1** to catch up **2** to grow up; настасаа децата the children grew up **3** to arrive in large numbers **II – се** to catch up with each other

настасува (се)   *impf of* настаса (се)

настигне   *pf* настигна *aor.* **I 1** to catch up **2** to arrive (*in large numbers*) **II – се** to catch up with each other

настигнува (се)   *impf of* настигне (се)

настин   *m* cold; од настин because of a cold

настине   *pf* настина *aor.* to catch a cold

настинка   *f see* настин

настинува   *impf of* настине

настиска   *pf* **I 1** to push, press **2** to squeeze, extract **II – се 1** to crowd in; се настискаа еден до друг they crowded in one next to the other **2** to tire of squeezing

настискува (се)   *impf of* настиска (се)

настојник   -ци *m* caretaker, janitor, *Am.* building superintendent; custodian; guardian; куќен настојник, настојник на зграда caretaker of a house, a building; црковен настојник sexton

настојница   *f* (*fem. form*) *see* настојник

настојува   *impf* to persist; to try hard, exert o.s.; to strive for; to be occupied with

настојчив   *adj* persistent, steadfast; stubborn

настојчивост   *f* persistence; stubbornness

настрада   *pf* **I** to suffer loss; to meet with an accident; to be ruined, destroyed; смртно настрада to perish, lose one's life **II – се** to have a bad time, go through hell

настрадува (се)   *impf of* настрада (се)

настрана   *adv* apart; aside; ❑ остава настрана to set aside (*saving*); шегата настрана joking apart; да го оставиме тоа настрана let us leave that aside! стои (се држи) настрана to keep to o.s., stand aloof

настрани   *pf* **I** to bend, tilt sideways *trans.* **II – се** to bend, lean, tilt *intrans.*

настранува (се)   *impf of* настрани (се)

настрвеност   *f* bloodthirstiness

настрви   *pf* **I 1** to make (*an animal*) hungry for blood; to flesh, make bloodthirsty **2** *fig.* to infuriate **II – се 1** to become bloodthirsty; да не се настрви пес на касапница *prov.* take care that s.o. doesn't develop bad habits **2** *fig.* to be infuriated

настрвува (се)   *impf of* настрви (се)

настроен   *pt* inclined, disposed, in the mood for; не сум настроен (*за нешто*) I'm not in the mood (*for s.th.*)

настроение   -ија *n* mood; disposition, frame of mind; во лошо настроение in a bad mood

настроеност   *f* disposition, inclination; mood, humour

настрои   *pf* настрои & настроја *aor.* **I 1** to put (*s.o.*) in a good/bad mood **2** to tune (*a musical instrument*) **II – се** to get into a mood

настројба   *f* mood; disposition, frame of mind

настројува (се)   *impf of* настрои (се)

насуво   *adv* dry; го избричи насуво he gave him a dry shave (*without lathering*); *fig.* he made a fool of him

насукува   *impf of* насуче

насуче   *pf* насука *aor.* **I** to roll (*layers of pastry in quantity*) **II – се** (*за брод*) to go aground

насучува   *impf of* насуче

насушен   -шна *adj* daily; essential, basic; urgent, pressing, imperative; насушен леб daily bread; насушна потреба urgent need, vital need

нат-   *see* над-

натаври (се)   *pf see* накити (се)

натаврува (се)   *impf of* натаври (се)

натажен   *pt* saddened, sad, depressed; bereaved

натажи   *pf* **I** to sadden, depress, distress, cause sadness **II – се** to become sad

натажува (се)   *impf of* натажи (се)

натака   *adv see* натаму; и така натака and so on, and so forth, et cetera (etc.)

натакај & **натаки**   *adv see* натака

наталитет   *m* birth rate, natality

наталожи   *pf* **I** to deposit **II – се** to be deposited, accumulate *intrans.*

наталожува (се)   *impf of* наталожи (се)

натамошен   -шна *adj see* понатамошен

натаму   *adv* that way, there, in that direction, to that side; further (*on*), onwards; in future; (*comparative:* понатаму) farther, further; погледна натаму he looked in that direction; не оди понатаму! don't go any farther! од линијата натаму не оди! don't go beyond the line! и така натаму and so on, and so forth, et cetera (etc.); отсега натаму from now on (in the future, henceforward); ❑ навaму-натаму to and fro, hither and thither

натега   *impf of* натегне

натегнато   *adv* tightly stretched, taut

натегне   *pf* натегна *aor.* **1** to tighten, pull tight **2** *see* натежне 3

натегнува   *impf see* натега

натежне   *pf* натежна *aor.* **1** to become heavy (heavier) **2** to become bent/twisted, lose shape (*under strain*); to become laden (*со – with*) **3** to tip (tilt) *intrans.* (*of scales*); терезијата натежна откај мене the scales tipped to my side **4** *fig.* to pressure, put pressure on, press, urge; to bother, pester; ти ќе му натежнеш да се согласи со тоа you'll put pressure on him to agree to that

натежнува   *impf of* натежне 1–3

натекне ми   *pf impers.* натекна ми *aor.* to remember, *see* текне[2] ми

натекува   *impf of* натече

натема   *in the expression:* натема го! damn him!

натепа   *pf* **I** to thrash, flog **II – се** to have one's fill of fighting

натепува (се)   *impf of* натепа (се)

натера   *pf* **I** to drive to, force, compel **II – се** to force o.s., compel o.s.

натерува (се)   *impf of* натера (се)

натече   *pf* натеков *1st p. sg aor.* to become swollen, swell; ми натече раката my hand/arm has swollen up

натимари   *pf* to groom, curry (*a horse*)

натимарува   *impf of* натимари

натиска   *impf of* натисне

натисне   *pf* натисна *aor.* **1** to press, pin down **2** to squeeze, crush **3** *fig.* to compel, force

натиснува   *impf of* натисне

натисок   *m see* притисок

наткаже   *pf* наткажа *aor.* to show, indicate more than the real weight (*of s.th.*)

наткажува   *impf of* наткаже; кантарот ваш наткажува your steelyard shows extra weight (does not give true measure)

наткасна   *f* bedside table

наткачи   *pf* to raise, add to (*e.g. price*)

наткачува *impf of* наткачи

натлак -ци *m &* **натлака** *f* deposit, silt, alluvium; mud

натлачи *pf* to deposit (*silt, sand, etc.*); to irrigate; реката го натлачи ова место the river deposited silt in this place

натлачиште *n* silt-bed, silt deposit

натлачува *impf of* натлачи

НАТО *abbr.* NATO

натовареност *f* I 1 state of being <over>loaded, busy

натовари *pf* I 1 to load 2 *fig.* to deceive, cheat; to make a fool of 3 *fig.* to force (*s.th. on s.o.*) 4 to impose s.th. (*as a duty*); to burden (*s.o. with s.th.*) II – **ce** 1 to load o.s. (*with*) 2 *fig.* to take upon o.s.

натоварува (ce) *impf of* натовари (ce)

натокми *pf* I 1 to arrange, put in order, fix; to decorate 2 to equip, get ready *trans.*; го натокми коњот he saddled his horse 3 to pay, settle, meet; не можам да ја натокмам целата сума I can't pay the full amount 4 to set, adjust, adapt II – **ce** 1 to put o.s. in order; to dress up *intrans.*; to adorn o.s. 2 to be quits, even (*со некого – with s.o.*)

натокмува (ce) *impf of* натокми (ce)

натопен *pt* soaked, saturated; земја натопена со крв ground soaked with blood

натопи *pf* I 1 to soak, wet; to moisten 2 to melt down (*in considerable quantity*) II – **ce** to get wet, be soaked

натопори се *pf* to throw out one's chest; to strut, show off

натопорува се *impf of* натопори се

натопува (ce) *impf of* натопи (ce)

наточи[1] *pf* to draw, tap, pour, decant; наточи вино to pour wine

наточи[2] *pf* to sharpen, grind, whet, hone

наточува[1] *impf of* наточи[1]

наточува[2] *impf of* наточи[2]

натпис *m* inscription; надгробен натпис inscription on a gravestone, tomb; epitaph; натпис на дуќан shop sign, signboard

натпише *pf* натпиша *aor.* to inscribe

натпишува *impf of* натпише

натплати *pf* to overpay; ќе платиме и ќе натплатиме we'll pay what's due and more

натплатува *impf of* натплати

натпревар *m* match; game; contest, competition

натпревари *pf* to pass, overtake; to surpass

натпреварува *impf* I *of* натпревари II – **ce** to compete

натпреварување *n* match; competition

натпреварувач *m* competitor, contestant

натпреварувачки *adj* competitive

натпретек 1 *m see* натпревар 2 *adv* playing; competing; surpassing

натприроден -дна *adj* supernatural

натрапи *pf* I 1 to come (*на некого – upon s.o.*), happen upon 2 to force, impose, foist (*на – on*) II – **ce** to force (*o.s.*) on, impose (*o.s.*) on, intrude on

натраплив *adj* intrusive, meddlesome

натрапливост *f* intrusiveness

натрапник -ци *m* intrusive, meddlesome man

натрапница *f* (*fem. form*) *see* натрапник

натрапува (ce) *impf of* натрапи (ce)

натрати *pf* I to knock; to damage; to bruise II – **ce** to hurt o.s.

натратува (ce) *impf of* натрати (ce)

натресе *pf* натресов *1st p. sg aor.* to shake down (*fruit, etc.*)

натреска се *pf colloq.* 1 to get drunk 2 to gorge, stuff (*o.s.*), guzzle *intrans.*

натрескува се *impf colloq. of* натреска се

натресува *impf of* натресе

натрива *impf of* натрие

натрие *pf* натри *aor.* to rub in; ❑ му го натрив носот I tore a strip off him, I gave him a piece of my mind

натриум *m Chem.* sodium; натриум хлорид sodium chloride, common salt; натриум хидроксид sodium hydroxide, caustic soda

натриев & **натриумов** *adj Chem.* sodium *attrib.*; натриумов карбонат sodium bicarbonate, soda

натроши *pf* to crumble, crush (*in quantity*)

натрошува *impf of* натроши

натрупа *pf* I 1 to amass, hoard, accumulate *trans.* 2 to cram, stuff in *trans.* II – **ce** 1 to accumulate *intrans.*; to pile up *intrans.* 2 to cram, pack *intrans.* (*into a room, etc.*)

натрупува (ce) *impf of* натрупа (ce)

натруфеност *f* state of being dressed up, overdressed

натруфи *pf* I to dress (*s.o.*) up; to overdress *trans.* II – **ce** to dress up *intrans.*; to overdress *intrans.*

натруфува се *impf of* натруфи се

натрча *pf* I to crowd, press, swarm, rush in II – **ce** 1 to tire of running 2 *see* I; луѓе се натрчаа да го видат people crowded in to see him

натрчува (ce) *impf of* натрча (ce)

натстрешник -ци *m* eaves; canopy; (*платнен*) awning

наттрча *pf* to outrun, surpass in running

наттрчува *impf* I *of* наттрча II – **ce** to compete in running

натупа се *pf colloq.* to gorge (*o.s.*)

натура *f* nature; ❑ плаќање во натура payment in kind

натурален -лна *adj* natural; in kind; натурално стопанство subsistence economy; натурална замена barter

натура (ce) *impf of* натури (ce)

натурализам -змот *m* naturalism

натуралист *m* naturalist

натури *pf* I 1 to pour; го натурила со вода she has poured water over him 2 to pour (*in quantity*) II – **ce** to pour (*water, etc.*) over o.s.; to get soaked

натуфка (ce) *pf see* натруфи (ce)

натучи *pf* to grease, smear with grease

натучува *impf of* натучи

натфрла *impf* I *of* натфрли II – **ce** to have a throwing contest

натфрли *pf* 1 to surpass in throwing 2 *fig.* to exceed, break (*a record, etc.*); ја натфрлија нормата they exceeded the production quota

натфрлува (ce) *impf see* натфрла (ce)

натцени *pf* to overvalue; to overestimate

натчовек *m* superman

наугоре *adv see* нагоре

наугорен -рна *adj see* нагорен

наудолен -лна *adj see* надолен

наудолу *adv see* надолу

наужива се *pf* to have one's fill of enjoyment

наука *f* 1 science, learning; општествените науки social sciences 2 *arch.* moral, lesson 3 *arch.* habit, practice

наум *adv* by heart

науми *pf* **1** to intend; to decide **2** to mention **3** to remind

наумува *impf of* науми

науст *adv arch.* by heart

науста *adv* orally, verbally

наут *m Bot.* chick-pea, gram, *see* слануток

наутика *m* maritime studies; maritime college

наутички *adj* nautical

наутро *adv* in the morning<s>, every morning

научен[1] *pt* accustomed to, used to

научен[2] -чна *adj* scientific; learned; scholarly; научен соработник senior research fellow; научен совет faculty board; university senate; research committee

научи *pf* **I 1** to learn; to get to know, find out; од него многу научив I learnt a lot from him; од каде научи за таа работа? where did you hear that? **2** to teach; to accustom; научи некого на нешто to teach s.o. s.th.; ❏ ќе те научам јас тебе! I'll teach you a lesson! **II – се** to learn; to get used to

научна-фантастика *f* science fiction

научник -ци *m* scientist; scholar, learned man

научно *adv* scientifically

научно-фантастичен -чна *adj* science-fiction *attrib.*

научува (се) *impf of* научи (се)

наушници *pl* ear-muffs; ear-flaps

нафати *pf* **I** to catch, seize a lot of **II – се 1** to bet, wager **2** to take on, agree to, undertake (*a job*); to set to

нафаќа *pf* **I** *see* нафати **I II – се** to stick to; to form on, spread over

нафаќа се *impf of* нафати се; сериозно се нафаќа за работа to get down to business

нафора *f Rel.* Orthodox Communion bread, eucharistic wafer

нафрла[1] *pf* **I** *see* нафрли **II – се 1** to tire of throwing **2** *see* нафрли се 1 & 3

нафрла[2] **(се)** *impf see* нафрлува (се)

нафрли *pf* **I 1** to throw on, pile on; *fig.* to remark, add; го нафрли ѓубрето во дупката he threw the rubbish into the hole **2** *fig.* to sketch, outline **II – се 1** to rush (*на – at*); to attack (*also fig.*); се нафрлија сите на него да го тепаат everybody rushed at him to beat him **2** *fig. see* напрати се 2 **3** to come out, break out (*in a rash, etc.*) **4** (*на*) to get down to

нафрлува (се) *impf of* нафрли (се)

нафта *f* oil, petroleum; naphtha; наидува на нафта to strike oil

нафталин *m* naphthalene; ❏ вади од нафталин to take s.th. out of mothballs

нафтоносен -сна *adj* oil-bearing; нафтоносни полиња oil fields

нахија -ии *f arch.* district (*in the Turkish administrative division of a country*)

нахрани *pf* **I** to feed *trans.* **II – се** to eat, feed *intrans.*

нахранува (се) *impf of* нахрани (се)

нацарува се *pf* to reign for a long time

нацврца се *pf colloq.* to get tipsy, get drunk

нацеди *pf* to squeeze, strain, extract; to fill by dripping

нацедува *impf of* нацеди

нацепи *pf* to chop (*a certain amount of*) firewood

нацепува *impf of* нацепи

нацизам -змот *m* Nazism

нација -ии *f* nation; Обединетите нации United Nations

национален -лна *adj* national; национална економија national economy; национално движење national movement

национализам -змот *m* nationalism

национализација *f* nationalization

национализира *pf & impf* to nationalize

националист *m* nationalist

националистички *adj* nationalistic

националност *f* nationality

националсоцијализам -змот *m* National Socialism

националсоцијалист *m* National Socialist

националсоцијалистички *adj* National Socialist

нацист *m* Nazi

нацистички *adj* Nazi

нацица *pf* **I** to suckle, nurse *trans.*, give suck to **II – се** to finish suckling, nursing *intrans.*; to suckle, nurse sufficiently

нацицува (се) *impf of* нацица (се)

нацрви *pf* **I 1** to make red, paint red **2** to smear with red **II – се 1** to put on rouge/lipstick **2** to soil o.s. with s.th. red

нацрвува (се) *impf of* нацрви (се)

нацрни *pf* **I** to blacken, darken; to cover with soot **II – се** to blacken o.s.; to soil o.s. with s.th. black; to get covered with soot

нацрнува (се) *impf of* нацрни (се)

нацрпе *pf* нацрпив *1st p. sg aor.* to draw, fetch (*water, etc.*); to ladle; to scoop

нацрпува *impf of* нацрпи

нацрт *m* sketch, draft, scheme, project; нацрт на закон *or* нацрт-закон bill, draft law

нацрта *pf* to draw, design, sketch

нацртен -тна *adj Math.* descriptive; нацртна геометрија descriptive geometry

нацртува *impf of* нацрта

начади *pf* to fill with smoke; to fumigate

начадува *impf of* начади

началник -ци *m* chief, head; prefect (*of police*)

началница & началничка *f* **1** (*fem. form*) *see* началник **2** chief's (head's)/prefect's wife

начало *n see* почеток

началство *n coll.* <the> authorities; prefecture

началствува *impf* **1** to be in charge; to officiate (*at church service*) **2** to command, direct

начас *adv* immediately, at once; in a moment

начасничав *adj* unstable, unsteady; fickle, unreliable

начек *m* **1** what can befall s.o., what s.o. may live to see **2** help (*in difficult circumstances*); salvation

начека *pf* **I 1** to catch, stop; to lie in wait for; ја начека топката со нога he stopped the ball with his foot; го начекаа кај бунарот they lay in wait for him by the well **2** to live to see; to experience; може ќе начекаме да нѐ молите perhaps we will live to see the day when you come begging to us **3** (*usu. of money*) to be of use, come in handy, be welcome; тие пари ќе ме начекаа I could have done with that money **II – се 1** to fall safely; се начека на нозе he landed on his feet **2** to wait for a long time; to be kept waiting; to get tired of waiting

начекува (се) *impf of* начека (се)

начелен -лна *adj* of principle; based on principle; basic, fundamental

начелно *adv* basically, fundamentally

начелност *f* adherence to principle<s>

начело[1] *n* principle, basis; во начело in principle

начело[2] & **на чело** *adv* at the head (*of*); начело (на чело) на софрата at the head of the table

наченка *f* first cut, first slice (*of a loaf, etc.*)

наченпе *pf* наченпна *aor.* **1** to bite into; to cut into; to break off (*a little of s.th.*) **2** *see* начне

наченпнува *impf of* наченпе

начесто *adv* **1** often **2** densely

начеток -ци *m see* наченка

начешла *pf* **I 1** to comb **2** to finish combing **II** – **се 1** to comb one's hair **2** to finish combing one's hair

начин *m* **1** way, manner, mode; *Cul.* style; на еден или на друг начин one way or another; на севозможни начини in all manner of ways; by all possible means; наоѓа начин да to find one's way to; на друг (поинаков) начин otherwise; на овој начин in this way; like this; thus; на секој начин by all means; at all costs; no matter what **2** <mode of> behaviour, manner<s>; начин на обнесување way of behaving **3** *Gram.* mood; глаголски начин verbal mood, mood of a verb

начисто *adv* clear, clean; да бидеме начисто по тоа прашање let us be clear on this question; биде со некого начисто to know where one stands with s.o.; препише начисто to make a clean copy

начита се *pf* to read a lot; to read one's fill

начитан *adj* well-read

начитаност *f* erudition

начитува се *impf of* начита се

начичка *pf* **I 1** to cover with burrs **2** to fill, stuff; небото беше начичкано со ѕвезди the sky was star-studded **II** – **се** to get covered with burrs

начичкан *pt* filled, crammed

начичканост *f* congestion, crush, jam

начкрта *pf* to scribble, scrawl

начне *pf* начна *aor.* to dip into, start using

начнува *impf of* начне

начпара *pf* to scratch; to scrape; to cut into, tear (*with a needle, with one's nails, with a thorn, etc.*)

начпарува *impf of* начпара

начуди се *pf* to be astonished, surprised; to wonder; не можам да ти се начудам како можеш да го трпиш I can't help wondering how you can stand him

начудува се *impf of* начуди се

начуе *pf* начу *aor.* to hear vaguely; to overhear; начув нешто за тебе I <over>heard s.th. about you

начука *pf* **I 1** to shake down (*apples, pears, etc.*) **2** to knock in, push in, shove in *trans.* **II** – **се 1** to push in, shove in *intrans.* **2** to tire of knocking (*with a hammer, etc.*) **3** *colloq.* to get sloshed (drunk)

начукува (се) *impf of* начука (се)

начули *pf* to prick up (*one's ears*)

начулува *impf of* начули

начумери *pf* **I** to crease, pucker, knit (*one's brow*) **II** – **се** to frown, scowl

начумерува (се) *impf of* начумери (се)

начури *pf see* начади

начурува *impf see* начадува

нацбара *pf* to find by groping (*in the dark*)

наш, наша, наше, *pl* наши *possessive pron* our; ours; нашиот народ our people; нашите our people; our family, our relations; our compatriots; ❑ наши сме feel free; be my guest; make yourself at home

наша се *impf f.p.* to restrain o.s.; to hold (hang) back

нашари *pf* to decorate; to colour; to doodle

нашарува *impf of* нашари

нашега & **на шега** *adv* joking, as a joke; му го реков тоа нашега I told him that as a joke

нашегува се *pf* to play a joke on, have a joke with

нашемаалец -лци *m* s.o. from our part (*of a town or village*)

нашепне *pf* нашепна *aor.* to whisper to (*s.o.*)

нашепнува *impf of* нашепне

нашета се *pf* to have a good walk; to tire of walking/travelling

нашетува се *impf of* нашета се

нашеќери *pf* to sweeten; to sugarcoat

нашеќерува *impf of* нашеќери

нашиба *pf colloq.* **1** to cram in, squeeze in *trans.* **2** to whip, flog, lash

нашибува *impf of* нашиба

нашива *impf of* нашие

нашивка *f* bordering, edging, trimming

нашие *pf* наши *aor.* **1** to sew (*in large quantities*) **2** to sew on

нашили *pf* to make pointed; to sharpen

нашилува *impf of* нашили

нашинец -нци *m* our fellow-countryman (compatriot)

нашинка *f* (*fem. form*) *see* нашинец

нашински[1] *adj* of/from our country/region

нашински[2] *adv* as in our country; in our way

нашир *adv* in width, in breadth

нашироко *adv* in a detailed manner; се расприкажа нашироко he started talking in great detail and at great length; ❑ надолго и нашироко thoroughly, exhaustively, fully, in detail; живее нашироко to live in <grand> style

нашлака *pf* **1** to slap, spank **2** (*боја*) to daub

нашлакува *impf of* нашлака

нашминка *pf* **I** to make up *trans.*, apply cosmetics to **II** – **се** to put on make-up, to make o.s. up

нашне *pf* нашна *aor.* to set on, incite (*на* – against) (*s.o. or s.th.*)

нашнува *impf of* нашне

наштеди *pf* to save up (*money, etc.*); to economize

наштедува *impf of* наштеди

наштети *pf* to harm, damage; to be bad for (*s.o. or s.th.*)

наштетува *impf of* наштети

наштрапа *pf* **1** to cut a large quantity of s.th. (*with scissors*) **2** *fig.* to scribble, scrawl; to daub; to doodle

наштрапува *impf of* наштрапа

наштрбен *adj* damaged, broken <off>, chipped; incomplete, defective

наштрби *pf* to damage, break off, chip; *fig.* to ruin, spoil

наштрбува *impf of* наштрби

наштрка *pf* to sprinkle, water sufficiently

наштркне *pf* наштркна *aor.* to bristle; to have goose-flesh

наштркнува *impf of* наштркне

наштркува *impf of* наштрка

нашуми *pf* to rustle; to make a loud noise

нашумува *impf of* нашуми

н.е. *abbr.* (*нашата ера*) AD

не *part* **1** no; така е, не? it's like that, isn't it? **2** not; да не си болен? you aren't ill by any chance?

не- (*prefix of negation*) un-, in-, mis-, dis-; non-; несреќа, недоверба, неразбирање misfortune, distrust, misunderstanding; нездрав, непослушен unhealthy, disobedient

нѐ *pron* (*short acc. form of* ние) us; нѐ виде he saw us

неа *pron* (*long form of* таа, она *for the oblique cases. Used for emphasis with short forms* ú, ja, *and with prepositions*) her; ja видов неа I saw her; од неа from her; за неа for/about her; со неа with her

неактивен -вна *adj* inactive; неактивен пазар sluggish market

неактуéлен -лна *adj* not topical; irrelevant; not current

неарен -рна *adj colloq*. **1** bad; wrong; неарен човек bad person **2** unwell, ill, sick; неарен сум денеска нешто I'm a bit unwell today

неарно *adv colloq*. **1** badly; wrongly; неарно стори денеска you acted wrongly today **2** неарно ми е I don't feel well

небаре *adv* as if

небен -бна *adj* **1** celestial, heavenly **2** *Phon*. palatal

небеса *pl* <the> heavens, sky, *see* небо

небесен -сна *adj* celestial, heavenly; небесно царство kingdom of heaven, heavenly kingdom; небесна синевина the blue of the sky

небески *adj see* небесен

небиденик -ци & **небидник** -ци *m* damned (accursed) man

небидница *f* **1** (*fem. form*) *see* небиденик **2** s.th. unrealizable, fantastic, impossible; a cock and bull story

небитница *f see* небидница

небичас & **не би час** *adv arch*. at once, immediately; that very moment; in a jiffy

неблагодарен -рна *adj* ungrateful

неблагодарник -ци *m* ungrateful man

неблагодарница *f* (*fem. form*) *see* неблагодарник

неблагодарност *f* ingratitude

неблагонадежен -жна *adj* disloyal; untrustworthy, unreliable

неблагонадежност *f* disloyalty; untrustworthiness

неблагопријатен -тна *adj see* неповолен

неблагороден -дна *adj* ignoble, mean, base

неблаготворен -рна *adj* harmful; bad; unpleasant

небо *n* sky; heaven; ❑ вишно небо sky high; под ведро небо in the open air; outdoors; крева (дига) некого до небо to think the world of s.o.; to praise s.o. to the sky; како да паднал од небо ill at ease; out of one's depth; на деветто (седмо) небо in seventh heaven; on cloud nine; happy as a lark; ветува и небо и земја to promise the earth (moon); отвори се отвори to rain cats and dogs; to come down in buckets; the heavens opened; ни на небо ни на земја hanging in the air; in limbo

неборец -рци *m* noncombatant, civilian

неборечки *adj* noncombatant, civilian; неборечки одред noncombatant unit/detachment

небосвод & **небосклон** *m* firmament; welkin, vault of heaven

небрат *m* enemy

небратски *adj* hostile

небрежен -жна *adj* careless, negligent; carefree

небричен *adj* unshaven

неброен *adj* countless, numberless, innumerable

неброеност *f* countless number

небудност *f* heedlessness, carelessness

небулóзен -зна *adj* nebulous, vague, unclear; incomprehensible

неважен -жна *adj* unimportant; insignificant; irrelevant

невалиден -дна *adj* invalid, void

невалидност *f* invalidity, lack of validity

неварен *adj* uncooked, raw

неваросан *adj* not whitewashed

невевче *n dim. of* невеста

невела *impf arch*. **1** (*only 3rd p. sg*) to feel unwell; to be sickly; детето нешто невела the child is not quite well **2** *impers*. it isn't good, it's not right; невела да се работи во недела it's wrong to work on Sundays

невен *n Bot*. (Calendula) <English> marigold

невенов *adj* marigold *attrib*.; китка невенова bunch of marigolds

невера *f poet*. breach of faith, disloyalty, treason, treachery

неверба *f* disbelief, doubt; incredulity

неверен -рна *adj* **1** unfaithful; неверен маж unfaithful husband **2** infidel; неверни Турци infidel Turks **3** doubting, uncertain; неверен Тома doubting Thomas **4** *rare* false, fake; неверна копија counterfeit copy

неверие *n* & **неверица** *f see* неверба

неверник -ци *m* adulterer; infidel; unbeliever

неверница *f* (*fem. form*) *see* неверник; adulteress

неверност *f* infidelity, unfaithfulness; disloyalty

неверојатен -тна *adj* incredible, unbelievable; improbable, unlikely

неверојатно *adv* incredibly; improbably

неверојатност *f* incredibility; improbability, unlikelihood

неверство *n* **1** disloyalty; treachery, treason **2** adultery, <marital> infidelity

невесел *adj* joyless, glum, morose; sad; depressing

невеста *f* **1** bride; ❑ млада невеста a new boy/girl; a freshwater sailor **2** young wife, spouse; jac ќе ja земам неа за невеста I will take her as my wife **3** daughter-in-law; sister-in-law

невестин *adj* bride's

невестински *adj* bridal; невестинското (оро) the bridal dance

невестулка *f Zool*. weasel

невешт *adj* clumsy, awkward; unskilled; inexperienced; not resourceful

невешто *adv* clumsily, awkwardly; unskilfully

невиделица *f* **1** darkness; невиделица да фатиш! go to hell! **2** од невиделица, *see* невидено 1

невиден *adj* unseen; unknown; unprecedented; невидена болест unknown illness

невиден -дна *adj* **1** nondescript, ordinary **2** invisible

невидено *n* **1** од невидено suddenly, unexpectedly; од невидено пред мене се создаде suddenly he appeared before me **2** s.th. unseen

невидлив *adj* invisible

невидно *adv* **1** invisibly **2** unobtrusively, in a nondescript way (manner)

невикан *adj* uninvited; невикан гост uninvited guest

невин *adj* **1** harmless; innocent, guiltless **2** naive, simple **3** virgin, pure; chaste, virtuous, innocent

невиност *f* **1** harmlessness; innocence, guiltlessness **2** naivety, simplicity **3** virginity, purity; chastity, virtue

невистина *f* untruth, lie

невистинит *adj* untrue, false

невистински *adj* unreal; bogus

невкусен -сна *adj* tasteless, insipid; in bad taste

невнимание *n* **1** lack of attention; thoughtlessness; carelessness **2** disrespect; discourteousness, inattentiveness

невнимателен -лна *adj* **1** inattentive; thoughtless, careless **2** disrespectful; discourteous, inattentive (*towards s.o.*)

невнимателност *f see* невнимание

невозбудлив *adj* unexciting

невоздржлив *adj* hot-tempered; ungovernable; unrestrained

невозможен -жна *adj* **1** impossible; unrealizable, improbable **2** unbearable, insufferable

невозможно *adv* impossibly

невозможност *f* impossibility

невола *f* **1** trouble, misfortune **2** need, want

неволен[1] -лна *adj* **1** wretched, unfortunate, miserable **2** weak, feeble; болните и неволните the weak and infirm

неволен[2] -лна *adj* involuntary; unintentional, unwitting; inadvertent; spontaneous

неволник -ци *m* unlucky, miserable person; wretch, poor devil

неволница *f* (*fem. form*) *see* неволник

неволничав *adj* wretched, unfortunate, miserable

неволно *adv* involuntarily; unintentionally, unwittingly; inadvertently, accidentally

невообичаен *adj* unusual

невоодушевен *adj* **1** unenthusiastic **2** inanimate

невооружен *adj* unarmed

невоспитан *adj* ill-bred, rude; spoilt; невоспитани деца bad-mannered children

невоспитаност *f* lack of breeding, bad manners, rudeness

невработен *adj* unemployed

невработеност *f* unemployment

невралгија -ии *f* neuralgia

невралгичен -чна *adj* neuralgic

неврамотежен *adj* unbalanced; неврамотежен развој unbalanced growth

неврамотеженост *f* disequilibrium

неврастенија *f* neurasthenia

неврастеник -ци *m* neurasthenic

неврастеничен -чна *adj* neurasthenic

неврат *m* place of no return; отиде во неврат he/it disappeared; во неврат! go to the devil!

невреден -дна *adj* incapable; unfit; тој е стар и невреден за работа he is old and unfit for work

невреме *n* bad weather, storm; inopportune moment; дојдовте во невреме you've come at a bad time

неврзан *adj* unbound, free; non-aligned; incoherent; rambling; неврзан разговор rambling conversation; неврзани земји non-aligned countries

неврит *m Med.* neuritis

невроза *f Med.* neurosis

невролог -зи *m* neurologist

неврологија *f* neurology

неврон *m* neuron

невротичен -чна *adj* neurotic

неврохирург -зи *m* neurosurgeon

неврохирургија *f* neurosurgery

неврстен -сна *adj* **1** weak **2** under age, juvenile; неврстен син an under-age son

невтасан *adj* unripe, green (*also fig.*)

невтасаник -ци *m colloq.* fool, idiot, dolt

нега *f* care, nursing; rearing, raising

негар -гри *m* Negro

негарка *f* Negress

негарски *adj* Negro

негасен *adj* негасена вар unslaked lime, quicklime

негатив *m Photography* negative

негативен -вна *adj* negative; негативен резултат negative result

негативец -вци *m* actor typecast in villainous roles

негативност *f* negativeness

негатор *m* negationist

негаторство *n* negativism; the role or activity of a negationist

негација -ии *f* **1** negation, rejection, denial **2** *Gram.* negation

негде *adv* **1** somewhere; негде далеку somewhere far away **2** approximately; негде кај Велигден some time towards (around) Easter

негде-годе *adv* here and there

негдека *adv see* негде

негибнат *adj* untouched; intact

негира *pf & impf* **1** to deny, refuse **2** to retract, repudiate; to negate

него *pron* (*long form for the oblique cases, except dat., of* тој, он *and* тоа, она. *Used for emphasis with short form* го *and with prepositions*) him; го видов него I saw him; од него from him; со него with him; за него about/for him

негов, негова, негово, *pl* негови *possessive pron* his; неговите his people; his family; his relations

негоден -дна *adj* unfit, unsuitable

негодник -ци *m* scoundrel, rascal; good-for-nothing, ne'er-do-well

негодница *f* (*fem. form*) *see* негодник

негодува *impf* to disapprove, express dissatisfaction; to be indignant

негостољубив *adj* inhospitable

недалеку *adv* not far, close by

недамна *adv see* неодамна

недамнешен -шна *adj see* неодамнешен

недарежлив *adj* ungenerous, mean, miserly, stingy

недвижен -жна *adj* immobile; недвижен имот real estate

недвижнина *f* real estate, realty

недвижност *f* **1** *see* неподвижност **2** real estate

недвосмислен *adj* unambiguous; clear, categorical, explicit

недвосмисленост *f* unambiguousness; clarity, explicitness

недела *f* **1** Sunday; в недела every Sunday **2** week; сирна недела Shrove-tide; од недела во недела week after week

неделен -лна *adj* **1** Sunday *attrib.*; неделен ден Sunday **2** weekly

неделив *adj* indivisible; неделиви трошоци indivisible costs

неделкан *adj* unhewn; rough; coarse, crude; неделкано дрво rough-hewn/coarse/saw timber

неделник -ци *m* weekly (*newspaper, magazine*)

неделно *adv* weekly

недело *n* misdeed, crime

недисциплиниран *adj* undisciplined

недоаѓање *n* nonappearance, failure to come, absence

недоапица *adv* од недоапица suddenly, unexpectedly

недоброен -јна *adj f.p.* countless

недобронамерен -рна *adj* malicious, spiteful

недоварен *adj* half-cooked, underdone

недоверба *f* mistrust, distrust; lack of confidence (*in s.o. or s.th.*)

недоверлив *adj* mistrustful, distrustful, suspicious

недоверливост *f* mistrustful, distrustful, suspicious attitude

недоверчив *adj see* недоверлив

недоветен -тна *adj* slow-witted, stupid, obtuse; ❏ се прави недоветен to play dumb

недоветност *f* slow wits, stupidity, obtuseness

недоволен -лна *adj* **1** insufficient; unsatisfactory; недоволна вработеност underemployment **2** *see* незадоволен[2]

недоволник -ци *m see* незадоволник

недоволница *f see* незадоволница

недоволство *n see* незадоволност & незадоволство

недовршен *adj* incomplete, unfinished

недовршеност *f* incompleteness

недоглед *m* infinity; as far as the eye can see; во недоглед infinitely

недогледа *pf* to overlook, miss, fail to observe/consider

недогледен -дна *adj* limitless, endless, boundless, infinite

недогледува *impf* **1** to see poorly (with difficulty) **2** *impf of* недогледа

недограден *adj* half-built, unfinished

недоделкан *adj* **1** incompletely trimmed **2** *fig.* uncouth, coarse, crude, half-hewn; недоделкан човек crude (uncouth, unpolished) person

недозволен *adj* impermissible, prohibited, unauthorized; недозволени средства impermissible methods

недозреан *adj* **1** unripe, not fully ripe **2** *fig.* immature, not ready

недозрелост *f* **1** unripeness **2** *fig.* immaturity

недоѕидан *adj* partly built, half-built, unfinished

недојаде *pf* недојадов *1st p. sg aor.* to under-eat

недојадува *impf of* недојаде; to go hungry

недокажан *adj* **1** unproven **2** *fig.* stubborn

недокажлив *adj* unprovable, indemonstrable

недоквакан *adj colloq.* **1** prematurely born **2** *fig.* immature; untrained

недолжен -жна *adj* guiltless, innocent, harmless

недоличен -чна *adj* **1** indecent; unbecoming **2** corrupt

недоловлив *adj* **1** unattainable, unreachable; inconceivable **2** imperceptible, subtle; elusive

недомаќин *m* **1** spendthrift, squanderer, prodigal **2** good-for-nothing, rascal, ne'er-do-well

недомаќинка *f* (*fem. form*) *see* недомаќин

недоновче & **недоносче** *n* **1** premature baby **2** *fig.* abortive effort

недоносен *adj* immature (*of a foetus*), abortive

недооден -дна *adj* immeasurable, endless, boundless, limitless; недоодна гора endless forest

недооран *adj* incompletely ploughed

недоострен *adj* not sharpened completely

недоотепан *adj* not completely killed, not finished off

недопадлив *adj* unpleasant; not likeable

недопечен *adj* **1** partly baked, underdone, rare **2** *fig.* half-baked, poorly planned

недопиен *adj* unfinished (*of a drink*)

недопица *adv see* недоапица

недопишан *adj* not written out completely

недоплатен *adj* not fully paid

недоплетен *adj* not knitted to the end

недоправен *adj* half-finished (*of a building, etc.*)

недопржен *adj* partly fried, underdone

недопустлив *adj* impermissible; inadmissible

недопуштен *adj* prohibited, not allowed; unauthorized

недоразберија -ии *f colloq.* misunderstanding

недоразбирање *n* **1** misunderstanding, misinterpretation **2** disagreement

недоразбран *adj* insufficiently understood; неговите зборови останаа недоразбрани his words were not properly understood

недоразвиен *adj* **1** undeveloped, underdeveloped **2** not fully blooming

недоразвиеност *f* underdevelopment

недораснат *adj* immature

недораснатост *f* immaturity

недоречен *adj* understated

недореченост *f* understatement

недосетлив *adj* unimaginative; slow-witted; not resourceful

недосетливост *f* lack of imagination, dullness; lack of resourcefulness

недоследен -дна *adj* inconsistent; inconsequent

недоследност *f* inconsistency; inconsequence

недослушува *impf* not to hear well; to be hard of hearing

недособран *adj* not completely collected; данокот остана недособран the tax was not collected completely

недосолен *adj* not sufficiently salted

недоспан *adj* lacking sleep, tired

недоспива *impf of* недоспие; овие неколку дена сè недоспивам I haven't had enough sleep lately

недоспие *pf* недоспа *aor.* not to sleep enough

недостапен -пна *adj* **1** inaccessible, unattainable **2** unapproachable, haughty; reserved, distant

недостапност *f* **1** inaccessibility **2** unapproachability; reserve, distance

недостаса *pf* **1** not to arrive, not to reach (*in time*); not to ripen; not to succeed, manage **2** *see* недостигне

недостасан *adj* **1** unripe, green **2** *fig.* immature

недостасаност *f* **1** unripeness **2** *fig.* immaturity

недостасува *impf of* недостаса

недостаток -ци *m* **1** shortage, lack; deficiency; во недостаток на (од) in the absence of; како недостаток на for lack of **2** defect; mistake, fault

недостаточен -чна *adj* insufficient

недостаточност *f* insufficiency

недостиг *m* shortage, lack; poverty, want

недостига *impf* to be short, be out of (*s.th.*); to be lacking, missing, in short supply; (*with dat.*) to miss (*s.o.*); што ти недостига? what do you lack? му недостигаат пари he is short of money; ми недостигаш I miss you

недостигне *pf* недостигна *aor.* to run low, run out of (*s.th.*)

недостигнува *impf see* недостига

недостижен -жна *adj* inaccessible, unreachable, unattainable, out of reach; тајна недостижна за човечкиот ум a mystery beyond human understanding

недостижност *f* inaccessibility

недостоен -јна *adj* 1 unworthy, undeserving; тој е недостоен за такво место he is unworthy of such a position 2 dishonest; wicked; недостоен човек dishonest person; scoundrel

недостојност *f* unworthiness

недосторен *adj* 1 partly pickled 2 unripe, under-ripe

недосушен *adj* insufficiently dried

недотеран *adj* unfinished, roughly made, imperfect

недоумева *impf* to be puzzled, perplexed, be at a loss, be in a quandary

недоумение *n see* недоумица

недоумица *f* bewilderment, perplexity, quandary; doubt, hesitation

недоучен *adj* semi-educated; ❏ Господ да те чува од учен недоучен man may the Lord preserve you from a semi-educated man

недофатен -тна *adj* unreachable, inaccessible; out of reach

недофатлив *adj* unattainable, inaccessible; (*недоловлив*) imperceptible

недофатливост *f* inaccessibility; imperceptibility

недохранет *adj* underfed, undernourished

недохранетост *f* malnourishment

недраг *adj* unloved, unwanted; disagreeable, ugly

недраго *adv* unhappily, disagreeably; тоа што рече ми падна недраго I didn't like what he said

недран *adj* unskinned

недругар *m* enemy, foe

недругарски *adj* unfriendly, hostile; недругарска постапка unfriendly act

недругарство *n* unfriendly act/behaviour; enmity

недружељубив *adj* unfriendly

недружељубивост *f* unfriendliness

недуг *m* 1 ailment, illness, infirmity 2 physical disability, defect

недугав *adj* sickly, infirm, feeble; crippled, disabled; lame

недугавост *f* infirmity, feebleness; lameness

неѓубрен *adj* not manured, unfertilized

нееднаков *adj* unequal; uneven

нееднаквост *f* inequality; unevenness; disparity

нееластичен -чна *adj* inelastic, inflexible

неефикасен -сна *adj* inefficient

нежен -жна *adj* 1 tender, gentle; delicate, fine; pleasant 2 weak, sickly, fragile; нежно здравје poor health

неженет *adj* unmarried (*of a man*), single

неженство *n* celibacy, unmarried (single) state (*of a man*)

нежничи *impf* to be excessively tender; to indulge in caresses

нежно *adv* tenderly, gently; mildly; fondly, affectionately

нежност *f* 1 tenderness, gentleness; affection 2 delicacy, refinement, sensitivity

незабавен -вна *adj* uninteresting, dull, tedious

незабележан *adj* unnoticed, unobserved

незабележано *adv* 1 unnoticed 2 imperceptibly

незабележлив *adj* imperceptible

незаборавен -вна *adj* unforgettable, memorable; unforgotten

незаверен *adj* uncertified; незаверен препис uncertified copy (transcript)

незавиден -дна *adj* unenviable; pitiable, wretched; незавидна состојба unenviable state (plight)

независен -сна *adj* independent, free; *Gram.* independent, coordinate

независно *adv* 1 independently, freely 2 irrespective, regardless; независно од irrespective of; even if/ though

независност *f* independence, freedom; финансиска независност financial independence

незавршен *adj* unfinished, incomplete

незавршеност *f* incompleteness

незагреан *adj* unwarmed; lukewarm, tepid

незадоволен[1] *adj* unsatisfied

незадоволен[2] -лна *adj* discontented, dissatisfied, unhappy

незадоволеност *f* discontent, dissatisfaction

незадоволителен -лна *adj* unsatisfactory

незадоволник -ци *m* malcontent; grumbler

незадоволница *f* (*fem. form*) *see* незадоволник

незадоволност *f* & **незадоволство** *n* discontent, dissatisfaction

незадоволувачки *adj* unsatisfactory

незадолжителен -лна *adj* optional, dispensable

незадржлив *adj* irrepressible, unrestrainable; irresistible

незаздравен *adj* unhealed; незаздравена рана unhealed wound

незаинтересиран *adj* 1 uninterested 2 disinterested, detached, impartial

незаинтересираност *f* 1 lack of interest 2 disinterestedness

незаинтересуван *adj see* незаинтересиран

незајакнат *adj* frail, weak, feeble

незајакнатост *f* frailty, weakness, feebleness

незаконие -ија *n* illegality, unlawfulness; unlawful act

незаконит *adj* illegal, unlawful; незаконита постапка unlawful act

незаконитост *f* illegality, unlawfulness

незаконски *adj* illegal, unlawful; незаконска продажба/трговија illicit sale/trade

незакрепнат *adj* feeble, weak, frail

незакрепнатост *f* feebleness, weakness, frailty

незаменлив *adj* irreplaceable

незаменливост *f* irreplaceability

незамислив *adj* unthinkable; inconceivable, unimaginable; egregious; незамислива глупост egregious folly

незанимлив *adj* uninteresting, boring, dull

незапалив *adj* incombustible; non-inflammable

незапаметен[1] *adj* unheard-of, unprecedented

незапаметен[2] -тна *adj* ancient, immemorial; од незапаметно време from time immemorial

незапирен -рна *adj* ceaseless, uninterrupted, continuous; незапирен дожд continuous rain

незапознат *adj* unacquainted; uninformed, unversed

незапомнет *adj see* незапаметен[1]

незасегнат *adj* unaffected; not concerned; *fig.* untouched

незаситен[1] *adj* unsatisfied, unsatiated

незаситен[2] -тна *adj* insatiable

незаситност *f* insatiability

незаслужен *adj* unearned, unmerited, undeserved

незастарен *adj* current, still in effect; still valid

незастареност *f* currency, validity

незастарлив *adj* permanent; ageless, enduring, abiding

незатоплен *adj* unheated; unwarmed

незафатен *adj* not busy; disengaged; vacant; незафатени места unoccupied/vacant places (seats)

незафатеност *f* freedom; disengagement (*from work, obligations, etc.*)

незаштитен *adj* undefended; defenceless; unprotected, open

незаштитеност *f* defencelessness

незгода *f* mishap, accident; trouble, difficulty, misfortune

незгоден -дна *adj* inconvenient, inopportune, awkward; uncomfortable; unpleasant; во незгодно време, во незгоден час at an inconvenient (inopportune) time, at a bad time

незгрижен *adj* neglected, not provided for

незгриженост *f* neglect, neglected state

нездрав *adj* unhealthy, sickly; unwholesome; *colloq.* crazy; нездраво време unhealthy weather; нездрави односи unhealthy attitudes

нездравост *f* ill health; unwholesomeness

нездржлив *adj* unrestrainable; unrestrained, unbridled

нездржливост *f* unrestrainable nature; lack of restraint/control

неземен -мна *adj* unearthly; elevated, sublime, exalted

незнаен -јна *adj* unknown; незнаен делија unknown warrior; ❑ незнајни пари untold riches; знајни и незнајни known and unknown (*people*)

незнаење *n* ignorance

незнајник -ци *m* stranger

незнајница *f* (*fem. form*) *see* незнајник

незнајно *adv* unknowingly; unknown

незнајност *f* unfamiliarity; uncertainty

незначителен -лна *adj* insignificant, unimportant

незрел *adj* unripe; immature, under age; незрел човек immature person

незрелост *f* immaturity

неизбежен -жна *adj* unavoidable; inevitable; certain

неизбежност *f* inevitability

неизбричен *adj see* небричен

неизбришлив *adj* indelible; неизбришливи траги indelible traces

неизброен -јна *adj* countless, innumerable

неизбројлив *adj* countless, innumerable

неизведлив *adj* impracticable, unfeasible

неизвежбан *adj* unpractised; untrained

неизвесен -сна *adj* uncertain; unsure; doubtful; vague, indefinite

неизвесност *f* uncertainty; doubtfulness; vagueness, indefiniteness; држи некого во неизвесност to keep s.o. in suspense; to keep s.o. guessing

неизвршлив *adj* impossible; impracticable, unfeasible

неизвршување *n* non-fulfilment, breach, default, non-compliance

неизгладлив *adj* indelible; permanent, lasting

неизговорлив *adj* unpronounceable

неизгорлив *adj* incombustible, non-inflammable

неиздаден *adj* unpublished

неизделкан *adj* **1** coarse, rough, rough-hewn, unpolished, unrefined (*also fig.*) **2** *fig.* unstudied, unresearched

неиздравен *adj see* неоздравен

неиздржан *adj* weak, poor; poorly made; incomplete; *fig.* half-baked; неиздржан стил poor, uneven style

неиздржаност *f* incompleteness

неиздржлив *adj* unbearable, unendurable; insupportable, intolerable

неизјаснет *adj* unexplained

неизјаснетост *f* inexplicability

неизлечив *adj* incurable

неизлечивост *f* incurability

неизменлив *adj* unchangeable, inalterable, immutable

неизменливост *f* immutability

неизмерен -рна *adj* immense, immeasurable; endless, vast; неизмерна радост immense joy

неизмерност *f* immensity, vastness

неизмиен *adj* unwashed

неизмирлив *adj* irreconcilable

неизоден -дна *adj* immense, vast, endless; неизодна гора vast forest

неизоставен -вна *adj* obligatory, compulsory

неизоставно *adv* compulsorily; without fail

неизразителен -лна *adj* indistinct, faint, unclear

неизразителност *f* indistinctness

неизразлив *adj* inexpressible, ineffable, unutterable; indescribable

неизречен *adj* unsaid, unexpressed

неимашен -шна *adj* poor, needy

неинтересен -сна *adj* uninteresting

неискажан *adj* **1** unexpressed, unsaid **2** *see* неискажлив

неискажлив *adj* inexpressible, unutterable, ineffable; indescribable

неискоренлив *adj* ineradicable; ingrained

неискористен *adj* unused, unexploited; неискористени средства unspent funds

неискрен *adj* insincere; hypocritical, feigned

неискреност *f* insincerity; hypocrisy; pretence

неискусен -сна *adj* inexperienced; unskilled, untrained

неискусност *f* inexperience; lack of training/skill

неиспан *adj see* ненаспан

неиспаност *f see* ненаспаност

неиспитан *adj* **1** untried, untested; unexplored **2** unquestioned, not interrogated

неиспишан *adj* **1** unwritten **2** clean, unmarked (*of paper*)

неисплатен *adj* unpaid; неисплатени долгови unpaid (outstanding) debts; неисплатена меница bill in abeyance

неисплатлив *adj* that cannot be repaid

неисползуван *adj* unused, unexploited

неисправен -вна *adj* **1** (*за човек*) lax, remiss; incorrigible **2** (*за машина*) defective; out of order

неисправност *f* **1** laxity; incorrigibility **2** defectiveness

неистреблив *adj* indestructible, ineradicable

неисцрпен -пна *adj* inexhaustible

нејавнат *adj* **1** unmounted, not yet ridden; нејавнат коњ a horse not yet broken in **2** (*за човек*) inexperienced in riding

нејаден *adj* hungry, not having eaten

нејак *adj* weak, feeble

нејасен -сна *adj* indistinct, unintelligible, unclear; vague

нејасност *f* indistinctness; vagueness; unintelligibility

нејатка *f* **1** day of total fasting **2** *Rel.* the eve of Epiphany (*18th January*)

нејзе *pron* (*long dat. form from* таа, она; *used with the short form* ú) <to> her; нејзе ѝ реков I told her

нејзин, нејзина, нејзино, *pl* нејзини *possessive pron* her, hers; нејзините her family, her relations

нејќе *impf* **1** not to want (*да – то*); нејќе да го земе he doesn't want to take it **2** not to love, not to desire

нека *part* (*expressing a wish, an order, a request, approval, etc.*) let . . . ; all right! нека дојде let him come! нека го! leave him alone! let him have it his own way! нека ти е алал! good luck to you! *Austral.* good on you!

некадарен -рна *adj* incapable, unable, unfit, worthless, feckless

некадарник -ци *m* incapable, unfit man

некадарница *f* (*fem. form*) *see* некадарник

некадарност *f* incapability, inability, unfitness, helplessness

некаде *adv* somewhere; некаде кај Скопје somewhere near Skopje; некаде кај Божиќ around Christmastime; одат некаде далеку they are going somewhere far away

неказнет *adj* unpunished

неказнето *adv* unpunished, with impunity

неказнив *adj* unpunishable

некако *adv* somehow, in some way; ќе излеземе некако на крај we'll manage somehow

некаков -ква *adj* some <sort of>, a, any <kind of>; некаков човек some person; се дружи со некаков си неранимајко he hangs around with some good-for-nothing

неканет *adj* uninvited; на неканети гости местото им е зад врата *prov.* in time every guest wears out his welcome

некастрен *adj* untrimmed; unpruned; дрво некастрено untrimmed tree; ❑ за него треба дрво некастрено he needs a good hiding

неквалификуван & **неквалифициран** *adj* unqualified; неквалификуван работник unqualified workman

некни *adv* the day before yesterday

некога *adv see* некогаш

некогаш *adv* at one time, once; sometimes; some time; ќе дојдам некогаш кога не ќе се надевате I'll come some time when you don't expect me; некогаш вели едно, некогаш друго sometimes he says one thing, sometimes another

некогашен -шна *adj* former, erstwhile, one-time

некого *pron* (*oblique case form, except dat., from* некој 2) somebody, someone; нашле некого they have found s.o.; со некого with s.o.

некој -кои *pron* **1** some, пред некој ден a few (some) days ago; по некое време after some time **2** (*only m; dat.* некому; *other cases* некого) someone, somebody; некој чука на врата s.o. is knocking at the door; ❑ некој и нешто person of consequence; a big shot

некојпат *adv see* некогаш

неколку *adv* some, a few; неколку луѓе some people; неколку дена a few days

неколкугодишен -шна *adj* of/lasting several years; *Bot.* perennial; неколкугодишна практика several years' practice

неколкудневен -вна *adj* of/lasting several (a few) days; неколкудневен одмор a few days' rest

неколкумесечен -чна *adj* of/lasting several (a few) months

неколкумина *adv see* неколцина

неколкучасовен -вна *adj* of/lasting several (a few) hours

неколцина *adv* (*of men and mixed company*) several, a few

некомпетентен -тна *adj* lacking competence; incompetent; not authoritative

некомпетентност *f* incompetence; lack of authority

некомпромитиран & **некомпромитуван** *adj* uncompromised

некому *pron* (*dat. form from* некој 2) <to/for> somebody; ❑ некому мајка, некому маштеа one law for the rich, another for the poor

неконвертибилен -лна *adj* non-convertible; неконвертибилна валута soft currency

неконсеквентен -тна *adj* inconsistent

неконсеквентност *f* inconsistency

некоректен -тна *adj* improper, incorrect; tactless; некоректна постапка improper act

некоректност *f* impropriety, incorrectness; tactlessness

некорисен -сна *adj* useless; vain; unprofitable

некорисност *f* uselessness; vainness

некористољубив *adj* unselfish, selfless; disinterested

некритичен -чна *adj* uncritical

некритичност *f* uncritical attitude

некролог -зи *m* **1** obituary **2** funeral oration

некрстен *adj* unbaptized, unchristened

некрстенко -овци *m* unbaptized person

нектар *m Bot., Myth.* nectar

некултурен -рна *adj* uncultured; vulgar, uncivilized, uncouth

некурентен -тна *adj* slow-moving, in low demand; некурентна стока slow-moving goods

нелегален -лна *adj* illegal

нелегалност *f* illegality

нели **1** (*interrogative part.*) така беше, нели? that's how it was, isn't it? нели ти реков да не одиш кај него? didn't I tell you not to go to his place? **2** *conj* as soon as; when; as, since, if; е, нели е таков, остави го well, if it's like that, leave it

неликвиден -дна *adj* insolvent; неликвидна актива unmarketable assets

нелогичен -чна *adj* illogical; senseless

нелогичност *f* illogicality; senselessness

нелојален -лна *adj* disloyal; unfair; нелојална конкуренција unfair competition

нелојалност *f* disloyalty

нелуѓе *pl* (*of* нечовек) monsters, brutes

нељубезен -зна *adj* unfriendly, unkind; impolite, discourteous; unhelpful

нељубезност *f* unfriendliness, unkindness; impoliteness, discourtesy; unhelpfulness

нем[1] *m* humidity, dampness; stale air

нем[2]   *adj* **1** mute, dumb; глув и нем deaf and dumb; ❏ нем како риба mute as a fish **2** tacit, unspoken, wordless; нема љубов unspoken love **3** *fig.* silent, noiseless; нокта е нема the night is silent

нема   *impf* (*see* има) **I 1** *impers.* there is no/not; нема никого there's no one; го нема he isn't here; нема ништо за јадење there's nothing to eat; нема зошто there is no reason why; (*in reply to thanks*) don't mention it! my pleasure! you're welcome! ❏ нема што no doubt; that's it; make no mistake; <има> да те нема! get lost! go away! го нема мајсторот nothing will come of it; крај му нема there is no end to it; нема гајле! don't worry! *Austral.* no worries; нема сметка it doesn't pay, it's not worth it; нема што нема you name it – we have it **2** not to have; нема време to have no time; to be out of time; тоа дете нема ни пет години that child isn't even five; вчера немавме состанок we didn't have a meeting yesterday; нема верба во него he doesn't trust him; нема намера he has no intention; ❏ немам скршен динар I haven't got a bean; I'm broke; немаше ни опинци на нозете he had nothing; немам абер I have no idea; search me! немам ништо против . . . I have nothing against . . . **II** *personal and impers.* (*as negative auxiliary verb for perfect and future tenses, corresponding to affirmative* има, *ќе*) нема работено во фабрика he has never worked in a factory; нема да дојдам I won't come

немажена   *adj* unmarried, single (*of a woman*)

немај-каде   *adv* **1** до немај-каде exceedingly, extremely; тој беше до немај-каде сиромав he was extremely poor **2** од немај-каде from sheer necessity; having no alternative

немак   -ци *m* dumb man, mute

немарен   -рна *adj* careless, negligent, inattentive; nonchalant

немарност   *f* carelessness, negligence, inattentiveness; nonchalance

нематен   -тна *adj* needy, poor

немачка[1]   *f* poverty, want

немачка[2]   *f* (*fem. form*) *see* немак

немачник   -ци *m f.p. see* немак

немаштија   *f* poverty, want, destitution, indigence, penury

немаштина   *f see* немаштија

немее   *impf* to be dumb, speechless; to be silent

неменлив   *adj* unchanging; invariable, immutable; *Gram.* non-inflected, indeclinable

неменливост   *f* invariability, immutability; *Gram.* lack of inflection

немерлив   *adj* immeasurable; immense, boundless

неметáл   *m* non-metal

немец   -мци *m see* немак

немечки   *adj* relating to a dumb person

немешање   *n*   non-interference;   non-intervention; немешање во внатрешните работи на една земја non-interference in the internal affairs of a country

немиен   *adj* unwashed; немиен отиде на работа he went to work without washing

немиенко   -овци *m colloq.* dirty person, sloven

немил   *adj* **1** unloved, unwanted **2** disagreeable, unpleasant, ugly

немилосрден   -дна *adj* merciless, pitiless

немилосрдност   *f* mercilessness, pitilessness

немилост   *f* disfavour; падне во немилост to fall into disfavour

немилуван   *adj* unloved

неминовен   -вна *adj* unavoidable, inevitable, ineluctable

неминовност   *f* inevitability

немир   *m* restlessness, disquiet, uneasiness; excitement; unrest, agitation

немирен   -рна *adj* **1** restless, agitated **2** mischievous, unruly, naughty; немирно дете naughty child

немирник   -ци *m* mischievous little boy

немирница   *f* (*fem. form*) *see* немирник

немирнотија   *f*   restlessness,   disquiet;   unrest; naughtiness

немислен   *adj* unexpected, unforeseen; (*as noun usu. n*) ❏ Господ да те чува од немислено God preserve you from unforeseen trouble

немислим   *adj see* незамислив

немлив   *adj* damp; немлив ѕид damp wall

неможен   -жна *adj* impossible; impracticable

неможно   *adv* impossibly

неможност   *f* impossibility

немој, *pl* немојте (*negative imperative, prohibition*) don't; ❏ ма немој! you don't say! no kidding!

неморал   *m* immorality; perversion

неморален   -лна *adj* immoral; perverted; amoral

неморалност   *f* immorality; perversion; depravity

немост   *f* dumbness, muteness

немоќ   *f* weakness, infirmity; helplessness; impotence

немоќен   -ќна *adj* weak, infirm; helpless; impotent; немоќен сум да ви помогнам I am unable to help you

немоќност   *f* weakness, infirmity; helplessness

немош   *f* weakness, infirmity, illness

немошен   -шна *adj* infirm, ill, sick; болеста го направи немошен his illness enfeebled him

немошница   *f* weakness, infirmity, illness

немски   *adv arch.* inarticulately

немтур   *m* gloomy, taciturn, sullen, surly person

немтурица   *f* **1** *see* немачка[2] **2** *see* немтурка

немтурка   *f* (*fem. form*) *see* немтур

нему   *pron* (*long dat. form from* тој, он *and* тоа, она; *used with the short form* му) <to> him; нему ништо немој да му кажеш don't say anything to him

немузикáлен   -лна *adj* unmusical

немузикáлност   *f* lack of talent for or interest in music

нена   *f child.* mummy, mum

ненавикнат   *adj* unaccustomed

ненавист   *f see* омраза

ненадарен   *adj* untalented, not gifted

ненадеен   -јна *adj* sudden, unexpected

ненадеж   *f* од ненадеж suddenly, unexpectedly

ненадежен   -жна *adj* unreliable, untrustworthy

ненадејно   *adv* suddenly, unexpectedly

ненадејност   *f* suddenness, unexpectedness

ненадлежен   -жна *adj* unauthorized, incompetent

ненадминат   *adj* unsurpassed; peerless, unrivalled, matchless, second to none

ненадоместлив   *adj* irreparable, irretrievable, irreplaceable; irredeemable

ненакриет   *adj* intact, whole, entire, unimpaired

ненакршен   *adj* intact; unbroken, whole; ненакршен леб unbroken loaf

ненамерен   -рна *adj* unintentional; chance, accidental

ненаоружан *adj see* невооружен

ненапаѓање *n* non-aggression; пакт за ненапаѓање non-aggression pact

ненапасен *adj* not <having> grazed; говедарот ги дотера говедата ненапасени the cowherd brought in the cattle ungrazed

ненаручан *adj* not having lunched/eaten (*sufficiently*); unfed

ненаселен *adj* uninhabited, empty, waste

ненаситен[1] *adj* unsatisfied

ненаситен[2] -тна *adj* insatiable; greedy, avid

ненаситник -ци *m* glutton; greedy person

ненаситница *f (fem. form) see* ненаситник

ненаситност *f* insatiability; greed, gluttony

ненаспан & ненаспиен *adj* sleepy

ненаспаност *f* sleepiness; lack of sleep

ненаучен -чна *adj* unscientific, unscholarly; ненаучни методи unscientific methods

ненахранет *adj* **1** unfed **2** not fattened

неначнат *adj* intact; uncut, whole, entire

ненормален -лна *adj* abnormal; insane, mad; ненормален раст abnormal growth

ненормалност *f* abnormality

неносен *adj* unworn; неносени алишта unworn (brand new) clothes

ненужен -жна *adj* unnecessary, superfluous, surplus, unwanted

необѕирање *n* disregard, neglect

необичен -чна *adj* unusual, strange; extraordinary, exceptional

необјаснив *adj* inexplicable

необлечен *adj* undressed, naked; partly dressed

необмислен *adj* imprudent; hasty, rash; ill-considered

необмисленост *f* imprudence; haste, rashness

необоснован *adj* unjustified, unfounded, groundless

необоснованост *f* groundlessness, baselessness

необработен *adj* uncultivated, unworked; unstudied; необработена земја untilled (uncultivated) land; необработено прашање unexplored issue

необработлив *adj* untillable; необработлива земја untillable land

необразован *adj* uneducated

необразованост *f* lack of education

необременет *adj* unburdened

необуздан *adj* unbridled; violent

необузданост *f* lack of restraint; violence

необучен *adj* untrained

неовенат *adj* not faded, fresh; неовенати цвеќиња/ лисја fresh flowers/leaves

неограничен *adj* unlimited, unrestricted; unbounded; неограничена власт unlimited power, authority; неограничени права unlimited rights

неограниченост *f* limitlessness

неодамна *adv* recently

неодамнешен -шна *adj* recent

неодбирлив *adj* indistinct; unintelligible

неодбранлив *adj* indefensible

неодговорен -рна *adj* irresponsible

неодговорност *f* irresponsibility

неодложен -жна *adj* urgent, pressing; неодложна работа urgent work (matter)

неодмерен *adj* uncontrolled; tactless; thoughtless, inconsiderate

неодобрителен -лна *adj* disapproving, *see* неодобрувачки

неодобрувачки *adj* disapproving; неодобрувачки поглед disapproving look

неодреден *adj see* неопределен

неодреденост *f see* неопределеност

неоженет *adj see* неженет

неоздравен *adj* not having recovered (*from an illness*)

неокупиран *adj* unoccupied (*by hostile forces*), free; неокупиран крај unoccupied region

неолит *m* the neolithic period

неологизам -зми *m* neologism

неомажена *adj see* немажена

неон *m Chem.* neon

неонски *adj* neon; неонска светлина neon light

неопарен *adj* not burned (scalded); uninjured, undamaged

неопасен -сна *adj* not dangerous, safe; harmless

неопеан *adj* unsung (*also fig.*)

неопиплив *adj* intangible

неопитен -тна *adj* inexperienced, unskilled, untrained

неопитност *f* inexperience

неопишан *adj* **1** undescribed **2** indescribable

неоплоден *adj* unfertilized; неоплодено јајце unfertilized egg

неоправдан *adj* unjustified; unjustifiable, inexcusable; неоправдан изостанок unexcused/unexplained absence

неопределен *adj* indefinite; vague; undecided; *Gram.* неопределен начин infinitive

неопределеност *f* indefiniteness; vagueness; uncertainty; undecidedness

неоптоварен *adj see* необременет

неопфатен -тна *adj* immense, immeasurable, endless

неопфатност *f* immensity, endlessness, boundlessness

неопходен -дна *adj* indispensable, essential; неопходна потреба pressing need

неопходно *adv* indispensably, urgently; неопходно потребно absolutely necessary, essential

неопходност *f* necessity; absolute need, emergency

неорганизиран *adj* **1** unorganized; disorganized **2** (*of a person*) who is not a member of an organization

неорганизираност *f* lack of organization

неоргански *adj* inorganic; неорганска природа inorganic nature; неорганска хемија inorganic chemistry

неориентиран *adj* disorientated

неосетен -тна *adj* **1** slight, imperceptible **2** *see* неосетлив

неосетлив *adj* insensitive, unfeeling, callous; insensible; imperceptible

неосетливост *f* insensitivity; insensibility; *Med.* душевна неосетливост mental insensitivity; полова неосетливост frigidity

неосквернет *adj* unprofaned, unsullied, pure

неоснован *adj* unfounded, groundless, unjustified

неоснованост *f* groundlessness

неоспорен -рна *adj* beyond dispute, indisputable; undisputed; неоспорни докази indisputable proofs

неоспорност *f* indisputability

неостварен *adj* unrealized, unfulfilled

неостварлив *adj* unrealizable; unfeasible

неоти *part colloq.* (*expressing mild doubt*) who knows,

I doubt that . . . ; неоти си прашал! I doubt whether you really asked!

неоткажлив *adj see* неотповиклив

неоткриен *adj* undiscovered; unrevealed; undetected

неотповикан *adj* unrevoked

неотповиклив *adj* irrevocable, unalterable, unconditional; peremptory, absolute; неотповиклива заповед peremptory command

неотповикливост *f* irrevocability

неотстапен -пна *adj* persistent, relentless; неотстапна мисла persistent (nagging, constant) thought

неотстаплив *adj* unyielding, unremitting, insistent

неотстапно *adv* persistently, relentlessly; unflinchingly; се бори неотстапно to fight doggedly

неотстранлив *adj* unavoidable, inevitable, ineluctable, certain; inalienable

неотстранливост *f* inevitability, certainty; inalienability

неотуѓив *adj* inalienable; неотуѓиво право inalienable right

неофицијáлен -лна *adj* unofficial, informal; неофицијален разговор unofficial talks

неоформен *adj* unformed; incomplete; неоформен карактер unformed character

неоформеност *f* unformed nature; incompleteness; *fig.* immaturity

неоценет *adj* not corrected, unmarked (*of schoolwork*)

неоценлив *adj* invaluable, precious; од неоценлива вредност of inestimable value

неочекуван *adj* unexpected, sudden, unforeseen

неоштетен *adj* unharmed, undamaged, intact

Непал *m* Nepal

Непалец -лци *m* Nepalese

Непалка *f (fem. form) see* Непалец

непалски *adj* Nepalese

непарен -рна *adj* odd; непарни броеви odd numbers

непечен *adj* not <sufficiently> baked/roasted; underdone, rare

непипнат *adj* not touched; intact

неписмен *adj* **1** illiterate; неписмени луѓе illiterate people; неписмен состав illiterate composition **2** *fig.* uneducated

неписменост *f* illiteracy

непишан *adj* unwritten; непишано правило unwritten rule

неплатен *adj* unpaid, overdue; неплатен одмор unpaid leave

непловен -вна *adj* unnavigable; непловна река unnavigable river

неплоден -дна *adj* infertile, sterile, barren

непобеден -дна *adj see* непобедлив

непобедлив *adj* invincible, unconquerable

непобедливост *f* invincibility

непобитен -тна *adj* irrefutable

непобитност *f* irrefutability

неповикан *adj* uncalled, uninvited, unasked

неповолен -лна *adj* unfavourable, unsuitable; unpleasant, bad

неповолност *f* unsuitability

неповрат *m see* неврат

неповратен -тна *adj* irretrievable, irreplaceable; irrevocable; неповратна загуба irretrievable loss

неповреден *adj* unharmed, unhurt

неповредлив *adj* invulnerable; inviolable

неповредливост *f* invulnerability; inviolability

неповторлив *adj* unique, unequalled

неповторливост *f* uniqueness

непогоден -дна *adj* inconvenient, unsuitable, unfavourable

непогодица *f* trouble, difficulty; mishap; inconvenience

непогрешен -шна *adj* unerring; infallible

непогрешност *f* infallibility

неподатлив *adj* inflexible; unmanageable; stubborn

неподатливост *f* inflexibility; unmanageableness; stubbornness

неподвижен -жна *adj* **1** immobile, immovable; motionless, stationary, fixed **2** sedentary

неподвижност *f* **1** immobility, motionlessness **2** sedentary nature, character

неподготвен *adj* unprepared; untrained

неподготвеност *f* unpreparedness; lack of training

неподелен *adj* undivided; unanimous

неподмитлив *adj* incorruptible

неподмитливост *f* incorruptibility

неподнослив *adj* unbearable; insufferable, intolerable

неподражлив *adj* inimitable

непожелен -лна *adj* undesirable, unwanted; непожелни последици undesirable consequences

непознат *adj* unknown

непозната *f Math.* unknown

непоклатлив *adj* strong, firm, unshakeable

непоколеблив *adj* immovable, unshakeable, firm; steady

непоколебливост *f* immovability, firmness; steadiness

непокорен -рна *adj* disobedient; unruly, rebellious

непокорност *f* disobedience

неполезен -зна *adj* useless, futile, vain

неполитички *adj* non-political; apolitical

неполн *adj* **1** not full **2** incomplete

неполнолетен -тна *adj* (*малолетен*) juvenile, underage

неполнолетност *f* (*малолетство*) minority

неполноправен -вна *adj* deprived of certain rights, disfranchised

непоматен *adj* undisturbed, untroubled, serene, unalloyed; непоматена радост unalloyed joy

непомирлив *adj* irreconcilable; непомирливи противречности irreconcilable contradictions

непомирливост *f* irreconcilability

непомрачен *adj* untroubled, serene; непомрачена среќа serene happiness

непонищтлив *adj* irrevocable, irreversible

непополнет *adj* unfilled

непоправлив *adj* incorrigible, incurable, habitual; irreparable; непоправлива грешка irreparable error

непоправливост *f* incorrigibility, incurability; irreparability

непопулáрен -рна *adj* unpopular

непопулáрност *f* unpopularity

непопустлив *adj* intransigent, unyielding; persistent; obstinate

непопустливост *f* intransigence; persistence; obstinacy

непорочен -чна *adj* irreproachable, unimpeachable, blameless; innocent

непорочност *f* irreproachability, blamelessness; innocence

непосветен *adj* undedicated; uninitiated; unordained; unconsecrated

непосилен -лна *adj* very difficult, beyond one's strength, superhuman; непосилни напори superhuman efforts

непослушен -шна *adj* disobedient; непослушно дете disobedient child

непослушност *f* disobedience

непосреден -дна *adj* direct, immediate, first-hand

непосредно *adv* directly, immediately, right near

непосредност *f* directness, immediacy

непостижен -жна *adj* unattainable; inaccessible; непостижна цел unattainable goal

непостојан *adj* changing; unstable, changeable, fickle

непостојаност *f* changeability, instability, fickleness

непостојанство *n see* непостојаност

непотеглив *adj* lazy, slow, sluggish; weak, irresolute, feckless; unenterprising

непотегливост *f* laziness, slowness, sluggishness; weakness of will, irresoluteness, fecklessness; lack of enterprise, initiative

непотткован *adj* 1 unshod (*of a horse*) 2 *fig.* unprepared; not ready; untrained, uneducated

непоткуплив *adj* incorruptible

непоткупливост *f* incorruptibility

непотполн *adj* incomplete

непотребен -бна *adj* unnecessary; useless; superfluous

непотстрижен *adj* (*за коса*) untrimmed; (*за овца*) unshorn

непочитание *n see* непочитување

непочитување *n* disrespect; disregard; dishonouring

неправ *adj* 1 false; counterfeit 2 unjust, unfair

неправда *f* injustice

неправдина *f see* неправда

неправеден -дна *adj* 1 unjust, unfair 2 wrong

неправедност *f* injustice

неправилен -лна *adj* 1 irregular (*in form, shape*); неправилен четириаголник irregular tetragon (quadrilateral) 2 inaccurate, incorrect, wrong; неправилен заклучок wrong conclusion

неправилност *f* irregularity; inaccuracy

неправина *f* injustice

неправо *adv* unjustly, unfairly

непрактичен -чна *adj* impractical; непрактичен човек impractical person; непрактични алишта impractical (unsuitable) clothes

непрактичност *f* impracticality

непран *adj* unwashed, dirty

непранко -овци *m* unwashed boy, man; dirty person

непрано *n coll.* dirty linen/clothes

непреводлив *adj* untranslatable

непрегледен -дна *adj* 1 confused, muddled; lacking clarity 2 immense, vast

непрегледност *f* 1 lack of clarity 2 immensity, vastness

непредвиден *adj* unforeseen, unexpected, sudden; непредвидени тешкотии unforeseen difficulties; непредвидени трошоци contingent costs

непредвидлив *adj* unforeseeable, unpredictable

непредвидливост *f* unpredictability

непреземлив *adj* impregnable, inaccessible

непрежален[1] *adj* unforgotten

непрежален[2] -лна *adj* unforgettable

непрекинат *adj* uninterrupted, continuous; permanent, enduring

непрекинато *adv* continuously; permanently

непрекинлив *adj* uninterrupted, uninterruptible, continuous

непремислен *adj* ill-considered; hare-brained; hasty, rash; inconsiderate

непремисленост *f* haste, rashness; inconsiderateness

непренослив *adj* not portable; untransferable; непреносливо право inalienable right; непренослива меница non-negotiable bill of exchange (draft)

непреоден -дна *adj Gram.* intransitive

непреодност *f* intransitivity

непреодолив *adj* invincible; insurmountable, insuperable

непреодоливост *f* invincibility; insuperability

непрестаен -јна *adj* continuous, uninterrupted; permanent

непрестајно *adv* continuously, uninterruptedly; permanently

непресушен -шна *adj* inexhaustible; непресушен извор inexhaustible source

непресушлив *adj* inexhaustible; непресушливи реки inexhaustible rivers; *see* непресушен

непретпазлив *adj* incautious, not careful, heedless, unwary

непретпазливост *f* incautiousness, heedlessness, unwariness

непречистен *adj* unrefined; not cleared up, unsettled; непречистен текст unrevised text; непречистени сметки unsettled accounts

неприбран *adj* disorderly, untidy; slovenly, sloppy

непривикнат *pt see* ненавикнат

непривлечен -чна *adj* unattractive

непривлечност *f* unattractiveness

непригоден -дна *adj* inappropriate, unsuitable; improper

неприготвен *adj* unprepared, unready

неприемлив *adj* unacceptable; inadmissible

непризнат *adj* unrecognized

непризнателен -лна *adj* ungrateful

непризнателост *f* ingratitude

непријавен *adj* undeclared; unsigned, unregistered; непријавени приходи undeclared income

непријател *m* enemy, foe; ❑ крвни непријатели sworn enemies

непријателка *f* (*fem. form*) *see* непријател

непријателски *adj* unfriendly, hostile

непријателство *n* unfriendliness; enmity, hostility

непријателствува *impf* to be enemies

непријатен -тна *adj* unpleasant

непријатност *f* unpleasantness; trouble, difficulty

неприкосновен *adj* inviolable, untouchable, immune; sacred, revered

неприкосновеност *f* inviolability, immunity; sacredness, sanctity

неприкриен *adj* unconcealed, open

неприлика *f* trouble; ❑ во неприлика in the mire; in hot water; запаѓа во неприлики to get into trouble; to get into hot water

неприличен -чна *adj* unseemly, indecent; inappropriate, unsuitable, inconvenient

неприличност *f* unseemliness, indecency; inconvenience

непринуден *adj* not forced, natural; unaffected

непринудено *adv* unaffectedly, sincerely; without embarrassment, unconstrainedly; се насмее непринудено to smile sincerely; се чувствува непринудено to feel at ease

непринуденост *f* ease; informality; naturalness

непринципиéлен -лна *adj* having no principles; inconsistent; unprincipled

неприроден -дна *adj* unnatural

неприспособен *adj* unadapted, unsuited (*to*)

непристапен -пна *adj* unapproachable; inaccessible; incomprehensible; непристапен за народните маси incomprehensible to the common people

непристапност *f* unapproachability; inaccessibility; incomprehensibility

непристоен -jна *adj* indecent; rude, crude, impolite

непристоjност *f* indecency; rudeness, impoliteness

непристрасно *adj* dispassionately, impartially; justly, fairly; objectively

непристрасност *f* impartiality; justness, fairness; objectivity

непристрастен -сна *adj* dispassionate, impartial; just, fair; objective

неприфатлив *adj* unacceptable

неприфатливост *f* unacceptability

непробоен -jна *adj* impenetrable; bullet-proof

непроверен *adj* unchecked, unverified; непроверени податоци unchecked data, information; непроверени вести unconfirmed news (reports)

непровиден -дна *adj* opaque, non-transparent; непровидно стакло opaque glass

непровидност *f* opaqueness

непродуктѝвен -вна *adj* unproductive

непродуктѝвност *f* unproductiveness

непроѕирен -рна *adj* opaque; non-transparent

непрокопсан *adj colloq.* bad, rotten, no-good; dissolute

непрокопсаник -ци *m colloq.* rascal, wretch, good-for-nothing

непрокопсаница *f colloq.* (*fem. form*) *see* непрокопсаник

непрокопсаност *f colloq.* rottenness

непрокопсиjа *f colloq.* rottenness

непроменлив *adj* unchangeable, stable, steady; unalterable; непроменливо време stable weather

непроменливост *f* stability, steadiness

непромислен *adj* ill-considered, hare-brained; hasty, rash; inconsiderate

непромисленост *f* haste, rashness; inconsiderateness

непрониклив *adj* undiscerning, obtuse; abstruse

непроникливост *f* obtuseness; abstruseness

непрооден[1] *adj, in the expression* непроодено дете crawling infant, toddler

непрооден[2] -дна *adj* impassable, impenetrable; непроодна шума impenetrable forest

непрописен -сна *adj* contrary to regulations; incorrect; illegal; непрописна брзина excessive speed

непропорционáлен -лна *adj* disproportionate

непропустлив *adj* waterproof, impermeable; essential, not to be missed

непропустливост *f* impermeability

непросветен *adj* uneducated, unenlightened

непросветеност *f* lack of education/enlightenment

непростим *adj* unpardonable, unforgivable; inexcusable

непростимо *adv* unpardonably, unforgivably; inexcusably

непушач *m* non-smoker

непце *n* palate (*also Phon.*); мекото непце the soft palate

непчен *adj* palatal; *Phon.* непчен глас palatal sound

неработен[1] *adj* unworked, untilled; unworked, raw

неработен[2] -тна *adj* idle; free; неработен ден day off, holiday

неработење *n* inactivity, idleness

неработник -ци *m* idler, slacker

неработница *f* (*fem. form*) *see* неработник

неработност *f* disinclination to work, idleness

неработоспособен -бна *adj* unable to work; incapable of work; disabled

нерадо *adv* reluctantly, unwillingly; нерадо прави нешто to do s.th. reluctantly

нерадосен -сна *adj* joyless, depressing, sad

нерадост *f* sadness; s.th. unpleasant; старост – нерадост *prov.* old age is no pleasure

неразбирање *n* incomprehension, lack of understanding; misunderstanding

неразбирлив *adj* unintelligible, unclear; incomprehensible

неразбориjа -ии *f* **1** unreasonableness; madness; lunacy **2** confusion, chaos; uproar **3** disagreement, quarrel

неразбран *pt & adj* **1** unreasonable, unjustified; obstinate, stubborn; ама неразбран човек! what an obstinate person! **2** not understood; неговото дело остана неразбрано his work was not understood **3** incomprehensible; unintelligible, unclear; зборува нешто неразбрано he is saying s.th. unintelligible

неразбраност *f* unreasonableness; intractability; obstinacy, stubbornness

неразвиен *adj* undeveloped; not yet in bloom

нераздел ен -лна *adj* inseparable; неразделни другари inseparable friends

неразделив *adj* **1** indivisible **2** unshared

неразделивост *f* indivisibility

неразделност *f* inseparability

неразработен **1** not elaborated, not developed; uncultivated, untilled **2** not run in (*of a car, engine, etc.*), not working smoothly

неразрешлив *adj* insoluble, problematic, puzzling

неразумен -мна *adj* unreasonable, not sensible; foolish, senseless

неразумност *f* unreasonableness; foolishness, senselessness

нерамен -мна *adj* **1** uneven; нерамен пат an uneven/rough road **2** unequal; нерамни сили unequal forces

нерамнина *f* uneven/rough spot, bump; unevenness

нерамномерен -рна *adj* uneven; нерамномерен развиток uneven development

нерамноправен -вна *adj* inequitable; not having equal rights

нерамноправност *f* unfairness; inequality (*of rights*)

нерамност *f* **1** *see* нерамнина **2** roughness, coarseness

неранимаjка -овци, **неранимаjко** -овци & **неранимаjковец** -вци *m colloq.* **1** rascal, good-for-nothing, ne'er-do-well, wretch **2** squanderer, spendthrift, prodigal

нераилив *adj* invulnerable

нерасипан *adj* **1** unspoiled; unsophisticated, naive;

uncorrupted **2** not rotting, not decomposing, not decaying

нераскинлив *adj fig.* unbreakable, permanent

нераскршен *adj colloq.* inexperienced, ill-prepared (*for life or work*)

нерасонет *adj* not awakened, sleepy, drowsy

нерасположба *f* bad mood, bad temper; moroseness, indisposition

нерасположен *adj* in a bad mood, morose, ill-disposed

нерасположеност *f* bad mood, bad temper; moroseness, indisposition

нераспукнат *adj f.p.* still in bud; бел трендафил нераспукнат a white rose still in bud

нерастворлив *adj* insoluble, indissoluble

нерастоплив *adj* insoluble, indissoluble

нерасчистен *adj* uncleared; untidy; not cleared up, unsolved; unsettled, unresolved; нерасчистено прашање unsolved question

нерационáлен -лна *adj* irrational; unpractical, uneconomical

нерв *m* nerve; ❏ губи нерви to lose one's temper; to hit the ceiling; оди на нерви to get on one's/s.o.'s nerves; игра на нерви war of nerves; има челични нерви to have nerves of steel

нервен -вна *adj* related to nerves, nervous; нервен систем nervous system; нервен слом nervous breakdown

нервира *impf* **I** to get on s.o.'s nerves, annoy **II** – се to get upset; to fret

нервоза *f* **1** nervousness **2** irritability; touchiness

нервозен -зна *adj* **1** nervous; irritable **2** irritated

нереален -лна *adj* unreal, fictitious, unrealistic

нерегулáрен -рна *adj* irregular

неред *m* **1** disorder, chaos; направи неред во собата he messed up the room; во неред in a mess **2** (*usu. pl*) riot, demonstration; прави нереди to cause disturbances

нередовен -вна *adj* **1** inaccurate; not in order, incorrect **2** not regular, irregular; part-time

нередовност *f* **1** irregularity **2** inaccuracy, incorrectness

нерез *m* entire (uncastrated) domestic animal (*usu. horse or pig*); stallion; boar

нерезина *f* untrimmed vine

нерентабилен -лна *adj* unprofitable, not lucrative, not viable

нерентабилност *f* unprofitability, unviability

нерешен *adj* unsolved, unsettled; undecided; *Sport.* tied

нерешено *adv* in a draw (tie); мечот заврши нерешено the match ended in a draw

нерешителен -лна *adj* indecisive, unsure, hesitant, vacillating

нерешителност *f* indecisiveness, hesitancy

нерешлив *adj* unsolvable, insoluble

нерешливост *f* insolubility

нероден -дна *adj* barren, sterile; неродна година barren year

неротка *f* barren woman; barren tree/soil

нерц -ови *m* mink

несамостоен -јна *adj* dependent

несамостојност *f* dependence

несачка *f* laying hen, good layer

несварлив *adj* indigestible

несвесен -сна *adj* **1** unconscious, comatose; во несвесна положба in a faint **2** unreasonable, irresponsible; mad **3** backward, <politically> uninformed

несвесност *f* unconsciousness

несвест *f* <state of> unconsciousness, faint, swoon; паѓа во несвест to faint, lose consciousness

несвестица *f* **1** *see* несвест **2** dizziness

несврзан *adj* unconnected, desultory, rambling; incoherent; несврзани мисли, реченици unconnected thoughts, sentences

несврзлив *adj* not joinable, separate, discrete

несврзливост *f* separateness

несвршен *adj* **1** unfinished, incomplete **2** *Gram.* imperfective

несе *impf* to lay (*eggs*)

несебичен -чна *adj* unselfish, generous, selfless; несебично залагање unselfish efforts

несебичност *f* unselfishness, selflessness

несериозен -зна *adj* not serious, frivolous, flippant; insignificant, trivial

несериóзност *f* lack of seriousness, frivolity

несесер *m* vanity bag (case)

несигурен -рна *adj* unreliable; uncertain, diffident, hesitant, unsure

несигурност *f* unreliability; diffidence, uncertainty

несиметричен -чна *adj* asymmetrical

несимпатичен -чна *adj* unpleasant, unattractive

несистематичен -чна, **несистематски** & **несистемен** -мна *adj* unsystematic

несистематичност & **несистемност** *f* unsystematic character

нескопен *adj* ungelded, uncastrated, entire

нескромен -мна *adj* immodest; boastful; ❏ ќе бидам нескромен . . . may I say in all modesty . . .

нескромност *f* immodesty; boastfulness

нескротлив *adj* untamable

нескротливост *f* untamability

нескрупулóзен -зна *adj* unscrupulous, ruthless; arrogant; inconsiderate

нескршлив *adj fig.* unbreakable; firm

неславен -вна *adj* inglorious, shameful

неслагање *n* disagreement, dissension, discord

неслога *f* discord, dissension

несмасен -сна *adj* **1** careless; slovenly **2** clumsy, awkward

несмасност *f* **1** carelessness; slovenliness **2** clumsiness, awkwardness

несмеќаван *adj* undisturbed, unhindered, free; несмеќаван развиток unhindered development

несносен -сна *adj* unbearable, unendurable; intolerable, insufferable

несовесен -сна *adj* unscrupulous, dishonest; unconscientious

несовесник -ци *m* blackguard, cad

несовесност *f* unscrupulousness, dishonesty

несовремен *adj* out-of-date; old-fashioned

несовршен *adj* imperfect, defective; primitive, crude

несогласен -сна *adj* **1** disagreeing **2** disharmonious, discordant

несогласие -ија *n* & **несогласица** *f* disagreement, quarrel; misunderstanding

несогласност *f* **1** disagreement **2** discord, disharmony

несогласување *n* **1** disagreement **2** discord

несолиден -дна *adj* not solid, weak; unreliable; shaky

несолидност *f* lack of solidity, weakness; unreliability; shakiness

несомнен *adj* undoubted, certain, undisputed, unquestionable, obvious

несоница *f* insomnia; sleeplessness

несоодветен -тна *adj* unsuitable, inappropriate; not corresponding; incompatible

несоодветност *f* discrepancy; disparity; lack of correspondence; incompatibility

несоодветство *n* discord; inadequacy

неспан *adj* not having slept; три ноќи сум неспан I haven't slept for three nights

неспастрен *adj* unkempt, slovenly

неспиење *n* **1** vigil, watch **2** insomnia; sleeplessness, lack of sleep

неспогодба *f* misunderstanding; disagreement

неспогодија -ии *f* misunderstanding

неспокоен -јна *adj* restless; turbulent

неспокојност *f* restlessness; turbulence, agitation

неспокојство *n see* неспокојност

неспоредлив *adj* incomparable

неспособен -бна *adj* incapable, unfit; неспособен човек unfit person; неспособен за работа incapable of work

неспособност *f* incapability; платежна неспособност insolvency

несправедлив *adj* unjust, unfair; partial, biased, prejudiced

несправедливост *f* injustice, unfairness; partiality

неспремен *adj* unprepared; се јави на испит неспремен he came to the examination unprepared; нè завари ја неспремни they caught us unprepared

неспремност *f* unpreparedness

несразмер *m* & **несразмера** *f* disproportion, disparity, incongruity

несразмерен -рна *adj* disproportionate, disparate, incongruous

несреден *adj* **1** disorderly; unregulated, unsettled; несреден живот disorganized life **2** *fig.* unbalanced

несреденост *f* disorder

несреќа *f* misfortune, bad luck; accident; disaster, calamity; ❑ за несреќа unfortunately; несреќата никогаш не доаѓа сама *prov.* misfortunes never come singly; it never rains but it pours

несреќен -ќна *adj* unfortunate, unlucky; unhappy

несреќник -ци *m* unlucky person, unfortunate; poor devil

несреќница *f* (*fem. form*) *see* несреќник

нестабилен -лна *adj* instable

нестабилност *f* instability, fluctuation; стопанска нестабилност business fluctuations

нестасан *adj* unripe, green; immature

нестасаност *f* unripeness; immaturity

нестрижен *adj* with uncut hair; unshorn

нестрплив *adj* impatient

нестрпливост *f* impatience

несфатлив *adj* incomprehensible; inconceivable

нетактичен -чна *adj* tactless

нетактичност *f* tactlessness

нето *adj indecl.* net<t>, clear; нето профит net profit; нето тежина net weight

нетолерáнтен -тна *adj* intolerant

нетолерáнтност *f* intolerance

нетоп *m* woman's silver ornament worn on the forehead

неточен[1] *adj* unsharpened, blunt; неточен молив unsharpened pencil; неточен нож blunt knife

неточен[2] -чна *adj* **1** irregular **2** incorrect, wrong, erroneous, untrue

неточност *f* inaccuracy

нетрпелив *adj* intolerant; impatient

нетрпеливост *f* intolerance; impatience

нетрпение *n* impatience

неубав *adj* not nice, ugly, bad; ❑ <тоа е> неубава работа, <тоа се> неубави работи that's a bad business; that's no way to behave

неубедлив *adj* unconvincing, unpersuasive

неуважавање *n* disrespect

неуверен *adj* uncertain, unsure; diffident

неувереност *f* uncertainty; diffidence

неуверлив *adj* unconvincing, unpersuasive

неуверливост *f* unpersuasiveness

неугасен -сна *adj see* неугаслив

неугаслив *adj* inextinguishable; unquenchable; insatiable

неугледен -дна *adj* nondescript, ordinary; unattractive

неугоден -дна *adj* unpleasant; uncomfortable

неугодност *f* unpleasantness; discomfort

неудобен -бна *adj* uncomfortable

неудобност *f* lack of comfort, discomfort

неудопство *n see* неудобност

неук *adj* uneducated, illiterate; ignorant

неукинлив *adj* irreversible, irrevocable

неукост *f* lack of education, illiteracy; ignorance

неуловлив *adj* elusive, *see* недоловлив

неумеење *n* inability; unskilfulness, clumsiness

неумерен *adj* immoderate, excessive

неумереност *f* immoderateness, excess

неумесен -сна *adj* inappropriate, irrelevant; misplaced; unsuitable; improper

неумесност *f* inappropriateness, irrelevance; unsuitability; impropriety

неумешен -шна *adj* unskilled; clumsy, awkward

неумешност *f* lack of skill; clumsiness

неумно *adv* unintelligently; unreasonably

неумолив *adj* inexorable, unyielding, merciless

неумоливост *f* inexorability, unyieldingness, mercilessness

неуморен -рна *adj* tireless, diligent, indefatigable, persistent; неуморен во работата persevering at work; неуморна работа strenuous work

неуништлив *adj* indestructible

неуништливост *f* indestructibility

неупатен *adj* uninformed, uninitiated, ignorant

неупатеност *f* ignorance

неупотреблив *adj* unusable, useless; inapplicable

неупотребливост *f* uselessness; inapplicability

неурамнотежен *adj* unbalanced (*also fig.*)

неурамнотеженост *f* lack of balance (*also fig.*)

неуреден -дна *adj* slovenly, sloppy; untidy, disorderly

неуредност *f* slovenliness, sloppiness; untidiness, disorderliness

неусетно *adv* imperceptibly; unnoticed; влезе неусетно во собата he entered the room unnoticed

неуслужлив *adj* disobliging, unhelpful

неуслужливост *f* disobliging manner, unhelpfulness

неуспех -си *m* failure

неуспешен -шна *adj* unsuccessful, futile

неуставен -вна *adj* unconstitutional

неустановен *adj* unestablished, unfounded

неутврден *adj* unfounded, unestablished; not fixed

неутешен -шна *adj* inconsolable, disconsolate, broken-hearted

неутешлив *adj see* неутешен

неутешливост *f see* неутешност

неутешност *f* disconsolateness

неутра́лен -лна *adj* neutral

неутрализација *f* neutralization

неутрализи́ра *pf & impf* to neutralize

неутра́лност *f* neutrality

неутро́н *m Phys.* neutron

неучество *n* lack of participation, non-participation

неучествување *n* non-participation

неучтив *adj* impolite, ill-mannered, discourteous; rude

неучтивост *f* impoliteness, discourtesy; rudeness

нефри́тис *m Med.* nephritis

нефроло́г -зи *m* nephrologist

нефрологија *f* nephrology

нефт *m see* нафта

нехигие́нски *adj* unhygienic; нехигиенски услови unhygienic conditions

нехуман *adj see* нечовечен

нехуманост *f see* нечовечност

нецеден *adj* unfiltered; нецеден мед unrefined (unprocessed) honey

нецелесообразен -зна *adj* not suitable, not fitting; unfitting, inexpedient

неценет *adj* invaluable

нечекан *adj see* неочекуван

нечепнат *adj* 1 intact, untouched 2 uncut, unbroken, whole

нечесен -сна *adj* 1 dishonest; corrupt 2 (*of a woman*) dishonoured

нечесност *f* dishonesty; corruptness

нечиј -ија, -ие, *pl* -ии *pron* someone's, somebody's

нечист *adj* 1 unclean, dirty, soiled 2 *fig.* dishonest 3 (*as noun*) нечистиот evil spirit, the devil

нечистота *f* dirt, filth; dirtiness, filthiness; *fig.* impurity

нечистотија -ии *f see* нечистота

нечитлив *adj* illegible

нечленуван *adj Gram.* нечленуван збор word without the <definite> article

нечовек *m* (*pl* нелуѓе) monster, brute

нечовечен -чна *adj* inhuman, monstrous, brutal; inhumane

нечовечки *adj* inhuman, monstrous, brutal; inhumane; нечовечка постапка monstrous (brutal) act

нечовечност *f* inhumanity, brutality

нечовештина *f* inhuman (brutal) act

нечувствителен -лна *adj* 1 imperceptible; insensible 2 insensitive, unfeeling; callous

нечувствителност *f* 1 imperceptibility; insensibility 2 insensitivity; callousness

нечуен -јна *adj* inaudible, quiet

нечујно *adv* inaudibly, quietly

нештедење *n* lavishness; prodigality; waste

нешто 1 *pron, n* something; (*pl*) нешта things; сакам нешто да те прашам I want to ask you s.th.; си ги купил потребните нешта he bought the things he needed; ❑ тоа нешто that; тоа нешто може секој да го поверува anybody can believe that; сè нешто everything, anything; на масата имаше од сè нешто по малку on the table there was a little of everything; многу нешто a lot; во многу нешто in many respects; ситуацијата во многу нешто се измени the situation has changed in many ways (respects) 2 *adv* somewhat, rather, a little, a bit; roughly, about; што си така нешто невесел? why are you so sad? нешто околу триста метри about three hundred metres; малу нешто постојал и си отишол he stood for a while then went on; ❑ чудно нешто! how strange! два без нешто just before two; два и нешто just past (after) two

ни[1] 1 *part* (*emphasizing a negative*) not even; немам ни грош I haven't even a cent (a sou); ни чекор понатаму! not a step further! 2 *conj* ни . . . ни . . . neither . . . nor . . . ; ни едното ни другото neither the one nor the other; ❑ ни жив ни умрен more dead than alive; ни пет ни шест suddenly, to my surprise

ни[2] *pron* 1 (*short dat. form from* ние) <to> us; ми рече дека ќе дојде he told us that he would come 2 (*as dat. of possession*) our; дедо ни our grandfather; тетка ни our aunt

нив *pron* (*long form for oblique cases, except dat., of* тие, они) them; нив да не ги гибаш don't touch them! од нив from them; со нив with them

нива *f* <cultivated> field

нивелација *f* levelling, making even, making smooth

нивели́ра *pf & impf* to level, make even, smooth

нивен -вна *possessive pron see* нивни

нивни -вна *possessive pron* their, theirs

ниво́ *n* level; нивото на морето sea level; културното ниво cultural level; се спушта на нечие ниво to sink to s.o.'s level; на најниско ниво е to be at a low ebb; to hit rock bottom

нивче *n dim. of* нива

нигде<ка> *adv see* никаде

Нигер *m* Niger

Нигерец -рци *m* Nigerien, person from Niger

Нигериец -ијци *m* Nigerian

Нигерија *f* Nigeria

Нигеријка *f* (*fem. form*) see Нигериец

нигериски *adj* Nigerian

Нигерка *f* (*fem. form*) see Нигерец

нигерски *adj* Niger attrib.

ние *pron* (*1st p. pl*) we; (*dat.* нам, ни; *other cases* нас, нè)

ниеден -дна *adj* 1 not one, not a single; ниеден човек not a single person 2 (*in expressions of indignation, contempt, etc.*) магаре ниедно! you ass! you idiot! ❑ во ниедна доба, во ниедно време at a bad time, at an inconvenient time, late

ниеднаш *adv* never, not once

ниет *m colloq.* intention, idea; со ниет е, има ниет he has the intention; стори ниет to decide; сторил ниет да бега he decided to run away

нижач *m* threader of tobacco leaves (*for drying*)

нижачка *f* (*fem. form*) see нижач

ниже *impf* I 1 to thread; ниже бисер to thread pearls; ниже тутун to string (thread) tobacco leaves 2 *fig.* to tell (*stories*) fluently, reel off; ниже приказни he tells stories (tales) one after another **II – се** to follow (*one after another*); to stand in a row

нижи *adj* lower, junior; ниже музичко училиште lower music school

низ *prep* through, across, along, about; помине низ едно село to pass through a village; говори низ носот to speak through one's nose; низ целиот живот throughout one's life; низ полиња и планини over hill and dale; едно сениште кружи низ Европа a spectre is haunting Europe

низа *f* **1** row, line, string; necklace; низа алтани a necklace of gold coins; низа тутун a string of tobacco leaves **2** series; range; низа настани a series of events **3** bunch, bundle; низа клучови bunch of keys

низаеден -дна *adj see* ниеден 2

низанка *f* necklace

низина *f* valley, lowland, depression

низок -ска *adj* low; short (*in stature*); *fig.* vile, base; ниски облаци low clouds; ниски цени low prices; ниска температура low temperature; низок глас low voice; ниска постапка low (vile) act

нијанса *f* nuance, shade

никаде *adv* nowhere; никаде го нема he is nowhere to be found; утре не одам никаде tomorrow I'm not going anywhere; ❏ за никаде very bad<ly>; worthless; се стори за никаде he disgraced himself; тој е за никаде (како никој никаде) he's no good

никаквец *m* scoundrel, rascal, good-for-nothing

никаквик -ци *m see* никаквец

никаквица *f* (*fem. form*) *see* никаквец

никако *adv* in no way, not at all; никако не можеа да се погодат they couldn't reach any kind of agreement; дождот никако да престане the rain showed no sign of stopping; (*emphasizing a negative reply*) никако! never! not at all!

никаков -ква *adj* **1** none at all; денеска немам никаква работа today I have no work at all **2** worthless, useless; срамота е за една никаква куќа да се карате it is disgraceful for you to quarrel over a house that isn't worth anything **3** (*as noun*) *see* никаквец; каде е книгата, бре никаков!? where's the book, you rascal!?

Никарагва *f* Nicaragua

Никарагванец -нци *m* Nicaraguan

Никарагванка *f* (*fem. form*) *see* Никарагванец

никарагвански *adj* Nicaraguan

никел *m* nickel; ❏ го бара и од татка си никелот he demands too much

никлен *adj* nickel; никлени пари nickel coins

никлува *pf & impf* to nickel

никне¹ *pf* никна *aor.* to sprout, shoot up; to appear; to originate, come into being, develop

никне² *impf see* никнува

никнува *impf of* никне; ❏ кај ќе мавне трева не никнува he destroys whatever he touches

никогаш *adv* never; ❏ како никогаш as never before; никогаш не е доцна it's never too late

никого *pron* (*oblique case form, except dat., of* никој) no one, nobody; никого не видов I didn't see anyone; нема никого there's no one there; со никого with no one, without anyone

никој **1** *pron* (*only m; dat.* никому; *other cases* никого) no one, nobody; никој не може да те види no one

can see you; нема никој there's no one there **2** *adj* никој -оја, -ое, -ои no, none; никоја од момите не се фати за оро none of the girls joined the dance; ❏ во никое време at a bad time, at an inconvenient time, late at night; во никој случај in (under) no circumstances, never; на никој начин in no way; никој жив not a soul; nobody under the sun; никој и ништо nonentity, nobody

никојпат *adv see* никогаш

николку *adv* (*of quantity*) none

никому *pron* (*dat. form from* никој 1) to no one, not to anyone

никотин *m* nicotine

никулец -лци *m* shoot, sprout, germ

Нил *m* the Nile

нилски *adj* Nile *attrib.*; ❏ нилски коњ hippopotamus

ним *pron* (*long dat. form from* тие, они) to/for them

нимфа *f* **1** nymph **2** *Zool.* pupa, chrysalis, nymph

нимфоманија *f* nymphomania

нимфоманка *f* nymphomaniac

ниско *adv* low; *fig.* basely; авионот лета ниско the plane is flying low; тоа е дрско и ниско that is shameless and vile

нискоглед *adj f.p.* with downcast/lowered eyes

нискост *f* baseness, vileness

нити *conj see* ниту 2

нитка *f see* нишка¹

нитна *f* stud; rivet

нитнува *impf* to stud; to rivet

нито *conj see* ниту

нитрат *m Chem.* nitrate

нитроглицерин *m* nitroglycerine

ниту **1** *part* (*emphasizing a negative*) not even, not a single; ниту збор не проговори he didn't utter a single word; ниту еднаш not once **2** *conj* ниту . . . ниту . . . ; ни . . . ниту . . . neither . . . nor . . . ; не дојде ниту мајка, ниту татко neither mother nor father came

нихилизам -змот *m* nihilism

нихилист *m* nihilist

ничиј -ија -ие -ии *pron* no one's, nobody's

ничко & ничком *adv dial. see* ничкум

ничкоса *pf* **I** to throw (*s.o.*) face downwards; to cast down; со очите ничкосани with downcast eyes **II – се** to fall face downwards (prone); to collapse, tumble <forwards>; to prostrate o.s.

ничкосува *impf of* ничкоса

ничкум *adv* prone, prostrate; падна ничкум he fell prone

ниша¹ *f* niche, recess, alcove

ниша² *impf* **I** to swing, rock, shake *trans.*; ниша дете to dandle a child; ги ниша нозете he is swinging his legs; ниша со главата, ниша глава to shake one's head; ❏ си ги ниша нозете he is doing nothing **II – се** **1** to swing, rock, sway *intrans.* **2** to be shaky, be loose **3** to heave, surge *intrans.*; се ниша сино море the blue sea heaves/surges

нишадор *m Chem.* sal ammoniac

нишалка *f* **1** swing **2** *dial. see* лулка¹

нишало *n* pendulum

нишан *m* **1** mark, sign **2** aim, goal, target; ❏ зема некого на нишан to take aim at s.o.; to be gunning for s.o.; застанува некому на нишан to play into s.o.'s hands **3** (*of a rifle*) front sight

нишани *impf* to aim (*at*)

нишанлија *adj indecl. colloq.* bearing some sign or mark

нишанџија -ии *m* 1 marksman 2 gunlayer (*in artillery*); gunner

нишевка *f* type of dark-red grape

нишесте *n* starch

нишка[1] *f* thread; ❏ црвена нишка motif; leitmotiv

нишка[2] *impf dim.* I to swing, rock a little *trans.* II – ce to swing, rock a little *intrans.*

нишне *pf* нишна *aor.* I to start rocking slightly *trans.* II – ce to start rocking slightly *intrans.*

нишнува (ce) *impf of* нишне (ce)

ништи[1] *impf* I to tie yarn (*into the threads of a loom*); to put threads (*into a loom*) II – ce to come out, fall out (*of threads in a loom*)

ништи[2] *impf* to annul; to destroy

ништо *pron* 1 nothing, not anything; ништо не видов I didn't see anything; од ништо не се плаши he's not afraid of anything; ❏ за ништо not for anything; for no reason; за ништо не го бидува he is good for nothing; it is no use; ништо за тоа never mind about that; пламнува за ништо to have a short fuse; за ништо на светов not for anything in the world; ништо не ми е (не ми фали) I'm all right; ништо не ми е (*moj, maa*) (*he, she*) is no relation to me; како ништо easily, as if it was nothing; никому ништо nobody is any the worse; <за> ништо не чини it's no good at all; <за> ништо живо in no way; absolutely nothing; ништо живо не го припуштал he wouldn't let anyone come near him; речиси ништо next to nothing; ништо посебно nothing to write home about; no big deal; ништо од so much for; ништо од него he won't make it; he is done for; ништо од тоа nothing doing; no way; ништо не менува it makes no difference; никому ништо <не сум направил> и пак кабаетлија *prov.* I've done no harm to anybody and still I get the blame 2 (*in reply to thanks*) you're welcome! my pleasure! don't mention it! (*in reply to apology*) it doesn't matter! no harm done!

ништовен -вна *adj Leg.* invalid, <null and> void; ништовна жалба invalid complaint

ништоверец -рци *m* non-believer, atheist; infidel; heathen

ништожен -жна *adj* insignificant, paltry, trifling; worthless

ништожество *n* 1 insignificance, worthlessness; worthless thing, trifle 2 insignificant person; worthless person

ништожност *f* worthlessness; insignificance; nothingness

но *conj* but, however

НОБ *abbr.* (*Народно-ослободителна борба*) National Liberation Struggle

нов *adj* new; нови алишта new clothes; Нова година New Year; ❏ што има ново? what's new? како нов brand new; as good as new; не е ништо ново news from nowhere; кине ново да закрпи старо to throw good money after bad

новак -ци *m* novice, beginner; newcomer

новáтор *m* innovator

новаторство *n* innovation

новéла *f* novella, short novel

новелúст *m* writer of novellas

Нов Зеланд *m* New Zealand

новина *f* 1 <piece of> news 2 novelty, innovation 3 new moon; ❏ од новина на погибел once in a blue moon

новинар *m* journalist, newspaper-man

новинарка *f* (*fem. form*) see новинар

новинарски *adj* journalistic; новинарска измислица canard, fabrication

новинарство *n* journalism

новинка *f dim. of* новина

новитéт *m* novelty, new item

новицијáт *m* novitiate

новиште *n* ground on which s.th. is sown for the first time

новка -вко *adj* (*no m form*) *dim. of* нов; quite new

ново- (*in compound words*) newly, new; ново-избрани одборници newly elected committee members; нововремски modern; новогрчки Modern Greek

нововерец -рци *m* New Believer (Nazarene)

нововерка *f* (*fem. form*) see нововерец

новогодишен -шна *adj* New Year's; новогодишен подарок New Year's Day present; новогодишни честитки New Year's greetings

новогрáдба *f* new building

новодојден *pt* newly arrived; (*as noun*) *m* newcomer

Новозеландец -дци *m see* Новозеланѓанец

новозеландски *adj* New Zealand *attrib.*

Новозеланѓанец -ни *m* New Zealander

Новозеланѓанка *f* (*fem. form*) see Новозеланѓанец

Новозелантка *f see* Новозеланѓанка

новоизграден *pt* newly built

новокуќник -ци *m* new householder

новооснован *pt* newly founded; newly organized, newly established

новооткриен *pt* newly discovered

новопокрстен *pt & adj* newly converted to Christianity, newly baptized

новороден *pt* new-born

новороденче *n* new-born infant, new-born babe

новоселец -лци *m* newcomer in a village

новосоздаден *pt* new, newly created; во новосоздадената ситуација in the new/changed situation

новост *f* 1 news item; филмски новости newsreel 2 newness

новота & новотија *f see* новост 2

нога *f, pl* нозе 1 leg; foot; ❏ нога за нога slowly, step by step; рипа на нозе to jump to one's feet; живее на широка (висока) нога to live in grand style; to live in clover, *Am.* to live high off the hog; со едната нога в гроб with one foot in the grave; со рамна нога со on equal terms (an equal footing) with; станува на лева нога to get out of bed on the wrong side; гори некому под нозе to be in dire straits; to be in hot water; добива нозе to disappear, vanish in thin air; застанува на свои нозе to stand on one's own two feet; како со нога в нога in a slapdash manner; jerrybuilt; колку што го држат нозете as fast as possible; to put one's best foot forward; копа и со нозе и со раце to move heaven and earth; му се тресат нозете to shake in one's boots; стои на стаклени нозе to stand on shaky ground; to have feet of clay; на цврсти нозе on a sound footing; од мали нозе from a tender age; испружи си ги нозете колку што ти е долга чергата *prov.* cut your coat according to your cloth **2** (*measure of length*) foot **3** *see* ногалка

ногавица *f* trouser leg

ногалка *f* leg (*of a table, chair, etc.*)

ноémври *m* November

ноемвриски *adj* November

нож -еви -ови *m* knife; ❑ клава сè под нож to criticize everything; <дошол> нож под грло (до коска) to be more than flesh and blood can bear; to reach screaming point; зарива некому нож в грб to stab s.o. in the back; става некому нож под грло to hold a gun to s.o.'s head; to force s.o. to the wall; на нож е со некого to be at daggers drawn with s.o.; to be at each other's throats

ножар *m* cutler

ножарница *f* **1** cutler's workshop **2** shop selling cutlery

ножарство *n* cutler's trade

ноже[1] *n dim. of* нога

ноже[2] *n dim. of* нож; џебно ноже penknife, pocket knife; ноже за бричење razor-blade; склопитно ноже folding knife

ножен -жна *adj* foot; ножна кочница (сопирачка) foot-brake

ножица *f & ножици pl* scissors

ножиче *n & ножичка f dim. of* ножица; nail scissors

ножичиња & ножички *pl dim. of* ножици; nail scissors

ножница *f* scabbard, sheath; трга меч од ножница to unsheathe one's sword

нозба *f* food and drink (*brought by guests*)

ноздра *f* nostril

нозе *pl see* нога

нoj -еви *m Zool.* (Struthio camelus) ostrich

нокаут *m* knockout

нокаутира *pf & impf* to knock out

нокот -кти *m* **1** <finger-/toe->nail **2** claw

нокте *n dim. of* нокот; ❑ едно нокте just a little; не се помрдна ни едно нокте he didn't so much as stir

ноктурно *n Mus.* nocturne

нокшир *m* chamber-pot, *colloq.* potty

номад *m* nomad

номенклатура *f* nomenclature

номер *m* number

номинален -лна *adj* nominal

номинатив *m Gram.* nominative

номинација *f* nomination

номинира *pf & impf* to nominate

ноншалантен -тна *adj* nonchalant

ноншалантност *f* nonchalance

нор -ови *m Zool.* (Phalacrocorax) cormorant; мал нор pygmy cormorant

Норвежанец -ни *m* Norwegian

Норвежанка *f* (*fem. form*) *see* Норвежанец

Норвешка *f* Norway

норвешки *adj* Norwegian

норка <се> *impf* to dive, plunge *intrans.*, *see* нурка <се> 1

норкач *m Zool. see* нор

норма *f* **1** norm, standard; rule, regulation<s> **2** quota; ги надминаа нормите they exceeded the production quotas (norms)

нормáла *f Math.* vertical, perpendicular

нормален -лна *adj* normal, sane; regular, ordinary; according to regulations

нормализација *f* normalization

нормализира *pf & impf* **I** to normalize **II** – се to become normal/normalized (*of political relations, etc.*)

норматив *m* scale (table) of norms

нормативен -вна *adj* normative; нормативна граматика normative grammar

нормира *pf & impf* to standardize

нормиран *pt & adj* standardized; нормирана работа standardized work

норне <се> *pf* норна <се> *aor. see* нурне <се>

нос *m* **1** nose; чпртав нос turned-up nose, pug-nose, snub nose; ❑ не гледа подалеку од носот to be unable to see beyond the end of one's nose; го дига (крева, прчи) носот to turn one's nose up; го обесува носот to be in low spirits; го пика носот во туѓи работи to put (poke) one's nose into other people's affairs; води (влече) некого за нос to lead s.o. by the nose; to lead s.o. a merry dance; има добар нос to have a good nose (flair for s.th.); му излезе низ нос тоа he paid through the nose for it; му го извади (истера) тоа низ нос to rub s.o.'s nose in it; под носот му е to be right under s.o.'s nose; да го помирисаш, носот ќе ти падне to stink like a polecat; да не му беше носон, трева ќе пасеше he is a fool (blockhead); добива по нос to burn one's fingers; со дигнат нос on one's high horse **2** (*на кораб*) bow<s>, prow **3** cape, head, headland, ness

носатен -тна *adj* носатно платно home-made cloth used as household linen

носач *m* **1** (*за човек*) porter; bearer **2** (*за брод*) carrier; носач на авиони aircraft carrier **3** *Architecture* beam, girder, strut

носе *n dim. of* нос

носен -сна *adj* nasal; носна преграда septum

носечки[1] *adj* supporting; носечки ѕидови supporting walls

носечки[2] *adv* on one's nose; падна носечки he fell on his nose, prone

носи *impf* **I** **1** to carry, bring, take; носи дрва на грбот he carries wood on his back; не носам пари I haven't any money on me; ❑ на раце го носат they make a great fuss over him; те носи редот <да го сториш тоа> etiquette requires you <to do that>; кој носи не проси better to have than wish; носи добивка to make a profit; носи камата to yield interest **2** (*за облека и обувки*) to wear; носи костум to wear a suit; носи црнина to wear mourning, mourn **3** (*за ветар, вода*) to blow away, carry away **4** to be pregnant (*with*), carry a child **5** (*за име, наслов и сл.*) to bear; таа го носи името на баба си she bears the name of her grandmother **II** – се **1** (*кон, спрема*) to act towards, behave towards, treat **2** (*за облека*) to dress *intrans.*; убаво се носи he dresses beautifully **3** (*за песна, глас и сл.*) to carry, resound

носивост *f* carrying capacity, tonnage

носија -ии *f* costume; народна носија traditional costume

носила *pl* stretcher

носилка *f* sedan chair; palanquin

носило *n* **1** bier **2** *see* носила

носител *m* **1** bearer; carrier; носител на нови идеи bearer of new ideas; носител на зараза vector, <disease> carrier **2** (*на орден, звање и сл.*) holder; recipient; носител на станарско право leaseholder, lessee

носителка *f* (*fem. form*) *see* носител
носиште *n augm. of* нос 1
после *n see* носе
нослест *adj* 1 long-nosed 2 nose-like
носло -овци *m colloq.* person with a prominent nose
носница *f* nostril
носовка *f Phon.* nasal vowel (*of Old Church Slavonic*)
носовост *f* nasality
носорог -зи *m Zool.* rhinoceros
носталгија *f* nostalgia
носталгичен -чна *adj* nostalgic
нострификација *f* recognition, validation (*of a foreign diploma, degree*)
нострифиц́ра *pf & impf* to recognize (*foreign diploma, degree*)
нота *f* 1 *Mus.* note 2 (*written*) note; дипломатска нота diplomatic note 3 (*нијанса во говорот*) note, inflexion (*in voice*)
нотариус *m* notary
нотен -тна *adj Mus.* of notes, from notes (printed music); нотен систем musical notation
нотес *m* notebook; memo pad
нот́ра *pf & impf* to note, write down, record (*in writing*)
ноторен -рна *adj* notorious; ноторен лажго notorious liar
ноќ -ќи *f* night; са ноќ all night <long>; добра (лека) ноќ! good night! ❑ до ниедно време во ноќта till late at night; ноќта ден ја прави to burn the midnight oil; преку ноќ <да се стане нешто> <to become s.th.> overnight
ноќви *pl* dough tray; kneading trough
ноќе *adv* at night, by night
ноќев *m* night's lodging; overnight shelter
ноќева *impf* to spend the night
ноќевалиште *n* 1 <overnight> shelter, night's lodging 2 overnight stay
ноќем *adv dial. see* ноќе
ноќен -ќна *adj* night; nocturnal; ноќна ламба night lamp
ноќеска *adv* tonight; last night
ноќешен -шна *adj* tonight's; last night's
ноќта *adv* that night
ноќува *impf see* ноќева
ноќувалиште *n see* ноќевалиште
ноќум *adv dial. see* ноќе
ношки *pl see* ножица
ношница *f* night-dress, night-gown
нуди *impf* I to offer (*нешто некому – s.th. to s.o.*); to ask (*некого нешто – s.o. to do s.th.*); to bid at an auction II – ce to offer <o.s.>; тој се нуди да помогне he offers to help

нуд́зам -змот *m* nudism
нуд́ст *m* nudist
нудистички *adj* nudist; нудистичка плажа nudist beach
нужда *f* need, necessity; poverty, want; при нужда if need be; во крајна нужда in urgent need; if the worst comes to the worst; живее во голема нужда to live in great poverty; врши нужда to relieve o.s.; голема и мала нужда defecation and urination
нужен -жна *adj* necessary; inevitable; indispensable, essential; со нужната претпазливост with the necessary caution; нужно сместување emergency accommodation
нужник -ци *m* lavatory, W.C., toilet; outdoor privy, *Austral. sl.* dunny; јавен нужник public lavatory
нужност *f* necessity, need
нуклеа́рен -рна *adj* nuclear; нуклеарен отпад <nuclear> fallout; nuclear waste; нуклеарна физика nuclear physics
нуклеи́нска *adj Chem.* нуклеинска киселина nucleic acid
нуклеус *m* nucleus
нула *f* naught, zero; под/над нулата below/above zero (*temperature, etc.*); ❑ од нула from scratch; at the bottom of the ladder
нулев *adj* zero
нумера́тор *m* numbering machine
нумерација *f* numbering
нумери́ра *pf & impf* to number
нумеро *n arch.* number
нумизматика *f* numismatics
нумизматичар *m* numismatist
нумизматички *adj* numismatic
нунка *f see* кума
нунко -овци *m see* кум
нура <се> *impf see* нурка <се>
нурец -рци *m see* нуркач 2
нурка <се> *impf* 1 to dive, plunge *intrans.* 2 *fig.* to roam, wander 3 *fig.* to move around, potter about 4 *fig.* to stagger, totter, stumble, trip
нуркач *m* 1 diver; scuba-diver 2 *Zool.* (Gavia) diver, *Am.* loon; (*also used for various mergansers, grebes and diving duck*)
нурне <се> *pf* нурна <се> *aor.* 1 to dive, plunge *intrans.* 2 *fig.* to start staggering, stumbling
нуспродукт & нуспроизвод *m* by-product
нутриме́нт *m* (*храна*) nutriment
нутрити́вен -вна *adj* (*хранлив*) nutrient, nutritive, nutritious
нутриција *f* (*исхрана*) nutrition
нутриционист *m* nutritionist
нутрологија *f* nutrition studies

Њ

О

њичево *adv colloq.* (*ништо*) nothing

њока *f* (*usu. pl*) dumpling

Њујорк *m* New York

њујорчанец -ни *m* New Yorker

њујорчанка *f* (*fem. form*) *see* њујорчанец

њујоршки *adj* New York *attrib.*

њути *m Phys.* newton

њуфаундлендер *m* (*вид куче*) Newfoundland <dog>

о *interj* (*expressing wonder, astonishment, joy, sorrow, pain, desire, etc.; adding emphasis; seeking attention*) о, колку е убаво! oh, how beautiful! о, јас сирота! oh, woe is me! о, Кузмане! hey, Kuzman! о, секако! о, се разбира! yes, certainly! yes, of course! о, никако! no, not at all! no, in no way!

о- *verbal prefix indicating* **1** *perfectivization*; обари to boil **2** *changes of state*; ослепи to blind **3** *contact*; огребе to scratch

оа́за *f* oasis (*also fig.*); оаза на мирот an oasis of peace

об- (*оп- before voiceless consonants*) *verbal prefix indicating* **1** *see* о- **2** *movement around; act of surrounding*; обиколи to surround; обземе to envelop; опкружи to encircle

обајцата *num* (*occurs only with the definite article, pertaining to male persons or mixed company*) both; *see* двајца; дојдете обајцата come here, both of you! обајцата браќа both brothers

обарен *pt* lightly boiled; обарени јајца soft-boiled eggs

обари *pf* to boil, simmer

обарува *impf of* обари

обата *num* (*m only; for f and n see* обете; *without the definite article only in folk poetry*) both

обаца *pf* **I** to dirty, soil **II – се** to get dirty, become soiled; што така си се обацал? why have you got so dirty?

обацува (се) *impf of* обаца (се)

обвива (се) *impf of* обвие (се)

обвивка *f* wrapping, cover; (*на книга*) dust cover (jacket)

обвидели *pf* to restore sight (*to s.o.*); ме обвидели he restored my sight

обвие *pf* обви *aor.* **I 1** to wrap <up>; to bind; обвие со платно to wrap in linen **2** to embrace, hug **3** to enwrap, envelop, entwine, wind (*around*); бршланот го обви дрвцето the ivy wound <itself> around the tree **II – се** to wrap/wind o.s. (*околу – around*); ќе се обвие во (со) трева it will be covered in grass

обвинение -ија *n* accusation, charge, incrimination, imputation; подигне обвинение против некого to bring a charge against s.o.; тој е под обвинение he is on a charge, he has been charged (*with a crime*)

обвинет *pt* **1** accused, charged **2** (*as noun*) обвинетиот *Leg.* the accused, defendant

обвини *pf* **I** to accuse (*за – of*), charge (*with*); to blame (*for*); to prosecute, indict; to incriminate; го обвини за предавство he accused him of treason; he charged him with treason **II – се** to accuse one another; тие еден со друг се обвинија they blamed each other

обвинител *m* accuser, plaintiff; prosecutor; јавен обвинител public prosecutor

обвинителен -лна *adj* accusing, charging; accusatory; обвинителен акт <bill of> indictment; обвинителни документи incriminating documents

обвинителство *n* prosecutor's office; јавно обвинителство public prosecutor's office

обвинува (се) *impf of* обвини (се)

обвинувач *m* accuser

обвинувачки *adj see* обвинителен; обвинувачки поглед accusing glance

обвиснат *adj & pt* flabby, hanging down, loose, drooping

обвисне <**се**> *pf* обвисна <се> *aor.* **1** to hang (*s.th.*), suspend; to throw one's arms (*around s.o./s.th.*); обвисне на нешто to hang (*s.th.*) on s.th.; му се обвисна на вратот she threw her arms around his neck **2** to gather *intrans.*; темни облаци <се> обвиснаа над градот dark clouds gathered over the town **3** to grow flabby; to hang loose; to grow soft; to droop *intrans.*, sag; му обвисна снагата he's gone to seed

обвиснува <**се**> *impf of* обвисне <се>

обврзан *pt* obliged, obligated, bound (*to do s.th.*); committed; indebted; обврзан е за нешто he is bound by something

обврзаност *f* obligation; commitment

обврзе *pf* обврза *aor.* **I** to put under an obligation; to bind; ме обврза со својата добрина he put me in his debt with his kindness **II – се** to undertake (*to*), give an undertaking; to bind o.s. (*to do s.th.*); to commit o.s.; тој се обврза да ја заврши задачата he undertook to carry out the task

обврзник -ци *m* person under obligation; даночен обврзник taxpayer; воен обврзник conscript

обврзница *f Comm.* bond; promissory note; обврзница на народен заем government bond; доходовни обврзници income bonds; приоритетни обврзници preference bonds; неосигурени обврзници debentures

обврзува (се) *impf of* обврзе (се); ова мене на ништо не ме обврзува this does not commit me to anything

обврзувачки *adj* binding

обврска *f* task, obligation, duty; *Comm.* liability; исполнува обврски to carry out one's duties; морална обврска moral obligation; воена обврска compulsory military service; *Comm.* се ослободи од обврските to be released from liability; *Comm.* неизвршени обврски outstanding liabilities; ❑ има обврска да to be under an obligation to; секојдневни обврски day-to-day duties; без обврски with no obligation

обгледа (се) *pf see* огледа (се)

обгледува (се) *impf of* обгледа (се), *see* огледува (се)

обгор *m* scorched place/thing

обгорен *pt* charred; scorched; (*од сонце*) sunburnt; гламна обгорена charred log

обгори *pf* to burn (char) on all sides; to scorch, singe; сонцето го обгори he got sunburnt

обгорува *impf of* обгори

огради *pf* **1** to fence in, enclose **2** to surround, encircle, hem in

оградува *impf of* огради

обгрне *pf* обгрна *aor.* to embrace, hug; to surround, crowd (cluster) around

обгрнува *impf of* обгрне

обдени се *pf impers.* to dawn, grow light; *see* раздени се

обденица *f f.p.* the morning star

обденува се *impf of* обдени се

обдува (се) *impf of* обдуе (се), *see* подува (се)

обдуе (се) *pf* обду *aor. see* подуе (се)

обдукција *f* autopsy, post-mortem <examination>

обдукционен -она *adj* post-mortem, autopsy *attrib.*; обдукциона сала autopsy room

обдуцира *pf & impf* to perform an autopsy (a post-mortem)

обе- *verbal prefix see* об-

обед *m dial.* **1** <main> meal, lunch **2** lunchtime; *see* ручек

обединет *pt* united; обединета република united republic; Обединетите нации the United Nations

обедини *pf* **I** to unite, unify, amalgamate, join together, incorporate *trans.*; ги обединија заедничките интереси they were united by their common interests **II – се** to unite *intrans.*; to join hands (*со – with*); неколку држави се обединија во една several states united into one

обединение -ија *n* union

обединител *m* unifier

обединува (се) *impf of* обедини (се)

обезбеден *pt* supplied (*with*), provided (*with*); protected, guarded; secure

обезбеденост *f* security; provision, supply

обезбеди *pf* **I** to provide; to supply (*со – with*); to reserve **2** to protect, guard; to secure, ensure; работата му обезбеди успех his work ensured success **II – се 1** to provide o.s. (*со – with*); to secure <for> o.s. **2** to make o.s secure, secure o.s. (*од – against*)

обезбедува (се) *impf of* обезбеди (се)

обезбедување *n* **1** provision, supplying; protecting, guarding **2** safeguarding, ensuring; мерки за обезбедување security measures

обезглавен *pt* **1** beheaded, decapitated **2** *fig.* beheaded, deprived of leadership **3** *fig.* confused; panic-stricken; crazed, frantic

обезглавеност *f* **1** headlessness (*also fig.*) **2** *fig.* panic

обезглави *pf* **I 1** to decapitate, behead **2** *fig.* to behead, deprive of leadership **II – се** *fig.* to lose one's head

обезглавува (се) *impf of* обезглави (се)

обезличи *pf* to deprive of individuality, depersonalize

обезличува *impf of* обезличи

обезнадежи *pf* **I** to deprive (*s.o.*) of hope **II – се** to lose hope

обезнадежува (се) *impf of* обезнадежи (се)

обезоружен *pt* disarmed, defenceless

обезоруженост *f* defencelessness

обезоружи *pf* **I** to disarm *trans.*, render helpless (*also fig.*) **II – се** to disarm *intrans.*, lay down one's arms (*also fig.*); *see* разоружи

обезоружува (се) *impf of* обезоружи

обезоружување *n* disarmament

обезумен *pt* confused; panic-stricken; crazed, frantic

обезуми *pf* **I 1** to drive mad, madden; to infatuate **2** *fig.* to confuse, embarrass, perplex, distract **II – се** to lose self-control; to go crazy, lose one's head

обезумува (се) *impf of* обезуми (се)

обелее *pf* обелеа *aor. see* обели

обележи *pf* to mark; to annotate

обележје *n* characteristic, feature, trait

обележува *impf of* обележи

обелен *adj & pt* **1** (*за коса*) grey; (*за човек*) grey<­haired> **2** faded (*by the sun*); обелен костум faded suit/costume

обели *pf* обели *or* обеле *aor.* **1** to turn white; обелеле планините од снег the mountains have turned white with snow **2** to turn grey; косата ми обеле my hair's gone grey; ❑ обелев I've grown old **3** to fade (*in the sun*); ти обеле фустанот your dress has faded **4** to make white, whiten; to bleach; ❑ му го обели образот to uphold s.o.'s honour **5** *dial.* to peel; to shell

обелиск -сци *m* obelisk

обелодени *pf* **I** to reveal, disclose, make public; обелодени сознание to publish evidence **II – се** to come to light, emerge; ќе се обелодени неговата невиност he will clear his name

обелува *impf of* обели & обелее

обем *m* volume; size; scope, extent; circumference, perimeter; *Math.* обем на круг circumference of a circle; голем по обем large in size; обем на знаења extent of knowledge; обем на производство volume of production/output

обемен -мна *adj* **1** voluminous; bulky; abundant, copious; long, detailed; обемен труд a voluminous work (book); обемна жетва abundant harvest **2** *Math.* circumferential; обемната должина на еден круг circumference of a circle

обемно *adv* voluminously; in abundance, to a great extent; abundantly

обемност *f* bulkiness; abundance, copiousness; length; size

обере *pf* обра *aor.* **1** to pick; обере лозје to pick grapes; ❑ го обрал бостанот he's fallen on hard times **2** *colloq.* to rob, plunder, fleece, *sl.* clean out

оберува *impf of* обере

обесвести *pf* **I** to render unconscious, knock (*s.o.*) out **II – се** to faint, swoon

обесвестува (се) *impf of* обесвести (се)

обесен -сна *adj f.p.* (*of tree*) <used> for hanging, serviceable as a gibbet

обесеник -ци *m* **1** hanged man **2** *fig.* villain, gallows-bird, scoundrel

обесеница *f* (*fem. form*) *see* обесеник

обеснички *adj* villainous

обеси *pf* **I 1** to hang *trans.*; to suspend; ја обеси торбата на едно дрво he hung the bag on a tree **2** to hang *trans.*, put to death by hanging; татко ми го обесија my father was hanged **3** to lower; ја обеси главата to duck one's head; *fig.* to hang one's head (*in shame*); ❑ го обеси носот to become despondent **II – се 1** to hang o.s., kill o.s. by hanging **2** to put one's arms round s.o.'s neck; му се обеси на вратот she flung her arms round his neck; *fig.* she became a burden to him **3** *fig.* to grow limp, feeble (*physically and mentally*); to get upset; to fall into depression

обескуражи *pf* **I** to discourage, dishearten, dismay **II – се** to become discouraged (disheartened), lose heart

обескуражува (се) *impf of* обескуражи (се)

обесмрти *pf* to immortalize

обесмртува *impf of* обесмрти

обесплоди *pf* to sterilize

обесплодува *impf of* обесплоди

обеспокои *pf* **I** to disturb, trouble, bother **II – се** to get upset

обеспокојува (се) *impf of* обеспокои (се); немој да ме обеспокојуваш don't disturb me!

обесправен *pt* deprived of rights; обесправени народи nations deprived of their rights, dispossessed peoples

обесправеност *f* lack of rights

обесправи *pf* to deprive of rights

обесправува *impf of* обесправи

обеспраши *pf* (*of tobacco, coal, etc.*) to clean of dust

обеспрашува *impf of* обеспраши

обессилен *pt* **1** weak, broken, crushed **2** revoked, annulled, cancelled, invalidated

обессили *pf* **1** to overpower; to exhaust, tire out, break, crush; тој уште со првиот удар го обессили he overpowered him with his very first blow **2** to invalidate, revoke; вишиот суд ја обессили пресудата the higher court revoked the decision

обессилува *impf of* обессили

обесува (се) *impf of* обеси (се)

обесхрабри *pf* to discourage, dishearten

обесхрабрува *impf of* обесхрабри

обесцени *pf* to devalue, cheapen *trans.*

обесценува *impf of* обесцени

обесчести *pf* to dishonour; to deflower; to disgrace, besmirch s.o.'s honour/image, shame

обесчестува *impf of* обесчести

обесштети *pf* to compensate, indemnify

обесштетува *impf of* обесштети

обете *num* (*for f and n gender*) both; обете нозе both legs; обете сестри both sisters

обетка *f* earring; едно рало обетки a pair of earrings

обетован *adj literary, only in the expression:* обетована земја promised land

обзема *impf of* обземе

обземе *pf* обзема & обзеде *aor.* to envelop, surround; to overcome, overwhelm; to consume; to seize, grip; огнот ја обзеде целата куќа the fire enveloped the whole house; го обзеде тага he was overcome by grief; ме обзеде силен студ I felt extremely cold; го обзема страв he was gripped by fear

обземен *pt* overcome (*од, со – by, with*); consumed (*with*); обземен од силни страсти possessed by violent passions; обземен од мисли engrossed in thought; обземен од ужас terror-stricken

обзори *pf* **I 1** (*only 3rd p. sg*) to dawn, grow light; зората обзори the day dawned, dawn broke **2** (*impers. or with* зората) <зората> ме обзори уште на пат dawn found me still on the road **II – се 1** *impers.* to dawn, grow light; се обзори dawn has broken **2** (*with* зората) зората се обзори day has dawned, dawn has broken

обзорува (се) *impf of* обзори (се)

обзрне се *pf* обзрна се *aor. see* обсрне се

обзрнува се *impf see* обсрнува се

обсида *pf* to wall in, surround with a wall

обсидува *impf of* обсида

обѕир *m* consideration, regard, respect; има обѕири спрема некого to have respect for s.o.; to be considerate of/towards s.o.; без никакви обѕири without any consideration; со обѕир на тоа with regard to that; ❑ земе во обѕир to take into account (consideration); земајќи во обѕир considering; taking into consideration; тоа не доаѓа во обѕир that is out of the question; доаѓа во обѕир to come into consideration; to be in the running; без обѕир на in spite of, regardless of

обѕира се *impf* 1 to look back; to look round; се обѕира лево-десно to look left and right 2 *fig.* to take (*s.th.*) into account; to show consideration (*за, на некого – for s.o.*), consider; тој не се обѕира на никого he has no consideration for anybody

обѕре се *pf* обѕри се *aor. see* обѕира се

обѕрне се *pf* обѕрна се *aor.* to look round; to turn round and look back; *see* обѕира се 1

обѕрнува се *impf of* обѕрне се

обигра *pf* to dance round (*s.o./s.th.*)

обигрува *impf of* обигра

обид *m* attempt, try; јалови обиди vain attempts; обид за убиство attempted murder; обид за бегство attempt to escape

обиде[1] *pf* I 1 to try, taste 2 to put to the test, test, try *trans.* II – се 1 to try, attempt *intrans.*; се обиде да ја помине границата he tried to cross the frontier; вреди да се обидеме it's worth a try; обиди се! have a go! have a shot at it! 2 to try one's strength; to compete (*со некого – with s.o.*)

обиде[2] *pf* 1 to visit; да дојдеш да ме обидеш come and visit me! 2 to go round, bypass, *see* обиколи, заобиколи

обидува[1] **(се)** *impf of* обиде[1] (се)

обидува[2] *impf of* обиде[2]

обиколен -лна *adj* roundabout, circuitous, indirect; devious; по обиколни патишта, по обиколен пат by a roundabout route; *fig.* in a roundabout way

обиколи *pf* 1 to go round, circle, pass round, orbit; сателитот ја обиколи земјата the satellite orbited the earth 2 to go round, avoid by a roundabout route, bypass; одредот го обиколи непријателот the detachment evaded the enemy 3 to travel the length and breadth (*of*), travel all over; обиколи цел свет to travel the <whole> world 4 to visit, call on (*in succession*); отиде да ги обиколи роднините he went to visit all his relatives

обиколка *f* tour, visit; (*на стражар и др.*) round<s>; (*на планета*) round, revolution, orbit; направи една обиколка околу градот to make a tour of the town; обиколка низ Италија a tour of Italy; обиколка на војска inspection of troops

обиколува *impf* 1 *of* обиколи 2 to surround; планини го обиколуваат селото mountains surround the village 3 to court, pay court to

обилен -лна *adj* plentiful, abundant, copious, ample; обилен дожд plentiful rain; обилна жетва abundant (bountiful) harvest; обилно јадење hearty meal

обилно *adv* plentifully, abundantly, copiously; лозјата обилно родија the vineyards have produced a good harvest

обилност *f* plenty, abundance

обилува *impf* to abound (*со – in*); овој крај обилува со руда this region is rich in ore

обир *m* 1 theft, stealing 2 stolen goods

обира *impf of* обере

обирач *m* thief, robber

обирачка *f* theft, stealing

обичаен -јна *adj* 1 customary, traditional; обичајно право common law 2 usual, ordinary, accepted; обичаен израз usual expression; *see* вообичаен

обичај -аи *m* 1 custom; tradition; народни обичаи folk customs; свадбени обичаи marriage (wedding) customs 2 habit; тој има обичај да . . . he is in the habit of (*doing s.th.*); според својот обичај according to his habit

обичајно *adv* usual<ly>; обичајно е да се каже . . . it is usual to say . . . , one usually says . . . ; *see* вообичаено

обичен -чна *adj* 1 ordinary, usual; обичен живот ordinary (daily) life; обична работа usual thing; обичен ден normal (working) day; обичното значење на зборот the usual meaning of the word 2 common; обичен врабец, обично врапче *Zool.* (Passer domesticus) house sparrow; обична слива *Bot.* (Prunus myrobalana) cherry plum, *see* џанка

обично *adv* usually; usual; подоцна од обично later than usual

обичност *f* usualness; everyday routine

објава *f* declaration; proclamation, announcement; објава на војна declaration of war; објава за патување, патна објава travel warrant, travel document

објави *pf* 1 to announce, declare, proclaim widely; објави наредба/заповед/закон to proclaim an ordnance/an order/a law; објави мобилизација to announce <general> mobilization 2 to publish, issue, print

објавител *m* announcer

објавува *impf of* објави

објавувач *m see* објавител

објагни *pf* I to produce, bring forth (*a lamb*), *arch.* yean; овцата објагни две јагниња the ewe produced two lambs II – се to lamb; овците се објагнија the ewes have lambed

објагнува (се) *impf of* објагни (се)

објало *n* (*usu. pl*) puttee

објаснение -ија *n* 1 explanation, explication; бараме објаснение we demand an explanation 2 argument, wrangling

објасни *pf* I to explain, explicate, clarify, elucidate II – се to have it out (*со некого – with s.o.*); to clear up a misunderstanding (*with s.o.*), talk things over; сакам да се објаснам со тебе I want to have it out with you

објаснив *adj* explainable, explicable; тоа е објасниво that can be explained

објаснивост *f* explicability

објаснител *m see* објаснувач

објаснителен -лна *adj* explanatory; објаснителен текст explanatory text

објаснува (се) *impf of* објасни (се)

објаснување *n* explanation

објаснувач *m* explainer, clarifier, commentator, interpreter

објаснувачки *adj* explanatory

објект *m* 1 object, thing, item 2 aim, task, object, objective 3 *Gram.* (*предмет*) object 4 building project, building under construction

објекти́в *m* object-glass, lens

објективациja *f see* објективизација

објекти́вен -вна *adj* objective; unbiased, impartial; објективна стварност (реалност) objective reality; објективна вистина objective truth; објективно оценување impartial evaluation

објективи́зам -змот *m Philos.* objectivism

објективизациja *f* objectivization

објективизи́ра & **објективи́ра** *pf & impf* **1** to objectify **2** to make objective

објективи́ст *m* objectivist

објективисти́чки *adj* objectivistic

објекти́вно *adv* objectively, truly, impartially

објекти́вност *f* objectivity, reality, impartiality

објектски *adj* pertaining to a building project; *Gram.* objective

облаг -зи *m f.p. see* облог

облага[1] *f f.p. see* облог

облага[2] *f* advantage, profit, gain; каква облага имам jac од тоа? what do I stand to gain from that?

облага[3] **(се)** *impf see* обложува[1] (се)

облагороди *pf* **I 1** to ennoble, dignify, refine **2** (*in plant/animal breeding*) to improve the strain/quality **II** – **се** to become noble

облагородува (се) *impf of* облагороди (се)

облажи *pf* **I 1** to sweeten **2** *dial. see* омрси **II** – **се 1** to eat s.th. sweet **2** *dial. see* омрси се

облажува (се) *impf of* облажи (се)

облази *pf* to crawl all over; ме облази гасеница a caterpillar crawled over me; ❑ ме облазија морници a shiver ran down my spine

облазува *impf of* облази

облак[1] -ци *m* cloud; црни и густи облаци се креваа од запад thick black clouds were rising in the west; градобитен (градоносен) облак hailcloud; се креваа облаци од прав clouds of dust rose; облак од грижа му помина по лицето a shadow of anxiety passed across his face; ❑ во облаци in the clouds; лебди во облаци to walk on air; to be woolgathering; sида кули во облаци to build castles in the air

облак[2] -ци *m* pommel (*on a saddle*)

облакоде́р *m* skyscraper, high-rise <building>

облакти се *pf* to lean one's elbows (*на нешто – on, against s.th.*); се облакти на масата he leant his elbows on the table

облактува се *impf of* облакти се

обла́нда *f* wafer; ❑ без обланди without mincing words; straight from the shoulder

област *f* **1** region, province; area, zone, belt; планинска област mountainous region; болки во областа на срцето pains in the region of the heart **2** *fig.* field, sphere, realm; во областа на науката in the field of science

областен -сна *adj* regional; обласни карактеристики regional characteristics (features); обласна управа regional administration

облаче *n dim. of* облак; cloudlet

облачен -чна *adj* cloudy, overcast; облачно небо cloudy sky; облачно време cloudy weather

облачи се *impf* to become overcast, cloud over

облачиште *n augm. of* облак

облачно *adv* cloudy; до пладне беше облачно till midday it was cloudy

облачност *f* cloudy condition<s>; cloud cover, cloudiness; облачноста ќе потрае неколку дена the cloudy conditions will persist for a few days

облева (се) *impf of* облее (се)

облега (се) *impf of* облегне (се)

облегалка *f* & **облегало** *n* back (*of a chair, etc.*); плетена облегалка на стол wicker chair-back

облегне *pf* облегна *aor.* **I 1** to lean *trans.*, prop; to rest (*on*) *trans.*; го облегна грбот на sидот he leant his back against the wall **2** *fig.* to put (exert) pressure on; to beleaguer; ме облегнаа од сите страни pressure was put on me from all sides **II** – **се 1** to lean *intrans.*; се облегне на стол to lean on a chair **2** to lie down, stretch out *intrans.*; се облегна на подот колку што е долг he lay down full length on the floor **3** *fig.* to have faith (*на – in*), rely (*on*); се облегнал на мене he's put his trust in me

облегнува (се) *impf of* облегне (се), *see* облега (се)

облее *pf* облеа *aor.* **I** to soak, drench; ме облеа студена пот I broke out in a cold sweat; месечината го облеа градот со своjата светлина the moon bathed the town in its light **II** – **се** to get soaked, drenched; се облеа во крв he was covered in blood

облека *f* clothes, clothing, dress; долна облека underclothes; цивилна облека civilian clothes; plain clothes, mufti; детска облека children's clothes

облекло *n* clothes, clothing

облекува (се) *impf of* облече (се)

облепи *pf* to paste, glue, cover by pasting; облепи sид со соопштениjа to cover a wall with announcements

облепува *impf of* облепи

облета *pf* to fly round; една пчела го облета неколку пати a bee flew round him/it several times

облетува *impf* **1** *of* облета **2** *fig.* to curry favour (*околу некого – with s.o.*); to court (*a girl*)

облече *pf* облече *aor.* облеков *1st p. sg aor.* **I 1** to put on; облече палто to put on a coat; ❑ облече мантиjа to become a priest; облече униформа to become a soldier/officer **2** to dress *trans.*; to clothe, supply with clothes; облече дете to dress a child; ме облече и нахрани he fed and clothed me **3** *fig.* to dress up *trans.* **II** – **се** to get dressed, clothe o.s.; за две минути се облеков I dressed in two minutes; со тие пари сите се облековме with that money all of us bought ourselves some clothes

облечен *pt* clothed, dressed; облечен во ново dressed in new clothes; облечена во црно clad in black

облечува (се) *impf of* облече (се)

облива (се) *impf see* облева (се)

облига́тен -тна *adj* obligatory, necessary; binding; облигатен договор binding agreement/contract

облигаторен -рна *adj* compulsory, mandatory; облигаторен предмет compulsory subject

облигациjа -ии *f* **1** obligation, duty; surety **2** bond, security, debenture

облигаци́онен -она *adj* contractual; облигационо право contract law

оближе *pf* оближа *aor.* **I** to lick; кравата го оближа телето the cow licked the calf; ❑ лиже некому газ *colloq.* to lick s.o.'s boots (*vulg.* arse) **II** – **се 1** to lick o.s.; мачката се оближа the cat licked itself **2** to lick one's lips

оближува (се) *impf of* оближе (се)

облизни <се> *pf* to bear (produce) twins

облизнува <се> *impf of* облизни (се)

облик -ци *m* 1 form, external appearance, contours; облик на квадрат form of a square; облиците на телото the contours of the body 2 manner of appearing, manifestation 3 *Philos.* manner of existence; *rare see* форма; облик и содржина form and content 4 *Gram.* граматички облици grammatical forms; *see* форма

обликува *impf* I to form, shape, give shape (*to s. th.*) II – се to take shape; to form *intrans.*

облина *f* roundness; curved surface; curve; облините на телото the curves of the body

облог -зи *m* bet, wager

облога *f* 1 compress, poultice; студена облога cold compress 2 covering, binding; lagging; cladding; жица со гумена облога rubber-insulated wire

обложи *pf* I to cover; to line; to lag, clad; обложи со штици to board up II – се to be covered; (*за цевки и сл.*) to get furred up

обложи се *pf* to bet, wager; се обложија по сто денари they bet one hundred denars each

обложува¹ (се) *impf of* обложи (се)

обложува² се *impf of* обложи се

обљуба *f* 1 sexual intercourse 2 rape; обљуба со малолетно лице child molesting, sexual abuse of minors

обљуби *pf* to have sexual intercourse (*with s. o.*)

обмислен *pt* considered, deliberate; premeditated

обмислено *adv* after careful consideration, deliberately

обмисленост *f* deliberateness

обмисли *pf* to think over, consider, ponder

обмислува *impf of* обмисли

обнадежи *pf* to inspire (*s. o.*) with hope; to encourage, give heart to

обниже *pf* обнижа *aor.* to string (*s. th.*) round with; ja обнижа капата со бисер he strung the cap round with pearls

обнижува *impf of* обниже

обнова *f* 1 renewal; restoration, reconstruction; обнова на зграда restoration of a building; обнова на стопанството economic recovery 2 revision, repetition; обнова на процес retrial

обнови *pf* I 1 to restore; to rebuild; to repair; to replace; обнови залихи to restock 2 to revive *trans.*, refresh; обнови спомени to revive memories 3 to revise, repeat *trans.*; to recover *trans.*; to renew; обнови процес to reopen a case (trial); обнови договор to renew an agreement/contract; обнови дипломатски односи to resume diplomatic relations II – се 1 to improve *intrans.*; здравјето ми се обнови I recovered my health 2 to revive *intrans.*; to remember; сите спомени од детството ми се обновија all my childhood memories came back to me 3 to recommence *intrans.*; се обновија старите кавги the old bickering started again

обновител *m see* обновувач

обновлив *adj* renewable

обновливост *f* renewability

обновува (се) *impf of* обнови (се)

обновувач *m* renovator, restorer; regenerator; reviver

обноска *f* (*usu. pl*) behaviour, manners; убави/лоши обноски good/bad behaviour; обноски со луѓе treatment of people

обносува се *impf* to behave (*кон, со – towards s. o.*), treat (*s. o.*)

обоа *f* обои *pl Mus.* oboe

обогати (се) *pf see* збогати (се)

обогатува (се) *impf see* збогатува (се)

обод *m* brim, edge; rim; шешир со широк обод broad-brimmed hat

ободри *pf* to encourage, cheer up *trans.*

ободрува *impf of* ободри

обоен *pt* coloured, painted; обоени метали/металургија non-ferrous metals/metallurgy

обоеност *f* colouring

обожава *impf* to worship, adore, idolize; учениците го обожаваа својот професор the pupils adored their teacher

обожавател *m* admirer, follower, fan

обожавателка *f* (*fem. form*) *see* обожавател

обои *pf* to colour, paint

обојст *m Mus.* oboist

обојува *impf of* обои

обопшти *pf* to generalize, summarize, crystallize

обопштува *impf of* обопшти

обор *m* pen, stall, stable; ❑ Авгиеви обори Augean stables

обори *pf* 1 (*кутне, собори*) to floor, throw to the ground 2 *fig.* to refute, rebut

оборува *impf of* обори

обоси <се> *pf* 1 to lose/wear out one's shoes; коњот ми <се> обоси my horse lost its shoes 2 *fig.* to grow poor

обоснование -ија *n* justification, explanation

обоснове *pf* обоснова *aor.* to base, establish

обосновува *impf of* обоснове

обособен *adj & pt* standing out, prominent

обособеност *f* prominence

обособи се *pf* to stand out, make o.s. different/prominent

обостран *adj* mutual, bilateral; обострана обврска mutual obligation; обострана полза mutual benefit

обостраност *f* mutuality

обосува <се> *impf of* обоси <се>

обр *or* обррр *interj* (*call to stop and turn horses*) whoa!

обрабен *pt* bordered, edged; hemmed

обраби *pf* to border, edge; to hem

обработи *pf* 1 (*за земја*) to cultivate, till 2 (*за сурови материјали*) to process; to treat (*s. th.*) (*со – with*) 3 (*за тема, проблем и сл.*) to discuss, treat, deal with

обработка *f* 1 (*на земја*) cultivation, tillage 2 (*на суров материјал*) processing 3 (*на тема и сл.*) treatment, discussion; adaptation; ❑ обработка на податоци data processing

обработлив *adj* 1 workable, adaptable; tractable 2 (*за земја*) cultivable, arable

обработливост *f* 1 workability 2 (*за земја*) cultivability, arability

обработува *impf of* обработи

обработувач *m* tiller (*of the soil*); process-worker

обрабува *impf of* обраби

образче *n dim. of* образ 1

образ *m* 1 cheek; face; бакне некого во образ to kiss s. o. on the cheek; ❑ имаш образ да го кажеш тоа you have the nerve to say that 2 appearance, image 3 *fig.* honour; бел образ unsullied honour; без образ shameless; ❏ обели образ to be a credit to; to do s.o. credit; to save the day; спаси образ to save face

образец -сци *m* **1** model, pattern; sample, specimen **2** formula; математички образец mathematical formula **3** form, blank; пополнува образец to fill in a form

образлага *impf see* образложува

образлест *adj* plump, cherubic, chubby-cheeked

образложение -ија *n* explanation, exposition; argumentation

образложеност *f* justification, explanation; argumentation

образложи *pf* to explain, justify; to put/make a case for

образложува *impf of* образложи

образован *pt* educated; високо образован highly educated

образование *n* education; ниже/средно/више/ високо образование elementary/ secondary/tertiary (college)/university education; стручно образование professional/vocational education; општо образование general education

образованост *f* <level of> education, learning

образува *pf & impf* **I** to form *trans.*, constitute; to create, set up, organize *trans.*; образувавме литературни дружини we organized literary associations; тие делови образуваат една целина these parts form a single whole **II** – **се** to form *intrans.*, be formed; се образуваат ситни капки droplets form (are formed)

обраснат *pt* overgrown (*co – with*); covered; unshaven

обрасне *pf* обрасна *aor.* to become overgrown (*co – with*); *fig.* to become covered (*with*); дворот обрасна со трева the yard became overgrown with grass

обраснува *impf of* обрасне

обрасте *pf see* обрасне

обрастен *pt see* обраснат

обраствува *impf of* обрасте, *see* обраснува

обрат *m* **1** turn, change; коренен обрат radical change; *see* пресврт **2** <turn of> phrase; прашален обрат interrogative phrase **3** *see* обраќање

обратен -тна *adj* reverse, opposite; во обратен правец in the opposite direction; обратна смисла opposite meaning

обрати *pf* **I 1** to turn, direct *trans.*; обрати внимание на нешто to draw (direct) attention to s.th.; to pay attention to s.th. **2** to convert *trans.*; го обрати во нова вера he converted him to a new faith **II** – **се 1** (*кај or with dat.*) to turn to, apply to; се обрати кај директорот, му се обрати на директорот to apply to the director **2** to change one's faith; се обрати во друга вера he <was> converted to another faith

обратно *adv* in the opposite direction; the other way; conversely; the other way round, vice versa; ❏ обратно на (од) contrary to; unlike

обраќа (се) *impf of* обрати (се)

обраќање *n* **1** turning (*кон некого – to s.o.*); address, approach **2** (*внимание на нешто*) drawing/paying attention (*to s.th.*) **3** (*во друга вера*) conversion (*to another faith*)

обрач *m* ring; hoop; *fig., Mil.* encirclement; железни обрачи iron hoops; од старо дрво обрач не се вие *prov.* a tree bends while it's young

обред *m* ritual, rite; религиозни (верски) обреди religious rituals (rites)

обреден -дна *adj* ritual; обредни молитви ritual prayers

обреже *pf* обрежа *aor.* **1** to trim back, prune, lop **2** to circumcise

обрежува *impf of* обреже

обрежување *n* **1** trimming, pruning, cutting off **2** circumcision

обрез *m* place where s.th. is cut off; trimmed edge

обрекува (се) *impf of* обрече (се)

обременет *pt* encumbered, burdened

обремени *pf* to burden, encumber, load; обремени некого со должности to burden s.o. with duties

обременува *impf of* обремени

обрецне се *pf* to snap (*на – at*), snarl (*at*)

обрецнува се *impf of* обрецне се

обрече *pf* обрече *aor.* обреков *1st p. sg aor.* **I** to promise (*s.o.*) in marriage; to betroth; тебе ти ја обрече ќерка си he promised you his daughter **II** – **се** to promise o.s. in marriage to s.o., promise to marry s.o.; обречи ми мене promise to marry me!

обречува (се) *impf see* обрекува (се)

обрешка *f* snippet, cutting

обричи (се) *pf see* избричи (се)

обрис *m* **1** silhouette, outline **2** sketch

обрише (се) *pf* обриша (се) *aor. see* избрише (се)

обрндави *pf* **I** to dirty, soil **II** – **се** to get dirty

обрне *pf* обрна *aor.* **I 1** (*внимание*) to draw, direct (*attention*); to pay (*attention*); to turn one's mind to; не му обрна никакво внимание he paid no attention to him/it **2** *dial.* (*сврти*) to turn; обрне глава to turn one's head **II** – **се 1** (*кон or with dat.*) to turn to, apply to; му се обрна на царот, се обрна кон царот he appealed to the emperor **2** to change (*во – into*) *intrans.*, become **3** *dial.* to turn round; to look round; обрни се, јас да те видам turn round so that I can see you!

обрнува (се) *impf of* обрне (се)

оброк -ци *m* **1** meal; portion, ration; по два оброка дневно two meals/portions a day **2** *see* оброчиште 2

оброни *pf* **I 1** to erode, wear away; to roll down, roll away *trans.*; to break off *trans.* **2** *f.p.* to shed (*tears*) **II** – **се** to roll down, roll away *intrans.*; to break off *intrans.*

оброшува (се) *impf of* оброни (се)

оброси *pf* **I** to bedew, cover with dew **II** – **се** to be covered with dew; полето се оброси the field was covered with dew

обросува (се) *impf of* оброси (се)

оброчиште *n* **1** site of former church, *see* црквиште 1 **2** place where a service is held for a patron saint

обрт *m* **1** turn, turn, revolution; обрти во минута revolutions per minute (r.p.m.) **2** *Finance* turnover, circulation; обрт на капиталот working capital; обрт на парите circulation of money; брз обрт quick returns

обртен -тна *adj Finance* circulating, turnover *attrib.*; обртни средства circulating funds

обружа *pf arch.* **I 1** (*подготви*) to fit out, prepare, get ready *trans.*; (*дотера*) to adorn **2** to arm, equip with arms **II** – **се 1** to fit o.s. out, prepare o.s., get ready *intrans.*; to adorn o.s. **2** to arm o.s. (*co – with*); *see* наоружа (се)

обружува (се) *impf arch. of* обружа (се), *see* наоружува (се)

ОБСЕ *abbr.* (*Организација за безбедност и соработка во Европа*) Organization for Security and Cooperation in Europe, OSCE

обува (се) *impf of* обуе (се)

обувало *n* (*only sg*) footwear

обувка *f* (*usu. pl*) footwear

обуе *pf* обу *aor.* I 1 *trans.* to put on (*shoes/socks*) 2 to shoe, supply with footwear II – **се** 1 to put on one's shoes/socks 2 to acquire footwear; се облеков и се обув I bought myself clothes and footwear

обуен *adj & pt* shod, wearing footwear/socks

обузди *pf* I 1 to bridle, restrain, curb; обузди коњ to bridle a horse 2 *fig.* to tame, subdue, restrain, master, hold in check, curb; обузди свои страсти to master one's passions II – **се** *fig.* to restrain o.s., control o.s.; to refrain (*од – from*)

обуздува (се) *impf of* обузди (се)

обука *f* training; предвојничка обука pre-conscription (military) training (*in secondary school*)

обусловеност *f* conditionality

обуслови *pf* I 1 to condition; to stipulate 2 to cause, call forth II – **се** to be conditioned (*од – by*), depend on, be conditional upon

обусловува (се) *impf of* обуслови (се)

обучен *pt* trained, qualified; *Mil.* drilled

обучи *pf* I to train, instruct *trans.*; *Mil.* to drill (*s.o.*) *trans.* II – **се** to train *intrans.*; *Mil.* to drill *intrans.*

обучува (се) *impf of* обучи (се)

обуш -шје *m & обушва* [*dial. see* обувало

ова *pron* (*n of* овој) this; ова дете this child; де ова де она now this, now that; (*as part.*) ова, што сакав да ти кажам? er . . . , what did I want to tell you?

оваа *pron* (*f of* овој) this

овал *m* oval

овален -лна *adj* oval, egg-shaped; elliptical; овално лице oval face

овалност *f* ovality, ovalness

оварда *adj indecl. colloq.* generous, open-handed

овација -ии *f* ovation; бурна овација great ovation, tumultuous (stormy) applause

овде & овдека *adv* 1 here; овдека кај нас among us; ❑ овде-онде here and there, in places; in dribs and drabs 2 hither, here; ела овде come here!

овдешен -шна *adj* local, from this place/area; овдешен човек a local <man>

овдовее *pf* to be widowed, lose one's spouse

овдовува *impf of* овдовее

овековечи *pf* to perpetuate, immortalize

овековечува *impf of* овековечи

овен -вни *m* 1 ram; *Astron.* Aries; чукан (кастриран) овен wether, gelded ram 2 *Hist.* battering-ram

овенат *pt* faded; овенати ружи faded roses

овене *pf* овена *aor.* 1 to fade, wilt, wither, waste away, droop (*also fig.*); лицето му овена his face has become lined (wrinkled) 2 *fig.* to become dispirited, lose heart

овенува *impf of* овене, *see* вене

овенча *pf* to crown (*also fig.*); to deck, decorate with wreaths (garlands), овенча со слава to crown with glory; овенча со успех to crown with success

овенчува *impf of* овенча

овери *pf* to verify, attest, certify; овери препис на документ to certify a copy of a document

оверува *impf of* овери

оверување *n* verification, attestation

оверувач *m* verifier

овес *m Bot.* oats

овесен -сна *adj* oaten, oatmeal; овесен леб oatmeal bread

оветвен *adj & pt* worn-out, shabby, threadbare; faded

оветвеност *f* shabbiness, threadbareness

оветви <**се**> *pf* to wear out *intrans.*, become shabby; алиштата ми се оветвија my clothes are worn-out

оветвува <**се**> *impf of* оветви <**се**>

овие *pron* (*pl of* овој) these

овисне *pf* овисна *aor. see* обвисне

овиснува *impf of* овисне

овистини се *pf* to come true, become a reality, be realized, be fulfilled

овистинува се *impf of* овистини се

овладее *pf* овладеа *aor.* to master, overcome; to seize, occupy; ја овладеа една мисла a thought took possession of her

овладува *impf of* овладее

овлажи *pf* I to dampen, moisten II – **се** to get damp; ѕидиштата се овлажија the walls got damp

овлажува (се) *impf of* овлажи (се)

овластеник -ци *m* authorized person, commissioner; proxy

овласти *pf* to authorize, entitle, empower

овластител *m see* овластувач

овластува *impf of* овласти

овластување *n* permission, authority, authorization, power of attorney

овластувач *m* authorizer

овнешки *adj* ovine; овнешко месо mutton; овнешка кожа sheepskin

ововче *n dim. of* овошка

овогодишен -шна *adj* this year's, *see* годинашен

овозможи *pf* to enable; тој ми овозможи да одам во странство he enabled me to go abroad

овозможува *impf of* овозможи

овој *m pron* this; овој човек this person; овој пат this time; овој сака едно, оној друго this one wants one thing, that one another

овоплоти *pf literary* to embody, incarnate (*also fig.*); to exemplify

овоплотува *impf of* овоплоти

овошен -шна *adj* fruit *attrib.*; овошен сок fruit juice

овошје *n* fruit; сушено овошје dried fruit; јужно овошје tropical and citrus fruit

овошка *f* fruit-tree

овоштар *m* fruit-grower; fruit-seller, fruiterer

овоштарник -ци *m* orchard

овоштарски *adj* fruit-grower's; fruit-growing; fruit *attrib.*; овоштарски крај fruit-growing district

овоштарство *n* fruit-growing, fruit-farming

овргали *pf* овргали очи во to stare at

оврши *pf* to thresh

овршува *impf of* оврши

овтика *f colloq. see* туберкулоза; ❑ ме фати овтика од тебе I'm sick and tired of you

овула *f ovum* (*pl ova*), egg cell

овулација *f* ovulation

овулира *pf & impf* to ovulate

овца *f Zool.* sheep; мерино овца merino <sheep>; ❑ од една овца две кожи сака to expect too much; му ги оставил овците на волкот да ги варди he left the sheep for the wolf to guard; брои овци to count sheep; црна овца the black sheep (*of the family*); не му се сите овци на број he has a screw loose, he's not all there; he is in a bad mood; не сме паселе овци заедно we're not on equal footing; со една овца бачило не бидува *prov.* one swallow doesn't make a summer; ако си овца, секој ќе те стриже *prov.* don't make yourself a mouse or the cat will eat you

овчар *m* shepherd; sheep breeder, sheep-farmer; (*куче*) sheepdog; на патникот патот, на овчарот стапот *prov.* to each his own

овчарин -ри *m f.p. see* овчар

овчарка *f* 1 shepherdess 2 shepherd's wife

овчарлак *m colloq. see* овчарство

овчарник -ци *m* sheepfold, sheep-cote

овчарски *adj* shepherd's; овчарски пес, овчарско куче sheepdog; овчарски стап shepherd's crook

овчарство *n* sheep farming, sheep breeding

овчарува *impf* to go in for sheep farming; to work as a shepherd

овчарче *n dim. of* овчар

овчи & овчки *adj* sheep's; овчо (овчко) млеко sheep's milk; овчо (овчко) сирење sheep's-milk cheese; овча (овчка) кожа sheepskin; овчо (овчко) месо mutton

овчица & овчичка *f dim. of* овца

овчуринка *f pejor.* wretched sheep

о.г. *abbr.* (*оваа година*) this year

оган -гнот, -гнови *m* 1 fire; огнот тлее the fire is smouldering; запали оган to light a fire; спотне оган to stoke a fire; *fig.* оган во очите fire in one's eyes; готви на тивок оган to simmer; логорски оган bonfire; camp-fire; ❏ бега како од оган to avoid (*s.o. or s.th.*) like the plague; to steer clear of; се фрла (рипа) в оган за некого; става рака во оган за некого to go through fire and water for s.o.; го разгорува огнот to fan the flames; <до>тура масло в оган to add fuel to the flames; со оган се игра со оган to play with fire; со оган шега се не се прави one doesn't play with fire; меѓу два огна between two fires; between the devil and the deep blue sea; *literary* вади костење од оган за друг to pull s.o. else's chestnuts out of the fire; to do s.o.'s dirty work; *literary* блуе (сипе) оган на некого to belch fire at s.o.; оган и пламен <е> 1. everything/life is terribly expensive 2. he's a live wire; бенгалски оган Bengal light 2 light, lighter; имаш ли оган? have you got a light? 3 *colloq.* high temperature, fever; има оган to have a high temperature 4 (*only sg*) gunfire; топовски (артилериски) оган artillery fire; митралески оган machine-gun fire; крстосан оган cross-fire

оганче *n dim. of* оган 1

огин *m see* оган

огинец & огинок *m poet. dim. of* огин, *see* оганче

оглав *m* 1 headstall; halter; *see* огламник 2 *dial.* (*свршувачка*) betrothal, engagement

огладни *pf* to become hungry

огладнува *impf of* огладни

огламник -ци *m* headstall; halter

оглас *m* 1 announcement, notice; advertisement; оглас во весник announcement/advertisement in a newspaper; табла за огласи notice-board; огласи (*рубрика во весник*) classifieds 2 (*одглас*) response; reception, reaction (*на нешто – to s.th.*) 3 (*ехо*) echo, reverberation

огласен -сна *adj* advertising, notice *attrib.*; огласна табла notice-board

огласи *pf* I 1 to announce; to advertise 2 to reverberate, echo; to resound, ring; борбени песни го огласија селото songs of battle resounded through the village II – се 1 to respond, reply; никој не се огласи no one replied 2 to echo; to resound

огласува (се) *impf of* огласи (се)

оглед *m* 1 experiment; врши огледи to carry out experiments 2 examination, inspection; visit to prospective bride 3 consideration, regard; со оглед на with regard to, taking account of; без оглед на regardless of, irrespective of

огледа *pf* I to examine, inspect, look at from all sides, look over II – се 1 to look at o.s. (*in a mirror, etc.*); to examine o.s. 2 to look back; to look round; to look right and left

огледало *n* mirror (*also fig.*), looking-glass; ѕидно огледало wall mirror; се гледа на огледало to look at o.s. in the mirror; очите се огледало на душата the eyes are a mirror of the soul

огледалце *n dim. of* огледало

огледен -дна *adj* experimental

огледува (се) *impf of* огледа (се)

оглода *pf* to gnaw

оглодува *impf of* оглода

оглувее *pf* to become deaf, *see* оглуви 2

оглуви *pf* 1 to deafen 2 to become deaf; ќе оглувам од оваа врева I'll go deaf from this racket

оглувне *pf* оглувна *aor. see* оглувее, оглуви 2

оглувнува *impf of* оглувне

оглувува *impf of* оглувее & оглуви

оглупавеност *f* stupefaction, *see* оглупеност

оглупави *pf* 1 to become (grow) stupid 2 to make (*s.o.*) stupid, stupefy

оглупее *pf* to become stupid, *see* оглупави 1

оглупеност *f* stupefaction

оглупи *pf* 1 to make (*s.o.*) stupid, stupefy 2 to become stupid

оглупува *impf of* оглупее & оглупи

оглуши *pf* to deafen, make (*s.o.*) <temporarily> unable to hear; не викај, ме оглуши don't shout, you're deafening me!

оглушлив *adj* deafening

оглушува *impf of* оглуши

огнар *m* fireman, stoker, furnaceman

огнарски *adj* stoker's; огнарска лопата stoker's shovel

огнаси *pf* I to dirty, soil; to besmirch; to defile II – се 1 to get dirty 2 to feel loathing (*од – for*), be disgusted (*by*)

огнасува (се) *impf of* огнаси (се)

огне *n dim. of* оган

огнебојка *f f.p.* пушка огнебојка fire-spitting (fire-breathing) gun

огнен *adj* 1 fire, fiery; огнено оружје firearms 2 *fig.* fiery, ardent, passionate; огнен приврзаник ardent supporter 3 *Rel.* Огнена Марија St. Marina, the Great Martyr

огненострелен -лна *adj see* огнострелен

огнило *n* (*секало*) steel (*for striking sparks*), flint and steel

огница *f* fever

огничав *adj* feverish

огниште[1] *n* **1** fireplace, hearth; си легнала крај огниште she lay down by the fire; огниште на локомотива firebox; решетка во огниште firedog; заштитна решетка пред огниште fire-guard, fire-screen **2** *fig.* the house, home, fireside; татково огниште hearth and home **3** focus; source; огниште на зараза/на болести nidus, seed (source) of infection/of illness; огниште на војна cause of war, hotbed of war **4** planting-hole, planting-place

огниште[2] *n augm. of* оган

огнодишен -шна *adj poet.* огнодишно оружје fire-breathing weapons, firearms

огномет *m* fireworks; firework display

огнометен -тна *adj* fireworks *attrib.*; огнометна приредба fireworks display

огноок *adj poet.* having blazing eyes; огнооки змејови fiery-eyed dragons

огноотпорен -рна *adj* fireproof; incombustible; fire-(heat-)resistant; огноотпорен материјал fireproof/incombustible material

огнопер *adj poet.* having fiery plumage; огнопер петел a cock with flame-coloured plumage

огнострелен -лна *adj* огнострелно оружје fire-arms

огњарка *f see* огнебојка

оговара *impf* to gossip about (*s.o. or s.th.*), find fault with, criticize, run down; *colloq.* to sling mud at; оговара некого to run s.o. down; *see* озборува

оговарач *m* gossip, gossipmonger, *see* озборувач

оговори *pf see* оговара

огојка *f Bot.* (Bryonia dioica) red (or white) bryony

оголее *pf* оголеа *aor. see* оголи (се)

оголеност *f* bare state, bareness

оголи *pf* **I 1** to bare, uncover, expose, reveal; to strip, denude; си ги оголи раменците she uncovered her shoulders; ги оголи забите he bared his teeth; ветрот ги оголи дрвјата the wind stripped the trees; берберот му го оголи вратот the barber shaved his neck; му ја оголија куќата his house was stripped bare **2** *fig.* to rob, plunder, ruin, fleece; *colloq.* to clean s.o. out; вчера ме оголија на коцка yesterday they cleaned me out at the gambling table **3** to leave naked, destitute; to impoverish, ruin; автомобилот нè оголи the car was the ruin of us **4** to grow bare; to lose vegetation, leaves; to lose one's hair; дрвјата оголеа the trees shed their leaves; ридиштата оголеа the hills grew bare **5** to be left without a stitch, with nothing to wear **6** *fig.* to be left destitute **II – се** *see* I 4

оологази *pf colloq.* **I** to bare one's buttocks **II – се** to undress, ungird *intrans.*; to uncover one's buttocks

оголува (се) *impf of* оголи (се)

огон -гнови *m see* оган

огори *pf* **1** to burn (*on all sides*) *trans.*; to scorch, singe **2** (*of nettles*) to sting

огорува *impf of* огори

огорчен *adj & pt* embittered, bitter; angry; resentful; irritated; offended

огорчено *adv* bitterly, angrily; се бореа огорчено they struggled (fought) bitterly

огорченост *f* bitterness; resentment

огорчи *pf* **I 1** to embitter, *fig.* poison; огорчи некому живот to poison s.o.'s existence **2** to insult, offend; твоите зборови ме огорчија your words offended

me **II – се** to become embittered; to be hurt (offended, insulted)

огорчува (се) *impf of* огорчи (се)

ограби *pf* to rob, plunder, loot

ограбува *impf of* ограби

ограбувач *m* greedy person, plunderer, looter

ограбувачки *adj* plundering; ограбувачка политика policy of plunder, exploitation

ограда *f* **1** fence, wall, enclosure; ограда од штици wooden fence; жива ограда hedge **2** enclosure, enclosed space, field, garden (*usu. on the outskirts of a village or town*); *pl* огради & ограѓе; во јужните огради на селото in the enclosures on the south-<ern> side of the village **3** *fig.* reservation, restrictions; ги прими нашите услови со извесни огради he accepted our terms with certain reservations **4** (*околу месечината*) ring, halo

огради *pf* **I 1** to fence <in>, enclose **2** *fig.* to protect, shield **II – се 1** to fence o.s. in; to put an enclosure round o.s. **2** *fig.* to dissociate o.s. (*од – from*); јас се оградив од неговите забелешки I dissociated myself from his remarks

оградува (се) *impf of* огради (се)

ограничен *adj & pt* **1** limited; ограничен простор limited space; ограничени права restricted rights; ограничено време limited time **2** (*за човек*) limited, narrow-minded; ограничени умствени способ-ности limited mental abilities

ограниченост *f* limitation; restriction; *fig.* narrow-mindedness

ограничи *pf* **I** to limit, set bounds, restrict, confine; ограничи средства to restrict funding; ограничи нечија слобода to restrict s.o.'s freedom **II – се** *fig.* to confine o.s.; ќе се ограничам на неколку факти I'll confine myself to a few facts

ограничува (се) *impf of* ограничи (се)

ограничување *n* limitation; limit; restriction; ограничување на брзината speed limit

огратче *n dim. of* ограда

огрден *pt* grown ugly; disfigured

огрденост *f* ugliness; disfigurement

огрди *pf* **I 1** to become ugly **2** to make ugly, disfigure **II – се** to make o.s. ugly, disfigure o.s.

огрдува (се) *impf of* огрди (се)

огребе *pf* огреба *aor.* **1** to scrape; огребе котел/тенџере to scrape a cauldron/pot **2** to scratch, make scratches on; мачката ме огреба the cat scratched me

огребува *impf of* огребе

огрев *m* **1** heating materials, fuel; дрва за огрев fire-wood **2** *f.p.* (*изгрев*) sunrise

огрева[1] *f f.p.* (*изгрев*) sunrise, dawn; од огрева до заоѓа from sunrise to sunset

огрева[2] **(се)** *impf of* огрее (се)

огревен -вна *adj* heating *attrib.*; огревен материјал heating material, fuel

огревиште *n* fuel, firewood

огрее *pf* огреа *aor.* **I 1** to warm; си ги огреав нозете I warmed my feet/legs **2** (*за сонцето и месечината*) to rise; огреа сонцето the sun has risen **3** (*за сонцето и месечината*) to light up; to shine on; огреан од сонце sunlit; ❏ сонцето го огреа fortune smiled on him **II – се** to warm o.s.

огрејсонце *n* sunrise; east; на огрејсонце at sunrise; откај огрејсонце from the east

огреши *pf* **I** to cause to sin, involve in sin **II** – **се** to sin, commit a sin

огрешува (се) *impf of* огреши (се)

огризе *pf* огриза *aor.* to gnaw; огризе коски to gnaw bones

огризина & **огризок** -ци *m* scraps, leavings, remnants of food

огризува *impf of* огризе

огрозни *pf* to become ugly, *see* огрди I 1

огрознува *impf of* огрозни, *see* огрдува

огромен -мна *adj* enormous, huge, immense; огромни згради enormous buildings

огруби *pf* 1 to become rough/coarse 2 to become ugly

огрубне *pf* огрубна *aor. see* огруби

огрубува *impf of* огруби

огули *pf* **I** to scratch, scrape (*the skin, etc.*); to dent **II** – **се** to get scratched; to peel off *intrans.*

од¹ *prep* 1 from; out of; излезе од собата he came out of the room; падна од коњот he fell off his horse; гледа од прозорецот he is looking out of the window; од сидот до масата from the wall to the table; од куќа в куќа from house to house; тој е од Скопје he comes from Skopje; производи од странство products from abroad; ❏ од коњ на магаре to come down in the world 2 (*indicating distance*) from; станицата е далеку од градот the station is a long way from the town; на два метра од него two metres from him 3 since; слеп е од раѓање he has been blind from birth; од денеска from today, henceforth 4 (*indicating date*) of; писмо од десетти март letter of 10th March 5 made of, consisting of, comprising; extracted from; куќа од камен a house built of stone; сок од малини raspberry juice; мармалад од сливи plum jam; од неколку делови consisting of several parts 6 (*possession, authorship*) of; куќата од мајка ми my mother's house 7 (*quantity, measure, value*) of; банкнота од илјада денари a thousand-denar note; прстен од илјада денари a ring worth a thousand denars 8 (*comparison*) than; јас сум помлад од тебе I am younger than you; тој е најбрз од сите нас he is the fastest of us all 9 (*indicating agent in passive constructions*) by; земја опустена од војна a country ravaged by war 10 (*cause*) from; умре од рак he died of cancer; се тресеше од страв he was trembling with fear; пееше од радост he sang from joy 11 (*with various verbs*) се крие од to hide from; има потреба од специјалисти specialists are needed; лиши од to deprive of; брани од to protect against

од² *m* 1 action of walking, way, step; забрзај го одот walk faster, step out! два часа од two hours' walk 2 manner of walking, gait, step; го познавам по одот I recognize him by his walk (gait) 3 operation, functioning; одот на иглата е неправилен the action of the needle is irregular; одот на стрелките на часовникот the movement of the hands of the watch/clock; празен од (*на мотор*) idling speed (*of an engine*) 4 play, freedom of movement, slack 5 course, development, progress; одот на востанието the course (development) of the uprising

од- (*от- before voiceless consonants*) *verbal prefix indicating* 1 *motion away, backward, from*; одбегне to run away 2 *negation of action* dis-, de-, un-; одврзе to untie 3 *completion of action*; одработи to finish a job

ода *f* ode

одава (се) *impf of* одаде (се)

одавник -ци *m* (*предавник*) traitor

одавница *f* (*предавница*) traitress

одаде *pf* **I** 1 to betray, give away; гласот го одаде his voice gave him away 2 to reveal; одаде тајна to reveal a secret **II** – **се** to give o.s. away

одаја -даи *f arch.* (*соба*) chamber, room; шарена одаја, голема одаја drawing-room, reception-room

одајче *n dim. of* одаја, *see* собиче, собичка

одамна *adv* 1 long ago; одамна беше тоа that was long ago 2 for a long time <*now*>; одамна сум тука I've been here for a long time now

одамнешен -шна *adj* olden, ancient; одамнешни настани events long past; одамнешни времиња days of old, bygone days; одамнешни соработници на списание long-standing contributors to a journal

одар -дри *m* 1 ledge along interior wall (*as fixed seat or bench*) 2 wooden bedstead, bunk; смртен одар catafalque, bier

одбашка *adv colloq.* (*башка, одделно*) apart, individually, separately

одбегне *pf* одбегна *aor.* 1 to run away, flee, escape *intrans.* 2 to avoid, evade, escape *trans.*

одбегнува *impf of* одбегне; одбегнува некого to give s.o. a wide berth; to give s.o. the slip; to steer clear of s.o.

одбележи *pf* 1 to mark; to celebrate; одбележи зборови во текст to mark words in a text; одбележи годишница to mark (celebrate) an anniversary 2 *fig.* to point out; to stress, underline, emphasize; треба да се одбележи дека . . . it ought to be pointed out that . . . , it should be emphasized that . . .

одбележува *impf of* одбележи

одбере *pf* одбра *aor.* **I** 1 to choose, select 2 *fig.* to understand, grasp, comprehend; ништо не одбрав I didn't understand anything 3 *in the expression:* одбере гајле to stop worrying; to free o.s. of cares **II** – **се** *fig.* (*see* I 2) to understand, grasp; ако си сетен, можеш да се одбереш if you're clever, you'll understand

одбив *m* 1 weaning; weaning time (*of animals*) 2 (*на река, на вода*) diversion

одбива (се) *impf of* одбие (се)

одбивање *n* 1 refusal, rejection 2 deduction; одбивање за данок tax deduction; одбивање за дара allowance for tare

одбивен -вна *adj* repulsive, unfriendly; disgusting; одбивен поглед unfriendly/scornful look

одбие *pf* одби *aor.* **I** 1 to ward off, repulse; to reflect; to deflect; одбие напад to repulse an attack; одбие удар to parry a blow; *Sport.* одбие топка to return the ball; стаклото ги одби сончевите зраци the glass reflected the sun's rays 2 to refuse, reject; одбие молба to refuse an application; одбие жалба to reject a complaint; одбие предлог to reject a proposal 3 to wean; мајката го одби детето на десет месеци the mother weaned the child at ten months 4 to deduct, reduce; ми одбија пет проценти од платата they deducted five per cent from my pay 5 to put off, repel; ги одби луѓето од себе he put people off 6 одбие на to attribute to; одбие на младост/ глупост/неискусност to attribute (put it down) to youth/ stupidity/inexperience; одбие едно кило на влагата to allow one kilo for moisture 7 to divert (*watercourse*), channel off; ја одби водата од јазот he diverted the water from the ditch/irrigation channel **8** to move off *intrans.*, get out of the way; одбиј! move off! get away! **9** to turn <off> *intrans.*; одбивме од патот во ливаѓето we turned off the road into the meadows **II – се 1** to bounce off, ricochet; to be reflected; топката се одби од ѕидот the ball bounced off the wall; зраците се одбија од огледалото the rays were reflected in the mirror **2** (*see* I 9) to turn <off> *intrans.* **3** to drop in, call on; се одбивме до старите we dropped in to see our parents

одбира (се) *impf of* одбере (се)

одбирач *m* selector

одбирачка¹ *f* (*fem. form*) *see* одбирач

одбирачка² *f colloq.* understanding, grasp; нема одбирачка he has/there is no understanding

одбиток -ци *m* deduction

одблесне *pf* одблесна *aor.* to be reflected (*of light*)

одблеснува *impf of* одблесне

одблесок -ци *m* reflection; gleam; сребрените одблесоци на росата the silvery gleam of the dew

одблизу & одблиску *adv* from nearby, from close at hand, at close range; го видов одблизу I saw him close up; ја запознав одблизу (одблиску) вистинската состојба на работите I got to know the true state of affairs at first hand

одбоен -јна *adj* blocking, checking; одбојна сила repelling force; одбоен вентил check-valve

одбој *m* **1** refusal; repulsion **2** *literary* withdrawal; signal for retreat

одбојка *f Sport.* volleyball

одбојност *f* repulsiveness; power of repulsion

одбор *m* **1** committee, board, council; управен/ извршен/надзорен одбор management/executive/ supervisory committee; училиштен одбор school council; претседател на одборот chairman of the committee/board/council **2** selection; elite; the pick of, a select group; одбор јунаци a heroic elite; одбор грозје a selection of grapes

одборник -ци *m* committee/council/board member; councilman, councillor

одборнички *adj* committee member's

одборски *adj* committee *attrib.*; одборска седница committee meeting

одборчи се *pf colloq.* (*оддолжи се*) to pay off a debt, repay

одборчува се *impf colloq. of* одборчи се

одбради *pf* **I** to untie, undo, take off (*a kerchief*) **II – ce** to untie, undo, take off one's kerchief

одбрадува (се) *impf of* одбради (се)

одбран *pt* chosen, selected; одбрани песни/раскази selected poems/tales

одбрана *f* defence; одбрана на земјата defence of the country; судска одбрана defence in court; има збор одбраната the defence has the floor; одбрана на докторска теза defence of a doctoral thesis

одбранбен *adj* defensive; одбранбена војна defensive war; одбранбен сојуз defensive alliance; одбранбена линија line of defence; одбранбени средства means of defence; одбранбена позиција defensive position

одбрани *pf* **I** to defend **II – ce** to defend, protect o.s.

одбранува (се) *impf of* одбрани (се)

одброи *pf* to count off; to count out

одбројува *impf of* одброи

одбули *pf* **I** to take off (*s.o.'s*) veil, unveil (*s.o.*) **II – ce** to take off one's own veil

одбулува (се) *impf of* одбули (се)

одвáj *adv* **1** with difficulty, hardly, scarcely, barely; одвај се држам на нозе I can hardly stand; ❏ одвај се спаси to have a narrow escape; одвај составува крај со крај to keep one's head above water; to make ends meet **2** (*usu. with adverbs of time, place, etc.*) only, not until; одвај тогаш почна да работи only then did he begin to work; одвај таму проговори only there did he start to speak **3** hardly, scarcely, just, no sooner, as soon as, the moment . . . ; одвај легнав да се одморам, ме повикаа на состанок no sooner had I lain down to rest, than I was called to a meeting

одвар *m* extract; одвар од смоквини лисја extract of fig leaves

одвева *impf of* одвее

одведе *pf* **1** to take (lead) s.o.; to drive; ме одведе на лекар he took/drove me to the doctor **2** to abduct **3** (*за вода*) to divert, channel

одведува *impf of* одведе

одвее *pf* одвеа *aor.* **1** to blow away; ветрот ми ја одвеа шамијата the wind blew off my kerchief **2** to winnow; го одвеавме житото we winnowed the grain

одвезе *pf* **I** to take, drive (*s.o. or s.th.*) (*in a vehicle*); *colloq.* to give a lift to **II – ce** to set out, leave, go off

одвезува (се) *impf of* одвезе (се)

одвејува *impf see* одвева

одвели *pf* to deny, refuse; to withdraw one's word, go back on a promise

одвелува *impf of* одвели; јас кога велам, не одвелувам when I say s.th., I stick to my word

одвери *pf* **I** to convert (*s.o.*); да вера ме одверивте you have converted me **II – ce** to change one's faith

одверува (се) *impf of* одвери (се)

одвет *m arch.* reply, response; *mainly in the expression:* не може одвет да си даде he has no reply to that, he cannot justify that to himself

одветрум *adv colloq.* (*of the onset of an illness*) suddenly, unexpectedly; одветрум му дошла болеста he suddenly fell ill

одвива (се) *impf of* одвие (се)

одвие *pf* одви *aor.* **I** to unwrap, unroll, untwist *trans.*; to unswathe; to unwind, uncoil *trans.*; одвие пакет to unwrap a parcel; одвие дете to undo a child's nappy (*Am.* diaper); одвие кабел to unwind a cable **II – ce 1** to become unwrapped, unrolled, untwisted; to unwrap, unroll *intrans.*; to unwind *intrans.* (*of mechanism, etc.*) **2** to develop, unfold *intrans.*; to happen, take place

одвик -ци *m &* **одвика** *f* breaking of a habit

одвикне *pf* одвикна *aor.* **I 1** to cure, break (*s.o.'s*) habit; таа го одвикна детето од мласкање she broke the child's habit of chewing noisily **2** to give up <a habit>, get out of the habit; одвикнав од пушење I've given up smoking **II – ce** *see* I 2

одвикнува (се) *impf of* одвикне (се)

одвинти *pf* **I** to unscrew **II – ce** to become loose/ undone; to unwind *intrans.*

одвинтува (се) *impf of* одвинти (се)

одвитка *pf* **I 1** to unwrap, untwist, undo **2** to straighten, unfold, unroll, unwind *trans.* **II – ce 1** to unwrap *intrans.*, become unwrapped, come undone **2** to straighten out, unfold, unroll, unwind *intrans.*

одвиткува (се) *impf of* одвитка (се)

одвише *adv dial.* too much, excessively

одвишен -шна *adj dial.* superfluous, excessive

одвишок *m* surplus, *see* вишок

одвлекува (се) *impf of* одвлече (се)

одвлече *pf* **I 1** to draw/lead/take away; to carry off, drag off; го одвлече сандакот he dragged the chest away **2** *fig.* (*за внимание, мисли и сл.*) to distract, divert **II – се** to drag o.s. off <with difficulty>

одвлечка (се) *pf see* одвлече (се)

одвлечкува (се) *impf of* одвлечка (се)

одвлечува (се) *impf see* одвлекува (се)

одвод *m* **1** (*на вода*) pipe, drain; (*на струја*) conductor, cable **2** sprout, shoot, new branch

одводен -дна *adj* drain, drainage *attrib.*; одводен канал drain; одводна цевка drain-pipe

одводни *pf see* одводнува

одводник -ци *m* conductor, cable; одводник на струја, електричен одводник conductor of electricity, power cable

одводнува *impf* to drain (*land*)

одвоен *pt* **1** separated; cut off; segregated; одвоен од светот cut off from society **2** divided, split; одвоени сили divided powers

одвоеност *f* **1** separateness; segregation **2** dividedness

одвои *pf* **I** to separate, divide, part *trans.*; to segregate; ❑ не може очи да одвои од неа he can't take his eyes off her **II – се** to separate, divide, part *intrans.*; to branch off; to break off *intrans.*; to come off; се одвоивме од групата we broke off from the group

одвојува (се) *impf of* одвои (се)

одвратен -тна *adj* revolting, horrible, disgusting; одвратен човек horrible person; одвратна мирозба revolting smell; одвратна постапка disgusting act

одврати *pf* **I 1** to pay back; to return *trans.*; ако го удриш, ќе ти одврати if you hit him, he'll hit you back; на насмевката ми одврати со насмевка he returned my smile **2** to reply, answer, answer back **3** to dissuade; одврати од крив пат to return (*s.o.*) to the straight and narrow **4** to repulse; to alienate, put off; ме одврати од себе he distanced himself from me **5** to turn aside, turn away *trans.*; одврати лице <настрана> to avert one's eyes; одврати нечие внимание to distract s.o.'s attention **6** to divert; одврати вода од поток to divert water from a stream **II – се 1** to withdraw, turn away, keep away (*од некој/нешто – from s.o./s.th.*) *intrans.* **2** *impers.* ми се одврати I felt disgusted, I felt revulsion

одвратно *adv* revoltingly, horribly, disgustingly; одвратно ми е да го гледам it makes me sick to see him

одвратност *f* disgust, repugnance, aversion; repulsiveness

одвраќа (се) *impf of* одврати (се)

одврже (се) *pf dial. see* одврзе (се)

одврзе *pf* одврза *aor.* **I 1** to untie, release; одврзе коњ to untie (untether) a horse; одврзе преврска од рана to undo a bandage on a wound **2** *fig.* to untie, free, release; одврзе јазик to find one's voice; одврзе некому јазик to loosen s.o.'s tongue **II – се 1** to become loose, untied; чевелот ми се одврза my shoelace has come undone **2** *fig.* (*usu. of the tongue*)

to be freed, loosened; јазикот му се одврза his tongue was loosened; he found his voice

одврзува (се) *impf of* одврзе (се)

одвркне *pf* одвркна *aor.* **I 1** (*see* одврати I 3) to dissuade; to cure (*s.o.*) of a habit; го одвркна од тутунот (од пушењето) he cured him of smoking **2** (*see* одврати I 4) to alienate, estrange (*од – from*); го одвркна од другарите he alienated him from his friends **II – се 1** (*od a habit*); to give up **2** to withdraw, turn away, keep away *intrans.* (*од – from*)

одвркнува (се) *impf of* одвркне (се)

одврти *pf* **I 1** (*одвинти*) to unscrew **2** *f.p.* (*of eyes*) to gouge out **II – се** to become loose/undone; to unwind *intrans.*

одвртува (се) *impf of* одврти (се)

одгатка *f* solution, answer to a riddle

одгатне *pf* одгатна *aor.* to guess, discover, figure out; to solve (*a riddle*)

одгатнува *impf of* одгатне

одглади *adv arch.* (*also* од глад) of/from hunger; ќе умреше одглади he would have died of hunger

одглас *m* **1** echo **2** response, reaction; наиде на убав одглас he/it got a good response (reception)

одгласи се *pf* **1** to echo; to resound; пукотот се одгласи на сите страни the firing resounded on all sides **2** to respond, reply

одгласува се *impf of* одгласи се

одгледа *pf* to raise, rear, bring up; to educate; сама си ги одгледала децата she brought up her children by herself

одгледува *impf* **1** *of* одгледа **2** to grow (*crops*)

одгледувач *m* guardian, tutor; breeder; grower

одговара *impf* **I 1** *of* одговори **2** to be proper; to suit; to agree with; to conform; тебе не ти одговара да играш на улица it's not right for you to play in the street; не ми одговара it doesn't agree with me; it doesn't suit me **3** to be accountable (responsible, answerable), bear the responsibility (*за нешто – for s.th.*) **II – се** *impf of* одговори се

одговор *m* reply, answer; reaction, rejoinder; response; одговорот е точен the answer is correct; брз/духовит одговор repartee; директен одговор straight answer; за сè има одговор to know all the answers; како одговор на in answer to

одговорен -рна *adj* responsible; answerable, accountable; одговорен уредник editor-in-chief; тешки и одговорни задачи difficult and responsible tasks

одговори *pf* **I 1** to answer, reply, respond; to retort; одговори на прашање to answer a question; му одговорив на писмото I replied to his letter **2** to fulfil, carry out, discharge; тој не одговори на своите обврски he didn't fulfil his obligations **II – се** *dial.* to respond, react

одговорник -ци *m* person in charge (*of*), responsible (*for*)

одговорно *adv* responsibly; не се однесува одговорно кон работата he does not take a responsible attitude to the work

одговорност *f* responsibility; accountability; liability; на моја одговорност on my responsibility; фрла одговорност на друг to put the responsibility on s.o. else; симнува секоја одговорност од себе to renounce all responsibility; повика на одговорност to call to account; презема одговорност за to claim responsibility for; чувство на одговорност sense of responsibility

одгоре *adv* 1 from above; on the top; ❑ одгоре додолу from top to bottom, from head to foot 2 from/on the outside; ковчегот беше одгоре бојадисан со црвена боја the chest was painted on the outside with red paint 3 (*of quantity, amount*) extra, in addition; уште триесет денари одгоре му дадов I gave him thirty denars extra

одгради¹ *pf* I to take down (remove) a fence; го одградивме дворот we took down the fence round the yard II – ce to get rid of one's fences

одгради² *pf* I to uncover s.o.'s chest/breast II – ce to uncover o.s., show one's chest/breast; тој се одгради за да му ги видат раните he uncovered his chest to let them see his wounds

одградува¹ **(ce)** *impf of* одгради¹ (ce)

одградува² **(ce)** *impf of* одгради² (ce)

одгризе *pf* одгриза *aor.* to bite off; одгриза парче сирење he bit off a piece of cheese

одгризува *impf of* одгризе

одгрли *pf* to loosen (*earth*), dig up, hoe, rake

одгрлува *impf of* одгрли

одгрне *pf* одгрна *aor.* I 1 to uncover, bare (*s.o.'s breast, etc.*) 2 to dig up II – ce 1 to uncover o.s.; to open <out> *intrans.*; небото се одгрна the heavens opened; it poured 2 to dig o.s. out; *f.p.* па се мртви одгрнале and the dead rose from their graves

одгрнува (ce) *impf of* одгрне (ce)

оддава (ce) *impf of* оддаде (ce)

оддаде *pf* I to pay (*one's respects to*); to give (*s.o. credit*), show (*recognition, etc. of*); оддаде почест на to pay homage to; оддаде признание to do justice to; to give credit to II – ce to devote, dedicate o.s. to; to give o.s. up (*на – to*), become addicted to; се оддаде на наука to devote o.s. to scholarship/science; се оддаде на алкохол to become addicted to alcohol

оддалеку *adv* 1 from far away, from afar; jac сум дојден оддалеку I have come from far away (afar); не слушам добро оддалеку I don't hear well at a distance; ❑ ни оддалеку nowhere near; ни оддалеку не личи на to be a far cry from 2 *fig.* (*with verbs of speaking*) indirectly, circuitously, in a roundabout way; ти многу оддалеку почна you've started in a very roundabout way

оддалечен *pt* distant, remote; оддалечени места, села remote places, villages

оддалеченост *f* 1 remoteness 2 distance; оддалеченоста на едната куќа од другата the distance from one house to the other

оддалечи *pf* I 1 to carry away; to remove 2 to put off, postpone, delay 3 to alienate, estrange (*од – from*); тој ги оддалечи пријателите од себе he alienated his friends II – ce 1 to go away, move away; (*од тема*) to digress 2 to become estranged (*from*), be alienated (*from*); to shun; се оддалечивме од роднините we've become estranged from our kinsmen; многу се оддалечија they drifted apart

оддалечува (ce) *impf of* оддалечи (ce)

оддел *m* 1 (*во установа, организација и сл.*) section, department 2 (*во книга, весник и сл.*) section, column 3 branch, area

одделен -лна *adj* 1 separate; special; одделна просторија separate room 2 some, certain; во одделни случаи in certain cases 3 individual; scattered, isolated, a few, odd; се слушаа само одделни довикувања only a few isolated calls were heard

одделение -ија *n* 1 department, section; (*во болница*) ward; *Mil.* detachment; одделение за печат press department; хируршко одделение surgical ward 2 (*во училиште*) class, form, grade

одделеност *f* 1 separateness; isolation 2 fragmentation; одделеност на силите dispersal of resources/effort/forces

оддели *pf* I 1 to set aside, select; оддели работи што се за продавање to put aside things that are for sale 2 to divide, separate *trans.*; ги оддели децата од родителите he/it separated the children from their parents 3 to establish separately; ќе ги женам синовите и ќе ги одделам I will marry off my sons and set them up on their own II – ce to separate *intrans.*; to part (*од – with*) *intrans.*; се оддели од нас he cut his ties with us; брат му се одделил од домаќинството his brother left the household

одделне *pf* одделна *aor.* to cut off, chop off

одделно *adv* 1 separately; specially; треба секој случај да се разгледа одделно every case must be examined separately 2 individually, one by one

одделнува *impf of* одделне

одделува (ce) *impf of* оддели (ce)

оддене *pf* оддена *aor.* I to unthread, pull out, take out II – ce to become unthreaded; to come out, fall out; се оддена конецот од иглата the thread has come out of the needle

одденува (ce) *impf of* оддене (ce)

оддесно *adv* from the right; оддесно и одлево from the right and from the left

оддив *m* & **оддивка** *f* rest, respite; pause, break; relaxation; цел ден таа оддив немаше she didn't have a break all day

оддивне *pf* оддивна *aor.* (*здивне*) *usu.:* оддивне си to catch/recover one's breath; to rest

оддивнува *impf of* оддивне

оддипли *pf* I to unfold, spread out, open *trans.*; оддипли ќебе to unfold a blanket II – ce to become unfolded, unfold, open *intrans.*

оддиплува (ce) *impf of* оддипли (ce)

оддише & **оддиши** *pf* оддиша *aor.* to catch/recover one's breath; to rest; *see* оддивне

оддишка *f* rest, respite; pause, break; *see* оддив; си дава оддишка to let off steam; to vent one's spleen

оддишува *impf of* оддише, *see* оддивнува

оддолжи *pf* I to release from debt II – ce 1 to pay one's debts 2 to return a favour; не можам никогаш да ти се оддолжам I can never repay you

оддолжува (ce) *impf of* оддолжи (ce)

оддоми *pf* I (*of a man*) to take to wife, marry II – ce (*of a girl*) to leave home, get married

одева *impf* to suffer (*from the actions of others*); коњите се клоцаат, магарињата одеваат *prov.* the powerful quarrel and the weak suffer in consequence

оеднаш *adv* suddenly, all of a sudden, unexpectedly; at once

одежда *f* 1 (*свештеничка*) priest's vestments 2 (*свечена облека*) robes, attire, *arch.* raiment

одек -ци *m poet.* (*одглас*) echo

одекне *pf* одекна *aor.* 1 to echo, reverberate, resound; гласот ѝ одекна како грмеж her voice echoed like thunder **2** to spread *intrans.*, resound; веста одекна во целата земја the news spread throughout the land

одекнува *impf of* одекне

одење *n* **1** departure; на одење on leaving; ❑ на/со едно одење at one swoop; while you're there; while you're at it **2** walk, gait, way of walking; го познав по одењето I recognized him by the way he walks

одере *pf* одра *aor.* **I 1** to skin; to flay; to graze, bark (*part of the body*); to rip, tear up; одере свиња to skin a pig; си го одра коленото he grazed his knee; ги одра панталоните he ripped his trousers; го одра грлото <викајќи> his voice became hoarse from shouting **2** *fig.* to fleece, rob; ме одраа адвокатите the lawyers fleeced me **II** – **ce 1** to graze (*part of one's body*) **2** се одра од викање he was yelling at the top of his voice

одерка *f* trellis, lattice; bower

одерува *impf of* одере

одживен *adj* outdated, obsolete, archaic

одзаден -дна *adj* **1** rear, back, hind **2** (*in the superlative*) hindmost, the very last; најодзадното девојче the very last <little> girl

одзади *adv* behind, at the rear (back); најодзади right at the back, last

одзве се *pf* одзви се *aor.* to respond, answer, *see* освие се

одзема *impf of* одземе

одземе *pf* одзема *aor.* **1** to take away; одземе имот to take away (confiscate) property **2** to shorten, reduce; одземе капут to shorten a coat **3** to deduct, subtract; одземи го вториот број од првиот take away (deduct) the second number from the first

одзив *m see* одсив

одзива се *impf see* освие се

одзивало *n* response, reply; reaction; *only in the expression:* мое одзивало, туѓо подуало I spoke up and I answered for it

одзове се *pf* одзва се *aor.* to respond, reply, *see* освие се

одзовува се *impf of* одзове се

одѕвива се *impf see* освива се

одѕвие се *pf* одѕви се *aor. see* освие се

одѕвони *pf* **1** to ring, strike (*of a clock*), chime **2** to resound, give a ringing echo

одѕвонува *impf of* одѕвони

одсив *m* **1** echo; јачеше одсив од сите страни an echo reverberated from all sides **2** answering call; на брегот се слушаа довикувања и одсиви cries and answering calls could be heard on the shore **3** *fig.* response, reaction; наиде на добар одсив to meet with a favourable response

одсива се *impf* (*освива се*) to respond, reply; to echo; ни жива душа не се одсива answer came there none

оди *impf* **1** to go, come; to proceed; to pass; to walk; to travel; to move; to make progress, advance; не можам да одам I can't walk; оди брзо to walk (go, move) fast; оди на гости (*кај*) to pay a call (*on*); оди на прсти to walk on tiptoe; одам во Белград I'm going to Belgrade; си одам дома I'm going home; јас си одам I'm leaving; ❑ оди аутопешки *joc.* to go on shanks' pony; оди на сѐ или ништо to go for all or nothing; оди по светот to roam the world; оди <во чекор> со времето to keep up with the times; оди војник to join the army; оди понадвор (по

нужда) to go to the toilet; сѐ оди добро everything's going well; не оди it's no good; не оди така it won't do; (*with dat.*) оди <за> напред to do fine; (*with dat.*) оди <за> назад to go downhill; тоа не ми оди од рака I can't get the hang of this; ни оди ни седи you can't please him, *colloq.* you can't win with him; како оди? how is it going? оди по ѓаволите! go to hell! **2** (*со*) to go with, associate with, keep company with; to support, back; to carry on with, have relations with; to go out with **3** (*по*) to follow, go after; to emulate; оди по неа he follows her; оди по последна мода to follow the latest fashion; оди по прописи to follow regulations; оди по другарите he does what his friends do **4** (*of road*) to lead; каде оди овој пат? where does this road lead? **5** to work, function, go; часовникот не оди точно the clock doesn't keep good time **6** to flow; реката оди низ шума the river flows through a forest; водата оди во каналот the water flows into the canal **7** to sell *intrans.*; тој производ не оди that product does not sell; <по> колку одат јаболката? how much are the apples? **8** (*со/на*) to suit, match, go with; не одат спортски чевли на црн костум sports shoes don't go with a black suit; не оди вино на овој ручек wine doesn't go with this lunch **9** to belong, fall into (*a category*); тие глаголи одат во посебна група these verbs fall into a separate group **10** *Math.* (*во*) to go into; шест во триесет оди петпати six goes into thirty five times **11** *impers.* (*with dat.*) ми се оди на море I feel like going to the seaside; денеска не ми се оди на работа I don't feel like going to work today **12** (*за/на*) to be spent on, go on; сто денари дневно ми одат за храна I spend a hundred denars a day on food **13** (*за боја – накај, кон*) to shade; оди накај зеленикаво shade into green **14** (*кон*) to strive for, aim at; оди кон поголема продуктивност to aim for greater productivity **15** to be in circulation, be accepted; доларот оди насекаде dollars are accepted everywhere

одигра *pf* **I** (*изигра*) to play <a role>; си ја одигра улогата he played his part **II** – **ce** to happen, occur, take place; тие настани се одиграа пред војната those events took place before the war

одигрува (се) *impf of* одигра (се)

одимне *pf* одимна *aor.* **I 1** to pass away, come to an end; гајлето/болеста ќе ти одимне your worry/sickness will pass **2** (*of worry, etc.*) to drive away, dispel, dissipate **II** – **ce** *see* I 1; ќе му се одимне лошотијата his anger (fury) will pass

одимнува (се) *impf of* одимне (се)

одисеја *f* odyssey

одјава *f* announcement/notice of departure; withdrawal of participation; close-down (*at the end of day's radio/TV broadcasting*), signing off

одјави *pf* **I** to announce s.o.'s departure/withdrawal of participation; to sign off (*radio/TV broadcasting*) **II** – **ce** to announce one's <own> departure/withdrawal of participation

одјавува (се) *impf of* одјави (се)

одјаде *pf* **1** to stop eating (*нешто – s.th.*), lose one's appetite for (*s.th.*); ги одјадов јајцата I don't eat eggs any more **2** *impers.* (*with dat.*) ми се одјаде I don't feel like eating any more, I've lost my appetite

одлага *impf of* одложи

одлагање *n* delay; postponement; adjournment

одлачи *pf* **I 1** to single out, set aside, separate *trans.* **2** to wean; одлачи јагне to wean a lamb **II – се** to separate *intrans.*

одлачува (се) *impf of* одлачи (се)

одлева *impf of* одлее

одлево *adv* from the left; одлево и оддесно from the left and from the right; четвртиот одлево the fourth from the left

одлее *pf* одлеа *aor.* **1** to pour off, pour out; ја одлеа чашата he poured some liquid out of the glass **2** to cast; одлее биста to cast a bust

одлежи *pf* одлежа *aor.* **1** to lie for a certain time, spend some time lying; (*за вино*) to lie in a cellar; една ноќ одлежав во паркот I spent one night sleeping in the park **2** to serve a sentence, do one's time, serve time; одлежи казна до крај to serve out one's full sentence

одлежува *impf of* одлежи

одлепи *pf* **I** to unstick, detach **II – се** to become unstuck, become detached; to come off; марката се одлепи the stamp came off; авионот се одлепи од земјата the plane lifted off the ground

одлепува (се) *impf of* одлепи (се)

одлета *pf* **1** to fly away, fly off, fly out; одлетаа врапците во нивјето the sparrows flew away into the fields; одлета кукавицата од дрвото the cuckoo flew out of the tree **2** *fig.* to fly, fly by; одлетаа годините the years have flown by

одлетне *pf* одлетна *aor. see* одлета

одлетнува *impf see* одлетува

одлетува *impf of* одлета

одлив *m* **1** low tide, ebb-tide; одлив и прилив low tide and high tide **2** flow; одлив на крв haemorrhage, bleeding, loss of blood **3** (*одливка*) casting, cast; бронзени одливи bronze casts **4** *Comm.* прилив и одлив на средства inflow and outflow of funds

одлива *impf see* одлева

одливка *f* casting, cast, moulding

одлие *pf* одли *aor. see* одлее

одлика *f* characteristic feature, characteristic, distinguishing mark; trait; distinction; ги поседува сите одлики да стане амбасадор to have the makings of an ambassador

одликува **I 1** *pf & impf* to decorate, give (*s.o.*) a decoration; ги одликуваа со орден на трудот they decorated them with the Order of Labour **2** *impf* to distinguish, set apart (*од – from*), mark out (*s.o.*) (*from*); искреноста го одликуваат него од другите луѓе his sincerity distinguishes him from the others **II – се** *impf* to distinguish o.s. (*by*); to stand out (*for, by, because of*)

одликување *n* **1** presentation of order **2** medal, order, decoration

одличен -чна *adj* excellent, outstanding, superb; одличен мајстор a superb craftsman; одличен ученик outstanding student

одличие -ија *n arch.* **1** *see* одлика **2** *see* одликување 2

одличник -ци *m* **1** outstanding pupil/student **2** distinguished (prominent, eminent) person

одлично *adv* excellently, superbly

одложи *pf* to delay, defer, postpone, put off; одложи судење to adjourn a trial; одложи плаќање to defer payment

одложлив *adj* deferrable, postponable

одложува *impf of* одложи

одломка *f* **1** fragment **2** passage, excerpt; одломка од роман/расказ excerpt from a novel/story

одлоши се *pf* to change/mend one's ways, reform (*o.s.*)

одлошува се *impf of* одлоши се

одлука *f* decision, resolution; донесе одлука to make a decision; судска одлука verdict

одлути се *pf* to calm down, cease being angry

одлутува се *impf of* одлути се

одлучи *pf see* реши

одлучува *impf of* одлучи

одлучување *n* decision-making

одлучувачки *adj* decisive; crucial

одлушне *pf* одлушна *aor.* **I** to break off, chip <off> *trans.*; ја одлушна чинијата he chipped the plate **II – се** to break off *intrans.*; се одлушна едно парче од статуата a piece broke off the statue

одлушнува (се) *impf of* одлушне (се)

одљуби *pf* to cease to love, stop loving

одљубува *impf of* одљуби

одмавне *pf* одмавна *aor.* to wave back <in reply>; to wave in refusal

одмавнува *impf of* одмавне

одмага *impf* (*with dat.*) to hinder, *see* одмогнува

одмагач *m* hinderer

одмазда *f* revenge, vengeance; reprisal; од одмазда in revenge, to get even; крвна одмазда blood feud; во (како) одмазда за in retaliation for

одмазди <се> *pf* to avenge o.s., take vengeance (*on*); ќе ти <се> одмаздам I'll get even with you

одмаздник -ци *m* avenger

одмаздница *f* **1** (*fem. form*) *see* одмаздник **2** *fig.*, *poet.* пушка одмаздница avenging gun

одмаздува <се> *impf of* одмазди <се>

одмаздувач *m* avenger, *see* одмаздник

одмаздувачка *f* **1** *see* одмаздница 1 **2** revenge, vengeance

одмалее *pf* одмалеа *aor.* to become exhausted, worn-out; to droop; to lose one's strength

одмален *adj & pt* exhausted, worn-out

одмаленост *f* exhaustion

одмалува *impf of* одмалее

одмара *impf* **I** to rest *trans.*, give rest to **II – се** to rest *intrans.*, take a rest; *see* одморува (се)

одмена *f* relief, replacement, surrogate, substitute

одмени *pf* to replace, relieve; требаше некој да те одмени someone should have stood in for you

одменува *impf of* одмени

одмерен *adj & pt* **1** steady; regular, measured, rhythmical; со одмерен чекор with measured step/tread **2** moderate, modest; temperate

одмерено *adv* steadily; moderately

одмереност *f* steadiness; moderation

одмери *pf* **1** to measure <out>; to determine by measuring; одмери парче земја to measure out a piece of land **2** *fig.* to look at attentively; to take/get the measure of; одмери некого од глава до петици to measure s.o. <up> from head to foot; одмери свои зборови to weigh one's words; одмери сили со to measure swords with

одмерува *impf of* одмери

одмести *pf* **I** to move, shift *trans.* **II – се** to move, shift *intrans.*

одместува (ce) *impf of* одмести (ce)

одметне *pf* одметна *aor.* to throw away, cast away; to throw, toss back; ја одметна главата назад he threw back his head

одметник -ци *m* **1** apostate, *literary* recreant; renegade **2** (*бунтовник*) rebel

одметнува *impf of* одметне

одмилее (ce) *pf* одмилеа *aor.* see одмили (ce) I 2 & II

одмили *pf* I **1** to cause to stop loving **2** (*with dat.*) to cease to please; му одмиле училиштето he no longer likes school **II – ce** *see* I 2; му се одмили и животот he is tired of life itself

одмилува (ce) *impf of* одмили (ce)

одмине *pf* I to pass, go by, miss; to evade; тој не може нас да нè одмине he cannot miss us (pass us by); сака да го одмине законот he wants to circumvent (evade) the law **II – ce** to pass each other; to miss each other, fail to meet each other; сме се одминале we missed each other

одминува (ce) *impf of* одмине (ce)

одмогне *pf* одмогна *aor.* (*with dat.*) to hinder

одмогнува *impf of* одмогне

одможува *impf see* одмага, одмогнува

одмоли *pf* I to plead forgiveness (*for s.o.*) **II – ce** to plead forgiveness (*for o.s.*); тие сакаа да го загубат, ама тој се одмоли they wanted to execute him, but he obtained their forgiveness

одмолува (ce) *impf of* одмоли (ce)

одмор *m* **1** rest; мене ми е потребен одмор I need a rest **2** (*кус*) break; (*подолг*) holiday, *Am.* vacation; половина час одмор half an hour's break; одмор меѓу часовите break (recess) between lessons; школски одмор school holidays

одмора (ce) *impf see* одморува (ce)

одморалиште *n* holiday home; corporate holiday centre; guest-house; работничко одморалиште workers' holiday home; детско одморалиште holiday camp for children; инвалидско одморалиште rest-house, sanatorium

одморен *pt* rested; вие сте секогаш најадени и одморени you are always well fed and rested

одмори *pf* I to rest *trans.*, give rest to; ги одморивме коњите we rested the horses **II – ce** to rest *intrans.*, take a rest

одмориште *n* landing (*on staircase*)

одморува (ce) *impf of* одмори (ce)

одмота *pf* I to unwind, uncoil, undo, unwrap *trans.*; одмота предено to unwind yarn **II – ce** to unwind *intrans.*; to become unwound, uncoiled, unwrapped; клопчето се одмота the ball (skein) unravelled

одмотува (ce) *impf of* одмота (ce)

одмрзне *pf* одмрзна *aor.* I to melt, thaw <out> *trans.*; to defrost; одмрзне месо to defrost meat; одмрзне торта to thaw a cake **II – ce** to thaw <out>, melt *intrans.*; реката се одмрзнала <the ice on> the river has thawed (melted)

одмрзнува (ce) *impf of* одмрзне (ce)

однавал & однавала *adv* intentionally, purposely, deliberately, on purpose; pretending; легна да спие однавала he lay down pretending to sleep; се разболе однавал he pretended to be ill; *see* навал[2]

однадвор *adv* from <the> outside; on the outside <exterior>; не бараме помош однадвор we are not seeking outside help; зградата однадвор изгледа добро the building looks all right from <the> outside

одназад *adv* from behind; from the end; in the rear, behind; почне одназад to begin from the end

однапред *adv* **1** in front; from the front **2** earlier, before, formerly **3** in advance; ти благодарам однапред I thank you in advance

однатре *adv* from <the> inside; on the inside; однатре се слушаше тропање a knocking sound came/could be heard from inside; *fig.* нешто го јаде однатре something is inwardly tormenting him

однегде *adv see* однекаде

однедопица *adv* suddenly, unexpectedly

однекаде *adv* from somewhere; се снабдуваат однекаде со оружје they are supplied with arms from somewhere

одненадеж *adv* suddenly, unexpectedly

однесе *pf* I **1** to take, bring; to convey, drive; однеси му ручек на татко ти take your father his lunch! ја однесов книгата во библиотеката I took the book to the library; го однесоа на доктор they took him to a doctor **2** to wash away; дотече реката и го однесе мостот the river rose and swept away the bridge **3** *fig.* (*of thought, the mind*) to take, carry; мислата ме однесе во јужните краишта my thoughts carried me away to the south **4** (*with the pronominal forms си го*) to suffer, *colloq.* pay for s.th.; ти ќе си го однесеш за сето тоа you'll pay for all this! **II – ce 1** to behave (*кон некого – towards s.o.*), adopt an attitude (*to*), treat; со иронија ќе се однесат кон моите надежи they will view my hopes with scepticism **2** to apply (*до некого – to s.o.*), turn to; срамота е да се однесете до него it is a disgrace for you to turn/appeal to him

однесен *adj in the expression:* будала однесен utter fool, hopeless idiot

однесува (ce) *impf* **1** *of* однесе (ce) **2** (*only in 3rd p.*) се однесува на (за, до) некого или нешто to refer to, relate to, concern s.o. or s.th.; тоа се однесува на (за) вашиот роднина this concerns your relative; ❏ што се однесува до мене as far as I'm concerned; внимава како се однесува to mind one's manners; недолично се однесува to misbehave; внимавај како се однесуваш! behave yourself! што се однесува до as for

однесување *n* **1** referral, referring **2** attitude, behaviour

одниже *pf* однижа *aor.* I to unstring, unthread; одниже бисер/тутун to unthread pearls/tobacco leaves **II – ce** to become unstrung, unthreaded

однижува (ce) *impf of* одниже (ce)

одникаде *adv* from nowhere; одникаде помош немал he had no help from anywhere

одново *adv* again, afresh; одново се фати за работа he took up his work again

однос *m* **1** attitude, conduct (*кон некого или нешто – towards s.o. or s.th.*); има неправилен однос кон работата he has the wrong attitude to his work; песимистички однос спрема (кон) животот a pessimistic attitude to life; ❏ во однос на нешто with regard to s.th., in respect of s.th.; in relation (proportion) to s.th.; во тој однос in this regard (respect) **2**

<relative> position, relationship; однос на слуга спрема господар a servant-master relationship **3** ratio, proportion; односот меѓу морталитетот и наталитетот the ratio of the mortality rate to the birth rate; во обратен однос in inverse proportion **4** (*usu. pl*) relations (*between people or things*); брачни односи marital (conjugal) relations; деловни односи business relations; другарски односи friendly relations; полови односи sexual relations (intercourse); во работен однос е to be in work/employed; ❑ во добри односи е со to keep up with; to be on good terms with

односен -сна *adj* **1** relative; concerned, appropriate, in question; relevant; односното прашање the matter in hand **2** *Gram.* relative; односни реченици relative clauses

односно *adv* or, that is to say; or rather

одобрение -ија *n* approval, assent, permission; писмено одобрение written permission; *Comm.* одобрение и задолжение credit and debit

одобри *pf* **1** to approve <of>; жената не ја одобри постапката на мажот the wife did not approve <of> her husband's action **2** to permit, allow; директорот ми одобри да го напуштам работното место the director permitted me to leave my post **3** to confirm, endorse, ratify; комитетот го одобри изборот на нов секретар the committee ratified the election of the new secretary **4** to meet, grant (*a request*); одобри кредит to grant credit; молбата ми е одобрена my application has been granted **5** *Comm.* to credit (*to, with*); одобри $20,000 на сметка to credit $20,000 to an account, credit an account with $20,000

одобрителен -лна *adj* approving; одобрителна насмевка approving smile

одоброволи *pf* **I 1** to cheer <up> *trans.*, put (*s.o.*) in a good mood **2** to win over (*s.o. to s.th.*) **II – се** to cheer up *intrans.*

одоброволува (се) *impf of* одоброволи (се)

одобрува *impf of* одобри

одобрување *n* **1** approval; подложен на одобрување subject to approval **2** *Comm.* permission **3** *Comm.* credit; одобрувања и задолженија credits and debits

одовде & *more rarely* **одовдека** *adv* **1** from here; одовде до станица има двесте метра from here to the station it's two hundred metres; одовде донде (дотаму) from here up to there; да бегаме одовде let's get away from here! тој не е одовде he's not from here; помини одовде pass by this way! ❑ одовде-одонде from here and there **2** from this point, from now on, henceforth; одовде почнува новиот период from this point the new period begins **3** from this, hence; одовде се гледа дека . . . from this it can be seen that . . . ; одовде следува from this it follows (*that . . .*)

одоглави *pf* to take off a halter/headstall; го одоглави коњот he took off the horse's halter

одоглавува *impf of* одоглави

ододзади *adv* behind, in the rear, една по друга ододзади one behind the other, one after the other

одозгора *adv* (*see* озгора) **1** from above; on the outside; from the top; (*од север*) from the north; ноќта тој слезе одозгора в село that night he came down into the village; дојде наредба одозгора, од штабот an order came from above, from headquarters; со жито ние се снабдуваме одозгора we get our grain from the north; тортата беше одозгора прелиена со чоколада the cake was covered with chocolate icing; третиот кат одозгора the third floor from the top **2** above; over and above; on top of; одозгора на сето тоа on top of all that, in addition to everything else

одоздола *adv* (*see* оздола) from below; underneath; from the bottom; (*од југ*) from the south; критиките доаѓаат одоздола the criticisms come from below; ветрот дува одоздола the wind is in the south; тој е одоздола, од Македонија he comes from the south, from Macedonia; што носиш ти одоздола, под кошулата? what are you wearing under your shirt?

одоколу *adv* **1** round, around; from around; од сите страни одоколу пукаа на нас they were shooting at us from all around **2** *fig.* in a roundabout way, circuitously; indirectly; почна полека, одоколу he started slowly, in a roundabout way

одолее *pf* одолеа *aor.* to overcome; to resist, withstand; одолее на искушение to resist the temptation

одолжи *pf* **I** to prolong, drag out *trans.*; to stretch out, lengthen, extend *trans.* **II – се** to drag on, stretch out, go on, extend *intrans.*; работата се одолжи the business dragged on; разговорот се одложи the conversation kept going

одолжува (се) *impf of* одолжи (се)

одоли *pf see* одолее

одолив *adj* surmountable, resistible

одолува *impf of* одоли & одолее

одоми *pf* **I 1** to house, provide a home (*for*) **2** (*удоми*) to marry off **II – се 1** to house o.s., acquire a house (a home) **2** (*удоми се*) to get married

одомува (се) *impf of* одоми (се)

одонде & *more rarely* **одондека** *adv* from <over> there, thence; on that side; одонде до сидов има пет метра from there to this wall it's five metres; дојде одонде it came from over there; одонде довде from there to here; помини одонде pass by on that side! ❑ одовде-одонде from here and there

одошто *conj* **1** because, as, since **2** than; тој е постар одошто јас мислев he is older than I thought

одработи *pf* to pay off (*s.th.*) by working, work off; to finish a job; to work (*for*); одработев пет дена I worked for five days

одработува *impf of* одработи

одраз *m* **1** reflection; одраз во огледало reflection in a mirror; одраз на стварноста reflection of reality **2** *fig.* response, result, consequence; тоа е одраз на лошото работење that is the result of bad management

одрази *pf* **I** to reflect (*also fig.*); езерото ја одрази светлината на огнот the lake reflected the light of the fire; романот верно го одрази тогашниот живот the novel faithfully reflected life at that time **II – се 1** to be reflected; to show, be visible; ѕвездите многу јасно се одразија во мирната вода the stars were very clearly reflected in the calm water **2** to influence, have an effect (*на – on*), have repercussions (*on*); тоа се одрази на неговото здравје it told on his health

одразува (се) *impf of* одрази (се)

одрами *pf* to take off one's shoulder<s>; одрами пушка to unsling a rifle

одрамува   *impf of* одрами
одрано   *adv* early, in good time
одрасне   *pf* одрасна *aor.* (*израсне, порасне*) to grow up
одраснува   *impf of* одрасне
одрасте   *pf see* одрасне
одрастува   *impf see* одраснува
одре   *n dim. of* одар
одред[1]   *m* detachment, unit; одред од сто војници detachment of a hundred soldiers (men); партизански одред partisan unit; извиднички одред reconnaissance detachment
одред[2]   *adv* in turn; right through; everything, everyone; сите одред every single one; bar none; across the board
одредба   *f* regulation, decree; clause (*in a law, bill, contract*); законска одредба ordinance, decree, legal provision
одреден   *adj & pt* (*see* определен 1 & 2) **1** fixed, definite, certain; одреден број a certain number; во одредено време at a certain time **2** destined, intended, earmarked (*за – for*); средства одредени за усовршување на кадри funds intended for staff-training
одреденост   *f see* определеност
одреди   *pf* (*see* определи) **1** to fix, establish, determine; одреди број/големина/ квалитет/квантитет/ мера на нешто to fix a number/size/quality/quantity/ measure of s.th.; одреди место и време to set a place and time (*for s.th.*); одреди поим to establish a concept **2** to prescribe, ordain; законот така одредил the law has so prescribed (determined) **3** to choose, select; to appoint; си го одреди својот наследник he chose his heir
одредлив   *adj* determinable
одредливост   *f* determinability
одредома   *adv f.p. see* одред[2]
одредува   *impf of* одреди
одреже   *pf* одрежа *aor.* (*пресече*) to cut off
одрежува   *impf of* одреже, *see* пресекува
одрекне (се)   *pf* одрекна (се) *aor. see* одрече (се)
одрекнува (се)   *impf of* одрекне (се), *see* одрекува (се)
одрекува (се)   *impf of* одрече (се), *see* откажува (се)
одреме   *pf* одрема *aor.* to doze
одрече   *pf* **I** **1** to retract, withdraw **2** to deny; to renounce, repudiate; не можам да му ја одречам способноста I can't deny his ability **3** *colloq.* to reply; to answer back; тој ништо не му одрече he didn't reply to him at all **II – се** (*откаже се*) to renounce; to give up, deny o.s.
одречен   -чна *adj* negative
одречно   *adv* negatively
одречува (се)   *impf see* одрекува (се)
одржи   *pf* одржа *aor.* **I** **1** to maintain, keep; одржи ред to keep (maintain) order; одржи врски со некого to keep in touch with s.o.; одржи пријателство со некого to keep up a friendship with s.o.; одржи нешто во исправна состојба to maintain s.th. in working order; одржи чекор (*со*) to keep up, keep pace (*with*) **2** to arrange, organize, hold; одржи состанок (седница) to hold a meeting; одржи предавање to give a lecture **3** to keep (*a promise*); си го одржа зборот he kept his word, he stuck

to his word **4** одржи победа to win a victory, emerge victorious **II – се 1** to be preserved; to survive, remain; обичајот се одржа the custom has survived **2** to hold out; се одржа во борбата против непријателот he held out in the fight against the enemy **3** to take place; конгресот ќе се одржи утре the congress will take place tomorrow
одржува (се)   *impf of* одржи (се)
одржување   *n* maintenance; одржување на патишта road maintenance; трошоци за одржување maintenance costs
одрина   *f* bower of vines on trellises (*usu. on veranda*)
одрод   *m* **1** (*изрод*) degenerate; freak; monster **2** *see* отпадник
одроди[1]   *pf* **I** to estrange, alienate (*s.o.*) from his relatives; жената го одроди од неговите роднини his wife alienated him from his relatives **II – се** to become estranged, alienated (*from one's relatives*); to estrange, alienate o.s.; to break family ties; to forget one's kinship with; се одродивме we've become alienated, we've forgotten that we are relatives
одроди[2]   *pf rare* **1** to stop bearing children; to become barren **2** to sterilize
одродува[1] **(се)**   *impf of* одроди[1] (се)
одродува[2]   *impf of* одроди[2]
одрони   *pf* **I** **1** to crumble, break off (*in small pieces*), chip off *trans.*; одрони малку малтер од ѕидот he chipped off a little mortar from the wall **2** to shed (*tears*); таа одрони една солза she shed a tear **II – се** to break off, fall *intrans.*
одронува (се)   *impf of* одрони (се)
одрпа   *pf* **I** to tatter, tear **II – се** to get tattered, torn; каде си се одрпал вака? where did you get your clothes torn like that?
одрпан   *pt* **1** (*за облека*) tattered, torn; ragged; одрпана кошула worn-out shirt **2** (*за човек*) shabby, ragged, down-at-heel; одрпан човек ragamuffin
одрпува (се)   *impf of* одрпа (се)
одртави   *pf colloq. pejor.* to grow old, reach one's second childhood
одруча се   *pf impers.* (*with dat.*) to lose one's appetite
одручек   **1** *adv* after midday, in the afternoon **2** -ци *m* (*попладне, поручек*) afternoon
одручува се   *impf of* одруча се
одука   *f* the breaking of a habit; на наука има и одука *prov.* every habit can be broken
одучи   *pf* **I** to make (*s.o.*) give up a habit, wean (*од – from*) **II – се** to lose a habit, get out of a habit
одучува (се)   *impf of* одучи (се)
одушевен   *pt* delighted, enthusiastic, enraptured; одушевен сум од тоа I am enthusiastic about that
одушевеност   *f* enthusiasm, ardour, fervour
одушеви   *pf* to fill with enthusiasm, inspire, excite; ме одушеви со своето знаење his knowledge inspired me
одушевува   *impf of* одушеви
одушевување   *n see* одушевеност
ожален   *pt dial., f.p.* distressed, sad
ождреби   *pf* **I** to foal, produce a foal **II – се** to foal
ождребува (се)   *impf of* ождреби (се)
ожебавен   *pt* wrinkled, furrowed, puckered, wizened; ожебавени образи wrinkled cheeks
ожег   -зи *m* poker

ожедни *pf* to grow thirsty

ождануна *impf of* ождни

оженет *pt* married (*of a man*), *see* женет

ожени *pf* **I** to marry off (*a son, etc.*) **II** – **се** to marry *intrans.*, get married (*of a man*); се ожени со (за) неа he married her; се ожени за пари he married for money; се оженив, се заробив; ожени се да си земеш беља на глава wedlock is a padlock

оженува (се) *impf of* ожени (се)

ожесточен *adj & pt* fierce, furious, violent, brutal; desperate; stubborn; ожесточена битка furious battle; ожесточена расправија violent quarrel

ожесточи *pf* **I** to anger, infuriate; to make (*s.o.*) cruel, merciless, brutal **II** – **се** to become angry, furious, cruel, merciless, brutal

ожесточува (се) *impf of* ожесточи (се)

оживее *pf* оживеа *aor. see* оживи 1, 2, 3

оживен *adj & pt* **1** agitated, excited **2** lively, merry, animated; оживен поглед merry look **3** full of noise, movement, life; lively; оживени улици busy streets

оживено *adv* excitedly

оживеаност *f* agitation, excitement; merriment; liveliness; animation

оживи *pf* оживи & оживе *aor.* **1** to revive, recover *intrans.*; to return to life **2** *fig.* to awake, reappear; старата омраза меѓу нив пак оживе their former mutual hatred was reawakened **3** *fig.* to become merry, livelier; градот оживе the town came to life **4** to revive *trans.*, resuscitate, bring back to life **5** *fig.* to rekindle, bring back to memory (mind), recall; оживи спомени to revive memories **6** *fig.* to enliven, breathe life into, make livelier (merrier), animate; железницата го оживи нашиот град the railway enlivened our town

оживотвори *pf* to realize, implement, carry out, carry (bring) into effect; to act upon; оживотвори решение to implement a resolution

оживотворува *impf of* оживотвори

оживотворувачки *adj literary* life-giving; оживотворувачкото сонце the life-giving sun

оживува *impf of* оживи

оживување *n* recovery, revival; animation, vivacity

ожнеа *impf of* ожнее, *see* ожнива

ожнее *pf* ожнеа *aor.* to reap, harvest; ја ожнеавме пченицата we reaped the wheat

ожнива *impf of* ожние

ожние *pf* ожни *aor. see* ожнее

ожолти *pf* ожолте *aor.* **1** to yellow, turn yellow *intrans.*; лисјата ожолтеа the leaves turned yellow **2** *colloq.* to grow pale; целиот ожолте he grew quite pale **3** to make yellow; to paint/dye yellow

ожолтува *impf of* ожолти

озаби се *pf* **1** to bare/show one's teeth, snarl **2** *fig.* to die (*of animals*)

озабува се *impf of* озаби се

озакони *pf* to give (*s.th.*) the force of law; to legalize, make (*s.th.*) legal, legitimate, legitimize

озаконува *impf of* озакони

озарен *adj & pt* radiant, beaming; озарено од радост лице a face beaming with joy

озареност *f* radiance

озари *pf* **I** to light up *trans.*, illuminate; ја озари светла мисла a bright idea occurred to her **II** – **се** to light up *intrans.*; лицето му се озари his face lit up

озарува (се) *impf of* озари (се)

озбори *pf* to gossip about, run down *trans.*

озборува *impf of* озбори

озборувач *m* gossip, gossipmonger

озвученост *f* acoustics; озвученоста на салата беше добра the hall had good acoustics

озвучи *pf* to wire for sound; to provide with a loudspeaker system

озвучува *impf of* озвучи

озглава *f f.p.* (*зглавје*) pillow, bolster; head of a bed

озгора *adv* **1** from above; on top; on the outside; from the top; (*од север*) from the north; директивите идат озгора the directives come from above; тие идеа озгора they came from up north; што ќе облечеш озгора? what will you wear on on top? прстенот беше само озгора прелиен со злато the ring was only gold-plated **2** (*на*) above, beyond; on top of, over and above; in addition (*то*); озгора на тоа on top of that, to cap it all

озгорен -рна *adj* (*горен*) upper, outer

оздола *adv* from below; underneath; from the bottom; (*од југ*) from the south; што облече оздола? what did you put on underneath?

оздравее *pf* оздравеа *aor. see* оздрави 1

оздрави *pf* оздраве *aor.* **1** to recover (*from an illness*); си оздраве детето the child recovered **2** to treat, heal, cure; таа ми ги оздраве очите she healed my eyes

оздравува *impf of* оздрави

оздравување *n* recovery

озимен -мна *adj in the expression:* озимна (зимна) пченица winter wheat

озимка *f* winter wheat

озимче *n* yearling calf

озлобен *adj* embittered (*на* – *against*), exasperated (*with*), bitter

озлобеност *f* bitterness, exasperation

озлоби *pf* **I** to anger, embitter, exasperate **II** – **се** to become angry, bitter, embittered, exasperated

озлобува (се) *impf of* озлоби (се)

озлобување *n* anger, bitterness, exasperation

озлогласен *pt* disreputable, infamous, notorious

озлогласи *pf* to defame, discredit, bring into disrepute

озлогласува *impf of* озлогласи

ознака *f* **1** sign, indication, mark; label, designation; ознака на вредноста sign of value; price tag **2** landmark

означи *pf* **1** to mark; to designate; означи на карта to map **2** to indicate; to represent; тие резултати означија крупен успех these results represented a great success **3** to signify, mean

означува *impf of* означи

озоба *pf* to peck up

озобува *impf of* озоба

озон *m Chem.* ozone

озонатор & **озонизатор** *m* ozonizer

озонизација *f* ozonization

озонира *pf & impf* to ozonize

озонски *adj* ozonic, ozone *attrib.*

осве се *pf* осва се *aor. see* освие се

осверен *pt* **1** savage; turned wild **2** surprised, amazed, bewildered; scared, frightened

озверено *adv* **1** savagely **2** in bewilderment; in fright

освери се *pf* **1** to become like a wild beast; to go wild **2** to be surprised, amazed, bewildered/scared, frightened

осверува се *impf of* освери се

освива се *impf of* освие се

освие се *pf* осви се *aor.* **1** to respond, answer; јас викав, но никој не се осви I was calling, but no one replied **2** to echo

осемне *pf* осемна *aor.* (*иземне*) to freeze *intrans.*, become frozen; му осемнале рацете his hands got frozen

осемнува *impf of* осемне

оивичен *pt* bordered, edged, framed

оивичи *pf* to border, edge, frame

оивичува *impf of* оивичи

ој *interj* **1** (*expressing fright, pain, sorrow, etc.*) oh! (*of pain*) ow! ој леле, леле, до Бога! *f.p.* alas, alas, my God! **2** (*addressing s.o.; usu. in poetry*) o! hey! **3** (*in response to calling*) yes! ay!

ојагни (се) *pf see* objaгни (се)

ојагнува (се) *impf of* ојагни (се)

ојалови *pf* **I** to sterilize **II – се** to become sterile (*also fig.*); се ојалови работата nothing came of it

ојаловува (се) *impf of* ојалови (се)

ојн *m & * **ојна** *f* game, match; да изиграме еден ојн let's play a game!

ојнак -ци *m see* којнак

ока[1] *f obs.* oka, measure of weight (*1282 grams*); ❑ ока маст – од кај нас if you side with us it'll be worth your while; за инает една ока сол јаде he would cut off his nose to spite his face; сто ока ќотек <изеде> <he got> an awful thrashing **2** *oka*, liquid measure (*1.5 litres*)

ока[2] *impf* to yell, scream, shout

окади *pf* to fumigate; to fill with smoke; to incense

окадува *impf of* окади

окае *pf* окаја *aor.* **1** to lament, bemoan **2** to repent; to expiate, atone for

окаен *pt* **1** wretched, desperate, miserable **2** (*as noun*) wretch, poor devil

окаже *pf* окажа *aor.* to inform upon, denounce, betray

окажува *impf of* окаже

окајува *impf of* окае

окали *pf* **1** to soil, dirty, stain (*with mud*) **2** *fig.* to spoil, mess up; ја окали работата he made a mess of things **3** *fig.* to stain (besmirch, sully) (*s.o.'s reputation*); to shame, put to shame

окалки *pl see* очила

окалува *impf of* окали

оканик -ци *m* **1** *see* оканица **2** weight for measuring one *oka*; сите камења оканици не се *prov.* all the fingers of a hand are not alike

оканица *f* metal vessel for measuring liquids of the quantity of one *oka*

окапан *adj* exhausted; feeble, decrepit; сиромав окапан poor wretch

окапаник -ци *m* **1** wizened, decrepit person **2** poor wretch

окапаност *f* exhaustion; decrepitude

окапе[1] *pf* окапа *aor.* **I** to bath, bathe *trans.* **II – се** to bathe *intrans.*, take a bath; *see* искапе[1] (се)

окапе[2] *pf* окапа *aor.* **1** to degenerate, decay; to break down *intrans.*; окапал веќе his health has broken

down; окапе в затвор to rot in prison; окапе од работа to work one's fingers to the bone **2** to fall <off/out>; лисјето окапаа the leaves have fallen

окапува[1] **(се)** *impf of* окапе[1] (се), *see* искапува[1] (се)

окапува[2] *impf of* окапе[2]

окара *pf* **1** to reprimand, rebuke, scold **2** to swear at, curse (*using bad language*)

окарактериса *pf* to characterize, describe

окарактерисува *impf of* окарактериса

окари́на *f Mus.* ocarina

окарува *impf of* окара

окат *adj* **1** having eyes, seeing; слепиот го направи окат he made the blind man see **2** *fig.* keen-sighted, sharp-eyed

окати се *pf* to grimace, make faces; to stare, gape

окашка *pf* **I** to dirty, soil; ❑ ја окашка работата you've made a mess of things, you've blown it **II – се** to get dirty; to soil o.s.

окашкува (се) *impf of* окашка (се)

океа́н *m* **1** ocean **2** *fig.* vast quantity

океаногра́ф *m* oceanographer

океанографија *f* oceanography

океанографски *adj* oceanographic<al>

океа́нски *adj* oceanic; (*за брод*) ocean-going; океански острови oceanic islands

окер **1** *m* ochre **2** *adj indecl.* ochreish, ochrous

оклети се *pf* to bring misery on o.s., become miserable, unhappy

оклетија -ии *f dial.* curse; damnation; оклетија ти оставам I adjure you; I implore (beg) you

оклешти се *pf* to grimace, scowl, make faces; to bare/show one's teeth

оклоп *m* armour; (*на брод, возило и сл.*) armour-plate; *Hist.* cuirass; челичен оклоп steel armour

оклопен -пна *adj* armoured

оклопник -ци *m* soldier in armour; *Hist.* cuirassier

оклопчест *adj* round, globular, ball-like, spherical

оклузи́в *m Phon.* occlusive

окнар *m* mine-shaft digger

окне *pf* окна *aor.* to give a yell, shout, scream; окнал да пукнал! *curse* go to blazes!

окно *n* **1** window; hatch **2** <window> pane **3** (*во воденица*) millstone **4** (*во амбар*) compartment, enclosed space **5** (*во рудник*) <mine> shaft

око *n*, очи *pl* eye; vision, sight; look; *Anat.* слепо око temple; крвјосани очи bloodshot eyes; ококори (ококоти) очи to goggle, gape, stare; има слаби/добри очи to have bad/good eyesight; расипе очи to ruin one's eyesight; сè во неа ти се очите you have eyes only for her; ❑ до каде ти досига окото (гледаат очи) as far as the eye can see; ништо не може да му избега од око (од очи) nothing escapes him; he doesn't miss a thing; тоа ми ги боде очите it offends my sight; истави ми се од очиве (од пред очи) get out of my sight! get lost! не сакам очите да му ги видам I don't want to set eyes on him; ако ти ме гледаш со едното око, јас ќе те гледам со двете if you will show me a little consideration, I will show twice as much for you; во четири очи in confidence, privately; гледа со криво око на некого to look at s.o. with a jaundiced eye; гледа од под око to glance furtively; to look with suspicion; гледа некого <право> в очи to look s.o. straight in the eye; гледа (чува, сака) некого како очите во главата to cherish s.o. like the apple of one's eye; й гледа на опасноста в очи to look danger in the face; каже некому нешто в очи to tell s.o. s.th. to his face; ми игра окото my eye is twitching; ми се стемни пред очите I saw red; не можам да го погледнам в очи <од срам> I can't look him in the face <for shame>; око не затвори; око на око не кладе he didn't have a wink of sleep; око не му трепнува he doesn't <even> bat an eyelid, he couldn't care a damn; he's as cool as cucumber; очите ми капнаа од срам I couldn't raise my eyes for shame; очите му играат he's a real devil; he has a roving eye; отворил очи како некои плочи his eyes popped out of his head; пред очите на некого before s.o.'s eyes; прст пред око не се гледа you can't see your hand in front of your face; си ги вадат очите еден со друг to get on like cat and dog; to be at daggers drawn; си остана бел во очите he didn't get anything, he was left empty-handed; остава некого бел во очите to bleed s.o. white; со голо око with the naked eye; со кои очи ќе ме погледне? how will he face me? со свои <сопствени> очи with one's own eyes; трн му е во окото на некого to be a thorn in s.o.'s side; фрли прав в очи на некого to throw dust in s.o.'s eyes, to deceive s.o.; шара со очите to look about one, to keep looking all around; to roll one's eyes; to have a roving eye; земе на око некого to have a grudge against s.o.; <издигне се/падне> во очите на некого <to go up/go down> in s.o.'s eyes (estimation); кај ми очи, таму и глава following my nose; му влезе (падна) в очи на некого to attract s.o.'s attention, to be noticed by s.o.; to catch s.o.'s eye; му ги отвори очите на некого to open s.o.'s eyes; на око (навидум) seemingly; as far as one can judge; на око е добар he seems all right; од око roughly, approximately; at a guess; отвори си ги очите open your eyes, have a good look; очите во неа му останаа she made a great impression on him, he liked her very much; очите не ги истава (одлепува) од некого not to take one's eyes off s.o.; паѓа в очи to stand out, be noticeable; to strike one; со други очи гледа на некого/на нешто to look at s.o./s.th. with different eyes; ми го фати окото he/it attracted me, caught my fancy; фрли око на to cast an eye over; to take a fancy to; лоши (урокливи) очи evil eyes; држи на око to keep an eye on; to keep under observation; за нечии црни очи for love; for nothing/free; затвора очи to pass away; to breathe one's last; to give up the ghost; затвора очи пред to close one's eyes to; to turn a blind eye to; има око за to have an eye for; лаже некого <право> в очи to lie through one's teeth; мачка некому очи to throw dust into s.o.'s eyes; to pull the wool over s.o.'s eyes; плакне очи to feast one's eyes on; to get an eyeful of; со заврзани очи blindfold; hands down; две очи поарно гледаат од едното *prov.* two pairs of eyes are better than one; и плетот има очи *prov.* walls have ears; око за око, заб за заб *prov.* an eye for an eye, and a tooth for a tooth; очите на страавот му се мошне големи *prov.* fear hath a hundred eyes; полни очи, празни раце *prov.* so near yet so far; во туѓото око ја гледа раската, во своето гредата не ја гледа *prov.* he sees the mote in another's eye and sees not the beam in his own

окован *adj & pt* **1** chained, shackled, fettered **2** set, mounted; окован со сребро set (mounted) in silver **3** *fig.* enslaved, in bondage

окове *pf* окова *aor.* **1** to shackle, manacle, fetter **2** to mount; to gold-plate; to fit out

окови *pl* chains, fetters, shackles; ропски окови fetters of slavery; slavery; скрши окови to smash one's shackles, sunder one's chains

оковува *impf of* окове

окози *pf* **I** (*of a goat*) to produce (bring forth) (*kids*) **II** – се **1** to kid **2** *fig.* to toil, slave, sweat (*to produce s.th.*)

окозува (се) *impf of* окози (се)

ококоли (се) *pf see* ококори (се)

ококорен *pt in the expression:* со ококорени очи goggle-eyed

ококори *pf* **I** *in the expression:* ококори очи to open one's eyes wide, stare, gape **II** – се **1** to stare, open one's eyes wide **2** (*of eyes*) to open wide *intrans.*, stare; му се ококорија очите his eyes opened wide

ококорува (се) *impf of* ококори (се)

ококотен *pt see* ококорен

ококоти (се) *pf see* ококори (се)

ококотува (се) *impf see* ококорува (се)

околен -лна *adj* neighbouring, nearby; surrounding; во околните села in the nearby villages

околија -ии *f* **1** district; Скопска околија district of Skopje **2** (*околина*) neighbourhood; surroundings

околина *f* **1** neighbourhood; surroundings, vicinity; во околината на Скопје in the neighbourhood of Skopje **2** *fig.* milieu, social environment; околината не ми чини the environment doesn't suit me

околиски *adj* district *attrib.*; околиски одбор (комитет) district committee

околност *f* **1** circumstance; олеснувачка/отежнувачка околност extenuating/aggravating circumstance; според околностите according to circumstances **2** (*only pl*) conditions; ние учевме при други околности we studied under different conditions; стек (сплет) на околностите coincidence

околу[1] *prep* **1** <a>round; сите седеа околу огнот everybody was sitting round the fire; земјата се врти околу својата оска the earth rotates on its axis **2** near; околу езерото near the lake; тој сè се врти околу неа he keeps following her all the time **3** (*of time*) <a>round, about; околу пладне about (round) midday; околу Божиќ/Велигден round Christmas/ Easter; дојди околу десет часот come about ten o'clock! **4** (*indicating approximate number, time, quantity*) about; околу пет дена/месеци/години about five days/months/years; ѕидот е висок околу три метри the wall is about three metres high; испивме околу десет литри вино we drank about ten litres of wine; околу илјада денари about a thousand denars **5** *fig.* concerning, about; се расправаат околу куќата they are arguing about the house

околу[2] *adv* (*rarely* наоколу) round, around; бара околу he is looking around; околу-наоколу all around; посednати околу-наоколу sitting all round

оконча *pf* to finish, end, complete; он го оконча животот to commit suicide

окончува *impf of* оконча

окоп *m* **1** *Mil.* trench **2** ditch; moat

окопили се *pf* to bear an illegitimate child

окопилува се *impf of* окопили се

окопити *pf* **I** to revive *trans.*, resuscitate, bring round **II** – **се** to recover, revive *intrans.*, come round/to; болниот малку се окопити the patient has recovered a little

окопитува (се) *impf of* окопити (се)

окопнет *pt* melted; окопнети снегови melted snows

окопни *pf* окопне *aor.* (*of snow*) to melt, thaw *intrans.*

окопнува *impf of* окопни

окорави <**се**> *pf* to harden *intrans.*; to form a crust/skin; to become hard/coarse; *fig.* to become insensitive; сосем окорави he's become quite callous

окоравува <**се**> *impf of* окорави <**се**>

окоси *pf* to mow; *fig.* to mow down; сено окосено mown hay

окосува *impf of* окоси

окоти *pf* **I** to bear, produce, bring forth (*young*) **II** – **се** **1** to cub, produce young, kitten **2** to be born (*of animals*) **3** *colloq.* to reproduce, multiply *intrans.*

окотува (се) *impf of* окоти (се)

окрвавен *pt* blood-stained; (*за очи*) bloodshot

окрвави *pf* **I** **1** to stain/bespatter with blood; ми ја окрвави кошулата he/it bespattered my shirt with blood **2** to scratch, draw blood; трњето ми ги окрвавија нозете the thorns scratched my legs **II** – **се** **1** to become covered in blood **2** (*крвјоса се*) to become bloodshot; очите му се окрвавија his eyes became bloodshot

окрвавува (се) *impf of* окрвави (се)

окрек *m Bot.* duckweed, conferva

окрепи *pf rare* to fortify; to strengthen, make firm

окрепне *pf* окрепне *aor.* (*закрепне*) to grow strong, firm; to recover

окрепнува *impf of* окрепне, *see* закрепнува

окрепува *impf of* окрепи

окриви *pf* **1** to become lame; to become deformed **2** to blame, accuse

окривува *impf of* окриви

окрилатен *pt see* окрилен

окрилати *pf see* окрили

окрилатува *impf of* окрилати, *see* окрилува

окрилен *pt* inspired, imbued with hope/enthusiasm; од млада среќа окрилен filled with youthful enthusiasm

окрили *pf* to motivate, inspire; to fill with enthusiasm

окрилува *impf of* окрили

окрка *pf colloq.* **1** to eat up; to gulp down, *colloq.* gobble up; сè окркаа they've gobbled up everything **2** *fig.* to be punished; to get a beating, *colloq.* cop it; ќе окркаш еден стап you'll get the stick; си го окрка he got a beating

окркува *impf of* окрка

окрни *pf* **1** to break off **2** to curtail, cut back; му ги окрнија правата на народот they curtailed the rights of the people

окрнува *impf of* окрни

окрои *pf* to trim, prune (*a vineyard*)

округ -зи *m* district; province; изборен округ constituency; воен округ military district

окружен[1] -жна *adj* district *attrib.*; окружен суд district court

окружен[2] *adj & pt* surrounded; вила окружена со ливади и овоштарници a villa surrounded by meadows and orchards

окружи *pf* to surround

окружница *f* circular <letter>

окружува *impf of* окружи

окрши *pf* **I** **1** to break, smash *trans.*; окрши шише to break a bottle **2** to break off *trans.*; окрши едно парче леб he broke off a piece of bread **II** – **се** to break *intrans.*, get broken, smashed; стаклото се окрши the glass (window pane) shattered

окршува (се) *impf of* окрши (се)

оксид *m Chem.* oxide; калциумов оксид calcium oxide

оксидација *f Chem.* oxidization

оксидира *pf & impf Chem.* **1** to rust, oxidize **2** to oxidize, apply a protective oxide coating **3** to dye (*hair*) a lighter colour, bleach

октав *m* octavo

октава *f* **1** *Mus.* octave **2** *Prosody* octet

октаедар -дри *m Geom.* octahedron

октаедарски *adj* octahedral

октан *m* octane

октет *m Mus.* octet

октомври *m* October; во октомври in October

октомвриски *adj* October; Октомвриската револуција the October Revolution (*in Russia*)

октопод *m Zool.* octopod

окубе *pf* окуба *aor.* **1** to pluck; ја окуба кокошката he plucked the chicken; ❏ попари, окуби to finish s.th. quickly **2** *fig.* to fleece; го окубаа на коцка they fleeced (skinned) him at the gambling table

окубува *impf of* окубе

окука *pf* to languish; to rot; окука по затвори he languished in prison

окулар *m* **1** ocular, eyepiece **2** (*двоглед*) binoculars; telescope

окулација *f* grafting, inoculation

окулира *pf & impf* to engraft, inoculate

окулист *m* oculist, eye specialist

окулистка *f* ophthalmology

окултација *f* occultation

окултен -тна *adj* occult, supernatural

окултизам -змот *m* occultism

окупатор *m* occupier

окупаторски *adj* occupying; окупаторски сили occupying forces

окупација *f* **1** occupation (*of foreign territory*) **2** occupation, employment, work

окупационен -она *adj* occupying, of occupation; окупационен режим regime of occupation

окупира *pf & impf* **1** to occupy (*space, territory*); to seize, take over **2** to engage, employ, occupy

окуражи *pf* **I** to encourage, cheer up *trans.* **II** – **се** to take courage, take heart, cheer up *intrans.*

окуражува (се) *impf of* окуражи

окучи *pf* **I** to bring forth, produce (*puppies*) **II** – **се** to whelp *intrans.*, have puppies

окучува (се) *impf of* окучи (се)

окце *n dim.* **1** small eye **2** hole (*in a net*)

олабавен *pt* loose, lax

олабавеност *f* looseness, laxness

олабави *pf* **I** **1** to loosen *trans.*, let go; ги олабави јажињата he loosened the ropes **2** to become loose, grow lax, slacken; to relax *intrans.*; олабавија врските ties/bonds have weakened; олабави човекот the man has grown lax **II** – **се** *see* I 2

олабавува (се) *impf of* олабави (се)

олади *pf* **I 1** to cool *trans.* (*also fig.*) **2** to freshen, refresh **II – ce 1** to get cold; to cool *intrans.* (*also fig.*); *fig.* (*за чувства*) to cool off, grow cold; чорбата се олади the soup has got cold; ce олади спрема мене he's cooled towards me **2** to refresh o.s., cool off

оладнее *pf* оладнеа *aor.* *see* оладни

оладни *pf* оладне *aor.* to become indifferent, cool off, grow cold; неговата љубов спрема мене оладне his love for me has grown cold; тој спрема мене оладне he's cooled towards me

оладнува *impf of* оладни

оладува (ce) *impf of* олади (ce)

олапа *pf colloq.* to eat everything; to bolt, *colloq.* wolf down

олапува *impf of* олапа

олеа́ндер -дри *m Bot.* (Nerium oleander) oleander

олеа́т *m* oil-painting

олеи́н *m Chem.* olein

олеи́нски *adj* oleic; олеинска киселина oleic acid

олеле *interj* oh! ow! ouch! alas!

олелија -ии *f* crying, lamentation; олелиите на жените the lamentations (wailing) of the women

олелика *impf* to cry out, wail, lament; to moan, howl, whine, scream

олеснение -ија *n* relief; discount, reduction, exemption; олеснение во плаќањето easy terms of payment; олесненија во работата relief at work; почувствува олеснение to be relieved; даночно олеснение tax exemption

олесни *pf* **I 1** to facilitate; to lighten *trans.*; to relieve; (*болки*) to alleviate, ease; to mitigate; ти ми ја олесни работата you've made my work easier **2** to become easier, lighter; веќе олеснив малку I have already lost a little weight **3** *fig.* to become senile **II – ce** *impers.* (*with dat.*) to feel better, easier; ми ce олесни <на душата, на срцето> I felt easier <at heart, in my mind>

олеснителен -лна *adj* extenuating, mitigating, *see* олеснувачки

олеснува (ce) *impf of* олесни (ce)

олеснување *n* relief; reduction, exemption; *Leg.* mitigation; commutation; даночно олеснување tax relief, tax reduction; посебно олеснување fringe benefit

олеснувачки *adj* extenuating, mitigating; олеснувачка околност extenuating circumstance

олига́рх -си *m* oligarch

олига́рхија *f* oligarchy; финансиска олигархија financial oligarchy

олига́рхиски *adj* oligarchic<al>; олигархиски систем oligarchical system

олиже *pf* олижа *aor.* to lick <all over>; си ги олижа прстите he licked his fingers

олижува *impf of* олиже

олимпија́да *f* Olympiad, Olympic games

олимписки *adj* Olympic; олимписки игри Olympic games

олицетворен *pt* personified; embodied; incarnate; олицетворен ѓавол the devil incarnate

олицетворение -ија *n* personification; embodiment; incarnation

олицетвори *pf* to personify, embody, incarnate

олицетворува *impf of* олицетвори

оличи *pf* to personify, represent, incarnate

оличува *impf of* оличи

оличување *n* incarnation; оличување на храброст incarnation of valour

олкав *adj* so (*big, small*), such a . . . , of such size; олкав маж such a big man; уште пет олкави книги another five books as big as these

олку *adv* (*of quantity and time*) so much, this much, so; што ce забави олку? why are you so late? не знаев дека е олку лесна работата I didn't know that the work was so easy; јас олку пари не сум видел I've never seen so much money; олку многу, олку малку so much, so little

оловат *adj f.p.* leaden; врати оловати leaden (heavy) doors

оловен -вна *adj* **1** lead; оловна руда lead ore; оловни плочи lead slabs; оловен куршум lead bullet; *Chem.* оловна вода (aqua plumbica) Goulard water **2** leaden; тешки оловни облаци leaden clouds; оловни (оловно-сини) очи grey-blue eyes

олово *n* **1** lead; a piece of lead **2** (*куршум*) bullet

олока *pf*; *see* излока to drink greedily, lap up

олокува *impf of* олока

оломлани *adv see* оломнани

оломнани *adv* the year before last

оломнански *adj* of the year before last; оломнанско вино wine from the year before last

олоши ce *pf* to fall out (*со некого – with s.o.*); ќе ce олошиш со муштериите you'll spoil relations with the customers

олтар *m* altar; светиот олтар the holy (sacred) altar; главниот олтар the main altar

олтарски *adj* altar *attrib.*

олук -ци *m* gutter; trough

олупи *pf* **I** to shell; to husk; to peel *trans.* **II – ce** to peel *intrans.*

олупува (ce) *impf of* олупи (ce)

олути *pf* **I 1** to make (*a dish*) hot, season with pepper; ја олути манџата he seasoned the food with pepper **2** (*with acc.*) to feel a burning sensation (*from highly spiced food*); ме олути пиперката the pepper (capsicum) burned my tongue **II – ce** to burn one's mouth (*on very spicy food*)

олутува (ce) *impf of* олути (ce)

олца *impf* to sob

ом *m Elec.* ohm

омадри *pf* **I** to bring (*s.o.*) to his senses; не можеше да ја омадри he couldn't bring her to her senses **II – ce** to come to one's senses

омадрува (ce) *impf of* омадри (ce)

омаѓоса *pf* (*маѓепса*) to bewitch, cast a spell on, charm

омаѓосан *pt* bewitched, spellbound

омаѓосува *impf of* омаѓоса, *see* маѓепсува

омае *pf* омаја *aor.* **I** to charm, cast a spell on, bewitch, carry away **II – ce** *fig.* to be carried away

омаен¹ *pt* spellbound, bewitched; *fig.* carried away, lost in thought

омаен² -јна *adj* charming; exhilarating; омајна свежина на шумата exhilarating freshness of the forest

омажена *pt* married (*of a woman*); омажена жена married woman

омажи *pf* **I** to marry off (*a daughter, etc.*) (*за некого – to s.o.*) **II – ce** to get married (*of a woman*)

омажува (се) *impf of* омажи (се)

омај -аи *m poet.* 1 charm, fascination 2 breeze; се леел омај a breeze was gently blowing

омајниче *n Bot.* (Dryas octopetala) mountain avens

омајност *f* charm, fascination, wonder

омајува (се) *impf of* омае (се)

омака *pf* I to dirty II – се to get dirty; *see* омаца (се)

омали *pf* (*премали*) to become weak, exhausted, worn-out

омаловажи *pf* to undervalue, neglect, underrate, underestimate, minimize

омаловажува *impf of* омаловажи

омалодушен *pt* 1 demoralized, discouraged, depressed 2 worn-out, enfeebled, exhausted

омалодуши *pf* I 1 to discourage, dishearten; to break s.o.'s spirit 2 to wear out *trans.*, enfeeble, exhaust II – се 1 to become discouraged, lose heart 2 to become exhausted, worn-out; to break down, collapse

омалодушува (се) *impf of* омалодуши (се)

омаломошти *pf* I to exhaust, wear out II – се to become exhausted, worn-out

омаломоштува (се) *impf of* омаломошти (се)

омалува *impf of* омали

омарнина *f* warm and humid air; sultriness

омаскари *pf colloq.* I to disgrace, bring shame on, dishonour; го омаскари пред целиот свет he shamed him before the whole world II – се to disgrace o.s.

омаскарува (се) *impf of* омаскари (се)

омасови *pf* I to spread <among the people> *trans.*, popularize, expand; омасови борба против алкохолизмот to broaden the campaign against alcoholism II – се to spread *intrans.*; нашето движење се омасови our movement has grown (assumed mass proportions)

омасовува (се) *impf of* омасови (се)

омаудрен *adj* astounded, stunned

омаца *pf* I to dirty, soil II – се to get dirty, soiled; to soil o.s.

омацува (се) *impf of* омаца (се)

омацулен & омацурен *adj & pt* dejected, sad, glum

омацури *pf* I to hang down *trans.*; го омацури носот he hung his head II – се to droop, bend down *intrans.*; to hang one's head, become dejected

омачи *pf* I to produce, bring forth (*kittens*) II – се to kitten, produce kittens; мачката се омачи the cat has had kittens

омачува (се) *impf of* омачи (се)

омега *f literary* omega; ❑ алфа и омега alpha and omega

омеѓи *pf* to delimit, demarcate

омеѓува *impf of* омеѓи

омекне *pf* омекна *aor.* 1 to soften *trans.*; тој крем ми ја омекна кожата that cream softened my skin 2 to soften *intrans.*, become soft/softer; му омекна кожата his skin grew soft 3 *fig.* to make docile, compliant; to tame, subdue 4 *fig.* to become soft, docile, compliant, subdued; му омекна срцето his heart softened 5 *fig.* (*of the weather*) to turn warmer, milder; to ease; времето омекна и мразот се стопи the weather became milder and the ice melted

омекнува *impf of* омекне

омелушен *adj* amazed, astounded, stunned

омелушеност *f* amazement

омелуши *pf* to amaze, astound, stun

омерка *f* measuring rod, yardstick, measuring cord, tape measure

омеси *pf f.p.* to knead

омечи *pf* I to bring forth, produce (*bear-cubs*) II – се to cub (*of a bear*)

омечува (се) *impf of* омечи (се)

омилен *adj literary* popular; favourite, beloved; омилено занимање favourite occupation; омилен во (кај) народот popular among the people, beloved of the people

омлет *m* omelette

омнибус *m* omnibus, bus

омодри *pf* омодре *aor.* 1 to turn blue; лицето му омодре his face turned blue (*with cold, etc.*); омодре целиот he went all blue 2 to paint/dye blue

омодрува *impf of* омодри

оморина *f see* омарнина

омот *m* wrapping; омот на книга book jacket, dust cover

омраз *m poet. see* омраза

омраза *f* 1 hatred 2 dissension, discord; quarrel

омразен -зна *adj* 1 hateful, odious, detestable; hated; таа му стана омразна she became odious to him 2 instilling, inspiring hatred

омрази *pf* I to cause to hate; тој нив ги омрази he made them hate each other II – се to take a dislike to one another; to start hating each other; to become estranged from one another; *see* замрази² (се)

омразија -ии *f* hatred; dissension, discord; да не стане некоја омразија помеѓу нас may no dissension/hatred arise between us

омразит *adj see* омразен 2

омразниче *n Bot. f.p. see* омајниче

омразува (се) *impf of* омрази (се)

омрзне *pf impers.* (*with dat.*) to be fed up (*with*), *colloq.* get sick (*of*); ми омрзна одењето на пазар I'm fed up with going to the market

омркне *pf* 1 to grow dark 2 *fig.* to become gloomy, depressed 3 (*with acc.*) to be overtaken by nightfall

омркнува *impf of* омркне

омрлушен *pt* exhausted, downcast, dispirited, discouraged, dejected; омрлушени глави bowed heads

омрлушеност *f* exhaustion, collapse; weakness

омрлуши *pf* I to hang, bow, lower *trans.*; ја омрлуши главата he hung his head II – се to hang, droop *intrans.*

омрлушува (се) *impf of* омрлуши (се)

омрси *pf* I 1 to feed (*s.o.*) meat or fats (*during fast*) 2 to feed (*s.o.*) well, richly; to give rich food (*to s.o.*) II – се 1 to break one's fast; се омрсив пред самоти празник I broke my fast on the eve of the festival 2 to have a treat

омрсува (се) *impf of* омрси (се)

омрцлавее *pf* омрцлавеа *aor. see* омрцлави (се) II

омрцлавен *pt* limp, flaccid, drooping; flabby

омрцлави *pf* I to lower, hang *trans.* II – се to grow limp, flaccid/flabby

омрцлавува (се) *impf of* омрцлави (се)

ОН *abbr.* (*Обединети нации*) United Nations, UN

он *m pron* (*usu.* тој) he

она *pron* 1 (*n of* оној) that; она дете that child 2 (*f of* он, *usu.* таа) she

онаа *pron* (*f of* оној) that; онаа жена that woman

онади *pf & impf colloq.* **I** (*verb denoting any action already known in context*) *usu.* to do, carry out, perform, finish, complete; го онади ли она? have you done it? **II – се** (*for any reflexive action*) што се карате, што се онадите? why are you bickering and carrying on?

онадува (се) *impf of* онади (се)

онака *adv* **1** like that, in that way; работи онака како што работат сите to work the same way as everybody else; вака-онака one way or another; вака-онака (вака или онака) ја свршивме работата we finished the work (job) somehow **2** (*to express indefiniteness*) without any particular purpose; го реков тоа онака, без врска I said it just like that, without meaning anything by it

онакваи (се) *pf & impf see* онади (се)

онаков -ква *pron* that kind of, like that; онаков капут како оној во излогон a coat like the one in the shop-window; ваков или онаков сè едно like this <one> or like that <one>, it's all the same; јас го сакам онаков каков што е I love him just as he is

онаму *adv* there; over there, in/to that place; along that road, that way; ваму-онаму, ја нареди работата one way or another he settled the matter

онани́зам -змот *m* onanism, masturbation

онанија -ии *f* masturbation

онани́ра *impf* to masturbate

онани́ст *m* masturbator, onanist

онани́стка *f* (*fem. form*) *see* онанист

онбаша & онбашија -ии *m arch.* corporal; squad leader

онде & ондека *adv* there; over there; <by> that way; оди онде горе go up there, go upstairs! овде-онде here and there

ондулација -ии *f* **1** (*hairdressing*) waving; трајна ондулација permanent wave, perm **2** undulation, rocking, swell (*of the sea*), wave-motion

ондули́ра *pf & impf* **1** to wave (*hair*), perm **2** (*only impf*) to heave, rock, swell

оневозможи *pf* to render impossible, prevent, frustrate, thwart; големиот снег го оневозможи преминувањето преку планината heavy snow made crossing over the mountain impossible

оневозможува *impf of* оневозможи

онегви (се) *pf & impf see* онади (се)

онемее *pf* онемеа *aor. see* онеми

онеми *pf* онеме *aor.* to become dumb, speechless; to fall silent; што онеме, говори! speak! have you lost your tongue?

онемоштен *pt* exhausted, worn-out, feeble

онемува *impf of* онеми

онеправда *pf* to deprive of rights; to do (*s.o.*) an injustice

онеправдува *impf of* онеправда

онерасположен *adj & pt* upset, distressed; dejected; in a bad mood

онерасположеност *f* distress; dejection; bad mood

онерасположи *pf* **I** to upset, distress, depress **II – се** to get upset, become distressed/dejected

онерасположува (се) *impf of* онерасположи (се)

онесвестен *adj & pt* in a faint, unconscious; knocked out

онесвести *pf* **I** to knock out, render unconscious **II – се** to become unconscious, faint, swoon

онесвестува (се) *impf of* онесвести (се)

онеспособи *pf* **I** to incapacitate, disable; го онеспособи за физичка работа it incapacitated him for physical work **II – се** to become incapacitated, disabled

онеспособува (се) *impf of* онеспособи (се)

они *pron* (*pl of* он, *usu.* тие) they

оние *pron* (*pl of* оној) those

оникс *m* onyx

онкологија *f Med.* oncology

онколошки *adj* oncological

оно *pron* (*n of* он, *usu.* тоа) it

оној *m pron* (*indicates remoteness in place or time and adds emphasis*) that <over there>; оној момент кога ќе видиш, кажи ми tell me the moment you see him! ❑ на оној свет in the next world

онолкав *adj* so big/small, of such a size; сакам онолкава топка I want a ball that size; онолкав ерген such a big chap

онолку *adv* so much/many, that much/many; as much/many; so; ќе добиеш онолку колку што ќе заслужиш you'll get as much as you deserve; онолку брзо so fast

онолку́нда & онолку́нѕa *adv dim. of* онолку, *see* онолкуцка

онолку́цка *adv dim.* (*of* онолку) so few, so little

онолку́цкав *adj dim.* (*of* онолкав) so small, such a small, that small

ономастика *f Ling.* onomastics

ономастички *adj Ling.* onomastic

ономатопе́ја *f* onomatopoeia

ономатопе́јски *adj* onomatopoeic

онтологија *f* ontology

онтолошки *adj* ontological

онцица *pron arch.* that man; such-and-such a person, so-and-so; умрел онцица so-and-so has died

ООН *abbr.* (*Организација на Обединетите нации*) United Nations Organization, UNO

оп- *verbal prefix see* об-

оп, оп *interj* jump! skip!

опа *interj child.* ups-a-daisy!

опавче *n dim. of* опашка

опаднат *pt* weak, feeble; depressed, downcast; impoverished

опаднатост *f* weakness, feebleness; depression; impoverishment

опадне *pf* опадна *aor.* **1** to fall; му опадна косата he's lost his hair; лисјата опаднаа the leaves have fallen **2** *fig.* to weaken in health, grow feeble, decline; моите родители сосем опаднаа my parents' health has failed **3** *fig.* to become poor; по војната тие многу опаднаа since the war they've become very poor

опаднува & опаѓа *impf of* опадне

опаѓање *n* fall, decline; ❑ во опаѓање in eclipse; on the wane

опак *adj* wicked, evil; ill-tempered, malicious; malevolent, pernicious

опаковка *f* wrapping, packaging

опаку *adv* (*see* наопаку) **1** the wrong way round, inside out; upside down; едниот чорап го обу опаку he put on one sock inside out **2** <from> behind; at the back, behind one's back; со врзани раце опаку with hands tied behind one's back **3** in the opposite direction, backwards, in reverse; колцето се вртеше опаку the wheel was going backwards **4** *fig.* in the opposite way; wrong, erroneously; опаку ме разбра you misunderstood me, *colloq.* you got me wrong

опал *m* opal

опален[1] -лна *adj* opal

опален[2] *pt* burnt, singed, scorched, seared; бега како опален he runs off like a scalded cat; опален од сонцето sunburnt; scorched by the sun; опалено лице sunburnt face; ❏ пес опален не ми втасува I could eat a horse

опали *pf* to burn, singe, scorch; го опали сонцето he's got sunburnt

опалува *impf of* опали

опамети *pf* **I** to make wiser; to bring (*s.o.*) to his senses; тој тебе ќе те опамети he'll make you see sense **II** – **ce** to become wiser, more sensible; to come to one's senses

опаметува (се) *impf of* опамети (се)

опарак -ци *m colloq.* uncouth person, boor; brute

опари *pf colloq.* **I** to cause (*s.o.*) to come into some money **II** – **ce** to come into some money; to earn <some> money

опасе *pf* to overgraze; овците ја опасија тревата the sheep ate all the grass

опасен -сна *adj* dangerous; (*гибелен*) disastrous, ruinous, perilous; опасен потфат risky venture

опасно *adv* dangerous<ly>; опасно е таму ноќе it is dangerous there at night; опасно за животот (по живот) life-threatening

опасност *f* danger; во опасност in danger (jeopardy); во случај на опасност in an emergency; in case of emergency; вон опасност out of danger; изложи (излага) се на опасност to expose o.s. to danger; изложува на опасност to place (put) in jeopardy; to endanger; укажува на опасност to sound a note of warning

опат *m* (*Catholic*) abbot

опатија -ии *f* **1** (*Catholic*) abbey **2** abbacy

опатица *f* (*Catholic*) abbess

опачен -чна *adj* **1** reversed, inside out; inverted; obverse; опачната страна на нешто the reverse side of s.th., *see* опачина **2** *fig.* wrong, incorrect, false; опачни сфаќања erroneous concepts; опачно поставување на работите incorrect presentation of affairs **3** *fig.* wicked, evil; ill-tempered, malicious; capricious, wilful; опачни луѓе queer people; evil people

опачина *f* reverse side, obverse, back; лице и опачина the front and reverse sides, both sides; опачината на работите the other side of the matter; опачината на животот the seamy side of life

опачки *adv* the wrong way round; inside out; upside down; backwards; wrongly; *see* опаку, наопаку

опачност *f* perversion; wickedness; spite, malice; malevolence; viciousness; опачноста на луѓето people's malice

опаш *m* tail, *see* опашка

опашалка *f* girdle, cord

опаше *pf* опаша *aor.* **I 1** to put on (*round the waist*); го опаша појасот he put on his belt; опаше сабја to gird on a sword **2** *fig.* to enclose from all sides; to surround, encircle **3** *fig.* to whip, lash, thrash **II** – **ce** to

gird o.s.; to put on a belt; се опаша со жажето he tied a rope round his waist

опашест *adj* having a tail, caudate; tail-like, caudal; опашеста ѕвезда comet

опашина *f* **1** (*доточка*) weak *raki* **2** husks, chaff, threshing-waste **3** remnants, waste (*from production processes*), tailings

опашка *f* **1** tail; опашка на магаре/на паун/на риба tail of a donkey/peacock/fish; коњска опашка tail of a horse; *fig.* pony-tail; мрда (мава) со опашката to wag one's tail; крене (напрчи) опашка to raise its tail; *fig.* to become arrogant, turn one's nose up; ❏ врти опашка to ingratiate o.s., fawn on; лаги со опашки bare-faced lies; му плукна под опашката he sent him packing, he showed him the door; свие опашка to put one's tail between one's legs; to get cold feet; дури не мрдне кучката со опашката, не трчаат кучињата по неа *prov.* somebody has to take the initiative **2** *fig.* queue, *Am.* line; опашки пред кината cinema queues **3** *fig.* last place in line/file/queue; tail-end, rear; се влече на опашката to bring up the rear; почне нешто од опашката to begin s.th. at the wrong end; фатил едно за глава, друго за опашка he hadn't yet finished one thing, when he began another **4** *fig.* train (*of a dress*) **5** *fig.* hanger-on **6** stem, stalk; секоја круша си има опашка *prov.* there's a reason for everything; there's no smoke without fire

опашкар *m* **1** *colloq.* the last dancer in an *oro* (line dance) **2** person who is one step behind events, who is out of touch

опашува (се) *impf of* опаше (се)

опева *impf of* опее

опее *pf* опеа *aor.* **1** to celebrate in song, sing the praises of, laud, glorify, extol; тој ја опеа љубовта кон татковината he sang of the love of the mother country **2** (*за свештеник*) to sing a requiem (*for the soul of the departed before burial*)

опекотина *f* burn; (*од врела вода*) scald

опекува (се) *impf see* опечува (се)

опело *n* funeral service, requiem

опера *f* **1** *Mus.* opera **2** opera-house

оператива *f coll.* **1** executive staff, personnel **2** (*operational*) practice

оперативен -вна *adj* **1** *Med.* surgical, operative; оперативно лекување surgical treatment; по оперативен пат by means of an operation, by surgery **2** operative, working; operational; оперативен план operational plan; **3** practical; оперативен човек practical person

оперативец -вци *m* operator, executive, operative

оперативно *adv* in a practical manner; efficiently, effectively; promptly; треба да се дејствува оперативно prompt action must be taken

оперативност *f* efficiency; оперативност во работата efficiency at work

оператор *m* **1** operator; (*во кино*) projectionist **2** *Med.* surgeon

операција -ии *f* operation (*also Med.*); ruse, stratagem; операција на срце heart operation; пластична операција plastic surgery; финансиска операција financial operation, transaction; математичка операција mathematical operation

операциóнен -она *adj* operating, surgical; operational; операциона маса operating-table; операциона сала operating theatre; операционен нож scalpel; операционен план plan of operation<s>; операциона база operational base/basis; операционен правец operational aim

опердаши *pf colloq.* (*испердаши*) to beat, thrash

опердашува *impf of* опердаши, *see* испердашува

опере *pf* опра *aor.* (*испере*) to wash (*clothes, etc.*), launder

оперен -рна *adj* opera; operatic; *see* оперски

оперета *f Mus.* operetta

оперетен -тна & **оперетски** *adj* operetta *attrib.*; оперетна музика operetta music; оперетен пеач operetta singer

оперира *pf & impf* **I 1** *Med.* to operate (*on*) **2** to act, operate; to conduct combat operations; to deal; *Comm.* to trade, speculate; флотата оперира во Средоземно Море the fleet operates in the Mediterranean; оперира со непроверени податоци to operate with (use) unconfirmed data **II – се** to undergo surgery

оперски *adj* opera; operatic; оперска пеачка opera singer

опет *adj* (*за човек*) conceited; arrogant, haughty

опето *adv* arrogantly, haughtily

опечали се *pf* to try, endeavour (*да – to*)

опечалува се *impf of* опечали се

опече *pf* **I 1** (*usu. of the sun*) to burn, scorch **2** (*испече*) to roast, bake; опече јагне to roast a lamb **II – се** to get sunburnt; to singe, burn o.s.

опечува (се) *impf of* опече (се)

опива (се) *impf of* опие (се)

опивен -вна *adj* intoxicating; narcotic; опивни испаренија intoxicating fumes

опие *pf* опи *aor.* **I 1** to intoxicate, make drunk; виното го опи the wine went to his head **2** *Med.* to anaesthetize, narcotize, drug s.o. **3** *fig.* to intoxicate, exhilarate; го опија успесите his successes went to his head; ме опи <со> нејзината убавина her beauty intoxicated me **II – се 1** to get drunk, become intoxicated **2** *Med.* to be drugged, anaesthetized **3** *fig.* to be carried away, exhilarated; се опи од успесите he was intoxicated by his successes

опиен *adj & pt* **1** drunk **2** drugged, anaesthetized, under sedation **3** *fig.* carried away, exhilarated, intoxicated; опиен од радоста, од љубовта и сл. intoxicated with joy, love, etc.

опиеност *f* **1** drunkenness, intoxication (*also fig.*) **2** *Med.* narcosis

опијанет *adj colloq. see* опиен, пијан

опијани (се) *pf colloq. see* опие (се)

опијанува (се) *impf of* опијани (се)

опили *pf* **I** to hatch (*eggs*); чавките опилија чавчиња the jackdaws hatched their young **II – се** to hatch *intrans.*; to be hatched; пилци се опилија the chicks were hatched

опилува (се) *impf of* опили (се)

опина (се) *impf* (*also* опнува (се)) *of* опне (се)

опинок -нци *m* peasant sandal, moccasin; гумени опинци rubber sandals, ☐ ќе ги ги земе опинците he will take everything you have; опинци! a fig for that!

опинчар *m* maker of *opinci*

опиња (се) *impf see* опина (се)

опипа *pf* **I** to feel, grope, touch *trans.* **II – се** *fig.* to be tangible, palpable

опиплив *adj* tangible, visible, palpable, real; опипливи резултати tangible results

опипливост *f* tangibility

опира (се) *impf of* опре (се)

опирен -рна *adj* опирна точка <point of> support

опис *m* description; точен опис an accurate description; личен опис personal description

описен -сна *adj* descriptive; описно изразување descriptive expression; описно излагање descriptive presentation; описен метод descriptive method

опит *m* **1** experience; животен опит experience of life; личен опит personal experience; знаеме од опитот we know from experience; горчлив опит bitter experience; разменува опити to compare notes **2** experiment, test, trial; врши опити to conduct experiments; лабораториски опити laboratory experiments

опитен -тна *adj* **1** experienced, skilled, expert **2** experimental; опитна станица experimental station

опитност *f* experience, skill, proficiency

опиум *m* opium

опиумски *adj* opium *attrib.*

опишан *pt* drawn, traced, circumscribed; described, portrayed

опише *pf* опиша *aor.* **1** to describe, portray, depict; to define; тоа не може да се опише it beggars description; опише нешто во најцрни бои to paint s.th. in the darkest colours **2** to draw, describe, trace, circumscribe; планетата ја опиша својата елипса околу сонцето the planet described its ellipse round the sun; *Math.* опише круг to describe a circle

опишува *impf of* опише

опишувач *m* describer

опкади *pf* to fumigate; to burn incense (*to*); to fill with smoke

опкадува *impf of* опкади

опкачи *pf* **1** to attach (fasten) barbs (*all round s.th.*) **2** to hang *trans.*

опкачува *impf of* опкачи

опкити *pf* **I** to decorate, adorn, deck out **II – се** to be decked (*со – with*); to adorn o.s. (*with*)

опкитува (се) *impf of* опкити (се)

опкова *f* **1** binding, band, hoop; ковчег со златна опкова a chest with hoops of gold round it **2** *pl* chains, fetters, shackles

опкова *impf see* опковува

опкован *pt* **1** reinforced with hoops, bands; опкован со злато reinforced, hooped with gold **2** shackled, fettered

опкове *pf* опкова *aor.* (*see* окове) **1** to reinforce with metal binding; to mount; to plate **2** to shackle

опковува *impf of* опкове

опколен *pt* surrounded, ringed; поле опколено со планини a plain ringed by mountains

опколи *pf* **1** to surround, fence in, enclose; *fig.* to hem in, press from all sides; сите го опколија детето everybody crowded round the child **2** *fig. f.p.* to overpower, overcome, seize; дремка ме опколи drowsiness overcame me **3** (*обиколи*) to pass round (*s.o./ s.th.*), go right round (*s.th.*), circumambulate; еден саат има да го опколиш езерото околу-наоколу it takes an hour to walk round the lake

опколува *impf of* опколи

опкопа *pf* to dig round, earth up; опкопа лози to dig round (earth up) vines

опкопува *impf of* опкопа

опкружен *pt* surrounded, encircled; ливада опкружена со шума a meadow ringed by woodland

опкружи *pf* to surround, encircle

опкружува *impf of* опкружи

оплакан *adj* tear-stained, distressed; оплакан во очите with tear-stained eyes

оплакне *pf* оплакна *aor.* (*исплакне*) **1** to rinse, wash out (*dishes, pots, etc.*) **2** to rinse (*one's throat, mouth*)

оплакнува *impf of* оплакне, *see* исплакнува

оплакува (се) *impf of* оплаче (се), *see* поплакува (се)

оплаче *pf* оплака *aor.* **I** to mourn; to bewail; си ја оплака ќерка си she mourned her daughter **II – се** (*поплаче се*) to complain, repine

оплачува (се) *impf of* оплаче (се)

оплеви *pf* (*исплеви*) to weed

оплевува *impf of* оплеви, *see* исплевува

оплени *pf* to rob, plunder, loot, pillage, ransack

опленува *impf of* оплени

оплеска *pf* **I 1** to soil, dirty, stain; *fig.* to spoil; ❏ ја оплеска работата you've made a mess of things, you've blown it **2** *fig. colloq.* to finish off, bump off, knock off **II – се** to get dirty; се оплеска целиот he got all dirty

оплескува (се) *impf of* оплеска (се)

оплете *pf* **I 1** (*за коса*) to plait, braid **2** to entwine (*s.th.*), weave round (*s.th.*); оплетено шише a bottle (flask) in wickerwork casing **II – се** to comb and arrange one's plaits

оплетува (се) *impf of* оплете (се)

оплоден -дна *adj* reproductive; оплодни органи reproductive organs; оплодна моќ (способност) reproductive capacity (ability)

оплоди *pf* **I** to impregnate, fertilize; to make fertile, fruitful; пчелата го оплоди цветот the bee fertilized (pollinated) the flower; оплоди јајце to fertilize an egg; оплоди земја to fertilize the soil **II – се** to become fertile

оплодува (се) *impf of* оплоди (се)

оплодување *n* insemination; pollination

опљачка *pf* to rob, plunder, loot, pillage, ransack

опљачкува *impf of* опљачка

опна *f* membrane, *see* мембрана, ципа

опнат *adj & pt* stretched tight, taut; outstretched; опната кожа taut skin; опнати раце outstretched arms

опне *pf* опна *aor.* **I 1** (*оптегне, затегне*) to pull tight, tense, tighten *trans.*; опне јаже to tighten a rope; опне узди to tighten the reins; опне ороз to cock a gunhammer; опне лак to draw a bow **2** (*протегне, истегне*) to extend, stretch out; опне рака to stretch out a hand/arm; опне врат to stretch one's neck **3** (*напрегне*) to exert, strain, exercise; опне мисла, ум to exert (apply) one's thoughts, mind; опне мускули to strain one's muscles **4** *colloq.* to put on, put up; опна бел тулбен she put on a white turban; ја опна пушката на рамо he slung the rifle on his shoulder; опне шатор to pitch a tent **5** *fig.* (*удри, тупне*) to strike, hit, thrash, wallop **6** *colloq.* (*with dat.*) to foist (*s.th. on s.o.*), force, impose (*on*) **7** *colloq.* to force (*s.o. to do s.th.*); ќе те опнат да работиш they'll force you to work here **8** *fig. colloq.* to drink down, drain in one draught; to eat up (*s.th.*) at one go, gulp down; опна

шише вино he downed a bottle of wine **9** to make an effort; опна сам да го крене каменот he tried to lift the stone himself **II – се 1** (*напрегне се*) to exert o.s., try, make an effort; треба јуначки да <му> се опнеме we must make an heroic effort **2** to tighten *intrans.*, fill out; му се опна кожата на лицето he's become fuller in the face **3** *colloq.* (*with dat.*) to intrude (*on s.o.*); to impose o.s. (*on s.o.*), barge in; му се опна на министерот he intruded on the minister

опнува (се) *impf* (*also* опина (се)) *of* опне (се)

опогани *pf* **I** to dirty, pollute; to profane, desecrate, defile **II – се** to become odious, vile

опоганува (се) *impf of* опогани (се)

опоен -јна *adj* intoxicating (*also fig.*); опојна пијачка an intoxicating drink; опојно средство narcotic, intoxicant; опојни дроги narcotic drugs; опоен мирис intoxicating aroma; опојната синотија на небото the intoxicating blue of the sky

опои *pf f.p.* to intoxicate

опожари *pf* to burn down; ги опожарија нашите села they burnt down our villages

опожарува *impf of* опожари

опозиција *f* opposition; resistance, antagonism

опозиционен -она *adj* opposition *attrib.*, oppositional; opposing; опозициона партија party in opposition, the opposition; опозиционен весник opposition newspaper

опозиционер *m* member of the opposition; opponent; critic

опој *m poet.* enchantment, intoxication

ополномоштеник -ци *m* representative, delegate; commissioner; <authorized> agent

ополномошти *pf* to authorize, empower

ополномоштува *impf of* ополномошти

ополномоштувач *m* authorizer

опомена *f* **1** reprimand; reproach, rebuke, admonition **2** (*предупредување*) warning, notice, reminder

опомене *pf* опомена *aor.* **1** to rebuke, admonish **2** (*предупреди*) to forewarn, warn **3** to dun

опоменува *impf of* опомене

опонент *m* opponent

опонира *impf* to oppose, resist; to object (*на – to*), disagree (*with*)

опора *f literary, fig.* support

опорен -рна *adj literary, fig.* support *attrib.*, supporting

опортун *adj* opportune, favourable, suitable, appropriate, fitting

опортунизам -змот *m* opportunism

опортунист *m* opportunist

опортунистка *f* (*fem. form*) *see* опортунист

опортунистички *adj* opportunist *attrib.*; опортунистичка политика opportunistic policy

опортуност *f* opportuneness

оправа (се) *impf see* оправува (се)

оправда *pf* **I 1** to acquit, find not guilty; судот го оправда обвинетиот the court acquitted the accused **2** to excuse; те молам да ме оправдаш пред другарите please convey my excuses to our friends **3** (*одобри*) to approve, endorse; оправда план to endorse a plan **4** to justify; тој не ја оправда нашата доверба he let us down; ги оправда надежите he lived up to expectations **5** to account for (*expenses*) **II – се** to justify o.s.; to make excuses

оправдан *adj & pt* justifiable, just, justified; excused, excusable; оправдани барања just demands; оправдан изостанок excusable absence

оправдание -ија *n* excuse; justification; докторско оправдание doctor's (medical) certificate (*for absence from work*)

оправданост *f* justifiability; justness

оправдува (се) *impf of* оправда (се)

оправдување *n* excuse; како оправдување за as an excuse for; in extenuation of

оправи¹ *pf* I to correct, put right; to repair, fix; ја оправи работата he settled the matter; ја оправи куќата he fixed up (repaired) the house II – ce 1 to improve, clear <up> *intrans.*; времето се оправи the weather cleared 2 *dial.* to equip o.s., prepare *intrans.*, fit o.s. out

оправи² *pf* I to direct, point, aim; to send on a mission II – ce to set out (*in a certain direction*); to get ready for a trip

оправија *f* putting in order, arranging, putting right; тука нема оправија this is beyond repair

оправува (се) *impf of* оправи¹ (се)

опраси *pf* I to farrow, produce (*pigs*) II – ce to farrow, produce pigs

опраши *pf* 1 to earth up; опраши лозје, афион и сл. to earth up a vineyard, poppies etc. 2 to pollinate; пчелата го опраши цветот the bee pollinated the flower

опрашува *impf of* опраши

опре *pf* I to lean *trans.*; ја опре главата на ѕидот he leant his head against the wall II – ce 1 to lean (*на нешто* – on, against *s.th.*) *intrans.*; се опре со лактовите на масата he leant his elbows on the table; се опре на ѕидот he leant against the wall 2 *fig.* to rely (*на некого/нешто* – on *s.o./s.th.*), trust (*s.o./s.th.*); to depend (*на* – on); ce опревме на традицијата we put our faith in the tradition

опрегач *m* (*скутник*) apron

определба *f* 1 definition, formulation 2 *Pol.* decision, choice 3 resolve, determination 4 *Gram.* attribute; modifier

определен *adj & pt* 1 fixed, appointed, set; certain; во определениот ден on the appointed day; во определено време at a certain time; тој нема определено звање he has no special (definite) vocation; во определени услови under certain conditions 2 clear, well-defined, definite; не можам ништо определено да ви кажам I can't tell you anything definite 3 committed, determined 4 *Gram.* определен начин indicative mood; определена придавка definite adjective (*in Serbo-Croatian*)

определеност *f* 1 clarity, definiteness 2 determination; decisiveness; commitment

определи *pf* I 1 to determine, fix, define; to indicate; to specify, stipulate; определи тежина to estimate weight; ситуацијата ја определи нашата тактика the situation determined our tactics; определи правец to indicate direction; определи ден на собрание to set the date for a meeting 2 (*избере*) to choose, select; си определи заменик he chose his deputy/successor 3 to award, assign, allocate (*a reward, prize, a task, duty, position, etc.*) II – ce to make a decision, make up one's mind; определи се за

нешто to decide on s.th.; определи се за некого to side with s.o.

определив *adj* determinable, definable

определивост *f* determinability

определува (се) *impf of* определи (се)

определувачки *adj* deciding, determining

опрема *f* equipment; gear; outfit

опреми *pf* to equip, furnish, fit out

опржи *pf* I to fry II – ce to burn, scorch o.s.

опржува (се) *impf of* опржи (се)

опресѝвен -вна *adj* oppressive

опресија *f* oppression

опрли¹ *pf* to scorch, singe; to tan

опрли² *pf* I (*of a donkey*) to foal, bring forth (*a foal*) II – ce to foal

опрлува¹ *impf of* опрли¹

опрлува² (се) *impf of* опрли² (се)

опрости *pf* I to pardon, forgive, excuse, absolve; to let off; to waive; опрости грев to forgive a sin; му ја опрости казната he let him off; опрости ми за невниманието forgive my thoughtlessness/ inattentiveness! опрости ми што не дојдов forgive me for not coming! II – ce to take leave (*of*), say goodbye (*to*); *see* прости (се)

опростува (се) *impf of* опрости (се)

опроштение *n* *arch.* pardon, apology; ❑ со опроштение with apologies; if you don't mind my saying so

опрска *pf* to splash, sprinkle; to spatter, bespatter; *fig.* to spoil; ❑ ја опрска работата he botched the job (affair); ја опрскавме we've made a mess of it

опрскан *pt* sprayed, splashed, spattered; сета со вода опрскана all splashed with water

опрскува *impf of* опрска

опрчи (се) *pf dial. see* напрчи (се)

опрчува (се) *impf dial. of* опрчи (се), *see* напрчува (се)

опсада *f* siege

опсаден -дна *adj* siege *attrib.*; опсадна состојба state of siege; опсадни топови siege-guns

опсади¹ *pf* to plant round, fill by planting

опсади² *pf* 1 to besiege 2 *fig.* to surround, build all round, shut in, enclose

опсадник -ци *m* besieger

опсадува¹ *impf of* опсади¹

опсадува² *impf of* опсади², *see* опседнува²

опсадувач *m* besieger, *see* опсадник

опсег *m* extent, range; sphere; широк опсег wide extent (range)

опсега *impf of* опсегне

опсегне *pf* опсегна *aor.* to include, embrace, comprise

опседла *pf* to harness

опседлува *impf of* опседла

опседнат *pt* obsessed (*co* – with)

опседне¹ *pf* опседна *aor.* to mount (*a horse*)

опседне² *pf* опседна *aor.* 1 *see* опсади² 2 *fig.* to take hold of, obsess; го опседна мисла an idea took possession of him

опседнува¹ *impf of* опседне¹

опседнува² *impf of* опседне²

опсежен -жна *adj* extensive, voluminous, detailed, abundant, long, large-scale

опсеклив *adj* sour, sharp; bitter, pungent, caustic

опсекува *impf of* опсече, *see* опсечува

опсен *m* **1** shadow, shade **2** apparition, spectre, ghost; illusion

опсени *pf* **1** (*засени*) to cast a shadow over, shade **2** (*заслепи*) to blind; to dazzle; to delude; to charm; to fascinate; to stun

опсенува *impf of* опсени

опсерва́т *m* suspect; person under police observation

опсерва́тор *m* (*набљудувач*) observer, viewer, onlooker

опсерваторија -ии *f* & **опсерваториум** *m* observatory; астрономска опсерваторија astronomical observatory

опсервација -ии *f* observation

опсерваци́онен -она *adj* observation; опсервациона точка, опсервационен пункт observation point

опсерви́ра *pf* & *impf* to observe

опсесија -ии *f* obsession

опсече *pf* to cut round, trim

опсечува *impf see* опсекува

опсипан *pt* covered with, strewn with; небо опсипано со звезди a sky studded with stars; опсипан со дамки covered with spots

опсипе I *pf* опсипа *aor.* to strew (*s. th.*) over (upon); to cover (*со – with*); to shower (*with*) (*also fig.*); опсипе нешто со снег/брашно/песок to sprinkle s.th. with snow/flour/sand; го опсипаа градот со бомби they rained bombs on the town; опсипе со светлина to bathe with light; опсипе со комплименти to shower with compliments; опсипе некого со прашања to bombard s.o. with questions **II – се** to become covered (*со – with*); се опсипа со дамки to come out in spots

опсипува *impf of* опсипе

опскокне *pf* опскокна *aor. see* опскокува

опскокува *impf* to jump round s.th.

опскура́нт *m* (*мракобесник*) obscurantist; reactionary; bigot

опскуранти́зам -змот *m* (*мракобесие*) obscurantism

опскурен -рна *adj* obscure, gloomy, unclear

опскурност *f* obscurity

опслужи *pf* to serve *trans.*; опслужи гости со пијалок to serve drinks to guests

опслужува *impf of* опслужи

опстане *pf* to survive, continue to exist

опстановка *f* situation, conditions, circumstances; во ваква опстановка не може да се работи in such conditions work is impossible

опстанок *m* survival; subsistence; борба за опстанок struggle for survival

опстанува *impf of* опстане

опстоен -јна *adj literary*, *rare* extensive, detailed, exhaustive, thorough

опструкција -ии *f* obstruction

опсуди *pf* to discuss; to examine, survey, consider

опсудува *impf of* опсуди

опсуче *pf* опсука *aor.* to twist, bend, roll *trans.*

опсучува *impf of* опсуче

оптати́в *m Gram.* optative mood

оптати́вен -вна *adj Gram.* optative

оптега (се) *impf see* оптегнува (се)

оптегари & **оптегарчи** *pf colloq.* to hit, strike, belabour (*with a stick*)

оптегарува & **оптегарчува** *impf of* оптегари & оптегарчи

оптегач *m* **1** (*на разбој*) bar, catch **2** ratchet; clamp, clasp, brace; ❑ за делачот оптегачот nothing left for the carver (*said when s.o. divides s.th. up among others, leaving nothing for himself*)

оптегне *pf* оптегна *aor.* **I 1** to stretch, tighten, tense *trans.*; оптегне јаже/жица to tighten a rope/wire; оптегне лак to draw a bow **2** to extend, stretch out *trans.*; оптегне раце to stretch out one's arms; оптегне врат to crane one's neck **II – се 1** to tighten, tense *intrans.*; кожата на лицето му се оптегна the skin on his face tightened **2** (*протегне се*) to stretch <out> *intrans.*; to sprawl; се оптегна на подот како мртов he stretched out on the floor as if dead

оптегнува (се) *impf of* оптегне (се)

оптек *m literary see* опток

оптекува *impf* **1** to flow round **2** to circulate

оптера *pf colloq.* to swear at, curse, abuse

оптече *pf see* оптекува 1

оптечува *impf of* оптече, *see* оптекува

оптика *f* **1** optics **2** optical instruments

оптима́лен -лна *adj* optimal, optimum

оптими́зам -змот *m* optimism

оптими́ст *m* optimist

оптимистичен -чна & **оптимистички** *adj* optimistic; оптимистични (оптимистички) идеи optimistic ideas

оптимистички & **оптимистично** *adv* optimistically

оптими́стка *f* (*fem. form*) *see* оптимист

оптичар *m* **1** specialist in optics **2** optician

оптички *adj* optic; visual, optical; оптички стакла optical lenses; оптички направи (уреди) optical appliances (instruments); оптичка измама optical illusion; mirage

оптовари *pf* **1** *literary* to load, burden; тој е оптоварен со многу должности he is burdened with many duties **2** *Comm.* to charge, debit; во сметката нè оптоварија (*со*) they've charged (*s.th.*) to our account

оптоварува *impf of* оптовари

опток *m literary* circulation (*of money*)

оптока *f* trimming (*of ribbon*), galloon, braid, piping

опточи *pf* to trim, border with braid

оптичува *impf of* опточи

оптрча *pf* to run round

оптрчува *impf of* оптрча

оптужба *f* accusation, charge, indictment, *see* обвинение

оптужи *pf* to accuse, charge; to bring a charge; *see* обвини

оптужница *f* <bill of> indictment, *see* обвинителен <акт>

оптужува *impf of* оптужи, *see* обвинува

опул *m dial.* (*поглед*) look, glance, gaze

опули¹ *pf dial.* **I** (*of eyes*) to open *trans.*; ги опули очите he opened his eyes **II – се 1** to look at; воопшто не ми се опули he didn't look at me at all; се опули вземи he looked at the ground **2** to open *intrans.*; му се опулија очите his eyes opened

опули² (се) *pf dial. see* опрли (се)

опулува (се) *impf of* опули¹ (се)

опус *m* opus, œuvre

опустен *pt* deserted; опустена куќа deserted house

опусти *pf* опусте *aor.* to become empty, deserted; селото опусте the village became deserted

опустошен *pt* devastated, ravaged, destroyed; опустошени села devastated (ravaged) villages

опустошеност *f* devastated, ravaged state; devastation

опустоши *pf* to lay waste, devastate, ravage

опустошителен -лна *adj* devastating, ruinous; опустошителна војна devastating war

опустошува *impf of* опустоши

опустува *impf of* опусти

опута *f* sandal strap, cord

опуштен *pt* relaxed, at ease

опуштеност *f* relaxation

опушти *pf* I to relax, loosen *trans.*; опушти мускули to relax one's muscles II – ce 1 to relax, loosen *intrans.* 2 to take the liberty

опфат *m* scope; volume; grasp

опфати *pf* 1 to embrace, envelop, engulf; to include, take in; to cover; (*обземе, фати*) to seize, grip; пожарот го опфати целото село the fire engulfed the whole village; опфати многу прашања to cover many questions; го опфати жал he was overcome by pity 2 *fig.* to scan, survey; го опфати со поглед полето his eyes scanned (surveyed) the field

опфаќа *impf of* опфати

опцуе *pf* опцу *aor.* to swear at

опчади *pf* to fill with smoke *trans.*

опчадува *impf of* опчади

опчекори *pf* to mount, straddle, bestride; to step over/across

опчекорува *impf of* опчекори

опчекува *impf* I to wait for, expect; to watch for II – ce to wait for, expect each other

опчури (се) *pf* I *see* опчади II – ce *fig.* to have a smoke

опчурува (се) *impf of* опчури (се)

опшета *pf* to visit, tour, do the rounds of; сите соседи ги опшетав I have called on all my neighbours

опшетува *impf of* опшета

опшива *impf of* опшие

опшивка *f* hem, border; trimming

опшие *pf* опши *aor.* to edge, hem; to border, trim (*with lace, braid, etc.*)

опширен -рна *adj* detailed; prolix; thorough; extensive; опширен извештај detailed report

опширно *adv* in detail, extensively, at length; изложи опширно to set forth in detail

опширност *f* extensiveness, <great> detail; prolixity

општ *adj* general, total, universal; common, shared, joint; општа мобилизација/амнестија general mobilization/amnesty; општо право на глас universal suffrage (franchise); општ незадоволство widespread/general discontent; општ лекар general practitioner; општа мана common fault; општ впечаток general impression; во општ лекар in general practitioner; општи фрази generalities, general phrases; општи интереси common interests; има нешто општо (*co*) to have s.th. in common (*with*)

општење *n* communication, communion, intercourse; немо општење mute communion

општополезен -зна *adj see* општополезен

општествен *adj* social; public; општествен строј, поредок, ред social structure, system, order; општествени односи social relations; општествена положба social position; општествен работник public figure; општествена сопственост public property; општествен имот public property; општествени простории public premises, public (meeting) rooms; општествена исхрана public catering

општественик -ци *m* public figure, public-spirited person

општество *n* society; наука за општеството sociology; првобитно општество primitive society; високо општество high society

општи *impf* to communicate (*co – with*); to associate (*with*), be friends (*with*)

општина *f* 1 municipality; district, township 2 town hall

општинар *m arch.* alderman; municipal worker

општински *adj* municipal, community; општински имот community property; општински одборник member of the municipal council; општински службеник town clerk

општо *adv* in general; generally; општо земено taken as a whole, generally speaking, *see* воопшто; општо позната работа common knowledge

општо- (*in compounds*) universally, common<ly>, widely; општословенски јазик Common Slavonic (*Am.* Slavic)

општокорисен -сна *adj* generally useful, beneficial, *see* општополезен

општонароден -дна *adj* nationwide; national; општонародно востание nationwide uprising; општонародна сопственост public property

општообразовен -вна *adj* of general education; општообразовни установи <high> schools providing a general education

óпштопóзнат *adj* well-known, widely known; општопознати работи well-known matters; општопознати факти well-known facts

општополезен -зна *adj* generally useful; општополезен труд, општополезна работа work useful/of benefit to all

општополезност *f* general usefulness, benefit

општораспространет *adj* widespread; well-known

општост *f* generality

општочовечки *adj* universal, common to all mankind; општочовечки идеали ideals shared by all mankind

ора *impf* to plough, till; ѓаволот ни ора, ни копа *prov.* the devil never rests

орав -си *m dial. Bot.* walnut, *see* орев

оравче *n dial. see* оревче

оражје *n rare see* оружје

орáкул *m* oracle; prophet

орален -лна *adj* oral, spoken

оралиште *n see* оролиште

орало *n* plough

оран *m* 1 ploughing 2 (*ораница*) ploughed land

орангутáн *m Zool.* (Pongo pygmaeus) orang-utan

орáнж *m* orange <colour>

оранжáда *f* orangeade

оранжерија -ии *f* greenhouse, glasshouse

ораница *f* 1 arable land no longer cultivated; wasteland; ораница беше угар го сторија it was wasteland, but they brought it under the plough 2 ploughed land 3 ploughing, tillage

орат *adj see* оратен

оратен -тна *adj* 1 arable; оратна земја ploughland 2 used for ploughing; оратни волови plough oxen

оратор *m* orator, speaker

ораториум *m Mus.* oratorio

ораторка *f* (*fem. form*) *see* оратор

ораторски *adj* oratorical; ораторска дарба gift for oratory; ораторска вештина oratorical skill

ораторство *n* oratory; rhetoric; eloquence

орач *m* 1 ploughman 2 *Astron.* Rigel, Beta Orionis

орачка *f* (*fem. form*) *see* орач 1

орачки *adj* ploughing

орација -ии *m colloq.* skilled oro dancer

орацика *f colloq.* (*fem. form*) *see* орација

орашина *f see* орешинка

орашков *adj dial. see* оревов

орбита *f* 1 orbit 2 *Anat.* eye-socket, orbit 3 *fig.* orbit, sphere of influence; range, field of action

орбитален -лна *adj* orbital; орбитален лет orbital flight

оргазам -змот *m* orgasm

орган[1] *m* 1 organ; говорни органи organs of speech; дишни органи respiratory organs; органи за варење digestive organs; полови органи sexual organs 2 organ; institutional body; законодавен/судски/синдикален орган legislative/judicial/trade union body (officials); органи за јавна безбедност security services; орган на власта authority 3 organ, mouthpiece; весникот е орган на Републиканската партија this paper is the organ of the Republican Party 4 human voice; има силен орган to have a powerful voice

орган[2] *m Mus.* organ, *see* оргула

организам -змот *m* organism; body; виши и нижи организми higher and lower organisms; тој има издржлив организам he has a robust constitution; државен организам state organism

организатор *m* organizer

организаторка *f* (*fem. form*) *see* организатор

организаторски *adj* organizational; организаторски способности organizational abilities; организаторска дејност organizational activity

организаторство *n* organizational activity, work; organizational ability

организација -ии *f* organization; организацијата на конгресот the organization of the congress; синдикална организација trade union organization; стопанска организација business concern, enterprise; Организација на обединетите народи United Nations Organization

организационен -она *adj* organizational; организациони прашања organizational matters

организациски *adj see* организационен

организира *pf & impf* to organize, set up, arrange; to bring order (*into*); организира концерт/екскурзија to arrange a concert/excursion

организиран *adj & pt* organized; planned; orderly; убаво организиран живот a well-ordered life

органист *m Mus.* organist, *see* оргулар 2

органографија *f* organography

органологија *f* organology

органски *adj* organic (*also fig.*); органски останки organic remains; органска хемија organic chemistry; органска омраза visceral (gut) hatred

оргија -ии *f* orgy

оргула *f Mus.* organ

оргулар *m* 1 organ-builder 2 *Mus.* organist

орда *f* horde (*Hist. & fig.*); host; Златната Орда the Golden Horde; Хитлеровите орди Hitler's hordes

ордевер *m* hors d'oeuvre

орден *m* order, decoration; орден на трудот Order of Labour

ордија -ии *f* army (*usu. Turkish*); *fig.* horde; царска ордија the czar's troops; турска ордија Turkish troops

ординарен -рна *adj* 1 ordinary, usual, daily, regular, average 2 plain, unsophisticated, vulgar, common

ординарец -рци *m Mil.* batman; orderly

ордината *f Math.* ordinate

ординатен -тна *adj Math.* ordinate; ординатна оска ordinate

ординација -ии *f* 1 *Med.* prescription 2 <doctor's> surgery, *Am.* office

ординира 1 *pf & impf* to direct; to prescribe, order 2 *impf* to receive patients (*for examination and treatment*); to practise (*of doctor, dentist*)

ордонанс *m Mil.* orderly; batman

орев -и *m Bot.* (Juglans regia) walnut (*tree and nut*); кокосов орев (Cocos nucifera) coconut (*tree and nut*); ❑ тврд орев a hard nut to crack; два лешника еден орев го кршат *prov.* there's strength in numbers

оревов *adj* walnut; оревово дрво walnut-tree; walnut timber; оревови јатки walnut kernels; оревова лушпа walnut shell, nutshell

оревовка *f* walnut cake

оревче *n* 1 *dim. of* орев; морско оревче (Myristica fragrans) nutmeg 2 *Zool.* (Troglodytes troglodytes) wren

орел -рли *m Zool.* eagle; сур орел (Aquila chrysaetos) golden eagle; крстатен (крстат) орел (Aquila heliaca) imperial eagle; речен орел (Pandion haliaetus) osprey; двоглав орел double (two-headed) eagle; ❑ смрди, орли збира to stink to high heaven, stink like a polecat (skunk); се собере како орли на мрша to gather like vultures round carrion

орелски *adj* eagle's, aquiline; орелски крилја eagle's wings

орен[1] -рна *adj* arable; орна земја arable land

орен[2] -рна *adj poet.* echoing, resounding

ореов *adj see* оревов

ореол *m* halo

орешинка *f* the outer, green shell of the walnut

ори се *impf* to echo, resound; сеореше песната the song rang out

оривче *n dim. of* ориз

оригинал *m* 1 original; чита некое дело во оригинал to read a work in the original 2 *fig.* eccentric, character

оригинален -лна *adj* 1 original, authentic 2 *fig.* strange, peculiar, original

оригиналничи *impf* to try to be original; to put on an act

оригиналност *f* originality

ориент *m* the Orient, the East

ориентален -лна *adj* oriental, eastern; ориентални народи oriental peoples

ориенталец -лци *m* Oriental

ориентализам -змот *m* orientalism

ориенталист *m* orientalist

ориенталистика *f* oriental studies

ориенталистка *f* (*fem. form*) *see* ориенталист

ориенталка *f* Oriental <woman>

ориенталски *adj* oriental; ориенталски стил oriental style

ориентација -ии *f* **1** orientation; има чувство за ориентација to have a sense of direction; губи ориентација to lose one's bearings **2** orientation, grasp, understanding

ориентационен -она *adj* **1** position-finding, <of> orientation, orientational; ориентациона точка point of orientation, landmark **2** approximate, tentative, giving guidance; ориентациони податоци approximate data

ориентир *m* landmark (*also fig.*), reference point; signpost

ориентира *pf & impf* **I** to orientate *trans.* **II – се 1** to orientate o.s., determine one's position **2** to direct one's efforts (*кон нешто – towards s.th.*); to aim towards **3** *fig.* to get one's bearings, find one's feet

ориз *m Bot.* (Oryza sativa) rice (*plant and grain*)

оризар *m* rice grower

оризарски *adj* rice grower's; rice-growing

оризарство *n* rice growing

оризен -зна *adj* rice; оризно брашно rice flour; оризно поле rice paddy, rice-field; оризно зрно grain of rice; оризна каша rice porridge; оризна вода rice-water

оризиште *n* rice-fields, paddies

оризник -ци *m* rice pie, pie with rice filling

оризов *adj see* оризен

оризоплеварка *f* (*woman*) rice-field worker

орисија *f literary* fate, lot, destiny

орјат & орјатин -ти *m* thief; cad, bounder; crude person, hick, boor

орјатка *f* (*fem. form*) *see* орјат

орјатски *adj* boorish; caddish

оркан *m* hurricane, cyclone

оркански *adj* cyclonic

оркестар -три *m* orchestra; симфониски оркестар symphony orchestra

оркестарски & оркестрален -лна *adj* orchestral; оркестарска придружба orchestral accompaniment

оркестрација *f* orchestration

оркестрира *pf & impf* to orchestrate, arrange

орле & орленце *n dim.* (*of* орел) eaglet

орлица *f Zool.* (*see* орел) female eagle

орлиште *n augm. of* орел

орлов *adj* eagle's; орлово крило, перо eagle's wing, feather; орлови нокти 1. eagle's talons (claws) 2. *Bot.* (Lonicera caprifolium) honeysuckle; ❑ орлово око eagle eye

орловски *adj* aquiline; орловски поглед eagle's (penetrating) look; орловски нос aquiline nose

орман[1] *m arch. colloq.* (*шума, гора*) forest, wood; орман да фати! *curse* the devil take him/it!

орман[2] *m* cupboard; wardrobe; орман за книги bookcase; орман за садови kitchen dresser; орман со огледало dresser, dressing-table; wardrobe with mirror

орнамент *m* ornament (*pictorial, sculptural, musical*), adornment

орнаментален -лна *adj* ornamental; орнаментални елементи ornamental elements

орнаменталист *m* ornamentalist

орнаментација *f* ornamentation

орнаментика *f coll.* ornaments, decorations

орнаментира *pf & impf* to ornament, adorn, embellish

орнитолог -зи *m Zool.* ornithologist

орнитологија *f Zool.* ornithology

орница *f see* ораница 1 *& 2*

орничка *f dim. of* орница

оро *n* oro, line-dance, round-dance, ring-dance; игра оро to dance the *oro*; се фати на оро to join the *oro*; *fig.* to join forces; води оро to lead the *oro*; *fig.* to rule the roost; to pull the strings; ❑ и оро ќе игра (на тепсија оро ќе игра; оро таратинско ќе игра) put that in your pipe and smoke it; си се фатил на оро, ќе играш in for a penny, in for a pound; гладна мечка оро не игра *prov.* you can't work on an empty stomach; кога ќе се фати сиромавиот на оро, ќе се скине тапанот *prov.* the poor must pay for all

ороводец -дци *m* leader of the oro (*also fig.*)

орографија *f* orography

орографски *adj* orographic<al>

орогуши *pf* to hit (*s.o.*) on the head and raise a large bump

ороди *pf* **I** to make (*s.o.*) a relative by marriage **II – се** to become related by marriage; *see* сроди (се)

ороз *m* trigger; cocking piece; повлече ороз to cock a gun, raise the hammer; to pull the trigger

оролиште *n* place where the oro is danced (*usu. in the middle of a village*); селско оролиште village dance floor

ороси *pf* to bedew; to moisten, sprinkle

оросница *f poet.* falling tear

ороспија -ии *f colloq.* slut, whore, trollop

оросува *impf of* ороси

орочи *pf* to deposit (*money*), make fixed-term deposits

орочува *impf of* орочи

ортак -ци *m* partner; fellow worker, workmate; accomplice

ортаклак *m colloq.* joint business, partnership; complicity

ортакува *impf* to work together, collaborate in a business, work as partners

ортачи *pf* **I** to appoint as a partner **II – се** to enter into a partnership (*со некого – with s.o.*), become a partner

ортачка *f* (*fem. form*) *see* ортак

ортачки *adj* partner's, shared (*in a business sense*)

ортогон *m* (*правоаголник*) rectangle, parallelogram

ортогонален -лна *adj* **1** (*правоаголен*) orthogonal, rectangular **2** (*вертикален*) vertical

ортографија -ии *f* orthography

ортографски *adj* orthographic<al>

ортодоксен -сна *adj* orthodox; ортодоксни марксисти orthodox Marxists

ортодоксност *f* orthodoxy

ортоепија *f* orthoepy, correctness of diction

ортоепски *adj* orthoepic

ортома *f* **1** rope, stout cord; ❑ од влакното ортома прави to make a mountain out of a molehill; суши просо на ортома he's doing nothing, he's wasting time **2** *fig.* gibbet, gallows; ❑ кој од кол, кој од ортома all sorts of riffraff; си ја влече ортомата <по себеси> he deserves to swing

ортомар *m* rope-maker; rope merchant

ортомарница *f* rope shop; rope walk

ортомиса *pf* to tether

ортомисува *impf of* ортомиса

ортопе́д *m* orthopaedist, orthopaedic surgeon

ортопедија *f* orthopaedics

ортопе́дски *adj* orthopaedic; ортопедски помагала orthopaedic aids; ортопедски чевли orthopaedic shoes

орудие -ија *n* implement, instrument, tool; земјоделски орудија agricultural tools; орудија на производството (за производство) implements of production; јазикот како орудие за разбирање меѓу луѓето language as a means of communication between people; *Mil.* тешко орудие <heavy> field gun, field piece

оружје *n* arms, weapons; атомско оружје atomic weapons; класично оружје conventional weapons; огнострелно оружје firearms; ладно (студено) оружје cold steel; ❑ грабне (дигне) оружје; фати се за оружје to take up arms; to rise up in arms; ѕвечка со оружје to rattle one's sabre; на оружје! to arms! под оружје <e> <to be> under arms; положи оружје to lay down one's arms; род оружје arm/ branch of the service; браќа по оружје brothers in arms

орхиде́ја -еи *f Bot.* orchid

оса *f* 1 *Zool.* wasp; ❑ лут како оса furious as a hornet; се собрале како оси на мед they've gathered like bees round a honey-pot 2 *fig.* waspish person (*usu. of a woman*), shrew

осакатен *pt* crippled, maimed, mutilated; disabled

осакатеност *f* mutilation; <physical> disability

осакати *pf* to cripple, maim, mutilate; to disable

осакатува *impf of* осакати

осамен *adj* alone, isolated, lonely; тој е секогаш осамен he is always alone

осамено *adv* alone, by oneself, in isolation; живее осамено to live by oneself (alone)

осаменост *f* loneliness, isolation; јас не ја сакам осаменоста I don't like loneliness (isolation)

осами *pf* I to make lonely, isolate II – **се** to isolate o.s.

осамне *pf* осамна *aor.* I 1 *impers.* to dawn, grow light; кога осамна, јас се разбудив when day broke, I woke up 2 to meet (greet) the dawn; осамнавме кај реката dawn found us by the riverside II – **се** *see* I 1

осамнува (се) *impf of* осамне (се)

осамотен *adj see* осамен

осамотеност *f see* осаменост

осамоти (се) *pf see* осами (се)

осамотува (се) *impf of* осамоти (се)

осамува (се) *impf of* осами (се)

осатка *f Bot.* (Hordeum murinum *or* secalinum) mouse-barley, wall barley, wild barley

осведочен *adj & pt* 1 proven 2 sure, confident, assured

осведочи *pf* I 1 to confirm, prove 2 to assure II – **се** to assure o.s.

осведочува (се) *impf of* осведочи (се)

освежен *pt* renewed, refreshed

освежи *pf* I to refresh, freshen *trans.*; to cool; to renew, renovate; to revive; дождот го освежи воздухот the rain freshened the air; освежи бои to freshen colours; освежи спомени to revive memories II – **се** to refresh o.s.; to freshen up *intrans.*; to become clean, fresh, cool

освежителен -лна *adj* refreshing; освежителни пијачки (пијалоци) refreshing drinks, refreshments; освежително дејство refreshing effect

освежува (се) *impf of* освежи (се)

освежувачки *adj see* освежителен

освен *prep* except, save, apart from; other than, besides, barring; сите освен тебе all except you; освен тоа that apart, apart from this; beside<s>; ништо друго освен nothing but; освен ако except if, unless; only if; освен кога except when; освен <тоа> што apart from the fact that; освен во среда except on Wednesdays; освен во случај да except if

освести *pf* I 1 to bring round, revive *trans.*; го освестивме со студена вода we revived him with cold water 2 to bring (s.o.) to his senses II – **се** 1 to come round, regain consciousness 2 to come to one's senses

освестува (се) *impf of* освести (се)

осветен *pt* sanctified, consecrated; осветена икона consecrated icon

освети *pf* to consecrate, make holy; to canonize; to sanctify; освети вода to bless water; освети црква, олтар to consecrate a church, an altar

осветлен *adj & pt* illuminated, lit up

осветление *n* lighting, illumination; осветлението беше слабо the lighting was poor; селото доби електрично осветление the village got electric lighting

осветли *pf* to illuminate, light up; to equip (supply) with lighting; осветли соба to light up a room; осветли село to bring power (electricity) to a village

осветлува *impf of* осветли

осветува *impf of* освети

освешта *pf literary* 1 *see* освети 2 *fig.* to affirm, establish

освештава *impf of* освешта

освештан *adj & pt literary* 1 sanctified, made holy, consecrated 2 *fig.* confirmed, established; освештани обичаи established customs; освештани правила time-honoured rules

освои *pf* 1 (присвои) to take over, appropriate, usurp; си ги освои сите ствари he appropriated everything 2 (заземе) to win; to occupy, take by force, conquer; освоивме неколку градови we captured several cities 3 (придобие) to gain; to win over; освои нечие срце to win s.o.'s heart; освои публика to captivate the public; освои на јуриш to take by storm

освојува *impf of* освои

освојувач *m* 1 usurper; appropriator 2 conqueror

освојувачки *adj* conquering, of conquest; освојувачка војна war of conquest

осврне се *pf literary* осврна се *aor.* to deal with, turn one's attention (на – то); to consider; to turn to; to take account of; не се осврна на тоа прашање he didn't address that question

осврнува се *impf literary of* осврне се

осврт *m* review; критички осврт critical review

оседла *pf* to saddle

оседлан *pt* saddled

оседлува *impf of* оседла

осека *f Geog. rare* (одлив) low tide, ebb-tide

осем *prep see* освен

осемени *pf* to inseminate

осеменува *impf of* осемени

осен -сна *adj* axial; осно лежиште axial bearing; осен притисок axial pressure; осна симетрија axial symmetry

осенча *pf literary* (*исенча*) to shade (*in painting*)

осенчува *impf of* осенча

осет *m* feeling; sensation; perception; губи осет за нешто to lose one's feel for s.th.

осетен -тна *adj* considerable; perceptible, appreciable; осетна разлика considerable difference

осети *pf* I to feel *trans.*; to sense; осети болка, тежина to feel pain, discomfort; осети радост to feel joy II – ce to feel *intrans.*; се осетив здрав и силен I felt fit and well; *impers.* веднаш се осети дека ќе дојде до караница one felt immediately that there would be a quarrel

осетлив *adj* 1 noticeable 2 sensitive, susceptible; touchy, tetchy; delicate; осетлив на светлост sensitive to light; осетлива кожа sensitive skin; осетливо место sensitive spot

осетливост *f* sensitivity, susceptibility; sensibility; irritability, touchiness

осетува (се) *impf of* осети (се)

осеќава (се) *impf see* осетува (се)

осиви *pf* 1 to turn (*s.th.*) grey 2 to go grey

осивува *impf of* осиви

осигурен *pt* 1 secure; protected; provided 2 insured; осигурен имот insured property

осигуреник -ци *m* the insured, policy holder

осигури *pf* I 1 to guarantee, assure; to ensure; осигури успех/победа to assure success/victory 2 to secure, provide for; to reserve; осигури живот на деца to provide for the future of one's children 3 to insure; осигури куќа to insure a house II – ce 1 to secure o.s.; се осигури од напад to guard against an attack 2 to provide o.s. (*co – with*); се осигуривме со храна за два месеца we've laid in provisions for two months 3 to assure o.s., make sure; се осигурив дека во куќата нема никого I assured myself that there was no one in the house 4 to insure o.s.

осигурителен -лна *adj* insurance, assurance *attrib.*; осигурително друштво insurance company; осигурителни мерки safety measures

осигурува (се) *impf of* осигури (се)

осигурување *n* insurance; осигурување од пожар fire insurance; животно осигурување life insurance; здравствено осигурување health insurance; завод за социјално осигурување department of social security; каско осигурување comprehensive insurance

осигурувач *m* 1 insurer, insurance company 2 *Elec.* fuse, safety-fuse; прегорен осигурувач burnt-out fuse 3 (*на оружје*) safety-catch

осил *m coll.* awn<s>, bristles

осилка *f* <single> awn

осило *n* 1 (*in bees, wasps etc.*) sting 2 *see* осилка

осин *adj* wasp's, vespine; осино гнездо wasps' nest; *fig.* hornets' nest

осип *m* rash

осипе се *pf* осипа се *aor.* (*срони се*) to crumble *intrans.*; to wear away, erode *intrans.*; to collapse *intrans.*; се осипа брегот the bank crumbled

осипнат *pt* (*засипнат*) hoarse; raucous; осипнат глас hoarse voice

осипне *pf* осипна *aor.* (*засипне*) to become hoarse; to lose one's voice

осипнува *impf of* осипне

осиромашен *pt* impoverished, poor

осиромашеност *f* impoverishment

осиромаши *pf* I 1 to impoverish 2 *intrans.* to become poor II – ce *see* I 2

осиромашува (се) *impf of* осиромаши (се)

осироти *pf* 1 to become an orphan; *fig.* to be deserted 2 *rare* (*of a woman*) to lose one's children

осиротува *impf of* осироти

осит *adj* 1 angry, cross 2 brisk, lively

осица & осичка *f dim. of* оса

оска *f* 1 axle, shaft; axis; подвижна оска movable axis; слободна/врзана оска free/fixed axis; оска на симетријата axis of symmetry; земјата се врти околу својата оска the earth rotates on its axis 2 *fig.* core, hub, centre

оскапи *pf* I 1 to grow dear, go up in price; лебот нема да оскапи bread won't go up in price 2 to make dearer, put up in price; фабриките ја оскапија хартијата the factories put up the price of paper II – ce *see* I 1; дрвата се оскапија firewood has gone up in price

оскапува (се) *impf of* оскапи (се)

осквернет *pt* 1 (*за црква итн.*) desecrated 2 (*за девојка*) raped, defiled, dishonoured

оскверни *pf* 1 to desecrate, dishonour; to profane, defile; оскверни црква to desecrate a church 2 to rape, violate

осквернител *m* desecrator

осквернителка *f* (*fem. form*) *see* осквернител

осквернува *impf of* оскверни

оскомина *f* (*скомина*) tartness, bitter taste

оскоруша *f Bot. see* оскруша

оскрби *pf arch.*, *literary* I to insult, offend; to distress, sadden II – ce to take umbrage, take offence, be offended, insulted; to be distressed, saddened; *see* навреди (се)

оскрбува (се) *impf of* оскрби (се)

оскруша *f Bot.* (Sorbus domestica) service tree; sorb<-apple>

оскубе *pf* оскуба *aor.* (*окубе, искубе*) to pluck, pull out, tear out

оскубува *impf of* оскубе, *see* окубува, искубува

оскуден -дна *adj* 1 inadequate, scant, meagre, insufficient; оскудни средства insufficient means; оскудни податоци inadequate data (information) 2 short (*of s.th.*); оскуден за пари short of money

оскудица *f* 1 poverty, need, destitution; живее во оскудица to live in poverty; во оскудица е за то be in need of 2 insufficiency, shortage, scarity; оскудица на муниција shortage of ammunition; оскудица на храброст lack of courage

оскудно *adv* poorly, meagrely

оскудност *f see* оскудица

оскудува *impf* to be in want (*од, co – of*), be short (*of*)

ослабен *pt* 1 weakened, thin, wasted; reduced, diminished; ослабени нозе weakened legs; ослабено интересирање, внимание и сл. diminished interest, attention, etc.; ослабена сила, моќ reduced strength, power 2 loose, loosened, relaxed; ослабени врски loose ties (connections, bonds, relations)

ослабеност *f* weakness

ослаби *pf* ослабе & ослаби *aor.* **1** to weaken, become weak (frail); to lose weight; ослаби во лицето (на лице) to grow thin in the face; ми ослабе видот my sight has dimmed; ми ослабе паметот my memory is failing **2** to diminish; to wane; to loosen *intrans.*; to relax, grow looser; неговата љубов спрема родителите ослабе his love for his parents has diminished; интересирањето и вниманието ослабеа interest and attention have waned **3** to weaken, reduce *trans.*; to loosen *trans.*; болеста многу го ослаби the illness greatly weakened him; вревата ми го ослаби вниманието the uproar distracted my attention

ослабува *impf of* ослаби

ослани *pf* to rime, cover with hoar-frost (rime); (*of frost*) to blacken, blight, scorch

осланува *impf of* ослани

ослепее *pf* ослепеа *aor.* to go blind; да ослепам <ако те лажам>! may I go blind <if I'm lying to you>!

ослепеник -ци *m* blind man; wretched person; *usu. in the voc.*: ослепенику! you poor wretch!

ослепи *pf* **1** to blind; сите заробеници ги ослепија they blinded all the prisoners **2** to dazzle; светлината ми ги ослепи очите the light dazzled me **3** to go blind

ослепува *impf of* ослепи

ослободен *pt* **1** freed, liberated; exempt; ослободена територија liberated territory; ослободени народи liberated nations; ослободено од царина exempt from duty; ослободено од данок tax free **2** encouraged, emboldened; relaxed, put at ease; сега е веќе ослободен now he has recovered his courage, now he is relaxed **3** (*as noun*) ослободениот released man; ослободената released woman

ослободи *pf* **I 1** to free, liberate, set free; to release; тие сакаа да ја ослободат Македонија they wanted to free (liberate) Macedonia; ги ослободи затворениците he freed the prisoners; ја ослободи едната рака he got one hand free; ослободете ме од него rid me of him! **2** to relieve, discharge, excuse, exempt; судот го ослободи he was acquitted by the court; ослободи од обврски/долгови/данок/ такса/ испит to excuse/exempt from duties/debts/tax/fees/an examination **3** to encourage, embolden; to put at ease **4** to vacate, clear; ослободи соба, просторија to vacate a room, premises; ослободи пат to clear the way/road **II – се 1** to win one's freedom, free o.s., rid o.s. (*од – of*) **2** to be relieved, dismissed, discharged; се ослободи од должности to be relieved of one's duties **3** to feel o.s. free, relax, take courage, gain confidence; детето не можеше брзо да се ослободи the child was slow to gain confidence

ослободител *m* liberator

ослободителен -лна *adj* <of> liberation, liberating; ослободителна војна war of liberation; ослободително движење liberation movement

ослободителка *f* (*fem. form*) *see* ослободител

ослободува (се) *impf of* ослободи (се)

ослободување *n* liberation; deliverance; exemption; ослободување од плаќање казна remission of penalty

ослободувачки *adj* releasing, relieving, excusing; ослободувачка пресуда acquittal

ослови *pf literary, rare* to turn to, address, talk to

ословува *impf literary, rare of* ослови

ослон *m* (*потпор*) prop; support

ослони се *pf* (*опре се, потпре се*) to rely (*на некого – on s.o.*), depend (*on s.o.*); to trust

ослонува се *impf of* ослони се

ослуша *pf see* ослушне, наслуша

ослушне *pf* ослушна *aor.* (*наслуша, наслушне*) to try to hear, overhear; to eavesdrop

ослушнува *impf of* ослушне

ослушува *impf of* ослуша

осмаден *pt* singed, scorched

осмади *pf* to singe, scorch

осмадува *impf of* осмади

осмак -ци *m* **1** measure for corn (*50 kg, c. 2.5 bushels*) **2** eight-year-old animal **3** s.th. comprising eight elements

османлија -ии *m Hist.* Ottoman Turk

османски *adj Hist.* Ottoman; османска империја the Ottoman (Turkish) empire

осмели се *pf* to dare, venture; to take the liberty; како се осмели да појде кај неа? how did he dare to go to her place?

осмелува се *impf of* осмели се

осми *adj num* eighth; осми ред eighth row; осмо одделение eighth grade (*final year of primary school*)

осмина¹ *f* **1** eighth **2** *Mus.* quaver, *Am.* eighth note **3** (*формат на книга*) octavo

осмина² *num* (*of men and mixed groups*) eight, *see* осуммина

осминка *f* eighth, *see* осмина¹ 1

осмисли *pf* to give meaning to; to make sense of; to interpret; осмисли живот to lend meaning to one's life

осмислува *impf of* осмисли

осмица *f dial. see* осумка

осмо́за *f* osmosis

осмокласник -ци *m obs.* eighth-former, pupil in the eighth form

осмокласничка *f obs.* (*fem. form*) *see* осмокласник

осмокрак *adj* **1** *f.p.* eight-legged; рак осмокрак eight-legged crayfish (crab, lobster) **2** eight-pointed; осмокрака ѕвезда eight-pointed star

осмолетка *f* eight-year primary (elementary) school

осмостран *adj* eight-sided, octagonal

осмрден *pt* stinking, smelly; внатре е сè осмрдено inside everything stinks

осмрди *pf* to make (*s.th./s.o.*) stink; ја осмрди сета сала he made the whole hall stink

осмрдува *impf of* осмрди

оснежен *pt* snow-covered, snow-capped; оснежени дрвја snow-covered (snow-clad) trees

основ *m literary, Leg.* basis, reason, *see* основа 4

основа¹ *f* **1** foundation, base (*also fig.*); basis; ѕидиштата имаат јака основа the ramparts have strong foundations; *Geom.* основа на триаголник base of a triangle; системот беше разнишан во својата основа the system was shaken to its foundations; ❏ во основата, во својата основа basically; врз основа на on the basis of **2** (*во ткаење*) warp **3** background, groundwork; на црвена основа on a red background **4** reason; grounds; немаш основа да се сомневаш во тоа you have no reason to doubt this; без основа groundless; uncalled-for **5** *fig.* (*only pl*) tenets, principles; elements; основите на марксизмот-ленинизмот the bases of Marxism-Leninism **6** *Gram.* stem; основа и завршок на еден збор stem and ending of a word **7** *Chem.* base, *see* база 2

основа² *impf of* основе, *see* основува

основан *pt* founded; established; justified; основана недоверба justified (justifiable) distrust

основател *m* founder, *see* основач 1

основателен -лна *adj* basic; (*основан*) justified

основателка *f* (*fem. form*) *see* основател, основачка

основач *m* **1** founder; основач на весник founder of a newspaper **2** promoter, organizer

основачка *f* (*fem. form*) *see* основач

основачки *adj* inaugural; основачко собрание inaugural meeting

основе *pf* основа *aor.* **1** to found; основе друштво to found a society **2** to base, construct (*one's argument, case*) (*на – on*)

основен -вна *adj* **1** basic, essential, main; primary; основна мисла central idea; основно правило basic (fundamental, main) rule; основно својство essential property (characteristic); основни потреби primary needs **2** thorough; radical; основна реорганизација far-reaching (thorough) reorganization; основно чистење thorough clean-up; radical purge **3** elementary; основно училиште elementary (primary) school; основно образование elementary education **4** (*as noun*) основното *n* the main thing, the most important part; the essence; основното во некое прашање the crux of a problem

основец -вци *m* primary-school pupil

основица *f* **1** *Geom.* base; основица на триаголник base of a triangle **2** *fig.* basis, foundation; даночна основица taxation basis

основно *adv* basically

основоположник -ци *m* founder; основоположник на Марксизмот founder of Marxism

основува *impf of* основе

основувач *m see* основач

основувачки *adj see* основачки

особа *f* (*лице*) person

особен *adj* special, distinct, particular; (*чуден*) odd, peculiar; ништо особено nothing special; особен човек odd fellow; queer chap; особени заслуги outstanding merits; со особено задоволство with particular pleasure; со особена почит very respectfully; особени мерки, закони special measures, laws

особено *adv* specially, particularly; remarkably

особеност *f* **1** feature, characteristic, peculiarity; стилски особености stylistic features **2** (*чудност*) oddity, eccentricity; idiosyncrasy; забележуваш ли некаква особеност во неговот држење? do you notice anything strange about his behaviour?

особина *f* characteristic property, distinctive trait, feature

особит *adj see* особен

особито *adv see* особено

осоен -јна *adj* **1** shaded, sheltered (*from the sun*); осојно место cool, dank, shady spot **2** осојна змија, *see* осојница 2

осој -ои *m* shady, cool, dank place, shade

осојка *f Zool.* (Garrulus glandarius) jay, *see* сојка

осојница *f* **1** shade; cool, dank, shady place; на осојница in the shade **2** *Zool.* (Vipera ammodytes) horned viper **3** *fig.* shrew, virago

осојничав *adj* **1** shady, cool, dank; осојничаво место shady place **2** *fig.* gloomy, cold, unpleasant

осоли *pf* to salt

осолува *impf of* осоли

оспори *pf* to contest, dispute, challenge; to deny, refute; моето право не може никој да го оспори no one can dispute my right

оспорлив *adj* disputable, debatable, contentious

оспорливост *f* contentiousness

оспорува *impf of* оспори

оспорувач *m* person who disputes, challenger

оспособен *pt* prepared; trained; qualified (*за нешто – for s.th.*)

оспособеност *f* readiness; training; competence

оспособи *pf* **I** to prepare, train *trans.*; to qualify *trans.*; си ги оспособи децата за живот he prepared his children for life **II** – ce to train o.s. (*за нешто – for s.th.*); to qualify *intrans.*

оспособува (се) *impf of* оспособи (се)

оспособување *n* training; стручно оспособување vocational training

осрамотен *pt* disgraced

осрамоти *pf* **I** to disgrace, dishonour, shame **II** – ce to bring shame upon o.s.

осрамотува (се) *impf of* осрамоти (се)

остава (се) *impf of* остави (се)

оставачка *f* **1** leaving, abandoning **2** divorce

оставен *pt* **1** left, abandoned; оставено дете abandoned child; ❑ оставен на милост и немилост left stranded/in the lurch **2** divorced; оставена <жена> divorced woman, divorcee

остави *pf* **I** to leave; (*во наследство*) to bequeath; (*напушти*) to abandon; (*настрана*) to set aside; (*откаже се*) to give up, quit, forego; (*пушти*) to let grow (*hair*); (*запусти*) to neglect; (*одложи*) to put off; го остави моливот he put down his pencil; ja остави жената he abandoned his wife; го оставив пенкалото дома I've left my pen at home; ja остави вратата отворена he left the door open; тој на мене остави силен впечаток he made a deep impression on me; го оставив пушењето I've given up smoking; остави брада to let one's beard grow; ❑ остави некого на пол пат (среде во калта, на цедило, на милост и немилост) to leave s.o. in the lurch; остави некого на место to thrash, beat up; to kill; ако те фатам, на место ќе те оставам if I catch you, I'll kill you (have your blood); остави коски некаде to die far away from home; to leave one's bones to bleach; да го оставиме тоа let's drop that! let's forget about it! let bygones be bygones; остави нерешено to leave open (unresolved); остави пари настрана to put money aside; остави некого на мира to leave s.o. in peace, to leave s.o. alone; не остави ни камен на камен to destroy, raze to the ground; to leave no stone unturned **II** – ce (*од*) to give up; (*со*) to leave, divorce; to part, separate *intrans.*; to allow, let; остави се од тутунот! give up smoking! се остави со жената he divorced his wife

оставина *f* inheritance; heritage; литературна оставина literary heritage

оставински *adj* hereditary; probate; оставинска расправа probate proceedings

оставител *m* depositor

оставка *f* resignation; retirement; даде оставка to resign; подаде (поднесе) оставка to submit (hand in) one's resignation; во оставка in retirement

останатиот *adj* (*most often as pl noun*) the others, the rest, the remainder (*more usu.:* другите)

остане *pf* остана *aor.* to stay, remain, be left <behind>; остане уште малку to stay a little longer; клучот остана на врата the key was left in the door; остане жив to stay alive, to save one's neck; остане незабележан to escape observation/notice; остане забележан/запамтен како to go down as; обичаите останаа the customs have survived; остане буден to wait up; остане назад to trail behind; остане на сила to remain in power; остане неповреден to come through unscathed; остане приврзан на to adhere to; to hold to; to stick to; тоа останува да се види that remains to be seen; ❑ меѓу нас да си остане between ourselves, between you and me; остане на улица (на пат) to be left homeless; остане на пол пат to get stuck half-way; остане бел во очите (со празни раце) to be left empty-handed; остане тешка (трудна, трудница) to become pregnant; остане со впечаток (*дека* . . .) to get the impression (*that* . . .); остане со прстот в уста to be disappointed (*in one's expectations*); to get nothing for one's pains; to get the worst of a bargain; пуст да остане! damn him/it! душа не ми остана I am worn out; атер да не ти остане I hope you won't regret this; си остане на зборот to keep to one's word; си остане на своето to stick to one's guns; остане на место to die, perish on the spot

останка *f* (*usu. pl*) remainder, remnant, residue, <the> rest; *pl* remains; останките од некогашната тврдина the ruins of the fortress; останки од минатото vestiges/relics of the past; посмртни останки mortal remains

останува *impf of* остане

останувачка *f* 1 remaining, staying 2 sojourn, stay 3 (*see* останка) remainder, remnant

остар -три *adj* 1 sharp; acute; остри заби sharp teeth; остар нож, меч sharp knife, sword; остар агол acute angle; остар завој sharp bend; остар судир sharp clash; остри црти sharp/angular features 2 *fig.* piercing, penetrating, biting, cutting, keen, shrill; incisive; остар ветар a biting/keen wind; остар воздух brisk air; остар звук shrill sound; остар слух acute hearing; остро око sharp/keen eye; остра миризба acrid/pungent smell; остар јазик sharp tongue; остра болка sharp pain 3 (*of manner*) abrupt, severe 4 coarse, stiff; остри влакна stiff bristles; остро брашно coarse flour

остарее *pf* остареа *aor.* to age, grow old, *see* остари I

остарен *pt* old, aged

остари *pf* остаре *aor.* 1 to grow old, age *intrans.*; to show wear and tear; книгата остаре the book is the worse for wear 2 to age *trans.*, make (*s.o.*) old

остарува *impf of* остари

остаток -ци *m* 1 the rest, the remaining part; остаток од пари the rest of the money; остатокот од денот the rest of the day 2 *Math.* remainder; колку изнесува остатокот? how much is the remainder? ❑ без остаток completely, fully 3 (*usu. pl*) remnants, *see* останка; остатоци од храна leftovers, scraps

оствари *pf* I to accomplish, achieve, carry out, implement, put into effect; оствари замисла to put an idea into practice; оствари профит (добивка) to make a profit; оствари доход to earn income; оствари план to carry out a plan II – се to be fulfilled; сонот ти се оствари your dream has been fulfilled (come true)

остварлив *adj* feasible, practicable, realizable

остварливост *f* feasibility, practicability

остварува (се) *impf of* оствари (се)

остварување *n* 1 implementation 2 (*постигање*) achievement; остварувања во литературата successes/achievements in literature

остен *m* 1 goad 2 *colloq.* stick (*about 1.5 m long, used to estimate time of day by the height of the sun above the horizon*)

остеологија *f* osteology

остер -тра *adj see* остар

острач *m* (*точач*) knife-grinder

острвен *pt* brutalized; infuriated

острвеност *f* bloodthirstiness

острви *pf* I to make bloodthirsty, brutalize; *fig.* to infuriate II – се to become bloodthirsty; *fig.* to be infuriated

острвува (се) *impf of* острви (се)

острелоуши се *pf* to prick up one's ears

острец *m* (*сечило*) blade, cutting edge

остри *pf* I 1 to sharpen, whet, hone; to grind; остри молив to sharpen a pencil; остри нож, сабја to sharpen a knife, a sabre; ❑ *colloq.* остри заби (*за*) 1. to have it in (*for*) 2. to hanker after, eagerly anticipate, lick one's lips 2 *fig.* to sharpen; остри слух/вид to sharpen one's hearing/sight II – се *fig.*, *colloq.* to prepare (*o.s.*) for a fight

острига *f Zool.* (Ostrea edulis) oyster

остригува (се) *impf see* острижува (се)

остриже *pf* острижа *aor.* I to cut, crop hair; (*овци*) to shear II – се to have a haircut

острижен *pt* cropped; shorn

острижува (се) *impf of* остриже (се)

острика *f Bot.* (Carex arenaria) sedge

острилец -лци *m* whetstone, grindstone, hone

острилка *f* pencil-sharpener

острило *n* 1 (*сечило*) blade, cutting edge 2 whetstone, grindstone, hone, *see* точило

острина *f* sharpness; acuity, acuteness; (*на вид, слух*) keenness; (*на мирис*) pungency, poignancy; острина на нож sharpness of a knife; острина на воздух freshness/briskness of air; острина на ум wit, mental acuity; острина на збор sharpness of speech

остринка & острица *f see* острило 1

остро *adv* sharply; остро свирне/писне to whistle/scream (squeal) shrilly; остро погледне to look at sternly; остро сврти to turn sharply; остро нападне to attack strongly; остро одговори to answer <back> sharply

остроаголен -лна *adj Geom.* acute-angled

остров *m* island

островски *adj* island<'s>, insular; островско население island population; островска држава island state

островче *n dim.* (*of* остров) islet, eyot

острозаб *adj* sharp-toothed

остроножица *f f.p.* (*folk name*) Morning Star (Venus)

острота *f see* острина

остроумен -мна *adj* witty, shrewd, sagacious; остроумен човек witty (clever) person; остроумна шега witty joke

остроумие *n see* остроумност

остроумност *f* wit, shrewdness

оструже *pf* остру́га *aor.* (*истружe*) to grind; to sharpen

осуда *f* **1** condemnation, sentence; осуда на смрт death sentence; осуда на робија sentence to hard labour **2** censure; condemnation; неговиот однос е за секаква осуда his attitude deserves utter condemnation

осуденик -ци *m* imprisoned criminal, convict

осуденичка *f* (*fem. form*) *see* осуденик

осуди *pf* **1** to condemn, convict; to sentence; осуди некого на смрт to condemn s.o. to death; осуди во отсуство to sentence in absentia; осуди со парична казна to fine **2** to censure, condemn; осуди нечии постапки to denounce (condemn) s.o.'s actions

осудува *impf of* осуди

осуети *pf* to thwart, foil, frustrate; осуети нечии планови to frustrate (foil) s.o.'s plans; осуети нечии намери to thwart s.o.'s intentions

осуетува *impf of* осуети

осука *pf* (*исука, исуче*) to roll (*a layer of pastry for a pita, etc.*)

осукува *impf of* осука, *see* исукува

осум *num* eight

осумаголен -лна *adj* octagonal

осумаголник -ци *m* octagon

осумгодишен -шна *adj* **1** eight-year-old; осумгодишно девојче a little girl of eight **2** lasting eight years; eight-year; осумгодишен план eight-year plan; осумгодишно школување eight years' schooling

осумдесет *num* eighty

осумдесетгодишен -шна *adj* **1** eighty-year-old; осумдесетгодишен старец an old man of eighty **2** lasting eighty years; eighty-year; осумдесетгодишно ропство eighty years of slavery (bondage)

осумдесетти *adj num* eightieth

осумка *f* **1** (*цифрата 8*) <figure> eight **2** (*во карти*) eight **3** (*студентска оцена*) eight (*out of ten*), distinction **4** (*автобус, трамвај итн*) <number> eight

осумкатен -тна *adj* eight-storey, of eight storeys

осумкатница *f* eight-storey building

осуммесечен -чна *adj* eight-month, of eight months

осуммина *num* (*of men and mixed groups*) eight

осумнаесет *num* eighteen

осумнаесетгодишен -шна *adj* **1** eighteen-year-old; осумнаесетгодишно момче a boy of eighteen **2** lasting eighteen years; eighteen-year; осумнаесетгодишна изградба an eighteen-year construction project

осумнаесетка *f* **1** <the figure> eighteen **2** No. 18 <tram, bus *etc.*>

осумнаесетмина *num* (*of men and mixed groups*) eighteen

осумнаесетти *adj num* eighteenth

осумстотини *num* eight hundred

осумчасовен -вна *adj* eight-hour, of eight hours; осумчасовен работен ден eight-hour day

осуши (се) *pf see* исуши (се)

осушува (се) *impf of* осуши (се), *see* исушува (се)

осцила́тор *m Elec.* oscillator

осцилаторен -рна *adj* oscillatory, oscillating; осцилаторно движење oscillating motion

осцилација *f* oscillation (*also fig.*)

осцилацио́нен -она *adj see* осцилаторен

осцили́ра *pf & impf* to oscillate (*also fig.*)

осцилограф *m* oscillograph

от- *verbal prefix see* од-

отаде *adv* **1** from there, from that place, *arch. literary* thence; отаде подобро се гледа you can see better from there; отаде натаму from there onward **2** from the other (the opposite) side; on the opposite side; го вртеше отаде одовде she turned it this way and that; ❏ дури отаде! you will jolly well have to! не одам таму – ќе одиш дури отаде I'm not going there – you damned well will! **3** hence; отаде произлегува (*дека*) hence it follows (*that*); отаде неговиот немир, страв hence his disquiet, fear **4** *prep* beyond, on the far side of; отаде река beyond the river, <on> the far side of the river

отаден -дна *adj* **1** from there, from that place; отадните деца the children from there **2** from/on the other side; отадните дрвја the trees on the other side

отапи *pf* **1** to blunt; to make dull **2** to grow blunt; to grow dull; *see* затапи

отапува *impf of* отапи, *see* затапува

отвор *m* **1** opening; aperture, orifice; (*дупка*) hole; (*на машина и сл.*) slot; *Anat., Zool.* foramen; влезен отвор inlet; излезен отвор outlet **2** *dial., f.p.* key

отвора (се) *impf of* отвори (се)

отворање *n from* отвора (се); свечено отворање inauguration

отворен *adj & pt* **1** open; unlocked; overt; отворен прозорец open window; ❏ отворено небо open sky; под отворено небо in the open air, out of doors; отворено писмо an open letter; отворена кола cabriolet; отворено море open sea; high seas; отворен рудник opencast (open-cut) mine; отворено заседание public meeting; игра со отворени карти to show one's cards (hand); дочека со отворени раце to receive with open arms (warmly); остане со отворена уста to gape in astonishment **2** unsolved, unresolved, open; отворено прашање open question **3** (*снаодлив*) enterprising, bright, resourceful **4** (*искрен*) sincere, frank, open, open-hearted; outspoken; jac сум со тебе секогаш отворен I'm always frank with you; отворено признание avowal, frank confession **5** light, pale; отворени бои light colours **6** (*as noun*) отворено *n* an open place; на отворено in the open <air>; out of doors

отворено *adv* frankly, openly, freely; ќе ти кажам отворено I'll tell you frankly; ❏ отворено кажано to be honest; се држи отворено to behave openly; признае отворено to admit (confess) openly, freely; се изјасни отворено to speak one's mind

отвореност *f* **1** frankness, openness; тој ме придоби со својата отвореност he won me over with his openness **2** outgoing nature, uninhibited behaviour; resourcefulness

отвори *pf* **I 1** to open *trans.*; to unlock; (*почне*) to begin; (*основе*) to found; отвори книга/кутија/писмо to open a book/box/letter; отвори шатор to pitch a tent; отвори дуќан to open a shop; to start a business; отвори изложба to open an exhibition; отвори собрание to open a meeting; отвори збор (разговор) за нешто to open (start) a conversation about s.th.; ❏ отвори очи to be careful; ги отвори дваесет и четири he was cautious day and night; отвори уста 1. to start talking 2. to get carried away; to let fly; отвори тефтери to bring up old scores; отвори карти to show one's hand (cards); to put one's cards on the table; отвори оган (на) to open fire (at/on); отвори апетит to whet the appetite **2** (пушти) to switch on, turn on; отвори чешма to turn on a tap **3** *fig.* to uncover, lay bare; отвори срце to open one's heart; отвори душа to bare one's soul **4** to look better, healthier **5** to become more outgoing, come out of one's shell **6** (за боја) to become lighter **II – се** to open *intrans.*; вратата се отвори the door opened; се отвори разговор a discussion began; ❏ се отвори небото the heavens opened; ми се отвори апетит I got up an appetite

отворува (се)   *impf see* отвора (се)

отврдне   *pf* отврдна *aor.* **I** to harden *trans.* **II – се** to harden *intrans.*, become hard, set; *see* стврдне (се)

отврднува (се)   *impf of* отврдне (се), *see* стврднува (се)

отежне   *pf* отежна *aor.* **1** to become heavy; од влагата тутунот отежнал the tobacco has become heavier owing to the moisture content **2** to grow lethargic, sluggish; му отежна снагата his body grew sluggish **3** to hinder, complicate, make more difficult; to aggravate; лошото време го отежна извршувањето на задачите the bad weather hampered operations

отежнува   *impf of* отежне

отежнувачки   *adj Leg.* aggravating; отежнувачки околности aggravating circumstances

отекува   *impf of* отече

отели   *pf* **I** to produce a calf **II – се** to calve

отелотвори   *pf see* олицетвори

отелотворува   *impf of* отелотвори, *see* олицетворува

отелува (се)   *impf of* отели (се)

отемни   *pf* отемне *aor.* **1** to grow dark, darken *intrans.*; целиот отемне he/it went all dark **2** to make dark, darken *trans.*

отемнува   *impf of* отемни

отепа   *pf* **I** to kill **II – се 1** to be killed; to commit suicide **2** *fig.* to wear o.s. out, become exhausted; се отепав од работа (работејќи) I worked myself to exhaustion

отепан   *adj & pt* **1** killed; (*as noun*) отепаните the dead; ❏ сиромав <дури> отепан poor devil **2** *fig.* utterly dejected, crushed, depressed; се врати дома отепан he returned home broken-hearted **3** *fig.* exhausted, *colloq.* dead beat; отепан од работа exhausted by work

отепува (се)   *impf of* отепа (се)

отепување   *n* **1** *from* отепува (се) **2** murder, violent death; *fig.* работев до отепување I worked myself to death

отепувачка   *f see* отепување; парите се отепувачка *saying* money spells ruin

отера   *pf* **1** to drive out/off/away; го отера добитокот на пасење he drove the cattle out to pasture **2** (истера) to expel; to dismiss, discharge; *colloq.* to

kick out **3** *fig.* далеку ја отера **1.** he went a long way, he had great success **2.** he exaggerated

отерува   *impf of* отера

отетерави се   *pf* to become lively (animated); to recover, recuperate (*from illness, tiredness, etc.*)

отец   -тци *m Rel. arch.* (*ecclesiastical title*) Father; црковните отци the Fathers of the Church

отече   *pf* to swell; ногата ми отече my foot/leg swelled up; беше отекол во лицето his face had swollen up

отечен   *pt* swollen; отечени жлезди swollen glands

отеченост   *f* swelling

отечува   *impf see* отекува

оти   *adv & conj* **1** *colloq.* (*зошто*) why; оти не дојде? why didn't you come? **2** *colloq.* (*зашто*) because, since, as; не одговорив, оти не знаев I didn't answer because I didn't know **3** *colloq.* (*дека*) that; слушнав оти си сакал да градиш куќа I've heard that you wanted to build a house **4** (*with* не, *usually indicates disbelief, doubt, etc.*) не оти I doubt if, who knows if; не оти ќе стане (биде) нешто од сета оваа работа who knows whether anything will come of all this business

отиде   *pf* отидов *1st p. sg aor. see* оди **1** to go; отиде кај нив he went off to their place; отиде на кино/на театар he went to the cinema (movies)/theatre; отиде на вода/на дрва he went to fetch water/firewood; отиде на работа he went to work; вчера отиде во Белград yesterday he went to Belgrade; отиде по него she went to pick him up; отиде за него she married him; отиде во пензија to retire **2** (*usu. with* си) to depart, go away, leave; вечерта си отиде he left (departed) in the evening; си отиде <дома> he went off (he went home); си отиде од Прилеп he left Prilep; ❏ си отиде пред време he passed away prematurely **3** to go by, pass; to disappear; си отиде младоста youth has passed; отидоа паричките the cash has gone; отидов! I'm off! I'm going! *fig.* I'm lost! **4** (*with nouns denoting profession, occupation, etc.*) to become; отиде калуѓер he became a monk; отиде војник he joined the army

отима   *impf* **I** to grab, seize **II – се** to struggle against, resist; to fight (*за – over*); му се отимаше и му се молеше she struggled with him and pleaded

отина   *impf see* отнува

откаже   *pf* откажа *aor.* **I 1** to cancel; to annul; откаже договор/порачка to cancel an agreement/order <for goods>; откаже работа to call off a deal **2** to deny, negate, retract; сето она што го призна во полицијата пред судот го откажа all that he confessed at the police station he denied in court; тоа не можам да го откажам I can't deny that; го откажа својот потпис he repudiated his own signature **3** (*одбие*) to refuse, renounce; to break off; ми ја откажа услугата he refused to do me this favour; откаже послушност to refuse to obey; откаже пријателство to break off a friendship; откаже помош на некого to refuse assistance to s.o.; откаже кредит на некого to refuse credit (a loan) to s.o. **4** to refuse, decline, turn down; ѝ предложија да се омажи, но таа откажа they suggested she should get married, but she refused **5** to fail, serve no longer; силите ми откажаа my strength failed me; нозете ми откажаа my legs failed me; моторот откажа the engine stalled **6** to misfire; пушката откажа the gun misfired **II – ce** to renounce; to abandon; to disown, relinquish; to give up; откаже се од својата вера/од светот/од наследство to renounce one's faith/the world/one's inheritance; се откажав од него I have disowned him; откаже се од тутун (пушење)/кафе to give up tobacco (smoking)/coffee; се откажа од поранешната намера he abandoned his earlier intention; откаже се од некое право to waive (renounce) one's right (*to s.th.*)

откажува (се) *impf of* откаже (се)

отказ *m* cancellation; notice; отказ на стан termination of tenancy of a flat; отказ на служба notice <at work>; отказ на договор cancellation of a contract; дава (*некому*) отказ to give notice, to sack (*s.o.*); добива отказ to get notice, get the sack, get one's marching orders

отказен -зна *adj* pertaining to cancellation, termination, dismissal, notice; отказен рок term of notice, cancellation, etc.

откај *prep* 1 from, out of, off, from the direction of; цитати откај Маркс quotations from Marx; откај реката from the direction of the river; откај север from the north; тој е откај него he is on his side 2 (*of time*) roughly from, <at> about; откај полноќ почна да врне about midnight it started to rain; откај Велигден наваму from about Easter until now

откако *adv & conj* 1 <ever> since, from the time that; откако заработи, не доаѓа кај нас since he started working, he hasn't visited us 2 *conj* after, when; откако се одморија малку, тие станаа when they had rested a little, they got up; откако ќе го прегледаше весникот after he had looked through the newspaper; *see* откога

откапе *pf* опкапа *aor.* to fall off; да би рака ти откапала! *curse* may your hand drop off!

откапува *impf of* откапе

откаршија *adv arch.* on the opposite side, *vis-à-vis*, *see* отспротива

откачи *pf* **I** 1 to detach, unhook, disconnect, unhitch; го откачија вагонот од локомотивата they uncoupled the carriage from the locomotive; ❏ *colloq.* откачи некого to dump s.o., give s.o. the boot 2 to take off, take down; откачи од закачалка to take (*s.th.*) off the peg/hook; го откачи медалот од палтото he took the medal off the coat 3 *fig.* to separate, keep off (*s.o. from s.o. else*); одвај го откачивме од неа we hardly managed to separate him from her 4 *fig.* to move away *intrans.*, move off; to progress; далеку откачија they had gone a long way **II – ce** 1 to become detached, break loose; to fall; куката се откачи од дигалката the hook became detached from the crane; сликата се откачи од куката the picture fell from its hook 2 *fig.* (*од*) to get rid of, rid o.s. of, shake off; не можам да се откачам од него I can't get rid of him

откачува (се) *impf of* откачи (се)

откине *pf* откина *aor.* **I** to save, free; to rid; ти ме откина од смртта you saved me from death **II – ce** to save o.s., free o.s., shake off (*s.o. or s.th.*); to get rid of, rid o.s. of; не можеме да се откинеме од нив we can't get rid of them

откинува (се) *impf of* откине (се)

откинувачка *f* salvation, saving; ridding; нема откинувачка од него there is no getting rid of him

отклик -ци *m literary* echo, *see* одглас

отклопи *pf* **I** 1 to remove the lid (*from s.th.*) 2 to uncover, open <up> *trans.* **II – ce** to open <up> *intrans.*

отклопува (се) *impf of* отклопи (се)

отклучен *pt* unlocked; отклучена врата unlocked door

отклучи *pf* to unlock; отклучи каса to unlock a till

отклучува *impf of* отклучи

откова *impf of* откове

откован *pt* unnailed, loose, detached; има една штица откована there's a loose board

откове *pf* откова *aor.* to detach by removing nails, unnail; откове шајки to pull out nails; откове штица to unnail a board

отковува *impf of* откове, *see* откова

откога *adv & conj* 1 since; поминаа четириесет години откога се ожени forty years have passed since he got married 2 after, when; откога го прегледа болниот, лекарот стана after he had examined the patient, the doctor stood up

отколку *conj* than, rather than; повеќе сакам да работам отколку да седам I prefer working to sitting around; подобро вака отколку никако better this way than not at all; отколку што than; тој има повеќе пари отколку што мислиш he has got more money than you think

откопа *pf* 1 to dig up, unearth, disinter; откопаа едно грне со пари they dug up a pot of coins 2 (*одгрне*) to rake away, clear; откопа огниште to rake out a fireplace

откопачи *pf* to dig up; to pull up, uproot, grub out; откопачи овошка to dig up a fruit tree; откопачи шини to tear up <railway> tracks

откопува *impf of* откопа

откопча *pf* to unbutton, unfasten, *see* отпетла

откопчува *impf of* откопча, *see* отпетлува

откорен *adv* radically; ситуацијата се измени откорен the situation has changed radically

откорнатик -ци *m* rogue, good-for-nothing; откорнатик ниеден! you rascal!

откорне *pf* откорна *aor.* **I** 1 to uproot; ветрот откорна неколку овошки the wind uprooted several fruit trees 2 to break off *trans.*; to tear (wrench) from its bearings; ја откорна вратата he tore the door off its hinges **II – ce** 1 to be uprooted 2 to fall off, break off *intrans.*; неколку парчиња од малтерот се откорнаа a few pieces of mortar fell off

откорнува (се) *impf of* откорне (се)

откос *m* 1 hay harvest 2 swathe

откоси *pf* to mow, reap a certain amount, mow off

откости *pf* **I** to trash, beat up; ако те фатам, ќе те откостам if I catch you, I'll give you a beating **II – ce** to smash o.s. up, get hurt badly; паднав и се откостив I fell and was badly hurt

откостува (се) *impf of* откости (се)

откосува *impf of* откоси

откочи *pf* to release the brakes; to unlock, slip off, release (*a safety-catch, etc.*)

откочува (се) *impf of* откочи (се)

откошне *pf* откошна *aor.* to kick aside

открадe & открадне *pf* открадна *aor.* **I** 1 to steal 2 (*за девојка*) to abduct, carry off (*a girl*) **II – ce** to steal away, get away unnoticed/by stealth

открад<н>ува (се) *impf of* откра<д>не (се)

открај *adv* **1** from the end; открај накрај from one end to the other, from end to end; открај до крај (открај-докрај) from beginning to end; throughout; completely; entirely; открај земја from the ends of the earth **2** (*of time*) always, from the <very> beginning, from the outset; открај си е <тој> таков he has always been like that; ❏ открај време from the beginning of time, since time began

открива (се) *impf of* открие (се)

откривач *m* discoverer

открие *pf* откри *aor.* **I 1** to uncover; откриј го лебот, побргу нека истине uncover the bread, so it cools quicker; открие споменик to unveil a statue **2** *fig.* to reveal, divulge, expose, lay bare; открие своја желба/ намера to reveal one's wish/intention; открие тајна/ заговор/вистина to reveal a secret/a plot/the truth **3** to discover, detect, find out; открие злочин/престап to detect a crime/an offence; Колумбо ја откри Америка Columbus discovered America; ❏ *iron.* ја откри Америка to invent gunpowder (retail stale news); повторно ја откри Америка to reinvent the wheel **II – се 1** to uncover o.s.; детето се открило the child has got uncovered **2** to open *intrans.*; се откри небото the heavens opened **3** *fig.* to confide (*пред некого – in s.o.*) **4** to show o.s., appear; пред мене се открија широки простори broad vistas/expanses opened up before me

откритие -ија *n* discovery; научно откритие scientific discovery

откровение -ија *n literary* revelation

открти *pf* **I** to break off, shear off *trans.*; ја открти вратата he broke down the door **II – се** to break off *intrans.*, fall off; се откртија неколку парчиња јаглен a few bits of coal broke off

откртува (се) *impf of* открти (се)

открши *pf* to break off *trans.*; открши парче леб to break off a piece of bread

откршува *impf of* открши

откуп *m* **1** ransom; redemption; repurchase **2** purchase; откуп на тутун/пченица purchase of tobacco/wheat

откупен -пна *adj* ransom/purchase *attrib.*; откупна цена purchase price

откупеник -ци *m* ransomed person, hostage

откупи *pf* **I 1** to pay ransom for (*s.o.*); го откупила да не го бесат she ransomed him to save him from hanging **2** to plead forgiveness (*for*), redeem **3** to buy up, purchase **4** to redeem (*pledge from pawnbroker*), buy back; си ги откупи златните предмети he redeemed the gold articles **II – се** to buy one's own freedom

откупнина *f* ransom money

откупува (се) *impf of* откупи (се)

откупувач *m* saviour; redeemer; purchaser

отме *pf* отми *aor.* **I** to seize, take away, grab **II – се** to get away, escape, free o.s.

отмен *adj* fine, noble, dignified; отмена дама fine lady; отмено држење dignified behaviour

отмено *adv* nobly, with dignity, in fine style

отменост *f* nobility; dignity

отне *pf* отна *aor.* **1** to unstop, unblock, unplug, clear (*blockage, pipe, etc.*); отне цевка to unblock a pipe/ drain **2** to uncork, open *trans.*; отне шише to uncork a bottle

отнува *impf of* отне

оток -ци *m* swelling

óтомáн *m* ottoman, sofa

отомáнски *adj* Ottoman; Отоманска империја Ottoman Empire

отопление *n* heating; парно отопление steam heating

оториноларинголóг -зи *m Med.* ear, nose and throat specialist

оториноларингологија *f Med.* otorhinolaryngology, study of the diseases of the ear, nose and throat

отпад *m* rubbish, refuse, *esp. Am.* trash; waste material, scrap, junk; нуклеарен отпад <nuclear> fallout; nuclear waste

отпаден -дна *adj* waste; отпадна вода waste water, effluent

отпадне *pf* отпадна *aor.* **1** to be left out (*од – of*), excluded (*from*); овој збор да отпадне this word should be omitted **2** to abandon, desert; to drop out (*of*); отпадне од движење to abandon a movement **3** to fall away/off; лисјата отпаднаа the leaves have fallen

отпадник -ци *m* **1** renegade, turncoat **2** (*од вера*) apostate

отпаднички *adj* apostatical

отпадништво *n* apostasy

отпаднува *impf of* отпадне, *see* отпаѓа

отпадок -ци *m* refuse, waste-product, tailings; отпадоци од јадење food scraps

отпадочен -чна *adj* waste; отпадочни материјали waste matter

отпаѓа *impf of* отпадне

отпара *pf* to unstitch, unpick, undo, rip off; отпара шев to unpick a seam

отпарува *impf of* отпара

отпатува *pf* to leave, start out, depart; гостите изутрина отпатуваа the guests left this morning

отпаше *pf* отпаша *aor.* **I** (*појас, колан, скутник*) to take off, untie, unfasten; (*сабја*) to ungird **II – се** to ungird o.s., unfasten one's belt

отпашува (се) *impf of* отпаше (се)

отпева *impf of* отпее

отпее *pf* отпеа *aor.* **1** to sing; отпее една народна песна to sing a folk song; ❏ си го отпеа своето to sing one's swansong **2** to sing a requiem for (*некого – s.o.*) **3** to consecrate, bless; го отпеа лебот he blessed the bread **4** *arch., colloq.* to understand, comprehend; не било чаре да се отпее тоа писмо it was impossible to understand that letter **5** to reply in song; една група испеа, друга отпеа one group sang, another replied in song

отпере *pf* отпра *aor.* to do a little washing; утре ќе отперам уште малку I'll wash a few more things tomorrow

отперува *impf of* отпере

отпетла *pf* to unbutton, unfasten

отпетлува *impf of* отпетла

отпечати[1] *pf* **I 1** to print; to issue, publish **2** to leave an imprint, mark, trace **II – се** to leave an imprint, a trace; прстите му се отпечатиле по ѕидот he left his finger-marks on the wall

отпечати[2] *pf* to unseal, open *trans.*; отпечати писмо to unseal (open) a letter

отпечаток -ци *m* **1** imprint; отпечаток од прсти, од стапала и сл. fingerprints, footprints, etc. **2** одделен отпечаток offprint **3** воден отпечаток watermark

отпечатува[1] **(се)** *impf of* отпечати[1] (се)
отпечатува[2] *impf of* отпечати[2]
отпива *impf of* отпие
отпие *pf* отпи *aor.* to take a sip
отпис *m* cancellation, writing off (*of a debt*)
отпише *pf* отпиша *aor.* **I** to erase, cross out, strike off, delete; to withdraw, deregister; to write off; отпише некого од список to withdraw (delete) s.o. from a list; отпише од училиште to withdraw from school; отпише долг to write off a debt **II – се** to withdraw *intrans.*; отпише се од факултет to withdraw from university
отпишува (се) *impf of* отпише (се)
отплата *f* **1** payment on account; на отплата by instalments; hire purchase; купи/продаде/даде на отплата to buy/sell/make available on credit **2** repayment; отплата на долг paying off (payment) of a debt; менична отплата payment of a bill of exchange **3** *fig.* (*вратка*; *одмазда*) repayment; vengeance, <act of> revenge, retribution, reprisal
отплати *pf* **I** **1** to pay off, pay off by instalments; to buy by hire purchase **2** to return, repay, take revenge upon, wreak vengeance on **II – се 1** to repay, return (*a kindness*); за оваа добрина твоја ќе ти се отплатам I shall repay you your kindness **2** *see* **I** 2
отплатлив *adj* repayable
отплатник -ци *m poet.* avenger
отплатува (се) *impf of* отплати (се)
отплаќа (се) *impf see* отплатува (се)
отплете *pf* to unknit, undo, unstitch; to unbraid, unravel; отплете коса to unbraid hair
отплетка *pf* **1** to disentangle, undo (*of yarn, thread, etc.*); отплетка конци to disentangle threads **2** *fig.* to clear up, arrange, sort out, put in order; како се заплеткаа работите, никој не може да ги отплетка matters have got so confused that no one can sort them out
отплеткува *impf of* отплетка
отплетува *impf of* отплете
отплива *pf* to swim away; to float away
отпливува *impf of* отплива
отплови *pf* (*of ships or their passengers and crew*) to sail, depart; sail off
отпловува *impf of* отплови
отповеќе *adv* too much/many
отповива (се) *impf of* отповие (се)
отповие *pf* **I** to unswathe **II – се** to unswathe o.s.
отповик *m literary* recall; cancellation, revocation; отповик на пратеник recall of an envoy; отповик на наредба cancellation/revocation of an order (command)
отповика *pf literary* to cancel, withdraw; to recall, revoke; отповика амбасадор to recall an ambassador; отповика договор to cancel a contract; отповика тестамент to revoke a will
отповиклив *adj literary* revocable
отповикливост *f literary* revocability
отповикува *impf literary of* отповика
отпоздрав *m* an answering greeting/salute
отпоздрави *pf* to return a greeting/salute
отпоздравува *impf of* отпоздрави
отпознае *pf* отпозна *aor.* **I** to forget, not to know s.o. any longer; ме отпозна веќе, дури и не ме

поздравува he's already forgotten me, he doesn't even say hello **II – се 1** to forget each other, no longer know each other; и јас самиот не можам да сфатам како се отпознавме and I myself cannot understand how we drifted apart **2** *f.p.* to know carnally
отпознат *pt f.p.* known, acquainted, familiar
отполу *adv* from the middle
отпор *m* opposition, resistance (*also Phys.*); дава отпор to offer resistance; наидува на отпор to meet with opposition; ❏ по линијата на најмалиот отпор along the line of least resistance; as a soft option
отпорен -рна *adj* **1** resistant, hardy, sturdy, durable; отпорен на студ/на влага resistant to cold/to damp (moisture-proof); отпорен на топлина heatproof, heat-resistant **2** pertaining to resistance; отпорна сила power of resistance
отпорник -ци *m Elec.* resistor; rheostat
отпорност *f* hardiness; resistance; отпорност на болести immunity
отпосле *adv* after that, later, after a certain time; се премажи отпосле и таа she too later remarried
отпослежен -жна *adj* later, subsequent
отпочине си *pf* отпочина си *aor.* to rest, have a rest; седнале да си отпочинат they sat down to rest
отпочинува си *impf of* отпочине си
отправа *impf of* отправи[1]
отправи[1] *pf* to undo, spoil; јас направи, тој отправи whatever I do, he ruins
отправи[2] *pf literary* **I** to send (*forth*), ship, dispatch, direct; отправи флота to dispatch a fleet; отправи зборови кон некого to direct one's words at s.o. **II – се** to set off, start <out>
отправник -ци *m literary* agent, representative; отправник на работите chargé d'affaires
отправнички *adj literary* pertaining to an agent/ chargé d'affaires
отправништво *n literary* representative's office; branch office; agency
отправува (се) *impf of* отправи[2] (се)
отпразни *pf* to pour off
отпразнува *pf* to celebrate
отпрвин & отпрво *adv* at first, at the beginning; from the beginning; at the start; отпрвин се двоумеше at first he hesitated
отпрега *impf see* отпрегнува
отпрегне *pf* отпрегна *aor.* to unharness (*oxen, horses, etc.*)
отпрегнува *impf of* отпрегне
отпреде *pf* to unwind (*yarn*), wind off into skeins
отпредува *impf of* отпреде
отпрета *pf* to unearth; to uncover, reveal; го отпретал сеното и го нашол детето he raked away the hay and found the child
отпретува *impf of* отпрета
отпришти *pf* to unblock, open (*blocked/dammed watercourse*)
отприштува *impf of* отпришти
отпрости се *pf f.p.* to take leave (*со – of*), say farewell (*to*), *see* опрости се
отпусница *f* discharge papers
отпуст *m* **1** discharge, dismissal; добие отпуст to receive notice **2** *Rel.* the end of a church service; доседи дури до отпуст he stayed till the end of the service

отпушта (се) *impf of* отпушти (се)

отпуштен *adj & pt* **1** loose, flabby, slack; *fig.* lax, easy-going, relaxed **2** dismissed

отпуштеност *f* looseness, flabbiness; slackness, laxness

отпушти *pf* **I 1** to let go, cease to hold; ако ми ја отпуштиш раката, ќе паднам if you let go my hand, I'll fall **2** to let fall, drop; ја отпушти од раце чинијата he dropped the plate **3** to release, set free; отпушти куче од синџир to let a dog off the chain **4** to loosen, slacken; to lower; отпушти узди to slacken the reins; отпушти раце to drop one's hands; отпушти глава to hang one's head **5** to dismiss; to discharge; отпушти од работа (од служба) to sack; (*привремено*) to lay off; отпушти од болница to discharge from hospital **6** to put into circulation, issue; отпушти кредит, заем to grant (approve) a credit, a loan **7** to unstop, allow to flow, unblock; ја отпуштија водата од каналот за да го наводнат полето they released the water from the channel (canal) to irrigate the field **II – се 1** to let go, relax one's grip **2** to free o.s., get untied; кучето се отпуштило од синџир the dog got off the chain **3** to slacken *intrans.*, hang limp, droop; јажињата и платната се отпуштија the ropes and sails slackened **4** (*за мускули и сл.*) to relax; (*за време*) to relent, let up, ease; *Cul.* to become soft, watery; времето се отпушти the weather has become milder **5** (*за вода*) to escape, get out; резервоарот се отпуштил the reservoir has run dry

отранчи *pf colloq.* to crush, smash

отранчува *impf of* отранчи

отрезни *pf* **I 1** to sober up *trans.* **2** to sober up *intrans.* **II – се** *see* I 2

отрезнителен -лна *adj see* отрезнувачки

отрезнува (се) *impf of* отрезни (се)

отрезнувачки *adj* sobering

откала *pf* **I** to roll away *trans.*; откала буре to roll a barrel away **II – се** to roll away *intrans.*; топката се откала во бавчата the ball rolled into the garden

откалува (се) *impf of* откала (се)

отров *m &* **отрова** *f* poison, venom, toxin (*also fig.*); силен (јак) отров strong poison; змиски отров snake's venom; отров и пелин да му стане may he choke to death!

отровен -вна *adj* poisonous (*also fig.*), venomous, toxic; noxious; отровни гасови poison<ous> gases; отровни печурки/билки poisonous fungi/plants; отровна змија poisonous (venomous) snake; отровни зборови venomous words

отровит *adj arch.* poisonous; билје отровито poisonous plants, *see* отровен

отровница *f* **1** *Zool.* (Vipera aspis) asp **2** *fig.* viper, shrew, termagant

отровност *f* toxicity, poisonousness

отроми *pf* to grow sluggish

отромува *impf of* отроми

отрпне *pf* отрпна *aor.* **1** to become numb; to grow stiff; раката ми отрпна my hand/arm has gone numb **2** *fig.* (*usu. of the skin*) to become insensitive (*to s.th. hard, harsh*) to get used to; ми отрпна кожата веќе my skin has already become insensitive

отрпнува *impf of* отрпне

отрув *m &* **отрува** *f f.p. see* отров, отрова

отрува (се) *impf of* отруе (се)

отрувач *m* **1** poisoner **2** poison, toxic agent, *see* отров, отрувачка 2

отрувачка *f* **1** (*fem. form*) *see* отрувач 1 **2** poison, *see* отров **3** poisoning

отрудни *pf* to conceive, become pregnant, *see* затрудни

отруднува *impf of* отрудни, *see* затруднува

отруе *pf* отру *aor.* **I 1** to poison; ни го отруја кучето they've poisoned our dog **2** *fig.* to poison, sour, render unbearable, ruin; ти ми го отру животот you've poisoned life for me **II – се 1** to poison o.s. **2** *fig.* to become embittered, exasperated

отрча *pf* to run off, run away; отрчал дома he ran off/away home

отрчува *impf of* отрча

отсвет *m literary* reflection; shine, gleam, glow; вечерен отсвет evening light

отсева *impf of* отсее

отсевки *pl* siftings, chaff (*left after sifting grain, etc.*)

отсега *adv* from now on, *literary* henceforward; отсега натаму from now on

отседла *pf* to unsaddle; отседла коњ to unsaddle a horse

отседлува *impf of* отседла

отседне *pf literary* отседна *aor.* to stop, stay; отседне во хотел to stay at a hotel

отседнува *impf of* отседне

отсее *pf* отсеа *aor.* to sift a certain amount

отсејува *impf see* отсева

отсек -ци *m* **1** (*оддел*) section; department **2** (*отсечок*) cutting, clipping, segment **3** sheer drop; cliff, bluff

отсекаде *adv* from everywhere, from/on all sides; селото е опколено отсекаде со шуми the village is surrounded on all sides by forests

отсекува (се) *impf of* отсече (се)

отсече *pf* **I 1** to cut off; му ја отсекоа главата they cut off his head **2** *fig.* to say sharply, abruptly, back **II – се** *fig.* (*of the hands/arms*) ми се отсекоа рацете my hands/arms went numb (gave way), hung helplessly; му се отсекоа нозете he was petrified; he was unable to move

отсечен -чна *adj* **1** decisive, firm; рече со отсечен глас he said firmly **2** distinct **3** abrupt

отсечка *f* (*отсечок*) cutting, clipping; segment (*also Math.*)

отсечок -ци *m* cutting, clipping, segment

отсечува (се) *impf see* отсекува (се)

отсјај -аи *m literary* reflection; shine; gleam, glint, sheen; зеленушкав отсјај greenish gleam, glint

отскок -ци *m* jump, leap; bounce, rebound; distance jumped

отскока *impf of* отскокне, *see* отскокнува

отскокне *pf* отскокна *aor.* **1** to jump, leap (*од – back, away from*); коњот отскокна назад the horse reared/shied away **2** (*одбие се*) to rebound, bounce off; (*за куршум и сл.*) to ricochet; секирата отскокна од цврстото дрво the axe bounced off the hard wood **3** *fig.* (*истакне се*) to stand out, distinguish o.s.; тој многу отскокна од своите другари he has far outstripped his friends **4** to jump/step back over

отскокнува *impf of* отскокне

отскоро *adv* (*неодамна*) recently

отскрива (се) *impf of* отскрие (се)

отскрие *pf* отскри *aor.* to uncover, lay bare

отскришем & **отскришум** *adv* secretly, stealthily; удри отскришум to strike (*s.o.*) by stealth

отслужи *pf* **1** to serve, complete one's service; отслужи воен рок to do one's military service **2** to celebrate (*a church service*); отслужи утрена/вечерна to celebrate matins/evensong (vespers) **3** to serve (*a sentence*); тој си го отслужи своето he has served his time

отслужува *impf of* отслужи

отсоли *pf* to desalt (*s.th. very salty, e.g. meat, cheese, etc.*)

отспива *impf of* отспие

отспие *pf* отспа *aor.* to sleep <for> a certain time; отспав два-три часа I slept for two or three hours

отспрвин *adv see* отпрвин

отспреден -дна *adj* (*преден*) front, frontal, leading; на отспредната страна on the front page

отспреди *adv* in front; отспреди и одзади in front and behind

отспротива *adv* on the opposite (other) side, across, opposite; отспротива стоеше една жена on the other side a woman was standing; шумот доаѓаше отспротива the noise was coming from the far side

отсрами *pf* **I** to save (*s.o.*) from shame, save s.o.'s face (*by making possible the discharge of a social or moral obligation*); to come in useful; виното нѐ отсрами the wine saved our social honour **II** – ce to save face

отсрамува (се) *impf of* отсрами (се)

отсрди се *pf* to recover from one's rage, calm down, *see* одлути се

отсрдува се *impf of* отсрди се, *see* одлутува се

отсреќа *adv* & *prep* (*with dat.*) *f.p.* towards, to meet; from the opposite direction; opposite; отсреќа му оди дете a child came towards him

отстап *m* retreat; deviation; concession

отстапен -пна *adj* retreating, withdrawing; отстапно движење retreating movement

отстапи *pf* **1** to step aside, step back **2** to withdraw, retreat; непријателската војска беше принудена да отстапи the enemy was forced to retreat **3** to yield, give in; ние не треба по никоја цена да отстапиме we must not give in at any price **4** to relinquish, abandon, give up; отстапи од свое мислење/убедување/решение to renounce one's opinion/conviction/decision; отстапи од своите поранешни позиции to renounce one's earlier views **5** to deviate, swerve, turn aside; отстапи од линијата to deviate from the policy; отстапи од правилата/од законот to break the rules/the law **6** to lower, cut, reduce (*price*); отстапи малку во цената to reduce the price a little **7** (*with dat.*) to be inferior to, fail to match, yield to; новите производи нема да им отстапат на старите the new products will not be inferior to the old ones **8** to hand over, give up, cede, yield (*нешто некому – s.th. to s.o.*); домаќинот му го отстапи својот кревет на гостинот the host let the guest have his bed; отстапи место/ред to give up one's place/turn

отстапка *f* **1** concession; прави отстапки to make concessions; заемни отстапки mutual concessions; отстапка во цена reduction in price, discount **2** deviation; отстапка од правила deviation from rules; отстапка од определена линија deviation/departure from a certain line (*of policy, etc.*)

отстаплив *adj* **1** accommodating; conciliatory; pliable, tractable **2** allowable

отстапливост *f* tractability, pliancy

отстапник -ци *m* renegade, turncoat; apostate

отстапница *f* **1** <route, direction of> retreat, withdrawal **2** rearguard **3** (*fem. form*) *see* отстапник

отстапнички *adj* apostatical

отстапништво *n* apostasy

отстапува *impf of* отстапи

отстори *pf* **I** to undo; тоа што е <веќе> сторено не може да се отстори what's done cannot be undone **II** – ce to return to one's original/previous state

отстрана *adv* **1** from one side, on one side; near, close by; ❏ гледа нешто отстрана to look on/observe s.th. from outside (disinterestedly) **2** askance, obliquely, sidelong; го погледна отстрана he gave him a sidelong glance

отстранет *adj* & *pt* **1** far from; отстранет од своите другари far away from his friends **2** banned, removed (*од – from*); отстранет од работа banned from work; отстранет од собрание expelled from parliament

отстранетост *f* distance (*од некого или нешто – from s.o. or s.th.*); isolation

отстрани *pf* **I** **1** to remove; отстрани пречки to remove obstacles **2** to dismiss; отстрани од работа to dismiss from work; отстрани од должност to remove from office **3** to alienate, estrange; таа ме отстрани од другарите she alienated me from my friends **II** – ce to distance o.s.; се отстрани од нас he has drifted away from us

отстранува (се) *impf of* отстрани (се)

отсуди *pf* **1** to judge, convict, pass judgement/sentence (*on*); како ќе отсуди судот as the court shall pronounce judgement **2** to decide; to judge, appraise; тој отсуди да си оди he decided to leave; брат ти инаку ќе отсуди your brother will express a different view

отсудува *impf of* отсуди

отсука *pf see* отсуче

отсукува *impf of* отсуче

отсуство *n* **1** absence; lack; отсуство на идеали lack of ideals; го осудија во отсуство he was condemned in his absence **2** leave; на отсуство on leave; добие отсуство од неколку дена to get a few days' leave

отсуствува *impf* to be absent/lacking

отсутен -тна *adj* **1** absent; колку души има отсутни? how many people are absent? **2** absent, vacant; отсутен поглед absent look; отсутен со духот absent in spirit, far away

отсутност *f* lack, absence, *see* отсуство 1

отсуче *pf* отсука *aor.* to unravel, untwist

отсучува *impf see* отсукува

оттаму *adv* **1** from there, that way, *arch.*, *literary* thence; и jac сум оттаму I come from there too; поминавме оттаму we passed that way **2** *literary* hence; оттаму произлегува (*дека*) hence (from this) it follows (*that*)

оттегли се *pf arch.*, *literary* to withdraw *intrans.*; се оттеглија војските the troops withdrew

оттекар *adv colloq.* again, *see* одново

оттиши *pf* to deflate *trans.*, let down (*e.g. tyre, balloon*)

оттишува (се) *impf of* оттиши (се)

оттогај & оттогаш *adv* from that time, since then; оттогаш навему ever since

оттргне се *pf* оттргна се *aor.* to get away, escape, break away; to free o.s., tear o.s. away

оттука *adv* **1** from here, from this place; оттука дотука from here to there; ај оттука! бегај оттука! get out of here! **2** *literary* hence; оттука произлегува (*дека*) hence it follows (*that*); *see* оттаму 2

оттура (се) *impf of* оттури (се)

оттури *pf* to pour off *trans.*

оттурне *pf* оттурна *aor.* **I** to push off, push away; to launch (*a boat, etc.*) **II** – **се 1** to break off *intrans.*; се оттурна една карпа од ридот a rock broke away from the mountainside **2** to move off *intrans.*; се оттурна лаѓата од брегот the boat pulled away from the shore

оттурнува (се) *impf of* оттурне (се)

оттурува (се) *impf of* оттури (се), *see* оттура (се)

оттуши се *pf* to vent one's anger (on), *see* истуши се

оттушува се *impf of* оттуши се, *see* истушува се

отуѓи *pf* **I 1** to alienate, estrange; жена му го отуѓи од нас his wife alienated him from us **2** to transfer ownership; отуѓи имот/земја to transfer (*Leg.* convey) property/land **II** – **се** to become alienated; to distance o.s. (*од – from*); се отуѓи од нас he distanced himself from us

отуѓува (се) *impf of* отуѓи (се)

отфркне *pf* отфркна *aor.* to fly off; to rush off (*noisily*)

отфркнува *impf of* отфркне

отфрла *impf of* отфрли

отфрли *pf* **1** to throw off, toss aside, fling away; to throw back; to repel, repulse; отфрли глава наназад to throw one's head back; отфрли противник, непријател to repulse the enemy **2** *fig.* to refute; to refuse, reject, cast out; to dismiss, brush aside; отфрли обвинение to reject an accusation; друштвото го отфрли society turned its back on him

отцеди *pf* to strain off (*a certain amount*), filter off

отцедува *impf of* отцеди

отцепи *pf* **I 1** to split off, chip off; отцепи парче дрво to split off a piece of wood **2** *fig.* to expel (*from an organization*) **II** – **се** to secede, break away (*from an organization, community, etc.*)

отцепува (се) *impf of* отцепи (се)

отцепување *n* **1** *from* отцепува (се) **2** secession

отчепи *pf* to unplug, unstop, clear; to open *trans.*

отчепува *impf of* отчепи

отчет *m literary* report, statement

отчешне *pf* отчешна *aor.* to dislocate, sprain, wrench; си го отчешна рамото he dislocated his shoulder

отчешнува *impf of* отчешне

отчкрапне *pf* отчкрапна *aor.* to open slightly, leave ajar; ја отчкрапна вратата he left the door ajar

отчкрапнува *impf of* отчкрапне

отчкрне *pf* отчкрна *aor. see* отчкрапне

отчовечи *pf* to dehumanize

отчовечува *impf of* отчовечи

отчука *pf* **1** to type out; отчука нешто на машина за пишување to type out s.th. on a typewriter **2** to strike; отчука дванаесет часот the clock struck twelve

отчукува *impf of* отчука

отшрафи *pf* **I** to unscrew *trans.* **II** – **се** to unscrew *intrans.*

отшрафува (се) *impf of* отшрафи (се)

отштета *f* compensation, damages; recompense, indemnity

отштетен -тна *adj* compensatory; recompensing

отштети *pf* to compensate

отштетува *impf of* отштети

оќелави *pf* **1** to make bald **2** to go bald

оќелавува *impf of* оќелави

оќорави *pf see* оќори

оќоравува *impf of* оќорави, *see* оќорува

оќоре *pf* to go blind, *see* оќори 2.

оќори *pf* **1** to make (*s.o.*) blind **2** to go blind

оќорува *impf of* оќори

оф *interj* (*expressing pain, sorrow, surprise, pleasure*) oh! ah! ow! оф, боли! ow (ouch), it hurts! оф леле! oh, my God!

офанзива *f Mil.* offensive

офанзивен -вна *adj* offensive, aggressive; офанзивно оружје offensive weapon; офанзивен план plan of attack; офанзивна политика offensive policy

офарда *adj indecl. colloq. see* оварда

офинка *f Bot. see* боровинка

офицер *m* officer

офицерка *f* **1** <woman> officer **2** officer's wife

офицерски *adj* officer's; офицерски чин officer's rank; офицерска униформа officer's uniform

офицерство *n* **1** the profession of military officer; него го привлекува офицерството he is attracted by (interested in) a career as a military officer **2** *coll.* the officer corps

офицерче *n dim. of* офицер

официјален -лна *adj* official; formal; официјални кругови official circles; официјални лица official persons, officials

официјалност *f* official nature (*of s.th.*)

официозен -зна *adj* semi-official

офка *impf* to moan, groan

офне *pf* офна *aor. see* офка

офнува *impf of* офне, *see* офка

оформен *pt* formed, shaped; developed; оформена личност mature person

оформи *pf* **I** to form, shape, create *trans.* **II** – **се** to form, develop *intrans.*

оформува (се) *impf of* оформи (се)

офсајд *m Sport.* offside

офсет[1] *m Print.* offset

офсет[2] *adj* offset *attrib.*; *Econ.* офсет програма offset purchase

офтамолог -зи *m* ophthalmologist

офтамологија *f* ophthalmology

офтика *f colloq.* consumption, tuberculosis, *see* туберкулоза

офтикаллија *adj indecl. colloq.* tuberculous, tubercular, *see* туберкулозен

офука *pf colloq.* to eat up, devour, gobble up

офукува *impf of* офука

ох *interj see* оф

охрабри *pf* **I** to encourage, cheer up *trans.* **II** – **се** to take courage; to cheer up *intrans.*

охрабрува (се) *impf of* охрабри (се)

охрабрувачки *adj* encouraging

Охрид *m* Ohrid

охридски *adj* Ohrid *attrib.*; Охридско Езеро Lake Ohrid

охриѓанец -ни *m* person from Ohrid

охриѓанка *f* (*fem. form*) *see* охриѓанец

оцапа *pf* **I** to dirty, soil; *fig.* to besmirch, sully; *fig.* ја оцапа работата he messed things up **II** – **се** to dirty o.s.

оцапува (се) *impf of* оцапа (се)

оцена *f* **1** valuation, evaluation; estimate, appraisal, opinion; assessment; оцена на покуќнина valuation of household furniture; според моја оцена according to my estimate; оцена за кредитна способност credit rating **2** *see* оценка 2

оцени *pf* **1** to value, assess, put a price on; to estimate, judge; to evaluate, appreciate; оцени производи to value products; оцени височина/длабочина to gauge height/depth; тој оцени дека работата не може да се заврши за два дена he estimated that the work could not be completed in two days; оцени песни to appreciate poetry **2** to mark, grade; ниеден ученик не е уште оценет none of the students (pupils) has been marked yet

оценка *f* **1** *see* оцена 1 **2** mark, grade; слаба оценка low mark; одлична оценка top mark (excellent)

оценлив *adj* assessable

оценува *impf of* оцени

оценувач *m* valuer; assessor; examiner

оцет *m* vinegar

оцетен -тна *adj* vinegar *attrib.*; оцетна киселина acetic acid

оцрни *pf* **1** to blacken, make black, stain; ми ги оцрни рацете it made my hands black **2** *fig.* to shame, disgrace, besmirch, humiliate; оцрни некому образ to sully s.o.'s honour **3** to become black, turn black *intrans.*

оцрнува *impf of* оцрни

оцрт *m* outline, contour

оцрта *pf* **I** to outline, sketch, describe briefly **II** – **се** to appear in outline/silhouette; to stand out against

оцртува (се) *impf of* оцрта (се)

очаблавен *adj* ragged; очаблавен во алиштата ragged, tattered; poorly dressed

очавчи *pf colloq. in the expression:* ја очавчи устата to open one's mouth wide; to gape

очае *pf* очаја *aor.* **I 1** to drive to despair; to cause (*s.o.*) to lose all hope; to discourage, disillusion; тоа мене ме очаја that drove me to despair **2** to despair, lose hope **II** – **се** *see* **I** 2

очаен[1] *adj & pt* despairing, disillusioned, desperate

очаен[2] -јна *adj* dreadful, terrible; времево е очајно this weather is awful

очаеност *f* despair; desperate state, desperation

очај *m* hopelessness, despair

очајник -ци *m* wretched, miserable person

очајница *f* (*fem. form*) *see* очајник

очајнички *adj* desperate, reckless; очајничка постапка desperate act

очајно *adv* desperately badly, dreadfully; очајно пее his singing is quite awful

очајува (се) *impf of* очае (се)

очапи *pf colloq.* to open wide; очапена врата wide open door

очапува *impf of* очапи

оче *n dial.* **1** *see* окце **2** *Bot. see* темјанушка, синоличка

очевиден -дна *adj* evident, obvious, *see* очигледен

очевидец -дци *m* eyewitness

очевидно *adv* evidently, obviously, *see* очигледно

очекори *pf* **1** to step; не може ни да очекори he cannot even take a step **2** to step over **3** to get on, straddle, mount (*a horse, etc.*); *see* опчекори

очекорува *impf of* очекори

очекува *impf* to expect, wait for; to count on; сите го очекуваа everybody was expecting him; очекувам вести од него I'm expecting news from him; такво нешто од него може и да се очекува I wouldn't put it past him; со нетрпение очекува to look forward to; очекувајќи да at the prospect of

очекување *n* expectation; ги исполнува очекувањата to be up to the mark; не ги исполнува очекувањата to fall short of expectations; над очекувањата beyond one's expectations/hopes; под очекувањата below the mark

очеличен *adj & pt* hardened, experienced, *see* закален, прекален

очеличеност *f* hardiness, experience, *see* закаленост, прекаленост

очеличи *pf* **I** to steel, temper; to toughen, harden *trans.*; очеличи мускули to harden one's muscles **II** – **се** to toughen, harden *intrans.*; to grow strong; се очеличи во борба to be tempered in battle

очеличува (се) *impf of* очеличи (се)

очен -чна *adj* ocular, optical; очниот нерв the optic nerve; очно јаболко eyeball; очна болест ocular (eye) disease; очен лекар oculist; очна клиника eye clinic

очеша *pf* **I** to graze, brush, scratch *trans.* **II** – **се** to brush (*од* – *against*)

очешла *pf* **I** to comb *trans.* **II** – **се** to comb one's hair; *see* исчешла (се)

очешлува (се) *impf of* очешла (се), *see* исчешлува (се)

очешува (се) *impf of* очеша (се)

очи *pl of* око

очигледен -дна *adj* evident, obvious, clear; очигледен доказ clear (obvious) proof; очигледна грешка obvious mistake

очигледно *adv* evidently, obviously, clearly; тој, очигледно, не сака да дојде he, clearly, doesn't want to come

очиклен *adj & pt* clever, resourceful, enterprising

очикли *pf* **I** to open <one's eyes> wide; ги очикли очите he opened his eyes wide **II** – **се 1** to stare (*with wide open eyes*) **2** *fig.* to become cleverer, shrewder, more resourceful, more enterprising, more capable

очиклува (се) *impf of* очикли (се)

очила *pl* spectacles, glasses; очила за сонце sunglasses; ❏ гледа на работите низ розови/темни очила to look at things through rose-tinted/dark spectacles

очилар *m* optician

очиларка *f Zool.* (Naja tripudians) spectacled Indian cobra

очиња   *pl dim. of* очи

очисти   *pf* to clean; to clear

очистува   *impf of* очисти

очобол   *m* pain in the eyes, eye ache; ophthalmia

очовечи   *pf* **I** to humanize, civilize **II** – **ce** to become civilized, humanized

очовечува (ce)   *impf of* очовечи (ce)

очув   *m* stepfather

очуди   *pf* to astonish, amaze

очудува   *impf of* очуди

очука   *pf* to knock down, beat down; градот ги очука лозјата the hail has flattened the vines

очукува   *impf of* очука

очумави   *pf* to devastate, ravage, lay waste

оџа   *m* khoja, Muslim cleric

оџак   -ци *m* **1** chimney **2** hearth

оџачар   *m* chimney-sweep

оџачарски   *adj* chimney-sweep's

ошав   *m arch.* stewed fruit, compote, *see* компот

ошлака   *pf* to dirty, bespatter; ошлака со кал to spatter with mud

ошлакува   *impf of* ошлака

ошмара   *f* porridge (*made of flour and fresh cheese*)

оштета   *f* damage

оштети   *pf* to damage; to harm, injure; to cause (*s.o.*) a loss, to short-change (*s.o.*)

оштетува   *impf of* оштети

оштетувач   *m* destroyer

оштрбави & **оштрби**   *pf* оштрбе *aor.* to lose one's teeth

оштрбува   *impf of* оштрби

оштур   *m in the curse:* оштурот те фатил! the devil take you!

оштури   *pf* to become deserted

оштурува   *impf of* оштури

ошугави   *pf* **I** to infect with mange **II** – **ce** to become infected with mange, become mangy

ошумоглавен   *adj* & *pt* stunned

ошумоглавеност   *f* stunned state, daze

ошумоглави   *pf* to stun

ошумоглавува   *impf of* ошумоглави

ошути   *pf* **I** **1** to make hornless, dehorn, poll **2** to make (*land*) barren **3** to become hornless; to lose/shed antlers/horns **4** to become barren (*of land*) **5** *fig.* to become stupid; to become senile **II** – **ce** *fig. see* **I** 5

ошутува (ce)   *impf of* ошути (ce)

па[1]   *conj* **1** and, then, so; прво ќе влезе тој, па ти first he will enter, then you **2** even; and yet; сите беа дојдени, па и тој everybody had come, even (including) him; па сепак мислам дека не си прав and yet I think that you are wrong

па[2]   *part* **1** (*for emphasis*) well; but; зошто да дојдам? – па знаеш why should I come? – you know why; па добро, ќе дојдам well, all right, I'll come **2** (*noncommittal response*) so so; fair to middling, not too bad; како си? – па ... how are you? – so so **3** (*as a question*) well? <and> what next? ќе ја свршам работата – па? I'll finish the job – and then what?

паберка   *f* (*usu. pl*) **1** aftercrop, fruit left for harvesting later; gleanings **2** *fig.* remnants, leavings **3** *fig.* fragments

паберкува   *impf* **1** to glean, gather remnants **2** *fig.* to compile, collect

павијан   *m Zool.* (Papio hamadryas) baboon

павилјóн   *m* pavilion

павит   *m Bot.* (Clematis vitalba) traveller's joy, old man's beard

павитарка   *f* small basket (*made from dry stems of clematis*)

павка   *impf* **I** **1** to wave (*a fan, etc.*) **2** *fig., colloq.* to yield, give in; туку го павка he continually gives in to him **3** (*за ветар*) to blow gently **II** – **ce** to cool o.s. (*with a fan, etc.*), fan o.s.

павкало   *n* **1** fan **2** *fig., colloq.* person who gives in; flatterer, toady

павлака   *f* **1** cream (*from milk*) **2** (*на око*) cataract; ❏ павлака му фатиле очите he can't see what's going on around him

павне   *pf* павна *aor.* **1** to wave (*a fan, etc.*) **2** (*за ветар*) to blow lightly (*once*)

павта   *impf* **1** to wave (*one's hands*) **2** to shake out (*bed linen, rugs, etc.*) **3** *see* павка 3

павтало   *n* fan

паган & **паганин**   -ани *m* pagan; polytheist

паганѝзам   -змот *m* paganism; polytheism

паганка   *f* (*fem. form*) *see* паган

пагански   *adj* pagan; polytheistic

паганство   *n see* паганизам

пагинација   *f* pagination

пагинѝра   *pf* & *impf* to paginate

пагода   *f* pagoda

пагур   *m* flat brandy flask

пагурче   *n dim. of* пагур

пад   *m* **1** fall, drop; слободен пад free fall; пад на цените fall in prices; пад на владата fall of the government; пад на вредноста depreciation; пад на производството decline in output **2** incline, gradient, slope

падавица *f* epilepsy

падавичар *m* epileptic

падар *m* (*полјак*) guardian of fields, vineyards; страв чува лозје, падар јаде грозје *prov.* fear guards the vineyard, the guardian eats the grapes

падарина *f* wages paid to a *padar*

падарница *f* hut of a *padar*

падарски *adj* of a *padar*

падеж[1] *m Gram.* case

падеж[2] *m dial.* fall; ruin, destruction; ако се надеваш на падеж, не ќе имаш вадеж *prov.* look on the bright side

падежен -жна *adj Gram.* case; падежна форма case form; падежна наставка case (inflexional) ending

пади *impf* to drive out, expel

падина[1] *f* **1** mountain slope; hillside, declivity **2** depression (*between two hills*)

падина[2] *impf dial. of* падне, *see* паднува; ❏ крушата под круша падина *prov.* like father, like son; a chip off the old block

падинка *f dim. of* падина[1]

падишах *m* padishah (*Turkish title*)

паднат *pt* fallen; паднат во борба fallen in battle; ❏ како од небо да е паднат he doesn't understand anything; не сме паднати од Марс we weren't born yesterday

падне *pf* падна *aor.* **1** to fall (*in various senses, lit. and fig.*); беше паднал голем снег a lot of snow had fallen; падне во борба to fall in battle; падна мрак darkness fell; падне в стапица to fall into a trap; падне во несвест to lapse into unconsciousness, to faint; падне на колена (коленици) to fall to one's knees; паднала цената на месото the price of meat has gone down; падна владата the government has fallen; паднале лисјата the leaves have fallen; празникот падна во среда the holiday fell on a Wednesday; ❏ паднаа в бунар! you can write that off! (*of lost money*); носот да му падне, не си го поткрева he's too lazy to scratch himself; паднавме на зборот while we're on the subject; паднавме во (на) разговор we started talking; му падна в очи (*дека*) it struck him (*that*), he noticed (*that*); му падна на ум (памет) it occurred to him; падне во постела; падне болен to fall ill; падна ред на него his turn came; му падна тешко he felt unwell; he felt hurt (offended); му падна грев (*за некого*) he took pity (*on s.o.*); му падна мака he felt regret; му падна жал he felt sorry; му паднал мрак пред очи he lost his temper, he saw red; крв ќе падне blood will be spilt; глави ќе паднат heads will roll; тој длабоко паднал he has sunk too deep (*in debt*); влакно нема да ти падне nothing will happen to you; не дава прав да падне на него he is very protective of him, he won't hear ill spoken of him; недраго ѝ паднало she was displeased; ако падне, пак ќе стане *prov.* he that falls today may rise tomorrow; каде падни, таму зобни *prov.* you have to make do **2** to happen, arise, take place; падна предлог a proposal was made; сега ќе падне еден говор now there will be a speech **3** to fall to one's lot; to go to (*by inheritance, etc.*); мене ми падна да ја свршам таа работа it fell

to me to finish the job; нему му паднало аутото the car went to him

паднува *impf of* падне

падобран *m* parachute; се спушта со падобран to come down by parachute, to parachute

падобранец -нци *m* parachutist; *fig.*, *colloq.* queue jumper

падобранка *f* (*fem. form*) *see* падобранец

падобрански *adj* parachute *attrib.*; parachutist's

падобранство *n Sport.* parachute jumping

паѓа *impf see* падне; тој празник паѓа во сабота that holiday falls on a Saturday; таа ми паѓа мене стрина she is my aunt on my father's side

паж *m Hist.* page-boy

пазар *m* **1** market, market-place; надворешен пазар foreign market; внатрешен (домашен) пазар home market; пазар на работна сила labour-market; зелен пазар farmers' market **2** market day; во сабота е пазар Saturday is market day **3** shopping; оди на пазар to go shopping **4** commerce; turnover, sales **5** business; bargain, deal; направивте пазар? have you done a deal? никој не се удирал на пазар no one wanted to do any business; дневен пазар day's takings, daily revenue, daily sales; ❏ таков ни беше пазарот that's what we agreed; добар пазар good bargain; good deal

пазарен -рна *adj* market; пазарен ден market day; пазарна цена market price

пазари *pf & impf* **I 1** to purchase (*various goods*); to buy; оди да пазари to go shopping **2** to fix the price (*of s.th.*); to make (do) a deal (*on s.th.*); ги пазаривте ли компирите? have you fixed the price of the potatoes? **3** to take on, hire (*labour*); пазари мајстор; to hire a builder **II** – **се 1** to bargain, haggle **2** to agree (*on terms of service and pay*); се пазари за цена to agree on a price; се пазарил да служи he has agreed to serve

пазариште *n* market-place, market-hall, market

пазариштен -шна *adj* market-place *attrib.*; пазаришна инспекција market<-place> inspection

пазарлак -ци *m colloq.* **1** negotiation; agreement; buying and selling; како ни беше пазарлакот? what did we agree to? направиле пазарлак they did a deal; ние сме на пазарлак we are negotiating **2** bargaining, haggling (*also fig.*)

пазарски *adj see* пазариштен

пазарува (се) *impf rare see* пазари (се)

пазарџија -ии *m* **1** market-goer **2** market trader

пазарџиски *adj see* пазарџија

пази *impf* **I 1** (*чува*) to take care of, look after; ❏ пази како очите to guard like the apple of one's eye **2** (*варди*) to watch out, take care, mind (*that s.th. does not happen*); пази да не згрешиш mind you don't make a mistake; пази! look out! ❏ *rare* пази Боже! God forbid! Lord save us! **II** – **се** (*чува се*) to be careful, look out; to take care of o.s.

пазува *f* bosom, breast; ❏ *iron.* од устата во пазувата! and the same to you! (*said in reply to a curse*); топла му е нему пазувата he is well off; чува змија во пазува to harbour a snake in one's bosom; ја љуби како снег в пазува he can't stand her; растен е како во мајкина пазува he's his mother's darling; нема пазува he has no protection

пазуварка *f* inside breast pocket

пајажина *f* cobweb, spider's web

пајажинен, пајажинест & **пајажинов** *adj* cobwebby, cobweb-covered; влакно пајажиново gossamer

пајак -ци *m* **1** *Zool.* spider; домашен (куќен) пајак (Tegenaria domestica) house spider **2** *fig.* cruel exploiter, bloodsucker **3** *colloq.* towing vehicle (*for towing away illegally parked vehicles*)

пајаков *adj* spider's; пајакова мрежа cobweb, spider's web

пајаче *n dim. of* пајак

пајва *f dial. see* патока

пајван *m* hobble (*on horse's legs*)

пајдушка & **пајдушката** *f*, **пајдушко** & **пајдушкото** *n* kind of *oro* (line dance)

пајка *f Zool.* duck

пајтон *m* coach, carriage; ❑ *joc.* ќе одел со на аџи-Пеша пајтонот he'll go on Shanks's mare

пајтонски *adj* coach, carriage; пајтонско тркало carriage wheel

пајтонџија -ии *m* coachman

пајтонџиски *adj* coachman's

пајче *n dim. of* duckling

пак¹ *adv* **1** <once> again, anew; ❑ еве пак here we go again **2** despite that, nevertheless, still; ❑ не и пак не no and no again; сè пак *see* сепак

пак² *conj* **1** but, however, still **2** *rare* and so; пак што ќе стане, нека стане (and) so let happen what may **3** (*with the conjunction и*) even <if>; пак и да не се вратиш even if you don't return

пак³ *part* **1** (*for emphasis*) зошто пак ти да не дојдеш? so why shouldn't you come too? или пак or <else> **2** (*expressing enthusiasm, surprise, disgust, exasperation*) пак луѓе што имаше, илјадници! there were thousands of people there! ❑ ти пак <што си бил>! you're no use at all!

пакет *m* packet, parcel; поштенски пакет postal packet, parcel by post; ❑ пакет аранжман package holiday (tour); пакет мерки package deal

пакетче *n dim. of* пакет

Пакистан *m* Pakistan

Пакистанец *m* Pakistani

Пакистанка *f* (*fem. form*) *see* Пакистанец

пакистански *adj* Pakistani

пакосен -сна *adj* **1** (*штетен*) harmful, noxious; пакосно животно harmful animal **2** (*злобен*) spiteful, malicious; пакосен поглед malevolent look

пакослив *adj see* пакосен

пакосник -ци *m* **1** pest, rascal; mischief maker, troublemaker; тој е голем пакосник it/he is a great nuisance **2** spiteful, malicious person; envious person

пакосница *f* (*fem. form*) *see* пакосник

пакоснички *adj* **1** pestilential **2** spiteful, malicious

пакосно *adv* **1** (*штетно*) harmfully; тутунот влијае пакосно на здравјето tobacco has harmful effects on health **2** (*злобно*) spitefully, maliciously, malevolently; го погледна пакосно he glanced at him malevolently

пакост *f* & *dial. m* **1** harm, damage; таа мечка правела големи пакости that bear was doing a lot of damage; ❑ црн пакост dreadful damage; само за пакост е роден he was born to be a nuisance; за пакост unfortunately; како за пакост just to spite one, as though deliberately **2** spite, malice; од пакост го стори тоа he did that out of spite

пакости *impf* **1** to harm, do damage (*to s.o.*); никому не му пакостеше he did no harm to anyone **2** to act maliciously

пакт *m* pact, treaty; пакт за ненапаѓање non-aggression pact; воени пактови military pacts

пактира *impf* to negotiate a pact; *colloq.* to scheme, plot

пакува *impf* **1** to pack; пакува куфери to pack one's bags **2** *colloq.* (*карти*) to stack

пала¹ *f arch.* kind of sword

пала² *f arch.* **1** happiness, good fortune; reign; ти ја начека палата good times have come for you **2** peace, rest

палав *adj* **1** naughty, restless, unruly; палаво дете naughty child; *poet.* палав ветрец frolicsome breeze **2** mad, crazy

палавец -вци *m see* палавник

палави се *impf* to do foolish things; to play pranks; to get up to mischief

палавина & **палавица** *f* **1** naughtiness; craziness; prank **2** madness **3** *f.p.* (*epithet for wind*) changeable, fickle wind **4** fool; Марко палавина Marko the madman

палавка *f see* палавница

палавко *m colloq. see* палавник

палавник -ци *m* mischievous boy

палавница *f* mischievous girl, hoyden

палаво *adv* naughtily; restlessly

палавост *f* naughtiness; restlessness

палавра *f colloq.* (*usu. pl*) lie, fib, tall story; ❑ продава палаври he is telling tall stories

палавштина *f see* палавост

паламарка *f* wooden hook (*with holes for the fingers, used in reaping*)

паламида¹ *f Zool.* (Palamys sarda) kind of salt-water fish of the mackerel family

паламида² *f Bot.* (Cirsium) thistle

паланечки *adj* small town *attrib.*, provincial; паланечки живот small town life

паланза & **паланса** *f dial.* balance, steelyard

паланка *f arch.* (*гратче*) small (provincial) town

паланчанец -нци *m* small town dweller; *pejor.* person with small-town mentality

паланчанка *f* (*fem. form*) *see* паланчанец

паларија -ии *f arch.* hat

паласка *f* ammunition pouch; brass box for gunpowder

палат *m arch.* **1** royal palace **2** *fig.* rich man's house

палата *f* large building (*usu. housing government institutions*); mansion; palace

палатал *m Phon.* palatal

палатален -лна *adj Phon.* palatal, "soft"; палатален глас palatal sound

палатализација *f Phon.* palatalization

палатализира *pf* & *impf Phon.* **I** to palatalize **II** – ce to be or become palatalized

палатализиран *pt Phon.* palatalized, "softened"; палатализирана согласка palatalized consonant

палачинка *f* crêpe; pancake

палеж *m* fire, conflagration; arson

палежен -жна *adj* cursed, damned; палежно време bad weather

пален & **пален** -лна *pt* & *adj see* палежен; ❑ палени соништа bad dreams

палента *f* polenta

палеограф *m* palaeographer

палеографија *f* palaeography

палеографски *adj* palaeographic<al>; палеографска анализа на текстот palaeographic<al> analysis of the text

палеозоик *m* <the> palaeozoic

палеозојски *adj* palaeozoic; палеозојска ера palaeozoic era

палеолит *m* the palaeolithic (period)

палеолитски *adj* palaeolithic; палеолитска пештера palaeolithic cave

палеонтолог -зи *m* palaeontologist

палеонтологија *f* palaeontology

палеонтолошки *adj* palaeontological; палеонтолошки атлас palaeontological atlas

Палестина *f* Palestine

Палестинец -нци *m* Palestinian

Палестинка *f* (*fem. form*) *see* Палестинец

палестински *adj* Palestinian

палета *f* palette (*also fig.*); богата палета a rich palette

палец -лци *m* 1 (*на рака*) thumb; (*на нога*) big toe; ❑ стиска палци to keep one's fingers crossed 2 *literary* inch

пали *impf* I 1 to light, set alight; пали оган/цигара to light a fire/cigarette 2 to destroy by fire, burn down 3 to turn on, switch on, light; пали свеќа/кандило to light a candle/an icon lamp; пали печка/ќумбе to light a furnace/stove 4 to start; пали мотор to start a motor 5 *Mil.* (*only imperative*) пали! fire! 6 (*жеже, пече*) to bake, scorch, burn; сонцето пали the sun burns 7 (*with acc.*) ме пали нешто в грло I have a burning sensation in my throat 8 to burn the mouth; овие пиперки палат these capsicums are very hot 9 *fig.* to inspire, delight; такви зборови палат such words inspire 10 ❑ тој пали, тој гаси he rules the roost, he's the boss; касно пали to be slow on the uptake; шегата не пали the joke misfired; тоа не пали it won't do/work; кој се фали, (тој) не пали *prov.* barking dogs seldom bite II – се *fig.* to become enthusiastic, get carried away; бргу се пали he's easily fired with enthusiasm

паливо *n see* палило

палијатив *m* palliative; half-measure

палијативен -вна *adj* palliative; палијативна мерка palliative measure, half measure

паликуќа -овци *m* arsonist, incendiary; убијци и паликуќовци murderers and arsonists

палило *n* tinder, kindling<s>

палимпсест *m* palimpsest

палир *m* building foreman

палисад *m* palisade

палисаден -дна *adj in the expression:* палисадно ткиво *Bot.* palisade layer

палица *f* stick, rod; club; *Sport.* bat; кој прави палица – за своја<та> главица *prov.* to make a rod for one's own back; he who does evil, does it to himself

паличник -ци & **палишник** -ци *m* (*лемеш*) plough-share

палјачо -вци *m* 1 circus clown 2 buffoon, wag 3 puppet

палка *f see* палица; ❑ гумена палка rubber truncheon

палма *f Bot.* palm <tree>

палмин & **палмов** *adj* palm *attrib.*; ❑ палмово гранче olive branch (*as peace offering*)

палне *pf* пална *aor.* to light; to switch on, turn on

палнува *impf of* палне

палто *n* (*кусо*) jacket; (*долго, зимно*) overcoat

палуба *f* deck

памет *f & m* 1 (*faculty of*) memory; тој има силна памет he has a good memory; ❑ на памет *see* напамет 2 (*usu. m*) mind; sense; ❑ ме извади од памет you amaze me; you gave me a fright; му дојде памет he's become more sensible; како ти фаќа паметот? what do you think? how do you think this should be done? кус е во паметот he hasn't much sense; уште му лета паметот he's still wet behind the ears; каде ти беше паметот? how could you? 3 (*usu. m*) thought; ❑ ти се чудам на паметот I'm surprised at your idea 4 advice; lesson, moral; од тебе памет нејќам I don't want advice from you; ова ќе му биде за памет this will teach him a lesson; ❑ продава памет to insist on giving advice; соли некому памет to give free advice 5 *rare, Rel.* (*памјат*) memory (*of one departed*)

паметен -тна *adj* 1 sensible; wise; reasonable; ❑ не е паметен not to know which way to turn; to be at a loss; паметниот попушта wisdom is better than strength; a wise man changes his mind, a fool never 2 *rare* long remembered; unforgettable; беа тоа паметни денови! those were unforgettable days!

памети *impf* to remember, recollect; тоа ќе го паметам дури сум жив I'll remember that as long as I live

паметлив *adj* having a good memory; паметлив човек person with a good memory

паметник -ци *m rare* (*споменик*) monument

паметно *adv* sensibly; wisely; reasonably; паметно зборува to talk sense

паметува *impf see* памети; ❑ да се знае и да се паметува let it be known and remembered

памјат *f Rel.* memory (*of one departed*); вечна му памјат! may his memory live for ever! may his soul rest in peace!

памполи *impf* to chatter, babble

пампур *m* 1 *dial.* sheet-iron stove 2 *arch.* train 3 *arch.* steamer, steamship

памтење *n* memory; има добро памтење he has a good memory

памти *impf see* памети; ❑ не памти што појадувал to have a memory like a sieve; памти како слон to have a memory like a sponge; памти па врати pay with the same dish you borrow

памтивека *adv in the expression:* од памтивека from time immemorial

памук *m* 1 *Bot.* (Gossypium herbaceum) cotton; ❑ мек како памук as soft as eiderdown 2 cotton <fabric>; блуза од памук cotton blouse; 3 cotton wool; ❑ како памук да има во ушите as though he has cotton wool in his ears

памуклија -ии *f* quilted garment

памуков *adj* <of> cotton (*plant*); памуково поле cotton field

памучен -чна *adj* cotton; памучни чорапи cotton socks; памучни стоки cotton goods; памучна индустрија cotton industry

памфлет *m* pamphlet

памфлетӣст *m* pamphleteer

памфлетски *adj* pamphlet-like; памфлетски тон pamphleteering tone, style

пан- (*in compounds*) pan-; панафрикански pan-African; панславизам pan-Slavism

пан *m* **1** *literary* gentleman (*in Polish and Czech*) **2** *Hist.* Polish, Ukrainian or Byelorussian landowner, nobleman

панагија *f Rel.* panhagia, panagia (*small, decorated icon worn by Orthodox bishops on the chest*)

панагон *m* load (*placed on back of pack-animal, between panniers*)

панаѓур *m* **1** fair **2** *fig.* disorder, confusion, chaos; scrimmage; crowd

панаѓуриште *n arch.* fairground

панаѓурски *adj* fair, fairground *attrib.*

панаѓурува *impf* to attend a fair; to revel

панама[1] *f* **1** kind of cotton material; cross-stitch fabric **2** panama hat

Панама[2] *f* Panama

Панамец -мци *m* Panamanian

Панамка *f* (*fem. form*) *see* Панамец

панамски *adj* Panama *attrib.*, Panamanian; Панамскиот Канал the Panama Canal

панго *n arch.* kind of cupboard or sideboard

пандан *m* (*sg only*) counterpart, opposite number; ❑ како пандан (*на некого, на нешто*) as a match for (counterpart to) (*s.o., s.th.*)

панделка *f* ribbon, bow (*for the hair, etc.*)

пандишпан *m* sponge layer; flan base

пандур *m arch.* watchman; constable; општински пандур municipal policeman

пандурски *adj arch.* police; пандурска служба police duty

панегӣрик -ци *m literary* panegyric, eulogy; hymn of praise; flattery

панегиричар *m literary* panegyrist; flatterer

панегиричен -чна & **панегирички** *adj* panegyric<al>, laudatory; панегиричен говор panegyrical speech

панел *m* **1** pavement **2** panel

пансир & **пансур** *m* **1** *see* панцир 1; да облече од пансур кошула to put on a shirt of mail **2** (*in traditional costumes*) decorations in the hair (*silver coins, etc.*)

пансирен -рна & **пансурен** -рна *adj see* панцирен

пансирлив & **пансурлив** *adj f.p. see* панцирен

пансиров & **пансуров** *adj f.p. see* панцирен

паника *f* panic; ❑ не кревај паника! don't panic! го фати паника he was panic-stricken

панихӣда *f* requiem

паница *f* **1** (*каленица*) earthenware bowl; еднему со лажица, другему со паница *prov.* mother to one, stepmother to the other **2** *dial.* dish, plate **3** *dial.* an old measure for grain

паничар *m* alarmist; panic-monger

паничен -чна *adj* panic; panic-stricken; панично бегство flight in panic

панкер *m* punk

панкреас *m Anat.* pancreas

панó -оа *n* panel

паноптикум *m* wax museum

панорáма *f* **1** panorama (*view*) **2** *fig.* panorama (*survey*); панорама на македонската поезија a survey of Macedonian poetry

панорáмен -мна & **панорáмски** *adj* panoramic

пансиóн *m* **1** boarding-school; students' hostel **2** boarding-house **3** board and lodging; ❑ цел (полн) пансион full board and lodging; пола пансион bed and breakfast

пансионáт *m see* пансион 1

пански *adj Hist.* landowner's, nobleman's; пански земји landowner's properties (lands)

панство *n Hist.* nobleman's status

панталони *pl* trousers, *Am.* pants

пантеӣзам -змот *m* pantheism

пантеӣст *m* pantheist

пантеистички *adj* pantheistic; пантеистички сфа-ќања pantheistic concepts

пантеóн *m* pantheon

пантер *m Zool.* (Felis pardus) panther

пантерски *adj* panther's; panther-like; пантерски скок panther-like leap

пантлика *f* ribbon; tape

пантличара *f see* тенија

пантомӣма *f* dumb-show, mime

пантомӣмен -мна, **пантомимички** & **пантомӣмски** *adj* <of> mime; со пантомимни средства by means of mime

пантофла *f* (*usu. pl*) slipper

панукла *f arch.* plague

пануклица *f dim. of* панукла

панцир *m* **1** armour (*of knight*) **2** armour plating (*of warship or vehicle*); armoured vehicle **3** *Zool.* cara-pace, shell

панцирен -рна & **панциров** *adj* of armour, armoured; панцирна кошула shirt of mail; <chain->mail tunic

папа, папа *interj* ho, ho!

папа[1] *m* pope, pontiff

папа[2] *m arch.* (*usu. preceding Christian name*) priest; папа-Никола Father Nikola

папавица *f Bot.* (Lycoperdon bovista) puff-ball, *see* пувка 5

папагал *m* parrot (*also fig.*)

папагалски *adj* parrot's; parrot-like; папагалско учење learning by rote

папагалство *n* & **папагалштина** *f* parrot-like imitation

папилóта *f* (*за коса*) curler, roller

папирус *m* **1** *Bot.* (Cyperus papyrus) papyrus **2** papyrus (*paper, manuscript*)

папка *f* file, folder

папо (*only sg*) *n child.* bread; ❑ на лебот уште папо му вика he's still wet behind his ears

папок -ци *m* navel, umbilicus; ❑ тука му е врзан папокот this is where he belongs; папокот му побегна за јадење <од стрвост> he's a glutton; не ти кладов жар на папокот! why are you yelling so?

папочен -чна *adj* umbilical; папочна врвца umbilical cord

папра, папрад & **папрат** -тта *f Bot.* (Aspidium (Nephrodium) filix mas) shield-fern; блага папрат (Polypodium vulgare) polypod<y>, wall fern

папрадник -ци *m* place overgrown with ferns/bracken

паприкаш *m Cul.* goulash, stew (*containing meat and capsicums*)

паприца *f dial. see* прплица 1

папса *pf* **1** to break down *intrans.*, collapse; to become exhausted; папсал од работа he got tired out with work **2** to shrink, dwindle; to weaken, calm down; папса морето the sea has calmed down; папса дождот the rain has eased **3** to tire, exhaust, wear out *trans.*; папса коњ to wear out a horse

папсан *pt* exhausted, worn out

папсаност *f* exhaustion

папски *adj* papal; папската држава papal state; папска була papal bull (edict)

папство *n* papal authority; pontificate; papacy

папсува *impf of* папса

Папуа Нова Гвинеја *f* Papua New Guinea

Папуанец -нци *m* Papuan

Папуанка *f* (*fem. form*) *see* Папуанец

папуански *adj* Papuan

папуча *f colloq.* (*влечка*) slipper

папучар *m colloq.* henpecked husband

папуџија -ии *m arch.* (*влечкар*) slipper-maker

папушкав & **папушлав** *adj* **1** (*за овошје*) soft; јаболко папушкаво soft apple **2** (*за човек*) of delicate health; delicate, frail

пар *m literary, rare* **1** (*рало, чифт; двојка*) pair, brace, couple; еден пар чорапи a pair of socks; брачен пар married couple; ❑ пар или непар, *see* чифт или тек **2** equal, match; тој не ти е пар he's no match for you

пара¹ *f* **1** steam; водна пара water vapour; заситена пара saturated steam; ❑ со полна пара full steam ahead **2** (*од јадење*) smell, aroma; се крева пара an aroma rises (spreads)

пара² *f* **1** para, hundredth part of a Yugoslav dinar **2** coin; стара пара an old coin; сребрена пара a silver coin; златна пара a gold coin; ❑ нема ни скршена (пукната) пара he hasn't got a brass farthing **3** *Hist.* fortieth part of a groat; ❑ две пари му е алот he's not getting on well; пет пари не дава he doesn't care tuppence **4** *colloq.* money, brass, dough; ❑ при пара е he's got some money; на пари лежи he's rolling in money; скапана пара има he's got money to burn; убава пара направи he made a tidy sum; парата на пара оди *prov.* money attracts money; парата и железна врата отвора; пуста пара сѐ отвора *prov.* money talks

пара³ *impf* **I** **1** to rip, tear, rend; to undo, unpick; пара шев to unpick a seam; ❑ ако не ми шиеш, <барем> не парај ми if you can't help, don't get in the way! **2** *fig.* to hurt, offend; пара уши to grate on the ears; пара очи to hurt s.o.'s eyes; пара <нечие> срце to break s.o.'s heart **II** – **се 1** to rip *intrans.*; to come undone **2** *fig.* to break *intrans.*; срцето ми се пара my heart is breaking

парабел & **парабелум** *m* Parabellum (*kind of pistol*)

парабола *f* **1** parabola **2** parable

параболичен -чна *adj* parabolic

параван *m* partition, screen (*also fig.*)

Парагваец -ајци *m* Paraguayan

Парагвај *m* Paraguay

Парагвајка *f* (*fem. form*) *see* Парагваец

парагвајски *adj* Paraguayan

парагон-блок *m* purchaser's invoice

параграф *m* **1** paragraph **2** *colloq.* the law, legal code; ❑ го фати параграфот he was caught by the law

парада *f* **1** parade; воена парада military parade; првомајска парада May Day parade **2** *Sport.* (in soccer) performance; убава голманска парада a fine performance by the goalkeeper

параден -дна *adj* parade; парадна униформа dress uniform; параден марш ceremonial march-past; goose-step; параден скок a spectacular jump

парадигма *f Gram.* paradigm

парадира *impf* **1** to parade, march in procession **2** to goose-step; to swagger **3** *fig.* to put on airs; to flaunt, show off, parade; парадира со своето знаење to parade (flaunt) one's knowledge

парадокс *m* paradox

парадоксален -лна *adj* paradoxical; парадоксален факт a paradoxical fact

паразит *m* parasite (*also fig.*); sponger

паразитизам -змот *m* parasitism (*also fig.*); sponging

паразитолог -зи *m* parasitologist

паразитологија *f* parasitology

паразитски *adj* parasitic<al>; паразитски растенија parasitical plants; паразитски начин на живеење parasitical way of life

паразитство *n see* паразитизам

параклис *m* wayside chapel, shrine

паралела *f* **1** *Math.* parallel line **2** *Geog.* line (parallel) of latitude **3** analogue; analogy, comparison

паралелен -лна *adj* parallel; паралелни линии parallel lines

паралелизам -змот *m* parallelism (*also fig.*)

паралелка *f* section, group (*of a school class*); stream; ученици од второ одделение се распределени во три паралелки the second-grade pupils are divided into three classes

паралелно *adv* in parallel; side by side; ❑ паралелно со тоа parallel with that

паралелност *f* parallelism

паралелограм *m Geom.* parallelogram; паралелограм на силите parallelogram of forces

паралелопипед *m Geom.* parallelepiped

парализа *f* **1** paralysis; парализа на ногата paralysis of the leg; детска парализа infantile paralysis, poliomyelitis **2** *fig.* slow-down, stoppage, stagnation

парализира *pf* & *impf* **I** to paralyse (*also fig.*) **II** – **се** to become paralysed

парализиран *pt* paralysed

паралитик -ци & **паралитичар** *m* person suffering from paralysis, paralytic

паралитичен -чна & **паралитички** *adj* paralytic; *Med.* паралитички удар paralytic stroke

параллија *adj indecl.* rich, wealthy

парамециум *m* paramecium

пара<м>парче *n* fragments, small pieces; ❑ скрши нешто на пара<м>парчиња (стори нешто пара<м>парчиња) to smash s.th. to smithereens

парангора *f f.p.* <waterproof> angora fabric

параноид & **параноик** -ци *m* paranoiac

параноја *f* paranoia

парапет *m* parapet, railing, balustrade

параспур *m* **1** *colloq.* disorderly person; worthless person; idler, loafer; параспур човек good-for-nothing **2** *arch.*, *dial.* voluntary co-operative work group **3** *arch.*, *dial.* field tilled by tenant farmer

парастас & **парастос** *m Rel.* requiem

паратифус *m Med.* paratyphoid

параф *m* initials

парафин *m Chem.* paraffin

парафи́нски *adj* paraffin; парафински свеќи paraffin candles

парафи́ра *f pf & impf* to initial

парафра́за *f* **1** paraphrase **2** *Mus.* elaboration (*of theme, usu. s.o. else's*)

парафрази́ра *pf & impf* to paraphrase

пардија -ии *f dial.* rough-hewn board, plank, slat

пардон & пардо́н 1 *m* pardon, forgiveness; mercy; молам пардон excuse me, I beg forgiveness **2** *interj* pardon! excuse me! ❑ ти давам пардон you're right

пардони́ра *pf & impf intrans.* to beg leave/pardon/ permission

пареа & парева *f see* пара¹; ❑ денеска нè има, утре нè нема, ќе загинеме како пареа here today, gone tomorrow; под полна пареа full steam ahead

парен¹ -рна *adj* steam; парен котел steam-boiler; парна машина steam-engine

парен² -рна *adj literary* even; парни броеви even numbers

пари¹ *pl* money; книжни пари banknotes, *Am.* bills; ковани пари coin<s>; готови пари cash, ready money; го купил за готови пари he paid cash for it; ситни (дробни) пари small change; враќање пари refunding; ❑ при пари e he's got some money; убави пари направи he made a tidy sum; си игра со пари (на пари лежи) to have money to burn; со пари не се купува unobtainable, out of reach; incorruptible; wonderful, priceless; со пари ли е или без пари? does one pay or is it free? за евтини пари го купил he bought it cheap; тешки пари bags of money; small fortune; колку пари чини? how much is it <worth>? знам колку пари чини I know what he's really like; носи добри пари to pay good money; парите не се важни money is no object; бели пари за црни дни savings for a rainy day; умот е пари *prov.* mind is money; ability is all; времето е пари *prov.* time is money; парите се отепувачка *prov.* money is the root of all evil

пари² *impf* **I 1** to steam *trans.*, expose to steam **2** to pour hot water over, scald **II – се 1** to be exposed to steam **2** to have a steam bath; to steam o.s.

пари³ *impf dial.* **1** *see* жеже **2** (*жури*) to sting **3** to burn, sting; ме пари грлово my throat is on fire **4** *f.p.* (*распарува*) to rip, tear; to break, split

Париз *m* Paris

парижанец -ни *m* Parisian

парижанка *f* (*fem. form*) *see* парижанец

париј -ии *m* pariah (*Hist. & fig.*)

парип *m dial.* horse, nag

парипка *f dial.* young (yearling) mare

пари́ра *pf & impf* to parry, ward off; to counter

париски *adj* Parisian

парите́т *m* parity; equality; девизен паритет par of exchange

парите́тен -тна *adj* based on parity, <of> parity; паритетен одбор parity board; врз паритетни принципи on principles of parity

парица & паричка *f dim. of* пара² **1** small coin **2** *colloq., hyp.* money, cash; парица треба за тоа one needs cash for that; ❑ убава парица направи he made a tidy sum; му ја лапна парицата he bled him dry; парица – царица *prov.* money is everything

париче *n* **1** small coin **2** *Bot.* (Bellis perennis) daisy

паричен -чна *adj* <in> money, cash; financial, mone-

tary; парична награда financial reward/cash prize; парична казна fine; парична пратка money order; парична единица monetary unit; парични средства funds

парички *pl hyp. of* пари¹; cash, *colloq.* brass, dough, lolly; парички си немал сиромавиот the poor fellow didn't have the lolly

парк *m* **1** park; градскиот парк municipal park, garden **2** depot, pool; возен парк motor depot, fleet of cars

парка¹ *impf in the expression:* што го парка? what's the matter with him? (what's eating him)? ништо не го парка there's nothing wrong with him

парка² *impf dial. see* пипа, фаќа

паркет *m* parquet

паркетар *m* parquetry worker

паркетен -тна *adj* parquet *attrib.*

паркети́ра *pf & impf* to parquet, lay parquet

паркинг *m* car-park, *Am.* parking-lot

парки́ра *pf & impf* **I 1** to landscape, lay out (*as parkland*) **2** to park (*a car*) **II – се** to park one's car

паркиралиште *n* car-park, *Am.* parking-lot

парламе́нт *m* parliament

парламента́р *m* negotiator, officer delegated to parley with enemy

парламента́рен -рна *adj* **1** parliamentary; парламентарни избори parliamentary elections **2** *fig.* polite; биди парламентарен! be civil!

парламента́рец -рци *m* member of parliament, M.P.

парламентари́зам -змот *m* parliamentary system, parliamentarism

парламента́рност *f* parliamentary character

парламента́рски *adj* negotiator's

парламе́нтски *adj* <of> parliament

парлив *adj dial.* hot, burning; парлива пиперка hot capsicum (pepper)

пармак -ци *m arch.* post, stake; railing

парне *pf* парна *aor. dial.* to scorch, burn; to sting

парник -ци *m literary, rare* member of a pair, partner, twin

парница *f* lawsuit, legal action; граѓанска парница civil suit

паричен -чна *adj* legal; парнична постапка legal procedure

парнува *impf dial. of* парне

пароброд *m* steamer, steamship; патнички пароброд passenger liner; товарен пароброд cargo steamer

пароброда́рски *adj see* паробродски

пароброда́рство *n* navigation by steamship; речно пароброда́рство river steamship navigation

пароброд́ски *adj* steamship's, steamer's; пароброд́ска сирена steamer's siren

парог -зи *m* **1** crook (*hooked staff*) **2** (*на вила*) prong **3** (*на еленски рог*) branch

пародија -ии *f* parody

пароди́ра *pf & impf* to parody

парожен -жна *adj* pronged, forked; парожна вила pitchfork with prongs

парожец -шци *m see* парог 3

парокси́зам -змот *m* paroxysm, fit (*also fig.*)

паро́ла *f* **1** motto; slogan; ❑ под паролата under the slogan; парола снајди се make the best of it **2** poster; лепи пароли to stick up posters **3** password

парса *f* **1** *colloq.* fee charged by musicians for playing *oros* **2** *arch.* sum collected by café owner or manager from customers playing cards (*per hour or more*)

парта *f* front upper part of a woman's blouse (*variously embroidered, detachable for laundering*)

партал *m* **1** rag; *pl* партали rags, tatters; *fig.* large, fluffy snowflakes; сиот во партали all in rags; ❑ собира партали to up sticks; сосе партали lock, stock and barrel **2** *fig. pejor.* ragamuffin, scamp; good-for-nothing **3** useless object

парталав *adj* ragged, tattered, shabby, frayed; парталаво палто tattered coat; парталав човек shabbily-dressed person

парталка *f* sloven, slattern

парталко -вци *m* ragamuffin; good-for-nothing

парталче *n dim. of* партал

партер *m* **1** *Theatre* stalls, pit **2** ground floor **3** *Gymnastics* floor; вежби на партер floor exercises

партиен -јна *adj rare see* партиски

партиец -јци *m* member of the <Communist> party, Party member

партизан *m* resistance fighter, partisan

партизанија *f colloq. fig.* territory liberated by the partisans

партизанка *f* (*fem. form*) *see* партизан

партизански *adj* **1** partisan's; resistance; партизанска војна partisan war; партизански одред partisan unit **2** *fig. iron.* hastily organized, unsystematic; haphazard; партизанско раководење reckless management policy

партизанство *n* **1** partisan activity **2** devil-may-care attitude

партизанштина *f* ill-organized, unsystematic work

партија -ии *f* **1** <political> party; комунистичка партија Communist party **2** group, party, side; тие се разделија во две партии they divided into two sides **3** *Mus.* part; партијата на Тоска the part of Tosca **4** game, match; партија шах a game of chess; ❑ отспива една партија to have a nap **5** (*marriage*) match, catch; испуштил добра партија he missed a good match **6** batch, consignment, shipment; нова партија чевли a new batch of shoes **7** *Book-keeping, Accountancy* heading, column; партија "Лични расходи" the "Personal Expenses" column **8** (*part of syllabus*) section, segment

партијка *f* (*fem. form*) *see* партиец

партијност *f* <Communist> party spirit (*accord with the principles of the <Communist> party*); партијноста во литературата (*degree of*) ideological conformity in literature

партикула *f Gram.* (честица) particle

партикуларизам -змот *m* particularism (*aspirations of separate parts of a state at the expense of nationwide interests*)

партикуларистички *adj* particularistic; партикуларистички тенденции particularistic tendencies

партиски *adj* of the <Communist> party; партиски конгрес Party congress; партиски стаж party experience; партиска книшка party booklet (record)

партитура *f Mus.* score; партитура на опера score of an opera

партицип *m Gram.* verbal adjective, participle

партиципант *m* participant

партиципација *f* participation

партиципира *pf & impf* to participate; to share

партиципски *adj Gram.* participial

партнер *m* partner; деловен партнер business partner

партнерка *f* (*fem. form*) *see* партнер

парфем *m* perfume, scent

парфимерија -ии *f* scents, perfumery; cosmetics shop

парфимериски *adj* perfumery; парфимериски производи perfumery products, scents

парфимира *pf & impf* **I** to spray with perfume; to scent, perfume **II** – се to scent o.s., perfume o.s.

пар-форфе *n & m Sport.* forfeit

парцела *f* plot, lot, parcel (*of land*); block

парцелизација *f* parcelling out (*of land*), sub-division

парцелизира *pf & impf* to sub-divide, parcel out (*lots for building, etc.*)

парцијален -лна *adj* partial, incomplete; парцијално решение partial solution

парче *n* **1** piece, bit; парче леб a slice of bread; ❑ направи парчиња 1. to smash to smithereens 2. to give a good hiding **2** item, individual piece; ❑ работи на парче to do piece-work; добро парче *sl.* nice bit of skirt (fluff, crumpet)

парченце *n dim. of* парче

парчоса *pf* **I 1** to break up *trans.*; to dismember **2** *fig.* to destroy, annihilate **II** – се **1** to break up *intrans.*, disintegrate **2** *fig.* to break *intrans.*; срцето му се парчоса his heart broke

парчосува (се) *impf of* парчоса (се)

пас *m Sport.* pass

пасаж *m* **1** passage; arcade; (*подземен*) subway **2** (*насус*) passage (*of text*)

пасе[1] *impf* **1** to graze *intrans.*; to feed *intrans.*; кравите пасеа the cows were grazing; ❑ пасе трева to be naive; to be stupid **2** to graze *trans.*, put out to grass (pasture) *trans.*; овчарот ги пасеше овците the shepherd was grazing the sheep; ❑ друг ги пасе овците, друг ја стриже волната one sows, another reaps

пасе[2] *impf* (*of a horse, donkey*) **I** to mount, mate with; пастувот ја пасе кобилата the stallion mounts the mare **II** – се to mate (*co – with*)

пасив *m Gram.* passive voice

пасива *f coll.* liabilities; актива и пасива assets and liabilities

пасивен -вна *adj* **1** passive, inactive; indifferent, apathetic, inert; пасивен учесник passive participant; пасивен посматрач passive onlooker (spectator); ❑ пасивен отпор passive resistance; пасивно избирачко право right to be elected **2** adverse, unfavourable, negative; пасивен трговски биланс adverse trade balance **3** *Gram.* passive

пасивизација *f* retirement

пасивизира *pf & impf* **I** to retire *trans.* **II** – се to retire *intrans.*

пасивност *f* passivity, inactivity, apathy, indifference; submissiveness

пасија -ии *f* passion, love, desire, craving

пасинок -ци *m* stepson

пасиониран *adj* passionate, avid, enthusiastic; пасиониран собирач на марки enthusiastic stamp collector

пасира *pf & impf* **1** to match, suit; to be appropriate, proper **2** to mash

пасиште *n* pasture

пасквил *m* & **пасквила** *f* lampoon, libel; pasquinade

пасменце *n dim. of* пасмо

пасмо *n* skein, hank; flock; ❑ не го гледа (жала) пасмото, туку го гледа (жала) влакното not to see the wood for the trees

пасне *pf* пасна *aor. dim. of* пасе¹ to graze for a while *trans & intrans.*

пасомце *n dim. of* пасмо

пасош *m colloq. see* паспорт

пасошки *adj colloq. see* паспортен

паспал *m* 1 mill-dust (*from wheat flour*) 2 waste from rags when reprocessed 3 *fig.* ragamuffin, tatterdemalion

паспалав *adj* 1 covered in wheat meal 2 *fig.* паспалав човек ragamuffin, tatterdemalion

паспорт *m* passport

паспортен -тна *adj* passport; паспортно одделение passport section/office

паспул *m* (*на облека*) piping, trimming

паста *f* paste; паста за чевли shoe polish; забна паста toothpaste

паства *f Rel.* flock, the faithful

пастел *m* pastel (*crayon or drawing*)

пастелен -лна *adj* pastel; пастелни моливи pastel crayons; пастелен пејзаж pastel landscape

пастеризација *f* pasteurization

пастеризира *pf & impf* to pasteurize

пастеризиран *adj* pasteurized; пастеризирано млеко pasteurized milk

пастир *m literary* 1 shepherd, herdsman; стадото и пастирот the shepherd and his flock 2 *Rel.* pastor

пастирка *f literary* shepherdess

пастирски *adj literary* shepherd's; pastoral; пастирска песна pastoral song; пастирска проповед pastoral sermon

пастирче *n dim. of* пастир 1

пастор *m Rel.* pastor, parson

пасторала *f* pastoral, pastorale

пасторален -лна *adj* pastoral; пасторална поезија pastoral poetry

пасторок -рци *m* stepson, *see* пасинок

пасторски *adj* pastor's

пасторче *n dim. of* пасторок; ❑ пасторче на судбината an unfortunate child

пастри *impf arch.* I (*чува*) to keep; to save; пастри некоја пара to save a little money; ❑ којшто си ја пастри устата, тој си ја пастри душата keep guard of your tongue, watch what you say II – се (*чува се*) to take care of o.s.

пастрма *f* smoked meat; лаана со пастрма sauerkraut with smoked meat; ❑ направи некого пастрма to make mincemeat of s.o.; to tear a strip off s.o.; волк пастрма не чува; за волк пастрма не треба *prov.* a glutton and a spendthrift don't think of the morrow

пастрмалија *adj indecl.* пита пастрмалија open pie with smoked meat, akin to pizza

пастрмица *f hyp. of* пастрма

пастрмка *f Zool.* (Salmo fario) trout

пастув *m* stallion

пастувски *adj* stallion's

пасува *pf & impf see* пасира 1

пасус *m* paragraph; passage (*of text*)

пат¹ -ишта, -тје & *f.p.* -и *m* 1 road, way; колски пат cart track; асфалтиран пат asphalt (sealed) road; споредем пат byroad, byway; сите патишта водат во (за) Рим all roads lead to Rome; ❑ од пат е it's far from the road; не сум го нашол на пат I had to make an effort to get it; остане на пат (на улица) to be left penniless 2 way, route; direction; водни патишта waterways; поморски пат sea route; воздушен пат air route; Млечен пат the Milky Way; скршне од патот to lose one's way; го знае патот he knows the way; оди по својот пат to go one's own way; фати убав пат; тргне по добар пат he's started off on the right track; на добар пат е (*да*) to be about (*to*); изведува некого на пат to bring s.o. up; му го пресече патот he/it crossed his path; пробива пат (*за*) to pave the way (*for*); to blaze the trail (*for*); му го даде патот he showed him the door; држи го патов keep to this track! заобиколен пат roundabout way; bypass; тајни патишта secret (mysterious) ways; остане на (пол) пат (насред пат) to get stuck half-way; една <чашка> за по пат one for the road; не знае кој пат да го фати to be at one's wit's end; to be at six and sevens; откако (кога) ќе се скрши (преврти) колата, патишта многу <се наоѓаат, се отвораат> *prov.* every cloud has a silver lining 3 passage, way; направете (сторете) пат да поминат make way for them to pass; иставете ми се од пат get out of my way! ❑ стои некому на патот to bar s.o.'s way 4 (*средство*; *начин*) means; manner, way; немавме друг пат we had no other way; го избира потешкиот пат to do s.th. the hard way; по судски пат by legal means; via the courts; по пат<от> на <нешто> by means of <s.th.> 5 journey; тргне на пат to start on a journey; до селото има три саата пат it takes three hours to get to the village; патот таму и назад the journey there and back; ❑ свадбен пат honeymoon; последен пат the last journey (*i.e. to the grave*); фати пат to set out; ќе тепа пат цел ден he'll be travelling all day; среќен (добар) пат! bon voyage! по пат on (along) the way; на пат е he's on his travels, he's away; службен пат on a business trip

пат² -и *m* time, occasion; два пати (двапати) twice; повеќе пати (повеќепати) several times; често пати (честопати) often; ❑ стопати сум ти рекол! I've told you a hundred times! еден пат 1. once; тие се собираат еден пат во неделата they meet once a week 2. once upon a time, at one time; живеел еден пат еден старец once upon a time there lived an old man; од еден пат suddenly, *see* одеднаш; идниот пат next time; друг пат (другпат), а не сега another time, not now; други пати (другипати) another time, on other occasions; едни пати (еднипати) sometimes; некој пат (некојпат) occasionally; по некој пат at times; на пати (напати) sometimes, occasionally; now and then; никој пат (никојпат) never; прв пат (првпат), први пат, првиот пат the first time; за прв пат (за првпат) for the first time; од првпат погоди he guessed straight away

пат³ *m Chess* stalemate

пата-карти *pl* draw, tie (*in card games*)

паталец -лци *m* poor devil, wretch; sufferer; ❑ не прашај гаталец (вражалец, старец), туку <прашај> паталец (паталца) *prov.* experience is worth more than wisdom патар *m* road maintenance worker, navvy

патарди́ја -ии *f colloq.* uproar, racket, hullabaloo; се крена една патардија a great hullabaloo started

патарина *f* <road> toll

патека *f* path; footpath; trail; track; route; <traffic> lane; runner <rug>; *Sport.* track; lane; distance; козја патека goat track; *Sport.* трчање на кратки/ средни/долги патеки sprinting/middle-distance/ long-distance running

патем & патема *adv* on the way; by the wayside; ❑ патем<a> кажано by the way, incidentally; in passing

патен -тна *adj* 1 travel, travelling; патни трошоци (разноски) travel expenses; патни и дневни travel and per diem allowance; патен лист itinerary; патен налог travel warrant; патна исправа passport 2 road, street *attrib.*; патна врата front door, front entrance; патна мрежа road network

пате́нт *m* 1 patent; управа за патенти patent office 2 zip-fastener, zipper

пате́нтен -тна *adj* <of> patent<s>; патентно право right of patent

патенти́ра *pf & impf* 1 to patent 2 to authorize, entitle, empower, privilege

патенти́ран *adj* 1 patented; патентирано средство patented instrument, patent remedy; патентиран производ proprietary product 2 *fig., iron.* genuine, well-known; тој е патентиран лаж he is an inveterate liar

патерица *f* 1 crutch; оди со патерици to walk on crutches 2 (*priest's, bishop's*) crook, crosier, staff; mace, sceptre 3 *colloq.* the day after a religious holiday 4 *dial.* forked tree

патетика *f* display of emotion; excitement

патетичен -чна *adj* emotional, passionate; agitated, excited; патетичен стил emotional style

пате-ќуте *interj* (*imitative of beating*) whack, whack

патец -тци *m* parting (*of the hair*), *Am.* part

пати[1] *impf* 1 to suffer, experience misfortunes; многу знаеш, многу ќе патиш it doesn't pay to know too much; ❑ тој од јазикот си пати his tongue gets him into trouble 2 to suffer (*од – from*), be prone (*to*); пати од чир во стомакот to suffer from a stomach ulcer

пати[2] се *impf* to grow, multiply *intrans.*

патика *f* (*usu. pl*) *Sport.* light sports shoe, tennis shoe, *Am.* sneaker, runner

патило *n* suffering, misfortune, misery; не прашај старо (старило), прашај патило *prov. see* паталец

патина *f* patina

патини́ра *pf & impf* to coat with anti-corrosion agent

патини́ран *adj fig.* having age, dignity, reputation

патица *f dial. see* патка[1], пајка, шатка

патка[1] *f Zool.* duck; ❑ новинарска патка canard

патка[2] *impf* I 1 to toddle, waddle (*of small children*) II – се *dial.* to wallow, splash about

патлиџан *m Bot.* (Solanum lycopersicum) tomato (*plant and fruit*), *see* домат; црвен патлиџан red tomato; црн (модар) патлиџан (Solanum melongena) aubergine, egg-plant

патник[1] -ци *m* traveller; (*редовен, на градско превозно возило*) commuter; (*во воз, на брод итн.*) passenger; трговски патник commercial traveller, travelling salesman; ❑ на патникот патот <кажи, му го>, на овчарот стапот *prov.* to each his own

патник[2] -ци *m rare* sufferer, victim, *see* страдалник

патнина *f* travel allowance

патница[1] *f* (*fem. form*) *see* патник[1]

патница[2] *f rare* (*fem. form*) *see* патник[2], страдалница

патничка *f see* патница[1]

патнички[1] *adj* 1 passenger; патнички воз passenger train 2 travelling; патничка чанта travelling-bag; патничка агенција travel agency; патнички чек traveller's cheque

патнички[2] *adj rare* sufferer's, victim's, *see* страдален, страдалнички

патоводен -дна *adj literary* leading, guiding; ❑ патоводна идеја guiding idea

патоген & патогенен -гена *adj Med.* pathogenic; патогени микроби pathogenic microbes

паток -ци *m dial. see* патор

патока *f* weak, poor-quality *raki*

патоказ *m* signpost (*also fig.*)

патоло́г -зи *m Med.* pathologist

патологија *f* 1 *Med.* pathology; општа патологија general pathology 2 *fig., literary* abnormality, deviation from the norm; degeneracy

патолошки *adj* pathological

патопис *m* travel notes; travel diary

патописен -сна *adj* of travel accounts; патописни белешки travel notes

патописец -сци *m* travel writer, author of travel stories

патор & *rare* паторок -ци *m Zool.* drake

патос *m* emotion, fervour, passionate enthusiasm; зборува со патос to speak with feeling; револуционерен патос revolutionary fervour

патрав *adj* 1 (*за човек*) bow-legged, bandy-legged 2 (*за нога*) crooked, curved, bandy; патрави нозе bandy legs

патраво *adv* оди патраво to sway when walking

патрија́рх -си *m* 1 *Rel.* patriarch; патријарх на Македонската православна црква Patriarch of the Macedonian Orthodox Church 2 *literary* doyen; патријарх на славистиката doyen of Slavonic studies

патријарха́лен -лна *adj* patriarchal

патријарха́т *m* patriarchy

патријаршија -ии *f Rel.* patriarchate

патријаршиски *adj Rel.* patriarch's

патрик -ци *m arch.* 1 *see* патријарх 1 2 *Hist.* popular title of the archbishop of Ohrid

патрика́на *f arch.* 1 *see* патријаршија 2 *Hist.* the Ohrid archbishopric (archdiocese)

патрио́т *m* patriot

патриоти́зам -змот *m* patriotism

патрио́тка *f* (*fem. form*) *see* патриот

патрио́тски *adj* patriotic

патри́циј -ии *m Hist.* patrician

патрициски *adj* patrician

патро́ла *f* patrol; воена патрола military patrol

патро́лен -лна *adj* patrol; патролен брод patrol vessel

патроли́ра *impf* to patrol

патро́н[1] *m* patron; protector

патро́н[2] *m* cartridge

патрона́жа *f* **1** patronage, protection, sponsorship **2** community health nursing

патрона́жен -жна *adj in the expression:* патронажна сестра community nurse, *Brit.* health visitor

патрона́т *m see* патронажа 1

патро́нен *adj in the expression:* патронен празник patronal holiday (*of a school, etc.*), founder's day

патува *impf* to travel; *fig.* to pass away; патува со воз/ автомобил/брод to travel by train/car/ship; патува за Загреб he's travelling to Zagreb; бродот патуваше накај Австралија the ship was bound for Australia; има долг пат да патува to have a long journey ahead of one

патување *n* travel; journey; trip; cruise; ❏ свадбено патување honeymoon; кружно патување round trip

патче *n dim. of* пат¹

пауза *f* pause, break, temporary stop, rest

паузи́ра *pf & impf* to pause; to rest; паузираше една година поради болест he took a year off because of illness

паун *m Zool.* (Pavo cristatus) peacock; ❏ оди, се шета како паун to strut like a peacock; to act the cock of the walk

пауница *f Zool.* peahen

паунов *adj* peacock<'s>; пауново перо peacock feather

паунски *adj rare see* паунов

паунче *n dim.* pea-chick

паупер *m literary* pauper

пауперизација *f literary* pauperization, impoverishment

пауша́л *m* flat rate; lump sum; работи со паушал to work for a flat rate (of . . .)

пауша́лен -лна *adj* rough, approximate; паушална сума <пари> rough total, approximate amount <of money>; паушална стапка flat rate

паушално *adv* roughly, approximately

пафта *f* (*usu. pl*) metal buckle (*in woman's traditional costume*)

паци́ент *m* patient

паци́ентка *f* (*fem. form*) *see* пациент

пацифи́зам -змот *m* pacifism

Пацифик *m* Pacific

пацификација -ии *f* pacification

пацифи́ст *m* pacifist

пацифистички *adj* pacifist; pacificatory

пацифистка *f* (*fem. form*) *see* пацифист

пацифички *adj* Pacific; Пацифички Океан Pacific Ocean

пача *f Cul.* aspic; brawn

пачавица *f* trouserleg, *see* ногавица

пачавра *f* **1** dishcloth **2** mop (*for cleaning baker's oven*) **3** *fig.* sloven, slattern

паша¹ *f* pasture, grazing

паша² *m* pasha; ❏ живее како паша to live like a lord

пашалак -ци *m* **1** *Hist.* pashalik (*pasha's province or jurisdiction*); Белградскиот пашалак the pashalik of Belgrade **2** *fig.* peaceful, free style of life; ергенлак – пашалак bachelorhood is like the life of a pasha (*free and untroubled*)

пашин *adj* pasha's; пашина ќерка pasha's daughter

пашиница *f* pasha's wife

пашински *adj* pasha's; of pashas; царски и пашински синови sons of tsars and pashas

пашит & пашитен -тна *adj* **1** (*за коњ, добиче*) free-grazing, untethered **2** *fig.* free; ❏ пашито добиче free; independent

пашица *f see* пашиница

пашка *impf* **1** to pursue, chase **2** to mistreat, abuse; to bully

пашов *adj see* пашин

пашовица *f see* пашиница

паштерка *f* stepdaughter; ❏ колне како маштеа паштерка she has a vicious tongue

паштета *f* meat/fish paste, pâté; свинска паштета pork pâté

паштрнак *m Bot.* (Pastinaca sativa) parsnip

ПДП *abbr.* (*Партија на демократскиот просперитет*) Party of Democratic Prosperity

пеан *pt* sung; *f.p.* learned; literate; пеан гроб grave over which a requiem has been sung

пеанија -ии *f* **1** *arch.* church singing (chanting) **2** *fig.*, *colloq.* homilies; preachifying

певец -вци *m literary* singer; chorister; оперски певец opera singer

певица *f* (*fem. form*) *see* певец

певница *f* choir (*section of church*), choir-stalls

пегла¹ *f* iron, flat-iron

пегла² *impf* **1** to iron, press **2** *fig.*, *colloq.* to scold, chide, berate

педа *f* span; nine inches; долг три педи three spans long; ❏ ни <за> педа не попушта not to yield an inch; педа човек a tiny person, dwarf, pigmy

педаго́г -зи *m* teacher, pedagogue

педагогија & rarely педагогика *f* pedagogy, teaching

педагошки *adj* pedagogical, teaching; педагошки кадри teaching staff

педа́л *m* pedal

педа́нт *m* pedant; hair-splitter

педа́нтен -тна *adj* pedantic; fastidious

педантерија *f see* педантност

педанти́зам -змот *m see* педантност

педа́нтност *f* pedantry; fastidiousness

педер & педера́ст *m* pederast; homosexual; *colloq.* gay

педерастија *f* pederasty; homosexuality

педесет *num* fifty

педесетгодишен -шна *adj* of fifty years; педесет-годишна жена a woman of fifty; педесетгодишна работа fifty years' work; a labour of fifty years

педесетгодишнина *f* fiftieth anniversary; педесет-годишнината на Илинденското востание the fiftieth anniversary of the *Ilinden* uprising (*St Elias' Day, 2nd August 1903*)

педесетина *num* about fifty; село со педесетина куќи a village with about fifty houses

педесетмина *num* a group of fifty

Педесетница *f Rel.* Pentecost, Whitsun

педесетти *adj num* fiftieth; во педесеттите години in the fifties (*of a given century*)

педигре́ *n* pedigree

педија́тар -три *m Med.* paediatrician

педијатрија *f Med.* paediatrics

педијатриски *adj Med.* paediatric

педике́р *m* chiropodist, *Am.* podiatrist

педике́рка *f* (*fem. form*) *see* педикер

педике́рски *adj* chiropodist's

педики́ра *pf & impf* to practise chiropody; to treat, take care of the feet

педику́ра *f* pedicure, chiropody

педофи́л *m* paedophile, child molester

педофили́ја *f* paedophilia

пее *impf* 1 to sing; *fig., literary* to praise in verse, hymn, sing of; пее песна to sing a song; *fig.* сѐ пееше во него his heart was singing; ❑ ако ти пее петлето 1. if things go well 2. if you have the knack, . . . ; рано пиле рано пее *prov.* the early bird catches the worm 2 to celebrate a requiem mass; пее гроб to perform requiem rites over a grave 3 *arch.* to read; го пеел весникот he was reading the newspaper 4 *arch.* to write *intrans.*; така пее книгата thus says the book 5 *colloq.* to scold, reprimand; to advise II – **се** (*with dat.*) ми се пее I feel like singing

пеење *n* 1 singing; хорско пеење choral singing 2 *literary* poem, canto 3 *arch.* reading; writing 4 celebration of a requiem over a grave 5 *arch.* prayer reading (*for health, recovery, etc.*)

пезевенк -ци *m* 1 *arch.* procurer, pimp 2 *colloq.* scoundrel

пезе́та *f* peseta

пејач *m* singer; оперски пејач opera singer

пејачка *f* (*fem. form*) *see* пејач, певица

пејачки *adj* singing; пејачки хор choir, chorus; пејачко друштво vocal group

пејза́ж *m* landscape; scenery; *Art* landscape

пејзажи́ст *m* landscape painter

пејовит *adj f.p.* that sings beautifully; ringing; пиле пејовито songbird

пејорати́в *m* *Gram.* pejorative

пејорати́вен -вна *adj* pejorative; abusive

пејсмејкер *m* pacemaker

пек *m* great heat, heatwave; ❑ Свети Илиев пек, илински пек great heat (*frequent in Macedonia round St Elias' Day, 2nd August*)

пека *impf* 1 (*with dat.*) to implore, beseech with tears; ѝ пекал на мајка си да му купи балон he begged his mother to buy him a balloon 2 *fig.* to long for, desire, cry out for; земјава пека за вода this earth is crying out for water; ❑ пека за ќотек he's asking for a beating

пекар *m* baker; pastry-cook

пекарница *f* bakery, bakehouse; градска пекарница town bakery; парна пекарница steam bakery

пекарски *adj* baker's; пекарски занает baker's trade

Пекинг *m* Peking (Beijing)

пекинѓанец -ни *m* person from Peking (Beijing)

пекинѓанка *f* (*fem. form*) *see* пекинѓанец

пекиншки *adj* Peking (Beijing) *attrib.*, Pekingese

пекмез *m* jam; пекмез од сливи plum jam

пекол *m* hell; inferno; рајот и пеколот heaven and hell

пеколен -лна *adj* hellish; пеколен оган hell-fire; пеколни маки hellish torment<s>

пеколски *adj* *see* пеколен

пексимид *m* Melba toast, fairy bread

пелена *f* baby's napkin (nappy), *Am.* diaper; дете во пелени a child in nappies; ❑ уште од пелени го знае he's known him since he was in nappies

пеленаче *n* (*бебе*) baby, newborn child

пеленица, пеленичка *f* & **пеленче** *n* *hyp. of* пелена

пелери́на *f* pelerine, cape

пеливан *m* 1 prize-fighter, all-in wrestler 2 hero,

knight 3 acrobat, tightrope-walker; ❑ повели ако си пеливан! go ahead, if you dare

пеливанлак -ци *m* *colloq.* *see* пеливанство; ❑ ќе ми продава пеливанлак he's trying to make a heroic impression

пеливански *adj* fighter's, wrestler's; пеливански борби wrestling matches; ❑ срце пеливанско heart of a hero

пеливанство *n* 1 fighting, wrestling 2 *fig.* skill, ability; political nous 3 heroism 4 acrobatics, tightrope-walking

пелика́н *m* *Zool.* (Pelecanus) pelican

пелин *m* 1 *Bot.* (Artemisia absinthium) wormwood ; ❑ горчи како пелин as bitter as wormwood; 2 *fig.* poison; bitterness; пелин му е во душава his soul is full of bitterness

пелинач *m* kind of vermouth (*flavoured with wormwood*)

пелинковец *m* wormwood brandy

пелинов *adj* wormwood *attrib.*; пелиново вино a kind of vermouth; пелинова вода wormwood-flavoured water (*folk remedy for loss of appetite, etc.*)

пелиноса *pf* *colloq.* I 1 to season (flavour) with wormwood 2 *fig.* to poison II – **се** *fig.* to become embittered

пелиносува *impf of* пелиноса I 1

пелцер *m* scion, shoot

пелцува *pf* & *impf* 1 to vaccinate 2 to graft

пелте *n* fruit jelly

пембе, пембелија *adj indecl.* & **пембен** *adj colloq.* pink, pale red; пембе боја peach colour

пен *m* 1 (*пенушка*, *ќутук*) tree-stump, short log; гнил пен rotten stump; ❑ како два пена like two tree-stumps (*said of a childless couple*); стариот пен посилно гори (*подолго тлее*) *prov.* there's many a good tune played on an old fiddle 2 *fig.* dolt, blockhead

пена *f* foam, froth, spume, lather; пена од пиво head on beer; пена од сапун soap-suds; вино без пена still wine; коњот е сиот в пена the horse is all in a lather; ❑ морска пена 1. spume, surf 2. (*минерал*) meerschaum; со пена на устата foaming at the mouth (*full of malice, enraged*); устата му фати пена he started fuming with rage/frustration/impatience

пена́л *m* 1 *Sport.* penalty kick 2 *pl Comm.* <penalty> fines

пендрек -ци *m* *colloq.* club, truncheon, *Am.* nightstick

пенест *adj* foamy, frothy

пенетраци́ја *f* penetration

пензи́ја -ии *f* pension; retirement; старосна/инвалидска пензија old-age/invalid pension; оди во пензија to retire

пензио́нен -она *adj* pension; пензионен фонд pension fund, superannuation fund

пензионе́р *m* pensioner

пензионе́рка *f* (*fem. form*) *see* пензионер

пензионе́рски *adj* pensioner's

пензиони́ра *pf* & *impf* I to pension; to pension off, retire *trans.* II – **се** to retire *intrans.* on a pension

пензиски *adj* pension; pensionable; pensionary; пензиски стаж pensionable period (*of service*)

пени *impf* I 1 to stir up; to cause to lather 2 *intrans. see* II 1 II – **се** 1 to foam, froth, bubble; to seethe; виното се пени the wine is sparkling; *fig.* се пени од јад (бес) to seethe with rage (fury) **2** *fig.* to grimace, make faces

пенис *m Anat.* penis

пеницили́н *m* penicillin

пеницили́нски *adj* penicillin; пеницилинска маст penicillin ointment

пенкало *n* (*со мастило*) fountain-pen; (*хемиско*) ball-point pen, Biro

пенлив *adj* foaming, frothy; bubbly; пенливо вино sparkling wine; пенлив сапун lathering soap

пенливост *f* foaming, lathering quality

пенушица *f Bot.* (Teucrium chamaedrys) wall germander

пенушка *f* **1** tree-stump **2** vine plant; vine stock **3** *fig.*, *colloq.* crone, hag **4** *fig.*, *colloq.* lonely, friendless person

пенче & *rarely* **пенце** *n* sole; удри пенчиња на чевли to resole shoes

пенчети́ра *impf* to sole, resole

пенцер *m f.p. see* пенцере

пенцере *n colloq.* window, *see* прозорец

пенцерче *n colloq. dim. of* пенцере; ❑ си оставил пенцерче he left himself a loophole

пења *f see* пена

пењави (се) *impf see* пени (се); ❑ пењави се, не пењави се, пари сум дал, ќе те јадам *joc.* like it or lump it

пењоа́р *m* (*woman's*) dressing-gown, peignoir

пењушка *f see* пенушка

пепел *m & f* **1** ashes; жарта и пепелта embers and ashes; ❑ тури му пепел (*на нешто*) give it up, write it off; му ја изгребал дури и пепелта од огништето he bled him white; го сторил (направил) прав и пепел 1. he reduced it to nothing 2. he crushed him; *literary* си ја потура (посипува) главата со пепел to put on sackcloth and ashes; му фрли пепел в<о> очи<те> he threw dust in his eyes; ни пепел нема во очите he is utterly destitute **2** *colloq.* dust

пепелав *adj* **1** covered with ashes; ❑ пепелаво жарче treacherous, underhand person; пепелаво жарче рана отвора *prov.* the hardest blow is dealt by a hidden foe **2** *rare* dusty **3** ash-grey, ashen

пепеланка *f Zool.* (Vipera berus) common adder, viper

пепелар *m arch.* ash-merchant

пепеларка *f arch.* ash-merchant's wife

пепелашка *f* <Мара> Пепелашка Cinderella

пеп<е>лиште *n* **1** site of a fire, burnt-out place; cinders **2** *fig.* family home, hearth and home **3** large dust-cloud, dust-storm

пепелник -ци *m* ash heap

пепелница *f* **1** lye, *see* лука **2** ashtray **3** rust fungus, wheat rust, *see* пламеница

пеп<е>лоса *pf* **I** **1** *arch.* to turn to ashes *trans.* **2** *fig.* to cause to turn pale **II** – **се** **1** *arch.* to turn into ashes *intrans.* **2** *fig.* to go as white as a sheet

пеп<е>лосан *adj fig.* very pale, as white as a sheet; ashen-faced

пеперуга *f* **1** *Zool.* butterfly; ноќна пеперуга moth; пеперуги (Lepidoptera) the butterfly family **2** *Bot.* (Iris germanica) blue (German) iris **2** *Bot. dial.* (Papaver rhoeas) red poppy, corn poppy

пеперуда *f dial. see* пеперуга, пеперутка

пеперуже *n dim. of* пеперуга

пеперужен -жна *adj rare* butterfly<'s>; butterfly-like; пеперужни крилја butterfly wings; пеперужни растенија *Bot.* (Papilionaceae) papilionaceous plants

пеперутка *f see* пеперуга

пеперутче *n dim. of* пеперутка

пеперушка *f* **1** *dim. of* пеперуга **2** *literary* bow-tie

пепито *n & adj indecl.* hound's-tooth (*pattern*)

пепсин *m* pepsin

пер *m Hist.* peer, nobleman

перален -лна *adj see* ператен; перална машина washing-machine

пералиште *n* washing (laundering) place (*on river bank*)

пералник -ци *m* copper, wash-boiler

пералница *f* laundry (*room*)

перало *n* **1** linen, laundry **2** *see* пералиште

пператен -тна *adj* washing; пператен сапун laundry soap; пературна машина washing-machine

перач *m* launderer, laundryman

перачка *f* laundress, washerwoman

перачница *f see* пералница

перваз *m* (*на прозорец*) ledge, sill; (*на ѕид*) cornice; (*на слика*) frame; (*на шешир*) brim; шешир со широк перваз broad-brimmed hat

перверзен -зна *adj* perverted

перверзија -ии *f* perversion

перверзност *f see* перверзија

пергаме́нт *m* parchment; greaseproof paper

пергаме́нтен -тна *adj* parchment; пергаментни листови parchment sheets; пергаментна хартија parchment paper

пердаши *impf colloq.* to batter, thrash, hammer, wallop

перде *n colloq.* **1** curtain; blind; drape **2** veil, *see* превез; ❑ му клале перде на очи they pulled the wool over his eyes **3** membrane; *fig.* maidenhood, virginity; innocence; ❑ нема ни срам, ни перде he is quite brazen; му пукнало пердето he's lost all sense of shame **4** *Med.* (*катаракт, мрежа*) cataract **2** *dial.* fence; бавча со перде fenced garden

пердув *m* feather<s>, down; *coll.* feathers, plumage; јорган наполнет со пердуви quilt stuffed with down; ❑ лесен како пердув light as a feather; ќе летаат пердуви there'll be trouble

пердувен -вна, **пердувест** & **пердушест** *adj* downy; fleecy

пердувче *n dim. of* пердув

пердушка *f* **1** *see* пердув **2** plume; tuft; feather duster

пере *impf* **I** to launder, wash; ❑ пере (*некому*) мозок to brainwash (*s.o.*); него ништо не го пере nothing can save him; не го пере ни Вардар ни Брегалница there's no hope for him **II** – **се** **1** to do one's washing; сам се пере he does his washing himself **2** to wash off, come out (*of a stain*)

перест *adj* (*за лисја*) pinnate

перестро́јка *f* perestroika (*restructuring process in former USSR*)

перештец *m Med.* dry eczema

периз *m arch.* diet; abstinence; држи периз to fast; ❑ нема периз <на устата> he doesn't take care what he says (he lacks tact)

перика *f* wig

перикарди́т<ис> *m Med.* pericarditis

периме́тар -три *m* perimeter

период *m* **1** period; повоениот период the post-war period; дождовен период rainy period; поминува низ тежок период to go through a bad patch **2** *Math.* period (*recurring decimal number*) **3** *Gram.* period (*long complex sentence*)

периода *f rare* period, time of menstruation, *see* менструација

периодизација *f* periodization

периодичен -чна *adj* periodic, periodical; периодични кризи periodic (recurrent) crises; *Chem.* периодичниот систем на елементите the periodic table of the elements; периодичен печат periodical press; периодично издание periodical <publication>

периодички *adj see* периодичен

периодично *adv* periodically

периодичност *f* periodical character

периодски *adj rare see* периодички

перипетија -ии *f* (*usu. pl*) peripeteia, vicissitude; troubles, problems

перископ *m* periscope

перистил *m* peristyle

перитони́т<ис> *m Med.* peritonitis

перифе́рен -рна *adj* peripheral; suburban; периферни центри suburban centres

периферија *f* periphery; outlying districts; на периферијата на градот on the outskirts of the city; периферија на круг circumference of a circle

перифериски *adj* peripheral; перифериски нервен систем peripheral nervous system

перифра́за *f* periphrasis, circumlocution

перифрази́ра <се> *pf & impf* to express o.s. at length, clumsily

перјан *adj* feather; перјани душеци feather mattresses

перјаница *f* feather head-dress; plume; *Hist.* panache

перка *f* **1** (*на риба*) fin **2** (*на воденично тркало*) paddle **3** (*на пченка*) leaf of maize **4** *rare* propeller **5** (*на тркало*) spoke **6** (*за пливање*) (*usu. pl*) flippers, fins

перкија *f Zool.* (Perca fluviatilis) perch

перкусија *f Med.* percussion

перкусио́нен -она *adj Med.* percussive

перкути́ра *pf & impf Med.* to percuss

перла *f* **1** pearl; beads; necklace **2** *fig., iron.* treasure

перлон *m* Perlon (*type of nylon*)

пермане́нтен -тна *adj* permanent

пермане́нтност *f* permanence

пермутација -ии *f* permutation

пернат[1] *adj* feathered; перната живина poultry

пернат[2] *adj* **1** crazy, dotty, mad **2** *see* напернат

перне *pf aor.* **1** to hit, strike (*usu. suddenly*) **2** *colloq.* to put; перни му на гравот две-три пиперки add to the beans two or three capsicums

перница *f* pillow; cushion

перниче *n dim. of* перница

пернува *impf of* перне

перо -а, -је, -ја *n* **1** (*pl* перје, перја) feather; plume; пауново перо peacock's feather; менување на перјето (перјата) moult; ❏ лесен како перо as light as a feather; *literary* се кити со туѓи перје (перја) to deck o.s. in borrowed plumes **2** (*pl* пера) pen; nib; челично перо steel nib; *Hist.* гускино перо quill <-pen>; ❏ со еден потег на перото with one stroke of the pen; има лесно перо he writes easily; од перото на Достоевски from the pen of Dostoyevsky; силен (јак) е на перо he is a very powerful writer; живее од перото he lives by writing; човек на перото a man of letters; сатирично перо satirical writer; продадено перо writer for money; venal journalist **3** (*pl* пера, перје, перја) green leaf (*of leek, garlic, onion, beetroot*) **4** (*pl* пера, перје, перја) fin, *see* перка 1

перодршка *f* penholder, pen

перон *m* <station> platform

пероноспо́ра *f* rust fungus

перонски *adj* platform; перонска карта, перонски билет platform ticket

перпендикула́р *m & перпендикула́ра* *f Geom.* perpendicular, vertical

перпендикула́рен -рна *adj* perpendicular, vertical, upright

перпе́рица *f dial., f.p. see* препелица

перпе́туум-мо́биле *m & n literary* perpetual motion, perpetuum mobile

Персиец -ијци *m* Persian

Персија *f* Persia

Персијка *f* (*fem. form*) *see* Персиец

персифла́жа *f literary* persiflage, banter

перси́ра *pf & impf* to address s.o. in second person plural (polite form)

персиски *adj* Persian

персо́на *f literary, iron.* person; personality; persona; персона грата *Diplomacy* persona grata

персона́л *m* staff, personnel; персонал на болница hospital staff; технички персонал technical staff

персона́лен -лна *adj* staff, personnel; personal; персонален состав personnel; персонална унија (*на две држави*) personal union (*of two states*)

персона́лец -лци *m colloq.* personnel manager

персонификација *f* personification; embodiment; incarnation, *see* олицетворение

персонификува & персонифици́ра *pf & impf* to personify, embody, *see* олицетвори, олицетворува

перспекти́ва *f* **1** perspective; од птичја перспектива from a bird's-eye view, from above; од жабја перспектива from below **2** vista, prospect **3** *fig.* prospect, outlook, perspective; перспективи за понатамошен развој perspectives of further development; ❏ во перспектива in the future, in prospect

перспекти́вен -вна *adj* **1** *Art* perspective **2** *fig.* forward-looking; prospective; перспективен план long-term plan **3** *fig.* promising, having prospects; перспективен студент promising student

перспекти́вно *adv* in prospect; ❏ перспективно гледано looking <optimistically> to the future

перспекти́вност *f* promising nature, promise

пертурбација -ии *f* perturbation; доживеал многу пертурбации he has experienced many upsets

Перу *n* Peru

Перуанец -нци *m* Peruvian

Перуанка *f* (*fem. form*) *see* Перуанец

перуански *adj* Peruvian

перуника *f Bot.* (Iris germanica) (*blue, purple*) iris

перустија -ии *f dial. see* пирустија

перу́кец *m dial. see* перештец

перушка *f* **1** *see* пердушка **2** *see* перка 1

перфект *m Gram.* perfect tense; (*in Macedonian*) past indefinite tense

перфектен -тна *adj* **1** (*совршен*) faultless, perfect, irreproachable, excellent, masterly, superb; перфектен учебник excellent textbook **2** *Gram.* perfect; перфектна основа perfect stem

перфекти́вен -вна *adj Gram.* (*свршен*) perfective; перфективни глаголи perfective verbs

перфе́ктно *adv* perfectly, irreproachably, excellently, superbly; зборува перфектно руски he speaks perfect Russian

перфи́ден -дна *adj* perfidious, deceitful; treacherous

перфи́дност *f* perfidy, deceit; treachery

перфора́тор *m* perforator; punch

перфора́ција *f* perforation

перфори́ра *pf & impf* to perforate

пер́це *n dim. of* перо

перце́пција -ии *f Psychol.* perception; observation, reception

перципи́ра *pf & impf* to perceive, observe, notice

пер́че *n* **1** tuft of hair; lock (*of hair*) **2** *Hist.* see перчин 1

пер́чи се *impf* to swagger, strut, puff o.s. up, show off, behave arrogantly

перчи́н *m* **1** *Hist.* plait (*on crown of head*), pigtail; ❑ го држи за перчин he's got him where he wants him **2** *fig.* silk (*silky styles of female maize-flower found on corn-cobs*), *Am.* corn silk

пес *m*, пци, пци́шта & *dial.* песо́ви *pl* (*see* куче) **1** *Zool.* dog; овчарски пес sheep-dog; верен пес faithful dog; ❑ тоа ни пците не го јадат no one would swallow that story; се јадат како пци they fight like cat and dog; кога беше волкот пес never; when pigs fly; пес да врзеш, не седи it's freezing; поминал како пците на Василица life was very hard for him; гладен како пес hungry as a wolf; уморен како пес dog-tired; пес од касапница мачно се одделува *prov.* old habits die hard **2** *fig.* cur; beast, brute

песими́зам -змот *m* pessimism

песими́ст *m* pessimist

песимисти́чен -чна & **песимисти́чки** *adj* pessimistic

песими́стка *f* (*fem. form*) see песимист

песја́к -ци *m* **1** canine tooth, eye-tooth **2** *fig.* cur **3** *fig.* stubborn, pig-headed person

песја́чка *f* (*fem. form*) bitch, see песјак 2

пес<ј>и -ја *adj* (*кучешки*) dog's; песја трага dog's tracks; *fig.* песји живот dog's life; ❑ песји син son of a bitch; песи́ нокти cuticle; песи́ дрен *Bot.* (Cornus sanguinea) common (red) dogwood

песна *f* **1** song; народна песна folk-song; црковни песни hymns, church singing; славеева песна nightingale's song; приспивна песна lullaby; ❑ си ја испеа песната his song is sung, his career is over; сè таа (сè една и иста) песна пее to harp on the same string; друга песна пее to change one's tune; лебедова песна swansong **2** poem; verse; canto; збирка песни collection of poems; првата песна на "Илијада" the first book of the "Iliad"; ❑ песна над песните Song of Songs; masterpiece

песна́рија -ии *m & f colloq.* see песнопоец, песнопо́јка

песна́рка *f* song-book

песна́тар *m see* песнопоец

песни́чка *f dim. of* песна; ditty, rhyme

песнопо́ец -јци *m* folk-singer

песнопо́јка *f* (*fem. form*) see песнопоец

песогла́в *adj* **1** ugly, hideous **2** *fig.* obstinate, headstrong; independent, self-willed

песогла́вец -вци *m* **1** (*во народните приказни*) monster (*with the head of a dog, one eye in its forehead and another in the back of its head*) **2** *fig.* obstinate, pigheaded person

песо́к -ци *m & more rarely f* sand; зрно песок a grain of sand; ❑ жив песок quicksand; *Med.* песок во бубрезите renal gravel; како песокот во море like the sands of the sea, innumerable; *f.p.* дробната песок број нема untold numbers; тура песок в море to waste time, plough the sands; му фрли песок (пепел) в очи he threw dust in his eyes; гради (прави кули) на песок he is building on sand

песо́клив *adj* sandy; песоклива земја sandy soil

песо́кливост *f* sandiness

песо́са се *pf fig.* to turn nasty, malicious

песо́сан *adj fig.* obnoxious, evil-tempered; песосан човек spiteful person

песо́саност *f* anger, ill temper, malice, malevolence

песо́сува се *impf of* песоса се

песо́ча *f arch. see* коритница

песо́чен -чна *adj* sand; песочно зрно grain of sand; песочни бури sandstorms; ❑ песочен саат sandglass, hourglass

песо́чина *f* sandy place; sand bar, sandbank

песо́чинка *f dim. of* песочина

песо́чиште *n* sandy terrain

песо́чник -ци *m* **1** sandstone; слој од песочник stratum of sandstone **2** sand-glass, hourglass

песо́чница *f Hist.* sandbox (*formerly used for drying ink*)

пет *num* five; пет пати five times; пет метра five metres; петте сестри the/all five sisters; во петте часот at five o'clock; пет години five years; два по пет прави десет twice five are ten; ❑ пет стечи, пет испечи spend according to your income; по пет за грош му оди he's afraid, he doesn't dare; ни пет ни шест without much thought, without any hesitation; wasting no time; пет пари не дава he doesn't care a fig; кога ќе дојдат моите пет минути when my turn comes

пета *f see* петица; ❑ *literary* Ахилова пета Achilles' heel, the weakest point

пета́к -ци *m arch. see* петаче

пета́ло *n arch.*, *dial. see* потковаı

пета́рда *f* firework, *Am.* firecracker, petard

пета́че *n arch.* five-para piece (coin)

петвеко́вен -вна *adj* five-century old; lasting five centuries

петгоди́шен -шна *adj* **1** five years old; петгодишно девојче a five-year-old girl, a girl of five **2** lasting five years; петгодишен план five-year plan

петгоди́шнина *f* fifth anniversary

петдне́вен -вна *adj* five-day; петдневен излет a five-day excursion

пе́тел -тли *m* **1** *Zool.* cock, rooster; петелот пее (кукурига) the cock crows; скопен петел capon; ❑ нему и петлите јајца му несат he has all the luck; <крај> кај што петли не пеат remote (out-of-the-way) place; му пее петелот his word is law; кога ќе ги стрижеме петлите never; when pigs fly; кај што петли пеат the back of beyond; стар петел old hand, man of the world; се дуе како петел на буниште to act the cock of the walk; два петла на едно буниште не пеат *prov.* a house can't have two masters; сто пари петел, пет гроша крчма *prov.* the game is not worth the candle **2** (*only pl*) cock-crow; ❑ легнува со кокошките, ама станува со петлите to rise with the lark and go to bed with the lamb **3** *see* калауз 5

петели се *impf* to show off, brag, strut

петелка *f* **1** (*илика*) buttonhole **2** stalk, stem

петен -тна *adj* heel; петни жили heel tendons; ❑ запне од петни жили to try with all one's might; to strain every nerve

петина *num* (*of men and mixed groups*) five; дома сме петина at home there are five of us; петина тетина Петка не чекаат *prov.* five people don't wait for one

петит *m* Print. brevier (*small printing font, 8-point*)

петица *f* heel; го доболеле петиците his heels started aching; гази на петици he walks on his heels; ❑ од глава до петици; од врв глава до петици from head to foot, completely; му слегло срцето в петици his heart sank to his boots; <коса> до петици <hair> to the floor; тој му е (му оди) по петиците he is at his heels, he follows him around; зад петици е некому to breathe down s.o.'s neck

петиција -ии *f* petition

петичен -чна *adj* of heels; петични стапалки traces of heels

петка *f* **1** five **2** *colloq.* <number> five (*bus, etc.*) **3** (*школска оценка*) top mark, 'A' (*in primary and secondary schools*), five (*out of five, hence = excellent*); сите оценки му се петки all his marks are 'A's **4** five (*out of ten*), Fail (*mark for an examination failure in tertiary institutions*) **5** (*во карти, на зар*) five

петкамен *m* five-stones, jacks (*children's game in which five pebbles are thrown into the air and caught in one hand*)

петкатен -тна *adj* **1** five-storey, five-floor; петкатна зграда five-storey building **2** fivefold; five-times; *Sport.* петкатен првенец five-times champion

петкатница *f* five-storey building

петла *impf* **I** to hook; to button up *trans.* **II** – ce to button up *intrans.*; *see* запетлува (ce)

петле *n* **1** (*dim. of* петел) cockerel; ❑ не му пее петлето 1. he's not having much luck 2. nobody takes any notice of him; ако ти пее петлето *see* пее 1; *joc.* кусо петле shorty (*s.o. short in stature*) **2** (*на пушка, револвер*) trigger **3** *colloq. napoleon* (*d'or*), old French gold coin

петленце *n dim. of* петле

петлетен -тна *adj literary* five-year, lasting five years; five years old

петлица *f* button; ❑ солзи како петлици large tears

петличе *n dim. of* петлица

петлиште *n augm. of* петел

петлов *adj* cock's; петлово перо 1. cock's feather 2. *Bot.* (Achillea coarctata) kind of yarrow (milfoil)

петлошиец *m colloq., iron.* man with a strong, thick neck

петмесечен -чна *adj* **1** of five months, five months old; петмесечно бебе a five-month-old baby **2** lasting, spanning five months; петмесечен извештај a five-monthly report

петмина *num see* петина

петнаесет *num* fifteen

петнаесетгодишен -шна *adj* **1** fifteen years old **2** lasting fifteen years

петнаесетгодишнина *f* fifteenth anniversary

петнаесетднèвен -вна *adj* **1** lasting fifteen days; петнаесетдневен семинар a fifteen-day (fortnight long) seminar **2** fortnightly; петнаесетдневен весник fortnightly newspaper

петнаесетина *num* about fifteen; петнаесетина куќи some fifteen houses

петнаесетмина *num* (*of men and mixed groups*) fifteen

петнаесетти *adj num* fifteenth

петнаести *adj num colloq. see* петнаесетти

петнеделен -лна *adj* lasting five weeks

петно *n literary* **1** spot, blot, stain, *see* дамка **2** *fig.* blemish, stain; ❑ фрли петно врз ... to cast a slur on ...

петоаголен -лна *adj* pentagonal

петоаголник -ци *m* pentagon

петоглав *adj literary* five-headed; петоглаво чудовиште five-headed monster

петоделен -лна *adj* five-part; *Mus.* петоделни тактови quintuple (five beat) time, five in a bar

петок -ци *m* Friday; во петок, во петоците on Fridays, every Friday; в петок on Friday, next Friday; во петокот last Friday; спроти петок on Thursday evening/night; ❑ вели петок, Велипеток Good Friday; ќе му дојде и нему црн петок he will meet his match (Waterloo); како петок и сабота like twins (bread and butter; horse and carriage)

петокнижие & петокнижје *n Rel.* Pentateuch

петокрак *adj* five-pointed; ❑ петокрака ѕвезда five-pointed star; (*as noun*) петокрака<та> <the> five-pointed star

петолетен -тна *adj literary see* петлетен

петолиние -ија *n literary, rare Mus.* five-line notation system

петолист & rarely петолистен -сна *adj Bot.* five-petal, pentamerous; петолист цвет five-petal flower

петопрсница *f & петопрст m Bot. see* јаглика, јагличе

петопрст & rarely петопрстен -сна *adj* five-finger<ed>

петорен -рна *adj* fivefold, *see* петкатен 2

петорка *f* group of five

петосложен -жна *adj* pentasyllabic; петосложен збор five-syllable (pentasyllabic) word

петособен -бна *adj* five-room; петособен стан a five-room flat

петострук *adj rare, dial.* fivefold; five-times, *see* петкатен, петорен

петочен -чна *adj* Friday; петочен ден Friday

петочлен *adj* five-member; петочлена комисија five-member committee

петпати *adv* (*see* пат[2]) five times

петрев & петров *adj* **1** *Bot.* (*part of the name of several mountain flowers*) петреви гаќи (Corydalis bulbosa/cava/solida) common fumatory; петров крст 1. (Paris quadrifolia) herb Paris 2. (Lilium bulbiferum) yellow (golden) lily **2** (*only as* петров) *see* петровденски, петровски; ❑ Петрова недела the week of St Peter's Day; Петрови жеги St Peter's Day heatwave

петрефàкт *m* petrifaction, fossil

петрифицѝра *pf & impf* to become fossilized, turn to stone; *fig.* to become obsolete, archaic; петрифицирана форма petrified, fossilized form (*in a language*)

Петровден *m Rel.* St Peter's Day (*12th July*)

петровденски *adj* St Peter's Day (*festivities, etc.*)

петровка *f* **1** early apple<s>, pear<s>, plum<s>, etc. (*which ripen about about 12th July, St Peter's Day*) **2** коковчица петровка pullet

петровски *adj rare see* петровденски; петровско јаболко *see* петровка 1; ❑ петровски жеги (горештини) *see* петрев 2, Петрови жеги

петрографија *f* petrography

петрографски *adj* petrographic<al>

петрол & петролеј *m* petroleum, oil; petrol (*Am.* gasoline); kerosene

петролејка *f* miner's lamp, Davy lamp

петролен -лна & **петролејски** *adj* petroleum, oil; петролејски извори oil wells

петстогодишнина *f* five-hundredth anniversary

петстотини *num* five hundred

петти *adj num* fifth; петти март fifth of March; петта глава fifth chapter; ❑ *Hist.* петта колона fifth column

петтина *f* fifth <part>; две петтини two fifths

петтокласник -ци *m obs.* fifth-form pupil

петтокласничка *f obs.* (*fem. form*) *see* петтокласник

петтоколонаш *m* fifth-columnist, traitor, spy

петтоколонаштво *n* fifth-column tendencies, activities

петчасовен -вна *adj* five-hour, of five hours; петчасовна борба five-hour battle

пет-шеесет *num* fifty to sixty

пет-шеснаесет *num* fifteen to (or) sixteen

пет-шест *num* five or six, a few; до селото има пет-шест километри it's a few (several) kilometres to the village; пет-шест милиони five to six million

пет-шестмина & пет-шестина *num* **1** <a group of> five or six men **2** (*of men and mixed groups*) five or six

пет-шестотини *num* five to six hundred

пехар *m* goblet, wineglass; *Sport.* cup

пецка *impf* **I** to sting, insult, be sarcastic (*to s.o.*) **II** – **се** to sting, insult one another

пецлив *adj* stinging, insulting, sarcastic, caustic

печал¹ *f arch., poet.* sorrow; longing; misery

печал² ** *m* & **печала *f arch. see* печалба

печалба *f* **1** emigration and work abroad; ❑ оди на печалба to go abroad to earn a living **2** (*заработка*) earnings, pay; имале голема печалба they earned good pay **3** *colloq.* (*добивка*) gain **4** *rarely* profit

печалбар *m* migrant worker; fortune-seeker

печалбари *impf* to work as a migrant worker

печалбарство *n* emigration and work abroad

печален -лна *adj arch., poet.* (*жален, тажен*) sad, gloomy; pitiful, miserable, wretched; печални останки pitiful remains

печали *impf* **I** **1** *intrans. & trans.* to earn, gain by work (labour); печали убава пара he earns good money; ❑ печали време to gain time; мачници печалеле, немачници јале *prov.* one sows, another reaps **2** to win in a game of chance **3** *see* **II** **II** – **се** to try, make an effort; to strive (*да – то*)

печалник -ци *m* good family man

печалница *f* good housewife, good home-maker

печат *m* **1** seal, stamp; postmark; ❑ чувар на државниот печат Keeper of the State Seal **2** *fig.* (*only sg*) trace, sign, imprint **3** print; ракописите се дадени во печат the manuscripts have been delivered to the printers; делото е излезено од печат the work is in print; готов за печат ready to print **4** <the> press; дневен печат daily press; слобода на печатот freedom of the press

печатар *m* printer

печатарски *adj* printer's, printing; печатарска машина printing-press; печатарска боја printer's ink

печатарство *n* the printing trade; typography

печатен -тна *adj* **1** printing; печатни <по>грешки misprints **2** printed; печатни и ракописни книги printed books and manuscripts; печатни букви capital letters, block capitals **3** sealing; печатен восок sealing-wax

печати *impf* **1** to print, publish **2** to stamp a seal; to seal

печатница *f* printing-office, print shop, printery; printing firm

печаторежач & печаторезач *m* seal engraver

печаторежачки & печаторезачки *adj* seal engraver's

печаторезница *f* seal-engraving workshop

пече¹ *n arch.*, black veil (*worn by Muslim women*)

пече² *impf* **I** **1** to bake; to roast; to grill *trans.*; пече леб to bake bread; пече месо to roast meat; ❑ вари го, печи го – тој си е he'll never change; не за кого е печено, ами за кого е речено *prov.* two dogs fight for a bone and a third runs away with it **2** to bake, fire, burn *trans.*; пече ќерамиди/тули to bake (fire) tiles/bricks; пече вар to heat (burn) lime **3** *dial.* (*вари*) пече ракија to distil *raki* **4** to burn, bake *trans.*; сонцето силно печеше the sun was very strong (fierce) **5** to sting, burn; раната ме пече my wound aches; пиперката ме пече во устава the capsicum burns my mouth **6** *fig.* совеста ме пече my conscience torments me **7** *impers.* (*with acc.*) ме пече во грлово I have a sore throat; ме пече во душава I feel very worried **8** to sun, warm (*one's body*) **II** – **се 1** to bake, roast, grill *intrans.* **2** to sun o.s., warm o.s.; ❑ *iron.* на едно сонце се печеле they're two of a kind; one's as bad as the other; they're cut from the same cloth

печен *pt* **1** baked, roast<ed>, grilled; печено јагне roast lamb; ❑ *iron.* да не сакаш печени кокошки? would you like that with caviar and cream? **2** (*as noun*) печено *n* roast, roast meat; свинско печено roast pork **3** baked, fired; печени тули fired bricks **4** *fig.* experienced, capable, skilled; ❑ печен, та дури препечен highly skilled, more than qualified **5** *fig.* finished; печен си you've had it, you're finished

печеник -ци *m dial. see* пешник

печеница *f Cul.* roast meat, roast

печенка *f dial. Bot.* (Cucurbita) kind of pumpkin

печиво *n* baked goods; roll, bun, croissant; прашак за печиво baking powder

печка *f* **1** (*heating or cooking*) stove; електрична печка electric heater; ја запалил печката he lit the stove **2** (*за руда и др.*) furnace; висока печка blast furnace; мартенов<ск>а печка open-hearth furnace

печок -ци *m* stunted, sickly person

печурка *f Bot.* mushroom, fungus; отровна печурка toadstool

печурник -ци *m* pie (*with spinach or other green vegetables and mushrooms*)

печурче *n* & **печурчица** *f dim. of* печурка

пеш[1] *m arch.* breast, front (*of an outer garment*); пешовите од антеријата the breast of a long-sleeved robe

пеш[2] *adj* pedestrian; оди пеш (*m*, пеша *f*, пешо *n*, пеши *pl*) to go on foot

пеш[3] *adv* on foot

пешадија -ии *f Mil.* infantry; поморска пешадија marines

пешадинец -нци *m Mil.* infantryman, *see* пешак 2

пешадиски *adj Mil.* infantry; пешадиски полк infantry regiment

пешак -ци *m* **1** pedestrian **2** *Mil.* infantryman **3** *Chess* pawn, *see* пион

пешачки *adj* pedestrian; infantry; пешачки премин pedestrian crossing

пеши *adv see* пеш[3]

пешкеш *m arch.* gift, present

пешки *adv see* пеш[3]

пешкир *m* **1** towel; ❑ фрла пешкир to throw in the towel **2** *dial.* apron **3** *colloq.* queer, fag, gay

пешник -ци *m* round flat loaf, foccacia, *Austral.* damper

пешт *m & f see* пештера

пештера *f* cave

пештерен -рна & **пештерски** *adj* cave *attrib.*; пештерно езеро underground lake; пештерни луѓе cave-dwellers; пештерска уметност cave paintings

пи-пи *interj* (*to call hens, etc.*) chick, chick, chick! chook! chook! chook!

пив *m* water-hole

пивара *f colloq. see* пиварница

пиварница *f* brewery

пиварски *adj* brewing; brewer's; пиварска индустрија brewing industry

пиварство *n* brewing

пивка[1] *adj* (*no m*) drinking, drinkable, potable; пивка вода drinking water; пивко вино palatable wine

пивка[2] *impf* to sip

пивка[3] *impf* (*usu. of chickens*) to cheep, peep, squeak

пивкост *f* potability

пивне *pf* пивна *aor.* to drink a little, sip; пивнал малку винце he drank a little wine

пивница *f* bar, pub, tavern

пивнува *impf of* пивне

пиво *n* **1** beer, ale; бело и црно пиво beer and stout **2** *dial.* drink (*usu. alcoholic*)

пивоквас *m* kvass

пивски *adj* beer *attrib.*; пивско шише beer bottle

пивтиест *adj* jelly-like, gelatinous

пивтија *f see* пача

пигмеј -еи *m* pygmy (*also fig.*)

пигмејски *adj* pygmy

пигмент *m* pigment

пигментација *f* pigmentation

пигментен -тна & **пигментски** *adj* pigmental; pigmentary

пие *impf* **I** **1** to drink; пие за нечија среќа to drink to s.o.'s happiness; ❑ во чаша да го пиеш he's gorgeous (really handsome); пие како смок to drink like a fish **2** *fig.* to absorb, soak up; сувата земја ја пие водата the dry earth soaks up the water; ❑ крвта ми ја пие he sucks my blood, he exploits me **3** *arch.* to smoke; пиеш тутун? do you smoke? **II – се** *impers.* (*with dat.*) to feel like drinking; ми се пие I feel like a drink

пиедеста́л *m* pedestal

пиење *n* **1** (*act of*) drinking; удриле едно пиење they started drinking heavily **2** *arch.* smoking; пиење тутун smoking **3** beverage, drink

пие́са *f* play; musical

пиете́т *m* esteem

пижа́ма *f* (*usu. pl*) pyjamas

пизма *f arch.* (*омраза*) hatred, spite; ❑ држи пизма, има пизма (*на некого*) to bear (nurse) a grudge (*against s.o.*)

пизми *impf arch.* **I** (*мрази*) to hate; to bear (nurse) a grudge against **II – се** to hate one another; правината и кривината се пизмат *prov.* justice and injustice don't agree

пијавица *f* **1** *Zool.* (Hirudo medicinalis) leech; ❑ се запил како некоја пијавица he started drinking heavily **2** *fig.* limpet **3** *fig.* exploiter, bloodsucker; leech **4** *Tech.* cramp-iron

пијалак -ци *m colloq.* drink (*usu. alcoholic*)

пијало *n colloq.* drink, beverage

пијан *adj* **1** drunk, intoxicated; пијан од радост drunk with joy; пијана состојба drunken state; ❑ мртов-пијан dead drunk; пијан како дрво (земја) drunk as a lord; пијан (дури) однесен blind drunk **2** (*as noun*) drunkard; drunk; ❑ се држи како пијан за плот he holds on like a drunk to a fence

пијанец *m Bot.* (Lolium temulentum) bearded darnel

пијани се *impf* to get drunk, become intoxicated

пијани́но *m Mus.* piano

пијанисимо *adv Mus.* pianissimo

пијани́ст *m Mus.* pianist

пијанистички *adj* pianist's; pianistic; piano; пијанистички концерт piano concert

пијани́стка *f* (*fem. form*) *see* пијанист

пијаница *m & f* drunkard, sot, tippler; голем пијаница heavy drinker

пијаничиште *n augm.* (*of* пијаница) heavy drinker

пијанка *f* **1** *Bot. see* пијанец **2** *colloq.* spree; *sl.* binge, booze-up

пија́но[1] *n Mus.* piano

пија́но[2] *adv Mus.* piano, softly

пијанство *n* drinking; drunkenness; intoxication; го сторил на пијанство he was drunk when he did it

пијач *m colloq.* drinker, drunkard, toss-pot

пијачка *f* **1** beverage, drink; алкохолни пијачки alcoholic drinks (liquor) **2** revelry, carousal

пик[1] *m* **1** pike, lance **2** spades; дама пик queen of spades

пик[2] *m* pique; *only in the expression:* има пик на некого to have a grudge against s.o.

пик[3] *m* **1** mountain peak **2** *Naut.* (*во клунот*) forepeak; (*во крмата*) after-peak

пика (се) *impf see* пикне (се); ❑ пика нешто некому под нос to shove s.th. under s.o.'s nose; не пикај си го носот! don't stick your nose in! му се пика под кожа he is trying to butter him up; не пикај се невикан! don't barge in when you're not invited!

пикадо́р *m* picador

пика́тен -тна *adj* **1** piquant, savoury **2** *fig.* spicy, racy, shocking, saucy, piquant; пикантни приказни *risqué* stories

пикантерија -ии *f* spicy story

пика́нтност *f* piquancy

пикет   *m* **1** piquet (*card-game*) **2** picket (*enforcing strike action*) **3** <surveyor's> stake

пики́ра   *pf & impf* **1** to dive (*of aircraft*) **2** пикира на некого to pick on s.o. **3** пикира на нешто to have one's eye on s.th.

пикне   *pf* пикна *aor.* **I 1** to cram, thrust, stuff in; *trans.*; ги пикнал рацете в џеб he pushed his hands into his pocket **2** *fig.*, *colloq.* to push s.o. (*into some position or job*) **II – се** to push (*o.s.*) in , shove in, intrude *intrans.*; ❑ во волов рог да се пикнеш, пак ќе те најдам wherever you hide I'll find you

пикник   -ци *m* (*излет*) picnic

пикнува (се)   *impf of* пикне (се)

пиков   *adj* <of> spades; пикова дама queen of spades

пикола   *f* **1** small mouth-organ, harmonica **2** piccolo

пила   *f* **1** saw; рачна (ракатна) пила handsaw **2** primitive sawmill

пилав   *m Cul.* pilaff (pilau, pilaw); со лаф (збор, зборови) пилав не се прави *prov.* actions speak louder than words

пила́на   *f* sawmill; парна пилана steam sawmill

пилаф   *m see* пилав

пиле   -иња, -лци & *rarely* -ишта *n* **1** *Zool.* chicken, chick; ❑ се заплеткал како пиле во колчишта he got tied in knots **2** *hyp. fig.* dear, darling; пиле мое my darling **3** (*usu. pl* пилци) nestling, baby bird, fledg<e->ling; *fig.* brood, children **4** (*usu. pl* пилци) bird (*usu. small*); шумско (горско) пиле woodland bird; седело без пилци empty nest (*also fig.*); ❑ млеко пигеон's milk; има од пиле млеко he has/ there is everything one could wish for; не дава пиле да прелета nothing can get past him; како пиле на гранче as free as a bird; каде пиле не пее the back of beyond; рано пиле рано пее *prov.* the early bird catches the worm **5** *colloq.*, *Cul.* chicken <meat> **6** *dial.* metal decoration (*in the form of a bird, worn by peasant women*)

пиленце   *n dim. of* пиле; ❑ секое пиленце на своето седелце <е најјако> *prov.* every cock crows on its own dunghill; every dog is a lion at home

пилешки   *adj* chicken's; (*as noun*) пилешко *n* chicken <meat>

пили¹   *impf* to saw

пили² се   *impf* **1** to hatch *intrans.*, be hatched **2** to produce young; таму змии се пилат snakes breed there

пилигрин   *m literary* **1** pilgrim **2** *fig.* traveller, wayfarer

пилигрински   *adj literary* pilgrim's; wayfarer's

пилило   *n* **1** brood; овие пилиња се од едно пилило these chicks are all from one brood **2** *fig.* stock, race, breed; не е тој од нивното пилило he is of different stock

пиличе *n* & **пиличка** *f dim. of* пила 1; fretsaw

пилиштарец   -рци *m* novice, greenhorn

пило   *n see* пијало

пилот   *m* pilot; пилот-ловец fighter-pilot

пилота́жа   *f* piloting; navigation; виша пилотажа aerobatics; aerobatic skill

пилоти́ра   *pf & impf* (*авион*) to pilot; (*брод*) to navigate

пилотски   *adj* pilot's; пилотска кабина cockpit, pilot's cabin

пилула   *f* (*анче*) pill, tablet; ❑ горчлива пилула bitter pill

пилчев   *adj poet.* (*птичји*) bird's; пилчев пој bird-song

пиљав   *m see* пилав

пиљар   *m* fruit and vegetable vendor, fruiterer, greengrocer

пиљара & **пиљарница**   *f* fruit and vegetable shop, greengrocer's

пимпла   *pf & impf* **1** (*with dat.*) to play up to, fawn on **2** *Sport.* to keep possession

пинакоте́ка   *f* picture and sculpture gallery

пингвин   *m Zool.* penguin

пинг-понг   *m Sport.* ping-pong, table tennis

пингпонгар   *m Sport.* ping-pong player

пингпонгарка   *f* (*fem. form*) *see* пингпонгар

Пинд   *m* the Pindus Mountains

пиндски   *adj* Pindus *attrib.*

пинија   -ии *m Bot.* (Pinus pinea) <Mediterranean> stone-pine

пинта   *f* pint

пинце́та   *f* forceps; tweezers

пинџур   *m* salad (*made of grilled capsicums, tomatoes, aubergines, garlic, etc.*); variety of paprika relish

пион   *m Chess* pawn (*also fig.*)

пионе́р   *m* pioneer (*also fig.*); Pioneer (*member of Macedonian children's organization*)

пионе́рка   *f* <girl> Pioneer

пионе́рски   *adj* pioneering; Pioneer's; пионерска работа pioneering work; *Mil.* пионерски единици engineering (road-building) units, pioneer corps; пионерски поздрав Pioneer salute

пионе́рство   *n* pioneering feat

пипа   *impf* **1** to feel, touch, handle; не пипај го овошјето don't handle the fruit; лекарот му го пипа пулсот the doctor is feeling his pulse; ❑ пипа некому пулс to gauge s.o.'s mood **2** to probe, grope; пипа по темница to grope in the dark **3** *fig.* (*испитува*) to try, test, probe **4** *colloq.* to steal, pilfer, pinch; му пипа раката he's given to stealing

пипав   *adj* sluggish, slow, clumsy; пипав е во рацете he's slow with his hands; пипава работа slow (laborious) work

пипало   *n* **1** *Zool.* feeler, tentacle; пипала на октопод tentacles of an octopus; *fig.* тој ги пуштил своите пипала кај нас he put out feelers towards us **2** *Bot.* tendril

пипер   *m* **1** *Bot.* (Capsicum, Piper) pepper; црвен пипер red pepper, paprika; црн пипер black pepper; ❑ толчи некому пипер на главата to treat s.o. like dirt; на секоја манџа црн пипер <се чини> <it seems as if> he turns up everywhere like a bad penny; вистината е <понекогаш> како пипер в очи *prov.* the truth can be painful **2** *fig.* irascible person, dragon

пиперица   *f Bot.* (Linaria) common toadflax

пиперка   *f Bot.* **1** (Capsicum annuum) pod pepper, red pepper, capsicum; лута пиперка hot pepper, chilli; блага пиперка mild (sweet) pepper (capsicum); ❑ како лута пиперка е he has a short fuse **2** *see* пиперица

пиперлив   *adj* peppery, very hot

пиперница   *f* **1** pepperpot, small pot for red pepper **2** *fig., joc.* noddle

пиперолист   *m Bot.* (Aegopodium podagraria) ground elder

пиперца   *f hyp. of* пипер 1

пипе́та   *f* pipette; <medicine> dropper

пипици   *pl* flies (*found in flour, grain and on poultry*)

пипка¹ *f* pip (*infectious disease in poultry*); пипката да те фати! *curse* a plague on you!

пипка² *impf dim. of* пипа

пипне *pf* пипна *aor.* **1** to feel (*briefly*), touch; го пипна по челото he touched him on the forehead **2** *sl.* to catch, grab; пипне криминалец to catch a criminal

пипнува *impf of* пипне

пир *m* banquet, feast

пирајка *f* **1** *see* пиралка **2** *dial.* spoke (*on a wheel*)

пиралка *f* battledore (*for laundering clothes*)

пирамида *f* pyramid

пирамидален -лна *adj* **1** pyramidal **2** *fig.* magnificent, majestic

пирамидон *m Med.* pyramidon

пират *m* pirate; пират од воздухот aircraft hijacker

пиратски *adj* piratical; пиратски напад piratical attack

пиратство *n* piracy

пирг -ови *m* **1** *arch.* (*столб, кула*) column; tower **2** *f.p.* kind of decoration

пире *n* purée; компир пире mashed potatoes

пиреј -еи *m Bot.* (Agropyrum repens, Triticum repens) couch grass

Пирин *m* Pirin, the Pirin Mountains

Пиринеи *pl* Pyrenees

пиринејски *adj* Pyrenean

Пиринец -нци *m* person from Pirin, person from the Pirin Mountains; person from Pirin Macedonia

Пиринка *f* (*fem. form*) *see* Пиринец

пирински *adj* Pirin *attrib.*; Пиринска Македонија Pirin Macedonia

пирит *m Chem.* pyrites

пироман *m* arsonist

пиротехник -ци & **пиротехничар** *m* specialist in pyrotechnics

пиротехника *f* pyrotechnics

пиротехнички *adj* pyrotechnical; пиротехнички завод pyrotechnical factory

пирошка *f Cul.* pasty, patty

пирува *impf* to feast; □ пир пирува to have a feast

пируета *f* pirouette

пирустија -ии *f* trivet

писа¹ *f* (*зифт*) pitch

писа² *f Zool.* (Scardinius erythrophthalmus scardafa) variety of carp (*found in Lake Ohrid*)

писалка *f rare* pencil

писан *pt & adj* **1** painted; many-coloured; писано јајце painted (coloured) egg; писани цвеќиња flowers of many colours **2** pretty; писани моми girls as pretty as pictures **3** *dial. see* пишан

писание -ија *n* **1** bad writing, scribbling; hack work **2** *arch.* (*спис*) document, writ **3** *Rel.* Свештеното писание Holy Scripture, the Bible

писанка *f colloq.* (*тетратка*) notebook

писар *m* clerk, scribe; општински писар municipal clerk; судски писар clerk of the court

писаринка *m pejor.* pen-pusher

писарка *f* (*fem. form*) *see* писар

писарски *adj* clerical, scribal; писарска грешка clerical (scribal) error

писател *m* writer; драмски писател playwright

писателка *f* (*fem. form*) *see* писател

писателски *adj* of a writer

писателство *n* writing (*as an occupation*)

писец -сци *m* **1** *arch.* pen, nib **2** *literary* scribe, copyist, transcriber

писка¹ *f Mus.* mouthpiece (*of wind instruments*)

писка² *f Anat.* shin-bone (tibia); fibula

писка³ *impf* to howl, scream; to squeal; to whistle; локомотивата пискаше the locomotive was whistling

пискав *adj see* писклив

пискавец -вци *m Bot.* (Succisa pratensis) devil's bit scabious

писклив *adj* squeaky, squealing, shrill; писклив глас squeaky voice

пискот *m* scream, howl, screech; whistle

пискотен -тна *adj poet.* squealing, screaming; пискотен плач violent sobbing

пискоти *impf see* писка³

пискотница *f see* пискот

пискул *m* **1** tassel; фес со пискул fez with a tassel **2** *dial., fig.* silk (*silky styles of female maize-flower*), *Am.* corn silk

писмен *adj* **1** written; писмен испит written examination **2** literate; музички писмен musically literate; политички писмен politically aware **3** correct, accurate; писмен цртеж accurate (correct) drawing **4** *rare* literary; писмени споменици literary monuments (landmarks)

писмено *adv* **1** in writing; писмено ќе му одговори he will answer him in writing **2** literately, correctly

писменост *f* **1** literacy; *fig.* политичка писменост political awareness **2** *rare* literature; старословенската писменост Old Slavonic literature

писменце *n dim. of* писмо; note

писмо *n* **1** letter; љубовни писма love letters; препорачано писмо registered letter; парично писмо <postal> money order; придружно писмо covering letter; *Comm.* shipping document; деловно писмо business letter; акредитивни писма letters of credit; отворено писмо 1. letter written on a postcard 2. open letter **2** script; словенско писмо Slavonic (Cyrillic or Glagolitic) script; глаголско писмо Glagolitic script **3** *rare, arch.* (*документ*) certificate; мајсторско писмо skilled craftsman's certificate **4** *arch.* (*ракопис*) handwriting; ситно писмо small handwriting **5** literacy; тој знае писмо he knows how to read and write **6** *arch.* (*usu. pl*) letters (*of the alphabet*)

писне *pf* писна *aor.* to scream, shriek; to squeal; сирената писна the siren wailed; □ да не си писнал! mum's the word

писнува *impf of* писне

писоар *m* pissoir, public urinal

писок -ци *m* whistle; scream; писок на локомотивата locomotive's (steam-engine's) whistle; писок на гајда the skirl of the bagpipes

писта *f* **1** *Sport.* track, race-track **2** (*на аеродром*) runway

пита¹ *f* **1** *Cul.* pita (*round pie made of layers of filo pastry with various fillings*); пита со праз leek pita **2** пита кашкавал <cake of> cheese; пита мед honeycomb

пита² *impf* **1** to beg; пита од куќа в куќа to beg from door to door **2** *f.p.* to ask for a girl's hand in marriage

питалец *m only in the prov.:* давалец – питалец generosity leads to poverty

питач *m* beggar

питачка *f* (*fem. form*) *see* питач

питачки *adj* beggar's; ❑ дотера до питачки стап 1. *trans.* to reduce to beggary 2. *intrans.* to be reduced to beggary

питачлак *m colloq.* beggary, penury, begging; ❑ *joc.* збогум сиромаштијо, повели питачлак things are going from bad to worse

питекáнтроп *m* pithecanthropus, ape-man, Homo erectus

питие -ија *n arch. Rel.* (*пијачка*) drink; ❑ јастие (јасје) и питие food and drink

питом *adj* 1 tame, domesticated; питом гулаб tame pigeon; питом зајак tame rabbit 2 gentle, approachable; питоми луѓе civilized people 3 cultivated; питоми овошки cultivated fruit-trees 4 productive, fertile; agreeable; питом крај fertile region

питомец -мци *m* pupil, student; воен питомец cadet

питоми *impf* to tame, domesticate

питомина *f* 1 (*питом крај*) fertile region 2 *see* питомост

питомица *f* (*fem. form*) *see* питомец

питомост *f* tameness; gentleness

питон *m Zool.* (Python reticulatus) python

питорéскен -кна *adj* picturesque

питулица *f* 1 *see* тиганица 2 kind of pancake

пица *f* pizza

пицаɟзла *f* crab-louse; *fig. colloq.* anal retentive

пицерија *f* pizzeria

пичка *f vulg.* cunt

пицáма *f see* пижама

пишан *pt & adj* 1 written; пишани закони written laws; пишани споменици literary landmarks, monuments (documents); ❑ пишан си you're finished, you've had it; било пишано thus it was written, it was fated thus 2 pretty; мома пишана a girl as pretty as a picture

пишанија *f* 1 *arch.* s.th. decreed (by fate), preordained; ❑ таква била пишанијата, пишанија било thus it was written 2 (*pl only*) *see* писание 2 & 3

пише[1] *pf* пиша *aor.* I 1 to write; пише писмо to write a letter 2 to write down, record, register; ❑ пиши го на мразот write it off as finished; му го пишале <за> грев it was a black mark against him; господ грев ќе ти пише don't do that, you'll be committing a sin 3 to fix, determine (*in writing*); to levy, exact; му пишале тежок данок they imposed a heavy tax on him 4 to bequeath, leave in one's will; пише некому куќа to leave a house to s.o. II – се *pf* to register, enlist, enrol *intrans.*

пише[2] *impf dial., f.p.* 1 (*пишува*) to write 2 to colour, paint, paint pictures

пишка *impf* 1 (*од болка*) to groan, moan 2 (*од умор, напор*) to pant, gasp

пишман *adj indecl. colloq.* sorry, regretful; ❑ пишман е (се сторил, се чинил) he is sorry, he repents

пишмани *impf colloq.* I to dissuade; го пишманиле да оди во странство he was dissuaded from going abroad II – се to be sorry, repent, regret; to change one's mind; to give up

пишталка *f* whistle

пиштало *n dial. see* пукало

пишти *impf* to scream, howl; to squeal; гајдите

пиштат the bagpipes are skirling; сирена пишти a siren is wailing

пиштол *m* large pistol, horse-pistol; ❑ гол како пиштол stark naked; penniless

пишува *impf* I 1 to write; пишува книга to write a book; пишува со молив/со мастило to write in pencil/in ink; си пишуваат често they often write to each other; пишува во весник he writes for a newspaper 2 *arch.* (*црта, шари*) to draw, paint; пишувал икони he painted icons; ❑ веѓи му пишува he's leading him by the nose II – се 1 to be written; овој збор се пишува со голема буква that word is written with a capital letter; како се пишува . . . ? how do you spell . . . ? ❑ лошо (слабо) ти се пишува hard times are in store for you 2 to register, enlist, enrol *intrans.*; се пишува за доброволец to register as a volunteer 3 *impers.* (*with dat.*) to have a wish, desire, inclination to write; to want to write; ми се пишува на таа тема I would like to write on that subject

пишување *n* writing; читање и пишување reading and writing; хартија за пишување writing paper; машина за пишување typewriter; пишување статии/книги writing of articles/books; за пишување не го бидува 1. he is incapable of writing; he is no good at writing 2. he does not want to write at all

пишувач *m* 1 writer, author (*of an article, a book, etc.*); ❑ *literary* пишувачот на овие редови the writer of these lines 2 *dial.* (*писар*) clerk, scribe

пишувачка *f colloq. see* пишување

пјат *m & rarely* **пјато** *n arch.* platter, shallow bowl

ПЈРМ *abbr.* (*Поранешна југословенска република Македонија*) Former Yugoslav Republic of Macedonia, FYROM

плавен -вна *adj literary* harmonious, measured, flowing, even, rhythmical; плавно движење flowing movement; плавна реч fluent speech; *Gram.* плавни согласки liquid consonants

плави *impf* 1 to rinse out (*laundry*), rinse (*suds out of washing*) 2 *dial.* to rinse rice 3 to flood (*land*); реката го плави полето the river is flooding the field

плавност *f literary* harmony, measure, fluency (*of speech*), rhythm, balance

плагијáт *m* plagiarism

плагијáтор *m* plagiarist

плагијаторски *adj* plagiaristic

плагѝра *pf & impf* to plagiarize

пладне *n* midday, noon; на пладне at midday; пред пладне in the morning; по пладне in the afternoon; ❑ ден до пладне a short (*usu. working*) day

пладневен -вна *adj* midday *attrib.*; пладневно сонце midday sun; пладневен одмор midday rest

пладнина *f* 1 (*пладне*) midday; кон пладнина around midday; насред пладнина in broad daylight 2 *dial.* midday meal, lunch

пладниште *n* place where cattle find shade at midday

пладнува *impf* 1 to rest at midday 2 *fig.* to be idle, do nothing; ❑ којшто лете пладнува, зиме гладува *prov.* he who is idle in the summer, goes hungry in winter

плажа *f* beach; оди на плажа to go to the beach

плаз *m* 1 (*на санка*) runner 2 (*на плугот*) ploughshoe (*holding ploughshare*) 3 (*only pl*) *dial.* hull-timbers (*of traditional boat on Lake Ohrid*)

плази *impf* **I** плази јазик to stick out one's tongue **II – ce** to stick out one's tongue

плазма *f Biol.* plasma; крвна плазма blood plasma

плак -ови *m f.p.* **1** *see* плач **2** *see* поплак (поплака)

плакар *m* built-in wardrobe; closet

плака́т *m* & **плака́та** *f* placard, poster

плаке́та[1] *f* **1** medallion (*commemorative bas-relief*) **2** certificate of honour

плакета[2] *f dial. see* мазник 1

плакне *impf* **I 1** to rinse <out>; плакне чаши to rinse glasses; си го плакне грлото to gargle; си ja плакне устата to rinse one's mouth; ❏ плакне очи to feast one's eyes on **2** *fig.* to lap, wash the shores of; море ja плакне Далмација the sea washes the Dalmatian shores **II – ce** to rinse one's mouth; to gargle; to splash o.s. (*with water*)

плам *m poet. see* пламен[1]; сред дим и плам amid smoke and flames

пламен[1] -и, -мни, -ење, -ења *m* **1** flame; куќата е во пламен the house is in flames; *Mil.* фрлач<ка> на пламен flame-thrower; *fig.* тој е пламен he's a live wire; ❏ оган и пламен **1.** enthusiastic **2.** passionate **3.** terribly expensive; на пазарот – оган и пламен prices are very high at the market **2** *fig.* passion, fervour, inspiration, thrill; во очите му гореше пламен his eyes were burning with passion

пламен[2] & **пламенен** -мена *adj* **1** fiery, blazing; пламени столбови pillars of flame; пламени јазици tongues of flame **2** *fig.* passionate; пламенен револуционер fiery revolutionary; пламен поглед passionate look

пламени се *impf rare see* пламти

пламенит *adj poet., rare see* пламен[2]

пламеница *f* (*пепелница*) wheat rust, rust fungus

пламенче *n dim. of* пламен[1]

пламне *pf* пламна *aor.* **1** to burst into flames; огинот пламна fire broke out **2** to wilt (*in the sun*); пламнало житото the wheat has been scorched by the sun **3** *fig.* to flash, light up; му пламнаа очите his eyes flashed **4** *fig.* to flush; to flare up, erupt, break out; тој пламна во лицето his face flushed; тој одеднаш ќе пламне he would suddenly flare up; борбите пламнаа со нова сила fighting broke out (flared) with renewed violence

пламнува *impf of* пламне

пламтеж *n poet., rare see* пламтење

пламтење *n* blazing

пламти *impf* to blaze; to rage; пламтеа огновите the fires were raging; образите му пламтеа his cheeks were blazing (glowing), his cheeks flushed; очите му пламтат од љубов/гнев/одмазда his eyes blaze with love/anger/revenge; сиот пламти од гнев he is blazing with anger

план *m* **1** plan; project; план на зграда plan of a building; урбанистички план urban development plan; петгодишен план five-year plan; перспективен план long-term plan; производствен план production plan; план за напад plan of attack; наставен план curriculum; спред планот on schedule; according to plan **2** plot; plan; план на роман plot of a novel **3** position; place <of importance>; standpoint; на психолошки план from a psychological standpoint; ❏ во крупен (преден) план in the foreground; избива во преден план to come to the fore; во заден план in the background; на преден (прв) план firstly, in the first place; на заден (втор) план secondly; least important

планер *m* planner

плане́та *f* planet

планета́рен -рна *adj rare see* планетен

планетариум *m* planetarium

планетен -тна & **планетски** *adj* planetary; Сончевиот планетен систем the solar system

планиглоб *m Geog.* world map

планиметрија *f* planimetry

планиметриски *adj* planimetric<al>

планина -и, -иње *f* mountain (*also fig.*); heap, pile; цели планини јаглен whole mountains of coal; ❏ еден човек – планина a mountain of a man

планинар *m* mountaineer, mountain-climber

планинари *impf* to go in for mountaineering

планинарка *f* (*fem. form*) *see* планинар

планинарски *adj* mountaineering; планинарско друштво mountaineering club

планинарство *n* mountaineering

планинец -нци *m* **1** highlander, mountain-dweller **2** *Sport. see* планинар

планиница & **планинка**[1] *f dim. of* планина; hill

планинка[2] *f* **1** (*fem. form*) *see* планинец 1 **2** *see* планинарка

планински *adj* **1** mountain; alpine; планинска верига mountain range/chain; планински воздух mountain air; планински цвеќиња alpine flowers; планински човек highlander; планински птици upland (game) birds **2** mountainous; планинска област mountainous region

планинче *n* **1** *dim. of* планина **2** *dim. of* планинец

плани́ра *pf* & *impf* to plan

планктон *m Biol.* plankton

планомерен -рна *adj rare* planned, systematic; планомерен развиток planned development

планомерно *adv rare* systematically

плански *adj* planned; planning; планска комисија a planning committee; планско стопанство planned economy; плански развиток planned development

планта́жа *f* plantation; плантажи на кафе coffee plantations

планта́жен -жна *adj* plantation *attrib.*; planting; плантажни работи plantation operations

плантаже́р *m* planter, plantation-owner

плапоти *impf* **1** to chatter, babble, gabble **2** *dial.* (*баботи*) to blaze; огинот плапоти the fire is blazing

плас *interj* plop! splash! flop! плас сторила she fell full length (went sprawling)

плаcи́ра *pf* & *impf* **I 1** to sell at a good price; to dispose of **2** to invest, place <capital> **II – ce** *colloq.* to establish o.s.; *Sport.* to place o.s., get a placing

пласка *impf* **1** *rare* to slap, clap, flap; пласка со крилја to flap one's wings, flutter **2** *fig.* to talk nonsense, babble

пласкоти *impf see* пласка

пласман *m Comm.* disposal; investment; *Sport.* placing; пласман на производи disposal of products

пласне *pf* пласна *aor.* **I 1** to throw down; to throw out, expel; пласне нешто наземи to dash s.th. to the ground **2** to slap; му пласнал некоја шлаканица he gave him a slap **3** *fig.* to blurt out, blab; пласне голема глупост to blurt out something stupid; ❏

ама ја пласна! he really put his foot in it! **II – се** to throw o.s.; to collapse, fall; to flop (*на/во – on/into*)

пласнува (се)   *impf of* пласне (се)

пласт   -ови, пласје *m* **1** пласт сено haystack, haycock **2** (*слој*) layer, stratum

пластелин   *m* Plasticine

пласти   *impf* **I 1** to stack; to pile up, heap up (*in layers*) *trans.*; пласти сено to stack hay **II – се** to accumulate, pile up *intrans.* (*also fig.*); се пластеа сè нови и нови тешкотии new difficulties kept piling up

пластика   *f* **1** (*во балет и танц*) fluidity of movement **2** *see* пластичност **3** plastic arts **4** plastic (*material*)

пластичен   -чна *adj* **1** plastic; **2** harmonious, fluid, graceful; пластични движења graceful movements **3** *fig.* (*сликовит*) striking, vivid; пластичен стил vivid style **4** modelling; пластична уметност plastic art **5** *Med.* plastic; пластична хирургија plastic surgery

пластичност   *f* plasticity

плата   *f* pay, wages, salary; месечна плата monthly pay (wages)

платан   *m Bot.* (Platanus orientalis) <oriental> plane<-tree>, *see* чинар

платежен   -жна *adj* <of> payment, paying; платежна (платна) способност solvency, ability to pay

платен[1]   *pt* **1** paid; платен годишен одмор paid annual leave (holiday); платен функционер paid official (functionary); ❏ платено "payment received" **2** bribed; hired; платен убиец hired killer, assassin

платен[2]   -тна *adj* <of> payment; платен список pay-roll; платна листа pay list; платна способност solvency, ability to pay

платеник   -ци *m* hireling, mercenary

плати   *pf* **I** to pay (*некому за нешто – s.o. for s.th.*); плати данок/долг to pay tax/a debt; ❏ плати во готово to pay cash; плати во натура to pay in kind; плати во рати to pay by instalments; плати од џеб to pay out of one's own pocket; му платил данок he paid the penalty; плати со глава<та> to pay with one's life; скапо плати to pay through the nose; плати па носи cash and carry **II – се** to settle, square accounts

платив   *adj* payable

платина   *f Chem.* platinum

платинест   *adj* platinum-like; платинеста коса platinum blonde hair

платински   *adj* platinum; платински прстен platinum ring

платица[1]   *f dim. of* плата

платица[2]   *f* thin plank

платичак   -ци *m see* лопув

платичка   *f see* платица[1]

платнар   *m arch.* cloth-maker; textile merchant

платнарка   *f arch.* **1** (*fem. form*) *see* платнар **2** wife of a cloth-maker/textile merchant

платнарница   *f* **1** textile factory <work>shop **2** *arch.* textile shop

платнарски   *adj* cloth-maker's; textile merchant's

платнен   *adj* cloth, linen; платнена кошула linen shirt; платнена стока linen goods

платненце   *n dim. of* платно

платниште   *n* **1** width (*of cloth*), panel **2** *rare* ground-sheet; flap of a tent **3** *augm. of* платно

платно   *n* **1** cloth; canvas; (*ленено*) linen **2** *see*

платниште **1 3** (*уметничко*) canvas; **4** филмско платно film screen **5** sail; чун со платно sailing-boat

платноса се   *pf colloq., fig.* to turn pale; сиот се платносал he went as white as a sheet

плато́   *m & n* **1** *Geog.* plateau, tableland **2** terrace, paved area

платонски   *adj* Platonic; платонска љубов Platonic love

платформа   *f* **1** platform (*also fig.*); изборна платформа election platform **2** (*основа*) basis; на таа платформа не може да се преговара it is impossible to negotiate on that basis

плаќа (се)   *impf of* плати се

плаќање   *n* payment; срок на плаќање date (term) of payment; плаќање однапред payment in advance; плаќање данок paying a tax; способност за плаќање (платежна способност) solvency (ability to pay); долг со плаќање, пат со барање <се свршува> *prov.* debts exist to be paid

плаќач   *m* client; payer

плафон   *m* **1** (*таван*) ceiling **2** *fig.* ceiling, uppermost limit; плафонот на платите ceiling of pay, wages limit

плафонски   *adj* ceiling *attrib.*

плах   *adj literary see* плашлив

плац   *m* <building> site; lot, block; слободен плац vacant site

плацдарм   *m Mil.* **1** bridgehead, beach-head; theatre of operations **2** base

плацента   *f Anat.* placenta

плач   -ови *m* crying, weeping, sobbing

плаче   *impf* **I** to cry, weep; викне да плаче to burst out crying; плаче над некого/нешто to cry about (weep over) s.o./s.th.; плаче над својата судбина to lament one's fate; плаче за некого to mourn s.o.; ❏ да го плаче човек one feels sorry for him; плаче на туѓ гроб to worry about s.o. else's affairs; плаче за . . . to be asking for (crying out for) . . . ; the time is ripe for . . . ; it's ideal for . . . ; ова место плаче за едно игралиште this site would be ideal for a playground; плаче за стап (ќотек) he needs a good hiding; работата плаче од него he lets the side down; де плаче, де се смее to blow hot and cold; заспива со плачење to cry o.s. to sleep **2** *colloq.* (*за око*) to run, water **3** (*за растенија*) to bleed, exude sap; лозата плаче the vine is bleeding **II – се 1** (*на, од – about*) to complain, grumble, *Austral.* whinge; сите се плачат од него everyone complains about him **2** *impers.* (*with dat.*) ми се плаче I feel like crying

плачен   -чна *adj* tearful

плачка[1]   *f colloq.* crying, weeping; имаше плачки tears were shed; ❏ играчка плачка <прават децата> this will end badly/in tears (*as a warning*)

плачка[2]   *f colloq.* (*fem. form*) *see* плачко

плачко   -вци *m colloq.* cry-baby

плачлив   *adj* given to crying; tearful; детето е плачливо the child cries easily; со плачлив глас in a tearful voice

плаши   *impf* **I** to frighten, scare, terrify; нè плашат неговите постапки his actions terrify us; ❏ деца плаши he scares only children, he doesn't scare anybody **II – се** to fear, be afraid; не му се плашам I'm not afraid of him; се плашам за неговото здравје

I fear for (am worried about) his health; ❑ му се плаши од сенката he's terrified of him

плашило *n* scarecrow (*also fig.*)

плашица *f Zool.* (Alburnus albidus alborella) variety of bleak (*found in Lake Ohrid*)

плашлив *adj* timid, fearful; плашливо дете a timid child; плашлив поглед frightened look

плашливост *f* shyness, timidity, bashfulness

плашт *m arch., fig.* cloak, mantle; veil, guise; ❑ под плаштот (*на нешто*) under the cloak (guise) (*of s.th.*)

плаштаница *f Rel.* shroud (*of Christ in tomb*)

плебеец -јци & **плебеј** -еи *m Hist., fig.* plebeian

плебејка *f* (*fem. form*) *see* плебеец & плебеј

плебејски *adj* plebeian; плебејско потекло plebeian birth (origin)

плебејство *n* 1 *Hist.* the Roman plebeian class, the Roman commoners 2 plebeian origin (birth) 3 *fig.* vulgarity, commonness, crudeness

плебисцит *m* plebiscite

плева *f* 1 chaff 2 *fig.* very many, heaps; *colloq.* oodles; ❑ како плева <има нешто> <there is> enough to burn; прст и плева very many, masses

плевач *m* weeder

плевачка *f* (*fem. form*) *see* плевач

плевел *m Bot.* (Lolium) darnel, rye-grass; weed

плеви *impf* to weed

плевна *f* barn; ❑ бара игла во плевна (во плева) to look for a needle in a haystack; на празна плевна покров не ѝ треба *prov.* don't waste good things on the undeserving; (*брзоговорка*) Петре плете плет пред Петревá плевна (*tongue-twister*) cf. Peter Piper picked a peck of pickled pepper

плевра *f Anat.* pleura

плеврит & **плеврѝтис** *m Med.* pleurisy

пледѝра *impf* to plead; пледира за толеранција to plead for tolerance

пледоајé -éа *n* plea, pleading; speech for the defence

плејáда *f literary* pleiad

плексиглас *m* & **плéкси-стáкло** *n* plexiglass, perspex

плексус *m Anat.* plexus

племе *n* tribe; словенски племиња Slav tribes

племеник -ци *m* tribesman, member of a tribe

племенски *adj* tribal; племенски односи tribal relations; племенски црти tribal features/characteristics

плен *m* 1 booty, loot, plunder; ❑ лен и плен much, many 2 (*на животно*) prey 3 *fig.* victim 4 robbery, plundering, looting, pillaging; enslavement

пленарен -рна *adj* plenary; пленарна седница plenary session

пленет *pt* taken prisoner, captive, captured; пленети војници prisoners of war (P.O.W.s)

плени[1] *pf* 1 to capture, take prisoner; ни пленија двајца војници they captured two of our soldiers 2 to seize, confiscate 3 *fig.* to charm, captivate, fascinate; актерите ја пленија публиката the actors captivated the audience 4 to rob; арамиите го плениле the robbers robbed him

плени[2] *impf rare, arch.* 1 to capture, seize; to plunder; село се плени, баба се чешла *prov.* Nero fiddles while Rome burns 2 *fig.* to captivate, charm

пленик -ци *m* (*заробеник*) captive, prisoner

пленица & **пленичка** *f* (*fem. form*) *see* пленик

пленички *adj* (*заробенички*) captive; prisoner's; пленички логор prison camp

пленство *n* 1 (*заробеништво*) captivity; се врати од пленство he returned from captivity 2 *f.p. see* плен 4

пленува *impf of* плени 1–3

пленум *m* (*заседание*) plenum, full assembly

плеонáзам -зми *m literary* pleonasm

плеонастичен -чна & **плеонастички** *adj* pleonastic; плеонастички израз pleonastic expression

плеска *impf* I 1 to slap; ја плескаше по образ he slapped her face 2 (*with dat.*) to clap, applaud; му плескавме на исполнителот we applauded the performer 3 (*место*) to roll, press, pat 4 *fig., rare* (*траска*) to talk nonsense, chatter, babble, twaddle 5 (*за вода*) to splash *intrans.*; брановите плескаа the waves were splashing II – ce to slap o.s.; сам се плеска по образи he is slapping himself on the cheeks

плескавица *f* <ham>burger

плесна *f* 1 spot (*on the face, body*) 2 lichen

плесне *pf* плесна *aor.* I 1 to slap, smack; го плеснал по образ he slapped his face 2 (*со рацете*) to clap one's hands 3 *fig.* to speak openly (frankly); плесне некому в очи to tell s.o. to his face 4 *fig.* to blurt out II – ce 1 to slap (hit) o.s.; to bump into (*briefly*); ce плесне во дрвото to bump into a tree

плесник -ци *m* woman's sleeveless jacket adorned with coins (*traditional costume in Debar district*)

плесница *f see* шлаканица

плесничав *adj* 1 spotty, freckled; pimply 2 covered with lichen

плеснува (ce) *impf of* плесне (ce)

плесок -ци *m* 1 clapping, applause; slapping, smacking; плесок во салата applause in the hall 2 splash; паѓа со силен плесок to fall with a splash

плет -ови, -ишта *m* (*плот*) wicker fence; ❑ жив плет <quickset> hedge; и плетот има очи walls have ears

плетало *n* knitting; yarn

плетач *m* knitter; weaver; basket-maker

плетачка *f* (*fem. form*) *see* плетач

плетачки *adj* knitting; weaving; knitter's; weaver's; basket-maker's; игла плетачка knitting-needle

плетва *f* weeding; во плетвата at weeding time

плете *impf* I 1 to knit; (*со една игла*) to crochet; to weave (*also fig.*); to plait; плете чорапи/џемпер to knit socks/a jumper; плете мрежа to weave a web; плете тантела to make lace; плете коса to plait hair 2 *fig.* плете (плетка) со нозете to stumble II – ce 1 to wind, entwine o.s. (*околу нешто* – round s.th.) 2 *fig. see* плетка[2] ce 2 3 *fig.* му се плете (плетка) јазикот to get tongue-tied; ❑ (*зборот, името*) ми се плете (плетка) на јазикот (*the word, name*) is on the tip of my tongue

плетен *pt* & *adj* knitted; wicker; плетен фустан knitted dress; плетен стол wicker chair

плетеница *f* 1 (*usu. pl*) plait, braid, tress 2 (*вид плетка*) cable 3 *see* плетка[1] 1 4 (*вид леб или печиво*) twist 5 bunch, string (*of onions, etc.*)

плетенка *f see* плетеница

плетење *n* knitting; weaving; машина за плетење knitting-machine; плетење кошници weaving of baskets

плетиво *n* 1 (*плетало*) knitting 2 *arch.* traditional ceremony of cutting a newborn baby's hair

плетина *f dial. see* плет, плот[1]

плетиплотка *f Bot.* (Lycium halimifolium) <quickset hedge of> box-thorn, prickly box

плетистол *m Bot.* (Sanguisorba minor) salad burnet

плетка[1] *f* **1** pattern **2** *see* плетеница 1 & 5

плетка[2] *impf* **I 1** to tangle, muddle; плетка конци to tangle threads **2** *fig.* to mix up, involve (*во – in*); мене не плеткај ме таму don't involve me in that! **3** *fig.* плетка со нозете to stumble **4** *fig.* плетка со јазикот to stutter (stammer); to stumble, fumble (*in speaking a foreign language*) **5** *fig.* to eke out a living, struggle, get by; плеткаше некако со платичката he was just managing on his paltry salary **II – се 1** to tangle *intrans.* **2** *fig.* to meddle, interfere (*во – in*); во cè се плетка he meddles in everything **3** *fig.* to roam; се плеткал по белиов свет to roam the wide world **4** (*with dat.*) to get in s.o.'s way; ми се плетка помеѓу нозе he/it gets under my feet, he/it trips me up **5** ❑ ми се плетка на јазикот it's on the tip of my tongue; му се плетка јазикот he gets tongue-tied, gets confused

плеќат & **плеќест** *adj* broad-shouldered

плеќи *pl* shoulders; <upper> back; го легна на плеќи he laid him flat on his back; спроти плеќите – и самарот *prov.* fit the burden to the shoulders; товар ми падна од плеќи a weight was lifted from my shoulders; даде плеќи to turn tail

плеќички *pl dim. of* плеќи

плешка *f Anat.* scapula, shoulder-blade; плешка со месо shoulder of meat; гледа (гата, врача) во плешка to tell (*s.o.'s*) fortune from his shoulder-blade (*folk custom*)

плива *impf* **1** to swim; плива на грб to swim on one's back; ❑ плива како риба to swim like a fish; плива во нечии води to be under s.o.'s influence; to be s.o.'s faithful follower **2** to float; маслото плива врз вода oil floats on water **3** *fig.* to be immersed (*во – in*); wallow; плива во раскош to wallow in luxury; месото плива во маст the meat is swimming in fat **4** *fig.* to be carried away; плива во радост/блаженство to be carried away with joy **5** *fig., colloq.* to flounder; to waffle; предавачот пливаше the lecturer was waffling **6** *dial., f.p.* (*плови*) to sail

пливалиште *n* swimming-pool

пливање *n* **1** swimming; floating; градно пливање breast-stroke; грбно пливање backstroke; кучешко пливање dog-paddle **2** *dial., f.p. see* пловење

пливач *m* swimmer

пливачица & **пливачка** *f* (*fem. form*) *see* пливач

пливачки *adj* swimming; floating; пливачки клуб swimming club; пливачки курс floating exchange rate

пливка *f* **1** (*за кандило*) wick **2** (*за ловење риба*) float

пливне *pf* пливна *aor.* **1** to start swimming/floating **2** *fig.* to appear in large numbers; козите пливнаа по сртот the goats appeared along the ridge **3** *fig.* to become bathed, soaked (*во – in*); пливне во светлина to be bathed in light; пливне во крв to be steeped in blood

пливнува *impf of* пливне

плик -ови *m* envelope

плима *f see* прилив

плипот *adv* crowds, masses; lots; на приредбата народ плипот at the show there were crowds of people

плисé *n* & *adj indecl.* plissé

плисира *impf* to pleat, pucker, make plissé (folds)

плисиран *pt* & *adj* plissé; плисирано здолниште plissé (pleated) skirt

плиска *impf* **I 1** to throw, splash (*water or other liquid*); (*од чун*) to bail out; си го плискаше лицето со вода he was splashing his face with water **2** *fig.* to spend recklessly; to splash money around; to squander; плиска пари за/на/по некого to lavish money on s.o. **3** (*за дожд*) to pour; цел ден плискаше дожд rain poured down all day long **4** to spill; to pour out *trans.* **5** (*за море, река*) to heave, surge, splash *intrans.* **6** (*за вода, море, река*) to water, wash, lap *trans.*; морето ги плиска бреговите the sea washes the shores **7** *fig., poet.* злоба од себе плиска to seethe with malice **II – се 1** to splash o.s. (*with water*) **2** *see* I 5 3 to run over, spill *intrans.* **4** *fig.* to be wasted; се плискаат и сили и време both time and energy are wasted

плискот *m rare, poet.* splashing; pouring

плискоти *impf see* плиска

плисне (се) *pf* плисна *aor. see* плиска (се)

плиснува (се) *impf of* плисне (се)

плисок *m rare, poet. see* плискот

плитак -ци *m* shallow<s>; shoal

плитар *m* adobe, sun-dried brick; тули и плитари brick and adobe; ❑ леб како плитар hard bread (*which has not risen*)

плитарен *adj* adobe *attrib.*; плитарена куќичка adobe cottage

плитарница *f arch.* brick-yard (*in which adobe bricks are made*)

плитвак -ци *m dial. see* плитак

плитка *f dial. see* плетеница, плетенка

плиткоумен -мна *adj* shallow-minded

плиткоумие & **плиткоумје** *n*, **плиткоумност** *f* shallow-mindedness

плиток -тка *adj* **1** shallow; плитка вода shallow water; плитка чинија shallow dish/plate; плитки чевли low shoes **2** *fig.* superficial; плитко знаење superficial knowledge; лагата е плитка; на лагата ѝ е плитко дното *prov.* lying gets you nowhere **3** (*as noun*) плитко *n* shallow <place>; се капе во плиткото to bathe in the shallows

плиш *m* plush

плишан *adj* plush

пловен -вна *adj* **1** navigable; пловна река navigable river **2** floating, sailing; пловни објекти vessels; ❑ пловен парк shipping fleet

пловење *n* sailing, navigation

пловец -вци *m* (*морепловец*) sailor, seaman, mariner

плови *impf* to sail; лаѓата пловеше на север the boat was heading north

пловидба *f* sailing, navigation; морска/речна/крајбрежна пловидба sea (marine)/river/coastal navigation; редот на пловидбата sailing timetable

пловидбен *adj* sailing

пловност *f* navigability; пловноста на реките the navigability of the rivers

плод *m* **1** fruit; *fig.* result; ❑ даде плод to bear fruit; ги собира плодовите на својата работа to reap the rewards of one's labour; забранет плод forbidden fruit; плод на имагинација figment of imagination **2** foetus, embryo

пловба *f Anat.* **1** womb, uterus **2** placenta

плоден -дна *adj* fruitful; fertile; prolific, productive;

плодна земја fertile land; плодна година bumper year; плоден писател prolific writer; плодна дејност productive work; плодни дни (*на жена*) fertile days (*of a woman*)

плоди *impf* **I** *rare, usu. fig.* to create, produce, bear **II – се** to multiply *intrans.*, reproduce, breed, propagate <itself>; тие животни многу се плодат these animals breed prolifically

плодник -ци *m Bot.* ovary

плодност *f* fruitfulness; fertility, fecundity

плодовит *adj rare see* плоден

плодоносен -сна *adj see* плоден

плодоред *m* crop rotation

плодороден -дна *adj* fruitful; fertile; productive; rich; плодородна земја fertile land

плодородие & плодородје *n rare* **1** *see* плодородност **2** bountiful crops; plenty; големо продородие bumper harvest

плодородност *f see* плодност

плодотворен -рна *adj literary, rare* fruitful

плодотворност *f literary, rare* fruitfulness

пломба *f* **1** (*за нешто спакувано/затворено*) <lead> seal; царинска пломба customs seal **2** (*за заб*) filling; златни пломби gold fillings

пломби́ра *pf & impf* **1** to seal; пломбира вагони to seal carriages (*Am.* cars), goods waggons (*Am.* freight cars) **2** (*за заб*) to fill

пломби́ран *pt* filled; sealed; пломбирани заби filled teeth

плоска *f* (*пагур*) flask, flat bottle

плоскав *adj see* плоскат

плоскат *adj* flat; плоската нога flat foot

плоскатост *f* flatness

плоскач *m see* лопув

плот[1] -ови, -ишта *m* fence; Петре плете плот да помине поп за едно зрно боб (*tongue-twister*) *cf.* Peter Piper picked a peck of pickled pepper

плот[2] -тта *f Rel. rare* the flesh, the body; ❑ плот и крв flesh and blood

плотски *adj Rel. rare* carnal, fleshly; плотски наслади carnal pleasures; плотска љубов carnal love

плотун *m* salvo, volley

плотунски *adj* in volleys, salvoes; плотунска стрелба firing in volleys (salvoes)

плоча *f* **1** slab; plaque; tablet; мраморна (мермерна) плоча marble slab; надгробна плоча gravestone; бетонска плоча slab of concrete; спомен-плоча commemorative plaque; ❑ отворил <едни> очи како плочи he opened his eyes as wide as dinner-plates **2** (*грамофонска*) record; ❑ смени плоча to change the subject **3** *arch.* slate, board (*for writing*) **4** horseshoe; ❑ ги фрли плочите *joc.* he's turned his toes up; од мртов коњ плочи ќе сака he's asking for the impossible **5** silver ornament worn on the breast (*in a woman's traditional costume*)

плочен *adj* of slabs, tiles, *Austral.* pavers; tiled; paved; плочен двор paved courtyard; плочна ивица edge of a slab

плочест *adj* **1** slab-like; tile-like **2** divisible into layers; плочеста земја shale **3** paved; tiled; плочест двор paved courtyard

плочка *f* **1** *dim. of* плоча **2** (*за на ѕид*) <wall> tile

плочник -ци *m* pavement

плошт -шје *m* broad, level place (ground)

плоштад *m* <city> square

плоштак -ци *m see* лопув

плоштатка & плоштинка *f dial. dim. of* плошт

плуг *m* plough, *Am.* plow; тракторски плуг tractor plough; без труд не се ора со плуг *prov.* no sweet without sweat

плуе *impf* **1** *rare see* гние **2** *fig.* (*кисне*) to hang around, idle, linger **3** *fig.* to sleep for a long time **4** *dial. see* плука

плужен -жна *adj* <of> plough, ploughing; плужен нож ploughshare

плужица & плужница *f* (small, wooden) plough

плука *impf* to spit, expectorate; to spit out; плука крв to spit blood; плука коски од цреша to spit out cherry stones; нов бунар копај, на стариот не плукај *prov.* when you make new friends, don't forget your old ones; не плукај угоре, да не падне на тебе *prov.* people who live in glass houses shouldn't throw stones

плукалник -ци *m* & **плукалница** *f* spittoon

плуканица & плуканка *f* saliva, spittle

плукнат *adj* spitting <image>, identical, extremely similar; плукнато на татка си the spitting image of his father

плукне *pf* to spit, spit out; му плукнал в лице he spat in his face; ❑ сега му ја плукнавме now we're in trouble; си плукна на рацете to spit on one's hands <and get down to work>; плукни си во пазува<та> pluck up your courage! кај си плукнал, не лижи *prov.* be true to your word

плукнува *impf of* плукне

плунка *f* saliva, spittle, spit; си ја голтне плунката to swallow hard; ❑ со плунки го удавија they gave him a thorough dressing-down; кој плука наугоре, на него паѓаат плунките *prov.* people who live in glass houses shouldn't throw stones

плунковен -вна *adj* salivary; плунковни жлезди salivary glands

плурал *m Gram.* plural

плурален -лна & **плуралски** *adj Gram.* plural; плурална наставка plural ending (suffix)

плурали́зам -змот *m* pluralism

плус *m* **1** benefit, plus; surplus; тоа е голем плус that is a great advantage (plus); ти си тука плус you are not needed here **2** *adv* plus; добив три плус на тестот I got three plus for the test; (*за температура*) плус осумнаесет plus eighteen <degrees> **3** *conj* plus; in addition to, on top of; осум плус три се единаесет eight plus three is eleven

плуска[1] *impf* **1** *fig.* to pour (*out, in*) *intrans.*; to explode **2** to blare, resound, reverberate **3** to lash, strike, whip **4** to break; to crack *intrans.*

плуска[2] *f* **1** blister; му излегле плуски на дланката blisters appeared on his palm **2** *fig.* (*usu. pl*) stories, idle chatter, gossip; плуски се тоа that's just gossip

плускав *adj see* плускавичав

плускавец -вци *m* **1** *see* плуска[2] 1 **2** (*usu. pl*) *see* пуканица & пуканка

плускавица *f see* плуска[2] 1

плускавичав *adj* blistered; плускавичави раце blistered hands

плускарец -рци *m see* плускавец

плусквампе́рфект *m Gram.* pluperfect

плускот *m* 1 banging, crashing, rumbling; blaring; uproar; ❏ 'рскот и плускот, 'рскоти-плускоти! what a hullabaloo! 2 *rare, fig.* pouring (*of rain*); exploding

плускоти *impf* to blare, resound, reverberate

плускотница *f see* плускот 1; ❏ 'рскотници-плускотници! what a hullabaloo!

плусне *pf* плусна *aor.* I 1 *see* плесне 1, 2 2 to break, crack *intrans.* 3 *see* лусне II – **се** *see* плесне се

плуснува (се) *impf of* плусне (се)

плута *f & плуто *n* 1 cork; затки од плута corks (cork stoppers); плутото не пропаѓа cork does not sink 2 pine bark used as float for fishing net (*on Lake Ohrid*)

плутократ *m* plutocrat

плутократија *f* plutocracy

плутократски *adj* plutocratic

пљампа *impf* to babble, chatter, gabble

пљампало *n* babbler, chatterbox, gabbler

пљачка[1] *f* 1 pillage, plunder, robbery 2 *rare* booty; воена пљачка spoils of war

пљачка[2] *impf* to plunder, pillage, rob; to fleece

пљачкаш *m* marauder

пљачки *pl dial.* belongings, chattels

пљачкоса *pf see* пљачка[2]

пљачкосува *impf of* пљачкоса

пневматичен -чна & **пневматички** *adj* pneumatic; пневматичко тркало pneumatic wheel; пневматичко оружје air rifle

пневмонија *f Med.* pneumonia

по *prep* 1 (*movement*) along; down; over; on; in; about; слегува по скали to go down the stairs; плови по небо to float in the sky; удри некого по глава to hit s.o. over (on) the head; оди по улица to go along the street; погледна по собата he looked round the room; шета по паркот to stroll in the park; оди некому по трагите to follow in s.o.'s footsteps; по реката угоре up river; по реката удолу down river 2 (*aim*) for, after; оди по невеста to go to get a bride; дојде по книги to come for books; прати по лекар to send for a doctor; оди по работа 1. to go looking for work 2. to finish a job 3 (*direction*) at; after; кучињата леја по нив the dogs were barking at them; полицијаците пукаа по илегалецот the policemen were shooting at the law-breaker 4 (*of mourning/longing, etc.*) for, about; тагуваше по (за) сина си she was mourning for her son; жал по младост regret for one's youth; се тресевме по него we were very worried about him 5 (*of sequence, order*) behind; after; вие сте по мене you are after me; парче по парче bit by bit; капка по капка drop by drop; малку по малку little by little; еден по еден one by one; по смртта на татка му after his father's death; по два дена in two days' time; по пристигнување on arrival 6 (*of duration*) по цел ден не е дома he's out all day; чека по цели саати to wait for hours; по цела ноќ работи he works all night 7 (*of weather conditions, etc.*) in; по магла и дожд in fog and rain; по сонце in the sunshine; по такво време in such weather; по лад<овина> while it was cool; по месечина in the moonlight 8 (*of distributed numbers, amount, size, price*) at; costing; по педесет денари килото at fifty denars a kilo; по три метра платно three metres of cloth each; седеа по

четворица they were sitting in groups of four; влегува по двајца to enter two at a time (two by two); по таа цена at that price; по жител per capita 9 (*in multiplication*) times; осум по пет се четириесет eight fives are forty 10 (*of manner, style, language*) in; like; by; in accordance with; облечен по селски dressed in peasant style; по српски in Serbian; по старо in the old way; по инерција by force of inertia; по војнички in military style; облечена по мода fashionably dressed; по закон by law; по правило as usual; ❏ по мое мислење in my opinion 11 (*of relationship*) by; in; другари по оружје comrades in arms; ❏ брат по Христа brother in Christ 12 (*of dress*) in; излегол по чорапи he went out in his stockinged feet; оди по палто to go about in one's coat 13 (*of intermediary, medium*) by; over, on; прати пари по човек to send money by messenger; зборува по (преку) радио to speak on (over) the radio; по (преку) телефон by telephone; по пошта/по железница by post/by rail 14 (*of cause, reason; occasion*) because of; in accordance with; by; по погрешка by mistake; ❏ по повод <на> тоа because of this; on the occasion of this 15 (*of science, scholarly discipline*) of; in; студент по философија philosophy student; учебник по историја history textbook; курс по физика physics course; испит по (од) политичка економија examination in political economy; специјалист по (за) внатрешни болести specialist in internal disorders 16 (*miscellaneous*) by; in; го познал по гласот he recognized him by his voice; ако се суди по изгледот judging by appearances; прв по важност first in importance; нежен по природа tender by nature; по народност е Македонец by nationality he is a Macedonian; ❏ се разбира само по (од) себе that goes without saying

по-[1] *verbal prefix indicating* 1 *action performed to a slight or lesser degree or for a short time*; поигра to play/dance for a while 2 *change of state*; побледи to turn pale; побугари to Bulgarize 3 *beginning of action*; потрча to start running 4 *completion*; поцрни to blacken; поарчи to spend 5 *action performed by many subjects*; поседне to sit down

по-[2] *prefix* 1 *forming the comparative degree*; поубав more beautiful; помек softer; по-на-север further north; (*sometimes used with nouns*) помајстор <од него> more skilled craftsman <than him> 2 (*with nouns*) foster-; помајка foster-mother; поќерка foster-daughter

поаѓа *impf of* појде to start out, leave, depart; кога поаѓа возот? when does the train leave? ❏ поаѓа од гледиштето (*дека . . .*) to start from the premise (*that . . .*); му поаѓа од (по) рака he succeeds, he manages

поаѓање *n* departure

поајдучи се *pf* to become a haiduk, an outlaw

поаловее *pf poet.* to turn red, flush, blush

поалови *pf poet.* I 1 to redden *trans.* 2 to blush, turn red II – **се** *see* I 2

поарчи (се) *pf colloq. see* потроши (се)

поарчува (се) *impf of* поарчи (се)

побаботи *pf* 1 to roar, boom, rumble 2 to make a noise; децата побаботија и си отидоа the children made a bit of noise and went away 3 (*за оган, печка*) to blaze for a while 4 *fig.* to babble, chatter a bit

побабува *pf* to be (act as) a midwife (*for a time*)

побара *pf* 1 to look for; to call up; побарај ме дома look me up at home 2 to demand, claim; to request, ask for; to seek, look for; побара решение to seek a solution; побаравме да се почитаат решенијата we demanded that the decisions should be abided by 3 *dial.* to search (*s.o.*) bodily, frisk

побарува *impf* 1 *of* побара 2 *Book-keeping* to credit

побарување *n* 1 demand; побарување различни стоки demand for various goods 2 crediting; credit; побарувања и должења crediting and debiting; ненаплативо побарување frozen credit 3 (*барање*) claim, demand; request

побарувач *m* creditor; claimant

побарувачка *f* demand; requirement; побарувачка на стоки demand for goods; понуда и побарувачка supply and demand

побегне *pf* побегна *aor.* to run away, escape, flee; to bolt; (*да се омажи*) to elope; побегне од затвор to escape from prison

побегнува *impf of* побегне

победа *f* victory, triumph; ❑ Пирова победа Pyrrhic victory

победен[1] *pt* defeated; conquered; (*as noun*) победниците и победените the victors and the vanquished

победен[2] -дна *adj see* победнички

победи *pf* to conquer, vanquish, win a victory (*over*); to win; *fig.* to overcome, master; кој победи на фудбалскиот натпревар? who won the football (soccer) match? победи страв to overcome one's fear; победи <свои> страсти to master one's passions

победлив *adj* vincible, conquerable

победливост *f* vincibility

победник -ци *m* victor, conqueror; winner

победница & **победничка** *f* (*fem. form*) *see* победник

победнички *adj* victorious, triumphant; of victory; победничка екипа winning (victorious) team

победоносен -сна *adj* conquering, victorious, triumphant; победоносен изглед triumphant appearance

победоносец -сци *m Rel.* victor

победува *impf of* победи

побелее *pf* побелеа *aor. see* побели 1

побели *pf* 1 to turn white, pale *intrans.*; to go grey; побелија полињата the fields turned white; сиот побелел во лицето his face went quite pale 2 to whiten

побелува *impf of* побели & побелее

побесни *pf* 1 to become rabid 2 *fig.* to lose one's temper, fly into a rage; побесни од јад to go mad with fury

побеснува *impf of* побесни

побива *impf of* побие

побие[1] *pf* поби *aor.* 1 *rare* (*забие*) to ram, drive in *trans.*; побие колје to drive in stakes 2 *fig.* to rebut, refute; побие нечие мислење to refute s.o.'s opinion

побие[2] се *pf* поби се *aor. in the expression:* побие се шега со некого to make fun of s.o. (*for a while*), have a bit of fun at s.o.'s expense

побирок *m dial.* gleanings (*after grape harvest*)

побледи & **побледне** *pf* побледи & побледна *aor.* to fade; to turn pale *intrans.*; побледне од бес to turn livid with rage

побожен -жна *adj* pious, devout; побожна жена pious woman; ❑ *literary* побожна желба pious wish

побожност *f* piety, devoutness, reverence

поболи *pf* I to cause (*s.o.*) to fall ill II – ce to fall ill (sick)

поболува (се) *impf of* поболи (се)

поборник -ци *m* advocate, champion, upholder; поборник на мир champion of the cause of peace

поборница & **поборничка** *f* (*fem. form*) *see* поборник

поборнички *adj* persevering, determined; active

побрати *pf arch. see* побратими

побратим *m* 1 blood-brother 2 (*најблизок пријател*) bosom friend 3 (*as a form of address*) brother, pal, *Brit., Austral.* mate 4 *dial.* best man; ❑ стар побратим witness at a wedding

побратими *pf* I to take (*s.o.*) as a blood-brother/close friend II – ce to swear brotherhood (*со некого – with s.o.*)

побратимица *f* wife of blood-brother/close friend

побратимка *f rare see* побратимица

побратимски *adj* of blood-brothers; close, intimate

побратимство *n* blood-brotherhood (*custom of forming blood-brother relationship; the relationship itself*)

побратимува (се) *impf of* побратими (се)

побрза *pf* I 1 to hurry, hasten *intrans.*; ❑ *joc.* побрзај пополека! make haste slowly! 2 *rare* (*забрза*) to hurry *trans.*; побрза работа to speed up work II – ce *dial. see* I 1

побрзува (се) *impf of* побрза (се)

побрка *pf* I 1 to confuse, muddle; to embarrass; сте им ги побркале имињата you have confused their names 2 to drive (*s.o.*) crazy; таа дури го побрка she drove him quite crazy 3 to mix (*a little, for a short time*) 4 to chase, pursue (*a little, for a short time*); *dial.* to chase off, drive off, drive away II – ce 1 to get confused 2 to go out of one's mind, go crazy, go mad 3 to chase each other (*for a short time*)

побркан *pt* 1 confused, perplexed; muddled; complicated; побркани сметки confused calculations 2 *rare* mad, off one's head, crazy

побрканост *f* muddle, confusion

побркува (се) *impf of* побрка (се)

побрлави & **побрливи** *pf* I 1 to give a sheep gid 2 *fig.* to make an idiot (*of s.o.*), drive (*s.o.*) crazy 3 to become affected with gid 4 *fig.* to become crazy, idiotic II – ce *see* I 3 & 4

побрлавува (се) & **побрливува (се)** *impf of* побрлави (се) & побрливи (се)

побугари *pf* I to Bulgarize II – ce to become Bulgarian

побугарува (се) *impf of* побугари (се)

побуда *f* incentive; initiative; impulse, impetus; incitement; родољубиви побуди patriotic intentions; од сопствени побуди for personal motives (reasons)

побудали *pf* I 1 to go mad, crazy; ќе побудали од вас човек you can drive a person mad; побудалел по неа he went crazy about her 2 to make (*s.o.*) mad, drive mad II – ce *see* I 1

побудалува (се) *impf of* побудали (се)

побуди *pf* 1 to prompt, impel, urge; тоа го побудило да ѝ пише that made him write to her; ❑ ce чувствувам побуден I feel impelled 2 to excite, call forth, awaken, arouse; неговиот предлог побуди внимание his proposal attracted attention

побудува *impf of* побуди

побуни *pf* **I** to incite to rebellion, stir up, arouse; to agitate *trans.*; ги побуни масите he stirred up the masses **II** – **се 1** to rebel; to revolt; во него се побуни нешто something inside him revolted **2** *rare* to be indignant (*for a while*); to complain (*a bit*)

повампирен *adj* re-emergent; renewed, resuscitated (*of s.th. evil*); повампирен шовинизам renewed chauvinism

повампири се *pf* **1** *arch.* to become a vampire **2** *fig.* (*of s.th. evil*) to reappear, resurface; to raise (rear) one's head

повампирува се *impf of* повампири се

поваса *pf colloq.* to overcome, master, defeat (*also fig.*); сонот пак ги поваса sleep overcame them again

повасува *impf of* поваса

повев *m poet.* **1** breath <of air>; никаде ни повев not a breath of air; првиот повев на пролетта the first breath of spring **2** waving, fluttering

повева (се) *impf of* повее (се)

поведе[1] *pf* **I 1** to lead, take, bring (*a person or animal*); to lead away; сина си го повел в Америка he took his son to America; полицајците ги поведоа студентите the policemen picked up the students; ги поведе во борба he led them in the struggle **2** (*in certain expressions*) to start; поведе борба to launch a campaign; поведе разговор to start (strike up) a conversation; поведе иницијатива to take the initiative; поведе оро to lead off an *oro* **II** – **се** *fig.* (*no*) to follow, imitate; се поведовме по нив we followed their example; се повел по умот на такви he followed (imitated) such ideas

поведе[2] **(се)** *pf dial. see* поведне (се)

поведение *n* behaviour, conduct; примерно поведение exemplary conduct

поведне (се) *pf dial.* поведна (се) *aor. see* наведе[1] (се), наведне (се)

поведнува (се) *impf of* поведне (се)

поведува[1] **(се)** *impf of* поведе[1] (се)

поведува[2] **(се)** *impf of* поведе[2] (се)

повее *pf* повеа *aor.* **I 1** to begin to blow; to start blowing gently (puffing); повеал ветар од море a breeze blew up from the sea **2** to blow a little, for a short time (*of the wind and of snow driven by the wind*); повеа и запре it blew a little and stopped **3** to winnow (*grain*) a little, for a short time **II** – **се** to wave <in the wind>, flutter a little, for a short time; се повеа знамето the flag fluttered for a while

повез *m* cover, binding (*of a book*)

повезден *adv* all day long

повеј -си *m poet. see* повев

повела[1] *f* **1** command; decree, edict; така било Божја повела so the Lord ordained; ❑ под моја повела under my command **2** *rare see* повелба 1

повела[2] *impf* to rule, lord it over, push (*s.o.*) around; коњ без узда не се повела *prov.* you can't control a horse without a bridle

повелач *m colloq.* master, boss

повелба *f* **1** charter; Повелбата на Обединетите нации Charter of the United Nations **2** *rare see* повела 1

повелбен *adj rare* authoritative; со повелбен тон in a commanding tone

повели *pf* **1** *rare* to order, command **2** welcome; help yourself! да повелите да дојдете на Велигден please come for Easter; повели седни please be seated

повелико *adv arch. see* повеќе 1

повелник -ци *m* master, ruler

повене *pf* повена *aor. see* овене

поверен *pt* entrusted

поверник -ци *m* **1** delegate; поверник на комитетот delegate of the committee **2** commissioner **3** representative, agent

повереница & **повереничка** *f* (*fem. form*) *see* поверник

поверенички *adj* delegate's, representative's

поверенство *n* commissariat; commission

повери (се) *pf see* довери (се)

поверлив *adj see* доверлив

поверливо *adv see* доверливо

поверува[1] *pf* to <start to> believe

поверува[2] **(се)** *impf of* повери (се)

повесмо *n see* пасмо

повест *f* story, novella, tale

повеќе *adv* **1** (*comparative of* многу) more; повеќе сака to prefer; ❑ сè повеќе more and more; колку повеќе толку поубаво the more the merrier; повеќе или помалку more or less; ни повеќе ни помалку (*ами* . . . , *туку* . . .) neither more nor less (*but* . . .); до толку повеќе (*што* . . .) all the more so (*that* . . .); нешто повеќе, од тоа more than that, on top of that; тоа и ништо повеќе that and nothing more; ако ништо повеќе . . . if nothing else; на ручекот повеќе зборуваа отколку што јадеа at lunch they talked more than they ate **2** (*with negation, веќе*) no more; no longer; никогаш повеќе нема да одам таму never again will I go there; немојте повеќе да се расправате stop arguing! **3** several, some, a few; повеќе луѓе several people **4** (*as noun, usu. with the article -то*) *n* majority; most; во повеќето случаи in most cases; повеќето од нив не дојдоа the majority of them didn't come; тоа се повеќето млади луѓе they are mostly young people

повеќе- (*in compounds*) many-, poly-; повеќегодишен of several years; повеќесложен polysyllabic

повеќегласен -сна *adj Mus.* for several/many voices/ instruments

повеќегодишен -шна *adj* of/lasting several years; повеќегодишни напори efforts lasting several years

повеќедневен -вна *adj* of/lasting several days

повеќемесечен -чна *adj* of/lasting several months

повеќемина & **повеќе мина** *adv* several people; more; ние бевме повеќемина there were several of us; повеќемина автори стојат на спротивно гледиште more authors hold the opposite view

повеќепати & **повеќе пати** *adv* several times

повеќечасовен -вна *adj* lasting several hours

повечера *pf* **1** to sup/dine, have supper/dinner; да повечераме и да си легнеме let's have supper and go to bed **2** *rare* to sup/dine in haste, lightly

повечерие -ија & **повечерје** *n* **1** *Rel.* (*вечерна*) evensong, vespers **2** *Mil.* lights out, tattoo, retreat, *Am.* taps; уште не свирело повечерје "lights out" hasn't sounded yet

повива (се) *impf of* повие (се)

повив\<а\>че *n see* пеленаче

повивка *f* 1 wrapping; napkin, nappy, *Am.* diaper 2 *Bot.* (Convolvulus arvensis) \<small/field\> bindweed

повие *pf* пови *aor.* **I 1** to swathe, swaddle; to wrap (*a child*) in nappies 2 *rare* (*наведне, свие*) to bend, bend down *trans.* **II – се** *rare* (*наведне се, свие се*) to bend down *intrans.*; гранките се повиле the branches bowed down

повик -ци *m* shout; call, appeal; vocation, profession; повик до граѓаните appeal to the citizens; им пратиле повик да се предадат they have sent them a call to surrender

повика *pf* **I 1** (*покани*) to invite; to call; to summon; повика некого на свадба to invite s.o. to a wedding; ❑ повика на одговорност to call to account; повика некого војник to be called up (drafted) into the army; повика на суд to summon \<to court\> 2 to shout, give a shout; повика колку го држи грл to shout at the top of one's voice 3 to shout a little, for a while **II – се** (*на*) to cite, refer to; се повика на сведоци to cite witnesses; се повика на законот to cite the law

повикува (се) *impf of* повика (се); се повикувам на вашето писмо in response to your letter, regarding your letter

повинува се *pf & impf literary* (*with dat.*) to obey; to submit to, abide by, comply with; им се повинува на прописите to comply with the regulations

повит *m see* павит

повишен *pt & adj* increased, raised; повишен глас (тон) raised voice (tone); повишен крвен притисок high blood pressure

повиши *pf* **I** to raise, increase *trans.*; повиши цени to raise prices **II – се** to rise, increase *intrans.*; се повишиле платите wages have gone up (risen); му се повишил крвниот притисок his blood pressure has risen

повишува (се) *impf of* повиши (се)

повјаса *pf colloq.* (*побрза*) to hurry, hasten, rush

повлада *pf* to overcome, take over; to cover; сета снага му ја повладале струпје sores spread all over his body

повладува *impf of* повлада

повластица *f* 1 reduced fare; concession; повластица за возење по железница concession on rail travel 2 *rare see* привилегија

повлекува (се) *impf of* повлече (се)

повлече *pf* повлеков *1st p. sg aor.* **I 1** to \<give a\> tug; to pull; повлече некого за ракав to tug s.o. by the sleeve 2 to haul, pull along; to drag; коњите ја повлекоа колата the horses pulled the cart; ветрот нè повлече на таа страна the wind dragged us in that direction; ❑ повлече нога to start the ball rolling; to make a start 3 to withdraw *trans.*; повлече војска to withdraw troops 4 *fig.* to take back, renounce, revoke, retract; повлече збор to take back one's word; повлече предлог to withdraw one's proposal; банката ги повлече старите банкноти the bank withdrew the old bankotes from circulation 5 to mark out, draw; повлече бразда to make a furrow; повлече линија/граница to draw a line/boundary 6 *fig.* to cause, produce, bring about; to lead to, entail 7 *fig., rare* to carry forward, inspire; сите ги повлече токму верата во победа it was precisely their belief

in victory that carried them all forward **II – се 1** to withdraw *intrans.*, retreat; непријателот се повлече од позициите the enemy retreated from his positions 2 to retire; се повлече од јавниот живот to retire from public life 3 to renounce; се повлече од својата кандидатура to withdraw one's candidacy

повлечен *adj* shy, withdrawn; повлечен човек reclusive person; повлечен карактер reserved nature

повлеченост *f* reserve; retirement (*from public life, etc.*)

повлечува (се) *impf see* повлекува (се)

повлијае *pf* повлијаа *aor.* to influence, exert an influence on; тоа ќе повлијае на нив that will influence them

повод¹ *m* cause, grounds, motive, pretext; бара повод to seek; божемен повод ostensible (professed) excuse (pretext); ❑ без секаков повод without any cause; користи повод to avail oneself of an opportunity (occasion); дава повод (*за разни заклучоци*) to give cause (grounds) (*for various conclusions*); по тој повод on that occasion; for that reason; по повод \<на\> нешто because of s.th., in the event of s.th.; по повод (на) неговата изјава regarding (with reference to) his announcement

повод² *m* 1 (*водило*) halter; headstall 2 *dial.* long shoot or leader on a vine (*dug into the ground to form a new vine*)

поводлив *adj* submissive, pliable; weak-willed

поводливост *f* pliability, submissiveness

поводник -ци *m see* водило, повод² 1

повоен *adj* post-war; повоени услови post-war conditions

повој -ои *m* 1 swaddling band; swaddling-clothes, nappies 2 *fig.* infancy; тој вид спорт е уште во повој (повои) that kind of sport is still in its infancy

повојница *f* 1 first presents (*for new-born baby*) 2 customary first visit to the mother and new-born baby (*with gift-giving*)

повојниче *n see* пеленаче

повојче *n dim. hyp. of* повој 1

поволен -лна *adj* favourable, propitious; поволни услови favourable conditions; поволна цена advantageous price

поврага *adv* to the devil (*with s.th.*); нека оди сè поврага! let everything go to the devil! to hell with it!

поврат *m* 1 restitution; recovery; со поврат на парите with repayment (refund) of money owed; поврат на долг debt redemption 2 *Leg.* repetition of an offence, recurrence; злосторството е сторено во поврат the crime has been perpetrated in repeated violation of the law

повратен -тна *adj* 1 returning; return; recurrent; повратна сила returning force; повратно дејство retroactive action; повратни информации feedback 2 *Gram.* reflexive; повратни глаголи reflexive verbs; повратна заменка reflexive pronoun 3 return; повратен \<возен\> билет, повратна \<возна\> карта return ticket

поврати¹ *pf* **I 1** to get back, recover *trans.*; си ги повратиле парите they got their money back 2 to bring back; to return *trans.*; to restore; тоа му ја повратило силата that restored his strength; му ја повратиле душата they helped him to get his breath back 3 to resuscitate, revive *trans.*; ❑ го повратиле во живот they brought him back to life **4** (*only in 3rd p.*) to return to *intrans.*; to recur; го повратила болеста his illness returned **5** (*with dat.*) to reply to; to retort **II** – **се 1** to return *intrans.*; to recur; му се поврати преѓешната сила his former strength returned; болеста пак му се повратила his illness returned **2** to recover, come round, come to, revive *intrans.*; онесвестениот се поврати the man who had fainted came to **3** *colloq.* (*in gambling*) to recover one's losses

поврати² *pf* to bring up, vomit; поврати сѐ што касна he brought up all he had eaten

повратник -ци *m* returnee

повратница & **повратничка** *f* **1** (*fem. form*) *see* повратник **2** redelivery note

повратува (се) *impf see* повраќа¹ (се)

повраќа¹ *impf* **I 1** *see* поврати¹ **2** (*impf only*) to use often, repeat (*certain words*) **II** – **се** *of* поврати¹ се

повраќа² *impf* **I** *of* поврати²; повраќа на пат to suffer from travel-sickness **II** – **се** *impers.* (*with dat.*) ми се повраќа I feel nauseous; I'm going to be sick

повраќање *n* vomiting; го тера на повраќање it makes him vomit; *Med.* средство за (против) повраќање travel-sickness pills; средство за (што предизвикува) повраќање emetic

повреда *f* **1** injury, wound; тешка телесна повреда serious injury; grievous bodily harm; повреда на работа work-related injury, accident at work **2** *fig.* infringement, violation; повреда на законот infringement of the law

повреди *pf* **I 1** to injure, hurt, wound; си ја повредил ногата he injured his foot/leg **2** *fig.* to offend, hurt; ја повредиле неговата чест they offended his honour **3** *fig.* to violate, infringe, break; повреди правило to break a rule **II** – **се** to injure o.s., hurt o.s.; падна од дрво и се повреди he fell from a tree and injured himself

повредува (се) *impf of* повреди (се)

повремен *adj* **1** occasional; повремени грмежи occasional thunder <claps> **2** periodical; повремено списание periodical journal

поврзаност *f* ties, links; деловна поврзаност business links

поврзе *pf* поврза *aor.* **I** to connect, join, unite, link *trans.*; поврзете ме со директорот please put me through to the director **II** – **се** *fig.* to contact, get in touch (*co – with*)

поврзло *n* (*of a bag, pot, etc.*) strap; handle; cord

поврзува (се) *impf of* поврзе (се)

површен -шна *adj* superficial; cursory; површен посматрач superficial observer; површна критика superficial criticism

површина *f* **1** surface; површината на водата the surface of the water; површината на земјата the surface of the earth; обработлива површина arable land ❏ излезе на површина to rise to the surface; се лизга (оди) по површината (*на нешто*) to slide (move) over the surface (*of s.th.*) **2** *Math.* area; површина на квадратот area of the square; површина и зафатнина area and volume

површински *adj* **1** superficial, outward, external; површинско ткиво surface tissue **2** *Math.* <of> area, square; површинска единица area (square) measure

површност *f* superficiality

повте *pf* **1** to want to; to feel like, fancy (*doing s.th.*); повте да го запраша he felt like asking him **2** to try to; to dare; повте да дојде дома to make an effort to get home

повтор *adv see* одново, повторно

повторен -рна *adj* repeated, renewed; повторен избор new election/re-election; повторна забелешка repeated (renewed) remark; повторен преглед second review/re-examination

повтори *pf* **I 1** to repeat *trans.*; повторете ги по мене овие зборови repeat these words after me! повтори клас to repeat a year **2** to echo; планината го повтори нивниот повик the mountain echoed their cry **3** to revise, *Am.* review **4** *literary* to reproduce, imitate **5** (*only in 3rd p.*) to recur; to start again; болеста му го повтори his illness returned; ќе повтори дождот it's going to rain again **II** – **се 1** to recur; to repeat o.s.; ❏ историјата се повтори history repeated itself **2** (*only in 3rd p.*) *see* I 5

повторлив *adj* **1** repeatable; repetitive; recurrent; успехот е лесно повторлив the success can easily be repeated **2** *Gram.* iterative; повторливи глаголи iterative (frequentative) verbs

повторливост *f* **1** repeatability; repetitiveness **2** *Gram.* iterativeness (*of verbs*)

повторно *adv* again, anew

повторува (се) *impf of* повтори (се)

повторување *n* repetition; ❏ повторувањето е мајка на знаењето practice makes perfect

повторувач *m colloq.* pupil who is repeating a year

повторувачка *f* (*fem. form*) *see* повторувач

повтува *impf of* повте

погаѓа *impf* **I** *of* погоди **II** – **се 1** to bargain, haggle **2** (*погодува се*) *impf of* погоди се

погаѓач *m* guesser, diviner; погаѓач на туѓи мисли diviner of other people's thoughts

погази *pf* **1** to tread, step (*briefly*) **2** *fig.* to transgress, break, violate; погази закон to break the law

погазува *impf of* погази

погали *pf* **I** to caress, stroke, pet, fondle (*for a while*) **II** – **се** to fondle each other, caress each other, hug each other a little

погалува (се) *impf of* погали (се)

поган *adj* unclean, dirty; foul, vile, repulsive, evil; погана уста foul mouth; поган јазик evil tongue; (*as noun*) *m* & *f* (*usu. of a snake*) vile creature

поганец -нци *m* evil person

погани *impf* **1** to dirty, soil **2** to dishonour, desecrate, profane

поганија -ии *f* **1** dirty thing; dirty trick<s> **2** evil person

поганица *f see* поган (*as noun*)

поганка *f* (*fem. form*) *see* поганец

поганштија -ии *f colloq.* **1** *coll.* scum, riffraff **2** *see* поганија 1

поганштина *f* base, mean act

погача *f Cul.* round flat loaf, focaccia; *Austral., N.Z.* damper; зрно по зрно погача *prov.* many a mickle makes a muckle; бара преку леб погача *prov.* no man is content with his lot; acorns were good till bread was found

погачар *m* idler; sponger, parasite

погачица *f dim. of* погача; small puff pastry, pasty

погибеж & **погибел** *m* last quarter of the moon; ❑ од новина на погибеж on rare occasions

погине *pf* погина *aor.* 1 to perish, be killed 2 *fig.* to vanish, disappear 3 *dial.* to kill 4 *dial., f.p.* to lose; прстенот го погинал he has lost the ring

погинува *impf of* погине

поглавар *m literary* head, chief, leader

поглед *m* 1 look, gaze; glance; длабок поглед penetrating look; поглед наназад backward glance; ❑ ведне поглед to lower one's eyes (avert one's gaze); управи (впери, насочи) поглед на, во to turn one's gaze towards; фрли поглед на to cast an eye over; крене поглед to look up, raise one's eyes; измери со поглед to look (*s.o.*) over/up and down; задржи поглед (*на*) to rest one's gaze (eyes) (*on*); на прв поглед at first glance (sight); со еден поглед at a glance; далеку од погледот (погледите) на некого far from s.o.'s eyes; погледот му падна на (*некого/ нешто*) his eyes (glance) fell on (*s.o./s.th.*); од птичји поглед (од птичја перспектива) from a bird's-eye view; пресекува со поглед to give (*s.o.*) a dirty look 2 *fig.* (*usu. pl*) attention, interest; погледите на јавноста се управени кон него he is in the public eye 3 view, vista; собата е со поглед на морето the room looks out towards the sea 4 point of view, regard, respect; во тој поглед in that respect; во поглед на with regard to; во секој поглед in every respect; во морален поглед from a moral standpoint 5 opinion, view; застарени погледи old-fashioned views 6 *f.p.* на поглед on the look-out, on the alert

погледне *pf* погледна *aor.* 1 to look at; не смееше да го погледне в очи he didn't dare to look him in the eye; ❑ погледне низ прсти to turn a blind eye; погледне некого под око to glance at s.o. furtively; погледне некого напорки (накриво) to look at s.o. askance 2 to start taking care of (*s.o.*), showing concern for (*s.o.*); на старост нема кој да те погледне in your old age there won't be anyone to look after you 3 *literary, fig.* (*на*) to take an attitude to, consider, regard; на своите обврски погледне сериозно to take one's obligations seriously

погледнува *impf of* погледне

погне *pf* погна *aor.* I to drive, chase; to rush *trans.*; го погнале од сите страни they harried him from all sides II – **се** 1 to drive, chase one another; се погнаа по полето they chased each other over the field 2 *rare see* загне се 1

погнува (се) *impf of* погне (се)

поговор *m* epilogue

поговори *pf see* позборува

поговорка *f* saying, byword

погодба *f* 1 (*спогодба*) agreement, pact; settlement; understanding; по заемна погодба by mutual agreement (consent) 2 condition; terms, stipulations; под погодба (*дека*) on condition (*that*)

погодбен *adj Gram.* conditional; погодбена (условна) реченица conditional clause; погодбен (условен) начин conditional mood

погоден[1] *pt* 1 offended, hurt; тој се почувствува погоден he felt offended 2 suitable, convenient; well-equipped; погодена куќа well-appointed house 3 agreed; погодена цена agreed price

погоден[2] -дна *adj* suitable, appropriate; convenient, favourable; под погодни услови under favourable

conditions; во погодниот момент at the appropriate moment

погоди *pf* I 1 to guess; to foretell 2 to hit <the target>; не погоди to miss 3 *fig.* to hit on, find; to choose (correctly) го погодиле патот they hit on the right road; го погодиле денот кога да дојдат they picked the right day to come 4 to agree a price for; колку го погоди куќата? what price did you agree on for the house? 5 to hire, engage (*labour*); погоди мајстори to take on craftsmen 6 *literary, fig.* to offend, hurt; ме погодија <в срце> неговите зборови his words cut me to the quick 7 to clean, put in order, tidy up; to fit out, kit out; погоди куќа to tidy up a house 8 (*with dat.*) to satisfy, please; не можеш секому да му погодиш you can't please everyone II – **се** 1 to come to terms, strike a bargain, reach agreement; се погодивте ли за куќата? have you come to an agreement on the house? 2 to happen to be; to find o.s.; во куќата се погодил син my his son happened to be in the house 3 *impers.* to happen; ова на мнозина им се погодило that has happened to many people 4 to be, prove to be, turn out to be; децата се погодија послушни the children proved to be obedient 5 (*with dat.*) to come out as one wished; to prove suitable, favourable; им се погодило времето they had ideal weather

погодност *f* 1 suitability, appropriateness; comfort 2 *literary* advantage; benefit, privilege; посебни погодности fringe benefits

погодок -ци *m* accurate shot, goal; полн погодок bull's-eye; jackpot

погодува (се) *impf see* погаѓа (се)

погодувач *m see* погаѓач

поголтне *pf* поголтна *aor.* 1 to swallow (*once*) 2 *fig.* to seize, steal, take by fraud; му ги поголтнаа паричките they robbed him of his money

поголтнува *impf of* поголтне

погон[1] *m* 1 motive power, propulsion; energy; operation; електричен погон electrical energy (power); млазен погон jet propulsion; стави во погон to start up (*an engine*), set in motion; пушти во погон to put into operation 2 workshop, section; фабрика со повеќе погони factory with several sections

погон[2] *m arch.* (*загон*) rood, dönüm (*square measure: 920 m²*)

погонски *adj* power, drive *attrib.*; погонска сила motive power, propulsion, thrust; погонски уреди engines, power units; погонско гориво engine fuel; погонски трошоци operating (running) costs

погордее се *pf* погордеа се *aor.* 1 to be arrogant, haughty for a while 2 to become arrogant, haughty

погорелец -лци *m* fire victim

погорешти *pf f.p. see* згорешти

погосподи се *pf* to become a gentleman, go up in the world; to become lordly, high and mighty

погосподува се *impf of* погосподи се

пограб *m f.p.* на пограб ready to snatch, waiting <for an opportunity> to steal

пограби *pf* to abduct, carry off (*a girl*)

пограѓани *pf colloq.* I to urbanize, gentrify, turn (*s.o., usu. a peasant*) into a townsman/woman, city-dweller II – **се** to become a townsman/woman, city-dweller; to become urbanized; to become gentrified

пограѓанува (се) *impf of* пограѓани (се)

пограничен -чна *adj* frontier, boundary, border; пограничен премин border crossing; пограничен столб border post; погранични инциденти border incidents

погрда *f* abuse, defamation; swear-word; outrage; mockery

погрден -дна *adj* abusive; nasty, disgusting; shameful; *Gram.* pejorative; погрдни зборови insulting words

погреб *m* burial, funeral, interment

погребален -лна *adj rare see* погребен

погребе *pf* погреба *aor.* to bury, inter; *fig.* to ruin; ги погребавте своите шанси you've ruined your chances

погребен -бна *adj* funeral, burial; погребна кола hearse; погребна процесија funeral procession; погребно претпријатие undertaker's <firm>, *Am.* funeral home (parlor); погребна реч funeral oration

погребува *impf of* погребе

погрешен[1] *pt* weak, run down, weakened

погрешен[2] -шна *adj* incorrect, wrong, mistaken; erroneous; погрешен одговор wrong answer; погрешни заклучоци erroneous conclusions; погрешен чекор false step/move

погреши *pf* **I 1** to make a mistake, err, be wrong **2** (*with dat.*) to cause harm (*to s.o.*) **II – се 1** to ail, suffer ill health, go downhill **2** to go wrong (awry)

погрешка *f* mistake, error; граматичка погрешка grammatical mistake; ❑ по погрешка by mistake (in error)

погрешно *adv* wrong; by mistake; го разбрале погрешно they misunderstood him, *colloq.* they got him wrong; погрешно известен misinformed; погрешно пресметано miscalculated

погрешува (се) *impf of* погреши (се)

погрижи се *pf* to take care (*за – of*), look after, see to; јас ќе се погрижам за таа работа I'll take care of that business

погрижува се *impf of* погрижи се

погром *m* pogrom

погруби *pf* **I 1** to disfigure **2** to become coarse/ugly **II – се** *see* **I** 2

погрубува (се) *impf of* погруби (се)

погрчи *pf* **I** to make Greek, Hellenize **II – се** to become Greek, be Hellenized

погрчува (се) *impf of* погрчи (се)

погубен -бна *adj literary* ruinous; dangerous, perilous; harmful; погубно влијание fatal influence

погуби *pf* **I 1** to kill, murder; to put to death, execute **2** to lose (*completely*); *f.p.* умот ќе си го погуби he'll go out of his mind **3** *fig.* to waste; to destroy, ruin; младоста си ја погубив I've wasted my youth **II – се** *fig.* to destroy o.s.; to bring misery, grief on o.s.

погубува (се) *impf of* погуби (се)

под[1] *prep* **1** under, below; под земја underground; под педесет години under fifty <years old>; три степени под нулата three degrees below zero; под раководство на under the leadership of; под знамето на under the banner of; под дејство на алкохол under the influence of drink; под влијанието на околината under the influence of the surroundings/milieu; се урнал под сопствената

тежина it collapsed under its own weight; статија под наслов ... article under the title ... ; познат под името ... known by the name <of> ... ; под добри услови in favourable/good conditions/circumstances; под закануваше under threat; од под from under; ❑ под секоја критика beneath all criticism; под нос ти е тоа it's right under your nose; под клуч under lock and key; in jail; под услов да ... on condition that ... ; под оружје under arms; под кирија (наем) rented out (on hire); под изговор (*дека*) on the pretext (*that*); под рака arm in arm; on the black market; под гаранција under guarantee (warranty) **2** right up to, as far as; дојдоа под самите ѕидишта they came right up to the ramparts

под[2] *m* floor; од подот до таванот from floor to ceiling; под со паркет parquet floor

под-[1] (под- *before voiceless consonants*) *verbal prefix indicating* **1** *action performed to a slight or lesser degree;* поджегне to sting, offend (*slightly*) **2** *action beneath, directed downward;* подвлече to underline; подвлече to drag under **3** *action performed furtively;* подговори to remind discreetly

под-[2] (под- *before voiceless consonants*) (*as prefix of nouns and adjectives*) sub-; under-; vice-; поткожен subcutaneous; подјармен subjugated; подгрупа subgroup; потполковник lieutenant-colonel

подава (се) *impf of* подаде (се)

подаде *pf* **I 1** to serve, offer; to hand, pass; подаде некому рака to offer s.o. one's hand; подаде топка to pass a ball **2** to show (*one's head*); тој подаде глава од прозорецот he showed his head at the window **3** *rare* to hand in, submit, lodge (*an application*); подаде молба to lodge an application **II – се 1** to show o.s., appear (*through an opening*); детето се подаде од прозорецот the child appeared at the window **2** (*with dat.*) to give o.s.; таа одбиваше да му се подаде she refused to give herself to him

подајник -ци & *usu.* **поданик** -ци *m arch.* (*државјанин*) subject, citizen; турски поданик Turkish subject; поданици на царот subjects of the emperor (tsar)

подајница & *usu.* **поданица, поданичка** *f arch.* (*fem. form*) *see* подајник, поданик

подајнички & *usu.* **поданички** *adj arch.* of a subject; поданичка верност a subject's loyalty

поданство *n arch.* (*државјанство*) citizenship; луѓе без поданство stateless persons

подари *pf* **1** to present, donate, give a present; ❑ подари некому живот to spare s.o.'s life; на подарен коњ (подарено магаре) забите не му се гледаат *prov.* one doesn't look a gift-horse in the mouth **2** to reward (*s.o. with s.th.*); подарам некого со подарок to reward s.o. with a gift;

подарок -ци *m* present, gift; свадбен подарок wedding present

подарува *impf of* подари

податлив *adj* flexible, pliant, yielding; податлив карактер compliant character

податливост *f* pliancy, flexibility

податок -ци *m* fact; datum, *pl* data; detail; биографски податоци biographical facts, personal details; важен податок important fact; собира податоци to collect data; врз основа на некои податоци on the basis of certain facts; обработка на податоци data processing

подбегне *pf* подбегна *aor.* to move away a little

подбел *m Bot.* (Tussilago farfara) coltsfoot

подбелее & **подбели** *pf* подбелеа & подбели *aor.* to turn slightly grey/white; to fade slightly; to turn slightly pale

подбере *pf* подбра *aor.* **1** (*забере*) to collect, round up, muster **2** *fig.* to begin to <pick a> quarrel; to attack, seize on, catch **3** *rare* (*избере*) to choose, select

подбив *m* mockery, derision; taunt, gibe; sneer; се бие подбив со некого to make fun of s.o.; ❑ ќе те земат на подбив they'll laugh at you

подбива <се> *impf of* подбие <се>

подбивач *m* joker; mocker; scoffer, sneerer

подбивен -вна *adj* derisive, mocking; taunting; sneering; подбивна насмевка sneer

подбие <се> *pf* подби *aor.* подбие <се> шега со некого to make fun of s.o.; to to mock (laugh at) s.o.

подбир *m* **1** *see* подбор **2** first harvest of tobacco

подбира *impf rare of* подбере 3

подбишег *m* & **подбишега** *f see* подбив; ❑ на подбишег<а>, за подбишег<а> in fun, as a joke

подбор *m* selection, choice; подбор на луѓе selection of people; врши подбор to make a selection; природен подбор natural selection

подбради *pf* **I** to put on (*a kerchief*) **II** – **се** to put on a kerchief

подбрадник -ци *m* **1** chin-cord, chin-strap **2** necklace of threaded coins

подбрадок -ци *m rare* double chin; (*на мисир*) wattle

подбрадува (се) *impf of* подбради (се)

подбуда *f rare see* побуда

подбуди *pf rare see* побуди

подбудува *impf of* подбуди

подбуни *pf* **I** to stir up, agitate, incite to revolt **II** – **се** to rebel, rise up

подбунува (се) *impf of* подбуни (се)

подбутне *pf* подбутна *aor.* **1** to push away slightly **2** *fig.* to reject, cease to take care of

подбуцне *pf* подбуцна *aor.* **I 1** to butt, spur; to prod, nudge; го подбуцна со лактот he nudged him with his elbow **2** *fig.* to egg on, incite **3** *fig.* to prick, sting a little, slightly **II** – **се** to push (shove) each other a little

подбуцнувач *m* agitator, rabble-rouser; воен подбуцнувач warmonger

подвари *pf* **I** to cook, boil (*briefly*) *trans.* **II** – **се** to go bad, go sour; млеково се подварило this milk's curdled

подварок *m* **1** (*изварка*) curds **2** cooked sauerkraut

подварува (се) *impf of* подвари (се)

подведе[1] *pf* **1** *literary* to reduce, bring down; to subsume (*под – into*); ❑ подведе под општ именител to reduce to a common denominator **2** (*некого на некого*) to procure (*s.o. for s.o.*)

подведе[2] **(се)** *pf dial. see* наведе[1] (се), наведне (се)

подведник -ци *m see* подведувач

подведница *f see* подведувачка

подведува[1] *impf of* подведе[1]

подведува[2] **(се)** *impf of* подведе[2] (се)

подведувач *m* procurer

подведувачка *f* procuress

подвене *pf* подвена *aor.* to fade, turn pale; to fade slightly, turn slightly pale

подвеска *f* (*usu. pl*) garter

подвива (се) *impf of* подвие (се)

подвиг -зи *m* exploit, deed; смел подвиг daring exploit; јуначки подвизи heroic deeds

подвид *m* subspecies

подвие *pf* подви *aor.* **I** to fold, tuck under; подвие ракави to roll up one's sleeves; ❑ подвие опаш<ка> to put one's tail between one's legs **II** – **се 1** to bend, bow **2** *fig.* to surrender **3** to curl up *intrans.*

подвижен -жна *adj* **1** movable, portable; подвижен мост drawbridge, lifting bridge; подвижни скелиња portable scaffolding; подвижна изложба travelling exhibition; *Phon.* подвижен акцент mobile accent (stress) **2** подвижен и недвижен имот personal estate (movable property) and real estate **3** mobile; agile, energetic, lively;

подвижник -ци *m Rel.* devotee, zealot; ascetic

подвижнички *adj Rel.* zealous; ascetic

подвижност *f* **1** agility; liveliness; energy **2** (*usu. pl*) movables

подвик -ци *m* shout; scolding

подвикне *pf* подвикна *aor.* **1** to call out, cry out, exclaim **2** (*with dat.*) to snap at; to scold, tell off **3** to call *trans.*

подвикнува *impf of* подвикне

подвитка (се) *pf see* подвие (се)

подвиткува (се) *impf of* подвитка (се)

подвластен *pt see* потчинет

подвласти *pf see* покори, потчини

подвластува *impf of* подвласти

подвлекува (се) *impf of* подвлече (се)

подвлече *pf* подвлеков *1st p. sg aor.* **I 1** to underline **2** to emphasize, stress **3** *rare* to drag under; подвлече нешто под кревет to drag s.th. under the bed **II** – **се** *fig.* (*with dat.*) to gain favour with

подвлечува (се) *impf see* подвлекува (се)

подводен -дна *adj* **1** swampy, marshy; <of> marshland, wetland подводно место marshy place **2** underwater; подводни карпи submerged rocks (reefs); подводно снимање underwater photography

подводи *pf* to flood (*land*)

подводник -ци *m see* подведувач

подводница *f see* подведувачка

подвоз *m rare* transport, haulage (*of goods, freight*); transportation (haulage) costs

подвозен -зна *adj rare* <of> transport, freight; подвозни трошоци haulage costs

подвозник -ци *m* underpass

подврзе *pf* подврза *aor.* **I 1** to tie, make fast, secure (*from below*) **2** to bind (*a book*) **II** – **се 1** to fasten (*one's belt*) tightly **2** *dial.* to bind o.s. with an agreement/promise/bet

подврзува (се) *impf of* подврзе (се)

подврне *pf* подврна *aor. usu. impers.* to rain, snow a little, slightly; ноќеска како да подврнало it seems that it rained a little last night

подврнува *impf of* подврне

подгази *pf* **1** to tread on <lightly> **2** *fig.* to go back on, break; си го подгази зборот to go back on one's word **3** *fig.* to insult, offend

подгазува *impf of* подгази

подговара *impf of* подговори

подговор *m* subdialect

подговори *pf* **1** (*with dat.*) to remind discreetly; to tell (*s.o.*) by hints, in a roundabout way; подговори му да не зборува веќе give him a hint not to talk any more! **2** *rare* (*наговори*) to persuade

подголтне *pf* подголтна *aor.* to swallow *intrans.*, gulp

подголтнува *impf of* подголтне

подгони *pf* to start chasing

подгонува *impf of* подгони

подгори *pf* **1** to burn, scorch, singe **2** to wilt, wither, fade

подгорјанин -ани *m f.p.* dweller of the foothills

подгорје *n* foothill region

подгорува *impf of* подгори

подготвен *pt* prepared; qualified, well versed (*за* – *in*); добро подготвен well-prepared; well-trained

подготвеност *f* qualification, training; fitness (*for a post*)

подготви *pf* **I** to prepare *trans.*; to train *trans.*; треба да се подготви теренот the ground has to be prepared **II** – **се** to prepare *intrans.*; се подготви за испит to prepare for an exam

подготвителен -лна *adj* preparatory, preliminary; подготвителни работи preparatory works (operations); подготвителен период preparatory period; подготвителен курс preparatory course

подготвува (се) *impf of* подготви (се)

подготовка *f* **1** preparation<s>; подготовки за избори preparations for elections; *Mil.* артилериска подготовка artillery preparation, "softening up" **2** training; стручна подготовка specialist training

подгради *pf* to reinforce, shore up, buttress

подградува *impf of* подгради

подгрбавен & **подгрбен** *pt* hunchbacked; bent, stooping

подгрбавеност & **подгрбеност** *f* stooping posture

подгрбави се & **подгрби се** *pf* to stoop; to become hunched (bent)

подгрбавува се & **подгрбува се** *impf of* подгрбави се & подгрби се

подгрева (се) *impf of* подгрее (се)

подгрее *pf* подгреа *aor.* **I 1** to warm up *trans.* **2** *fig.* to revive; подгрее стари кавги to reignite old quarrels **II** – **се** to warm up *intrans.*; млекото нека се подгрее let the milk warm up

подгризе *pf* to bite, gnaw into (*from below*); to corrode, eat away; to undermine

подгризува *impf of* подгризе

подгрлник -ци *m* **1** necklace; string of coins round the neck **2** hollow in the neck below the throat; larynx

подгрупа *f* subgroup

подгушен -шна *adj* sublaryngeal; subtracheal

подгушка *f* & **подгушник** -ци *m* **1** (*подбрадок*) double chin **2** dewlap

поддава (се) *impf of* поддаде (се)

поддаде *pf* **I** to give a little (*usu. secretly, furtively*); поддаде некому некој денар to slip s.o. a few denars **II** – **се** to give o.s. over (*на* – *to*); to succumb (*to*), give o.s. up (*to*); се поддаде на чувство на жал he succumbed to grief

поддоаѓа & **поддојдува** *impf* to come occasionally (from time to time); јас ќе гледам да поддојдувам понекогаш I'll see that I drop in now and then

поддоговор *m* subcontract

поддоговорувач *m* subcontractor

поддржи *pf* поддржа *aor.* **I** to support, back <up>;

предлогот никој не го поддржа no one supported the proposal **II** – **се** to support one another

поддржува (се) *impf of* поддржи (се)

поддршка *f* (*потпрена*) support, help; дава поддршка на to stand up for

поддувне *pf* поддувна *aor.* to blow a little; поддувна ветре a light breeze blew

поддувнува *impf of* поддувне

подева *impf* **I** of подене **II** – **се** *dial. see* задева се

подејствува *pf* (*with dat.*) to affect, influence; одморот убаво му подејствувал the holiday did him good

поделба *f* division; поделба на трудот division of labour; братска поделба share and share alike

подели *pf* **I 1** to deal out, distribute; to divide up *trans.*; to share; им ги подели парите he distributed the money to them **2** to confer (*on*); to award; подели награди to award prizes **3** *Math.* to divide **II** – **се 1** to divide up *intrans.*; тие се поделија во групи they divided up into groups **2** to share an inheritance; браќата се поделија the brothers shared the estate

поделува (се) *impf of* подели (се)

подем *m literary* rise, upsurge, boom; подем на културата cultural upsurge

подене *pf* подена *aor.* **1** *f.p.* to begin, start, strike up **2** *dial.* (*задре*) to tease, needle; to provoke

поденува (се) *impf see* подева (се)

подетинее & **подетини** <**се**> *pf* подетинеа & подетини <се> *aor.* to become like a child; to behave like a child

подетинува <**се**> *impf of* подетини <се>

поджджригне *pf* поджджригна *aor.* to belch (*slightly*)

поджджригнува *impf of* поджджригне

поджегне *pf* поджегна *aor.* **1** to sting, offend (*slightly*); to tease, torment a little **2** *impers.* (*with acc.*) to pierce, stab

поджегнува *impf of* поджегне

поджолтнат *adj* sallow

поджолтнатост *f* facial pallor

поджолтне *pf* поджолтна *aor.* to turn slightly yellow (sallow) *intrans.*

поджолтнува *impf of* поджолтне

поджугне *pf* поджугна *aor.* **1** (*за растенија*) to sprout **2** (*за деца*) to get a bit stronger, grow a little **3** (*по болест*) to recover to a certain extent **4** to become somewhat livelier **5** *dial.* to whisper a little

подзаборава (се) *impf of* подзаборави (се)

подзаборавен *pt* <somewhat> carried away; absent-minded

подзаборави *pf* **I** to forget (*partially*) **II** – **се** to forget o.s. (*a little*); to become carried away

подзаврати *pf* **1** to roll up (*slightly*), tuck in (*sleeves, apron, etc.*) **2** to turn (*slightly*)

подзаврне *pf* подзаврна *aor.* to rain/drizzle/snow a little; подзаврна дождец a little rain fell

подзагори *pf* to get slightly burnt

подзадре <**се**> *pf* подзадра <се> *aor.* to tease, needle

подзакачи *pf fig.* **I** to sting a little; to irritate, annoy **II** – **се** to start bickering, quarrelling

подзакрпи *pf* **I** to patch up (*a bit*); to repair, reinforce **II** – **се 1** to smarten (*o.s.*) up (*a little*) **2** *fig.* to recover somewhat

подзакуп *m* sub-lease, sub-tenancy

подзалади *pf* **I 1** (*3rd p. only*) to cool off (down) a little *intrans.*; времево како да подзалади the weather seems to have cooled off a little **2** *rare* to cool (*slightly*) *trans.* **II – се** *see* I 1

подзалаже *pf* подзалажа *aor.* **1** to deceive (*partially*) **2** *fig.* to distract, amuse (*briefly*) **II – се 1** to deceive, fool o.s. (*partially*) **2** to take a mild interest (*co – in*); to amuse o.s.

подзамачка *pf* I **1** to smear (*slightly*); *fig.* му ги подзамачка очите he pulled the wool over his eyes **2** *fig.* to hush up, suppress **II – се** to smear o.s., dirty o.s. (*slightly*)

подзамислен *adj* preoccupied, thoughtful; worried

подзамисли се *pf* to become <somewhat> concerned; to become rather absorbed in thought

подзанемарен *adj* somewhat neglected, overlooked

подзанемари *pf* I to neglect somewhat, overlook **II – се** to neglect o.s. somewhat, let o.s. get run down

подзанемарува (се) *impf of* подзанемари (се)

подзаниша *pf* I to swing, rock slightly *trans.* **II – се 1** to swing, rock slightly *intrans.* **2** *fig.* to be a little concerned (*за – about*); to do something (*about*)

подзанишува (се) *impf of* подзаниша (се)

подзаостава (се) *impf of* подзаостави (се)

подзаостави (се) *pf* подзаостава (се) *aor. see* подзанемари (се)

подзаостанат *adj* somewhat backward; (*за деца*) mildly retarded

подзаостане *pf* подзаостана *aor. see* заостане; тие подзаостанаа, а ние отидовме напред they have fallen behind, while we have gone ahead

подзаостанува *impf of* подзаостане

подзаострен *pt* somewhat strained, rather tense

подзаостри *pf* I to sharpen a little; to make stricter, more tense, more strained **II – се** *rare* to become stricter, more tense, more strained

подзаострува (се) *impf of* подзаостри (се)

подзапира (се) *impf of* подзапре (се)

подзаплаши *pf* **1** to startle, scare **2** to threaten a little

подзаплашува *impf of* подзаплаши

подзапре *pf* подзапра *aor.* I **1** to stop *trans.*, detain, hold up; to shut off; му ја подзапреле водата they cut off his water for a time **2** to pause; подзапре пред куќата he paused in front of the house **3** (*with ∂а and verb*) to suspend (*action*); подзапреа да даваат дозволи they've suspended the issuing of permits **II – се** *see* I 2

подзапрен *pt* detained, held up

подзасегнат *pt* somewhat concerned; rather offended (upset)

позасега (се) *impf of* позасегне (се)

подзасегне *pf* подзасегна *aor.* I **1** to touch lightly; to brush against, graze **2** *fig.* to touch, arouse a little **3** *fig.* to slight, irk **4** *fig.* (*прашање*) to touch on, broach **II – се** to feel slighted; to be marginally affected; to be somewhat concerned

подзасегнува (се) *impf see* подзасега (се)

подзасили *pf* I **1** to strengthen, increase somewhat, step up; подзасили напори to step up efforts **2** to reinforce, consolidate; подзасили своја позиција to consolidate one's position somewhat **II – се** to intensify; to become a little stronger, more powerful

подзасилува (се) *impf of* подзасили (се)

подзасипнат *adj* rather hoarse; somewhat raucous

подзасолнат *pt* **1** partially hidden, concealed **2** partially sheltered

подзасолне *pf* подзасолна *aor.* I **1** to hide, conceal (*partly*) *trans.* **2** to shelter, protect, shield (*partly*) **II – се** to hide *intrans.*, conceal o.s., take cover (*briefly*)

подзасолнува (се) *impf of* подзасолне (се)

подзасрамен *pt* somewhat ashamed, mildly embarrassed/shamefaced

подзастарен *pt* **1** somewhat old-fashioned, outdated, obsolescent; подзастарено правило an outdated rule **2** elderly

подзастари *pf* **1** to become old-fashioned, outdated, obsolescent; подзастарија тие учебници those textbooks are rather out of date **2** to age

подзастарува *impf of* подзастари

подзатвора (се) *impf of* подзатвори (се)

подзатвори *pf* I to close partly, push (*a door*) to; ја подзатвори вратата he left the door ajar; ❏ подзатвори некому уста to make s.o. pipe down **II – се** *rare* to close partly *intrans.*; to be left ajar

подзатскрива (се) *impf of* подзатскрие (се)

подзатскрие *pf* подзатскри *aor.* I to cover, hide, shield (*partly*) *trans.* **II – се** to hide *intrans.*, find refuge (*briefly*)

подзема *impf of* подземе

подземе *pf* подзема *aor.* **1** to take, pick up **2** (*песна*) to take up, pick up; to chime in **3** *rare* to take in; подземе сирачиња to take in orphans **4** *fig.* to ask (*s.o.*) indirectly **5** to take a small amount

подземен -мна *adj* subterranean; underground (*also fig.*); подземни води subterranean waters; подземна железница underground <railway>, *Am.* subway; *Myth.* подземен свет underworld; подземна организација clandestine organization

подземи *adv* underground, under the ground

подземје *n* **1** basement, cellar **2** *Myth.* the underworld **3** *fig.* <criminal> underworld:

подземница *f* underground dwelling; *Mil.* dug-out

подсида *pf* to underpin, shore up, buttress

подсидува *impf* **1** *of* подсида **2** *colloq.* to do a little building (*from time to time*)

подсирне *pf* подсирна *aor.* I **1** to glance at; to look (*s.o.*) up, drop in on (*s.o.*) **2** to peep, peer furtively, spy **II – се** to peer, peep at each other

подсирнува (се) *impf of* подсирне (се)

подивее *pf* подивеа *aor. see* подиви 1

подивен *pt* <that has> run wild; подивени страсти rampant passions

подивеност *f* state of having gone wild, wildness

подиви *pf* **1** to go wild **2** *see* здиви

подивува *impf of* подиви

подига (се) *impf of* подигне (се)

подигање *n* uplift, upswing; raising; духовно подигање spiritual uplift; подигање на стандардот raising of the standard

подигне *pf* подигна *aor.* I **1** to raise, lift up, pick up; to elevate; подигне глава to raise one's head, look up; *fig.* to rebel; подигне очи to raise one's eyes; ❏ *Math.* подигне број на квадрат/куб to raise a number to the second/third power, to square/cube a number; подигне рака на себе to attempt suicide; го подигна нивниот дух it/he raised their spirits; подигне глас to raise one's voice; подигне кредит to raise credit (a loan) **2** to erect, construct, build; подигне куќа to build a house; подигне споменик to erect a monument **3** to raise, rear, bring up; подигне ново поколение to raise a new generation **4** (*земе*) to withdraw; to collect *trans.*; подигне пари од банка to draw money from a bank; подигне пакет to collect (pick up) a parcel **5** *fig.* (*предизвика*) to create, raise, cause; подигне тужба (*против*) to bring an indictment (a charge) (*against*); подигне врева to cause a commotion; подигне прашање to raise a question **6** *fig.* (*поведе*) to start; подигне востание (бунт, буна) to raise a rebellion (a riot) **7** *fig.* (*поправи*) to restore, revive (*s.th. neglected*); to improve; го подигнаа земјоделството they revived agriculture **II – се 1** to rise; се подигне од масата to get up from the table **2** *fig.* to recover financially **3** *fig.* to improve *intrans.*; се подигна настроението the mood improved **4** *fig.* to rise in rebellion

подигнува (се) *impf see* подига (се)

подигра *pf* **I 1** *f.p.* to make (*a horse*) dance, prance (*briefly*) **2** *rare* to make fun of (*s.o.*); to laugh at (*s.o.*) **II – се** (*co*) to make fun of

подигравка *f rare, dial.* (*подбив*) clowning; joking; mockery, ridicule

подигрува *impf* **I 1** подигрува си to play/dance now and then, from time to time **2** *of* подигра **II – се** *of* подигра се

подидува *impf* to come, go (*somewhere*) occasionally; тој подидуваше често кај нас he used to come and see us quite often

подизвлекува (се) *impf of* подизвлече (се)

подизвлече *pf* **I** to extricate (*partly*) (*also fig.*) **II – се** to extricate o.s. (*partly*)

подизгасне *pf* подизгасна *aor.* **1** to quench, extinguish (*partly*) **2** to be quenched; (*за оган*) to die down

подизгаснува *impf of* подизгасне

подизгледа *pf* **1** to measure with the eye, look over (*quickly*); ме подизгледа малку и се сврти he looked me up and down and turned away **2** to raise, rear, bring up (*for a period*)

подизгледува *impf of* подизгледа

подисправа (се) *impf of* подисправи (се)

подисправен *pt* straightened; restored to a <near-> vertical position

подисправи *pf* **I** to straighten (*partly*) *trans.*, make erect; подисправи ја главата lift your head up a bit! **2** *fig.* to amend, make corrections to **II – се 1** to straighten up a bit *intrans.* **2** *fig.*, *rare* to correct o.s. (*slightly*)

подистава (се) *impf of* подистави (се)

подистави *pf* **I** to move slightly away *trans.* **II – се** to move away, move off, move a little *intrans.*

подиставува (се) *impf see* подистава (се)

подиум *m* podium, platform

подише & **подиши** *pf* подиша & подиши *aor.* to breathe (*for a while*); излезе да подише малку чист воздух to go out for a breath of fresh air

подишува *impf of* подише

подјаде *pf* **1** to eat away (*from below*) **2** to undermine, erode (*also fig.*); тешкотиите му го подјадоа здравјето the difficulties undermined his health **3** to consume (*a certain amount*) **4** *colloq.*, *fig.* to cheat out of; ми подјаде педесет денари he did me out of fifty denars

подјаден *pt* undermined; подјадено место an undermined spot

подјадува *impf of* подјаде

подјазичен -чна *adj Anat.* sublingual; подјазична жлезда sublingual gland

подјармен *pt fig.* subjugated; enslaved; подјармени народи subjugated peoples

подјарми *pf* to subjugate, subdue; to enslave

подјармува *impf of* подјарми

подлага (се) *impf of* подложи (се) I 2 & II

подлаже *pf* to deceive; to cheat, defraud

подлажува *impf of* подлаже

подланица *f Bot.* **1** (Turgenia latifolia) great bur-parsley **2** (Caucalis daucoides) bastard-parsley, hen's foot

подлева *impf of* подлее

подлегне *pf* подлегна *aor.* **1** to lie down for a while, take a nap **2** *rare, literary* to succumb (*на – to*); подлегна на повредите he succumbed to his injuries

подлегнува *impf of* подлегне

подлее *pf* подлеа *aor.* **1** to pour under; to penetrate from below; ❑ подлее (пушти) вода некому под рогузина to flatter s.o. **2** to water; подлее цвеќиња to water flowers

подлежи *impf literary* to be subject (*на – to*), open to; решението не подлежи на ревизија the decision is not subject to review; ❑ тоа не подлежи на сомнение that is not in doubt

подлепи *pf* **I** to stick under *trans.* **II – се** to stick under *intrans.*

подлепува (се) *impf* **1** *of* подлепи (се) **2** *colloq.* подлепува to glue up, patch up

подлеск *m arch.*, *f.p. Bot.* (Viola odorata) violet

подлесков *adj f.p.* of violets

подлесница *f* small plait, braid

подлетаче *n dial.* fledgling; орле подлетаче fledgling eaglet

подлец *m* rascal, scoundrel

подлива *impf see* подлева

подлие *pf see* подлее

подлизурко -овци *m* lickspittle

подлисник -ци *m* newspaper supplement

подлога *f* **1** foundation, base; ground; backing, support; златна подлога gold backing **2** stock for grafting

подложен -жна *adj* prone, liable, subject, susceptible (*на – to*); подложен на болести susceptible to illness

подложи *pf* **I 1** *rare* to place under **2** *literary* to subject (*на – to*), expose to; ❑ подложи на критика to subject to criticism **II – се** to undergo *trans.*, submit o.s. (*на – to*); се подложи на операција to undergo an operation

подложност *f* susceptibility

подлока *pf* (*за вода*) to erode, wear away; водата го подлокала сидот the water undermined the wall

подлокува *impf rare of* подлока

подлост *f* baseness; meanness; villainy

подлошка *f* (*подлога*) base, support; (*за чаша*) coaster; *Tech.* washer

подлути *pf* **I 1** to aggravate, inflame **2** *rare, Cul.* to season (*food*) with hot spices **II – се 1** (*за рана*) to become inflamed **2** to get angry, irritated

подмама & **подмамка** *f* **1** deceit; ruse **2** enticement

подмами *pf* **1** to deceive, swindle, trick **2** to lure, entice, decoy

подмамува *impf of* подмами

подмачка *pf* **1** to oil, grease, lubricate (*lightly*) **2** *fig.* to pay (*s.o.*) a bribe; to oil the wheels

подмачкува *impf of* подмачка

подмеси *pf* to prepare, mix (*yeast*)

подмести *pf rare, f.p.* **I** to move *trans.* **II** – **ce** to move *intrans.*

подместува (ce) *impf of* подмести (ce)

подмет *m Gram.* subject

подметне *pf* подметна *aor.* **I 1** to place under; ❑ подметне некому нога <да падне> to trip s.o. up **2** *fig.* to plant (*s.th. on s.o.*) **3** *dial.* to have a miscarriage **II** – **ce** (*with dat.*) to give a leg up; to provide support for (*by offering one's back as a step*)

подметнува (ce) *impf of* подметне (ce)

подметов *adj Gram.* subject *attrib.*

подмигне *pf* подмигна *aor.* (*with dat.*) to wink (*at*)

подмигнува *impf of* подмигне

подмилкува ce & *rare* **подмиткува ce** *impf* (*with dat.*) to ingratiate o.s. (*with*)

подмладен *pt* rejuvenated; renewed

подмлади *pf* to rejuvenate; to renew

подмладок -ци *m literary* the younger generation, youth

подмладува *impf of* подмлади

подмол *m* **1** hollow; cavity; fissure **2** *f.p.* ditch, trench

подмолен -лна *adj* **1** undermined; having caverns/cavities; подмолно место undermined spot; place of underground caverns **2** *fig.* undermining, destabilizing, subversive; secret **3** *fig.* treacherous, perfidious

подмолит *adj see* подмолен 1

подмолиште *n see* подмол

подмолник -ци *m* treacherous, perfidious person

подмолница *f* (*fem. form*) *see* подмолник

подмолност *f* treachery, perfidy

подморница *f* submarine

подморнички *adj* <of a> submarine; подморничка посада submarine crew

подморски *adj* submarine, undersea, underwater

подмрежица *f f.p. Zool.* (Parus caeruleus) blue tit

подмрзнат *pt* touched by frost

подмрзнатица *f* black ice, *Am.* glaze

подмрзне *pf* подмрзна *aor.* to become superficially frozen; to freeze slightly; *impers.* нокта подмрзнало there was a slight frost at night

подмрзнува *impf of* подмрзне

поднапие ce *pf* поднапи ce *aor.* to to get tipsy, slightly drunk

поднапиен *pt* tipsy, slightly drunk

поднаслов *m* subtitle; subheading

поднаучен *pt* partially accustomed

поднаучи *pf* **I 1** to learn a little; to brush up; to study a little **2** to train; to accustom **3** to find out, get to know (*a little*); поднаучи некои работи to find out a few things **II** – **ce 1** to gain a little knowledge **2** to grow partially accustomed (*на* – *to*)

поднаучува (ce) *impf of* поднаучи (ce)

поднебесен -сна *adj rare, poet.* lofty, heavenly; поднебесни вишини lofty heights

поднебесје *n rare, poet.* firmament, welkin

поднебје *n literary* climate, clime (*also fig.*)

поднесе *pf* **I 1** to present; to hand in; поднесе сметка to present a bill (account); поднесе тужба to level a charge; поднесе оставка to hand in (tender) one's resignation; поднесе документи to submit documents **2** *rare* to offer (*food, hospitality*) **3** to endure, bear, withstand; поднесе горештина to withstand heat **II** – **ce** to stand (put up with) one another

поднесок -оци *m* submission, application

поднесува (ce) *impf of* поднесе (ce)

поднесувач *m* applicant, proposer

подниже *pf* поднижа *aor.* to trim with pearls, beads, *etc.*

поднижува *impf of* подниже

подник -ци *m* **1** shoot, sucker **2** *fig.* descendant, scion **3** *dial.* enclosure, pen

подникне *pf* подникна *aor.* **1** to begin to sprout **2** *f.p.* to look down

подникнува *impf of* подникне

подница *f* earthenware dish (pan)

поднова *f* **1** new acquisition **2** new-born baby

поднови *pf* **I 1** to buy s.th. new (*for*); го подновиле детето со костумче they bought the child a costume **2** to renew (*partly or completely*); to replenish; to replace; си го подновил алатот he replaced his toolkit **3** *rare* to start again, renew, resume; поднови експерименти to resume experiments **II** – **ce 1** to buy s.th. new for o.s. **2** (*за рана*) to reopen

подновува (ce) *impf of* поднови (ce)

подножје *n* **1** foot (*of mountain*); foothill<s> **2** pedestal, base; footing **3** footrest

подноктица *f* (*usu. pl*) whitlow, *Med.* paronychia

подносител *m see* поднесувач

поднослив *adj* bearable, endurable, tolerable

подношка *f* **1** footrest, footboard, footstool **2** *pl* (*на разбој*) treadles

подобава *impf literary, rare* (*with dat.*) to befit, behove

подобен -бна *adj* **1** similar (*на* – *to*); like; и други подобни работи and so on; and the like **2** fitting, suitable (*за* – *for*)

подобност *f* **1** similarity **2** capability; fitness; suitability

подобри *pf* **I** to improve *trans.*; подобри услови за работа to improve working conditions **II** – **ce** to improve *intrans.*; ce подобри ситуацијата the situation has improved

подобрува (ce) *impf of* подобри (ce)

пододбор *m* subcommittee

пододдел *m* section; subsection

подозира *impf literary* to suspect

подозрение -ија *n* suspicion; причини за подозрение grounds for suspicion

подозрив *adj* suspicious, suspect; distrustful

подои *pf* to suckle, nurse (*for a while*)

подојница *f* foster mother (*of nurseling lamb or calf*)

подојува *impf of* подои

подол -дла *adj* base, vile, despicable

подопашник -ци *m* & **подопашница** *f* crupper <strap>

подорешка *f Bot.* **1** (Crocus biflorus) mauve ("blue") crocus **2** (Colchicum autumnale) meadow saffron, autumn crocus

подотворен *pt* ajar, slightly open

подотвори *pf* **I** to open slightly *trans.*; to leave ajar **II** – **ce** to open slightly *intrans.*

подотера *pf* **I** to smarten up a little, titivate slightly **II** – **ce** to smarten o.s. up, dress up a bit

подотсек -ци *m* subsection
подофицéр *m Mil.* non-commissioned officer (N.C.O.)
подофицéрски *adj* <of an> N.C.O.
подочен -чна *adj* subocular; подочни сенки shadows (bags) under the eyes
подочници *pl* shadows (bags) under the eyes
подработи *pf* to do a bit of work
подработува *impf of* подработи
подражава *impf* to imitate, mimic
подражавач *m* imitator, mimic
подражавачки *adj* imitative
подразбере *pf* подразбра *aor.* to begin to grasp/ sense; to find out; to infer
подразбира *impf* **I** to grasp; to sense; to infer **II** – **се 1** to be meant, understood; ❑ се подразбира само по (од) себеси it goes without saying **2** to understand each other
подраздел *m* subsection
подраздели *pf literary* to sub-divide
подразделува *impf of* подраздели
подрака & под рака *adv* **1** by the arm; arm in arm; ❑ дава (продава) подрака to sell on the black market **2** to hand, at hand
подрамни *pf* **I** to even up, level off, smooth off **II** – **се** *rare* to line up *intrans.*, *Mil.* to dress *intrans.*
подрамнува (се) *impf of* подрамни (се)
подрани *pf* **1** to get up early **2** to arrive early
подранува *impf of* подрани
подрачен -чна *adj* regional; подрачните органи regional bodies
подрачје *n* **1** region, area; zone; економско подрачје an economic region **2** *rare, fig.* sphere, field; на подрачјето (во областа) на општествените науки in the sphere of the social sciences
подреден *pt* arranged, put in order, tidy
подреденост *f* tidiness, good order; lucidity, clarity
подреди *pf* to arrange, put in order, tidy up
подредува *impf of* подреди
подрек *m* (*sg only*) <evil> spell, charm; ❑ да не му е за подрек touch wood, *Am.* knock on wood
подреси *pf* to adorn, decorate, embellish with tassels
подресува *impf of* подреси
подрече *pf* **1** to hint; to whisper; ми подрече за таа работа he told me a little about that business; подречи му некој збор have a quiet word with him **2** *rare* to bewitch, cast a spell on
подржави *pf* to nationalize
подржавува *impf of* подржави
подржи *pf* to hold for a while *trans. & intrans.*; вака ако подржи времево . . . if the weather holds . . .
подржува *impf of* подржи
подрива *impf of* подрие
подривачки *adj see* подривен
подривен -вна *adj* subversive; подривна дејност subversive activity
подрие *pf* подри *aor.* to undermine, erode; to subvert
подробен -бна *adj* detailed, precise; подробен план detailed (exact) plan; подробни информации detailed information
подробно *adv* in detail, exactly, precisely; thoroughly; расправа подробно to give a full (detailed) account
подробност *f* **1** detail, particular, fine point; се впушта во подробности to go into detail **2** exhaustiveness; thoroughness

подрони *pf* to undermine, erode *trans.*; водата го подронила брегот the water has undermined the bank
подронува *impf of* подрони
подруг *adj* different, other; во подруга ситуација in a different situation; сега е подруго времето times have changed
подружница *f* branch
подува¹ *pf* to blow for a while
подува² (се) *impf of* подуе (се)
подуе *pf* поду *aor.* **I** to inflate, blow up *trans.* **II** – **се** to inflate *intrans.*, swell up
подуен *pt* swollen
подузди *pf* to bridle *trans.*
подума <**се**> *pf dial.* to think for a while
подуши *pf* **1** to smell, sniff *trans.* **2** *fig.* to sense, gather
поевтини *pf* **1** to make cheaper, reduce in price **2** to become cheaper, fall in price
поевтинува *impf of* поевтини
поединец -нци *m* individual
поединечен -чна *adj* individual; isolated
поединечно *adv* individually, singly
поединечност *f* individuality
поезија *f* poetry
поéма *f* narrative poem; epic poem
поен¹ *m Sport.* point; победа на поени a win (victory) on points
поен² -јна *adj in the expression:* појна птица songbird
поéнта *f* <main> point (*of a story, joke*)
поентéр *m* **1** referee, umpire; scorer, marker **2** production supervisor, checker
поет *m* poet
поетéса *f* <woman> poet, poetess
поетизúра *pf & impf* to poeticize
поетика *f* poetics, theory of poetry, prosody
поетичен -чна *adj* poetic<al>
поетски *adj* poetic<al>, poetic; ❑ поетска слобода poetic licence
пожали & пожала *pf* **I** **1** to pity, take pity on, feel sorry for; Господ ја пожали the Lord took pity on her **2** to spare (*expense*), stint **3** to mourn *trans.* **II** – **се** to complain (*на – то/about*); му се пожали на директорот he complained to/about the director; се пожали на работата he complained about the work
пожалува (се) *impf of* пожали (се)
пожар *m* fire, conflagration; гаси пожар to fight a fire
пожарен -рна *adj* **1** fire-fighting; fire *attrib.*; пожарна команда (чета) fire brigade **2** (*as noun*) пожарниот *m* night watch; пожарна *f* fire-engine
пожари *pf f.p.* to destroy by fire, burn down/up, consume
пожариште *n* site of a fire
пожарник -ци & **пожарникар** *m* fireman, firefighter
пожарникарски & пожарнички *adj* fireman's
пожелен -лна *adj* desirable; desired
пожели *pf* пожели & пожела *aor.* **1** to want, wish for **2** (*with dat.*) to wish (*s.o. s.th.*); пожела некому многу здравје to wish s.o. good health
пожелност *f* desirability
пожелува *impf of* пожели
поживее *pf* поживеа *aor.* to live for a while; поживеа осумдесет години he lived to the age of eighty; колку време поживеа в град? how long did you live in town?

поживи *pf* to grant long life to; ❏ Господ (Бог) да те поживи! may the Lord grant you long life!

пожиговина *f see* жиговина

пожнева & **пожнива** *impf of* пожнее & пожние

пожнее & **пожние** *pf* пожнеа & пожни *aor.* **1** to harvest, reap (*also fig.*) **2** to reap for a while

пожолтее *pf* пожолтеа *aor. see* пожолти 2

пожолтен *pt* yellowed; pale; sallow; пожолтени лисје yellow leaves; пожолтено лице pale face; sallow complexion

пожолти *pf* **1** to make yellow, turn yellow **2** to turn yellow *intrans.*; лисјето пожолтија the leaves turned yellow

пожолтува *impf of* пожолти & пожолтее

пожртвува (се) *pf rare see* жртвува (се)

пожртвуван *pt* self-sacrificing, committed, selfless; пожртвувани борци dedicated fighters

пожртвуваност *f* self-sacrifice; selflessness

поза *f* pose, posture; posturing; ❏ зеде поза to strike a pose

позаврти *pf* позаврти, позаврте *aor.* **I 1** to turn a little *trans.* **2** (*за пари*) to save up a little **II – се 1** to turn a little *intrans.* **2** to stay for a while

позагрижи *pf* **I** to perturb, put out **II – се** to take care (*за – оf/over/about*); to worry *intrans.*; to give some thought (*за – to*)

позадлабочи *pf* **I** to make deeper, more profound **II – се** to go deeper (*во нешто – into s.th.*)

позборува *pf* to have a talk, chat, natter

поздрав *m* greeting; прати поздрави to send greetings; многу поздрави best regards; прощален поздрав farewell; срдечен поздрав warm greetings; војнички поздрав salute; *Mil.* поздрав надесно/ налево eyes right/left!

поздравен -вна *adj* welcoming; <of> greeting; поздравен говор, поздравна реч speech of welcome

поздрави *pf* **I** to greet; to welcome; ќе го поздравиш од нас give him our greetings **II – се 1** (*со*) to greet; to shake hands; се поздравил со сите he greeted everybody **2** to greet each other, exchange greetings

позелени *pf* позелени, позелене *aor.* **1** to make green, turn green **2** to turn green *intrans.*; позелени во лицето од јад to turn green with rage

позеленува *impf of* позелени

позема *impf of* поземе

поземе *pf* позема *aor. see* подземе 1

поземи *adv* along the ground, over the ground

позен -зна *adj rare* late; позна есен late autumn

позер *m* poseur

позерски *adj* poseur's

позив *m* **1** (*за на суд*) summons, subpoena, citation **2** (*професија*) profession, vocation, calling **3** *Mil.* levy; call-up **4** *rare see* покана **5** *rare* cry, call

позивница *f rare* invitation

позира *impf* to pose; to strike an attitude

позитив *m* **1** *Photography* positive **2** *Gram.* positive form (*of adjective*)

позитивен -вна *adj* positive; affirmative; позитивен одговор answer in the affirmative; позитивна критика constructive criticism; позитивни резултати positive results; позитивен биланс a positive balance

позитивизам -змот *m* positivism

позитивист *m* positivist

позитивистички *adj* positivistic

позиција -ии *f* position; stance; attitude; артилериски позиции gun positions; исходни (излезни) позиции starting points; непријателски позиции hostile views; ❏ земе позиција to take up a position

позициóнен -она *adj Mil.* position-dominated; stationary; позициона војна trench warfare

позјапа *pf* to stare for a while

позлата *f* gold leaf, gilding, gilt

позлатен *pt* gilded; gold-plated; позлатено огледало gilded mirror

позлати *pf* to gild, to gold-plate; *fig.* сонцето ги позлати вршјето од дрвјата the sun gilded the tree-tops

позлатува *impf of* позлати

позлаќен & *rare, arch.* **позлаштен** *adj f.p., dial. see* позлатен

познава *impf* **I 1** to know, be acquainted with; го познава законот to know the law; тука никого не познавам I don't know anyone here **2** to sense, tell, realize; по очите познаваше дали го лажат he could tell by people's eyes whether they were lying **II – се 1** to be acquainted (*со – with*), know **2** *impers.* one can tell (*дека – that*), it is clear

познавање *n* knowledge; cognition

познавач *m* expert, authority (*на – on*)

познае *pf* позна *aor.* **I 1** to recognize, identify; го познав од еден опул I recognized him at first glance **2** *rare, literary* to experience; to endure **II – се 1** to recognize each other **2** *impers.* it is clear (plain) (*дека – that*)

познак -ци *m* late-ripening chestnut

познајник -ци *m* acquaintance

познајница *f* (*fem. form*) *see* познајник

познание -ија *n* **1** cognition, comprehension; теорија на познанието theory of cognition **2** *rare* knowledge, recognition; learning, erudition

познаник -ци *m see* познајник

познаница *f see* познајница

познанство *n* acquaintanceship; кругот на моите познанства the circle of my acquaintances

познат *adj* **1** known; познато е дека . . . it is known . . . ; како што е познато as is <generally> known **2** (*as noun*) познат и позната *m* & *f see* познајник & познајница; *Math.* позната a known (value, quantity); две познати и една непозната two known quantities and one unknown one **3** well-known, celebrated, famous; познат научник famous scientist/ scholar

позно *adv* late; рано или позно sooner or later

позновит *adj f.p., dial. see* познат 1

позове (се) *pf* позва *aor. dial., rare, literary see* повика (се)

пои *impf* **1** to give to drink; to water; пои коњ to water a horse **2** (*usu. fig.*) to water, irrigate; со крв ја пои земјата to water the land with blood

поигра *pf* to play/dance for a while

поигрува *impf of* поигра

поило *n* water trough; watering-place

поим *m* concept, notion, idea; поимот слобода the concept of freedom; ❏ немам поим (*за тоа*) I have no idea (notion) (*about that*)

поима *impf rare* to understand, comprehend, grasp

поимен -мна *adj* conceptual

поименичен -чна *adj* nominal; of names

поименчен *pt Gram.* substantivized; поименчена придавка substantivized adjective

поименчи *pf Gram.* to substantivize

поименчува *impf Gram. of* поименчи

поименчување *n Gram.* substantivization

поимлив *adj rare* conceivable; comprehensible, understandable

поинаков *adj* different; other; поинакви услови different conditions (circumstances)

поинаку *adv* differently; otherwise; ❑ поинаку речено (кажано) in other words

поита *pf* to hurry, hasten; ајде поитај малку get a move on

поиште *n see* поило

пој *m poet.* singing, song; пилчев пој bird-song

појава *f* **1** phenomenon, occurrence; појави во природата, природни појави natural phenomena; случајна појава chance occurrence **2** person, figure; извонредна појава outstanding figure **3** scene (*in a play*) **4** emergence, appearance

појавен *pt* shown, demonstrated; manifested

појави *pf* **I** *rare* to show *trans.* **II** – **се** to appear, emerge, arise; to show o.s.; to come to light; се појави на врата to appear at the door

појавува (се) *impf of* појави (се)

појаде *pf* **1** to have breakfast **2** to eat for a while **3** *dial.* to eat up

појадок -ци *m* breakfast

појадува *impf of* појаде

појас *m* **1** belt; ❑ појас за спасување, спасителен појас lifebelt **2** waist, middle; брада до појас waist-length beard; танок во појасот narrow-waisted; ❑ кантарот си го носи за појас he is a calculating fellow **3** *Geog.* zone, belt; умерениот појас temperate zone; зелен појас green belt

појасен -сна *adj* zonal, regional

појасни *pf* to explain, elucidate, interpret

појаснува *impf of* појасни

појде *pf* **1** to go; ❑ како дошло, така пошло easy come, easy go; му појде нему в уши word reached him **2** *rare, dial.* to start out, depart; појде на пат to set out on a journey

појдува *impf see* поаѓа

појми *pf rare* to conceive, grasp; ти не можеш да појмиш you can't imagine

појцина *adv dial. see* повеќемина; бевме појцина there were several of us

покае *pf* покаја *aor.* **I** *Rel. rare* to repent <of>; си ги покајал гrevовите he repented <of> his sins **II** – **се** to repent; to regret; to confess

покаже *pf* покажа *aor.* **I 1** to show; to display, demonstrate; иднината ќе покаже time will tell; ❑ му ја покажа вратата he showed him the door; ќе ти покажам јас тебе! I'll show you! **2** to point (*на – to*) **3** to show, register, read; колку покажа термометарот? how much did the thermometer show? **II** – **се 1** to appear, come into view; to show o.s.; се покажа на врата to appear at the door **2** *fig.* to prove one's mettle; се покажавме храбри we showed what we were made of

покажува (се) *impf of* покаже (се)

покажувач *m* pointer, indicator, signal

покажувачка *f* **1** *see* показалка 1 **2** display, demonstration

показ *m* **1** *rare* demonstration, display; ❑ на показ 1. on show; тие факти се на показ these facts are plain to see 2. *rare* impending; about to begin; на показ се нови сили new forces are about to appear **2** sign; symbol; omen, portent

показалец -лци *m* **1** index finger, forefinger **2** *rare* index, list

показалка *f* **1** pointer, fescue **2** *arch.* indication

показател *m* indicator, index; економски показатели economic indices

показателен -лна *adj literary, rare* telling, revealing, significant

показен -зна *adj Gram.* **1** demonstrative; показна заменка demonstrative pronoun **2** indicative; показен начин indicative mood

покајан *pt* penitent, having repented

покајание -ија *n Rel.* repentance, confession; отиде на покајание to go to confession

покајник -ци *m* penitent

покајница *f* (*fem. form*) *see* покајник

покајнички *adj* penitent; penitential; remorseful

покајува (се) *impf of* покае (се)

покалуѓери *pf* **I** to receive as a monk/nun **II** – **се** to take monastic vows

покалуѓерува (се) *impf of* покалуѓери (се)

покана *f* **1** invitation; invitation card **2** *rare* summons; судска покана subpoena, summons to appear in court

покани *pf* **1** to invite **2** to treat (*со – to*); ги поканила со чај she offered them tea

поканува *impf of* покани

покатоличи *pf* **I** to catholicize **II** – **се** to become a Catholic, embrace Catholicism

покатоличува (се) *impf of* покатоличи (се)

покаури *pf arch.* **I** to make (*s.o.*) an infidel, cause to renounce Islam **II** – **се** to become an infidel, renounce Islam

покачи *pf* **I** to lift, raise (*slightly*); покачи цени to raise prices **II** – **се** to climb up; to rise; цените се покачија prices have risen (gone up)

покачува (се) *impf of* покачи (се)

покер *m Cards* poker

покисне *pf* покисна *aor.* **I 1** to ferment slightly **2** *rare* to get wet; ми покисна облеката my clothes got wet **3** *fig., rare* to wait some time, hang around **II** – **се** to get damp

покиснува (се) *impf of* покисне (се)

покити *pf* to decorate, adorn a little

покладен -дна *adj Rel.* Shrovetide

поклади *pl Rel.* Shrove Tuesday, Mardi Gras; сирни, месни поклади Shrovetide

покладува *impf Rel.* to observe Shrove Tuesday

поклекне *pf* поклекна *aor.* **1** *rare* to bend one's knee **2** *literary* to decline, weaken

поклекнува *impf of* поклекне

поклон *m* **1** bow; длабок поклон low bow **2** present, gift **3** *poet., rare* homage, act of paying homage

поклонение -ија *n* **1** worship, veneration **2** pilgrimage; оди на поклонение to go on a pilgrimage

поклони *pf* **I** to give (*as a gift*), make a present **II** – **се** (*with dat.*) to bow

поклоник -ци *m* **1** pilgrim **2** devotee, admirer; поклоник на класична музика devotee of classical music; поклоник на Шекспира admirer of Shake-speare **3** *literary, rare* suitor; worshipper

поклоница & (*usu. pl*) **поклоничка** *f* (*fem. form*) *see* поклоник 1, 2

поклонува (се) *impf of* поклони (се)

поклоп *m see* поклопка

поклопи *pf* **I 1** to cover, put a lid on **2** to smother; to envelop; to overwhelm **3** *fig.* to silence s.o.; to quash, quell; со два збора го поклопи he put him in his place with two words **II – се** to coincide; интересите не им се поклопија their interests did not coincide

поклопка *f* lid, cover; ако му ја сакаш (бараш) поклопката, ќе ти го сака (бара) и грнето *prov.* give him an inch and he'll take a mile

поклопче *n dim. of* поклоп & поклопка

покоен -јна *adj* **1** deceased, late; неговиот покоен татко his late father **2** (*as noun*) покојниот, покојната *m, f* the deceased **3** *rare* calm, tranquil, serene

покој *m* rest, repose; peace; за покој на душата на . . . for the repose of the soul of . . . ; тела во покој и во движење bodies at rest and in motion

покојник -ци *m* the deceased, the departed

покојница *f* (*fem. form*) *see* покојник

покојнички *adj* of a deceased person

поколеба *pf* **I** to cause to hesitate; to sway, dissuade; to deter; неуспехот не го поколеба his failure did not deter him **II – се** to hesitate, waver, vacillate; to pause

поколебан *pt* shaken; wavering, doubtful

поколебува (се) *impf of* поколеба (се)

поколение -ија *n* generation; младо поколение younger generation; ❑ од поколение на поколение from generation to generation

покор *m literary, rare* shame, disgrace; ❑ срам и покор for shame!

покорен[1] *pt* subjugated, conquered, subjected; subdued; покорени народи subjugated peoples

покорен[2] -рна *adj* obedient, submissive; ❑ *literary, arch.* слуга <сум> покорен <I am> your humble servant

покори *pf* **I** to subdue; to conquer, surmount, vanquish; ги покори природните сили to tame the forces of nature **II – се** (*with dat.*) to obey; to resign o.s. to one's fate; се покори на законот to obey the law

покорител *m* conqueror

покорност *f* & *rare* **покорство** *n* obedience, submission, submissiveness; држи во покорност to keep in submission

покорува (се) *impf of* покори (се)

покорувач *m see* покорител

покоси *pf* **1** to mow, cut; покоси сено to mow hay **2** *fig.* to wipe out, mow down **3** to mow for a while

покосница *f* (*usu. pl*) goose-flesh, goose-pimples; покосница ми иде по снагата shivers run down my spine

покосува *impf of* покоси

покраина & *rare* **покрајнина** *f* district, provinces, region; outlying provinces

покраински *adj* provincial, regional, district; покраински комитет provincial committee

покрај *prep* & *adv* **1** beside, by, near; покрај огнот by the fire; еден покрај друг side by side **2** along;

through; покрај брегот along the bank (shore); покрај ниви through the fields **3** in addition to, besides, apart from; покрај грчкиот, го познаваше и францускиот besides Greek, he knew French; ❑ покрај другото among other things; покрај тоа that apart; покрај сувото ќе изгори и суровото *prov.* the baby may be thrown out with the bath water **4** и покрај in spite of, despite; и покрај сето тоа in spite of everything **5** *adv* <of one side

покрив *m* roof; shelter, protection; ❑ остане без покрив над глава to be left homeless

покрива (се) *impf of* покрие (се)

покривало *n* covering, cover

покривач *m* **1** *see* покривка **2** покривач на покриви roofing worker, roofer

покривен -вна *adj* <of a> roof

покривка *f* **1** cover, covering, bedspread **2** head covering, head-scarf, kerchief **3** *fig.* cloak, mantle, shroud; снежна покривка covering of snow

покрие *pf* покри *aor.* **I 1** to cover; to roof; снегот ги покрил полињата the snow has covered the fields; заврнаа снегови, покрија трагови *prov.* all traces were buried; all tracks were covered **2** to cover, settle, pay off; покрие трошоци to cover costs **3** *fig.* to hush up, cover up, suppress **4** *fig.* to drown <out>; моторот го покри неговиот глас his voice was drowned by the engine **5** *Sport.* to cover, mark **II – се** to cover o.s.; се покрие преку глава to pull the covers over one's head

покриен *pt* covered; покриен пазар covered market; покриена чаршија covered shopping centre

покритие -ија *n* <financial> cover; чек без покритие overdrawn cheque

покров *m* **1** *see* покривка; ❑ остане без покров to be left homeless; покровот ми е кус I have limited means; колку ти е покровот толку пушти си ги нозете *prov.* cut your coat according to your cloth **2** shroud, winding sheet **3** *rare* roof

покровец -вци *m* horse-cloth

покровител *m* patron, protector, sponsor

покровителка *f* (*fem. form*) *see* покровител; patroness

покровителски *adj* patron's; protective; покровителски однос protective attitude/relationship

покровителство *n* patronage, protection; sponsorship

покровителствува *impf literary, rare* to offer patronage, help, protection; to patronize, support

покроце *adv* slowly; quietly; steadily; сè покроце врват they keep going steadily along

покрстен *pt* **1** christened, baptized **2** initiated

покрстеник -ци *m* <Christian> convert

покрсти *pf* **I 1** to christen, baptize **2** to initiate **II – се** to be christened, baptized

покрстува (се) *impf of* покрсти (се)

покуда *f* censure, reproach; тоа е за покуда that is to be condemned; нема покуда there's no denying it

покуди *pf* to reprimand, censure

покудува *impf of* покуди

покуќешка & **покуќешница** *f* gossip, tittle-tattler

покуќнина *f coll.* household furnishings

пол[1] *adv* half; пол кило шеќер half a kilo of sugar; осум и пол half past eight; пол саат (*also* полсаат) half an hour; пол пат (*also* полпат) half-way; ❑

остане на полпат to get stuck half-way; јал, не јал – три и пол it's all the same; it makes no difference

пол² *m* sex; машки и женски пол male and female sex; без разлика на пол irrespective of sex; ❏ убавиот (нежниот, слабиот) пол the fair (gentle, weaker) sex

пол³ *m* -ови, -ла *pl Geog., Phys., fig.* pole; Северниот пол the North Pole; позитивен пол positive pole; спротивни полови opposite poles

пола *f* **1** lap, flap, skirt; ❏ тресе поли to avoid involvement; се држи за полите од мајка си to cling to one's mother's skirts **2** (*на врата*) wing **3** separately woven part of a rug (floor-mat); черга од две поли a rug with two parts **4** *fig., literary* (*pl only*) foothills; во полите од планините in the foothills of the mountains

полага *impf rare of* положи; ❏ полага испит to take (sit for) an examination; полага (има) надеж<и> to place one's hopes (*во – in*); полага (има) право (*на*) to lay claim (*to*); многу полага на to set great store by

полагач *m rare* depositor; полагач на сметки (сметкополагач) renderer of an account; *Mil.* полагач на мини minelayer

полазен *pt* infested, tainted

полази *pf* **1** to creep, crawl for a while **2** to crawl over; to swarm over; мравки го полазиле ants were swarming over him/it; ❏ морници (мравки) ме полазија shivers ran down my spine

полазува *impf of* полази

полакоми *pf* **I** *rare* to tempt **II** – **се** to be tempted, develop a craving (*за – for*)

полакомува (се) *impf of* полакоми (се)

полани *adv* (*преклани*) the year before last

полански *adj* (*преклански*) of the year before last; поланската зима the winter before last

поларен -рна *adj* **1** polar; поларна светлина Northern/Southern Lights; aurora borealis/australis; поларна мечка polar bear; поларна лисица arctic fox **2** *fig., literary* opposite, contrary; opposing

поларизација *f* polarization

поларизира *pf & impf* **I** to polarize *trans.* **II** – **се** to polarize *intrans.*

поласка *pf* to compliment; to flatter

полатини *pf* **I** **1** to Latinize **2** *Rel.* to convert to Catholicism **II** – **се** to be converted to Catholicism

полатинува (се) *impf of* полатини (се)

полв *m Zool.* (Myoxus glis) dormouse

полвец -вци *m* cuckoo-spit (*protective froth secreted by froghopper larvae*)

полвосан *pt* fly-blown, tainted

полден *m* midday; (*as adv*) (*also* пол ден) half a day; работи полден to work <for> half a day

поле -иња, *poet.* -ja & *dial.* -ишта *n* **1** field; plain; фудбалско поле football field; ❏ бојно поле battle-field; видно поле field of vision; магнетско поле magnetic field; рудно поле ore-bearing deposit; нафтоносни полиња oilfields; на полето на честа on the field of honour; поле окато, гора ушата walls have ears **2** *fig.* field, sphere; на полето на културата in the cultural sphere **3** background, base, field; на бело поле on a white background **4** (*usu. pl*) margin; белешки на полињата marginal notes

полева (се) *impf of* полее (се)

полега *impf see* полегне 2

полегне *pf* полегна *aor.* **1** to lie down for a while, have a rest **2** to bend down, bend over, bow down; житото полегнало од дождот the corn was lodged (laid) by the rain

полегнува *impf of* полегне

поледица *f* black ice

полее *pf* полеа *aor.* **I** **1** to pour; полее некому вода да се измие to pour water for s.o. to wash in **2** to pour water over; to hose down; полее улица to wash a street; полее цвеќиња to water flowers **II** – **се** to spill, pour s.th. on o.s.; се полеал со мастило he spilt ink over himself

полежи *pf* to lie for a while

полежина *f* **1** lodged (laid) crops (*beaten down by rain*) **2** *f.p.* idleness

полежува *impf of* полежи

полезен -зна *adj* useful, beneficial; полезен труд useful work; полезен за здравјето good (beneficial) for one's health

полезност *f* usefulness

полека *adv* **1** slowly, unhurriedly; gently, carefully; оди полека to walk slowly; ❏ полека-лека (лека-полека) gradually, little by little; полека, та далеку slowly but surely **2** quietly; зборува полека to speak quietly

полелеј -еи *m Rel.* chandelier (*in an Orthodox church*)

полемизира *impf* to polemize, enter into polemics, dispute (*со – with*)

полемика *f* polemics, controversy

полемичар *m* polemicist, polemist, controversialist

полемичен -чна & **полемички** *adj* polemical, controversial; полемичен напис polemical article

полен *m Bot.* pollen

поленка *f see* полено

полено *n* log, billet (*usu. of pinewood*)

поленце *n dim. of* поле

полет *m* **1** take-off; upward flight **2** *fig.* upsurge, upswing, surge, boom; полет во стопанството a boom in the economy **3** *fig.* inspiration, enthusiasm; elation; поетски полет poetic inspiration

полета *pf* **1** to fly for a while **2** to fly off; to take off; авионот полета the plane took off

полетарче *n* **1** fledgling **2** *fig.* beginner, novice, tyro

полетен -тна *adj* **1** <of, for> take-off **2** *fig.* inspired, enthusiastic

полетува *impf of* полета

полецка *adv dim. of* полека

полжав *m* **1** *Zool.* snail; slug; ❏ оди како полжав to move at a snail's pace **2** *Anat.* cochlea

полза *f* use, advantage, benefit, profit; тоа е од полза that is useful; извлече полза од нешто to profit from s.th.; ❏ во полза (*на некого, на нешто*) to the advantage (*of s.o., of s.th.*), on behalf of (*s.o., s.th.*); се откажувам во негова полза I resign in his favour; во полза на пострадните on behalf of the victims

ползач *m* reptile

ползи *impf* to creep, crawl (*also fig.*); детето ползи the child is crawling; мракот ползеше darkness was coming on; бршланот ползи по ѕидот the ivy climbs up the wall; ползи пред некого to grovel before s.o.

ползува *impf* **I** **1** (*with dat.*) to help, be of use (*to*) **2** *rare* to use, exploit; to take advantage of; тој вас ве ползува he's exploiting you **II** – **се** **1** to use, exploit, make use (*од – of*); се ползува од своето право (*да . . .*) to exercise (avail o.s. of) one's right (*to . . .*); се ползува од случајот to take the opportunity (*to . . .*) **2** (*со*) to enjoy, possess, have; се ползува со популарноста to enjoy popularity

ползувач *m* user; beneficiary

полиандрија *f* polyandry

полива (се) *impf see* полева (се)

поливинил *m Chem.* polyvinyl

поливинилски *adj Chem.* <of> polyvinyl

полигамија *f* polygamy

полиглот *m* polyglot

полигон *m* testing (training, proving) ground; артилериски полигон firing range

полиелеј -еи *m see* полелеј

поликлиника *f* polyclinic

поликлинички *adj* polyclinical

поликолор *m* emulsion paint

полилеј -еи *m see* полелеј

полиморфизам -змот *m Biol., Chem.* polymorphism

полином *m Math.* polynomial, multinomial

полип *m* **1** *Zool.* polyp, sea anemone **2** *fig.* leech **3** *Med.* (*usu. pl*) polypus

полира *pf & impf* to polish, varnish

полиран *pt* polished, varnished

полисемија *f* polysemy

политбиро -оа *n* politburo (*political bureau; executive body of the central committee of many Communist parties*)

политеизам -змот *m* polytheism

политехника *f* polytechnic

политехнички *adj* polytechnic<al>; политехничко образование polytechnic education

политизира *impf* to play politics

политика *f* **1** policy; внатрешна политика domestic policy; надворешна политика foreign policy **2** politics; се занимава со политика to go in for politics; ❏ прави некому политика to play up to s.o.

политикант *m pejor.* unprincipled politician; intriguer, schemer, political hack

политиканство *n* politicking, scheming

политиколог *m* political scientist

политира *pf & impf see* полира

политиран *pt see* полиран

политичен -чна *adj* political, politically minded, interested in politics

политички *adj* political; политичка економија political economy

политура *f* polish, varnish; *fig.* refinement, veneer

полифонен -она *adj Mus.* polyphonic

полифонија *f Mus.* polyphony

полифоничен -чна & **полифонички** *adj see* полифонен

полица[1] *f* **1** shelf; орман со три полици cupboard with three shelves **2** ledge, terrace, shelf

полица[2] *f* <insurance> policy

полицаец -ајци *m* policeman

полиција *f* police

полициски *adj* police; полициска станица police station; полициски час curfew

полјак[1] -ци *m* field ranger, field guard, warden

Полјак[2] -ци *m* Pole

полјана *f* glade; clearing

полјанец -нци & **полјанин** -ани *m* plainsman; countryman

полјанка[1] *f* plainswoman; countrywoman

полјанка[2] *f dim. of* полјана

полјански *adj* <of a> plainsman, countryman; rustic

полјанче *n dim. of* полјана

Полјачка *f* (*fem. form*) *see* Полјак

полјачки *adj* <of a> field guard, warden

полјоделство *n* grain growing

полјоделски *adj* agricultural; rural

полк *m* regiment

полка *f* polka

полковник -ци *m* colonel

полковнички *adj* colonel's; полковнички чин rank of colonel

полковски *adj* regimental; полковско знаме regimental colours

полн *adj* **1** full; complete, total, entire, utter; полна чаша full glass; полн мев full belly; полна <со> ужас filled with horror, horror-stricken; ❏ со полни гради with open arms; во полн состав at full strength; во полна тишина in complete silence; полн опис full description; со (под) полна пареа full steam ahead; полн-полничок filled to the brim **2** plump, fleshy; полни образи chubby cheeks **3** (*за пушка*) charged, loaded

полнеж *m rare* **1** electrical charge; process of charging **2** (*за полнење перници и др.*) flock

полнет *pt Cul.* filled, stuffed; полнети пиперки stuffed capsicums (peppers)

полнетица *f* **1** stuffing, padding, quilting **2** *dial.* village house with filled cavity walls

полни *impf* **I** to fill *trans.*; to stuff; to load; to charge; полни базен to fill a swimming-pool; полни душеци to stuff mattresses; полни пушка to load a gun; ❏ полни некому глава to brainwash s.o.; мене ли ќе ми ја полниш главата? whose leg are you trying to pull? **II** – **се** to fill *intrans.*; to be charged (*of batteries*); очите му се полнеа <со> солзи tears welled in her eyes; ❏ окото никако не му се полнеше he always wanted more

полничок -чка *adj* **1** fairly full **2** rather plump, fleshy

полно *adv* much, many, a lot; полно народ a lot of people

полноважен -жна *adj* valid, sound; полноважно решение valid decision

полноважност *f* validity, soundness

полновластен -сна *adj* absolute, arbitrary; authorized, plenipotentiary; полновластен господар absolute ruler, sole master

полновластие *n* unlimited authority; absolutism

полноводен -дна *adj rare* (*за река*) deep

полновреден -дна *adj* of full value; valid; полновредна храна nutritious food

полновредност *f* validity

полногласен -сна *adj* pleophonic

полногласие & **полногласје** *n Phon.* full vocalism, pleophony

полнозвучен -чна *adj literary* full, resonant, sonorous

полнокрвен -вна *adj* **1** full-blooded; полнокрвен коњ thoroughbred <horse> **2** ruddy, florid; полнокрвно лице ruddy face **3** *fig.* eventful; vigorous, hearty; полнокрвен живот life lived to the full

полнолетен -тна *adj* adult, major; тој е веќе полнолетен he's of age, he's attained his majority

полнолетност *f* & **полнолетство** *n* <age of> majority

полномасен -сна & **полномаслен** *adj* whole, un-skimmed, full-cream, rich; полномасно сирење full-cream cheese

полномошен -шна *adj* **1** plenipotentiary, authorized, empowered; полномошен министер minister pleni-potentiary **2** (*as noun*) полномошно *n colloq. see* полномоштво

полномошник -ци *m* plenipotentiary; legal represen-tative, agent; proxy

полномоштво & **полномоштие** -ија *n* proxy, autho-rity, power of attorney, mandate; competence; дава некому полномоштие to empower (authorize) s.o.; напише некому полномоштие to sign a power of attorney for s.o.; <из>вонредни полномоштија emergency powers

полноправен -вна *adj* enjoying full rights; полно-правен член full member

полноправност *f* full rights

полнота *f* **1** plenitude, abundance; fullness, complete-ness **2** corpulence; plumpness

полноќ *f* midnight; на полноќ at midnight

полноќен -ќна *adj* midnight; полноќен час midnight hour

полов *adj* sexual; sex; полова зрелост puberty; полов живот sex life

половак -ци *m arch.*, *dial.* **1** *see* половник **2** vessel holding half an *oka* of liquid

половен -вна *adj* second-hand; половни книги second-hand books

полови *impf* **I** to cut into halves **II** – се to split in two, in half *intrans.*

половин *adv dial. see* пол[1], половина

половина *f* **1** half; половина ден (*also* пол ден, полден) half a day; ❑ *joc.* мојата подобра половина my better half; половина човек infirm (incapacitated) person; со половина уста (*му рече*) (*he told him*) reluctantly **2** middle; кон половината на април around the middle of April **3** small of the back, *Med.* sacrum **4** waist; танка половина thin (slim) waist

половичен -чна *adj literary* partial; половични мерки half measures; половичен успех partial success

половник -ци *m* **1** *arch.* measure of capacity of about 5.6 gallons **2** half a sack (bag)

половница *f in the expression:* нема ни пара ни половница he hasn't got a brass farthing

половост *f* libido, sexual drive

полог[1] -зи *m* nest-egg

полог[2] -зи *m* bundle

положба *f* **1** position, situation, location **2** position, pose, posture; незгодна положба uncomfortable position **3** position, status; state, situation, condition; социјална положба social position; службена положба official position (post); висока положба high standing; меѓународната положба the inter-national situation; опсадна положба state of siege

положение *n* (*sg only*) *colloq. see* положба; ❑ жената е во положение the woman is pregnant; влезе некому во положение to put o.s. in s.o. else's shoes (place)

положи *pf rare* to place, put, lay; ❑ положи (стави) основи, темели to lay the foundations; to establish the base; положи (предаде) сметки to present (ren-der) accounts; положи (даде) заклетва (клетва) to

take (swear) an oath; положи испит to pass an examination

положит *adj* sloping, inclined, slanting

положито *adv* aslant, obliquely, slantwise

положува *impf of* положи

полока<р>ник -ци *m*, **полока<р>ница** *f* & *hyp.* **полока<р>ниче** *n* tin vessel holding half an *oka* (*1282 grams*) of liquid

поломи (се) *pf dial. see* искрши (се), сокрши (се)

поломува (се) *impf dial. see* искршува (се), сокршува (се)

полонéза *f* polonaise

полошка *f. Zool.* (Caprimulgus europaeus) nightjar

полпат *m* half-way; сме на полпат we are at the half-way point; ❑ остане на полпат to get stuck half-way

полсаат *m* (*also* пол саат) half an hour; за полсаат ќе се вратам I'll be back in half an hour

Полска *f* Poland

полски[1] *adj* field; полски пат country (unsealed) road; полски цвеќиња wild flowers; полски глушец *Zool.* (Apodemus agrarias) field-mouse; полска кујна field kitchen; полска болница field hospital

полски[2] *adj* Polish

полти *impf* to leak, drip

полтрон *m* poltroon, coward; flatterer, toady, fawner

полтронски *adj* cowardly; spineless

полтронство *n* cowardice, poltroonery

полу- (*in compounds*) half-, semi-, demi-

полубог -ови *m* & **полубожество** *n* demigod

полубогиња & **полубожица** *f* demigoddess

полубрат -аќа *m rare* half-brother, step-brother

полувековен -вна *adj* lasting half a century, of fifty years

полувистина *f* half-truth

полувóкал *m Ling.* semivowel

полувокален -лна *adj Ling.* semivocalic

полувóлнен *adj* wool-blend

полувреме *n Sport.* half, half-time; игравме само едно полувреме we played only one half

полуглáден -дна *adj* half-starved

полуглас -ови *m* **1** *Ling. see* полувокал **2** low voice

полугласен -сна *adj* **1** *Ling. see* полувокален **2** soft-voiced

полугласно *adv* in a low voice, softly

полугнил *adj rare* half-rotten

полугодие -ија *n* half-year, semester

полугодишен -шна *adj* half-yearly, bi-annual; полуго-дишна претплата half-yearly subscription

полугодиште *n* semester, half-year

полугол *adj* half-naked

полугóтов *adj* semi-finished; полуготови производи semi-finished products

полуден *adj* mad, crazy; полуден по (за) некого mad about s.o.; madly in love with s.o.

полуди *pf* **1** to go mad; полуди по некого to go crazy about s.o.; ❑ да полуди човек it's enough to drive one mad **2** to make (drive) mad

полудив *adj* half-savage

полудúвјак -ци *m* half-savage

полудневен -вна *adj* lasting half a day

полудува *impf of* полуди

полужив *adj* half-dead

полузатворен *adj rare* half-closed, ajar

полузрел *adj* half-ripe

полукат -ови *m* mezzanine

полукруг -ови *m* semicircle

полукружен -жна *adj* semicircular

полумéсец *m* half-moon; crescent

полумесечен -чна *adj* fortnightly

полумесечник -ци *m* fortnightly publication

полумрак *m* semi-darkness, twilight, dusk; penumbra

полумрачен -чна *adj* semi-dark, half-lit

полумртов -тва *adj* half-dead

полунов *adj* second-hand

полуóстров *m* peninsula; Балканскиот Полуостров the Balkan Peninsula

полуостровски *adj* peninsular

полуотворен *adj rare* half-open, ajar

полуофицијáлен -лна *adj* semi-official; полу-официјални извори semi-official sources

полупúсмен *adj* semi-literate

полупрáзен -зна *adj* half empty

полупрéчник -ци *m* radius

полусвест *f* semi-consciousness

полусвет *m literary, rare* demi-monde

полусéнка *f* <partial> shade, penumbra

полусéстра *f* half-sister, step-sister

полуслýжбен *adj* semi-official

полусон *m* drowsiness, somnolence

полустих -ови *m Prosody* hemistich, half line

полусýров *adj* half-cooked

полута *pf* to wander, roam for a while

полутéжок -шка *adj Sport.* light heavyweight

полутéмен -мна *adj* half-dark, semi-obscure, penumbral

полутемнина & *rare* полутемница *f* half-light, semi-darkness, penumbra

полутина, полутинка, полутица *f* <cut> half; полутина леб half a loaf of bread

полутка *f* 1 *see* полутина, полутинка, полутица 2 *Sport.* inside forward, inside left/right

полутон -ови *m* 1 *Mus.* semitone, half-tone 2 nuance, shade

полутóпка *f Geog.* hemisphere

полуфабрикáт *m* semi-finished product, ready-to-cook food

полуфинáл *m* & полуфинáле *n Sport.* semifinal

полуфинáлен -лна *adj Sport.* semifinal; полуфинален натпревар semifinal <match>

полуција *f Med.* nocturnal emission

полуцилиндер -дри *m* bowler <hat>, *Am.* derby

полуцúра *impf & pf Med.* to emit sperm during sleep

полуцрн *adj* half black; полуцрни букви semi-bold letters

получасовен -вна *adj* lasting half an hour; получасовен разговор half-hour conversation

полчас *m* (*also* пол час) half an hour

полчиште *n* horde; crowd, mass

полька *f arch.* woman's hip-length jacket

польуби *pf f.p.* to kiss

помага (се) *impf* (*also* помогнува & поможува) *of* помогне (се) & поможе (се)

помагалка *f* stout forked stave used by pack-horse handlers

помагало *n* 1 manual, handbook 2 aid, help; учебно помагало teaching aid

помагач *m* helper, assistant

помагачка *f* (*fem. form*) *see* помагач

помáда *f* pomade, ointment, cream

помаже *pf Rel.* to anoint; помаже за цар to anoint king

помазан *pt* anointed

помазник -ци *m Rel.* anointed person; божји помазник the Lord's Anointed

помазница *f Rel.* (*fem. form*) *see* помазник

помајка *f* foster-mother

помајчима *f see* помајка

помак -ци *m* Macedonian convert to Islam

помама *f* 1 rage, fury 2 lust, craving, passion 3 *rare see* помамица

помамен -мна *adj* 1 crazy, mad 2 lustful, lascivious

помами *pf* I 1 to madden, enrage, infuriate 2 to trick, cheat, dupe (*for a while*) 3 to entice, lure (*briefly*) II - се to become enraged, infuriated; се помами ветрот the wind became violent

помамица & помамка *f* ruse, fraud, trick

помамност *f* rage, fury, madness, violence, frenzy; lust

поматен *pt* troubled; dimmed; ruined; поматени односи soured relations

помати *pf* 1 rare to make turbid, stir up 2 *fig.* to trouble, disturb, mar, cloud; тоа ни ја помати радоста it marred our joy

поматува *impf of* помати

помачи се *pf* to make an effort, strive

помеѓу *prep* between, among; ❑ помеѓу два огна between two fires; помеѓу другото among other things, by the way, incidentally; помеѓу нас between ourselves

помен *m* 1 memorial service, requiem 2 trace, remnant; mention; ни помен не остана од него no trace of him was left; нема ни помен there's no mention

помене *pf rare* помена *aor.* to mention; *see* спомене, спомне

поменик -ци *m Rel.* bead-roll, *see* споменик

поменува *impf rare of* помене

померен *pt* deranged, mad, insane

помери се *pf* to go mad, crazy; се померил од умот he's lost his mind

померува се *impf of* помери се

помести *pf* I 1 rare to displace, move, remove, shift *trans.* 2 *literary, rare* to publish, print (*in a newspaper*); весникот ја поместил неговата статија the newspaper printed his article II – се 1 to move, shift, remove *intrans.*; никако да се помести од место nothing would shift him 2 *dial. see* помери се; ми се чинеше, ќе се поместам I thought I would go crazy

поместува (се) *impf of* помести (се)

помете *pf* 1 to sweep for a while 2 (*измете*) to sweep up; помете двор to sweep a courtyard

пометне *pf* пометна *aor.* to miscarry, have a miscarriage

пометнува *impf of* пометне

пометнување *n* miscarriage

помешечки *adv* lying face down

помија -ии *f* slop, swill, dish-water

помилува¹ *pf* to fondle, caress, pat for a while

помилува² *pf* to pardon, grant amnesty; to have mercy on, show mercy

помилување *n* pardon, clemency; amnesty

помин *m* 1 life; existence, livelihood; ❑ помин поминува to enjoy life; to have a good time 2 *literary* pastime, recreation, amusement, fun; мојот неделен помин *my* weekend (Sunday) recreation **3** passing; ending

помине *pf* помина *aor.* **I 1** (*trans. or* низ, *покрај*) to go by, pass, traverse, cross (*over*); *fig.* to go through, endure, undergo, experience; помине мост to cross a bridge; помине низ тешкотии to endure difficulties; тој арно помина he got off lightly; ќе поминеме некако we'll manage somehow; ❏ сум поминал јас по тој пат I've gone through that; не можеше пиле да помине (прелета) nothing could get past; колку да помине на редот only for the sake of appearances; купи ден, помини live from day to day; live from hand to mouth **2** (на испит) to pass **3** (време) to spend; помине одмор to spend one's holidays; помине век to spend one's life **4** to transfer; to send over (across) **5** to elapse, pass, come to an end; помина зимата the winter is over; помина оттогаш три месеци three months have passed since then; ми помина гладот I am not hungry any more; ❏ како на куче му помина <болеста> he got better in no time **6** to happen; што ќе помине, ќе видиме we'll see what happens **II – се** to pass away, die

поминлив *adj* passing, transitory, transient

поминок *m see* помин 1; нема поминок со него he's difficult to live with

поминува *impf of* помине

поминување *n* **1** passing; crossing; забрането е поминувањето no trespassing **2** life; какво ви е поминувањето? how are you getting on? how's life treating you? **3** pastime, recreation, amusement, fun; убаво поминување pleasant pastime; have fun!

поминувач *m* passer-by

поминувачка *f colloq. see* помин 1

помирен *pt* reconciled, resigned (со – то); помирен со судбината resigned to one's fate

помиреност *f* reconciliation; resignation

помири *pf* **I** to reconcile; помири различни погледи to reconcile differing views **II – се 1** to be reconciled, make one's peace (со – with) **2** to resign o.s. (со – то); to accept; ❏ се помири со судбината to resign o.s. to one's fate; to accept one's lot

помириса *pf* to smell *trans.*, sniff; ❏ не е цвеќе да го помирисаш it takes time to get to know a person; и не сум помирисал I haven't a clue

помирисува *impf of* помириса

помирител *m* peacemaker, conciliator

помирлив *adj* conciliatory; reconcilable

помирува (се) *impf of* помири (се)

помирување *n* reconciliation; peace-making

помирувач *m* peacemaker, conciliator

помисла *f* idea; intention; thought; далеку сум од помислата far be it from me

помисли *pf* **I** to think (на/за – of); to think for a while **II – се 1** to think for a while **2** to regard o.s. as; се помислил веќе учен he already considered himself educated

помислува (се) *impf of* помисли (се)

помнење *n* memory; remembrance

помни *impf* **1** to memorize **2** to remember, recollect; слабо помни he has a bad memory

помножи *pf* to multiply *trans.*; помножи пет со десет to multiply five by ten

помножува *impf of* помножи

помогне *pf* помогна *aor.* **I 1** (*with dat.*) to help, to assist, aid **2** (*trans. or with dat.*) to support financially, help **II – се 1** to help each other **2** (со) to find a use for

помогнува (се) & **помможува (се)** *impf of* помогне (се)

помоден -дна *adj* fashionable; помоден збор vogue-word

помодри *pf* **1** to turn blue *intrans.* **2** to make (turn) blue

помодрува *impf of* помодри

поможе (се) *pf* поможа (се) *aor. see* помогне (се)

поможувач *m rare see* помагач

помози *interj arch. in the expression:* помози Бог! God be with you! may God protect you! (*in reply:* дал ти Бог добро! may God bless you!)

помолба *f usu. in the expresssion:* оди на помолба to go begging

помоли *pf* **I** to plead with; to beg, beseech, entreat **II – се 1** (*with dat.*) to ask, request; to beg, beseech, entreat **2** to plead for a while **3** to pray

помолува (се) *impf of* помоли (се)

помолчи *pf* to keep silent for a while

помолчува *impf of* помолчи

помор *m* **1** pestilence; mass death from plague or famine **2** slaughter, massacre, annihilation

поморец -рци *m* sailor, seaman

помори *pf* to annihilate, slaughter

поморје *n* seaboard

поморлив *adj f.p.* поморлива земја infertile (barren) land; поморлива вода undrinkable water

поморница *f f.p.* чума поморница fatal plague (pestilence)

поморски *adj* maritime, nautical, naval; поморско право maritime law; поморски офицер naval officer

поморство *n* seafaring, navigation

поморува *impf of* помори

помоча *pf* **I** to wet with urine **II – се** to urinate, wet o.s.; ❏ *colloq.* се помоча од смеење to wet o.s. laughing

помочува (се) *impf of* помоча (се)

помош *f* помошти *pl* help, aid, assistance; морална помош moral support; парична помош financial assistance; станица за брза помош emergency (casualty) station; прва помош first aid; ❏ дојде некому на помош to come to s.o.'s aid; со помошта на with the help of (by means of)

помошен -шна *adj* auxiliary; accessory, subsidiary; помошна служба auxiliary/subsidiary service; помошен персонал (состав) auxiliary personnel (staff); *Gram.* помошен глагол auxiliary verb

помошник -ци *m* assistant, aide, helper; deputy; помошник-министер deputy minister

помошница & **помошничка** *f* (*fem. form*) *see* помошник; куќна (домашна) помошница home (domestic) help

помпа[1] *f* pomp, splendour

помпа[2] *f see* пумпа[1]

помпа[3] *impf see* пумпа[2]

помпезен -зна *adj* pompous

помрачи *pf* **I** to obscure; to eclipse; *fig.* to cast a pall over; облаци го помрачија небото clouds covered the sky **II – се** to become obscure, dark; to be eclipsed; умот му се помрачил he has lost his mind

помрачува (се) *impf of* помрачи (се)

помрачување *n* darkening; eclipse; помрачување (потемнување, затемнување) на сонцето eclipse of the sun; помрачување на умот mental breakdown

помрдне *pf* помрдна *aor.* **I** to move, shift, displace (*slightly*) *trans.* **II – се 1** to move *intrans.*; тој не се помрдна од местото he didn't budge **2** *dial., fig.* to lose one's head, go crazy; се помрдна по неа he went crazy for love of her

помрднува (се) *impf of* помрдне (се)

понавлезе *pf* to go in, penetrate further; понавлезе во работата he made more progress with the matter

понада *f* gifts of food (*usu. for the sick*); летна лепешка – зимна понада *prov.* all things have their uses

понадвор *adv* **1** to/in the lavatory **2** *rare* out; outside

понади *pf* to bring gifts (*of food, to the sick*); го понадија болниот they brought food for the patient

понадица *f dim. of* понада

поназира *impf of* поназре

поназре *pf see* назре

понамали (се) *pf see* поднамали (се)

понапред *adv* earlier, before; further forward

понапрежен -жна *adj* former, erstwhile; понапрежен учител former teacher

понатака *adv see* понатаму

понатамошен -шна *adj* further; subsequent; понатамошни напори further efforts; понатамошни страници subsequent pages

понатаму *adv* (*comparative of* натаму) further, farther; onward<s>; не оди понатаму don't go any further!

поначесто *adv* quite often

понаша се *impf dial., f.p.* **1** to say "no"; to restrain o.s. **2** to be proud (*со – of*)

понашува се *impf see* понаша се

пондила *pl* stable, stall for livestock (*part of traditional peasant house*)

поне- *verbal prefix* (*with imperfective verbs only*) indicating action performed to a lesser extent than previously; понеболи to hurt (ache) less than before; понегреши to err less than before

понѐгде & *rare* понегдека (*also* по негде<ка>) *adv* here and there, in places

понеделник -ци *m* Monday; во еден понеделник one Monday; в понеделник on Monday (this Monday); во понеделник every Monday (on Mondays); во понеделникот last Monday; чисти понеделник the first Monday of Lent; Велипонеделник Easter Monday

понеделнички *adj rare* referring to Monday, Monday's; понеделнички средби Monday meetings; (*as adv*) on Monday; on Mondays; понеделнички фати да работи he started work on Monday

понекаде *adv* (*also* по некаде) *see* понѐгде

понекогаш *adv* at times, occasionally, now and then

понѐкој -ои *pron rare* (*usu.* по некој) **1** some, any, an occasional; понекоја книга an occasional book **2** someone; понекој доаѓа someone may call

понекојпат *adv* occasionally, now and then, from time to time

понемчи *pf* **I** to Germanize, make German **II – се** to become German, be Germanized

понемчува (се) *impf of* понемчи (се)

понесе *pf* **I** to carry off, take away **II – се** *literary, fig.* to resound, ring out

понесува (се) *impf of* понесе (се)

пони *m indecl.* pony

понижен *pt* humiliated

понижи *pf* to humiliate

понижува *impf of* понижи

понижување & понижение *n* humiliation

понижувачки *adj* humiliating

понизен -зна *adj* humble, submissive

понизи *pf see* понижи

понизно *adv* humbly, submissively; ❑ понизно молам I humbly request

понизност *f* humility

понизува *impf see* понижува

понизување *n see* понижување

понизувачки *adj see* понижувачки

поникне¹ *pf* поникна *aor.* to spring up, arise; поникна трева grass has sprouted; поникна ново движење a new movement has sprung up

поникне² *pf f.p.* поникна *aor.* to lower one's eyes, look down

поникнува *impf of* поникне¹

понира *impf* (*за вода*) to soak into the ground; *fig.* to penetrate

поништи *pf* **1** to annul, revoke, cancel, rescind; поништи решение to revoke a decision **2** *dial.* to destroy

поништува *impf of* поништи

понор *m* **1** swallow-hole, sink-hole **2** abyss

понорница *f Geog.* watercourse beginning on the surface and continuing underground

поносечки *adv in the expression:* падне поносечки to fall flat, on one's face

поноси *pf* to wear/carry for a while

понтон *m* pontoon

понтонски *adj* pontoon; понтонски мост pontoon bridge

понуда *f* offer; bid; даде, поднесе понуда to make an offer; понуда и побарувачка supply and demand

понуди *pf* **I** to offer; понуди некому место to offer s.o. a post **2** to treat s.o. (*со – to*); го понуди со бонбони he offered him sweets **II – се** to offer one's services; to offer (*да – to*); се понудил тој да ја сврши работата he offered to finish the job

понудува (се) *impf of* понуди (се)

поодамна *adv* for a long time; од поодамна те немам видено I haven't seen you for a long time

пооддело *adv* separately, singly; individually

пооди *pf* to walk/go for a while; to function, operate, run for a while; саатот пооде десетина дена точно this watch kept good time for about ten days

поора *pf* **1** to plough for a while **2** to plough up; поора бразда to plough a furrow

поорува *impf of* поора

поп *m* **1** priest; ❑ праќа од попа до ковача to send from pillar to post; попот во црквата греши to err is human **2** *Cards* king **3** heart of a water-melon

попадиин *adj* belonging to a priest's wife

попадија -ии & *rare* **попадика¹** *f* priest's wife; ❑ еден му се радува на попот, друг на попадијата one man's meat is another man's poison

попадика² *f* & **попадиче¹** *n Bot.* **1** (Tanacetum parthenium) feverfew **2** (*loosely*) camomile, marigold, daisy, etc.

попадиче² *n hyp. of* попадија & попадика¹

попадне *pf* попадна *aor.* **1** *rare, literary* to find o.s., come to be; попаднале под неговото влијание they fell under his influence; попаднале во едно мочуриште they found themselves in a morass **2** to fall

попалави *pf* I to drive insane; to madden **II – се** to go mad; се попалави по неа he lost his head over her

попара *f* bread pap; bread and milk; ❑ тој ja jaл попарата he paid the price; не сркај со деца попара *prov.* this is not a matter for children; тој ja надроби таа попара he got us into this mess

попарен *pt* **1** scalded; ❑ скокна како попарен he jumped like a scalded cat **2** (*од слана*) blackened, blighted **3** *fig.* crushed, broken, shattered

попари *pf* I **1** to scald **2** (*за слана*) to blight, blacken **3** *fig.* to destroy, crush **II – се 1** to scald o.s.; кој се попарил од пресно млеко, дува и на матеницата *prov.* once bitten, twice shy **2** *fig.* to be crushed, broken in spirit

попасок *m* short grazing (*of stock before milking*)

попатен -тна *adj* **1** on the way, local; попатна станица local station **2** by the way, incidental, casual; marginal; попатни белешки casual remarks, asides

попива *impf* **1** to absorb, soak up **2** *rare* to drink a little, from time to time

попивач *m & попивка f* blotting pad, blotter; blotting-paper

попивен -вна *adj in the expression:* попивна хартија blotting-paper

попие *pf* попи *aor.* **1** *f.p.* (*испие*) to drink up **2** to absorb, soak up

попис *m* list, inventory, register; попис на имот inventory of property; попис на имиња list (register) of names; попис на населението census of the population

пописен -сна *adj* <of a> register, census, inventory; пописни комисии census commissions; stock-taking committees

попише *pf* попиша *aor.* to list, inventorize; попише имот to inventorize property; попише населението to conduct a census of the population

попишува *impf of* попише

попишувач *m* recorder; stock-taker; попишувач на населението census-worker

поплав *m & поплава f* flood, inundation; deluge (*also fig.*); цела поплава од зборови torrent of words

поплавен *pt* flooded

поплави *pf* to flood, inundate (*also fig.*)

попладне *n* afternoon; (*as adv*) in the afternoon

поплак -ци *m & поплака f* complaint; биро за жалби и поплаки office of appeals and complaints

поплакува (се) *impf of* поплаче (се)

поплаче *pf* поплаче & поплака *aor.* I to cry (weep) for a while **II – се** to complain

попленец -нци *m f.p.* plunderer; robber

поплени *pf* **1** to pillage, plunder; му го попленија рувото they robbed him of his clothes **2** to capture, take prisoner

поплочи *pf* to pave, tile

поплочува *impf of* поплочи

поплука *pf* **1** to spit (*briefly*) **2** to spit on (*all over*)

попов *adj* priest's; *Zool.* попово прасе (Gryllotalpa vulgaris) mole-cricket

поповски *adj* priest's; priestly

поповство *n* office (position) of priest; priesthood

поповштина *f* *pejor.* priestly dogma; religious superstition

пополека *adv see* полека

пополни *pf* to occupy, fill; to fill in (fill out); пополни место to occupy a place (seat); пополни формулар to fill in a form

пополнува *impf of* пополни

попопи *pf* I to ordain as a priest **II – се** to enter the priesthood

попосле *adv see* после

поправ *m in the expression:* нема поправ it's beyond repair

поправа (се) *impf of* поправи (се)

поправач *m* corrector; repairer; *Elec.* rectifier, transformer

поправен -вна *adj* corrective, correcting; поправен дом house of correction; поправна казна corrective punishment (detention)

поправи *pf* I **1** to repair; to correct; to tidy; поправи куќа/кола to repair a house/car; поправи граматички грешки to correct grammatical mistakes; поправи фризура to tidy one's hair **2** to cure, set right, restore **II – се 1** to improve *intrans.*; to correct o.s.; се поправи времето the weather has improved **2** to recover, recuperate **3** to put on weight

поправка *f* **1** repair; поправки на куќа house repairs **2** correction; поправка на задачи correction of tests **3** improvement

поправлив *adj* repairable; corrigible

поправо *adv* really; actually, in fact; exactly

попраг -зи *m* (*also* потпраг) saddle-girth

попраже *n dim. of* попраг

попражи *pf* to put on a girth, fasten a saddle-girth on; to saddle

попражува *impf of* попражи

попрати *pf* to accompany, escort; to see off

попратува & попраќа *impf of* попрати

попраша *pf* **1** to ask, inquire; to question **2** to keep asking for a while

попраши (се) *pf see* напраши (се)

попрашува *impf of* попраша

попрашува (се) *impf of* попраши (се)

попрвин *adv* first of all

попрво *adv see* попрвин

попреде *pf* to spin for a while; ❑ ако ми попредеш, ќе ти поткаам you scratch my back, I'll scratch yours

попредок -ци *m & попретка f* traditional outdoor spinning party

попрекршен *adj* elderly

попреку *adv rare see* напреку, напорки

попрелка *f* spinning bee

попречен -чна *adj* transversal, diagonal

попречи *pf* (*usu. with dat., rarely trans.*) to prevent, hinder; болеста му попречи да дојде his illness prevented (kept) him from coming

попречува *impf of* попречи

поприште *n literary* **1** scene; location; поприште на битка scene of a battle **2** career, walk of life, field, profession; литературно поприште literary career

попрска *pf* I **1** to spatter (*lightly*); to sprinkle a little **2** (*за дожд*) to drizzle, spit **II – се** *colloq., sl.* to boast, brag a little

попски & поповски *adj* of a priest; priestly

попство *n see* поповство

попува *impf* **1** to serve as a priest **2** to preach

попука *pf* **1** to shoot for a while, fire a few shots **2** to break up *intrans.*; сидовите попукаа the walls cracked **3** to upset, anger for a while

популáрен -рна *adj* popular; популарна песна a popular song

популаризáтор *m* popularizer

популаризација *f* popularization

популаризúра *pf & impf* to popularize

популáрност *f* popularity

попуст *m* discount, price-reduction; патува со попуст he travels at reduced fares; се продава со попуст it's being sold at a discount; попуст од десет проценти ten percent discount

попустлив *adj* yielding, compliant

попусто *adv* in vain, vainly

попушта *impf* **1** *of* попушти; паметењето му попушта his memory is failing **2** *f.p.* to send (*a letter*); пушта, попушта книга по книга he keeps sending letter after letter

попуштање *n* **1** slackening, loosening; easing, weakening; попуштање на уздата slackening of the reins; попуштање на дисциплината slackening of discipline; попуштање на меѓународната затегнатост easing of international tension (*détente*); попуштање на сид weakening of a wall **2** (*попуст*) discount, price reduction

попушти *pf* **1** to relax *trans.*, to loosen, slacken *trans.*; попушти ремен to loosen a strap **2** to offer at reduced price; to discount; колку денари ќе ми попуштиш? how many denars' discount will you give me? **3** to give in, yield *intrans.*; to give way; попушти сидот the wall gave way; здравјето ми попушти my health deteriorated **4** to diminish, ease, abate; му попуштија болките his pains have eased

попче *n* **1** *dim. of* поп **2** *Zool.* обично попче (Prunella modularis) hedge sparrow, dunnock

пор *m* *Zool.* (Mustela putorius) polecat; ❑ смрди како пор to stink like a polecat

пора¹ *f* pore

пора² *f dial.* age; generation

пораб *m* hem; selvedge

пораби *pf* to hem

порабува *impf of* пораби

поради *prep* because of, by reason of, owing to, as a consequence of; поради тоа for that reason, therefore

пораѓа (се) *impf of* породи (се)

пораз *m* defeat; трпи пораз to suffer defeat

поразговара & поразговори *pf* **I** to comfort, cheer; to entertain with conversation **II** – **се** to get talking; седнале и се поразговориле they sat down and got into conversation

поразен -зна *adj* destructive; disastrous; поразна критика crushing criticism; поразен впечаток overwhelming impression

порази *pf* **1** to defeat **2** to strike down; to kill **3** *rare* to appal, dismay, terrify, shock; глетката ме порази the sight shocked me

поразува *impf of* порази

порака *f* message; order; по порака на раководството by order of the management; порака на писателот a writer's message

порамни *pf* **I** to level, even <out> **II** – **се** *Leg.* to reach a settlement; to agree

порамнува (се) *impf of* порамни (се)

поранешен -шна *adj* former, previous

порани *pf* **1** to get up early **2** to arrive early

поранува *impf of* порани

пораснат *pt* grown big, increased; пораснати нужди (потреби) increased needs (demands)

порасне *pf* пораснá *aor.* **1** to grow up, grow *intrans.*; to increase; тревата пораснала the grass has grown; децата пораснаа the children have grown up; ❑ му пораснаа акциите his stock has risen **2** to bring up, raise, rear

пораснува *impf of* порасне

пораст *m* growth, increase; пораст на населението population growth; пораст на цените increase in prices

порасте *pf see* порасне

порастен *pt see* пораснат

порача *pf* **1** to order; си порачав чевли I ordered some shoes for myself **2** to send a message; татко ти порача да дојдеш your father sent word for you to come

порачка *f* order; направи порачка за нешто to place an order for s.th.

порачува *impf of* порача

порачувач *m* purchaser, client, customer; sender of message

порева се *impf of* порне се

поредба *f* comparison; *Gram.* поредба на придавките comparison of adjectives

поредбен *adj* comparative

пореди¹ *pf* (*спореди*) to compare

пореди² *pf* **I** to line up *trans.*, arrange in rows; to arrange partially **II** – **се** to line up *intrans.*

поредница *f dial.* plague; epidemic; *f.p.* црна чума поредница Black Death

поредок -ци *m literary* order, system, regime; установен поредок established order; во боен поредок in battle order

поредува¹ *impf of* пореди¹

поредува² (се) *impf of* пореди² (се)

поредум *adv f.p. usu.* in the expression: ред поредум in a row; consecutively, one after the other

порез *m* (*данок*) tax

порезник *m* tax-collector

поречје *n* river basin

поречка се *pf colloq.* to get into an argument; to start squabbling

поречканица *f colloq.* squabble, quarrel, wrangle

пори *impf literary, poet.* to rend, cleave; небото го пореа молњи flashes of lightning rent the sky

пориби *pf* to stock with fish; пориби езеро to stock a lake with fish

порибува *impf of* пориби

порив *m literary* impulse, drive, urge

порне се *pf* порне се *aor.* to lurch, stagger, totter; to trip

порнографија *f* pornography

порнографски *adj* pornographic

пороби *pf* **1** to enslave **2** *rare* to rob; to plunder **3** *rare* to capture, take prisoner

поробува *impf of* пороби

поробувач *m* enslaver, oppressor

пороганија -ии *f colloq.* scandal, scene; shame, disgrace

пород *m* progeny, issue, offspring; ❑ (*in arch. form* порода) за него нема ни рода ни порода he doesn't care about anyone

порода *f* breed, stock; descent, extraction; коњи арапска порода Arab horses

породи *pf* I 1 to assist at a birth; to deliver; породи некого да деливер s.o.'s baby 2 *f.p.* to bear, give birth to 3 *literary* to arouse, awaken, give rise to, engender; породи незадоволство to give rise to dissatisfaction II – се 1 to give birth 2 *literary* to arise; се породија сомненија doubts arose

породилен -лна *adj* (*родилен*) maternity, labour; *Med.* породилни маки labour pains, *fig.* birth pangs; породилна треска puerperal fever; ❑ породилен дом maternity home, maternity hospital

породилиште *n* maternity home (hospital)

породува (се) *impf rare see* пораѓа (се)

пороен[1] -јна *adj* 1 torrential; поројна вода flash-flood water; пороен поток torrential stream; пороен дожд torrential rain; downpour 2 torrent-prone; поројни подрачја flood-prone regions

пороен[2] -јна *adj f.p.* swarming (*of bees*)

пороже *n* horn rope, tether attached to horns

порожи *pf* to tether (*cattle*) by the horns

порожница *f see* пороже

порожува *impf of* порожи

порозен -зна *adj* porous

порозност *f* porosity

пороит *adj rare, f.p. see* пороен[1]

пороиште *n* 1 *augm. of* порој 2 flood-prone area

порој -ои *m* torrent, deluge, downpour, cloudburst; порој од зборови a torrent of words; порој од луѓе hordes of people

поројник *m poet.* in the expression: дожд поројник downpour

поројница *f* in the expression: река поројница river swollen by melt-water

порок -ци *m* vice, weakness

порота *f* jury

поротен -тна *adj* jury; поротен суд a jury court

поротник -ци *m* juror, juryman; судија-поротник juror

порочен -чна *adj* 1 immoral, depraved 2 *literary, rare* порочен круг vicious circle

порочност *f* immorality; depravity, vice

порта *f* gate; front door; *Hist.* Високата порта the Sublime (Ottoman) Porte

портабл *adj indecl.* portable; портабл-машина за пишување portable typewriter

портал *m* portal

портар *m arch.* door-keeper, porter, gatekeeper

портарка *f colloq., iron.* a woman who gossips at her gate

порте *n dim. of* порта; small gate on to the street

портик -ци *m* portico

портир *m* house-porter; desk clerk; security guard

портирка *f* (*fem. form*) *see* портир

портирница *f* porter's room/cabin

портирски *adj* porter's

портмоне́ -еи, -еа *m & n* purse

портокал *m Bot.* (Citrus aurantium) orange (*tree and fruit*)

портокалов *adj* 1 orange; портокалово дрво orange tree 2 orange-coloured

Порторика́нец -нци *m* Puerto Rican

Порторика́нка *f* (*fem. form*) *see* Порториканец

порторика́нски *adj* Puerto Rican

Порторико *n* Puerto Rico

портпаро́л *m* spokesman

портрет *m* portrait

портрети́ра *pf & impf* to portray, depict

портрети́ст *m* portrait artist, portraitist

портре́тски *adj* <of a> portrait; portrait-like

Португалец -лци *m* Portuguese

Португалија *f* Portugal

Португалка *f* (*fem. form*) *see* Португалец

португалски *adj* Portuguese

портфе́љ -ли *m* portfolio; министер без портфељ minister without portfolio

поруга[1] *f* mockery; стане за поруга to become a laughing-stock

поруга[2] *pf* I to mock, deride, ridicule, make fun of II – се to ridicule, make fun (*co – of*)

порумене *pf rare* порумена *aor. see* порумени 1

порумени *pf* 1 to blush slightly 2 *rare* to make pink, rosy

порумунува *impf of* порумене & порумени

поруси[1] *pf* to Russify, Russianize

поруси[2] *pf* (*за коса*) to become lighter, fairer

поруча *pf* to breakfast, have breakfast

поручан *pt* having breakfasted

поручек -ци *m* afternoon; (*as adv*) in the afternoon, after lunch; поручек сум дома I'll be at home after lunch

поручник -ци *m* lieutenant

порфир *m* porphyry

порфи́ра *f* <ceremonial> purple, purple robe<s>

порфирен -рна *adj* 1 <of> porphyry; порфирни столбови porphyry columns 2 purple; порфирен плашт purple mantle

порхет *m* fustian

порхетен -тна *adj* fustian; порхетен фустан a fustian dress

порцела́н *m* porcelain

порција -ии *f* 1 portion 2 mess tin

посада *f literary* 1 garrison 2 crew

посади *pf* to plant; посади цвеќиња to plant flowers

посадува *impf of* посади

посака *pf* 1 to ask for, request; посака прочка to ask forgiveness 2 to want, wish for; имавме сè што ќе ни посака душа we had everything we could wish for 3 to ask for the hand (*of*); ја посакал момата he asked for the girl's hand

посаклив *adj* demanding; посакливо дете demanding child

посакува *impf of* посака

посакум *adv arch.* deliberately, specially

посатка *f* crockery

посвати се *pf* to become related by marriage

посведочи *pf* I to testify, give evidence (*дека – that*); to demonstrate, give proof of; ја посведочи својата приврзаност to prove one's loyalty II – се *rare* to assure o.s.

посведочува (се) *impf of* посведочи (се)

посвета *f* dedication, inscription; посвета од авторот a dedication from the author

посветен   pt (often as noun) initiate<d>

посвети¹   pf I 1 to dedicate, devote, give; посвети некому песна to dedicate a poem to s.o.; посвети внимание на нешто to turn one's attention to s.th. 2 to initiate; го посветил во својата тајна he revealed his secret to him II – се to devote o.s., dedicate o.s. (на – то); се посветил на литературна дејност he devoted himself to literary activity (work)

посвети²   pf to canonize; to sanctify

посветува¹ (се)   impf of посвети¹ (се)

посветува²   impf of посвети²

посвири   pf to play (an instrument) for a while

посвоен   -јна adj Gram. possessive; посвојна заменка possessive pronoun

посвоеник   -ци m adopted son

посвоеница   f adopted daughter

посвои   pf 1 to appropriate 2 to adopt

посвојност   f Gram. possession

посвојувач & посвоител   m adoptive parent

посвојче   n adopted child

посврши   pf f.p., dial. I 1 to betroth 2 rare to finish; посврши работа to finish a job II – се to get engaged

посвршува (се)   impf of посврши (се)

посебен   -бна adj particular, special; separate

посебно   adv specially; separately

посебност   f separateness; peculiarity

посев   m 1 sowing, seeding 2 seed for sowing 3 (usu. pl) sown fields; crops

посева   impf of посее

посевен   -вна adj <of/for> sowing; посевни површини cultivated land; sown area; посевно семе seed for sowing

посега (се)   impf of посегне (се)

посегне   pf посегна aor. I 1 to reach out 2 to encroach (на/врз – on); to assail; to impinge (on); посегне врз (на) честа to tarnish (s.o.'s) honour; ❑ посегне на својот живот (на себеси) to attempt suicide II – се rare to reach into one's pocket

посегнува (се)   impf see посега (се)

посед   m property, real estate; земјишен посед landed property

поседа   f see поседок

поседи   pf to sit for a while

поседне   pf поседна аор. (за многу народ) to sit down one by one

поседник   -ци m landowner

поседок   -ци m spinning/sewing bee

поседува¹   impf of поседи

поседува²   impf to own, possess

посее   pf посеа aor. 1 to sow; fig. посее раздор to sow discord 2 to sow for a while

посејува   impf see посева

посеклив   adj Bot. посеклива (секлива) трева (Achillea millefolium) yarrow, milfoil

посекува (се)   impf of посече (се)

поселани   pf I to countrify (s.o., by dress, etc.) II – се to become a countryman/peasant

поселанува (се)   impf of поселани (се)

посен   -сна adj 1 lenten; посна храна lenten fare; посни дни fast days 2 meatless; посна чорба vegetable soup 3 lean, having little fat; посно месо lean meat 4 (за земја) poor in nutrients; посна земја poor soil

посесѝвен   -вна adj Gram. (посвоен) possessive; посесивни придавки possessive adjectives

посестри   pf I to take (adopt) as a sister II – се to become like sisters

посестрима   f bosom friend; "blood-sister"

посестрими (се)   pf see посестри (се)

посестримува (се) & посеструва (се)   impf of посестрими (се), посестри (се)

посета   f visit, call; направи посета to pay a call; лекарска посета doctor's call (visit), house call

посетеност   f popularity (with visitors, customers); attendance

посети   pf 1 to visit; to pay a call on; ме посети син ми my son visited me; ја посетивме изложба we visited an exhibition 2 fig., literary, rare to overcome (of a feeling); го посети сонот sleep overcame him

посетител   m 1 visitor 2 participant; student; курсот има триесет посетители the course has thirty students

посетителка   f (fem. form) see посетител

посетница   f (визит-карта) visiting-card

посетува   impf 1 of посети to attend, go regularly to; посетува курс to attend a course

посече   pf I 1 rare, f.p. to cut up, cut to pieces; to cut off; ❑ чесен крст да ме посече ако кажам may I drop dead if I tell 2 to cut for a while II – се rare to cut o.s.

посечува (се)   impf see посекува (се)

посивее   pf посивеа aor. see посиви 2

посиви   pf 1 to make grey, turn grey trans. 2 to go grey

посивува   impf of посивее & посиви

посига (се)   impf of посигне (се)

посигне   pf посигна aor. I 1 to reach <out>; посигне в џеб to reach into one's pocket 2 rare see посегне I 2 II – се rare to reach into one's pocket

посигнува (се)   impf see посига (се)

посиненик   -ци m adopted son, foster-son

посини¹   pf to adopt (as a son)

посини²   pf 1 to make blue, to blue 2 to go (turn) blue

посинува¹   impf of посини¹

посинува²   impf of посини²

посипе   pf посипа aor. I to sprinkle; to pour trans. II – се to shower/sprinkle o.s. (со – with); ❑ се посипе со пепел to admit one's guilt

посипка   f dial. poker; coal shovel

посипува (се)   impf of посипе (се)

поскапи   pf 1 to make dearer, more expensive; поскапи книга to raise the price of a book 2 to become more expensive; to go up

поскапува   impf of поскапи

поскапување   n price increase, price rise

поскара   pf I to scold, rebuke (briefly) II – се to quarrel for a while

поскок¹   m jump, hop; ❑ на поскок ready to jump

поскок²   -ци m Zool. (Vipera ammodytes) horned viper

поскока   pf to jump, hop a little, for a short time

поскура   f host, Communion bread

поскурник   -ци m stamp for imprinting the cross onto the Communion bread

послание   -ија n epistle; missive

после   adv 1 later, afterwards, then 2 after all, besides 3 (reinforcing prep. по) по два дена после two days later; после него after him; по тоа после after that, afterwards

последен -дна *adj* **1** last, final; последниот ред last row; ❑ до последниот здив to one's dying breath; за прв и последен пат for the first and last time; оддаде последна почит to pay one's last respects; до последен (ќе се бориме) (*we will fight*) to the last; до последната капка крв to the last drop of blood **2** recent; во последниве години in recent (the last few) years; ❑ во последно време, последново време in recent times, recently (lately) **3** (*as noun*) the latter **4** extreme, uttermost; последното средство extreme means; последната инстанција the highest instance **5** newest, latest; последни вести the latest news; последна мода latest fashion; ❑ последен крик на модата the very latest fashion (*le dernier cri*); последен збор на техниката the last word in technology **6** worst, lowest

последица *f* effect, result, consequence; причините и последиците the causes and effects; сè помина без последици everything passed without trace

последичен -чна *adj Gram.* consecutive; последична реченица consecutive clause

последовен -вна *adj rather rare* **1** consecutive, uninterrupted, continuous, successive; последовни напади continuous attacks **2** consistent; последовна политика consistent policy **3** *fig.* unswerving; последовен борец determined advocate (*of a cause*)

последовност *f rather rare* **1** continuity; successiveness **2** consistency

последок -ци *m Anat.* (*плацента*) placenta

последува *impf literary, rare* **1** to follow *trans.* **2** to imitate, emulate; ти ќе го последуваш неговиот пример you will follow his example **3** to ensue

пословени *pf* to Slavicize

пословенува *impf of* пословени

пословечки *adj in the expression:* пословечки говор secret language, private (personal) language (*created by adding a given syllable to every syllable of a word*)

пословица *f* proverb

пословичен -чна *adj* proverbial

послуга *f* **1** use; даде некому нешто на послуга to give s.o. s.th. to use **2** staff; service; послуга во хотел service in a hotel

послужи *pf* **I 1** to serve, wait on; домаќинката нè послужи <со> вино the hostess served us wine; ❑ среќата го послужи luck was on his side **2** (*with dat.*) to be of service, come in handy; ова ќе ни послужи во работата this will help us in our work **3** to serve for a while **II – се 1** to help o.s., serve o.s. **2** to use, utilize, avail o.s. (*со – of*); се послужив со тие извори I used those sources

послужува (се) *impf of* послужи (се)

послуша *pf* **1** to listen <то> for a while **2** to obey

послушен -шна *adj* obedient, dutiful

послушност *f* obedience

посматра *impf* to watch; to observe

посматрачки *adj literary* observant; посматрачка дарба gift of observation

посмее *pf* посмеа *aor.* **I 1** to make s.o. laugh a little **2** *dial.* to laugh at; може да ја посмеат perhaps they'll laugh at her **II – се 1** to laugh for a while **2** (*with dat.*) to laugh at s.o., mock s.o.

посмртен -тна *adj* posthumous; посмртна слава posthumous fame; посмртен говор funeral oration, *Am.* eulogy

посмртнина *f* funeral allowance

посмртница *f* death certificate

посмрче & посмртче *n* child born after the death of its father, posthumous child, orphan

посник -ци *m* **1** monk of an ascetic order; anchorite **2** (*usu. pl*) fast days **3** (*popular name for*) December

посница *f* **1** nun of an ascetic order **2** monk's cell

поснички *adj* of fasting; ascetic, austere; поснички живот life of fasting

поснопица *adv* like ninepins; сите паднаа поснопица they all dropped like ninepins

посока *f see* правец

посоли *pf* **1** to salt; посоли чорба to salt soup **2** to scatter, sprinkle; посоли пепел to scatter ashes

посомнева се *pf* to entertain doubts/suspicions

посоп *m* flour used for sprinkling dough

посочи *pf literary* to show; to indicate, point out; to mention

посочува *impf of* посочи

поспие *pf* поспа *aor.* to doze, catnap, take a nap

посрами *pf* **I** to bring shame upon; to shame; to embarrass **II – се** to be embarrassed

посрамоти *f* **I** to put to shame; to disgrace, dishonour **II – се** to be shamed, dishonoured; to disgrace o.s.

посрамотува (се) *impf of* посрамоти (се)

посрамува (се) *impf of* посрами (се)

посрби *pf* to Serbianize

посрбува *impf of* посрби

посред & rare посреде *prep* in the middle (midst) of; посреде полето in the middle of the field; посред бел ден in broad daylight

посреде *adv* at bottom, basically, essentially, fundamentally

посребри *pf* **I** to silver; to silver-plate **II – се** *fig., rather rare* to go grey

посребрува (се) *impf of* посребри (се)

посреден -дна *adj* **1** indirect; посреден пат indirect route; посреден данок indirect tax **2** (*за брат, сестра*) middle

посредник -ци *m* mediator, intermediary, middleman, go-between

посредница & посредничка *f* (*fem. form*) *see* посредник

посреднички *adj* mediating; посредничка мисија mediating mission

посредништво *n* mediation, arbitration

посредство *n literary usu. in the expression:* со посредство<то> на by means of, with the aid of

посредува *impf* to mediate, arbitrate

посрете & посретна *pf rather rare* посрете & посретна *aor.* **I 1** to welcome **2** to meet *trans.* **3** to intercept **II – се** (*со*) to meet *trans.*

посретнува (се) & посреќава (се) *impf of* посретне (се) & посрете (се)

пост -и *m* fast, fasting; велици пости Lent, Lenten Fast

поста *f* swathe (*of reaped grain crop*); lot, job

постава[1] *f* lining; свилена постава silken lining

постава[2] **(се)** *impf see* поставува (се)

поставен *pt* placed, positioned; established; добро поставен well established, stable

поставеност *f* stability

постави[1] *pf* **I 1** to put, place, lay; постави споменик to erect a monument **2** to appoint; постави некого

<за> учител, судија to appoint s.o. <as> teacher, judge **3** to post, place; постави стражи to post sentries **4** to set; си постави <за> задача, цел to make it one's task, aim; постави рокови to set time-limits (dates) **5** to pose, present; постави проблем to pose a problem; постави прашање to put (pose) a question **6** (*драма*) to stage; to direct **II – се 1** to establish o.s. **2** to adopt a standpoint (position); зависи од тоа како ќе се поставиш it depends what attitude you take; добро се поставил he is well established

постави² *pf* to line; постави палто со кожа to line a coat with leather

поставка *f* principle; tenet; филозофски поставки philosophical principles

поставува (се) *impf of* постави¹ (се)

постамент *m* pedestal

постанат *adj* exhausted, worn-out

постанатост *f* exhaustion, fatigue

постане *pf* постана *aor.* to become exhausted, worn out

постанува *impf of* постане

постапен *-пна adj see* постепен

постапи *pf* **1** to behave, act; постапи по својата совест to act according to one's conscience **2** *rare* to take up (start) a job; постапи на занает to take up a trade

постапка *f* act; action; behaviour, conduct; procedure, proceedings

постапува *impf of* постапи

постара се *pf* to take pains (*да – то*), take care; to try, endeavour, make efforts

постела *f* **1** bed; стане од постела to get out of bed; својата постела е најмека *prov.* there's no place like home **2** *dial.* mattress

постеле *pf* посла *aor.* **1** to spread <out>, lay; постеле постела to make a bed; како ќе си постелеш така ќе си легнеш *prov.* as you make your bed, so you must lie in it **2** to carpet; to cover; постеле соба to carpet a room

постелен *-лна adj* <of/for a> bed; постелни работи bedclothes, bed-linen

постелува *impf see* постила

постење *n* fasting

постепен *adj* gradual; постепен развој gradual development

пости *impf* to fast; to abstain

постига *impf of* постигне I 1

постигне *pf* постигна *aor.* **I 1** to attain, achieve, accomplish, reach; постигне цел to achieve one's goal **2** *f.p.* to bear, bring forth **II – се** *f.p.* to be born

постигнува *impf see* постига

постила *impf of* постеле

постилач *m* **1** *see* постилка **2** cover; coverlet, bedspread

постилка *f* carpet, rug

постоен *-jна adj* existing, existent, current, present; во постојните услови in the existing conditions

постоење *n* existence; survival; борбата за постоење struggle for survival

постои¹ *pf* постоја *aor.* to stand for a while; to wait a moment

постои² *impf* to exist, be

постојан *adj* constant, permanent, continuous, steady; постојана грижа constant worry; постојан

посетител regular visitor; постојана служба permanent employment/service; постојана работа permanent work; постојан жител permanent resident; постојана војска regular (standing) army; постојана вредност constant value; постојан карактер stable character

постојаност *f* constancy, regularity

постојанство *n* firmness, steadiness; persistence; steadfastness (*of character*)

пострада *pf* **1** to be damaged, come to harm; to suffer *intrans.* **2** to suffer for a while

пострадува *impf of* пострада 1

пост-рестант *m* poste restante, *Am.* general delivery

постриг *m Rel.* tonsure; taking of monastic vows

постриже *pf* пострижа *aor.* **I 1** *Rel.* to tonsure, receive as a monk **2** to shear, clip (*sheep*) for some time; to cut, trim hair for some time **II – се** *Rel.* to be tonsured, become a monk

пострижува (се) *impf of* постриже (се)

построи *pf* **I 1** to line up, form into ranks *trans.* **2** *rare* to build **II – се** to form ranks, form up *intrans.*

постројка *f* installation, factory, plant

постројува (се) *impf of* построи (се)

пост-скриптум *m* postscript, PS

постулат *m* postulate

постхумен *-мна adj* posthumous

пот *f & rarely m, pl rare* потови sweat, perspiration; студена пот беше го избила he broke out in a cold sweat (all over); потови од мене да течат sweat was simply pouring from me; кај нема пот има глад; кај има пот нема глад *prov.* no sweat without sweat; ❏ со пот (*спечалено*) (*earned*) by honest toil; сака пот it takes hard work

пот- *verbal prefix see* под-

потаен *-jна pt & adj* **1** covered, hidden; secret; потајно место secret place; потаен јаглен (жар) повеќе жеже *prov.* a hidden foe is twice as dangerous **2** furtive, secretive **3** *fig.* mysterious

потаи *pf poet.* to hide, conceal

потај *m poet.* secrecy, mystery; чува во потај to keep secret

потајник *-ци m* **1** secretive person **2** *poet.* dagger

потајница *f* **1** (*fem. form*) *see* потајник 1 **2** *f.p.* сабја (пушка) потајница concealed weapon

потамина *adv* at random, blindly; пука потамина to fire blindly

потамошен *-шна adj* (*понатамошен*) further, subsequent; потамошните чекори further steps

потаму *adv* (*понатаму*) further, farther; onwards

потврда *f* confirmation; acknowledgement; receipt; note; certificate; evidence

потврден *-дна adj* positive, affirmative; потврден одговор affirmative reply (answer)

потврди *pf* **I 1** to confirm; to bear out; to acknowledge; to certify; потврди прием to confirm receipt **2** to sanction, ratify, endorse; потврди договор to ratify an agreement **II – се** to prove correct; to be confirmed

потврдува (се) *impf of* потврди (се)

потег *-зи m* **1** line; stroke; во големи потези in broad outline; ❏ со еден потег на перото with one stroke of the pen **2** *Chess* move; ти си на потег it's your move **3** *fig.* stroke, move; погрешен потег false move; генијален потег stroke of genius

потега *impf of* потегне

потегне *pf* потегна *aor.* **1** to tug, pull; потегне некого за ракав to tug at s.o.'s sleeve **2** *f.p.* to set off, start out **3** to pull slightly, for a short time **4** *fig.* to suffer for some time

потегнува *impf see* потега

потекло *n* origin, descent; Македонец по потекло Macedonian by origin

потекува¹ *impf of* потече¹ 1

потекува² *impf of* потече²

потем **1** *adv* afterwards, later; then **2** *prep* after; потем некое време after some time; потем малу a little later

потемнее *pf* потемнеа *aor. see* потемни 3

потемни *pf* **1** to darken *trans.* **2** *fig.* to obscure; to cast a shadow over **3** to darken *intrans.*; лицето му потемнело his face darkened

потемнува *impf of* потемни & потемнее

потен -тна *adj* **1** sweaty, perspiring; of sweat, perspiration; потни жлезди sweat-glands; потни капки drops of sweat; ❑ потен ручек е секогаш поблаг *prov.* food tastes sweeter when earned by hard work **2** *fig.* misted, clouded by condensation; потен џам steamed-up window pane

потенција *f* potency; possibility, potential; полова потенција sexual potency

потенцијал *m* potential; воен/економски потенцијал military/economic potential

потенцијален -лна *adj* potential, latent; потенцијален противник potential opponent; потенцијална енергија potential energy

потенцѝра *pf & impf* to emphasize, stress

потепа *pf* **I 1** to beat, pummel, for a short time **2** *rare*, *dial.* to give a good hiding **II** – **ce** *rare* to fight, brawl

потера¹ *f* **1** search party; posse **2** pursuit; ce крене <во> потера по to set off in pursuit of

потера² *pf* **1** to start chasing, driving; потера непријател to drive out an enemy **2** (*за растение*) to put forth, sprout *trans.* **3** to spring up, begin to grow; тутунот потера the tobacco has started growing **4** детето потера десета година the child has turned nine **5** to continue (go on) for a short time; не можеме да си потераме работа we can't get on with our work; потера инает to persist; to be stubborn

потерница *f* arrest warrant

потерува *impf of* потера

потече¹ *pf* **1** to start flowing; ❑ ми потекле лигите my mouth started watering **2** to flow, run a little, for a short time

потече² *pf* to swell <up>

потечен *pt see* отечен

потечува¹ *impf see* потекува¹

потечува² *impf see* потекува²

поти се *impf* **1** to sweat, perspire; *fig.* to take pains; ce потам над задача to sweat over a problem **2** to mist over, steam up

потир *m Rel.* chalice

потиска & потискува *impf of* потисне

потиснат *pt* oppressed

потисне *pf* потисна *aor.* **1** to crush; to displace **2** *fig.* to oppress, hold down **3** *fig.* to stifle, curb, suppress **4** to put pressure on; to squeeze

потисник -ци *m* oppressor, tyrant, exploiter

потисница *f rare* (*of a woman, country*) *see* потисник

потиснички *adj rare* oppressing; oppressive

потиснува *impf of* потисне

поти<х>ом *adv f.p.* quietly, gently, slowly, imperceptibly

потиштен *pt literary* depressed, disheartened, dejected, downcast

потиштеност *f literary* depression, dejection

потишти *pf literary* to discourage, dishearten, depress

потка *f* boundary marker

поткаже *pf* поткажа *aor.* **1** to denounce; поткаже некого на полицијата to denounce s.o. to the police **2** (*with dat.*) to prompt; ми поткажа, што да кажам he told me what to say **3** to hint, suggest

поткажува *impf of* поткаже

поткажувач *m* **1** informer **2** person who prompts (supplies information)

поткани *pf* to urge, encourage (*s.o. to do s.th.*)

потканува *impf of* поткани

поткаса *pf* **I** to bite slightly; си го поткаса јазикот to bite one's tongue **II** – **ce** to bite one's tongue/lip

поткасне *pf* поткасна *aor.* **1** *see* поткаса **2** *rare* to have a bite to eat

поткаснува *impf of* поткасне

поткастри *pf* **1** to prune, clip, trim; to cut off **2** *fig.*, *colloq.* to reduce, cut, cut back; поткастри фондови to reduce funding

поткаструва *impf of* поткастри

поткачи¹ *pf* **I 1** to sting, bite, prick **2** *colloq.* to hit, strike, wallop; to kick **II** – **ce** to start quarrelling

поткачи² *pf* **I** to lift up, raise slightly; поткачи цени to increase prices a little **II** – **ce** to rise, climb a little

поткачува¹ (**ce**) *impf of* поткачи¹ (ce)

поткачува² (**ce**) *impf of* поткачи² (ce)

поткашлува *impf* to cough slightly, occasionally

потккваси *pf* to leaven (*dough*), sour (*milk*)

поткквасува *impf of* поткваси

поткине *pf* поткина *aor.* **1** to break off; to cut off **2** *rare* to reduce, cut; поткине некому платата to cut s.o.'s pay; *fig.* крилата ѝ ги поткина he clipped her wings

поткинува *impf of* поткине

поткисели *pf* **I** to flavour with vinegar **II** – **ce** to turn slightly sour

поткиселува (**ce**) *impf of* поткисели (ce)

поткисне *pf* поткисна *aor.* (*за леб*) to rise slightly

поткиснува *impf of* поткисне

поткклава *impf of* поткладе; на распален оган не поткклавај борина *prov.* don't add fuel to the flames

поткладе *pf* поткла *aor.* **1** to place, put under **2** to add a little of s.th.

поткклекне *pf* поткклекна *aor.* **1** to bend one's knee slightly **2** *fig.* to give up, give in

поткклекнува *impf of* поткклекне

потков *m* **1** heel-plate, toe-cap **2** (*на кундак*) buttplate

потккова¹ *f* **1** horseshoe **2** heel-plate, toe-cap

потккова² (**ce**) *pf see* поткове (ce)

потккова³ (**ce**) *impf of* поткове (ce)

потковало *n coll.* tools for shoeing horses

потккован *pt* **1** shod; потковани коњи shod horses **2** *fig.* well prepared, well versed

потковач *m* farrier

поткове *pf* потккова *aor.* **I 1** to shoe (*a horse*) **2** to reheel/re-toe (*a shoe, with metal caps*) **3** *fig.* to instruct, train, prepare **II** – **ce** to prepare o.s.

потковен *pt see* поткован
потковица *f see* поткова 1
потковичав *adj* horseshoe-shaped
потковка *f* 1 horseshoe, *see* поткова 1, потковица; ❑ од пцовисан коњ бара потковка *prov.* to ask the impossible 2 *see* потков 1, налче 3 *see* потков 2
потковува *impf of* поткове 1 & 2
потковувач *m rare* farrier, *see* налбат, потковач
поткожен -жна *adj* subcutaneous; поткожно ткиво subcutaneous tissue
поткожури се *pf (за кожа)* to swell slightly
потколеница *f* 1 lower leg, shin 2 garter
поткомисија -ии *f* subcommission
поткомитет *m* subcommittee
поткоп *m* tunnel, underground passage, sap
поткопа *pf* to undermine (*also fig.*); реката го поткопала брегот the river undermined its bank; поткопа некому здравје to undermine s.o.'s health
поткопува *impf* 1 *of* поткопа 2 *rare* to dig a little, from time to time
поткоси *pf* I 1 to cut down, lay low, mow down 2 *fig.*, *rare* to exhaust; поткоси некому сили to sap s.o.'s strength II – се ❑ ми се поткосија нозете my legs gave way under me
поткосува (се) *impf of* поткоси (се)
поткошнат *pt* pushed to one side
поткошне *pf* поткошна *aor.* 1 to kick (*lightly*) 2 *fig.* to push aside; to reject
поткошнува *impf of* поткошне
поткошула *f Am.* undershirt
поткрад\<н\>е *pf* поткрад\<н\>а *aor.* I *rare* to filch, pilfer *trans.* II – се to creep up, steal up, slip in; ❑ ми се поткрала грешка (*во текстот*) a mistake crept in (*into the text*)
поткрад\<н\>ува (се) *impf of* поткрад\<н\>е (се)
поткрева (се) *impf of* поткрене (се); ❑ ни лостови не го поткреваат nothing can shift him
поткрене *pf* поткрена *aor.* I 1 to lift (raise) slightly; поткрене глава to raise one's head; поткрене раменици to shrug one's shoulders 2 to restore s.o.'s health II – се to recover (*partly*) *intrans.*, get back on one's feet; ❑ косата му се поткрена his hair stood on end
поткренува (се) *impf see* поткрева (се)
поткрепа *f* support, backing, help; материјална и морална поткрепа material and moral support; во поткрепа на нашиот став in support of our stance
поткрепи *pf* I 1 to support, prop up, bolster; to confirm, corroborate; поткрепи тврдење to support (substantiate) an assertion 2 to strengthen, revive *trans.*, restore II – се 1 to support one another 2 to recover *intrans.*, grow stronger
поткрепува (се) *impf of* поткрепи (се)
поткришум *adv* secretly
поткрпи *pf* I to patch up II – се *fig.* to manage, get by (*with minimal funds*)
поткрпува (се) *impf of* поткрпи (се)
поткрши *pf* I 1 to break off, snap off *trans.* 2 *rare* to damage slightly II – се to break slightly *intrans.*
поткршува (се) *impf of* поткрши (се)
поткум & **поткумник** -ци *m* chief witness at a wedding
поткуп *m* bribe; bribery, graft; зема поткуп to take bribes

поткупен *pt* bribed, corrupt
поткупи *pf* to bribe; to corrupt
поткуплив *adj* venal, bribable
поткупливост *f* venality
поткупува *impf of* поткупи
поткупувач *m* bribe-giver
поткуси *pf* 1 to shorten a little *trans.*; поткуси палто to shorten a coat 2 *fig.* to give short measure; to withhold; ми поткуси нешто he withheld something from me
поткусува *impf of* поткуси
потлачи *pf* to tread underfoot, trample down
потоа *adv* afterwards, then
поток -ци *m* stream, brook, *Am.*, *Austral.*, *N.Z.* creek
потокми *pf dial.* 1 to prepare *trans.*, make ready II – се to prepare *intrans.*, get ready
потокмува (се) *impf rare of* потокми (се)
потомка *f* (*fem. form*) *see* потомок
потомок -мци *m* descendant; нашите потомци our offspring
потомори *pf colloq.* to conceal, cover up
потоморува *impf of* потомори
потомство *n* posterity
потон[1] *m* basement, cellar
потон[2] *m* sink-hole, swallow-hole; ❑ потон фати the earth has swallowed him up; he's nowhere to be found
потоне *pf* потона *aor.* to sink *intrans.*; *fig.* to disappear; ❑ како земи да потонале as though the earth had swallowed him up; потоне во долгови to be up to one's neck in debts; потоне во мисли to sink \<deep\> in thought
потонува *impf of* потоне
потоп *m* flood, deluge; ❑ уште од пред потопот from time immemorial; по мене – и потоп *après moi le déluge*
потопен -пна *adj* \<of a\> flood
потопи *pf* I 1 to sink, scuttle *trans.*; потопи брод to sink a ship 2 to flood, inundate 3 (*за перење*) to soak II – се 1 to get wet 2 *rare* to drown *intrans.* 3 to sink *intrans.*
потопница *f Zool.* (Aythya nyroca) ferruginous duck
потопува (се) *impf of* потопи (се)
поточе *n dim. of* поток; streamlet, rivulet
поточен -чна *adj* \<of a\> stream, brook
поточина *f* mud, deposit, silt
потпадне *pf* потпадна *aor.* to come under; работата потпадна под дирекцијата the matter fell under the competence of the head office; тие краишта потпаднаа под \<власта на\> Турците those regions fell under Turkish rule
потпаднува & **потпаѓа** *impf of* потпадне
потпали *pf* I 1 to light, kindle; to set fire to; потпали куќа to set fire to a house 2 *fig.* to incite; потпали војна to stir up war 3 *fig.* to infuriate, provoke II – се to catch fire; *fig.* to get excited, enthusiastic; *fig.* to get angry, flare up
потпалува *impf of* потпали
потпалувач *m* incendiary (*also fig.*), firebrand; потпалувач на војна warmonger; потпалувач на пожар arsonist
потпаше *pf* потпаша *aor.* I to gird II – се to gird o.s., put on a belt
потпашник -ци *m dial. see* подопашник

потпашува (се) *impf of* потпаше (се)

потпева *impf* to hum; to sing (*a little, from time to time*)

потпива *impf* to tipple; кој винце потпива, без капица останува *prov.* drink spells ruin

потпика & **потпикне** *pf colloq.* потпика & потпикна *aor.* I to insert, thrust in (*also fig.*) II – **ce** to ingratiate o.s.; ❑ му се потпикнал под кожа he wormed his way into his favour

потпикнува (се) *impf of* потпикне (се)

потпир *m poet. see* потпор

потпира (се) *impf of* потпре (се)

потпирач *m see* потпор, потпорка

потпис *m* signature

потписник -ци *m* signatory; потписник на договорот signatory to the agreement

потписница & **потписничка** *f* (*fem. form*) *see* потписник; земјите потписници the signatory countries

потпише *pf* потпиша *aor.* I to sign *trans.* II – **ce** to sign one's name, append one's signature *intrans.*; ce потпише на меница to sign a bill of exchange

потпишува (се) *impf of* потпише (се)

потплати *pf* (*поткупи*) to bribe

потплатува & **потплаќа** *impf of* потплати

потполковник -ци *m* Mil. lieutenant-colonel

потполковнички *adj Mil.* lieutenant-colonel's

потполошка *f* 1 *Zool.* (Coturnix coturnix) quail, *see* препелица 2 *Bot.* (Hordeum murinum) mouse barley, wall-barley

потпомага (се) *impf of* потпомогне (се)

потпомогне & *rare* **потпоможе** *pf* потпомогна & потпоможа *aor.* I to support; to back; потпомогне акција to support a campaign II – **ce** to support/help each other

потпомогнува (се) & **потпоможува (се)** *impf see* потпомага (се)

потпор *m* support, strut, prop; *Mech.* fulcrum; ❑ потпор на куќата bread-winner

потпора *f* maintenance, support

потпорасне *pf* потпорасна *aor.* to grow up a little; *fig.* to grow a bit stronger

потпорен -рна *adj* supporting; потпорен столб supporting column; потпорен фонд maintenance fund

потпорка *f* support, strut, prop

потпорошка *f* pole for support (*when loading a donkey or pack-horse*)

потпоручник -ци *m Mil.* second lieutenant

потправа *impf of* потправи

потправи *pf rare* to adjust, put right; to patch up

потпраг -зи *m* saddle-girth

потпраша *pf* to ask, question in a roundabout way

потпрашање *n* subsidiary question; further question

потпрашува *impf of* потпраша; to keep asking, enquiring

потпре *pf* потпра *aor.* I to support (*also fig.*); to prop up; to buttress; потпре предлог to support a proposal; ja потпре главата на рамото од другарот he leant his head on his friend's shoulder II – **ce** 1 to support o.s.; to lean; ce потпрел на (со) бастунот he leant on his walking-stick (cane) 2 *fig.* (*на, врз*) to rely on, trust in; ce потпревме врз вас we have relied on you

потпретседател *m* vice-president; vice-chairman

потпретседателски *adj* vice-presidential; vice-chairman's

потпркне *pf* потпркна *aor.* 1 to flutter; to flit a short distance 2 *fig.* to grow fast, shoot up; to grow up a bit, become stronger; децата потпркнаа the children have shot up

потпркнува *impf of* потпркне

потпури *m* & *n Mus.* pot-pourri

потпушти *pf* 1 (*попушти*) to loosen/slacken slightly 2 to send secretly

потрага *f* enquiry, investigation; search; ❑ во потрага по in search of

потрае[1] *pf* потраja *aor.* (*помолчи*) to keep silent for a while

потрае[2] *pf* потраja *aor.* to last for a while; ако потрае убаво време if the weather holds

потргне *pf* потргна *aor.* I 1 to tug, pull; потргне некого за ракав to tug at s.o.'s sleeve 2 to shift, move slightly *trans.*; потргне столица to move a chair 3 *f.p.* (*сабја*) to draw II – **ce** to withdraw, move slightly away *intrans.*

потргнува (се) *impf of* потргне (се)

потреба[1] *f* need, necessity; потребите на животот the necessities of life; ❑ без потреба unnecessarily; имаме потреба (*од нешто*) we have need (*of s.th.*)

потреба[2] *pf* to become necessary, be needed; ❑ *iron.* тоа ми потребало! that's the last thing I needed!

потребен -бна *adj* necessary, needed; вие сте ми потребни I need you; сите потребни подготовки all necessary preparations

потребува *impf of* потреба[2]

потрес *m* shock; earth tremor; shudder; *Med.* потрес на мозокот cerebral concussion

потресе *pf* I to shake *trans.*; *fig.* to shock; to horrify II – **ce** to be shaken; to be shocked; ce потресе од вестите to be shocked by the news

потресен[1] *pt* 1 shaken, shocked 2 anxious; таа беше потресена по (за) сина си she was very worried about her son

потресен[2] -сна *adj* shattering; stirring; moving; потресни настани shattering events; потресна слика shocking picture

потресија *f in the expression:* вересија – потресија; *see* вересија

потресува (се) *impf of* потресе (се)

потрети *pf* to repeat for a third time

потретува *impf of* потрети

потрива *impf rare of* потрие

потрие *pf* потри *aor.* 1 to massage/rub for a while 2 *f.p.* to wear down, scrub away

потроа *adv* (*also* по троа) a little, a bit; од сè потроа ќе каснам I'll taste a little of everything

потропа *p* 1 to start knocking; потропа на портата to knock at a door 2 to bang/knock for a short time

потрошен -шна *adj* usable, consumable; потрошна стока consumer goods

потроши *pf* 1 1 to spend; потроши пари to spend money 2 *f.p.* to wear out with use II – **ce** 1 to be spent, used (up) 2 to spend a lot

потрошлив *adj* expendable; consumable, usable

потрошливост *f* expendability

потрошува (се) *impf of* потроши (се)

потрошувач *m* spender; buyer; consumer; потрошувачите на електрична енергија electricity users

потрошувачка *f* consumption, use; стоки за широка потрошувачка consumer goods

потрошувачки *adj* consumer<'s>; потрошувачки кредит consumer credit; потрошувачки задруги consumer co-operatives

потрпи *pf* to endure for a while *trans. & intrans.*; to be patient

потруди се *pf* to try, take pains (*да – то*)

потруса *pf* to squander, waste

потрча *pf* 1 to run about for a while 2 to start running

потрчува *impf of* потрча

потсвест *f* the subconscious; subconsciousness

потсвесен -сна *adj* subconscious

потсвитка *pf* I 1 to fold, bend under, tuck up *trans.*; потсвитка колена to tuck one's feet under o.s. 2 to fold, turn up slightly *trans.* II – се to fold up, bend down *intrans.*, stoop

потсвиткува (се) *impf of* потсвитка (се)

потседла *pf* to saddle

потсекретар *m* under-secretary

потсектор *m* subsector

потсекува (се) *impf of* потсече (се)

потсекција -ии *f* subsection

потсети *pf* I 1 to remind (*за, на – of, about*) 2 *rare* to have a presentiment/sense (*дека – that*) II – се to remind o.s.; to remember

потсетник -ци *m* memo pad, notebook; aide-memoire

потсетува (се) & **потсекава (се)** *impf of* потсети (се)

потсече *pf* потсеков *1st p. sg aor.* I to trim, prune, clip; потсече дрво to prune a tree II – се *in the expression:* ми се потсекоа нозете my legs gave way under me

потсечува (се) *impf see* потсекува (се)

потсири *pf* to curdle *trans.*

потскаже *pf* потскажа *aor. see* поткаже

потскок -ци *m* hop, skip

потскокне & **потскочи** *pf* потскокна & потскочи *aor.* to hop, skip; потскокне од радост to jump for joy

потскрати *pf* (*поткуси*) to shorten a little; to trim; потскрати фустан to shorten a dress; потскрати коса to trim hair

потслизне *pf* потслизна *aor.* I 1 to deceive, cheat 2 to cause to slip, stumble (*also fig.*) II – се to slip, skid slightly; *fig.* to make a mistake, slip up

потслушне *pf* потслушна *aor.* to hear vaguely, get wind of

потсмев *m* sneer; mockery; taunt, jibe

потсмева се *impf of* потсмевне се & потсмее се; ❏ се потсмева под мустак to laugh up one's sleeve

потсмевне се & **потсмее се** *pf* потсмевна се & потсмеа се *aor.* (*with dat.*) to make fun of, laugh at, mock; to sneer at

потсмешлив *adj* mocking, derisive, quizzical; ironic

потспотина *impf see* потспотнува

потспотне *pf* потспотна *aor.* (*оган*) to stoke up; (*разговор*) to stir up

потспотнува *impf of* потспотне

потстакне *pf literary, rare* потстакна *aor.* to incite, instigate, agitate; to initiate, launch (*a discussion, an initiative*)

потстакнува *impf of* потстакне

потстане *pf* потстана *aor.* to rise slightly; потстана од место he made to get up

потстег -зи *m f.p. see* попраг, потпраг

потстрешник -ци *m* eaves; penthouse

потстриг -зи *m* 1 *Rel.* tonsure 2 poor-quality wool

потстриже *pf* потстрижа *aor.* I 1 (*коса*) to trim, cut; (*овци*) to clip, shear 2 *Rel.* to tonsure, receive as a monk II – се to have one's hair trimmed/cut

потстрижува (се) *impf of* потстриже (се)

поттекст *m* sub-text; implication

поттик -ци *m literary* incentive, stimulus, inducement; impulse; благороден поттик a noble impulse

поттикне *pf* поттикна *aor.* to impel, prompt, incite; ме поттикна кон тоа I felt impelled to do that

поттикнува *impf of* поттикне

потточка *f literary* subsidiary point (item)

поттура *impf of* поттури

поттури *pf* 1 to push/place under *trans.*; кукавицата му го поттури јајцето на славејот the cuckoo laid its egg in a nightingale's nest 2 *rare* to decant, pour off (*in small quantities*)

поттурка *impf* I 1 to push, shove (*lightly, occasionally*) 2 *fig.* to drive away, chase off, reject II – се 1 to push, shove a little *intrans.* 2 *fig.* to wander, roam; се поттурка по светот to roam the world

поттурнат *pt* cast aside, rejected

поттурне *pf* поттурна *aor.* to push lightly, nudge; to displace

потуѓи *pf colloq.* to snaffle, pinch

потули *pf* 1 to extinguish, put out 2 *fig.* to muffle, stifle; ги потули своите чувства to suppress one's feelings

потур & **потурјак** *m* convert to Islam

потура (се) *impf of* потури¹ (се)

потури¹ *pf* I to pour *trans.*; to scatter, strew; потури некому вода to pour some water for s.o.; потури со пепел to shower with ashes II – се to pour/spill over o.s.; ❏ се потури со пепел to don sackcloth and ashes

потури² *pl* baggy peasant breeches

потурјак -ци *m see* потур

потурнат *pt see* поттурнат

потурне *pf* потурна *aor. see* поттурне

потурчен *pt* Turkized, made Turkish; Muslimized; (*as noun*) потурчените forced converts to Islam

потурчи *pf Hist.* to convert to Islam *trans.*

потфат *m* project, undertaking, enterprise

потфати *pf* I 1 to grasp, seize, take hold of; ❏ камен му ги потфатил нозете he is in serious trouble 2 *fig.* to undertake; to set about 3 *rare* to accept II – се 1 to make a come-back; to recover 2 *rare* to become embroiled in a quarrel

потфака *impf* I 1 *of* потфати 2 to stutter, stammer II – се *impf of* потфати (се)

потфрла *impf of* потфрли

потфрлен *pt* 1 dumped, abandoned; planted (*by stealth*); потфрлено дете abandoned child 2 failed, unsuccessful

потфрли *pf* 1 to toss; to toss in, put in; потфрли некому парче леб to toss s.o. a piece of bread; потфрли некој збор за мене put in a word for me! 2 to place surreptitiously; to dump, to abandon; потфрли дете to abandon a child 3 *rare* to under-supply 4 to fail; потфрли план to fail to meet a plan; to fall short of one's target

потхрани *pf* 1 to feed additionally, feed up; потхрани стока to fatten cattle 2 *fig.* to nourish, nurture

потхранува *impf* 1 *of* потхрани 2 to feed inadequately, underfeed, undernourish

потцени *pf* to undervalue; to underestimate

потценува *impf of* потцени

потцрта *pf* 1 to underline 2 *fig.* to stress, emphasize

потчинет *pt* subjugated; (*with dat.*) subordinate to; subservient <to>; потчинета улога subordinate role

потчинетост *f* subordination, subjugation

потчини *pf* I to subjugate; to subordinate; потчини некого на својата волја to subordinate s.o. to one's will; своите интереси ги потчини на нивните he subordinated his own interests to theirs II – **се** to submit *intrans.*

потчинува (се) *impf of* потчини (се)

потчуе *pf* потчу *aor.* (*потслушне*) to hear vaguely, get wind of

потшепне *pf* потшепна *aor.* to whisper; to prompt

поќерчи *pf* to adopt (*as a daughter*)

поќути *pf* (*помолчи*) to be silent for a while

поузрее *pf* поузреа *aor.* to ripen/mature a little; поузреа работата the matter came to a head

поука *f* 1 advice, hint, tip 2 lesson, moral

поулавен *pt* mad, crazy; *fig.* поулавен од радост crazy with joy

поулави *pf* I 1 to drive (*s.o.*) mad 2 to go mad; to become wild II – **се** *see* I 2; *fig.* се поулави од радост to go crazy with joy

поулавува (се) *impf of* поулави (се)

поуми се *pf* to ponder, reflect, think for a while

поучен -чна *adj* instructive, edifying; поучни примери edifying examples

поучи *pf* I 1 to teach, instruct; to teach for a while 2 to study for a short time; поучив француски I studied French for a while II – **се** to study for a while; to learn a little; to become accustomed; се поучи од своите грешки to learn from one's mistakes

пофала *f* praise

пофалба *f* praise, commendation, plaudit; за пофалба praiseworthy

пофален -лна *adj* 1 laudatory; пофални зборови words of praise 2 praiseworthy

пофали *pf* I to praise; учителот го пофали ученикот the teacher praised the pupil II – **се** to boast, brag

пофалува (се) *impf of* пофали (се)

пофати *pf* 1 to take hold of (*lightly*); to touch, feel (*with the hands*); ❏ пофати работа to get busy, get down to work 2 to reach out; пофати да земе нешто to reach out to take s.th.

пофаќа *impf of* пофати; ❏ му пофаќа раката; тој пофаќа he has light fingers

похвала *f literary* eulogy

похвален -лна *adj literary* laudatory; похвална песна song of praise

поход *m Mil., fig.* campaign; expedition; excursion, outing; тргне на поход to set out on an expedition

похота *f* lust, lasciviousness

похотен -тна & **похотлив** *adj* lustful, lascivious, wanton; похотливи погледи lustful (lascivious) glances

похотливост & **похотност** *f* lustfulness, lasciviousness, wantonness

похристијани *pf* to convert to Christianity; to baptize

поцинкува *pf* & *impf* to plate with zinc; to galvanize

поцрвенее *pf* поцрвенеа *aor.* to turn red, blush

поцрвени *pf* I 1 to redden *trans.* 2 (*поцрвенее*) to turn red, blush; му поцрвенија образите his cheeks flushed II – **се** *see* I 2

поцрвенува (се) *impf of* поцрвени (се)

поцрнее *pf fairly rare* поцрнеа *aor.* to turn black

поцрни *pf* I 1 to blacken *trans.* 2 *fig.* to bring shame on, disgrace 3 *fig.* to ruin, make miserable 4 to turn black *intrans.* II – **се** *rare* 1 to turn black *intrans.* 2 to make o.s. unhappy, make o.s. suffer

поцрнува (се) *impf of* поцрни (се)

почва *f* 1 soil, earth, ground 2 *fig.* foundation, basis, ground; подготви почва за to prepare the ground for

почвен *adj* of the soil, earth, ground

почек *m in the expression:* на почек on credit

почека *pf* to wait a little; to wait for

почест *f* honour, homage; укаже некому почести to pay homage to s.o.; to award honours to s.o.

почести *pf* I 1 to treat (*s.o. to s.th.*); го почестиле гостинот со кафе they served the guest coffee 2 to honour II – **се** to give o.s. a treat

почестува (се) *impf of* почести (се)

почетен -тна *adj* initial; почетна брзина initial speed; muzzle velocity; почетен удар kick-off

почетник -ци *m* beginner, novice, tyro

почетница & **почетничка** *f* (*fem. form*) *see* почетник

почетнички *adj* beginner's

почетништво *n* elementary work

почеток -ци *m* beginning, start

почива *impf* 1 (*одмора се*) to rest (*also fig.*); овде почива here lies 2 to be based (*врз, на – on*)

почивалиште *n* resting-place; вечно почивалиште eternal resting-place

почин *m poet. see* починка

починалиште *n* 1 *see* почивалиште 2 (*in burial rites*) platform on which coffin is laid while requiem is sung

починат *pt* <the> late, deceased

почине *pf* почина *aor.* I 1 to rest; седне да си почине to sit down to rest 2 to die, pass away 3 to rest *trans.*; почине коњи to rest the horses II – **се** *see* I 1

починка *f* & **починок** -ци *m* rest, repose; break, pause; без починка without a break; вечниот починок eternal rest

починува (се) *impf of* почине (се)

почисти *pf* 1 to clean for a short time 2 *rare, f.p.* to clean up; почисти соба to tidy a room

почит *f* respect, esteem, regard; остануваме со почит respectfully yours, yours sincerely

почита[1] *impf see* почитува

почита[2] *pf* to read a little, for a short time

почитан *pt* (*почитуван*) respected, esteemed; почитан<и> колега esteemed colleague, (*formula beginning letter*) dear colleague

почитање *n see* почитување

почитател *m* devotee, admirer, follower

почитателка *f* (*fem. form*) *see* почитател

почитува *impf* to respect, esteem

почитуван *pt* respected, esteemed

почитување *n* respect; почитувањето на нивните интереси respect for their interests

почкива *pf sl.* to take a quick look

почне *pf* почна *aor.* to begin, start *trans.* & *intrans.*;

почне говор to begin a speech; почна да врне дожд it's started raining; ❑ почне оддалеку to begin in a roundabout way

почнува *impf of* почне; ❑ почнувајќи од (*денеска*) starting from (*today*)

почувствува *pf literary* **I** to <start to> feel *trans.*; почувствува болка to feel pain **II – се** *rare* to <start to> feel *intrans.*; се почувствував одговорен I felt responsible

почуден *pt* **1** astonished, amazed; ❑ *f.p.* чудо почудено wonder of wonders **2** delighted

почуденост *f* **1** astonishment, amazement **2** delight

почуди *pf* **1** to astonish, amaze **2** to delight

почудува *impf of* почуди

почуе *pf* почу *aor.* **1** to listen for a while **2** *f.p.* to obey, heed

пошегува се *pf* **1** to joke, jest **2** to trifle (*co – with*)

пошета *pf* **I 1** to take a stroll **2** to take (*s.o./s.th.*) for a stroll (walk); пошета деца to take the children for a walk **II – се** *see* **I** 1

пошта *f* post, mail; post office; ❑ по пошта by post; со обратна пошта by return <of> post; весела пошта Chinese whispers

поштар *m* postman, *Am.* mailman; postal worker

поштарина *f* postage; платена е поштарината postage paid

поштарка *f* (*female*) postal worker; postman's wife

поштација -ии *m arch. see* поштар

поштеда *f* exemption; consideration; без поштеда (беспоштедно) without mercy (mercilessly); sick-leave

поштеди *pf* to spare; поштеди некому живот to spare s.o.'s life; нема да ги поштедам своите сили I shall spare no effort

поштенски *adj* postal; поштенски жиг postmark; поштенски марки postage stamps

пошти *impf* to delouse

пошто *conj dial.* (*бидејќи*) because, since

поштозашто *adv* cheaply, at almost no cost, for almost nothing

поштоми *pf* **I 1** *colloq.* to pinch, snaffle **2** *rare* to drive mad **II – се** *see* поштукне се

поштук *m usu. in the expression*: поштукот му го нема, поштукот не му се знае there is no trace of him

поштукнат *pt* crazed, maddened, hysterical

поштукне *pf* поштукна *aor.* **I 1** to disappear, vanish; ❑ му поштукнал умот (*no неа*) he's lost his head (*over her*) **2** to go mad, lose one's senses **3** *rare* to madden, drive mad, crazy **II – се** *see* **I** 2

поштукнува (се) *impf of* поштукне (се)

поштури *pf* **1** to madden, drive mad **2** to go mad, crazy

поштурува *impf of* поштури

пошумен *pt* wooded; пошумен рид a wooded hill

пошуми *pf* to afforest, forest

пошумува *impf of* пошуми

пошумување *n* afforestation

пра- *prefix* **1** great; прадедо great grandfather **2** proto-; прајазик protolanguage; прасловенски Common Slav (Common Slavic, Proto-Slavic)

прабаба *f* great grandmother

прав[1] *m* -ови & *f, pl* правови, *rare* правој **1** dust; ❑ фрли прав некому в очи to throw dust in s.o.'s eyes, to deceive s.o.; прав не дава да падне на некого to take great care of s.o.; колку прав на тапан <остана> there's nothing left; прав и пепел dust and ashes; стори некого прав и пепел to make mincemeat of s.o. **2** powder; ❑ цветен прав pollen

прав[2] *adj* **1** straight; upright; права линија straight line; прав агол right angle; ❑ прав како свеќа as straight as a die; прав како јаже во торба as crooked as a snake **2** right, correct; на прав пат on the right track; вие сте прав you are right; ❑ за права Бога, на права Бога blamelessly, through no fault of our own **3** (*вистински*) true, genuine, real; exact; прав Македонец a true Macedonian; ❑ во правата смисла на зборот in the true sense of the word; на права полноќ on the stroke of midnight **4** *literary* just, rightful, fair; право дело a just cause **5** *dial.* права рака right hand

правда *f* **1** justice; дели правда to dispense justice; суди по правда to judge according to the law; министер на правдата Minister of Justice **2** *literary, rare* truth

правдина *f* justice, right; правдината е откај нас right is on our side; правдини rights; борец за човечки правдини fighter for human rights

правдољубив *adj* righteous

правдољубивост *f*, **правдољубие** & **правдољубје** *n* righteousness

праведен -дна *adj* **1** just, fair; праведно барање just demand; праведно дело just cause; праведна осуда just verdict **2** righteous

праведник -ци *m Rel.* righteous man; ❑ заспа со сон на праведник he fell asleep and slept the sleep of the just

праведница *f* (*fem. form*) *see* праведник

праведност *f* **1** fairness, justice **2** righteousness

правен[1] *pt colloq.* артифициал; правени заби false teeth

правен[2] -вна *adj* legal; правните науки jurisprudence; правно лице lawyer; правен факултет faculty of law

правец -вци *m* **1** direction; во правец на Скопје in the direction of Skopje **2** trend, direction; нови правци во науката new trends in science

прави *impf* **I 1** to do; to make; to act; to form, constitute; to perform; што да правам? what am I to do? ❑ прави шега to make a joke; прави посета to pay a visit; прави разговор to carry on a conversation; прави пречки to create obstacles; прави кисело лице to make a face; прави некому услуга to do s.o. a favour; ми прави чест it is a <great> honour for me **2** to make, produce, create; прави куќа to have a house built; ❑ прави пари to make money; прави капитал од нешто to make capital out of s.th.; кој прави палица – за своја главица *prov.* to make a rod for one's own back **3** to make, cause to become; to turn (*s.o., s.th.*) into; прави будала to make a fool of; ❑ и ноќта ден ја прави to work round the clock **4** to make, amount to; тоа прави илјада денари that comes to (makes) a thousand denars; пет и пет прават десет five and five make ten **5** to adjust, fix, set aright; си ги правам забите I'm having my teeth seen to **II – се 1** to become; to act; to feign, pretend; се прави важен to show off; се прави глупав to play dumb; се прави удрен to feign madness; се правиш како да не знаеш you're acting as if you didn't know; ❑ за една игла се правиш! what a fuss-pot you are! крвта вода не се прави *prov.* blood is thicker than water **2** *impers.* (*with dat.*) to feel like doing, want to do; ми се прави куќа I would like to build a house

правилен -лна *adj* **1** correct, right; правилно решение correct decision/solution **2** regular; правилно дишење regular (even) breathing; правилни глаголи regular verbs; правилни црти на лицето regular facial features; правилен нос a straight nose **3** *Math.* regular; правилни многуаголници regular polygons

правилник -ци *m* rule-book; statute

правилност *f* correctness; правилност на дишењето regular breathing

правило *n* rule, regulation; граматичко правило grammatical rule; исклучок од правилото exception to the rule; правилата на друштвото the rules of society; ❑ по правило, како правило as a rule, usually

правина *f* right, justice; правината и кривината right and wrong; кај кого е правината? who is in the right? ❑ осуди на правина to convict wrongfully; правина планина поместува *prov.* the truth can move mountains; оди по правината to follow the right path

правичен -чна *adj see* праведен 1

правичност *f literary, rare see* праведност 1

правник -ци *m* lawyer, specialist in law; law student

правнички *adj* lawyer's

правнук -ци *m* **1** great grandson **2** (*usu. pl*) descendants

правнука *f* great granddaughter

правнуче *n hyp.* great grandchild

право[1] *n* **1** law; граѓанско право civil law; по меѓународното право according to international law; ❑ право на граѓанство right of citizenship **2** right, entitlement; право на глас right to vote, voting rights; со кое право? by what right? со право with good reason

право[2] *adv see* прав[2]; ❑ право да ви кажам to tell you the truth

правоаголен -лна *adj* right-angled; rectangular; правоаголен триаголник right-angled triangle

правоаголник -ци *m* rectangle

правобранител *m* barrister, *Am.* attorney; procurator

правобранителски *adj* barrister's, *Am.* attorney's; procuratorial

правобранителство *n* office of procurator general

правоверен -рна *adj* orthodox; правоверен католик a strict Catholic; (*as noun*) правоверните the faithful, *i.e.* Muslims

правоверец -рци & **правоверник** -ци *m* believer, follower

правоверка & **правоверница** *f* (*fem. form*) *see* правоверец & правоверник

правоверност *f* orthodoxy

правоговор *m* correct pronunciation, orthoepy

правоговорен -рна *adj* orthoepic; правоговорна норма orthoepic norm (standard), standard of literary pronunciation

правоземец -мци *m* (*usu. pl*) *Zool.* (Archamphybia) primitive amphibians

правокрилец -лци *m* (*usu. pl*) *Zool.* orthopteran

праволинеен -јна *adj* **1** rectilinear; праволинејно движење rectilinear motion **2** *fig.* straightforward

праволинејност *f* straightforwardness

праволиниски *adj see* праволинеен 1

правопис *m* orthography, standard spelling

правописен -сна *adj* orthographic<al>; правописен речник orthographical dictionary

правосилен -лна *adj* effective, in force, in effect

православен -вна *adj* Orthodox; православната црква the Orthodox Church; (*as noun*) православни Orthodox believers

православие & **православје** *n* Orthodoxy, the Orthodox faith

правосмукалка & **правосмукачка** *f* vacuum cleaner

правоспособен -бна *adj Leg.* legally competent

правоспособност *f Leg.* legal competence

правосуден -дна *adj* justiciary; правосудна управа department of justice

правосудство *n* administration of justice

праг -ови, *rare* -oj *m* **1** threshold (*also fig.*), doorstep, sill; на куќниот праг at the front entrance; на прагот на нова ера on the threshold of a new era **2** (*железнички*) sleeper, *Am.* tie **3** (*usu. pl*) (*на речно корито*) rapids **4** (*usu. pl*) (*на чун*) ribs (*framework of hull of boat*)

Прага *f* Prague

прагматѝзам -змот *m* pragmatism

прагматичен -чна & **прагматички** *adj* pragmatic

прадедо -овци, -и *m* **1** great grandfather **2** (*only pl*) ancestors, forbears

прадедовина *f rare* (*прародина*) ancestral homeland

прадедовски *adj* ancestral

пражанец -ни *m* person from Prague

пражанка *f* (*fem. form*) *see* пражанец

праживотно *n* (*usu. pl*) *Zool.* protozoan

праз *m Bot.* (Allium porrum) leek; главица праз a bulb of a leek; ❑ на бавчанција праз му продава to teach one's grandmother to suck eggs

празен -зна *adj* **1** empty, vacant, spare, unoccupied; празен ден free day; празен лист blank page; празна соба vacant room; празно шише empty bottle; ❑ на празен стомак on an empty stomach; со празни раце empty-handed **2** idle, unladen; стои празен to stand idle **3** *fig.* pointless, futile, idle; празни зборови empty words; празни надежи vain hopes

празнење *n* discharge; електрично празнење electrical discharge

празни *impf* **I** to empty *trans.*; to drain; to vacate; *Elec.* to discharge; празни шише to empty a bottle; публиката ја празни салата the audience is leaving the hall **II** — се to empty *intrans.*

празник -ци *m* holiday, festival, festive occasion; национален празник national holiday; ❑ не знае делник, празник he knows no rest; и на нашата улица ќе биде празник our day will come

празнина *f* **1** gap, space; void, vacuum **2** *fig.* omission; рефератот имаше празнини there were omissions in the report

празничен -чна *adj* festive, holiday; празничен ден a holiday; празнично расположение holiday (festive) mood

празноверен -рна *adj rare* superstitious

празноверие, **празноверје** & **празноверство** *n* superstition

празноглав *adj* empty-headed

празнословен -вна *adj literary* verbose, wordy; празнословен човек windbag;

празнослови *impf* to talk idly

празнословие & празнословје *n* verbiage, idle talk, hot air

празнува *impf* 1 to celebrate, mark; празнува Први мај to celebrate May Day 2 not to work; в среда ќе празнуваме Wednesday is a day off

праизведба *f literary* premiere, opening night

праизвор *m* original source

праискона *adv literary, arch.* from time immemorial, since time began

праисконски *adj literary* primordial, primeval

праисторија *f* prehistory

праисториски *adj* prehistoric

прајазик -ци *m* protolanguage

прајазичен -чна *adj* protolinguistic

практика *f* practice; professional work; во практика in practice; пет години практика five years' experience; приватната лекарска практика private medical practice

практика́нт *m* trainee

практика́нтка *f (fem. form) see* практикант

практика́нтски *adj* trainee's

практикува *impf* 1 (*се вежба*) to practise *trans.*, apply in practice 2 (*за адвокат, лекар*) to be in practice; практикува како адвокат to practise law 3 to act, behave; како практикувате во вакви случаи? how do you act in such cases?

практикум *m* practical training; lab class; хемиски практикум a chemistry practical

практици́зам -змот *m* 1 emphasis on practice (*at expense of theory*) 2 practical sense, savvy

практицистички *adj* pragmatic, having a practical outlook

практичар *m* practitioner; лекар-практичар a practising doctor, medical practitioner

практичен -чна *adj* practical; практична математика applied mathematics; практичен ум practical mind

практички *adj* practical

практично *adv* in practice

прамајка *f literary* original ancestress, mother of the race

праматерија *f* primeval material

прамен -мни *m* lock, tuft (*of hair, etc.*); *fig.* прамен светлина a pencil of rays; димни прамни wisps/ plumes of smoke

пран *pt (from* пере) washed, laundered

пранги & прангии *pl* shackles, fetters, chains; го кладоа во пранги they clapped him in irons; *fig.* во прангите на смртта in the jaws of death

прање *n* 1 washing, laundering 2 purging; menstruation; бело прање leucorrhoea

праобразец -сци *m* prototype

праоснова *f* original basis

праотец -тци *m literary* progenitor, oldest ancestor; праотци for<e>bears

прапорец -рци *m* harness bell, cow-bell, sleigh-bell

прапорче *n dim. of* прапорец

прапочеток -ци *m* origin; прапочетокот на животот the origin of life

прапрабаба *f* great great grandmother

праправнук -ци *m* great great grandson

праправнука *f* great great granddaughter

прапрадедо -овци & -и *m* great great grandfather

прапричина *f* original (primary) cause

прародина *f (прататкови́на)* original homeland

прародител *m literary* progenitor, oldest ancestor

прародителски *adj literary* ancestral; прародителскиот грев original sin

прасе *n* 1 pig, hog; sucking-pig; боцливо прасе (Hystrix cristata) porcupine; морско прасе (Cavia porcellus) guinea-pig; попово прасе (*also* коњоштип) (Gryllotalpa vulgaris) mole-cricket 2 (*usu. pl*) calf (*of leg*)

прасенце *n dim. of* прасе; piglet

прасење *n* farrowing

прасец -сци, -вци *m (usu. pl)* 1 pig 2 calf (*of the leg*)

прасешки *adj* pig's, of a pig; прасешко <месо> pork

праси *impf* I to produce, bring forth (*piglets*) 2 to breed (raise) pigs II – се to farrow

прасило *n* 1 farrow, litter of pigs 2 *fig.* breed, stock; од едно прасило се they are of the same breed, from the same stable

праска *f Bot.* peach (*tree and fruit*)

прасков *adj* peach; прасково дрво peach-tree

праслика *f (прототип)* prototype

прасловенски *adj* Common Slav, Common Slavic, Proto-Slavic

прасна *adj see* спрасна

прасостојба *f literary* primeval state

прастар *adj* ancient, primeval; од прастари времиња from ancient times

прат -ови, -тје *m* rod, switch; ❑ се тресе како прат to tremble like a leaf

прататкови́на *f* original homeland

пратеник -ци *m* envoy, emissary; delegate

пратенички *adj* envoy's

пратеништво *n* legation, mission

пратец -тци *m* ramrod, cleaning-rod (*for gun-barrel*)

прати *pf* to send, dispatch; прати писмо to send a letter; прати помош to send help; прати поздрав to send greetings

пратка *f* parcel, package; shipment, consignment; пратка лекови consignment (shipment) of medicines; поштенска пратка postal packet/package

пратока *f Bot.* (Ricinus communis) castor oil plant

пратче *n dim. of* прат

праќа¹ *f* catapult, *Am.* sling-shot, *Austral.* shanghai

праќа² *impf of* прати

праќица¹ *f & праќиче n dim. of* праќа¹

праќица² *f* side ropes (*securing a pack-saddle*)

праушка *f* small fossil

прах *m* mortal remains, dust, ashes; ❑ мир на прахот негов! may he rest in peace!

прачка *f* 1 rod, switch; twig; wand; железна прачка iron bar (rod) 2 stem/stump (*of a vine*); лозова (лозинкова) прачка vine cutting (*for propagation*)

прачовек *m, pl* пралуѓе primitive man

праша *impf & pf* I to ask; to question; to examine; праша за цената на нешто to ask the price of s.th.; праша ученик to examine a pupil; не прашај гаталец (вражалец), туку <прашај> паталец *prov.* experience is worth more than wisdom II – се 1 to wonder, ask o.s.; to ask each other 2 to be answerable; јас се прашам овдека I'm in charge here 3 (*usu. pf*) to seek advice (*на, кај, до – from*); се праша на лекар to consult a doctor

прашален -лна *adj* interrogative, inquiring; прашален знак question mark

прашалник -ци *m* **1** questionnaire **2** question mark; ❑ под прашалник in doubt, in question

прашанка *f literary* riddle

прашање *n* **1** question; постави некому прашање to ask s.o. a question; to pose a question to s.o. **2** problem, question, matter, issue; ❑ болно прашање vexed question; подига прашање to raise a question; прашање на вкус a matter of taste; **3** consultation

прашен -шна *adj* (*прашлив*) dusty; powdery; прашни патишта dusty roads

прашец *m dim. of* прав; цветен прашец (*прав*) pollen

праши¹ *impf* **I** to raise dust; to sprinkle with powder; to dust **II – се** to get dusty

праши² *impf* to earth up, loosen the soil (*round vines, etc.*)

прашина *f colloq. see* прав¹ 1

прашинка *f* speck, fleck of dust

прашки *adj* Prague *attrib.*

прашлив *adj* dusty

прашник -ци *m Bot.* stamen

прашница *f Bot.* anther

прашок -ци *m* **1** pollen **2** powder; прашок за болви flea powder

прашти *pf in the expression:* ја прашти to run off, beat it, make o.s. scarce

праштило *n* string, cord (*on a bag, apron, etc.*)

прашува (се) *impf see* праша (се)

прашума *f* primeval forest, jungle; ❑ законот на прашумата the law of the jungle

прв *adj num* first (*in various senses*); most important, primary; earliest, former, previous; прва награда first prize; прво чедо first child; првиот . . ., вториот (последниот) . . . the former . . . , the latter; ❑ во прв ред in the first place (first of all); на прва линија in the front line; за прв пат (за првпат) for the first time; прва брзина first (bottom) gear; на прв поглед at first glance (sight); прва помош first aid; *Gram.* прво лице first person; при прва можност at the first opportunity; на прв (преден) план in the foreground; in the first place

прва *impf see* првне; *fig.* срцето ѝ прва од радост her heart is aflutter with joy

првак -ци *m* **1** champion; front-runner; leader **2** first-ling, first-born child **3** first-distilled <and strongest> alcohol **4** premiere (*of opera, etc.*)

прваче *n* **1** *dim. of* првак **2** **2** *colloq., hyp.* pupil of the first form (*Am.* grade)

првен¹ -вна *adj see* прв

првен² *adv see* првин

првенец -нци *m* **1** eminent person; политички првенец political leader **2** champion; првенец (првак) во фудбалот soccer champion **3** *literary* first male child, first-born son

првенка *f* (*fem. form*) *see* првенец; првенка на операта prima donna

првенствен *adj* **1** most important, primary, main, chief; првенствена задача main task **2** *Sport.* championship *attrib.*; првенствен натпревар championship match

првенствено *adv* in the first place, above all; chiefly

првенство *m* **1** precedence; preference; priority **2** *Sport.* (*шампионат*) championship

првенче *n dim. of* првенец 3

првескинка & **првестија** -ии *f dial. see* првестинка, првостинка

првестинка & **првостинка** *f* primipara (*woman or female animal giving birth for the first time*)

први *adj num see* прв

првин *adv* first, firstly

првина & *rare* **првица** *f* **1** first act, s.th. done for the first time; не му е првина it's not his first time; (*as adv*) for the first time **2** *see* првнина 2

првиче *n* traditional first visit by the bride's parents to the newly-weds' home

првичен -чна *adj* **1** primary, original **2** most important; main

првичност *f* primacy

првне *pf* првна *aor.* to flutter

првнина *f* **1** s.th. done for the first time **2** *f.p.* first love

првнува *impf of* првне

прво *adv* first, firstly, first of all; види го прво дрвото, после седни под него *prov.* first consider, then act; ❑ прво и прво first of all, first and foremost

првобитен -тна *adj* original, primeval, primordial, primitive; првобитната смисла на збор the original meaning of a word

првоборец -рци *m Hist.* partisan in action from the outbreak of hostilities (*in World War II*)

првовенчан *adj Hist.* first-crowned

првоизвор *m literary* original source

првокатегорник -ци *m Sport.* first-class (top) player

првокласен -сна *adj* first-class, prime; првокласна техника first-rate technology

првомајски *adj* May-Day; првомајска парада May-Day parade

првообразец -сци *m* prototype

првооснова *f* (*праоснова*) original basis

првопрестолен -лна *adj literary*, *arch.* cathedral; првопрестолен град cathedral city

првопричина *f* (*прапричина*) original cause, reason

прворазреден -дна *adj literary* first-class, first-rate; прворазредни резултати first-class results

првороден -дна & -ена *adj literary* first-born

првородство *n Hist.* primogeniture; право на прво-родство right of primogeniture

прворотка *f* primipara, woman giving birth for the first time

првосвештеник -ци *m* archpriest

првостепен *adj* **1** primary; првостепен суд court of primary jurisdiction (of first instance) **2** first-class, first-rate; првостепена важност first-rate importance

првостинка *f see* првестинка

првоучител *m* (*usu. pl*) first teacher; словенските првоучители the First Teachers of the Slavs (*i.e. Saints Cyril and Methodius*)

првут *m* dandruff, scurf

пргав *adj* **1** nimble, agile, active; пргав ум quick mind **2** hard-working, diligent, industrious

пргавост *f* **1** agility **2** diligence at work

прдеж *m vulg.* fart, farting

прди *impf vulg.* to fart

прдла *f vulg.* (*fem. form*) *see* прдло

прдло -овци *m vulg.* farter

прдне *pf vulg.* прдна *aor.* to fart; ❏ ем стисни ем прдни – не бидува you can't do two things at once

прднува *impf of* прдне

пре¹- *prefix* **1** *with adjectives, as intensifier or formant for superlative degree;* пребогат extremely rich; премил very dear; преблаг very sweet; предобар most kind **2** (*with kinship terms, alternative to* пра-) great; пребаба great grandmother; превнук great grandson

пре²- *verbal prefix with various senses, including* **1** (*repetition*) re-, препише to rewrite; преизбира to re-elect **2** (*action to excess, surpassing limits*) over-, преполни to overfill; прејаде to overeat; престигне to surpass **3** *motion across, over, through;* предаде to transfer; премине to pass through (across); префрли to throw over **4** *change of position or state;* пресели to resettle; премести to relocate *trans.*

преамбула *f* preamble

преангажиран *adj* too busy, occupied; over-committed

преапе *pf* преапа *aor.* to bite <through>; ❏ си го преапе јазикот to bite one's tongue

преати *pf* **I** to upset, overturn *trans.* **II – се** to capsize, overturn *intrans.*

преатува (се) & **преаќа (се)** *impf of* преати (се)

пребаба *f see* прабаба

пребавен -вна *adj literary, rare* too slow

пребара *pf* **I 1** to search through; to comb through, ransack; полицијата ја пребара сета околина the police combed the district **2** *rare* to seek (look for) again; to demand, apply again **II – се** *dial.* to turn out one's pockets <again>

пребарува *impf* **I 1** *of* пребара **2** to demand too much; to find fault; to cavil **II – се** *impf of* пребара се

пребега & **пребегне** *pf* пребега & пребегна *aor.* **1** to run across (over); пребегне преку граница to flee across the border **2** to desert

пребегнува *impf of* пребегне

пребел *adj* pure white; grey-haired

пребели *pf* **1** to bleach/whitewash <over> again **2** *rare, colloq.* to bleach/whitewash too much, more than necessary

пребере *pf* пребра *aor.* **1** *in the expression:* му го пребрав гајлето he's/it's off my hands; it's out of my hands **2** *f.p., dial.* to select, pick out **3** *rare, colloq.* to gather, collect again

пребива¹ (се) *impf of* пребие (се)

пребива² & **пребивава** *impf literary, rare see* престојува

пребивалиште *n literary, rare* place of residence, dwelling, residence, domicile

пребие *pf* преби *aor.* **I 1** *rare* to beat up **2** to snap, break in two *trans.* **3** to refract **4** *Econ.* to settle, balance *trans.*; пребие трошоци to balance expenses **II – се 1** to hurt o.s. badly **2** *Econ.* to balance; to cancel each other out

пребира *impf* **1** to select, pick out; ❏ уште и ќе пребира! he's hard to please **2** to look through thoroughly (*when choosing*) **3** пребира жици to strum on the strings (*of a guitar, etc.*)

пребирач *m* fastidious person

пребирлив *adj* choosy, fastidious, fussy

преблаг *adj* very mild; too sweet

пребледи & **пребледнее** *pf* пребледи & пребледнеа *aor.* to grow very pale

пребледнува & **пребледува** *impf of* пребледи & пребледнее

пребликне *pf* пребликна *aor.* to pour over, overflow; to boil over; пребликнале чувства emotions boiled over; ❏ му дошло до носот и му пребликнало he got fed up and gave vent to his feelings

пребликнува *impf of* пребликне

пребогат *adj* **1** very rich **2** abundant, extensive; copious

пребои *pf* to repaint, redye

пребој *m* coarse flour

пребојадиса & *rare* **пребојоса** *pf* to redye, recolour

пребојадисува & **пребојосува** *impf of* пребојадиса & пребојоса

пребојува *impf of* пребои

преболи *pf* преболи & преболе *aor.* **1** to recover, be restored to health **2** to get over (*an illness*) *trans.*; го преболе тифусот he recovered from typhus **3** *fig.* to cease to mourn; не може да го преболи синот she cannot get over the loss of her son **4** (*за болка*) to stop hurting, aching

преболува *impf of* преболи

пребори се *pf* to wrestle/fight again

преборува *impf of* пребори се

пребрго & **пребргу** *adv* very quickly; too quickly, too soon

пребрз *adj literary* very fast; too quick

пребрише *pf* пребриша *aor.* to wipe clean; to rub out; to wipe again

пребришува *impf of* пребрише

преброва (се) *impf see* пребројува (се)

преброди *pf* **1** to ford; преброди река to ford a river **2** *fig.* to overcome; преброди тешкотии to overcome difficulties

пребродлив *adj literary* surmountable

пребродува *impf of* преброди

преброи *pf* преброи & преброја *aor.* **I 1** to count, enumerate **2** *rare* to count again, re-count **II – се** to number off

пребројува (се) *impf of* преброи (се)

превади *pf* to transfer (*pictures, patterns, etc.*)

превадува *impf of* превади

превал & **превалец** *m Geog.* (*преслап, преслоп*) (*mountain*) saddle, col

превапса *pf colloq. see* пребојадиса, пребојоса

превапсува *impf of* превапса

превар *m dial. in the expression:* на превар suddenly; hastily

превара *f* **1** *arch., f.p.* deception, deceit; fraud **2** *rare see* превар

преварен *pt* **1** over-cooked, over-boiled **2** double-distilled; преварена ракија double-distilled brandy

превареница *f* double-distilled brandy

превари¹ *pf* **1** to over-cook, over-boil, overdo **2** to re-boil, re-cook **3** to double-distil

превари² *pf* to outrun, outstrip; to surpass; кој превари, тој товари *prov.* first come, first served

превари³ *pf arch., f.p.* (*измами*) to deceive

преварува¹ *impf of* превари¹

преварува² *impf of* превари²

превева *impf of* превее

преведе *pf* **1** to lead, guide, take (*преку – over, across*) (*also fig.*); ги преведе преку преслапот he guided them over the pass **2** to transfer (*money*); to remit

3 to translate, interpret; преведе од француски на македонски to translate from French into Macedonian; ❑ преведено на обичен јазик in plain language **4** to move up *trans.*; to promote; преведе ученик во погорен клас to move a pupil to a higher form (grade)

преведува   *impf of* преведе

преведувач   *m* translator, interpreter

преведувачки   *adj* translating; преведувачка дејност translation work

превее   *pf* превеа *aor.* **1** to winnow again **2** (*за ветар и сл.*) to die down

превез   *m* veil; ❑ под превезот на under the veil (cloak) of

превезе¹   *pf* превеза *aor.* to embroider again

превезе²   *pf literary* превеза *aor.* to transport, convey, move, transfer

превезува¹   *impf of* превезе¹

превезува²   *impf of* превезе²

превејува   *impf rare see* превева

превели   *pf rare see* прекаже

превене   *pf* превена *aor.* to lie down to rest

превенти́вен   -вна *adj* preventive; превентивни мерки preventive measures

превенува   *impf of* превене

превери   *pf f.p.* **1** to convert (*to a new faith*) *trans.* **2** to break one's word

превива   *impf* **I 1** to fold <in two>; to bend *trans.*; to twist *trans.*; превива врат to bend one's neck **2** to wrap again; to wind on *trans.*; to overwind **3** *rare, literary* (*преврзува*) to bandage; превива рана to bandage a wound **II – се 1** to bend *intrans.* **2** to writhe, squirm; се превива од болки to squirm with pain

превид   *m* oversight; error

превиди   *pf* **1** to experience, suffer, endure (*pain, suffering, etc.*) **2** *literary* to overlook

превидува   *impf of* превиди

превие (се)   *pf* преви (се) *aor. see* превитка (се)

превира   *impf of* преврие

превитка   *pf* **I 1** to fold, bend *trans.* **2** *fig.* to convince **3** to wind on (*thread, etc.*) **4** *rare* to wind too much, overwind **II – се 1** to bend down *intrans.*, lean down **2** to become hunchbacked

превиткува (се)   *impf see* превива (се)

превиши   *pf* **1** to outgrow **2** *literary* to surpass, exceed; ги превиши своите компетенции to exceed one's powers

превишува   *impf of* превиши

превласт   *f* dominance, supremacy

превнук   -ци *m see* правнук

превнука   *f see* правнука

превод   *m* translation; буквален, дословен превод literal, word-for-word translation

преводен   -дна *adj* <of> translation, interpreting; преводна литература literature in translation; translated literature

преводлив   *adj* translatable

превоз   *m* transport, transportation

превозвишен   *adj literary* exalted, most high (*as a title*)

превозен   -зна *adj* <of> transport; превозно средство means of transport; превозни трошоци transport costs

превознесе   *pf literary, rare* to praise, glorify, exalt

превознесува   *impf of* превознесе

превозува   *impf of* превезе²

превој   -ои *m literary* **1** *rare see* преслап **2** curve, bend **3** *Gram.* apophony, ablaut, vowel gradation

превооружи   *pf* **I** to rearm *trans.* (*also fig.*) **II – се** to rearm *intrans.* (*also fig.*)

превооружува (се)   *impf of* превооружи (се)

превоспита   *pf* to re-educate

превоспитува   *impf of* превоспита

превосходен   -дна *adj* excellent, superb, outstanding, superior, superlative

превосходно   *adv literary* **1** superbly, excellently **2** predominantly, mainly

превосходност   *f literary* **1** excellence, outstanding quality **2** prevalence, predominance

превосходство   *n literary* superiority, dominance, ascendancy

преврат   *m* revolution; државен преврат *coup d'état*; преврат во науката scientific breakthrough

превратен   -тна *adj* **1** revolutionary **2** *rare, literary* fickle, inconstant; превратна судбина perverse fate

преврати   *pf* **I 1** *see* преврти **2** *dial.* to answer back **II – се** *rare, dial.* to turn over *intrans.*; to capsize, overturn *intrans.*

превратник   -ци *m* revolutionary

превратнички   *adj* revolutionary

превратност   *f literary, rare* vicissitude; reverse, setback

превратува (се) & **превраќа (се)**   *impf of* преврати (се)

преврзе   *pf* преврза *aor.* **I 1** to tie <up>; to wrap, enclose; преврзе пакет to wrap a parcel **2** (*рана*) to bandage **3** to tie again, retie **II – се 1** to tie, bind o.s. **2** to bandage/dress one's own wound

преврзок   -ци *m* strip of cloth with coins sewn into it (*in traditional costume*)

преврзува (се)   *impf of* преврзе (се)

преврива   *impf of* преврие

преврие   *pf* преври *aor.* **1** (*ферментира*) to ferment *intrans.* **2** *fig.* to settle **3** to boil over

преврне   *pf* преврна *aor.* to stop raining/snowing (*also impers.*); <дождот> преврна the rain has stopped

преврнува   *impf of* преврне

преврска   *f* **1** bandage, dressing; стави преврска на рана to bandage (dress) a wound **2** *dial.* kerchief; apron

преврти   *pf* преврти & преврте *aor.* **I 1** to overturn *trans.*; to turn <round, over> *trans.*; преврти чун to overturn a boat; ❑ ја превртивме куќата we turned the whole house upside-down; превртивме сѐ живо we went through everything; преврти (сврти) лист to turn over a new leaf **2** to wind more than necessary, overwind (*a watch*) **3** *fig.* to win over, convince; ме преврте he converted me (I joined his group) **II – се 1** to overturn, roll over *intrans.*; to turn <round, over> *intrans.*; кога ќе се преврти колата, патишта многу *prov.* every cloud has a silver lining **2** *fig.* to change one's views, attitude

превртлив   *adj* fickle, inconstant

превртливец   -вци *m literary, rare* fickle, inconstant person

превртливка   *f literary, rare* (*fem. form*) *see* превртливец

превртливост *f* inconstancy, fickleness

превртува (се) *impf of* преврти (се)

превртува *pf* to demolish; to destroy; to smash

преврушува *impf of* превруши

преврши *pf f.p.* to win over, steal (*s.o. else's fiancée*)

превтаса *pf* 1 to outrun, overtake; to surpass 2 (*наваса, навакса*) to manage, cope; to keep up 3 (*за овошје*) to become over-ripe

превтасува *impf of* превтаса

прега (се) *impf of* прегне (се)

прегази *pf* 1 to walk across, step over; to ford, wade through; прегази река to ford a river 2 to run over, knock down; автомобил го прегази he was run over by a car 3 *fig.* to destroy, crush; to trample underfoot 4 *fig., dial.* to break one's word

прегазува *impf of* прегази

прегален *pt* pampered, spoilt

прегали *pf* to pamper, spoil

прегар *m* arid, barren land

прегатен -тна *adj usu. in the expression:* прегатен вол draught ox

прегладнет *pt* starving, starved, famished

прегладнетост *f* starvation

прегладни *pf* 1 to get very hungry; to starve *intrans.* 2 to lose one's appetite 3 *rare* to starve *trans.*

прегладнува *impf of* прегладни

преглас *m Phon.* vowel gradation

прегласи *pf Phon.* I to cause ablaut (vowel gradation) II – се to undergo ablaut

прегласува (се) *impf of* прегласи (се)

преглед *m* 1 review, inspection, check-up; examination; лекарски преглед medical examination; преглед на печатот press review 2 survey; преглед на македонската граматика survey of Macedonian grammar 3 outlook, aspect, view 4 *rare, dial.* model; pattern

прегледа *pf* I 1 to look through, mark, correct; прегледа задачи to mark homework 2 to scan, glance through; прегледа весник to glance through a <news>paper 3 to examine, scrutinize; прегледа ракопис to examine a manuscript; лекарот го прегледа the doctor examined him 4 to copy, use as a model II – се to have a <medical> check-up; оди прегледај се <на лекар> go and have a <medical> check-up!

прегледен -дна *adj* lucid, clearly written

прегледност *f* lucidity

прегледува *impf* I 1 *of* прегледа 2 *colloq.* to begrudge, hold against; to take offence at; ние треба да не си прегледуваме на некои зборови we must not take offence at a few words II – се *impf of* прегледа се

прегледувач *m* examiner, inspector

прегна́тен -тна *adj* pithy; succinct

прегне *pf* прегна *aor.* I 1 to harness, hitch 2 *fig.* to enlist *trans.* II – се to get busy with s.th.; to get involved

прегнува (се) *impf see* прега (се)

преговара *impf* to negotiate

преговарач *m* negotiator

преговори *pl only* negotiations; трговски преговори trade talks

прегозба *f* traditional feast arranged by newly-weds for the bride's parents on the Thursday after their wedding

прегозбар *m* participant in a *pregozba*

преголем *adj* too big; excessive

преголтне *pf* преголтна *aor.* to swallow (*also fig.*)

преголтнува *impf of* преголтне

прегор *m* 1 arid, barren place 2 *poet., fig.* self-sacrifice

прегори *pf* прегори & прегоре *aor.* 1 to burn *intrans.*, burn out, burn through; светилката прегоре the bulb has gone 2 to cease to burn, stop burning, burn out 3 to burn *trans.*, scorch, sear; сонцето ја прегорело тревата the sun has scorched the grass 4 to burn *intrans.*, be scorched; прегоре пченицата the wheat has been scorched by the sun 5 (*за крава*) to cease giving milk 6 *fig.* to get over; to cease to mourn (*s.o.*)

прегорува *impf of* прегори

прегости *pf* I (*often iron.*) to treat to lavish hospitality II – се to over-indulge

преграб *m* 1 grasp, embrace 2 armful; еден преграб сено an armful of hay

преграби *pf* to hug, embrace, take in one's arms

преграбува *impf of* преграби

преград *f poet. see* прегратка[1]

преграда *f* 1 partition, screen; просторијата е одделена со преграда a partition divides the room 2 *fig.* barrier, obstacle 3 compartment, *see* прегратка[2]

преграден -дна *adj rare* of a partition/fence

прегради *pf* 1 to partition off; to fence; *fig.* (*препречи*) to obstruct; прегради двор to fence a courtyard; *fig.* прегради некому пат to bar s.o.'s way 2 to rebuild

преградица *f dim. of* преграда 3, *see* прегратка[2]

преградува *impf of* прегради

прегратка[1] *f* embrace, hug; grasp; во мајчина прегратка in his mother's embrace; во прегратките на смртта in the jaws of death

прегратка[2] *f* small compartment

прегрбави & прегрби *pf* I *rare* to make (*s.o.*) hunchbacked; to bend, bow; годините го прегрбавија old age bent his back II – се to become hunchbacked, stoop

прегрбавува (се) & прегрбува (се) *impf of* прегрбави (се) & прегрби (се)

прегрева (се) *impf of* прегрее (се)

прегрее *pf* прегреа *aor.* I 1 to overheat *trans.* 2 to warm up, reheat *trans.* 3 *rare* to keep warm through winter *trans.* II – се to warm o.s. too much; to get overheated

прегрешение -ија *n Rel.* transgression, sin

прегреши *pf rare* to sin, transgress; (*with dat.*) to trespass against, give offence

прегрешува *impf of* прегреши

прегризе *pf* прегриза *aor.* to bite through/off

прегризува *impf of* прегризе

прегрми *pf* to cease thundering; *fig.* to stop shouting

прегрмува *impf of* прегрми

прегрне *pf* прегрна *aor.* 1 to embrace, hug, take in one's arms 2 *literary, fig., rare* to embrace, espouse, take up; го прегрна делото на слобода to embrace the cause of freedom

прегрнува *impf of* прегрне

прегрупи́ра *pf & impf* I to regroup *trans.* II – се to regroup *intrans.*

прегушне *pf* прегушна *aor. see* прегрне

прегушнува *impf of* прегушне

пред- *prefix* pre-, fore-

пред *prep* **1** (*spatial, fig.*) before, in front of; in the presence of; compared with (to); пред куќа in front of the house; пред законот before the law; пред тешкотии in the face of difficulties; пред сите in front of everybody **2** (*temporal*) before; токму пред вечера just before supper; пред самоти војна just before the war; пред зори before dawn; пред неколку години a few years ago; пред време (предвреме) early, prematurely, before time; ❏ пред cè first of all; above all **3** пред да (*as conjunction*) before; уште пред да огрее сонцето before sunrise

предава *impf* **I 1** *of* предаде **2** to lecture, deliver lectures; to teach **II – се** *impf of* предаде се

предавање *n* **1** delivery; предавање телеграма delivery of a telegram; предавање молба submission of an application; предавање на страстите abandonment to passions **2** lecture; држи предавање to give a lecture

предавател *m* transmitter

предавач *m* lecturer; виш предавач senior lecturer

предавачки *adj* lecturing; lecturer's

предавник -ци *m* traitor; предавник на делото traitor to the cause

предавница *f* traitress

предавнички *adj* traitorous; treacherous

предавство *n* betrayal, treason, treachery

предаде *pf* **I 1** to hand in, hand over; to submit, present; to send in; to convey, pass on; предаде молба to submit an application; предаде свои акредитиви to present one's credentials; предаде должност to relinquish one's duties; предаде поздрави to convey greetings; ❏ предаде на заборавот to consign to oblivion; предаде Богу душа to give up one's soul to God **2** to surrender *trans.*, give up, concede; непријателот ја предаде тврдината the enemy surrendered the fortress **3** *literary* to portray, play, present; предаде улога to play a part **4** *rare* to transmit, broadcast; радиото предаде соопштение the radio broadcast an announcement **5** to betray **II – се 1** to give o.s. up, surrender, yield *intrans.*; се предаде без борба to surrender (give up) without a fight **2** to devote o.s. (*на – to*); to abandon o.s. (*to*); й се предаде сиот на борбата he devoted himself wholly to the struggle; им се предал на своите страсти he abandoned himself to his passions

предаден *pt* devoted, dedicated (*на – to*); тој е предаден на работата he is devoted to the work

предајник -ци *m rare see* предавник

предајница *f rare see* предавница

предајнички *adj rare see* предавнички

предало *n* collective term for yarn and loom

предан *pt* devoted, loyal; предана служба devoted service; предан кон дело devoted to a cause

предание -ија *n* tradition; по предание by tradition

преданост *f* devotion, loyalty

предач *m* spinning worker

предачен -чна *adj* (*предилен*) spinning; предачна машина spinning-machine

предачка *f* (*предилка*) **1** (*fem. form*) *see* предач **2** spinning-machine

предачница *f* (*предилница*) spinning-mill

предварди *pf rare see* претпази

предвардлив *adj rare see* претпазлив

предвардува *impf rare of* предварди (се)

предвесник -ци *m* herald; omen; предвесници на пролетта harbingers of spring

предвесница *f see* предвесник

предвест *f & rarer* **предвестие** -ија *n* **1** prediction, forecast; announcement **2** omen, sign

предвести *pf* to predict, forecast; to announce; to foretell, presage

предвестува *impf of* предвести

предвечер *f poet.* early evening

предвечерен -рна *adj poet.* <of> early evening

предвечерие -ија *n*, **предвечерина** *f & * **предвечерје** *n* eve; во предвечерието на војната on the eve of the war

предвид *adv in the expressions:* иде (доаѓа) предвид to come into consideration; зема нешто предвид to take s.th. into consideration; има нешто предвид to have s.th. in mind

предвиди *pf* **1** to foresee; to expect, envisage; ги предвидовме сегашните настани we foresaw the present events **2** to anticipate, make provision for

предвидлив *adj* **1** foreseeable; predictable **2** clairvoyant; discerning, penetrating

предвидува *impf of* предвиди

предводи *impf* to lead, head; предводи делегација to head a delegation

предводник -ци *m* leader

предводница *f* (*fem. form*) *see* предводник

предводнички *adj* leading

предводништво *n* leadership, management

предводува *impf see* предводи

предвоен *adj* pre-war; предвоениот период the pre-war period

предвои *pf* **I** to divide (split) in two *trans.*; to halve **II – се** to divide (split) in two *intrans.*

предвојнички *adj* pre-conscription, pre-draft; предвојничка обука pre-conscription training

предвојува (се) *impf of* предвои (се)

предворје *n* vestibule, hall, lobby, antechamber

предвреме *adv* ahead of time (schedule), early

предвремен *adj* premature; предвремена смрт premature death

предговор *m* preface, prologue, foreword; предговор кон третото издание preface to the third edition

предговорник -ци *m* previous speaker

предговорница & предговорничка *f* (*fem. form*) *see* предговорник

предгорје *n* foothills

предградие -ија *n* outlying urban district; outskirts; suburb

преде *impf* **1** to spin (*wool*) **2** (*за мачка*) to purr

предело -овци, -и *m see* прадедо

пределовски *adj see* прадедовски

предел *m* **1** (*usu. pl*) area, region **2** (*usu. pl*) landscape, scenery **3** *literary, rare* frontier, boundary

предела *f* **1** *f.p.* flock; предела овци flock of sheep **2** *see* пасиште

предели *pf* **1** to redivide *trans.* **2** to fence off **3** *arch.* to assign, allocate

пределува *impf of* предели

преден[1] *pt* spun; предена волна spun wool

преден[2] -дна *adj* front, first, foremost, leading; предни заби front teeth; предни нозе front legs, forepaws; откај предната страна from the front; ❏ преден одред vanguard; на преден план in the foreground

преденка *f* spinning bee

предено *n (преѓа)* yarn

преденува *pf* to spend the day

предзнаење *n* foreknowledge, previous knowledge

предзнак -ци *m* sign; omen; сигурен предзнак a sure sign

предзори *adv* before dawn (daybreak)

предивен -вна *adj poet.* extremely beautiful; предивни гори extremely beautiful forests

прединво *n rare* yarn

предигра *f* 1 *Mus.* prelude, *see* прелудиум 2 *(во театар)* prologue *(also fig.)*; lead-in, lead-up 3 *Sport.* preliminary match

предизборен -рна *adj* pre-election; предизборна кампања election campaign

предизвик -ци *m literary, rare* challenge, provocation

предизвика *pf* 1 to evoke, call forth; to cause; предизвика болка to cause pain 2 to provoke, incite; предизвика некого to provoke s.o. 3 to challenge; предизвика некого на двобој to challenge s.o. to a duel

предизвиклив *adj see* предизвикувачки

предизвикува *impf of* предизвика

предизвикувач *m* 1 pathogen; предизвикувач на болест carrier of an illness 2 challenger; inciter, instigator; *agent provocateur*

предизвикувачки *adj* challenging; provocative; defiant; предизвикувачки став provocative attitude

предика́т *m Gram.* predicate

предика́тски *adj Gram.* predicative

предилен -лна *adj* spinning; предилна машина spinning-machine

предилка *f* 1 female spinning worker 2 spinning-machine

предилница *f* spinning-mill

предимно *adv* mainly, mostly, particularly

предимство *n (предност)* advantage; priority, preference

предиспит *m* preliminary examination

предиспитен -тна *adj* pre-examination

предисторија *f* prehistory

предисториски *adj* prehistoric

предише се & предиши се *pf* предиша се & предиши се *aor.* to recover one's breath, get one's breath back

предишка *f* pause, break; без предишка without a break

предишува се *impf of* предише се & предиши се

предјадење *n* appetizer, hors-d'oeuvre, *Austral., N.Z.* entrée

предлага *impf of* предложи

предлагач *m* proposer; bidder

предлог -зи *m* 1 proposal, suggestion 2 *Gram.* preposition

предложен -жна *adj Gram.* *(предлошки)* prepositional

предложи *pf* 1 to propose; to suggest 2 to nominate; предложи кандидат за претседател to nominate a presidential candidate 3 *rare (понуди)* to offer; предложи свои услуги to offer one's services

предложува *impf rare see* предлага

предлошки *adj Gram.* prepositional

предмет *m* 1 thing, object, article 2 theme, subject; topic; предмет на испитување subject of research; предмет за шеги butt of jokes, object of ridicule 3 <school> subject; наставни предмети teaching subjects 4 case, file, dossier 5 *Gram.* object; подмет и предмет subject and object

предметен -тна *adj* object/subject *attrib.*; предметен регистар register of subjects; предметна настава departmentalized teaching

предмугрен *adj usu. in the expression:* предмугрен час the hour before dawn

предмугри *adv* at daybreak, at dawn

предназначи *pf literary, rare* to intend, earmark *(s.th. for s.th.)*; тие предмети се предназначени за вас these things are intended for you

предназначува *impf of* предназначи

преднина *f (предност)* advantage, superiority; priority, preference; дава некому преднина to give s.o. priority (precedence)

предница *f* front part; yoke of a dress; предница на кола front of a car/cart; *(на чун)* bow

предност *f* advantage, superiority; priority, precedence; има предност над to take priority over

предоволен -лна *adj* more than adequate (sufficient)

предоволно *adv* more than enough

предодреден *pt* predestined, preordained, predetermined

предодреденост *f* predestination

предодреди *pf* to predetermine, predestine, preordain

предодредува *impf of* предодреди

предок -дци *m* forebear, ancestor

предомина́нтен -тна *adj literary* predominant, prevalent

предопределен *pt see* предодреден

предопределеност *f see* предодреденост

предопредели *pf see* предодреди

предопределува *impf of* предопредели

предосети *pf* to have a presentiment (premonition) of; предосети опасност to sense danger

предосетува & предосеќава *impf of* предосети

предостава *impf of* предостави; тоа ви го предоставам I leave that to you

предостави *pf literary* to allow, grant; to leave *(s.th. to s.o.)*

предоставува *impf literary see* предостава

предостатен -тна *adj see* предоволен

предостатно *adv see* предоволно

предочи *pf literary* to confront *(s.o. with s.th.)*, point out; предочи некому опасност to point out a danger to s.o.

предочува *impf of* предочи

предрасполага *impf of* предрасположи

предрасположен *pt* predisposed *(кон, за – to)*, inclined *(to)*; susceptible *(to)*; предрасположен кон (за) болест susceptible to illness

предрасположение -ија *n & предрасположеност* *f* predisposition, tendency; susceptibility

предрасположи *pf* I to predispose, persuade, incline II – се to feel an inclination *(кон – towards)*, get into a mood *(да – to)*

предрасположува (се) *impf of* предрасположи (се)

предрасуда *f & предрасудок* -ци *m* prejudice, bias

предрекува *impf of* предрече

предреме *pf* предрема *aor.* to doze for a while

предремува *impf of* предреме

предрече *pf* предреков *1st p. sg aor.* 1 to foredoom (*to failure*) 2 *rare* to foretell, predict

предречува *impf see* предрекува

предрешава *impf of* предреши

предреши *pf literary, rare* to predetermine, decide in advance

предрешува *impf see* предрешава

предручек *adv colloq. see* претпладне

предубеден *pt* prejudiced

предубедување *n* prejudice, bias

предума *pf dial.* I 1 to think over, consider 2 to dissuade 3 *rare, f.p. see* проговори 1 II – **се** to change one's mind

предупреди *pf* 1 to forewarn, warn 2 *rare* to prevent, forestall, avert; предупреди несреќа to prevent an accident

предупредува *impf of* предупреди

предупредувачки *adj* warning

предусети *pf see* предосети

предусетува & **предусекава** *impf of* предусети

предуслов *m* pre-condition; prerequisite

предучилиштен -шна *adj* pre-school; деца од предучилишна возраст children of pre-school age

преѓа *f* yarn; домашна преѓа homespun yarn

преѓе & **преѓеска** *adv* before, earlier; recently, a moment ago; преѓеска беше овде he was here a moment ago

преѓешен -шна *adj* previous, former; преѓешниот стопан на куќата the previous owner of the house

преемник -ци *m literary, rare* successor, heir

преемница *f literary, rare* (*fem. form*) *see* преемник

преемствен *adj literary, rare* successive, repeated; consecutive; continuous

преемственост *f literary, rare* succession; continuity

прежали *pf* 1 to get over (*a loss*); to cease to mourn (*s.o.*) 2 to sacrifice (*s.th.*), give up

прежалува *impf of* прежали

прежен -жна *adj see* преѓешен; во прежни времиња in former times

прежени *pf* I to arrange s.o.'s remarriage II – **се** to get married again, remarry *intrans.*

преженува (се) *impf of* прежени (се)

прежива *impf* to chew the cud, ruminate; зборот дури не го предумаш и преживаш арно, не вели го *prov.* weigh your words well

преживар *m Zool.* ruminant

преживеан & **преживен** *adj* 1 surviving; преживеан борец veteran, old soldier 2 *rare* outdated, obsolete

преживее *pf* преживеа *aor.* 1 to live through, experience; to endure, suffer; ги преживее ужасите на војната to experience the horrors of war 2 to survive; to last out, pull through 3 *rare* to survive *trans.*, outlive

преживелица & **преживеница** *f* 1 experience; adventure 2 *rare* old-fashioned object, relic of the past

преживува *impf of* преживее; to live one's part; артистот треба да ја преживува својата улога the actor must live his part

прежили *pf* to cut into (*of a string, etc.*); ременот од пушката му го прежили рамото the strap of his rifle cut into his shoulder

прежилува *impf of* прежили

през *prep dial.* 1 at the time of, during; през целиот период throughout the period; през ден (презден) every other day 2 (*низ*) through; мине през поле to cross a field

презадолжи се *pf* to incur large debts, sink deep into debt

презадолжува се *impf of* презадолжи се

презакаже *pf* презакажа *aor.* to reconvene, arrange again; to make revised arrangements for (*a meeting, conference, etc.*)

презакажува *impf of* презакаже

презапише *pf* презапиша *aor.* I to re-enrol, re-register; презапише некого to re-enrol s.o.; го презапише вториот семестар to re-enrol for the second semester II – **се** to re-enrol *intrans.*

презапишува (се) *impf of* презапише (се)

презаситен *pt* 1 *Chem.* supersaturated; презаситен раствор supersaturated solution 2 *fig.* sated

презаситеност *f* supersaturation; satiety

презасити *pf* I 1 *Chem.* to supersaturate 2 to sate II – **се** 1 *Chem.* to become supersaturated 2 to over-indulge *intrans.*

презаситува (се) *impf of* презасити (се)

презбира *impf f.p.* to collect, gather *trans.*

презборок -ци *m dial.* reproach

презборува *impf* 1 to reproach, rebuke, find fault with 2 to answer back

презвитер *m Rel.* presbyter, elder

презвитерски *adj Rel.* presbyterian

презден *adv dial.* every other day, on alternate days

презема *impf of* преземе

преземе *pf* презема *aor.* 1 to take over; преземе должност to take up (over) a post; преземе одговорност to assume responsibility; преземе на (врз) себеси to take upon o.s. 2 *dial.* to imitate, copy 3 *dial.* to occupy, capture, conquer, seize 4 *rare fig.* to overcome, consume, possess; преземен од користољубие consumed by greed 5 to undertake; преземе офанзива to take the offensive; преземе чекори to take steps

презент[1] *m Gram.* present tense

презент[2] *m* gift, present

презентација *f* presentation

презентен -тна *adj Gram. see* презентски

презентира *pf* & *impf* to present

презентски *adj Gram.* <of the> present tense; презентски наставки present endings

презерватив *m* condom, contraceptive sheath

презива се *impf* to be called (*by a surname*); to have as a surname; како се презива? what is his surname?

президент *m rare see* претседател

президиум *m* presidium

презиме *m* 1 surname, family name 2 *f.p.* nickname

презими *pf* to winter, over-winter, spend the winter; (*за животни*) to hibernate

презимува *impf of* презими

презир *m* contempt, disdain, scorn

презира *impf of* презре

презоба *pf* I to overfeed (*livestock*) II – **се** to overeat; се презобале грозје they've eaten too many grapes

презобува (се) *impf of* презоба (се)

презрамка *f* (*usu. pl*) *arch. see* прерамка

презре *pf* to despise; to scorn, disdain

презреан *pt* over-ripe

презрева *impf of* презрее

презрее *pf* презреа *aor.* to become over-ripe

презрен *adj* contemptible, despicable

презрение *n see* презир

презрив *adj* contemptuous, scornful; презрив однос scornful attitude

пресида *pf* **1** to rebuild, restructure **2** to partition

пресидува *impf of* пресида

преигра *pf* to play again, replay

преигрува *impf of* преигра

преизбере *pf* преизбра *aor.* to re-elect; to re-appoint

преизбира *impf of* преизбере

преизбор *m* re-election; re-appointment

преизборност *f* eligibility for re-appointment

преиздава *impf of* преиздаде

преиздаде *pf* to republish, reprint (*a book*)

преименува *pf & impf* **I** to rename **II** – **се** to change one's name

преиначи *pf* to distort, twist; to spoil; преиначи нечии зборови to distort s.o.'s words

преиначува *impf of* преиначи

преиспита *pf* to recheck, test again; to review, reinvestigate

преиспитува *impf of* преиспита

преjаде *pf* **I** to feed too much, overfeed **II** – **се** to overeat

преjаден *pt* replete; overfed

преjадува (се) *impf of* преjаде (се)

преjде *pf* (*помине*) **1** to cross <over> *trans.*; преjде река to cross a river **2** to move, transfer *intrans.*; преjе во друг воз to change trains **3** *fig.* to pass on (over) *intrans.*, go on (*на* – *to*), proceed (*to*); ќе преjдеме на друго прашање we'll pass on to another matter

преjдува *impf see* преоѓа

преjудици́ра *pf & impf* to prejudice, prejudge; не сакаме да ja преjудицираме работата we do not wish to prejudge the issue

прек *adj* **1** straight, direct; прек пат short cut; *Gram.* прека реч direct speech **2** speedy; sudden; прек суд drumhead court martial **3** urgent, pressing; прека потреба urgent need

прекади *pf* to censer, sprinkle with incense <again>

прекадува *impf of* прекади

прекажан *adj Gram.* renarrated, retold

прекажаност *f Gram.* the category of renarration (*in the Macedonian verb*)

прекаже *pf* прекажа *aor.* to retell, renarrate, relate

прекажува *impf* **1** *of* прекаже **2** to gossip about (*s.o.*), malign, run down

прекален *pt literary* tough, seasoned, hardened

прекаленост *f literary* hardiness, toughness

прекали *pf* **1** to temper more than necessary **2** to temper, steel again **3** *literary, fig.* to toughen, harden *trans.*

прекалува *impf of* прекали

прекапе[1] *pf* прекапа *aor.* to stop dripping/leaking

прекапе[2] **& прекапне** *pf* прекапа *& прекапна *aor.* to grow weak (*from exhaustion*); to grow numb (*with cold*)

прекапнува *impf see* прекапува[2]

прекапува[1] *impf of* прекапе[1]

прекапува[2] *impf of* прекапе[2] *& прекапне

прекар[1] *m* **1** nickname; како го викаат на прекар? what is his nickname? **2** surname, last name

прекар[2] *m f.p.*, *dial.* reproach, rebuke

прекарба *f* reproach, rebuke

прекардаши *pf colloq.* to exaggerate, go too far, exceed the bounds

прекардашува *impf of* прекардаши

прекарува[1] *impf of* прекори; црен шутаре прекарува *prov.* the pot calls the kettle black

прекарува[2] **се** *impf colloq.* **1** to have a nickname **2** to have a surname, be called; како се прекаруваш? what's your surname?

прекаса *pf* (*прегризе*) to bite through/off

прекасува *impf of* прекаса

преквалификациjа *f* retraining, requalification; change of profession

преквалификува & преквалифици́ра *pf & impf* **I** to retrain *trans.* **II** – **се** to retrain *intrans.*, requalify; to change one's profession

прекин *m* interruption, break; pause; прекин на струjа power failure; прекин на односите severance of relations; без прекин without a break/pause

прекине *pf* прекина *aor.* **I** **1** to interrupt, cut off, cut short, conclude; струjата ja прекинале the power was cut off; прекине разговор to end a conversation; прекине молчење to break the silence; прекине предавач to interrupt a lecturer; прекине односи to break off relations; прекине со некого to break with s.o. **II** – **се** **1** to break, snap *intrans.*; to tear *intrans.*; jажето се прекина the rope snapped **2** to break down; снагата ми се прекина my strength failed me

прекинува (се) *impf of* прекине (се)

прекинувач *m Tech.* <electric> switch

прекипи *pf* **1** (*за млеко, кафе*) to boil over **2** *fig.*, *impers.* (*with dat.*) to erupt, explode (*with rage*); му прекипе his anger boiled over **3** *rare* to finish boiling/fermenting; to settle *intrans.*

прекипува *impf of* прекипи

прекисели *pf* to make (*s.th.*) too sour; to flavour excessively with vinegar

прекиселува *impf of* прекисели

прекисне *pf* прекисна *aor.* to ferment (rise) to excess; лебот прекиснал the dough has risen too much

прекиснува *impf of* прекисне

преклава *impf of* прекладе

прекладе *pf* to place (lay, stand, set) again

преклани *adv* the year before last

преклански *adj* of the year before last

прекласи́ра *pf & impf* to reclassify

прекласификациjа *f* reclassification

прекласификува & прекласифици́ра *pf & impf see* прекласира

преклина *impf see* преколнува

преклони *pf literary* **I** **1** to bow, bend, lower *trans.*; ❑ преклони глава to bow one's head (*in submission*) **2** (*за време*) to pass *intrans.*; пладнето беше преклонило midday had passed **II** – **се** **1** (*with dat.*) to bend, bow down (*to*); *fig.* to submit (*to*); не ѝ се преклони he did not submit to her **2** *rare* (*пред*) to pay homage (tribute) to, bow down before; **се** преклони пред нивниот подвиг he honoured their exploit

преклонува (се) *impf of* преклони (се)

преклоп *m* **1** covering; flap (*of a garment*) **2** lid, top

преклопен -пна *adj* folding; преклопен нож folding knife, penknife; преклопна постела folding bed

преклопи *pf* **I 1** to cover; to fold over *trans.* **II – ce** to fold over, close, overlap *intrans.*

преклопка & **преклопница** *f Elec.* circuit-breaker

преклопува (се) *impf of* преклопи (се)

прекова & **прекове** *pf* прекова *aor.* to forge anew, to reforge; to mint again (*coins*); прекова коњ to reshoe a horse

прековува *impf of* прекова & прекове

преколе *pf* прекла *aor.* to butcher, slaughter

преколие *pf* преколна *aor.* **I 1** to swear in; to extract a promise from; ја преколна да дојде he made her promise to come **2** *f.p.* to swear an oath **3** *rare* to curse, swear at **II – ce 1** to swear an oath **2** to curse o.s.

преколнува *impf* **I 1** to implore, entreat, beseech **2** *rare* to curse, swear at **II – ce** to swear an oath

преколува *impf of* преколе

прекопа *pf* **1** to dig over (through); to dig over once more **2** to hoe, loosen soil (*round vines, maize, etc.*); прекопа лозје to hoe a vineyard

прекопира *pf & impf* to copy; to trace

прекопне *pf* прекопна *aor.* to desire fervently; прекопнавме чекајќи be we got quite desperate waiting for you; прекопна да биде на неговото he insisted on having his own way

прекопнува *impf of* прекопне

прекопува *impf of* прекопа

прекор[1] *m* reproach, rebuke, reprimand

прекор[2] *m dial.* (*прекар*) nickname

прекорен -рна *adj* reproachful

прекори *pf* to reproach, rebuke, reprimand

прекорува[1] *impf of* прекори

прекорува[2] се *impf dial. see* прекарува[2] се

прекоси *pf* **1** to scythe, mow <again> **2** *fig.* to cut across; прекоси улица to cross a street

прекосува *impf of* прекоси

прекрасен -сна *adj* beautiful, fine, wonderful, marvellous, superb; прекрасен случај splendid opportunity

прекрати *pf literary* **1** to stop, cease *trans.*, interrupt, suspend; прекрати работа to stop work **2** *rare* прекрати време to kill time

прекратува *impf of* прекрати

прекрива *impf of* прекрие

прекривач *m* bedspread

прекривка *f* sheet

прекрие *pf* прекри *aor.* to cover

прекров *m* (*превез*) bridal veil

прекрова *impf see* прекројува

прекровка *f see* прекров

прекрои *pf* to alter *trans.*, remake, rearrange; прекрои фустан to alter a dress; прекрои карта to redraw a map

прекројува *impf of* прекрои

прекрсти *pf* **I 1** to place crosswise **2** to make the sign of the cross over; прекрсти дете to make the sign of the cross over a child **3** to convert to Christianity **4** to rename, rechristen **II – ce 1** to cross o.s. **2** to change one's name, take a new name

прекрстува (се) *impf of* прекрсти (се)

прекршен *pt* elderly, advanced in years

прекрши *pf* **I 1** to break off *trans.* **2** to break *trans.*; to smash *trans.*; прекрши нога to break a leg **3** (*зраци*) to refract **4** *fig.* to convince, persuade, win over **5** (*закон, пропис*) to break, violate, transgress, infringe;

прекрши наредба to disobey an order **6** *Print.* to make up <into> pages **7** (*во години*) to age *intrans.*, grow old, get on in years **8** (*за време*) to pass *intrans.*; денот беше прекршил the day was well advanced **II – ce 1** to break *intrans.* **2** to be refracted **3** *fig.* (*се реши*) to decide, make up one's mind **4** (*се свитка*) to bend down *intrans.*; to twist, turn *intrans.*

прекршок -ци *m* violation, infringement; стори прекршок to commit an offence; судија за прекршоци magistrate

прекршува (се) *impf of* прекрши (се)

прекршувач *m* offender, lawbreaker

прексиноќа *adv* the evening before last

прексиноќен -ќна *adj* of the evening before last

преку- *prefix* over-; прекумерен excessive; прекуноќ overnight; прекуморец person living overseas

преку *prep* **1** across; on the far side of; помине преку мост to cross a bridge; помине преку фактите to disregard the facts; преку Вардар on the other side of the Vardar **2** through, via, by way of; оди за Охрид преку Битола to go to Ohrid by way of (via) Bitola; јави некому преку некого to let s.o. know through s.o. else **3** over, more than; over and above; преку (над) сто души more than (over) a hundred people; има преку (над) сто години he is over 100 years old **4** during; преку неделата during the week; преку летото during the summer **5** contrary to, against; преку волја against one's will; ❑ прекуред out of turn; прекумера (преку мера) excessively; beyond measure; прекусила at the most; прекутрупа by a short cut

прекуброен -јна *adj* supernumerary; superfluous

прекубројност *f* superfluity

прекувремен *adj* overtime; прекувремена работа overtime work

прекуглава *adv* head over heels (*also fig.*); sick and tired (*of s.o. or s.th.*); се преметне прекуглава to turn a somersault

прекуден *adv* (*also* преку ден) during the day, by day

прекум *adv* across; direct, by a short cut

прекумера *adv* beyond measure, excessively, too much

прекумерен -рна *adj* excessive

прекуморец -рци *m* foreigner

прекуморка *f* (*fem. form*) *see* прекуморец

прекуморски *adj* overseas; прекуморска трговија overseas (foreign) trade

прекумче *n f.p.* godson

прекуноќ *adv* during the night, by night, overnight; не станува тоа прекуноќ that doesn't happen overnight (all at once)

прекуокеански *adj* transoceanic; ocean-going; прекуокеански бродови ocean-going vessels

прекупец -пци *m* middleman; profiteer

прекупи *pf* to buy up for resale

прекупува *impf of* прекупи

прекуред *adv* out of turn

прекусила *adv* **1** with difficulty **2** at most, at best

прекутре *adv* the day after tomorrow

прекутрешен -шна *adj* of the day after tomorrow

прекутрупа *adv* by a short cut; cross-country

прекуутре *adv see* прекутре

прекуутрешен -шна *adj see* прекутрешен

прекучуди се *impf* to be astounded

прекчера *adv* the day before yesterday

прекчерашен -шна *adj* of the day before yesterday

прелаже *pf* прелажа *aor.* **I** to cheat, deceive, mislead **II – се** to be mistaken; to be deceived, misled

прелажува (се) *impf of* прелаже (се)

прелаз *m* garden gate, archway, lych-gate

прелазен *adj f.p.* blocked, barred; closed

прелакѝра *pf & impf* to lacquer, varnish, polish again

прелат *m Rel.* prelate

прелева (се) *impf* 1 *of* прелее (се) 2 to glisten, glitter

прелее *pf* прелеа *aor.* **I** 1 to pour *trans.*; to transfer by pouring 2 to overfill, pour too much; прелее чашка to overfill a glass 3 to sprinkle (*co – with*); *Cul.* to glaze; (*торта*) to ice; (*месо*) to baste 4 to recast, reforge 5 to overflow; Вардар прелеал the Vardar has burst its banks; ❑ чашата (на трпението) прелеа that was the last straw 6 to flood *trans.*, swamp, inundate **II – се** 1 to overflow *intrans.* 2 *rare* (*за боја*) to shade (*во – into*)

прележи *pf* прележа *aor.* 1 to lie for a while 2 to get over, recover (*from an illness*); прележи маларија to get over a bout of malaria 3 to lie fallow

прележува *impf of* прележи

прелез *m* entrance, wicket-gate, lych-gate

прелепи *pf* to stick, glue on again

прелепува *impf of* прелепи

прелест *f literary* beauty, splendour

прелестен -сна *adj literary* beautiful, splendid, superb

прелет *m* overflight

прелета *pf* 1 to fly over (across); to fly past; над градот прелетаа авиони some planes flew over the city; прелета океан to fly across the ocean 2 *fig.* to scan, look through; прелета книга со очи (поглед) to glance through a book 3 *fig.* (*за време и сл.*) to fly by; младоста наша прелета our youth has flown by

прелетен -тна *adj rare in the expression:* прелетна (преселна) птица migratory bird, bird of passage

прелетува *impf of* прелета

прелив *m* 1 (*action of*) sprinkling (*with sugar, etc.*) 2 nuance; iridescence; play of colours

прелива (се) *impf see* прелева (се)

прелие (се) *pf* прели (се) *aor. see* прелее (се)

прелимина́рен -рна *adj* preliminary

прелиста *& rare* **прелисти** *pf* to glance through, skim through, leaf through

прелистува *impf of* прелиста *&* прелисти

прелка *f* 1 (*female*) spinning worker 2 distaff; spinning-wheel for flax and hemp

прело *n* spinning (*wool, yarn*)

прелог -зи *m* fallow land

прелом *m literary* 1 watershed, reversal, turning-point 2 *rare* fracture; прелом на коска fracture of a bone 3 *Print.* <page> make-up

преломен -мна *adj literary* decisive, critical, crucial; преломен момент critical moment, turning-point, watershed

преломи (се) *pf literary see* прекрши (се)

преломува (се) *impf of* преломи (се)

прелудиум *m* prelude

прељуб *m &* **прељуба** *f literary* adultery

прељубник -ци *m literary* adulterer

прељубница *f literary* adulteress

прељубнички *adj literary* adulterous

прељубодејство *&* **прељубочинство** *n literary* adultery

премава *pf* (*usu. in a game*) to hit, strike again

премавне *pf literary, rare* премавна *aor.* to overcome, surmount; to defeat; to thrash, beat; премавне пречки to overcome obstacles

премавнува *impf of* премавне

премажи *pf* **I** to marry off (*usu. a daughter*) a second time **II – се** to remarry *intrans.* (*fem. form*)

премажува (се) *impf of* премажи (се)

премален *pt* exhausted, worn-out; weakened

премаленост *f* exhaustion

премали *pf* премале *aor.* to weaken *intrans.*; to tire, become exhausted

премалува *impf of* премали

премама *f* deception, ruse, ploy

премами *pf* to mislead, deceive, cheat

премамка *f see* премама

премамлив *adj* 1 deceitful, false 2 alluring, attractive, seductive

премамува *impf of* премами

премачка *pf* to re-coat, re-stain

премачкува *impf of* премачка

премеле *pf* премеле *&* премле *aor.* to grind (mill) again

премелува *impf of* премеле

премер *m* measuring; remeasuring; measure, measurement

премери *pf* **I** 1 to measure; to measure out (*a definite quantity*); to weigh; to survey; *fig.* to size up; премери некого со очи to look s.o. up and down; ❑ си ги премери силите to try one's strength 2 to measure again, remeasure **II – се** to match, equal, rival, measure up

премерлив *adj* measurable

премерува (се) *impf of* премери (се)

премеси *pf* to knead again

премести *pf* **I** to move *trans.*, shift, transfer **II – се** to move *intrans.*; to change places; (*се пресели*) to move house

преместува (се) *impf of* премести (се)

премесува *impf of* премеси

премет[1] *m rare Ling.* metathesis

премет[2] *m dial.* broom (*for sweeping straw during threshing*)

premete *pf* to sweep again

преметка (се) *impf see* преметнува (се)

преметне *pf* преметна *aor.* **I** 1 to put over, throw over; преметне сако преку рамо to throw one's jacket over one's shoulder 2 to upset, overturn 3 (*пари*) to place in circulation **II – се** 1 to somersault 2 to overturn *intrans.* 3 to get across, scramble across, jump across; се преметне преку ограда to scramble over a fence

преметнува (се) *impf of* преметне

преметува *impf of* премете

премива (се) *impf of* премие (се)

премие *pf* преми *aor.* **I** 1 to wash again *trans.* **II – се** to wash o.s.

премие́р *m* premier, prime minister

премие́ра *f* premiere <performance>

премие́рен -рна *&* **премие́рски** *adj* of a premiere; премие́рна претстава premiere performance

премија -ии *f* premium, bonus, bounty; first prize, jackpot

премин *m* 1 crossing, crossing point; border crossing

2 mountain pass, col **3** (*за боја*) shift, shading off **4** (*преод*) transition; преминот од социјализам во комунизам the transition from socialism to communism; на преминот од XX во XXI век at the turn of the century

премине *pf* премина *aor.* **1** to pass <over>, cross; to go over (*на – то*); to pass/move on (*to*); премине <преку> река/мост/граница to cross a river/bridge/frontier; премине од еден воз во друг to change trains; премине на страната на непријателот to go over to the enemy camp; наследството премина на синот the inheritance passed to the son; ❏ премине <молкома> преку to pass over in silence **2** to change into *intrans.*; квантитетот ќе премине во квалитет quantity will change into quality **3** to carry across; премине некого преку река to carry s.o. across a river **4** *f.p.* to pass away, die, breathe one's last

преминува *impf of* премине

премира[1] *impf of* премре

премѝра[2] *pf & impf* to award a prize/premium/reward to

премѝса *f* premise, premiss

премиски *adj* <of a> bonus, premium

премислен *pt* well thought out

премисли *pf* **I** to think out/over/through **II – се 1** to ponder, reflect, consider *intrans.* **2** to change one's mind

премислува *impf* **I 1** *of* премисли **2** to hesitate, waver **II – се** *impf of* премисли се

премногу *adv* **1** very much, very many; too much, too many **2** too, excessively; премногу важен too important

премолчи *pf* to say nothing, keep quiet, hold one's tongue; премолчи нешто to pass over s.th. in silence

премолчува *impf of* премолчи

премор *m & rare* **премора** *f* exhaustion

преморен *pt* exhausted

премореност *f* exhaustion

премори се *pf* to exhaust o.s., wear o.s. out

преморува се *impf of* премори се

премости *pf* **1** to bridge, span; премости река to bridge a river **2** *fig.* to surmount, overcome; премости пречки to overcome obstacles

премостува *impf of* премости

премота *pf* to wind/wrap up again; to rewind; to rewrap

премотува *impf of* премота

премоќен -ќна *adj literary* dominant, superior

премре *pf* **1** to faint, swoon, pass out **2** to be alarmed/terrified

премреже *n* **1** misfortune, mishap **2** danger, peril (*usu. avoided*), pitfall, ordeal

премрежен *pt* (*за очи, поглед*) dim, blurred, misty

премрежи *pf* **I 1** *f.p.* to net, enmesh **2** (*за дим, солзи*) to dim, blur, cloud one's vision *trans.*; густиот дим му ги премрежи очите the thick smoke dimmed his eyes; силна му тага око премрежи he was blinded by grief **3** *rare* (*очи*) to half-close, narrow; премрежив очи I half-closed my eyes; **II – се** (*за очи, поглед*) to grow dim

премрежува (се) *impf of* премрежи (се)

премрзнат *pt* frozen through, thoroughly frozen

премрзне *pf* премрзна *aor.* to freeze, freeze solid

премрзнува *impf of* премрзне

премудар -дра *adj literary* exceedingly wise; премудри Соломон Solomon the Wise

пренапина се *impf of* пренапне се

пренапнат *pt* too/extremely taut; overstrained; пренапната атмосфера very tense atmosphere

пренапне се *pf* пренапна се *aor.* to overstrain o.s., overwork

пренапнува се *impf see* пренапина се

пренапрега се *impf of* пренапрегне се

пренапрегнат *pt see* пренапнат; пренапрегнати нерви overstrained nerves

пренапрегнатост *f* strain; tension

пренапрегне се *pf* пренапрегна се *aor. see* пренапне се

пренапрегнува се *impf see* пренапрега се

пренаселен *adj* overpopulated, overcrowded

пренаселеност *f* overpopulation, overcrowding

пренасели *pf* to overpopulate

пренаселува *impf of* пренасели

пренебреглив *adj literary, rare see* пренебрегнувачки l

пренебрегне *pf literary* пренебрегна *aor.* to disregard, ignore, neglect

пренебрегнува *impf literary* **1** *of* пренебрегне **2** to look down on, have no respect for

пренебрегнувачки *adj literary* **1** neglectful **2** scornful; пренебрегнувачки однос scornful attitude

пренесе *pf* **I 1** to take, carry (*преку – across, over*); пренесе кревет во друга соба to carry a bed into another room **2** to transfer *trans.* **3** (*емитува*) to transmit, broadcast *trans.*; радиото пренесе соопштение the radio broadcast an announcement **4** (*болест и др.*) to pass on, convey, transmit; патници ја пренесле епидемијата the epidemic was carried by some travellers; пренесе опит to hand on one's experience **5** to carry over (*a word to a new line*) **6** *Book-keeping* to carry forward **7** *Mil.* пренесе оган to redirect fire **II – се 1** to move, shift *intrans.*; (*пресели се*) to move house **2** *fig.* to think back, cast one's mind back (*во – то*) **3** (*за болест*) to spread *intrans.*; (*за звук*) to travel; болеста се пренесе брзо the illness spread rapidly

пренесен *pt & adj* figurative, metaphorical; пренесена смисла figurative sense

пренесува (се) *impf of* пренесе (се)

пренесувач *m* (*на зараза*) carrier, bearer; (*на гласини*) gossip; (*поткажувач*) informer

прениже *pf* пренижа *aor.* to rethread

пренижува *impf of* прениже

пренос *m* **1** transport; transportation **2** *Tech.* transmission; пренос на сила transmission of power, drive **3** *Leg.* transfer; судски пренос legal transfer, conveyance; пренос на власт transfer of power/authority **4** *Book-keeping* transfer **5** (*на радио, ТВ*) broadcast, transmission **6** *colloq.* hyphen

преносен -сна *adj* **1** transfer; преносни трошоци transfer costs; преносен ремен transmission belt **2** *see* пренослив **3** (*пренесен*) metaphorical, figurative

пренослив *adj* portable; transportable; transferable

преноќева *pf & impf* to spend the night; to stay overnight (*regularly*)

преноќи *pf rare see* преноќева

преноќува *pf & impf see* преноќева

преоблекува (се) *impf of* преоблече (се)

преоблече *pf* **I 1** to change (*s.o.'s*) clothes **2** to disguise; го преоблече во офицер he disguised him as an officer **II – ce 1** to change one's clothes **2** to disguise o.s.

преоблечува (се)　*impf see* преоблекува (се)

Преображение & **Преображење**　*n Rel.* Transfiguration

преобразба　*f* transformation, change

преобрази　*pf* **I** to transform, change *trans.* **II – ce** to change *intrans.*

преобразува (се)　*impf of* преобрази (се)

преобразувач　*m rare* reformer; person who brings change

преобразувачки　*adj* transforming, transformative

преобрати　*pf literary, rare* **1** to change, transform *trans.* **2** to convert *trans.*; преобрати некого во правата вера to convert s.o. to the true faith

преобратува & **преобраќа**　*impf of* преобрати

преоптоварен　*pt* overburdened

преоптовари　*pf* **I** to overburden **II – ce** to overburden o.s.; to take on too much

преоптоварува (се)　*impf of* преоптовари (се)

преобува (се)　*impf of* преобуе (се)

преобуе　*pf* преобу *aor.* **I** to change (*s.o.'s*) footwear (shoes) **II – ce** to change one's footwear (shoes)

преовладее & **преовлада**　*pf* преовладеа & преовлада *aor.* to prevail, win out

преовладува　*impf of* преовладее & преовлада

преод　*m* (*премин*) transition; преод од тврда во течна состојба transition from a solid to a liquid state

преоден　-дна *adj* **1** transitional; преоден период transitional period; ❏ преодно знаме (знаменце) challenge banner; travelling trophy **2** *Gram.* transitive; преоден глагол transitive verb **3** passing, transitory, transient; преодна појава a transitory phenomenon

преодиште　*n* crossing-point; ford

преодолее　*pf literary* преодолеа *aor.* to overcome, surmount

преодолив & **преодолим**　*adj literary, rare* surmountable

преодолува　*impf of* преодолее

преоѓа　*impf of* прејде

преоѓалиште　*n* crossing-point; passage; ford

преокупација　-ии *f literary* preoccupation

преокупира　*pf* & *impf literary* to preoccupy; to be of concern to

преокупиран　*pt literary* preoccupied

преопачи　*pf* **1** *dial.* to distort, twist **2** to turn round, turn upside down

преопачува　*impf of* преопачи

преора　*pf* **I** **1** to plough again, replough **2** to plough up; to finish ploughing **II – ce** *colloq.* (*usu. iron.*) to tire o.s. out by ploughing

преориентација　*f* reorientation

преориентира　*pf* & *impf* to reorientate, reorient

преорува (се)　*impf of* преора (се)

преосвештен　*adj Rel.* right reverend; преосвештениот епископ the right (most) reverend bishop

преосвештеност　*f rare* & **преосвештенство** *usu. n Rel.* (*addressing a bishop*) Eminence, Grace; Ваше преосвештенство Your Eminence, Your Grace

преосетлив　*adj* over-sensitive

преосетливост　*f* over-sensitivity

преосмисли　*pf literary* to reinterpret; to give a different sense to

преосмислува　*impf of* преосмисли

преостане　*pf* преостана *aor.* to remain, be left <over>

преостанува　*impf of* преостане

преотима　*impf of* преотме

преотме　*pf dial.*, *f.p.* преотме & преотма *aor.* to seize, wrest; царството сакал да му го преотме he wanted to rob him of his kingdom

преоцена　*f* re-evaluation, reappraisal, reassessment; revision, review

преоцени　*pf* to revalue, reassess; to review

преоценка　*f see* преоцена

преоценува　*impf of* преоцени

препад　*m* surprise attack

препакува　*pf* & *impf* to pack again, repack

препала　*f f.p.* **1** love **2** love's torments **3** beloved (*girl*)

препален　*pt* terrified

препаленост　*f* terror

препали　*pf* **1** to overheat *trans.* **2** *f.p.* to burn up *trans.* **3** to frighten, terrify

препалува　*impf of* препали

препарат　*m Chem., Med.* preparation; remedy

препаратор　*m* laboratory assistant, demonstrator; taxidermist

препараторски　*adj* laboratory assistant's, demonstrator's; taxidermist's

препарира　*pf* & *impf* **1** to prepare (*as in a laboratory*) **2** to stuff, mount **3** *fig.* to soften up (*by persuasion*) **4** *fig.* to doctor, massage (*e.g. a text*)

препати　*pf* to suffer greatly

препатува　*impf of* препати

препаше　*pf* препаша *aor.* **I** to gird on, put on (*round the waist*); си препаше унечка to put on an apron; си препаше сабја to put on a sword **II – ce** to tie s.th. round one's waist; to gird o.s. (*co – with*); ce препашаа со унечки they put on aprons

препашка　*f* woman's woollen belt (sash)

препашува (се)　*impf of* препаше (се)

препев　*m* verse translation; poetic rendition

препева (се)　*impf of* препее (се)

препевач　*m* verse translator

препее　*pf* препеа *aor.* **I** **1** to render in verse, make verse translations **2** to sing again *trans.* **3** *arch.* to read; to reread **II – ce** *colloq.* to sing too much, get tired of singing

препек　*m* double-distilled *raki* (brandy)

препека　*pf* to cease pleading (imploring)

препелица　*f Zool.* (Coturnix coturnix) quail

препеличин　*adj* quail's; препеличини јајца quails' eggs

препере　*pf* препра *aor.* to wash (launder) again

препечати　*pf* to reprint

препечатува　*impf of* препечати

препече　*pf* **I** **1** to overdo, roast/bake too long **2** *dial.* to double-distil **3** *colloq.* to sun (*part of the body*) too much **II – ce** *colloq.* to sunbathe too long; to get sunburnt; to get overdone

препечен　*pt* **1** overdone; overbaked; ❏ препечен леб overbaked bread; burnt toast; shrewd operator **2** *dial.* double-distilled; препечена (преварена) ракија double-distilled *raki* (brandy)

препеченица　*f colloq. see* препек

препива (се)　*impf of* препие (се)

препие *pf* препи *aor.* **I 1** to make drunk; to ply with <excessive> drink **2** to drink to excess; to get drunk; многу вино препил he drank too much wine **II – се** *see* **I** 2

препили *pf* to saw through, saw in half

препилува *impf of* препили

препина (се) *impf of* препне (се)

препира се *impf* to quarrel, squabble, bicker

препирка *f* squabble; quarrel

препис *m* copy, transcript; препис од диплома copy of a degree certificate

преписка *f* correspondence; води преписка со некого to correspond with s.o.

препише *pf* препиша *aor.* **1** to rewrite; to copy, transcribe; препише на чисто to make a fair copy **2** to copy, crib **3** *Leg.* to bequeath; to make over (*property to s.o.*); му ја препишал куќата he bequeathed the house to him **4** to prescribe; ми препиша лекарот некакви апчиња the doctor prescribed some pills for me

препишува *impf of* препише

препишувач *m* **1** copyist, transcriber; scribe **2** cheat

препишувачки *adj* scribal

препка *f* trip; кладе некому препка to trip s.o.

преплави *pf* **1** to flood, inundate; *fig.* to fill, crowd **2** to rinse again (*laundry*)

преплавува *impf of* преплави

преплакне *pf* преплакна *aor.* **I** to rinse again **II – се** to rinse one's mouth/throat again

преплакнува (се) *impf of* преплакне (се)

преплати *pf* to overpay, pay too much (*за – for*)

преплеви *pf* to weed again

преплет *m rare* interlacing, weave, mesh

преплете *pf* **I 1** to intertwine, interlace *trans.* (*also fig.*) **2** to reknit; преплете џемпер to reknit a sweater **II – се** to intertwine, interlace *intrans.*; *fig.* to blend, merge *intrans.*; се преплеле разни интереси various interests intertwined

преплетка (се) *pf see* преплете (се)

преплеткува (се) *impf of* преплетка (се)

преплетува (се) *impf of* преплете (се)

преплива *pf* **I** to swim across; преплива река to swim across a river **II** *dial.*, *f.p.* (преплови) to sail across, cross by boat

преплови *pf* to sail across, cross by boat; преплови океан to sail across the ocean

препне *pf* препна *aor.* **I 1** to trip *trans.* **2** to hobble (*livestock*) **3** *fig.* to thwart, balk, frustrate; еден камен ме препна one obstacle proved my undoing **II – се** to stumble, trip *intrans.* (*also fig.*); се препнав на (од) еден камен I tripped over a stone

препнува (се) *impf see* препина (се)

преповива *impf of* преповие

преповие *pf* препови *aor.* to change a baby's nappies (*Am.* diapers)

преповтори *pf* to repeat/recite again

преповторува *impf of* преповтори

преподобен -бна *adj Rel.* (*title of canonized monk*) saint; venerable

преподобие *n Rel.* (*title of archimandrite*) reverence; Ваше преподобие Your Reverence

препозиција -ии *f Gram.* (*предлог*) preposition

препознава (се) *impf of* препознае (се)

препознае *pf* препозна *aor.* **I** to recognize; по гласот те препознав I recognized you by your voice **II – се** to make a mistake of recognition; to mistake s.o. for s.o. else

препокрива *impf of* препокрие

препокрие *pf* препокри *aor.* to re-roof; препокрие куќа to re-roof a house

преполн *adj* overfull; преполна сала overcrowded hall; срце преполно радост a heart brimming with joy

преполнет *pt see* преполн

преполни *pf* to fill to overflowing; to overfill *trans.*; ❏ ја преполни чашата <на трпението> to try one's patience

преполнува *impf of* преполни

преполови *pf* **I 1** to cut in half, divide into two, halve **2** *fig.* to break; *f.p.* мене срце преполови he broke my heart **3** to half-finish; преполови шише to half-finish a bottle **II – се** to break in two *intrans.*; ❏ срцето ми се преполовило my heart was broken

преполовува (се) *impf of* преполови (се)

препомине *pf rare* препомина *aor.* to pass by again

препон *m* & **препона** *f* obstacle, stumbling-block

препорака *f* recommendation; собранието донесе препораки the assembly passed recommendations; по препораката на мојот професор at the recommendation of my professor

препорача *pf* **I** to recommend, commend; ми го препорачаа овој хотел this hotel was recommended to me **II – се** to commend o.s.

препорачан *pt* registered; препорачано писмо registered letter

препорачлив *adj* commendable; advisable

препорачува (се) *impf of* препорача (се); ❏ *literary* се препорачувам yours faithfully

препотёнтен -тна *adj* overbearing, arrogant, presumptuous

препотёнтност *f* arrogance

препотёнција *f* arrogance

преправа *impf* **I** *of* преправи **II – се** **1** *of* преправи се **2** to pretend; се преправа дека е болен to pretend to be ill

преправи *pf* **I 1** to remake, re-do, change, alter *trans.*; си го преправила фустанот she altered her dress **2** to distort, twist *trans.*; преправи нечии зборови to twist s.o.'s words **3** to change, reform *trans.* **4** to disguise **II – се** to assume a new guise; to disguise o.s.; се преправи во (на) старец to disguise o.s. as an old man

преправка *f* alteration

препрати *pf* **1** to forward; to send on; to redirect (*mail*) **2** to see off

препраќа & *more often* **препратува** *impf of* препрати

препраша *pf* to question, interrogate again

препрашува *impf of* препраша

препреде *pf* to spin again; to respin (*yarn*)

препреден *adj* cunning, crafty; canny, shrewd

препреденост *f* cunning, craftiness; shrewdness

препредува *impf of* препреде

препречи *pf* **I 1** to block, obstruct; ми го препречија патот they barred my way **2** to intercept; to accost **II – се** (*with dat.*) to get in the way; ми се препречи една река my way was blocked by a river

препречува (се) *impf of* препречи (се)

препржи *pf* **1** to fry, roast, toast too much **2** to fry, roast, toast again

препржува *impf of* препржи

препродава *impf of* препродаде

препродавач *m* middleman; profiteer; pedlar

препродаде *pf* to resell

препродажба *f* resale

препрочита *pf* to read again, reread

препрочитува *impf of* препрочита

препрчали *pf* **I 1** to upset, overturn *trans.* **2** to put over, throw over **II – се 1** to overturn *intrans.* **2** to somersault; to fly head over heels, go flying

препрчалува (се) *impf of* препрчали (се)

препукне *pf* препукна *aor.* (*од болка, жал*) to break, burst, break down *intrans.*; од жал срце ѝ препукна her heart broke from grief

препукнува *impf of* препукне

препушта *impf of* препушти

препушти *pf* **1** to allow, grant; to leave, let; препушти ми го тоа мене leave that to me! **2** *f.p.* to let go; to leave alone

преработи *pf* **I 1** to revise, rework; to adapt; преработи статија to revise an article **2** to process, treat **II – се** *colloq.* to overwork, overdo it

преработка *f* **1** processing; преработка на тутун processing of tobacco **2** adaptation; преработка на роман adaptation of a novel **3** manufactured product

преработува (се) *impf of* преработи (се)

преработувач *m* processing works; process worker

преработувачки *adj* processing; преработувачка индустрија processing industry

прераѓа (се) *impf of* прероди (се)

преразгледа *pf* to review, re-examine, reconsider; to reinvestigate

преразгледува *impf of* преразгледа

прерами & прерамчи *pf* to shoulder; прерами пушка to shoulder a rifle

прерамка *f* (*usu. pl*) braces, *Am.* suspenders; shoulder straps

преран *adj* premature, untimely; прерана смрт premature death

прерани (се) *pf colloq. see* прехрани (се)

преранува (се) *impf of* прерани (се)

прераскаже *pf* прераскажа *aor.* to recount, to retell

прераскажува *impf of* прераскаже

прерасказ *m* retelling, exposition

прерасне *pf* прерасна *aor.* **1** to change, develop (*во – into*) *intrans.* **2** *rare see* надрасне

прераснува *impf of* прерасне

прераспределба *f* redistribution

прераспредели *pf* to redistribute

прераспределува *impf of* прераспредели

прерасте *pf see* прерасне

прерастува *impf of* прерасте

пререди *pf* **I 1** to rearrange; пререди соба to rearrange a room **2** to get ahead of (*in a queue*) **II – се** to line up again *intrans.*

переудува (се) *impf of* пререди (се)

пререже *pf* прережа *aor.* **I** *rare* to cut **II – се** *rare* to cut o.s.

прережува (се) *impf of* пререже (се)

пререкува *impf of* пререче

пререче *pf* пререков *1st p. sg aor.* **1** to reproach, reprimand, chide **2** *rare* to repeat

преречува *impf of* пререче

пререшава *impf of* пререши

пререши *pf* to come to a new decision

пререшува *impf see* пререшава

прерипа & прерипне *pf* прерипа & прерипна *aor.* to jump over; прерипа <преку> ѕид to jump over a wall

прерипнува & прерипува *impf of* прерипне & прерипа

прерија -ии *f* prairie

прериски *adj* prairie; прериски волк coyote, prairie wolf

прерогатив *m* prerogative

преродба *f* rebirth, revival; Renaissance, renascence

преродбеник -ци *m* activist in the Macedonian national revival movement

преродбенски & преродбенички *adj* **1** Renaissance **2** regenerating

прероди *pf* **I 1** to change, transform *trans.*; to regenerate, revive *trans.* **2** *rare* to bear abundant fruit, give a good yield **II – се 1** to revive *intrans.*; to be transformed **2** to be reborn

преродува (се) *impf see* прераѓа (се)

прероси *pf* to stop drizzling; прероси дождот the drizzle has stopped

преросува *impf of* прероси

преса *f* **1** press; рачна преса hand press; хидраулична преса hydraulic press; преса за вино winepress **2** *literary, rare* printing press; the press; слободна преса free press

пресад *m* seedling (*tree*)

пресади *pf* to transplant (*also fig.*); пресади дрво to transplant a tree; пресади бубрег to transplant a kidney

пресадува *impf of* пресади; старо дрво не се пресадува *prov.* you can't teach an old dog new tricks

пресакува *impf* to make excessive demands

прес-биро -оа *m* press bureau

пресвет *adj* **1** (*also* пресвети) (*of saints, etc.*) most holy, blessed; пресвета богородица Most Holy Mother of God **2** most sacred; пресвето место sacred site

пресвета *f Rel.* offering of bread (*in church*)

пресветлост *f* Reverence (*as title of church dignitary*); Ваша пресветлост Your Reverence

пресветол -тла *adj usu. in the form:* пресветли (*за цареви*) most illustrious

пресврт *m literary* turnabout, reversal

пресврти (се) *pf see* преврти (се)

пресвртница *f literary* watershed, turning-point

пресвртува (се) *impf see* превртува (се)

пресева *impf of* пресее

пресега (се) *impf of* пресегне (се)

пресегне (се) *pf* пресегна (се) *aor.* to reach out (*to take s.th.*)

пресегнува (се) *impf see* пресега (се)

преседан *m literary* precedent; направи преседан to set a precedent

преседи *pf* to stay for a while; to sit through; преседи докај полноќ to stay till midnight; преседи ноќта to stay up all night

преседне *pf* пресéдна *aor.* (*3rd p. only, with dat.*) **1** преседне ми I've eaten my fill **2** ми преседна во грлото it stuck in my throat; ❏ ќе ти преседне! you'll pay dearly for it!

преседнува *impf of* преседне

преседува *impf of* преседи

пресее *pf* пресеа *aor.* **1** to sift (*also fig.*); to select, sort out **2** *rare* to sow again, resow **3** *rare* to sift again, resift

пресек -ци *m* cut; section; точка на пресек point of section; попречен (напречен) пресек cross-section; пресек на една епоха end of an era; *arch.* на пресек (payment) at a flat rate

пресека *f Geog.* <mountain> pass; saddle, col

пресекне *pf* пресекна *aor.* to dry up *intrans.*, run dry (*also fig.*); пресекнаа изворите на инспирација the sources of inspiration dried up

пресекнува *impf of* пресекне

пресекува (се) *impf of* пресече (се)

преселба *f* moving house, relocation; migration; *Hist.* големата преселба на народите the great migration of peoples

преселен -лна *adj* migratory; преселна птица migratory bird, bird of passage

преселеник -ци *m* immigrant; migrant

преселеница *f* (*fem. form*) *see* преселеник

преселенички *adj* immigrant's, migrant's

пресели *pf* **I** to help (*s.o.*) move; to resettle, rehouse **II** – **се 1** to move house **2** to emigrate; ❑ се пресели во вечноста to depart this life

преселник -ци *m see* преселеник

преселница *f see* преселеница

преселнички *adj see* преселенички

преселува (се) *impf of* пресели (се)

пресен -сна *adj* fresh; new; пресна вода fresh water; пресен (свеж) воздух fresh air; пресно млеко fresh (unfermented) milk; со пресни (свежи) сили with renewed vigour

пресени се *pf see* присени се

пресенува се *impf see* присенува се

пресече *pf* пресеков *1st p. sg aor.* **I 1** to cut, cut up, slice, cut in two, bisect; to cut off (*also fig.*); пресече леб to slice bread; си го пресече прстот to cut one's finger; пресече некому отстапница to cut off s.o.'s retreat **2** to cross, cut across; пресече улица to cross a street **3** *fig.* to cut short, put an end to; to interrupt, silence (*s.o.*) **4** to take a short cut **5** (*вино*) to cause to stop fermenting **6** (*млеко*) to curdle *trans.* **7** *arch.* (*пари*) to mint **8** *f.p.* to kill; to cut down **II – се 1** to cross, intersect *intrans.* **2** to cut o.s. **3** to give way; ми се пресекоа нозете my legs gave way under me

пресечен -чна *adj* intersecting

пресечува (се) *impf see* пресекува (се)

пресија *f literary* pressure; се наоѓа под пресија to be under pressure

пресил *m* excessive strain, exertion

пресилен *pt literary* **1** forced, strained; пресилена насмевка forced smile **2** exaggerated, excessive; пресилена оцена <excessively> high estimate

пресили *pf* **I** to overstrain; to overwork *trans.*; пресили коњ to overwork a horse **II – се** to overstrain o.s., overwork *intrans.*

пресилува (се) *impf of* пресили (се)

пресипе *pf* пресипа *aor.* to pour, decant (*from one vessel to another*)

пресипка *f* (*dairy product resembling*) sweetened yog<h>urt

пресипнат *pt see* засипнат

пресипнатост *f see* засипнатост

пресипне *pf* пресипна *aor. see* засипне

пресипнува *impf of* пресипне

пресипува *impf of* пресипе

пресири *pf* **I** to cause to vomit, make sick (*usu. a baby*) **II – се** (*за бебе*) to bring up suckled milk

пресирува (се) *impf of* пресири (се)

пресита *f* satiety

преситен[1] *pt* sated, replete; *Chem.* преситен раствор supersaturated solution

преситен[2] -тна *adj literary, rare* very fine, minute; преситен песок very fine sand

пресити *pf* to satiate, sate; *Chem.* to supersaturate

преситува (се) *impf of* преситен (се)

прескака (се) *impf dial. see* прескока (се)

прескакулица *f* leap-frog

прескок -ци *m* leap, jump, vault; ❑ на прескок (прегледа, прочита) cursorily (*to glance through, skim*)

прескока (се) *impf of* прескокне (се)

прескокне *pf* прескокна *aor.* **I 1** to jump; to jump over, leap across; прескокне <преку> ѕид to jump over a wall; прескокнав преку ендек I jumped over a ditch **2** to omit, leave out, miss out, skip; прескокне страница to skip a page; прескокне предавање to miss (skip) a lecture **3** (*посети*) to drop in, call in; прескокнете докај нас come and see us **II – се** to jump over one another

прескокнува (се) *impf of* прескокне (се)

прескочи (се) *pf dial. see* прескокне (се)

прескочува (се) *impf of* прескочи (се)

преслага[1] *impf of* преслoжи

преслага[2] *pf dial.* to reckon up, tot up

преслади *pf* to oversweeten

прескладок -тка *adj* too sweet; very sweet (*also fig.*); very nice, delightful

пресладува *impf of* преслади

преслап *m & f Geog.* pass, saddle, col

преследува *impf literary, rare* **1** to pursue; to persecute **2** *fig.* to strive after, aim for, pursue; преследува цел to pursue a goal

преслека *f* change of clothes/linen

преслекува (се) *impf of* преслече (се)

преслече *pf* преслеков *1st p. sg aor.* **I** to change (*s.o.'s clothes*) *trans.*; to change bedding/covers; преслече дете to change a child's clothes; преслече постела to change sheets **II – се** to change <one's clothes> *intrans.*

преслечува (се) *impf see* преслекува (се)

преслика *pf* **I** to copy (*a picture*); to rephotograph **II – се** to be photographed again

пресликува (се) *impf of* преслика (се)

преслица *f Bot.* (Equisetum arvense) horse-tail

пресло *n dial. see* преѓа

преслoжи *pf* **1** to rearrange; to re-stack; to lay out, arrange differently **2** *Print.* преслoжи текст to recompose a text

преслoжува *impf see* преслага[1]

преслoп *m & f Geog. see* преслап

преслуша *pf* **I** to question, quiz; to examine; to interrogate **II – се** to test o.s. (*on homework, etc.*)

преслушува (се) *impf of* преслуша (се)

пресмета *pf* **I 1** to calculate *trans.*, reckon up, estimate, work out; пресмета раздалечина to calculate a distance **2** to balance, settle *trans.* **3** to include, allow for, take into account **4** to recalculate **II** – **се** to fight, clash; to settle a score

пресметка *f* settlement; squaring of accounts; направи пресметка to settle accounts

пресметлив *adj* **1** calculable **2** responsible, accountable

пресметливост *f* accountability, responsibility

пресметне (се) *pf* пресметна (се) *aor. see* пресмета (се)

пресметува (се) & **пресметнува (се)** *impf of* пресмета (се) & пресметне (се)

преснег -зи *m see* преснец

преснец *m* kind of *pita*; од просо преснец не се прави *prov.* you can't make a silk purse out of a sow's ear

пресник -ци *m see* преснец

пресними *pf* to rephotograph, film again, refilm; to re-record

преснимува *impf of* пресними

преснина & **преснота** *f* freshness

пресоздава *impf of* пресоздаде

пресоздаде *pf literary* to create anew, re-create

пресол *m* brine, pickle

пресоли *pf* **1** to oversalt **2** *fig., colloq.* to go too far, overstep the mark

пресолува *impf of* пресоли

преспа *f* snowdrift

Преспа *f* Prespa; Lake Prespa

Преспанец -нци *m* person from <Lake> Prespa

Преспанка *f* (*fem. form*) *see* Преспанец

преспански *adj* Prespa *attrib.*; Преспанско Езеро Lake Prespa

преспива *impf of* преспие

преспие *pf* преспа *aor.* **1** to sleep through; to hibernate; преспие ручек to miss lunch (*by failing to wake*); преспие зима to sleep through the winter **2** to have a rest, have a nap; преспие еден сон to take a nap; така ја преспаа ноќта thus they passed the night; преспа и замина he had a rest and left **3** to spend the night; преспавме во село we spent the night in a village

пресрами *pf* **I** to embolden, give courage to **II** – **се** to overcome shyness/shame

пресрамува (се) *impf of* пресрами (се)

пресрет *m* meeting, encounter; ❑ во пресрет на (*Први мај*) to celebrate (*the 1st of May*); излезе некому во пресрет to oblige s.o., meet s.o.'s wishes

пресрета *f see* пресрет

пресрете *pf* пресрете & пресрети *aor. see* пресретне

пресретлив *adj* obliging, helpful

пресретливост *f* helpfulness; hospitality

пресретне *pf* пресретна *aor.* to meet, encounter, face; to intercept

пресретнува, пресретува & **пресреќава** *impf* **I** *of* пресретне & пресрете **II** – **се** *rare* to meet, coincide; нашите интереси се пресретнуваат our interests coincide

пресреќа *f dial. see* пресрет

престави се *pf* **1** *arch.* to pass away, depart this life **2** *dial.* to present o.s., appear

преставува се *impf of* престави се **2**

престан *m* stop, end; pause; без престан without a pause, break; continually

престане¹ *pf* престана *aor.* **1** to stop, cease; престане да свири to stop playing; дождот престана it has stopped raining **2** *dial., f.p.* (*пресуши*) to dry up; to run dry

престане² *pf* престана *aor. see* преостане

престанува¹ *impf of* престане¹

престанува² *impf of* престане²

престап *m* **1** crime, felony, offence; стори престап to commit an offence **2** *rare* crossing; exceeding

престапалка *f* & **престапалник** -ци *m* kind of *pita* (*customarily made when a child begins to walk; custom of making this*)

престапен -пна *adj* **1** criminal, felonious; престапна дејност criminal activity; престапни елементи criminal elements **2** leap<-year> *attrib.*; престапна година leap year

престапи *pf* **1** to step across (over); престапи праг to cross the threshold **2** to set foot **3** (*прекрши*) to break, violate (*a law*); to disobey (*an order*); престапи правила to break the rules **4** *rare* to deviate (*од* – *from*)

престапник -ци *m* criminal, felon, offender; малолетен престапник juvenile delinquent

престапница *f* (*fem. form*) *see* престапник

престапнички *adj* criminal; of an offender

престапува *impf of* престапи

престарава се *impf literary, rare* to try too hard

престарее *pf* престареа *aor. see* престари

престарен *pt* aged, ancient; too old

престареност *f* old age

престари *pf* to grow old

престарува *impf of* престарее & престари

престаса *pf colloq.* **1** to overtake; to outrun; to surpass **2** (*за тесто*) to rise too much; (*за овошје и сл.*) to over-ripen, pass its best **3** to manage, succeed **4** (*преостане*) to be left over, remain

престасува *impf* **I** *of* престаса **II** – **се** to overtake/surpass one another

престега (се) *impf of* престегне (се)

престегне *pf* престегна *aor.* **I** to draw tight, pull in (*belt*) **II** – **се** to tighten one's belt

престегнува (се) *impf see* престега (се)

престига *impf of* престигне; како престигаш? how are you managing?

престигне *pf* престигна *aor.* **1** to overtake; to outrun; to surpass **2** *colloq. see* престаса **3** to be left over, remain **4** *f.p.* to reach, arrive at; престигне Струга to reach Struga

престигнува *impf see* престига

престиж *m* prestige

престо *adv Mus.* presto

престои *pf* престоја *aor.* **1** to stand for a while; престои еден саат to stand for an hour **2** to stand through (*for the duration of*); целата литургија ја престојале they stood throughout the whole service **3** to stay, remain; to sojourn

престој -ои *m* stay, sojourn; научен престој study leave

престојува *impf of* престои; to stay, sojourn, live temporarily

престол *m* **1** throne; стапи на престолот to ascend the throne; наследник на престолот heir to the throne **2** *Rel.* светиот престол Communion table

престолен -лна *adj* <of a> throne; престолна беседа speech from the throne; престолен град capital <city>

престолнина *f* capital <city>

престолонаследник -ци *m* heir to the throne

престолонаследнички *adj* of the heir to the throne

престорен *pt* pretended, feigned, insincere, false; престорена љубов feigned love

престореност *f* pretence, insincerity, hypocrisy

престори *pf* I 1 to transform, change *trans.* 2 *rare* (*препознае се*) to mistake (*s.o. for s.o. else*); те престорив сестра ти I took you for your sister II – се 1 to change <o.s.> (*во – into*) *intrans.* 2 to disguise o.s. 3 *rare* to pretend; се престори болен to feign sickness

престорува (се) *impf of* престори (се)

престраши *pf* I 1 to free (*s.o.*) from fear (fright) 2 to horrify II – се to cease being afraid; to overcome one's fear

престрашува (се) *impf of* престраши (се)

престрели *pf f.p.* (*устрели*) to shoot <dead>

престрелка *f literary* exchange of fire; skirmish

престриг *m* renewed sheep shearing

престриже *pf* престрижа *aor.* 1 to shear again 2 *rare* to cut, trim s.o.'s hair again

престрижува *impf of* престриже

престрои *pf Mil.* I to form up again *trans.*; to rearrange, re-form II – се to form up again, re-form *intrans.*

престројник -ци *m* member of bridegroom's family (*serving at wedding*)

престројува (се) *impf of* престрои (се)

преступи *pf see* престапи 3

преступува *impf of* преступи

пресува *impf* to press, compress, squeeze

пресуда *f* judgement, verdict; sentence; opinion; смртна пресуда death sentence; ослободувачка пресуда acquittal

пресуден -дна *adj literary* decisive, crucial; пресуден момент crucial moment

пресуди *pf* 1 to judge, pass judgement on 2 to condemn; пресуди на смрт to condemn to death

пресудно *adv literary* decisively

пресудува *impf of* пресуди

пресука & **пресуче** *pf* to twist/spin again *trans.*

пресуши *pf* I 1 to run dry, dry up (*also fig.*) *intrans.*; to come to an end, be exhausted; пресушила реката the river has run dry; пресушија изворите на приходи the sources of revenue have come to an end 2 to dry more than necessary, overdry *trans.* II – се 1 *see* I 1 2 to dry more than necessary *intrans.*

пресушлив *adj* exhaustible, finite; subject to drought

пресушува (се) *impf of* пресуши (се)

прета *impf* 1 to stir *trans.*; to scrape, to scratch about, rummage; прета пепел to rake the ashes 2 to struggle, lash out 3 *fig.* to complain; ❏ не туку претај! don't make such a fuss! 4 *fig.*, *colloq.* to stir *intrans.*, give signs of life; уште прета he's still alive

претарашува *pf* & *impf* to search *trans. and intrans.*; to rummage; претарашува по таванот to rummage in the attic; си ги претарашува џебовите to turn one's pockets out

претвора (се) *impf of* претвори (се)

претворач *m* converter, transformer

претвори *pf* I to convert, transform, change *trans.* II – се to change, turn (*во – into*) *intrans.*

претворлив *adj* transformable, convertible

претворливост *f* transformability, convertibility

претег *m literary* preponderance, ascendancy

претега *impf of* претегне

претегне *pf* претегна *aor.* 1 to draw tight 2 *f.p.* to pull off, take off 3 to win, prevail 4 to lean, tend, incline; кај претегнаа неговите симпатии? where did his sympathies lie?

претегнува *impf see* претега

претежен -жна *adj literary* prevalent, predominant; preponderant; претежно влијание predominant influence

претежност *f literary, rare* predominance, prevalence

претек *m usu. in the expression:* на претек in competition

претекст *m rare* pretext, excuse; под претекст на . . . under (on) the pretext of . . .

претекува[1] *impf of* претече[1]

претекува[2] **(се)** *impf of* претече[2] (се)

претендéнт *m* claimant; pretender; претендент за (на) престолот pretender to the throne

претендúра *impf* to lay claim (*на/за – to*); to aspire (*to*); претендира на место to aspire to a position

претензија -ии *f* demand; claim

претенција -ии *f see* претензија

претенциóзен -зна *adj* 1 exacting, demanding 2 pretentious

претепа *pf* I to thrash, beat, beat up; to trounce II – се *fig.* to work o.s. to exhaustion

претепува (се) *impf of* претепа (се)

претера *pf* I 1 to go too far, exaggerate; to overdo; to overstate 2 to drive (*cattle*) from one place to another 3 *rare* to pass (put) (*s.th.*) through; ги претерав алиштата низ две води I washed the clothes twice 4 *dial.* to spend (*time*); претера лето to spend the summer 5 *dial.* to get on; to enjoy o.s.; како претеравте на свадба? how did you get on at the wedding? 6 *dial.* to suffer, experience, endure; претера многу болести to suffer many illnesses II – се to rush past

претеран *pt* exaggerated, overdone; excessive; претерана работа overwork

претераност *f* excess

претерува (се) *impf of* претера (се); претерува во пиење to drink to excess; се претеруваат волци по планињето wolves roam the mountains

претеча *m literary, arch. see* преттеча

претече[1] *pf* (*only in 3rd p.*) 1 to stop flowing; to run out 2 to overflow 3 *dial.* to flow past, through

претече[2] *pf* претеков *1st p. sg aor.* I to outrun, outstrip, overtake II – се *dial. see* притече се

претечува[1] *impf see* претекува[1]

претечува[2] **(се)** *impf see* претекува[2] (се)

преткаже *pf* преткажа *aor.* I to foretell, predict; ми ја преткажа иднината he foretold my future II – се *impers.* (*with dat.*) to have a presentiment, premonition; му се преткажало дека ќе умре he had a premonition of his death

преткажува (се) *impf of* преткаже (се)

преткажувач *m* prophet; soothsayer

преткомора *f Anat.* atrium; срцева преткомора cardiac atrium

претне *pf* претна *aor. dim. of* прета; to stir slightly *trans. and intrans.* ❑ и не претна he didn't even budge

претнува *impf of* претне

претовар *m* trans-shipment, transfer; handling

претовара (се) *impf of* претовари (се)

претоварен[1] *pt* overloaded, overburdened (*also fig.*)

претоварен[2] -рна *adj* <of> trans-shipment; пре-товарна станица handling facility

претовари *pf* **I 1** to overload, overburden (*also fig.*); претовари некого со одговорности to overburden s.o. with responsibilities **2** to trans-ship, shift **3** to reload, load again **4** *colloq., dial.* (*за коњ*) to throw off, lose the load; коњот паднал и претоварил the horse fell and lost its load **II – се 1** *fig.* to overload (overburden) o.s. **2** *colloq., dial. see* I 4

претоварува (се) *impf see* претовара (се)

претопи *pf* **I 1** to melt down/render <again>; (*руда*) to re-smelt **2** *fig.* to absorb, assimilate **II – се** *fig.* to change one's nationality, be assimilated; се претопи во Француз to become a Frenchman

претопува (се) *impf of* претопи (се)

претор *m Hist.* praetor

преторијанец -нци *m Hist.* praetorian

преторијански *adj Hist.* praetorian; преторијанска гарда praetorian guard

преторски *adj Hist.* praetor's, praetorian

преточи[1] *pf* **1** to pour off *trans.*; to decant **2** *fig.* to recast, refashion, remould; to translate

преточи[2] *pf* to sharpen excessively, oversharpen

преточува[1] *impf of* преточи[1]

преточува[2] *impf of* преточи[2]

претпазен -зна *adj* protective; preventive, precaution-ary; defensive; претпазни мерки preventive/protective measures

претпази *pf* to protect, preserve; претпази од болест to protect from illness

претпазлив *adj* **1** careful, cautious, prudent **2** pre-cautionary; warning; претпазлива постапка precau-tionary measure; претпазлив глас a warning voice

претпазливост *f* care, caution, prudence

претпазува *impf of* претпази

претпладне *n* morning; (*as adv*) in the morning, before lunch

претпладневен -вна *adj* morning; претпладневна настава morning classes

претплата *f* subscription; претплата на весник sub-scription to a newspaper

претплатен -тна *adj* <of a> subscription; претплатна цена subscription charge

претплати *pf* **I** to subscribe, pay (*s.o.'s*) subscription; ќе те претплатам на весникот I shall pay your sub-scription to the newspaper **II – се** to subscribe, pay one's subscription; се претплати на "Нова Македонија" to subscribe to "Nova Makedonija"

претплатник -ци *m* subscriber

претплатува (се) & претплаќа (се) *impf of* претплати (се)

претполага *impf of* претположи

претположи *pf* to suppose, assume; да претположиме дека си прав let us suppose that you are right

претпоследен -дна *adj* penultimate, last but one, sec-ond to last

претпоставен *pt* **1** senior, superior; претпоставена власт higher authority **2** (*as noun*) претпоставен<иот> officer-in-charge, superintendent; претпоставени superiors

претпостави *pf* **1** to put in charge **2** to suppose, assume; да претпоставиме дека е така let us assume that it is so **3** *rare* to give precedence (preference) to

претпоставка *f* **1** supposition, assumption, con-jecture; hypothesis **2** *rare* precondition

претпоставува *impf of* претпостави

претпотопен -пна **& претпотопски** *adj* antediluvian (*also fig.*); antiquated, outdated

претпочита & rarely претпочитува *impf* to prefer

претприемач *m* entrepreneur; contractor

претприемачки *adj* entrepreneurial; contractual

претприеме *pf literary, rare* to undertake; пре-тприеме мерки, чекори to take measures, steps

претприемчив *adj literary* enterprising

претприемчивост *f literary* enterprise; drive

претпријатие -ија *n* **1** enterprise, firm, business; индустриско претпријатие industrial enterprise **2** *rare, arch.* (*потфат*) project, undertaking

претрга *pf* to suffer, bear, endure *trans.*; претрга маки to suffer torments

претрес *m* **1** search, raid **2** inquiry, investigation; dis-cussion; судски претрес trial

претресе *pf* **1** to ransack; to search; го претресоа таванот they searched the attic **2** to discuss, debate; to examine; претресе прашање to debate an issue **3** to shake out; претресе постела to shake bedding **4** *impers.* (*with acc.*) to stop shaking *trans.*; го претресе his fever passed

претресува *impf of* претресе

претрива (се) *impf of* претрие (се)

претрие *pf* претри *aor.* **1** to saw/file through **2** (*за јаже и сл.*) (*with dat.*) to burn; јажето му ја претрило раката the rope burned his arm

претрпи *pf* **1** to suffer, endure; to hold out <to the end>; претрпи маки to suffer torments **2** to experi-ence, undergo, be subjected to; претрпи влијание to be subject<ed> to an influence; претрпи измени to undergo changes; претрпи неуспех to suffer failure

претрпне *pf* претрпна *aor.* **1** (*за болка*) to stop hurt-ing **2** *fig.* to lose sensitivity; to grow dull; to flag (*of feelings, enthusiasm*)

претрпнува *impf of* претрпне

претрпува *impf of* претрпи

претрупа *pf* **I** to overload (*also fig.*) **II – се** *fig.* (*со работа*) to overload o.s. (*with*); to take on too much

претрупан *pt* overloaded; претрупан со работа over-loaded (swamped) with work

претрупи *pf* to chop <up>

претрупува (се) *impf of* претрупа (се)

претрча *pf* to run (*a certain distance*); to run (*to a certain point*); претрча сто метра за дванаесет секунди he ran 100 metres in 12 seconds

претрчува *impf of* претрча

претседава *impf* to chair, preside; претседава на седница to preside at (over) a session

претседавач *m* chairman, presiding officer

претседател *m* chairman; president; претседател на одборот chairman of the committee; Претседа-телот на Републиката President of the Republic; Претседател на владата Prime Minister, Premier

претседателка   *f* (*fem. form*) *see* претседател
претседателски   *adj* presidential; chairman's; претседателски избори presidential elections
претседателство   *n* presidency; chairmanship
претседателствува   *impf* to preside, act as chairman/ president
претскаже   *pf* претскажа *aor.* to foretell, forecast, predict
претскажува   *impf of* претскаже
претскажувач   *m* prophet; soothsayer
претсметка   *f* provisional estimate
претсметковен   -вна *adj* <of an> estimate; projected
претсмртен   -тна *adj* occurring immediately before death; last; dying; претсмртен час last hour; претсмртни маки death agony; претсмртни грчови death throes
претсобје   *n* entrance-hall, lobby, ante-room
претсрете & претсретне   *pf* претсрете & претсретна *aor. see* пресретне
претсретнува, претсретува & претсрекава   *impf of* претсрете & претсретне
претстава   *f* **1** show, performance; театарска претстава theatrical (stage) performance **2** idea, concept, notion
претстави   *pf* **I 1** to introduce; им го претстави гостинот на присутните he introduced the guest to those present **2** to represent; претстави своја земја to represent one's country **3** to present; поинаку ги претстави работите to present matters differently **4** *rare* to perform; претстави пиеса to perform a play **5** си претстави to imagine; to envisage; вие не можете тоа да си го претставите you can't imagine it! **6** to produce, show; претстави свој пасош to show one's passport **II – се 1** to introduce o.s.; чест ми е да ви се претставам I have the honour of introducing myself **2** to pretend to be; се претстави како богат човек he pretended to be rich **3** *rare* (*престави се*) to die, pass away **4** to appear, present o.s.
претставка   *f* **1** written submission **2** *Gram.* prefix
претставник   -ци *m* **1** representative, spokesman; дипломатски претставник diplomatic representative **2** biological specimen
претставница & претставничка   *f* (*fem. form*) *see* претставник
претставнички   *adj* representative
претставништво   *n* **1** representation; agency, office, branch; дипломатско претставништво diplomatic mission, embassy **2** assembly; народно претставништво national representatives
претставува (се)   *impf of* претстави (се)
претстоен   -јна *adj* imminent; impending, approaching, forthcoming
претстои   *impf* to lie ahead; (*with dat.*) to be in store (*for*); ни претстои тешка борба we have a hard struggle ahead
претстража   *f* advance guard, vanguard (*also fig.*)
преттеча   *m literary, arch.* precursor, forerunner
претури (се)   *impf of* претури (се)
претури   *pf* **I 1** to decant **2** to fill to the brim (to overflowing) **3** to produce an abundant harvest; сливите туриле и претуриле the plum trees have produced an abundant crop **4** *dial.* (*преврти*) to overturn *trans.* (*a cart, car*) **II – се** *dial.* to overturn *intrans.*; колата се претури the car/cart overturned

претходен   -дна *adj* preceding; preliminary; претходни разговори preliminary talks
претходи   *impf* (*with dat.*) to precede
претходник   -ци *m* predecessor; precursor
претходница   *f* **1** (*fem. form*) *see* претходник **2** *Mil.* (*претстража*) advance guard
претходно   *adv* previously, earlier; first of all
претхристијански   *adj* pre-Christian
претчувство   *n* presentiment; foreboding
претчувствува   *impf* to have a presentiment (foreboding) of; to sense (*in advance*)
преувеличен   *pt* exaggerated; overstated
преувеличи   *pf* to exaggerate, overstate; преувеличи значење на нешто to exaggerate s.th.'s importance
преувеличува   *impf of* преувеличи
преуми (се)   *pf see* премисли (се)
преумора   *f* exhaustion
преуморен   *pt* exhausted
преувмореност   *f* exhaustion
преумори   *pf* **I** to wear out, tire out, exhaust **II – се** to exhaust o.s., wear o.s. out
преуморува (се)   *impf of* преумори (се)
преумува (се)   *impf of* преуми (се)
преуреди   *pf* to rearrange, reorganize; to remodel, restructure; преуреди соба to redecorate a room
преуредува   *impf of* преуреди
преустрои   *pf* to reorganize
преустројство   *n* reorganization; reform
преустројува   *impf of* преустрои
префазонира   *pf & impf* to restyle
префали   *pf* to praise excessively, overpraise
префалува   *impf of* префали
префати   *pf* **1** to put one's arms round, embrace **2** to retain, keep back (*money; part of debt*) **3** (*за болест*) to infect; to catch **4** *in the expression*: чини фати префати to fidget, fiddle
префатлив   *adj* contagious; infectious; префатлива болест contagious disease
префака   *impf of* префати
префект   *m* prefect
префектура   *f* prefecture
преферанс   *m Cards* preference, Swedish whist
префикс   *m Gram.* prefix
префиксиран   *adj Gram.* prefixed
префинет   *pt & adj* **1** refined, polished; префинет вкус sophisticated taste **2** *rare see* препреден
префинетост   *f* refinement
префини   *pf* to refine
преформулира   *pf* to formulate differently, reformulate, re-word, re-phrase
префрла (се)   *impf of* префрли (се)
префрлачка   *f dial.* shawl
префрли   *pf* **I 1** to throw across (over); префрли нога преку (врз) нога to cross one's legs; ❑ префрли некого преку девет планини to pull the wool over s.o.'s eyes **2** to throw again **3** to outdo in throwing, throw further than **4** *fig.* to transfer *trans.*; to shift *trans.*; префрли пари во странство to transfer money abroad; ја префрлил куќата на жена си he made over the house to his wife; префрли вина/ одговорност на некого to shift the blame/ responsibility onto s.o. **5** to reproach, admonish, rebuke **6** to cross; to pass (*a limit*); префрли граница to cross a border; ја префрли триесеттата to pass

the age of thirty **7** *rare, dial.* to cover (*a distance*); префрли десет километри to travel ten kilometres **II – ce 1** to cross (*преку – over*); се префрли преку река to cross a river **2** to move *intrans.*; се префрли од едно место на друго to move from one place to another

префтаса *pf colloq. see* превтаса, престаса

префтасува (се) *impf colloq. see* превтасува (се), престасува (се)

прехрана *f* fare, board; nourishment, subsistence

прехранбен *adj* alimentary

прехрани *pf* **I 1** to feed; to provide for, maintain, keep **2** to overfeed; си го прехранила детето, затоа повраќа you've overfed the child, that's why it is vomiting **II – ce** to maintain o.s.; to feed o.s.; to subsist

прехранува (се) *impf of* прехрани (се)

прецапа *pf* to wade through (*mud, water*)

прецвета *pf* **1** to fade, wither; трендафилите процветаа the roses have faded **2** to cease to flower

прецветува *impf of* прецвета

прецедéнт *m literary rare see* преседан

прецеди *pf* to filter, strain; to strain again; ❑ прецеди низ заби to speak through clenched teeth; првин прецеди го зборот weigh your words carefully

прецедува *impf of* прецеди

прецени *pf* **1** *see* оцени **2** *see* натцени

преценка *f see* оцена

преценува *impf of* прецени

прецизен -зна *adj* precise, exact; прецизна механика precision mechanics; прецизни одредби precise (strict) regulations

precизи́ра *pf & impf* to state precisely, specify

прецизност *f* precision, accuracy; со прецизност на часовник with clockwork regularity

прецрта *pf* **1** to redraw; to copy; to trace over **2** to cross out, delete **3** to criss-cross

прецртува *impf of* прецрта

прецути *pf see* прецвета

прецутува *impf of* прецути

пречек -ци *m* welcome, reception; му излегоа на пречек they came out to greet him

пречека *pf* **1** to welcome, receive, greet **2** to lie in wait for; to ambush

пречеклив *adj* hospitable, welcoming

пречекливост *f* hospitality

пречекори *pf* **1** to take a step; пречекори понапред to step forward **2** to cross, step over; пречекори праг to cross the threshold **3** *fig.* to exceed; to violate; to overstep; ги пречекори своите права to exceed one's rights

пречекорува *impf of* пречекори

пречекува *impf of* пречека

пречи *impf* (*with dat.*) to prevent, hinder; си пречат they get in each other's way

пречисти *pf* **I** to cleanse, purify, refine; to purge; ❑ си ги пречистиле сметките they settled accounts **II – ce** to relieve o.s.

пречистува (се) *impf of* пречисти (се)

пречита *pf* to read again, reread

пречитува *impf of* пречита

пречка[1] *f* obstacle, hindrance; прави пречки некому to place obstacles in s.o.'s way

пречка[2] *f* cross beam; crossbar; rung; rail

пречка[3] *f rare* squabble

пречка се *impf* to squabble, bicker, quarrel

пречканица *f see* пречка[3]

пречкрта *pf see* прецрта 2

пречкртува *impf of* пречкрта

пречник -ци *m* **1** diameter **2** crosspiece, cross-member (*linking runners of a sled*)

пречувствителен -лна *adj literary* over-sensitive, hypersensitive; touchy

пречувствителност *f literary* hypersensitivity, touchiness

пречуе *pf* пречу *aor.* **I** to fail to hear; to mis-hear **II – ce** *dial., f.p.* (*прочуе се*) to become famous (*со/за – for*)

пречука *pf* **1** to knock in again (*a nail, etc.*) **2** *colloq.* to retype; пречука страница to retype a page **3** to beat up

пречукува *impf of* пречука

прешива *impf of* прешие

прешие *pf* преши *aor.* to sew again, resew

прешлен *m* **1** *Anat.* vertebra **2** weight on a spindle **3** *Bot.* node

прешленест *adj* vertebrate

прешленски *adj* vertebral

прешленце & прешленче *n dim. of* прешлен

пржа *f dial.* fried chitterlings

пржајка *f* **1** *see* полжав 1 **2** shell

пржал, пржел *m & пржелика* *f* dry, sandy soil

пржалка *f* frying-pan

пржалница *f* **1** *see* пржалка **2** *fig.* smoky hovel

пржен *pt* fried

прженица *f* fried meat

прженко *adj hyp. dim. of* пржен; прженки лепчиња pieces of fried bread/French toast

пржи *impf* **I** to fry **II – ce** *colloq. fig.* to toil

пржол *m see* пржал, пржел & пржелика

прзгал *f* barren land on a hillside

при- *verbal prefix indicating* **1** *movement towards, attachment to;* пристапи to approach; пришие to sew on; приврзе to tie to **2** *addition;* придаде to add, give extra **3** *limited extent; limited time;* придигне to lift a little; причека to wait for a while

при *prep* **1** at; near, by; при вратата by the door **2** attached to; with; in possession of; институт при министерство institute attached to a ministry; при пари in funds; having money; ❑ си останувам при (на) своето мислење I haven't changed my mind/opinion **3** at; during, at the time of; given; with; при заоѓањето на сонцето at sunset; при видело during daylight, with open windows; при (под) оние услови given (in) those conditions **4** (*in time expressions*) towards; при вечер (привечер, приквечер) towards evening; при крајот на векот towards the end of the century **5** beside, despite; при тоа beside that, besides; при сето тоа for all that; при тоа at the same time; despite this; при сè што although; despite the fact that; при сè што беше болен although he was ill **6** beside, compared to (with) **7** *literary, rare* during the reign of, in the time of, under; при Наполеон during Napoleon's reign **8** *literary* with, to the accompaniment of; резолуцијата се прими при френетичен аплауз the resolution was carried with stormy applause **9** *rare* at/to the home of; при татка си at/to one's father's house

прибавен -вна *adj rare* surplus; прибавна вредност surplus value

прибави *pf* **1** to acquire, obtain, procure **2** *rare* (*додаде*) to add **3** provide, supply; прибави храна to provide food

прибавка *f rare* (*додаток*) addition, supplement; increase

прибавува *impf of* прибави

прибегне *pf* прибегна *aor.* to resort (*кон – то*); прибегне кон други средства to resort to other means

прибегнува *impf of* прибегне

прибежиште *n* refuge, shelter, asylum

прибележи *pf* to note <down>, make a note of

прибележува *impf of* прибележи

прибелешка *f rare* note

прибере *pf* прибра *aor.* **I 1** to collect, pick up, gather up *trans.*; to take in; to harvest; to receive; прибере документација to collect documentation; прибере мисли to collect one's thoughts; ❑ Бог си го прибра he was called to his maker **2** to put away; tidy up, arrange; прибере коси to tidy one's hair **3** to tuck (pull) in (*arms, legs*); прибере нозе to tuck one's feet under one **4** *f.p.* to start, begin; прибере да чита to start reading **II – ce 1** to find lodgings, somewhere to stay **2** (*дома*) to return home, go home; ce прибере во своја соба to withdraw (retire) to one's room **3** to pull in one's arms and legs **4** *fig.* to come to one's senses; to settle down **5** to congregate, assemble, gather *intrans.* **6** *f.p., dial.* to approach, draw close (*до – то*) **7** *rare, literary* to compose o.s.; to recover *intrans.*; ce прибере од возбуда to get over the excitement

прибира (ce) *impf of* прибере (ce)

прибирач *m* collector, gatherer

приближен[1] *pt* (*usu. pl as noun* приближени) entourage

приближен[2] -жна *adj* approximate; приближни резултати approximate results; приближна вредност approximate value

приближи *pf* приближив & приближав *1st p. sg aor.* **I 1** to bring nearer (*до – то*); го приближи лицето до прозорецот she brought her face closer to the window **2** (*до, крај*) to approach, draw near; приближи до село to approach a village **II – ce** *see* I 2

приближно *adv* roughly, approximately, about

приближува (ce) *impf of* приближи (ce)

приблуе ce *pf* приблу ce *aor. impers.* (*with dat.*) to feel sick (nauseous); ми ce приблу I felt sick

прибор *m* set, equipment, gear, kit; utensils; прибор за бричење shaving kit; прибор за јадење cover (plates and cutlery)

прибран *pt* **1** neat, tidy; прибрана коса well-groomed hair **2** *fig.* composed, collected, calm

прибрат -аќа *m* half-brother

прибрежен -жна *adj* (*крајбрежен*) coastal, littoral; прибрежен појас coastal belt (zone)

прибрежје *n rare* (*крајбрежје*) coast, coastal region, littoral

прибрза *pf* **1** to act hastily, rashly **2** to hurry, make <excessive> haste

прибрзан *pt* hasty, rash; premature; прибрзано решение hasty decision

прибрзаност *f* haste, rashness; prematurity

прибрзува *impf of* прибрза

приварди *pf* **I** to look after, take care of for a while; приварди дете to mind a child **II – ce** to be careful; to watch out

привардува (ce) *impf of* приварди (ce)

приватен -тна *adj* private; приватна сопственост private property; приватен сектор private sector

приватник -ци *m* private tradesman, person in private business; self-employed person

приведе *pf* **1** *rare* to bring <in>; приведе кон крај to bring to a close; приведе во дело to bring into play **2** *literary* (*наведе*) to quote, cite; приведе пример to give an example; приведе докази to adduce evidence

приведува *impf of* приведе

привее *pf* привеа *aor.* **1** (*за ветар*) to spring up suddenly **2** (*за снег*) to start falling heavily

привезе *pf* привеза *aor.* to embroider (*a little more*)

привезува *impf of* привезе

привива (ce) *impf of* привие (ce)

привид *m* optical illusion

привиден -дна *adj* apparent, seeming, illusory; привиден мир illusory peace

привидение -ија *n* apparition, spectre, ghost, phantom; hallucination

привиди *pf* **I** *rare* to catch a glimpse of **II – ce** (*with dat.*) to seem; привиди ми ce дека . . . it seems to me that . . . ; тоа им ce привидело they only imagined it

привидно *adv* seemingly, apparently

привидност *f* illusoriness

привидува (ce) *impf of* привиди (ce)

привие *pf rare* приви *aor.* **I** to tie, attach by tying (binding) **II – ce** *fig.* to snuggle up (*кон – то*)

привика *pf* **I** to summon, call *trans.* **II – ce** (*with dat.*) to hail; to call out to

привикне *pf* привикна *aor.* **I** to grow accustomed, get used (*на – то*) **2** to acclimatize, accustom **II – ce** *see* I 1

привикнува (ce) *impf of* привикне (ce)

привикува (ce) *impf of* привика (ce)

привилегија -ии *f* privilege, favour, advantage

привилегира *pf & impf* to grant privileges to, bestow favours upon

привилегиран *pt* privileged; привилегирана положба privileged position

привјавне *pf f.p.* пријавна *aor. see* пријавне

привкус *m* after-taste; flavour (*also fig.*)

привлекува (ce) *impf of* привлече (ce)

привлече *pf* привлеков *1st p. sg aor.* **I** to draw close; to attract; to win over; привлече на своја страна to win over to one's side; привлече интерес to arouse interest, curiosity; привлече внимание to attract attention **II – ce** *rare* to steal up (*кон – то*), sneak up (*то/он*)

привлечен -чна *adj* attractive; *Phys.* привлечна сила attractive force (attraction); привлечно патување interesting journey; привлечна жена attractive woman

привлечност *f* charm, attraction, attractiveness,

привлечува (ce) *impf see* привлекува (ce)

привнесе *pf literary, rare* to add; привнесе нов елемент to introduce a new element

привнесува *impf of* привнесе

привремен *adj* temporary; provisional; привремени правила provisional rules

привременост *f* transience

приврзан *pt* **1** loyal, devoted (*кон – to, or with dat.*); приврзан кон дело devoted to a cause **2** attached, bound, tied; приврзан за постела bedridden

приврзаник -ци *m* advocate, adherent; devotee; admirer

приврзаница *f* (*fem. form*) *see* приврзаник

приврзаност *f* devotion

приврзе *pf* прицрза *aor.* **I** to attach, bind, tie (*also fig.*); приврзе коњ за дрво to tie a horse to a tree **II – се** *fig.* to become attached, devoted; се приврзавме кон (за) него we became attached to him

приврзува (се) *impf of* приврзе (се)

приврши *pf* **I 1** to complete; to finish *trans.*; приврши работа to finish a job **2** to use up, exhaust **3** to end, finish *intrans.*; to run out **II – се** to end, finish *intrans.*; to run out; се приврши работата the job is done

привршува (се) *impf of* приврши (се)

привсени се *pf see* присени се

привсенува се *impf of* привсени се

привтаса *pf colloq. see* пристигне

привтасува *impf of* привтаса

пригласува *impf rare* to accompany <musically> *trans.*

пригласување *n rare* <musical> accompaniment

пригледа & пригледне *pf* пригледа & пригледна *aor.* to look after, take care of, mind

пригледнува & пригледува *impf of* пригледне & пригледа

приглув *adj see* наглув

приглувост *f see* наглувост

приглуп *adj* rather stupid, obtuse

пригмечи *pf* to pin down, press on

пригмечува *impf of* пригмечи

приговара *impf of* приговори

приговор *m* reproach, reprimand; objection; нема приговор there is no objection

приговори *pf* (*with dat.*) to rebuke, reproach; му приговори дека не зборува вистина she reproached him for not telling the truth

приговорка *f* catchword, repeated expression

пригода *f* **1** convenience, comfort; домаќинска куќа со сета пригода a home with all conveniences **2** opportunity, occasion, chance

пригоден -дна *adj literary* appropriate, fitting, suitable

пригоди *pf* **I 1** to arrange, get ready, prepare *trans.* (*за – for*) **2** *rare* to adapt (*кон – to*) *trans.*; пригоди нешто кон нови услови to adapt s.th. to new conditions **II – се 1** to prepare, get ready *intrans.* **2** *rare* to happen to be; to find o.s. (*somewhere*)

пригодија -ии *f see* пригода 1

пригодува (се) *impf of* пригоди (се)

приготви *pf* **I** to prepare *trans.* (*за – for*); приготви пречек за некого to prepare a welcome for s.o. **II – се** to prepare, get ready *intrans.*; се приготви за пат to prepare for a journey

приготвува (се) *impf of* приготви (се)

приграби *pf rare, literary* (*грабне*) to seize; приграби власт to seize power

приграбува *impf of* приграби

пригради *pf* **1** to build on, add (*кон – to*) **2** *rare* to build s.th. small, hastily

приградски *adj* suburban; приградски населби suburbs

приградува *impf of* пригради

пригрева *impf of* пригрее

пригрее *pf* пригреа *aor.* **1** to warm slightly **2** (*за сонце*) to burn; to get hot

пригрми *pf rare see* згрми

пригрмува *impf of* пригрми

пригрне *pf* пригрна *aor.* **1** to embrace, hug **2** *fig.* to embrace, adopt, espouse; пригрне дело to espouse a cause

пригрнува *impf of* пригрне

прид *m* **1** dowry **2** extra gift, bonus

придава *impf of* придаде

придави *pf* to strangle, throttle, choke

придавка *f Gram.* adjective; глаголска придавка past participle passive

придавски *adj Gram.* adjectival

придавува *impf of* придави

придаде *pf* to add; to attach (*кон – to*); to impart, lend; to ascribe; придаде важност на нешто to attach importance to s.th.; ❑ Господ (Бог) да ви придаде! may the Lord be bountiful!

придаток -ци *m literary* supplement; appendage

придвижи *pf literary, rare* **I** to bring closer, nearer **II – се** (*до*) to approach

придвижува (се) *impf of* придвижи (се)

придворен -рна *adj* court; придворен поет court poet; (*as noun*) придворните courtiers

придига (се) *impf of* придигне (се)

придигне (се) *pf rare see* поткрене (се)

придигнува (се) *impf see* придига (се)

придих *m Phon.* aspiration

придоаѓа *impf of* придојде

придобива *impf of* придобие

придобивка *f* advantage; gain; acquisition; *fig.* prize, achievement

придобие *pf* придоби *aor.* **1** to gain, acquire; придобие значење to gain importance; придобие опит to gain experience **2** to win over

придодава *impf of* придодаде

придодаде *pf rare* **1** to add **2** to transfer, secónd

придојде *pf* **1** to come, arrive (*after others*); придојде уште народ more people came **2** (*за вода, порој*) to rise; придојдоа потоците the streams rose

придојдува *impf see* придоаѓа

придонес *m* contribution

придонесе *pf* to contribute

придонесува *impf of* придонесе

придреме *pf* придрема *aor.* **I** to doze off; to take a nap **II – се** *impers.* (*with dat.*) to feel sleepy; to nod off

придремува (се) *impf of* придреме (се)

придржи *pf* придржа *aor.* **I 1** to support, hold up **2** *fig.* to reserve, retain, uphold; си придржи право to reserve a right **II – се** to support o.s., hold o.s. up; (*кон*) to adhere (*кон – to*), abide (*by*)

придржува (се) *impf of* придржи (се)

придружба *f* **1** entourage, retinue, escort, suite, party; претседателот и неговата придружба the president and his party (entourage) **2** accompaniment; со придружба на пијано (клавир) with piano accompaniment

придружен -жна *adj* accompanying, concomitant; придружна појава concomitant phenomenon; придружен ескадрон escort squadron; придружно писмо covering letter

придружи *pf* **I 1** to see off; to accompany, go with; ќе ве придружам до станица I'll see you to the station **2** *rare, Mus.* to accompany **3** (*сврзе, соедини*) to annex; to unite with *trans.*; придружи краиште кон татковината to annex a region to one's country **II** – **се** (*with dat.*) to unite (join) (*со/кон* – *with*) *intrans.*; им се придружив I joined them

придружник -ци *m* companion, escort; satellite

придружница & **придружничка** *f* **1** (*fem. form*) *see* придружник **2** runner-up in a beauty contest

придружнички *adj* accompanying, companion

придружува (се) *impf of* придружи (се); се придружувам кон вашето мислење I share your opinion

придушен -шна *pt* muted, muffled; придушен глас/ шум muffled voice/noise; придушена смеа muffled laughter

придуши *pf* **1** to choke *trans.*, throttle, stifle **2** to mute, muffle; to silence, suppress; придуши вистина to suppress the truth

придушува *impf of* придуши

прием *m* **1** admittance; admission; receipt; прием на молби receipt of applications; прием на болни admission of patients; потврди прием на писмо to acknowledge receipt of a letter **2** reception (*formal gathering*) **3** welcome, reception; срдечен прием warm welcome **4** *Tech.* <radio/television> reception

приемен -мна *adj* reception; admission; *Tech.* приемна антена receiving aerial; приемни испити entrance examinations; (*as noun*) приемна (гостинска) *f* drawing-room

приемлив *adj* acceptable, admissible; приемливо решение acceptable solution; приемливи предлози acceptable proposals

приемливост *f* acceptability

приемник[1] -ци *m Tech.* <radio/television> receiver

приемник[2] -ци *m literary, rare see* преемник

приемница *f literary, rare see* преемница

приемственост *f literary, rare see* преемственост

приемчив *adj* receptive; impressionable

приемчивост *f* receptiveness; impressionability

приет *m arch. usu. in the expression:* на приет! *bon appétit!*

прижежа *pf* прижежа *aor.* (*за сонце*) to burn, bake <slightly>; *impers.* (*with dat.*) ми прижежа I've got a bit hot

прижежува *impf of* прижеже

призавитка *pf* to wrap hastily

призамачка *pf* to smear over; *fig.* to hush up, cover up

призатвори *pf* to close <incompletely/hurriedly>

призвук -ци *m* harmonic; overtone (*also fig.*); призвук на меланхолија overtone of melancholy

приземен -мна *adj* ground-floor; приземна куќа one-storeyed house; приземен стан ground-floor (*Am.* first-floor) flat, apartment

приземје *n* ground floor, *Am.* first floor

приземјен *pt* earthbound

приземји *pf* **I** to land, put down (*an aircraft*) *trans.* **II** – **се** to land *intrans.*, put down

приземјува (се) *impf of* приземји (се)

приземница *f* single-storey house

призети *pf* **I** to accept as one's son-in-law **II** – **се** (*за маж*) to move into the home of one's in-laws

призеток -ци *m see* домазет

призетува (се) *impf of* призети (се)

призма *f* prism; ❏ гледа низ призмата на нешто to view from a certain angle, in a certain light

призматичен *adj* prismatic

признава[1] *impf of* признае

признава[2] *impf dial.* (*разбира*) to be knowledgeable about; таа признава од тие работи she knows a bit about those matters

признае *pf* призна *aor.* **1** to confess, admit *trans.*; признае своја вина to admit one's guilt **2** to recognize, acknowledge; признае вистина to acknowledge the truth; признае нова влада to recognize a new government **3** to be grateful for, express gratitude for

признаен *pt* recognized, acknowledged, respected; признаен експерт acknowledged expert

признак -ци *m rare* (*белег, знак; симптом*) sign, symptom; признаци на живот signs of life; признаците на болест symptoms of a disease

признание -ија *n* **1** admission, confession; признание на вина confession of guilt **2** recognition, acknow-ledgement; признание на нечии заслуги recognition of s.o.'s merits

признаница *f rare* receipt (*for payment*)

признат *pt see* признаен

признателен -лна *adj literary, rare see* благодарен

признателност *f literary, rare see* благодарност

призне *pf dial.* to peep, peer

признува *impf of* призне

призове *pf literary, poet., rare* призва *aor.* to call; to invite

призори *adv* at dawn (daybreak)

призори (се) *pf rare see* обзори (се)

призорува (се) *impf of* призори (се)

призрак -ци *m literary* (*привидение*) ghost, spectre, phantom, spirit, apparition

призрачен -чна *adj literary, rare* illusory, deceptive; ghostly

присида *pf* to build on (*кон* – *to*)

присидува *impf of* присида

присира (се) *impf of* присира (се)

присне *pf dial. see* призне

приснува *impf of* присне

присре *pf* **I** to peep, peer **II** – **се** to dawn, grow light

приспре (се) *pf see* присре (се)

приидува *impf see* придоаѓа; водата уште приидуваше the water was still rising

пријава *f* **1** registration; registration form; application form **2** denunciation **3** declaration, statement

пријавен -вна *adj* <of> registration

пријави *pf* **I** to register for; to report; to declare; пријави испит to register for an examination **2** to denounce, report, inform against; пријави виновник to report a culprit **II** – **се 1** to announce o.s.; to report *intrans.*; се пријави дека дошол he reported that he had arrived **2** to sign up (*за* – *for*); to register, enrol *intrans.*

пријавне *pf f.p.* пријавна *aor.* to mount (*a horse, etc.*)

пријавница *f* **1** application form; registration form **2** registry, registration office; reception

пријавува (се) *impf of* пријави (се)

пријавувач *m* **1** applicant **2** informer

пријаде *pf* **I** (*usu. with part of the body as subject*) to start itching (suddenly); го пријаде грбот his back started itching; ❏ го пријаде јасникот to feel a draught; to sense danger **II – се** *impers.* (*with dat.*) to feel hungry

пријадува (се) *impf of* пријаде (се)

пријае *impf dial.* (*with dat.*) to please; тоа јадење ми пријае I like this food

пријател *m* **1** friend; <си> фати некого за пријател to make friends with s.o.; пријателот е требен во нужда; пријателот се познава во нужда како златото во огнот *prov.* a friend in need is a friend indeed **2** devotee; пријател на музиката music-lover

пријателка *f* (*fem. form*) *see* пријател

пријателски *adj* friendly; пријателски однос friendly attitude/relationship

пријателство *n* friendship

пријателче *n dim. hyp. of* пријател

пријателштина *f colloq. see* пријателство

пријатен -тна *adj* pleasant, agreeable, nice; enjoyable; пријатен вкус nice taste; ❏ пријатен ручек! enjoy your meal! пријатно спиење! sleep well! пријатен сон! sweet dreams!

пријатно *adv* pleasantly, nicely; ❏ пријатно! 1. enjoy your meal! *bon appétit!* 2. goodbye! see you!

пријатност *f* pleasure; pleasantness; чувство на пријатност feeling of pleasure

пријде *pf* **1** (на, кон) to approach, draw near **2** to set about, embark upon; пријде кон проучувањето на филозофија to embark upon the study of philosophy

пријдува *impf see* приоѓа

прикажан *adj* famous, noted, illustrious, glorious

прикаже *pf* прикажа *aor.* **I 1** to narrate, relate, tell (*a story*) **2** *rare* to add, say more **3** to review; прикаже книга to review a book **II – се 1** to introduce o.s., present o.s.; to make an appearance **2** to appear; ❏ ми се прикажа 1. it seemed to me 2. I had a foreboding

прикажиште *n see* привидение

прикажлив *adj* talkative; loquacious, garrulous

прикажливост *f* talkativeness; loquacity, garrulity

прикажува (се) *impf of* прикаже (се)

прикажувач *m* **1** narrator, story-teller **2** reviewer

прикажувачка *f* **1** *see* прикаска **2** (*fem. form*) *see* прикажувач

приказ *m* **1** *usu. in the expressions:* за приказ; за чудо и приказ astonishingly, amazingly, to everyone's amazement; тоа е за приказ it's amazing **2** review, summary; приказ за книга/филм book/film review

приказен -зна *adj literary* fabulous, fantastic; enchanting

приказма *f dial. see* приказна

приказна *f* story, tale; народни приказни folk-tales; за приказна as in a fairy-tale, fabulously; лична за приказна fabulously beautiful, as pretty as a picture

приказница & приказничка *f dim. hyp. of* приказна

прикаска *f* **1** *see* приказна **2** (*usu. pl*) gossip, talk; празни прикаски empty talk, nonsense; светски прикаски chit-chat, gossip

прикасне *pf* прикасна *aor.* to have another bite (*of s.th.*); to eat a little more; прикасне сиренце to have a little more cheese

прикаснува *impf of* прикасне

прикачи[1] *pf* to attach, affix, hitch on, hook on; прикачи вагон to hitch on a carriage; прикачи натпис на врата to put a sign on a door

прикачи[2] *pf rare* **I** to raise, lift a little more **II – се** to climb, rise a little more

прикачува[1] *impf of* прикачи[1]

прикачува[2] **(се)** *impf of* прикачи[2] (се)

приквечер[1] *adv* towards evening, in the <early> evening

приквечер[2] *f rare* late afternoon, early evening; една приквечер early one evening

приквечерен -рна *adj literary* <of> early evening

приквечерина[1] *f* late afternoon, early evening; eve (*day before*); ❏ во приквечерината на празникот on the eve of the holiday

приквечерина[2] *adv see* приквечер[1]

приклава *impf of* приклаДе

приклаДе *pf* to add <on>

приклеД *m* pantry; cellar

приклекне *pf* приклекна *aor.* **1** to kneel <for a moment> **2** *rare* to submit

приклекнува *impf of* приклекне

приклешти *pf* **1** to pinch *trans.* **2** to pin, press, squeeze; приклешти некого до ѕид to pin s.o. against a wall **3** *fig.* to pin down, nail down

приклештува *impf of* приклешти

приклони *pf literary* **I** to bend down *trans.*; to bow; to incline *trans.*; ја приклони главата to bow one's head **II – се 1** to bend down *intrans.* **2** *fig.* to incline (кон – to); се приклони кон некое мислење to incline to a view

приклонува (се) *impf of* приклони (се)

приклука *pf* **1** (*страна*) to start knocking, banging **2** (*за рана*) to start stinging, throbbing; ме приклука раната my wound started throbbing

приклучен -чна *adj* connecting

приклучение -ија *n rare* adventure

приклучи *pf* **I 1** to attach, join *trans.*; to annex; приклучи земји кон свое царство to annex lands to one's empire **2** to connect *trans.*; приклучи куќа на (кон) електричната мрежа to connect a house to the grid (mains) **II – се 1** (*with dat. or кон*) to join; се приклучи кон движењето to join a movement; се приклучи кон нечие мислење to share s.o.'s opinion **2** *rare* to end, finish *intrans.*; борбата се приклучи the struggle came to an end

приклучок -ци *m* connection; connector; plug; terminal; електричен приклучок electrical connection; electrical socket, power point

приклучува (се) *impf of* приклучи (се)

прикова & прикове *pf* прикова *aor.* to nail, fasten with nails; to chain; to fix (*also fig.*); прикова нешто за греда to nail s.th. to a rafter; прикова некого со поглед (очи) to fix one's eyes on s.o.

приковува *impf of* прикова & прикове

приколка *f* trailer; side-car; мотоцикл со приколка motor cycle with side-car

прикраДе се *pf literary* to creep up (*до/кон – on*), steal up (*to*)

прикрадува се *impf of* прикраде се; *fig.* се прикрадуваше денот dawn was approaching

прикрај *adv* **1** along the side (edge) **2** at the end (*of s.th.*); веќе сме прикрај we've nearly finished

прикрепи *pf rare* **I 1** to fix, attach, bind, make fast; to connect **2** to hold on to; to seize **II – се 1** to register (кон – with) *intrans.*; to attach o.s. to (*an organization*) **2** to hold on to (*s.th. or s.o.*), support o.s. *or* each other

прикрепник -ци *m* breadwinner, mainstay

прикрепува (се) *impf of* прикрепи (се)

прикрива (се) *impf of* прикрие (се)

прикрие *pf* прикри *aor.* **I** to conceal, hide, cover up; прикрие свои намери to mask one's intentions **II** – се **1** to hide *intrans.* **2** *fig.* to disguise o.s.

прикриен *pt* hidden; covert; furtive; прикриен непријател hidden enemy

прикриеност *f* furtiveness, stealth

прикрпи *pf* **I** to patch up, repair **II** – се (*usu. fig.*) to cope, get by, manage *intrans.*

прикрпува (се) *impf of* прикрпи (се)

прикупи *pf* to buy a little more

прикупува *impf of* прикупи

прилага *impf of* приложи

прилева *impf of* прилие

прилега *impf* **1** (*на*) to look like, resemble; ќерката прилега на мајка си the daughter looks like (resembles) her mother; ❑ си прилегаат како две капки вода they are as like as two peas; на што прилега ова! this is an outrage! **2** (*with dat.*) to suit, be suitable, fitting (*for*); (*за алишта и др.*) to fit; капелата ти прилега убаво that hat suits you; ❑ како што прилега fittingly **3** *impers.* (*with acc.*) to be suited (*to a position*), capable; го прилега за учител he would make a good teacher

прилеган *adj* **1** *colloq.* decent, proper; civil, polite **2** *rare* beautiful; wonderful

прилегне *pf* прилегна *aor.* **1** to lie down; to lie down for a while; to take a nap; прилегни до мене lie down next to me **2** (*with dat.*) to fit snugly

прилегнува *impf of* прилегне

прилее *pf* прилеа *aor.* to pour a little more

прилежен -жна *adj* industrious, diligent, hardworking

прилежи *pf see* прилегне

прилежност *f* diligence

прилепи *pf* **I** to stick on (*на, до, врз, кон – то*), glue on; прилепи нешто на ѕид to paste s.th. on a wall **II** – се to cling, stick *intrans.*; се прилепи до прозорец to press up against a window

прилепува (се) *impf of* прилепи (се)

прилесно *adv rare* lightly; easily; решението го донесе прилесно he made the decision easily

прилив *m* **1** <high> tide; прилив и одлив high and low tide **2** onrush, surge, influx; прилив на чувства a rush of emotion; прилив на крв <во главата> rush of blood <to the head>

прилива *impf see* прилева

прилие *pf* прилиа *aor. see* прилее

прилика *f* **1** match, equal, mate; не си му прилика you are no match for him; ❑ лика и прилика perfect likeness; perfect match **2** (*usu. pl*) condition; circumstance; приликите беа тешки conditions were difficult; историјски прилики historical circumstances **3** occasion, opportunity

приличен -чна *adj* considerable, quite large; приличен број луѓе a large number of people, a good many people; прилична големина a fair size

прилично *adv* fairly, quite; прилично добар резултат a fairly good result, quite a good result; пишува прилично he writes quite well

прилог -зи *m* **1** supplement; прилог кон весникот supplement to a newspaper **2** <press> article **3** enclosure (*in a letter*); во прилог на ова писмо

enclosed with this letter **4** donation; contribution; доброволен прилог a voluntary contribution **5** *rare* advantage, benefit; favour; тоа ти оди во прилог that is to your advantage **6** *Gram.* adverb; глаголски прилог verbal adverb

приложи *pf* **1** to add; to supplement **2** to enclose; кон молбата ги приложив бараните документи with the application I enclosed the required documents **3** to contribute, donate

приложува *impf of* приложи

прилошки *adj Gram.* adverbial

прилути *pf impers.* (*with dat.*) to feel a burning sensation in the mouth

прилутува *impf of* прилути

прим *m Mus.* **1** kind of mandolin; soprano *tambura* **2** first violin

прима (се) *impf of* прими (се)

примабалери́на *f* prima ballerina

примадо́на *f* prima donna

примајка *f* foster-mother

примами *pf* to entice, tempt, lure

примамлив *adj* enticing, tempting; примамливи зборови enticing words

примамува *impf of* примами

примање *n* **1** acceptance, reception; welcome; часови за примање (прием) surgery hours, reception hours; примање на резолуција adoption of a resolution **2** (*pl only*) примања income; месечни примања monthly income

примарен -рна *adj* primary; most important

примариус *m* chief medical officer

примат *m literary* primacy, pride of place, precedence

примат눻ка *f* (*fem. form*) *see* примач

примач *m* receiver, recipient

примаш *m* first violin, leader (*usu. of a gypsy band*)

приме伀дба *f* objection

примена *f* application, use; практична примена practical application

применет *pt* applied; применета наука applied science

примени *pf* to apply *trans.*, use, utilize; примени нов метод to apply a new method

применлив *adj* applicable, usable

применливост *f* applicability

применува *impf of* примени

пример *m* example, instance; sample; земе некого за пример to take s.o. as an example; даде некому пример to set an example for s.o.; ❑ на пример for example

примерен -рна *adj* exemplary; примерно поведение exemplary conduct (behaviour)

примерок -ци *m* copy (*of a book, etc.*); issue, number; specimen, sample; тираж од илјада примероци print-run of a thousand copies

примес *m* ingredient; admixture; alloy

примеша *pf* **I** to mix (*s.th.*) in **II** – се *rare* to get involved; се примеша во разговор to break into a conversation

примешува (се) *impf of* примеша (се)

прими *pf* **I 1** to receive, accept; to take; прими одговорност to accept responsibility; прими нова вера to accept (adopt) a new faith; прими резолуција to adopt a resolution **2** to take over, take up, assume; прими должност to take up a position **3**

to welcome, receive, take in; прими студено to give a cool reception to **4** to assume, take on; прими различни форми to assume different forms (guises) **5** *rare* to accommodate, hold; собата може да прими дваесетина души the room can hold twenty people **II – се 1** (*за*) to accept, take on; се прими за раководител to accept the post of manager **2** (*да*) to agree to; се прими да прави нешто to agree to do s.th. **3** *rare* (*за растение, вакцина*) to take

примига & **примигне** *pf* примига & примигна *aor.* to start blinking/winking suddenly

примигнува *impf of* примига & примигне

примижан *pt* **1** with half-closed eyes, squinting; примижан поглед squinting look **2** *fig.* twinkling, blinking; примижаните улични светилки flickering street lights

примижи *pf* примижа *aor.* to narrow (half-close) one's eyes; to squint; примижа од дремката his eyelids drooped from weariness

примижува *pf of* примижи

примира *impf of* примре

примирен *pt literary* (*помирен*) reconciled, resigned (*со – то*); примирен со судбината resigned to one's fate

примиреност *f literary* (*помиреност*) resignation

примири *pf* **I 1** to pacify, calm, quieten *trans.* **2** *rare, literary* to reconcile **II – се 1** to calm down **2** *literary* to reconcile o.s., resign o.s. (*со – то*)

примириса *pf* **I 1** to scent, catch a scent; *fig.* to suspect; тој и не го примирисал тоа he had no inkling of that **2** (*with dat., 3rd p. only*) ми примириса нешто I caught a whiff of s.th.

примирје *n* truce, armistice; склучи примирје to conclude a truce

примирува (се) *impf of* примири (се)

примити́вен -вна *adj* primitive; примитивен живот primitive life

примити́вец -вци *m* crude person; philistine

примитиви́зам -змот *m* primitivism; the Primitive school (*of painting*)

примка *f* **1** *see* јамка **2** *fig.* trap, snare **3** buttonhole

примоли *pf* **I** *rare* to ask, beg *trans.* **II – се** (*with dat.*) to plead with, entreat

примолува (се) *impf of* примоли (се)

примопредавање *n* hand-over (*of duties, files, etc.*)

приморец -рци *m* inhabitant of a coastal region

приморје *n* coastal region, coast

приморка *f* (*fem. form*) *see* приморец

приморски *adj* coastal, littoral

примоча се *pf impers.* (*with dat.*) to need to urinate

примочува се *impf of* примоча се

примрак *m* (*самрак*) dusk, twilight

примре *pf* примра *aor.* to become petrified; to become paralysed; to fall in a coma

примрен *pt* unconscious

примула *f Bot.* (Primula veris) primula

примус *m* primus <stove>

принадлежност *f* **1** *literary, rare* (*припадност*) membership; affiliation **2** (*pl only*) income, salary, pay

принаправи *pf* **1** to do up, make partial repairs to; принаправи куќа to do up a house **2** to make more (*of s.th.*)

принесе *pf* **I 1** to bring; принесе жртва to sacrifice,

make (offer) a sacrifice **2** to bear, yield; *fig.* принесе полза to be of use **II – се** се принесе жртва to sacrifice o.s.

принесува (се) *impf of* принесе (се)

принижен *adj literary, rare* low; принижен стил low style

принова *f* & **приновче** *n* new-born baby; принова во семејството an addition to the family

принос *m* **1** contribution, donation **2** harvest; приносот на пченицата the wheat crop (harvest)

принуда *f* compulsion, coercion; без принуда without compulsion; под принуда under duress

принуден -дна *adj* forced; compulsory; принудна работа forced labour; принудни мерки coercive measures

принуди *pf* **I** to force, compel, coerce **II – се** to force o.s.

принудно *adv* compulsorily; under duress; авионот принудно се спушти the plane made a forced landing

принудува (се) *impf of* принуди (се)

принц -ови *m* prince

принцéза *f* princess

принцип *m* principle; tenet; ❑ во принцип, по принцип in principle; theoretically speaking; од принцип on principle

принципиéлен -лна & **принципен** -пна *adj* basic, fundamental; principled; принципиелно прашање basic question; принципиелен човек person of principle

принципиéлност *f* adherence to principles; correctness

приобиде *pf f.p.* to arrange, smarten up a little

приоблекува (се) *impf of* приоблече (се)

приоблече *pf* **I** to put on (*hastily*); to throw on (*clothes*) **II – се** to dress (*o.s.*) (*hastily, carelessly*)

приоблечува (се) *impf see* приоблекува (се)

приод *m* **1** approach; access; на приодите на градот in the approaches to the city **2** approach, attitude; нашиот приод кон тоа прашање our approach to that question

приоден -дна *adj* <of> approach, access; приодни патишта approach roads

приоѓа *impf of* пријде

приопшти *pf* **I** to include, win over, involve (*s.o. in s.th.*); приопшти некого кон движење to involve s.o. in a movement **II – се** (*кон*) to join; се приопшти кон некого to join s.o.

приопштува (се) *impf of* приопшти (се)

приоритéт *m* priority, precedence

приоритéтен -тна *adj* priority *attrib.*

припадне¹ *pf* припадна *aor.* (*with dat.*) to fall to, go to; победата му припадна нему the victory was his

припадне² *pf* припадна *aor.* **1** to faint, pass out, swoon; to have an epileptic fit **2** (*with dat.*) to rush at, fall on *fig.*; му припадна на лебот he fell on the bread

припадник -ци *m* member

припадница & **припадничка** *f* (*fem. form*) *see* припадник

припадничав *adj* epileptic; prone to fainting fits

припадност *f* membership; affiliation; национална припадност nationality

припаѓа¹ *impf* (*with dat.*) to belong; куќата им припаѓа ним the house belongs to them; вие припаѓате таму you belong there

припаѓа[2]   *impf of* припадне[2]

припази   *pf* to keep an eye on; to mind

припари   *pf (до)* to approach, draw near; не му давам да припари I don't let him come near

припарува   *impf of* припари

припев   *m* refrain

припее се   *pf* припеа се *aor. impers.* (*with dat.*) to feel like singing

припек   -ци *m* **1** heat (*of the sun*); ❏ на припек in the heat of the sun; како волк на припек restless **2** sunny side (*of a building*)

припекува   *impf of* припече

припече   *pf* **1** to bake, roast, scorch (*of the sun*) *intrans.*; сонцето припече the sun has got hot **2** to bake/roast more (*of s.th.*)

припечува   *impf see* припекува

припива се   *impf of* припие се

припие се   *pf* припи се *aor. impers.* (*with dat.*) to grow thirsty

припис   *m & * **приписка** *f* marginal note, gloss

припитоми   *pf* **I** to tame, domesticate **II** – ce to become tame (*also fig.*)

припитомува (се)   *impf of* припитоми (се)

припише   *pf* припиша *aor.* **1** to annotate; to gloss **2** to attribute, ascribe; авторството му го припишале на друг authorship was attributed to s.o. else

припишува   *impf of* припише

припка   *impf* to gambol, frolic, caper

приплаши   *pf rare, f.p.* to scare

приплашува   *impf of* приплаши

приплеска   *pf* **1** to make, mix (*bakery products*) **2** *colloq. fig.* to do for, do in, kill

приплескува   *impf of* приплеска

приплете   *pf* to knit on more

приплетува   *impf of* приплете

приплод   *m* issue, increase (*in cattle numbers*); breeding; коњ за приплод stud horse

приплоден   -дна *adj* breeding; приплоден добиток breeding stock

приплука   *pf* to spit several times

приплукува   *impf of* приплука

припознава   *impf of* припознае

припознае   *pf* припозна *aor. rare* **1** to admit, confess; си го припознала кабаетот she admitted her guilt **2** to acknowledge, recognize, be grateful for

припомага   *impf of* припомогне

припомни   *pf* **1** to remind; припомни некому нешто to remind s.o. of s.th. **2** to remember; си припомни нешто to remember (recall, call to mind) s.th.

припомнува   *impf of* припомни

припомогне & припоможе   *pf* припомогна & припоможа *aor.* (*with dat.*) to lend a hand; to help

припомош   *f rare* help, assistance; дојде некому на припомош to come to s.o.'s aid

приправа   *impf of* приправи

приправи   *pf* **1** to make more (*of s.th.*) **2** to repair; to extend (*a house*)

приправник   -ци *m* new employee, trainee; адвокатски приправник law clerk

приправнички   *adj* beginner's; training *attrib.*; приправнички стаж <on-the-job> training period

припрати се   *pf see* напрати се

припратува се   *impf of* припрати се

припрост   *adj* rather plain, simple

припука   *pf* to start shooting, open fire

припуши се   *pf impers.* (*with dat.*) to feel a desire to smoke

припушта   *impf of* припушти

припушти   *pf* **1** to allow to approach; to admit *trans.*, let in **2** *rare, f.p.* to drive hard, drive faster (*a horse*)

приработува   *impf* to do a little work (*occasionally*)

прираѓа   *impf of* природи

прирамни   *pf literary* **I** **1** to equalize *trans.*; to level out *trans.*, make even; прирамни загуби to even out losses **2** to straighten *trans.*, put right **II** – ce to become equal; to level out *intrans.*

прирамнува (се)   *impf of* прирамни (се)

прирасне & прирасте   *pf* прирасна & прирасте *aor.* **1** to grow (*за, на – onto*); *fig.* (*with dat.*) to become dear to; ми прирасна за срце I've become very fond of him **2** to increase, grow, increase *intrans.*; прирасна населението the population has increased

прираснува & прирастува   *impf of* прирасне & прирасте

прираст   *m* increase, growth; прираст на населението population growth

прирачен   -чна *adj* handy; прирачна книга handbook, manual

прирачник   -ци *m* handbook, manual

приредба   *f* **1** party, celebration, function; show, performance **2** *rare* editorial work (*on a book*)

приреден   *adj Gram. rare* coordinate; приредени (независни) реченици coordinate clauses

приреди   *impf of* to organize, arrange; to prepare *trans.*; приреди пречек to organize a reception; приреди ново издание (*на книга*) to prepare a new edition (*of a book*)

приредува   *impf of* приреди

приредувач   *m* **1** organizer **2** editor (*of a book*)

приречe   *pf* приреков *1st p. sg aor.* to add, say s.th. more

приречица   *f* favourite saying or phrase, watchword

при'ржи   *pf rare, f.p.* to start neighing/whinnying suddenly

природа   *f* **1** nature, the natural world; scenery; силите на природата the forces of nature; ❏ мајка природа Mother Nature; мртва природа 1. inanimate nature 2. *Art* still life **2** character, nature; природата на човекот human nature; тој е мека природа he has a gentle nature; ❏ втора природа second nature; во природата на стварите in the nature of things

природен   -дна *adj* natural; природни богатства natural resources; природни појави natural phenomena; природен гас natural gas

природи   *pf* to bear children by a second (*or subsequent*) husband

природно   *adv* **1** naturally; се држи природно to behave naturally **2** of course, certainly

природонаучен   -чна *adj* of natural sciences, natural history; природонаучен музеј natural history museum

природонаучник   -ци *m* naturalist

прирок   -ци *m Gram.* predicate; подмет и прирок subject and predicate

прироков   *adj Gram.* predicative; прироков додаток complement

приручa се   *pf impers.* (*with dat.*) to feel hungry, feel a need for lunch

присад *m* grafted fruit-tree; graft

присака *pf* **I** to want, wish for <more> **II – се** *impers.* (*with dat.*) to want, feel like; ми се присака чаша вода I should like a glass of water

присакува (се) *impf of* присака (се); не присакувам ништо I don't want anything more

присвоен -jна *adj Gram.* possessive; присвоjна заменка possessive pronoun

присвои *pf* to appropriate, annex; to arrogate, usurp; си присвои право to usurp a right

присвоjност *f Gram.* possession

присвоjува *impf of* присвои

присебен -бна *adj* self-possessed, calm, collected, composed

присебност *f* calmness, coolness, composure; загуби присебност to lose one's composure

приседне *pf* приседна *aor.* to sit down for a moment

приседнува *impf of* приседне

присен -сна *adj literary* very close, intimate; присен приjател close (bosom) friend; присна соработка close cooperation

присени се *pf* 1 *impers.* (*with dat.*) to seem, appear, look; ми се присени it seemed to me 2 to be noticed; to catch s.o.'s attention (eye)

присенува се *impf of* присени се

присестра *f* half-sister, step-sister

присети се *pf* (*за, на*) to remember, recall

присетува се & присеќава се *impf of* присети се

присилен -лна *adj* forced; compulsory; присилна работа forced labour; присилни мерки coercive measures

присили *pf* **I** to force, compel, coerce; го присилиле да каже they forced him to tell **II – се** to force o.s.

присилно *adv* compulsorily; under duress

присилува (се) *impf of* присили (се)

присламчи се *pf colloq.* to force o.s., impose o.s. (*кон – upon*)

присламчува се *impf of* присламчи се

прислужник -ци *m rather rare* 1 (*во училиште*) janitor; cleaner 2 (*во манастир*) servant

прислушен -шна *adj* (for) listening; прислушна служба telephone-tapping service

прислушува *impf* **I** to eavesdrop (*on s.o.*), listen in; (*телефонски разговори*) to tap **II – се** to be heard (audible) (*at intervals*)

присмади *pf* to get singed

присмадува *impf of* присмади

присмев *m* sneer; taunt, jibe; mockery, derision; земе некого на присмев to make fun of s.o.

присмева се *impf of* присмее се

присмее се *pf* присмеа се *aor.* (*with dat.*) to make fun of, laugh at, mock; се присмеал цреп на шутар *prov.* the pot calls the kettle black

присмрди *pf* to emit a slight odour; нешто му присмрдело he caught a whiff of s.th.; *fig.* he smelt a rat

присмрдува *impf of* присмрди

присност *f literary* intimacy, closeness

присобере *pf* присобра *aor.* **I** to collect a little more **II – се** to pull o.s. together, collect one's wits

присобира (се) *impf of* присобере (се)

присоедини *pf* **I** to annex; to add on; присоедини краиште кон царство to annex a region to a kingdom **II – се** to unite *intrans.*; (*кон or with dat.*) to join;

да ви се присоединам let me join you; се присоедини кон предлог to subscribe to a proposal

присоединува (се) *impf of* присоедини (се)

присоен -jна *adj* 1 sunlit, sunny 2 присоjна змиja *see* присоjница 1

присоj -ои *m* sunny side; sunny spot

присоjница *f* 1 viper 2 *rare* sunny, dry place

присоjничав *adj see* присоен 1

присони *pf* (*with dat.*) to dream of; ми се присони . . . I dreamt of . . .

присонува се *impf of* присони се

приспива (се) *impf of* приспие (се)

приспивен -вна *adj* soporific; lulling; приспивна песна lullaby

приспие *pf* приспа *aor.* **I** 1 to put/lull to sleep 2 *fig.* to dull *trans.*; to wear down, erode *trans.*; приспие нечиjа волja to wear down s.o.'s will **II – се** *impers.* (*with dat.*) to feel sleepy

приспособен *adj* adapted

приспособи *pf* **I** to adapt, adjust *trans.*; приспособи нешто кон своите потреби to adapt s.th. to one's needs **II – се** to adapt *intrans.*; се приспособи кон нова ситуациja to adapt to a new situation

приспособлив *adj* adaptable; adjustable

приспособливост *f* adaptability

приспособува (се) *impf of* приспособи (се)

присрце *adv* to heart, seriously; земе нешто присрце to take s.th. to heart; to put one's heart into s.th.

пристави *pf* to put, place

приставува *impf of* пристави

пристан *m* 1 landing-stage, mooring; quay 2 *fig.*, *literary* refuge, haven

пристане[1] *pf* пристана *aor.* to get up, rise (*for a while*)

пристане[2] *pf rare* пристана *aor.* (*за кораб, чун*) to tie up, moor *trans.*

пристаниште *n* 1 landing-stage; port; harbour 2 *fig.* refuge, haven

пристанишен -шна *adj* port, harbour; пристанишни работници dockers

пристанува[1] *impf of* пристане[1]

пристанува[2] *impf of* пристане[2]

пристап *m* 1 approach, access; пристапите кон градот the approaches to the city 2 *fig.* approach, attitude; пристап кон прашање attitude to a question

пристапен -пна *adj* 1 approach, access; пристапни патишта approach roads 2 *rare* introductory; пристапно предавање introductory lecture

пристапи *pf* 1 (*with dat.*) to approach, draw near 2 (*with dat.*) to join, become a member of; му пристапи на клуб to join a club 3 *fig.* (*кон*) to embark upon, set about, begin; пристапи кон излагањето he started his explanation/report; пристапи кон работата to get down to work

пристапница *f* application form

пристапува *impf of* пристапи

пристар *adj* elderly

пристаса *pf colloq. see* пристигне

пристасува *impf* пристаса

пристега (се) *impf of* пристегне (се)

пристегне *pf* пристегна *aor.* **I** to tighten, draw tight *trans.*; *fig.* to discipline, bring into line, rein in **II – се** to tighten one's belt (*a little more*); *fig.* to rein o.s. in, discipline o.s.

пристегнува (се) *impf see* пристега (се)

пристига *impf of* пристигне

пристигне *pf* пристигна *aor.* **1** to arrive; to come; возот пристигна на станицата the train has arrived at the station **2** to catch up with

пристигнува *impf see* пристига

пристоен -јна *adj literary* proper, decent; fitting; polite

пристојност *f* decency

пристори се *pf* (*with dat.*) to seem, appear; ми се присторило дека . . . it seemed to me that . . .

присторува се *impf of* пристори се

пристрасен -сна *adj* biased, prejudiced; пристрасна оцена prejudiced assessment

пристрасност *f* bias, prejudice, partiality

пристуди *pf* пристуде *aor* **1** (*за време*) to turn cold **2** *impers.* (*with dat.*) to begin to feel cold/chilled

пристудува *impf of* пристуди

присуство *n* presence; attendance; ❏ во присуство на in the presence of; присуство на духот presence of mind

присуствува *impf* to be present

присутен -тна *adj* present; (*as noun*) присутните those present

присутност *f see* присуство

присушт *adj literary* (*својствен*) characteristic, typical; нему му е тоа присушто that is typical of him

прит *m see* прид

притаен *pt* secret, hidden; со притаен здив with bated breath

притаеност *f* secrecy, stealth

притаи *pf* **I** to conceal, hide *trans.*; to keep secret; ја притаи својата желба he kept his wish to himself; го притаи здивот to hold one's breath **II** – **се** to hide *intrans.*; to take shelter

притајува (се) *impf of* притаи (се)

притатко *m* foster-father

притвор *m* custody; стави во притвор to remand in custody

притвора *impf of* притвори

притвори *pf* **1** to take into custody; to detain **2** (*врата и сл.*) to close partially

притега *impf of* притегне

притегне *pf* притегна *aor. see* пристегне

притегнува *impf see* притега

притекне[1] *pf* притекна *aor.* (*with dat.*) to come to mind; ќе ми притекне it will come back to me; it's on the tip of my tongue

притекне[2] (**се**) *pf* притекна (се) *aor. see* притече (се)

притекнува[1] *impf of* притекне

притекнува[2] (**се**) *impf of* притекне (се)

притекува (се) *impf of* притече (се)

притемни *pf* to grow dark, darken *intrans.*; ❏ ми притемне пред очите I saw red

притемнува *impf of* притемни

притеснет *pt* **1** cramped, squashed **2** *fig.* hard pressed; anxious, apprehensive

притесни *pf* **I 1** to cramp, squeeze, squash **2** to inconvenience, put out **3** *fig., rare* to oppress **II** – **се 1** to be cramped, squeezed **2** to be inconvenienced **3** to feel anxiety

притеснува (се) *impf of* притесни (се)

притече *pf* **I 1** (*дотече*) to flow in; to rise (*of water*) **2** to run in, rush in; притече некому на помош to hurry to the rescue/aid of s.o. **II** – **се** *rare see* **I** 2

притечува (се) *impf see* притекува (се)

притивне *pf* притивна *aor.* to grow quiet, quieten down, subside, settle down *intrans.*

притивнува *impf of* притивне

притиска (се) *impf of* притисне (се)

притисне *pf* притисна *aor.* **I 1** to exert pressure on; to press, squeeze; ❏ притисне до ѕид to corner, pin down, pin to the wall **2** *fig.* to oppress, worry **3** to overrun, swarm over; народ го притисна плоштадот the crowd swarmed over the square **II** – **се** to huddle together; to snuggle up; детето се притисна до мајка си the child pressed up against its mother

притиснува (се) *impf see* притиска (се)

притисок -ци *m* pressure; атмосферски притисок atmospheric pressure; крвен притисок blood pressure; врши притисок to exert pressure; ❏ качува некому притисок to get under s.o.'s skin, raise s.o.'s blood pressure

притка *f* stake (*to support plants*)

приткае *pf* приткаја *aor.* to weave on, attach by weaving

притоа *adv* besides; at the same time

приток -ци *m* **1** tributary; притоците на Вардар the tributaries of the Vardar **2** inflow

притока *f see* приток 1

притокми *pf* **I** to get ready, prepare *trans.* **II** – **се** to get ready, prepare *intrans.*

притокмува (се) *impf of* притокми (се)

притопори се *pf* **1** to throw out one's chest **2** (*with dat.*) to threaten; му се притопори со нож he threatened him with a knife

притопорува се *impf of* притопори се

притреба *pf* (*with dat.*) to be needed, become necessary; ќе ми притреба добар работник I shall need a good worker; ❏ *iron.* ми притребало! much good it did me! си ми притребал! I don't need you!

притребува *impf of* притреба

притресе се *pf* to make threatening gestures

притресува се *impf of* притресе се

притропа *pf* to start knocking, banging

притропува *impf of* притропа

притрпи се *pf* to be patient

притрпува се *impf of* притрпи се

притрча *pf* to run up (*до*/*кон – to*)

притрчува *impf of* притрча

притули *pf* **I 1** to hide *trans.*; to shelter *trans.* **2** to shade (*a light, lamp*) **3** *fig.* to suppress; притули желба to suppress a desire **II** – **се 1** to hide *intrans.*; to take shelter **2** to crouch, nestle, squat; to cower; се притулиле селата во планината the villages nestled in the mountains

притулува (се) *impf of* притули (се)

притура *impf of* притури

притури *pf* **1** to pour a little more **2** *rare* to add

прика *f*, **прике** *n* & **прикија** *f dial.* (*чеиз, мираз*) dowry

прикоса *pf* **1** *dial.* прикоса прике to bring a dowry **2** *colloq.* to squander, waste **3** *dial.* to destroy, ruin; прикоса некого to be the ruin of s.o.

прикосува *impf of* прикоса

приука *pf* to <start to> hoot/howl

приучен *pt* partly trained

приучи *pf* **I 1** to teach, train, instruct (*partly*); to accustom **2** to study (*a little more*) **II – се** to train o.s.; to become accustomed

приучува (се) *impf of* приучи (се)

прифати *pf* **1** to take hold of, grasp; ❑ го прифатиле мајките; го прифатило he's not all there **2** *literary* to take in, give shelter to; прифати бегалци to take in refugees **3** to accept, adopt; прифати предлог to adopt a proposal

прифатилиште *n* refuge

прифатлив *adj literary* acceptable; прифатливо решение acceptable decision

прифаќа *impf of* прифати

приход *m* income, revenue

прихрани *pf* **I** to sustain (*for a while*) **II – се** to maintain o.s.

прихранува (се) *impf of* прихрани (се)

прицврсти *pf* to fasten, strengthen, fix

прицврстува *impf of* прицврсти

причека *pf see* почека

причесна & причест *f Rel.* the Sacrament, Eucharist, Holy Communion

причести *pf Rel.* **I** to administer the Sacrament to, give Communion to; попот ги причестил the priest gave them Communion **II – се** to take Communion; *sl.* to have a few drinks

причестува (се) *impf of* причести (се)

причина *f* cause; reason; причини и последици causes and effects; нема причина да се жали he has no cause for complaint

причини *pf* to cause; причини несреќа to cause an accident; причини некому штета to cause s.o. harm; ми причини задоволство he/it gave me pleasure; I was glad to . . .

причини се *pf* (*with dat.*) to seem, appear; ми се причини дека . . . it seemed to me that . . .

причинител *m* doer; cause; factor; причинител на болест carrier of a disease

причиност *f* causality

причински *adj* causal; причинска врска causal connexion

причинува *impf of* причини

причинува се *impf of* причини се

причува *pf rare* **I** to mind, look after for a while **II – се** to look after o.s., be careful, watch out

причука *pf rare* to hammer on/in

пришепне *pf* пришепна *aor.* to whisper; to add in a whisper

пришепнува *impf of* пришепне

пришествие *n Rel. usu.* второ пришествие <the> second coming (*of Christ to earth*)

пришива *impf of* пришие

пришие *pf* приши *aor.* **1** to sew on; пришие копчиња to sew on buttons **2** *fig., rare* to impute (*нешто некому – s.th. to s.o.*)

пришт *m* boil, ulcer; ❑ црн пришт anthrax; зол пришт stomach ulcer

приштав *adj* covered in boils, pimply

приштоса се *pf* to come out in boils

прка *impf* to flutter

пркне *pf* **1** to flutter; to fly off, flit away **2** to sprout *intrans.*, spring up, come up

пркнува *impf of* пркне

пркос *m literary* defiance; stubbornness; со пркос defiantly

пркосен -сна *adj literary* defiant; stubborn

пркоси *impf literary* (*with dat.*) to defy

прле *n* donkey foal; ❑ како магарето и прлето inseparable; не трчај како прле пред магаре *prov.* **1.** look before you leap **2.** don't put the cart before the horse

прли *impf* to singe

прли се *impf* (*of a donkey*) to foal

прлица *f dial. see* потполошка, препелица

прлок -ци *m Bot.* (Crocus moesiacus) yellow crocus

прлушка *f Zool.* mollusc; oyster

прлушци *pl Bot.* (Trapa natans) water-caltrop, water-chestnut

прнар *m Bot.* **1** (Quercus coccinea) scarlet oak **2** (Quercus ilex) holm-oak **3** (Quercus pubescens/lanuginosa) downy oak **4** *coll.* bushes, scrub, undergrowth

пр.н.е. *abbr.* (*пред нашата ера*) BC

про *adv* for; про и контра for and against (pro and contra)

про-[1] *prefix* pro-; профашистички pro-Fascist

про-[2] *verbal prefix indicating* **1** *beginning of action;* проговори to start talking; проработи to start working **2** *brief duration; hasty action;* пророси to drizzle for a while; прокасне to have a quick snack **3** *movement through, by, past;* провлече to pull through; прободе to pierce **4** *action carried to completion;* прочита to finish reading; протера to drive out

проаѓа *impf* (*mainly dial.*) *of* пројде

проаѓач *m see* минувач, поминувач

проанализира *pf* to analyse

проба *f* **1** experiment, trial, test; ❑ земе на проба to take on approval; става на проба to put on trial **2** rehearsal; генерална проба dress rehearsal

проба *pf & impf* **I** **1** to try *trans.*, to test; (*облека*) to try on; (*јадење и сл.*) to taste; проба мотор to test an engine; проба костум to try on a suit; проба вино to try (taste) wine; уште не сте ја пробале мусаката you haven't yet tasted the moussaka **2** to attempt, try, endeavour (*да – to*) ; проба да учи to try to study **II – се** **1** *see* I 2 **2** (*usu. pl*) to compete in a trial of strength; to pit o.s. against another

пробаботи *pf* **1** to boom, rumble, roar (*for a while*) **2** to begin to roar/rumble **3** *fig.* to babble for a while

пробае *pf* пробаја *aor.* to dabble in sorcery

пробандори *pf* to babble, chatter (*for a while*)

пробања *pf* **I** to bathe quickly, hastily *trans.* **II – се** to bathe quickly, hastily *intrans.*

пробара *pf* to search through hurriedly, superficially

пробари *pf* to steam superficially, hastily

пробдее *pf* пробдеа *aor.* to keep vigil (*for a period*); целата ноќ ја пробдеал he kept vigil through the night

пробелее & пробели *pf* пробелеа & пробели *aor.* to go (turn) white/grey *intrans.*

пробен -бна *adj* experimental; trial; пробно летање test flight; пробен балон trial balloon; ❑ пушта пробен балон to fly a kite; пробен камен touchstone

пробере *pf* пробра *aor.* **1** to pick over, go through **2** to gather *trans.*, harvest (*in haste; for a while*)

пробесен *pt* hanging down, drooping; пробесени уши drooping ears, lop-ears

пробеси *pf* **I** to dangle *trans.* **II – се** to dangle *intrans.*, hang down, droop

пробесува (се) *impf of* пробеси (се)

пробив *m* opening, gap, breach, breakthrough (*also fig.*); научен пробив scientific breakthrough

пробива (се) *impf of* пробие (се); ❑ тешко се пробива низ животот his life is an uphill struggle

пробивен -вна *adj* 1 penetrating, piercing; punching; пробивна сила penetrating force 2 *fig.* thrusting, *colloq.* pushy; go-ahead

пробие *pf* проби *aor.* **I 1** to break through, pierce, penetrate, breach; реката го пробила насипот the river has burst its banks; ❑ пробие мраз to break the ice; пробие некому глава to get on s.o.'s nerves **2** to clear/beat (*a path*) **3** (*за чир*) to burst, break open *intrans.* **II – се 1** (*низ*) to break through; се пробие низ непријателски редови to break through enemy lines **2** *fig.* to succeed, make one's way; добро се проби he managed well; he has gone far

пробира *impf of* пробере

пробирач *m rare* fastidious person

пробистри *pf colloq.* to clarify (*partly*), shed some light on

проблем *m* problem; проблеми за решавање problems to be solved

проблематика *f coll.* problems

проблематичен -чна *adj* problematic<al>

проблемски *adj* problem, consisting of problems; проблемски шах problem chess

проблесне *pf* проблесна *aor.* to gleam, glint, flash; ми проблесна во главата дека … it flashed through my mind, it occurred to me that …

проблеснува *impf of* проблесне

проблесок -ци *m* glimmer (*also fig.*); проблесок на надеж glimmer (ray) of hope

прободе *pf* to stab (*also fig.*); *fig.* неговите зборови ме прободија в срце his words came as a stab in the heart; ме прободе нешто во градиве I felt a stabbing pain in the chest

прободува *impf of* прободе

пробоен -јна *adj see* пробивен

пробој -ои *m see* пробив

пробрбори *pf* 1 to blurt out 2 to chat for a while

пробричи *pf* to shave (*hurriedly*) *trans.*

пробрсти *pf* to browse for a while

пробрчи *pf* (*за мотор*) 1 to throb/roar for a short time 2 to start roaring (*usu. after stalling*)

пробуда *f literary* awakening; национална пробуда national awakening

пробуди *pf* **I** to waken, wake <up> *trans.*; *fig.* (*предизвика, возбуди*) to evoke, arouse; пробуди чувства to awaken feelings **II – се** to awake, wake up *intrans.* (*also fig.*)

пробудува (се) *impf of* пробуди (се)

пробуричка *pf* **I** 1 to stir (*carelessly, hurriedly*) *trans.* 2 to turn over, search, rummage in (*briefly*) **II – се** 1 to rummage in one's pockets (*for a while*) 2 to splash/wallow (*for a while*)

провади *pf* to sprinkle, water (*hastily, briefly*)

провала¹ *pf* to roll (*hastily, briefly*) *trans.*

провала² *f* 1 betrayal (*of an illegal organization*) 2 burglary, break-in 3 *rare see* пробив 4 *rare* eruption; провала на вулкан eruption of a volcano 5 *dial.* chasm, abyss

провали *pf* **I** 1 to betray, give away 2 *dial.* to break down/into *trans.* провали врата to break down a door 3 to break (*во – in*); to burst in, invade; арамии провалиле во дуќанот thieves broke into the shop 4 to rupture, burst *intrans.*; чирот му провалил his boil/ulcer burst 5 *literary* to ruin; провали претстава to ruin a performance **II – се** to collapse, give way, fail; се провали планот the plan foundered

провалија *f* gorge; chasm, abyss

провалник -ци *m* 1 traitor 2 burglar, housebreaker

провалува (се) *impf of* провали (се)

проварди *pf* **I** to watch, guard, mind (*for a while*) *trans.* **II – се** to keep watch (guard) (*for a while*)

провари *pf* to boil/cook for a while *trans.*; to digest partly

провев *m* draught, *Am.* draft

провева *impf* 1 *of* провее **I** 2 *fig.* to exude; од неговото држење провева незадоволство his bearing exuded discontent

проведе *pf* 1 *dial.* to lead, guide 2 to carry out, conduct; проведе избори to hold elections

проведри *pf* **I** to clear (*partly*) *trans.*; ветрот го проведри небото the wind partly cleared the sky **II – се** to clear up (*partly*) *intrans.*; се проведри <времето> the weather has cleared up a bit; *fig.* лицето му се проведри his face brightened

проведува *impf of* проведе

провее *pf* провеа *aor.* 1 (*за ветар, снег*) to begin to blow/fall; to blow/fall for while 2 (*жито*) to winnow

провејува *impf see* провева

провенча *pf* to marry (*perform/arrange a marriage*) in haste *trans.*

провери *pf* to check, verify

проверка *f* check, verification, inspection; test; проверка на документи inspection of documents

проверува *impf of* провери

провесели се *pf* to revel, celebrate (*for a while*) *intrans.*

проветри *pf* **I** to air, ventilate; проветри соба to air a room; ❑ *colloq.* си го проветри мозокот to clear one's head **II – се** 1 to be aired 2 *fig.* to take the air, get some fresh air

проветрува (се) *impf of* проветри (се)

провечера *pf* to sup/dine hastily, finish one's supper/dinner

провиден -дна *adj see* просирен

провидение *n* Providence

провиди *pf rare* **I** 1 (*прогледа*) to regain one's sight 2 (*npospe*) to see through 3 (*погледне*) to glance at **II – се** 1 (*види се*) to have a brief meeting (*со – with*) 2 *impers.* to become visible; се провидело it became light enough to see 3 to be transparent

провидност *f see* просирност

провидува (се) *impf of* провиди (се)

провизија -ии *f* commission, agent's fee

провизо́рен -рна *adj* provisional; temporary; провизорни мерки temporary measures

провија́нт *m rare* victuals, provisions, supplies

провика *pf* to cry out, yell (*for a while*)

провикне <се> *pf* провикна <се> *aor.* to cry out, give a shout

провикнува <се> *impf of* провикне <се>

провинција -ии *f* province; the provinces, the country; тој е од провинција he's a provincial

провинциа́лен -лна *adj see* провинциски

провинциа́лец -лци *m* provincial, rustic

провинцијали́зам -зми *m* provincialism

провинција́лка *f* (*fem. form*) *see* провинцијалец

прови́нциски *adj* provincial; провинциски град provincial town; провинциски менталитет provincial mentality

про́вира (се) *impf of* провре (се); ❑ провира некого низ прстен (увце) to give s.o. a hard time

прови́рач *m colloq.* artful dodger, slyboots

про́вирен -рна *adj* 1 (*за храна*) easily digestible 2 *fig.* transparent, translucent; провирно небо azure sky; провирна пролет a spring full of sun and freshness 3 (*за земја*) loose, friable

про́влак -ци *m Geog.* isthmus

провлече́ку́ва (се) *impf of* провлече (се)

про́влече *pf* провлеков *1st p. sg aor.* **I 1** to drag *trans.* **2** (*песна, зборување*) to drag out *trans.*; to drawl **3** *fig.* to delay, draw out **II – се 1** to trudge along; to straggle past **2** *fig.* to just manage, get by; се провлече на испит to scrape through an exam **3** *fig.* to drag on *intrans.*; ноќта се провлече the night wore on

про́влечен *pt* **1** careless, slovenly in dress **2** (*за глас, песна*) drawling; dragging out

провлече́чу́ва (се) *impf see* провлеку́ва (се)

про́вне (се) *pf* провна (се) *aor. see* провре (се)

про́внува (се) *impf of* провне (се)

прово́ден -дна *adj see* споводен

про́води *pf* **I** to accompany, take (*s.o. somewhere*) **II – се** to enjoy o.s.; to revel

прово́дник -ци *m see* споводник

провока́тивен -вна *adj* provocative

провока́тор *m* agent provocateur

провока́ција -ии *f* provocation

провоци́ра *pf & impf* to provoke

про́вре *pf* провра *aor.* **I** to draw, poke, pull (*низ – through*); провре прст низ една пукнатица to push one's finger through a crack; провре конец во игла to thread a needle **II – се 1** (*низ*) to squeeze through; се провре низ отвор од ѕид to squeeze through a gap in a wall **2** to just manage, get by

про́врева *pf* **1** to start making a noise; to start shouting, yelling **2** *dial.* to start talking; to talk a little **3** *rare* to make a noise, shout for a short time

про́вреска *pf* to squeal/scream/yell for a while

про́врне *pf impers.* проврна *aor.* (*за дожд и снег*) to rain/snow for a while

про́врти *pf* **I 1** to bore a hole in/through **2** *rare, colloq.* to turn, twist, spin (*for a while; hastily*) *trans.* **II – се 1** to twist, spin, turn (*for a while*) *intrans.* **2** to stay for a while, spend some time; се проврти трошка кај нас he spent a little time with us

про́вртка се *pf see* проврти се 2

провртýва (се) *impf of* проврти (се)

про́глас *m* proclamation; manifesto; declaration

про́гласи *pf* to announce, proclaim, declare; принцот го прогласиле <за> цар the prince was proclaimed emperor

прогласýва (се) *impf of* прогласи (се)

про́гледа *pf* **1** to begin to see, recover one's sight **2** *fig.* to see the light **3** to overlook, close one's eyes to; ❑ прогледа некому низ прсти to turn a blind eye to s.o.'s faults **4** *fig.* to start a better life

прогледýва *impf of* прогледа

про́глода *pf* **1** to gnaw into/through **2** *rare, colloq.* to gnaw for a short time

про́гние *pf* прогни *aor.* to rot through *intrans.*; to decay completely

прогно́за *f* forecast; prognosis; прогноза на времето weather forecast; спортска прогноза sporting prediction, tip

прогнозе́р *m* forecaster

прогнози́ра *pf & impf* to forecast, predict

прогова́ра *impf of* проговори

прого́вори *pf* **1** to begin to speak; to speak up, speak out; девојчето проговори the little girl started talking **2** to say, utter; ни збор не можеше да проговори he couldn't utter a single word; ❑ не му проговорил ни црна, ни бела he didn't say a single word to him

прого́лта *pf* to swallow (*also fig.*); to gulp down in a hurry, bolt

про́гон *m* pursuit, expulsion; (*судски*) persecution

прого́ни *pf rare, literary* to banish, expel, drive out; (*судски*) to persecute

прого́нство *n* banishment, exile

прогонýва *impf of* прогони

прого́ри *pf* **1** to burn holes in, burn through *trans.* **2** to burn through *intrans.* **3** *rare* to burn for a while

прогорýва *impf of* прогори

програ́ма *f* programme, *Am.* program; наставна програма curriculum; телевизиска програма television programme

програ́мер *m* <computer> programmer

програми́ра *pf & impf* to programme

програ́мски *adj* programme, programmatic; програмски материјал programme material; програмска статија programmatic article

про́грес *m* progress; општествен прогрес social progress

прогреси́вен -вна *adj* progressive

прогреси́ја -ии *f* progression; аритметичка прогресија arithmetical progression

прогреси́ра *pf & impf rare* to progress, advance, move ahead

прогри́зе *pf* прогриза *aor.* **1** to bite through, gnaw through **2** *Chem.* to corrode *trans.*; 'рѓа го прогризала металот rust has corroded the metal **3** to start biting/chewing **4** *rare* to bite/gnaw/chew for a while

прогризýва *impf of* прогризе

про́грми *pf* прогрме *aor.* **1** *impers.* to thunder; прогрме there was a peal of thunder **2** *rare* to bellow, thunder **3** *fig.* to rush by; прогрмеа годините the years sped (rushed) by **4** *poet., fig.* to echo, resound, reverberate; прогрме неговата слава his fame spread

прогýга *pf* to start cooing

про́дава (се) *impf of* продаде (се); ❑ на бостанцијата краставици му продава don't teach your grandmother to suck eggs; мене ум ќе ми продава! I don't need your advice; продава чалами (фалби) to boast, brag, show off; арната стока сама се продава *prov.* good wares make quick markets

прода́вање *n* sale; за продавање for sale; ум продавање giving unsolicited advice; чалами (фалби) продавање boasting, bluster

прода́вач *m* **1** seller; vendor; уличен продавач street vendor, hawker **2** shop assistant, salesman

продава́чка *f* **1** (*fem. form*) *see* продавач 1 **2** saleswoman, saleslady, salesgirl

продавен -вна *adj* selling, sale; продавна цена selling (sale) price

продавница *f* shop, *Am.* store; продавница за чевли shoe shop

продаде *pf* **I 1** to sell; ❏ скапо/евтино ја (го) продаде својата кожа (својот живот) to sell one's life dearly/cheaply **2** *fig.* to betray; продаде татковина to betray one's country **II** – **се 1** to sell *intrans.*; добро ќе се продаде стоката these goods will sell well **2** *fig.* to sell o.s., sell one's soul

продаден & *literary* **продан** *pt* sold; corrupt; продадена (продана) душа venal person

продажба *f* sale; тоа не е за продажба that is not for sale; продажба на големо и на мало wholesale and retail trade

продажен -жна *adj see* продавен

продекан *m* sub-dean

продемонстрира *pf see* демонстрира

продефилира *pf* to parade, file past, march past

продискутира *pf* to discuss thoroughly

продлаби & **продлабочи** *pf* to deepen *trans.*; *fig.* продлабочи прашање to explore a question in greater depth

продлабочува & **продлабува** *impf of* продлабочи & продлаби

продолжение -ија *n* continuation; instalment; роман во продолженија novel <published> in instalments; во продолжение на in the course of; продолжение на виза extension of a visa; продолжение на меница renewal of a bill of exchange; продолжение за струја (electrical) extension cord; *Sport.* продолжение на натпревар extra time

продолжи *pf* **I 1** to lengthen, prolong, extend *trans.* **2** to continue *trans.*; to resume; продолжи борба to continue a struggle; продолжи работа to get on with one's work; го продолжи патот to continue one's journey, go on one's way; продолжи да зборува to go on talking **3** to continue *intrans.*, go on; претставата ќе продолжи the performance will continue **II** – **се 1** to be extended; to stretch *intrans.* **2** to continue *intrans.*, go on; to last; разговорот се продолжи the conversation continued/went on and on

продолжува (се) *impf of* продолжи (се)

продолжувач *m literary* successor, heir (*fig.*)

продреме *pf rare* продрема *aor.* to snatch a little sleep

продува *pf* **1** to clean by blowing, blow out (*pipes, etc.*) *trans.* **2** to blow through, cut through; го продувал ветерот the wind blew right through him; *impers.* ме продува I was in a draught **3** to blow for a while *intrans.*

продукт *m* **1** product, result; индустриски продукти industrial products **2** (*usu. pl*) *colloq.* foodstuffs, groceries; млечни продукти) dairy produce

продуктивен -вна *adj* productive; продуктивен труд productive work; продуктивен писател productive writer; *Gram.* продуктивна наставка productive suffix

продуктивност *f* productivity; продуктивност на трудот productivity of labour

продукција *f* **1** production, output; manufacture; годишна продукција annual output **2** performance; concert

продукционен -она *adj* <of> production

продума *pf dial.*, *f.p.* to start speaking

продупи *pf* **1** to prick, pierce; to punch; to perforate; продупи тунел to bore a tunnel **2** to stab, knife, pierce; продупи некому срце to stab s.o. in the heart; го продупи со очите he gave him a piercing look

продупува *impf of* продупи; од многу капење капавицата и камен продупува constant dripping wears away stone

продупчи *pf* to make small holes (*in s.th.*); to puncture, perforate

продуховен *adj literary* spiritual; inspired, saintly

продуховеност *f literary* spiritual quality, spirituality

продухови *pf literary* to make spiritual; to inspire

продуцент *m* producer; филмски продуцент film producer

продуцентски *adj* <for> production; продуцентска куќа film <production> company

продуцира *pf* & *impf* **1** to produce, manufacture **2** to perform, present; to produce

проект *m* **1** plan, project, scheme **2** draft, outline; проект на устав draft constitution

проектант *m* architect; draughtsman; planning engineer; designer

проектантски *adj* planning; design; проектантско биро planning office

проектил *m* projectile, missile

проектира *pf* & *impf* **1** to plan; to design *trans.*; проектира зграда to design a building **2** to plan, intend (*да – то*)

проектор *m* projector

проекција -ии *m* projection

проекционен -она *adj* <of> projection; проекционен апарат projector

прожени *pf* to marry off (*a son*)

проживее *pf* проживеа *aor.* to live (dwell) for a period; две години проживеал на село he spent two years in the country

проживува *impf of* проживее

проза *f* prose

прозавитка *pf rare* to wrap/roll up (*hurriedly, carelessly*)

прозаврзе *pf* to tie/bind (*hurriedly, carelessly*)

прозаик -ци & **прозаист** *m* prose-writer

прозаичен -чна *adj* prosaic

прозакрпи *pf* **I** to patch up **II** – **се 1** to patch one's clothes **2** *fig.* to grow slightly stronger

прозамазни *pf* **I** to level; to smooth down **II** – **се** to smooth down one's hair, comb o.s. (*hastily*)

прозбори *pf see* прозборува

прозборува *pf* **1** to start speaking, talking; детето уште не прозборувало the child hasn't started talking yet **2** to say, utter; ни збор не прозборувал he didn't utter a word **3** to make (*s.o.*) speak, get (*s.o.*) talking

прозвучи *pf see* зазвучи

прозен -зна *adj* prose; прозен писател prose-writer

прозива *impf rare of* прозове

прозивка *f* roll-call; изврши прозивка to call the roll

прозове *pf* прозва *aor.* to summon, call by name, call (*s.o.*) out

прозодија *f* prosody

прозодиски *adj* prosodic

прозорец -рци *m* window; window pane; *fig.* loophole, way out

прозори се *pf* to dawn; <зора> се прозори dawn has broken

прозорски *adj* <of a> window; прозорско окно window pane; прозорско стакло window glass

прозорува се *impf of* прозори се

прозорче *n dim. of* прозорец

прозрачен -чна *adj* transparent

прозрачност *f* transparency

просева се *impf of* просевне се

просев<ав>ица *f see* просевка

просевка *f* yawn, yawning; ❑ оди како просевка од уста на уста it's spreading like wildfire; it's highly infectious

просевне се *pf* просевна се *aor.* to yawn

просира *impf* **I 1** to peer, peep (низ – *through*); просира низ клучалка to peep through a keyhole **2** to see through (*also fig.*); ги просираме неговите намери we see through his intentions **II – се 1** to be visible (perceptible) **2** to be transparent; ❑ уште му се просираат he is wasting away, he's a walking skeleton

просирен -рна *adj* transparent, translucent; clear, limpid; просирна хартија transparent paper; tracing-paper; просирно небо clear sky; просирни намери transparent intentions

просирец -рци *m f.p. see* прозорец

просирка *f* crack, chink

просирност *f adv* transparency

проспре *pf literary* проспра *aor.* to see through (*also fig.*); ги проспрела неговите намери she guessed/ understood his intentions

проигра *pf* **1** to start dancing/playing **2** to gamble away; го проиграл имотот he gambled away his property **3** *fig.* to waste, squander, fritter away; to lose

произведе *pf* **1** to manufacture, make; to produce; to generate; произведе ран зеленчук to produce early vegetables **2** to promote; произведе <за> мајор to promote to <the rank of> major **3** *rare, literary* to produce, make; произведе впечаток to make an impression

произведува *impf of* произведе

произведувач *m* producer; manufacturer

производ *m* product; млечни производи dairy products/produce

производител *m see* произведувач

производителски *adj* producer's, <of, for> production

производствен *adj* <of, for> production; производствени трошоци production costs; производствен план production plan

производство *n* **1** production, output, manufacture; средства за производство means of production; производство на јаглен coal production **2** *Mil.* promotion

произволен -лна *adj literary* **1** arbitrary; unfounded, unsubstantiated; произволно тврдење unfounded assertion **2** unspecified, selected at random; произволна точка any point; произволна количина random amount **3** *rare* self-willed, high-handed

произлегува *impf of* произлезе

произлезе *pf* **1** to come (од – *from*), stem from, derive from *intrans.*; македонскиот јазик произлезе од старословенскиот Macedonian is derived (de-

scended) from Old Church Slavonic **2** to follow (result) (од – *from*)

произнесе *pf literary* **I** to state, say, utter; to pronounce **II – се** to state one's opinion, to speak one's mind

произнесува (се) *impf of* произнесе (се)

проицира *pf & impf* **1** *Math., fig.* to project **2** (на екран) to project

пројава *f* **1** manifestation, display **2** act, action; conduct; некултурни пројави uncivilized behaviour

пројави *pf* **I** to manifest, show *trans.*, display; пројави талент to show ability **II – се 1** to show *intrans.*, show up, become apparent **2** to stand out; to distinguish o.s.; се пројави со своите успеси to distinguish o.s. by one's achievements/successes

пројавува (се) *impf of* пројави (се)

пројаде *pf* **I 1** to start eating; болниот уште не пројал the patient has not yet started eating **2** to bite through; to corrode *trans.* **3** to eat up (consume) quickly **II – се 1** to wear thin/out *intrans.*; јажево се пројало this rope has worn thin **2** *impers. (with dat.)* to feel hungry; ми се пројаде **I** <suddenly> felt hungry

пројадува (се) *impf of* пројаде (се)

пројасни *pf* **I 1** to clarify *trans.*, explain, elucidate **2** *rare* (разведри) to clear up *trans.* **II – се 1** to become clear/clearer; сега се пројасни ситуацијата the situation has now become clear **2** *rare* (разведри се) to clear up *intrans.*; времето како да се пројасни the weather appears to have cleared up

пројаснува (се) *impf of* пројасни (се)

пројде *pf* to pass

прокаже *pf rare* прокажа *aor.* to give away, inform on, betray

прокажува *impf of* прокаже

прокапе *pf* прокапа *aor.* **1** to spring a leak, begin to leak (drip); чешмата прокапа the tap has started dripping; *fig.* прокапа веста the news leaked out **2** to leak (drip) for a while; *impers.* to drizzle/spit for a while *intrans.*

прокасне *pf* прокасна *aor.* to take (have) a snack

прокастри *pf rare* **1** to prune/trim (*hurriedly*) **2** *fig.* to reproach, admonish

прокисне *pf* прокисна *aor.* to get soaked

прокламација *f* proclamation

прокламира *pf & impf* to proclaim, announce, make known

проклет *adj* **1** cursed, accursed, damned, wretched **2** evil; bad-tempered; malicious

проклетија *f* **1** *see* проклетство **2** scoundrel, villain **3** malice

проклетник -ци *m* wretch; scoundrel

проклетница *f* (*fem. form*) *see* проклетник

проклетство *n* **1** curse, oath **2** perdition, damnation **3** (*as interj*) damnation! damn!

проклина *impf rare see* проколнува

проклитика *f Gram.* proclitic

проклитички *adj* proclitic

проклука *pf* **1** to start banging, knocking (*at a door*) **2** *f.p.* to start banging (*of a door*)

прокнижи *pf Book-keeping* to enter *trans.*, record, log

прокнижува *impf of* прокнижи

прокоба *f poet.* foreboding, presentiment; evil prophecy

прокобен -бна *adj* ominous, foreboding, sinister; прокобен сон ominous dream

прокоби *pf* to foretell (predict) misfortune, prophesy ill; to bode ill, augur ill

прокобник -ци *m* prophet of doom, evil augur

прокобница *f* bird of ill omen, evil augur

прокобува *impf of* прокоби

проколнат *pt* cursed, accursed

проколне *pf* проколна *aor.* to curse *trans.*

проколнува *impf of* проколне

прокоментира *pf* to comment on

проконтролира *pf* to check

прокоп *m* trench, ditch

прокопа *pf* to dig through; to dig, cut, drive; прокопа тунел to dig a tunnel

прокопса *pf colloq.* **1** to do well, get on, thrive; ❑ нема да прокопса no good will come of it **2** *fig., iron.* to make a mess of one's life; to fail, go to the wall; to come to a sticky end

прокопсан *pt colloq.* **1** well-bred, polite **2** *iron.* good-for-nothing; mischievous

прокопсаник -ци *m colloq.* **1** decent person, good fellow **2** *fig., iron.* good-for-nothing, ne'er-do-well

прокопсаница *f (fem. form)* see прокопсаник

прокопува *impf of* прокопа

прококца *pf rare, literary* to gamble away; to squander

прокуда *f colloq.* bad habit

прокуди *pf* I to lead astray; to spoil *trans.*; прокуди дете to spoil a child **II – се** to fall into bad habits

прокудлив *adj* easily led, weak-willed, suggestible

прокудува (се) *impf of* прокуди (се)

пролева (се) *impf of* пролее (се)

пролее *pf* пролеа *aor.* I **1** to spill *trans.*; to shed; пролее крв to shed blood; пролее солзи to shed tears **II – се** to spill *intrans.*, be spilt/shed

пролет -тта *f* пролети *pl* & **пролетје, пролеќе** *n* **1** *f.p.* spring; на пролет in spring; со една ластовица пролет не иде *prov.* one swallow does not make a summer; **2** *(as adv)* in spring

пролета *pf* **1** to fly past/over; to rush (hurry) past; пролета кола a car sped past; ми пролетаа разни мисли various thoughts flashed through my mind; летото пролета the summer flew by **2** to start flying; to learn to fly

пролетаризација *f* proletarianization

пролетаризира *pf* & *impf* to proletarianize

пролетаријат *m* proletariat

пролетен -тна *adj* spring, springlike, vernal; пролетни цвеќиња spring flowers; пролетна пченица spring wheat

пролетер *m* proletarian

пролетерка *f (fem. form)* see пролетер

пролетерски *adj* proletarian

пролетнина *f* spring crops

пролето *n in the expression: f.p.* лето-пролето spring and summer; warm weather; кога ќе дојде лето-пролето when the warm season comes

пролетоска *adv* **1** last spring **2** *rare* next spring

пролетошен -шна *adj* <of> last/next spring

пролетува *impf of* пролета

пролив *m* **1** *Med.* diarrhoea **2** *rare* spillage, spilling; *fig.* shedding

пролог -зи *m* prologue

проломоти *pf* **1** to start mumbling **2** to make a noise *(for a while)*; to grumble/chatter *(for a while)*

пролонгира *pf* & *impf* to prolong, extend *trans.*

промажи *pf* to marry off *(a daughter, hurriedly)*

промена *f* **1** change, exchange; ситуацијата е без промени the situation is unchanged; промена на воздух change of air **2** *Gram.* inflexion; глаголска промена conjugation; именска промена declension **3** change of clothes

променет *pt* dressed up; ❑ променет нецеливан all dressed up and nowhere to go

промени *pf* I **1** to change, alter *trans.*; ❑ го промени мислењето to change one's mind; промени стан to move house **2** to dress *(s.o.)* in new clothes **II – се 1** to change *intrans.*; животот се промени life has changed **2** to exchange, swap; се променија со становите to exchange (swap) flats **3** to put on new clothes; to change one's clothes

променица *f f.p. dim. of* промена 3

променлив *adj* **1** changeable, variable; променлив ветар variable wind; *Math.* променлива величина variable **2** fickle, capricious **3** *Gram.* inflected, declinable

променливост *f* changeability, variability; *Gram.* inflexion

променува (се) *impf of* промени (се)

промет *m* trade, traffic, sale<s>; промет на стоки turnover of goods

промете *pf* to sweep out *(hurriedly)*

прометен -тна *adj* **1** busy; прометна улица busy street **2** circulating; прометен капитал turnover

прометува *impf of* промете

промеша *pf* I to mix, stir, blend, shuffle *(hurriedly) trans.* **II – се 1** to meddle *(во – in) (briefly)* **2** to be friendly *(со – with)*, mix *(for a while) intrans.*

промил *m* thousandth part; пет промила five per mil

промовира *pf* & *impf* to confer a degree *(usu. doctoral)* upon; to promote *(to)*; to publicize, advertise; го промовираа за шеф на катедра he was promoted to head of department

промоција -ии *f* conferring of a *(usu. doctoral)* degree; promotion; celebration; промоција на книга book launch

промрда *pf* I **1** to begin to move (shift) again *trans.* **2** to move (shift) slightly *trans.* **II – се** to move (stir) for a while *intrans.*

промрмори *pf* to mumble; to mutter; to murmur

пронајде *pf* **1** to discover, invent **2** *rare* to find, seek out

пронајдок -ци *m* discovery; invention

пронајдувач *m see* пронаоѓач

пронајдувачки *adj see* пронаоѓачки

пронаоѓа *impf of* пронајде

пронаоѓач *m* inventor; discoverer

пронаоѓачки *adj* inventor's; discoverer's; inventive

проневера *f* embezzlement; misappropriation

проневери *pf* to embezzle, misappropriate

проневерува *impf of* проневери

проневерувач *m* embezzler

пронесе[1] *pf* I **1** to carry through/by *trans.* **2** *(глас, вест)* to spread *trans.*; тие пронесоа глас дека победиле they spread a rumour that they had won **II – се** *(за глас, вест)* to spread *intrans.*

пронесе[2] *pf* (*за птица*) to start laying <eggs>

пронесува[1] **(се)** *impf of* пронесе[1] (се)

пронесува[2] *impf of* пронесе[2]

прониже *pf* пронижа *aor. rare, literary* **1** to pierce, transfix; to stab; прониже со куршуми to riddle with bullets; (*за звук*) прониже уши to shatter s.o.'s ear-drums **2** *fig.* (*за чувство, мисла*) to come over *trans.*; ме пронижа мисла an idea took hold of me

пронижува *impf of* прониже

пронизлив *adj* shattering, ear-splitting, piercing, shrill

прониклив *adj* penetrating, perceptive, discerning

проникливост *f* perspicacity, insight, acumen

проникнат *pt* rapt; imbued; проникнат од чувство на љубов filled with loving feelings

проникне[1] *pf* проникна *aor.* **I 1** (*низ, во*) to penetrate; to breach; to force an entry into; проникне во суштината на нешто to get to the essence of s.th. **2** *fig.* (*за мисла, чувство*) to come over *trans.*, take hold of; to imbue **II – се** to be filled with; to be imbued with

проникне[2] *pf* to germinate, sprout, come up

проникнува[1] **(се)** *impf of* проникне[1] (се)

проникнува[2] *impf of* проникне[2]

проносена *adj in the expression:* проносена кокошка chicken which has started laying

проноси[1] *pf* to start wearing/using

проноси[2] *pf see* пронесе[2]

проод *m* passage; aisle; gangway

прооден -дна *adj* passable (*of road, track*)

проодено *adj in the expression:* проодено дете toddler

прооденче *n* toddler

прооди *pf* **1** (*за дете*) to start walking, learn to walk; ❏ прооди гол to be reduced to penury **2** *rare* to cross, pass *trans.*; планината ја проодиле they crossed the mountain

проодува *impf of* прооди

пропага́нда *f* **1** propaganda; advertising **2** *Hist.* (*usu. pl*) activities by Balkan states to gain positions of influence in Macedonia

пропага́нден -дна *adj* <for> propaganda; advertising; пропаганден материјал propaganda/advertising material

пропаганди́ст *m* propagandist

пропагандисти́чки *adj* <for> propaganda; propagandistic; пропагандистичка дејност propaganda work

пропага́тор *m* propagandist; proponent

пропаги́ра *pf & impf* to promote; to propagate

пропади *pf rare* **1** *see* испади, напади **2** *see* прогони, протера

пропаднат *pt* ruined; debauched, degraded; broken; пропадната жена fallen woman

пропадне *pf* пропадна *aor.* **1** to fall; to collapse *intrans.*; пропадне во дупка to fall into a hole **2** *fig.* to vanish, disappear; to get lost; како земи да пропаднал it's as if the earth had swallowed him up **3** *fig.* to fail, collapse, go bankrupt; сите планови му пропаднаа all his plans came to nothing; сè пропадна all is lost; здравјето му пропадна his health is ruined **4** (*во вода*) to sink *intrans.* **5** to sink *trans.*, send to the bottom (*also fig.*); пропадне пари to throw money away

пропаѓа *impf of* пропадне

пропаст *f* **1** abyss, precipice; chasm, gorge, ravine **2** *fig.* rift, cleft, division; нè дели длабока пропаст there is a gulf between us **3** *fig.* destruction, ruin; ги спасија од сигурна пропаст they saved them from certain disaster; ❏ вечна му пропаст! **1.** woe betide him! **2.** you can write that off (kiss that goodbye)!

пропасти (се) *pf see* упропасти (се)

пропастува (се) *impf of* пропасти (се)

пропатува *pf* to travel through/around; пропатува цела Европа to travel all over Europe

пропева *impf of* пропее

пропее *pf* пропеа *aor.* **1** to start singing <again>; ❏ и моето пиле ќе пропее my turn will come **2** (*за поет*) to start writing poetry

пропека *pf* **1** to start pleading, imploring **2** *rare* to scream (cry) a little

пропеле́р *m Tech.* propeller; screw

пропере *pf* пропра *aor.* to wash (launder) hastily

пропива се *impf of* пропие се

пропие се *pf* пропи се *aor.* to take to drink

пропис *m* regulation; order; ordinance; prescript; законски пропис legal regulation; според прописите according to the regulations

пропишен -сна *adj* legal, lawful

прописка *pf see* пропишти

пропита *pf* to become a beggar, start begging

пропише *pf* пропиша *aor.* to order, prescribe

пропишти *pf* to start screaming/squealing/weeping

пропишува *impf of* пропише

проплаче *pf* **1** to start crying a little **2** to cry for a while **3** to start screaming

проплеска *pf* **1** to slap lightly; to <begin to> clap (applaud) a little **2** (*тесто*) to pat, knead (*lightly, hurriedly*)

проплете *pf* to <start to> knit; to resume knitting

проплива *pf* to start swimming <again>

проплиска *pf* **1** to start splashing/spattering **2** (*за дожд*) to spit, drizzle; проплиска малку дожд there was a light shower

проплука *pf* to start spitting; ❏ крв проплука to go through hell

проповед *f* sermon

проповеда *pf & impf see* проповедува

проповедник -ци *m* preacher

проповедни́чки *adj* <of> preaching; propagandistic; moralizing; evangelizing, missionary

проповедни́штво *n* preaching

проповедува *impf* to preach; *pejor.* to sermonize, hold forth

пропозиција -ии *f* **1** (*предлог*) suggestion, proposition **2** (*изјава*) presentation; announcement **3** *Sport.* (*usu. pl.*) rules of a game

пропорција -ии *f* proportion, ratio; scale

пропорциона́лен -лна *adj* proportionate; proportional; пропорционален изборен систем proportional representation

пропорциона́лност *f* proportional relationship

пропржи *pf* to fry lightly

пропрска *pf* **1** to splash/spray (*lightly*) **2** (*за дожд*) to stop

пропусница *f* pass, permit

пропуст *m* **1** admission; free passage **2** passageway; ford; mountain pass **3** omission, oversight; lapse

пропустлив *adj* porous; permeable; leaky

пропустливост *f* porosity; permeability

пропуши *pf* to start (take up) smoking <again>

пропушта (се) *impf of* пропушти (се); чунот пропушта вода the dinghy is taking water

пропушти *pf* **I 1** to admit *trans.*, let in/out/through **2** to miss *trans.*; пропушти предавање to miss a lecture **3** to leave out, omit, overlook, fail to notice; пропушти збор to leave out a word; пропушти момент to let an opportunity slip **4** to neglect (*да – то*); пропушти да се потпише to neglect to sign **II – се** to slip down *intrans.*; to droop *intrans.*; му се пропуштиле чорапите his socks slid down

проработи *pf* to start working/operating/functioning; to resume work; ❑ му проработи среќата fortune smiled upon him; he had a stroke of luck

проработува *impf of* проработи

проред *m Print.* space, interval <between lines>; новинарски проред double spacing

прореди (се) *pf see* проретчи (се)

проредува (се) *impf of* прореди (се)

прореже *pf* to cut <through>, slice

прорежува *impf of* прореже

прорез *m* cut; slit; (*деколте*) low-cut neckline, *décolletage*

проректор *m* deputy vice-chancellor

проретчи *pf* **I** to thin <out> *trans.*; to dilute **II – се** to thin <out> *intrans.*; му се проретчила косата his hair has thinned; се проретчија редовите the ranks have thinned

проретчува (се) *impf of* проретчи (се)

пророк -ци *m* prophet

пророкува *impf* to prophesy, foretell, predict

пророни *pf literary, rare* to utter, say; to shed, drop, let fall; пророни солзи to start shedding tears; to shed a few tears; пророни слово to utter (breathe) a word

проронува *impf of* пророни

пороси *pf* (*usu. impers.*) **1** to begin to form (*of dew*); to begin to drizzle (*of rain*); роса пороси dew began to form **2** to drizzle for a while

проросува *impf of* пороси

пророчица *f* prophetess

пророчиште *n Hist.* oracle; Делфиското пророчиште Delphic oracle

пророчки *adj* prophetic

пророштво *n* prophecy

про'рти *pf* to germinate, sprout *intrans.*

про'ртува *impf of* про'рти

просаска *pf* **1** (*за змија и др.*) to start hissing **2** *fig.* to hiss, growl, snarl, snap

просвета *f* enlightenment; education; здравствена просвета health education

просветен *adj* enlightened; *Hist.* просветениот апсолутизам enlightened despotism

просветен -тна *adj* educational; просветна работа educational work

просветеност *f* enlightenment; education, learning; culture

просвети *pf* **I** to enlighten; to educate **II – се** to become enlightened; to receive an education

просветител *m literary* enlightener; educator, teacher

просветителски *adj* enlightening, instructive; teacher's

просветителство *n* enlightenment/education

просветлен *adj literary* clear, lucid; просветлен ум enlightened mind

просветление *n literary* enlightenment

просветли *pf literary* to illuminate, explain, elucidate, clarify *trans.*

просветлува *impf of* просветли

просветува (се) *impf of* просвети (се)

просвири *pf* to start playing *intrans.*; просвири виолина a violin began to play; виолинистот просвири the violinist began to play

просвирува *impf of* просвири

просева *impf of* просее

просее *pf* просеа *aor.* to sift (*also fig.*)

просек -ци *m* **1** cut, slice **2** *see* просека **3** average, mean; во просек on the average; под просек below average

просека *f* forest path, ride

просекува *impf of* просече

просен *adj* millet; просено брашно millet flour

просеник -ци *m* millet bread (loaf)

просец -сци *m f.p.* suitor, wooer

просече *pf* to cut through, cut a swathe/path

просечен -чна *adj* average; ordinary; просечна брзина average speed; просечен човек man in the street

просечно *adv* on average

просечува *impf see* просекува

проси *impf* to beg, seek alms; to ask for, request

просија *f* begging, mendicancy

просјак -ци *m* beggar, mendicant

просјачка *f* (*fem. form*) *see* просјак

просјачки *adj* beggar's; ❑ дотера до просјачки стап to ruin, reduce to beggary; to be reduced to poverty

проскита *pf* **I 1** to roam (rove, wander) for a while; го проскита градот; проскита по (низ) градот to stroll around town **2** to start wandering **II – се** *see* I 1

проскура *f see* покскура

проскурник -ци *m see* поскурник

прослава *f* celebration; party

прославен *pt* famous, celebrated, well-known; glorious, illustrious

прослави *pf* **I 1** to celebrate *trans.*; го прослави Први мај to celebrate May Day **2** to glorify, bring glory to **II – се** to become famous, win renown

прославува (се) *impf of* прослави (се)

проследен *pt* accompanied (*co – by*)

проследи *pf* **1** to accompany; проследи предавање со проекции to illustrate a lecture with slides **2** to trace back, go over, review

проследува *impf of* проследи

просне се *pf* просна се *aor. see* пласне се

проснува се *impf of* просне се

просо *n Bot.* (Panicum miliaceum) millet; алвациско просо (Sorghum vulgare) sorghum; common (African, back) millet, *Am.* broom corn; диво просо 1. (Leersia oryzoides) *also* оризарско просо rice grass, cut-grass 2. (Lithospermum arvense) corn gromwell; ❑ суши просо на ортома to waste time

просолзи *pf* (*за очи*) to fill with tears *intrans.*

прослончи се *pf* (*usu. impers.*) to clear up, become sunny; се прослончи времево the weather has cleared

проспект *m* prospectus, brochure

просперира *pf & impf* to prosper, flourish, thrive

просперитёт *m* prosperity; стопански просперитет economic prosperity

прост *adj* **1** simple, easy, uncomplicated; unadorned, plain; проста работа simple matter; *Gram.* проста реченица simple sentence; прости броеви prime numbers; ❑ со просто око with the naked eye **2** ordinary; common; vulgar, coarse; прост војник a common soldier; прост народ common (ordinary) people; просто држење crude (vulgar) behaviour **3** simple-hearted; simple-minded; artless; ingenuous; проста душа simple soul; просто срце kind/open heart; ❑ прост како лека (грав) 1. slow on the uptake 2. (*of things*) as easy as pie

простак -ци *m* boor, lout, ruffian

простачки *adj* boorish, loutish, crude, vulgar

простен *pt* **1** forgiven **2** *arch.* <of> farewell, parting; простена молитва prayer for the dying

прости *pf* **I** to forgive, pardon; to absolve; to condone; му ја простиле грешката they forgave him his mistake (excused his mistake); простете excuse me! <I beg your> pardon; да простите if you will forgive me; ❑ Бог да го прости! 1. God rest his soul! 2. *iron.* you can write that off! за Бог да прости 1. in (*s.o.'s*) memory 2. *iron.* for nothing, for peanuts; не работам за Бог да прости I don't work for nothing **II** – **се 1** to say goodbye (*со, од – то*), part with, take one's leave of **2** to forgive each other

простира (се) *impf of* простре (се)

простирка *f see* покривка

проституира *pf & impf* **I** to prostitute *trans.* (*also fig.*) **II** – **се** to prostitute o.s. (*also fig.*)

проститутка *f* prostitute, whore

проституција *f* prostitution

простичко *adv rare dim. of* просто[1]

простичок -чка *adj dim. of* прост

просто[1] *adv* simply, plainly; merely, just; ❑ просто напросто simply (in plain terms); nothing but

просто[2] *adv see* простум

просто[3] *adv in the expressions:* просто да му е, нека му е просто may he be forgiven! let us forget it! од Бога нека му е просто may God forgive him!

простодушен -шна *adj* open-hearted; good-natured, kindly

простодушност *f* open-heartedness; good nature, kind(li)ness

простонароден -дна *adj* of the common people

простор *m* **1** space, expanse; *fig.* scope; бесконечен (бескраен) простор infinite space; празен простор empty space (void); vacuum; ❑ бришан простор danger zone, no man's land **2** enclosure; field; site

просторен -рна *adj* **1** spatial **2** *rare, literary* spacious, roomy; extensive, vast

просторија -ии *f* room; premises; општествени простории public premises; communal rooms

простосмртен -тна *adj literary in the expression:* простосмртен човек mere mortal

простосрдечен -чна *adj* sincere, straightforward; artless, ingenuous; kindly

простосрдечност *f* sincerity; artlessness, ingenuousness; kind<li>ness

простота *f* **1** simplicity; plainness; sincerity; artlessness, ingenuousness; ❑ света простота ignorance is bliss **2** *rare see* простотија 2

простотија *f* **1** ignorance; illiteracy **2** vulgarity, boorishness; coarse speech; ill-breeding

простран *adj* spacious, roomy; ample, vast

пространствен *adj see* просторен 1

пространство *n see* простор 1

простре *pf* простра *aor.* **I 1** to spread *trans.*; to strew; to extend; (*алишта*) to hang out; простре своја власт to extend one's power; ❑ како ќе си простреш така ќе си легнеш *prov.* as you make your bed, so you must lie in it **2** to knock down, lay out, send sprawling **II** – **се 1** to spread out, extend *intrans.*; се прострело пред нив големо поле a large field stretched before them **2** to reach, extend *intrans.*; далеку се простре неговата власт his power extended far and wide **3** to sprawl, stretch out *intrans.*; се прострел на креветот he sprawled on the bed

прострели *pf* to shoot through, pierce with a shot; to riddle with bullets/arrows; ❑ прострели со поглед to transfix with a glance

прострелува *impf of* прострели

простру́и *pf literary* to spread, circulate (*of rumours*) *intrans.*

простуди́ра *pf* to study, examine, peruse

простум *adv* upright, standing; стои простум to stand straight; оди простум to walk erect

просфора *f Rel. see* поскура

просце *n hyp. dim. of* просо

протагони́ст *m* protagonist

протатни *pf* to rumble/roar by/past; to speed past; авионите протатнија the planes roared overhead; протатнија годините the years flew by

протега (се) *impf of* протегне (се)

протегавица *f* spontaneous (involuntary) stretching

протегнато *adv rare* at length, extendedly; drawlingly

протегне *pf* протегна *aor.* **I** to stretch, extend *trans.*; *fig.* to apply *trans.*; протегне раце to stretch out one's arms; протегне правило на сите случаи to apply a rule to all instances **II** – **се** to extend/reach/stretch *intrans.*; се протегне на кревет to stretch out on a bed; неговата власт се протегнала на други земји his power has extended to other countries

протегнува (се) *impf see* протега (се)

протеже́ -éи *m* protégé, (*fem. form*) protégée

протежи́ра *pf & impf* to give patronage to; to patronize

проте́за *f* **1** prosthesis, prosthetic appliance; artificial limb; denture **2** *Phon.* prothesis; prothetic consonant

протеи́н *m* protein

проте́ктор *m* protector, defender; patron, friend at court

протектора́т *m* protectorate

протекува *impf* **1** to leak, fail to hold water **2** *rare* (*за река*) to flow <through/by> **3** *fig.*, *literary* (*за време*) to go by, pass, elapse **4** *impf of* протече 1

протекција *f* protection, preferential treatment

протекциона́ш *m colloq.* careerist, hanger-on

протекциона́шки *adj colloq.* time-serving, careerist

протекциони́зам -змот *m* protectionism

протекциони́ст *m* **1** protectionist **2** *rare see* протекционаш

протепа *pf* **I** to give (*s.o.*) a quick beating, spanking **II** – **се** to have a short brawl

протепка *pf* to stammer (stutter); to start stammering

протера *pf* **1** to drive out, expel, banish **2** *colloq.* (*3rd p. only, often impers.*) (*with acc.*) to cause diarrhoea; го протерал гравот the beans have given him the runs **3** *colloq* to spend (*time*); кај ќе ги протераш празниците? where are you going to spend your holidays? **4** *fig.*, *colloq.* to live (get) through, survive; протера зима to get through the winter

протерува *impf of* протера

протест *m* protest

протеста́нт *m* Protestant

протестанти́зам -змот *m* Protestantism

протеста́нтка *f* (*fem. form*) *see* протестант

протеста́нтски *adj* Protestant; протестантска вера Protestant faith

протеста́нтство *n see* протестантизам

протестен -стна *adj* protest, protesting; протестен митинг protest meeting

протести́ра *pf & impf* to protest

протети́чки *adj* prosthetic; prothetic

протече *pf* (*3rd p. only*) **1** to start flowing; to start leaking; вода протече water started flowing; протече таванот the ceiling has started leaking **2** *fig.*, *literary* (*за време*) to pass, elapse; протекоа два месеца оттогаш two months have passed since then

протечува *impf see* протекува

против *prep* **1** against; contrary to; против своја волја against one's will; лек против (за од) кашлица cough medicine **2** *dial.* (*спроти*) opposite

против- *prefix* counter-; anti-

противавио́нски *adj* anti-aircraft; противавионска артилерија anti-aircraft artillery; противавионска заштита anti-aircraft defence

противакција *f* counteraction

противатомски *adj* anti-atomic, anti-nuclear; противатомска заштита anti-nuclear defence

противвредност *f* equivalent value, countervalue

противдејство *n* counteraction; reaction; counter-effect

противдржавен -вна *adj* anti-state, seditious; противдржавни елементи subversive elements

противен -вна *adj* **1** contrary, adverse; противен ветар head wind; ❏ во противен случај if the opposite is the case; otherwise **2** opposed, in opposition to; јас сум противен на тоа I am against (opposed to) that **3** opposite; противната страна the opposite side; the opposing party (opponent)

противзаконит *adj* illegal; противзаконита постапка illegal act

противзаконски *adj see* противзаконит

противзаразен -зна *adj* antiseptic

противи се *impf* (*на*) to offer resistance; to oppose, object to **2** to run counter (*на – to*), be at variance with, contradict; тоа му се противи на законот that is against the law

противнароден -дна *adj* unpatriotic

противник -ци *m* **1** opponent **2** enemy, adversary

противников *adj* enemy; opposing

противница & противничка *f* (*fem. form*) *see* противник

противнички *adj* hostile, enemy; opposing; противнички сили enemy forces

противно *adv* contrary (*на – to*), against; противно на очекувањата contrary to expectations

противност *f* contrast, opposition; contrariness

противофанзи́ва *f* counter-offensive

противо́тров *m* antidote, antivenene, serum

противпожарен -рна *adj* fire-fighting; противпожарни средства fire-fighting equipment; противпожарна команда fire brigade, *Am.* fire department

противпра́вен -вна *adj* illegal

противпре́длог -зи *m* counter-proposal

противреформација *f* Counter-reformation

противречен -чна *adj* contradictory

противречи *impf* (*на*) to contradict, *literary* gainsay; to run counter to; противречи на политика to run counter to a policy; си противречи to contradict o.s./ one another; тие две работи си противречат these two things are contradictory

противречие -ија & **противречје** *n* contradiction, discrepancy, dichotomy; conflict

противречност *f* contradiction, disjuncture; contrariety; противречност меѓу зборовите и делата disjuncture between words and actions

противстави *pf* **I** (*нешто на нешто*) to oppose (to), contrast (with) *trans.*, set s.th against s.th. **II – се** to oppose, resist *intrans.*

противставува (**се**) *impf of* противстави (се)

противте́жа *f* counterweight (*also fig.*)

противтенковски *adj* anti-tank; противтенковска пушка anti-tank rifle

противту́жба *f* counter-charge, counter-accusation

противу́дар *m* counter-blow

противуслуга *f* return favour, favour in return

противуставен -вна *adj* unconstitutional

противхемиски *adj* anti-gas; противхемиска заштита protection against chemical weapons

протина (**се**) *impf of* протне (се)

проткае *pf* проткаја *aor.* **1** to weave (*s. th.*) into s.th. **2** to decorate by weaving **3** *fig.* to permeate *trans.*, pervade **4** to weave (*hurriedly*)

проткајува *impf of* проткае

протне (**се**) *pf see* провре (се)

протнува (**се**) *impf see* протина (се)

протоје́реј -еи *m Rel.* <Orthodox> archpriest

протојерејски *adj Rel.* <Orthodox> archpriest's

проток -ци *m Geog.* straits; channel; flow

протокол *m* protocol

протокола́рен -рна *adj* protocol; протоколарна посета protocol visit

протолкува *pf* to interpret *trans.*, explain

протон *m* proton

протопла́зма *f* protoplasm

протопла́змен *adj* protoplasmal, protoplasmic

протоси́нгел *m Rel.* Orthodox cleric

прототип *m* prototype, archetype

прототипски *adj* prototypal, prototypical

проточка се *pf* to rush past (by) in large numbers; кај него се проточкаа многу луѓе many people have visited his house

протрбуши *pf* to eviscerate, disembowel

протресе *pf* to shake out/up, jolt *trans.*; to shake slightly *trans.*; *impers.* (*with acc.*) ме протресе малку I had a slight bout of fever

протресува *impf of* протресе

протрива (**се**) *impf of* протрие (се)

протрие *pf* протри *aor.* **I** to rub, scrub a little (slightly); протрие очи to rub one's eyes **II – се 1** to rub o.s. a little (*with ointment, etc.*) **2** to rub, scrub o.s. a little

протрча *pf* to run past; to run (*низ – through*) *intrans.*

протрчува *impf of* протрча

протуѓер *m arch.* town crier

протурен *pt* **1** (*за овошка*) fruiting heavily, fruitful **2** (*за човек*) very fat, obese; inept, clumsy

протури *pf* **I 1** to rupture *trans.*, give (*s.o.*) a hernia; to harm **2** to tangle, entangle, mess up **II** – **се 1** to burst open *intrans.* **2** (*за овошка*) to be laden with fruit **3** to rupture o.s., get a hernia

протурка *pf* **1** to push/shove through **2** *fig.* to manage *intrans.*; to survive; така го протурка веков that's how he got through life

протутне *pf fig.* протутна *aor.* to manage, get along/through, survive *intrans.*

проумре *pf* to come close to death, almost die

проусти *pf poet.* to utter

проучи *pf* to investigate, study thoroughly, research *trans.*

проучува *impf of* проучи

проучување *n* study, investigation, research

профан *adj* **1** profane; профана литература secular literature **2** uninitiated, ignorant **3** uncouth, common

профанира *pf & impf* to profane, defile, desecrate, debase

професија -ии *f* profession; occupation

професионален -лна *adj* professional

професионалец -лци *m* (*usu. Sport.*) professional

професионализам -змот *m* (*usu. Sport.*) professionalism

професор *m* **1** professor; вонреден професор associate professor **2** secondary-school teacher (*with a university degree*); професор по хемија chemistry teacher

професорка *f* (*fem. form*) *see* професор

професорски *adj* professorial; teaching; професорски колегиум teaching staff

професура *f* chair, professorship

профил *m* profile (*also fig.*); cross-section; type

профилакса *f see* профилактика

профилактика *f* prophylaxis; preventive medicine, treatment, measures

профилактички *adj* prophylactic

профит *m* profit, gain

профитира *pf & impf* to profit, make a profit, gain advantage (*од – from*)

профучи *pf* to rush past/by; to fly by/past; профучи куршум a bullet whistled past; профучија дните the days flew by

прохибиција *f* prohibition

прохибиционизам -змот *m* prohibitionism

прохибиционист *m* prohibitionist

процвета *pf see* процути

процветува *impf of* процвета

процвили *pf* **1** to start whining **2** to whine from time to time, for a moment

процвркоти *pf see* цвркоти

процеди *pf see* прецеди

процедува *impf of* процеди

процедура *f* procedure; судска процедура legal procedure

процедурален -лна *adj* procedural

процена *f* estimate, valuation

процени *pf* to value, evaluate, estimate

процент *m* **1** percent, percentage **2** interest

процентен -тна *adj* **1** of percent **2** *see* процентуален

процентуален -лна *adj* percental, percentile; процентуален однос percentages

проценува *impf of* процени

проценувач *m* valuer, valuator, appraiser

процеп *m* crevice, fissure

процес *m* **1** process; ❑ во процесот на (*нешто*) in the process of (*s.th.*) **2** судски процес trial

процесија -ии *f* procession; column; mass procession; погребна процесија funeral procession, cortège

процесуален -лна *adj in the expression:* процесуално право procedural law

процитира *pf rare* to quote, make a quotation

процут *m* flourishing, flowering, blossoming (*also fig.*); процут на културата flourishing of culture

процути *pf* to flourish *intrans.*, blossom, bloom, flower (*also fig.*); процути културниот живот cultural life flourished

процутува *impf of* процути

прочепка *pf* **1** to pick, clean by picking; прочепка заби to pick one's teeth **2** *fig.* to probe, investigate; ја прочепка работата to look into the matter

прочисти *pf* **I** to clear, clean out *trans.*; to purge **II** – **се 1** to relieve o.s., evacuate one's bowels **2** to clear up *intrans.*

прочистува (се) *impf of* прочисти (се)

прочита *pf* **I** to read **2** *fig.*, *sl.* to understand, fathom (*s.o.*)

прочитува *impf of* прочита

прочка *f* **1** *see* прошка **2** Shrovetide

прочрчори *pf* to start chirruping, twittering

прочуе *pf* прочу *aor.* **I** to regain one's hearing **II** – **се** to become famous/notorious; се прочул во целиот крај he won fame throughout the land

прочуен *pt* famous, celebrated, illustrious; notorious; прочуен мајстор famous craftsman

процавка *pf* **1** to start yapping; to yap for a while **2** *fig.* to start shouting, yelling **3** *fig.*, *iron.* to tire of shouting

прошари *pf* **I 1** to add colour to; to dapple, mottle, stipple; to blotch **2** (*коса*) to cause to turn grey *trans.* **II** – **се 1** to take on <patchy> colour; to become stippled, mottled, blotchy **2** (*за коса*) to begin turning grey **3** (*за грозје*) to start ripening

прошарува (се) *impf of* прошари (се)

прошепоти *pf* to <say in a> whisper

прошепотува *impf of* прошепоти

прошета *pf* **I 1** to take for a walk; прошета куче to walk a dog; прошета дете to take a child for a walk **2** to go for a walk; *fig.* прошета со поглед to run one's eye over **3** to pass/travel through; тој ја прошетал франција he has travelled all over France **II** – **се** *see* **I** 2

прошетка *f* **1** stroll, walk; излезе на прошетка to go out for a walk **2** outing

прошетува (се) *impf of* прошета (се)

прошива *impf of* прошие

прошие *pf* проши *aor.* to sew up, stitch

проширен *pt* extended; expanded, broadened; widened

прошири *pf* **I** to extend, widen, expand, broaden *trans.*; прошири свој репертоар to extend one's repertoire; прошири свои знаења to broaden one's knowledge **II** – **се** to spread, extend, widen, expand *intrans.*

проширува (се) *impf of* прошири (се)

прошка *f* forgiveness; бара (моли за) прошка to ask <for> forgiveness

прошлака *pf* I 1 to slap, smack repeatedly 2 *fig.* to slap on paint 3 *fig.* to blurt out II – **се** to wash o.s. hurriedly

прошлапа *pf* 1 to wade (splash) <through mud/water> for a while 2 *fig. see* прошлака I 3

прошлапка *pf see* прошлапа 1

проштава *impf of* прости

проштавање *n* 1 act of forgiving 2 act of bidding goodbye, farewell; на проштавање in parting

проштален -лна *adj* <of> farewell; проштално писмо farewell letter; suicide note

проштење *n arch. see* прошка

прпа *impf* 1 (*за птица*) to flutter 2 *fig.* to tremble, quiver; срцето му прпа his heart is all aflutter 3 *see* прпори 2

прпела *impf* I to roll (*s. th.*) on the ground II – **се** to roll/writhe/wriggle on the ground

прпелка (се) *impf dim. of* прпела (се)

прплица *f* 1 water-mill spindle 2 *fig.* babbler, chatterbox

прпне *pf* прпна *aor.* to fly off; to flutter

прпори *impf* 1 to murmur, rustle, hum; to mumble, mutter 2 (*за пламен*) to play, flicker

прпот *m* trembling, quivering

прпоти *impf see* прпори

прпулав *adj* stunted, underdeveloped

ррр *interj* (*sound of a bird flying off*) prrr!

прсиплева *adv* much, many, countless, masses, heaps

прска *impf see* прсне I 1 to spray, sprinkle, splash, hose; прска улица to hose the street; прска лозјето to spray a vineyard 2 to gush, spurt, squirt; искри прскаат sparks fly 3 *dial. see* дрска 4 to burst, blow up, explode; прскаат гранати grenades are exploding; ❏ ми прска (пука) главава my head is splitting II – **се** 1 to splash o.s. or each other 2 *colloq., sl.* to brag, boast *intrans.*

прскал *n see* прскалка

прскалка *f* sprinkler; spray, atomizer; nozzle; spray-gun

прскач *m* 1 sprayer 2 *sl.* boaster, braggart 3 *Zool.* (Otis tetrax) little bustard

прскот *m* sprinkling, crackling

прскоти *impf see* прска I 2 & 4

прсне *pf* прсна *aor.* I 1 to splash, spatter, sprinkle, hose; прсне некого со кал to splash s.o. with mud; му прснало нешто во очи s.th. spattered in his eyes 2 to burst, break, snap *intrans.*; прсна жицата the wire snapped; ќе му прсне срцето his heart will break 3 (*побегне*) to flee, run away 4 (*with да*) to start, burst into; прсне да се смее to burst out laughing; прсне да бега to start running 5 to gush, spurt, squirt; прсна вода од цевката water gushed from the pipe 6 to burst, blow up, explode II – **се** 1 to spatter o.s. 2 *rare* to scatter, disperse; се прсне по светот to scatter all over the world

прснува (се) *impf of* прсне (се)

прст[1] *m* (*на рака*) finger; (*на нога*) toe; малиот прст little finger; домалиот прст the ring-finger; средниот прст the middle finger; *dial.* големиот прст *see* палец 1; стои на прсти to stand on tiptoe; ❏ гледа некому низ прсти to overlook s.o.'s faults;

брои на прсти to count on one's fingers; има <замешано> прст во таа работа he has a finger in that pie; со прст покажува (*на*) to point one's finger (*at*); на малиот прст не можеш да му се фатиш you aren't worth his little finger; остане со прстот во уста to be left empty-handed; прст пред око не се гледа you can't see your hand in front of your face; од прсти го исцица to concoct, invent; си го клал прстот на умот he started thinking; тоа е прст божји the writing is on the wall; врата кај што скрца, прст не клавај *prov.* don't plunge into dangerous waters

прст[2] *f arch.* soil; *only in the expression:* прст и плева masses, heaps, crowds

прсте *n dim. of* прст[1]

прстен[1] -и, -ње, -ња *m* ring; венчан (венчален) прстен wedding-ring; прстен мененик engagement ring; Сатурновите прстени Saturn's rings

прстен[2] -стна *adj* <of the> finger/toe; прстен зглоб knuckle, finger-joint; toe-joint

прстенест *adj* annular, ringlike; *Zool.* прстенести глисти annulated worms

прстени (се) *pf & impf dial. see* прстенува (се)

прстенува *pf & impf* I to betroth II – **се** to get engaged (*со – то*)

прстенување *n* engagement

прстенце *n see* прсте

прстенче *n dim. of* прстен[1]

прт *m* path, track (*in snow*)

пртен *adj* flaxen; of coarse linen

пртеница *f* 1 thick homespun 2 homespun foot-cloths; knee socks

прти *impf* to make a path through the snow

пртина *f see* прт

пруга *f* track, line; железничка пруга (линија) railway line

пругав *adj* lined, striped

пругоре *adv see* нагоре, угоре

пругорен -рна *adj see* нагорен, угорен

пругорнина, **пругорница** *f & пругорниште* *n see* нагорнина, нагорница, нагорниште & угорнина, угорница, угорниште

прудолен -лна *adj see* надолен, удолен

прудолнина, **прудолница** *f & прудолниште* *n see* надолнина, надолница, надолниште & удолнина, удолница, удолниште

прудолу *adv see* надолу, удолу

пружи *pf* I to stretch, stretch out, extend *trans.*; (*алишта*) to hang out; пружи си ги нозете спроти јорганот (ќуберот) *prov.* cut your coat according to your cloth 2 to spreadeagle; to lay out II – **се** to stretch out *intrans.*, sprawl

пружина *f* 1 spring, coil; пружина на саат watch/clock spring 2 (*на мадрац*) inner spring

пружува (се) *impf of* пружи (се)

пруса *impf* to mince *intrans.*; to trot

прцел -цли *m* plait, braid

прцле *n dim. of* прцел

прч *m* 1 male goat, billy-goat; ❏ како прч е he's as fit as a fiddle 2 *joc.* bearded man 3 fornicator; braggart 4 *see* прчко

прчи *impf* I 1 (*усни*) to pout 2 (*опашка и сл.*) to raise, stick out II – **се** 1 (*за кози*) to mate *intrans.* 2 *fig.*, *colloq.* to put on airs, be conceited; to boast *intrans.*

прчка *f* (*fem. form*) *see* прчко

прчко -овци *m fig.*, *colloq.* boaster, braggart

прчовина *f* **1** goat-like odour **2** goat meat, kid; unappetizing meat

пршута *f* smoked ham, prosciutto

псала *impf see* пцала

псали *impf see* пцали

псалм -и *m Rel.* psalm

псалт *m see* пцалт

псалтир *m Rel.* **1** the Book of Psalms **2** psalter

псевдо- (*in compounds*) pseudo-

псевдоним *m* pseudonym

психа *f* psyche; mentality

психијáтар -три *m* psychiatrist

психијатрија *f* psychiatry

психијатриски *adj* psychiatric; психијатриско оделение psychiatric ward

психички *adj* psychic<al>, spiritual; mental; психички растројства psychic derangements

психоанали́за *f* psychoanalysis

психоаналитички *adj* psychoanalytic<al>; психоаналитички испитувања psychoanalytical tests

психóза *f* psychosis; воена психоза war psychosis

психолóг -зи *m* psychologist

психологија *f* psychology; детска психологија child psychology

психолошки *adj* psychological; психолошка анализа psychological analysis

психопáт *m Med.* psychopath

психопатија *f Med.* psychopathy

психопатолóг -зи *m Med.* psychopathologist

психопатологија *f Med.* psychopathology

психопатолошки *adj Med.* psychopathological

психопáтски *adj Med.* psychopathic

психотерапија *f Med.* psychotherapy, psychotherapeutics

психотераписки *adj Med.* psychotherapeutic

психофизика *f* psychophysics

психофизиологија *f* psychophysiology

психофизиолошки *adj* psychophysiological

психофизички *adj* psychophysical; психофизички својства psychophysical properties

псомор *m Bot.* (Periploca graeca) silk vine

пст *interj* hush! shush!

птица *f* bird; појна птица songbird; преселна птица migratory bird; bird of passage (*also fig.*); граблива птица bird of prey; ❑ го знам што птица е I know what sort of bird he is

птичар *m* **1** bird-catcher, fowler **2** gun dog; pointer; setter

птичарник -ци *m* aviary

птичарски *adj* bird-catcher's; gun dog's

птиче *n* **1** *dim. of* птица **2** *rare* young bird, fledgeling, nestling

птиченце -а *n dim. of* птиче

птичиште *n augm. of* птица

птичји, -ја, -је *adj* bird's; birdlike; птичје гнездо bird's nest; ❑ од птичји поглед, од птичја перспектива from a bird's-eye view

птичка *f dim. hyp. of* птица; birdie

ПТТ *abbr.* (Пошта Телеграф Телефон) postal and telephone service

пубертéт *m* puberty

пубертéтски *adj* pubertal

публика *f* audience; public; отворено за публиката open to the public; ❑ широката публика the general public

публикација -ии *f* publication

публикува *pf & impf* to publish; to make known, publicize

публици́ст *m* publicist; columnist, public-affairs commentator

публицистика *f* socio-political comment (*in the press*)

публицистички *adj* of current affairs commentary

публицитéт *m* publicity

пувка *f* **1** (на пантофли) pompom **2** (кај птица) crest **3** (пуканка) <single> popcorn **4** (колаче) kind of macaroon **5** *Bot.* (Lycoperdon bovista) puffball

пувкав *adj* soft, downy, fluffy; пувкав снег soft snow; пувкава земја friable/loose soil

пувче[1] *n dim. of* пувка

пувче[2] *n dim. of* пушка 1

пудер *m see* пудра

пудинг -зи *m* custard

пудла *f* poodle

пудлица *f dim. of* пудла

пудра *f* <cosmetic> powder; face-powder

пудри *pf* to powder

пудриéра *f* powder compact

пуза *f* hot coals, embers (*used for warming compresses*)

пуздер *m* powder; ❑ пуздер стори to smash to smithereens; прав и пуздер dust and ashes

пуздра *f* lean meat

пузе & **пуземаже** *n dial. see* кепец, џуџе

пуземажест *adj rare see* џуџест

пука (се) *impf see* пукне (се)

пукало *n* **1** *colloq.* gun **2** popcorn-maker (*device*)

пуканица & **пуканка** *f* (*usu. pl*) popcorn

пукачка *f* worry, trouble

пукнат *pt* cracked; ❑ пукнат грош (пукната пара) brass farthing

пукнатик -ци *m see* небидник, проклетник

пукнатина *f* **1** crack, crevice; сидот беше сиот со пукнатини the wall was all cracked **2** gap; пукнатини во знаењето gaps in one's knowledge

пукнатица[1] *f* **1** *see* пукнатина **2** death

пукнатица[2] *f see* небидница 1, проклетница

пукне *pf* пукна *aor.* **I 1** to break, burst, crack, split, snap *intrans.*; му пукнал чирот his ulcer burst; пукне од смеа to die of laughter; *fig.* пукна зора dawn broke; пукнала пролетта spring has come **2** to fire, shoot **3** to burst, break, crack; пукна балонот the balloon burst **4** *fig.*, *sl.* to peg out, croak **II – се** to burst <out> *intrans.*; се пукне од смеа to split one's sides laughing

пукнува (се) *impf see* пука (се)

пукот *m* gunfire; explosions, detonations

пукоти *impf* **1** to blare, roar **2** to fire, shoot *intrans.*

пукотница *f see* пукот

пулејка *f* (*usu. pl*) tinsel

пулен *m usu. Sport.* protégé, pupil

пули *impf dial.* **I 1** to look at (за дрвја) to come into leaf **II – се 1** to look (на – at) **2** *rare* to open one's eyes wide, gape **3** *impers.* (*with dat.*) to want to look; не ми се пули I'd rather not look

пулка *f* young hen, pullet

пуловер　*m* pullover

пулс　*m* pulse (*also fig.*); пипа некому пулсот to take s.o.'s pulse; *fig.* му го опипа пулсот he sounded him out (*about s.th.*)

пулсúра　*impf* to pulsate, throb

пулт　*m* 1 *Mus.* stand; rostrum; диригентски пулт conductor's podium 2 control panel

пумпа¹　*f* pump

пумпа²　*impf* to pump <up>

пумпен　-пна *adj* pumping; пумпна станица pumping station

пункт　*m* point, dot; centre; избирачки пункт polling station

пунктúра　*impf* 1 to draw a dotted/broken line 2 *Med.* to draw (drain) a liquid, tap

пункција　*f Med.* tapping

пунч　*m* punch (*drink*)

пупе　*n child.* tummy

пупи　*impf* 1 to bud (*also fig.*); пролет е, дрвјата веќе пупат it is spring, the trees are budding already 2 to swell *intrans.*; ногата ми пупи my foot is swelling up

пупка　*f* 1 bud 2 *dial.* lace

пупулец　-лци *m see* пупка

пупули се　*impf* 1 to stand on tiptoe 2 *fig.* to put on airs, show off

пупунец　-нци *m Zool.* (Upupa epops) hoopoe

пупунче　*n dim. of* пупунец

пупурник　-ци *m dial.* s.o. stunted, underdeveloped; sickly, feeble person

пура　*f* type of cigar

пургатúв　*m Med.* purgative, strong laxative

пурева　*f* 1 evaporation 2 *dial.* smoke, mist, dust (in the air)

пури　*impf* to steam; to emit smoke; to evaporate

пурúзам　-змот *m* purism

пурúст　*m* purist

пуристички　*adj* puristic<al>; пуристички тенденции puristic tendencies

пуритáн & пуритáнец　-нци *m* puritan

пуританúзам　-змот *m see* пуританство

пуритáнка　*f* (*fem. form*) *see* пуритан & пуританец

пуритáнски　*adj* puritanic<al>

пуритáнство　*n* puritanism

пурпур　*m* purple

пурпурен -рна　*adj* purple

пусија　-ии *f colloq., arch.* ambush; стави пусија to set an ambush; фати пусија to wait in ambush

пуст　*adj* 1 desert, deserted, desolate, waste, barren; пуст град deserted town 2 futile, vain, empty, void; пусти ветувања empty promises 3 damned, cursed; wretched; □ пусто <и штуро> да остане! damn it all! пусто дрво! you'll get a good hiding! 4 wonderful, marvellous

пустее　*impf rare* to become empty

пустелија　-ии *f* wasteland, abandoned place, wilderness (*also fig.*)

пустелник　-ци *m* destructive person, destroyer

пусти　*impf* I 1 to lay waste, destroy, devastate, ravage 2 to squander; пусти пари to spend money recklessly 3 (*in emphatic function, semantically void*) што да кажам (чинам), што да пустам? what can I say (do)? how can I manage? □ пусти штури to move heaven and earth, spare no effort II – се 1 to be abandoned 2 to be ruined, destroyed

пустикуќа　-овци *m & f* squanderer, spendthrift

пустикуќство　*n* prodigality

пустина　-и, -ње *f* 1 desert; пустината Сахара the Sahara desert; □ глас <на вопијуштиот> во пустина voice <of one crying> in the wilderness 2 cursed thing 3 (*as interj*) in God's name, for goodness' sake; кај си, пустиње? in God's name, where are you? 4 по пустина 1. in vain; троши пари по пустина he wastes money 2. without a trace; to an unknown place; фати да бега по пустина he started running God knows where

пустиник　-ци *m* hermit

пустинички　*adj* hermit's

пустиништво　*n* life of a hermit

пустински　*adj* 1 desert, lifeless, deserted; пустински песок desert sand 2 cursed, damned

пусто　1 *adv* empty, emptily 2 *interj* blast <it>! damn <it>! 3 *interj* alas!

пустовина　*f* emptiness; lifelessness; кога ќе си заминеа другарите, таа секаваше пустовина whenever her friends went off, she used to feel a certain desolation

пустокуќник　-ци *m* squanderer, spendthrift

пустокуќница　*f* (*fem. form*) *see* пустокуќник

пустота　*f see* пустелија; *fig.* духовна пустота spiritual desolation

пустош　*f & m* 1 *see* пустелија 2 desolation, devastation; emptiness, void; *fig.* пустош во душата spiritual desolation

пустошен　-шна *adj* 1 neglected, deserted; пустошно место deserted place 2 devastating, destructive; пустошен оган devastating fire

пустоши　*impf rare see* пусти

пустошник　-ци *m* devastator, destroyer

путер　*m colloq.* butter

пуфка　*impf* 1 (*за човек*) to puff; to pant 2 (*за животно*) to snort; to snarl 3 (*за машина*) to throb; to puff

пуч　-еви, -ови *m* putsch, coup d'état

пучúст　*m* rebel

пучистички　*adj* <of a> putsch, rebel

пушач　*m* smoker; купе за пушачи smoking compartment

пушачки　*adj* smoker's, smoking; пушачки прибор smoking accessories

пушење　*n* smoking; забрането е пушењето no smoking

пуши　*impf* I to smoke II се *impers* (*with dat.*) пуши ми се I feel like smoking (would like a smoke)

пушилница　*f* smoking-room

пушка　*f* 1 rifle, gun, shotgun; ловечка (ловџиска) пушка sporting gun, shotgun; □ пукна пушка the moment of truth has arrived; тој е пушка he's in top form; од празна пушка двајца се страшат *prov.* uncertainty increases fear 2 shot; фрли пушка he fired a single shot; се чу пушка a shot was heard; □ со една пушка два зајака to kill two birds with one stone

пушкар　*m* gunsmith

пушкарница　*f* 1 gunsmith's shop 2 loophole

пушкарски　*adj* gunsmith's

пушкомет　*m* gunshot range

пушкомитралéз　*m* light machine-gun

пушкомитралéзец　-сци *m* light-machine-gunner

пушкомитралéски *adj* <of a> light machine-gun

пуш<т> *m arch., colloq.* corrupt, venal person; *sl.* villain

пушта (се) *impf of* пушти (се)

пуштен *adj* generous, giving freely; spending lavishly; ❑ пуштена рака generous/free-spending person

пушти *pf* **I 1** to release, set free, let go, let out; to let fall, drop; ❑ пушти ветар to break wind; пушти вода to pass water; пушти глас to start a rumour; пушти душа to pass away; пушти крв to let blood; пушти куршум to fire a shot; пушти солзи to shed tears; пушти чекор to quicken one's step; пушти во продажба to put on sale, offer for sale; пушти во погон (експлоатација) to put into operation, bring into service; пушти на слобода to set free **2** (*олабави*) to slacken, loosen, relax *trans.*; пушти узда to slacken the reins (*also fig*) **3** (*дозволи*) to let, allow, permit; admit, let in; пушти некого да зборува to let s.o. speak; пушти му го прстот, ќе ти ја фати раката *prov.* give him an inch and he'll take a mile **4** (*брада, коса*) to let grow; пушти брада to grow one's beard **5** to put forth; пушти корење to put down roots **6** to start, set in motion, turn on; пушти радио to turn on the radio **7** (*брод*) to launch; (*издаде*) to put out, issue, publish **8** (*испрати*) to send; пушти писмо/поздрав to send a letter/greeting **9** to set on (*of dogs*); to pair, mate (*of domesticated animals*); пушти куче на некого to set a dog on s.o.; пушти пастув на кобила to pair a stallion with a mare **10** to give; кравата ни пушти три литра млеко the cow gave us three litres of milk **11** (*пропушти*) to leak (*of boat, container*) **II – се 1** to relax *intrans.*; to let o.s. drift, be carried; to let o.s. go; се пушти веков what's the world coming to? **2** to stretch out *intrans.* **3** to rush off **4** to go down, descend, lower o.s. **5** to go in (*во – for*); се пушти во трговија to go into business **6** *dial.* to free o.s. (*од – from, of*); to get rid (*of*)

пушчен *adj* <of a> gun; ❑ пушчено месо cannon-fodder

пфу<ј> *interj* (*expressing disgust, contempt etc.*) ugh! yuck!

пцала *impf see* пцали

пцали *impf* **1** to sing in church **2** *fig.* to babble; (*за дете*) to whimper, whine

пцалт *m arch.* chorister

пци *pl of* пес

пцовиса *pf* (*of animals, also colloq. of humans*) to die; *fig.* to croak

пцовисан *pt* dead; пцовисаното магаре од волкот нема гајле *prov.* a dead mouse feels no cold

пцовисува *impf of* пцовиса

пцоглав *adj dial. see* песоглав

пцоглавец -вци *m dial. see* песоглавец 2

пцоменик -ци *m* bread made from bran; *fig.* bread of very poor quality

пцост *f* oath, curse, swear-word

пцуе *impf* to swear at, abuse; to blaspheme

пчела *f* bee; рој пчели a swarm of bees; секоја пчела не дава (бере) мед *prov.* it takes all sorts to make a world

пчелар *m* bee-keeper, apiarist

пчеларка *f Zool.* (Merops apiaster) bee-eater

пчеларник -ци *m* **1** apiary **2** *Bot. see* пчелник 1

пчеларски *adj* bee-keeper's, apiarist's

пчеларство *n* bee-keeping, apiculture

пчелен -лна & **пчелин** *adj* <of a> bee, bees'; пчелен (пчелин) восок beeswax

пчелинок *m Bot.* (Marrubium vulgare) white horehound

пчелица & пчеличка *f dim. of* пчела

пчелник *m* **1** *Bot.* (Melissa officinalis) lemon balm **2** *see* пчеларник 1

пченица *f* wheat (*plant and grain*); boiled wheat (*used in various church services*); зимна (озимна) пченица winter wheat; пролетна (јара) пченица spring wheat; ❑ со пченицата в уста е; си ја носи пченицата в уста; пченицата си ја каснал he's at death's door

пченичен -чна *adj* wheat, wheaten; пченично зрно a grain of wheat

пченичица *f hyp. of* пченица

пченичиште *n* **1** wheatfield **2** *pejor.* soiled/unclean wheat

пченка *f Bot.* (Zea mays) maize (*plant and grain*), *Am.* <Indian> corn; змиина пченка, мечкина пченка *Bot.* (Arum maculatum) lords and ladies, cuckoo-pint, wild arum

пченкан & пченкарен -рна *adj* maize; пченкано (пченкарно) брашно maize flour, cornflour

пченканик -ци & **пченкарник** -ци *m* maize bread

пченкариште *n* maize field

пченковина & пченковица *f* maize stalks, *Am.* corn stalks (fodder)

пченкушка *f* (*кочан<ка>*) corn-cob

пченчиште *n* maize stubble field

пчошки *adj* dog's; пчошка храна dog food; пчошки живот a dog's life

пшт *interj* hush! shush!

Р

раат *colloq.* **1** *m* peace, quiet; comfort; остави ме на раат leave me alone! ❏ трга раат to enjoy peace and quiet **2** *adj indecl. & adv* peaceful, quiet, carefree; спие раат to sleep peacefully

раатиса *pf colloq.* **I** to free; to relieve (*from cares*) **II** – ce to free o.s. of worries; ми се раатиса главата од нив I'm not worrying about them

раатисува (се) *impf of* раатиса (ce)

раатлак *m colloq.* peaceful life, quiet; comfort

раб¹ *m* edge; margin; (*на материјал*) hem; seam; ❏ на работ на пропаста on the brink of the abyss

раб² *m Rel.* servant of God

рабат *m* (*попуст*) discount, rebate, deduction; allowance

рабаџија -ии *m dial. see* арабаџија

рабен -бна *adj* of the edge/border/boundary; рабна линија hem-line; seam

рабест *adj* having many edges

раби *impf* (*порабува*) to hem

рабин *m* rabbi

рабина *f Rel.* (*fem. form*) *see* раб²

раболепен -пна *adj literary, arch.* servile, cringing

работа -и, (*rare* -оќе) *f* **1** work; job; task; домашна (куќна) работа housework; испитувачка (истражувачка) работа research work; присилна работа forced labour; градежни работи building works; пушти во работа to set in motion; се фати за работа to get down to work; си ја знае работата to know one's job, know what one's about; без работа unemployed; стапи на работа to start a job; по службена работа on official business; тоа не е моја работа that isn't my job; that's none of my business; работа во смени shift work; работа на норма piecework, job work; работа на црно moonlighting; работа со полно работно време full-time work; работа со скратено работно време part-time work; нередовна работа casual work; odd job; рачна работа handicraft (*manual art/skill*); ќе си има работа со него he'll have trouble with him; ❏ му отвори работа he kept him busy; he caused him trouble; Сизифова работа labour of Sisyphus; лета од работа to get the sack; работата го фали мајсторот actions speak louder than words; волкот сам си ја врши работата, та затоа му е дебел вратот well done is self done; добрата работа сама се пофалува *prov.* good wine needs no bush; немал ѓаволот работа <та си ги давел децата> *prov.* the Devil finds work for idle hands; не оставај ја сегашната работа за утре don't leave to the morrow what you can do today **2** work of art/literature/

scholarship; <student's> assignment; дипломска работа final examination paper (*at university*); домашна работа homework; писмена работа test paper **3** (*usu. pl*) thing, object; купивме многу работи за дома we bought a lot of things for the house **4** thing, affair, matter, business; состојба на работите state of affairs; како стојат работите? how are things? работата дојде до таму matters have reached this point; да минеме на работата let's get to the point! страшна работа! 1. what a terrible business! 2. (*also* голема работа!) *sl.* big deal! so what? гледај си ја работата! mind your own business! министерство за внатрешни/надворешни работи ministry of internal/foreign affairs; вршител на работите chargé d'affaires; ❏ ветер работа a trifling matter; лесна работа an easy matter; лоша му е (не му чини) работата his business is going badly; he's not too well at all; му прави работа to engage in match-making; не му е чиста работата his hands are not clean (there's s.th. fishy about him); тука е работата (работата е) the question is this (the matter is . . .); that's the point; чудна работа! how strange! бркај работа off you go! get on with it! готова работа a sure thing; има поважна работа to have better things to do; ја подмачкува работата to oil the wheels; сериозна работа no laughing matter

работен -тна *adj* **1** diligent, hard-working, industrious **2** work, working; работните луѓе the working people; работна сила (рака) work-force (labour force); работно време working hours (business hours); работен ден working day; работна маса work bench; desk; работна соба work-room (study); работна облека working clothes; school uniform; работни навици work habits; во работен однос employed, in work

работење *n* **1** work; лошо работење bad workmanship **2** operations; финансиско работење financial transactions

работи *impf* **I 1** to work; работи како ѕидар to work as a builder; работи на книга to work on a book; работи за некого to work for s.o.; работи како мравка (коњ, вол) to work like a Trojan; ❏ работи на своја рака he acts on his own; среќата (касметот) му работи fortune favours him; работи како вол за слама to work for peanuts **2** to do; што работиш? what are you doing? **3** to function, operate, work; моторот работи добро the engine is running well; музејот не работи the museum is closed; не работи to be out of order; часовникот работи точно the clock keeps perfect time **4** to till, work; работи земја to till the soil **II** – ce **1** *impers.* се работи за . . . it's a question of . . . **2** *impers.* (*with dat.*) не ми се работи I don't feel like working

работилиште *n* work site; building site

работилница *f* workshop

работиче *n dim. of* работа **1** little job **2** little thing

работичка *f dim. of* работа

работлив *adj* industrious, diligent, hard-working

работливост *f* industriousness, diligence

работник -ци *m* worker; hard-working man, good worker; метални работник metalworker; наемен работник hired worker; научен работник research fellow/scholar; општ работник unskilled labourer

работница *f* (*fem. form*) *see* работник

работничка *f* (*fem. form*) *see* работник

работнички *adj* workers'; labour; работничка класа working class

работништво *n coll.* the working class

работност *f* industriousness, diligence

работоводител *m* works manager, site manager, superintendent of works; operational manager; foreman

работода́вач *m see* работодавец

работода́вец -вци *m* employer

работода́тел *m see* работодавец

работоспособен -бна *adj* fit for (capable of) work, able-bodied

работоспособност *f* capacity for work

рабуш *m Hist.* tally board; ❏ разбира колку магаре од рабуш he can't make head or tail of it; на рабуш on tick; on the slate

рабушлија *adj indecl.* notched (*as on a tally board*)

раван *m* **1** (*вид коњско одење*) amble, easy pace **2** *dial.* ambler **3** (*as adv*) оди раван to amble

раванија -ии *f* kind of oriental sweet

равен -вна *adj dial. see* рамен

равенка *f Math.* equation; равенка со една непозната equation with one unknown

равенство *n see* еднаквост

рагби *m Sport.* rugby <football>

рагби́ст *m Sport.* rugby player

раглан *m* raglan

рагу *n Cul.* ragout

рад *adj f.p.* glad; willing

радар *m* radar; <police> radar trap

радарски *adj* radar; радарска станица radar station

радија́лен -лна *adj* radial

радија́лка *f* radial-ply tyre

радијан *m Geom.* radian

радија́тор *m* radiator

радија́ција *f* radiation; сончевата радијација solar radiation

радика́л *m* **1** *Math., Chem.* radical **2** *Pol.* radical

радика́лен -лна *adj* radical; радикални промени radical changes

радика́лец -лци *m Pol.* radical, *see* радикал 2

радикали́зам -змот *m* radicalism

радика́лски *adj see* радикален

радио *n* radio; (*радиоапарат*) radio receiver; (*радиостаница*) radio station

радиоактивен -вна *adj* radioactive; радиоактивни елементи radioactive elements

радиоактивност *f* radioactivity

радиоамате́р *m* radio amateur, *sl.* radio ham

радиоапара́т *m* radio receiver

радиобран -ови *m* radio wave

радиове́сник -ци *m* radio news bulletin

радиогра́м *m* & **радиогра́ма** *f* radio-telegram

радиографија *f* radiography

радиогра́фски *adj* radiographic

радиодифузија *f* radio coverage; radio broadcasting

радиодра́ма *f* radio play

радиоемисија -ии *f* radio broadcast<ing>

радиоло́г -зи *m Med.* radiologist

радиологија *f Med.* radiology

радиоло́шки *adj Med.* radiological; радиолошки институт radiological institute

радиомеханичар *m* radio repairer (repairman)

радиооркестар -три *m* radio orchestra

радиопредавател *m* radio transmitter

радиопре́нос *m* radio broadcast

радиопретплата *f* radio licence, subscription

радиопретплатник -ци *m* radio subscriber, licensee

радиоприемник -ци *m* radio receiver

радиопрогра́ма *f* radio programme

радиоскопија *f Med.* radioscopy

радиоско́пски *adj Med.* radioscopic

радиослушател *m* (*radio*) listener

радиосонда *f* radiosonde, radio sounding balloon

радиостаница *f* radio station

радиостудио *n* broadcasting studio

радио-телевизија *f* radio and television

радиотелегра́ма *f* radio-telegram

радиотелегра́ф *m* radio-telegraph

радиотелеграфија *f* radio-telegraphy

радиотелеграфи́ст *m* radio-telegraphist, radio operator

радиотелеграфи́стка *f* (*fem. form*) *see* радиотелеграфист

радиотелегра́фски *adj* radio-telegraphic; радиотелеграфска станица radio-telegraphy station

радиотелефо́н *m* radio-telephone

радиотелефонија *f* radio-telephony

радиотелефо́нски *adj* radio-telephonic; радиотелефонска служба radio-telephonic service

радиотерапија *f Med.* radiotherapy

радиотехник -ци *m see* радиотехничар

радиотехника *f* radio engineering

радиотехничар *m* radio technician

радиотехнички *adj* telecommunications; radio-engineering *attrib.*

радиофикација *f* radio installation

радиофонија *f* radiophonics

радиофоничен -чна *adj* radiophonic; радиофоничен глас radiophonic voice

радиохо́р *m* radio choir

ради́ст *m see* радиотелеграфист

радиум *m Chem.* radium

радиумов *adj radium attrib.*; радиумов сулфат radium sulphate; радиумова руда radium ore

радиус *m* radius; радиус на дејство radius of action

радо *adv* gladly

радосен -сна *adj* joyful, joyous; glad; радосни чувства joyous feelings; радосна вест joyful news

радосница *f* солзи радосници tears of joy

радост *f* joy, gladness; излета од радост to be carried away with joy; со голема (неискажана) радост with great pleasure; моја радост my darling

радува *impf* **I** to gladden, make happy **II** – се to rejoice (*на – at*), be glad/pleased; многу се радувам I am very glad

радување *n* joy, rejoicing

раѓа (се) *impf of* роди (се); брзата кучка слепи кучиња раѓа *prov.* haste makes waste

раѓање *n* birth; *fig.* beginning; предвремено раѓање premature birth; раѓање на сонцето sunrise

раѓачка *f* birth; у кого има раѓачка – ќе има и умирачка *prov.* all men are mortal

ражен -жни *m* spit (*for roasting*); зајакот в планина, а раженот на оган *prov.* don't count your chickens before they're hatched

раженче *n* **1** *dim. of* ражен **2** kebab

ражне *n dim. of* ражен, *see* раженче

раз- (*pa-* before с *and* ш, *pac-* before other voiceless consonants) *verbal prefix indicating* **1** (*division into two or more parts*) dis-, un-; раздели to divide; разбие to break up; расече to cut into pieces **2** (*dispersion, scattering*) dis-; растури to disperse; расфрли to strew **3** (*action in reverse; change of state*) dis-, de-, un-; разведе to divorce; распара, раше to unstitch **4** *beginning of an action or state* (*often with* ce); расплаче се to start crying **5** *intensification of action*; разбунтува to stir up; разбесни to enrage

разбаботи *pf* **I** *trans.* to stoke up (*stove, fire*) **II** – **се 1** (*of a stove, fire*) to roar, blaze <up> **2** *fig.* to start making a noise **3** *fig.* to get talking, start chattering

разбаботува (се) *impf of* разбаботи (се)

разбандори се *pf colloq.* to babble, start babbling

разбашкари се *pf* to lounge around

разбега <се> *pf* to scatter, disperse *intrans.*; to run away

разбегува <се> *impf of* разбега <се>

разбере *pf* разбра *aor.* **I 1** to understand, comprehend; to grasp; разбра? have you understood? *colloq.* got it? погрешно разбере to misunderstand **2** (*узнае*) to find out, learn; разбрав дека сте биле на излет I learnt that you were on an excursion **3** to realize (*дека – that*) **4** to experience; разбере глад to experience hunger **II** – **се 1** to understand each other (one another); to reach an understanding/agreement; да се разбереме let's get this straight **2** to become clear (obvious) **3** *colloq.* to come to one's senses; to pull o.s. together

разбесни *pf* **I** to infuriate, enrage **II** – **се** to fly into a rage

разбеснува (се) *impf of* разбесни (се)

разбива (се) *impf of* разбие (се)

разбивач *m* destructive person, destroyer

разбивачки *adj* destructive; разбивачка политика destructive policy

разбие *pf* разби *aor.* **I 1** to break, smash, crush *trans.*; ❏ разбие мраз to break the ice; топ не може да го разбие he/it is very strong **2** *Mil., Sport.* to defeat, beat **3** *fig.* to demolish, destroy, ruin; му ја разби последната надеж he destroyed (wrecked) his last hope **4** to divide up, break up *trans.*; (*за пари*) to change; разбие голема група to break up a large group; разбие илјадарка to change a thousand-denar note **II** – **се 1** to break up, smash *intrans.*; брановите се разбија од брегот the waves broke against the shore **2** to hurt o.s. badly **3** to split up *intrans.*; одредот се разби на неколку групи the unit broke up into several groups

разбира (се) *impf of* разбере (се); разбира од музика to be knowledgeable about music; разбира турски to understand Turkish; ❏ разбира колку свиња од дињa he can't make head or tail of it; разбира дури отаде! he doesn't understand at all; не разбира шега to have no sense of humour; *Mil.* разбирам! yes, sir! се разбира it goes without saying, of course (naturally)

разбирање *n* **1** understanding, grasp; agreement; sympathy **2** conviction; opinion, view; напредни разбирања progressive views

разбирателство *n arch. see* разбирање

разбирачка *f colloq. see* разбирање

разбирлив *adj* understandable, intelligible; тешко разбирлив hard to understand; ❏ разбирлива работа an understandable matter; understandably (naturally)

разбирливо *adv* understandably; intelligibly; зборува јасно и разбирливо to speak clearly and intelligibly; разбирливо of course (certainly)

разбирливост *f* intelligibility

разбистри *pf* **I** to clarify, make clear **II** – **се** to become clear; небото се разбистри the sky cleared; се разбистри малу ситуацијата the situation has become a little clearer

разбиструва (се) *impf of* разбистри (се)

разблажи *pf* **1** to dilute **2** *fig.* to pacify, calm

разблажлив *adj* amenable to dilution (thinning)

разблажува *impf of* разблажи

разблее *pf* разблеа *aor.* **I 1** to make sheep bleat **2** *see* **II II** – **се** to start bleating

разблејува (се) *impf of* разблее (се)

разблуда *f* lust, carnal desire; perversion, vice

разблуден -дна *adj* **1** lustful, lecherous, sensual; perverted; dissolute, wanton **2** rebellious, restless; разблудно време troubled time

разблуди *pf* **I** to pervert, corrupt **II** – **се** to become dissolute

разблудник -ци *m* lecher, debauchee, fornicator

разблудница *f* hussy, slut, wanton

разблудност *f* lustfulness; dissoluteness, debauchery

разблудува (се) *impf of* разблуди (се)

разбој -ои *m* **1** loom **2** *Gymnastics* parallel bars

разбојник -ци *m* **1** robber; bandit, brigand **2** good-for-nothing; scamp, rascal

разбојница & разбојничка *f* (*fem. form*) *see* разбојник

разбојнички *adj* robber's; разбојничка чета a band of robbers

разбојништво *n* robbery; banditry

разбојче *n dim. of* разбој 1

разболи *pf* разболе *aor.* **I 1** to cause to fall ill; to make ill **2** *colloq.* (*заболи*) to start aching; срце ја разболе her heart started aching **II** – **се** to fall ill

разболува (се) *impf of* разболи (се)

разбор *m colloq.* choice; без разбор without <any> choice

разборит *adj* reasonable, sensible

разборитост *f* common sense, reasonableness

разбради *pf* **I** *rare* to untie, take off (*s.o.'s*) kerchief **II** – **се** to untie, take off one's own kerchief

разбрадува (се) *impf of* разбради (се)

разбран *pt* **1** understood **2** intelligible, comprehensible, understandable **3** reasonable, sensible

разбрани *pf see* разбранува

разбрано *adv* **1** understandably; sensibly, intelligibly **2** (*usu. in answer to a question, order, etc.*) yes, sir!

разбраност *f* reasonableness, common sense

разбранува *pf* **1** to disturb, agitate; to ruffle; ветрот го разбранува морето the wind ruffled the sea **2** *fig.* (*вознемири*) to alarm, upset, perturb; таа вест многу го разбранува that news upset him a great deal

разбрануван *pt* disturbed, agitated; aroused

разбрбори се *pf* разбрборе се *aor.* to start babbling, chattering

разбрборува се *impf of* разбрбори се
разбременет *pt* unburdened, relieved
разбремени *pf* to unburden; to relieve (*од – of*); разбремени некого од обврски to release s.o. from his duties
разбременува *impf of* разбремени
разбрза се *pf* to start hurrying
разбрка *pf* to disperse *trans.*, scatter; to chase away
разбркува *impf of* разбрка
разбркување *n* dispersal, expulsion
разбрмчи се *pf* to start buzzing/humming
разбуди *pf* **I 1** to wake <up>, awaken *trans.* **2** (*предизвика*) to arouse, evoke, awaken *trans.*; разбуди чувства to awaken feelings **II – се** to wake up, awaken *intrans.*
разбудува (се) *impf of* разбуди (се)
разбунтува *pf* **I** to stir up **II – се** to rebel, rise in rebellion
разбунцави (се) *pf dial. see* разбушави (се)
разбуричка *pf* to disarrange, displace, turn over (*while rummaging for s.th.*)
разбуричкува *impf of* разбуричка
разбута *pf* **1** to push (shove) aside/away, disperse (*by pushing*) *trans.* **2** *dial.* (*растури*) to destroy, demolish
разбутка *pf see* разбута
разбуткува *impf of* разбутка
разбутува *impf of* разбута
разбушавен *pt* dishevelled, unkempt, tousled; разбушавена коса dishevelled hair; разбушавени деца dishevelled children
разбушави *pf* **I** to tousle, ruffle; ветрот ми ја разбушави косата the wind ruffled my hair **II – се** to become dishevelled
разбушавува (се) *impf of* разбушави (се)
развари *pf* **I** to boil down *trans.*; to overcook **II – се** to boil down *intrans.*; to be overcooked
разварува (се) *impf of* развари (се)
развева (се) *impf of* развее (се)
разведе *pf* **I 1** to take (lead) round; разведе гости низ градот to show guests round the town **2** to break up a marriage, cause a divorce; to divorce **II – се** to get divorced
разведен *pt* divorced; (*as noun*) divorcee
разведеник -ци *m* divorcee
разведеница *f* (*fem. form*) *see* разведеник
разведри *pf* **I 1** to clear *trans.*; to brighten *trans.*; ветер го разведри небото a breeze cleared the sky **2** *fig.* to cheer up *trans.*; to hearten **II – се 1** (*of sky, weather*) to clear *intrans.* **2** *fig.* to cheer up, brighten up *intrans.*
разведрува (се) *impf of* разведри (се)
разведува (се) *impf of* разведе (се)
разведувач *m see* разводник 2
развее *pf* развеа *aor.* **1** to unfurl *trans.*; развее знаме to unfurl a flag **2** to drive away, blow away; to disperse *trans.*; ветер го развеа снегот a wind blew the snow away **II – се** to disperse *intrans.*
развезе *pf* развеза *aor.* **I 1** to unstitch (*embroidery*) **2** *fig.* to hold forth **II – се** to start embroidering, get carried away with embroidering
развезува (се) *impf of* развезе (се)
развејува (се) *impf see* развева (се)
развенча *pf* **I 1** to discredit; тогаш го развенчале

како поет then he was discredited as a poet **2** to divorce, grant a divorce to **II – се** to get divorced
развенчава (се) *impf of* развенча (се)
развенчан *pt* **1** discredited **2** divorced; (*as noun*) divorcee
развесели *pf* **I** to cheer up *trans.* **II – се** to cheer up, brighten up *intrans.*
развеселува (се) *impf of* развесели (се)
разветрее (се) *pf see* разветри (се)
разветри *pf* **I** to air, ventilate; разветри соба to air a room **II – се** to take the air
развива (се) *impf of* развие (се)
развивач *m Photography* developer
развигор *m* warm breeze, zephyr
развигора & развигорец *m see* развигор
развидели (се) *pf see* раздени (се); ❑ ми се развидели пред очите it dawned on me (I realized); I saw the light
развиделува (се) *impf of* развидели (се)
развие *pf* разви *aor.* **I 1** to unfurl; to unwrap; to unroll; unfold **2** to develop *trans.*; to build up; развие интерес to develop an interest; развие свои мисли to develop one's thoughts; развие полна брзина to build up speed; развие филм to develop a film **3** (*of trees, etc.*) to put out (*leaves*) **4** *Mil.* to deploy *trans.* **II – се 1** to develop *intrans.*; to unfold *intrans.*; момата се разви the girl developed; индустријата се разви the industry developed; настаните брзо се развија the events developed rapidly **2** to put out leaves **3** (*разврзе се, размота се*) to unwind *intrans.*
развиен *pt* developed; well-developed; развиена земја developed country
развика се *pf* to start shouting, yelling, screaming, bellowing (*loudly*); ми се развика he started shouting at me
развикува се *impf of* развика се
развинти *pf* to unscrew *trans.*
развинтува *impf of* развинти
развиори *pf poet.* **I** to stir up, raise, evoke; развиори радосен трепет to arouse a joyful flutter **II – се** to rise up; to soar
развиорува (се) *impf of* развиори (се)
развиска се *pf* to start neighing, whinnying; to start screaming
развискува се *impf of* развиска се
развитка *pf* **I** to untwist *trans.*; to unroll *trans.*; to unwrap; to remove bandages (*from*); развитка рана to remove bandages from a wound **II – се** to unravel *intrans.*; to unroll *intrans.*
развиткува (се) *impf of* развитка (се)
развитли *pf* **I 1** to untie (*sheaves*) **2** to arouse **3** to whirl, spin *trans.* **II – се 1** to <start to> rage, blaze; се развитли востание rebellion burst forth **2** to swirl, whirl, spin *intrans.*
развитлува (се) *impf of* развитли (се)
развиток *m* development; growth; evolution; развитокот на науката the development of science/ learning; земја во развиток developing country
развиши се *pf* to rise high; to fly up; to soar
развишува се *impf of* развиши се
развладичи *pf* to unfrock (*a bishop*)
развладичува *impf of* развладичи
развластен *pt* deposed; dispossessed
развласти *pf* to dispossess; to depose, strip of power

развластува *impf of* развласти
развлеклив *adj* elastic, extendible, flexible
развлекува (се) *impf of* развлече (се)
развлече *pf* развлеков *1st p. sg aor.* **I 1** to stretch *trans.* **2** to scatter, disperse *trans.*; развлече разни работи на подот to scatter things on the floor **3** to protract; to drag out; to prolong **II – се 1** to stretch *intrans.* **2** to drag on *intrans.*
развлечен *pt* stretched; protracted; *fig.* verbose; (*за говор*) drawling
развлечува (се) *impf see* развлекува (се)
развод *m* **1** divorce **2** deployment; distribution; разводот на стражата mounting (posting) of the guard
разводен -дна *adj* **1** divorce; разводно дело divorce case **2** <of> distribution; разводен мост drawbridge; разводна табла switchboard; разводна мрежа switching network (*for TV, radio, electricity, water-supply, etc.*)
разводни *pf* to dilute; to thin (*also fig.*); разводни боја to thin paint
разводник -ци *m* **1** *Mil.* corporal of the guard **2** (*во кино, театар*) usher **3** *Tech.* governor
разводница & разводничка *f* usherette
разводнува *impf of* разводни
развоен -jна *adj* developmental; developing; evolutionary; развојниот процес the evolutionary process
развој *m see* развиток; стопански развој economic development; умствен развој mental development; развој на настани turn/unfolding of events
развража <се> *pf* to start milling around; to swarm
развражува <се> *impf of* развража <се>
разврат *m* debauchery, depravity
развратен[1] *adj* dissolute, corrupt, debauched; развратено момче dissolute youth
развратен[2] -тна *adj* wanton, dissolute, debauched
разврати *pf* to corrupt, debauch
развратник -ци *m* rake, libertine, debauchee
развратница & развратничка *f* hussy, wanton
развратнички *adj* dissolute
развратност *f* debauchery
развратува *impf of* разврати
разврака *pf see* развратува
развреви се *pf* **1** to kick up an awful noise (din) **2** *dial.* to start talking a great deal
развредни се *pf* to become diligent; to start working
развреднува се *impf of* развредни се
разврека се *pf* to start squealing/bleating
разврекува се *impf of* разврека се
развреска се *pf* to start screaming
разврескува се *impf of* развреска се
разврзе *pf* разврза *aor.* **I 1** to unfasten, loosen, untie, undo; to unleash *trans.*; ❑ го разврза јазикот he started speaking freely; му го разврзе јазикот to loosen s.o.'s tongue **2** *fig.* to hold forth; to strike up (*conversation*) **II – се** to come undone; to loosen *intrans.*
разврзува (се) *impf of* разврзе (се)
развриска се *pf see* развреска се
разврискува се *impf see* разврескува се
разврне се *pf* разврна се *aor.* (*of rain, snow, hail*) to start falling heavily; силен дожд се разврнало heavy rain started to fall

разврнува се *impf of* разврне се
разврска *f* dénouement, outcome; трагична разврска tragic outcome
разврти *pf* **I 1** to loosen *trans.*; to untwist; to unscrew; to ream **2** to <start to> spin *trans.*; разврти тркало to spin a wheel **II – се** to become fidgety (restless)
развртува (се) *impf of* разврти (се)
разгази *pf* **1** to stamp down, trample on; разгази снег to stamp down snow **2** (*за чевли*) to wear in
разгазува *impf of* разгази
разгален *pt* spoilt, pampered; разгалено дете spoilt child
разгали *pf* to spoil *trans.*, pamper
разгалува *impf of* разгали
разгалче *n dim.* spoilt child; мамино разгалче mother's darling
разгаштен *pt* untidy, unkempt, sloppy; unbridled, undisciplined; разгаштено дете unruly child (brat)
разгашти *pf* **I 1** to ungird, unbridle, unbelt **2** *fig.* to spoil, allow to become unruly **II – се 1** to ungird o.s. **2** *fig.* to let o.s. go
разгаштува (се) *impf of* разгашти (се)
разгласен -сна *adj* public-address *attrib.*; разгласна станица public-address system
разгласи *pf* **I** to make public, announce, publicize, trumpet forth **II – се** to become known, (*of news*) spread *intrans.*
разгласува (се) *impf of* разгласи (се)
разглед *m literary* observation, examination, consideration; разгледи discussions
разгледа *pf* **1** to look at, examine, inspect; разгледа градот to see the sights of the town **2** to consider, evaluate, review
разгледница *f* picture postcard
разгледува *impf of* разгледа
разгледување *n* examination; consideration; sightseeing предмети за разгледување exhibits (*in court*); topics for discussion; зема во разгледување to take into consideration
разгледувач *m* examiner, assessor
разглези *pf dial. see* разгали
разглоби *pf* **I 1** to dismantle, disassemble, take apart; разглоби мотор to dismantle a motor **2** *fig.* to break down *trans.*, analyse; убаво ги разглоби своите принципи he clearly analysed his principles **II – се** *see* раскости се **3**
разглобува (се) *impf of* разглоби (се)
разгмечи *pf* to mash
разгмечува *impf of* разгмечи
разгневен *pt* enraged, infuriated; разгневен глас furious voice
разгневеност *f* fury, rage
разгневи *pf* **I** to infuriate, enrage **II – се** to fly into a rage, flare up
разгневува (се) *impf of* разгневи (се)
разговара (се) *impf of* разговори (се)
разговор *m* **1** conversation, talk, chat; (*телефонски*) call; ❑ без разговори no more talking! don't argue! води разговори to carry on a conversation; to conduct talks (discussions); врзе (заврзе) разговор to start (strike up) a conversation; нема разговор there's no dispute (question) about that **2** *colloq.* companion, pal

разговорен -рна *adj* **1** colloquial, spoken; разговорен јазик colloquial language **2** conversational; разговорен речник phrase-book **3** *colloq.* talkative, chatty

разговори *pf* **I 1** to enter into conversation (*co – with*); to start talking to **2** to entertain with conversation; to comfort; to set at ease **II – ce** to talk/chat, get talking

разговорка *f* **1** chat; дојдоа на разговорка they came for a chat **2** *see* разговорник 2

разговорлив *adj* talkative, chatty

разговорник -ци *m* **1** phrase-book **2** companion (*to talk to*)

разговорува (се) *impf see* разговара (се)

разговорче *n dim. of* разговор

разголен *pt* bared, exposed; naked; разголен грб bare back

разголеност *f* nudity; nakedness

разголи *pf* **I 1** to bare, expose; to strip *trans.*; го разголи грбот to bare one's back **2** to clothe lightly **3** *fig.* to uncover, expose, reveal **II – ce 1** to undress, strip *intrans.*; се разголи до половина to strip to the waist **2** to dress lightly *intrans.* **3** *fig.* to reveal o.s., show o.s. in one's true colours

разголува (се) *impf of* разголи (се)

разгон *m Bot.* (Veronica officinalis) common speedwell

разгони *pf* to chase away, drive off, scatter, disperse; (*демонстранти*) to break up *trans.*; (*мисли, облаци*) to dispel, disperse, scatter

разгонува *impf of* разгони

разгор *m* climax, peak; во разгорот на жетвата at the height of the harvest; ❑ во разгорот на младоста in the prime of youth; во разгорот на настаните at the climax of events, in the heat of the moment

разгорештен *pt* excited, worked-up

разгорештеност *f* excitement

разгорешти *pf* **I** to heat, warm up *trans.*; *fig.* to kindle, ignite, inflame **II – ce** to warm up *intrans.*; to get hot; *fig.* to get excited

разгорештува (се) *impf of* разгорешти (се)

разгори *pf* разгоре *aor.* **I** to kindle, ignite (*also fig.*); to inflame, arouse; разгори оган to get a fire going; разгори омраза to fan (foment) hatred **II – ce** to burn, flare up (*also fig.*); се разгоре пожарот the blaze spread; борбата се разгоре the struggle intensified

разгорува (се) *impf of* разгори (се)

разграба *pf* **I 1** to plunder, pillage **2** to buy up, snap up **II – ce** to start snatching things up/plundering

разграбува (се) *impf* разграба (се)

разграден[1] *pt* **1** ruined, wrecked, demolished **2** unfenced; разградена градина an unfenced garden

разграден[2] *pt* unbuttoned at the breast/chest, bare-chested

разгради[1] *pf* **1** to remove a fence from; го разградија дворот they took down the fence round the yard **2** to destroy, wreck, demolish, ruin

разгради[2] *pf* to unbutton at the chest; to bare one's chest; разгради кошула to unbutton one's shirt

разградува[1] *impf of* разгради[1]

разградува[2] *impf of* разгради[2]

разграка се *pf* to start cawing/croaking loudly

разгракува се *impf of* разграка се

разгранет *pt* **1** extended, ramified, branching out **2** jagged, indented; разгранет брег jagged shore-<line>

разграни *pf* **I 1** to branch out, put out branches; to ramify *intrans.* **2** *fig.* to develop *trans.*; to expand *trans.*; разграни културни врски to build cultural links **II – ce 1** to branch out **2** *fig.* to develop, expand *intrans.*

разграничи *pf* to delimit, define, demarcate

разграничува *impf of* разграничи

разгранок -ци *m* branch

разгранува (се) *impf of* разграни (се)

разгранчи (се) *pf see* разграни (се)

разгребе *pf* разгреба *aor.* to rake

разгребува *impf of* разгребе

разгрева (се) *impf of* разгрее (се)

разгрее *pf* разгреа *aor.* **I** to heat, warm up *trans.* **II – ce** to heat, warm up *intrans.*

разгрејува (се) *impf see* разгрева (се)

разгрли *pf* **I 1** to unbutton/undo (*s.o.'s*) clothing **2** to untie; to disentangle, unravel **II – ce 1** to unbutton/undo one's clothing; to bare one's breast **2** to untie o.s.; to free o.s.

разгрне *pf* разгрна *aor.* **I 1** to uncover, expose; to bare; to turn over **2** to stretch out, spread out *trans.*; разгрне раце to open one's arms **3** to throw aside, sweep aside; разгрне снег to shovel snow **4** *fig.* to manifest; to develop *trans.*; разгрне енергична дејност to embark on energetic activity

разгрнува *impf of* разгрне

разгром *m* utter defeat, rout

разгроми *pf* to rout, crush; разгроми непријател to rout an enemy

разгромува *impf of* разгроми

разгуга се, разгугука се & разгугутка се *pf see* разгука се

разгука се *pf* to start cooing (*loudly*)

разгукува се *impf of* разгука се

раздава *impf of* раздаде

раздавач *m* distributor, deliverer

раздаде *pf* to distribute, hand out, dispense

раздалек *m see* раздалечина; на раздалек at a distance

раздалеченост *f* distance

раздалечи *pf* **I** to move apart, separate *trans.* **II – ce** (*оддалечи се*) to go away, move away

раздалечина *f* distance; interval

раздалечува (се) *impf of* раздалечи (се)

раздвиженост *f* agitation; unease, disquiet; раздвиженоста на морето the roughness of the sea; се чувствуваше некаква раздвиженост a certain uneasiness could be felt

раздвижи *pf* **I 1** to set in motion, activate, move *trans.*; ги раздвижи нозете to move one's legs; раздвижи машина to activate a machine **2** *fig.* to arouse, stir up; to ruffle *trans.* **II – ce** to bestir o.s., start moving <about, around> *intrans.*

раздвижува (се) *impf of* раздвижи (се)

раздвоен[1] *pt* divided, separated, disunited

раздвоен[2] -јна *adj* dividing, separating; раздвојна линија dividing line; раздвоен ѕид dividing wall

раздвоеност *f* disunity; dissension

раздвои *pf* **I** to divide, split in two *trans.*;

(*сопружници*) to divorce, separate *trans*. **II – се** to separate, split up *intrans*.; to part company (*со – with*); to get divorced

раздвој *m* division, separation

раздвојува (се) *impf of* раздвои (се)

раздел *m* **1** part; section **2** barrier; dividing line; division

разделба *f* parting; separation; leave-taking; на разделба in parting

разделбен *adj* of parting; разделбен час hour of parting

разделен -лна *adj Gram.* disjunctive; разделен сврзник disjunctive conjunction

разделение -ија *n* (*делба, поделба*) division

разделеност *f* division; separation

раздели *pf* **I 1** to divide up *trans*.; to share out, distribute **2** to divide, split *trans*.; раздели број на четири to divide a number by four **3** to separate *trans*.; to sever; (*разведе*) to divorce **II – се 1** to divide, split up *intrans*.; to disperse *intrans*. **2** to separate *intrans*.; to get divorced; to part company (*солод – with*), take one's leave (*of*)

разделив *adj* (*делив*) divisible

разделница *f* dividing line, limit; мине разделница to overstep the mark

разделува (се) *impf of* раздели (се)

разделувач *m see* раставувач

раздене *pf* раздена *aor. see* оддене

раздени *pf* **I** impers. (*of daybreak*) to catch, reveal; го разденило на патот dawn found him on the road **II – се 1** to dawn, grow light; ❏ ми се раздени it dawned on me (*дека – that*)

разденува (се) *impf of* раздени (се)

раздере *pf* раздра *aor.* **I 1** to tear, rip <up>; си ја раздра кошулата to tear one's shirt **2** to scratch; си ја раздрав ногата I scratched my leg **3** (*with dat.*) to <start to> shout (*at s.o.*) **II – се 1** to get scratched **2** *fig.* to start shouting

раздерува (се) *impf of* раздере (се)

раздига *pf* **I 1** to tidy up *trans*.; (*маса*) to clear **2** to remove, carry off **3** to steal; to plunder **4** to buy up, snap up **II – се** to start snatching things up/ plundering

раздигне *pf* раздигна *aor. see* раздига

раздигнува *impf see* раздигува

раздигува *impf of* раздига

раздипли *pf* to unfold, spread out *trans*.

раздиплува *impf of* раздипли

раздира (се) *impf see* раздерува (се)

раздирлив *adj* piercing, shrill, penetrating; раздирлив вик penetrating cry

раздобје *n* epoch

раздолжи[1] *pf* **I** to release from a debt **II – се** to pay off one's debt, settle up (*со – with*)

раздолжи[2] **(се)** *pf see* развлече (се)

раздолжува[1] **(се)** *impf of* раздолжи[1] (се)

раздолжува[2] **(се)** *impf of* раздолжи[2] (се)

раздоми *pf* **I** to break up a home/marriage **II – се** to end one's marriage

раздомува (се) *impf of* раздоми (се)

раздор *m* strife, discord; ❏ сее раздор to sow the seeds of discord; јаболко на раздорот bone of contention

раздразлив *adj* **1** irritable, touchy **2** irritating,

provocative; раздразливо држење provocative behaviour

раздразливост *f* **1** irritability **2** provocativeness

раздразнет *pt* irritated, annoyed, tetchy

раздразнетост *f* irritation, tetchiness

раздразни *pf* **I 1** to annoy, irritate **2** to stimulate, arouse, excite **II – се 1** to get annoyed, lose one's temper **2** to get excited, become aroused

раздразнува (се) *impf of* раздразни (се)

раздрапа *pf* **I** to scratch (*all over*); to start stratching vigorously *trans*. **II – се 1** to start scratching vigorously *intrans*. **2** *fig.* to start clowning, playing the fool

раздрапува (се) *impf of* раздрапа (се)

раздрдори се *pf* to start chattering ceaselessly

раздрдорува се *impf of* раздрдори се

раздреме (се) *pf see* расони (се)

раздремува (се) *impf of* раздреме (се)

раздрмоли *pf* **I 1** to shake <up>, jolt *trans*.; to move violently *trans*.; to loosen *trans*.; ударот ми го раздрмоли забот the blow loosened my tooth **2** *fig.* to cause (*s.o.*) anxiety; to put into a flutter **II – се** to become shaky (wobbly); to start wobbling, shaking *intrans*.

раздрмолува (се) *impf of* раздрмоли (се)

раздрнда се *pf* **1** to start working hard, get down to work **2** *fig.* to start babbling, chattering

раздрндува се *impf of* раздрнда се

раздрнка *pf* **I 1** to start ringing/rattling *trans. & intrans.*; to start making a noise **2** *colloq.* (*раѕне*) to ruin; to wreck; раздрнка автомобил to wreck a car **II – се 1** to start ringing/rattling *intrans*. **2** *fig.* to start babbling, chattering **3** *fig.* to start strumming/playing; се раздрнка на гитара to start strumming a guitar

раздрнкува (се) *impf of* раздрнка (се)

раздробен *pt* **1** crushed, crumbled; раздробен камен crushed stone **2** fragmented, divided

раздробеност *f* fragmentation; factionalism, division

раздроби *pf* **1** to crush, pulverize **2** *fig.* to fragment; to break down *trans*.; to analyse

раздробува *impf of* раздроби

раздрум *m* (*раскрсница*) crossroads, intersection

раздруса (се) *pf see* растресе (се)

раздува *pf* **I 1** to disperse *trans*.; to blow about; ветрот ги раздува облаците the wind scattered the clouds **2** to fan *trans*.; to blow *trans*.; раздува оган to fan the flames **II – се 1** to start blowing hard *intrans*. **2** *dial.* to get angry

раздувува (се) *impf of* раздува (се)

раздупи *pf* to perforate *trans*., make holes in

раздупува *impf of* раздупи

разединет *pt* disunited, divided

разединето *adv* separately

разединетост *f* disunion, disunity; dissension

разедини *pf* **I** to divide *trans*.; to separate *trans*. **II – се** to split up, break up *intrans*.

разединува (се) *impf of* разедини (се)

разедначи *pf* to make different, differentiate <between> *trans*.; *Gram.* to dissimilate

разедначува *impf of* разедначи

разен -зна *adj* **1** different, unlike, dissimilar **2** different, various, diverse; на разни страни on different sides; in different directions; разни стоки miscellaneous goods **3** (*as noun*) разно *n* miscellaneous; (*на дневен ред*) any other business

разжаби *pf* I (*за нозе*) to spread (*too far apart*) *trans.*; (*за уста*) to open wide *trans.* II – **се** to sprawl

разжабува (се) *impf of* разжаби (се)

разжали *pf* I to sadden *trans.* II – **се** to become sad

разжалости (се) *pf see* разжали (се)

разжалостува (се) *impf of* разжалости (се)

разжалува (се) *impf of* разжали (се)

разжари *pf* 1 to make (*s. th.*) red-hot; to set fire to 2 *fig.* to inflame, arouse

разжарува *impf of* разжари

разжени *pf* I to divorce, separate *trans.* II – **се** to get divorced

разженува (се) *impf of* разжени (се)

разжешти (се) *pf see* разгорешти (се)

разжештува (се) *impf of* разжешти (се)

раззаби *pf* to open (*one's mouth*) wide

раззборува се *pf* to get deep into conversation; to start talking too much

раззеленее <**се**> *pf* раззеленеа <**се**> *aor.* to turn (grow) green; (*за дрво*) to come into leaf

раззелени <**се**> *pf see* раззеленее <**се**>

раззеленува <**се**> *impf of* раззелени <**се**>

раззема *impf of* разземе

разземе *pf* раззема *aor.* to buy up, snap up, snatch up

раззине *pf* раззина *aor.* to open (*one's mouth*) wide *trans.*; раззине уста to gape

раззинува *impf of* раззине

раззори <**се**> *pf impers.* to dawn, break (*of the day*); <**се**> раззори dawn has broken

раззорува <**се**> *impf of* раззори <**се**>

раззида *pf* to demolish

раззидува *impf of* раззида

разигра *pf* I 1 to cause to dance; (*за коњ*) to cause to prance 2 (*за срце*) to beat faster *intrans.*; срцето му разигра his heart sang II – **се** 1 to start dancing/ playing/prancing 2 (*за море*) to be ruffled, churned up, agitated

разигрува (се) *impf of* разигра (се)

разиде се *pf see* разотиде се

разјаде *pf* I to eat away; to destroy; to corrode *trans.*; to make (*s. o.*) start eating, give (*s. o.*) an appetite II – **се** to start eating greedily (voraciously)

разјадлив *adj* corrodible, corrosive

разјадливост *f* corrodibility

разјадоса *pf* I (*разгневи*) to infuriate, enrage II – **се** to fly into a rage

разјадосува (се) *impf of* разјадоса (се)

разјадува (се) *impf of* разјаде (се)

разјарен *pt* enraged, furious, infuriated

разјареност *f* rage, fury

разјари (се) *pf see* разјадоса (се)

разјарува (се) *impf of* разјари (се)

разјасни *pf* I 1 to explain, clarify, elucidate 2 (*небо, време*) to clear *trans.*; to clear up *trans.*; ветрето го разјасни небото the breeze cleared the sky II – **се** to become clear; to clear up *intrans.*; се разјасни небото the sky cleared; се разјасни состојбата the situation has become clear; ❑ се разјасни со to have it out with; to have a word with

разјаснител *m* explainer, clarifier

разјаснителен -лна *adj* explanatory

разјаснува (се) *impf of* разјасни (се)

разјаснувачки *adj see* разјаснителен

разјужи *pf* (*of the weather*) to get warmer

разјужува *impf of* разјужи

разјуначи се *pf* 1 to pluck up one's courage 2 to boast; to show off

разјуначува се *impf of* разјуначи се

разјури *pf f.p.* to urge on (*horses*)

разлабави *pf* I to loosen, slacken *trans.*; ги разлабави малу веригите he made the chains a bit looser II – **се** 1 to work loose, loosen, slacken *intrans.* 2 to become lax

разлабавува (се) *impf of* разлабави (се)

разлава *impf* to become unruly/restless; to run wild

разлавачка *f* unruliness, disobedience, recalcitrance

разлага (се) *impf of* разложи[1] (се)

разлагач *m* presenter; analyst

разладен -дна *adj* refrigeration, cooling; разладни уреди cooling appliances (*refrigerators, freezers, air-conditioners*)

разлади *pf* I to cool *trans.* II – **се** to cool *intrans.*; се разлади времево the weather has cooled

разладува (се) *impf of* разлади (се)

разлае *pf* разлаја *aor.* I to excite, provoke (*a dog, so that it starts barking*) II – **се** 1 (*за куче*) to start barking a lot 2 *fig.* to start chattering (babbling)

разлази се *pf* 1 (*за дете*) to start crawling 2 *fig.* to crawl in all directions

разлазува се *impf of* разлази се

разлајува (се) *impf of* разлае (се)

разлапа се *pf* to start eating greedily

разлапува се *impf of* разлапа се

разласка *pf f.p.* to start sparkling

разлатен -тна *adj* broad and shallow

разлачи *pf* 1 to separate, part *trans.* 2 to wean

разлачува *impf of* разлачи

разлеан *pt* 1 spilt 2 *fig.* wandering, rambling, desultory; разлеан говор a rambling speech

разлева (се) *impf of* разлее (се)

разлее *pf* разлеа *aor.* I 1 to spill *trans.* 2 to decant, pour <**out**> *trans.*; разлее вино во чаши to pour wine into glasses 3 to melt down; разлее сребро to melt down silver II – **се** 1 to spill over; to spread *intrans.*; (*за река*) to overflow; секоја пролет реката ќе се разлееше the river overflowed every spring 2 (*за боја и сл.*) to run *intrans.*

разлежи се *pf* to lie (recline) for a long time

разлежува се *impf of* разлежи се

разлејува (се) *impf see* разлева (се)

разлелее *pf* разлелеа *aor.* to start rocking/swinging/ ruffling *trans.*

разлелека се *pf* to start howling/whining

разлепи *pf* 1 (*плакати и сл.*) to put up (*in various places*) 2 (*одлепи*) to unstick, detach

разлепува *impf of* разлепи

разлета се *pf* 1 to fly away (*in different directions*), disperse (*flying*) *intrans.* 2 *fig.* to run away; to hurry away; scatter *intrans.*

разлетува се *impf of* разлета се

разлива (се) *impf see* разлева (се)

разлигави се *pf* to start snivelling/slobbering; to burst into tears

разлигавува се *impf of* разлигави се

разлие (се) *pf* разли (се) *aor. see* разлее (се)

разлиже *pf* разлижа *aor.* I to wear out *trans.*; to make shabby II – **се** 1 to wear out *intrans.* 2 to start licking

разлижува (се) *impf of* разлиже (се)

разлика *f* difference; за разлика од in contrast to; не прави разлика it makes no difference; класни разлики class distinctions; ❑ без разлика (на) indifferently; regardless (of); no matter what

разликува (се) *impf of* различи (се); не се разликуваат меѓу себе there is no difference between them

разлипа се *pf* to start crying/sobbing a great deal

разлипува се *impf of* разлипа се

разлисне <се> *pf* разлисна <се> *aor. see* разлисти <се>

разлиснува <се> *impf of* разлисне <се>

разлисти <се> *pf* разлиста <се> *aor.* to put out leaves

разлистува *impf* I 1 *of* разлисти 2 (прелистува) to turn pages, leaf through II – се *see* I 1.

различен -чна *adj* 1 different, unlike, dissimilar 2 different, various, diverse

различи *pf* I 1 to tell apart; to distinguish, make out; to differentiate *trans.* 2 (разубави) to embellish, beautify, improve the appearance of II – се 1 to differ (од – from) 2 (разубави се) to become more beautiful

различно *adv* differently

различност *f* difference, variety

различува (се) *impf see* разликува (се)

разлог -зи *m* (причина) cause, reason; без разлог without cause; приведе разлози to give reasons

разложен -жна *adj rare* rational, reasonable, sensible

разложи[1] *pf* I 1 to break up *trans.*, dismantle; to break down *trans.* 2 *fig.* to undermine; разложи организација to undermine an organization 3 *fig.* to justify, explain, give grounds for II – се to break up/down, disintegrate, decompose, rot *intrans.*

разложи[2] *pf* to clear away (round a fire before extinguishing it)

разложува[1] **(се)** *impf of* разложи[1] (се)

разложува[2] *impf of* раложи[2]

разлока *pf* to undermine, wash away; водата го разлока брегот the water undermined the bank II – се to start drinking heavily

разлокува (се) *impf of* разлока (се)

разломоти се *pf* to start babbling (chattering), get talking

разлоши *pf* I to make wicked, evil II – се to become wicked, evil, contrary

разлошува (се) *impf of* разлоши (се)

разлула & разлулее *pf* разлула & разлулеа *aor. see* разлелее

разлулува *impf of* разлула

разлутен *pt* enraged, infuriated, furious

разлутеност *f* rage, fury

разлути *pf* I 1 to make (a dish) peppery, hot 2 (рана, болест) to aggravate, make worse 3 *fig.* to enrage, infuriate II – се 1 to fly into a rage 2 (за рана, болест) to get worse, deteriorate

разлутува (се) *impf of* разлути (се)

разљуби *pf f.p.* to cease to love

размав *m* breadth, scope, range; зема размав to escalate

размава[1] *impf literary* 1 to sweep by; to be in full swing 2 *fig.* to call forth, cause, evoke; неговиот говор размава бура his speech caused a storm

размава[2] **се** *pf* to start hitting hard

размавне *pf literary* размавна *aor.* to flare up; востанието размавна the uprising flared

размавнува *impf of* размавне, *see* размава[1]

размавта *pf* I to brandish, start brandishing/swinging/waving *trans.*; ги размавта рацете to start gesticulating, to saw the air II – се (со) to start swinging/waving

размавтува (се) *impf of* размавта (се)

размавува се *impf of* размава се[2]

размаже (се) *pf* размажа (се) *aor. see* размачка (се)

размажува (се) *impf of* размаже (се)

размати *pf* to dilute; to stir/mix/blend; размати боја to dilute paint

разматува *impf of* размати

размачка *pf* I to spread *trans.*; to smear, daub *trans.* II – се (за боја и сл.) to spread unevenly, run *intrans.*

размачкува (се) *impf of* размачка (се)

размеѓи *pf* (земја) to divide, mark boundaries on/between; *fig.* to delimit, demarcate, define; размеѓи сфери на влијание to determine spheres of influence

размеѓува (се) *impf of* размеѓи (се)

размекне *pf* размекна *aor.* I to soften *trans.* (also fig.); to mellow *trans.*; размекне некому душа to melt s.o.'s heart II – се to grow soft, soften *intrans.*; *fig.* to mellow *intrans.*

размекнува (се) *impf of* размекне (се)

размекчи (се) *pf see* размекне (се)

размекчува (се) *impf of* размекчи (се)

размена *f* exchange; во размена (за) in exchange (for); размена на погледи exchange of views; размена на материјата metabolism; стоковна размена trade, commerce; (трампа) barter

размени *pf* I 1 to exchange, swap *trans.*; размени впечатоци to swap impressions 2 to take by mistake (mistaking one thing for another); си го разменив палтото I took the wrong overcoat 3 (пари) to change, break; размени илјадарка to change a thousand-denar note II – се to exchange, swap *intrans.*

разменлив *adj* exchangeable

разменува (се) *impf of* размени (се)

размер *m* 1 dimensions; scale; size; во широки размери on a large scale 2 *Prosody* metre

размерен -рна *adj* regular, measured, proportionate

размерност *f* regularity; steadiness

размеси *pf* to knead

размести *pf* I 1 to distribute, dispose *trans.*, place; to rearrange, transpose, shift *trans.*; (војници) to billet II – се to shift *intrans.*; to change places

разместува (се) *impf of* размести (се)

разместување *n* shift, movement; разместување на кадри rotation of personnel

размесува *impf of* размеси; сама меси, сама размесува she does everything herself

размете *pf* I to sweep, sweep up/out; размете двор to sweep a yard II – се to start sweeping

разметува (се) *impf of* размете (се)

размеша *pf* to mix, blend; to stir *trans.*

размешува *impf of* размеша

размине *pf* размина *aor.* I *colloq.* (помине) to come to an end, pass; младоста ќе размине youth will pass II – се 1 to pass each other; нашите писма се разминаа our letters crossed 2 to miss, fail to meet (s.o.)

разминува (се) *impf of* размине (се)

размир *m poet. see* размирица

размирен -рна *adj* restless, turbulent; размирни времиња troubled times; размирен дух rebellious spirit

размириса <се> *pf* to start smelling strongly; <се> размирисаа ружите the roses spread their scent

размирисува <се> *impf of* размириса <се>

размирица *f* discord, dispute, quarrel

размисла *f* thought, reflection

размисли *pf* **I** to reflect (*за – upon*), deliberate, think; to consider; размисли малу, па се согласи he thought for a moment, then agreed; размисли за некоја работа to consider a matter **II – се** to reflect (*за – upon*)

размислува (се) *impf of* размисли (се)

размислување *n* reflection, thought, cogitation; без размислување without thinking;

размјаука се *pf* to start mewing a lot

размножи *pf* **I** 1 to multiply *trans.*; размножи овци to breed sheep 2 to duplicate; to reproduce *trans*; размножи реферат to make copies of a report **II – се** to increase in number, reproduce *intrans.*; to multiply *intrans.*

размножува (се) *impf of* размножи (се)

размножување *n* multiplication; reproduction; органи за размножување reproductive organs

размолскоти *pf* to start sparkling/gleaming

размолскотува *impf of* размолскоти

размота *pf* **I** to unwind *trans.*; to unroll *trans.*; to unwrap **II – се** to unwind *intrans.*; to come undone

размотува (се) *impf of* размота (се)

размрда *pf* **I** to move, stir *trans.*, agitate; (*море*) to ruffle *trans.*; размрда нозе to stretch one's legs; to take a stroll **II – се** 1 to limber up, loosen up *intrans.* 2 *fig.* to get moving, get busy

размрдува (се) *impf of* размрда (се)

размрзне *pf* размрзна *aor.* to unfreeze *trans.*; to defrost **II – се** to thaw, melt *intrans.*

размрзнува (се) *impf of* размрзне (се)

размрмори се *pf* to start mumbling/grumbling

размрморува се *impf of* размрмори се

размрси *pf* **I** 1 to untwist, disentangle, unravel *trans.*; to undo; размрси коса/конци to untangle hair/thread 2 *fig.* to explain, make clear **II – се** 1 to unwind, unravel *intrans.* 2 *fig.* to become clear (comprehensible, understandable)

размрсува (се) *impf of* размрси (се)

размука се *pf* to start mooing

размукува се *impf of* размука се

разнебити *pf* to wreck, ruin, destroy (*also fig.*); to wear out

разнебитува *impf of* разнебити

разнежен *pt* touched, moved

разнежи *pf* 1 to pamper, spoil 2 to touch, move *trans.*; to appeal to (*s.o.'s*) emotions песната многу ме разнежи that song moved me deeply

разнежува *impf of* разнежи

разнеможе се *pf* to fall ill

разнеможува се *impf of* разнеможе се

разнервира *pf* **I** to get on s.o.'s nerves, irritate **II – се** to get upset, get agitated

разнесе *pf* **I** 1 to deliver; to distribute; разнесе писма to deliver letters 2 (*развее*) to blow away; to scatter, disperse *trans.*; ветрот ги разнесе облаците the wind has dispersed the clouds 3 *fig.* to disseminate; to spread *trans.*; разнесе болест to spread an illness; разнесе вест to spread news, spread the word 4 (*разграба*) to seize, grab, take possession of 5 to destroy, wreck; to blow up *trans.*; бомба ја разнесе банката a bomb blew up the bank **II – се** 1 (*за вест и сл.*) to spread *intrans.* 2 (*за звук*) to resound, ring; to reverberate; се разнесе екот the echo resounded

разнесува (се) *impf of* разнесе (се)

разнесувач *m* messenger, courier; разнесувач на млеко milkman

разниже *pf* разнижа *aor.* to unstring

разнижува *impf of* разниже

разниша *pf* to loosen *trans.*; to <start to> rock *trans.*, make (*s.th.*) shaky/wobbly; to <start to> shake *trans.*; ветрот ги разниша дрвјата the wind rocked the trees

разнишува *impf of* разниша

разно *adv rare see* различно

разно- (*in compounds*) many-, multi-, hetero-

разнобоен -јна *adj* variegated, motley, colourful

разновиден -дна *adj* various, diverse; разновидни јадења various dishes

разновидност *f* variety, diversity

разногласен -сна *adj* discordant, jarring; разногласна песна discordant song

разногласие -ија & **разногласје** *n* 1 disagreement, discord, dissonance; разногласие на мислења difference of opinion 2 discordant singing/music

разногласица *f* disagreement, differences

разногласност *f see* разногласие

разноимен *adj* variously named

разнојазичен -чна *adj* polyglot, multilingual; разнојазични песни songs in various languages

разнолик *adj* heterogeneous, diverse; разнолика природа varied nature

разноликост *f* diversity, variety

разнообразен -зна *adj* diverse, heterogeneous, dissimilar; разнообразна храна varied diet

разнообрази *pf* to vary, diversify *trans.*; децата им го разнообразија животот their children brought variety to their life

разнообразие & **разнообразје** *n see* разнообразност

разнообразност *f* diversity, variety; заради разнообразност for variety's sake

разнообразува *impf of* разнообрази

разнороден -дна *adj* different, heterogeneous; разнородно население heterogeneous population

разнородност *f* heterogeneity, variety

разнос *m* delivery, shipping; distribution

разносен -сна *adj usu. in the expression:* разносна книга delivery book

разносител *m see* разнесувач

разносителка *f* (*fem. form*) *see* разносител

разноски *pl* (*расход*) expenses

разностран *adj* 1 *Math.* scalene; разностран триаголник scalene triangle 2 *fig.* multilateral, many-sided; versatile; разностран талент all-round talent

разносува (се) *impf see* разнесува (се)

разобеси *pf* to hang *trans.*; to hang in different places *trans.*; to hang in large numbers; разобеси слики по сидовите to hang pictures on the walls

разобесува *impf of* разобеси

разоблачи се *pf rare* (*разведри се*) to clear *intrans.*

разоблачува се *impf of* разоблачи се

разоблече (се)   *pf see* расоблече (се)
разобличи   *pf* to unmask, expose, lay bare
разобличува   *impf of* разоблични
разоглавен   *pt* unbridled (*also fig.*); разоглавени страсти unbridled passions
разоглавено   *adv* unrestrainedly
разоглави   *pf* I to unbridle (*also fig.*); to unleash, give free rein to II – се *see* разузди (се)
разоглавува (се)   *impf of* разоглави (се)
разоден   *pt* run in (*of motors, etc.*)
разоди се   *pf* 1 to start walking/moving/travelling (*after a period of inactivity*) 2 (*за машина*) to be run in
разодува се   *impf of* разоди се
разонода   *f* recreation, leisure; fun; во часовите на разонода in one's spare time
разоноди   *pf* I to entertain, amuse II – се to amuse o.s., have fun
разонодува (се)   *impf of* разоноди (се)
разопина (се)   *impf see* разопнува (се)
разопне   *pf* разопна *aor.* I (*платно, мрежа и сл.*) to unfurl, open out *trans.*; (*шатор*) to pitch II – се to stretch, spread out *intrans.*
разопнува (се)   *impf of* разопне (се)
разора   *pf* to plough up
разоран   *pt* ploughed; разорана ледина virgin soil upturned
разорен[1]   *pt* (*разурнат*) ruined, destroyed, demolished
разорен[2]   -рна *adj* destructive, ruinous; разорно дејство destructive action/effect
разори   *pf* to destroy, lay waste, ruin; to blow up *trans.* (*also fig.*)
разорлив   *adj* destructible
разорливост   *f* destructibility
разорност   *f* destructiveness
разортачи   *pf* I to separate, part *trans.*; to dissolve *trans.* II – се to separate, part *intrans.*
разортачува (се)   *impf of* разортачи (се)
разорува[1]   *impf of* разора
разорува[2]   *impf of* разори
разорувач   *m* 1 wrecker, destroyer 2 *Naut.* destroyer
разоружен   *pt* disarmed
разоружи   *pf* to disarm *trans.* (*also fig.*)
разоружува   *impf of* разоружи
разоружување   *n* disarmament
разотвора (се)   *impf of* разотвори (се)
разотвори   *pf* I to open up, open wide *trans.* II – се to open up, open wide *intrans.*
разотиде се   *pf* to scatter, disperse *intrans.*; се разотидоа по куќите they dispersed to their houses
разотидува се   *impf of* разотиде се
разоткрива (се)   *impf see* открива (се)
разоткрие (се)   *pf* разоткри (се) *aor. see* открие (се)
разофка се   *pf* to start moaning, groaning/sighing
разофкува се   *impf of* разофка се
разочара   *pf* I to disappoint; to disillusion II – се to be disappointed (*во – in*); to be disillusioned
разочаран   *pt* disappointed; disillusioned
разочараност   *f* disappointment; disillusionment
разочарува (се)   *impf of* разочара (се)
разочарување   *n* disappointment
разработен   *pt* tried and tested, established; (*за механизам и сл.*) smooth-running, run in
разработеност   *f* efficiency; smooth-running

разработи   *pf* I 1 to work; to exploit; разработи рудник to work a mine; разработи земја to till (work) the land 2 to put in working order; to get (*s.th.*) running; to make (*s.th.*) run well; разработи мотор to run in an engine 3 *fig.* to develop; to elaborate; to treat; разработи тема to develop a theme II – се (*за човек*) to get down to work; (*за нешто*) to start working smoothly
разработка   *f* running in; *fig.* development; elaboration; drafting
разработува (се)   *impf of* разработи (се)
разрадува   *pf* I to gladden, delight II – се to be glad, delighted
разрани   *pf* 1 to scratch; to injure, wound; си го разрани лицето to scratch one's face 2 (*рана*) to scratch open (*also fig.*); разрани стара рана to reopen an old wound
разранува   *impf of* разрани
разрасне <се>   *pf* разрасна <се> *aor.* to grow, spread *intrans.*; to become larger/taller; <се> разрасна градот the town has grown; му разрасна семејството his family has grown; се разрасна движењето the movement has grown
разраснува <се>   *impf of* разрасне <се>
разраст   *m* growth
разрасте <се>   *pf see* разрасне <се>
разрастува <се>   *impf of* разрасте <се>
разреве се   *pf* разрева се *aor. see* разрика се
разревува се   *impf of* разреве се
разред   *m* class, category, group
разредба   *f* classification; arrangement, disposition
разреден   *pt* rarefied; diluted; thinned; разредена шума thinned woodland
разреди[1]   *pf* 1 to spread out *trans.* 2 (*со течност*) to dilute, thin *trans.*; разреди боја to thin paint 3 (*воздух, гас*) to rarefy *trans.*
разреди[2]   *pf* to spoil *trans.*, mess up
разредлив   *adj* rarefiable
разредува[1]   *impf of* разреди[1]
разредува[2]   *impf of* разреди[2]
разреже   *pf* разрежа *aor.* 1 to cut, cut up; to separate *trans.* 2 to determine, apportion; разреже данок to set tax levels
разрежува   *impf of* разреже
разрез   *m* 1 cut, slit; надолжен разрез lengthwise cut; ❏ во разрез со in contrast to 2 setting; apportionment; разрез на данок apportionment of tax
разрезува   *impf of* разреже, *see* разрежува
разретчи   *pf see* разреди[1]
разретчува   *impf of* разретчи
разрешава   *impf of* разреши
разрешавање   *n* solution; разрешавање на прашање solution to a problem
разреши   *pf* 1 to solve, settle *trans.*; разреши проблем to solve a problem 2 to dismiss, discharge; to acquit (*од – of*); to exonerate (*from*); разреши од должност to sack; разреши некого од обврски to release s.o. from his obligations
разрешлив   *adj* solvable, soluble
разрешница   *f* 1 dismissal notice 2 exoneration; clearance
разрешува   *impf see* разрешава
разрива   *impf of* разрие
разрига се   *pf* to start belching/vomiting

разригува се *impf of* разрига се

разрие *pf* разри *aor.* to dig up; to undermine

разриеност *f* friability

разрика се *pf* to start roaring/bellowing/howling/ weeping

разрикува се *impf of* разрика се

разрине *pf* разрина *aor.* to shovel

разринува *impf of* разрине

разрипа *pf* I *rare* to cause to jump II – се to start jumping a lot

разрипува (се) *impf of* разрипа (се)

разрита се *pf dial. see* расклоца се

разружа *pf* I to ungird, unsaddle II – се to ungird o.s.

разружува (се) *impf of* разружа (се)

разрумени *pf* I to turn (*s.o./s.th.*) pink II – се to blush, flush

разруменува (се) *impf of* разрумени (се)

разрушен[1] *pt* wrecked; ruined; demolished

разрушен[2] *pt* (*разбушавен*) dishevelled

разруши[1] *pf* I to wreck, ruin, demolish; *fig.* to dash II – се to collapse *intrans.*, go to ruin; се разрушија неговите илузии his illusions were dashed (shattered)

разруши[2] *pf* I to ruffle II – се to become dishevelled

разрушител *m* wrecker, destroyer

разрушлив *adj* destructible

разрушливост *f* destructibility

разрушува[1] **(се)** *impf of* разруши[1] (се)

разрушува[2] **(се)** *impf of* разруши[2] (се)

разубави *pf* I to beautify, embellish II – се to grow more beautiful

разубавува (се) *impf of* разубави (се)

разубеди *pf* I to dissuade; to change (*s.o.'s*) mind II – се to change one's mind

разубедува (се) *impf of* разубеди (се)

разувери *pf* I to dissuade; to disillusion II – се to lose one's faith; to change one's mind

разуверува (се) *impf of* разувери (се)

разуздан *pt* unbridled (*also fig.*)

разузданост *f* dissoluteness, licentiousness

разузда (се) *pf see* разузди (се)

разузди *pf* разузда *aor.* I to unbridle; *fig.* to unleash, give free rein to II – се to run wild, run amok

разуздува (се) *impf of* разузди (се)

разузнава *impf of* разузнае

разузнавање *n* 1 recognition 2 intelligence service; intelligence gathering

разузнавач *m* intelligence officer; scout

разузнавачки *adj* intelligence; разузнавачка служба intelligence service; разузнавачка работа intelligence work

разузнае *pf* разузна *aor.* 1 to distinguish; to recognize 2 to find out

разуларен *pt see* разоглавен, разуздан

разулари (се) *pf see* разоглави (се), разузди (се)

разум *m* sense, reason; mind intellect; здрав разум common sense

разумен -мна *adj* sensible, reasonable, rational; разумни предлози reasonable proposals; разумно решение sensible decision

разумник -ци *m rare* sensible person

разумница *f* (*fem. form*) *see* разумник

разумност *f* reasonableness, reason, sense

разурнат *adj* wrecked, ruined, demolished, destroyed

разурне *pf* разурна *aor.* I to wreck, ruin, demolish; destroy II – се to collapse *intrans.*, fall down

разурнува (се) *impf of* разурне (се)

разурнувач *m* 1 destroyer, wrecker 2 destroyer (*warship*)

разурнувачки *adj* destructive; damaging; разурнувачко дејство destructive action/effect

рај *m* heaven, paradise, Eden; земен рај heaven on earth, earthly paradise

раја *f* 1 *coll.* infidels 2 *see* рајатин

рајатин -ти *m* Christian subject of the Ottoman empire; peasant; village elder; *pejor.* giaour

рајатски *adj* infidel

рајбер *m* upright bolt

Рајна *f* the Rhine

рајнски *adj* Rhine *attrib.*, Rhenish

рајски *adj* heavenly, divine; blissful; рајски порти heavenly gates; рајска птица *Zool.* (Paradisea apoda) bird of paradise

рак -ци; -ови *m* 1 *Zool.* crustacean; морски рак (Cancer pagurus) hermit crab; (Nephoridae) lobster; речен рак (Astacus fluviatilis) crayfish; ❑ ни риба, ни рак neither fish, nor flesh <nor good red herring>; црвен како рак as red as a lobster 2 *Med.* cancer; рак на белите дробови lung cancer; рак на дојка breast cancer; рак-рана fatal wound; dangerous disease 3 *Astron.* Cancer

рака -це *f* arm; hand; со прекрстени раце with arms folded; цврста рака firm hand; вешта рака skilled hand; ❑ во најмала рака at least; во некоја рака somehow; врзан (фатен) е во рацете to be all thumbs; врзе раце некому to tie s.o.'s hands; горе рацете! hands up! десна рака е некому to be s.o.'s right hand <man>; дига (крева) рака (раце) од некого или од нешто to abandon s.o. or s.th.; долна́ рака lower order (rank); дупена́ рака spendthrift; измие раце to wash one's hands (*of s.th.*); има долги раце to be light-fingered; има златни раце to be very skilled, able to do anything; има лесна рака to manage things easily, be successful; има полни раце работа to have one's hands full; мавне со рака to wave (flap) one's hand (*signalling disagreement*); минува низ раце<те> на некого to pass through s.o.'s hands; му се тресе раката he is a miser; на брза рака hastily; на своја рака in one's own way; носи некого на раце to make a fuss of s.o.; одврзе некому раце to leave s.o. a free hand; од втора (трета *и сл.*) рака second- (third-, etc.) hand (*goods, information, etc.*); оди од рака на рака to pass from hand to hand; оди на (по) рака некому to suit s.o., be useful to s.o.; оди под рака to walk arm in arm; рака за рака hand in hand; остане <како> без раце to be left helpless; падне в рака (раце) некому to fall into s.o.'s hands; плукне на рацете to roll up one's sleeves; под рака underhandedly; предаде на раце некому to hand over to s.o./s.o.'s care; при рака е (се наоѓа) to be on hand; работи (прави) на рака to do (make) (*s.th.*) by hand (manually); работна рака workforce; рака на срце hand on my heart, honestly; скрсти раце to fold one's arms; стисне (стегне) рака некому to shake/squeeze s.o.'s hand; трие раце to rub one's hands (*with glee, pleasure*); пара на рака, Мара под рака cash and carry

ракав *m* 1 sleeve; ❑ засуче (запрегне) ракави to roll

up one's sleeves; истура како од ракав to give ready/ glib advice/answers; to answer off the cuff **2** (*на река*) arm, branch, tributary

раавица *f* glove; (*со еден прст*) mitten; заштитни ракавици protective gloves; ❑ работи со ракавици to handle with kid gloves; фрли ракавица to throw down the gauntlet; прими ракавица to take up (accept) a challenge

ракавичар *m* glove-maker, glover

ракавичка *f dim. of* ракавица

ракавче *n dim. of* ракав

ракатен -тна *adj see* рачен

ракатка *f* handful; bunch; ракатка жито a handful of wheat; ракатка цвеќиња a bunch of flowers

ракѐта¹ *f* rocket, missile; сигнална ракета a signal flare

ракѐта² *f Sport.* racket, racquet

ракѐтен -тна *adj* rocket; ракетен мотор rocket engine; ракетна рампа rocket-launching pad

ракида *f see* ракита

ракиден & ракидин *adj see* ракитов

ракиен *adj* brandy (*raki*) *attrib.*; ракиена чаша a *raki* glass

ракиица & ракиичка *f hyp. of* ракија

ракија -ии *f raki*, brandy (*usu. home-made*); сливова ракија plum brandy (slivovitz)

ракијар *m see* ракиџија

ракијарка *f* (*fem. form*) *see* ракијар

ракита *f Bot.* (Salix purpurea) purple osier

ракитак -ци *m* osier-bed

ракитен -тна *adj see* ракитов

ракитка *f dim. of* ракита

ракитник -ци *m see* ракитак

ракитов *adj* osier; ракитови кошници osier baskets

ракитовина *f see* ракита

ракиџија -ии *m* **1** *raki* producer/seller **2** *raki* drinker

ракиџијница *f see* ракиџилница

ракиџика *f* (*fem. form*) *see* ракиџија

ракиџилница *f raki* distillery

раков *adj* lobster's/crab's/crayfish's; ракова супа lobster soup

раковиден -дна *adj see* ракообразен

раковина *f* shell, carapace

раководен -дна *adj* leading; directing; managing; раководен кадар management; раководна улога leading role

раководење *n* management; leadership; методи на раководење management methods

раководец -дци *m see* раководител

раководечки *adj see* раководен

раководи *impf* I to lead, direct, manage, run *trans.* (*or with co*); to guide **II** – **се** to be guided (*од – by*)

раководител *m* director; manager; head

раководителка *f* (*fem. form*) *see* раководител

раководителски *adj* leader's; manager's, managerial

раководство *n* **1** leadership; management; direction; партиско раководство party leadership; под раководство на under the direction of **2** directive; guide **3** manual, handbook; раководство по латински јазик Latin primer (textbook)

раководелен -лна *adj* handmade

раководелец -лци *m* handicraftsman; craftsman

раководелски *adj* craftsman's; <of> handicraft

раководелство *n* handwork; needlework, embroidery

ракомет *m Sport.* handball

ракометар *m Sport.* handball player

ракометен -тна *adj* handball; ракометен турнир handball tournament

ракообразен -зна *adj* crablike; lobsterlike

ракопашен -шна *adj only in the expression:* ракопашен бој hand-to-hand fighting (combat)

ракопис *m* **1** manuscript **2** handwriting; читлив ракопис legible <hand>writing

ракописен -сна *adj* manuscript, handwritten; ракописна збирка manuscript collection

ракописно *adv* in manuscript, in handwriting; напишан ракописно written by hand; не пишувајте ракописно write in block capitals

ракоплеска *impf* (*with dat.*) to applaud, clap; им ракоплескаа на артистите they applauded the actors

ракополага *impf of* ракоположи

ракополагање *n* ordination

ракоположи *pf* to ordain; ракоположи за свештеник to ordain as priest

ракотворба *f* handicraft product; сребрени ракотворби silver artefacts

ракотворец -рци *m* handicraftsman; craftsman

ракува *impf* I (*со*) to handle, work, operate; знае да ракува со оружје to know how to handle weapons **II** – **се** to shake hands

ракување *n* **1** ракување со пари/оружје handling of money/weapons **2** handshake

ракувач *m* operator (*of a machine*)

ракун *m Zool.* raccoon

ракче *n dim. of* рак

ралица *f* plough handle

ралник -ци *m* ploughshare

рало *n* **1** plough **2** acre; пет рала земја five acres of land **3** pair, brace, couple; рало обетки a pair of earrings **2** *Astron.* the Plough, Ursa Major

рам *m see* рамка

рамазан *m* Ramadan

рамазански *adj* <of> Ramadan; рамазанска пита Ramadan flat bread

раме -ена, (*dial.* -ења; -иња) *n see* рамо

рамен -мна *adj* **1** flat, level, even; рамен пат level road **2** straight; рамна линија straight line **3** equal; similar; сите сме рамни we are all equal; не му е рамен he is not his equal; ❑ во рамна мера in equal measure, in kind; на рамна нога on an equal footing, on equal terms; му нема рамен he has no equal, he is peerless

рамен -мена *adj* shoulder; рамена коска shoulder-blade

рамница *f* shoulder; ❑ крене (дигне, собере, свие) рамници to shrug one's shoulders

рамење *n dim. of* рамо

рами *impf poet.* (*нарамува*) to shoulder *trans.*, take on one's shoulders; рами пушка to shoulder a rifle

рамификација *f* ramification

рамка *f* **1** frame; рамка на слика picture frame **2** framework; limits; ги натфрли рамките to exceed the bounds; излезе од рамките to go beyond the limits; во рамките на законот within the law

рамни *impf* I to level *trans.* **II** – **се** to compare o.s. (*со – to/with*)

рамнило *n* spirit-level

рамнина *f* **1** plain; lowland **2** *Math.* plane

рамница *f see* рамнина 1

рамничар *m* plainsman

рамничарски *adj* lowland; plainsman's; рамничарска клима lowland climate

рамниште *n* **1** *see* рамнина 1 **2** *fig.* level; на исто рамниште on the same level

рамно¹ *n* **1** level ground **2** kind of *oro* (*line-dance*)

рамно² *adv* **1** evenly; on the level; ❑ сѐ ми е рамно it's all the same to me **2** horizontally; лежи рамно to lie horizontally **3** exactly; рамно пет саат exactly five o'clock

рамно- (*in compounds*) equi-; рамностран equilateral

рамноаголен -лна *adj Math.* equiangular

рамноапостол *m* (*epithet of some saints*) equal to the apostles

рамноглав *adj* flat-headed

рамноденица *f* equinox; пролетна/есенска рамноденица vernal/autumnal equinox

рамнодневица *f see* рамноденица

рамнодушен -шна *adj* indifferent (*кон – to, towards*); apathetic

рамнодушност *f* indifference

рамнозначен -чна *adj* equivalent (*со – to*); рамнозначни зборови synonymous words

рамнокрак *adj* having equal sides/branches; *Math.* рамнокрак триаголник isosceles triangle

рамномерен -рна *adj* regular; even; рамномерен развиток uniform development; рамномерно движење regular movement; uniform motion

рамномерност *f* regularity; uniformity; evenness

рамнообразен -зна *adj* identical

рамноправен -вна *adj* equal, enjoying equal rights; рамноправен член full member

рамноправие *n arch. see* рамноправност

рамноправност *f* equality; рамноправност на народи equal rights of nations; рамноправност на жената и мажот equality of the sexes

рамносилен -лна *adj* equivalent; tantamount (*со – to*)

рамност *f* smoothness, evenness

рамностран *adj Math.* equilateral; рамностран триаголник equilateral triangle

рамнотéжа *f* balance, equilibrium; equanimity; загуби рамнотежа to lose one's balance; душевна рамнотежа balance of mind; исфрли од рамнотежа to unbalance, upset

рамо -ена; -ења; - иња *n* **1** shoulder; ❑ дигне рамена to shrug one's shoulders; рамо до рамо shoulder to shoulder; side by side **2** shield; рамо на топ gun shield

рампа *f* **1** proscenium, apron; *fig.* footlights **2** lifting barrier, swing-beam

рамстек *m Cul.* rump steak

ран *adj* early; рана пролет early spring; ран зеленчук early vegetables; рано породување premature birth; рано пиле рано пее *prov.* the early bird catches the worm

рана *f* wound, injury; жива рана running sore; отворена рана an open wound

ранг *m* rank; grade; најстар по ранг senior in rank; писател од прв ранг a first-rate writer; ❑ ранг-листа order of precedence; *Sport.* <list of> seeds

рангúра *pf & impf* to rank *trans.*; to determine, award a rank (*to*)

рандевý *m & n* rendezvous, assignation, *colloq.* date; ми закажа рандеву he made a date with me

раненик -ци *m dial. see* храненик

ранениче *n dim. see* хранениче

ранет *pt* **1** wounded, injured **2** (*as noun*) *m* casualty; wounded/injured person

ранец¹ *m* early ripening vine

ранец² -нци *m see* раница¹

ранжúр *m* arrangement, disposition; shunting, marshalling

ранжúра *pf & impf* to arrange; to shunt *trans.*; ранжира вагони to shunt trucks

ранжúрен -рна *adj* shunting, marshalling; ранжирна станица marshalling yard

рани *pf* to wound, injure; to hurt (*also fig.*); го раниле во ногата he was wounded in the leg/foot

рани¹ *impf* to get up early

рани² (се) *impf see* храни (се)

ранина *f* early morning; на (од, в) ранина early in the morning; ❑ од ранина до доцнина from early morn to late at night

раница¹ *f* haversack, knapsack; ❑ празна раница не варди граница an army marches on its stomach

раница² & **раничка** *f dim. of* рана

ранко *adv dim. of* рано

ранлив *adj* **1** vulnerable **2** wounded, sore

рано *adv* early; рано изутрина early in the morning; јавете ми порано let me know beforehand (in advance); рано рани to get up early; ❑ што порано as early as possible; рано (порано) или доцна (подоцна) sooner or later; рано пиле рано пее *prov.* the early bird catches the worm

ранобуда *m dial. see* ранобудник

ранобуден -дна *adj* early rising

ранобудник -ци *m* early riser

ранобудница *f* (*fem. form*) *see* ранобудник

ранува (се) *impf of* рани (се)

ранч *m* ranch, farm

ранчер *m* rancher, farmer

рапав *adj* **1** rough, coarse; рапава штица rough board; рапава кожа rough skin **2** hoarse, harsh; со рапав глас in/with a hoarse voice; рапава смеа raucous laughter **3** *fig.* coarse, uncultivated; рапави изрази coarse expressions; рапав стил unpolished style

рапавина *f rare see* рапавост

рапавост *f* roughness; hoarseness

рапиден -дна *adj* rapid, quick; рапиден напредок rapid advance

раплав *adj* (*врглест*) knotty, gnarled

рапорт *m* report; јави се на рапорт to report, present o.s.

рапортúра *pf & impf* to report, deliver a report

рапсод *m* rhapsodist, bard

рапсодија -ии *f* rhapsody

раритет *m* rarity

раса¹ *f* race; breed; коњ од чиста раса thoroughbred horse; крстосување на раси cross-breeding

раса² *f* cassock; ❑ фрли раса to leave the priesthood

расад *m coll.* seedlings, nursery plants

расади *pf* to transplant, plant out

расадник -ци *m* **1** nursery; шумски расадник tree nursery **2** *fig.* source, seat; hotbed; расадник на зараза hotbed of infection; расадник на просвета centre of education

расадува *impf of* расади

расветли *pf* **1** to illuminate, light up *trans.* **2** *fig.* to explain, interpret, clarify

расветлува *impf of* расветли

расвири се *pf* to start playing (*an instrument*), be carried away playing

расвирува се *impf of* расвири се

расеан *pt* **1** scattered, dispersed **2** *fig.* absent-minded, distracted; расеан поглед distracted gaze

расеаност *f* absent-mindedness

расед *m Geog.* fault

раседла *pf* to unsaddle

раседлува *impf of* раседла

расее *pf* расеа *aor.* **I 1** to disperse, scatter *trans.*; to dispel; расее страв to dispel fear **2** *fig.* to distract **II – се 1** to disperse, scatter *intrans.* **2** to become absent-minded

расејува (се) *impf of* расее (се)

расек -ци *m* slit

расекува *impf see* расечува

расели *pf* **I** to resettle *trans.*; to evacuate; to deport **II – се** to settle *intrans.*; to migrate

раселува (се) *impf of* расели (се)

расен -сна *adj* **1** racial; расни разлики racial differences; расна дискриминација racial discrimination **2** pure-bred; расна крава a pedigree cow

расече *pf* to cut; to chop (slice) up; расече јагне to quarter a lamb; си го расече лицето he cut his face

расечува *impf of* расече

раси *impf* to besprinkle, sprinkle upon; to sprinkle (*dust, sand, ash*) on

расизам -змот *m* racism, racialism

расипан *pt* rotten (*also fig.*), spoilt; corrupt; damaged; расипано јадење rotten food; расипани заби decayed teeth; расипани односи soured relations; ❏ расипан телефон Chinese whispers, Russian scandal; расипана душа corrupt soul

расипаник -ци *m* corrupt person; pervert

расипаница *f* (*fem. form*) *see* расипаник

расипанко -овци *m see* расипаник

расипе *pf* расипа *aor.* **I 1** to wreck, ruin (*also fig.*); to mar; расипе односи to spoil relations; расипе настроение to spoil a mood; расипе дете to spoil a child **2** to squander; расипе имот to squander an estate **3** to change (*banknotes, coins*) **4** *fig.* to corrupt *trans.*, debauch **II – се 1** to break down *intrans.*; to deteriorate, decay; to spoil *intrans.*; (*за храна*) to go off; се расипа времето the weather has deteriorated **2** to become corrupt/debauched

расипикуќа *m & f see* растурач 2, расипник

расиплив *adj* perishable; расиплива храна perishable food; лесно расиплив easily spoilt

расипливост *f* perishability

расипник -ци *m* spendthrift, wastrel, prodigal

расипница *f* (*fem. form*) *see* расипник

расипнички *adj* prodigal, spendthrift

расипништво *n* prodigality

расипокуќник -ци *m see* расипник

расипува (се) *impf of* расипе (се)

расист *m* racist

расистички *adj* racist; расистичка теорија racist theory

расистка *f* (*fem. form*) *see* расист

раситни *pf* to break up *trans.*; to chop up; раситни ја земјата to break up the soil; раситни една стотка to change a hundred-denar note

раситнува *impf of* раситни

раска *f* bit, scrap, speck; ❏ раска во око a thorn in the flesh; mote in the eye

раскае се *pf* раскаја се *aor.* to repent (*од – of*)

раскаже *pf* раскажа *aor.* **I** to tell, recount, narrate **II – се 1** (*за вест*) to spread *intrans.*; се раскажало по светот it was noised abroad **2** *rare see* расприкаже се

раскажлив *adj* **1** skilled at story-telling **2** talkative **3** (*за текст*) narrative

раскажник -ци *m colloq.* storyteller; babbler, prattler;

раскажница *f* (*fem. form*) *see* раскажник

раскажува (се) *impf of* раскаже (се)

раскажувач *m* narrator; storyteller; raconteur

раскажувачки *adj* storytelling; раскажувачки талент storytelling talent

расказ *m* story, tale; збирка раскази collection of stories

расказен -зна *adj* narrative; расказна форма narrative form

раскајаник -ци *m* penitent

раскајува се *impf of* раскае се

раскака се *pf see* раскока се

раскакува (се) *impf of* раскака (се)

раскалуѓер *m* unfrocked (defrocked) monk

раскалуѓери *pf* **1** to defrock, unfrock (*a monk*) **II – се** to leave a monastic order

раскалуѓерува (се) *impf of* раскалуѓери (се)

раскапан *pt* worn-out; decrepit, dilapidated; *fig.* exhausted

раскапаник -ци *m* worn-out, decrepit person

раскапаност *f* dilapidation; exhaustion, decrepitude, feebleness

раскапе[1] *pf* раскапа *aor.* **I 1** to tear to pieces; to break up *trans.* **2** to overwork *trans.* **II – се 1** to disintegrate; to rot, decay **2** се раскапе од работа to overwork *intrans.*, work o.s. to exhaustion

раскапе[2] **се** *pf* раскапа се *aor.* to start dripping heavily

раскапува[1] **(се)** *impf of* раскапе (се)

раскапува[2] **се** *impf of* раскапе се

раскара *pf* **I** to cause to quarrel; to set at odds **II – се 1** to quarrel, fall out (*co – with*) **2** to start quarrelling

раскарува (се) *impf of* раскара (се)

раскасапи *pf* to cut up; to butcher (*also fig.*)

раскасапува *impf of* раскасапи

раскати се *pf* to open <up>, split open *intrans.*

раскатува се *impf of* раскати се

раскашави *pf* **I** to soften *trans.*; to overcook; to make mushy **II – се** to become soft, soften *intrans.*; to weaken *intrans.*; to become milder; to go wrong; се раскашави времево the weather's turned milder; планот се раскашави the plan went awry

раскашавува (се) *impf of* раскашави (се)

раскашла се *pf* to start coughing a lot

раскашлува се *impf of* раскашла се

расквака се *pf* to start croaking/quacking loudly

расквакува се *impf of* расквака се

раскваси *pf* to moisten; раскваси уста to wet one's whistle

расквасува *impf of* раскваси

расквичи се *pf* (*за куче, свиња*) to start yelping/squealing

расквичува се *impf of* расквичи се
раскива се *pf* to start sneezing
раскикоти *pf* **I** to make (*s.o.*) giggle **II** – **ce** to burst into giggles
раскикотува (се) *impf of* раскикоти (се)
раскилави *pf* **I 1** to rupture *trans.* **2** *fig.* to exhaust, tire out, overwork *trans.* **II** – **ce 1** to rupture o.s. **2** *fig.* to overwork *intrans.*, tire o.s. out
раскилавува (се) *impf of* раскилави (се)
раскин *m* severance, break-up; раскин на договор breach of contract
раскине *pf* раскина *aor.* **I 1** to break up *trans.*, tear up, rend asunder **2** to abrogate, annul, cancel; раскине односи to break off (sever) relations; раскине договор to cancel an agreement/contract **3** *fig.* to tire out, exhaust; to overwork *trans.* **II** – **ce 1** to exhaust o.s., tire o.s. out; to overwork **2** *fig.* to break *intrans.*; од жал срцето ѝ се раскина her heart broke with grief
раскинлив *adj* severable; раскинлив договор a severable agreement/contract
раскинува (се) *impf of* раскине (се)
раскинувач *m* breaker, severer (*of a contract, etc.*)
раскинувачки *adj* tearing, rending; раскинувачки липања heart-rending sobs
раскисели *pf* **I 1** to sour *trans.*, make sour **2** *fig.*, *colloq.* to upset, distress, annoy **II** – **ce 1** to go sour, turn sour **2** *fig.*, *colloq.* to get into a bad mood, get irritated, annoyed
раскиселува (се) *impf of* раскисели (се)
раскисне *pf* раскисна *aor.* **I** to soak *trans.*, drench **II** – **ce** to get soaked, drenched
раскиснува (се) *impf of* раскисне (се)
расклања се *pf* to start bowing
расклапа *pf* **I** to make shaky/wobbly/rickety **II** – **ce** to become shaky/wobbly/rickety
расклапан *pt* shaky; wobbly; rickety; расклапана врата a wobbly door
расклапува (се) *impf of* расклапа (се)
раскласи *pf* *poet.* to start forming ears (*of cereals*)
раскласува *impf of* раскласи
расклати *pf* **I** to make shaky/wobbly/rickety; to loosen *trans.* *fig.* to shake, undermine; ни го расклати уверението he shook our confidence **II** – **ce** to loosen *intrans.*; to become shaky/wobbly/rickety; *fig.* (*за здравје*) to deteriorate; to get worse; се расклати дисциплината the discipline grew lax
расклатува (се) *impf of* расклати (се)
расклепа се *pf* **1** to start rattling, clattering **2** to start beating out (sharpening)/hammering **3** to start chiselling, sculpting **4** to start babbling, chattering **5** (*со очи*) to start blinking
расклепува се *impf of* расклепа се
расклешти се *pf* to start grinning/laughing a lot
расклештува се *impf of* расклешти се
расклика се *pf* (*за орел и некои др. птици*) to start calling, screaming loudly
раскликува се *impf of* расклика се
расклинка се *pf* to start hopping
расклинкува се *impf of* расклинка се
расклокоти се *pf* (*за река, поток; за течност*) to start gurgling/babbling
расклокотува се *impf of* расклокоти се

расклони се *pf* (*за дрво*) to spread *intrans.*
расклонува се *impf of* расклони се
расклопи *pf* **1** to dismantle, take apart **2** (*обично книга*) to open *trans.*; to unfold *trans.*
расклоплив *adj* demountable
расклопува *impf of* расклопи
расклоца се *pf* to start kicking
расклоцува се *impf of* расклоца се
расксове *pf* расксова *aor.* **I** to unfetter, unnail; to unshoe (*horses*) **II** – **ce** to start forging
расковува *impf of* расксове
раскока се *pf* to start jumping
раскокорави се *pf* to start strutting
раскокоравува се *impf of* раскокорави се
раскокори се *pf see* раскокорави се
раскокорува се *impf of* раскокори се
раскокува се *impf of* раскока се
раскол *m* discord; dissent, schism
расколеба *pf* **I** to shake, unsettle; ништо не можеше да го расколеба nothing could shake him **II** – **ce** to waver, hesitate
расколебаност *f* wavering, hesitation
расколебува (се) *impf of* расколеба (се)
расколник -ци *m* dissenter, schismatic
расколница & **расколничка** *f* (*fem. form*) *see* расколник
расколнички *adj* schismatic; расколничка дејност schismatic activity
расколништво *n* dissent
раскомати *pf* to break into pieces *trans.*; to crumble *trans.*
раскоматува *impf of* раскомати
раскомоти *pf* **I** to make comfortable **II** – **ce** to make o.s. comfortable; to settle down/in; to make o.s. at home
раскомотува (се) *impf of* раскомоти (се)
раскопа *pf* to dig up; to excavate; (*гроб*) to disinter, exhume
раскопачи *pf* (*за шума*) to clear *trans.*, grub out
раскопачува *impf of* раскопачи
раскопина *f* excavation, excavated site; find, excavated object
раскопка *f see* раскопина
раскопне[1] *pf* раскопна *aor. dim. of* раскопа
раскопне[2] *pf* раскопна *aor.* to thaw *intrans.*; to melt *intrans.*
раскопнува *impf of* раскопне[2]
раскопува *impf of* раскопа
раскопча *pf* **I** to unbutton, undo **II** – **ce 1** to unbutton one's clothes **2** to come undone
раскопчува (се) *impf of* раскопча (се)
раскоси[1] **се** *pf* to start mowing, scything
раскоси[2] **се** *pf* to get angry, furious; to get annoyed, worried
раскостен *pt* exhausted, worn-out, decrepit
раскостеност *f* exhaustion, feebleness, decrepitude
раскости *pf* **I 1** to dismember; to crush; раскости од ќотек to thrash, give (*s.o.*) a good hiding **2** *fig.* to tire out, exhaust, overwork *trans.* **II** – **ce 1** to shatter *intrans.*, fall to pieces **2** to decompose **3** *fig.* to wear o.s. out, overwork *intrans.*
раскостува (се) *impf of* раскости (се)
раскош *m* luxury; splendour
раскошен -шна *adj* luxurious, sumptuous, splendid;

раскошен живот life of luxury; раскошни цвеќиња delightful flowers

раскоштравен *pt see* разбушавен

раскоштрави (се) *pf see* разбушави (се)

раскоштравува (се) *impf of* раскоштрави (се)

раскрака се *pf* to start clucking (cackling)

раскракува се *impf of* раскрака се

раскрачи *pf* **I** раскрачи нозе to place one's feet apart **II** – **се** to place one's feet apart

раскрачува (се) *impf of* раскрачи (се)

раскрвави *pf* **I** to cause to bleed, draw blood **II** – **се** to bleed (*profusely*)

раскрвавува (се) *impf of* раскрвави (се)

раскрева *impf of* раскрене

раскрека се *pf* **1** (*за жаба*) to start croaking **2** *fig.* to start screaming

раскрекува се *impf of* раскрека се

раскрене *pf* раскрена *aor. see* раздига 1 & 2

раскренува *impf of* раскрене

раскрепости *pf* to emancipate from serfdom

раскрепостува *impf of* раскрепости

раскреска се *pf* to start shrieking/screaming/squealing

раскрескува се *impf of* раскреска се

раскрили *pf* раскрили крилја to spread one's wings

раскрилува *impf of* раскрили

раскрои *pf* **I** **1** to cut out/up (*leather, cloth, etc.*) **2** to break down *trans.*, tear down **II** – **се** to collapse *intrans.*, fall down; се раскрои ѕидот the wall collapsed

раскројува (се) *impf of* раскрои (се)

раскрпи *pf* to rip open *trans.*

раскрпува *impf of* раскрпи

раскрсница *f* crossroads, intersection

раскрсти *pf* to break off (*co – with*); to give up (*s. th.*) *trans.*

раскрстува *impf of* раскрсти

раскрши *pf* **I** **1** to break up *trans.*; to shatter *trans.*; to crumble *trans.* **2** (*снага*) to limber up *trans.*; to start swaying, bending the body (*when walking*) **II** – **се 1** to break up *intrans.*; to shatter *intrans.*; to crumble *intrans.* **2** to limber up *intrans.*; to start swaying, bending the body (*when walking*); to <start to> stretch one's limbs

раскршува (се) *impf of* раскрши (се)

раскупи *pf* to buy up, snap up

раскуќи *pf* **I** to destroy, break up (*a family*); to squander, fritter away **II** – **се** to fall apart, break up *intrans.* (*of a family*)

раскуќува (се) *impf of* раскуќи (се)

раскуштри (се) *pf dial. see* разбушави (се)

раслои *pf* to divide into layers *trans.*; to stratify

раслојува *impf of* раслои

расмева (се) *impf see* расмејува (се)

расмее *pf* расмеа *aor.* **I** to make (*s. o.*) laugh **II** – **се** to burst out laughing

расмејува (се) *impf of* расмее (се)

расмрди се *pf* to start stinking

расмрдува се *impf of* расмрди се

расне *impf see* расте

расност *f* pedigree, pure breed

расо *n see* раса²

расоблекува (се) *impf of* расоблече (се)

расоблече *pf* **I** to undress *trans.* **II** – **се** to undress *intrans.*

расоблечува (се) *impf see* расоблекува (се)

расобува (се) *impf of* расобуе (се)

расобуе *pf* расобу *aor.* **I** to take off (*s. o.'s*) shoes, boots, socks, etc.; расобуе дете to take off a child's shoes **II** – **се** to take off one's shoes, boots, socks, etc.

расов *adj see* расен

расол *m* sauerkraut (pickled cabbage)

расолзи *pf* **I** to bring tears to (*s. o.'s*) eyes, make (*s. o.*) cry **II** – **се** to start crying

расолзува (се) *impf of* расолзи (се)

расоли *pf see* отсоли

расолка *f* leaf of pickled cabbage

расолник -ци *m* puff pastry with pickled cabbage

расолница *f* brine

расолува *impf of* расоли

расони *pf* **I** to wake *trans.* **II** – **се** to wake (up) *intrans.*

расонува (се) *impf of* расони (се)

распавта се *pf* to start waving (*one's arms, etc.*)

распавтува се *impf of* распавта се

распад *m* decomposition, decay; disintegration, break-up; crumbling

распади *pf* to disperse, chase away, drive away *trans.*

распадлив *adj* frail, fragile

распадливост *f* frailty, fragility

распаднат *pt* decayed, decomposed

распаднатост *f* disintegration, decomposition

распадне се *pf* распадна се *aor.* to fall apart, disintegrate; to decompose, break down *intrans.*

распаднува *impf of* распадне се

распадува *impf of* распади

распаѓа се *impf see* распаднува се

распаѓање *n* decomposition; disintegration, collapse

распакува *pf & impf* **I** to unpack *trans.*; распакува сандак to unpack a trunk **II** – **се** *colloq.* to unpack one's bags

распалавен *adj* naughty, mischievous; распалавено дете naughty child

распалавеност *f* naughtiness, mischievousness

распалави се *pf* to start misbehaving/acting mischievously

распалавува се *impf of* распалави се

распален *pt* blazing; *fig.* aroused; inflamed

распалено *adv* hotly, heatedly, excitedly; angrily

распали *pf* **I** **1** to kindle; to light *trans.* **2** *fig.* to incite, arouse, excite, inspire; распали некому фантазија to fire s.o.'s imagination **II** – **се 1** to blaze up, flare **2** *fig.* to become aroused/impassioned

распалив *adj* irascible, quick-tempered

распалува (се) *impf of* распали (се)

распара *pf* **I** **1** to unpick, undo, unstitch; to rip open, rip up; to cut up **2** *fig.* to rend; to break *trans.*; срцето ми го распара it broke my heart; распара тишина to rend the silence **II** – **се 1** to come undone, become unstitched **2** *fig.* to break *intrans.*; му се распара срцето his heart broke

распарлив *adj literary* harsh, grating

распартали *pf* **I** to tear to pieces, tear up *trans.* **II** – **се 1** to become tattered **2** to relax, *colloq.* let one's hair down; to let o.s. go

распарталува (се) *impf of* распартали (се)

распарува (се) *impf of* распара (се)

распарча & распарчи *pf* **I** to break up, break into

pieces *trans.*; to tear to pieces **II – ce** to break up *intrans.*, smash, shatter *intrans.*; *fig.* to get hurt

распарчаност & **распарченост** *f* fragmentation, fragmentariness

распарчува (се) *impf of* распарча (се) & распарчи (се)

распасе се *pf* to start grazing

распасува се *impf of* распасе се

распати *pf* **I** to breed *trans.*, raise, rear; распати пилиња to breed chickens **II – ce** to breed, multiply *intrans.*

распатува (се) *impf of* распати (се)

распаќе *n* crossroads, intersection

распашан *adj* undisciplined, unruly

распашаност *f* unruliness, indiscipline

распаше *pf* распаша *aor.* **I 1** to ungird **2** *fig.* to allow to get out of hand; to lose control of **II – ce 1** to ungird o.s. **2** to relax **3** to let o.s. go; to run riot

распашува (се) *impf of* распаше (се)

распеан *adj* singing easily, freely; распеан глас melodious voice; распеана мелодија catchy tune

распева (се) *impf of* распее (се)

распее *pf* распеа *aor.* **I 1** to cause to sing **2** распее глас to exercise/train one's voice **II – ce** to start singing; to reach one's best singing form

распејува (се) *impf see* распева (се)

распени се *pf* to foam, froth

распенува се *impf of* распени се

распердаши <се> *pf colloq.* to start hitting, thumping, walloping

распердашува <се> *impf of* распердаши <се>

распердуши *pf* **1** to pluck; распердуши кокошка to pluck a chicken **2** *fig.* to pull to pieces

распердушува *impf of* распердуши

распетие -ија *n* **1** crucifix **2** crucifixion

распетла *pf* to unbutton, undo

распетлан *pt* unbuttoned; uncovered; распетлан врат open neck

распетлува (се) *impf of* распетла (се)

распечати *pf* **I** to unseal, break the seal of **II – ce** to open *intrans.*; to become unsealed

распечатува (се) *impf of* распечати (се)

распие се *pf* распи се *aor.* to start drinking heavily

распина (се) *impf see* распнува (се)

распис *m* circular, notice, announcement; распис до сите установи circular to all institutions

расписка¹ *f* receipt; acknowledgement

расписка² се *pf* to start screaming, shrieking (*loudly*); (*за локомотива и сл.*) to start whistling

распискува се *impf of* расписка² се

распит *m* hearing, inquiry; interrogation

распита *pf* **I** to question, interrogate; to ask, inquire; распита сведок to question a witness **II – ce** to make enquiries

распитува (се) *impf of* распита (се)

распише *pf* распиша *aor.* **I 1** to declare in writing, announce; распише конкурс to announce a competition/vacancy; распише лицитација to invite tenders **2** *colloq.* (*перо, молив*) to cause to write properly, get working **II – ce** to start writing busily

распишти се *pf see* расписка² се

распиштоли се *pf colloq.* to relax, *colloq.* let one's hair down; to let o.s. go

распиштолува се *impf of* распиштоли се

распиштува се *impf see* расписк ва се

распишува (се) *impf of* распише (се)

расплакува (се) *impf see* расплачува (се); ❏ расплакува дете во мајка to be cruel, merciless

распламти *pf* распламти & распламте *aor.* **I 1** to set alight, set fire to; to whip up; ветрот го распламте огнот the wind fanned the blaze **2** *fig.* to arouse, inspire; to inflame; ја распламти борбата he inflamed their struggle; распламти страст to fuel a passion **II – ce 1** to start burning, burst into flames; to flare up **2** *fig.* to erupt, burst out; се распламте востание rebellion broke out

распламтува (се) *impf of* распламти (се)

расплапоти се *pf colloq.* **1** *see* раздрдори се **2** *see* разбаботи се 1

распласка се *pf* **1** to start striking, clapping hard; to start flapping **2** *fig.* to start talking nonsense

расплата *f* settling of accounts; reckoning; *fig.* revenge, vengeance; ❏ часот на расплатата the day of reckoning

расплати се *pf* to settle (square) accounts (*co – with*); *fig.* to repay, take revenge (*co – on*), exact vengeance; се расплатиле со востаниците they took their revenge on the rebels

расплатува се *impf of* расплати се

расплаче *pf* **I** to make (*s.o.*) cry, reduce to tears **II – ce** to start crying uncontrollably

расплачува (се) *impf of* расплаче (се)

расплеска *pf* **I** to flatten *trans.* **II – ce 1** to become flat **2** to start clapping hard

расплескува (се) *impf of* расплеска (се)

расплет *m literary* outcome, result; dénouement

расплете *pf* **I** to unravel *trans.*, unpick, undo, unplait **II – ce 1** to unravel *intrans.* **2** *fig.* to be resolved; to become clear; брзо ќе се расплете ситуацијата the situation will be speedily resolved **3** to start knitting/weaving busily

расплетува (се) *impf of* расплете (се)

распливнат *adj* vague; rambling

распливне <се> *pf* распливна <се> *aor.* **1** to spread, spill *intrans.*; to run; <се> распливна маслото the oil spread **2** *fig.* to become confused, muddled

распливнува <се> *impf of* распливне <се>

расплиска *pf* **I** to splash, spill *trans.*; расплиска вода to splash water about **II – ce** to start pouring (*of rain*); се расплиска дожд the rain started to pour

расплискува (се) *impf of* расплиска (се)

расплод *m* breeding; reproduction; добиток за расплод breeding stock

расплоден -дна *adj* breeding; расплоден коњ stud horse

расплоди *pf* **I** to breed *trans.*; расплоди пилиња to breed chickens **II – ce** to breed *intrans.*

расплодлив *adj* fertile

расплодливост *f* fertility

расплодник -ци *m* sire; stud horse; stallion; stud bull

расплодува (се) *impf of* расплоди (се)

расплука се *pf* to start spitting copiously

расплукува се *impf of* расплука се

распљампа се *pf colloq.* to start babbling, chattering

распљампува се *impf of* распљампа се

распне *pf* распна *aor.* **I 1** to tighten; to stretch out *trans.*; to unfurl *trans.*; распне шатор to pitch a tent;

распне јаже to tighten a rope **2** *Hist.* to crucify **3** *fig.* to torment **II** – **се** to tighten *intrans.*; to stretch, spread out *intrans.*; се распнаа платната the sails billowed

распнува (се) *impf of* распне (се)

расповива *impf of* расповие

расповие *pf* распови *aor.* to unwrap; to remove nappies from

расподелба *f* distribution

расподели (се) *pf see* раздели (се), распредели (се)

расподелува (се) *impf of* расподели (се)

распознава (се) *impf of* распознае (се)

распознае *pf* распозна *aor.* **I 1** to recognize, identify; не можеше да ги распознае во темнината he couldn't recognize them in the dark **2** to get to know, become thoroughly familiar with **II** – **се 1** to recognize one another **2** to get to know each other, become acquainted

распојаса (се) *pf see* распаше (се)

распојасан *adj see* распашан

распојасува (се) *impf of* распојаса (се)

располага *impf* **1** to have at one's disposal, possess; to control; располага со средства to command resources **2** *colloq.* to be well off

располагање *n* disposal; ❏ има на располагање to have available, at one's disposal, at hand; на располагање е некому to be at s.o.'s disposal

расползи се *pf* to start swarming, crawling

располови *pf* **I** to cut in two (in half); to halve **II** – **се** to break, split in two *intrans.*

располовува (се) *impf of* располови (се)

расположба *f* **1** position; site; градот имаше убава расположба the city had a beautiful position **2** mood, frame of mind; лоша расположба bad mood; свечена расположба festive mood

расположен *pt* **1** situated, located, sited; градот е расположен во рамнина the city is situated on a plain **2** disposed; не сум расположен I am not in the mood (*за* – *to*); лошо расположен in a bad mood; расположен е за работа he is in the mood for work

расположение -ија *n see* расположба 2

расположеност *f* **1** good mood **2** situation

расположи *pf* **I 1** to place, dispose, arrange; to billet **2** *fig.* to win over, gain the favour of **3** *fig.* to put in a good mood; to cheer <up> *trans.* **II** – **се 1** to take up position; to make o.s. comfortable **2** to get into a good mood; to cheer up *intrans.*

расположив *adj* available; расположиви средства available means

расположивост *f* availability

расположува (се) *impf of* расположи (се)

распон *m* span; range; распон на мост span of a bridge; распон на плати range of salaries

распоп *m* unfrocked priest

распопи *pf* to unfrock, defrock

распопува *impf of* распопи

распоред *m* schedule; timetable; programme; распоред на часовите class timetable

распоредба *f* **1** *see* распоред **2** *arch. see* заповед, наредба 1

распореди *pf* **I** to arrange, organize, put in order; to billet **II** – **се** to place o.s., arrange o.s.

распоредува (се) *impf of* распореди (се)

распоредувач *m* usher

распори *pf* **I 1** to cut/rip open **2** *fig.* to destroy; to rend, break; распори тишина to rend the silence

распорне *pf* распорна *aor. dim. of* распори; to cut partly; to open partly (*by cutting*)

распорнува *impf of* распорне

распорува *impf of* распори

распостеле *pf* распосла *aor.* (*распростре*) to spread out *trans.*

распостелува *impf of* распостеле

распостила *impf see* распостелува

распра *f see* расправија

расправа[1] *f* (*court*) hearing; treatise; discussion

расправа[2] **(се)** *impf of* расправи (се)

расправи *pf* **I 1** to tell, recount, relate **2** to straighten, disentangle; си ја расправи косата to do one's hair **3** to settle, sort out, clear up *trans.*; расправи проблем to resolve a problem; расправи двор to clear up a yard; расправи пат to clear the way **II** – **се 1** to settle accounts (*со* – *with*) **2** (*за време*) to clear <up> *intrans.*; времето се расправи the weather cleared

расправија -ии *f* **1** squabble, quarrel, wrangle **2** talking; без расправии without discussion; no talking!

расправува (се) *impf of* расправи (се)

распрати *pf* to send out/off, despatch (*several/many people; to various places*)

распраќа *impf of* распрати

распраша *pf* **I** to question, interrogate **II** – **се** to ask, enquire (*за* – *about*)

распрашува (се) *impf of* распраша (се)

распрди *pf* **I** *colloq.* to spoil *trans.*, pamper; распрди дете to spoil a child **II** – **се 1** to start farting **2** *colloq.* to become spoilt, pampered

распрдува (се) *impf of* распрди (се)

распрега *impf see* распрегнува

распрегне *pf* распрегна *aor.* to unharness; to unyoke

распрегнува *impf of* распрегне

распреде *pf* **1** to untwist, unravel; ја распреде свилата she untwisted the silk **2** *fig.* to hold forth

распределба *f* distribution, allocation

распредели *pf* **I** to distribute, allot, allocate; to arrange **II** – **се** to arrange o.s., place o.s.; се распредели по групи to break up into groups

распределува (се) *impf of* распредели (се)

распредува *impf of* распреде

распремени (се) *pf see* распромени (се)

распременува (се) *impf see* распроменува (се)

распрета *pf* to stoke; *fig.* to stir up, arouse

распретува *impf of* распрета

распријатели *pf* *rare* to alienate, estrange **II** – **се** to break (*со* – *with*); to terminate a friendship

распријателува (се) *impf of* распријатели (се)

расприкаже *pf* расприкажа *aor.* **I** to induce to talk **II** – **се** to start talking at length; to warm to one's theme

расприкажува (се) *impf of* расприкаже (се)

распродава *impf of* распродаде

распродаде *pf* to sell out *trans.*

распродажба *f* sale, clearance sale; распродажба на текстил a sale of textiles

распромени *pf* **I** to change (*s.o.'s*) clothes; to change *trans.*; распромени дете to change a baby **II** – **се** to change one's clothes

распроменува (се) *impf of* распромени (се)

распростира (се) *impf of* распростре (се)

распространет *adj* widespread; распространето мислење widely held opinion

распространи *pf* **I 1** to extend, widen *trans.*; распространи граници to extend frontiers **2** to spread, disseminate, diffuse *trans.* **II – се 1** to extend, widen *intrans.*; да се распространи царството твое *biblical* Thy Kingdom come! **2** to spread, diffuse *intrans.*, become widespread

распространува (се) *impf of* распространи (се)

распространувач *m literary* disseminator, propagator

распростре *pf* распростра *aor.* **I** to spread, spread out *trans.*; распростре платно to spread out a cloth; распростре свое влијание to extend one's influence **II – се** to spread <out> *intrans.*; се распростре неговата слава his fame spread

распрска *pf* **I** *see* распрсне **I II – се 1** *see* распрсне (се) **2** to start splashing vigorously

распрскува (се) *impf of* распрска (се)

распрснат *pt* dispersed, scattered

распрсне *pf* распрсна *aor.* **I** to drive away, dispel, scatter, disperse *trans.*; распрсне тешки мисли to banish gloomy thoughts **II – се 1** to explode *intrans.*; to burst, blow up *intrans.* **2** to disperse, scatter *intrans.*

распрснува (се) *impf of* распрсне (се)

распрчка *pf dial.* to scatter *trans.*; to toss about; to mess up

распрчкува *impf of* распрчка

распука *pf* **I 1** to break up, fall apart, crack *intrans.*; земјата распукала the earth has cracked **2** to break up *trans.* **II – се 1** to crack, break up *intrans.*; карпите се распукаа the rocks cracked; од жал срцето ѝ се распука her heart broke with grief **2** to start shooting a lot **3** *dial.* to get angry, lose one's temper **4** to bud

распукне (се) *pf* распукна (се) *aor. see* распука (се)

распукнува (се) *impf see* распукува (се)

распукува (се) *impf of* распука (се)

распупи *pf* to bud

распупува *impf of* распупи

распуст *m* holiday, *Am.* vacation; распустот на собранието parliamentary recess

распуфка се *pf* to start panting heavily

распуфкува се *impf of* распуфка се

распуши *pf* **I** to cause to smoke heavily **II – се** to start smoking heavily

распушта (се) *impf of* распушти (се)

распуштен *adj* undisciplined, unruly

распуштеник -ци *m* divorcee

распуштеница *f* (*fem. form*) *see* распуштеник

распуштенички *adj* divorcee's

распуштеност *f* dissoluteness; полова распуштеност licentiousness

распушти *pf* **I 1** to dismiss *trans.*; to dissolve, adjourn *trans.*; распушти собрание to adjourn Parliament **2** (*отпушти*) to dismiss, discharge, sack *trans.* **3** to make loose, slacken *trans.* **4** to pamper, spoil *trans.*; распушти дете to spoil a child **II – се 1** to break up *intrans.*; to dissolve, adjourn *intrans.*; се распушти соборот the assembly dissolved **2** to stretch *intrans.* **3** to let o.s. go **4** to get out of hand; to become unruly

распушува (се) *impf of* распуши (се)

расрден *pt* angry, furious

расрди *pf* **I** to anger, enrage **II – се** to get angry, lose one's temper

расрдува (се) *impf of* расрди (се)

рассали се *pf* **1** to melt *intrans.* **2** to smear o.s. with fat **3** to chafe (*one's skin*) to rawness

рассалува се *impf of* рассали се

раст *m* **1** stature, size, height; среден раст medium height **2** growth

растава (се) *impf of* растави (се)

раставен -вна *adj Gram.* (*разделен*) disjunctive

растави (се) *pf see* раздели (се)

раставка *f see* разделба

раставува (се) *impf see* растава (се)

раставувач *m* separator (*person*)

растаженост *f* grief

растажи *pf* **I** to sadden, grieve **II – се** to grow sad

растажува (се) *impf of* растажи (се)

растане[1] *pf* растана *aor.* (*of many people*) to get up (*all together or one after another*)

растане[2] **се** *pf* растана се *aor.* to separate, part *intrans.*

растанува[1] *impf of* растане[1]

растанува[2] **се** *impf of* растане[2] се

растанчи (се) *pf see* растенчи (се)

растанчува (се) *impf see* растенчува (се)

растапани се *pf colloq.* (*за срце*) to start beating hard, pounding

растараши се *pf colloq.* to start rummaging

растарашува се *impf of* растараши се

раствор *m* solution; раствор на сол salt solution

раствора (се) *impf of* раствори[1] (се)

растворен -рна *adj* solvent; растворно средство solvent

раствори[1] *pf* **I** to open *trans.*; раствори очи to open one's eyes; раствори прсти to spread one's fingers **II – се** to open *intrans.*; небото се раствори the heavens opened

раствори[2] *pf* **I 1** to dissolve *trans.* **2** to dilute **II – се** to dissolve *intrans.*

растворлив *adj* soluble, dissoluble; растворливи соли soluble salts

растворливост *f* solubility, dissolubility

растворува[1] **(се)** *impf of* раствори[1] (се)

растворува[2] **(се)** *impf of* раствори[2] (се)

растворувач *m* solvent

расте *impf* **1** to grow *intrans.*; to grow up; ❏ расте во очите на некого to rise in s.o.'s esteem **2** to increase *intrans.*; цените растат prices are rising

растег -зи *m* (*approximately*) fathom

растега (се) *impf of* растегне (се)

растеглив *adj* extensible, elastic, flexible; adaptable; растеглив метал tensile metal; растеглив поим elastic concept

растегливост *f* tensility; flexibility; elasticity

растегнат *pt* stretched; protracted; verbose; tedious; растегнат стил verbose style

растегнатост *f* verbosity; tediousness

растегне *pf* растегна *aor.* **I 1** to stretch *trans.*; to lengthen *trans.*; to extend *trans.* **2** *fig.* to drag out *trans.*, prolong **II – се 1** to stretch *intrans.*; пуловерот ти се растегнал your pullover has stretched **2** to drag on *intrans.*; се растегна денот the day wore on

растегнува (се) *impf of* растегне (се)

растеж *m* growth, increase; растеж на стопанството growth in the economy; културен растеж cultural development

растекува се *impf see* растечува се

растение -ија *n* plant; едногодишно растение annual

растенчи *pf* **I** to thin <out> *trans.* **II** – **се** to become thinner, grow thin

растенчува (се) *impf of* растенчи (се)

растера *pf* to disperse, drive off *trans.*; ветрот ги растера облаците the wind dispersed the clouds

растерува *impf of* растера

растече се *pf* to start leaking

растечува се *impf of* растече се

растила *impf* **1** to spread *trans.*; to lay **2** *fig.* to exude, radiate *trans.*

растителен -лна *adj* vegetable; растителен свет vegetable kingdom; растително масло vegetable oil

растителност *f* vegetation; бујна растителност luxuriant vegetation

расткае се *pf* расткаја *aor.* **1** to unravel *intrans.*; to fall to pieces **2** to start weaving a lot

растовар *m* unloading

растовара *impf see* растоварува

растоварен *pt see* разбременет

растовари *pf* **1** to unload *trans.*; растовари воз to unload a train **2** *fig.* to unburden, relieve (*од* – *of*)

растоварува *impf of* растовари

растојание -ија *n* distance; ❏ држи на <извесно> растојание to keep at a distance; се држи на растојание to keep one's distance (*од* – *from*)

растока *f* fork (*in a river*)

растолкува *pf* to explain, interpret

растопи *pf* **I** to melt *trans.*; to thaw *trans.*; (*руда*) to smelt; сонцето го растопи снегот the sun melted the snow; го растопи неговото срце she melted his heart **II** – **се** to melt *intrans.*; мразот се растопи the ice melted

растоплив *adj* meltable; soluble; *Chem.* liquefiable; *Metallurgy* fusible

растопува (се) *impf of* растопи (се)

расторбеши *pf colloq.* **I** to mess up (*s.o.'s*) clothing **II** – **се** to mess up one's clothing; to loosen one's clothing

расторбешува (се) *impf of* расторбеши (се)

расточи *pf* (*расука*) to roll (*dough*)

расточина *f Bot.* (Serpula lacrymans) dry-rot fungus

расточува *impf of* расточи

растрака се *pf* to start clattering loudly; to start chattering

растракоти се *pf see* растрака се

растракотува се *impf see* растракува се

растракува се *impf of* растрака се

растрбушен *pt* **1** ungirded; bared **2** sloppily dressed

растрбуши *pf* **I 1** to gut, clean *trans.*; to disembowel; растрбуши риба to gut fish **2** *fig.* to wreck, ruin, play havoc (*with*) **3** *see* расторбеши **II** – **се** *see* расторбеши се

растрбушува (се) *impf of* растрбуши (се)

растрга (се) *pf see* растргне (се)

растргне *pf* растргна *aor.* **I 1** to tear to pieces, pull apart, dismember **2** *fig.* to exhaust, wear out, work to exhaustion *trans.* **II** – **се** *fig.* to wear (tire) o.s. out; to overwork *intrans.*

растргнува (се) *impf of* растргне (се)

растреби *pf* to clean, shell, husk

растребува *impf of* растреби

растревожен *pt literary* worried, alarmed

растревоженост *f literary* anxiety

растревожи *pf literary* **I** to disturb, worry, alarm **II** – **се** to grow worried (alarmed)

растревожува (се) *impf of* растревожи (се)

растрезни *pf* **I** to sober up *trans.* **II** – **се** to become sober, sober up *intrans.*

растрезнува (се) *impf of* растрезни (се)

растрел *m literary* execution by firing squad

растрела *pf literary* to shoot, execute by shooting

растрелува *impf of* растрела

растреперен *pt* quivering, trembling; excited; растреперен глас quavering voice

растрепери *pf* **I** to stir *trans.*; to alarm, agitate; to shake *trans.*; веста ги растрепери the news shook them **II** – **се** to begin trembling (quivering); се растрепери неговото срце his heart fluttered

растреперува (се) *impf of* растрепери (се)

растресе *pf* **I 1** to shake *trans.*; експлозија ја растресе земјата an explosion shook the ground **2** *fig.* to alarm; to move, stir, touch *trans.*; му го растресе срцето she touched his heart **II** – **се** to <start to> shudder (shake, tremble); земјата се растресе the ground shuddered

растресит *adj* (*ровит*) friable; растресита земја friable soil

растреситост *f* friability

растреска се *pf* to start banging, knocking loudly; се растрескаа прозорци и врати windows and doors started banging

растрескува се *impf of* растреска се

растресува (се) *impf of* растресе (се)

растрешти се *pf* to start blaring, roaring

растрештува се *impf of* растрешти се

растрива (се) *impf of* растрие (се)

растрие *pf* растри *aor.* **I** to rub; to massage; си ги растрие очите to rub one's eyes **II** – **се** to chafe one's skin to rawness; се растрие лежејќи to get bedsores

растроен *pt* **1** disarranged; disorganized; растроени планови disrupted plans **2** upset; disturbed; растроен желудник upset stomach **3** *Mus.* out of tune

растроеност *f* disorder; derangement; душевна растроеност mental derangement

растрои *pf* **I 1** to disorganize, disrupt; to unsettle, upset; растрои некому здравје to damage s.o.'s health; растрои план to frustrate (thwart) a plan **2** *Mus.* to put out of tune, detune **II** – **се 1** to fall into confusion; to become disorganized; планот се растрои the plan fell through **2** *fig.* to become upset; нервите му се растроија his nerves have gone to pieces **3** *Mus.* to get out of tune, lose pitch

растрој *m poet. see* растројство

растројство *n* derangement, disorder, breakdown; растројство на стопанството breakdown (collapse) of the economy; нервно растројство nervous breakdown

растројува (се) *impf of* растрои (се)

растропа се *pf* to start banging, knocking

растропан *adj colloq.* lively, active

растропува се *impf of* растропа се

раструби *pf* to trumpet <abroad>; to spread *trans.*; раструби новости to spread news

раструбува *impf of* раструби

растрча *pf* I to cause to run about II – **се** to <start to> run about

растрчува (се) *impf of* растрча (се)

раступа се *pf* to start banging, knocking, pounding; ми се раступало срцето my heart is thumping

раступка *pf* I (*за срце*) to cause to beat hard II – **се** *see* раступа се

раступкува (се) *impf of* раступка (се)

раступува се *impf of* раступа се

растур *m* 1 distribution; dispersal 2 waste, wastage

растура (се) *impf of* растури (се)

растурач *m* 1 distributor; растурач на весници newspaper boy 2 spendthrift, wastrel

растурен *pt* scattered, spilt; disordered; disbanded

растури *pf* I 1 to disarrange, disturb, make untidy; to scatter *trans.*; to spill *trans.*; си ја растури косата to let down one's hair 2 to wreck, destroy, tear down, upset; растури план to upset a plan 3 to disband, dissolve *trans.*; растури организација to disband an organization; растури собир to dissolve an assembly 4 to spread *trans.*, disseminate; растури вести to spread word 5 to squander, dissipate *trans.* II – **се** 1 to break up *intrans.*; to fall to pieces 2 to disband, disperse *intrans.*; to break up *intrans.* 3 to spread *intrans.*; се растурија разни гласови various rumours spread

растурник -ци *m see* растурач

растуфка се *pf* to start worrying/complaining

расудба *f* reasoning

расуден -дна *adj see* расудлив

расуди *pf* to pass judgement (*on*), express an opinion (*on*), to reason (*дека – that*); to judge

расудлив *adj* sensible, judicious

расудливост *f* reasonableness, sense; judiciousness, discretion

расудник -ци *m* reasonable person

расудност *f see* расудливост

расудок *m* reason, judgement, sense

расудува *impf of* расуди

расукува *impf see* расучува

расуче *pf* расука *aor.* 1 to unwind, unravel *trans.* 2 to roll (*pastry, dough*)

расучува *impf of* расуче

расформира *pf & impf* I to disband, break up *trans.* II – **се** to break up *intrans.*

расфрла *impf* I *of* расфрли II – **се** 1 to be wasteful; се расфрла со пари to squander money 2 to boast, brag *intrans.* 3 to start throwing things; се расфрла со камења to start throwing stones

расфрлен *pt* scattered; untidy, disorderly; расфрлена постела unmade bed

расфрли *pf* расфрла *aor.* 1 to scatter *trans.*, spread, toss about 2 to squander, waste

расфрлува (се) *impf see* расфрла (се)

расфрчи се *pf* to flutter (flit) in various directions

расфучи се *pf* 1 to start whistling, blowing hard 2 *fig.* to get angry, lose one's temper

расфучува се *impf of* расфучи се

расход *m* expense<s>; expenditure, outlay; лични расходи personal expenses; покрие расходи to cover expenses

расходен -дна *adj* <of, for> expenses; расходна книга expenses book

расходник -ци *m* expenses book

расходува *pf & impf* 1 to spend, expend; to use up, consume; автомобилот расходува многу гориво the car uses a lot of fuel 2 to write off

расцапа *pf* I to trample; to dirty, soil II – **се** to start trampling; to start spreading dirt

расцар -еви, -ови *m* deposed monarch

расцари *pf* to depose, dethrone

расцвет *m see* расцут

расцвета & расцвети *pf* расцвета *aor. see* расцути

расцветува *impf of* расцвета & расцвети

расцвили се *pf* to start whining/squealing/neighing

расцвилува се *impf of* расцвили се

расцвичи се *pf* to start squealing/yelping

расцврка се & расцвркоти се *pf* to start chirping loudly

расцеп *m* rift, crack, cleft, fissure; расцеп во организација rift in an organization

расцепи *pf* I to chop up; to split *trans.*; to divide *trans.*; расцепи дрва to chop wood; расцепи политичка партија to split a political party II – **се** to split up *intrans.*, fragment; to separate, divide *intrans.*

расцепка (се) *pf dim. of* расцепи (се)

расцепкан *pt* disunited, divided, split up

расцепканост *f* disunity, split

расцепкува (се) *impf of* расцепка (се)

расцепува (се) *impf of* расцепи (се)

расцивка се *pf* to start cheeping/squeaking

расцимоли се *pf* to start whimpering

расцрка се *pf* to start shouting, shrieking

расцркува се *impf of* расцрка се

расцрта се *pf* to start drawing, sketching

расцрцори се *pf* to start chirping

расцут *m* flowering; flourishing; blooming; heyday; расцут на уметноста/стопанството flourishing of art/the economy

расцути *pf* to flower, bloom (*also fig.*)

расцутува *impf of* расцути

расчекор *m* discrepancy, divergence; ❏ оди во расчекор to be out of step

расчекори се *pf* to place one's feet apart

расчекорува се *impf of* расчекори се

расчепати (се) *pf see* расчепи (се)

расчепатува (се) *impf of* расчепати (се)

расчепи *pf* I 1 to open wide *trans.*; расчепи уста to gape 2 *fig.* to overwork, work (*s.o.*) to exhaustion II – **се** 1 to place one's feet apart 2 to overwork o.s., work one's fingers to the bone

расчепиуста *f & m colloq.* babbler, chatterbox; gossip

расчепка *pf* I 1 to scratch open/scratch through/pick (*at*) 2 *fig.* to analyse, examine

расчепкува *impf of* расчепка

расчепува (се) *impf of* расчепи (се)

расчеречи *pf* 1 to cut up, quarter; to tear apart; расчерепи јагне to quarter a lamb 2 *fig.* to overwork *trans.*, overtax (*with demands*), overburden

расчеречува *impf of* расчеречи

расчет *m literary, arch.* (*сметка*) reckoning, calculation

расчеша *pf* I to scratch open (*a wound*) II – **се** to start scratching o.s.

расчешла *pf* I to comb II – **се** to comb one's hair

расчешлува (се) *impf of* расчешла (се)

расчешува (се) *impf of* расчеша (се)

расчини[1] *pf* to melt *trans.*, dilute, water down; to dissolve *trans.*

расчини[2] *pf literary*, *rare* to demote, degrade, reduce in rank

расчини[3] *pf f.p.* to light, kindle; расчини оган to light a fire

расчинува[1] *impf of* расчини[1]

расчинува[2] *impf of* расчини[2]

расчисти *pf* **I** **1** to clear; to clean; расчисти двор to sweep a yard; ветрот веднаш ги расчисти облаците the wind drove the clouds away; расчисти пат to clear a path; *fig.* to pave the way **2** *fig.* to solve, resolve, settle; расчисти прашање to resolve a matter; ❑ расчисти сметки со некого to settle accounts with s.o. **II – се** **1** to clear <up> *intrans.*; времето се расчисти the weather cleared **2** to start clearing up, cleaning thoroughly

расчистува (се) *impf of* расчисти (се)

расчита се *pf* to start reading a lot; to become engrossed in reading

расчитува се *impf of* расчита се

расчлени *pf* to analyse, dissect

расчленува *impf of* расчлени

расчовечи се *pf* to become a monster/inhuman; to go astray

расчовечува се *impf of* расчовечи се

расчувствува *pf* to touch, move, stir (*feelings, etc.*); расчувствува некого до солзи to move (*s.o.*) to tears

расчувствуван *pt* touched, moved; stirred, aroused

расчуе се *pf* расчу се *aor.* to be heard/rumoured; (*за вест*) to spread *intrans.*; се расчуло по целиот град word spread all over the town

расчука се *pf* to start banging, knocking

расчукува се *impf of* расчука се

рата *f* instalment; купува на рати to buy by hire purchase; плати на рати to pay by instalments

ратификација *f* ratification; ратификација на договор ratification of a treaty

ратификационен -она *adj* <of/for> ratification; ратификациони документи documents of ratification

ратификува *pf & impf* to ratify

ратифицира *pf & impf see* ратификува

ратник -ци *m* fighter, warrior; protagonist

ратнички *adj* warrior's

ратоборен -рна *adj* warlike, belligerent, militant

ратоборец -рци *m rare see* ратник

ратоборност *f* militancy, belligerence

рафал *m* burst (*of gunfire*)

рафија *f Bot.* (Raphia vinifera) raffia

рафинер *m* refiner, refinery worker

рафинерија -ии *f* refinery; рафинерија за нафта petroleum (oil) refinery

рафинира *pf & impf* to refine; *fig.* to polish; рафинира шеќер to refine sugar

рафиниран *pt* refined; *fig.* polished, sophisticated

рафинираност *f* refinement, sophistication

рафт *m* shelf; stand (*for music, etc.*)

рахитис *m Med.* rickets, rachitis

рахитичар *m* rickets sufferer

рахитичен -чна *adj* **1** rachitic **2** *fig.* weak, puny, feeble; rickety

рација -ии *f* police round-up (raid)

рационален -лна *adj* rational, reasonable, sensible; suitable, appropriate; рационално користење на средствата appropriate use of resources; *Math.* рационален број rational number

рационализам -змот *m* rationalism

рационализатор *m* rationalizer

рационализаторски *adj* rationalizer's

рационализаторство *n* rationalizing, rationalization

рационализација -ии *f* rationalization; рационализација на производството rationalization of production

рационализира *pf & impf* to rationalize

рационалист *m* rationalist

рационалистичен -чна *adj see* рационалистички

рационалистички *adj* rationalistic

рационалност *f* rationality

рационира *pf & impf* to ration

рача *impf f.p.* (*usu. with* порача) рача порача to place an order, ask for s.th. to be brought

раче[1] *n dim. of* рака

раче[2] *n dim. of* рак

рачен -чна *adj* manual; hand/arm *attrib.*; рачен часовник wrist-watch; рачен багаж hand luggage; рачна преса hand press; рачна граната, бомба hand grenade; ❑ рачна аптека first aid kit; рачна работа handwork, handicraft

рачест *adj* long-armed

рачец -чци *m dim. of* рак

рачешки *adj* crab's; lobster's; рачешка чорба lobster soup; ❑ рачешка брзина snail's pace

рачина *f dial. see* рид

рачица & рачичка *f dim. of* рака & рачка

рачка *f* handle, knob, grip; ❑ наоѓа рачки <и мрдалки> to find excuses

рачник -ци *m* towel, hand towel

рачно *adv* manually, by hand

рашета *pf* **I** to take for a walk; to take (*s.o.*) sightseeing **II – се** to go for a walk; to go travelling; се рашета низ Европа he toured Europe

рашетка *f* walk, stroll

рашетува (се) *impf of* рашета (се)

рашива *impf of* рашие

рашие *pf* раши *aor.* to unstitch, unpick, undo

раширен *pt* widespread, widely held; раширено мислење widely held opinion

рашири *pf* **I** to widen *trans.*; to spread, extend, expand *trans.*; рашири свое влијание to extend one's influence; рашири зараза to spread an infection; рашири раце to fling one's arms wide **II – се** to widen *intrans.*; to spread, extend, expand *intrans.*; фабриката се рашири the factory has expanded

раширува (се) *impf of* рашири (се)

раштима *pf Mus.* to put out of tune

раштимува *impf of* раштима

раштрака се *pf* to start clicking/rattling/clattering; раштракале пушки rifles started firing

раштракува се *impf of* раштрака се

раштрка *pf* **I** to disperse, scatter *trans.* **II – се** to disperse, scatter *intrans.*

раштркан *pt* scattered, dispersed; раштркани села scattered villages

раштркува (се) *impf of* раштрка (се)

’рбел *m only in the prov.*: се насмеал (посмеал) ’рбел на штрбел the pot called the kettle black

’рбет *m* **1** *Anat.* spine, backbone; *fig.* ’рбетот на движењето the pillar of the movement; ❑ без 'рбет е to be spineless; свие (свива) 'рбет to give in 2 (*на рид*, *бран*) ridge, crest

'рбе́тен -тна *adj* spinal; 'рбетен столб spinal column; 'рбетен мозок spinal cord

'рбе́тник -ци *m* 1 *see* 'рбет 2 *Zool.* vertebrate

'рбе́тница *f see* 'рбет 1

'рва́јчи *impf dial.* to squeal, yap, yelp

'рве́ник -ци *m* well; донесе вода од 'рвеник to fetch water from a well

'рга *impf* 1 to hit; to push, shove 2 *fig.* to work hard, toil, slave away

'рга́ч *m* toiler, hard worker

'ргне *pf* 'ргна *aor.* to hit; to shove

'ргну́ва *impf of* 'ргне

'рдо́ква *f Bot.* (Raphanus sativus) radish

'рдо́квен *adj* radish; 'рдоквена салата radish salad

'рѓа[1] *f* 1 rust; фалбата е 'рѓа *prov.* self-praise is no recommendation 2 rust (*disease of crops*); mildew 3 *fig., rare* worthless person, good-for-nothing

'рѓа[2] *impf see* 'рѓосува

'рѓо́са *pf* to rust *intrans.*, start rusting

'рѓо́сан *adj* rusty

'рѓо́сува *impf of* 'рѓоса

ре *n Mus.* D

ре́а *f* smell, odour, stench

реаги́ра *pf & impf* to react (*на – to; со – with*); to respond; сулфурната киселина реагира со некои метали sulphuric acid reacts with certain metals

реакти́в *m Chem., Phys.* reagent

реактива́ција *f* reactivation

реакти́вен -вна *adj* 1 reactive; реактивни материи reactive substances 2 jet; реактивен мотор (двигател) jet engine; реактивен авион jet plane

реактивизи́ра (се) *pf & impf see* реактивира (се)

реактиви́ра (се) *pf & impf* to reactivate, return to service *trans.*

реакти́вност *f* reactivity

реа́ктор *m* reactor; нуклеарен реактор nuclear reactor

реа́кција -ии *f* 1 reaction, response (*на – to*) 2 *Pol. coll.* reactionaries; силите на реакцијата the forces of reaction

реакцио́нен -она *adj* 1 reactive 2 reactionary

реакционе́р *m* reactionary; obscurantist

реакционе́рен -рна *adj* reactionary; реакционерна политика reactionary policy

реакционе́рски *adj* reactionary; реакционерски сфаќања reactionary ideas

реакционе́рство *n Pol.* reaction

реа́лен -лна *adj* 1 real, actual; реалниот свет the real world 2 realistic, practical; feasible; реален план realistic plan; реална политика *realpolitik*; realistic policy; ❑ реална плата real wages; реална гимназија secondary school (*with emphasis on mathematics and science); Math.* реални броеви real numbers

реа́лец -лци *m* secondary-school pupil

реали́зам -змот *m* realism

реализа́ција *f* fulfilment, implementation, realization; реализација на план implementation of a plan

реализи́ра *pf & impf* to put into effect, implement, fulfil

реализира́ње *n* fulfilment, implementation, realization

реали́ст *m* realist

реалисти́чен -чна *adj see* реалистички

реалисти́чки *adj* realistic

реа́лка *f see* реална гимназија

реа́лно *adv* really, in reality

реа́лност *f* reality; чувство на реалност sense of reality

реанима́ција *f* resuscitation

реаними́ра *pf & impf* to resuscitate; to revive

реафирма́ција *f* reaffirmation

ребала́нс *m* rebalance, readjustment; ребаланс на буџет readjustment of a budget

ре́брен *adj Anat.* costal; ребрена коска costal bone; ребрени мускули costal muscles

ре́бренце *n dim. of* ребро

ре́брест *adj* ribbed; rib-like; corrugated

ре́бри се *impf* to be afraid, frightened; to worry

ре́бро *n* 1 *Anat., Tech.* rib; ❑ го чеша (му игра) некое ребро he is asking for a spanking; му се бројат ребрата you can count his ribs; he's all skin and bone 2 slope, mountainside

ре́бус *m* rebus

ребу́ски *adj* rebus-like, enigmatic

рев *m* 1 roar; howl; scream; рев на ветер howling of the wind 2 weeping, crying; ревот на деца the weeping of children

ревакцина́ција *f* revaccination

ревакцини́ра *pf & impf* to revaccinate

ревалва́ција & ревалориза́ција *f* revaluation

рева́нш *m* 1 revenge, retaliation; *Sport.* return match 2 *fig.* return of a favour; ти должам реванш за услугата I owe you a repayment for your kindness

реванши́зам -змот *m* revanchism

реванши́ра се *pf & impf* to take revenge (*на – on*), pay back

реванши́ст *m* revanchist

реванши́стички *adj* revanchist<ic>

реве́ *impf* 1 to roar, bellow; to howl, yell 2 *colloq.* to cry, weep

ре́вер *m* lapel

реве́рс *m* 1 (*обврзница*) written obligation 2 (*признаница*) receipt 3 (*во библиотека*) call card 4 (*опачина*) obverse side

реви́дира *pf & impf* 1 to audit (*accounts*); to inspect 2 to revise; to review

реви́зија *f* 1 inspection; audit (*of accounts*) 2 review; revision 3 proofreading; checking of page proofs

ревизио́нен -она *adj* revisory; auditing; review *attrib.*; ревизиона комисија committee of inspection; auditing commission

ревизиони́зам -змот *m* revisionism

ревизиони́ст *m* revisionist

ревизиони́стички *adj* revisionist

реви́зиски *adj* revisionary, revisory

реви́зор *m* inspector; auditor

реви́зорски *adj* inspector's; ревизорски обврски inspector's duties

реви́ја -ии *f* 1 inspection of troops; parade; review; модна ревија fashion parade/show 2 periodical publication 3 theatrical review; музичка ревија a musical review

ревија́лен -лна *adj see* ревиски

ревир *m* area, region, district; basin (*of a river, etc.*)

ревиски *adj* review *attrib.*; ревиски оркестар light orchestra

ревитализација *f* revitalization, recovery; ревитализација на стопанството economic recovery

ревлив *adj* 1 noisy; vocal 2 tearful; ревливи деца whining children

ревливост *f* tearfulness

ревматӣзам -змот *m see* реуматизам

ревматичар *m* rheumatic

ревматичен -чна *adj* rheumatic

ревне *pf* ревна *aor.* 1 to roar, bellow 2 to <start to> cry (weep)

ревнив *adj arch.* jealous; envious

ревнивец -вци *m arch.* jealous man

ревнивка *f arch.* jealous woman

ревнивост *f arch.* jealousy

ревнител *m arch.* supporter, zealot, champion (*of a cause*)

ревносен -сна *adj* zealous, earnest, devoted (*to a cause*)

ревносност *f see* ревност 1

ревност *f* 1 zeal, dedication, industry; conscientiousness 2 *arch.* jealousy, envy

ревнува¹ *impf of* ревне

ревнува² *impf (with dat.)* to be jealous; to be envious

револвӗр *m* revolver

револверӑш *m* gunslinger, cowboy

револвӗрски *adj* revolver *attrib.*; револверски истрел revolver shot; ❏ револверски печат gutter press

револт *m* 1 indignation 2 revolt

револтӣра *pf & impf* I to disgust; to infuriate; to arouse (*s.o.'s*) indignation II – се to get angry; to revolt, rebel

револуција -ии *f* revolution

револуциӧнен -она *adj* revolutionary

револуционӗр *m* revolutionary

револуционӗрен -рна *adj* revolutionary

револуционӗрка *f (fem. form) see* револуционер

револуционӗрство *n* revolutionary activity

револуционизӣра *pf & impf* to revolutionize

револуциски *adj see* револуционерен, револуционен

регӑл *m* 1 *Print.* composing frame; standing type rack 2 shelves; bookcase; wall unit 3 portative organ, regal

регалии *pl* regalia, insignia; царски регалии imperial regalia, insignia

регӑта *f* regatta

регенерӑт *m* 1 *Tech.* recycled material 2 *Biol.* regenerated tissue

регенератӣвен -вна *adj* regenerative; регенеративен циклус regenerative cycle; *Tech.* регенеративна печка regenerative furnace

регенерӑтор *m* regenerator

регенерација *f* 1 regeneration; регенерација на црвените крвни зрнца regeneration of red blood corpuscles 2 recycling

регенерӣра *pf & impf* I to regenerate *trans.*; to recycle II – се to regenerate *intrans.*

регент *m* regent

регентски *adj* regent's; регентски совет regent's council

регентство *n* regency

регентствува *impf* to rule as regent

регија -ии *f* region

региӧн *m see* регија

региона́лен -лна *adj* regional

регӣстар -стри *m* 1 register, list 2 *Mus.* register, range, compass 3 *Mus.* organ stop, register 4 *Tech., Print.* register, regulator; keyboard; регистар-ка́са cash register, till

регистарски *adj* register; регистарски (регистарска) тон<а> register ton (tonne)

регистра́тор *m* registrar; register, recorder; recording device

регистратӯра *f* registrar's office, registry

регистрација *f* registration; registry-office marriage

регистрациӧнен -она *adj* registration, registrative; регистрациона комисија registrative commission

регистрӣра *pf & impf* I to register *trans.*; to record; to note down; апаратот регистрира земјотрес the apparatus registered an earthquake II – се 1 to register *intrans.* 2 to get married

регрес *m* 1 regression 2 damages; compensation; bonus; се одобри регрес од 30 проценти damages of up to 30% were awarded; регрес за годишен одмор holiday bonus (loading) 3 subsidy, reduction; recourse, legal remedy; право на регрес right of recourse, right of recovery

регресӣвен -вна *adj* regressive; backward-looking

регресија *f* 1 regression 2 *Geol.* marine regression

регресӣра *impf* to retreat, regress, retrogress

регрут *m* recruit, conscript

регрутација *f* recruitment, conscription

регрутен -тна *adj* recruiting, conscription *attrib.*; регрутна комисија recruiting committee, *Am.* draft board

регрутӣра *pf & impf* to recruit, enlist, conscript

регрутски *adj* recruit's

регрутува *pf & impf see* регрутира

регула *f* rule, measure

регула́рен -рна *adj* regular, normal, usual; ❏ регуларна армија regular army

регула́рност *f* regularity

регулатива *f* regulation, article of law

регулатӣвен -вна *adj* regulative, regulatory

регула́тор *m Tech.* governor, regulator; регулатор на температура temperature regulator

регулаторски *adj see* регулативен

регулација *f* regulation, control; регулација на градот town planning

регулациӧнен -она *adj* regulatory

регулӣра *pf & impf* to regulate; to adjust; регулира цени to regulate prices; регулира сообраќај to regulate traffic; регулира правилник to revise a rulebook

ред *m* 1 row, rank, line; layer; пишува неколку реда to write a few lines; ред месо layer of meat; три години по ред three years running, three years in succession; ред по ред row upon row; ❏ сплоти редови to close ranks; чита меѓу редови to read between the lines 2 order, sequence; system; азбучен ред alphabetical order; без ред in confusion (disorder); општествен ред social order; стариот ред the old regime; ред на возење timetable; ред на летања flight schedule; ❏ дневен ред agenda; сè е во ред everything is in order; нешто не е во ред something is wrong; в ред all right, OK; чини ред некому to show respect for s.o.; ред е it would be right (proper); it would be nice; it's about time **3** turn; ми дојде редот my turn came; сите по ред each in turn; кој е на ред whose turn is it? оди преку ред to jump the queue **4** series, number; ред прашања a number of questions; ❑ и ред други работи and the like **5** category, class; прв ред first class; во прв ред in the first place, primarily

редактѝра *pf & impf* **1** to edit; редактира ракопис to edit a manuscript **2** (*impf only*) to serve as editor of; редактира весник/списание to edit a newspaper/journal

редáктор *m* editor; главен и одговорен редактор editor-in-chief

редакторка *f (fem. form) see* редактор

редакторски *adj* editorial

редакторство *n* editorship

редакција -ии *f* **1** editing; revision **2** editorship; editorial board; editorial office **3** redaction, edition, version

редакциóнен -она *adj see* редакциски

редакциски *adj* editorial; редакциски колегиум <meeting of> editorial staff; редакциска статија editorial article

редар *m* **1** steward **2** <school> prefect, monitor

редарица *f see* редница

редарка *f* **1** (*fem. form*) *see* редар **2** *see* редница

редарски *adj* steward's; monitor's; редарска служба stewarding service

редарство *n* stewardship; monitoring

редачка *f* epidemic

редба *f* lament, dirge

реден -дна *adj* Gram. ordinal; реден број ordinal number

реденик -ци *m* cartridge-belt

реди *impf* **I 1** to put in order; to arrange; to stack; реди дрва to stack wood; си ги реди работите to put one's affairs in order **2** to enumerate; to recount, recite **3** to prepare; to dress up *trans.*; to adorn **4** to lament, mourn **5** *colloq.* to be in charge **II – се 1** to line up *intrans.*, stand in line, fall in **2** to prepare *intrans.*; to smarten up *intrans.*; to preen o.s.; се редеше за директор he was grooming himself for the post of director

редигѝра *pf & impf see* редактира

редигува *pf & impf see* редактира

редица *f* **1** row, rank, file; queue; во предните редици in the front ranks **2** (*sg only*) series, sequence; редица проблеми a series of problems; редица статии a series of articles

редник -ци *m see* реденик

редница *f* temporary housekeeper

редно *adv usu. in the expression:* редно е one should; it's high time; редно е и јас да појдам I should go too

редов[1] *m* private <soldier>

редов[2] *adj only in the expression:* редова недела the week before All Souls' Day

редоват *adj* редовата недела, *see* редов[2]; редоват петок Friday of the week before All Souls' Day

редовен -вна *adj* regular; редовни лекции regular lessons; редовно дежурство regular tour of duty; редовни приходи regular income; редовен студент full-time student

редовност *f* regularity

редок -тка *adj* rare, scarce; sparse; ретки влакна thin hair; ретко млеко thin milk; ретки свезди scattered stars; ретка птица rare bird

редосејалка & редосејачка *f* seed-drill

редослед *m* order, sequence, succession; по редослед in order, in succession

редува се *impf* arch. to take turns running a household

редување *n* Ling. alternation

редукција *f* reduction; редукција на персоналот staffing cuts; Phon. редукција на самогласките vowel reduction

редукциóнен -она *adj see* редукциски

редукциски *adj* reductive, reducing

редум *adv* one after another; one by one; на сите редум to each in turn; ❑ ред по редум one after another

редупликација *f* Ling. reduplication

редуцѝра *pf & impf* to reduce *trans.*; редуцира средства to reduce (cut) funding

редуцѝран *pt* reduced; Phon. редуцирани самогласки reduced vowels

редушка *f see* редачка

рее *impf poet.* **I** (*за око*) to wander, stray **II – се** (*за птици, облаци*) to glide, float, soar

режало *n* small knife

режач *m see* резач

реже *impf* **1** to cut (*also fig.*); to slice; to trim; to chop; to hew; реже леб to slice bread; реже лозја to prune vines; реже уво to grate on the ear; експлозии го режат воздухот explosions rend the air **2** to carve; to engrave **3** *fig.* to have a tart taste; to tingle on the tongue **4** *fig.* (*за ветер*) to cut, bite **5** *fig., colloq.* to speak candidly (plainly)

режија *f* **1** supervision; direction; режијата на филм direction of a film **2** overheads; administration costs

режим *m* **1** regime; демократски режим democratic regime **2** Med. regimen; diet; болнички режим hospital regimen

режимлија -ии *m colloq.* pro-government citizen/politician

режимски *adj* <of the> regime

режѝра *pf & impf* to direct; to stage; to organize

режисéр *m* **1** director (*of play, film*) **2** manager, accounts-keeper

режисéрски *adj* director's

режиски *adj* of overhead costs; режиски трошоци (издатоци) overhead expenses, disbursements; режиска карта concession ticket/card

режовит *adj (за вино)* dry

рез *m* **1** blade **2** cut; incision; notch; ❑ царски рез Caesarean section

реза *f dial. see* резе

резанка *f* piece, slice (*usu. of water melon, melon, etc.*)

резанки *pl* noodles; супа со резанки noodle soup

резач *m* cutting tool; penknife; secateurs

резачка *f* cutting machine/tool

резба *f* carving, wood-engraving

резбар *m* carver, wood-engraver

резбарски *adj* carver's, sculptor's, carving

резбарство *n* sculpting, sculpture, xylography, <the art of> carving

резе *n* bolt, latch

резе́да *f* 1 *Bot.* (Reseda lutea) mignonette, reseda 2 pale green colour

резен *m* & **резенка** *f see* резанка

резе́рва *f* 1 (*usu. pl*) reserves, stocks, supplies; резерви во храна reserves of food; ❏ внатрешни резерви inner reserves; скриени резерви hidden reserves 2 *Mil., Sport.* reserve; игра во резерва to play as a reserve; префрли во резерват to transfer to the reserve 3 *fig.* caution, restraint, reserve; reservation; зема со резерва to have reservations about; зборува со извесна резерва to speak with a certain reserve; прифаќа нешто со резерва to take s.th. with a pinch of salt

резерва́т *m* nature reserve; reservation; ловен резерват hunting reserve

резервација *f* reservation, booking; резервација на соба room reservation

резе́рвен -вна *adj* 1 spare, emergency; резервни делови spare parts; резервна гума spare tyre; резервен фонд reserve fund 2 *Mil.* reserve; резервна единица reserve unit; резервен офицер officer of the reserve

резерви́ра *pf* & *impf* to reserve; to book; резервира билети to reserve tickets

резерви́ран *pt* 1 reserved, booked; резервирана маса reserved table 2 reserved, reticent; резервиран став reserved attitude

резервираност *f* reticence, reserve

резерви́ст *m Mil.* reservist

резервоа́р *m* 1 reservoir; tank; резервоар за вода water tank 2 *fig.* pool, reserve; резервоар за приходи funding pool

резец[1] -сци *m see* резач

резец[2] -сци *m* incisor

резигнација *f* resignation

резигни́ра *pf* & *impf* to resign; резигнира на судбината to resign o.s. to one's fate; резигнира од служба to resign one's post

резигнирано *adv* with resignation

резиде́нт *m* 1 resident<-minister> 2 foreign resident, expatriate 3 intelligence agent, resident

резиденција *f* residence

резил[1] *m colloq.* disgrace, shame; стане за резил to disgrace o.s.

резил[2] *adj indecl. colloq.* shameful, disgraceful; disgraced

резилак -ци *m colloq. see* резил[1]

резилење *n colloq.* disgraceful behaviour

резили *impf colloq.* I to disgrace; to shame II – се to disgrace o.s.

резиме́ *n* résumé, summary, précis

резими́ра *pf* & *impf* to summarize, précis; to sum up

резистенција *f* resistance, opposition; пасивна резистенција passive resistance

резлив *adj* 1 sharp; резлив нож sharp knife 2 (*за вино*) dry 3 *fig.* (*за звук*) piercing, sharp; резлив глас shrill voice 4 (*за ветер*) cutting, biting

резник -ци *m* tree-stump

резок -ска *adj see* резлив

резолуција -ии *f* resolution, decision

резо́н *m* 1 reason, motive 2 reason, sense, wits

резона́нс *m* 1 *Phys.* resonance; good acoustics 2 *fig.* echo, response

резонанција *f see* резонанс

резона́тор *m Tech.* resonator

резоне́р *m* 1 philozophizer; moralizer 2 *Literature* author's mouthpiece

резоне́рски *adj* philosophizing, moralizing, theorizing

резоне́рство *n* theorizing

резони́ра *impf* to theorize, reason, philosophize

резо́нски *adj* rational, reasonable, sensible

резулта́нта *f Math.* resultant

резулта́т *m* result; outcome; *Sport.* score; нерешен резултат draw, tie; ❏ во (како) резултат на (од) . . . as a result of . . .

резулта́тен -тна *adj* successful, fruitful

резулти́ра *impf* to result (*од – from*)

ре́зус-фа́ктор *m* Rhesus factor

реинкарнација *f* reincarnation

реис *m arch.* 1 head, chief 2 ship's captain (master)

рејс *m colloq. see* автобус

рејтинг -зи *m* rating, standing

река *f* river; нагоре по реката upstream; надолу по реката downstream; реки <од> луѓе streams of people

рекапитулација *f* 1 recapitulation; revision 2 audit

рекапитули́ра *pf* & *impf* to recapitulate; to revise

реквием *m* requiem

реквизи́ра *pf* & *impf see* реквирира

реквизи́т *m* 1 (*usu. pl*) requisites, accessories; stage properties, props; sports equipment 2 *Leg.* formal requirement

реквизи́тер *m* property man, props man

реквизиција -ии *f* requisition; реквизиција на жито requisition of grain

реквизицио́нен -она *adj* requisitioning; реквизициона комисија requisition board

реквизициски *adj see* реквизиционен

реквири́ра *pf* & *impf* to requisition, commandeer

рекет *m see* ракета[2]

рекица & **речичка** *f dim. of* река; stream, brook, rivulet

рекла́ма *f* 1 advertising, publicity 2 poster; advertisement; signboard; <TV/radio> commercial

рекламација -ии *f* claim for compensation; complaint

рекламацио́нен -она *adj* <of a> claim/complaint; рекламационо барање complaint

рекла́мен -мна *adj* advertising, publicity, promotional; рекламно одделение advertising department; рекламна табла hoarding, *Am.* billboard

реклами́ра[1] *pf* & *impf* to advertise; to publicize; рекламира стоки to advertise one's wares

реклами́ра[2] *pf* & *impf* to lodge a protest; to file a complaint/claim

рекогносци́ра *pf* & *impf* 1 *Mil.* to reconnoitre 2 to survey

реко́лта *f* harvest, yield; богата реколта good harvest

рекомандација -ии *f* recommendation, reference

рекоманди́ра *pf* & *impf* to recommend

рекомпензација *f* compensation, indemnity; revenge, punishment

рекомпензи́ра *pf* & *impf* to compensate, indemnify; to punish

реконвалесце́нт *m* convalescing patient, convalescent

реконвалесце́нтен -тна *adj* convalescent

реконвалесценција *f Med.* convalescence

реконструѝра *pf & impf* 1 to reconstruct, rebuild 2 to re-enact 3 (*влада*) to reshuffle

реконструктѝвен -вна *adj* reconstructive

реконструкција -ии *f* 1 reconstruction 2 re-enactment

рекóрд *m* record; постави нов рекорд to set a new record; натфрли/собори рекорд to break a record

рекóрден -дна *adj* record *attrib.*; рекордна брзина record speed

рекордéр *m* record-breaker, record-holder

рекордéрски *adj* record-holder's; record *attrib.*

рекордéрство *n* record-breaking/holding

рекреација *f* recreation, relaxation

рекреациóнен -она *adj* recreational; рекреациона сала recreation hall

рекреацѝски *adj see* рекреационен

рекрейра се *pf & impf* to relax; to entertain o.s.

ректор *m* rector, vice-chancellor, *Am.* president (*of a university*)

ректорáт *m* rectorship; rector's office; rector's position and duties

ректорски *adj* rector's, rectorial; ректорски додаток rector's allowance

ректорство *n* rectorship

рекуперација *f* recycling

релаксација *f* relaxation

релаксѝра *pf & impf* I 1 to relax *trans.* 2 *Leg.* to reduce, mitigate II – се to relax *intrans.*

релаксѝран *adj* relaxed, at ease

релатѝвен -вна *adj* relative; релативна вистина relative truth; *Math.* релативни броеви relative numbers; *Gram.* релативни заменки relative pronouns; релативни реченици relative clauses

релативѝзам -змот *m* relativism

релативѝст *m* relativist

релативѝстички *adj* relativistic

релативитéт *m* relativity; теорија на релативитетот theory of relativity

релација -ии *f* 1 (*сообраќајна линија*) route; релација Скопје-Лондон the Skopje-London route 2 (*растојание*) distance; релацијата меѓу Скопје и Битола the distance between Skopje and Bitola 3 (*однос*) relation<s>; релацијата помеѓу вработените и студентите staff-student relations 4 (*извештај*) report, account, statement 5 *Mil.* citation

релевáнтен -тна *adj* relevant, pertinent

релéен -јна *adj Tech.* relay; релејна радиостаница translator, relay (broadcasting) station

релéј -еи *m* 1 *Tech.* relay 2 *Mil.* signaller, member of a signals unit

релѝ *n & m Sport.* rally

религија -ии *f* religion, faith, confession; христијанската религија the Christian faith

религиóзен -зна *adj* religious; pious, devout

религиóзност *f* piety

религиски *adj* religious, denominational

реликвија -ии *f* relic

релѝкт *m* relic; relict, survival

релјеф *m Art, Geol., Geog.* relief

релјефен -фна *adj Art., Geol., Geog.* 1 <in> relief; релјефна карта relief map 2 *fig.* graphic, lucid, vivid; релјефен стил graphic style

релјефно *adv* in relief; vividly, graphically

релса *f* 1 rails, track 2 *fig.* route; во кои релси се движиш? which route are you taking?

рема *f see* хрема

ремек-дело *n* masterpiece

ремен -и, -ње *m* strap; belt; sling

ременче *n see* ремче

реми[1] *n & m Chess* draw; партијата заврши реми the game ended in a draw

реми[2] *n & m Cards* rummy

ремизѝра *pf & impf* to draw, tie; ремизира партија to end a game with a draw (tie)

ремилитаризација *f* remilitarization

ремилитаризѝра *pf & impf* to remilitarize *trans.*

реминисценција -ии *f* reminiscence

ремис *m* discount

ремник -ци *m see* ремен

ремонт *m* repair<s>; overhaul; maintenance

ремонтен -тна *adj* repair; ремонтни работи repair works

ремонтѝра *pf & impf* to repair; ремонтира кола to repair a car

реморкéр *m* tugboat, tug

ремче *n dim. of* ремен; watch-strap

ренда *impf see* рендосува

рендген *m* X-ray (Roentgen) machine; оди на рендген to go for an X-ray

рендгенов *adj see* рендгенски

рендгенгрáм *m* & **рендгенгрáма** *f* X-ray <photograph>

рендгенографија *f* radiography, roentgenography

рендгенолóг -зи *m* radiologist

рендгенологија *f* radiology

рендгенолошки *adj* radiological

рендгеноскопија *f* radioscopy

рендгенотерапија *f* radiotherapy

рендгенски *adj* X-ray; рендгенски зраци X-rays; рендгенски преглед X-ray examination; рендгенска снимка X-ray <photograph>

ренда *impf* 1 to plane 2 to grate *trans.*; ренда сирење to grate cheese

ренде *n* 1 (*струг*) plane 2 grater; ❏ го направи ренде he destroyed him/it

рендоса *pf* to plane

рендосува *impf of* рендоса

ренегáт *m* renegade

ренегáтски *adj* renegade's, apostatical

ренегáтство *n* apostasy

ренесáнс *m* & **ренесáнса** *f* 1 *Hist.* Renaissance 2 rebirth, revival

ренесáнсен -сна *adj* Renaissance; ренесансна литература Renaissance literature

ренса *impf* to whimper, snivel; to sob, moan

ренсало *n* cry-baby

реновѝра *pf & impf* to renovate

реномé *n* reputation; renown

реномѝран *adj* renowned; реномирана фирма a well-known firm

рента *f* rent; revenue; annuity; годишна рента annuity; земјишна рента ground rent

рентабѝлен -лна *adj* profitable

рентабѝлност *f* profitability, economic viability

рентен -тна *adj* rental

рентиéр *m rentier*

рентиéрка *f* (*fem. form*) *see* рентиер

рентѝра се *pf & impf* to be profitable, to pay *intrans.*

реон *m* region, area, district; zone; *fig.* field;

земјоделски реон agricultural region; работнички реон working-class district; реонот на станицата the area of the railway station; тоа не е во негов реон that is not in his field

реонизација *f* regionalization; division into districts

реонѝра *pf & impf* to regionalize

реонски *adj* regional; district *attrib.*; реонски комитет regional/district committee

реорганизáтор *m* reorganizer

реорганизација *f* reorganization

реорганизѝра *pf & impf* to reorganize

реостат *m Elec.* rheostat

репа *f see* репка

репарација -ии *f* 1 war reparations 2 compensation 3 repair<s>

репарациóнен -она *adj* reparative, reparation *attrib.*; репарациона комисија reparation committee

репарѝра *pf & impf* 1 to compensate (*for damage*) 2 to repair, restore

репатријација *f* repatriation

репатрѝра *pf & impf* to repatriate

репатрѝрец -рци *m* returnee, repatriate

реперкусија -ии *f* 1 repercussion; reverberation; response 2 *Mus.* variation <on a theme>

репертоáр *m* repertoire

репертоáрен -рна *adj see* репертоарски

репертоáрски *adj* repertoire *attrib.*; репертоарска политика repertoire policy

репетé *n* second helping, *colloq.* seconds

репетéнт *m* 1 tutor, coach 2 pupil/student repeating a grade/year

репетѝра *impf* 1 to rehearse *trans.*; репетира драма to rehearse a play 2 to revise, repeat 3 (*пушка*) to cock

репетѝтор *m see* репетент 1

репетиториум *m* revision course; crammer

репетиторски *adj* coaching; репетиторска работа tutorial work

репетиција -ии *f* rehearsal; генерална репетиција dress rehearsal

репетициóнен -она *adj* rehearsal *attrib.*; репетициона сала rehearsal hall

репка *f Bot.* (Brassica rapifera) turnip; шеќерна репка (Beta vulgaris) sugar beet

реплика *f* 1 retort, rejoinder; *Leg.* replication 2 (*во театар*) cue 3 *Mus.* reprise 4 replica, copy

репне *pf* репна *aor. colloq.* to hit, thump; to poke

репнува *impf of* репне

репортáжа *f* reportage, report, story; звучна репортажа sound reportage

репортáжен -жна *adj* reporter's; reporting

репортéр *m* reporter, journalist; спортски репортер sports reporter

репортéрски *adj* reporter's

репортéрство *n* reporting; journalism

репортѝра *impf* to report

репрезентáнт *m* representative

репрезентатѝвен -вна *adj* representative; репрезентативен хотел first-class hotel; *Sport.* репрезентативен играч international; репрезентативна форма good form

репрезентатѝвец -вци *m Sport.* star player; international

репрезентатѝвка *f* (*fem. form*) *see* репрезентативец

репрезентација -ии *f* 1 representation 2 *Sport.* државна репрезентација national team

репрезентѝра *pf & impf* to represent

репресалија *f* (*usu. pl*) reprisals

репресѝвен -вна *adj* repressive; репресивни мерки repressive measures

репресија -ии *f* repression

репрѝза *f Theatre, Film, TV,* repeat; *Mus.* reprise

репрѝзен -зна *adj* reprise; репризна изведба repeat performance

репродуктѝвен -вна *adj* reproductive; репродуктивни органи reproductive organs

репродуктѝвец -вци *m* reproducer

репродуктѝвка *f* (*fem. form*) *see* репродуктивец

репродукува *pf & impf see* репродуцира

репродукција -ии *f* 1 *Art, Print.* reproduction; duplication 2 *Biol.* reproduction, propagation

репродукциóнен -она *adj* reproducing, duplicating, copying *attrib.*; репродукционен апарат copying machine

репродуцéнт *m* 1 reproducer 2 *Leg.* counter-witness, opposing evidence 3 imitator

репродуцѝра *pf & impf* to reproduce *trans.*

репроматеријал *m* raw material; semi-finished material

република *f* republic

републикáнец -нци *m* republican

републикáнски *adj* republican; републиканска партија republican party

републички *adj* republican

репутација *f* reputation, good name

рерна *f* oven

реса *f* 1 catkin; врбова реса a willow catkin 2 fringe; tassel<s>; чаршав со реси fringed tablecloth

ресав *adj* fringed; tasselled; ресав фустан fringed dress

ресен -сна *adj see* ресав

ресест *adj see* ресав

реси¹ *pf arch.* to cross out, erase

реси² *impf* I 1 to put forth catkins 2 to cause to wear out, fray II – се to fray *intrans.*

ресица *f Anat.* uvula

реска¹ *f see* рецка

реска² *impf* to notch, nick

рескир *m see* ризик

рескѝра *impf see* ризикува

ресне *pf* ресна *aor. see* рецне

ресор *m* profession; sphere, field; competence; <government> department; министер без ресор minister without portfolio

ресорбѝра *pf & impf* to reabsorb, resorb

ресорен -рна *adj see* ресорски

ресорпција *f* reabsorption, absorption

ресорски *adj* professional; special; ресорски додаток salary increment/bonus (*Austral.* loading)

респект *m* respect, esteem, consideration; има респект спрема некого to respect s.o.

респектабилен -лна *adj* respectable

респектабилност *f* respectability

респектѝвен -вна *adj* respective, corresponding

респектѝра *impf* to respect

респиратор *m* respirator (*also Med.*)

респирација *f* respiration

респирациóнен -она *adj* respiratory; респирациони органи respiratory organs

респири́ра *pf & impf* to respire
реставра́тор *m* restorer
реставраторски *adj* restorer's; restoration; реставраторски работи restoration works
реставрација *f* restoration
реставри́ра *pf & impf* to restore
рест́о *n* 1 (*кусур*) change 2 remainder, rest
ресторан *m* restaurant
рестора́нски *adj* restaurant *attrib.*; ресторански цени restaurant prices
рестора́нт *m see* ресторан
ресторација -ии *f see* ресторан
рестрикти́вен -вна *adj* restrictive
рестрикција *f* restriction
рестува *impf* to cook in oil
ресува *impf arch. of* реси[1]
ресу́рс *m* (*usu. pl*) resources; природни ресурси natural resources
ретина *f* retina
реткач *m* sparse wood
ретко *adv* uncommonly, seldom, rarely; ретко убав глас a voice of rare beauty
реткост *f* rarity; библиографска реткост bibliographical rarity
ретор *m* rhetorician, teacher of rhetoric
реторика *f* rhetoric
реторичар *m* rhetorician
реторичен -чна *adj* rhetorical
реторички *adj* rhetorical; реторичко прашање rhetorical question
рето́рта *f Chem.* retort
ретро- (*in compounds*) retro-
ретроактивен -вна *adj* retroactive
ретроград *m* reactionary, die-hard
ретрограден -дна *adj* backward-looking, retrograde, reactionary
ретроградност *f* backwardness
ретроспекти́ва *f* retrospection, retrospective; flashback
ретроспекти́вен -вна *adj* retrospective; ретроспективен поглед retrospective view
ретроспекција *f see* ретроспектива
рету́р *m* return; ретур-билет return ticket
рету́ш *m* touch-up, retouching (*of photograph, painting, etc.*)
ретуше́р *m* retoucher
ретуши́ра *pf & impf* to retouch, touch up (*photograph, painting, etc.*)
ретче *n dim. of* ред 1
ретчи се *impf* to thin <out> *intrans.*; се ретчат облаците the clouds are thinning
реума *f Med. see* реуматизам
реумати́зам -змот *m Med.* rheumatism
реуматичар *m* rheumatic, rheumatism sufferer
реуматичарка *f* (*fem. form*) *see* реуматичар
реуматичен -чна *adj* rheumatic; реуматични болки rheumatic pains
рефера́т *m* report, paper; воведен реферат keynote address
рефере́ндум *m* referendum
рефере́нт *m* 1 conference speaker 2 official; administrator; кадровски референт personnel officer
рефери́ра *pf & impf* to read a report on; to report on
рефлекс *m* reflex; ❏ условни рефлекси conditioned reflexes

рефлексен -сна *adj see* рефлексивен
рефлекси́вен -вна *adj* 1 reflex; рефлексивно движење reflex action 2 *Gram.* reflexive; рефлексивни глаголи reflexive verbs 3 reflective, contemplative; рефлексивна лирика meditative poetry
рефлексија -ии *f* 1 reflection 2 *fig.* reflection, contemplation
рефлекта́нт *m* applicant, candidate; рефлектант на работно место applicant for a post (position, job)
рефлекти́ра *impf* 1 (*светлина, звук*) to reflect *trans.* 2 to reflect (*на – on, upon*) 3 to aspire (*на – то*)
рефлектор *m* 1 reflector 2 spotlight; searchlight; floodlight
рефлекторски *adj* reflecting; рефлекторско огледало reflector mirror
рефо́рма *f* reform; аграрна реформа land reform
реформа́тор *m* reformer
реформаторски *adj* reformer's
реформаторство *n* reform, reforming activity
реформација *f Hist.* the Reformation
реформи́зам -змот *m* reformism
реформи́ра *pf & impf* to reform *trans.*
реформи́ст *m* reformist
реформистички *adj* reformist; реформистичка политика reformist policy
рефрен *m* refrain
рефунда́ција *f* refund, reimbursement
рефунди́ра *pf & impf* to refund, reimburse
рехабилитација -ии *f* rehabilitation
рехабилитаци́онен -она *adj* rehabilitative, rehabilitation *attrib.*
рехабилити́ра *pf & impf* I *Med., Leg.* to rehabilitate II – се 1 to recover 2 to vindicate o.s.
рецензе́нт *m* reviewer, critic; театарски рецензент theatre critic
рецензе́нтски *adj* reviewer's
рецензија -ии *f* review, notice
рецензи́ра *pf & impf* to review; рецензира книга to review (write a review of) a book
рецепис *m* receipt; acknowledgement
рецепт *m* 1 recipe (*also fig.*) 2 (*за лекови*) prescription; без рецепт over the counter
реце́пта *f see* рецепт
рецепти́вен -вна *adj* receptive
рецептор *m* receiver
рецепција *f* 1 reception 2 reception room/desk; front office
рецеси́вен -вна *adj* retiring, withdrawn; recessive; рецесивни гени recessive genes
рецесија *f* recession
рециди́в *m* 1 recurrence; *Med.* relapse 2 *Leg.* repeat offence
рецидиви́зам -змот *m* 1 *Med.* relapse 2 *Leg.* recidivism
рецидиви́ра *pf & impf Med.* to relapse; *Leg.* to re-offend
рецидиви́ст *m* recidivist
реципроците́т *m* reciprocity; принципот на реципроцитет the principle of reciprocity
реципрочен -чна *adj* reciprocal; mutual; *Math.* реципрочна вредност на број reciprocal value of a number
реципрочност *f* reciprocity

рецита́л *m* recital

рецитати́в *m Mus.* recitative

рецитати́вен -вна *adj* recitative; рецитативна изведба recitative performance

рецита́тор *m* reciter

рецита́торски *adj* reciter's

рецита́ција -ии *f* recitation, declamation

рецити́ра *pf & impf* to recite

рецка[1] *f* line, mark; notch; perforation; ❑ пишува рецка на нешто to write s.th. off

рецка[2] *impf dim. of* реже

рецне *pf* рецна *aor.* to notch, nick

реч *f* **1** speech; language, tongue; човечка реч human speech/language; му се растрои речта his speech was impaired; македонска реч Macedonian language **2** speech, oration, address **3** *colloq.* word; со една реч in a word; слаткатa реч и железна врата отвора *prov.* a soft answer turneth away wrath

рече *pf* **1** to say, utter; to tell; ❑ речи го so to speak; кажи-речи roughly, more or less; речено-сторено no sooner said than done; да (нека) речеме дека . . . let's say . . . , let's suppose . . . ; не речи два пати don't be too sure; don't bet on it; рече и остане жив to drop a brick; to put one's foot in it; така да се рече in a manner of speaking **2** *colloq.* to decide; реков да ве видам I decided to call on you **3** *colloq.* to do, go; речи вака go like this **4** (*with following verb*) to start; рече паѓа it started raining

речел *m* preserve

речен[1] -чна *adj* riverine, fluvial, river; речно корито river bed; *Zool.* речен орел (Pandion haliaetus) osprey

речен[2] *pt* spoken; ❑ благо речено to put it mildly; грубо речено at a rough estimate; од реченото не се бега no flying from fate

речениja *f colloq.* fate, destiny, lot

реченица *f* sentence; clause; проста реченица simple sentence; зависна реченица subordinate clause; независна реченица main clause

реченичен -чна *adj* <of a> sentence/clause; реченични знаци punctuation marks

реченички *adj see* реченичен

речено *n colloq.* fate, destiny, lot

речина *f* fine sieve, strainer

речиси *adv* almost, nearly; речиси цел ден almost all day; ❑ речиси ништо next to nothing; речиси секогаш nine times out of ten

речит *adj see* речовит

речитати́в *m see* рецитатив

речитост *f see* речовитост

речица & речичка *f dim. of* река; stream, rivulet

речник -ци *m* **1** dictionary; glossary; правописен речник orthographical dictionary **2** vocabulary, lexis; богат речник large (rich) vocabulary; слаб речник limited vocabulary

речникар *m colloq.* lexicographer

речникарски *adj colloq.* lexicographical; речникарска работа lexicographical work

речникарство *n colloq.* lexicography

речница *f* (*usu. pl*) *see* наречница 1

речниче *n dim. of* речник 1

речнички *adj* lexical

речовит *adj* talkative; eloquent

речовитост *f* eloquence

речува *impf rare of* рече

рецба *f f.p.* word

реш *adj* crisp, crunchy

решава (се) *impf of* реши (се)

решавачки *adj* decisive, crucial, critical; во решавачкиот момент at the crucial moment; решавачка борба decisive struggle

решение -ија *n* **1** decision; resolution; (*судско*) judgement, verdict; решенијата на конгресот the resolutions of the congress **2** solution, answer; решение на проблем solution to a problem

решеност *f* decisiveness, resolve; determination

решетар *m* sieve-maker

решетарка *f* (*fem. form*) *see* решетар

решети *impf* to make holes in; to riddle; решети со куршуми to riddle with bullets

решетка *f* lattice; grating, bars; ❑ зад решетки behind bars (in prison)

решеткав *adj* barred, latticed; решеткав прозорец barred window; решеткава ограда latticework fence

решето *n* sieve, colander; ❑ носи вода во решето to waste time and effort; to beat the air; помине и сито и решето to go through thick and thin

решетце & решетче *n dim. of* решето

реши *pf* **I 1** to decide (*да – то*), make up one's mind (*to*); resolve **2** to decide, resolve, settle *trans.*; реши спор to resolve a dispute; ❑ реши судбина на некого to decide s.o.'s fate **3** to solve (*a problem*) **II – се 1** to decide (*to*), make up one's mind (*to*); се решив да му се доверам I decided to confide in him **2** to be settled, solved, resolved

решителен -лна *adj* **1** resolute, determined; решителен противник a resolute opponent; решителен тон firm tone <of voice> **2** crucial, critical, deciding; во решителниот момент at the crucial moment

решително *adv* decisively, resolutely

решителност *f* decisiveness, resolve; determination

решлив *adj* (*разрешлив*) solvable; проблемот е лесно решлив the problem is easy to solve

решка[1] *f* stroke; mark; line; *fig.* feature, trait

решка[2] *f* reverse side (*of a coin*); tails

решо *n* hotplate

решува (се) *impf see* решава (се)

'рж *f Bot.* (Secale cereale) rye; ближната 'рж е поблага (поарна) од далечната пченица *prov.* a bird in the hand is worth two in the bush

'ржан *adj see* 'ржен

'ржаник -ци *m see* 'рженик

'ржаница *f see* 'рженица

'ржанов *adj rare see* 'ржен

'ржен *adj* rye; 'ржени полиња rye fields; 'ржен леб rye bread

'рженик -ци *m* rye bread

'рженица *f* rye straw

'ржи *impf* **I 1** (*за коњ*) to neigh, whinny **2** (*за куче*) to growl, snarl

'ржиште *n* rye field

'ржлив *adj* whining; 'ржлив глас whining voice

'ржца *f hyp. of* 'рж

'рзне[1] *pf* 'рзна *aor.* to <start to> beat *intrans.*; to <start to> bang *intrans.*; to <start to> knock *intrans.*; 'рзнаа тапани drums started beating

'рзне[2] *pf* 'рзна *aor.* to neigh

'рзнува *impf of* 'рзне[1,2]

риба *f* 1 fish; *Astron.* Pisces; морска риба salt-water fish; слатководна риба freshwater fish; оди на риба to go fishing; лов на риби fishing; ❑ <се чувствува> како риба во вода to be in one's element; ситна риба small fry; во матно (матна вода) фаќа риба to fish in troubled waters; нем (молчи) како риба as quiet as a mouse; ни рак, ни риба neither fish, nor flesh <nor good red herring>; добра риба *colloq.* nice bit of fluff; рибата во вода (в море), тавата на оган *prov.* don't count your chickens before they are hatched; first catch your hare; рибата смрди од главата *prov.* the rot starts at the top 2 slice, piece (*usu.* bread)

рибар *m* 1 fisherman, angler; fishmonger; lover of fish 2 *Zool.* (Pandion haliaetus) osprey

рибари *impf* to fish, angle

рибарина *f* fishing tax

рибарник -ци *m see* рибник

рибарница *f* fishmonger's shop; fish market

рибарски *adj* fisherman's; fishing; рибарски чун fishing boat; рибарски прибор fishing tackle; рибарска мрежа fishing net

рибарство *n* fishing, fishery; fishing industry; завод за рибарство fish<-processing> factory, fish cannery

рибарче *n* 1 *dim. of* рибар 2 *Zool.* (Alcedo atthis) kingfisher

рибен -бна *adj* fish; рибен ресторан fish/seafood restaurant

рибенце *n dim. of* риба

рибизла *f Bot.* (Ribes rubrum) red currant

рибин *adj* fish *attrib.*; рибина чорба fish soup; рибино масло cod-liver oil; ❑ рибина коска herring-bone

рибица *f* & **рибиче** *n dim. of* риба

рибичка *f dim. of* риба

рибиште *n augm. of* риба 1

рибји *adj see* рибен, рибин

рибник -ци *m* fish hatchery; fish-pond

рибовиден -дна *adj* fish-like

риболик *adj see* рибовиден

риболов *m* fishing, angling; слатководен риболов freshwater fishing

риболовен -вна *adj* fishing; риболовна сезона fishing season

риболовец -вци *m* angler; fisherman; страстен риболовец an enthusiastic angler; спортски риболовец a sporting fisherman

риболовски *adj see* риболовен

риболовство *n* fishing

рива *f* promenade (*along beach or river bank*)

ривал *m* rival, competitor

ривалитет *m* rivalry, competition, opposition

ривалство *n see* ривалитет

ривиера *f* riviera

рига[1] *f* stripe, line, streak, band; панталони на риги striped trousers

рига[2] *impf* 1 to belch 2 to bring up, vomit, spew; рига крв to vomit blood; рига пламен to belch flame

Рига *f* Riga

ригест *adj* striped; ригест штоф striped material

ригне *pf* ригна *aor.* (*see* рига)

ригнува *impf of* ригне

ригорозен -зна *adj* rigorous, uncompromising, strict, unbending

ригорозност *f* rigorousness, rigour, strictness

рид -ови, -је, -ишта *m* hill; по ридот угоре uphill; по ридот удолу downhill; по ридови и по долови over hills and dales

рида *f* towel; kerchief

риден -дна *adj* hilly; ридно место hilly place

ридиште *n augm. of* рид

ридски *adj* hilly, hill; ридска патека a hill path; ридска трка hill race

рие *impf* to dig, burrow

рижанец -нци *m* person from Riga

рижанка *f* (*fem. form*) *see* рижанец

риза[1] *f dial.* 1 shirt 2 *see* рида

риза[2] *impf dial.* 1 to obey 2 *fig.* to do (*s.o.*) a favour

ризик -ци *m* risk; се изложи на ризик to take a risk; ❑ на свој ризик at one's own risk

ризикува *impf* to take a risk; to risk *trans.*; го ризикува животот to risk one's life; ❑ кој ризикува, тој добива nothing ventured, nothing gained

ризичен -чна *adj* risky; ризичен потег a risky move

ризлинг *m* Riesling

ризница *f* 1 *Rel.* vestry 2 *fig.* treasure house, treasury; repository; ризница на знаења treasure house of knowledge

ризничар *m* custodian, curator (*of a museum*)

ризото *n Cul.* risotto

рик *m* 1 roar, bellow; yelling 2 crying, weeping, howling; рикот на сирени the wailing of sirens

рика *impf* 1 to roar, bellow; (*за говеда*) to moo; (*за магаре*) to bray 2 *colloq.* to weep, wail, lament, howl

рикавица *f* whooping cough

рикне *pf* рикна *aor. see* рика

рикнува *impf of* рикне

рикоше *n* ricochet

рикша *m* & *f* rickshaw

рила *impf* to trench (*vines*)

рилач *m* trenching worker

рилест *adj* 1 long-nosed, snouted 2 *dial.* thick-lipped

рилка *f* 1 snout; *Zool.* proboscis 2 *fig. see* усна

рилкар *m Zool.* (*usu. pl*) proboscidean

рило *n see* рилка 1

рилце *n dim. of* рило

Рим *m* Rome

рима *f* rhyme

Римјанин -ни *m* Roman

Римјанка *f* (*fem. form*) *see* Римјанин

римски *adj* Roman; римско царство Roman Empire; ❑ римската црква the Roman <Catholic> Church; римски броеви (цифри) Roman numerals

римува *pf* & *impf* to rhyme

римуван *pt* rhymed

ринг *m Sport.* ring

рингишпил *m* merry-go-round

рингла *f* ring, hotplate; burner (*of cooking stove*)

рине *impf* to shovel

ринка *impf* to scratch about, root

ринта *impf* to toil, labour, slave away

рипа *impf* to jump <about>, *see* скока

рипач *m see* скокач

рипачка *f* jump, jumping, *see* скок

рипида *f Rel.* icon (*mounted on a wooden staff*)

рипка¹ *f dim. of* риба; *Zool.* златна рипка (Carassius auratus) goldfish

рипка² *impf* to skip about, frolic, gambol

рипне *pf* рипна *aor.* to skip, jump; рипне на нозе to jump to one's feet; *see* скокне

рипнува *impf of* рипне

рипс *m* rep\<p\>, fine-corded material

рипсен *adj* \<of\> rep; ribbed

рипче *n dim. of* риба 1; ❏ фрли рипче да фатиш крапче (дава рипче, зема крапче) throw a sprat to catch a mackerel

рис¹ *m Zool.* (Felis lynx) lynx; ❏ лут како рис mad as a hornet

рис² *m* ream (*usu. 500 sheets*)

рискантен -тна *adj see* ризичен

рискува *impf see* ризикува

рисов & **рисовски** *adj* lynx, lynx's

рита (се) *impf see* клоца² (се)

ритам -тми *m* rhythm

ритамски *adj* rhythmic\<al\>

ритер *m* knight (*also fig.*)

ритерски *adj* knightly, chivalrous; ритерска чест knightly honour; ритерска постапка chivalrous act

ритерство *n* chivalry; gallantry

ритка (се) *impf see* клоца² (се)

ритмика *f* **1** *Literature* rhythm system; rhythmicity **2** eurhythmics

ритмичен -чна *adj* rhythmic\<al\>; ритмични движења rhythmical movements

ритмички *adj see* ритмичен

ритне (се) *pf* ритна (се) *aor. see* клоцне (се)

ритнува (се) *impf of* ритне (се)

ритуал *m* ritual, rite

ритуален -лна *adj* ritual, ceremonial; ритуална свеченост ritual celebration

ритче *n dim. of* рид; hillock, mound

рицар *m see* ритер

рицарски *adj see* ритерски

рицарство *n see* ритерство

рицино *n colloq. see* рицинус

рицинов *adj colloq. see* рицинусов

рицинус *m Bot.* (Ricinus communis) castor oil plant

рицинусов *adj* \<of\> castor oil plant; рицинусово масло castor oil

ричка *f see* ритче

ришки *adj* Riga *attrib.*

'рка *impf* to snore

'ркавица *f* snore\<s\>, snoring

'ркач *m* snorer

'ркне *pf* 'ркна *aor.* to snore

'ркнува *impf of* 'ркне

'ркулец -лци *m see* 'ртулец

РМ *abbr.* (*Република Македонија*) Republic of Macedonia

'рика *f* (*usu pl*) nostril, *see* ноздра, носница

роб -ови, -је, -ја *m* **1** slave, bondsman; *fig.* роб на страста a slave of passion **2** captive, prisoner

роба *f* robe; dressing-gown

роби *impf* to enslave

робија -ии *f* penal servitude, hard labour; forced labour

робијаш *m* convict

робијашки *adj* convict's

робијашница *f* prison, gaol, jail

робина & **робинка** *f* (*fem. form*) see роб

робинчица *f dim. of* робина & робинка

робовладелец -лци *m see* робовладетел

робовладетел *m* slave-owner, *Am.* slaveholder

робовладетелски *adj* slave-owning; робовладетелско општество slave-owning society

робовладетелство *n* slave-owning regime (system)

робот *m* robot

робува *impf* to live as a slave, live in slavery (*also fig.*); им робува на страстите he is a slave to his passions

робувачка *f* slavery

робустен -сна *adj* **1** robust, tough **2** unpolished, coarse, rough-hewn

ров *m* trench

рови *impf* **1** (копа) to dig **2** (за река) to erode, undermine, wear away *trans.* **3** *fig.* to rummage; рови по библиотеки to rummage in libraries **4** *dial.* (боде) to butt

ровина *f* gully (*formed by erosion*)

ровит *adj see* ровок

ровитост *f see* ровкост

ровја *f* thunderbolt; ❏ како ровја од ведро небо like a bolt from the blue

ровјоса *pf usu. in the expression:* ровја те ровјосала! go to hell!

ровкав *adj see* ровок

ровкавост *f see* ровкост

ровкост *f* fragility; friability; softness; ровкоста на земјата the friability of the soil

ровок -вка *adj* **1** soft; fragile; tender, delicate; friable; ровок снег soft snow; ровка земја friable soil; ровко дете delicate child **2** (за јајце) soft-boiled

ровче *n dim. of* ров

рог *m* **1** horn; antler; рог за барут powder horn; ❏ бара рогови to ask too much; втера во козји рог to make s.o. knuckle under; како рогови во вреќа (*to fight*) like cat and dog; лаги со рогови bare-faced lies; ги скрши роговите на некого to break s.o.'s pride; си ги покаже (пушти) роговите to show one's true colours; \<про\>даде рог за свеќа to sell s.o. a pig in a poke; набива некому рогови to cuckold s.o.; рог на изобилието *literary* horn of plenty, cornucopia; темно како во рог pitch-dark **2** *colloq.* bump, swelling **3** horn, bugle; ловечки рог hunting horn

рога¹ *f only in the expression:* баба рога old witch

рога² *impf see* 'рга¹ 1, фраска, бие

рогат **1** *adj* horned; рогат добиток cattle **2** (*as noun*) рогатиот *m* the devil, Satan

рогач *m* **1** *Bot.* (Ceratonia siliqua) carob, locust bean **2** *poet.* crescent moon

рогачка *f Bot.* (Ceratonia siliqua) carob\<-tree\>; locust bean

рогле -вци *m* longhorn, long-horned animal; *fig.* cuckold

роглец *m see* полжав 1

рогов *adj see* рожен

роговиден -дна *adj* hornlike, horn-shaped

рогожа *f see* рогозина

рогожар *m see* рогозинар

рогоз *m Bot.* (Typha latifolia) reed-mace, cat's-tail

рогозен -зна *adj* reed

рогозина *f* reed mat; ❏ не ми гори рогозина it's none of my business; видела свињата рогозина, па посакала и постела *prov.* give them an inch and they'll take a yard

рогозинар *m* mat-maker, mat-seller
рогозинарка *f* (*fem. form*) *see* рогозинар
рогозинка *f dim. of* рогозина
рогоносец -сци *m colloq.* cuckold
рогоска *f see* рогозина, рогозинка
рогужина & рогузина *f dial. see* рогозина
рогуша & рогушка *f* horned sheep
род *m* 1 kin, family, clan; race; од добар род of good family; од господски род of upper-class family; ние сме близок род we are closely related; човечки род the human race, mankind 2 progeny, offspring; crop, yield, harvest; богат, обилен род plentiful, abundant crop; прв род first offspring; даде род to bear fruit 3 *Bot., Zool.* genus, family; родот на мачките the cat family; felines 4 kind, sort, type; од ист род of the same type; род <на> оружје type of weapon; род <на> војска arm of the service 5 *Gram.* gender
рода *f see* род 1
родака се *impf dial.* to become related (*by marriage*)
родан *m* spindle; distaff; spinning-wheel
родбина *f see* роднина 2
роделив *adj f.p.* fertile, fruitful
роден[1] *pt* 1 born; роден поет a born poet 2 own (*by blood relationship*); роден брат blood-brother (brother-german); родена сестра sister-german; мојот роден татко my own father; ❑ роден ден birthday; родено име Christian/first name
роден[2] -дна *adj* 1 fertile, fruitful; родна земја fertile ground 2 native; home; familiar; неговото родно место his birthplace; роден град native town
роди *pf* I 1 to bear, bring forth 2 to give rise to, engender II – се 1 to be born; ❑ таков човек повеќе нема да се роди second to none 2 (*за сонце*) to rise 3 *fig.* to appear, arise
родилен -лна *adj* <of> childbirth; ❑ родилен дом maternity home/hospital; родилна треска puerperal fever; родилни маки labour pains, birth pangs (*also fig.*)
родилиште *n* maternity home, maternity clinic (hospital)
родилка *f* nursing mother; woman in childbirth
родина *f* native land
родител *m* parent, father
родителка *f* <female> parent, mother
родителски *adj* parental
родлив *adj* fruitful, fertile, productive
родливост *f see* родност
роднина -и, -ње *m & f* 1 relative, relation; не му е роднина they are not related 2 *coll.* relatives, kin; сета моја роднина all my relatives (relations)
роднински *adj* family; kindred; роднински врски ties of kinship
роднинство *n* <family> relationship
родница *f* 1 fertile land (soil) 2 fruitful tree; дрво родница fruitful tree
родност *f* fertility; родноста на земјата the fertility of the land
родобитен -тна *adj see* родлив
родов *adj see* родовски
родовит *adj see* родлив
родовски *adj* family/clan/race *attrib.*; родовски старешина head of a family (clan); родовско уредување clan structure

родозаштитник -ци *m literary, rare* defender of one's country
родољуб *m* patriot
родољубен -бна *adj see* родољубив
родољубец -пци *m see* родољуб
родољубив *adj* patriotic
родољубивост *f* patriotism
родољубие & родољубје *n see* родољубивост
родољубност *f see* родољубивост
родољупка *f* (*fem. form*) *see* родољуб
родоначалник -ци *m* forebear, ancestor; *fig.* father, founder; родоначалник на движење founding father of a movement
родоотстапник -ци *m* traitor
Родопи *pl* Rhodopes, Rhodope Mountains
родопис *m see* родословје
родопски *adj* Rhodope *attrib.*
родоскврнавење *n* incest
родословен -вна *adj* genealogical; родословно дрво (стебло) genealogical (family) tree
родословие & родословје *n* genealogy
родствен *adj* related, kindred; cognate
родственост *f literary, rare see* родство
родство *n* kinship; affinity
родум *adv* by birth/origin; родум Македонец Macedonian by birth; тој е родум од Источна Македонија he is a native of Eastern Macedonia
роен -јна *adj f.p.* reddish
рожба *f* 1 child; progeny, offspring 2 *coll.* young, baby animals/birds 3 crop 4 *fig.* product, creation; рожба на природата product of nature
рождество *n Rel.* Рождество Христово Christmas
рожен -жна *adj* horn; рожен чешел comb of horn; рожни украси horn ornaments
рожница *f Anat.* cornea
роза *f see* ружа[1]
розéт<к>а *f* rosette
розмарин *m see* рузмарин
розов *adj* 1 *see* ружин 2 pink; rosy
рои се *impf* to swarm (*also fig.*); to crowd
роиште *n augm. of* рој
рој -еви *m* swarm (*also fig.*); mass, crowd; во роеви in swarms
ројак -ци *m see* рој
ројализам -змот *m* royalism
ројалист *m* royalist
ројалистички *adj* royalist
ројче *n dim. of* рој
рок *m* term, time limit; краен рок deadline; рок на доспевање maturity; гарантен рок guarantee period; во краток рок at short notice
рокáда *f* 1 *Chess* castling; ❑ растури рокада to thwart a plan 2 *fig.* rotation; reshuffle
рокáден -дна *adj* castling
рокенрол *m* rock and roll, rock 'n' roll
рокер *m* rocker, devotee of rock music
рокира <се> *pf & impf* 1 *Chess* to castle 2 to rotate, reshuffle
роковен -вна *adj see* сроковен, срочен
роковник -ци *m see* сроковник
рококо *n* rococo
рокче *n* 1 *dim. of* рог 2 *see* козирог, рогачка
ролат *m* roulade (*kind of sweetmeat*)
ролéтка *f dim. of* ролетна

ролéтна *f* blind, shutter; венецијански ролетни Venetian blinds

ролја -лји *f* role, part; главна ролја leading part; ❑ игра важна (голема) ролја to play an important part

ролна *f* roll; scroll; roller; една ролна хартија a roll of paper

роло *n* roller door

роломобил *m see* тротинет

ролшуа *f* (*usu. pl*) roller skate

Ром *m* Romany, gypsy, Rom

роман *m* novel

Романец -нци *m* Romanian, Rumanian

романѝзам -змот *m* Romance borrowing

романизација *f* **1** romanization **2** novelization

романѝра *pf & impf* **1** to romanize **2** (*романсира*) to adapt as a novel; to novelize

романизува *pf & impf rare see* романизира 1

Романи *pl* Romance peoples

Романија *f* Romania, Rumania

Романка *f* (*fem. form*) *see* Романец

романѝст *m* **1** specialist in Romance philology **2** specialist in Roman law **3** *rare* novelist

романистика *f* Romance philology

романистички *adj* <of> Romance studies

романѝстка *f* (*fem. form*) *see* романист 1

ромáнса *f Mus.* romance

романсиéр *m* novelist

романсиéрка *f* (*fem. form*) *see* романсиер

романсиéрски *adj* novelistic, novelist's

романсѝра *pf & impf* to adapt as a novel, to novelize

романски *adj* **1** Roman; Romance; Romanic; романски јазици Romance languages; романска филологија Romance philology; романски стил Romanesque **2** Romanian, Rumanian

романтѝзам -змот *m* romanticism

романтизѝра *pf & impf* to romanticize

ромáнтик -ци *m see* романтичар

романтика *f* romance

романтичар *m* romantic; romanticist; dreamer

романтичен -чна *adj* romantic; романтична поема romantic poem; романтични места romantic places

романтички *adj* romantic

ромб *m Geom.* rhombus

ромбичен -чна *adj* rhombic; ромбична антена rhombic aerial

ромбовиден -дна *adj* rhombic

ромбойд *m Geom.* rhomboid

ромбойден -дна *adj* rhomboid<al>

ромобѝл *m* scooter

ромол *m see* ромон

ромоли *impf see* ромони

ромон *m* murmur

ромони *impf* to murmur

ромонлив *adj* murmuring; ромонливи води murmuring waters

ромор *m see* ромон

ромори *impf see* ромони

ронатица *f* eroded ground

роначка *f* maize-husker, hulling machine

рондо *n Mus.* rondo

рони *impf* **I 1** to husk, hull; рони пченка to husk maize **2** to crush, crumble *trans.*; to wear away *trans.*; ❑ рони солзи to shed tears; тивка вода брег рони *prov.* still waters run deep **II – се 1** to crumble *intrans.*; to wear away *intrans.*; лебот се рони the bread is crumbling **2** *fig.* to weaken *intrans.*, ail

ронка *f* crumb (*also fig.*); ❑ до ронка to the last crumb, completely; една ронка just a crumb, very little

ронкичка *f dim. of* ронка

ронлив *adj* (*за леб и сл.*) crumbly; (*за тесто*) short; (*за земја*) friable; erosion-prone

ропот *m* mutter, grumble; без ропот without a murmur

ропски *adj* slavish; ропски труд slave labour; ропска послушност slavish obedience

ропство *n* **1** slavery; servitude **2** captivity; падне во ропство to fall into captivity

роптае *impf* to grumble, murmur

ропче *n dim. of* роб

роса *f* **1** dew; утринска роса morning dew **2** shower, drizzle; ситна роса заросила it started drizzling

росен -сна *adj* dewy, dew-covered; росни капки dewdrops

роси *impf* **1** to drizzle **2** to bedew

росица & росичка *f dim. of* роса

росопас *Bot.* (Chelidonium majus) celandine

ростбиф *m* roast beef

ростфрај *adj indecl.* stainless steel

ротација *f* **1** rotation **2** rotary press

ротациóнен -она *adj* rotary; ротациона машина rotary machine/press

ротѝра *pf & impf* **I** to turn *trans.*; to rotate *trans.* **II – се** to turn *intrans.*; to rotate *intrans.*

ротóнда *f* rotunda

ротор *m Tech.* rotor

роторен -рна *adj* rotor *attrib.*

рото-хартија *f* newsprint

рофја *f dial. see* ровја

рочен -чна *adj see* сроковен, срочен

рочиште *n see* срочиште

рошав *adj* dishevelled; (*за лице*) pockmarked

рошка *impf* to rummage

рошне *pf* рошна *aor. see* рошка

'рпалец -лци *m* dry twig

'рска *impf* to crunch; to munch

'рскав *adj* crunching, crunchy

'рскавица *f* cartilage; gristle

'рскавичав *adj* cartilaginous; gristly; 'рскавичаво месо gristly meat

'рскавичен -чна *adj see* 'рскавичав

'рскот *m* bang, banging, crashing, rumbling; се слушна 'рскот a bang was heard; ❑ 'рскот и плускот loud crash, din

'рскоти *impf* to bang, crash *intrans.*; 'рскоти, плускоти to crash around, make a din

'рскотница *f see* 'рскот

'рсне *pf* 'рсна *aor. see* 'рска

'рснува *impf of* 'рсне

'рт *m* **1** hound; greyhound **2** *Geog.* promontory, cape, headland; 'рт Добра Надеж Cape of Good Hope

РТВ *abbr.* (*радио-телевизија*) Radio and Television

'рти *impf* to germinate, sprout; *fig.* to develop *intrans.*

'ртица & 'ртка *f* hound/greyhound bitch

'ртулец -лци *m* germ, embryo; shoot; *fig.* first sign

'ртулче *n dim. of* 'ртулец

Руáнда *f* Rwanda

Руандец -дци *m* Rwandan

руандски *adj* Rwandan

Руанѓанец -нци *m see* Руандец

Руанѓанка *f see* Руантка

руанѓански *adj see* руандски

Руантка *f* (*fem. form*) *see* Руандец

руба *f* **1** clothes, attire, dress, garments; ❏ руба краси, руба гнаси fine feathers make fine birds **2** bride's trousseau; dowry

рубео̀ла *f Med.* rubeola, measles

рубиичка *f Bot.* (Leucanthemum vulgare) ox-eye daisy

рубин *m* ruby

рубинен *adj* ruby; ruby coloured

рубинов *adj see* рубинен

рубински *adj see* рубинен

рубља -бли *f* rouble

рубо *n see* руба

рубрика *f* <newspaper> column; heading; rubric

руво *n* dress, attire; невестинско руво bride's trousseau

руга[1] *f arch.* wage of a village servant

руга[2] *impf* **I** to scold, rebuke **II** – се to quarrel

руд *adj* **1** (обично за јагне) young, lively, fresh **2** reddish-brown **3** curly; руда коса curly hair

руда[1] *f* ore; железна руда iron ore

руда[2] *f* shaft (*of cart*), thill

рудар *m* miner

рударски *adj* miner's; mining; рударска капа miner's helmet; рударска ламба Davy lamp; рударски инженер mining engineer

рударство *n* mining

рудее *impf* to turn reddish, ruddy; to glow red; рудее зората dawn is breaking

руден -дна *adj* ore; рудна жица lode, ore vein; рудни наоѓалишта ore deposits; рудно богатство mineral wealth

руди *impf see* рудее

рудимѐнт *m* rudiment

рудиментѝрен -рна *adj* rudimentary

рудина *f* mountain pasture; meadow, clearing

рудища *f* reddish sheep

рудник -ци *m* mine; pit; рудник за јаглен coalmine, coal pit; рудник за злато gold-mine, placer

руднички *adj* mining, mine *attrib.*; рудничко раководство mine administration

рудокоп *m see* рудник

руе *impf* **1** dial. (за куче) to growl **2** to hum, buzz

руен -јна *adj f.p.* red; reddish; рујно вино red wine; руен коњ fiery steed; рујни образи rosy cheeks

руж *m* **1** lipstick **2** rouge

ружа[1] *f Bot.* (Rosa) rose; дива ружа *Bot.* (Rosa canina) dog-rose, wild rose; питома ружа cultivated rose; ❏ не му цутат ружи his life is no bed of roses

ружа[2] *impf* **I** to saddle **II** – се to get ready, prepare *intrans.*; се ружа за пат to prepare to set out

ружест *adj* rose-like

ружин *adj* rose; ружина вода rose-water; ружино масло attar of roses

ружица *f* **1** *dim. of* ружа **2** (за вино) *rosé*

ружичка *f dim. of* ружа

рузмарин *m Bot.* (Rosmarinus officinalis) rosemary

руина *f* ruin (*also fig.*)

руинѝра *pf & impf* to ruin, wreck

руј *m Bot.* (Rhus cotinus) sumac, young fustic

рука *impf see* рукне 1, 2

рукне *pf* рукна *aor.* **1** to shout, yell, bellow **2** to gush forth; to burst out; рукна вода од чешмата water gushed from the tap **3** to crowd in **4** to flare up, burst forth

рукнува *impf of* рукне

рула̀да *f Mus.* roulade

рулек -лци *m see* рулче

рулѐт *m* roulette

рулѐтка *f see* рулет

рулец -лци *m see* сугурец

рулче *n* baby

рум *m* rum

румба *f* rumba

румее *impf see* руменее <се>

румен[1] *m poet. see* руменило, руменина

румен[2] *adj* ruddy; rosy; румени образи rosy cheeks; румени јаболка red apples

руменее <се> *impf* to blush; to show red; руменееше зората dawn was breaking

руменило *n* **1** *see* руменина **2** rouge

руменина *f* redness; rosiness; ruddiness; руменина на лице rosy complexion

руменикав *adj* reddish

руменолик *adj poet.* rosy-cheeked

руменост *f* ruddiness, rosiness; blush

руна *f* rune

рунда *f Boxing* round; рунда пиво round of beers; рунда разговори round of talks

рунест *adj* fleecy, woolly

руно *n* fleece; ❏ златно руно golden fleece; прави од влакно – руно to make a mountain out of a molehill

рунски *adj* runic; рунски натписи runic inscriptions

рунтав *adj* shaggy; furry; hairy, hirsute; рунтаво куче shaggy dog; рунтави гради hairy chest

рунтавее *impf* to grow shaggy/hairy

рунтавко *m* shaggy dog

рунтее *impf see* рунтавее

рунце *n dim. of* руно

рупа[1] *f* ravine, gorge; hollow

рупа[2] *impf* to crunch, munch, champ

рупија -ии *f* rupee

рупка *impf dim. of* рупа[2]

рупне *pf* рупна *aor. see* рупа[2]

рупнува *impf of* рупне

рупоти *impf see* рупа[2]

рус *adj* fair-haired, blond; руса коса fair hair; ❏ руса среда *f Rel.* the fourth Wednesday between Easter and Whitsun

Рус *m see* Русин[2]

русалија -ии *m* participant in ritual sword-dance

русалка *f* water-nymph, naiad

русвај *m* chaos, mayhem

русее *impf* to become fair

русѝзам -змот *m* Russianism

Русија *f* Russia

русин[1] *m Bot.* (Dictamnus albus) dittany, fraxinella, hart's-eye

Русин[2] *m*, Руси *pl* Russian

Русинка *f* (*fem. form*) *see* Русин[2]

русист *m* specialist in Russian studies

русистика *f* Russian studies, Russian philology

русификација *f* Russification, Russianization

русифицѝра *pf & impf* to Russify, Russianize

руска *impf see* рупа²

рускавица *f dial.* kind of early apple

руски *adj* Russian

русокос *adj* fair-haired, blond

русолик *adj* fair of face, comely; bright

русоок *adj* blue-eyed

русофи́л *m* Russophil<e>

русофи́лка *f* (*fem. form*) *see* русофил

русофи́лски *adj* Russophile

русофи́лство *n* Russophilism

рути *impf rare* **I** to demolish, raze to the ground, tear down **II** – **се** to collapse, tumble down

рутина *f* routine

рутина *impf see* рути

рутине́р *m* **1** slave to routine, person set in his ways (of fixed habits) **2** skilled worker; professional

рутине́рство *n* **1** routine work **2** efficiency, professionalism

рутини́ран *adj* skilled; wily, canny

рутиште *n dial.* (*usu. pl*) clothes, apparel, garb

руфет *m colloq.* **1** (*облека*) clothes **2** fashion

руча *pf & impf* **1** to have lunch **2** *dial.* (*jаде*) to eat

ручек -ци *m* lunch; lunch-time

ручка *impf child.* to eat

ручок -ци *m see* ручек

рушвет *m colloq.* tip; bribe, graft

рушветчија -ии *m colloq.* bribe-taker

рушење *n* demolition

руши *impf* **I** to wreck, demolish, pull down; *fig.* to be the ruin (downfall) of; (*надежи*) to dash **II** – **се** to collapse, crumble, tumble down *intrans.*

рушител *m* destroyer, wrecker

рушки *adj f.p. see* фрушки

'рчи *impf see* 'рка

'рчка *impf colloq.* to tease, badger; не ме 'рчкај leave me alone!

'рчпал *m colloq.* boor, oaf, clod, blockhead

C

с *prep dial., f.p. see* со

с- & **со-** *verbal prefix indicating* **1** *unification, movement together*; собере to collect; сврзе to bind **2** *downward direction*; слезе to climb down; спушти to lower **3** *beginning of action*; списка to start squealing; срупа to chew, champ **4** *brief duration, with completion*; стапне to tread on **5** *completion, with definite result* согради to build (finish building); сошие to sew up

са *pron* (*only with certain nouns*) са зима all winter; са ноќ all night; *see* сиот

саан *m* large copper dish (bowl)

сaaнче *n dim. of* саан

саат *m colloq.* **1** hour; половина (пол) саат half an hour; ❏ му дојде саатот his turn/time came; со саати for hours on end; во ситни саати in the small hours **2** (*часовник*) clock; watch; саатот е точен the watch/clock is right; саатот оди напред the watch/clock is fast; ❏ види (разбере) колку е саатот to see the point, get the message; точен како саат as regular as clockwork **3** moment; во овој саат at this moment; во истиот саат at the same moment

саатчија -ии *m colloq.* (*часовничар*) clockmaker; watchmaker

саатчиски *adj colloq.* (*часовничарски*) clockmaker's; watchmaker's; саатчиски дуќан clockmaker's/watchmaker's shop

саба́јле *n & adv colloq.* (*утро*) morning; in the morning; ❏ утре сабајле never; pigs may fly!; that'll be the day!

сабајлина *f & adv colloq. see* сабајле

сабја *f* sword, sabre; јазикот е поостар од сабја *prov.* the pen is mightier than the sword; наведена (покорна, сложена) глава сабја не ја сече *prov.* better bend than break

сабјест *adj* sabre-shaped, sabre-like; сабјест лист falcate leaf

сабјиче *n & сабјичка f dim. of* сабја

сабјиште *n augm. of* сабја

сабјоклун *m Zool.* (Recurvirostra avosetta) avocet

сабјолик *adj see* сабјест

сабота *f* Saturday; Велја (Велика) сабота Holy Saturday, Easter Saturday; мртва сабота All Souls' Day; Тодорова сабота the feast of St Theodore, Theodore's Day (*first Saturday in Lent*); ❏ тие се петок и сабота they are inseparable

сабота́жа *f* sabotage

сабота́жен -жна *adj* sabotage; саботажни акции acts of sabotage

саботен -тна *adj* Saturday; саботен ден Saturday

саботéр *m* saboteur

саботéрски *adj* saboteur's

саботéрство *n see* саботажа

саботúра *pf & impf* to sabotage

саботјанин *m Rel.* Sabbatarian; Seventh-day Adventist

саботјански *adj Rel.* Seventh-day Adventist

саботнина *f* **1** memorial service (*held on Saturdays*) **2** newly-weds' traditional Saturday visit to relatives

Сава *f* the <River> Sava

савак -ци *m* sluice-gate

саван *m arch.* (*покров*) shroud, winding-sheet

савáна *f* savannah

савáнски *adj* savannah

савски *adj* Sava *attrib.*

саглам *adj indecl. colloq.* good; honest, decent, steady

САД *abbr.* (*Соединети американски држави*) United States of America, USA

сад¹ *m* **1** vessel, container; земјан сад earthenware pot; измие садови to wash the dishes (wash up) **2** *Biol.* vessel, duct, canal; крвни садови blood-vessels

сад² *m* **1** newly planted vineyard (*up to three years*) **2** (*овоштарник*) orchard

садач *m* planter

саде¹ *n dim. of* сад¹

саде² *adv colloq.* (*само*) only

сади *impf* **1** to plant **2** сади јајца/кокошка to set eggs/a hen (*to hatch eggs*)

садúзам -змот *m* sadism

садилка *f see* садило

садило *n* planting stick, dibble, dibber

садúст *m* sadist

садистички *adj* sadistic; sadistically

садúстка *f* (*fem. form*) *see* садист

садница *f* seedling; sapling

садно *n* saddle sore

садноса *pf* to develop saddle sores (*of horse, donkey*)

садносува *impf of* садноса

садовина *f* hard soil

садразам *m arch.* Grand Vizier (*Ottoman prime minister*)

садријазам *m see* садразам

саѓа *f* (*usu. pl*) soot; smut; fly ash; црн како саѓи black as soot

саѓав *adj* sooty, covered with soot

саѓинка *f* black sheep/cow

саѓоса *pf* to cover/blacken with soot

саѓосан *pt see* саѓав

саѓосува *impf of* саѓоса

саем *m* fair, show, exhibition; трговски саем trade fair; саем на книгата book fair

саемски *adj* <of a> fair; саемски денови fair-days; show-days

сажен -жни *m arch.* sazhen (*2.13 metres*)

саја -аи *f* saya, cloak

сајбија -ии *m colloq.* (*стопан*) master, head of household, householder

сајдиса *pf colloq.* to take into consideration, take account of; to respect

сајдисува *impf of* сајдиса

сајла *f* wire cable

сајмиште *n* fairground; show-ground, exhibition centre

сак *m* **1** (*за риба*) fishing-net **2** (*за на пазар*) <shopping> bag

сака *impf* **I 1** to want; сака да јаде to be hungry; ако сакаш if you want; if you wish; како што сакаш as you like (wish); ❑ без да сака unwittingly; unwillingly; сакаш-нејќеш whether you like it or not; willy-nilly; што сака нека биде! што сакало било! come what may! сакам да кажам I mean **2** to like; to love; си ја сака работата he loves his work; ❑ така те сакам that's my boy/girl; now you're talking **3** to wish; ти сакам сè најубаво I wish you all the best **4** to need; сака да се јаде one has to eat; месо не сака да јадеш you shouldn't eat meat **5** *dial.* to ask for; to look for; му сакал сто денари he asked him for a hundred denars; го сакам детето I'm looking for the child **II** – се **1** *impers.* (*with dat.*) to feel like; ми се сака I want to, I would like to; така му се сакаше that's what he wanted **2** to be in love, love each other

сакагија *f* glanders; farcy

сакаглив *adj* infected with glanders, glanderous; сакаглив коњ glanderous horse

сакалдиса *pf colloq.* **I** to upset; to annoy, irk **II** – се to get upset

сакалдисува (се) *impf of* сакалдиса (се)

сакан **1** *pt* beloved; longed for, coveted; сакано дете beloved child; сакано патување eagerly awaited (longed for) trip **2** (*as noun*) саканиот, саканата loved one, beloved

сакана *adv* на сакана on purpose, deliberately; не беше на сакана it was not intentional (deliberate)

саканик -ци *m* beloved; favourite; lover

саканица *f* (*fem. form*) *see* саканик

сакање *n* from сака; *arch.*, *literary* wish, will; сакањето Божје God's will

сакат *pt* **1** crippled; mutilated; lame; сакат човек cripple; сакат во ногата lame **2** *fig.* faulty, defective; сакато решение bad (unsound) decision

сакати *impf* **1** to cripple; to mutilate, maim; to disable **2** *fig.* to ruin, wreck

сакатиса *pf dial. see* осакати

сакатник -ци *m* cripple

сакатница *f* (*fem. form*) *see* сакатник

сакатост *f* disability; *fig.* defective state, imperfection

саке *n* sake (*Japanese alcoholic drink*)

саклет *m colloq.* worry, anguish, uneasiness, discomfort; саклет ми е I feel uneasy/uncomfortable

саклетиса (се) *pf colloq. see* сакалдиса (се)

саклетисува (се) *impf of* саклетиса (се)

сакó *n* jacket

сакрамéнт *m Rel.* sacrament

сакраментáлен -лна *adj* sacramental

саксиче *n* & **саксиица, саксиичка** *f dim. of* саксија

саксија -ии *f* flowerpot; ❑ не растел в саксија he's no fool (you can't fool him)

саксофóн *m Mus.* saxophone

саксофонúст *m Mus.* saxophonist

сакуле *n colloq. dim. of* сако

сал¹ *m arch.* float, raft

сал² *adv colloq. see* саде, само

сала *f* hall; сала за играње ballroom; изложбена сала exhibition hall (showroom)

салáма *f* salami

саламáндер -дри *m* & **саламáндра** *f Zool.* (Salamandra maculosa) salamander, *see* дождалец

саламура *f* (*солило*) brine, souse; стави во саламура to salt in brine

саламурен -рна *adj* salted (*in brine*)

саламџија -ии *m* salami maker/seller

салана *f* wooden structure for curing meat

салата *f* 1 *Bot.* (Lactuca sativa) lettuce 2 salad; салата од зелка cabbage salad; coleslaw; руска салата Russian salad 3 *fig.* jumble; mess

салатник -ци *m* salad bowl

салва *f* salvo (*also fig.*); салви на смеа peals (roars) of laughter

Салвадóрец -рци *m* Salvadorean, Salvadoran, Salvadorian

Салвадóрка *f* (*fem. form*) *see* Салвадорец

салвадóрски *adj* Salvadorean, Salvadoran, Salvadorian

салвéта *f see* салфета

салдúра *pf* & *impf* to balance accounts (the books)

салдиса *pf colloq.* to send off, send on one's way

салдисува *impf of* салдиса

салдо *n Book-keeping* balance; ❏ во позитивно салдо in the black; во негативно салдо in the red; црвено салдо overdraft

салеп *m* salep

салепчија -ии *m* salep-vendor

салицúл *m* salicylic acid (canning preservative)

салицúлен -лна & **салицúлов** *adj* salicylic; салицилна (салицилова) киселина salicylic acid

сало *n* fat; lard

салóн *m* 1 hall; салон на театар house, auditorium of theatre 2 salon; drawing-room, parlour; литературен салон literary salon; салон за дами beauty parlour; hairdresser's salon

салóнски *adj* salon; салонски живот society life; салонско воспитание good breeding (society manners); салонски кавалер ladies' man; ❏ салонски политичар armchair politician; салонски социјалист champagne socialist

салтанат *m colloq.* pomp, splendour; ❏ продава салтанати to show off

салтанатлија *adj indecl. colloq.* pompous, showy

салто *n* 1 somersault; двојно салто double somersault 2 *fig.* turning-point

салтомортáле *n* 1 somersault 2 *fig.* risky move

салýт *m Mil.* salute

салутúра *pf* & *impf* to salute

салфéта *f* serviette, <table->napkin

салфéтка *f dim. of* салфета

салца *f* tomato sauce/purée/paste; ketchup

салце *n dim. of* сало

салџија -ии *m arch.* raftsman

сам *pron* & *adj* 1 oneself, itself; самиот директор the director himself; самата чесност the soul of integrity; ❏ зборува сам со себе to talk to o.s.; сам од (по) себе of one's (it's) own accord; сам за себе живее to keep to o.s. 2 alone, on one's own; живее сам to live alone; сам – самичок (сам – сам сам) all alone 3 the very; на самиот раб on the very edge, right on the edge

самак -ци *m see* самец

самар *m* 1 pack-saddle; имаш ли грб, самари триста *prov.* there's always work for the willing;

спроти самарот и зобницата *prov.* to cut one's coat according to one's cloth 2 hod-carrier's shoulder-pad 3 *fig.* (*бреме, товар*) burden

самарен -рна *adj* pack-saddle

самари *impf* 1 to saddle; самари магаре to saddle a donkey 2 *colloq., fig.* to make a fool, make (*s.o.*) look silly

самариште *n augm. of* самар

самарјанин -јани *m* Samaritan; милостивиот самарјанин the good Samaritan

самарјанка *f* (*fem. form*) *see* самарјанин

самарјански *adj* compassionate, benevolent, philanthropic

самарјанство *n* philanthropy, compassion, benevolence

самарче *n dim. of* самар

самарџија -ии *m* saddler

самарџилница *f* saddlery

самарџиски *adj* saddler's; самарџиски дуќан saddler's shop; самарџиска игла saddler's bodkin (packing needle)

самба *f* samba

самец -мци *m* 1 bachelor, single man 2 solitary person

самечки *adj* 1 bachelor's, single; самечки живот single life; самечки стан bachelor flat, *colloq.* bed-sitter 2 solitary

самит *m* summit, summit conference

самица *f* 1 single woman 2 (*во затвор*) solitary confinement cell

самицок -цка *adj.* alone, on one's own

самне *pf* самна *aor.* 1 *impers.* to dawn, grow light; ❏ ми самна it dawned on me; I saw the light; на еден дури не му се стемни, на друг не може да му самне *prov.* it's an ill wind that blows nobody good 2 *impers.* (*with acc.*) to meet (greet) the dawn; нè самна кај реката dawn found us by the riverside

самнува *impf of* самне

самнување *n* dawn, daybreak

само *adv, conj* 1 only, merely, just; nothing but; ❏ само и само just, simply; само да . . . just to . . . ; не само . . . , туку (но, ами) и . . . not only . . . but also; само еден момент just one moment; само кал е he's covered in mud 2 constantly, all the time; тие само зборуваат they talk all the time 3 само што only just, scarcely, hardly; само што влезе he's just come in 4 but, however; куќата е убава, само скапа the house is beautiful, but expensive

само- (*in compounds*) auto-, self-

Самоа *f* Samoa

самоанализа *f* self-analysis, introspection

Самоанец -нци *m* Samoan

Самоанка *f* (*fem. form*) *see* Самоанец

самобитен -тна *adj* original, distinctive; distinct

самобитност *f* originality

самовар *m* samovar

самовила *f* 1 (*добра*) fairy; nymph; (*лоша*) elf 2 *Zool.* (Pavonia pavonia) emperor moth

самовилски *adj* nymph/fairy *attrib.*, elfin

самовласник -ци *m* autocrat

самовласнички *adj* autocratic; самовласничко управување autocratic rule

самовласт *f see* самовластие

самовластен -сна *adj* autocratic; despotic

самовластие *n* absolute rule, autocracy; despotism; чиновничко самовластие bureaucracy

самовљубен *adj* self-centred, narcissistic; самовљубени луѓе self-seekers

самовљубеност *f* self-love, narcissism, self-worship

самоволен -лна *adj* 1 wilful, headstrong, wayward; arbitrary 2 unauthorized; irresponsible; самоволно изостанување absence without leave

самоволие -ија *n* licence; self-will; arbitrariness

самоволја *f see* самоволие

самоволник -ци *m* self-willed/wayward person; a law unto himself

самоволница & **самоволничка** *f* (*fem. form*) *see* самоволник

самоволност *f see* самоволие

самоволство *n see* самоволие

самовоспита се *pf* to educate o.s.

самовоспитание *n* self-education

самовоспитува се *impf of* самовоспита се

самоглавец -вци *m see* самоглавник

самоглавник -ци *m* solitary person

самоглавница *f* (*fem. form*) *see* самоглавник

самогласен -сна *adj* Phon. vocalic

самогласка *f* Phon. vowel; акцентирани самогласки accented vowels

самодеен -јна *adj* amateur; самодеен хор amateur choir

самодеец -јци *m* amateur

самодејност *f* 1 independent action, spontaneous activity; initiative 2 amateur performances/activities; amateur art

самоделен -лна & **самоделски** *adj* home-made

самодива *f see* самовила

самодивски *adj see* самовилски

самодисциплѝна *f* self-discipline

самодоволен -лна *adj see* самозадоволен

самодржавен -вна *adj* autocratic; самодржавно устројство autocratic system

самодржавие & **самодржавје** *n* autocracy

самодржец -шци *m* autocrat

саможив & **саможивен** -вна *adj* selfish, self-centered; саможивни трговци ruthless businessmen

саможивец -вци *m see* саможивник

саможивник -ци *m* egoist, selfish person, self-seeker

саможивност & **саможивост** *f* selfishness, egoism

саможртва *f* self-sacrifice

самозаборав *m* oblivion; stupor; abandon; пие до самозаборав to drink o.s. into a stupor; се сака до самозаборав to be blindly in love

самозаборава се *impf of* самозаборави се

самозаборави се *pf* to forget o.s.; to become presumptuous; to become conceited

самозаборавува се *impf see* самозаборава се

самозадоволен -лна *adj* self-satisfied, complacent, smug

самозадоволи се *pf* 1 to be self-sufficient 2 to masturbate

самозадоволност *f* & **самозадоволство** *n* self-satisfaction, smugness

самозадоволува се *impf of* самозадоволи се

самозадоволување *n* 1 self-sufficiency 2 masturbation

самозалаже се *pf* самозалажа се *aor.* to deceive (delude, fool) o.s.

самозалажува се *impf of* самозалаже се

самозаљубен *adj see* самовљубен

самозаљубеност *f see* самовљубеност

самозапалив *adj* self-igniting

самозаштита *f* self-defence; убиство во самозаштита murder in self-defence

самозаштити се *pf* to defend (protect) o.s.

самозаштитува се *impf of* самозаштити се

самозван *pt* self-styled, false, would-be; самозван министер self-styled minister

самозванец -нци *m* impostor; pretender

самоизградба *f* self-development, self-education

самоизгради се *pf* to develop (educate) o.s.

самоизградува се *impf of* самоизгради се

самоиздржи се *pf* to support (keep, maintain) o.s.

самоиздржува се *impf of* самоиздржи се

самоиздршка *f* self-support, self-maintenance

самоизмама *f* self-delusion, self-deception

самоизмами се *pf see* самозалаже се

самоизмамува се *impf of* самоизмами се

самоизмачи се *pf* to torment (torture) o.s.

самоизмачува се *impf of* самоизмачи се

самоиницијатѝва *f* initiative; drive

самоиницијатѝвен -вна *adj* enterprising, *colloq.* go-ahead

самоиницијатѝвност *f* initiative; drive

самоисклучи се *pf* to exclude o.s., cut o.s. off (од – *from*)

самоисклучува се *impf of* самоисклучи се

самоистребување *n* self-destruction, self-annihilation

самојски *adj* Samoan

самоквас *m* sour (curdled) milk

самокиш *m see* самоквас

самоков *m* steam-hammer

самоконтрѓла *f* self-control

самокритика *f* self-criticism

самокритикува се *pf & impf* to criticize o.s.

самокритичен -чна *adj* self-critical

самокритички *adj see* самокритичен

самокритичност *f* self-criticism

самокуќник -ци *m* solitary man, *see* самоглавник

самокуќница *f* (*fem. form*) *see* самокуќник

самољѓубец -пци *m* self-centred person, self-admirer

самољѓубив *adj* self-centred, self-admiring

самољѓубивост *f* egoism, self-love, self-admiration

самољѓубие *n see* самољѓубје

самољѓубје *n* pride, egoism, self-love, self-admiration; повреди нечие самољубје to hurt s.o.'s pride

самонабљудение *n see* самонабљудување

самонабљудува *impf* to observe o.s.

самонабљудување *n* self-observation, self-analysis; introspection; метод на самонабљудување introspective method

самонадеан *adj* self-assured, *see* самоуверен

самонадеаност *f* self-assurance

самоник -ци *m* self-sown plants/trees

самообвинение -ија *n* self-accusation; self-reproach

самообвини се *pf* to accuse/reproach/blame o.s.

самообвинува се *impf of* самообвини се

самообразова се *pf & impf see* самообразува се

самообразование *n* self-education, self-instruction

самообразованост *f see* самообразуваност

самообразовен -вна *adj* <of, for> self-instruction,

self-taught; **самообразовен курс** teach-yourself course

самообразува се *pf & impf* to educate (teach) o.s.

самообразуваност *f* self-education, self-instruction

самоограничи се *pf* to limit (confine) o.s.; to restrain o.s.

самоограничува се *impf of* самоограничи се

самоодбрана *f* self-defence

самоодреди се *pf see* самоопредели се

самоодредува се *impf of* самоодреди се

самоодржување *n* self-preservation; self-sustenance

самооплодување *n* self-fertilization, *Bot.* autogamy

самооправдание *n* self-justification

самоопределба *f Pol.* self-determination; **право на самоопределба** right to self-determination

самоопредели се *pf* to determine one's own future

самоопределува се *impf of* самоопредели се

самоосвести се *pf see* самосвести се

самоосвестува се *impf of* самосвести се

самоосознава се *impf of* самоосознае се

самоосознае се *pf see* самосвести се

самоосуда *f* self-condemnation

самооткажување *n* self-denial, self-sacrifice

самопожртвуван *adj* self-sacrificing, self-denying; selfless; **самопожртвуван труд** selfless toil; **самопожртвувана љубов** self-effacing (devoted) love

самопожртвуваност *f* self-sacrifice, self-denial

самопознавање *n* self-knowledge

самопоканет *pt* uninvited

самопо́мош *f* self-help

самопонижување *n* self-abasement, self-deprecation

самопослуга *f see* самопослужување

самопослужување *n* **1** self-service; cafeteria **2** supermarket

самопосматрање *n* self-observation, self-analysis; introspection

самопо́чит *f* self-respect

самопре́гор *m* selflessness, self-sacrifice; dedication

самопрегорен *-рна adj see* самопожртвуван

самопрегорност *f* self-sacrifice; unselfishness, selflessness

самопре́зир *m* self-contempt

самопридонес *m* self-imposed tax, voluntary tax

самопризнание *-ија n* confession, admission

самопрогонство *n* self-banishment, self-exile

саморазвиток *m* self-development

самораст *m see* самоник

саморачен *-чна adj see* своерачен

саморекла́ма *f* self-advertisement

самороден *-дна adj rare* **1** (*чист*) pure; **самородно злато** pure (native) gold **2** (*роден*) natural; **самороден мајстор** born craftsman

самосвесен *-сна adj* self-conscious

самосвесност *f* self-awareness; self-consciousness

самосвест *f* self-awareness, consciousness

самосвести се *pf* to become self-aware

самосвестува се *impf of* самосвести се

самосовладување *n* self-control, self-possession

самосознавање *n* consciousness

самост *f see* самотија

самостоен *-јна adj* **1** independent, self-governing; **самостојна држава** independent state **2** independent, self-reliant, self-supporting, self-employed;

самостоен занаетчија self-employed tradesman; **самостојни работници** free-lance workers; **самостоен поглед** independent view

самостојност *f* independence; self-reliance

самота *f see* самотија

самотвор & самотворен *-рна adj* self-made, spontaneously generated

самотен *-тна adj* **1** lonely; lone; alone; **самотен човек** recluse; lonely person **2** isolated, secluded

самоти *pron* **пред самоти војна** just before the war

самотија *f* **1** solitude; isolation; loneliness; **сака самотија** to like one's own company **2** privacy, seclusion, peace and quiet **3** isolated/remote/deserted place, back of beyond, godforsaken place

самотник *-ци m* recluse, hermit, loner

самотница *f* (*fem. form*) *see* самотник

самотнички *adj* lonely; solitary; **самотнички живот** solitary life

самотност *f* solitude; loneliness

самоток *m* (*за вино*) must; (*за мед*) virgin honey

самотува *impf see* самува

самоубеден *adj* self-confident, self-assured

самоубеденост *f* self-confidence, self-assurance

самоубедување *n see* самоубеденост

самоубива се *impf of* самоубие се

самоубие се *pf* **самоуби се** *aor.* to commit suicide

самоубиец *-јци m* suicide

самоубиствен *adj* suicidal

самоубиство *n* suicide; *fig.* self-destruction

самоуважение *n* self-respect, self-esteem

самоуверен *adj* self-confident, self-assured

самоувереност *f* self-confidence, self-assurance

самоук[1] *adj* self-taught, self-educated

самоук[2] *-ци m* self-taught (self-educated) person

самоунижи се *pf* to demean o.s., humiliate o.s.

самоунижува се *impf of* самоунижи се

самоунижување *n see* себеунижување

самоуништување *n* self-destruction, self-annihilation

самоуправа *f* self-government, autonomy

самоуправен *-вна adj* <of, for> self-government/self-management

самоуправува се *impf* to govern o.s., manage one's own affairs

самоуправување *n* self-management; **работничко самоуправување** workers' self-management

самоуче *n dim. of* самоук[2]

самоуштво *n* self-instruction, self-education

самофалбација *-ии m see* самофалец

самофалец *-лци m* boaster, braggart

самофалка *f* (*fem. form*) *see* самофалец

самофалство *n* self-praise, boastfulness, braggartism

самохипно́за *f* self-hypnosis

самоцел *f* end in itself

самоцелен *-лна adj* as an end in itself; **самоцелна уметност** art for art's sake

самочувство *n* feeling; **самочувство на нерешителност** feeling of uncertainty

самоштина *f colloq.* isolation; solitude; loneliness

самрак *m* (*no pl*) twilight, dusk

самрачен *-чна adj* dim, shadowy; twilight

самски *adv f.p.* alone, on one's own, separately; **одеше самски напред** he went on ahead on his own

самува *impf* to live alone; to lead a solitary life, shun company, live in seclusion

самур *m Zool.* (Mustela zibellina) sable (*animal and fur*)

самур<лија> *adj indecl.* sable; самур-калпак sable cap

санаториум *m Med.* sanatorium

санација *f* **1** *Med.* rehabilitation; recuperation **2** *fig.* stabilization; renovation; financial rehabilitation, financial recovery; санација на финансиската состојба stabilization of the financial situation; санација на оштетени згради renovation of damaged buildings; мерки за санација remedial measures; заем за санација consolidation/rehabilitation loan

санациóнен -она & **санациски** *adj* <of, for> rehabilitation; <of, for> stabilization/renovation; санациони работи renovation

сангвѝник -ци *m* sanguine person

сангвиничар *m see* сангвиник

сангвиничен -чна *adj* sanguine

сангвиничка *f (fem. form) see* сангвиник

сангвинички *adj see* сангвиничен

сангвиничност *f* sanguine disposition

сандак -ци *m* **1** trunk; chest; box; сандак пиво crate of beer; ❑ турне некому сандак to trip s.o. up **2** coffin; мртовечки сандак coffin

сандала *f* sandal

сандалија[1] -ии *f colloq.* (стол) chair

сандалија[2] -ии *f colloq., dial. see* сандала

сандаче *n dim. of* сандак; casket; поштенско сандаче letter-box, *Am.* mailbox

сандвич *m see* сендвич

сандолѝна *f* canoe

санѝра *pf & impf* **1** *Med.* to rehabilitate **2** *fig.* to consolidate; to renovate; to rehabilitate financially, restore financial soundness; санира зграда to renovate a building; санира положба to stabilize a situation

санита́р *m* hospital attendant, medical orderly

санита́рен -рна *adj* sanitary; sanitation; санитарна инспекција food/sanitary inspection; санитарен јазол lavatory, washing and toilet facilities

санита́рка *f (fem. form) see* санитар

санитéт *m* **1** health-care services; *Mil.* medical corps **2** medical orderly

санитéтски *adj* <of, for> public health; *Mil.* <of, for> medical corps

санка[1] *f* sledge, sled; детски санки toboggan

санка[2] *impf* **I** to give (*s.o.*) a ride on a sledge **II** – се to sledge, toboggan

санки *adv colloq. see* санким

санким *adv colloq.* as though, as if

санкција -ии *f* **1** *Leg.* sanction, approval **2** *pl* sanctions; економски санкции economic sanctions

санкционѝра *pf & impf* to ratify; to sanction

Санмаринец -нци *m* person from San Marino

Санмаринка *f (fem. form) see* Санмаринец

Сан Марино *n* San Marino

санмарински *adj* San Marinese

санс *m Cards* Swedish whist

санскрит *m* Sanskrit

санскритѝст *m* Sanskrit scholar

санскритски *adj* Sanskrit

сантиграм *m* centigram

сантилѝтар -три *m* centilitre

сантим *m* **1** centime **2** *colloq. see* сантиметар 1

сантимéтар -три *m* **1** centimetre **2** tape-measure

сантимка *f see* сантим

сантрач *m colloq.* **1** (*вид скара*) gridiron, barbecue **2** (*карирано платно*) chequered cloth **3** (*ограда*) enclosure, fence

санцак -ци *m Hist.* sanjak

сања *f* **1** *see* санка[1] **2** type of cart (*used in certain mountain regions*)

сап *m* helve, haft

сапи *pl* crupper, croup

сапраг -зи *m see* запрега[1]

сапун *m* soap; калап сапун bar (cake) of soap; сапун за перење laundry soap; сапун за бричење shaving soap

сапунар *m* soap-maker; soap vendor

сапунарка *f (fem. form) see* сапунар

сапунарница *f* soap-works; soap shop

сапунарски *adj* <of> soap-making; soap-maker's; soap vendor's

сапунарство *n* soap production

сапунен *adj* soap; сапунен меур soap-bubble

сапунéрка *f* soap-dish

сапунест *adj* soapy

сапунец *m hyp. of* сапун

сапуниса *pf* to soap

сапунисува *impf of* сапуниса

сапуница *f* suds, lather; меур од сапуница soap-bubble

сапунски *adj.* soap *attrib.;* сапунска серија soap opera

сапунче *n dim. of* сапун

сапунџија -ии *m colloq. see* сапунар

сапунџилница *f colloq. see* сапунарница

сапунџиски *adj colloq. see* сапунарски

сарага *f Zool.* (Alburnus) bleak

Сараево *n* Sarajevo

сараевски *adj* Sarajevo *attrib.*

сараевчанец -ни *m* Sarajevan, person from Sarajevo

сараевчанка *f (fem. form) see* сараевчанец

сарај -аи *m* seraglio

сарајлија[1] -ии *f* type of round flat loaf; type of sweetmeat

сарајлија[2] *m see* сараевчанец

сарајлика *f see* сараевчанка

сарајски *adj* seraglio; сарајски порти seraglio gates

сарак -ци *m dial.* (*драг*) pole, bar

сарандар *m colloq.* forty-day prayers for the dead

сараф *m arch.* money-changer

сарафин -фи *m arch. see* сараф

сарафлак *m arch.* money-changer's trade

сарач *m* saddler; harness-maker; leather-worker

сарачки *adj* saddler's; harness-maker's; leather-worker's; сарачки дуќан saddlery; harness shop

сарачлак *m* saddler's/harness-maker's/leather-worker's trade

сарачница *f* saddlery; harness shop

сараца *f colloq.* (*non-specific name applied to various diseases*) dysentery; scrofula; glanders; farcy

сараџица *f Bot.* (Polygonatum multiflorum) Solomon's seal

сардéла *f see* сардина

сардѝна *f Zool.* (Sardina pilchardus) sardine; ❑ стиснати како сардини packed like sardines

сардиница & сардинка *f dim. of* сардина

сардиса *pf colloq.* to surround, besiege

сардисан *pt colloq.* surrounded, besieged; ❑ од сите страни Ѓорѓи сардисан to be up against the wall; to have no choice

сардисува *impf of* сардиса

сардонски *adj* sardonic; сардонска смеа sardonic laugh/laughter

сарикана *f arch.* depilatory, mixture for removing hair

саркáзам -змот *m* sarcasm; sarcastic remark

саркастичен -чна *adj* sarcastic

саркастички *adj see* саркастичен

саркастичност *f* sarcasm

саркóма *f Med.* sarcoma

саркофáг -зи *m* sarcophagus

сарма *f Cul.* stuffed cabbage/vine leaves; дроб-сарма lamb's caul stuffed with liver and rice, *cf.* haggis

саска *impf colloq.* to set (*a dog, etc.*) (*на – on to*); to egg on; немој да го саскаш don't egg him on!

сатана *m* **1** Satan, the Devil; ❑ бегал од ѓаволот, паднал на сатаната he jumped from the frying-pan into the fire **2** *fig.* fiend, malevolent person

сатански *adj* satanic, diabolical; fiendish

сатар *m* chopper, cleaver

сателúт *m* **1** satellite; вештачки сателит artificial satellite **2** *fig.* stooge, *colloq.* hanger-on, yes-man

сателúтски *adj* satellite; сателитска влада satellite government

сатен *m* satin; sateen; свилен/памучен сатен satin, sateen

сатенски *adj* satin/sateen; сатенска јака satin/sateen collar

сатинéт *m* satinette

сатинúран *adj* satin<ed>; сатинирана хартија satin paper

сатир *m Myth.* satyr

сатúра *f* satire

сатúрик -ци *m see* сатиричар

сатиричар *m* satirist

сатиричен -чна *adj* satirical

сатирички *adj see* сатиричен

сатисфакција -ии *f* satisfaction; бара сатисфакција to demand satisfaction

сатрап *m* satrap

сатрапски *adj* satrap's; despotic

саудиарабиски *adj see* саудиски

Саудиец -ијци *m* Saudi Arabian, Saudi

Саудијка *f (fem. form) see* Саудиец

Саудиска Арабија *f* Saudi Arabia

саудиски *adj* Saudi-Arabian, Saudi

сауна *f* sauna

сафа *f colloq.* jug, pitcher, ewer

сафари *n* safari

сафир *m* sapphire

сафра *f colloq.* nausea; weariness, tedium; ме фати сафра I felt sick/faint; *colloq.* I was fed up; сафра е to be a pain in the neck

сафт *m* sauce; gravy; juice; ќофте во сафт rissoles in sauce

сафтен *adj* in sauce/gravy

сафтијáн *m* morocco <leather>

сафче *n dim. of* сафа

Сахара *f* the Sahara <Desert>

Сахарец -рци *m* Saharan

сахарúн *m* saccharin

сахарúнски *adj* <of> saccharin; сахарински прашок saccharin powder

Сахарка *f (fem. form) see* Сахарец

сахарски *adj* Saharan

сач *m* iron lid covering dough during baking; ❑ надвор е сач it's baking hot outside

сачица *f see* сачка

сачка *f* stick, switch

сачма *f* fine shot

сачмен *adj* <of> fine shot

сацаде *n see* сецаде

сацак -ци *m colloq.* trivet

саштиса *pf colloq.* to confuse; to stupefy; to stun

саштисува *impf of* саштиса

св. *abbr. (свети)* Saint, St

свадба *f* wedding; ❑ сребрена/златна/дијамантска свадба silver/gold/diamond wedding; би свадба и мина all good things come to an end; по свадба тапани what's done cannot be undone; it's too late to call back yesterday; it's no use crying over spilt milk

свадбар *m* wedding-guest

свадбарина *f* marriage fee

свадбарка *f (fem. form) see* свадбар

свадбарски *adj* <of> wedding-guest, wedding; свадбарска песна wedding-song

свадбен *adj* wedding; свадбен фустан wedding-dress; свадбена веселба wedding celebration; ❑ свадбен пат, свадбено патување honeymoon

свадбува *impf* to celebrate a wedding

свалка *pf* **I** to knock down, fell; to topple *trans.* **II** – **се** to roll *intrans.*; to fall down; to topple *intrans.*

свалкува (се) *impf of* свалка (се)

свампири се *pf* **1** to turn into a vampire *intrans.* **2** *fig.* to go mad

свампироса се *pf* to turn into a vampire *intrans.*

свампиросува се *impf of* свампироса се

свампирува се *impf of* свампири се

свари *pf* **I** **1** to cook/boil/stew *trans.*; to distil *trans.*; свари кафе to brew (make) coffee; ❑ го свари гравот he fell ill **2** (*за желудник*) to digest **3** *fig.* (*сфати*) to grasp, understand; ова не можам никако да го сварам I can't grasp this at all **II** – **се** to cook/boil/stew *intrans.* (*also fig.*); (*за кафе*) to brew *intrans.*; се свари ли веќе јадењето? is the meal done (ready) yet?; ❑ се свари the heat is killing him

сварлив *adj* digestible

сварливост *f* digestibility

сварува (се) *impf of* свари (се)

сват *m* **1** son's/daughter's father-in-law; kinsman by marriage **2** wedding-guest

сватица *f see* сваќа

сватовен -вна *adj see* сватовски

сватовски *adj* **1** related by marriage **2** wedding; сватовска песна wedding-song

сватовство *n* kinship by marriage

сватовштина -и, -ње *m & f* kinsman/kinswoman by marriage

сватоса се *pf* to become relatives by marriage

сватосува се *impf of* сватоса се

сватува *impf* to attend a wedding

сваќа *f* **1** son's/daughter's mother-in-law; kinswoman by marriage **2** loaf (*traditionally baked by the bridegroom's guests for the bride's mother*)

сведбина *f see* светлост 1

сведе *pf* **I 1** to bring down, lead down; (*вода*) to drain off *trans.* **2** to reduce; ❏ сведе на нула to bring to nought (nothing) **II – се 1** to come down (*на – то*); to boil down (*то*); неговата улога се сведе на неколку реченици his role amounted to a few sentences **2** (*сведне се*) to bend, lean (*forward, over*) *intrans.*

своден -дни *m* festival; patron saint's day

сведлив *adj* reducible; сведлив број reducible number

сведливост *f* reducibility, reducibleness

сведне *pf* сведна *aor.* **I** to incline, bend, bow *trans.*; to lower, bring down; сведне глава to bow one's head **II – се** to lean, bend (*over, forward*), bow down *intrans.*; to stoop

сведнува (се) *impf of* сведне (се)

сведок -ци *m* witness; повика за сведок to call as witness; ❏ жив сведок a living witness (proof)

сведочење *n* testimony; лажно сведочење perjury; false witness

сведочи *impf* to testify, bear witness, attest (*дека – that*); неговата популарност сведочи за неговиот талент his popularity is evidence of his talent

сведоштво *n* **1** testimony, evidence; proof **2** *see* свидетелство

сведува (се) *impf of* сведе (се)

сведување *n* reduction; сведување на минимум (на најмала мера) reduction to the bare minimum

свеж *adj* fresh; свежа риба fresh fish; на свеж воздух in the fresh air; свежи бои fresh (bright) colours; свежо лице fresh complexion; свежи новости recent news

свежест *f see* свежина

свежина *f* freshness

свежост *f see* свежина

свекло *n Bot.* (Beta vulgaris) beet, beetroot, *see* цвекло

свеклов *adj* beet<root>

свекор *m* father-in-law (*husband's father*)

свекрва *f* mother-in-law (*husband's mother*)

свекрвин *adj* mother-in-law's; свекрвин јазик *Bot.* (Sansevieria trifasciata) mother-in-law's tongue

свекров *adj* father-in-law's; свекрова глава *Bot.* (Echinocactus tortuosus) hedgehog cactus, barrel cactus

свенат *pt* faded; withered (*also fig.*); свенати цвекиња faded flowers; свенати лисје withered leaves; свенато лице wizened face

свене *pf* свена *aor.* to wilt, wither *intrans.*; to fade *intrans.* (*also fig.*)

свенува *impf of* свене

свесен -сна *adj* **1** conscious, aware; deliberate **2** conscientious, responsible

свеси *pf poet. see* сведне

свеска[1] *f* sister-in-law (*wife's sister*)

свеска[2] *f* **1** (*тетратка*) exercise book, notebook **2** (*том, број*) volume, number, issue, fascicle

свесност *f* consciousness; deliberateness

свест *f* consciousness; загуби свест to lose consciousness; му се врати свеста he regained consciousness; ❏ ми се вие (врти) свеста I feel giddy (dizzy)

свести *pf* **I 1** to revive *trans.* **2** *fig.* to bring (*s.o.*) to his senses **II – се 1** to regain consciousness, revive *intrans.*, come to **2** *fig.* to come to one's senses, see reason

свестува (се) *impf of* свести (се)

свесува *impf of* свеси

свет[1] *m* **1** world; страни на светот cardinal points <of the compass>; пропаст на светот the end of the world; ❏ бел свет the world, the whole wide world; Божји свет the world, God's earth; видел свет he has seen the world, he has knocked about the world; види <бел> свет to appear; to be born; го испрати на тој свет he dispatched him, he did him in, he launched him into eternity; за сè на светот for everything in the world; за ништо на светот not for anything in the world; на крај <на, од> свет<от> at/to the end of the world; на овој свет in this world; Новиот свет the New World; од крај <на> свет<от> from the end<s> of the earth; пушти на свет to start, put into circulation; to release; свет (село) се плени, баба се чешла *prov.* Nero fiddles while Rome burns; Стариот свет the Old World; тие се два света they are worlds apart **2** society; people; world; чуден свет strange people; многу свет lots of people; христијанскиот свет Christian people, Christendom; словенскиот свет Slavdom, the Slavs; животински и растителен свет animal and plant kingdom **3** life; ❏ светов (веков) е скала life has its ups and downs

свет[2] *adj* **1** holy, sacred; *fig.* cherished; светиот дух the Holy Ghost (Spirit); свето евангелие the gospel; свет долг sacred duty **2** saint; свети Петар St Peter; свето лице holy man/woman

Свéта Гóра & Светá Гóра *f* <Mount> Athos

светало *n* small domestic lamp

свете *n dim. of* светало

светен *pt* sanctified, hallowed; светена вода holy water; светено лице baptized person

светец -тци *m* saint; животот на светците the life of the saints; прогласи за светец to canonize; ❏ се прави светец to look as if butter wouldn't melt in one's mouth; никој не е светец nobody is perfect; каков светец, таков венец (спроти светецот и клепалото) everyone gets his just deserts; to each according to his merits

светечки *adj* saintly

свети[1] *impf* **1** to shine, glow (*also fig.*); to glisten; сонцето свети the sun is shining; свеќата свети the candle is burning; свети од среќа to beam (glow) with happiness; свети од чистота to be sparkling clean **2** to illuminate, light <up> *trans.*; (*with dat.*) to hold a light (*for s.o.*) **3** to be lit up (lighted); прозорецот му светеше there was light in his window **4** *fig., colloq.* to stand idly by

свети[2] *impf* to bless, consecrate, hallow; свети вода/ масло to bless water/oil; ❏ ќе му свети масло he's going to kill him

свети[3] *adj see* свет[2] 2

светија -ии *m colloq. see* светец

светилен -лна *adj* **1** illuminating; luminous; illuminated; светилна фирма illuminated sign **2** *dial.* (*светол*) bright, shining; светилна ноќ moonlit night

светилиште *n* temple (*also fig.*); светилиште на науката a temple of learning

светилка *f* light, lamp; електрична светилка electric lamp

светилник -ци *m* **1** *see* светало **2** lighthouse **3** *fig.* beacon, luminary, leading light

светило *n* **1** *see* светало **2** *see* светилник **3** **3** *fig.* (*usu. pl*) sight, eyes; му се зеде светилото he has lost his sight (gone blind)

светина *f see* светиња

светиња *f* **1** shrine **2** sacred object/site; ❑ чува како светиња to cherish as the apple of one's eye; смета некого за светиња to worship the ground s.o. walks on

светител *m* saint, holy man

светителка *f* (*fem. form*) *see* светител

светителски *adj* saintly; holy; светителска икона holy icon

светица *f* (*fem. form*) *see* светец; ❑ се прави светица she pretends to be the Virgin Mary

светка *impf* to flash; to sparkle; to gleam, glint; светкаат светкавици lightning is flashing; очите му светкаа his eyes glinted

светкав *adj* gleaming; glittering; светкава ноќ starlight/moonlit night

светкавица *f* lightning

светкавичен -чна *adj* <of> lightning; as quick as lightning; светкавичен удар lightning strike; со светкавична брзина with the speed of lightning; светкавична војна blitzkrieg

светли *impf see* свети[1]

светлив *adj* bright, shining; glittering; shiny

светликав *adj* twinkling, glistening; shimmering, gleaming; светликави ѕвезди twinkling stars; светликава слика glossy photo

светлина *f* light (*also fig.*); lightness; brightness; сончева светлина sunlight, sunshine; по светлина на (од) свеќа by candlelight; дневна светлина daylight, light of day; вклучи светлина to turn (put, switch) on the light; ❑ во вистинска светлина in its true light (colours); во друга светлина in a different light; во светлината на . . . in the light of . . . ; излезе на светлина, види светлина to come to light, come out; фрли светлина врз нешто to throw (shed) light on s.th.

светлинка *f dim. of* светлина

светличав *adj see* светликав

светло[1] *n* light; beam; headlight; запали светло to turn on a light; ❑ дава зелено светло to give the all-clear, give the go-ahead

светло[2] *adv* light, bright

светло- (*in compounds*) light, pale; светложолт pale yellow, light yellow

светлокос *adj* fair-haired

светлолик *adj* fair-skinned

светлоносец -сци *m* torch-bearer; *fig.* luminary

светлоок *adj* blue-eyed/green-eyed

светлосен -сна *adj* <of> light; светлосни зраци rays of light; светлосни сигнали light signals; flashing lights; traffic lights; *Astron.* светлосна година light-year

светлост *f* **1** (*светлина*) light<ness>; brightness **2** Highness, Serene Highness

светлота *f rare see* светлост 1

светне *pf* светна *aor.* **1** to flash; to shine (*also fig.*); светкавица светна lightning flashed; му светнаа очите his eyes lit up; ❑ ми светна мисла a thought occurred to me (flashed through my mind) **2** to clean, polish, make shiny; светне чевли to shine (polish) shoes; светне куќа to clean a house thoroughly **3**

(*with dat.*) to hold/flash a light (*for s.o.*); светни ми малу со свеќата hold the candle for me for a moment! **4** *fig.* to strike *trans.*; to slap; to stab

светник -ци *m* brazier (*for illumination*)

светнува *impf of* светне

световен -вна *adj* secular, temporal; worldly; световни песни secular songs; световни лица lay people

светоглед *m* world view, *Weltanschauung*

светогорски *adj* of/from Mount Athos

светол -тла *adj* **1** bright (*also fig.*); light, illuminated; светли ѕвезди bright stars; светла соба light (bright) room; светла иднина bright future; светли спомени happy memories; светло лице radiant face; светол поглед cheerful look; светли царе Your Majesty! Serene Highness! **2** (*no боја*) light, pale; светол костум a light-coloured suit; светла коса fair hair **3** clear; светли солзи sparkling tears; светол глас silvery (ringing) voice

светост *f* **1** sanctity, holiness; saintliness; светоста на црквата the sanctity of the Church **2** (*ecclesiastical title*) Grace; ваша светост Your Grace, My Lord!

светрум *adv* at once, in a flash, in no time

светски *adj* **1** world; worldwide; светска војна world war; светско првенство world championship; светски глас worldwide reputation **2** genteel; refined; светско воспитание genteel upbringing; светски човек a man of the world

светулка[1] *f Zool.* (Lampyris noctiluca) firefly; glow-worm

светулка[2] *impf see* светка

свеќа *f* **1** candle; taper; восочна свеќа wax candle; ❑ прав како свеќа straight as a ramrod; <про>даде рог за свеќа to sell s.o. a pig in a poke; си го бара со свеќа he's looking for trouble **2** *Tech.* spark<ing>-plug **3** candela; candle power; ламбичка од пет свеќи lamp of five candle power **4** *Gymnastics* shoulder stand (balance)

свеќава *impf see* свети[2]

свеќалник -ци *m see* свеќник

свеќар *m* chandler; candle-maker/-seller

свеќарка *f* (*fem. form*) *see* свеќар

свеќарник -ци *m see* свеќник

свеќарница *f* chandler's shop, chandlery

свеќарски *adj* chandler's; свеќарски занает the trade of a chandler

свеќарство *n* chandlery

свеќица *f* spark<ing>-plug

свеќиче *n dim. of* свеќа 1

свеќичка *f dim. of* свеќа 1, 2

свеќник -ци *m* candlestick

свечен *adj* solemn; festive; formal; свечен ден festive day; свечена облека formal attire, gala dress; свечен глас solemn voice; свечена клетва solemn oath

свеченост *f* **1** solemnity **2** celebration<s>, festivity (festivities), ceremony

свечери *pf* *impers.* (*of nightfall*) to overtake (*s.o.*), descend (*on s.o.*); нè свечери во шумата nightfall found us in the wood **II – се** to get dark; *impers.* (*of darkness*) to fall; се свечери night has fallen; *see* стемни (се)

свечерува (се) *impf of* свечери (се)

свечерум *adv* towards evening; *see* квечер, квечерина[2], квечерум

свешник -ци *m see* свеќник

свештен *adj* (*свет*) holy, sacred; свештено лице priest, clergyman; свештена книга Bible; holy book, Scripture

свештеник -ци *m* clergyman, priest

свештенички *adj* priestly; priest's; свештенички одежди priest's vestments, sacerdotal robes; свештеничкиот сталеж the priesthood

свештенодејство *n* religious rite, office

свештенодејствува *impf* to officiate (*at a church service/ceremony*)

свештенство *n* clergy, priesthood; православното свештенство the Orthodox priesthood

свештилник -ци *m dial. see* свеќник

свива (се) *impf of* свие (се)

свивка *f* 1 roll, ball (*of string, etc.*) 2 *dial.* (*свијок*) bend, curve

свиден -дна *adj* dear, cherished; свидни спомени fond memories

свидетел *m see* сведок

свидетелство *n* certificate; diploma; матурско свидетелство matriculation certificate, school-leaving certificate

свидетелствува *impf see* сведочи

свиди се *pf* (*with dat.*) to please; му се свиди девојката he liked the girl

свидлив *adj* pleasing, pleasant, agreeable, likeable

свидува се *impf of* свиди се, *see* свиѓа се

свиѓа се *impf see* свиди се

свие *pf* сви *aor.* I 1 *see* свитка²; ❑ свие гнездо to build a nest 2 to turn *intrans.*; свие десно to turn right 4 (*with acc., заболи*) to ache, cause pain; ме сви стомакот my stomach began to ache II – се *see* свитка² се

свијок -ци *m* curve, bend (*in road, river*)

свика¹ *pf* to shout, cry out; (*with dat.*) to shout at, tell off, scold

свика² *pf* to call together, assemble *trans.*, summon; to convene *trans.*; свика седница to call a meeting; свика конгрес to convene a congress

свикнат *pt* accustomed (*на – to*), used to; свикнат е веќе he has got used to it already

свикне *pf* свикна *aor.* I 1 to accustom (*на – to*), habituate; to train *trans.* 2 to get used (*на – to*), become accustomed; свикне на нова средина to get used to new surroundings II – се *see* I 2

свикнува (се) *impf of* свикне (се)

свикува¹ *impf of* свика¹

свикува² *impf of* свика²

свикување¹ *n* shouts, cries, shouting

свикување² *n* convocation, assembly

свила *f* silk; фустан од свила silk dress; вештачка свила artificial silk, rayon

свилар *m* silk-producer; silk-merchant

свиларка *f Zool.* (Bombycilla garrulus) waxwing

свиларница *f* silkworm farm; silk factory

свиларски *adj* silk-producer's/-trader's; свиларски занает sericulture

свиларство *n* silk trade, silk manufacture

свилее се *impf* to shine like silk; се свилее тревата the lawn has a silky sheen

свилен *adj* 1 silken; silky; silk; свилен конец silk<en> thread; свилен фустан silk dress; свилена постава silk lining; свилена буба silkworm 2 *fig.* timid; gentle

свиленикав & свиленкав *adj* silky

свилест *adj* silky

свили *impf f.p.* to dress in silk *trans.*

свилокос *adj* silky-haired

свилорун *adj* silky-fleeced

свинг *m* 1 *Boxing* swing 2 (*танц*) swing

свински *adj* 1 <of a> pig, pig's; pork; свинска кожа pigskin; свинска чекутина hog's bristle; свинска маст lard; свинско месо pork; свинско печено roast pork; свинска кочина pigsty; ❑ на свински стриг when pigs fly 2 *colloq.* piggish, swinish; свински постапки contemptible acts, dirty tricks 3 (*as noun*) свинско *n* pork

свинче *n dim. of* свиња; piglet

свинштина *f* 1 mess; каква свинштина! what a mess! 2 *fig.* base act; dirty trick

свиња *f* 1 *Zool.* pig; swine; hog; sow; дива свиња (Sus scrofa) wild boar, feral pig; ❑ му прилега како звонец (самар) на свиња he has as much use for it as a cow has for side pockets; разбира колку свиња од диња (знае свиња што е диња) he doesn't know the first thing about it; убавите (зрелите) круши свињите ги јадат the devil's children have the devil's luck; fortune favours fools; видела свињата рогозина, па посакала и постела *prov.* give him an inch and he'll take a mile 2 *fig., colloq.* swine, cad

свињар *m* swineherd; pig-breeder

свињарка *f* (*fem. form*) *see* свињар

свињарник -ци *m* pigsty (*also fig.*)

свињарница *f see* свињарник

свињарски *adj* swineherd's/pig-breeder's

свињарство *n see* свињогојство

свињарче *n dim. of* свињар

свињогојство *n* pig-breeding

свињски *adj see* свински

свињче *n see* свинче

свињштина *f see* свинштина

свиок -ци *m see* свијок

свирајка *f see* свирка¹, свирол

свиралка *f see* свирка¹, свирол

свирач *m* musician

свирба *f* music

свиреп *adj* fierce; savage; furious; свирепа борба fierce struggle; свирепи мерки drastic measures

свирепост *f* ferocity, viciousness; severity, harshness

свирепство *n see* свиреп(ост)

свирец¹ -рци *m rare see* свирач

свирец² -рци *m Zool.* (Gryllus campestris) cricket, *see* жужалец, прцорец

свири *impf* 1 to play; свири на пијано to play the piano; музиката престана да свири the music stopped; ❑ како ќе ти свират, така ќе играш you will have to dance to their tune; свири втора виолина to play second violin; *fig.* to play second fiddle 2 to whistle; to sound a horn, honk, hoot; локомотивата свири the locomotive whistles; ветрот свири the wind howls; свири <со уста> to whistle 3 to chirp, hum; to chirrup; свират прцорци crickets are chirping

свирка¹ *f* 1 whistle; siren; horn; pipe; shepherd's flute 2 music

свирка² *impf* 1 (*со уста*) to whistle 2 (*за публика*) to hiss, boo 3 (*на инструмент*) to play

свиркар *m dial. see* свирач

свирне *pf* свирна *aor.* **1** to whistle **2** *fig.* to whack

свирнува *impf of* свирне

свирол *m Mus.* pipe (*traditional flute*)

свиролче *n dim. of* свирол

свирче *n dim. of* свирка² 1

свириија -ии *m dial. see* свирач

свиснат *pt* hanging <down>, drooping; flabby

свисне¹ *pf* свисна *aor.* to sag, droop; to deteriorate; свисне глава to hang one's head

свисне² *pf* свисна *aor.* to whistle

свиснува¹ *impf of* свисне¹

свиснува² *impf of* свисне²

свисти *impf* (*свири*) to whistle; to howl, bluster; свистат куршуми bullets are whizzing (whistling) by

свита¹ *f* suite, retinue, escort

свита² *f* thick woollen cloth

свита³ *f Mus. see* суита

свитен *adj* made of thick woollen cloth

свитка¹ *f see* светулка¹

свитка² *pf* **I 1** to bend *trans.*; to crook *trans.*; to fold *trans.*; свитка колена to bend one's knees; свитка писмо to fold a letter; ❏ свитка глава пред некого to bow to s.o.; свитка грб to bob, duck, bow and scrape; свитка опашка to put one's tail between one's legs; свитка раменици to shrug one's shoulders **2** to twist *trans.*; to roll <up> *trans.*; свитка некому рака to twist s.o.'s arm; свитка цигара to roll a cigarette; свитка ракави to roll up one's sleeves (*also fig.*); ❏ свитка некому врат to wring s.o.'s neck **3** (*завитка*) to wrap; свитка подарок to wrap a present **II – се 1** to bend (*down, over*); to stoop; се свитка од тежината на нешто to bend/sag under the weight of s.th.; дрвото се свитка на ветрот the tree bent in the wind **2** to curl <up> *intrans.*; to wriggle *intrans.*; to twist *intrans.*; to roll *intrans.*; (*од болки и сл.*) to squirm, writhe

свиткува (се) *impf of* свитка² (се)

свитлив *adj* **1** pliable, flexible; свитливо дрво supple tree **2** *fig.* malleable, compliant; лесно свитлив easily manipulated

свитливост *f* flexibility; pliancy

свиток -ци *m see* свивка 1

свлекува (се) *impf of* свлече (се)

свлече *pf* свлеков *1st p. sg aor.* **I 1** to drag down; *fig.* свлече товар од себе to free o.s. of a burden **2** (*соблече*) to undress *trans.*; to strip; свлече угул гол to strip s.o. naked **II – се 1** to slide (slip) down *intrans.*; му се свлекле чорапите his socks slipped down **2** (*соблече се*) to undress *intrans.*, get undressed

свлечка *pf* to <start to> drag down

свлечкува *impf of* свлечка

свлечува (се) *impf see* свлекува (се)

свод *m* arch, vault; *fig.* firmament; небесниот свод the vault of heaven

сводена -дна *adj* arched

сводест *adj* arched; vaulted; сводест ходник vaulted passage

своди (се) *impf see* сведува (се)

сводник -ци *m* pander, pimp, procurer

сводница & сводничка *f* (*fem. form*) *see* сводник

своднички *adj* pander's, pimp's, procurer's

сводништво *n* procurement, pimping

сводообразен -зна *adj see* сводест

своевиден -дна *adj* distinctive, original, peculiar

своевидност *f* peculiarity; originality; oddness; uniqueness

своеволен -лна *adj* self-willed, wilful; capricious; wayward, arbitrary, irresponsible; своеволни постапки irresponsible actions

своеволие *n* self-will, wilfulness; arbitrariness

своеволник -ци *m* self-willed person

своеволничи *impf literary* to be self-willed; to act wilfully/irresponsibly

своеволничка *f* (*fem. form*) *see* своеволник

своеволност *f see* своеволие

своевремен *adj* timely, opportune; well-timed; своевремена акција well-timed action

своевремено *adv* in time, in good time, opportunely

своевременост *f* timeliness, opportuneness

своеглав *adj* headstrong, obstinate, stubborn

своеглавост *f* obstinacy, stubbornness

своеобразен -зна *adj* distinctive, original, peculiar

своеобразност *f* peculiarity; originality; oddness, uniqueness

своерачен -чна *adj* made with one's own hands; hand-written; своерачен потпис personal signature

своера́чно *adv* (*направен*) with one's own hands; (*напишан*) in one's own hand

своетина *f* kith and kin, one's family/relations; ние сме своетина we are related

своештина *f see* своетина

своина *f rare see* сопственост

своински *adj rare* property; ownership

свој, своја, свое, *pl* свои **1** *pron* one's (*my, your, etc.*) own; седне на свое место to sit down in one's seat; си ја сака својата работа he likes his work; има своја куќа he has his own house, he has a house of his own; ❏ за своја сметка at one's own expense; на свој начин in one's own way; на своја глава (рака) by oneself; in one's own way; умре со своја смрт to die a natural death; оди по свој пат to go one's own way; сè во свое време one thing at a time, all in good (due) time; со свои зборови in one's own words; со свои очи with one's own eyes; свои луѓе сме we're not strangers **2** (*as noun*) свои *pl* one's family/relatives; one's own people; ние сме свои we are related **3** (*as noun*) свое *n* one's bit; one's own (way); ❏ си го каже своето to say one's piece; to speak one's mind; остане на своето to insist on one's own point of view; to stick to one's guns; го стори своето he did his bit, he did what he could; секој си го фали своето there's nothing like one's own, one's own is always best; тера по свое to turn a deaf ear to s.th; to have a mind of one's own

својствен *adj* typical, characteristic (*за – of*); својствени особини characteristic features; тоа е својствено за него that's typical of him

својствено *adv* in one's own way

својственост *f* peculiarity, idiosyncracy

својство *n* **1** property, quality, trait, characteristic, attribute **2** *fig.* role, capacity; во својството на претседател in his capacity as chairman

својштина *f see* своетина

сворче *n* whistle; pipe; shepherd's flute

сврака *f Zool.* (Pica pica) magpie

свракин *adj see* сврачешки

сврачешки *adj* magpie's; сврачешко гнездо magpie's nest

сврачка *f see* сврака

сврби *impf dial.* (*only in 3rd p.*) to itch, *see* чеша 2

сврбогаска *f Bot.* (Rosa canina) dogrose

свргав *adj* **1** (*за дрво*) knotty **2** *fig.* (*за време*) harsh, severe

сврдел -дли *m* **1** (*бургија*) auger; gimlet; borer; (*шило*) bradawl; drill; *Med.* burr; сврдел в торба не се крие *prov.* love and a cough cannot be hid; со сврдел ум не се става *prov.* he that is born a fool is never cured **2** *fig., colloq.* fidgety person; *colloq.* go-getter **3** *dial. see* вител 1

сврдлар *m* maker or seller of awls/drills

сврдле *n dim. of* сврдел

св020000рдли *impf* to bore, drill

сврдло *n see* сврдел

сврели *pf* **I** to heat <up>, warm up *trans.* **II – се 1** to warm up, heat up *intrans.* **2** *fig.* to get angry, lose one's temper

сврелува (се) *impf of* сврели (се)

свреска *pf* to cry out, shriek

врескува *impf of* свреска

свржи *impf* (*of the wind*) to sting, cut

сврзан *pt* joined, connected, linked; (*за говор*) coherent, cogent

сврзано *adv* coherently

сврзе *pf* сврза *aor.* **I 1** to tie together, bind up, join *trans.* **2** to link, connect *trans.*; новиот пат ќе го сврзе селото со градот the new road will link the village with the town **3** (*по телефон, радио и сл.*) to connect *trans.*, put through **4** *fig.* to put (*s.o.*) in touch (*co – with*) **II – се 1** to connect, combine *intrans.*; to link up *intrans.* **2** to make contact, get in touch (*co – with*); to switch over, cross *intrans.* се сврзав со поштата I got through to the post office **3** *fig.* to establish close/intimate ties (*со некого – with s.o.*); to unite *intrans.*, join forces

сврзлив *adj* joinable

сврзник -ци *m Gram.* conjunction

сврзува (се) *impf of* сврзе (се)

сврска *f* link, connexion; tie, bond; coupling; *Sport.* <left/right> inside forward, inside left/right

сврталиште *n* meeting place, club; сврталиште на уметници a gathering place for artists

сврти *pf* сврте *aor.* **I 1** to turn *trans.*, direct; сврти глава to turn one's head; сврти страница to turn a page; сврти пушка на некого to turn one's gun on s.o.; ❏ сврти некому ум to turn s.o.'s head; сврти внимание на то turn (direct) attention to; сврти лист to turn over a new leaf; не може пара да сврти he can't save a penny **2** to turn *intrans.*; сврти лево to turn left; ❏ сврти на подобро to take a turn for the better **3** to change; to switch; сврти разговор to change the subject; сврти на играње they started dancing **II – се 1** to turn (*кон – to*) *intrans.*; to appeal (*кон – to*); се сврти на друга страна to face the other way; to turn over; to turn away; се сврти кон некого to turn/appeal to s.o.; ❏ нема каде да се свртиш there's no room to move; се сврти за 180 степени to do an about-face; се сврти во гробот to turn in one's grave **2** *fig.* to turn, change (*на – into*) *intrans.*; жалоста се сврти на радост sorrow turned to joy

свртиште *n see* сврталиште

свртува (се) *impf of* сврти (се)

свруќи (се) *pf see* сврели (се)

свруќува (се) *impf of* свруќи (се)

свршен *pt* **1** finished, complete, *colloq.* over and done with; свршена работа finished work, completed task; *fig.* closed matter **2** *Gram.* perfective; свршен вид на глаголот the perfective aspect of the verb; минато свршено време aorist

свршеник -ци *m* fiancé, betrothed

свршеница *f* (*fem. form*) *see* свршеник; fiancée

свршенички *adj* engagement; свршенички прстен engagement ring

свршиI *pf* **I 1** to finish, end *trans.*; to complete; to accomplish; to terminate, conclude *trans.*; to close, wind up *trans.*; сврши медицина to graduate in medicine; сврши работа to finish a job; ❏ сврши работа! *iron.* well done!; сврши нашето! *colloq.* we've had it! *colloq.* we're done for!; сврши со некого to finish with s.o.; to break up with s.o. **2** to finish, use up, consume; ги сврши парите he spent all his money **3** to finish, end *intrans.*; to come to an end; *sl.* to come **4** to perish, end one's life; to end up; сврши на улица to end up in the street **II – се** *see* **I** 3; добро се сврши it ended well

свршиII *pf* **I** to engage, betroth **II – се** to get engaged

свршок -ци *m rare see* завршок²

свршуваI (се) *impf of* сврши¹ (се)

свршуваII (се) *impf of* сврши² (се)

свршувачкаI *f colloq. see* крај 1

свршувачкаII *f* engagement, betrothal

СДСМ *abbr.* (*Социјалдемократски сојуз на Македонија*) Social-Democratic Union of Macedonia

сеI *3rd p. pl pres. of* сум

сеII *reflexive pron* oneself; се мие to wash o.s., wash *intrans.*

сèI *pron n* everything, all; ❏ дава сè од себе to do one's best; не е сè изгубено all is not lost; тоа не е сè that's not the whole story; you ain't seen nothing yet; па сè до ... down to; подготвен на сè ready for anything; пожелува некому сè најубаво to wish s.o. all the best; пред сè in the first place; сè е можно anything could happen; сè живо <и диво> everything under the sun; сè и сешто odds and ends; сè или ништо all or nothing; double or quits; сè на сè all in all; all things considered

сèII *adv* **1** always, constantly; сè тоа го зборува he is forever saying that; ❏ сè уште still; при сè што ... although ... **2** nevertheless, all the same, in spite of everything; ти сè ќе наминеш кај нас you'll still come to see us **3** (*for emphasis in comparison*) even more, more and more; сè пострашен more and more terrifying/frightening; ❏ сè повеќе more and more; сè помалку less and less

се- (*in compounds*) all-, pan-, omni-; сесилен all-powerful; сеопфатен all-inclusive; сенароден national; севластен omnipotent

сеалка *f see* сејалка

сеа́нса *f* meeting; seance

сеач *m see* сејач

сеачка *f see* сејачка

себап *m colloq.* **1** good turn, kindness, favour; направи некому себап to do s.o. a favour **2** motive, reason

себаплија *adj indecl. colloq.* helpful, kind

себапчија -ии *m colloq.* helpful (kind) person

себе<си> *reflexive pron (dat. себе<си>; other cases себе<си>, се)* oneself; ❏ си рече сам со себе (си рече себеси) to say to o.s.; се убие себеси to kill o.s.; дојде на себе<си> to come to, come round; to come to one's senses; надвор од себе<си> е to be beside o.s.; не е на себе<си> he is not quite himself; се најде себеси to find o.s.; to get one's bearings; сам по себе by oneself/itself; владее со себе to be in control of o.s.; to behave; затвори се во себе to become introverted, withdraw into one's shell; земе на себе to take upon o.s.; работи над себеси to work beyond one's capacity; гледа само за себе to look after number one

себељубец -пци *m* egoist, self-centred person

себељубив *adj* self-centred, selfish, self-admiring, self-seeking

себељубивост *f* egoism, selfishness, self-love, self-admiration

себељубие *n see* себељубивост

себељубје *n see* себељубивост

себеунижување *n* self-abasement, self-deprecation

себечки *adv dial.* selfishly, for o.s.

себичен -чна *adj* selfish, self-centred

себичник -ци *m* egoist, selfish person, self-seeker

себичница *f (fem. form) see* себичник

себичност *f* selfishness, egoism

себлаг *adj usu. in the expression:* себлаг Господ most gracious (benign) Lord

севастокра́тор *m Hist.* Prince

севда *f colloq.* 1 love, passion 2 *fig.* sweetheart

севдалија *adj indecl. colloq.* enamoured; passionate

севдалинка *f* love-song

севдалиски *adj colloq.* passionate, romantic

севдоса *pf colloq.* 1 to fall in love with; севдоса една девојка to fall in love with a girl **II** – се to fall in love; тие се севдосаа they fell in love

севдосува (се) *impf of* севдоса (се)

севезден *adv see* везден

север *m* north; дува северот the north wind is blowing

северен -рна *adj* north, northern; northerly; северен пол North Pole; северна полутопка northern hemisphere; северен ветер north<erly> wind; северен елен reindeer

северец *m see* северник

северко *m see* северник

северлив *adj* of/exposed to the north wind

северник -ци *m* north<erly> wind

северница *f* 1 *Astron.* North Star, pole star 2 (на компас) compass needle

северно- (*in compounds*) north-; северноатлантски North Atlantic; северноамерикански North American

северњак -ци *m* northerner

северњачка *f (fem. form) see* северњак

северњачки *adj* northerner's; северњачки темперамент northern temperament

северозапад *m* north-west

северозападен -дна *adj* north-west<ern>; north-westerly; северозападен ветер nor'-wester<ly>

североисток *m* north-east

североисточен -чна *adj* north-east<ern>; north-easterly; североисточен ветер nor'-easter<ly>

севидлив *adj* all-seeing; севидливо око all-seeing eye

севишен -шна *adj* almighty, omnipotent; (*as noun*) *m* севишниот the Almighty

севкупен -пна *adj* total, entire; overall, general

севласт *f* omnipotence

севластен -сна *adj* omnipotent, almighty

севозможен -жна *adj* 1 of every kind; various; севозможни пречки all sorts of obstacles 2 *rare* (*семожен*) omnipotent, almighty; севозможен владетел omnipotent ruler

севозможност *f* variety; omnipotence

севте *n see* сефте¹

сега¹ *adv* now, at present; in a moment; сега дојде he has just come; сега ќе дојде he'll be here shortly; ❏ ами сега? what now? what next? сега за сега for the time being; сега едно, сега друго now one thing, now another

сега² *impf* to reach (*no – for*)

сегашен -шна *adj* present, current, present-day; сегашна мода today's fashion; ❏ сегашно време the present; *Gram.* present tense; сегашната работа не оставај ја за утре *prov.* don't leave to the morrow what you can do today!

сегашнина *f* the present

сегашница *f see* сегашнина

сегашно *n rare see* сегашнина

сегашност *f* the present, present (modern) times; во сегашноста in the present; at present

сегде<ка> *adv see* секаде

сегмент *m* segment

сегментација *f* segmentation

сегментен -тна *adj* segmental, segmentary; segmented

сегне *pf* сегна *aor. see* сега²

сегнува *impf of* сегне

сегрега́т *m* s.th. segregated (separated); segregate

сегрегација *f* segregation; расна сегрегација racial segregation

сегреги́ра *pf & impf* to segregate, separate

сед & седав *adj* grizzled, grey; со седа коса grey-haired

седалиште *n see* седиште

седалка *f see* седало

седало *n* 1 seat; стол со плетено седало a chair with a wicker seat 2 *see* седело

седалче *n dim. of* седело

седба *f* crop<s>; sowing

седелиште *n see* седиште

седелка¹ *f see* седело

седалка² *f see* седенка

седело *n* nest; <hen's> roost; ❏ и на ѓаволот седелото му го знае he is well-informed; ќе дојде кокошката на седело my turn will come

седелце *n dim. of* седело

седенка *f* party; приреди седенка to arrange a party

седеф *m* 1 mother-of-pearl, nacre 2 *Bot.* (Ruta graveolens) rue

седефен -фна *adj* mother-of-pearl; седефно копче mother-of-pearl button

седефлија *adj indecl.* mother-of-pearl

седечки *adj* sitting, seated; sedentary; седечки став sitting position, sedentary posture

седи *impf* 1 to sit; седи на стол to sit on a chair; седи на маса to sit at table; ❑ ни оди, ни седи there's no pleasing him; седи како на игли (трње, клинци) to be on tenterhooks; седи на два стола to sit on the fence; седи <по> турски to sit cross-legged (tailor-fashion); седи без работа to sit idle; седи дома to stay at home **2** *colloq.* to live, reside; седи в град to live in town; село фали, в град седи *prov.* to play it safe; to hedge one's bets **3** (*with dat.*) to suit; како ми седи палтово? how does this coat suit me?

седимéнт *m* sediment, deposit; dregs

седиментáција *f* sedimentation

седимéнтен -тна *adj* sedimentary, sedimental; седиментни карпи sedimentary rocks

седимéнтски *adj see* седиментен

седиште *n* **1** seat, place; слободно седиште vacant seat **2** (*на власт и сл.*) seat; (*на претпријатие и сл.*) head office, headquarters, main office; седиштето на Обединетите нации the seat of the United Nations

седла *impf* to saddle; седла коњ to saddle a horse

седлар *m* saddler

седларница *f* saddlery

седларски *adj* saddler's; седларски занает saddler's trade

седларство *n* saddler's trade

седленце *n dim. of* седло

седлест *adj* saddle-shaped

седло *n* **1** saddle; seat **2** (*на планина*) col, saddle

седловина *f see* седло 2

седма *num see* седмина 1

седмак -ци *m* **1** seven-year-old animal **2** *see* седмаче

седмаче *n dim.* premature baby (*born in the seventh month of pregnancy*)

седмерец -рци *m Prosody* seven-syllable line

седми *num adj* seventh; ❑ седма сила the Fourth Estate, the press

седмина *num* **1** seventh; пет седмини five sevenths **2** (*of men and mixed groups*) seven

седмица[1] *f literary* (*недела*) week

седмица[2] *f see* седумка

седмоаголен -лна *adj see* седумаголен

седмоаголник -ци *m see* седумаголник

седмоглав *adj* seven-headed; седмоглаво чудовиште seven-headed monster

седмогодишен -шна *adj see* седумгодишен

седмокатница *f see* седумкатница

седмокласен -сна *adj obs.* of seven classes (forms); седмокласно образование seven years' schooling

седмокласник -ци *m obs.* seventh-former

седмокласничка *f* (*fem. form*) *see* седмокласник

седмокрак *adj* seven-pointed; seven-legged; with seven branches

седмокрил *adj* seven-winged

седмолетка *f* **1** seven-form primary school **2** seven-year plan

седмолист *adj Bot.* heptamerous, seven-petal; седмолисно растение heptamerous plant

седмомесече *n see* седмаче

седморен -рна *adj* sevenfold, septuple

седморка *f see* седумка

седмосложен -жна *adj see* седумсложен

седмостран *adj Math.* seven-sided, heptagonal

седмочлен *adj* of seven members; седмочлена комисија a seven-member committee

седне *pf* седна *aor.* **1** to sit down *intrans.*, take a seat; *fig.* to get down to a job **2** to seat *trans.*; седне некого на стол to seat (sit, put) s.o. on a chair

седница *f* meeting; session; assembly; држи седница to hold a meeting; пленарна седница plenary session

седнува *impf of* седне

седокос *adj* grey-haired

седржител *m* God Almighty

седум *num* seven; седум години seven years

седум- (*in compound*) seven-, hept<a>-, sept<i>-

седумаголен -лна *adj Math.* heptagonal

седумаголник -ци *m Math.* heptagon

седумгодишен -шна *adj* **1** seven-year-old; седумгодишно девојче seven-year-old girl **2** lasting seven years, septennial; seven-year; седумгодишна војна Seven Years War; седумгодишен план seven-year plan

седумгодишник -ци *m* seven-year-old

седумгодишнина *f* seventh anniversary

седумгодишница *f see* седумгодишнина

седумдесет *num* seventy; седумдесет дена seventy days

седумдесетгодишен -шна *adj* **1** seventy-year-old, septuagenarian **2** lasting seventy years; seventy-year **3** <of a> seventieth anniversary; седумдесетгодишен јубилеј a seventieth jubilee

седумдесетгодишник -ци *m* seventy-year-old, septuagenarian

седумдесетгодишнина *f* seventieth anniversary

седумдесетгодишница *f see* седумдесетгодишнина

седумдесетина *num* **1** seventieth **2** group of about seventy people

седумдесетмина *num* (*of men and mixed groups*) seventy

седумдесетти *adj num* seventieth; седумдесетти роден ден seventieth birthday; во седумдесеттите години in the seventies

седумдневен -вна *adj* <of/for> seven days; седумдневен престој seven-day stay

седумка *f* **1** (*цифрата* 7) <figure> seven **2** (*во карти*) seven **3** (*автобус, трамвај итн.*) <number> seven **4** (*студентска оцена*) seven (*out of ten*), credit

седумкатница *f* seven-storey building

седумкратен -тна *adj* seven-times; sevenfold; седумкратен првак seven-times champion

седуммесечен -чна *adj* seven-month, of seven months; седуммесечно бебе seven-month-old baby; седуммесечен план seven-month plan

седуммина *num* (*of men and mixed groups*) seven

седумнаесет *num* seventeen

седумнаесетгодишен -шна *adj* **1** seventeen-year-old; седумнаесетгодишно момче a boy of seventeen **2** lasting seventeen years; seventeen-year **3** <of a> seventeenth anniversary; седумнаесетгодишен јубилеј seventeenth jubilee

седумнаесетгодишник -ци *m* seventeen-year-old

седумнаесетгодишнина *f* seventeenth anniversary

седумнаесетгодишница *f see* седумнаесетгодишнина

седумнаесетина *num* **1** seventeenth **2** *see* седумнаесетмина

седумнаесетка *f* seventeen, number seventeen

седумнаесетмина *num* (*of men and mixed groups*) seventeen

седумнаесетти *adj num* seventeenth

седумнеделен -лна *adj* seven-week

седумниче *n see* седмаче

седум-осумдесет *num* seventy or eighty

седум-осумнаесет *num* seventeen or eighteen

седумсложен -жна *adj* seven-syllable, heptasyllabic; седумсложен стих heptasyllabic verse

седумсто *num see* седумстотини

седумстогодишен -шна *adj* **1** seven-hundred-years-old **2** lasting seven hundred years; seven-hundred-year **3** <of a> seven-hundredth anniversary

седумстогодишнина *f* seven-hundredth anniversary

седумстогодишница *f see* седумстогодишнина

седумстотен -тна *adj num* seven-hundredth

седумстотини *num* seven hundred

седумчасовен -вна *adj* seven-hour; of seven hours; седумчасовно работно време seven-hour working day

сее *impf* **1** to sow (*also fig.*); сее пченица to sow wheat; сее раздор to sow discord; сее гласови to spread rumours; ❑ кај не го сееш, таму никнува to turn up like a bad penny; како ќе сееш, така ќе жнееш as you sow, so you reap **2** to sift *trans.*; сее брашно to sift flour

сеедно *adv* **1** constantly, incessantly, always **2** all the same; мене ми е сосем сеедно it's all the same to me

сезнаен -јна *adj* all-knowing, omniscient

сезнајко -овци *m colloq.* know-all

сезналец -лци *m literary* polymath

сезо́на *f* season; театарска сезона theatre season; туристичка сезона tourist season; сезона на годишни одмори holiday season; ❑ мртва сезона dead season, off-season; главна сезона high (peak) season; вон сезона out of (off) season; во сезона in season

сезо́нски *adj* seasonal; сезонски работник seasonal worker, casual labourer; сезонска облека seasonal clothing; сезонска распродажба clearance sale

сеидба *f* sowing, seeding; sowing-season; есенска сеидба autumn sowing (seeding)

сеидбен *adj* sowing, seeding; сеидбен план sowing (seeding) plan

сеиз *m arch.* (коњушар) stable-hand, groom

сеизмички *adj* seismic; сеизмички области earthquake zones

сеизмичност *f* seismicity

сеизмогра́ма *f* seismogram

сеизмогра́ф *m* seismograph

сеизмогра́фски *adj* seismographic; сеизмографска станица seismographic station

сеизмоло́г -зи *m* seismologist

сеизмологија *f* seismology

сеизмолошки *adj* seismological; сеизмолошки извештај seismological report

сеир *m colloq.* sight, spectacle, show; marvel, wonder; гледа сеир to sit and watch; to enjoy a spectacle; чини сеир to put on a show

сеирџија -ии *m colloq.* spectator, onlooker

сеирџика *f* (*fem. form*) *see* сеирџија

сејалка *f* seed-drill

сејанина *f* seed, crop<s>

сејач *m* sower; *fig.* disseminator

сејачка *f* **1** (*fem. form*) *see* сејач **2** *see* сејалка

сејачки *adj* sower's; sowing; сејачка машина seed-drill

сејмен *m arch.* gendarme (*in Ottoman empire*)

сејменски *adj* gendarme's

Сејшели *pl* Seychelles

сејшелски *adj* Seychellois; Сејшелски Острови Seychelles

сек. *abbr.* (*секунда*) sec.

сек¹ *m* cutting; cut; длабок сек a deep cut

сек² *m dial. see* сак

сека *impf* **1** to flash; to sparkle; секавици секаат lightning is flashing; им секаат очите their eyes light up **2** *fig.* (*за болка*) to pierce, stab; ме сека во слабините I have stabbing pains in my sides (loins) **3** to strike sparks (*with flint and steel*)

секавица¹ *f* lightning; брз како секавица as quick as lightning

секавица² *f dial. see* секира¹

секавичен -чна *adj* lightning; секавичен удар a lightning strike; секавичен воз express train; секавична војна blitzkrieg

секавичност *f* lightning speed

секаде *adv* everywhere; бара секаде to search high and low

секадешен -шна *adj arch.*, *literary* general, ubiquitous

секако *adv* in any case; in every way; anyway, in any/every way; of course, by all means, certainly; ќе дојдеме секако we'll come whatever happens (in any case)

секаков -ква *pron* of all kinds; ❑ има секакви <луѓе> it takes all sorts to make a world

секал *m see* трад

секало *n* tinder-box, flint and steel

секанс *m Math.* secant

секач *m* cutter; hacksaw; chisel; браварски секач metalworker's chisel

секве́нца & секвенција -ии *f* sequence

секве́стар -три *m* **1** *Leg.* sequestration; наложи секвестар to sequestrate, distrain **2** *see* секвестратор **3** *Med.* sequestrum

секвести́ра *pf & impf see* секвестрира

секвестра́тор *m Leg.* sequestrator, receiver

секвестрација *f* **1** *Leg.* sequestration **2** *Med.* sequestrotomy

секвестри́ра *pf & impf Leg.* to sequester, sequestrate, distrain

секи сека *pron dial. see* секој

секидневен -вна *adj see* секојдневен

секидневие -ија & **секидневје** *n see* секојдневје

секидневност *f* everyday life/routine

секира¹ *f* axe; hatchet; poleaxe; ❑ му паднала секирата в мед he had a stroke of luck

секира² *impf* **I** to upset, worry *trans.* **II** – се to be upset, worry *intrans.*; to fret

секирица *f dim. of* секира¹

секириште *n aug. of* секира¹

секирче *n dim. of* секира¹

секне¹ *pf* секна *aor. see* сека

секне² *pf* секна *aor.* to run dry, stop flowing; чешмата секна the fountain has dried up

секне³ *impf* **I** to wipe (*s.o.'s*) nose **II** – се to blow one's nose

секнотина *f* (*usu. pl*) mucus, snivel, *vulg.* snot

секнува¹ *impf of* секне¹

секнува² *impf of* секне²

секога *adv see* секогаш

секогаш *adv* always; еднаш за секогаш once and for all

секогашен -шна *adj* continual, constant

секого *pron see* секој

секој секоја, секое, *pl* секои *pron* (*m & n dat.* секому; *acc.* секого) each, every; everyone; секое утро every morning; ❏ на секој чекор at every step, constantly, everywhere; секој човек си има своја среќа every dog has his day; за секој случај just in case; по секоја цена at any price (cost), at all costs; секое зло за добро every cloud has a silver lining

секојдневен -вна *adj* daily, everyday, routine, regular; секојдневна работа day's work, daily routine; regular occurrence; секојдневен весник daily newspaper

секојдневие -ија *n see* секојдневје

секојдневје *n* daily round (routine); everyday event

секојдневник -ци *m* daily <newspaper>

секојдневно *adv* every day

секојпат *adv see* секогаш

секому *pron see* секој

секрет[1] *m* **1** (*тајна*) secret, *literary* arcana; секретот на успехот the secret of success **2** concealed mechanism **3** *Mil.* concealed observation post

секрет[2] *m* secretion

секретар *m* secretary; секретар на суд court clerk; личен секретар personal (private) secretary; генерален секретар Secretary General; државен секретар Secretary of State

секретаријат *m* secretariat

секретарка *f* (*fem. form*) *see* секретар

секретарски *adj* secretarial; secretary's

секретарство *n* secretaryship; secretarial work

секретарствува *impf* to work as <a> secretary, be a secretary

секретен[1] -тна *adj* (*таен*) secret; секретни документи classified/top-secret documents; секретна брава combination lock; секретно копче press-stud, patent stud

секретен[2] -тна *adj* secreting, secretory; секретни жлезди glands, secretory organs

секретно *adv* secretly, in secret, covertly

секретност *f* secrecy

секреција *f* secretion; внатрешна секреција internal secretion

секс *m* sex; без секс sexless, without sex; ❏ секс-бомба sex kitten, sexpot

сексапил *m* sex appeal

сексапилен -лна *adj* sexy

сексапилност *f* sex appeal

секста *f Mus.* sixth

секстант *adj* sextant

секстет *m Mus.* sextet

сексуален -лна *adj* sexual; сексуален однос <sexual> intercourse

сексуалност *f* sexuality

секта *f* **1** sect; верска секта religious sect **2** *fig.* faction, splinter group, camp

сектант *m see* секташ

секташ *m* sectarian, schismatic; faction member

секташи *impf* to follow a sect; to be partial (partisan)

секташки *adj* sectarian; секташка група sectarian group

секташтво *n* sectarianism, sectionalism, factiousness

сектор *m* sector; *Math.* рамен сектор congruent sector; приватен сектор private sector; државен сектор state sector; сектор за продажба sales department, sales division

секторски *adj* sectional, divisional

секунда *f* second; ❏ само една секунда just a second (moment); точен во секунда punctual to the second

секундант *m* second (*at duel, boxing match, etc.*)

секундарен -рна *adj* secondary, subordinate

секундарник -ци *m* second hand (*of a watch/clock*)

секунден -дна *adj* <of, for a> second; секундна стрелка second hand

секундира *pf & impf* to second, act as a second

секција[1] -ии *f* section

секција[2] -ии *f Med.* autopsy, post-mortem

секцира *pf & impf* to dissect

секциски *adj* sectional

селамет *m colloq.* safety; help; success, luck; Господ на селамет да ти е! God be with you!

селанец -ани *m* peasant; countryman; *colloq. pejor.* rustic, yokel

селанин -ани *m see* селанец

селаниште *n augm. of* селанец

селанка *f* (*fem. form*) *see* селанец

селански *adj* peasant's, peasant; rural; rustic; boorish, uncouth

селанство *n* peasantry, peasants; country people

селанче *n dim.* **1** *of* селанец, селанин **2** *of* селанка

селанштина *f* boorishness, uncouthness, bad manners

селвија -ии *f Bot.* (Cupressus) cypress

селектор *m* selector

селекција -ии *f* **1** selection; (*plant, animal*) breeding; ❏ природна селекција natural selection, survival of the fittest **2** *Sport.* selection; chosen team

селекционен -она *adj* <of, for> selection; селекциона станица plant/animal research centre; селекциона комисија selection committee

селекционер *m* **1** selector, breeder **2** *see* селектор

селекциски *adj see* селекционен

селенит *m* **1** moon-dweller **2** selenite

селење *n see* селидба

сели *impf* **I** to move, relocate *trans.*; сели некого од куќа to move s.o. out of a house **II** – се **1** to move *intrans.*, move house; ❏ сели се на оној свет to depart this life **2** (*за птици*) to migrate

селидба *f* removal, (*act of*) moving house

селидбен *adj* removal; селидбени трошоци removal expenses, costs of moving

селица *f see* преселник

селиште *n* **1** *augm. of* село **2** (*населено место*) settlement

село *n* village; the country; ❏ шпански села double Dutch; секое село – свој закон when in Rome do as the Romans do; село се плени, баба се чешла *prov.* Nero fiddles while Rome burns

селски *adj* village; country; rural; rustic; селско училиште village school; селски воздух country air; селско стопанство agriculture; farming; rural economy

селскостопански *adj* agricultural; селскостопанско производство agricultural produce

селце *n* **1** *dim. of* село; убаво селце pretty little village **2** hamlet; села и селца villages and hamlets

семазиологија *f see* семантика

семантика *f Gram.* semantics
семантичар *m Gram.* semantician, semanticist
семантичен -чна *adj Gram.* semantic
семантички *adj see* семантичен
семафор *m* **1** traffic-lights; затворен семафор red light **2** semaphore, signal-station
семе -иња *n* **1** seed; (*сперма*) sperm, semen **2** *fig.* germ, genesis; семе на раздор seed<s> of discord; семето на бунтот the germ of the uprising **3** *fig.* (*потомство*) progeny, issue, offspring; ѓаволско семе seed of the Devil, satanic brood
семевод *m* **1** (*на сејалка*) seed canal, delivery tube **2** *Anat.* seminal (spermatic) duct
семеен -јна *adj* **1** family; domestic; семеен албум family album; семејна среќа domestic bliss **2** (*as noun*) семеен *m*, семејна *f* married man/woman
семејно *adv* with the family, *en famille*
семејство *n* family; глава на семејството head of the household; семејство на словенските јазици the Slavonic language family
семенар *m* seed merchant; seed producer
семенарница *f* seed shop
семенарски *adj* seed merchant's (producer's)
семенарство *n* seed production
семенен -мена *adj* seminal, spermatic; семенен канал seminal (spermatic) duct; семена течност seminal fluid, semen
семеник -ци *m Bot.* pericarp, seed capsule (vessel)
семениште *n* seed-bed; nursery
семенски *adj* <of, for> seed; семенски резерви seed reserves
семенце *n dim. of* семе
семестар -три *m* semester
семестарски *adj* semester; семестарски распуст semester break
семестрáлен -лна & **семестријáлен** -лна *adj see* семестарски
семилостив *adj* all-merciful, most gracious
семинар *m* **1** seminar, tutorial; course; семинар по македонски јазик seminar on Macedonian; Macedonian-language tutorial **2** seminar room **3** department
семинарија -ии *f* (*богословија*) seminary
семинарѝст *m* seminarist
семинáрски *adj* <of a> seminar; семинарски вежби seminar, tutorial
семир *m* (*вселена*) the universe; space; лет во семирот space flight
семирен -рна *adj* universal, worldwide; <of, in> space
семитски *adj* Semitic; семитски јазици Semitic languages
семка *f* **1** seed, pip; stone; семки од лубеница watermelon seed<s>; семки од кајсии apricot stones **2** (*usu. pl*) pumpkin seed
семкар *m* seller of pumpkin seeds
семожен -жна *adj* **1** of every kind; семожни шпекулации all sorts of speculation **2** *rare* (*семоќен*) omnipotent, almighty
семожност *f* endless variety; omnipotence
семоќ *f* omnipotence
семоќен -ќна *adj* omnipotent, almighty; семоќен владар all-powerful ruler
семоќност *f* omnipotence

семошен -шна *adj see* семоќен
семудар -дра *adj* all-wise, all-knowing, omniscient
семудрост *f* omniscience
сен[1] *m & f* **1** shade, shadow **2** *literary* (*дух*) ghost, shade, phantom; сените на предците the shades of one's ancestors
сен[2] *m* (*во воденица*) mill spindle
сенар *m* hay-merchant
сенарник -ци *m* barn, hayloft
сенарница *f see* сенарник
сенароден *adj* national; nationwide; of/for all the people; сенародно дело the work of the entire nation; сенародно движење national (popular) movement
сенат *m* senate
сенатор *m* senator
сенаторски *adj* senator's, senatorial
сенатски *adj* <of the> senate
сендвич *m* sandwich
Сенегал *m* Senegal
Сенегáлец -лци *m* Senegalese
Сенегáлка *f* (*fem. form*) *see* Сенегалец
сенегáлски *adj* Senegalese
сенештар *m* **1** scrap merchant; rag-and-bone man **2** *iron.* jack of all trades and master of none, dabbler; *colloq.* know-all
сенештарница *f* junk shop; variety store
сенештарски *adj* scrap merchant's
сенештарство *n* junk trade
сенешто *pron* odds and ends
сензáл *m* broker; берзански сензал stockbroker
сензација -ии *f* sensation; направи (предизвика) сензација to create (provoke) a sensation
сензационáлен -лна *adj* sensational, startling
сензациóнен -она *adj see* сензационален
сензибѝлен -лна *adj* sensitive; сензибилно прашање delicate matter
сензибѝлност *f* sensitivity; tenderness
сензитѝвен -вна *adj see* сензибилен
сени *impf* **1** to shade *trans.*, cast shadow over; не сени ми! don't stand in the light! **2** (*за светлина*) to dazzle, blind (*temporarily*); светлината ми ги сени очите the light is dazzling me
сенилен -лна *adj* senile
сенилност *f* senility
сениор *m* **1** senior; elder; provost **2** feudal landowner, seigneur
сениорски *adj* senior, senior's
сеница[1] *f* **1** bower, arbour **2** *arch.* (*шатор*) marquee, tent, pavilion
сеница[2] *f Zool.* (Parus) titmouse
сениште *n* ghost, phantom, spectre
сеништен -шна *adj* ghostly, spectral; eerie
сенка *f* **1** shade, shady place; седи на (во, под) сенка to sit in the shade; меѓу светлина и сенка between light and shade; шарена сенка patchy shade, chequered light and shade ❑ дебела сенка 1. deep shade 2. sinecure, easy (*colloq.* cushy) job; држи се (стои) во сенка to stay in the background; to keep a low profile; следи како сенка to follow like a shadow; падне сенка на некого to be under a cloud; фрли <лоша> сенка на некого to cast a shadow over s.o.; фрла некого во сенка to put s.o. in the shade; to run rings round s.o.; to take the shine off s.o.; **сенка му е**

to live in s.o.'s shadow **2** shadow; outline; ❏ му се плаши (бега) од сенката he is afraid of his shadow; нема ни сенка од него there's no trace of him; сенка од човек a shadow of a person, a shadow of his former self **3** phantom, shade, ghost **4** *dial.* peak (*of a cap*)

сенкар *m colloq.* idler, lazybones, loafer, malingerer, *Austral., N.Z.* bludger

сенлив *adj* shady

сено *n* hay; пласт (стог) сено haystack; haycock

сенокос *m* **1** haymaking; haymaking season **2** (*folk name for*) June

сенокосач *m see* косач

сенокосачка *f* **1** (*fem. form*) *see* косач **2** mower, mowing machine

сенокосен -сна *adj* haymaking

сенокосец -сци *m see* косач

сентенција -ии *f* **1** (*изрека*) maxim, aphorism **2** *Leg.* (*пресуда*) sentence, verdict **3** (*мислење*) opinion

сентенциозен -зна *adj* aphoristic, pithy

сентенциозност *f* pithiness

сентимент *m* sentiment

сентиментален -лна *adj* emotional, sentimental

сентиментализам -змот *m* sentimentalism

сентименталност *f* sentimentality, emotion

сенува *impf see* сени

сенф *m* mustard

сенце *n dim. of* сено

сенче *n dim. dial. of* сенка 4

сенчест *adj* shady; сенчеста градина a shady garden

сенчи *impf* to shade; сенчи слика to shade a picture

сеоддаен -јна *adj see* предан

сеопфатен -тна *adj* all-embracing, all-encompassing, all-inclusive, comprehensive; сеопфатна анализа comprehensive analysis

сеопфатност *f* comprehensiveness, inclusiveness

сеопшт *adj* general, universal; сеопшто избирачко право universal suffrage

сеопшто *adv* generally, universally; сеопшто примено generally accepted

сепак *conj* yet, however, nonetheless; па сепак all the same, even so

сепарат *m* offprint

сепаратен -тна *adj* separate, special, individual

сепаративен -вна *adj see* сепаратен

сепаратизам -змот *m* separatism

сепаратист *m* separatist

сепаратистичен -чна *adj see* сепаратистички

сепаратистички *adj* separatist; сепаратистичко движење separatist movement

сепаратност *f* separateness, discreteness

сепаратор *m* separator, centrifuge

сепарација *f* separation; сепарации (*во рудник*) separation section

сепаре *n* private dining-room; booth

сепија -ии *f* **1** *Zool.* (Sepia officinalis) cuttlefish **2** (*боја*) sepia

сепне *pf* сепна *aor.* **I** to startle; to arouse, wake up *trans.* **II** – се **1** to wake up with a start *intrans.*; to give a start **2** to come to one's senses

сепнува (се) *impf of* сепне (се)

сепобеден -дна *adj* all-conquering

сепса *f* sepsis

септември *m* September

септемвриски *adj* September; септемвриско сонце September sun

септима *f Mus.* seventh

септина *f Prosody* seven-line stanza, heptastich

септичен -чна *adj* septic

септички *adj see* септичен

сербез *adj indecl. colloq.* casual, relaxed, happy-go-lucky; blithe

сервер *m Sport.* server

сервета *f see* салфета

сервилен -лна *adj* servile

сервилност *f* servility

сервира *pf & impf* **1** to serve; сервира вечера to serve dinner **2** *Sport.* to serve

сервис *m* **1** service; сервис за перење облека laundry service; авто-сервис automobile (motor-vehicle) repairs **2** service, set; кристален сервис за ликер crystal liqueur service **3** *Sport.* service

сервисен -сна *adj* service; сервисна работилница repair shop, garage

сервус *interj* hello

серген *m arch.* (*ѕиден долап*) wardrobe, closet

сергија -ии *f arch.* stall, stand

сергиџија -ии *m arch.* stallholder

сердар *m arch.* sirdar, commander-in-chief

сердарија -ии *f arch.* sirdar's territory

сердарски *adj arch.* sirdar's

сердарство *n arch.* <rank of> sirdar

середум *adv* one after another

сереј *m* **1** fat content of colostrum/beestings **2** grease in a sheep's fleece

серејлив *adj* rich, containing fat/grease; серејливо млеко full cream milk; серејлива волна greasy wool

серенада *f* serenade; прави серенади to serenade

сержант *m* sergeant

сержантски *adj* sergeant's; сержантско звање rank of sergeant

серија -ии *f* series

сериозен -зна *adj* serious, earnest; grave; solemn; considerable; сериозен кандидат serious candidate; сериозни успеси significant successes; substantial progress; сериозна опасност grave danger; сериозна болест serious (grave) illness

сериозно *adv* seriously, in earnest; gravely; solemnly; сериозно се зафаќа со to get to grips with

сериозност *f* seriousness; gravity; solemnity; сериозност на ситуацијата gravity of the situation; со нужната сериозност with due solemnity

сериски *adj* serial; сериско производство serial production; сериски трактори mass-produced tractors

серкме *n see* сертме

сермија -ии *f colloq.* capital, property; investment; му остана сета сермија his entire capital was saved; ❏ (*се напие се, се најаде и сл.*) на сермија (*to drink, eat*) one's fill

серологија *f* serology

серотерапија *f Med.* serotherapy

серпентина *f* winding road; double bend

серт *adj indecl. colloq.* hot-tempered; bad-tempered; peppery; ❏ серт тутун strong tobacco

сертме *n* type of fishing net

серум *m Med.* serum

сесветски *adj* worldwide, universal

сесија -ии *f* session; sitting; term; вонредна сесија extraordinary session; испитна сесија examination session

сесилен -лна *adj* all-powerful, omnipotent; сесилен владар all-powerful ruler

сесловенски *adj* pan-Slav<ic>

сесрден -дна *adj* hearty, cordial; сесрден прием cordial (warm) welcome

сесрдност *f* heartiness, cordiality

сестина *f Prosody* six-line stanza, hexastich

сестра *f* **1** sister; ❑ милосрдна сестра Sister of Mercy; медицинска сестра nurse **2** nun; манастирски сестри nuns

сестран *adj* comprehensive; all-round; сестран развиток comprehensive development

сестрано *adv* comprehensively, thoroughly, closely; сестрано надарен човек a man of universal talents

сестраност *f* comprehensive quality; versatility, universality

сестрин *adj* sister's

сестрински *adj* sisterly; сестринска љубов sisterly love

сестринство *n* sisterly love; sisterhood

сестрица *f* **1** *dim. of* сестра **2** *dial.* sister-in-law (*husband's sister*)

сестриче *n hyp.* little sister, *colloq.* sis

сестриченик -ци *m* type of children's game

сестричка *f dim. of* сестра

сестрична *f* niece (*sister's daughter*)

сестричник -ци *m* nephew (*sister's son*)

сестричница *f see* сестрична

сестроубиец -јци *m literary* sororicide

сестроубиство *n literary* sororicide; изврши сестроубиство to commit sororicide, murder one's sister

сет¹ *m Sport* set

сет² *pron dial. see* сиот

сетен -тна *adj dial.* (*последен*) last; за сетен пат for the last time

сети *pf* I **1** to feel, sense; сети болка to feel pain **2** to realize, grasp, guess **3** *rare* to remember; to mention II – се **1** to feel *intrans.* **2** to become apparent **3** to remember, recall (*дека – that*); се сети на нешто/некого to remember s.th./s.o.; не се сетив да го викнам и него it didn't occur to me to invite him as well

сетиво *n see* сетило

сетики *adv colloq.* (*секако*) probably; surely; of course

сетилен -лна *adj* sensory; sensual; palpable, perceptible; сетилни центри sensory centres, sensoria; сетилниот свет the world of the senses, the tangible world

сетило *n* sense; сетило за вкус <sense of> taste

сетне *adv dial.* (*после*) later, afterwards; најсетне finally, in the end, at last

сетнина *f dial. usu. in the expression:* на сетнина later, afterwards

сетува (се) *impf dial. of* сети (се)

секава (се) *impf of* сети (се)

секавало *n colloq.* feeling; нема секавало to be insensitive (thick-skinned)

секавање *n* **1** memory; секавањето му беше поматено his memory was dimmed; his recollection was blurred **2** reminiscence; за долго секавање long to be remembered

Сеул *m* Seoul

сеулски *adj* Seoul *attrib.*

сеф *m* (*долап*) safe, strongbox; (*просторија*) strongroom

сефа *f colloq.* good mood; fun; peace, ease; не од сефа not for the fun of it

сефте¹ *n colloq.* beginning, start; ❑ по сефтето се познава денот a good beginning makes a good ending; прави сефте to make a start; to make one's debut; to break the ice; to try one's hand at s.th.; to draw first blood; од сефте from the first; at the first go

сефте² *adv colloq.* for the first time; не ни е сефте it's nothing new for us

сефтоса *pf colloq.* **1** to make a start **2** to wear (*s.th.*) for the first time

сефтосува *impf of* сефтоса

сецело *adv literary* entirely, completely; сецело сам all alone

сецесија *f* secession

сецесионизам -змот *m* secessionism

сецесионист *m* secessionist

сецесионистички *adj* secessionist, breakaway

сецесионистка *f* (*fem. form*) *see* сецесионист

сеч *f poet.* (*сеча*) massacre, slaughter, carnage

сеча *f* **1** wood-cutting; tree-felling **2** (*колеж*) slaughter, massacre

сечач *m* woodcutter; lumberjack

сече *impf* **1** to cut, cut through; to cut up; (*дрво*) to fell; to hew; сече леб to slice bread; сече месо to carve meat; сече дрва to chop firewood; ❑ сече данок to apportion taxes; сече пари to make money; сече турски/руски to speak fluent Turkish/Russian; сече карти to cut cards **2** *fig.* (*за пат, река и сл.*) to cut through; to intersect; бродот ја сече водата the ship cuts through the water; патишта ја сечат планината roads cut through the mountains **3** *fig.* (*за ветер*) to cut, bite, sting II – се to intersect *intrans.*; линиите се сечат the lines intersect

сечиво *n see* сечило

сечиј -ија, -ие, *pl* -ии *pron* everyone's, everybody's

сечилиште *n see* сечиште

сечило *n* blade; ❑ меч со две сечила a two-edged (double-edged) sword

сечиште *n* **1** coppice, copse, felling area **2** clearing

сечка *impf* to chop <up>, cut <up>, dice; сечка месо to chop meat

сечко *m* (*folk name for*) February

сечник -ци *m* chopping block, log; tree-stump

сеџаде *n* prayer mat

сешто *pron* (*сенешто*) all sorts of things; everything; anything, odds and ends

СЗО *abbr.* (*Светска здравствена организација*) World Health Organization, WHO

си¹ *2nd p. sg pres. of* сум

си² *pron* **1** (*short dat. form of* себе) <to, for> oneself (myself, yourself, etc.); си помисли to think to o.s.; (*also with the long form*) си рече себеси to say to o.s. **2** (*as dat. of possession*) one's own (my, his, her, etc.); си ги зеде книгите he took his books; и рече на мајка си he said to his mother **3** (*with certain verbs, esp. of motion*) си дојде дома he came home; си отидоа they left **4** (*after некој, as part., often with pejorative* *nuance; not translated*) дојде некоја си жена some woman <or other> arrived

си³ *pron arch.* (*сиот*) all, every

си⁴ *n Mus.* B

Сибир *m* Siberia

Сибирец -рци *m* Siberian

Сибирка *f* (*fem. form*) *see* Сибирец

сибирски *adj* Siberian

сив *adj* grey; *fig.* drab, dull; сив сокол (Falco peregrinus) peregrine falcon; сив коњ grey horse; сива стварност tedious reality

сивак *m* grapes that do not ripen

сивее *impf* I 1 to turn grey *trans.* 2 to turn grey *intrans.*, go grey 3 *fig.* to wither; to fade *intrans.* II – се to appear grey; карпите се сивеат во далечината the rocks look grey in the distance

сивило *n* greyness; *fig.* drabness, dullness

сивина *f see* сивило

сивка *f* (*of a female animal*) *see* сивчо

сивкав *adj* greyish; grizzled

сивокос *adj* grey-haired

сивомаслинест *adj* greyish-green, olive-green

сивоок *adj* grey-eyed

сивопер *adj poet.* with grey feathers (plumage)

сивост, сивота & сивотија *f see* сивило

сивоќа *f dial. see* сивило

сивчо -овци *m* grey bull/ox/stallion, etc.

сига *f* stalagmite; stalactite

сигла *f* (*во стенографијата*) logogram, grammalogue

сигнал *m* signal, sign; *fig.* warning, alarm bell; звучни сигнали sirens; alarms; светлосни сигнали signal lights, warning lights; flares; traffic lights; даде сигнал to give a signal

сигнален -лна *adj* signal; signalling; сигнални уреди signalling devices; сигнална труба bugle; сигнална ламбичка signal lamp; warning light

сигнализатор *m* 1 signalling apparatus; signal generator; автоматски сигнализатор automatic signalling device 2 *rare see* сигналист

сигнализација *f* signalling; signal system; alarm system; железничка сигнализација railway signals

сигнализира *pf & impf* to signal; (*предупреди*) to tip off; to give warning of

сигналист *m* signaller, signalman; bugler

сигнатура *f* 1 *Print.* signature 2 (*во библиотека*) call number, shelf-mark, pressmark 3 (*знак*) label

сигнатурен -рна *adj* <of/for a> signature; сигнатурен знак signature mark; shelf-mark; сигнатурен број signature number; call number

сигнира *pf & impf* to mark; to sign; to catalogue; to initial

сигур *adv colloq. see* сигурно

сигурен -рна *adj* 1 sure, confident, certain; сигурен во себе sure of o.s.; со сигурен чекор with resolute steps, resolutely; не биди така сигурен don't bet on it 2 reliable, dependable, trustworthy 3 (*безбеден*) safe, secure; сигурно место safe place; сигурна служба secure job 4 (*неизбежен*) inevitable, sure, certain; сигурна смрт certain death; сигурен успех sure success

сигурно *adv* certainly, surely; for sure; safely; ❑ сигурното си е сигурно better sure than sorry; полека но сигурно slowly but surely; оди на сигурно to play it safe; на сигурно out of harm's way; home and dry

сигурносен -сна *adj* <of/for> safety/security; сигурносни вентили safety-valves

сигурност *f* certainty; safety, security; confidence; зборуваше со голема сигурност he spoke with great confidence; тие се грижат за неговата сигурност they are responsible for his security (safety); заради секоја сигурност just to be on the safe side; сигурност на работа safety at work, industrial safety; материјална сигурност material (financial) security

СИДА *abbr.* AIDS

сиднеец -ејци *m* person from Sydney

Сиднеј *m* Sydney

сиднејка *f* (*fem. form*) *see* сиднеец

сиднејски *adj* Sydney *attrib.*

сидро *n* (*котва*) anchor

сиже *m & n* subject, plot, topic; сиже на роман subject (theme) of a novel

сижетен -тна *adj* <of the> subject; сижетен развој the development of the subject (plot)

сијалица *f* <light->bulb

сика *impf see* цика

сикне *pf* сикна *aor. see* цикне

сиктер *interj colloq.* get out! go to hell! сиктер одовде! get out of here! go away!

сиктердиса *pf colloq. see* сиктериса

сиктердисува *impf see* сиктерисува

сиктериса *pf colloq.* to throw (drive, kick) out

сиктерисува *impf of* сиктериса

сиктерманца *f colloq.* (*usu. of coffee served to guests*) cue to leave

сила *f* 1 strength; power; force; сила на ветрот strength of the wind; сила на звукот sound intensity; ❑ во полна сила at the height of one's powers; со сета (полна) сила with all one's might; *Tech.* at full power/speed; коњска сила horsepower; преку сила at most, at the outside; според своите сили to the best of one's ability, as best one can; Големите сили the Great Powers; куповна сила purchasing power; сила на волја will-power; со сила by force; сила на навикот force of habit; работна сила manpower, labour; жива сила personnel; движечка сила prime mover; собира сила to summon up courage; супер сила superpower; седма сила the Fourth Estate (the press); човечки сили human resources; по силата на . . . by force of . . . , by virtue of . . . ; кај има сила, нема правина (правда); у кого е власта, у него е и силата *prov.* might is right 2 *Leg., Tech.* сила на закон force of law; центрифугална сила centrifugal force; ❑ во сила valid; става вон сила to make void; to declare null and void; влезе (стапи) во сила to come into effect 3 (*pl only*) вооружените сили armed forces; воздухопловни сили air force; сувоземни сили land forces, ground troops 4 *colloq.* (*as adj and adv*) excellent, great, superb; сила работа hot stuff; како си? – сила <сум>! how are you? – on top of the world!

силабичен -чна *adj* syllabic; силабични стихови syllabic verse

силажа *f* ensilage

силажира *pf & impf* to ensile, ensilage

силен *adj* strong, powerful, potent; силна волја

strong will; силна струја strong current; силно кафе strong coffee; силна болка severe pain; силен дожд heavy rain; силна желба keen desire; силен ученик capable pupil; силен по математика good at mathematics; силна страна (*на некого*) (*s.o.'s*) forte (strong point); силна храна nourishing food

силеџија -ии *m colloq.* ruffian; bully; thug

силеџиски *adj* ruffianly, thuggish

сили *impf* I 1 (*присилува*) to force, compel; сили некого да работи to force s.o. to work 2 *see* забрзува, засилува II – се 1 to exert o.s., try 2 to swagger, brag, strut 3 *see* забрзува се, засилува се

силикат *m* (*usu. pl*) silicate

силикатен -тна *adj* silicate; силикатен раствор silicate solution

силина[1] *f* strength, power, force; со сета силина with all one's might; with full force

силина[2] *f Bot.* (Isatis tinctoria) woad

силициум *m Chem.* silicon

силициумов *adj* silicon

силник -ци *m* rowdy, bully; tyrant, despot

силнички *adj* rowdy, bullying; tyrannical, despotic; силничко друштво rowdy friends

силно *adv* strongly; вика силно to shout loudly; силно возбуден greatly disturbed; very excited

силовит *adj see* силен

силовитост *f see* силина[1]

силогизам -змот *m* syllogism

силогистички *adj* syllogistic; силогистички расудувања syllogistic reasoning

силомер *m* dynamometer

силос *m* silo

силува *impf* to rape, violate

силување *n* rape, violation

силуета *f* silhouette

силум *adv* forcibly, by force

симбиоза *f Biol.* symbiosis

симбол *m* symbol

симболизам -змот *m* symbolism

симболизира *pf & impf* to symbolize

символика *f* symbolism

символист *m* symbolist

символистички *adj* symbolist; символистичка поезија symbolist poetry

символистка *f* (*fem. form*) *see* символист

символичен -чна *adj* symbolic; символично значење symbolic meaning; символичен подарок token (symbolic) gift

символички *adj see* символичен

символ *m Rel.* символ на верата creed

симетрала *f* centre line

симетрија *f* symmetry

симетричен -чна *adj* symmetrical; симетрични фигури symmetrical figures

симид *m* simid, bread roll, bun

симина (се) *impf of* симне (се); ❑ не симина очи (поглед) од некого/нешто not to take one's eyes off s.o./s.th.; симина ѕвезди од небо to promise (*s.o.*) the earth; симина шапка (капа) некому *colloq.* to take one's hat off to s.o.

симит *m see* симид

симитче *n dim. of* симид

симитчија -ии *m* baker/seller of *simids*

симиџија -ии *m see* симитчија

симиџиски *adj see* симитчиски

симне *pf* симна *aor.* I 1 to take down; to take off; to lower *trans.*; симне книга од полица to take a book down from a shelf; ❑ симне маска некому to unmask s.o. 2 *rare* симне некому глава to cut off s.o.'s head 3 *fig.* to depose, bring down; to dismiss, sack II – се 1 to descend, come/go down 2 to dismount 3 (*за боја*) to peel/flake off

симнува (се) *impf see* симина (се)

симпатизер *m* sympathizer, follower

симпатизерски *adj* <of a> sympathizer; симпатизерска група group of sympathizers

симпатизира *pf & impf* 1 to sympathize/be in sympathy (*co – with*) 2 to like (*s.o.*), feel drawn (*to s.o.*)

симпатија -ии *f* 1 sympathy; liking 2 (*f and more rarely m*) beloved, sweetheart; favourite

симпатичен -чна *adj* likeable, attractive, nice; congenial; симпатично лице a nice face; *Anat.* симпатичен нервен систем sympathetic nervous system

симплификација *f* simplification

симплифицира *pf & impf* to simplify

симплицизам -змот *m* simple-mindedness

симпозиум *m* symposium

симптом *m* symptom; *fig.* indication, pointer; симптоми на големи сипаници symptoms of smallpox; симптоми на војна harbingers of war

симптоматичен -чна *adj* symptomatic

симс *m* barge-board

симулант *m* malingerer

симулантка *f* (*fem. form*) *see* симулант

симулантски *adj* malingerer's; malingering

симулантсво *n see* симулација

симулатор *m* <flight> simulator

симулација *f* malingering

симулира *impf* to simulate, feign, sham; to malinger; симулира дека е болен (симулира болест) he is feigning illness

симултан *adj* simultaneous; симултан превод simultaneous interpreting

симултанка *f Chess* simultaneous match

симфониета *f Mus.* sinfonietta

симфонија -ии *f* symphony

симфониски *adj* symphonic; симфониски концерт symphony concert; симфониски оркестар symphony orchestra

симфоничар *m* 1 symphonist, composer of symphonies 2 member of a symphony orchestra

син[1] *m* son; ❑ блудниот син the prodigal son; духовен син spiritual son; кучешки (песји) син *sl.* son of a bitch; *colloq.* мамин син mummy's boy, sissy, milksop; каков што е таткото, таков е и синот *prov.* like father, like son; страдна мајка за слепаго сина *prov.* half a loaf is better than no bread

син[2] *adj* (*модар*) blue; сини очи blue eyes; сино море blue sea; ❑ син камен bluestone, blue vitriol, copper sulphate; сини колца под очите rings under the eyes; син патлиџан eggplant, aubergine; сина крв blue blood

синагога *f* synagogue

синап *m Bot.* (Sinapis arvensis, *also* Brassica arvensis & Brassica nigra) mustard; див синап charlock

синапов *adj* mustard *attrib.*; синапово зрно mustard seed

Сингапур *m* Singapore

Сингапу́рец -рци *m* Singaporean

Сингапу́рка *f (fem. form) see* Сингапурец

сингапу́рски *adj* Singaporean

сингел *m Rel.* <Orthodox> syncellus, church dignitary

сингл *m Sport.* singles

сингула́р *m Gram. (еднина)* singular

сингула́рен -рна *adj Gram. (еднински)* singular; сингуларни форми singular forms

синдик -ци *m* syndic, advocate, legal agent

синдика́лен -лна *adj* syndicalist; <of/for a> syndicate/trade union; синдикално движење trade-union movement

синдикали́зам -змот *m* syndicalism

синдикали́ст *m* syndicate member; trade-unionist

синдикалистички *adj* <of a> syndicalist; синдикалистичка струја syndicalist movement

синдика́т *m* trade union; syndicate

синдрак -ци *m colloq.* mummy's boy (pet, darling); milksop

синдром *m Med.* syndrome

сине *n dim. of* син¹

сине́ст *m* film director; cineaste, film-buff

синевина *f* blue, blueness; небесна синевина the blue of the sky

синевица *f* 1 *see* синевина 2 *see* модрица

синегдо́ха *f* synecdoche

синее *impf* I to make blue II – се to turn blue *intrans.*; to look blue

синеку́ра *f* sinecure

синеку́рен -рна *adj* <of/as a> sinecure

синемаско́п *m* cinemascope (wide-screen) theatre

синец -нци *f* type of pear

синииче *n dim. of* синија 1

синија -ии *f arch.* 1 round metal tray; flat baking tray 2 round table

синило *n* washing blue, *Am.* laundry bluing

синина *f see* синевина

сининка *f dim. of* синина

синкав *adj* blueish; синкав чад blueish smoke

синко -овци *m (only in the voc.) see* син¹

синковец -вци *m* rogue, ne'er-do-well, good-for-nothing

синко́па *f* 1 *Mus.* syncopation 2 *Med.* syncope 3 *Gram.* syncope

сино *n* blue

синов *adj* son's

синовски *adj* filial; синовски долг filial duty

синод *m* synod

синода́лен -лна *adj see* синодски

синодски *adj* synodical, synodal

синокрил *adj poet.* blue-winged

синоличка *f Bot.* (Viola) violet, *see* теменуга, темјануга

синоло́г -зи *m* sinologist

синологија *f* sinology, Chinese Studies

синолошки *adj* sinological; синолошки испитувања studies in sinology

синони́м *m* synonym

синони́мен -мна *adj* synonymous; синонимен израз a synonymous expression

синонимика *f* synonymy

синоок *adj* blue-eyed

синопсис *m* synopsis; trailer

синоптика *f* meteorology, weather forecasting

синоптичар *m* meteorologist, weather forecaster

синоптички *adj* synoptic; синоптичка карта synoptic chart

синор *m* boundary<-line>; balk; pale; precinct<s>; манастирски синор monastery precinct (close); во синорот на селото within the bounds of the village; волкот на синорот не дави *prov.* it is a foolish bird that fouls its own nest

синорен -рна *adj* <of a> boundary/precinct; синорен камен landmark

синост *f see* синевина

синотија *f see* синевина

синоќа *adv* yesterday evening, last night

синоќашен -шна *adj see* синоќен

синоќен -ќна & *(more usu.)* **синоќешен** -шна *adj* last night's

синоубиец -јци *m literary* filicide

синоубиство *n literary* filicide

синтагма *f Ling.* syntagma

синтакса *f Ling.* syntax

синтаксичен -чна *adj see* синтактичен

синтактичен -чна *adj* syntactic; синтактична анализа syntactic analysis

синтактички *adj see* синтактичен

синте́за *f* synthesis

синтетизи́ра *pf & impf* to synthesize; *Chem.* to obtain by synthesis

синтетика *f* synthetic methods; synthetic materials

синтетичен -чна *adj* synthetic; синтетично влакно synthetic fibre; синтетични јазици synthetic languages

синтетички *adj see* синтетичен

синус *m* 1 *Math.* sine 2 *Med.* sinus; воспаление на синусите sinusitis

синусен -сна *adj* <of a> sine; <of the> sinuses; синусна функција <function of a> sine; синусно воспаление sinusitis

синусов *adj* <of a> sine

синхрони́зам -змот *m* synchronism

синхрониза́тор *m* synchronizer

синхронизација *f* synchronization

синхронизацио́нен -она *adj* <of> synchronization; синхронизациона камера synchronization camera

синхронизи́ра *pf & impf* to synchronize *trans.*

синхроничен -чна *adj* synchronous, contemporaneous; synchronic; синхронична таблица synchronic table; синхроничен метод synchronic method

синче *n dim. of* син¹; sonny

синчец *m Bot.* (Centaurea cyanus) cornflower, bluebottle

синџир *m* chain; *pl* fetters, shackles, manacles

синџирлија *adj indecl. colloq.* <like a> chain

синџирче *n dim. of* синџир; синџирче за саат watch chain

синџирџија -ии *m arch.* 1 chain-maker 2 jailer, *Brit.* gaoler; warder

сињ *adj see* син²

сињак *m* hoar-frost, rime

сињелко *m dial.* the Lord

сињоличка *f see* синоличка

сиот, сета, сето, *pl* сите *pron* all; сиот народ the

whole nation; all the people; од сите страни from all sides; ❏ не е со сиот ум; не е со сите he's not quite right in the head, he is not all there; сите до еден to the last man; сите како еден as one man

сип *m* scree

сип, сип *interj* cheep, cheep (*imitating bird call*)

сипа *f see* сепија

сипак -ци *m see* сипка[1]

сипаница *f* pox; мали сипаници measles; chickenpox; големи сипаници smallpox, variola

сипаничав *adj* 1 suffering from chickenpox/measles/smallpox 2 pock-marked; сипаничаво лице pock-marked face

сипе[1] *pf* сипа *aor.* I to pour *trans.*; сипе една чаша вода to pour a glass of water II – ce 1 to spill *intrans.*; to fall apart, crumble *intrans.*; to scatter, disperse *intrans.*; стадото се сипало the flock has scattered 2 to come out in a rash; се сипале децата по снагата the children have broken out in a rash all over their bodies 3 *fig.* (*with dat.*) to attack (*s.o.*)

сипе[2] *impf* I 1 to pour *trans.*; to decant; сипе вино to pour wine 2 to pour *intrans.*, fall; сипе <непрекинато> дожд it is pouring with rain 3 *fig.* сипат искри showers of sparks are falling; сипе навреди to heap insults (*на – on*); сипе цитати to spout II – ce 1 to spill *intrans.*; to leak *intrans.* 2 to pour forth, shower, strew *intrans.*; куршуми се сипат bullets are flying in all directions 3 to wear out *intrans.*; to crumble *intrans.*; се сипат килимите the carpets are wearing thin; се сипе земјата the ground is giving way

сипка[1] *f* pimple, pock, pustule

сипка[2] *f Zool.* (Parus) tit<mouse>; голема сипка (Parus major) great tit; мала (модроглава) сипка (Parus caeruleus) blue tit

сипкав *adj* 1 *see* сиплив 2 hoarse; сипкав глас hoarse voice

сипкавост *f* hoarseness

сиплив *adj* loose, friable; сиплива земја loose soil

сипливост *f* friability

сир *m* a <ball (cake) of> cheese

сирак -ци *m* orphan; *fig.* friendless person; остане сирак to be orphaned

сираче *n dim. of* сирак

сираченце *n hyp. of* сирак

сирачка *f* (*fem. form*) *see* сирак

сирачки *adj* orphan's

сирен -рна *adj in the expression:* Сирна недела Shrovetide, carnival week

сире́на *f* 1 *Myth., fig.* siren (*seductive woman*) 2 siren, hooter; автомобилска сирена horn, hooter; фабричка сирена factory whistle (hooter)

сиренце *n hyp. of* сирење[1]

сирењар *m* cheese-maker; cheesemonger

сирењарка *f* (*fem. form*) *see* сирењар

сирењарски *adj* <of/for> cheese-making; cheesemonger's; сирењарско производство cheese production

сирењарство *n* cheese-making

сирење[1] *n* cheese; младо сирење fresh cheese; овчо сирење sheep's-milk cheese; ❏ брат за брат<а>, сирење за пари business is business

сирење[2] *n* curdling (*of milk into cheese*); сирење на млекото curdling of milk

сири *impf* I to curdle, turn into cheese *trans.*, make cheese II – ce to curdle *intrans.*, to turn into cheese *intrans.*

Сириец -ијци *m* Syrian

Сирија *f* Syria

Сиријка *f* (*fem. form*) *see* Сириец

сириски *adj* Syrian

сириште *n* rennet

Сирница[1] *f* (*Сирна недела*) Shrovetide

сирница[2] *f* cheese-tub, cheese-making vat

сирњача *f Bot.* (Boletus edulis) cep

сироват *adj usu. in the expression:* сировата урда curds (*left after making cheese*)

сиромав[1] -ци *m* poor man, pauper, down-and-out; кога ќе се фати сиромавиот на оро, ќе се скине тапанот the poor devil; the poor suffer all the wrong

сиромав[2] *adj* (*m only*) poor, destitute, wretched

сиромавче *n dim. of* сиромав[1]

сиромашен -шна *adj* poor, destitute; *fig.* feeble, bland; сиромашна фантазија feeble imagination; сиромашна природа monotonous landscape

сиромашец -шци *m dim. of* сиромав[1]

сиромаши <ce> *impf* to become impoverished, be reduced to poverty

сиромашија *f see* сиромаштија

сиромашка *f* (*fem. form*) *see* сиромав[1]

сиромашки *adj* poor, wretched, meagre; ❏ сиромашко лето Indian summer

сиромашност *f* poverty; сиромашност на мислата poverty of thought; сиромашност на духот spiritual poverty

сиромаштво *n see* сиромаштија 1

сиромаштија *f* 1 poverty; penury; ❏ сиромаштија до шија utter (grinding) poverty, hand-to-mouth existence; сиромаштија и кашлица не можат да се скријат *prov.* poverty and a cough cannot be hid; сиромаштијата од болест е полоша *prov.* health without wealth is half a sickness 2 *coll.* the poor, the destitute, *colloq.* the have-nots

сиромашче *n see* сиромавче

сиропиталиште *n arch.* orphanage; *Brit. Hist.* workhouse, poorhouse

сироса се *pf see* засири се

сиросан *pt see* засирен

сиросува се *impf of* сироса се

сирота[1] *f* poor woman

сирота[2] -о, -и *adj not usu. m, see* сиромав[2]

сиротен -тна *adj see* сиромав[2], сиромашен

сиротински *adj see* сиромашки

сиротица *f* 1 orphan girl; lonely woman/girl 2 unfortunate, wretched woman

сиротност *f see* сиромашност, сиромаштија 1

сируп *m* syrup; малинов сируп raspberry syrup

сисавец *m Bot.* (Juncus communis) rush

систем *m* system; сончевиот систем the solar system; нервен систем nervous system; енергетски систем power grid; изборен систем electoral (voting) system

система *f see* систем

систематизација -ии *f* systematization; reorganization; rationalization; систематизација на работните места rationalization of positions

систематизи́ра *pf & impf* to systematize, set in order, reorganize, rationalize *trans.*

систематика *f* 1 systematization 2 taxonomy

систематичар *m* 1 taxonomist 2 methodical person

систематичен -чна *adj see* систематски

система́тски *adj* systematic; methodical; regular; систематско учење systematic study; систематска контрола regular checks

системен -мна *adj* systematic, methodical; systemic

сит *adj* 1 satisfied, satiated, replete, full; ❑ и волкот сит, и овците на број all parties are satisfied; сит гладен не верува half the world doesn't know how the other half lives 2 lavish, bountiful; сита трпеза hearty meal; lavish spread; сита година a fat (good) year 3 *fig.* fed up (*од – with*); сит од животот tired of life

ситар *m* sieve-maker/-dealer

ситарка *f* (*fem. form*) *see* ситар

ситен¹ -тна *adj* 1 fine; small; ситен дожд light rain, drizzle; ситно стопанство small farming, smallholding; ❑ ситен добиток sheep and goats; ситен од mincing gait; ситни пари small change; petty cash; ситна риба small fry; ситна кражба petty larceny 2 minor, insignificant, petty, small; ситен чиновник minor civil servant; petty official

ситен² -тна *adj arch. see* сит 2

ситенце *n dim. of* сито

ситест *adj* sievelike, *Anat.*, *Bot.*, *Zool.* cribriform; *Anat.* ситеста коска ethmoid bone; *Bot.* ситеста цевка sieve tube

сити *impf* I (*наситува*) to satisfy, satiate, sate II – се 1 (*наситува се*) to eat one's fill; to get (become) saturated; земјата се сити the ground is waterlogged (saturated) 2 *fig.* (*with dat.*) to gloat over (*s.o.'s*) misfortune, crow over (*s.o.*)

ситнак -ци *m Bot.* (Quercus lanuginosa *or* pubescens) downy oak

ситнеж *m* 1 odds and ends, knick-knacks; trifles; ситнеж од кокошка giblets 2 (*пари*) small change; petty cash

ситни *impf* 1 to chop up; to divide up *trans.*; (*пари*) to break, get change 2 to walk with a mincing gait; to scurry; to dance briskly, trip *intrans.*; ситни оро to dance a folk-dance briskly

ситнина *f see* ситнеж

ситница *f* 1 trinket, knick-knack; oddment 2 trifle, bagatelle; до ситници to the last detail; ❑ се фаќа за ситници to carp, cavil 3 small fruit<-tree>

ситничав *adj* meticulous; hair-splitting, cavilling; ситничав дух petty mind

ситничар *m* 1 *obs.* dealer in sundries 2 *fig.* perfectionist, nit-picker

ситничари *impf* to carp, cavil, split hairs

ситничарка *f* (*fem. form*) *see* ситничар

ситничарски *adj* petty, petty-minded; hair-splitting, cavilling, nit-picking

ситничарство *n* pettiness, petty-mindedness; meticulousness; hair-splitting, nit-picking, pedantry

ситно¹ *n see* ситнеж, ситнина

ситно² *adv* finely; daintily; ❑ продава на ситно to <sell> retail

ситнобуржоа́ски *adj* petty bourgeois

ситнозрнест *adj* small-seed; small-grained, fine-grained

ситноклас *adj in the expression:* ситнокласа пченица small-ear wheat

ситнолик *adj* dainty-faced, small-faced

ситноод *adj* mincing, tripping

ситносопственик -ци *m* small proprietor; smallholder

ситносопственички *adj* small proprietor's; smallholder's

ситнотија *f* 1 smallness, fineness 2 sundries; odds and ends, knick-knacks

ситнурија -ии *f* sundries; knick-knacks; разни ситнурии various odds and ends

сито *n* 1 sieve; ситно сито fine sieve; ❑ поминал <и> сито и решето he has been through the mill (through thick and thin) 2 *fig.*, *colloq.* hurdle; obstacle

ситовиден -дна *adj see* ситест

ситост *f* satiety, satiation, repletion; до ситост to satiety; држи ситост (*of food*) to be satisfying (filling)

ситуација -ии *f* situation; site plan, layout; ❑ дораснат на ситуацијата equal to the occasion; спасува ситуација to save the day; проценува ситуација to size up a situation

ситуацио́нен -она *adj* <of> layout, site plan; ситуационен план site plan

ситуи́ра *pf & impf* to place; to set up, situate

ситуи́ран *pt* located; well-to-do, well-off

ситце *n dim. of* сито

сифилис *m Med.* syphilis

сифилитичар *m Med.* syphilis patient, syphilitic

сифилитичарка *f* (*fem. form*) *see* сифилитичар

сифилитичен -чна *adj see* сифилитички

сифилитички *adj* syphilitic

сифо́н *m* siphon

сифо́нски *adj* <of a> siphon

сицил *m arch.* court register, judicial record<s>

сицим *m colloq.* cord, rope

сицимка *f colloq. see* сицим

сјагна *adj* (*f only*) pregnant (*of a sheep*), with lamb

сјае *impf* I to shine, gleam, sparkle; to twinkle; to beam; месечината сјае the moon is shining; сјае од радост to be radiant with happiness II – се to shine *intrans.*; езерото се сјае на сонце the lake shines in the sunlight

сјаен -јна *adj* brilliant (*also fig.*), bright, shiny; *fig.* splendid, magnificent; сјајно сонце the bright sun; сјајни бои bright colours; сјаен пример shining example; сјаен талент a brilliant talent; сјаен доказ compelling proof

сјаи (се) *impf see* сјае (се)

сјај *m* radiance, glow; lustre, twinkle; *fig.* splendour; сјај во око twinkle in the eye; ❑ во сиот сјај in all one's glory

сјајност *f* brilliance; brightness

скади (се) *pf see* задими (се), зачади (се)

скадува (се) *impf of* скади (се)

сказ *m poet. see* сказна

сказна *f* tale, folk-tale, myth, fable

скај *m* imitation leather

скака *impf see* скока

скакал *m see* скакулец

скакалец -лци *m see* скакулец

скакарака *f see* сврака, страчка 1

скакне *pf* скакна *aor. see* скокне

скакулец -лци *m Zool.* (Locusta) locust, grasshopper; рој скакулци a swarm of locusts

скала¹ *f* ladder; (*usu. pl*) steps, stairs, staircase; ❑

светов (веков) е скала times change, life has its ups and downs; општествена скала social ladder (hierarchy)

скала² *f* scale; dial; пее скали to sing scales; скалата на радиоапарат dial of a radio; скала на термометар scale of a thermometer

скала³ *f dial.* rock, boulder

скалапи *pf* **I 1** to mould, form, shape *trans.* **2** to slap together, cobble together; to dash off *trans.* **II – се** (*of people*) to fit in

скалапува (се) *impf of* скалапи (се)

скалест *adj dial.* rocky

скалило *n* rung, step; *fig.* stage, level; ниско скалило на култура low level of culture

скалица & скаличка *f dim. of* скала¹

скалиште *n augm. of* скала¹

скалп *m* scalp

скалпел *m* scalpel

скалпира *pf & impf* to scalp

скалун *m &* **скалунка** *f* **1** leek **2** *fig.* tall, lanky man; beanpole

скама *f see* сапуница

скаменет *pt* **1** petrified, fossilized; скаменета шума petrified forest; скаменети животни fossilized animals; скаменета останка fossil **2** *fig.* callous, insensitive; скаменето срце heart of stone

скаменетост *f* **1** petrification, fossilization **2** insensitivity, lack of feeling

скамени *pf* **I** to turn to stone, petrify *trans.* **II – се 1** to turn into stone, petrify *intrans.*; to become fossilized **2** *fig.* to freeze *intrans.*; се скамени од чудо to freeze in wonder **3** *fig.* to become callous; му се скамени срцето his heart grew cold

скаменува (се) *impf of* скамени (се)

скамија *-ии f arch.* school desk

скандал *m* **1** scandal **2** rumpus, rowdy scene

скандализира *pf & impf* to scandalize, shock

скандалозен *-зна adj* **1** scandalous **2** *colloq.* notorious; rowdy; скандалозен човек reprobate; trouble-maker, *enfant terrible*

Скандинавец *-вци m* Scandinavian

Скандинавија *f* Scandinavia

Скандинавка *f* (*fem. form*) *see* Скандинавец

скандинавски *adj* Scandinavian

скандира *pf & impf* **1** to declaim, recite **2** to chant (*e.g. slogans*); го скандираа неговото име they chanted his name

скап *adj* **1** dear, expensive, costly; скапи подароци expensive gifts; скап хотел an expensive hotel **2** valuable, precious; скап опит valuable experience **3** *literary, rare* dear, cherished, beloved; скапи спомени cherished memories; скап гостин welcome guest

скапан *pt* **1** rotten; скапано овошје rotten fruit; скапано дрво rotten tree; ❑ има скапани пари to have a lot of money, be swimming in money **2** *fig.* worn out, tired out, exhausted; сиот е скапан he's completely exhausted

скапаник *-ци m see* скапаница

скапаница *f & m* **1** (*гниеж*) rot, decay **2** *fig., colloq.* blockhead, dunce

скапаност *f* **1** rottenness **2** *fig.* exhaustion

скапе *pf* скапа *aor.* **I 1** to rot, decay; to disintegrate; скапе в затвор to rot in prison **2** *fig.* to overwork

trans. **3** to beat up *trans.* **II – се 1** *see* **I** 1 **2** to work o.s to death, sweat blood

скапен *-пна adj arch. see* скап 3

скапец *-пци m* ridge, spur

скапија *f see* скапотија

скапнат *adj see* капнат, скапан 2

скапнатост *f* exhaustion

скапне *pf* скапна *aor.* to get tired, worn out, exhausted

скапнува *impf of* скапне

скапнувачка *f* exhaustion; не знае за скапнувачка he never gets tired

скапо *adv* dear<ly>; ❑ кој не го знае, скапо ќе го плати appearances are deceptive; you can't tell a book by its cover

скапотија *f* expensiveness, high prices, high cost of living

скапоцен *adj* precious, expensive, priceless; скапоцен камен precious stone

скапоценост *f* jewel, piece of jewellery (*Am.* jewelry), gem; скапоцености valuables, items of value

скапува (се) *impf of* скапе (се)

скапчија *-ии m colloq.* extortioner

скапчика *f* (*fem. form*) *see* скапчија

скара¹ *f* grill, barbecue; grilled meat; електрична скара electric grill

скара² *pf* **I 1** to set at odds (at loggerheads); to estrange **2** to tell off, scold, reprimand **II – се 1** to pick a quarrel, fall out (*co – with*); се скара со зелката he doesn't like (doesn't eat) cabbage **2** *see* **I** 2; му се скара he told him off

скарлатина *f Med.* scarlet fever

скарува (се) *impf of* скара² (се)

скарувачка *f* quarrel, fight

скаса се *pf* to start fighting, squabbling

скаска *f see* сказна

скастри *pf* **1** to prune, trim; скастри дрво to trim a tree **2** *fig.* to cut, curtail, reduce; скастри буџет to cut a budget **3** *fig.* to cut (*s.o.*) off (prevent s.o. speaking), cut short, interrupt **4** *fig.* to reprimand, scold, tick off

скаструва *impf of* скастри

скафандер *m* diving suit; space suit

скачи¹ (се) *pf see* искачи (се)

скачи² *се pf* **1** to become involved (*co – with*); to become intimate **2** *fig.* to pick a quarrel (fight) (*co – with*)

скачка *f Zool. see* скакулец

скачува¹ (се) *impf of* скачи¹ (се)

скачува² *се impf of* скачи² (се)

скашка *pf* **I** to dirty, soil **II – се** to dirty, soil o.s.; ❑ се скашка работата things got messed up

скашкува (се) *impf of* скашка (се)

скашла се *pf* to <start to> cough

скашлува се *impf of* скашла се

сквер *m* <town> square

сквернавење *n* sacrilege; blasphemy

сквернави *impf* to defile, desecrate; to sully

сквернење *n see* сквернавење

скверни *impf see* сквернави

скеј<т>борд *m* skateboard

скела *f see* скеле

скеларина *f* ferry toll

скеле *n* **1** scaffolding; stage frame **2** ferry; raft

скелет *m* **1** skeleton **2** *fig.* frame, framework; shell;

outline, bare bones; **скелет на зграда** frame of a building

скелетен -тна *adj* skeletal

скелецuja -ии *m* ferryman

скелецински *adj* ferryman's

скенер *m* scanner

скепса *f see* скептицизам

скептик -ци *m* sceptic

скептици́зам -змот *m* scepticism

скептичар *m rare see* скептик

скептичен -чна *adj* sceptical

скептички *adj* sceptical

скептичност *f* scepticism, sceptical attitude

скерцо *n Mus.* scherzo

скеч *m Theatre, Art* sketch

ски-лифт *m* ski-lift

скија *f* (*usu. pl*) ski<s>

скија се *impf* to ski

скијач *m* skier

скијачки *adj* skier's; skiing; **скијачка опрема** skiing equipment; **скијачки спорт** skiing

скимне *pf* скимна *aor.* (*with dat.*) to cross (*s.o.'s*) mind, occur (*to s.o.*); **му скимна да си отиде** he took it into his head to leave; **ми скимна** I've had an idea

скимнува *impf of* скимне

скинат *pt* 1 torn, ragged, in tatters (shreds) 2 *fig.* worn out, exhausted

скине *pf* скина *aor.* I 1 to tear, rip; to tear up; to tear off; ❏ **скине конци** to kick the bucket; **скине некому конци** to thwart (frustrate) s.o.'s plans 2 to pick, pluck; **скине цвеќиња** to pick flowers; ❏ **ја скине зелена** to botch (*s.th.*) 3 (*пат, врски*) to block, cut off 4 *fig.* to exhaust, wear out; **скине некого од работа** to work s.o. to death; **скине некого од ќотек** to give s.o. a good hiding II – **се** 1 to tear, to rip *intrans.*; to get torn 2 (*за патишта, врски*) to be blocked, cut 3 to drop off, fall off 4 *fig.* to wear o.s. out, exhaust o.s.; **се скине од работа** to work o.s. to death

скинува (се) *impf of* скине (се)

скинувачка *f* exhaustion; ruin; **таа работа е скинувачка** that job is back-breaking

скипи *pf* скипе *aor.* to boil *intrans.*, seethe (*also fig.*); **скипи водата во него** the water boiled; **скипе од лутина** to seethe with rage

скипне *pf* скипна *aor.* to subside, recede, ebb; *fig.* to fade away, die down

скипнува *impf of* скипне

скиптар -три *m* sceptre; **под скиптарот на некого** under s.o.'s rule

скипува *impf of* скипи

скисели *pf* I to turn sour *trans.*; (*млеко*) to curdle *trans.*; (*зеленчук*) to pickle II – **се** 1 to go sour; (*за млеко*) to curdle *intrans.*; (*за зеленчук*) to be pickled; (*за тесто*) to rise; (*расипе се*) to go bad (off) 2 *fig.* to get upset/depressed

скиселува (се) *impf of* скисели (се)

скиснат *pt* upset, out of sorts; dejected, depressed; in a bad mood

скиснатост *f* annoyance; ill humour

скисне <**се**> *pf* скисна <**се**> *aor.* to go bad (off); to turn sour *intrans.*; (*за тесто*) to rise; *fig.* to get upset, become distressed/dejected

скиснува <**се**> *impf of* скисне <**се**>

скита <**се**> *impf* to wander, roam, rove; to gad about;

скита по светот to roam the world; **кој пита, не скита** *prov.* better to ask the way than go astray

скиталец -лци *m see* скитач

скитач *m* wanderer, roamer; vagrant, tramp, vagabond; nomad

скитачки *adj see* скитнички

скитне *pf* скитна *aor.* to wander, rove, roam (*for a while*)

скитник -ци *m see* скитач; **светски скитник** globetrotter

скитница *f* (*fem. form*) *see* скитник

скитнички *adj* roving, roaming; nomadic

скитништво *n* nomadic life; vagrancy

скиф *m* skiff; racing shell; **натпревари во скиф** single sculls

скифи́ст *m* sculler

скица *f* sketch; sketch-plan; musical study; outline, draft; **скица на град** street-plan; **скица на реферат** draft report

скици́ра *pf & impf* to sketch; to draft

склад[1] *m* store, storehouse, warehouse, depot; storeroom; **склад за дрва** timber-yard; ❏ **има на склад** to have (keep) in stock

склад[2] *m literary* (*хармонија*) harmony, accord; **во склад со** in accordance (agreement) with

складен -дна *adj literary* (*хармоничен*) harmonious

склади́ра *pf & impf* to store; to stockpile

складиште *n see* склад[1]

складиштен -тна *adj* store, storing, storage; **складиштен простор** warehouse capacity, storage space

складност *f literary* (*хармоничност*) harmony, accord

склек -ци *m Sport.* sit-up

склепа *pf* to throw together, cobble together, slap together

склепува *impf of* склепа

склеро́за *f Med.* sclerosis; **склероза на крвните садови** arteriosclerosis

склеро́зен -зна *adj Med.* sclerotic, indurated; **склерозни појави** signs of sclerosis

склеро́тик -ци & **склеротичар** *m Med.* sclerosis patient, sclerotic

склеротичен -чна *adj Med.* sclerotic; **склеротични крвни садови** sclerotic (indurated) arteries

склечка се *pf* to become involved (*со – with*); to become intimate

склечкува се *impf of* склечка се

склештен *pt* wedged in, clamped; cornered; **склештени раце** clenched hands; locked arms

склешти *pf* I 1 to grip, clamp; to wedge in; to clench; **склешти вилици** to clench (grit) one's teeth II – **се** to squirm, writhe, double up

склештува (се) *impf of* склешти (се)

склобурец -рци *m* (*клобурец*) bubble

склон *adj* inclined, disposed; **склон кон пиење** inclined to drink; **склон кон музиката** fond of music

склони *pf* I 1 (*наклони*) to bend, incline, tilt *trans.* 2 *fig.* to persuade, dispose, induce; **го склонила да отиде со нив** she persuaded him to go with them 3 *fig.* to consent, agree II – **се** 1 (*наклони се*) to bend <over>, lean <over> *intrans.* 2 *fig. see* I 3

склоност *f* inclination, tendency; liking, partiality; taste; propensity; **склоност кон дебелење** tendency to corpulence; склоност кон пиење partiality to drink; склоност кон (за) штедење propensity to save

склонува (се) *impf of* склони (се)

склоп *m* structure, composition; *Tech.* fit (*as of machine parts*); ❏ во склопот на as part/member of, within

склопец -пци *m* container (*esp. for cheese*)

склопи *pf* **1** to put together, assemble; to fit *trans.*; to fold up *trans.* **2** (*очи, клепки*) to shut, close **3** to conclude; склопи сојуз to form an alliance; склопи брак to contract a marriage, get married

склопит *adj see* склопитен

склопитен -тна *adj* folding, collapsible; ноже склопитно penknife, pocket knife; jack-knife

склопува *impf of* склопи

склопчи се *pf* to curl up *intrans.*

склопчува се *impf of* склопчи се

склоца *pf* to start kicking *intrans.*

склоцува *impf of* склоца

склука *pf* **1** (*strona*) to start knocking (banging); склука на порта to start knocking at a door **2** to start stinging/throbbing; ме склука раната my wound began to throb

склукува *impf of* склука

склупица *f see* склупца

склупца *f* **1** mousetrap; trap, snare; ❏ се фати в склупца to fall into a trap

склупчи се *pf see* склопчи се

склупчува се *impf see* склопчува се

склучен *pt* (*за раце*) folded, clasped; (*за вилици*) clenched; contracted; склучени веѓи puckered brows; со склучени раце with folded arms; with clasped hands

склучи *pf* **I 1** to join, link *trans.*; (*за раце*) to fold; to clasp; (*за веѓи*) to pucker; ги склучи рацете he folded his arms; he clasped his hands **2** to conclude, contract; склучи сојуз to form an alliance; склучи брак to contract a marriage, get married; склучи мир to conclude a peace/treaty, make peace **II** – **се 1** to unite, join together *intrans.* **2** to curl up *intrans.* **3** to freeze, go numb

склучува (се) *impf of* склучи (се)

скобичка *f see* желевце 2

скобуст *m Zool.* (Chondrostoma nasus Ochridanum) Lake Ohrid carp

скова *pf* **I 1** to forge; to fashion **2** *fig.* to fabricate, concoct **3** *fig.* to pin down, restrain; to transfix **II** – **се** *fig.* to go stiff; to become petrified; се скова од чудо to be dumbfounded

скован *pt* frozen, benumbed; transfixed; скован поглед fixed gaze

скованост *f* stiffness; rigidity; awkwardness; скованост на мислата mental block; скованост на животот confined conditions of life

скове (се) *pf see* скова (се)

сковува (се) *impf of* скова (се) & скове (се)

скожури се *pf* to become wrinkled

скожурува се *impf of* скожури се

скожурчи се *pf* **1** *see* скожури се **2** *fig.* to withdraw into one's shell

скожурчува се *impf of* скожурчи се

скозна *adj* (*f only*) pregnant (*of a goat*)

скок *m* **1** jump, leap, bound; со еден скок at (in) one bound; *Sport.* скок во вода dive; diving; скок во

далечина long jump; скок во височина high jump; скок со стап pole-vault **2** *fig.* rise; surge; leap forward; скок на цените sharp rise in prices; скок на температурата sharp rise in temperature

скока *impf* **1** to jump, leap, spring; to hop; to caper, frolic; to skip; скока со падобран to parachute; to bale out; скока во височина to perform a high jump; скока на една нога to hop (*on one leg*) **2** *fig.* to rise, go up; скокаат цените prices rise sharply

скокалиште *n Sport.* jumping pit

скокалница *f Sport.* ski-jump; diving board; ❏ мамутска скокалница high ski-jump/diving board

скокалче *n* marble; игра со скокалчиња to play marbles

скоканица *f see* прескакулица

скокарка *impf dial.* (*potскокнува*) to hop, skip

скокач *m Sport.* high/long-jumper; pole-vaulter; diver

скокачка *f* (*fem. form*) *see* скокач

скокле -евци *m colloq.* jack-in-the-box, frisky person/animal

скоклест *adj colloq.* long-legged, long-shanked; скоклесто момче beanpole, lanky fellow

скоклив *adj* lively, frisky, nimble

скокне *pf* скокна *aor.* to jump, leap; to make a dash; скокнаа цените the prices have shot up; прво скокни, после речи "оп"! *prov.* don't count your chickens before they're hatched!; look before you leap!

скокнеж *m rare see* скок

скокнува *impf of* скокне

скоковит *adj* uneven, unsteady, erratic; скоковит развој rapid/uneven development; *Bot., Zool.* saltatory evolution; скоковит растеж rapid/uneven growth

скоковито *adv* unevenly, unsteadily; by leaps and bounds

скокообразен -зна *adj see* скоковит

скокот *m* tickle; ticklishness; titillation; има скокот to be ticklish

скокотка¹ *f see* скокот

скокотка² *impf* to tickle; to titillate; мислата му го скокоткаше самољубјето the thought tickled his vanity

скокоткав *adj see* скокотлив

скокотлив *adj* **1** ticklish **2** titillating; racy, spicy, erotic **3** ticklish, delicate, tricky; скокотлива тема delicate matter

скокотливост *f* ticklishness; spiciness, raciness

скокум *adv poet.* in one bound; with a jump

сколастика *f see* схоластика

сколастичар *m see* схоластик, схоластичар

сколастички *adj see* схоластичен, схоластички

сколеници *adv* on one's knees, kneeling

сколободија *f colloq.* chaos, disorder

сколовранец -нци *m Zool.* (Sturnus vulgaris) starling

скомина *f* tartness; bitter taste

скомраз *m colloq.* disgust, loathing; скомраз му е he is disgusted

сконтира *pf & impf* to grant a price reduction, discount

сконто *n* discount

сконцентрира (се) *pf & impf see* концентрира (се)

сконачние *n arch. see* сконачило

сконачи *pf arch. usu. in the expression:* сконачи со животот 1. he passed away 2. he took his own life

скончило *n arch.* 1 conclusion; end; скончилото на светот the end of the world 2 death; му дошло скончилото he met his end

скончува *impf of* скончи

скопа *pf (ископа)* to dig <up, over>

скопак -ци *m* 1 *(евнух)* eunuch 2 castrated animal

скопец[1] -пци *m see* скопак

скопец[2] -пци *m (копец)* clasp; buckle; hook and eye

скопи *impf* to castrate; to geld

скопјанец -ни *m* person from Skopje

скопјанка *f (fem. form) see* скопјанец

Скопје *n* Skopje

скопне *pf* скопна *aor.* to melt, thaw *intrans.*; скопна снегот the snow has thawed

скопнува *impf of* скопне

скопски *adj* Skopje *attrib.*

скопува *impf of* скопа

скопчи *pf* to join, link *trans.*; to clasp, interlock *trans.*; си ги скопчија рацете they joined hands

скопчува *impf of* скопчи

скор *adj rare (скорашен)* forthcoming; early; speedy; скоро оздравување speedy recovery; ❑ во <нај>скоро време <very> soon; до скоро видување see you again soon!

скорави *pf* I to cover with a hard crust/skin; to dry out *trans.*; to toughen; to coarsen; ветерот го скорави снегот the wind hardened the snow II – се to become covered with a hard crust/skin; to dry out *intrans.*; to harden, toughen *intrans.*

скоравува (се) *impf of* скорави (се)

скорашен -шна *adj* 1 recent; new, fresh 2 coming, approaching; impending; early; скорашна посета forthcoming visit

скорбут *m Med.* scurvy

скорбутен -тна *adj Med.* <of> scurvy; скорбутни симптоми symptoms of scurvy

скорен *m arch. (usu. pl)* boot; едно рало скорни a pair of boots

скорешен -шна *adj see* скорашен

скорива *impf of* скорне

скорија *f* slag, dross

скорне *pf* скорна *aor.* 1 to wake up, awaken *trans.* 2 *fig.* to provoke, engender, arouse; скорне јадови to arouse *(s.o.'s)* sorrow, rub salt into a wound 3 to make *(s.o.)* stand up

скорнува *impf of* скорне

скоро *adv* 1 *(неодамна)* recently; the other day 2 *(набрзо)* soon; ајде поскоро! come on, hurry up! колку <што> може поскоро as soon as possible; поскоро ќе умрам I'd rather (sooner) die 3 *(речиси)* almost, nearly; скоро готов nearly ready; беше скоро пладне it was almost midday

скороевец -вци *m literary* upstart, parvenu, *nouveau riche*

скорозрејка *f see* скорозрелка

скорозрелка *f* early crop, early-ripening fruit; скорозрелки кајсии early apricots; скорозрелка пченка early maize

скорпија -ии *f* 1 *Zool.* scorpion 2 *fig., colloq.* shrew; *sl.* bitch 3 *Astron.* Scorpio

скоруша *f Bot.* (Sorbus domestica) service tree; service-berry, sorb-apple; *see* оск<о>руша

скорчав *adj* knotty; gnarled; скорчаво дрво knotty wood; gnarled tree

скоси *pf* to cut down, mow; to reap; *fig.* to mow down

скосува *impf of* скоси

скот *m* beast, brute *(also fig.)*; ❑ живее како скот to lead a dog's life

скотна *adj (f only)* pregnant *(of cats, rabbits, hares)*

скотски *adj fig.* swinish, brutish

скотство *n colloq.* brutishness; base act

скотштина *f see* скотство

скочанет *pt* frozen; stiff; lifeless; скочанети прсти stiff fingers

скочани *pf* I to freeze *trans.*; to stiffen with cold II – се 1 to stiffen *intrans.*, go stiff with cold; to go numb 2 *fig.* to be petrified *(with fear)*; to be taken aback

скочанува (се) *impf of* скочани (се)

скраен -јна *adj see* краен

скраја *adv* far away, distant *(од – from)*; ❑ скраја нека е! скраја да е! 1. God forbid! 2. good riddance!

скрака *pf* to <start to> cackle, quack, crow

скрама *f* skin; scum

скрапла *f see* скорпија

скрастави *pf see* крастоса <се>

скраставува (се) *impf of* скрастави (се)

скрастоса (се) *pf see* скрастави (се)

скрастосува (се) *impf of* скрастоса (се)

скратен *pt* shortened; reduced; curtailed; abbreviated; скратено работно време reduced working hours

скратеница *f* abbreviation

скрати *pf* I 1 to shorten *trans.*; to cut short, curtail; to abbreviate; to take a short cut; скрати постапка to curtail proceedings; скрати напис to abridge a report; ❑ скрати малку! *colloq.* stop bragging! 2 to reduce, cut <down>; to retrench; скрати приходи to reduce income; скрати број на работници to make staffing cuts 3 *Math.* to cancel II – се 1 to get shorter; to shrink *intrans.*; се скратија деновите the days became shorter 2 to be reduced (cut), go down; расходите се скратија our expenses have been cut

скратува (се) *impf of* скрати (се)

скрб *f literary* grief, sorrow; со скрб во душата with a heavy heart

скрбен -бна *adj literary* sorrowful, sad, mournful; скрбна вест sad news; скрбен поглед mournful expression

скрби *impf literary* to be sad; to grieve, mourn; скрби по некого to mourn s.o.

скрвавен *pt* covered with blood, bloody; bloodshot; скрвавени очи bloodshot eyes

скрвави *pf* I to stain (smear) with blood; to cause to bleed, draw blood II – се 1 to become covered in blood; to start bleeding; *(за очи)* to become bloodshot 2 *fig. (with dat.)* to irk, weary, bore; ми се скрвави оваа работа I'm sick and tired of this business

скрвавува (се) *impf of* скрвави (се)

скрви се *pf* to quarrel; to become mortal enemies

скрвничи се *pf (with dat.)* to irk, bore; to become unbearable; тој ми се скрвничи веќе I can't bear him any more

скрвува се *impf of* скрви се

скрди *pf* I to round up *(usu. sheep)* II – се to get together, gather *intrans.*

скрдува (се) *impf of* скрди (се)

скреба *f Bot.* (Clematis vitalba) traveller's joy, old man's beard

скреж *m* hoar-frost, rime
скрежен -жна *adj poet.* <of> hoar-frost, rime
скрежец -шци *m see* црцорец, штурец
скрека *pf* 1 (*за жаба*) to <start to> croak 2 *fig.* to <start to> shout
скрекува *impf of* скрека
скреска *pf* to <start to> scream/shriek
скрескува *impf of* скреска
скржав *adj* 1 mean, miserly, stingy 2 *fig.* meagre, scanty; скржава светлина faint (poor) light 3 *fig.* moderate, restrained; скржав на зборови taciturn, tight-lipped
скржавец -вци *m* skinflint, miser
скржави *impf* to be miserly
скржавко -овци *m see* скржавец
скржавост *f* meanness, miserliness, stinginess, avarice
скржавштина *f see* скржавост
скржец -шци *m see* скржавец
скривалиште *n see* скривница
скриви *pf* to do wrong; (*with dat.*) to offend, harm, wrong
скривница *f* hiding-place; shelter, *colloq.* hide-out; *Mil.* bunker, dugout; (*за драгоцености*) cache
скрие *pf* скри *aor.* I to hide *trans.*, conceal; to keep secret II – **се** 1 to hide *intrans.*; се скриле во шумата they hid in the forest 2 to disappear, vanish; месечината се скри зад облаците the moon disappeared behind the clouds
скриен *pt* hidden, concealed; secret; скриена опасност a hidden danger; скриени можности latent possibilities
скријалиште *n dial. see* скривница
скрипец[1] -шци *m* windlass, winch; pulley, block
скрипец[2] -шци *m Bot.* (Silene vulgaris) bladder campion
скрипта *f* (*usu. pl*) 1 manuscript, paper 2 lecture notes
скришем<а> *adv see* скришум
скришен -шна *adj* secret, clandestine, covert; hidden; скришни работи clandestine activities
скришно *adv* secretly, in secret; работи скришно to work clandestinely
скришност *f* secrecy, covertness, furtiveness
скришум *adv* secretly, in secret, furtively
скрка *f* barren soil, stony ground
скркори *pf* 1 to <start to> wheeze 2 (*за црева*) to <start to> rumble 3 *dial.* (*скрека*) to <start to> croak 4 (*за’рка*) to <start to> snore
скркорува *impf of* скркори
скрнави *impf see* сквернави
скроб *m* starch
скробен -бна *adj* starch, starchy; скробно брашно starchy flour
скроби *impf* to starch
скрои *pf* 1 to cut out; скрои фустан to cut out a dress; ❑ скрои некому капа to cook s.o.'s goose; како се скроил, така ќе се искине *prov.* the leopard cannot change his spots; уште Петко нероден, капа му скроиле *prov.* don't count your chickens before they're hatched 2 *fig.* to think up, concoct, *colloq.* cook up; скрои лага to concoct a lie
скројува *impf of* скрои
скромен -мна *adj* modest, humble, unpretentious; скромни примања modest income; скромни успеси modest achievements

скромничи *impf* to be overmodest; to behave humbly/demurely
скромност *f* modesty; humility; frugality
скроти *pf* I 1 (*животно, човек*) to tame 2 (*чувства*) to curb, to subdue; скроти свој гнев to overcome one's anger; скроти свои страсти to curb one's passions II – **се** 1 to become submissive, obedient 2 to calm down *intrans.*; to calm o.s.; се скроти ветрот the wind has dropped
скротител *m* tamer; trainer; скротител на лавови lion tamer
скротлив *adj* tameable; trainable; лесно скротливо животно easily trained animal
скротливост *f* tameability; amenability to training
скротне (се) *pf see* скроти (се)
скротнува (се) *impf of* скротне (се)
скротува (се) *impf of* скроти (се)
скротувач *m see* скротител
скрофули *pl Med.* scrofula
скрофулóза *f Med.* scrofula, king's evil
скрофулóзен -зна *adj Med.* scrofulous
скрпи *pf* 1 to put (slap) together; (*пари*) to scrape together 2 *see* скрои 2; скрпи некому обвинение *sl.* to frame s.o.
скрпува *impf of* скрпи
скрснозе *adv* cross-legged; седи скрснозе to sit tailor-fashion
скрсти[1] *pl see* крсти[1]
скрсти[2] *pf* (*раце*) to fold; (*нозе*) to cross; ❑ седи со скрстени раце to sit on one's hands
скрстува *impf of* скрсти
скртала (се) *impf see* стркала (се)
скрупец -шци *m* lump (*usu. of salt*)
скрупула *f* scruple; нема скрупули за to have no scruples about, make no bones about
скрупулóзен -зна *adj* scrupulous
скрупща *f see* скрупец
скрц *interj see* крц
скрца *pf see* скрцка
скрцка *pf* 1 to <start to> creak; скрцкаа штиците the floorboards creaked 2 (*со заби*) to gnash (grind) (*one's teeth*); ❑ скрцка некому со заби to threaten s.o.
скрцкува *impf of* скрцка
скрцлив *adj* creaky; squeaky
скрцне *pf* скрцна *aor. see* скрцка
скрцнува *impf of* скрцне
скршен *pt* 1 broken; ❑ нема ни скршена пара he hasn't got a penny to his name 2 *fig.* exhausted, worn-out; сиот сум скршен I'm dead beat
скрши *pf* I 1 to break *trans.*; to shatter *trans.*, smash, crush; си го скрши носот he broke his nose; ❑ го скрши мразот to break the ice; скрши некому рогови to break s.o.'s pride; to humiliate s.o.; скрши глава (врат) to vanish without trace; скрши некому ќеф not to comply with s.o.'s wish 2 *fig.* to kill, destroy; скрши некого од работа to overwork s.o.; скрши некого од ќотек to beat s.o. up 3 *colloq.* *see* скршне[2] II – **се** 1 to break *intrans.*; to shatter *intrans.*; откако ќе се скрши колата, многу патчиња се отвораат *prov.* every cloud has a silver lining 2 *fig.* to wear o.s. out, kill o.s.; се скрши од работа to work o.s. to exhaustion 3 *fig., colloq.* to hurt o.s.

скршне[1] *pf* скршна *aor.* to break off (*a little*) *trans.*; скршне едно парче леб to break off a piece of bread

скршне[2] *pf* скршна *aor.* to turn, turn off/away *intrans.*; to deviate (*од – from*); скршне од главниот пат to turn off the main road

скршнува *impf of* скршне[2]

скршува (се) *impf of* скрши (се)

скубач *m colloq.*, *fig.* leech, bloodsucker

скубе *impf* **I 1** to pluck, pull out *trans.*; скубе кокошка to pluck a chicken; скубе веѓи to pluck one's eyebrows; скубе трева/плевел to pull out grass/weeds; ❑ ги скубе косите to tear one's hair out **2** *fig.* to fleece, rook, rob, overcharge **II** – **се** to pull out one's hair; to pluck one's eyebrows

скубне *pf* скубна *aor.* **1** to pluck, pull out *trans.*, pick; скубне магдонос to pick parsley **2** *fig.* to fleece, rook **3** *fig.* to run away, bolt; скубне од затвор to break out <of prison>

скубнува *impf of* скубне

скуден -дна *adj* **1** meagre, scant; скудна сончева светлина wan sunlight; скудни податоци scant data **2** lacking, short of; не сум скуден за ништо I don't want for anything

скудност *f* poverty; scarcity, meagreness; paucity; скудноста на средствата financial stringency; shortages

скудост *f see* скудност

скудоумен -мна *adj literary* obtuse, feeble-minded

скудоумје *n see* скудоумност

скудоумност *f literary* feeble-mindedness

скудоумство *n literary see* скудоумност

скукали *pf* **I** to cause to waste away, make haggard **II** – **се** to waste away

скукалува (се) *impf of* скукали (се)

скукулен *pt* stooped, bent

скукули се *pf* to stoop; to bend *intrans.*

скулптор *m* sculptor

скулпторка *f* <woman> sculptor, sculptress

скулпторски *adj* sculptor's

скулптура *f* sculpture; statue

скулптурен -рна *adj* <of> sculpture, sculptural; *fig.* vivid; скулптурно дело a sculpture

скумрија -ии *f Zool.* **1** (Scomber scombrus) mackerel **2** *see* гугутка 1

скупчи се *pf* to curl up *intrans.*

скупштина *f* parliament

скупштински *adj* <of the> parliament

скуси *pf* **I 1** *see* скрати **I** 1 & 2; ми ги скуси ли панталоните? did you shorten my trousers? му го скуси животот he cut his life short **2** to give short weight, *Am.* to short-weight; to short-change (*also fig.*); му скуси малу he didn't give him full value **II** – **се** *see* скрати се

скусува (се) *impf of* скуси (се)

скут *m* **1** lap; му седнало на деда си в скут he sat on (in) his grandfather's lap **2** skirt **3** lapful; еден скут круши a lapful of pears

скутер *m* motor scooter

скутина *f see* скутник

скутник -ци *m* apron

скутниче *n dim. of* скутник

скутоносец -сци *m* **1** page-boy **2** *fig.* lackey, flunkey, toady

скучна *adj* (*f only*) pregnant (*of bitches, vixens, she-wolves*)

слаб *adj* **1** weak, puny; feeble; faint; slight; poor; слабо срце weak heart; слаб пол the weaker sex; слабо место weak point; слаба волја weak will; слаб раствор weak solution; слаб пулс weak pulse; слаби траги faint traces; слаба земја poor soil; слаб дожд light rain; слаба утеха cold comfort; слаба дисциплина lax discipline; слаб спрема виното fond of wine; слаба валута soft currency; слаба продажба slack sale **2** thin, lean, slim

слабак -ци *m* thin person; weakling

слабее *impf* **1** to weaken *intrans.*, get weaker; слабее ветрот the wind is easing; ми слабее паметењето my memory is getting worse **2** to lose weight

слабеж *m see* слабак

слабикав *adj* weakly, sickly; spare, frail

слабикавост *f* weakliness, sickliness; puny stature; spareness, frailty

слабина -ни, -ње *f Anat.* (*кај човек*) groin; (*кај животно*) flank

слабинка *f see* јоргован, лилјак[2]

слабински *adj* inguinal, of the groin

слабичок -чка *adj see* слабикав

слабнее *impf see* слабее

слабо *adv* weakly, feebly, faintly; poorly, badly; гори слабо to burn feebly; слабо развиен poorly developed

слабоволен -лна *adj* weak-willed

слабоволие *n* irresolution, lack of will-power

слабодушен -шна *adj* pusillanimous; faint-hearted

слабодушност *f* faint-heartedness

слабокарактерен -рна *adj* weak-willed, milk-and-water, *colloq.* weak-kneed

слабокарактерност *f* weakness of character

слабоквалитётен -тна *adj* poor-quality

слабокрвен -вна *adj* anaemic (*also fig.*)

слабокрвност *f* anaemia

слабокултурен -рна *adj* uncouth

слабонаселен *adj* thinly settled, sparsely populated

слабописмен *adj* semi-literate, barely literate; unschooled, untrained; unscholarly; слабописмен реферат half-baked report

слабосилен -лна *adj* weak, feeble

слабосилност *f* weakness

слабост *f* **1** weakness, feebleness; drawback; човечки слабости human foibles **2** fondness, weakness (*кон – for*)

слабота *f see* слаботија

слаботија *f* **1** *see* слабост 1 **2** *see* слабак

слабоумен -мна *adj* feeble-minded

слабоумје *n* feeble-mindedness, imbecility; вродено слабоумје congenital imbecility; старечко слабоумје senility

слабоумник -ци *m* feeble-minded person, imbecile

слабоумност *f* feeble-mindedness, imbecility

слабуњав *adj see* слабикав

слабуњавост *f* sickliness; puny stature; frailty; thinness

слабушен -шна *adj see* слабикав

слабушкав *adj see* слабикав

слава *f* **1** fame; glory; овенчан со слава crowned with glory; тој е нашата слава he is our pride and joy; ❑ за чест и слава for honour's sake; glory to … !

слава му! may he rest in peace! may his memory live! слава Богу (на Бога)! thank God! стекнува слава to make a name <for o.s.> **2** (*сведен*) *slava*, family/village feast (*in honour of its patron saint*)

славеj -еи *m Zool.* (Luscinia megarhynchos) nightingale

славеjски *adj* nightingale's; славеjска песна nightingale's song

славеjче *n dim. of* славеj

славен -вна *adj* renowned, famous, celebrated; glorious; славно дело glorious enterprise/achievement

слави *impf* to celebrate; to honour, extol; слави победа to celebrate a victory

славина *f* tap, *Am.* faucet; отвори славина to turn on a tap

славист *m* Slavist

славистика *f* Slavonic (*Am.* Slavic) studies

славистички *adj* <of a> Slavist; Slavonic, *Am.* Slavic

славистка *f* (*fem. form*) *see* славист

славjанизира *pf & impf see* словенизира

славољубец -пци *m* ambitious person

славољубив *adj* ambitious; vain; славољубив владар a vainglorious ruler

славољубивост *f* ambition; vanity

славољубје *n see* славољубивост

славопоjка *f* glorification, eulogy

слага[1] **(се)** *impf see* сложува (се)

слага[2] *impf colloq.* **1** to consider; слага нешто за свето to consider s.th. sacred **2** to respect; to have regard for **3** to get on (*co – with*)

слагалиште *n see* склад[1]

слагалка *f* jigsaw puzzle

слагач *m Print.* typesetter, compositor

слагачки *adj Print.* typesetter's; <of> typesetting; слагачки сандак type case

слагачница *f Print.* typesetting (composing, case) room

слад *m* malt

слади *impf* **I** to sweeten *trans.*; слади тесто со мед to sweeten dough with honey **II – ce** *fig.* to enjoy o.s.; се слади jадеjќи he enjoys eating

сладина *f* **1** sweetness, sweet taste **2** pleasant (nice) taste, tastiness **3** *fig.* delight, joy

сладникав *adj* **1** sweetish; сладникаво вино medium-sweet wine **2** sickly, luscious; сладникава миризба heavy scent **3** *fig.* insipid, sentimental, sugary; сладникави романи sentimental novels

сладникавост *f* sweetness; mawkishness, sentimentality; sickliness

сладок -тка *adj* **1** sweet; sugary; слатко вино sweet wine **2** tasty, delicious; слатка вечера a nice supper; слатка вода fresh water **3** *fig.* pleasant; delightful; charming; sweet; сладок живот pleasant life; сладок сон sweet dream; сладок глас sweet voice; слатката реч и железна врата отвора *prov.* a soft answer turneth away wrath

сладолед *m* ice-cream

сладолетчиjа -ии *m colloq.* ice-cream man

сладосен -сна *adj* sweet, delicious; сладосни чувства pleasurable feelings

сладост *f see* сладина

сладострастен -сна *adj* lascivious, lustful, sensual, voluptuous; сладострасна природа sensual nature; сладострастен поглед lascivious look

сладострастие *n see* сладострастjе

сладострастjе *n* **1** lust, lasciviousness, sensuality, voluptuousness **2** delight

сладун *m see* благун

сладуњав *adj see* сладникав

слае *pf* слаjа *aor.* to <start to> bark

слаjд *m Photography* slide

слаjува *impf of* слае

слалом *m Sport.* slalom; патека за слалом slalom course

слама *f* straw; спие на слама to sleep on straw; ❑ Кумова слама Milky Way; работи како вол за слама to work for a pittance; чука празна слама to beat the air; чукање празна слама a dead-end job; оган со слама не се гаси *prov.* don't add fuel to the flames

сламарица *f* straw mattress

сламарка *f see* сламеница

сламен *adj* <of> straw; *rare* straw-coloured; сламен покрив thatched roof; сламена коса straw-coloured hair; сламен шешир straw hat

сламеник -ци *m see* сламарица

сламеница *f* house/hut with thatched roof

сламка *f* (*single stalk of*) straw; drinking straw; ❑ од сламка се препнува to trip over a straw; тоj што се дави и за сламка се фаќа a drowning man will clutch at a straw

сламник -ци *m see* сламарица

сламница *f see* сламарица

сламњак -ци *m dial. see* сламарица

сламче *n dim. of* сламка

слана *f* hoar-frost

слани *impf see* сланосува

сланина *f* bacon; fat; пушена сланина smoked bacon

сланица & сланинка *f dim. of* сланина

сланлив *adj* frosty, covered with hoar-frost

сланоса *pf* (*of frost*) **1** to form *intrans.* **2** to cover with rime/hoar-frost **3** to blacken, blight

сланосува *impf of* сланоса

слануток -ци *m Bot.* (Cicer arietinum) chick-pea

слап *m* **1** wave **2** spasm **3** *see* водопад

сласт *f see* сладина **2 & 3**

сластен -сна *adj* delightful; delicious

слатина *f* salty ground; salt-marsh; salt-pan

слаткар *m* **1** pastry cook; confectioner; pastry-shop owner **2** person with a sweet tooth

слаткарка *f* (*fem. form*) *see* слаткар

слаткарница *f* pastry (cake) shop; confectionery <shop>; ice-cream parlour; coffee-shop, sweetshop

слаткарски *adj* confectioner's/pastry-cook's; <of/for> confectionery/pastry-making; слаткарска работилница confectionery shop; слаткарски занает confectioner's/pastry-cook's trade/craft

слаткарство *n* confectioner's trade/craft; pastry-making

слатки *pl* pastries, sweets, sweetmeats; confectionery

слатко[1] *n slatko*, preserve<s>, conserve; слатко од цреши cherry preserve; вари слатко to make preserve<s>

слатко[2] *adv* sweetly; спие слатко to sleep sweetly

слатководен -дна *adj* freshwater; слатководни риби freshwater fish

слаткогласен -сна *adj* sweet-voiced, melodious, mellifluous

слаткозвучен -чна *adj* melodious, mellifluous; слаткозвучна песна melodious song

слаткопоен -jна *adj see* слаткогласен

слаткоречив *adj* eloquent; voluble; smooth-tongued, glib

слаткоречивост *f* eloquence; glibness, volubility

слач *f & m see* сладина

слачен -чна *adj see* сластен

слачина *f see* сладина

слачица *f Bot.* (Solanum dulcamara) bitter-sweet, woody nightshade

слеан *pt* **1** cast<-iron> **2** composite; combined; blended; *Mus.* slurred

слеано *adv* together; се пишува слеано, како еден збор it is written together, as one word

слева (се) *impf of* слее (се)

слегува *impf of* слезе

следа *f see* трага

следбеник -ци *m* **1** successor **2** adherent, follower

следбеничка *f (fem. form) see* следбеник

следбенички *adj* successor's; follower's

следбеништво *n* **1** sequence; succession; successors **2** adherence; followers, adherents

следен -дна *adj* next; following; следната недела next week; следниот пат next time; под следниот наслов under the following title (heading)

следени (се) *pf see* смрзне (се)

следи *impf* **1** to follow; to watch; to track *trans.*; to shadow; следи со поглед to follow with one's eyes; следи пример to follow suit **2** to keep up with, follow; следи печат to follow the press; to keep up with world affairs

следствено *conj* consequently, therefore, so; that is

следува *impf* **1** to follow; по првиот напад следуваше втор a second attack followed the first **2** to result (*од – from*), follow *intrans.*; од тоа следува дека . . . from that it follows that . . . **3** (*with dat.*) to be fitting, appropriate; не му следува по законот he is not legally entitled to that

слее *pf* слеа *aor.* **I 1** to cast (*molten metal*) **2** *fig.* to join, merge, combine, unite, blend *trans.*; *Mus.* to slur *trans.* **II – се** to merge, blend *intrans.*; to join together *intrans.*; to join forces; to coalesce; to combine *intrans.*

слез *m Bot.* (Malva sylvestris) common mallow

слезе *pf* слегов *1st p. sg aor.* **1** to go/come down, descend; слезе од планина to come down from a mountain **2** to get out/off; to get down; to dismount *intrans.*; to alight; слезе од воз to get off a train; слезе од коњ to dismount

слезена & слезенка *f see* слезина

слезина *f Anat.* spleen

слезинка *f see* слезина

слекува *impf* **I** to undress *trans.*; to take off *trans.* **II – се** to undress *intrans.*

слелее *pf* слелеа *aor.* **I** to <begin to> ruffle, agitate *trans.*; ветер го слелеа морето a breeze ruffled the sea **II – се** to <begin to> sway, ripple, wave *intrans.*

слелејува (се) *impf of* слелее (се)

слелека *pf* to <start to> wail

слеме *n* **1** (*на покрив*) ridge **2** (*на планина*) mountain top/peak

слеп *adj* blind (*also fig.*); слеп роден blind from birth; слеп за нечии грешки blind to s.o.'s faults; ❏ се држи

како слеп за стап to hang on for dear life; слепо око temple; *Anat.* слепо црево caecum, appendix; слепа послушност unquestioning obedience; слеп лет flying blind, instrument flight; слепо пишување (*на машина*) touch-typing (*on a typewriter*); слепа улица blind alley, cul-de-sac; слеп сид blank wall; слеп патник stowaway; брзата кучка слепи кучиња раѓа *prov.* haste makes waste; меѓу слепите, тој со едно око е цар *prov.* in the country of the blind the one-eyed man is king; на слепото пиле Господ му го прави седелото *prov.* heaven takes care of children, sailors and drunken men

слепак¹ -ци *m Zool. see* слепок

слепак² -ци *m* (*also* слеп чир) carbuncle

слепач *m Zool. see* слепок

слепачка *f (fem. form) see* слепец, слепица

слепее *impf* **1** to go blind **2** *rare* to blind *trans.*

слепелница *f see* слепачка

слепеник -ци *m see* слепец

слепец -пци *m* **1** blind man; ❏ бара од слепец очи to ask the impossible; to get blood from a stone; се водат како слепци they are like the blind being led by the blind **2** *fig.* unfortunate person, wretch; pauper; ignorant person

слепечки *adj* of/for a blind man; слепечко писмо Braille

слепи¹ *impf f.p. see* слепее 2

слепи² (**се**) *pf rare see* залепи (се)

слепило *n see* слепота

слепица *f* blind woman

слепичок -чка *adj dim. of* слеп

слепок -ци *m Zool.* (Anguis fragilis) blindworm, slow-worm

слепоочен -чна *adj* temporal, <of the> temple; слепоочна коска temporal bone

слепоочница *f* (*слепо око*) temple

слепороден *adj* blind from birth

слепост *f see* слепота

слепота *f* blindness; ❏ кокошкина слепота night blindness; снежна слепота snow blindness

слепотија *f see* слепота

слепува¹ *impf see* слепи¹

слепува² (**се**) *impf of* слепи² (се)

слепуток -ци *m see* слепок

слепчо -овци *m iron.* ignoramus

слеска *f see* слезина

слет *m* rally, jamboree

слета *pf* **I 1** (*летне*) to fly away, take flight **2** *fig.* (*на некого*) to fly (*at s.o.*), round (*on s.o.*) **3** to fly down, land *intrans.* **II – се 1** to fly away **2** to attack, fly (*на – at*); се слетаа сите по него they all went for him

слетува *impf of* слета

слече *pf* слеков *1st p. sg aor.* **I** to undress *trans.*; to take off *trans.* **II – се** to undress *intrans.*

слечува (се) *impf of* слече (се)

слив *m* basin; gutter; слив на река river basin

слива¹ *f* **1** *Bot.* (Prunus domestica) plum (*tree and fruit*) **2** *rare, colloq.* slivovitz, *see* сливовица

слива² (**се**) *impf see* слева (се)

сливак -ци *m see* сливарник

сливар *m* plum grower; plum seller; *colloq.* lover of plums

сливарник -ци *m* plum orchard

сливарски *adj* plum grower's/seller's

сливарство *n* plum growing/selling

сливица *f dial.* (*usu. pl*) tonsil<s>; воспаление на сливиците tonsillitis; *see* крајник

сливка *f* 1 *dim. of* слива¹ 1 2 *colloq.* slivovitz

сливник *m* gutter

сливов *adj* plum; сливово дрво plum tree; сливов мармалад plum jam; сливова ракија plum brandy, slivovitz

сливовица *f* plum brandy, slivovitz

сливче *n dim. of* слива¹

слие (се) *pf* сли (се) *aor. see* слее (се)

слизга (се) *impf see* лизга² (се)

слизгав *adj* slippery (*also fig.*); слизгав пат slippery road; слизгава тема delicate subject

слизгалиште *n* skating-rink

слизне *pf* слизна *aor.* I to cause to trip, stumble (*usu. fig.*) II – се 1 to slip, skid 2 *fig.* to slip up; поарно е да се слизнеш со нога одошто со збор *prov.* better the foot slip than the tongue

слизнува (се) *impf of* слизне (се)

слик *m Prosody* rhyme, *see* рима

слика¹ *f* 1 picture, painting; галерија на слики picture-gallery; ❑ во најдобра слика at one's best; слика и прилика (на) mirror image (*of*); a chip off the old block; убав како слика as pretty as a picture 2 (*пејзаж*) view, scene 3 (*фотографија*) photograph, picture, snapshot 4 *Theatre* scene 5 *Math.* figure; геометриска слика geometrical figure

слика² *impf* I 1 to draw; to paint; to depict, picture, portray (*also fig.*) 2 *fig.* слика си to picture, imagine; си ја сликаше во фантазијата средбата со неа he conjured up in his imagination the meeting with her 3 (*со апарат*) to photograph II – се 1 to draw/paint o.s.; ❑ можеш да се сликаш over my dead body; never 2 to be reflected; дабот се сликаше во водата the oak was reflected in the water 3 *fig.* to appear in one's mind's eye 4 to have one's picture taken

сликар *m* 1 artist, painter; сликар на пејзажи landscape artist 2 *colloq.* photographer

сликарка *f* (*fem. form*) *see* сликар

сликарница *f* picture gallery

сликарски *adj* artist's; photographer's

сликарство *n* art, painting; современо сликарство modern art

сликиче *n &* **сликичка** *f dim. of* слика

сликовит *adj* vivid, picturesque, graphic; сликовит стил vivid style

сликовница *f* picture-book

слина *f* saliva; ми течат слини my mouth is watering

слинка *f see* слина

слисан *pt see* смајан

слисне *pf* слисна *aor. dial.* to slap

слисти *pf* (*збрише*) to destroy; слисти непријател to crush an enemy; слисти имот to squander a fortune

слистува *impf of* слисти

сличен -чна *adj* similar; многу се слични they are very much alike

слично *adv* like; similarly; ❑ нема ништо слично there is no resemblance; и <на тоа> слично and the like; and so on (forth)

сличност *f* likeness, similarity

слобода *f* freedom; liberty; слобода на волја free will; слобода на движење freedom of movement; слобода на мислење freedom of thought; слобода на печатот freedom of the press; слобода на совеста freedom of conscience; слобода на трговијата free trade; поетска слобода poetic licence; пушти на слобода to release, set free; си зема слобода да стори нешто to take (allow o.s.) the liberty to do s.th.; лишува од слобода to put under arrest; to take into custody; на слобода at large; at liberty; се брани од слобода to be out on bail

слободарство *n* freethinking; liberalism; libertarianism

слободен -дна *adj* 1 free; слободен избор free choice; слободен стих free verse; слободни цени unregulated prices; слободно паѓање free fall; црта со слободна рака to draw freehand; со слободна професија freelance 2 easy, casual; outgoing; слободно држење free and easy manner 3 free, vacant; unoccupied; вие сте слободни попладне? are you free this afternoon? слободен стан vacant flat; слободно место empty place; слободно време spare time; слободен ден day off; слободен удар free kick; слободно работно место vacancy, job opportunity

слободи *impf* I to embolden, urge on; to reassure; to put at ease II – се to dare, pluck up courage

слободија -ии *f* 1 *arch.* freedom; liberty 2 licence, excessive liberty

слободица & **слободичка** *f dim. hyp. of* слобода

слободник -ци *m literary, rare* freeman

слободништво *n literary, rare* liberalism; freethinking

слободно *adv* 1 freely 2 (*in response to a knock at the door*) слободно! come in! 3 *Mil.* stand at ease!

слободољубец -пци *m literary, rare* freedom-loving person

слободољубив *adj* freedom-loving

слободољубивост *f* love of freedom

слободољубје *n see* слободољубивост

слободоумен -мна *adj* freethinking

слободоумје *n see* слободоумност

слободоумник -ци *m* freethinker

слободоумност *f* freethinking

Словак -ци *m* Slovak

Словакија *f* Slovakia

Словакинка *f* (*fem. form*) *see* Словак

Словачка *f see* Словакија

словачки *adj* Slovak, Slovakian

Словенец -нци *m* Slovene

словенечки *adj* Slovenian

Словени *pl* Slavs; Јужни Словени South Slavs

словенизам -змот *m* Slavonicism

словенизација *f* Slavonicization

словенизира *pf & impf* to Slavonicize, *Am.* Slavicize

Словенија *f* Slovenia

Словенка *f* (*fem. form*) *see* Словенец

словенофил *m* Slavophile

словенофилка *f* (*fem. form*) *see* словенофил

словенофилски *adj* Slavophile; словенофилски идеи Slavophile ideas

словенофилство *n* Slavophilism

словенски *adj* Slavonic, *Am.* Slavic; словенска филологија Slavonic philology

Словенство *n* Slavdom, the Slav peoples

слово *n* 1 *see* буква 2 *arch.* word; ❑ чесно слово word of honour **3** *arch.* speech; посмртно слово funeral oration

слог¹ *m* ridge between two furrows

слог² *m Phon.* syllable

слог³ *m Print.* type, typeface

слога *f* harmony, accord, agreement; живее во слога to live in harmony

слоговен -вна *adj Phon.* syllabic

слоготворен -рна *adj see* слоговен

слоевит *adj* stratified; layered

слоевитост *f* stratification

сложен¹ *adj* **1** compound; composite; complex; сложени реченици complex/compound sentences; сложени броеви complex numbers; сложени зборови compound words **2** complicated, complex, intricate; сложена операција complicated operation; сложена ситуација complicated situation

сложен² -жна *adj* harmonious; unanimous, in agreement

сложен³ -жна *adj* gently sloping

-сложен -жна *adj* (*in compounds*) -syllabic; двосложен збор dis<s>yllabic word; повеќесложен polysyllabic

сложеница *f see* сложенка

сложенка *f Gram.* compound <word>

сложеност *f* complexity; intricacy

сложи *pf* **I 1** to arrange, order; to stack; сложи дрва to stack timber **2** to assemble, put together **3** *Print.* to set *trans.* **4** to reconcile; to harmonize **II** – **се 1** to reach agreement **2** to match, blend *intrans.*; to harmonize *intrans.*; сметките се сложија the accounts balanced; ќе се сложат боите the colours will match

сложно *adv* harmoniously, in harmony; живее сложно to live in harmony

сложност *f* agreement, harmony, unanimity

сложува (се) *impf of* сложи (се); се сложува со to get along (on) with;

слој -еви *m* layer, stratum; на слоеви in layers; вишиот слој на општеството the higher circles of society

слом *m* disaster, ruin, collapse, rout; нервен слом nervous breakdown

сломи *pf f.p. see* скрши

слон *m* **1** *Zool.* elephant; ❑ прави од мувата слон to make a mountain out of a molehill; како слон во стакларница like a bull in a china shop **2** *fig., colloq.* ungainly, hulking person

слоница *f* she-elephant

слонов *adj* elephantine; слонова кожа elephant hide; слонова коска ivory

слонски *adj* elephant-like, elephantine; слонска сила the strength of an elephant; слонски од elephantine gait

слонче *n dim. of* слон

слофокс *m* slow foxtrot

слоши се *pf* **1** *impers.* (*with dat.*) to feel ill/nauseous/faint; ❑ ќе (да не) ти се слоши! you've had your share; you're asking too much; you're overdoing it **2** (*излоши се*) to get worse, deteriorate, worsen *intrans.*

слошува се *impf of* слоши се

слуга¹ *m* **1** servant, manservant; valet; footman; *fig.* flunkey, lackey; ❑ слуга покорен your humble servant **2** *see* служител, прислужник

слуга² *f arch. see* служба 2

слугарка *f* tray, salver

слугинка *f* maid, maidservant, housemaid

слугинче *n dim. of* слугинка

слугува *impf colloq. see* служи

слугувач *m colloq.* servant

служавник -ци *m* tray, salver

служанка *f literary, arch. see* слугинка

служач *m see* слугувач

служба *f* **1** service, work; стапи на служба to start a job; воена служба military service; државна служба civil (public) service; напушти служба to resign **2** liturgy; Божја служба divine service; црковна служба church service **3** office, bureau, service; метеоролошка служба weather-forecasting service; разузнавачка служба intelligence service

службен *adj* official; business; службен пат business trip; по службена должност in the line of duty; службена кола official/company car; службен весник government gazette; службена белешка memorandum; службено лице (an) official

службеник -ци *m* **1** employee, white-collar worker; clerk; civil (public) servant; работници и службеници blue-collar and white-collar workers **2** *see* службеник

службеничка *f* (*fem. form*) *see* службеник 1

службенички *adj* clerical; службенички однос salaried employment

службено *adv* officially; on business; ex officio; патува службено to travel on business

службодавец -вци *m* employer

службува *impf* to work for a salary

служебник -ци *m Rel.* prayer-book; missal

служи *impf* **I 1** to serve, work; служи во морнарица to serve in the navy; служи војска to do one's military service **2** to celebrate the liturgy, officiate **3** to wait on; to serve; служи гости to wait on guests; служи вино to serve wine **4** to work, function, be of use; to serve; како те служи телевизорот? how is your television working? служи за пример to serve as an example **II** – **се 1** to serve o.s., help o.s. **2** (*with co*) to use, make use of, employ; ❑ се служи со ниски удари to hit below the belt

служител *m* attendant

служителка *f* (*fem. form*) *see* служител

служителски *adj* attendant's

служува *impf f.p. see* слугува, служи

слуз *f* mucus; phlegm; slime

слузен -зна *adj* mucous; mucoid; slimy; слузна материја mucous matter

слузест *adj* mucous; слузести жлезди mucous glands

слузница *f* mucous membrane

слузокожа *f see* слузница

слупи *pf* **I 1** to peel; to shell; to husk; to hull **2** *fig.* to squander; слупи пари to waste money **II** – **се** to peel <off> *intrans.*; to flake off; се слупила крастата the scab flaked off

слупува (се) *impf of* слупи (се)

слух *m* **1** hearing; ear; остар слух keen (acute) hearing; нема слух (*за музика*) to have no ear (*for music*); ❑ апсолутен слух perfect pitch; напрега слух to prick up one's ears; пее/свири на (по) слух to sing/play by ear **2** *rare* (*usu. pl*) rumour; шири слухови to spread rumours

слухов *adj* auditory, acoustic; <of, for> hearing; слуховни органи organs of hearing

случаен -jна *adj* chance, fortuitous, accidental, casual; coincidental; random; случајна средба chance meeting; случајна работа 1. odd job 2. coincidence; случајни гости unexpected guests; случаен успех fluke; ❏ случаен човек a nobody

случај -аи *m* **1** instance, case; occasion; event; ❏ во краен случај if the worst comes to the worst; во најдобар/најлош случај at best/worst; во никој случај under no circumstances; во секој случај in any case; во случај да/на . . . in the event that/of . . . , in case . . . ; во таков случај in that case; за секој случај just in case; несреќен случај accident; по случај . . . on the occasion of . . . ; смртен случај death, fatality; тежок случај a serious case; hopeless case; queer customer **2** opportunity, chance; искористи случај to seize the opportunity **3** coincidence, chance; среќен случај a stroke of luck; игра на случајот coincidence; остави нешто на случајот to leave s.th. to chance; ако дојде по некој случај if he should happen to come; по игра на случајот by some quirk of fate

случајно *adv* by chance, accidentally; at random

случајност *f* chance, coincidence

случи се *pf* **1** to happen, take place; се случи несреќа an accident occurred **2** to happen, <chance> to be; се случив на улица I found myself (happened to be) in the street

случка *f* event, occurrence, incident; вистинска случка a true occurrence (story); сека случка за научка *prov.* experience is the best teacher; live and learn

случува се *impf of* случи се

слуша *impf* **I 1** to listen to; слуша музика to listen to music **2** to attend (*classes*), study; слуша предавања to attend lectures; слуша македонска граматика to study Macedonian grammar **3** to listen to, obey; никого не слуша he won't listen to anyone **4** to hear; слабо слуша to be hard of hearing **5** to hear, gather, know from hearsay; слушам дека си бил во странство I gather you've been abroad **6** *colloq. see* слугува **II – се 1** to hear o.s., listen to o.s. **2** *colloq.* to listen to each other **3** to be heard; се слушаше смеа laughter rang out **4** it is said, rumoured; they say; се слуша дека . . . rumour has it that . . .

слушалка *f* **1** (*лекарска*) stethoscope **2** (*телефонска*) receiver; спушта слушалка (*некому*) to hang up (*on s.o.*) **3** (*usu. pl*) earphone, headphone, headset

слушална *f see* слушалница

слушалница *f* lecture theatre (room, hall)

слушател *m* **1** listener **2** student

слушателка *f* (*fem. form*) *see* слушател

слушателски *adj* listener's; слушателски состав audience

слушач *m* earphone, headphone; listening device

слушен -шна *adj see* слухов; слушен нерв auditory nerve; слушни органи organs of hearing; слушен апарат hearing-aid

слушне *pf* слуша *aor.* **1** to hear; не слушнав I beg your pardon **2** to listen to; не сакаше ни да ме слушне he would not even listen to me

слушнува *impf of* слушне

см *abbr.* (*сантиметар*) cm

смагли се *pf impers.* to become misty, foggy

смаглува се *impf of* смагли се

смад *m* smell of burning

смаден -дна *adj* burnt, charred, smelling of burning

смади *impf* to scorch, singe *trans.*

смадоса *pf see* смади

смадосува *impf of* смадоса

смадри *pf colloq.* to bring (*s.o.*) to (*his*) senses; to calm <down> *trans.*

смадрува *impf of* смадри

смае *pf* смаја *aor.* to stun, daze; to astound

смајан *pt* stunned, dazed; dizzy

смајаност *f* astonishment, stupefaction; dizziness

смајува (се) *impf of* смае (се)

смали *pf* **I** to reduce *trans.*, cut down, diminish, decrease *trans.*; смали расходи to reduce expenditure **II – се** to go down, diminish *intrans.*; се смалија цени prices have fallen

смалува (се) *impf of* смали (се)

смандори *pf colloq.* **1** (*некого*) to hoodwink, hoax, outwit; to fleece **2** (*нешто*) to slap (cobble) together

смандорува *impf of* смандори

смарагд *m* emerald

смарагден -дна *adj* emerald; смарагден килим emerald-green rug

смасен -сна *adj* nimble, adroit, skilful, deft

сматен -тна *pt* unclear, vague, nebulous; misty; сматна слика blurred picture; сматни претстави vague ideas; со сматен поглед dull-eyed

смати *pf* **I 1** to stir up; to make muddy (turbid) **2** to spoil *trans.*; to disturb; to confuse; to make misty; смати некому настроение to spoil s.o.'s mood **II – се 1** to become muddy/turbid/troubled; to cloud over; се смати водата the water became turbid **2** *impers.* (*with dat.*) ми се смати <во главата> I feel dizzy

сматкоса се *pf* (*за јајце*) to go bad

сматкосува се *impf of* сматкоса се

сматок -ци *m* **1** rotten egg **2** *fig.* bad egg (*corrupt, immoral person*)

сматува (се) *impf of* смати (се)

смачи се *pf impers.* (*with dat.*) to irk, bore; to sicken; ми се смачи I felt sick; му се смачи од чекање he got tired of waiting

смачка *pf* **1** (*столчи*) to crush; to trample; to smash, break *trans.*; смачка јајце to break an egg **2** *colloq.* (*убие*) to kill, do in **3** *fig.* (*уништи*) to destroy; to crush, shatter *trans.*; to ruin, lay waste **4** *fig.* (*изеде*) to eat up, polish off **5** (*смандори*) to slap (cobble) together **II – се 1** to break, smash *intrans.* **2** to hurt o.s. badly

смачкан *adj* shabby, *colloq.* scruffy; смачкан изглед shabby appearance

смачкува (се) *impf of* смачка (се)

смачна *adj* (*f only*) pregnant (*of a cat*)

смачува се *impf of* смачи се

сме *1st p. pl pres. of* сум

смеа *f* **1** laughter; ❏ на смеа as a joke; не му е до смеа it is no laughing matter for him; пукне (скине се, умре) од смеа to split (burst one's sides) with laughter, die laughing **2** laughing stock, object of derision; служи за смеа to be a laughing stock; го зедоа на смеа they made fun of him

смеачка *f colloq.* laugh, laughter

смеаџија -ии *m colloq.* (*шегаџија*) comedian, comic, joker

смев *m see* смеа

смее¹ *impf* **I** to make (*s.o.*) laugh, cause to laugh; ги смееше децата he kept the children laughing **II – се 1** to laugh; to smile; се смее во себе to laugh to o.s.; очите ѝ се смееја her eyes were smiling; ❑ се смее под мустаќ to laugh up one's sleeve **2** (*with dat.*) to laugh at; to make fun of, ridicule, mock; немој да му се смееш don't make fun of him! **3** *impers.* ми се смее I feel like laughing

смее² *impf* **1** to dare; не смееше да излезе he didn't dare go outside **2** to be allowed; не смее да пуши he is not supposed to smoke; смеам ли да ве прашам? may I ask you?

смејач *m* cheerful (jolly) person

смекнат *pt* **1** softened; mellowed; mollified **2** *Phon.* palatalized; смекнати согласки palatalized consonants

смекнатост *f* softening, softness; *Phon.* palatalization

смекне *pf* смекна *aor.* **1** to soften *trans.*; to tone down; to mollify; смекне некому срце to melt s.o.'s heart; смекне боја to tone down a colour **2** *Phon.* to palatalize

смекнува *impf of* смекне

смел *adj* bold, audacious; fearless; intrepid

смеле *pf see* сомеле

смелост *f* boldness, bravery; audacity

смелува *impf of* смеле

смена *f* **1** change; (*замена*) replacement, *Mil.* relief; *fig.* rising generation; successors; младината е наша смена the young are our successors; смена на раководство change of management; смена на стража changing of the guard; ❑ на смена in turns **2** shift; работи во смени to work shifts; дневна смена day shift

смени *pf* **I** to change *trans.*; to exchange, swap; to replace, take the place of; смени кошула to change one's shirt; смени стан to move house; смени стража to relieve a sentry; ноќта ја смени ден night gave way to day; смени сто денари to change a hundred denars **II – се 1** to replace (relieve) one another **2** to change *intrans.*; му се смени изгледот на лицето his expression changed **3** to exchange, swap; се сменија со марки they exchanged stamps

сменува (се) *impf of* смени (се)

смерен -рна *adj see* смирен²

смес & смеса *f* mixture, combination, blend; смеса од сребро и бакар alloy of silver and copper

смесник *m* mixed flour

смести *pf* **I 1** to put, place; to store **2** to place, accommodate, find room for; го сместија во интернат they placed him in a boarding-school **II – се 1** to take one's seat; to find a seat (place), make o.s. comfortable; се сместивме во првиот ред we took our seats in the front row **2** to move (settle) in *intrans.*

сместува (се) *impf of* смести (се)

сместување *n* accommodation, lodgings; ❑ нужно сместување emergency accommodation; сместување и храна room and board

смет *m* rubbish, *Am.* garbage; канта за смет rubbish bin, dustbin, *Am.* trash can

смета *impf* **1** to reckon; to count, add up, calculate; смета до сто to count to one hundred; смета напамет (во себе) to do mental arithmetic; смета на прсти to count on one's fingers **2** *fig.* to take into account (consideration); to reckon with; to count (*на – on*); смета на некого to count on s.o.; смета со (на) тоа to count on that; to take that into consideration; не сметајќи not including, not counting **3** *fig.* to deem, regard; to consider; to think; го сметаше тоа за свој долг he considered it his duty; смета нешто за чест to consider s.th. an honour; сметам дека нема да дојде I don't think he'll come **II – се** to consider o.s.

сметалка *f* abacus

сметанка *f colloq.* arithmetic textbook

сметање *n* counting, arithmetic, reckoning; лекции по сметање arithmetic lessons

сметач *m* **1** mathematician **2** (*направа*) calculator; computer

сметачка *f* **1** (*fem. form*) *see* сметач 1 **2** *see* сметалка

смете¹ *pf* to sweep <away/up/out>; смете соба to sweep a room; смете ѓубре to sweep up rubbish

смете² *pf* **I** to disturb, interrupt; to hamper, hinder; to distract **II – се** to get confused, muddled

сметен *pt* **1** mixed up, confused **2** swept

сметеник -ци *m literary rare* confused person; scatterbrain

сметина (се) *impf see* сметнува (се)

сметка¹ *f* **1** arithmetic, *colloq.* sums; calculation; грешка во сметката arithmetical error, miscalculation; прави сметка to calculate **2** account; bill, *Am.* check; извод од сметка statement <of account>; дава сметка to render (submit) an account **3** books, accounts; текушта (тековна) сметка current account; чековна сметка cheque (*Am.* check) account; расчисти сметки to settle (square) accounts; сметка загуби loss statement; жиро-сметка giro account **4** (*usu. pl*) mutual financial relations; *fig.* mutual grudges, account; score; имаме уште стари сметки we still have old scores to settle; лични сметки personal grudges **5** intention; дојде со таква сметка he came with that intention **6** *colloq.* profit, benefit, advantage, interest; има сметка да го држи дуќанот it is in his interest to keep the shop; без сметка for nothing; without an ulterior motive; води сметка to take account of; to watch out for; *fig.* to give an account; ❑ за своја/туѓа сметка at one's own/s.o. else's expense; расипе некому сметките to upset s.o.'s apple-cart; не му оди во сметка it doesn't suit him; на нова сметка all over again; прави сметка без крчмар to reckon without one's host; со сметка (*живее*) (*to live*) frugally (economically); чиста сметка, долга љубов *prov.* short reckonings make long friends

сметка² *pf* to muddle, tangle, mix up *trans.*; to complicate, confuse; сметка конци to tangle threads; *fig.* to get everything mixed up

сметкаџија -ии *m colloq.* calculating person; schemer; skinflint, *colloq.* money-grubber; self-seeker

сметкаџиски *adj* calculating, mercenary, venal; сметкаџиска политика opportunistic policies; venal politics

сметковен -вна *adj* arithmetical; <of an> account; сметковна операција financial transaction; arithmetical operation

сметководен -дна *adj* accounting; сметководни

книги <accounts> books; сметководен период accounting period

сметководител *m* book-keeper; accountant

сметководителски *adj* of/for a book-keeper/ accountant; сметководителски курсеви accountancy courses

сметководствен *adj see* сметководен

сметководство *n* book-keeping; accountancy; трговско сметководство commercial accountancy; општествено сметководство auditing

сметкополагач *m* **1** person who renders an account **2** book-keeper

сметкорасписка *f colloq.* receipt

сметкува *impf of* сметка²

сметне (се) *pf* сметна (се) *aor. see* симне (се)

сметнува (се) *impf of* сметне (се)

сметува *impf of* смете¹

смеќа *f colloq.* hurdle, difficulty

смеќава *impf of* смете²

смеурија -ии *f colloq.* **1** funny story; joke **2** laughing stock

смеша *pf* **1** to mix *trans.*; to blend *trans.*; to mix up, shuffle; смеша вино to blend wine; смеша карти to shuffle cards **2** to confuse, fluster, muddle; неговите прашања ме смешаа his questions confused me **3** *colloq., fig.* to make s.o. acquainted with **II – се 1** to combine, mix *intrans.*; to blend *intrans.* (*co – with*) **2** to get mixed up, become confused; ми се смешаа мислите my thoughts became confused **3** to interfere, meddle (*во – in*) **4** *colloq. fig.* to mix *intrans.*, socialize

смешен -шна *adj* funny, comical; absurd, ridiculous

смешка¹ *f* **1** joke; anecdote; prank; *colloq.* wisecrack; прави смешки to crack jokes; to play pranks **2** *dial. see* смеа

смешка² се *impf* to smile (*на – at*); ❑ му се смешка среќата fortune is smiling upon him

смешлив *adj* jolly, gay, merry

смешник -ци *m literary* (*шегаџија*) joker, jester

смешува (се) *impf of* смеша (се)

смива (се) *impf of* смие (се)

смивка *f dial.* (*помија*) slops, dishwater

смие *pf* сми *aor.* **1** to clean, wash clean; смие крв од кошула to wash blood from a shirt **2** to wash away, erode; реката го сми брегот the river washed away the bank **II – се** to wash away/off *intrans.*; ќе се смие бојата the paint will wash off

смил *m* **1** *Bot.* (Helichrysum arenarium) immortelle, yellow everlasting **2** yellow soil

смилен -лна *adj* of yellow everlasting<s>

смили *pf* **I** to cause to be merciful, move to pity **II – се 1** *impers.* (*with dat.*) to wish to, feel like; му се смилило да оди со нив he felt like going with them **2** to have (take) pity, show mercy (*за – on*); му се смилило срцето his heart softened

смилица *f* place with yellow soil

смилов *adj see* смилен

смилоса се *pf* to turn yellow *intrans.*

смилостиви (се) *pf see* смилува (се)

смилосува се *impf of* смилоса се

смилува (се) *pf see* смили (се) I & II 2

смирен¹ *pt* calm, serene; смирен глас calm voice

смирен² -рна *adj* humble, unassuming, submissive, meek

смиреност *f* calm, serenity

смири *pf* **I 1** to calm, subdue, pacify, restrain **2** to relieve, soothe, ease; смири болка to soothe pain **3** to reconcile **II – се 1** to calm down *intrans.*; to fall silent **2** to ease, abate; се смири болката the pain eased **3** to make peace, make up

смириса *pf* **I 1** to smell *intrans.*, emit a smell, begin to smell; смириса месото the meat began to smell; смириса на темјан there came a scent of incense **2** to smell *trans.*, catch the scent of, sniff **II – се** to smell (stink), begin to smell (stink)

смирисува (се) *impf of* смириса (се)

смирност *f* humility; meekness

смирува (се) *impf of* смири (се)

смисла *f* **1** sense, meaning; смислата на статија the gist of an article; вникне во смисла to grasp the meaning; во буквалната смисла на зборот in the strict (literal) sense of the word; во потесна смисла strictly speaking **2** sense, purpose, point; нема смисла there's no point; it's not fair **3** sense, feel, feeling; смисла за музика gift for music; ❑ здрава смисла common sense

смисли *pf* **1** to think of; to remember; смисли две реченици to think of two sentences **2** to decide, conclude; to intend; смисли да отиде to decide to leave

смисловен -вна *adj* semantic; смисловна нијанса nuance, shade of meaning; смисловна врска logical connexion

смислува *impf of* смисли

смлачи *pf* **I** to warm <up> *trans.* **II – се** to warm up *intrans.*; се смлачила веќе водата the water is now lukewarm

смлачува (се) *impf of* смлачи (се)

смог *m* smog

смогне *pf* смогне *aor.* to be able (*да – to*); to manage; to succeed

смогнува *impf of* смогне

смок -ови, (*rare* -ци) *m Zool.* any snake of the genus Coluber; планински смок (Coronella austriaca) smooth snake; ❑ пие како смок to drink like a fish; цица како смок to suck well, feed well (*of a baby*)

смоква *f Bot.* (Ficus carica) fig (*tree and fruit*); слатко од смокви fig preserve

смокварник -ци *m* fig-tree grove

смоквен & смоквин *adj* fig; смоквено дрво fig-tree; смоквин лист fig-leaf

смокинг -зи *m* dinner-jacket, *Am.* tuxedo

смоков *adj see* смоквен

смоковница *f* fig-tree

смола *f* resin; turpentine; gum; течна смола liquid pitch/tar; борова смола pine resin

смолар *m* resin collector; *N.Z.* gum-digger; pitch maker

смолари *impf* to extract resin; to produce pitch

смолен -лна *adj* resinous; pitchy

смолест *adj* resinous; resin-like; pitch-like; смолести дрвја resinous trees; смолеста коса pitch-black hair

смолец *m Bot.* (Bolboschoenus maritimus) sea club-rush

смоли *impf see* смолоса

смолкне *pf* смолкна *aor.* **I 1** to drag/pull down; to slide down *trans.* **2** *colloq.* to take off (*clothing*) **II – се 1** to slide down *intrans.* **2** *colloq.* to come down, slip off *intrans.* (*of clothing*) **3** *fig.* to lose weight

смолкнува (се) *impf of* смолкне (се)

смолник *m see* смолница

смолница *f* clay soil

смолоса *pf* to tar; to smear with resin; to coat with pitch

смолосува *impf of* смолоса

смолчи *pf rare* to fall silent

смолчува *impf of* смолчи

смота *pf* **I 1** to wind <up> *trans.*; to roll up *trans.*; to wrap; смота преѓа to wind yarn **2** *fig.* to steal, *sl.* pinch **3** *fig.* to cheat, hoodwink, hoax **II – се** to curl up *intrans.*; *colloq.* to get confused

смотра *f* **1** review; inspection; смотра на војска review of troops; врши смотра to carry out an inspection **2** show, exhibition; смотра на младоста youth festival; смотра на техничките достигања exhibition of techological achievements

смотува (се) *impf of* смота (се)

смрамори (се) *pf* **I** to turn to stone, petrify *trans.* **II – се** to turn to stone, petrify *intrans.*

смраморува (се) *impf of* смрамори (се)

смрачи *pf* **I 1** *impers.* (*of darkness*) to catch, overtake (*s. o.*); го смрачи близу до селото darkness overtook him close to the village **2** to darken *trans.*; to blot out; авиони го смрачија небото the sky was black with planes **II – се** to get dark; се смрачи веќе it is already dark, darkness has fallen; се смрачи небото the sky went black

смрачува (се) *impf of* смрачи (се)

смрачување *n* dusk, nightfall; onset of darkness

смрда *pf* to start moving (*suddenly*)

смрдеа *f* stench, stink, <bad> odour

смрдеж *m* **1** stench, stink, <bad> odour **2** stinker, malodorous person

смрделика *f Bot.* (Juniperus sabina) savin

смрди¹ (се) *pf see* засмрди (се)

смрди² *impf* to smell bad, stink, reek; ❏ смрди – корне (трује) it/he stinks like a polecat

смрдивранка *f Zool.* (Coracias garrulus) roller

смрдија *f* stench, stink

смрдла *f* (*fem. form*) *see* смрдле

смрдле -евци *m* **1** smelly creature, stinker **2** *dial.* idler, loafer, *colloq.* lazybones

смрдлив *adj* **1** evil-smelling, stinking, smelly; rank; смрдлив воздух fetid air **2** *dial.* lazy

смрдливец *m Bot.* (Cicuta virosa) water hemlock, snake root

смрдло -овци *m see* смрдле

смрдува¹ *impf of* смрда

смрдува² (се) *impf of* смрди (се)

смрѓа, смрѓава & смрѓија *f see* смрдеа

смрежи *pf* **I 1** to enmesh; to net **2** to blur *trans.*; to dazzle **3** *fig.* to ruffle **II – се** to cloud over, become befogged; му се смрежија очите his spectacles misted over

смрежува (се) *impf of* смрежи (се)

смрека *f Bot.* (Juniperus communis) juniper

смрекарка *f Zool.* (Turdus pilaris) fieldfare

смреков *adj* juniper; смреков дрозд *see* смрекарка

смрековина *f* juniper wood (timber)

смрзнат *pt* frozen; frostbitten; deep-frozen; смрзнато езеро frozen lake; смрзната кокошка frozen chicken

смрзне *pf* смрзна *aor.* **I 1** to freeze *intrans.*; to get cold; *fig.* to be terrified, to become numb with fear; смрзна реката the river has frozen; ќе смрзнат децата the children will freeze; ми смрзнале прстите my fingers were frostbitten; ❏ му смрзна крвта во жилите his blood froze in his veins **2** to freeze *trans.*; *fig.* to terrify; смрзне месо to freeze meat **II – се** *see* I 1

смрзнува (се) *impf of* смрзне (се)

смрзнување *n* freezing; ❏ точка на смрзнувањето freezing-point

смрлушен *pt* unconscious; stunned

смрлуши *pf* **I** to stun; to knock out; ракијата го смрлуши the *raki* went to his head **II – се** to lose consciousness, faint, pass out

смрлушува (се) *impf of* смрлуши (се)

смрмори *pf* смрмори & смрморе *aor.* to start muttering

смрморува *impf of* смрмори

смрси *pf* (*конци, коса и сл.*) to tangle *trans.*; (*коса*) to ruffle

смрсува *impf of* смрси

смрт *f* death; ненадејна смрт sudden death; осуди на смрт to condemn to death; предвремена смрт premature death; ❏ бела смрт death of cold/exposure; црна смрт the Black Death; блед како смрт as pale as death; борба на живот и смрт a fight to the death; ѝ гледа на смртта во очи to stare death in the face; меѓу животот и смртта more dead than alive; на смрт е to be at death's door; прашање на живот и смрт a matter of life and death; *colloq.* смрт ми е тоа that's s.th. I hate; смртта не прашува (гледа) стар и млад *prov.* all men are mortal

смртен -тна *adj* **1** fatal, lethal, mortal; смртен удар deathblow; смртна рана fatal wound; смртна опасност deadly danger; смртна казна capital punishment; смртна пресуда death sentence; смртна досада deadly boredom; смртен грев mortal sin; сите луѓе се смртни all men are mortal **2** (*as noun*) ordinary mortal

смртник -ци *m* ordinary mortal

смртница *f* (*fem. form*) *see* смртник

смртно *adv* fatally; greatly, extremely; смртно вљубен head over heels in love; смртно погоден cut to the quick; смртно ранет fatally injured, mortally wounded

смртност *f* mortality; death rate; смртноста кај децата infant mortality

смртовница *f* death certificate

смртоносен -сна *adj* deadly, fatal, lethal, mortal; смртоносен удар deathblow; смртоносна рана fatal wound; смртоносно оружје lethal (deadly) weapon

смртоносно *adv* fatally, lethally, mortally; го удри смртоносно he dealt him a fatal blow

смрштен *pt* frowning; with wrinkled brows; смрштени веѓи puckered brow

смршти *pf* **I** to furrow, wrinkle, pucker; смршти чело to frown **II – се** to become puckered (furrowed); to frown, scowl

смрштува (се) *impf of* смршти (се)

смук *m Sport.* downhill skiing

смука *impf see* шмука

смукалка *f see* шмукалка

смуртен *pt* gloomy; sullen, surly; *fig.* overcast

смурти се *pf* **1** to frown; to sulk, glower **2** *fig.* to cloud over

смуртува се *impf of* смурти се

смут *m literary* discord; unrest; disorder, chaos, turmoil; intrigue; ❑ сее смут to sow discord

смутен -тна *adj literary* troubled, turbulent; restless; rebellious; смутно време time of troubles

смути *pf literary* **I** to stir up, agitate *trans.*; го смути народот he incited the populace to revolt **II – се** to revolt, rebel, rise up

смутител *m literary* troublemaker, *agent provocateur*

смутка *f* rotten egg; *fig.* bad egg/apple

смуткоса се *pf see* сматкоса се

смуткосува се *impf of* смуткоса се, *see* сматкосува се

смутува (се) *impf of* смути (се)

смуча се *impf* to ski

смучар *f* skier

смучарски *adj* skiing

смучарство *n* skiing

смучка *f* (*usu. pl*) ski

смушне се *pf* смушна се *aor.* to sneak, creep (*во/низ – in/by/past*)

смушнува се *impf of* смушне се

снаа *f* **1** daughter-in-law **2** sister-in-law (*brother's wife*) **3** (*mode of address to a younger woman*) my dear, my lass

снабден *pt* well-supplied; well-stocked

снабди *pf* **I** to supply, furnish, provide; to equip; снабди некого со месо to supply s.o. with meat **II – се** to stock up (*co – with*) *intrans.*; to fill up *intrans.*; се снабди со гориво to take on fuel; се снабди со билети to acquire tickets

снабдител *m* supplier, purveyor; victualler

снабдува (се) *impf of* снабди (се)

снабдување *n* supply; provisioning

снабдувач *m* supplier, purveyor; victualler

снага *f* body, figure, form; тенка/вита снага slender/lithe figure

снажен -жна *adj* well-built; sturdy, robust, strapping

снаин *adj* daughter-in-law's; sister-in-law's

снаица *f*, **снаиче** *n* & **снаичка** *f dim. of* снаа

снајде *pf* **I** *impers.* (*with acc.*) to befall; to happen to; го снајде голема несреќа s.th. terrible has happened to him; што те снајде? what happened to you? **II – се** to cope, manage; умее да се снајде во секоја ситуација he can cope with any situation

снајдува (се) *impf of* снајде (се), *see* снаоѓа (се)

снајпер *m* **1** sniper's rifle **2** sniper, sharpshooter

снајперист *m see* снајпер 2

снајперски *adj* <of a> sniper/sniper's rifle; снајперски оган sniper fire

снаодлив *adj* resourceful, clever; adaptable

снаодливост *f* resourcefulness; adaptability

снаоѓа (се) *impf of* снајде (се)

сневесели се *pf* to grow sad

сневиде се *pf usu. in the expression:* да ти се сневиди! to hell with you!

снег *m* snow; врне снег it is snowing; грутка снег snowball; ❑ бел како снег as white as snow, snow-white; го жали (љуби, сака) како снегот лански she doesn't care two hoots for him

снегар *m Zool.* (Fringilla coelebs) chaffinch

снегов<**ен**> *adj see* снежен; грутка снегова snowball

снеговит *adj* <of> snow; snowy; снеговито место snowy place; снеговита зима snowy winter

снегочистачка *f* snowplough

снегулка *f* snowflake

снежен -жна *adj* <of> snow; snowy; снежна топка snowball; снежни соспи snowdrifts; снежен човек snowman; снежни височини snow-covered peaks; снежна бура snowstorm, blizzard; снежна чистота extreme cleanliness

снежест *adj poet. see* снежен

снежец *m dim. hyp. of* снег

снежи *impf* to fall (*of snow*); to snow

снежинка *f see* снегулка

снежовица *f f.p.* грутка снежовица snowball

снекбар *m* snackbar

снема *pf* **1** (*impers. with acc.*) to disappear, vanish; одеднаш го снема he suddenly disappeared **2** to run out of; снемавме пари we ran out of money **3** to run out, come to an end; снема брашно there is no flour left

снеможе *pf* to feel weak/faint/ill

снеможеност *f see* истоштеност

снеможува *impf of* снеможе

снемува *impf of* снема

снесе *pf* to lay (*eggs*); кокошката снесе јајце the hen laid an egg

снесува *impf of* снесе

снешко -овци *m* snowman

снижи *pf* **I** to lower, reduce, diminish *trans.*; снижи цени to reduce prices **II – се** to decrease, diminish *intrans.*; to fade; се снижија цените prices have fallen; се снижи звукот the sound faded

снижува (се) *impf of* снижи (се)

снизи (се) *pf rare see* снижи (се)

снизок -ска *adj see* низок

снима (се) *impf of* сними (се)

снимател *m* cameraman

снимач *m* **1** camera **2** *rare see* снимател

сними *pf* (*со камера*) to film; (*со апарат*) to photograph; (*на магнетофон*) to tape-record; (*на рентген*) to X-ray

снимка *f* photograph, snapshot; X-ray; tape recording; магнетоскопска снимка video recording; магнетофонска снимка tape recording

снисходлив *adj* **1** lenient, indulgent **2** obliging, gracious; condescending

снисходливост *f* leniency, indulgence; condescension

сноб *m* snob

снобизам -змот *m* snobbery

снобовски *adj* snobbish

снова (се) *impf see* snove (се)

сновалка *f* spool, cone, bobbin

сновачка *f* warper (*in weaving*)

snove *impf* **I** **1** *Weaving* to warp **2** *fig.* to walk to and fro, shuttle **II – се** *see* I 2

сновидение -ија *n arch.* dream

сноп *m* sheaf; bundle; bunch; сноп банкноти a wad of notes; снопови светлина beams of light

снопи *impf* to bind into sheaves; снопи пченица to sheaf wheat

снопче *n dim. of* сноп

сносен -сна *adj literary* bearable, tolerable

снослив *adj literary see* сносен, поднослив

сноќева (се) *impf of* сноќи (се)

сноќи *pf* **I** *impers.* (*of darkness*) to overtake (*s.o.*); го сноќи близу до селото night overtook him close to the village **II – се** to get dark

сноќува (се) *impf of* сноќи (се)

сношген -шна *adj see* синоќен, синоќешен

сношти *adv see* синоќа

снужден *adj literary* sad, sorrowful; dejected

снужденост *f literary* sadness, sorrow

снужди се *pf literary* to grow sad; to become depressed

снуждува се *impf of* снужди се

со[1] *m Mus.* G

со[2] *prep* **1** (*company, accompaniment*) with; and; таа дојде со мајка си she arrived with her mother; дожд со снег sleet; чекори со песна to sing as one marches **2** (*manner*) with; со радост with joy; со полно право with full justification; со болно срце with an aching heart **3** (*instrument*) with; by means of; сече со нож to cut with a knife; пишува со молив to write with a pencil; градовите се сврзани со добри патишта the towns are linked by good roads **4** (*possession, properties, contents*) with, of; човек со талент a man of talent; супа со зеленчук vegetable soup; сандак со книги a chest full of books **5** (*in time expressions*) with; for; in; со години for years; со годините with the years; со време разбере to realize in good time **6** (*with numerals*) in; by; со стотици by the hundred; со илјадници in thousands **7** (*miscellaneous senses*) with; доста со тие разговори enough of that talk; со поздрав with kind regards; со убави желби with best wishes; лице со лице face to face

соа *f dial. see* скала[1]

соавтор *m* co-author, joint author

соавторство *n* co-authorship, joint authorship

соаре *n* soirée

соба *f* **1** room; гостинска соба parlour, drawing-room; guest-room; соба за спиење bedroom; ❑ ја чува собата to be confined to one's room **2** *dial.* (*печка*) stove

собарица *f* <chamber> maid

собен -бна *adj* room; собна врата door to a room; собна температура room temperature; собни растенија indoor plants

собер *m f.p. see* собор

собере *pf* собра *aor.* **I 1** to gather, collect *trans.*; собере податоци to gather (collect) information; собере мисли to collect one's thoughts; собере пари to raise money **2** to assemble, muster, bring together, gather *trans.*; to rally *trans.*; to round up (*animals*); собере стадо to gather a flock; собере народ to rally people **3** to add <up>; собере броеви to add numbers **4** to place together; to draw in; собере веѓи to knit (pucker) one's brows; собере нозе to put one's feet together; ❑ собере (собира) раменици to shrug one's shoulders **5** to accommodate, hold; собава ќе собере десет души this room will hold ten people **II – се 1** to gather, muster, collect; to meet *intrans.* **2** *colloq.* to get together; to move in (*co – with*) **3** to contract; to shrivel; to shrink **4** to fit <in> *intrans.*; се собраа сите книги all the books fitted in

собеседник -ци *m* interlocutor, conversation partner

собеседница & собеседничка *f* (*fem. form*) *see* собеседник

собеси *pf* to take down, remove; собеси слика од сид to take down a picture from a wall

собесува *impf of* собеси

собир *m* assembly, meeting; свика собир to call a meeting

собира (се) *impf of* собере (се)

собиралиште *n* meeting place; кај ви е собиралиштето? where do you usually meet?

собирач *m* collector

собирачки *adj* collector's; collecting

собирен -рна *adj* <of/for> collection; collecting; собирен центар collection point (*for crops*)

собица *f see* собиче, собичка

собиче *n & собичка f dim. of* соба 1

собиште *n augm. of* соба 1

соблазан *f see* соблазна

соблазна *f* temptation; воведе во соблазна to lead into temptation

соблазни *pf* **I** to tempt; to seduce, lead astray; го соблазни нејзината убавина her beauty turned his head **II – се** to succumb to temptation

соблазнив *adj* tempting; seductive; exciting; соблазниви новини exciting news

соблазнител *m* tempter; seducer

соблазнува (се) *impf of* соблазни (се)

соблекува (се) *impf of* соблече (се)

соблекувална *f* dressing-room, changing room, locker-room; ❑ го прати во соблекувалната *Sport.* he was sent off

соблече *pf* соблеков *1st p. sg aor.* **I 1** to undress *trans.*; to take off (*clothing*) **2** *fig., colloq.* to fleece, *sl.* skin, rip off **II – се** to undress *intrans.*

соблечува (се) *impf see* соблекува (се)

собор *m* **1** assembly; convention; council; црковен собор synod; вселенски собор ecumenical council **2** fair, festival; feast day; собор на селото village fair

собора *impf of* собори

соборен -рна *adj* assembly; synodal; соборен ред synod standing orders; ❑ соборна црква (*Orthodox*) cathedral

соборец -рци *m* fellow soldier, brother-in-arms; comrade

собори *pf* **1** to knock over/down, throw down, push over; to fell, floor **2** to overthrow, bring down; to depose, topple *trans.*; собори власт to bring down a government **3** to demolish, tear down, pull down; собори зграда to demolish a building **4** *fig.* to overwhelm; сон ме собори sleep overcame me

соборише *n* meeting place; fairground

соборски *adj* assembly; festival; council *attrib.*

соборува *impf of* собори

собрание -ија *n* **1** meeting; годишно собрание annual general meeting; собранието ја осуди неговата постапка the meeting condemned his action **2** assembly; parliament; законодавно собрание legislative assembly; уставотворно собрание constituent assembly; градско собрание town assembly; (*зграда*) town hall **3** *literary, arch.* (*збирка*) collection; собрание од народни песни collection of folk-songs

собрат *m* confrère; opposite number; counterpart

собува (се) *impf of* собуе (се)

собуден *adj literary* conscious, aware; alert

собуди *pf* **I 1** to provoke, arouse, excite; собуди желба to excite desire **2** *literary, fig.* to bring (*s.o.*) to his senses; to enlighten **II – се** to give a start *intrans.*; *fig.* to wake up *intrans.*

собудува (се) *impf of* собуди (се)

собуе *pf* собу *aor.* **I** to take off (*usu. shoes, socks*) **II – се** to take off one's shoes/socks

собуен *pt* barefoot; unshod

совалка *f Weaving* shuttle

совесен -сна *adj* conscientious; совесна работа conscientious work

совесност *f* conscientiousness

совест *f* conscience; човек без совест unscrupulous person; ❑ гласот на совеста the promptings of one's conscience; гризење на совеста pricks (pangs) of conscience, remorse; го мачи совеста he has a guilty conscience; оди (постапува) против својата совест to go (act) against one's conscience; слобода на совеста freedom of conscience; со мирна (чиста) совест with a clear conscience

совет *m* **1** advice, counsel; даде совет to give advice **2** council; conference; семеен совет family council; советот на институтот the council of the institute; куќен совет tenants' council **3** soviet

советник -ци *m* **1** adviser, counsellor; consultant; правен советник legal counsel (adviser); советник на амбасада <embassy> counsellor **2** councillor; советник на градското собрание city councillor; ❑ научен советник senior research fellow

советница & советничка *f (fem. form) see* советник

советнички *adj* adviser's

советодавен -дна *adj* advisory, consultative; consultative body

советодавец -вци *m* adviser, counsellor; consultant

советува *impf* **I** to advise; советува некого како да постапи to advise s.o. how to act **II – се 1** to seek advice; to consult (*co – with*); се советува со правник to consult a lawyer **2** to confer *intrans.*; to deliberate

советувалиште *n* counselling service; citizens' advice bureau; брачно советувалиште marriage-guidance counselling service

советување *n* **1** counselling; advice **2** conference; deliberation; се свика советување a conference was convened **3** discussion, deliberation

совземе (се) *pf* совзема (се) *aor. dial. see* соз눔e (се)

совие (се) *pf* совие (се) *aor. dial. see* свие (се)

совлада *pf* **I** to overcome, surmount, master; совлада непријател to defeat an enemy; совлада пречки to overcome (surmount) obstacles; совлада тешкотии to surmount difficulties; го совлада сонот sleep overcame him; совлада техника to master a technique **II – се** to contain o.s.

совладлив *adj* surmountable; manageable

совладува (се) *impf of* совлада (се)

совпадне се *pf* совпадна се *aor.* **1** to coincide (*co – with*) **2** to correspond, concur, tally; нивните мислења се совпаднаа their opinions concurred **3** *Geom.* to be congruent

совпаѓа се *impf of* совпадне се

совреме *adv* punctually, on time; in good time; дојде совреме to come on time; совреме извести to inform in good time

современ *adj* **1** contemporary, modern, up-to-date; современи писатели contemporary writers; современа техника today's technology; modern

equipment **2** *rare* (*истовремен*) contemporaneous (*with*)

современик -ци *m* contemporary

современица & современичка *f (fem. form) see* современик

современост *f* **1** modernity; contemporaneity **2** modern times, the present

соврзе (се) *pf* соврза (се) *aor. see* одврзе (се), разврзе (се)

соврзува (се) *impf of* соврзе (се), *see* одврзува (се), разврзува (се)

совршен *adj* **1** perfect **2** complete, total; совршена тишина complete silence; совршено поклопување complete agreement; совршена спротивност complete opposite

совршено *adv* **1** perfectly; зборува совршено француски to speak flawless French **2** *colloq.* completely, utterly, fully

совршеност *f* perfection

совршенство *n* perfection; се стреми кон совршенство to strive for perfection

согласен[1] -сна *adj* **1** in agreement (*co – with*) **2** harmonious, coordinated; unanimous; согласна работа harmonious work; согласни движења harmonious movements

согласен[2] -сна *adj Ling.* consonantal; согласни групи consonant clusters

согласи *pf* **I** *rare* to reconcile; to harmonize, coordinate **II – се 1** to agree, consent (*да – to*); to consent; се согласи да одржи предавање he agreed to give a lecture **2** to agree, concur (*co – with*); се согласи со предлог to agree with a suggestion

согласка *f Ling.* consonant; тврди согласки hard consonants

согласно *adv* in agreement, harmoniously; ❑ согласно со in accordance with

согласност *f* **1** consent, agreement, assent; даде согласност to give one's consent **2** accord, agreement, harmony; harmoniousness; најде согласност to reach accord; со заемна согласност by common consent; согласност на погледите identity of views; согласност на движењата harmony of movement; ❑ во согласност со in keeping with, in accordance with

согласува (се) *impf of* согласи (се)

согледа *pf* **1** to see, notice, catch sight of **2** to realize, grasp, understand; брзо ја согледа ситуацијата he took in the situation immediately; согледа дека . . . to realize that . . .

согледува *impf of* согледа

соговорник -ци *m* interlocutor, conversation partner

соговорница & соговоричка *f (fem. form) see* соговорник

соголен *pt* **1** naked, bare, uncovered, nude; соголени дрвја trees bare of leaves **2** *fig.* cheated, defrauded, fleeced

соголеност *f* nakedness, nudity

соголи *pf* **1** to strip *trans.*, denude; ветерот ги соголи тополите the wind stripped the leaves from the poplars **2** *fig.* to fleece, cheat, defraud **II – се 1** to strip *intrans.* **2** to lose (shed) leaves; се соголиле гранките the branches lost their leaves

соголува (се) *impf of* соголи (се)

согради *pf* **1** to build; согради куќа to build a house **2** to fence <in>; согради лозје to fence a vineyard

соградува *impf of* согради

сограѓанин -ани *m* fellow townsman

сограѓанка *f* fellow townswoman

согреши *pf* to sin, commit a sin; (*with dat.*) to offend; to err, make a mistake

согрешува *impf of* согреши

сода *f* **1** soda; сода за прање (перење) washing soda; сода бикарбонат bicarbonate of soda, baking-soda, sodium bicarbonate; каустична сода caustic soda; сапун со сода soda soap **2** (*газирана вода*) soda; една чаша сода a glass of soda; сода-вода soda water

содаџија -ии *m colloq.* soda-water seller/producer

содаџика *f (fem. form)* see содаџија

содаџиски *adj colloq.* soda-water seller's/producer's; содаџиски дуќан soda fountain

содејство *n* cooperation, assistance, aid; укаже содејство to assist, render assistance

содејствува *impf* to co-operate (*со – with*)

содере *pf* содра *aor.* **1** to tear off, strip off; содере кожа to skin, flay **2** to rip, tear *trans.*; to wear out *trans.*; ги содрал панталоните he tore his trousers; he wore out his trousers

содерува *impf of* содере

содира *impf of* содере, *see* содерува

содомија *f* sodomy; bestiality

содомит *m* sodomite

содржаен -јна *adj* pithy; substantial, full, detailed; содржајна книга informative book

содржај -аи *m literary rare* content<s>, *see* содржина

содржание -ија *n arch.* see содржина

содржи *impf* **I** to contain; зеленчукот содржи различни витамини vegetables contain various vitamins **II – се** to form part of; to be contained (*во – in*); *Math.* се содржи без остаток it goes into it without remainder

содржина *f* **1** contents; содржината на шишето the contents of the bottle **2** subject matter, essence, substance; содржината на разговорот the subject of the conversation **3** content; component; percentage; содржината на злато во рудата the gold content in the ore

содржински *adj* <of the> content; содржинската страна на текстот the substantive burden of the text

содржител *m Math.* multiple; denominator; заеднички содржител common denominator

содружи се *pf* to unite, associate (*со – with*) *intrans.*; to make friends

содружува се *impf of* содружи се

соединение -ија *n* **1** *Chem.* compound; азотни соединенија nitrogen compounds **2** *arch.* joining, junction; union; unity; combination

соединет *pt* united, joint; amalgamated; consolidated; соединети сили combined strength; Соединетите Американски Држави the United States of America

соедини *pf* **I 1** to connect, join, link; соедини цевки to connect pipes **2** to mix *trans.*; to blend *trans.*; to combine *trans.*; to merge *trans.*; to unite *trans.* **II – се 1** to link up, join, unite (*со – with*) *intrans.*; to contact *intrans.* **2** to combine; to merge, blend *intrans.*; to unite *intrans.*; се соединил кислородот со водородот the oxygen combined with the hydrogen

соединува (се) *impf of* соедини (се)

сожалба *f literary rare* sympathy; pity

сожали *pf* **I** to take pity on; го сожали и му помогна he took pity on him and helped him **II – се** to feel regret

сожалив *adj* compassionate; pitying; сожалив човек compassionate person; сожалив поглед a look of pity

сожаливост *f* compassion, pity

сожалува *impf* **I 1** to pity, feel sorry for **2** to feel regret, feel sorry; сожалувам, но не е така I'm sorry, but that it is not the case **II – се** to feel sorry, feel regret

сожвака *pf see* соцвака

сожвакува *impf of* сожвака, *see* соцвакува

соживее се *pf* соживеа се *aor.* to become accustomed, get used (*со – to*); to make friends (*со – with*); се соживее со работата to get used to a job; се соживее со улога to get the feel of a role

соживи *pf* **I** to revive *trans.*, resuscitate **II – се 1** to revive *intrans.* **2** *see* соживее се

соживува (се) *impf of* соживи (се)

сожител *m* fellow resident; fellow citizen

сожителка *f (fem. form) see* сожител

сожителство *n arch.*, *literary* living together, coexistence; cohabitation

сожнее *pf* сожнеа *aor. see* сожние

сожние *pf* сожни *aor. f.p.* (*ожнее*) to reap, harvest

созбори се *pf* to reach agreement

созборува се *pf of* созбори се

созвучен -чна *adj* harmonious

созвучје *n* **1** *Mus.*, *fig.* chord; harmony, accord **2** assonance

созвучност *f* harmony; assonance

создава (се) *impf of* создаде (се)

создавање *n* creation; создавањето на светот the creation of the world; литературно создавање a work of literature; во фаза на создавање in the making

создавачки *adj* creative, artistic; создавачка работа creative work

создаде *pf* **I** to create, make, produce; to set up, found; ми создаде грижа he caused me anxiety; создаде име to make/win a name for o.s.; создаде погрешна претстава to give the wrong idea/ impression **II – се** to spring up, appear; to arise; се создаде тешка ситуација a difficult situation arose

создание -ија *n arch.* **1** creation; work of art **2** creature, living being; human being; живо создание living creature

создател *m arch. see* творец

создроби *pf f.p. see* здроби

созема (се) *impf of* созeме (се)

созeме *pf* **I 1** to accommodate, hold, have room for; не може да ги созeме сандакот they will not fit in the trunk **2** to muster, collect, gather *trans.*; созeме сила to regain one's strength **II – се 1** to recover *intrans.*; to recuperate **2** to come to, regain consciousness; to give a start *intrans.* **3** to get back on one's feet; to pull o.s. together; to compose o.s.

созива *impf arch.*, *literary see* свикува[2]

сознава *impf of* сознае

сознае *pf* созна *aor.* **1** to realize, grasp, understand; сознае вистина to realize the truth **2** *rare* (*узнае*) to find out, learn

сознание *n* **1** fact<s>, evidence **2** perception, cognition, comprehension **3** *arch. see* свест

созове *pf* созва *aor. arch., literary see* свика²

созрева *impf of* созрее

созревање *n rare* maturation, maturing; ripening; полово созревање puberty

созрее *pf rare* созреа *aor.* **1** to mature, to grow up; to ripen; созреала пченицата the wheat is ready to harvest **2** *fig.* to assume final form, take shape; созреаја условите conditions are ripe

соѕвездие -ија & **соѕвездје** *n* constellation; соѕвездието Колата Ursa Major, the Great Bear, the Plough, Charles's Wain; Ursa Minor, the Little Bear

соѕвечи *pf f.p. see* ѕвекне

соѕида *pf* (*изѕида, изгради*) to build

соѕидува *impf of* соѕида

соѕира *impf of* созре

созре *pf* to see, notice, catch sight of

соиграч *m* fellow player, team-mate

сој -еви *m colloq.* ancestry, origin; breed; sort; од ист сој 1. of the same stock 2. birds of a feather; риби од разен сој different sorts of fish; ❏ од <господски> сој of good family; од долен сој of humble origins; кучешки (кучински) сој ill-bred lot

соја¹ *f Bot.* (Soja hispida) soya <bean>

соја² *f dial.* trellis

соjаде се *pf see* пријаде се

соjадува се *impf of* соjаде се

соjка *f Zool.* (Garrulus glandarius) jay; ❏ брка соjки to waste time

соjкин *adj* <of a> jay; соjкино крило a jay's wing

соjлија *adj indecl. colloq.* of a good family/breeding; соjлија жена a woman of breeding; соjлија крава thoroughbred cow

соjуз *m* **1** union; league, federation; Советски Соjуз Soviet Union; Соjуз на младината Youth League **2** alliance; coalition; склучи соjуз to form an alliance/coalition; троен соjуз Triple Alliance

соjузен -зна *adj* union/alliance *attrib.*; federal; соjузна република federal republic

соjузи *pf literary* **I** to unite *trans.*, bring together as allies **II** – **се** to ally o.s., form an alliance, unite *intrans.*

соjузник -ци *m* ally

соjузница & **соjузничка** *f* (*of a woman or a state*) *see* соjузник

соjузнички *adj* ally's; allied

соjузништво *n* alliance, coalition

соjузува (се) *impf of* соjузи (се)

сок *m* **1** juice; sap; желудочен сок gastric juice; овошни сокови fruit juices **2** *fig.* essence, pith; cream; сокот на дискусиjата the gist of the discussion

сокаj -аи *m* woman's hood (*in traditional costume*)

сокак -ци *m* street; alley; ❏ ќор сокак blind alley, dead end, cul-de-sac; наjде се во ќор сокак to have reached an impasse

сокапе *pf* сокапа *aor.* **I** *colloq.* to beat up **II** – **се** to hurt o.s. badly

сокапува (се) *impf of* сокапе (се)

сокачарка *f colloq.* slattern; slut; whore

сокачарски *adj colloq.* slatternly; sluttish

сокаче *n dim. of* сокак

сокачки *adj* street *attrib.*; сокачка песна ribald song

сокине (се) *pf* сокина (се) *aor., see* скине (се)

сокинува (се) *impf of* сокине (се), *see* скинува (се)

сокласник -ци *m* classmate

сокласничка *f* (*fem. form*) *see* сокласник

сокле *n dim. of* сокол; falcon chick; сиво сокле juvenile peregrine <falcon>

сокол -кли, -и *m* **1** *Zool.* (Falco) falcon; tercel; мал сокол (Falco columbarius) merlin; сив сокол (Falco peregrinus) peregrine <falcon>; сокол ловец (Falco rusticolus) gyrfalcon; ❏ гол како сокол as poor as a church mouse **2** *fig.* knight, stout fellow

соколар *m Hist.* falconer; falcon-trainer

соколе & **соколенце** *n dim. of* сокол, *see* сокле

соколи *impf* **I** to encourage, embolden; to rally *trans.*, inspire, urge on **II** – **се 1** to take courage, show fight **2** to strut

соколина *f augm. of* сокол

соколица *f* (*of a female*) *see* сокол

соколов *adj* falcon's; соколово крило falcon's wing; соколово гнездо falcon's eyrie; ❏ око соколово eagle eye

соколски *adj* falcon's

соколче *n dim. of* сокол, *see* сокле

сократи (се) *pf see* скрати (се), скуси (се)

сократува (се) *impf of* сократи (се), *see* скратува (се), скусува (се)

сокрива (се) *impf of* сокрие (се)

сокрие (се) *pf see* скрие (се)

сокровишница *f arch., literary* treasury, depository; treasure-house, repository

сокровиште *n arch., literary* treasure (*also fig.*)

сокрши (се) *pf see* скрши (се)

сокршува (се) *impf of* сокрши (се)

сол *f* **1** salt; англиска сол Epsom salts; калиумови соли potassium salts; камена сол rock-salt, table salt, common salt; sodium chloride; куjнска сол cooking salt; морска сол sea salt; ❏ направи сол to make mincemeat of, beat the life out of; to smash to smithereens; за инает и вреќа сол се jаде to cut off your nose to spite your face; трие (толчи) некому сол на главата to rub salt into s.o.'s wounds **2** *fig.* essence, heart <of the matter>; солта на прашањето the point <of the question>, nub of the matter; солта на животот the spice of life

солáна *f* **1** salt mine **2** saltern, salting

солар *m* salt producer; salt merchant

соларник -ци *m* salt-cellar, *Am.* salt-shaker

соларница *f see* солана

соларниче *n dim. of* соларник

соларство *n* salt production

солба *f* stalk; shoot

солдат *m arch.* (*воjник*) soldier; го зедоа солдат he was conscripted

солдатéска *f colloq.* soldiery; mob of soldiers

солдатски *adj arch.* soldier's; military; soldierly

солен¹ *adj* **1** salt *attrib.*, saline; солени извори salt springs; солени езера salt lakes; солено море salty sea **2** salted; salty; savoury; солено jадење salted food **3** pickled; (*of beef, etc.*) corned; солени риби salted fish; kippers **4** *fig. colloq.* pricey, expensive; малку е солен овоj штоф this material is a bit pricey; му излезе солено he had to pay through the nose

солен² -лна *adj Chem.* salt *attrib.*, saline; солна киселина hydrochloric acid

соленик -ци *m see* соларник

сoleникав *adj* rather salty

соленина *f* saltiness; salinity

соленица *f see* соларник, соленик

соленка¹ *f* cheese straw; bread stick, grissino

соленка² -о *adj dim. (only f and n)* rather salty; *colloq.* pricey

соленост *f* saltiness; salinity

солза *f* tear; ❑ доведе до солзи to reduce to tears; рони (лее) солзи to shed tears; полни очи солзи eyes brimming with tears; се капе во солзи to cry one's eyes out; бистар (чист) како солза crystal-clear; крокодилски солзи crocodile tears; момина солза *Bot.* (Convallaria majalis) lily of the valley

солзавец -вци *m* tear-gas

солзен -зна *adj* **1** tear *attrib.*, lacrimal, lachrymal; солзни жлезди lacrimal glands; солзни канали lacrimal canals, tear-ducts **2** tearful; со солзни очи with eyes brimming with tears **3** *colloq.* piteous, heart-rending; солзни молби heart-rending pleas

солзи *impf* **1** to water, run *intrans.*; ми солзат очите my eyes are watering **2** *literary* to shed tears, weep **3** to ooze; to leak; солзи лозата the vine is oozing sap; солзат стаклата the windows are misting over

солзица & солзичка *f dim. of* солза

солзлив *adj see* солзен

солзница *f* lacrimal gland

соли *impf* **1** to salt; соли јадење to salt food; ❑ му соли ум (памет) to lecture s.o. **2** to salt <down>; to souse *trans.*; to corn (*beef, etc.*); to cure *trans.*; to pickle; соли риба to salt (souse) fish **3** *fig.* to sprinkle, dust; соли некого/нешто со прав to shower s.o./s.th. with dust

солидáрен -рна *adj* **1** making common cause (*co – with*); in solidarity; солидарен со говорникот in agreement with the speaker **2** *Leg.* solidary, joint and several; солидарни обврски solidary obligations; солидарна одговорност joint liability

солидаризúра се *pf & impf* to make common cause (*co – with*); to stand by, side with; to unite, stick together *intrans.*; to sympathize

солидáрност *f* **1** solidarity **2** *Leg.* joint liability

солиден -дна *adj* **1** solid, sound, sturdy; солидна градба sturdy construction **2** *fig.* reliable; sound; солиден човек trustworthy person; солидни знаења profound knowledge **3** reputable; солидно претпријатие established firm **4** *colloq.* considerable, substantial; солидна заработка decent wage; солидна заштеда considerable savings; солидно јадење square (hearty) meal

солидност *f* solidity; soundness; reliability; respectability

солило *n* **1** brine **2** salt-lick (*for livestock*)

солúст *m* **1** soloist **2** *colloq.* show-off; prima donna; one-man band

солистички *adj* solo; soloist's; солистички концерт solo concert

солúстка *f (fem. form) see* солист

солитéр *m* **1** skyscraper **2** *sl.* lanky person, *colloq.* beanpole

солиште *n see* солило 2

солне <се> *pf colloq.* солна <се> *aor.* to take cover, shelter *intrans.*; *see* засолне се

солник -ци *m see* соларник

солница *f* **1** salt-marsh; salt-pan **2** *see* соларник

солнува <се> *impf of* солне <се>

соло¹ *n Mus.* solo <piece>; соло за виолина violin solo

соло² *adv* solo, on one's own, alone; пее соло to sing solo

Соломóни *pl* Solomon Islands

соломонски *adj* Solomon *attrib.*; Соломонски Острови Solomon Islands

сол-пипер *m colloq.* salt with crushed paprika/chilli

Солун *m* Salonika, Salonica, Thessaloniki

солунец -нци *m* person from Salonika; Thessalonian

солунка *f (fem. form) see* солунец

солунски *adj* Salonika *attrib.*

солуњанин -ни *m see* солунец

солуњанка *f see* солунка

солупи *pf* **I** to peel, skin; to shell **II** – се (*за боја*) to peel *intrans.*

солупува (се) *impf of* солупи (се)

солуција -ии *f* solution; dénouement; најде солуција to find a solution

солфеж *m Mus.* solfeggio, tonic sol-fa

солца *f dim. of* сол

сом *m* **1** *Zool.* (Silurus glanis) sheatfish, European catfish **2** *fig.* blockhead, dolt

Сомалиец -ијци *m* Somali

Сомалија *f* Somalia

Сомалијка *f (fem. form) see* Сомалиец

сомалиски *adj* Somali

соматологија *f Med.* somatology

соматски *adj Med.* somatic, corporeal

сомбрéро *n* sombrero

сомеле *pf* сомле *aor.* **1** to grind, mill; to mince; to chew; сомеле жито to mill grain; сомеле кафе to grind coffee; сомеле месо to mince meat; сомеле во устата to chew **2** *fig.* to thrash, to make mincemeat of **3** to digest **4** *fig., colloq.* to grasp, understand, master; to take in, cope with

сомелува *impf of* сомеле

сомилосен -сна *adj* compassionate; sympathetic

сомилост *f* pity, compassion, sympathy

сомисленик -ци *m* **1** like-minded person; kindred spirit; ние сме сомисленици we share the same views **2** adherent, follower

сомисленица *f (fem. form) see* сомисленик

сомиште *n augm. of* сом

сомнамбýл *m Med.* sleepwalker, somnambulist

сомнамбýлен -лна *adj Med.* somnambulant; somnambulistic; сомнамбулни признаци signs of somnambulism

сомнамбулúзам -змот *m Med.* sleepwalking, somnambulism

сомнева се *impf* (*во*) to doubt; to distrust; to suspect; се сомневаше со право во него he had reason to distrust him

сомневање *n* doubt; suspicion; uncertainty; misgiving; ❑ без <секакво> сомневање without <any> doubt; нема сомневање no doubt; надвор од секое (секакво) сомневање beyond the shadow of a doubt

сомнеж *m poet. see* сомневање

сомнение -ија *n see* сомневање

сомнителен -лна *adj* doubtful, dubious, questionable; сомнителна вредност questionable value; сомнително лице suspicious person; suspect; сомнителен поглед sceptical/suspicious look; сомнително познанство dubious acquaintance

сомов *adj* catfish's

сомовина *f* catfish <flesh>

сомовски *adj see* сомски

сомот *m* velvet; (*ребрест*) corduroy; фустан од сомот velvet dress

сомотен -тна *adj* velvet; corduroy

сомотски *adj* velvet; corduroy; сомотски панталони corduroys

сомски *adj* catfish's; сомско месо catfish <flesh>

сомун *m colloq.* loaf; топол сомун hot bread

сомуниште *n augm. colloq. of* сомун

сомунче *n dim. colloq. of* сомун

сомунџија -ии *m colloq.* baker

сомче *n dim. of* сом

сон[1] *m* **1** sleep, *poet.* slumber; *fig.* torpor; длабок сон deep sleep; лесен сон light sleep; тврд сон sound sleep; ❏ зајачки сон light sleep; зимски сон winter sleep, hibernation; како на сон (*се секава и сл.*) (*to remember, etc.*) vaguely; летаргичен сон lethargic sleep; ни на сон (*не се надевал, мислел и сл.*) not in his wildest dreams (*had he hoped, thought, etc.*) **2** (*pl* соништа, сонови, *less often* сништа) dream; сони (виде) сон to have a dream; ѝ се исполни сонот her dream came true; реализирани соништа dreams made flesh

сон[2] *m colloq.* (*во карти*) talon, stock

сонант *m Ling.* sonant, sonorant

сонантен -тна & **сонантски** *adj Ling.* sonant, sonorant *attrib.*

сонароднник -ци *m* fellow-countryman, compatriot

сонароднница & **сонароднничка** *f* fellow-country-woman

сонаследник -ци *m* joint heir, parcener

сонаследница & **сонаследничка** *f* joint heiress

соната *f Mus.* sonata

сонатен -тна *adj Mus.* sonata *attrib.*; сонатна форма sonata form

сонатина *f Mus.* sonatina

сонда *f* **1** *Geol.* bore; sounding-line **2** *Med.* probe; stomach-pump/-tube; catheter **3** weather balloon, sonde; space probe

сондажа *f Med., fig.* probing; sounding<s>; drilling; exploratory talk

сондевче *n dim. f.p. of* сонце

сондира *pf & impf Med., Geol., fig.* to sound *trans.*; to drill; to probe, take soundings of; ❏ сондира мислење to probe (sound out) (*s.o.'s*) opinion; сондира терен to see how the land lies

соне *n dim. of* сон, *see* сонче

сонет *m* sonnet

сонетен -тна *adj* sonnet *attrib.*; сонетен венец sonnet sequence

сони[1] *pf* **I** to dream; сон сони to have a dream **II – се** *impers.* (*with dat.*) to dream; му се сони he had a dream

сони[2] *impf dial. see* сонува

сонлив *adj* sleepy, drowsy; somnolent; torpid; сонлив израз sleepy expression; сонлива состојба lethargic state

сонливец -вци *m* sleepyhead

сонливица & **сонливка** *f* (*fem. form*) *see* сонливец

сонливост *f* sleepiness, drowsiness

соновник -ци *m* dream book

сонок *m dim. of* сон, *see* сончок

сонометар -три *m* sonometer; audiometer

сонорен -рна *adj* sonorous

сонорност *f* sonority

сонува *impf* **1** to dream (*of/about*); сонува некого to dream of s.o. **2** *fig.* to day-dream, imagine; тоа немој да го сонуваш don't even think about it!

сонце *n* sun; sunshine, sunlight; ❏ затемнување на сонцето eclipse of the sun; заод на сонцето sunset; изгрев на сонцето sunrise; се грее на сонце to bask in the sun; сонце со заби winter sun

сонцев *adj see* сончев

сонцуле *n dim. of* сонце, *see* сонченце

сонча *impf* **I** to sun *trans.*; си сонча рацете to sun one's arms **II – се** to sun o.s., sunbathe

сончан *adj rare see* сончев

сончаница *f* sunstroke

сонче *n hyp. of* сон[1]; sweet sleep, slumber

сончев *adj* **1** solar; ❏ сончева топлина solar energy; сончева светлина sunlight; сончеви зраци sunbeams; сончевиот систем the solar system; сончев удар sunstroke, a touch of the sun; сончев часовник sundial **2** sunny; сончев ден sunny day; сончево време sunny weather **3** *fig.* joyful, happy; сончеви слики happy pictures; сончева насмевка bright smile; сончева иднина rosy future

сончевина *f* sunlight

сонченце *n dim. of* сонце

сончоглед *m Bot.* (Helianthus annuus) sunflower; семе од сончоглед sunflower seeds

сончогледов *adj* sunflower; сончогледово масло sunflower oil

сончок *m dim. hyp. of* сон[1]; nap, forty winks; sweet sleep

сообразен -зна *adj literary* appropriate; suitable; adequate; consistent (*co – with*)

сообрази *pf literary* **I** to reconcile, harmonize; to adapt *trans.* **II – се** to conform (*co – to, with*); to adapt *intrans.*; се сообрази со нечии желби to fall in with s.o.'s wishes; не се сообрази со условите to take no account of the circumstances

сообразителен -лна *adj literary* quick-witted, sharp, bright; resourceful

сообразителност *f literary* quick wits, quickness of mind; resourcefulness; tact

сообразно *adv literary* accordingly; ❏ сообразно со законот in accordance (conformity, compliance) with the law

сообразност *f* conformity; ❏ во сообразност со in accordance (conformity, compliance) with

сообразува (се) *impf of* сообрази (се)

сообраќа *impf* to run, operate *intrans.* (*of transport*); автобусите не сообраќаат the buses are not running

сообраќаен -јна *adj* traffic *attrib.*; (of/for) communication; сообраќајно средство means of transport; сообраќајни врски lines of communication

сообраќаец -јци *m* traffic policeman

сообраќај *m* **1** transport; traffic; железнички сообраќај rail traffic/transport; воздушен сообраќај air traffic; градски сообраќај public transport; city traffic; пречки во сообраќајот traffic hold-ups; жив сообраќај heavy traffic **2** circulation; trade, traffic; паричен сообраќај circulation of money; turnover

сообраќајка *f* traffic accident, road accident

сообраќајница *f* arterial road, trunk road; главните сообраќајници во градот the main thoroughfares of the city

соодветен -тна *adj* appropriate, suitable; corresponding; презеде соодветни мерки to take appropriate measures

соодветно *adv* appropriately, suitably; соодветно екипирани луѓе suitably equipped people; ❑ соодветно со in keeping (harmony, accordance) with

соодветност *f* correspondence; congruence; conformity

соодветство *n* accordance; congruence; conformity, compliance; ❑ во соодветство со in keeping (harmony, accordance) with

соодветствува *impf* (*with dat.*) to correspond (*со, на – to*), conform (*to*) *intrans.*, be in line (*with*); to harmonize (*with*) *intrans.*; to be suitable (*for*); тоа им соодветствуваше на неговите сфаќања that was in keeping with his views

соодговорен -рна *adj* jointly responsible

соодговорност *f* joint responsibility

соодос *m* correlation; interrelation; proportion; соодносот на силите *Phys.* correlation of forces; *Pol.* balance of power; во соодос со in relation (proportion) to

соодносен -сна *adj* corresponding; correlative; balanced

соопштение -ија *n* announcement; report; notice; научно соопштение scholarly article; официјално соопштение official announcement; communiqué

соопшти *pf* to announce; to report; to let (*s.o.*) know; соопшти податоци to release details; соопшти некому вест to comunicate (pass on) news to s.o.

соопштува *impf of* соопшти

сооснивач *m* co-founder

соотечественик -ци *m arch.* fellow-countryman, compatriot

соотечественица & соотечественичка *f arch.* fellow-countrywoman

сопа *f* stick; staff; club, cudgel

сопази *pf see* забележи

сопазува *impf of* сопази, *see* забележува

сопатник -ци *m* **1** travelling companion, fellow-traveller **2** *fig.* partner, companion; associate; неразделен сопатник во животот lifetime companion **3** satellite

сопатница & сопатничка *f* (*fem. form*) *see* сопатник 1, 2

сопатнички *adj* companion's

сопаше *pf* сопаша *aor.* **I** to undo, loosen *trans.*; to ungird; сопаше појас to unfasten a belt; сопаше дете to undress a child; сопаше сабја/меч to remove one's sabre/sword **II** – ce to undress *intrans.*; to loosen one's clothes

сопашува (се) *impf of* сопаше (се)

соперник -ци *m literary* rival; equal, match; немаше соперник he had no equal

соперница *f literary* (*fem. form*) *see* соперник

соперничи *impf literary* to compete, vie (*со – with*); (*with dat.*) to rival

соперничка *f literary see* соперница

соперички *adj literary* rival *attrib.*, rival's

соперништво *n literary* rivalry; соперништво меѓу држави rivalry between states

сопива се *impf of* сопие се

сопие се *pf* сопи се *aor. impers.* (*with dat.*) to feel thirsty

сопина (се) *impf of* сопне (се)

сопира (се) *impf of* сопре (се)

сопирачка *f* (*кочница*) brake (*also fig.*); воздушна сопирачка air brake; рачна сопирачка handbrake; ножна сопирачка footbrake; сопирачка на развојот obstacle to development

сопка[1] *f* hobble (*on legs of livestock*); trip-wire; stumbling block; кладе некому сопка to trip s.o. up

сопка[2] **(се)** *impf see* сопина (се)

соплеменик -ци *m* fellow-tribesman

соплеменица & соплеменичка *f* fellow-tribeswoman

соплеменички *adj* fellow tribesman's/tribeswoman's

соплете (се) *pf see* сплете (се)

соплетува (се) *impf of* соплете (се), *see* сплетува (се)

сопне *pf* сопна *aor.* **I 1** to trip *trans.* **2** to hobble *trans.*; сопне коњ to hobble a horse **II** – ce to trip *intrans.*, stumble; внимавај да не се сопнеш mind you don't trip!

сопнува (се) *impf of* сопне (се)

сопнување *n* stumble; ❑ камен на сопнување stumbling block

сопостави *pf literary* **I** to compare *trans.*, juxtapose **II** – ce to compare *intrans.*

сопоставува (се) *impf of* сопостави (се)

сопотпис *m literary* co-signature; counter-signature

сопотписник -ци *m literary* co-signatory

сопразни (се) *pf see* испразни (се)

сопразнува (се) *impf of* сопразни (се)

сопра́н *m Mus.* soprano; колоратурен сопран coloratura soprano

сопрани́ст *m* boy soprano

сопрани́стка *f* girl soprano

сопра́нски *adj* soprano *attrib.*; сопранска партија soprano part (voice)

сопрво *adv* first; сопрво промисли па после речи think before you speak!

сопре *pf* сопра *aor.* **I** to stop *trans. & intrans.*; to hold <back/up>; сопре автобус to stop a bus; нешто го сопре кај нас something kept him at our place; му сопреле од хонорарот they kept back part of his honorarium; сопреле кај мостот they stopped at the bridge; сопре локомотивата the engine stopped; сопре трговијата trade has come to a standstill **II** – ce to stop *intrans.*, come to a halt

сопровод *m literary rare see* придружба 2

сопроводува *impf literary rare see* придружува

сопротива *f literary rare* (*omnop*) resistance

сопруг· -зи *m* **1** husband, spouse **2** *pl* married couple

сопруга *f* wife, spouse

сопружник -ци *m rare see* сопруг

сопружнички *adj* matrimonial; marital; conjugal; сопружнички односи conjugal relations; сопружничка врска marital bond

сопружништво *n* married life, matrimony

сопрушки *adj see* сопружнички

сопствен *adj* <one's> own; сопствен стан one's own flat (apartment); по сопствена желба at one's own request; со своите сопствени очи with one's own eyes; сопствена тежина <own> weight; empty weight, tare; net weight; dead weight (load); сопствена вредност one's own worth (dignity); *Math.* intrinsic value

сопственик -ци *m* owner, proprietor; ❑ ситен сопственик smallholder; голем сопственик landowner

сопственица & **сопственичка** *f* proprietress

сопственички *adj* owner's; proprietor's; proprietary; сопственички права proprietary rights

сопствениство *n rare see* сопственост

сопственост *f* 1 property; туѓа сопственост s.o. else's property; општествена сопственост public property; приватна сопственост private property; општонародна сопственост common property 2 ownership

сопче *n dim. of* соба 1

соп *m* pruning hook; pruning knife; billhook

соработка *f* collaboration, co-operation

соработник -ци *m* 1 collaborator; associate; ❑ научен соработник research fellow; стручен соработник research assistant 2 contributor; соработник на весникот contributor to the newspaper; newspaper correspondent

соработница & **соработничка** *f* (*fem. form*) *see* соработник

соработнички *adj* collaborator's; collaborative, co-operative; соработнички колектив working group, team; соработнички хонорар contributor's fee

соработниство *n rare see* соработка

соработува *impf* 1 to collaborate; to co-operate (*co – with*) 2 to contribute; соработува во списание to contribute to a journal

сорта *f colloq.* 1 sort; variety; нова сорта јаболка new variety of apple 2 quality, grade; brand; полоша сорта lower grade

сортачи *pf colloq.* I to take as one's associate; to befriend II – се to become partners; to make friends

сортачува (се) *impf of* сортачи (се)

сортен -тна *adj* best-quality; choice; сортни семиња select seeds; сортно вино fine wine

сортира *pf & impf* to sort; to grade; сортира јаглен/ руда to sort/grade coal/ore

сортирач *m* 1 sorter, classifier, sizer 2 sorting (grading) machine

сортирачка *f* 1 (*fem. form*) *see* сортирач 2 sorting (grading) machine

сортирка *f see* сортирач 2

сортирница *f* sorting room/space

соружи *impf f.p.* to saddle

сорче *n dim. of* сор

сос *m* sauce; gravy; *fig.* mess, trouble; доматен сос tomato sauce; ❑ се наоѓа во сос *colloq.* to be in the soup

соса се *pf* 1 to get away, escape 2 to be used up; to come to an end

сосвати се *pf see* сватоса се

сосватува се *impf of* сосвати се

сосе *prep* with, together with; дојде сосе децата he came with all his children

сосед *m* neighbour

соседен -дна *adj* neighbouring; next; adjoining; соседна куќа house next door; соседна соба adjoining room

соседов *adj* neighbour's

соседски *adj* 1 neighbour's; соседски деца neighbour's children 2 neighbourly; соседски односи neighbourly relations

соседство *n* 1 neighbourhood; proximity; седи во соседство to live in the vicinity; во соседство на огнот near/next to the fire 2 neighbourliness 3 *colloq., coll.* the neighbours; целото соседство го знае all the neighbours know him

сосекува *impf of* сосече

соселанец -ни *m* fellow-villager

соселанка *f* (*fem. form*) *see* соселанец

сосем *adv* completely, entirely; заборави сосем to forget completely; сосем така absolutely; сосем не јаде he won't eat anything at all

сосема *adv see* сосем

сосетка *f* (*fem. form*) *see* сосед

сосеткин *adj* neighbour's (*of women*)

сосече *pf* to cut up; сосече на парчиња to cut into pieces

сосечува *impf see* сосекува

сосила *adv* 1 forcibly, by force; влезе сосила во соба to force one's way into a room; сосила отвори врата to force a door 2 scarcely, with difficulty, hardly

сосипе[1] *pf* сосипа *aor.* I to devastate, ruin, lay waste, ravage; го сосипа болеста the illness broke him II – се to be ruined; то go to the wall; се сосипа од многу работа he worked himself to death

сосипе[2] **(се)** *pf rare* сосипа (се) *aor. see* истури (се)

сосипија *f colloq.* ruin; devastation; destruction

сосипува[1] **(се)** *impf of* сосипе[1] (се)

сосипува[2] **(се)** *impf of* сосипе[2] (се)

сосири *pf* I to cause to congeal; to thicken *trans.*; to curdle *trans.* II – се to curdle *intrans.*; to thicken *intrans.*; ❑ му се сосири крвта the blood froze in his veins

сосирува (се) *impf of* сосири (се)

сословие -ија *n* <social> class

сослуша *pf* 1 to interrogate; to question 2 *rare* (*ислуша*) to listen to; to hear out, hear to the end; не сакаше ни да го сослуша he would not even listen to him

сослушува *impf of* сослуша

сосна *f* snowdrift

соспива се *impf of* соспие се

соспие се *pf* соспа се *aor. impers.* (*with dat.*) to feel sleepy; брзо ми се соспа I soon felt sleepy

сосредоточен *pt* 1 concentrated; сосредоточено внимание rapt attention; сосредоточен поглед fixed look; сосредоточен оган concentrated fire 2 intent; engrossed; сосредоточен ученик attentive pupil

сосредоточеност *f* <degree of> concentration; сосредоточеност на вниманието concentration of attention

сосредоточи *pf* I to concentrate *trans.*, focus; сосредоточи внимание to focus attention; сосредоточи оган to concentrate fire II – се 1 to converge, come together; to focus *intrans.*; сето внимание се сосредоточи на него all attention was focused on him 2 to concentrate *intrans.*, focus one's attention (*на – on*)

сосредоточува (се) *impf of* сосредоточи (се)

сосрете *pf rare (сретне)* to meet, encounter, come upon, meet with

состав *m* 1 composition, make-up, structure; compound; хемиски состав chemical compound; составот на комитетот the composition of the committee 2 staff; members; раководен состав managerial cadres, management; професорски состав professorial staff 3 composition, essay; писмен состав <written> composition 4 joint, join

составен -вна *adj* component, constituent; составен дел integral part; составни елементи component parts; *Gram.* составни реченици coordinate clauses; составни сврзници coordinating conjunctions

состави *pf* I 1 to join, put together; состави маси to put tables together <side by side>; состави нозе to put one's feet together 2 to assemble, form; состави влада to form a government; состави машина to assemble a machine 3 to compose, compile; состави речник to compile a dictionary; состави список to make a list; состави договор to draw up (draft) a contract II – се to unite, link up *intrans.*; to merge *intrans.*

составител *m rare see* составувач

составка *f* 1 component 2 joint; junction; составките на коските joints

составува (се) *impf of* состави (се); ❑ одвај составува крај со крај to have difficulty making ends meet

составувач *m* compiler; composer; assembler; составувач на речник compiler of a dictionary; составувач на учебник textbook author

составувачки *adj* compiler's; compiling *attrib.*; составувачка работа work of compiling

состане се *pf* состана се *aor. (со)* to meet *intrans.*; to join, link up *intrans.*; утре ќе се состане комисијата the commission will meet tomorrow

состанок -ци *m* 1 meeting, gathering; партиски состанок party meeting; таен состанок clandestine meeting 2 meeting, encounter; rendezvous, *colloq.* date; имам состанок со другарите I am meeting my friends; закаже некому состанок to make a date with s.o.; случаен состанок a chance meeting

состанува се *impf of* состане се

состари *pf see* остари

состарува *impf of* состари

состои се *impf* 1 to consist (*од – of*), comprise; рефератот се состои од неколку дела the paper consists of several parts 2 to consist (*во – in*), lie in; разликата се состои во тоа herein lies the difference

состојба *f* state, condition; position; status; во добра состојба in good condition; состојбата на работите state of affairs; бројна состојба number, numerical strength; економска состојба economic situation; здравствена состојба state of health; состојба на готовност a state of readiness; имотна состојба property status; assets; семејна состојба marital status; течна состојба liquid state; цврста состојба solid state; ❑ во состојба е да to be in a position to

состојка *f* component; ingredient; хранливи состојки nutritious ingredients

сосуштествува *impf literary* to coexist

сосуштествување *n literary* coexistence

сот *m* honeycomb

сотатковник -ци *m rare see* сонародник

сотира (се) *impf of* сотре (се); се сотираат меѓу себе there is friction between them

сотирачка *f colloq.* friction; destruction; exhaustion

соткае *pf see* исткае

соткајува *impf of* соткае

сотона *m see* сатана

сотре *pf* I to destroy; to crush (*also fig.*); сотре непријател to defeat an enemy; сотре муви to swat flies; ги сотре од работа he worked them to death; го сотре болеста the illness broke him II – се to perish; to destroy o.s.; to work o.s. to death

сотрува (се) *impf of* сотре (се), *see* сотрува (се)

соумева *impf of* соумее

соумее *pf literary* соумеа *aor.* to contrive, manage (*да – то*)

соученик -ци *m* schoolmate, fellow pupil, classmate

соученичка *f (fem. form) see* соученик

соучесник -ци *m* collaborator; (*во злочин*) accomplice, accessory

соучесница *f (fem. form) see* соучесник

соучеснички *adj* collaborator's; joint; collaboration *attrib.*; (*as adv*) in league, hand in glove

соучеништво *n rare see* соучество

соучество *n* 1 complicity; collaboration; соучество во злочин complicity in crime 2 *rare see* сочувство

соучествува *impf* 1 to co-operate, collaborate 2 *rare see* сочувствува

софа *f* sofa

софизам -змот *m* sophism

Софија *f* Sofia

софијанец -нци *m* person from Sofia

софијанка *f (fem. form) see* софијанец

софиски *adj* Sofia *attrib.*

софист *m* sophist

софистика *f* sophistry

софистички *adj* sophistic<al>; софистички аргументи sophistical arguments

софистка *f (fem. form) see* софист

софра *f colloq.* 1 low wooden dining table 2 *fig.* meal, food; богата софра feast

софта *m arch.* softa (*Muslim theological student*)

софтвер *m* software

софтински *adj arch.* softa's; софтински алишта softa's robes

социјалдемократ *m* social democrat

социјалдемократија *f* social democracy

социјалдемократски *adj* social-democratic

социјален -лна *adj* social; societal; социјални науки social sciences; социјален прогрес social progress

социјализам -змот *m* socialism

социјализација *f* nationalization; социјализација на индустрија nationalization of industry

социјализира *pf & impf* to nationalize, socialize *trans.*

социјалист *m* socialist

социјалистички *adj* socialist; социјалистичко општество socialist society

социјалистка *f (fem. form) see* социјалист

социолог -зи *m* sociologist

социологија *f* sociology

социолошки *adj* sociological

сочен -чна *adj* 1 juicy, succulent; сочна трева lush grass; сочно јаболко juicy apple 2 *fig.* rich; full; vivid; сочни бои rich colours; сочна слика vivid picture;

сочни усни full lips; сочен глас mellow/fruity voice; сочна игра lively performance

сочиво *n* 1 *dial. see* лека 2 *see* лупа

сочини *pf literary rare* 1 (*направи, образува*) to create; to assemble *trans.* 2 (*состави*) to draw up; to compose; сочини договор to draw up a contract; сочини песна to compose a song

сочинител *m literary rare* (*творец, составувач*) creator; composer; author

сочинува *impf of* сочини

сочност *f* succulence, juiciness; freshness; richness; vividness; vigour, liveliness

сочува (се) *pf rare see* зачува (се), запази (се)

сочувствен *adj literary* sympathetic; compassionate; сочувствени зборови words of sympathy

сочувственост *f literary* sympathetic manner; compassion

сочувство *n literary* sympathy, fellow-feeling; compassion; condolences; му изрази сочувство he offered him his condolences

сочувствува *impf literary* to sympathize (*со – with*); сочувствува со нечија болка to sympathize with s.o.'s suffering

соцвака *pf* 1 to chew <up> 2 *fig.* to master, assimilate *trans.*; to digest, take in

соцвакува *impf of* соцвака

сошива *impf of* сошие

сошие *pf* сошии *aor.* to sew up/together; to stitch <up>; *Med.* to suture; сошие фустан to make a dress

спадне *pf* спадна *aor.* 1 to go down; to subside; to drop, fall; водата спадна the water has subsided; спадна веке отокот the swelling has subsided; спаднаа цените prices have fallen 2 *dial.* to get off; to get down; to go down; спадне од автобус to get off a bus; спаднав малу в град I went into town for a while

спаднува *impf of* спадне

спаѓа¹ *impf of* спадне, *see* спаднува

спаѓа² *impf* to belong (*во – in*); to come under; тоа не спаѓа во мојата струка that is not my field

спази *pf literary* to abide by, comply with, observe, respect; спази закон to obey the law; спази куќен ред to observe the house rules

спазма *f* spasm, convulsion; twitch

спазматичен -чна *adj* spasmodic, convulsive

спазува *impf of* спази

спаија -ии *m Hist.* 1 spahi (*Ottoman feudal cavalryman*) 2 Ottoman landlord

спаијка *f Hist.* landlord's wife, spahi's wife, lady of the manor

спаилак -ци *m* 1 rank of spahi 2 fief

спаиски *adj* spahi's; landlord's

спаиство *n see* спаилак 1

спакува *pf* I 1 to wrap <up>; to pack <up> *trans.*; брзо ги спакував книгите I quickly wrapped up the books 2 *fig.* to play a dirty trick on; to set (*s.o.*) up; to land (*s.o.*) with s.th. II – ce *colloq.* to pack one's bags

спалави (се) *pf rare see* спопалави (се)

спалавува (се) *impf of* спалави (се), *see* спопалавува (се)

спален -лна *adj* sleeping *attrib.*; спална соба bedroom; спална кола, спален вагон sleeping-car, sleeper

спална *f* bedroom; dormitory

спанак *m Bot.* (Spinacia oleracea) spinach

спанка *f* (*fem. form*) *see* спанко

спанко -овци *m colloq.* sleepyhead

спање *n see* спиење

спарен -рна *adj* sultry, muggy, humid; спарно време sultry weather

спари¹ *pf* I 1 to pair, couple, match *trans.*; to put together in pairs 2 to mate *trans.*, pair, couple *trans.* II – ce 1 to get together, pair up, join forces 2 to mate *intrans.*, copulate

спари² (се) *pf see* спури (се)

спарина *f* sultriness, mugginess

спа́ринг-па́ртнер *m Sport.* sparring partner

сларингува *impf Sport.* to act as a sparring partner; to spar

спарнина & спарнотија *f see* спарина

спартанец -нци *m* Spartan (*also fig.*)

спартанка *f* (*fem. form*) *see* спартанец

спартански *adj* spartan

спарува¹ (се) *impf of* спари¹ (се)

спарува² (се) *impf of* спари² (се)

спаруши (се) *pf dial. see* спури (се)

спас *m* salvation; deliverance; нема спас there is no way out

спасение *n arch.* (*see* спас) спасение на душите redemption of souls; ❑ трпение – спасение everything comes to him who waits

спаси *pf* I to rescue, save; to retrieve; to redeem; спаси некому животот to save s.o.'s life; ❑ си ја спаси кожата to save one's skin II – ce 1 to save o.s.; to flee; to escape; ce спаси од сигурна пропаст he escaped certain death 2 *Rel.* to be absolved; ce спаси од сите гревови he was absolved of all his sins

спасител *m* 1 rescuer 2 *Rel.* Saviour, Redeemer

спасителка *f* (*fem. form*) *see* спасител 1

спасителски *adj* rescuer's, saviour's

Спасовден *m Rel.* Ascension Day

спасовденски *adj* Ascension Day *attrib.*; спасовденски собор Ascension Day fair; спасовденски петок Friday before Ascension

спасоносен -сна *adj* life-saving; salutary, beneficial

спасоносно *adv* 1 beneficially 2 as a last resort

спастира (се) *impf see* спаструва (се)

спастра *f colloq.* 1 order, tidiness; лоша спастра untidiness, mix-up, mess 2 (*влошка*) sanitary towel (*Am.* napkin)

спастри *pf colloq.* I (*прибере, среди*) to put in order; tidy up; спастри соба to tidy a room II – ce to smarten/spruce o.s. up

спаструва (се) *impf of* спастри (се)

спасува (се) *impf of* спаси (се); ce спасуваа кој како што знаеше it was every man for himself

спасување *n* rescue, salvation; екипа за спасување rescue squad; кола за спасување rescue vehicle

спасувач *m* rescuer; (*на плажа и сл.*) lifeguard, *colloq.*, *Austral. & N.Z.* life-saver; first-aid attendant

спасувачки *adj* rescue; rescuer's; lifeguard's; спасувачка служба rescue service; спасувачка екипа rescue squad

спатија -ии *f Cards* clubs

спашка *pf colloq. pejor.* to throw out, send packing

спашкува *impf of* спашка

спев *m literary* canto

спевува *impf of* спее

спее *pf literary* спеа *aor.* to write, compose (*poem, song*)

спектакл -кли *m* performance; play; show; балетски спектакл ballet performance

спектакуларен -рна *adj* spectacular

спектар *m* spectrum

спектрален -лна *adj* spectrum *attrib.*, spectral; спектрална анализа spectrum analysis

спектроскоп *m* spectroscope

спекулира *impf see* шпекулира

спелеолог -зи *m* speleologist

спелеологија *f* speleology

спелеолошки *adj* speleological; спелеолошки испитувања speleological exploration

спепели *pf* to reduce to ashes, incinerate

спепелува *impf of* спепели

сперлив *adj* peculiar, odd, eccentric; perverse; сперлив човек eccentric, crank

сперливост *f* peculiarity, eccentricity, oddity; perversity

сперма *f* sperm, semen

сперматозоид *m* spermatozoon

спермацет *m* spermaceti

спермацетен -тна *adj* spermaceti *attrib.*, spermacetic

спец *m colloq.* (специјалист) ace

специјален -лна *adj* special

специјализација *f* specialization; специјализација на производството specialization of production

специјализира *pf & impf* I 1 to train in a specialized field *trans.*; to provide specialist training to; специјализира студенти за хирургија to train students in surgery 2 to classify according to speciality; to earmark (*for special purposes*) II – се to specialize (*за/во – in*)

специјализиран *pt* specialized; специјализирана единица specialized unit

специјалист *m* specialist; специјалист за нервни болести specialist in nervous disorders

специјалистички *adj* specialist *attrib.*

специјалистка *f* (*fem. form*) *see* специјалист

специјалитет *m* speciality; специјалитети на македонската кујна specialities of Macedonian cuisine

специјално *adv* specially; especially; deliberately; работи специјално на таа тема he is working on that very topic

специјалност *f* speciality, specialism; работи на својата специјалност to work in one's own field

специфика *f* specificity, specifics; спецификата на селото the specific character of the village

спецификација *f* specification

спецификум *m* specificity; special feature, peculiarity

специфицира *pf & impf* to classify; to inventory, compile an inventory of

специфичен -чна *adj* specific; специфични услови specific conditions; ❑ специфична тежина specific gravity, relative density

специфички *adj rare see* специфичен

специфичност *f* specificity, specific character

спечали *pf* 1 to earn, gain; спечали многу пари to make a lot of money 2 *joc.* to catch, end up with, *sl.* cop; спечали болест to catch a disease

спечалува *impf of* спечали

спече се *pf* to become stunted

спечен *pt* stunted; спечени растенија stunted plants

спечок -ци *m* runt; stunted plant

спечува се *impf of* спече се

спечурчен *adj see* спечен

спечурчи се *pf see* спече се

спида *f* stormy weather; blizzard

спие *impf* I to sleep; спие тврдо to sleep soundly; ❑ спие како зајак to be a light sleeper; спие како заклан/топ to sleep like a log/top II – се *impers.* (*with dat.*) to feel sleepy; му се спие he feels sleepy

спие се *pf* спи се *aor. impers.* (*with dat.*) to feel thirsty; ми се спи вода I'd like a drink of water

спиење *n* sleep; пријатно спиење! sleep well (tight)! sweet dreams! кола за спиење sleeping-car, sleeper; вреќа за спиење sleeping-bag; ❑ затече некого на спиење to catch s.o. unawares; to catch s.o. napping

спија *f usu. in the expression:* прва спија beauty sleep

спијач *m* sleepyhead

спика *pf* I to put, stick, stuff, cram; го спика писмото в пазува he shoved the letter into his shirt; кај ги спикал билетите? where did he put the tickets? II – се to crawl in, sneak in; to squeeze in *intrans.*; to hide *intrans.*; кај се спикал? where has he got to?

спикер *m* newsreader; announcer

спикерка *f* (*fem. form*) *see* спикер

спикерски *adj* newsreader's; announcer's

спикира *impf* to read the news; to announce, present

спикува (се) *impf of* спика (се)

спила *f* cliff; bluff; crag

спилест *adj* craggy; спилести ридови rocky hills

спипиле *n colloq.* (спанко) sleepyhead

спир *m poet.* stop; rest; без спир without stopping; нема спир there is no rest; there is no end <to it>

спирала *f* spiral; coil; spring; спирала на часовник watch-spring

спирален -лна *adj* spiral

спирант *m Ling.* spirant

спирантски *adj Ling.* spirant

спири се *pf colloq.* to insist; to be determined, bent on; се спирил да отиде he was determined to go

спиритизам -змот *m* spiritualism

спиритист *m* spiritualist

спиритистички *adj* spiritualist, spiritualistic; спиритистичка сеанса <spiritualist> seance

спиритистка *f* (*fem. form*) *see* спиритист

спиритуал *m* spiritual father, father confessor

спиритуален -лна *adj literary* spiritual; спиритуален живот spiritual life

спиритуализам -змот *m Philos.* spiritualism

спиритуалист *m Philos.* spiritualist

спиритуалистички *adj Philos.* spiritualistic; spiritualist *attrib.*; спиритуалистичко учење spiritualist doctrine

спиритуалистка *f Philos.* (*fem. form*) *see* спиритуалист

спирт *m* (шпиритус) spirit, alcohol

спиртен -тна *adj* (шпиртусен) alcoholic; spirit *attrib.*; *see* шпиртен

спирува (се) *impf of* спири (се)

спис -и *m* statement, document; deed; во неговите списи in his writings/papers

списание -ија *n* magazine; journal; месечно списание monthly <magazine>

списка *pf* to start shrieking/crying

спискува *impf of* списка

список -ци *m* list; roll; register; избирачки списоци electoral rolls, *Am.* voter registration list; платен список payroll

спитомен *pt* tamed, domesticated; well-bred; спитомени животни domesticated animals

спитоменост *f* 1 tameness 2 polish, breeding

спитоми *pf* to tame, domesticate; to train *trans.*; (*за куче*) to house-train; (*за коњ*) to break in

спитомува *impf of* спитоми

спица¹ *f* spoke

спица² *f* splinter; chip, sliver

спишти *pf see* списка

сплав *m* raft

сплавар *m* raftsman

сплави *impf* to convey by raft; to raft

сплавне *pf* сплавна *aor. see* спласне

сплавнува *impf of* сплавне

сплакне *pf* сплакна *aor.* 1 (*исплакне*) to splash; to rinse 2 *dial.* (*спласне*) to go down; to subside

сплакнува *impf of* сплакне

спласне *pf* спласна *aor.* to subside; to go down, abate, diminish *intrans.*; спласна отокот the swelling has gone down; спласна водата the water level has dropped; спласна еланот enthusiasm has waned

спласнува *impf of* спласне

спласти *pf* (*напласти*) to stack, pile up *trans.*; спласти сено to stack hay

спластува *impf of* спласти

сплашен *pt* frightened, terrified; alarmed

сплашеност *f* fright, alarm

сплаши *pf* I (*исплаши*) to frighten to death, terrify II – се (*исплаши се*) to take fright

сплашува (се) *impf of* сплаши (се)

сплеска¹ *pf* 1 to flatten *trans.*; to crush; to squash *trans.* 2 *fig.* to eat up; to polish off 3 *fig.* to beat to death

сплеска² *pf* (*заплеска*) to start clapping

сплескан *pt* flattened <out>; flat; crushed; сплескана чинија shallow dish

сплескува *impf of* сплеска

сплесне *pf* сплесна *aor. see* сплеска

сплет *m* 1 tangle; braid; (*за јаже*) splice; *Anat.* plexus; interlacing, knotwork; сплет на артерии plexus of arteries 2 *fig.* cluster, bunch; web; сплет на околности coincidence; сплет <на> лаги tissue (web) of lies; сплет на народни ора medley of folk-dances

сплете *pf* I 1 to knit; to braid, plait; to weave; сплете џемпер to knit a jumper; сплете кошница to weave a basket 2 *fig.* to invent, compose, think up; сплете песна to compose a song 3 *fig.* to confuse, perplex II – се 1 to plait one's hair 2 to become entangled/interwoven; to get mixed up with one another 3 *fig.* to become confused, perplexed

сплетен *pt* tangled; confused; intertwined; interwoven

сплетка¹ *f* intrigue, scheme; gossip; slander; прави сплетки to scheme

сплетка² *pf* I 1 to intertwine *trans.*; to entangle 2 *fig.* to confuse, perplex II – се 1 to become entangled/interwoven 2 *fig.* to become perplexed, confused

сплеткан *pt* perplexed, confused

сплетканост *f* confusion, uncertainty, bewilderment, perplexity

сплеткар *m* gossip, scandalmonger; intriguer

сплеткари *impf* to gossip; to intrigue, scheme

сплеткарка *f* (*fem. form*) *see* сплеткар

сплеткарски *adj* gossip's; intriguer's

сплеткарство *n* gossip, scandalmongering; intriguing, scheming

сплеткува (се) *impf of* сплетка (се)

сплетува (се) *impf of* сплете (се)

спливна *pf f.p.* спливна *aor.* to start swimming; to set sail

сплиска *pf* 1 to start pouring (*with rain*); сплиска еден дожд a sudden downpour started 2 *fig.* to squander; сплиска наследство to squander an inheritance

сплискува *impf of* сплиска

сплит *m Bot.* (Cuscuta) dodder

сплотен *pt* combined, unified, united; со сплотени сили with united efforts

сплотено *adv* with united efforts; in serried ranks; with one accord

сплотеност *f* unity, cohesion; solidarity

сплоти *pf* I to unite, unify, rally *trans.*; сплоти редови to close ranks II – се to unite, rally <round> *intrans.*; се сплоти околу раководството to rally around the leadership

сплотува (се) *impf of* сплоти (се)

сплуе се *pf colloq.* to rot, decompose; оди и сплуј се! go to hell!

сплуска *pf* to start slapping/clapping

сплускува *impf of* сплуска

СПМ *abbr.* (*Социјалистичка партија на Македонија*) Socialist Party of Macedonia

спобрка *pf* to send/drive/shoo away

спобркува *impf of* спобрка

спобудали *pf* I to drive mad (crazy); to madden; to infuriate; парите го спобудалија the money has gone to his head II – се to go mad (crazy); to take leave of one's senses; to run wild; се спобудали по една мома to lose one's head over a girl

спобудалува (се) *impf of* спобудали (се)

спогодба *f* agreement, accord; contract; treaty; covenant; постигне спогодба to reach agreement; трговска спогодба trade agreement; врз основа на спогодба on the basis of an agreement

спогодбен *adj* contractual; treaty *attrib.*

спогодбено *adv* by agreement/treaty; работи спогодбено to work by consensus; се разведоа спогодбено they divorced by mutual consent

спогоди се *pf* to reach agreement (*за – on*); to come to terms

спогодува се *impf of* спогоди се

сподавен *pt* stifled, suppressed; сподавен вик a stifled cry; сподавен глас muffled voice

сподави *pf* (*задави, задуши*) to suppress, repress; to stifle, muffle; to smother

сподели *pf* to share; сподели мисли со некого to share one's thoughts with s.o.; сподели болка to share s.o.'s pain

споделува *impf of* сподели

споен -јна *adj* connecting; connective; copulative; *Mech.* спојни лостови connecting-rods

спознава *impf of* спознае

спознае *pf literary* to realize; to acknowledge; to learn *trans.*; спознае вистина to learn/realize the truth

спознание -ија *n literary, Philos., Psychol.* cognition

спои *pf* **I** to join, link, connect *trans.*; to integrate, combine *trans.*; *Tech.* (*завари*) to weld; to solder; (*на телефон*) to put through; ja спои теоријата со практиката he combined theory with practice **II – се** to link up, join *intrans.*; to combine *intrans.*; to cohere; to blend *intrans.*

споив *adj* joinable

спој -еви *m* **1** joint; juncture; connexion; ◻ краток спој short circuit; погрешен спој mismatch; (*на телефон*) wrong number **2** weld, join, joint

спојка *f* link, connexion; join; *Tech.* tie, coupling; *Mil.* intercommunication, signals, liaison

спојлив *adj* joinable

спојме *pf colloq.* спојми *aor.* to decide (*да – to*)

спојмува *impf of* спојме

спојник -ци *m see* спојница 1

спојница *f* **1** link, connexion; *Tech.* tie; axle; *Elec.* coupler; (*на шина*) fishplate; coupling **2** paper-clip

спојува (се) *impf of* спои (се)

спокоен -јна *adj* calm, placid, composed; tranquil; unruffled; untroubled; спокоен глас calm voice; спокоен живот quiet/uneventful life; спокојно море calm sea; ◻ биди спокоен! keep calm! don't worry! relax! делени круши, спокојни заби *prov.* short reckonings make long friends

спокој *m poet. see* спокојство

спокојно *adv* calmly; tranquilly; живее спокојно to lead a quiet life

спокојство *n* **1** calm, calmness; tranquillity; stillness **2** composure, sang-froid; placidity; загуби спокојство to lose one's composure

сполај *colloq.* (*with dat.*) thanks (*за – for*), *colloq.* ta; сполај ти што ми помогна thanks for helping me; сполај му на Господа (сполај Богу) thanks be to God (thank God, thank goodness); сполај ти за услугата thank you for the favour

спомага *impf of* спомогне, споможе

спомагало *n* aid

спомагач *m see* помагач

спомен *m* **1** memory, recollection; remembrance; спомени од детството childhood memories; му останаа верни на неговиот спомен they remained faithful to his memory **2** souvenir, memento **3** (*usu. pl*) memoir, reminiscence

спомене *pf* спомена *aor.* **1** to mention; to refer to **2** (*with dat.*) to remind (*за – of*); спомене некому за обврска to remind s.o. of a promise

споменик -ци *m* **1** monument, statue; memorial; надгробен споменик headstone; пишан споменик literary monument **2** *colloq.* death-bill (*list of deceased family members for whom prayers are to be said*)

споменица *f* **1** commemorative volume **2** certificate of service (*in army or partisans*)

спóмен-плóча *f* memorial plaque

споменува *impf of* спомене

спомина *impf see* споменува

спомне *pf* спомна *aor. see* спомене

спомне си *pf* спомна си *aor. see* сети се 3; си спомнав за него I remembered him

спомнува *impf of* спомне

спомнува си *impf of* спомне си, *see* секава се

спомогне *pf* спомогна *aor.* (*with dat.*) to help, to aid, assist

спомогнува *impf of* спомогне

споможе *pf* спомогов *1st p. aor. see* спомогне

споможува *impf of* споможе

спомош *f see* помош

спондеј -еи *m Prosody* spondee

спонтан *adj* spontaneous; спонтан аплауз spontaneous applause; *Med.* спонтана гангрена idiopathic gangrene

спонтаност *f* spontaneity

спопалави (се) *pf see* спобудали (се)

спопалавува (се) *impf of* спопалави (се)

спор *m* **1** dispute; argument; quarrel; нема никаков спор there is no argument **2** *Leg.* lawsuit; води спор to be engaged in a lawsuit

спорадичен -чна *adj* sporadic

споразумение -ија *n arch. see* спогодба

според *prep* **1** according to; според законот according to the law, by law; според обичајот according to custom; според мене to my mind, in my opinion; ◻ според тоа consequently **2** *rare* compared with/to

споредба *f* **1** comparison; parallel; ◻ во споредба со by analogy with; in contrast to; прави споредба to draw a comparison (parallel) **2** simile

споредбен *adj* comparative; споредбен метод comparative method; *Gram.* споредбен степен comparative degree

спореден -дна *adj* subsidiary, secondary; subordinate; споредна улога supporting part; *fig.* tangential role; спореден колосек siding; branch line; споредно занимање sideline; споредна личност minor character (*in a novel, play etc.*); *fig.* unimportant person; спореден производ by-product; споредно прашање side issue

спореди *pf* **I** to compare *trans.*; to juxtapose (*со – with*) **II – се** to compare o.s.; to compare *intrans.*; кој може да се спореди со него? who can compare with him?

споредлив *adj* comparable; тешко споредлив difficult to compare

споредливост *f* comparability

споредност *f* triviality

споредува[1] *impf dial.* to talk to, have dealings (*со – with*)

споредува[2] (се) *impf of* спореди (се)

споредум *adv f.p. see* спроти

спорен -рна *adj* debatable; disputed, contentious; controversial; спорно прашање moot point; vexed question; спорно место debatable point; contested zone

спори *impf* **I** to argue; to quarrel **II – се** *Leg.* to pursue legal action; to go to court

спорија -ии & **спорја** *f* pumpkin seeds

спорјација -ии *m* pumpkin-seed vendor

спорт *m* sport; пријател на спортот sports enthusiast (fan)

спортѝст *m* sportsman, athlete

спортѝстка *f* sportswoman, athlete

спортски *adj* sport<s>; sporting; спортски клуб sports club; спортски терен sports ground; спортска кола sports car

спортува *impf* to go in for sport, practise sport

способен -бна *adj* **1** gifted, talented; capable, able **2** fit (*за – for*); capable (*за – of*); способен за војска fit for military service; способен за сè capable of anything

способност *f* 1 ability, capability; faculty; способност за зборување power of speech 2 (*usu. pl*) talent, gift, aptitude; музички способности musical abilities; ретки способности rare abilities

спотаен *pt* hidden, concealed; suppressed; спотаен гнев suppressed anger

спотаи *pf* I to hide, conceal; to suppress; не можеше да ги спотаи своите чувства he could not conceal his feelings II – се to hide *intrans.*; to lurk, skulk

спотајува (се) *impf of* спотаи (се)

спотера *pf* to urge on, goad; to hurry *trans.*; спотера коњи to whip up the horses; ❏ му спотера сушина he gave him a hard time

спотерува *impf of* спотера

спотина *impf of* спотне[1]

спотне[1] *pf* спотна *aor.* 1 (*огин*) to stoke/stir up 2 *fig.* to egg on, incite, goad, prod; to arouse; to set in motion; тој ја спотна целата работа he got (set) the whole thing rolling

спотне[2] *pf* спотна *aor.* I to make (*s.o.*) sweat (perspire) II – се to break into a sweat, work up a sweat

спотнува *impf of* спотне[1], *see* спотина

спотнува (се) *impf of* спотне[2], *see* спотина

споулави (се) *pf see* спобудали (се)

споулавува (се) *impf of* споулави (се)

справа *f* apparatus; implement; appliance; <piece of> equipment; справа за прислушкување listening device; bug; гимнастичка справа gymnastics apparatus

справедлив *adj* 1 fair, just; impartial; справедлив судија impartial judge; справедлив учител even-handed teacher 2 justified, just; equitable; справедлива казна well-deserved punishment; справедлива делба equitable distribution

справедливост *f* justice, fairness, equity; impartiality; справедливоста на претензија the justice of a claim

справи[1] *pf* I to prepare, get ready *trans.*; справи коњ to saddle a horse II – се to prepare, get ready *intrans.*; се справи за пат to prepare for a journey

справи[2] се *pf literary rare* to cope (*co – with*), manage

справува[1] (се) *impf of* справи[1] (се)

справува[2] се *impf of* справи[2] се

спрасна *adj* (*f only*) pregnant (*of a pig*)

спрасност *f* pregnancy

спраши[1] *pf rare* (*испраши*) to cover with dust, make dusty

спраши[2] *pf* (*испраши*) to loosen the soil round (*a plant*); го спрашија лозјето they loosened the soil around the vines

спрашти *pf colloq. usu. in the expression*: ја спрашти to bolt *intrans.*, *sl.* beat it

спраштува *impf of* спрашти

спрега[1] *f* 1 yoke, pair, team; коњска спрега pair (team) of horses; воловска спрега team of oxen 2 *fig.* combination, union; неразбирлива спрега puzzling combination

спрега[2] (се) *impf of* спрегне (се)

спрегне *pf* спрегна *aor.* 1 to yoke, hitch, harness; спрегне волови to harness oxen 2 *fig. colloq.* to enlist, involve (*s.o.*) with s.th. II – се *colloq.* to buckle down; се спрегне да работи to set to work

спрегнува (се) *impf of* спрегне (се)

спреде *pf* to spin *trans.*; спреде волна to spin wool

спреј *m* aerosol, spray

спрема[1] *f* 1 training, preparation; школска спрема schooling; стручна спрема specialist/technical training/qualification 2 equipment; armament, munitions 3 dowry

спрема[2] *prep* 1 to, towards; патот води спрема селото the road leads to the village; се сврти спрема нив he turned to them 2 towards; for; љубов спрема татковината love for the motherland; омраза спрема непријателот hatred for the enemy 3 according to; спрема законот according to the law; спрема него in his opinion 4 compared with/to 5 *rare* on the eve of; спрема Велигден the day before Easter; во сабота спрема недела on Saturday night

спрема[3] (се) *impf of* спреми (се)

спремен -мна *pt* ready, prepared; спремен на/за ready for; спремен на/за сè ready for anything

спреми *pf* I to prepare, get ready *trans.*; to prepare for; спреми испит to prepare for an exam II – се to prepare, get ready *intrans.*; to prepare o.s.; се спреми за пат to get ready for a journey; се спреми за испит to prepare for an exam

спремност *f* preparedness, readiness; willingness

спрепина (се) *impf see* спрепнува (се)

спрепне *pf* спрепна *aor.* I 1 to trip <up> *trans.* 2 *fig.* to hinder, hamper; to get in s.o.'s way 3 to hobble (*a horse*) II – се 1 to trip *intrans.*, stumble; се спрепне на камен to trip over a stone 2 *fig. colloq.* to stumble, fall; to fail; се спрепне на испит to fail an exam

спрепнува (се) *impf of* спрепне (се)

спрета *pf* 1 to <start to> kick, thrash about 2 *fig. iron.* to <start to> protest; to bridle; to whinge

спретува *impf rare of* спрета

спречи *pf* to prevent, hinder, impede, hamper; дождот ги спречи да дојдат the rain prevented them from coming; спречи ширење на зараза to prevent the spread of infection

спречка *pf* I to set at odds (loggerheads); to cause to fall out II – се to fall out, quarrel (*co – with*); се спречка за ништо to quarrel over nothing

спречкува (се) *impf of* спречка (се)

спречува *impf of* спречи

спржи *pf* I 1 (*испржи*) to fry, roast *trans.*; спржи јајце to fry an egg 2 *fig.* to parch *trans.*; to scorch *trans.*; горештината ги спржи лисјата the heat has dried up the leaves II – се 1 (*испржи се*) to fry, roast *intrans.* 2 *fig.* to dry up (out) *intrans.*; to become parched/scorched; тревата се спржила the grass has turned yellow

спржува (се) *impf of* спржи (се)

спријатели *pf* I to cause to become friends; to bring together; ги спријатели заедничката несреќа their shared misfortune drew them together II – се to make friends (*co – with*) ; to strike up a friendship

спријателува (се) *impf of* спријатели (се)

спринт *m Sport.* sprint

спринтер *m Sport.* sprinter

спринтерица *f Sport.* (*fem. form*) *see* спринтер

спринтерка *f Sport.* 1 (*fem. form*) *see* спринтер 2 (*usu. pl.*) spiked running shoes, track-and-field shoes

спринтерски *adj Sport.* sprint<ing> *attrib.*; sprinter's

спринтува *impf Sport.* to sprint

сприпука *pf* (*припука*) to start firing (shooting)

сприпукува *impf of* сприпука

спрли *pf* to singe *trans.*; to scorch *trans.*

спроведе *pf* **1** to conduct; to escort; to accompany; го спроведоа низ селото they took him through the village **2** to install, put in; спроведе вода to lay on water; спроведе електрична енергија to connect electricity **3** *fig.* to carry out; to put into effect, implement; спроведе план to carry out a plan; ❑ спроведе во живот to put into practice; спроведе во дело to put into effect

спроведува *impf of* спроведс; спроведува своја волја to impose one's will

спровира (се) *impf of* спровре (се); ❑ ти кај што шиеш, јас се спровирам you can't fool me

спровод *m* escort; воен спровод military escort

спроводен -дна *adj* conductive; спроводна цевка pipe, duct; спроводна жица wire, lead, conductor

спроводлив *adj* feasible, practicable

спроводливост *f* feasibility, practicability

спроводник -ци *m* **1** escort; guide; conductor; bodyguard; спроводник на воз train conductor; спроводник на уапсени escort for prisoners **2** *fig.* conduit; exponent; mouthpiece; спроводник на политика conduit for a policy **3** *Elec.* conductor; спроводник на електроенергијата conductor of electricity

спроводница & **спроводничка** *f* (*fem. form*) *see* спроводник 2

спровре *pf* **I 1** to push/pass/squeeze (*s.o./s.th.*) through; ja спроврел главата низ оградата he stuck his head through the fence; спровре конец во игла to thread a needle **2** *fig.* to get (*s.o.*) in; to clear the way for; го спровре без билет he got him in without a ticket **II** – **се** to squeeze through *intrans.*; to sneak in *intrans.*; ❑ се спровре низ иглина дупка to pass through the eye of a needle

спроврува (се) *impf see* спровира (се)

спростира (се) *impf of* спростре (се)

спростре *pf* **I 1** to put out to dry; to hang out/up *trans.*; спростре алишта to hang out the washing **2** to lay down; to spread out *trans.*; спростре килими to lay carpets; како ќе спростреш, така ќе си легнеш *prov.* as you make your bed, so you must lie in it **3** to extend, spread *trans.*; јаболкницата ги спростре своите гранки во дворот the apple tree spread its branches over the yard; спростре свое влијание to extend one's influence **4** to send sprawling; to spread-eagle **II** – **се 1** to spread out, extend, stretch *intrans.*; to expand *intrans.*; далеку се спрострела неговата власт he casts a long shadow, he has a lot of pull **2** to stretch out, sprawl *intrans.*; to fall prostrate

спострува (се) *impf of* спростре (се)

спростур *m* frame for drying fishing nets

спроти *prep* **1** opposite; спроти нас opposite us **2** towards; гледа спроти сонцето to look into the sun; тргне спроти ветрот to head into the wind **3** in accordance with, according to; спроти неговите зборови in his words; спроти адетот according to custom, following the custom, as custom will have it **4** compared with/to, in comparison with, next to **5** on the eve of, the day before; спроти недела on Saturday evening

спротив *prep* & *adv* opposite; against; compared with; кој ќе му стане спротив? who can stand up

to him? застана спротив нив he stopped opposite them

спротива *adv* (*отспротива*) opposite, over there; ене го спротива! there he is over there!

спротивен -вна *adj* **1** opposite; спротивен ветер headwind; спротивен правец opposite direction **2** opposed, conflicting; opposing, antagonistic; *Math.* inverse; спротивни мислења conflicting/contrary opinions; ❑ во спротивен случај otherwise

спротиви се *pf* to oppose, resist; to object (*на – то*); се спротиви на решение to oppose a decision; се спротиви некому to stand up to s.o.

спротивно *adv* in contrast to, as opposed to, unlike; спротивно од договореното contrary to what was agreed

спротивност *f* **1** contradiction; conflict; спротивност на погледите conflict of views **2** opposite, contrast; мајката беше полна спротивност на таткото the mother was the exact opposite of the father

спротивстави <**се**> *pf* to oppose, resist; to object (*на – то*)

спротивставува <**се**> *impf of* спротивстави <се>

спротивува се *impf of* спротиви се

спротина (се) *impf of* спротне (се)

спротне (се) *pf* спротна (се) *aor. see* спровре (се)

спротнува (се) *impf see* спротина (се)

спрпа *pf* to start fluttering/throbbing; му спрпа срцето his heart started racing

спрпела *pf* **I** to knock down, push over **II** – **се** to fall over (down)

спрпелува (се) *impf of* спрпела (се)

спрпори & **спрпоти** *pf* **1** to start droning/humming/ whirring **2** (*за оган*) to start crackling

спрсне *pf* спрсна *aor.* **1** (*да*) to start; спрсна да бега he took to his heels; децата спрснаа да бегаат the children ran away; спрсне да се смее to burst out laughing **2** *rare* to splash (*s.o./s.th.*)

спружи *pf* **I 1** to stretch out, extend *trans.*; to spread out *trans.*; to hang out/up *trans.*; спружи рака да се здравува to offer one's hand in greeting **2** to send sprawling; to floor; to spread-eagle **II** – **се** to stretch out *intrans.*; to spread out *intrans.*; се спружи на кревет to stretch out on a bed

спружува (се) *impf of* спружи (се)

спука *pf* **1** to start shooting (firing) **2** *fig.* to shout

спукоти *pf* **1** to start shooting (firing) **2** to make a sudden noise **3** *fig.* to shout

спукува *impf of* спука

спулна *adj* (*f only*) pregnant (*of a donkey*)

спурен *pt* shrivelled, wilted; wrinkled; спурена трева sun-dried grass; спурено лице wrinkled face

спурен -рна *adj* sultry, humid

спури *pf* **I 1** to shrivel *trans.*; to wither *trans.*; to wrinkle *trans.* **2** to rub, chafe *trans.* **II** – **се 1** to shrivel, wilt *intrans.*; to wrinkle *intrans.* **2** to rub, chafe *intrans.*

спурнина *f* sultry weather

спурува (се) *impf of* спури (се)

спусти *pf* **1** to desert, abandon **2** to lay waste, devastate, ravage

спустува *impf of* спусти

спушта (се) *impf of* спушти (се)

спушти *pf* **I 1** to lower, pull down; to reduce; спушти знаме to lower a flag; спушти цени to cut prices; спушти глас to lower one's voice **2** (*за брод*) to

launch **3** (*with dat.*) to slight, snub **II – се 1** to go/
come down, descend; to land; завесата се спушти
the curtain came down; се спушти по Вардар to sail
down the Vardar; се спушти мрак darkness fell;
температурата се спушти the temperature dropped/
fell **2** to rush, dash; се спушти да помогне некому to
rush to s.o.'s aid **3** (*with dat.*) to attack, pounce on, fly
at

с.р. *abbr.* (*своерачно*) signed, sgd.

сработи *pf* **1** to make; to finish *trans.*; сработи
работа to finish a job **2** *rare* (*стори, направи*) to do **3**
dial. (*заработи*) to earn

сработува *impf of* сработи

сразмер *m* **1** proportion, ratio, relation **2** size, scale,
magnitude

сразмерен -рна *adj* proportional; proportionate;
сразмерни сили well-matched forces; сразмерно
покачување на платите proportional pay increment

сразмерно *adv* proportionately, proportionally; to
scale; relatively; сразмерно мала сума relatively
small sum; сразмерно на вложениот труд in proportion to the work done

сразмерност *f* proportionality; строга сразмерност
strict proportionality (relation)

срам *m* shame; чувствува срам to feel ashamed;
поцрвени од срам to blush with shame; ❑ за срам,
за триста срамови! it's a disgrace! it's a crying
shame! не ти е срам! shame on you! си го загуби
(касне) срамот to bring shame upon oneself; срам
да ти е! you should be ashamed of yourself! срам не
срам however awkward it may be; ни срам, ни перде
completely shameless

срамеж *m rare see* срам; нема срамеж to have no
shame

срамежлив *adj* shy, retiring; bashful, timid; среме-
жлив поглед timid glance

срамежливец -вци *m rare see* срамежливко

срамежливка *f* (*fem. form*) *see* срамежливко

срамежливко -вци *m* shy person, shrinking violet

срамежливост *f* shyness, timidity, bashfulness

срамежниче *n see* срамниче 1

срамен -мна *adj* shameful, disgraceful; срамно дело
disgraceful deed/business; *Anat.* срамна коска pubic
bone; ❑ срамна болест venereal disease; срамни
делови на телото private parts

срами *impf* **I** to shame, put to shame; to embarrass; to
disgrace **II – се 1** to be ashamed; to feel shy; to be
embarrassed; се срами да признае нешто to be
ashamed to admit s.th. **2** to disgrace o.s.

срамлив *adj see* срамежлив

срамливка *f see* срамежливка

срамливко -вци *m see* срамежливко

срамливост *f see* срамежливост

срамни *pf* **I 1** to level; to smooth, even out *trans.*;
работниците го срамнија теренот the workmen
levelled the ground; ❑ срамни со земја<та> to level;
to raze to the ground **2** *rare* to compare *trans.* **II – се**
rare to compare *intrans.*

срамник -ци *m* shameless person; cad

срамница[1] *f* (*fem. form*) *see* срамник; hussy

срамница[2] *f Anat.* vulva

срамниче *n* **1** last piece of food (*which politeness forbids one to take*) **2** *Bot.* (Daucus carota) wild carrot,
Queen Anne's lace

срамно *adv* shamefully; disgracefully, in disgrace,
ignominiously

срамнува (се) *impf of* срамни (се)

срамота *f* disgrace; dishonour; стори некому
срамота to bring discredit on s.o.; ❑ од работа нема
срамота *prov.* honest work is no disgrace

срамотен -тна *adj* shameful, disgraceful; срамотни
зборови swear-words

срамоти (се) *impf see* срами (се)

срамотија *f colloq.* **1** *see* срамота **2** private parts

срамотилак -ци *m colloq. see* срамота

срамотник -ци *m rare see* срамник

срамотно *adv see* срамно

срамува (се) *impf see* срами (се)

срамувалка *f obs.* kerchief (*with which the bride hides
her face at her wedding*)

срамулец -лци *m see* срамниче 1

сраснат *pt* fused, joined; (*за коски*) knitted; сраснати
рани healed wounds

срасне *pf* срасна *aor.* **I 1** to join, fuse *intrans.*; to grow
together; (*за коски*) to knit *intrans.*; (*за рана*) to heal
intrans.; *Bot.*, *Anat.*, *Geol.* to accrete *intrans.* **2** *fig.* to
become accustomed, to get used (*со – то*); срасне со
идеја to get used to an idea **II – се** *see* I 1

сраснува (се) *impf of* срасне (се)

срасте *pf see* срасне

срастува *impf of* срасте

срба *impf dial. see* срка

србизам -змот *m* Serbianism, Serbian word/ex-
pression

србизира *pf & impf* to Serbianize

Србија *f* Serbia

Србијанец -нци *m* Serbian, person from Serbia proper

Србијанка *f* (*fem. form*) *see* Србијанец

србијански *adj* Serbian, from Serbia proper

Србин -би *m* Serbian

Србинка *f* (*fem. form*) *see* Србин

србне *pf dial.* србна *aor. see* сркне

србоман *m pejor. see* србофил

србомански *adj pejor. see* србофилски

србоманство *n pejor. see* србофилство

србофил *m* Serbophile

србофилка *f* (*fem. form*) *see* србофил

србофилски *adj* Serbophile; србофилска политика
Serbophile policies

србофилство *n* Serbophilism

СРГ *abbr.* (*Сојузна Република Германија*) Federal
Republic of Germany

срдба *f* anger, wrath; vexation, annoyance

срдеж *m see* срдба

срдечен -чна *adj* hearty, cordial, heartfelt; warm,
warm-hearted; срдечни луѓе friendly people;
срдечна благодарност heartfelt gratitude; срдечен
прием hearty welcome; срдечен поздрав kindest
regards; срдечна смеа hearty laugh

срдечност *f* heartiness, cordiality

срдешница *f colloq.* diarrhoea, *sl.* the runs

срди *impf* **I** to anger, irritate, vex **II – се** to be/get
angry (cross); се срди за ништо to get angry over
nothing; му се срди he is angry with him

срдина *f see* срдба

срдит *adj* angry, cross, *Am.* mad; grumpy, disgruntled;
срдит човек grumpy person; срдито писмо angry
letter

срдитост *f* anger; vexation

срдлив *adj* irascible, irritable; short-tempered

срдост *f rare see* срдба

сребрар *m* silversmith

сребрее *impf* **I 1** to turn grey **2** to appear silvery **II** – **ce** *see* **I 2**

сребрен *adj* silver, silvery; сребрени пари silver coins; сребрени садови silverware; *Zool.* сребрена рипка (Atherina mochon pontica) sand smelt, atherine; сребрена свадба silver wedding

сребренее (се) *impf literary rare see* сребрее (се)

сребреник -ци *m arch.* silver coin

сребреникав *adj dim.* silvery; сребреникава коса silvery hair; сребреникав тон silvery tone

сребреница *f* silver goblet/chalice

сребренов *adj f.p. see* сребрен

сребрест *adj rare see* сребреникав

сребри *impf* **I 1** to silver, coat with silver **2** to appear silvery **II** – **ce** *see* **I 2**

сребро *n* **1** silver; ❑ живо сребро quicksilver, mercury **2** silver plate; silverware; silver coins

сребробел *adj literary* silvery-grey (-white); сребробели коси silvery-grey hair

среброглав *adj literary* silver-haired; среброглав старец silver-haired old man

среброкос *adj literary* silver-haired

среброљубен -бна *adj see* среброљубив

среброљубец -пци *m* miser, *colloq.* money-grubber

среброљубив *adj* avaricious, money-grubbing, rapacious

среброљубивост *f* avarice, cupidity

среброљубје *n* avarice, cupidity

среброљупка *f (fem. form) see* среброљубец

среброрун *adj literary* silver-fleeced

сред *prep* in the middle/midst of; amidst, among; сред село in the middle of the village; сред ноќ in the middle of the night; сред смеата amidst the laughter; сред народот among the people; ❑ сред бел ден in broad daylight

среда *f* Wednesday; ❑ Велјасреда Ash Wednesday

средба *f* **1** meeting, encounter; rendezvous, date; непредвидена средба unforeseen encounter; родителска средба parents' meeting; љубовна средба assignation, *arch.* tryst; закаже средба to arrange a meeting; to make an appointment; to make a date; ❑ средба во четири очи tête-à-tête **2** *Sport.* game, match, meet, sporting fixture; пливачка средба swimming competition

среде[1] *n (средина)* middle; средето на лебот the soft (inner) part of the bread; во средето на минатиот век the middle of the last century; ❑ уште крајот и средето there is still a lot to be done, there is still a long way to go

среде[2] *adv rare (насреде)* in the middle; точно среде right in the middle

среде[3] *prep see* сред

среден[1] *pt* settled; composed; steady, reliable; well-organized; средена состојба settled state, stable situation; среден одговор measured response

среден[2] -дна *adj* **1** middle; medium, intermediate; middling fair, average; среден прст middle finger; средна категорија intermediate category; *Sport.* middleweight; ❑ нешто средно s.th. in between; среден век Middle Ages; Среден Исток Middle East; *Gram.* среден род neuter gender; среден сталеж middle class; средна рака човек man of modest abilities; средни години човек a middle-aged person; средно образование secondary schooling/education; средно училиште secondary school **2** average, mean; средна годишна температура mean annual temperature; средна цена average price

среденост *f* stability, steadiness; settled state; composure

среденоќ *f see* средноќ

средзимен -мна *adj* midwinter; wintry

среди *pf* **I** to arrange, tidy, put in order; to classify; to organize; си ги среди работите to put one's affairs in order; ❑ среди мисли to collect one's thoughts **II** – **ce 1** to get ready *intrans.*; се средивте ли? are you ready? **2** *fig.* to compose o.s.; to calm down *intrans.*; to get settled

средина *f* **1** middle; средината на улицата the middle of the street; во средината на мај in mid-May; ❑ се држи до средината to steer a middle course; кај него немаше средина there were no half-measures with him; there were no shades of grey with him; златна средина golden (happy) mean **2** milieu, environment; circle, sphere; семејна средина family circle; family background; професорска средина academic circles

срединка *f dim.* soft part of a loaf

средишница *f Chess* middle game

средиште *n* centre; во средиштето на престолнината in the centre of the capital; културно средиште cultural centre

средишен -шна *adj* central, middle; средишна точка central point

средлетен -тна *adj* midsummer; средлетна жега midsummer heat

средник -ци *m literary* middling peasant, peasant of average means

среднист *m literary* person with secondary-school education, *Am.* high-school graduate

среднистка *f (fem. form) see* среднист

средно *adv* on average; средно двапати на ден twice a day on average

среднoазиски *adj* Central Asian

средновековен -вна *adj* medi<a>eval

средновековие *n see* средновековје

средновековје *n* Middle Ages; периодот на средновековјето the medieval period

средностав *adj poet.* of medium height/build

средноќ *f* midnight

средноќен -ќна *adj* midnight *attrib.*; средноќен час midnight hour; средноќна тишина still\<ness\> of the night

средношколец -лци *m* secondary-school pupil, high-school student

средношколка *f (fem. form) see* средношколец

средношколски *adj* secondary-school, high-school *attrib.*; средношколски учебник secondary-school textbook

средњак -ци *m see* средник

средобежен -жна *adj* centrifugal; rotary

средовечен -чна *adj* middle-aged

средовечност *f* middle age

Средоземно Море *n* Mediterranean \<Sea\>

средоземноморски *adj* Mediterranean

средопосен -сна *adj* Mid-Lent *attrib.*; средопосна недела *Brit.* Mothering Sunday

средопосница *f* Mothering Sunday

средопост *m* Mid-Lent

средорек -ци *m* point of land (*at river confluence*); eyot, ait

средочен -чна *adj* Wednesday *attrib.*; средочен ден Wednesday

средство *n* **1** means, way; measure; единствено средство the only way; last resort; воспитно средство pedagogical measure; нема друго средство there is no other way; ❏ целта ги оправдува средствата the end justifies the means; не бира средства to stop at nothing; сите средства се дозволени with no holds barred **2** (*usu. pl*) facilities, means; tools; средства за производство means of production; превозни (сообраќајни, транспортни) средства means of transport; средства за врска means of communication **3** remedy; средство против главоболие headache remedy; средство за прочистување aperient, purgative, laxative; дезинфекционо средство disinfectant **4** (*only pl*) <financial> means, funds, capital, wherewithal; <о>скудни средства scant resources, straitened means; со свои сопствени средства at his own expense; парични средства financial resources, funds; ❏ не жали средства to spare no expense

средува (се) *impf of* среди (се)

средувач *m* organizer; arranger

средувачки *adj* organizational; средувачка работа organizational work

среже *pf* срежа *aor.* **1** to cut off, chop off **2** *fig. colloq.* to reduce, cut; среже буџет to cut a budget **3** *fig.* to interrupt, cut off

срежува *impf of* среже

срета *f f.p. see* средба

срете (се) *pf see* сретне (се)

сретне *pf* сретна *aor.* **I 1** to meet *trans.*; *colloq.* to run/bump into; сретне некого на улица to meet s.o. in the street **2** to come across, find, discover; to meet with, encounter; ги сретна нејзините очи (*намерно*) he caught her eye; (*случајно*) their eyes met; не го сретна неговото име во весникот he did not come across his name in the newspaper; сретне отпор to meet with resistance; сретне тешкотии to encounter difficulties **II – се 1** to meet *intrans.*; се сретне со другар to meet a friend; погледите им се сретнаа their eyes met; се сретнаа очи со (во) очи they met face to face **2** to be found/encountered; to occur; таков човек ретко може да се сретне you don't come across a man like that very often; ќе се сретнат тешкотии there will be difficulties

сретнува (се) *impf of* сретне (се)

среќа¹ *f* **1** happiness **2** <good> luck, <good> fortune; среќа во карти luck at cards; среќа во игра luck in sport; во сè има среќа he has all the luck; fortune smiles upon him; ❏ за среќа fortunately, as luck would have it; камо среќа! if only! на среќа (*оди, работи, игра и сл.*) to take a chance, leap in the dark; to go somewhere on the off-chance; to work randomly; среќата му работи luck is on his side; воена среќа the fortunes of war; добра среќа! good luck! држи среќа to keep one's fingers crossed; има повеќе среќа отколку памет to have more luck than sense;

more by luck than judgement; има среќа колку што е тежок to have the devil's own luck; лоша среќа bad (hard, *colloq.* tough) luck; носи добра/лоша среќа to bring good/bad luck; не било среќа it wasn't meant to be; повеќе среќа следниот пат better luck next time! си ја бара среќата to seek one's fortune; си ја проба среќата to try one's luck; среќа во несреќа a blessing in disguise; среќата ги прати храбрите fortune favours the brave; среќата му се насмевнува fortune smiles upon him; не носи среќа *colloq.* he/it is bad news; трета среќа third time lucky; тркалото на среќата the wheel of fortune; кој рано рани, две среќи граби *prov.* the early bird catches the worm; first come, first served **3** *colloq.* destiny, fate; секој со својата среќа everyone has his cross to bear

среќа² *f colloq.* meeting; на среќа му излегол he came out to meet him

среќа³ *f Bot.* (Hemerocallis fulva) day lily

среќава (се) *impf of* срете (се); птицава се среќава во јужните области that bird is found in the southern regions

среќавање *n* **1** meeting, encounter; неочекувано среќавање unexpected meeting **2** *Sport.* fixture; пријателско среќавање friendly match

среќен -ќна *adj* **1** happy, merry; беше сиот среќен he was overjoyed; ❏ среќен пат! *bon voyage!* Среќен Божиќ! Merry Christmas! среќен роденден! happy birthday! среќен исход happy ending; среќен и пресреќен on top of the world **2** lucky, fortunate; ❏ среќен е колку што е тежок to have the luck of the devil; среќен број lucky number; се роди под среќна звезда to be born under a lucky star

среќка¹ *f literary rare (лоз)* lottery ticket

среќка² *f dial.* lamb's shoulder-bone (*used in telling fortunes*)

среќлија *adj indecl. colloq.* lucky, fortunate

среќник -ци *m* lucky fellow, *colloq.* lucky devil

среќница *f (fem. form) see* среќник

срж *f* **1** *Anat.* marrow; core; до сржта на коските to the marrow; ❏ расипан до сржта rotten to the core **2** *Bot.* pith; сржта на дрвото heartwood **3** *fig.* essence, core, heart; сржта на проблемот the crux of the problem

сржи *pf* **1** (*за коњ*) to start neighing <suddenly> **2** (*за куче*) to start growling <suddenly> **3** *fig.* (*за човек*) to bark, snarl

сржува *impf of* сржи

срика *pf* to start roaring/braying/bellowing; *colloq.* to kick up a shindy

срикува *impf of* срика

срине *pf* срина *aor.* **I** to rake/shovel away; to raze; *colloq.* to do away with **II – се** to collapse *intrans.*, fall down

сринува (се) *impf of* срине (се)

срипа *pf* to jump up

срипува *impf of* срипа

срита *pf* **I 1** to kick *trans.* **2** to start kicking *intrans.* **II – се** *see* I 2; се сритаа коњите the horses started kicking

срица *impf see* срича

срича *impf* to spell; to spell out, read haltingly

CPJ *abbr.* (*Сојузна република Југославија*) Federal Republic of Yugoslavia

срка *impf* (*тивко*) to sip; (*гласно*) to slurp; to drink noisily, lap <up>; срка супа to eat soup; како дробил, така и ќе срка *prov.* as you sow, so shall you reap

сркне *pf* сркна *aor.* to sip

сркнува *impf of* сркне

срма *f* tinsel; silver-gilt thread

срмајлија & срмалија *adj indecl. colloq. see* срмен

срмен *adj* **1** <embroidered with> silver-gilt **2** *fig.* (*сребрен*) silver; срмени коси silver hair

срмоса *pf* to decorate/embroider with silver-gilt thread

срмосува *impf of* срмоса

срна *f Zool.* (Capreolus capreolus) roe deer

срндак -ци *m* roebuck

срнешки *adj* roe-deer's; срнешка кожа roe-deer hide; срнешко месо venison

срнче *n* **1** *dim. of* срна **2** fawn

сроден¹ *pt* accustomed, used to; сроден со работното место accustomed to one's work

сроден² -дна *adj* **1** related, kindred; akin; cognate; сродни народи kindred peoples; сродни јазици cognate languages **2** similar; similar in meaning

сроди *pf* **I 1** rare to make (*s.o.*) a relative by marriage **2** to bring <close> together; to join *trans.* **II** – **ce 1** *rare* to become related by marriage **2** to make friends (*co – with*); to get used to; набрзо се сроди со сите работници he soon made friends with all his work-mates; се сроди со градот he became used to the town

сродник -ци *m* relative, relation

сродница & сродничка *f* (*fem. form*) *see* сродник

сроднички *adj* kinship *attrib.*; сроднички врски ties of kinship

сродност *f* kinship, affinity; similarity, resemblance; сродност по смисла similarity in meaning

сродствен *adj literary rare see* сроден²

сродство *n* **1** kinship; се наоѓа во сродство to be related **2** similarity; affinity; полно сродство на идеите complete identity of ideas

сродува (се) *impf of* сроди (се)

срок *m* period; term; time limit, closing date, deadline; испитен срок examination period; кадровски срок traineeship; во најкраток срок as soon as possible; во срок од една недела within a week; пред срокот ahead of time (schedule); срокот помина the deadline has passed

сроковен -вна *adj see* срочен

сроковник -ци *m* journal; diary

срони *pf* **I** to chip off, break off, crumble *trans.*; to wear away, erode *trans.* **II** – **ce** to crumble *intrans.*; to collapse *intrans.*; to wear away, erode *intrans.*; се срони брегот the bank crumbled

сронува (се) *impf of* срони (се)

-срочен (*in compounds*) -term; краткосрочен short-term; долгосрочен long-term

срочен -чна *adj* **1** urgent **2** prompt **3** fixed-term; срочен заем fixed-term loan

срочиште *n literary* day of <court> hearing; беше закажано срочиште the day of the hearing was fixed

срочно *adv* urgently; promptly; in <good> time

срп *m* sickle; ❑ срп и чекан hammer and sickle

српест *adj* crescent-shaped; *Anat.* falcate; српеста месечина crescent moon

срповиден -дна *adj see* српест

српообразен -зна *adj see* српест

српски *adj* Serbian

српство *n* the Serbs

српче *n dim. of* срп

срска *pf* to start champing (chomping)/crunching

срскоти *pf* to start blaring (roaring)

срт *m* ('рбет) spine; ridge; срт на животно spine of an animal; срт на планина mountain ridge

срти *impf* to growl

срупа *pf* to start champing (chomping) <suddenly>

срути (се) *pf rare see* сруши (се)

срутува (се) *impf of* срути (се)

сруши *pf* **I 1** to bring down; to tear (pull) down *trans.*; to demolish; (*владетел*) to depose, topple *trans.*; (*влада*) to overthrow **2** *fig.* to ruin; to upset, thwart, frustrate; алкохолот му го сруши здравјето alcohol ruined his health; сруши план to thwart a plan **II** – **ce 1** to crumble, collapse *intrans.* **2** *fig.* to be upset/ thwarted/dashed; им се срушија соништата their dreams were shattered

срушува (се) *impf of* сруши (се)

срце *n* heart; *Cards* hearts; *fig.* core, centre; болно срце weak heart; ❑ цврсто срце stout heart; широко срце generous spirit; срце на зелка cabbage heart; срце на Земјата the centre of the earth; срце мое my darling; што му е на срце, тоа му на уста he wears his heart on his sleeve; срце му застана his heart missed a beat; пушти срце to dip into one's pocket; на гладно срце on an empty stomach; без срце heartless; му лежи на срце it's very important to him; на драго срце willingly, gladly; од длабочината на срцето from the bottom of one's heart; in one's heart of hearts; од сè срце heart and soul, with all one's heart; со срце wholeheartedly; ми се кине срцето my heart bleeds; земе на (при) срце to take to heart; срце го изело! to hell with him! срцето му преврте it turned his stomach; далеку од очите, далеку од срце *prov.* out of sight, out of mind

срцебиење *n literary* palpitations, *Med.* tachycardia

срцебол *m literary* heart pains; *fig.* heartache

срцев *adj* heart; *Med.* cardiac; срцев удар heart attack; срцева мана heart defect

срцевиден -дна *adj* heart-shaped; *Bot.* cordate; срцевиден лист cordate leaf

срцевина *f see* срж

срцелик *adj see* срцевиден

срценце *n dim. of* срце

срцест *adj see* срцевиден

срча *f colloq.* **1** glass; свети како срча it glistens like glass **2** *rare* (*скокалче*) marble

срчен¹ *adj* **1** *see* срчовен **2** *see* срцев

срчен² *adj colloq.* glass; glassy; срчени чаши glass tumblers

срченица *f colloq. see* срдешница

срченост *f* audacity; pluck

срчест *adj colloq.* glassy; срчест поглед glassy (glazed) look

срчка *f colloq. see* срдешница

срчовен -вна *adj colloq.* **1** brave, bold; plucky **2** agile, quick, nimble

СССР *abbr.* (*Сојуз на Советските Социјалистички Републики*) USSR

сст *interj* sh! shush!

стабилен -лна *adj* stable; steady; sturdy; стабилни цени stable prices; *Phys., fig.* стабилна рамнотежа stable equilibrium

стабилизáтор *m* stabilizer; стабилизатор на електричната енергија equalizer; вертикален стабилизатор fin, vertical stabilizer; хоризонтален стабилизатор horizontal stabilizer

стабилизација *f* stabilization

стабилизи́ра *pf & impf* I to steady, stabilize *trans.*; стабилизира цени to stabilize prices II – **се** to steady, stabilize *intrans.*; веќе се стабилизира стопанството the economy has now stabilized

стабилитéт *m see* стабилност

стабилност *f* stability

став *m* 1 posture, pose, stance; неприроден став на телото unnatural posture; *Mil.* во став мирно standing at attention 2 view, opinion; непријателски став unfriendly attitude; заземе цврст став to take a firm stand; менува став to change one's mind; to have a change of heart 3 paragraph 4 *Mus.* movement

става[1] *f* 1 build; figure; вита става slim figure 2 stook

става[2] **(се)** *impf of* стави (се)

ставелка *f* bunch of grapes hung up to dry; ❏ се исушил како ставелка he is nothing but skin and bone

стави *pf* I 1 to put, place, lay; стави нож на масата to put a knife on the table; ❏ стави точка (крај) на нешто to put a end to s.th.; to bring s.th. to a close; стави потпис на (под) нешто to affix one's signature to s.th.; стави срок to set a time-limit; стави на гласање to put to a vote; стави некого во задача to set s.o. a task; стави на проба to put to the test; ја стави главата во торба to risk one's neck; стави некого на свое место to put s.o. in his place; стави сè (животот) на коцка to risk/stake/hazard everything (one's life) 2 to instal, fit, fix; стави чешма to put in a tap 3 to apply *trans.*; to administer; стави инјекција to give an injection 4 to put on, don; стави капа to put on a cap; стави нараквици to put on gloves; *rare* си ги стави чевлите he put on his shoes 5 *colloq.* to serve; стави вода/вино to pour water/wine; стави софра to serve a meal 6 *colloq.* to bring (*people*) together; ги стави децата he arranged for the children to meet II – **се** 1 to put, place o.s.; се стави во нечија положба to put o.s. in s.o. else's position (shoes) 2 to meet; се стави со него to meet s.o.

ставина *f see* става[1] 2

ставит *adj* (*за маж*) well-built, (*за жена*) comely; shapely

ставица *f dim. of* става[1] 2

ставјало *n colloq.* refuge

ставка *f* 1 rate, pay scale; тарифна ставка tariff rate; наголеми ставки to raise wages 2 paragraph

ставор & створец *m Zool.* rat

ставрофор *m Rel.* archpriest

ставува (се) *impf of* стави (се)

стагнација *f* stagnation

стагни́ра *impf* to stagnate

стаден -дна *adj* gregarious; herd *attrib.*; стадно животно gregarious animal

стадио́н *m* stadium

стадиум *m* stage; стадиум на развитокот stage of development

стадо *n* herd, flock (*also fig.*); стадо овци flock of sheep; стадо коњи a herd of horses; викај по волкот дури не влегол во стадото *prov.* prevention is better than cure; старо куче стадо варди *prov.* an old ox makes a straight furrow

стаен *pt* (*притаен*) muted, quiet, silent; hidden, secret

стаеност *f* silence; concealment, secrecy

стаж *m* 1 length of service, experience, practice; стаж во струката professional experience 2 probation, probationary period; practice; <on-the-job> training; (*во болница*) *Brit.* housemanship, *Am.* internship, *Austral.* residency

стажáнт *m* probationer; trainee; лекар стажант *Brit.* houseman, *Am.* intern, *Austral.* resident medical officer (R.M.O.)

стажáнтка *f* (*fem. form*) *see* стажант

стажáнтски *adj* probationer's; trainee's; (*во болница*) houseman's, *Am.* intern's, *Austral.* resident's

стажи́ра *impf* to work on probation, be a probationer; to be in training; (*во болница*) to work as a houseman (*Am.* intern, *Austral.* resident)

стажи́ст *m rare see* стажант

стаза *f* path; пешачка стаза footpath

стаи́[1] *pf* I to conceal, suppress; стаи здив to hold one's breath II – **се** to hide *intrans.*, lie low; to skulk, lurk

стаи́[2] **се** *pf* 1 to deposit a sediment; to settle *intrans.*; to become clear; се стаи виното the wine has settled 2 *fig.* to abate; ми се стаија болките my pains have eased

стаja *f dial.* 1 (*коњушница*) stable 2 (*соба*) room

стаjува[1] **(се)** *impf of* стаи[1] (се)

стаjува[2] **се** *impf of* стаи[2] се

стакáто *adv Mus.* staccato

стаклар *m* glass-maker; glass-worker; glass-blower; glass merchant; glazier

стакларија *f* glass, glassware; glass-work; продавница за стакларија glassware shop

стакларница *f* glassware shop

стакларски *adj* glass-worker's; glazier's; стакларски дукáн glassware shop

стакларство *n* glass-work, glass manufacture, glassmaking

стаклен *adj* 1 glass *attrib.*; glassed; glazed; стаклена маса glass-topped table; стаклена чаша glass; стаклена бавча greenhouse, glasshouse; ❏ стаклена волна glass wool; стаклена хартија glass-paper 2 *fig.* glassy; стаклен блесок glassy sheen; стаклен поглед glassy stare; ❏ <стои> на стаклени нозе <to be> on slippery ground; <to have> feet of clay

стакленица *f rare* glass vessel; (*за вода, вино*) carafe; (*за вино, алкохол*) decanter

стакленце *n* 1 *dim. of* стакло 2 splinter <of broken glass>

стаклест *adj see* стакловиден

стакли се *impf* to glisten; to shimmer; to glitter; се стакли езерото the lake glints like glass

стакло *n* glass; матно стакло frosted glass; стакла на очила spectacle lenses

стакловиден -дна *adj* glassy; vitreous

стаклорезец -сци *m* glass-cutter

стаклорезечки *adj* glass-cutter's; стаклорезечки занает glass-cutter's trade

стаклорезница *f* glassworks

сталагми́т *m* stalagmite

сталакти́т *m* stalactite

стала́жа *f* rack

сталеж *m* class; profession; trade; *Hist.* estate; духовен сталеж the clergy; среден сталеж the middle class; чиновнички сталеж civil servants

сталешки *adj* class *attrib.*; professional; social; сталешка организација professional organization; сталешки интереси class interests; сталешки разлики social differences; class distinctions

сталка *f see* статив

сталожен *adj* calm, composed, cool; сталожен човек calm person

сталоженост *f* calmness, sang-froid, nonchalance; composure

сталожи *pf* **I** *fig.* to calm, quieten *trans.*; to subdue **II** – **се 1** to settle *intrans.*; to become clear **2** *fig.* to calm down *intrans.*; to regain one's composure; to pull o.s. together; to rally *intrans.*

сталожува (се) *impf of* сталожи (се)

стамболка *f* **1** variety of fruit tree (*e.g. pear, apple, cherry*) **2** pumpkin, winter squash

стамен *adj* hard, firm, steady; стамен камен hard rock

стан *m* **1** flat, apartment; наместен стан furnished flat; стан и храна board and lodging **2** seat, headquarters (HQ); станот на врховната команда headquarters of the supreme command

станар *m* tenant

станарина *f* rent

станарка *f* (*fem. form*) *see* станар

станарски *adj* tenant's; станарско право tenant's right

станбен *adj* housing *attrib.*; лоши станбени услови poor housing; станбена изградба housing construction

стандард *m* standard, norm; benchmark; pattern; утврдени стандарди established patterns; ❑ животен стандард (стандард на животот) standard of living

стандарден -дна *adj* standard<ized>; stock, trite; conventional; стандарден мебел standard furniture; стандардни одговори stock replies

стандардизација *f* standardization

стандардизи́ра *pf & impf* to standardize

стане[1] *pf* стана *aor.* **1** to stand up, get up, arise; стане од стол to rise from a chair; **2** to revolt, rebel, take up arms, rise in rebellion; стане во борба против непријателот to take up arms against the enemy; стане во нечија одбрана to rise to s.o.'s defence

стане[2] *pf* стана *aor.* **1** to become; to turn; стане профессор to become a professor; стане голем to grow up; лицето му стана модро од студ his face turned blue with cold **2** *colloq.* to be arranged, set right; стана работава that business has turned out well **3** to occur, arise, take place; to become of; што стана со куќата? what has become of the house? не стана збор за тоа it wasn't mentioned; ако стане потреба if the need arises **4** *impers.* (*with dat.*) to become; му стана јасно (*дека*) it became clear to him (*that*); ми стана непријатно I felt uncomfortable; ќе ти стане смешно you will find it funny; што ти стана? what's got into you? what was/is wrong with you?

станио́л *m* tin foil, silver paper

станица *f* station; шеф на станица station master; автобуска станица (*градска*) bus stop; (*меѓуградска*) bus (coach) station; железничка станица railway (*Am.* railroad) station; здравствена станица medical centre; метеоролошка станица weather station; полициска станица police station; станица за итна помош first-aid post; ambulance station

станичен -чна *adj* station *attrib.*; станично бифе station buffet

станка *f literary* interruption, pause; interval; без станка without a break (without stopping)

становит *adj see* стамен

становиште *n* stance, standpoint, attitude; stand, point of view

станодавец -вци *m* landlord

станодавка *f* landlady

станува[1] *impf of* стане[1]

станува[2] *impf of* стане[2]

станувачка *f* getting up; дошло времето за станувачка it is time to get up

станчи *pf* **I** to make thin, thin out **II** – **се** to grow thin, lose weight; to grow weak; to wear thin *intrans.*

станчува (се) *impf of* станчи (се)

стаорец *m Zool. see* ставор & створец

стап *m* stick, staff; cudgel, club; овчарски стап shepherd's crook; *Sport.* скок со стап pole-vault; ❑ дотера до питачки стап 1. *trans.* to reduce to beggary (penury); 2. *intrans.* to be reduced to beggary; се држи како слеп за стап to hold on for dear life; се тресе како стап во вода to shake like a leaf; како стап да голтнал <as> stiff as a poker (ramrod); за стап плаче he is asking for it; го крка стапот to take the rap; со стап не му се плаќа beating would be too good for him; стапот има два краја *prov.* that can go either way; it's a two-edged sword

стапалка *f* **1** footprint **2** foot; sole

стапало *n* **1** foot; sole **2** (*на скала*) step; rung **3** (*на/во возило*) running-board **4** *fig.* degree; stage; стапало на развитокот stage of development

стапец -пци *m* (*на разбој*) cross-beam

стапи *pf* **1** to tread, step, set foot; стапи во соба to enter a room; стапи во задруга to join a cooperative; стапи во борба to enter the fray; стапи во брак to get married; стапи во врска to get in touch **2** (*на*) to assume, take up; стапи на должност to take up a position; стапи на престол to ascend the throne; стапи на (во) сила to come into force (effect)

стаписа *pf* **I** to startle; to take aback; to confuse **II** – **се 1** to step back, retreat **2** *fig.* to be astonished, stunned; to be confused; (*обично за коњ*) to shy

стаписува (се) *impf of* стаписа (се)

стаписа *f* trap, snare; стави стаписи to set traps

стаписте *n augm. of* стап

стапка *f* **1** step; footstep; направи неколку стапки to take a few steps; се слушаа стапки footsteps were heard; ❑ на секоја стапка at every step (turn); стапка по стапка step by step **2** (*како мера*) yard, pace **3** pace, gait; војничка стапка marching pace **4** footprint; trail, spoor; остави стапки зад себе to leave a trail; ❑ следи некого в стапка to follow s.o. closely; му оди по стапките he is following in his footsteps **5** *Prosody* foot; стапка јамб iamb<ic> **6** rate; каматна стапка interest rate

стапне *pf* стапна *aor.* 1 *see* стапи 2 to tread on; ме стапна he trod on my foot

стапнува *impf of* стапне

стапува *impf of* стапи

стапче *n dim. of* стап; ❏ волшебно стапче magic wand; диригентско стапче conductor's baton

стар¹ *m* <film> star

стар² *adj* 1 old, aged, elderly; ancient, former; Стариот завет Old Testament; во стариот век in the olden days; ❏ од стара мајка дете an old fox; стар волк old dog; стара мома spinster, old maid; пак старата песна the same old story; стариот пен посилно гори *prov.* there's many a good tune played on an old fiddle; стар пријател и старо вино не пуштај *prov.* old friends and old wine are best 2 (*as noun*) old man/woman; *pl* old people; *colloq.* parents; grandparents; старо и младо young and old; по старо<то> in the traditional fashion; пак на старо<то> back to square one

старател *m* carer; guardian; trustee

старателка *f (fem. form) see* старател

старателски *adj* custodial; carer's; guardian's; trustee's; trusteeship *attrib.*; старателски совет board of trustees; Trusteeship Council <of the UN>

старателство *n* care, custody; guardianship; trusteeship; детето е под старателство the child is in the care of a guardian

старачка *f* old sheep

стареа *m arch.* elder; senior; chief

старее *impf* to grow old

старејко -овци *m dial. see* старосват

старејковица *f dial. see* старосватица

старец -рци *m* old man; дрт старец decrepit old man; old fool

старечки *adj literary* of old age; old man's/woman's; senile; старечка болест senility

старешина *m* elder; chief; head; *Mil.* warrant officer; non-commissioned officer

старешински *adj* elder's; senior's; chief's; head's

старешинство *n* seniority; по старешинство by seniority

старешиње *pl arch. of* старешина

старикав *adj* elderly

старило *n* old man

старина *f literary* 1 ancient/historical monument; antique; relic 2 old times; olden days; ancient times, antiquity

старинар *m* second-hand/antique dealer; junk dealer; antiquary, antiquarian

старинарница *f* antique shop; second-hand shop; junk shop

старинарски *adj* antiquarian, second-hand; старинарски дуќан antique shop

старинец -нци *m* aborigine, native; original resident

старински *adj* 1 ancient; antique; old; old-time 2 outdated, outmoded; old-fashioned; obsolete; (*за збор*) archaic; historical

старица *f* old woman

старичка *f hyp. of* старица

старичок -чка *adj dim. of* стар

старка *f see* старичка

староверен -рна *adj* traditional, orthodox

староверец -рци *m* Old Believer

староверски *adj* traditional, orthodox; староверски обичај time-honoured custom

старовина *f colloq. see* старина 1

старовремски *adj* antiquated, old-fashioned; antique; ancient; old-time

старогрчки *adj* Ancient Greek; старогрчката литература Ancient Greek literature

стародревен -вна *adj* ancient

старозаветен -тна *adj* Old-Testament *attrib.*

старолик *adj* old-looking; тој е старолик he looks old

старомоден -дна *adj* old-fashioned; out of date; outmoded; dated

старосват *m* second witness (*at a wedding*)

старосватец -тци *m see* старосват

старосватица *f* wife of старосват; second witness (*at a wedding*); matron of honour

старосватски *adj* second witness's

старосватство *n* status/duties of second witness

староседелец -лци *m* aborigine, native; original resident; *see* старинец

старосен -сна *adj* old-age; старосна пензија old-age pension

старословенски *adj* Old <Church> Slavonic, *Am.* Old <Church> Slavic

старост *f* old age; ❏ длабока старост advanced age, ripe old age; на старост in one's old age; збирај на младост, да имаш на старост *prov.* an idle youth, a needy age

старски *adj* old people's; старски дом old people's home, nursing home, rest-home

старт *m* 1 *Sport.* start; (*во фудбал*) kickoff 2 beginning, start 3 *Sport.* tackle

стартен -тна *adj Sport.* start *attrib.*; starting; стартен број starting number

стартер *m Sport.* starter

стартува *impf* 1 to start (*also Sport.*) 2 *Sport.* to attack, tackle

старудија -ии *f* old things; junk; rubbish

старче *n dim. of* старец

старчиште *n augm. of* старец

стас *m* stature

стаса *pf colloq. see* втаса

статив *m* stand; easel; tripod

статива *f Sport.* goalpost

статија -ии *f* article; уводна статија leader, leading article; директивна статија guidelines

статика *f* 1 statics 2 *fig.* (*мирување*) state of rest; standstill

статира *impf* 1 *Theatre, Film* to be an extra 2 *fig.* to play a minor role, play second fiddle; to be insignificant

статист *m* 1 *Theatre* walk-on, supernumerary; *Theatre, Film* extra 2 *fig.* nonentity, dummy

статистика *f* statistics

статистичар *m* statistician

статистички *adj* statistical; статистички податоци statistical information

статистка *f (fem. form) see* статист

статичен -чна *adj* static

статички *adj see* статичен

статни *pf* статни, статна *aor.* 1 to thunder 2 *fig.* to bark; to bawl

статнува *impf of* статни

статуа *f* statue

статуе́тка *f dim.* statuette

статус *m* **1** staff complement, strength **2** status; статус кво status quo

статусен -сна *adj* status *attrib.*; статусен симбол status symbol; статусни права civil/statutory rights

статут *m* statute<s>; by-law; по статутот according to the statute<s>

статута́рен -рна *adj* statutory; статутарни измени statutory changes

стафид *m (usu. pl)* currant; raisin; sultana

стафилоко́ка *f (usu. pl) Med.* staphylococcus (*pl* staphylococci)

стациона́р *m* infirmary

стациона́рен -рна *adj* in-patient *attrib.*; стационарно лекување in-patient treatment

стационе́р *m* patrol vessel

стациони́ра *pf & impf* to station

ствар *f (colloq. m)* thing

ствaрен -рна *adj Leg.* real; material, tangible; factual; стварно право property law

ствaрност *f* reality

створ *m* creature

ствoри (се) *pf see* создаде (се)

стврднат *pt* hardened, hard; стврдната земја hard ground

стврдне *pf* стврдне, стврдна *aor.* **I** to harden *trans.* **II** – се to go (turn) hard, harden *intrans.*

стврднува (се) *impf of* стврдне (се)

сте *2nd p. pl pres. of* сум; како сте? how are you?

стеари́н *m Chem.* stearin

стеари́нски *adj* stearic; stearin *attrib.*; стеарински свеќи stearin candles

стеблак -ци *m* tree top, crown <of a tree>

стебленце *n dim. of* стебло

стеблест *adj* **1** (*за дрво*) having many branches; having a stout trunk/bole; стеблесто дрво mighty tree; forked tree **2** having a stalk; stalk-like

стеблиште *n augm. of* стебло

стебло *n* **1** stem, stalk; trunk <of a tree>; bole **2** *fig.* stock, lineage; descent; родовско стебло family tree

стег *m colloq. see* стега

стега[1] *f* **1** discipline, iron hand; држи под стега to keep on a short lead **2** *Mech.* clamp, vice

стега[2] *impf* **I** **1** *see* стегне **2** (*за облека, чевли*) to be tight (too small); (*за чевли*) to pinch *trans.*; палтото ме стегаше the coat was too small for me **II** – се **1** *see* стегне се **2** *fig.* to be afraid; to be shy; to be coy; не стегај се help yourself; feel free **3** to scrimp <and save>

стегнат *adj* thrifty; ❑ стегната рака skinflint, miser

стегне *pf* стегна *aor.* **I** **1** to tighten *trans.*; to press, grip, clamp; to constrict; to close (*ranks*); *Med.* (*вена*) to strangulate; стегне шраф to tighten a screw; ❑ стегна студ there is a hard frost; cold weather has set in; си го стегне ременот to tighten one's belt **2** to hoop **3** *fig.* (*за болка*) to stab; ме стегна околу срцето I felt a stabbing pain in the heart **4** *fig.* to discipline; to take in hand; *fig.* to put pressure upon **5** *fig.* to prepare *trans.* **II** – се **1** to tighten *intrans.*; се стегнаа јажињата the ropes tightened **2** to shrink *intrans.*; чевлите ми се стегнаа my shoes have shrunk **3** to harden *intrans.*; to congeal; to contract **4** *fig.* to become more disciplined; to brace o.s.; to pull

o.s. together; to close ranks **5** *fig.* to get ready, prepare *intrans.*; се стегне за на пат to pack for a journey

стегнува (се) *impf of* стегне (се)

стежер *m see* стожер

стежне *pf* стежна *aor.* to become heavy/heavier

стежнува *impf of* стежне

стек[1] *m f.p.* gain, profit; goods, possessions

стек[2] *m* concurrence, coincidence; стек на околности coincidence

стек[3] *m (при кладење)* stake

стек[4] *m Cul. (бифтек)* steak

стекне *pf* стекна *aor.* to acquire, get, gain; стекне уверение дека…to become convinced that…; стекне пријатели to make friends

стекнува *impf of* стекне

стела *f* pack-saddle pad

стелна *adj (f only)* pregnant (*of a cow*), in calf

стемни *pf* **I** *impers.* (*of darkness*) to overtake (*s.o.*); нè стемни на патот darkness overtook us on the way **II** – се to get dark; *impers.* (*of darkness*) to fall; се стемни darkness fell; ❑ ми се стемни пред очи 1. I saw red 2. I felt faint

стемнува (се) *impf of* стемни (се)

стен *m poet.* moan, groan; howl, wailing, lament<ation>

стена *f* **1** (*карпа*) rock, boulder; cliff, face; escarpment; **2** *dial.* wall

стеница *f dial. see* дрвеница[1]

стенка *impf* to moan, groan

стеновит *adj (карпест)* rocky, craggy

стенограм *m see* стенограма

стеногра́ма *f* shorthand report/record, verbatim report; notes in shorthand; стенограма на лекциите shorthand lecture notes

стенограф *m* stenographer

стенографија *f* shorthand, stenography

стенографи́ра *pf & impf* to take down in shorthand

стенографка *f (fem. form) see* стенограф

стенографски *adj* shorthand *attrib.*, stenographic; стенографски белешки shorthand notes

стенодактилогра́ф *m* shorthand typist

стенодактилогра́фка *f (fem. form) see* стенодактилограф

стенодактилогра́фски *adj* shorthand *attrib.*, stenographic

стено́за *f Med.* stenosis

стенокардија *f Med.* angina pectoris

стенотипија *f* stenography (*by machine*)

стенотипи́ст *m* machine stenographer

стенчи (се) *pf see* станчи (се)

стенчува (се) *impf of* стенчи (се), *see* станчува (се)

степ *m* step dance

степа[1] *f* steppe

степа[2] *pf* **I** to cause to fight **II** – се to fight, have a fight

степен *m (rare f)* **1** level; degree; extent; степен на продуктивност level of productivity; степен на култура cultural level; ❑ до извесен степен to some extent; up to a point **2** <academic> degree; *Mil.* rank; висок степен high rank; академски степен academic degree; степен на доктор doctoral degree, PhD **3** (*на температура, агол*) degree **4** *Math.* power; exponent; шести степен на бројот осум eight to the power of six, eight to the sixth <power>

степенува *impf* **1** to grade, rate; to class, classify **2** *Math.* to raise to the (*second, third, etc.*) power

степски *adj* steppe; степска клима steppe climate

степува¹ *impf* to dance the step dance

степува² **(се)** *impf of* степа² (се)

стереометрија *f Math.* stereometry

стереометриски *adj* stereometric<al>

стереоскоп *m* stereoscope

стереоскопски *adj* stereoscope *attrib.*; stereoscopic

стереотип *m Print.* stereotype

стереотипен -пна *adj* stereotyped; *fig.* stock, trite; стереотипен израз conventional (trite) expression

стереотипија *f Print.* stereotype, stereotypography, stereotyping

стереотипира *pf & impf Print.* to stereotype

стерилен -лна *adj* **1** sterile; (*за млеко*) pasteurized; стерилен памук sterile cotton wool **2** barren, infertile *also fig.*

стерилизатор *m* sterilizer; sterilizing machine; (*за млеко*) pasteurizer

стерилизација *f* sterilization; (*за млеко*) pasteurization

стерилизационен -она *adj* sterilizing; (*за млеко*) pasteurizing; стерилизационен апарат sterilizing apparatus

стерилизира *pf & impf* to sterilize; (*млеко*) to pasteurize

стерилизиран *pt* sterilized; стерилизирано млеко pasteurized milk

стерилитет *f* sterility

стерилност *f* sterility

стерлинг *m only in the combination:* фунта стерлинг pound sterling

стерлиншки *adj* sterling *attrib.*; стерлиншка зона sterling area

стеснет *pt* embarrassed; shy, bashful; self-conscious

стеснетост *f* embarrassment; shyness, bashfulness; self-consciousness

стесни *pf* **I 1** to narrow *trans.*; to constrict; to take in (*a garment*); to thin out *trans.* **2** *fig.* to limit; to reduce **3** to cramp; to crowd *trans.*; to cause crowding **II – се 1** to narrow *intrans.*; to shrink *intrans.* **2** to crowd together *intrans.*; to be cramped, feel crowded **3** *fig.* to feel embarrassed/shy

стеснува (се) *impf of* стесни (се); ❏ не се стеснувај! feel free! don't stand on ceremony!

стетоскоп *m Med.* stethoscope

стетоскопија *f Med.* stethoscopy

стетоскопски *adj* stethoscopic

стечаен *adj* insolvent, bankrupt

стечаец *m* bankrupt, insolvent person

стечај *m* bankruptcy; insolvency; падне под стечај to go bankrupt/into receivership

стече¹ *pf* стеков *1st p. aor.* to acquire, get, gain; стек стече to make a profit; пет стече, пет испече *prov.* what you lose on the swings, you gain on the roundabouts

стече² *pf* стеков *1st p. aor.* to start flowing, gush forth, well up; стече вода water gushed forth

стивне *pf* стивна *aor.* to die down; to fall silent; to fade; to abate; гласовите стивнаа the voices fell silent; ветрот стивна the wind dropped; болките стивнаа the pain subsided

стивнува *impf of* стивне

стига¹ *adv* (*доста*) enough; стига со таа викотница! that's enough of that noise!

стига² *impf of* стигне

стигне *pf* стигна *aor.* **1** to catch up with **2** to succeed, manage; стигне да заврши нешто to manage to finish s.th. **3** to arrive; to reach; to get as far as; стигне во Скопје to reach Skopje; стигна на час he got to class **4** to be enough, suffice; ако нешто не ти стигне if you are short of anything; јадењево нема да ни стигне this food will not be enough for us **5** *fig.* to touch, affect, hit <home>; to befall **6** *arch.* to give birth to; десет синови стигнала she gave birth to ten sons

стигнува *impf of* стигне; ❏ далеку стигнува (дотуркува) to go a long way; to come a long way

стија -ии *f f.p.* (*добра*) fairy; nymph; (*лоша*) elf

стијоса *pf only in the expression:* стија те стијосала! go to hell!

стил *m* style; готски стил Gothic style; новинарски стил journalese; ❏ во стилот на in the style of, in the manner of, à la; во голем стил in grand style; со стил with style; stylishly; по нов стил New Style, according to the Gregorian calendar; по стар стил Old Style, according to the Julian calendar

стилизатор *m* stylist

стилизаторски *adj* stylist's; stylistic; стилизаторски способности stylistic skill

стилизација -ии *f* stylization

стилизира *pf & impf* to style, stylize, form

стилизиран *pt* stylized, styled, formed; стилизирана повест polished novella

стилист *m* stylist; style editor

стилистика *f* stylistics

стилистички *adj* stylistics *attrib.*

стило *n see* пенкало

стилски *adj* style *attrib.*, stylistic; elegant; стилска грешка stylistic mistake; стилска фигура figure of speech, trope; стилски мебел period furniture; стилска облека elegant clothes

стимари *pf* **1** to groom, curry, comb (*a horse*) **2** to tidy/spruce up

стимарува *impf of* стимари

стимул *m* stimulus

стимуланс *m see* стимул

стимулација *f* stimulation

стимулира *pf & impf* to stimulate

стине *impf* to cool down *intrans.*

стинее *impf see* стине

стипендија -ии *f* scholarship, bursary; grant; fellowship

стипендијант *m* scholarship holder, holder of a bursary; fellow

стипендијантка *f* (*fem. form*) *see* стипендијант

стипендира *impf* to grant (award) a scholarship (bursary, fellowship)

стипендист *m see* стипендијант

стипендистка *f see* стипендијантка

стипл-чез *m Sport.* steeplechase

стипса *f* **1** alum **2** *fig., colloq.* miser, skinflint, tightwad

стипсоса *pf* to add alum; to treat (paint) with alum

стипсосува *impf of* стипсоса

стипца *f see* стипса

стипцоса *pf see* стипсоса

стиска *f see* грст

стиска *impf* **I 1** *see* стисне **2** (*за чевли*) to pinch **II – се** *see* стисне се

стиснат *adj* tight, miserly; стиснат човек skinflint

стиснатост *f* miserliness, avarice; parsimony

стисне *pf* стисна *aor.* **I 1** to squeeze; (*заби, тупаници и др.*) to clench; to press, compress; to hold tight, grip; стисне некому рака to shake hands with s.o.; to squeeze s.o.'s hand **2** to close tightly; стисне усни to purse one's lips **II – се** to huddle together; to snuggle up

стиснува (се) *impf of* стисне (се)

стисок -ци *m* to grip, squeeze; стисок на раце a firm handshake

стих *m* **1** verse; line of verse **2** (*only pl*) poetry

стихар *m Rel.* surplice, alb, cassock

стихиен -jна *adj see* стихиски

стихиja -ии *f* element; водната стихиja носеше сè пред себе the floodwaters swept everything away; во својата стихиja in one's element

стихиjно *adv see* стихиски

стихиjност *f* spontaneity; unplanned work; lack of organization

стихира *f Rel.* hymn, canticle

стихиски *adj* elemental; spontaneous; unplanned; стихиски сили elemental forces

стихозбирка *f* collection of verses

стихотворба *f* poem

стихотворен -рна *adj* verse, poetry *attrib.*; стихотворна збирка collection of verse

стихотворење *n* the writing of poetry

стихотворец -рци *m* **1** poet **2** *pejor.* rhymester, poetaster

стихотворство *n* versification; poetry; *pejor.* verse-making

стихуван *adj* rhymed, in verse; во стихувана форма in verse form

стихче *n dim. of* стих

стиши (се) *pf see* стивне

стjуард *m* steward (*on a ship or aeroplane*)

стjуардéса *f* stewardess; air-hostess

сто *num* hundred; сто денари one hundred denars; пет од (на) сто five per cent; сто на сто one hundred percent; *fig.* definitely, for sure; entirely; ❑ сто пари петел, пет гроша крчма *prov.* the game is not worth the candle; сто стапа по туѓ грб ништо не се *prov.* it's no skin off my/your *etc.* nose

стовари *pf* **I 1** to unload; *fig.* to drop, dump (*s.o.*) **2** to off-load (*нешто на некого – s.th. on to s.o.*), burden (*s.o. with s.th.*); jа стовари вината на нив he put the blame on them **II – се** to collapse, drop *intrans.*; се стовари на креветот he collapsed on to the bed

стоварИште *n* store<house>, warehouse; depot

стоваришТен -шна *adj* store<house>, warehouse *attrib.*

стоварува (се) *impf of* стовари (се)

стог *m* stack, haycock, rick

стогодишен -шна *adj* one hundred years old; lasting a hundred years; centennial; стогодишен jубилеj centenary, one-hundredth anniversary

стогодишник -ци *m* centenarian

стогодишнина *f* centenary, one-hundredth anniversary

стогодишница *f see* стогодишнина

стоденарка *f* hundred-denar note

стодинарка *f obs.* hundred-dinar note

стодневен -вна *adj* one-hundred-day *attrib.*; стодневни резерви reserves/supplies for one hundred days

стодрам *m arch.* hundred drams

стодрамница *f arch.* vessel holding a hundred drams, hundred-dram vessel

стоенката *adv colloq.* standing, on one's feet

стоење *n from* стои; место за стоење standing-room; забането стоење standing prohibited; no standing

стоечки *adv see* стоенката

стожер *m* **1** centre post in threshing-floor **2** *fig.* pillar, mainstay; стожер на движење mainstay of a movement

стои *impf* **1** to stand; стои на место to stand still; ❑ стои добро со to be on good terms with; како стои работата? how do things stand? стои зад некого to back s.o., stand behind s.o.; стои здраво на нозете to stand on one's own two feet; стои како на трње (игли) he is on tenterhooks (edge); стои на зборот to keep one's word; стои на своето 1. to stand one's ground 2. to insist on getting one's own way; стои на стража to be on guard; стои настрана to stand aside **2** *fig.* to stand idle; работата ми стои my work is at a standstill; часовникот ми стои my watch has stopped **3** to be located (situated); книгите стоеjа во чантата the books were in the bag **4** (*of a means of transport*) to stop *intrans.* **5** (*with dat.*) to suit; добро ѝ стои фустанот the dress suits her well

стоик -ци *m* stoic

стоилjаден -дна *adj* of one hundred thousand; стоилjаден град a town of one hundred thousand inhabitants

стоицѝзам -змот *m* stoicism

стоички *adj* stoic<al>

стоjалиште *n* position; location; vantage point; standpoint, point of view

стоjалка *f* baby-walker

стока *f* **1** goods, wares; commodity; merchandise, article <of trade>; индустриски стоки industrial products; стока за широка потрошувачка consumer goods; ❑ не е стока ни тоj he is no saint either; што стока, штостока! great! wonderful! што стока е овоj човек? what sort of fish is he? готова стока - готови пари cash on the nail; business is business; убавата стока сама се продава *prov.* good ware makes quick markets; quality sells well **2** <live>stock; jадра стока horses and cattle; ситна стока sheep and goats

стокми *pf* **I 1** to prepare, get ready *trans.*; to fit out, equip; стокми коњ to saddle a horse **2** *fig.* to arrange, *colloq.* fix, cook up; тоj ми jа стокми оваа работа he landed me in this mess **3** to place (put) together; стокми ги нозете! put your feet together! **II – се** to prepare, get ready *intrans.*; се стокми да си оди to get ready to leave

стокмува (се) *impf of* стокми (се)

стоковен -вна *adj* goods *attrib.*; стоковна куќа department store; стоковна размена commodity exchange

стократен -тна *adj* <one->hundredfold

Стокхолм *m* Stockholm

стокхолмски *adj* Stockholm *attrib.*

стол *m* **1** (*со наслон*) chair; (*без наслон*) stool; ❑ седи на два стола to sit on the fence; to wear two hats **2** *arch.* throne

столар *m* carpenter; joiner; cabinet-maker

столарија *f* woodwork, carpentry

столарница *f* carpenter's/joiner's/cabinet-maker's workshop

столарски *adj* carpenter's; joiner's; cabinet-maker's; столарски занает carpenter's/joiner's/cabinet-maker's trade; carpentry; joinery

столарство *n* carpentry; joinery

столб *m* **1** pillar, column; post; pylon; support; сала на столбови columned hall; граничен столб border post; landmark (*also fig.*); телефонски столб telephone pole; 'рбетен столб spinal column, backbone; *Hist., fig.* срамниот столб pillory **2** *fig.* mainstay

столба *f* **1** stairs, staircase **2** <step>ladder

столбец -пци *m* **1** *dim. of* столб 1 **2** <newspaper> column

столбица *f dim. of* столба

столбиште *n* staircase, stairs; stairway, flight of stairs

столбовиден -дна *adj* column-like; pillar-like

столбообразен -зна *adj see* столбовиден

столетен -тна *adj* one hundred years old; lasting a hundred years; centennial; столетен старец centenarian; столетен јубилеј centenary

столетие *n see* столетје

столетје *n* **1** century **2** *rare* centenary

столетник -ци *m* centenarian

столетница *f* (*fem. form*) *see* столетник

столица *f* **1** *see* столница **2** *see* стол; ❏ жешка столица hot seat; загрева столица to burn the midnight oil **3** *Med.* stool; тврда столица constipation

столнина *f* **1** capital <city>, metropolis **2** *rare* throne; ❏ седне на столнината to ascend the throne

столовит *adj* **1** having a stem/stand; столовита чаша wineglass **2** (*за дрво*) branched

столче *n dim. of* столб 1

столче[1] *n dim. of* стол 1; ❏ земи столче take/have a seat!

столче[2] **& столчи** *pf* столчи *aor.* **1** to smash, shatter *trans.* **2** to crush, destroy, kill **3** *fig.* to break *trans.*; го столчи болеста the illness broke him **4** *fig.* to do (*s.th.*) hastily; to knock (*s.th.*) together

столчува *impf of* столче[2] & столчи

стомак -ци *m* stomach; belly; го боли стомак he has a stomach-ache; чир во стомакот stomach ulcer; полн/празен стомак full/empty stomach; ❏ има ламја во стомакот to have a huge appetite; му се преврте <во> стомакот; му се крена стомакот his gorge rose; нема стомак за to have no stomach for

стоматолог -зи *m* dentist

стоматологија *f* stomatology, dental medicine

стоматолошки *adj* stomatological; стоматолошка клиника stomatological (dental) clinic (practice)

стомаче *n dim.* tummy

стомачен -чна *adj* stomach, *Med.* gastric; стомачен сок gastric juice; стомачни болки stomach ache, gastric pains; стомачни киселини gastric acids; heartburn, acid dyspepsia, brash

стомачиште *n augm. of* стомак

стометраш *m Sport.* hundred-metre sprinter

стомина *num* (*of men or mixed groups*) one hundred

стомна *f* pitcher, ewer, earthenware jug

стомнар *m* pitcher-maker

стомниче *n* & **стомничка** *f dim. of* стомна

стонога *f see* стоногалка

стоногалка *f Zool.* (Chilopoda *or* Myriapoda) centipede

стоножица *f see* стоногалка

стоп *interj* stop!

стопан *m* **1** owner, proprietor; landlord; farmer **2** householder, master of the house **3** *fig.* master **4** *colloq.* husband

стопанисува *impf* **1** to manage (run, operate) a firm (*etc.*) **2** to earn one's living; почне да стопанисува to start earning

стопаница *f see* стопанка

стопанка *f* **1** owner, proprietress; landlady **2** housewife, mistress of the house; farmer's wife **3** *fig.* mistress **4** *colloq.* wife

стопански *adj* **1** economic; business, trade *attrib.*; стопанско право commercial (business) law; стопанска делегација trade delegation **2** proprietor's

стопанственик -ци *m* tradesman; merchant; businessman

стопанственички *adj* tradesman's; merchant's; businessman's

стопанство *n* **1** economy; селско стопанство agriculture and animal husbandry; rural economy; шумско стопанство forestry; plantation; forest estate; ученик во стопанството apprentice **2** farm; земјоделско стопанство farm; сточарско стопанство cattle/sheep farm

стопаре *n Hist., colloq.* fifty *paras*, fifty-*para* coin

стопати *adv* a hundred times

стопи *pf* **I** **1** to melt, thaw *trans.*; (*руда*) to smelt; (*метал*) to fuse; сонцето го стопи снегот the sun melted the snow **2** *fig.* to emaciate, reduce to skin and bone **3** *fig.* to upset, thwart, foil; стопи план to frustrate a plan **II** – **се** **1** to melt, thaw *intrans.* **2** *fig.* to lose weight; to waste away *intrans.* **3** *fig.* to dwindle; (*за надежи, желби и сл.*) to evaporate, come to nothing **4** *fig.* to merge (*со – with*) **5** *dial.* to step aside

стопира *pf & impf* to stop *trans.*; to thumb a lift; to hitchhike

стопли *pf* **I** to warm <up> *trans.*; to heat *trans.*; *fig.* to please; стопли соба to heat a room; веста му го стопли срцето the news warmed his heart **II** – **се** to warm o.s., warm up *intrans.*; to grow warmer

стоплува (се) *impf of* стопли (се)

стопроцентен -тна *adj* one-hundred-percent, complete; out-and-out; стопроцентно присуство one-hundred-percent attendance

стопува (се) *impf of* стопи (се)

стори *pf* **I** **1** to do; to make; ништо не можам да сторам there is nothing I can do; ❏ *colloq.* стори абер to send word; сѐ би сторил за . . . I'd do anything for . . . ; стори пет/десет години to turn five/ten; што ќе сториш, тоа ќе најдеш *prov.* as you sow, so shall you reap; стореното е сторено *prov.* there's no use crying over spilt milk **2** to make, turn (*s.o./s.th.*) into; го стори генерал he made him a general **3** to mistake (*s.o. for s.o. else*); те сторив дека си Петко I thought you were Petko; сторив дека чука некој I thought I heard s.o. knocking **II** – **се** **1** to become; се стори богат to get rich **2** to change (turn into *intrans.* **3** *f.p.* to happen; така се сторило that's how it happened **4** (*of pickles*) to go sour; ❏ краставици сторени! rubbish! **5** to ferment *intrans.*; се стори виното the wine is ready **6** *impers.* (*with dat.*) to seem; ми се стори дека . . . it seemed to me that . . . **7** ❏ се стори! 1. agreed! it's a deal! 2. the damage is done; there's no use crying over spilt milk; од тој ден жив не се стори from that day on he has not been seen

сторни́ра *pf & impf* to cancel; (*исплати*) to stop; (*поништи*) to annul, revoke (*a decree, act, etc.*)

сторно *n* reversal (*of a ledger entry*); cancellation (*of an order*)

стота *f* one-hundredth <part>

стотен -тна *adj* hundredth; стотен дел hundredth part; minute part

стотина *num* hundred; about a hundred

стотинка *f obs.* **1** *para*; cent **2** *see* стота

стотица *f* hundred; купува со стотици to buy by the hundred

стотка *f* hundred-denar/-dollar (*etc.*) note

стотница *f see* стотица

сточар *m* stock-breeder, *Am.* cattleman

сточари *impf* to raise <live>stock

сточарски *adj* stock-breeding *attrib.*

сточарство *n* stock-raising, stock-breeding, animal husbandry

сточен -чна *adj* <live>stock *attrib.*; сточна храна stock feed, forage; fodder

стр. *abbr.* (*страна*) page, p.

страв *m* fear, dread (*од – of*); apprehension; од страв out of fear, for fear; ❏ ме фати страв I felt scared, I was seized by fear; мечка страв, мене не страв! here goes! му го има стравот he is scared of him; живее во страв и трепет to live in fear and trembling; тој е страв и трепет he is a terror; страв ми е I'm scared; од страв да не би; од страв да не/дека lest; for fear of; <се> смрзнува од страв to be scared stiff, to be frightened to death; очите на стравот му се мошне големи *prov.* fear has big eyes; страв лозје чува *prov.* wise fear begets care

стравотен -тна *adj* terrifying, horrifying; terrible, horrible; стравотни болки terrible pains

стравотија -ии *f* terror, horror; стравотиите на војната the horrors of war

страда *impf* to suffer; страда за дело to be a martyr to a cause; страда за леб to go hungry; страда од срце to suffer from a bad heart; страда работата the work is being <adversely> affected

страдален -лна *adj see* страдалнички

страдалец -лци *m see* страдалник

страдалник -ци *m* sufferer; sick person; victim; martyr; wretch

страдалница *f* (*fem. form*) *see* страдалник

страдалнички *adj* full of suffering, miserable, pained; martyred; страдалничко лице tormented face; страдалнички живот a life of suffering

страдалнички *adv* with suffering, miserably; painfully; with a martyred/sorrowful look

страдање *n* suffering, misery; hardship

страден -дна *adj* **1** suffering; miserable **2** *fig.* wanting, lacking; не сум страден за ништо I am not wanting for anything

страеше *impf* (*only imperfect tense*) *impers.* (*with acc.*)

to be afraid (scared, frightened) (*од – of*); ме страеше од него I was afraid of him

страж *m poet. see* стража

стража *f* guard; watch; escort; постави стража to mount a guard; ❏ под стража under guard; почесна стража (*ceremonial escort*) guard of honour; стои на стража to stand guard; чува стража to keep watch; телесна стража bodyguard

стражар *m* **1** guard; watchman; escort; prison warder; sentry, sentinel **2** *literary* defender, champion

стражари *impf* **1** to keep watch; to stand guard, be on guard (sentry) duty **2** to watch over, guard; to defend, champion

стражарница *f* guardhouse; watch-tower, lookout; sentry-box

стражарски *adj* guard *attrib.*; watch *attrib.*; patrol *attrib.*; *Mil.* sentry's; стражарско место guard post

стражарчи *impf see* стражари

страк *m* **1** spray, sprig; switch; stalk, stem; blade (*of grass*); страк босилек sprig of basil **2** vine plant; vine stock

стракче *n dim. of* страк

страна *f* **1** side; flank; bank; планинска страна mountainside; mountain slope; лева страна left-hand side; ❏ влече на своја страна to work in one's own interest; другата страна на медалот the other side of the coin; од една страна . . . , on the one hand . . . ; љубезно од ваша страна it's very kind of you; од моја страна for my part, as for me; од страна на некого on the part of, by s.o.; on behalf of s.o.; става на страна to set aside **2** side, aspect, feature; тоа му е слабата страна that is his weak point, that is his Achilles heel; нечии добри и лоши страни s.o.'s good and bad points; јака страна strong point **3** (*правец*) direction; way; point of the compass; ❏ на сите страни in all directions; all over the place **4** page; насловна страна (*на книга*) title page; (*на весник*) front page; ❏ доаѓа на прва страна to make the front page, *colloq.* hit the headlines; на следната страна overleaf; од прва до последна страна from cover to cover **5** *fig.* point of view, standpoint; aspect, respect; од политичка страна from a political point of view **6** *fig.* party; заинтересирана страна interested party; трета страна a third party

странец -нци *m* foreigner; alien; stranger

страни[1] *impf* to avoid, shun

страни[2] *impf* to arrange in rows, line up *trans.* (*cut firewood*)

страница *f* **1** page; ❏ отвори нова страница to turn over a new leaf **2** (*на разбој*) side frame; (*на кола*) side board

страници *pl* tonsils, *see* крајник, сливица

страничен -чна *adj* **1** side *attrib.*, lateral; странична улица side street **2** *fig.* secondary, incidental, accessory; chance *attrib.*; external, outside, extraneous; странично прашање side issue

странка *f Administration* member of the public; client

странски *adj* foreign; странски јазик foreign language

странство *n* abroad, foreign countries

странствува *impf* to travel abroad

страсник -ци *m* sensualist; lecher, sex maniac

страсница *f* sensualist; nymphomaniac

страсно *adv* passionately; vehemently, ardently; зборува страсно to speak with feeling

страсност *f* passion; vehemence

страст *f* **1** passion; lust; vehemence, zeal, ardour; обузда свои страсти to curb one's passions; распалени страсти consuming passions; човечки страсти human foibles **2** hobby-horse; mania, obsession

страстен -сна *adj* passionate; enthusiastic, ardent, fervent; vehement; страстен бакнеж passionate kiss; страсна жена passionate woman; страстен пушач ardent (inveterate) smoker; *Rel.* страсна недела Holy (Passion) Week

стратег -зи *m* strategist

стратегија -ии *f* strategy

стратегиски *adj* strategic; стратегиски план strategic plan

стратешки *adj* **1** strategist's **2** *see* стратегиски

стратор *m Bot.* (Amaranthus paniculatus) amaranth

страторов *adj* amaranthine, amaranthaceous; китка страторова bunch of amaranths

стратосфера *f* stratosphere

стратосферски *adj* stratospheric

страхопочит *m* veneration; awe

страхува *impf see* плаши се

страч *m Zool.* male magpie

страче *n Zool.* (Lanius) shrike; мало страче (Lanius collurio) red-backed shrike; големо страче (Lanius excubitor) great grey shrike

страчка *f* **1** *Zool.* (Pica pica) magpie **2** *fig.* tall, thin, bedraggled person **3** *sl.* the runs; го фати страчка *colloq.* he was caught (taken) short

страчкин *adj* magpie's; ❑ умот му е по страчкини седела his head is in the clouds

страшен -шна *adj* **1** terrifying, frightening; terrible, awful; dreaded; wild, savage; *Rel.* страшниот суд Doomsday, Day of Judgement, the Last Judgement; страшна болка terrible pain **2** *fig., colloq.* tremendous, terrific; страшен филм terrific film

страши (се) *impf see* плаши (се)

страшилиште *n see* страшило 2, 3

страшило *n* **1** scarecrow **2** horror, horrible thing, horrible scene **3** *fig.* ghost; monster

страшла *f see* страшливка

страшле -евци *m see* страшливец

страшлив *adj* timid, fearful, faint-hearted

страшливец -вци *m* coward

страшливка *f (fem. form) see* страшливец

страшливост *f* timidity, fearfulness, faint-heartedness

страшло -овци *m see* страшливец

стрв *f* **1** bait; carrion **2** bloodthirstiness, rapaciousness **3** gluttony, voracity

стрвен -вна *adj* **1** bloodthirsty; rapacious, grasping; predatory; стрвни птици birds of prey **2** *fig.* gluttonous, voracious; insatiable

стрвла *f (fem. form) see* стрвло

стрвле -евци *m see* стрвло

стрвло -овци *m* glutton; greedy/ambitious man; extortioner; greedy animal

стрвник -ци *m* **1** carnivore; man-eating beast; волци стрвници man-eating wolves **2** *fig.* glutton; greedy/ambitious man; extortioner

стрвница *f* **1** *usu. in the expression:* мечка стрвница

flesh-eating bear **2** *fig.* glutton; greedy/ambitious woman; extortioner; greedy animal

стрвнички *adj see* стрвен

стрвост *f* **1** bait; carrion **2** bloodthirstiness; rapaciousness **3** gluttony, voracity

стреа -еи *f* **1** eaves; awning **2** *fig.* roof, shelter, home; под таткова стреа in one's father's house

стрела[1] *f* arrow, *Hist.* bolt; shaft; ❑ брз како стрела as swift as an arrow; пушта стрели против некого to aim one's barbs at s.o., draw a bead on s.o.; прав како стрела straight as an arrow

стрела[2] **1** *impf* to shoot, fire; to shoot (fire) at; to take aim, aim at; to hit; стрела со лакови to shoot with a bow and arrow **2** *fig.* (со очи) to stare at; to shoot a glance at, dart a look at; ја стрелаше со очи момата he kept stealing glances at the girl **3** *pf & impf* to shoot, execute **4** *impf Sport.* to shoot; стрела на гол to shoot at goal

стрелан *pt* shot, executed <by firing squad>

стрелање *n* death by firing squad (shooting)

стрелач *m see* стрелец

стрелаштво *n* shooting; archery

стрелба *f* shooting; gunfire, firing; брза стрелба rapid fire

стрелест *adj* arrow-shaped; *Bot., Zool.* sagittate; стрелест лист sagittate leaf

стрелец -лци *m* marksman; sniper; *Aviation* gunner; *Mil.* rifleman; (со лак) archer, bowman; *Astron.* Sagittarius, the Archer; *Sport.* scorer, goal-getter; ❑ волшебниот стрелец Cupid

стрелечки *adj* rifle *attrib.*; infantry *attrib.*; shooting; archery *attrib.*; стрелечка организација rifle club

стрелица **& стреличка** *f dim. of* стрела[1]

стрелиште *n* shooting-range, rifle-range, butts; shooting-gallery

стрелка[1] *f dim. of* стрела[1]; pointer, needle, arrow; стрелките го покажуваат патот the arrows mark the route; стрелка на часовник clock/watch hand

стрелка[2] *impf* **I** *dim. of* стрела[2]; стрелка со очи to shoot a glance (*at*), dart a look (*at*) **II – се** to pop up, turn up unexpectedly *intrans*

стрелне *pf* стрелна *aor. see* стрела[2]; стрелне со очи to shoot a glance (*at*), dart a look (*at*)

стрелнува *impf of* стрелне

стреловиден -дна *adj see* стрелест

стреловит *adj* of an arrow; swift; стреловита брзина the speed of an arrow

стрелуши се *impf* to be afraid, fear; to be worried

стрем[1] *m* horse-drawn cart/waggon

стрем[2] *m* upturned virgin soil

стремеж *m* longing, yearning; aspiration, striving (кон – *for*); pursuit (*of*)

стремен *m* stirrup; *Anat.* stirrup bone, stapes

стреми[1] *impf* to trench-plough

стреми[2] **се** *impf* to long, crave (кон – *for*); to aspire (*to*); to strive (*for*); *colloq.* to be after, out for

стрепери *pf see* стрепети

стреперува *impf of* стрепери

стрепети *pf* to start trembling (quivering); стрепети птица со крилјата the bird began to flutter

стрепетува *impf of* стрепети

стрепка *pf* to blink; стрепка со очите he blinked

стрепкува *impf of* стрепка

стрепти *pf see* стрепети

стрептокóка *f* (*usu. pl*) *Med.* streptococcus (*pl* streptococci)

стрептокóкен -кна *adj* streptococcal; стрептококна ангина streptococcal tonsillitis

стрептомицѝн *m Med.* streptomycin

стрес *m* stress

стресе *pf* **I 1** to <start to> shake *trans.* **2** *impers.* (*with acc.*) ме стресе I'm feverish **II – се** to start shivering (trembling, shuddering); се стресе од страв to quake with fear

стресен -сна *adj* stressful; <of> stress; стресна ситуација stressful situation

стресува (се) *impf of* стресе (се)

стрефи *pf colloq.* **I 1** to hit (*one's target*) **2** to hit on, find; to guess (*correctly*); го стрефивме патот we found the way **II – се 1** to happen to be (*somewhere*); to find o.s.; не се стрефив дома кога дошле I happened to be out when they came **2** (*with dat.*) to turn out well (*for s.o.*); им се стрефи времето they had ideal weather

стрефува (се) *impf of* стрефи (се)

стреш[1] *m* caution; на стреш alert, on guard, on the qui vive

стреш[2] *m* **1** water used by goldsmiths and silversmiths to wash metal **2** *fig.* sense; logic; нема ни капка стреш во главата he does not have a grain of sense in his head

стриг *m* shearing; ❏ на свињски стриг when pigs fly

стригарница *f* shearing shed; shearing place

стрижба *f see* стриг

стриже *impf* (*овци*) to shear; (*луѓе*) to cut s.o.'s hair; ❏ кога ќе ги стрижеме петлите when pigs fly; ако си овца, секој ќе те стриже *prov.* don't make yourself a mouse or the cat will eat you

стрико -овци *m* **1** uncle (*father's brother*) **2** (*mode of address used for a man one generation older than the speaker*) uncle

стриков *adj* uncle's

стриктен -тна *adj* strict

стрина *f* **1** aunt (*uncle's wife*) **2** *colloq.* (*mode of address to older woman*) auntie **3** *fig.* weakling, coward, *colloq.* chicken

стринин *adj* aunt's

стринка *f hyp. of* стрина

стринкин *adj hyp. see* стринин

стрип *m* comic strip

стрихнѝн *m* strychnine

стркала *pf* **I** to roll <down> *trans.*; to bowl *trans.*; to trundle *trans.*; to wheel *trans.* **II – се** to roll <down> *intrans.*; (*гласно, за кола*) to rumble *intrans.*

стркалува (се) *impf of* стркала (се)

стрм *adj see* стрмен

стрмен -мна *adj* steep; стрмен брег steep bank/hill

стрмец *m* west wind on Lake Ohrid

стрмина *f see* стрмнина

стрмнина *f* **1** steep slope, steep incline **2** steepness, gradient

стрмниште *n* steep slope, steep incline, steep bank/ road

стрниште *n* stubble field

строг *adj* strict; stern; severe; exacting; строг критичар a severe critic; строг тон severe tone; строга диета strict diet; строга казна severe sentence; <нај>строгиот центар the very centre

строгост *f* strictness; severity; rigidity; stringency

строеж *m* **1** building, construction; building site; construction project **2** system, *see* строј[2] **3** structure; texture; строежот на јазикот the structure of the language

строен -јна *adj* **1** (*за маж*) well-built; (*за жена*) shapely **2** harmonious; orderly

строи[1] *impf* **I 1** to form <up>, line (draw) up *trans.*; строи во два реда to line (*e.g. soldiers*) up in two rows **2** *fig.*, to upbraid; *colloq.* to tick off; *colloq.* to carpet **II – се** to form up, line up *intrans.*

строи[2] *impf see* стројува

строи[3] *impf see* гради[2]

строј[1] -оеви *m* **1** formation, order; line; array; стрелечки строј line of riflemen; излезе од строј to break ranks; во строј! fall in! ❏ исфрли од строј to disable, put out of action; to take out of service; вон строј out of order **2** system; order; régime; општествен строј social system

строј[2] -оеви, -ови *m* engagement/marriage agreement

стројник -ци *m* matchmaker, go-between

стројница *f* (*fem. form*) *see* стројник

стројничица *f see* стројница

стројност *f* **1** shapeliness; grace **2** harmoniousness; orderliness; harmony, order

стројоса *pf* to matchmake, arrange a match

стројосува *impf of* стројоса

стројува *impf* to matchmake, arrange a match

стропа *pf* to <start to> knock; ми стропа срцето my heart started racing

стропори се *pf* to throw one's chest out; to square up (*for a fight*)

стропорува се *impf of* стропори се

стропува *impf of* стропа

строфа *f* stanza

строши *pf* **I 1** to crumble *trans.*, crush **2** *dial.* to break, shatter, smash *trans.* **II – се** *dial.* to break, shatter, smash *intrans.*; to collapse, crash down

стрпи се *pf* to be patient; to hold on, hold out

стрплив *adj* patient; long-suffering

стрпливост *f* patience

стрпува се *impf of* стрпи се

струг *m* lathe; machine tool; plane; метален струг metal lathe

струга *impf dial. see* струже

стругалка *f see* струшка 1

стругало *n* lathe; machine tool; plane

струганица *f* (*usu. pl*) chips, shavings, filings; sawdust

стругар *m* turner, lathe operator

стругарница *f* turnery; sawmill

стругарски *adj* turner's; стругарски нож chisel

стругарство *n* turner's trade

стругне *pf* стругна *aor.* **I 1** to plane, turn (*wood*) **2** *fig.* to bolt *intrans.*, *sl.* beat it **3** *fig.*, *colloq.* to shave **II – се** *fig.*, *colloq.* to shave *intrans.*

стругнува (се) *impf of* стругне (се)

струготина *f see* струганица

струготинка *f dim. of* струготина

струен -јна *adj* **1** swift-flowing **2** *Ling.* fricative; струјни гласови fricatives, fricative consonants

струење *n* circulation; струење на крвта <blood> circulation; струење на животот the round of life

струже *impf* **1** to plane/turn (*wood*); to file, rasp; to saw; to fret *trans.* **2** to scrape; to scrub; *Med.* to scarify **3** *fig.* to grate (*on the ear*), rasp *intrans.* **4** to snore **5** to rub, chafe; ме струже јажево this rope is chafing me

струи *impf* to flow, stream, gush; почнаа да струјат нови идеи new ideas began to circulate

струја *f* **1** stream; current; морска струја ocean current; студена воздушна струја cold front **2** electrical current, power; едносмерна струја direct current; наизменична струја alternating current **3** *fig.* trend, movement, tendency

струјник -ци *m Ling.* fricative

струјоказ *m* current-meter, current-gauge (*for water*)

струјомер *m* electricity meter

струка¹ *f* <special> field, speciality, specialism

струка² *f* type of cloth (*of goat's hair, wool, etc.*); cloak; rug

струкови *pl Med.* children's eczema

структу́ра *f* structure; организациона структура organizational framework

структура́лен -лна *adj* structural

структурали́зам -змот *m* structuralism

структурали́ст *m* structuralist

структуралисти́чки *adj* structuralist

структу́рен -рна *adj* structural

струна *f* **1** horsehair **2** string (*of musical instrument*)

струнен *adj* horsehair; струнена торба horsehair bag

струненица *f* horsehair bag

струп -пје *m* scab, crust (*on a wound*)

струпа *pf* **I 1** to pile; to dump **2** to off-load (*на – on to*); сета работа ја струпаа на него they piled (heaped) all the work on to him **II – се 1** to pile up *intrans.*; to crowd *intrans.* **2** (*of work*) to fall to, land (*на – on*); работата се струпа на мене the task fell to me

струпјоса *f* **I** to make scabby **II -се** to become scabby

струпка *f see* струп

струплив *adj* scabby

струполи *pf* **I** to knock down **II – се** to fall, collapse, tumble (*heavily*); се струполи во фотелја to collapse into an armchair

струполува (се) *impf of* струполи (се)

струпува (се) *impf of* струпа (се)

струпче *n dim. of* струп, струпка

стручен -чна *adj* specialized; expert *attrib.*; стручен испит qualifying examination; стручен учител specialist teacher; стручно усовршување specialized training; стручно училиште technical college; стручно мислење expert opinion

стручњак -ци *m* expert, specialist

стручка *f* **1** scraper (*usu. for dough*) **2** *see* струганица **3** (*usu. pl*) scraps (*of dough*)

стрча *pf* **I** to <start to> run **II – се** to flock, swarm; се стрчаа децата the children came running

стрчи *impf* **1** to project, protrude, stick (jut) out; (*нагоре*) to stick up *intrans.*; (*за коса*) to stand on end, bristle *intrans.* **2** to tower, rise (*од – over/above*); карпите стрчеа над морето the cliffs towered above the sea **3** *fig.* to stand out; тој стрчи меѓу другарите he stands out among his friends

стрче (се) *pf* стрчна (се) *aor. see* стрча (се)

стрчнува (се) *impf of* стрчне (се), *see* стрчува (се)

стрчува (се) *impf of* стрча (се)

стршел -шли *m see* стршен

стршен -шни *m* **1** *Zool.* (Vespa crabro) hornet **2** *fig.* frisky child, *colloq.* scamp

студ *m* cold <weather>; се тресе од студ to shiver with cold; ❏ камен пука од студ it's bitterly cold; сув студ black frost

студен¹ *adj* cold; cool, chilly; frigid; студен појас frigid zone; студен бран cold spell; cold front; ❏ ме облеа студена пот I broke out in a cold sweat; студено оружје cold steel; студен пречек cool reception

студен² -дна *adj f.p. see* студен

студенец -нци *m* well; spring

студеникав *adj* cool, chilly

студенило *n see* студенина

студенина *f* cold, coldness; frigidity; bleakness; coolness; умре од студенина to die of cold; пречека некого со студенина to receive coolly

студенокро́вен -вна *adj Zool.* cold-blooded

студеност *f see* студенина

студе́нт *m* <university> student, undergraduate; вонреден студент external student; part-time student; редовен студент full-time student; студент по право law student

студе́нтка *f* (*fem. form*) *see* студент

студе́нтски *adj* student's; student; студентски дом hall of residence, *Am.* dormitory; студентска задруга student union

студе́нтство *n* **1** the student body **2** student life, student days

студи *impf impers.* to be cold; денеска ќе студи it will be cold today; многу ми студи I'm freezing

студија -ии *f* **1** study, scholarly work **2** study, sketch **3** (*only pl*) studies, learning

студио *n* **1** <artist's or photographer's> studio **2** art school **3** <broadcasting> studio

студио́зен -зна *adj* painstaking; studious; studied, purposeful

студи́ра *impf* to study *trans. & intrans.*

ступка *pf* **1** (*за срце*) to start racing **2** (*со нозе*) to begin stamping one's feet

ступоти *pf* to start tramping (stamping)

ступотува *impf of* ступоти

стурен *adj* fruitful

стури се *pf* to bear (*fruit*) abundantly

стурува се *impf of* стури се

стутка *pf* **I 1** to crumple *trans.*, crush **2** to pull in; to stoop *trans.*; ја стуткал главата he pulled his head in **II – се 1** to crumple, crease *intrans.* **2** to cower

стуткан *pt & adj* **1** crumpled, creased; стуткани панталони creased trousers **2** wrapped up, enveloped; стуткан во шинела wrapped in an overcoat **3** clumsy, awkward; confused, perplexed

стуткува (се) *impf of* стутка (се)

стутулен *adj see* стуткан 2

стутули (се) *pf see* стутка (се) I 2, II 2

стуфка (се) *pf* to start worrying, fretting

стушен *adj* **1** cloudy, overcast **2** *fig.* frowning, scowling, sullen; dejected

стушеност *f* gloom; dullness; *fig.* sullenness

стуши се *pf* **1** to turn cloudy, cloud over; се стуши небото the sky clouded over **2** *fig.* to knit one's brows, frown; to become gloomy (dejected)

стушува се *impf of* стуши се

скелави *pf see* окелави

субаша *m arch.* police superintendent (*in Ottoman Turkey*)

субвенција -ии *f* subsidy

субвенционира *pf & impf* to subsidize

субверзивен -вна *adj* subversive

субверзија -ии *f* subversion

субјект *m* **1** *Philos.* subject, ego, self **2** individual, character **3** *Leg., Med.* subject **4** *Gram.* (*подмет*) subject

субјектен -тна *adj Gram.* subject *attrib.*; субјектна реченица subject clause;

субјективен -вна *adj* subjective; субјективна оценка subjective assessment

субјективизам -змот *m* **1** *Philos.* subjectivism **2** subjectivity

субјективист *m Philos.* subjectivist

субјективистички *adj Philos.* subjectivist *attrib.*

субјективност *f* subjectivity

сублимат *m Chem.* sublimate

сублимација *f Chem.* sublimation

сублимен -мна *adj* sublime

сублимира *pf & impf Chem.* to sublimate, sublime *trans.*; to sublime *intrans.*

субординација *f* subordination

сув *adj* **1** dry; arid; stale; суви сливи prunes; сувó грозје raisins; sultanas; суво овошје dried fruit<s>; суво месо smoked meat; ❑ по сув пат (по суво) by land, overland; сув како барут as dry as tinder; сув леб stale bread; сува храна picnic lunch, cold meal; сув студ black frost; остане сув to receive nothing; покрај сувото и суровото гори *prov.* the rain falls on the just and unjust; сува пола риба не јаде *prov.* no sweet without sweat **2** dry, withered; сува гранка dead branch **3** *fig.* lean, thin, spare; slight **4** *fig.* laconic, arid; cold, dry; сув пречек cool reception; cold shoulder; сув стил dry style **5** *fig.* pure; сувó злато pure gold **6** (*as noun*) dry place; dry land; излезе на суво to go ashore; ❑ како риба на суво like a fish out of water

суварак -ци *m* dead wood; dry twigs; kindling

суварка *f* dead wood; dry twig<s>; kindling

сувенир *m* souvenir, keepsake

суверен¹ *m* sovereign, ruler

суверен² *adj* sovereign; supreme; суверена држава sovereign state; суверена волја supreme will; суверени права sovereign rights

суверенитет *m* sovereignty

сувереност *f* sovereignty

сувикав *adj dim. of* сув 3; сувикаво дете skinny child

сувичок -чка *adj dim. of* сув 1 (*за човек*) skinny, lean, slight **2** dryish

суводолица *f* dry valley/gorge

сувоземен -мна *adj* land *attrib.*; overland; сувоземен пат overland route; сувоземна граница land border; *Zool.* сувоземно животно terrestrial animal; сувоземна војска land forces, ground troops

сувосидица *f* dry-stone wall

сувомесен -сна *adj* delicatessen *attrib.*; сувомесни производи delicatessen, *Austral., N.Z.* smallgoods

сувомразица *f* black frost; black ice

сувопарен -рна *adj* dry, arid, dull; laconic

сувост *f* dryness; aridity

сувота *f* dryness; aridity

сувотија *f* **1** dryness; aridity **2** *fig.* hard times; poverty, penury

сувотува *impf* to live frugally, lead a frugal life

сугаре *n* (*за јагне*) late-born suckling; *fig.* baby; latecomer, straggler

сугарен -рна *adj* sucking; baby *attrib.*; јагне сугарно sucking lamb; ❑ сугарен Велигден late Easter

сугари се *impf dial. see* сугурчи се

сугерира *pf & impf* to suggest

сугестивен -вна *adj* suggestive; *Psychol.* hypnotic; сугестивно прашање leading question

сугестија -ии *f* suggestion; influencing; assertion; *Psychol.* hypnosis; тој е под сугестија he is under hypnosis; лекување со сугестија hypnotherapy

суградица *f* fine hail; sleet

сугреб *m* (*usu. pl*) **1** dug-up earth (*as by an animal*) **2** hives, nettle rash, *Med.* urticaria; prurigo

сугурен *adj* bent, stooped

сугурец -рци *m* **1** (*usu. pl*) dirt **2** small lumps of dough (*which form on the skin during kneading*) **3** tangled thread

сугурчи се *impf* (*of thread*) to get tangled, tangle *intrans.*

суд *m* **1** court <of law>; law-court; суд на честа court of honour; граѓански суд civil court; истражен суд court of inquiry; суд за прекршоци magistrate's court; воен суд court martial; покана за на суд summons, subpoena; повика на суд to summon to court; тужи некого на суд to take s.o. to court; ❑ страшниот суд the Last Judgement **2** trial; legal proceedings; оди на суд to go to court **3** opinion, estimation; judgement; discretion; судот на критиката critical opinion; судот на публиката public opinion

Судан *m* Sudan

Суданец -нци *m* Sudanese

Суданка *f* (*fem. form*) *see* Суданец

судански *adj* Sudanese

судба *f see* судбина

судбина *f* fate, destiny; fortune; ❑ игра на судбината a whim of fate; на произвол на судбината at the mercy of fate; си ја предизвикува судбината to tempt fate; му ја запечатува судбината на некого to seal s.o.'s fate, sound the <death> knell of; се помирува со судбината to resign o.s. to one's fate

судбински *adj* of fate (destiny); fateful; судбински пријател companion in misfortune; судбинско прашање fateful question

судбоносен -сна *adj* fateful, ominous, portentous; crucial

суден¹ *pt* **1** foreordained, decided by fate; тоа му било судено that was his destiny **2** (*as noun*) *n* destiny

суден² -дна *adj* judgement *attrib.*; судни маки great suffering; судниот ден Day of Judgement, Doomsday; day of reckoning

суди *impf* **I** **1** to judge (*a case*); to try **2** to sue **3** *Sport.* to referee; to umpire; to adjudicate; суди натпревар to referee a match **4** *colloq.* to berate, scold **5** *fig.* to judge, pass judgement; to stand in judgement; судејќи по фустанот judging by her dress; суди по изгледот to judge by appearances **II** – се to go to court; јас ќе се судам со него I am going to sue him; со богат не суди се, со рогат не боди се *prov.* be not bold with your biggers and betters

судија -ии *m* **1** judge; magistrate; судија на окружен суд district magistrate; мировен судија Justice of the Peace, JP **2** *Sport.* umpire; referee; помошен судија linesman

судилиште *n see* суд 1

судир *m* **1** collision; crash; судир на возови train crash; директен судир head-on collision **2** conflict; clash; воен судир military conflict; skirmish; <во>оружен судир armed conflict; дојде во судир to come into conflict (*co – with*)

судира се *impf of* судри се

судиски *adj* judge's

судник -ци *m arch. see* судија

судница *f* court<room>

судри се *pf* to collide (*co – with*); to run (bump) into, encounter; to clash with; to bump into each other; се судри со тешкотии to run into difficulties

судрува се *impf see* судира се

судски *adj* court *attrib.*; judicial; forensic; по судски пат by legal action, through the courts; судска медицина forensic medicine; судски извршител bailiff; officer of the court; sheriff; судски писар clerk of the court; судски процес legal proceedings, lawsuit, case; trial; судски трошоци costs <of an action>; судска пракса legal practice

судство *n* **1** judiciary, judicial system; legal officers; the courts **2** profession/position of a judge; judge's term of office

суеверен -рна *adj* superstitious

суеверец -рци *m* superstitious person

суеверие *n* superstition

суеверје *n* & **суеверство** *n see* суеверие

суета *f* **1** bustle, flurry, ado; суетата на градот the hustle and bustle of the city **2** vanity, conceit

суетен -тна *adj* vain; суетен човек vain person; суетна надеж vain hope

суетност *f* vanity

Суец *m* Suez

суецки *adj* Suez *attrib.*; Суецки Канал Suez Canal

сужен -жни *m* prisoner; slave

сузбива *impf of* сузбие

сузбие *pf* сузби *aor.* to eradicate, stamp out

сузбивање *n* eradication, elimination; борба за сузбивање на болест struggle to stamp out disease

суздаде се *pf* to appear in the distance, arise

суинг -зи *m* dandy

суйта *f Mus.* suite; балетска суита ballet suite

суйтен -тна *adj* suite *attrib.*

сук *m* thick thread (*made up of many strands*)

сука *impf see* суче

сукалка *f see* сукало

сукало *n* rolling-pin

сукано *n see* сучено

сукар *m* cable; thick chain

сукнар *m* maker/vendor of woollen cloth

сукнарство *n* manufacture of woollen cloth

сукнен *adj* woollen; broadcloth *attrib.*; felt *attrib.*; сукнени панталони woollen trousers

сукно *n* woollen cloth; (*фино*) broadcloth; (*грубо*) felt

сукрвица *f Med.* sanies; ichor

сукрвичав *adj Med.* sanies *attrib.*; ichorous; сукрвичава течност watery discharge

сукцесивен -вна *adj* successive

суложи *pf* **1** to lay down (*arms*) **2** *fig.* to fell, spread-eagle **3** to spread out *trans.*

суложува *impf of* суложи

султан *m* sultan

султана *f* sultana (*lady of sultan's harem*)

султанáт *m* sultanate

султанка *f see* султана

султанов *adj* sultan's; султановата ќерка the Sultan's daughter

султански *adj* sultan's; султански ферман Sultan's edict, firman

сулудничав *adj* foolish; crazy

сулфамúд *m Med.* (*usu. pl*) sulphanilamide; sulpha drug

сулфáт *m Chem.* sulphate; натриумов сулфат sodium sulphate; Glauber salt

сулфатијазóл *m Med.* sulphathiazole

сулфúд *m Chem.* sulphide; сребрен сулфид silver sulphide, argentite

сулфúт *m Chem.* sulphite; натриумов сулфит sodium sulphite

сулфур *m Chem.* sulphur, *arch.* brimstone

сулфурводород *m Chem.* hydrogen sulphide

сулфурдиоксид *m Chem.* sulphur dioxide

сулфурен -рна *adj* sulphur *attrib.*; sulphuric; сулфурна киселина sulphuric acid

сулфурест *adj* sulphureous; sulphurous; сулфуреста киселина sulphurous acid

сум *impf pres.* си, е, сме, сте, се; *past pt active* бил to be

сума[1] *f* sum, amount; општата сума sum (grand) total; ❑ сума сумáрум all in all

сума[2] *adv* a lot of, lots of; сума пари a tidy sum; сума луѓе lots of people

сумален -лна *adj see* сумалочен

сумалочен -чна *adj* smallish, shortish, (*за жена*) petite

сумарен -рна *adj* **1** total, sum; сумарен резултат sum total **2** summary; сумарен преглед summary review

сумарно *adv* in total; summarily

суми *pf* **I 1** to think (*дека – that*); to think of **2** to notice; не те сумив кога си дошол I did not hear you arrive **II** – **се** (*with dat.*) to occur to s.o., cross s.o.'s mind

сумúра *pf* & *impf* **1** to count (add) up, tally **2** to sum up, summarize

сумица & **сумичка** *f dim. of* сума[1]

сумпор *m see* сулфур

сумрак *m see* самрак

сумрачен -чна *adj see* самрачен

сумти *impf* to breathe heavily <and noisily> through the nose; to snort

сумува *impf of* суми

сунѓер *m* **1** *Zool.* (Euspongia officinalis) sponge **2** <bath *etc.*> sponge; <blackboard> duster

сунѓерлив *adj* spongy

сунѓерлија *adj indecl. f.p.* foaming, seething

сунѓерче *n dim. of* сунѓер

сунет *m Islam* circumcision

сунизок -ска *adj* (*за човек*) rather short, shortish; (*за куќа*) rather low

суп *m Zool.* (Gyps fulvus) griffon vulture

супа *f* soup; broth; пилешка супа chicken soup

супен *adj* soup *attrib.*; супена лажица soup-spoon; tablespoon

суперио́рен -рна *adj* superior

суперио́рност *f* superiority

суперлати́в *m Gram.* superlative

суперлати́вен -вна *adj Gram., fig.* superlative

перо́ксид *m Chem.* peroxide

суперреви́зија -ии *f* **1** double check **2** *Print.* final proofreading

суперфосфа́т *m Chem.* superphosphate

суперфосфа́тен -тна *adj* superphosphate *attrib.*; суперфосфатно ѓубре superphosphate fertilizer

супица & **супичка** *f dim. of* супа

супле́нт *m* secondary-school teacher (*who has not yet passed the state examination*); trainee teacher; teaching assistant

супле́нтка *f* (*fem. form*) *see* суплент

супле́нтски *adj* trainee teacher's

суплете *pf f.p.* to plait

супра́ва[1] *f* order, tidiness

суправа[2] *impf of* справи

суправи *pf* **1** to tidy up **2** *fig.* to kill, get rid of, *colloq.* fix, do in

супрашка *f* hot ashes

супстанти́в *m Gram.* substantive, noun

супстанти́вен -вна *adj* substantival

супстантиви́ра *pf & impf* to substantivize

супста́нца *f see* супстанција

супстанци́ја *f* substance

супстанција́лен -лна *adj* substantial

супстра́т *m* substratum

супти́лен -лна *adj* subtle

суптилност *f* subtlety

суптро́пи *pl* subtropics

суптро́пски *adj* subtropical; суптропска клима subtropical climate

сур *adj* **1** light-grey, ashen; сура нишевка type of dark-red grape **2** *fig.* sombre; суро лице sombre expression

сура́т *m colloq.* face, *sl.* mug; expression; убав сурат pretty face; ❑ има сурат да . . . to have the nerve (gall, cheek, hide) to . . .

сурди́на *f Mus.* mute, sordino; под сурдина with muted strings, with a mute on; *fig.* under one's breath; quietly

сурди́са *pf colloq.* **I 1** to imprison; to banish, exile **2** to purge, administer a laxative to **II – се** to purge o.s., take a laxative

сурдисува (се) *impf of* сурдиса (се)

суре́дба *f* **1** well-appointed house/office **2** furnishings; household appliances; office equipment

суре́ди *pf* **1** to tidy up, put in order; to fix up, decorate; to adjust, adapt *trans.*; суреди нешто по нечиј вкус to adapt s.th. to s.o.'s taste **2** *fig.* to deal with, sort out, fix; јас ќе го суредам него I'll see to him **3** *fig.* to eat <up>, *colloq.* clean up, polish off; го суредија сиот леб they polished off the whole loaf

суредува *impf of* суреди

сури́ја -ии *f colloq.* <large> herd, pack, flock, rabble, mob; сурија деца crowd of children

Сурина́м<е> *n* Surinam

Сурина́мец -мци *m* person from Surinam, Surinamese, Surinamer

Сурина́мка *f* (*fem. form*) *see* Суринамец

сурина́мски *adj* Surinamese, Surinam *attrib.*

сурка *f* grey cow/goat, etc.

сурла[1] *f* **1** trunk; сурлата на слонот elephant's trunk **2** *pejor.* snout, big nose

сурла[2] *f Mus. see* зурла

сурлари *pl Zool.* Proboscidea

сурнопарно *adv* superficially, hastily, shoddily; ја сврши работата сурнопарно he made a bad job of it

суров *adj* **1** raw, uncooked; unseasoned; untreated; crude; coarse; сурово месо raw meat; сурова кожа rawhide; сурова нафта crude oil; сурово железо pig-iron; сурови дрва damp timber; green timber; ❑ пишало и суво и сурово од него everyone is fed up with him; сурова суровица, весела годиница! сурова година! Happy New Year! (*traditional form of New Year greeting*) **2** stern, severe, austere; сурово лице stern expression; сурово воспитание strict upbringing **3** harsh, inclement; сурова зима severe winter; сурова клима harsh climate **4** *dial.* sick, ill

суровар *m* (*usu. pl*) *see* бабар, василичар

суровина *f* raw material

суровински *adj* raw-material *attrib.*; суровинска база source of raw material; raw-material base

суровица *f* **1** green firewood **2** cudgel, club, bludgeon **3** *fig.* lanky person, *colloq.* beanpole **4** *see* суров 1

суровост *f* sternness; crudeness; rudeness; harshness

сурога́т *m* surrogate; сурогат на шеќер sugar substitute

суртук -ци *m colloq.* **1** vagabond **2** good-for-nothing

сурутка *f* whey

су́ршка *f* maslin (*mixture of wheat and rye*)

сусам *m Bot.* (Sesamum indicum) sesame, gingili

сусамка *f see* сусамче

сусамов *adj* sesame *attrib.*; сусамово масло sesame oil, gingili

сусамче *n* sesame bar; sesame snap

сусвати се *pf* to become related by marriage

сусватува се *impf of* сусвати се

сусерка *f Bot.* (Marrubium peregrinum) <white> horehound

суспенди́ра *pf & impf* to suspend

суспенди́ран *pt* suspended; суспендиран играч suspended player

суспензи́вен -вна *adj* suspensive, suspension *attrib.*

суспензи́ја -ии *f* suspension

сутере́н *m* basement room/flat

сутере́нски *adj* basement *attrib.*; сутеренска просторија basement room

сутина *impf of* сутне

сутли́јач & **сутли́јаш** *f* rice pudding

сутне *pf* сутна *aor.* to win, gain

суфикс *m Gram.* suffix

суфиксен -сна *adj Gram.* suffixal; suffixed

суфици́т *m* surplus

суфицита́рен -рна & **суфици́тен** -тна *adj* surplus; суфицитарни <факултетски> кадри surplus graduates

суфлер *m* **1** <theatre> prompter **2** *fig.* (*поткажувач*) prompter; informer

суфлерка *f* (*fem. form*) *see* суфлер

суфлерница *f* prompt-box

суфлерски *adj* prompter's; суфлерска куќичка prompt-box

суфле́рство *n* prompting, prompter's work/position

суфли́ра *pf & impf* **1** to act as prompter; (*with dat.*) to prompt (*s.o.*) **2** *fig.* to inform (*за – on/against*), denounce; суфлира на полицијата за некого to denounce s.o. to the police

суче *impf* **I 1** to spin; to twist, twirl, wind *trans.*; суче конци to spin yarn; си ги суче мустаците to twirl one's moustache; ❑ пред него не сукам мустаќ I don't talk big in front of him **2** to roll, roll up, roll out *trans.*; суче ракави to roll up one's sleeves; суче кори to roll dough

сучено *n* pastry (*made of filo*)

сучка *f dial. see* сачка, деланка

сучкоса се *pf* to grow thin, lose weight

сучкосува се *impf of* сучкоса се

суџук -ци *m* **1** savoury dried sausage (*made of mutton or beef*) **2** type of Turkish sweetmeat (*made of grape juice and nuts in the form of a sausage*)

суша[1] *f* drought; од голема суша и на глад благодари се *prov.* beggars can't be choosers

суша[2] *f* land, earth, dry land, mainland

сушална *f see* сушница, сушилница

сушелка *f* dried fruit (*usu. plums, pears, apples*)

сушен[1] *pt* dried; сушени сливи prunes

сушен[2] -шна *adj* dry; drought-stricken; drought-prone

сушец *m* dry snow

суши *impf* **I 1** to dry *trans.*; to dehydrate; to dessicate; (*земјиште и сл.*) to drain *trans.*; (*месо*) to smoke, <dry->cure; суши алишта to dry clothes; суши мочуриште to drain a marsh; суши сено to ted hay; ❑ суши просо на ортома to talk hot air **2** *fig.* to cause to lose weight; to make thin; болеста сè повеќе го сушеше the illness was sapping his strength **II – се 1** to dry <out> *intrans.*, get dry **2** *fig.* to waste away

сушилка *f see* сушило

сушилница *f* drying room (chamber); (*за цигли*) drying shed

сушило *n* drier; (*за тутун*) drying rack; (*за облека*) clothes-horse; (*за плодови*) evaporator; *Tech.* drying-oven; (*за храна, Chem.*) desiccator

сушина *f* **1** shelter, shed **2** land, earth, dry land, mainland; ❑ му тера сушина, му спотера сушина he has it in for him

сушица *f* consumption, tuberculosis, TB

сушичав *adj* consumptive, tubercular

сушлак *m see* сушец

сушница *f* drying room

сушност *f* essence

сушт *adj* absolute; the very; itself; сушта вистина the absolute truth; сушта спротивност the very opposite; сушта нежност the soul of kindness

суштерлав *adj* lean, slight, scrawny

суштествен *adj* essential, vital, material; important; fundamental; crucial; суштествен елемент an essential element; суштествена слабост fundamental weakness

суштественост *f* essence; *Leg.* materiality

суштество *n* being, creature; human being

суштествува *impf* to exist; to live; суштествуваат разни погледи there are different schools of thought

суштествување *n* existence; life

суштина *f* essence; влезе во суштината на работата to get to the heart of the matter; ❑ во суштина essentially; at bottom; the bottom line <is>; суштината е во the point is; the fact of the matter is

суштински *adj* essential, vital

сфати *pf* to grasp, understand; to master; сфати лекција to master a lesson

сфатлив *adj* **1** understandable, comprehensible **2** bright, clever, perceptive, astute; сфатливо дете bright child

сфатливост *f* **1** intelligibility **2** perceptivity; acumen; intelligence

сфаќа *impf of* сфати; не ме сфаќај погрешно don't get me wrong

сфаќање *n* **1** understanding **2** view, standpoint; idea; погрешни сфаќања erroneous views; според сопствени сфаќања according to one's own lights

сфера *f* **1** sphere; Земјината сфера the globe **2** *fig.* realm, province; circle<s>; ❑ тоа не спаѓа во мојата сфера that's not my field; сфера на влијание sphere of influence

сферен -рна *adj see* сферичен; сферна геометрија spherical geometry; *Optics* сферна аберација spherical aberration

сферичен -чна *adj* spherical; сферично огледало convex/concave mirror

сфероид *m Geom.* spheroid, ellipsoid of revolution

сфероиден -дна *adj Geom.* spheroidal; сфероидно тело spheroidal body

сфинга *f* sphinx

сфинкс *m see* сфинга

СФРЈ *abbr.* (*Социјалистичка Федеративна Република Југославија*) Socialist Federative Republic of Yugoslavia

схема *f see* шема

схематизам -змот *m see* шематизам

схематизација *f see* шематизација

схематизи́ра *pf & impf see* шематизира

схематичен -чна *adj see* шематичен

схематичност *f see* шематичност

схематски *adj see* шематичен, шематски

сходен -дна *adj literary arch. see* сличен

сходно *adv only in the expression:* сходно со in accordance with; сходно со законот in accordance with the law

схола́стик -ци *m* **1** Scholastic, Schoolman **2** pedant

схоластика *f* **1** Scholasticism **2** scholasticism, pedantry

схоластичар *m see* схоластик

схоластичен -чна *adj* **1** Scholastic **2** scholastic, pedantic

схоластички *see* схоластичен

сцена *f* **1** stage; theatre, the boards **2** scene; episode **3** *fig.* (*скандал*) scene, row; прави сцена to make a scene

сценарио -ија *n* **1** *Film* screenplay, screen version; *Radio, TV* script book **2** scenario **3** cast in order of appearance, dramatis personae

сценарист *m* screenplay-/script-/scenario-writer

сценарија *f* (*rarely pl*) set; scenery, props; general equipment

сценограф *m* scenographer, set designer

сценографија *f* scenography

сценографски *adj* scenographic

сценски *adj* stage *attrib.*, scenic; stageworthy; stageable; dramatic, theatrical; сценски ефект stage effect; сценска импровизација stage improvisation; сценско дело stageworthy/stageable work; сценска уметност dramatic art

сцрви *pf* **I** to cause to blush **II – се** to blush

сцрвува (се) *impf of* срви (се)

сцрка *pf* to start bellowing/bawling/screaming

сцркува *impf of* сцрка

счудовиденост *f* surprise, astonishment; (*непри-јатна*) shock

счудовиди се *pf* to be astonished; (*непријатно*) to be shocked

счудовидува се *impf of* счудовиди се

счудоневиди се *pf see* счудовиди се

счука *pf* to <start to> knock/bang

счукува *impf of* счука

Т

т *abbr.* (*тона*) t.

та *conj* **1** and; and so, so **2** (*adding emphasis*) та дури indeed, even **3** та да in order to, so as to **4** та . . . та . . . now . . . , now . . . ; та ова, та она now this, now that

таа *pron* (*f of* тоj) **1** (*dat.* нejзе, *ú; other cases* неа, *ja*) she; it **2** that

табак[1] -ци *m* **1** sheet (*of paper*); еден табак хартија one sheet of paper **2** *Print.* signature; авторски (печатарски) табак printer's sheet, 16 pages

табак[2] -ци *m* tanner

табакéра *f* cigarette case; tobacco case/pouch; snuffbox

табан *m* sole <of foot/shoe>; рамни табани flat feet

табáна *f* tanning yard/workshop, tannery

табарина *f f.p.* homespun peasant coat

табачки *adj* tanner's; табачки занает tanner's trade

табéла *f* **1** board; scoreboard; timetable; второ место на табелата second place in the table **2** (*листа*) table; graph; chart; schedule; табела на седиментација на урина urine sediment chart

табелáрен -рна *adj* tabular, in tabular form; табеларен преглед tabular summary

табиет *m colloq.* character, nature; custom, habit; има лош табиет he is bad-tempered/ ill-mannered

табиетлиja *adj indecl. colloq.* **1** good, decent **2** capricious, freakish; лимон-табиетлиja crotchety, irritable; табиетлиja човек queer customer, odd fish

табла[1] *f* **1** wide and shallow basket **2** tray, salver **3** hawker's tray

табла[2] *f* **1** blackboard **2** panel, board; plate; табла на кревет headboard; табла на дуќан shop sign, signboard; табла за цртање drawing board; огласна табла notice-board, *Am.* bulletin board; разводна табла switchboard; шоферска табла dashboard, fascia; контролна табла instrument panel; рекламна табла hoarding, *Am.* billboard; табла со осигурувачи fuse-box; шаховска табла chessboard; *Sport.* табла на кош backboard **3** block; табла чоколада bar (block) of chocolate **4** point scored in *tablanet* (*when a player takes all the cards on the table*) **5** backgammon; backgammon board

табланéт *m* kind of card game

таблациja -ии *m colloq.* backgammon player

табле & табленце *n dim. of* табла[1]

таблéта & таблетка *f* (*анче*) tablet, pill, lozenge, pastille

таблица *f* **1** *dim. of* табела **2** *arch.* (*ученичка*) slate **3** table; логаритамска (логаритмична) таблица logarithm <table>; таблица на (за) множење multiplication table **4** регистарска таблица number-plate, *Am.* license plate

табличка *f arch.* (*ученичка*) slate, *see* таблица 2

табло́ *n* **1** tableau (*in theatre*); dumb show; *fig.* astonishment **2** alumni memorial board (*with class photographs*)

табор *m* **1** camp; противничкиот табор the enemy/ opposing camp (*lit. and fig.*); цигански табор gypsy camp **2** *arch.* battalion (*in Ottoman army*)

таборски *adj* camp *attrib.*; таборски живот camp life

табу *n* taboo; табу-тема taboo subject

табуре́т *m* <low> stool

табут *m arch.* bier (*on which Muslims carry a corpse*)

тава *f* **1** large baking tin; frying-pan; уште рибата в море, тавата на оган *prov.* first catch your hare; don't count your chickens before they're hatched **2** casserole dish **3** casserole, stew; турли-тава stew (*dry, with meat, okra and other vegetables*), hotpot

таван *m* **1** (*во просторија*) ceiling **2** (*под покрив*) attic, garret; loft; ❑ до таван sky-high; пробива таван to go through the roof

тавански *adj* ceiling *attrib.*; attic, garret *attrib.*; таванска соба (просторија) attic room; тавански прозорец attic window; skylight

таверна *f* tavern, pub

тавиче *n dim. see* тавче

тавмина *adv colloq.* roughly, approximately; at a guess; *see* тамина

тавминција -ии *m arch.* **1** casual employee **2** assessor

тавминцилак -ци *m arch.* casual employment

тавра *f colloq.* dandified style of dress

таврација -ии *m colloq.* dandy, snappy dresser

таври *impf colloq.* **I** to dress up, doll up *trans.* **II – ce** to put on one's finery; to act/dress like a dandy, deck o.s. out, doll o.s. up

тавтабита *f Zool.* (Cimex lectularius) bedbug

тавтологија *f* tautology

тавтолошки *adj* tautological

тавче *n dim. of* тава; грав на тавче, гравче тавче, тавче гравче bean stew, baked beans

тавчија -ии *m arch.* (*каменорезец*) stonemason

тага *f* sadness; melancholy; sorrow, grief; тага за родниот крај homesickness

тагар *m obs.* **1** drum (*for measuring grain*) **2** *see* тагарче & тагарчик **3** kind of brazier

тагари *impf* **I** to swell *trans.*; to blow (puff) up *trans.* **II – ce 1** to swell *intrans.*; to puff up *intrans.* **2** *fig.* to show off, put on airs

тагарче *n*, **тагарчик** -ци *m* & **тагарчица** *f* kind of leather bag

таговен -вна *adj* (*see* тажен) sad, melancholy, sorrowful; wistful; таговна песна a doleful song; таговни солзи tears of grief

тагува *impf* to be in mourning, mourn, grieve; to be sad; to be homesick; цел ден плаче и тагува all day he cries and grieves; тагува за (по) некого to grieve for s.o.

таен -јна *adj* **1** secret, clandestine; closed; confidential; covert; secretive; тајна седница closed meeting (*for members only*); private/secret session; *Leg.* meeting in camera; тајни преговори secret negotiations; тајна работа undercover work; тајна дејност clandestine activity; ❑ тајната вечера *Rel.* the Last Sup-

per; таен советник privy counsellor; таен агент secret agent; plain-clothes man; тајно гласање secret ballot **2** secret, concealed, hidden; mysterious, cryptic, occult; тајна врата secret door; таен влез secret entrance

тажачка *f* **1** lament, dirge; wail, keen **2** <professional> mourner (wailer), keener **3** grieving, mourning

тажен -жна *adj* **1** sad, melancholy, despondent, sorrowful; wistful; dismal; тажни новости sad news **2** unfortunate, wretched

тажи *impf* **1** *see* тагува; мајка ти тажи по тебе your mother misses you **2** to lament, bewail, bemoan, weep for; плакала и го тажела she kept weeping and wailing for him

тажник -ци *m* <poor> wretch, *see* клетник

тажница *f* (*fem. form*) *see* тажник; *see* клетница

тажновина *f* **1** sadness, sorrow; mourning; тажновина беше му паднала he felt sad **2** (*as adv*) sadly, sorrowfully; woefully; пее тажновина to sing wistfully; to sing a dirge

тажовен -вна *adj see* таговен, тажен 1

тазе *adj indecl. colloq.* (*свеж*) fresh; тазе леб fresh bread; тазе вода fresh water

таи[1] *impf* **I** to hide *trans.*; таи нешто во себе to keep s.th. to o.s. **II – ce** to hide *intrans.*, lie low; to be secretive

таи[2] *impf intrans.* **1** to leak, ooze; to seep out **2** to melt <away>

таим & таин *m arch.* <daily> ration; small loaf (*issued to soldiers*)

таинствен *adj* mysterious, enigmatic, inscrutable, occult; таинствен поглед inscrutable look

таинственост *f* mysteriousness, mystery

таинство *n* mystery

таинција -ии *m arch.* quartermaster

Тајван *m* Taiwan

Тајванец -нци *m* Taiwanese

Тајванка *f* (*fem. form*) *see* Тајванец

тајвански *adj* Taiwanese

тајга *f* taiga

Тајланд *m* Thailand

тајландски *adj* Thai

Тајланѓанец -ни *m* Thai

Тајланѓанка *f* (*fem. form*) *see* Тајланѓанец

тајна *f* **1** secret; тајните на природата the secrets of nature; службена тајна official secret; државна тајна state secret; јавна тајна open secret; деловна тајна trade secret; чува тајна to keep a secret; оддава тајна to reveal a secret; to give the game away; носи тајна в гроб to take a secret to the grave **2** (*сакрамент*) sacrament; света тајна the Holy Sacrament

тајност *f* secrecy; confidentiality; secretiveness; mysteriousness; држи нешто во тајност to keep s.th. secret; во тајност secretly

тајфа *f* gang, band, bunch; guild

тајфун *m* typhoon

так *m* <billiard> cue

така **1** *adv* thus, in that way, like that, so; како што му рече, така постапи he did as he was told; така и мислев just as I thought; тоа е така (толку) просто it is that simple; ❑ така да се рече so to speak; in a manner of speaking; така <ти> е тоа that's the way things go; that's how it is; that's life; така и ти треба it serves you right; исто така also, as well; и така anyway; како така how come? и така натаму (итн.) and so on, et cetera (etc.); и вака и така so-so, not too bad; така нешто sort of; something along those lines; така од прилика roughly, something like; туку така for no reason; *see* тукутака **2** (*in compound conjunctions*) како . . . , така и . . . both . . . and . . . ; тоа беше добро како за нас, така и за вас it was good both for us and for you; така што so that; so; и така and so **3** *part* да, така е yes, that's right; ❏ баш (токму) така! exactly! precisely! **4** *interj.* simply, just; just for the sake of it ; ете, така, излегов да се прошетам I just went out for a walk

такам *m arch.* **1** gear; tackle; kit **2** clothes, suit, *colloq.* gear

такаречи *adv see* тукуречи 1

таква *pron f see* таков

такво *pron n see* таков

таков -ква, -кво, *pl* такви *pron* such, such a . . . ; of that kind; like that; таков човек a man like him; таква убава зграда such a beautiful building; ❏ таков ти е животот (светот)! such is life! такво нешто such a thing, something like that; на таков начин in that way; thus, in such a manner; каков-таков so-so; и такви работи and such like; таков и таков such and such; такви како нас the likes of us; каков таткото, таков и синот *prov.* like father like son

такс *m rare* promise, *see* ветување

такса¹ *f* statutory price; duty, tax; fee, dues; fare; плати такса to pay a tax; испитна такса examination fee; такса за уверение stamp-duty for a certificate

такса² *pf colloq.* **I** to promise *trans.* **II** – ce to commit o.s., promise; *see* вети (се)

таксативен -вна *adj* by name; таксативно набројување classification by name

таксен *adj* duty *attrib.*; таксена марка duty stamp

такси *n* taxi, cab, taxi-cab

таксиметар *m* taximeter

таксир *m arch. see* таксират

таксира¹ *pf & impf* **1** to tax; to assess tax (*on s.th.*); to rate, estimate, value, appraise **2** to affix duty stamps to, put duty stamps on (*a document*)

таксира² *impf* to drive a taxi; to take by taxi

таксират *m colloq.* misfortune; за таксират unfortunately; за мој таксират to my great misfortune

таксиратлија *adj indecl. colloq.* unfortunate

таксува (се) *impf of* такса (се), *see* ветува (се)

таксување *n colloq. see* ветување; од таксување куќа не се расипува *prov.* promises are like pie-crust, made to be broken

таксувачка *f see* таксување

такт *m* **1** *Мus.* (*ритмичка мерка*) measure; time; (*раздел во пишувана музика*) bar; дводелен такт common time; троделен такт triple time; удира такт to beat time; пее/игра по такт to sing/dance in time **2** *Mus.* (*редење на рамномерни движења*) rhythm, tempo, beat; ❏ вади од такт to throw s.o. off his balance; to put s.o. off his stride/stroke **3** *fig.* tact; има такт to be tactful

тактизира *impf* to use subtle tactics

тактика *f* tactics

тактира *impf* to keep/beat time

тактичар *m* **1** tactician **2** *colloq.* tactful person

тактичен -чна *adj* tactful

тактички *adj* tactical; тактичка грешка tactical error

тактички & тактично *adv* tactfully

тактичност *f* tactfulness, tact

такуѓере *adv* (*исто така*) also

такшава (се) *impf of* такса (се), *see* таксува (се)

талаз *m arch., colloq.* wave, *see* талас

таламбас *m* kettledrum

талас *m see* бран

таласам *m colloq.* goblin, hobgoblin, bogy, bogle; ghost

талент *m* talent; gift; талент за музика talent for music; тој е вистински талент he is very gifted

талентиран *adj* talented, gifted; талентиран писател talented writer

талер *m* wooden plate

талерче *n dim. of* талер

талига *f see* кочија

талисман *m* talisman, amulet, charm

талк *m* talc; talcum powder

талка *impf* to wander, rove, roam about; jac сум талкал по друмови десет години I have been on the road for ten years

талмуд *m* the Talmud

талне *pf* тална *aor.* to wander off/away; to drift off/away

талнува *impf of* талне

талог -зи *m* dregs (*also fig.*); sediment, deposit; sludge; *Chem.* precipitate; талог од кафе coffee grounds; талог од песок deposit of sand; талог на (од) општеството the dregs of society

таложи *pf* **I** to deposit **II** – ce to pile up, accumulate *intrans.*; to settle *intrans.*

талон *m* **1** counterfoil, stub (*of a ticket*) **2** *Comm.* talon **3** (*во карти*) talon, stock

талпа *f* thick board, plank, beam

таљувче *n dim. dial. see* талерче

таљур *m dial. see* талер

тамавќар *m colloq. see* тамаќар

тамам *adv colloq.* just, exactly, precisely; just right; тамам на полноќ exactly at midnight; дојде дома тамам кога вечеравме he arrived just as we were having supper; чевлите ми се тамам the shoes fit me perfectly; ❏ тамам работа! *iron.* not likely!

таман *adv colloq. see* токму

тамаќар *m colloq.* skinflint; *Am.* tightwad

тамаќарка *f* (*fem. form*) *see* тамаќар

тамбур *m* drum, tambour

тамбура *f* tamboura, oriental mandolin

тамбураш *m* tamboura player

тамбурашки *adj* tamboura, mandolin *attrib.*; тамбурашки оркестар mandolin orchestra

тамбурица *f hур. of* тамбура; тамбурице, денгубице *prov.* time spent in vice or folly is doubly lost

тамина *adv colloq.* roughly, round about; (*usu. with the prep no, less often на*) по (на) тамина at random, by chance

тамо & тамока *adv dial. see* таму

тамошен -шна *adj* of that place, local; тамошни обичаи local customs

тампо́н *m* **1** *Med.* tampon, wad, swab; ❏ тампон држава/зона buffer state/zone **2** stamp pad, ink-pad

тампони́ра *pf & impf* **1** *Med.* to tampon, wad, swab **2** to plug/block/cork <up>

таму *adv* **1** there; over there; ❏ ваму-таму here and there; не е ни ваму ни таму he doesn't know whether he's coming or going **2** (*as emphatic part.*) *colloq.* дај таму нешто, што и да било! give us whatever you have!

тан *m* sesame paste

тана́лва *f* halva

тана́ника *impf colloq.* to hum

тангар-мангар *interj see* тандар-мандар

та́нгенс *m Math.* tangent

танге́нта *f Math.* tangent

танге́нтен -тна *adj* tangential; contact *attrib.*

танги́ра *impf* **1** to touch *trans.* **2** to concern; тоа тебе воопшто не те тангира that's none of your business

танго *n* tango

тандар-мандар & **тандара-мандара** *interj* nonsense!

танец -нци *m colloq.* (*оро*) dance; води (трга) танец to lead a dance

Танзаниец -ијци *m* Tanzanian

Танзанија *f* Tanzania

Танзанијка *f* (*fem. form*) *see* Танзаниец

танзаниски *adj* Tanzanian

танин *m* tannin

танкер *m* tanker (*ship or railway wagon*); танкер за нафта oil tanker

танки́ра *pf & impf* **I** to load (*a tanker*) with oil **II – се** *colloq.* to get drunk (tanked up)

танко *adv* **1** thin, thinly; finely; танко насече нешто to cut s.th. thin; танко намачка to spread thin<ly> *trans.*; танко преде 1. to spin finely 2. ❏ to go into great detail **2** in a high-pitched/thin voice; танко пее to sing in a high-pitched voice; танко свири 1. to play softly and at a high pitch 2. ❏ to have a hard time

танковрат *adj* slim-necked

танколик *adj* (*of hay*) fine

танконог *adj* thin-legged

танкост *f* **1** thinness; fineness; slimness, slenderness **2** delicacy, subtlety **3** fine point; minute detail

танкотија *f* thinness, slimness

танок -нка *adj* **1** thin; fine; танка хартија thin/fine paper; танок слој thin layer; танок фустан light dress; *Anat.* танко црево small intestine; ❏ каде е <нај>тенко, таму се кине a chain is as strong as its weakest link; тука сум најтанок I'll bet you anything **2** thin; weak; watery; rarefied; танко млеко thin milk; танки облаци light (wispy, airy) clouds **3** high<-pitched>, thin; танок глас thin voice; танко свиркање high-pitched whistle **4** slim, slender; танка половина slim waist **5** *fig.* keen; discriminating; танок слух keen ear; танок вкус discriminating taste **6** *fig.* subtle, fine, nice; delicate; tenuous; танка разлика subtle distinction; најтанки детали minutest details

тантал *m Chem.* tantalum

тантела *f* lace; бриселска тантела Brussels lace (*pillow lace*); венецијанска тантела Venetian lace (*point lace*)

тантелен *adj* lace *attrib.*; тантелена блуза lace blouse; тантелена завеса lace curtain

тантур *m Bot. see* кантарион

танур *m dial. see* тарун

танц *m* dance; модерен танц modern dance

танцмајстор *m* dancing teacher

танцов *adj* dance *attrib.*; танцова музика dance music

танцува *impf* to dance

танцувач *m* dancer

танцувачка *f* (*fem. form*) *see* танцувач

танчар *m see* танцувач

танчарија -ии *f see* танчарка

танчарка *f* (*fem. form*) *see* танчар

танчи *pf* **I** **1** to make thin/thinner; to hammer thin; to beat out **2** *fig.* to refine, polish **3** *fig.* to go into detail; to split hairs; ти многу ја танчиш you're going into too much detail **II – се** **1** to get thin/thinner; (*за облека и сл.*) to wear thin *intrans.*; му се танчат лактовите на палтото his jacket is wearing thin at the elbows **2** *fig.* to become stretched; правината се танчи, ама не се кине *prov.* truth and oil are ever above

тап *adj* **1** blunt, dull; тап нож blunt knife; тап нос flat (broad) nose **2** *fig.* dull, muffled; тап глас hollow voice; тапа болка dull ache; тап слух poor hearing, dull ear **3** *fig.* obtuse, stupid, slow, dull; тап ум slow wit; тап човек dullard; тап ученик dunce; тап поглед vacant expression **4** *Math.* obtuse; тап агол an obtuse angle

тапа *f* **1** stopper, cork **2** cork bullet (*for toy pistol*) **3** *fig.* dullard; ❏ глуп како тапа as thick as two short planks; прост како тапа boorish, common as muck **4** *fig. colloq.* (*as adj*) plastered, sloshed

тапан *m* <large> drum; ❏ се надул како еѓупски тапан he is puffed up like a turkey-cock; he is throwing his weight around; кога ќе се фати сиромавиот на оро, ќе се скине тапанот *prov.* the poor suffer all the wrong

тапанар *m* **1** drummer **2** *fig.* dullard; boor

тапанарски *adj* drummer's

тапанче *n* **1** *dim. of* тапан **2** *Anat.* eardrum

тапаци́ра *pf & impf* **1** (*ѕидови*) to <wall>paper, *see* тапетира **2** (*мебел*) to upholster

тапе́т *m* **1** <green> tablecloth on conference table, green baize; ❏ стави на тапет to table (bring up) s.th. for discussion; to carpet s.o. **2** wallpaper; пластични тапети fabric wallcoverings; самолепливи тапети prepasted wallpaper

тапета́р *m* **1** (*на ѕидови*) paper-hanger, decorator **2** (*на мебел*) upholsterer

тапета́рски *adj* paper-hanger's, decorator's; upholsterer's; тапетарска работилница paper-hanger's workshop

тапети́ра *pf & impf* to <wall>paper; to upholster

тапеци́рунг *m* wallpapering; upholstery

тапи *impf* **I** *trans.* to blunt *trans.* **II – се** to get (go) blunt

тапија -ии *f* title-deed

тапир *m Zool.* (*Tapirus*) tapir

тапи́ра *impf* (*коса*) to tease

таписерија -ии *f* **1** tapestry/tapestries, wallcovering<s> **2** tapestry-making (manufacture) **3** wallpapering, paper-hanging

тапка *impf* **I** **1** to stamp (*one's feet*); to walk with heels tapping, patter; тапка со нозете за да се затопли to stamp one's feet to get warm; ❏ тапка на едно место to mark time **2** to tap; тапка некого по рамо to tap s.o. on the shoulder; тапка по маса to rap on a table; тапка тесто to pat dough **3** to tread on, trample <on>, stamp on **4** to cram in; to stamp down; *fig.* to cram, stuff (*s.o.*) (*with food*) **II – се 1** to worry, fret **2** *fig.* to gorge, stuff o.s. (*with food*), guzzle *intrans.*

тапоаголен -лна *adj Math.* obtuse-angled; тапоаголен триаголник obtuse-angled triangle

тапоглав *adj* dull, stupid, thick-headed

тапоглавец -вци *m* dullard, numskull, blockhead, dolt

тапоглавост *f* dullness, stupidity, thick-headedness, slow wit

тапоса *pf colloq.* **I** to slip, give (*a bribe*); тапосај му нешто, ќе те пушти slip him s.th. and he'll let you go **II – се** to get plastered (sloshed)

тапост *f* **1** bluntness **2** dullness **3** *fig.* stupidity, foolishness, obtuseness

тапосува *impf of* тапоса

тапоумен -мна *adj see* тапоглав

тапоумност *f see* тапоглавост

таптиса *pf colloq.* to <begin to> stare (gape)

таптисува *impf of* таптиса

тараба *f* plank (wooden) fence

тарабука *f Mus.* earthenware kettledrum

тарак -ци *m* comb (*for dressing flax*)

тарамбука *f see* тарабука

тарана *f* granular pasta

тарапа́на *f arch.* **1** mint (*where money is coined*) **2** *fig.* large numbers; дојдоа луѓе тарапана lots of people came

таратински *adj in the expression*: оро таратинско ќе игра he will dance to my tune, he will do as I tell him

таратур *m* tzatziki (*cold dish made of yoghurt, chopped cucumber and garlic*)

тарашка *impf see* тарашува

тарашмаалка *f* (*of a woman*) gadabout

тарашува *impf* to search/rummage through; to ransack

тарга *f rare see* тезгере

тарифа *f* **1** rate<s>; tariff; wage-rate; (*за возни карти*) fare<s> **2** <rail/bus, *etc.*> timetable

тарифен -фна *adj* tariff; тарифна ставка tariff rate; тарифен договор tariff agreement; тарифни цени regular charges

тарун *m* **1** round board (*for kneading bread*) **2** round dining-table **3** platter

тас *m* **1** (*во црква*) collection plate **2** <metal> basin, bowl/cup (*for fetching water for washing*) **3** (*послужавник*) tray **4** (*подлошка за чаша и др.*) coaster **5.** (*на вага*) pan **6** *Mus.* ride cymbal, top cymbal

тастер *m* telegraph key

татар & **татарин** -ри *m arch.* **1** messenger; herald; harbinger **2** Tartar

татарка *f* (*fem. form*) *see* татар 2

татарник -ци *m arch.* crossbow

татарски *adj* **1** messenger's **2** Tartar

тате *m hyp. see* тато

татев *adj* dad's; (*as noun*) татеви dad's relatives

татенце *n hyp.* daddy

татин *adj* dad's, daddy's; детенце татино daddy's little boy

таткин *adj f.p.* father's; во таткини скутови in one's father's lap

татко -овци *m* **1** father; *colloq.* dad, daddy; тој е цел како татка си he is just like his father; метне (истера) се на татка си to take after one's father; каков таткото, таков и синот *prov.* like father, like son **2** (*usu. pl*) forefather, ancestor **3** *fig.* originator, initiator; patriarch, father; protector

татков *adj* father's; paternal; таткова куќа, татков дом father's house

татковина *f* **1** homeland, native land, motherland; падне за татковината to die for one's country **2** *see* татковнина

татковински *adj* **1** of the homeland, native **2** patriotic

татковнина *f* inheritance, patrimony

татковски *adj rare* fatherly; paternal; татковски чувства paternal feelings

татковски *adv* paternally, like a father, in a fatherly way; се грижи татковски за мене he looks after me like a father

татковство *n* fatherhood, parenthood, paternity; признае татковство на некое дете to admit paternity for a child; *Leg.* to affiliate a child to s.o.

татли *adj indecl. arch.* sweet

татлија -ии *f* sweetmeat (*small sweet butter cake with sugar icing*)

татнеж *m* rumble, rumbling; (*на топови и сл.*) thunder, roar, boom; (*на тапани и сл.*) drumbeat

татни *impf* to rumble; (*топови и сл.*) to roar, boom; земјата татнеше од експлозии the earth reverberated with explosions

тато *m colloq.* dad, daddy

татони *impf see* татни

татула *f Bot.* (Datura stramonium) thorn-apple, stramonium, *Am.* jimson weed

татче *n hyp.* daddy

тафра *f see* тавра

тафри (се) *impf see* таври (се)

тафт *m* taffeta

тафтен *adj* taffeta *attrib.*; тафтена блуза taffeta blouse

Тахити *pl* Tahiti

Тахиќанец -ни *m* Tahitian

Тахиќанка *f* (*fem. form*) *see* Тахиќанец

тахиќански *adj* Tahitian

Таџик -ици *m* Tajik

Таџикиста́н *m* Tajikistan

таџикиста́нски *adj* Tajik

Таџичка *f* (*fem. form*) *see* Таџик

таџички *adj see* таџикистански

ташак -ци *m* **1** *vulg.* ball<s> **2** clapper; hanging object; *see* маде 1 & 2

ташаклија *adj indecl. vulg.* spunky, husky; *see* мадлест

ТБЦ *abbr.* (*туберкулоза*) ТВ

ТВ *abbr.* (*телевизија*) ТV

твар *m* **1** matter, substance **2** *colloq.* healthy (rosy) complexion; децата немаат твар the children have no colour

таровит *adj* with a healthy complexion, rosy-cheeked

твој, твоја, твое, *pl* твои *pron* **1** your, yours, *arch.* thy, thine; куќата е твоја the house is yours; на твое место in your position, in your shoes; ❏ твое е да . . . it's up to you to . . . **2** (*as noun*) твоето *n* your things; твоите *pl* your family; ❏ нека биде на твоето as you wish; so be it

творба *f* creation, work; литературна/музичка творба literary/musical work

творец -рци *m* **1** creator; author; architect **2** *Rel.* the Creator, our Maker

творечки *adj* creative; творечка работа creative work; творечка сила creative power, creativity

творештво *n* **1** creativity, creative activity **2** creation; works, *oeuvre*; народното творештво popular art; folklore

твори *impf* to create, make; to work creatively

творчество *n arch. literary see* творештво

тврд *adj* **1** hard; tough; тврдо легло hard bed; тврдо месо tough meat; тврдо дрво hardwood; ❏ тврд орев 1. (*за човек*) tough (hard) nut 2. (*за проблем*) hard nut to crack; тврда столица constipation; тврдо срце hard heart; има тврда глава 1. to have a thick skull 2. to be pigheaded; тврд на солзи unfeeling, cold; тврд на уши hard of hearing; тврди согласки hard consonants; тврда рака e he is tight-fisted (hard-fisted); тврда вода hard water **2** firm, solid; тврда состојба solid state **3** *fig.* strong, sound, staunch; firm, steady, unwavering; тврда вера firm faith; тврдо убедување firm conviction; тврд карактер strong character; тврд сон sound sleep; тврда валута hard currency

тврдење *n* **1** assertion, affirmation **2** contention, claim; statement; по тоа прашање има различни тврдења on that question opinions differ

тврди *impf* to maintain, assert, claim; to contend; тврди дека не бил тука he claims that he was not here; тврди решително to assert firmly

тврдина *f* stronghold; bulwark; fortress, citadel

тврдо *adv* stubbornly; staunchly; firmly; heavily; тврдо чекори to tread resolutely; тврдо одговори to reply firmly; тврдо спие to sleep soundly (deeply); тврдо варено јајце hard-boiled egg

тврдоглав *adj* pigheaded, stubborn; headstrong

тврдоглавец -вци *m* mule, pigheaded/headstrong person

тврдоглавост *f* pigheadedness, obstinacy, stubbornness

тврдокорен -рна *adj* **1** (*за плод*) hard **2** *fig.* hardbitten, tough

тврдокорност *f* toughness

тврдокрил & **тврдокрилен** -лна *adj* coleopterous

тврдокрилци *pl Zool.* coleoptera (*sg* coleopteron)

тврдоперки *pl Zool.* (*order of fish*) acanthopterygii (*sg* acanthopterygian)

тврдост *f* hardness; strength, firmness, steadiness; steadfastness

т.е. *abbr.* (*то ест*) that is to say, i.e.

те *pron* (*short acc. form of* ти) you, *arch.* thee; те молам please; I beg you, I beseech you

театар -три *m* theatre; playhouse; ensemble; народен театар National Theatre; куклен театар puppet theatre; оди на театар to go to the theatre

театарски *adj* theatre; театарска претстава theatre performance; театарски персонал theatre staff; театарска публика theatre-going public

театрален -лна *adj* theatrical, dramatic

театро *n arch. see* театар

тебабија *f arch.* retinue

тебдил *m* & *adv arch.* disguised, in disguise, incognito; се сторил тебдил he disguised himself

тебе *pron* (*long form of* ти *for the oblique cases. Used for emphasis with short forms* ми, ме, *and with prepositions*) you, *arch.* thee; тебе те виде he saw *you*; тебе ти даде he gave it to *you*; за тебе 1. for you 2. about you; до тебе near you; по тебе after you

тебека *pron dial. see* тебе

тебешир *m arch. see* креда 2

тевна *f colloq.* peace, quiet, silence; да поразговараме на тевна let's have a quiet chat

тевнадиса се *pf colloq.* to stop work

тевница *f f.p.* prison, jail, *see* темница 2

тег *m* weight; (*на часовник*) bob (*weight on a pendulum*); дигање тегови weight-lifting

тегав *adj* tough, sinewy; тегаво месо tough meat

тегавец *m Bot.* (Plantago) plantain; rib-grass

тегави *impf* **I** to draw (drag) out, drag one's feet; (*при зборување*) to drawl; ја тегави работата he is dragging this matter out **II** – **се 1** (*се протега*) to stretch *intrans.* **2** (*се влече*) to take one's time, dally, dawdle; немој да се тегавиш get a move on! **3** (*се колеба*) to waver, dither

тегавица *f* urge/need to stretch (*one's limbs*)

тегет *adj indecl.* navy blue

тегла *f* jar

тегли *impf* **I 1** to draw, haul, pull; (*со јаже и др.*) to tow; to drag *trans.*; тегли кола to haul a cart; тегли сабја to draw a sword **2** (*за кабел и сл.*) to unwind *trans.* **3** *fig.* to suffer *intrans.*; ние си теглиме we have a hard life **4** *dial.* (*тргнува*) to set off (out); утре теглиме за Куманово tomorrow we set off for Kumanovo **II** – **се** to stretch *intrans.*

теглилен -лна *adj poet.* burdensome; теглилен живот a hard life

теглило & **тегло** *n* suffering, hardship

тегне *impf* **I 1** to stretch *trans.* **2** to pull, drag, haul **3** *rare* (*of cloud, dusk, etc.*) to close in, fall; над Пелистер тегне мрак darkness is falling over Pelister **4** *f.p.* to move/head/walk (*кон, в – towards*) **II** – **се 1** to stretch *intrans.* **2** to dawdle, dally, linger **3** *dial.* to weigh o.s.

тегоба *f* pain; suffering, hardship; тој чувствува тегоби кога дише he feels discomfort when he breathes

тегобен -бна *adj* **1** difficult; burdensome, severe, full of suffering **2** pregnant, expecting, with child

тегобност *f* difficulty; severity; suffering, heaviness of heart

теговен -вна *adj rare see* тегобен

тежа *f literary* gravity; земјината тежа the earth's gravity

тежест *f literary see* тежина

тежи *impf* **1** to weigh *intrans.*; пакетот тежи две кила the parcel weighs two kilos **2** to be heavy; to be a burden (*also fig.; with dat. – on*); ми тежи оваа должност this job is too hard for me

тежина *f* **1** weight; *fig.* burden; тежината на плодот the weight of the fruit; *Phys.* специфична тежина specific gravity; *Leg.* тежината на доказите the weight of the evidence; ❏ има тежина it carries much weight **2** *fig.* suffering, hardship; ache; <degree of> difficulty; severity; тежината на задачата the difficulty of the problem; тежината на казната the severity of the punishment

тежиште *n* **1** centre of gravity **2** *fig.* gravity, significance; essence

тежнее *impf literary rare* to aim/strive/long for

тежок -шка *adj* **1** heavy; (*масивен*) massive; тешка артилерија heavy artillery; тешка индустрија heavy industry; тежок чекор heavy footfall, heavy tread; тој е тежок 60 кг he weighs 60 kg; тешка храна rich/stodgy food; **2** *fig.* heavy, oppressive; тешка миризба overpowering smell; тешки даноци high (*Brit.* swingeing) taxes; тешки мисли gloomy thoughts **3** hard, difficult; onerous; тешки времиња hard times; тешка работа hard work, toil; тешко прашање difficult question **4** *fig.* grave, serious, severe; тешка болест grave illness; тешка грешка serious mistake; тежок злочин serious crime; тешки последици serious consequences; тежок удар severe (*Brit.* swingeing) blow; тешка загуба grave loss; тежок грев deadly sin **5** trying, awkward, difficult (*of character*); тежок човек difficult person; тежок во разговор difficult to talk to **6** *fig.* serious, solid, respectable; тежок граѓанин respectable citizen **7** clumsy, slow, ponderous; тежок од ponderous gait **8** *fig.* strong, potent; тешко вино strong wine; ❏ има тешка рака за мавање to have a strong arm, to command respect **9** *colloq.* (*only f*) тешка pregnant, *see* трудна **10** ❏ тешка ми е главата I have a <splitting> headache; очите му се тешки he can hardly keep his eyes open; среќен е колку што е тежок he has the luck of the devil; со тешко срце with a heavy heart; тешка вода *Chem.* heavy water; тешки метали *Metallurgy* heavy metals; има тешка рака за нешто to be clumsy (heavy-handed) at s.th.; тежок збор harsh word, bitter reproach; тежок пијаница heavy drinker; тешка должност onerous position; тешко дишење heavy (laboured) breathing; panting; тежок сон oppressive dream; restless sleep, tossing and turning; тешка судбина grim fate

теза *f* thesis

тезга & **тезге** *n* **1** (*на пазар*) stand, stall; (*во продавница*) counter; ❏ под тезга under the counter **2** <joiner's/carpenter's> bench **3** *fig.* a second job; има тезга to moonlight, have a job on the side

тезгере *n* wooden litter (*for carrying building materials*)

тей́зам -змот *m* theism

тей́ст *m* theist

теисти́чки *adj* theist *attrib.*, theistic

тей́ко *m dial. see* татко

тек¹ *m* **1** (*на вода*) current **2** (*на река*) course, reach; горниот тек на реката the upper reaches of the river **3** (*за време*) course; во текот на оваа година during (in the course of) this year; во текот на целиот свој живот throughout his life; со текот на времето in due course, eventually **4** (*за процес на извршување*) progress; работите се во тек the work is in progress; ❏ во тек ongoing; in progress; under way; во тек е to be informed (*au courant*) **5** (*правец, развој*) course, direction; измени <свој> тек to change course (direction); тек на мисли train of thought

тек² *adj indecl. colloq.* (*of a number*) odd; тек број odd number; ❏ тек или чифт (*при игра*) odd<s> or even<s>

текар *adv arch.* <once> again

текија -ии *f arch. see* теќе

теклиф *m arch.* **1** invitation; стори теклиф to issue an invitation **2** ceremony, etiquette, protocol; биди без теклиф don't stand on ceremony! ич теклиф не ти фаќам feel free!

теклифи *pf arch.* to invite

теклифсиз *adv arch.* without ceremony; free-and-easy, familiar, unconstrained

текне¹ *n arch.* trough

текне² *pf* текна *aor.* (*only in 3rd p. with dat.*) **1** to occur to, enter s.o.'s mind; to dawn on; ми текна it occurred to me, I remembered; сè што ќе му текне whatever he wants **2** *interj* (*in oral narrative*) ти текна you see, you know; ти текна? do you see? are you with me?

текнефес *adj indecl. arch.* (*of a horse*) short-winded, broken-winded; текнефес коњ *sl. dial.* piper

текнеж *m* fancy, caprice

текнува *impf of* текне

текнувало *n* sensitivity; ingenuity; *in the expression:* има текнувало to be sensitive/bright; нема текнувало to be insensitive/stupid

текст *m* text; одбрани текстови selected readings; текст на песна lyrics <of a song>; текст за опера libretto; ❏ остане без текст to be speechless

текстил *m coll.* fabrics, textiles

текстилен -лна *adj* textile; текстилна фабрика textile mill; текстилни стоки textiles

текстилец -лци *m* textile worker, mill-hand

текстуа́лен -лна *adj* **1** textual; текстуални разлики textual differences **2** (*буквален*) literal, word-for-word

тек-тук *adv* here and there; небото беше украсено тек-тук со бели облаци the sky was dotted with white clouds

текушт *adj* current; present; текушти работи work in progress; current developments; текушта сметка current account; текушта вода running water

тел. *abbr.* (*телефон*) Tel., ph.

телал & **телалин** -ли *m arch.* **1** town crier **2** second-hand dealer

телалка *f arch.* (*fem. form*) *see* телал 2

телалски *adj* town crier's; second-hand dealer's; телалска работа! rubbish!

телар *m dial. see* телал

теле -иња, -лци *n* **1** calf; крава со теле a cow with a calf; ❏ гледа како теле <во шарена врата> to stand agape **2** *fig.* dolt

телевизија *f* television, TV; радио-телевизија radio and TV

телевизиски *adj* television, TV; телевизиски апарат (приемник) TV set; телевизиска емисија television programme (broadcast); телевизиски пренос telecast

телеви́зор *m* television set, *colloq.* telly, the box (*Am.* the tube)

телеграм *m rare see* телеграма

телегра́ма *f* telegram, cable<gram>, *colloq.* wire

телеграф *m* telegraph

телеграфија *f* telegraphy; безжична телеграфија wireless telegraphy

телеграфи́ра *pf* & *impf* to telegraph, cable, *colloq.* wire

телеграфи́ст *m* telegrapher, telegraphist

телеграфи́стка *f* (*fem. form*) *see* телеграфист

телеграфски *adj* telegraphic; telegraph *attrib.*; телеграфски кабел telegraphic cable; телеграфска служба (агенција) news agency; wire service; *fig.* телеграфски стил telegraphic style, *colloq.* telegraphese

телекомуникации *pl* telecommunications

телен *adj* wire *attrib.*; телена мрежа wire netting, *Mil.* barbed wire entanglement; телена ограда wire fence

теленга *f f.p.* (*кочија*) kind of horse-drawn peasant cart

теленгар *m f.p.* cart (wagon) driver

теленце *n dim. of* теле

телеологија *f* teleology

телеолошки *adj* teleological; телеолошки сфаќања teleological concepts

телепат *m* telepathist

телепатија *f* telepathy

телепатски *adj* telepathic

телепринтер *m* teleprinter

телесен -сна *adj* body *attrib.*; bodily, physical, corporeal; corporal; телесна тежина/температура body weight/temperature; телесен недостаток physical handicap; телесно воспитување physical education, PT; телесно уживање sensual pleasure; телесна казна corporal punishment; *Leg.* <тешка> телесна повреда <aggravated> assault and battery, grievous bodily harm

телескоп *m* telescope

телескопски *adj* telescopic

телесно *adv* in body; bodily; physically; corporally; душевно и телесно in body and soul

телефон *m* telephone, phone; по телефон by telephone; over the telephone; стави телефон to install a telephone; викне некого на телефон to <tele>phone s.o.; to call s.o. to the <tele>phone; се јави на телефон to answer the <tele>phone; □ црвен телефон hot line; расипан телефон Chinese whispers

телефонира *pf & impf* to <tele>phone, *colloq.* ring <up>, *Am.* call

телефонист *m* telephone operator, *Brit.* telephonist

телефонистка *f (fem. form) see* телефонист

телефонски *adj* <tele>phone; telephonic; телефонски разговор, претплатник, број, именик telephone conversation, subscriber, number, directory; телефонска врска telephone line; телефонска централа telephone exchange; телефонска говорница telephone box (booth); public telephone; телефонски повик <tele>phone call; меѓународен телефонски повик international call; меѓуградски телефонски повик STD (trunk) call, *Am.* long-distance call

телешки *adj* calf; veal; телешки бут leg of veal; телешко <месо> veal

тели *impf* **I** to give birth to (*a calf*); секоја година кравата ни тели по едно теленце every year our cow gives birth to a calf **II** – **се** to calve *intrans.*; кравата се телеше the cow was calving

тело *n* **1** body; (*труп*) trunk, torso; делови на телото parts of the body; душа сака, ама тело не може the spirit is willing but the flesh is weak; во здраво тело здрав дух a sound mind in a sound body; □ туѓо тело foreign body **2** *Phys., Chem., Math., Astronomy* substance; body; цврсто тело solid substance; небески тела heavenly (celestial) bodies; геометриски тела geometrical bodies **3** corpse, cadaver, dead body **4** (*на кораб*) hull; (*на авион*) fuselage **5** *fig.* staff, body; законодавно тело legislative body; управно тело governing body

телољубец -пци *m arch. literary* sensualist, hedonist

телохранител *m literary* bodyguard

телце *n* **1** *dim. of* тело 1 & 3 **2** (*зрнце*) <blood> corpuscle; бели и црвени крвни телца white and red blood corpuscles, *Med.* leucocytes and erythrocytes

телци *pl of* теле

телчар *m* calf-breeder/-tender

телчарче *n dim. of* телчар

тел -ови *m* **1** *Mus.* string **2** wire; бодлив тел barbed wire **3** *rare* clothes-line **4** (*pl only*) silver lace; tinsel

телоса *pf* (*за невеста*) to decorate (adorn) with silver lace, deck out in tinsel

тема[1] *f poet.* darkness, *see* темница, темнина

тема[2] *f* **1** subject, topic, theme; се оддалечува од темата to stray from the subject, to digress; тема на денот talk of the town; менува тема to change the subject; пишува состав на дадена тема to write an essay on a given topic **2** *Mus.* theme; тема со варијации theme and variations **3** *Gram.* (*основа*) stem, theme

темане *n arch.* Turkish greeting (*bringing the fingers of the right hand to the lips and then to the forehead*); прави (чини) темане to greet in the Turkish manner

тематика *f* subject matter

тематски *adj* thematic; тематска разнообразност thematic variety; *Gram.* тематска самогласка thematic vowel

тембр *m* (*боја на звук, глас*) timbre; мек тембр mellow timbre; резлив тембр harsh timbre

теме *n* **1** crown <of the head>, *Anat.* vertex; *Anat.* sinciput; голо теме bald spot; удри некого по теме to strike s.o. on <the top of> the head; □ ќе падне на теме he'll get the surprise of his life **2** *Math.* apex, vertex; теме на триаголник apex of a triangle; теме на пирамида vertex of a pyramid

темел *m* foundation (*also fig.*); basis; удри темел на зграда to lay the foundations of a building; темелите на новото општество the foundations of the new society; □ од темел from the ground up; урне до темел to raze to the ground

темелен -лна *adj* **1** foundation *attrib.*; basic; темелен камен foundation-stone, corner-stone **2** *fig.* fundamental; thorough, solid; темелно познавање thorough knowledge

темели *impf literary* **1** to found **2** to base (*на – on*)

темелиште *n augm. of* темел

темелница *f literary* counterfoil, stub (*of a money order*)

темелност *f* thoroughness, solidity

темен[1] *adj Anat.* coronal; parietal; sincipital; темена коска parietal bone; темена површина coronal surface

темен[2] -мна *adj* **1** dark; gloomy, murky, dim; темна ноќ dark night; темни зори the small hours; темни облаци dark clouds; □ на темно in the dark; од темно до темно from dawn till dusk; темно стакло tinted glass **2** dark, swarthy; темен тен dark complexion; темна боја dark colour **3** *fig.* sinister;

suspicious; shady; темно минато shady past; темен поглед suspicious look; темни сили dark forces

теменуга & **теменушка** *f Bot. see* темјанушка

темерук -ци & **темерут** *m colloq.* surly fellow

темјан *m* incense, frankincense; кади со темјан to burn incense; to incense; ❑ бега како ѓавол од темјан to avoid like the plague

темјанка *f Bot. poet. see* темјанушка

темјанов *adj* incense *attrib.*; темјанов чад scent of incense, trail of incense

темјановина *f in the expression:* мириса <на> темјановина it smells of incense; *fig.* he is at death's door

темјаноса *pf colloq.* to incense, perfume/fumigate with incense; to burn incense

темјануга *f Bot. see* темјанушка

темјанугав & **темјанужен** -жна *adj* violet; темјанужна боја violet <colour>

темјанушка *f Bot.* **1** (Viola odorata) sweet (garden) violet **2** (Viola altaica, Viola tricolor) pansy; heart's-ease; love-in-idleness

темјанче *n Bot.* (Asarum europaeum) asarabacca

темнее *impf* **I 1** to go dark, darken *intrans.*; небото темнее the sky is going dark; среброто темнее silver gets tarnished **2** to get dark; темнее, денот помина it's getting dark, the day is over **II – се** to show/look/appear/loom dark; нешто се темнееше во далечината something loomed dark in the distance; му се темнее пред очи his vision is clouded; *fig.* he sees red

темник -ци *m* dark place

темникав *adj* rather dark, gloomy, darkish

темнило *n* darkness, gloom

темнина *f* dark<ness> **1** gloom; obscurity; ноќна темнина dark (gloom) of night; по темнина at (by) night; во темнина in the dark<ness>; at (by) night **2** *fig.* ignorance; живее во темнина to live in ignorance

темница *f* **1** darkness; црна темница е it's pitch-dark **2** dungeon; jail, prison

темничав *adj* rather dark, gloomy

темничар *m* **1** jailer, prison warder **2** prisoner, *sl.* jailbird **3** blind man **4** *f.p.* south wind, sirocco

темничарка *f (fem. form) see* темничар 1–3

темничен -чна *adj* prison

темничешки *adv* in the dark; како одиш темничешки? where are you going in the dark?

темничиште *n augm. see* темница

темно *adv* darkly; во собата беше темно it was dark in the room; ме погледна некако темно he gave me a rather sinister look

темно- (*in compounds*) dark-; темнозелен dark-green

темножолт *adj* buff

темнозелен *adj* dark-green, deep-green, bottle-green

темнокрил *adj poet.* with dark wings

темнолик *adj* dark, swarthy

темноок *adj* dark-eyed; темноока девојка dark-eyed maiden

темноса се *pf* to darken *intrans.*

темносив *adj* dark-grey; темносив облак dark-grey cloud

темносин *adj* dark-blue, deep-blue; navy-blue

темнотија *f* <impenetrable> darkness

тѐмноцр̀вен *adj* dark-red; crimson; russet

темпера *f* distemper; tempera; темпера-бои distemper paints

темпераме́нт *m* temperament; spirit, verve; буен темперамент fiery temperament; човек без темперамент person lacking spirit

темпераме́нтен -тна *adj* temperamental; excitable; fervent; темпераментна музика lively music

температу́ра *f* temperature; (*висока*) fever; имам температура I have a temperature; мери некому температура to take s.o.'s temperature

температу́рен -рна *adj* temperature; температурни промени changes in temperature; температурен лист на болен patient's temperature-chart

темпи́ра *pf & impf* **1** to prime (*a bomb*); to set a time-fuse, timing device **2** *fig.* to time, choose a time

темпи́ран *pt* **1** primed, timed to explode (detonate); темпирана бомба time bomb **2** *fig.* well-timed

темпо *n* **1** speed; rate; со брзо темпо briskly, rapidly; успори темпо to slacken the pace; темпо на развиток rate of growth **2** *Mus.* tempo; time

темпора́лен -лна *adj* temporal; *Gram.* темпорални (временски) реченици temporal clauses

тен *m* complexion

тенденција -ии *f* **1** trend, tendency; inclination, leaning, bent; bias; тенденции во уметноста trends in art; има тенденција кон to tend towards; роман со тенденција a tendentious novel **2** purpose, aim; неговите зборови имаа определена тенденција his words had a definite purpose

тенденцио́зен -зна *adj* tendentious; biased; prejudiced; тенденциозна литература tendentious literature; тенденциозни вести biased reports

тенденцио́зност *f* tendentiousness; bias

тендер *m Rail* tender

тенекија -ии *f colloq.* **1** tin, tin plate **2** tin, can; тенекија со петрол a can of petrol (*Am.* gasoline)

тенекиен *adj colloq.* tin; тенекиена конзерва tin can

тенеќе *n see* тенекија

тенеќен *adj see* тенекиен

тенеќеџија -ии *m colloq.* tinsmith

тенеќеџилница *f colloq.* tinsmith's shop

тенеќеџиски *adj colloq.* tinsmith's; тенеќеџиски ножици tinsmith's shears, tinsnips

тенеќеџиство *n colloq.* tinsmith's trade

тенија -ии *f Zool.* (Taenia solium) tapeworm, *Med.* taenia

тенис *m* tennis

тенисер *m* tennis player

тенисе́рка *f (fem. form) see* тенисер

тениски *adj* tennis *attrib.*; тениско игралиште tennis court; тениско првенство tennis championship<s>

тенк *m Mil.* tank

тенки́ст *m Mil.* member of tank crew

тенко *adv see* танко

тенковски *adj* tank; тенковско одделение tank detachment; armoured unit

тенок -нка *adj see* танок

тенор *m Mus.* tenor

теноpи́ст *m* tenor (*singer*)

тенористички *adj* tenor *attrib.*

тенорски *adj* tenor *attrib.*; тенорска партија tenor part; тенорски глас tenor voice

тенџере *n* pot; се истркала тенџерето, си го најде поклопчето *prov.* birds of a feather flock together

тенџерче *n dim. of* тенџере

теозóф *m* theosophist

теозофија *f* theosophy

теозóфски *adj* theosophical

теокрáт *m* theocrat

теократија *f* theocracy

теокрáтски *adj* theocratic; теократска организација на државата theocratic organization of the state

теолóг -зи *m* theologist

теологија *f* theology

теолошки *adj* theological; теолошки студии theological studies; теолошки факултет Faculty of Theology

теорéма *f* theorem; Питагорина теорема Pythagoras' theorem

теоретизúра *impf* to theorize

теоретичар *m* theorist; theoretician; thinker

теоретски[1] *adj* theoretical; теоретска физика theoretical physics

теоретски[2] *adv* theoretically, in theory

теорија -ии *f* theory; теорија на музиката, на литературата theory of music, of literature; теорија на релативитетот theory of relativity; теорија на веројатноста probability theory; ❑ *colloq.* нема теорија not a chance; out of the question

теориски *adj see* теоретски

тепа *impf* **I 1** *trans.* to beat; (*силно*) to thrash; to defeat, *colloq.* lick; на свој терен тие секогаш нè тепаат on their home ground they always beat us; ❑ тепа време to kill time **2** *intrans.* to win; во овој натпревар ние ќе тепаме we're going to win this match **II – се 1** to fight; се тепа со непријателот to fight the enemy bravely

тепаница *f* fight, brawl, fisticuffs

тепач *m* thug, brawler

тепачка *f see* тепаница

тепе *n arch.* summit, tip, top; hillock; rise

тепих -си *m* carpet, rug

тепка[1] *f only in the expression:* од тепка a lucky strike/guess; a shot/leap in the dark

тепка[2] *impf see* тептави

тепсија -ии *f* pan; baking tin; ❑ на тепсија оро ќе игра he will dance to my tune, he will do as I tell him

тепсиче *n dim. of* тепсија

тептав *adj* stuttering

тептави *impf* to stutter, stammer

тептиса *pf colloq.* to waver, slip, lose one's balance

тептисува *impf of* тептиса

тера *impf* **I 1** to drive *trans.*; тера стока to drive cattle; тера кола to drive a car; тера велосипед to ride a bicycle **2** to drive, power, move *trans.*; водата ја тера воденицата the mill is powered by water **3** (*with да*) to force, make; (*with на*) to induce, make; тера некого да работи to make s.o. work; тера некого да чека to keep s.o. waiting; ова вино тера на спиење this wine makes one sleepy; тера некого да полуди to drive s.o. mad; ❑ ни се тера, ни се води he is an awkward customer **4** (*брка*) to drive out *trans.*, expel; тера некого од школо to expel s.o. from school; клин клин тера *prov.* like cures like **5** (*гони*) to chase, pursue; to hunt *trans.*; тера дивеч to hunt game **6** to continue (*trans. and intrans.*); to pursue, carry on

(*with*); нека тера понатаму let him carry on! jac ќе ja терам работата I shall carry on with the job; тера правина to tell (stick to) the truth; ❑ си ja тера работата he goes about his own business; тера инает to be spiteful; to be pigheaded; тера шега со некого to poke fun at s.o.; to pull s.o.'s leg; не тера долго he is at death's door; тера по свое to insist on having one's way **7** to put forth, sprout; тера пупки to bud **8** to carry on, do s.th. to excess; тера живот to live it up **9** to be getting on for, reaching the age of; ja тера четвртата година he is nearly four **10** to develop, grow; тутунот тера добро the tobacco is coming on well **11** (*за пушка*) to carry *intrans.*, have a certain range; оваа пушка тера далеку this gun has a long range **II – се 1** to urge one another on **2** to race *intrans.* **3** (*за животни*) to mate; to be in heat

терапéвт *m* therapist

терапија *f* therapy; физикална терапија physiotherapy; работна терапија occupational therapy

терαписки *adj* therapeutic

терáса *f* **1** (*веранда*) veranda; terrace **2** (*покрив*) porch; terrace roof **3** (*хоризонтални рамнини*) terrace

терасовúден -дна *adj* terraced

терач *m* (*на стока*) herdsman, cattle driver, drover; (*на дивеч*) beater

терачка *f* (*fem. form*) *see* терач

терезија -зии *f* **1** scales; ❑ рака не е терезија it is difficult to be fair **2** *colloq.* (*либела*) spirit level **3** *Astron.* Libra

терен *m* terrain, landscape; ground; territory, area; планински терен mountainous terrain; лизгав терен slippery ground (*also fig.*); фудбалски терен football field; непријателски терен hostile/enemy territory; ❑ заеднички терен common ground; испитува терен to investigate the situation; to see how the land lies; излегува на терен *Sport.* to take to the field; на свој терен е he is in his element; подготвува терен за to set the scene for; теренот е чист the coast is clear

теренец -нци *m* fieldworker; man on the spot

теренски *adj* field *attrib.*; теренска работа fieldwork; (*doctor's*) house calls; теренски проучувања field studies; теренски додаток per diem travel allowance

терзија -ии *m arch.* tailor

терзилак *m arch.* tailor's trade; работи терзилак he works as a tailor

терзиски *adj arch.* tailor's; терзиски ножици tailor's shears

терзиче *n dim. (usu. f.p.) of* терзија

територија -ии *f* territory; територија на град metropolitan area

територијáлен -лна *adj* territorial; територијални води territorial waters; територијални претензии territorial claims; територијална одбрана territorial defence, home reserve, territorial army, home guard, militia

терк *m colloq.* (*дезен, цртеж*) pattern; (*мостра, примерок*) sample

терлик -ци *m arch.* (*usu. pl*) embroidered leather slipper, mule

термален -лна *adj* thermal; термален извор thermal spring; geyser; термална бања spa

термин[1] *m* <technical> term

термин² *m* appointment; appointed (fixed) date; term; time-limit, deadline, closing date; *Leg.* date of trial

терминологија *f* terminology

терминолошки *adj* terminological; терминолошки речник specialized dictionary

термински *adj* urgent; scheduled <for completion by a certain date>

термити *pl Zool.* (Termitidae) termites, white ants

термички *adj* thermal, thermic; термичка струја heat flow; термичка изолација thermal insulation, heat protection

термоген *adj* thermogenic, heat-generating

термогенéза *f* thermogenesis

термодинамика *f* thermodynamics

термодинамички *adj* thermodynamic; термодинамички процес thermodynamic process

термомéтар -три *m* thermometer

термонуклеáрен -рна *adj* thermonuclear; термонуклеарна војна thermonuclear war

термос *m* Thermos <flask>, vacuum flask

термостáт *m* thermostat

термофор *m* hot-water bottle

термоцентрáла *f* thermal power station

терор *m* terrorism, terror; фашистички терор fascist terror; врши терор над населението to terrorize the population

терорѝзам -змот *m* terrorism

терорѝзира *impf* to terrorize

терорѝст *m* terrorist

терористички *adj* terrorist *attrib.*

терорѝстка *f* (*fem. form*) *see* терорист

терпентѝн *m* turpentine

терпентѝнски *adj* turpentine *attrib.*; терпентинско масло oil of turpentine, *colloq.* turps

терсене *colloq.* 1 *adj indecl.* (*of a person*) awkward; difficult, contrary 2 *adv* awkwardly

тертип *m colloq.* habit; му го знам јас тертипот I know his way of doing things

терца *f* 1 *Mus.* (*трет степен од дијатонската скала*) mediant; (*интервал*) third 2 *Fencing* tierce

терцéт *m* trio

терцијáна *f Med.* tertian <fever>

терцијар *m Geol.* Tertiary <Period>; помлад терцијар Pliocene; постар терцијар Palaeocene

терцијáрен -рна *adj* 1 Tertiary; терцијарен слој (пласт) Tertiary layer 2 tertiary; *Med.* терцијарен стадиум tertiary stage (*usu. of syphilis*)

терцѝна *f Literature* terza rima

тесен -сна *adj* 1 narrow; тесна улица narrow street; ❏ тесна победа close win 2 small, cramped, confined; тесен стан small (*colloq.* poky) flat; тесен простор confined space 3 tight; close-fitting; чевлите ми се многу тесни the shoes are too small for me; тесен фустан tight/close-fitting dress 4 *fig.* narrow; limited; narrow-minded; тесни сфаќања narrow<-minded> views; <по>тесното значење на зборот the strict meaning of a word 5 *fig.* close, intimate; close-knit; тесно пријателство close friendship 6 (*as noun*) тесно *n*; ❏ се најде во тесно to find o.s. in a fix (mess)

тескере *n arch.* 1 document, identity card; certificate 2 invitation

тесла *f* adze; мајсторска тесла carpenter's adze; bricklayer's hammer; алвациска тесла pastry knife

(*for cutting halva*); ❏ <му сече умот> како алвациска тесла *iron.* he is as thick as a brick

тесле *n dim. of* тесла

тесличе *n* & **тесличка** *f dim. of* тесла

теснец *m* (*only sg*) 1 gorge, ravine, *see* клисура, теснина 2 (*морски*) straits, narrows 3 *fig.* straits, <tight> corner; доведе некого во теснец to drive s.o. into a corner

тесни *impf* I to narrow *trans.*; to make smaller; (*облека*) to take in; *fig.* to restrict, limit II – се to narrow *intrans.*; *fig.* to become restricted (limited)

теснина *f* gorge, ravine

тесничок -чка *adj dim. of* тесен

тесно *adv* narrowly; tightly; closely; во станот е тесно the flat is crowded; тој тесно ги сфаќа работите he takes a narrow view of things; тесно победува/губи to win/lose by a whisker

тесноград *adj* 1 narrow-chested 2 *fig.* narrow-minded

тесноградост *f* narrow-mindedness

теснота & **теснотија** *f* narrowness; tightness; smallness; close quarters

тест¹ *m* father-in-law (*wife's father*)

тест² *m* test; ❏ го положува (издржува) тестот на времето to stand the test of time; тест на издржливост endurance test

тестав *adj* doughy

тестамéнт *m* will; legacy; bequest

тестаментáрен -рна *adj* testamentary

тестáтор *m* testator; legator; bequeather

тесте *n arch.* dozen; packet; bunch

тестемел *m arch.* towel; kerchief

тестен *adj* dough *attrib.*; doughy, dough-like; тестени производи pasta; pastries

тестикул & **тестис** *m Anat.* testicle, testis (*pl* testes)

тестѝра *pf* & *impf* to test, put to the test

тестирање *n* testing

тесто *n* 1 dough; pastry; (*за палачинки*) batter; нараснато (збунато) тесто dough that has risen; вала (валка) тесто to roll <out> dough; кисело тесто sourdough; лиснато тесто flaky (puff) pastry 2 (*од гипс и др.*) paste

тета *f usu. child.* auntie

тетанус *m* tetanus; lockjaw, *Med.* trismus

тетерави се *impf* to stagger, totter

тетѝва *f* 1 (*жица на лак*) bowstring 2 *Math.* chord 3 *Anat.* tendon; sinew

тетин¹ *m* uncle (*aunt's husband*)

тетин² *adj hyp.* auntie's

тетинов *adj* uncle's

тетка *f* 1 (*father's/mother's sister*) aunt, *colloq.* auntie 2 (*form of address used for a woman one generation older than the speaker*) auntie; madam

теткин *adj* aunt<ie>'s

теткица *f hyp.* (*of* тетка) auntie

тетовѝра *pf* & *impf* to tattoo

тетраéдар -дри *m Math.* tetrahedron

тетралогија *f* tetralogy

тетрамéтар -три *m Prosody* tetrameter

тетратка *f* notebook, exercise book; music-book

тетреб *m Zool.* (Lyrurus tetrix) black grouse

теќе *n arch.* 1 dervish lodge 2 mausoleum (*of a Muslim holy man*)

теферич *m arch.* picnic

тефтер *m* register, book of accounts, account-book;

ledger; ❑ запише некого во црниот тефтер to black-list s.o., put s.o. on the black list

тефтерче *n colloq.* notebook

техника *f* **1** technology; engineering; наука и техника science and technology; студира техника to study engineering **2** machinery, equipment, plant; воена техника military hardware, *matériel*; бела техника household appliances **3** technique, method; skill

техниколóр *m* technicolour

техникум *m* technical school; vocational school

техничар *m* **1** technician; mechanic **2** technical-school pupil/graduate

техничарка *f* (*fem. form*) *see* техничар

технички *adj* **1** technical, technological; mechanical; технички прогрес technological progress; техничко училиште technical school; технички израз technical term; технички преглед mechanical check (inspection); технички директор technical director; техничка грешка technical fault; *Sport.* technical foul **2** industrial; технички метали/масла industrial metals/oils

технолóг -зи *m* technologist; engineer

технологија *f* technology

технолошки *adj* technological

тече¹ *impf* **1** to flow (*also fig.*); to run *intrans.*; to pass; to ooze; течат солзи tears flow; носот му тече he has a runny nose; мислите му течеа глатко his thoughts flowed easily; годините си течат the years pass; му тече пот he is sweating; му тече крв од носот his nose is bleeding; интересот тече од почетокот на годината the interest is calculated from the beginning of the year; платата му тече од први март his salary begins on the first of March; ❑ каде што тече мед и млеко the land of milk and honey; мед му тече од устата he speaks honeyed words; лиги му течат his mouth is watering; ако не тече, капе there's enough to keep the pot boiling; кај текла вода (река) пак ќе тече *prov.* 1. old habits die hard 2. money makes money **2** to leak *intrans.*; чешмата/бурето тече the tap/barrel is leaking; чевлите ми течат my shoes leak

тече² *impf arch.* to win, gain, earn, make one's fortune; кој се мачи, тој течи *prov.* diligence is the mother of good fortune

течен -чна *adj* **1** liquid; течна состојба liquid state; течно олово molten lead **2** *fig.* fluent, eloquent; smooth; течен стил fluent style

течение -ија *n arch. see* тек¹

течно *adv* fluently; говори течно to speak fluently

течност *f* fluid; liquid

тешачка *f dial.* solace

теши *impf* **I** to console; to calm **II** – **се** to find solace; to calm down *intrans.*

тешка *adj* (*only f*) *colloq.* pregnant

тешко *adv* **1** heavily; weightily, with dignity; gravely; seriously; тешко оди to tread heavily; се држи тешко to bear o.s. with dignity; тешко ранет gravely wounded; тешко ми е 1. I feel wretched (ill) 2. I feel miserable (sick at heart) **2** with difficulty; hardly; barely; тешко може да се верува it is hard to believe; тешко спечалено богатство hard-earned wealth; тешко дише to breathe heavily, (*многу тешко*) to labour for breath; ❑ тешко е да се рече (каже) it's

hard to say (tell); **3** тешко мене! woe is me! I'm in trouble; тешко на децата one feels sorry for the children

тешконосен -сна *adj rare* arduous, burdensome, gruelling

тешкотија -ии *f* **1** difficulty, trouble; прави тешкотии to cause (make) trouble **2** crux; тешкотијата на проблемот the nub of the problem

тешта *f* mother-in-law (*wife's mother*)

ти¹ *pron* (*2nd p. sg*) you, *arch.* thou (*dat. тебе ти*; *other cases тебе те*); со некого е на ти to be on familiar (first-name) terms with s.o.

ти² *pron* **1** (*short dat. form of* ти¹) <to> you, *arch.* thee; ти реков I told you; (*also with the long form*) тебе ти велам it's you I'm telling, I'm telling *you* **2** (*as dat. of possession*) your; син ти, сестра ти your son, your sister; точно ли ти оди часовникот? is your watch keeping good time?

Тибет *m* Tibet

тибетски *adj* Tibetan

Тибеќанец -ани *m* Tibetan

Тибеќанка *f* (*fem. form*) *see* Тибеќанец

тивко *adv* quietly, softly; peacefully; (*за време*) still, calm

тивкотија *f* quiet, calm; silence; serenity

тивне *pf* тивна *aor.* to quieten down *intrans.*, fall silent; to calm down *intrans.*; ветрот тивна the wind has died down

тивнува *impf of* тивне

тивок -вка *adj* **1** quiet, soft; (*слаб*) faint; со тивок глас in a soft (low) voice, under one's breath; тивко смеење faint laughter; тивко тропање gentle knock<ing>, tap<ping> **2** calm, serene; still, quiet, silent; тивка ноќ still night; тивко време calm weather; тивок живот quiet life; тивок човек taciturn/retiring person

тиган *m* (*тава*) frying-pan

тиганица *f* kind of doughnut (*usu. savoury*)

тиганичар *m* doughnut maker/vendor

тиганче *n dim. of* тиган

тигар *m Zool.* (Panthera tigris) tiger

тигарски *adj* tiger's; tiger *attrib.*; tigerish; тигарски скок tiger-like leap

тигарче *n dim.* tiger cub

тигрица *f Zool.* tigress

тие *pron* (*pl of* тој) **1** (*dat. ним, им*; *other cases нив, ги*) they **2** those

тизап *m Chem. colloq.* nitric acid, *see* ќезап

тизе<ка> *pron dial. see* ти¹

тиква *f* **1** (Cucurbita) pumpkin; squash; gourd; тиква стамболка (Cucurbita pepo, maxima, moschata) pumpkin, winter squash; тиква тврдокорка (Cucurbita melo, melopepo) pumpkin, summer squash; ❑ тикви <со расол>! nonsense! my foot! **2** *fig.* head, *colloq.* noddle, pate; тиквата му е зелена he is a greenhorn; добива по тиква to get it in the neck **3** *fig.* dolt, cabbage-head, numskull

тиквар *m* **1** vendor of baked pumpkin **2** lover of pumpkin

тикварка *f* (*fem. form*) *see* тиквар

тикварник -ци *m* pumpkin pie

тикве *n Bot.* (Cucurbita pepo) <vegetable> marrow; (*мало*) courgette, *Am. & Austral.* zucchini; *Cul.* полнети тиквиња stuffed marrows

тиквен *adj* pumpkin/marrow *attrib.*; тиквена ластунка pumpkin vine (stalk)

тиквеник -ци *m* pumpkin pie

Тиквеш *m* Tikvesh

Тиквешанец -ани *m* person from Tikvesh

Тиквешанка *f* (*fem. form*) *see* Тиквешанец

тиквешки *adj* Tikvesh *attrib.*

тиквиче *n* & **тиквичка** *f see* тикве

тиквиште *n augm. of* тиква

тики *conj* so, and so; тој беше многу сиромав, тики само леб јадеше he was very poor, so he only ate bread

тик-так *interj* tick-tock

тил *m* 1 back of the head, *Anat.* occiput; nape, back of the neck; ❑ кога ќе си го видам тилот when hell freezes over (*literally* when I see the back of my neck); мачка некому мед по тилот *colloq.* to butter s.o. up 2 *Mil.* rear, rear lines; *fig.* home front, interior; фронт и тил front and rear; ❑ од тилот from the rear 3 (*на нож*) flat; (*на секира*) butt

тилен -лна *adj Anat.* occipital; тилна коска occipital bone

тилје *pl of* тил 3

тилници *pl dial.* braids, plaits

тим *m* team

тимар[1] *m arch.* (*спаилак*) estate, fief; тимари ќе си заложам *f.p.* I shall mortgage my estates

тимар[2] *m* grooming; harness

тимари *impf* to groom, curry (*a horse*)

тимпан *m* 1 *Mus.* kettledrum; timpani (*pl*); *see* таламбас 2 *Architecture* tympanum 3 *Anat.* tympanum, tympanic membrane, eardrum

тимски *adj* team *attrib.*; тимска (групна) работа teamwork

тинејџер *m* teenager

тинктура *f* tincture; јодна тинктура tincture of iodine

тинтири-минтири *colloq.* rubbish, hot air, nonsense

тиња *f* silt, mud; slime; ooze; sludge

тињест *adj* silty; mud *attrib.*; muddy; slimy

тип[1] *m* 1 type, kind, sort; model, pattern; make; нов тип автомобили a new model/make of motor car 2 *colloq.* (*особен човек*) fellow, character; интересен тип an interesting character; чуден тип an odd fish

тип[2] *m Sport.* tip

типизација *f* 1 standardization; типизација на технолошките процеси standardization of technological procedures 2 classification 3 typification

типизира *pf* & *impf* 1 to standardize 2 to classify, type 3 to typify

типичен -чна *adj* typical; типичен пример a typical example

типограф *m* typographer, printer

типографија *f* 1 typography, printing 2 printing-press (-house, -shop)

типографски *adj* typographic, printing *attrib.*

типологија *f* typology

типоса *pf arch.* to print, print off; to finish printing

типосува *impf of* типоса

типски *adj* standard; типски мебел standard furniture

тип-топ *adj, adv indecl. colloq.* tiptop, super

типува *pf* & *impf Sport.* to tip

тирада *f* tirade

тираж *m* 1 print run; printing; (*на весник*) circulation 2 draw (*of a lottery*)

тиран *m* 1 tyrant 2 *fig.* bully

Тирана *f* Tirana

тиранизира *impf* 1 to tyrannize 2 *fig.* to bully; to torment

тиранија *f* 1 tyranny 2 *fig.* bullying behaviour

тиранин -ни *m see* тиран

тиранка *f* (*fem. form*) *see* тиран

тирански[1] *adj* tyrannical; тиранска власт tyrannical power

тирански[2] *adj* Tirana *attrib.*

тиранство *n* (*see* тиранија) tyranny

тиранствува *impf* to rule as/like a tyrant

тиранчанец -ни *m* person from Tirana

тиранчанка *f* (*fem. form*) *see* тиранчанец

тире *n Gram.* dash

тиса *m Bot.* 1 (Taxus baccata) yew 2 (Juniperus excelsa; Juniperus foetidissima) juniper

тиска *impf* I to push, press; to squeeze in *trans.* II – се to push (press) forward *intrans.*; to crowd, throng; to squeeze in *intrans.*

тисканица *f* crowd, throng

тисов *adj* yew; тисово дрво yew tree

титан[1] *m* 1 *Myth.* Titan 2 *fig.* (*гигант, великан*) titan, giant; superman

титан[2] *m Chem.* titanium

титанит *m* 1 titanite, sphene 2 powerful explosive

титански *adj* titanic; gigantic; титански напори titanic efforts

титиз *m colloq.* miser, skinflint, *Am.* tightwad

титл -ови *m Film* subtitle

титла *f* tittle (*diacritic mark denoting an abbreviation, as in Old Church Slavonic*)

титлува *impf Film* to subtitle

титовка *f* partisan's cap (*with a five-pointed star*)

титула *f* title; *Leg.* (*поседовен лист*) property title; title-deed; грофовска титула title of count; почесна титула honorary title; докторска титула PhD; академска титула academic title; титула на светски шампион (*во*) world title (*in*)

титуларен -рна *adj* titular

титулира *pf* & *impf* 1 to address (*s.o.*) by title 2 to confer a title upon, entitle

тиќе *n colloq.* vermin (*also fig.*)

тифус *m Med.* typhus; црвен тифус abdominal typhus, typhoid (enteric) fever; пегав тифус epidemic typhus fever, classical typhus, spotted fever

тифусар *m* typhus patient

тифусен -сна *adj* typhus *attrib.*; typhoid; тифусна треска typhoid (enteric) fever

Тихи Океан *m* Pacific Ocean

тихо *adv poet. see* тивко

тихоокеански *adj* Pacific *attrib.*

тиши се *impf* 1 to lose air, go down; гумата се тиши the tyre is going down 2 (*за ветер*) to ease *intrans.*

тишина *f* silence, stillness, quiet; calm; ноќна тишина still of the night; наруши тишина to disturb/break the silence; ❑ кобна тишина an ominous silence; мртва тишина dead silence; мир и тишина peace and quiet

тишка *f f.p. see* птица

тишлер *m* (*столар*) carpenter

тишлерај *m* (*столарство*) carpentry

тишти *impf* **1** to weigh down (*on*), worry, depress, bother; мисли го тиштеа his thoughts weighed heavily on him; што те тишти? what is bothering you? **2** to <scrimp and> save

ткаач *m see* ткајач

ткаачка *f see* ткајачка

ткаачки *adj see* ткајачки

ткаачница *f see* ткајачница

ткае *impf* to weave; ткае платно to weave cloth

ткаенина *f* <woven> fabric; textile, cloth; памучна ткаенина cotton fabric

ткаеница *f see* ткаенина

ткаење *n* **1** weaving **2** texture; ткаењето на килимот the texture of the rug **3** fabric

ткајач *m* weaver

ткајачка *f* (*fem. form*) *see* ткајач

ткајачки *adj* weaving; weaver's; ткајачки занает weaver's trade, weaving

ткајачница *f* weaving workshop

ткиво *n* tissue; мускулно ткиво muscle tissue; спојно (соединувачко, соединително) ткиво connective tissue

тлака *f* **1** (*поседок*) working bee **2** (*кулук*) socage, statute labour, corvée, compulsory labour; *fig.* drudgery

тланик -ци *m* fireside (*in a peasant house*)

тласок -ци *m literary rare* stimulus, impetus

тлее *impf* **1** to glow, glimmer; огнот тлееше the fire was glimmering **2** *fig.* to smoulder; омразата тлее hatred smoulders **3** *fig.* to wither away, languish, pine away

т.н. *abbr.* (*таканаречен*) so-called

тоа *pron* (*n of* тој) **1** it **2** that; тоа и тоа this and that; тоа утро that morning; ❑ тоа е она! that's it! that's the answer! при тоа moreover; furthermore; <и> покрај тоа besides; освен тоа furthermore, besides that; поради тоа therefore, because of that; и без тоа anyway, anyhow; тоа <ти> е тоа that's the way things go

тоалет *m* & **тоалета** *f* **1** dress, attire; dressing, toilet; вечерна тоалета evening dress **2** dressing-table, toilet table **3** toilet, lavatory, W.C., *Am.* bathroom, restroom; powder-room; тоалет за жени Ladies; тоалет за мажи Gentlemen **4** (*за артисти*) dressing-room, make-up room

тоалетен -тна *adj* toilet *attrib.*; тоалетен сапун toilet soap; тоалетна хартија toilet paper (tissue); (*за раце*) paper towelling

Тобаго *n* Tobago

тобагошки *adj* Tobagonian

тобоган *m* toboggan; slide

товар *m* **1** load; *Comm.* freight; (*на брод, авион*) cargo; симне товар од кола to unload a cart; ❑ си направи товар to make a packet **2** load; cartload; containerful; пет товари дрва five loads of wood **3** *fig.* burden, cross; тоа ми е голем товар that/he is my cross; оди на товар на to be attributed to; to fall to the account of; to be due to

товарач *m* loader; (*на пристаниште*) stevedore, docker

товарен -рна *adj* **1** load *attrib.*, of lading; (*за животно*) of burden, pack *attrib.*; (*за брод*) cargo *attrib.*; товарно животно, товарен добиток beast of burden, pack animal; товарен лист (*за брод*) bill

of lading; (*за авион*) air waybill; (*за воз*) waybill; товарни трошоци freight charges **2** goods *attrib.*; freight *attrib.*; товарна кола lorry, *Am.* truck; (*покриена*) van; *Rail* <goods> wag<g>on, *Am.* freight car; товарен воз goods (*Am.* freight) train **3** *dial.* (*only f*) pregnant; товарна жена pregnant woman

товари *pf* & *impf* **I 1** to load **2** *fig.* to burden (*со нешто – with s.th.*); to work (*s.o.*) hard **3** to denounce; товари некого пред полицијата to denounce s.o. to the police **II – се 1** to load/burden o.s. (*со нешто – with s.th.*) **2** *fig.* to force (impose) o.s. (*на – on*); to intrude (*on*) **3** to board; (*на брод*) to embark *intrans.*; се товарија на бродот they took ship

товарит *adj rare* of burden, pack *attrib.*; товарити добици pack animals

тога *f* **1** toga **2** (*на судија, професор и др.*) gown; robe

тога *dial.* & **тогај** *adv see* тогаш

тогаш *adv* **1** then, at that time **2** then, next, after that, later **3** then, in that case, (*or not translated*); ако одиш, тогаш и јас ќе дојдам if you are going, I'll come too

тогашен -шна *adj* of that time; тогашните услови the conditions at that time; тогашно време that time/era

Того *n* Togo

Тогоанец -нци *m* Togolese

Тогоанка *f* (*fem. form*) *see* Тогоанец

тогоански *adj* Togolese

тозлуци *pl* leggings; gaiters

тој *m pron* (*3rd p.*) **1** (*dat. нему, му*; *other cases него, го*) he; it **2** that; тој ден <on> that day; тој час (тојчас) at that moment; ❑ тој и тој such and such; so and so

тојага *f see* стап

ток *m see* тек²

тока¹ *f* toast by clinking glasses; прави тока to clink (touch) glasses

тока² *f* buckle, clasp; sequin

токата *f Mus.* toccata

токиец -ијци *m* person from Tokyo

токијка *f* (*fem. form*) *see* токиец

Токио *n* Tokyo

токиски *adj* Tokyo *attrib.*

токмак -ци *m* **1** *arch.* mace **2** *arch.* mallet, beetle **3** *fig.* fool, blockhead

токмеж *m* preparation, grooming

токми *impf* **I 1** to prepare *trans.*; to groom *trans.*; to intend (*за – for*); токми коњ за некого to saddle a horse for s.o.; токми син за нечија ќерка to groom a son for s.o.'s daughter **2** to dress up *trans.*; ја токмат невестата they are dressing up the bride **3** to compare (*со – with*), put on a level; токми една работа со друга to compare one job with another **II – се 1** to get ready *intrans.*; to intend (*to do s.th.*); се токмеа за на свадба they were getting ready to go to the wedding; се токмевме да одиме we were about to leave **2** to dress up *intrans.* **3** to compete (*со – with*), rival; ние не можеме со вас да се токмиме we can't compete with you

токмо *adv see* токму

токмоглав *adj* of the same height

токмонога & **токмонозе** *adv* with one's feet together; застане токмонозе to stand with one's feet together

токму *adv* **1** right, just, exactly, precisely; токму тоа сакав да го кажам that's exactly what I meant; токму во овој момент at this very moment; ти стоеше токму до него you were standing right next to him; ❏ токму како exactly as; токму така како ... just as ... ; just like ... ; токму тоа! just the thing! just the job! токму така! exactly! that's right! тој е токму како татко му he's a chip off the old block **2** (*as adj*) (*за човек*) normal, all right; тој човек не е токму that man is not right in the head; токму човек a clear-headed person

токо & **току** *adv arch. see* туку

токсикологија *f* toxicology

токсиколошки *adj* toxicological

токсин *m* (*usu. pl*) toxin

токсичен -чна *adj* toxic

толерантен -тна *adj* tolerant

толерантност *f* toleration, tolerance, forbearance

толеранција *f* toleration, tolerance

толерира *impf* to tolerate

толкав *adj pron* of that size; that big; that small; толкав останал колкав што беше he has stayed the same height

толковен -вна *adj* explanatory; толковен речник explanatory (monolingual) dictionary

толку *adv* **1** as much/many; so much/many; толку години so many years; толку пари so much money; двапати по толку twice as much; колку имам толку ти давам I am giving you all I have; толку и очекував I thought as much; ❏ колку-толку at least a little; толку и толку such-and-such a number (*of*); и толку and that's all there is to it, and that's that; толку од прилика approximately **2** (*with adj or adv*) so, as; толку добар so good; толку добро so well; ❏ толку побргу all the more so; толку подобро/полошо all (so much) the better/the worse; колку побргу толку подобро the quicker the better

толкува *impf* **1** to interpret; толкува закон to interpret a law **2** to explain, explicate, comment on; толкува текст to explicate a text

толкувач *m* interpreter; commentator; толкувач на законот legal commentator

толкумина *adv* (*of men or mixed groups*) so (that) many; пак сме толкумина колку што бевме вчера there are as many of us as there were yesterday

толкунса & **толкуцка** *adv* so (that) little; a tiny bit; само толкуцка зедов I only took a tiny bit

толкуцкав *adj* so (that) little (small)

толмач *m see* толкувач

толпа *f literary* crowd; mob

толче & **толчи** *impf* **I** **1** to crush; to pound; толчи лук to crush garlic **2** *fig.* (*град*) to buffet; to beat, thrash; градот го толчеше полето the hail was buffeting the field; толчи непријател (*во борба*) to thrash an opponent (*in a fight*) **3** *fig.* to win; ќе толчиме во натпреварот we will win the match **II** – **се 1** to fight (*со некого – with s.o.*) **2** *arch.* to slap o.s.

толчило *n see* толчник 1

толчник -ци *m* **1** pestle **2** *Bot.* pistil

том *m* volume; првиот том volume one

томбак *m* copper-zinc alloy

томбола *f* **1** raffle; *Brit.* tombola **2** first prize in a raffle/tombola

томбрук -ци *m dial. see* томрук

томрук *m* wooden shackle

тон[1] *m* **1** *Mus., fig.* note; tone; висок тон high note; висина на тонот pitch; повишен тон sharp; снижен тон flat; пријателски тон friendly tone; ❏ во тон е (*со*) to match, suit; дава тон to set the tone (*with dat. – for*); to lead the way; добар тон *bon ton*, good manners (breeding, form) **2** *fig.* tone, tint, hue, shade, tinge; нежен тон delicate tint; светли тонови bright tones

тон[2] *m* тона *pl* tonne, metric ton; еден тон јаглен a tonne of coal

тона *f see* тон[2]

тонажа *f* tonnage

тоналитет *m* **1** *Mus.* key, mode, tonality **2** colour scheme

Тонга *f* Tonga

Тонгаец -ајци *m* Tongan

Тонгајка *f* (*fem. form*) *see* Тонгаец

тонгаски *adj* Tongan

тоне *impf* to sink, founder *intrans.*, go down (*also fig.*); to drown ; бродот тоне the ship is sinking; тоне во мисли he is absorbed in thought

тонок -нка *adj f.p. dial. see* танок

тонски *adj* (*of verse*) accentual, tonic

топ[1] *m* cannon, gun; *Chess* castle, rook; полски/опсаден/противавионски топ field/siege/anti-aircraft gun; ❏ глув како топ as deaf as a doorpost; в топ ќе те стави (фрли) he'll give you a blast; топ не го бие (разбива) he is sitting pretty; he is well-to-do; го фрли топот 1. he has finished <the job> 2. he is finished, *sl.* he has kicked the bucket

топ[2] *m* **1** roll, bolt; три топа басма three rolls of cotton print **2** (*хартија*) ream; packet (*1000 sheets*) **3** (*бала*) bale

топаз *m* topaz

топал *m colloq.* lame person, cripple

топен *adj* melted, molten; топена маст rendered/melted fat; топено сирење processed cheese, cheese spread; *Cul.* fondue

топеница *f* fried breadcrumbs

топи[1] *impf* to dip (*в – into*); to dunk; to soak *trans.*

топи[2] *impf* **I** **1** to melt *trans.*; (*маст*) to render; (*руда*) to smelt; (*метали*) to fuse *trans.*; (*растворува*) to dissolve *trans.*; *Chem.* to liquefy *trans.*; сонцето го топи снегот the sun melts the snow **2** *fig.* to waste *trans.*; to torment; некаква мака него го топи something is worrying him **3** *fig. poet.* to suppress, crush, drown *trans.*; to overwhelm; топи тага to drown one's sorrow **II** – **се 1** to melt, dissolve *intrans.*; (*метали*) to fuse *intrans.*; *Chem.* to liquefy *intrans.*; мразот се топи the ice is melting; се топи в уста it melts in one's mouth (it's delicious); солта се топи во вода salt dissolves in water **2** *fig.* to waste away *intrans.*, pine **3** *fig.* to be overwhelmed; се топи од среќа to be overwhelmed with happiness

топилница *f* smeltery; foundry, forge; топилница на железо iron smeltery

топилничар *m* smelter; foundry worker

топилничарство *n* smelting

топило *n* **1** place in river etc. where hemp is soaked (*for making rope*) **2** *Metallurgy* flux

топка *f* **1** globe; sphere; Земјината топка the globe **2** ball; топка за фудбал/кошарка football/basketball;

❏ меч топка match-point (*tennis*); префрла топка to pass the ball; *sl.* to pass the buck

топли *impf* **I 1** to warm <up> *trans.*; to heat *trans.*; to keep warm *trans.*; топли вода to heat water; сонцето нè топли the sun warms us; ова палто многу топли this coat is very warm **2** *fig.* to delight *trans.*, regale; нејзиното писмо му го топли срцето her letter warms his heart **II – се** to warm up *intrans.*; to warm o.s.; се топли на сонце to warm o.s. in the sun; времето се топли the weather is getting warmer

топлив *adj* meltable; soluble; *Chem.* liquefiable; *Metallurgy* fusible

топлик -ци *m dial.* sunny spot

топлина *f* heat; warmth; *fig.* cordiality; единица за топлина thermal unit; топлина на чувствата warm feelings; душевна топлина warm-heartedness

топлинки *pl* warm slippers; warm winter boots

топлински *adj see* топлотен

топличок -чка *adj* (*dim. of* топол) warmish, lukewarm, tepid

топлица *f* hot (thermal) spring

топло *adv* warmly; овде е многу топло it is very warm here; топло ме поздрави he greeted me warmly; топло облечен warmly dressed

топлокрвен -вна *adj* warm-blooded, *Anat.*, *Zool.* homoiothermic; топлокрвни животни warm-blooded animals

топлокрвност *f* warm-bloodedness

топломер *m* clinical thermometer

топлота *f see* топлина

топлотен -тна *adj* heat *attrib.*; warmth *attrib.*; thermic, thermal; calorific; топлотни зраци heat rays; топлотен спроводник heat conductor; топлотна единица thermal unit; топлотна енергија thermal energy; *Meteorology* топлотен бран heatwave; *Med.* топлотен удар heatstroke

топовски *adj* cannon *attrib.*; топовски оган bombardment, cannon (artillery) fire, cannonade; топовско зрно cannon-ball; топовска граната artillery shell; *fig.* топовска храна cannon-fodder

топограф *m* topographer

топографија *f* topography

топографски *adj* topographical; топографска карта topographical map; топографски знак topographical symbol

топол -пла *adj* warm (*also fig.*); топли алишта warm clothing; топло време warm weather; топла зима mild winter; топол прием warm (cordial) reception

топола *f Bot.* (Populus) poplar; бела топола (Populus alba) white poplar, abele; црна топола (Populus nigra) common black poplar; ❏ висок колку топола as tall as a beanpole

тополов *adj* poplar *attrib.*; тополово дрво poplar

топоним *m* toponym

топонимија *f* toponymy

топономастика *f* study of place-names, toponomastics

топори *impf* **I** to brandish; топори нож to brandish a knife **II – се** to strut, swagger; to act haughtily; to be self-important, give o.s. airs

топот *m* thud; tramp; *see* тупот

топоти *impf* to thud; to tramp, stamp; *see* тупоти

топтан *adv colloq.* wholesale; in bulk; all together;

colloq. the whole caboodle; продаде нешто топтан to sell s.th. wholesale/in bulk

топтанџија *m arch.* wholesale dealer

топувче *n dim. of* топуска

топуз *m arch.* **1** (*боздоган*) mace **2** (*на кантар*) weight

топук -ци *m* heel (*of a shoe*)

топуска *f* **1** (*шпенадла*) pin **2** *see* топуз 2

топче¹ *n dim. of* топ¹; црешовото топче little cherry-wood cannon (*symbol of the Ilinden Uprising*)

топче² *n dim. of* топ² **1** (*платно*) roll **2** (*врска*) wad; топче пари (банкноти) wad of banknotes

топче³ *n dim. of* топка 2

топчест *adj* ball-shaped, globular; rotund; spherical

топчија -ии *m* gunner, artilleryman

торба *f* bag; sack; pouch; патна торба travelling bag; ловџиска торба gamebag; ❏ си ја стави (кладе) главата в торба to put one's neck in the noose; прав е како јаже в торба *iron.* crooked; секое месење, торба тресење living from hand to mouth; циганска торба mixed bag

торбар *m* (*usu. pl*) *Zool.* marsupial

торбе *n dim. of* торба; pouch

торбенце *n & ***торбичка** *f dim. see* торбе

торбеш *m* Macedonian Muslim

тореадор *m* toreador

торзо *n* torso, trunk

торлак -ци *m colloq.* simpleton, country bumpkin, boor, hick

тормоз *m literary* torment, ill treatment, harassment

тормози *impf literary* to torment, ill-treat, harass; to bully; to badger; to tease

торнадо *m* tornado

торпеден -дна *adj* torpedo; торпеден чамец torpedo boat

торпедира *pf & impf* to torpedo

торпедо *n* torpedo

торпилер *m* torpedo boat

торпилира *pf & impf see* торпедира

торта *f* cake; torte; роденденска торта birthday cake

тортура *f* torment; torture

тоска *f f.p.* smock, long shirt

тост¹ *m* (*препечено парче леб*) toast

тост² *m* (*здравица*) toast

тостер *m* toaster

тотален -лна *adj* total; ❏ тотална војна total war; тотално затемнување total eclipse

тотализатор *m* totalizator, totalizer, *colloq.* tote

тотализација *f* adding up; summing up; totalization

тотализира *pf & impf* **1** to add up *trans.*, totalize **2** to round off, bring to round figures

тоталитарен -рна *adj* **1** total; comprehensive **2** totalitarian; тоталитарен режим totalitarian regime; тоталитарна држава totalitarian state

тоталитаризам -змот *m* totalitarianism

тоталитарист *m* totalitarian, adherent/advocate of totalitarianism

тоталитаристички *adj* totalitarian

тоталитет *m* totality

тотално *adv* totally

тоталност *f* totality

тотем *m* totem

тотемизам -змот *m* totemism

точак *m colloq.* bicycle, bike

точач¹ *m* bartender

точач[2] *m* sharpener; (*на ножови*) knife-grinder; (*на стакла*) glass-cutter, (*на драгоцени камени*) gem-cutter, lapidary; (*на дијаманти*) diamond-cutter

точен -чна *adj* 1 exact, accurate; precise; точен препис exact copy; точен одговор correct answer; точно време the right time; точен кантар accurate scales 2 reliable; punctual; точен службеник reliable employee

точи[1] *impf* I 1 to pour <out> *trans.*; to decant; to tap *trans.*; точи вино to serve wine; точи пиво to tap beer, serve draught beer; ❏ точи пари to have money on tap, to be rolling in money 2 to spin *trans.*; точи свила to spin silk II – се 1 (*за солзи и др.*) to trickle *intrans.*; (*за вино, пиво и сл.*) to be on tap; ❏ парите не се точат money doesn't grow on trees 2 *fig.* to come and go, pass by, flow; се точат гости guests come and go; се точат деновите the days pass

точи[2] *impf* 1 to sharpen; (*на точило*) to grind; (*на брус*) to whet; (*на ремен*) to strop; точи молив to sharpen a pencil; точи нож to sharpen (whet) a knife; ❏ *colloq.* точи заби (*за*) 1. to have it in (*for*) 2. to hanker after, eagerly anticipate, lick one's lips 2 to turn *trans.*

точило *n* whetstone; grindstone; steel

точка[1] *f* 1 spot, dot; speck; фустан со црни точки dress with black polka dots 2 *Gram.* full stop, *Am.* period; dot; точка и запирка semicolon; две точки colon; три точки suspension points; ❏ стави точка на . . . to put an end to . . . 3 *Tech., fig.* point; точка на пресек point of intersection; точка на замрзнување freezing point; точка на вриење boiling point; точка на дневен ред an item on the agenda; план од осум точки an eight-point plan; ❏ излезна точка point of departure, starting-point; мртва точка dead point, dead centre; на мртва точка at a standstill; допирна точка point of contact; common ground; врвна точка high point, apogee; climax; потпорна точка *Phys.* fulcrum; *Tech.* bearing; слепа точка a blind spot; гледна точка point of view; точка! that's enough! period! full stop! тргнува од мртва точка to get the ball rolling; доведува/доаѓа до точка на кулминација to bring/come to a head; достигне најниска точка to hit an all-time low; допира во болна точка to touch a sore point; to touch a nerve; слаба точка weak point (spot); soft spot

точка[2] *f.f.p.* *see* чешмурка

точка[3] се *impf* 1 *see* точи[1] (се) II 2 2 to move about aimlessly; to mill around; to fuss about; to snoop/sneak about

точно *adv* 1 exactly, accurately; precisely; punctually; on the dot; точно препише to copy accurately; точно преведе to translate faithfully; точно во минута to the minute; точно осум часот exactly eight o'clock; точно на време dead on time; часовникот работи точно the clock/watch keeps good time 2 reliably; точно ги врши своите должности he carries out his duties meticulously

точност *f* accuracy; precision; punctuality; correctness

Тошо *in the expression*: се прави на Тошо to feign innocence; to play dumb

траба *f* roll, bolt (*of material*); навие (навитка) на траба to roll up (*material*)

трава *f dial.* *see* трева

траве́рза *f* 1 *Rail* sleeper, *Am.* tie 2 *Building* traverse; cross-beam 3 *Mil.* traverse 4 wall of sandbags, embankment, *Am.* levee

траг *m see* трага

трага *f* 1 footprint, imprint; track; trail; (*од тркала и сл.*) rut, groove; трага од волк, зајак итн. wolf's, hare's, *etc.* tracks (spoor); трага од колски тркала trace (tracks) of wagon wheels; ❏ му влезе на некого или на нешто во трагата to be on s.o.'s trail; тргне по трагата на некого to set off in pursuit of s.o.; изгуби трага to lose track (*of s.o.*); прикрива траг<и> to cover one's tracks; на прав траг on the right track; on the right scent 2 trace, sign; траги од војна traces of war; нема ни трага од селото there is no sign of the village; носи траги од to bear/give/show evidence of; остава траги to make one's mark

трагедија -ии *f* tragedy

траги́зам -змот *m* tragedy

трагик -ци *m see* трагичар

трагика *f* 1 (*чувство на потресеност*) sense of tragedy 2 (*несреќа, суштината на трагедијата*) tragedy, tragic essence (*of s.th.*)

трагикомедија -ии *f* tragicomedy

трагикомичен -чна *adj* tragicomic<al>

трагичар *m* tragedian, writer of tragedies; tragic actor

трагичарка *f* (*fem. form*) *see* трагичар

трагичен -чна *adj* tragic; трагична смрт tragic death; трагична судбина tragic fate

трад *m* tinder

традиција -ии *f* tradition; по традиција as a rule; as it always happens; раскинува со традицијата to break with tradition

традициона́лен -лна *adj* traditional

традиционали́зам -змот *m* traditionalism

традиционали́ст *m* traditionalist

трае *impf* 1 to last, go on, continue; ништо не трае вечно nothing lasts forever; додека трае светот forever 2 (*за храна*) to keep *intrans.*; (*за облека*) to wear well; овие продукти не траат многу these products don't keep 3 to endure, put up with; to be patient; тој не трае горештина he can't stand the heat; ❏ кожа не го трае he is impatient 4 to keep quiet, *colloq.* keep mum

траен -јна *adj* lasting, enduring, permanent; durable; continual; траен мир lasting peace; траен спомен enduring memory; трајна ондулација permanent wave, *colloq.* perm

траенката *adv dial.* *see* молкома

тражи *impf dial.* *see* бара[2]

трајно *adv* lastingly, enduringly, permanently; continually

трајност *f* permanence

трак *interj* click! knock!

трака[1] *f literary* tape; ribbon

трака[2] *impf* 1 to rattle, clatter *intrans.*; to click *intrans.*; to snap *intrans.*; трака со заби his teeth are chattering 2 (*чука*) to knock (*at a door*)

тракатанец -нци *m* 1 (*ѕвонец*) bell; cowbell 2 *fig.* chatterbox; тракатанци! nonsense!

трака-трука *interj* (*see* трак) трака-трука на портата knock, knock!

Тракиец -ијци *m* Thracian

Тракија *f* Thrace

Тракијка *f* (*fem. form*) *see* Тракиец
тракиски *adj* Thracian
тракне *pf* тракна *aor. see* трака²
тракта́т *m* **1** (*расправа, студија*) treatise, paper **2** (*меѓународен договор*) treaty
трактор *m* tractor
тракторист *m* tractor driver
трактористка *f* (*fem. form*) *see* тракторист
тракторски *adj* tractor *attrib.*; тракторски мотор tractor engine
трамбулина *f* **1** trampoline; springboard **2** *fig.* stepping-stone, jumping-off place, launching pad
трамвај -аи *m* tram, *Am.* streetcar
трамвајски *adj* tram; трамвајска пруга tramline<s>
трамвајџија -ии *m colloq.* tram driver/conductor
трампа *f* barter<ing>; swap<ping>
трампи *pf & impf* to barter; to swap
транзистор *m* transistor <radio>
транзит *m* transit
транзитен -тна *adj* transit; транзитна стока goods in transit; транзитна виза transit visa
транзитивен -вна *adj Gram.* transitive; транзитивни глаголи transitive verbs; *see* преоден
транзитивност *f Gram.* transitivity
транс *m* trance; падне во транс to fall into a trance
трансакција -ии *f* transaction
трансатлантик -ци *m* transatlantic liner
трансатлантски *adj* transatlantic
трансверза́ла *f* transversal
трансверза́лен -лна *adj* transverse, transversal
трансгресија *f* transgression (*also Geol.*)
транскрибира *pf & impf* to transcribe
транскрипција -ии *f* transcription
транслитерација *f* transliteration
трансмисија -ии *f Tech.* transmission
трансмисио́нен -она *adj Tech.* transmission *attrib.*; трансмисионен ремен transmission belt
транспаре́нт *m* **1** banner (*with a political slogan or picture*) **2** *Photography* transparency
транспаре́нтен -тна *adj* transparent
трансплантација *f* (*пресадување, esp. Surgery*) transplant
трансплантира *pf & impf* (*пресади, пресадува, esp. Surgery*) to transplant
транспозиција *f* transposition
транспонира *pf & impf* to transpose
транспорт *m* **1** transport; transportation; железнички транспорт rail transport **2** consignment, shipment; автомобилски транспорт road transport; транспорт со текстилна стока consignment (shipment) of textiles **3** *Mil.* convoy; supply units, field train **4** *Mil.* (*see* транспортер 2) transporter; troop-carrier; десантен транспорт landing-craft
транспортен -тна *adj* transport; транспортни средства vehicles, conveyances, means of transport; транспортни трошоци transport costs, *Comm.* freight charges, carriage; транспортно претпријатие forwarding agency, shipping firm
транспортер *m* **1** (*уред*) conveyor **2** *Mil.* transporter, carrier **3** (*лице*) transporter, conveyor, shipping (forwarding) agent
транспортира *pf & impf* to transport
трансфер *m* transfer

трансфери́ра *pf & impf* to transfer *trans.*
трансфер-ли́ста *f Sport.* transfer list
трансфигурација *f* transfiguration
трансформа́тор *m Elec.* transformer
трансформација -ии *f* transformation
трансформира *pf & impf* to transform
трансфузија *f* <blood> transfusion
транше́ја -еи *f Mil.* trench
траор *m see* траур
трап *m* **1** ditch; pit; ако баба лаже, трап не лаже *prov.* actions speak louder than words **2** furrow
трапез *m* **1** *Geom.* trapezium **2** *Gymnastics* trapeze
трапеза *f see* трпеза
трапезойд *m Geom.* trapezoid
трапезойден -дна *adj Geom.* trapezoid<al>; трапезоидна форма trapezoid shape
трапка *impf* to tread lightly, trip along, patter
траса *f* route, line (*marked out for construction*)
траси́ра¹ *pf & impf Tech.* to mark out, trace; трасира железничка пруга to mark out a route for a railway line
траси́ра² *pf & impf Comm.* to write a bill of exchange
траска *impf* **1** to bang; to slam; to rattle *intrans.*; to clatter *intrans.*; шишињата траскаат the bottles are rattling; сабјата му траскаше по подот his sword clattered on the floor **2** *colloq.* to smack, wallop; траска дете to smack a child **3** *fig.* to chatter, babble; немој да траскаш! don't talk nonsense!
траскот *m Bot.* (Andropogon ischaemum) beard grass, bluestem, broom sedge, *see* троскот
трасне *pf* трасна *aor.* **1** to crack, crash *trans. & intrans.*; to bang; to slam; трасна пушка a gun went off; трасне врата to slam a door **2** *colloq.* to smack, wallop **3** *fig.* to blurt out (*s. th. nonsensical*); ❑ трасна и остана жив *colloq.* he dropped a brick (clanger)
траснува *impf of* трасне
трат *m Bot.* (Polyporus fomentarius) tinder
трати *pf* **1** to dash to the ground *trans.*, strike down **2** to jilt, leave
трака́ се *impf* to sleep restlessly, toss and turn
траур *m* crape, crepe (*as a sign of mourning*); black clothes; widow's weeds; *poet.* sables
траурен -рна *adj* mourning; grieving; траурна облека black clothes (*as a sign of mourning*)
трафика *f* <tobacco> kiosk; tobacconist's <shop>
трафика́нт *m* tobacconist
трафо-станица *f Elec.* transformer
трбув -си *m* (*мев*) belly
трбушен -шна *adj* abdominal; трбушен тифус abdominal typhus, *Med.* typhoid <fever>
трбушка *f* tripe
трга *impf* **I 1** *see* тргне I; ❑ трга по малку to tipple; трга напред, трга назад to waver; не го трга срце за нешто his heart is not in it **2** to weigh; to weigh out; ❑ лош е, кантар не го трга he is evil beyond measure **3** to suffer; трга маки to suffer torments **4** трга живот to enjoy life; трга раат to lead a quiet life **II – се 1** *see* тргне (се) II **2** to weigh o.s. **3** (*usu. in negative*) не се трга he is unbearable; it is intolerable
тргач *m colloq.* (*локач, пијач*) drunkard, boozer
тргне *pf* тргна *aor.* **I 1** to set out, leave, depart; возот тргна the train left (departed); тргна за Белград he set off for Belgrade; тргна да налее вода he went to draw water; ❑ тргне по лош (крив) пат to go astray;

тргне по трагата на некого to follow in s.o.'s footsteps; тргне од некоја гледна точка to proceed from a certain assumption **2** to fall in (*co – with*), start keeping company (*with*); тргне со лоши другари to fall into bad company **3** to start; to start working; to start prospering; тргне оро to start dancing; тргне на училиште to start school; тргна трговијата business has picked up **4** to pull *trans.*; to draw, pull out; to remove; тргне за уво to pull s.o.'s ear; тргне јаже to pull a rope; тргне сабја (меч) to draw a sword; тргне нешто (*од*) to remove s.th. (*from*) **5** (*пијалок*) to sip; (*цигара*) to pull on, draw on **6** to mark, draw; тргне граница to mark a boundary; тргне линија (црта) to draw a line; тргне бразда to plough/cut a furrow **II – се 1** to withdraw *intrans.*; to recoil; се тргна настрана he moved aside; пушката се тргна the gun recoiled **2** to flinch, start; се тргна од страв he gave a start; се тргна од сон he awoke

тргнува (се) *impf of* тргне (се); тргнува надолу to go downhill; ❏ тргнувај! get moving!

трговец -вци *m* merchant, trader, dealer; businessman

трговија *f* trade; commerce; business; трговија на големо (јадро) wholesale trade; трговија на мало (ситно, дробно) retail trade; трговија со кожи leather trade; слободна трговија free trade; внатрешна/надворешна трговија domestic/foreign trade

трговиште *n f.p.* market, *see* пазар

трговски *adj* trade *attrib.*; commercial; business *attrib.*; трговски врски trade links; трговски односи trade relations; трговско претпријатие firm; трговски сталеж traders; businessmen; трговски патник (агент) travelling salesman, commercial traveller; трговски претставник trade representative; трговска комора chamber of commerce; трговски договор commercial treaty; трговски преговори trade negotiations/talks; трговска морнарица merchant navy, *Am.* merchant (mercantile) marine; трговска куќа department store; трговски центар shopping centre, *Am., Austral., N.Z.* mall

трговче *n dim. usu. f.p. of* трговец

тргува *impf* to trade; to buy and sell; to do business, deal (*co – in, with*)

трдулав *adj* (*usu. of water melon, rock melon, pumpkin*) stunted; misshapen; squashed

треба *impf* (*with dat.*) **1** *impers.* it is necessary (*that*), it is fitting (*that*); треба да знаете you should know; не е како што треба it is not as it should be; така треба that's right! требаше да дојдете you should have come; овој човек треба да е некој странец this man must be a foreigner; ❏ така и му треба <нему> that serves him right! he asked for it! ако треба if need be; ми треба I need **2** to be needed (necessary); ако ти требам, викај ме if you need me, call me! му требаат многу пари he needs a lot of money; ❏ уште тоа ми требаше that is the last straw! that's all I needed!

требен -бна *adj colloq.* needed, necessary; не си ми требен I don't need you

треби *impf* **I** to clean *trans.*, pick, sort; треби грав/ориз/леќа/пченица to clean (pick, sort) beans/rice/lentils/wheat; треби бунар to clean out a well **II – се** to clean o.s. (*of*), remove (*lice, etc.*); to <de>louse o.s.;

кокошките се требеа од вошки the hens were pecking lice off one another

требник -ци *m Rel.* missal; prayer-book

требува *pf & impf Administration, Mil.* to requisition; требува месо to requisition meat

трева *f Bot.* **1** grass; (*тревник*) lawn; ливадска трева meadow grass; морска трева seaweed; sea grass; не газете ја тревата! keep off the grass! ❏ не пасе трева he's no fool; каде што ќе удри трева не расте he is very strong; не умри, коњу, до зелена трева *prov.* you can wait till doomsday **2** *colloq.* (*билка*) herb; лековити треви medicinal herbs

треварство *n* herbal lore, knowledge of herbs

тревен[1] -вна *adj* **1** grassy; covered (overgrown) with grass; тревни терени grassed areas; тревна ливада field of grass **2** grasslike; herbaceous; тревни растенија grasslike/herbaceous plants **3** grass *attrib.*; тревни семиња grass seeds

тревен[2] *m* (*popular name for*) April

тревица *& тревичка f dim. of* трева

тревиште *n augm. of* трева

тревјоса *pf* to grow over with grass, become covered (overgrown) with grass; нивана тревјосала сета that field is completely overgrown with grass

тревјосан *adj* grassy; covered (overgrown) with grass

тревјосува *impf of* тревјоса

тревка *f* blade of grass

тревлив *adj* grassy; overgrown with grass

тревливи *impf* to stutter, stammer

тревник -ци *m* lawn, grass

тревога *f literary* alarm; anxiety, uneasiness; alert; ❏ дава знак за тревога to raise (sound) the alarm; лажна тревога false alarm; воздушна тревога air-raid warning

тревожен -жна *adj literary* alarming, disturbing; alarm, alert *attrib.*, troubled, anxious, uneasy; тревожни гласови anxious voices; тревожен сигнал alarm signal; тревожни вести alarming news

тревожи *impf literary* to alarm, worry, trouble

тревожно *adv literary* anxiously, in great alarm; alarmingly

тревопасен -сна *adj* herbivorous; тревопасно животно herbivorous animal

тревче *n dim. of* тревка

трегер *m* **1** *Building* main beam, main spar **2** (*pl*) braces, *Am.* suspenders

трезвен *adj* sober; *fig.* sensible, sober-minded; трезвен суд a sober judgement

трезвеник -ци *m* teetotaller, total abstainer, non-drinker

трезвеништво *n* temperance movement

трезвеност *f* sobriety; (*воздржливост*) temperance

трезен -зна *adj* sober (*also fig.*)

трезни *impf* **I** to sober up, dry out *trans.*; *fig.* to sober up, bring (*s.o.*) to his senses **II – се** to sober up, dry out *intrans.*; *fig.* to come to one's senses

трем *m* **1** porch, verandah; corridor; doorway **2** (*предворје*) entrance-hall; antechamber; lobby

трема *f* stage fright; butterflies in the stomach

трембет *m arch. see* трембете

тремен -мна *adj* porch *attrib.*; antechamber *attrib.*; lobby *attrib.*; тремни столбови verandah posts; porch columns

тремпете *n arch.* (*барабан*) drum; бие тремпете to beat a drum

тремче *n dim. of* трем

трендафил *m Bot.* rose; ❑ црвен како трендафил rose-red

трендафилов *adj* rose; трендафилов мирис scent of roses

тренер *m Sport.* trainer, coach

тренерка *f* 1 (*fem. form*) *see* тренер 2 track-suit, sweatsuit

тренерски *adj* trainer's, coach's; training *attrib.*; тренерска школа training school

тренинг -зи *m Sport.* training, practice

тренира *pf & impf Sport.* I to train *trans. & intrans.*; to coach II – се to train *intrans.*

тренирка *f* (*usu. pl*) *see* тренерка 2

трепери *impf* 1 to shake *intrans.*, tremble, quiver; to vibrate; to shiver; (*за мускул*) to twitch; лисјето треперea the leaves were trembling; гласот му трепери his voice quavers 2 (*со крилја*) to flutter 3 (*за ѕвезди*) to twinkle; (*за светлина, ламба, пламен*) to flicker 4 *fig.* to be in terror (dread) (*од – of*); трепери од мене he is terrified of me

треперлив *adj* shaking, trembling; tremulous; shaky; flickering; треперлива рака trembling hand; треперлив глас quavering voice; треперлива светлина flickering light

трепет *m* shaking, trembling, quivering; (*возбуда*) thrill, excitement; trepidation; vibration; (*на мускул*) twitch; радосен трепет a quiver of joy; ❑ страв и трепет fear and trembling

трепетен -тна *adj* anxious; eager; trembling, tremulous; радосни и трепетни солзи tears of joy and excitement; со трепетен глас in a tremulous voice

трепети *impf* to tremble, quiver; to vibrate; to twinkle; to flicker; ❑ трепети како срна to tremble like a leaf; ѕвездите трепетеа the stars were twinkling

трепетлив *adj* trembling; tremulous; shaky; flickering; трепетлив пламен flickering flame; трепетлив глас tremulous voice

трепетлика *f Bot.* (Populus tremula) aspen

трепетулчица *f f.p. see* трепетуша

трепетуша & трепетушка *f* sparkler, pin (*costume jewellery*)

трепка[1] *f* (*клепка*) eyelash

трепка[2] *impf* 1 to blink; трепка со очите to blink 2 (*светка*) to flicker; (*за ѕвезда*) to twinkle; кандилцето трепка the icon lamp is flickering 3 (*трепери*) to tremble; to flutter; трепка со крилјата to flutter its wings

трепкав *adj* 1 (*светкав*) flickering 2 (*треперлив*) quivering, trembling; трепкав лист trembling leaf

треплив *adj see* трепкав

трепне *pf* трепна *aor.* 1 to blink; трепне со очите to blink; ❑ око нема да му трепне he won't bat an eyelid; дури <со око> да трепнеш in the twinkling of an eye; додека <да> трепнеш before you can say Jack Robinson (*затрепери*) to start shaking (trembling)

трепнеж *m poet.* shaking, trembling; quivering; (*возбуда*) thrill

трепнува *impf of* трепне; ❑ око не му трепнува he doesn't bat an eyelid

трепнување *n of* трепнува; само за едно трепнување in the twinkling of an eye

тресајка *f dial. see* тресалка 2

тресалка *f* 1 carpet-beater, rug-beater 2 (*во воденица*) shoe, trough, spout 3 *fig.* skinflint

тресе *impf* I 1 to shake *trans.*; тресе сливи/јаболка од дрво to shake (knock down) plums/apples from a tree; ❑ тресе глупости to talk nonsense 2 to beat *trans.*; to shake out; тресе килим to beat a rug; тресе постела to shake out the bedding 3 *impers.* (*with acc.*) ме тресе I have a fever II – се 1 to shake *intrans.*; to tremble, quiver; рацете му се тресеа his hands were shaking; се тресе од студ he is shivering with cold 2 to jolt, jerk *intrans.*; колата се тресеше по селскиот пат the cart was jolting along the country road 3 to worry, be worried (*над – about*); се тресе над децата she is worried about the children; she dotes on the children; се тресе над секој денар to grudge every penny

тресет *m* peat

треска[1] *f* fever; треска ме тресе I have a fever, I am feverish; ме фаќа треска I am catching a fever; скришна треска chronic fever (*esp. tuberculosis*); тригодишна треска intermittent fever, remittent <fever>; блатна треска malaria, swamp fever; жолта треска yellow fever; тропска треска tropical fever; тифусна треска typhoid <fever>

треска[2] *f* (*usu. pl*) kindling; собира трески to collect kindling

треска[3] *impf* 1 *see* тресне 1–3 2 *f.p.* to upset, distress; не трескај ми го срцево don't upset me! 3 *fig.* to make a pig of o.s., gorge

трескав *adj* feverish (*also fig.*), febrile; frantic, frenzied, frenetic; трескави подготовки feverish preparations

трескот[1] *m* crash<ing>, bang<ing>; clap <of thunder>; викот и трескот hue and cry

трескот[2] *m Bot. see* троскот

трескоти *impf* to bang, crash *intrans*; to go bang (crash); to thunder

трескотница *f see* трескот[1]

трескулав *adj f.p.* (*трескав*) feverish; thin; sickly

треслив *adj literary* trembling, shaking; shaky; тресливо плачење convulsive sobbing

треснатик -ци *m* good-for-nothing, scoundrel

треснатица *f* (*fem. form*) *see* треснатик

тресне *pf* тресна *aor.* I 1 to hit, strike; to slam; to whack; to slap; (*нешто*) to bang *trans.*; to crash *trans.*; ѝ тресна една шлаканица he slapped her face; ја тресна колата he crashed the car; тресне нешто одземи to knock s.th. to the ground; тресне врата to slam a door 2 *fig.* to blurt out; тресне глупост to make a stupid remark 3 to come down with a crash; (*за гром*) to crash; тресна на подот he crashed to the floor 4 *colloq.* to kick the bucket, croak; да треснеш! damn you! II – се to hit o.s., bump into; си ја тресна главата he hit his head

треснува (се) *impf of* тресне (се)

тресок -ци *m see* трескот[1]

тресопатка *f Zool.* (Motacilla alba) pied wagtail

тресотија *f rare* 1 earthquake; tremor 2 roar, rumble, boom

трет *adj num* third; на трето место in the third place; thirdly; на третиот ден on the third day; ❑ трета рака third picking (*of tobacco*); од трета рака third-hand; трето нема there is no third way; преку трето лице from/through a third party; третиот сталеж *Hist.* (*in France*) the third estate; трето лице 1. *Gram.* third person 2. third party (person); патува со трета класа to travel third-class; *Med.* од трет степен third-degree; *see* трети

трета *f see* третина

трети *adj num* third; трети клас third form (*of secondary school*); трети кат third floor; на трети мај on the third of May; *see* трет

третина *f* third <part>; две третини two thirds

третинка *f dim. of* третина

третира *impf* 1 to treat; добро третира некого to treat s.o. well 2 to deal with, treat; оваа книга третира познати прашања this book treats well-known issues

третјак -ци *m see* треќак

третман *m* treatment; третман на прашање treatment of an issue; лекарски третман medical treatment; козметички третман beauty treatment

третокласен -сна *adj* third-class, third-rate

третокласник -ци *m* pupil in the third form (*of secondary school*), third-former

третосложен -жна *adj Phon.* (*of stress*) on the third syllable, third-syllable

третостепен *adj* 1 third-class; minor; inferior, mediocre; третостепена улога supporting role 2 third-level; tertiary; третостепена настава third-level instruction; третостепено образование tertiary education

треќак *m* three-year-old animal; елен треќак three-year-old deer

треќ & **треќи** *adj num dial. see* трет, трети

трешница *f* 1 slap; smack; удри некому трешница to slap s.o. 2 (*беља*) blow, misfortune

трештен *adj* wild, crazy; dazed

трешти[1] *impf* to blare; to roar; to rumble, thunder; радиото трешти the radio is blaring; топовите трештат the cannons are roaring

трешти[2] *pf* 1 (*of thunder and lightning*) to strike 2 to start (*running*), bolt *intrans.*; трешти да бега he took to his heels

тржествен *adj literary see* свечен

тржество *n literary* 1 celebration, *see* свеченост 2 triumph

тржествува *impf literary* to celebrate; to triumph

трзалица *f* (*за гитара и сл.*) plectrum

три *num* three; во три часот at three o'clock; два-три дена two or three days; три пати three times, *arch.* thrice; ❏ се прави на три и пол to play the innocent; секое чудо за три дена a nine days' wonder

триаголен -лна *adj* triangular, three-cornered

триаголник -ци *m* triangle

триангл -гли *m Mus.* triangle

триангулација *f* triangulation

триангулационен -она *adj* triangulate

трибина *f* rostrum, speaker's platform, tribune; *fig.* forum; свечена трибина official stand; новинарска трибина (*на натпревар*) stand for the press; (*во парламент*) press gallery

трибун *m* tribune; *fig.* leader, champion

трибуна *f see* трибина

трибунал *m* tribunal

трибунски *adj* tribune's

трибут *m* tribute

тривиден -дна *adj* of three sorts

тривијален -лна *adj* trivial, banal; hackneyed

тривијалност *f* triviality

триглав *adj* three-headed; триглава ламја three-headed dragon

тригодински *adj f.p. see* тригодишен

тригодишен -шна *adj* 1 three-year-old 2 three-year, for/of three years; triennial; тригодишен план three-year plan; тригодишна треска intermittent fever, remittent <fever>; тригодишно растение triennial plant

тригодишнина *f* third anniversary

тригонометрија *f Math.* trigonometry

тригонометриски *adj Math.* trigonometric; тригонометриски функции trigonometric functions

тридневен -вна *adj* lasting three days; three days old; тридневен престој three-day stay; тридневна треска tertian fever

трие *impf* 1 to rub *trans.*; to massage; to scrub, scour; трие очи to rub one's eyes; трие раце to rub one's hands (*also fig.*); трие под to scrub the floor 2 to grate, grind, mash; трие грав to mash beans; ❏ трие некому сол на главата to rub s.o.'s nose in it 3 (*жули*) to chafe *trans.*; торбата ми го трие вратот this bag chafes on my neck **II** – **се** 1 to rub (*од нешто* – *against s.th.*) *intrans.* 2 to rub, scrub o.s.; to massage o.s.

триенале *n* triennial festival, *triennale*

триење *n* friction (*also fig.*); rubbing

триер *m* sorting/sampling machine (*for grains*)

триесет *num* thirty

триесетгодишен -шна *adj* 1 thirty years old; триесетгодишен човек thirty-year-old <person> 2 lasting thirty years; триесетгодишна војна Thirty Years' War

триесетгодишнина *f* thirtieth anniversary

триесетдневен -вна *adj* thirty-day, lasting thirty days

триесетина 1 *num* (*of men or mixed groups*) thirty, *see* триесетмина 2 *num* about thirty, thirty odd 3 *f* thirtieth <part>

триесетка *f* <the figure> thirty; no. 30 bus/tram, etc.

триесетмина *num* (*of men or mixed groups*) thirty

триесетти *adj num* thirtieth

триж, трижд & **трижди** *adv dial. see* трипати

тризаб *adj* three-toothed; three-pronged, three-tined; тризаба вила trident, three-pronged fork

тријада *f* triad; triple

тријажа *f* triage

тријазичен -чна *adj* trilingual

тријазичност *f* trilingualism

тријач *m* bath-house attendant

тријачка *f* (*fem. form*) *see* тријач

трик *m* trick; stunt; акробатски трик acrobatic feat; ❏ му ги научив трlicте I know his tricks

трикатен -тна *adj* of three storeys; трикатна зграда three-storey building

трикатница *f* three-storey building

трико *n* 1 (*ткаенина*) tricot; stockinet; jersey 2 leotard; <pair of> tights, fleshings, leggings

трикотажа *f* knitwear

трикотажен -жна *adj* knitwear; knitted; трикотажна индустрија knitwear industry; трикотажна облека knitted garment

трикрак *adj* three-legged; tripod

трикратен -тна *adj* threefold, triple; three-time; трикратна загуба threefold loss; трикратен шампион three-time champion

трикрилен -лна *adj* three-winged/-leaved; трикрилна врата three-leaved door

трилер[1] *m* thriller

трилер[2] *m Mus.* trill

трилио́н *m* trillion

трилистен -сна *adj* three-leaved, *Bot.* trifoliate; трилисна детелина trefoil, three-leaved clover

трилогија -ии *f* trilogy

трима *num dial. see* тројца

тримесечен -чна *adj* **1** lasting three months; тримесечен престој three-month stay **2** quarterly; тримесечно списание quarterly journal

тримесечје *n* quarter; trimester; three-month term; прво тримесечје на една година first quarter of a year

тримесечник -ци *m* quarterly <publication>

тримесечно *adv* quarterly, <once> every three months; списанието излегува тримесечно the journal is published quarterly

тримéстар -три *m* (*see* тримесечје) quarter; trimester; three-month term

триместрáлен -лна *adj* quarterly; trimester *attrib.*; term *attrib.*

тримина *num see* тројца

тримир *m* three-day fast (*at the beginning of Lent*); држи тримир to observe the three-day fast

тримири *impf* to fast for three days

тримоторен -рна *adj* three-engine; тримоторен авион three-engine aeroplane

тринаесет *num* thirteen

тринаестогодишен -шна *adj* **1** thirteen years old **2** lasting thirteen years

тринаесетдневен -вна *adj* lasting thirteen days

тринаесетина **1** *num* (*of men or mixed groups*) thirteen, *see* тринаесетмина **2** thirteenth <part>

тринаесетка *f* <the figure> thirteen; no. 13 bus/tram etc.

тринаесетмина *num* (*of men or mixed groups*) thirteen

тринаесетти *adj num* thirteenth

тринеделен -лна *adj* lasting three weeks

тринитротолуол *m* TNT, trinitrotoluene, trinitrotoluol, *see* тротил

триногарник -ци *m* three-legged stool; tripod; *see* триножник

триножен -жна *adj* three-legged; триножно столче small three-legged stool

триножник -ци *m* three-legged stool; tripod

трино́м *m Math.* trinomial

трио *n Mus.* trio

триод *m Rel.* liturgical book for Lent

трио́да *f* triode

триоден -дна *adj* triode; триодна цевка triode valve

трио́ла *f Mus.* triplet

триолéт *m Prosody* triolet

трипати *adv* three times, *arch.* thrice; трипати потежок three times as heavy; трипати по два three times two

трипер *m* gonorrhoea

трипликáт *m* triplicate

трипроцентен -тна *adj* three-percent *attrib.*

триреден -дна *adj* of/in three rows

трирог *adj* three-horned, tricorn<e>; трирога шапка tricorne hat, cocked hat

трироден -дна *adj Gram.* of three genders

трисагија *f* threefold prayer to the Holy Trinity

трисложен -жна *adj* of three syllables, trisyllabic; трисложни зборови trisyllabic words

трисобен -бна *adj* of three rooms; трисобен стан three-room flat

триста *num* three hundred; ❏ триста маки, триста бели видов (претрпев) I have been through untold suffering; триста стравови dread, mortal terror, *colloq.* blue funk; триста чуда wonder upon wonder

тристапен -пна *adj Prosody* consisting of three feet; тристапен јамб iambic trimeter

тристепен *adj* on three levels; тристепена настава three-level instruction

тристих -си *m Literature* tristich

тристран *adj* **1** three-sided, trilateral; тристрана пирамида three-sided pyramid **2** tripartite; тристран договор tripartite treaty; тристрана спогодба tripartite agreement

тритолку *adv colloq.* three times as much

тритомен -мна *adj* in three volumes; тритомен речник three-volume dictionary

тритон *m Zool.* (Triton *or* Triturus) newt

тритонски *adj* three-tonne; тритонски камион three-tonne lorry (*Am.* truck)

триумви́р *m* triumvir

триумвирáт *m Hist., fig.* triumvirate

триумф *m* triumph

триумфáлен -лна *adj* triumphal; triumphant; триумфална порта triumphal arch; триумфален поглед triumphant air

триумфално *adv* triumphantly, in triumph

триумфáтор *m* conqueror; conquering hero; victor; winner; champion

триумфи́ра *pf & impf* to triumph (над – over); to exult

трихи́на *f* trichina

трици *pl* **1** bran; chaff **2** *fig.* nonsense; trifles

трици́кл *m* tricycle

тричав *adj* containing bran/chaff; тричаво брашно flour with high bran content, coarse flour

тричасовен -вна *adj* lasting three hours; тричасовен марш three-hour march

тричекор *m* triple jump; hop, step and jump

тричетвртински *adj Mus.* three-four; тричетвртински такт three-four time

три-четириесет *num* thirty or forty; три-четириесет кила thirty or forty kilos

три-четиринаесет *num* thirteen or fourteen

трички *pl dim. of* трици

тричленен -лена *adj* of three members (parts); тричлена комисија three-member committee; тричленен израз *Math.* trinomial, *see* трином

трк *m* run; ајде, трк! come on! ready, steady, go!

трка *f* **1** run **2** race; коњски трки horse races; ❏ мртва трка dead heat; трка со време race against time; трка во вооружувањето arms race

трка се *impf* to race

тркала *impf* **I** to roll, bowl, trundle, wheel *trans.*; to roll down *trans.* **II** – се **1** to roll, tumble *intrans.*; to trundle *intrans.*; to roll down *intrans.*; to wallow **2** to lie about (around), be scattered about, litter

тркалезен -зна & **тркалест** *adj* round; circular; rotund; тркалезно лице round face; ❑ разговори на тркалезна маса round-table talks

тркалиште *n* track; racetrack; (*за коњи*) racecourse

тркалка *impf dim. of* тркала

тркалне *pf* тркална *aor.* to roll *trans.* (bowl, trundle, wheel) for a while

тркало *n* wheel; ќе дојде коло на тркало *prov.* my day will come

тркалообразен -зна *adj* round-faced, chubby

тркалце *n dim. of* тркало

тркач *m* runner, athlete; коњ тркач, тркачки коњ racehorse

тркачица *f (fem. form) see* тркач

тркачки *adj* race *attrib.*; тркачки коњ racehorse; тркачки велосипед racing cycle

тркне *pf* тркна *aor.* to run, sprint; to drop in (*кај - он*); *Brit. colloq.* to nip out

тркнува *impf of* тркне

трла (се) *impf dial. see* трие (се)

трлав & **трлив** *adj dial.* rotten; трлава бука а rotten beech; *see* гнил

трлинка *f Bot. see* трненка

трло *n* <sheep>fold; sheepcote

трмка *f dial. see* улиште

трн *m*, трње *coll.* **1** *Bot.* (Paliurus aculeatus, Sanguisorba spinosa, Prunus spinosa, etc.) Jerusalem thorn, Christ's thorn; blackthorn; thistle; од трн та на глог *prov.* out of the frying-pan into the fire **2** thorn, spine; prickle; ❑ клава си трн во здрава нога to shoot o.s. in the foot; седи како на трње to be on tenterhooks; трн му е во окото на некого to be a thorn in s.o.'s side/flesh

трнарче *n Zool.* (Carduelis carduelis) goldfinch

трненка & **трнинка** *f Bot.* (Prunus spinosa) blackthorn; (*плодот*) sloe

трница *f dial. see* трњак

трнка *f* **1** *Bot.* (Crataegus oxyacantha) common hawthorn, whitethorn **2** *Bot.* (Prunus spinosa) *see* трненка **3** *see* трнче

трнлив *adj* thorny; *fig.* arduous; трнлив терен thorny ground; трнлив пат а life full of hardship; трнлив венец crown of thorns

трнов *adj* thorn *attrib.*, made of thorns; трнов венец crown of thorns

трноса *pf* **1** to become overgrown with thorns/thistles **2** to enclose (*s.th.*) with a thorny hedge

трносува *impf of* трноса

трнче *n* prickle, spine, spinule, thorn

трњак -ци *m* thicket of thorn-bushes

троа *adv* a little; троа солца a pinch of salt; троа пари a little money; троа подобар a little better; по троа a little at a time; троа по троа little by little, bit by bit; *see* трошка 2

тробоен -јна *adj* of three colours, tricolour<ed>; тробојно знаме tricolour flag

тробојка *f* tricolour <flag>

трова *f dial. see* трошка

тровче *n dim. of* трошка

трога *impf of* трогне; ни ги трога срцата it touches our hearts

трогателен -лна *adj literary* touching, moving; pathetic; трогателни зборови touching words

троглодѝт *m (usu. pl)* troglodyte

трогнат *adj literary* touched, moved; трогнат до солзи moved to tears

троглив *adj see* трогателен

трогне *pf* трогна *aor. literary* to touch, move, affect *trans.*; to hurt, wound, upset; тоа ме трогна до солзи that moved me to tears

трогнува *impf of* трогне

троделен -лна *adj* triple; *Mus.* троделен такт triple time

тродимензионáлен -лна *adj* three-dimensional, 3-D; тродимензионален филм three-dimensional film

троен -јна *adj* **1** triple; treble; triplicate; three-ply; тројни синџири triple chains; троен сојуз Triple Alliance; *Math.* тројно правило the rule of three **2** three times as much, threefold; тројна сума пари three times as much money, a threefold sum of money

трозаб *adj see* тризаб

трои *adj num f.p. see* трети

троица *f Rel.* Trinity; света троица Holy Trinity

тројка *f* **1** (*цифрата* 3) <figure> three **2** (*школска оцена*) three (*out of five, hence = good*), credit **3** (*во карти*) three; тројка и кец a three and an ace **4** (*трамвај, автобус итн.*) <number> three **5** (*запрега*) troika, three-horse carriage/sleigh, three-in-hand **6** (*група*) three; trio

тројкаџија -ии *m colloq.* average (fair) pupil/student

тројно *adv* three times, threefold; тројно посилен three times as strong; тројно повеќе three times as much/many

тројноглав & **тројоглав** *adj arch. & f.p.* three-headed; змија тројноглава (тројоглава) a three-headed serpent

тројство *m* trinity

тројца *num (group of three men or mixed group)* three; сите тројца загинаа all three died; тројца синови three sons

тројче *n dim. of* тројка

трокатен -тна *adj see* трикатен

трокатница *f see* трикатница

трокрак *adj see* трикрак

трократен -тна *adj see* трикратен

трокрилен -лна *adj see* трикрилен

трола *f Tech.* trolley

тролејбус *m* trolleybus

тролејбуски *adj* trolleybus; тролејбуска станица trolleybus stop

тролистен -сна *adj see* трилистен

тром & **тромав** *adj* clumsy; sluggish; lumbering; тром човек oaf

тромаво *adv see* тромо

тромавост *f see* тромост

тромб *m Med.* thrombus

тромблóн *m Mil.* grenade launcher

тромбóза *f Med.* thrombosis

тромбóн *m Mus.* trombone

тромбоцѝт *m (usu. pl)* thrombocyte

тромеѓа *f literary* junction of three borders

тромесечен -чна *adj see* тримесечен

тромесечје *n see* тримесечје

тромесечник -ци *m see* тримесечник

тромесечно *adv see* тримесечно

тромо *adv* clumsily; sluggishly

тромост *f* clumsiness; sluggishness

тромоторен -рна *adj see* тримоторен

тромпе́та *f Mus.* trumpet

трон *m* throne

тронsа *adv* a little, a dash; тронsа леб a morsel of bread; тронsа вода a drop of water; *see* трошичка

троножен -жна *adj see* триножен

тронта *f* clumsy woman, bungler, blunderer

тронтав *adj* clumsy, gauche, bungling

тронтавост *f* clumsiness, gaucherie, bungling

тронтак -ци *m* clumsy child

тронталест & тронтест *adj see* тронтав

тронь *m dial.* wooden bed (*in village houses*)

тропа¹ *f Literature* trope

тропа² *impf see* тропне

тропаница *f* banging; rattling; knock<ing>; beat<ing>

тропар *m Rel.* Orthodox anthem for Saint's day; според светецот и тропарот *prov.* everyone gets his just deserts

тропи *pl* tropics

тропика́л *m* light synthetic material

тропка *impf dim. of* тропа

тропне *pf* тропна *aor.* 1 to make a noise; to thud, bang; тропне со нозете to stamp one's feet 2 to knock; тропне на врата to knock at a door 3 to beat *intrans.*; срцето му тропна посилно his heart started beating faster 4 *fig.* to blurt out; ❏ тропне и остане жив to drop a clanger

тропнува *impf of* тропне

тропот *m* 1 clatter, rattle; тропот на кола rattle of a cart 2 thud; stamping; тропот на чекори heavy foot-falls, tramping of feet; stamping

тропоти *impf* 1 to clatter, rattle 2 to thud; to stamp one's feet

тропотница *f* clatter<ing>, rattle; banging, crashing; stamping; тропотница на звонци clanging of bells

тропроцентен -тна *adj see* трипроцентен

тропски *adj* tropical; тропска клима tropical climate; тропски појас torrid zone

трореден -дна *adj see* триреден

тророг *adj see* трирог

тророден -дна *adj Gram. see* трироден

троска *f Bot.* (Polygonum aviculare) knot-grass

троскот *m Bot.* (Andropogon ischaemum) beard grass, bluestem, broom sedge

тросложен -жна *adj see* трисложен

трособен -бна *adj see* трисобен

троспратен -тна *adj see* трикатен

троспратница *f see* трикатница

тростран *adj see* тристран

троти́л *m* TNT, trotyl, *see* тринитротолуол

тротине́т *m* <child's> scooter

тротоа́р *m* pavement, footpath, *Am.* sidewalk

тротоа́рски *adj* pavement, footpath, *Am.* sidewalk *attrib.*

трофе́ен -јна *adj* captured; trophy *attrib.*; трофејно оружје captured weapons

трофе́ј -еи *m* trophy; booty

трохе́ј -еи *m Prosody* trochee

трохе́јски *adj Prosody* trochaic; трохејска стапка trochee

трошарина *f* excise; toll-house

трошарински *adj* excise *attrib.*; трошаринска станица excise (customs) post

трошач *m* spender, squanderer

трошен -шна *adj literary* dilapidated, tumbledown

троши *impf* I 1 to crumble *trans.* 2 to spend; to waste *trans.*; троши пари to spend money; троши преку мера to live beyond one's means 3 to consume, use; таа кола троши многу бензин that car uses a lot of petrol II – се 1 to crumble *intrans.* 2 to wear out *intrans.*; моторот се троши the motor is wearing out

троширало *n Bot.* (Colutea arborescens) bladder senna, *see* зајачковина 1

трошичка *f dim. of* трошка (*also as adv*); трошичка леб a wee bit of bread

трошка *f* 1 crumb; small piece; трошка од леб a breadcrumb; a crumb of bread; трошка земја a tiny bit of land 2 a little, a bit (*also as adv*); помрдни се трошка move over a bit! ❏ дај ми трошка мегдан give me a little time! give me a little longer! трошка по трошка little by little, bit by bit; ни трошка not a bit; нема ни трошка сомнение there is not a shadow of a doubt

трошлив *adj* 1 crumbly; crumbling; friable 2 dilapidated, *see* трошен

трошок -ци *m* cost, expense; expenditure; судски трошоци court costs; сноси (поднесува) трошоци to bear (meet, defray) the costs; надомести трошоци to reimburse (*s.o.*) for costs; to refund (repay) expenses; прави трошоци to incur (run up) expenses; изложува некого на трошок to put s.o. to the expense (*of*); трошоци за одржување maintenance costs; на свој трошок at one's own expense; ❏ со ист трошок while you are about it; while you are there

трошоли *impf* (*of a child*) to burble, prattle, babble *intrans.*

трпеж *m* patience; ❏ трпеж му е мајката! take it easy! крпеж трпеж два века; крпеж и трпеж куќа врти *prov.* a stitch in time saves nine

трпеза *f* 1 dining-table; стави трпеза to set the table; на чело на трпезата at the head of the table 2 (*синија*) round metal tray

трпезарија -ии *f* 1 dining-room; (*во одморалиште или манастир*) refectory; (*во воз*) dining-car 2 *colloq.* (*трпеза*) dining-table; dining-room suite

трпезариски *adj* dining-room/refectory *attrib.*; трпезариски мебел dining-room furniture (suite)

трпезен -зна *adj* table *attrib.*; трпезно вино table wine

трпезница *f dial.* kind of large dining-table

трпелив *adj* patient; tolerant

трпеливо *adv* patiently; tolerantly

трпеливост *f* patience; tolerance

трпение *n* patience; endurance; forbearance; испроба нечие трпение to try s.o.'s patience; изгуби трпение to lose one's patience; ја преполни чашата на трпението to exasperate s.o.; ❏ трпение спасение everything comes to him who waits

трпи *impf* I 1 to endure, bear, suffer (*trans. and intrans.*); to undergo; to put up with; to take, stand, abide; трпи болка to endure pain; трпи пораз to suffer a defeat; мораш да трпиш you must grin and bear it; тој може многу да трпи he can take a lot; не можам него да го трпам I can't abide him; I can't stand it; ❏ *prov.* хартијата сѐ трпи paper won't blush 2 (*допушта*) to permit, stand for, tolerate, brook; работата не трпи одлагање the matter brooks no delay; книгата не трпи критика the book is above criticism **3** to have patience **II – се** to tolerate s.o.; to get on together; тие двајца не се трпат there is no love lost between those two

трпкавица *f* numbness; ногата ми фати трпкавица my foot has gone to sleep

трпки *pl* shudder, shiver; goose-flesh, goose-pimples; pins and needles; му поминаа трпки по снагата a shiver ran through him

трпкост *f* astringency, acerbity, tartness, sourness

трпне & **трпнее** *impf* **1** to have goose-flesh; to shiver; трпне од студ to shiver (shudder) with cold; to have goose-flesh **2** to go numb; рацете ми трпнат (трпнеат) my hands are going numb **3** to be afraid/worried

трпнеж *m* shiver; pins and needles

трпок -пка *adj* astringent, acerbic, tart, sour; трпко вино sour wine; трпок збор harsh word

трска *f* **1** *Bot.* (Phragmites communis) <common> reed; (Juncaceae) rush; шеќерна трска (Saccharum officinarum) sugar cane **2** *pl* reed-bed, reed-marsh **3** walking-stick; cane; трска за тресење carpet-beater, rug-beater; трска за риби fishing-rod; ❏ танок како трска <as> thin as a rake **4** drinking straw; пие со трска to drink through a straw

трстика *f* *Bot.* **1** *see* трска **2** (Arundo donax) giant reed

трти се *impf* **1** to stoop <down> **2** to strut, put on airs

тртка *f* **1** *see* тртник **2** (брадавица) wart; (здебелена кожа) callus

тртник -ци *m* rump (*of bird, etc.*)

тртори *impf* to burble, babble, prattle

труба *f* **1** *Mus.* trumpet; (рог) bugle; horn **2** *fig.* roll; завитка нешто во <вид на> труба to roll s.th. up

трубадур *m* troubadour

трубадурски *adj* troubadour's; трубадурски песни troubadour's songs

трубач *m* trumpeter; (со рог) bugler

трубачки *adj* trumpeter's; trumpet *attrib.*

трубен -бна *adj* trumpet; bugle; horn; трубен сигнал clarion call

труби *impf* **1** to play the trumpet **2** *fig.* to trumpet <forth>, trumpet about, blare forth

трубичка *f dim. of* труба

труд *m* **1** work, labour, toil; физички труд manual labour; продуктивност на трудот labour productivity **2** *pl* -ови (*scholarly*) works **3** effort, trouble; вложи труд во нешто to put great effort into s.th.; ❏ со голем труд with great effort; with great difficulty; не жали труд to spare no effort; без труд не се ора no gain without pain

трудбеник -ци *m* worker, toiler; *see* работник

трудбеничка *f* (*fem. form*) *see* трудбеник

трудбенички *adj* worker's

труден -дна *adj* **1** *only f* (бремена) pregnant, expecting, with child; трудна жена pregnant woman **2** (тежок) hard, difficult; трудна работа hard work

труди *impf* **I** *f.p. see* уморува, мачи¹ **II – се 1** to toil, exert o.s. **2** to try <hard> (*да – то*); to make an effort; се трудев да го убедам I tried to convince him; не се ни труди he doesn't even bother

трудница *f* pregnant woman, expectant mother

трудно *adv* with difficulty; hard

трудност *f* **1** (*only sg*) pregnancy, pregnant condition **2** difficulty

трудов *adj* labour, work *attrib.*; трудова медицина industrial medicine

трудоден -дни *m obs.* day's work; one day's wage

трудољубив *adj* hard-working, industrious

трудољубиво *adv* industriously, conscientiously

трудољубивост *f* & **трудољубие** *n* industriousness, conscientiousness, diligence

труе *impf* **I** to poison (*also fig.*); to pollute, contaminate; труе глувци to poison mice; труе воздух to pollute the air; тој ми го труе животот he is the bane of my life **II – се** to take poison

труженик -ци *m literary* worker; working man; toiler, zealous worker

труженичка *f literary* (*fem. form*) *see* труженик

труженички *adj literary* toiling; of hard work; труженички живот a life of hard labour; an active life

труженищво *n literary* toil, hard work; labour

трујач *m* poisoner

трујачка *f* poisoning; poison

трумбук -ци *m see* труп 3

трунтест *adj dial. see* тронтест

труп¹ *m* **1** (на човек) body; trunk, torso; (мртов) corpse, cadaver **2** body; (на авион) fuselage, hull; (на брод) hull; (на размонтиран брод) hulk; (на столб) shaft **3** (од дрво) log; stump <of a tree> **4** *fig.* blockhead

труп² *interj* (при паѓање) thud! труп-труп! (за чекори) tramp, tramp! thud, thud!; stamp! (за чукање) knock, knock!

трупа¹ *f* **1** (*only pl*) troops; смотра на трупите inspection of the troops; parade **2** *Mil.* unit; инженерска трупа engineering unit; construction unit **3** troupe, company, ensemble; патувачка трупа travelling company

трупа² *f* kind of card game

трупа³ *interj in the expressions:* рупа-трупа, трапа-трупа (за лесни чекори) pitter-patter! pit-a-pat! (за тешки чекори) tramp, tramp! thud, thud! (за старо возило и сл.) clatter-bang; (силно) thump! thump!

трупа⁴ *impf* **I** to amass; to hoard, pile up; to concentrate, build up *trans.*; трупа богатство to amass/hoard wealth; трупа војски to concentrate troops **II – се** (за нешто) to accumulate, pile up *intrans.*; (за луѓе) to congregate, gather, throng *intrans.*

трупа⁵ *impf of* трупне I

трупав *adj dial.* simple, stupid

трупач *m see* сечач

трупен -пна *adj* troop *attrib.*; трупна единица army unit

трупец -пци *m* log

трупечки *adv* with one's legs together; рипа, скока трупечки to jump with one's legs together; *see* токмонога, токмонозе

трупиште *n augm. of* труп¹

трупка *f Bot.* (Raphanus sativus) radish

трупне *pf* трупна *aor.* **I 1** to tread heavily **2** to knock, bang **II – се** to fall, drop; се трупна право в кревет he fell straight into bed

трупче *n dim. of* труп¹

труска *impf* **I** to shake, jolt *trans.* **II – се** to shake, jolt *intrans.*

труст *m Comm.* trust; ❏ труст на мозоци brains trust

трут *m* drone (*also fig.*)

труцка (се) *impf see* труска (се)

трча *impf* to run *intrans.*; to hurry; to rush about; трча по некого to run after s.o.; трча по куќата to bustle about the house; трча некому на помош to hasten to s.o.'s aid; не трчај! take your time! не трчај како прле пред магаре *prov.* look before you leap

трчана & **трчанка** *adv* at a run, running; до дома си дојде трчанка he came running home

трчаница **1** *f* run; со трчаница running; со трчаница отиде дома he ran home **2** *adv* running; *Mil.* at the double

трчилаж *m* rumour-monger, gossip

трчка *impf dim. of* трча

трчкало *m* errand-runner, cat's-paw

трчне *pf* трчна *aor.* to run for a while; трчна по неа he ran after her

трчнува *impf of* трчне

ту[1] *conj* ту . . . ту now . . . now . . . ; ту едно ту друго now one thing, now another

ту[2] *interj* alas! woe! ту што сторив! oh dear, what have I done!

туба *f* **1** tube (*for toothpaste, etc.*) **2** glass tube **3** *Mus.* tuba

туберкулóза *f Med.* tuberculosis, TB, consumption; белодробна туберкулоза pulmonary tuberculosis; брзотечна туберкулоза galloping consumption

туберкулóзен -зна *adj* tubercular; consumptive; туберкулозен процес tubercular process; туберкулозен човек tubercular (consumptive) (patient)

туберóза *f Bot.* (Polianthes tuberosa) tuberose

тува *adv dial. see* тука

туѓ *adj* **1** someone else's; туѓ имот someone else's property; без туѓа помош unaided; without outside help; (*as noun*) туѓо<то> s.o. else's property; ❏ на туѓ грб at s.o. else's expense; по туѓ грб не боли no skin off my nose; под туѓо име under an assumed name; се кити со туѓи перје to deck o.s. in borrowed plumes; тоа е туѓо масло s.o. else is behind it; туѓата кокошка поголеми јајца снесла *prov.* the grass is always greener on the other side of the fence **2** foreign, alien; unknown, strange; туѓ човек outsider; туѓи луѓе strangers; туѓ јазик foreign language; туѓи обичаи alien ways; интригите му се туѓи he is a stranger to scheming; туѓо влијание external influence

туѓин *m see* туѓинец

туѓина *f* foreign parts; оди на туѓина to go abroad (*Austral.* overseas)

туѓинец -нци *m* **1** foreigner **2** *colloq., arch.* stranger, outsider

туѓинка *f* (*fem. form*) *see* туѓинец

туѓински *adj* alien; foreign; туѓински обичаи alien ways

туѓинче *n usu. in f.p. dim. of* туѓинец

туѓоземен -мна *adj see* странски

туѓоземец -мци *m see* странец

туѓоземка *f* (*fem. form*) *see* туѓоземец

туѓоземски *adj see* туѓоземен

туѓоземство *n see* странство

тужба *f Leg.* (кривично право) charge<s>, indictment; prosecution; (граѓанско право) lawsuit; поднесе (подаде, подигне) тужба против некого (кривично право) to bring charges against s.o.; (граѓанско право) to file a lawsuit against s.o., to sue s.o.

тужбен *adj Leg.* of a charge (indictment); of a lawsuit; тужбено барање lawsuit; case for the prosecution

туженик -ци *m Leg.* defendant; prisoner at the bar

тужи *impf Leg.* **I** (кривично право) to bring charges against s.o.; to prosecute; (граѓанско право) to file a lawsuit against s.o.; to place on trial, arraign **II** – **се** to be at law (*co – with*), go to court

тужител *m Leg.* (граѓанско право) plaintiff; (кривично право) prosecutor, prosecution

тужителка *f Leg.* (*fem. form*) *see* тужител

тук[1] *m* fat, grease; sauce

тук[2] *adv f.p. see* тука

тука *adv* **1** here; тука негде somewhere here **2** тука . . . тука now . . . now . . . ; тука во Скопје, тука во Битола now in Skopje, now in Bitola

тукашен -шна *adj* **1** (овдешен) from here, local; тукашни обичаи local customs **2** (тамошен) from there

туку *conj* **1** but; only; anyway; не тоа, туку ова not this but that; не само . . . туку и . . . not only . . . but also . . . ; туку, ќе видиме што ќе стане anyway, we'll see what happens **2** (*as adv*) just, only; сè туку вика all he does is shout

тукурéчи *adv* **1** almost; тукуречи сите луѓе almost all the people **2** maybe; I suppose; surely; for all I know

тукутака *adv* for no reason, just like that

тукушто *adv* just <now>; a moment ago; тукушто излезе he has just left; тукушто не to be about to; to be on the brink/verge/point of

тукче *n dim. of* тук[1]

тул[1] *m* leather quiver

тул[2] *m* (материјал) tulle

тула *f* brick; пече тули to bake bricks; непечена тула adobe

тулáна *f see* туларница

тулар *m* **1** brickmaker **2** owner of brickworks **3** brick vendor

туларница *f* brickworks, brickyard

туларски *adj* brickmaker's; brickmaking *attrib.*

туларство *n* brickmaking

тули *impf* **I** to cover; to conceal, hide *trans.* **II** – **се** to cover o.s., cover up *intrans.*; to hide *intrans.*

тулипан *m Bot.* tulip, *see* лале

тулум *m* **1** (мешина) wineskin **2** feudal rent (*paid by a wine-grower*)

тулумба *f* **1** tulumba (*sweetmeat made of dough soaked in syrup*) **2** tin, can; една тулумба масло a tin of oil **3** *arch.* hose; pump; пожарникарска тулумба fire-hose

тулумбиче *n dim. of* тулумба 1

тулумина *f augm. of* тулум

тулуп *m* ball of raw cotton; ❏ бел како тулуп <as> white as snow

туљбен *m* woman's kerchief, headscarf

тумба *f* **1** bump; rise; hillock; тумби и длапки bumps and potholes **2** bulge; hump

тумбест *adj* **1** bumpy, uneven, rutted; тумбест терен bumpy ground **2** bulging, round, rotund

тумбури *impf colloq.* **I** to force (нешто некому – s.th. on s.o.); to thrust (s.th. at s.o.); to push (s.th. down s.o.'s throat) **II** – **се** to push o.s. forward

тумор *m Med.* tumour; доброкачествен тумор benign tumour; злокачествен тумор malignant tumour

тумрук -ци *m* fetter, *see* томрук

туна *f Zool.* (Scombridae) tuna, tunny

тундра *f* tundra

туне *impf see* тоне

тунел *m* tunnel

тунелски *adj* tunnel *attrib.*; тунелски влез tunnel entrance

туника *f* tunic; pinafore <dress>

Тунис *m* Tunisia

туниски *adj* Tunisian

Тунишанец -ни *m* Tunisian

Тунишанка *f (fem. form) see* Тунишанец

тунтурест *adj* rotund; stocky, thickset; plump, chubby

тунтурици *pl* braids/tresses adorned with silver ornaments and coins (*above the temples*)

тупа *impf* **I 1** to hit, beat, knock; тупа килим to beat a carpet (rug) **2** (*со нозе*) to stamp (*one's feet*) **3** (*за срце, тапан*) to beat *intrans.*; срцето силно му тупа his heart is racing; тапаните тупаат the drums are beating **4** (*по рамо, грб*) to slap/tap (*s.o. on the shoulder, back*) **II – ce** (*в гради*) to thump one's chest; to boast, brag

тупалка *f* & **тупало** *n* carpet-beater, rug-beater, *see* тресалка 1

тупаница *f* fist; удар со тупаница punch; му ја покажа тупаницата he threatened to hit him

тупка (ce) *impf dim. of* тупа (ce)

тупне *pf* тупна *aor.* **I 1** to hit, beat, knock **2** (*со нозе*) to stamp (*one's feet*) **3** (*за срце, тапан*) to beat *intrans.*; му тупна срцето his heart missed a beat; тапанот тупна the drum thundered **4** (*по рамо, грб*) to slap/tap (*s.o. on the shoulder, back*) **II – ce 1** (*в гради*) to thump one's chest; to boast, brag **2** *colloq.* (*with dat.*) to impose upon, intrude on; им се тупна he burst in upon them **3** to fall; to collapse; се тупна во фотелјата he collapsed into the armchair

тупнува (ce) *impf of* тупне (ce)

тупот *m* stamping; thud; тупот на нозе stamping of feet; тупот на коњски копита clatter of horse's hooves

тупоти *impf* to stamp one's feet

тура[1] *f arch.* ball (*of thread*), skein; тура ибришим a ball of thread

тура[2] *f arch.* Sultan's monogram; imperial signature; царската тура imperial signature

тура[3] *f* tour; round; да направиме една тура let's take a turn/stroll! let's stretch our legs! една тура пиво a round of beer

тура[4] *impf* **1** to pour *intrans.*; ❑ врне тура it's pouring, it's raining cats and dogs **2** to put, place

тура́жа *f* engine speed (*in revolutions per minute*), *colloq.* revs

турач *m* cupbearer

турбан *m* turban

турби́на *f* turbine

турбински *adj* turbine *attrib.*

турбогенера́тор *m* turbogenerator

тури *pf* **I 1** to pour *trans.*; to add; тури вода/вино to pour water/wine; тури сол во јадење to add salt to food; ❑ тури му пепел <на тоа> forget it! **2** to put, place **II – ce 1** *dial.* (*втури ce*) to bear fruit abundantly **2** *dial.* (*на коњ*) to mount

турива *impf dial. see* тура[4]

тури́зам -змот *m* tourism; (*со пешачење*) hiking; (*планински*) mountaineering; (*воден*) boating; (*морски*) cruising

туриле́ќа -ќовци *m colloq.* irascible (short-tempered) person

тури́ка *f dial.* crackling, *see* цимиринка

тури́ст *m* tourist; hiker; mountaineer

туристички *adj* tourist *attrib.*; туристичко место tourist resort

тури́стка *f (fem. form) see* турист

турка *impf of* турне **I 1** *see* турне I; турка количка to push a pram; турка со лактот to nudge **2** *fig.* to pursue; to see (*s.th.*) through; турка нешто до крај to pursue a matter to the end **II – ce 1** to jostle *intrans.*; to elbow one's way (*во – through*); немој да се туркаш don't push! **2** *fig.* to roam, rove, wander; се турка по светов to roam the world

турканица *f* **1** hustle; го истера со турканица he hustled him out **2** crush, scrum, crowding; таму има голема турканица it is very crowded there

туркиџија -ии *m arch.* singer, troubadour, *see* песнарија

Туркменија & **Туркмениста́н** *m* Turkmenistan

туркмениста́нски *adj* Turkmenistan *attrib.*

Туркмен *m* Turkmen

Туркменка *f (fem. form) see* Туркмен

туркменски *adj* Turkmen

турлија -ии *m arch.* kind, sort

турлитава *f* stew, casserole (*dry, with meat, okra and other vegetables*)

турли-турли *adj indecl. colloq.* all sorts; турли-турли цвеќиња all sorts of flowers

турлоса *pf* to throw; to push, shove *trans.*; to knock

турлосува *impf of* турлоса

турма *f* throng, crowd; group of people

турне *pf* турна *aor.* **I 1** to push, shove *trans.*; to jostle, hustle *trans.*; турне врата to push open a door; ме турна во вода he pushed me into the water **2** to pull down, demolish; турне куќа to demolish a house **3** *fig.* to bring down, overthrow, depose, topple; турне крал од престол to depose a king; турне влада to overthrow a government **II – ce** to push one another/each other; to nudge one another

турне́ја -еи *f* tour

турнир *m Hist., Sport.* tournament; шаховски турнир chess tournament

турнирски *adj* tournament *attrib.*

турпија -ии *f* file; rasp; турпија за нокти nail-file

тур-ретур *m* return ticket

турски *adj* Turkish; турско кафе Turkish coffee; турско Ottoman times; турски <јазик> Turkish <language>

туртулици & **туртурици** *pl see* тунтурици

турунка *f dial.* orange, *see* портокал

турфанда *f colloq.* early<-ripening> fruit or vegetables

турци́зам -змот *m* Turkism

Турција *f* Turkey

турчи *impf* to make Turkish, Turkicize

Турчин -рци *m* Turk; ❑ нема па да убиеш еден Турчин not one blessed thing; пуши како Турчин to smoke like a chimney

Турчинка *f (fem. form) see* Турчин

туршија   -ии *f* pickled vegetables, pickles

тутале   *n* ball (*of dough or some other substance*)

тутенка   *f Bot.* (Papaver rhoeas) field (corn, Flanders) poppy, *see* божурига

тутка[1]   *f* ball (*of yarn, etc.*); (*за коса*) chignon; тутка си го направил панталонот you've creased your trousers badly

тутка[2]   *impf* **I** to crumple, crease *trans.*; тутка кошула to crumple a shirt **II – се 1** to crumple, crease *intrans.*; овој материјал многу се тутка this material creases badly **2** to writhe, squirm; се тутка од срам to squirm with shame

тутка[3]   (се) *impf see* тутне (се)

туткал   *m* carpenter's glue

туткалиса   *pf* to glue; to smear with glue

туткалисува   *impf of* туткалиса

туткун   *m colloq.* clumsy/impractical person; *colloq.* butter-fingers

тутне   *pf* тутна *aor.* (*with dat. or* на *and noun*) **I 1** to set (sick) (*a dog*) (*on s.o.*); му го тутна кучето he set (sicked) the dog on him **2** to foist (*s.th. on s.o.*); to impute (*s.th. to s.o.*); *colloq.* to plant (*s.th. on s.o.*); му го тутна детето she foisted the child on him **II – се 1** (*за куче*) to attack; му се тутна кучето the dog attacked him **2** *fig.* to force (thrust) o.s. (*on s.o.*), intrude (*on s.o.*), impose o.s. (*on s.o.*); to descend (burst, drop in) (*on s.o.*); му се тутна право в канцеларија he burst into his office

тутнува (се)   *impf of* тутне (се)

тутор   *m* (*на деца*) guardian; coach, tutor; (*на болен или стар човек*) carer; ❏ црковен тутор patron of a church community

туторка   *f* (*fem. form*) *see* тутор

туторство   *n* guardianship, tutelage; tutorship; carer's duties/position

тутулав   *adj* clumsy, sluggish, slow

тутуле   *n colloq.* slow-witted person

тутули   *impf* **I** to dress (*s.o.*) too warmly, overdress *trans.* **II – се** to dress too warmly, overdress *intrans.*, put on too many clothes

тутун   *m Bot.* (Nicotiana) tobacco (*plant and product*); лут тутун strong tobacco; пие тутун *colloq.* to smoke

тутунар   *m* **1** tobacco-grower; tobacco-worker; tobacco-picker **2** smoker; голем тутунар heavy smoker

тутунарка   *f* (*fem. form*) *see* тутунар

тутунарски   *adj* tobacco-growing *attrib.*; тутунарски крај tobacco-growing area

тутунарство   *n* tobacco growing; tobacco industry

тутунешка   *f* **1** picked tobacco stalk **2** *see* кочанка

тутуниште   *n* tobacco field

тутунов   *adj* tobacco; тутунов комбинат tobacco factory; тутунов лист tobacco leaf; тутунов чад tobacco smoke

тутунски   *adj* tobacco; тутунско ќесе tobacco pouch

тутунџија   -ии *m* **1** tobacco-grower **2** tobacconist

тутунџица   *f* (*fem. form*) *see* тутунџија

тутур & **тутурка**   *f* paper funnel

туф   *interj colloq.* alas! oh! oh dear!

туфек   -ци *m arch.* musket, flintlock

туфекчија   -ии *m arch.* **1** gun-maker, gunsmith; gun-seller **2** foot-soldier; musketeer **3** *Hist.* guard at the Imperial Palace (*in Ottoman times*)

туфекчиски   *adj arch.* musket; musketeer's; imperial guard's

туфка   *f dial.* bunch; туфка цвеќиња bouquet <of flowers>

туфка (се)   *impf* to complain; to fret, worry; to <weep and> wail; немој да <се> туфкаш don't fret!

туфне (се)   *pf* туфна (се) *aor. of* туфка (се)

туч   *m* bronze

тучалник   -ци *m* (*esp. Christmas*) feast-day

тучен   *adj* bronze *attrib.*

тучен   -чна *adj* (*of food*) rich; тучна манџа rich food

тучи   *impf* **1** to smear with fat; to add fat **2** to feed, fatten

тучница   *f Bot.* (Portulaca oleracea) <common> purslane

туџар   *m arch.* merchant, trader

туџарка   *f arch.* (*fem. form*) *see* туџар

туџарски   *adj arch.* merchant's, trader's

туш[1]   -еви, -ови *m* Indian ink

туш[2]   -еви, -ови *m* **1** shower **2** shower <bath>; студен туш cold shower; *fig.* shock, unpleasant surprise

туш[3]   *m* fanfare; оркестарот ги поздрави гостите со туш the band greeted the guests with a fanfare

туш[4]   *m Wrestling see* туше

туше   *n Wrestling* wrestling (pinning down)

туши   *impf* to emit gas<es>, *vulg.* to fart; to stink

туши се   *impf* to vent one's rage, take out one's frustrations/anger (*на – on*)

туши́ра   *pf & impf* **I 1** to give (*s.o.*) a shower **2** to draw in Indian ink **3** *Wrestling* to wrestle (pin) down **II – се** to take (have) a shower

Ќ

ќај (*pl* ќаи) *m* & ќаја¹ (*pl* ќаи) *f* small cheese cake, cheese scone

ќаја² (*pl* ќаи) *m arch.* 1 chief herdsman/shepherd 2 wealthy cattle breeder 3 estate manager

ќајџија -ии *m* baker

ќар *m colloq.* gain, advantage, benefit, profit; никаков ќар нема од тоа there's no profit in that; it's useless; ❑ ни ќар ни зијан neither profit, nor loss; ќарот и зијанот се браќа *prov.* what you gain on the swings, you lose on the roundabouts

ќари *pf colloq.* to gain, profit

ќарлија *adj indecl. arch.* winner; јас излегов ќарлија од таа работа I came out <the> winner from that affair

ќарува *impf colloq. of* ќари

ќарџија -ии *m colloq.* 1 middleman, trader, merchant 2 profiteer

ќе *part* (*formant for future and related tenses*) shall, will; should, would; should/would have; was/were going to; таму ќе ноќуваме we shall spend the night there; ќе одеа в град they were going to go to the city; кога ја виде, ќе паднеше во несвест when he saw her, he nearly fainted; младичот не ќе имаше повеќе од шеснаесет години the young man couldn't have been more than sixteen years old; одвреме навреме ќе пукнеше пушка occasionally a rifle would fire; кажа дека утре ќе ни дојдел учителот he said that tomorrow the teacher would visit us; викни ме кога ќе дојде call me when he comes! штом ќе разбереш, јави ми веднаш as soon as you find out, let me know immediately!

ќебап *m Cul.* kebab; shashlik; тас-ќебап *tas kebab* (*stewed chopped meat with onions*); шиш-ќебап shish kebab 2 *see* ќебапче

ќебапче *n Cul.* (*usu. pl*) kjebapche, small kebab

ќебапчија -ии *m* kjebapche seller

ќебапчилница *f* kjebapche rotisserie

ќебапчиски *adj* kebab *attrib.*; ќебапчиски дуќан kebab shop

ќебе *n* woollen blanket/rug; counterpane

ќебенце *n dim. of* ќебе

ќезап *m* nitric acid (*used for separating gold and silver*)

ќеиф *m see* ќеф

ќела *f* bald patch

ќелав *adj* bald; ќелава глава bald head

ќелави *impf* to become bald

ќелавко -овци *m* baldhead, *colloq.* baldy

ќелавост *f* baldness

ќелавче *n dim. of* ќелавко

ќелезанка *f hyp.* bald head

ќелепош *m* skullcap

ќелепур *m* bargain

ќелеш *m* 1 *see* ќелавко 2 *fig., pejor.* worm, louse, wretch; ќелеш ниеден! you louse!

ќелибар *m* amber

ќелибарен -рна *adj* amber

ќелиен -јна *adj* (*from* ќелија 1) <of a> cell; *Hist.* ќелијно училиште church school, convent school

ќелија -ии *f* 1 cell; манастирска ќелија monastery cell; затворска ќелија prison cell 2 cell, structural unit 3 *fig.* cell; партиска ќелија party cell

ќелијка *f dim. of* ќелија

ќелиски *adj* cell *attrib.*; ќелиски систем cell system; ќелиско јадро nucleus of a cell

ќелосан *adj* bald; ќелосана глава bald head

ќемане *n arch.* 1 *Mus.* fiddle, *see* виолина 2 *fig.* head (*of a person*), *colloq.* pate

ќеманеџија -ии *m arch. Mus.* fiddler

ќемер *m* 1 belt; се опаша со ќемерот he put on his belt 2 vault, arch; мост на ќемер arched bridge

ќемерлија *adj indecl.* arched; vaulted; мост ќемерлија arched bridge

ќенев *m arch.* outdoor privy, *Austral. sl.* dunny, *see* нужник

ќепе *n* 1 felt cap 2 felt waistcoat

ќепенок -нци *m* large pull-down shutter (*of shop window*)

ќепче *n* 1 ladle 2 landing-net

ќерал *m* pantry

ќерамида *f* <roof> tile

ќерамиден -дна *adj* <roof> tile *attrib.*; tiled; ќерамиден покрив tiled roof

ќерамидница *f arch.* <roof->tile works, tilery

ќерамиџија -ии *m arch.* <roof> tiler

ќерамитка *f see* ќерамида

ќерамитче *n dim. of* ќерамитка

ќерáна *f* bakery

ќерата *m colloq.* good-for-nothing; cad, bounder

ќердоса *pf colloq.* I 1 *intrans.* to gain, get, earn 2 to succeed, have luck, do well 3 *trans.* to marry (*of a man*), take to wife II – ce to succeed, prosper; да се ќердосаш may you be happy!

ќердосува (се) *impf of* ќердоса (се)

ќересте *n arch.* timber

ќерестеџија -ии *m arch.* timber merchant

ќерка *f* daughter; говорам (зборувам) ти, ќерко, сеќавај (дошикај) се, снао *prov.* she scolds her daughter in order to reproach her daughter-in-law; a word to the wise is enough

ќеркин *adj* daughter's

ќеркински *adv* like/as a daughter

ќеркиче *n* & ќеркичка *f dim. of* ќерка

ќерпич *m* adobe, unbaked brick

ќесе *n* 1 purse; wallet; ❑ не посигај ми во ќесето mind your own business! не ми влегува в ќесе there's nothing in it for me 2 hair-glove (*for rubbing the body*); loofah 3 pouch; bag; едно ќесе тутун a pouch of tobacco; пластично ќесе plastic bag

ќесеџија -ии *m arch.* brigand, highwayman

ќесија -ии *f arch.* (*вреќа*) sack

ќеф *m colloq.* 1 wish; fancy, whim; стори му го ќефот do as he wishes! do as he says! make him happy! 2

good mood; gladness; со голем ќеф with great joy/ pleasure; од ќеф for sheer pleasure; for the hell of it; for kicks; ❑ гледај си го ќефот suit yourself!

ќефледиса *pf colloq.* **I** to put in a good mood, cheer (*s.o.*) up *trans.* **II** – **ce** **1** to get into a good mood, cheer up *intrans.* **2** *fig.* to get tipsy, get a bit tight

ќефлија *adj indecl. colloq.* **1** in a good mood **2** *fig.* tipsy, merry

ќече *n* **1** Albanian white felt cap **2** felt, thick cloth **3** nappy (*made of this or similar material*), *Am.* diaper

ќешки *part colloq.* if only . . . ; ќешки да е така if only it were so!

ќоле *n* **1** *arch.* servant; slave **2** *fig.*, *pejor.* ruffian, boor

ќопав *adj* lame, crippled

ќор *adj* **1** blind; ќоро и сакато blind and lame; ❑ пијан ќор, ќор-ќутук *sl.* blind drunk, plastered; ќор фишек blank cartridge **2** (*as noun*) ќоро *n colloq.* good opportunity; bargain; ❑ му се погоди на ќорото, удри на ќорото, најде ќоро he had good luck; *colloq.* he hit the jackpot; he struck a good bargain

ќорав *adj see* ќор 1

ќорави *impf* to go blind

ќоравост *f* blindness

ќорле -евци *m see* ќорчо

ќорлеме & **ќорлемечки** *adv colloq.* **1** blindly, *see* слепечки; оди така ќорлемечки he walks like a blind man **2** recklessly, headlong; ќорлемечки дотрча he came running headlong

ќорсокак -ци *m* **1** blind alley, cul-de-sac **2** *fig.* dead end, impasse, hopeless situation; дојдовме во ќорсокак we've come to a dead end; се најдовме во ќорсокак we reached an impasse

ќорчо -овци *m colloq.* blind person

ќос *adj* beardless; (*as noun*) *m* beardless youth/man, *see* ќосе

ќосави *impf* to become beardless

ќосавост *f* beardlessness

ќосе *n* beardless youth/man

ќотек -ци *m colloq.* beating, thrashing, hiding, spanking; ❑ му удри ќотек he gave him a good hiding; плаче за ќотек he's asking for it; ќотекот е од рај<от> излезен *prov.* spare the rod and spoil the child

ќофте *n Cul.* rissole; hamburger; meatball; meatball stew; ќофте на кромид hamburger with onion; ❑ *colloq.* алал ти ќофте! well done! bravo! good on you!

ќофтенце *n dim. of* ќофте

ќош -еви, -ови *m colloq.* corner; angle; *fig.* retreat, out-of-the-way place; на ќошот од улицата at the street corner; извиткани ќошови на книга dog-eared pages of a book; ❑ натера некого в ќош to drive s.o. into a corner; to bring s.o. to bay; в ќош е to be cornered; to be up against the wall

ќоше *n colloq. see* ќош

ќошлест *adj colloq.* **1** cornered; angular **2** *fig.* peevish, irascible, abrasive

ќуд *m* **1** nature, character, temper; волкот влакното го менува, ама ќудот не *prov.* the leopard cannot change his spots **2** whim, caprice

ќулав *m* & **ќулавка** *f* **1** conical cap; ❑ ќе му го скрои ќулавот *colloq.* he'll fix him **2** hood

ќумез *m dial.* (*печка*) stove

ќумез *m* **1** chicken coop; dovecote **2** *fig.* small, cramped room; den; hut, shack

ќумур *m colloq.* (*јаглен*) coal; дрвен ќумур charcoal; камен ќумур hard coal

ќумурџија -ии *m colloq.* (*јагленар*) coal merchant; charcoal burner; charcoal pedlar; stoker

ќумурџилница *f colloq.* (*јагленарница*) coal yard; charcoal kiln

ќунк -нци *m* (*за вода*) pipe, drainpipe; sewer; (*за чад*) flue; funnel

ќуп -ови *m* earthenware pot; ќуп злато pot of gold

ќупче *n dim. of* ќуп

ќурк -ови *m* fur-lined coat; pelisse, fur-lined cloak; ❑ ќе му го скрои ќуркот he will make him toe the line, *colloq.* he'll fix him

ќурче *n dim. of* ќурк

ќурчија -ии *m* furrier, *see* кожувар

ќурчилак *m* furrier's craft, furrier's trade

ќурчиски *adj* furrier's; ќурчиски дуќан furrier's shop

ќускија -ии *f* **1** crowbar, lever **2** *fig.* dolt, blockhead

ќуспе *n* oil extract from plant seeds; oilcake

ќутење *n* **1** *from* ќути **2** silence; ❑ ќутењето е злато silence is golden

ќути *impf* to be silent, *see* молчи; ❑ ќути и трај grin and bear it!

ќутлив *adj see* молчалив & молчелив

ќутливост *f see* молчаливост & молчеливост

ќутук -ци *m* **1** tree-stump; log; ❑ ќутук пијан blind drunk **2** *fig.* clod, dullard, blockhead

ќуќур *m arch.* sulphur, *see* сулфур

ќушка *f* the thick end of a shepherd's crook

у¹ & у-у *interj* (*expressing amazement, displeasure, disgust*) ooh! ooh-ooh! oh! ugh! (*expressing pain*) ouch! у, страшно! oh, that's terrible! у, боли! ouch, that hurts!

у² *prep* (*каде, кај*) at, in; у нас at our place; in our country

у³ *prep dial. see* во

уа *interj* (*expressing disapproval, indignation*) boo!

уапе *pf* уапа *aor.* (*касне*) to bite; to sting; го уапа змија he was bitten by a snake

уапси *pf* to arrest, imprison, lock up; to take into custody

уапува *impf of* уапе

убав *adj* beautiful, lovely, pretty, (*обично за маж*) handsome; fine, good; nice; убава жена beautiful woman; убав маж handsome man; убав ден fine (nice) day; убава прошетка nice stroll; убави совети good advice; убава служба good (well-paid) job; убава парица доби he earned good money; ❑ убава литература belles-lettres; *iron.* убава работа a fine state of affairs! a pretty kettle of fish! ви пожелувам сè најубаво I wish you all the best; убавата мома сама се мажи *prov.* who is born fair is born married; убавите круши свињите ги јадат *prov.* the more knave the better luck; убавата стока сама се продава *prov.* good ware makes quick markets; (*as noun*) убавото *n* the beautiful, beauty

убавее *impf* **I** to become more beautiful/handsome **II** – се to be, look beautiful/handsome; како се убавее градината how beautiful the garden looks!

убавест *adj see* убавичок

убавец -вци *m* handsome (good-looking) man, good-looker; beautiful thing

убавина *f* **1** beauty; убавината пазар собира, а груботијата куќа врти *prov.* beauty won't make the pot boil **2** quality, virtue **3** beautiful thing

убавица *f* beautiful woman, beauty; beautiful thing; beauty queeen; Заспаната убавица the Sleeping Beauty

убавичок -чка *adj* pretty

убавка -вко *adj* (*with no m gender*) beautiful, pretty; убавко девојче pretty little girl

убавко *adv* fine, pretty well, quite well

убаво *adv* beautifully; nicely; fine, well; убаво изгледаш you look beautiful; убаво звучи it sounds beautiful; убаво живее he lives well; убаво постапи he did the right thing; убаво го истепа he gave him a good thrashing; убаво од тебе it's nice of you

убавост *f see* убавина 1

убеден *adj & pt* convinced, persuaded; staunch; убеден противник/приврзаник staunch opponent/ adherent

убедено *adv* staunchly; with conviction

убеденост *f* conviction, persuasion

убеди *pf* **I** to convince, persuade, assure; убеди некого во нешто to convince s.o. of s.th. **II** – се to become convinced, persuaded (*во – of*); to make sure/certain (*во; дека – of; that*)

убедлив *adj* convincing, persuasive; убедлив доказ convincing (conclusive) proof, cogent argument; убедлив говорник persuasive speaker

убедливо *adv* convincingly, persuasively

убедливост *f* persuasiveness, cogency

убедува (се) *impf of* убеди (се)

убедување *n* **1** *from* убедува (се); persuasion, assurance; по пат на убедување by means of persuasion **2** conviction, belief; според моето убедување according to my belief; против своето убедување against one's conviction; промени свое убедување to change one's opinion, take a different view of things

убедувачки *adj* convincing, persuasive; убедувачка моќ persuasive power

убежиште *n* asylum, sanctuary, refuge

убива (се) *impf of* убие (се); ❑ убива време to kill time; се убива од работа to be worked off one's feet

убие *pf* уби *aor.* **I 1** to kill (*also fig.*), murder; (*позната личност*) to assassinate; убие нечиј глас (углед) to destroy s.o.'s reputation; убие нечија волја to crush s.o.'s will/enthusiasm; го убија грижите worries destroyed him; ме убиваат чевлите my shoes pinch terribly; Бог да те убие! may God strike you down! **2** (*of hail, frost, ice, etc.*) to destroy, blight, kill off; градот ги уби полињата the hail ruined the crops **3** to injure, hurt; падна и си ја уби ногата he fell and hurt his leg/foot **II – се 1** to commit suicide, kill o.s.; ❑ тоа <ти> е да се убие човек it's enough to drive you mad **2** *fig.* to wear o.s. out, kill o.s.; се убив од работа (работејќи) I worked myself to exhaustion; се убив од докажување (докажувајќи) I nearly killed myself trying to prove it **3** to hurt o.s.; се убив во ногата I hurt my leg/foot

убиен *pt* **1** killed, murdered; assassinated **2** *fig.* dejected, despairing; се врати дома скинат и убиен he returned home exhausted and crushed **3** injured, hurt; убиено место tender (sore) spot

убиец -јци *m* murderer, killer; assassin

убиствен *adj* murderous (*also fig.*); devastating, ruinous; fatal; exhausting; убиствен скок fatal leap; убиствена работа backbreaking toil; убиствена жега murderous (terrible) heat

убиствено *adv* murderously; ruinously; fatally

убиственост *f* murderousness

убиство *n* killing; homicide; (*со умисла*) murder; (*ненамерно*) manslaughter; (*атентат*) assassination; обид за убиство attempted murder/ assassination; изврши убиство to commit murder

ублажи *pf* **I 1** (*ублажи*) to sweeten **2** to alleviate, soothe; ублажи болка to alleviate (ease) pain **3** to reduce, mitigate; му ја ублажија казната they reduced his sentence **II – се 1** (*ублажи се*) to eat s.th. sweet **2** to be alleviated, soothed; to calm down *intrans.*, die down; to be reduced

ублажува (се) *impf of* ублажи (се)

убод *m* stab; prick; sting; рана од убод a stab wound

убоде *pf* I (*со нож и сл.*) to stab; (*со боцка и др.*) to prick; (*со осило*) to sting *trans.*; (*со рогови*) to butt *trans.*; извади нож и го убоде he drew a knife and stabbed him **II – се** to stab o.s.; to prick o.s.

убодува (се) *impf of* убоде (се)

убоен -jна *adj* murderous, deadly; убојно оружје deadly weapon

убои се *pf* to become afraid, take fright; се убои од непријателот he feared the enemy

убојува се *impf of* убои се

уболни се *pf f.p.* to fall ill, become sick

убори *pf f.p.* (*кутне*) to topple *trans.*, knock down

убосник -ци *m see* убавец

убосница *f see* убавица

убост *f* beauty, *see* убавина

уброва (се) *impf see* убројува (се)

уброи *pf literary* I to count (*во, меѓу – among*); го уброи во најдобрите другари he counted him among his best friends **II – се** to count o.s. (*among*), include o.s., consider o.s.

убројува (се) *impf of* уброи (се)

убрус *m* 1 face towel 2 kerchief, head-scarf

уважен *adj & pt* esteemed; уважени професоре esteemed professor; (*во писмо*) Dear Professor

уважение *n see* почит; со уважение with respect; (*во писмо*) yours faithfully

уважи *pf* (*земе во предвид*) to consider, take into consideration; (*прифати*) to accept; ја уважиле твојата молба your application has been accepted

уважува *impf* 1 *of* уважи 2 *see* почитува

уважување *n from* уважува; уважување на оставката acceptance of (*s.o.'s*) resignation; уважување постари respect for old people, respect for one's elders

увари *pf f.p.* to cook, boil (down) *trans.*

увезе *pf* to import; увезе производи за широка потрошувачка to import consumer goods

увезува *impf of* увезе; ние увезуваме разни стоки we import various goods

увеличи *pf* I 1 to enlarge *trans.*; to magnify; увеличи фотографија to enlarge a photograph; увелича под микроскоп to magnify under a microscope 2 to exaggerate **II – се** to expand, increase, multiply, enlarge *intrans.*

увеличителен -лна *adj* magnifying; увеличително стакло magnifying glass

увеличува (се) *impf of* увеличи (се)

увенча *pf see* овенча

увенчува *impf of* увенча

уверен *adj & pt* 1 confident, assured 2 (*predicatively only*) sure, positive, certain; цврсто уверен fully (firmly) convinced; уверен во себе sure of oneself, self-confident, self-reliant

уверение -ија *n* 1 assurance, conviction 2 certificate; лекарско уверение medical (doctor's) certificate; уверение за имотна состојба assets and liabilities certificate

уверено *adv* confidently, assuredly, with certainty

увереност *f* confidence, sureness, certainty

увери *pf* I to assure, convince **II – се** 1 to assure o.s., convince o.s.; to become convinced (*во – of*); се

уверив во тоа со свои очи I was convinced by what I saw with my own eyes 2 to rely on; to make sure of; се уверил во својето искуство he put faith in his own experience

уверлив *adj* convincing, persuasive

уверливо *adv* convincingly, persuasively

уверливост *f* persuasiveness

увертира *f Mus.* overture (*also fig.*)

уверува (се) *impf of* увери (се)

уверува се *pf* to assure o.s. (*во, дека – of, that*); to start believing/trusting

уверување *n* 1 *from* уверува (се); assurance, attempts to convince/persuade 2 conviction, belief

уви *interj* alas!

увива (се) *impf of* увие (се)

увид *m* inspection, review; insight; investigation; има увид во нешто to have insight into s.th.; се изврши увид an inspection was conducted

увиди *pf* to realize; си ја увиде грешката he realized his mistake; увиде дека сум прав he saw that I was right

увидува *impf of* увиди

увие *pf* уви *aor.* I 1 to envelop, wrap; го уви детето во ќебе she wrapped the child in a blanket 2 to wind *trans.*; to coil, curl *trans.*; to weave, twist *trans.*; увие венец to weave a garland; увие коса to curl one's hair; увие мустаќи to twist one's moustache **II – се** 1 to wrap o.s.; се уви во чаршаф to wrap o.s. in a sheet 2 to gird o.s.; се уви со појас to put on a belt 3 to wind (wrap) o.s. (*околу нешто – round s.th.*); to wind *intrans.*; to curl *intrans.*; to coil *intrans.*; лозата се уви околу столбот the vine wrapped itself around the post

увилен *adj* distressed, upset; downcast, sad; што си толку увилена? why are you so sad?

увиленост *f* distress, sadness, sorrow

увили се *pf* to become upset, saddened

увилно *adv f.p.* sadly, sorrowfully

увилува се *impf of* увили се

уво (*pl* уши) *n* 1 ear; (*слух*) hearing; надворешно, средно и внатрешно уво external, middle and inner ear; *Med.* воспаление на увото inflammation of the ear; otitis; со едното уво не слуша he doesn't hear with one ear; музикално уво musical ear; пара уши to grate on one's ears; со свои уши го чув тоа I heard that with my own ears; ми бучат ушите my ears are buzzing; шум во ушите buzzing in the ears; ми ги оглуши ушите it deafened me; затне уши to block (close) one's ears; ❏ начули (нададе, наостри) уши to prick up one's ears; тргне <некого> за уво to pull s.o. by the ear; се вцрви до уши to blush to one's ears; допре до нечии уши to come to s.o.'s attention, reach s.o.'s ears; се вљуби до уши to fall head over heels in love; до уши up to one's ears; седи на уши to be inattentive; цел се претвора во уво to be all ears; шепнува на уво to whisper in s.o.'s ear; тврд на уши hard of hearing; тепа некого по уши to give s.o. a box on the ear; од едното уво му влегува, од другото му излегува it goes in one ear and out the other; *colloq.* ме боли уво за . . . I don't give a damn about . . .; му влезе вода в уши success went to his head; од уши в уши (од уста в уста), на царот в уши *prov.* word gets about; и ѕидовите имаат уши *prov.* walls have ears 2 (*usu. pl*) flat (*of an axe, hoe,* *etc.*) **3** (*usu. pl*) eye (*of a needle*) **4** (*only pl*) plough handle

уволболка *f* earache

увод *m* introduction; увод на книга prologue, introduction to a book; увод во лингвистиката introduction to linguistics

уводен -дна *adj* introductory; уводен збор preface; уводна статија editorial, leading article, leader

уводник -ци *m* editorial, leading article, leader

увоз *m* import, importation; стоки од увозот imported goods

увозен -зна *adj* import; увозна царина import duty; увозна трговија import trade; увозна стока imported goods

увозлив *adj* importable

увозник *m* importer; земја увозник importing country

увознина *f* import tax

увозница *f* import licence

увце *n dim. of* уво

увула *f Anat.* uvula

угаѓа *impf of* угоди

Угаѓда *f* Uganda

Угандец -дци *m* Ugandan

угандски *adj* Ugandan

Уганѓанец -ни *m see* Угандец

Уганѓанка *f see* Угантка

Угантка *f* (*fem. form*) *see* Угандец

угар *m* **1** fallow <land> **2** *see* угарка

угарен -рна *adj* fallow; угарна нива fallow field

угари *impf* to fallow, plough and leave fallow

угарка *f* & **угарок** -ци *m* burnt/smouldering brand; ❑ како угарок се сторил he's a shadow of himself, a burnt-out shell

угарче *n dim. of* угарка

угаси (се) *pf see* угасне (се)

угаслив *adj* extinguishable

угаснат *adj* & *pt* extinguished, faded; *fig.* lifeless; угаснат поглед, угаснати очи lifeless eyes; угасната младост lost youth

угасне *pf* угасна *aor.* **I 1** to extinguish, put out; угасна оган to put out the fire; угасне ламба to turn off a lamp **2** *fig.* to smother, stifle *trans.*, crush; ѝ ги угасна сите благородни чувства he crushed all her finer feelings **3** *fig.* to quench, slake; лимонот ми ја угасна жедта the lemon quenched my thirst **4** to be extinguished, go out; огнот угасна the fire went out; ❑ ѕвездата му угасна his star faded **5** *fig.* to fade, wane, die down; љубовта во него угасна his love faded; славата му угасна his glory faded; тој угасна (умре) he passed away **II – се** *see* 4 & 5

угаснува (се) *impf of* угасне (се)

угич *m* bell-wether

углав *m* & **углава** *f dial.* **1** (*свршувачка*) betrothal, engagement **2** (*главеж*) employment contract

углавеник -ци *m dial. see* свршеник

углавеница *f dial. see* свршеница

углави *pf dial.* **I 1** (*глави*) to employ, hire (*for a certain period*) **2** (*свр ши*) to betroth **II – се 1** (*глави се*) to take work, enter service (*кај – with*) **2** (*свр ши се*) to get engaged, announce one's engagement

главник -ци *m dial.* **1** *see* стројник **2** *see* свршеник

главница *f dial.* **1** *see* стројница **2** *see* свршеница

угладен *adj* polished, refined, well-bred, polite, urbane

угладеност *f* refinement, polish, civility, politeness, urbanity

углед *m* **1** reputation; prestige; ужива углед to enjoy a <good> reputation; изгуби углед to lose one's reputation; ѝ го уби угледот he/it ruined her reputation **2** example, model; служи за углед to serve as an example; ❑ по углед на ... following (after) the manner/pattern of

угледа се *pf* (*на*) to emulate (*s.o.*), take (*s.o.*) as a model; се угледа на татко му he emulated his father; се угледа на добар/лош пример to follow a good/bad example; се угледа на некого to take one's cue from

угледен -дна *adj* respected, honoured, prominent; well-known; угледен граѓанин eminent citizen

угледник -ци *m* (*стројник*) matchmaker

угледност *f* prestige; reputation; respect

угледува се *impf of* угледа се

угнетен *adj* oppressed, downtrodden; угнетените маси the oppressed masses

угнетеност *f* oppression

угнетува *impf* to oppress, keep down

угнетувач *m* oppressor, exploiter

угнетувачки *adj* oppressive

угоден -дна *adj* (*пријатен*) pleasant, pleasing, agreeable; (*погоден*) favourable; opportune; (*удобен*) comfortable

угоди¹ *pf* (*with dat.*) to please, oblige, satisfy; само да му угоди just to please him

угоди² се *pf f.p.* to happen, take place, occur; се угодило на ден Велигден it happened on Easter Day

угодлив *adj* **1** helpful, obliging **2** servile, obsequious

угодливост *f* **1** helpfulness, consideration **2** servility, obsequiousness

угодник -ци *m* **1** *Rel.* righteous man, saint, holy man; Божји угодници (светци) the Lord's elect **2** flatterer, toady

угодница *f* (*fem. form*) *see* угодник

угодничи *impf* to flatter, fawn (*on*)

угоднички *adv* flatteringly, servilely, slavishly, obligingly

угодништво *n* obsequiousness, servility

угодно *adv* obligingly, pleasantly; comfortably

угодност *f* agreeableness; comfort

угодува *impf of* угоди

угои (се) *pf see* згои (се)

угојка *f Bot.* (Bryonia dioica) red bryony

угојува (се) *impf of* угои (се), *see* згојува (се)

угоре *adv see* нагоре

угорен -рна *adj see* нагорен; угорно место upward slope; (*as noun*) угорно *n* rise, climb

угори *pf* **I** to heat, make red-hot/white-hot **II – се** to become red-hot/white-hot; *see* усвити (се)

угорнина & **угорница** *f see* нагорниште

угорничав *adj see* нагорен 1

угорниште *n see* нагорниште

угорува (се) *impf of* угори (се), *see* усвитува (се)

угости *pf* to entertain, serve (*with food*)

угостител *m* caterer; waiter; cook; restaurant keeper; hotelier; innkeeper

угостителка *f* (*fem. form*) *see* угостител

угостителски *adj* catering; угостителски услуги

catering services; **угостителски дуќан** restaurant/hotel

угостителство *n* catering; hospitality industry; restaurant/hotel management

угостува *impf of* угости

уготви *pf dial.* (*зготви*) to prepare food, cook

уготвува *impf dial. of* уготви

угрева (се) *impf of* угрее (се)

угрее *pf* угреа *aor.* **I 1** *trans.* to shine on; to warm; **сонцето нè угреа** the sun warmed us; **си ги угреав рацете** I warmed my hands; **сонце да не те угрее!** *curse* may the sun never warm you! **2** *intrans.* to rise, begin to shine; **угреа летното сонце** the summer sun rose **II – се** to warm o.s.; *see* огрее (се)

угрижи *pt dial.* worried, *see* загрижен

угрижи *pf* **I** to worry *trans.* **II – се** to get worried; *see* загрижи (се)

угрижува (се) *impf of* угрижи (се), *see* загрижува (се)

угриз *m* scrap of food

угул *adv colloq.* completely, quite; **угул гол** stark naked

угурсуз *m colloq.* rowdy, rascal; good-for-nothing

угурсузлак -ци *m colloq.* rowdiness, rowdyism

угурсуски *adj colloq.* rowdy, rascal's

удава се *impf impers. of* удаде се

удавеник -ци *m* drowning person

удавеница *f* (*fem. form*) *see* удавеник

удави *pf* **I 1** (*задуши*) to choke, suffocate *trans.*, strangle **2** (*во вода*) to drown *trans.* **3** *colloq.* to sink *trans.*, scuttle; to submerge *trans.*; **за малку ќе ја удавел гемијата** he nearly sank the boat **II – се 1** to choke, suffocate *intrans.* **2** (*во вода*) to drown *intrans.*

удаде се *pf impers.* (*with dat.*) to be successful, succeed (*in doing s.th.*), manage (*to*); **му се удаде да ја фати** he managed to catch her; **не ми се удаде** I didn't succeed; **ако ми се удаде случај** if I get a chance (opportunity)

удар *m* **1** blow, stroke; (*со камшик*) lash; (*со тупаница*) punch; (*со нога*) kick; **удари на чекан** hammer blows; **удари на часовник** chimes of a clock; **смртоносен удар** deathblow (*also fig.*); ❑ **удар на гром** thunderclap, thunderbolt; **зададе** (**нанесе**) **удар** to strike a blow; to deal (*s.o./s.th.*) a blow; **зададе последен удар** to go in for the kill; **разменува удари со** to exchange blows with; **ублажува удар** to soften a blow; to absorb shocks; **одбива удар** to parry a blow; **низок удар** below the belt; **на удар е** to bear the brunt; **со еден удар** at/with a single blow; at a stroke; at (in) one fell swoop; **со еден удар убива две муви** (**два зајака**) to kill two birds with one stone **2** *Mil.* blow, attack, assault, thrust; **удар од воздух** air raid **3** *fig.* blow, shock; **неговата смрт беше за неа тежок удар** his death was a heavy blow for her **4** coup; **државен удар** *coup d'état*, putsch; **воен удар** military coup **5** *Sport.* kick; stroke; strike; **казнен удар** penalty; **слободен удар** free kick; **почетен удар** kickoff; **удар од аголот** corner kick **6** *Med.* stroke, apoplexy; **сончев удар** sunstroke; **топлотен удар** heatstroke; **срцев удар** heart attack; **електричен удар** electric shock

ударен -рна *adj* striking; shock; *Tech.*, *Mus.* percussion, percussive; **ударна сила** striking force; force of impact; **ударна бригада** shock-brigade (elite work team); **ударна работа** shock work; **ударни** <**воени**> **единици** shock troops

ударник -ци *m* shock-worker

ударничка *f* (*fem. form*) *see* ударник

ударнички *adj* shock-worker's

ударништво *n* shock work

удвоеност *f* duality

удвои *pf* **I** to double *trans.*, duplicate **II – се** to double *intrans.*

удвојува (се) *impf of* удвои (се)

удел *m* part, share; **има удел во нешто** to have a share in s.th.; to participate in s.th.; **нема удел во** to have nothing to do with; to have no share in

удина *f* boneless meat

удир *m see* удар 1

удира (се) *impf of* удри (се)

удиралки *pl Mus.* percussion instruments

удобен -бна *adj* comfortable, cosy; convenient, suitable; **удобен живот** comfortable life

удобно *adv* comfortably, cosily; conveniently, suitably

удобност *f* comfort, cosiness; convenience; **му ја расипа удобноста** he disturbed his comfort

удобри *pf colloq. see* одобри

удобрува *impf colloq. of* удобри, *see* одобрува

удоволствие -ија *f see* задоволство

удолен -лна *adj see* надолен

удолнина & **удолница** *f* & **удолниште** *n see* надолниште

удолу *adv see* надолу

удоми *pf* **I** to marry off **II – се** to settle down, get married

удомува (се) *impf of* удоми (се)

удопство *n* comfort; convenience

удостои *pf* **I** (*некого со нешто*) to grant (*s.th. to s.o.*), bestow (*s.th. on s.o.*); to deign; to honour (*with*); **удостои некого со внимание** to pay attention to s.o.; **удостои некого со доверба** to bestow one's trust on s.o.; **не ме удостои ни со поздрав** he didn't even deign to say hello to me **II – се 1** to be granted (*to s.o.*) **2** to deign, condescend (*to do s.th.*); **не се удостои ни да ми одговори на писмото** she didn't even deign to answer my letter

удостојува (се) *impf of* удостои (се)

удраска *pf* to scratch; **си го удраска прстот** he scratched (grazed) his finger

удрен *adj* crazy, mad, *colloq.* dotty; **тој е малку удрен** he is a bit dotty; **се прави удрен** to play dumb

удреник -ци *m* madman, fool

удри *pf* **I 1** to strike, hit, bump, deal a blow to (*also fig.*); to hurt; (*силно*) to wallop; to bang; to smash; (*со нога*) to kick; (*со тупаница*) to punch; (*со камшик*) to lash; **удри по глава** to hit (*s.o.*) on the head; **удри шлаканица** to slap s.o.'s face; **автомобилот удри во ѕидот** the car hit the wall; **непријателот удри на градот** the enemy struck at (attacked) the town; **удри камбаната** the church bell struck; **болеста го удри во нозете** the illness affected his legs; **си ја удрив главата** I've bumped my head; **го удри дамла** he had a stroke; *fig.* he was astounded (thunderstruck); **удри гром** there was a clap of thunder; **удри некого по прсти** to rap s.o. on the knuckles ❑ **му удри во глава** to go to s.o.'s head; **удри клоца некому** to dump s.o.; to give s.o. the boot; **удри како со копито** to pack a hard punch; **удри прв** to fire the first shot;

to draw the first blood; го удри одземи he struck him to the ground; he smashed it on the ground; *colloq.* му удри еден убав ќотек (едно убаво тепање) he gave him a good thrashing **2** (*на врата*) to knock **3** to turn *intrans.*, turn off; to turn to; удри влево to turn left **4** to set off, start out; й удри по трагата he set off after her; удри по патеката to take a path **5** to begin, start; удри да пие to start drinking; удри да плаче to burst into tears; удри дожд it started to rain; му удри крв од носот his nose started bleeding **6** to impose, levy; to inflict; удри данок на нешто to impose a tax on s.th.; удри цени to fix prices **7** to apply paint/polish; to paint; to polish; му удри жолта боја на сидот he painted the wall yellow; им удри боја на чевлите he polished his shoes **8** *colloq.* to snatch, filch, grab **9** to place, put, lay *trans.*; удри печат to affix a seal; to stamp; удри темел to lay a foundation; *colloq.* удри шатори to pitch camp (tents); удри пенчиња на чевли to put soles on shoes; удри шајка во сид to drive a nail into a wall; ќе ти удри на кантарот he'll give you short measure; удри клуч на куќа to lock up the house **10** to attack; удри на некого to attack s.o. **II – се 1** to strike (hit) o.s., hurt o.s.; се удри во/по глава од маса to bump one's head on a table; се удри ли? have you hurt yourself? чамецот се удри во карпа the boat struck <against> a rock **2** to clash, collide; војските се удрија the armies clashed; возовите се удрија the trains collided **3** (*only impf*) се удира в гради to beat one's breast

удрува (се) *impf of* удри (се)

удрување *n from* удрува; impact; blow

уѓе *adv in the expression:* нека му е уѓе! serves him right!

еедначен *pt* standardized, equalized; квалитетот е веќе еедначен the quality has now been standardized

еедначеност *f* uniformity

еедначи *pf* **I** to standardize, equalize *trans.* **II – се** to equalize *intrans.*, become equal

еедначува (се) *impf of* еедначи (се)

уем *m* miller's fee (*paid in flour*)

ужален *pt* bereaved, in mourning; ужалена фамилија bereaved family

ужаленост *f* bereavement

ужали *pf* to bereave

ужалува *impf of* ужали

ужас *m* terror, horror; ме фати ужас I was seized by terror; се потресе од ужас he was shaken by terror; ужасите на војната the horrors of war

ужасен¹ *pt* terrified, horrified, horror-struck

ужасен² -сна *adj* terrible, dreadful, horrible; ужасна глетка terrible (horrible) sight; ужасен крик terrible scream; ужасна скапотија terribly high cost <of everything>

ужасеност *f* horror, terror

ужаси *pf* **I** to horrify, terrify **II – се** to be horrified, terrified

ужасија -ии *f* horror

ужасно *adv* terribly, dreadfully, horribly; на фронтот беше ужасно it was terrible at the front; ужасно скап terribly expensive; ужасно убав extremely beautiful; (*as interj*) ужасно! terrible! dreadful! awful!

ужасува (се) *impf of* ужаси (се)

ужива *impf* **1** to enjoy o.s.; (*во нешто*) to enjoy (*s.th.*),

derive pleasure (*from*); тој ужива во играње шах he enjoys playing chess **2** (*во нешто*) to be addicted to, take (*drugs, etc.*) **3** to enjoy, possess; ужива свои права to enjoy full rights; ужива голема почит to enjoy great respect; ужива нечија благонаклоност to be in s.o.'s favour

уживанција *f colloq.* enjoyment, fun

уживање *n* **1** *from* ужива **2** enjoyment, pleasure; delight

уживател *m* **1** possessor, holder (*of a right*) **2** addict; уживател на дроги drug addict

ужина¹ *f* tea, snack

ужина² *pf & impf* to have tea, a snack

уз *prep dial.* **1** up, along; уз река up river, upstream **2** by, near, next to, beside; ја стави торбата на земја уз него he put the bag on the ground beside him **3** <together> with; виното оди многу подобро уз јадење wine goes much better with food

узакони *pf* to legalize, legitimize

узаконува *impf of* узакони

Узбек -еци *m* Uzbek

Узбекистáн *m* Uzbekistan

узбекистáнски *adj* Uzbekistan *attrib.*; Uzbek

Узбечка *f* (*fem. form*) *see* Узбек

узбечки *adj* Uzbek

узда *f* rein, bridle, curb; ❑ му ги стегна/пушти уздите на некого to tighten/release the reins on s.o.; држи <некого> за узда to keep s.o. in check (under control); ги држи уздите to hold the reins

уздичка *f dim. of* узда

узенгија -ии *f* stirrup

узнава *impf of* узнае

узнае *pf* to find out, hear, learn (*за – of, about*); за тоа никој не смее да узнае no one must find out about that

узреан *adj & pt* ripe, mature

узрева *impf of* узрее

узрее *pf* узреа *aor.* **1** to mature, ripen *intrans.* (*also fig.*); грозјето узреа the grapes are ripe; девојчето рано узреа the girl matured early **2** *fig.* (*of a boil, etc.*) to come to a head, *Med.* maturate

узур *m arch.* leisure, break, rest, *see* уsyp

узурпáтор *m* usurper

узурпаторски *adj* usurping, of a usurper

узурпација *f* usurpation

узурпѝра *pf & impf* to usurp

узус *m* **1** *Leg.* usage **2** custom, habit, practice

уsyp *m arch.* leisure, spare time

ујаден *pt* saddened, unhappy, distressed

ујади *pf* **I** to sadden, make unhappy, distress **II – се** to become saddened, distressed

ујадува (се) *impf of* ујади (се)

ујгун *adj indecl. arch.* pleasant; suitable, appropriate; ујгун работа just the right thing

ујдиса *pf colloq.* **I 1** *trans.* to arrange; to adjust *trans.*; ја ујдиса работата he arranged/settled the matter **2** *trans.* to fit, adapt *trans.*; го ујдиса клучот и отвори he inserted the key and opened the door **3** *intrans. see* II 1 **II – се 1** to fit; клучот се ујдиса the key fitted <in the keyhole> **2** to get along (*со некого – with s.o.*), suit one another; to fit in (*with s.o.*)

ујдисува (се) *impf of* ујдиса (се)

ујдурма *f colloq.* trick, ruse; fraud, deceit

ука¹ *f* **1** learning, education; lesson, advice; ука ја учеше she used to advise her (give her advice) **2** habit; ука и одука habit and breaking of a habit **3** learning; science

ука² *impf* **1** to blow, puff *intrans.*; ука во рацете to blow into one's hands **2** to hoot *intrans.*; бувот ука the owl is hooting **3** to groan, call out, howl; дервишите укаат the dervishes are howling

укаже *pf* укажа *aor.* **1** to point (на – to), point out; укаже на грешки to point out s.o.'s mistakes; укаже на некои факти to point to certain facts **2** to show *trans.*; му укажаа голема почит they showed him great respect; укаже некому внимание to pay attention to s.o. **3** to render, offer; студентите му укажаа помош the students helped him **II – се** to appear, arise; ако ми се укаже случај if I get an opportunity; ако се укаже потреба if the need arises

укажува (се) *impf of* укаже (се)

указ *m* order, decree

указание -ија *n* instruction; information; notification

укаса *pf* **I** (касне) to bite *trans.*; to sting *trans.*; го укаса змија a snake bit him **II – се** to bite o.s. (*one's lip, etc.*); to bite one another

укасува (се) *impf of* укаса (се)

укач *m* howling dervish

укине *pf* укина *aor.* to abolish; to revoke, rescind, repeal, discontinue; укине закон to repeal a law; укине договор to revoke (abrogate) an agreement; укине некое место, некоја установа to abolish a post, an institution

укинлив *adj* revocable

укинува *impf of* укине

укит *m* hoar-frost; укит време season of hoar-frost

укне *pf* укна *aor. see* ука² 1 & 2

укнижи *pf Accounting* to log, register, record

укнижува *impf of* укнижи

укнува *impf of* укне

укове *pf f.p.* **1** *see* поткове I **2** to hammer, knock in nails; to nail down

укор¹ *m* reprimand, reproach, reproof

укор² *m* **1** wretched creature **2** ill omen **3** monster, freak

укорен -рна *adj* reprimanding, reproachful; укорни зборови words of reproach

укори *pf* to rebuke, reprimand, reproach; укори некого поради нешто to reproach s.o. for/with s.th.

укоричи *pf* (*of a book*) to bind *trans.*

укоричува *impf of* укоричи

укориште *n see* укор²

укорува *impf of* укори

укотви *pf* **I** to anchor *trans.* **II – се** to cast anchor, drop anchor

укотвува (се) *impf of* укотви (се)

украде *pf* **I** to steal *trans.* **II – се** to slip away, run off, steal away

украдува *impf of* украде I; ❑ дете од мајка украдува he's a cunning thief, he could steal anything

Украина *f* Ukraine

Украинец -нци *m* Ukrainian

Украинка *f* (*fem. form*) *see* Украинец

украински *adj* Ukrainian

украс *m* decoration, adornment; ornament; поетски украс poetic embellishment

украсен -сна *adj* decorative, ornamental; украсна придавка epithet

украси *pf* to decorate, adorn, embellish

украсува *impf of* украси

укрива (се) *impf of* укрие (се)

укрие *pf* **I** to conceal, hide *trans.*, keep secret **II – се** to conceal o.s., hide *intrans.*; *see* скрие (се), сокрие (се)

укрили *pf* to shelter, protect; to take under one's wing; чесен крст да нè укрили may the Holy Cross protect us!

укрилува *impf of* укрили

укроти *pf* **I** to tame; to train *trans.*; укроти лав to tame a lion; укроти куче to train a dog **II – се** to be tamed; to become meek, quieten down *intrans.*; *see* скроти (се)

укротител *m* tamer; укротител на лавови lion tamer; укротител на змии snake-charmer

укротителка *f* (*fem. form*) *see* укротител

укротлив *adj* tameable; tractable

укротливост *f* tameability; tractability

укротува (се) *impf of* укроти (се), *see* скротува (се)

укруп *m* sorrow; anguish, torment; укруп на срцето му паднало sorrow seized his heart

укутари се *pf* to crouch, squat; to cower

ул. *abbr.* (улица) Street, St

ула *f* blasphemy; ула на Бога, на верата reviling God, one's faith

улав *adj* mad, insane, crazy; ❑ од улав ум не барај don't expect sense from a madman!

улави се *impf* to be mad; to rage, fume; не улави се don't do anything silly!

улавко -овци *m* madman, fool, crazy fellow

улавски¹ *adj* mad, crazy, crack-brained; улавски работи crazy things

улавски² *adv* madly, crazily; немој така улавски да постапуваш don't be so foolish!

улавчо -овци *m see* улавко

улавштина *f* madness, craziness, foolishness; foolish behaviour

улегне <се> *pf* улегна <се> *aor.* to settle down; to subside; to sink, sag; улегна земјата the earth has settled; подот <се> улегна the floor sagged

улегнува <се> *impf of* улегне <се>

уленик -ци *m see* улјаник

улера *f arch.* cholera; улерата да те фати (да те истреби)! *curse* go to hell!

ули *impf* to blaspheme, curse, swear; ули на Бога to blaspheme against God

улит *m Med.* (воспаление на непцата) gingivitis

улител *m* blasphemer

улица *f* street; главна улица main street; споредна улица side-street; жива улица busy street; на улица in the street; од дома, outside; ❑ исфрли некого на улица to dismiss (sack) s.o.; остане на улица to be left homeless/on the streets; мери улици to walk the streets; лета на улица to get the sack; to be laid off; to be thrown out; слепа улица cul-de-sac

уличар *m* street urchin, guttersnipe, street Arab; lout, tough

уличарка *f* **1** (*fem. form*) *see* уличар **2** streetwalker, whore, prostitute

уличен -чна *adj* street; улично осветление street lighting; улични борби street fights; улично куче stray dog; улични зборови vulgar words; улична жена streetwalker, prostitute; уличен продавач hawker; pedlar

уличка *f dim.* (*of* улица) alley

уличник -ци *m see* уличар

улиши *pf* (*од*) to deprive (*s.o. of s.th.*), take (*s.th.*) away (*from s.o.*)

улиште *n* 1 beehive 2 (*poj*) swarm (*of bees*) 3 *fig.* monster, *colloq.* scarecrow; улиште едно! you monster!

улишува *impf of* улиши

улјаник -ци & **улјарник** -ци *m* apiary

улка *f colloq.* madwoman, crazy woman

улкус *m Med.* ulcer

улови *pf* 1 to catch; улови риба to catch a fish 2 *fig.* to hear, catch; улови некој збор to catch a few words; улови нови вести to hear fresh news

уловува *impf of* улови

улог -зи *m* cripple

улога[1] *f* role, part; function; главна улога leading role; споредна улога supporting role; ❑ игра важна улога во нешто to play an important role in s.th.; игра споредна улога to take a back seat; to play second fiddle

улога[2] *m f.p. see* улогавец & улогар

улогав *adj* crippled, lame

улогавец -вци & **улогар** *m* cripple

улогар *m* cripple

улогарка *f* (*fem. form*) *see* улогар

улогори *pf* I to encamp *trans.* II – **ce** to encamp *intrans.*, set up camp

улогорува (ce) *impf of* улогори (ce)

уложје *n Anat.* placenta

ултимати́вен -вна *adj* 1 decisive, final, last 2 ultimatum *attrib.*; испрати ултимативна нота to issue an ultimatum

ултима́тум *m* ultimatum; даде (постави) ултиматум to present an ultimatum

ултра- *prefix* ultra-

у́лтравиоле́тен -тна & **у́лтравиоле́тов** *adj* ultraviolet; ултравиолетни (ултравиолетови) зраци ultraviolet rays

ултразвук *m* ultrasound

улути (ce) *pf f.p. see* налути (ce)

ум -ови, -ишта *m* 1 mind, wits; intelligence; brain; sense; ❑ според мојот ум to my mind, in my opinion; има на ум to bear/have in mind; на ум му е to be on one's mind; му изветреал умот he's become senile; голем ум great mind (thinker); загуби ум to go mad, to take leave of one's senses; извади некому ум <од главата> to drive crazy; сврти некому ум to turn s.o.'s head; to sweep s.o. off his/her feet; мати (брка) некому ум to trouble, confuse s.o.; дотера некому ум, научи некого на ум to teach s.o. a lesson; му дојде умот <во главата> he came to his senses; толку му сече (фаќа) умот he can grasp that much <but no more>; не е <токму> со умот he's not all there; he's not quite right in the head; ми се меле умот my head is reeling (spinning); кај ти е умот? where's your common sense? кус во умот not very bright; паѓа (доаѓа) некому на ум to occur to s.o.; to cross one's mind; to come to mind; умот да ти зајде (застане) it's beyond belief, it beggars description, it's out of this world; бери ум, ум в глава take care! be careful! bear in mind! клај го тоа на ум get that into your head! му штукна умот 1. his mind was unhinged 2. he was amazed; на ум се

стори he was astounded; си рече (вели) со (во) умот to say to o.s.; на еден ум сме двајцата we both have the same idea; со кој ум го стори тоа? what made you do that? how could you? уште му лета умот <по чавките> his head's still full of fantasies, he's still wet behind the ears; му влезе нешто во умот he remembered s.th.; ова ќе ми биде за ум this will be a good lesson for me; чавка умот му го испила he's taken leave of his senses; како ти фаќа умот? what do you think? ми се врти во умот 1. it's on my mind, I keep thinking 2. I feel giddy; еден ум (е), дали за зиме дали за лете I can't remember everything; со друг ум е to have a change of heart; што на ум, тоа на друм to call a spade a spade; ќе му дојде умот, кога ќе си појде кумот *prov.* he will get some sense when it is too late; главата му обеле, умот не му дојде *prov.* old age doesn't protect from folly 2 advice; бара ум од некого to seek advice from s.o.; продава ум to give unwanted advice

ума *f* argil, potter's clay

умее *impf* to know how to; не умее да готви she doesn't know how to cook; како знаеш и умееш to the best of your ability

умеење *n* skill, capability; know-how, knack

умен -мна *adj* sensible, clever, wise; умна жена intelligent woman; умни деца sensible children; умна постапка sensible action

умение *n see* умеење

умерен *adj* moderate, reasonable; temperate; abstemious; modest; frugal; умерен во сè moderate in all things; умерена клима temperate climate; умерен појас temperate zone; умерени барања modest demands

умерено *adv* moderately; frugally; умерено топол moderately warm; умерено се храни he eats in moderation; умерено живее he lives frugally

умереност *f* moderation

умери *pf* to hit, find one's mark

умерува *impf of* умери

умеси *pf f.p.* to knead, *see* меси

умесно *adv* appropriately; aptly; opportunely

умесност *f* appropriacy; aptness

уместен -сна *adj* appropriate, sensible, reasonable; apt; timely; уместен предлог sensible proposal; умесна молба sensible request

уметен -тна *adj see* умешен; девојчето е уметно the girl is clever

уметник -ци *m* artist

уметница & **уметничка** *f* (*fem. form*) *see* уметник

уметнички *adj* 1 artistic; уметничка игра artistic dancing; уметничка дарба artistic gift; уметничко лизгање figure skating 2 of art, of the arts; уметничка академија academy of art; уметничка галерија art gallery; уметнички слики paintings

уметништво *n* artistry

уметност *f* art; ликовна уметност fine art; историјата на уметноста the history of art; драмска уметност theatrical art, the theatre

умешен -шна *adj* skilled, clever, adroit

умешно *adv* cleverly, adroitly, skilfully

умешност *f* skill, cleverness, adroitness

уми се *impf* to think over, reflect (*on*), ponder (*over*); што се умиш? what are you thinking about?

умилен[1] *pt* distressed, sad, sorrowful

умилен² -лна *adj* sweet, lovable, tender; touching, moving; умилен поглед tender look; умилна песна moving/tender song/poem

умилено *adv* sadly, sorrowfully

умиленост *f* distress, sadness, sorrowfulness

умили *pf* **I** to distress, sadden, upset **II** – **се** to become distressed, saddened

умилкува се *impf* to play up to, flatter *trans.*, fawn on

умилно *adv* tenderly, touchingly, movingly; sweetly

умилност *f* tenderness, sweetness, lovableness; power to touch (move)

умилува (се) *impf of* умили (се)

умир *m poet.* peace; calming

умира *impf of* умре; само еднаш се умира *saying* a man can die but once

умирање *n* dying, death; на умирање е he is on his deathbed; ❑ не е болка за умирање it's not fatal, it's nothing serious

умирачка *f* (*умирање*) death, dying; на умирачка е he is dying; ❑ не е болка за умирачка it's not so bad, you'll survive; иде (има) умирачка life is short

умири *pf* **I 1** to calm <down> *trans.*, pacify, soothe; to appease **2** to subdue **II** – **се** to calm down, quieten down *intrans.*; *see* смири (се)

умирува (се) *impf of* умири (се)

умисла *f* premeditation, intention (*also Leg.*)

умислен *adj Leg.* premeditated, deliberate

умислено *adv Leg.* with malice aforethought, deliberately, with evil intent

умисленост *f Leg.* premeditation, evil intent

умјазува *impf* to look like, resemble

умник -ци *m* **1** clever person, wise man, sensible person **2** wisdom tooth

умнина *f see* умнотија

умница *f* (*fem. form*) *see* умник

умно *adv* sensibly, wisely, intelligently; умно постапи he acted wisely

умножи *pf* **I** to multiply, increase *trans.*; to duplicate **II** – **се** to multiply, increase *intrans.*; *see* намножи (се)

умножлив *adj* multipliable

умножливост *f* multipliability

умножува (се) *impf of* умножи (се), *see* намножува (се)

умност *f* wisdom

умнотија *f* wisdom; reason; личотија и умнотија good looks and good sense

умоболен -лна *adj* insane, mad, mentally ill, deranged

умоболник -ци *m* madman, lunatic

умоболница *f* (*fem. form*) *see* умоболник

умоболност *f* insanity, madness, lunacy

умовит & **умовитен** -тна *adj* wise, sensible, *see* умен

умодавец -вци *m* adviser; *iron.* would-be scholar; даскали умодавци teachers

умолен -лна *adj* imploring, entreating; со умолна гестикулација with pleading gestures

умоли *pf* to move by entreaties

умолува *impf of* умоли

умор *m* & **умора** *f* **1** exhaustion, weariness, tiredness, fatigue; капнав од умора I collapsed from exhaustion; умствен умор mental fatigue/exhaustion **2** *f.p.* (*умирачка*, *смрт*) dying, death; на умор dying, at death's door

уморен¹ *adj* & *pt* weary, tired, exhausted; уморен од работа exhausted by/from work; уморена од трчање tired out by running

уморен² -рна *adj* tiring, exhausting, hard, strenuous; уморна работа strenuous work

умореност *f* tiredness, exhaustion

умори *pf* **I 1** to tire *trans.*, exhaust, wear out; таа работа многу ме умори that work wore me out **2** *f.p.* to kill, put to death **II** – **се 1** to get tired, tire *intrans.* **2** *f.p.* to get killed; to kill o.s.

уморнина *f* (*запурнина*) sultriness, stuffiness

уморност *f* tiredness, weariness

уморува (се) *impf of* умори (се)

умотворба *f* creation, work of art; народни умотворби folklore, folk literature

умре *pf* **1** *intrans.* to die, pass away; умре за татковината to die for one's country; умре со природна смрт to die a natural death; умре од болест to die of an illness; ❑ умре без време (ден) to die before one's time; to come to an untimely end; умре од досада to be bored to death; умре од мака to be bitterly disappointed; умре од смеа to die laughing; умре од срам to die of shame; умре за to be dying for; умрев за јадење I'm starving; умре за (по) неа he was dying for her; секој што се родил <и> ќе умре *saying* death comes to us all **2** *trans.* to kill; *fig.* to torment, be the death of; ме умре со своите молби he wore me down with his requests

умрен *adj* **1** dead **2** *fig.* (*за*) dying for; умрен за вода dying for water; умрена за убав збор dying for a kind word **3** (*as noun*) умрен<иот> *m* the deceased

умртви *pf* **I 1** to kill, put to death **2** *fig.* to deaden *trans.*; to benumb; умртви нерв to deaden/destroy a nerve **3** to soothe, ease; умртви болка to soothe pain **II** – **се 1** to kill o.s. **2** to calm down, quieten down *intrans.*, die down

умртвува (се) *impf of* умртви (се)

умски *adj see* умствен

умствен *adj* mental; intellectual; <of the> brain; умствен труд mental/intellectual work; умствен работник intellectual, brainworker; умствени напори mental/intellectual efforts

умува *impf* to philosophize, theorize, speculate

умут *m arch. see* надеж

умштина *f* **1** cleverness, sense, brains **2** slyness, craftiness; ruse; му текнала една умштина he hit on a scheme (ruse)

уназади *pf* **1** to obstruct, hold back, set back **2** to degrade, demote (*an officer, etc.*)

уназадува *impf of* уназади

унапреди *pf* to advance *trans.*; to promote; го унапредија за генерал he was promoted to general

унапредува *impf of* унапреди

Унгарец -рци *m* Hungarian

Унгарија *f* Hungary

Унгарка *f* (*fem. form*) *see* Унгарец

унгарски *adj* Hungarian

унер *m arch.* **1** wonder, miracle **2** skill, mastery

унерџија -ии *m arch.* miracle-worker

унес *m* (*занес*) enthusiasm, rapture; trance; reverie; fanaticism; absent-mindedness

унесен *pt* (*занесен*) carried away

унесено *adv* with rapture; absent-mindedly, dreamily

унесеност *f see* унес

унесреќи *pf* **I** to hurt *trans.*, cause (*s.o.*) suffering **II** – **се** to become distressed; to bring misery on o.s.

унесреќува (се) *impf of* унесреќи (се)

унечка *f* apron; опашан со унечка wearing an apron

универзален -лна *adj* universal; all-purpose; универзален лек panacea, universal remedy; универзално образование many-sided/liberal education

универзалност *f* universality

универзитет *m* university; народен универзитет adult education centre; работнички универзитет workers' college

универзитетски *adj* university *attrib.*; универзитетски професор university professor; универзитетска библиотека university library; универзитетски совет university council

универзум *m* universe

унижен *adj see* понижен

унижи *pf* **I** to humiliate, demean, abase **II** – **се** to humiliate o.s., abase o.s., demean o.s.

унижува (се) *impf of* унижи (се)

унижувачки *adj* humiliating, *see* понижувачки

унија *f* **1** union, alliance **2** *Hist.* Union (*alliance of the Orthodox and Catholic Churches under papal rule*)

унијат *m Hist.* Uniat<e>

уникат *m* unique item, specimen

уникатен -тна *adj* unique

уникум *m* unique object

унисон *m usu. in the expression:* во унисон со . . . in unison with . . .

унификација *f* unification, union

унифицира *pf & impf* to unify, unite *trans.*; to standardize

униформа *f* uniform

униформен -мна *adj* uniform, the same, similar

униформизам -змот *m* conformism

униформира *pf & impf* **1** to dress in uniform *trans.* **2** to equalize *trans.*, standardize, unify

униформност *f* uniformity

уништи *pf* **1** to destroy, annihilate; to exterminate; to obliterate **2** *fig.* to ruin, crush; to butcher; критиката го уништи the critics were the ruin of him **3** (*укине*) to abolish, annul, revoke, cancel; уништи пресуда to quash a verdict

уништлив *adj* destructible

уништува *impf of* уништи

уништување *n* destruction; annihilation; abolition

уништувач *m* destroyer, annihilator, exterminator

унција -ии *f* ounce; jot, small amount

уобичаен *adj see* вообичаен

уобичаеност *f see* вообичаеност

уочи *pf* to notice, observe

уочлив *adj* noticeable, observable; marked

уочува *impf of* уочи

упад *m* **1** invasion; intrusion; forced entry; упад на непријателот the enemy invasion **2** interruption, heckling

упадлив *adj* conspicuous; obvious, evident; упадлив е фактот (*дека . . .*) it is evident (*that . . .*)

упадливо *adv* conspicuously; evidently

упадливост *f* conspicuousness

упадне *pf* упадна *aor.* **1** to invade, burst into; to intrude; жандармите упаднаа во салата the police burst into the hall **2** to interrupt, heckle; to come in; ѝ упадна во зборот he interrupted her speech; трубата упадна прерано the trumpet came in too early

упадок *m* decline, decay; *Art, Philos.* decadence

упаѓа *impf of* упадне

упаѓач *m* intruder; invader; heckler

упази *pf dial.* to observe, notice

упат *m* **1** referral; општиот лекар му даде упат за специјалист his GP gave him a referral to a specialist **2** reference; упат на друга страна reference to another page

упатен *pt* directed; instructed; initiated; (*as noun*) *m* initiate

упатеник -ци *m* initiate

упати *pf* **I** **1** to direct, send, dispatch; to refer; ја упати војската на југ he sent his army south; упати писмо to send a letter; ❑ упати на погрешен пат to put s.o. on the wrong track; ги упати читателите кон новата литература he referred the readers to the new publications; го упати на специјалист he referred (sent) him to a specialist; упати <некому> прашање/молба to direct (address) a question/ request to s.o. **2** to instruct, direct; јас постапив онака како што ме упати ти I acted as you instructed me **3** to initiate (*во – into*); го упати во сите тајни he initiated him into all the secrets **II** – **се** **1** to set out *intrans.*, set off (*за – for*); се упатија накај мене they set out to visit me **2** to be initiated (*во – into*); се упати во таа работа he acquainted himself with that matter

упатница *f* covering letter; referral; order; телеграфска упатница telegraphed money order

упатство *n* instruction<s>, direction<s>; упатство за употреба (*на нешто*) instructions for <the> use (*of s.th.*); упатство за работа directions for work

упатува (се) *impf of* упати (се)

упатување *n* direction<s>, instruction<s>; reference

упечок -ци *m* stunted child, plant, etc.; *see* спечок

упика (се) *pf dial. see* втера (се), пикне (се)

упис *m* registration, enrolment; admission; услови за упис admission (entrance) requirements; упис во матичната книга на родените registration of a birth

уписен -сна *adj* registration *attrib.*; уписна такса registration fee

уписнина *f* registration fee

уписница *f* registration form

управ *m* fright, terror, fear, alarm; болен од уплав sick with fear

уплакан *adj* tearful, crying; уплакани очи tear-stained eyes

уплата *f* payment

уплати *pf* to make a payment, pay (*на – in*)

уплатлив *adj* payable

уплатница *f* deposit form; postal (money) order

уплатува *impf of* уплати

уплачен *adj see* уплакан

уплашен *pt* frightened, terrified

уплашено *adv* fearfully

уплашеност *f* <state of> fear, terror

уплаши *pf* **I** to frighten, terrify; ме уплаши he frightened me **II** – **се** to get frightened, terrified; многу (силно) се уплашив I got a terrible fright

уплашува (се) *impf of* уплаши (се)

уплете *pf dial. see* исплете

уплив *m* influence, *see* влијание

упоен -јна *adj poet.* fervent, ecstatic; упојна љубов fervent love

упој *m poet.* ecstasy, thrill, rapture

упокои *pf* I to calm *trans.*, soothe II – ce to calm down *intrans.*, calm o.s.; *see* успокои (се)

упокојува (се) *impf of* упокои (се)

упорен -рна *adj* determined, persistent, steadfast, tenacious; obstinate, stubborn; упорни напори determined efforts; упорен во своите барања insistent in his demands

упорит *adj see* упорен

упорито *adv see* упорно

упоритост *f see* упорност

упориште *n* stronghold, bastion, bulwark

упорно *adv* determinedly, persistently; stubbornly, steadfastly; упорно работи he works persistently; упорно се бореа they fought stubbornly

упорност *f* persistence, determination; obstinacy

упорство *n* persistence, determination, *see* упорност

упорствува *impf literary* to be persistent/obstinate; to persist (*во – in*)

употреба *f* use; application; употреба на сила use of force; употреба на оружје use of arms; исфрли од употреба to discard; to pension off; употреба на лекови taking of medicines; начин на употреба usage, manner of use; за употреба for application; излезе од употреба to fall into disuse; to fall out of use; погрешна употреба misuse; прекумерна употреба overuse

употребен *pt* used

употребен -бна *adj Econ.* in use; употребна вредност use value

употреби *pf* to use, make use of, employ; употреби оружје to use firearms; го употреби своето влијание he used his influence; употреби лекови to take medicines

употреблив *adj* usable; in use; употребливи зборови generally used words

употребливост *f* usability

употребува *impf of* употреби

употребуван *pt* used (*regularly, usually*)

управа *f* administration, management; control; government; управата на земјата the government of the country; управа на училиште administration of a school; градска управа city administration, town hall; даночна управа tax office; управа за безбедност на сообраќајот traffic authority; принудна управа receivership

управен -вна *adj* administrative; управни органи administrative bodies; управен одбор administrative committee

управеност *f* direction, aim

управи *pf* I to direct, point to/at, aim at, turn (*on/to*) *trans.*; ги управија топовите во црквата they aimed the guns at the church; го управи погледот кон небото he turned his gaze heavenward II – ce to point at, turn (*on/to*) *intrans.*; иглата се управи кон север the needle pointed north

управија *f arch.* administration, order, rule, law; автономна управија autonomy, self-rule; турската управија Turkish rule

управител *m see* управник

управителка *f* (*fem. form*) *see* управител

управителски *adj see* управнички

управник -ци *m* administrator; director; manager; head

управничка *f* (*fem. form*) *see* управник

управнички *adj* administrative, managerial

управува[1] *impf* I *of* управи I II – ce 1 *of* управи (се) II 2 to adapt (*со, според – to*), conform (*to*); to behave (*according to*); тој се управува според времето he takes the time/weather into account

управува[2] *impf* 1 to govern, rule; управува држава to rule a state 2 to manage, run *trans.*; управува претпријатие to manage an enterprise 3 (*автомобил*) to drive; (*брод, возило, авион*) to steer; (*авион*) to fly; (*машина*) to operate

управување *n* 1 aiming, directing; governing, ruling 2 management; control; работничко управување workers' management; далечинско управување remote control; управување со копче pushbutton control

управувач *m* 1 (*владетел*) ruler 2 (*управник*) administrator; manager; head 3 (*на возило*) driver; (*на брод*) helmsman; (*на машина*) operator 4 (*на велосипед*) handlebars; (*на автомобил*) steering wheel

упражнува *impf* to practise, train (*at*), engage in; упражнува скијање to ski; упражнува фискултура to exercise

упразнет *adj* vacant; упразнето место vacancy, vacant position

упразни *pf* I to vacate II – ce to fall vacant, be vacated; се упразни местото на шефот на одделението the post of section head fell vacant

упразнува (се) *impf of* упразни (се)

упрек -ци *m* rebuke, reproach

упрекне *pf* упрекна *aor.* to rebuke, reproach

упрекнува *impf of* упрекне

упропастен *pt* ruined, spoilt, wrecked; упропастени посеви ruined crops; упропастено здравје ruined health

упропастеност *f* ruined state (*of s.th.*)

упропасти *pf* I to spoil *trans.*, ruin, destroy, wreck; (*девојка*) to deflower; си го упропасти здравјето he ruined his health; ја упропасти работата he ruined the work II – ce to ruin o.s.

упропастител *m see* упропастувач

упропастува (се) *impf of* упропасти (се)

упропастувач *m* wrecker, destroyer

упростен *pt* simplified

упростеност *f* simplicity

упрости *pf* to simplify

упростлив *adj* reducible

упростува *impf of* упрости

упростувач *m* simplifier

ура *interj* hurrah! hurray! трипати ура за three cheers for

уравнилóвка *f* levelling; wage-levelling

ураган *m* hurricane; tornado

урагански *adj* <of a> hurricane, hurricane-like; <of a> tornado

урами *pf* to frame

урамнотежен *adj & pt* stable, well-balanced; steady, even-tempered; урамнотежен буџет balanced budget

урамнотеженост *f* balance, stability, peace, composure; steadiness, even temper

урамнотежи *pf* I to bring into balance, balance *trans.*, counterbalance II – **се** to balance *intrans.*

урамнотежува (се) *impf of* урамнотежи (се)

урамува *impf of* урами

уран & **ураниум** *m Chem.* uranium

ураниумов & **уранов** *adj* uranic, uranium

урбанѝзам -змот *m* town planning

урбанизација *f* urbanization

урбанизѝра *pf* & *impf* to urbanize

урбанѝст *m* town planner, city architect

урбанистика *f* town-planning studies/practices

урбанистички *adj* urbanistic

урбанѝстка *f* (*fem. form*) *see* урбанист

урва[1] *f* ravine, chasm, abyss; <steep> slope, precipice

урва[2] **(се)** *impf dial. see* урива (се)

урвен *adj* made of/with vetch; fed on vetch

урвест *adj* steep

урви *pf dial.* I 1 *see* урне I 2 to pick, break off *trans.*, remove; урви сосе корен to root out 3 to come down, go down II – **се** *see* урне се II

урвокос *f* malice, evil; колку за урвокос out of sheer spite

ургѐнтен -тна *adj* urgent, pressing

ургѐнтност *f* urgency

ургенција -ии *f* 1 urgent demand; urgency, insistence 2 intervention

ургѝра *pf* & *impf* 1 to urge, press *trans.* 2 to intervene

урда *f* (*изварка*) curds

урѐа *f* urea

уред *m* 1 office, bureau; матичен уред registry office 2 device, gadget; appliance; електрични уреди electrical appliances

уредба *f* 1 *Leg.* regulation; decree; by-law, enactment, statute 2 arrangement, order; disposition, deployment; уредба на војска deployment of troops 3 (*суредба*) furniture, furnishings; household appliances

уреден[1] *pt* arranged, orderly, tidy

уреден[2] -дна *adj* tidy, neat, orderly; regular; уреден човек orderly person; уредно плаќање regular payment; уредна куќа tidy house

уреденост *f* tidiness

уреди *pf* I 1 to arrange, put in order, tidy up; уреди своја куќа to tidy up one's house 2 to settle, see to, conclude *trans.*; тој ја уреди работата he settled the matter 3 to edit; го уреди првиот број на списанието he edited the first number of the journal II – **се** to settle down *intrans.*; to put o.s. (one's things) in order

уредник -ци *m* (*редактор*) editor; главен и одговорен уредник editor-in-chief

уредничка *f* (*fem. form*) *see* уредник

уреднички *adj* (*редакторски*) editorial; уредничка работа editorial work

уредништво *n* (*редакција*) editorship; editorial staff

уредно *adv* neatly; in an orderly manner; reliably; punctually; methodically; уредно живее to live an orderly life; уредно плаќа to pay regularly

уредност *f* orderliness, tidiness; уредност во животот order in life

уредски *adj* office, bureau *attrib.*; уредски простории office premises

уредува (се) *impf of* уреди (се)

уредување *n* 1 *from* уредува; уредување на излог window dressing 2 organization, order, system, structure; државно уредување state structure/system

уредувач *m* 1 organizer 2 *see* уредник

уредувачки *adj* 1 (*редакциски*) editorial; уредувачки одбор editorial committee 2 organizing; уредувачка акција clean-up

уремија *f Med.* uraemia

урива (се) *impf of* урне (се)

уривач *m* demolition worker; wrecker; уривач на општествен поредок disturber of public order

урина *f* urine

уринар *m* bedpan

урка *f* distaff; spinning-wheel

урма *f Bot.* (Phoenix dactylifera) date (*fruit and tree*)

урна *f* 1 (*за пепел*) urn 2 (*за гласање*) ballot-box 3 (*за лотарија*) lottery-wheel

урнатина *f* ruin, wreck

урне *pf* урна *aor.* I 1 to knock down, demolish, wreck; *fig.* to bring down, overthrow; урне ѕид to demolish a wall; урне влада to bring down a government; го урнаа стариот систем they overthrew the old system; урне аргумент to refute (rebut) an argument; урне некому чест to ruin s.o.'s reputation 2 to push off, knock off *trans.*; урне некого од коњ to knock s.o. off his horse 3 to erode, wear away *trans.*; водата го урна брегот the water eroded the bank 4 *fig.* to reduce, lower; му ја урна цената he reduced the price II – **се** 1 to collapse, fall, fall to pieces, fall down; ѕидот се урна the wall collapsed; авионот се урна the aeroplane has crashed; се урна од коњот he fell off his horse 2 to erode *intrans.*, be worn away; брегот се урна the bank has been eaten away 3 to throw o.s., rush *intrans.*; се урна во собата he rushed into the room 4 to attack, fall upon; се урнаа сите на него they all fell upon him 5 *fig.* to fall, sink (*morally*), lower o.s.; сосем се урна he has gone right downhill 6 *dial.* to come out, come down; урни се долу come down! come out!

урнебес *m* 1 din, rumpus, racket, clamour; урнебес да фатиш! *curse* the devil take you! 2 disorder, chaos; направи урнебес во собата he messed up the room; ❑ урнебес салата tossed salad 3 uproar, disturbance; шефот направи урнебес the boss hit the roof

урнебесен -сна *adj* noisy, riotous; chaotic; урнебесни викотници loud shouting

урнек -ци *m arch.* model, example, sample

урниса (се) *pf see* урне (се); го урниса човекот you've ruined the man; се урниса to go to rack and ruin

урнисува (се) *impf of* урниса (се)

урнува (се) *impf of* урне (се), *see* урива (се)

уров *m Bot.* (Vicia sativa) common vetch

урок[1] *m more often* **уроци** *pl* evil spell; да не го фаќаат уроци touch wood!

урок[2] -ци *m* lesson; го научи урокот he learned the lesson

уроклив *adj see* урочлив

уролог -зи *m Med.* urologist

урологија *f Med.* urology

уролошки *adj Med.* urological

урони (се) *pf f.p. see* изрони (се)

урочен *adj* bewitched, under a spell

урочи *pf* **I** to cast a spell on, bewitch **II** – **се** to fall under a spell

урочлив *adj* **1** easily captivated (spellbound) **2** evil-looking; урочливи (лоши) очи evil eyes

урочува (се) *impf of* урочи (се)

Уругваец -ајци *m* Uruguayan

Уругвај *m* Uruguay

Уругвајка *f* (*fem. form*) *see* Уругваец

уругвајски *adj* Uruguayan

усамен *adj & pt* isolated; усамен човек lonely person; усамено селце isolated hamlet

усамено *adv* alone, by oneself; живее усамено he lives alone

усаменост *f* loneliness, isolation

усами *pf* **I** to isolate **II** – **се** to isolate o.s., withdraw *intrans.*

усамува (се) *impf of* усами (се)

усвитен *adj* **1** red-hot, glowing red; усвитено железо red-hot iron **2** *fig.* hotheaded; усвитена глава hothead

усвитеност *f* red heat

усвити *pf* **I** to heat *trans.*, make (*s.th.*) red-hot **II** – **се** to become red-hot

усвитува (се) *impf of* усвити (се)

усвитување *n* red heat; точка на усвитување red heat (*the temperature at which s.th. becomes red-hot*)

усвоеник -ци *m* *Leg.* (*посвоеник, посвојче*) adopted son, child

усвои *pf* to adopt; усвои дете to adopt a child; усвои предлог to adopt a proposal

усвоител *m* *Leg.* (*посвоител, посвојувач*) adoptive parent

усвојлив *adj* adoptable, acceptable

усвојливост *f* adoptability, acceptability

усвојува *impf of* усвои

усвојување *n from* усвојува; усвојување на закон adoption (passing) of a law; усвојување на понуда acceptance of a tender

усвојувач *m* *see* усвоител

усекне (се) *pf* усекна *aor.* *see* исекне (се)

усекнува (се) *impf of* усекне (се), *see* исекнува (се)

усели *pf* **I** to move (*s.o.*) into, settle (*s.o.*) in *trans.* **II** – **се** to move in, settle in *intrans.*; се уселивме во нов стан we've moved into a new flat (apartment)

уселува (се) *impf of* усели (се)

усет *m* **1** feeling; усет за музика feeling for music; има усет за to have an eye for; to have the touch; to be versed in **2** *fig.* scent, sense of smell; има добар усет to have a good sense of smell

усета *f* presentiment, foreboding; му дојде усета he had a foreboding (presentiment)

усети *pf* **I** **1** to feel, sense; to notice, perceive; to scent, get wind of; усети дека зад него стои некој he sensed s.o. standing behind him **II** – **се** **1** to figure out, guess; веднаш се усети he figured it out immediately **2** to remember, think (*за – of*); се усети за сестра си he remembered his sister

усетува (се) *impf of* усети (се)

усече *pf poet.* to engrave, inscribe, carve

усилба *f* effort; со големи усилби with great effort<s>

усилен[1] *pt* stepped-up, intensified, vigorous

усилен[2] -лна *adj* strenuous, heavy, difficult; усилна работа strenuous work

усилено *adv* intensively, at full speed; работиме усилено we are working intensively

усили *pf* **I** **1** (*засили*) to strengthen, intensify *trans.*, step up; усили од (чекор) to speed up, step up the pace **II** – **се** **1** (*засили се*) to strengthen, intensify *intrans.*, grow stronger **2** to gather momentum, gather speed, speed up

усилно *adv* strenuously, hard; требало усилно да се работи we had to work hard

усилува (се) *impf of* усили (се)

усклади *pf* **I** to match *trans.*; to coordinate *trans.*; to reconcile **II** – **се** to coincide; to match *intrans.*; *see* усогласи (се)

ускладува (се) *impf of* усклади (се), *see* усогласува (се)

ускрати *pf* to refuse, deny; банката му ускрати кредит the bank refused him credit (a loan); ускрати некому право to deprive s.o. of his right/entitlement; си ускрати од нешто to deny o.s. s.th.

ускратува *impf of* ускрати

услагоди *pf* to arrange, put in order, tidy up; услагоди куќа to put a house in order

услагодува *impf of* услагоди

услади <ми> се *pf* to enjoy

усладува <ми> се *impf of* услади ми се

услани *pf impers.* to cover with rime (hoar-frost)

уеланува *impf of* услани

услачи *pf* to sweeten *trans.*, make sweeter

услачува *impf of* услачи

уследи *pf* to follow <as a consequence>, ensue; потоа уследија разговори talks followed (ensued)

услекне *pf* to die (*of animals*)

услекнува *impf of* услекне; фатија да му услекнуваат добиците his cattle started dying off

услиши *pf literary* to grant; услиши молба to grant a request

услишува *impf literary of* услиши

услов *m* **1** condition; stipulation; terms; услови за развиток conditions for progress; условите на капитулацијата the terms of the capitulation (surrender); прифатливи услови easy terms; услови за упис admission requirements; животни услови living conditions; ❑ под услов (*да, ако*), со услов (*да*) on condition (*that*), provided (*that*); под еден услов on one condition; под никакви услови on no account; под еднакви услови on equal terms **2** (*only pl*) circumstances, conditions, situation; тој е во добри услови he is in a good situation (comfortably off); според условите according to the conditions; станбени услови housing conditions

условен[1] *pt* restricted, dependent; predetermined, defined; conditioned; stipulated; условен рефлекс conditioned reflex

условен[2] -вна *adj* conditional, prearranged; условен термин agreed term; условни знаци conventional signs; условна пресуда suspended sentence; условна согласност conditional agreement; *Gram.* условен начин conditional mood

условеност *f* dependence, restriction; convention; conditionality; заемна условеност mutual restriction

услови *pf* **1** to condition, lay down, stipulate; restrict, regulate; make conditional upon; услови со договор to restrict by an agreement **2** to cause, bring about, call forth, lead to

условно *adv* conditionally; условно осуден given a suspended sentence, put on probation; условно пуштен на слобода <released> on parole

условност *f* conditionality

условува *impf of* услови

усложнет *pt* complicated, complex; усложнета ситуација complicated situation

усложнетост *f* complexity

усложни *pf* **I** to complicate *trans.*; тој секогаш ги усложнува работите he always complicates matters **II – се** to become complicated; работите се усложнија matters became complicated

усложнува (се) *impf of* усложни (се)

услуга *f* service; favour; good turn; прави некому услуга to do/render s.o. a service; to do s.o. a favour; во овој хотел услугата е брза и добра in this hotel the service is fast and efficient; занаетчиски услуги craftsmen's services; ❑ на твоја услуга сум I am at your service; мечешка услуга disservice; action well intended but having adverse consequences; ill turn; без никакви противуслуги no strings attached; услуга за услуга you scratch my back and I scratch yours; комунални услуги public utilities

услужен -жна *adj* **1** *see* услужлив **2** service *attrib.*; услужен шалтер service counter (desk); услужни дејности service industry; услужна такса service charge

услужи *pf* to do (*s.o.*) a favour, oblige, render a service, attend (*to*), serve, wait on; to cater (*for*); услужи гостин to wait on a guest; услужи муштерија to serve a customer; како можам да ве услужам? what can I do for you?

услужлив *adj* obliging, helpful, complaisant

услужливост *f* obligingness, helpfulness, complaisance

услужност *f see* услужливост

услужува *impf of* услужи

услуп *m* shapeliness

услупен -пна *adj* shapely, beautiful; well-built, good-looking; услупна уста beautiful, well-shaped mouth

усмев *m* & **усмевка** *f* smile

усмевнат *adj* smiling

усмевнато *adv* smilingly, with a smile

усмевне се *pf* to smile

усмевнува се *impf of* усмевне се

усмири *pf* **I 1** to pacify, calm, soothe; to put at ease; си ја усмири совеста to ease one's conscience **2** to quell, put down, suppress; усмири востание to crush a rebellion **II – се** to calm down, quieten down *intrans.*

усмирува (се) *impf of* усмири (се)

усмрти *pf* **I** to put to death, kill **II – се** to kill o.s.

усмртува (се) *impf of* усмрти (се)

усна *f* lip; горна и долна усна upper and lower lip; со танки усни thin-lipped; прчи усни to pout; ❑ си ја прекаса усната to bite one's lip

уснен *adj Phon.* labial; уснени согласки labial consonants

усни *pf f.p. see* заспие

усно *adv* orally, by word of mouth; усно и писмено orally and in writing

усност *f Leg.* orality; принципот (начелото) на усноста the principle of orality

усоврешн *pt* perfected, improved; усоврешни орудија improved implements

усоврешност *f* perfection; improved state (*of s.th.*)

усоврши *pf* **I** to perfect, improve *trans.* **II – се** to perfect o.s.; to improve one's qualifications; to be perfected, improved; стручно се усоврши to receive advanced training

усовршлив *adj* perfectible, improvable

усовршува (се) *impf of* усоврши (се)

усовршување *n* **1** improvement; perfection **3** advanced study/training

усовршувач *m* improver

усогласи *pf* **I** to bring into accord, harmonize; to match *trans.*; to coordinate *trans.*; to reconcile; усогласи бои to match colours; усогласи мислења to reconcile <conflicting> opinions; усогласи време to arrange one's time; усогласи напори to co-ordinate efforts **II – се** to coincide; to match *intrans.*; тие се усогласија they agreed (came to an agreement)

усогласува (се) *impf of* усогласи (се)

усоен -јна *adj* sunless, shaded, shady, dank; усојно место shady spot; *Zool.* змија усојна *see* усојница 2

усој -ои *m* shaded side; shaded, dank place

усојница *f* **1** shade; shady, dank place; на усојница in the shade **2** *Zool.* (Vipera ammodytes) horned viper **3** *fig.* evil/malicious woman, shrew, viper

усојничав *adj* **1** shaded, dank; усојничаво место shady spot **2** gloomy, cold, unpleasant

усомни се *pf see* посомнева се

успева *impf of* успее; пченицата успева the wheat is growing well

успее *pf* успеа *aor.* to succeed (*во, со – in*) *intrans.*; to be successful, manage; to prosper, thrive, do well; не успеав да ја свршам работата I didn't manage to finish the work; успеа да постигне гол he succeeded in scoring a goal; обидот успеа the attempt succeeded; не успеа he failed, he missed the mark; ❑ успеа да истурка докрај <со нешто> to make do <with s.th.>

успех -си *m* **1** success; успеси во работата successes at/in work; ❑ доживува успех, жнее успеси to be successful, enjoy success; to come out on top; постигне успех со to make a hit with; на пат е да постигне успех to be on the road to success; успеси и неуспеси ups and downs **2** result<s>; ја заврши гимназијата со одличен успех he completed high school with excellent results (with distinction); учениците покажаа слаб успех the pupils showed poor results

успешен -шна *adj* successful; prosperous; успешен крај successful conclusion

успешно *adv* successfully; борбата заврши успешно the fight/struggle ended successfully

успешност *f* successfulness, degree of success

успива (се) *impf of* успие (се)

успивач *m* **1** person who lulls (*a child*) to sleep **2** *fig.* soporific

успивен -вна *adj* soporific; успивно средство soporific drug, sleeping-pill; успивна песна lullaby, cradle song

успие *pf* успа *aor.* **I** to put (lull) to sleep; успие дете to put a child to sleep; ова вино ќе те успие this wine will send you to sleep; успие совест to salve one's conscience **II – ce** to fall (heavily) asleep; to oversleep, sleep in, lie in

успокои *pf* **I** to calm, quieten *trans.*, soothe **II – ce** to calm down, quieten down, settle down *intrans.*

успокоителен -лна *adj see* успокојувачки

успокоително *adv* soothingly; овие гласови дејствуваат успокоително these voices have a calming effect

успокојува (се) *impf of* успокои (се)

успокојување *n* tranquillity, peace; средство за успокојување tranquillizer

успокојувачки *adj* calming, quietening, soothing; успокојувачко средство tranquillizer; успокојувачки вести reassuring news

успори *pf* to slow down; успори темпо to slacken <speed or pace>

усрами *pf* **I** 1 to shame, embarrass 2 to disgrace, bring shame on **II – ce 1** to feel ashamed, embarrassed 2 to be disgraced, humiliated; to disgrace o.s.; *see* посрами (се)

усрамоти (се) *pf see* усрами (се)

усрамува (се) *impf of* усрами (се)

усреќи *pf* **I** to make happy **II – ce** to become happy

усреќител *m* bringer of joy, happiness

усреќителка *f* (*fem. form*) *see* усреќител

усреќува (се) *impf of* усреќи (се)

уста¹ *m f.p.* (*mode of address*) Master; уста Ѓуро Master Djuro

уста² *f* 1 mouth; ❑ земе некому залак од уста to take the food from s.o.'s mouth; на волкот в уста му влезе (му отиде) to stare death in the face; не ми се клава залак в уста I have no appetite; уста не му се отвора to be off one's food; ништо не сум клал в уста I haven't eaten anything; си дели од устата, одвојува од уста to deny o.s. for the sake of others, to pinch and scrape; си ја носи пченицата в уста to have one foot in the grave; остане со прстот в уста to be left empty-handed; to get the worst of a bargain; устата му мириса на млеко he is still wet behind the ears; устата му мириса на мед и млеко butter wouldn't melt in his mouth; блага (слатка, златна, медена) уста има to be smooth-tongued; в уста ми е <зборот> I have it (the word) on the tip of my tongue; зар уште има уста да зборува? does he still have the nerve to speak? затвори <си> ја устата shut your mouth! shut up! ни уста не отвора not to say a word, to keep silent; отворил една уста до уши he started talking endlessly; he opened his mouth wide (*when laughing or yawning*); кажи, нема да ти се изеде устата tell me, it won't hurt you; лоша (погана) уста foul mouth; evil tongue; многу си ја отворил устата you talk too much; земе некому збор од уста to take the words out of s.o.'s mouth; сè што ми дојде до уста everything that came to mind; затне (зачепи) некому уста to stop s.o.'s mouth, to gag s.o.; од уста в уста by word of mouth; од твоја уста во Божји уши may your prayers be answered! со која уста го рече тоа? how could you say that? how dare you say that? со половина (празна) уста unwillingly, reluctantly; со полна уста gladly, with all one's heart; со уста те канам I'm inviting you personally; уста има, јазик нема he's very shy; his lips are sealed; has the cat got your tongue?; фали ме, усто, зашто ќе те раскинам stop shooting your

mouth off! има перис на уста to bridle one's tongue; мртва уста не зборува dead men tell no tales; пена му доаѓа на уста to foam at the mouth; устата пена да ти фати <од зборување> you could talk until you're blue in the face; сам <себе> си скока в уста to cut off one's nose to spite one's face; to put one's foot in it; уста како чорапа a big mouth; зборува на цела уста to speak plainly, pull no punches; остане со отворена уста to gape; слуша со отворена уста to listen intently, be all ears; многу раце благословени, многу усти колнати *prov.* many hands make light work, but too many cooks spoil the broth; многу усти капеле *prov.* too many cooks spoil the broth; медената уста железни врати отвора *prov.* there is a great force hidden in a sweet command 2 *fig.* (на оружје) muzzle 3 (*see* усна) lips; ја бакна в уста he kissed her on the lips; со нацрвена уста with lipstick on; ❑ си ја прекаса устата to bite one's lip 4 (*see* утока 1) mouth (*of a river*), estuary

уста³ *f Bot.* (Antirrhinum majus) antirrhinum, snapdragon, *see* чавкин: чавкина уста

устабаша & устабашија -ии *m arch.* head of a guild

устав¹ *m* constitution; повреда на уставот violation of the constitution; врз основа на уставот on the basis of the constitution; според уставот according to the constitution

устав² *m* uncial script, majuscules (*early writing in Cyrillic capitals*)

уставен¹ -вна *adj* constitutional; уставна монархија constitutional monarchy; уставно право constitutional law

уставен² -вна *adj* uncial, majuscule; уставно писмо uncial script

уставност *f* constitutionality

уставобранител *m Hist.* constitutionalist, defender/advocate of constitutionalism

уставотворен -рна *adj* constituent; уставотворно собрание constituent assembly

уставотворец -рци *m* constitutor, framer of the/a constitution

установа *f* institution; establishment; државна установа state institution; здравствена установа health centre; кредитна установа bank

установен *adj* confirmed; established, fixed, set; установени норми established norms (standards, patterns); установен ред established order

установеност *f* stability

установи *pf* 1 to establish, found, institute; установи дипломатски односи to establish diplomatic relations 2 to confirm, determine, fix; to ascertain, find out, establish; комисијата установи дека тука нема никаква руда the commission established that there was no ore here; судот установи дека е крив the court found him guilty; установи вистина to establish the truth

установува *impf of* установи

устат *adj* 1 thick-lipped 2 *fig.* talkative, garrulous

усталија *adj indecl. arch. see* устат

усташ *m Hist.* Ustashi (*member of the Croatian Fascist organization*)

усташки *adj Hist.* Ustashi *attrib.*; усташка организација Ustashi organization

усте *n dim. of* уста¹

устен -сна *adj* oral; усна празнина oral cavity; усна

хармоника mouth-organ, harmonica; устен испит oral exam<ination>; усна покана spoken invitation

устие -ија *n see* утока

устина & устинка *f* neck (*of bottle*)

устиче *n Bot.* (Antirrhinum majus) antirrhinum, snapdragon

устои *pf* to withstand, resist, stand up (*против, на – то, against*), hold out (*against*) (*also fig.*); to hold one's own

устојува *impf of* устои

устраши *pf* **1** to frighten **II – се** to be frightened, scared; *see* уплаши (се)

устрашува (се) *impf of* устраши (се), *see* уплашува (се)

устрел *m* **1** devil, imp, demon; vampire **2** name of several acute illnesses including stroke (apoplexy), erysipelas; устрелот да го фати (да го устрели)! *curse* a plague on him!

устрелато *adv* swiftly

устрели *pf* **1** to shoot *trans.* **2** *fig.* (*за болест*) to attack, bring down, kill, destroy

устрелува *impf of* устрели

устрем *m* enthusiasm, inspiration, *élan*, dash

устремен¹ *pt* directed, aimed at

устремен² -мна *adj* enthusiastic, carried away

устременост *f* enthusiasm, zest, *élan*, dash

устреми *pf* **I** to aim (*во – at*) *trans.*, direct; го устреми својот поглед во него he fixed his eyes (gaze) on him **II – се** to aim (*во – at*) *intrans.*, strive for

устремува (се) *impf of* устреми (се)

устрои *pf* to organize, arrange, put in order

устројство *n* **1** <mode of> construction, mechanism; устројството на моторот the mechanics of the engine **2** arrangement, order, system, organization; општествено устројство social organization

устројува *impf of* устрои

устрпне *pf* устрпна *aor.* (*здрви се*) to become numb, grow stiff; раката ми устрпнала my hand is numb

устрпнува *impf of* устрпне

устрчник -ци *m* (*in marriage ritual*) herald announcing bride's arrival at bridegroom's house

усука (се) *pf see* усуче (се)

усукува (се) *impf of* усука (се), *see* усучува (се)

усул *m colloq.* cleverness, skill; cunning; со усул adroitly, cleverly; со поусул with great<er> skill

усуче *pf* **I** **1** to twist *trans.*; усуче конец to twist thread; усуче мустаќ to twist (twirl) one's moustache **2** to roll *trans.*; усуче пита to roll out <layers of> pastry **II – се 1** to twist, roll, curl *intrans.*; хартијата се усучила од влагата the paper curled from the damp **2** *fig.* to become upset **3** *fig.* to become thin, lose weight

усучува (се) *impf of* усуче (се)

ут *m* **1** *Zool.* owl (*various species*); ❏ <му дојде> како на утот <he got it> without lifting a finger; чека како утот to make no effort **2** *fig.* dullard, blockhead; clumsy person

ута¹ *impf* (*of an owl*) to hoot; to screech

ута² *f* (*унечка, престилка*) apron, pinafore

утаен -јна *pt* hidden, secret

утаи *pf* **I** to conceal, hide *trans.*, keep secret **II – се 1** to conceal o.s., hide *intrans.* **2** to fall silent

утајува (се) *impf of* утаи (се)

утајум *adv see* скришно

уталожи *pf* **I** to calm, settle, compose *trans.* **II – се** to calm o.s., settle down *intrans.*; (*of liquids*) to settle *intrans.*

уталожува (се) *impf of* уталожи (се)

утаре *n dim. of* ута²

уташин *m f.p. see* ут 1

утвари *pl* eucharistic vessels, utensils; chalices

утврда *f* fortification, fortress

утврден *pt* **1** fortified; утврден град fortified city **2** set, fixed; established; confirmed; утврдени цени fixed prices

утврди *pf* **I 1** to fortify; го утврдија градот they fortified the city **2** to strengthen, consolidate *trans.*; ја утврди својата власт he consolidated his authority **3** to establish; to fix; утврди ден на конференција to fix the day of a conference **4** to confirm, endorse, ratify; утврди план to ratify a plan; утврди договор to endorse an agreement **5** to ascertain, establish; комисијата ја утврди вистинската положба the committee established the real situation; утврдивме дека тој ден не дошол на работа we established (confirmed) that on that day he didn't come to work **II – се** to fortify o.s.; *fig.* to gain a foothold; to become firmly established

утврдува (се) *impf of* утврди (се)

утека *f* weir (*for fishing*), arm of river or stream dammed for fishing

утелиса *pf colloq.* to iron

утелисува *impf colloq. of* утелиса

утепа (се) *pf dial. see* отепа (се)

утепува (се) *impf dial. of* утепа (се), *see* отепува (се)

утерус *m Anat.* (*матка*) uterus

утеха *f* consolation, comfort, solace; синот ми е единствената утеха my son is my only consolation; ❏ наоѓа утеха во to take comfort in; бара утеха во to seek consolation in; слаба утеха cold comfort; poor consolation

утече *pf f.p.* to run away, flee, escape

утешен -шна *adj* **1** comforting, consoling, consolatory; утешна награда consolation prize; утешни зборови comforting words **2** (*утешлив*) consolable; утешна вдовица consolable widow

утеши *pf* **I** to comfort, console **II – се** to be comforted, put at rest; to calm down *intrans.*; to find consolation, take comfort (*во – in*); to console o.s.

утешител *m* consoler, comfort<er>

утешителен -лна *adj* comforting, consoling; утешителни зборови comforting words (words of comfort); *see* утешен 1

утешителка *f* (*fem. form*) *see* утешител

утешително *adv see* утешно

утешлив *adj* consolable

утешно *adv* consolingly

утешува (се) *impf of* утеши (се)

утија -ии *f colloq.* (*пегла*) <smoothing> iron, flat-iron

утилитарен -рна *adj* utilitarian

утилитаризам -змот *m* utilitarianism

утилитарист *m* utilitarian

утилитаристички *adj* utilitarian

утина *impf of* утне²

утиса *pf see* сутне

утисува *impf of* утиса, *see* сутина

утица *f Zool.* owl, *see* утка¹ 1

утка¹ *f* **1** *Zool.* owl (*various species*); живее сама како утка she lives all alone; ❑ му се отворија очите како на утка his eyes opened wide **2** *fig.* blockhead, idiot, fool

утка² *f sl.* miss (*at games, etc.*), boss-shot

уткае *pf* утка *aor.* to weave in; to insert

уткајува *impf of* уткае

утлеиса *pf colloq. see* утелиса

утлеисува *impf of* утлеиса, *see* утелисува

утман *m colloq.* dullard, dunce; clumsy person; *see* ут 2

утмански *adj colloq.* referring to a dullard, etc.

утне¹ *pf* утна *aor.* (*of an owl*) to hoot

утне² *pf* утна *aor.* **1** *f.p.* to drain, empty (*a glass, etc.*) *trans.* **2** *colloq.* to miss (*one's aim or target, etc.*)

утока *f* **1** mouth (*of a river*), estuary **2** *see* утека

уткоми *pf f.p.* **I** to prepare *trans.*; to arrange; to adorn **II** – **се** to prepare (*o.s.*) *intrans.*; to adorn o.s., smarten (*o.s.*) up *intrans.*; *see* натокми (се)

уткомува (се) *impf of* уткоми (се), *see* натокмува (се)

утоне *pf* утона *aor.* **1** to sink, drown *intrans.*; утонал до гуша he sank up to his neck **2** *fig.* to become engrossed/absorbed; утоне во грижи to be overwhelmed with cares/worries; утоне во мисли to become lost in thought

утонува *impf of* утоне

утоп *m* soaking; утоп стане, утоп се стори to get wet through (drenched)

утопи *pf* **I** to soak, drench **II** – **се** to get wet through, get drenched

утопѝзам -змот *m* utopianism

утопѝја -ии *f* utopia

утописки *adj* utopian; утописки социјализам utopian socialism

утопѝст *m* utopian

утопистички *adj* utopian

утопува (се) *impf of* утопи (се)

уточни *pf* to formulate, specify exactly, state clearly/ precisely; to elaborate; to stipulate

уточнува *impf of* уточни

утре *adv* tomorrow; the morrow, the future; утре изутрина tomorrow morning; утре на пладне tomorrow at noon; со денеска, со утре from day to day, with every passing day; ❑ утре сабајле never! pigs may fly; that'll be the day; од денес<ка> до утре a day-to-day affair; <што можеш денес> не оставај за утре don't leave until tomorrow what you can do today! денеска-утре <ќе биде готово> today or tomorrow <it will be ready>, any day now; денеска нѐ има, утре нѐ нема here today, gone tomorrow; и утре е нов ден; и утре има ден tomorrow is another day

утревечер *adv* tomorrow evening/night

утревно *n dial. see* утрена

утредента *adv* <on> the next day, the following day; утредента си замина од Скопје the next day he left Skopje

утреж *m in the prov.:* утреж куќа не рани (не крепи) never put off till tomorrow what you can do today!

утрен *adj* morning; утрен пурпур morning glow; утрена молитва morning prayer; утрено сонце morning sun

утрена *f Rel.* matins

утрешен -шна *adj* **1** of tomorrow, tomorrow's;

утрешниот ден tomorrow **2** morning; утрешна роса morning dew **3** *fig.* future; тој е мојот утрешен наследник he is my future heir/successor **4** *colloq.* (*as noun*) утрешен the morrow, the future; ќе видиме што ќе каже утрешен (утрешниот) we shall see what the future holds

утрешнина *f* the future, the morrow; за поарна утрешнина for a better future

утрина¹ *f* morning, early morning; станал една утрина рано he got up early one morning; на утрина in the morning

утрина² *f* **1** pasture, grazing land; селска утрина village pasture **2** herdsman's pay (*for grazing cattle*)

утрината *adv* **1** <on> that morning **2** tomorrow morning, the next morning

утринен -ина *adj* morning; утринен воздух morning air; *see* утрен, утрински

утрински *adj* morning; утрински магли morning mists; утринска гимнастика morning exercises

утркала *pf f.p.* (*истркала*) to roll away, roll off *trans.*

утро *n* morning; секое утро every morning; станал едно рано утро he got up early one morning; од утро до вечер from morning till evening; на утро in the morning, *see* наутро; добро утро! good morning! вчера утро yesterday morning, *see* вчераутро; ❑ од утро до мрак from dawn till dusk; по утрото се познава денот *prov.* a good beginning makes a good ending; well begun is half done

утроба *f* **1** womb, uterus **2** entrails, insides; ми се слоши дури во утробата I felt sick to my stomach **3** *fig.* bowels, depths; во утробата на земјата in the bowels of the earth

утробен -бна *adj* uterine, of the womb; internal

утроен *pt* tripled, trebled, increased threefold

утрои *pf* **I** to triple, treble *trans.* **II** – **се** to triple, treble *intrans.*

утројува (се) *impf of* утрои (се)

утрото *adv* **1** that morning; утрото не дојде на работа that morning he didn't come to work **2** next morning, in the morning; вечерта дојде а утрото си замина he came by night and the next morning he left

утрошен -шна *adj* this morning's; утрошен леб this morning's bread

утрчник -ци *m see* устрчник

утски *adj* owl's; owlish; owl-like

уттиса *pf arch. see* сутне

уттисува *impf of* уттиса, *see* сутина

уќумат *m arch.* **1** state authority **2** administrative headquarters

уу *interj* (*expressing surprise*) o-oh!

уф *interj* oh! (*expressing weariness, boredom, discomfort, fear*) ooh! phew! gee!

уфилен *pt see* увилен

уфили се *pf see* увили се

уха¹ *interj* yes, indeed! *colloq.* uh-huh!

уха² *impf intrans. & trans.* to blow; ги ухаше рацете за да ги стопли he was blowing into his hands to warm them

ухлебие *n literary* livelihood

ухне *pf* ухна *aor. intrans. & trans.* to puff, blow; to give a puff

ухнува *impf of* ухне

уцена *f* **1** blackmail, extortion; ransom **2** reward

уцени *pf* 1 to blackmail 2 to set a price on <s.o.'s head>; му ја уценија главата со огромна сума пари they put a high price on his head 3 *arch.* to evaluate, estimate; го уценила оти има голема дарба she thought he had a great talent

уценува *impf of* уцени

уценувач *m* blackmailer

уценувачка *f (fem. form) see* уценувач

уценувачки *adj* blackmailing

учасок -ци *m Hist.* Bulgarian police station

учебен -бна *adj* school; учебна година school year; учебни помагала teaching aids; учебен материјал syllabus

учебник -ци *m* textbook; primer; учебник по физика physics textbook

учебникар *m* author of textbooks

учебникарка *f (fem. form) see* учебникар

учебникарски *adj* of textbook production and authors; учебникарска работа working on, writing, producing textbooks

учебникарство *n* textbook production (*compilation, as a trade*)

учебнички *adj* (of/for a) textbook; книгата има учебнички карактер the book is in the nature of a textbook

учен *adj* 1 erudite, learned, scholarly; учени луѓе learned people, scholars; ❑ никој учен не се родил no man is born wise and learned; учена глава an egghead 2 accustomed (*на – to*), used (*to*); трained; тој не е учен на горештина he is not used to heat

учение *n arch. see* учење

ученик -ци *m* 1 pupil, schoolboy; learner; ученик по пливање learner swimmer 2 (*следбеник*) follower, disciple; Фројдови ученици followers of Freud 3 (*чирак*) apprentice; ученици во стопанството industrial apprentices

ученичка *f (fem. form) see* ученик

ученички *adj* pupil's; ученичка книшка pupil's record book; ученичка кошула school shirt; ученичка претстава school performance

ученштво *n* school-days

учено *adv* learnedly, in a scholarly manner; прашањето е учено обработено the problem/ question is treated in a scholarly way

ученољубив *adj* studious, diligent

ученољубивост *f* studiousness, diligence

ученост *f* learning, erudition

учење *n from* учи 1 teaching 2 learning, studying, study; учење на француски јазик the study of French 3 rote-learning, learning by heart; учење на улога, на стихотворба learning one's part (lines), learning a poem by heart 4 getting used to, acclimatization; треба учење и на студ и на горештина one has to get used to both the cold and the heat 5 teachings; Марксовото учење the teachings of Marx

учесник -ци *m* 1 participant; (*натпреварувач*) competitor; учесник на конкурс applicant for a position/ scholarship, etc.; учесник во заговор a party to a plot 2 shareholder

учесница & учесничка *f (fem. form) see* учесник

учество *n* 1 participation; учество во дискусија participation in a discussion; учество во борбата taking part in the struggle; земе учество во нешто to take part in s.th. 2 share, portion; учество во добивката sharing the profit 3 *fig.* (*соучество*) sympathy, condolence<s>; искрено учество во жалоста sincere condolences in your bereavement 4 (*капар, депозит*) deposit

учествува *impf* to participate, take part (*во, на – in*); to have a share/hand (*in*); учествува на конференција to take part in a conference; секој учествува во расподелбата на доходот everyone shares in the distribution of the proceeds

учетвори *pf* I to quadruple *trans.* II – ce to quadruple *intrans.*

учетворува (се) *impf of* учетвори (се)

учи *impf* I 1 to teach, train, instruct; го учи да чита he's teaching him to read; ме учи дека . . . he teaches me that . . . 2 to learn; to study; учи француски <јазик> to study French; учи да тера автомобил he is learning to drive; учи улога to learn one's lines; учам за доктор I am studying to be a doctor; уште учи he's still at school; учи напамет to learn by heart; денеска не учиме today we don't go to school; учи занает to be apprenticed; ❑ има уште многу да учи he has a lot to learn; учи од свои грешки to learn by one's own mistakes 3 (*некого на нешто*) to accustom, prepare; учи дете на студ to get a child used to cold weather 4 to find out, hear, learn; од каде ги учиш овие новини? where did you hear this news? II – ce 1 to learn; се учи да чита he's learning to read; се учи на шиење to learn to sew; помладите се учат од постарите the young learn from the old; ❑ цел век се учиме live and learn 2 to get used; се учи на студ to get used to the cold

училиште *n* school; основно училиште primary (elementary) school; средно техничко училиште secondary technical school; оди на училиште to go to school; бега од училиште to run away from school, play truant; се запише на училиште to enrol at school

училиштен -шна *adj* school *attrib.*; училишна зграда school building; училиштен инспектор school-inspector

училница *f* classroom

учило *n* teaching aid/material<s>; training appliances

учини *pf dial.* (*направи, стори*) to do

учител *m* teacher; учител по пливање swimming teacher (instructor); учител по музика music teacher; учител за танцување dancing-master; приватен (домашен) учител <home> tutor

учителка *f (fem. form) see* учител

учителски *adj* teacher's; schoolmasterly, school-mistressy; учителска соба staff room; учителска школа teacher-training college

учителски *adv* in a schoolmasterly fashion

учителство *n* the teaching profession; цел живот му помина во учителство he spent his whole life teaching; да се подобри положбата на учителството to improve the position of teachers

учителствува *impf* to work as a teacher

учкур *m* waistband

учкурлак -ци *m* waistband casing (*in traditional costume trousers*),

учтив *adj* polite, courteous; учтив човек polite (courteous) person

учтиво *adv* politely, courteously; најучтиво молам I beg you; may I ask you . . .

учтивост *f* politeness, courtesy

уччува *pf arch.* (*зачува*) to preserve, keep, spare

уччуди *pf arch.* **I** to amaze **II – се** to be amazed

уцере *n* inner partition; dividing wall

уш *interj* gee up!

ушат *adj* eared

уше *n dim. of* уво, *see* увце

ушен -шна *adj* ear *attrib.*, otic; ушни жлезди ear glands; ушна клиника ear (otological) clinic; ушни болести ear (otic) diseases; ушна кал earwax; ушна ресичка ear lobe; ушно тапанче eardrum; ушна школка auricle

уши *pl of* уво

ушка *adv in the expression:* на ушка piggyback

ушла *f* (*fem. form*) *see* ушле

ушле -вци *m* large-eared man

ушлест *adj* large-eared

ушло -вци *m see* ушле

ушник -ци *m* (*more usu. pl*) earring, *see* обетка

ушника *f see* ушник

уште *adv* **1** still, yet; уште јаде he's still eating; уште не знае he doesn't know yet; уште не not yet; cè уште still; тој сè уште седи тука he's still sitting here; ❑ уште само тоа ни треба! that's the last straw! that's all we needed! **2** some more, another; else; уште една чаша вино another glass of wine; тури уште малку pour a little more! уште еднаш once more; once again; yet again; уште два дена two more days; кој уште? who else? чекај уште малку wait a little longer! уште двапати по толку twice as much; и што уште не and what not; ќе прашаш има ли уште that's the end of the matter **3** as long ago as, as far back as; already; even; уште како дете even as a child; уште од мал from childhood; from a tender age; уште истиот ден on the very same day **4** (*with comparative*) even more, still more; уште поубав even more beautiful; уште подобро even better; so much the better; better still; уште повеќе still more; what is more

уштип *m* crescent moon

Ф

фа *f Mus.* F

фабрика *f* factory, mill, plant; текстилна фабрика textile factory; фабрика за кожи tannery; фабрика за конзерви cannery; фабрика за стакло glass-works; фабрика за шеќер sugar refinery

фабрикáнт *m* factory-owner, manufacturer

фабрикáнтски *adj* factory-owner's, manufacturer's

фабрикáт *m* manufactured article; finished product

фабрикација *f* **1** manufacturing, production **2** *fig.* invention, fabrication

фабрикува *impf* **1** to produce, manufacture **2** *fig.* to invent, forge, fabricate; фабрикува вести/лаги to fabricate news/false stories

фабричен -чна & **фабрички** *adj* factory *attrib.*; industrial, manufacturing; фабричен дефект manufacturing defect; фабрична марка trade mark; фабрична цена factory price; фабрички комитет factory committee

фабула *f Literature* plot; расказ со убава фабула a story with a fine plot

фабулен -лна *adj* pertaining to a plot; фабулни сличности similarities in the plot

фабулúра *impf* to tell stories, spin tales; to fantasize

фаворизација *f* favouritism

фаворизúра *impf* to favour, give preference to

фаворúт *m* favourite

фаворúтка *f* (*fem. form*) *see* фаворит

фагóт *m Mus.* bassoon

фаготúст *m Mus.* bassoonist

фагоцúт *m* phagocyte

фагозитóза *f* phagocytosis

фаза *f* phase; stage; војната влезе во нова фаза the war entered a new phase; фази на месечината phases of the moon; *Elec.* струја со три фази three-phase current

фазан *m Zool.* (Phasianus colchicus) pheasant

фазанерија -ии *f* pheasantry

фазанов *adj* pheasant's; фазаново перо pheasant's feather

-фазен -зна *adj* (*in compounds*) -phase; *Elec.* трифазна струја three-phase current; *Elec.* многуфазен polyphase

фазла *adv colloq.* (*повеќе*) too much/many; немаме фазла жито we haven't any wheat to spare; тој има фазла пари he has too much money

фазон *m* fashion, style

фазонúра *pf & impf* to fashion, shape

фајáнс *m* faience, pottery, glazed earthenware

фајáнсен -сна & **фајáнсов** *adj* faience *attrib.*; фајáнсна ваза glazed earthenware vase

фајде *n colloq.* **1** use, good; какво фајде виде од тоа? what good did that do you? нема фајде it's no use; ако е за фајде, доста е enough is enough! **2** interest; дава пари на фајде to lend money on interest

фајделив *adj arch.* useful, beneficial

фајдица & **фајдичка** *f dim. of* фајде; имаше фајдица од тоа it helped you a bit

фајрон *m colloq.* closing time

фак *m* snare, trap; mousetrap; ❑ влезе во фак he fell into a trap; *see* склупша

факел -кли *m* **1** torch, burning brand **2** *fig.* beacon; torch; се издигна како факел во борбата he stood out like a beacon in the struggle

факир *m* fakir (*also fig.*)

факирски *adj* fakir-like; of a magician; факирска вештина magical skill

факла *f see* факел

факлин & **факлов** *adj usu. in the combination:* факлина (факлова) борина torch

факсимил *m* **1** facsimile **2** fax <machine>

факт *m* fact; ги извртува фактите he distorts the facts; неоспорен факт indisputable fact; ❑ свршен факт *fait accompli*; го стави пред свршен факт he confronted him with a *fait accompli*; факт! true! that's right!

фактичен -чна *adj* factual, actual, true, real; фактична состојба actual state

фактички *adj* & *adv see* фактичен, фактично

фактично *adv* in fact, really, actually; фактично, тие ништо не добиле as a matter of fact, they didn't get anything

фактичност *f* reality, actual state; factual state

фактограф *m* recorder of facts

фактографија *f* recording of facts

фактографски *adj* based on facts and figures; fact-finding

фактор *m* **1** factor; важен фактор an important factor; *Math.* разложува на фактори to factor<ize> **2** influential figure; decision maker; leader; не сум јас никаков фактор I have no influence; раководните фактори the leading figures; надлежни фактори competent authorities

фактура *f* **1** *Art, Poetry* texture; style, technique **2** invoice, bill

фактурен -рна *adj* invoice *attrib.*; фактурна книга invoice book

фактурира *pf* & *impf* to invoice

фактурист *m* invoice clerk

факултативен -вна *adj* optional, elective; германски се учи како факултативен предмет German is studied as an optional subject

факултативно *adv* optionally, not obligatorily

факултативност *f* optionality

факултет *m* faculty, school (*of university*); правен факултет Faculty of Law; природно-математички факултет Faculty of Mathematics and Science

факултетлија -ии *m colloq.* graduate

факултетски *adj* faculty *attrib.*; university *attrib.*; факултетско образование university education; факултетски совет Faculty Board

фала *colloq.* thanks (*за, на – for*); фала ти многу за услугата thank you very much for the favour! фала Богу! thank goodness!

фаланга *f* phalanx; Falange

фалангист *m* phalanx member; Falangist

фалангистички *adj* phalanx *attrib.*; Falangist *attrib.*

фалба *f* **1** praise, commendation; само фалби можеш да чуеш за него no one has anything but praise for him **2** boasting, bragging; ❑ фалби продава to blow one's own trumpet; фалбата е 'рѓа (краста) *prov.* self-praise is no recommendation **3** threat; не ти се плашам на фалбите I'm not afraid of your threats

фалбаџија -ии *m* boaster, braggart, *see* фаленичар

фалбаџика *f* (*fem. form*) *see* фалбаџија

фалбен *adj* praiseworthy, laudable; laudatory; фалбени песни songs of praise

фален *adj iron.* wonderful; тоа ни го направи твојот многу фален син that's what your wonderful son has done to us; фалени јаготки, празни кошници *prov.* praises fill not the belly

фаленица *f* (*usu. pl*) boasting, bragging; доста со тие фаленици enough of those boasts!

фаленичар *m* boaster, braggart; тој беше голем фаленичар he was a great boaster

фали[1] *impf* **I** to praise; учителот многу го фалеше the teacher praised him highly; работата го фали his work is a credit to him; ❑ не да го фалам, туку . . . I don't want to praise him, but . . . ; секој си го фали своето everyone praises his own; село фали, во град седи play it safe! have it both ways! *iron.* умре Циганката (Гупката) што те фалеше all right! don't harp on it! фали ме, усто, зашто (оти) ќе те раскинам stop shooting your mouth off! **II** – се **1** to boast, brag; ❑ не да се фалам, туку in all modesty . . . ; доброто само се фали *prov.* good wares make quick markets; good wine needs no bush; кој се фали, <тој> не пали *prov.* barking dogs seldom bite **2** to threaten, bluster; доста се фалеше, никој не ти се плаши that's enough blustering, you don't scare anyone

фали[2] *impf colloq.* to be missing, lacking; to be needed; што ти фали? 1. what do you need? 2. *fig.* what's wrong with you?

фалимент *m* (*банкрот*) bankruptcy

фалира *pf* & *impf* (*банкротира*) to go bankrupt

фалител *m literary* flatterer, adulator

фаличен -чна *adj* faulty, defective; deficient; handicapped; фаличен штоф defective material

фаличност *f* faultiness, defectiveness; deficiency; handicapped condition

фалсификат *m* forgery; counterfeit; falsification

фалсификатор *m* forger; falsifier; фалсификатор на историјата falsifier of history

фалсификаторка *f* (*fem. form*) *see* фалсификатор

фалсификаторски *adj* forging; falsifying; фалсификаторска група group of forgers

фалсификација -ии *f* falsification, forgery; фалсификација на свидетелство falsification of a certificate; фалсификација на историјата falsification of history

фалсификува *pf* & *impf* to forge; to counterfeit; to falsify; го фалсификувал потписот на директорот he forged the director's signature

фалсификување *n* **1** *from* фалсификува **2** forgery; фалсификувањето се казнува по законот forgery is punishable by law

фалсифицира *pf & impf see* фалсификува

фалта *f* fold; pleat; tuck

фалц *m less freq. also* **фалца** *f* (*in ball games, marbles, etc.*) side <spin>; го удри со фалц he gave it a spin

фалцет *m Mus.* falsetto

фалцетен -тна *adj Mus.* falsetto *attrib.*; фалцетен глас falsetto voice

фалш **1** *m* lie, deceit **2** *adj see* фалшлив **3** *adv see* фалшливо

фалшлив *adj* **1** false, sham, fake; insincere; фалшливи пари counterfeit money; фалшлива насмевка a false smile **2** out of tune; таа пее со фалшлив глас she sings out of tune

фалшливо *adv* falsely; deceitfully; hypocritically

фалшливост *f* falseness, falsity; deceit; hypocrisy

фама *f* hearsay, rumour; се шири фама a rumour spreads

фамилен -лна *adj see* фамилијарен

фамилија -ии *f* family; глава на фамилијата head of the family; видна фамилија a prominent family; фамилија брези the birch family

фамилијарен -рна *adj* **1** family *attrib.*; тој е фамилијарен човек he is a family man; фамилијарен албум family album; фамилијарна гробница family tomb, vault **2** intimate, close; familiar; татко ми беше фамилијарен со него my father was on close terms with him; фамилијарниот тон на дискусијата the familiar tone of the discussion; фамилијарни односи familiar relations **3** (*as noun*) married person; фамилијарен *m* married man; фамилијарна *f* married woman

фамилијарно *adv* **1** with the family; дојдовме фамилијарно we came with the family **2** familiarly, intimately; зборуваше фамилијарно со него he was talking to him in a familiar manner; истапи фамилијарно he behaved/spoke in an unconstrained manner

фамилијарност *f* familiarity; having a family; state of being married

фамозен -зна *adj* famous (*also iron.*); well-known; notorious; infamous

фанариот *m Hist.* (*usu. pl*) phanariot<s> (*Greeks from the Phanar district of Constantinople, known as bitter opponents of the reawakening of nationalities in Turkey in the 19th century*)

фанариотски *adj* phanariot; фанариотско ропство phanariot yoke

фанатизам -змот *m* fanaticism

фанатизира *pf & impf* **I** to make fanatical, blind (*s.o. to s.th.*) **II** -се to become fanatical

фанатизиран *pt* fanaticized, frenzied, fanatical; фанатизиран дух fanatical spirit

фанатик -ци *m* fanatic

фанатичен -чна *adj* fanatical; фанатичен човек a fanatical person; фанатична омраза fanatical hatred

фанатичка *f* (*fem. form*) *see* фанатик

фанатички[1] *adj* fanatical; фанатична упорност fanatical persistence

фанатички[2] *adv* fanatically; ги бранеше фанатички своите идеи he defended his ideas fanatically

фанатично *adv* fanatically

фанатичност *f* fanaticism; exultation

фанела *f colloq.* **1** vest, singlet, *Am.* undershirt **2** sweater, pullover, jumper

фанелка *f* **1** *dim. of* фанела **2** T-shirt; tank top; *Sport.* црвена фанелка red sports jersey

фантазер *m* dreamer; visionary

фантазерка *f* (*fem. form*) *see* фантазер

фантазерски *adj* dreamer's; visionary's

фантазерство *n* day-dreaming, escapism; idealism

фантазија -ии *f* **1** fantasy, imagination; фантазијата многу му работеше his imagination was very active **2** dream, day-dream; тој негов предлог беше фантазија his proposal was just a pipedream **3** *Mus.* fantasia; фантазија на тема fantasy on a theme

фантазира *impf* **1** to fantasize, day-dream, be carried away, imagine **2** to improvise, extemporize

фантаст *m* fantast; dreamer; visionary

фантастика *f* fantasy; научна фантастика science fiction

фантастичен -чна *adj* fantastic; fabulous; фантастичен роман fantastic novel; фантастичен нацрт a fantastic drawing; фантастични цени fantastic prices

фантастично *adv* fantastically

фантастичност *f* fantastic quality; fantasy; во тие легенди има многу фантастичност in those legends there is a lot of fantasy

фантом *m* phantom, ghost, spectre

фанфара *f* **1** *Mus.* bugle, trumpet **2** fanfare, flourish **3** *fig.* ostentation, fanfare, flourish

фар *m* **1** lighthouse **2** headlight **3** *fig.* luminary, beacon, light; фар на народниот друм a beacon on the nation's path

фара *f colloq.* origin, race, family; од која фара е of what origin/extraction

фарак *m see* варак

фараон *m* **1** Pharaoh **2** *iron.* (*see* Циган) Gypsy

фараонски *adj* pharaoh's; фараонска пирамида pharaoh's pyramid

фараш *m rare* dustpan, *see* ѓубрарник

фарба[1] *f see* боја

фарба[2] *impf see* бојосува, вапсува

фарисеј -еи *m* Pharisee (*also fig.*); *fig.* hypocrite

фарисејка *f* (*fem. form*) *see* фарисеј

фарисејски *adj* Pharisaic<al>; фарисејска скромност Pharisaical modesty

фарисејство *n* Pharisaism

фарисејштина *f* Pharisaism

фарма *f* farm; сточарска фарма cattle-breeding farm, *Am.* ranch, *Austral.* cattle station

фармаколог -зи *m* pharmacologist

фармакологија *f* pharmacology

фармаколошки *adj* pharmacological

фармакопеја *f* pharmacopoeia

фармацевт *m* chemist, pharmacist

фармацевтка *f* (*fem. form*) *see* фармацевт

фармацевтски *adj* pharmaceutical; фармацевтска индустрија pharmaceutical industry; фармацевтски препарат pharmaceutical preparation

фармација *f* pharmacy; студент по фармација pharmacy student

фармер *m* farmer

фармерки *pl* jeans

фармерски *adj* farmer's

фарса *f* farce (*also fig.*)

фасада *f* facade (*also fig.*)

фасáден -дна *adj* front; фасадната страна the facade

фасадéр *m* facade painter/plasterer

фасóнка *f Elec. colloq.* socket

фасул *m Bot. dial. see* грав

фасцикла *f* folder, fascicle

фасцинáнтен -тна *adj* fascinating

фасцинација *f* fascination; delight, enchantment

фасцинира *pf & impf* to fascinate, delight, bewitch

фат *m* има фат во работата to have a professional touch

фатáлен -лна *adj* fatal (*also fig.*); фатална грешка fatal mistake; фатални срокови impossible deadlines

фатализам -змот *m* fatalism

фаталист *m* fatalist

фаталистички[1] *adj* fatalistic

фаталистички[2] *adv* fatalistically

фаталистка *f (fem. form) see* фаталист

фатáлно *adv* fatally; тоа беше фатално за него that was fatal for him

фатáлност *f* fatality, inevitability

фатаморгáна *f* illusion, mirage, fata Morgana

фатен *pt* stiff; paralysed; лежеше фатен he lay paralysed; со фатени нозе with paralysed legs; ❏ фатен е во рацете he is all thumbs

фатеност *f* stiffness; paralysis

фати *pf* **I 1** to seize, grab, grasp, catch; to trap; to arrest; to overcome, take possession of; to occupy; to take *trans.*; to take by surprise, catch unawares; го фати за рака he took him by the hand; го фати перото he took up his pen; го фати за опашка he grabbed it by the tail; ја фати топката he caught the ball; фати неколку рипчиња he caught a few tiddlers; ништо не фативме we didn't catch anything; ❏ го фати на дело he caught him in the act, he caught him red-handed; фати воз to catch a train; го фатиле ридот they took/seized the hill; фати работа to get a job **2** to seize, strike, overcome; (*за болест*) to affect; ме фати грч I got cramp; ме фати дремка I was overcome by sleepiness; I felt drowsy, sleepy; ме фати мака I felt sick/sorry; ме фати грип I caught flu; ме фати виново this wine has gone to my head; фати кајмак млекото cream/skin formed on the milk; ме фати досада I got bored; ме фати криза I had a crisis; ме фати страв I took fright; ме фати сонце I caught a touch of the sun; I got sunburnt; нè фати дожд на патот rain caught us on the road **3** to set, harden; to take *intrans.*; фати бетонот the concrete set; не фати бојата the paint did not take **4** to stitch, mend; to join *trans.*; ги фати конците he joined the threads **5** to understand, grasp, *colloq.* get; to catch *trans.*; ја фати смислата to grasp the meaning **6** to set in, begin; фати лето summer came on; фати голем студ extreme cold set in **7** (*with да*) to start, begin; фати да зборува he started talking; фати да се смее he burst out laughing; фати да плаче he burst into tears **8** to set off, set out; фати патот he set out, took to the road; he left **9** *colloq.* to hire, take on; фати работници to hire workers; фати адвокат to hire a lawyer **10** *colloq.* to catch, become infested with; фати вошки to get lice **11** to charge *trans.*; фати му за работата charge him for the work! ми го фати по десет денари килограм he charged me ten denars a kilogram **12** *colloq.* to reach, attain; фати голем чин he reached high rank; фати

пари (камен, камче) he struck it rich **13** to catch fire, light *intrans.*; дрвата беа влажни и не фати огнот the logs were damp and the fire wouldn't light; кибритот не фати the match didn't light **14** *colloq.* (*за радио и сл.*) to get, pick up; to tune into *trans.*; синоќа успеавме да ја фатиме Москва last night we managed to pick up Moscow; ја фатив италијанската телевизија I picked up Italian TV **15** ❏ го фати за гуша he put him on the spot; he called him to account; го фати за зборот he held him to his word; го фати крстот 1. he had a stroke of luck 2. he got roaring drunk; го фатија мајките (неговите) *colloq.* he flew off the handle; го фати на спиење he caught him nodding; чини едно фати, друго пушти he's fooling around; ми фати око it caught my fancy, took my eye; фати нечии конци 1. to catch s.o.'s drift 2. to pull the strings; му ја фати танката he got the gist of it; му ја фати трагата he got on his trail; не можеш да го фатиш ни за глава, ни за опаш<ка> he is hard to understand/please; не можеш да му го фатиш крајот he's hard to please; you can't make head or tail of it; орман фатил! get lost! clear out! пустина, вид виделија фати he's run off, disappeared; фати вера со некого to secure s.o.'s promise; фати корен to take root; фати Бога за очи to achieve the impossible; фати магла to take to one's heels; фати место 1. to find a seat 2. to find its place 3. to take effect; фати позиција to take up a position; што ќе фати – фатено е a dab hand **II – се 1** to take hold (*за – of*), catch hold (*of*), seize, take up; to undertake; to seize on, pick on; to get down to, set about; to join (*на – in*); to focus on; се фатија за раце they joined hands; се фати за оружје he grabbed his gun; се фати за работа to get down to work; се фати да чита to start reading; се фати на оро to join the *oro*; се фати да го направи тоа he undertook to do that; се фати лимонот the lemon tree took root; се фати бојата the paint took; се фати за предлогот на планот he addressed the draft plan; ❏ се фатија гуша за гуша they flew at each other's throats; се фати за зборот he seized on the word **2** to get caught; се фати крапот the carp was hooked; се фати в стапица to be trapped (*also fig.*) **3** to keep company (*со – with*); to fall in (*with*); се фатил со лошо друштво he fell in with bad company **4** to clash (*со – with*); се фатија со секретарот околу извештајот they clashed with the secretary over the report **5** (*of limbs, etc.*) to go stiff, become paralysed; to seize up; му се фатија нозете he lost the use of his legs; ми се фати гласот I lost my voice; ми се фати грлото I have gone hoarse; I got a sore throat **6** *impers.* (*with dative*) to cost; ми се фати многу скапо it cost me dear **7** *impers.* (*with dat.*) to fit, be just right; ми се фатија твоите чевли your shoes fitted me well **8** ❏ се фати за глава 1. to be at a loss 2. to be amazed; се фатија в костец they were at loggerheads; се фати на бас to bet; се фати на јадица to swallow the bait; можеш да ми се фатиш! *vulg.* you can kiss my arse; screw you! нема за што да се фати not to have a leg to stand on; кога ќе се фати сиромавиот на оро, ќе се скине тапанот *prov.* it's the poor that get the blame; the poor suffer all the wrong; се фатил на оро, ќе го игра *prov.* in for a penny, in for a pound; се фатила царица за работа, па ѝ се исприштиле рацете *prov.* manual work doesn't suit everybody; фати се за даб, а не за трн *prov.* rely on solid support!

фатка *f* handful

фаќа *impf* **I 1** *of* фати; ❑ како ти фаќа умот? what do you think? ми фаќа умот it seems to me; I can understand; место не го фаќа he can't sit still; to strain at the leash; to be on tenterhooks; не фаќај му <за> кусур! don't pay any attention to him! око не ги фаќа you can't take in the whole scene; (*of an alcoholic drink*) фаќа без раце it is strong stuff **2** to hold; оваа бочва фаќа сто литра this barrel holds one hundred litres **II – се** *of* фати се; ❑ се фаќа за сламка to clutch at a straw; исто ти се фаќа it comes to the same thing

фаќање *n* catching; мрежа за фаќање риби fishing net; фаќање на бас betting; фаќање кусур *colloq.* nit-picking

фаќач *m* catcher

фаул *m Sport.* foul; играчот беше исклучен поради груб фаул the player was sent off because of a serious foul

фаулира *pf & impf Sport.* to commit a foul

фауна *f* fauna; македонските планини имаат богата фауна the mountains of Macedonia are rich in fauna

фаунски *adj* faunal; фаунски испитувања wildlife research

фах *m* **1** field of specialization, speciality; (*универзитетски, училишен предмет*) subject **2** shelf, box, pigeonhole; поштенски фах post<-office> box

фаша *f colloq.* **1** broad strip of leather; piece of leather (*usu. for moccasins*) **2** piece of s.th. woven for mending socks

фашизам -змот *m* fascism

фашизација *f* making fascist; фашизација на војската making the army fascist

фашизира *pf & impf* to impose fascism, make fascist, run on fascist lines *trans.*

фашира *pf & impf Cul.* to mince

фаширан *pt Cul.* minced, mince *attrib.*; фаширано месо mince; фаширана шницла rissole

фашиски *adj see* фашистички

фашист *m* fascist

фашистички *adj* fascist; фашистичката војска fascist army; фашистички режим fascist régime

фашистка *f* (*fem. form*) *see* фашист

февруари *m* February; во февруари in February

февруарски *adj* February *attrib.*; февруарски ден a February day; февруарски студ February cold (weather)

февче *n dim. of* фес; црвено февче little red fez

федер *m colloq.* (*пружина*) spring; федерот на часовникот the spring in the watch/clock; федерите на мадраците the springs in the mattresses

федерален -лна *adj* federal; федерална единица federal unit

федерализам -змот *m* federalism

федералист *m* federalist

федеративен -вна *adj* federative, federal; федеративна република federative (federal) republic; врз федеративни принципи on federative principles; федеративно устројство federative structure

федерација -ии *f* federation; светска синдикална федерација World Federation of Trade Unions

федерира[1] *pf & impf* to enter into a federation; to federate *intrans.*

федерира[2] *pf & impf* to spring back

феја -еи *f* fairy

фекален -лна *adj* effluent; faecal; фекални води effluent

фекалии *pl* sewage, effluent; faeces

фела[1] *f* kind, sort

фела[2] *impf arch.* (*only in 3rd p. sg with* не) *see* невела

фелах -си *m* fellah

фелдмаршал *m* Field Marshal

фелдфебел *m* sergeant major

фелер *m* defect, fault, flaw

фелеричен -чна *adj* flawed, defective, faulty; штофов е фелеричен this material is flawed

фелија -ии *f* (*usu. of bread or fruit*) piece, slice; една фелија леб a slice of bread

фељтон *m* feuilleton

фељтонист *m* feuilletonist, feuilleton writer

фељтонистка *f* (*fem. form*) *see* фељтонист

фељтонски *adj* feuilleton *attrib.*; фељтонски стил feuilleton style

феминизам -змот *m* feminism

феминист *m* feminist

феминистички *adj* feminist *attrib.*; феминистичко списание a feminist journal

феминистка *f* (*fem. form*) *see* феминист

фенер *m* lantern, lamp

фенерче *n dim. of* фенер

фенерџија -ии *m arch.* lamplighter

Феникија *f* Phoenicia

феникиски *adj* Phoenician

Феничанец -ни *m* Phoenician

Феничанка *f* (*fem. form*) *see* Феничанец

феникс *m* phoenix (*also fig.*)

фенол *m Chem.* phenol

фенологија *f* phenology

фенолошки *adj* phenologic<al>

феномен *m* phenomenon (*also fig.*); prodigy

феноменален -лна *adj* phenomenal; феноменално паметење phenomenal memory

феноменализам -змот *m* phenomenalism

феноменалност *f* phenomenal quality

феноменологија *f* phenomenology

фер *adj indecl.* fair, correct, honest, nice; фер плеј fair play

фереџе *n* veil, yashmak

ферибот *m* ferry

ферии *pl* holidays, *Am.* vacation; за време на фериите during the holidays

феријален -лна *adj* holiday (*Am.* vacation) *attrib.*; феријален сојуз Student Holiday Association

феријалец -лци *m* Student Holiday Association member

феријалка *f* (*fem. form*) *see* феријалец

ферма *impf colloq.* to respect, care about, *colloq.* give a damn; не ферма ни татко, ни мајка he has no respect for anybody

ферман *m Hist.* firman, edict; царски ферман emperor's decree; ферман му дојде од царот he received a firman from the emperor

фермене *n* waistcoat, *Am.* vest

фермент *m* ferment

ферментација *f* fermentation; ферментација на алкохол fermentation of alcohol; ферментација на тутун fermentation of tobacco

ферментацио́нен -она *adj* fermentative; ферментационен процес fermentative process

ферменти́ра *pf & impf* to ferment *intrans.*

феро- (*in compounds*) ferro-; ferrous; фероалуминиум ferro-aluminium

феромагнетски *adj Phys.* ferromagnetic

феро́оксид *m* ferrous oxide, iron oxide

фес *m* fez

фесиште *n augm. of* фес

фестива́л *m* festival; фестивал на забавни мелодии/на народни песни festival of light music/of folk-songs; филмски фестивал film festival

фестива́лски *adj* festival *attrib.*; фестивалска значка festival badge

фетиш *m* fetish (*also fig.*)

фетиши́зам -змот *m* fetishism (*also fig.*)

фетиши́ст *m* fetishist (*also fig.*)

феуд *m Hist.* fief, feud

феуда́лен -лна *adj* feudal; феудално право feudal right; феудално устројство feudal system

феуда́лец -лци *m Hist.* feudal lord

феудали́зам -змот *m* feudalism

фибри́н *m* fibrin

фигура *f* 1 figure, form, shape, silhouette; pattern; нејасно се гледаа фигурите на куќите the outlines of the houses could be dimly discerned; килимот беше ишаран со разни фигури the rug was decorated with various figures; се истакнуваше неговата фигура his figure stood out; бронзени фигури bronze figures; централна фигура a central figure; фигура во рамнина *Geom.* plane figure 2 *Mus., Dance, Literature* figure; movement; изведуваа разни фигури they performed/executed various figures; поетска фигура trope 3 *Chess* chessman, piece (*excluding pawns*)

фигура́нт *m* 1 (*во пиеса*) extra, a walk-on, supernumerary 2 *fig.* nonentity, dummy

фигура́нтка *f* (*fem. form*) *see* фигурант

фигурати́вен -вна *adj* figurative, metaphorical; фигуративно значење на зборо; figurative meaning of the word

фигурати́вно *adv* figuratively

фигурати́вност *f* figurativeness

фигури́ра *impf* 1 to figure; to appear 2 *fig.* to be a figurehead

фигури́ст *m* 1 figure painter; sculptor 2 figure dancer; figure skater

фигурка *f dim. of* фигура; figurine

фидан & фиданка *f* sapling; *fig.* scion; ❏ прав<а> како фидан straight as a ramrod

фиданбо́јли<ја> *adj indecl. colloq.* tall and slender

фиданче *n dim. of* фидан & фиданка

фиде *n* noodles, vermicelli; супа со фиде noodle soup

фиде́јзам -змот *m* fideism

фиде́јст *m* fideist

физика *f* 1 physics 2 *rare* physique

физика́лен -лна *adj* physical; физикална терапија physical therapy; *see* физички

физиокра́т *m Hist.* physiocrat

физиократи́зам -змот *m Hist.* physiocracy

физиократија *f Hist.* physiocracy

физиоло́г -зи *m* physiologist

физиологија *f* physiology

физиолошки *adj* physiological; физиолошки испитувања physiological research; физиолошка појава physiological phenomenon

физиономија *f* physiognomy, countenance, face; *fig.* appearance; непозната физиономија unfamiliar face; селото ја измени својата физиономија the village has changed its appearance

физиономи́ст *m* physiognomist

физиотерапе́вт *m* physiotherapist

физиотерапија *f* physiotherapy

физиотераписки *adj* physiotherapeutic

физичар *m* physicist

физички *adj* 1 physical, physics *attrib.*; физички закони и појави physical laws and phenomena; физичка лабораторија physics laboratory; физичка хемија physical chemistry 2 physical, bodily; manual; физичка болка physical pain; физичко здравје physical health; физичко пресметување fisticuffs; *Leg.* assault and battery; физичка работа manual labour; физички работник manual labourer; физичка сила physical strength; физичка култура exercise, physical training 3 *Leg.* физичко лице natural (physical) person

физички *adv* physically; in body; сакаше да се пресмета физички со него he wanted to beat him up

фија́ско *n* fiasco, crash, collapse, failure; претрпе фијаско he suffered a fiasco

фиксати́в *m* fixative

фиксати́вен -вна *adj* fixative

фиксација *f* fixation

фиксен -сна *adj* fixed; фиксна плата fixed pay; фиксна цена fixed price; фиксни трошоци fixed costs

фикс-иде́ја -еи *f idée fixe*, obsession

фикси́ра *pf & impf* 1 to set, fix; фиксира датум to set a date 2 to record; таму беа фиксирани сите негови искажувања all his statements were recorded there 3 *fig.* to stare at; ја фиксираше младата жена he was staring at the young woman; фиксира поглед (*на*) to fix one's eyes (gaze) (*on*) 4 *Photography* to fix; ја фиксира сликата he fixed the negative

фиктивен -вна *adj* fictitious, pro-forma, bogus; imaginary; decoy; фиктивна борба sham fight; фиктивен брак fictitious (bogus) marriage; фиктивен капитал fictitious capital

фиктивно *adv* fictitiously; ostensibly; on paper

фиктивност *f* fictitiousness

фикус *m Bot.* (Ficus elastica) indiarubber tree, rubber plant, ficus

фикција -ии *f* fiction, invention

-фил (*in compounds*) -phil<e>; словенофил Slavophil<e>; филмофил film-lover, cineaste

фил[1] *m Cul.* (*за торта*) filling; (*за пиперки, кокошка и др.*) stuffing

фил[2] *m arch.* elephant, *see* слон

филантро́п *m* (*човекољубец*) philanthropist

филантропија *f* (*човекољубие*) philanthropy

филантро́пски *adj* philanthropic

филателија *f* philately

филатели́ст *m* philatelist

филателистички *adj* philatelic; филателистичка изложба exhibition of postage stamps

филателѝстка *f* (*fem. form*) *see* филателист

филдиш *m arch.* (*слонова коска*) ivory

филдишен -шна *adj* ivory *attrib.*; филдишен чешел ivory comb

филигран *m* filigree

филигрански *adj* 1 filigree, filigreed 2 *fig.* meticulous; delicate

филија -ии *f see* фелија

филијála *f* branch (*of institution or firm*); филијала на Народната банка branch of the National Bank

филипика *f* philippic (*Hist., fig.*)

Филипѝнец -нци *m* Filipino

Филипѝни *pl* the Philippines

Филипѝнка *f* (*fem. form*) *see* Филипинец

филипѝнски *adj* Filipino, Philippines *attrib.*

филистер -стри *m* philistine, narrow-minded person

филистерски *adj* philistine, narrow-minded; филистерска ограниченост philistine narrow-mindedness

филистерство *n* philistinism, narrow-mindedness

филм *m* 1 *Photography* film; развивање на филм developing; ❑ му пукна филмот he flew off the handle; he has had enough 2 film, motion picture, *Am.*, *colloq.* movie; документарен филм documentary <film>; долгометражен филм feature-length film; кусометражен филм short film; научно-популарен филм educational film; нем филм silent film; цртан филм cartoon; ❑ тој филм нема да го гледаш forget it!

филмаџија *m* 1 film-maker 2 film-lover, cineaste

филмофѝл *m* film-lover, cineaste, *Am., colloq.* movielover

филмски *adj* film *attrib.*; филмска лента film-strip; филмски артист film actor; филмско платно cinema screen; ❑ со филмска брзина at the speed of light

филмува *impf* to film *trans.*; филмувана приказна a filmed story

филов *adj arch.* (*from* филм²) ivory *attrib.*; ❑ филови заби да има, па не може ништо да направи even if he had ivory teeth he wouldn't be able to do anything!

филозóф *m* philosopher; ❑ дрвен филозоф *colloq.* know-it-all, wiseacre

филозофија *f* 1 philosophy; историјата на филозофијата the history of philosophy 2 *colloq.* outlook, philosophy; се држи до некоја филозофија to embrace a certain philosophy 3 *pl* -ии, *colloq., iron.* philosophizing; доста со тие ваши филозофии that's enough philosophizing!

филозофѝра *impf* 1 to study philosophy 2 *iron.* to philosophize

филозофски *adj* philosophical; филозофски факултет Philosophy Faculty, Arts Faculty, *Am.* School of Humanities; филозофски размислувања philosophical reflections

филозофски *adv* philosophically; треба да погледнеш филозофски на работите you should look at things philosophically

филоксéра *f Zool.* phylloxera

филолóг -зи *m* philologist

филологија *f* philology; класична/романска/словенска филологија classical/Romance/Slavonic philology

филолошки *adj* philological; филолошки факултет School of Languages and Literatures; филолошка анализа philological analysis

филтер *m* filter; песочен филтер sand filter; електричен филтер electrical filter; цигари со филтер filter-tipped cigarettes

филтер-хартија -ии *f* filter-paper

филтрáт *m* filtrate

филтрација *f* filtration

филтрѝра *pf & impf* 1 to filter, strain 2 *fig.* to screen, vet, check

филува *impf* 1 *Cul.* (*за слатки*) to fill *trans.*; (*за пиперки, кокошка и др.*) to stuff 2 *fig.* to adorn, decorate, embellish; to gild

филхармонија *f* 1 philharmonic society 2 philharmonic orchestra

филхармониски *adj* philharmonic; филхармониски оркестар philharmonic orchestra

филц *m* felt

филџан *m* small cup (*for Turkish coffee*); филџан кафе cup of coffee; ❑ очи-филџани large beautiful eyes, saucer-like eyes

филџанче *n dim. of* филџан

фиљан *pron indecl. colloq.* a certain, such and such; фиљан планина some mountain or other; фиљан човек a certain person, so-and-so

фин *adj* 1 fine, refined, delicate; sophisticated; фин човек refined person; фини црти fine features; фино држење refined behaviour; финиот свет beau monde 2 fine, thin; фина хартија fine paper; фино брашно fine flour

финáл *m* 1 end 2 *Mus.* finale 3 *Sport.* final<s>; влезе во финалот he got into the finals

финále *n see* финал

финáлен -лна *adj* 1 final, concluding, finishing; финален производ end product; финална средба final meeting 2 *Gram.* purpose *attrib.*; финална реченица purpose clause

финалѝст *m Sport.* finalist

финалѝстка *f* (*fem. form*) *see* финалист

финáнс *m* tax-collector; commissioner of taxation

финансиéр *m* 1 financier 2 financial expert

финансии *pl* finance<s>; министер за финансии Finance Minister 2 *colloq.* money; нема финансии за тоа there isn't any money for that

финансѝра *pf & impf* to finance; to fund; банката ја финансираше изградбата the bank was financing the construction; тој го финансираше додека студираше he supported him while he was studying

финансиски *adj* financial; fiscal; финансиска криза financial crisis; финансиска ревизија audit; checking the books; финансиски план financial plan; финансиски инспектор financial inspector, auditor; финансиски капитал finance capital; финансиски тешкотии financial difficulties

финансѝст *m* financier; financial expert

финéса *f* finesse

Финец -нци *m* Finn

финиш *m Sport.* finish, finishing post; во финишот на трката at the end of the race, at the finish

Финка *f* (*fem. form*) *see* Финец

финост *f see* финеса

Финска *f* Finland

фински *adj* Finnish

финта *f Sport.* feint; направи финта и го мина противничкиот играч he made a feint and slipped past the opposing player

фиока *f* drawer

фира *f* loss in weight (*of goods due to evaporation, damage, etc.*); wastage, allowance for waste; shrinkage; spoilage; ullage

фиран *adj indecl. only in the expression:* фиран стори (направи) to destroy, ruin, lay waste

фирка *impf impers.* to blow strongly; овде многу фирка it's very draughty here

фирма *f* 1 firm; company; concern; голема, угледна фирма a large, prominent firm 2 sign, signboard (*of company, etc.*) 3 *fig., colloq.* guise; под фирмата на љубовта under the guise of love

фирмописец -сци *m* sign-painter, sign-writer

фирнајс *m* varnish, lacquer, shellac

фирца *impf* to tack, baste *trans.*; го фирца палтото he is tacking the coat

фис[1] *m colloq.* tribe; clan

фис[2] *interj* whack! slap!

фисија *f* fission

фисионен -она *adj* fission *attrib.*; fissive

фиск *m* 1 exchequer; fisc, fisk 2 fiscal, treasury official

фискал *m* fiscal, treasury official

фискален -лна *adj* fiscal; фискална година fiscal (financial) year

фискултура *f* physical training (PT), physical education (PE); фискултура и спорт PT and sport

фискултурен -рна *adj* physical training/education *attrib.*, PT/PE *attrib.*

фискултурник -ци *m* athlete, gymnast, sportsman

фискултуричка *f* (*fem. form*) *see* фискултурник

фистула *f* 1 *Med.* fistula 2 *Mus.* falsetto

фит[1] *adj Sport.* fit, in good form

фит[2] *adv colloq.* quits, even; сега сме фит now we are quits

фитил *m see* фитиљ

фитилен -лна *adj* (*from* фитиљ) wick *attrib.*; фитилен пламен burning wick

фитилник -ци *m* old-fashioned earthenware lamp with a wick, *see* виделце

фитилче *n dim. of* фитиљ

фитиљ -ли *m* 1 wick; taper 2 fuse; ❏ му пушта фитили he puts him up to s.th.; he puts the cat among the pigeons

фитопатологија *f* plant pathology, phytopathology

фиу *interj* (*indicates the whistling of the wind or of the sound of an object moving fast through the air*) whiz!

фиука *impf see* фрчи 1, фучи 1

фифти-фифти *adv* fifty-fifty

Фиџи *n* Fiji

Фиџиец -ијци *m* Fijian, Fiji

Фиџијка *f* (*fem. form*) *see* Фиџиец

фиџиски *adj* Fijian, Fiji

фиша *f* card, slip (*for card index*)

фишек -ци *m* 1 cartridge, round <of ammunition>, *Am.* shell; имаше само пет фишеци he had only five rounds; ❏ стегнат како фишек stiff as a ramrod; фрла фишеци he is shooting 2 <ice-cream> cone 3 *colloq.* roll, rouleau; conical paper wrapper; витка пари во фишеци to wrap coins in rouleaus

фишеклак -ци *m* cartridge pouch; cartridge-belt

фишече *n dim. of* фишек

фјорд *m Geog.* fiord

флагрантен -тна *adj* flagrant, blatant, obvious, open; флагрантна спротивност glaring contrast

фламинго *m & n Zool.* (Phoenicopterus) flamingo

фланг *m Mil.* flank, wing

фланел *m* flannel

фланелски *adj* flannel

фластер *m* 1 adhesive bandage, Band-Aid, *Brit.* <sticking->plaster 2 *fig.* pest; ❏ ми се залепи како фластер he clung to me like a leech

флаута *f Mus.* flute, *see* флејта

флебит *m Med.* phlebitis

флегма 1 *f* phlegm, apathy; sang-froid; со својата флегма тој запусти сè with his nonchalance he ruined everything 2 *m colloq.* (*see* флегматик) phlegmatic person

флегматик -ци *m* phlegmatic person

флегматичен -чна *adj* phlegmatic; флегматично движење phlegmatic/leisurely movement

флегматично *adv* phlegmatically, nonchalantly

флегматичност *f* phlegm, phlegmatic character, nonchalance

флејта *f Mus.* flute

флејтист *m Mus.* flautist, *Am.* flutist

флека *f* 1 stain; blot 2 patch (*on footwear*)

флекав *adj* stained; флекави панталони soiled trousers

флексивен -вна *adj Gram.* inflected; флексивни јазици inflected languages

флексија *f Gram.* flexion, inflexion; внатрешна флексија internal inflexion

флерт *m* coquetry, flirting

флертува *impf* to flirt *intrans.*

флеш[1] *m Photography* (блиц) flash

флеш[2] *m* flush (*in some card-games*)

флигорна *f Mus.* bugle<-horn>; cornet; flugelhorn

флигорнист *m Mus.* bugler

флинта *f colloq.* whore, streetwalker

флирт *m see* флерт

флисне *pf* флисна *aor.* to slap, hit, whip, strike; му флисна една шлаканица he slapped his face; *see* фрасне

флиспапир *m* wrapping tissue

фломастер *m* felt-tip pen

флор *m* 1 crepe (*material*) 2 (*see* превез) veil 3 crape, crepe; black armband

флора *f* flora

флорет *m Sport.* foil

флорист *m* florist; floriculturist

флористика *f* floristics, the study of flora

флота *f* fleet; воена флота navy; воздушна флота air force; трговска флота merchant fleet; Средоземноморската флота the Mediterranean fleet

флотација *f* flotation

флотен -тна *adj* fleet *attrib.*; naval

флотила *f* flotilla

флувијален -лна *adj* fluvial

флуид *m* 1 fluid 2 *fig.* aura

флуиден -дна *adj* flowing, fluid; fluent; флуиден стил fluid style

флуктуација *f* fluctuation (*also fig.*); флуктуација на работната сила fluctuation in the workforce

флуор *m Chem.* fluorine

флуоресце́нтен -тна *adj* fluorescent; флуоросцентно осветление fluorescent lighting

флуоресце́нија *f* fluorescence

флуоресци́ра *impf* to fluoresce, be fluorescent

флуорогра́фија *f* fluoroscopy

флуорогра́фски *adj* fluoroscopic

фљо́нго *n* (*пантлика, кордела*) ribbon; со фљонго на главата with a ribbon in her hair

фоаје́ *n* foyer

-фо́б (*in compounds*) -phobe; англофоб Anglophobe; женофоб misogynist

фоби́ја *f Med.* phobia

фо́дул *adj colloq.* 1 proud 2 conceited, *colloq.* stuck-up

фоду́лен -лна *adj colloq. see* фодул

фоду́ли се *impf colloq.* 1 to be proud (*co – of*); to pride o.s. (*on s.th.*) 2 to be conceited, have a swelled head, *sl.* be too big for one's boots

фоду́лштина *f colloq.* 1 pride 2 conceit, *colloq.* swelled head

фо́ја *f Bot. see* смрека

фо́ка *f Zool.* (Phoca vitulina) seal

фока́лен -лна *adj* focal

фо́кс *m see* фокстрот

фокстро́т *m* foxtrot

фо́кус *m* focus (*Phys., Photography, Med.*); *fig.* centre, mid-point, locus

фоку́сен -сна *adj* focal; фокусна раздалеченост focal distance (length)

фол *m colloq.* lie; trick, ploy; не му успеа фолот his ploy did not work

фоли́ја *f* foil; алуминиумска фолија aluminium foil

фолија́нт *m & фо́лио *n* folio

фоли́ра *impf colloq.* to pretend; to pose, put on a show

фолкло́р *m* folklore

фолкло́рен -рна *adj* folkloric, folkloristic; folklore *attrib.*; folk *attrib.*; фолклорни материјали folkloric materials; фолклорен ансамбл folk ensemble; фолклорни песни folk-songs

фолклори́ст *m* folklorist

фолклори́стика *f* study of folklore

фолклори́стка *f* (*fem. form*) *see* фолклорист

фолкло́рност *f* folkloric character, local colour

фолксдо́јчер *m Volksdeutscher*

фон *m* background (*also fig.*)

-фо́н (*in compounds*) -phone; телефон telephone; саксофон saxophone

фонд *m* 1 fund; инвестиционен фонд investment fund; ❏ златен фонд capital, most valuable possession 2 reserves, resources, stock; книжен фонд (*of a library, etc.*) holdings; ❏ основен речнички фонд basic vocabulary 3 foundation; фонд за научна работа science foundation

фонда́ција *f* foundation, *see* фонд 3

фоне́м & фоне́ма *f Gram.* phoneme

фоне́тика *f* phonetics

фонети́чар *m* phonetician

фонети́чки *adj* phonetic, *see* фонетски

фоне́тски *adj* phonetic; фонетски закони phonetic laws; фонетски испитувања phonetic research; фонетски правопис phonetic orthography; фонетско писмо phonetic script

фоногра́ма *f arch.* phonogram

фоно́граф *m arch.* phonograph

фоногра́фија *f* phonography

фоногра́фски *adj* phonographic

фоноло́г -зи *m* phonologist

фоноло́гија *f Ling.* phonology

фоноло́шки *adj* phonological; фонолошки испитувања phonological research

фономе́тар -три *m* phonometer

фономе́трија *f* phonometry, phonometrics

фоноте́ка *f* record and tape library/collection, sound archive

фонта́на *f* fountain

фор *m Sport.* 1 attack, *Am.* offense, offensive line; имаме слаб фор we have a weak attack 2 forward pass; му даде фор he made a forward pass to him

фо́ра *f* 1 advantage, lead; даде фора to cede the advantage; to give a start; to accept a handicap 2 ❏ тој е главна фора he is cock-of-the-walk; he is the boss

фо́ринт *m & фо́ринта *f* 1 (*парична единица во Унгарија*) forint 2 florin

фо́рма *f* 1 form, shape, appearance; physique; гробницата имаше форма на пирамида the tomb had the shape of a pyramid; форма на владеење form of government; *Philos.* форма и содржина form and content; во форма на извештај in the form of a report; граматичка форма grammatical form; само про форма only pro forma; for form's sake; merely for the sake of appearances; ❏ во одречна форма in the negative; во форма на in the shape of; in the form of; in effigy; доведува во форма to lick (knock) into shape; поприма форма to begin to take shape 2 *Sport.* condition, fitness; екипата не е во форма the team is out of practice; во добра/лоша форма in good/bad form/shape 3 *Tech.* mould; *Print.* chase; форми за колца (при лиење) moulds for wheels (when casting) 4 (*униформа*) uniform; учениците мора да носат форма the pupils had to wear uniform

форма́лен -лна *adj* formal; формална логика formal logic; формална должност formal duty; формален договор formal contract

формали́зам -змот *m* 1 formalism 2 *fig.* formality, red tape

формали́н *m* formalin

формали́ст *m* 1 formalist 2 *fig.* stickler for form

формалисти́чки *adj* formalistic; formalist *attrib.*; формалистичка уметност formalist art; формалистички однос formalistic attitude

формали́стка *f* (*fem. form*) *see* формалист

форма́лно *adv* formally

форма́лност *f* formality; без никакви формалности without any formalities; да се исполнат формалностите in order that the formalities be observed/completed

форма́нт *m Ling.* derivational affix, formant

форма́т *m* 1 format; џебен формат pocket size 2 stature, standing; научник од голем формат scholar of great stature

форма́ција -ии *f* 1 formation, stage of development; општествено-економска формација socio-economic formation 2 *Mil.* body of troops, formation; непријателските формации the enemy's formations 3 *Geology* formation; терцијарна формација Tertiary formation; кредна формација Cretaceous formation

формациски *adj* formational

форми́ра *pf & impf* **I** to form *trans.*, mould; to shape; to set up, organize; формира свој поглед на светот to form one's own outlook; тоа го формира карактерот that moulds the character; формира влада to form a government **II** – **се** to be formed, form *intrans.*

формула *f* formula; готови формули set formulas; политичка формула political formula; математичка/хемиска формула mathematical/chemical formula

формула́р *m* form; questionnaire; го пополни формуларот he filled in the form

формулација -ии *f* formulation

формули́ра *pf & impf* to formulate

формули́ро́вка *f see* формулација

форси́ра *pf & impf* **1** to speed up *trans.*; ja форсираа работата they pressed ahead with the work, *colloq.* they rushed things **2** *fig.* to back, support, favour; тој го форсира и затоа напредува he supports him strongly (*colloq.* he's behind him) and that's why he gets on **3** *Mil.* to force; to cross, negotiate *trans.*; ja форсираа реката they forced a crossing over the river

форси́ран *pt* forced; accelerated; со форсирано темпо with accelerated tempo; форсиран марш forced march; форсиран мат *Chess* forced mate

форте *adv & n Mus.* forte

фортепија́но *n Mus.* fortepiano

фортисимо *adv & n Mus.* fortissimo

фортификација -ии *f Mil.* fortification; fortress, strong point, stronghold

фортификацио́нен -она *adj Mil.* fortification *attrib.*, fortifying; фортификациони работи fortification works

фортуна *f* snowstorm; rainstorm; gale

форум *m* forum

форхенд *m Sport.* forehand

форца *f colloq.* energy, impetus, force, power; ❏ дај му форца give him a push! hurry him up!

фосил *m* fossil (*also fig.*)

фосилен -лна *adj* fossil (*also fig.*); фосилни останки fossilized remains

фосфа́т *m Chem.* phosphate

фосфа́тен -тна *adj* phosphatic; phosphate *attrib.*; фосфатни ѓубриња phosphate fertilizers, phosphates

фосфор *m Chem.* phosphorus

фосфорен -рна *adj* phosphorous; фосфорни руди phosphate ores; фосфорна светлина phosphorous light

фосфоресценција *f* phosphorescence

фосфоресци́ра *impf* to phosphoresce

фосфори́т *m Chem.* phosphorite, rock phosphate

фота *f* forfeits; играат фота they are playing forfeits

фоте́лја -лји *f* armchair, easy chair

фото- (*in compounds*) photo-

фотоаматёр *m* amateur photographer

фотоаматёрски *adj* of/for amateur photographers; фотоаматерски курс a course for amateur photographers

фотоапара́т *m* camera

фотогеничен -чна *adj* photogenic; фотогенично лице a photogenic face

фотогеничност *f* photogenic quality

фотограф *m* photographer

фотографија -ии *f* **1** photography **2** snapshot, photograph; момент<ал>на фотографија instantaneous exposure; fast photo

фотографи́ра *pf & impf* **I** to photograph **II** – **се** to have one's photo taken

фотографски *adj* photographic; фотографски апарат camera; фотографска снимка photograph, snapshot; фотографска точност photographic accuracy

фотоелемёнт *m* photoelectric cell

фото-љубител *m see* фотоаматер

фотомётар -три *m* photometer; light meter

фотометрија *f* photometry

фотомонта́жа *f* photomontage

фотомонта́жен -жна *adj* photomontage *attrib.*

фотóн *m* photon

фоторепорта́жа *f* photo-report, picture story

фоторепортёр *m* press photographer

фоторепортёрски *adj* press photographer's

фотос *m* photograph, photo

фотосинтёза *f* photosynthesis

фотосфёра *f* photosphere

фототёка *f* photo archive/file

фототерапија *f* phototherapy

фототераписки *adj* phototherapeutic

фототи́пен -пна *adj* phototypographical; prototype *attrib.*; фототипно издание phototype edition

фототипија -ии *f* phototype; phototypography

фотохемија *f* photochemistry

фотохемиски *adj* photochemical

фото-цинкогра́ф *m* <photo>zincographic printer

фото-цикнографија *f* <photo>zincography; photo-etching

фото-цинкогра́фски *adj* <photo>zincographic

фрагмёнт *m* fragment; detail; фрагменти од керамика ceramic fragments; фрагмент од роман fragment from (excerpt from) a novel

фрагмента́рен -рна *adj* fragmentary; incomplete; фрагментарно излагање fragmentary presentation

фрагмента́рно *adv* fragmentarily

фрагмента́рност *f* fragmentary character

фраер *m colloq.* **1** playboy, rake; idler, lout, *colloq.* lazybones **2** cool/trendy fellow, *Am. sl.* dude

фраерски *adj colloq.* **1** rakish; loutish **2** cool; trendy

фраза *f* phrase; празни фрази empty phrases; почетните фрази на симфонијата the opening phrases of the symphony

фразеологија *f* **1** phraseology; фразеологијата на македонскиот јазик the phraseology of the Macedonian language; фразеологијата на минатиот век the phraseology of the last century **2** *fig.* verbiage, claptrap

фразеолошки *adj* phraseological; фразеолошки израз idiom, phraseological expression; фразеолошки речник phraseological dictionary, dictionary of idioms

фразер *m* phrasemonger, *colloq.* windbag

фразерски *adj* phrasemonger's; фразерски говор empty talk, *sl.* hot air

фразерство *n* phrasemongering, empty rhetoric, bombast

фразира *impf* to talk in clichés; to be glib; *Brit. colloq.* to waffle

фрак *m* tailcoat, evening dress, *colloq.* tails

фрактура *f Med.* fracture; фрактура на виличната коска fracture of the jawbone

фракција -ии *f Pol.* faction, splinter group

фракционер *m* factionary, factionist

фракционерски *adj* factional; factious, divisive; фракционерски борби factional struggle (infighting); фракционерски истап factional provocation; divisive speech

фракционерство *n* factionalism

фракциски *adj* factional; фракциски борби factional struggle (infighting); *see* фракционерски

франк -ови, -ци *m* franc

франко *adv Comm.* (*usu. in compounds*) prepaid, carriage paid; (*при испорачување*) f.o.b. (free on board), f.o.r. (free on rail); (*при пристигнување*) ex ship; франко станицата free station; франко-вагон free on rail; франко-железница carriage paid; франко-царина customs duty prepaid; порто-франко free port

Франција *f* France

Француз & **Французин** -зи *m* Frenchman

Французинка *f* Frenchwoman

француски *adj* French; францускиот јазик the French language; учам француски I am learning French; на/по француски in French; по француски, на француски начин à la française; ❏ француски клуч adjustable spanner, monkey wrench

фрапантен -тна *adj* striking, remarkable, unusual

фрапантно *adv* strikingly, remarkably, unusually

фрапантност *f* strikingness, remarkableness, unusualness

фрапира *pf & impf* to amaze, strike, astonish, astound

фрас *m* 1 numbness, shock, paralysis 2 fit; convulsion

фраска *impf* I to whip, flog, beat *trans.*; постојано го фраскаше коњот he kept whipping the horse; ветрот му фраскаше в лице the wind was lashing his face II – се to whip one another

фрасне *pf* фрасна *aor.* I to strike *trans.*, *colloq.* whack; го фрасна со прачката he whacked him with the stick; добро го фрасна he whacked him hard II – се to hit o.s. hard; to deal o.s. a blow

фраснува (се) *impf of* фрасне (се)

фратар -три *m* Catholic monk, brother, friar

фратарски *adj* brother's, friar's; monastic

фратрија -ии *f Hist.* phratry

фрба *impf* to sip; to slurp; *see* срка, шрка

фрегата *f* 1 frigate 2 *Zool.* (Fregata) frigate-bird, hurricane-bird

фрегатен -тна *adj* frigate *attrib.*, frigate's

фрезер *m* milling-machine operator

фрезмашина *f* milling machine

фреквентен -тна *adj* frequent; accelerated; *Med.* фреквентен пулс rapid pulse

фреквенција *f* frequency

френгија[1] *f colloq. see* френгуз

френгија[2] *adj f.p. only in the expression:* сабја френгија thin long sword

френгуз *m colloq.* syphilis

френетичен -чна *adj* frenetic; френетичен аплауз frenzied applause

френетички *adv see* френетично

френетично *adv* frenetically; го поздравија френетично they greeted him enthusiastically

фреска *f* fresco

фреско *n* 1 light woollen fabric 2 (*see* фреска) фреско-слика fresco; фреско-сликарство fresco mural painting

фриволен -лна *adj* frivolous

фриволност *f* frivolity

фригиден -дна *adj* 1 frigid, <sexually> cold, unresponsive 2 apathetic, indifferent

фригидност *f Med.* frigidity

фрижидер *m* refrigerator, *colloq.* fridge

фризер *m* hairdresser; (*за мажи*) barber

фризерка *f* (*fem. form*) *see* фризер

фризерски *adj* hairdressing *attrib.*, hairdresser's; фризерски салон hairdresser's shop

фризира *pf & impf* I 1 to do s.o.'s hair 2 *colloq.* to spruce up, dress up, touch up, *colloq.* do up *trans.*; *colloq.* to doctor *trans.*; to do some window-dressing; ја фризира изјавата he touched up the statement II – се to have one's hair done; *sl.* to dress up *intrans.*, *colloq.* do o.s. up

фризура *f* hairstyle, coiffure, *colloq.* hairdo

фрикативен -вна *adj Phon.* fricative; фрикативни согласки fricative consonants, fricatives

фрикативност *f* fricative quality/status

фрка *impf* 1 to flash; to penetrate; веди фркаат lightning is flashing; ме фркаат коленициве I have stabbing pains in my knees; *see* молска, жега[2] 2 *see* фрчи, фучи

фркат *adj dial.* flying, winged; фркато пиле bird that can fly

фркне *pf* фркна *aor.* 1 to fly off, flutter off; фркна пилето the bird flew off 2 to strike *trans.*, hit; to stab, pierce; ме фркна со прачката he hit me with the rod; пушка те фркнала! may you get shot! 3 to gush <forth>; фркна водата the water came gushing out 4 *dial.* to get angry, *colloq.* blow up *intrans.*; тате ќе фркне по некој пат Dad blows his top sometimes

фркнува *impf of* фркне

фрковат *adj rare* flying, winged, *see* фркат

фрла (се) *impf of* фрли (се); ❏ фрла <со> кал врз to fling/sling/throw mud at

фрлање *n* 1 throwing; throw; фрлање отпадоци throwing away rubbish; *f.p.* фрлање камен од рамо (*rural sport*) throwing large stones in shot-putting style; *Sport.* фрлање диск/кладиво/копје throwing the discus/the hammer/the javelin; фрлање ѓуле putting the shot; ❏ не е за фрлање not too bad 2 *dial.* divorcing, divorce

фрлач *m* thrower; *Mil.* фрлач на бомби grenade-launcher; *Naut.* depth-charge gun; фрлач на мини mortar, *see* минофрлач<ка>; фрлач на пламен flame-thrower; *Sport.* фрлач на диск discus thrower

фрлачка *f* 1 throwing 2 *dial.* divorce

фрлачки *adj Sport.* throwing; фрлачки дисциплини throwing events (*discus, javelin etc.*)

фрли *pf* I 1 to throw, cast, hurl, fling; (*исфрли*) to throw away/out, *colloq.* chuck out; to throw off, toss *trans.*; to give up; го фрли каменот далеку he threw the stone a long way; го положи испитот и ги фрли книгите he passed the exam and he threw out his books; ги фрли цигарите he gave up smoking; ❏ фрли мрежа to cast a net; фрли оружје to lay down one's arms; фрли во борба to throw into battle; фрли во војна to plunge into war *trans*.; фрли во воздух to blow up; фрли (пушти) котва to cast anchor; фрли во зандана (во затвор, во темница) to clap in prison; фрли во старо железо to scrap; фрли в постела to make s.o. ill; фрли една чашка (една ракија, едно вино и сл.) to have a drink; фрли ждрепка to draw (cast) lots; фрли вина на некого to put (lay) the blame on s.o.; фрли на ветер to squander; фрли пари на нешто to put a lot of money into s.th.; фрли поглед (*на/кон/врз*) to cast a glance at, steal a glance at; фрли сенка (*на/врз*) to cast a shadow (*over*); фрли светлина (*врз*) to shed light (*on*); фрли ракавица to throw down the gauntlet; фрли раса to give up the priesthood; фрли икра (*of fish*) to spawn; фрли мерак, *see* фрли око 1; фрли око (*на некого или на нешто*) 1. to take a fancy (*to s.o./s.th.*); to set one's heart (*on s.th.*) 2. to cast an eye (*over s.o./s.th.*); фрли прав (пепел) в очи на некого to throw dust in s.o.'s eyes; фрли <му> пепел! let bygones be bygones! wipe the slate clean! го фрли во грижи he caused him a lot of worry/trouble; *colloq.* го фрли топот 1. he kicked the bucket 2. he finished the job; ги фрли плочите, *see* го фрли топот 1; нема игла каде да фрлиш there is no room to swing a cat; фрли камен по нас he's stopped visiting us; роди ме, мајко, со касмет, па фрли ме на буниште *prov. see* буниште; фрли глиста, фати јагула *prov.* throw a sprat to catch a mackerel; фрли го во морето, тој ќе ти излезе со стадо овци; фрли го на буниште, ќе го најдеш на огниште *prov.* he bounces back every time, *cf.* he that endures is not overcome; фрли зад себе, да најдеш пред себе *prov.* give and spend, and God will send 2 *colloq.* to fire; фрли пушка to fire a gun; фрли еден куршум he fired a single shot 3 *colloq.* to yield, produce (*profit, income*); не ми фрли занаетот my trade didn't bring me much 4 *dial.* to abandon, divorce *trans*.; ја фрли жената he left his wife II – ce 1 to throw o.s., leap, rush, plunge *intrans*.; ce фрли на помош to rush to help; ce фрли на колена to fall to one's knees; ce фрли во морето to dive into the sea; ce фрли во работата to plunge into work; му ce фрли в прегратка she flung himself into his arms; *Sport.* му ce фрли в нозе he tripped him 2 *dial.* to get divorced; to separate *intrans*.

фрлокрил *adj f.p.* fleet of foot; коњче фрлокрило little steed with wingèd feet

фронт *m Mil. fig.* front; ❏ го напушти фронтот he deserted; на два фронта on two fronts; на широк фронт on a broad front; Источниот фронт the Eastern Front; идеолошкиот фронт the ideological front; народен фронт Popular Front

фронта́лен -лна *adj* frontal; фронтален удар frontal blow; фронтален напад frontal attack

фронта́лно *adv* frontally; напаѓавме фронтално we used to attack from the front

фротир *m* <cotton> terry

фротирски *adj* terry; фротирско ќебе terry blanket

фртуна *f see* фортуна

фруглица *f* traditional marriage banner; *cf.* хоругва

фругличар *m* person who carries the marriage banner

фрушки *adj f.p.* (*as a fixed epithet with the noun ноже*) фрушко ноже small sharp knife

фрфало *n* children's toy, kind of rattle

фрцка (ce) *impf colloq.* to mince *intrans*.; to play around; *colloq.* to pussyfoot <around>; *see* врцка (ce)

фрча *f colloq.* brush; фрча за алишта clothes-brush; фрча за чевли shoe-brush; *see* четка[1]

фрчи *impf* 1 *colloq.* to whistle, whiz, fly; каменот фрчи the stone whizzes <through the air>; искри фрчат sparks crackle; орелот фрчи со крилјата the eagle flaps its wings; си фрчи времето! how time flies! 2 to snort 3 to rage, fume, fulminate; *see* фучи

фрчиче *n* & **фрчичка** *f colloq. dim. of* фрча; фрчиче за заби toothbrush; *see* четкиче, четкичка

фуга *f Mus.* fugue

фудбал *m Sport.* 1 football, soccer 2 soccer ball, football

фудбале́р *m Sport.* soccer player, footballer; врвен фудбалер top soccer player

фудбалски *adj Sport.* football (soccer) *attrib*.; фудбалски натпревар football match; фудбалски судија referee

фузија *f* fusion, merging, amalgamation; merger

фузиони́ра *pf* & *impf* I to fuse, merge (*s.th. with s.th.*); to amalgamate *trans*. II – ce to merge, combine (*co – with*), join *intrans*., fuse *intrans*.; to amalgamate *intrans*.

фука (ce) *impf of* фукне (ce)

фукара *f* & *m colloq.* 1 wretch; што бараш од тој фукара what do you want with that poor wretch? 2 *pejor.* scoundrel, cad, *colloq.* heel

фукарлак *m colloq.* misery, poverty, misfortune

фукне *pf* фукна *aor.* I 1 to hit, *colloq.* whack, *sl.* wallop; to shove *trans*.; го фукна силно по вилици he punched him in the jaw 2 *fig.* to eat greedily, bolt, gulp; го фукна <наеднаш> јадењето he bolted his food; *see* офука II – ce 1 to bump into (*во – into*); to hurt o.s. 2 *fig.* to barge in, burst in; ce фукна од малата врата внатре he barged in by the side door

фунд *m dial.* end; на фундот од селото at the end of the village; *see* крај

фундаме́нт *m* foundation (*also fig.*), basis; моите тврдења имаат цврст фундамент my assertions are well-founded

фундамента́лен -лна *adj* fundamental, basic; фундаментални испитувања basic research; фундаментална библиотека main library

фунди́ра *pf* & *impf* 1 to establish, found 2 *fig.* to substantiate

фунди́ран *adj* 1 firm, well-founded 2 funded; фундиран доход funded income; фундирани заеми consolidated annuities

фундус *m* 1 (*почва, земја*) soil, earth 2 (*имот*) estate, property 3 (*фонд, резерви*) funds

функција -ии *f* function (*also Math.*); functioning; врши функција to perform a function; функцијата на срцето the functioning of the heart; *Math.* тригонометриски функции trigonometric functions

функциона́лен -лна *adj* functional; practical; функционален додаток functional increment; функционален мебел functional furniture

функционе́р *m* functionary; партиски функционер party functionary

функционе́рка *f* (*fem. form*) *see* функционер

функциони́ра *impf* to function, work *intrans.*; машината функционира добро the machine runs well

фунта *f* **1** (*за тежина*) pound **2** (*парична единица*) pound; фунта стерлинг pound sterling

фураж *m* forage, feed, fodder

фуражен -жна *adj* forage *attrib.*; фуражни култури fodder crops

фура́шка *f* peak cap, service cap

фургон *m* **1** (*железнички*) luggage-van; service van **2** (*товарна кола*) lorry, *Am.* truck; caravan; removal van **3** *Mil.* <supply> truck **4** (*мртовечка кола*) hearse

фурда *f colloq.* **1** scraps, waste **2** poor-quality goods, rejects

фурија -ии *f* **1** *Myth.* Fury **2** tempest, violent storm **3** *fig.* fury, shrew, termagant; се спушти како фурија he descended like a fury

фурио́зен -зна *adj* furious

фурка *f* **1** distaff; галената жена не преде со фурка *prov.* the foot on the cradle and hand on the distaff is the sign of a good housewife **2** *fig.* lickspittle, toady

фурке́та *f* hairpin, *see* шнола

фурна *f* **1** oven; ovenful, batch; месила девет фурни леб she made nine batches of bread; ❏ има да јадеш уште многу фурни леб you must grow up a bit **2** bakery

фурнација -ии *m colloq.* baker

фурнацика *f colloq.* (*fem. form*) *see* фурнација

фурнациски *adj colloq.* baker's

фурнир *m* veneer; оревов фурнир walnut veneer

фурни́ра *pf & impf* to veneer

фуртуна *f see* фортуна

фусно́та *f* footnote

фуста *f colloq.* skirt; petticoat

фустан *m* <woman's> dress; невестински фустан wedding dress; свилен фустан silk dress

фустанче *n dim. of* фустан

фута *f* apron, pinafore, *see* скутник, унечка

футро́ла *f* case; футрола за очила spectacle case; футрола за виолина violin case; футрола за пиштол holster

футур *m Gram.* future <tense>

футури́зам -змот *m* futurism

футури́ст *m* futurist

футуристички *adj* futurist *attrib.*; futuristic; футуристичко списание futurist journal; футуристички стихови futuristic verse

футури́стка *f* (*fem. form*) *see* футурист

футурски *adj Gram.* future

фукне се *pf* фукна се *aor.* to slip out, escape unnoticed; се фукна надвор he slipped out

фуфул *m* comb, crest (*of a cock*)

фуцеле *n* small barrel, keg; едно фуцеле вино a cask of wine

фучи *impf* **1** to whistle, howl; надвор ветерот фучеше outside the wind was whistling **2** *fig.* to snort; коњот фучи the horse is snorting **3** *fig.* to get angry; to fume, fulminate; to quarrel; to foam at the mouth; to snarl; цел ден само фучи he has been foaming at the mouth all day

фучииче *n colloq. dim. of* фучија

фучија -ии *f colloq.* barrel; vat, cask

фушер *m colloq.* bungler, botcher

фушерај *m* shoddy work

фушерски *colloq.* **1** *adj* shoddy; фушерска работа shoddy work **2** *adv* shoddily; ми го соши фушерски костумот he made a bad job of my suit

фушкија *f colloq.* dung, excrement, droppings; ❏ фушкија го направи he made mincemeat of him; he smashed it to smithereens

ха & **хаа** *interj* **1** (*expressing surprise, pleasure, displeasure, approval, etc.*) ha! aha! hah! good heavens! **2** (*repeated – indicating laughter*) ha ha!

хабанéра *f* habanera

хабилитација -ии *f* habilitation

хабилитациóнен -она *adj* habilitation *attrib*.; хабилитациона работа, хабилитационен труд habilitation thesis

хабит *m* **1** *arch.* (*монашка облека*) habit **2** (*облека на судија и др.*) gown, robe

хабитáт *m* habitat

хаварија -ии *f* **1** damage; breakdown **2** *Leg.* average **3** (*бродолом*) shipwreck

Хаг *m* the Hague

хагиогрáф *m* hagiographer

хагиографија -ии *f* hagiography

хагиографски *adj* hagiographic<al>; хагиографска книжнина hagiographical literature

хаѓанец -ни *m* person from the Hague

хаѓанка *f* (*fem. form*) *see* хаѓанец

хазард *m* **1** gambling; dice; *see* комар[2] **2** *fig.* gamble

хазарден -дна *adj* gambling *attrib*.; хазардна игра game of chance

хазардéр *m* gambler

хазардúра *impf* to gamble, *colloq.* chance it

хазардно *adv* on a gamble; riskily; играше хазардно he was playing recklessly

хазéна *f Sport.* <women's> handball

Хáйти *m* Haiti

хаитски *adj* Haiti *attrib*., Haitian

Хаиќанец -ни *m* Haitian

Хаиќанка *f* (*fem. form*) *see* Хаиќанец

хаиќански *adj* Haitian

хај-фај *m colloq.* hi-fi

хајка *f* **1** hunt, chase; shooting party; *battue*; хајка на диви свињи wild boar hunt **2** *fig.* manhunt, drag-net; witch-hunt; полициска хајка police raid; кренаа хајка they are out to get s.o.

хајкач *m* beater; member of a posse

хајкаџија -ии *m see* хајкач

хала *f* hall

халогéн[1] *m Chem.* halogen

халогéн[2] *adj Chem.* halogenic

халуцинација -ии *f* hallucination

халуцинúра *impf* to hallucinate *intrans.*

халф *m Sport.* half-back, *colloq.* half; халф-линија half-back line

халф-тајм *m Sport.* half-time

хамбург *m* Hamburg <grapes/wine>

хамбургер *m* hamburger

хангар *m* hangar; хангар за авиони aircraft hangar

ханоец -ојци *m* person from Hanoi

Ханој *m* Hanoi

ханојка *f* (*fem. form*) *see* ханоец

ханојски *adj* Hanoi *attrib*.

хаос *m* chaos; во собата беше хаос the room was in total disorder; хаос во главата confused thoughts

хаотичен -чна *adj* chaotic; хаотична состојба chaotic state; хаотични мисли chaotic thoughts

хаотично *adv* chaotically; ми идеа хаотично разни мисли various unconnected thoughts were coming into my mind

хаотичност *f* chaotic nature/character; chaos; хаотичност во зборувањето disjointed way of speaking

хаплологија *f Ling.* haplology

харакúри *n* hara-kiri

характер *m see* карактер

харанга *f* harangue

харангéр *m* haranguer; agitator, troublemaker

харангúра *impf* to harangue

хардвер *m Computers* hardware

харем *m* harem

харемски *adj* harem *attrib*.; харемска робинка odalisque

харизма *f Rel.* charisma (*also fig.*)

харинга *f Zool.* (Clupea harengus) herring

хармонизација -ии *f Mus.* harmonization

хармонизúра *pf & impf Mus.* to harmonize

хармонија *f* **1** harmony; хармонијата на песната the harmony of the song **2** *fig.* harmony, accord, concord; хармонија на интересите harmony of interests; во хармонија со барањата in accordance with the demands; во хармонија со времето in keeping with the times; живеат во хармонија they live in harmony

хармоника *f Mus.* accordion, concertina; ❑ како хармоника concertina-like; (*за ѕид*) accordion wall; (*за врата*) folding door; усна хармоника harmonica, mouth-organ

хармоникáш *m Mus.* accordionist, concertina player

хармоникáшки *adj Mus.* accordion, concertina *attrib*.; хармоникашки оркестар accordion orchestra

хармониски *adj* (*from* хармонија) harmonious; *Mus.* harmonic; *see* хармоничен

хармонúст *m* harmonist, harmonizer

хармониум *m Mus.* harmonium

хармоничен -чна *adj* **1** harmonious (*also fig.*), sweet-sounding, melodious; *Mus.* harmonic; хармонични гласови melodious voices; хармоничниот шум на реката the melodious murmur of the river; хармоничен развој harmonious development **2** well-built; хармонична снага shapely body

хармонично *adv* harmoniously; хармонично развиен harmoniously developed

хармоничност *f* harmoniousness, harmony; хармоничноста на линиите the harmony of the lines; хармоничноста на развојот на стопанството the balanced development of the economy

харпија *f* harpy

харпун *m* harpoon

харпуне́р *m* harpooner

хартиен *adj* paper *attrib.*; хартиена вреќа paper bag; фабрика за хартиена и картонска амбалажа factory for paper and cardboard wrapping materials; paper-mill

хартија -ии *f* paper; (*ракопис, документ*) manuscript, document; амбалажна хартија wrapping paper; Лакмусова хартија litmus paper; пергаментна хартија <vegetable> parchment; печатарска хартија printing paper, newsprint; попивна хартија blotting-paper; просирна хартија tracing paper; санитарна, тоалетна, хигиенска хартија toilet paper; paper towelling; хартија за ноти music-paper; хартии од вредност (вредносни хартии) securities; ги стави своите мисли на хартија he put his thoughts down on paper; свиткај го в хартија wrap it <up> in paper! ❑ хартијата трпи paper won't blush; мртва буква на хартија dead letter

хартијка *f dim. of* хартија; slip of paper; му напиша на хартијка he wrote it out for him on a slip of paper

харфа *f Mus.* harp; свири на харфа to play the harp

харфист *m Mus.* harpist, harper

харфи́стка *f Mus.* (*fem. form*) *see* харфист

хатихума́јун *m Hist.* Hatt-i Humayun (*Sultan's decree of 1856 on the equal rights of all subjects of the Ottoman Empire irrespective of their religious faith*)

хатише́риф *m Hist.* Hatt-i Sherif (*Sultan's decree of 1839 by which Christians were given rights in the Ottoman Empire*)

хауба *f* 1 (*на кола*) bonnet, *Am.* hood 2 (*во фризерница*) <wall> hair-drier, swivel-mounted drier

хаубиша *f Mil.* howitzer

хаубички *adj Mil.* howitzer *attrib.*

хаузма́јстор *m* caretaker, janitor

ха-ха & **ха-ха-ха** *interj see* ха

хаџи *indecl.* (*title*) hajji, hadji; хаџи Томо hadji Tomo

хаџија -ии *m see* аџија

хашиш *m* hashish; marijuana, cannabis

хашки *adj* <of/from> the Hague *attrib.*

хе[1] *interj* (*sometimes also repeated* хе-хе *and* хе-е-е *to express doubt, displeasure, indignation, etc.*) hum! huh! хе, кој знае дали ќе биде добро huh, who knows whether it'll be all right? хе-е-е, не оди тоа така huh . . . , that won't do

хе[2] *part see* е[1]

хегемонија *f* hegemony; хегемонијата на пролетаријатот the leading role of the proletariat

хегемони́ст *m* hegemonist

хегемонистички *adj* hegemon<ist>ic, hegemonist *attrib.*

хедони́зам -змот *m* hedonism

хедони́ст *m* hedonist

хеј *interj* 1 (*also* хе-е-еј *expressing joy, sorrow, surprise, doubt*) ah! oh! hey; hello 2 (*to attract attention*) hey! хеј, елате ваму! hey, come over here! *see* ej

хека́томба *f* 1 *Hist.* hecatomb (*Greek sacrifice of 100 oxen*) 2 *fig.* wholesale slaughter

хексаго́н *m Geom. see* шестаголник

хексае́дар -дри *m Geom.* (*коцка*) hexahedron

хексаме́тар -три *m Prosody* hexameter

хектар *m* hectar

хекто- (*in compounds*) hecto-

хектограм *m* hectogram<me>

хектограф *m* hectograph

хектоли́тар -три *m* hectolitre

хектоме́тар -три *m* hectometre

хелени́зам -змот *m* Hellenism

хеленизација *f* Hellenization

хелени́ст *m* Hellenist

хелидром *m* heliport

хелико́птер *m* helicopter

хелиогра́ф *m* heliograph

хелиоме́тар *m Astronomy* heliometer

хелиотерапија *f Med.* heliotherapy

хелиотераписки *adj* heliotherapeutic; хелиотераписко лекување heliotherapy

хелиотропи́зам -змот *m Bot.* heliotropism

хелиоцентричен -чна *adj* heliocentric

хелиум *m Chem.* helium

хелиумов *adj* helium *attrib.*; хелиумови соединенија helium compounds

Хелсинки *m* Helsinki

хелсиншки *adj* Helsinki *attrib.*

хемати́т *m* haematite

хематоло́г -зи *m* haematologist

хематологија *f* haematology

хематурија *f Med.* haematuria

хемизација *f* utilization of chemical products (*in industry and agriculture*); chemicalization; хемизација на земјоделството the chemicalization of agriculture

хемија *f* 1 chemistry; аналитичка хемија analytical chemistry; неорганска и органска хемија inorganic and organic chemistry; испит по хемија chemistry exam; хемијата на крвта the chemical composition of blood 2 *colloq.* chemistry textbook; излегоа нови хемии new chemistry textbooks have been published

хемикалија -ии *f* chemical

хемиски *adj* 1 chemical; хемиска анализа chemical analysis; хемиска реакција chemical reaction; хемиска формула chemical formula; хемиски обид chemical experiment; хемиски состав chemical composition; хемиска индустрија chemical industry; хемиско бојадисување и чистење chemical dyeing and dry-cleaning; хемиски молив indelible pencil; хемиско пенкало ball-point pen; хемиска војна chemical warfare; хемиско оружје chemical weapons 2 chemistry *attrib.*; хемиска лабораторија, хемиски кабинет chemistry laboratory

хемисфе́ра *f* hemisphere

хемичар *m* chemist; chemistry student; employee in the chemical industry

хемичарка *f* (*fem. form*) *see* хемичар

хемичарски *adj* chemist's; chemical

хемоглоби́н *m* haemoglobin

хеморо́иди *pl Med.* haemorrhoids, piles

хемотерапија *f Med.* chemotherapy

хемото́ракс *m Med.* haemothorax

хемофилија *f Med.* haemophilia

хемофиличар *m Med.* haemophiliac

хендикеп *m* 1 *Sport.* handicap; odds 2 *fig.* disadvantage

хендикепи́ра *pf & impf* to handicap, impede, hamper; to place at a disadvantage; лошото време ги хендикепира работниците the bad weather hampered the workers

хендс *m Sport.* hands, handling

хепиенд *m* happy ending (*to a film, novel, etc.*)

хералдика *f* heraldry

хералдички *adj* heraldic; хералдички знаци heraldic symbols (figures, charges)

хербар *m see* хербариум

хербариум *m Bot.* herbarium

херкул<ес> *m* **1** Hercules; man of outstanding strength **2** Hercules (*constellation in the northern hemisphere*)

херкулски *adj* Herculean, Hercules *attrib.*

хермафродит *m* hermaphrodite

хермафродитски *adj* hermaphroditic; хермафродитски црти hermaphroditic characteristics

хермелин *m* **1** *Zool.* (Mustela erminea) ermine; stoat **2** (*крзно*) ermine

хермелински *adj* ermine *attrib.*; хермелинска наметка ermine cape

херметичен -чна *adj* hermetic, airtight, hermetically sealed; watertight; херметичен сад airtight container; pressure cooker; херметична врата airtight (hermetically sealed) door

херметички[1] *adj see* херметичен

херметички[2] *adv* hermetically; вратата беше затворена херметички the door was airtight (hermetically sealed); херметички затворен часовник waterproof watch

херметично *adv see* херметички[2]

херметичност *f* airtightness; watertightness

хернија *f Med.* hernia, rupture

хероизам -змот *m* heroism; личен хероизам personal heroism

хероика *f* heroics; heroic style/ethos; хероиката на периодот the heroic spirit of that period

хероин *m* heroin

хероиња *f* heroine

херој -ои *m* **1** hero; падна со смртта на херој he died a hero's death; народен херој national hero; херој на нашето време a hero of our time **2** (*лице во уметничко дело*) character; главните херои на романот the central figures of the novel

херојски[1] *adj* heroic; херојски подвиг heroic exploit; херојско дело heroic deed; херојска поема a heroic poem

херојски[2] *adv* heroically; сите се држеа херојски пред непријателот they all behaved heroically in the face of the enemy

херојство *n* heroism

херпес *m Med.* herpes

херувика *f Rel.* cherubikon (*sung at the Orthodox eucharistic celebration*)

херувим *m Rel.* cherub, *pl* cherubim; сите серафими и херувими all the seraphim and the cherubim

херувимски *adj Rel.* cherubic; херувимска песна hymn to the cherubim

херц[1] *m Phys.* hertz

херц[2] *m* (*во карти*) heart<s>

херцег -зи *m* duke

херцегиња *f* duchess

Херцеговец -вци *m* Hercegovinian

херцеговина[1] *f* duchy

Херцеговина[2] *f* Hercegovina

Херцеговка *f* (*fem. form*) *see* Херцеговец

херцеговски *adj* Hercegovinian

херцешки *adj* ducal, duke's; херцешки дворец ducal palace

хетера *f literary* hetaera, hetaira, courtesan

хетероген *adj* heterogeneous; хетероген состав heterogeneous composition

хетерогеност *f* heterogeneity; хетерогеноста на организацијата the heterogeneity of the organization

хет-трик *m Sport.* hat trick

хи *interj* (*often doubled* хи, хи *or tripled* хи-хи-хи; *denotes soft laughter*) hee-hee

хибрид *m Bot., Zool., Gram.* hybrid

хибриден -дна *adj* hybrid; хибридна пченка hybrid maize; хибридно растение hybrid plant; хибриден јазик hybrid language

хибридизација *f Bot., Zool.* hybridization, cross-breeding, crossing

хигиена *f* hygiene, hygienics; хигиена на устата oral hygiene; хигиена на трудот occupational health

хигиеничар *m* hygienist

хигиенски[1] *adj* hygienic; (*за мерки*) sanitary; хигиенски навици hygienic habits; хигиенски услови hygienic conditions; ❑ хигиенска влошка sanitary towel, pad (*Am.* napkin, tampon); хигиенска гумичка condom

хигиенски[2] *adv* hygienically; живее хигиенски to live hygienically

хигрометар -три *m* hygrometer

хигроскопичен -чна *adj* hygroscopic; хигроскопична вата hygroscopic cotton-wool

хигроскопичност *f* hygroscopic quality

хидра *f* **1** *Myth.* hydra (*also fig.*); *Zool.* (Hydra viridis) hydra **2** *Astron.* Hydra, the Water Snake, the Sea Serpent

хидрант[1] *m* hydrant

хидрант[2] *m Zool.* hydranth

хидрат *m Chem.* hydrate; јагленородни хидрати carbohydrates

хидратен -тна *adj* hydrated

хидраулика *f* hydraulics

хидрауличен -чна *adj* hydraulic; хидраулични проучувања hydraulic research; хидраулична преса hydraulic press; хидраулична сопирачка (кочница) hydraulic brake; хидрауличен малтер hydraulic cement

хидро- (*in compounds*) hydro-

хидроавијација *f* seaplane operations; seaplane fleet

хидроавион *m* seaplane, flying boat, *see* хидроплан

хидробаза *f* seaplane base

хидробиологија *f* hydrobiology

хидробиолошки *adj* hydrobiological; хидробиолошки испитувања hydrobiological research; хидробиолошки завод hydrobiological institute

хидробус *m* water bus

хидроген *m Chem.* (*водород*) hydrogen

хидрогенски *adj* hydrogen *attrib.*; хидрогенска бомба hydrogen bomb

хидроглисер *m* hydrofoil

хидрографија *f* hydrography

хидрографски *adj* hydrographic; хидрографска карта hydrographic map

хидродинамика *f* hydrodynamics

хидроенергетика *f* hydroelectric power engineering

хидроенергија *f* 1 hydroelectric energy 2 water-power

хидролиза *f Chem.* hydrolysis

хидрологија *f* hydrology

хидрометар -три *m* hydrometer

хидрометеорологија *f* hydrometeorology

хидрометереолошки *adj* hydrometeorological; хидрометеоролошки податоци hydrometeorological data

хидромеханика *f* hydromechanics

хидроним *m Ling.* hydronym

хидроплан *m* seaplane, flying boat

хидросфера *f* hydrosphere

хидротерапија *f Med.* hydrotherapy; water cure, hydropathy

хидротехника *f* hydraulic engineering; applied hydraulics; coastal engineering; water management

хидротехнички -чка *adj* hydraulic-engineering *attrib.*; хидротехнички објекти water-conservation projects; flood-control projects

хидрофобија *f* 1 hydrophobia, fear of water 2 *Med.* hydrophobia, rabies

хидроцентрала *f* hydroelectric power station

хиена *f Zool.* (Hyaena) hy<a>ena (*also fig.*); *fig.* bloodsucker, jackal; пегава хиена spotted hyena

хиерархија *f* hierarchy; *fig., pejor.* pecking order; службеничката хиерархија official hierarchy; по хиерархија by hierarchy, on the basis of seniority

хиерархиски *adj* hierarchical

хиероглифи *pl* hieroglyphics (*also fig.*)

хиероглифски *adj* hieroglyphic (*also fig.*); хиероглифско писмо hieroglyphic script

хијат *m Phon.* hiatus

хилус *m Anat.* 1 hilum 2 chyle

хилусен -сна *adj Anat.* hilar; chyl<ace>ous; хилусни жлезди hilar glands

Хималаи *pl* the Himalayas

хималајски *adj* Himalayan

химен *m Anat.* hymen

химера *f* 1 *Myth.* Chim<a>era 2 *fig.* chimera, mirage

химеричен -чна *adj* chimeric<al>, wildly unrealistic; химерични желби fantastic desires

химна *f* hymn, anthem; народна (национална) химна national anthem; химна на мирот a hymn of peace; ❏ пее химни (*за некого*) to sing (*s.o.'s*) praises

хинин *m* quinine, *see* кинин

хининов *adj* quinine *attrib.*; cinchona *attrib.*; хининово дрво cinchona tree

хипер- (*in compounds*) hyper-

хипербола[1] *f Literature* hyperbole, exaggeration

хипербола[2] *f Geom.* hyperbola

хиперболика *f Literature* (*cf.* хипербола[1]) hyperbolism, exaggeration

хиперболичен[1] -чна *adj Literature* hyperbolic<al>; хиперболичен израз hyperbolic<al> expression

хиперболичен[2] -чна *adj Geom.* hyperbolic; хиперболични функции hyperbolic functions

хиперболички *adj see* хиперболичен[1]

хиперболично *adv* hyperbolically; ликот е претставен хиперболично the character is presented hyperbolically

хиперболичност *f* hyperbolical quality, hyperbolism; хиперболичноста на неговите аргументи his hyperbolic style of argument

хиперболоид *m Geom.* hyperboloid

хиперманган *m* permanganate

хиперпродукција *f* overproduction; oversupply

хипертензија *f* 1 *Med.* hypertension, high blood pressure 2 *fig.* hypertension, extreme tension

хипертонија *f Med.* 1 (*на крвниот притисок*) hypertension, high blood pressure 2 (*на мускулите*) hypertonia, hypertonicity

хипертоничен -чна *adj Med.* hypertensive; hypertonic; хипертоничен желудник hypertonic stomach

хипертрофија *f Med.* hypertrophy; хипертрофија на срцето hypertrophy of the heart

хипертрофиран *adj* hypertrophied, hypertrophic, enlarged; хипертрофиран бубрег hypertrophic kidney

хипноза *f* hypnosis; *fig.* mesmerism

хипнотизам -змот *m* hypnotism; hypnosis; *fig.* mesmerism

хипнотизер *m* hypnotist

хипнотизира *pf & impf* to hypnotize; *fig.* to mesmerize

хипнотички *adj* hypnotic; *fig.* mesmerizing; хипнотичка сила, состојба hypnotic power, state; хипнотичко влијание mesmerizing influence

хипо-[1] (*in compounds*) hypo-

хипо-[2] (*in compounds*) hippo-

хиподром *m* racecourse, racetrack; *Hist.* hippodrome

хипокористик -ци *m Gram.* hypocoristic

хипокористички *adj Gram.* hypocoristic; хипокористички збор hypocoristic word

хипокризија *f* hypocrisy, *see* лицемерство

хипокрит *m* hypocrite, *see* лицемер

хипокритски *adj* hypocritical, *see* лицемерен

хипоплексија *f Med.* apoplexy

хипопотам *m Zool.* hippopotamus

хипотеза *f* hypothesis; speculation; supposition

хипотека *f* mortgage

хипотекарен -рна *adj* mortgage *attrib.*; хипотекарна банка mortgage bank

хипотензија *f Med. see* хипотонија 1

хипотенуза *f Geom.* hypotenuse

хипотетичен -чна *adj* hypothetical; хипотетични судови hypothetical judgements; *Gram.* хипотетична реченица conditional clause

хипотетички & хипотетски *adj see* хипотетичен

хипотетично *adv* hypothetically

хипотетичност *f* hypothetical nature; хипотетичноста на неговите оцени the hypothetical quality of his assessments

хипотонија *f Med.* 1 (*на крвниот притисок*) hypotension, low blood pressure 2 (*на мускулите*) hypotonia, hypotonicity

хипотоничен -чна *adj Med.* hypotensive; hypotonic

хипофиза *f Anat.* hypophysis, pituitary gland

хипохондрија *f* hypochondria

хипохондрик -ци *m* hypochondriac

хипохондричен -чна *adj* hypochondriac<al>

хипоцентар -три *m* hypocentre

хирург -зи *m* surgeon

хирургија *f* surgery

хирургиски *adj see* хируршки

хируршки *adj* surgical; хируршка помош surgical help; хируршка интервенција surgical operation; хируршка клиника surgical clinic; хируршки нож scalpel, lancet

хисар *m arch.* castle, fort

хистерија *f* hysteria; падне во хистерија to go into hysterics

хисте́рик -ци *m* hysteric, hysterical person

хистеричен -чна *adj* hysterical; хистерична жена hysterical woman; хистерична смеа hysterical laughter

хистерички *adv see* хистерично

хистерично *adv* hysterically; се насмеа хистерично he laughed hysterically

хистеричност *f* hysterical quality/manner; hysteria

хистологија *f* histology

хистолошки *adj* histological; хистолошки испитувања histological research

хит *m* hit, hit song

хитон *m* (*старогрчка облека*) chiton

хит-парада *f colloq.* hit parade, top of the pops

хлор *m Chem.* chlorine

хлора́т *m Chem.* chlorate

хлорен -рна *adj* chlorine; хлорна вар chlorinated lime, chloride of lime, bleaching powder; хлорни соединенија chlorine compounds

хлори́д *m Chem.* chloride

хлори́ра *pf & impf* to chlorinate; хлорира вода to chlorinate water

хлороводород *m Chem.* hydrogen chloride

хлороводороден -дна *adj* hydrochloric; хлороводородна киселина hydrochloric acid

хлорофи́л *m* chlorophyll

хлорофо́рм *m Chem.* chloroform

хм *interj* (*often reduplicated and lengthened* хм-хм! хм-м! – *expressing doubt, hesitation, diffidence, irony, reflection, surprise, disapproval*) h'm, hum, hem

хмелен -лна *adj* hop *attrib.*; хмелно брашно hop meal (flour)

хмељ *m Bot.* (Humulus lupulus) (*растението*) hop vine; (*плодот*) hops; одгледување хмељ hop-growing; маја, квасец од хмељ hop yeast; берење хмељ hop-picking

хо *interj* (*often reduplicated and lengthened* хо-хо! хо-о!) **1** (*expressing surprise, satisfaction*) oho! aha! ho-o! хо-о! кој ни дошол на гости oho! look who's come to visit us! **2** (*representing laughter*) ho ho! ha! ha!

хоби *m & n* hobby; шахот му е хоби chess is his hobby

ходник -ци *m* corridor, passage; подземен ходник underground passage; *Mil., Mining* gallery; таен ходник secret passage

хокеар *m Sport.* hockey-player

хокеј *m Sport.* hockey; хокеј на мраз ice-hockey; хокеј на трева field hockey

хокејски *adj Sport.* hockey *attrib.*; хокејски клуб hockey club

хокуспокус *m* hocus-pocus

хол *m* hall<way>; vestibule; lobby

Холандија *f* Holland, the Netherlands

холандски *adj* Dutch, Netherlands *attrib.*

Холан́ганец -ни *m* Dutchman

Холан́ганка *f* Dutchwoman

холестеро́л *m Biochemistry* cholesterol

хомоген *adj* homogen<e>ous; хомогена организација homogeneous organization; хомогена целина homogeneous whole; хомогена влада homogeneous (one-party) government

хомогеност *f* homogeneity

хомологен -гна *adj* homologous; хомологни органи *Biol.* homologous organs; хомологен ред *Chem.* homologous order

хомони́м *m Ling.* homonym

хомони́мен -мна *adj Ling.* homonymous; хомонимни зборови homonymous words

хомосексуа́лен -лна *adj* homosexual; хомосексуални црти homosexual characteristics

хомосексуа́лец -лци *m* homosexual

хомосексуали́зам -змот *m* homosexuality

хомосексуа́лка *f* lesbian, *see* лезбејка

хомосексуа́лност *f* homosexuality

хомофонија *f Mus.* homophony

Хонгконг & Хонг Конг *m* Hong Kong

Хонгкон́ганец -ни *m* person from Hong Kong

Хонгкон́ганка *f* (*fem. form*) *see* Хонгкон́ганец

хонгкошки *adj* Hong Kong *attrib.*

Хондурас *m* Honduras

Хондурашанец -ни *m* Honduran

Хондурашанка *f* (*fem. form*) *see* Хондурашанец

хондурашки & хондурски *adj* Honduran

хонора́р *m* fee; payment; honorarium; авторски хонорар author's fee; (*за секоја продадена книга*) royalties; хонорар за прекувремена работа overtime payment

хонора́рен -рна *adj* **1** paid; fee-for-service *attrib.*; хонорарна работа freelance work **2** casual; part-time; хонорарен службеник casual employee; хонорарен предавач part-time lecturer

хонори́ра *pf & impf* **1** to pay a fee/honorarium (*for*); to remunerate; статиите се хонорираат fees are paid for the articles **2** to appreciate, recognize; го хонорираа со пофалница за долгогодишна работа they recognized his long service with a certificate of merit **3** *Comm.* to honour (*a cheque*)

хор *m* **1** (*in ancient Greek drama*) chorus **2** (*певачки колектив*) choir; аматерски хор amateur choir; детски хор children's choir; мешан хор mixed choir; црковен хор church choir **3** *Mus.* (*песна*) chorus; хор од операта "Продадена невеста" a chorus from the opera *The Bartered Bride*; ❑ зборува во хор to speak in chorus

хоре́ј -еи *m Prosody* trochee

хоризо́нт *m* horizon (*also fig.*); skyline; *fig.* perspective, outlook; видлив хоризонт visible horizon; се скри зад хоризонтот he disappeared below the horizon; на хоризонтот ништо не се гледаше on the horizon nothing was visible; дојде од странство со раширени хоризонти he arrived from abroad with broadened horizons; се отворија нови хоризонти new perspectives opened up; ❑ се појави на хоризонтот to appear on the horizon; исчезне од хоризонтот to disappear from view (the public eye)

хоризонта́ла *f* horizontal <line>; (*на карта*) contour line; по хоризонталата horizontally; in the horizontal plane

хоризонта́лен -лна *adj* horizontal; (*рамен*) flat, level; хоризонтална линија horizontal line; хоризонтална оска horizontal axis; *Math.* x-axis; хоризонтална положба horizontal position; ❑ хоризонтална (кадровска) ротација rotation of personnel

хоризонта́лно *adv* horizontally, in a horizontal position; (*во крстословка*) across

хори́ст *m* chorister

хори́стка *f* (*fem. form*) *see* хорист

хормо́н *m* Biochemistry hormone

хормонски *adj* hormonal; hormone *attrib.*; хормонски таблети hormone pills; хормонско пореметување hormonal disorder

хорна *f* Mus. <French> horn

хорни́ст *m* Mus. horn player, bugler

хорографија *f* chorography, topography

хороскоп *m* horoscope

хорски[1] *adj* choral; хорска група choral group; хорска рецитација choral recital; хорско пеење choral singing

хорски[2] *adv* in chorus, at the same time; одговараат хорски they answer in chorus

хортензија *f* Bot. (Hydrangea macrophylla) hortensia, hydrangea

хортикултура *f* horticulture, *cf.* градинарство, цвеќарство

хоругва *f* Rel. banner

хоспита́нт *m* attendant at observation (demonstration) classes; observer at lessons

хоспитација *f* observation, attendance at observation (demonstration) classes; attendance at classes as an observer

хоспити́ра *impf* to attend observation (demonstration) classes; to attend lessons as an observer

хотел *m* hotel; отседна в хотел, појде на хотел to stay at a hotel, go to a hotel

хотелие́р *m* hotel-keeper; hotel owner (proprietor), hotelier

хотелие́рка *f* (*fem. form*) *see* хотелиер

хотелие́рски *adj* hotel-keeper's; hotel owner's (proprietor's), hotelier's; hotel-industry *attrib.*

хотелие́рство *n* hotel management, the hotel business; hotel/tourist industry

хотелски *adj* hotel *attrib.*; хотелска соба hotel room

хохштаплер *m* impostor, fraud, phony; swindler, con man; snob, status-seeker; adventurer

хохштаплерка *f* (*fem. form*) *see* хохштаплер

хохштаплерски *adj* phony; хохштаплерска постапка fraud, confidence trick; snobbish act

хоџа *m* khoja, *see* оџа

хоџабашија -ии *m dial. arch. see* коџабашија

храбар -бра *adj* brave, courageous, valiant; храбар човек a brave man; лудо храбар audacious; rash, foolhardy; даваше храбар вид he made a courageous impression; he put a brave face on it

храбрец *m literary* brave person, hero, man of mettle

храбри *impf* I to inspire, encourage; to urge on, embolden; со својот пример тој ги храбреше своите луѓе by his example he would rally his men II – ce to take (pluck up) courage, steel o.s.

храбро *adv* bravely, courageously; сите се држеа храбро they all behaved bravely; само храбро напред courage! *colloq.* keep your chin up! храбро се бори to put up a good fight

храброст *f* courage, bravery, valour; немаше храброст да го стори тоа he did not have the courage (*colloq.* nerve, guts) for it; орден (медал) за храброст order (medal) for valour; собира храброст to muster (screw up) courage

храм *m* 1 temple, church, place of worship; биле ограбени сите храмови all the places of worship were desecrated 2 church festival (*in honour of its patron saint*); на манастирот храмот му бил Св. Никола the monastery's feast-day was St Nicholas's day 3 *fig.* temple; храм на културата a temple of culture

храна *f* food, nourishment; снабди со храна to provide with food; го прими на стан и храна he gave him food and lodgings (bed and board); млечна храна dairy food<s>; сточна (добиточна) храна stock feed, fodder; сува храна dried food<s>; резерви <од> храна reserves of food; здрава храна healthy food (fare); душевна (духовна) храна spiritual nourishment; ❑ топовска храна cannon fodder

хранарина *f* meal allowance; deduction for meals; *Sport.* food supplement

храненик -ци *m see* хранениче

храненица *f* foster-daughter

хранениче *n* foster-child

хранење *n from* храни (се); хранењето на детето feeding the child; вештачко хранење bottle-feeding; artificial/intravenous feeding; force-feeding; хранење со лажиче spoon-feeding; хранењето на семејството supporting the family

хранет *pt* fed; nourished, sustained; fattened, fatted; хранета стока fat<tened> cattle; store (fattening) cattle; само со шеќер хранета fed on sugar alone

храни *impf* I 1 to feed *trans.*; храни добиток to feed the cattle; храни вештачки to bottle-feed; to feed intravenously; to force-feed; храни куче да те лае *prov.* don't bite the hand that feeds you! 2 *fig.* to support, sustain, maintain; татко му уште го храни his father is still supporting him; дуќанот нè хранеше the shop kept us; учителството ме храни teaching keeps the wolf from the door II – ce 1 to eat; to feed (*on s.th.*) *intrans.*; *Mil.* to mess together; се хранеше само со риба he ate only fish; се храни диетално to be on a diet; се храни в ресторан to take one's meals in a restaurant; веќе сама се храни she can feed herself now 2 *fig.* to earn one's living, make a living; работеше и се хранеше he worked and earned a living; се храни со својата пот to make a living by the sweat of one's brow

хранилиште *n arch.* depository, depot, storehouse, repository; (*на мошти*) feretory

хранител *m* 1 bread-winner, provider, sustainer 2 guardian, foster-parent 3 *arch.* defender, protector; ангел-хранител guardian angel

хранителен -лна *adj* 1 food *attrib.*; хранителни продукти foodstuffs; *see* прехранбен 2 nutritious, nourishing; јајцата се многу хранителни eggs are very nourishing; *see* хранлив

хранителка *f* (*fem. form*) *see* хранител

хранителност *f see* хранливост

хранлив *adj* nutritious, nourishing; хранливи сокови nourishing juices; *Biol.* nutrients; млекото е мошне хранлив производ milk is a very nourishing product; хранливи материи nutrients; хранлива средина culture medium, nutrient medium; хранлив раствор nutrient solution

хранливост *f* nutritiousness, nutritional value, food value; хранливоста на зеленчукот и на овошјето the nutritional value of fruit and vegetables; слаба хранливост poor nutritional value

храновод & **хранопровóд** *m Anat.* gullet, oesophagus; заболување на хранопроводот infection of the oesophagus

Хрват *m* Croat<ian>

Хрватка *f* (*fem. form*) *see* Хрват

Хрватска *f* Croatia

хрватски *adj* Croatian

хрема *f* cold in the head

хремав *adj* suffering from a cold <in the head>; with a runny nose

хрестоматија -ии *f* chrestomathy, reader

хризантéма *f Bot.* (Chrysanthemum) chrysanthemum

хрисовул *m Hist.* royal decree

христијанизација *f* Christianization, baptism

христијанизи́ра *pf* & *impf* **I** to baptize; to convert to Christianity *trans.*; to Christianize *trans.*; тогаш беа христијанизирани сите племиња што живееја таму at that time all the tribes living there were baptized **II** – **се** to be baptized; to convert to Christianity *intrans.*; to become <a> Christian; *see* покрсти (се)

христијанин -јани *m* Christian

христијáнка *f* (*fem. form*) *see* христијанин

христијáнски *adj* Christian; христијанска црква Christian church; христијанската наука Christian Science; по христијанските закони according to the laws of Christianity; христијанскиот свет Christendom

христијáнски *adv* as a Christian, in a Christian way; се држи христијански he behaves as a Christian

христијáнство *n* **1** Christianity, Christian religion; Christian faith; проповеда христијанство to preach Christianity **2** Christendom; сето христијанство стана против тоа the whole of Christendom rose against that

христољу́бец -пци *m arch.* pious (God-fearing) person; *cf.* богољубец

христољу́бив *adj* pious, God-fearing; *cf.* богољубен

хром *m Chem.* chromium, chrome

хромати́зам -змот *m* **1** *Phys.* chromatism **2** *Mus.* chromatic scale

хроматичен -чна *adj Phys., Mus.* chromatic; хроматични интервали chromatic intervals

хромен -мна *adj* chromium, chrome *attrib.*; хромни соединенија chromium compounds; хромна руда chromite

хроми́ра *pf* & *impf* to chromium-plate; to plate/coat with chromium

хроми́ран *pt* chromium-plated; хромиран сад chromium-plated vessel

хромов *adj see* хромен

хромозóм *m Biochemistry* chromosome

хромолитографија *f* **1** chromolithography **2** chromolithograph

хроника *f* **1** *Hist.* chronicle; средновековните хроники the medi<a>eval chronicles **2** *Literature* chronicle; saga; семејна хроника family saga **3** *Journalism* news in brief; report; спортска хроника sports news, sporting round-up; судска хроника court report **4** *Film* chronicle; newsreel

хроничар *m* chronicler, historian; annalist, diarist

хроничарски *adj* chronicle *attrib.*; chronicler's

хроничен -чна *adj* chronic; хронично воспаление chronic inflammation; хроничен бронхитис chronic bronchitis

хронички *adj see* хроничен

хроничност *f* chronic character; хроничноста на воспалението chronic character of the inflammation

хронологија *f* chronological record; time sequence; (*наука*) chronology; Грците од таа година почнале да ја водат својата хронологија the Greeks began to keep their historical records from that year on; the Greeks began to trace their history from that year on

хронолошки[1] *adj* chronological; хронолошки датуми chronological dates; по хронолошки ред in chronological order

хронолошки[2] *adv* in chronological order; настаните беа дадени хронолошки the events were presented in chronological order

хрономéтар -три *m* chronometer, master-clock; *Sport.* stop-watch

хубертус *m* loden coat

хула *f literary* insult; blasphemy; грозна хула terrible insult; grave blasphemy

хулахоп *m* **1** hula hoop **2** хулахоп чорапи, хулахопки pantihose

хули *impf literary* to blaspheme; не хули <на> Бога do not commit blasphemy! *see* ули

хулител *m literary* blasphemer, *see* улител

хулник -ци *m literary see* хулител, улител

хуман *adj* humane; kind; compassionate; хуман човек humane person; хумани постапки humane deeds; хумани цели humane goals

хумани́зам -змот *m* **1** *Hist.* Humanism **2** humanism; социјалистички хуманизам socialist humanism

хумани́ст *m* **1** *Hist.* Humanist **2** humanist

хуманистички *adj* humanist *attrib.*; humanistic

хумани́стка *f* (*fem. form*) *see* хуманист

хуманитáрен -рна *adj* **1** humanistic; humanist *attrib.*; хуманитарно образование humanistic education, the liberal arts; хуманитарни науки the humanities; the classics **2** *rare* humanitarian; хуманитарна акција humanitarian action

хумано *adv* humanely; kindly; compassionately; постапува хумано со сите he treats everyone kindly

хуманост *f* humaneness, humanity; kindness; compassion

хумор *m* **1** humour; има голема смисла за хумор he has a great sense of humour; добродушен, лесен хумор kind, gentle humour **2** humorous contribution/interlude; sketch; funny story; хумор и сатира humour and satire

хуморéска *f* **1** sketch; funny (humorous) story **2** *Mus.* humoresque; музичка хумореска humoresque

хумори́ст *m* humorist; comic

хумористика *f literary* humorous literature (writing)

хумористичен -чна *adj* humorous, comical; хумористичен тон humorous tone; хумористичен расказ funny story

хумористички *adj* comic; хумористички театар comedy theatre

хумористично *adv* humorously, comically, in a humorous vein/spirit

хумори́стка *f* (*fem. form*) *see* хуморист

хумус *m* humus

хумусен -сна *adj* humus *attrib.*, rich in humus; хумусна почва humus-rich soil

хунта *f* junta; воена хунта military junta

хуриет *m colloq. obs.* freedom, liberation, emancipation

хурија -ии *f* houri

хусар *m* hussar

хусарски *adj* hussar *attrib.*; хусарски полк hussar regiment

цајтнот *m Chess* time trouble, lack of time (*also fig.*); се наоѓа во цајтнот to be short of time

цак *interj* click! clack! ping! цак! пукна нешто во моторот click! something snapped in the engine

цака *f colloq.* trick, dodge, knack; ways, style; не му ja знае цаката (*за лице*) he doesn't know his ways; (*за нешто*) he doesn't have the hang of it

цакне *pf* цакна *aor.* **1** *intrans.* to click, clack; ❏ пукнало, цакнало! *curse* I hope it blows up! **2** *trans. fig.* to hit; to smack, *colloq.* whack; го цакнал малу момченцето he slapped the little boy

цакнува *impf* to go click

цакумпакум *adv* all together

цанцаре *n Bot.* (Cucurbita ovifera) courgette, *Am., Austral.* zucchini, *see* гргуле 1

цап[1] *m dial.* (*japeц*) billy-goat

цап[2] *interj* splash! plop!

цапа *impf* **1** to tread; to wade **2** *see* цапне 2 & 3

цапалка *f* (*стапалка*) <foot>step; гази по цапалките to follow s.o., tread in s.o.'s footsteps

цапне *pf* цапна *aor.* **1** to step, tread; цапне во кал to step in mud **2** to leave dirty marks; цапнаа по килимот they left dirty marks on the rug **3** *fig., colloq.* to put one's foot in it, blot one's copybook; пак jac цапнав I have put my foot in it again **4** to tread, set foot; една деценија човечка нога не цапнала во дворот for a decade no one has set foot in the yard

цапнува *impf of* цапне

цапоти *impf see* цапа 1

цапутка *impf dim. of* цапа

цар -еви, -ови *m* emperor; king (*also fig.*); lord (*also fig.*); *Chess* king; турски цар Turkish Emperor; руски цар Russian Tsar (Czar); си бил еднаш еден цар once upon a time there was a king; честити царе Your Majesty! ❏ живее како цар to live like a lord; цар далеку, Бог високо between the devil and the deep blue sea; you're on your own; царот на мувите lord of the flies; што нема и царот не jaдe any port in a storm; one has to cut one's coat according to one's cloth; make the best of it; каде царот оди пеш<ки> lavatory, toilet; цар на животните king of beasts; *Zool.* змиски цар boa constrictor; на царот данокот, на попот колакот *prov.* render unto Caesar that which is Caesar's and unto God that which is God's; сред слепи и ќорав е цар *prov.* in the country of the blind the one-eyed man is king

царев *adj* emperor's; king's; lord's; царев син emperor's son, prince; царева војска the emperor's army; царевиот имот emperor's lands (property, estate)

царевен -вна *adj* (*пченкарен*) maize, *Am.*, *Austral.* corn *attrib.*; царевен леб corn-bread; царевно брашно maize meal, maizina, cornflour

царевина¹ *f* empire, *see* царство

царевина² *f dial. see* царевка

царевица *f dial. see* царевка, пченка

царевка *f Bot.* (*растението*) (Zea mays) maize, Indian corn, *Am.*, *Austral.* sweet corn; (*плодот*) corn-cob; maize kernels; ги копаат царевките they are hoeing the maize; *see* пченка

царевковина *f* (*пченковина*) maize (*Am.* corn) stalk

царевница *f* (*пченка<р>ник*) corn-bread, Indian bread

царее *impf see* цари, царува

цари *impf see* царува; цареле цареви emperors reigned

Цариград *m* Constantinople

цариградски *adj* of/from Constantinople

царѝзам -змот *m* tsarism, czarism

царина *f* customs; customs duty; подлежи на царина it is dutiable (liable to customs duty); ослободува од царина to exempt from duty; ослободено од царина duty-free

царинарница *f* customs post, custom-house

царини *impf* to charge (levy) duty (*on*); to assess the duty (*on*); не ми ја царинеа машината they did not charge me duty on the machine

цариник -ци *m* customs officer

царински *adj* customs *attrib.*; царински преглед customs inspection; царинска тарифа customs duty (tariff)

царѝст *m* tsarist, czarist

царистички *adj* tsarist, czarist *attrib.*; царистичка Русија Tsarist Russia

царица *f* (*сопруга на цар или жена цар*) empress; (*in Russia*) Tsarina, Czarina; *Chess, fig.* queen; царот и царицата the Emperor and the Empress; за време на владеењето на царица Елеонора during Empress Eleonora's reign; царица на цвеќињата the queen of flowers; царица на балот the queen of the ball; ❑ a царица, а магарица in the dark all cats are grey; Ѓупката и царица да биде, па ќе проси *prov.* it is harder to change human nature than to change rivers and mountains; се фатила царица за работа, па ѝ се исприштиле рацете *prov.* manual work isn't for everyone

царичин *adj* empress's; царичин прстен the Empress's ring

царски¹ *adj* emperor's; imperial (*also fig.*); regal, royal; kingly; царски двор<ец> the Emperor's palace; царска круна the Emperor's crown; царски престол imperial throne; царска титула emperor's title; царски указ imperial/royal decree; царска власт monarchy; царски род the imperial line/family; царско величество imperial/regal majesty; царски довереник a confidant of the Emperor; царската влада His Majesty's government; царска Русија Imperial (Tsarist) Russia; царски подарок regal gift; царско јадење a dish fit for a king; ❑ неговото/нејзиното царско величество His/Her Majesty; *Chem.* царска вода aqua regia; *Med.* царски рез Caesarean section

царски² *adv* like a lord, splendidly; живееле царски и господарски they lived in grand style

царство *n* 1 empire; kingdom; realm; македонското царство the <ancient> Macedonian empire; римското царство the Roman Empire; турското царство the Turkish (Ottoman) Empire; ❑ *Rel.* земно и небесно царство the earthly and heavenly kingdom<s> 2 reign; <reins of> power; за време на царството на цар Александар in the reign of Alexander the Great; му го предаде царството he handed him the reins of power; му мина (сврши) царството his day is done 3 *fig.* kingdom, realm, world; животинско царство the animal kingdom; растително царство the vegetable kingdom; царство на сказните in the realm of fiction (stories); ❑ во царството на соништата in the land of Nod

царува *impf* to reign (*also fig.*), rule; to prevail, hold sway; кога царувал цар Константин in the reign of Emperor Constantine; царува длабока тишина complete silence reigns

царување *n* reign; царувањето на цар Самоил Emperor Samuel's rule (reign); во текот на неговото царување during his reign

царче *n dim. of* цар; родила царче she gave birth to a little prince

царштина *f* 1 *colloq.* empire; kingdom, realm; во нашава царштина in this kingdom of ours 2 *colloq.* reign; му дојде царштината негова he came to the throne 3 *arch.* tax<es>

цацка *impf dial.* 1 (*за дрва*) to hew, hack, chop; цацка дрва to chop wood 2 (*за месо, зеленчук и сл.*) to chop <up>, dice *trans.*; цацка месо to dice (*mince*) meat

цацко *m colloq.* devil; the Devil; ❑ го дупнал цацко the Devil put him up to it; кој цацко те тераше? what <the devil> got into you? му влегол цацко the Devil got into him; he kicked over the traces; цацко го бараше? who/what the devil (hell) were you looking for? цацко ќе го знае the Devil only knows! who <the hell> knows?

цванцик -ци *m* 1 *arch.* twenty-kreutzer coin; ❑ немам ни цванцик I haven't got a penny, *Am.* I don't have a red cent 2 *fig.* (*кепец, џуџе*) dwarf, midget

цвекло *n Bot.* (Beta vulgaris) beetroot, *Am.* red beet

цвекне *pf* цвекна *aor.* 1 *intrans.* to clink, jingle, jangle 2 *trans.* to hit; to smack; го цвекнал по глава he cracked him on the head; *see* свекне

цвет *m* 1 flower; blossom; липов цвет lime blossom; *see* цут 2 *fig.* (*usu. with article*) elite, pick, cream; цветот на интелигенцијата the flower (cream) of the intelligentsia 3 *fig.* blossom, bloom, prime; во цветот на младоста in the blush of youth; во цветот на годините in the prime of life, in one's prime; во цветот на силите at the peak of one's powers

цветеж *m poet.* blossom<ing>, blooming, flowerage; во пролетен цветеж in vernal blossom

цветен¹ -тна *adj* 1 flower *attrib.*; floral; цветен прав pollen; цветна круничка floral crown, corolla 2 flowery, flowered; цветна ливада flowery meadow; цветна леа flower-bed

цветен² -тна *adj* (*cf.* Цветници) Palm Sunday *attrib.*; Цветна недела Palm Sunday; Цветен петок Friday before Palm Sunday

цветење *n from* цвети; време на цветење flowering/blossom season; efflorescence; цветење на праските season of peach-tree blossom

цветец *m dim. of* цвет blossom, floweret; *Bot.* floret

цвети *impf* **1** (*see* цути) to blossom, bloom, flower (*also fig.*); цвеќиња цветат flowers are blooming; цветат веќе ружите the roses are already in flower; лицето ѝ цветеше како цвеќе her face was radiant; ❑ не им цветаат ружи life is not a bed of roses for them **2** *fig.* to thrive; to flourish, prosper; претпријатието цвети the firm is flourishing

цветне *pf poet.* цветна *aor.* **1** to burst into blossom, flower; памукот цветна the cotton flowered **2** *fig.* to bloom; во дните нови животот цветна life blossomed in the new times; *see* расцвета, расцвети, расцути

цветник -ци *m* flower garden, *see* цвеќник, цвеќарник

Цветници *pl Rel.* Palm Sunday

цветнува *impf of* цветне

цветоносен -сна *adj* flowering, flower-bearing, *Bot.* floriferous; цветоносни растенија flowering plants

цветче *n dim. of* цвет, *see* цветец

цвеќар *m* **1** florist; (*уличен*) flower-seller; (*лице што одгледува цвеќиња*) flower-grower, floriculturalist **2** flower-lover

цвеќарка *f* (*fem. form*) flower-girl, *see* цвеќар

цвеќарник -ци *m* flower garden; nursery garden; glass-house

цвеќарница *f* **1** (*дуќан*) flower-shop, florist's <shop> **2** *see* цвеќарник

цвеќарски *adj* florist's; цвеќарски занает florist's trade; цвеќарски дуќан florist's shop

цвеќарство *n* flower trade; floriculture

цвеќе -иња, *coll.* цвеќе *n* **1** flower<s>; цвеќињата уште не развиле the flowers have not yet come out; одгледува цвеќиња to grow flowers; планинско, полско, собно цвеќе alpine, wild, indoor flowers; венец од цвеќиња floral wreath; букет од цвеќиња bouquet; вештачки и природни цвеќиња artificial and fresh flowers; ❑ твојата мака е цвеќе според мојата your problem is nothing compared with mine; и тој не е цвеќе <за мирисање, да го помирисаш> he is a skunk too; цвеќето се бере дури е росно gather ye rosebuds while ye may, make hay while the sun shines; како цвеќе без вода all forlorn; со едно цвеќе лето не иде *prov.* one swallow doesn't make a summer **2** *colloq.* <woman's> period **3** *colloq.* (*мали сипаници*) measles

цвеќенце *n dim. of* цвеќе

цвеќник -ци *m see* цвеќарник

цвеќуле *n dim. of* цвеќе, *see* цвеќенце

цвик *m* (*сурутка*) whey

цвикери *pl* **1** pince-nez **2** *colloq.* specs

цвикне *pf* цвикна *aor.* **1** *intrans.* to clink, clang, jingle, jangle; герданот ми цвикна my necklace clinked **2** *trans.* to hit; to smack; *see* свекне

цвикнува *impf of* цвикне, *see* свекнува

цвиковина *f* whey-like substance

цвилба *f* whinny<ing>; whining; screeching; wailing, wail<s>

цвили *impf* **1** (*за коњ*) to whinny; (*за куче*) to whine **2** (*за птици*) to screech, squawk; to peep; во гнездото цвилеа малите орлиња the little eaglets were screeching in the nest **3** *fig.* to lament, <weep and> wail; to whine; цвили старата за синот the old woman is mourning for her son; цвили за секоја ситница he whinges about every trifle **4** (*за змија*) to hiss

цвилне *pf* цвилна *aor. see* цвили

цвилнува *impf of* цвилне

цвителен -лна *adj f.p.* (*светликав, светкав*) bright; twinkling; glittering; зацвитлела ми, зацвитлела ми /цвителна звезда a bright star began to shine

цвитен -тна *adj f.p.* (*светол*) bright, shining; цвитно руво shining raiment

цвитка *f Zool.* (Lampyris noctiluca) firefly; glow-worm; *see* светулка[1]

цвитли *impf f.p.* (*светли*) to shine; to glow

цвитлив *adj f.p.* shiny, bright, gleaming, nitid

цвичи *impf* (*за куче*) to whine, yelp; (*за прасе*) to squeal; *see* квичи

цволи *impf dial.* (*'рти*) to germinate; to sprout, bud

цволка *f dial.* (*'ркулец*) germ, embryo; shoot, bud

цврка *impf see* цвркоти 1

цвркот *m* chirp<ing>, chirrup, cheep, twitter, peep; врабечки цвркот twitter of sparrows

цвркотен -тна *adj poet.* chirruping, twittering; цвркотни пилци twittering birds

цвркоти *impf* **1** to chirrup, chirp, cheep, twitter, peep; врапчињата едностојно цвркотеа the little sparrows twittered continually **2** *fig., poet.* to warble, chirrup; срце во град му цвркоти his heart is singing in his breast

цвркотник -ци *m poet.* chirruping (twittering) bird; над нив шират цвркотници лет twittering birds circle above them

цвркотница *f see* цвркот; се слушаше цвркотница a twitter <of birds> could be heard

цврст *adj* **1** firm; sturdy, robust; hard; solid; sound; од цврсто дрво of hardwood; на цврста почва on firm ground; цврста прегратка firm embrace; цврст сон sound sleep **2** *Chem.* solid; цврсти тела solids **3** firm, steady, stable; цврст стол a steady (firm) chair **4** *fig.* firm, resolute; цврста волја firm will; цврсто решение firm decision; цврст карактер firm character; цврста рака a firm hand

цврстина *f* firmness; sturdiness, robustness; hardness; solidity; steadiness

цврсто *adv* firmly, steadily; стегни го јажето цврсто make the rope fast! масата стои цврсто the table is standing steady; верува цврсто во него he believes firmly in him; држи цврсто to grasp firmly; се држеше цврсто he was holding on tight; he was holding fast; цврсто граден thickset (stocky); цврсто ја прегрна he hugged her tight; цврсто спие to sleep soundly

цврстота *f* firmness; sturdiness, robustness; hardness; solidity; steadiness; *see* цврстина

цврцалче *n* spout; шишенце со цврцалче a little flask with a drinking spout

цврцка *impf colloq.* (*пивка*) to tipple, drink a little; to nip; секој ден си цврцкаше he used to drink every day

цврцнат *adj & pt colloq.* tipsy

цврцне *pf* цврцна *aor. colloq.* (*пивне*) to take a nip; цврцне една ракија to have a <nip of> brandy; цврцне од нога to have a drink standing up; убаво си цврцнал, ти се познава по лицето you've had a few drinks, one can tell from your face

цврцнува *impf colloq.* (*пивнува*) *of* цврцне, *see* цврцка; си цврцнува ракија he often has a glass of brandy

цврчи *impf see* цркоти 1 & црцори 1

цевка *f* **1** (*од разбој*) cone, bobbin, spool; моташе цевки she was winding thread on to spools **2** pipe; tube; reed; valve; (*на клуч*) shank; железна цевка <metal> pipe; оловна цевка lead pipe; стаклена цевка glass pipe; цевка за дишење breathing tube; snorkel; пие со цевка to drink through a straw; to be fed through a tube; водоводна цевка water pipe; (*подземна*) water main; одводна цевка drainpipe; издувна цевка exhaust pipe; одливна цевка overflow pipe; вентилациона цевка ventilation duct; флуоресцентна цевка fluorescent light tube; катодна цевка cathode ray tube; триодна цевка triode <valve> **3** (*на оружје*) barrel; ❑ *colloq.* ќе дувне в цевка he's going to be done in, his number's up

цевче *n dim. of* цевка

цегер *m* shopping bag

цедалка *f* strainer; colander

цеди *impf* **I 1** to strain *trans.*, sieve; цеди млеко to strain milk **2** to squeeze *trans.*; to wring out; цеди лимон to squeeze a lemon; цеди мед to extract honey; цеди алишта to wring out clothes **3** *fig.* to be very exacting; to test rigorously, grill *trans.*; to put (*s.o.*) through the hoops (wringer); професорот ги цедеше многу кандидатите the professor grilled the examinees **4** *fig.* to mutter; одвај ги цеди зборовите he speaks through clenched teeth **II – се** to drip, drop *intrans.*; водата се цедеше во садот the water dripped into the basin

цедилка *f* **1** *see* цедалка **2** cheesecloth **3** *dial.* baby sling

цедило *n* **1** cloth (*for covering dough while it is rising*) **2** *see* цедилка 2; ❑ остави на цедило to leave in the lurch; остане на цедило to be left in the lurch

цедилце *n dim. of* цедило, цедилка

цеѓ *f* (*пепелница*) lye, *obs.* buck, buck-water

цеѓалница *f see* цеѓ

цезура *f* **1** *Prosody* caesura **2** *Mus.* rest

Цејлон *m* Ceylon

Цејлонец -нци *m* Ceylonese

Цејлонка *f* (*fem. form*) *see* Цејлонец

цејлонски *adj* Ceylonese

цел¹ *f* **1** goal, aim, purpose, objective; intention; цел во животот aim in life; си ја постигна целта he achieved his goal; со каква цел? with what aim? со таа цел with that aim <in mind>; за таа цел for that purpose; благодарни, добротворни, хумани цели noble, charitable, humane objectives; со цел да се постигне нешто with the aim of achieving s.th., in order to achieve s.th.; остварува цел to attain one's end; цел <сам> по себе an end in itself; без цел aimlessly; ❑ животна цел mission in life; целта ги оправдува средствата the end justifies the means; има задни цели to have ulterior motives **2** *Mil., Sport.* target, mark; bull's-eye; finish; погоди во целта to hit the bull's-eye (*also fig.*); ја промаши целта to miss the target (mark) (*also fig.*); далеку од целта wide of the mark (*also fig.*); лесна цел an easy target; сите атлетичари пристигнаа заедно на целта all the runners reached the finish together

цел² *adj* **1** whole, untouched, intact; лебот остана цел the loaf was untouched; ми падна шишето и пак остана цело I dropped the bottle but it didn't break; ❑ цел-целеничок and цел-целеличок safe and sound, untouched, unscathed; as large as life **2** whole, entire; all; целиот собир ги прифати неговите предлози the entire meeting accepted his proposals; целиот град the whole town; цел ден all day; цела ноќ all night; ❑ цел божји ден the whole day long; цела вечност an eternity; for all of eternity **3** real; цел маж си станал you have become a real man **4** (*as a noun*) *n* 1. *literary* whole, unit, entity 2. *Math.* whole number, integer; едно цело и две десетти one point two

целвоѓле *n* staple fibre

целеличок -чка *adj see* целеничок

целеничок -чка *adj usu. in the expression*: цел-целеничок safe and sound, untouched, unscathed; as large as life

целер *m Bot.* (Apium graveolens) celery; celeriac; салата/супа со целер celery salad/soup

целесообразен -зна *adj* appropriate; expedient, advisable; целесообразни мерки/постапки appropriate measures/steps; целесообразно користење на средствата appropriate use of resources

целесообразно *adv* appropriately; средствата се користеа најцелесообразно the resources were used most appropriately

целесообразност *f* appropriateness

цели *impf* to aim (*at*); to be after, seek; не знам што целеше со тоа I don't know what he was trying to achieve with that; I don't know what he was driving at; целеше во групата he aimed at the group; целеше многу високо he was aiming very high (*also fig.*)

целибат *m* celibacy

целив *m poet. see* целув

целива (се) *impf of* целивне (се), *see* бацува (се)

целивка *f* (*бакнеж, бацувка*) kiss

целивне *pf* целивна *aor.* **I** to kiss *trans.*, give a kiss **II – се** to kiss *intrans.*; *see* бакне (се)

целивок -ци *m see* целивка

целина¹ *f see* целост

целина² *f* (*ледина, здравица*) virgin soil; разорана целина virgin soil upturned

целинка¹ *f dim. of* целина¹

целинка² *f dim. of* целина², *see* лединка

целисходен -дна *adj see* целесообразен

целисходно *adv see* целесообразно

целисходност *f see* целесообразност

цело *n* **1** *see* цел² 4 **2** *arch.* old coin, medallion

целовечерен -рна *adj* full-length; целовечерен филм full-length film, feature <film>

целовка *f see* целивка

целодневен -вна *adj* day, all-day, full-day, day-long *attrib.*; целодневен излет day-trip; целодневни вежби all-day exercises; целодневна градинка day-care centre

целокупен -пна *adj* complete; entire; целокупните дела the complete works; целокупното население the entire population

целокупно *adv* all <together>

целокупност *f* totality

целосен -сна *adj* (*полн*) **1** comprehensive, complete, all-embracing; full; *Philos., Psychol.* holistic; **целосен** преглед на настаните comprehensive review of the events; **целосен** успех complete success **2** mature, rounded, all-round, overall; **целосен** лик rounded character (*in a work of art*); **целосна** личност rounded personality

целосно *adv (наполно)* fully, completely; comprehensively, in an all-embracing fashion; извештајот беше разгледан **целосно** the report was examined comprehensively

целосност *f* completeness; comprehensiveness, all-embracing quality

целост *f* **1** whole, ensemble; entirety, wholeness, completeness, totality; завршена **целост** complete whole; во **целост** in full; in its entirety; земено во **целост** on the whole **2** (*see* цел[2] 4) unit; entity; integrity; територијална **целост** territorial unit; territorial integrity; *Phon.* акцентска **целост** accentual (stress) unit

целофа́н *m* cellophane

целофа́нски *adj* cellophane *attrib.*; **целофанска** хартија cellophane wrapping

целув *m poet.* (*бакнеж*) kiss

целува (се) *impf dial. see* целива (се), бацува (се)

целувка *f rare see* целув, бакнеж

целуло́за *f* cellulose; pulp

целуло́зен -зна *adj* cellulose *attrib.*; **целулозна** хартија cellulose paper

целуло́йд *m* celluloid

целуло́йден -дна *adj* celluloid *attrib.*

цемент *m* cement; фабрика за **цемент** cement factory

цементен -тна *adj* cement *attrib.*; **цементен** сид cement wall

цементи́ра *pf & impf* to cement (*also fig.*); *fig.* to solidify, consolidate

цементи́ран *pt* cemented; куќа со **цементиран** двор house with a cemented yard; нашето братство е **цементирано** со крв our brotherhood has been cemented with blood

цена *f* **1** price; cost; charge; високи и ниски **цени** high and low prices; набавна **цена** purchase price; по намалени **цени** at reduced prices, at a discount; набивање на **цените** driving up prices; паѓање на **цените** drop (fall) in prices; покачување на **цените** price rise; increasing prices; последна **цена** best (final) price; продажна **цена** selling price; фабричка **цена** factory (ex works) price; утврдени **цени** fixed prices; максимални **цени** ceiling prices; пазарна **цена** market price; малопродажна **цена** retail price; ❑ на **цена** е it is in demand/vogue; нема **цена** it is priceless; по никоја **цена** not at any price, not for anything; under no circumstances; по секоја **цена** at any price (cost); по **цена** на . . . for (at) the price of . . .; по **цена** на животот at the cost of one's life; продава под **цена** to sell cut-price **2** (*only sg*) value, worth; животот немаше никаква **цена** за нив life had no value for them; неговото мислење нема **цена** за мене his opinion is of no value to me; си ја знае **цената** he knows his worth

ценач *m* valuer, valuator; appraiser; assessor

ценет *adj* **1** valuable; **ценета** кожа valuable hide **2** *fig.* appreciated, valued, dear; esteemed, respected; **ценетиот** профессор the highly regarded professor **3** highly valued; во вашето **ценето** писмо in your

kind/esteemed letter; **ценета** соработка highly valued cooperation

ценз *m* **1** *Hist.* census (*in ancient Rome for taxation purposes*) **2** census (*for demographic study*) **3** qualification, right, entitlement

цензор *m* censor (*also Hist.*)

цензорски *adj* censor's; **цензорски** права censor's rights

цензорство *n* censor's position

цензу́ра *f* censorship (*also Roman Hist.*); censor's office; **цензурата** го забрани филмот the censor (censor's office) banned the film

цензу́рен -рна *adj* censorship *attrib.*; **цензурни** услови censorship conditions

цензури́ра *pf & impf* to censor; во воено време се **цензурираат** писмата in times of war letters are subject to censorship

цензус *m see* ценз

цени *impf* **1** to value, assess; to estimate, appraise; еднакво ги **ценеше** сите производи he put the same value/price on all the products; штетата ја **цена** на неколку милиони денари they put (estimated) the damage at several million denars; ❑ **цени** од око to give a rough estimate **2** to appreciate, esteem <highly>; to treasure; високо **цени** некого to have a very high opinion of s.o.; добрите дела секој ги **цени** everyone appreciates good deeds; го **ценеа** како професор they regarded him highly as a professor; ја **ценам** твојата помош I appreciate your help

ценка се *pf* to haggle

ценовник -ци *m* price-list; (*за автобуски, железнички карти*) list of fares; **ценовник** на услугите tariff, scale of charges; максимиран **ценовник** inflated price-list

ценост *f literary, arch.* (*вредност, драгоценост*) value

цент *m* cent

цента *f* **1** *see* цент **2** hundredweight (112 lb. = 50.8 kg.); (*квинтал*) quintal (100 lb. *or* 100 kg.); метричка **цента** quintal (100 kg.)

центар -три *m* centre, middle; focus; *Sport.* (*кошарка*) centre; (*фудбал – центарфор*) centre forward; **центар** на круг centre of a circle; во **центарот** на градот in the city centre, *Am.* downtown; културен **центар** cultural centre; трговски **центар** shopping centre, *Am., Austral.* mall; телевизиски **центар** TV centre; индустриски **центар** industrial centre/heartland; стопански **центар** centre of trade; ❑ *Anat.* **центар** на рамнотежата centre of balance, inner ear; **центар** на вниманието centre (focus) of attention

центарфо́р *m Sport.* centre forward

центарха́лф *m Sport.* centre half

центаршу́т *m Sport.* centre <kick>

центра́ла *f* **1** head (main) office, headquarters; **централата** на фирмата беше во Скопје the head office of the firm was in Skopje **2** *colloq.* електрична **централа** power station **3** телефонска **централа** telephone exchange

централен -лна *adj* central, middle; focal; **централна** точка central point, mid-point; **централниот** дел на градот the city centre, central business district (CBD), *Am.* downtown; **централна** фигура central figure; **Централен** комитет Central Committee; **централно** греење central heating; *Anat.* **централен** нервен систем central nervous system

централи́зам -змот *m* centralism; ❑ *obs.* демократски централизам democratic centralism

централизаци́ја *f* centralization; централизација на капиталот centralization of capital

централизи́ра *pf & impf* to centralize; ја централизираат управата they are centralizing the administration

централизи́ран *pt* centralized; централизирано стопанство centralized economy

центра́лист *m* centralist

централисти́чки *adj* centralized; centralist *attrib.*; centralistic; централистичко раководење centralized administration; централистичка политика centralistic policy

ЦЕИ *abbr.* (*Централноевропска иницијатива*) Central European Initiative

центрипета́лен -лна *adj* centripetal; ❑ центрипетална сила centripetal force

центри́ра *pf & impf* **1** to centre, adjust *trans.*; to align, true <up>; центрира инструмент to adjust an instrument; центрира тркало to align a wheel **2** *Sport.* to centre; крилото убаво центрираше the wing<er> centred the ball beautifully

центрифу́га *f* centrifuge; (*за млеко*) <milk> separator; (*за мед*) extractor

центрифуга́лен -лна *adj* centrifugal; центрифугална машина centrifuge; ❑ центрифугална сила centrifugal force

центрума́ш *m Pol.* centrist; sympathizer/member of the Centre Party

центу́рија -ии *f Hist.* **1** century (*in the Roman Army*), 100 soldiers **2** (*in the Roman electorate*) century, 100 voters

центурио́н *m Hist.* centurion

цену́ва (се) *impf of* цени (се), *see* главува (се), пазарува (се)

цеп *m* **1** (*see* цепнатина) crack, chink; cleft; fissure; ѕирка низ цепови to peep through cracks **2** (*во облека*) slit; tear, rip

цепани́ца *f see* цепеница

цепа́ч *m* woodcutter; цепач на дрва woodcutter

цепели́н *m* airship, dirigible, zeppelin

цепени́ца *f* **1** <split> log, billet; куп цепеници a pile (heap) of logs **2** *fig. colloq.* lout, oaf, clod; цепеница беше и цепеница си остана once an oaf, always an oaf **3** *fig. colloq.* lanky fellow, *colloq.* beanpole

цепе́ње *n* **1** *from* цепи **2** *Phys., Biol.* fission; цепење на јадро nuclear fission; цепење на атом splitting the atom

це́пи *impf* **I** to cut, hew, chop, hack; to cleave, split *trans.*; to tear *trans.*; to sever *trans.*; to rend; *fig.* to plough, furrow; цепи дрва to chop wood; истрели ја цепеа ноќта shots rent the night; несогласиците ја цепат партијата the party is torn (riven) by discord; коработ ги цепеше мирните води the boat furrowed the peaceful waters; ❑ цепи влакно to split hairs; го цепи умот to rack one's brains; како ти цепи умот? what do you reckon? *dial.* цепи шамија to get divorced **II – се** to split *intrans.*; to cleave *intrans.*; to tear *intrans.*; платното убаво се цепи the material tears easily; партијата се цепеше на помали групи the party was disintegrating into smaller groups

цепивла́кно *m* hair-splitter, pedant, *colloq.* nit-picker

це́пка[1] *f see* цеп

це́пка[2] *impf dim. of* цепи **I** to splinter, sliver *trans.*; to chop up; цепка дрва to split firewood; to cut (chop) kindling; ми го цепка слободното време it cuts into my spare time **II – се** to split *intrans.*; to splinter, sliver *intrans.*; лесно се цепкаат дрвата the wood splits easily

це́плив *adj* cleavable; fissile; scissile; *Mineralogy* sectile

цепли́вост *f* fissility; scissility; *Mineralogy* sectility; цепливоста на кристалите the sectility of crystals

цепнати́на *f* crack, fissure, cleft; *Geol.* break, joint; (*во почва*) crevice; (*длабока во глечер*) crevasse

це́пне *pf* цепна *aor.* to chop, hack, hew; to split *trans.*

цепну́ва *impf of* цепне

цепу́тка *f see* цеп

цер[1] -ови, -је *m Bot.* (Quercus cerris) Turkey oak

цер[2] *m colloq.* (*лек*) remedy, cure; за неа веќе цер нема nothing can help her any more; ❑ нема ни за цер he doesn't have a blessed thing; there isn't a blessed thing

цера́да *f* (*платно*) oilcloth; (*облека на поморци*) oilskins; (*навлака на коли*) tarpaulin; canvas cover, canvas, tilt

церебра́лен -лна *adj Anat.* cerebral; церебрална парализа cerebral palsy

церемо́нија -ии *f* **1** ceremony; погребна церемонија burial (funeral) ceremony **2** (*usu. pl*) ceremony; тој не сака многу церемонии he does not much like ceremony; ❑ без церемонии without ceremony, informally; without further ado

церемонија́л *m* ceremonial

церемонија́лен -лна *adj* **1** ceremonial; official; церемонијален марш parade, march-past **2** *fig.* formal, ceremonious; тој беше многу церемонијален во своите односи со луѓето he was very formal in his relations with people

церемонија́л-ма́јстор *m* master of ceremonies

церемонија́лно *adv* ceremonially, officially; formally, ceremoniously; тој се држеше многу церемонијално he behaved very formally

церемонија́лност *f* ceremonial/official manner; formality; церемонијалност на пречекот ceremonial nature of the reception; непотребни церемонијалности unnecessary formalities

це́ри[1] *impf arch.* **I** to treat; цери тешки рани to treat severe injuries **II – се** to treat o.s.; to take (undergo) treatment; мораше да се цери самата she had to treat herself; *see* лекува (се)

це́ри[2] **се** *impf dial.* **1** to laugh **2** to grin; to grimace, make grimaces, make a wry face; to bare (show) one's teeth; *see* клешти се

цери́ка *f see* цер[1]

цериу́м *m Chem.* cerium

це́ров *adj* Turkey oak *attrib.*; дрво церово бесплодно a barren oak tree; церови стари греди old oak beams

це́сар *m literary see* цар

цех[1] *m* **1** *Hist.* guild, corporation; чевларскиот цех the shoemaker's guild **2** (*во фабрика и сл.*) <work>shop

цех[2] *m* bill, *Am.* check; направија голем цех they ran up a big bill; ❑ тој го плати цехот he paid the piper

це́ховски *adj* **1** guild, corporation *attrib.*; цеховски организации guild organizations, corporations;

цеховски закони guild law<s> **2** shop, group *attrib.*; цеховски интереси <narrow> group interests

цеца   *f* (*form of address to older sister*) sister, *colloq.* sis

цеце   *Zool.* (*usu. in the combination* мувата цеце *f*) tsetse fly

цибрина   *f* bitter cold; cold but clear weather; *see* јасник

цивил   *m* **1** civilian; имаше само неколку цивили there were only a few civilians **2** civilian life; во војската не е како во цивилот army life is not like civilian life **3** civilian clothing, plain clothes, mufti, *sl.* civvies; беше во цивил he was in plain clothes **4** civil law

цивилен   -лна *adj* **1** civil; civilian; in civilian clothing, in plain clothes; цивилна заштита civil defence; Home Guard; цивилен одред civil-defence unit; цивилна облека civilian clothing, plain clothes; цивилен агент plain-clothes agent; ❑ цивилен брак civil marriage; цивилна листа civil list; цивилна служба civil service, *Austral.* public service **2** *Law* civil, *see* граѓански **3** (*rare as a noun*) цивилен *m* civilian; двајца војници и петмина цивили two soldiers and five civilians; *see* цивил 1

цивилиза́тор   *m* civilizer

цивилизаторски   *adj* civilizing, civilizatory; цивилизаторска политика civilizing policies

цивилизација   *f* civilization

цивилизи́ра   *pf & impf* **I** to civilize; го цивилизира месното население to civilize the indigenous population **II** – се to become civilized; племињата брзо се цивилизираа the tribes rapidly became civilized

цивилизи́ран   *pt* civilized; цивилизиран човек civilized person; цивилизирано општество civilized society

цивилизираност   *f* civilized state; degree of civilization; цивилизираноста на населението the people's degree of civilization

цивили́ст   *m* civil-law specialist

цивка   *impf* (*за глувци*) to squeak; (*за пилиња*) to cheep, peep

Циган<ин>   -ани *m* Gypsy, Rom; *pejor.* gypsy

Циганка   *f* (*fem. form*) *see* Циган<ин>

цигански[1]   *adj* Gypsy's; gypsy; Rom, Romany (*also as a noun m*); Bohemian; циганско маало gypsy quarter; цигански живот gypsy life; знаеше да зборува цигански he could speak Romany; ❑ циганско лето Indian summer

цигански[2]   *adv* like a gypsy; in a mean/sponging way; *colloq.* on the cheap; живеат цигански they live like gypsies

циганчи се   *impf colloq.* to be stingy (niggardly); to haggle; to beg for a living; се циганчи за една банка he grudges even ten denars

циганштија   *f colloq. see* циганштилак

циганштилак   -ци *m colloq.* stinginess, niggardliness

цигара   *f* cigarette; запали цигара to light a cigarette; пуши (пие) цигари to smoke cigarettes; една кутија цигари a pack<et> of cigarettes; фабрика за цигари cigarette factory; свитка една цигара to roll a cigarette

цигарлак   -ци *m* (*чибук*) cigarette holder; пушеше со цигарлак he smoked with a cigarette holder

цигаре   *n colloq.* smoke, *sl.* fag

цигарче   *n dim. of* цигара

цигла   *f* brick, *see* тула

циглар   *m* brickmaker, *see* тулар 1

цигларница   *f* brickworks, brickyard, *see* туларница

цигларски   *adj* brickmaker's; brickmaking *attrib.*; цигларскиот занает brickmaker's trade; *see* туларски

цигларство   *n* brickmaking, *see* туларство

цигува   *impf* to gather (*material*) *trans.*

цијан   *m Chem.* cyanogen

цијанводород   *m Chem.* hydrogen cyanide

цијанводороден   -дна *adj Chem.* цијанводородна киселина hydrocyanic acid

цијани́д   *m Chem.* cyanide

цијанкалиум   *m Chem.* <potassium> cyanide

цика   *impf of* цикне

цикла́ма   *f Bot.* (Cyclamen) cyclamen

цикличен   -чна *adj* cyclic<al>; цикличен развиток cyclic<al> development; циклично движење cyclical movement; циклични музички форми cyclic<al> musical forms

циклички   *adj see* цикличен

цикличност   *f* cyclic<al> nature (quality), recurrence

циклон   *m* **1** *Meteorology* cyclone; depression, low-pressure area, low; силен циклон ја зафати нашата земја the country is in the grip of a deep depression **2** *Tech.* cyclone dust separator

цикло́на   *f Meteorology* depression, low-pressure area, low

циклостил   *m* cyclostyle, duplicator; умножи на циклостил to duplicate on a cyclostyle

циклотрон   *m* cyclotron

циклус   *m* cycle; series; course; производствен циклус production cycle; биолошки циклус biological cycle; циклус на народни песни cycle of folksongs; циклус на предавања series of lectures

цикне   *pf* цикна *aor.* **1** (*за птица*) to squawk; пилето цикна и летна the chicken squawked and took flight **2** *fig.* to squeal; to shriek; цикна преплашено жената the woman shrieked in fear; цикна да плаче she started weeping and wailing

цикнува   *impf of* цикне

цикорија   *f Bot.* (Cichorium intybus) chicory; кафе со цикорија coffee with chicory

цикцак   *adv* zigzag; пијаниот одеше цикцак the drunken man was walking in a zigzag

цикцак-црта & цикцак-линија   *f* zigzag

цили́ндар   -дри *m* **1** cylinder; tube; drum; roll; обемот на цилиндарот the circumference of the cylinder; парен цилиндар cylinder (*on a steam engine*) **2** glass, chimney (*on an oil-lamp*) **3** top (silk) hat

цилиндричен   -чна *adj* cylindrical, tubular; цилиндрично тело cylindrical body; цилиндрична печка cylindrical stove

цимбал   *m Mus.* dulcimer, cimbalom

цимбали́ст   *m Mus.* dulcimer (cimbalom) player

цимент   *m see* цемент

цименто   *n* **1** *see* цемент **2** cement floor/path

цимер   *m* room-mate

цимет   *m Bot.* (Cinnamomum zeylanicum) (*дрво и мирудија*) cinnamon

циметов   *adj* cinnamon *attrib.*; циметово дрво cinnamon tree

цимоли   *impf* to sob; што туку цимолиш! why on earth are you sobbing?

цимолка *impf dim. of* цимоли; to whimper

цини́зам -змот *m* cynicism; *Hist.* Cynicism

циник -ци *m* cynic; *Hist.* Cynic

циничен -чна *adj* cynical; цинична насмевка cynical smile; цинични зборови cynical words

цинички 1 *adj see* циничен **2** *adv see* цинично; го погледна цинички she gave him a cynical look

цинично *adv* cynically; постапува цинично to act cynically

циничност *f* cynicism, cynical quality/nature; циничноста на неговите постапки the cynical nature of his actions

цинк *m Chem.* zinc

цинквајс *m* zinc (Chinese) white, zinc oxide

цинков *adj* zinc *attrib.*; цинкови руди zinc ore; цинкова маст zinc ointment; цинкова труба zinc trumpet

цинкогра́ф *m* zincograph

цинкографија *f* **1** zincography **2** zincographer's shop

цинкографски *adj* zincographic; zincograph's; цинкографски занает zincograph's trade; цинкографско клише zincographic plate

цинкува *impf* to zinc, zincify

цинкуван *adj* zinc-coated

цинобер *m* cinnabar; vermilion

цинцарка *f* kind of pumpkin, *see* тиква 1

циони́зам -змот *m* Zionism

циони́ст *m* Zionist

ционистички *adj* Zionist *attrib.*

циони́стка *f* (*fem. form*) *see* ционист

ципа *f Anat.* **1** groin; болки во ципите pains in the groin **2** membrane; мозочна ципа meninx; velamen

цирада *f see* церада

цирка¹ *f Bot.* (Zizyphus jujuba) jujube

цирка² *impf dial.* to trickle *intrans.*; циркаше вода од кладенецот water was trickling from the well

цирка³ *adv* approximately, circa; цирка десет проценти about ten per cent

циркли *pl Geom.* <pair of> compasses

циркула́р *m* **1** circular <letter>; циркуларот на Секретаријатот the circular from the Secretariat **2** *Tech.* circular saw, *Am.* buzz-saw

циркула́рен -рна *adj* circular; циркуларно писмо circular letter; циркуларна пила circular saw

циркулација *f* circulation; циркулацијата на крвта the circulation <of the blood>; циркулација на воздухот circulation of air, convection; циркулацијата на новите банкноти the circulation of the new banknotes

циркулацио́нен -она *adj* circulation *attrib.*; circulatory; circulating; *Comm.* циркулациони хартии securities

циркули́ра *pf & impf* to circulate *intrans.*; крвта циркулира во вените the blood circulates in the veins; писмото веќе циркулираше the letter was already circulating; овие пари веќе не циркулираат this money is no longer in circulation

циркумфлекс *m Gram.* circumflex <accent>

циркус *m* **1** circus; circus ground; circus tent **2** *fig.* fuss; каков циркус е ова? what is all this about? ❏ прави циркус to fool around; to make an exhibition of oneself

циркуса́нт *m* **1** circus artist **2** clown; *fig.* buffoon

циркуски *adj* circus *attrib.*; *fig.* circus-like, buffooning, clownish; циркуски артист circus artist; циркуски игри circus acts (stunts)

циро́за *f Med.* cirrhosis; цироза на црниот дроб cirrhosis of the liver

цирон *m &* циронка *f Zool.* (Cobitis) loach

цирус *m* (*usu. pl*) *Meteorology* cirrus <cloud>

циста *f Med.* cyst

цисте́рна *f* **1** cistern, tank; во цистерните немаше ни капка вода in the tanks there was not a drop of water; цистерна за нафта oil tank **2** tanker, tank-truck, *Brit.* tank-lorry; street-washing (-watering) lorry; вагон-цистерна tank wagon, *Am.* tank-car; брод-цистерна tanker; камион-цистерна tanker <vehicle>

цитаде́ла *f* citadel

цита́т *m* quotation, citation, *colloq.* quote; ракописот обилуваше со цитати од класиците the manuscript was full of quotations from the classics

цити́ра *pf & impf* to quote, cite

цитопла́зма *f* cytoplasm

цитра *f Mus.* zither

цитра́т *m Chem.* citrate

цитрон *m Bot.* (Citrus medica) citron, *cf.* лимон

цитрона́да *f* (*лимонада*) lemonade; студена цитронада cold lemonade

цитронка *f Bot.* (Citrus paradisi) grapefruit

циун *m dial.* stopper, plug; тече низ циунот the stopper is leaking

цифарски *adj see* цифрен

цифра *f* figure; (*број*) numeral, number, digit, cipher; *colloq.* (*сума*) sum; целиот лист беше покриен само со цифри the whole page was covered with numbers; арапски и римски цифри Arabic and Roman numerals; бара астрономски цифри he is asking astronomical sums

цифрен *adj* (*броен*) figure *attrib.*; numerical; digital; цифрени податоци numerical data, figures; цифрен преглед examination of the figures; statistical report

цифреник -ци *m* (*на часовник*) face, dial; (*на телефон*) dial, key-pad

циц¹ *m* printed calico, cretonne; chintz; фустан од циц chintz dress

циц² *interj* (*usu.* циц, циц to call goats) here!

цица¹ *f see* цицка¹

цица² *impf* **1** to suck; детето сака да цица the child wants the breast; цица мајчино млеко he feeds on his mother's milk; детето си го цица прстот the child is sucking his thumb; ❏ му ја цица крвта he is bleeding him white; кротко јагне од две мајки цица *prov. cf.* kindness is the noblest weapon to conquer with **2** to draw, imbibe *trans.*; од пазувите на земјата цицаат хранителни сокови they draw nourishment from the depths of the earth **3** *fig.* to squeeze *trans.*; разни аги и бегови го цицаа народот various agas and beys were squeezing the populace

цицалче *n* suckling; (*бебе*) infant, babe in arms; јагне цицалче suck<l>ing lamb

цицање *n from* цица; цицање на мајчино млеко breast-feeding; одбивање на децата од цицање weaning the children

цицач *m* **1** *Zool.* (*usu. pl*) mammal **2** *less freq.* sucker, a person or thing that sucks

цицаче *n see* цицалче

цице *n dim. of* цица

цицен¹ *adj* printed-calico, cretonne *attrib.*; chintz *attrib.*; цицен фустан chintz dress

цицен² -цна *adj* mammary; цицни жлезди mammary glands

цицер *m Print.* **1** point **2** pica, em, pica em, 12 point

циција -ии *m colloq.* (*скржавец*) skinflint, tightwad

цицина *f dial.* swelling

цицингарец -рци *m dial. see* црцорец

цициште *n* (*usu. pl*) *augm. of* цица¹

цицка¹ *f* **1** breast; teat, nipple; (*на животно*) udder, dug; уште е на цицка he is still being breast-fed; плаче детето, дај му цицка the child is crying, give him the breast! **2** *fig.* mother's milk; мајчината цицка ја проколнуваше во тој момент at that moment she cursed her mother's milk

цицка² *f colloq.* (*срчка, срдешница*) diarrhoea, *colloq.* the runs

цицка³ *f Bot.* (Sedum) sedum

цицлест *adj* (*за жена*) full-bosomed, big-bosomed, bosomy, buxom; (*за животно*) having large/many teats

цицне *pf* цицна *aor.* to suck (feed) a little; to start sucking (feeding); детето цицна малу и ја пушти цицката the baby drank a little and let go of the breast

цицнува *impf of* цицне

ЦК *abbr.* (*Централен комитет*) Central Committee

цоиса *pf dial. see* пцовиса

цокле *n Architecture* socle, plinth

цокула *f* **1** army boot; heavy boot; hob-nailed boot **2** clog

цол -ови, цола *m obs.* inch (*26 mm*)

црв -је, црви *m* worm (*also fig.*); maggot; larva; бараше црвје и ловеше со нив риби he looked for worms and caught fish with them; зар моиве црви ќе станат некогаш луѓе will these children of mine ever turn into people? црвот на сомневањето почна да го гризе the worm of doubt began gnawing at him; црвот на каењето the worm of repentance; ❏ го јаде црв something is eating him; се витка (вие) како црв <во дрво> he is trying to worm his way into s.o.'s favour; работи како црв to work like a beaver, to be a hard worker; црвите го јадат he is food for worms; како да има црви he has ants in his pants

црвен *adj* **1** red; црвен молив red pencil; црвено знаме red flag; црвено мастило red ink; ❏ црвен ветер erysipelas, ergotism, St Anthony's fire; црвен восок sealing wax; Црвен крст Red Cross; црвен пипер paprika; (*лут*) cayenne pepper; црвен телефон, црвена линија hot line; црвено салдо overdraft, in the red; црвено светло red light; црвени крвни зрнца red blood cells (corpuscles); црвена аспра не гине (не загинува) *prov.* the more wicked, the more lucky; the more knave, the better luck **2** pink; ruddy; reddish; девојката е бела и црвена the girl is peaches and cream; ❏ црвен како крв, рак, јаболко <as> red as a <boiled> lobster, peony **3** *fig.* Red; <pro->communist, radical, revolutionary; *Hist.* Црвената армија the Red Army; црвена република red republic; црвените чети the red units **4** (*in certain botanical and zoological names*) црвен багрем (Robinia hispida) rose acacia; црвена боровинка (Vaccinium myrtillus) cowberry, mountain cranberry, red bilberry; црвена врба (Salix

purpurea) purple willow (osier); црвен кантарион (Centaurium umbellatum *or* Erythraea centaurium) centaury; црвена клека (Juniperus oxycedrus) prickly cedar; црвена ракита *see* црвена врба; црвени корали red coral **5** *Heraldry* gules **6** (*as noun*) 1. црвено<то> *n* jac сум за црвеното I like red; црвеното секогаш добива red always wins; секогаш носи црвено she always wears red 2. црвен *m* (*see* 3) тој беше познат како црвен he was a notorious red

црвендалест *adj* red-cheeked, ruddy, rubicund; црвендалест млад човек a ruddy-faced young man

црвенее (се) *impf* to be/appear (look) red; to turn red *intrans.*; to blush; во далечината се црвенееја покривите на куќите in the distance the red roofs of the houses could be seen; црвенееше зората dawn was breaking; се црвенее од срам he's blushing <for shame>

црвени *impf* **I** to redden, turn red *trans.*; to colour/paint red **II** – **се 1** *see* црвенее (се), црви (се) **II** 1 **2** *see* црви (се) **II** 2

црвеник *m* (*folk name for*) June/July

црвеникав *adj* reddish; црвеникава убава куќа pretty, reddish house

црвенило *n* **1** redness; red glow; rosy complexion; blush<ing>; црвенило му го облеа лицето he blushed all over his face **2** lipstick; rouge; ќе си купам белило и црвенило I'll buy <myself> some powder and rouge; *see* црвило

црвенина *f see* црвенило 1; црвенината на изгревот the red glow of the sunrise

црвеница *f* **1** (*болест*) erysipelas, ergotism, St Anthony's fire **2** (*земја*) loam, clay

црвенка *f* **1** red wheat **2** red wine

Црвенкапа *f* Little Red Riding Hood

црвено *adv* red; in red; собата ја бојадисаа црвено they painted the room red; го означи со црвено he marked it <in> red

црвенобра́д<ест> *adj* red-bearded

црвеноко́ж *adj* red-skinned

црвеноко́жец -шци *m* **1** red-skinned person **2** American Indian, Red Indian, *colloq.* redskin

црвенко́с *adj* (*лисест*) red-haired, red-headed

црвеноперка *f Zool.* (Scardinus erythrophthalmus) rudd

црвеноса (се) *pf rare see* вцрви (се), поцрвени (се), сцрви (се)

црвенотија *f see* црвенина

црвеношијка *f Zool.* (Erithacus rubecula) robin

црвенузлав *adj see* црвеникав

црвенушка *f* kind of red apple

црвенушкав *adj see* црвеникав

црвец -вци *m* worm; бели црвци larvae, maggots, grubs; *see* црв

црви *impf* **I** to colour/paint red; црви јајца за Велигден to colour eggs red for Easter; веќе го црви лицето she is using make-up already **II** – **се 1** to turn red *intrans.*; се црви од срам to blush **2** to put rouge/lipstick on; не се бели, Маре мори, не се црви *f.p.* don't powder your face, Mara, don't put rouge on your face!

црвило *n* lipstick; rouge; без црвило нацрвена rosy-cheeked without rouge

црвилце *n dim. of* црвило

црвјоса *pf see* црвоса

црвлив *adj* wormy, full of worms, worm-ridden, worm-eaten; maggoty; црвливи јаболка worm-eaten apples

црвливост *f* worminess, worm-eaten/maggoty state

црвојадина *f see* црвојаднина

црвојаднина *f* worm-hole

црволик *adj* wormlike, vermiform

црвообразен -зна *adj see* црволик

црвоса *pf* **1** to become infested with worms/maggots, go wormy/maggoty; to become worm-eaten; црвосал гравот the beans are full of maggots; да би му уста црвосала! may he never speak again! (*literally* may his mouth fill up with worms!) **2** *fig.* to get tired of sitting; to go stiff from sitting <about>; to get bored, have enough of (*s.th.*); црвоса од седење на едно место he got stiff from sitting in one place; црвоса во канцеларијата he has gone stale <working> in the office

црвосан *adj* wormy, full of worms, worm-ridden, worm-eaten; maggoty; *see* црвлив

црвосаница *f* worm-eaten piece of fruit, tree etc.

црвосува *impf of* црвоса; црешите црвосуваат секоја година the cherry-trees get worm-eaten every year

црвоточина *f* **1** infestation of worms in a tree; residue left by worms **2** worm-hole, *see* црвојаднина

црвул *m dial. see* опинок

црвче *n dim. of* црв<ец>; се храни со црвчиња it feeds on maggots

цревар *m* gut-cleaner; gut-dealer; offal-merchant

цреварски *adj* gut-cleaner's; gut-dealer's; offal-merchant's; gut-cleaning/selling *attrib.*; цреварска работилница gut-cleaning shop

цреварство *n* gut-cleaning; gut trade; offal trade

цревен -вна *adj* intestinal, enteric, bowel *attrib.*; цревен тифус enteric fever, typhoid <fever>; цревни жлезди intestinal glands

црево *n* **1** *Anat.* bowel, gut, intestine; дванаесетпрсно црево, дванаесетпрсник duodenum; дебело црево colon, large intestine; тенко црево small intestine; задно црево rectum; слепо црево blind gut, caecum; воспаление на цревата enteritis, intestinal catarrh; преплет на цревата intestinal constriction; ❏ се влечат (точат) како црева 1. they're moving slowly in a long line 2. they are inseparable; се влече како црево (*за човек*) he's dragging his feet; he is a slow-coach; (*за нешто*) it's dragging along the ground; се влече како црево по него he sticks to him like a leech; цревата ми кркорат (гргорат) my stomach is rumbling, I'm starving **2** hose; гумено црево rubber hose; платнено црево fire-hose **3** skin, casing (*for processed meat*)

цревоугодник -ци *m* glutton

цревоугодница *f* (*fem. form*) *see* цревоугодник

цревце *n dim. of* црево; *pl* цревца chitterlings

црека *impf* to bawl, yell, howl, bellow, roar; вечно црекаат во дворот they are forever shouting in the yard

црекало *n* noisy person

црекаица *f* howling, howls; clamour; му здодеа таа црекаица he grew tired of that shouting

црекне *pf* црекна *aor.* **1** to bellow, shout, cry out; ќе црекнеше некој одвреме-навреме someone would

cry out from time to time **2** to squirt <out>; црекни некоја капка млеко squirt out a drop or two of milk!

црекнува *impf of* црекне

црен *m* black horn; horn knife handle

ценче *n dim. of* црен

цреп *m* **1** flowerpot **2** shard, crock; broken earthenware; цреп шутаре прекарува *prov.* the pot calls the kettle black

црепка *f dial. see* цреп 2

црепна *f* earthenware lid (*used in baking bread*); оваа црепна пече убаво the bread bakes well under this lid; очи имал колку една црепна he had eyes as big as saucers

црепналка & **црепнарка** *f* cloth for wiping a *црепна*

црепнарски *adj* црепнарска пачавра, *see* црепналка, црепнарка

црепче *n dim. of* цреп

цресло *n* coulter

цреша *f* (Prunus avium) <sweet> cherry; се качи на црешата he climbed the cherry tree; бели цреши yellow cherries; сок од цреши cherry juice; слатко од цреши cherry preserve

црешак -ци *m* cherry grove; cherry orchard

црешар *m* **1** cherry vendor; cherry lover **2** (*folk name for*) May

црешна *f see* цреша

црешнар *m see* црешар

црешница *f* cherry tree

црешов *adj* cherry *attrib.*; црешово дрво cherry tree/wood

црка *impf see* црека

цркавец -вци *m dial. see* црцорец

црканица *f see* црекаица

црква *f* church; се венчаа в црква they got married in church; соборна црква cathedral; денеска нема црква there is no church (service) today; служи црква to conduct a service, celebrate the liturgy; чука за на црква the bells are tolling for church; Македонската православна црква the Macedonian Orthodox Church; ❏ нашол црква кај да се крсти he has come to the wrong shop; од врата мандало, од црква клепало a distant relative; црква направи to do a good deed; црква расипа to ruin everything, ruin s.o.'s plans

црквар *m* churchgoer

цркварка *f* (*fem. form*) *see* црквар

црквен *adj see* црквин

црквенски *adj* church *attrib.*, *see* црквински

црквин *adj* church *attrib.*; пред црквина врата at the church door

црквински *adj* church *attrib.*; на црквинска врата at the church door

црквица *f dim. see* црквичка

црквичка *f dim.* (*of* црква) chapel

црквиче *n see* црквичка

црквиште *n* **1** site of a former church **2** churchyard

цркне *pf* цркна *aor.* **1** (*of animals*) to die, *see* пцовиса 1; коњот му цркна одненадеж his horse died suddenly **2** *colloq.* to conk out; to burst *intrans.*; цркна гумата the tyre burst **3** *fig. colloq.* (*of people*) to peg out; *sl.* to croak; цркна додека не ја исполни задачата he pegged out before he could finish the job; цркна од глад he died of hunger; цркна од мака he was very cut up about it; цркна од смеење he split his sides laughing; цркнал та пукнал! *curse* go to hell!

цркнува *impf of* цркне

црковен -вна *adj* church *attrib*.; ecclesiastical; црковен суд ecclesiastical (church) court; црковна историја church history; црковна литература church literature; црковни книги liturgical books; црковно учење teachings of the church, church dogma; црковен собор synod; црковна земја church land; црковен имот patrimony; црковна врата church door; црковни двери church doors; ❑ сиромав како црковен глушец <as> poor as a church mouse

црковиште *n see* црквиште

црковнословенски *adj* Church Slavonic; црковнословенски јазик Church Slavonic language; црковнословенски ракописи Church Slavonic manuscripts

црн *adj* **1** black; dark; swarthy, olive-skinned; <sun-> tanned; црно мастило black ink; црн флор crape; црна лента black band; *Sport.* црн појас black belt; црно лице swarthy complexion; црн леб rye (black) bread; црно вино red wine; црно кафе Turkish coffee; black coffee; црни облаци black clouds (*also fig.*) **2** *fig.* dark, sombre; sinister; loathsome; disastrous; црни мисли dark thoughts; црни вести bad news; црни денови/години hard times; го опишува животот со црни бои he paints life in sombre hues; остана црна вдовица she was left a widow; црна судбина sorry fate; црни дела dark deeds; *f.p.* црна се чума зададе a terrible plague broke out; црн хумор black humour; ❑ црн ми е пред очиве I can't bear the sight of him **3** dirty, soiled, filthy; црни раце dirty hands **4** unskilled, manual; црн труд manual labour; црна работа dirty (heavy) work; legwork, spade work **5** (*in botanical and zoological names*) црн даб (Quercus petraea *or* sessiliflora) sessile (durmast) oak; црна дреновица variety of black grapes; црна црница (Morus nigra) black mulberry; црн пипер (Piper nigrum) black pepper; црна мечка black bear **6** (*as noun*) 1. Црни, Црниот *m* nickname for a dark-skinned person; црни, црниот *m* Chess black; црниот е на потег it's black's move 2. црно *n* black, black colour; black clothing; носи црно to wear black, be in mourning **7** ❑ биволицата е црна, ама бело млеко дава; и кафето е црно, ама е слатко a black hen lays a white egg; a black plum is as sweet as white; за нечии црни очи for the sake of s.o.'s blue eyes, for love, for nothing; не прозбори ни црна ни бела he didn't say a word; црн петок Black Friday; Friday the 13th; ќе му дојде црн петок he will meet his match (Waterloo); црн ден 1. second day after St Athanasius, i.e. 7 July 2. black day; *Anat.* црн дроб liver; црн поп kind of card-game; црн список blacklist; црн фонд slush fund; црн како гавран, гламња, Ѓуптин, јаглен, катран, ќумур, ќутук, Циган <as> black as a raven, coal, ink, pitch; <as> black as the ace of spades, jet-black, pitch-black; црна берза black market; црна кашлица whooping-cough; црна крв venous blood; црна металургија ferrous metallurgy; црни метали ferrous metals; црно духовенство regular clergy; црно злато 1. black diamonds, coal 2. oil, *Am. colloq.* black gold; црно на бело in black and white, in writing, on paper; црна

магија black magic, the black art; црна овца black sheep; не баш така црн како што се прикажува not as black as one is painted; црното бело, а белото црно го прави he will swear that black is white and white is black; црното бело не бидува black is black and white is white; чувај бели пари за црни дни save for a rainy day!

црнава *f see* црнотија

црнавица *f see* црневица

Црна Гóра & **Црнá Горá** *f* Montenegro

црнгалест *adj* dark, olive-skinned, swarthy; црнгалеста мома olive-skinned young woman; *see* црномурен

црнева *f see* црнотија

црневица *f* blackness, darkness; по улиците – црневица од луѓе the streets were thick with people

црнее *impf* **I 1** to go black, turn black *intrans.*; црнее брзо на сонце it soon turns black in the sun **2** *fig.* to mourn, grieve; to lead a miserable life; ете вака кај живеам и црнеам 35 години I've been living in this misery for 35 years; ќе црнеам по тебе I will grieve for you **II** – *ce* to be/look (appear, show, loom) black; се црнееја високите тополи the tall poplars loomed black

црнец -нци *m* **1** Black; African, Negro; поцрнел како црнец he turned as brown as a berry **2** *fig.* sweated labourer; работи како црнец to work like a horse (slave) **3** *rare* swarthy (olive-skinned) person

црнечки *adj* black; sweated; црнечки народни песни Negro spirituals; црнечка работа sweated labour

црни *impf* **1** to blacken *trans.*, colour (dye, paint) black; си ја црни косата he dyes his hair black **2** *fig.* to blacken *trans.*, denigrate, run (put) down, belittle; не пропушташе ниедна можност а да не го црни пред луѓето he did not miss a single opportunity to run him down in front of everyone **3** *fig.* to spoil *trans.*, mar; to poison, make (*s.o./s.th.*) unhappy; сама си го црнеше животот she poisoned her own life, she made her own life a misery

црникав *adj* blackish; dark

црнилка *f see* црнка 2

црнило¹ *n* **1** black dye/paint; (*за шминкање*) mascara; eye-brow pencil; (*за чевли*) black shoe polish **2** *fig.* misery, miserable life; *f.p.* венчило – пусто црнило *saying* wedlock is a padlock **3** crape, black clothes; black; ти в црнило си го свила you've caused him to wear black; *fig.* you've cooked his goose

црнило² *n Bot. see* гламна²

црнина *f* **1** blackness, black/dark quality; tan; црнината на кожата е добра a suntan is a good thing **2** crape, black <clothes>; носи црнина to wear black, be in mourning; ја симна црнината he stopped mourning (wearing black), *poet.* he cast off the sables

црница *f* **1** *Bot.* (Morus alba) mulberry; се качи на црницата he climbed the mulberry tree; јаде црници he is eating mulberries **2** *see* црнозем

црничка *f dim. of* црница 1

црничов *adj* mulberry *attrib.*; црничови лисја mulberry leaves; црничова шума mulberry grove; црничова ракија mulberry brandy

црничок -чка *adj dim. of* црн

црнка *f* **1** dark-skinned woman, brunette; се сакаше

со една црнка he was in love with a dark-skinned woman **2** *Anat.* pupil; ❏ чувај го како црнката во окото guard it like the apple of your eye!

црнкавест *adj* blackish; dark; *see* црникав

црнкиња *f (fem. form)* Negress, *see* црнец 1

црно *adv* black<ly>; *fig.* bleakly, dismally, gloomily, in the worst possible light; прегаа ја бојадисаа црно they dyed the yarn black; ти гледаш многу црно на животот you take a very bleak view of life, you always look on the dark side of life; ❏ црно ми е, црно ми стана/станува пред очиве 1. I feel faint 2. I see red

црноберзијáнец -нци *m* black marketeer

црноберзијáнка *f (fem. form)* see црноберзијанец

црноберзијáнски *adj* black-market *attrib.*; црно-берзијанска цена black-market price

црнобрад<ест> *adj* black-bearded; црнобрадо момче young man with a black beard

црногледец -дци *m literary see* песимист

Црногорец -рци *m* Montenegrin

црногорка[1] *f* kind of folk-dance

Црногорка[2] *f (fem. form) see* Црногорец

црногорски *adj* Montenegrin

црнозем *m* black earth, chernozem

црноземен -мна *adj* black-earth, chernozem *attrib.*

црнок *m Bot.* (црн даб) sessile oak

црнокапец -пци *m pejor.* cleric, priestling

црноклас *adj* black-awned; црнокласа пченица black-awned wheat

црнокласица *f* black-awned wheat

црнокож *adj* dark-skinned; Black

црнокос *adj* black-/dark-haired

црнокошулец -лци *m Hist.* blackshirt

црнокошулски *adj Hist.* of the blackshirt<s>

црнокрил *adj* black-winged

црномурен -рна *adj* dark<-skinned>, swarthy

црноок *adj* black-/dark-eyed

црноперка *f f.p.* arrow with a black feather

црноризец -сци *m* monk

црнослива *f Bot.* (Prunus insititia) bullace, damson <plum>

црност *f see* црнотија

црнотија *f* 1 black<ness>, darkness; црнотијата на јагленот the blackness of coal; во црнотијата на ноќта in the darkness of the night, in the dead of night **2** *fig.* misery, miserable life; despair; болна од својата црнотија sick with black despair

црноцрен *adj (see* црен) black horn; horn knife handle; ноже црноцрено little knife with a horn handle

црнулав *adj* blackish, dark; црнулава коса blackish hair; *see* црникав

црнулест *adj see* црникав; црнулесто лице dark face

црнче *n dim. of* црнец 1

црњак *m* red wine

црпалка *f see* црпка[1]

црпе *impf* 1 to draw *trans.*, scoop up; to ladle out; црпе вода од бунар to draw water from a well; црпе песок со рака he is scooping up sand with his hands; ❏ со лопата црпел пари he was making money by the shovelful **2** *fig.* to gather, collect *trans.*; to obtain; црпе податоци од книги to collect data from books **3** *fig.* to draw *trans.*; оттаму црпеше нови сили from there he drew new strength; црпе мудрост to absorb wisdom

црпка[1] *f* 1 ladle; bailer; scoop; pump; наполни црпка со вода to fill a scoop with water! **2** *Bot.* gourd, cucurbit **3** *fig. colloq.* noddle, *sl.* nut, block, *Am.* bean; десетпати му ја полнев црпката и ништо I have tried to get it through his skull ten times without any result; празна му е црпката his head is empty

црпка[2] *impf* to draw a little at a time *trans.*; to scoop up a little at a time

црпне *pf* црпна *aor. see* црпе 1

црпнува *impf of* црпне

црпче *n dim. of* црпка

црта[1] *f* 1 line; trace; notch, nick; stripe; streak; *Math.* vinculum; повлече една дебела црта he drew a thick line; крива/права црта crooked/straight line; вертикална/хоризонтална црта vertical/horizontal line; ❏ во кратки црти in short (brief); во главни (општи, основни) црти in outline; broadly speaking; не повлече ни црта he didn't lift a finger; повлече црта to draw the line; to stop, leave off; ниеден ден – без црта *prov.* not a day without a line **2** boundary, pale, line; не може да се повлече реска црта помеѓу нив one cannot draw a clear line between them **3** (*usu. pl*) trait, feature, lineament (*also fig.*); имаше правилни црти на лицето he had regular features; негативни црти на неговиот карактер negative traits in his character; карактеристична црта a characteristic feature **4** *Gram.* dash, *see* тире

црта[2] *impf* 1 to draw, sketch; to design; го црташе детето во природна големина he was drawing the child life-size; црта планови to draw up plans **2** *fig.* to depict; ги црташе до најмали подробности нивните квалитети he depicted their qualities in the finest detail; во мислите си ја црташе татковата куќа in his thoughts he would picture his father's house; го црта животот со црни бои he depicts life in dark colours

цртанка *f* drawing-book, sketching pad, sketch-book

цртање *n* 1 drawing, sketching; сала за цртање drafting/sketching room; хартија за цртање drawing-paper; техничко цртање technical drawing **2** *fig.* depiction; цртање на подробности depiction of details

цртач *m* artist; sketcher; draughtsman; беше најдобар цртач во класот he was the best artist in the class

цртачка *f (fem. form) see* цртач

цртачки *adj* drawing *attrib.*; sketching *attrib.*; artistic; draughtsman's; цртачки талент artistic talent, talent for drawing; цртачки прибор drawing materials (kit)

цртеж *m* sketch, drawing; design, pattern; draft, outline; аматерски цртеж amateur drawing

цртица & цртичка *f* 1 (*dim. of* црта) short line; повлече цртица to draw a short line **2** (*usu. pl*) notes; цртици од патот по Италија notes from the journey around Italy **3** *Gram.* hyphen; таа сложенка се пишува со цртица that compound word is written with a hyphen; *cf.* тире

црца *impf see* цврцка

црцорец -рци *m Zool.* (Gryllus campestris) <field> cricket

црцори *impf* 1 (*of crickets*) to chirp; црцорец црцори a cricket is chirping **2** to drip *intrans.*; чешмата црцори the tap (*Am.* faucet) is dripping **3** to sizzle

цуг *m colloq. see* голтка 1

цулуф *m* (*usu. pl*) (*на жена*) side locks of hair, love-locks; (*на маж*) side-burns

цуне *pf* цуна *aor. dial.* **I** to kiss *trans.*; цуни му рака kiss his hand! **II – се** to kiss *intrans.*; *see* бакне (се)

цунка *impf child.* to kiss

цунува (се) *impf dial. of* цуне (се), *see* бакнува (се)

цупка *impf colloq.* **1** *intrans.* to hop, frisk, gambol; to bob up and down (*while dancing*) **2** *trans.* to bounce a child on one's knees **3** *fig.* to dote on, dance attendance (*on*)

цурајка *f dial.* **1** (*обетка*) earring; ear-clip **2** *Bot.* (Fuchsia) fuchsia

цурајче *n dim. of* цурајка

цурак -ци *m dial.* (*обетка*) earring; ear-clip ❑ цурак да ставиш! make a knot in your handkerchief!

цурачка *f see* цурајка

цурко *n dial. see* девојченце, момиче

цут *m* (*see* цвет) flower; цутот на интелигенцијата the flower (cream) of the intelligentsia; во цутот на младоста in the flower of youth

цутеж *m poet.* (*see* цветеж) blossom<ing>, bloom<ing>

цути *impf* (*see* цвети) to flower, blossom, bloom; јаболкницата цутеше the apple-tree was in blossom; нека цути и нека се развива! may he/it prosper!; десница да му цути! God bless him!; уста му цутела! God bless him! ❑ многу раце цутеле, многу усти капеле many hands make light work, but too many cooks spoil the broth

цутка¹ *f see* цут

цутка² *impf see* цути

цутне *pf* цутна *aor.* to <come into> flower (blossom, bloom); цутнало цвеќе the flowers are in bloom

цутче *n dim. of* цут

цуце *n* dwarf, *see* џуџе

цуцка *f* (*на птица*) crest, tuft; (*на човек*) tuft, wisp, shock; tassel; *Geog.* conical peak, hilltop

цуцла *f Brit.* dummy, *Am.* pacifier; (*на шише*) nipple, teat

цуцул *m Zool.* (Upupa epops) hoopoe, *see* пупунец

цуцулига *f* (*летачка*) kind of kite

цуцулка *f see* цуцка

цушпајз *m Cul.* cooked vegetables

Ч

ч. *abbr.* (*час*) hour, h.

чабав *adj* **1** darkened **2** sooty, smutty **3** musty; foxed (*of paper*); чабав том musty tome

чабур *m &* **чабура** *f arch.* large wooden tub; *f.p.* чабур чаша kind of large wine goblet

чабурлија *adj f.p. in the expression:* чаша чабурлија kind of large wine goblet

чавка *f Zool.* (Corvus monedula) jackdaw; ❑ чавка умот му го испила he's taken leave of his senses; уште му лета умот по чавките he is still wet behind the ears; зјапа по чавките he stares at the ceiling, he is with the fairies, he is miles away; чавка со чавка очите не си ги вадат *prov.* hawks will not pick out hawks' eyes; there is honour among thieves

чавкин *adj* jackdaw's; чавкино седело jackdaw's nest; чавкина уста *Bot.* (Antirrhinum majus) snapdragon

чавче *n dim. of* чавка

чад¹ -ови, -дје *m* smoke; мириса на чад it smells of smoke; ❑ ако ми е оцакот крив, чадот нека ми оди право even if I am foolish, may my business prosper

Чад² *m* Chad

чадар *m dial. see* чадор

чаден *adj* smoked; чадено месо smoked meat

чади *impf* **I** **1** *intrans.* to emit smoke; оцакот чади the chimney is smoking; каде што чади, има и оган *prov.* there's no smoke without fire **2** *trans.* to cure by smoking; чади суво месо to smoke dried meat **II – се** **1** to be smoked; сувата риба се чади the dried fish gets smoked **2** to get sooty (smutty), get covered with soot; немој да се чадиш mind you don't get covered in soot!

чадлив *adj* smoking, smoky; smoke-filled; sooty; чадливо огниште smoking hearth; чадлива светлина smoky light; чадливи дрва smoky wood; чадлива (зачадена) соба smoke-filled room; чадливи греди sooty beams

чадовина *f* smoke; мириса на чадовина to smell of smoke

чадор *m* **1** umbrella; parasol **2** *arch. see* шатор² 1

чадорче *n dim. of* чадор

чадорџија *m* umbrella-maker; umbrella vendor

чадски *adj* Chadian

Чаѓанец -ни *m* Chadian

Чаѓанка *f* (*fem. form*) *see* Чаѓанец

чаен -јна *adj* tea *attrib.*; чајно печиво biscuits, *Am.* cookies; teacake

чаир *m arch.* meadow; pasture

чај чаеви *m* tea; *Bot.* (Camellia sinensis); сто грама чај one hundred grams of tea; едно пакетче руски чај a packet of black tea; чаша чај cup of tea; липов чај lime tea; планински чај herbal tea

чајанка *f* tea party

чајарник -ци & **чајник** -ци *m* teapot

чај-шеќер *m colloq.* lump sugar

чакал[1] *m Zool.* (Canis aureus) jackal

чакал[2] *m* **1** (*кршен камен*) crushed stone, rubble; road-metal, ballast **2** (*крупен песок*) gravel

чакален -лна *adj* rubble/gravel *attrib.*; чакална покривка layer of crushed stone

чакалест *adj* gravel *attrib.*; pebbly, full of pebbles; чакалеста земја stony soil

чакарест *adj* (*of eyes*) of different colours; (*of a person*) having eyes of different colours

чакија -ии *f* pen-knife, pocket-knife

чакиче *n dim. of* чакија

чакмак *m colloq.* **1** tinder-box, flint<stone> and steel; <cigarette> lighter **2** *Naut.* stay

чакнат *adj colloq.* crazy, *Brit. colloq.* daft, *sl.* crackers, nuts

чакрест *adj see* чакарест

чактиса <ce> *pf colloq.* to go crackers (off one's rocker); <ce> чактиса од умот he has lost his marbles

чактисува <ce> *impf of* чактиса <ce>

чакшири *pl* baggy-bottomed calf-hugging Turkish trousers; trousers (*in traditional costume*); *see* бечви

чалам *m colloq.* airs and graces; ❑ продава (крева, дига) чалам to have a big mouth, put on airs, brag, *sl.* shoot one's mouth off, *Austral.* skite

чаламџија -ии *m colloq.* big-mouth, boaster, braggart, *colloq.* loud-mouth, *Austral.* skite

чалга (се) *impf of* чалне (се)

чалгаџија -ии *m arch.* musician

чалгија -ии *f arch. Mus.* **1** instrument **2** band

чалдиса *pf colloq.* **I** to singe, scorch, burn (*esp. when ironing*) *trans.*; ми ги чалдиса панталоните you have scorched my trousers **II** – ce **1** to get singed (burnt) **2** to go crazy

чалдисува (се) *impf of* чалдиса (се)

чалма *f* turban

чалмиче *n dim. of* чалма

чалмиште *n augm. of* чалма

чалнат *adj* mad, crazy, *Brit. colloq.* daft, *sl.* crackers, nuts

чалне *pf* чална *aor.* **I 1** (*топка*) to kick *trans.*; ја чална топката со десната нога he kicked the ball with his right foot **2** *fig.* (*некого*) to reproach, blame **II** – ce to have a row

чам *m* pine (*tree and timber*)

чамец -мци *m* boat; dinghy; чамец за спасување life-boat; моторен чамец motor-boat; торпеден чамец torpedo boat; гумен чамец rubber dinghy; ❑ во чамец ли си се родил? were you born in a barn (stable, tent)?

чамов *adj* pine<wood>, deal *attrib.*; чамови штици pinewood planks, deal; чамово дрво, чамов материјал deal; чамова маса pinewood table

чамовина *f* pine<wood>, deal

чампари *pl Mus.* cymbals

чам-саказ *m colloq.* pine resin, colophony

чамче *n see* чапче

чанак -ци *m* wooden bowl

чаначе *n dim. of* чанак

чанкир *m* ulcer; chancre; canker

чанта *f* **1** bag; женска (дамска) чанта <lady's> handbag; патничка чанта travel<ling> bag **2** *pejor.* bitch; baggage

чантар *m* bag-maker, leather-worker

чанте *n* **1** *dim. of* чанта **2** purse; wallet

чантиче & **чантичка** *f see* чанте

чанче *n* **1** *dim. of* чанак **2** *see* чапче

чапа[1] *f dial. see* мотика, копачка 2

чапа[2] *f dial. see* чапја

чапанка *f* hoof

чапарда *f colloq.* large hand

чапја -пји *Zool.* (Ardea) heron; чапја лажичарка (Platalea leucorodia) spoonbill; како некоја чапја e she is lanky, *iron.* she has all the grace of a stork; ja отворил устата како некоја чапја he stood there with his mouth agape, his jaw dropped <a mile>; he looked aghast

чапкан *m colloq.* **1** swift horse **2** *fig.* good-for-nothing, wastrel; rake

чапканлак *m colloq. fig.* wild life, loose living; тој е познат по пијанство и по чапканлак he is notorious for his drinking and womanizing

чапкански *adj* **1** swift; чапкански коњ swift horse **2** *fig.* wild, loose; чапканска работа filthy business

чапканува *impf colloq. fig.* to lead a loose (wild) life

чапкун *m colloq. see* чапкан

чапкундар *m arch. fig. see* чапкан 2

чапкунлак *m colloq. see* чапканлак

чапкунски *adj see* чапкански

чаплок -ци *m Zool. dial. see* чапја

чапне *pf* чапна *aor.* to grab, seize; to snatch; тие ja чапнале од мајка й they snatched her from her mother

чапнува *impf of* чапне

чапорешка *f see* чепорошка

чапраз *m* (*usu. pl*) *arch.* clasp; buckle

чапунка *f see* чапанка

чапче *n* scoop; drinking cup

чар -и *f* & *m* charm, fascination; allure, magic; glamour

чардак -ци *m* **1** veranda, *Am.* porch; balcony, loggia; *f.p.* високи чардаци high balconies; ❑ чардак ни на небо ни на земја cloud-cuckoo-land **2** *Hist.* watch-tower, guardhouse

чардак-боја *f* kind of yellow paint (*for wooden floors*)

чардаклија[1] *adj indecl.* having a veranda/balcony; balconied; куќа чардаклија house with a veranda

чардаклија[2] *f dial.* **1** house with a veranda **2** *see* лозница **3** *Hist.* border guard

чардаче *n dim. of* чардак 1

чардаш *m Mus.* csardas

чаре *n colloq.* ways and means, remedy, solution, cure, help; ами чаре, бре домаќине? what now, boss? нема чаре there is no way out, there is nothing for it; there is no hope; it is beyond repair; најде чаре to find a solution (way out); нема друго чаре there is no other way; за чаре сум дојдена I've come for help, I've come to ask your help; чарето да си го бара to seek help; to seek one's fortune; не било чаре да го види there was no way he could see him

чарк *m* **1** cog-wheel, toothed wheel; *Tech.* gear, pinion; чаркови на часовник clockwork; чарк на воденица, воденичен чарк mill-wheel, water-wheel **2** reel; winch; crank; (*на бунар*) windlass; чарк за гајтан cord reel; чарк за режење штици circular saw for cutting planks **3** (*на пиштол и сл.*) cocking piece, hammer

чарлстон *m Mus.* charleston

чартер *m* charter; чартер авион charter aircraft

чаршаф *m* <bed> sheet; cloth; јоргански чаршаф quilt cover; чаршаф за на маса tablecloth

чаршафски *adj* sheet/cloth *attrib.*

чаршија -ии *f* **1** market<place>, bazaar; shops **2** *fig.* local merchants (traders) **3** *fig.* street politics; lower middle class, philistines

чаршијуузлија *m arch. see* чаршуузлија

чаршиски *adj* market<place>, bazaar *attrib.*; shop *attrib.*; *fig.* street *attrib.*; *fig.* philistine; чаршиски човек *see* чаршуузлија

чаршуузлија -ии *m arch.* trader, merchant

час *m* **1** hour; состанокот траеше два часа the meeting took (lasted) two hours; половина час half an hour; (*as a measure of distance*) до врвот имаше уште два часа одење it was still two hours' walk to the top **2** (*sg only and with the article*) o'clock; дојди во три часот come at three <o'clock>! возот трггнува во осум часот и десет минути the train departs at eight ten (at ten past eight) **3** class, lesson, period; час по математика mathematics class (lesson); по третиот час, го напушти одделението after the third lesson he left the class; тој дома дава часови he gives lessons at home; распоред на часови <school> timetable; оди на часови to attend classes **4** moment, minute, instant; овој час at this <very> instant; <во> истиот час at the same moment (time); од тој час from that moment on; и не би час instantly, in the twinkling of an eye; и тој час at that <very> moment; и тој час станал домаќинот и излегол at that very moment the master got up and left; на часот (*less often* на час, часот) straight away, immediately, in a moment; on the dot; еден час for a moment; дојди еден час кај мене call in for a moment! ❏ секој час all the time; смртен (претсмртен) час the hour of <one's> death; на добар час *bon voyage!* во лош час in an evil hour, at the wrong time; час поскоро as soon as possible, the sooner the better; му удри часот, му дојде часот his hour (time) has come; his time is up; во дванаесеттиот час at the eleventh hour; at the last moment, in the nick of time; дванаесеттиот час удри, удри часот it is high time; до последниот час up to the last moment; полициски час curfew; час сака, час не сака now he wants to, now he doesn't

часкум *adv* **1** straight away, immediately; in a flash (moment); часкум излета низ врата immediately he ran out through the door **2** for a moment; види часкум дали е тука have a quick look and see if he's here!

часовник -ци *m* clock; watch; џебен часовник pocket-watch, fob watch; рачен часовник <wrist> watch; ѕиден часовник <wall> clock; стрелка на часовник hand on a clock/watch; градски часовник town clock; песочен часовник hourglass; навие часовник to wind a watch/clock; намести часовник to set one's clock/watch; провери часовник to check one's watch/clock

часовникар *m* watchmaker

часовникарски *adj* watchmaker's; watchmaking *attrib.*; часовникарски занает watchmaker's trade

часовникарство *n* watchmaking

часом & часум *adv see* часкум

часослов *m Rel.* diurnal, Book of Hours

част *f in the expression:* нека му е част и чест all honour to him; нека ти е част и чест congratulations! *iron.* thank you!

частица *f see* честица, честичка

чатал *m* fork (*of a tree*)

чаталест *adj* forked

чатално *adv* in the form of a fork; in the shape of a V; in V formation; две гранки чатално се шират two branches fork

чати *impf arch. see* чита

чатија -ии *f* wooden roof structure, truss

чатиса *pf colloq.* (*in the tailor's trade*) to tack/baste together

чатисува *impf of* чатиса

чатма *f Carpentry* join, joint

чатма-веѓи *pl colloq.* beetle brows

чатмалија *adj indecl.* веѓи чатмалии *see* чатма-веѓи

чат-пат *adv colloq.* **1** now and then; occasionally; доаѓа кај нас чат-пат he comes to see us from time to time **2** little; very little; знае турски чат-пат he speaks broken Turkish, he has a smattering of Turkish

чауш *& less often* **чаушин** -ши *m* **1** *Hist.* sergeant (*in the Ottoman army*) **2** *Hist.* armed guard; bodyguard; policeman **3** *colloq.* boss, VIP

чаша *f* glass; tumbler; cup; mug; glassful, cupful; винска чаша wineglass, goblet; пивска чаша beer glass; ракиена чаша spirit glass; чаша за чај tea glass; teacup; чаша чабурлија *see* чабур чаша; кристална чаша crystal glass; пластична чаша plastic glass/cup; чаша за миење заби tooth glass (mug); чаша за коцкање dice-box, dice cup; испив неколку чаши вино I drank a few glasses of wine; чаша чај glass/cup of tea; чаша вода glass of water; ја испи чашата до крај he drained the cup to the dregs (*also fig.*); ❏ во чаша да го/ја пиеш (испиеш) he/she is a delight; крева (дига, пие) чаша to raise one's glass, toast; горчлива чаша poisoned chalice, bitter pill

чаше & чашенце *n dim. of* чаша; чаше коњак, ракија и сл. a glass of brandy, *raki*, etc.

чашка *f* **1** *dim. of* чаша **2** *Bot.* calyx, envelope **3** *Anat.* 1. (*на колено*) kneecap, patella 2. (*на бубрег*) renal calyx 3. (*на зглоб*) glenoid cavity **4** *Elec.* porcelain insulator (housing)

чашурка *f* **1** *see* чашка 1 & 2 **2** demitasse, coffee-cup **3** scallop shell

чвркне *pf colloq.* чвркна *aor.* **1** to burn, scorch, singe *trans.*; сонцето го чвркна тутунот the sun scorched the tobacco **2** to hit

чвркнува *impf of* чвркне

чврчори *impf see* црцори

чевел -вли *m* shoe; обуе чевли to put on one's shoes; собуе чевли to take off one's shoes; ниски чевли court shoes, *Am.* pumps; високи чевли ankle-high boots; дрвени чевли clogs; лачени чевли patent-leather shoes; планинарски чевли hiking boots; чевли на врзување lace-up shoes; чевли за танцување dancing shoes, pumps; чевли за бебиња bootees; боја за чевли shoe polish; четка за чевли shoe-brush; лажица за чевли shoehorn; едно рало чевли a pair of shoes

чевла *f dial. see* чевел

чевлар *m* shoemaker, cobbler

чевларница *f* 1 cobbler's workshop 2 shoe shop

чевларски *adj* shoemaker's; shoemaking *attrib.*; чевларски занает shoemaker's trade

чевларство *n* shoemaking

чевле & чевленце *n dim. of* чевел

чевличе *n dim. of* чевла, *see* чевле

чевол -вли *m dial. see* чевел

чевре *n* embroidered kerchief

чедник -ци *m dial.* father

чедница *f dial.* mother

чедо *n* child; му даде Господ чедо the Lord gave him a child

чедоубиец -јци *m* infanticide, murderer of a child

чедоубиство *n* infanticide, murder of a child

чеза *f* gig, cabriolet

чезне *impf* to languish, pine, (за, no – for) waste away

чеиз *m arch.* trousseau, dowry

чек *m Comm.* cheque; бариран чек crossed (*Am.* certified) cheque; наплати чек to cash a cheque; плати <по> чек to honour a cheque

чека *impf* 1 to wait (for), await; чекај ме тука! wait for me here! чекај! hang on! wait a moment! сите овие работи тебе те чекаат all this work is waiting for you; ❏ чека во ред за нешто to queue up for s.th.; чека во заседа to lie in wait (for); не чекајќи straight away, without delay; чека месец обесен to twiddle one's thumbs; чека поволна прилика to bide one's time; кој чека, ќе дочека *prov.* everything comes to him who waits 2 (очекува) to expect; to look forward to; не го чекав тоа од тебе I didn't expect that from you; одвај чекам да те видам I am looking forward to seeing you, I can hardly wait to see you

чекален *m dial.* person who waits; person who welcomes s.o.

чекалиште *n* waiting spot (place)

чекална *f see* чекалница

чекалница *f* waiting-room

чекан *m* hammer; дрвен чекан mallet; тежок чекан sledgehammer

чеканче *n* 1 *dim. of* чекан 2 gavel; докторско чеканче plexor, plessor 3 *Anat.* (коска во средното уво) hammer, malleus

чекање *n* (*from* чека) waiting; листа на чекање waiting-list

чекач *m* person who waits

чекич *m dial. see* чекан

чеклас *m* awn, beard

чекмеже & чекмеце *n colloq.* drawer; (за пари) till

чековен -вна *adj* cheque *attrib.*; чековна сметка cheque account; чековна книшка cheque-book

чекор *m* step; pace; (голем) stride; (звук на чекори) footsteps; *fig.* move, step, demarche; со брз чекор, со брзи чекори with quick steps; два чекори понатаму two steps further on; чекор напред a step forward; дипломатски чекор diplomatic move, demarche; ❏ погрешен чекор a false move, a step in the wrong direction; презема заеднички чекори со/против to make common cause with/against; преземе

решителен чекор to take a decisive step; чекор по чекор step by step; држи (оди во) чекор со некого to keep in step with s.o., keep abreast of s.o.; оди во чекор со времето to move with the times; на секој чекор at every step, on every hand; губи чекор to fall (lag) behind; to be out of step; следи некого во чекор to tail (tag) s.o.; to be hard on s.o.'s heels; не отстапува ни чекор not to yield an inch; прави прв чекор to take the first step, make the first move; тој е чекор пред другите he stays one jump ahead; he leads the field

чекора *f see* чекор

чекори *impf* I 1 *intrans.* to step; (со големи чекори) to stride; чекори ситно to mince, take mincing steps; чекори напред to move forward (*also fig.*) 2 *trans.* to walk over, cross; чекори праг to cross the threshold II – се to place one's feet wide apart, splay one's legs

чекрек -ци & **чекрк** -ци *m* 1 *see* родан 2 (на бунар и др.) winch, windlass; pulley

чекулец -лци *m* speck <of dirt>, mote

чекутина *f* stunted grass/grain

чекутка *f see* чекутина

челад *f coll.* 1 children, offspring; машка челад sons; женска челад daughters 2 members of a household, family, clan; домаќинот и челадта the master and his household

челадија *f coll. colloq.* people; children; members of a household

челебија -ии *m arch.* sir, master; young master

челебиче *n f.p. dim. of* челебија

челен -лна *adj* 1 *Anat.* frontal; челна коска frontal (coronal) bone 2 *Mil.* frontal; челен одред vanguard 3 *fig.* leading, foremost; high-ranking; челно место leading position

челенка *f arch.* ornamental silver headgear (*as a sign of heroism*)

челик[1] *m* steel (*also fig.*); пречистен челик fine (refined) steel; кален челик tempered steel; тврд како челик as hard as steel; фабрика за челик steelworks, steel mill

челик[2] -ци *m* 1 (дрвцето) cat, tipcat 2 (играта) tipcat; игра челик to play tipcat

челиков *adj* steel *attrib.*, of steel; порти челикови steel gates; *see* челичен 1

челист *m Mus.* cellist

челистички *adj Mus.* cellist's

челистка *f Mus.* (*fem. form*) *see* челист

челичана *f* steelworks, steel mill

челичен -чна *adj* 1 steel *attrib.*; челични прачки steel rods; челична жица steel wire 2 *fig.* steely, of steel; челичен дух spirit of steel; челично здравје iron constitution; челични нерви nerves of steel, iron nerves

челичи *impf fig.* I to steel, harden, inure to hardship; челичи карактер/дух to steel the character/spirit II – се to steel (harden) o.s., become inured to hardship; во тешкотиите се челичиме we are tempered by hardship

челник -ци *m* leader; front-ranker; head shepherd; chieftain; *Mil.* file-leader

чело[1] *n* 1 forehead, *poet.* brow; го бакна в чело he kissed him on the forehead; високо чело high forehead; ниско чело low forehead; намуртено чело furrowed (puckered) brow; ❏ со ведро чело serenely,

with a serene look; with a clear conscience; со кренато чело with flying colours; со крстот на челото е he wears his heart on his sleeve; he is very honest/sincere **2** *fig.* front, head; чело на одред/ баталјон *и сл.* head of detachment/battalion, *etc.*; на чело на војската at the head of the troops, in the vanguard; на чело на државата at the head of the state; на чело на трпезата at the head of the table; ❏ на чело е to lead the way, be in the van; to be a ringleader; застанува на чело to come to the fore

чело² *n Mus.* cello

челуз *m* one side of a ridge between furrows, *see* слог¹

челуст *f Anat.* jaw, maxilla; (*на животно исто и*) chop; mandible

челустен -сна *adj Anat.* jaw *attrib.*, maxillary; mandibular; челусна коска jawbone

челце *n dim. of* чело¹

чембер¹ *m arch.* **1** iron hoop **2** strip iron

чембер² *m arch.* veil; <silk> kerchief

чемер *m* bitterness; gall, wormwood; distress, affliction, heartbreak, wretchedness

чемерен -рна *adj* full of gall (wormwood); distressed, heart-sick, wretched; чемерни зборови bitter words

чемерика *f Bot.* (Veratrum album) <white> hellebore, <false> hellebore

чемрее *impf* to pine (long) (*за, по – for*), miss; to be homesick; to mourn, grieve (*for*)

ченгел *m* metal hook

ченгија -ии *f arch.* dancing-girl; се крши (се витка) како некоја ченгија she sways like a Gypsy dancer

чеп *m* (*на каца и сл.*) spigot; cork; stopper; plug; (*на чешма*) tap, stopcock; *Med. colloq.* tampon, wad; gag

чепати *impf* **I** to open wide *trans.*; чепати уста to gape **II – се 1** to splay one's legs; to do the splits **2** *fig.* to exert o.s., make an effort, strain, strive; (*премногу*) to overexert (overwork) o.s. **3** *fig. colloq.* to pull a face; to put on an act; to fool around

чеперест *adj see* чепорест

чеперок -ци *m* (*педа*) span (*the distance from the tip of the thumb to the tip of the forefinger*)

чепи се *impf colloq.* to try to get out (*of s.th.*), try to wriggle out (*of s.th.*); to stall, hedge, beg off, invent excuses

чепка *impf* **I 1** to poke about, scratch <in> the ground, dig (*for worms*); кокошките си чепкале на буниште the hens were picking about the dungheap **2** to pick; чепка заби to pick one's teeth; чепка нос to pick one's nose **3** *fig.* (*буцка*) to pick (poke) about; to tinker (*with s.th.*); to rummage (*through s.th.*); to poke (*into s.th.*); to potter <about> *intrans.*; не чепкај тука don't poke about here! чепка по бавчата to potter in the garden; чепка каде што не му е работа to poke one's nose into s.th.; to meddle in s.o.'s affairs **4** to card, pick, tease; чепка волна to card wool **II – се 1** (*see* I 2) to pick (*one's nose, teeth, skin, etc.*) **2** to stir up trouble; to tease; не се чепкај! stop messing about! let sleeping dogs lie!

чепкалка *f* toothpick

чепкало *n* **1** *colloq.* snooper, busybody; *Brit. colloq.* Nosey Parker, *Austral.* stickybeak **2** card (*for wool, etc.*)

чепкен *m arch.* a kind of short overcoat (*the sleeves of which are slit, leaving the arms free*)

чепне *pf* чепна *aor.* **1** to pick, poke **2** to touch; to brush (*against s.th.*); to glance, graze

чепнува *impf of* чепне

чепорест *adj* forked

чепорок -ци *m see* чеперок

чепорошка *f* forked stick

чепур *m see* шопур

чепче *n dim. of* чеп

червиш *m colloq.* gravy, juice

черга *f* **1** rag-carpet, rough carpet **2** small makeshift tent, gypsy tent **3** *dial. see* јамболија

чергар *m* wanderer, traveller; *colloq.* Gypsy

чергарка *f* (*fem. form*) *see* чергар

чергарски *adj* traveller's; *colloq.* Gypsy's; чергарски живот nomadic life

чергиче *n dim. of* черга

черевиз *m Bot. colloq. see* целер

черек -ци *m colloq.* quarter; quarter of an hour; исече на череци to quarter; во еден и черек at one fifteen, at a quarter past one

черен *m arch* above the hearth

череп *m* **1** *dial. see* црeп **2** *literary Anat.* skull, cranium

черепна *f dial. see* црепна

речи *impf* **1** to quarter, divide (cut up) into quarters **2** *fig.* to torment; to overload (*s.o. with duties*)

черешна *f dial. see* црeшa

черешнар *m* (*folk name for*) May

черчеве *n colloq.* frame (*esp. of a door, window*)

чесен¹ -сни *m* clove <of garlic>

чесен² -сна *adj* **1** decent, fine; honest; honourable; chaste; чесна душа honest soul; чесни намери honourable intentions; чесна постапка honourable deed; ❏ чесен и поштен fair and square; чесен збор! upon my honour! word of honour! honest to God! cross my heart! дава чесен збор to pledge one's word of honour; чесно име никогаш не гине honesty is the best policy **2** *arch.* holy, venerable; чесен крст holy cross (rood); чесна сестра nun; чесен суде! Your Honour! (*addressing a magistrate or judge*)

чесно *adv* decently; honestly; honourably, with honour; morally; fairly; чесно мисли to think honourably; чесно работи to work honestly

чесност *f* decency; honesty; honour; morality; fairness; chastity

чест¹ *f* **1** honour, reputation; virtue; изгуби чест to be disgraced; гледа многу на својата чест to be jealous of one's honour; суд на честа public esteem, court of honour; смета за чест to consider (*s.th.*) an honour; тоа ми прави чест I am honoured; имам чест (ja имам честа) да . . . I have the honour to . . . ; во чест на некого/нешто in honour of s.o./s.th.; во чест на празникот on the occasion of the holiday; чест на девојка a young woman's virtue (virginity); земе чест на девојка to dishonour (deflower) a maid; ❏ чест да немам <ако те лажам> <it's the truth,> upon my word of honour! cross my heart! за чест и слава just for the glory of it; секоја чест congratulations! well done! good for you! секоја чест на присутните present company excepted; тоа му е под чест that's beneath his dignity; му служи на чест that does him credit; *iron.* he should be ashamed of himself; прашање на честа point of honour; част и чест *see* част; чест секому, вересија никому *prov.* business is business; honour and profit lie not in one sack; поарно да си без пари, отколку без чест *prov.* honesty is the best policy; better beg than steal **2** respect; стекне чест, здобие се со чест to gain respect; направи (стори) чест на некого to show s.o. respect; to be a credit to s.o.; to wine and dine s.o.; оддаде некому чест to pay one's respects to s.o.

чест² *adj* **1** frequent; честа појава frequent occurrence; чести патувања frequent trips **2** thick, dense; честа гора (шума) dense forest

честак -ци *m* dense (thick) forest

честар *m* thicket; heart of the forest

чести¹ *impf* **I 1** to treat (*s.o. to s.th.*), stand (*s.o.*) a treat/drink, invite (*s.o.*) for a drink/treat, *Austral., N.Z. colloq.* shout (*s.o. a drink, etc.*); to foot the bill; ќе те честам една чаша вино let me buy you a glass of wine! чести кафе to invite (*s.o.*) to have coffee, treat (*s.o.*) to coffee; денеска јас честам today it is my treat, *colloq.* today it's on me **2** to honour, respect, like; тебе сите те честат you are always popular **3** to congratulate; ти го честиме името we wish you a happy name-day **II – се** to treat o.s. (*to s.th.*); to treat one another

чести² *impf f.p.* to go/come (*somewhere*) often, be a frequent visitor; што честом честиш на хоро? why do you come to the dances so often?

честина *f* fine sieve

честит *adj* **1** happy, *only in expressions such as:* честит именден! happy name-day! честита Нова година Happy New Year! честит син! congratulations on the birth of your son! честита ви работа! good luck in your work! **2** *arch. in the expressions:* честити царе, честита царице! Your Majesty!

честита *impf* to congratulate; честита на некого победа/успех to congratulate s.o. on a victory/on a success; честита некому именден/роденден to wish s.o. a happy name-day/birthday; <ти> честитам! congratulations! good for you! well done!

честитка *f* **1** congratulations; good wishes; новогодишни честитки season's greetings **2** greeting card, Christmas/New-Year card

честито *adv* congratulations!

честитост *f* happiness

честица *f* **1** fragment; fraction, particle, jot, tittle **2** *Gram.* particle

честичка *f see* честица 1

често *adv* often, frequently; често пати *see* честопати

честољубец -пци *m literary* ambitious person

честољубив *adj literary* **1** (*кој држи многу до својата чест*) self-respecting; (*кој не трпи никакви навреди*) touchy **2** ambitious; (*премногу*) nakedly ambitious

честољубивост *f literary* self-respect; touchiness; ambitiousness; naked ambition

честом *adv see* често

честопати *adv* often, frequently

честоред *adj* densely arranged; closely packed/spaced; in serried ranks

честота *f* frequency

чета *f* **1** *Mil.* company; (*коњска*) troop; вод, чета и баталјон a platoon, a company and a battalion **2** unit, work-gang **3** *Hist.* comitadji unit; комитска чета band of komitadjis **4** band, gang; разбојничка чета band of robbers

четворен -рна *adj* **1** quadruple, fourfold; четворен успех fourfold success **2** quadruple; четворна кола *see* четворкола; четворен конец four-ply yarn; четворно платно quadruple cloth, cloth consisting of four layers **3** *fig.* veritable, real, four-square; четворен маж a man-and-a-half, a real man **4** four-sided, quadrilateral; quadripartite; four-man; четворен сојуз *Hist.* Quadruple Alliance

четворица *num* (*of men or mixed groups*) <group of> four, foursome; четворица браќа four brothers

четворка *f* **1** (*цифрата* 4) <figure> four; мојот број завршува на две четворки my number ends in two fours **2** (*школска оцена*) four (*out of five, hence = 'very good'*), 'В'; тој е наполно одличен, нема ни една четворка he is a first-class student, he does not have even one four ('В') **3** (*во карти*) four; кец и четворка an ace and a four **4** <group of> four, foursome; поделете се на четворки divide up into groups of four! **5** (*автобус, трамвај итн.*) <number> four; кај него се оди со четворката you can get to his place with the number four

четворкола *f* four-wheeled carriage, four wheeler; coach and four, four-in-hand, four-horse carriage; wagon drawn by four bullocks

четворно *adv* fourfold, four times over; ќе ти платам тројно и четворно I'll repay you three and four times over

четворогласен -сна *adj see* четиригласен

четворокатен -тна *adj see* четирикатен

четворокатница *f see* четиркатница

четворократен -тна *adj see* четирикратен

четворокрилен -лна *adj see* четирикрилен

четворолистен -сна *adj see* четирилистен

четворомоторен -рна *adj see* четиримоторен

четвороножен -жна *adj see* четириножен

четворореден -дна *adj see* четириреден

четворосложен -жна *adj Gram. see* четирисложен; четворосложен збор tetrasyllable, word of four syllables

четворособен -бна *adj see* четирисобен; четворособен стан four-room flat (*Am.* apartment)

четворостран *adj see* четиристран; четворострана пирамида four-sided pyramid

четврт¹ *m* quarter; четврт кило a quarter <of a> kilo; еден четврт шеќер 250 gram<me>s of sugar; три четврти сол three quarters of a kilo of salt, 750 gram<me>s of salt; еден и четврт a quarter past one

четврт² *f* quarter; градска четврт city quarter

четвртест *adj* square; *Geom.* rectangular; четвртеста шамија square kerchief

четврт<и> *adj num* fourth; на четвртиот кат on the fourth floor; четвртиот ден the fourth day; четврти дел од нешто <the> fourth part of s.th., quarter; ❏ четврта рака <тутун> fourth picking <of tobacco>

четвртина *f* **1** quarter **2** *Print.* quarto **3** *Mus.* crochet, *Am.* quarter note

четвртинка *f dim. of* четвртина 1

четврток -ци *m* Thursday; вели четврток (*also* величетврток) Maundy Thursday

четвртокласник -ци *m* pupil in the fourth form (*of secondary school*), fourth-former

четвртокласничка *f* (*of a girl*) *see* четвртокласник

четврточен -чна *adj* Thursday *attrib.*; секој четврточен ден every Thursday

четвртчија -ии *m arch.* tenant farmer (*who pays over*

three quarters of the crop as rent), *Am.* sharecropper, *Austral.* share farmer

чете *impf dial. see* чита

четен -тна *adj* company *attrib.*; unit *attrib.*; detachment *attrib.*; band *attrib.*; четен командир company commander; group leader; komitadji leader, *condottiere*; captain

четиво *n* reading; extract; reading matter

четина *f* bristle<s>; свинска четина hog's bristles

четинар *m* conifer

четинест *adj* bristly

четири *num* four; на сите четири страни in all directions; оди на четири нозе to crawl on all fours, crawl on hands and knees; ❑ отвори си ги на <дваесет и> четири <очите> keep your eyes peeled, keep your weather-eye open; во четири очи face to face; confidentially; between you and me; ги дигнал сите четири he's idling his time away; he's taking it easy; седи помеѓу четири ѕида to be cooped up at home; повеќе гледаат четири очи отколку две *prov.* four eyes are better than two

четириаголен -лна *adj* rectangular; square; quadrangular; four-cornered

четириаголник -ци *m* rectangle; square; quadrangle

четирибоен -јна *adj* four-colour, four-tone *attrib.*

четиривалентен -тна *adj Chem.* quadrivalent

четиригласен -сна *adj Mus.* four-part; четиригласна хорска песна four-part choral song, song arranged for four voices

четиригодишен -шна *adj* 1 four years old; четиригодишно дете four-year-old <child>; четиригодишно вино four-year-old wine 2 four-year *attrib.*, of/for four years; lasting four years; quadrennial; четиригодишно школување four years' schooling

четиригодишнина *f* fourth anniversary

четиридневен -вна *adj* of/for four days, four-day *attrib.*

четириесет *num* forty

четириесетгодишен -шна *adj* 1 forty years old 2 of/for forty years, forty-year *attrib.*

четириесетгодишнина *f* fortieth anniversary

четириесетдневен -вна *adj* of/for forty days, forty-day *attrib.*

четириесетина *num* 1 (*of men or mixed groups*) <group of> forty, *see* четириесетмина 2 about forty 3 *f* fortieth <part>; две четириесетини two fortieths

четириесетмина *num* (*of men or mixed groups*) forty

четириесетти *adj num* 1 fortieth; четириесеттиот ден 1. the fortieth day 2. on the fortieth day 2 во четириесеттите години in the <nineteen/eighteen *etc.*> forties

четириесетчасовен -вна *adj* forty-hour *attrib.*; четириесетчасовна работна недела forty-hour week

четирикатен -тна *adj* four-storey<ed>; четирикатна куќа four-storey house

четирикатница *f* four-storey house

четирикратен -тна *adj* fourfold; quadruple; four-time<s> *attrib.*

четирикрилен -лна *adj* four-leaved/-winged; четирикрилна врата four-leaved door; четирикрилен прозорец four-paned, four-light window

четирилистен -сна *adj* four-leaf, *Bot.* quadrifoliate; четирилисна детелина (Marsilia quadrifolia) four-leaf clover

четиримесечен -чна *adj* 1 lasting four months, four-month *attrib.* 2 four months old

четиримоторен -рна *adj* four-engined *attrib.*; четиримоторен авион four-engined aircraft

четиринаесет *num* fourteen

четиринаесетгодишен -шна *adj* 1 lasting fourteen years, fourteen-year *attrib.* 2 fourteen years old

четиринаесетмина *num* (*of men or mixed groups*) fourteen

четиринаесетти *adj num* fourteenth

четиринеделен -лна *adj* 1 lasting four weeks, four-week *attrib.* 2 four weeks old

четириножен -жна *adj* four-legged; четириножно животно four-legged animal, quadruped; четириножно столче four-legged stool

четирипати *adv* four times; четирипати дојде he came four times; четирипати поголем four times larger (as large)

четириреден -дна *adj* four-rowed; four-tiered; four-deep

четирисложен -жна *adj* tetrasyllabic, four-syllable *attrib.*; четирисложен збор tetrasyllable

четирисобен -бна *adj* four-room *attrib.*; четирисобен стан four-room flat (*Am.* apartment)

четириспратен -тна *adj see* четирикатен

четириспратница *f see* четирикатница

четиристапен -пна *adj Prosody* of four feet; четиристапен јамб iambic tetrameter

четиристишен -шна *adj Prosody* of four lines; четиристишна строфа four-line stanza

четиристишие -ија *n Prosody* quatrain

четиристотини *num* four hundred

четиристран *adj* four-sided, quadrilateral; четиристрана пирамида four-sided pyramid

четиритактен -тна *adj Mech.* four-stroke; четиритактен мотор four-stroke engine

четиритонски *adj* 1 weighing four tonnes 2 holding four tonnes, four-tonne *attrib.*; четиритонски камион four-tonner

четиричасовен -вна *adj* of/for four hours, four-hour *attrib.*; четиричасовен одмор four-hour break

четири-четвртински *adj Mus.* четири-четвртински такт four-beat, four-stroke

четиричлен & четиричленен -лена *adj* of four members (parts), four-member/-man *attrib.*; четиричлено семејство family of four

четка[1] *f* brush; четка за алишта clothes-brush; четка за чевли shoe-brush; четка за кал hard shoe-brush; четка за рибање scrubbing-brush; четка за варосување whitewash-brush; четка за коса hairbrush; четка за чистење broom

четка[2] *impf* 1 to brush *trans.*, give a brushing; четка алишта/чевли to brush clothes/shoes 2 *fig.* to fool *trans.*, pull the wool over s.o.'s eyes; те четка he is lying to you

четкар *m* brush-maker; brush-seller

четкарник -ци *m* brush-holder (*a wall holder for clothes-brushes and hairbrushes*)

четкиче *n & ***четкичка** *f see* четче

четник -ци *m Hist.* 1 comitadji, komitadji, komitaji 2 chetnik

четнички *adj Hist.* comitadji *attrib.*; chetnik *attrib.*

четништво *n Hist.* comitadji/chetnik movement; comitadji/chetnik activities; comitadjis/chetniks

четче *n dim. of* четка; четче за заби toothbrush; четче за цртање/боење paint-brush

Чех -еси *m* Czech

Чехинка *f (fem. form) see* Чех

чечка *impf see* чепка 1 & 2

чечкало *n colloq. see* чепкало 1

чечне *pf* чечна *aor. see* чепне

чечнува *impf of* чечне

чеша *impf* **I 1** (*with person as subject*) to scratch *trans.*; ❑ си го чеша јазикот he's just talking, he's wagging his tongue; си ги чешаат јазиците they are shooting the breeze; кај што те чеша твоја рака, не те чеша туѓата; туѓата рака не чеша како твојата *prov.* if you want a thing well done, do it yourself **2** (*with part of body as subject*) to itch; го чеша грбот 1. his back is itchy 2. *fig.* he is looking for trouble, he is asking for it; ❑ го чеша јазикот to be itching (dying) (*to say s. th.*) **II – се** to scratch o.s.; to scratch one another; не се чешај кај што не те јаде let sleeping dogs lie!

чешалка *f* & **чешало** *n* curry-comb

чешел -шли *m* **1** comb **2** *see* чешалка & чешало

чешелче *n dim. of* чешел

чешен -шни *m dial. see* чесен[1]

чешит[1] *m colloq.* sort, kind; разни чешити different sorts

чешит[2] *adj indecl. colloq.* mischievous, impish; чешит човек roguish fellow

Чешка[1] *f* the Czech Republic

чешка[2] (**се**) *impf dim. of* чеша (се)

чешки *adj* Czech

чешла *impf* **I** to comb **II – се** to comb o.s.; to preen o.s.; селото гори, бабата се чешла *prov.* Nero fiddles while Rome burns

чешлар *m* comb-maker; comb-seller

чешларка *f (fem. form) see* чешлар

чешларница *f* comb workshop; comb shop

чешларски *adj* comb-maker's; comb-seller's

чешле & **чешленце** *n dim. of* чешел

чешлика *f Bot.* (Dipsacus silvestris) <wild> teasel

чешлиште *n augm. of* чешел

чешма *f* **1** spring, fountain; drinking fountain; оди на чешма да донесе вода she is going to the fountain to fetch water **2** tap, *Am.* faucet; затвори ја чешмата turn off the tap!

чешмен *adj* fountain *attrib.*; tap, *Am.* faucet *attrib.*; чешмена вода tap water

чешмеџија -ии *m* fountain-maker/repairer; tap- (*Am.* faucet) maker; plumber

чешмиче *n* & **чешмичка** *f dim. of* чешма

чешмурка *f* tap, *Am.* faucet; spout (*of a fountain*)

чешмурче *n dim. of* чешмурка

чешне[1] (**се**) *pf* чешна (се) *aor. see* чешка[2] (се)

чешне[2] *impf* to tear off *trans.*

чешоглава *f (fem. form) see* чешоглавец

чешоглавец -вци *m colloq.* lazybones, layabout

чибук -ци *m* **1** pipe-stem; chibouk, long-stemmed pipe **2** long cigarette-holder **3** *Hist.* tax paid in cattle to the Ottoman Sultan

чибукар & **чибукчија** -ии *m Hist.* **1** servant in charge of tobacco-pipes **2** chibouk maker/seller **3** tax collector, *see* чибук 3

чибуче *n* **1** *dim. of* чибук 1 **2** cigarette-holder

чивија -ии *f* nail; wedge; pin, peg, bolt; (*дрвена*) nog; (*на тркало*) linchpin; чивија чивија чука *prov.* one nail drives out another; you have to fight fire with fire

чивит *m* **1** *Bot.* (Indigofera tinctoria) indigo <plant> **2** *colloq.* indigo <blue>

чивитар *m arch.* indigo vendor

чизија -ии *f arch.* line

чизма *f* boot; чизми за јавање riding boots; војнички чизми army boots; jackboots; гумени чизми gumboots; wellington boots; ❑ под фашистичка чизма under the fascist heel

чизмар *m* bootmaker

чизмарка *f (fem. form) see* чизмар

чизмарски *adj* bootmaker's; bootmaking *attrib.*

чизмарство *n* bootmaking

чизмичка *f dim. of* чизма

чиј -ја, -ие *pron* whose; (*as a relative pron. with or without* што; *see also* чијшто) чие е ова девојче? whose daughter is this? човекот чија беше куќата не беше присутен the man whose house it was was not present; веднаш се сетив чиј син е тој I remembered straight away whose son he was

чијшто, чијашто, чиешто *pron* whose, *see* чиј

чик *interj dial.* (*see* ајде, ајде де) come on!

чик-чирик *interj* (*of birds*) chirrup! chirp! cheep!

чиле[1] *n* (*волница*) skein, hank; (*конец*) reel, spool

Чиле[2] *n* Chile

Чилеанец -нци *m* Chilean

Чилеанка *f (fem. form) see* Чилеанец

чилеански *adj* Chilean

чин *m* **1** rank; во чин на офицер of officer's rank; as an officer **2** *Theatre* act; пиеса во три чина a play in three acts **3** *literary* act, deed; ❑ го стави пред свршен чин he confronted him with a *fait accompli*

чина *f dial. see* стрина

чинар *m Bot.* (Platanus orientalis) <oriental> plane <tree>

чинéли *pl Mus.* cymbals

чини *impf* **I 1** *colloq.* to do, act; што да чинам? what am I to do? чини злости to commit atrocities; чини кавга to start a fight; чини метании to bow <down>; *fig.* to grovel; to kow-tow; *f.p.* чини зговор to arrange an engagement; чини лакрдии (*со*) to have a chat; to make fun of; *f.p.* чини свадба to celebrate a wedding; чини дикат (мукает) to watch out, be careful **2** to be worth; to cost; колку чини шапкава? how much does this hat cost? ❑ чини пари to be valuable; тоа ти чини пари that's worth a fortune; колку <пари> чини 1. what use is it? 2. what's it worth? ни пет пари не чини it's not worth a brass farthing (*Am.* red cent); ќе те чини како на свети Петар кајганата it will cost you an arm and a leg **3** to be of use, of help; тоа не ти чини that won't do you any good; that won't help you; you shouldn't do/ say that; ❑ за ништо не чини (*за нешто*) it's useless, it's no use; (*за човек*) he's completely wrong; (*за човек*) he's not well, he is in poor health **4** *f.p.* to change into *trans.*; чини ме еден крал turn me into a king! **5** *impers.* (*with dat.*) to want, feel like; ако ми чини if I feel like it; ако ти чини as you like! take it or leave it! **6** *impers.* (*usu. negated*) one should, one ought; не чини така да зборуваш you shouldn't talk like that **7** *impers.* чини! all right! fine! **8** (*with following imperative of* *perfective verb*) to keep <on>; чини фати ја и пак пушти ја he keeps grabbing her and letting her go **9** to think, consider, believe; чинев дека спиеш I thought you were asleep; чинам дека немаш право I do not think you're right; го чинев будала I took him for a fool; чиниш . . . apparently, you might think **II – се 1** *impers.* (*with dat.*) to seem; ми се чини дека . . . it seems to me that . . . ; I think that . . . ; така ти се чини that's what you think; се чини <дека> . . . it looks as though . . . ; времево, се чини, ќе се расипе it looks as though the weather's going to deteriorate; како што се чини to all appearances **2** *colloq.* to pretend (*to be*); to regard o.s. (*as*); се чинел поумен од другите he thought himself cleverer than the rest **3** *colloq.* to become; од ден на ден сè полош се чинеше he was getting worse day by day **4** *colloq.* to become; to turn into *intrans.*; се чини калуѓерка to become a nun, take the veil

чинија -ии *f* plate; (*за сервирање*) dish; bowl; (*количество*) plateful; длабока чинија soup-plate; плитка чинија dinner plate; ❑ дава некому нешто на чинија to give s.o. s.th. on a plate

чининачалствува *impf Rel.* to officiate

чиниче *n* (*dim. of* чинија) dessert plate; side plate; saucer

чиновник -ци *m* office worker, white-collar worker, clerk; (*во државна служба*) civil (*Austral.* public) servants

чиновникува *impf* to work in an office; to be (work as) a civil (*Austral.* public) servant

чиновничка *f* (*fem. form*) *see* чиновник

чиновнички *adj* office, white-collar *attrib.*, clerical; civil (*Austral.* public) servants

чиновништво *n* white-collar work; civil (*Austral.* public) service; civil (*Austral.* public) servants

чинодејствува *impf literary Rel.* to officiate, conduct the service (liturgy)

чип & чипав *adj see* чпрнтав & чпртав

чипаво *adv* weakly, feebly; faintly; poorly; чипаво фати he grasped it feebly

чипчи *impf* **1** to press, squeeze *trans.*, clench; таа ми ја чипчеше раката she was squeezing my hand **2** *fig.* to be mean, scrimp <and save>; многу чипчиш you're very mean

чир *m* **1** (*надворешен*) boil, *Med.* furuncle; blain **2** (*внатрешен*) ulcer; чир во стомакот stomach ulcer

чирав *adj* covered with boils; suffering from ulcers

чирак -ци *m* apprentice

чираклак -ци *m* apprenticeship

чиракува *impf* to serve one's apprenticeship, be (work as) an apprentice; to be apprenticed (*кај – to*)

чираче *n dim. of* чирак

чирачки *adj* apprentice's, of an apprentice

чирика & чирилика *impf* to chirrup, chirp, cheep; врабците чириликаа the sparrows were chirruping

чириш *m* shoemaker's glue

чирче *n dim. of* чир

число *n arch. see* број

чист *adj* **1** clean; (*уреден*) tidy, orderly; чисти алишта clean clothes; чисти раце clean hands; чиста куќа clean house; чист воздух clean (fresh) air; ❑ има три чисти to have a nerve, have the gall; to have the guts; нема три чисти to lack the nerve, *colloq.* chicken out

2 pure; unadulterated, unalloyed, fine, native; чисто злато pure (native, solid, fine) gold; чисто сребро pure (sterling) silver; чиста раса pure race; чиста наука pure science; чиста филозофија/математика *и сл.* pure philosophy/mathematics *etc.*; на чист македонски јазик in pure Macedonian **3** clear; crisp; чисто (јасно) небо clear sky; чисто лице, чист тен на лицето clear complexion; чист звук clear sound **4** clear; clean, honest, fair, straight; above board; чиста сметка clear reckoning; чиста работа 1. everything is clear; everything is fine 2. honest business; работата не ти е чиста your business is not honest; this is not a straight (honest, fair) deal; тоа не е чиста работа, тоа не се чисти работи there is something fishy about this; сметките не ти се чисти your accounts are not clear/honest **5** *Finance* clear, net<t>; чиста печалба clear (net) profit; чист приход net income; чиста загуба clear/dead loss; sheer waste; чиста штета net damage; dead loss **6** *fig.* innocent, with clean hands, with a clear conscience; spotless; chaste, undefiled; тој излезе чист од борбата he came out of the struggle with clean hands (with a clean slate); чиста ми е совеста my conscience is clear; човек со чисто срце a man with a guileless heart; чиста девица immaculate virgin **7** *fig.* pure, sheer, downright, blatant; чиста љубов true love; чиста клевета out-and-out (unqualified) slander; чиста лага a downright (blatant) lie; чист случај pure chance, sheer coincidence **8** *Rel.* чисти понеделник first Monday in Lent

чистач *m* cleaner; чистач на чевли shoeblack; чистач на улици street-sweeper, *Am.* street cleaner

чистачка *f* **1** (*fem. form*) *see* чистач **2** cleaning machine, cleaner; чистачка за снег snowplough; чистачка за улици street-sweeper

чистачки *adj* cleaner's; cleaning *attrib.*

чистеница *f dial. see* чистотница

чистење *n from* чисти; пролетно чистење spring-cleaning; хемиско чистење dry-cleaning; *fig. sl.* abortion; *Pol.* етничко чистење ethnic cleansing

чисти *impf* **I** to clean; to cleanse/purify/refine/clear (*also fig.*); чисти куќа/улица/ алишта/чевли/заби to clean a house/the street/clothes/shoes/one's teeth; чисти дрво од гасеници to remove caterpillars from a tree; чисти оџак to sweep a chimney; чисти канал to dredge a canal; чисти риба to clean (scale) fish; чисти ораси to shell walnuts; чисти земја (држава) од крадци to clear a country (state) of thieves **II – се 1** to wash *intrans.*, clean o.s.; (*за птици*) to preen **2** to clear <up> *intrans.*; небото се чисти the sky is clearing; времето се чисти the weather is clearing up; гласот ми се чисти my voice is improving **3** *fig.* to be freed (cleansed, rid) (*од – of*) **4** to clear out, clear off; морам да се чистам одовде I'll have to get out of here; *colloq.* чисти се! clear off!

чистилиште *n literary Rel.* purgatory

чистина *f* **1** clearing; open space; ❑ да се изведе работата на чистина to bring the matter out into the open **2** *see* чистота

чистинка *f dim. of* чистина 1

чистка *f Pol.* purge

чисто *adv* **1** cleanly; clearly; purely; внатре беше чисто и уредно inside it was clean and tidy; таа држи многу чисто she keeps things very tidy, she runs a tidy household; чисто македонски збор pure<ly> Macedonian word; говори чисто to speak clearly; свири чисто to play faultlessly; тоа е чисто твоја грешка that is purely your mistake; ❏ чисто – сол да макаш it's so clean you can eat off the floor **2** (*нето*) clear, net<t>; десет килограма чисто ten kilos net **3** ❏ тој е на чисто he knows where he stands; сакам со тоа да бидеме на чисто I want this to square our accounts; изведе нешто на чисто to bring s.th. out into the open; чисто и јасно plainly; чисто и просто purely and simply

чистокрвен -вна *adj* (*за животни*) pure-bred, pure-blooded; (*особено за коњи*) thoroughbred; (*за луѓе*) pure, full-blood; чистокрвен арапски коњ a thoroughbred Arab horse

чистокрвност *f* (*за животни*) pure-bloodedness; (*особено за коњи*) thoroughbred quality, pedigree; (*за луѓе*) pure line

чистосрдечен -чна *adj* candid, frank, open-hearted

чистосрдечно *adv* candidly, frankly, open-heartedly

чистосрдечност *f* candour, frankness, open-heartedness

чистота *f* cleanness, cleanliness; tidiness, neatness; purity; чистота на град cleanliness of a town; градска чистота *Brit.* corporation cleansing department, *Am.* municipal sanitation department; чистота на воздух cleanness/clarity/purity of the air; чистота на јазик purity of a language; морална чистота moral purity; chastity; чистота на обичаи/стил purity of customs/style; чистота на ракопис neatness of (*s.o.'s*) handwriting; чистотата е половина здравје *saying* cleanliness is next to godliness

чистотија *f see* чистота

чистотник -ци *m* **1** stickler for clean<li>ness **2** *fig.* paragon of virtue **3** *fig.* purist

чистотница *f* (*fem. form*) *see* чистотник

чистотништво *n* scrupulous/excessive cleanliness; *fig.* purism

чита *impf* to read; тој знае да чита и да пишува he can read and write; чита книга/писмо/роман to read a book/letter/novel; чита предавање to deliver a lecture; чита в₀ себе to read silently, read to o.s.; чита на глас to read aloud; чита на брзина to scan; чита буква по буква to spell; чита ѕвезди to read the stars; чита ноти to read music; чита карта to read a map; чита нечии мисли to read s.o.'s thoughts; му чита на некого од очите to see (read) s.th. in s.o.'s eyes; чита меѓу редовите to read between the lines; ❏ чита на некого лекција (молитва, евангелие, буквица) to read s.o. the riot act, give s.o. a piece of one's mind

читав *adj in the expression:* здрав и читав safe and sound

читак -ци *m colloq. pejor.* Turk

читалиште *n Hist.* community cultural centre (*with a library*)

читална & **читалница** *f* reading-room

читаник -ци *m dial. see* љубовник

читанка *f* reader, primer; spelling-book

читанче *n dim. of* читанка

читател *m* reader; читателите на нашиот весник the readers (readership) of our newspaper;

библиотеката е полна со читатели the library is full of readers

читателка *f* (*fem. form*) *see* читател

читателски *adj* reader's; reading; читателска публика reading public

читач *m* **1** reader (*who reads aloud*); announcer; lecturer **2** *see* читател

читачки[1] *adj* reading *attrib.*, reader's; читачка група study group

читачки[2] *adj colloq. pejor.* (*see* читак) Turk's; Turkish

читлив *adj* legible; читлив ракопис legible manuscript/handwriting; читлив потпис legible signature

читливо *adv* legibly; тука беше сѐ јасно и читливо напишано here everything was written clearly and legibly; пишува читливо to write legibly

читливост *f* legibility

читок -тка *adj see* читлив

читко *adv see* читливо

чифлиг -зи *m* **1** *Hist.* feudal agricultural estate **2** farm; (*мал*) *Brit.* smallholding; манастирски чифлиг monastery farm

чифлигар *m Hist.* serf; farm-hand; tenant farmer, *Am.* sharecropper

чифлигарски *adj Hist.* serf's; farm-hand's; tenant farmer's, *Am.* sharecropper's

чифлигарство *n Hist.* feudal agricultural system

чифлигија -ии & **чифликсајбија** -ии *m Hist.* feudal lord, landowner

чифлишки *adj Hist.* feudal; farming *attrib.*

чифт *m* **1** pair, brace; yoke; (*дивеч*) brace; two, a couple; два чифта чорапи two pairs of socks/stockings; чифт пиштоли a brace of pistols; еден чифт промена a change of clothes; два чифта волови two pairs of bullocks; чифт по чифт in pairs, two by two **2** even number; чифт или тек, чифт-тек odd<s> or even<s>

чифте *n* **1** double-barrelled gun **2** ❏ фрла чифте (чифтиња) to kick <out>, lash out **3** pair; чифте пиштоли a brace of pistols, *see* чифт 1

чифтелија *adj indecl. arch.* double; чифтелија пиштоли double-barrelled pistol

чифтоса *pf* **I** (*за животни*) to mate, pair <for breeding> *trans.*; to couple *trans.*; (*за предмети*) to match, mate *trans.* **II** – ce to pair off *intrans.*; to copulate, mate *intrans.*

чифтосува (ce) *impf of* чифтоса (ce)

чифчија -ии *m Hist.* **1** *see* исполичар **2** *see* чифлигар

чифчилак *m Hist. see* чифчиство

чифчиски *adj Hist. see* чифлигарски

чифчиство *n Hist.* serfdom; farm labour

чиче -евци *m* **1** (*only sg*) *dim. hyp. of* чичо, чичко (*usu. as form of address*) **2** (*only pl*) uncle's house/family (household); ќе одиме кај чичевци we're going to uncle's

чичев *adj see* чичов

чичек -ци *m Bot. see* чичка

чиченце *n dim. of* чиче, чичко, чичо

чичин *adj see* чичов 2

чичка *f Bot.* **1** (Carduus nutans) <musk> thistle **2** bur<r>

чичко -овци *m see* стрико **1** father's brother **2** (*mode of address to a man one generation older than the speaker*) **1.** (*with a name*) чичко Петре Uncle Peter;

чичко Никола Uncle Nicholas 2. (*without a name*) mister

чичков *adj* uncle's

чичо -овци *m see* чичко

чичов *adj* 1 *see* чичков 2 (*mode of address to nephew, niece or any other child*) my boy/girl, son

чиш *interj* child. (*when a child wishes to urinate*) има чиш? are you going to pee?

чиша <ce> *impf child.* to piddle, pee

чишка <ce> *impf dim. of* чиша <ce>

чкембар *m colloq. see* шкембар

чкембарка *f colloq. see* шкембарка

чкембарница *f colloq. see* шкембарница

чкембарски *adj colloq. see* шкембарски

чкембе *n colloq. see* шкембе

чкембелија *adj indecl. colloq. see* шкембелија

чкембест *adj colloq. see* шкембест

чкембеџија -ии *m colloq. see* шкембеџија

чкембеџилница *f colloq. see* шкембеџилница

чкето *n colloq. see* шкето

чкива *impf sl.* to see; to look at; го чкиваш? can you see him? не му се чкива he can't bear the sight of him/it

чколија -ии *f* & **чколо** *n dial. see* училиште

чкор -ови *m* tree stump

чкорка *f* small tree stump

чкорлав *adj* hard

чкорче *n* 1 *dim. of* чкорка 2 (*кибритче*) match

чкота *impf dial.* (*буричка, буцка*) to rummage (*in, through*), poke about (*in*); to tinker (*with*)

чкрап *interj* click!

чкрапа *impf see* чкрапне

чкрапја *f Zool.* (Scorpio) scorpion

чкрапне *pf* чкрапна *aor.* 1 to click, go click; бравата чкрапна the lock clicked 2 to grind, gnash (*one's teeth*); чкрапне со забите to gnash one's teeth 3 (*со кибрит*) to strike (*a match*); (*со запалка*) to flick (*a lighter*); чкрапна со огнилото he struck the flint with the steel 4 *fig.* to wink; чкрапне со окото to wink

чкрапнува *impf of* чкрапне

чкрбот *m* gnashing, grinding

чкрботи *impf* to gnash, grind

чкрипи *impf see* чкрипне

чкриплив *adj* creaking, creaky, squeaky; чкрипливи скали creaking (creaky) stairs

чкрипне *pf* чкрипна *aor.* 1 to creak, squeak; вратата чкрипна the door creaked 2 (*со заби*) to gnash, grind (*one's teeth*)

чкрипнува *impf of* чкрипне

чкрка *f see* скрка

чкрт *m* creaking, squeaking; crunching; (*со заби*) gnashing

чкрта *impf* 1 to creak, squeak; вратата чкрта the door creaks 2 to gnash, grind; чкрта со заби to gnash one's teeth 3 to scribble; to daub

чкртка *impf dim. of* чкрта

чкртне *pf* чкртна *aor.* 1 to creak, squeak 2 (*со заби*) to gnash, grind 3 to cross out; to scrawl out

чкртнува *impf of* чкртне

чкулав *adj* crippled; lame

чкунка *f* stump (*of an arm or a leg*)

чл. *abbr.* (*член*) 1 *see* член 1 2 (*во закон и сл.*) art.

член *m* 1 member; (*на научно друштво*) fellow; нашето семејство се состои од три члена our family consists of three members; член на партијата party member; член на друштво (здружение) member of a society (association); член на управниот одбор member of the management committee; <дописен> член на академијата <corresponding> member of the Academy 2 *Anat.* (*usu. pl*) limb, part of the body, member 3 *Anat., Zool.* joint; *Bot.* node 4 article; нашиот правилник се состои од 12 члена our statutes consist of 12 articles 5 *Math.* member, term; член на прогресија/сразмер/бином/трином member (term) of a progression/proportion/binomial/trinomial 6 *Gram.* article; определен и неопределен член definite and indefinite article

членарина *f* membership dues, *Brit., Austral.* subscription; собирање членарина collecting members' dues

членест *adj* articulate, articulated, segmented; членесто тело на стоногалка the segmented body of a centipede

членка *f* (*of a woman or a feminine noun*) member; Грција е членка на НАТО Greece is a member of NATO

членконошци *pl Zool.* Arthropoda

членовиден -дна *adj* articulate, articulated, *see* членест

членоразделен -лна *adj* articulate; членоразделна реч articulate speech

членски *adj* 1 member's, membership *attrib.*; членска карта membership card; членски влог *see* членарина 2 *Gram.* of the article; членската форма the form of the article

членство *n* membership

членува *impf* 1 to be a member (*of an organization*), belong (*to an organization*) 2 *Gram.* (*also pf*) to add the article (*to a noun, etc.*), use (*a noun, etc.*) with the article

членуван *adj Gram.* with the article, definite; членувана именка a noun with the article

членче *n dim. of* член 3

членчест *adj see* членест

чмае *impf* to languish, pine (*по, за – for*); чмае по родниот крај to pine for one's native country, to be homesick

чмај *m poet.* languishing, pining

чобан *m* (*mainly in f.p.*) shepherd

чобанка *f* (*fem. form*) shepherdess

чобанов *adj* shepherd's

чобански *adj* shepherd *attrib.*; чобанска песна shepherd's song; чобанско куче sheepdog

чобанче *n dim. of* чобан

човек *m*, луѓе *pl* 1 man, *pl* men; person, *pl* people/persons; human being; виден човек eminent person; угледен човек man of distinction; фамилијарен човек family man; искусен човек man of experience; деловен човек businessman; светски човек man of the world; душа човек a delightful (lovely) person; чесен човек man of honour; градски човек 1. city dweller, *pejor.* city slicker 2. urbane person; селски човек villager, person from the country, *pejor.* country bumpkin, rustic; човек на уметноста artist; човек на перото man of letters; човек од дело man of action; човек од збор man of his word; човек на полицијата police agent; police informer; ❏ големите луѓе the high and mighty; малиот човек the little man; обичен човек the man in the street, ordinary/average man; **човек на <свое> место** a man who knows his place; a decent/honest person; **оган од човек** *colloq.* a go-getter; **божји човек** a quiet person; a holy man; **човече божји!** for God's sake! for crying out loud! **жив човек нема** there's nobody around; **педа човек** manikin; undersized man; *pejor.* shrimp of a man; **половина човек** a wreck of a man; **свој човек** one's own master; **човек од крв и месо** a man of flesh and blood; **таков човек повеќе не се раѓа** he is one in a million; **стане човек** 1. to mend one's ways 2. to get on in the world, make good; **стане друг човек** to become a new man; **направи некого човек** to make a man of s.o. **2** Man, humanity, mankind, humankind; **потеклото на човекот** the origin of mankind **3** one, they, you, *pl* people; **човек би рекол** one might say; **тоа жив човек не може да го поднесе** no one can stand that; **како може човек да се сложи со тоа** how can anyone agree with that? **човек не може сè да знае** one can't know everything

човеков *adj* of man<kind>; man's; human; **човековото потекло** the origin of man<kind>; **човекова средина** the human environment

човекојадец -дци *m* **1** man-eater, cannibal **2** *fig.* cut-throat, savage; ogre

човекојадство *n* cannibalism

човеколик *adj* anthropoid; **човеколик мајмун** anthropoid <ape>

човекољубец -пци *m* philanthropist

човекољубив *adj* philanthropic

човекољубивост *f* & **човекољубие** *n* philanthropy

човекомрзец -сци *m* misanthropist

човекоубиец -ијци *m* murderer, killer

човекоубиствен *adj* murderous, homicidal

човекоубиство *n* murder, homicide

човече *n dim. of* **човек 1** little man, manikin; undersized man **2** *dial. Anat.* pupil

човечен -чна *adj* **1** human **2** humane; **човечна постапка** humane step **3** kind-hearted, decent; noble; **човечна постапка** noble act

човечество *n arch. literary see* човештво

човечец *m (only sg) dim. hyp. (of* човек*)* little fellow; **кутриот човечец!** poor fellow!

човечиште *n augm. (of* човек*)* hulk of a man, hulking fellow, hulk

човечки¹ *adj* **1** human; **човечко тело** human body; **човечки живот** human life; **човечки дела** human deeds; **човечко достоинство** human dignity **2** of people; **човечка маса** mass of people; **човечкото општество** human society **3** humane

човечки² *adv* like a human being; decently, intelligently; properly; **разговара човечки** to talk like reasonable people

човечно *adv* **1** humanely **2** kind-heartedly, decently, nobly

човечност *f see* човештина

човешки *adj & adv see* човечки

човештво *n* humanity, mankind, humankind; **во целото човештво** in all of humankind; **во интерес на човештвото** in the interest<s> of humanity

човештилак *m colloq. see* човештина

човештина *f* humaneness, humanity; kindness

чоен *adj* broadcloth *attrib.*, made of woollen broadcloth

чоиче *n* & **чоичка** *f dim. hyp. of* чоја

чоја *f* woollen broadcloth; **зелена чоја** baize

чојадар *m arch.* footman

чојар & **чојаџија** -ии *m* woollen-broadcloth maker/seller

чок *adv arch.* very; very much; ❏ **чорба чок, месо јок** *iron.* much juice, little meat, *i.e.* the stew is a bit thin

чоканче *n raki* flask

чокој -ои *m* owner of a large estate (*formerly in the Rumanian lands*); ❏ **живее како некој чокој** to live like a lord

чоколада *f* **1** chocolate **2** chocolate bar, block of chocolate; **млечна чоколада** <a bar/block of> milk chocolate

чоколаден¹ -дна *adj* <made of> chocolate; **чоколадни бонбони** chocolates

чоколаден² *adj* chocolate *attrib.*; **чоколадена фабрика** chocolate factory; **чоколадена боја** chocolate colour

чолак *adj indecl. colloq.* one-armed/handed

чолн -ови *m see* чун

чолта *f* **1** large knuckle-bone (*usu. from an old large animal*) **2** *fig.* thin ugly fellow, monstrosity; **чолто една!** you freak!

чолтар *m see* чултар

чолтарче *n dim. of* чолтар, *see* чултарче

чомак -ци *m arch.* mace; spiked club; cudgel; hub, nave of a wheel

чомбаз *m arch. see* перчин

чомлек *m* meat stew (*with onions and garlic*)

чому *pron arch. see* чуму

чопенка *f dial.* piece of meat

чопка (се) *impf dial. see* чепка (се)

чорап *m* (*кус*) sock; (*долг*) stocking; **машки чорапи** men's socks; **женски чорапи** women's stockings; **спортски чорапи** sports socks; **волнени чорапи** woollen socks; **свилени чорапи** silk stockings; **најлон чорапи** nylon stockings; **мрежести чорапи** mesh (net) stockings; **хулахоп чорапи** tights, pantihose; **чорапи доколеници** knee-high socks/stockings; **едно рало чорапи** a pair of socks/stockings; **обуе чорапи** to put on socks/stockings; **собуе чорапи** to take off socks/stockings; ❏ **мавнат со чорап** a bit daft, not all there; **уста како чорап** big mouth

чорапар *m* sock/stocking maker; hosiery manufacturer

чорапарница *f* sock/stocking shop; sock/stocking department of a factory

чорапарски *adj* sock *attrib.*; stocking *attrib.*; hosiery *attrib.*; **чорапарски занает** hosiery trade; **чорапарски дуќан** hosiery shop

чорапен -пна *adj* sock *attrib.*; stocking *attrib.*; **чорапна плетка** sock pattern; **чорапна игла** needle for knitting socks

чорапиште *n augm. of* чорап

чорапче *n* **1** *dim. of* чорап **2** (*на ламба*) mantle

чорба *f Cul.* <thick> soup, broth, *Am.* chowder; **пилешка/јагнешка чорба** chicken/lamb soup; **рибина чорба** fish soup; **прас-чорба** leek soup; **шкембе-чорба** tripe soup; ❏ **запржува чорба некому** to cook s.o.'s goose

чорбалак -ци *m* **1** tureen **2** watery (thin) stew

чорбар *m* soup-lover

чорбаци *m* **1** (*voc. of* чорбаџија) sir! master! повели, чорбаци! come in, sir! те молам, чорбаци! I beg you, sir! чорбаци Митко! Mr Mitko! **2** (*title of a notable*) Mr, Master; чорбаци Теодос Master Teodos

чорбаџија -ии *m* rich man, lord, master

чорбаџилак *m see* чорбаџиство 2

чорбаџиски *adj* wealthy man's, lord's, master's; lordly, grand; тој е чорбаџиски син he is a son of a wealthy man; чорбаџиска куќа grand house

чорбаџиство *n* **1** the rich **2** position/status of a master (rich man)

чорбаџица *f* **1** rich woman, lady, mistress **2** rich man's (lord's, master's) wife

чорбаџиче *n dim. hyp.* (*usu. in f.p.*) *of* чорбаџија

чорбест *adj* soupy, thin, watery; чорбесто јадење watery food (dish), gruel

чорбица & **чорбичка** *f dim. hyp. of* чорба

чорбиште *n augm. of* чорба

чорла *f colloq.* dishevelled woman/girl

чорлав *adj colloq.* dishevelled, unkempt; scruffy; (*за брада*) shaggy, bushy

чорлавост *f* dishevelled (unkempt/scruffy) state; (*за брада*) shaggy (bushy) state

чорло -вци *m colloq.* scruff, dishevelled man/boy

чочек -ци *m* **1** belly-dance **2** belly-dancer

чочечки *adj* **1** belly-dance *attrib.* **2** belly-dancer's

чпирто *n* **1** *colloq. see* шпиритус **2** *see* кибрит

чпиртоса *pf* **I** to preserve (*with formalin*) **II** – **се** *fig.* to get a fright, turn pale <with fright>

чпиртосува (се) *impf of* чпиртоса (се)

чпота се *impf colloq. see* шпота се

чпотало *n see* шпотало

чпрнтав & **чпртав** *adj* (*of a nose*) pug, snub, turned-up

чпрт *adj see* чпрнтав, чпртав

чрчори *impf see* чврчори

чубрика & **чубрица** *f Bot.* (Satureia hortensis) savory

чува *impf* **I 1** to look after, mind, watch over, take care of, keep an eye on; to guard, safeguard, protect (*од – from, against*); to tend *trans.*; to nurse, care for; чува куќа to look after a house; чува деца to mind children; чува заробеници to guard prisoners; чува овци to tend sheep; чува овошки од мраз to protect fruit trees from frost; тој си го чува здравјето he looks after his health; чува некого од лошо друштво to keep s.o. out of bad company; ❑ чува тајна to keep a secret; чува стража to keep watch, stand guard; нив Господ ги чува the Lord is watching over them; Господ да чува <и да брани> God forbid! чува како зеница во око to cherish like the apple of one's eye; си ја чува кожата to save one's skin; не сум чувал (пасел) овци со тебе you and I are not so close; we're not on an equal footing **2** to keep, save; чува пушка во визба to keep a gun in the cellar; чува стари писма to save old letters; ❑ чувај бели пари за црни дни save for a rainy day **3** *dial. see* слуша **II** – **се** to take care of o.s.; to watch out, beware (*од – of*); to protect o.s.; чувај се! take care! be careful! look out! watch out! beware! чувај се од него beware of him! чувај се од настинка take care not to catch cold! чувај се да не те види некој mind no one sees you!

чувадар *m arch. see* чувар

чувалиште *n* stor<ag>e room; (*за багаж*) left-luggage room; (*за мебел и др.*) depository

чувар *m* guard, watchman, security guard, janitor; guardian, custodian; (*на зграда*) caretaker; (*на паркинг*) attendant; (*на заробеници*) warder; (*на животно*) keeper; (*заштитник*) protector; чувар на магазините store watchman; музејски чувар museum curator (custodian); ноќен чувар <night> watchman; шумски чувар forest ranger; затворски чувар prison guard (warder); чувари на редот guardians of public order, policemen; чувар на печатот *Hist.* Keeper of the Seal, (*U.K.*) Lord Privy Seal; ангелот чувар guardian angel

чуварина *f* storage charge

чуварка *f* (*fem. form*) *see* чувар

чувач *m see* чувар

чувачка *f see* чуварка

чувствен *adj* feeling *attrib.*; emotional; sensual; чувствен живот life of the senses, emotional life

чувствено *adv* emotionally, with the senses, in relation to the senses

чувственост *f* sensuality; emotionality

чувствителен -лна *adj* **1** delicate, sensitive, tender; sentimental; compassionate; тој е поетска, чувствителна природа he has a poetic, sensitive nature; чувствително срце a soft heart; чувствителна душа a sensitive soul **2** sensitive, thin-skinned, touchy, irritable; tender; susceptible (*на – то*); со тебе човек не може да се пошегува, многу си чувствителен you can't take a joke, you are very sensitive; чувствителна кожа a sensitive skin; чувствителен стомак an irritable stomach; чувствително место a tender spot **3** sensitive, delicate; precision *attrib.*; чувствителен на светлина light-sensitive; чувствителен механизам a delicate mechanism **4** *fig.* perceptible, appreciable, considerable; чувствително покачување на температурата appreciable rise in temperature; чувствително подобрување a considerable improvement; чувствителна загуба a painful/deeply-felt loss

чувствително *adv* emotionally; touchily; perceptibly, appreciably, considerably

чувствителност *f* emotional nature; sensitivity; sentimentality

чувство *n* **1** feeling, sentiment, emotion; sense; благородни чувства noble sentiments; чувство на пријатност good feeling<s>; чувство на одговорност a sense of responsibility; нема чувство he is unfeeling; човек без чувство a man without feeling<s>, hard<-hearted> man; има поделени чувства to have mixed feelings; има чувство дека ... to have a feeling that ... **2** (*усет*) sensation; чувство на болка feeling of pain; чувство на опаднатост feeling of weariness

чувствува *impf* **I 1** to feel *trans.*; to experience; чувствува радост/мака/жал to feel joy/suffering/sorrow; чувствува омраза (*кон*) to feel hatred (*to, towards*), bear malice (*towards*); чувствува физичка болка to feel a physical pain; чувствува глад to feel hungry; чувствува премореност to feel exhausted; чувствува мирис to notice a scent; чувствува вртоглавица to feel giddy (dizzy); чувствува на своја кожа to experience firsthand **2** to sense, feel; тој чувствуваше дека не ќе може да издржи до крај he felt that he could not hold out to the end; чувствував дека стоиш зад мене I could sense you standing behind me **II – се** to feel *intrans.*; како се чувствуваш? how do you feel? се чувствува болен/ здрав/способен/среќен to feel ill/well/able/happy; се чувствува погоден/навреден to feel hurt/offended; не се чувствува баш најдобро not to feel quite up to the mark; чувствувај се слободно да ... feel free to ... ; се чувствува како дома to feel at home; се чувствува како риба во вода to be in one's element; се чувствувам како будала I feel <like> a fool

чудак -ци *m* crank, eccentric, *colloq.* odd fish; *colloq.* freak; *colloq.* crotchety fellow

чудачки *adj* eccentric, odd, queer, peculiar, *colloq.* cranky; crotchety; чудачки карактер odd/crotchety character

чудаштво *n* eccentricity, oddity; crotchety character

чудба *f* **1** *see* чудење **2** *dial. see* чудо, чудесија

чуден -дна *adj* **1** odd, strange; bizarre; чуден сон strange dream; што е најчудно при тоа ... the strangest thing about it is ... ; чуден вкус odd taste; чудна работа odd (*Brit. colloq.* rum) business; чуден човек odd fellow; чудно чудо, чудна чудесија a miracle; a big surprise, the strangest thing **2** marvellous, wonderful; чудно лето е ова this is a marvellous summer **3** amazing, astonishing; чудна убавина astonishing beauty; тоа тој го сврши со чудна брзина he did that with amazing speed; тој покажа чудна истрајност he showed amazing determination **4** *dial.* (*зачуден*) astonished, amazed; таа остана чудна she was astonished (got a big surprise)

чудење *n from* чуди; тоа е за чудење! good heavens! I don't believe it! well I never! *Austral. colloq.* you wouldn't read about it! *Gram.* знак на чудење exclamation mark

чудесен -сна *adj* **1** marvellous, wonderful, lovely; чудесно место a wonderful place; чудесна работа something wonderful **2** *rare arch.* strange; miraculous

чудесија -ии *f* miracle, wonder, marvel; чудесии правеа they performed miracles, they worked wonders; *iron.* they were on the rampage; ти да видиш чудни чудесии you will be amazed; чудесија! it's miraculous!

чудесно *adv* wonderfully, delightfully; miraculously; чудесно свири he plays divinely; чудесно убав beautiful beyond words

чудесност *f* **1** wonderful (lovely) nature **2** miraculous/ extreme quality

чуди *pf* **I** to surprise, astonish, amaze; тоа никого не го чуди that doesn't surprise anyone; ме чуди што не пишува I am surprised that he does not write, I wonder why he does not write; што те чуди you shouldn't be surprised **II – се 1** to be surprised; се чудам како можеше тоа да го речеш I am surprised that you could say that; нема зошто да се чудиш there's no reason to be surprised; ❏ ти се чудам на умот I am astonished how clever you are; *iron.* what gave you that idea? **2** to marvel, be amazed (delighted) **3** to wonder, rack one's brains, be at a loss; се чудам како ќе излеземе на крај I wonder how we are going to get out of this; I wonder how we are going to manage; се чуди што да прави he is wondering what to do

чудија -ии *f colloq. see* чудо, чудба, чудесија

чудило *n* wonder, marvel

чудно *adv* (*see* чуден 1–3) **1** oddly, strangely; се држи чудно to behave strangely; многу ми е чудно I find it very odd; не е чудно! it's quite possible! навистина чудно strange to say, curiously enough; не е ни чудно small wonder; чудно ми чудо! *colloq.* so what! *iron. sl.* big deal! **2** marvellously, wonderfully **3** amazingly, astonishingly

чудноват *adj see* чуден 1 & 3

чудновато *adv* oddly, strangely; amazingly, astonishingly

чудноватост *f* oddness, oddity, strangeness; amazing/ astonishing quality

чудност *f* oddness, oddity, strangeness; amazing/ astonishing quality

чудо *n* **1** miracle; Св. Наум правел многу чуда Saint Naum is supposed to have worked many miracles **2** (*позитивно*) miracle, marvel; (*негативно*) horror, disaster, calamity; нашите борци прават чуда our fighters are performing miracles; ❏ чудо големо! **1.** wonder of wonders! **2.** *colloq.* so what! *iron. sl.* big deal! за чудо големо! *colloq.* so what! *iron. sl.* big deal! стане на чудо *colloq.* to be surprised; најде се во чудо to get into a fix; to be in a quandary, be at one's wits' end; како по чудо as if by some miracle; за чудо funnily (strangely, oddly) enough; направи триста чуда he worked miracles; *iron.* he made a mess of it; знае триста чуда he knows many things; Алиса во земјата на чудата Alice in Wonderland; секое чудо за три дена *prov.* it's a nine days' wonder **3** (*as adj*) marvellous; чудо дете an infant prodigy; чудо девојка a marvellous girl **4** (*as adv*) very much; таму имаше чудо народ there were masses of people there; едно чудо tons of, lots of, piles, *see* едночудо; чудо, да не се јави уште it's odd (I'm surprised) that he has not yet called

чудовишно *adv* monstrously

чудовишност *f* monstrosity, enormity

чудовиште *n* **1** monster; морско чудовиште sea monster **2** *fig.* monstrosity, terror

чудовиштен -шна *adj* monstrous

чудотворен -рна *adj* wonder-working, miraculous; чудотворна икона wonder-working icon; чудотворна вода holy water; чудотворен лек miraculous remedy

чудотворец -рци *m* worker of wonders, miracle worker, thaumaturge

чудотворка *f* (*fem. form*) *see* чудотворец

чудотворно *adv* miraculously, as if by a miracle

чудотворност *f* **1** miraculousness, miraculous quality **2** ability to work wonders

чуе *pf* чу *aor.* **1** to hear; ја чу ли трубата? did you hear the trumpet? се чу пукот a shot was heard; не чуе на едното уво he is deaf in one ear; не се чуе ни жива душа she is very quiet; не сакам ни гласот да му го чујам I don't want even to hear his voice; ❏ да не чуе злото (лошото) touch wood, *Am.* knock <on> wood! **2** to hear, learn; чув дека си тука I heard that you were here; ја кажи, да чујам come on, tell me, I want to hear <about it>; за тоа не сака ни да чуе he won't hear of it; **3** *colloq.* (*as interj*) чуја! (*as an answer*) yes, I heard you!; yes, I'm listening! *see* слушне

чуен[1] *adj in the expression:* ни виден ни чуен completely unheard-of; дојде некој ни виден ни чуен some completely unknown person turned up

чуен[2] -јна *adj* audible; чујно шепотење audible whisper; (*во театар*) stage whisper

чујно *adv* audibly; срцето чујно ѝ чукаше you could hear her heart beating

чујност *f* audible quality, audibility

чук[1] *m see* чекан

чук[2] *interj* knock! knock!

чука[1] *f* rocky hill/peak; висока чука high stony peak

чука[2] *impf* **I 1** to knock; to hammer; (*за дожд*) to beat *intrans.* (*по – against*); (*за срце*) to beat *intrans.*; to thump *intrans.*; (*за часовник*) to tick *intrans.*; to strike *trans.*; (*со прсти*) to rap, tap; чука со чекан to hammer, strike with a hammer; чука на порта to hammer/knock at the door; ❏ си ја чука главата 1. he is sorry 2. he's looking for a way out; чукна последниот час the final (eleventh) hour has come **2** to knock down (*fruit from a tree*); чука јаболка to knock apples down from a tree **3** to geld; чука овен to castrate a ram **4** *see* чукне I **5** **II – се** *see* чукне (се) II 1 & 2; се чукаат со јајца на Велигден they are cracking eggs for Easter

чукајдрвец -вци *m Zool. see* клукајдрвец

чукало *n* door-knocker

чукан *adj* gelded; чукан овен castrated ram, wether

чукар *m see* чука[1] *f*

чукнат *adj* silly, foolish, crazy, *Brit. colloq.* daft; чукнат в глава, чукнат од умот not right in the head; ❏ чукнат со мокар чорап he has a screw loose, he is not all there

чукне *pf* чукна *aor.* **I 1** to hit, strike; to knock; to rap; (*полека*) to tap; (*силно*) to slap; *Med.* to percuss; го чукна по глава he hit (cracked) him on the head; си ја чукна главата he bumped his head (*од нешто – on s.th.*); чукне со чекан to hammer, strike (hit) with a hammer; чукне на врата to knock at a door **2** to drive (hammer) in *trans.*; чукни му уште една шајка hammer another nail into it! **3** to hit *trans.*; to smack *trans.*; to slap *trans.* **4** *see* чука I **5** *fig.* to put; to add; чукни му уште малку сол на јадењето put a little more salt on the food! го чукнаа в затвор they clapped him in jail **II – се 1** to bump (*во, на, од нешто – into s.th.*); to bump one's head (*во, од нешто – on s.th.*); to stub one's toe (*во, на, од нешто – on s.th.*); to bump (*во некого – into s.o.*); се чукнав од каменон I bumped into that rock; I stubbed my toe on that stone **2** to clink (touch) glasses; ајде да се чукнеме! let's clink glasses! **3** to go crazy (*Brit. colloq.* daft); чукнал целиот he has a screw loose **4** *fig.* (*with на or dative*) to drop in on s.o.; ќе му се чукнам I'll drop in on him

чукнува (се) *impf of* чукне (се)

чукче *n dim. of* чук, *see* чеканче

чукш *interj* (*used to urge on a donkey*) come on!

чул *m* horse-cloth

чулав *adj* having small ears, crop-eared

чулашник -ци *m see* чул

чуле -вци *m* person with small ears

чули *impf* чули уши to prick up one's ears

чуло *n literary see* сетило; има шесто чуло to have a sixth sense

чултар *m* **1** *see* чул **2** kind of apron

чултарче *n dim. of* чултар

чулче *n dim. of* чул

чулчинка *f dim. of* чул

чума *f* plague; bubonic plague, pestilence, *Hist.* the Black Death; ❏ бега од некого/нешто како од чума to avoid s.o./s.th. like the plague; чумата да те изеде! чумата да те удри! *curses* a plague (pox) on you! go to the devil!

чумав *adj* **1** suffering from the plague **2** plague-stricken, pestilential (*also fig.*); чумава година plague year

чумак -ци *m arch. see* чомак

чумба *f* & **чумбаз** *m arch. see* чомбаз

чумбер *m see* чембер[2]

чумен -мна *adj* plague *attrib.*; чумна зараза plague infection

чуметина *f f.p. pejor.* plague

чумоса *pf* **I** *in the curse:* чума да те чумоса! <a> plague on you! **II – се** *colloq.* to catch the plague

чумосува (се) *impf of* чумоса (се)

чуму *pron* (*arch. dat. of* што) what for?

чун *m* rowing-boat, (*Am.* row-boat), dinghy

чунка *f dial.* ball of wool

чунки & **чунким** *colloq.* **1** *part* it is as if; чунки не знае дека сум тука it's as if he didn't know that I was here **2** *conj dial.* because, as; чунки баеги беше скраја од нив as he was quite a distance from them

чунче *n dim. of* чун

чупа *f dial.* girl, *see* девојка, мома 1

чупале *n dial. dim. of* чупа; *see* чупе

чупе *n dial. dim. of* чупа, *see* девојченце

чупенще *n dial. dim. of* чупа, *see* чупе

чупинство *n dial.* girlhood, *literary* maidenhood, *see* девојчинство, моминство

чупиште *n dial. augm. of* чупа, *see* девојчиште, момиште

чупка *impf dial. see* колве

чупче *n dim. dial. see* чупе

чур *m see* чад[1]

чурек -ци *m* special Easter bread

чури *impf see* чади I; оџакот чури the chimney is smoking

чурилка *f* & **чурило** *n* snout

чурилче *n dim. of* чурилка & чурило

чурлава *f dial.* smoking, smoke

чурудиса *pf colloq.* to go bad (rotten); to go from bad to worse

чурудисува *impf of* чурудиса

чурук *adj indecl. colloq.* rotten, faulty, poor, bad, worthless; чурук стока worthless wares; чурук работа poor work

чуруклак *m colloq.* rottenness, faultiness, poor quality, worthlessness

чурулика *impf* to twitter, chirp; to warble

чуруликне *pf* чуруликна *aor.* to twitter (chirp)/warble once, give a twitter (chirp)/warble

чурулка *f see* чурилка

чут *pt of* чуе, *see* чуен[1]

чутура *f* water-bottle, canteen; hip-flask

чутурица *f* & **чутурче** *n dim. of* чутура

чучи *impf* (*usu. child.*) to sit

чучне *pf* чучна *aor.* (*usu. child.*) to sit down; си чучна до мене he sat down next to me

чучулига *f Zool. see* чучурлига

чучур *m dial.* spout (*on fountain*), *see* шопур &
шопурка

чучурка *f dial. see* шопур & шопурка, чешмурка

чучурлига *f Zool.* lark; цуцул чучурлига (Galerida
cristata) crested lark; полска чучурлига (Alauda
arvensis) skylark

чушка *f* **1** (*мешунка*) pod **2** *Bot. dial. see* пиперка

чушкар *m* capsicum (pepper) lover

џаба *adv f.p. see* џабе

џабалак *m colloq.* **1** hand-out, freebie **2** cut prices;
bargain **3** useless effort

џабе *adv colloq.* (*see* бадијала) **1** for nothing, free,
gratis; џабе е it's dirt cheap **2** to no purpose, in vain;
џабе зборува to waste one's breath; to kick against
the pricks; дошол тука за џабе he's come here on a
fool's errand; џабе се мачиш your efforts are in vain,
colloq. you're wasting your time; џабе <ти> е it's no
use

џавка *impf* to bark, yap, yelp

џавне *pf* џавна *aor.* to bark (*once*), give a yap

џавнува *impf of* џавне

џаволи *impf* to chat, prattle, yack, *colloq.* yap; to
make small talk

џагара-магара *interj* what a racket (row, hullabaloo,
brouhaha)! *colloq.* rhubarb! rhubarb!

џагор *m* racket, row

џагори *impf* to make a racket, raise a shindig

џаде *n colloq.* street, main road; ❑ фаќа џаде to take
to one's heels; фаќај џаде! *sl.* beat it!

џадија -ии *f colloq.* fury, shrew

џака *impf colloq.* (*врви*) to make a racket

џам -ови *m colloq.* **1** (*стакло*) glass; window-pane **2**
(*прозорец*) window

џамадан *m arch.* double-breasted waistcoat (*usu. of
embroidered velvet*)

џамаданче *n dim. of* џамадан

џамбаз *m arch.* **1** equestrian <acrobat> **2** horse-
breaker; horse-trader **3** *fig.* wheeler-dealer; cheat

џамбаски *adj* equestrian's; horse-breaker's; horse-
trader's; horse-trading *attrib.*; џамбаски коњ an
acrobat's horse

џамија -ии *f* mosque; ❑ нека влезе свињче у џамија
come hell or high water; come what may

џамлак -ци *m colloq.* **1** shop-window, show-window;
showcase, glass case **2** window-frame

џамлија **1** *adj indecl. colloq. see* стаклен **2** (*as noun*)
џамлија -ии *f see* скокалче; ❑ кога/тогаш <ти> уште
си играше џамлии when you were just a little boy

џамџија -ии *m colloq.* glazier

џамџиски *adj* glazier's; glazing *attrib.*

џан *m arch.* spirit; soul; life

џанам *part arch.* my darling, my dear

џангарак -ци *m arch.* large bell; gong

џандар *m colloq. see* жандарм

џандарски *adj colloq. see* жандармски

џандрлив *adj* cantankerous, quarrelsome, *colloq.*
crabby; peevish, petulant, grumbling; џандрлива
жена nagging (shrewish) wife/woman

џандрливост *f* cantankerousness, quarrelsomeness; peevishness, petulance, grumbling mood

џанка *f Bot.* (Prunus myrobalana) cherry plum, myrobalan

џан-џин *colloq. in the expression:* нема џан-џин there's not a living soul about

џапа *impf of* џапне

џапне *pf* џапна *aor.* to tug, pull

џари се *impf* to stare (peer) at; се џареше во него he was staring at him

џбара *impf* to grope (*for*); џбара по темница to grope in the dark

џбарне *pf* џбарна *aor. see* џбара

џбарнува *impf of* џбарне

џбитак -ци *m* stocky (thickset) person

џбун *m & џбунка f* bush, shrub, *see* грмушка

џбура (се) *impf colloq. see* џбурне (се)

џбурка (се) *impf colloq. see* џбурне (се)

џбурне *pf* џбурна *aor. colloq.* **I 1** to rummage (*in s.th.*), stick one's hand (*into s.th.*); џбурна во торбата he stuck his hand into the bag **2** to put (*s.th. into s.th.*), add (*s.th. to s.th.*); to throw, toss *trans.*; to plunge *trans.*; многу сол си му џбурнала во јадењето you put a lot of salt in his meal; кој знае кај го џбурнала клучот goodness knows where she tossed the key **II** – **се** to plop, plunge, dip *intrans.*; се џбурна во вода he jumped into the water

џбурнува (се) *impf colloq. of* џбурне (се)

џвака *impf* **1** to chew; to munch; џвака леб to chew <on a piece of> bread; џвака гума to chew gum; џвака тутун to chew tobacco **2** *fig.* to chatter <idly>, babble; to grumble; не туку џвакај stop babbling! *colloq.* shut up!

џвакне *pf* џвакна *aor. of* џвака 1

џвакнува *impf of* џвакне

џвало *n* **1** jaws, mouth (*of an animal*), maw **2** *dial.* sting (*of a bee, wasp*)

џврка *impf see* џвркне

џвркало *n* water-pistol, *Am.* water gun

џвркло -вци *m colloq.* halfwit, *vulg.* shithead

џвркне *pf* џвркна *aor.* **1** to gush, spurt, spray, squirt **2** *fig. colloq. see* дрсне

џвркнува *impf of* џвркне

џган *m* **1** riff-raff, rabble, scum <of the earth>, unsavoury characters **2** crowd, mob

џгапа *impf* to tramp, tread heavily/clumsily

џгура[1] *f see* згура

џгура[2] *impf colloq.* to wander/roam about; to ramble; to dart about; џгура по темницата to grope in the dark

џеб -ови, -а *m* pocket; мал џеб fob; заден џеб hip-pocket; надворешен џеб patch pocket; внатрешен џеб inset pocket; inside pocket; кладе (стави) нешто в џеб (во џебот) to put s.th. in one's pocket, pocket s.th.; ❑ џебот му е полн; има длабок џеб he is well-off, he is rolling in money; плати од својот џеб to pay <for s.th.> out of one's own pocket; има некого в џеб (во џебот) to have s.o. in one's pocket, hold s.o. in the palm of one's hand; има нешто в џеб to have s.th. in the bag; си ги полни џебовите to line one's pockets; му го наполни џебот на некого to help s.o. get rich; to help s.o. feather his nest; му ги испразни џебовите he fleeced him; гледа само за свој џеб to

feather one's nest; има плиток џеб to be short of cash; познава нешто како својот џеб to know s.th. like the back of one's hand; се фати за џеб to put one's hand in one's pocket; удира некого по џеб to impose a fine on s.o.; ни в џеб ни од џеб it's no skin off my nose

џебáна *f see* џепане

џебен -бна *adj* pocket *attrib.*; џебен часовник fob watch; џебно шамиче handkerchief; џебен формат pocket format, (*за книга*) paperback; џебно ноже pocket knife, penknife

џева *f colloq.* racket, rumpus, shindy, row; прави/стори џева to make a fuss; не дигај џева! don't make a fuss about it! cut it out!

џеваир *m arch.* jewel, gem; precious thing; valuable

џевап *m colloq.* answer; даде џевап to answer

џез *m* **1** jazz **2** jazz band, big band

џеза *f arch.* (*глоба*) fine, penalty

џезве *n see* ѓезве

џезов *adj* jazz *attrib.*; џезов оркестар jazz band, big band

џелат *m* **1** executioner, hangman **2** *fig.* killer, butcher, thug, cutthroat; bully

џелатов *adj* hangman's

џелатски *adj* hanging *attrib.*; *fig.* slaughter, carnage *attrib.*; џелатска работа massacre

џелатство *n* slaughter, carnage; massacre

џелеп & џелепин -пи *m arch.* cattle-dealer

џелепски *adj arch.* cattle-dealer's

џем *m* jam

џембос *m in the expression:* џембос да (нека) фати to hell with him!

џембоса се *pf colloq.* to go to hell, go to the devil

џембосува се *impf of* џембоса се

џемпер *m* jumper; cardigan

џенабет *m arch.* poor wretch

џенáза *f* **1** corpse, mortal remains **2** funeral; џеназа намаз a funeral prayer

џенарика *f see* џанка

џенем *m colloq. arch.* hell; ❑ џенем да се стори (да фати, да иде, да оди) to hell with him/it!

џенк -ови *m arch.* battle, combat; war; strife

џентлемéн *m see* џентлмен

џентлемéнски *adj see* џентлменски

џентлемéнство *n see* џентлменство

џентлмéн *m* gentleman

џентлмéнски *adj* gentlemanly, courteous, noble; џентлменски однос gentlemanly behaviour; џентлменска спогодба gentlemen's agreement

џентлмéнство *n* gentlemanliness, gentlemanly behaviour

џепане *n colloq. arch.* **1** munitions depot **2** ammunition

џепче *n dim. of* џеб

џепчија -ии *m colloq.* pickpocket

џереме *n arch. see* џеза

џефа *f arch. see* џева

Џибутáнец -нци *m* Djiboutian

Џибутáнка *f* (*fem. form*) *see* Џибутанец

џибутански *adj* Djiboutian

Џибути *n* Djibouti

џивка *impf* (*of a sparrow*) to chirp, chirrup, peep; врапчињата џивкаат the little sparrows are cheeping

џивџан *m Zool. see* врабец

џивџанче & **џивџаре** n Zool. dim. of џивџан, see врапче

џигер m see дроб; бел џигер lung; црн џигер liver; воспаление на црниот џигер hepatitis; ❑ му го изеде џигерот he drove him to distraction; he worked him to death

џигерче n 1 dim. of џигер 2 (usu. pl) lamb's fry

џида f arch. spear, lance, javelin

џидне (се) pf џидна aor. see џитне (се)

џиднува (се) impf of џидне (се)

џилит m Hist. blunt-pointed wooden lance for jousting

џимберица f f.p. see ластовица

џимиринка f crackling

џимрија adj indecl. colloq. fussy person; miser

џин¹ -ови m giant; ❑ џин на стаклени нозе a giant with feet of clay

џин² m gin, geneva

џинка f 1 kind of small chicken; bantam 2 see џинороз 2 3 pepperone, kind of small hot pepper

џиновски adj gigantic, enormous; џиновска работа enormous task; џиновска сила gigantic strength

џинороз m 1 kind of small cock; bantam 2 fig. dwarf; manikin, puny little fellow, runt

џинс¹ m colloq. clan, family, stock

џинс² m jeans

џинче n dim. of џин¹˒²

џип m jeep

џипче n dim. of џип

џитка (се) impf see џитне (се)

џитне pf colloq. џитна aor. I to throw, toss trans.; to brandish, flourish, swing II – ce to throw (hurl) o.s. (во, на, по некого – at s.o.); to fly at; to fall (во нечии раце – into s.o.'s arms); (во вода) to jump; кучето се џитна по него the dog rushed at him

џитнува (се) impf of џитне (се)

џиџан adj child. beautiful

џиџе n child. <baby's> rattle; toy; s.th. beautiful

џиу-џицу n ju-jitsu

џиш interj child. it's hot! (when warning a child)

џишне се pf џишна се aor. child. to burn o.s., scorch o.s., scald o.s.

џишнува се impf of џишне се

џогинг m jogging

џогира pf & impf to jog

џока¹ f arch. kind of tight-fitting jacket

џока² impf colloq. to drink deep; to carouse, booze

џокеј -еи m jockey

џокер m Cards joker; fig. gatecrasher; fly in the ointment

џоница f see суница 1

џонка f junk (Chinese boat)

џотка (се) impf colloq. see џотне (се)

џотне pf colloq. џотна aor. I to put/drive (во – in) trans.; to pull trans.; to push (shove, thrust) (во – into) trans. II – ce to push (во – into) intrans.; to thrust o.s. (во – into)

џотнува (се) impf of џотне (се)

џоџе n dial. see џуџе

џрџа impf see грга

џрџне pf џрџна aor. see грџне

џрџнува impf of џрџне

џубе n arch. 1 robe, kaftan 2 type of long cloak (worn by Muslim clergy)

џубокс m jukebox

џувап m colloq. see џевап

џудист m Sport. judoist, judoka

џудо n Sport. judo

џул m Phys. joule

џумбуш m colloq. 1 fun, merrymaking 2 fig. mess, mix-up, confusion; racket, row; прави џумбуш to make a mess

џумбушлија 1 adj indecl. merry, jolly, humorous, playful, jocular 2 m joker, jester, wag

џумка f knob, gnarl; bump, lump, swelling, welt; главата му беше само џумки his head was covered in welts

џумкалест adj knobbly; knotty; bumpy

џунгла f jungle; ❑ законот на џунглата the law of the jungle; вистинска џунгла absolute bedlam; a pretty kettle of fish

џунка f see џонка

џунџуле n Bot. (Narcissus pseudonarcissus) daffodil

џурка (се) impf see џурне (се)

џурлив adj stinging; џурлива коприва stinging nettle<s>

џурне pf џурна aor. I (of nettles) to sting; коприватa ме џурна the nettles stung me II – ce to get stung (by nettles)

џурнува (се) impf of џурне (се)

џус m juice, orange juice

џуџе n dwarf; Снежана и седумте џуџиња Snow White and the Seven Dwarfs

џуџест adj dwarf attrib.; dwarfed; stunted; џуџести растенија dwarf plants; џуџест раст stunted growth

ш *interj* **1** (*молчи*) sh! shush! **2** (*еј*) psst!

шаблон *m* **1** pattern, mould, template; (*за цртеж*) stencil **2** *fig.* stereotype; cliché; работи по шаблон to work by rote (unimaginatively); to be in a rut

шаблонизација *f* formalization

шаблонизира *pf* & *impf* to render commonplace/banal; to reduce to a <set> formula

шаблонски *adj* **1** *Tech.* pattern, template *attrib.* **2** *fig.* stock, hackneyed, commonplace; conventional; шаблонски фрази trite expressions, hackneyed phrases

шаблонски *adv* conventionally; mechanically, un-originally; работи шаблонски to work by rote (unimaginatively); to be in a rut

шава *impf* **1** to stir, move about *intrans.*; лисјето шаваат the leaves are stirring **2** *fig. colloq.* to stir, move about *intrans.*; to wander about; to loiter; to fidget *intrans.*; младината почна да шава навамунатаму the young people are up and about; кај туку шаваш цел ден? where do you hang about all day? **3** *fig. colloq.* to gad (*colloq.* gallivant) about; to sleep around; иако е женет, тој шава по малку although he is married he likes to play around a bit

шавар *m Bot.* (Carex) sedge; (Scirpus) bulrush, club-rush; (Phragmites communis) reed, <common> rush

шаварлија *adj indecl. only in the expression:* сабја шаварлија *joc.* paper tiger

шаваспур *m arch.* gauze

шавне *pf* **1** to move, stir, budge *intrans.*; нешто шавна во сламата something moved in the straw **2** *fig. colloq.* to go for a walk; to pop out; вечер ќе шавнам малку this evening I'll go for a walk **3** *fig. colloq.* to start gadding about; to start sleeping around; *see* шава

шавнува *impf of* шавне

шадрван *m arch.* **1** fountain **2** tank (*attached to mosques, for ablutions*)

шаек -ци *m see* шајак

шаечки *adj see* шајачен

шажбој -ои *m* string of old silver coins worn on plaits

шаин *m Zool. arch.* peregrine falcon

шаит *m arch.* witness

шајак -ци *m* homespun

шајачен -чна *adj* homespun; шајачни панталони homespun trousers

шајбна *f Tech.* washer

шајка[1] *f* nail

шајка[2] *f arch.* boat, small vessel, dinghy

шајка[3] *f* gang, band, pack

шајкача *f* Serbian military cap

шајкаџија -ии *m colloq.* member of a gang, bandit, gangster

шајкаџиски *adj colloq.* bandit's, gangster's; band *attrib.*; brutal

шајче *n dim. of* шајка[1]

шака *f* joke; не знае за шака he can't take a joke; без шака no joking; joking apart; остави ја шаката *colloq.* cut the cackle! нема шака it's no joke; не е шака it's no laughing matter; it's no trifle

шакаџија -ии *m* joker, wag, jester; голем шакаџија a great joker

шал *m* scarf, muffler; shawl; stole; волнен шал woollen scarf

шалав *adj* restive, unruly; шалави деца unruly children

шалави *impf* to be restive (unruly); to be on the rampage

шалавост *f* restiveness, unruliness

шалварест *adj* wearing baggy trousers

шалвари *pl* baggy Muslim trousers, pantaloons; свилени шалвари silk pantaloons

шалваришта *pl augm. of* шалвари

шалварчиња *pl dim. of* шалвари

шалган *m Bot.* (Helianthus tuberosus) Jerusalem artichoke, topinambour

шалитра *f Chem.* saltpetre

шалитрен *adj* nitric; шалитрена киселина nitric acid

шалтер *m* **1** (*на пошта, мала продавница*) counter, window; (*на станица*) ticket office, *Brit.* booking-office; (*во театар и сл.*) box office **2** *Elec.* switch; circuit breaker

шалче *n dim. of* шал

шам- (Шам – *arch.* Damascus; Syria) Damascene; damascene; *in the combinations:* шам-шалвари damask pantaloons; шам-кутија damascene box; шам-кајсија damask apricot

шамак *m Bot. see* шавар

шамар *m dial. see* шлаканица; ❑ врзува (залепува) шамар некому to give s.o. a slap in the face; to slap s.o.'s face; to give s.o. a thick ear

шамата *f dial. see* врева

шамати *impf dial. see* врви

шамија -ии *f* kerchief, scarf; црна шамија black scarf

шамиче *n* handkerchief

шамот *m* fireclay

шамотен -тна *adj* fireclay *attrib.*; шамотни тули fire-bricks

шампањ *m* champagne

шампањски *adj* champagne *attrib.*, sparkling; шам-пањско вино sparkling wine

шампињон *m Bot.* (Agaricus campestris) champignon, edible mushroom

шампион *m Sport.* champion

шампионат *m Sport.* championship

шампионка *f* (*fem. form*) see шампион

шампон *m* shampoo

шан *m arch. colloq.* honour, reputation, dignity; ❑ му го скрши шанот на некого to impugn s.o.'s reputation; to shame (disgrace) s.o.; му се скрши шанот his reputation has been tarnished, his honour has been sullied

шандало *n see* мандало

шандан *m see* свешник

шанец -нци *m* trench, *see* ров, окоп

шанк *m* bar; пие на шанк to have a drink at the bar

шанса *f* chance; ❏ има шанса <да направи нешто> he has a chance <of doing s.th.>; дава некому шанса to give s.o. a chance (break); животна шанса chance of a lifetime; има еднакви (фифти-фифти) шанси he has an even (a fifty-fifty) chance; нема шанса to stand no chance; not a chance; нема ама баш никакви шанси he hasn't a ghost of a chance

шансо́на *f* popular song

шансоне́тка *f* singer of popular songs

шанта се *impf* to totter, stagger, reel; to limp

шантав *adj* 1 not all there, off one's head, *Brit. colloq.* daft; тој е шантав *colloq.* he has bats in the belfry 2 lame

шантавост *f* 1 craziness, *Brit. colloq.* daftness 2 lameness, limp

шантан *m arch.* café chantant, bar

шантански *adj arch.* bar *attrib.*; шантанска пеачка bar singer

шантра се *impf see* шанта се

шантрав *adj see* шантав

шантунг *m* (*вид материјал*) shantung

шап *m* foot-and-mouth disease

шапирогра́ф *m* duplicating machine, mimeograph <machine>

шапка *f* 1 hat; (*женска, старомодна*) bonnet; црна шапка black hat; му симина шапка на некого 1. to raise one's hat to s.o. 2. *fig.* to take off one's hat to s.o. 2 poppy-head 3 *dial. see* бабушка 1

шапкар *m* (*за мажи*) hatter; (*за жени*) milliner

шапкарка *f* (*fem. form*) *see* шапкар

шапкарница *f* hatter's/milliner's <shop>, hat shop

шапкарски *adj* hatter's; milliner's; hat *attrib.*; шапкарска работилница hatter's/milliner's workshop, hat workshop

шапкарство *n* hatter's/milliner's trade

шаплив *adj* suffering from foot-and-mouth disease

шапче *n dim. of* шапка

шар¹ *m* 1 hue, tinge, tint, shade (*of colour*) 2 motley, variety (diversity) in colour; пролетен шар spring colour<s>

шар² *m* (*топка*) globe, sphere, ball; земниот шар the globe

шара¹ *f see* шарка¹

шара² *f dial. see* пила

шарабија *adj indecl. f.p.* wine-coloured, crimson

шара́да *f* charade

шаран *m Zool.* (Cyprinus carpio) carp, *see* крап

шарба *f* 1 scribbling, scratching 2 *see* шарка¹ 3 decoration, ornament, gem

шарве́та *f dial.* kerchief

шарен *adj* 1 variegated, multicoloured, motley; (*премногу*) gaudy; (*за сенка*) dappled; (*за животни*) piebald; dappled; brindled; (*за куче*) spotted; шарено јајце brightly coloured Easter egg; шарен килим patterned rug 2 *fig. colloq.* mixed; motley; шарена група mixed group, motley crew; шарено оро mixed folk-dance (*final dance, in which all dance together*) 3 *fig.* light, loose; шарена жена loose woman, *pejor. colloq.* floozie 4 шарен грав *Bot.* (Phaseolus coccineus) scarlet runner bean

шаренее се *impf* 1 to look variegated (multicoloured) 2 *see* шари (се) II 1

шаренило *n* 1 variegated (multicoloured) appearance, mottle, mottling 2 *fig.* varied (mixed) nature; medley; jumble; шаренилото на програмата the variety of the programme

шаренина *f see* шаренило

шареница *f* gaudiness

шарец -рци *m* dappled/piebald horse

шаржер *m* clip, magazine (*for firearm*)

шари *impf* I 1 to variegate, dapple; to colour/paint in different colours; шари џемпер/чорап to knit a jersey/sock in different colours; шари јајце to colour (paint) an Easter egg 2 to scribble; шари хартија to scribble (scrawl) all over a piece of paper 3 *fig.* to wander, rove 4 *fig.* (*за сопружници*) to be unfaithful, play (*colloq.* sleep) around 5 *fig.* to move about *intrans.*; шари со очите to let one's eye wander (rove, dart about) II – се 1 to appear multicoloured; to appear (show up) in the distance, be a dot in the distance; се шари нешто онаму there is s.th. visible over there 2 to have measles

шарило *n* dye; paint

шарка¹ *f* pattern, design; stencil; (*на гуми*) tread pattern

шарка² *f* dappled/piebald sheep; dappled/piebald goat

шарка³ *f* hinge

шарка⁴ *f* measles

шарка⁵ *f Zool.* (Vipera berus) adder

шарка⁶ (се) *impf dim. of* шари (се)

шарко *m* spotted dog; dappled/piebald/brindled animal

шарконог *adj f.p.* with dappled/piebald legs

шарлаган *m arch.* vegetable oil

шарлаганџија -ии *m arch.* producer/purveyor of vegetable oil

шарлаганџилница *f* oil shop

шарлаганџиски *adj* oil-producer's/-seller's; шарлаганџиски коњ oil-seller's horse

шарлата́н *m* 1 cheat, impostor 2 charlatan; quack

шарлата́нка *f* (*fem. form*) *see* шарлатан

шарлата́нски *adj* 1 cheating, fraudulent 2 charlatan's; quackish; amateurish; шарлатанско лечење quackish treatment

шарлата́нство *n* charlatanry; quackery

шарлатанствува *impf* to play the charlatan (mountebank)

шарлах *m Med.* scarlet fever

шарм *m* charm

шарма́нтен -тна *adj* charming

шарма́нтно *adv* charmingly

шарма́нтност *f* charm, charming manner

шармер *m* charmer; seducer

шарми́ра *pf & impf* to charm; to seduce

шарнир *m see* шарка³

шаро *m see* шарко

Шар Планина *f* the Shar Mountains

шарпланински *adj* Shar *attrib.*

шасија -ии *f Tech.* 1 chassis, frame (*of a vehicle*) 2 undercarriage, landing gear (*of an aircraft*)

шати́ра *pf & impf* 1 to shade, hatch 2 (*коса*) to streak *trans.*; to highlight

шатка *f Zool.* duck; питома (домашна) шатка domestic duck; дива шатка (Anas platyrhynchos) wild duck, mallard

шаткин *adj* duck's, duck *attrib*.; шаткино јајце duck egg

шаток -ци *m Zool. see* шатор¹

шатор¹ *m Zool.* drake

шатор² *m* **1** tent; (*голем*) marquee, pavilion; распне шатор to pitch a tent; колче за шатор tent-peg **2** *see* чадор 1

шаторест *adj* tent-like; umbrella-shaped; дрво шаторесто umbrella-shaped tree

шаторски *adj* tent *attrib*.; шаторско крило tent flap

шаторче *n* **1** *dim. of* шатор² **2** *Bot.* (Convolvulus) bindweed

шат-пат *adv* from time to time, occasionally; here and there; *colloq.* in dribs and drabs

шатра *f* **1** *see* шатор² 1 **2** log cabin; shanty; tent stall, booth

шафран *m Bot.* (Crocus sativus) crocus; saffron

шах¹ *m* shah; Shah

шах² *m* **1** chess; check; игра шах to play chess; даде шах to check (*s.o.*); даде шах-мат to checkmate (*also fig.*); ❏ држи некого во шах to hold s.o. in check, have s.o. over a barrel **2** chess set, set of chessmen

шахист *m* chess player

шахистка *f* (*fem. form*) *see* шахист

шаховски *adj* **1** Shah's **2** chess *attrib*.; шаховска табла chessboard

шахта *f* **1** mine shaft, pit **2** manhole

шашав *adj see* шашлив

шашардиса *pf colloq.* **1** to stun; to take aback; to scare **2** to confuse, nonplus, perplex; го шашардиса детето he confused the child

шашардисува *impf of* шашардиса

шашарма *f colloq. see* шашма

шашка *f arch. see* сабја

шашкан *m* foolish (crazy, *Brit. colloq.* daft) person

шашлив *adj* (*see* кривоглед) cross-eyed, *Med.* strabismal; squinting; шашливо дете cross-eyed child; шашливи очи crossed/squinting eyes

шашливо *adv* with crossed eyes, with a cast in the eye; squinting, with a squint; гледа шашливо to look with crossed eyes, look with a cast in the eye; to squint

шашливост *f* cross-eye, cast in the eye, *Med.* strabismus; squint

шашма *f colloq.* confusion, muddle; ❏ на шашма lucky guess; at random

шаштиса *pf colloq. see* шашардиса

шаштисува *impf of* шаштиса, *see* шашардисува

швајсер *m* welder

швајсува *pf & impf* to weld

Швајцарец -рци *m* Swiss

Швајцарија *f* Switzerland

Швајцарка *f* (*fem. form*) *see* Швајцарец

швајцарски *adj* Swiss

швалер *m sl.* (*see* љубовник) lover; playboy, lady-killer, lady's man

швалерисува се *impf sl.* to sleep around

швалерка *f sl.* (*see* љубовница) mistress; good-time girl; fast woman, vamp

шваргла *f Cul.* brawn, head cheese

Шведска *f* Sweden

шведски *adj* Swedish

Швеѓанец -ни *m* Swede

Швеѓанка *f* (*fem. form*) *see* Швеѓанец

шверц *m* smuggling; black marketeering; black market

шверцер *m* smuggler

шверцерка *f* (*fem. form*) *see* шверцер

шверцува *pf & impf* **1** to smuggle, work as a smuggler, deal in smuggled goods; to deal on the black market **2** to travel (*on public transport*) without a ticket, dodge the fare, steal a ride

шврка (се) *impf see* швркне (се)

швркне *pf* **I** to flog, birch, whip *trans.*; to flagellate **II** – **се** to flog (birch, whip)/flagellate o.s.

швркнува (се) *impf of* швркне (се)

шворц *adj indecl. sl.* penniless; шворц е he doesn't have a penny to his name, *colloq.* he is broke (*Brit. sl.* skint)

шебек -ци *m arch.* monkey, ape

шебој -ои *m Bot.* (Cheiranthus cheiri) wallflower

шев *m* **1** seam; *Med.* suture; *Tech.* join<t>, seam; шев на цевка join on a pipe/tube **2** sewing, needlework; needlecraft; ситен шев fine needlework

шевен -вна *adj* sewing *attrib*.; having a seam (*Tech.* join<t>); *Tech.* joined; шевни цевки seamed tubing

шевиот *m* serge, cheviot

шевро *n* kidskin

шега *f* **1** joke; practical joke, prank, lark; trick; тој ни правеше шеги he cracked jokes with us; ❏ несолена шега practical joke; невкусна шега dirty joke; знае за шега he has a sense of humour, he can take a joke; не знае за шега he has no sense of humour, he can't take a joke; прифаќа (сфаќа) шега to see (get) the joke; без шега seriously, *sl.* no kidding; каже нешто на шега to say s.th. in jest (for fun); нема тука шега this is no joking (laughing) matter; this is no joke; нема <повеќе> место за шега this is beyond a joke; шегата настрана joking apart; бие (тера) шега со некого to make fun of s.o., pull s.o.'s leg; во секоја шега има пола вистина *saying* there is many a true word spoken in jest **2** <мере> trifle; тоа е шега за него it's a piece of cake for him

шегајлив *adj see* шеговит

шеган *m* kind of peasant dress of white homespun

шегарка *f f.p. see* шегртка

шегарче *n f.p. see* шегртче

шегач *m* joker, wag, jester; banterer; mocker, derider, scoffer

шегачи се *impf* to joke, make a joke; to speak in jest, *sl.* kid; to play tricks (*with s.o.*)

шегачка *f* (*fem. form*) *see* шегач

шегачки *adj* joker's, wag's, jester's; joking

шегаџија -ии *m see* шегач

шегаџиски *adj see* шегачки

шегобиен -јна *adj* joking, jesting; bantering, chaffing; mocking, derisive, scoffing; шегобијни зборови banter

шегобиец -јци *m see* шегач

шегобиство *n* joking, jesting; banter, chaffing, persiflage; mockery, scoffing

шеговит *adj* jocular, funny, facetious, playful; waggish; bantering; шеговит човек jocular (playful) person, joker; шеговити прикаски humorous stories; шеговит тон jocular tone

шеговито *adv* jokingly, facetiously, playfully; waggishly; banteringly

шеговитост *f* jocularity, facetiousness, playfulness; waggery; banter

шегрт *m* apprentice, *see* чирак

шегртка *f* (*fem. form*) *see* шегрт

шегртски *adj* apprentice's

шегрче *n dim. of* шегрт & шегртка

шегува се *impf* 1 to make a joke; to crack jokes; сношти беше тој многу весел: раскажуваше, се смееше, се шегуваше last night he was in very good spirits: he told stories, laughed <a lot>, told jokes; ❑ се шегува на туѓа сметка to joke at s.o.'s expense 2 to trifle, play (*co – with*); to make fun (*co – of*); јас не дозволувам со мене да се шегувате I won't let you trifle with me 3 to joke; се шегува, нема да те казни he's joking, he won't punish you 4 (*only with negation*) to fool around; не шегувај се! don't fool around! ❑ не се шегува he means business

шедба *f* walk, stroll; шедба шета *f.p.* to go for a walk

шеесет *num* sixty

шеесетгодишен -шна *adj* 1 sixty years old 2 lasting sixty years; sixty-year *attrib.*

шеесетгодишнина *f* sixtieth anniversary

шеестина 1 *num* about sixty 2 *f* sixtieth <part>

шеесетмина *num* (*of men or mixed groups*) sixty

шеесетти *adj* sixtieth

шеик -ци *m* sheikh, sheik

шеј *m arch. dial.* thing, chattel; сите шејови што ги донесе невестата all the goods and chattels that the bride brought with her

шејтан *m arch.* (*see* ѓавол) 1 the Devil, Satan 2 *fig.* clever devil, crafty customer, *colloq.* slyboots

шејтански *adj arch.* 1 the Devil's, Satan's; devilish 2 *fig.* devilishly clever

шекне *pf sl.* I to drive s.o. mad II – ce to go crazy (mad); *colloq.* to go off the deep end

шекнува (се) *impf sl. of* шекне (се); се шекнува за (по) to be crazy (mad) about

шекспировски *adj* Shakespearian

шекспиролог *m* Shakespeare specialist, Shakespearian

шекспирологија *f* Shakespeare studies

шекспиролошки *adj of* Shakespearian studies

шема *f* 1 (*нацрт*) plan; chart; diagram; set-up; *Phys.* circuit; *Elec.* circuitry; шема на телефон a wiring diagram of a telephone 2 (*скица*) sketch; design; outline, plan; шема на рефератот an outline of the paper 3 *fig.* (*шаблон*) routine, set form, beaten track, schematic behaviour (way of thought), <behaviour> pattern; drill; stock example; cliché; работи/мисли по шеми he works/thinks in conventional patterns; ❑ му се вклопува во шема to suit (fit) s.o.'s book

шематизам -змот *m* oversimplification; schematic way of thought, conventionalism, conventionality, conformity, formalism

шематизација *f* oversimplification; formalization; sketchy/oversimplified representation

шематизира *pf & impf* to oversimplify, reduce to conventional models; to formalize; to represent as a diagram

шематичен -чна *adj* 1 schematic; sketchy; oversimplified 2 routine *attrib.*, conventional, stock

шематичност *f* 1 schematic/oversimplified quality, sketchiness 2 conventional quality, stock character

шематски 1 *adj see* шематичен 2 *adv* in an oversimplified/conventional manner

шемет *f* giddiness, dizziness, vertigo

шеметен -тна *adj* dizzy, vertiginous, staggering; со шеметна брзина at a vertiginous (dizzy) speed, like greased lightning

шеметно *adv* vertiginously, at a vertiginous (dizzy) speed, like greased lightning

шемизет *m* linen cupboard; drawer for underwear

шен *adj indecl. arch. see* шенлив

шенга се *impf colloq.* to joke; to play (*co – with*); ce шенга со тебе he's having you on

шенголка се *impf dim. of* шенга се

шенгуле *colloq. in the expression:* си игра шенгуле со некого to play jokes (pranks, tricks) on s.o., pull s.o.'s leg

шени се *impf colloq.* to have fun (a good time), enjoy o.s.

шенлив *adj f.p.* in good spirits, cheerful, happy

шепа *f* hollow <of the hand>; cupped hand<s>; (*на животно*) paw; (*количество*) handful (*of*); ❑ има некого во своите шепи to have s.o. in one's clutches

шепетајка *f f.p.* (*epithet for a duck*) четири пајки шепетајки four waddling ducks

шепина *impf see* шепне

шепкач *m* 1 person who speaks in a whisper 2 (*во театар и др.*) prompt<er>, *see* суфлер 3 *fig.* gossip, gossip-monger

шепне *pf* шепна *aor.* 1 to whisper; му шепна нешто на уво he whispered something in his ear 2 (*во театар и др.*) to prompt, *see* суфлира

шепни-покров *m colloq.* (*said of a wife who stirs up her husband against the rest of the family*) шепни-покров куќа запустува *prov.* a backbiter ruins a house

шепнува *impf of* шепне

шепот *m* 1 whisper 2 *fig.* murmur

шепоти *impf* 1 to whisper; (*во театар и др.*) to prompt 2 *fig.* to murmur

шепотлив *adj* whispering; со шепотлив глас in a whisper, *sotto voce*

шепурка *f see* шопурка

шербет *m* 1 (*напивка*) sherbet 2 (*густо растопен шеќер*) syrup

шербетлија *adj indecl.* syrupy

шервета & шерветка *f dial. see* шарвета

шерет *m* little scamp; crafty customer, *colloq.* slyboots

шеретлак -ци *m* scampish behaviour/nature; craftiness, slyness

шеретски *adj* scampish; crafty, sly

шеретува *impf* to behave like a little scamp, play pranks; to be crafty (sly)

шеријат *m* sharia

шеријатски *adj* sharia *attrib.*; шеријатско право sharia

шериф¹ *m* sheriff

шериф² *m* sharif, shereef, sherif

шерифов *adj* sheriff's

шерифски *adj* sheriff's

шеснаесет *num* sixteen

шеснаестгодишен -шна *adj* 1 sixteen years old 2 lasting sixteen years; sixteen-year *attrib.*

шеснаесетгодишнина *f* sixteenth anniversary

шеснаесетдневен -вна *adj* lasting sixteen days; шеснаесетдневен одмор a sixteen-day holiday

шеснаесетина *f* sixteenth <part>

шеснаесетка *f* 1 <the figure> sixteen 2 No. 16 <tram, bus *etc.*>

шеснаесетмина *num* (*of men and mixed groups*) sixteen

шеснаесетник -ци *m Sport.* penalty area

шеснаесетти *adj* sixteenth

шеснаестинка *f Mus.* semiquaver, *Am.* sixteenth note

шест *num* six

шеста *impf colloq.* (*only with дума*) to think over; *in the expression:* дума, шеста *or* мисли, шеста to think and think, rack one's brains; думале, шестале, какво чаре да бараат they were racking their brains over what to do

шестаголен -лна *adj* hexagonal

шестаголник -ци *m Geom.* hexagon

шестак -ци *m f.p.* six-groat coin

шестар *m* pair of compasses

шестгодишен -шна *adj* 1 six years old 2 lasting six years; six-year *attrib.*

шестгодишнина *f* sixth anniversary

шестдневен -вна *adj* lasting six days; шестдневен престој six-day stay

шести *adj* sixth; шесто одделение sixth form, *Am.* sixth grade; шести кат sixth floor; шести по ред sixth <in order>; на шести март on the 6th (sixth of) March, *Am.* on March 6

шестина 1 *num* (*of men and mixed groups*) six, *see* шестмина 2 *f* sixth <part>; две шестини two sixths

шестиса (се) *pf dial. see* шаштиса (се)

шестка *f* 1 (*цифрата* 6) <figure> six 2 (*во карти, на зар*) six 3 (*студентска оцена*) six (*out of ten*), pass 4 (*автобус, трамвај итн.*) <number> six

шесткатен -тна *adj* six-storey *attrib.*, of six storeys

шесткатница *f* six-storey building

шесткрилат *adj see* шестокрил

шестмесечен -чна *adj* six-month *attrib.*, of six months; шестмесечно списание six-monthly, bi-annual journal/magazine

шестмина *num* (*of men and mixed groups*) six

шестнеделен -лна *adj* six-week *attrib.*, of six weeks; шестнеделен пост six-week fast

шестокатен -тна *adj see* шесткатен

шестокатница *f see* шесткатница

шестокласник -ци *m* sixth-former, pupil in the sixth form

шестокласничка *f* (*fem. form*) *see* шестокласник

шестокрил *adj* six-winged, having six wings

шесторед *adj* (*of wheat*) six-awned

шесторедица *f f.p.* (*epithet of six-awned wheat*) бела пченица шесторедица white six-awned wheat

шесторен -рна *adj* sixfold; six times greater

шесторно *adv* sixfold

шестосложен -жна *adj* six-syllable *attrib.*, of six syllables

шестостран *adj* hexagonal; шестострана призма hexagonal prism

шестоти *adj* six-hundredth

шестотини *num* six hundred

шесточлен & **шесточленен** -на *adj* six-member *attrib.*, of six members; шесточлена комисија six-member commission

шестпати *adv* six times

ше́ст-седум *num* six or seven; шест-седум души six or seven people

шест-седумдесет *num* sixty or seventy; шест-седумдесет килограми sixty or seventy kilograms

шест-седумнаесет *num* sixteen or seventeen; шест-седумнаесет дена sixteen or seventeen days

шест-седумстотини *num* six or seven hundred; шест-седумстотини денари six or seven hundred denars

шестчасовен -вна *adj* six-hour *attrib.*, of six hours; шестчасовен работен ден six-hour working day

шета *impf* I 1 *intrans.* to stroll, <go for a> walk; (*со коњ*) to go for a ride; (*со кола*) to go for a drive; секоја вечер шетаа по паркот every evening they would stroll in the park; шета на чист воздух to take the air 2 to walk to and fro, walk up and down; to pace the room; ние седевме, а тој шеташе низ дворот we were seated but he walked up and down in the yard; волкот шеташе низ шумата the wolf was prowling about in the forest 3 to wander (roam) about; to trip/gad about; шета по дуќани to wander round the shops, go shopping; тој шеташе на коњ по селата he roamed round the villages on horseback, he rode round the countryside 4 *fig.* (*of eyes, thoughts, etc.*) to wander; очите му шетаа по движењата на гостинот his eyes followed the guest's movements 5 *trans.* to take for a walk; ги шетав децата I took the children for a walk 6 to wander about, visit; сум ги шетал јас тие места I have wandered about these places II – се *see* I 1

шеталиште *n* promenade; walk; park; <public> gardens; esplanade

шетан *adj* <much->travelled; јас сум шетан човек I've been around, I've knocked about

шетаница *f* walk, stroll, turn; trip; (*со коњ*) ride

шетање *n* 1 *from* шета (се) 2 walk, stroll; excursion, trip; (*со коњ*) ride; (*со кола*) drive; ќе одиме на шетање we're going out

шетач *m* person who goes walking, promenader, stroller

шетачка *f* 1 (*fem. form*) *see* шетач 2 *see* шетање 2

шетка (се) *impf dim. of* шета (се)

шетне (се) *pf* шетна (се) *aor.* to go for a short walk, take a turn; шетни малку 1. take a turn outside! 2. *pejor.* go away!

шетнува (се) *impf of* шетне (се)

шеќер *m* sugar; чај-шеќер *colloq.* lump sugar, cube sugar; ситен шеќер castor sugar; шеќер во прав icing (*Am.* confectioner's) sugar; жолт шеќер brown sugar; кристал шеќер granulated sugar; млечен шеќер milk sugar, lactose; фабрика за шеќер sugar mill (refinery); сладок како шеќер <as> sweet as sugar, sugary

шеќера́на *f* sugar mill (refinery)

шеќераш *m colloq.* diabetic

шеќерен -рна *adj* 1 sugar *attrib.*; шеќерна фабрика sugar mill (refinery); шеќерна коцка sugar cube, lump of sugar; шеќерен раствор sugar solution, syrup; шеќерна трска sugar cane; шеќерна репка (репа), шеќерно цвекло sugar beet 2 *Med.* шеќерна болест diabetes 3 *fig.* sweet, sugary; шеќерна уста cajolery, honeyed words, *colloq.* sweet talk; *f.p.* шеќерно грло flatterer, cajoler, *colloq.* sweet talker

шеќерка *f* sugar-apple

шеќерлеме *n arch.* sugarplum

шеќерлија *adj indecl. arch.* sugary, sugar-sweet

шеќерлиса се *pf* to go sugary; to crystallize; слат-кото се шеќерлисало the preserve has crystallized

шеќерлисува се *impf of* шеќерлиса се

шеќеров *adj f.p. see* шеќерен 1; грутка шеќерова lump of sugar

шеќерче *n colloq.* sweet, sweetmeat, sugarplum

шеќерџија -ии *m colloq.* confectioner; pastry-cook

шеќерџилница *f colloq.* confectioner's <shop>; pastry shop

шеќерџиски *adj colloq.* confectioner's; confectionery *attrib.*

шеф *m* head, director, manager, *colloq.* boss; шеф на одделение departmental head; шеф на отсек section head; шеф на кабинет Head of the Cabinet; шеф на катедра Head of Department, Professor; шеф на продажба sales manager; шеф на станица station master

шефица *f* 1 (*fem. form*) *see* шеф 2 *colloq.* head's (director's, manager's) wife

шефовски *adj* head's, director's; managerial; шефо-вско место headship, director's/managerial position

шефовство *n* headship, director's position; management

шефтелија -ии *f Bot.* variety of peach

шефува *impf* to be the head (director, manager), carry out the duties of a director (manager)

шех *m* (*only sg*) *Chess* check (*of the queen*)

шеш-беш *m* backgammon; game of chance

шешери се *impf* to put on airs, strut <about>, swagger

шешерлав *adj* (*за дрво*) with a spreading, rambling crown

шешир *m* hat; сламен шешир straw hat; шешир со широк первaз broad-brimmed hat

шиба *impf* I 1 to lash, beat, belabour; (*со нога*) to kick; (*со тупаници*) to pummel, punch; (*со стап и сл.*) to flog; to lash; to cane; (*со камшик*) to whip, scourge; шиба со клоци to kick; студен ветер нѐ шибаше в лице a cold wind lashed our faces 2 *fig. colloq.* to put, push, *colloq.* shove (*во – into s.th.*); to slip *trans.* (*во – into s.th.*); to toss *trans.* (*во – into s.th.*); само шиба в торба сѐ што ќе му дојде до рака he just shoves into the bag everything that he comes across II – се *see* шибне (се) II

шиблинка *f* rod, switch

шибне *pf* шибна *aor.* I *see* шиба I II – се 1 to hit o.s. 2 *fig. colloq.* to push, shove *intrans.* (*во – into*); to duck/sneak (*во – into*); се шибна во еден дуќан he ducked/sneaked into a shop

шибнува (се) *impf of* шибне (се)

шивач *m* tailor

шивачка *f* dressmaker, seamstress

шивачки *adj* tailor's; dressmaker's; sartorial; шива-чки салон tailor's/dressmaker's shop

шие *impf* 1 to sew, stitch; *Med.* to sew, stitch, suture, *see* сошива; to sew on; шие петлица (копче) to sew on a button; шие на рака to sew by hand; шие на машина to sew on a machine; шие фустан/костум to make a dress/suit; to have a dress/suit made; ❏ пред да шиеш, треба да кроиш don't put the cart before the horse! 2 *fig. colloq.* to beat (*s.o. at/in s.th.*); го шијам jac него <во тоа> I run rings round him, I beat him hands down <at that>

шизи *impf sl.* to go off one's rocker, go nuts; не шизи! don't go mental! шизи по to go mad about, be wild about

шизма *f* schism

шизматик -ци *m* schismatic

шизматички *adj* schismatic

шизофренија *f* schizophrenia

шизофрéник -ци & **шизофреничар** *m* schizophrenic

шизофренички *adj* schizophrenic

шија -ии *f rare* neck; му ја свитка шијата she wrung his neck (*also fig.*); ❏ не по врат, по шија six of one and half a dozen of the other;

шијак -ци *m dial.* 1 man with a thick/long neck 2 stiff-necked person

шијарка *f* sewing needle

шијач *m see* шивач

шијачка *f* 1 *see* шивачка 2 sewing; needlework

шијачки *adj* 1 *see* шивачки 2 sewing *attrib.*; шијачка игла sewing needle; шијачка машина sewing-machine

шик¹ *m* 1 gold leaf, tinsel 2 *as adj indecl.* with gold leaf/braid; adorned with tinsel; gilded; шик перници pillows with gold braid

шик² 1 *m* style; без шик without any style 2 *adj indecl.* stylish, elegant; шик дама an elegant lady; шик шапка a chic hat 3 *adv* stylishly, elegantly, smartly; шик облечена stylishly dressed; се носи шик to dress elegantly

шика¹ *impf* (*see* шикне¹) to gush out (forth), well up, squirt <out>; крв му шикаше од раната blood gushed from his wound

шика² *impf of* шикне²

шикáна *f literary* chicanery, nasty trick, harassment

шиканúра *pf & impf* to persecute, torment, harass, bully

шикла *f* 1 oak-apple (-gall), nutgall, gall-nut; мастило од шикли nutgall/oak-gall ink; ❏ шикли! nonsense! 2 nutgall/oak-gall dye

шикло *adj f.p.* gilded; шикло седло gilded saddle, *see* шикосан; шикло сребро silver gilt

шиклоса *pf* 1 to colour (tint) with nutgall/oak-gall dye; си ја шиклоса косата she dyed her hair with nutgall/oak-gall dye 2 *see* шикоса

шиклосан *adj* 1 coloured (tinted) with nutgall/oak-gall dye 2 *see* шикосан

шиклосува *impf of* шиклоса

шикне¹ *pf* шикна *aor.* to gush out (forth) suddenly; шикна вода од чешмата water gushed out of the tap

шикне² *pf* шикна *aor.* to shush *trans.*; шикни му да молкне tell him to be quiet!

шикнува¹ *impf of* шикне¹

шикнува² *impf of* шикне²

шикоса *pf* to gild; to tinsel

шикосан *adj* gilded; adorned with tinsel; седло шикосано gilded saddle; налани шикосани gilded clogs

шикосува *impf of* шикоса

шиле *n see* шилеже 1

шилегар *m* shepherd

шилегарче *n dim. of* шилегар

шилеже *n* 1 weaned lamb 2 *see* сугаре

шилер *m* sort of wine made from green and black grapes

шилест *adj* sharp; pointed; шилести карпи jagged rocks; шилест нос pointed nose; шилест кол sharp-<ened> stake

шилец -лци *m* **1** point, sharp end **2** wooden awl

шилешки *adj* lamb *attrib.*, lamb's; шилешка кожа lambskin

шили *impf* to sharpen, taper <off> *trans.*

шилинг -зи *m* (*англиска монета*) shilling; (*австриска монета*) Schilling

шило *n* **1** (*за кожа*) awl; (*за платно*) stiletto, bodkin; (*за дрво*) bradawl; чевли крпи со игла и шило to repair shoes with a needle and an awl **2** *fig.* busybody, meddler; го знам што шило е тој I know what a busybody he is

шилте *n* thin cushion

шилче *n dim. of* шилец & шило

шилчест *adj see* шилест

шилчи *impf see* шили

шимпанзо *n Zool.* (Pan troglodytes) chimpanzee

шимшир *m* **1** *Bot.* (Buxus sempervirens) box **2** *as adj indecl.* boxwood *attrib.*; шимшир-порти *f.p.* boxwood portal

шимширов *adj* box *attrib.*; boxwood *attrib.*; шимширова лажица boxwood spoon; шимширова гранка box branch; шимширово дрво boxwood

шина *f* **1** rail; railway (*Am.* railroad) track; tramlines, tram (*Am.* streetcar) track; излегува од шини to jump the rails/track **2** (*обрач*) <wheel> rim **3** *Med.* splint

шинат *adj* sprained, dislocated

шиндра *f* shingle, lath, board

шине *pf* шина *aor.* **I** to sprain, wrench, dislocate; си ја шинав ногата I have sprained my ankle **II** – се **1** to sprain (*one's wrist, one's ankle*) **2** *fig.* to overdo things, do one's back in, suffer from overwork (*also iron.*); се шинав работејќи I overdid things at work

шинел *m* & **шинела** *f* <heavy military> overcoat, greatcoat

шиник -ци *m* **1** wooden drum for measuring grain **2** quarter bushel

шинобус *m* rail-bus

шинтер *m* **1** dog catcher **2** *fig.* bloodsucker

шинува (се) *impf of* шине (се)

шип -ови, -је *m Bot.* **1** *see* шипка¹ **1 2** bush, shrub

шипинка *f see* шипка 2

шипка¹ *f* **1** *Bot.* (Rosa canina) dogrose **2** rose-hip; мармалад од шипки rose-hip jam; ❑ (*only pl*) шипки! nonsense! *sl.* rhubarb!

шипка² *f* <metal> bar, rod

шипков *adj* rose-hip *attrib.* шипков чај rose-hip tea шипкова грмушка rose-hip bush

Шиптар *m pejor.* Albanian

Шиптарка *f* (*fem. form*) *see* Шиптар

шиптарски *adj pejor.* Albanian

шир *f* & *m poet.* expanse, space; морската шир the open sea, the high seas; небесниот шир the vault of heaven

шира *f* must

ширден *m* rennet-bag, abomasum (*fourth stomach of ruminants*); *Cul.* полнети ширдени stuffed rennet-bag (*dish like haggis*)

ширен -рна *adj* wide, extensive, vast; ширни полиња large fields

шири *impf* **I 1** to widen, enlarge, extend *trans.*; to broaden *trans.*; (*за зеници*) to dilate *trans.*; шири некаков отвор to enlarge an opening; патувањето ги шири погледите travel broadens the mind **2** to open <wide> *trans.*; to spread *trans.*; шири раце to open one's arms; *fig.* to shrug one's shoulders, make a helpless gesture; шири прсти to spread one's fingers; шири крилја to spread one's wings; дрвото ги шири гранките the tree spreads its branches **3** to spread, propagate, circulate *trans.*, disseminate; to distribute *trans.*; шири лажни вести to spread false rumours; шири идеи/заблуди to spread ideas/errors **II** – се **1** to widen *intrans.*; to broaden *intrans.*; to expand *intrans.*; to spread out *intrans.*; to dilate *intrans.*; сите тела на топлината се шират all bodies expand in the heat; неговото царство почна да се шири his empire began to expand **2** to open <wide> *intrans.*; очиве слатко се шират *poet.* my eyes open wide **3** to spread <out>, spread out far and wide, extend *intrans.*; пред мене полето се шири the field extends in front of me **4** to spread *intrans.*; болеста се шири the disease is spreading; се шират гласови rumours are circulating; се шират вести news is spreading; нашите идеи се шират our ideas are taking hold; модата се шири the fashion is catching on **5** to spread o.s.; сам се шири во тросовен стан he lives by himself in a three-room flat

ширина *f* **1** width, breadth; size; ширина на улицата width of the street; во должина и во ширина in length and breadth, lengthwise and sideways; ширина на облека size of clothing **2** open space; децата играа на една ширина the children were playing on open ground **3** *Geog.* latitude; географска ширина geographic latitude; на 38° северна/јужна ширина at 38° north/south, on the 38th parallel **4** *fig.* (*only sg*) breadth; latitude; ширина на поим breadth of a concept; ширина на погледи/сфаќања breadth of views/mind

ширински *adj* of latitude, latitudinal; ширински степен degree of latitude

ширит *m* braid, ribbon, galloon

ширнограден -дна *adj fig. poet.* broad-breasted, wide; над селото лежат ширноградни ридој above the village lie broad hills

широк *adj* **1** wide, broad; spacious; large, ample; (*за облека*) loose<-fitting>, baggy; широка улица wide street; широко чело broad forehead; широки раменици broad shoulders; широк екран wide screen; патот е широк седум метра the road is seven metres wide; палтото ти е многу широко your coat is too big for you; широк фустан loose-fitting dress; широки панталони baggy trousers **2** *fig.* broad, extensive, considerable, varied; широк поим broad concept; широка програма varied programme; широка обработка wide-ranging discussion; во широк размер on a large scale; широки познанства/врски extensive acquaintances/contacts; широките народни маси the bulk of the population; широка мрежа од библиотеки extensive network of libraries; производи за широка потрошувачка consumer goods; широк замав large scale; широк асортиман wide range (choice); широки можности considerable possibilities; во широката (пошироката) смисла на зборот in the broad sense of the word; ❑ долг и широк lengthy and detailed; долга и широка расправа a long-winded story; таа е долга и широка that's a long story **3** *fig.* broad-minded; easy-going; generous; широк човек broad-minded person; широко срце generous heart; има (е со) широка рака to be generous (open-handed); живее на широка нога to live in <grand> style **4** *Phon.* open; широко *a* open (broad) *a*

широко[1] *adv* wide; widely; ја отвори широко вратата he opened the door wide, he threw open the door; гледа широко на работите to take a broad view of things; ❏ на долго и на широко, *see* надолго <и нашироко>; вратата е широко отворена the door is wide open; широко му е околу вратот he has a great deal of latitude, he takes it easy; he is making himself at home; he has no problems

широко[2] *n* sirocco

широкогра́д *adj* easy-going, broad-minded; generous

широкогра́д<н>о *adv* generously; with open arms; неа примени широкоградно they were welcomed with open arms

широкогра́дост *f* easy-going nature, broadmindedness; generosity

широкообразен -зна *adj* large-scale *attrib.*, on a large scale

широкотрупен -пна *adj* wide-bodied; широкотрупен авион wide-bodied aircraft

широчи *impf dial. see* шири

широчина *f see* ширина

ширум *adv* wide; ширум отворена врата wide open door

шитка *impf colloq. see* шитне

шитне *pf* шитна *aor. colloq.* **1** to throw away, *colloq.* chuck out, *see* цитне **2** to get rid of, sell off, *colloq.* unload; го шитнав велосипедот за десет илјади денари I got rid of my bicycle for ten thousand denars

шитнува *impf of* шитне

шифон *m* chiffon

шифоњер *m* wardrobe, cupboard

шифра *f* code, cipher

шифра́нт *m* code clerk, cipher clerk

шифри́ра *pf & impf* to encode

шифри́ран *adj* <en>coded, in code, code *attrib.*; шифрирано писмо coded letter; шифрирана телеграма coded telegram

шиш -еви, -ови *m* spit, broach; skewer

шишарка *f* **1** <fir->cone **2** (*мешунка*) pod

шише *n* **1** bottle; шише од (за) пиво a beer bottle **2** bottle<ful>; испи две шишиња пиво he drank two bottles of beer **3** <lamp-> chimney

шишенце *n dim. of* шише; (*за лекови*) vial, phial; (*за оцет и сл.*) cruet

шишка *f see* шишарка 1

шишкав *adj colloq.* fat, plump, chubby

шишкавост *f colloq.* fatness, plumpness, chubbiness

шишко -вци *m colloq.* fatty, *sl.* fatso

шишман *m* **1** *see* шишко **2** *f.p. as adj indecl.* fat, plump

шкарпа *f dial. see* карпа

шкарт *m* **1** rejects; spoilage, waste; junk **2** *fig.* reject, good-for-nothing

шкарти́ра *pf & impf* to reject, discard, sell off

шкаф *m* cupboard; locker; *see* орман[2]

шкафче *n dim. of* шкаф

шкембар *m* **1** tripe seller **2** lover of tripe

шкембарка *f* (*fem. form*) *see* шкембар

шкембарница *f* tripe shop

шкембарски *adj* tripe *attrib.*; шкембарски дуќан tripe shop

шкембе *n* **1** *Anat. Zool.* <ruminant's> first stomach, paunch, rumen; *Cul.* tripe; шкембе-чорба tripe soup **2** *fig. colloq.* fatty, dumpling

шкембелија *adj indecl. see* шкембест

шкембест *adj* **1** loose; soft, spongy, flabby, floppy **2** potbellied, paunchy

шкембеџија -ии *m see* шкембар 1

шкембеџилница *f see* шкембарница

шкето *n Cul.* dish of meat with gravy

шкоба *f* scraper

шкобав & шкоблест *adj* thinnish, spare, lean, meagre; gaunt; шкобави раце bony hands

школа *f* **1** school; балетска школа ballet school; виша педагошка школа teachers' college, pedagogical institute; школата се наоѓа во центарот на градот the school <building> is in the centre of the town **2** *fig.* training, schooling; школата на животот the school of life; има добра школа *iron.* he's been in bad company **3** *fig.* group; school of thought; Рафаеловата школа the Raphael school; основе (создаде) школа to found a school; приврзаник на старата школа a man of the old school **4** *Mus.* musical workbook (primer), manual, school; школа за клавир (пијано) piano textbook

школарина *f* school fees, *Am.* tuition

школија -ии *f dial. see* школа 1

школка *f* **1** *Zool.* mussel; oyster **2** shell; (*голема*) conch **3** *Anat.* concha, helix

школник -ци *m literary* pupil, schoolboy

школо *n colloq. see* школа 1

школовка *f* training

школски *adj* **1** school *attrib.*; школски двор school yard; школски инспектор school inspector; школска дисциплина school discipline; школски другар school friend, schoolfellow, schoolmate; школска клупа school desk; школски распуст school holiday (*Am.* vacation) **2** schoolboyish; elementary, raw, crude, unskilled; школска дефиниција working definition; школска интерпретација primitive interpretation

школство *n* schooling, school system, public education, primary and secondary education

школува *impf* **I** *trans.* to school, educate; <ги> школува своите<те> деца to send one's children to school **II** – се to go to school, get one's schooling; каде си се школувал? where did you go to school?

школуван *adj* educated

школувано *adv* in an educated manner

школуваност *f* education, being educated

школување *n from* школува (се); за време на школувањето in one's school-days

шкорка *f see* чкорка

шкорлав *adj see* чкорлав

шкорче *n dim. see* чкорче

Шкот & Шкотланѓанец *m* Scot, Scotsman

Шкотланѓанка *f* Scot, Scotswoman

Шкотска *f* Scotland

шкотски   *adj* Scottish, Scots

шкрапја & шкрапла   *f Zool. see* чкрапја

шкрапне   *pf* шкрапна *aor. see* чкрапне

шкрапнува   *impf of* шкрапне, *see* чкрапнува

шкрботи   *impf see* чкрботи

шкрга   *f see* жабра; ❏ *sl.* диши на шкрги! it stinks to high heaven, it stinks like a polecat; it is stuffy/sultry/oppressive

шкрилест   *adj literary* slate, slaty, shale *attrib.*, schistose; шкрилест пласт schist

шкрилец   -лци *m literary* slate, shale, schist; нафта од шкрилци shale oil

шкрипи   *impf see* чкрипи

шкрипне   *pf* шкрипна *aor. see* чкрипне

шкрипнува   *impf of* шкрипне, *see* чкрипнува

шкропне   *pf* шкропна *aor. see* шкрипне

шкропоти   *impf see* шкрботи, чкрботи

шкрта   *impf see* чкрта

шкртне   *pf* шкртна *aor. see* чкртне

шкртнува   *impf of* шкртне, *see* чкртнува

шлаг   *m* cream, whipped cream; сладолед со шлаг ice-cream with cream

шлагер   *m* hit tune, pop song

шлајм   *m* phlegm; *Med.* sputum, expectorated matter

шлајфер   *m* knife sharpener

шлајфува   *impf* **1** to slip *intrans.*; тркалото шлајфува во калта the wheel is slipping/spinning in the mud **2** to finish, burnish, grind *trans.*; to file; (*со камен*) to whet; (*остри*) to sharpen *trans.*; (*со чакија*) to hone; (*мазни*) to polish

шлак   *interj* slap! (*со/во вода*) splat! splash!

шлака¹   *f* dross; slag

шлака² (се)   *impf of* шлакне (се)

шлаканица   *f* cuff, slap, smack; удри (врзе, залепи, плесне, тресне, шлакне) шлаканица to slap s.o., give s.o. a slap in the face; добие шлаканица to get a slap in the face

шлаке   -вци *m colloq.* crazy fellow; fool, idiot, imbecile, *colloq.* moron

шлакнат   *adj colloq.* crazy, *Brit. colloq.* daft; foolish, idiotic

шлакне   *pf* шлакна *aor.* **I 1** (*силно*) to slap (*s.th.*); (*полека*) to pat (*s.th.*) **2** to clap, applaud; шлакна со раце he clapped <his hands> **3** to box (*s.o.'s*) ears; to slap (*s.o.*) in the face; to smack, cuff; кога го шлакна еднаш! he gave him a mighty slap! **4** (*со вода*) to splash, splatter *trans.*; го шлакна в лице со вода he splashed water over his face **5** *fig.* to blurt out (*something stupid*), *colloq.* drop a brick; шлакна една глупост he dropped a brick **II – се 1** to slap o.s.; to slap one's own face **2** (*со вода*) to splash (splatter) o.s.; (*во вода*) to plop *intrans.*; to jump/plunge (*into*)

шлакнува (се)   *impf of* шлакне (се)

шлакутница   *f* <state of> being splashed (splattered)/awash with water; што е ова, сè шлакутница сте направиле what's this, everything is sopping wet

шланк   *adj indecl.* slim

шлап   *interj* шлап-шлуп! **1** splash! squish! *cf.* шлапа 1 **2** smack! slurp! *cf.* шлапа 2

шлапа   *impf* **1** (*гази по вода, кал, мек снег и сл.*) to wade, squelch, slosh *intrans.*; to splash, slop *intrans.*; (*во плитка вода*) to dabble *intrans.*; шлапа по калта to wade through mud **2** (*при јадење*) to

champ *intrans.*, chew noisily; to smack one's lips **3** *see* шлапне 3

шлапа-шлупа   *interj see* шлап!

шлапка   *impf dim. of* шлапа

шлапне   *pf* шлапна *aor.* **1** to splash, plop *intrans.*; шлапна во вода he plopped into the water; he trod in a puddle **2** *see* шлапа 2 **3** (*шлакне*) to slap

шлапнува   *impf of* шлапне

шлафрок   -ци *m* dressing-gown, housecoat, *Am.* <bath>robe; smoking-jacket

шлем   *m* helmet

шлеп   *m* **1** (*пловен објект*) barge **2** (*опашка на свечен фустан*) train

шлепер   *m* **1** tugboat **2** tow truck **3** articulated lorry, *Austral.* semi-trailer

шлепува   *impf* **I** (*влече*) to tow **II – се** *fig.* to hang out (*со некого – with s.o.*); to sponge (*некому – on s.o.*)

шлиба   *impf* **1** to shake, jolt **2** to slurp; to guzzle

шлибне   *pf* шлибна *aor. see* шлиба

шлибнува   *impf of* шлибне

шлиф   *m* politeness, courtesy, polish; good manners, breeding

шлифува   *impf* **1** (*остри*) to sharpen *trans.*; (*изгладува*) to polish; (*делка*) to trim *trans.* **2** *fig.* to teach (*s.o.*) good manners

шлиц   *m* (*на фустан*) slit; (*на панталони*) fly

шличуи   *pl* <ice->skates

шлог   *m* stroke; го удри шлог 1. he had a stroke 2. *fig.* he got a shock

шлогира   *pf* **I** *fig.* to shock *trans.* **II – се** to have a stroke; *fig.* to shock *intrans.*

шлогиран   *adj* struck down by a stroke; *fig.* shocked

шлука   *f Zool.* snipe; sandpiper, stint; барска шлука (Philomachus pugnax) ruff; голема шлука (Limosa limosa) black-tailed godwit; шумска шлука (Scolopax rusticola) woodcock; шлука бекасина (Gallinage gallinago) common snipe

шлуп   *interj see* шлап!

шлупка¹   *f dial. see* лушпа

шлупка²   *impf see* шлапка

шљахта   *f* Polish gentry

шљахтич   *m* Polish nobleman

шмајзер   *m Mil.* submachine-gun

шмеќар   *m* cheat, dodger

шмеќарија   -ии *f &* шмеќарлак   -ци *m see* шмеќарство

шмеќарски   *adj* slick, tricky, crafty; шмеќарски работи monkey business

шмеќарство   *n* artifice, trick, ruse, swindle; sleight of hand

шмеќарува   *impf* to swindle, hoax, pull the wool over (*s.o.'s*) eyes, lead (*s.o.*) up the garden path; (*во игра*) to cheat

шмизла   *f colloq.* **1** vain woman, fashion plate **2** chatterbox, *colloq.* windbag, *sl.* gasbag

шминка¹   *f* make-up

шминка²   *impf* **I** to make (*s.o.*) up **II – се** to make o.s. up

шминкер   *m* make-up man

шмиргла   *f* sandpaper, glass-paper, emery-paper

шмиргла   *impf* to sandpaper

шмрк   *m* hose; пожарникарски шмрк fire-hose

шмрка   *impf* **1** to sniff *intrans.*, sniffle; само шмрка, настинал he just sniffs all the time, he must have caught cold **2** to sniff *trans.*; шмрка бурмут to take snuff **3** to pump **4** to sip; шмрка кафе to sip coffee

шмркне *pf* шмркна *aor. see* шмрка

шмркнува *impf of* шмркне

шмугне се *pf* шмугна се *aor.* to steal (sneak, slink) away (off); некои веднаш се шмугнаа низ една странична врата some immediately sneaked away through a side-door

шмугнува се *impf of* шмугне се

шмука *impf* to suck; шмука бонбонче to suck a sweet; си ги шмука прстите to suck one's fingers; шмука прав to vacuum; ❑ му ја шмука крвта на некого <со памук> to suck s.o. dry; to bleed s.o. white; to work s.o. to death

шмукалка *f &* **шмукало** *n* **1** pump **2** insect's proboscis

шмукне *pf* шмукна *aor.* to suck up, imbibe

шмукнува *impf of* шмукне

шнајдер *m colloq. see* шивач

шнајдерка *f colloq. see* шивачка

шнајдерски *adj colloq. see* шивачки

шнајдерство *n colloq.* tailor's trade, tailoring; dressmaking; *colloq.* rag trade

шнира *impf* to tie up; (*чевли*) to do (lace) up

шнит *m* **1** pattern (*for sewing*) **2** piece, slice (*of bread, bacon, etc.*)

шницла *f Cul.* schnitzel, escalope

шнола *f* **1** hairpin; hair clip, *Brit.* hair-slide **2** buckle

шнур *m* **1** string; cord, lace **2** *Elec.* cord, flex **3** (*во карти*) bank

шовинизам -змот *m* chauvinism, jingoism

шовинист *m* chauvinist, jingoist

шовинистички *adj* chauvinist, jingoist *attrib.*; chauvinistic, jingoistic; шовинистичка пропаганда chauvinist propaganda

шовинистка *f* (*fem. form*) *see* шовинист

шогавче *n f.p.* mangy little boy/girl

шок[1] *m* shock (*Med. & fig.*); *colloq.* jolt

Шок[2] *m pejor.* Albanian

шокантен -тна *adj* shocking

шок-соба *f* intensive care unit

шок-терапија *f* shock therapy (treatment)

шокира *pf & impf* to shock *trans.*, scandalize; *colloq.* to jolt, give s.o. a shock

шол *m see* шолја

шолја -лји *f* **1** cup; mug; шолја за млеко cup/mug for milk; шолја за чај teacup; ❑ гледа во шолја to tell s.o.'s fortune by reading coffee grounds, read s.o.'s coffee cup **2** клозетска шолја lavatory bowl

шоп[1] *m* provincial fellow

Шоп[2] *m* inhabitant of NE Macedonia

шопа *impf* **1** to flow, run; (*силно*) to gush **2** *fig. colloq.* to pee, piddle

шопне *pf* шопна *aor.* **1** to start flowing (running); (*силно*) to gush out **2** *fig. colloq.* to have a pee, *sl.* take a leak

шопнува *impf of* шопне

шопски *adj* provincial; from NE Macedonia

шопур *m &* **шопурка** *f* spout

шора *impf see* шопа

шорне *pf* шорна *aor. see* шопне

шорнува *impf of* шорне, *see* шопнува

шота се *impf colloq. see* шпота се

шотало *n colloq. see* шпотало

шоу *n* show

шоумен *m* showman

шофер *m* driver; chauffeur; ❑ пцуе како шофер to swear like a trooper

шоферски *adj* driving *attrib.*; driver's; chauffeur's; шоферски испит driving test; шоферска табла dashboard

шоферство *n* driving, chauffeur's work

шофершајбна *f* windscreen

шофира *impf* to drive (*a motor vehicle*)

шошница *f f.p. see* кошница 1

шпага *f* **1** sword, rapier **2** *Gymnastics* splits

шпагети *pl* spaghetti

шпајз *m* pantry

шпалир *m* **1** lane <of people>, double row; cordon **2** row (*of vines, etc.*); espalier

шпалта *f Print.* (*набран текст*) galley, pull; (*за коректура*) galley proof

Шпанец -нци *m* Spaniard

Шпанија *f* Spain

Шпанка *f* (*fem. form*) *see* Шпанец

шпански *adj* Spanish

шпарта *impf* **1** to line, rule, cover with lines; шпарта хартија to line paper; шпартана хартија lined (ruled) paper **2** *colloq.* to walk, stroll

шпационира *pf & impf Print.* to space

шпедитер *m* forwarding agent, forwarder; shipping company, shipper

шпедитерски *adj* forwarding *attrib.*; forwarding agent's; shipping *attrib.*; shipper's; шпедитерско одделение shipping department; шпедитерско претпријатие forwarding firm, shipping firm; шпедитерски услуги shipping services

шпедиција *f* **1** *see* шпедитер **2** forwarding; shipping

шпекула *f see* шпекулација 1

шпекулант *m* speculator, profiteer, *colloq.* shark

шпекулантка *f* (*fem. form*) *see* шпекулант

шпекулантски *adj* profiteer's; speculative

шпекулантство *n* **1** speculation, profiteering, jobbery **2** *Philos.* speculation

шпекулативен -вна *adj* **1** speculative, profiteering *attrib.* **2** *Philos.* abstract, conjectural

шпекулација -ии *f* **1** speculation, profiteering **2** *Philos.* theorizing, abstract thought, conjecture

шпекулира *pf & impf* **1** to speculate (*co – in*), profiteer (*by*), take unfair advantage (*of s.th.*) **2** *Philos.* to theorize, pursue abstract thought, conjecture

шпенадла *f* pin

шперплоча *f* plywood

шпигл *m* **1** *see* огледало **2** *Print.* layout, face, type area

шпил *m* deck, pack (*of cards*)

шпион *m* spy; eavesdropper

шпионажа *f* spying, espionage

шпионира *impf* to spy, conduct espionage; to eavesdrop, pry

шпионка *f* **1** (*fem. form*) *see* шпион **2** peep-hole (*in a door*)

шпионски *adj* spy<ing>, espionage *attrib.*

шпионство *n see* шпионажа

шпиритус *m Chem.* spirit; denatured (methylated) alcohol

шпиритусен -сна *adj* spirit *attrib.*; of/for/with denatured (methylated) alcohol

шпирт *m see* шпиритус

шпиртен *adj see* шпиритусен

шпирто *n* **1** *colloq. see* шпиритус **2** *see* кибрит, чпирто 2

шпиртоса (се) *pf see* чпиртоса (се)

шпиртосува (се) *impf of* шпиртоса (се), *see* чпиртосува (се)

шпиц *m* **1** *see* шилец, врв **2** *as adj indecl.* pointed, pointy; jagged; шпиц чевли pointed shoes **3** шпиц време rush hour **4** spitz <dog>

шпица *f Film* cast and credits

шпицест *adj* pointed; jagged; sharp

шпора *f literary see* мамуза

шпорет *f* stove, *Am.* range

шпота се *impf colloq.* to mock, make fun (*of*); немој да се шпоташ со мене don't make fun of me!

шпотало *n colloq.* scoffer, mocker, banterer

шприц *m* **1** needle, syringe **2** hose

шприца *impf* to squirt, spray, sprinkle

шприцер *m* wine with soda; ❏ ладен како шприцер <as> cool as a cucumber

шрапнел *m &* **шрапнела** *f Mil.* shrapnel

шраф *m Tech.* screw; bolt; ❏ <само> еден шраф во машината just a cog in the wheel; му фалат неколку шрафа he has a screw loose

шрафцигер *m* screwdriver

шрафче *n dim. of* шраф

Шри Ланка *f* Sri Lanka

Шриланканец -ни *m* Sri Lankan

Шриланканка *f* (*fem. form*) *see* Шриланканец

шриланкански *adj* Sri Lankan

шрифт *m* script

шрка *impf see* срка

штаб *m* **1** *Mil.* general staff, supreme command; главен (генерален) штаб *see* генералштаб **2** *Mil.* headquarters; depot **3** management, direction, headquarters; штаб на работни бригади work-brigade headquarters

штабен -бна *adj* staff *attrib.*; supreme; management *attrib.*

штава *f* tannic acid, tannin, tan

штаве *n Bot. see* штавеj

штавеj *m Bot.* (Rumex) dock, sorrel; сарма од штавеj stuffed dock <leaves>

штави *pf & impf* **1** (*кожа*) to tan *trans.* **2** *fig. colloq.* to thrash, beat up, *sl.* rough up; *sl.* to tan (*s.o.'s*) hide; ако те фатам, убаво ќе те штавам if I catch you I'll give you a good hiding

штавоса *pf see* штави

штавосува *impf see* штави

штавува *impf of* штави

штавувач *m see* кожар, табак[2]

штала *f* stall; (*коњска*) stable; (*за крави*) cowshed

шталски *adj* stall *attrib.*; шталско ѓубре stable dung (manure)

штама *f* <profound> silence; ноќна штама silence of the night; зацари (завладеа) штама a profound silence descended

штамбил *m* stamp, seal

штампа *f arch.* **1** (*на хартија*) print, wood-cut **2** (*на штоф*) print

штампоса *pf arch. see* отпечати[1], напечати

штампосува *impf arch. of* штампоса

штанга & **штангла** *f* metal bar (rod, lever)

штанд *m* stand, stall; counter

штапски *adj see* штабен

штафелаj -аи *m* easel

штафета *f Sport.* **1** baton **2** relay <race>

штафетен -тна *adj* relay *attrib.*; штафетна палка baton

штедар -дра *adj* generous, open-handed; ungrudging

штедач *m* depositor, client (*of a savings bank*)

штеди *impf* **I 1** to save, spare; to use sparingly; to be thrifty (*with*); to economize (*on*); штеди пари to save money; штеди за старост to save for one's old age; штеди време to save time; to make the most of one's time; си ги штеди своите сили to conserve one's powers; to save one's energy; не штеди труд to spare no effort; си го штеди здравјето, си ги штеди очите to take care of one's health/eyes; штедете ги дрвата use the wood sparingly! **2** to treat leniently, indulgently; (*за деца*) spoil; тоj човек треба да се штеди he is to be handled with kid gloves; he is to be excused; таа не штеди никого she spares no one **II –** **се** to spare o.s., conserve one's energy, husband one's resources, look after o.s.; тоj многу се штеди he takes good care of his health

штедилница *f* savings bank; поштенска штедилница postal savings bank

штедлив *adj* thrifty, economical, careful; (*умерен*) frugal; (*скржав*) parsimonious

штедливец -вци *m* thrifty person

штедливо *adv* sparingly, thriftily, economically; frugally; parsimoniously; живее штедливо to live thriftily, lead a modest life

штедливост *f* thrift, thriftiness; economy; frugality; parsimony

штедро *adv* generously, lavishly, liberally; unstintingly

штедрост *f* generosity, lavishness, liberality

штедрота *f see* штедрост

штекер *m Elec.* plug; socket, *Brit.* power-point

штекол *m dial.* rod (*used to lead a vicious dog to prevent it from biting the person leading it*)

штелува *pf & impf* to adjust, fix *trans.*; штелува кочници to adjust the brakes; штелува мотор to tune the engine

штеп *m* stitch

штепува *impf* to darn, sew up

штерна *f dial. see* цистерна

штета *f* damage, loss; нанесе штета на некого to cause s.o. damage/harm; претрпи штета to incur a loss; надомести штета to compensate for damages (loss); to make amends (*to s.o.*) for an injury; на сопствена штета to one's own disadvantage, at one's own expense, to one's cost; без штета по (за) without detriment to; на штета на to the detriment of; чиста штета an outright loss; <прави> повеќе штета отколку добро to do more harm than good; to throw good money after bad; штетата е сторена the damage is done; штета! what a pity!

штетен -тна *adj* detrimental, harmful, damaging; noxious; pernicious; dangerous; штетен за здравјето bad for one's health

штети[1] *pf colloq. trans.* (*нешто*) to damage; (*човек*) to harm, injure; to cause (*s.o.*) a loss, short-change; го штетивме човекот we've caused him a big loss; we've done him a lot of harm; *see* оштети

штети[2] *impf intrans.* to be harmful; тоа му штети на здравјето that is bad for one's health

штетник -ци *m* harmful person; pest, parasite, vermin

штетно *adv* adversely, detrimentally; дејствува штетно to have a detrimental effect, be dangerous (harmful)

штетност *f* adverse (detrimental) nature, harmfulness; dangerous quality

штеточинец -нци *m see* штетник

штиглец & штиглиц *m Zool.* (Carduelis carduelis) goldfinch, *see* трнарче

штик *m see* бајонет

штикла *f* heel (*on woman's shoe*); високи тенки штикли stiletto heels

штиклира *pf & impf* to tick

штикличе *n dim. of* штикла

штим¹ *m* combings

штим² *m Mus.* style (*of tuning for guitar*); руски/италијански штим Russian/Italian-style guitar

штима *impf see* штимува

штимер *m Mus.* tuner

штимка *f see* штим¹

штимува *impf* 1 *Mus.* to tune *trans.*; штимува клавир to tune a piano 2 *fig.* to be right; тука нешто не штимува (штима) something is not right here 3 *pejor.* to chat up, wine and dine (*a woman*)

штимунг *m* mood, spirits; high spirits; atmosphere

штипалка *f see* штипка¹ 3

штипало 1 *m* person who pinches 2 *n see* штипка¹ 3

штипе *impf* I 1 to pinch *trans.*; to tweak; немој да го штипеш детето don't pinch the child! 2 to pinch (*pieces*) off (*s.th.*); си штипеше по малку од лебот he was picking bits off the bread 3 to prick, bite, sting; to prickle; нешто ме штипе по снагава something is pricking me in the back 4 *fig.* to burn, sting; to prickle; остриот ветар му го штипеше лицето the bitter wind stung his face; чадот штипе во очите the smoke stings one's eyes; виното штипе по устата the wine is tart on the palate II – **се** 1 to pinch o.s. 2 to pinch one another

штипка¹ *f* 1 (*за алишта*) <clothes->peg, *Am.* clothespin 2 (*за хартија*) clip; (*за коса*) hair clip, *Brit.* hairslide 3 *Zool.* pincer, claw 4 pair of tongs

штипка² *f* 1 (*количество*) pinch 2 pinch, <act of> pinching; prick

штипка³ (се) *impf dim. see* штипе (се)

штиплив *adj* (*see* штипе I 4) biting, stinging; prickly; ветрот веќе не беше толку штиплив the wind was no longer so keen

штипливост *f* (*see* штипе I 4) sting; prickle; (*за студ*) bite, nip; (*за ветар*) keenness

штипне *pf* штипна *aor.* I *see* штипе I 1–3 II – **се** to pinch o.s.

штипнува (се) *impf of* штипне (се)

штир¹ *m Bot.* (Amaranthus) amaranth, love-lies-bleeding

штир² *adj* barren, sterile, infertile; штира жена barren woman

штирак *m* starch, *see* кола²

штираквица *f f.p.* barren animal; овца штираквица barren sheep; *see* штирка 1

штирен *adj* prepared with amaranth

штирка¹ *f* 1 barren animal 2 barren woman, *see* неротка

штирка² *impf* (*see* колосува) to starch; штирка кошула/чаршаф и сл. to starch a shirt/sheet etc.

штит *m* shield (*also fig.*); *Tech.* guard; *Bot.* umbel; *Zool.* scutum

штитеник -ци *m* 1 protégé 2 ward

штитеничка *f* (*fem. form*) *see* protégée

штитенички *adj* protégé's; protégée's; ward's

штити *impf* I 1 to protect; to shield, screen, guard; штити од муви/комарци to protect from flies/mosquitoes; штити од студ/ветар to protect from the cold/wind 2 to favour, patronize, champion; тој го штити него he looks after him II – **се** to guard *intrans.*, protect o.s. (*од – against*)

штитовиден -дна *adj* shield-shaped, scutiform, peltate; штитовидна жлезда *Anat.* thyroid gland

штитоносен -сна *adj* штитоносна вошка *Zool.* (Coccus) scale insect, *Am.* scale bug

штитоносец -сци *m* shield-bearer

штих *m* 1 stab, thrust 2 (*во карти*) court-card, ten *or* ace; ❑ јак штих *colloq.* a big noise (bug, pot, shot); *sl.* a big cheese 3 bad smell, stench 4 tinge

штица *f* board; дебела штица <thick> plank; танка штица thin board; штица за месо chopping board; штица за месење pastry board; ❑ со три штици е he has a screw loose; на гнила штица не гази don't tread on thin ice! како штица е he is as thin as a rake; рамен како штица <as> flat as a board (pancake); штици што живот значат "the boards", the stage, the theatre

штиче *n dim. of* штица

штичка *f* 1 *dim. of* штица 2 *colloq., dial.* ruler

што I *interrogative pron* 1 what? што сакаш? what do you want? што ти е? what's wrong with you? што има ново? што има што нема? what's new? од што се плашиш? what are you afraid of? за што станува збор? what's it about? what are you talking about? што чини (вреди) ова? how much is this? what is it worth? how much does it come to? и што? па што? што дека? so what? what about it? знаеш што? do you know what? I say! што правиш, како си? how are you, how are things? што сум јас крив? what have I done? ❑ нема што there's nothing for it; no doubt about it; што ќе правиш! what can one (you) do! не е којзнае што it's nothing special; nothing to write home about; што е, тука е that's it; it cannot be helped; that's the way it goes 2 (*каков*) what sort of? what a . . . ! што човек е тој? what sort of man is he? што зборови слушна од него? what did he say to you? што човек беше тој! what a man he was! 3 (*exclamatory*) what . . . ! what a . . . ! what a lot of . . . ! how <much> . . . ! што е убаво! how beautiful! што е прав! what a lot of dust! што сме се смееле! how we laughed! 4 (*зошто*) if only; што не е тука татко ти? if only your father were here II *relative pron* 1 which; who; куќата што ја купи брат ми the house that my brother bought; сите што беа на свадба all who were at the wedding; ❑ што трезен мисли, пијан зборува what soberness conceals, drunkenness reveals; in vino veritas 2 that which, what<ever>; кажи ми сè што знаеш tell me all you know! 3 (*often* што и да . . .) whatever; ❑ што сака нека биде whatever happens, no matter what; што <и> да е, што <и> да било whatever it may be, anything at all, no matter what; што и да правиш whatever you do; што и да кажеш нема да ти верува whatever you say he won't believe you; било што било come what may; what's done is done! што не, што ли не all sorts of things; што е, тука е it can't be helped; што е уште полошо what is even worse **III** *conj* **1** that; прости ми, што не дојдов порано forgive me for not coming earlier; мило (драго) ми е што . . . I am glad that . . . ; толку побргу, што . . . the more so as . . . ; затоа што because; така што, така . . . што so that; во куќата имаше доволно храна, така што не моравме да излегуваме надвор there was enough food in the house, so we did not need to go out; тој зборуваше така (толку) досадно, што никој не сакаше да го слуша he was so boring that no one wanted to listen to him; таков . . . што such . . . that; сликата беше таква, што не смеевме ни да ја покажеме the picture was so awful that we didn't dare show it; толку што, толку . . . што so much . . . that **2** (*with comparative adj or adv*) as . . . as; што побргу as soon/ fast as possible; што подобро as well as possible; што поголем as big as possible; ❏ што побрзо, тоа подобро the sooner the better **IV** *interrogative adv* (*зошто*) why, what for; што си замислен? a penny for your thoughts; што ме гледаш така? why are you looking at me like that? **V** *part* (*with a repeated verb denoting action performed for a short time*) чекал што чекал, па си отишол he waited for a while and then left

штогоде *pron* **1** whatever, anything at all, no matter what; тој не сака да јаде штогоде he won't eat just anything **2** (*adjectivally*) any sort of; штогоде човек just anyone; anybody at all; штогоде работа any sort of work <at all>

штом *conj* **1** (*temporal*) as soon as; штом ќе се најадеше добро, ќе легнеше да спие as soon as he had had a good meal he would go to bed; штом дојде потерата, тој се скри as soon as the posse arrived he hid **2** (*conditional*) as, since; штом го нема него, работата не врви since he is not here the work is not progressing; штом не сака, немој да го молиш since (if) he doesn't want to, don't ask him! штом веќе now that

штопер *m* timekeeper

штоперица *f* stopwatch

штопува *pf & impf* to time (*with a stopwatch*)

штос *m* **1** blow **2** wad; извади штос пари he took out a wad of money **3** gag, stunt, joke

штостока *adv* how nice, how beautiful

штотуку *conj* (*see* штом 1) as soon as, hardly, scarcely; штотуку ти излезе, тој се јави no sooner had you left than he arrived; штотуку влезе, пак излезе he had scarcely come in when he left again

штоф *m* cloth, material

штофен *adj* cloth, material *attrib.*

штрајк -ови *m* strike; штрајк со глад hunger strike; ❏ предупредувачки штрајк token (warning) strike; организира штрајк to stage a strike; стапува во штрајк to go on strike, walk out, down tools

штрајкач *m see* штрајкувач

штрајкачки *adj see* штрајкувачки; штрајкачки одбор (комитет) strike committee; штрајкачко движење strike movement

штрајкбрехер *m* strikebreaker, *pejor. colloq.* scab, *Brit. pejor.* blackleg

штрајкува *impf* to <be/go on> strike

штрајкувач *m* striker, striking worker

штрајкувачки *adj* strike *attrib.*; striker's

штрак *interj* click! snap! (*за ножици*) snip!

штрака *impf* **1** to click; (*со ножици*) to snip; (*со очи*) to blink; (*со прсти*) to snap; штрака со заби his teeth are chattering **2** *colloq.* to clap <one's hands>, applaud; луѓето викаа, тропаа и штракаа the people were shouting, stamping and clapping **3** to rattle, clatter

штракало *n* <baby's> rattle

штракне *pf* штракна *aor.* **1** *see* штрака 1; клучот штракна во бравата the key went click in the lock **2** *colloq.* to start clapping <one's hands>; to clap <one's hands> once **3** *see* штрака 3

штракнува *impf of* штракне

штрап *interj* (*со ножици*) snip!

штрап-штруп & штрапа-штрупа *interj* **1** (*со нозе*) tramp! slip-slop! slosh! **2** (*со ножици*) snip!

штрапа *impf* **1** to tramp; (*во вода, кал*) to slosh; штрапаа боси по дворот they tramped barefoot across the yard **2** to cut, snip; многу брзо штрапа со ножиците he works very fast with the scissors

штрапне *pf* штрапна *aor. see* штрапа

штрапнува *impf of* штрапне

штрас *m* paste, strass; rhinestone; накит од штрас paste jewellery

штрб & штрбав *adj* **1** broken, chipped; jagged; штрбава стомна broken pitcher; штрбава секира jagged axe **2** gap-toothed, with teeth missing; toothless; штрбава баба gap-toothed old woman

штрбавост *f* broken (chipped) state; jagged quality; gap-toothed state; toothlessness

штрбел *m see* штрбол

штрбла *f* gap-toothed woman/girl

штрбло -вци *m* gap-toothed man/boy

штрбне *pf* штрбна *aor.* to break <a piece off s.th.>, chip; to truncate

штрбнува *impf of* штрбне

штрбол *m* **1** crock; jagged tool; tool with teeth missing; се посмеал 'рбол на штрбол *prov.* the pot calls the kettle black **2** *see* штрпка[1] 1 & 2

штрбуле *n dim. of* штрбол; смее се штрбуле на 'рбуле *prov.* the pot calls the kettle black; *see* шутаре

штрек *m in the expression:* на штрек е to be on the alert, be on the qui vive, be on one's guard, watch out

штрека *impf* **I 1** to hurt, be painful; to twinge; раната штрека, бере гној the wound is tender, it is festering; ме штрека нешто во крстот I have stabbing pains in the lower back **2** to gush <out/forth>; од дупката штрекаше вода water was gushing from the hole **II – се** to be afraid (in a flap), quiver, shake <with fear>

штрекнат *adj & pt* **1** scared, quivering, shaking <with fear>; *see* штрекне I 3 **2** штрекнат со умот crazy, out of one's mind

штрекнатост *f* alarm, fright, fear, *Brit. colloq.* blue funk

штрекне *pf* штрекна *aor.* **I 1** to hurt, be painful; to twinge; ме штрекна нешто во прстот I felt a sharp pain in my finger **2** to start gushing <out/forth>; штрекна вода од дупката water started gushing out of the hole **3** *trans.* to give (*s.o.*) a fright, scare, startle; to make (*s.o.*) flinch; го штрекна гласот на мајка му his mother's voice startled him **II – се 1** to get a fright, start quivering, start shaking <with fear>; to flinch; to wake with a start **2** *in the expression:* штрекне се со умот to go crazy (out of one's mind)

штрекнува (се) *impf of* штрекне (се)

штрингла *f see* чиле[1]

штрих *m* line

штрк *m Zool.* (Ciconia) stork; штрковите кљакаат the storks are displaying (*clattering their bills*); висок како штрк tall as a maypole

штркал *m Zool. dial. see* штркел

штркел -кли *m Zool.* (Hypoderma bovis) gadfly, warble fly, ox-warble, bot-fly; го фати штркелот 1. he was bitten by a warble fly 2. *fig.* he's got a bee in his bonnet, s.th. has bitten him; he has gone off his rocker

штркле -вци *m colloq.* long-legged (lanky) fellow, *colloq.* beanpole

штрклее *impf* to go berserk; to be goaded into fury; *fig.* to rage, go on the rampage; говедата беа мирни, па овците штрклееја the cattle were quiet but the sheep were running wild

штрклест *adj* long-legged, lanky

штркне (се) *pf* штркна *aor.* to show, appear *intrans.*; (*за стеблика и др.*) to rise, stand upright (erect); (*за коса*) to stand on end, bristle

штркнува (се) *impf of* штркне (се)

штрков *adj* stork's, stork *attrib.*; штрково гнездо stork's nest; штрково цвеќе *Bot.* (Narcissus) daffodil

штркол -кли *m Zool. dial. see* штркел

штркче *n dim. of* штрк

штрпка[1] *f* **1** (*откршено место*) chip, chipped spot **2** gap <in a row of teeth>; stump <of a tooth>; broken tooth **3** (*штрбнато парче*) broken piece, shard, fragment

штрпка[2] *impf* to break off a piece; штрпка леб (од лебот) to break off a piece of bread

штрпне *pf* штрпна *aor. see* штрбне

штрпнува *impf of* штрпне, *see* штрбнува

штрудла *f* strudel; штрудла со јаболки apple strudel

штрче *n dim. see* штркче

штука[1] *f Zool.* (Esox lucius) pike, (*млада*) jack

штука[2] *f* Stuka (*German dive bomber*)

штука[3] *impf see* штукне

штукне *pf* штукна *aor.* to disappear; to get lost; to run away; кој знае кај отиде, кај штукна, никаде го нема who knows where he went, where he disappeared to, he's nowhere to be found; ❏ да му штукне умот на некого to drive s.o. mad

штукнува *impf of* штукне

штур *adj* **1** empty, vain; во ноќта штура *poet.* in the dead of night; пусто и штуро да остане! *curse* damn it! **2** empty-headed, obtuse, stupid

штура се *impf* to hang about, loiter; to roam, wander <about>; уште ли се штураат таму? are they still hanging about there?

штурелија *f* bleakness; bleak spot; ❏ штура штурелија empty wastes

штурец -рци *m Zool.* cricket; полски штурец (Gryllus campestris) field-cricket; домашен штурец (Gryllus domesticus) house-cricket

штури[1] *impf* to chirp; штурците штурат the crickets are chirping

штури[2] *impf in the expression:* пусти штури spare no effort, move heaven and earth, go all out, leave no stone unturned! прави што ќе правиш, пусти

штури, само куќа да имаш do whatever you can, go all out to get a house!

штурина *f pejor.* (*of women or animals*) bitch

штурка *impf see* штури[1]

штурм *m Mil.* assault, storm, attack

штурмовик -ци *m Mil.* ground-attack aircraft

штуро *adv* **1** emptily, vainly; штуро напишано blandly written **2** empty-headedly, vacuously, stupidly

штурост & **штуротија** *f* **1** emptiness, vainness **2** empty-headedness, vacuity, vapidity, stupidity

штурче *n dim. of* штурец

штутка се *impf* **1** to wander, roam <about>; to stray, lose one's bearings; се штуткал, се плеткал по белиов свет *poet.* he wandered over the whole wide world **2** to be shy **3** to hesitate, vacillate

шуба *f* fur coat

шубара *f* fur cap; fur cap with ear-flaps; (*на гардист*) busby, bearskin

шубе *n colloq.* **1** qualm; има шубе, со шубе е he is uneasy, he has qualms; без шубе without doubt, doubtless; да не ти е шубе, да бидеш без шубе don't worry! го фати шубе he began to feel uneasy, he got cold feet

шубелија *adj indecl. colloq.* **1** doubtful, uneasy, hesitant **2** *m* (*as noun*) doubting Thomas

шуга[1] *f* **1** mange; scabies; фати шуга to get the mange **2** tag (*children's game*)

шуга[2] **се** *impf* to become mangy, get the mange; to get scabies; to get lichen/eczema

шугав *adj* affected with scabies; scabby; mangy; шугава овца mangy sheep; *fig.* black sheep

шугавост *f* manginess, mangy condition; scabbiness

шугоса *pf* **I 1** to infect with mange **2** to get the mange, become mangy **II** – **се** *see* I 2

шука[1] *impf see* шукне

шука[2] **се** *impf/see* шуга[2] се 2

шуканица *f* има шуканица he has lichen/eczema; целиот е со шуканици he has eczema all over his body

шукне *pf* шукна *aor.* **I 1** to shove (push) away; ја шукна топката he pushed/kicked the ball away **2** to push, shove, shift, manhandle, trundle (*into*); to put, stick; го шукнала момчето внатре she hustled the young man inside **II** – **се** to push one's way in, push in *intrans.*; to sneak in

шукнува (се) *impf of* шукне (се)

шук-шук *adv colloq.* easily, just like that, with one's eyes closed; со шук-шук сака да си помине he wants to get by with no effort

шуко & **шукоштекер** *m Elec.* power point (*for a stove*)

шум *m* noise; murmur; hubbub; од соседниот двор се слушаше некаков шум there was a noise coming from the next yard; ❏ дигне шум околу нешто to make a lot of noise about s.th., make a fuss about s.th.; *Med.* шум на срце heart murmur

шума *f* **1** (*лисје*) leaves, foliage; greenery; тие колје се фатиле и пуштиле шума these cuttings have taken root and come into leaf **2** (*гора*) wood<s>; (*поголема*) forest; борова/букова/дабова шума pine/beech/oak forest; густа/ретка шума dense/open forest; ❏ ја фати шумата he took to the hills (forest); од шумата не се гледаат дрвјата not to see the wood for the trees **3** (*зимна храна за добиток*) dry (winter) feed, forage; насече шума за добиток he cut winter feed for the livestock; шума, волна, дупка полна *prov.* the best food is that which fills the belly **4** (*пченковина, царевковина*) maize (*Am.* corn) stalks

шумар[1] *m see* шумјак

шумар[2] *m* **1** ranger **2** forester

шумарина *f* forest tax

шумарка *f* (*fem. form*) *see* шумар[2]

шумарски *adj* **1** (*see* шумар[2] 1) ranger's; шумарско куче ranger's dog; шумарска куќа ranger's house **2** (*see* шумар[2] 2) forester's; forestry *attrib.*; шумарска школа forestry school; земјоделско-шумарски факултет Faculty of Agriculture and Forestry

шумарство *n* forestry

шумен -мна *adj* **1** noisy; loud; (*за човек*) *colloq.* loud-mouthed; (*за поток*) babbling; шумна река murmuring river; шумна пења sparkling froth **2** noisy; tumultuous; шумна сала noisy hall; шумни расправии noisy altercations **3** *fig.* sensational, spectacular, celebrated; topical; шумен процес *cause célèbre*

шуменица *f f.p.* leaves (*as a pillow, bed or blanket*)

шуми *impf* **1** (*издава шум*) (*за лисје*) to rustle, whisper; (*за шампањ*) to sparkle; (*за поток*) to murmur, babble; дрвјата шумат the trees are rustling; Вардарот шуми the Vardar is murmuring **2** (*дига шум*) to make a noise; to be noisy; to raise a racket; ти многу шумиш you are making a lot of noise, you are very noisy

шумичка *n dim. of* шума 2

шумјак -ци *m* copse, coppice; thicket; *see* горичка

шумка[1] *f* **1** bush, shrub **2** maize (*Am.* corn) plant

шумка[2] *impf dim. of* шуми 1

шумкар *m pejor.* guerrilla, partisan (*agent of the Bulgarian fascist authorities in World War II*)

шумлив *adj see* шумен 1

шумнат *adj* **1** *see* шумовит **2** leafy; шумнато дрво leafy tree

шумне *pf* шумна *aor. see* шуми; шумна ветерчок a breeze started blowing

шумно *adv* noisily; loudly; sensationally; шумно се расправаат they are arguing loudly

шумнува *impf of* шумне

шумовит *adj* well-wooded, <heavily> forested; шумовит крај, шумовита месност well-wooded region, heavily-timbered area

шумовитост *f* extent of forest cover

шумоглавен *adj see* ошумоглавен

шумоглави (се) *pf see* ошумоглави (се)

шумоглавува (се) *impf of* шумоглави (се), *see* ошумоглавува (се)

шумоли *impf* to rustle, murmur, whisper; (*ромони*) to ripple, babble; (*за платно*) to rustle, crinkle; дрвјата шумолат the trees are rustling; поточето ја шумоли својата песна the little brook is babbling

шумот *m* (*see* шум) rustle, rustling

шумоти *impf* **1** *see* шуми 1 **2** (*за луѓе*) to whisper; to murmur

шумски *adj* forest *attrib.*; шумски поток forest stream; шумски пат forest track; шумско дрво forest tree; шумска управа forest administration; шумско стопанство forest; plantation; forest estate; forestry; шумски пожар forest fire, bushfire; шумски

работник lumberjack, *Am.* logger; шумски расадник tree nursery; шумски јагоди wild strawberries; шумски лепешкар dung-fly; dung-beetle

шунд *m literary* trash; шунд-литература pulp literature, pulp fiction

шунка *f* ham

шупа *f* shed

шупелка *f* **1** *Mus.* kind of flute **2** small hole; сирење со шупелки cheese with holes

шупелкав *adj* full of holes; porous

шупелкавост *f* state of being full of holes; porosity

шупи *impf dial.* to play the flute

шуплив *adj* **1** hollow; шупливо дрво rotten (hollow) tree **2** full of holes; worm-eaten; шуплив орев empty <husk of> nut; шупливо јаболко rotten apple; шуплив заб decayed (rotten) tooth **3** *fig.* empty; шуплива глава empty head; шуплива фраза empty phrase **4** (*as noun*) empty-headed person, num<b>skull; само шупливите така си поминуваат that only happens to numskulls

шупливец -вци *m* empty-headed person, numskull

шупливица *f f.p.* tree that bears worthless fruit

шупливост *f* hollowness; state of being full of holes; emptiness; *fig.* empty-headedness

шуплика *f dial.* hollow (rotten) tree

шуплина *f* hollow, cavity; усна шуплина oral cavity

шуплоса се *pf* to go bad; to rot; to become worm-eaten

шуплосан *pt* rotten; worm-eaten; шуплосани ореви empty nutshells

шуплосува се *impf of* шуплоса се

шупне[1] *pf dial. see* шупи

шупне[2] ce *pf see* шукне[2] се

шура *m* brother-in-law (*wife's brother*)

шурка[1] *impf* to ransack, rummage through, search through; бараше, шуркаше, но ништо не најде he searched and rummaged but didn't find anything

шурка[2] *impf see* блика, шурти

шурна *f see* шурнеа

шурне *pf* шурна *aor.* to gush out (forth); шурна крв blood gushed forth; *see* бликне

шурнеа *f* (*see* шура) sister-in-law (*brother-in-law's wife*)

шурнува *impf of* шурне

шурти *impf* to gush forth, pour out; од чешмата шуртеше бистра вода clear water was pouring from the fountain

шуруп *m colloq.* syrup, *see* сируп

шут[1] *adj* **1** having a broken horn; hornless; шута коза hornless goat; шута се шути ем боде *prov.* the pot calls the kettle black **2** with a broken handle; with a chipped spout; шута стомна jug with a broken handle; jug with a chipped spout **3** *fig.* short, incomplete, deficient, defective; некако шуто ми изгледа сето ова овде somehow something seems to be missing here; ❑ шуто ми е I feel uneasy; I miss (*s.o.*); I am short (*of s.th.*) **4** *fig.* a button short, weak in the upper storey; шут човек blockhead

шут[2] *m* court jester; *fig.* fool

шут[3] *m Sport.* kick, shot; силен (јак)/слаб/добар шут powerful/feeble/good shot

шут[4] *m* rubble

шутак -ци *m dial.* cotton waistcoat

шутар *m* broken/chipped vessel; цреп шутара прекарува *prov. see* шутаре

шутаре *n dim. of* шутар; цреп шутаре прекарува *prov.* the pot calls the kettle black

шутарка *f* **1** *see* шутар **2** *Bot.* variety of awnless wheat

шутѝра *pf & impf Sport.* to shoot (*at the goal*)

шутка[1] *f* **1** *see* шутар, шутарка **2** hornless cow/goat etc. **3** *fig. vulg.* cunt

шутка[2] *impf* **I** to throw out; (*топка и сл. или некого*) to kick; (*исфрла некого*) to kick out; (*преместува некого*) to shunt around *trans.*; само го шуткаат наваму-натаму they keep shunting him around **II –** **се 1** to kick one another **2** to hang about

шутко -вци *m see* шутрак 1

шутлак -ци *m see* шутрак 2

шутлачка *f see* шутрачка 2

шутне (се) *pf see* шутка (се) I & II 1

шутовски *adj* (*see* шут[2]) court jester's; *fig.* foolish; шутовска облека court jester's garb

шутрак -ци *m* **1** hornless ox **2** *fig.* blockhead, num<b>skull; шутрак еден! you numskull!

шутрачка *f* **1** hornless cow/goat **2** (*fem. form*) *see* шутрак 2

шукур *part colloq. arch.* thank goodness; шукур што те најдов thank goodness I found you! шукур на Бога thank goodness!

шушка[1] *f* scrap; speck

шушка[2] *f dial.* dried capsicum

шушка[3] *impf* **1** to rustle *intrans.*; нешто шушка во сеното something is rustling in the hay; банкнотите беа нови, шушкаа во рацете the banknotes were new, they rustled in one's hand **2** *see* шушука

шушкав *adj* rustling; шушкави лисје dry leaves; шушкаво сено dry hay

шушкавец -вци *m* plastic raincoat

шушки *pl* **1** *see* шушка[1] **2** dry leaves; sawdust **3** *sl.* dough, loot, readies, *pejor.* lucre

шушкот *m* rustling

шушлак -ци *m see* шутлак, шутрак 2

шушлачка *f see* шутлачка, шутрачка 2

шушлее *impf see* шушка[3] 1

шушлек *m* **1** *see* шушки[1] **2** granular snow

шушлив *adj see* шушкав

шушлоп *m see* шушлек 1

шушне *pf* шушна *aor.* **1** to make a rustling sound, *see* шушка[3] 1; нешто шушна во житото something rustled (made a rustling sound) in the grain **2** to whisper; видов дека му шушна нешто I saw her whisper something in his ear

шушнува *impf of* шушне

шушолка *impf dim. of* шушка[3]

шушука *impf* to whisper; нешто се шушука за него there is a rumour going round about him; си шушукаат they are whispering to each other

шушукне *pf* шушукна *aor.* to whisper; за него се шушукна не една работа people whispered different things about him, there was more than one rumour about him

шушумига *f & m* **1** timid person, mouse **2** oaf, *sl.* clod, jerk **3** stay-at-home, home-body

шш *interj* sh! shush!